1989 CATHOLIC ALMANAC

Felician A. Foy, O.F.M.
EDITOR

Rose M. Avato
ASSOCIATE EDITOR

DISCARD

**Our Sunday Visitor Publishing Division
Our Sunday Visitor, Inc.**
HUNTINGTON • INDIANA

University of Charleston Library
Charleston, WV 25304

ACKNOWLEDGMENTS: NC News Service, for coverage of news and documentary texts; *The Documents of Vatican II,* ed. W. M. Abbott (Herder and Herder, America Press: New York 1966), for quotations of Council documents; *Annuario Pontificio* (1988); *Statistical Yearbook of the Church* (1986); *The Official Catholic Directory* (P. J. Kenedy & Sons, 1988); *The Papal Encyclicals,* 5 vols., ed. C. Carlen (McGrath Publishing: Wilmington, NC 1981); Newsletter of the U.S. Bishops' Committee on the Liturgy; The United States Catholic Mission Assoc. (3029 Fourth St. N.E., Washington, D.C. 20017), for U.S. overseas-mission compilations and statistics; *Catholic Press Directory* (1988); *Annuaire/Directory 1988* (copyright© Concacan Inc., 1988; reproduced with permission of the Canadian Conference of Catholic Bishops) for Canadian Catholic statistics; Rev. Thomas J. Reese, S.J., for names of dioceses for which U.S. bishops were ordained; other sources as credited in particular entries.

1989 Catholic Almanac

Copyright © Our Sunday Visitor Publishing Division, Our Sunday Visitor, Inc., 1988
Published annually, with ecclesiastical permission, by Our Sunday Visitor Publishing Division, Our Sunday Visitor, Inc., 200 Noll Plaza, Huntington, Indiana 46750. Address inquiries to the Publisher.

ISBN 0-87973-259-8 (paper edition)
ISBN 0-87973-262-8 (cloth edition)
Library of Congress Catalog Card No. 73-641001
International Standard Serial Number (ISSN) 0069-1208

TABLE OF CONTENTS

Index	4-30
Special Reports	31-62
On Social Concerns: Encyclical	31-35
200th Anniversary of the American Hierarchy	35
One Canonization, Two Beatifications	36
Pope John Paul in Austria	36-37
Pope John Paul in South America	38-41
The Lefebvre Schism	42-44
Marian Year in Retrospect	44-45
Euntes in Mundum: Apostolic Letter	45-47
Magnum Baptismi Donum: Apostolic Letter to Ukrainians	47-48
Events of Medjugorje	48-49
Biblical Fundamentalism	49-51
Partners in the Mystery of Redemption: Pastoral Letter on Women	51-52
Humane and Dignified Death Act	52-54
Abortion-Related Court Decisions	54-55
School-Based Clinics: Bishops' Statement to Youth	56-57
The Many Faces of AIDS: A Gospel Response	57-59
Mass for Homosexuals	59-61
The Church and the Housing Problem	61-62
News Events (October 1987 to September 1988)	63-108
Pope John Paul in Africa	107-08
Pope John Paul II	109-11
Dates, Events in Church History	112-22
Ecumenical Councils	122-24
Popes	125-35
Canonizations	135-36
Encyclicals	137-42
Hierarchy of the Catholic Church	143-46
Synod of Bishops	145-47
Roman Curia	147-53
Cardinals	153-70
Representatives of the Holy See	170-73
Diplomats at the Vatican	173-74
U.S.-Vatican Relations	174-75
Vatican City	175-78
Doctrine of the Catholic Church	179-207
Constitution on the Church	179-82
The Pope, Teaching Authority, Collegiality	182-83
Constitution on Revelation	183-86
The Bible	186-96
Apostles and Evangelists	196-98
Fathers and Doctors	198-200
Social Doctrine	202-07
The Challenge of Peace	207-08
Liturgy	209-22
The Mass	212-15
Liturgical Developments	217-22
Sacraments	222-37
Marriage Doctrine	230-34
Church Calendar	238-50
Saints	250-60
The Mother of Jesus	261-65
Ecumenical Common Statement	264-65
Apparitions of Mary	265
Eastern Catholic Churches	266-73
Separated Eastern Churches	274-75
Eastern Ecumenism	275-76
Protestant Churches	276-81
Ecumenism	281-90
Judaism	290-91
Catholic-Jewish Relations	291-93
Islam, Non-Abrahamic Religions	293-95
Glossary	295-332
The Church in Countries	333-68
Catholic World Statistics	367
Episcopal Conferences	368-71
International Catholic Organizations	371-74
The Catholic Church in Canada	374-85
Missionaries to the Americas	385-88
Shrines and Places of Historic Interest	388-90
History, Chronology of the Church in the U.S.	391-409
Church-State Supreme Court Decisions	409-14
U.S. Hierarchy, Jurisdictions	415-24
U.S. Catholic Statistics	425-34
Cathedrals, Minor Basilicas, Chancery Offices	434-39
National Conference of Catholic Bishops, U.S. Catholic Conference	439-43
State Catholic Conferences	443-44
Biographies of American Bishops	444-69
American Bishops of the Past	470-85
Black Catholics	486-87
Hispanics	487-88
Religious, Men and Women	489-516
Secular Institutes	517-19
Secular Orders	520
Missionary Activity of the Church	520-24
Catholic Education, U.S.	525-37
Statistics	526-30
Colleges and Universities	530-35
Seminaries	535-37
Pontifical Universities, Institutes	537-39
Pontifical Academy of Sciences	540-41
Social Services	541-58
Facilities for Retired and Aged	541-51
Facilities for Handicapped	551-55
Retreats, Renewal Programs	558-64
Lay Persons and Their Apostolate	565-76
Rights and Obligations	565-66
Special Apostolates	566-68
Associations, Movements, Societies	569-76
Communications	577-93
Catholic Periodicals in U.S.	577-87
Catholic Writers' Market	589-91
Radio, Television, Theatre	592-93
Economic Justice	593-94
Honors and Awards	595-600
Deaths	600

INDEX

A

Abbacies, 144
  World Statistics, 367
Abbacy, 295
Abbess, 295
Abbey (Monastery), 319
Abbot, 295
Abelard, Peter (1140), 117
Abington v. Schempp (Prayer in Public Schools), 410
Ablution, 295
Abortion (Moral Principles), 295
  See also Life, Respect for
Abortion, Canada, Europe, 71, 78, 86
Abortion, U.S., Developments, 54-5, 72-3, 76, 77, 81, 84, 89, 92, 100, 414
  Court Rulings, 54-5, 72-3, 100
  Hyde Amendment, 54-5
  March for Life, 77
  Multifetal Births, 89
  Operation Rescue, 92, 101
  Statistics, 55
  Supreme Court Decisions, 54, 55
Abramowicz, Alfred L., Bp., 444
Absolution, 227, 295-96
  See also Penance (Penitential Celebrations)
Absolution, General, 227, 442
  U.S. Bishops' Proposal, 104
Absolution, General (Blessing), 296
Abstinence, Days of, 239
Acacius, Patriarch (484), 114
Academic Freedom, 104
Academy of American Franciscan History, 569
Acadians, see Canada, Church in
Accessory to Sin, 296
Accommodated Senses (Bible), 195
Acerra, Angelo Thomas, O.S.B., Bp., 444
Ackerman, Richard, C.S.Sp., Bp., 444
Acolyte, 229
Act of Supremacy (1533), 118
Acta Apostolicae Sedis, 177
Acta Sanctae Sedis, 177
Actors' Guild, Catholic, 592
Acts of the Apostles, 193
Actual Grace, 312
Actual Sin, 328
Acuna Cardenas, Victor, Rev., 74
Adamek, Joseph V., Bp., 444
Ad Gentes (Mission Decree), 124
Ad Limina Visit, 144
  1988 Directory, 129
Addresses of John Paul II, see John Paul II
Adjutor, St., 250
Adolescent Family Life Act, 76, 97
Adoptionism (787), 115
Adoration, 296
Adorers of the Blood of Christ, 499
Adorno Fathers (Clerics Regular Minor), 491
Adultery, 296
Advent, 238
Advent, First Sunday, Dates (1989-2012), 246
Advent Wreath, 296
Adventists, 296
Afghanistan, 333
Africa
  American Missionary Bishops, 425
  Bishops' Concerns, 66
  Cardinals, 169
  Catholic Statistics, 367
  Eastern Rite Jurisdictions, 270
  Episcopal Conferences, 371
  John Paul II Foundation for Sahel, 101
  Refugees, 91
Africa, Missionaries of, 489
Africa, Missionary Sisters of Our Lady, 499

African Missions, Society of, 489
Agape, 296
Agatha, St., 250
Agca, Mehmet Ali, see John Paul II, Biography
Age of Reason, 296
Aged, Eucharistic Fast, 310
Aged, Facilities for (U.S.), 541-51
Aggiornamento, 296
Agnes, St., 250
Agnes, Sisters of St., 499
Agnosticism, 296
Agnus Dei, 296
Agrimissio, 332
Aguilar v. Felton (Remedial Classes Decision), 413
Ahern, Patrick V., Bp., 444
Ahr, George William, Bp., 444
AIDS (Acquired Immune Deficiency Syndrome), 57-9, 65, 72, 78, 83, 89, 442
  Administrative Board Statement, USCC, 57-9, 72, 442
Akathist Hymn, 83
Alabama, 388, 394, 427, 431, 432, 436, 527, 541-42, 553, 555, 559
Alaska, 394, 429, 431, 433, 529, 559
Alb, 214
Albania, 333
  Plea for Religious Freedom, 91
Albanian Byzantines, 268
Albanian Catholic Information Center, 569
Albert the Great, St., 198
Albigensianism (1179), 117
Alcoholics, Social Services, 556
Alcoholism, National Catholic Clergy Conference, 574
Alexandrian Rite, 267
Alexian Brothers, 496
Alexis de Toqueville Society Award, 85
Alfonso Rodriguez, St., 40, 387
Alfrink, Bernard Jan, Card., 600
Algeria, 333
Alhambra, Order of, 574
Aliens, Undocumented (Illegal), Amnesty, 65, 92
All Saints, 247
All Souls, 247
Alleluia, 296
Allocution, 296
Allouez, Claude, 385
Alms, 296-97
Aloysius Gonzaga, St., 250
Alpha and Omega, 297
Alpha Sigma Nu, 569
Alphonsus Liguori, St., 198
Altar, 214, 216
  Dedication, New Rites, 220
  Relics, 214
Altar Cloth, 215
Altham, John, 385
Amand, St., 250
Ambo (Pulpit), 216
Ambrose, St., 198
Ambrosian Rite (Rites), 211
Ambrozic, Aloysius, Bp., 380
Ambry, 216
Amen, 297
America, see United States
American Benedictine Academy, 569
  Board of Catholic Missions, 77
  Catholic Correctional Chaplains Association, 569
  Catholic Historical Association, 569
  Catholic Philosophical Association, 569
  Committee on Italian Migration, 569
  Friends of the Vatican Library, 569
American College, Louvain, 485

American Heresy, 392-93
American Lutheran Church, see Lutheran Churches
Americans Against Human Suffering, 52, 54, 93
Amice, 214
Amnesty International, 78
Amos, 192
Anabaptism, 276
Analogy of Faith, 185
Anaphora (Canons, Eucharistic Prayers), 300
Anathema, 297
Anchieta, Jose de, Bl., 385
Anchorite, 297
Ancient Churches of the East, 274-75
Ancient Order of Hibernians in America, 569
Anderson, Floyd, 600
Anderson, Moses B., S.S.E., Bp., 444
Anderson, Paul F., Bp., 470
Andorra, 333
Andre Bessette, Bl., 250
  St. Joseph's Oratory, 384
Andre Grasset, Bl., 250
Andreis, Felix, 385
"Andres Bello" Catholic Univ. (Venezuela), 538
Andrew, St. (Apostle), 196
Andrew Bobola, St., 251
Andrew Corsini, St., 251
Andrew Fournet, St., 251
Andrew Kim, Paul Chong and Companions, Sts., 251
Angela Merici, St., 251
Angelic Salutation (Hail Mary), 312
Angelica, Mother, 592
Angelico, Fra (Bl. Angelico), 251
Angelicum, 539
Angell, Kenneth A., Bp., 444
Angels, 297
Angels, Guardian, 248
Angelus, 297
Anger, 297
Anglican Communion, 277
  Ecumenical Reports, Statements, 287, 288-89
  Lambeth Conference, 106
  See also Episcopal Church, U.S.
Anglican Orders, 297
Anglican-Roman Catholic Consultation U.S. (Episcopal), Dialogues, Statements, 285, 288, 289
Anglican-Roman Catholic International Commission, 287, 288, 289-90
Angola, 333, 368
Anguilla, 333
Ann (Anne), St., 249
Ann, Sisters of St., 499
Anne, Sisters of St., 499
Anne de Beaupre, St., Shrine, 384
Anne Mary Javouhey, Bl., 251
Annuario Pontificio, 177
Annulment, 235, 237
Annulments, Rota Decrees (1987), 88
Annunciation, 247
Anointing of the Sick, 223, 227-28
Anselm, St., 198
  Pontifical Athenaeum, 539
Ansgar, St., 251
Ansgar's Scandinavian Catholic League, St., 575
Anthony, St. (Abbot), 251
Anthony, St. (of Padua), 198
Anthony, St., Missionary Servants of, 499
Anthony Claret, St., 251
Anthony Daniel, St., 386
Anthony Gianelli, St., 251
Anthony House, 557
Anthony Zaccaria, St., 251

Index

Antichrist, 297
Anticlericalism (Clericalism), 303
Antigua, 333-34
Antilles, Episcopal Conference, 368
Antilles, Netherlands, 354
Antimension, 273
Antioch Program, 564
Antiochene Rite, 267-68
  in United States, 271
Antiphon, 297
Antipopes, 128-29
Anti-Poverty Grants, 64-5
Anti-Semitism, 291
  and Criticism of Israel, 68, 89
  and Passion Plays, 85
  in Italy, 89, 94
Antonelli, Ferdinando G., O.F.M., Card., 154, 168, 169
Antonianum, Pontifical Athenaeum, 539
Aparicio, Sebastian, Bl., 385
Apartheid (South Africa), 67
  See also South Africa
Apocalyptic Book, New Testament (Revelation), 194
Apocrypha, 188
Apollonia, St., 251
Apologetics, 297
Aponte Martinez, Luis, Card., 154, 168, 169
Apostasy (Apostate), 298
Apostles, 197-98
Apostles' Creed, 200
Apostleship of Prayer, 569
  Prayer Intentions (1989), 240-45
Apostleship of the Sea, 566
Apostolate, 298
  See also Laity; Lay Apostolate
Apostolate, Sisters Auxiliaries of the, 499
  Society of the Catholic, see Pallottines
Apostolate for Family Consecration, 569
Apostolates, Special, 566-68
Apostolic
  Administrator, 144
  Chamber, 153
  Constitution, 304
  Delegates, 169, 170-72
  Fathers, 198
  Nuncios, Pro-Nuncios, 170-72
  Penitentiary, 150
  Signatura, 150
Apostolic Life, Societies, 489
  Congregation for 149-50
Apostolic See (Holy See), 312
Apostolic Succession, 298
Apostolicae Curae, see Anglican Orders
Apostolicam Actuositatem (Lay Apostolate Decree), 124
Apostolos, 272
Appalachia, Catholic Committee, 524
Apparitions of the BVM, 265
  Medjugorje, 48-9, 70
Apuron, Anthony Sablan, O.F.M. Cap., Abp., 444
Aquinas, Thomas, St., see Thomas Aquinas, St.
Aquinas Medal, 597
Arab Countries, Episcopal Conference, 368
Arabian Peninsula, 334
Arabic and Islamic Studies, Pontifical Institute, 539
Arabs in Occupied Territories, 78
Aramburu, Juan Carlos, Card., 154, 168, 169
Archangel, 297
Archangels (Michael, Gabriel, Raphael), Feast, 249
Archbishop, 144
  ad Personam, 144
  Titular, 144
Archbishops, 144
  Canada, 375-76
  United States, 416-24

Archbishops
  World Statistics, 367
Archconfraternity of Christian Mothers, 569
  Holy Ghost, 569
Archdiocese, 298
Archdiocese for the Military Services Seminary Fund, 569-70
Archdioceses
  Canada, 375-76
  United States, 416-24
  World Statistics, 367
Arche (L') Communities, 372
Archeology, Pontifical Commission, 152
  Pontifical Institute, 539
Archimandrite, 295
Architecture, see Church Building
Archives, 298
Archives, Ecclesiastical, Italy, Commission, 152
Archives, Vatican II, 153
Archivists, Association of Catholic Diocesan, 570
Archpriest, 298
Argentina, 334, 368
Arianism (325), 113
Arias, David, O.A.R., Bp., 444
Arias, Oscar, Pres., Central American Peace Plan, 70, 74, 81-2
Arinze, Francis A., Card., 154-55, 169
Arizona, 388, 394, 428, 431, 433, 436, 443, 529, 542, 559
Ark of the Covenant, 298
Arkansas, 394-95, 428, 431, 433, 528, 542, 559
Arkfeld, Leo, S.V.D., Abp., 444
Arliss, Reginald, C.P., Bp., 445
Armenian Rite, 268
  in United States, 271
Arminianism, 276
Arms Control, INF Treaty, 72
Arms Race, 207, 208
Arnold Reche, Bro., Beatification, 68
Arns, Paulo E., O.F.M., Card., 155, 168, 169
Art, Byzantine, 272
Art, Liturgical (Sacred), 211
Art, Religious, 79
Artificial Insemination, 315
Arzube, Juan A., Bp., 445
Ascension (May 4, 1989), 242, 247
  Dates (1989-2012), 246
Asceticism, 298
Ash Wednesday (Feb. 8, 1989), 240, 247
  Dates (1989-2012), 246
Ashes, 298
Asia
  American Missionary Bishops, 425
  Cardinals, 169
  Catholic Statistics, 367
  Eastern Rite Jurisdictions, 269-70
  Federation of Bishops' Conferences (FABC), 93, 371
Asmara University (Ethiopia), 537
Aspergillum, 298
Aspersory, 298
Aspiration, 298
Assemblies of God, 281
Association
  for Religious and Value Issues in Counseling, 570
  for Social Economics, 570
  of Catholic Diocesan Archivists, 570
  of Catholic Trade Unionists, 570
  of Contemplative Sisters, 517
  of Marian Helpers, 570
  of Permanent Diaconate Directors, 231
  of Romanian Catholics, 570
Associations, Catholic, U.S., 569-76
Assumption, 247
Assumption, Augustinians of, 489
  Little Sisters of, 499
  of Blessed Virgin, Sisters of, 499
  Religious of, 499
Assumptionists, 489

Asteriskos, 273
Athanasian Creed, 201
Athanasius, St., 198
Atheism, 298-99
  John Paul II, on 67
  See also Non-Believers, Secretariat
Atonement, 299
Atonement, Day of (Yom Kippur), 291
Atonement, Franciscan Friars of, 489
Attila (452), 114
Attributes of God, 299
Attrition, see Contrition
Audet, Lionel, Bp., 380
Audet, Rene, Bp., 380
Audiences, Papal, 177
  See also John Paul II
Augsburg, Peace of (1555), 119
Augsburg Confession (1530), 118
Augustine, Order of St., 489
Augustine, Third Order of St., 520
Augustine of Canterbury, St., 251
Augustine of Hippo, St. (430), 114, 198
Augustinian Cloistered Nuns, 499
Augustinian Recollects, 489
Augustinian Sisters, Servants of Jesus and Mary, 499
Augustinian Volunteers, 566
Augustinians, 489
Australia, 334, 368
Austria, 334, 368
  Papal Visit, 36-7
Authority
  Encyclicals, 137
  of Councils, 122
  Papal, 182-83
Authority, Teaching, of Church (Magisterium), 182-83, 184
Autograph Letter (Chirograph), 303
Auxiliaries of Our Lady of the Cenacle, 567
Auxiliary (Titular) Bishop, 144
Avarice, 299
Ave Maria (Hail Mary), 312
Avignon Residency of Papacy, 129
Awards, Catholic, 597-600
Azores, 334

B

"Baby M" Decision, 80
  See also Surrogate Motherhood
Badin, Stephen, 385
Bafile, Corrado, Card., 155, 168, 169
Baggio, Sebastiano, Card., 155, 168, 169
Bahamas, 334
Bahrain, 334
Baker, Nelson, Rev., Canonization Process, 64
Baldachino, 299
Balearic Islands, 334
Balke, Victor, Bp., 445
Ballestrero, Anastasio Alberto, O.C.D., Card., 155, 168, 169
Baltakis, Paul Antanas, O.F.M., Bp., 445
Baltimore, Plenary Councils, 392
Bangladesh, 334-35, 368
Banks, Robert J., Bp., 445
Banneaux, 265
Baptism, 222, 223-24
  Rite of Initiation of Adults, (RCIA), 222, 224
"Baptism, Eucharist and Ministry," 68, 289
Baptism of the Lord, Feast (Jan. 9, 1989), 240, 247
Baptisms, Catholic, U.S., 432-33
  World, 367
  See also Individual Countries
Baptistery, 216
Baptists, 277
  Churches, U.S., 277-78
  Ecumenical Dialogues, U.S., 285
  International Catholic-Baptist Colloquium, 287
Baraga, Frederic, 385
Barbados, 335

Barbuda, 333-34
Barnabas, St., 196
Barnabites, 489
Barrera Case, see Wheeler v. Barrera
Bartholomew, St., 196
Bartolomea Capitania, St., 251
Baruch, 191
Basel, Council of (1431-1449), 118
Base Ecclesial Communities, 299
Basil, St., Congregation of Priests, 490
Basil the Great, St., 198-99
Basil the Great, St., Order, 489-90
Basil the Great, Srs. of the Order of St., 499
Basilian Fathers, 490
Basilian Order of St. Josaphat, 489-90
Basilian Salvatorian Fathers, 490
Basilica, 436
  St. John Lateran, 176, 247-48
  St. Mary Major, 248
  St. Peter, 176
Basilicas, Minor, U.S. and Canada, 436-37
Baudoux, Maurice, Abp., 380
Baum, William W., Card., 155, 168, 169
Beatific Vision, 299
Beatification, 299
Beatifications (1987, 1988), 36, 63, 68, 87
Beatitude, 299
Beatrice da Silva Meneses, St., 251
Beatty, Chester A., 600
Beauraing, 265
Bede the Venerable, St., 199
Beginning Experience, 570
Begley, Michael J., Bp., 445
Belgium, 335, 368
Belief, Catholic, see Doctrine, Catholic
Belisle, Gilles, Bp., 380
Belize, 335
Bellarmine, Robert, St., 200
Bellarmine Medal, 597
Beltran, Eusebius J., Bp., 445
Benedict, St. (of Nursia), 251
Benedict, St., Order of, 490
Benedict, St., Sisters of Order of, 499
Benedict XIV, Pope, Encyclicals, 137
Benedict XV, Pope, 131
  Canonizations, 135
  Encyclicals, 140-41
Benedict Joseph Labre, St., 251
Benedict the Black (il Moro), St., 251
Benedictine Congregation of Solesmes, 499
Benedictine Monks, 490
Benedictine Nuns of Primitive Observance, 499
Benedictine Sisters, 499-500
Benedictines, Olivetan, 490
Benedictines, Sylvestrine, 490
Benediction of Blessed Sacrament, 309-10
Benedictus, 299
Benedik, Fidelis, C.P., 600
Benemerenti Medal, 597
Benin, 335, 368
Bennett, William J. (Catholics in Presidents' Cabinets), 408
Berakah Award, 597
Beran, Josef, Abp., see Czechoslovakia
Beras Rojas, Octavio, Card., 155, 168, 169
Berengarius (1079), 116
Bermejo, Aloysius M., S.J., 86
Bermuda, 335
Bernadette Soubirous, St., 251
  Lourdes Apparitions, 265
Bernard of Clairvaux, St., 199
Bernard of Montjoux (or Menthon), St., 251
Bernardin, Joseph L., Card., 59-61, 65, 81, 88, 155, 168, 169
  Mass for Homosexuals, 59-61
Bernardine of Feltre, Bl., 251

Bernardine of Siena, St., 251
Bernardine Sisters, 505
Bernarding, George, S.V.D., Abp., 441, 600
Berthelet Jacques, C.S.V., Bp., 380
Bertie, Andrew Willoughby Ninian, 87
Bertoli, Paolo, Card., 155, 168, 169
Bertran, Louis, St., 385
Betancur, Pedro de San Jose, Bl., 385
Bessette, Andre, Bl., 250, 384
Bethany, Brothers of, 496
Bethany, Sisters of, 500
Bethlehem Missionaries, Society of, 490
Bethlehem Univ., Israel, 78, 82
Bethlemita Sisters, 500
Better World Movement, 567
Bevilacqua, Anthony J., Abp., 445
Bhutan, 335
Bible, 183-96
  Canons, 186-87
  Federation, 188
  First Printed (c. 1456), 118
  Inerrancy, 185
  Interpretation, 184-85, 194-96
  Pontifical Commission, 152
  Studies, 186, 195-96
  Vatican II Constitution, 183-86
  See also Tradition
Bible, Mary in, 261
Bible and Fundamentalism, 49-51
Bible Reading in Public Schools, see Church-State Decisions
Biblical Apostolate, World Federation, 188
Biblical Commission, Pontifical, 152
Biblical Fundamentalism, NCCB Statement, 49-51
Biblical Institute, Pontifical, 539
Biblical Studies, 186, 195-96
Biffi, Giacomo, Card., 155, 168, 169
Biglietto, 299
Bigotry, Racial and Religious, 76
Bilock, John M., Bp., 445
Bination, 213, 218-19
Bioethics Congress on Issues in Morality and Medicine, 90
Biographies
  Apostles, Evangelists, 196-98
  Bishops (Canadian), 380-84
  Bishops (U.S.), 444-69
  Bishops (U.S.), of Past, 470-85
  Cardinals, 154-68
  Fathers and Doctors, Church, 198-200
  John Paul II, 109-11
  See also John Paul II
  Missionaries to the Americas, 385-88
  Popes, Twentieth Century, 130-35
  Saints, 250-52
Biretta, 299
Birth Control, Catholic Teaching (Humanae Vitae), 232-34
  John Paul II on, 84
  See also Contraception
Birth Control Clinics, Programs in Schools, 56-7
Birthright, 55
Bishops, 144, 228
  and Ecumenical Councils, 122
  and Religious Orders, Relations, 91
  Collegiality, 183, 303-04
  Conferences, 368-71
  Congregation, 149
  First, see Apostles
  Nomination, 144
  Statistics, World, 367
  Synod, 64, 145-47
  Titular, 144
Bishops, Canadian, 376-77, 380-84
  Conference, 378-80
Bishops, U.S., 416-24, 444-69, 470-85
  Anniversary of Hierarchy (200th), 35
  Black, 487
  Blood Brothers, 469

Bishops, U.S.
  "The Challenge of Peace: God's Promise and Our Response," 207-08
  Committee, Secretariat for Black Catholics, 77, 486-87
  Committees, 439-40
  Conferences, 439-41
  Conferences, Court Case, 96-7
  "Economic Justice: A Pastoral Message," 593-94
  Ecumenical Affairs Committee, 283
  General Absolution, 104
  Hispanic, 487
  Humane and Dignified Death Act (Calif. Bishops' Statement), 52-4
  "Many Faces of AIDS" Statement, 57-9, 72, 442
  Meeting (1987), 441-42
  Meeting (1988), 97, 442-43
  of the Past, 470-85
  Pastoral on Women, Draft Statement, 51-2
  Retired, 469-70
  School-Based Clinics, Pro-Life Committee, 56-7
  Secretariat, Catholic-Jewish Relations, 292, 293
  Native American, 92
  See also Pelotte Donald E.
  Serving Overseas, 425, 469
  War and Peace Pastoral, 207-08
Black and Indian Mission Office, 73, 524
Black Catholics, U.S., 73, 77, 80, 84, 88, 486-87
  Bishops, 487
  First Archbishop, 84
  National Congress, Pastoral Plan, 73, 486
  National Office for, 486
  Sisters Conference, 517
  Statistics, 486
Black Death (1347-1350), 118
Blais, Leo, Bp., 380
Blanchet, Bertrand, Bp., 380
Blandina Marten, Beatification, 68
Blas Rolon, Ismael, Abp., 82, 102
Blase, St., 251
Blasphemy, 299
Blasphemy of the Spirit, 299
Blessed Sacrament, see Eucharist, Holy
Blessed Sacrament, Exposition, 309-10
Blessed Sacrament (Religious)
  and Our Lady, Religious of the Order of, 515
  Congregation of, 490
  Missionary Sisters of Most, 515
  Nuns of Perpetual Adoration, 515
  Oblate Sisters of, 515
  Religious Sisters of, 515
  Servants of, 515
  Srs. of, for Indians and Colored People, 515
  Srs. Servants of, 515
Blessed Virgin Mary, 261-64
  Annunciation, 247
  Apparitions, 265
  Assumption, 247
  Birth, 247
  First Saturday Devotion, 310
  Immaculate Conception, 248
  Immaculate Heart, 249
  Joys (Franciscan Crown), 310-11
  Purification (Presentation of the Lord), 249
  Queenship, 250
  Rosary (Devotion), 325-26
  Rosary (Feast), 249
  Solemnity, 250
  Sorrows (Feast), 249
  Visitation, 250
  See also Marian Year; Mary
Blessed Virgin Mary (Religious)
  Institute of, 500
  Sisters of Charity, 502

Index

Blessed Virgin Mary (Religious) Sisters of Presentation of, 514
Blessing, 299
Blind, Catholic Facilities, Organizations, 555, 557
Blind, International Federation for Catholic Associations, 373
Blue Army, 576
Shrine, 389
Boat, 299
Boccella, John H., T.O.R., Abp., 445
Boland, Ernest B., O.P., Bp., 445
Boland, Raymond J., Bp., 445
Bolivarian Pontifical University (Colombia), 537
Bolivia, 335, 368
Land Claims, 93-4
Papal Visit, 38-9
Bollandists (1643), 119
Bonnel, Ferdinand, S.J., 102
Bon Secours, Sisters of, 500
Bonaventure, St., 199
Bonaventure, St., Pontifical Theological Faculty, 539
Boniface, St., 251
Bonilla, Pietro, Beatification, 87
Book Clubs, Catholic, 587
Book of Common Prayer (1549), 119
Book of Kells, 115
Books, 587
Awards (1988), 599, 600
Censorship, 301-02
Index of Prohibited, 314
Liturgical, see Lectionary; Sacramentary
Books of the Bible, 188-94
Booths, Festival, 291
Borders, William D., Abp., 445
Borecky, Isidore, Bp., 380
Borromeo, Charles, St., 252
Borromeo Award, 597
Bosco, Anthony G., Bp., 445
Bosco, John, St. (Don Bosco), 75, 77, 255
Bossilkoff, Eugene, Bp., see Bulgaria
Botswana, 335-36
Papal Visit to Africa, 107-08
Boudreaux, Warren L., Bp., 445
Bourgeoys, Marguerite, St., 385
Boy Scouts, 568
Boys Town (Nebraska), 552
Braga Rite, (Rites), 211
Brandsma, Titus, Bl., 258
Brazil, 336, 368
Social Programs, 74
Brebeuf, John de, St., 386
Breitenbeck, Joseph M., Bp., 445
Brendan, St., 251
Brennan, Francis (U.S. Cardinals), 170, 471
Brennan, Peter J. (Catholics in Presidents' Cabinets), 408
Brennan, William (Catholics in Supreme Court), 409
Brent Award, 597
Breviary, 210
Bridget (Birgitta), St. (of Sweden), 251
Bridget (Brigid), St. (of Ireland), 251
Brief, Apostolic, 299-300
Brigid, Congregation of St., 500
Brigittine Monks, 490
Brigittine Sisters, 500
British Honduras, see Belize
Brizgys, Vincas, Bp., 445
Broderick, Edwin B., Bp., 446
Brom, Robert H., Bp., 446
Brothers, 489
World Statistics, 367
Brothers, U.S., 496-97
National Assembly, 517
Statistics, 425-29
Brown, Charles A., M.M., Bp., 446
Brown, Robert McAfee, Rev., 68
Brunei, 336
Brunini, Joseph B., Bp., 446
Bruno, St., 251
Brust, Leo J., Bp., 446

Brzana, Stanislaus, Bp., 446
Buddhism, 294-95
Buechlein, Daniel M., O.S.B., Bp., 446
Bulgaria, 336, 368
Appointment of Bishop, 99
Bulgarian Catholics (Byzantine Rite), 268
Bull, Bulla, Bullarium, 300
Bull of Demarcation (1493), 118
Bullock, William H., Bp., 446
Bureau of Catholic Indian Missions, 524
Burial, Ecclesiastical, 300
See also Funeral Rites
Burke, Austin-Emile, Bp., 380
Burke, James C., O.P., Bp., 446
Burkina Faso (Upper Volta), 336, 368
Burma, 336, 368-69
Isolated Catholics, 82
Burse, 215
Burundi, 337, 369
Religious Rights, 70, 74
Violence, 103
Buswell, Charles A., Bp., 446
Butler, Pierce (Catholics in Supreme Court), 409
Byelorussians, 268, 271
Byrne, James J., Abp., 446
Byzantine Rite (Catholic), 268-69
in U.S., 270-71
Liturgy, Calendar, Features, Vestments, 271-73

C

Cabrini, Mother (St. Frances Xavier Cabrini), 253
Cabrini Sisters, (Sacred Heart Missionary Sisters), 515
Caesar, Raymond R., S.V.D., 472
Cajetan, St., 251
Calabria, Giovanni, Beatification, 87
Calendar, Church, 238-46
Byzantine, 271-72
Gregorian (1582), 119
Califano, Joseph A. (Catholics in Presidents' Cabinets), 408
California, 388-89, 395, 429, 431, 433, 436, 443, 529, 535, 542, 551, 553, 559
Abortion Ruling, 2
Hispanics and Sects, 97
Humane and Dignified Death Act, 52-4, 89, 93
Calix Society, 570
Callistus I, St., 251
Callo, Marcel, Beatification, 63
Calumny, 300
Calvary, 300
Calvin, John, 277
Camacho, Tomas Aguon, Bp., 446
Camaldolese Congregation, 490
Camaldolese Hermits, 490
Cambodia (Kampuchea), 66, 94, 337, 369
Cambodian Catholics, 94
Camerlengo, (Chamberlain), 302
Cameroon, 336, 369
Camillian Fathers and Brothers, 490
Camillus de Lellis, St., 251-52
Camp Fire, Inc., 568
Campaign for Human Development, 429
Anti-Poverty Grants, 64-5
Campbell, Colin, Bp., 380
Campbell, James (Catholics in Presidents' Cabinets), 408
Campinas, University of (Brazil), 537
Campion, Edmund, St., 253
Campion Award, 597
Campus Ministry, 535
Canada, 337, 374-85
Abortion Legislation, 78, 102
Agriculture, 70
Basilicas, 437
Bishops (Biographies) 380-84
Bishops' Conference, 379-80
Catholic Press Statistics, 577
Catholic Publications, 384-85
Eastern Rite Catholics, 379

Canada
Homeless, 74
Shrines, 384
Statistics, 337, 377-79
Universities, Catholic, 537
Canadian Conference of Catholic Bishops, 379-80
Canary Islands, 337
Cancer de Barbastro, Louis, 386
Cancer Homes and Hospitals, 556
Candle, Paschal, 322
Candlemas Day (Presentation), 249-50
Candles, 216
Canestri, Giovanni, Card., 155, 168, 169
Canon, 300
of Bible, 186-87, 300
of Mass, (Eucharistic Prayer), 213, 218, 221, 300
Canon Law, Code of, 300
Authentic Interpretation, Commission, 151
Canon Law, Oriental Code, Commission for Revision, 152
Canon Law Society of America, 65, 570
Canonization, 300
Canonizations (Leo XIII to Present), 135-37
See also John Paul II
Canons Regular of Holy Cross (Crosier Fathers), 491
Canons Regular of Premontre (Premonstratensians), 495
Canticle, 300
Cap-de-la-Madeleine, Shrine, 384
Cape Verde, 337
Capital Punishment, 300
Capital Sins, 300-01
Capitalism and Marxism, Vatican Survey, 86
Cappa Magna, 215
Caprio, Giuseppe, Card., 155-56, 169
Capuchin Sisters of St. Clare, 505
Capuchins, 492
CARA, 566
Carberry, John, Card., 156, 168, 169
Cardinal, 153
Bishops, 154, 168
Deacons, 154, 169
in Pectore (Petto), 154
Patriarch, 154
Priests, 154, 168
Cardinal Gibbons Award, 597
Cardinal Mindszenty Foundation, 570
Cardinal Patrick O'Boyle Award, 597
Cardinal Spellman Award, 597
Cardinal Virtues, 301
Cardinal Wright Award, 597
Cardinals, 153-70
American, 169-70
Biographies, 154-68
Categories, 154, 168-69
Chamberlain, 302
College, 153-54
Council of, 152
Dean, 154
Geographical Distribution, 169
New, 91, 95
Retirement Age, 153-54
Seniority (Categories), 168-69
Voting Eligibility, 169
Carew, William A., Abp., 380
Caritas, 519
Caritas Christi, 518
Caritas Internationalis, 73, 372
Carlson, Robert J., Bp., 446
Carmel, see Mt. Carmel
Carmel Community, 500
Carmelite Missionaries of St. Theresa, 500
Carmelite Nuns, Discalced, 500-01
Carmelite Nuns of Ancient Observance, 501
Carmelite Sisters, 501
for Aged and Infirm, 501
of Charity, 501

Carmelite Sisters
  of Corpus Christi, 501
  of St. Therese of the Infant Jesus, 501
  of the Divine Heart of Jesus, 501
  of the Sacred Heart, 501
Carmelites (Men), 490-91
Carmelites, Secular Orders, 520
Carney, James F., Abp., 380
Carolines and Marshalls, The, 337
Carpatho-Russians (Ruthenians), 268, 270
Carpino, Francesco, Card., 156, 168, 169
Carroll, Beverly, 77, 80
Carroll, Charles, 387
Carroll, John, Bp., 387, 472
Carroll, Mark K., Bp., 472
Carroll Center for the Blind, 557
Carter, Alexander, Bp., 380
Carter, Gerald Emmett, Card., 156, 168, 169
Carter, Samuel E., Abp., 94
Carthusians, Order of, 491
Casaroli, Agostino, Card., 80, 95, 168, 169
Casey, Luis Morgan, Bp., 446
Casimir, St., 252
Casimir, Sisters of St., 501
Casoria, Giuseppe, Card., 156, 169
Cassata, John J. Bp., 446
Cassian, St., 252
Cassock, 215
Castel Gandolfo, 175
Castillo, John de, St., 40, 386
Castillo Lara, Rosalio Jose, Card., 156, 169
Castro, Fidel, Meeting with Cardinal O'Connor, 90
  See also Cuba
Catacombs, 301
Catala, Magin, 386
Catechesis, 301
Catechetics (Bishops' Synod), 145
Catechism, 301
Catechism Commission, 152
Catechisms, Development of, 64
Catechists, Role in Evangelization, 71
  World Statistics, 367
Catechumen, 301
  See also Baptism
Catechumenate, 224
Catechumens, Mass, 212
Catechumens, Oil of, 320
Catharism, **see** Manichaeism
Cathedra, 301
  See also Ex Cathedra
Cathedral, 434
Cathedrals, U.S., 434-36
Cathedraticum, 301
Catherine Labouré, St., 252
  Miraculous Medal, 265
Catherine of Bologna, St., 252
Catherine of Siena, St., 199
Catholic, 301
  Action, **see** Lay Apostolate
  Actors' Guild of America, 592
  Aid Association, 570
  Alumni Clubs International, 570
  Associations, 569-76
  Awards, 597-600
  Baptisms, **see** Baptisms
  Belief, **see** Doctrine, Catholic
  Biblical Assn. of America, 570
  Book Publishers Association, 570
  Center, 570
  Central Union, 566
  Charities, USA, 541
  Chronology in U.S., 394-408
  Church Extension Society, 524
  Colleges, U.S., 530-35
  Commission on Intellectual and Cultural Affairs, 570
  Communications Foundation, 593
  Conferences, State, 443-44
  Conferences, U.S., 439-43
  Converts, American, **see** Converts
  Daughters of the Americas, 101, 570

Catholic
  Daughters of the Americas, Junior, 568
  Dictionary, **see** Glossary
  Doctrine, **see** Doctrine, Catholic
  Eastern Churches, 266-73
  Education, **see** Education, Catholic
  Family Life Insurance, 570
  Forester Youth Program, 568
  Golden Age, 570
  Guardian Society, 570
  Health Association, 97, 541
  Hierarchy, **see** Hierarchy
  History in the U.S., 391-409
  Home Bureau for Dependent Children, 570
  Hospitals, **see** Hospitals, Catholic
  Interracial Council of New York, 570
  Knights of America, 570
  Knights of Ohio, 570
  Kolping Society, 570
  Laity, National Council, 574
  League, 570
  League for Religious and Civil Rights, 576
  Library Association, 570
  Medical Mission Board, 566
  Men, National Council of, 574
  Missions, 520-24
  Movement for Intellectual and Cultural Affairs, 566
  Near East Welfare Association, 570
  Negro-American Mission Board, 524
  News Agencies, 588
  One Parent Organization, 570
  Order of Foresters, 570-71
  Organizations (U.S.), 569-76
  Organizations, International, 371-74
  Pamphlet Society, 571
  Peace Fellowship, 571
  Periodicals, Foreign, 587-88
  Periodicals, U.S., 578-87
  Population, **see** Statistics, Catholic
  Press, **see** Press, Catholic
  Press Association, 93, 571
  Press Month, 80
  Radio Programs, U.S., 592
  Relief Services, 94, 105, 443
  Schools, **see** Schools, Catholic
  Social Doctrine, 31-5, 202-07
  Social Service Facilities, World, 367
  Social Services, U.S., 541-58
  Societies in U.S., 569-76
  Statistics, **see** Statistics, Catholic
  Supreme Court Justices, 408
  Telecommunications Network of America, 64, 593
  Television Network, 593
  Television Programs, 592, 593
  Theatre, U.S., 592
  Theological Society of America, 571
  Universities, Pontifical, 537-38
  Universities, U.S., 530-35
  University of America, 64, 531, 538, 597
  War Veterans, 571
  Women, National Council of, 574
  Worker Movement, 69, 571
  Workman, 571
  Writers' Market, 589-91
  Youth Organization (CYO), 568
  Youth Organizations, 568-69
  See also Church, Catholic
Catholic Evangelization, 77
Catholic-Jewish Relations, 291-94
  and Criticism of Israel, 89
  Commission (Vatican), 152, 292
Catholic-Moslem Relations, Commission, 152
Catholic-Orthodox Relations
  Communion-Confirmation Problem, 68-9
  Declarations of Popes, Other Prelates, 285, 286
  Dialogues, U.S., 288, 289

Catholic-Orthodox Relations
  International Theological Commission, 68-9, 95-6, 288
  Statement (1988), 95-6
    See also Orthodox Churches, Eastern
Catholics
  in Presidents' Cabinets, U.S., 408
  in Supreme Court, U.S., 409
  in Statuary Hall, 408
  Statistics, **see** Statistics
Catholics, Lapsed, 67, 81
Catholics United for Spiritual Action, 571
Catholics United for the Faith, 571
Catoir, John T., Rev., 105
Causality, **see** Existence of God
Causes of Saints, Congregation, 149
Cavasoz, Lauro, 105, 408
Cayenne, **see** French Guiana
Cayman Islands, 337
Cé, Marco, Card., 156, 168, 169
Cecilia, St., 252
Cecilia Medal, 597
CELAM (Latin American Bishops' Conference), 81-2, 271
Celebret, 301
Celebrezze, Anthony (Catholics in Presidents' Cabinets), 408
Celibacy, 301
  John Paul II on, 83
Cenacle, 301
Cenacle, Congregation of Our Lady of Retreat in the, 501
Cenobitic Life (318), 113
Censer, 301
Censorship of Books, 301-02
Censures, 302
Center for Applied Research in the Apostolate, (CARA), 566
Center of Concern, 568
Central African Republic, 337, 369
Central America
  American Missionary Bishops, 425
  Cardinals, 169
  Episcopal Conferences, 371
  FBI Probe, 80
  Peace Plan, 70, 74, 81-2
    See also El Salvador; Guatemala; Nicaragua
Central Association of the Miraculous Medal, 571
Central Statistics Office, 153, 177
Ceremonies, Master of, 302
Cerularius, Michael (1043-1059), 116
Ceuta, 337-38
Ceylon, **see** Sri Lanka
Chabanel, Noel, St., 386
Chad, 338, 369
Chair of Peter (Feast), 246
Chalcedon, Council of (451), 114, 123
Chaldean Rite, 269
  in U.S., 271
Chalice, 215
"The Challenge of Peace: God's Promise and Our Response" (U.S. Bishops' Pastoral), 207-08
Chamber, Apostolic, 153
Chamberlain, 302
Chancellor, 302
Chancery, 302
Chancery Offices, U.S., 437-39
Chant, Gregorian, 210-11
Chapel, 302
Chaplain, 302
Chaplains, National Association of Catholic, 541
Chaplains Aid Association, 571
Chaplet, 302
Chapter, 302
Chaput, Charles J., O.F.M. Cap., Bp., 446
Charbonneau, Paul E., Bp., 380
Charismatic Renewal, Catholic, 93, 302
Charisms, 302-03
Charities, Catholic National Conference, **see** Charities USA

Index

Charities, Pontifical Council, Cor Unum, 151
Charities USA, Catholic, 541
Charity, 303
　Heroic Act, 312
Charity, Brothers of, 99, 496
　Institute of (Rosminians), 495
　Servants of, 491
Charity, Daughters of, Divine, 501
Charity, Sisters of (List), 501-02
Charles, Missionaries of St., Congregation, 494
Charles Borromeo, St., 252
Charles Borromeo, St., Missionary Sisters of, 503
Charles Garnier, St., 386
Charles Lwanga and Comps., Sts. (Uganda Martyrs), 252
Charles of Sezze, St., 252
Chastity, 303
　Texas Bishops' Pastoral, 76
Chasuble, 214
Chasuble-Alb, 214
Chatham, Josiah G., Msgr., 600
Chaumonot, Pierre J., 386
Chavez, Cesar, 105
Chavez, Gilbert, Bp., 446
Chedid, John, Bp., 446
Cherubim (Angels), 297
Chiang Ching-Kuo, Pres., 600
Chiasson, Donat, Abp., 380
Child Jesus, Sisters of the Poor, 503
Children, Mass for, 219
Chile, 106, 338, 368
　Protests, 94
　Vicariate of Solidarity, 73, 86, 106
Chimy, Jerome, Bp., 380
China, 66, 74, 77, 85, 97-8, 106, 338
　Bishops Freed, 77
　Dissident Church, 74, 85
　Religious Worship, 66
Chinese Rites (1704), 119-20
Chirograph, 303
Choirs of Angels (Angels), 297
Chretienne, Sisters of Ste., 503
Chrism, see Oils, Holy
Christ, 303
　Annunciation, 247
　Ascension, 247
　Baptism, 247
　Circumcision (Solemnity of Mary), 250
　Epiphany (Theophany), 248
　in Gospels, 193
　Kingship, 247
　Mystical Body, 180-81
　Nativity (Christmas), 247
　Passion, 249
　　See Stations of the Cross
　Presentation, 249
　Resurrection (Easter), 248
　Sacred Heart, 250
　Seven Last Words, 328
　Transfiguration, 250
　Virgin Birth, 261
Christ, Society of, 491
Christ, United Church of, 280
Christ Child Society, National, 568
Christ the King (Feast) (Nov. 26, 1989), 245, 247
Christ the King, Rural Parish Workers, 519
Christ the King, Sister Servants, 503
Christ the King, Sisters of St. Francis, 507
Christian, see Christians
Christian Brothers, 496
Christian Charity, Franciscan Sisters of, 506
　Sisters of, 502
Christian Church, U.S. (Disciples of Christ), 280
　Ecumenical Dialogues, 285, 289
Christian Culture Award, 597
Christian Doctrine, Confraternity of, 530
Christian Doctrine, Sisters of Our Lady, 503
Christian Education, Religious of, 503

Christian Family Movement, 566
Christian Initiation (Baptism), 223-24
Christian Instruction, Brothers of, 496
Christian-Jewish Relations, National Workshop, 68
Christian Life Communities, 566-67
Christian-Moslem Tension, South Africa, 94
Christian Schools, Brothers, 496
Christian Science, 303
Christian Students, Young, 569
Christian Unity, 75
Christian Unity, Week of Prayer for, 75, 76, 332
　See also Ecumenism
Christian Unity Secretariat, 151
Christian Witness, 75, 332
Christianity, 303
Christianity and Social Progress (Social Doctrine), 202
Christians, 303
Christians, Baptized, Reception into Church, 224
Christmas, 247
　Message, John Paul II, 72
Christmas Nativity Scenes, see Church-State Decisions
Christmas Season, 238
Christopher, St., 252
Christopher Movement, 571
　Awards, 600
　Radio-TV Work, 592
Christos (Christ), 303
Christus Dominus, 124
Chronicles (Books of Bible), 189
Chronology
　Church History, 112-22
　Church in U.S., 394-408
　Ecumenical Councils, 122-24
　Old Testament, 192
　Popes, 125-28
　U.S. Episcopates, 416-24
Chrysostom, John, St., 198
Church, 303
Church (Catholic), 179-82
　and Unity, see Ecumenism
　and Homeless, 61-2
　and World Council of Churches, 283-84, 286-87
　Apostolic Succession, 298
　Authority (Magisterium), 182-83, 184
　Belief, see Doctrine
　Constitution on (Vatican II), 122, 179-82, 182-83, 212, 222-23, 228-29, 302-03, 310, 326
　Creeds, 200-01
　Doctrine, 179-207
　Eastern, 266-73
　Hierarchy, 143-46
　History, Dates, 112-22
　in Canada, 374-85
　in Countries of the World, 333-68
　　See also Individual Countries
　in Modern World, Constitution (Vatican II), 124, 202-04, 205-07, 230-31
　in U.S., 391 ff
　Infallibility, 182
　Languages, 317
　Liturgy, see Liturgy
　Marriage Doctrine, Laws, see Marriage
　Ministries, 229
　Moral Obligations, 201-02
　Mystery of, 179-80
　Politics and IRS, 101
　Precepts, 201-02
　Prophetic Office, 180-81
　Relations with Other Churches, see Ecumenism; Catholic-Jewish Relations
　Rites, 211-12, 267-70
　Sacraments, 222-34
　Salvation, 326
　Social Doctrine, 202-07
　Statistics, see Statistics
　Treasury, 332
　Year (Calendar), 238-46

Church, Daughters of the, 503
Church and State (U.S.)
　Court Decisions, 409-14
　Legal Status of Catholic Education, 525
　Wall of Separation, 414
Church Building, 216-17
Church of England, Embryo Research, 82
Churches, Eastern (Separated), 274-75
Churches, National Council, 69, 76, 284
Churches, Orthodox, 274
Churches, Protestant, in U.S., 277-81
Churches, U.S., Membership Statistics, 104-05
Churches, World Council, see World Council of Churches
Ciappi, Mario Luigi, O.P., Card., 156-57, 169
Ciborium, 215
Cimichella, Andre, O.S.M., Bp., 380
Cincture, 214
Circumcision, 303
　Feast, see Solemnity of Mary
Circumincession, 303
Cistercian Nuns, 503
Cistercian Nuns of Strict Observance, 503
Cistercians, Order of (Men), 491
Cistercians of the Strict Observance (Trappists), 491
Citizens for Educational Freedom, 571
Civardi, Ernesto, Card., 157, 169
Civil Rights League, Catholic, 576
Civil Rights Restoration Act, U.S., 85
Civiletti, Benjamin (Catholics in Presidents' Cabinets), 408
Clairvaux Abbey (1115), 116
Clancy, Edward Bede, Card., 157, 168, 169
Clare, St., 252
　Patroness of Television, 80, 259
Clare, St., Order of, see Poor Clare Nuns, Franciscan
Clare, St., Sisters of, 503
Claretians, 491
Clark, Mark, Gen.(U.S.-Vatican Relations), 175
Clark, Matthew H., Bp., 446
Clarke, Maura, M.M., Sr., 78
Clavel Mendez, Tomas Albert, Abp., 447
Claver, Peter, St., 386
Clement Hofbauer, St., 252
Clement I, St., 252
Clement XIII, Pope, Encyclicals, 137-38
Clement XIV, Pope, Encyclicals, 138
Clergy, 303
　Congregation, 149
Clergy, Byzantine, 273
Clergy, Congr. of Our Lady Help of the, 503
Clergy, Servants of Our Lady Queen of, 503
Clericalism, 303
Clerics of St. Viator, 496
Clerics Regular, Congregation of (Theatines), 496
Clerics Regular Minor, 491
Clerics Regular of St. Paul (Barnabites), 489
Clinch, Harry A., Bp., 447
Cloister, 303
Clune, Robert B., Bp., 380
Cluny Abbey (910), 116
Coadjutor, Archbishop, Bishop, 144
Code, 303
　See also Canon Law
Coderre, Gerard M., Bp., 380
Coggin, Walter A., O.S.B., Abbot, 447
Cohill, John E., S.V.D., Bp., 447
Coins, Vatican, 176
College of Cardinals, 153-68
Colleges, Catholic, U.S., 530-35

Colleges and Universities, Association of Catholic, 93
Collegiality, 183, 303-04
  See also Synod of Bishops
Collettines (Franciscan Poor Clare Nuns), 506
Colombia, 338-39, 369
Colombo, Giovanni, Card., 157, 168, 169
Colorado, 395, 428, 431, 433, 436, 443, 529, 535, 542, 551, 559-60
Colors, Liturgical, 214-15
Colossians, 194
Columba, St., 252
Columban, St., 252
Columban, St., Missionary Sisters, 503
Columban, St., Society of, 491
Columbian Squires, 568
Columbus, Knights of, **see** Knights of Columbus
Comber, John W., M.M., Bp., 447
Comboni Missionaries of the Sacred Heart (Verona Fathers), 491
Comboni Missionary Sisters (Missionary Srs. of Verona), 503
Comillas, Pontifical Univ. (Spain), 538
Commandments of God, 201
Commissariat of the Holy Land, 304
Commission for Catholic Missions among Colored and Indians, 524
Commissions, Roman Curia, 151-52
  Reorganization, 147
Common of Mass, 213
Communications, U.S., 577-93
  See also Press, Catholic
Communications Commission, Papal, 151
Communion, Holy (Holy Eucharist), 223, 225-26
  Fast before Reception, 310
  First, and First Confession, 225
  Guidelines for Reception, 221
  In-Hand Reception, 220
  Intinction, 316
  Ministers, Special, 219, 221
  Reception Outside of Mass, 226
  Reception More than Once a Day, 226
  under Forms of Bread and Wine, 226
  Viaticum, 332
  See also Eucharist, Holy
Communion of Mass, 213
Communion of Saints, 304
Communione of the Faithful, 304
"Communione e Liberazione" Fraternity, 372
Communism, 304
  Ostpolitik, 321
"Communist Manifesto" (1848), 120
Community (Social Doctrine), 202-04
Comoros, 339
Company of Mary, 511
Company of Mary, Little, 511
Company of St. Paul, 518
Company of St. Ursula, 518
Compostela Award, 597
Comunidades de Base, 299
Concelebration, 304
  Inter-Ritual, 219
Concerts in Churches, 72, 222
Conciliarists (1438-45), 118
Conclave (Papal Election), 321-22
Concord, Formula of (1577), 119
Concordance, Biblical, 304
Concordat, 304
  of Worms (1122), 117
Concordat, Vatican-Italy, 178
Concupiscence, 304
Conewega Chapel (Penn., 1741), 405
Conference of Major Superiors of Men in U.S., 104, 517
Confession (Penance), 223, 226-27, 304
  First, and First Communion, 225
  Frequent, 227

Confession (Penance)
  Individual, after General Absolution, 227
  Revised Rite, 219, 226-27
  Seal, 327
  Synod of Bishops' Theme, 145
  See also General Absolution; Penance
Confessional, 216-17
Confessor, 304
Confirmation, 223, 224-25
  Sponsor, 225
Confraternity, 304
  of the Immaculate Conception, 571
Confraternity Home Study Services, 571
Confraternity of Catholic Clergy, 571
Confraternity of Christian Doctrine, 530
Confucianism, 295
Congo, 339, 369
Congregationalists, 277
Congregations, Curial, 148-50
  Reorganization, 147
Congresses, Eucharistic, 308-09
Connare, William G., Bp., 447
Connecticut, 389, 395, 425, 430, 432, 443, 526, 536, 542, 551, 553, 560
Connery, John R., S.J., 600
Connolly, Thomas A., Abp., 447
Connolly, Thomas J., Bp., 447
Connor, John (Catholics in Presidents' Cabinets), 408
Connors, Ronald G., C.SS.R., Bp., 447
Conrad of Parzham, St., 252
Conscience, 304
  Examination of, 304
Conscientious Objectors, 206, 208
Consecrated Life, Institutes, 489
Consecration (Dedication) of Church, 306
Consecration of the Mass, 213
Consistory, 304
Consolata Missionary Sisters, 503
Consolata Society for Foreign Missions, 491
Consortium Perfectae Caritatis, 517
Constance, Council (1414-18), 118, 123
Constantinople I, Council (381), 114, 123
Constantinople II, Council (553), 114, 123
Constantinople III, Council (680-81), 115, 123
Constantinople IV, Council (869-70), 116, 123
Constantinople, Fall of (1453), 118
Constitution, 304
Consubstantiation, 304
Consultation on Church Union, 284
Contardo Ferrini, Bl., 252
Contemplative Institutes (Religious), 489
Contraception, 304-05
  See also *Humanae Vitae*
Contraceptives, Availability in Schools (School-Based Clinics), 56-7
Contrition, 305
Contumely, 305
Conventuals (Franciscans), 492
Conversion of St. Paul (Feast), 247
Convert Movement Our Apostolate, 571
Converts (Rite of Christian Initiation), 224
Converts (U.S.), 432-33
Cook Islands, 339
Cooke, Terence J. (U. S. Cardinals), 170, 472
Cooney, Patrick R., Bp., 447
Cooray, Thomas B., O.M.I., Card., 157, 168, 169
Cope, 215
Coptic Orthodox Pope Shenouda III — Paul VI Declaration, 286
Copts, Catholic, 267
Cor Unum, 151

Cordeiro, Joseph, Card., 157, 168, 169
Corinthians, 193-94
Cornelius, St., 252
Corporal, 215
Corporal Works of Mercy, 305
Corporate Responsibility, Interfaith Center, 77
Corpus Christi (May 28, 1989), 242, 247
  John Paul II Observance, 95
Corrada del Rio, Alvaro, S.J., Bp., 447
Corripio Ahumada, Ernesto, Card., 157, 168, 169
Coscia, Benedict D., O.F.M., Bp., 447
Cosgrove, John E., 600
Cosgrove, William M., Bp., 447
Cosmas and Damian, Sts., 252
Costa Rica, 339, 369
Costello, Thomas J., Bp., 447
Côte d'Ivoire (Ivory Coast), 349, 369
Cotey, Arnold R., S.D.S., Bp., 447
Couderc, St. Therese, 258
Council, Second Vatican, 124
  and Mary, 261
  Excerpts from Documents, 122, 179-82, 182-83, 183-86, 202-04, 205-07, 209-11, 212, 222-23, 228-29, 230-31, 238, 266-67, 281-82, 291, 294, 302-03, 306, 310, 326, 517-18
Council of Europe, 83
Council of European Bishops, 371
Councils of the Church (Catholic)
  Ecumenical, 122-24
  Plenary, 305
  Plenary, Baltimore, 392
  Provincial, 305
Counsels, Evangelical, 305
Counter-Reformation, 305
Countries, Church in, 333-68
  See also Individual Countries
Countries, Patrons, 259-60
Couple to Couple League, 231
Court, Supreme, **see** Supreme Court, U.S.
Cousins, William E., Abp., 447
  Death, 600
Couture, Jean-Guy, Bp., 380
Couture, Maurice, R.S.V., Bp., 380
Couturier, Gerard, Bp., 380
Covenant, 305
Covenant, Old, **see** Revelation, Constitution
Covenant House, 557
  Toll Free Hot Line, 69
Covetousness (Avarice), 299
Creation, 305
Creator, 305
Creature, 305
Creed of the Mass (Nicene), 200-01, 213
Creeds of the Church, 200-01
Cremation, 305
Crete, **see** Greece
Crib, 305
Crispin and Crispinian, Sts., 252
Crispin of Viterbo, St. 252
Criticism, Biblical, 195
Croatians (Byzantine Rite), 269
Cromwell, Oliver (1649), 119
Cronin, Daniel A., Bp., 447
Crosier, 305
Crosier Fathers, 491
Cross
  Pectoral, 322
  Sign of the, 328
  Stations of the, 329-30
  Triumph (Exaltation), 250
Cross, Canons Regular of Holy, 491
  Congregation of Holy (Brothers), 496
  Congregation of Holy (Priests), 491
  Daughters of, 503
  Sisters, Lovers of the Holy, 503
  Sisters of the Holy, 503
Cross and Passion, Sisters of the, 503
Croteau, Denis, O.M.I., Bp., 380
Crowley, Joseph R., Bp., 447
Crowley, Leonard P., Bp., 380
Crown, Franciscan, 310-11

Index

Crowned Shrine, 328
Crucifix, 217
Crucifix, Stations (Stations of the Cross), 330
Cruets, 217
Crusades (1097-1099), 116
Crypt, 305
Cuba, 77, 86, 90, 103, 106, 339, 369
  Changes in, 86
  Emigration, Bishops' Statement, 77
  Visit of Cardinal O'Connor, 90
Cult of Saints, 326
Culture, 67
Culture, Pontifical Council, 75, 152
Cum Gravissima, **see** Cardinals, College
Cummins, John S., Bp., 447
Cura Animarum, 305
Curacao, **see** Netherlands Antilles
Curia, 305-06
Curia, Roman, 147-53
  Internationalization, 153
  Reform, 95, 147-48
Curran, Charles E., Rev., 88, 93
Cursillo Movement, 567
Curtis, Walter W., Bp., 447-48
Curtiss, Elden F., Bp., 448
Cushing, Richard J. (U.S. Cardinals), 170, 473
Custos, 306
Cyprian, St., 252
Cyprus, 339
Cyril and Methodius, Sts., 252

See also Czechoslovakia
Cyril and Methodius, Srs. of Sts., 503
Cyril of Alexandria, St., 199
Cyril of Jerusalem, St., 199
Czech Catholic Union of Texas, 571
Czechoslovakia, 63, 78, 86, 90, 91, 94, 97, 340-41
  Bishops, New, 91, 97
  Religious Freedom Petition, Protests, 78, 86, 94
  Women Religious, 90
Czestochowa, Our Lady of, Shrine (Pa.), 390

D

Daciuk, Myron, O.S.B.M., Bp., 381
Dadaglio, Luigi, Card., 68, 157, 169
Dahomey, **see** Benin
Daily, Thomas V., Bp., 448
Dalmatic, 214
Dalmau, Eduardo, Bp., 600
Daly, Cahal, Bp., 98
Daly, James, Bp., 448
Damasus I, St., 252
Damian, St. (Sts. Cosmas and Damian), 252
Damien, Father (Joseph de Veuster) (Hawaii, 1873), 397
Damien-Dutton Society, 571
  Award, 597
Dancing and Worship, 220
Danglmayr, Augustine, Bp., 448
Daniel, 191
Daniel, Anthony, St., 386
Danneels, Godfried, Card., 157, 168, 169
D'Antonio, Nicholas, O.F.M., Bp., 448
D'Arcy, John M., Bp., 448
Darmojuwono, Justin, Card., 157, 168, 169
Darwin, Charles (1882), 121
Das Kapital (1867), 121
Dates, **see** Chronology
D'Aubisson, Roberto, 70
Daughters of Isabella, 571
Daughters of Our Lady of Fatima, 519
Daughters of St. Paul, 513
David, **see** Historical Books of Bible
David, St., 252
Davis, James P., Abp., 473, 600
Day, Dennis, 600
Day of Atonement, 291
Deacon, 228-29
Deaconess, 307
Deacons, 228-29

Deacons, First Seven, 229
Deacons, Permanent, 77, 228, 229-30
  United States, 229-30, 425-29
  World Statistics, 367
Dead, Masses for, 214
Dead Sea Scrolls, 188
Deaf, 551, 557-58
  Facilities for, 551
Dean, 307
Dean of College of Cardinals, 154
De Araujo Sales, Eugenio, Card., 165, 168, 169
Dearden, John F., Card., 424, 440, 473, 600
Death Act, California, 52-4, 89
Death of God, **see** Atheism
Death Penalty, **see** Capital Punishment
Deaths (September, 1987 to September, 1988), 600
Debt, International, 38
Decalogue (Ten Commandments), 201
Decision, Apostolic, 306
Declaration, 306
Decosse, Aime, Bp., 381
Decourtray, Albert, Card., 157, 168, 169
Decree, 306
Decree of Nullity (Annulment), 88, 235, 237
Decretals, False (847-852), 115
Dedication of a Church, 306
Dedication of Basilica of St. Mary Major, 248
  of Lateran Basilica, 247-48
Defensor Pacis (1324), 117
De Furstenberg, Maximilien, Card., 157, 168, 169
Dei Verbum (Divine Revelation Constitution), 124, 183-86, 331
Deism, 306
Deksnys, Antanas L., Bp., 448
Delaquis, Noel, Bp., 381
Delaney, Joseph P., Bp., 448
De La Salle Medal, Manhattan, 598
Delaware, 395-96, 426, 430, 432, 526, 542, 551, 560
Delegates, Apostolic, **see** Apostolic Delegates
Delta Epsilon Sigma, 569
De Lubac, Henri, S.J., Card., 157-58, 169
Democrats, Convention, 100-01
Democrats, Platform, 93
De Mojana di Cologna, Angelo, Fra, 600
Dempsey, Michael J., O.P., Bp., 448
Denis, St., 252
Denmark, 341
Denning, Joseph P., Bp., 448
De Palma, Joseph A., S.C.J., Bp., 448
De Paoli, Ambrose, Abp., 448
De Porres, Martin, St., 387
De Rojas, Simon, Canonization, 99
De Roo, Remi J., Bp., 381
DeSales, Francis, St., 199
DeSales Secular Institute, 518
De Simone, Louis, A., Bp., 448
'Deskur, Andrzej Marie, Card., 158, 169
De Smet, Pierre, 386
Despair, 306
Despatie, Roger A., Bp., 381
Detraction, 306
Deusto, Catholic University (Spain), 538
Deuterocanonical Books, 187
Deutero-Isaiah (Isaiah), 191
Deutero-Zechariah (Zechariah), 192
Deuteronomy, 189
Development, Human, **see** Campaign for Human Development
Development of Peoples, **see** Social Doctrine
Developmentally Handicapped, Catholic Facilities, 553-55
Devil, 306

Devotion, 306
Devotion, Eucharistic, 226
Devotions. 306-07
Diabolical Obsession, 320
Diabolical Possession, 323
Diaconate, **see** Deacons, Permanent
Dialogue in Pluralistic Societies, 91
Dialogues, Ecumenical, U.S., 285
Dictionary, **see** Glossary
Didache (Second Century), 113
Didymus (Thomas), 197
Diego, Juan (Guadalupe Apparition), 265
Dies Natalis, 238
Dignitatis Humanae (Religious Freedom Declaration), 124, 311
Dignity (Homosexual Organization), 60, 61, 72
Di Lorenzo, Francis X., Bp., 448
Dimitrios I, Ecumenical Patriarch
  Meeting with John Paul II, 71
Dimino, Joseph T. Bp., 448
Dimmerling, Harold J., Bp., 473, 600
Dingman, Maurice J., Bp., 448
Diocesan Laborer Priests, 517
Diocese, 307
  Curia, 305-06
  Synod, 331
Dioceses, Canadian, 376-77
Dioceses, U.S., 416-24
  Chancery Office Addresses, 437-39
  Eastern Rite, 270-71
  with Interstate Lines, 429
Dioceses, World, 367
Diocletian (292, 303), 113
Dion, Georges E., O.M.I., Bp., 448
Dionne, Gerard, Bp., 381
Dionysius Exiguus (c. 545), 114
Diplomacy, Papal, 170
Diplomats at Vatican, 173-74
  Dean, 173
Directory for Ad Limina Visit, 100
Disabled, Facilities, Organizations for, 551-55, 557-58
Disarmament, 95, 207, 208
Disasters, 72, 100, 104
Discalced, 307
Discalced Carmelites (Nuns), 500-01
  Carmelites, Order of (Men), 491
Disciple, 307
Disciples of Christ (Christian Church), 280-81, 285, 287, 289
Disciples of the Divine Master, Sister, 503
Disciplina Arcani, 307
Diskos, 273
Dismas, St., 252
Dispensation, 307
District of Columbia, 389, 396, 426, 430, 432, 526, 536, 542, 553, 560
Divination, 307
Divine Compassion, Sisters, 503
Divine Love, Oblates to, 503
Divine Office, **see** Liturgy of the Hours
Divine Positive Law, **see** Law
Divine Praises, 307
Divine Redeemer, Sisters, 514
Divine Revelation, Constitution, 124, 183-86, 331
Divine Savior, Sisters, 516
Divine Spirit, Congregation, 503
Divine Word, Society of, 491
Divine Worship, Congregation, 149
Divino Afflante Spiritu (Biblical Studies), 196
Divorce, 235
Divorce and Family, 96
Divorced and Remarried Catholics, Ministry for, 236-37
  Good Conscience Procedure, 237
Djibouti, 341
Docetism (c. 125), 112
Doctors, Church, 198-200
Doctrine, Catholic, 179-207
  Development, 184
  Marian, 261-64
  Marriage, 230-34

Doctrine, Catholic
　Social, 31-5, 202-07
Doctrine of the Faith, Congregation, 148
Dolinay, Thomas V., Bp., 448-49
Dolors, see Sorrows of BVM
Dominations (Angels), 297
Dominic, St., 252
Dominic, St., Sisters of, 504
　See also Dominicans
Dominic Savio, St., 252
Dominic Savio Club, St., 569
Dominica, 341
Dominican Laity, 520
Dominican Nuns, 503-04
Dominican Republic, 341, 369
Dominicans (Men), 491-92
Dominicans (Women), 503-04
Dominguez Recinos, Evelio, Bp., 600
Don Bosco Volunteers, 518
Donaghy, Frederick, M.M., Bp., 473, 600
Do Nascimento, Alexandre, Card., 158, 168, 169
Donation of Pepin (754), 115
Donatism (314), 113
Donnellan, Thomas A., Abp., 473, 600
Donnelly, Robert William, Bp., 449
Donoghue, John F., Bp., 449
Donohoe, Hugh A., Bp., 473, 600
Donovan, Jean, 78
Donovan, John A., Bp., 449
Donovan, Paul V., Bp., 449
Donovan, Raymond J., (Catholics in Presidents' Cabinets), 408
Dorothy, Institute of Sisters of St., 504-05
Dorsey, Norbert M., C.P., Bp., 449
Dos Santos, Alexandre Maria, O.F.M., Card., 165, 168, 169
Douay-Rheims Bible, 187
Double Effect Principle, 307
Dougherty, Dennis (U.S. Cardinals), 170, 473-74
Doxology, 307
　Mass, 213, 220
Doyle, James L., Bp., 381
Doyle, W. Emmett, Bp., 381
Drainville, Gerard, Bp., 381
Drexel, Katharine, Beatification, 36
Drory, Mordechai, 72
Drug Abuse, Rehabilitation Centers, 556
Drug Trafficking, John Paul II on, 39
Drury, Thomas, Bp., 449
Duarte, Jose Napoleon, Pres., 64, 70
Duchesne, Rose Philippine, St., 386
　Canonization, 36
Dudick, Michael J., Bp., 449
Dudley, Paul, Bp., 449
Duhart, Clarence J., C.SS.R., Bp., 449
Dukakis, Michael S., Gov., 100
Dulia, 307
Du Maine, Roland Pierre, Bp., 449
Dumouchel, Paul, O.M.I., Abp., 381
Dunn, Francis J., Bp., 449
Dunstan, St., 252-53
Durick, Joseph A., Bp., 449
Durning, Dennis, C.S.Sp., Bp., 449
Durocher, Marie Rose, Bl., 256
Durrant, Mignonette Patricia, Ambassador, 75
Dutch Guiana, see Suriname
Duty, 307
Duty, Easter, 308
Duval, Leon-Etienne, Card., 158, 168, 169
Dymphna, St., 253

E

East Germany, 344, 369
Easter, 248
　Controversy, 307-08
　Dates (1989-2012), 246
　Duty, 308
　Season, 238
　Time, see Easter Duty
　Triduum, 238

Easter
　Vigil, 248
　Water, 308
Easter Message (John Paul II), 88
Easter Observance, Jerusalem, 90
　Russia, 90
Eastern Churches, Catholic, 266-73
　Celibacy, 301
　Clergy, 273
　Decree (Vatican II), 124, 266-67, 275-76
　Inter-Ritual Concelebrations, 219
　Jurisdictions, 269-70
　Liturgical Traditions, 83
　Liturgy, Byzantine Rite, 271
　Marriage Laws, 236
　Patriarchs, 266
　Rites and Faithful, 267-70
　Sacraments, 266-67
　Sacred Congregation, 148-49
　Statistics, Canada, 379
　Statistics, U.S., 270-71, 429, 433, 529
　Synods, Assemblies, 270
　Worship, 267
　See also Byzantine Rite
Eastern Churches, Separated, 274-75
　Intercommunion, 226
　See also Ecumenism; Orthodox Churches, Eastern; Orthodox Church, Oriental
Eastern Ecumenism, 275-76
　See also Ecumenical Reports
Ebacher, Roger, Bp., 381
Ecclesiastes, 190
Ecclesiastical
　Burial, 300
　Calendar, 238-46
　Honors, 595-97
　Jurisdictions, World (Statistics), 367
　Provinces, Canada, 375
　Provinces, U.S., 415-16
Ecclesiasticus, see Sirach
Ecclesiology, 308
Economic Affairs, Prefecture, 153
"Economic Justice: A Pastoral Message," 493-94
Ecstasy, 308
Ecthesis (649), 115
Ecuador, 341, 369
　Catholic University, 537
Ecumenical Councils, 122-24
　See also Council, Second Vatican
Ecumenical Statement on Mary, 265-66
Ecumenical Reports, Statements, 285-90
Ecumenism, 275-76, 281-90, 308
　Agencies, 283-84
　and Intercommunion, 226, 315
　and Mary, 264
　and Separated Eastern Christians, 275-76
　Declarations of Popes, Other Prelates, 285-86
　Decree on, 281-83
　Dialogues, U.S., 285
　Interfaith Statements, 287-89
　International Consultations, 286-87
　International Bilateral Commissions, 286-87
　Participation in Worship, 282
　Reports, International, 285-88
　Vatican Secretariat, 151, 283
　Week of Prayer for Christian Unity, 75, 76, 332
　World Council of Churches 283-84, 286-87
　See also Catholic-Jewish Relations; Catholic-Moslem Relations
Eddy, Mary Baker (Christian Science), 303
Edict of Milan (313), 113
Edith Stein, Bl., 253
Edith Stein Guild, 571
　Award, 598
Edmund, Society of St., 492

Edmund Campion, St., 253
Education, Catholic, Congregation, 150
Education, Catholic, U.S., 525-37
　Campus Ministry, 535
　Facilities for Handicapped, 551-55
　Legal Status, 525
　　See also Church-State Decisions
　Religious Dimension, 79
　Seminaries, 535-37
　Statistics, 526-29, 530
　Universities and Colleges, 530-35
　　See also Schools, Catholic; Seminaries
Education, Religious, 530
　Pupils Receiving Instruction, 530
Educational Association, National Catholic, 525
Edward the Confessor, St., 253
Edwin Vincent O'Hara Institute (Rural Ministry Institute), 524
Egan, Edward M., Bp., 449
Egypt, 341
Eileton, 273
Eire, see Ireland
Ejaculation, (Aspiration), 298
Ekandem, Dominic, Card., 158, 168, 169
Elections, Papal, 321-22
　Eligibility of Cardinals, 153-54, 169
Elevation, 308
Eligius, St., 253
Elijah (Kings), 189
Elisha (Kings), 189
Elizabeth of Hungary, St., 253
Elizabeth of Portugal, St., 253
Elizabeth Seton, St., 253
Elko, Nicholas T., Abp., 449
Elmo (Erasmus), St., 253
El Salvador, 70, 77, 78, 86, 342, 369
　Death Squads, 77
Elvira, Council (306), 113
Elya, John A., B.S.O., Bp., 449
Emblems of Saints, 260
Embolism (Prayer for Deliverance), 213
Embryos, Human, Experimentation, 82
Emily de Rodat, St., 253
Emily de Vialar, St., 253
Emmanuel D'Alzon Medal, 598
Emotionally Maladjusted, Catholic Facilities, 551-55
Employment, 91
Encuentro, see Hispanics
Encyclical Letter (1987), "On Social Concerns," 31-5
Encyclicals, 137
　Authority, 137
　List, Benedict XIV to John Paul II, 137-42
　Social, 31-5, 202, 204-06
End Justifies the Means, 308
Engaged Encounter, 237
England, 342, 369
　Catholic Relief Act (1926), 122
　Church of England Synod, 82
　Popish Plot (1678), 119
　Test Act (1673), 119
England and Wales, Bishops, Papal Addresses, 67, 79
English Martyrs, Beatification, 68
Enlightenment, Age, 120
Enrique y Tarancon, Vicente, Card., 158, 168, 169
Enthronement of the Sacred Heart, 571
Environment, Protection of, 75
Envy, 308
Eparch, 144
Ephesians, 194
Ephesus, Council (431), 114, 123
Ephesus, "Robber" Council (449), 114
Ephraem, St., 199
Epikeia, 308
Epimanikia, 273
Epiphany, 248

Index

Episcopal Church, see Anglican Communion; Anglicans
Episcopal Church in U.S., 280
  Ecumenical Dialogues, Statements, 285
  See also Ecumenism
Episcopal Conferences, 368-71
  Vatican Draft Statement, 93
Episcopal Vicar, 144
Episcopate, 308
Epistles (Letters), 193-94
Epitrachelion, 273
Equality (Social Doctrine), 203
Equatorial Guinea, 342, 369
Equivocation, 308
Erasmus, St., 253
Eritrea, see Ethiopia
Eschatology, 308
Escriva de Balaguer, Jose Maria (Opus Dei), 320
Essenes, see Dead Sea Scrolls
Esther, 190
Estonia, 342
Etchegaray, Roger, Card., 158, 168, 169
Eternal Word Network, 443, 592
  Coverage of U.S. Papal Visit, 64
Eternity, 308
Ethelbert, St., 253
Ethics, 308
  Situational, 329
Ethiopia, 88, 342-43, 369
  Aid for, 73
  CRS Food Program, 94
Ethiopian Rite Catholics, 267
Euangelion (Gospel), 193
Eucharist (Holy), 223, 225-26
  Administration to Non-Catholics, 226
  Devotion Outside of Mass, 226
  Exposition, 221, 309-10
  Fast, 310
  Ministers, Special, 219, 221
  Reservation of, see Tabernacle
  Sacrifice, see Mass
  See also Communion, Holy; Transubstantiation
Eucharist, Peace-Giving and Unifying Power, 83
Eucharist, Religious of, 505
Eucharistic Congresses, 308-09
Eucharistic Liturgy, 213
Eucharistic Missionary Sisters, 505
Eucharistic Prayers (Mass), 213, 218
Eudes, John, St., 255
Eudists (Congregation of Jesus and Mary), 492
Eugenics, 309
Euntes in Mundum: Apostolic Letter, 45-7
Euphrasia Pelletier, St., 253
Europe
  Bishops' Conference, 371
  Cardinals, 169
  Catholic Statistics, 367
  Eastern Rite Jurisdictions, 269
  Missionary Bishops (U.S.), 425
Eusebius of Vercelli, St., 253
Eustochia Smeralda Calafato, Beatification, 95
Euthanasia, Legalized, 52-4, 65, 76, 85, 93, 309
  Physician-Assisted Suicide, 52-4, 85, 93
  Withdrawal of Food and Water, 65, 76, 85
Eutychianism (451), 114
Evangelical Counsels, 305
Evangelicalism, 281
Evangelion, 272
Evangelists, 193, 196-97
Evangelization, 145, 309
Evangelization of Peoples, Congregation of, 150
Everson v. Board of Education (Bus Transportation), 410
Evolution, 309

Ex Cathedra, 182
  See also Infallibility
Exaltation (Triumph) of the Holy Cross, 250
Examen, Particular (Examination of Conscience), 304
Exarch, 144
Exceptional Children, see Handicapped, Facilities for
Excommunication, 309
Excommunication, Abp. Lefebvre, 44
Exegesis, 194
Existentialism, 309
Exner, Adam, O.M.I., Abp., 381
Exodus, 189
Exorcism, 309
Exorcist, 229
Exposition of the Blessed Sacrament, 309-10
Extended Periods of Time, 221
Extension Society, 524
External Forum, 310
Extreme Unction, see Anointing of the Sick
Eymard League, 571
Ezekiel, 191
Ezra, 189-90

F

Fabian, St., 253
Faculties, 310
  of Ecclesiastical Studies, 538-39
Faith, 310
  Congregation for Doctrine of, 148
  Congregation for Propagation of, 150
  Mysteries, 319
  Privilege of (Petrine Privilege), 235
  Promoter of, 324
  Rule of, 310
  See also Creed; Doctrine
  Society for Propagation of, 575
Faithful, Communion of, 304
Faithful, Mass of, 212
Faithful, Prayer of the, 213
Falcao, Jose Freire, Card., 158, 168, 169
Falkland Islands, 343
False Decretals (847-852), 115
Families for Prayer, 571
Family, Council for, 151-52
Family, Holy (Feast), 248
Family Movement, Christian, 566
Family Rosary, Inc., 571
Family Theater, Father Peyton's, 592
Fan Xueyan, Peter Joseph, Bp. (China), 77
Farley, James A. (Catholics in Presidents' Cabinets), 408
Farley, John (U.S. Cardinals), 170, 474
Farmer, Ferdinand, 386
Farms, Small, 63
Faroe Islands, 343
Fasani, Francis, St., 253
Fast, Eucharistic, 310
Fast Days, 239
Father, 310
Father Flanagan's Boys Town, 552
Father McKenna Award, 598
Fathers, Church, 198
Fathers of Mercy, 494
Fatima, 265
Faulkner, Paul, M.H.M., 600
Favalora, John C., Bp., 449-50
Fear, 310
Feast Days, 239, 247-50
Feast of Weeks, 291
Feasts, Movable, 239, 246
Febres Cordero, Miguel, St., 256
Febronianism (1764), 120
Federal, Joseph L., Bp., 450
Federal Aid to Education, 525
  See also Church-State Decisions
FBI Probe, 80
Federation of Diocesan Liturgical Commissions, 572

"Feeding and Hydrating the Permanently Unconscious and Other Vulnerable Persons," 85
Felici, Angelo, Card., 158, 169
Felician Sisters (Sisters of St. Felix), 505
Felicity, St. (Perpetua and Felicity, Sts.), 257
Fellowship of Catholic Scholars, 572, 597
Ferdinand III, St., 253
Fernando Po, see Equatorial Guinea
Ferrario, Joseph A., Bp., 450
Ferraro, Barbara, Sr., Resignation, 100
Ferre, M. Isolina, Sr., 85
Festival of Evangelization, Chicago, 104
Festival of Lights (Hanukkah), 291
Fiacra, St., 253
Fidelis of Sigmaringen, St., 253
Fidelitas Medal, 598
Fides (Mission News Service), 588
Fiji, 343
Filevich, Basil (Wasyl), Bp., 381
Filippini, Religious Teachers, 505
Films, Catholic, see Television
Finger Towel, 215
Finland, 343
Fiorenza, Joseph A., Bp., 450
First Amendment (Wall of Separation), 414
  See also Church-State Decisions
First Catholic Slovak Ladies Association, 69, 572
First Catholic Slovak Union (Jednota), 572
First Friday, 310
First Saturday, 310
Fisher, Carl, S.S.J., Bp., 450
Fisher, Eugene, Dr., see Catholic-Jewish Relations
Fisher, John, St., 255
Fisherman's Ring, 310
Fitzpatrick, John J., Bp., 450
Fitzsimons, George K., Bp., 450
FitzSimons, Thomas, 391
Flag, Papal, 176
Flaget, Benedict, 386
Flahiff, George B., C.S.B., Card., 158, 168, 169
Flanagan, Bernard J., Bp., 450
Flavin, Glennon P., Bp., 450
Fliss, Raphael M., Bp., 450
Florence, Council (1438-45), 118, 123
Flores, Patrick, Abp., 450
Flores Reyes, Gerardo Humberto, Bp., 82
Florida, 389, 396, 426, 430, 432, 436, 443, 527, 536, 542-43, 553, 560
Floyd, John B. (Catholics in Presidents' Cabinets), 408
Flynn, Harry J., Bp., 450
Focolare Movement, 92, 519
Foi et Lumiere, 372
Foley, David E., Bp., 450
Foley, John Patrick, Abp., 450
  on Catholic Press, 80, 93
Food and Liquid, Morality of Withholding, 65, 76, 85
Food Supply, Imbalance, 67
Ford, Ita, M.M., Sr., 78
Foreign Mission Society of America, Catholic (Maryknoll), 494
Foreign Missions, U.S. Personnel, 520-23
  American Bishops, 425
Foreign Missions, Consolata Society for, 491
  St. Joseph's Society for (Mill Hill Missionaries), 494
Forester Youth Program, 568
Foresters, Catholic Order of, 570-71
Forgiveness of Sin, 310
  See also Confession; Penance
Formosa, see Taiwan
Forst, Marion F., Bp., 450
Fortier, Jean-Marie, Abp., 381

Fortitude, 310
Fortune Telling, 310
Forty Hours Devotion, 310
Forum, 310
Foster Care, New York, 96
Four Books of Sentences (1160), 117
France, 343, 369
  Bishops, Ad Liminia Visit, 71
  Interfaith Council, 78
  In Vitro Fertilization, 65
  Moral Health, 90
  Religious Sanctions (1901), 121
  Revolution (1789), 120
Frances of Rome, St., 253
Frances Xavier Cabrini, St., 253
Francis, Joseph A., S.V.D., Bp., 450
Francis, St., Assisi, 253
  See also Crib; Portiuncula
Francis, St. (Religious)
  Brothers of the Poor, 497
  Little Brothers of, 497
  Secular Order, 520
  Sisters of (List), 505-08
  Third Order Regular (Men), 492
  See also Franciscans; Friars Minor
Francis Borgia, St., 253
Francis Caracciolo, St., 253
Francis de Sales, St., 199
Francis de Sales, St. (Religious)
  Oblate Sisters, 505
  Oblates of, 492
  Society of (Salesians), 495
Francis de Sales, St., Award (CPA), 599
Francis Fasani, St., 253
Francis of Paola, St., 253
Francis Solanus, St., 387
Francis Xavier, St., 253
  Brothers of, 497
  Catholic Mission Sisters, 516
Francis Xavier Bianchi, St., 253
Franciscan Advertising and Media Enterprises, 592
Franciscan Apostolate of the Way of the Cross, 572
Franciscan Brothers of Brooklyn, 497
Franciscan Brothers of Christ the King, 497
Franciscan Brothers of the Good News, 497
Franciscan Brothers of the Holy Cross, 497
Franciscan Communications, 592
Franciscan Crown, 310-11
Franciscan Friars of the Atonement, 489
Franciscan International Award, 598
Franciscan Missionary Brothers, 497
Franciscan Missions (California), 388
Franciscan Sisters (List), 505-08
Franciscans (Friars Minor), 492
Franciscans, Capuchins, 492
  Conventuals, 492
  Third Order Regular, 492
Franciscans, Secular, 520
Franco, Francisco (1936), 122
Franklin, William Edwin, Bp., 450
Franz, John B., Bp., 450
Franzetta, Benedict C., Bp., 451
Frassinetti, Paola, St., 257
Free the Fathers, 572
Free Will, 311
Freedom, Academic, 104
Freedom, Religious, 311
Freedom Sunday Rally, 72
Freeman, James D., Card., 158, 168, 169
Freemasons, 311
Freking, Frederick W., Bp., 451
French Guiana, 343
French Polynesia, 344
Fresno Larrain, Juan Francisco, Card., 158, 168, 169
Frey, Gerard L., Bp., 451
Friar, 311

Friars Minor, Order of (Franciscans), 492
Friars Preachers, Order of (Dominicans), 491-92
Friend, William B., Bp., 451
Frontier Apostolate, 567
Frosi, Angelo, S.X., Bp., 451
Fruits of the Holy Spirit, 311
Fruits of the Mass, 213-14
Fu Jen University (Taiwan), 538
Fulda, Monastery (744), 115
Fulton, Thomas B., Bp., 381
Fundamentalism, 49
Fundamentalism, Biblical, 49-51
Fundamentalists, 281
Funeral Mass, Rites, Vestments, 214
Furlong, Philip J., Bp., 451
Futuna Islands, 366

G

Gabon, 73, 344, 369
Gabriel (Archangel), 249
Gabriel Lalemant, St., 386
Gabriel of the Sorrowful Mother, St., 253
Gabriel Richard Institute, 572
Gabris, Julius, Bp., 600
Gagnon, Edouard, P.S.S., Card., 63, 84-5, 158, 169
  Lefebvre Investigation, 63
Galatians, 194
Galician Ruthenian Catholics, 268
Galilei, Galileo (1642), 119
Gallagher, Raymond J., Bp., 451
Gallegos, Alphonse, O.A.R., Bp., 451
Gallican Articles (1682), 119
Gallitzin, Demetrius, 386
Gambia, The, 344, 369
Gambling, 311
Ganter, Bernard J., Bp., 451
Gantin, Bernardin, Card., 158-59, 168, 169
Garland, James H., Bp., 451
Garmendia, Francisco, Bp., 451
Garmo, George, Abp., 451
Garner, Robert F., Bp., 451
Garnier, Charles, St., 386
Garrone, Gabriel, Card., 159, 168, 169
Gaspar del Bufalo, St., 253
Gaston, William (North Carolina), 403
Gathering for Christians, Texas, 92
Gaudete Sunday, Vestments, **see** Liturgical Colors
Gaudium et Spes (Church in Modern World), 124, 202-04, 205-07, 230-31
Gaughan, Norbert F., Bp., 101, 451
Gaumond, Andre, Bp., 381
Gehenna (Gehinnom), 311
Gelasian Guild, 572
Galasius I, Pope, St. (494), 114
Gelineau, Louis E., Bp., 76, 451
Gemma Galgani, St., 253
Gendron, Odore, Bp., 451
General Absolution, 227
  U.S. Bishops' Proposal, 104
Genesis (Bible), 188-89
Genesius, St., 253
Genetic Experiments, Manipulation, 71
Genevieve, St., 253
Genuflection, 311
George, St., 253
George M. Cohan Award, 598
Georgetown University, 531, 538
  Homosexual Student Groups, 84
Georgia, 396-97, 426, 430, 432, 443, 526, 551, 560
  Franciscan Martyrs, (Georgia, 1597), 396
Georgian Byzantine Rite, 268
Gerard Majella, St., 254
Gerber, Eugene, Bp., 451
Gerbermann, Hugo, M.M., Bp., 451
Gerety, Peter L., Abp., 451
Germany, 344-45, 369
  Kulturkampf (1871), 121

Germany
  Surrogate Mother Center (West Germany), 77-8
Gerrard, James J., Bp., 451-52
Gerry, Joseph, O.S.B., Bp., 452
Gertrude, St., 254
Gervais, Marcel A., Bp., 381
Gethsemani, 311
Ghana, 345, 369
Gibault, Pierre, 386
Gibbons, James (Catholic History of U.S.), 392, 475
Gibraltar, 345
Gifts, Preternatural, 323-24
Gifts of the Holy Spirit, 311
Gilbert, Arthur J., Bp., 381
Gilbert Islands (Kiribati), 350
Giordano, Michele, Card., 159, 168, 169
Girl Scouts, Catholic, 568
Glasnost, 66
Glemp, Jozef, Card., 159, 168, 169
  See also Poland
Glenmary Missioners, 105, 493, 523
  Sisters (Home Mission Sisters of America), 509
  See also Home Missions
Glenn, Laurence A., Bp., 475
Glennie, Ignatius, S.J., Bp., 452
Glennon, John (U.S. Cardinals), 170, 475
Glory to God (Mass), 212
Glossary, 295-332
Gluttony, 311
Gnosticism (c. 125), 112
God, 311-12
  Attributes, 299
  Commandments, 201
Godparents, 223-24
God-Spell (Gospel), 193
Golden Bull (1338), 118
Golden Spur, Order of, 596
Gonzalez Martin, Marcelo, Card., 159, 168, 169
Gonzalez, Roberto O., O.F.M., Bp., 452
Gonzalez, Roch, St., 40, 386
"Good Conscience" Procedures (Marriage), 237
Good Friday (Mar. 24, 1989), 241, 248
Good Samaritan Award, 598
Good Shepherd Sisters, 508
Good Shepherd, Society of Brothers, 497
Gorbachev, Michail, Gen. Sec., 72
Gorman, John R., Bp., 452
Gospel, 193
Gospel (Mass), **see** Readings
Gospels, 185-86, 193
  Synoptic, 193
Gossman, F. Joseph, Bp., 452
Gottwald, George J., Bp., 452
Goudrault, Henri, O.M.I., Bp., 381
Goupil, Rene, St., 386
Gouyon, Paul, Card., 159, 168, 169
Government, Church, 143-44
  See also Roman Curia
Grace, 312
  at Meals, 312
Gracida, Rene H., Bp., 452
Grady, Thomas J., Bp., 452
Graham, John J., Bp., 452
Grahmann, Charles V., Bp., 452
Grail, 567
Grasset de Saint Sauveur, Andre, Bl., 250
Gratian (1160), 117
Gratton, Jean, Bp., 381
Graves, Lawrence P., Bp., 452
Gravier, Jacques, 386
Gravissimum Educationis, 124
Gray, Gordon J., Card., 159, 168, 169
Graymoor Institute, 284
Graymoor Sisters (Franciscan Srs. of the Atonement), 506
Graziano, Lawrence, O.F.M., Bp., 452
Great Britain
  Episcopal Conferences, 369

Index

Great Britain
　See also England, Scotland, Wales
Greece, 345, 369
Greek Byzantine Rite Catholics, 268
Greek Melkites, 268
　in U.S., 271
Green, Francis J., Bp., 452
Greenland, 345
Gregoire, Paul, Card., 159, 168, 169
Gregorian Calendar (1582), 119
Gregorian Chant, 210-11
Gregorian Masses, 214
Gregorian University, Pontifical, 539
Gregory, Wilton D., Bp., 452
Gregory Barbarigo, St., 254
Gregory Nazianzen, St., 199
Gregory of Nyssa, St., 254
Gregory I, the Great, St., 199
Gregory VII, St. (Hildebrand), 254
Gregory XVI, Pope, Encyclicals, 138
Gregory Thaumaturgus, St., 254
Gregory the Great, Order of St., 596
Gregory the Illuminator, St., 254
Grenada, 345
Greschuk, Martin, Bp., 381
Grey Nuns, see Charity, Sisters of
Grey Nuns of the Sacred Heart, 508
Griffin, James A., Bp., 452
Groër, Hans, Hermann, O.S.B., Card., 159, 168, 169
Gronouski, John (Catholics in Presidents' Cabinets), 408
Grutka, Andrew G., Bp., 452
Guadalupe, Our Lady of, 265
　Feast (U.S.), 249, 442
Guadalupe Shrine, Mexico, Pilgrims, 74
Guadalupe, Sisters of, 508
Guadeloupe, 345
Guam, 345
　Minor Basilica, 436
Guard of Honor of the Immaculate Heart, 572
Guardian Angels, 248
Guardian Angels, Sisters of Holy, 508
Guatemala, 345-46, 369
　Catechists and Sects, 102
　Sanctuary for Indians, 82
Guerri, Sergio, Card., 159, 168, 169
Guiana, Dutch, see Suriname
Guiana, French, 343
"Guideline," 592
Guild of Our Lady of Ransom, 572 of St. Paul, 572
Guilfoyle, George H., Bp., 452
Guillory, Curtis J., S.V.D., 453
Guinea, 346, 369
Guinea, Equatorial, 342, 369
Guinea-Bissau, 346
Gulbinowicz, Henryk, Card., 159, 168, 169
Gumbleton, Thomas J., Bp., 453
Gunpowder Plot (1605), 119
Gutenberg, Johann (c. 1456), 118
Gutierrez, Gustavo, Rev., 100
Guyana, 346
Guyot, Louis J., Card., 600
Gypsies, Italy, 70

H

Habakkuk, 192
Habit, 312
Habit, Religious, 215
Habitual Grace, 312
Hacault, Antoine, Bp., 381
Hacker, Hilary B., Bp., 453
Hackett, John F., Bp., 453
Haggai, 192
Hagiography, 312
Haig, Alexander M. (Catholics in Presidents' Cabinets), 408
Hail Mary, 312
Haiti, 346, 369
　Bishops Praised, 103
　Unconstitutional Actions, 73-4
Hakim, Michel, Abp., 381
Halpin, Charles A., Abp., 381

Ham, J. Richard, M.M., Bp., 453
Hamelin, Jean-Guy, Bp., 381
Hamer, Jean Jerome, Card., 159-60, 169
Hammes, George A., Bp., 453
Handicapped, Catholic Facilities, Organizations, 551-55, 557-58
Handmaids of Divine Mercy, 518
　of Mary Immaculate, 508
　of the Precious Blood, 508
Hanifen, Richard C., Bp., 453
Hannan, Philip M., Abp., 453
Hannegan, Robert E. (Catholics in Presidents' Cabinets), 408
Hanselmann, Johannes, Bp. (Lutheran), 83
Hanukkah, 291
Hanus, Jerome George, O.S.B., Bp., 453
Harper, Edward, C.SS.R., Bp., 453
Harrington, Timothy J., Bp., 453
Harris, Vincent M., Bp., 476, 600
Harrison, Frank J., Bp., 453
Hart, Daniel A., Bp., 453
Hart, Joseph, Bp., 453
Hastrich, Jerome J., Bp., 453
Hawaii, 397, 429, 431, 433, 529
Hayes, James M., Abp., 381
Hayes, Nevin W., O.Carm., Bp., 476, 600
Head, Edward D., Bp., 453
Health Association, Catholic, 541
Health Care Facilities (Aged), 541-51
Health Care Workers, Pontifical Commission, 152
Healy, James A. (Maine, 1875), 399, 476
Heart of Jesus, Institute of, 518
Heart of Mary, Daughters of, 511
Heart of the Nation, 592
Heaven, 312
Hebrews (Letter), 194
Heckler, Margaret (Catholics in Presidents' Cabinets), 408
Hedwig, St., 254
Hegira (622), 115
Hegumen (Abbot), 295
Heim, Capistran F., O.F.M., Bp., 453
Helena, St., 254
Hell, 312
Helmsing, Charles H., Bp., 453
Helpers, Society of, 508
Helpless, Mothers of the, 507
Helsinki Conference Follow-Up, 86
Hemlock Society (Humane and Dignified Death Act), 52-4
Hengsbach, Franz, Card., 160, 168, 169
Hennepin, Louis, 386
Henoticon (484), 114
Henry, Frederick, Bp., 381
Henry, St., 254
Henry VIII, King (1533), 118
Heresy, Heretic, 312
Herman, Woody, 600
Herman Joseph, St., 254
Hermanas Catequistas Guadalupanas, 508
Hermanas Josefinas, 509
Hermaniuk, Maxim, C.SS.R., Abp., 381
Hermeneutics, 194
Hermit (Anchorite), 297
Hermit Sisters of Christ in Solitude, 509
Heroic Act of Charity, 312
Herrmann, Edward J., Bp., 454
Herzig, Charles E., Bp., 454
Heterodoxy, 312
Hettinger, Edward G., Bp., 454
Hickey, Dennis W., Bp., 454
Hickey, James A., Card., 160, 168, 169
　Installed as Cardinal, 95
Hierarchy, 143-44
Hierarchy, Canadian, see Bishops, Canadian
Hierarchy, U.S., see Bishops, U.S.
High Schools, Catholic, U.S. (Statistics), 526-29, 530

High Schools, Catholic, U.S.
　Thirty-One Honored, 64
Higi, William L., Bp., 454
Hilary, St., 199
Hildebrand (Gregory VII, St.), 254
Hinduism, 294
Hines, Vincent J., Bp., 454
Hinton, Mary, 600
Hippolytus, St., 254
Hirsch, Richard H., 85
Hispanic Telecommunications Network, 592
Hispanics, U.S., 487-88
　Loss to Sects, Los Angeles, 97
　Pastoral Program for Ministry, 442
　Vocations Project, 65
　Youth Congress, Los Angeles, 105
Historical Association, American Catholic, 569
Historical Books of the Bible, 189-90
Historical Sciences, Commission, 152
History
　Catholic, Canada, 374-75
　Catholic, U.S., 391-408
　Church, Significant Dates, 112-22
　See also Individual Countries
Hitler, Adolf (1933), 122
　See also Germany
Hoch, Lambert A., Bp., 454
Hodapp, Robert, S.J., Bp., 454
Hoeffner, Joseph, Card., 64, 600
Hoey Awards, 598
Hoffman, James R., Bp., 454
Hogan, James J., Bp., 454
Hogan, Joseph L., Bp., 454
Holiness Sects, 281
Holocaust, Cardinal John O'Connor on, 69
Holocaust, John Paul II on, 36
Holocaust Memorial Day, 291
Holy Child Jesus, Society, 509
Holy Childhood Association, 568
Holy Communion, see Communion, Holy; Eucharist
Holy Days, 239, 247-50
　Byzantine Rite, 272
Holy Eucharist, see Eucharist, Holy
Holy Eucharist, Brothers of, 497
Holy Faith, Sisters of the, 509
Holy Family (Feast), 248
Holy Family (Religious)
　Congregation of Missionaries of, 493
　Congregation of Sisters of, 505
　Little Sisters of, 505
　of Nazareth, Sisters of, 505
　Sisters of, 505
　Sons, 493
Holy Father, see Pope
Holy Ghost, see Holy Spirit
Holy Ghost Fathers, 493
Holy Heart of Mary, Servants, 509
Holy Innocents, 248
Holy Land, Commissariat, 304
Holy Land, Emigration of Christians, 82
Holy Name Society, 572
Holy Name Society, Natl. Assn., 572
Holy Names of Jesus and Mary, Srs. of, 509
Holy Office, see Doctrine of the Faith, Congregation
Holy Oils, 320
Holy Orders, 223, 228-29
Holy Saturday, 248
Holy See, 312
　Publications, 177
　Representatives, 170-73, 178
　See also Vatican
Holy Sepulchre, Order of, 596
Holy Spirit, 312-13
　Blasphemy of, 299
　Fruits of, 311
　Gifts of, 311
　Sins Against, 329
Holy Spirit (Religious)
　and Mary Immaculate, Sister Servants of, 509
　Community of, 509

Holy Spirit (Religious)
  Daughters of, 509
  Mission Sisters, 509
  Missionaries of, 493
  Missionary Sisters, Servants, 509
  Sisters of, 509
Holy Spirit of Perpetual Adoration, Sister Servants of, 509
Holy Thursday, 248
  Papal Letter to Priests, 83
Holy Trinity, 250
Holy Trinity, Missionary Servants of the Most, 496
  Order of Most, 496
  Sisters of Most, 516
Holy Water, 313
Holy Week, 220, 238, 272
  Liturgy of, 222
Holy Year, 313
Home Mission Sisters (Glenmary), 509
Home Missioners of America, 105, 493, 523
Home (Rural) Missions, U.S., 523-24
  Financial Support, 77
  See also Hispanics
Home Visitors of Mary, 509
Homeless
  Canada, 74
  Church and Housing Problem, Justice and Peace Commission Statement, 61-2, 80
  United States, 62
  United States, Shelters, 556, 557
  Vatican Shelters, 92
Homes for Aged and Retired, 541-51
Homily, 213
  Reserved for Priest or Deacon, 222
Homosexuality, 313
Homosexuals
  Mass for, Chicago, 59-61
  Protests, New York, 72
  Student Group, Georgetown Univ., 88
  See also Dignity
Honduras, 346, 369
Hong Kong, 346
Honor et Veritas Award, 598
Hope, 313
Horan, Dennis J., 600
Hosanna, 313
Hosea, 191
Hospitaller Order of St. John of God, 497
Hospitals, Catholic, U.S., 434
  and Sterilizations, 65
  Mission to Poor, 93
  See also Cancer Homes, Hospitals; Health Care Facilities
Hospitals, Catholic, World, 367
Host, Sacred, 313
  See also Communion, Holy
Houck, William Russell, Bp., 454
Hours, Liturgy of, 210, 220
Housing Problem, Church and, 61-2, 80
Howard R. Marraro Prize, 598
Howze, Joseph Lawson, Bp., 454
Hubbard, Howard J., Bp., 454
Hubert, Bernard, Bp., 381
Hubert, St., 254
Hugh of Cluny, St., 254
Hughes, Alfred C., Bp., 454
Hughes, Edward T., Bp., 454
Hughes, William A., Bp., 454
Human Development Campaign, 429
Human Life, Dignity of, 80-1
Human Rights, see Various Countries
Humanae Vitae, 84, 232
  20th Anniversary Statement (U.S. Bishops), 232-34
Humane and Dignified Death Act, Calif. 52-4
Humani Generis (Authority of Encyclicals), 137
Hume, George Basil, O.S.B., Card., 68, 160, 168, 169
Humeral Veil, 215

Humility, 313
Humility of Mary, Congregation of, 509
  Sisters of, 509
Hungarian Byzantine Catholics, 268
Hungarian Catholic League of America, 572
Hungary, 346-47, 369
  Invitation to Pope, 103
Hunthausen, Raymond G., Abp., 101, 454
  Seattle Ministry, 81
Hurley, Denis, Abp., 94
Hurley, Francis T., Abp., 85, 454
Hurley, Mark J., Bp., 454-55
Hus, John, 276
Hussein, King, 80, 104
Hussey, Patricia, Sr., Resignation, 100
Hyde Amendment, 54-5
Hyperdulia, 313
Hypnosis, 313
Hypostatic Union, 313

I

Ibrahim, Ibrahim N., Bp., 455
Iceland, 347
Iconoclasm (731, 787), 115
Iconostas, 273
Icons, 313
Idaho, 397, 428, 431, 433, 529, 560
Idolatry, 313
Ignatius of Antioch, St., 254
Ignatius of Laconi, St., 254
Ignatius of Loyola, St., 254
IHS, 313
Illegal Aliens, Registration, 65, 92
Illinois, 389, 397, 427, 430, 432, 436, 443, 527, 536, 543, 551, 553, 560
  Abortion Ruling, 72-3
  Mass for Homosexuals, Chicago, 59-61
  Pornography Boycott, Chicago, 88
Imesch, Joseph L., Bp., 455
Immaculate Conception, 248, 262-63
Immaculate Conception (Religious)
  Little Servant Sisters, 509
  Missionary Sisters, 507
  of BVM, Sisters, 509
  Sisters of, 509
Immaculate Conception Shrine, 260
Immaculate Heart of Mary, 249
Immaculate Heart of Mary, (Religious)
  Brothers, 497
  Congregation of (Missionhurst), 494
  Missionary Sisters, 509
  Missionary Sons (Claretians), 491
  Sisters, 509
  Sisters, Servants, 509
Immersion, see Baptism
Immigration Policies, U.S., and Political Refugees, 68
Immigration Reform Act, 65, 92
Immortality, 313
Impanation, (Consubstantiation), 304
Impediments, Matrimonial, 235
Imprimatur, 301
Impurity, 313
In Pectore, see Cardinal in Pectore
In Sin, 315
In Vitro Fertilization, 65, 82
Incardination, 313
Incarnate Word and Blessed Sacrament, Cong., 509
Incarnation, 313-14
Incense, 314
Incest, 314
Inculturation, 39, 75, 314
Index of Prohibited Books, 314
India, 347-48, 369
  Anti-Christian Attitudes, 98, 101-02
  Bishops' Conference, Single, 90
  Theologian Barred from Teaching, 86
Indiana, 389, 397-98, 426, 430, 432, 436, 443, 527, 536, 543-44, 551, 553, 560
  Sisters' Salary, Indianapolis, 73

Indians (Native Americans), Organizations, 524
  Bishop Appointed, 92
  Native Languages, Liturgy, 220
  Statistics, 524
Indifferentism, 314
Indonesia, 348, 369
  Pancasila Philosophy, 69
Indulgence, 314-15
Indulgence, Portiuncula, 323
Indult, 315
Inerrancy of the Bible, 185
INF Arms Control Treaty, 72
Infallibility, 182
Infant Jesus, Congregation of the, 509
Infant Jesus of Prague, 315
Infused Virtues, 315
Infusion, see Baptism
Innocent III, Pope (1198-1216), 117
Innocenti, Antonio, Card., 160, 169
Inquisition, 315
Inquisition, Spanish, 315
INRI, 315
Insemination, Artificial, 315
Insignis Medal, 598
Inspiration, Biblical, 184-85
Institute of Apostolic Oblates, 519
Institute of Blessed Virgin Mary, 500
Institute of Charity (Rosminians), 495
Institute of Judaeo-Christian Studies, 65
Institute of Secular Missionaries, 518
Institute of the Heart of Jesus, 518
Institute on Religious Life, 517
Institutes, Secular, 517-19
Institutes and Universities, Pontifical, 537-38, 539
Institutes of Consecrated Life, 489
Institutes of the Christian Religion (1536), 119
Institutions, Catholic, see Social Services, Catholic
Instruction, Apostolic, 315
Intercommunion, 226, 315
Interdict, 315
Interfaith Center on Corporate Responsibility, 77
Interfaith Reports, Statements, 68, 287-90
Inter Mirifica (Communications Document), 124
Internal Forum, 310
International
  Anti-Euthanasia Task Force, 65
  Catholic Deaf Association, 557-58
  Catholic-Jewish Liaison Committee, 293
  Catholic Migration Commission, 70, 97, 372
  Catholic-Orthodox Theological Commission, 68-9, 95-6, 288
  Catholic Union of the Press, 372-73
  Eucharistic Congresses, 308-09
  Federation of Catholic Medical Associations, 373
  Institute of the Heart of Jesus, 572
  Liaison, 567
  Organizations, Catholic, 101, 371-74
  Organizations, Vatican Representatives, 178
  Theological Commission, 152
  Union of Superiors General, 517
Internuncio, see Representatives, Vatican
Interpretation, Biblical, 184-85, 194-96
  Teaching Authority of Church, 184
Interracial Council, Catholic, 570
Interracial Justice, National Catholic Conference, 573
Interregnum, 315-16
Intinction, 316
Iowa, 389, 398, 427, 431, 433, 436, 443, 528, 536, 544, 560
  School Preference Survey, 81
Iran, 348
  Airline Disaster, 100
Iran-Iraq War, 83, 88, 99, 104
Iraq, 348

Index

Ireland, 348, 369
　Partitioning (1920-22), 121
　　See also Northern Ireland
Irenaeus of Lyons, St., 254
Irenicism, 316
Irish Republican Army (IRA), **see** Northern Ireland
Irregularity, 316
Isaac Jogues, St., 386
Isaiah, 191
Iscariot (Judas), 197-98
Isidore of Seville, St., 199
Isidore the Farmer, St., 254
Islam, 293-94
　Catholic-Moslem Relations Commission, 152
Israel, 68, 71, 76, 78, 82, 86, 89, 102, 349
　Criticism of Policies, 68, 89
　Liaison Officer to Vatican, 76
　Plight of Arabs, 78, 86
Italian Catholic Federation of California, 572
Italo-Albanians, 268
Italy, 70, 86, 89, 94, 95, 349, 369
　Abortion, 86
　Anti-Semitism, 89, 94
　Concordat with Vatican, 178
　Papal Visits, 95
Itinerarium, 316
"It's Over, Debbie," 85
Ivory Coast, 349, 369

J

Jakubowski, Thad J., Bp., 455
Jamaica, 75, 349
　Workers Rights, Pastoral Letter, 94
James the Greater, St., 196
James the Less, St., 196
　Letter, 194
Jane Frances de Chantal, St., 254
Jansenism, 316
Januarius, St., 254
Japan, 106, 350, 369
Japanese Martyrs, **see** Paul Miki, St.
Jaricot, Pauline (1822), 120
Javierre Ortas, Antonio Maria, S.D.B., Card., 160, 169
Jeanne d'Arc, Sisters of St., 510
Jeanne Delanoue, St., 254
Jeanne de Lestonnac, St., 254
Jeanne de Valois, St., 254
Jeanne Elizabeth Bichier des Anges, St., 254
Jeanne Jugan, Bl., 254
Jehovah's Witnesses, 316
Jeremiah, 191
Jerome, St., 199
Jerome Emiliani, St., 254
Jerusalem, 350
Jerusalem Bible, 188
Jerusalem Council (51), 112
Jesuit North American Martyrs, 386
　Shrine at Auriesville, 390
Jesuit Martyrs' Shrine (Canada), 384
Jesuit Volunteer Corps, 567
Jesuits, 493
　Suppression (1773), 120
Jesus, 316
　See also Christ
Jesus, Daughters of, 510
　Daughters (Filles de Jesus), 510
　Little Brothers of, 497
　Little Sisters of, 510
　Servants of, 510
　Society of, **see** Jesuits
　Society of Sisters, Faithful Companions, 510
Jesus Caritas — Fraternity of Priests, 519
Jesus Crucified, Congregation of, 510
　and Sorrowful Mother, Poor Sisters, 510
Jesus-Mary, Religious of, 510
Jesus, Mary and Joseph, Missionaries of, 510
Jesus Prayer, 316
Jews
　Canon of Scripture, 187

Jews
　Judaism, 290-91
　Nazi Persecution and Pius XII, 73
　Persecution, Germany (1933), 122
　Relations with Catholics, 291-93
　See also Anti-Semitism; Israel
Joachim, St., 249
Joan Antida, Sisters of Charity of St., 502
Joan Antida Thouret, St., 254
Joan of Arc, St., 254
Joaquina de Vedruna de Mas, St., 254
Job (Bible), 190
Joel, 192
Jogues, Isaac, St., 386
John, St. (Apostle), 197
　Gospel, 193
　Letters, 194
John Baptist de la Salle, St., 254
John Berchmans, St., 254-55
John Bosco, St., 255
　Anniversary of Death, 75, 77
John Bosco, Salesians of St., 495
John Capistran, St., 255
John Carroll Society, 572
John Chrysostom, St., 199
John Courtney Murray Award, 598
John Damascene, St., 199
John de Brebeuf, St. 386
John de Castillo, St., 386
　Canonization, 40
John de Massias (Macias), St., 387
John de Ribera, St., 255
John Eudes, St., 255
John Fisher, St., 255
John Gilmary Shea Prize, 598
John Gualbert, St., 255
John Kanty, St., 255
John LaFarge Memorial Award, 598
John Lalande, St., 386
John Lateran Basilica, St., 176
　Feast of Dedication, 67, 247-48
John Leonardi, St., 255
John Nepomucene, St., 255
John Neumann, St., 255
John of Avila, St., 255
John of Britto, St., 255
John of God, St., 255
John of God, St., Hospitaller Order of, 497
John of Matha, St., 255
John of the Cross, St., 200
John Ogilvie, St., 255
John I, St., 254
John Paul I, Pope, 135
John Paul II, 31-5, 36-41, 43-4, 45-8, 63-4, 67-8, 71-2, 75-6, 79-80, 83-4, 87-8, 91-2, 95-6, 99-100, 103-04, 107-08, 109-11, 136, 142, 204-06, 292-93
　Africa Visit, 108-09
　Austria Visit, 36-7
　Beatifications, 36, 63, 68, 87
　Biography, 109-11
　Canonization of Rose Duchesne; Beatification of Junipero Serra and Katharine Drexel, 36
　Canonizations, 36, 40, 63, 95, 99, 136
　Ecumenical Statements, 286
　Encyclicals, 31-5, 142, 204-06
　"Euntes in Mundum," Apostolic Letter, 45-7
　Foundation for the Sahel, 101
　General Audience Topics, 63, 67, 72, 75, 79-80, 84, 88, 92, 96, 99-100, 103-04
　Laborem Exercens Excerpts, 204-06
　Lefebvre Schism, 42-4
　"Magnum Baptismi Donum," Apostolic Letter to Ukrainians, 47-8
　Marian Year, 44-5
　"On Social Concerns," Encyclical Letter, 31-5
　Roman Curia Reform, 147-48
　South America Visit, 38-41
　Statement on Humanae Vitae, 84

John Paul II
　Statements on Relations with Jews, 292-93
John the Baptist, St., 249
John the Baptist, St., Sisters of, 510
John XXIII, Pope
　Biography, 133-34
　Canonizations, 136
　Encyclicals, 142
　Second Vatican Council, 124, 133
　Social Encyclicals, 202
John Vianney, St., 255
Jolson, Alfred, S.J., Bp., 455
Jonah, 192
Jordan, 350
Josaphat, St., 255
Joseph, St., 249
Joseph, St. (Religious)
　Congregation of, 99, 493
　Missionary Servants of, 510
　Oblates of, 493
　Poor Sisters of, 510
　Religious Daughters of, 510
　Religious Hospitallers, 510
　Sisters of (List), 510
　Society for Foreign Missions (Mill Hill Missionaries), 494
　Society of the Sacred Heart (Josephites), 493
Joseph Benedict Cottolengo, St., 255
Joseph Cafasso, St., 255
Joseph Calasanz, St., 255
Joseph of Cupertino, St., 255
Joseph Pignatelli, St., 255
Josephinism (1760s), 120
Josephites (Baltimore), 493
　Pastoral Center, 487
Josephites (California), 493
Joshua, 189
Joyce, Robert F., Bp., 455
Joys of the Blessed Virgin Mary (Franciscan Crown), 310-11
Jubany Arnau, Narciso, Card., 160, 168, 169
Judaism, 290-91
Judaizers (51), 112
Judas, 197-98
Jude Thaddeus, St., 197
　Letter, 194
Judean Society, 572
Judges, 189
Judgment, Last and Particular, 316
　Rash, 325
Judith, 190
Jugan, Jeanne Bl., 254
Julia Billiart, St., 255
Julian the Apostate (361-363), 114
Junior Catholic Daughters of the Americas, 568
Jurisdiction, 316
Justice, 316
Justice and Peace Commission, 151
　Document on Homeless, 61-2
Justification, 316
Justin, St., 255
Justin de Jacobis, St., 255

K

Kaffer, Roger L., Bp., 455
Kalisz, Raymond P., S.V.D., Bp., 455
Kampuchea (Cambodia), **see** Cambodia
Kaniecki, Michael Joseph, S.J., Bp., 455
Kansas, 398, 428, 431, 433, 443, 528, 544, 553, 560
Kappa Gamma Pi, 569
Karma, **see** Buddhism
Kateri Tekakwitha, Bl., 255
　Shrine, 390
Katholicos, 143
Kazel, Dorothy, M.M., Sr., 78
Keating, John Richard, Bp., 455
Keeler, William H., Bp., 455
Keleher, James P., Bp., 455
Kells, Book of, 115
Kelly, Thomas, O.P., Abp., 455
Kemon, George, Jr., 600

Kennedy, Anthony M., Supreme Court Justice, 81, 409
Kennedy, John F. (Catholic History in U.S.), 392
Kennedy, Robert F. (Catholics in Presidents' Cabinets), 408
Kenney, Lawrence J., Bp., 455
Kenny, Michael H., Bp., 455
Kentucky, 398, 427, 430, 432, 436, 443, 527, 544, 551, 553, 561
Kenya, 350, 369
Kerner Commission Report, 84
Kerygma, 316-17
Keys, Power of, 317
Khan, I., 94
Khoraiche, Antoine Pierre, Card., 160, 168, 169
Kievan Rus, Millennium of Christianity, 45-7, 89
Kim, Stephen Sou Hwan, Card., 160, 168, 169
King Award, 598
King James Bible, 188
Kingdom of God, 179
Kingdom of Heaven (God), 312
Kings, Books of, 189
Kingship of Christ, Missionaries, 518
Kinney, John, Bp., 455
Kino, Eusebio, 386
Kiribati (Gilbert Islands), 350
Kitbunchu, Michael Michai, Card., 160, 168, 169
Kmiec, Edward U., Bp., 455
Knights of Columbus, 576
Knights of Lithuania, 572
Knights (Order) of Malta, 87, 596-97
Knights of Peter Claver, 572
Knights of St. Gregory, 596
Knights of St. John, 572
Knights of the Altar, 568
Knights of the Immaculata, 572
Kocisko, Stephen, Abp., 455
Koenig, Franz, Card., 160, 168, 169
Koester, Charles R., Bp., 456
Kokud, Selcuk, 96
Kolbe, Maximilian, St., 256
Kolping Society, Catholic, 570
Korea, 350, 369
Korea, North, 102
Korea, South, 350
Korean Martyrs (Sts. Andrew Kim and Comps.), 251
Kozak, Joseph K., 600
Krawczak, Arthur H., Bp., 456
Krol, John J., Card., 160, 168, 169
Kucera, Daniel, O.S.B., Bp., 456
Kuharic, Franjo, Card., 160, 168, 169
Kuchmiak, Michael, C.Ss.R., Bp., 456
Kulturkampf (1871), 121
Kung Pin-Mei, Ignatius, Bp., 77, 85, 101
Kupfer, William, M.M., Bp., 456
Kuwait, 350
Kuzma, George M., Bp., 456

L

Laborem Exercens, 204-06
Labrie, Jean-Paul, Bp., 382
Lacey, Michael Pearse, Bp., 382
Lacroix, Fernand, C.J.M., Bp., 382
Ladies of Charity in the U.S., 572
Ladislaus, St., 255
Laetare Medal, 598
Laghi, Pio, Abp., 173
  See also U.S.-Vatican Relations
Lahey, Raymond, Bp., 382
Laicization, 317
Laity
  Council for, 151
  in Missions Abroad, 521-23
  National Center for, 574
  National Council of (U.S.), 574
  Priesthood of, 324
  Rights and Obligations, 567-68
  Role of, 87, 146-47, 567-68
  Special Ministers (Eucharist), 219, 221
Laity
  Vocation and Mission (1987 Assembly of Synod of Bishops), 146-47
Lalande, John, St., 386
Lalemant, Gabriel, St., 386
Lamb of God (Mass), 213
Lamb of God, Sisters of, 510-11
Lambeth Conference, 106
Lambert, Francis, S.M., Bp., 456
LaMennais Brothers (Bros. of Christian Instruction), 496
Lamentations, 191
Lamy, Jean (John) Baptiste, 386
Landazuri Ricketts, Juan, O.F.M., Card., 160-61, 168, 169
Landriault, Jacques, Bp., 382
Landrieu, Moon (Catholics in Presidents' Cabinets), 408
Langevin, Louis-de-Ganzague, Bp., 382
Languages, Liturgical, 317
  Native American, 221
  Spanish, U.S., 221
Languages of the Bible, 187
Laos, 350, 369
  Church-State Relations, 82
Lapsi (249-251), 113
Larkin, W. Thomas, Bp., 456
LaRocque, Eugene, Bp., 382
LaSalette, Missionaries of, 493
LaSalette, Our Lady of, 265
Las Casas, Bartolome, 386
Last Judgment, 316
Last Temptation of Christ, The (Film), 105
Lateran, Canons Regular of, 493
Lateran Agreement (Roman Question), 132, 176
  1985 Concordat, 178
Lateran Councils I-IV (1123, 1139, 1179, 1215), 117, 123
Lateran Council V (1512-17), 118, 123
Lateran University, 539
Latin (Languages of Church), 317
  Mass in, 219
  See also Tridentine Mass
Latin America
  Bishops' Conference (CELAM), 81-2, 371
  Confederation of Religious, 517
  Pontifical Commission, 152
  See also Individual Countries
Latin Liturgy Association, 572
Latin (Roman) Rite, 211
Latria, **see** Adoration
Latvia, 350-51, 369
Laval, Francoise de Montmorency, Bl., 386
Laval University (Canada), 537
Lavigerie, Charles (Missionaries of Africa), 489
Law, 317
Law, Bernard F., Card., 161, 168, 169
Law, Canon, **see** Canon Law
Law, Civil, 317
Law, Divine, 317
Law, Natural, 317
Lawrence, St., 255
Lawrence of Brindisi, St., 200
Lawrence Ruiz and Companions, Sts., 63, 255
Lay Apostolate, **see** Laity; Organizations
Lay Brothers, **see** Brothers
Lay Carmelites, 520
Lay Institutes of Men, 489
Lay Mission-Helpers, 567
Lay Persons, **see** Laity
Lazarists (Vincentians), 496
Leadership Conference of Women Religious, 104, 517
Lebanon, 70, 74, 79, 351
  Christians, 70
  Corruption, 74
Lebel, Robert, Bp., 382
LeBlanc, Camille A., Bp., 382
Lebrun Maratinos, Jose Ali, Card., 161, 168, 169
Leclerc, Marc, Bp., 382
Lectionary, 218
Lector, 229
Lefebvre, Marcel, Abp., 42-4, 63, 74, 84, 96
  Reconciliation Efforts, 42, 63
  Schism (Chronology of Events) and Excommunication, 42-4, 96
  Seminary, U.S., 84
Legare, Henri, O.M.I., Abp., 382
Legates, Papal, **see** Representatives, Vatican
Leger, Paul Emile, S.S., Card., 161, 168, 169
Legion of Mary, 567
Legionaries of Christ, 493
Leguerrier, Jules, O.M.I., Bp., 382
Leibrecht, John J., Bp., 456
Lemieux, Marie Joseph, O.P., Abp., 382
Lent, 238
  Byzantine Rite, 272
  John Paul II on, 79
Leo I, the Great, St., 200
Leo III, the Isaurian (726), 115
Leo IX, St. (1049-54), 116
Leo XII, Pope, Encyclicals, 138
Leo XIII, Pope (1878), 121, 130
  Canonizations, 129
  Document on Anglican Orders, 297
  Encyclicals, 138-40
  Social Teachings, 130, 202
Leonard, Vincent M., Bp., 456
Leonard Murialdo, St., 255
Leonard of Port Maurice, St., 255
Leopold Mandic, St., 255-56
Lepanto (1571), 119
Lessard, Raymond W., Bp., 456
Lesotho, 351, 369-70
  Papal Visit to Africa, 107-08
Letters (Epistles), 193-94
Letters, Papal, **see** Encyclicals
Levada, William J., Abp., 456
Levesque, Louis, Abp., 382
Leviticus, 189
Lewis, Thomas A.J., 600
Liberalism, 317
Liberation Theology, 38, 100, 317
Liberia, 351, 369
Libya, 351
Lichten, Joseph, 600
Liechtenstein, 351
Life, Respect for, 65, 77, 87
  and Withdrawal of Food and Water, **see** Euthanasia
Life, Sanctity of, Presidential Proclamation, 77
Life, March for, 77
Life in Outer Space, 317
Lille, Catholic University (France), 537
Limbo, 317
Linens, Altar, 215
Lipscomb, Oscar H., Abp., 64, 456
Litany, 317-18
Literary Criticism, Bible, 195
Literary Forms of Bible, 195
Lithuania, 70, 87, 94, 102, 351-52, 370
  Government Concessions, 94
  Priest Released, 102
  Restrictions, 87, 106
Lithuanian Catholic Alliance, 573
Lithuanian Catholic Federation Ateitis, 572
Lithuanian Catholic Religious Aid, 573
Lithuanian Roman Catholic Federation, 573
Lithuanian Roman Catholic Priests' League, 573
Little Brothers of Jesus, 497
Little Brothers of St. Francis, 497
Little Flower, **see** Therese of Lisieux, St.
Little Flower Mission League, 573
Little Flower Society, 573
Little Sisters of Jesus, 510

Index

Little Sisters of the Holy Family, 505
Little Sisters of the Poor, 513
Liturgical
  Art, 211
  Colors, 214-15
  Conference, 573
  Developments, 217-22
  Music, 210, 220
  Year (Church Calendar), 238-39
Liturgy, 209-22
  Constitution, 124, 209-11, 212, 238, 306
  Dancing and Worship, 220
  Developments, 217-22
  Eastern Churches, 271
  Eucharistic, 213
  Popular Piety, 221
  See also Mass
Liturgy of the Hours, 210, 220
Liturgy of the Word, 212-13
Living Word, Sisters of, 511
Lobsinger, Thomas, O.M.I., Bp., 382
Lodge, Henry Cabot, 175
Lohmuller, Martin J., Bp., 456
Lombard, Peter (1160), 117
Lopez Contreras, Carlos, 76
Lopez Trujillo, Alfonso, Card., 161, 168, 169
Lord's Prayer, 213
Lorenzo (Lawrence) Ruiz and Companions, Sts., 63, 255
Loreto, House of, 318
Loretto at the Foot of the Cross, Sisters, 511
Lorscheider, Aloisio, O.F.M., Card., 161, 168, 169
L'Osservatore Romano, 177, 587
Losten Basil, Bp., 456
Lotocky, Innocent Hilarius, O.S.B.M., Bp., 456
Louis, Congregation of Sisters of St., 511
Louis Bertran, St., 385
Louis de Montfort, St., 256
Louis Moreau, Bl., 256
Louis IX of France, St., 256
Louise de Marillac, St., 256
Louisiana, 389, 398-99, 428, 431, 433, 436, 443, 528, 536, 544, 551-52, 553-54, 561
Lourdes, Our Lady of, Feast, 79
Lourdes Apparition, Shrine, 265
Lourdusamy, D. Simon, Card., 161, 169
Louvain, University, 537
  American College, 485
Loverde, Paul S., Bp., 456
Loyal Christian Benefit Association, 573
Lubachivsky, Myroslav J., Card., 100, 161, 168, 169
Lubbock, Tex., Events, 105
Lubich, Chiara, **see** Focolare Movement
Lublin, Catholic University (Poland), 538
Luce, Clare Booth, 600
Luciani, Albino, **see** John Paul I, Pope
Lucker, Raymond A., Bp., 456
Lucy, St., 256
Lucy Filippini, St., 256
Luecke, Janemarie, Sr., 600
Luke, St., 197
  Acts of the Apostles, 193
  Gospel, 193
Lumen Christi Award, 598
Lumen Gentium, **see** Church, Constitution
Lumen Vitae Center, 373
Luna (Lunette, Lunula), 215
Lust, 318
Lustiger, Jean-Marie, Card., 90, 106, 161, 168, 169
Luther, Martin, 276
Lutheran-Catholic Dialogue, U.S., 285, 289

Lutheran-Roman Catholic Commission, 287
Lutheran Churches, U.S., 278-79
Lutheran World Federation, 83, 287
Luxembourg, 352
Lyke, James P., O.F.M., Bp., 457
Lynch, George E., Bp., 457
Lyne, Timothy J., Bp., 457
Lyon, Catholic Faculties, 537
Lyonnaise Rite, **see** Rites
Lyons, Councils (1245, 1274), 117, 123
Lyons, Thomas W., Bp., 478, 600

M

Macau (Macao), 352
McAuliffe, Michael F., Bp., 457
MacBride, Sean, 600
Maccabees, 190
McCann, Owen, Card., 161, 168, 169
McCarrick, Theodore E., Abp., 457
  RENEW Revision, 88-9
McCarthy, Edward A., Abp., 457
McCarthy, John E., Bp., 457
McCloskey, John (U.S. Cardinals), 170, 479
McClurg, Patricia Ann, Rev., 69
McCollum v. Board of Education (Released Time), 410
McCormack, William, Bp., 457
McCormick, J. Carroll, Bp., 457
McDonald, Andrew J., Bp., 457
MacDonald, James H., C.S.C., Bp., 382
MacDonald, Joseph F., Bp., 382
McDonald, William J., Bp., 457
McDonough, Thomas J., Abp., 457
McDowell, John B., Bp., 457
Macedonianism (381), 114
McFarland, Norman F., Bp., 457
McGann, John R., Bp., 71, 457
McGarry, Urban, T.O.R., Bp., 457
McGivney, Michael J., **see** Knights of Columbus
McGranery, James P. (Catholics in Presidents' Cabinets), 408
McGrath, J. Howard (Catholics in Presidents' Cabinets), 408
McGrath, Marcos, Abp., 82
Macharski, Franciszek, Card., 161-62, 168, 169
McHugh, James T., Bp., 457-58
McInerney, Ralph, 81
McIntyre, James F., Card. (U.S. Cardinals), 170, 479
McKeever, Paul E., Rev., 600
McKenna, Joseph (Catholics in Presidents' Cabinets), 408
McKinney, Joseph C., Bp., 458
McLaughlin, Ann Dore (Catholics in Presidents' Cabinets), 408
McLaughlin, Bernard J., Bp., 458
McManus, William E., Bp., 458
McNabb Conway, John C., O.S.A., Bp., 458
McNamara, Lawrence J., Bp., 458
McNaughton, William, M.M., Bp., 458
MacNeil, Joseph N., Abp., 382
McRaith, John Jeremiah, Bp., 458
McShea, Joseph M., Bp., 458
Madagascar, 352, 370
Madeira Islands, 352
Madeleine Sophie Barat, St., 256
Madera, Joseph J., M.Sp.S., Bp., 458
Madonna House Apostolate, 519
Magazine Awards, CPA, 599
Magazines, Catholic, Canada, 385, 577
Magazines, Catholic, Foreign, 587-88
Magazines, Catholic, U.S., 577, 580-87
Magi, 318
Magisterium (Teaching Authority), 182-83
  and Interpretation of Bible, 184
Magnificat, 318
Magnum Baptismi Donum, Apostolic Letter (Ukrainian Millennium), 47-8
Maguire, John J., Abp., 458
Maguire, Joseph F., Bp., 458

Maher, Leo T., Bp., 458
Mahoney, James, Bp. (Canada), 382
Mahoney, James P., Bp. (U.S.), 458
Mahony, Roger M., Abp., 458
Maida, Adam J., Bp., 458
Maillat, Eugene, Bp., 600
Maine, 399, 425, 430, 432, 526, 544, 555, 561
Mainz Council (848), 115
Major Orders, **see** Holy Orders
Malabar Rite, **see** Chaldean Rite
Malachi, 192
Malachy, St., 256
Malachy, St., Prophecies, 324
Malagasy Republic, **see** Madagascar
Malankarese (Malankara Rite), 267-68
Malawi, 352, 370
  Refugees, 103
Malaysia, 352, 370
Maldives, 352
Mali, 352, 370
Malone, James W., Bp., 458
Maloney, Charles G., Bp., 458
Maloney, David, Bp., 458
Malta, 80, 352, 370
Malta, Order of, 596-97
Malula, Joseph, Card., 162, 168, 169
Malvinas, **see** Falkland Islands
Manchuria, **see** China
Mandela, Nelson, 100
Mandic, Leopold, St., 255-56
Manichaeism (c. 242), 113
Manning, Thomas R., O.F.M., Bp., 459
Manning, Timothy, Card., 162, 168, 169
Manogue, Patrick, 386-87
"Many Faces of AIDS," U.S. Bishops' Statement, 57-9, 72, 422
Manzini, Raimondo, 600
Marcellinus and Peter, Sts., 256
March for Life, 77
Marcinkus, Paul C., Abp., 96, 459
Marcionism (c. 144), 112
Marconi, Dominic A., Bp., 459
Marcus Aurelius (161-180), 112
Margaret Clitherow, St., 256
Margaret Mary Alacoque, St., 256
  Promises of the Sacred Heart, 326
Margaret of Cortona, St., 256
Margaret of Hungary, 256
Margaret of Scotland, St., 256
Margeot, Jean, Card., 162, 168, 169
Margil, Antonio, 387
Marguerite Bourgeoys, St., 385
Maria Goretti, St., 256
Marialis Cultus, 261
Marian Devotion, 261-64
Marian Fathers and Brothers, 493
Marian Library Medal, 598
Marian Movement of Priests, 573
Marian Sisters of Diocese of Lincoln, 511
Marian Society of Dominican Catechists, 511
Marian Union of Beauraing, 265
Marian Day Celebration, U.S. Vietnamese, 105
Mariana Paredes of Jesus, St., 256
Marianas, The, 353
Marianist Award, 598
Marianists (Priests), 493
Marianites of the Holy Cross, Sisters, 511
Mariannhill Missionaries, 493
Marianum Theological Faculty, 539
Marie-Leonie Paradis, Bl., 256
Marie of the Incarnation, Bl., 387
Marie Rose Durocher, Bl., 256
Marino, Eugene A., S.S.J., Abp., 84, 96, 100-01, 459
Mariological Society of America, 573
Mariology, **see** Mary
Marist Brothers, 497
Marist Fathers, 493-94
Marist Sisters, 511
Mark, St., 197

Mark, St.
  Gospel, 193
Markiewicz, Alfred J., Bp., 459
Maronite Antonine Sisters, 511
Maronite Monks, 494
Maronites, 268
  in U.S. (Antiochene Rite), 271
Marquesas Islands (French Polynesia), 344
Marquette, Jacques, 387
Marriage (Matrimony), 223, 230-37
  Doctrine on, 230-32
  Laws of the Church, 234-36
  Mixed, 236
Marriage Encounter, 237
Marriages, Invalid, and Sacraments, 236-37
Marriages, Catholic Statistics (U.S.), 434
  World, 367
Marshall, John A., Bp., 459
Marsilius of Padua (1324), 117
Marten, Blandina, Beatification, 68
Martha, St., 256
Marthe, Sisters of Sainte, 511
Martin, Albertus, Bp., 382
Martin, Jacques, Card., 162, 168, 169
Martin de Porres, St., 387
Martin of Tours, St., 256
Martin I, St., 256
Martinez Somalo, Eduardo, Card., 162, 169
Martini, Carlo Maria, S.J., Card., 162, 168, 169
Martinique, 353
Martino, Renato R., Abp., 70
Marty, Francois, Card., 162, 168, 169
Martyr, 318
Martyrology, 318
Marxism and Capitalism, Vatican Survey, 80
Mary
  Catholic Teaching, 261-64
  Ecumenical Common Statement, 264-65
  Marian Year, 44-5, 68, 104
  Role of, 91
  See also Blessed Virgin Mary
Mary (Religious)
  Company of, 511
  Daughters of Heart of, 511
  Little Company of, 511
  Missionaries of Company (Montfort Missionaries), 494
  Missionary Sisters of Society, 511
  Missionary Sons of Immaculate Heart (Claretians), 491
  Servants of, 511
  Servants of, Secular Order, 520
  Sisters of St., 511
  Sisters, Servants of, 511
  Society, 493-94
  Third Order Secular, 520
Mary, Legion of, 567
Mary and Joseph, Daughters, 511
Mary Domenica Mazzarello, St., 256
Mary Help of Christians, Daughters, 511
Mary Immaculate (Religious)
  Daughters, 511
  Oblates of, 494
  Religious, 511
  Sisters, Servants, 511
Mary Josepha Rossello, St., 256
Mary Magdalen Postel, St., 256
Mary Magdalene, St., 256
Mary Magdalene dei Pazzi, St., 256
Mary Major, Basilica of St., Dedication, 248
Mary Michaela Desmaisieres, St., 256
Mary of Immaculate Conception, Daughters, 512
Mary of Namur, Sisters of St., 511
Mary of Providence, Daughters of St., 511
Mary Productions, 592
Mary Queen, Congregation of, 512
Mary Reparatrix, Society of, 512

Maryheart Crusaders, 573
Maryknoll, 494
Maryknoll Sisters, 80, 504
Maryland, 389, 399, 426, 430, 432, 436, 443, 526, 536, 544-45, 552, 554, 561
Masons (Freemasons), 311
Mass, The, 213-14, 218-19
  Byzantine Rite, 271
  Canon, 213, 218, 221
  Changes, 218-19
  Children's, 219
  Concelebration, 304
  Dancing and Worship, 220
  Doxology, 213, 220
  Eucharistic Prayers, 213, 218, 221
  for Deceased Non-Catholics, 220
  for People, 318
  Homilist, 222
  Inter-Ritual Concelebration, 219
  Home (Mass for Special Groups), 218
  Latin, 219
  Lectionary, 218
  Missal (Sacramentary), 218
  Nuptial, and Blessing, 214
  Places and Altars, 214
  Saturday Evening, 218
  Special Eucharistic Ministers, 221
  Stipends, 330
  Study, 220
  Tridentine, 221
  Trination, 218-19
  Vestments, Vessels, 214-15
Mass for Homosexuals, 59-61
Massachusetts, 389, 399-400, 425, 430, 432, 436, 443, 526, 536, 545, 551, 552, 554, 561
Massias (Macias), John de, St., 387
Master of Ceremonies, 302
Master of Novices, 318
Mater et Magistra Award, 598
Materialism, 318
Matrimony, **see** Marriage
Matthew, St., 197
  Gospel, 193
Matthias, St., 197
Matthiesen, Leroy T., Bp., 459
Maundy Thursday, **see** Holy Thursday
Maurer, Jose Clemente, C.SS.R., Card., 162, 168, 169
Mauritania, 353
Mauritius, 353
Mauthausen Concentration Camp, 37
Maximilian Kolbe, St., 256
May, John L., Abp., 459
May Laws, **see** Kulturkampf
Mayotte, 353
Mazzarello, Mary Domenica, St., 256
Mazzuchelli, Samuel C., 387
Medal, Miraculous, 265
Medal, Scapular, 327
Medals, Papal, 597
Medals, (Awards), Catholic, 597-600
Medeiros, Humberto (U.S. Cardinals), 170, 480
Media (John Paul II on), 83
Medical Mission Sisters, 512
Medical Missionaries of Mary, 512
Medical Sisters of St. Joseph, 512
Medicus Mundi Internationalis, 373
Meditation, 318
Medjugorje, Yugoslavia, Events, 48-9, 70
Meek v. Pittenger (Auxiliary Services, Schools), 412
Meisner, Joachim, Card., 162, 168, 169
Mekhitarist Order of Vienna, 494
Melczek, Dale J., Bp., 459
Melilla, 353
Melkite Byzantine Rite, 268
Melkites, U.S., 270
Membre, Zenobius, 387
Men, Conference of Major Superiors, 517
Men, Religious Institutes, Membership, 498-99

Men, Religious Institutes, U.S., 489-97
Men of the Sacred Heart, 573
Menaion, 272
Mendel Medal, 598
Mendez, Alfred, C.S.C., Bp., 459
Mendicants, 318
Mennonites, **see** Anabaptism
Menologion, 272
Mentally Retarded Persons, National Apostolate with, 553-55
Mentally Retarded, Facilities for, 559
Mercedarian Missionaries of Berriz, 512
Mercedarian Third Order, 520
Mercedarians, 494
Mercy
  Corporal Works, 305
  Divine, 318
  Spiritual Works, 329
Mercy (Religious)
  Brothers of, 497
  Daughters of Our Lady of, 512
  Fathers of, 494
  Missionary Sisters of Our Lady of, 512
  Order of Our Lady of, 494
  Sisters of, 512
  Sisters of, of the Union, 512
Merit, 318
Mesena, Antonio, Beatification, 63
Messiah, **see** Christ
Mestice, Anthony F., Bp., 459
Metempsychosis, 318
Methodist Churches, U.S., 278
  Dialogues, 285
Methodist-Roman Catholic Commission, 287
Methodists, 277
Methodius, St. (Cyril and Methodius, Sts.), 252
  See also Czechoslovakia
Metropolitan, 144
Mexican Americans, 487-88
  Mexican American Cultural Center, 488
  PADRES, 488
  See also Hispanics
Mexico, 74, 90, 98, 353, 370
  Evangelical Sects, 90
  Missionaries of Charity, 98
  Problems, 74
Mexico, Twelve Apostles, 387
Meyer, Albert (U.S. Cardinals), 170, 480
Micah, 192
Michael, Archangel, 249
Michaels, James E., S.S.C., Bp., 459
Michigan, 400, 427, 430, 432, 436, 443, 527, 536, 545, 552, 554, 561
Middle East, 71, 72
  See also Iran-Iraq, Israel, Lebanon
Mieszko (966), 116
Migrant Workers, Rights, 67
Migration, Pontifical Commission, 151
Miguel Febres Cordero, St., 256
Milan, Edict (313), 113
Military Ordinariates, World Statistics, 367
Military Service, 206, 208
Military Services, Archdiocese for, U.S., 424
Militia of Our Lord Jesus Christ, 595-96
Mill Hill Missionaries, 494
Millennium, 318
Milone, Anthony, Bp., 459
Minder, John, O.S.F.S., Bp., 459
Mindszenty, Jozsef, Card. (Hungary), 347
Minim, Sisters of Mary Immaculate, 512
Ministries of the Church, 229
Minnesota, 400-01, 427, 431, 433, 436, 443, 528, 536, 545-46, 552, 554, 561-62
Minorities (U.S.), **see** Blacks; Hispanics

Index

Minton, Sherman (Justices of the Supreme Court), 408
Miracles, 318-19
Miraculous Medal, 265
Mirari Vos (1832), 120
Misericordia Sisters, 512
Missal, 319
Missiology, 319
Mission, 319
Mission, Congregation of (Vincentians), 496
Mission Association, U.S., 523
Mission Doctors Association, 567
Mission Helpers of the Sacred Heart, 512
Missionaries, American, 520-24
  Bishops, 425
  in Foreign Countries, 520-23
  in Home Missions, 523
Missionaries of Africa, 489
Missionaries of Charity, 92, 501
Missionaries of Sacred Heart, 495
Missionaries of St. Charles, 494
Missionaries of the Holy Apostles, 494
Missionaries of the Kingship of Christ the King, 518
Missionary Association of Catholic Women, 573
Missionary Catechists of the Sacred Hearts of Jesus and Mary, 512
Missionary Cenacle Apostolate, 573
Missionary Sisters of the Catholic Apostolate, 512
Missionary Union in the U.S., Pontifical, 575
Missionary Vehicle Association, 573
Missionhurst, 494
Missions, Catholic (U.S.), 523
  See also Hispanics
Mississippi, 401, 427, 431, 433, 527, 546
Missouri, 389, 401, 427, 431, 433, 436, 443-44, 528, 536, 546, 551, 552, 554, 562
Mitchell, James P. (Catholics in Presidents' Cabinets), 408
Mitre, 215
Mixed Marriages, 235
Modalism (c. 260), 113
Modern World, Constitution (Vatican II), 124, 202-04, 205-07, 230-31
Modernism, 319
  Syllabus of St. Pius X, 131, 331
Mogrovejo, Turibius de, St., 387
Mohammed (622), 115
Monaco, 353
Monarchianism (c. 260), 113
Monastery, 319
Monasticism (Sixth Century), 115
Mongolia, 353
Monica, St., 256
Monk, 319
Monophysite Churches, **see** Ancient Churches of the East
Monophysitism (451), 114
Monotheism, 319
Monothelitism (680-81), 115
Monsignor (Honorary Prelate), 144
Monstrance, 215
Montana, 401, 428, 431, 433, 444, 529, 536, 562
Montanism (156), 112
Monte Cassino (c. 529), 114
Montfort Missionaries, 494
Montrose, Donald, Bp., 459
Montserrat, 353
Mooney, Edward (U.S. Cardinals), 170, 480
Mooney, Silvester, Rev., 600
Moore, Emerson John, Bp., 459
Moral Obligations, 201-02
Morality, 319
Morality in Media, Inc., 573
Moran, William J., Bp., 459
Morand, Blaise, Bp., 382
Moravian Church, **see** Hus, John
More, Thomas, St., 258
Moreau, Louis, Bl., 256
Moreno, Manuel D., Bp., 459

Morin, Laurent, Bp., 382
Morissette, Pierre, Bp., 382
Morkovsky, John Louis, Bp., 459-60
Mormons, 319
Morneau, Robert F., Bp., 460
Morocco, 353
Morosini, Pierina, Beatification, 63
Moscati, Giuseppe, Canonization, 63
Mortal Sin, 328
Mortification, 319
Moskal, Robert, Bp., 460
Moslems (Muslims), 293-94
Mother Co-Redemptrix, Congregation of, 494
Mother of God, **see** Mary, Catholic Teaching
Mother of God, Missionary Sisters, 512
Mother of God, Sisters, Poor Servants, 512
Mother Carmel (Religious)
Mount Carmel, BVM of (July 16), 243
Mount Carmel (Religious)
  Congregation of Our Lady of, 500
  Institute of Our Lady of, 500
  Order of Our Lady, 490-91
  See also Carmelites
Mouton, Charles B., Msgr., 70
Movement for a Better World, 567
Movimiento Familiar Cristiano USA, 567
Mozambique, 82, 87, 107-08, 354, 370
  Papal Visit to Africa, 107-08
  Seminary Returned to Church, 106
Mozarabic Rite (Rites), 211
Mubarek, Hosmi, Pres., 80
Muench, Aloysius (U.S. Cardinals), 170, 480
Mugavero, Francis J., Bp., 460
Mulcahy, John J., Bp., 460
Mullor Garcia, Justo, Abp., 89
Mulqueen, Harold, S.J., Rev., 600
Mulrooney, Charles R., Bp., 460
Mulvee, Robert, Bp., 460
Mundelein, George (U.S. Cardinals), 170, 480
Mundo, Michael P., Bp., 460
Munoz Vega, Pablo, S.J., Card., 162, 168, 169
Muratorian Fragment, 186
Murphy, Frank (Catholics in Presidents' Cabinets), 408
Murphy, Michael J., Bp., 460
Murphy, Philip F., Bp., 460
Murphy, T. Austin, Bp., 460
Murphy, Thomas J., Abp., 81, 101, 460
Murphy, Thomas W., C.SS.R., Bp., 460
Muscat, **see** Arabian Peninsula
Music, Sacred, 210-11, 220
  Pontifical Institute, 539
Muskie, Edmund S. (Catholics in Presidents' Cabinets), 408
Muslims, **see** Moslems
Myers, John Joseph, Bp., 460
Mysteries of Faith, 319
Mysteries of Rosary, **see** Rosary
Mysterii Paschalis (Calendar), 238
Mysterium Fidei, **see** Transubstantiation
Mystery of Church, 179
Mystery of Eucharist, **see** Mass
Mystical Body, 179-80

N

Nahum, 192
Namibia (South West Africa), 354
  Church Bombing, 66
Napoleon (1789, 1809), 120
Nasalli Rocca di Corneliano, Mario, Card., 162, 168, 169
Nascimbeni, Giuseppe, Beatification, 87
Nathaniel (Bartholomew), 196
National
  Apostolate with Mentally Retarded Persons, 558

National
  Assembly of Religious Brothers, 517
  Assembly of Religious Women, 573
  Association of Catholic Chaplains, 541
  Association of Church Personnel Administrators, 573
  Association of Diocesan Ecumenical Officers, 573
  Association of Pastoral Musicians, 573
  Association of Permanent Diaconate Directors, 230
  Association of Priest Pilots, 573
  Bible Week, 69
  Black Catholic Congress, **see** Black Catholics
  Black Sisters Conference, 517
  Catholic Bandmasters' Association, 573
  Catholic Cemetery Conference, 573
  Catholic Conference for Interracial Justice, 573
  Catholic Conference for Seafarers, 566
  Catholic Development Conference, 573
  Catholic Disaster Relief Committee, 573
  Catholic Educational Association, 88, 525
  Catholic Forensic League, 568
  Catholic Office for Persons with Disabilities, 558
  Catholic Office for the Deaf, 558
  Catholic Pharmacists Guild, 573
  Catholic Rural Life Conference, 524
  Catholic Society of Foresters, 573-74
  Catholic Stewardship Council, 574
  Catholic Student Coalition, 569
  Catholic Women's Union, 574
  Catholic Young Adult Ministry Association, 568
  Catholic Youth Conference, 69
  Center for the Laity, 574
  Center for Urban Ethnic Affairs, 574
  Christ Child Society, 568
  Clergy Conference on Alcoholism and Related Drug Problems, 574
  Committee of Catholic Laymen, The, 574
  Conference of Airport Chaplains, 574
  Conference of Catholic Bishops, 439-43
  Conference of Diocesan Directors of Religious Education, 574
  Conference of Diocesan Vocation Directors, 574
  Conference of Religious Vocations Directors (National Religious Vocation Conference), 517
  Conference of Vicars for Religious, 517
  Council for Catholic Evangelization, 574
  Council of Catholic Laity, 574
  Council of Catholic Men, 574
  Council of Catholic Women, 69, 574
  Council of Churches of Christ, 69, 76, 284
  Federation for Catholic Youth Ministry, 568-69
  Federation of Catholic Physicians Guilds, 574
  Federation of Priests' Councils, 89, 574
  Federation of Spiritual Directors, 574
  Guild of Catholic Psychiatrists, 574
  Office for Black Catholics, **see** Black Catholics
  Organization for Continuing Education of Roman Catholic Clergy, 574

Index

National
  Religious Vocation Conference, 517
  Sanctity of Human Life Day, 77
  Sisters Vocation Conference (National Religious Vocation Conference), 517
NC News Service (Catholic News Service), 588
Native Americans, **see** Indians
Nativity, Blessed Virgin Mary, 247
Nativity, Christ (Christmas), 247
Nativity, St. John the Baptist, 249
Natural Law, 317
Natural Virtue, **see** Virtue
Nauru, 354
Navarra, Catholic University (Spain), 538
Nazareth, Poor Sisters of, 512
Ncube, Bernard, Sr., 66
Nebraska, 401, 428, 431, 433, 444, 528, 546, 552, 554, 562
Necromancy, 319
Nehemiah, 189-90
Nelson, Knute, O.S.B., Bp., 460
Nepal, 354
Nereus and Achilleus, Sts., 256
Nerinckx, Charles, 387
Nero (64), 112
Nestorian Churches, **see** Ancient Churches of the East
Nestorianism (431), 114
Netherlands, 354, 370
  Polarization in Church, 75
  Roman Catholic University, 538
Netherlands Antilles, 354
Network, 574
Neumann, John, St., 255
Nevada, 401-02, 428, 431, 433, 529, 552
Neves, Lucas Moreira, O.P., Card., 162, 168, 169
Nevins, John J., Bp., 460
New American Bible, 187-88
New Beginnings, Pittsburgh Diocese, 92
New Caledonia, 354
New English Bible, 188
New Guinea, **see** Papua New Guinea
New Hampshire, 389, 402, 425, 430, 432, 526, 546, 562
  AIDS Policy, Manchester Diocese, 89
New Hebrides (Vanuatu), 365
New Jersey, 389-90, 402, 426, 430, 432, 444, 526, 536, 546-47, 552, 554, 562
  Moment of Silence Ruling, 72
  Racial Attacks on Asian Indian Community, 65
  Surrogate Mother Contracts, 80
New Mexico, 390, 402, 428, 431, 433, 529, 536, 547, 554, 562
New Testament, 185-86, 193-94
New York, 390, 402-03, 425-26, 430, 432, 436, 444, 526, 536, 547, 551, 552-53, 554, 555, 562-63
  Homosexual Protests, St. Patrick's Cathedral, 72
  Surrogate Mother Contracts, 96
New Zealand, 354-55, 370
Newman, John H. (1833), 120
Newman, William C., Bp., 460
News Agencies, Catholic, 588
News Events (1987-1988), 63-108
News Services, U.S., 588
News Stories, Top (1987), 73
Newspaper Awards, CPA, 599
Newspapers, Catholic, U.S., 577-80
Neylon, Martin J., S.J., Bp., 460
Niagara Univ. (U.S.), 532, 538
Nicaea I, Council (325), 113, 123
Nicaea II, Council (787), 115, 123
  Anniversary, 79
Nicaragua, 66, 70, 81-2, 93, 355, 370
  Peace Efforts, 70, 103
  Radio Catolica, 66, 106
  Sandinistas Criticized, 105
Nicene Creed, 200-01
Nicholas, St., 256
Nicholas of Flue, St., 256

Nicholas of Tolentino, St., 256
Nicholas Tavelic and Companions, Sts., 256
Niedergeses, James D., Bp., 461
Niger, 355, 368
Nigeria, 355, 370
Nihil Obstat (Censorship of Books), 301
Niue, 355
Noble Guards, 176
Nobrega, Manoel, 387
Nocturnal Adoration Society of U.S., 574
Noel, Laurent, Bp., 382
Noel Chabanel, St., 386
Nolan, John G., Bp., 461
Nolker, Bernard C., C.SS.R., Bp., 461
Noll, John F., Abp., 481
Non-Abrahamic Religions, 294-95
Non-Believers, Secretariat, 151
Non-Christian Religions, Declaration (Vatican II), 124, 291, 294
Non-Christians, Secretariat, 151
Non-Expedit, 320
Norbert, St., 256-57
Norbert, Third Order of St., 520
Norbertines (Premonstratensians), 495
Noriego, Manuel, Gen., 82, 86, 90
North America, Cardinals, 169
  Catholic Statistics, 367
  Eastern Rite Jurisdictions, 270
North American Academy of Liturgy, 574
North American College, 558
North American Conference of Separated and Divorced Catholics, 574
North American Martyrs, Jesuit, 386
North Carolina, 403, 426, 430, 432, 526, 547, 555, 563
North Dakota, 403-04, 427, 431, 433, 444, 528, 536, 547-48, 552, 563
Northeast Hispanic Catholic Center, 488
Northern Ireland, 348
  Violence, 68, 69-70, 77, 86, 98
  See also Ireland
Norway, 355
Nostra Aetate (Non-Christian Religions Declaration), 124, 291, 294
Notre Dame (Religious)
  de Namur, Srs. of, 513
  de Sion, Congregation, 513
  School Sisters, 512-13
  Sisters, 513
  Sisters of Congregation, 513
Notre Dame University, 533
Novak, Alfred, C.SS.R., Bp., 461
Novalis Marriage Preparation Center, 373
Novatian (249-51), 113
Novena, 320
Novice, 320
Novices, Master, 318
Novitiate, **see** Novice
Nsubuga, Emmanuel, Card., 162-63, 168, 169
Nuclear Deterrence, 75
Nuclear War (U.S. Bishops Pastoral), 207-07
Nuclear Weapons Treaty, 97
Nulla Celebrior, **see** Patriarchs
Nullity Decree (Annulment), 235, 237
Numbers, 189
Nun, 320
Nunc Dimittis, 320
Nuncios, 170-73
Nuptial Mass, Blessing, 214

O

O Salutaris Hostia, 321
Oath, 320
Oath of Succession (1563), 119
Obadiah, 192
Obando Bravo, Miguel, Card., 70, 76, 103, 163, 168, 169
Obedience, 320
Obedience of Faith, 310

Oblate Missionaries of Mary Immaculate, 518-19
Oblate Sisters of
  Blessed Sacrament, 515
  Providence, 514
  St. Francis de Sales, 505
Oblates of
  Mary Immaculate, 494
  Most Holy Redeemer, 514
  St. Benedict, 520
  St. Francis de Sales, 492
  Virgin Mary, 494
Obligations, Moral, 201-02
O'Boyle, Patrick A. (U.S. Cardinals), 170, 481
O'Brien, Brendan M., Bp., 382
O'Brien, Lawrence (Catholics in Presidents' Cabinets), 408
O'Brien, Thomas Joseph, Bp., 461
Obsession, Diabolical, 320
O'Byrne, Paul J., Bp., 382
Occasions of Sin, 329
Occultism, 320
Oceania
  American Bishops, 425
  Cardinals, 169
  Catholic Statistics, 367
  Eastern Rite Jurisdictions, 270
Ochoa, Armando, Bp., 461
O'Connell, Anthony J., Bp., 461
O'Connell, William (U.S. Cardinals), 170, 481
O'Connor, Hubert P., O.M.I., Bp., 382
O'Connor, John J., Card., 163, 168, 169
  View of Holocaust, 69
  Visit to Cuba, 90
Octave, 320
Octave of Birth of Our Lord (Solemnity of Mary), 249
Oddi, Silvio, Card., 163, 168, 169
Odilia, St., 257
O'Donnell, Cletus F., Bp., 461
O'Donnell, Edward J., Bp., 461
Of Human Life (Humanae Vitae), 84, 232
  Twentieth Anniversary Statement, 232-34
Offertory, 213
Office, Divine (Liturgy of the Hours), 210, 220
Offices of the Roman Curia, 153
O'Fiaich, Tomas, Card., 163, 168, 169
  on IRA Bombing, 69-70
O'Grady, John F., O.M.I., Bp., 382
O'Hara, John F. (U.S. Cardinals), 170, 481-82
Ohio, 390, 404, 426, 430, 432, 436, 444, 527, 536, 548, 551, 552, 555, 563
  Hospital Status Changed, Akron, 65
  Office of Public Affairs, USCC/NCCB, 588
Oil of Catechumens, 320
Oil of the Sick, 320
Oils, Holy, 320
O'Keefe, Gerald, Bp., 461
O'Keefe, Joseph Thomas, Bp., 461
Oklahoma, 390, 404, 428, 431, 433, 528, 548, 563
Oktoechos, 272
Old Catholics, 320
Old Testament, 185, 186, 188-92
  See also Bible
O'Leary, Edward C., Bp., 461
Olga, St. (955), 116
Oliver Plunket, St., 257
Olivetan Benedictine Sisters, 499
O'Malley, Sean, O.F.M. Cap., Bp., 461
Oman, 355
O'Mara, John A., Bp., 382
O'Meara, Edward T., Abp., 73, 461
"On this Rock," 592
O'Neil, Leo E., Bp., 461
O'Neill, Arthur J., Bp., 461
Operation Rescue, 92, 101
Operation Rice Bowl, 81
Optatam Totius, 124
Opus Dei, 320-21
Opus Spiritus Sancti, 519

Index

Oratorians, 494
Oratory, 321
Oratory of St. Philip Neri, 494
Order of the Alhambra, 574
Orders, Anglican, **see** Anglican Orders
Orders, Holy, **see** Holy Orders
Orders, Religious, 489
Orders of Knighthood, 595-96
Ordinariate, 321
Ordinary, 144
Ordination, 321
  See also Deacons, Permanent; Holy Orders
Ordo Paenitentiae, **see** Penance
Oregon, 390, 404-05, 429, 431, 433, 444, 529, 536, 548, 552, 555, 563
O'Reilly-Conway Medal, 598
Organ Transplants, 321
Organizations, Catholic, 569-76
Oriental Church, Orthodox, Dialogues, 285
Oriental Churches, Sacred Congregation, 148-49
Oriental Studies, Pontifical Institute, 539
Orientalium Ecclesiarum, 124
  See also Eastern Churches, Catholic
Original Sin, 321
O'Rourke, Edward W., Bp., 461
Ortega, Daniel, Pres. (Nicaragua), 75
  See also Nicaragua
Orthodox Churches, Eastern, 274
  Catholic-Orthodox Theological Commission, 68-9, 96-7, 288
  Conference of Bishops, 274
  Dialogues, U.S., 285
  Ecumenical Statements, 285, 286, 288
  Ecumenism, 275-76
  Jurisdictions, 274
Orthodox Churches, Oriental (Ancient Churches of the East), 274-75
  Dialogues, 285
  Ecumenical Statements, 285, 286
Ortiz Miranda, Carlos, 68
Osservatore Romano (L'), 177
Ostensorium, 215
Ostpolitik, 321
Ott, Stanley J., Bp., 461
Ottenweller, Albert H., Bp., 461-62
Otto I (962), 116
Otunga, Maurice, Card., 163, 168, 169
Ouellet, Gilles, P.M.E., Abp., 382
Ouellette, Andre, Bp., 383
Our Father (Lord's Prayer), 213
Our Lady, **see** Apparitions of BVM; Blessed Virgin Mary
Our Lady of Charity, North American Srs. of Union of, 513
Our Lady of LaSalette, Missionaries, 493
Our Lady of Mercy, Missionary Sisters, 512
Our Lady of Sorrows, Sisters, 513
Our Lady of the Garden, Sisters, 513
Our Lady of the Way, Society, 519
Our Lady of Victory Homes, 64
Our Lady of Victory Missionary Sisters, 513
Oxford Movement, 321
Ozanam, Frederic (St. Vincent de Paul Society), 541

P

Pacem in Terris, **see** Social Doctrine
Pacem in Terris Priests, Czechoslovakia, 86
Pachomius, St. (318), 113
Pactum Callixtinum (1122), 117
Padilla, Juan de, 387
Padiyara, Anthony, Card., 163, 168, 169
PADRES, 488
Paenitemini, **see** Penance

Paganism, 321
Pakistan, 355, 370
Palaeologus, Michael (1281), 117
Palatine Guard of Honor, 176
Palazzini, Pietro, Card., 163, 168, 169
Palestinians, 69, 86, 89
Pall, 215
Pallium, 215
Pallottine Sisters, 513
Pallottines, 494
Palm Sunday (Sunday of the Passion), 249
Palms, 321
Palou, Francisco, 387
Palou y Quer, Francisco, Beatification, 87
Panama, 82, 86, 90, 355, 370
  U.S. Economic Sanctions, 90
Pancasila, 69
Pancras, St., 257
Pange Lingua, 321
Pantheism, 321
Paola Frassinetti, St., 257
Papacy, **see** Pope
Papal
  Addresses, **see** John Paul II
  Audience, 177
    See also Vatican in News Events
  Election, 321-22
  Flag, 176
  Medals, 597
  Representatives, 75, 170-73, 178
  Secretariat of State, 148
  States (1870), 121, 176
    See also Apostolic; Pontifical; Pope; Vatican
Pappalardo, Salvatore, Card., 163, 168, 169
Pappin, Bernard F., Bp., 383
Papua New Guinea, 356, 370
Paraclete, 322
Paraclete, Servants of the, 494
Paraguay, 356, 370
  Papal Visit, 40-1
  Tension, 82, 85, 102, 106
Paraliturgical Services, **see** Devotions
Pare, Marius, Bp., 383
Paredes de Jesus, St. Mariana, 256
Parents, Duties, 322
Paris, Catholic Institute, 537
Paris Foreign Mission Society, 494
Pariseau, Mother Joseph, 387
Parish, 322
Parish Visitors of Mary Immaculate, 513
Parishes (Statistics), U.S., 425-29
  World, 367
Parker, Matthew, **see** Anglican Orders
Parochial Schools, **see** Schools, Catholic
Parousia, 322
Particular Examen, **see** Conscience
"Partners in the Mystery of Redemption," Pastoral on Women, 51-2
Paschal Baylon, St., 257
Paschal Candle, 322
Paschal Precept, 322
Paschal Season (Easter Season), 238
Paschal Vigil (Easter Vigil), 248
Paschang, John L., Bp., 462
Paskai, Laszlo, O.F.M., Card., 163, 168, 169
Passion, Congregation of, 494
Passion of Christ, 322
Passion (Palm) Sunday, 249
Passion Plays, 85
Passionist Communications, 592
Passionist Nuns, 513
Passionist Sisters, 503
Passionists, 494
Passover, 291
Pastor, 322
Pastor Aeternus (Primacy of Pope), 182
Pastor Bonus (Curia Reform,) 95, 147-48

Pastors, 64
Pataki, Andrew, Bp., 462
Paten, 215
Pater Noster, 322
Patriarchates, Catholic, 143-44, 266
Patriarchates, Orthodox, 274
Patriarchs, Catholic, 143-44, 266
  Cardinals, 154
  Eastern, 266
  Synods, 270
Patrick, St., 257
Patrick, St., Brothers of (Patrician Brothers), 497
Patrick's Missionary Society, St., 494
Patrimony of the Holy See, 153
Patriotic Association of Chinese Catholics, 74, 106
  See also China
Patripassianism (c. 260), 113
Patron Saints, 258-60
Paul, John J., Bp., 462
Paul, St. (Apostle), 197
  Feast, Conversion, 247
  Feast (Peter and Paul), 249
  Letters (Epistles), 193-94
Paul, St. (Religious)
  Angelic Sisters of, 513
  Daughters of, 513
  for Apostolate of Communications, Society of, 495
  of Chartres, Sisters of, 513
  the Apostle, Missionary Society of, 495
  the First Hermit, Order of, 494-95
Paul Miki and Companions, Sts., 257
Paul of the Cross, St., 257
Paul VI, Pope
  Anniversary of Death, 103
  Biography, 134
  Canonizations, 136
  Ecumenical Meetings, 285, 286
  Encyclicals, 142, 232
Pauline Fathers (Doylestown), 494-95
Pauline Fathers and Brothers, 495
Pauline Letters, 193-94
Pauline Privilege, 235
Paulinus of Nola, St., 257
Paulist Award for Lay Evangelization, 598
Paulist Communications Services, 593
Paulist National Catholic Evangelization Association, 575
Paulist Productions, 593
Paulists, 495
Paupini, Giuseppe, Card., 163, 168, 169
Pavan, Pietro, Card., 163-64, 168, 169
Pax Christi International, 373
Pax Christi USA, 568
Pax Christi (Pious Association), 519-20
Pax Christi Award, 598
Pax Romana, 373
Pax Romana, U.S., 566
Peace, 207-08
  Commission for, 151
  Central America, Efforts, 70, 74, 81-2, 103
  Iran-Iraq Cease Fire, 103
  John Paul II Appeals, 71, 72, 75, 88, 103
  World Peace Day Message (John Paul II), 76
  U.S. Bishops' Pastoral, 207-08
Peace, Sign of (Mass), 213, 322
Peace Award, 598
Peace Prayer, Mass, 213
Pearce, George H., S.M., Abp., 462
Pechillo, Jerome, T.O.R., Bp., 65, 462
Pectoral Cross, 322
Pednault, Roch, Bp., 383
Pelagianism (431), 114
Pellegrino, Edmund, Dr., 90
Pelotte, Donald E., S.S.S., Bp., 462
Pena, Raymundo J., Bp., 462
Penance (Penitence), 322
Penance (Sacrament), 223, 226-27
  First, and First Communion, 225
  Norms on General Absolution, 227

Penance
  Penitential Celebrations, 227
Penitential Rite, Mass, 212
Penitentiary, Apostolic, 150
Penney, Alphonsus L., Abp., 383
Pennsylvania, 390, 405, 426, 430, 432, 436, 444, 526, 536-37, 548-49, 551, 552, 555, 563-64
  Abortion Ruling, 73
  New Beginnings, Pittsburgh Diocese, 92
Pentateuch, 188-89
Pentecost, 249
  Dates (1989-2012), 246
Pentecost '88, 92
Pentecost (Jewish Festival), 291
Pentecostal Churches, 281
Pentecostal-Roman Catholic Consultation, 288
Pentecostarian, 272
People of God, 180
Pepin (754), 115
Peregrine, St., 257
Perfect Contrition, 305
Perfectae Caritatis, 124
Perfectionist Churches, 281
Periodicals, Catholic, 577-87
Perjury, 322
Permanent Diaconate, 77, 229-30
Perpetua and Felicity, Sts., 257
Perpetual Eucharistic Adoration, 575
Perry, Harold R., S.V.D., Bp., 462
Persecution, Religious, 322
Persia, see Iran
Personal Prelature, 322
  Opus Dei, 320
Peru, 356, 370
  Papal Visit, 39-40
  Priest Murdered, 74
  Violence, 98
Peter, St. (Apostle), 197
  Feast (Chair of St. Peter), 247
  Letters, 194
Peter and Paul, Sts. (Feast), 249
Peter Canisius, St., 200
Peter Chanel, St., 257
Peter Chrysologus, St., 200
Peter Claver, St., 386
Peter Claver, St., Missionary Sisters, 513
Peter Damian, St., 200
Peter Fourier, St., 257
Peter Gonzalez, St., 257
Peter Guilday Prize, 598
Peter Julian Eymard, St., 257
Peter Nolasco, St., 257
Peter of Alcantara, St., 257
Peter of Ghent, 387
Peter's Pence, 322
Petition, 323
Petrilli, Savina, Beatification, 87
Petrine Privilege, 235
Pevec, A. Edward, Bp., 462
Pews, 216
Pfeifer, Michael, O.M.I., Bp., 462
Phantasiasm (c. 125), 112
Pharisees, 323
Phelonian, 273
Phi Kappa Theta Fraternity, 569
Philangeli, 575
Philemon, 194
Philip, St. (Apostle), 197
Philip Benizi, St., 257
Philip Neri, St., 257
Philip Neri, St., Congregation of Oratory of, 494
  Missionary Teachers, Sisters, 507
Philip of Jesus, St., 257
Philippians, 194
Philippines, 72, 81, 98, 356, 370
  Apparition, Alleged, 81
Philosophical Association, American Catholic, 569
Phoebe (Deaconess), 306
Photius (857), 115
Piarists, 495
Picachy, Lawrence Trevor, S.J., Card., 164, 168, 169

Piche, Paul, O.M.I., Bp., 383
Picpus Fathers (Sacred Hearts Fathers), 495
Pierce v. Society of Sisters, 409, 525
Pilarczyk, Daniel E., Abp., 81, 462
Pilgrimages, Papal, see John Paul II
Pilla, Anthony M., Bp., 462
Pimenta, Ignatius, Card., 164, 168, 169
Pinger, Henry A., O.F.M., Bp., 462
Pious Fund, 323
Pious Schools, Order of, 495
Pious Schools, Sisters of, 513
Pious Union
  of Prayer, 575
Piovanelli, Silvano, Card., 166, 168, 169
Pironio, Eduardo, Card., 164, 168, 169
Pisa, Council (1409), 118
Pius IV, Creed, 201
Pius V, St., 257
Pius VI, Encyclicals, 138
Pius VII (1809), 120
  Encyclical, 138
Pius VIII, Encyclical, 138
Pius IX (1864, 1870), 120, 121
  Encyclicals, 138-39
  Order of, 596
  Syllabus, 331
Pius X, St. (1903-14), 121
  Biography, 130-31
  Canonizations, 135
  Encyclicals, 140
  Liturgical Movement, 217
  Syllabus (*Lamentabili*), 131, 331
Pius X, St., Brothers of, 497
  Secular Institute of, 519
Pius XI (1922-39), 121-22
  Biography, 131-32
  Canonizations, 135
  Encyclicals, 141
Pius XII, Pope
  and Nazi Persecution of Jews, 73
  Biography, 132-33
  Canonizations, 135-36
  Encyclicals, 141-42
  Liturgical Movement and, 132-33, 217
Pius XII Marian Award, 598
Planned Parenthood and United Way, Seattle, 101
Plenary Councils, 305
Plenary Councils, Baltimore, 392
Pliny the Younger (112), 112
Plouffe, Jean-Louis, Bp., 383
Plourde, Joseph A., Abp., 383
Plunket, Oliver, St., 257
Poland, 71, 82, 92, 93, 98, 356-57, 370
  Labor Unrest, 92, 93, 103
Poletti, Ugo, Card., 164, 168, 169
Polish National Catholic Church, Dialogue, 285
Political Responsibility, 64
Politics, Church Involvement and IRS, 101
Polycarp, St., 257
Polygamy, 67
Polyglot Press, Vatican, 177
Polynesia, French, 344
Polytheism, 323
Pompei, Loreto and Bari, Sanctuaries, Comm. for, 152
Pontian, St., 257
Pontiff see Pope
Pontifical
  Academy of Sciences, 540-41
  Assn. of the Holy Childhood, 568
  Biblical Commission, 152
  College Josephinum, 539
  Commissions, 151-52
  Ecclesiastical Faculties, 538-39
  Household, Prefecture, 153
  Institute for Foreign Missions, 495
  Letters, see Encyclicals
  Mission for Palestine, 69, 575
  Missionary Union, 575
  Orders of Knighthood, 595-96
  Universities, 537-38, 539
    See also Papal

Poor, Little Sisters of, 513
Poor, Option for, 34
Poor Box, 323
Poor Clare Missionary Sisters, 513
Poor Clare Nuns, 506
Poor Clares of Perpetual Adoration, 507
Poor Handmaids of Jesus Christ, 513
Pope, 143
  Authority, Infallibility, Primacy, 183-84
  Election, 321-22
  See also John Paul II
Pope Joan, 323
Popes (List), 125-29
Popes, Encyclicals (List), 137-42
Popes, False (Antipopes), 128-29
Popes, Twentieth Century, 130-35
"Popish Plot" (1678), 119
Popp, Bernard, Bp., 462
Population, Catholic
  Canada, 337, 377-79
  Countries of World, 333-68
  United States, 97, 425-31, 434
  World Totals, 367
Populorum Progressio, 20th Anniversary, 80
  See also *Sollicitudo Rei Socialis*
Pornography
  Boycott Urged, Chicago, 88
  Wisconsin Bishops' Statement, 81
Porres, Martin de, St., 387
Porter, 229
Porter, William, 600
Portiuncula, 323
Portugal, 357-58, 370
Possession, Diabolical, 323
Postulant, 323
Poterion, 273
Poupard, Paul, Card., 164, 169
Poverello Medal, 598
Poverty, 323
Povish, Kenneth J., Bp., 462
Power, Cornelius M., Abp., 462
Power, William E., Bp., 383
Power of the Keys, 317
  See also Infallibility; Primacy
Powers (Angels), 297
Pragmatic Sanction (1438), 118
Pragmatism, 323
Prague, Infant Jesus of, 315
Praises, Divine, 307
Prayer, 323
Prayer Intentions, Monthly, see Calendar, 1989
Prayer of the Faithful, 213
Prayer over the Gifts, 213
Precept, Paschal, 322
Precepts, 323
Precepts of the Church, 201-02
Predestination, see Calvin, John
Preface, 213
Prefect Apostolic, 144
Pregnancy, Teen, and School-Based Clinics, 56-7
Premontre, Order of Canons Regular (Premonstratensians), 495
Presbyterian Churches, U.S., 279
Presbyterians, 277
Presbyterians, Reformed, Dialogue, 285
Presbyterium Ordinis, 124
Presence of God, 323
Presentation (Feast), 249
Presentation (Religious)
  Brothers, of Mary, 497
  of Mary, Sisters, 514
  of the BVM, Sisters, 514
Press, Catholic, U.S., 577-87
  Statistics, 577
Press, International Catholic Union, 372-73
Press, Vatican, 177
Press Association, Catholic, 571, 599-60
  St. Francis de Sales Award, 599
Press Office, Vatican, 177
Presumption, 323

Index

Preternatural Gifts, 323-24
Pride, 324
Prie-Dieu, 324
Priest, 228
Priesthood (Synod of Bishops), 145
Priesthood Candidates, U.S., 68
Priesthood of the Laity, 324
Priestly Society of St. Pius X, **see** Lefebvre, Marcel, Abp.
Priests, Holy Thursday Letter (John Paul II), 83
Priests, Canada (Statistics), 377-79
Priests, U.S. (Statistics), 425-29
  in Foreign Missions, 520-21
Priests, World (Statistics), 367
  See also Individual Countries
Priests' Councils, National Federation (U.S.), 89, 574
Priests' Eucharistic League, 575
Primacy of Pope, 143, 182
  and Unity, 71
Primary Option, 324
Primate, 144
Primatesta, Raul Francisco, Card., 164, 168, 169
Primeau, Ernest, Bp., 462
Principalities (Angels), 297
Prior, 324
Privilege, 324
Privilege of Faith (Petrine Privilege), 235
Probabilism, 324
Pro-Cathedral, 324
Pro Comperte Sane, **see** Roman Curia
Pro Ecclesia et Pontifice Medal, 597
Pro Ecclesia Foundation, 575
Pro Maria Committee, 575
Promoter of the Faith, 324
Pro-Nuncio, 170
Propagation of the Faith, Cong. of, 150
  Society of, 575
Proper of the Mass, 213
Prophecies of St. Malachy, 324
Prophecy, 324
Prophets, 191-92
Pro Sanctity Movement, 373, 575
Prost, Jude, O.F.M., Bp., 462-63
Protestant
  Canon of the Bible, 187
  Churches in the U.S., Major, 277-81
  See also Ecumenism
Protestants and Intercommunion, 226
Protocanonical Books (Canons of Bible), 187
Proulx, Amedee W., Bp., 463
Proverbs, 190
Providence, Sisters of, 514
Providence, Sons of Divine, 495
Providence Association of Ukrainian Catholics, 575
Province, 324
Provinces, Ecclesiastical, Canada, 375
  United States, 415-16
Provincial Councils, 305
Providentissimus Deus, 196
Prudence, 324
Psalms, 190
Pseudepigrapha, 188
Public Affairs of Church, Council for, 148
Public Schools
  Contraceptive Programs, (School-Based Clinics), 56-7, 441-42
  Released Time, 525
Publications, Vatican, 177-78
Publishers, 594-95
Puerto Rico, 358, 370
  Dates in Catholic History, 407-08
  Episcopal Conference, 370
  Minor Basilica, 436
Puerto Rican Catholics in U.S., **see** Hispanics
Pulpit, 216
Punishment Due for Sin, 324
Purgatory, 324-25

Purification (Presentation of the Lord), 249
Purificator, 215
Purim, 291
Puritans, 277
Pursley, Leo A., Bp., 463
Puscas, Louis, Bp., 463
Pyx, 215

Q

Qatar, 358
Quakers, 277
Quam Singulari, **see** Communion, First and First Confession
Quanta Cura (1864), 120
Quartodecimans (Easter Controversy), 307-08
Queenship of Mary, 250
Quinn, Alexander James, Bp., 463
Quinn, Francis A., Bp., 463
Quinn, John R., Abp., 463
Quiroga, Vasco de, 387
Qumran Scrolls (Dead Sea Scrolls), 188

R

Racial Discrimination, John Paul II on, 83
Racism, 325
Racism, U.S., Attacks on Asian Indian Community, 65
  Kerner Report, 84
Radio, Catholic, U.S., 592
Radio, Vatican, 176
Rafaela Maria Porras y Ayllon, St., 257
Ramirez, Ricardo, C.S.B., Bp., 463
Ramousse, Yves Georges-Rene, Abp., 94
Ramsey, Michael, Abp. (Anglican), Death, 87, 600
Raphael, Archangel, 249
Rash Judgment, 325
Raskob Foundation, 575
Rationalism, 325
Ratzinger, Joseph, Card., 59, 63, 64, 78, 164, 168, 169
  Lefebvre Schism, 42-4
Ravalli, Antonio, 387
Raya, Joseph M., Abp., 463
Raymbaut, Charles, 387
Raymond Nonnatus, St., 257
Raymond of Penyafort, St., 257
Razafimahatratra, Victor, S.J., Card., 164, 168, 169
RCIA (Rite of Christian Initiation of Adults), 222, 223-24
Reader (Lector), 229
Readings, Mass, 212
Readings, Office of (Liturgy of Hours), 210
Reagan, Ronald, Pres., 72, 77
  National Sanctity of Human Life Day Proclamation, 77
Reason, Age of, 296
Reche, Arnold, Beatification, 68
Recollection, 325
Recollects, Augustinian, 489
Reconciliation, **see** Penance
Reconciliation Room, 216-17
Red Mass, Washington, D.C., 64
Redemptorists, 495
Reformation (1517), 118
  Men, Doctrines, Churches, 276-77
Reformed Churches-Roman Catholic Conversations, 288
Refuge, Sisters of Our Lady of Charity, 513
Refugees, 70
  African, 91
  Palestinian, 69
  Political, U.S., 68
Regan, Joseph, M.M., Bp., 463
Regimini Ecclesiae Universae (Roman Curia), 147
Regina Caeli (Angelus), 297
Regina Medal, 599
Regis College Lay Apostolate, 568

Regular Clergy, 303
Reh, Francis, Bp., 463
Reilly, Daniel P., Bp., 463
Reilly, Thomas F., C.SS.R., Bp., 463
Reiss, John C., Bp., 463
Relativism, 325
Released Time, 525
  See also Church-State Decisions
Relics, 325
Relief Services, Catholic, 94, 105, 443
Religion, 325
Religions, Non-Abrahamic, 294-95
Religious, 489
  Congregation for, 149-50
  John Paul II Advice, 99
  Latin American Confederation, 517
  Retired, Needs of, 93
  Superiors, Internatl. Union, 517
  Vicars of, 517
Religious, Men, 489
  Brothers National Assembly, 517
  Brothers (World Statistics), 367
  Conference of Major Superiors, U.S., 104, 517
  in U.S. (List), 489-97
  in U.S. (Statistics), 425-29
  Priests (World Statistics), 367
  Relations with Bishops, 91
  World Membership, 498-99
Religious, Women U.S., 499-516
  Organizations, 517
  Retirement Fund, Needs, 72, 93
  Salaries, Indianapolis Archdiocese, 73
  Statistics, 425-29
  Teachers, Catholic Schools, 530
Religious, Women (World Statistics), 367
Religious Education, U.S., 530
  Pupils Receiving Instruction, 530
Religious Formation Conference, 517
Religious Freedom, 311
Religious Indifference, Baltic Countries, 70
Religious Liberty, 87
  Violations, 70
Religious Life, Institute on, 517
Religious News Service, 588
Reliquary, 325
Remedial Education Classes (Aguilar v. Felton), 413
Rene Goupil, St., 386
RENEW, Revised Program, 88-9
Reparation, 325
Representatives, Vatican, 170-73, 178
Requiem Mass, 214
Rescript, 325
Reserved Case, 325
Restitution, 325
Resurrection (Easter), 248
Resurrection, Congregation, 495
Resurrection, Sisters of, 514
Retarded, Facilities for, 553-55
Retired, Facilities for, 541-51
Retired Religious, Needs, 72, 93
Retreat Houses, U.S., 559-64
Retreats International, 558
Reunion, 358
Revelation (Dogmatic Constitution), 124, 183-86, 331
  See also Bible
Revelation, Book of, 194
Revised Standard Version (Bible), 188
Revollo Bravo, Mario, Card., 164, 168, 169
Revolution, American, **see** Catholic History of U.S.
Rheims, Synod (1148), 117
Rhode Island, 405, 425, 430, 432, 526, 537, 549, 564
Rhodes, 358
Rhodesia, **see** Zimbabwe
Riashi, Georges, B.C.O., Bp., 463
Ribeiro, Antonio, Card., 164-65, 168, 169
Ricard, John, S.S.J., Bp., 73, 463
Ricci, Matteo (1610), 119

Richard, Arsène, Bp., 383
Richard, Gabriel, 387
Rieve-Estrella, Gary, S.V.D., 65
Rigali, Justin, Abp., 463-64
Righi-Lambertini, Egano, Card., 165, 169
Right to Die, 52-4
Riley, Lawrence J., Bp., 464
Ring, 325
  Fisherman's, 310
Rio de Janeiro, University, 537
Rio Grande do Sul, University, 537
Rita, St., Sisters of, 514
Rita of Cascia, St., 257
Rites, 211-12
Rites, Eastern, 267-69
Ritter, Joseph (U.S. Cardinals), 170, 483
Ritual, 325
Rivera Damas, Arturo, Abp., 76, 77
Roach, John R., Abp., 464
Robert Bellarmine, St., 200
Robert Southwell, St., 257
Roch, St., 257
Roch Gonzalez, St., 386
  Canonization, 40
Rochet, 215
Rodimer, Frank J., Bp., 464
Rodrigo, Miguel, O.M.I., Rev., Death, 70
Rodriguez, Alfonso, St., 40, 387
Rodriguez, Miguel, C.SS.R., Bp., 464
Rodriguez, Placido, C.M.F., Bp., 464
Roe v. Wade, 54
Rogationist Fathers, 495
Rogito, 325
Role of Law Award, 599
Roman, Agustin, Bp., 464
  and Siege at Federal Detention Center, 69
Roman Catholic Church, see Church
Roman Curia, see Curia, Roman
Roman Martyrology, 318
Roman Missal (Sacramentary), 218, 319
Roman Pontiffs, see Popes
Roman Question, see Lateran Agreement
Roman Rite, 211
Romania, 358
Romanian Byzantine Rite, 268
  in the United States, 271
Romans, 193
Romero, Oscar, Abp., Anniversary of Assassination, 86
  Suspects in Death, 70
Romuald, St., 257
Rooney, Arthur J., Sr., 600
Roque, Francis, Bp., 464
Roque (Roch) Gonzalez, St., 40, 386
Rosary, 325-26
  Feast, 249
  Franciscan Crown, 310-11
Rosary, Family, 571
Rosary Apostolate, 575
Rosary Congress, American National, 96
Rosary League, 575
Rosary Rally, Washington, D.C., 64
Rosati, Joseph, 387
Rosazza, Peter A., Bp., 464
Rose, Robert John, Bp., 464
Rose of Lima, St., 257
Rosminians (Institute of Charity), 495
Rosh Hashana, 291
Rossi, Agnelo, Card., 165, 168, 169
Rossi, Opilio, Card., 165, 168, 169
Rota, Roman, 150
  Marriage Cases (1987), 88
Rouleau, Reynold, O.M.I., Bp., 383
Routhier, Henri, O.M.I., Abp., 383
Roy, Raymond, Bp., 383
Rubin, Wladyslaw, Card., 165, 168
Rubrics, Mass, 218
Rudin, John J., M.M., Bp., 464
Rueger, George E., Bp., 464
Rugambwa, Laurean, Card., 165, 168, 169

Ruggieri, George D., S.J., Rev. 600
Rule of Faith. 310
Runcie, Robert, Abp. (Anglican), 87, 286
Rural Life Conference, 524
Rural Ministry Institute, 524
Rural Parish Workers of Christ the King, 519
Rusnak, Michael, C.SS.R., Bp., 383
Russell, John J., Bp., 464
Russia, see Union of Soviet Socialist Republics
Russian Byzantine Rite, 268
  in the United States, 271
Russian Orthodox, Celebration of Millennium of Christianity, 45-7, 98
Ruth, 189
Ruthenian Byzantine Rite, 268
  in the United States, 270
Rwanda, 359, 370
Ryan, Daniel L., Bp., 464
Ryan, James C., O.F.M., Bp., 464
Ryan, Joseph F., Bp., 383
Ryan, Joseph T., Abp., 464

S

Sabatini, Lawrence, C.S., Bp., 383
Sabattani, Aurelio, Card., 165, 169
Sabbah, Michel, Patriarch (Jerusalem), 71, 78, 82, 89, 102
Sabbath, 326
Sabbath (Jewish), 290
Sabellianism (c. 260), 113
Sacrament, Blessed, see Blessed Sacrament
Sacrament, Sisters of Most Holy, 515
Sacramental Forum, see Forum
Sacramentals, 209-10
Sacramentary, 218, 326
Sacramentine Nuns, 515
Sacraments, 222-32
  Congregation, 149
  Eastern Churches, 266-67
  Grace, 312
  Liturgical Developments, 219
Sacrarium, 326
Sacred Heart (June 2, 1989), 250
  Enthronement, 326
  Promises, 326
Sacred Heart Catholic Univ. (Italy), 538
Sacred Heart League, 575
Sacred Heart of Mary, Religious, 515
Sacred Heart Program, 592
Sacred Hearts, Fathers of, 495
Sacred Scripture, see Bible
Sacrifice of Mass, see Mass
Sacrilege, 326
Sacristy, 326
Sacrosanctum Concilium, 124
  See also Liturgy Constitution
Sacrum Diaconatus Ordinem, see Deacon, Permanent
Sadducees, 326
Sahagun, Bernardino de, 387
Sahel, John Paul II Foundation, 102
Saint
  Anne de Beaupre, Shrine, 384
  Ann's Church, Vatican City, 176
  Ansgar's Scandinavian Catholic League, 575
  Anthony's Guild, 575
  Bonaventure University Medal, 599
  Christopher and Nevis, 359
  Francis de Sales Award, 93, 599
  Francis Xavier Medal, 599
  Helena, 359
  Joan's International Alliance, 373
  Joseph's Oratory Shrine, 384
  Joseph's University of Beirut, 538
  Jude League, 575
  Lucia, 359
  Margaret of Scotland Guild, 575
  Martin de Porres Guild, 575
  Patrick's College, Maynooth (Ireland), 537
  Paul's University, Ottawa, 537

Saint
  Pierre and Miquelon, 359
  Thomas Aquinas Foundation, 575
  Thomas of Villanueva Univ. (Cuba), 537
  Vincent and Grenadines (West Indies), 359
  Vincent de Paul Medal, 599
  Vincent de Paul Society, 541
Saint-Antoine, Jude, Bp., 383
Saint-Gelais, Raymond, Bp., 383
Saints, 326
  Biographical Sketches, 250-58
  Canonization, 300
  Canonizations (1987, 1988), 36, 40, 63, 95, 99, 136
  Canonized since Leo XIII, 135-36
  Commemorations in Calendar, 238-39, 240-45
  Communion of, 304
  Congregation for Causes of, 149
  Cult, 326
  Emblems, 260
  Patrons, 258-60
  Veneration. 326
  See also Proper Names of Individual Saints
Salamanca, University of (Spain), 538
Salatka, Charles, Abp., 464
Salazar Lopez, Jose, Card., 165, 168, 169
Sales, Eugenio de Araujo, Card., 165, 168, 169
Salesian Cooperators, 373
Salesian Sisters (Daughters of Mary Help of Christians), 511
Salesians of St. John Bosco, 495
Salesianum, Pontifical University, 539
Salgado, Ernesto, Bp., 98
Salvation, 326
Salvation History, 326-27
Salvation outside the Church, 327
Salvatorian Fathers, Basilian, 490
Salvatorians, 495
Sammon, Sean, S.M., Bro., 104
Samoa, American, 359
Samoa, Western, 359
Samuel, 189
San Marino, 359
Sanchez, Robert, Abp., 464
Sanctifying Grace, 312
  See also Sacraments
Sanctuary, 216
Sanctuary Lamp, 217
Sandinistas, see Nicaragua
San Pedro, Enrique, S.J., Bp., 464
Sanschagrin, Albert, O.M.I., Bp., 383
Santo Tomas University (Philippines), 538
Santos, Alexandre Maria dos, O.F.M., Card., 165, 168, 169
Sao Paulo University (Brazil), 537
Sao Tome and Principe, 359
Satan (Devil), 306
Satanism, 327
Satowaki, Joseph Asajiro, Card., 166, 168, 169
Saudi Arabia, 359
Saul (Historical Books of the Bible), 189
Savior, see Jesus
Scalabrinians (Missionaries of St. Charles), 494
Scalia, Antonin (Catholic Justice, Supreme Court), 409
Scandal, 327
Scandinavia, Episcopal Conference, 370
Scanlan, John J., Bp., 465
Scapular, 327
  Medal, 327
  Promise, 327
Scarpone, Gerald, O.F.M., Bp., 465
Schad, James L., Bp., 465
Scherer, Alfred Vicente, Card., 166, 168, 169

Index

Scheut Fathers, **see** Immaculate Heart Missioners
Schism, Schismatic, 327
Schism, Lefebvre, **see** Lefebvre, Marcel, Abp.
Schism, Western, 129
Schladweiler, Alphonse, Bp., 465
Schlaefer Berg, Salvator, O.F.M. Cap., Bp., 465
Schlarman, Stanley G., Bp., 465
Schlotterback, Edward, O.S.F.S., Bp., 465
Schmidt, Firmin M., O.F.M. Cap., Bp., 465
Schmidt, Matthias W., O.S.B., Bp., 465
Schmitt, Bernard W., Bp., 465
Schmitt, Mark, Bp., 465
Schmitz, Carl, C.P., Rev., 600
Schmitz, Paul, O.F.M. Cap., Bp., 465
Schoenherr, Walter J., Bp., 465
Schoenstatt Sisters of Mary, 519
Scholastica, St., 257
Scholasticism, 327
School-Based Clinics, 56-7, 441-42
Schools, Catholic (U.S.), 525-37
  Among Exemplary School Award Winners, 64, 92
  Aid, 525
  Colleges and Universities, 530-35
  for Handicapped, 551-55
  Legal Status, 525
  Remedial Education (Aguilar v. Felton), 413
  See also Church-State Decisions of Supreme Court
  NCEA, 88, 525
  Shared Time, 525
  Statistics, 526-29
  Value Education, 81
  See also Religious Education; Seminaries
Schools, Public, **see** Public Schools
Schuck, James A., O.F.M., Bp., 465
Schulte, Francis B., Bp., 465
Schuster, Eldon, Bp., 465
Science and Morality, 90
Science and Respect for Human Dignity, 67
Sciences, Pontifical Academy, 540-41
Scotland, 359-60, 369
Scribes, 327
Scripture, **see** Bible
Scruple, 327
Sea, Apostleship of, 566
Seal of Confession, 327
Seasons, Church, 238
Seattle Archdiocese, 81
Sebastian, St., 257
Sebastian Aparicio, Bl., 385
Second Vatican Council, **see** Council, Second Vatican
Secretariat for Black Catholics, 77
  See also Black Catholics
Secretariat of State, Vatican, 148
Secretariats (Roman Curia), 151
Sects, 38, 84
  Hispanic Loss to, 97
  Mexico, 90
Secular (Diocesan) Clergy, 303
  Statistics (World), 367
  See also Individual Countries
Secular Institutes, 517-19
  Congregation, 149-50
Secular (Third) Orders, 520
Secularism, 327
Sede Vacante, **see** Interregnum
See, 327
Seelos, Francis X., 387
Seghers, Charles J., 387
Seminarians
  Countries of the World, 333-68
  United States, 68, 434
  World (Summary), 367
Seminaries, U.S., 535-37
  Enrollment, Los Angeles, 65
  Study Report, 497
Seminary, 327

Semi-Pelagianism (431, 529), 114
Sendero Luminoso, Peru, 74, 98
Senegal, 68, 360, 370
Senses of the Bible (Interpretation), 195
Sensi, Giuseppe Maria, Card., 166, 168, 169
Separated and Divorced Catholics, Pastoral Ministry, 236-37
Separation, Marriage, 235
Septuagint Bible, 187
Seraphim (Angels), 297
Serbs (Byzantine Rite), 269
Sermon on the Mount, 328
Serra, Junipero, 72, 387
  Beatification, 36
Serra Award of the Americas, 599
Serra International, 575
Servite Sisters, 511
Servites, 495
Servitium Christi Secular Institute, 519
Setian, Nerses Mikail, Bp., 465
Seton, Elizabeth Bayley, St., 253
Seven Holy Founders, 257
Seven Joys of the Blessed Virgin Mary, **see** Franciscan Crown
Seven Last Words of Christ, 328
Seventh Day Adventists (Adventists), 296
Sex Education, 84-5
Sexuality, Human, 56-7, 58
Seychelles, 360
Sfeir, Nasrallah, Patriarch, 74
Shaheen, Elias, Abp., 383
Shakespeare, Frank, **see** U.S.-Vatican Relations
Sharbel Makhlouf, St., 257
Shea, Francis R., Bp., 465
Sheehan, Daniel E., Abp., 465
Sheehan, Michael J., Bp., 105, 466
Shehan, Lawrence J., Card. (U.S. Cardinals), 170, 484
Sheldon, Gilbert I., Bp., 466
Shenouda III, Pope (Coptic Orthodox), 286
Sherbrooke University (Canada), 537
Sherlock, John M., Bp., 383
Shinto, 295
Shrine, Crowned, 328
Shrine, Immaculate Conception, 260
Shrines, Canada, 384
Shrines, U.S., 388-90
Shroud of Turin, 328
  Tests, 81, 87
Shubsda, Thaddeus A., Bp., 466
Shultz, George, Sec. of State, 88
Sick, Anointing of, **see** Anointing of Sick
Sick, Eucharistic Fast, 310
Sick, Oil of, 320
Sick Calls, 328
Sierra Leone, 360, 369
Sign of Cross, 328
Signatura, Apostolic, 150
Signs of the Times, 328
Signum Fidei Medal, 599
Silva Henriquez, Raul, S.D.B., Card., 166, 168, 169
Silvestrini, Achille, Card., 166, 169
Simon, St. (Apostle), 197
Simon, William (Catholics in Presidents' Cabinets), 408
Simon Bolivar Prize, 86
Simonis, Adrianus J., Card., 75, 166, 168, 169
Simony, 328
Sin, 328
  Accessory to, 296
  Original, 321
  Punishment, 324
Sin, Jaime L., Card., 166, 168, 169
Singapore, 360
Sins
  against Holy Spirit, 329
  Capital, 300-01
  Forgiveness, 310
  See also Penance (Sacrament)

Sins
  Occasions, 329
  That Cry to Heaven for Vengeance, 329
Sirach, 191
Siri, Giuseppe, Card., 166, 168, 169
Sister, 329
Sisterhood, 329
Sisters, Archbishops Fund, Los Angeles, 81
Sisters, United States, 499-516
  Retirement Needs, 72, 93
  Statistics. 425-29
  See also Religious, Women
Situation Ethics, 329
Sixtus II, St., 257
Skinner, Patrick J., C.J.M., Abp., 383
Sklba, Richard J., Bp., 466
Skylstad, William, Bp., 466
Sladkevicius, Vincentas, Card., 166, 168, 169
  See also Lithuania
Slander, 329
Sloth, 329
Slovak Byzantine Catholics, 268
Slovak Catholic Federation of America, 575
Slovak Catholic Sokol, 575
Slovakia, Persecution (Czechoslovakia), 340
Smith, Alfred E. (Catholic History in U.S., Bigotry), 391-92
Smith, John M., Bp., 466
Smith, Philip M., O.M.I., Abp., 466
Snyder, John J., Bp., 466
Social Communications Commission, 151
  See also Communications
Social Doctrine of the Church, 31-5, 202-07
"On Social Concerns," Encyclical Letter, 31-5
Social Service, Sisters of, 516
Social Services, Catholic, U.S., 541-57
  World Statistics, 367
Socially Maladjusted, Facilities for, 551-53
Societies, Catholic, in U.S., 569-76
Societies, Religious, **see** Religious, Men, Women, in U.S.
Society for the Propagation of the Faith, 575
Society of St. Paul, 495
Society of St. Peter the Apostle, 576
Society of St. Vincent de Paul, 541
Society of the Divine Attributes, 576
SODEPAX (Society for Development and Peace), 284
Soenneker, Henry J., Bp., 484, 600
Soens, Lawrence D., Bp., 466
Solanus, Francis, St., 387
Solemnity of Mary, 250
Solidarity, **see** Poland
Sollicitudo Omnium Ecclesiarum (Representatives of the Holy See), 170
Sollicitudo Rei Socialis (On Social Concerns), Encyclical Letter, 31-5, 80
Solomon (Kings 1 and 2), 189
Solomon Islands, 360, 370
Somalia, 360
Somascan Fathers, 496
Song of Songs (Bible), 190
Sons of Mary Missionary Society, 496
Sophia, Catholic University (Japan), 538
Sorcery, 329
Sorin, Edward F., 387
Sorrows (Dolors) of the Blessed Virgin Mary, 249
Soteriological Award, 599
Soteriology, 329
Souls, Holy, **see** All Souls
South Africa, 66, 67, 82, 85, 94, 102, 360-61, 368
  Christian-Moslem Tension, 94

South Africa
  Protests Against Apartheid, 82, 85, 102
South America
  Cardinals, 169
  Catholic Statistics, 367
  Eastern Rite Jurisdictions, 270
  Episcopal Conferences, 371
  Missionary Bishops, 425
  Papal Visit, 38-41, 92
South Carolina, 405, 426, 430, 432, 526, 549, 564
South Dakota, 405-06, 427, 431, 433, 528, 549, 564
South Korea, 350
South West Africa, see Namibia
Southern Africa Bishops' Conference, 66, 368
Southern Baptist Convention, 277, 285
Southwell, Robert, St., 257
Southwest Volunteer Apostolate, 568
Sowada, Alphonse, O.S.C., Bp., 466
Spain, 361, 370
  Civil War (1936), 122
  Inquisition, 315
  Persecution (1931), 122
  Terrorist Bombing, Zaragoza, 72
Spanish Sahara, see Western Sahara
Spanish-Speaking in U.S., see Hispanics
Species, Sacred, 329
Spellman, Francis J. (U.S. Cardinals), 170, 484
Speltz, George H., Bp., 466
Spence, Francis J., Abp., 383
Speyrer, Jude, Bp., 466
Spiritism, 329
Spiritual Crisis, World, 89
Spiritual Life Institute of America, 576
Spiritual Works of Mercy, 329
Sponsor, see Confirmation
Spoon, 273
Sri Lanka, 361, 370
  Commemorative Stamp, 102
  Missionary Murdered, 70
Stafford, James F., Abp., 466
Stamps, Vatican, 176
Stanggassinger, Kaspar, Rev., Beatification, 87
Stanislaus, St., 257
State and Church, see Church-State
State Catholic Conferences, 443-44
State of Grace, see Grace
Stational Churches, Days, 329
Stations of the Cross, 329-30
Statistics, Catholic
  Canada, 337, 377-79
  Countries of World, 333-68
  Men Religious, 498-99
  United States, see Statistics, Catholic, U.S.
  World (Summary), 367
Statistics, Catholic, United States
  Baptisms, 432-33, 434
  Black Catholics, 486
  Brothers, 425-29, 434
  Converts, 432-33, 434
  Eastern Rite, 270-71, 429, 433, 529
  Missionary Personnel Abroad, 520-23
  Permanent Deacons, 229, 425-29, 434
  Population, 425-31, 434
  Press, 577
  Priests, 425-29, 434
  Schools and Students, 526-29, 530
  Seminarians, 68, 434
  Sisters, 425-29, 434
  Summary, 434
Statistics Office, Central, 153
Statuary Hall, U.S., Catholics in, 408
Statues, 216
Statutes, 330
Steib, J. (James) Terry, S.V.D., Bp., 466
Stein, Edith, Bl., 253
Steinback, Leo, M.M., 106
Steinbock, John T., Bp., 105, 466

Steiner, Kenneth D., Bp., 466
Stephen, St. (Deacon), 257
Stephen, St. (King), 258
Stepanavicius, Julijonas, Bp. (Lithuania), 351
Stepinac, Aloysius (Yugoslavia), 366
Sticharion, 273
Stickler, Alfons, S.D.B., Card., 166, 169
Stigmata, 330
Stigmata, Congregation of Sacred (Stigmatine Fathers and Brothers), 496
Stipend, Mass, 330
Stole, 214
Stole, Use of, Confirmation, 219
Stole Fee, 330
Stoup, 330
Straling, Phillip F., Bp., 466
Strecker, Ignatius, Abp., 466
Stritch, Samuel (Cardinals in U.S.), 170, 484
Stroessner, Alfredo, Gen., 40, 41, 82, 102
  See also Paraguay
Students, Catholic
  United States, 526-29, 530
  University, College, U.S., 530-35
  World (Catholic World Statistics), 367
Subdeacon, 229
Sudan, 65, 75, 79, 102, 361, 370
  Civil War, 75, 102
Suenens, Leo J., Card., 166, 168, 169
Suffragan See, 330
Suicide, 330
  Physician-Assisted, 52-4, 85, 93
  See also Euthanasia; Life, Respect for
Sullivan, James S., Bp., 466
Sullivan, John J., Bp., 466
Sullivan, Joseph M., Bp., 467
Sullivan, Sharon, O.S.F., Sr., 600
Sullivan, Walter F., Bp., 89, 467
Sulpice, Society of Priests of St. (Sulpicians), 496
Sulyk, Stephen, Abp., 467
Sunday, 239
  Celebration in Absence of Priest, 96, 124
Sunday Mass on Saturday, 218
Supererogation, 330
Supernatural, 330
Supernatural Virtue, 332
Superstition, 330
Supremacy, Act of (1533), 118
Supreme Court, U.S.
  Abortion Rulings, 54-5, 72-3, 414
  Church-State Decisions, 409-14
  Decisions and Actions (1987, 1988), 72, 72-3, 96-7, 97, 414
Supreme Court, U.S., Catholics in, 409
Supreme Order of Christ, 595
Suquia Goicoechea, Angel, Card., 166, 168, 169
Suriname, 361
Surplice, 215
Surrogate Motherhood, 73, 77-8, 80, 96
Suspension, 330
Sutton, Peter A., O.M.I., Bp., 383
Swaziland, 362
  Papal Visit to Africa, 107-08
Swearing, 330
Sweden, 362
Swedenborgianism, 330-31
Swiss Guards, 176
Switzerland, 362, 370
Sword of Loyola Award, 599
Syllabus, 331
Sylvester, Order of St., 596
Sylvester I, St., 258
Sylvestrine Benedictines, 490
Symbols, see Emblems of Saints
Symons, J. Keith, Bp., 467
Synaxis, 272
Synod, Diocesan, 331
Synod of Bishops, 64, 145-47
  1987 Assembly, 146-47

Synod of Whitby (664), 115
Synods, Patriarchal, 270
Synoptic Gospels, 193
Syria, 362
Syrian Orthodox-Catholic Joint Statements, 285, 286
Syrian Rite Catholics 268
Syro-Malabar Rite Catholics, 269
Szoka, Edmund C., Card., 166, 168, 169
  Installation as Cardinal, 95

T

Tabernacle, 216
Tabernacles, Festival, 291
Tafoya, Arthur N., Bp., 64-5, 467
Tahiti, (French Polynesia), 344
Taiwan, 362, 369
Taney, Roger Brooke (Catholic Justice, Supreme Court), 409
Tanner, Paul F., Bp., 467
Tanzania, 363, 370
  Evangelization, 71
Taofinu'u, Pio, S.M., Card., 166, 168, 169
Taoism, 295
Tarcisius, St., 258
Tawil, Joseph, Abp., 467
Tax Exemption, Churches, 413-14
  and Political Involvement, 101
Taylor, Myron C., 175
Te Deum, 331
Teachers, Lay, Catholic Schools, 530
Teachers, Religious, Catholic Schools, 530
Teaching Authority of the Church (Magisterium), 182-83
  and Interpretation of Bible, 184
Teen-Age Pregnancy, see School-Based Clinics
Teens Encounter Christ, 93
Tekakwitha, Kateri, Bl., 255
Tekakwitha Conference, 524
Telecommunications Network, Catholic, 593
Television, 65, 592
  Coverage of Pope's U.S. Visit, 64
  Effects of, 80
Television Network, Catholic, 593
Television Networks, Church Participation in Public Policy Debates, 85
Temperance, 331
Templeton Foundation Prize, 94
Temporal Punishment, 324
Temptation, 331
Ten Commandments, 201
Tennessee, 406, 427, 430, 432, 527, 549, 552, 555, 564
Teresa, Mother, (of Calcutta), see Mother Teresa
Teresa Margaret Redi, St., 258
Teresa (Theresa) of Jesus (Avila), St., 200
Teresa of Jesus, Society of St., 516
Teresa of Jesus Jornet Ibars, St., 258
Teresian Institute, 519
Terrorism, 69, 72, 98
Tertullian (206), 113
  See also Montanism
Tessier, Maxime, Bp., 383
Testament, Old and New, see Bible
Texas, 390, 406, 428, 431, 433, 436, 444, 528, 537, 549-50, 555, 564
  Events at Lubbock, 105
  Gathering for Christians, 92
Thaddeus, Jude, St., 197
Thailand, 363, 370
Thanksgiving, 331
That's the Spirit Productions, 593
Theatines, 496
Theatre, Catholic, 592
Theism, 331
Theodosian Code (438), 114
Theological Commission, International, 152
  Deaconess Statement, 306
Theological Virtues, 331
Theology, 331

Index

Theology of Liberation, **see** Liberation Theology
Theophany, **see** Epiphany
Therese Couderc, St., 258
Therese of Lisieux, St., 258
Theresians of the United States, 576
Thessalonians, 194
Thiandoum, Hyacinthe, Card., 166-67, 168, 169
Third Order Regular of St. Francis, 492
Third Orders (Secular Orders), 520
Thirty-Nine Articles (1563), 119
Thirty Years' War (1648), 119
Thomas, St. (Apostle), 197
 See also India
Thomas Aquinas, St., 200
 Pontifical University (Angelicum), 539
Thomas Becket, St., 258
Thomas Christians, **see** Syro-Malabar Catholics
Thomas More, St., 258
Thomas of Villanova, St., Congregation of Srs., 516
Thorlac, St., 258
Thrones (Angels), 297
Thurible, **see** Censer
Timlin, James C., Bp., 467
Timor, Eastern (Indonesia), 348
Timothy, St., 258
 Letter, 194
Tiso, Joseph, Msgr. (Czechoslovakia), 340
Tithing, 331
Titular Archbishop, Bishop, 144
Titular Sees, 331
Titus, St., 258
 Letter, 194
Titus Brandsma, Bl., 258
Tobago, 363
Tobin, Maurice J. (Catholics in Presidents' Cabinets), 408
Tobit, 190
Todadilla, Anthony de, 387
Togo, 363, 370
Tokelau, 363
Toleration Act, England (1689), 119
Tomasek, Frantisek, Card., 94, 167, 168, 169
Tomko, Jozef, Card., 167, 169
Tonga, 363
Tonnos, Anthony, Bp., 383
Tonsure, **see** Holy Orders
Toulouse, Catholic Institute, 537
Tourism, Commission, 151
Tradition, 184
Transfiguration, 250
Transfinalization, 331
Transignification, 331
Transkei, **see** South Africa
Translations, Bible, 187-88
Transplants, Organ, 321
Transubstantiation, 331-32
 See also Miracles
Trappists, 491
Trautman, Donald W., Bp., 467
Treasury of the Church, 332
Treinen, Sylvester, Bp., 467
Tremblay, Gerard, P.S.S., Bp., 383
Trent, Council of (1545-63), 119, 123
 and Bible, 187, 196
 and Celibacy, 301
 Doctrine on Mass, 212
Tribunals of Roman Curia, 150
Tri-Conference Retirement Project, 93
Tridentine Mass, 221
Triduum, 332
Trination, 218-19
Trinh Van Can, Joseph Marie, Card., 167, 168, 169
Trinidad, 363
Trinitarians, 496
Trinity, Blessed, Missionary Servants of Most, 516
Trinity, Holy, 250
Trinity Missions, 496

Triodion, 272
Triumph of the Cross, 250
Troy, J. Edward, Bp., 384
Truce of God (1027), 116
Truman, Pres. Harry S., 175
Tschoepe, Thomas, Bp., 467
Tumi, Christian Wiyghan, Card., 167, 168, 169
Tunisia, 363
Turcotte, Jean-Claude, Bp., 384
Turibius de Mogrovejo, St., 387
Turin, Shroud of, **see** Shroud of Turin
Turkey, 363-64, 370
 Ambassador to Vatican, 96
Turks and Caicos Islands, 364
Tuvalu (Ellice Islands), 364
Twelve Apostles of Mexico, 387
"Type" (649), 115
Typical Sense (Bible), 195
Tzadua, Paulus, Card., 167, 168, 169

U

Uganda, 364, 370
Uganda Martyrs (Sts. Charles Lwanga, Companions), 252
Ukraine (USSR)
 Appeal for Religious Freedom, 89, 92
 Public Mass, 102
Ukrainian Byzantine Rite Catholics, 268
 in the United States, 270
Ukrainian Millennium Celebration, 45-7, 47-8, 83, 100
Ulrike Nische, Beatification, 68
Unam Sanctam (1302), 117
Unbaptized, 181
Unda-USA, 593
Union of Soviet Socialist Republics, 66, 70, 83-4, 87, 89, 90, 98, 99, 364
 Treaty with U.S., Nuclear Weapons, 72, 97
Union of European Conferences of Major Superiors, 517
Union of Superiors General, 517
Unitarianism, 277
Unitatis Redintegratio, 124
 See also Ecumenism Decree
United Arab Emirates, 364
United Brethren Church (John Hus), 276
United Church of Christ, 280
United Methodist Church, 278
 Dialogues, 285
United Nations, 67, 95
 Vatican Representation, 178
United Societies of U.S.A., 576
United States
 Apostolic Delegates, 173
 Bishops, **see** Bishops, U.S.
 Catholic Historical Society, 73, 576
 Catholic Population, 425-29, 434
 Eastern Rite Catholics, 270-71, 429, 433, 529
 History, Catholic, 391-408
 Jurisdictions, Hierarchy, 416-24, 444-69
 Liturgical Developments, 217-22
 Missionaries, 425, 520-23
 Pontifical Ecclesiastical Faculties, 539
 Pontifical Universities, 538
 Protestant Churches, Major, 277-81
 Social Services, Catholic, 541-58
 Statistics, Catholic, **see** Statistics
 Supreme Court, **see** Supreme Court
 Universities and Colleges, 530-35
 Vatican Relations, 174-75
U.S. Catholic Award, 599
United States Catholic Conference, 96-7, 440-41
 Secretariat for Hispanic Affairs, 487-88
United States Catholic Mission Association, 523
United States-Vatican Diplomatic Relations, 174-75

United Way and Planned Parenthood, Seattle, 101
Unity, Christian, **see** Ecumenism
Universalism, 277
Universities, Pontifical, 537-38
Untener, Kenneth E., Bp., 467
Unterkoefler, Ernest L., Bp., 467
Upper Volta, **see** Burkina Faso
Ursi, Corrado, Card., 167, 168, 169
Ursula, Company of St., 518
Ursula of the Blessed Virgin Mary, Society of Srs., 516
Ursuline Nuns, 516
Ursuline Sisters, 516
Uruguay, 364-65, 370
 Papal Visit, 38
Ustrzycki, Matthew, Bp., 384
Usury, 332
Utah, 406, 428, 431, 433, 529, 550, 564

V

Vachon, Louis-Albert, Card., 167, 168, 169
Vaivods, Julijans, Card., 167, 168, 169
Valdivia, Luis de, 388
Valentine, St., 258
Valero, Rene A., Bp., 467
Vallee, Andre, P.M.E., Bp., 384
Valois, Charles, Bp., 384
Valparaiso, Pontifical University (Chile), 537
Vanuatu (New Hebrides), 365
Varela, Felix, Rev., 90
Vasques de Espinosa, Antonio, 388
Vatican City, 175-78
 Basilica of St. Peter, 176
 Budget Deficit, 64, 84
 Commission, 152
 Diplomats at, 173-74
 Employees, 80, 148
 Financial Report, 80
 Italian Concordat, 178
 Labor Office, 148
 Library, 176
 Office for U.S. Visitors, 177
 Press Office, 177
 Radio, 176
 Representatives, 170-73, 178
 Secretariat of State, 148
 Television, 177
Vatican Bank Officials, Immunity, 96
Vatican Council I (1869-70), 121, 123-24
Vatican Council II, **see** Council, Second Vatican
Vaughan, Austin B., Bp., 92, 467
Veigle, Adrian, T.O.R., Bp., 467
Veil, 215, 273
Veil, Humeral, 215
Veillette, Martin, Bp., 384
Venerini Sisters, 516
Venezuela, 365, 370
Venial Sin, 328
Vercelli Medal, 599
Vermont, 390, 406-07, 425, 430, 432, 526, 550
Verona, Italy, Papal Visit, 87
Veronica, 332
Vessels, Sacred, 215
Vestments, 214-15
 Byzantine, 273
Viaticum, 332
Viator, Clerics of St., 496
Vicar Apostolic, 144
Vicar General, 332
Vicariate of Solidarity, Chile, 73, 86, 106
Vicariates Apostolic, World, 367
Vicenta Maria Lopez y Vicuna, St., 258
Victor Emmanuel II (1870), 121
Victory, Missionary Sisters of Our Lady of, 513
Vidal, Ricardo, Card., 167, 168, 169
Vienne, Council (1311-12), 123
Vieira, Antonio, 388
Vietnam, 63, 66, 73, 97, 98, 365, 370
 Catholics in, 66

Vietnam
 Church-State Climate, 73
 Persecution, 97
 See also Vietnamese Martyrs, Canonization
Vietnam Catholics, U.S., Marian Day Celebration, 105
Vietnamese Congregation of the Mother Co-Redemptrix, 105, 494
Vietnamese Martyrs, Canonization, 95, 97, 98
Vigil, Easter, 248
Vincent, St., 258
Vincent de Paul, St., 258
Vincent de Paul, St. (Religious)
 Daughters of Charity, 502
 Sisters of Charity, 502
Vincent de Paul, St., Society, 541
Vincent Ferrer, St., 258
Vincent Pallotti, St., 258
Vincent Strambi, St., 258
Vincentian Sisters of Charity, 502
Vincentians, 496
Vincenza Gerosa, St., 258
Virgin Birth of Christ, 262-63
Virgin Islands, 365
Virgin Islands, British, 365
Virginia, 407, 426, 430, 432, 526, 550, 555, 564
 Outreach to Lapsed Catholics, 81
Virginity, 332
Virtue, 332
Virtues (Angels), 297
Virtues, Cardinal, 301
Virtues, Infused, 315
Virtues, Theological, 331
Visitation, 250
Visitation Nuns, 516
Visitation Sisters, 516
Vitus, St., 258
Vladimir, St., Baptism, **see** Ukrainian Millennium Celebration
Vlazny, John G., Bp., 467
Vocation, 332
Vocation Conference, National Sisters, **see** National Religious Vocations Conference
Vocationist Fathers, 496
Vocation Sisters, 516
Vocationist Sisters, 516
Volk, Hermann, Card., 600
Volpe, John (Catholics in Presidents' Cabinets), 408
Voluntas Dei, 519
Von Balthasar, Hans Urs, 95, 98, 600
Vonesh, Raymond J., Bp., 467
Vote, Responsibility to, 64
Votive Mass, 214
Vow, 332
Vulgate Bible, 187
 Commission for Revision, 152

W

Wagner, Robert E., 175
Walburga, St., 258
Waldensianism (1179), 117
Waldheim, Kurt, Pres., **see** Austria, Papal Visit
Waldschmidt, Paul E., C.S.C., Bp., 468
Wales, 365-66
Walker, Frank (Catholics in Presidents' Cabinets), 408
Wall, Leonard J., Bp., 384
Wall of Separation (First Amendment), 414
Wallis and Futuna Islands, 366
Walsh, Daniel F., Bp., 468
Walsh, Nicolas E., Bp., 468
Walters, David, 175
Walters, Vernon, 64
Walz v. Tax Commission of New York, 411, 413-14
War
 Church Teaching (Vatican II), 206-07
 U.S. Bishops Pastoral, 207-08
Ward, John J., Bp., 468

Washington, 407, 428, 431, 433, 444, 529, 537, 550, 552, 564
Washington for Jesus '88, 89
Water, Easter, 308
Water, Holy, 313
Watson, Alfred M., Bp., 468
Watters, Loras J., Bp., 468
Watty Urquidi, Ricardo, M.Sp.S., Bp., 468
Way of the Cross (Stations of the Cross), 329-30
Weakland, Rembert, O.S.B., Abp., 468
Weber, Jerome, O.S.B., Abbot, 384
Week of Prayer for Christian Unity, 75, 76, 332
Weekdays (Church Calendar), 239
Weigand, William K., Bp., 468
Weitzel, John Quinn, M.M., Bp., 468
Welsh, Lawrence H., Bp., 468
Welsh, Thomas J., Bp., 468
Wenceslaus, St., 258
Wesley, John, 277
West, Catholic University of (France), 537
West Germany, 344-45
 Air Show Disaster, 104
West Virginia, 407, 426, 430, 432, 526, 550, 564
Western Catholic Union, 576
Western Sahara, 366
Western Samoa, 359
Western Schism, 129
Westphalia Peace (1648), 119
Wetter, Friedrich, Card., 167, 169
"What Have You Done to Your Homeless Brother," Justice and Peace Commission Document, 61-2
Whealon, John F., Abp., 468
Wheeler v. Barrera (Student Aid), 411
Whelan, Robert L., S.J., Bp., 468
Whitby, Synod (664), 115
White, Andrew, 388
White, Edward Douglass (Catholic Justices of Supreme Court), 409
White Fathers (Missionaries of Africa), 489
White Russian Byzantines, 268
Whitsunday (Pentecost), 249
Wildermuth, Augustine F., S.J., Bp., 468
Wilhelm, Joseph L., Abp., 384
Will, Free, 311
Willebrands, Johannes, Card., 167, 168, 169
Williams, Edward Bennett, 600
Williams, James Kendrick, Bp., 468
Williams, Thomas Stafford, Card., 167-68, 169
Wilson, William A., 174, 175
Wimmer, Boniface, 388
Windle, Joseph R., Bp., 384
Wirz, George O., Bp., 468
Wisconsin, 390, 427, 430, 432, 436, 444, 527, 537, 550-51, 553, 555, 564
 Pornography, Bishops' Statement, 81
Wisdom, Daughters of, 516
Wisdom Books (Bible), 190-91
Wiseman, Nicholas (1850), 120
Witness, Christian, 332
 John Paul II on, 75
Witnesses, Jehovah's, 316
Wojtyla, Karol, **see** John Paul II, Pope
Wolman v. Walter (Textbook Loans), 412
Women, Draft of Pastoral Letter, U.S. Bishops, 51-2
Women, Ordination, Lambeth Conference, 106
Women for Faith and Family, 576
Women's Organizations, Catholic, World Union, 374
Word, Liturgy of, 212-13

Word of God Institute, 576
Work, Encyclical on (*Laborem Exercens*), 204-06
World Apostolate of Fatima (Blue Army), 389, 576
World Communication Day, 91
World Conference of Secular Institutes, 517
World Council of Churches, 283-84, 286-87
World Food Day, 63
World Lutheran Federation, Interfaith Statements, 287
World Statistics, Catholic, 367
 Men Religious, 498-99
 Population, 99, 367
Worldwide Marriage Encounter, 237
Worms, Concordat (1122), 117
Worship, **see** Adoration
Worship, Divine, Congregation, 149
Worship, Eastern Rite, 267
Worship, Liturgical, **see** Liturgy
Wright, John J. (U.S. Cardinals), 170, 485
Writers' Market, Catholic, 589-91
Wu Cheng-Chung, John Baptist, Card., 168, 169
Wuerl, Donald, Bp., 104, 468
 on Academic Freedom, 104
 New Beginnings Program, 92
Wycislo, Aloysius J., Bp., 468
Wycliff, John, 276
Wyoming, 407, 428, 431, 433, 529, 553
Wyszynski, Stefan, Card. (Poland), 356-57

X

Xaverian Brothers, 497
Xaverian Missionary Fathers, 496
Xaverian Missionary Society of Mary, 516
Xavier Mission Sisters, 516
Xavier Society of the Blind, 557

Y

Yago, Bernard, Card., 168, 169
Year, Church (Calendar), 238-39
Yemen, North, 366
Yemen, South, 366
Yom HaShoah, 291
Yom Kippur, 291
Young Christian Students, 569
Young Ladies' Institute, 576
Young Men's Institute, 576
Youth, Bishops' Statement to (School-Based Clinics), 56-7
Youth Organizations, 568-69
Youville, Marie D', Bl., 388
Yugoslav Byzantines, 269
Yugoslavia, 366, 371
 Events at Medjugorje, 48-9, 70
 Restrictions on Religious Freedom, 78

Z

Zaire, 87, 367-68, 371
Zakka I, Syrian Orthodox Patriarch, and John Paul II, Joint Statement, 286
Zambia, 368, 371
 Refugees, 99
Zanzibar (Tanzania), 363
Zayek, Francis, Abp., 469
Zechariah, 192
Zechariah, Canticle (Benedictus), 299
Zephaniah, 192
Zerr, Bonaventure, O.S.B., 600
Ziemann, G. Patrick, Bp., 469
Zimbabwe (Rhodesia), 368, 371
 Papal Visit to Africa, 107-08
Zita, St., 258
Zorach v. Clauson (Released Time), 410
Zone, 273
Zoungrana, Paul, Card., 168, 169
Zucchetto, 215
Zumarraga, Juan de, O.F.M., 388
Zwingli, Ulrich, 276

SPECIAL REPORTS

ON SOCIAL CONCERNS: ENCYCLICAL LETTER

Pope John Paul commemorated the 20th anniversary of Paul VI's encyclical letter, "Populorum Progressio" ("On the Development of Peoples"), with an encyclical of his own entitled "Sollicitudo Rei Socialis" ("On Social Concerns"). The letter, dated Dec. 30, 1987, was issued Feb. 19, 1988.

The following coverage deals principally with sections of the encyclical concerning authentic human development, a theological reading of modern problems, and some guidelines for action. Quotations are from the Vatican's English-language text circulated by the NC Documentary Service, Origins, Mar. 3, 1988 (Vol. 17, No. 3). Subheads and lead lines have been added.

Purpose

"The aim of the present reflection is to emphasize, through a theological investigation of the present world, the need for a fuller and more nuanced concept of development.... Its aim is also to indicate some ways of putting it into effect."

SURVEY OF THE CONTEMPORARY WORLD

Negative Impressions: In "a brief review of some of the characteristics of today's world," the encyclical cites a number of negative impressions with respect to the following and other subjects: the prevalence of poverty, the widening gap between have and have-not nations, the sense that the unity of the human race is compromised, widespread illiteracy, lack of opportunity for higher education, various types of exploitation (economic, social, political), religious oppression, discrimination, suppression of economic initiative and deprivation of rights.

Positive Factors: Coexistent with negative factors are such positive aspects as: increasing awareness of human dignity, conviction about the radical interdependence and solidarity of society, concern for peace and ecology, actions of international and regional organizations, and new moral concern regarding human problems like development and peace.

Responsibility: Responsibility for the deterioration of society rests with developed as well as developing nations, and with disordered functioning of economic, financial and social mechanisms.

Signs of Underdevelopment: Secific ones are: the housing crisis, unemployment and underemployment, the burden of international debts, political causes, neo-colonialism and economic imperialism, arms production and traffic, the plight of hundreds of thousands of refugees, terrorism on various levels and anti-birth campaigns.

East-West Blocs: The encyclical directed special attention to the fact and effects of the tension existing between antagonistic blocs of Eastern and Western nations.

"In the West, there exists a system which is historically inspired by the principles of the liberal capitalism which developed with industrialization during the last century. In the East, there exists a system inspired by the Marxist collectivism which sprang from an interpretation of the condition of the proletarian classes made in the light of a particular reading of history."

Critical Attitude: "The Church's social doctrine adopts a critical attitude toward both liberal capitalism and Marxist collectivism; for, from the point of view of development, the question naturally arises: In what way and to what extent are these two systems capable of changes and updating such as to favor or promote a true and integral development of individuals and peoples in modern society?"

AUTHENTIC HUMAN DEVELOPMENT

(From this point on, excerpts are given without quotation marks.)

Development is not a straightforward process, as it were automatic and in itself limitless; as though, given certain conditions, the human race were able to progress rapidly toward an undefined perfection of some kind.

Such an idea — linked to a notion of "progress" with philosophical connotations deriving from the Enlightenment — now seems to be seriously called into doubt, particularly since the tragic experience of the two world wars, the planned and partly achieved destruction of whole peoples and the looming atomic peril. A naive mechanistic optimism has been replaced by a well-founded anxiety for the fate of humanity.

Better Understanding: At the same time, however, the "economic" concept itself, linked to the word *development*, has entered into crisis. In fact, there is a better understanding today that the mere accumulation of goods and services, even for the benefit of the majority, is not enough for the realization of human happiness. Nor, in consequence, does the availability of the many real benefits provided in recent times by science and technology, including the computer sciences, bring freedom from every form of slavery. On the contrary, the experience of recent years shows that, unless all the considerable body of resources and potential at man's disposal is guided by a moral understanding and by an orientation toward the true good of the human race, it easily turns against man to oppress him.

Consumerism: A disconcerting conclusion about the most recent period should serve to enlighten us. Side-by-side with the miseries of underdevelopment, themselves unacceptable, we find ourselves up against a form of superdevelopment, equally inadmissible; because, like the former, it is contrary to what is good and to true happiness. This superdevelopment, which consists in an excessive availability of every kind of material goods for the benefit of certain social groups, easily makes people slaves of "possession" and of immediate gratification, with no other horizon than the multiplication or continual replacement of the things already owned with others still better. This is the so-called civilization of "consumption" or "consumerism," which involves so much "throwing away" and "waste."

All of us experience firsthand the sad effects of this blind submission to pure consumerism: in the first place, a crass materialism, and at the same time a radical dissatisfaction because one quickly learns . . . that the more one possesses the more one wants, while deeper aspirations remain unsatisfied and perhaps even stifled.

Having and Being: The encyclical of Pope Paul VI pointed out the difference, so often emphasized today, between "having" and "being." To "have" objects and goods does not in itself perfect the human subject unless it contributes to the maturing and enrichment of that subject's "being," that is to say, unless it contributes to the realization of the human vocation as such.

Of course, the difference between "being" and "having," the danger inherent in a mere multiplication or replacement of things possessed compared to the value of "being," need not turn into a contradiction. One of the greatest injustices in the contemporary world consists precisely in this: that the ones who possess much are relatively few and those who possess almost nothing are many. It is the injustice of the poor distribution of the goods and services originally intended for all.

This then is the picture: There are some people . . . who do not really succeed in "being" because, through a reversal of the hierarchy of values, they are hindered by the cult of "having"; and there are others — the many who have little or nothing — who do not succeed in realizing their basic human vocation because they are deprived of essential goods.

Matter of Orientation: The evil does not consist in "having," as such, but in possessing without regard for the quality and the ordered hierarchy of the goods one has. Quality and hierarchy arise from the subordination of goods and their availability to man's "being" and his true vocation.

This shows that, although development has a necessary economic dimension since it must supply the greatest possible number of the world's inhabitants with an availability of goods essential for them "to be," it is not limited to that dimension. If it is limited to this, then it turns against those whom it is meant to benefit.

Development, which is not only economic, must be measured and oriented according to the reality and vocation of man seen in his totality, namely, according to his interior dimension.

Development cannot consist only in the use, dominion over and indiscriminate possession of created things and the products of human industry, but rather in subordinating the possession, dominion and use to man's divine likeness and to his vocation to immortality. This is the transcendent reality of the human being, a reality which is seen to be shared from the beginning by a couple, a man and a woman (cf. Gn. 1:27), and is therefore fundamentally social.

Man the Protagonist: It is logical to conclude, at least on the part of those who believe in the word of God, that today's "development" is to be seen as a moment in the story which began at creation, a story which is constantly endangered by reason of infidelity to the Creator's will and especially by the temptation to idolatry. But this "development" fundamentally corresponds to the first premises. Anyone wishing to renounce the difficult yet noble task of improving the lot of man in his totality, and of all people, with the excuse that the struggle is difficult and that constant effort is required, or simply because of the experience of defeat and the need to begin again, that person would be betraying the will of God, the Creator. In this regard, in the encyclical *Laborem Exercens* I referred to man's vocation to work in order to emphasize the idea that it is always man who is the protagonist of development.

Church's Concern: The concept of faith makes quite clear the reasons which impel the Church to concern herself with the problems of development, to consider them a duty of her pastoral ministry and to urge all to think about the nature and characteristics of authentic human development. Through her commitment she desires, on the one hand, to place herself at the service of the divine plan which is meant to order all things to the fullness which dwells in Christ (cf. Col. 1:19) and which he communicated to his body; and, on the other hand, she desires to respond to her fundamental vocation of being a "sacrament," that is to say, "a sign and instrument of intimate union with God and of the unity of the whole human race."

Church's Vocation: Thus, part of the teaching and most ancient practice of the Church is her conviction that she is obliged by her vocation — she herself, her ministers and each of her members — to relieve the misery of the suffering, both far and near, not only out of her "abundance" but also out of her "necessities." Faced by cases of need, one cannot ignore them in favor of superfluous church ornaments and costly furnishings for divine worship; on the contrary, it could be obligatory to sell these goods in order to provide food, drink, clothing and shelter for those who lack these things. As has been already noted, here we are shown a "hierarchy of values" — in the framework of the right to property — between "having" and "being," especially when the "having" of a few can be to the detriment of the "being" of many others.

Imperative for All: The obligation to commit oneself to the development of peoples is not just an individual duty and still less an individualistic one, as if it were possible to achieve this development through the isolated efforts of each individual. It is an imperative which obliges each and every man and woman as well as societies and nations. In particular, it obliges the Catholic Church and the other churches and ecclesial communities, with which we are completely willing to collaborate in this field. In this sense, just as we Catholics invite our Christian brethren to share in our initiatives, so too we declare that we are ready to collaborate in theirs and we welcome the invitations presented to us. In this pursuit of integral human development we can also do much with the members of other religions.

Collaboration in the development of the whole person and of every human being is in fact a duty of all toward all; and must be shared by the four parts of the world: East and West, North and South; or, as we say today, by the different "worlds." If, on the contrary, people try to achieve it in only one part or in only one world, they do so at the expense of the others; and, precisely because the others are ignored, their own development becomes exaggerated and misdirected.

Rights to Full Development: Peoples or nations too have a right to their own full development which, while including ... the economic and social aspects, should also include individual cultural identity and openness to the transcendent. Not even the need for development can be used as an excuse for imposing on others one's own way of life or own religious belief.

Nor would a type of development which did not respect and promote human rights — personal and social, economic and political, including the rights of nations and of peoples — be really worthy of man.

Today, perhaps more than in the past, the intrinsic contradiction of a development limited only to its economic element is seen more clearly. Such development easily subjects the human person and his deepest needs to the demands of economic planning and selfish profit.

Development-Respect Connection: The intrinsic connection between authentic development and respect for human rights once again reveals the moral character of development: the true elevation of man in conformity with the natural and historical vocation of each individual is not attained only by exploiting the abundance of goods and services or by having available perfect infrastructures.

When individuals and communities do not see a rigorous respect for the moral, cultural and spiritual requirements based on the dignity of the person and on the proper identity of each community, beginning with the family and religious societies, then all the rest — availability of goods, abundance of technical resources applied to daily life, a certain level of material well-being — will prove unsatisfying and, in the end, contemptible.

True development, in keeping with the specific needs of the human being, ... implies, especially for those who actively share in this process and are responsible for it, a lively awareness of the value of the rights of all and of each person. It likewise implies a lively awareness of the need to respect the right of every individual to the full use of the benefits offered by science and technology.

Respect for Rights: On the internal level of every nation, respect for all rights takes on great importance, especially: the right to life at every stage of its existence; the rights of the family as the basic social community or "cell of society"; justice in employment relationships; the rights inherent in the life of the political community as such; the rights based on the transcendent vocation of the human being, beginning with the right of freedom to profess and practice one's own religious belief.

On the international level, that is, the level of relations between states or, in present-day usage, between the different "worlds," there must be complete respect for the identity of each people, with its own historical and cultural characteristics.

In order to be genuine, development must be achieved within the framework of solidarity and freedom, without ever sacrificing either of them under whatever pretext. The moral character of development and its necessary promotion are emphasized when the most rigorous respect is given to all the demands deriving from the order of truth and good proper to the human person.

True development must be based on the love of God and neighbor, and must help to promote the relationships between individuals and society. This is the "civilization of love" of which Paul VI often spoke.

Ecology: Nor can the moral character of development exclude respect for the beings which constitute the natural world, which the ancient Greeks — alluding precisely to the order which distinguishes it — called the "cosmos."

A true concept of development cannot ignore the use of the elements of nature, the renewability of resources and the consequences of haphazard industrialization — three considerations which alert our consciences to the moral dimension of development.

THEOLOGICAL CONSIDERATIONS

Precisely because of the essentially moral character of development, it is clear that the obstacles to development likewise have a moral character.

The main obstacles to development will be overcome only by means of essentially moral decisions. For believers, and especially for Christians, these decisions will take their inspiration from the principles of faith, with the help of divine grace.

Structures of Sin: If the present situation can be attributed to difficulties of various kinds, it is not out of place to speak of "structures of sin" which ... are rooted in personal sin and thus always linked to the concrete acts of individuals who introduce these structures, consolidate them and make them difficult to remove. And thus they grow stronger, spread and become the source of other sins, and so influence people's behavior.

"Sin" and "structures of sin" are categories which are seldom applied to the situation of the contemporary world. However, one cannot easily gain a profound understanding of the reality that confronts us unless we give a name to the root of the evils which afflict us.

Spiritual Attitudes: One would hope that ... men and women without an explicit faith would be convinced that the obstacles to integral development are not only economic but rest on more profound attitudes which human beings can make into absolute values. Thus, one would hope that all those who, to some degree or other, are responsible for ensuring a "more human life" for their fellow human beings, whether or not they are inspired by a religious faith, will become fully aware of the urgent need to change the spiritual attitudes which define each individual's relationship with self, with neighbor, with even the remotest human communities and with nature itself; and all of this in view of higher values such as the common good or . . . the full development "of the whole individual and of all people."

Sin and Conversion: For Christians, as for all who recognize the precise theological meaning of the word *sin*, a change of behavior or mentality or mode of existence is called *conversion*, to use the language of the Bible (cf. Mk. 13:3, 5; Is. 30:15). This conversion specifically entails a relationship to God, to the sin committed, to its consequences, and hence to one's neighbor, either an individual or a community.

On the path toward the desired conversion, toward the overcoming of the moral obstacles to development, it is already possible to point to the positive and moral value of the growing awareness of interdependence among individuals and nations.

Interdependence, Solidarity: It is, above all, a question of interdependence, sensed as a system determining relationships in the contemporary world in its economic, cultural, political and religious elements, and accepted as a moral category. When interdependence becomes recognized in this way, the correlative response as a moral and social attitude, as a "virtue," is solidarity.

Interdependence must be transformed into solidarity, based upon the principle that the goods of creation are meant for all. That which human industry produces through the processing of raw materials, with the contribution of work, must serve equally for the good of all.

Solidarity, therefore, must play its part in the realization of this divine plan, both on the level of individuals and on the level of national and international society. The "evil mechanisms" and "structures of sin" of which we have spoken can be overcome only through the exercise of the human and Christian solidarity to which the Church calls us and which she tirelessly promotes. Only in this way can such positive energies be fully released for the benefit of development and peace.

Some Particular Guidelines

The Church does not have technical solutions to offer for the problem of underdevelopment as such. For the Church does not propose economic and political systems or programs, nor does she show preference for one or the other, provided that human dignity is properly respected and promoted, and provided she herself is allowed the room she needs to exercise her ministry in the world.

Whatever affects the dignity of individuals and peoples, such as authentic development, cannot be reduced to a "technical" problem. If reduced in this way, development would be emptied of its true content, and this would be an act of betrayal of the individuals and peoples whom development is meant to serve.

Church Contribution: The Church offers her first contribution to the solution of the urgent problem of development when she proclaims the truth about Christ, about herself and about man, applying this truth to a concrete situation.

As her instrument for reaching this goal, the Church uses her social doctrine.

Not a Third Way: The Church's social doctrine is not a "third way" between liberal capitalism and Marxist collectivism nor even a possible alternative to other solutions less radically opposed to one another: Rather, it constitutes a category of its own. Nor is it an ideology, but rather the accurate formulation of the results of a careful reflection on the complex realities of human existence, in society and in the international order, in the light of faith and of the Church's tradition. Its main aim is to interpret these realities, determining their conformity with our divergence from the lines of the Gospel teaching on man and his vocation, a vocation which is at once earthly and transcendent; its aim is thus to guide Christian behavior. It therefore belongs to the field, not of ideology, but of theology and particularly of moral theology.

The teaching and spreading of her social doctrine are part of the Church's evangelizing mission. It will not be superfluous to re-examine and clarify the characteristic themes and guidelines dealt with by the magisterium in recent years.

Option for the Poor: Here I would like to indicate one of them: the option or love of preference for the poor. This is an option or a special form of primacy in the exercise of Christian charity to which the whole tradition of the church bears witness. It affects the life of each Christian inasmuch as he or she seeks to imitate the life of Christ, but it applies equally to our social responsibilities and hence to our manner of living, and to the logical decisions to be made concerning the ownership and use of goods.

Property under Social Mortgage: It is necessary to state once more the characteristic principle of Christian social doctrine: The goods of this world are originally meant for all. The right to private property is valid and necessary, but it does not nullify the value of this principle. Private property, in fact, is under a "social mortgage," which means that it has an intrinsically social function based upon and justified precisely by the principle of the universal destination of goods.

Likewise, in this concern for the poor, one must not overlook that special form of poverty which consists in being deprived of fundamental human rights, in particular the right to religious freedom and also the right to freedom of economic initiative.

International Trade: In this respect I wish to mention specifically: the reform of the international trade system, which is mortgaged to protectionism and increasing bilateralism; the reform of the world monetary and financial system, today recognized as inadequate; the question of technological exchanges and their proper use; the need for a review of the structure of the existing international organizations, in the framework of an international juridical order.

Initiative and Collaboration: Development demands above all a spirit of initiative on the part of the countries which need it.

The development of peoples begins and is most appropriately accomplished in the dedication of each people to its own development, in collaboration with others.

None of what has been said can be achieved without the collaboration of all — especially the international community — in the framework of a solidarity which includes everyone, beginning with the most neglected. But the developing nations themselves have the duty to practice solidarity among themselves and with the neediest countries of the world.

An essential condition for global solidarity is autonomy and free self-determination, also within associations such as those indicated. But at the same time solidarity demands a readiness to accept the sacrifices necessary for the good of the whole world community.

More than Economic Development: Development which is merely economic is incapable of setting man free; on the contrary, it will end by enslaving him further. The principal obstacle . . . to authentic liberation is sin and the structures produced by sin.

200TH ANNIVERSARY OF THE U.S. HIERARCHY

Commemoration of the 200th anniversary of the establishment of the hierarchy in the United States will take place from the latter part of 1989 into 1990. One of the key events in the celebraton will occur at the site of the diocese where it all started, in Baltimore. The event will be the annual meeting of the National Conference of Catholic Bishops and the U.S. Catholic Conference in November.

In a papal bull issued late in 1789, Baltimore was designated the first U.S. diocese and John Carroll was named its first bishop. That year is usually considered the starting point of the hierarchy of the continental United States even though Father Carroll was not ordained a bishop until Aug. 15, 1790, in Dorsey, England, and did not take possession of the diocese until Dec. 12 of the same year.

At the time of writing, no list of commemorative events was available. However, no matter how many or how great such events might eventually be, they will hardly be able to measure up to the 200-year record of accomplishments not only of the bishops but of all the people of the Church in this country.

Aspects of this record are covered in standard and current articles of the Almanac under such headings as: The Catholic Church in the United States, Background Dates in U.S. Catholic Chronology, Biographies of U.S. Bishops (from 1789 to 1988), and a wide variety of specific titles. Repetition is not considered necessary in this brief article.

The bishops and faithful were praised by Pope Pius XII in his encyclical letter, *Sertum Laetitiae,* of Nov. 1, 1939, in which he commemorated the 150th anniversary of the U.S. hierarchy. Along with praise, he called attention to problems in the Church and American society in general.

Pope John Paul did the same thing during his visit to this country in 1987. He also reviewed a number of salient points in talks with U.S. bishops during their ad limina visits in 1988. In one talk, before a group of bishops from the West, he spoke Sept. 2 about approaches to their ministry. His observations could well serve to guide present and future bishops of this country as they move into the beginning of the third century of the hierarchy of the United States.

"Our program calls us to reflect together on our ministry and on the profound pastoral solicitude that we as bishops must have for humanity and for every human being. To be authentic, our episcopal ministry must truly be centered on man. At the same time, it must be centered on God, whose absolute primacy and supremacy we must constantly proclaim and urge our people to recognize in their lives."

Anthropocentrism and Theocentrism

"The (Second) Vatican Council has invited us to adopt both of these approaches — anthropocentrism and theocentrism — and to emphasize them together, linking them in the only satisfactory way possible; that is, in the divine Person of Christ, true God and true man. This task for us is both formidable and exhilirating. The effect it can have on the local churches is profound. In my encyclical on God's mercy, I stated that the deep and organic linking of anthropocentrism and theocentrism in Jesus Christ is perhaps the most important principle of the Second Vatican Council. The basic reason for this is the pastoral effectiveness of this principle.

"In concentrating on Christ, the Church is able to exalt human nature and human dignity, for Jesus Christ is the ultimate confirmation of all human dignity. The Church is also able to concentrate on humanity and on the well-being of each human being because of the fact that, in the Incarnation, Jesus Christ united all humanity to himself. In Christ, God the Father has placed the blueprint of humanity. At the same time, in concentrating on Christ, the Church emphasizes the centrality of God in the world; for in Christ — through the hypostatic union — God has taken possession of man to the greatest possible degree.

"To proclaim Christ to the full extent willed by the Second Vatican Council is to exalt man supremely and to exalt God supremely. To proclaim Christ fully is to proclaim him in the Father's plan of the Incarnation, which expresses man's greatest glory and God's greatest accomplishment in the world. Anthropocentrism and theocentrism truly linked in Christ open the way for the Church to a proper understanding of her pastoral service to humanity, for the glory of God."

ONE CANONIZATION, TWO BEATIFICATIONS

Rose Philippine Duchesne, missionary to the United States, was canonized July 3, 1988. She was born Aug. 29, 1769, in Genoble, France. She joined the Visitation Nuns in 1788 but was forced to leave the convent four years later during the hectic course of the atheistic French Revolution. She became a Religious of the Sacred Heart in 1804 and established the first convent of the order in Paris. In May, 1818, she arrived in New Orleans to take up missionary work. She started the first convent of her order in this country, as well as the first free school west of the Mississippi River, at St. Charles, Kan. At age 72 she founded a mission school for girls at Sugar Creek, Mo. Active missionary work was beyond her physical abilities, and she was unable to learn the language of the Potawatami Indians; they called her "the woman who always prays." She was recalled to St. Charles in 1842 where she died 10 years later. During the canonization ceremonies, Pope John Paul praised her "radical commitment to the poor." Her feast day is Nov. 17.

California missionary **Junipero Serra** was beatified Sept. 25, 1988, in solemn ceremonies at the Vatican. He was born Nov. 24, 1713, on the Island of Majorca. He joined the Order of Friars Minor in 1730, was ordained to the priesthood eight years later, taught philosophy and theology and discharged other duties as well in Spain before being assigned in 1749 to missionary work in Mexico. Between 1769 and 1782, he established nine in the chain of Franciscan missions in Upper California and is credited with introducing Indians to sound methods of agriculture, animal husbandry and various crafts. He died Aug. 28, 1784, at Carmel. His statue, representing California, is in National Statuary Hall.

Mother Katharine Drexel, whose beatification took place Nov. 20, 1988, was born Nov. 26, 1858, in Philadelphia. Daughter of a wealthy family, she devoted her inheritance of $12 million to the establishment in 1891 and the works of the Sisters of the Blessed Sacrament for Indians and Colored People. She retired as superior of the society in 1937 and died Mar. 3, 1955, at Cornwells Heights, Pa. At the time of her death, the order had 49 foundations in the Northeast, Midwest and Deep South.

The relevant Seattle announcement said: "Everything connected with this ministry to and with gay and lesbian people must be in accord with church teaching and discipline."

POPE JOHN PAUL IN AUSTRIA

Pope John Paul visited Austria June 23 to 27, 1988, on the 38th trip outside Italy since the beginning of his pontificate. Following are highlights of the pastoral tour along with the Holy Father's own account of the trip.

JUNE 23

On arrival at Schwechat-Vienna Airport, the Pope exchanged greetings with President Kurt Waldheim.

At Vespers in St. Stephan's Cathedral, the Holy Father urged Austrians to take the lead in re-evangelizing Europe. Among other things, he told them to use their democratic freedoms to promote pro-life causes and stable family life.

"What kind of society is this," he asked, "in which old age is often regarded as a disease, where the sick are sometimes seen as a hindrance to a comfortable life, where marriages are contracted irresponsibly and dissolved even more irresponsibly, where tens of thousands of children are killed each year even before they see the light of day?"

Democracy and European Renewal: In the evening, the Pope met privately with President Waldheim.

Afterwards, in an address to government officials and diplomats, he called for strengthening democracy as a guarantee against tyranny. He pledged the Church's "cooperative partnership" with government efforts to promote human rights, aid refugees and foster development in the Third World.

He also said: "The entire continent needs a creative process of renewal to achieve a united Europe. . . . The Church endeavors to make its contribution to a re-evangelization of the peoples of Europe. . . . Europe was born out of Christianity, and European nations, in all their diversity, have embodied Christian existence. We have to rediscover this Christian identity and the inner unity of Europe."

JUNE 24

Holocaust: This was the theme of the Pope's remarks at a meeting with members of the Jewish community.

"You and we are weighed down by memories of Shoah, the murder of millions of Jews in camps of destruction. It would be unjust and wrong to attribute these unspeakable crimes to Christianity. Much to the contrary, these events show us the horrifying face of a world without God, of a world even inimical to God, of a world whose stated intent it was to destroy not only the Jewish people but also the faith of those who venerate the Redeemer of the world in the Jew Jesus of Nazareth. Solemn protests and appeals on the part of a few individuals only served to nurture this fanaticism."

"From these cruel sufferings may rise even deeper hope, a warning call to all of mankind that may serve to save us all. Remembering Shoah means hoping that it will never happen again, and working to ensure that it does not."

Constructive Discussions: "It is imperative that we promote constructive discussions between Jews, Christians and Moslems so that our common testimony to our faith in the 'God of Abraham, the God of Isaac and the God of Jacob' (Ex. 3:6) may become fruitful in our search for mutual understanding and fraternal living together without detriment to the rights of any person or group.

"It is in this spirit that any initiative of the Holy See should be seen when it endeavors to seek recognition of the same dignity for the Jewish people in the state of Israel and for the Palestinian people. The Jewish people has a right to a country of its own, as any other nation has under international law. The same, however, holds for the Palestinian people, many of whom have become homeless and are refugees. Through mutual understanding and compromise, solutions will finally have to be found which result in just, comprehensive and permanent peace in the region. If only forgiveness and love are abundantly sown, the weeds of hatred will no longer be able to grow; they will be choked. To remember Shoah also means to stand up against the seed of violence and to protect and nurture, patiently and persistently, any tender shoot of peace and freedom."

Mauthausen: At the concentration camp where some 122,000 persons, including 14,000 Jews, were put to death, the Pope said: "In this place here in Mauthausen there were men who, in the name of an insane ideology, set in motion an entire system of contempt and hatred against other human beings. They performed tortures, broke bones and cruelly mistreated bodies and souls. They persecuted their victims with their cruelty."

Criticism: The Pope was the target of Jewish criticism: (1) for not making explicit mention of Jews who were killed at Mauthausen; (2) for not establishing diplomatic relations between the Vatican and Israel; (3) for his 1987 visit with President Waldheim who, it was alleged, had been involved in Nazi brutality against Jews during World War II.

Rejection of God: During Mass at Trausdorf, the Pope said the rejection of God was the cause of "bitter" problems of the 20th century: "the mechanized death of two world wars, the persecution and annihilation of whole groups of people because of their ethical and religious background, the ongoing nuclear arms race, the helplessness of man confronted with unspeakable misery in many parts of the world."

He also told Austrians to remain faithful to "their function as a link ... with the peoples of Eastern Europe. ... You are ready to cultivate contacts wth them. ... The many guests that have come today from your neighboring countries (60,000 from Hungary and about 15,000 from Yugoslavia) are living proof of this."

Superficial Faith: In an address to bishops in Salzburg, the Holy Father called Catholicism in Austria a "superficial and petrified" faith in need of a "vast re-evangelization. ... The faith has lost its force in concrete, everyday life. ... The dimensions of secularization, caused by well-being and religious indifference, have grown among you in the life of the individual, the family, and especially in public life. ... The bishops must engage in a vast re-evangelization which begins with the individual, the family and the community."

June 25

Crisis of Faith: Christians must reinforce their faith if they are to overcome the current "hour of darkness" marked by wars, oppression and injustices," said the Pope during a Liturgy of the Word attended by 80,000 people in Enns. While encouraging efforts to overcome political and economic problems, he was strong in declaring that social progress and spiritual conversion "walk hand in hand, one sustaining the other."

During a Mass at Gurk, he said Europe was facing "a crisis of faith" and had "urgent need of a new evangelization." He called on his listeners to "begin anew to talk of faith, and transmit it in dialogue between generations."

JUNE 26

Faith Overcomes Fear: At a morning Mass in Salzburg, the Holy Father said in a homily that faith helps to overcome "the fear of that dark abyss within ourselves, the fear of death and nothingness. ... The tedious cycle of working, earning one's living, consuming, working again, does not yet provide an answer to the question of what ultimate purpose all this may serve."

Deal with Mistakes: He told youths at an afternoon meeting to take responsibility for the future by dealing with their mistakes. "Do not simply sweep the remains of your failures, your faults and your unkept resolutions under the carpet. If you do, they will poison your spiritual environment or make you find scapegoats for your own mistakes."

Science and Values: Mankind must return to belief in God in order to overcome "the ambivalence of progress" and the mistaken search for scientific means of escaping death, the Pope said at a meeting with scientists and artists. He warned against the "sorry idea that one might have himself copied by genetic engineering in the vain hope of escaping death." He criticized "the killing of so many unborn" and "the problems resulting from genetic engineering. ... It is high time to call into question the practice of regarding scientific work as being free from considerations of value."

Ecumenism: At an interfaith prayer meeting, the Pope noted that ecumenical developments had resulted in greater theological understanding, but said that "convergence, however, does not yet mean consensus. ... It is most painful also for the Pope and the Catholic bishops" to experience "the division among Christians at the very table of the Lord."

JUNE 27

The Holy Father spent the last day of his Austrian visit in Innsbruck, where he celebrated Mass, addressed an assembly of youths, and took part in Marian Vespers in the local basilica dedicated to the honor of Mary.

Fear: During Mass, he told a throng of 80,000 persons that many people in recent years "have been aroused by a fear fed constantly by political earthquakes, threats to the environment, and an apparent feeling of senselessness both inside themselves and in the world. ... An excessively naive sense of progress in recent decades has led to a painful loss of significance. This new atmosphere has paralyzed many. Others live for the moment, without thinking about tomorrow."

POPE JOHN PAUL IN SOUTH AMERICA

Pope John Paul, on the 37th foreign pastoral trip of his pontificate May 7 to 18, 1988, visited Bolivia and Paraguay (for the first time), Uruguay and Peru (for the second time).

The trip took place in the context of a years-long novena of preparation, already under way, for the celebration in 1992 of the introduction of Christinity in Latin America. Its overall theme was the need for renewed evangelization throughout the region.

The following excerpts from papal addresses are from texts circulated by the NC News Documentary Service, Origins (Vol. 18, Nos. 2 and 3), and English editions of *L'Osservatore Romano*, (June 6, 13, 20, 27, July 4).

URUGUAY
May 7 to 9

The Pope spent about 48 hours in Uruguay, from the time of his arrival May 7 at the Montevideo Airport until his departure for Bolivia on the 9th. In the most secularized country in South America, he stressed the need for a "public profession of Christianity."

He spoke about employer-employee relations, support for labor unions and a civilization of work, at Melo; addressed the bishops in Montevideo; ordained 13 priests and consecrated the nation to Mary at Florida; and at Salto emphasized evangelization for the promotion of justice.

Civilization of Work: "The construction of a civilization based on work is an ethical necessity because of man's supernatural vocation and is at the same time a challenge to his creative capacity." It "brings with it an invitation for a peaceful dialogue among those who have different opinions on possible solutions to the problems at hand. There is no single solution to these, and no one has the right to describe his solution as the 'Catholic' solution, since the principles put forward by the Church allow for various types of practical application."

Evangelization: While this was the main thrust of the Pope's remarks to the bishops of Uruguay, he also underscored two needs: (1) for the spiritual development of all members of the Church, and (2) for "teaching the truths of the faith without reductionism or dubious interpretations."

Regarding evangelization, he said: "The new stage of evangelization of each faithful Christian should have repercussions in his entire social life, impregnating all the aspects of culture. It is not enough just to see to it that some keep the faith; it is necessary . . . that the very life of the country in all its manifestations be in conformity with the principles of the Gospel."

Priests: The Holy Father called on the newly ordained and other priests to "be witnesses of this God who is Love and who manifested himself in Christ his Son as the Good Shepherd who gives up his life for love. You are to be servants of the love which God infuses in our hearts by the indelible 'seal' of the Spirit of love. In the name of this friendship with which Christ has marked you, do not refuse this beautiful task of being servants of Love."

BOLIVIA
May 9

Fundamentalist sects and liberation theology were among subjects of the Pope's remarks at a meeting with the bishops of Bolivia May 9 in La Paz.

Sects: He urged the bishops to provide people with the "doctrinal guidance" they need in order to "defend themselves in the face of the active proselytizing of sects" which undermine the coherence and unity of the evangelical message."

More than 150 churches and sects were legally registered in the country. Some of them were heavily subsidized by sources in the United States, and many of them were blatantly anti-Catholic in the substance and rhetoric of their preaching and teaching.

Liberation Theology: An "authentically evangelical liberation theology contains positive values," said the Pope, while warning at the same time against "dangers of deviations" from church doctrine which do not take adequate account of spiritual liberation from sin. The Church "cannot limit itself to offer merely temporal aspirations or partial liberations from ills which are solely terrestrial. . . . We cannot confine people within the bounds of a solely material liberation. . . . Personal sin, especially selfishness, is at the root of unjust social structures."

May 10

The Pope celebrated Mass May 10 at the El Alto Airport outside La Paz before a throng of 600,000.

Family and Moral Themes: While mixing praise and criticism of the customs of the Aymara Indians, the Pope restated, as on many other occasions, the oposition of the Church to divorce, abortion, artificial birth control, trial marriages and flight from family resonsibilities. He said, among other things:

• "The anti-conception mentality is a falsification of conjugal love."

• "Do not flee from family obligations, putting your heart into other objectives such as labor problems, the problems of society and politics."

• Women should not seek refuge "in a female liberation which does not promote, but only subjugates, women even more."

Serving the Poor: He encouraged nuns to continue their educational work among the poor, and to serve as well "the new poor and the new marginal people, fruit of a materialistic society" which stresses the "unchained desire for comfort, profit and dominance."

International Debt: Through diplomats, he appealed to political leaders and heads of state to lift the "onerous weight of the foreign debt" on poor countries. "The unevenness between the amount of this debt and the capacity to pay it, the difference between the sums loaned to borrowers and the amount of repayment required by creditors, are causing grave damage to many poor countries.

... The abysmal differences between rich and poor countries are incompatible with the divine plan for an equitable and just participation in all the goods of creation."

May 11

In the morning of May 11, the Pope addressed about 150,000 farmers, miners and other workers at Oruro, nearly 14,000 feet above sea level in the Andes. Later, he celebrated Mass in Cochabamba where he also met with priests, seminarians and Religious, and addressed a gathering of youths.

Hope and Justice: The Holy Father said in Oruro: "I come to bring you a message of hope, which does not mean remaining passive in the face of poverty that grows with every passing day."

He called for the equitable distribution of farm lands and for non-violent solutions to the serious problems of the poorest nation in South America. "The criteria to be adopted in the noble struggle for justice must never degenerate into a confrontation of brother against brother. You must always be inspired and moved by the evangelical principles of collaboration and dialogue, excluding all forms of violence. ... Violence and hatred are pernicious needs, incapable of producing anything but violence and hatred."

He also warned against a tendency to overlook the defects of an economic system that has "profit as its main goal" and which subordinates the human person to the vast machinery of production."

In conclusion, he said: "I would like to invite all of you to live in the hope of a better tomorrow, knowing that it is a tomorrow that you must work to build yourselves, each one according to his gifts and possibilities."

No Moral Blackmail: At Mass, the Pope said that measures to resolve problems of the country should not include "prohibited methods of birth control or sterilization or abortion. . . . Do not give in to the moral blackmail of those who subjugate health and material aid to illicit plans for limiting births."

Inculturation: He told priests, seminarians and Religious that inculturation "is not limited to absorbing sociological data. . . . Genuine inculturation brings the light and force of the Gospel, which is above the manifestations of all cultures, thus making possible the discernment of all authentic values, their purification, transformation and elevation."

Before an assembly of youths, the Pope warned against drug and alcohol abuse, and "the absence of moral norms in sexual conduct." He urged them not to be seduced by the "easy enrichment" of drug trafficking, and not to succumb to "fictitious solutions" to problems.

Latin American Bloc: At a gathering of intellectual, business and civic leaders, the Pontiff said Lain American countries should "overcome national selfishness and create a common front capable of dialogue on a level of equality with industrialized countries." This would allow them to seek conditions "which respect the economic initiative and proper identity of each nation."

May 12

Tribute to Missionaries: At Mass May 12 in Sucre, the Pope defended the work of the missionaries who brought Christianity to Latin America nearly 500 years earlier. They endured "great sacrifices (and) reached the heart of the people through the means of catechesis, the sacraments, popular piety and works of charity. They firmly established the basis for your cultural identity, oriented toward maturity in Christ."

Brain Drain: In Santa Cruz, he called the "flight of brains and capital" from Latin America "a serious problem." Many professionals, "instead of contributing to the progressive development of the nation, prefer to leave national ties and look for other more prosperous places to establish themselves." He said they should, rather, commit themselves "in all generosity to make Bolivia a peaceful and stable nation."

May 13

The Pope began May 13 with an address at the airport in Tarija, where he said that education and health care for children, the first victims of poverty, are an obligation in justice.

Committed Lay Persons: With members of apostolic movements at the cathedral in Santa Cruz, he spoke about their union with Christ, their bishops and each other in efforts to consecrate the world to its Creator and Savior.

Social Gospel: Some of its principles were the subjects of papal remarks at Mass. The Holy Father emphasized the primacy of persons over things, stating that people are "the criterion for evaluating the concrete forms which human community and social progress take." He called on Christians to live "the virtue of solidarity" and to resist the temptation to violence as "a means of breaking up those structures which are considered to be unjust."

Drug Traffic: In Santa Cruz, a major crossroads of cocaine traffic, he referred to a "deterioration in basic ethical values" and urged action to end it. "Commerce in drugs . . . leads to the most terrible form of slavery and sows corruption and death in your soul." It has dire "domestic and foreign consequences." It is vital "to protect the young from using drugs and to fight the trafficking itself, because we are dealing with an activity that is infamous in every way."

BOLIVIA — PERU
May 14

The Holy Father celebrated a last Mass on Bolivian soil at Trinidad. Love as the point of departure for the vocation and mission of the Church was the main point of his homily.

Enroute to Lima, as he flew by the national Bolivian shrine of Our Lady of Copacabana, he broadcast an appeal that children be taught to live together in peace.

In the capital city of the extremely violent nation of Latin America, he told priests, deacons, seminarians and Religious that the Gospel of Christ judges the world, consecrated the nation to Our Lady of Evangelization, and spoke about the evangelizing work of lay missionaries.

May 15

One of the exceptional highlights of the pastoral tour of Latin America was the Pope's presence and celebration of Mass at the closing of the Fifth Eucharistic and Marian Congress of the Bolivarian nations (Peru, Bolivia, Colombia, Ecuador, Panama and Venezuela).

Eucharist and Union with Christ: "Every time that we participate in the Eucharist, we are more closely united to Christ and, in him, to all people, with a more perfect bond than any natural union. Thus united, we are sent into the whole world to be a witness to God's love through faith and works of service to others, preparing for the coming of his kingdom and anticipating it in the shadows of this present time. We also discover the profound sense of our action in the world in favor of development and peace, and we receive from him the energy to pledge ourselves to this mission more generously each time. . . . Thus, we will construct a new civilization: the civilization of love. . . . A civilization which, on (the) basis of love of the person who is near us — our neighbor — will transform structures and the whole world."

Sacrament of Mission: The Pope summoned the people to mission as he said: "Church of Peru! Church of the Bolivarian nations! Church of Latin America! Christ speaks to you in the same words which he spoke then and sends you to preach the Good News to every creature just as he sent the Apostles on the day of the Ascension." "The Eucharist . . . is the sacrament of mission, of sending. From it is born the mission of all: bishops, priests, Religious, lay persons, all the people of God."

New Evangelization: This was one of the subjects of the Pope's remarks at a meeting with the bishops of Peru. "As we now approach the third millennium of Christianity and, closer still, on the eve of the fifth centenary of the evangelization of Latin America, I wish to remind you of the need for a renewed effort in . . . a new evangelization."

"Certainly, the seed of the message of Christ has penetrated deeply in Peruvian soil, has germinated with pesistent vigor and has produced abundant fruits of holiness. . . . However, the Lord calls us to press on with this evangelization which . . . has to be new in its ardor, methods and expression, while remaining always faithful to that Good News which the Gospel is in any moment of history.

"This new or renewed evangelization, while proclaiming Jesus Christ where he is still unknown, will place greater demands on those who already belong to his flock. . . . We cannot be satisfied with the goals already achieved. . . . Without doubt, much has already been achieved but, at the same time, it is little if we think of the extensive horizons of possible expansion and deepening in Christian life which open before our eyes."

The Pope also addressed:

• Women Religious: "Your ecclesial witness should enlighten the world."

• Business and cultural leaders: "You have the responsibility of making Peru a place where all can live in conformity with human dignity."

• Youths: "Christ and his message are the answer to the ills of our time."

PARAGUAY
May 16 to 18

Before leaving Peru for the flight to Asuncion, Paraguay, the Holy Father reminded well-wishers at the Jorge Chavez Airport that only the Gospel and its social teaching can bring salvation to Latin America.

Canonization: The highlight of the Pope's first day in Paraguay was the canonization of three Jesuit priests who were martyred there during an Indian uprising in 1628. The priests were Roque Gonzalez, a native Paraguayan, and his Spanish confreres, Alfonso Rodriguez and Juan del Castillo. They were pioneer founders of reductions among Guarani Indians in areas which are now parts of Paraguay, Uruguay, Argentina and Brazil.

The reductions were mission settlements for the evangelization and general development of the Indians; they dated from 1609 to 1768, when the Jesuits were expelled from Spanish-ruled South America by King Carlos III; at their peak, they numbered 54 and had an exclusively Indian population of about 150,000.

Challenge of the Martyr: In his homily, the Holy Father said that St. Roque Gonzalez, who served at the Asuncion cathedral, "comes back and talks to us once again:

• "to exhort you to keep your faith alive . . .

• "to inspire you to make this faith really operative so that your love for God will bring forth a love for your neighbors capable of breaking down all barriers of division, and of creating a feeling of real solidarity and of charity in today's Paraguay;

• "to invite you to be faithful to the most authentic traditions of your people and of your land, which are imbued with a real sense of authentic Christianity;

• "to give you an example of love for the Virgin Mary, who will guide you in your lives as she guided the steps of St. Roque in his apostolic pilgrimage among you."

Solidarity and Human Rights: The Pope emphasized the ethical dimension of politics in an address to President Alfredo Stroessner, other government officials and members of the diplomatic corps. "The attainment of the common good of all people presupposes that certain conditions of peace and justice, security and order are present."

"Solidarity is a Christian virtue intimately related to charity. We are all obliged to contribute, through our collaboration, to the common good. Your task, as part of a government, will be immensely facilitated and will reach an unsuspected efficiency if at all times you search for the means to an easier dialogue and greater participation of all in everything to do with public affairs. Your task will be better fulfilled within a just administration which is zealous in its operations, so that the rights of the most underprivileged are always upheld."

Respect for human rights, as is well known, is not a question of political convenience, but is derived from each person's individual dignity by virtue of being a creature of God called to a transcendent destiny. Therefore, every offense to a human being is also an offense to the Creator. The inevitable demands of moral issues must inform the managers in public places of their options for truth and justice within freedom, which must be reflected in the institutional and legal systems which regulate civil life."

Catechetics: This was the key subject of the Pope's address to the bishops of Paraguay.

"The Word of God must be sown everywhere by means of a continuous, extensive and intensive preaching and catechetical activity. . . . It is a task which should be given top priority, an indispensable task. It is an activity that, in order to be effective, demands not only the dedication of priests and other pastoral workers but also the serious concern of parents for the religious formation of their children.

"You should keep watch . . . over the adequate doctrinal and human preparation of those you have entrusted to catechize, so that they teach systematically and profoundly the totality of the mysteries of the faith with the correct criteria, piety and competency. it is not enough to teach doctrine you must make it your objective that those who receive religious instruction will be strongly motivated to put into practice what they learn."

May 17

The first of several meetings of the day was with priests, Religious and seminarians at the cathedral in Asuncion; he told them their work for total liberation must be inspired by criteria and methods of the Gospel.

During Mass at Villarica Airport, he said in a homily that public authorities must recognize their obligation to seek solutions for the problems of farmers.

With Indians at Santa Teresita Mission in Mariscal Estigarriba, he called on all Paraguayans to collaborate in efforts to integrate natives into the national community.

Call for Democracy: This was the theme of an address by the Pope before a gathering of 3,000 civic leaders known as the Builders of Society.

The government of Alfredo Stroessner had canceled the meeting but was constrained to rescind the cancellation in response to adverse criticism and publicity. The Pope's remarks, in addition to being a statement of basic principles, were a rebuttal of Stroessner's stated claim that Paraguay, under his control for 34 years, was a model of social justice, well-being and democracy.

Following are salient points of the papal address.

• The social doctrine of the Church "is characterized by optimism and hope because it is based on the person; and, from the standpoint of humanity, it wants to make its voice heard within social, political and economic institutions. It is inspired by the person, and views people as the main actors in building up society. It means that people . . . were created in the image and likeness of their Creator and are called upon to mold themselves in God's image in their personal and communal life."

• "This social doctrine proposes an ideal of society characterized by solidarity and openness to people and to transcendence."

• "All social relations, in their ethical substance, consist precisely in recognizing the dignity of every person, recognizing in each one his real humanity."

• "Truth must be the fundamental foundation, the solid cement of all social building. . . . We should not reflect in a sterile way about truth, but accept it as the criterion which, applied to civil society, ought to characterize actual relations. . . . A society founded on truth is opposed to any form of corruption; therefore, your bishops . . . have made a call for 'the moral healing of the nation.' "

• "A crisis in public morality, apart from creating serious difficulties for the members of society, can also compromise the destiny of salvation. . . . Where there is a lack of morality, not only is the realization of . . . ideals inhibited, but the confidence in institutions is lost, thus generating passivity and a loss of social dynamism."

• "The simultaneous observance of and solidarity with values such as peace, freedom, justice and participation are essential requisites if we want to speak of an authentically democratic society based on the free consensus of the citizens. It is not possible, therefore, to speak of real freedom and even less of democracy, where there is no real participation by all the citizens in making decisions which involve the life and future of the nation. While adopting an attitude of agreement and dialogue, it is necessary to seek out those types of participation which are most suitable for expressing the deepest aspirations of all citizens."

Basis for Dialogue: "The Christian roots of your people, toward which human and spiritual reserves of hope converge, must inspire solidarity, generous sacrifice and mutual respect in everyone, providing the basis for a permanent dialogue enabling Paraguay to progress more and more along the road toward peace, agreement and equality of all its citizens, without distinction of race or social condition."

May 18

On the last day of his pastoral tour, the Holy Father urged people attending a Liturgy of the Word at Encarnacion to make the multifaceted love of Christ present in society.

At Mass in Caacupe, he consecrated the nation to Mary and prayed in a homily for justice to the poor.

Back in Asuncion, he told an assembly of youths that God calls on them to commit themselves to the defense of human rights; he also spoke about the liberating force of the Ten Commandments.

Late in the evening, the Holy Father bade farewell at the Asuncion airport, with an expression of hope that Paraguayans might devote themselves to efforts for reconciliation among all sectors of society.

THE LEFEBVRE SCHISM

Swiss Archbishop Marcel Lefebvre, after 15 or more years of open dissent from the authority of the Pope and enactments of the Second Vatican Council, formally excommunicated himself from the Church June 30, 1988, as he ordained four bishops without proper authorization. By so doing, he created the first formal schism from the Church in more than a hundred years.

The following statement, issued by the Vatican June 16, is an account of efforts by the Vatican to forestall the schismatic action.

This statement, with subheads added, was circulated by the NC Documentary Service, Origins, June 30, 1988 (Vol. 18, No. 7).

Archbishop Marcel Lefebvre, founder of the Society of St. Pius X, made public Wednesday, June 15, 1988, his decision to proceed June 30 with the ordination of four bishops chosen by himself without the necessary papal mandate.

Having noted with profound sorrow this gesture of a schismatic nature, the Holy See considers it necessary to provide the following information for the benefit of the bishops and their faithful.

CHRONOLOGY OF EVENTS

Following Cardinal Gagnon's apostolic visit to the Society of St. Pius X (November-December, 1987), the Holy Father, in his letter of April 8, 1988, to Cardinal Ratzinger, prefect of the Congregation for the Doctrine of the Faith, clearly expressed his desire that everything possible be done to respond to the readiness that Archbishop Lefebvre apparently has shown to reach a solution which would allow the society to obtain a regular place within the Church in full communion with the Apostolic See. Meetings between expert theologians and canonists of the congregation and of the society were held April 12-15, 1988, with such an aim in view. The satisfactory progress made during these conversations allowed for a further meeting May 4, with the participation of Cardinal Ratzinger and Archbishop Lefebvre themselves. At the end of this meeting, a protocol note was drawn up and signed by both participants May 5. This document, drawn up in common agreement and meant to be used as a basis for reconciliation, was then to be given to the Pope for a final decision.

The protocol note of May 5, 1988, contained a declaration of a doctrinal kind and a plan for some type of juridical disposition as well as measures for regulating the canonical situation of the society and of those concerned with it.

In the first part of the text, Archbishop Lefebvre declared in his name and in that of the Priestly Society of St. Pius X that they would:

• Promise to be faithful to the Catholic Church and to the Roman Pontiff, head of the body of bishops.

• Accept the doctrine contained in No. 25 of Vatican II's Dogmatic Constitution, *Lumen Gentium*, on the ecclesiastical magisterium and the need to adhere to it.

• Commit themselves to a studious and communicative attitude toward the Apostolic See, avoiding any polemics so far as those points taught by Vatican II or appearing in subsequent reforms are concerned, and which seemed difficult for them to reconcile with tradition.

• Recognize the validity of the Mass and of the sacraments celebrated with the requested intention and following the rites of the typical editions promulgated by Paul VI and by John Paul II.

• Promise to respect the common discipline of the Church and the ecclesiastical laws, especially those contained in the 1983 Code of Canon Law, except for that special discipline conceded to the society by particular law.

Measures Proposed

In the second part of the text, apart from the canonical reconciliation of people, the following measures were taken:

• The Priestly Society of St. Pius X would be erected as a society of apostolic life under pontifical right with appropriate statutes following Canons 731-746, and also benefiting from a certain amount of exemption as far as public worship, spiritual care and apostolic activities are concerned, taking into consideration Canons 679-683.

• The society would be allowed to use the liturgical books in use up to the post-conciliar reform.

• In order to coordinate the relationships among the various departments of the Roman Curia and the diocesan bishops, and also for resolving any problems or disputes, the Holy Father would set up a Roman commission. The commission would include two members of the society and be provided with the necessary faculties.

• Finally, taking into account the particular situation of the society, it was suggested to the Holy Father that a bishop should be chosen from among its members who, normally, should not be the superior general.

Lefebvre Objections

However, on May 6, Archbishop Lefebvre wrote to Cardinal Ratzinger and, without taking into account the free will of the Pope recognized by the protocol note, insisted that the episcopal ordination of a member of the society take place June 30; and added that, if the reply were negative, he would be obliged in all conscience to go ahead with this consecration all the same. Cardinal Ratzinger replied to him immediately, inviting him to reconsider his proposal, which was contrary to the protocol note signed only the day before.

Finally, the two prelates met for the second time in Rome on Tuesday, May 14. At this meeting, Cardinal Ratzinger communicated to Archbishop Lefebvre that the Holy Father was willing to nominate, following the criteria and the normal procedure of the Church, a bishop chosen from within the society and to make it possible for his ordination to take place Aug. 15, 1988, for the closing of the Marian Year, but on the condition that the founder of the society put forward to him a real re-

The Lefebvre Schism

quest for reconciliation on the basis of the protocol note already signed, and that he submit himself to the Pope's decision so far as the ordination of a bishop was concerned. For his part, Archbishop Lefebvre provided two letters, one to the Holy Father and one to Cardinal Ratzinger, in which he insisted on the date of June 30 and in which he proposed once again his previous request to nominate three bishops in order to guarantee the life and the activities of the society; he also requested that the society be allowed the majority of members in the future Roman commission. It was decided, at this point, to begin a period of reflection on both sides.

Contents of Ratzinger Letter

Following the indications given by the Holy Father, Cardinal Ratzinger replied to Archbishop Lefebvre May 30. In this letter, he pointed out:

- That, for the Roman commission, a structure of the Holy See at the service of the society and of a consultative nature, the question of a majority did not arise since, in point of fact, the final decisions belonged to the Supreme Pontiff; and that those principles laid down in the protocol note of May 5 should be adhered to.

- That, so far as the ordination of a bishop was concerned, Archbishop Lefebvre should give up his idea of consecrating one June 30, "with or without Rome's consent," and that he should show full obedience to the decision of the Holy Father, who, it was well known, had been very understanding.

Lefebvre Letter

On June 2, Archbishop Lefebvre sent the Holy Father the following letter.

Econe, June 2, 1988

Most Holy Father,

The conversations and meetings with Cardinal Ratzinger and his assistants, although they took place in an atmosphere of courteousness and charity, have convinced us that the moment for frank and effective collaboration has not yet arrived.

In effect, if each Christian has the right to ask the competent church authorities to guard the faith in which he was baptized, what about priests and men and women Religious?

It is in order to keep intact the faith in which we were baptized that we felt obligated to oppose the spirit of Vatican II and the reforms inspired by it.

That false ecumenism which is the origin of all the innovations of the Council — in the liturgy, in the new relations between the Church and the world, in the concept of the Church itself — is leading the Church to ruin and Catholics to apostasy.

Radically opposed to this destruction of our faith and resolved to stay within the traditional doctrine and discipline of the Church, especially in that which concerns the training of priests and religious life, we feel the absolute need to have church authorities who take up our concerns and help us to guard against the spirit of Vatican II and the spirit of Assisi.

That is why we are asking for several bishops, chosen from within the tradition, and a majority of members in the Roman commission, so that we may be protected against all compromise.

In view of the refusal to consider our requests and since it is evident that the aim of this reconciliation is not at all the same for the Holy See as it is for us, we think it preferable to wait for a more propitious moment, when Rome returns to tradition.

That is why we will ourselves provide the means for carrying on the task that Providence has assigned to us, assured by the letter of His Eminence Cardinal Ratzinger, dated May 30, that the episcopal consecration is not contrary to the will of the Holy See, because it was agreed on for Aug. 15.

We shall continue to pray that modern Rome, infested by modernism, will once again become Catholic Rome and will once again find its 2,000-year-old tradition. Then the problem of reconciliation will no longer have a reason to exist, and the Church will find a new youth.

Deign to accept, Most Holy Father, my very respectful wishes, filially devoted in Jesus and Mary.

Archbishop Marcel Lefebvre
archbishop-bishop emeritus of
Tulle, founder of the Society
of St. Pius X.

Vatican Clarification

It is necessary, with reference to this letter, to point out that the arguments used by Archbishop Lefebvre are absolutely groundless when, taking up once again, in complete contrast to what was accepted in the protocol note of May 5, his radical polemic against Vatican II, he affirms that the episcopal ordination would not be contrary to the will of the Holy See. So far as this is concerned, it is evident — as can be seen from the protocol note — that the proposed episcopal ordination could only take place after the formal act of reconciliation and within the framework of a global canonical solution, and that the choice of a candidate and his nomination would only be decided by the Pope himself. Taking this into account, the date of Aug. 15 was indicated. Now, since Archbishop Lefebvre's letter expressly interrupts the process of reconciliation, it is clear that an episcopal ordination carried out by him would be contrary to the will of the Holy See.

Papal Letter

On June 9, the Holy Father sent the following letter to Archbishop Lefebvre.

To His Excellency, Archbishop Marcel Lefebvre, archbishop-bishop emeritus, of Tulle,

It is with heartfelt and deep pain that I take note of your letter of June 2.

Guided only by my solicitude for the unity of the Church in fidelity to revealed truth — an imperative obligation imposed on the successor of the Apostle Peter — last year I set up an apostolic visit to the Society of St. Pius X and its works, which was carried out by Cardinal Edouard Gagnon. Discussions followed, first with the experts of the Congregation for the Doctrine of the Faith, then between yourself and Cardinal Joseph Ratzinger. During these meetings, solutions were drawn up, accepted and signed by you on May 5, 1988. These permitted the Society of St. Pius X to exist and operate within the Church in full communion with the Pope, the guardian of unity in the truth. For its part, the Apostolic See only had one aim during its discussions with you: that of favoring and safeguarding this unity in obedience to divine revelation, transmitted and interpreted by the magisterium of the Church, notably in the 21 ecumenical councils from Nicea to Vatican II.

In your letter to me, you appear to reject all that which was accomplished in the previous discussions, because you clearly show your intention to "provide yourselves with the means for carrying on with your task," notably by going ahead very shortly and without an apostolic mandate with one or more episcopal ordinations, this being in flagrant contradiction not only to what is prescribed by Canon Law, but also to the protocol note signed May 5 and the indications relative to this problem contained in the letter Cardinal Ratzinger wrote to you May 30 at my request.

With a paternal heart, but gravely concerned by the seriousness of the present circumstances, I exhort you, Venerable Brother, to give up your project which, if it were carried out, would only look like a schismatic act whose inevitable theological and canonical consequences are already known to you. I ardently invite you to return, in humility, to full obedience to the Vicar of Christ.

I not only invite you to do his, but I ask it of you in the name of the wounds of Christ, our Redeemer, in the name of Christ, who on the eve of his passion prayed for his disciples, "so that they may all be one" (Jn. 17:21).

To this request and to this invitation, I add my daily prayer to Mary, Mother of Christ.

Dear Brother, do not permit the year dedicated in a special way to God's Mother to bring yet another wound to her Mother's heart!

From the Vatican, June 9, 1988.

John Paul II.

CONSEQUENCES OF ORDINATIONS

In conclusion, it is not superfluous to underline that, within all the phases of the process described above, the Pope was constantly informed and he himself provided the fundamental guidance on the position of the Apostolic See. Also, upon his request, the cardinals who are heads of dicasteries and the presidents of the episcopal conferences most interested in the problem of reconciliation of the Society of St. Pius X were informed in a precise way by the cardinal prefect of the Congregation for the Doctrine of the Faith.

Should Archbishop Lefebvre actually proceed with the announced episcopal ordinations, thus sealing the break with the Apostolic See, there would be grave canonical consequences, and in line with these the interested parties have been sent a *monitum,* as provided for in the ecclesiastical legislation.

The Holy See, upon presentation of this informative note, is also anxious to make an urgent appeal to the members of the society and to the faithful connected with it, to reconsider their position and to remain united to the Vicar of Christ, and it wishes to assure them that all measures will be taken to guarantee their identity in full communion with the Catholic Church.

DECREE OF EXCOMMUNICATION

The Congregation for Bishops issued the following decree of excommunication July 1, 1988.

Archbishop Marcel Lefebvre, archbishop-bishop emeritus of Tulle, notwithstanding the formal canonical warning of last June 17 and the repeated appeals to desist from his intention, has performed a schismatical act by the episcopal consecration of four priests without pontifical mandate and contrary to the will of the Supreme Pontiff, and has therefore incurred the penalty envisaged by Canon 1364,1 and Canon 1382 of the Code of Canon Law.

Having taken account of all the juridical effects, I declare that the above-mentioned Archbishop Marcel Lefebvre and Bernard Fellay, Bernard Tissier de Mallerais, Richard Williamson and Alfonso de Galarreta have incurred ipso factor excommunication *latae sententiae* reserved to the Apostolic See.

Moreover, I declare that Bishop Antonio de Castro Mayer, bishop emeritus of Campos, since he took part directly in the liturgical celebration as co-consecrator and adhered publicly to the schismatical act, has incurred excommunication *latae sententiae* as envisaged by Canon 1364,1.

The priests and faithful are warned not to support the schism of Archbishop Lefebvre; otherwise they shall incur ipso facto the very grave penalty of excommunication.

From the office of the Congregation for Bishops, July 1, 1988, Cardinal Bernardin Gantin, prefect.

MARIAN YEAR IN RETROSPECT

As Pope John Paul brought the 14-month Marian Year observance to its conclusion Aug. 15, 1988, he called the period a "pilgrimage of faith" on the eve of the third millennium of Christianity. Addressing himself to Mary, he said: "We have begun to walk with you: we, a generation which bears a certain resemblance to that first Advent when, on the horizon of human longing for the coming of the Messiah, a mysterious light was enkindled."

The concluding Mass in St. Peter's Basilica was attended by a throng of thousands. Like other Vatican celebrations during the period, it included elements of Eastern Rite liturgies replete with Marian tradition; final ceremonies of the year, in fact, began the previous evening with the Coptic ceremony of the Prayer of Incense.

The Vatican celebration was matched in Israel with a Mass and accompanying rites in the Basilica of Gethsemane.

Vatican Events

Many special events took place in Rome between June 7, 1987, and Aug. 15, 1988: Masses, congresses of one kind or another and lectures, along with the comings and goings of pilgrims from all over the world.

Pope John Paul issued his sixth encyclical letter entitled "Mary, Mother of the Redeemer." He addressed a letter to members of religious orders and secular institutes in which he urged them to seek in and through Mary inspiration and renewal in their personal and community lives. A letter from the Congregation for Catholic Education underlined the need for Marian theology in courses of study for the priesthood.

Eighty-seven pastoral letters by bishops in various countries were made public during the year. Also published were numerous translations of the Holy Father's encyclical letter on Mary. Hundreds of articles on Mary appeared in Catholic newspapers and periodicals.

Other Observances

The Central Committee for the Marian Year received reports on local church events in 50 countries. Great enthusiasm was reported in countries of Africa and Latin America, with significant participation in pilgrimages and attendance at sanctuaries. Basic catechetical programs were reported in some Asian countries. Among ecumenical events were congresses and prayer gatherings of Roman Catholics, Orthodox and other Christians in Syria, Turkey, Egypt, Greece and Kevelaer, West Germany.

Pilgrims to such Marian shrines as Lourdes and Fatima were more numerous than usual.

In the United States, local celebrations were numerous and of considerable variety. Diocesan pilgrimages from most dioceses brought thousands of people to the National Shrine of the Immaculate Conception in Washington.

Concluding Ceremonies

Hundreds of thousands of Catholics around the world gathered at famous shrines and in small churches to attend ceremonies marking the end of the year on Aug. 15 — at the Vatican, at Fatima and Lourdes, in Paris, at Knock in Ireland, at the Jasna Gora Monastery in Czestochowa, in Managua, Mexico City and Manila. Ceremonies at these and other places testified to the truth of the prophecy that all generations will call Mary blessed.

Concluding ceremonies of the year attracted thousands of people to the National Shrine of the Immaculate Conception in Washington. Marian scholar Father Eamon Carroll said in a homily: "As we conclude the Marian Year, we can rejoice in our American Catholic heritage, in our devotion to Mary Immaculate.... She is the witness to the divine plan" who, as the Mother of Jesus, "testifies to his human reality.... The wonderful truth is that no one fails to find room under her wing. Mary is the mother of us all."

Father Timothy Cloutier, a staff member of the Central Committee for the Marian Year, observed as the committee ended its work that the 14-month observance had brought about "a rebirth of Marian awareness in the life and the prayers of the Church."

EUNTES IN MUNDUM: APOSTOLIC LETTER

Pope John Paul, in an apostolic letter dated Jan. 25 and released Mar. 22, 1988, commemorated the 1,000th anniversary of the baptism of Vladimir the Great and his people in Kievan Rus. The commemoration was of special interest to Ukrainian Catholics under oppression in the Soviet Union and in freedom in other countries. The event was also commemorated by the Russian Orthodox Church.

The Vatican's English text of the letter was circulated by the NC Documentary Service, Origins, Mar. 31, 1988 (Vol. 17, No. 42). Subheads have been added.

I desire with this letter to offer praise and gratitude to the ineffable God — Father, Son and Holy Spirit — for having called to faith and to grace the sons and daughters of many peoples and nations who accepted the Christian heritage of the baptism administered at Kiev. They belong, first of all, to the Russian, Ukrainian and Byelorussian nations in the eastern regions of the continent of Europe. Through the Church's service, which was begun in the baptism at Kiev, this heritage reached, beyond the Urals, many peoples of northern Asia, as far as the coasts of the Pacific and even beyond.

Baptism of Vladimir and His People

We desire to take part in the celebrations and in the joy of the millennium of the baptism of Kievan Rus. We recall that event in the manner proper to the Church of Christ; namely, in a spirit of faith. That event was one of enormous importance.... Kievan Rus entered into the context of salvation and itself became such a context. Its baptism began a new wave of holiness. It became a significant moment of the Church's missionary commitment, a new and important stage in the development of Christianity. The whole Catholic Church turns its gaze to that event and shares spiritually in the joys of the heirs of that baptism.

Vladimir (was) the protagonist of the baptism in 988 who accepted the Christian faith and brought about the permanent and definitive conversion of the people of Rus. Vladimir and the new converts experienced the beauty of the liturgy and religious life of the Church of Constantinople. And so it happened that the new Church of Rus drew from Constantinople the entire patrimony of the Christian East and all the treasures peculiar to it in the fields of theology, liturgy, spirituality, ecclesial life and art.

Slavic Inculturation

The word of God and the grace flowing from it reached the Eastern Slavs in a form culturally and geographically closer to them. Those Slavs, accepting the word with total obedience of faith, desired at the same time to express it in their own forms of thought and in their own language. There thus took place that particular 'Slav inculturation' of the Gospel and of Christianity which is connected with the great work of Sts. Cyril and Methodius, who from Constantinople brought Christianity, in the Slav version, into Greater Moravia and . . . to the peoples of the Balkan Peninsula.

The old Slavonic language became an important instrument in the baptism of Rus, in the first place for evangelization, and subsequently also for the original development of the future cultural patrimony of those peoples, a development which became in many areas a treasure of the life and culture of the whole human race.

Byzantine Tradition

It must be emphasized quite firmly, in fidelity to historical truth, that in the eyes of the two holy brothers from Thessalonika there was introduced into Rus with the Slav language the style of the Byzantine Church, which at that time was still in communion with Rome. And this tradition was subsequently developed in an original and perhaps unrepeatable way on the basis of its indigenous culture and also thanks to contacts with the neighboring peoples of the West.

Through the new center of ecclesial life which Kiev became from the moment of its baptism, the Gospel and the grace of the faith reached those populations and those lands which today are linked, as regards the Orthodox Church, with the Patriarchate of Moscow, and with the Ukrainian Catholic Church, whose full communion with the See of Rome was renewed at Brest.

The baptism of Kievan Rus marks the beginning of a long historical process in which there develops and expands the original Byzantine-Slav form of Christianity in the life of the Church, of society, and of the nations which, down the centuries, have found in that form and still find in it today the foundation of their own spiritual identity.

Desire for Full Communion

The baptism of Rus took place, as I have already pointed out, at a time when the two forms of Christianity had already developed: the Eastern form, linked with Byzantium, and the Western, linked with Rome, while the church continued to remain one and undivided. This consideration, as we celebrate the millennium of the baptism received by the Eastern Slav peoples at Kiev, cannot fail to enkindle in us an even greater desire for full communion in Christ with these sister churches, and to impel us to undertake fresh studies and take new steps to favor it.

This anniversary is not merely an historical remembrance and an occasion for preparing scientific explanations and evaluations; but it is also, and above all, an incentive to turn our pastoral and ecumenical sensibilities from the past toward the future, to strengthen our longing for unity and to intensify our prayer.

Yes, both churches, the Catholic and the Orthodox, despite the difficulties born of age-old misunderstandings, today more than ever are determined to rediscover communion around the eucharistic table and are looking with particular attention and hope in this millennium to all the spiritual sons and daughters of St. Vladimir.

What an advantage this would be for the whole people of God if the Orthodox and Catholic heirs of the baptism of Kiev, stirred by a renewed awareness of their original communion, would take up its challenge and repeat for the Christians of our time the ecumenical message which flows therefrom, urging them to hasten their steps toward the goal of the full unity willed by Christ! More than anything else, this would have a beneficial influence also in that process of detente in the civil sphere which is evoking such great hopes in those working for peaceful coexistence in the world.

May the rich experience of the full communion lived in the first millennium, but forgotten for so many centuries by both sides, be for us and for our ecumenical efforts a light, an encouragement and a constant point of reference.

Conditions for World Peace

True peace can only exist on the basis of a process of unification in which each people is able to choose, in freedom and truth, the paths of its own development. Moreover, such a process is impossible if there is no agreement on the original and fundamental unity which is manifested in different forms, not opposed but complementary, which need one another and seek one another. For this reason we are profoundly convinced that the path of true peace can, in an incomparable way, be made straight in people's minds, hearts and consciences through the presence and service of that sign of peace which is, by her nature, the church as she is obedient to Christ and faithful to her vocation.

We express complete confidence in all human efforts which aim at removing occasions of tension and conflict through the peaceful path of patient dialogue, agreements and mutual understanding and respect.

It is the vocation of Europe, born upon Christian foundations, to exercise particular care for peace in the whole world. In many parts of the world peace is lacking or is gravely threatened. What is needed, therefore, is a constant and harmonious cooperation on the part of the European continent with all nations which are in favor of the peace and well-being to which every person has a sacrosanct right.

Sister Church

In particular, we join with all the heirs of this baptism, whatever their religious confession, nationality or dwelling place; with all our Orthodox and Catholic brothers and sisters. In a special way we join with all the beloved sons and daughters of the Russian, Ukrainian and Byelorussian nations.

In a special way, of course, this is the feast of the Russian Orthodox Church, which has its center in Moscow and which we call with joy "Sister Church." It is precisely she who has received in great part the inheritance of ancient Christian Rus, linking herself with and remaining faithful to the Church of Constantinople.

This Church, like the other Orthodox churches,

has true sacraments, particularly — by virtue of the apostolic succession — the Eucharist and the priesthood, whereby she remains united to the Catholic Church with very close links. And together with the churches mentioned she makes intense offers "to perpetuate in a communion of faith and charity those family ties which ought to thrive between local churches as between sisters."

At this solemn moment in history the Catholic community prays and meditates upon "the mighty works of God" (cf. Acts 2:11), and sends to her 1,000-year-old Sister Church, through the bishop of Rome, the kiss of peace as a manifestation of the ardent desire for that perfect communion which is willed by Christ and inscribed in the nature of the Church.

BACKGROUND

Backgrounding the apostolic letter are these facts.

1. The baptism of Vladimir and his people in 988 marked the beginning of Christianity in the territory of Kievan Rus, which eventually became part of Russia in virtue of the Union of Ukraine in 1654.
2. The Eastern-Rite (Byzantine) Church established in Kievan Rus was in communion with the Pope until the second half of the 11th century, when most of the Eastern-Rite Churches severed relations and became known as Orthodox Churches.
3. The Russian Orthodox Church, with several exceptions — one of which is lack of communion with Rome — retains the spiritual heritage of the Byzantine Church from which it came — in doctrine, discipline, liturgy and traditions. In view of this heritage, the Russian Orthodox Church is called a Sister Church.
4. The Ukrainian Catholic Church — which lacked communion with Rome for many years — is distinct from the Russian Orthodox Church because of its union with the Pope. It has been suppressed and underground in its own territory in the Soviet Union since the late 1940s. There are Ukrainian Catholics in countries outside the Soviet Union, including more than 150,000 in four jurisdictions of their own in the United States.

MAGNUM BAPTISMI DONUM: APOSTOLIC LETTER TO UKRAINIANS

"The Great Gift of Baptism" is the title of a second letter issued in 1988 by Pope John Paul to commemorate the 1000th anniversary of the conversion and baptism in 988 of St. Vladimir and the people of Kiev, which subsequently became part of Russia. This letter was addressed Apr. 19 directly to Ukrainian Catholics, especially the 3.5 million practicing the faith underground in the Soviet Union. The earlier letter, "Euntes in Mundum" (see separate entry), was addressed to all heirs of the original baptism of Kiev, including the Russian Orthodox.

The following excerpts from "Magnum Baptismi Donum" are from the Vatican's English-language text circulated by the NC Documentary Service, Origins, May 5, 1988 (Vol. 17, No. 47). Subheads have been added.

It is at this moment in the history of salvation, a moment so rich in hopes, that it is granted to us to celebrate the millennium with the Ukrainian Catholic community, which has taken the place assigned to it by Providence in the universal Church side by side with so many particular churches of both East and West.

In Full Communion of Faith

I greet the whole Ukrainian Catholic community, which sees the roots of its own existence in the baptism of the people of Kiev and which today lives in full communion of faith and of sacramental life with the Bishop of Rome.

I greet you, brothers in the episcopate, under the leadership of Cardinal Myroslav Ivan Lubachivsky, major archbishop of Lvov of the Ukrainians; I greet you, the priests, Religious and faithful who are celebrating the thousandth anniversary of the birth of your people to the life of grace in the baptism of Kievan Rus. I greet you all with the fraternal kiss of peace, as your brother and as the first Pope of Slav origin in the history of the Church.

In the hour of your great jubilee I feel spiritually united with you and, from the heart of the Church, I wish to hold you in a fraternal embrace in the sight of all believers in Christ. In the name of the Most Holy Trinity — Father, Son and Holy Spirit — the Church of Rome bows with singular understanding and love before all the spiritual sons and daughters of St. Vladimir, especially those who pray and suffer for unity with the universal Church.

Confirmation of Ukrainian Features

At this extraordinary moment in history for your church, which has been tried by such great adversity in recent decades, I wish to confirm once again that her Catholic dimension, as well as her particular features, merit every respect. This is demanded by fraternal love. It is demanded by the ecumenical vocation of the holy brothers Cyril and Methodius who, by their example, remind us of the right of every member of the faithful to be respected in his or her tradition and rite and in the identity of the people to which he or she belongs.

With all our heart, we express the hope that in the future you will be granted the joy of seeing misunderstandings and mutual distrust overcome, and that recognition will be given to the full right of every person to his or her own identity and profession of faith. No one ought to consider membership in the Catholic Church as incompatible with the good of the homeland and with the heritage of St. Vladimir. May your great numbers of faithful enjoy true freedom of conscience and respect for their religious right to give public worship to God according to many different traditions, in their own rite and with their own pastors.

Fidelity to Rome

The Apostolic See feels a singular affection for your church, for throughout history she has given so many proofs of her attachment to Rome, not excluding the supreme test of martyrdom. For this reason the principal celebration of the millennium of your church in the diaspora will take place in Rome. Gathered at the tomb of St. Peter, near which there rest the remains of your own dear St. Josaphat, we shall give thanks together for all the fruits that come from participation in the divine mysteries in the communion of the same faith and in the bond of the same love.

Your church cannot fail to be present, in the concert of the entire Catholic Church, at the celebration of this special anniversary; nor at the solemn celebration of the millennium can the bishop of Rome be absent, he who so ardently desires to sing in your language, in the Basilica of St. Peter, together, with all the bishops and faithful, the *Te Deum* of thanksgiving.

I entrust to the one and triune God the thousandth anniversary event that belongs to your church and to your people. With confidence, I place in the hands of the Lord of history the celebration of the millennium. I desire to begin it together with all the Ukrainian Catholic bishops, priests, Religious and faithful throughout the world, and then to continue it together with them under the watchful eyes of holy Mary, whose presence pervades the whole history of your church.

To Mary we owe the birth of Christ. She was present also at the birth of the church of Kievan Rus. Therefore I go in spiritual pilgrimage to the feet of Our Lady of Vladimir . . . I go to the Cathedral of St. Sophia, to the feet of the praying Virgin, of the "Indestructible Wall," to whom 950 years ago Prince Yaroslav the Wise entrusted the city of Kiev and the whole of Rus.

Entrustment to Mary

I prostrate myself before you, O dearest Mother, and to you I entrust the whole history of the Ukrainian Catholic community.

O Mother of Christian Unity, show us the sure paths toward that goal. Grant that on the way of this great work we may ever more frequently meet our brothers and sisters in the faith and rediscover together the divine features of that unity for which Christ himself prayed.

O Mother of Consolation, I place in your hands all the centuries of pain and suffering, the prayers and living witness of so many of your children; to you I entrust the hopes and expectations of the heirs of the baptism of Rus, who through your intercession hope that the ancient Christian stock will know the splendor of a new flowering.

Draw to your breast, O Mother, the people who suffer at the memory of what they have lost, but who do not cease to hope for the coming of better times. Help these faithful followers of yours so that, together with their pastors and in spiritual communion with the successor of Peter, they may celebrate with joy the millennium and sing with fervent soul the hymn of thanksgiving to God and to you, the most holy Mother of the Redeemer, to you *Theotokos!*

Invoking the intercession of the holy apostles Peter and Paul, of the apostles of the Slavs Sts. Cyril and Methodius, of St. Olga and St. Vladimir, St. Josaphat and all the saints, I entrust you to the protection of the Most Holy Trinity — brothers in the episcopate, with your head the major archbishop of Lvov of the Ukrainians, as well as the priests, Religious and faithful. And I cordially impart to each and every one my apostolic blessing in the name of the Father, and of the Son and of the Holy Spirit.

EVENTS OF MEDJUGORJE

Alleged apparitions of Mary to six young people at Medjugorje, Yugoslavia, have been the center of interest and controversy since they were first reported in June, 1981, initially in a neighboring hillside field and subsequently also in the village church of St. James.

Reports say the alleged visionaries have seen, heard and touched Mary during visions, and that they have variously received several or all of 10 secret messages related to world events and urging a quest for peace through prayer, penance and personal conversion. Since the initial report of apparitions, some of the visionaries have left the village. One of them, at least, Marija Pavlovic, said she still had daily visions, according to an article in the NC news releases of Mar. 7, 1988.

An investigative commission appointed by Bishop Pavao Zanic of Mostar-Duvno reported in March, 1984, that the authenticity of the apparitions had not been established and that cases of reported healings had not been verified. He called the apparitions a case of "collective hallucination" exploited by local Franciscan priests at odds with him over control of a parish.

Archbishop Frane Franic of Split-Makarska, on the other hand, said in December, 1985: "Speaking as a believer and not as a bishop, my personal conviction is that the events at Medjugorje are of supernatural inspiration." He based his conviction on the observation of spiritual benefits related to the reported events, such as the spiritual development of the six young people, the increases in Mass attendance and sacramental practice at the scene of the apparitions, and the incidence of reconciliation among people.

"Further exploration" of the events at Medjugorje on the national level, as distinguished from the earlier diocesan investigation, was announced in a communique published in the official bulletin of the Archdiocese of Zagreb, dated Jan. 29, 1987, as follows.

Text of Communique

In conformity with the canonical norms concerning the discernment of alleged apparitions and private revelations, the diocesan commission instituted for this purpose by the Bishop of Mostar, Ordinary of the place, has conducted an inquiry into the events of Medjugorje.

In the course of the investigation, it emerged that the events in question went far beyond the diocese in question. Consequently, on the basis of the abovementioned norms, it seemed fitting to continue the investigation on the level of the episcopal conference with the institution of a new commission for that purpose.

The Congregation for the Doctrine of the Faith was informed. It expressed its appreciation for the work carried out by the diocesan commission under the responsibility of the local Ordinary, and it encouraged the continuance of the work at the national episcopal level.

The episcopal conference, therefore, is establishing a commission to continue the investigation of the events at Medjugorje. While awaiting the results of the commission's investigation and the Church's judgment, pastors and faithful should observe an attitude of prudence customary in such situations. Therefore, it is not permissible to organize pilgrimages and other manifestations motivated by the supernatural character attributed to the facts of Medjugorje. Legitimate devotion to Our Lady, recommended by the Church, must conform to the directives of the magisterium, and especially to those contained in the apostolic exhortation *Marialis Cultus* of 2 February, 1974.

The communique, which appeared in the Feb. 22, 1987, English edition of *L'Osservatore Romano*, was signed by Cardinal Franjo Kuharic, president of the Yugoslav Episcopal Conference, and Bishop Pavao Zanic of Mostar-Duvno.

Spiritual Development

While the authenticity of the reported visions remains an open question, there is no doubt about positive spiritual developments in the experience of persons who have visited Medjugorje: personal conversion, reconciliation, return to the sacraments and practice of the faith, renewed fidelity to personal obligations and opportunities for doing good, strength to cope with spiritual struggle and to bear crosses of all kinds.

Between 1981 and early 1988, it was estimated that eight million people visited Medjugorje; one million visitors were expected in 1988. The Yugoslav National Tourist Office in New York reported that 235,000 persons from the United States visited Yugoslavia in 1987; it was assumed that most of them visited Medjugorje.

BIBLICAL FUNDAMENTALISM: PASTORAL STATEMENT

This statement was composed by the Ad Hoc Committee on Biblical Fundamentalism, National Conference of Catholic Bishops, under the chairmanship of Archbishop John Whealon of Hartford. The statement, dated Mar. 26 and released Sept. 30, 1987, notes that fundamentalism regards the Bible as the "single rule for living," seeks to "find in the Bible all the direct answers for living," and "eliminates from Christianity the Church as the Lord Jesus founded it."

This text was circulated by the NC Documentary Service, Origins, Nov. 5, 1987 (Vol. 17, No. 21). Paragraphing has been changed in some instances and subheads have been added.

This is a statement of concern to our Catholic brothers and sisters who may be attracted to biblical fundamentalism without realizing its serious weaknesses. We Catholic bishops, speaking as a special committee of the National Conference of Catholic Bishops, desire to remind our faithful of the fullness of Christianity that God has provided in the Catholic Church.

Fundamentalism indicates a person's general approach to life which is typified by unyielding adherence to rigid doctrinal and ideological positions — an approach that affects the individual's social and political attitudes as well as religious ones. Fundamentalism in this sense is found in non-Christian religions and can be doctrinal as well as biblical. But in this statement we are speaking only of biblical fundamentalism, presently attractive to some Christians, including some Catholics.

Bible Only

Biblical fundamentalists are those who present the Bible, God's inspired word, as the only necessary source for teaching about Christ and Christian living. This insistence on the teaching Bible is usually accompanied by a spirit that is warm, friendly and pious. Such a spirit attracts many (especially idealistic young) converts.

With ecumenical respect for these communities, we acknowledge their proper emphasis on religion as influencing family life and workplace. The immediate attractions are the ardor of the Christian community and the promises of certitude and of a personal conversion experience to the person of Jesus Christ without the need of church.

As Catholic pastors, however, we note its presentation of the Bible as a single rule for living. According to fundamentalism, the Bible alone is sufficient. There is no place for the universal teaching Church — including its wisdom, its teachings, creeds and other doctrinal formulations, its liturgical and devotional traditions. There is simply no claim to a visible, audible, living, teaching authority binding the individual or congregations.

Fundamentalist Inerrancy

A further characteristic of biblical fundamentalism is that it tends to interpret the Bible as being always without error or as literally true in a way quite different from the Catholic Church's teaching on the inerrancy of the Bible. For some biblical fundamentalists, inerrancy extends even to scientific and historical matters. The Bible is presented without regard for its historical context and development.

In 1943, Pope Pius XII encouraged the church to promote biblical study and renewal, making use of textual criticism. . . . In 1965, the Second Vatican Council, in its *Constitution on Divine Revelation*, gave specific teaching on the Bible. Catholics are taught to see the Bible as God's book — and also as a collection of books written under divine inspiration by many human beings.

The Bible is true — and to discover its inspired truth we should study the patterns of thinking and writing used in ancient biblical times. With Vatican II, we believe that "the books of Scripture must be acknowledged as teaching firmly, faithfully and without error that truth which God wanted put into the sacred writings for the sake of our salvation" (*Dogmatic Constitution on Divine Revelation*, No. 11).

Biblical Truth: Catholic View

We do not look upon the Bible as an authority for science or history. We see truth in the Bible as not to be reduced solely to literal truth, but also to include salvation truths expressed in varied literary forms.

We observed in biblical fundamentalism an effort to try to find in the Bible all the direct answers for living — though the Bible itself nowhere claims such authority. The appeal of such an approach is understandable. Our world is one of war, violence, dishonesty, personal and sexual irresponsibility. It is a world in which people are frightened by the power of the nuclear bomb and the insanity of the arms race, where the only news seems to be bad news. People of all ages yearn for answers. They look for sure, definite rules for living. And they are given answers — simplistic answers to complex issues — in a confident and enthusiastic way in fundamentalist Bible groups. . . .

Problem of Answers

The appeal of finding *the answer* in a devout, studious, prayerful, warm, Bible-quoting class is easy to understand. But the ultimate problem with such fundamentalism is that it can give only a limited number of answers and cannot present those answers, on balance, because it does not have Christ's teaching Church nor even an understanding of how the Bible originally came to be written and collected in the sacred canon, or official list of inspired books.

Church Tradition and Teaching

Our Catholic belief is that we know God's revelation in the total Gospel. The Gospel comes to us through the Spirit-guided tradition of the church and the inspired books: "This sacred tradition, therefore, and Sacred Scripture of both the Old and New Testament are like a mirror in which the pilgrim church on earth looks at God" (*Dogmatic Constitution on Divine Revelation*, No. 7).

A key question for any Christian is, Does the community of faith which is the Lord's Church have a living tradition which presents God's word across the centuries until the Lord comes again? The Catholic answer to this question is an unqualified yes. That answer was expressed most recently in the *Constitution on Divine Revelation* of the Second Vatican Council. We look to both the Church's official teaching and Scripture for guidance in addressing life's problems. It is the official teaching or magisterium that in a special way guides us in matters of belief and morality that have developed after the last word of Scripture was written. The Church of Christ teaches in the name of Christ and teaches us concerning the Bible itself.

Non-Church Fundamentalism

The basic characteristic of biblical fundamentalism is that it eliminates from Christianity the Church as the Lord Jesus founded it. That Church is a community of faith, worldwide, with pastoral and teaching authority.

This non-church characteristic of biblical fundamentalism, which sees the church as only spiritual, may not at first be clear to some Catholics. From some fundamentalists they will hear nothing offensive to their beliefs, and much of what they hear seems compatible with Catholic Christianity. The difference is often not in what is said — but in what is not said. There is no mention of the historic, authoritative Church in continuity with Peter and the other apostles. There is no vision of the Church as our mother — a mother who is not just spiritual, but who is visibly ours to teach and guide us in the way of Christ.

Unfortunately, a minority of fundamentalist churches and sects not only put down the Catholic Church as a "man-made organization" with "man-made rules," but indulge in crude anti-Catholic bigotry with which Catholics have long been familiar.

We believe that no Catholic properly catechized in the faith can long live the Christian life without those elements that are had only in the fullness of Christianity: the Eucharist and the other six sacraments, the celebration of the word in the liturgical cycle, the veneration of the Blessed Mother and the saints, teaching authority and history linked to Christ, and the demanding social doctrine of the Church based on the sacredness of all human life.

The Church's Book

It is important for every Catholic to realize that the Church produced the New Testament, not vice versa. The Bible did not come down from heaven, whole and intact, given by the Holy Spirit. Just as the experience and faith of Israel developed its sacred books, so was the early Christian Church the matrix of the New Testament. The Catholic Church has authoritatively told us which books are inspired by the Holy Spirit and are therefore canonical. The Bible, then, is the Church's book. The New Testament did not come before the Church, but from the Church. Peter and the other apostles were given special authority to teach and govern before the New Testament was written. The first generation of Christians had no New Testament at all — but they were the Church then, just as we are the Church today.

Belonging to the Church

A study of the New Testament, in fact, shows that discipleship is to be a community experience with liturgy and headship and demonstrates the importance of belonging to the Church started by Jesus Christ. Christ chose Peter and the other apostles as foundations of his Church, made Simon Peter its rock foundation and gave a teaching authority to Peter and the other apostles. This is most clear in the Gospel of Matthew, the only Gospel to use the word *church*. The history of 20 Christian centuries confirms our belief that Peter and the other apostles have been succeeded by the bishop of Rome and the other bishops, and that the flock of Christ still has, under Christ, a universal shepherd.

For historical reasons, the Catholic Church in the past did not encourage Bible studies as much as she could have. True, printing (the Latin Bible was the first work printed) was not invented until the mid-15th century, and few people were literate during the first 16 centuries of Christianity. But in the scriptural renewal the Church strongly encourages her sons and daughters to read, study and live the Bible. . . .

Use of the Bible

At the present time, two decades after Vatican II, we Catholics have all the tools needed to become Christians who know, love and live the Holy Bible. We have a well-ordered Lectionary that opens for us the treasures of all the books of the Bible in a three-year cycle for Sunday and holy day Masses, and a more complete two-year cycle for weekday Masses. Through the Lectionary the Catholic becomes familiar with the Bible according to the rhythm of the liturgical seasons and the Church's experience and use of the Bible at Mass. We have excellent translations (with notes) in The New American Bible and The Jerusalem Bible. We have other accurate translations with an imprimatur. We have an abundance of commentaries, tapes, charts and Bible societies.

We Catholics have excellent Bible resources and scholars of international repute. Our challenge now is to get this knowledge into the minds, hearts and lives of all our Catholic people. We need a pastoral plan for the word of God that will place the Sacred Scriptures at the heart of the parish and individual life.

Pastoral Considerations

Pastoral creativity can develop approaches such as weekly Bible study groups and yearly Bible schools in every parish. We need to have the introduction to each Bible reading prepared and presented by the lector in a way that shows familiarity with and love for the sacred text. In areas where there is a special problem with fundamentalism, the pastor may consider a Mass to which people bring their own Bibles and in which qualified lectors present a carefully prepared introduction and read the text — without, however, making the Liturgy of the Word a Bible study class.

We need better homilies, since the homily is the most effective way of applying biblical texts to daily living. We need a familiar quoting of the Bible by every catechist, lector and minister. We have not done enough in this area.

The neglect of parents in catechetics and the weakness of our adult education efforts are now producing a grim harvest. We need to educate — to re-educate — our people knowingly in the Bible so as to counteract the simplicities of biblical fundamentalism.

In addition to that, we Catholics need to redouble our efforts to make our parish Masses an expression of worship in which all — parishioners, visitors and strangers — feel the warmth and the welcome and know that here the Bible is clearly reverenced and preached. The current trend toward smaller faith-sharing and Bible-studying groups within a parish family is strongly to be encouraged.

PARTNERS IN THE MYSTERY OF REDEMPTION: PASTORAL LETTER ON WOMEN

"Partners in the Mystery of Redemption: A Pastoral Response to Women's Concerns for Church and Society," is the title of a pastoral letter in the process of development by a six-member committee of bishops with the assistance of seven women, five consultants and two experts. The first draft of the letter was released Apr. 12, 1988; it was a subject of discussion at the semiannual meeting of the U.S. bishops in June.

Backgrounding the draft are views on issues brought forth at listening sessions attended by about 70,000 women in 100 dioceses, on 70 college campuses and 40 military bases in the U.S. Among those consulted were representatives of 25 organizations of Catholic women.

Some of the Subjects

The focus of participants in the listening sessions and of writers of the draft was on the relation of women's experience to the teaching and practice of the Church. The wide range of subjects is covered in four chapters entitled "Partners in Personhood," "Partners in Relationships," "Partners in Society" and "Partners in the Church."

The draft calls sexism a sin, urges equal treatment of women in the Church and society, and calls for affirmative action to correct past injustice.

It calls on men, especially church officials, to become sensitive to the concerns of women and to recognize ways in which women are exploited, ignored or dismissed, or are otherwise treated as unequal to men.

Equal Access

Within the Church, the draft calls for women to have the same access as men to all positions not requiring ordination, including full access to lay ministries from which they are currently excluded. It does not call for the ordination of women to the priesthood, although it notes that many women consider ordination fundamental to real equality in the Church; it does ask, however, for study of the possibility of ordaining women as deacons.

Bishops at the semiannual meeting asked for expansion and development of a number of topics, including: the treatment of sexism as a sin; the treatment of husband-wife relationships; the discussion of women of minority groups; the issue of patriarchy, or the domination of cultural and social structures by men and their views; greater attention to Christian anthropology; more emphasis on church teaching opposing the ordination of women to the priesthood, and on the difference between deacons and priests.

Reactions

Reactions of lay persons to the draft were mixed. Some thought the draft was unduly influenced by feminist ideology and expressive of priest-bashing. But this was not the view of Bishop Joseph L. Imesch of Joliet, chairman of the writing committee. Speaking of the women who expressed views reported in the draft, he said at the bishops' meeting:

"I do not consider these women to be radical in any sense of the term, as some have charged. They were ordinary women, if such a term may be used: wives, mothers, single women, women Religious, women who are involved in their own parishes, women who have never been asked before about their experiences in the Church, women who love the Church and work generously for the Church, women who are determined to live in the Church, but women who are anxious to see the Church accept them as equals and treat them as equals."

More To Come

It was reported that the draft text would be subject to further discussion and amendment in the course of consultations still to be held. It was also expected that the contents of the final text of the pastoral letter would be affected by a forthcoming document on women announced by Pope John Paul in the summer of 1988. The time of the bishops' approval and publication of the final text of the letter was not known at the time of writing.

HUMANE AND DIGNIFIED DEATH ACT OPPOSED

Efforts to place a "Humane and Dignified Death Act" on the November, 1988, ballot in California failed for lack of a requisite number of signatures in support of a referendum. As signature-gathering was under way, the state's 22 bishops issued Apr. 22 the following statement of unqualified opposition to the measure. The act in question proposed to exempt doctors from criminal liability for giving a lethal injection to consenting terminally ill adults certain to die within six months.

The following text was circulated by the NC Documentary Services, Origins, May 5, 1988 (Vol. 17, No. 47). Subheads have been added.

The Catholic Church benefits from 20 centuries of reflection on the value and meaning of human life. It also supports hundreds of hospitals and other institutions for care of the sick and the dying. Therefore, it cannot be a matter of indifference to the Church that efforts are well under way in this country to legalize active euthanasia for terminally ill patients.

Misleading Descriptions

The immediate focus of our attention is a ballot initiative called the "Humane and Dignified Death Act" proposed for inclusion on the November (1988) ballot in California. The true nature of this act has been obscured by euphemisms and misleading descriptions advanced by its proponents — the Hemlock Society and its political arm, Americans Against Human Suffering. But its legal effect would be quite straightforward: If approved by a majority of California voters in November, it would carve out an exception to our state laws against homicide and assisted suicide, so that terminally ill patients could be killed on request by lethal injections or other active means.

Three Moral Principles

As moral teachers, we have evaluated this proposal in light of principles which we believe can be appreciated not only by Catholics but also by people of good will generally. Three principles are especially relevant.

First, human life is sacred and hence should not be subjected to direct attack. As Christians, we believe men and women are made in the image and likeness of God, and that destroying God's image is an offense against the Creator. But even non-denominational statements affirming human dignity, such as our nation's Declaration of Independence, have proclaimed the right to life as first among human beings' unalienable rights. Life is indeed the most fundamental right, in the sense that it is the condition for exercising all other rights and freedoms. Therefore, to demean respect for life never advances human rights, because other rights will ultimately lose their meaning if life itself is continually diminished in value.

Second, we human beings have stewardship over life but not absolute dominion. We hold life in trust, and have a solemn responsibility to help it achieve its potential for love and service to others. As faithful stewards, we must take reasonable steps to preserve life and health, but we are not obligated to fend off death with every means at our disposal. In the final stages of terminal illness, we respect the dignity of the dying person by providing comfort and care when we can no longer cure.

In stark contrast with this attitude of respect and compassion is an approach that denigrates the dying person's life, treating it as valueless or as too great a burden upon others to warrant care and support.

Third, we are in solidarity with one another as members of one human family. We are not isolated individuals in a social or economic system, joined only by commercial transactions. Rather, we depend upon one another in order to live and flourish. Those who are most helpless and most dependent upon us for their needs merit more protection, not less, for their fundamental rights. In a civilized society, that protection demands a system of legal justice which upholds the inherent worth of every human being. If the law allows one class of humanity to fall outside its protection, the rights of all are endangered. It is both shortsighted and unjust to claim that such legal changes are of interest only to those most immediately affected. They deeply affect us all.

Unalterable Opposition

Because we are committed to this vision of human dignity and solidarity, we must be unalterably opposed to the deceptive proposal called "The Humane and Dignified Death Act." This act in no way serves the legitimate rights to refuse disproportionate treatment or to receive comfort and relief from pain during a terminal illness — rights which are well established in California law. The only solution to human suffering which it proposes is direct killing of the human being who suffers. To kill persons who need our love and support can be called neither "humane" nor "dignified." It is precisely the inherent dignity of human life that this proposal violates.

Spurious Claims

The Hemlock Society and its allies deny this charge, claiming that approval of the ballot initiative would vindicate human freedom. This claim is spurious for several reasons.

First, respect for human freedom will become meaningless if life itself can be destroyed with impunity. To kill an innocent person — even at that person's request — is to take away all of that person's present and future earthly freedoms. In our view, the freedom to be killed is not the ultimate exercise of free choice but its ultimate self-contradiction.

Second, this campaign ultimately is not based on "freedom of choice" as such, because its supporters offer the "choice" of death only to certain seriously ill persons. They claim to have no plans, at least at present, to extend this "choice" to other suffering individuals who may be tempted to commit suicide — the depressed teen-ager, the adult with serious physical disabilities, the lonely senior citizen. The Hemlock Society's director assures us that assisted suicide will not be "misused by the wrong people." And it is easy to see why he feels such assurances are necessary, for few voters would support such an unlimited license to take life.

But, if our society is to continue saying that some people are "the wrong people" to receive help in committing suicide, this can only suggest that those granted this freedom are the "right" people to receive such assistance. Would we not then be saying to some of our most helpless citizens that society no longer recognizes any objective worth in their lives? And if their lives can be judged to lack objective worth, what is to guarantee society's recognition of objective worth in any life?

Hindrance to Respect, Support

We wish to address these questions especially to individuals who may be tempted to support this initiative in the belief that they themselves will benefit from it. With all due respect, we ask them to consider that the Hemlock proposal may be a hindrance rather than a help in their struggle for respect and support from others. We appeal with special urgency to persons diagnosed as having AIDS or other terminal illnesses: In a society which may be all too grudging in its recognition of your human dignity, would it not be tragic if the right most enthusiastically granted you is the "right" to be killed?

Targets of the Act

We mention individuals in these groups because they are targeted for special attention by proponents of the "Humane and Dignified Death Act." Indeed, because depression and even suicidal feelings are common experiences in coming to terms with a diagnosis of incurable illness, persons with AIDS and similar conditions are especially vulnerable to the propaganda of euthanasia advocates. Those who would exploit the suffering and depression of these persons to serve a political campaign for euthanasia cannot be described as advocates for human rights.

But we are also convinced that this campaign will not stop at authorizing assisted suicide for the terminally ill. The current initiative's restriction to patients expected to die in six months is clearly arbitrary, and will lead to demands that the same "right" be granted to those who fall just beyond this boundary. It scarcely matters where such lines are initially drawn; once "aid in dying" is established as a basic human right, physicians' freedom to terminate their patients' lives will override all meaningful limits. This is already apparent in The Netherlands, where permissive policies on killing terminally ill patients have expanded in a few short years to encompass non-terminal elderly residents of nursing homes.

Right Equals Duty To Die

Furthermore, our pastoral experience suggests that the so-called "right to die" will quickly become the "duty to die." Society will become immersed in an atmosphere where older, suffering and debilitated people will surely feel internal and external pressure to die. This would be one of the most tragic consequences if this proposal were to become law.

To its credit, the California Medical Association has opposed this initiative as an attack on the ethical foundations of the healing professions. In one sense, physicians would be even more grievously harmed by legalized euthanasia than their patients; for as the Second Vatican Council reminded us, crimes against human life "debase the perpetrators more than the victims" (*Gaudium et Spes*, 27). All of us, as citizens and voters, must also choose whether to share responsibility in such crimes or to protect the vulnerable among us. If our society chooses to encourage healers to become killers, it will become less truly human.

Christian Attitude

With other Christians we observe Easter this month to celebrate the triumph of life over death in Jesus Christ. Those of us who wish to live this resurrection faith should not hesitate to provide companionship and comfort to the dying person, confident that dying in Christ will bring us to new life in him. Nor should we hesitate to oppose initiatives which dishonor the Creator by seeking prematurely to end the lives of human beings made in his image. By accompanyig dying persons on their difficult spiritual journey and by protecting them from the false promises of euthanasia, we will best serve him who joined us on earth that we "might have life and have it to the full" (Jn. 10:10).

EUTHANASIA ADVOCATES

Leaders in efforts for the legalization of mercy killing and assisted suicide are the **Hemlock Socie-** ty, founded by Derek Humphry in 1980, with an estimated membership of 21,000 in 26 chapters; and its political arm, **Americans Against Human Suffering** under the leadership of Robert Risley of Los Angeles, which conducted the unsuccessful campaign to get the euthanasia issue on the California ballot in November, 1988.

In The Netherlands, courts have permitted physician-assisted suicide, and formal legalization of euthanasia is under consideration by the government. It is estimated that 5,000 physician-assisted suicides take place annually in the country, considered the euthanasia capital of the world.

ABORTION-RELATED COURT DECISIONS

Following is a chronological list of abortion-related decisions handed down by the U.S. Supreme Court and other courts since Jan. 22, 1973. For most recent developments see items in News Events.

• In Roe v. Wade, the Court ruled, 7 to 2, Jan. 22, 1973: (1) During the first three months of pregnancy a woman's right to privacy is paramount. Accordingly, she has an unrestricted right to abortion with the consent and cooperation of a physician. (2) In the second trimester, the principle controlling legislation on abortion is the health or welfare of the mother, understood in the widest possible sense. (3) In the "state subsequent to viability," the controlling principles are the State's "interest in the potentiality of human life" and "the preservation of the life or health of the mother." These rulings canonized the absolutely private right of a woman to have an abortion and denied to the unborn the right to life.

• In Dole v. Bolton, also decided Jan. 22, 1973, the Court ruled, 7 to 2, against restrictions on facilities that could be used in performing abortions.

• In Danforth v. Planned Parenthood, the Court ruled, 6 to 3, July 1, 1976, against the constitutionality of state laws requiring spousal (in the case of a married woman) or parental (in the case of a minor) consent for an abortion.

Restrictive Amendment

• (The first of several versions of the Hyde Amendment was adopted by Congress Sept. 30, 1976, in an appropriations measure for the Department of Labor and the Department of Health, Education and Welfare. The amendment provided for limiting federal funding of abortions under Medicaid to cases of danger to the life of a mother and to cases of rape or incest reported in a required manner. See below.)

• An injunction against the amendment was issued Oct. 22, 1976, by U.S. District Court Judge John F. Dooling Jr., in a suit originally filed by Cora McRae.

• In Maher v. Roe, the Court ruled, 6 to 3, June 20, 1977, that the Constitution does not require states to pay for non-therapeutic (elective) abortions and does not require public hospitals to provide them.

• The Court set aside June 19, 1977, Judge Dooling's injunction against the Hyde Amendment and ordered him to restudy his ruling of the previous October in the light of its decision in Maher v. Roe.

• Funding restrictions of the Hyde Amendment went into effect Aug. 4, 1977, and the McRae case went back to the Dooling courtroom.

• The Court ruled, 6 to 3, Jan. 9, 1979, in Colautti v. Franklin against the constitutionality of a 1974 Pennsylvania law because of its vagueness about the timing of fetal viability. The decision had the effect of meaning that a woman exercising a legal right to have an abortion had the right to a dead fetus and that the doctor performing the abortion could not be charged civilly or criminally for the death of the fetus.

• In Bellotti v. Baird, the Court ruled, 8 to 1, July 2, 1979, against the constitutionality of a Massachusetts law requiring a minor to consult with her parents before having an abortion. In the absence of parental consent (which the Court ruled in 1976 was not required) or parental consultation (not required either), a court could clear the way for the abortion of a minor judged to be mature enough to have one.

• Judge Dooling ruled Jan. 15, 1980, against the constitutionality of the Hyde Amendment but stayed enforcement of his decision to permit an appeal to the Supreme Court.

• The Court responded Feb. 19, 1980, to Judge Dooling's action with a one-sentence order requiring federal and state governments to provide Medicaid funding for abortions deemed "medically necessary." The Court also agreed to rule on the constitutionality of the Hyde Amendment, in connection with another case (Williams v. Zbaraz) that originated in Illinois.

Hyde Amendment Constitutional

• In Harris v. McRae, the Court, with a 5-to-4 decision June 30, 1980, upheld the constitutionality of the Hyde Amendment and its restrictions on Medicaid abortion funding. The decision overturned the Dooling ruling, of Jan. 15, 1980.

While deciding that neither the federal government nor state governments are required to provide funding for "medically necessary" abortions, the Court noted that "abortion is inherently different from other medical procedures because no other medical procedure involves the purposeful termination of a potential life."

The Hyde Amendment provided: "None of the funds provided for in this paragraph shall be used to perform abortions except where the life of the mother would be endangered if the fetus were carried to term; or except for such medical procedures necessary for the victims of rape or incest, where such rape or incest has been reported promptly to a law enforcement agency or public health service."

About two-thirds of the states dropped elective abortion funding from their Medicaid programs after the 1977 decision of the Supreme Court. As of January, 1986, 14 states permitted the use of Medicaid funds to subsidize abortions.

Additional Decisions

• The Supreme Court, by a 6-to-3 vote in H.L. v. Matheson, upheld Mar. 23, 1981, the constitutionality of a Utah law requiring physicians to notify the parents of an unmarried, immature minor daughter seeking an abortion.

• With another 6-to-3 vote in Gary-Northwest Indiana Woman v. Orr, the Court ruled Apr. 27, 1981, that states may outlaw the performance of abortions outside of hospitals for women more than three months pregnant.

• The Court struck down, 6 to 3, June 15, 1983, major provisions of a Dayton, O., ordinance regulating the practice of abortion; in so doing, it reaffirmed its key decisions of 1973 against any such constraints.

The Court also struck down a Missouri law requiring that abortions after 12 weeks of pregnancy be performed in hospitals.

At the same time, the Court upheld two Missouri laws: one requiring the presence of a second physician during abortions after viability, the other requiring a pathology report for each abortion performed.

• The Pennsylvania Commonwealth Court ruled Mar. 9, 1984, that a 1980 state law prohibiting public funding of abortion violated the equal protection clause of the state's constitution and equal rights amendment.

• The 3rd U.S. Circuit Court of Appeals struck down May 31, 1984, some regulatory provisions of Pennsylvania's Abortion Control Act, but upheld the requirement that a child born alive through abortion be protected.

• In Thornburgh v. American Society of Obstetricians and Gynecologists, the Court ruled 5 to 4 against the constitutionality of the Pennsylvania Abortion Control Act of 1982. The five-Justice majority contended that requirements of the Pennsylvania law violated the Constitution because they posed an "unacceptable danger" of deterring women from choosing an abortion. Chief Justice Warren Burger said in dissent: "The Court astonishingly goes so far as to say that the state may not even require that a woman contemplating an abortion be provided with accurate medical information concerning the risks." He also said: "The Court's astonishing rationale . . . is that such information might have the effect of 'discouraging abortion,' as though abortion is something to be advocated and encouraged."

• The three-judge 8th U.S. Circuit Court of Appeals ruled Aug. 27, 1987, that Minnesota cannot require minors to notify both parents before they undergo an abortion. The court declared: "Because it frequently does more harm than good, on balance the present statute fails to further the state's asserted interests" of fostering communication within the family and protecting pregnant minors by promoting parental involvement in a girl's decision to have an abortion.

Statistics on legal abortions performed in the U.S. each year from 1972 to 1979 provide reliable indices of the magnitude of the challenge facing right-to-life proponents. The rising numbers of abortions and years, as reported by the Center for Disease Control, U.S. Department of Health and Human Services, were: 586,760 (1972), 615,831 (1973), 763,476 (1974), 854,853 (1975), 988,267 (1976), 1,079,430 (1977), 1,157,776 (1978), 1,251,921 (1979), 1,297,606 (1980), 1,303,890 (1982), 1,268,987 (1983). It is estimated that 20 million or more abortions were performed between 1973 and 1988.

The total number of abortions performed annually worldwide is estimated in the range of 30 to 35 million.

Charges Against the Church

The Catholic Church is the largest and strongest institutional opponent of abortion, because of its firm teaching and practice on the subject, and also because of the number of its members who are against it.

Because this is so in a cultural climate favoring abortion and moral liberalism, the Church has been accused and charged with:

• dominating the pro-life movement;

• trying to force its views on others who do not share its faith;

• violating a peculiar interpretation of the principle of separation of Church and state.

These accusations have been implicit and explicit in reporting of the abortion controversy ever since it began.

The Church insists, however, on its right to speak and act on moral issues on an equal basis with others who claim rights of conscience and freedom to influence others in a society which is subject not only to the laws of man but, above all, to universal moral law.

BIRTHRIGHT

Birthright is an interdenominational guidance and referral service organization offering pregnant women alternatives to abortion, in line with the motto, "It is the right of every pregnant woman to give birth and the right of every child to be born." Started by Mrs. Louise Summerhill of Toronto, Canada, in 1968, it has chapters in Canada, the United States, the United Kingdom, Ireland, New Zealand, Australia, Hong Kong, Ghana, Nigeria and South Africa. The executive director of Birthright, U.S.A., is Mrs. D. Cocciolone, 686 N. Broad St., Woodbury, N.J. 08096. Birthright is independent and interdenominational. Birthright operates a national 800 number.

SCHOOL-BASED CLINICS: BISHOPS' STATEMENT TO YOUTH

This statement, written by the Committee for Pro-Life Activities, was published with the approval Mar. 23, 1988, of the Administrative Committee of the National Conference of Catholic Bishops. Its publication followed the release of a report on such clinics during the November, 1987, meeting of the NCCB and of the U.S. Catholic Conference.

The text was circulated by NC News Service.

We are writing to you, the youth of our country, about a very important concern that touches your life.

Human sexuality is a gift from God and an important part of your total personality. Integrating your sexuality with all the facets of your life is a lifelong process that can be most difficult in the teen years when you face so many changes and challenges.

Human sexuality is also a gift that is designed for the total union of a man and woman in marriage. This union expresses the deepest form of human intimacy and is meant to enrich the life-giving love and commitment of married couples.

Pressures

We know the pressures you face every day to become involved in sexual activity. We know that some young people do become sexually involved and that a number of teen-age girls become pregnant each year.

You may also be aware of an effort to set up clinics in your schools to provide contraceptive services as a solution to teen-age pregnancies. This is something that is happening all over the country. Many people think that the only way to help you cope with your sexuality is to provide you with contraceptives. They assume that young people will be involved in sexual activity and cannot achieve the self-control that will lead to healthy physical and spiritual growth.

We know that there are better solutions. Because we care about you and your growth and development, we would like to help you develop healthy attitudes abut sexuality. We want you to understand that school-based clinics will present real dilemmas that you must face. We want to support you in living in a way that will lead to true and lasting happiness for you.

Claims and Responses

Let's look at some of the claims made by supporters of school-based clinics.

Claim No. 1: School-based clinics assume that you will be sexually active and cannot learn how to make wise and responsible choices about sexuality. Their solution is to give you contraceptives.

Response: We do not believe that sexual activity among young people is inevitable. In fact, clinics may even promote the attitude that everyone is sexually active. That is certainly not true. We believe in your ability to choose another way of living — to learn the positive values of honesty, responsibility, promise-keeping, self-control, commitment and respect for the other person that will help you to reserve your sexual activity for marriage.

Claim No. 2: School-based clinics claim that making contraceptives available to you will reduce teen-age pregnancy.

Response: Even though contraceptives are widely promoted in our society, especially through commercials and advertisements, they have not led to fewer teen-age pregnancies. We believe that the wide availability of contraceptives confirms teen-agers in their harmful sexual behavior. You are being told to deal with your sexuality by using pills and devices, instead of learning about the beauty of sexuality in God's plan and the responsible values that will help you grow as a sexual person. The only 100 percent safe way to avoid an unwanted pregnancy is to reserve sexual activity for marriage.

Claim No. 3: School-based clinics lead you to believe that contraceptives can prevent all of the negative consequences of teen-age sexual activity.

Response: Premarital sexual activity has adverse consequences for you. There are serious medical, emotional, moral and spiritual consequences of premature sexual activity. Clinics deceive you by not telling you about the physical and emotional realities of sexuality and by failing to teach you about the responsibilities of sexual intimacy. Please remember: for unmarried teen-agers, the only sure way to avoid the sexual transmission of AIDS or any other sexually transmitted disease is to refrain from sexual activity.

Claim No. 4: School-based clinics say they must give young people information about abortion and refer them to abortion clinics in order to provide a comprehensive answer to teen-age pregnancy.

Response: Abortion is not the answer! Abortion not only destroys the unborn child, but it also has severe emotional and physical consequences for the teen-age mother, and may have emotional consequences for the father as well. In a society that already contains far too much violence, adults should be helping young people to deal with the problems of pregnancy without promoting the violent solution of abortion.

Claim No. 5: School-based clinics lead you to believe that once you have become sexually active you will always be sexually active.

Response: Teachers and counselors do not assume that teen-agers cannot understand the harm of drugs and alcohol simply because they have experimented with them. In fact, people are encouraged to "Say No to Drugs!" and are helped to overcome drug and alcohol abuse. The same is true for teen-agers who have been sexually active. They can learn responsible values and change their behavior. We believe in your ability to change for the better, to open yourself to a morally responsible way of life.

Premarital sexual intercourse is a risky venture, a behavior that will violate your moral principles and your hopes for happiness. We know that pressures from our society to become sexually active are great. We encourage you to resist these pressures — to say NO to premarital sexual activity.

Challenges for Action

We challenge local communities across the country to drop the idea of school-based clinics. In their place, we encourage schools, parents and churches to:

• Provide you with the best information about human sexuality — how it is a marvelous gift from God that should not be abused.

• Help you to think critically about the sexual messages you find on television, in songs, in music videos, in advertisements, and to compare these messages with the positive understanding of human sexuality that you are learning.

• Teach you honesty, moral responsibility, promise-keeping, self-control, commitment and respect for other persons to help you reserve sexual activity for marriage.

• Support you in living these positive, healthy values.

We the Catholic bishops of the United States pledge our energies in working with you, your families and your schools to help build a society in which the positive values of human sexuality will be lived and appreciated.

THE MANY FACES OF AIDS: A GOSPEL RESPONSE

This is the title of a statement issued Dec. 11, 1987, by the Administrative Board of the U.S. Catholic Conference regarding pastoral concern about persons affected by acquired immune deficiency syndrome, facts and commentary about the disease, and preventive measures against it.

The following excerpts are from the text circulated by the NC Documentary Service, Origins, Dec. 24, 1987 (Vol. 17, No. 28).

Summary of Reflections

Our reflections may be summarized in this way:

• As with all other diseases, AIDS is a human illness to which we must respond in a manner consistent with the best medical and scientific information available.

• As members of the church and society, we have a responsibility to stand in solidarity with and reach out with compassion and understanding to those exposed to or experiencing this disease. We must provide spiritual and pastoral care as well as medical and social services for them and support for their families and friends.

• As members of the church we must offer a clear presentation of Catholic moral teaching with respect to human intimacy and sexuality.

• Discrimination or violence directed against persons with AIDS is unjust and immoral.

• As a society, we must develop educational and other programs to prevent the spread of the disease. Such programs should include an authentic understanding of human intimacy and sexuality as well as an understanding of the pluralism of values and attitudes in our society.

• Those who have been exposed to the virus are expected to live in a way that does not bring injury or potential harm to others.

Facts and Commentary

The AIDS phenomenon is complex. We do not intend to review all of the pertinent facts. The surgeon general of the United States and others have provided careful analysis of the causes of AIDS, the ways in which it is transmitted and the various dangers or risks of contracting the disease. Some of those facts are simply highlighted here.

• At the present time, AIDS is an incurable disease. Not restricted to the United States, it is found throughout the world. Currently two-thirds of the persons afflicted with AIDS in the United States are homosexual or bisexual men. Some estimate that the number of heterosexual persons with AIDS will increase significantly in the next five years. At present, nearly one out of four persons with AIDS is a drug user who used contaminated intravenous needles or other drug paraphernalia infected with the AIDS virus. Four hundred twenty-three hemophiliacs and people with blood-coagulating disorders and 2,955 women have been diagnosed as having AIDS.

• AIDS is a disease which cuts across all racial and ethnic lines.

• AIDS is not merely an "adult disease" in the United States. As of Oct. 12, 1987, 595 children have been reported as having contracted the disease.

• At this time, after extensive research there is no evidence that AIDS can be contracted through ordinary casual contact.

• AIDS can be contracted through certain forms of intimate sexual contact and encounters with tainted blood. It can also be transmitted from a mother to her child during pregnancy as well as through artificial insemination and by organ transplants.

AIDS, in other words, is a human disease whose spread, according to the best available scientific knowledge, is limited to identifiable modes of communication and contact.

Observations

1. We encourage all members of our society to relate to its victims with compassion and understanding, as they would to those suffering from any other fatal disease.

2. We strongly condemn violence directed against gay and lesbian people.

3. We oppose the enactment of quarantine legislation or other laws that are not supported by medical data or informed by the expertise of those in the health care or public health professions.

4. We oppose the use of the HIV-antibody tests for strictly discriminatory purposes.

5. We call upon all in the health care and support professions to be mindful of their general moral obligation, while following acceptable medical standards and procedures, to provide care for all

persons, including those exposed to the AIDS virus. Similarly, although funeral directors may find it necessary to take appropriate precautions, they are not justified in refusing to accept or prepare for burial the bodies of deceased persons with AIDS. Nor are they justified in unnecessarily charging more for the funeral of persons with AIDS.

6. To the extent possible, persons with AIDS should be encouraged to continue to lead productive lives in their community and place of work. They also have the right to decent housing, and landlords are not justified in denying them this right merely because of their illness.

7. We support collaborative efforts by governmental bodies, health providers and human service agencies to provide adequate funding and care for persons with AIDS.

8. Because of the virtually epidemic proportions of AIDS, we acknowledge the need for cooperative efforts by private and public entities to discover ways to treat and cure this disease and to commit adequate funding for basic research, applied research and general education.

9. We call on the federal government to provide additional funding for the care of those infected with the HIV virus who do not have health insurance as well as expanded income support for those impoverished by illness related to the AIDS virus.

10. Current programs and services need to be expanded to assist the families of those with AIDS while they are alive and also to support them in their bereavement.

11. Hospitals, because of their responsibility to care for the sick, and Catholic hospitals, because of their special mission and philosophy, have a unique call and role in caring for persons with AIDS.

12. As a society, we need effective educational media programs to help reduce fear, prejudice and discrimination against persons with AIDS, ARC, antibody-positive persons and those perceived to be in high-risk groups.

Prevention

Consistent with the insights and values found in the Scriptures, our religious tradition and a philosophy of the human person that is consonant with both, we believe that the best source of prevention for individuals and society can only come from an authentic and fully integrated understanding of human personhood and sexuality, and from efforts to address and eliminate the causes of intravenous drug abuse. We are convinced that the only measures that will effectively prevent this disease at present are those designed to educate and to change behavior.

In our society we must offer everyone a fully integrated understanding of human sexuality. Every person, made in God's image and likeness, has both the potential and the desire to experience interpersonal intimacy that reflects the intimacy of God's triune love. This reflection in human love of the divine love gives special meaning and purpose to human sexuality. Human sexuality is essentially related to permanent commitment in love and openness to new life. It is most fully realized when it is expressed in a manner that is as loving, faithful and committed as is divine love itself. That is why we call upon all people to live in accord with the authentic meaning of love and sexuality. Human sexuality, as we understand this gift from God, is to be genitally expressed only in a monogamous heterosexual relationship of lasting fidelity in marriage.

In light of this understanding of the human person, we are convinced that unless, as a society, we live in accord with an authentic human sexuality, on which our Catholic moral teaching is based, we will not address a major source of the spread of AIDS. Any other solution will be merely short term, ultimately ineffective and will contribute to the trivialization of human sexuality that is already so prevalent in our society.

No to "Safe Sex"

That is why we oppose the approach to AIDS prevention often popularly called "safe sex." This avenue compromises human sexuality — making it "safe" to be promiscuous — and, in fact, is quite misleading. As the National Academy of Sciences has noted in its study of AIDS, "many have argued that it is more accurate to speak in terms of 'safer' sex because the unknowns are still such that it would be irresponsible to certify any particular activity as absolutely safe."

Since AIDS is transmitted through intravenous drug use, we support and urge increased public support for drug treatment programs, the elimination of the importation of illicit drugs and every effort to eliminate the causes of addiction in all communities, especially those of the poor.

Since AIDS is also transmitted through sexual practices, legislation and public guidelines should encourage private and public institutions to go beyond mere biological education. Such legislation or guidelines must respect, however, the inalienable right of parents to be the first educators of their children regarding the meaning and purpose of human sexuality.

Public Educational Programs

Because we live in a pluralistic society, we acknowledge that some will not agree with our understanding of human sexuality. We recognize that public educational programs addressed to a wide audience will reflect the fact that some people will not act as they can and should; that they will not refrain from the type of sexual or drug abuse behavior which can transmit AIDS. In such situations educational efforts, if grounded in the broader moral vision outlined above, could include accurate information about prophylactic devices or other practices proposed by some medical experts as potential means of preventing AIDS. We are not promoting the use of prophylactics, but merely providing information that is part of the factual picture. Such a factual presentation should indicate that abstinence outside of marriage and fidelity within marriage as well as the avoidance of intravenous drug abuse are the only morally correct and medically sure ways to prevent the spread of AIDS. So-called "safe sex" practices are at best only partially effective. They do not take into account either the real values that are at stake or the fundamental good of the human person.

In sum, it is our judgment that the best approach to the prevention of AIDS ought to be based on the communication of a value-centered understanding of the meaning of human personhood. Such a perspective provides a suitable context for the consideration of legislation or educational policy.

Catholic Educational Programs

We also encourage our Catholic elementary schools, high schools, colleges and universities, and religious education programs to develop curricular guidelines and educational materials to educate their students about the prevention of AIDS. All guidelines and educational materials should stress the importance of chastity and the power of God's love which enables us to live a chaste life. Of course, such guidelines and materials must be developed in collaboration and consultation with parents as much as possible.

Responses of Bishops

The responses of bishops to the statement were generally positive with respect to its primary thrust and substance. Objection was voiced, however, regarding the portion of the text in which it was said that, under certain circumstances, providing information or prophylactics could be tolerated in public educational programs. The objectors included Cardinals John J. O'Connor of New York and Bernard F. Law of Boston, Archbishops Theodore E. McCarrick of Newark and James F. Stafford of Denver, the bishops of New England and others.

Cardinal Joseph Ratzinger, prefect of the Congregation for the Doctrine of the Faith, expressed his views in a letter to Archbishop John L. May, president of the National Conference of Catholic Bishops. He said, in part, as follows.

Ratzinger View

"One must keep in mind the problem posed by the worldwide reaction which accompanies certain documents issued by various episcopal conferences. This requires a particular sense of responsibility and prudence in the choice of themes to be treated and in the manner in which these statements are published, not to mention a careful composition of the texts themselves. At least in some cases, when the subjects under discussion are of interest to the universal Church, it would seem advisable to consult in advance with the Holy See.

"Secondly, regarding the precise moral issue in question here. I want to draw attention to the clarification which appeared in the March 10 edition of *L'Osservatore Romano*, in an unsigned article entitled 'Prevention of AIDS: Christian Ethical Aspect,' and I quote, 'To seek a solution to the problem of infection by promoting the use of prophylactics would be to embark on a way not only insufficiently reliable from the technical point of view but also, and above all, unacceptable from the moral aspect. Such a proposal for 'safe' or at least 'safer' sex — as they say — ignores the real cause of the problem, namely, the permissiveness which, in the area of sex as in that related to other abuses, corrodes the moral fiber of the people.'

"In the case here under discussion, it hardly seems pertinent to appeal to the classical principle of tolerance of the lesser evil on the part of those who exercise responsibility for the temporal common good of society. In fact, even when the issue has to do with educational programs promoted by the civil government, one would not be dealing simply with a form of passive toleration but rather with a kind of behavior which would result in at least the facilitation of evil."

Second Statement To Come

Bishops at the June, 1988, meeting of their conference voted to stand by the statement issued by the Administrative Board (without a vote by the entire conference) the previous December. At the same time, they opted for a new statement in approving the following motion brought forward by Cardinal Joseph L. Bernardin of Chicago.

"I move that the president appoint an ad hoc committee to prepare a new, updated statement on the AIDS crisis which will respond to the new facts, fears and efforts which have emerged in recent months. The committee, in preparing the new statement, will have the benefit of the extant board statement on AIDS, the discussions which have taken place since its publication, dialogue with the Congregation for the Doctrine of the Faith, and participation by all the bishops in open, plenary session."

Statistics

The Federal Centers for Disease Control reported 38,541 deaths nationwide from AIDS, as strictly defined by the agency. Also reported were 68,229 cases diagnosed. The figures were cited in an article in the July 22, 1988, edition of *The New York Times*.

MASS FOR HOMOSEXUALS

Cardinal Joseph L. Bernardin, in a statement issued May 15, 1988, announced that the Archdiocese of Chicago would assume sponsorship of a weekly Sunday Mass for homosexuals. Such a Mass had been celebrated in the archdiocese under the never-formally-recognized auspices of Dignity, an organization of homosexuals at odds with the teaching and practice of the Church. The purposes of the Cardinal's action were: (1) to provide pastoral care for homosexual persons in accord with the teaching and practice of the Church, and (2) to dispel any implication of church approval of Dignity views on the morality of homosexual behavior.

This text was circulated by the NC Documentary Service, Origins, June 9, 1988 (Vol. 18, No. 4). Subheads have been added.

For more than 17 years there has been a Sunday evening Mass at St. Sebastian Church that has served Catholics who are gay and lesbian. This Mass was begun by the parish itself as an outgrowth of the apostolate of the Legion of Mary among the members of the gay community. Subsequently, Dignity/Chicago assumed sponsorship for this Mass. Nonetheless, the Mass has always been considered by the pastor and parish council as an important part of the ministerial life of the parish. Moreover, as a regularly scheduled Mass, it has attracted some worshipers who are not members of the gay community.

Dignity at Variance with Church Teaching

Since its inception, the archdiocese has been aware of the Mass at St. Sebastian. The sponsorship/involvement of Dignity/Chicago has been monitored by the pastor of the parish. The archdiocese, however, never formally recognized the sponsorship of Dignity/Chicago because it saw an ambiguity in the position taken by Dignity with regard to Church teaching on human sexuality. Its statement of purpose could be read either as being in conformity with Church teaching or at variance with it. Last August, however, that ambiguity was eliminated when Dignity/National adopted a resolution which called for an "openness to discussion on the morality of homosexual acts." The context of this resolution clearly indicates that its intent is to change some fundamental teachings of the Church on human sexuality as reaffirmed recently by the Congregation for the Doctrine of the Faith in its instruction "The Pastoral Care of Homosexual Persons."

I am very concerned that gay and lesbian Catholics receive the pastoral care of their Church. That pastoral care involves in one way or another elements of acknowledgment, support and direction. This new development, however, has required that the status of Dignity/Chicago's sponsorship of the Mass at St. Sebastian be reconsidered. It is my responsibility, as pastor of the Church of Chicago, to make sure that the Church's teaching on human sexuality is presented clearly and without any ambiguity. Moreover, it would be inappropriate to endorse an organization which officially advocates a position which is contrary to that of the Church or to allow such an organization to assume a position of leadership in one of our parishes or agencies.

In order to resolve this dilemma in a way which will be doctrinally correct and pastorally sensitive, I have been meeting for over a year with the pastors of a number of parishes that have a significant number of gay and lesbian members. These pastors are already ministering in various ways to their gay and lesbian members. They are eager to develop this ministry, in collaboration with the archdiocese, in a way that will be both faithful to Catholic teaching and effective in their parishes.

Basic Principles

The pastors and I have agreed on some basic principles upon which our ministry to the Catholic gay and lesbian community should be based:

- 1. The archdiocese strongly affirms the teaching of the Church on the rights and dignity of all persons and the fact that these rights should be respected and protected.

- 2. The archdiocese condemns arbitrary discrimination and prejudice, violence and harassment against a person because of his or her sexual orientation.

- 3. The archdiocese fully supports the Church's teaching on human sexuality, which rejects as immoral homosexual acts as distinguished from the person who is homosexual.

- 4. Accordingly, the archdiocese reaffirms its commitment to minister spiritually to its brothers and sisters who are homosexual. To that end, the archdiocese should pursue ways in which it can do this more effectively.

- 5. The archdiocese does not endorse any organization which assumes a position of advocacy against church teaching.

In the context of these principles, I wish now to address the matter of the Sunday evening Mass at St. Sebastian. The importance and significance of this Mass go beyond the question of "sponsorship" by Dignity/Chicago. The Mass is an important part of the parish's ministry and is supported by the parish pastoral council. The Mass has become a point of return to the life of the Church for many persons, whether homosexual or not, whether members of Dignity or not. It has met a pastoral need that exists at St. Sebastian and other parishes. To cancel the Mass would be a serious pastoral mistake.

Archdiocesan Responsibility

For this reason, I have decided that the archdiocese will assume responsibility for this Mass and have asked the pastors of neighboring parishes to collaborate with the pastor of St. Sebastian in this responsibility. They will have direct responsibility for the Sunday evening liturgy, celebrating Mass on a regular basis. This understanding does not preclude, however, their inviting other priests to preside and preach on occasion.

In the future the archdiocese, rather than Dignity/Chicago, will be the sponsor of the Mass. All of those who have been participating in the Mass are invited to continue. All who have been involved in the planning and celebration of the Sunday Eucharist are invited to continue sharing their experience and talent. It will be the responsibility of the pastors to ensure that everything connected with the Mass and any events which might take place before or after the liturgy be in accord with Church teaching and discipline.

Father John Flavin, as pastor of St. Sebastian and dean of the area, will serve as coordinator of this pastoral project. Periodically, I will review the situation with him and the other pastors. In addition, I will continue to dialogue with them and other interested people as to how we can extend further, as the authentic teaching of the Church directs, our pastoral outreach to gay and lesbian Catholics throughout the archdiocese.

END OF DIGNITY-SPONSORED MASSES

The Archdiocese of Seattle joined more than 20 other dioceses June 30, 1988, in discontinuing celebrations of Mass sponsored by Dignity, an organization of homosexuals who do not accept church teaching regarding the immorality of homosexual activity. Directly influencing the bishops in halting these celebrations was a letter on "the pastoral care of homosexual persons" from Cardinal Joseph Ratzinger, prefect of the Congregation for the Doctrine of the Faith. He said in a letter of October, 1986:

"The Archdiocese (of Seattle, as well as other dioceses) should withdraw all support from any group which does not unequivocally accept the teaching of the magisterium concerning the intrinsic evil of homosexual activity. ... A compassionate ministry must be developed that has as its clear goal the promotion of a chaste lifestyle."

In other developments, a number of U.S. bishops have gone on record against homosexual rights bills proposed in state and other lawmaking bodies. They call such legislation unnecessary because of existing anti-discrimination statutes. They also say such bills pose threats to the good of society and would tend to give legitimacy to an unacceptable lifestyle.

THE CHURCH AND THE HOUSING PROBLEM

"What Have You Done to Your Homeless Brother? The Church and the Housing Problem," is the title of a document issued by the Pontifical Justice and Peace Commission Feb. 2, 1988. It was written as a complement to other initiatives undertaken in line with the dedication of 1987 as The International Year of Shelter for the Homeless.

The following excerpts are from the Vatican's English-language text circulated by the NC Documentary Service, Origins, Feb. 11, 1988 (Vol. 17, No. 35). Subheads have been added.

Political authorities, religious leaders and, in general, public opinion, all recognize that a situation in which millions of human beings lack adequate housing is a serious problem.

Urgent measures must be taken (to cope with the problem because) a fundamental human right is, in reality, being violated.

The Church appeals to governments and to those with social responsibilities to take the necessary decisions and set up economic programs that will adequately meet the need for housing, particularly for the poorest and the most marginalized.

Statistics

A few figures will suffice to give an idea of the extent of the problem. A billion people, one-fifth of the human race, do not have decent housing. One hundred million quite literally do not have a roof over their head. In Western Europe, for example, more than a million people are seeking adequate housing. In Latin America, it is estimated that 20 million children sleep in the street. In 1986, more than 600 million people — 45 percent of the total urban population of the world — lived in zones of misery around big cities, in shantytowns or in slum neighborhoods. (Among the homeless are) individuals (who are) often the victims of personal problems. . . young people and engaged couples who want to get married (but lack) the amount of money needed to acquire a decent home, (and people in) the social category of the marginalized, in both rural and urban milieus.

The lack of housing . . . constitutes, without a doubt, one of the most tragic indications of that underdevelopment which strikes so many people, or, to be more precise, which affects a large part of humanity.

Structural Crisis

This situation is not simply a fact to which those with responsibilities in the field and, indeed, all persons are called to react. Rather, from an ethical point of view, it is a scandal and one more indication of the unjust distribution of goods originally destined for the use of all.

The lack of sufficient housing must be considered a structural crisis rising from multiple causes but ending inevitably in poverty. . . . This poverty lays bare those socio-economic inequalities that have given rise to an inhuman separation denoted by the expression North-South or rich nations-poor nations. These same gaps and inequalities are also found today in the North.

At the source of the problem of housing . . . lie unemployment, low salaries, the rural exodus and . . . rapid industrialization . . . accelerated population growth in certain regions and . . . the phenomenon of urbanization, (along with political factors, the displacement of populations and racial discrimination).

Result of Poverty

All of the root causes of the housing problem . . . point to a generalization of relative or absolute poverty, particularly in the Third World countries. In general terms, the situation of homelessness is the result of poverty and of social marginalization. In other words, it is the result of a whole series of economic, social, cultural, physical, emotional and moral factors that specifically bear down on those who have never been integrated into the current social system. Without substantial changes and modifications within societies marked by this fault, such integration will remain difficult or even impossible.

Any discernment concerning the complex situaton of the homeless . . . must include an ethical evaluation of the new challenge presented by this modern-day poverty.

Any person or family that, without any direct fault on his or her part, does not have suitable housing, is the victim of an injustice. . . . This injustice is clearly a structural injustice, caused and perpetuated by personal injustices. It is likewise, however, an autonomous and independent phenomenon, with its own interior unjust and disordered dynamism.

Obligation of Society and State

The injustice of which homeless persons and families are victims can be laid at the door of a social organization or political will which is, at times, either deficient or powerless.

Society, as well as the state, has the obligation to guarantee for its citizens and members those living conditions without which they cannot achieve fulfillment, either as persons or as families.

Anything which does not meet the basic needs of a person — alone or in a family — cannot be considered part of an authentic culture. . . . The right to housing is a universal right.

Property at Service of Persons

Those goods without which it is impossible for a person to lead a decent human life must be equitably provided to those who lack them. In the light of the teaching of the Church on the universal destination of goods, one can understand that property has a specific social function, subordinated to the right to common use. In reflecting on this principle, we can better see that housing constitutes a basic social good and cannot simply be considered a market commodity.

Property is at the service of the human person. Any speculative practice which diverts property use from its function of serving the human person should be considered an abuse.

Each one of us should feel obliged to do what he or she can do, either directly or indirectly, through various existing organizations, so that others (without homes) can also enjoy a right of which they have been deprived.

Action by the Homeless

This by no means excludes the action of the men and women who are homeless. On the contrary! Once informed of their rights, and if necessary with adequate legal assistance to defend these rights, the homeless should be encouraged to form grass-root associations for the purpose of procuring housing. In the same way, society must not be allowed to forget a tragedy that we are only too often ready to ignore. A lack of housing can . . . even accustom people and families to subminimal conditions of existence.

For each Christian and for the Church, as the people of God, the stark reality of homeless persons and families is at one and the same time an appeal to conscience and an exigency to do something to remedy the situation.

Concern of the Church

The concern of the Church for housing and its insistence in calling for decent housing for all flows from three considerations:

• Adequate housing is important if a person is to find fulfillment, both as an individual and as a member of a family and society.

• The witness that the Church seeks to give in collaborating in the search for a solution to the problem of the poor is a sign of the presence of the kingdom of salvation and liberation.

• The mission of the Church also consists in helping to make society more human.

In many countries, the number of the homeless presents a problem of vast proportions. The efforts of the local churches to procure decent housing for those who have none . . . go far beyond simple material gestures. The aim of these actions is to promote the dignity of persons as well as the stability of the family and its intimacy, and the education of children, in addition to assuring the minimum conditions of health and hygiene that are indispensable for the normal development of family life.

An analysis of the various housing programs indicates that the local churches address the problem in three ways:

• material help to provide shelter to homeless families;

• education and community development;

• dialogue with authorities in view of legislation and housing policies that are favorable to the poor.

Commitment of Society and Church

The commitment of all the active forces of society is absolutely necessary if a radical and definitive solution to the housing crisis is to be found. The problem has its roots in poverty, which depends in turn on the dialectic between development and underdevelopment, and the truly scandalous division which exists between rich and poor countries. Choices must be made and political and economic measures taken that change for the better the causes of the problem.

The commitment of the Church to the homeless is a humanitarian and evangelical commitment; it is also an expression of a preferential love for the poor. At the same time, it is an indication of the Church's support for the objectives and programs of the U.N. International Year of Shelter for the Homeless. The Church's presence and its charitable action are always a sign of that solidarity, salvation and liberation that anticipates the kingdom of God among us.

HOMELESSNESS IN THE U.S.

It is estimated that there are three million homeless persons in the U.S. The world total is thought to be about 100 million.

Concern for the homeless was the substance of testimony given before a House of Representatives subcommittee June 15, 1988, by Auxiliary Bishop Joseph M. Sullivan of Brooklyn and Bishop James W. Malone of Youngstown.

Bishop Sullivan said: "The Churtch is deeply involved in the housing issue. But we know our efforts cannot be, and should not be, substitutes for effective and just public policies to deal with the crisis of homelessness and the urgent, desperate need for decent housing in our communities and country."

Bishop Malone testified: "It is appropriate and necessary that Congress provide emergency relief funds to private and public agencies to care for those living in the streets; but this cannot, and will not, and should not substitute for federal action also to help provide permanent, affordable housing."

NEWS EVENTS — OCTOBER 1987 TO SEPTEMBER 1988

OCTOBER 1987

VATICAN

Repression in Czechoslovakia — Pope John Paul, in an unusual public indictment of religious repression in Czechoslovakia, said Catholics there should have the right to bishops, independent seminaries, religious education and a free religious press. Speaking Oct. 1 to Cardinal Frantisek Tomasek of Prague, he said the communist government's restrictions on the faithful were "without parallel" in traditionally Christian countries. The Pontiff's remarks came two weeks after a group of Catholics published a 16-point "Charter for Believers" that called on the regime to end religious discrimination, allow the building of new churches and seminaries, and agree to the naming of bishops free of government control.

Singular Moment of Vatican II — The Second Vatican Council was a "singular moment" for the Church, providing it with a "program of action for the Christians of our time." So stated the Pope Oct. 11 during a Mass commemorating the 25th anniversary of the opening of the council. Quoting Pope John XXIII at that time, he said the purpose of the council was to take the "certain and unchangeable doctrine" of the Church and present it "in a way that responds to the needs of our time." Enactments of the council, Pope John Paul said, threw "new light on the perennial truths of the Christian mystery," resulting in "a vast program of renewal with regard to almost every area of Christian action, on the personal as well as on the communitarian level."

Small-Farm Owners — In a letter addressed Oct. 16 to Edouard Saouma, director general of the U.N. Food and Agriculture Organization, the Pope appealed for efforts to improve conditions for small-farm owners and workers in Third World countries. "Small-farm owners often live in precarious situations," he said. "They are not favored by health-care plans, in means of information and education, and even in expressing their opinions in social and political life." The occasion for the letter was the observance of World Food Day.

New Financial Framework — At a meeting with Peru's new ambassador to the Vatican, the Pope cited Oct. 17 the need for a "new international financial framework" to help solve the economic and social problems of Third World countries. The weight of such problems, he said, "is so heavy that it puts into difficulty the free and responsible direction and progress" of countries. International financial reforms should stress the "solidarity of nations."

Vietnamese Families — "Vietnamese families, including those in the diaspora, should be schools of faith and places of prayer, human formation and apostolic spirit," the Pope told 25 Vietnamese priests Oct. 28. He also said that vocations to the priesthood and religious life should be pastoral priorities for Vietnamese Catholics, including those outside their native country.

Saints Canonized — On Mission Sunday, Oct. 18, Pope John Paul canonzied 16 Catholics martyred for their faith between 1633 and 1637 in or near the Japanese city of Nagasaki. They included Lorenzo Ruiz, the first Filipino saint, nine Japanese, four Spaniards, one Italian and one Frenchman. Two hundred and 31 other Catholics killed during the late 16th century and the 17th century had already been declared saints.

On Oct. 25, the Holy Father canonized Dr. Giuseppe Moscati, a physician and scientist, who died in 1927 at age 46. He called the saint, who practiced his profession in Naples, a leader in the "humanization of medicine."

On Oct. 4, the Pope beatified three young people of the 20th century: Marcel Callo, a Frenchman who organized religious activities in German labor camps during World War II, and two victims of attempted rape — Pierina Morosini, an Italian factory worker beaten to death in 1957, and Antonia Mesina, known as the "martyr of Purity" in Sardinia, who was killed in 1935.

Lefebvre Reconciliation? — Pope John Paul named Cardinal Edouard Gagnon as his investigating delegate to the Priestly Society of St. Pius X, headed by dissident Archbishop Marcel Lefebvre. Announcement of the appointment was made Oct. 29 by Cardinal Joseph Ratzinger, prefect of the Congregation for the Doctrine of the Faith. He said Cardinal Gagnon would be in charge of gathering information which might contribute to efforts toward "canonical regulation" of the society, whose status had been irregular since 1975.

The appointment was the latest in a series of developments related to reports that reconciliation might be accomplished between Archbishop Lefebvre and the Church. The Archbishop was suspended from the exercise of holy orders in 1976 for ordaining priests without proper authorization. He also refused to accept enactments of the Second Vatican Council on a variety of critical subjects.

The Priestly Society of St. Pius X, founded by Archbishop Lefebvre, was reported to have a membership of about 250 priests, 300 seminarians, five seminaries, and 90 priories and houses in 28 countries.

Cardinal Ratzinger, speaking about Vatican-Lefebvre dialogue, said: "Clearly, the hoped-for definitive solution is founded on the presupposition of a necessary obedience to the most holy Pontiff and of fidelity to the Church's magisterium."

General Audience Topics — These included:
• "The revealed truth that Jesus has the power to forgive sins, a power that is closely linked with his authority as God to judge the living and the dead" (Oct. 7).
• "The truth that Jesus is the divine lawgiver" (Oct. 14).
• "The fact that Jesus is truly God, one in being with the Father" (Oct. 21).

The Pope Also:
- Told regents and students from The Catholic University of America that universities play a "special role" in fulfilling "the Church's mission of evangelization." The academic community "is linked in a vital way with the Gospel's impact on the evolution of thought and culture, and with the integral development of society."
- Called West German Cardinal Joseph Hoeffner, who died Oct. 16, a "great man of the Church, of culture and of science."
- At the opening of the academic year Oct. 20, told Catholic university students that they should integrate their knowedge with their faith, declaring that "such a synthesis is demanding but, at the same time, attractive."
- Met with Salvadoran President Jose Napoleon Duarte and U.S. Ambassador to the United Nations Vernon Walters in separate private sessions, Oct. 24.

Vatican Briefs:
- Cardinal Joseph Ratzinger, speaking Oct. 1 before the assembly of the Synod of Bishops, reported that the Vatican would seek comments from bishops throughout the world on a draft of guidelines for use in the development of local catechisms. The purpose of the compendium would be to provide "an organic and summarized exposition of essential and fundamental points of Catholic teaching in the areas of faith and customs."
- Worldwide contributions ($35.8 million) to the Vatican to cover its annual budget deficit more than doubled by the end of September but were still "far from sufficient," according to Cardinal Agostino Casaroli, secretary of state.

Synod of Bishops

"The Vocation and Mission of the Laity in the Church and in Society 20 Years after the Second Vatican Council" was the theme of the seventh ordinary assembly of the Synod of Bishops held Oct. 1 to 30. The number of voting delegates — representatives of 101 episcopal conferences and papal appointees — was about 230. The three-phased assembly produced more than 200 expressions of bishops' views, a message to the people of God and a set of 54 recommendations submitted to Pope John Paul II for consideration relative to a papal statement on the theme of the assembly.

(See separate article.)

NATIONAL

Pastors Praised — Pastors of parishes "should experience a well-deserved sense of satisfaction" because of their leadership and adaptability in the 20 years of parish renewal and change since the Second Vatican Council. This was the theme of an 84-page book, *A Shepherd's Care: Reflections on the Changing Role of Pastor*, issued early in the month by the U.S. bishops' Committee on Priestly Life and Ministry.

Establishment of Non-Religion — U.S. society is "perilously close" to the establishment of "non-religion" in the legal system when the wall of separation between church and state is treated as an absolute, Archbishop Oscar H. Lipscomb of Mobile told judges and lawyers attending a Red Mass Oct. 4 in Washington. He asked: "Does the No Establishment Clause (of the Constitution) dominate the Free Exercise Clause, or stand in service to it? By reason of the First Amendment, do the rights of unbelief weigh more heavily than the right to believe in our land today?" If the "wall" separating church and state "is as absolute as some judicial opinion would have it, then we have come perilously close, in some sensitive areas, to the enactment of laws, or their interpretation, that effectively 'establish' non-religion." Three Justices of the U.S. Supreme Court — William Rehnquist, John Paul Stevens and Antonin Scalia — were among those at the Mass.

Catholic High Schools Honored — Thirty-three Catholic schools were honored by President Reagan and U.S. Education Secretary William J. Bennett Oct. 5 at the White House. They were among 271 public and private secondary schools cited for academic goals, high expectations for students, development of character and values, positive climate and administrative leadership.

Canonization Process — Bishop Edward D. Head announced Oct. 7 that the Vatican had granted permission for the Diocese of Buffalo to begin the process for the possible canonization of Father Nelson Baker, founder of Our Lady of Victory Homes in Lackawanna, N.Y. Father Baker, ordained in 1876, died in 1936 after decades in service to handicapped children, pregnant teen-agers and adolescent boys in trouble with the law.

TV Coverage of the Pope's Visit — Live coverage on cable television of Pope John Paul's visit to the U.S. in September was the "most significant electronic media activity that the Church in this country has ever engaged in." So stated Richard Hirsch, secretary of the Department of Communications, U.S. Catholic Conference. The 10-day broadcast of Papal Visit '87 was co-produced by the Eternal Word Television Network and the Catholic Telecommunications Network of America. The broadcast was carried by about 700 cable outlets in 44 states, and had a potential audience of 20 million homes.

Political Responsibility: Choices for the Future — This was the title of a 23-page statement released Oct. 14 by the Administrative Board of the U.S. Catholic Conference. Key policy issues "laden with moral content" were the subjects of the statement, in which the bishops said they repudiated "the formation of a religious voting bloc" and did not intend "to instruct persons on how they should vote for particular candidates" in November elections. They said their public policy role was to advocate peace, justice and the common good, to promote human rights and denounce their violation, and to "call attention to the moral and religious dimension of secular issues."

Anti-Poverty Grants — The Campaign for Human Development reported 1987 awards totaling $6.5 million in grants to 216 self-help projects across the country. Bishop Arthur N. Tafoya, chairman of the oversight committee, said the "grants help build human solidarity to enable millions of poor Americans abandoned by an economic system that is excessively motivated by individual self-interest to gain basic human rights — housing, employment and education. Campaign grants to more than 2,800 anti-poverty projects since 1970 amounted to $100 million.

Alien Registration — The Archdiocese of Los Angeles announced Oct. 27 a reduction, from 18 to 12, in the number of its alien legalization processing centers because of a decrease in the number of clients. Father R. David Cousineau, executive director of Catholic Charities, said the centers, set up in July, had been staffed by 270 persons and were equipped to serve 4,000 clients a week. The weekly average for the previous three months was 1,500 clients.

Racially Motivated Attacks — Auxiliary Bishop Jerome A. Pechillo of Newark said late in the month that racially motivated attacks on members of Jersey City's Asian Indian community were "intolerable as far as we Christians are concerned. Our Gospel, given to us by Christ, is a Gospel of love, tolerance, forbearance and acceptance." Catholics should be aware of their "moral responsibility to champion the needs of all people."

Hospital Status Changed — Auxiliary Bishop Gilbert I. Sheldon of Cleveland announced that St. Thomas Hospital and Medical Center in Akron could no longer be considered a Catholic hospital because it allowed the performance of sterilizations, a practice not in line with Catholic medical-moral directives. The hospital, although independent of church sponsorship and administration, was perceived to be a Catholic institution. The Bishop said in his statement: "Inasmuch as the board of trustees of St. Thomas Medical Center has elected to depart (from Catholic directives), the hospital can no longer be considered a Catholic hospital." He added that the diocese would continue to minister to patients at the hospital.

Meetings: Meetings included those of:

• Ninety Protestant, Orthodox and Catholic mission specialists, Sept. 27 to Oct. 3 in Madison, Conn.; they committed themselves to seek ways and means of greater interfaith cooperation in their work.

• Canon Law Society of America, Oct. 12 to 15 in Nashville; approved was a report urging church agencies to respect the rights of their employees to join unions and other collective bargaining associations.

National Briefs:

• The Archdiocese of Los Angeles announced that its three seminaries had an enrollment of 355 students, the largest student body in 15 years.

• Father Gary Rieve-Estrella, S.V.D., was named Oct. 1 director of the U.S. bishops' vocation project, "Hispanic Vocations and Formation: Project 13."

• Three hundred and 50 persons took part in a Rosary Rally for Peace Oct. 12 at the Washington Monument in the nation's capital.

• The Institute of Judaeo-Christian Studies at Seton Hall University established an academic chair named for Msgr. John M. Oesterreicher, its founder and director since 1953.

• The first television station owned and operated by a U.S. diocese was placed on sale because of cost and concern over programming. The intent to sell KDTU, Channel 18, was announced by the Diocese of Phoenix Oct. 22.

Respect for Life

Advocates of euthanasia and "rational suicide" for AIDS victims "lose sight of the equal dignity of every human being." So stated Cardinal Joseph L. Bernardin in a message for the observance of Respect Life Sunday, Oct. 4. "Some propose euthanasia, either by active intervention or the deliberate withholding of ordinary and customary life-sustaining measures for the purpose of causing death, as a means of avoiding the responsibilities of caring for the disabled and helpless. . . . Some advocate 'rational suicide' as a response to the suffering of persons dying from AIDS. Such proposals lose sight of the equal dignity of every human being, regardless of age or condition."

In a related development, the International Anti-Euthanasia Task Force, based at the Human Life Center at the University of Steubenville, said in a statement: "We categorically reject euthanasia in American society as it masquerades under the euphemisms of a 'right to die,' 'aid in dying,' and 'death with dignity.' . . . There is no dignity in starvation or dehydration unto death, nor any shining mercy."

INTERNATIONAL

Bishops Ready To Cooperate in Sudan — Msgr. Macram Max Gassis, apostolic administrator of the Diocese of El Obeid, said at a Washington luncheon Oct. 8 that the bishops of Sudan had told the government they were "ready to support" its efforts for peace if they were founded on "justice and respect for human rights." Specifically, he said the Moslem-dominated regime should provide Christians with opportunities to participate in public affairs, should reject efforts to make the Islamic Penal Code the law of the land, and should lift restrictions on Christian missionaries. He reported that Christians and other non-Moslems were suffering in the civil war between the Arab-Moslem North and black Christians and animists in the South. Among other things at issue were demands of government opponents for setting aside the strictures of Islamic law and for equitable division of political power between North and South.

Hospital Bans In Vitro Fertilization — Our Lady of Good Help Hospital in Paris, where six test-tube babies had been born since June, 1986, banned any further use of in vitro fertilization. The hospital's administrative council made the decision at mid-month. Father Robert Perrelet, a member of the council and representative of the Archdiocese of Paris, told French journalists that Cardinal Jean-Marie Lustiger had reminded responsible parties of the necessity to respect the "true character" of the hospital. Backgrounding his concern was a document issued the previous March in which the Congregation for the Doctrine of the Faith said that in vitro fertilization is illicit because it separates procreation from the conjugal act.

Caught in South African Crossfire — The Church is being pressured "by conflicting secular agendas" and is "caught in the crossfire between oppressor and liberator, between one ideology of liberation and another," said Bishop Wilfred F. Napier, head of the Southern African Bishops' Conference.

Addressing the Synod of Bishops Oct. 6, he said: "Criticized on one side, the Church finds herself exploited by another; expressing concern for all, she satisfies none. . . . On the one hand, her task is to Christianize the secular political order. On the other hand, the political order threatens to secularize her Christianity. . . . Secularism shows itself especially in the demands on her allegiance made by the opposing political forces and ideologies of the country. . . . From without, she is pressured to choose between ideologies; from within, she is tempted to yield to the pressure."

Glasnost Is for Western Consumption — The Soviet policy of glasnost, or openness, "is only for the West," according to a Ukrainian Catholic activist who spent more than 20 years in Soviet prisons. Josyp Terelya, speaking in Toronto, said he saw no evidence of glasnost in the Soviet Union, where Christians "were still praying in secret" and "being arrested for their faith." Since January, he said, persecution and suppression of the Church in the Ukraine had been worse than it had been before. He accused the government-sponsored Russian Orthodox Church of being the "unofficial agent of Soviet Russification of the Ukraine."

Outdoor Masses Oct. 11 — More than 1,000 persons attended a special outdoor Mass Oct. 11 in the town of Omulukila, Namibia, near the ruins of a church destroyed by a bomb Sept. 20. As Bishop Bonifatius Hauxiku of Windhoek celebrated the Mass, thousands of other Catholics in the northern and central parts of the country took part in similar services. Priests called the bombing "devilish destruction" and expressed "deepest shock" over the incident. They said it touched "the very nerve of the Church" because a church building is "not only the center of our ministry, the symbol of our very existence, but even more . . . the holy place where the Eucharist, the highest act of worship of our Christian religion, is celebrated and where the Blessed Sacrament is kept and revered by the people."

No Priests in Cambodia — "In Cambodia, there have been no eucharistic celebrations since 1976. All the priests were killed during the Pol Pot revolution, and all the churches and other buildings were either destroyed or confiscated. The laity themselves took charge of their communities." So stated Bishop Yves-George-Rene Ramousse, head of the Paris-based Office for the Promotion of the Apostolate among Cambodians, at a session of the Synod of Bishops. He also said that Pol Pot initiated a repressive government which killed an estimated two to four million people and tried to destroy all religious institutions. Speaking of his own ministry, Bishop Ramousse called for the development of more effective pastoral programs for Cambodians living outside their native country. He said there were about 500,000 Cambodian refugees, and that approximately half of them were living in difficult conditions in refugee camps.

African Concerns — African bishops spoke about specific concerns of their local churches in addresses during the first phase of the Synod of Bishops. The wide range of topics included the dowry system, witchcraft, family-centered worship, basic Christian communities, lay parish administrators, basic as well as advanced religious education and formation, catechists, lay ministries and reciprocal relations between local churches and the Church universal.

No News Broadcast — Nicaragua's Radio Catolica, reopened Oct. 2 after being off the air since January, 1986, was prohibited from airing its first news broadcast Oct. 19. A government censor called the station that day and said a news program could not be aired without government permission. Msgr. Bismarck Carballo, director of the station, told NC News Oct. 20 that permission had not been sought because it was assumed it was implicit in a freedom-of-expressin clause in the Central American peace plan signed Aug. 7 at Esquipulas, Costa Rica.

International Briefs:

• *New Nation*, a newspaper published by the Southern African Bishops' Conference, was warned by the government that copy in three of its issues violated media regulations and could be subject to action by the government.

• Sister Bernard Ncube, a member of the Companions of St. Angela, detained in South Africa since June, 1986, on charges of subversion, sedition and assault, was released on bail, on conditions that she may not participate in political or civic organizations and must report to police twice a week.

• Fides, the news agency of the Congregation for the Evangelization of Peoples, reported in September that Chinese authorities appeared to be loosening some restrictions on religious worship under the auspices of the government-controlled Patriotic Association of Chinese Catholics. It was said that about 1,900 churches had been reopened. Ministry by priests and practice of the faith by Catholics in union with the Pope remained under ban.

• Representatives of the Catholic Church and the Russian Orthodox Church, in a "theological conversation" Oct. 11 to 16 in Venice, expressed "deep agreement" that total nuclear disarmament and the peaceful use of space are needed, and called for a common study of problems related to human rights.

Catholics in Vietnam

Vietnamese Catholics "have won the sympathy of all, even the atheist authorities, with their radiant charity, their honesty and their justice," said Auxiliary Bishop Francois Nguyen Van Sang of Hanoi during a session of the Synod of Bishops. Despite government restrictions on religious assembly, education and movement, he said lay persons had found a way to "live the Gospel in the heart of the nation" by organizing communities of prayer and charity and by celebrating the Liturgy of the Word.

NOVEMBER 1987

VATICAN

Polygamy — "The Church clearly teaches that the communion of love constituted by marriage is contradicted by polygamy," said the Pope Nov. 6 at a meeting with bishops from Ghana. "We need to insist that the conjugal communion of marriage is characterized by its unity and also by its indissolubility." He encouraged the bishops to explain to their people "with great pastoral love" that "the practice of polygamy directly negates the plan of God which was revealed from the beginning."

Scientific Respect for Human Dignity — In an address Nov. 12 at a Vatican-sponsored conference on "Humanization and Medicine," the Pope urged an international group of medical experts to resist modern "solutions and strategies" that offend human dignity. "The questions raised by experimentation, by the relationship between population and resources, by irreversible illnesses, are more pressing now that technical progress has made it easy to use solutions and strategies that offend the dignity of life and the human being. ... There are forms of scientific advancement that do not coincide with the authentic well-being of man. In those cases, scientific progress dissolves into a human regression" with dire consequences.

Participants in the conference said in a statement: "The most modern (technological) means can be put in use without ever jeopardizing the absolute respect due to the patient." Rejection or exploitation of a human being, "from conception to ultimate old age," is against the nature of medicine.

Tragic Imbalance in Food Supply — The Pope, describing the world food-supply imbalance as a "tragic situation," called on governments to develop and adopt a better system of distribution based on justice and concern for the weak. He told members of the United Nations Food and Agriculture Organization Nov. 13 that there was a glaring contrast between the surplus of cereals in some countries and the "real danger of death through starvation" in others. ... In responding to this tragic situation, there is an urgent and inescapable need for international solidarity. There exists a duty, now and in the future, to make resources available to those whose lives and welfare are the most threatened."

In a related development, the Pontiff appealed for emergency food aid for Ethiopians. On Nov. 18, he invited "everyone to participate in initiatives which aid organizations, especially Catholic ones, have begun to implement to avoid the threat of famine."

Immigrants and Their Families — Society must appreciate "the importance of the family in the migration phenomenon," declared the Pope in comments marking Italy's National Migration Day, Nov. 15. He expressed hope that "interested governments would pay greater attention to the rights of the families and not only to the productive capacity" of migrant workers.

Christian-Inspired Culture — Pope John Paul called for the creation of a "Christian-inspired culture" in which "liberty and co-responsibility, autonomy and interdependence, efficiency and solidarity would be wisely joined." Such a culture would be a "sign of contradiction" to individualism and collectivism," both of which lack a "perception of the transcendent dimension of the human person." So stated the Holy Father Nov. 20 in an address to 1,000 participants in a meeting on the theme, "Men, New Technologies, Solidarity: The Service of the Italian Church."

Reach Out to Lapsed Catholics — The Pope encouraged bishops from England and Wales Nov. 23 to reach out to Catholics who have ceased to practice the faith. Factors contributing to the fall-off in religious practice included "the pressures of modern living" and "atheistic" secularism. Also, he noted, doctrine and sacraments "are often replaced by individual religious sentiment or a vague and illusory search for the divine or the sacred. ... Some would seek to justify themselves by claiming that one can be a good Christian apart from the Church. With Scripture and tradition, however, we must insist on the unbreakable bond that exists between Christ and his Church."

Atheism and Materialism — The Pope told a group of East German bishops Nov. 27 that Catholics in their country should unite with other Christians in efforts to overcome "the danger of an atheism" which "ideologically permeates every sector of society and considers religion an absurdity." A godless ideology cannot adequately meet "the necessities of humanity and the important problems of the present and the future," he said. He also asked the bishops to counteract "the daily practical materialism" which "hardens the hearts and blinds the eyes."

Apartheid — In an appeal "to all those who hold power to recognize the rights of the oppressed," the Pope told bishops from South Africa and Namibia that apartheid should be overcome by a "conversion of hearts" which includes "sincere dialogue" and a willingness "to pardon, to be just and to be reconciled." He also said Nov. 27 that it is necessary to work for "liberation not only from structures that violate human dignity, but liberation from sin itself." He added: "Reason itself still pleads that violence not be accepted as a solution to violence."

General Audience Topics:

• "Jesus reveals himself as the Son of God who establishes God's kingdom in history" (Nov. 4).

• The miracles of Christ were "facts that actually happened. ... Whoever approaches them with intellectual honesty and scientific skill cannot get rid of them with a few words, as if they were pure inventions that came later" (Nov. 11).

• "The mighty works and wonders and signs" by which God affirmed the divine Sonship of Jesus (Nov. 18).

• How the "mighty works and wonders and signs" which he performed reveal his power to save the human family from evil and to restore it to communion with God (Nov. 25).

The Pope Also:

• Encouraged Catholics of Senegal Nov. 3 to engage in "friendly dialogue" with their Moslem countrymen.

• Condemned as an "outrage" an Irish Republican Army bombing Nov. 8 that killed 11 people attending a ceremony in Northern Ireland for British war dead.

• Told a group of Catholic family experts Nov. 16 that the physical and spiritual happiness of marriage is incomplete without self-control and self-sacrifice.

• Celebrated a traditional memorial Mass Nov. 17 for eight cardinals and 92 bishops who died since November, 1986.

Vatican Briefs:

• In an official critical appraisal of a major interfaith statement, "Baptism, Eucharist and Ministry," the Secretariat for Promoting Christian Unity called it a "remarkable achievement." The critique expressed reservations on numerous aspects of the document but said, however: "There is much that we can affirm, and we must build on these positive achievements." (See separate entry under Ecumenism.)

• Cardinal Luigi Dadaglio, president of the committee for the celebration of the Marian Year, called on charitable and health institutes affiliated with Marian shrines to provide care for AIDS victims and drug addicts.

• The U.S.-Soviet accord to remove intermediate-range nuclear missiles from Europe was highly praised Nov. 29 by *L'Osservatore Romano*, which called it the first step in real nuclear disarmament.

Beatifications

Pope John Paul beatified two German nuns and a French brother on All Saints' Day — Sisters Blandina Marten (d. 1918) and Ulrike Nisch (d. 1913), and Christian Brother Arnold Reche. During the ceremonies, he said living the Beatitudes is the way to sainthood.

Three weeks later, on Nov. 22, the Holy Father beatified 85 martyrs killed because of "hatred of the faith between 1584 and 1689" in the British Isles. In a joint statement issued three days before the beatification ceremony, Cardinal George Basil Hume of Westminster and Anglican Archbishop Robert Runcie of Canterbury said the faith of the martyrs "can serve as an inspiration even to those whose spiritual forebears held different Christian convictions."

NATIONAL

Inadequate Asylum Rules — In comments submitted to federal immigration officials, Carlos Ortiz Miranda said Nov. 6 that refugees were being offered insufficient protection under proposed rules for political asylum. The assistant general counsel of the U.S. Catholic Conference said the conference objected to: (1) the elimination of immigration judges to accept and review applications for asylum, and (2) the use of State Department country reports on human rights practices as the primary source of information on conditions in the nations of asylum-seekers. The comments stated that procedural safeguards in proposed rules would not guarantee a fair hearing to refugees who, if forced to return to their nations, might face "loss of life or freedom."

Criticism of Israel — Christians should be able to criticize the government of Israel without being labeled anti-Semitic, the Rev. Robert McAfee Brown told a gathering of interfaith activists Nov. 11. Addressing the 10th National Workshop on Christian-Jewish Relations in Minneapolis, the prominent Protestant theologian said Christians need to and can speak up against injustices they see Israel committing because Jews themselves need to and do so. "The internal debate in Israel should be a model for all nations," he said, adding that it is the "prophetic tradition" of the Jewish and Christian faith which mandates the voicing of concern when justice is at issue.

Marian Pilgrimage — More than 6,000 people from the Archdiocese of Newark took part Nov. 14 in a pilgrimage to the National Shrine of the Immaculate Conception in Washington. Archbishop Theodore E. McCarrick told those participating in the Marian Year observance: "There hasn't been a crowd like this since they built the shrine."

Seminary Enrollment — The total number of students for the priesthood in the U.S. dropped below 10,000 for the first time in decades, according to figures compiled by Benedictine Father Adrian Fuerst of the Center for Applied Research in the Apostolate. The drop was from 10,373 in 1986-87 to 9,410 in the current year.

Communion-Confirmation Problem — The Catholic practice of administering first Communion before confirmation to baptized persons is an obstacle to Catholic-Orthodox union. So stated the International Commission for Theological Dialogue between the Roman Catholic Church and the Orthodox Church in a document approved in June, 1987, and released this month. The commission observed that, in the early Church, the three sacraments of initiation — baptism, confirmation and the Eucharist — were administered in that order "in the course of a single, complex liturgical celebration," whose "pattern remains the ideal." Eastern Churches retained this unity of celebration, whereas the Latin-Rite Church placed Communion before, and separate from, confirmation. The commission called for "deep theological and pastoral reflection" on the matter.

Clinics Promote Promiscuity — School-based clinics which promote the use of contraceptives and provide abortion referrals convey "the strong message (that) sex outside of marriage is OK," said the 21 bishops of California in a statement entitled "Parental Primacy in the Raising of Children." By trying to stem "the tide of unwed parenthood among our children" through birth control, advocates of contraception overlook the real causes of teen pregnancy. Promotion of contraception rather than chastity also "sells children short by implying that they are incapable" of understanding the spiritual and moral dimensions of

News Events — November 1987

life. Several state Catholic conferences and a number of other bishops were also on record in opposition to school-based clinics.

The Center for Population Options, based in Princeton, N.J., reported that there were 61 clinics operating by the summer of 1986, and that an additional 100 were in the process of development. The Robert Wood Johnson Foundation was a major contributor to the School-Based Adolescent Health Care Program.

The Bishop and the Siege — Auxiliary Bishop Agustin A. Roman of Miami played a key role in developments leading to termination Nov. 29 of the state of siege at the federal detention center at Oakdale, La. He was instrumental in convincing Cuban detainees to release 26 hostages and to accept a government agreement to deal with problems related to the threat of their deportation.

Holocaust Can Be Viewed as Redemptive — "In my perspective, if the suffering of the crucifixion was infinitely redemptive, the suffering of the Holocaust, potentially conjoined with it, is incalculably redemptive. ... If suffering with patience and resignation and hope and faith and love inspires others, and simultaneously gives the sufferer a sense of compassion and new understanding toward others, then Jews must be perceived as grace-filled models. If suffering can ennoble, then Jews offer the world a nobility unsurpassed by any other people." So stated Cardinal John J. O'Connor in an article written for the winter edition of *Face to Face*, a quarterly journal published by the Anti-Defamation League. The cardinal wrote the article in order to explain the meaning of a definition of the Holocaust he framed in January, 1987: "The Holocaust is the greatest gift the Jewish people could give to the world." Many Jews — but not the Anti-Defamation League nor Agudath Israel — had been critical of the description.

Meetings: Meetings included those of:
• The Governing Board of the National Council of Churches, Nov. 4 to 6 in Jacksonville; the Rev. Patricia Ann McClurg was elected president for 1988-89.
• Nearly 400 members of the Catholic Worker movement, Nov. 6 to 8 in Las Vegas; to commemorate the 90th anniversary of the birth of Dorothy Day and to demonstrate in protest at the nuclear test site in Nevada.
• The 10th National Workshop on Christian-Jewish Relations, Nov. 8 to 11 in Minneapolis; attended by approximately 1,500.
• The National Council of Catholic Women, Nov. 8 to 12 in Minneapolis; attended by about 1,500.
• The National Catholic Youth Conference, Nov. 12 to 15 in Pittsburgh; attended by 3,500; the theme was "Love Is Our Shelter — Together We Build"; the plight of the homeless was a major subject of discussion.

National Briefs:
• The Covenant House ministry for runaways established a toll-free hot line (800-999-9999) for help from anywhere in the United States. Father Bruce Ritter reported that 2,500 calls were received the first day the line was open.

• Announced Nov. 13 was the decision of the First Catholic Slovak Ladies Association to contribute $500,000 toward construction of the new headquarters building for the National Conference of Catholic Bishops and the U.S. Catholic Conference.
• National Bible Week was observed Nov. 15 to 22, "to emphasize the importance of prayerful reading, reflection and study of the Word of God, and of application of its message in private and public life."

NCCB-USCC Meeting

About 300 bishops attended the annual meeting of the National Conference of Catholic Bishops and the U.S. Catholic Conference Nov. 16 to 19 in Washington, D.C.

Actions at the meeting included approval of: a statement critical of public school-based clinics providing contraceptive and abortion services; an appeal for peaceful settlement of conflicts in Central America; a national pastoral plan for ministry among Hispanics.

(See 1987 Meeting of the U.S. Bishops.)

INTERNATIONAL

Palestinian Refugees — Msgr. Antonio Franco, speaking Nov. 2 on behalf of the Vatican delegation to the United Nations, called Palestinian refugees "victims of a dramatic situation that has persisted for too many years." He quoted Pope John Paul to the effect that Palestinians "have a right to a homeland, as does any civil nation, according to international law." Msgr. Franco also told participants in debate on refugee relief that the Pontifical Mission for Palestine distributed in 1986 some $6.1 million in support of programs and projects which included the sponsoring of 7,856 needy children and support for: the Center for the Blind in Gaza, Egypt; the Mission du Sacre Couer in Haifa, Israel, for victims of birth defects; and clinics, refugee camps and public libraries.

Pancasila — The Indonesian bishops' conference was given a new legal identity — as a religious organization rather than a mass organization — and, with this identity, release from adherence to Pancasila, a national philosophy ordered to be the sole guiding principle of mass organizations. While the Church in Indonesia recognized basic principles of Pancasila, the bishops' conference held that the Church should not be forced to place the national philosophy above its own religious principles.

Murder Most Terrible — Cardinal Tomas O'Fiaich of Armagh condemned the bombing Nov. 8 at a ceremony for Britain's war dead which left 11 persons dead and 55 wounded. Most of the victims were in a crowd gathering for traditional Remembrance Sunday events in Enniskillen, Northern Ireland. The cardinal said the bombing "was deliberately designed to cause the maximum destruction of human life. ... Those who planned this deed, those who carried it out and those who in any way gave willing assistance to its execution, each and every one, are guilty of murder most horrible." The bishops of Ireland, England and Wales concurred with the prelate's characterization of the crime.

Violations of Rights — "Flagrant violations" of religious and other human rights were continuing in many countries, according to a U.N. report cited Nov. 12 by Archbishop Renato R. Martino, Vatican representative to the United Nations. Without mentioning names, he indicated that two of the countries guilty of violations of religious rights were Czechoslovakia (failure to grant the Church freedom in the choice of bishops) and Romania (where the Church was not recognized by the State because "it did not accept the law").

Christians in Lebanon — The struggle for survival of Christianity in Lebanon was the theme of talks by Emile Rahme in various parts of the United States during the month. He claimed to be head of the Christian Solidarity Movement, an organization which he said was comprised as an "elite" corps of approximately 500 doctors, lawyers, engineers and other professionals seeking to preserve the "last bastion" of Christianity in the Middle East.

Canadian Agriculture — The bishops of Saskatchewan, declaring that Canadian agriculture was suffering from a lack of "stewardship," urged Catholics to seriously consider alternative approaches to farming. "Any system which puts profit and 'efficiency' before the health of the land and the well-being of all its citizens must be seriously questioned," they said in a statement released in the middle of the month.

Religious Indifference — Children in Soviet Baltic countries were called "indifferent" to religion because their parents are forbidden to teach them religion, according to Vytautas Skuodis, a Catholic dissident recently permitted to emigrate from Lithuania. Children in Lithuania, Latvia and Estonia "don't despise Catholicism," he told reporters in Toronto. But, "since they're not taught about spiritual matters, they have no interest." He also said Communists intended to "destroy the Catholic Church in Lithuania" and to "suppress Lithuanian nationalism.... There is an intensive effort under way to deny Lithuanian culture and to Bolshevikize the nation"

More Refugees, Less Refuge — Dr. Elizabeth Winkler, secretary general of the International Catholic Migration Commission, predicted that in the 1990s there would be more refugees and fewer host countries willing to receive them. The attitude of most governments, except a few in Africa, appeared to be against acceptance,

Religious Rights in Burundi — The government which gained control of the country in a September, 1987, coup announced a number of measures affecting the practice of religion, including:

• restoration of weekly religious services, which had been banned;

• reopening of religious schools and seminaries, which had been expropriated;

• legalization of activities by catechists and other lay Catholics who had been responsible for weekly services in more than 600 places of worship;

• legalization of parish councils and meetings on church property;

• authorization for the use of mass media by religious associations;

• permission for foreign missionaries to work in the country.

The government rules were circulated Nov. 11 by *Fides*, the information agency of the Congregation for the Evangelization of Peoples.

Anti-Gypsy Demonstrations — Neighborhood demonstrations against government plans to build permanent camps for gypsies in Rome suburbs were "an alarming episode of intolerance toward a minority," said *L'Osservatore Romano* in a front-page eidtorial Nov. 22. It said the demonstrations had to be viewed in the context of "a systematic mentality of rejection and marginalization" against migrant workers and other large minorities in cities like Paris, London and New York, as well as Rome.

D'Aubuisson Accused of Romero Murder — Salvadoran President Jose Napoleon Duarte accused prominent right-wing legislator Roberto D'Aubuisson of ordering the assassination of Archbishop Oscar Arnulfo Romero as the prelate celebrated Mass in a hospital chapel Mar. 24, 1980. The charge had been leveled against D'Aubuisson several times in the past, but the Nov. 23 accusation was the first by Duarte, who said he based his statement on testimony by the driver of the assassin's getaway car.

International Briefs:

• Despite a ban imposed by the local bishop, pilgrimage Masses were still being celebrated at the site of alleged apparitions of Mary at Medjugorje, Yugoslavia.

• Oblate Missionary Father Miguel Rodrigo was shot to death while celebrating Mass Nov. 10 in Buttala, Sri Lanka. He had been a supporter of a controversial plan to end the violence of ethnic clashes which resulted in more than 90 deaths in the early part of the month.

• For services on behalf of French language and culture, Msgr. Charles B. Mouton, a native of Louisiana and former Vatican diplomat, was honored Nov. 18 by the French government with the Cross of Knight of the National Order of Merit.

Cardinal Obando, Mediator

Without changes in mind and heart, "we are going to face unvarying fixed positions; and, without a certain flexibility, mediation will continue for months on end." So stated Cardinal Miguel Obando y Bravo Nov. 8, in reference to his role in seeking peace in Central America, especially in his native Nicaragua. He was named in September to head the four-member National Reconciliation Commission charged with monitoring the Arias peace plan, signed Aug. 7 by Central American political leaders.

Success of the peace-seeking process was open to question. But, according to Gustavo Parajon, an independent member of the commission: Cardinal Obando is "the ideal person to serve as mediator because he has the confidence of the contras, and it now seems he has the confidence of the government as well."

DECEMBER 1987

VATICAN

Evangelization in Tanzania — Christians must proclaim the Gospel as well as set a good example in fulfilling their responsibility to evangelize, the Pope declared Dec. 4 at a meeting with Tanzanian bishops. Evangelization is "the baptismal responsibility of all. ... The witness of an exemplary Christian life is already an act of evangelization. (But) I hasten to add that the witness of Christian living through example is not enough in itself. It has to be preceded and accompanied by the proclamation of the Good News of salvation in Christ, which is at the heart of all the Church's action of evangelization." The Pontiff praised lay catechists for their "important contribution to the proclamation of the Gospel" in Tanzania.

Law and Genetic Manipulation — Pope John Paul called for legal restriction on non-therapeutic forms of genetic manipulation as a measure to protect human life and the unborn. He did so Dec. 5 at a meeting with 100 Italian Catholic legal experts discussing "juridical problems of biomedicine." He said: A "utilitarian culture" has legalized abortion and is now seeking to legalize euthanasia and human experimentation. "It is an alarming fact that the health field cannot, alone, confront (these developments) without the help of the law."

Pope and Patriarch — Pope John Paul and Ecumenical Patriarch Dimitrios I of Constantinople issued a joint statement Dec. 7 in which they pledged collaboration and continuing efforts toward church unity while rejecting "every form of proselytism" and "every attitude that would be, or could be perceived as, a lack of (mutual) respect." The statement also said that work of the International Catholic-Orthodox Theological Commission had shown that both churches express a common faith with respect to the mystery of the Church and the link between faith and sacraments. Differences of expression of a common faith do not represent an obstacle to communion. One substantial difference, however, is the status and ministry of the pope. Unlike the Orthodox, who attribute only a primacy of honor to the pope, the Catholic Church believes that the pope has primacy of jurisdiction over the whole Church and is infallible when formally proclaiming doctrine on faith or morals.

During the Patriarch's Vatican visit of Dec. 3 to 7, he was invited to join the Pope in blessing a throng of 50,000 people from the central balcony of St. Peter's Basilica.

Catholic Presence in Society — Pope John Paul urged bishops from southern France Dec. 14 to promote a more active Catholic presence in society, especially by lay persons. "Too often, it seems, Christians do not feel themselves personally responsible for this superior mission (to evangelize the world where one lives), leaving the task to the clergy or to some lay 'apostles' who are admired but not followed." He praised church movements for bringing the Gospel to the home and work place, and said the Church in France needed to be stimulated toward a "more courageous" demonstration of the faith. Invigoration of the sacramental life of local church communities was stressed by the Pope in meetings with French bishops making *ad limina* visits to the Vatican during the year.

Crisis in Poland — The Pope told a group of Polish bishops Dec. 17 that the current economic and social crisis in their country "cannot be cured superficially," and warned that the government should be careful not to destroy private economic initiative. He said it was a symptom of Poland's "deep crisis" that "the system can turn a man from his own workbench, annihilate economic initiative and indirectly deprive him of the very sense of work." He also stated that religious liberty, restricted in Poland, is so important that it cannot "remain isolated among all the other rights of the human being, the human community and society."

Abortion in Europe — The Church's concern about legalized abortion was the theme of the Pope's remarks Dec. 18 before a gathering of 450 persons attending a meeting on the right to life in Europe. "When the Church calls the state to task, it does not want to introduce a Christian state. It simply wants to promote a human state. ... It is easy to note the strident contradiction that exists between abortion legislation, already passed, unfortunately, throughout almost all of Europe and that which constitutes the greatness of European culture. ... In this incomparable cultural patrimony (of Europe), legalized abortion inserts itself as a foreign element, carrying with it the germ of corruption. On this point, Europe is gambling its destiny, because it is giving signs of moral decadence and even demographic impoverishment." The Pontiff encouraged those struggling in defense of the right to life: "Do not be frightened by the difficulty of the task. Do not be stopped by the realization that you are a minority. You are working to restore to Europe its proper dignity."

Acquittals — On grounds of "insufficient proof," an Italian appeals court announced Dec. 19 the acquittals of three Bulgarians and three Turks accused of complicity in the shooting of Pope John Paul in May, 1981.

Violence in Gaza and West Bank — Speaking 12 days after the outbreak of new fighting in Israeli-occupied territories, the Pope called Dec. 20 for an urgent end to violence and injustice there. "That land cannot continue to be treated as a theater of violence, confrontation and injustice, with suffering for those populations with whom I feel particularly close. ... We ask God in prayer that all the parties involved, and those in a position to collaborate, may put an end to this violence."

Arab Named Patriarch — The Vatican announced Dec. 28 that Pope John Paul had appointed the first-ever Arab Latin-Rite Patriarch of Jerusalem — Nazareth-born, 54-year-old Father Michel Sabbah, president of the Catholic University of Bethlehem.

General Audience Topics:
- The miracles of Jesus are signs of his power over creation, and give proof of his "saving power" and promise of redemption (Dec. 2).
- The miracles of Jesus were "real actions," and "it is clear" that the "true obstacle" to belief in the miracles recounted in the Gospels "is antisupernatural prejudice" (Dec. 9).
- A "spiritual atmosphere" should reign in families before Christmas (Dec. 16).
- Christians were urged to "find Jesus" at Christmas by turning away from "compromises, duplicity and selfishness" (Dec. 23).
- At year's end, "reflect on the loving providence of God and ... examine how well we have responded to the Lord's goodness and mercy to us" (Dec. 30).

The Pope Also:
- Met Dec. 4 with Mordechai Drory, Israeli ambassador to Italy, with whom he discussed conditions in the Middle East, Catholic-Jewish history and the State of Israel, according to an embassy spokesman.
- Advanced the canonization cause of Franciscan Father Junipero Serra, with acknowledgment of a miracle attributed to his intercession.
- Decried the terrorist bombing in Zaragoza, Spain, Dec. 11 in which 11 people were killed and 40 were wounded.
- Expressed "great sadness" at the deaths of perhaps 1,500 persons who drowned when two ships collided off the coast of Mindoro, the Philippines.
- Told nearly 25,000 persons that he was concerned about the lack of unity among Christians: "Like you, I am constantly distressed to see that Christians are not all united in the full communiion of faith and charity."

Vatican Briefs:
- Msgr. Fernand Franck, general secretary of the Pontifical Mission Aid Society, reported that in 1987 the agency sent more than $100 million in aid to institutions and projects in over 900 mission jurisdictions throughout the world.
- The Congregation for Divine Worship, in a letter made public Dec. 5, stated that concerts of religious or sacred music, but not of secular music, could be held in churches, on a limited basis and free of charge to the general public.

Christmas Message

In his Christmas message "To the City and the World," the Holy Father called for rejection of the idea that man can gain salvation by himself. While extending greetings of the season in 52 languages, he said:

"Will people know how to make use of such power (to become children of God)? Will they know how to welcome the extraordinary chance offered them in the Babe of Bethlehem to transcend the limits of their finiteness, the heavy dullness of their egoisms, in order to enter into the marvelous reality of the life of God, which is the fullness of light, joy and love? The question has been asked for every generation in history. But it returns with particular intensity in this our time, in the technologial age; because never, so much as today, has man been tempted to believe that he is self-sufficient, capable of building with his own hands his own salvation."

NATIONAL

Moment of Silence Appeal Rejected — The U.S. Supreme Court unanimously rejected Dec. 1 an appeal by New Jersey legislators to restore a daily "moment of silence" law in the state's public schools. The Court did not rule on the law itself, which had been called unconstitutional by two lower courts. The appeal was denied on grounds that the legislators who filed it no longer had legal standing to make the appeal. Left open to a possible future Supreme Court decision was the validity or invalidity of laws in about 25 states which, like the New Jersey statute, called for a moment of reflective silence but made no mention of prayer.

Funds for Nuns — The proceeds of special retirement-fund collections for nuns were reported by two dioceses in New York. In Albany, $912,000 was contributed by 198 parishes Nov. 7 and 8. Syracuse reported the receipt of more than $4 million in cash and pledges in the first stage of a five-year effort to realize an $8.4 million diocesan fund for retired sisters.

Freedom Sunday, INF Treaty — On the eve of the U.S.-Soviet summit meeting of President Reagan and Soviet General Secretary Mikhail Gorbachev, 200,000 persons participated in an interfaith Freedom Sunday rally Dec. 6 in Washington, in support of appeals for religious freedom in the Soviet Union and peace on earth. Bishop William H. Keeler, representing the National Conference of Catholic Bishops, and Archbishop James A. Hickey of Washington addressed the crowd assembled on the Mall of the nation's capital.

The INF arms control treaty signed by the President and General Secretary Dec. 8 provided for the elimination of U.S. and Soviet intermediate-range and shorter-range nuclear missiles. Ratification of the treaty was still required.

Homosexual Protests — Eleven persons were arrested during Sunday Mass Dec. 6 at St. Patrick's Cathedral, New York, while protesting against the Church's opposition to homosexual activity. They were among 35 individuals who remained standing during the homily and refused to sit down or leave the church when requested to do so. The arrests were the first in the course of monthly demonstrations that began in the cathedral in March, 1987, when the Archdiocese of New York ordered an end to Dignity-sponsored Masses celebrated at St. Francis Xavier Church in Lower Manhattan. Dignity was a nominally Catholic association of homosexuals with a policy at serious odds with the teaching and practice of the Church regarding homosexuality.

AIDS — "The Many Faces of AIDS: A Gospel Response," was the title of a statement produced by the 50-member Administrative Board of the U.S. Catholic Conference and released Dec. 11, 1987. (See separate entry.)

Abortion Developments — The U.S. Supreme Court, ruling 4-to-4 Dec. 14, upheld a lower court decision that struck down an Illinois law requiring a girl under age 18 to notify both parents 24 hours before having an abortion.

Catholic officials in Pennsylvania expressed surprise and criticism after Governor Robert P. Casey vetoed Dec. 17 the state's Abortion Control Act of 1987 on the grounds that it was probably unconstitutional. Provisions of the law required: that the unborn child's father be notified before the mother had an abortion; that the consent of parents or court be obtained before girls under age 18 could have abortions; that pregnant victims of rape or incest report those crimes before obtaining state-funded abortions; that hospitals report information on abortions; that government funds for legal services not be used for abortion-rights efforts.

In California, Superior Court Judge Morton Colvin granted an injunction Dec. 28 against a state law, scheduled to take effect Jan. 1, that would have required an unmarried girl under age 18 to get written consent from one parent or a court before obtaining an abortion.

Nun Salaries — Archbishop Edward T. O'Meara of Indianapolis directed that nuns working for the archdiocese be paid salaries equivalent to those of their lay counterparts, beginning July 1, 1989. "Past methods of compensation (currently $9,840 annually) for members of religious communities are not adequate to meet the needs of today," he said in announcing the pay increase. He also directed that retirement compensation for nuns working in the archdiocese be increased from the current amount of $800 to $2,000 annually, beginning in fiscal year 1989.

Surrogate Motherhood Rejected — With a resolution calling for an end to "profit-making and brokering of women, tissues or embryos," the 10,000-member American Medical Women's Association became the first organization of medical personnel to officially reject the business of surrogate motherhood.

It was reported that about 70 bills dealing with various aspects of surrogacy had been introduced in 27 states since the landmark Baby M decision was handed down in March, 1987, in New Jersey.

Support for Black Pastoral Projects — Auxiliary Bishop John H. Ricard of Baltimore told representatives of 112 dioceses at a meeting in St. Louis that a grant of $100,000 from the Black and Indian Mission Office would be helpful in putting into effect recommendations made the previous May by the National Black Catholic Congress. Recommendations included those for a workshop for priests, a conference on evangelization in the black community, and a leadership development program for lay volunteers.

National Briefs:

• The Chilean Vicariate of Solidarity was the recipient of the second annual Carter-Menil Human Rights Prize of $100,000; it was accepted by Cardinal Juan Francisco Fresno Larrain of Santiago, in ceremonies Dec. 10 in Atlanta.

• The United States Catholic Historical Society announced a plan to publish a comprehensive body of source materials on the response of Pope Pius XII to the Nazi persecution of the Jews. (The purpose of the venture was to counteract one-sided attacks on the Pope, who — despite widely publicized adverse assertions — was influential in providing refuge and aid to thousands of Jews in danger of their lives.)

• "There is nothing so important to the life of the Church and to the individual lives of its members as good liturgical worship," declared Bishop Joseph A. Fiorenza of Galveston-Houston in a pastoral letter entitled "Sunday: The Original Feast Day."

Leading 1987 News Stories

Thirty-eight U.S. and Canadian editors ranked the following news stories of 1987.
1. The visit of Pope John Paul to the U.S. in 1987.
2. The 1987 assembly of the Synod of Bishops.
3. Central American conflicts and the Arias peace plan.
4. Women's issues in the Church.
5. Catholic-Jewish relations, related to Waldheim and Cardinal Ratzinger incidents and other factors.
6. The "Instruction on Respect for Human Life in Its Origin and on the Dignity of Human Procreation," issued by the Congregation for the Doctrine of the Faith.
7. AIDS, a subject of pastoral and moral concern.
8. The Marian Year and the papal encyclical "Mother of the Redeemer."
9. Financial needs for the retirement of nuns.
10. Pastoral concern for Hispanic Catholics in the U.S.

The leading newsmaker was Pope John Paul.

INTERNATIONAL

Aid for Ethiopia — Caritas Internationalis appealed Dec. 1 to member aid agencies in 13 countries to raise a total sum of nearly $14 million to provide food and other assistance for thousands of people in Ethiopia. Once again, the country was reported to be "sitting right on the brink of a severe famine."

Conditions in Vietnam — The "climate of distrust" between Church and state in Vietnam seemed to be diminishing. "One senses a certain climate of openness and thus catches a glimpse of the possibility that the Church can undertake social programs and contribute to the reconstruction of the country." So stated Bernard Holzer, vice president of Catholic International Cooperation for Development and Solidarity, Dec. 2 on Vatican Radio.

On the negative side in 1987, a priest and 20 other Catholics were arrested and jailed, and the government exerted pressure against the canonization of 117 Vietnamese martyrs.

Unconstitutional Action in Haiti — The bishops of Haiti said in a statement Dec. 4 that it was unconstitutional for the government to disband the country's independent electoral council, and announced that they would not name a representative to a new election board. The bishops also condemned election "atrocities" which resulted in cancellation of the nation's first free national election in 30 years. The official death toll for Nov. 29

was 34, but journalists estimated that more than 200 persons had died. Churches and a Catholic-run radio station were among targets of violence attributed to members of the terrorist Tontons Macoutes, supporters of former President Jean-Claude Duvalier.

Brazilian Social Programs Defended — The Permanent Council of the Brazilian Bishops' Conference defended the prelates' social action programs, saying that social change must be "founded upon great moral and religious values." The council also warned Christians not to participate in groups supporting "scandalous concentration of lands for the big landowners," because such support was "in clear opposition to the social teachings of the Church." The council's statement, "At the Service of Truth, Justice and Life," was issued late in November, following a series of newspaper accusations which resulted in a congressional investigation of the bishops' Indigenous Missionary Council and its work with Indians.

Millions at Guadalupe Shrine — A spokesman for the Archdiocese of Mexico City reported that more than three million people visited the Basilica of Our Lady of Guadalupe during the several days around the Dec. 12 feast of the Patroness of the Americas. Cardinal Ernesto Corripio Ahumada prayed during a feast day Mass that Mary would intercede for the Church in Mexico, so that it might be "the conscience of a people who have always been believers, but who lately have lost their way." He was critical of social injustice in the country and warned Mexicans that hard times lay ahead. "We won't be able to have what we've had, to spend what we've spent, to waste as we have in the past."

Central American Peace Plan — The Central American peace plan, signed Aug. 7, was called a "house of cards" that was likely to topple without U.S. and guerrilla support, according to Auxiliary Bishop Juan Gerardi Conedera of Guatemala City. Nevertheless, he called the Arias plan a "beacon of hope" because it had drawn international attention to conditions in Central America.

Hope in Burundi — Cardinal Jozef Tomko, interviewed on Vatican Radio Dec. 23 after a trip to Burundi, said he found in the country an atmosphere of "relaxation, joy and hope" in place of previously existing restrictions on church activity. The prefect of the Congregation for the Evangelization of Peoples said the government in power since September had restored nearly all of the traditional rights of the Church.

Corruption in Lebanon — In a message released Dec. 24, Maronite Patriarch Nasrallah Pierre Sfeir said that foreign occupying forces, power-seeking politicians and corruption had combined to shatter Lebanon. "The country is cut up into small pieces. The occupying forces are numerous, with a foot on the chest of the people. The state is nothing but an aggregate of mini-powers imposing themselves on the citizens."

Problems in Mexico — As Mexicans prepared for the celebration of Christmas:

• Archbishop Adolfo Suarez Rivera of Monterrey called for a more democratic electoral system. He said the government, "in not complying with its duty to respect the vote of the citizenry and to create conditions of security for voters, has removed from them the serious obligation of casting their votes."

• Archbishop Juan Jesus Posadas Ocampo of Guadalajara called attention to the "widening gap between the superfluous possessions of the minority and the subhuman needs of the majority."

Homelessness in Canada — "Homelessness in our richly endowed country is a social evil, a social sin, because the knowledge, the talent and the resources to correct it exist if we, as Canadians, have the political will to act." So stated Archbishop James M. Hayes, president of the Canadian Bishops' Conference, in a Christmas message. He said homelessness was as real in Canada as in Third World countries. He cited as powerless "the elderly, single parents with small children, native people, unemployed young people, mentally or physically handicapped persons who are unable to care for themselves and cannot get institutional help. . . . In addition, refugees . . . are knocking at our doors, seeking safe haven. Like Mary, Joseph and the Christ Child, these people have found no room at the inn, but this time the inn is called Canada."

In another development, a coalition including the bishops' Social Affairs Commission called Dec. 8 for nationwide opposition to what it said were market-oriented government policies and private-industry trends which had increased unemployment and made life harder for the poor. In a 17-page document, the interfaith Working Committee for Social Solidarity appealed for full employment, economic controls to assure the creation of jobs, revitalized government, equal pay for equal work, improved social programs and increased taxation of the wealthy.

International Briefs:

• Father Victor Acuna Cardenas, archdiocesan welfare director, was shot to death while celebrating Mass Dec. 3 in Ayacucho, Peru. The Ayacucho area was the center of operations of Marxist *Sendero Luminoso* guerrillas.

• A "good number" of Catholics in Gabon were coming under the influence of dissident Archbishop Marcel Lefebvre's Priestly Society of St. Pius X. So stated Bishop Felicien-Patrice Makouaka of Franceville Dec. 7 during a meeting with the Pope at the Vatican.

Dissident Church in China

A report appearing in *Ming Pao*, a Chinese-language newspaper published in Hong Kong, said the ordination of two more bishops early in the month brought to 53 the number of illicitly consecrated bishops serving the government-controlled Patriotic Association of Chinese Catholics not in communion with the Pope and the Catholic Church. Also reported were 220,000 baptisms since 1980 and more than 2,700 religious personnel in service in 112 dioceses and 2,100 restored churches.

The number of people maintaining fidelity to the Catholic Church was not known.

JANUARY 1988

VATICAN

Racism — It is "a grave violation of the dignity of the human person and his fundamental rights," declared the Pope Jan. 4 during a meeting with Wilted Joseph Phiri, Zambian ambassador to the Vatican. The remark was interpreted as criticism of South Africa and its rigid policy of racial discrimination.

Civil War in Sudan — At a meeting Jan. 7 with Sudan's ambassador to the Vatican, the Pope appealed for efforts of "mutual understanding and dialogue" to end five years of civil war in the southern part of that country. He expressed "grave concern" over the conflict while asking for more international assistance for the nation.

Critique of Nuclear Deterrence — "The fear of 'mutually assured destruction,' which is at the heart of the doctrine of nuclear deterrence, cannot constitute, in a lasting way, a viable base for security and peace." Nuclear deterrence must be replaced by a strategy in which mutual security is based on an "intertwining of vital interests and relations ... in a context of detente and cooperation." So stated the Pope in an annual address Jan. 9 to diplomats accredited to the Vatican. He praised the "political will" of the U.S. and the U.S.S.R. "to physically destroy an entire class of weapons." He noted, however, that the accord signed by President Reagan and Soviet leader Mikhail Gorbachev Dec. 8, 1987, covered "a very limited portion of their (nations') arsenals."

Environmental Concern — Exploiting natural resources solely for economic reasons has led to increasing pollution and the danger of turning the earth into an "abandoned desert," the Pope told a group of young Italian farmers Jan. 9. He called for "rational management of the environment, with due regard for human as well as economic values.

Inculturation — Helping Christians understand what it means to evangelize cultures is a "complex and arduous task," but one of "primary importance." So stated the Holy Father before participants in the Jan. 14-to-17 plenary meeting of the Pontifical Council for Culture. Lay persons must make the Gospel "more present in the living tissues of cultures: the family, work, school, the university, the means of social communication. ... The problems concerning faith and inculturation ... assuredly merit a deep study to illuminate a proper pastoral approach" to the subject.

Polarization in Holland — The Holy Father agreed with Cardinal Adrianus Simonis that the Church in The Netherlands remained deeply divided despite seven years of effort by the Vatican to promote unity. The Cardinal said: "We bishops are trying to adapt the Church's mission in a society which is rapidly changing. Spreading secularization and individualism have changed traditional society." The Pope, concerned about "polarization within the ecclesiastical community," told the bishops to:

• dialogue with dissident Catholics;

• improve the training of priests, so they might retain the "transcendental dimension" of their ministry;

• impart a profound knowledge of the Church's spiritual dimension in catechetical programs.

The Pope called for the avoidance of anything "which could lead to the formation of a parallel (rival) clergy" in conflict with the authentic clergy. He also urged action to "prevent religious institutions (especially religious orders) from becoming a form of alternative church, a refuge for those who find it difficult to accept the legitimate authority of the bishops."

Christian Unity — Pope John Paul began the Week of Prayer for Christian Unity Jan. 18 with an appeal to Catholics to pray more intensely for that intention. At week's end, he expressed hope that the celebration later in the year of the 1000th anniversary of the baptism of St. Vladimir, King of Kievan Rus, would stimulate efforts toward unity between Catholics and Russian Orthodox.

Christian Witnesses — In an address Jan. 28 to a group of bishops from West Germany, the Pope urged West German Catholics to present their Christian witness as an antidote to the "strong tendency to secularization in your society." The Church must be "strong and spiritually prepared if it wants to change the world with its faith witness," he said.

John Bosco's 100th Anniversary — In a letter commemorating the 100th anniversary of the death of St. John Bosco, the Pope called on educators to help develop a "critical conscience" in students by offering them religious values, sympathy and patience. The letter, addressed to about 17,000 Salesians in more than 1,200 schools and other institutions throughout the world, was published Jan. 30, a day before the actual date of the death of the founder of the Society of St. Francis de Sales.

General Audience Topics:

• "The miracles performed by Jesus during his earthly ministry are signs of God's power and love" (Jan. 13).

• "Ecumenism is a response in faith to the will of Christ himself, who desires us all to be one" (Jan. 20).

• "The mystery of Jesus Christ as true God and true man is central to our faith and the key to Christology" (Jan. 27, at the start of a new series of talks).

The Pope Also:

• Told future diplomatic officers of the Vatican that they should serve the Church with self-sacrifice and dedication, without using their positions to gain "honor or personal advantage."

• At a meeting Jan. 22 with Jamaican Ambassador Mignonette Patricia Durrant, said international peace and justice required that no nation be excluded from the "good things" — political, social or economic — of the world.

• At the end of the month, as talks got under way for peace in Central America, met with Nicaraguan President Daniel Ortega, Cardinal Miguel

Obando Bravo of Managua, Salvadoran Archbishop Arturo Rivera Damas, and Honduran Foreign Minister Carlos Lopez Contreras.

Vatican Briefs:

• Israel downgraded, from full- to part-time, the status of its liaison officer to the Vatican. The action was viewed as an expression of Israeli displeasure with the existing state of its relations with the Vatican.

• The Congregation for the Doctrine of the Faith was said Jan. 18 to be studying the moral aspects of non-payment of taxes by Catholics who object to the way in which the revenue is used.

Peace Day Message

"Religious freedom, an essential requirement of the dignity of every person, is a cornerstone of the structure of human rights, declared the Pope in a message for the 20th annual observance of World Peace Day, Jan. 1.

He developed the theme, "Religious Freedom: Conditions for Peace," with considerations regarding the dignity and freedom of the hunan person, religious freedom and peace, the responsibility of religious people, and the commitment of the followers of Christ.

This was the 20th annual commemoration of World Peace Day. The observance was begun by Pope Paul VI, to emphasize the need for peace.

NATIONAL

Chastity — In a pastoral statement on human sexuality issued Jan. 4, the 16 bishops of Texas called the observance of chastity "perhaps one of the greatest needs of our time.... Our sexuality is a beautiful and magnificent gift from God," but all forms of sex outside marriage "pervert" the gift. "Sexual permissiveness and promiscuity" are a form of "slavery" and "an enemy of love.... The virtue of chastity does not ... seek to suppress one's sexuality" but, rather, "frees us to live joyfully as the masters, not slaves, of our natural inclinations and desires."

Wrongful Birth Suit — A three-judge panel of the District of Columbia Court of Appeals reinstated Dec. 31 a "wrongful birth" suit brought against an obstetrician by the mother of a child with Down's syndrome. The woman claimed that her doctor deprived her of the right to decide whether to have an abortion and thus avoid the birth of her daughter. Richard Doerflinger, assistant director of the U.S. bishops' Office for Pro-Life Activities, said Jan. 6 in comment on the decision: Courts "unintentionally make themselves into tools of pro-abortion advocacy" by upholding such suits against physicians "who fail to facilitate the abortion of a mentally disabled child.... These suits could make it legally and financially impossible for pro-life physicians to practice obstetrics."

Withdrawal of Nutrition and Hydration — A bishop's endorsement of discontinuing food and water for a woman in an irreversible coma sparked debate between those viewing the withdrawal as a first step toward legalized euthanasia and those regarding it as ending extraordinary medical treatment. Bishop Louis E. Gelineau of Providence said Jan. 11 that it would be in accord with Catholic moral teaching to allow nutrition and hydration to be stopped for a woman who had been in a coma for two years. The statement was not in accord with one issued by the Pontifical Academy of Sciences in 1985, that treatment of a person in a permanent irreversible coma "is not required, but all care should be lavished on him, including feeding." The American Academy of Medical Ethics was authority for a statement saying that it is "never right and ought never legally be permitted" to deny food and water for those permanently unconscious or seriously debilitated "as a means of securing their deaths."

Bigotry — Nationwide proliferation of religious and racial bigotry in recent years was the subject of "They All Don't Wear Sheets: A Chronology of Racist and Far-Right Violence 1980-1986," a report compiled under the auspices of the National Council of Churches. Kenyon Burke, a staff member of the NCC, said at a Washington press conference Jan. 13: "Either we learn to live as brothers and sisters in an open society, or ultimately we will destroy ourselves and perish as fools." A total of 2,919 incidents of violence included 121 murders, 145 shootings, 301 cross-burnings and 302 assaults.

Adolescent Family Life Act Program — The U.S. Catholic Conference and other groups urged the U.S. Supreme Court to allow participation by religious organizations in a federal program aimed at curbing teen-age sexual activity. The conference contended in a brief that the decision of the U.S. District Court in Washington against participation demonstrated "hostility toward religion that is itself a threat to religious liberty," and encouraged unnecessary church-state "antagonism." In a separate brief, the Legal Defense Fund of Americans United for Life argued that "to exclude an otherwise eligible organization from participation in a government program merely because of its religious affiliation raises serious constitutional questions." At issue was participation by Catholic agencies in implementation of the 1981 Adolescent Family Life Act. It was noted that Congress had specifically called for involvement by "religious and charitable organizations" in the program.

Week of Prayer for Christian Unity — God's love can help Christians face a world fraught with fear, cynicism and despair, said a message for the observance of the Week of Prayer for Christian Unity, Jan. 18 to 25. The theme of the Week was "Love Casts Out Fear" (1 Jn. 4:18). The message, by officials of the National Council of Churches and the National Conference of Catholic Bishops, said: "There is fear of rejection simply because one is different.... There is fear which arises out of hatred and suspicion between nations and races and classes of people.... There is fear of war of such catastrophic proportions that any future for humanity cannot be envisioned.... This quest for Christian unity is a vital component of the quest for human unity. Both are more urgent and more necessary than ever before."

News Events — January 1988

Permanent Deacons — The Secretariat for the Permanent Diaconate, National Conference of Catholic Bishops, reported Jan. 19 that there were 8,443 permanent deacons and 1,885 candidates for the permanent diaconate in the U.S. as of Oct. 31, 1987. The statistics were based on information received from 140 dioceses.

Corporate Responsibility — One hundred and 55 resolutions, filed by about 100 church groups with 125 companies, were reported in "Church Proxy Resolutions 1988," published by the Interfaith Center on Corporate Responsibility. Among the resolutions were those seeking the withdrawal of business relations with South Africa, equal opportunity for employment in Northern Ireland, equal employment opportunity for women and members of minority groups in the U.S., negotiated debt settlement for Third World countries and reduced manufacture of military weapons. Companies to which stockholder resolutions were directed included American Brands, Data Design, DuPont, TRW, United Technologies, Ford, General Motors and IBM.

National Briefs:

• Beverly Carroll, executive director of the Urban Commission of the Archdiocese of Baltimore, took office Jan. 4 as the first director of the Secretariat for Black Catholics, National Conference of Catholic Bishops.

• A report disclosed Jan. 12 that home mission activities received $10.2 million in support from the American Board of Catholic Missions during a recent 18-month period.

• The Paulist Fathers issued the first edition of a magazine entitled *Catholic Evangelization in the United States of America*. Father Kenneth Boyack, the editor, said: "With 53 million active Catholics and 19,400 parishes, Catholics are now in a position to make a significant difference in the evangelization of people in the United States."

• The 100th anniversary of the death of St. John Bosco was celebrated Jan. 31 by Salesians at a solemn Mass in St. Patrick's Cathedral in New York. January 31 was also the first day of an international holy year for youth, proclaimed by Pope John Paul.

March for Life, Presidential Proclamation

An estimated 50,000 persons from across the country converged on Washington Jan. 22 to join the March for Life, in a demonstration of opposition to legalized abortion and of support for the right of the unborn to life. The march, with counterpart demonstrations in many cities, marked the 15th anniversary of the U.S. Supreme Court's decision in Roe v. Wade, which legalized abortion, and the toll of at least 22 million abortions since 1973.

President Reagan, while designating Jan. 17 to be National Sanctity of Human Life Day, issued the following proclamation.

Now, therefore, I, Ronald Reagan, President of the United States of America, by virtue of the authority vested in me by the Constitution and laws of the United States, do hereby proclaim and declare the unalienable personhood of every American, from the moment of conception until natural death, and I do proclaim, ordain, and declare that I will take care that the Constitution and laws of the United States are faithfully executed for the protection of America's unborn children. Upon this act, sincerely believed to be an act of justice, warranted by the Constitution, I invoke the considerate judgment of mankind and the gracious favor of Almighty God. I also proclaim Sunday, January 17, 1988, as National Sanctity of Human Life Day. I call upon the citizens of this blessed land to gather on that day in their homes and places of worship to give thanks for the gift of life they enjoy and to reaffirm their commitment to the dignity of every human being and the sanctity of every human life.

In witness whereof, I have hereonto set my hand this fourteenth day of January, in the year of our Lord nineteen hundred and eighty-eight, and of the Independence of the United States of America the two hundred and twelfth.

— Ronald Reagan

INTERNATIONAL

Cubans Urged To Stay Home — While praising U.S.-Cuba accords permitting greater emigration from the island, the bishops of Cuba invited "Catholics to discard easy or selfish motives in any emigration plan," and to stay home in order to "announce the Gospel here. . . . Love of country demands at times our efforts and sacrifices." The prelates said dialogue had eased church-state tension to some extent, but that "instability and conflicts" continued to exist. The bishops' statement was read at Masses the weekends of Dec. 20 and 27.

Death Toll in Northern Ireland — Political violence in Northern Ireland in 1987 took a toll of 93 lives, including 11 slain in a single bombing. Responsibility for 60 of the killings was claimed by the outlawed Irish Republican Army, an organization roundly condemned by bishops of the country.

Death Squads in El Salvador — Archbishop Arturo Rivera Damas called Jan. 3 an apparent resurgence of death squads in the country a "nefarious sin" and pledged to seek ways to stop it. He appealed for "an end to this practice, which threatens the consolidation of a true democracy as well as being a nefarious sin that goes against the Christian spirit." In December, 1987, alone, 25 civilians were reported killed in death squad-type fashion.

Chinese Bishops Freed — Bishop Ignatius Kung Pin-mei of Shanghai, 87, who was imprisoned on treason charges for nearly 30 years before being paroled in 1985, was pardoned by the Chinese Communist government Jan. 5. Also announced was the release in November, 1987, of 80-year-old Bishop Peter Joseph Fan Xueyan of Paoting who had been serving a 10-year prison sentence on charges related to his duties as a bishop. Both prelates were in communion with the Pope.

Surrogate Center Banned — A West German court ordered Jan. 6 the immediate closing of a Frankfurt surrogate motherhood center, stating that it was contrary to the nation's adoption laws and to basic moral principles. The center had been operated by United Families International, an American company. Its work was called an affront to human dignity by a government official.

Amnesty Denied Killers — Judge Consuelo Salazar Alvarenga de Revelo of the 1st Criminal Court of Zacatecoluca rejected the amnesty appeal of five former national guardsmen convicted of murdering four U.S. churchwomen Dec. 2, 1980, in El Salvador. In a ruling handed down Jan. 8, she said: "The court finds the appeal for amnesty to be without grounds and therefore rejects it," without right to further appeal. The murdered missionaries were Maryknoll Sisters Ita Ford and Maura Clarke, Ursuline Sister Dorothy Kazel and lay missionary Jean Donovan.

French Interfaith Council — It was reported Jan. 8 that the bishops of France voted 106 to 2 on Nov. 9, 1987, to join with representatives of Protestant and Orthodox churches in forming the country's first Council of Christian Churches. A statement said activities of the council would be related to Christian witness, charitable service, and social issues such as unemployment, racism and problems connected with AIDS and its victims. Catholic representatives on the council were led by Cardinals Albert Decourtray of Lyons and Jean-Marie Lustiger of Paris.

No Arab Authority — Troubles in Israeli-occupied territories stemmed from the fact that Arab residents had no share in authority over the regions, according to Latin-Rite Patriarch Michel Sabbah of Jerusalem. In an interview published Jan. 10 in the Italian Catholic newspaper *Avvenire*, he spoke about discrimination against Arab Christians in occupied areas. "Discrimination? There is this fact: the Arabs are an occupied people. These Arabs do not participate in authority. Especially in the occupied territories, this is a reality." The question of social difficulties "depends entirely on this juridical position: The Arabs are not in control. They are governed and live in (Israeli) administered territories."

Ratzinger Lectures — "Consumer Materialism and Christian Hope" were themes addressed by Cardinal Joseph Ratzinger in the annual Fisher Lecture Jan. 25, at the invitation of the divinity faculty of Great Britain's Cambridge University. He said the modern age rejects objective moral values. "The opposing world views of today have a common starting point in the rejection of the natural moral law and the reduction of the world to mere facts." But moral values and laws give people dignity. And, "the moral law which the Church teaches is not a special burden for Christians, but man's defense against attempts to reduce him to nothing." He said the awareness of values such as freedom and justice was high but cautioned against letting it evaporate into romanticism. "It is easier to demonstrate for rights and freedom than to practice in everyday life the discipline of freedom, or to bind oneself to service by the sacrifice of the greater part of one's freedom."

Biblical studies and interpretation were the subjects of the Cardinal's Emmaus Lecture Jan. 27 in New York. The address was sponsored by the Rockford Institute's Center on Religion and Society, under the leadership of the Lutheran Rev. Richard J. Neuhaus.

New Abortion Legislation Needed in Canada — The head of the Canadian Conference of Catholic Bishops called for new legislation against abortion following a Supreme Court decision that the nation's restrictive law was unconstitutional. Archbishop James M. Hayes said the decision was "a dramatic challenge to all lay members of the Church and to all of us, their pastors," because "the sacredness of life is being violated. . . . The situation of 'abortion on demand' that follows from the court's decision must be corrected legislatively as soon as possible. . . . This is our common task now, and the future of our human society depends on how soon and how well it is done. . . . The need for responsible political action was never more urgent," because "God's law condemning abortion is not changed by the Supreme Court decison." The court ruled 5-to-2 Jan. 28 that the existing law was in violation of the Canadian Charter of Rights and Freedoms, declaring: "Forcing a woman by threat of criminal sanctions to carry a fetus to term unless she meets certain criteria unrelated to her own priorities and aspirations is a profound interference with a woman's body and thus an infringement of security to the person."

International Briefs:

• Amnesty International cited 18 countries in which "the most basic rights" of children were violated, Jan. 5.

• Vatican Radio reported Jan. 12 that the bishops of Yugoslavia had complained to the government about restrictions on religious freedom in the armed forces and the withdrawal of passports from priests and members of religious orders.

• Christian Brother Anton De Roeper reported that turbulent conditions in the Israeli-occupied West Bank were "destroying" Catholic-run Bethlehem University.

• A Vatican official, Archbishop Fiorenzo Angelini, speaking during a conference on AIDS in London, said Jan. 27 that efforts to stop the spreading disease and care for its victims must be based on "the safeguarding of ethical principles which cannot be renounced."

Petition for Religious Liberty

More than 90,000 persons signed a petition calling for full restoration of religious liberty in Czechoslovakia, Vatican Radio reported Jan. 16. The 31-point petition urged the Communist-controlled government to end restrictions on the appointment of pastors and bishops, the enrollment of students for the priesthood, activities by religious orders, association by lay persons, religious instruction, and religious television and radio broadcasting. The petition also proposed:

• an end to government jamming of Vatican Radio programs;

• permission to build new churches;

• restoration of church goods and property;

• an end to government removal of religious symbols from roadsides;

• permission for people to travel outside the country on religious pilgrimages.

FEBRUARY 1988

VATICAN

Religious Art — In an apostolic letter commemorating the Second Council of Nicea (787), the Pope asked bishops to "maintain firmly the practice of proposing to the faithful the veneration of sacred images in the churches," and to "do everything possible so that more works of truly ecclesial quality may be produced." He also said: "The believer of today, like the one yesterday, must be helped in his prayer and his spiritual life by seeing works that attempt to express the mystery (of faith) and never hide it." The council, recalled in the letter made public Feb. 4, upheld the use of sacred images against the Iconoclasts who contended that their use was a form of idolatry.

Politicians' Commitment — Pope John Paul told a group of Italian politicians Feb. 6 that they should be dedicated to a commitment of "service and love." Because of the many difficulties and human needs which constantly challenge local leaders, a politician must always keep strong and clear his "moral conscience, social sensibility and political farsightedness." These strengths, combined with "technical competence," can help resolve problems and meet the requests of citizens. In addition, the Pope called politics not only "the art of the possible" but also the "science and art of service."

Message for Lent — In a Feb. 8 message to the faithful, the Holy Father said: "I strongly urge you, in this liturgical period of Lent, to allow the Spirit of God to take hold of you, to break the chains of selfishness and sin. In a spirit of solidarity, share with those who have fewer resources than yourselves. Give, not only things you can spare but things you may perhaps need, in order to lend your generous support to the actions and projects of your local church, especially to ensure a just future for (abused) children who are least protected. . . . May our faithfulness to our Lord and our generous deeds bear witness to our obedience to his commandment."

A special appeal for repentance and conversion in Western Society was made by the Pope on Ash Wednesday, Feb. 17.

Meeting with U.S. Congressmen — "Your public service is aimed at the unity and common good of all," declared the Pope Feb. 10 during a meeting with 11 members of Congress. "And it demands that you make every effort to safeguard and enhance the rights and dignity of every human person, from the moment of conception until natural death. . . . You have a particularly serious responsibility to promote justice and to overcome the scandalous inequalities that exist between the rich and the poor, the powerful and the powerless."

Our Lady of Lourdes — The Holy Father marked the feast of Our Lady of Lourdes Feb. 12 with Mass in St. Peter's Basilica. He called the apparitions of Mary in 1858 a "special sign" of her presence in the mission and work of the Church." He also said: "The miracles of Lourdes are the miracles of Christ, obtained by the intercession of Mary." At Lourdes, a "privileged place of Christian experience, . . . We learn to know Christ through Mary. . . . One learns that the faith alleviates suffering, in that it makes it acceptable as a means of expiation and as an expression of love." The Lourdes shrine is visited by more than four million people a year.

For Religious Freedom in Sudan — The Pope criticized the government of Sudan because of its efforts to restrict religious freedom, at a meeting with bishops of the nation Feb. 13. Even in a country where a particular religion (Islam) has "special status" because it represents the beliefs of a majority (73 per cent), the state "cannot claim to impose that religion on all of its people or restrict the religious freedom of other citizens or of foreigners living within its territory." Since religious freedom "touches the most intimate sphere of the human spirit," no group or state "can claim authority in the sphere of religious convictions." The Pontiff also called for a "negotiated settlement" of the bloody, five-year civil war that would respect "the just aspirations of the people involved."

For Peace in Lebanon — The Holy Father appealed Feb. 28 for peace and solidarity for the "beloved people" of Lebanon during an address to visitors and pilgrims in St. Peter's Square. "We unite with the Lebanese in invoking from the Madonna peace, solidarity and a rapid solution of the problems that so test that land," he said. In addition, he noted that Orthodox and Moslems as well as Catholics in Lebanon "feel profoundly bound to Mary. . . . In 13 years of grave sufferings, the invocation of all Lebanese to the most holy Virgin, 'Our Lady of Lebanon,' has been continuous and intense."

At the beginning of the month, the Pope said Feb. 2 that Lebanon was trapped in a "fury of destruction."

Religious Dimension in Education — "If religion is neglected or set aside in the educational process that forms a nation's heart and soul, then a morality worthy of man will not survive. Justice and peace will not endure." So stated the Pope Feb. 29 in an address to 10 members of the Bishops' Conference of England and Wales. While praising their efforts on behalf of Catholic schools, he said they must safeguard the "Catholic character" of the schools, particularly through the proper training of teachers. Backgrounding the papal remarks was a British government proposal to eliminate religion from the "core subjects" taught in the nation's schools.

General Audience Topics:

• "In continuity with Sacred Scripture and the tradition of the Church, the Second Vatican Council repeated the doctrine of Jesus' true humanity and emphasized the new relationship that the Incarnation initiates between Jesus, the Word of God, and every human being" (Feb. 3).

• "Jesus draws near to sinners in order to free them from sin. He shows great love and profound solidarity toward every person, who is created in

God's image and likeness" (Feb. 10).

• "In his self-emptying, Jesus shows the truth of what it means to be human." While Adam and Eve sought to be like God, Christ became man "in order to restore men and women to their original dignity" (Feb. 17).

The Pope Also:
• Discussed Middle East issues with King Hussein of Jordan, Feb. 1, and Egyptian President Hosni Mubarak, Feb. 5.

• During a private meeting with Maltese Prime Minister Edward Fenech Adami Feb. 12, said that church-state relations, long troubled, were "on the road to solution."

Vatican Deficit — In a first-ever officially released annual financial report, the Vatican disclosed that its 1986 deficit amounted to a record $56.7 million. The three major entries in the report were $57,258,223 in income, $113,981,595 in expenses and the deficit of $56,723,375. The deficit was liquidated from funds realized in the 1986 Peter's Pence collection and from reserves in hand from previous contributions.

Vatican Briefs:
• "What Have You Done for Your Homeless Brother? The Church and the Housing Problem," was the title of a document issued Feb. 2 by the Pontifical Commission on Justice and Peace. (See separate entry).

• Television offers "almost unthinkable possibilities of information, but also of disinformation; of the spread of culture, but also of its betrayal." It can help in the formation of youth, yet also offer "subtle forms of diseducation, particularly in the sector of recreation and entertainment." This was the tenor of remarks by Cardinal Agostino Casaroli Feb. 14 during the commemoration of the 30th anniversary of the proclamation of St. Clare as the patron saint of television.

• The Congregation for Divine Worship issued Feb. 20 a "Circular Letter concerning the Preparation and Celebration of the Easter Feasts," calling for appropriate instruction for greater appreciation of the Holy Week liturgy.

• Ninety percent of the lay persons employed by the Vatican took part in a work slowdown Feb. 29 in protest against what they considered to be unilateral management decisions affecting them in an adverse manner.

Sollicitudo Rei Socialis

This is the title ("On Social Concerns") of Pope John Paul's seventh encyclical letter, commemorating the 20th anniversary of *Populorum Progressio* ("The Development of Peoples"), the encyclical of Pope Paul VI, and extending the reach of its social teaching. (See separate entry.)

NATIONAL

The Catholic Press — It "remains the most effective instrument we have for ongoing formation in a timeless faith and for continuing stimulation to ever-needed charity," said Archbishop John P. Foley in a statement about the February observance of Catholic Press Month. "Catholics need a dependable source of authentic information about Christ's Church, their Church, and about the moral questions which fill their lives every day. They need to know how they can live close to God in their families and in their work. They need to know about the needs of others . . . so that they can help in the name of Christ and so that they don't become selfish themselves." Archbishop Foley was president of the Pontifical Commission for Social Communications.

Surrogate Contracts Illegal — The New Jersey Supreme Court ruled Feb. 3 that surrogate contracts involving payment for a woman to bear a child were illegal and "perhaps criminal." Ruling in the "Baby M" case, the court awarded custody of the child, Melissa Elizabeth Stern, to her father, William Stern, and his wife, Elizabeth, and restored parental rights to the child's surrogate mother, Mary Beth Whitehead-Gould. William F. Bolan, Jr., executive director of the New Jersey Catholic Conference, said in comment about the decision: "The court embraced the argument which we had advanced, that money paid by a couple in connection with the baby born to a surrogate mother violates our state law." He added, however: "We cannot agree with that portion of the ruling which would permit surrogacy where there is no payment, because that arrangement would also, in our judgment, violate Catholic moral theology."

Black Catholics — Director Beverly Carroll said early in the month that the newly created Secretariat for Black Catholics, of the National Conference of Catholic Bishops, would "fill a void" in the Church's recognition of black Catholics and would ensure "a black voice at the highest level" of the Church. She called 1987 "a banner year" of developments for black Catholics, including:

• deliberations of the National Black Catholic Congress in May, which produced a national pastoral plan;

• the appointment of members of the new NCCB Committee on Black Catholics;

• Pope John Paul's meeting with black Catholics in New Orleans in September;

• appointment of the 12th black U.S. Bishop, the Most Rev. Curtis J. Guillory, S.V.D., auxiliary of Galveston-Houston.

Violation of Rights — Representatives of church groups named in a five-year FBI probe of organizations opposed to Reagan administration policy in Central America expressed dismay at what they called a violation of their constitutional rights. What began as a probe of the Committee in Solidarity with the People of El Salvador apparently developed into an investigation of hundreds of individuals and groups, including members of at least two orders of nuns, three Catholic parishes and a Milwaukee-based food program run by the Society of St. Vincent de Paul. One of the groups, the Maryknoll Sisters, issued a statement Feb. 2 in which they said the probe endangered "the democratic principles on which this country is founded."

Vatican Instruction a Sure Guide — The Vatican's 1987 "Instruction on Respect for Human Life in Its Origin and the Dignity of Procreation" is "a sure guide on how respect for human life in its origin can be shown and the dignity of procreation preserved." So stated Notre Dame University philosophy professor Ralph McInerney at a medical-moral conference attended by about 200 bishops early in the month in Dallas. The instruction, by the Congregation for the Doctrine of the Faith, said that procreation techniques that do not involve sexual intercourse between husband and wife are morally wrong and a threat to humanity. It condemned in vitro fertilization, surrogate motherhood and other procreative techniques, and warned against genetic engineering, the freezing of human embryos, fetal experimentation and the immoral application of prenatal diagnostics. McInerny said dissent from the contents of the instruction stemmed from moral relativism.

Pornography — Pornography is "loveless" and "glorifies sex for its own sake," said the 13 bishops of Wisconsin Feb. 10 in a statement urging passage of a state anti-pornograpy bill. They called it "an evil that desensitizes and degrades all who use it, insults and victimizes all women, promotes sexual violence and violates the minds and bodies of innocent children." The title of the statement was "An Ethical Evaluation of Pornography and a Call for Legislative Action." Wisconsin was one of eight states without obscenity statutes.

Value Education Rated First — Parents surveyed in the Archdiocese of Dubuque chose Catholic elementary schools for their children primarily because of their value-oriented mission, according to Sister Mary Leanne Welch, curriculum director of the archdiocese. Her dissertation focused on 23 factors that parents believed important to the moral and academic growth of their children. The highest rated items were the development of "a healthy self-concept," basing decisions on "Christian values," learning "self-discipline," mastery of mathematics and "respectful response to authority."

Fund for Sisters — The Archbishop's Fund for Sisters in Los Angeles opened a grant-review process during the month to award more than $2 million to congregations of women Religious around the world to assist them in their work. Sister of Charity Barbara Garland, executive director of the fund, said it was supported by the Hilton Foundation and had $2.5 million to distribute annually. In the first funding period, from November, 1986, to October, 1987, a total of $1,710,002 in 76 grants was approved for projects in nine countries and 25 states in this country.

Abortion Violates Founding Principles — The legalization of abortion in the U.S. violates some of the basic tenets upon which this country was founded, said Archbishop Daniel E. Pilarczyk in an article in the Feb. 26 edition of the archdiocesan *Catholic Telegraph*. By legalizing abortion, the government exempted unborn children from equal protection under the law and "made every unborn child legally vulnerable. . . . In doing so, government posited a threat against us all. If unborn human beings can be left legally unprotected, what about human beings at the other end of life: the terminally ill, the senile, those who have lived out their 'usefulness'? If society can take away the protection of life from one group, it can take that protection away from us all. Here we are dealing not with theology but with simple social logic."

Return to Practice of the Faith — An estimated 1,000 individuals, and families living within the Diocese of Arlington returned to practice of the Catholic faith in response to a September-to-December media outreach campaign, according to Ellen McCloskey, communications director of the diocese. The campaign focused attention on the theme: "There was a time when we were together; perhaps it's time to be together again."

National Briefs:

• The University of Arizona was named one of three test sites for determining the age of the Shroud of Turin; the other two sites were Oxford University in Great Britain and the Federal Institute of Technology in Zurich, Switzerland.

• World Marriage Day was observed Feb. 14, under the sponsorship of Worldwide Marriage Encounter.

• "Building Self-Reliance" was the theme of Operation Rice Bowl, sponsored annually during Lent by Catholic Relief Services to raise funds for the needy.

• Anthony M. Kennedy was sworn in Feb. 18 as the 104th Justice of the U.S. Supreme Court and the third Catholic on the current Court.

Progress in Seattle

Cardinal Joseph L. Bernardin reported Feb. 26 that Seattle's Archbishops — Raymond G. Hunthausen and Coadjutor Thomas J. Murphy — were "progressing quite well" in addressing Vatican concerns about earlier reported pastoral irregularities in the archdiocese. The subjects of concern were operations of the archdiocesan tribunal, the acceptance of church teachings, ecclesiology, Christology, seminary programs, the role of conscience in decision-making, general absolution and intercommunion, liturgy and ministry to homosexuals.

Cardinal Bernardin was one of three prelates appointed in 1987 by the Vatican to monitor remedial developments in the archdiocese. The other two members of the commission were Cardinal John J. O'Connor of New York and Archbishop John R. Quinn of San Francisco.

INTERNATIONAL

Alleged Vision — Cardinal Jaime Sin of Manila ordered an investigation of an alleged appearance of the Blessed Virgin Mary Feb. 2 before a crowd in the back yard of a private residence in Quezon City. People at the scene said they had seen the sun spinning and giving off different colors; one person said the vision of Mary was "in the center of the sun, reaching out her hand."

Problems Greater than Yes or No to Contra Aid — The general secretary of the Latin American Bishops' Conference warned Feb. 8 that resolution of the problems of Nicaragua and the rest of Central America was not a simple matter of a U.S. Congressional vote for or against contra aid. Auxiliary Bishop Oscar Andres Rodriguez said the

Church favored "non-violent solutions," and that "we're all" in favor of the peace plan of Costa Rican President Oscar Arias. But the success of the plan would depend on the development of true democracy. "Without democracy, it will not be possible to have peace."

Embryo Ban Rejected — At a meeting Feb. 8 to 11 in London, the General Synod of the Church of England rejected a total ban on embryo experimentation. In another action, the synod supported a proposal that all surrogate motherhood arrangements should be left outside the protection of the law, in order to discourage the practice.

Panama's Need for Reform — In a Vatican Radio interview Feb. 9, Archbishop Marcos McGrath of Panama City said the Church had been trying "to orient our government since the military takeover of 1968 toward a form of civil democracy." He added that the process "had come along quite far" until about six months earlier when major divisions surfaced in the military and people began demonstrating in the streets against the regime of Gen. Manuel Noriego. Under such circumstances, the Church defended the right of people to express themselves, "but insisted on non-violence." Gen. Noriega was under indictment in the United States for trafficking in drugs.

Terror in Mozambique — A Christmas letter from religious superiors to 800 missionaries in Mozambique painted a portrait of death, fear, hunger and homelessness in the war-torn country. "The minds and the wills of the people are paralyzed by fear. Only those who live on location are aware of the killings, the theft, the vengeance, the arbitrary accusations, the hunger, the suffering, the sickness, the nakedness, the lack of housing and the insecurity." The letter described burned-out "no man's lands" between warring government and anti-government forces, widespread flight to the cities by "terrified" villagers, and the breakup of families. Isolated missionaries were at risk of ambush and abduction.

In Vitro Fertilization — Four Catholic university hospitals in Western Europe were still performing in vitro fertilizations despite a 1987 declaration by the Congregation for the Doctrine of the Faith that the procedure is immoral. The hospitals were associated with the universities of Nijmegen, The Netherlands; Louvain and Leuven, Belgium; and Lille, France. The practice was reported by Theo Palstra, a spokesman for the Dutch Bishops' Conference, several days after the Vatican issued a statement saying it would not tolerate practices in Catholic hospitals that violate moral principles.

Indians Sheltered from the Army — It was reported late in the month that a Guatemalan bishop had turned a 17th-century monastery into a sanctuary for Indians who believed their lives were threatened by the army in its search-and-destroy missions against rebel forces. Bishop Gerardo Humberto Flores Reyes said he thought the Indians had good reason to fear the troopers because of massacres perpetrated by the army between 1978 and 1985, when more than 100 of their villages were wiped out.

Protest in South Africa — South African church leaders raised a chorus of protest over the government's latest, wide-ranging clampdown on 17 leading anti-apartheid groups, including the umbrella-like United Democratic Front. The Southern African Bishops' Conference, for its part, called the use of curbs and other restrictions on anti-apartheid activists a "malignant cancer" in South African society and urged the government to stop the practice "before it is too late." Under the ban imposed Feb. 25, affected organizations remained legal but were forbidden to carry out any activity without permission from the government. The ban also muzzled the press.

More Room for Unions and Private Enterprise — The bishops of Poland, in a sharp critique of government economic policies, called for more space for private enterprise and independent labor unions. Strengthening the role of private enterprise, they said, would help individuals and society at large. At the same time, they said collectivist sectors of the nation's economy should be depoliticized. The prelates' statement, published in the Feb. 28 edition of *L'Osservatore Romano*, was issued several weeks after the government increased prices for many goods, in the latest of a series of unpopular measures to deal with a chronic economic crisis.

International Briefs:

• Bethlehem University, the only Catholic university in Israeli-occupied West Bank, was ordered closed indefinitely by Israeli military authorities Feb. 1.

• Visiting foreign priests heard confessions and celebrated Mass recently for about 50 isolated Catholics in Burma who had not been able to receive the sacraments for more than 12 years.

• Bishop Jean Khamse Vithavong of the Vientiane Vicariate said Feb. 3 that church-state relations in Laos had improved: "I am satisfied with the church situation at present and with the government policy toward the Catholic Church."

• Archbishop Ismael Blas Rolon of Asuncion called the reelection Feb. 14 of Gen. Alfredo Stroessner to an eighth term as president a "farce" which "changes nothing" and "will serve to increase tensions" in Paraguay.

• Thousands of persons marched in protest Feb. 27 in Mexico City against an art exhibit they called "sacrilegious" because of its blatant offensiveness to religious sensibility and reverence.

Christians Leaving the Holy Land

The emigration of educated Christians from the Holy Land for a more prosperous and peaceful life elsewhere threatens the future of the Catholic Church in the region, according to Latin-Rite Patriarch Michel Sabbah of Jerusalem. "We can't guarantee that the Christian world will always be represented in the Holy Land," he said in an interview with *The Southern Cross*, newspaper of the San Diego, Calif., Diocese. "People are going to the (United) States and elsewhere, trying to escape the minority situation." He estimated that each year 20 to 30 percent of the 300 graduates of Bethlehem University leave the country in search of jobs and better opportunities.

MARCH 1988

VATICAN

Fearless Media — In an address Mar. 3 to members of the Pontifical Commission for Social Communications, the Pope said he hoped "every Catholic in the communications media will be fearless in the presentation and defense of truth, even when that truth may be unpopular at a particular time or in a particular place." He encouraged communicators to stand for "the rights and dignity of every human being" Such rights include the right to life, housing, education, a just wage and freedom to express one's religious belief.

Spiritual Development and Ecumenism — Christian churches can hope to achieve "full communion" only by deepening their spiritual foundations, declared the Holy Father Mar. 4 at a meeting with Bishop Johannes Hanselmann, president, and other officials of the Lutheran World Federation. While viewing the visit of the Lutherans to the Vatican as "a sign of commitment to the deepening of our relationship," he spoke in praise of progress in Catholic-Lutheran theological dialogue and of efforts to "bear common witness on pressing social concerns."

Iran-Iraq Bombardment — "We are dealing with babies, women and the elderly, defenseless people," stated the Pope Mar. 6 as he condemned the bombing of civilians by warring Iran and Iraq. The attacks, which "violate the norms of international humanitarian law, . . . should provoke firm condemnation." He called on the nations' leaders to take "initiatives to finally put an end to this terrible conflict," in the wake of reciprocal missile attacks on the Iraqi capital of Baghdad and the Iranian capital of Teheran.

AIDS Problem: Christian Response — Christians should respond to the AIDS problem by proclaiming chastity and marital fidelity while offering compassion to victims, but not by promoting the use of condoms, declared an article in the Mar. 10 edition of *L'Osservatore Romano*. "To seek the solution to the disease in the promotion of the use of prophylactics is to take a path that is not only unreliable from a technical point of view but also, and above all, unacceptable from a moral point of view."

Eucharist — The Pope spoke about the "peace-giving and unifying" power of the Eucharist Mar. 11 at a meeting with planners of the 1989 International Eucharistic Congress to be held in Seoul, South Korea. The peace of the Eucharist is, in the first instance, "an individual's acceptance of Christ and the divine will." "Subsequently, this peace extends to social relations. . . . By means of the boundless love which he communicates to human hearts, Christ in the Eucharist urges the faithful to foster warm and constructive relationships with everyone, and to work untiringly for the spread of peace throughout the world." People who live by eucharistic love are "convinced that conflicts can be resolved and that social justice can prevail."

European Unity and Christian Values — "It is my profound conviction that, if Europe wishes to regain its fundamental unity, it must turn to the values which Christianity caused to emerge in European society and culture from the beginning." So stated the Pope Mar. 17 in remarks to members of the Council of Europe. "With its achievements and failures," he said, "Europe has left an indelible mark on the course of history," and added: Today the Continent must discover the "common patrimony and civilization of its peoples and nations," despite "physical, political and ideological divisions."

1,000 Years of Christianity — In a 40-page apostolic letter made public Mar. 22, the Holy Father commemorated the millennium of the baptism of St. Vladimir and the people of Kievan Rus. He urged Russian Orthodox as well as Ukrainian Catholics to celebrate the event in an ecumenical spirit and for the sake of peace between the churches and in the world. The title of the letter was *Euntes in Mundum* ("Go into All the World"). (See separate entry for excerpts.)

Racial Discrimination — The Pope condemned racial discrimination Mar. 20, calling it a "painful wound that still exists in various parts of the world, sometimes even under particularly cruel forms." He said Christians should avoid any behavior favoring or maintaining any form of racial discrimination. He noted that church teaching about the dignity and rights of people as children of God should be affirmed "always" and "forcefully."

Priestly Celibacy — In a letter to priests throughout the world, the Holy Father reaffirmed Mar. 25 celibacy "for the whole of our lives" and told priests to have recourse to Mary in times of difficulty. "We freely renounce marriage and establishing our own family, in order to be better able to serve God and neighbor. . . . Our priestly choice of celibacy . . . should . . . be placed within (Mary's) heart. We must have recourse to the Virgin Mother when we meet difficulties along our chosen path."

Eastern Liturgical Tradition — The Holy Father paid tribute Mar. 25 to the liturgical tradition of Eastern churches during a Slavic-Byzantine ceremony that included the singing of a venerable 1,500-year-old Marian hymn. During his sermon on the Solemnity of the Annunciation of the Lord, he praised "the splendors of the Byzantine liturgy" and said the Akathist hymn reminds Christians "how indissoluble is the event of the Mother of God from the entire economy of salvation."

Religious Life in Russia — The Pope complimented participants in a Mar. 25-26 meeting in Rome for "turning (their) attention to believers living in difficulty." While not naming the Soviet Union, he complained of parts of the world where religious liberty is "badly interpreted or openly trampled upon. . . . Believers become objects of suspicion and distrust, almost as if they were less trustworthy than other citizens." Instead, they are "a factor for peace, development and cooperation for the common good" because they are "stimulated to live in goodness, justice and truth." One of the sponsors of the meeting was the Russian Ecumenical Center in Rome.

General Audience Topics:
• New Testament accounts of the life, death and resurrection of Jesus "reflect firsthand knowledge" and provide the basis of the Church's faith in his divinity (Mar. 2).
• The definition of the divinity of Jesus by the Council of Nicea in 325 — against the heretical opinion of Arius — "continues to be relevant today in the face of tendencies, both old and new, to see Christ as only an extraordinary man, but not God" (Mar. 9).
• "The Council of Ephesus (431) . . . condemned Nestorius and insisted that the eternal Word of God and the Son of Mary are one and the same. Therefore, Mary can rightly be called 'Mother of God' " (Mar. 16).
• "The early ecumenical councils insisted on the full humanity of the Incarnate Word, while at the same time teaching that Christ's human actions and his knowledge and will, as well as his capacity for suffering and death, belong to a divine Person" (Mar. 23).
• "In union with the suffering Christ, we must accept what God sends, confident that there is a reason for our crosses. . . . We must also pray for those who, through lack of faith, do not understand why they must suffer" (Mar. 30).

The Pope Also:
• Asked Mar. 13 for prayers that "in the land of St. Patrick the political and terroristic violence, which for almost 20 years has caused death and suffering in both Catholic and Protestant communities, may cease."
• Said Mar. 17 he hoped that "difficulties of application (regarding religious education in Italy) will find solutions fair and satisfying for all," in the context of the 1984 revision of the concordat between the Vatican and Italy.

Vatican Briefs:
• In an article appearing in the Mar. 2 edition of *L'Osservatore Romano,* Cardinal Paul Poupard wrote that sects generally "present themselves as perfectly compatible with belief in Christianity. In reality, the re-figuring of Christ which these present has nothing to do with the Jesus of the Gospel nor the God he revealed. . . . Christ is shattered into many sectarian pieces and disseminated according to the religious ideology of each one." The Cardinal's comment had special reference to the Unification Church of the Rev. Sun Myung Moon.
• Contributions in 1987 for reduction of the Vatican's annual budget deficit amounted to more than $50 million; the amount was $9 million short of the total needed for complete coverage.

Humanae Vitae Is Not Debatable

Pope Paul VI's condemnation of artificial birth control in the encyclical letter *Humanae Vitae* is "a teaching which belongs to the permanent patrimony of the moral doctrine of the Church. . . . The uninterrupted continuity with which the Church has proposed (this teaching) is born from its responsibility for the true good of the human person." So stated the Pope Mar. 14 in an address to participants in the Fourth International Congress for the Family in Africa and Europe.

He took exception to pastors and theologians who challenge *Humanae Vitae,* calling its teaching open to debate.

NATIONAL

Abortion Counseling and Referral — The Reagan administration suspended implementation Mar. 3 of regulations barring abortion counseling and referral in federal family planning programs. The suspension was announced after a U.S. District Court in Boston issued an injunction against enforcement of the rules nationwide. The stated purpose of the rules was to prohibit programs, known as Title X, "from encouraging, promoting or advocating abortion as a method of family planning," and "to require that Title X programs maintain physical and financial separation from prohibited abortion activities." Judge Walter Jay Skinner said the regulations violated the First Amendment right to freedom of speech.

Kerner Report 20 Years Later — Twenty years after the Kerner Commission warned that the nation, fueled by racism, was rapidly "moving toward two societies — one black, one white — separate and unequal," a group of experts on racism and urban affairs said the "Kerner Report is coming true. . . . The country isn't as different as it should be." Auxiliary Bishop Joseph A. Francis of Newark agreed. He said Mar. 4 that the report "was absolutely correct in its prophetic statements," and added: "Education, employment and housing remain the greatest sources of irritation and injustice for blacks."

Lefebvre Seminary Moving — Followers of dissident and suspended Archbishop Marcel Lefebvre were reported to be moving their St. Thomas Aquinas Seminary from Ridgefield, Conn., to Stockton, Minn., because more room was needed to accommodate an increasing number of students for the Priestly Society of St. Pius X. Bishop John G. Vlazny, within whose Diocese of Winona the seminary would be located, said the move was being made "neither in consultation" with him "nor with our approval." The move was announced Mar. 15 by Father Richard N. Williamson, rector of the seminary.

Nation's First Black Archbishop — Bishop Eugene A. Marino, auxiliary of Washington for 14 years, was appointed Archbishop of Atlanta Mar. 15. At a press conference shortly after his appointment by Pope John Paul was announced, he said: "I come to proclaim the Gospel of Jesus Christ . . . to bring good news to the poor, and the poorest are those who do not know Christ." Proclaiming the Gospel "must be supported by visible witness through education, advocacy and works of service" in continuance of past efforts in the archdio-

Parental Right To Control Children's Education — Catholic parents have a right and duty to control the education of their children, particularly with respect to sexuality, said Cardinal Edouard

News Events — March 1988

Gagnon in an interview with the *Arlington Catholic Herald*. The president of the Pontifical Council for the Family said he was "amazed that the country which speaks so much about freedom would not recognize the freedom of anyone to say what he thinks about certain textbooks." In 1986, the Cardinal was criticized for describing as a "travesty of sex education" a textbook series used in many U.S. dioceses.

Networks Seeking To Oust Church from National Debate — Richard H. Hirsch, secretary of communication for the U.S. bishops, declared that TV networks are trying to "privatize religion" and oust the church from participating in public-policy debate on such issues as nuclear disarmament and the economy. The networks reflect a movement which seeks to remove from the public arena religious groups which feel "an obligation to be a part of the national debate that's forming the values of society." Part of society "tends to want the church to stay inside of the sanctuary." And, with television, "you see the same thing happening — that attempt to privatize religion and somehow get it out of the national debate." Hirsch made his comments during the "Christopher Closeup" TV program Mar. 20.

Anti-Semitic Passion Plays — Because Christ's passion "touches upon the most sacred and central mysteries of the faith," depictions of the events surrounding his death must "conform to the highest possible standards of biblical interpretation and theological sensitivity.... Any presentations which explicitly or implicitly seek to shift responsibility from human sin onto this or that historical group, such as the Jews, can only be said to obscure a core Gospel truth." So stated the Bishops' Committee for Ecumenical and Interreligious Affairs Mar. 24 in a statement entitled "Criteria for the Evaluation of Dramatizations of the Passion."

Civil Rights Act — Congress overrode Mar. 22 President Reagan's veto of the Civil Rights Restoration Act. The law overturned the 1984 Supreme Court ruling in the Grove City College case, in which the Court declared that only the federally funded program in such institutions as universities, not whole institutions, could be penalized for violations of civil rights. The U.S. Catholic Conference supported the bill after it was amended to include (1) a provision to prevent its use to demand abortion coverage and (2) a "religious tenets" exemption to prevent religious organizations from being unduly burdened.

Not Right To Withhold Food, Water — In a statement released Mar. 24, about 100 theologians and ethicists rejected on moral and legal grounds the withholding or withdrawing of food and water from non-competent, non-dying patients. Except in rare circumstances, it "is not morally right nor ought it be legally permissible" to withhold food and fluid from patients in irreversible comas or who are otherwise debilitated. "Food and fluids are universally needed for the preservation of life, and can generally be provided without the burdens and expense of more aggressive means of supporting life. Both morality and law should recognize a strong presumption in favor of their use." The statement, entitled "Feeding and Hydrating the Permanently Unconscious and Other Vulnerable Persons," was released in *Issues in Law and Medicine*, a publication of the National Legal Center for the Medically Dependent and Disabled, in Terre Haute, Ind.

National Briefs:

• Archbishop Francis T. Hurley of Anchorage urged priests of the archdiocese during Lent "to remind our people of the spiritual experience (of the sacrament of penance) so many are missing."

• Puerto Rican Sister M. Isolina Ferre, 73, known for her work with juvenile delinquents in New York and Puerto Rico, was named 1988 recipient of the United Way of America's Alexis de Toqueville Society Award.

"It's Over, Debbie"

Cardinal Joseph L. Bernardin, among others, was shocked at an account in the *Journal of the American Medical Association* of a physician-assisted suicide of a 20-year-old terminal cancer patient. The doctor's action "can only be described as immoral," the Cardinal said in a guest editorial column in the Mar. 10 edition of *The Chicago Tribune*.

In the article, entitled "It's Over, Debbie," an unnamed gynecology resident in a large, private hospital was requested late one night to attend a patient he had never seen before. She was a 20-year-old woman reportedly dying of ovarian cancer, in extreme pain, suffering "unrelenting vomiting," and unable to sleep. She said to the doctor, "Let's get this over with." He wrote: "I could not give her health, but I could give her rest." He did so, in death, with a fatal overdose of morphine.

INTERNATIONAL

Patriotic Chinese Bishop — Auxiliary Bishop Aloyisus Jin Luxian of Shanghai was elected to head the diocese by the government-sanctioned Patriotic Association of Chinese Catholics. The Vatican-appointed Bishop of Shanghai was Ignatius Kung Pin-mei. Bishop Kung, after 30 years in detention, was released on parole in 1985; his parole was lifted and his political rights were restored in January, 1988, but the government would not permit him to function as a bishop.

Tension in Paraguay — Pro-government mobs disrupted Masses in a small Paraguayan town as church-state tension continued rising less than two months before Pope John Paul's scheduled visit to the country. A mob of 200 civilians armed with clubs and guns, and led by a local official of the pro-regime Colorado Party, broke into a church Mar. 6 in Carapegua during a Mass at which a statement denouncing a similar incident was to have been read, according to news reports. Archbishop Ismael Blas Rolon of Asuncion was quoted as saying that the Church was having problems with the Stroessner government, in power for more than 30 years. He also declared that the

South African Protest — Four archbishops and four bishops escalated their protest against the banning of anti-apartheid organizations with an unprecedented public demonstration Mar. 11.

Change in Cuba — "In general, one can speak of a change of atmosphere (in Cuban church-state relations), even if they are not sensational facts." So stated Msgr. Carlos Manuel de Cespedes Mar. 12 in a Vatican Radio broadcast. Welcome changes included government authorization for the admission of 20 missionaries into the country and the importation of 30,000 Bibles in 1987. Individual rights remained restricted, however, and: "In the field of religious liberty," the Church hoped for "more access to the mass media" and the "construction of new churches."

Israeli Repression — An influential Jesuit magazine described Israel's violent repression of the four-month-old Palestinian revolt as a "vendetta." An article in the Mar. 19 edition of *La Civilta Cattolica* said the killing and maiming of Palestinian protesters and innocent bystanders by occupation troops in Gaza and the West Bank were "brutal" and "horrendous." Three thousand Palestinians were under detention at the end of the month.

Romero Anniversary — In El Salvador, a crowd of more than 40,000 jammed downtown San Salvador Mar. 24 in a demonstration commemorating the eighth anniversary of the death of Archbishop Oscar Romero, who was shot to death while celebrating Mass in a hospital chapel. The crowd was reported to be larger than in previous years, and the masking of many paraders, to avoid identification, was thought to be a sign of a new wave of political repression in the volatile country.

Unorthodox Views — Father Saturnino Dias, deputy secretary of the Indian Bishops' Conference, rejected charges that the Vatican had acted improperly in barring Jesuit theologian Father Aloysius M. Bermejo in 1987 from teaching at an Indian seminary because of unorthodox published views regarding:
• the identity of the Catholic Church as the true Church of Christ;
• the role of Scripture in understanding Christian revelation;
• the nature and infallibility of ecumenical councils;
• papal infallibility and primary jurisdiction over the whole Church.

Czech Demonstration Broken Up — Riot police prevented about 2,000 people in Bratislava from holding a protest demonstration Mar. 25 that had been banned by the government; hundreds of demonstrators were beaten and arrested. One demand of the demonstrators was for government clearance for the appointment of bishops by the Vatican. The regime was opposed to Vatican efforts to name as bishops priests who did not belong to the *Pacem in Terris* association of priests favored by the government.

No Progress on Rights — A conference on European security and humanitarian issues was recessed Mar. 26 after reporting some progress on new negotiations on conventional arms but no significant movement on human rights. The 16-month-long conference was one of several provided for by the 1975 Final Act of the Helsinki Conference on Security and Cooperation. The Vatican was a signatory of the Final Act, along with the Soviet Union, the United States, Canada, and all European nations except Albania. The Soviet Union was said to be stonewalling movement on human rights.

Bishops Ask for Noriega Resignation — Because of "the urgent need to clarify the legitimacy of the executive authority of the nation, as it remains unrecognized at present by large sectors within and outside the country," the bishops of Panama called for the resignation of Gen. Manuel Noriega, the country's military chief and de facto ruler. The prelates asked Noriega in their statement of Mar. 29 to "separate himself from his position as soon as possible." At the same time, they said: "The Church has always been ready to offer its services in the search for peaceful and constructive solutions. For this reason, the Panamanian Bishops' Conference is willing to support this initiative, if both sides acccept it positively." Noriega was the target of U.S. efforts for his ouster from Panama and legal action against him on charges of drug trafficking and related corruption.

Caritas, the charitable agency of the Archdiocese of Panama, reported that it had distributed food to more than 6,000 families affected by the nation's economic and political turmoil.

International Briefs:
• Irish and English Catholic officials reacted with anger and horror to the rash of sectarian killings in Northern Ireland over the previous month. The latest victims were two British soldiers, killed Mar. 19 in Belfast during a funeral.
• The Constitutional Court of Italy upheld Mar. 31 Article 5 of the nation's 1978 law on abortion, permitting a married woman to have an abortion without informing or consulting with her husband.
• The Chilean Vicariate of Solidarity was named recipient of the 1988 Simon Bolivar Prize for its activities benefitting human freedom, dignity and independence, by UNESCO.

Marxism and Capitalism

Findings of a Vatican survey released Mar. 4 indicated that Marxism and capitalism were declining ideologies in the East and West but were still potent and antagonistic forces in the Third World.
• In Soviet-bloc countries, "ideology based on historical and dialectical materialism seems to be irreversibly in decline," leaving people "deprived of the freedom necessary to feel responsible and respected in their dignity and their right to exercise initiative in their private lives and public commitments."
• The industrialized West is marked "by hedonism, the loss of the sacred character of life and utilitarian pragmatism." Technological progress "is one of the factors that most strongly shapes contemporary mentalities."
• In Third World countries of Latin America, Africa and Asia, Marxism and liberal economics have strong holds as competing ideologies promising social progress.

The survey, begun in 1985 and based on 170 responses from around the world, was conducted by the Secretariat for Non-Believers.

APRIL 1988

VATICAN

New Head of Knights of Malta — Pope John Paul approved the election of Andrew Willoughby Ninian Bertie as the new head of the Sovereign Military Order of the Knights of Malta. Bertie was elected during a conclave Apr. 8 at the Knights' headquarters on Rome's Aventine Hill. (See Knights of Malta.)

Respect for Innocent Life — Doctors must oppose "the ominous temptation to interrupt innocent life, especially when it is not perfect and not completely healthy," declared the Pope Apr. 14 in an address to 1,300 physicians attending an international congress on prenatal and postnatal health care. "The existence of an eventual deformation cannot constitute the motive for a death sentence, not even if it is by the parents themselves, filled with emotion and wounded in their hopes, who request euthanasia through the suspension of medication and nutrition."

Cultivating Peace in Mozambique — Pope John Paul called on the bishops of Mozambique Apr. 15 to "cultivate peace" in their war-torn country by aiding the victims of violence and by promoting social development. "Authentic peace and collective security, indispensable for the development of a people, are inseparable from justice and freedom," he said. While decrying a "mentality of violence" in the country, he told the bishops they should continue "development initiatives as an impartial service to society."

Visit to Verona — During an Apr. 16-17 visit to the northern Italian city of Verona, the Pope appealed for tight controls on arms sales, criticized excessive consumerism and urged industrial leaders to develop a "scale of priorities" for the production of goods more beneficial to society. In speeches to priests, Religious, young people and pastoral workers, he stressed the need to penetrate with Christian values "a climate of secularism in which every search for transcendence becomes irrelevant." He said the goal of Christians "is to create an ever-broader social environment, inspired by the great values of the Gospel."

The Pope beatified two local priest-founders of religious communities Apr. 17, Msgr. Giuseppe Nascimbeni (d. 1922) and Father Giovanni Calabria (d. 1954).

Religious Liberty — The Pope said the "winds of renewal" blowing through the Soviet Union should affect the restoration of religious liberty — specifically, the right of the Church to worship, to carry out pastoral programs and to maintain a full force of bishops and priests. In a talk to Lithuanian bishops Apr. 18, he said the Church in their country was struggling against government restrictions in a "decidedly atheistic" environment. He cited limitations on the number of candidates for the priesthood, the illegal status of religious orders, and restrictions on pastoral ministry, religious instruction and the organization of church property.

In another appeal, the Holy Father urged the Soviet Union to grant Catholics in the Ukraine the right to worship publicly "in their own rite and with their own pastors." (See *Magnum Baptismi Donum*.)

Address to Anglican Bishops — In a pre-Lambeth Conference address to a group of Anglican bishops Apr. 22, the Pope said: "You will deal with the difficult and delicate issues which touch on essential aspects of your relationship with the Catholic Church as well as your Orthodox brothers and sisters. I pray that when you are together (in July) you will give full weight to the importance of maintaining and strengthening the bonds of that real though imperfect communion in which Anglicans and Catholics are united." The Pope did not mention any specific issues in his speech, but it was known that the ordination of women to the priesthood in some provinces of the Anglican Communion was cause for serious concern.

Death of Archbishop Ramsey — The Pope, in a message to Anglican Archbishop Robert Runcie, expressed his sympathy on the death Apr. 23 of his predecessor. "I have learned with deepest sorrow of the death of Lord Ramsey, an outstanding spiritual leader and pioneer of ecumenical relations between the Catholic Church and the Anglican Communion. Be assured of my prayers and sincere sympathy. May he rest in peace and receive the reward of his great labors."

Evangelization in Africa — In an address Apr. 23 to bishops of Zaire, the Holy Father called evangelization the "heart" of their ministry and stressed the importance of inculturation in worship — "expressing the Christian mystery according to the African genius." With a word of caution, however, he said that efforts to affirm African cultural identity risked encouraging the rise of "certain customs averse to Christian marriage, like polygamy," and procreation, "without the intention of a stable matrimonial union." The Pontiff expressed concern over the "proliferation of sects and their corrosive action" against the teaching and practice of the Church. He urged the prelates to "develop the catechetical formation of the faithful and living ecclesial communities."

Beatifications — The Pope beatified Apr. 24 Redemptorist Father Kaspar Stanggassinger and three founders of religious congregations: Pietro Bonilla (Holy Family Sisters of Spoleto), Savina Petrilli (Poor Sisters of St. Catherine of Siena), and Francisco Palau y Quer (two congregations of Carmelite missionaries).

Defense of Life — West Germans must "defend inalienable values against the fashion of the moment," declared the Pope Apr. 30 as he urged 120 Christian Democrats from that country to promote the right to life from conception until death. "Every man has the right to life. This right belongs to the unborn child from the moment of conception as well as to the child already born, and to the elderly and to the sick as well as the healthy." He called on the government officials to help "reawaken the consciences of men and to save the lives of children not yet born."

General Audience Topics:
• Since "every Sunday is a small Easter," the Solemnity of Easter should be more than an "isolated episode" in the lives of the faithful (Apr. 6).
• "We are certainly not prohibited from seeking new ways of expressing the mystery of the Incarnate Word," but attempts to explain the mystery of Christ "must be in accord with the deposit of the faith" (Apr. 13).
• Christian hope, which involves "self-denial and sacrifice," is more than "a superficial philosophy of earthly happiness" (Apr. 20).
• "The Father's invitation to the heavenly feast" of the kingdom of God "is a call to everyone, but each person must decide whether to accept the invitation and abide by its requirements or to refuse it" (Apr. 27).

The Pope Also:
• During a meeting Apr. 2 with U.S. Secretary of State George Shultz,' encouraged him on his latest mission for peace in the Middle East.
• Called Apr. 10 for peace in Ethiopia, where food aid for thousands of people was jeopardized by civil war operations, and in Iran and Iraq, where people were in danger because of the "particularly cruel" use of chemical weapons.
• Called catechists "missionary figures" and said contemporary Europe was in need of re-evangelization, Apr. 25.

Vatican Briefs:
• Catholic media have the responsibility to present authentic teaching of the Church alongside dissent, and to correct errors about the Church in the secular media.
• The Roman Rota, known for its appellate role in marriage cases, passed judgment on 194 cases and issued 113 decrees of nullity in 1987.

Easter Message

The Holy Father dedicated his traditional Easter address *Urbi et Orbi* ("To the City and to the World") Apr. 3 to Mary as a witness to the suffering and resurrection of Jesus.

"The whole Church shares in your Easter joy; the whole Church knows that on this day the Lord has made you 'go before' in a singular way along this path of the pilgrimage of faith in the paschal mystery. Pray for us! During this Marian Year, be present in a special way in the Church . . . along all the paths of the people of God, paths upon which shines the light of Christ. Let this light never leave anyone, this light of the new life which is he himself, the Risen One!"

NATIONAL

Georgetown-Homosexuals Agreement — Georgetown University, according to an Apr. 4 report, formalized an agreement Mar. 29 with homosexual student groups providing them with the same benefits enjoyed by other student organizations while affirming the school's right to refuse granting them official recognition. The signing of the consent order by District of Columbia Superior Court Judge Sylvia Bacon ended eight years of litigation over alleged discrimination by the university. The order provided that the Gay People of Georgetown University and the Lesbian and Gay Association at Georgetown University Law School would have the right to meet on campus, use campus facilities and apply for student government funds. However, a university statement said: "The university will not recognize or endorse these student groups and will be able to continue to make clear that it does not share their views." The signing of the consent order, for precautionary reasons, meant that Georgetown would not ask the U.S. Supreme Court for a hearing of the case.

NCEA Convention — More than 16,000 persons attended sessions of the 85th annual convention of the National Catholic Educational Association Apr. 4 to 7 in New York. Topics on the agenda included a wide variety of subjects related to the financial condition of Catholic schools, the emotional health of their most vulnerable students, and the moral health of the society they serve. "Catholic Education: Gift to the Nation" was the theme of the convention.

Father Curran's Lost License — The Board of Trustees of The Catholic University of America stripped Father Charles E. Curran of his church license to teach theology Apr. 12 but said he still held tenure and could teach outside the university's Vatican-accredited theology department. The action came nearly two years after the Congregation for the Doctrine of the Faith declared that Father Curran was not fit to teach Catholic theology because of his continuing dissent from church teaching on sexual ethics, the indissolubility of marriage and other moral issues.

A week before the board's action, the Superior Court of the District of Columbia denied a motion by the university to dismiss a suit brought by Father Curran in seeking to retain his position at the university.

Pornography Boycott — Cardinal Joseph L. Bernardin of Chicago urged citizens Apr. 13 to boycott stores that rent or sell sexually-oriented videos and magazines, and to tell shop owners why they were doing so. He made the appeal at an archdiocesan conference on pornogrpahy, saying: "We must and do oppose pornogrpahy because it exploits and degrades the human person. Children are victimized; women are exploited; men are perverted; the young and insecure are seduced; families are undermined; personal and social relations are twisted. God's gift of sexuality is stripped of personal dignity."

Black Catholics — The "pentecostal experience" of the National Black Catholic Congress held in May, 1987, resulted in an agenda for the 1980s and 1990s with evangelization, the study of black culture, leadership training in pastoral ministry, and community outreach as priorities. So stated Auxiliary Bishop Joseph A. Francis of Newark Apr. 18 at a workshop sponsored by the National Black Catholic Congress and the U.S. bishops' Secretariat for Black Catholics. The workshop, held in Houston, was attended by about 300 persons.

RENEW Renewed — The RENEW program for the spiritual renewal of people and parishes, revised in response to criticism of doctrinal and related shortcomings, will be "richer and more helpful (than before) to dioceses and parishes," announced Archbishop Theodore E. McCarrick of Newark Apr. 18 in a letter to bishops across the country. He said efforts would continue "to present a challenging and well-balanced program directed toward the important goal of renewed life and vitality in our parish communities." RENEW, introduced in the Newark Archdiocese in 1978, had been used in more than 100 dioceses in the U.S., Canada and other countries. It involves a series of six-week programs in parishes aimed at deepening faith, developing lay leaders and bringing lapsed Catholics back to practice of the faith.

Selective Abortion — A Catholic pro-life official called it "tragic" that some doctors were using selective abortion to reduce the number of fetuses in women who were pregnant with several. "And it is all the more tragic in light of the advances that could be made if the relentless effort to destroy were re-channeled into an equally relentless effort to help every mother and every child. . . . We have reached a point where some in the medical community will not only kill, but seemingly suffer no embarrassment of conscience when they detail in learned journals how the killing was accomplished." The comments were made in response to a report in the Apr. 21 edition of the *New England Journal of Medicine*, on the "selective reduction of multifetal pregnancies in the first trimester of a pregnancy."

Death Act Opposed — The 22 bishops of California said in a statement Apr. 22 that they were "unalterably opposed" to an initiative to include on the state ballot in November "The Humane and Dignified Death Act" which would legitimize "direct killing" to end human suffering. (See separate entry for text.)

Appeal for Ukrainians, Religious Freedom — "An Appeal for Religious Freedom in the Soviet Union on the Occasion of the Millennium of Christianity in Kievan Rus" was the title of a five-page document signed by 240 U.S. religious and political leaders and released Apr. 27 at a press conference in Washington. Legalization of the Catholic Church in the Ukraine was one of the principal subjects of the appeal directed to Soviet leader Mikail Gorbachev. Other subjects were:
• return to religious groups of expropriated church buildings and religious items;
• restoration of the right to build churches;
• lifting the ban against charitable activities by religious groups;
• ending of registration for religious associations and clergy;
• declaration of general amnesty for prisoners of conscience;
• freedom of religious communities to preach and publish;
• permission for Soviet believers to leave the country for religious reasons;
• permission for believers to maintain contacts with other believers throughout the world.

National Briefs:
• The Church is challenged "to be consistent in proclaiming justice," Bishop Walter F. Sullivan of Richmond told participants in the 1988 Heartland Conference Apr. 11 to 13 in Kansas City, Mo.
• Two hundred and 50 priests attended the 20th annual convention of the National Federation of Priests' Councils Apr. 25 to 29 in Louisville. Subjects of resolutions included the permanent diaconate for women, optional celibacy for priests, "reconciliation and restoration" for resigned, married priests.
• Catholics were among the 35,000 participants in the "Washington for Jesus '88" prayer rally Apr. 29 on The Mall of the capital city.

AIDS Policy

Upholding teachings of the Church on homosexuality, sex outside of marriage and drug abuse does not eliminate responsibility to minister to people with AIDS, according to a policy statement of the Diocese of Manchester.

"We will continue to teach forcefully our conviction that the basic meaning of human sexuality requires a commitment in love and openness to life in a permanent and faithful marriage of a man and woman. We will continue to emphasize the beauty and importance of chastity outside of the relationship of marriage. These convictions, however, do not prevent us from reaching out in love to those who are suffering."

The statement said clearly that "persons with AIDS have the right to the sacraments and to Christian burial in accordance with the provisions of the Code of Canon Law."

INTERNATIONAL

Criticism of Israel — Religious bonds between Catholics and Jews are not a barrier to Catholic criticism of Israeli political policies, wrote Bishop Alberto Ablondi of Leghorn in the Apr. 2 edition of *Avvenire*, the Italian Catholic newspaper published in Milan. The Bishop called for a clear distinction between religion and politics in Catholic-Jewish relations. He criticized "dissonant Catholic voices" in Italy which ignore the Church's rejection of anti-Semitism, and said such voices "do not have an influence in ecclesial circles."

Way of the Cross — Holy Week 1988 was a "Way of the Cross" for Palestinians living in Israeli-occupied territories, said Latin-Rite Patriarch Michael Sabbah of Jerusalem in an article appearing in the Apr. 3 edition of *L'Osservatore Romano*. "Every Palestinian carries the cross. They have carried it for so many years. It is carried by the wounded, by the people in jail." It is "a social, collective and individual cross."

Spiritual Crisis — The world faces a spiritual crisis as serious as the economic crisis afflicting developing nations and needs a "universal moral philosophy," declared Archbishop Justo Mullor Garcia Apr. 8 at an international conference in Lisbon. "The primacy of money over life and of matter over spirit has led all over the world to a sort of psychological and moral tempest which is shaking mankind to the very roots," said the Vatican permanent observer to the Office of the United Nations and Specialized Institutions.

Less Women Religious — Vatican Radio reported Apr. 11 that the number of women Religious in the Czechoslovakian provinces of Bohemia and Moravia was expected to decline and that the government had not given religious orders permission to accept new members. It was estimated that the membership of 2,811 in 1986 would shrink to about 1,400 by the year 2000.

One Conference of Indian Bishops — At a meeting in Kottayam, the bishops of India decided to form one conference for bishops of the Latin Rite and two Eastern Rites, Syro-Malabar and Syro-Malankara. The action was considered significant because it was made after Pope John Paul issued a directive that would have permitted them to form three separate conferences along with a national conference for dealing only with matters of a national or doctrinal character. Syro-Malankarese Archbishop Benedict Varghese Gregorios Thangalathil was elected conference president.

Aggressive Sects in Mexico — The activities of evangelical sects was a recurring theme at the 42nd semiannual assembly of the Mexican bishops Apr. 12 to 16. The issue was the focus of a discussion entitled "The Catholic Church in the Face of the New Religious Groups." At a press conference during the meeting, the prelates told reporters that about 350 sects, with a total membership of between three and five million, were operating in the country. They made a distinction between traditional Protestant churches and the sects, noting that "these religious sects are much more aggressive." They called them divisive and said that some of them could not even be considered Christian. The sects included Jehovah's Witnesses, Light of the World Church and the Summer Institute of Linguistics.

Laws on Religion To Change? — The Soviet government wishes to "improve" its 1929 "ecclesiastical legislation" because it "does not correspond to the spirit and to the level reached by the state today," according to Konstantin Kharchev, chairman of the Department of Religious Affairs. Interviewed for the Apr. 19 edition of an Italian daily, he also said his department was printing more Bibles and that the government would allow the importation of 50,000 copies at the request of Pope John Paul. However, he said laws against the religious education of children would probably remain in force.

Moral Health of France — On the eve of French presidential elections, Cardinal Jean-Marie Lustiger of Paris expressed concern for the moral health of the nation and defended the right of the Church to address specific moral issues. "If the norms of social life, dictated by political and administrative power, do not permit the Church and Catholics to express themselves, it is the nation which is in danger.... We think that this liberty is necessary for the life of the nation, for its future." In an interview published Apr. 22 in the Italian Catholic daily *Avvenire,* he said he was particularly concerned about the breakdown of family structures, the need for mutual respect among peoples, and the necessity of moral education. Moral values are not passively inherited by each generation, he said, but must be actively taught.

End Sanctions against Panama — The bishops of Panama called for an immediate end to U.S. economic sanctions against their country, calling the measures "a threat to the life of our people." In a statement issued late in the month, they also denounced the "apathy and incompetence of many government organisms" in Panama, and expressed concern about "the increased militarization of civil groups and the 'national system of information.' " Economic sanctions had been imposed by the U.S. in an effort to topple the regime of strongman Gen. Manuel Antonio Noriega, who was accused of rigging presidential elections in 1984 and was under a U.S. indictment for trafficking in drugs.

International Briefs:

• A week after cancellaton of the traditional outdoor procession of Palm Sunday, the celebration of Easter in Jerusalem took place in the shadow of developments related to ongoing Palestinian-Israeli conflict.

• Speculation about the possibility of change in the Soviet Union's hard-line attitude toward religion was prompted, among other things, by the apparent freer-than-ever celebration of Easter by the Russian Orthodox Apr. 10. A part of the liturgy celebrated in St. Vladimir's Cathedral in Kiev was broadcast on television.

• Cardinal John J. O'Connor told reporters Apr. 21 in Havana that he and Cuban President Fidel Castro had talked about "building bridges for peace" during a meeting the previous night. The Cardinal was in Cuba to participate in ceremonies marking the 200th anniversary of the birth of Father Felix Varela, a Cuban hero who served in the Archdiocese of New York after being exiled from Cuba in the early 1800s.

Morality and Science

Moral theologians should uphold their right to raise questions about science despite the increasing array and complexity of ethical issues spawned by scientific advances, said a leading U.S. bioethicist at an international gathering on morality and medicine. "I fear many theologians, being non-scientists, allow themselves to be overwhelmed by the technical knowledge and are not sufficiently critical" of scientific proposals and developments." So stated Dr. Edmund Pellegrino, director of Georgetown University's Kennedy Institute of Ethics. He was one of 250 ethicists, moral theologians and scientists attending the Apr. 5 to 8 International Bioethics Congress on Issues in Morality and Medicine, sponsored by the Redemptorist Order's Alphonsian Academy of Moral Theology. Developments of concern to the moralists and scientists were:

• advances in genetic engineering,

• embryo and fetal experimentation and the use of fetal tissues,

• legalization of direct, voluntary euthanasia,

• allocation and commercialization of health care.

MAY 1988

VATICAN

Employment Outranks Profit — Employment is a right never to be sacrificed to the "law of profit" or to new production techniques, declared the Holy Father on the feast of St. Joseph the Worker, May 1, during a one-day visit to the central Italian city of Civita Castellana.

Dialogue but Don't Compromise — In pluralistic societies, the Church should dialogue with other sectors of society without compromising Catholic beliefs, said the Pope in an address May 3 during the annual general assembly of the bishops of Italy. "It would be an illusion, with possible dizzying consequences for the faith of our people, to hold that it is possible to evangelize by modifying the profile of the faith, Christian ethics and the social doctrine of the Church." Frank proposals of Christian truth must be given priority in "the cultural confrontations and efforts to reach understandings among diverse positions, which in reality are often irreconcilable." Christians must have "a strong ability to listen and to dialogue," but this "does not mean that they should not express and give witness to, with clarity and integrity," religious truth and "the ethical demands which derive from it."

African Refugees — The Holy Father called on the bishops of Zambia and international agencies to do all they could to help hundreds of thousands of refugees in southern Africa. In a talk to the bishops May 5, he said he was "deeply concerned" and: "I commend you in all the initiatives which you have undertaken to provide for their physical and spiritual well-being. ... It is my fervent prayer that the international community will continue to respond generously in helping you to meet the difficult problem of refugees in your region." It was estimated that nearly 900,000 Mozambicans had left their country, and that hostilities there had taken a toll of more than 100,000 lives since 1986.

Helping Missionaries — All Christians can participate in the missionary work of the Church through prayer and "the offering of their own sufferings." The Church has "an absolute need" for such support, which provides an "enormous reserve of spiritual energy" and contributes "a powerful impetus to the diffusion of the Gospel" throughout the world. So stated the Pope May 6 before 200 participants in the annual plenary assembly of the Superior Council of the Pontifical Missionary Works.

For Religious Freedom in Albania — In an address to 200 pilgrims from Albania May 6, the Holy Father appealed for religious freedom in their officially atheistic country. He shared their hope that the Church, with centuries-long roots "in Albanian soil, may be able to enjoy freedom once more." He paid tribute to Albanian Catholics for their fidelity to the Church "even in the most difficult and painful circumstances" of their "often tormented history."

Bishop-Religious Relations — In a letter dated May 14, the Vatican asked bishops and members of religious orders to review, and report on by the end of the year, their mutual relations, in light of "Mutual Relations," a document issued 10 years earlier on the subject. The letter said progress had been made in promoting "greater collaboration" between bishops and religious orders, and in developing a "more intense and operative church communion." At the same time, it added that there was need for a "serious examination of current problems." Although the nature of the problems was not mentioned specifically, it was thought they had reference to the balance between the autonomy of religious orders and the authority of the bishops in places where the orders were located. The letter was signed by Cardinals Bernardin Gantin and Jerome Hamer, prefects, respectively, of the Congregation for Bishops and the Congregation for Religious and Secular Institutes.

Social Communications — Fraternity and solidarity were keys to the Pope's message for the observance May 15 of the 22nd World Communications Day. Regarding the role of the Church, he said: It "reminds men and women that fraternity and solidarity cannot be regarded merely as conditions for survival. They are essentials of their vocation, a vocation which the exercise of social communication permits them to realize freely."

Three Bishops for Czechoslovakia — The Pope's appointments of three bishops for Czechoslovakia, the first such appointments in more than a decade, was announced May 19. The appointees were: Father Jan Sokol, 54, apostolic administrator of the Archdiocese of Trnava; Msgr. Jan Lebeda, 75, and Father Antonin Liska, 63, auxiliary bishops of Prague. The appointments came at the conclusion of several months of delicate negotiations between the Vatican and the communist government.

Role of Mary — In a message issued in advance of the observance of Mission Sunday, Oct. 18, the Pope asked Catholics to reflect on "the presence and influence of the Mother of Jesus (which) has always accompanied the missionary activity of the Church. ... Everywhere the Church performs missionary activity among peoples, Mary is present." In turn, evangelized peoples "enrich the cult and devotion" of Mary "with new titles and expressions, responding to their needs and in their own religious spirit." The Pontiff called Mary "a perfect model of dedication and fidelity" for the missionary "heralds of the Gospel" who are "often ignored, forgotten or persecuted" while working in the "outposts of the missions of the Church."

New Cardinals — Pope John Paul announced May 29 that 25 new members would be inducted into the College of Cardinals June 28. Two Americans were among those named, Archbishops James A. Hickey of Washington and Edmund C. Szoka of Detroit. (See additional entries.)

General Audience Topics:
- "The Second Vatican Council teaches that everyone is obliged to seek the truth, especially in matters concerning God and his Church, and to accept and persevere in the truth once it is known. But the Council also teaches that the truth cannot be imposed by coercion" (May 4).
- "Today, a new evangelization is called for in keeping with the teachings of the Second Vatican Council, particularly as these apply to the Church in the world, the vocation of the laity and the Church's social doctrine" (May 25, after returning from his May 7 to 18 trip to South America).

The Pope Also:
- Expressed concern about spreading labor unrest in Poland, saying that workers and communist authorities should seek a Gospel-based resolution to their differences.
- Said May 5 that Ukrainian Catholics in the Soviet Union should be granted freedom of religion and worship.
- Officially opened May 21 a new Vatican shelter for homeless people living in the shadow of St. Peter's Basilica; the hostel was to be staffed by Mother Teresa's Missionaries of Charity.
- Told 2,000 priests that Mary is the model of the Church's "fundamental vocation" of presenting Jesus to the world, May 26 at an international meeting sponsored by the Italian-based Focolare Movement.
- Encouraged 25,000 members of Italy's national police force to continue defending justice.

Vatican Brief:
- "The Church and University Culture" was the title of a document being circulated by the Congregation for Catholic Education, the Pontifical Council for the Laity and the Pontifical Council for Culture. The document said: "What is at stake is of fundamental importance: the inculturation of the Gospel and the evangelization of cultures."

Trip to South America

The Holy Father, on the 37th foreign trip of his pontificate May 7 to 19, visited cities in Uruguay, Bolivia, Peru and Paraguay. Feature events of the pastoral visitation were his canonization of three martyrs — Roque Gonzalez de Santa Cruz, Alfonso Rodriguez and Juan de Castillo — and his participation in closing ceremonies of the Marian Eucharistic Congress of the Bolivarian nations. (See separate entry.)

NATIONAL

Second Native American Bishop — The appointment May 3 of the second American Indian bishop brought "rejoicing on the reservations in South Dakota," said Bishop-designate Charles J. Chaput, 43, who was named by Pope John Paul to head the Diocese of Rapid City.

Alien Registration — Registration of undocumented aliens for the purpose of obtaining permanent residency and eventual citizenship ended at midnight of May 4. By that time, it was estimated that 2.1 million had registered, and that more than 920,000 had been granted temporary residency cards. Registration had been in process for a year, according to provisions of the 1986 Immigration Reform and Control Act. Eligible for residency were immigrants who had resided illegally in the United States since before Jan. 1, 1982. About 100 diocesan offices and church agencies participated in the registration program as qualified designated entities.

New Beginnings — Bishop Donald W. Wuerl of Pittsburgh called on people throughout the diocese to take part in New Beginnings, an educational and planning program intended to address the needs and services of the Church. The declining number of Catholics in the six counties of southwestern Pennsylvania, a $2.6 million diocesan deficit in 1987-88 and the diminishing number of priests called for "gradual steps" to ensure a healthy future for the diocese, he said. He noted: "It's time to move to the future. We must prepare ourselves in the best possible way to continue to pass on the faith."

Operation Rescue — Organizers of a week-long Operation Rescue abortion protest reported May 6 more than 1,650 arrests for disrupting business at three New York abortion clinics. Juli Loesch, media coordinator for the protest, said the clinics were closed for three out of four days. She stated also that the peaceful conduct of those arrested during four separate protests "set a standard for the way non-violent, direct action should be carried out." Among those arrested were New York Auxiliary Bishop Austin B. Vaughan, at least a dozen priests, four women Religious, more than 20 Protestant ministers and two Orthodox rabbis.

Exemplary Schools — Thirty-one Catholic elementary schools were among the 287 elementary schools named to receive the 1988 Exemplary School Award of the U.S. Department of Education. Each of the 31 schools "had strong programs in values development, active parental and parish support, and teachers committed to helping students achieve their best," according to Christian Brother Robert J. Kealey, executive director of the Department of Elementary Schools, National Catholic Educational Association.

Gathering of Christians — About 1,500 Catholics, Orthodox and Protestants came together for a Gathering of Christians May 20 to 25 in Arlington, Texas. They joined in prayer, reflection and discussion of a variety of subjects including "explorations in spirituality," Hispanic forms of devotion to Mary, periods in the life of Jesus, and the activity of people of all religious faiths in matters of public policy.

Pentecost '88 — Thousands of Catholics gathered at more than 250 sites in 85 or more U.S. dioceses May 21, the eve of Pentecost, "to discover the best and most effective ways to share the good news of Christ." The teleconference, which originated in Washington, focused on practical ways of motivating and supporting lay persons in efforts to share their faith with the estimated 90 million people in the U.S. who do not attend church regularly. It was estimated that some 16 million Catholics did not attend church regularly.

In another development, Redemptorist Father Thomas Forrest told nearly 7,000 people that spreading the Gospel is the "greatest kindness" a

News Events — May 1988

person can perform because "Jesus is the greatest gift." The director of the international Evangelization 2000 project spoke during the May 27-to-29 National Conference on the Charismatic Renewal in the Catholic Church, at the University of Notre Dame.

Catholic Press Convention — Members of the Catholic Press Association held their 77th annual convention May 25 to 27 in Boston. St. Francis de Sales Awards were presented to Henry P. Libersat, Jr., editor-manager of *The Florida Catholic*, and James A. Doyle, retiring after 30 years of service to the association. First place in the general excellence category for national newspapers was won by *The National Catholic Register*. Archbishop John P. Foley, president of the Pontifical Commission for Social Communications, told the journalists that the Catholic press should "reflect the universality of the Church" and cultivate understanding of Catholics and their culture.

Retirement Deficit — A survey conducted under the auspices of the Tri-Conference Retirement Project indicated that religious orders in the United States needed at least $2.9 billion more than they had in order to provide for the retirement needs of their members. The survey report put the average annual retirement cost for members over 70 at approximately $10,123 and the average Social Security benefit at $2,603. As a result, it was estimated that orders needed an additional average of $7,520 annually to support each retired member. The retirement project was sponsored by the National Conference of Catholic Bishops, the Conference of Major Superiors of Men and the Leadership Conference of Women Religious.

Organization Meetings — Meeting during the month were:
• National Convocation of Jail and Prison Ministers, attended by more than 250 May 14 to 18 in Arlington, Va.
• Association of Catholic Colleges and Universities, attended by 100 May 23 to 26 in St. Paul, Minn.; under discussion was "The Church and American Culture in the Post-Vatican II Era: The Challenge to the Catholic Intellectual Community."
• Teens Encounter Christ, attended by nearly 350 May 27 to 30 in Bismarck, N.D.; the theme of the meeting focused on the paschal mystery of Christ's death, resurreciton and mission.

National Briefs:
• The U.S. Catholic Conference urged the platform committee of the Democratic Party May 10 to oppose abortion with a human life amendment, support agreements on nuclear arms, assist parents who send their children to Catholic schools, create a more equitable immigration policy, and "take stock" of U.S. economic life "in the broadest possible measure."
• Father Charles E. Curran said May 17 that he and The Catholic University of America could not agree on a way for him to return to a professorship at the university and that, therefore, he was asking the Superior Court of the District of Columbia to enforce his teaching contract.

• Catholic hospitals must keep themselves financially solvent, but not at the expense of their mission to the poor. So stated Archbishop John R. Roach of St. Paul-Minneapolis May 15 in New York.

Physician-Assisted Suicide
Backers of a physician-assisted suicide measure failed to get enough signatures in support of their effort to include the proposal in the California ballot in November. By the deadline date of May 9, the number of signatures obtained was 285,928, short of the required 372,128 by 86,200. The legislative initiative would have provided that a terminally ill person, likely to die within six months in the judgment of two medical experts, could request a lethal injection from a physician, who would not be subject to prosecution. The initiative was sponsored by Americans Against Human Suffering. It was opposed by bishops of the state, various religious groups and the California Medical Association. It appeared that backers of the measure would try again to get it on the ballot in 1990.

INTERNATIONAL

Objections to Vatican Draft Statement — The Theological Advisory Commission of the Federation of Asian Bishops' Conferences recommended rejection of the Vatican's draft statement on the nature and authority of episcopal conferences. The commission said the draft adopted positions "difficult to reconcile" with the development of bishops' conferences since the Second Vatican Council and which could "foreclose" their further development. "The bishops would be justified in responding (to a request from the Vatican for comment) that this text, as it now stands, should not be used as a basis on which to continue the study of the status of episcopal conferences."

This reaction to the Vatican draft was similar to those expressed by other episcopal conferences.

Labor Mediation Stymied — The bishops of Poland were frustrated in efforts to mediate a mounting labor crisis after riot police attacked striking workers May 5 at a giant steel mill near Krakow. The bishops had urged the government to meet with the opposition to seek a broad solution to labor problems. "The situation in the country dictates that formal considerations be set aside and an intensive search be made for common solutions serving the good of the entire nation," they said. "New concern for the nation's fate should incline us to jointly seek new roads leading to a meeting and cooperation between the authorities and society."

Church Efforts for Peace — Enrique Bermudez, the controversial military commander of the contras, credited the Church in Nicaragua May 6 for seeking peace, but added that the Sandinists had raised a "barrier" to that effort. "Cardinal Obando has been trying hard to bring peace . . . The Church has always been looking for peace and for human rights . . . and some basic freedoms." But, "the Sandinists have repressed many bishops, many priests."

Bolivian Land Claim — German Quiroga Galdo, Bolivian ambassador to Mexico, reported that his government had asked the Vatican for help in pressing its claim to access to four Pacific Ocean ports through a land corridor. He released a series of letters exchanged between the Bolivian government and the Vatican which indicated that Pope John Paul might be willing to intercede in the dispute over land lost to Chile in 1883 as a result of the four-year War of the Pacific. The possibility of Vatican intervention recalled Vatican mediation of the Beagle Channel dispute between Argentina and Chile several years earlier.

Easing of Christian-Moslem Tension — A midmonth exchange of messages between the Vatican and the Moslem community of Durban, South Africa, eased some interfaith tensions, declared Archbishop Denis Hurley of Durban. He said it was a "real joy" to relay to the local Moslem community a message from the Vatican for celebrations of the end of Ramadan, the holy month of fasting and prayer. He called the reply of the secretary-general of the Islamic Council of South Africa "very impressive and very heartwarming. . . . I think this heals some of the hurts we have experienced in Durban from the rather aggressive attitude of certain Moslem people and institutions. . . . This heals hurts and really offers a good way ahead for close collaboration between the Christian and Moslem faiths."

Progress in Lithuania? — Soviet authorities, during a rare meeting with several bishops May 17, pledged that the government would (1) restore to Catholics on July 1 the Church of Our Lady, Queen of Peace, in Klaipeda, and (2) enlarge the main diocesan seminary in Kaunas. An unnamed Vatican official thought the meeting represented "a positive sign that indicates small progress is in the offing — and which might indicate big progress in the future."

Food for Ethiopians — Paul Cunningham reported May 17 that, although civil war in the Ethiopian provinces of Eritrea and Tigre had severely disrupted feeding programs of Catholic Relief Services, the programs were continuing in parts of the provinces under government control. Cunningham, a CRS desk officer for Ethiopia, said that "at no time did we suspend or terminate operations in either of the regions." Relief supplies were always "more than the trickle" falsely reported by U.S. officials.

Workers' Rights — In a pastoral letter marking the 50th anniversary of the labor movement in Jamaica, Archbishop Samuel E. Carter of Kingston listed five "fundamental principles" of Catholic social teaching related directly to human labor: the primacy of the person over profit, equitable distribution of the world's goods, preferential option for the poor, the Gospel character of the struggle for justice, the priority of labor. Among other things, he said: "Human labor should not be treated as a commodity to be simply bought and sold in the marketplace." It "takes precedence over both capital and technology in the productive process."

Cardinal's Demand Rejected — The Czechoslovakian government rejected a demand by Cardinal Frantisek Tomasek for religious freedom as sought in a petition signed by more than 500,000 citizens the previous April. Deputy Prime Minister Matej Lucan told priests the demand was rejected because it was "confrontational" in tone. Three of the 31 points in the petition were for permission to build new churches, the restoration of church goods and property, and unrestricted access by priests to Catholic patients in hospitals.

Concern over Anti-Semitism in Italy — The Italian Bishops' Conference expressed profound concern May 23 over recent anti-Semitic incidents and reiterated church opposition to anti-Jewish prejudice. They said: "Episodes of intolerance against Jews and Jewish institutions" and "attitudes of hostility and prejudice" are of "profound concern" to the Catholic community. They quoted an address delivered by Pope John Paul at the Synagogue of Rome in 1986: "Acts of discrimination, unjustified limitation of religious freedom, oppression also on the level of civil freedom in regard to Jews were, from an objective point of view, gravely deplorable manifestations."

International Briefs:
• In Santiago, Chile, military police broke up a rally by priests, nuns and lay persons protesting against the use of torture by government agencies, May 6.
• Moslem Inamullah Khan, chairman of the Executive Committee of the World Conference on Religion and Peace, was awarded May 10 the 1988 Templeton Prize for Progress in Religion. The award of $369,000 was given in view of his "tireless work as a coordinator for peace between Moslems, Christians and Jews."
• English and Welsh bishops called May 10 for major reduction in world armaments and the use of resources saved for the alleviation of world poverty.
• Families must be given top priority in pastoral and social planning if they are to have renewed vitality. So stated Cardinal Edouard Gagnon, president of the Pontifical Council for the Family, May 20 in Dublin at a seminar on "Progress through the Family," sponsored by Family Solidarity, an Irish organization.

Cambodian Catholics

Three categories of Cambodian Catholics were described in an address by Archbishop Yves-Georges-Rene Ramousse, papal representative to Cambodian Catholics throughout the world. The address, reported by NC News May 13, was delivered Apr. 28 at the fourth annual meeting of Cambodian, Hmong, Kmhmu and Laotian apostolates in Irving, Texas.
• He called the Church in Cambodia the "Church of silence (trying) to make her voice heard outside."
• In refugee camps, "she is the Church of the poor, and she is expecting hands for help from outside."
• Among communities scattered in different parts of the world, "she is the Church of foreigners, and she is looking for hearts to welcome" her.

JUNE 1988

VATICAN

Corpus Christi Observances — The Holy Father marked the Italian observance of the solemnity of Corpus Christi June 2 with a Mass at the Basilica of St. John Lateran and a procession through the streets of Rome to the Basilica of St. Mary Major. He said the procession "symbolically expresses" the Christian's "pilgrimage" of faith.

Disarmament — Security is essential for peace. But, "all are aware that the type of security on which our planet has depended for the last several decades — a balance of terror based on nuclear deterrence — is a security with a far-too-high risk-level." So stated the Pope in an address delivered June 2 on his behalf by Cardinal Agostino Casaroli, at the U.N. General Assembly's third special session on disarmament. "The progressive, balanced and controlled elimination of weapons of mass destruction, and the stabilization at the lowest possible level of the defensive weapon systems of countries, is an objective that should garner the necessary consensus as a first step toward increased security.... Of course, as long as countries are obliged to have adequate means of self-defense in order to repel possible aggression, they will inevitably be obliged to modernize and replace their weapons. But, beyond this limit, any increase in or improvement of armaments would mortgage the very possibility of reaching the desired aim and must, therefore, be decisively avoided."

In Northern Italy — The Pope made a five-day swing June 3 to 7 through nearly a dozen cities of the region of Emilia-Romagna, preaching a message of social justice and religious transcendence.

• In Carpi June 3, he said he wanted to reach out especially to persons who had left the Church "in a desire for social justice" or because of "anti-clerical traditions that are now largely unjustified."

• Appealing June 4 to non-believers and fallen-away Catholics in Modena, he urged them to "continue to look for God until you have found him."

• In Piacenza June 5, he said that, without spiritual guidelines, genetic technology held the potential threat of outdoing the Industrial Revolution in "savage and dehumanizing practices." In another address the same day, he declared that the state should provide social benefits to homemakers in order to help them perform their "specific activity" as mothers.

• At a meeting with pastoral workers June 6 in Reggio Emilia, he said they faced a mentality that was "perhaps more dangerous" than open persecution and martyrdom, a mentality which "does not want to create martyrs but wants to make men 'free' — free, that is, from all religion and morality. It does not suffocate the idea of God through violence, but through the accumulation of consumer goods and in the satisfying of natural instincts. It does not combat the Christian idea but ignores it, placing it among the myths of the past."

Visit to Southern Italy — On a June 11 and 12 trip to southern Italy, the Pope canonized St. Eustochia Smeralda Calafato, a Claretian nun who lived in the 15th century, addressed a Eucharistic Congress and denounced organized crime in the region. In Reggio Calabria, he said before a throng of tens of thousands: "Do not let yourselves be corrupted by the attractions of drugs and consumerism. Do not fall into the snares of criminal and Mafia organizations." He also said "Every form of abuse of power, of corruption, of unjust oppression and of organized criminality" is "radically opposed to human dignity" and must be opposed by Christians.

Vietnam Martyrs — On June 19, Pope John Paul canonized 117 persons martyred in Vietnam in the 18th and 19th centuries — 96 Vietnamese, 11 Spanish missionaries and 10 French missionaries. With objections of the Vietnamese government in mind, the Pontiff said "The search for the common good of the homeland is a sincere obligation of the Christian citizen, within the freedom to proclaim the truth of God, in communion with his pastors and his brothers in the faith.... The Vietnamese Church, with its martyrs and through its witness, has been able to proclaim its desire and commitment not to reject the traditional culture and legal institutions of the country. Instead, it has declared and demonstrated that it wishes to be incarnated in the country, contributing... to the construction of the homeland."

Trip to Austria — Pope John Paul visited Austria June 23 to 27 on the 38th foreign pastoral trip of his pontificate. (See Pope John Paul in Austria.)

Curia Reform — In an apostolic constitution entitled *Pastor Bonus* ("The Good Pastor"), Pope John Paul announced June 28 changes in the Roman Curia, the complex of agencies serving the Vatican and local churches throughout the world. The document said the mini-reform would go into effect Mar. 1, 1989. (See Roman Curia.)

New Cardinals — The Pope installed 24 new cardinals in the College of Cardinal June 28, bringing the total membership to 160. The new cardinals were from 17 countries: there were four from Italy; two each from the United States, Brazil, India and Spain and one each from Australia, Austria, Cameroon, Canada, Colombia, France, Hong Kong, Hungary, Lithuania, Mauritius, Mozambique and West Germany. The two new American cardinals, Archbishops James Hickey of Washington and Edmund Szoka of Detroit, raised U.S. membership in the college to 11. Father Hans Urs von Balthasar of Switzerland, also named a cardinal, died June 26, before the installation ceremonies.

Catholic-Orthodox Statement — The Pope announced June 29 that the international Catholic-Orthodox Theological Commission had approved a joint statement, "The Sacrament of Orders in the Sacramental Structure of the Church." He said the approval was "good news" and called it a sign of continuing progress in dialogue. "Let us thank the Lord who, through his Spirit, leads us toward the realization of our much-desired goal; the full unity between Orthodox and Catholics." The Pontiff made the announcement in the presence of Greek

Orthodox Metropolitan Damaskinos of Switzerland, Bishop Spyridon of Apamea and Archimandrite Vassilios Drosses.

General Audience Topics:
- "Jesus reveals God in the most authentic way, ... based on the single source that is absolutely certain and without doubt: the very essence of God. The testimony of Christ thus has the value of absolute truth" (June 1).
- "Jesus is demanding — not tough or inexorably severe, but strong and unambiguous in calling everyone to life in the truth" (June 8).
- "The one flock of Christ, the Church, is universal in scope, made up of people of every nation" who come to "sit at table in the kingdom of God. ... All the preachings of Christ, all of his messianic mission, revolves around assembling the flock" (June 15).
- "Let us go back to the prayer of Christ who at the Last Supper exhorted his apostles to be one single thing. As we pray the Our Father at the end of this audience, let us do so with this particular intention" (June 22, several days before Archbishop Marcel Lefebvre went into schism).

The Pope Also:
- Said divorce and marital instability are "seeds of death" threatening the modern family, June 10 at a meeting with members of the Pontifical Council for the Family.
- At a meeting June 13 with Selcuk Kokud, Turkey's new ambassador to the Vatican, said that governments have the responsibility to defend religious liberty because it is "one of the important foundations of peace."
- Told five Soviet journalists June 30 that Soviet reforms promoting greater public participation in society are in harmony with teachings of the Church. At the same time, he criticized religious restrictions in effect in the Soviet Union, and expressed hope that they might be relaxed.

Vatican Briefs:
- A ruling by the Constitutional Court of Italy confirmed that officials of the Vatican Bank were immune from prosecution for alleged involvement in the collapse of Banco Ambrosiano in 1982. The immunity of Archbishop Paul Marcinkus and two lay officials was based on the Vatican's "sphere of sovereignty," stipulated in its 1929 treaty with Italy.
- "What is perceived as a technological crisis in contraception is really a crisis in ethics, caused by a ruthless and insensitive contraceptive imperialism." So stated a document prepared by the Vatican for presentation at a conference sponsored by the World Health Organization June 19 to 24 in Bangkok, Thailand.
- The Congregation for Divine Worship issued June 30 a set of directives for prayer services in place of Mass on priestless Sundays.

Schism

Archbishop Marcel Lefebvre, after at least 15 years of open dissent from enactments of the Second Vatican Council and the authority of the Pope, formally excommunicated himself from the Church June 30 as he ordained four bishops (also excommunicated) without proper authorization. By so doing, he created the first formal schism from the Church in nearly 100 years. (See separate entry.)

NATIONAL

Backing for Ban on Commercial Surrogate Contracts — The New York State Catholic Conference expressed support June 3 for recommendations that the state ban commercial surrogate-mother contracts. The Task Force on Life and Law, organized by Gov. Mario Cuomo, said the state should declare such contracts unenforceable as contrary to public policy, and urged that criminal penalties be imposed against surrogates and those who arrange surrogacy contracts. The state's bishops, in earlier testimony, called surrogacy a "psychological minefield" and a "moral disaster" that "seriously damages the integrity of marriage" and "threatens the child produced."

New York Foster Care Rules — A federal appeals court rejected June 8 efforts by Catholic and Jewish foster-care agencies to block a New York City policy limiting the role of religion in the foster-care system. Among other things, the policy required agencies to provide abortion referral and birth control services to children. In 1987, Cardinal John J. O'Connor threatened to drop archdiocesan foster-care services rather than comply with the policy at issue.

Rosary Congress — "Mary reminds us even today that we can never have true peace among nations until there is peace in homes and families. And there can be no peace in homes and families until individuals have peace in their hearts." So stated Archbishop Eugene A. Marino of Atlanta June 11 in a homily during Mass for participants in the first American National Rosary Congress. He said "the life, the worship, and the mission of the Church cannot be understood apart from Mary." He called her "an eminent and singular exemplar of the Church, who has given birth to all those baptized in Christ and instructed them with the word of God uncontaminated by error." Daily events of the congress from June 6 to 11 were attended by an average of 1,500 or more people. The congress was sponsored by *Apostolatus Uniti*, the Marian Movement of Priests and the Rosaries for Peace prayer crusade. It featured continuous recitation of the Rosary, devotion of the brown scapular, personal consecration to the Immaculate Heart of Mary, and devotion focused on divine mercy.

Mother Teresa Speaking of the Poor — The poor need more than food, clothing and shelter, Mother Teresa of Calcutta told an estimated 20,000 people June 13 at the National Blue Army Shrine in Washington Township, N.J. She spoke about the ministry of her Missionaries of Charity to the "hungry, who hunger not only for a piece of bread, but to feel wanted and loved; the naked, who are naked not only from a lack of a piece of cloth, but from the loss of purity; and the homeless, who suffer not only from not having a home, but from being unwanted, unloved by society, having no one to call their own."

Challenge Upheld in ARM Case — On an 8-to-1 vote, the U.S. Supreme Court upheld the right of the U.S. Catholic Conference to challenge subpoenas for financial records brought by Abortion Rights Mobilization and sent the case back to a lower court for further action. The decision continued o spare the conference and the National Conference of Catholic Bishops from fines of $50,000 a day each for non-compliance with subpoenas, but did not end the underlying court case. In the litigation, ARM was seeking to force the Internal Revenue Service to revoke the tax exemption of virtually every Catholic church entity in the U.S. for alleged violations of laws and regulations forbidding political activity by tax-exempt groups.

Loss of Hispanics to Sects — The loss of Hispanic Catholics to other denominations is often the result of "an aggressive and disrespectful proselytism," said the Hispanic bishops in California in a pastoral letter. Factors contributing to the alienation of Hispanics from the Church included:

* confusion resulting from visits by members of sects antagonistic to the Church;
* problems with a priest or Religious;
* difficulty in finding Spanish-speaking clergy and Spanish-language liturgies;
* feeling that there is a lack of emphasis on the Bible in the Catholic tradition.

The bishops' letter, released in May, was in circulation among the Spanish-speaking in California.

Persecution in Vietnam — The Church in Vietnam "always grows with persecution," said Father Tran Dinh Nhi, several days before the canonization of 117 Vietnamese martyrs June 19. The pastor of Blessed Vietnamese Martyrs Church in Arlington, Va., said "the persecution now under the communist regime is much more delicate" than persecutions of the 18th and 19th centuries. "The communist government tries to create difficulties for the people to practice their faith," for example, by scheduling community meetings at Mass time, by limiting seminary enrollment, by preventing Catholics from holding government jobs and their children from entering universities. Buddhists and Protestants were also subject to persecution. From 1580 to 1885, it was estimated that more than 130,000 Vietnamese Catholics were martyred for their faith.

CHA Assembly — About 1,000 delegates attended the 73rd annual assembly of the Catholic Health Association June 19 to 22 in Nashville. Harvard professor Robert Blendon told delegates that Catholic hospitals should ride the current wave of public concern for social issues, such as health care for the uninsured poor. He also said that the safety net for the poor was unraveling with reductions in Medicare coverages and federal and state grants, and lack of direct support for "charity care" from business and labor. The association reported that exenditures for health care at Catholic institutions accounted for 16.5 percent, or $23 billion, of the $143.5 billion spent in the U.S. in 1987.

Bishops' Meeting — Nearly 300 bishops attended the semiannual meeting of the National Conference of Catholic Bishops and the U.S. Catholic Conference June 23 to 27 at Collegeville, Minn. (See separate entry.)

Religious Groups in Chastity Program — The U.S. Supreme Court upheld June 29 the role of religious organizations in a federal program to fight teen-age sexual activity. In a 5-to-4 decision in Bowen v. Kendrick, the Court found that the role given religious groups in the Adolescent Family Life Act of 1981 does not violate the U.S. Constitution. "In sum," said the majority opinion, written by Chief Justice William H. Rehnquist, "we have concluded that the statute has a valid secular purpose, does not have the primary effect of advancing religion, and does not create an excessive entanglement of church and state."

National Briefs:

* The U.S.-Soviet intermediate-range nuclear weapons treaty signed by President Reagan and Mikhail S. Gorbachev June 1 in Moscow had the support of U.S. bishops; they called it an important step toward nuclear disarmament.
* Andre Nguyen Van Chau, a Vietnamese refugee to the U.S. in 1975, became secretary general of the International Catholic Migration Commission June 1.
* "Spiritual resources" to deal with problems surrounding addiction to drugs and alcohol "are abundant in the Catholic faith," declared the bishops of New Jersey in a pastoral statement, "Called To Live in Freedom," released June 8.
* Scientists at the University of Arizona completed dating tests of a sample piece of the Shroud of Turin and sent the results to the British Museum for further study, June 10.

Catholic Population Statistics

The Official Catholic Directory reported that, as of Jan. 1, 1988, there were nearly 53.5 million U.S. Catholics, about 600,000 more than reported the previous year. There was a slight increase in the number of priests, but declines were reported in the numbers of women Religious, brothers, seminarians, and teachers and students in Catholic schools. (See statistical entries.)

INTERNATIONAL

Three bishops for Czechoslovakia — The first new bishops for Czechoslovakia in more than a decade were ordained June 11 and 12. They were: Auxiliary Bishops Jan Lebeda, 75, and Antonin Liska, 63 of Prague, and Bishop Jan Sokol, 54, apostolic administrator of Trnava. Archbishop Francesco Colasuonno, the Vatican's special envoy for Eastern Europe, said at the ceremony in Trnava that he hoped the appointments might be the beginning of a wider process of religious liberalization in the communist country. Before 30,000 people, he spoke June 12 about the "necessity to have bishops in all the dioceses" of the country. (Nine of the nation's dioceses were still without ordinaries or Vatican-approved apostolic administrators.) Existing dialogue between the government and the Vatican, he said, "should not end with the nominations of bishops, but should go far beyond. . . . The religious dimension, when it enjoys full citizenship in civil society, does no damage to public life but, on the contrary, contributes to the progress and prosperity of all."

Ban on Import of Religious Materials — The

Chinese government barred the importation of religious materials, except of small amounts for personal use, according to a report by the semi-official China News Service. Also barred were materials that criticize the nation's constitution and current national policies; libel the Chinese Communist Party and state leaders; advocate subversive activities and create national divisions; advocate "Two Chinas" or "Taiwan independence." The new regulations went into effect June 15.

Anti-Christian Attitude in India — Amid reports in the secular press of illegal conversions by Catholic missionaries, the Indian Catholic Press Association announced it would establish a monitoring group to counteract what it called anti-Catholic polemics. The association also said it would study the feasibility of publishing a national weekly to help correct what it said was unbalanced coverage of church-related news. Press sources said anti-Christian reports had appeared in the central State of Madhya Pradesh, where a bishop was arrested for allegedly converting local residents. In Bihar in the North, the Church had been accused of supporting the Jharkhand Movement for a separate state for tribal people. Bishop Frederick D'Souza of Jhansi was authority for the view that the secular press was engaged in a systematic campaign against the Church.

No Vietnamese Bishops at Canonizations — The Vietnamese government prevented the nation's bishops from attending the canonizations June 17 of 117 martyrs of Vietnam. The government was on record in protest against the canonizations, saying they were an offense to non-believers, would damage church-state relations, and might be the pretext for anti-government rallies (which did not happen). The bishops' conference said in a message to Pope John Paul: "We have fervently prayed in union with all those who attended the Mass (during the canonization ceremonies). In the name of the bishops' conference, we express our gratitude to the Pope, and the attachment of the Christian people of Vietnam, asking for your apostolic blessing."

Meanwhile, a new wave of Vietnamese refugees, driven by harsh economic conditions and the threat of famine, was swelling the numbers in Asian refugee camps. Boat people were also subject to untold hardships.

For Reforms in Poland — The bishops of Poland called for sweeping government reforms and blamed communist authorities for the public's "lack of feeling of participation" in national life. They issued the statement after authorities reported a turnout of 56 percent, a new low, in elections June 19 for provincial and local council seats. Opposition sources said the poor turnout indicated that Poles felt increasingly unafraid of expressing their apathy, alienation from authorities, and disinterest in political activities that offered no choice to voters.

Warning of Backlash of Nature — Church leaders in the Cordillera Mountains of Northern Luzon warned of a "backlash of nature" from continuation of the current rate of forest destruction by logging companies and "slash and burn" farmers. Bishop Ernesto Salgado of the Mountain Provinces Vicariate said he believed logging had to be stopped in order to protect the rain forest that serves as home for thousands of tribal people and as a watershed for most of the river systems of the region. He blamed logging operations for the floods in Kalinga Apayao Province that killed 30 people in 1988.

Religious Freedom for Ukrainian Catholics — This was among topics brought forward at a meeting of representatives of the Vatican Secretariat for Promoting Christan Unity and their counterparts from 14 Orthodox Churches, including the Russian Orthodox Church. The meeting was held June 19 to 26 in Finland.

Missionaries of Charity in Mexico — Mother Teresa of Calcutta was on hand June 25 to greet five priests and 20 students for the priesthood when they arrived at their new headquarters in poverty-stricken Tijuana. The mission of the priests, seminarians and Sisters of the Missionaries of Charity was to run a soup kitchen and infirmary. The former headquarters of the priests was in the South Bronx, New York City.

Death of Outstanding Theologian — Father Hans Urs von Balthasar, 82, died June 26, two days before he was scheduled to become a cardinal. Bishop Otto Wust of Basel, called him "one of the century's greatest theologians."

International Briefs:

• Bishop Cahal Daly of Down and Connor denied June 19 that the Catholic community as a whole was responsible for the serious violence in the Belfast area. He did so during a Mass in Lisburn, Northern Ireland, 10 miles from Belfast, where six British soldiers were killed June 15 by a bomb attached to their van by partisans of the outlawed Irish Republican Army.

• Two Peruvian bishops struck out at continuing violence in the country. Auxiliary Bishop Augusto Beuzeville Ferro of Lima said: "We must reject the violence of 'Shining Path' (*Sendero Luminoso*) just as much as the massacre of defenseless campesinos by military troops." Bishop Luis Bambaren Gastelumendi of Chimbote called on Peruvians to "eject the ideologies of death and destruction put forward by terrorism."

Russian Orthodox Celebration

A 16-member Vatican delegation attended Russian Orthodox Church-sponsored ceremonies June 5 to 15 marking the 1,000th anniversary of the introduction of Christianity in what is now, but was not then in 988, part of Russia. Heading the delegation was Cardinal Agostino Casaroli, Vatican secretary of state.

Cardinal Casaroli, speaking June 10 at the Bolshoi Theater in Moscow, told government officials that the Christian vision of the world is in "complete opposition" to the Marxist view that human reason can eliminate religion.

On June 13, at a meeting with Mikhail Gorbachev, the Cardinal gave the Soviet leader a letter in which Pope John Paul stated his desire for regular contacts with Soviet officials.

JULY 1988

VATICAN

Briefing on Soviet Congress — Pope John Paul received a briefing by Nikolai M. Lunkov July 12 on proceedings of the reform-minded congress of the Soviet Communist Party which ended July 1. Lunkov, the Soviet ambassador to Italy, had attended the congress and "wished to inform the Holy Father of it," said Joaquin Navarro-Valls, the Vatican spokesman. He said it was "a courtesy call and another occasion of dialogue between the Soviet Union and the Holy See."

An editorial in the July 3 edition of *L'Osservatore Romano* said the congress was a sign of "good intentions" on the part of the nation's leaders to make important political and economic reforms. However: "It is premature to issue an operative judgment on the historic assembly," but "the good intentions are recognized."

The editorial cautioned that Soviet political rules "are and remain very different from classical democratic systems." Substantial change in Soviet society requires "a mutation which, overcoming old ideologies, raises the searching to the level of the real and global demands of the contemporary world so gravely conditioned by the opposition between East and West, as well as that between North and South.'

Catholic World Population — As of Dec. 31, 1986, there were approximately 879.4 million Catholics in the world, according to the 1986 *Statistical Yearbook of the Church*. The figure, nearly 13 million higher than that reported the previous year, included an estimated 15 million Catholics in countries under communist control. Countries with the largest numbers of Catholics were: Brazil (122.67 million), Mexico (76.49 million), Italy (56.11 million), the U.S. (53.55 million), France (46.18 million).

Advice to Religious — The Holy Father encouraged religious orders to carry on with their works of evangelization and to ensure the proper formation of their own members. Such formation, he stressed, holds the key to "true renewal."

• He encouraged participants in the general chapter of the Congregation of St. Joseph July 11 to continue envangelization with troubled youths and workers. "The youths of today are mixed up in their conscience and disturbed in their ability to reason. . . . At times, they are even wounded and scandalized by the society in which they live: an agnostic and secularized society." With respect to ministry among working people, he said: "For too long, Catholics have left to the freethinkers, to the revolutionaries and to the enemies of society and religion, the leadership of the labor movement."

• On the same day, the Pontiff praised the Viatorian Fathers for their pastoral work, and especially for the manner in which they involved lay persons in their catechetcial and liturgical programs; he called this a sign of "clarity and wisdom."

• "Initial and permanent formation" of their members is a matter of "extreme importance," the Pontiff told delegates to the general chapter of Capuchin friars July 12. He urged the Franciscans to develop a "continuous maturation process" characterized by the "specific features of Capuchin spirituality." He spoke about a "triple commitment" for the order: awareness of Capuchin identity, realism in daily life, and discernment — the ability to make right choices and priorities. He said they should imitate St. Francis in "his concern not to remain on the level of words but to go on to deeds."

• Fidelity to the charism of "service to the smallest, the weakest, the most abandoned," was the theme of the Pope's address to chapter members of the Brothers of Charity.

Vacation — Pope John Paul spent July 13 to 22 in the foothills of the Dolomite Mountains in northern Italy. He made several public appearances, however, on the weekend of July 16 and 17, when he spoke during Mass about communion with God through communion with nature. He said it was a message people need to absorb if they are to enjoy spiritual and international peace. "The mountains have always had a special fascination. . . . They invite you to be uplifted, not only materially but also spiritually. . . . Nature is a perpetual hymn to the greatness of the Creator" and an invitation "to submerge yourself in prayer. . . . The majestic peace of Adamello Mountain invites us and obliges us to construct and consolidate a society free of slavery, war and hate."

Canonizations — The Holy Father canonized two saints July 3: Sister Rose Philippine Duchesne (1769-1852), French foundress of the Religious of the Sacred Heart and missionary in the U.S. for 34 years (see separate entry); and Spanish Trinitarian Father Simon de Rojas (1552-1624), theologian and promoter of devotion to the Holy Name of Mary.

Cease-Fire Hopes — The Pope told reporters July 22 that he hoped efforts for peace and an end to the long war between Iran and Iraq would be successful. He called Iran's decision to accept a U.N. cease-fire resolution a consolation. "Certainly, this is a consolation after many years of efforts on various levels, including those of the Church, to convince the two warring states to cease war operations and return to peace. . . . Truly this war has brought with it many victims, many massacres, and has continued for so long. . . . We must thank God if this move toward peace is fully realized."

Appointment of Bulgarian Bishop — The Pope appointed Father Gheorghi Ivanov Jovcev apostolic administrator of the Diocese of Sofia-Plovdiv and designated Archbishop Francesco Colasuonno to ordain him bishop July 31 in Sofia. Officials of the atheistic government, along with Orthodox prelates, were invited to attend the ordination ceremonies. The diocese had been without a bishop or apostolic administrator since 1983.

General Audience Topics:
• "The salvific liberation effected by Christ . . .

contains in itself . . . two dimensions: liberation 'from' evil and liberation 'for the' (good), which are intimately united, and mutually condition and complete each other" (July 3).

• "Divine mysteries are made present in the life of the Church, especially through the sacraments . ., . (which) are visible signs that confer the new life of grace" (July 13).

• "When Christ established the Church, he wished her to be holy by sharing in his own divine life. . . . Holiness is to be the mark of all members of the Church in every walk of life" (June 23).

• "It is through the blood of Christ that the work of salvation takes place, that humanity is liberated from the evil of sin, that the kingdom of God draws near and human history has a new beginning" (July 27, at Castelgandolfo).

The Pope Also:

• Expressed his concern and sympathy: over the deaths of 290 people aboard the Iranian airliner shot down by the U.S.S. Vincennes July 3: on the deaths of some 160 persons who died in an oil platform explosion July 6 in the North Sea; on the deaths of about 250 people in a train wreck July 8 in India.

• Praised imprisoned South African anti-apartheid leader Nelson Mandela for the "greatness" of his character in suffering "so much for the rights of his people."

Vatican Briefs:

• The Congregation for Bishops released July 1 a new set of guidelines for the mandatory ad limina visits which heads of dioceses make to the Vatican every five years. (see "Directory for the Ad Limina Visit.")

• The Pontifical Commission for the Authentic Interpretation of the Code of Canon Law issued a statement July 19 saying that lay ministers of the Eucharist should not be used for the distribution of Communion when enough priests or deacons are available. The statement was a reiteration of existing regulations which have sometimes been disregarded in practice.

Celebration of Ukrainian Millenium

Climactic ceremonies July 9 and 10 marked the end of the Ukrainian Rite celebration of the 1,000th anniversary of the baptism of St. Vladimir and the people of Kievan Rus in 988, and the introduction of Christianity in what is now, but was not then, part of Russia.

The Ukrainian hierarchy led the celebration of the Moleben, a solemn act of thanksgiving in honor of the Mother of God, July 9 in front of the Pro-Cathedral of St. Sophia in Rome. Pope John Paul took part in the Liturgy of the Word and delivered a homily based on the theme of the Magnificat. He said that "Mary accompanies the Ukrainian people, sharing their destiny throughout their history."

The final major event of the millenial observance was the celebration of the Divine Liturgy in the Byzantine-Ukrainian Rite July 10 in St. Peter's Basilica. Concelebrating with the Pope were Cardinal Myroslav Ivan Lubachivsky, the highest ranking Ukrainian prelate, 20 Ukrainian metropolitans and bishops, and over 100 priests. In a homily, the Holy Father lamented the "sadness" felt by Ukrainians attending the ceremonies that many of their "brothers and sisters (perhaps four million or more) do not enjoy religious liberty" in their homeland under communist control. He also said:

"The celebration of the millenium must revive in all Christians an ecumenical commitment, and push the Catholic Church and the Orthodox Church to rediscover in the Ukraine their ancient historical bonds." He asked Catholics and Russian Orthodox "to work with renewed enthusiasm for the cause of union." At the same time, he called for recognition by the Soviet government of the rights of Ukrainian Catholics to practice their faith, declaring that "membership in the Catholic Church should not be considered by some as incompatible with the good of one's own earthly country and with the inheritance of St. Vladimir."

(See apostolic letters: *Euntes in Mundum, Magnum Baptismi Donum.*)

NATIONAL

Abortion Decisions — A federal district court in New York upheld July 1 the Reagan administration's regulations removing abortion-related services from the Federal Title X Family Planning Program. U.S. District Court Judge Louis L. Stanton found that the regulations' ban on abortion referrals and counseling did not violate rights of free speech. U.S. District Judge June L. Green in Washington struck down July 5 a ban on U.S.-funded international family planning agencies providing abortion-related services with their own money.

Pro-Abortion Nuns Resign — Sisters Barbara Ferraro and Patricia Hussey announced July 13 their resignations from the Sisters of Notre Dame de Namur, which had refused a Vatican request to expel them from the community because of their unacceptable views on abortion. The resignations followed four years of controversy triggered by their signing of an advertisement in *The New York Times* which stated that there is more than one legitimate Catholic position on abortion.

Liberation Theologian Honored — Twenty years after coining the term, "liberation theology," Father Gustavo Gutierrez, its foremost proponent, was honored July 17 during a month-long Summer Institute for Justice and Peace conducted by the Maryknoll School of Theology. In an interview July 11, he said he accepted Vatican critiques of some forms of liberation theology as "relevant observations for myself," and that he had modified some expressions of his views. The author of *A Theology of Liberation* said his "big question, theologically and pastorally, is to try to relate social justice and our experience of the gratuitous love of God."

Convention Prayer — Archbishop Eugene A. Marino of Atlanta was one of several dignitaries who offered public prayer during the July 18-to-21 convention of the National Democratic Party which nominated Massachusetts Governor Michael S. Dukakis for the presidency. He prayed for divine assistance "to renew our convictions that the American democracy, despite its failings and shortcomings, remains the world's last best hope" at a time when so many other nations live in oppression.

Planned Parenthood and United Way — The archbishops of Seattle, saying the local United Way was "one of the strongest pro-life activities" in the area, asked Planned Parenthood to either drop plans to provide abortion services in King County or relinquish its United Way funding. The decision to offer abortions "has become the source of dangerous division in our community and threatens to undermine United Way and the work it does on behalf of the needy," stated Archbishops Raymond G. Hunthausen and Coadjutor Thomas J. Murphy in a letter July 21 to local directors of Planned Parenthood.

Catholic Daughters of America — Twelve hundred women attended the 42nd biennial convention of the Catholic Daughters of America in San Diego. Delegates approved resolutions to help retired Religious, assist AIDS victims and fight abortion. They voted to support "any legislation that prohibits in vitro fertilization, embryo transfer and experimentation, and surrogate motherhood. They agreed to continue financial assistance to the Eternal Word Television Network, to contribute $300,000 to the North American College in Rome and $300,000 for the new building under construction in Washington for the National Conference of Catholic Bishops.

Operation Rescue — More than 1,200 persons were arrested during the month for taking part in Operation Rescue in the Philadelphia area July 5 and 6 (850), Atlanta July 19 during the convention of the National Democratic Party (134), and Williamsville, N.Y. July 29 (250). Among those arrested was Auxiliary Bishop Austin B. Vaughan of New York, for the fourth time. The purpose of the non-violent protest demonstrations at abortion clinics was, in the words of the founder, Randall A. Terry: "To save children from death, women from being exploited, and to inspire more vision and hope so that this type of activity will occur all across the country.

National Briefs:
• The Wisconsin Catholic Conference called for full respect for the fishing-treaty rights of Chippewa Indians in the northern part of the state.
• More than 150 delegates from 30 nations attended the general assembly of the International Apostolate Movement of the Independent Social Milieux July 2 to 10 in Baltimore. Key subjects under discussion were urbanization, bioethics, international debt, cults and Islam.
• In proposals for raising $25 million for its schools, the Archdiocese of Baltimore asked all parishes to give amounts equal to "at least 20 percent of their annual Offertory collection" for education.
• In a July 15 letter to priests of the Diocese of Gary, Bishop Norbert F. Gaughan prohibited the use of church facilities for partisan political gatherings.
• A spokesperson for the Federal Communications Commission repeated, again, July 18, that there was no truth to a rumor that atheist Madalyn Murray O'Hair had asked the government to ban religious broadcasts.
• Mother Teresa of Calcutta underwent successful eye surgery for cataract removal July 25 at St. Vincent's Hospital, New York.
• Bishop Ignatius Kung Pin-Mei of Shanghai, after 30 years of imprisonment and detention in China, was residing with a nephew in Stamford, Conn.

Church, Politics and the IRS

Mark E. Chopko, general counsel to the U.S. Catholic Conference, released July 26 an advisory on the Church vis-a-vis political involvement in the light of Section 501(c)3 of the Internal Revenue Service Code. As tax exempt organizations, the conference and some 28,000 other Catholic entities cannot be involved in partisan politics without risking loss of their tax exempt status. They are forbidden to "participate in, or intervene in — including the publishing or distributing of statements — any political campaign on behalf of — or in opposition to — any candidates for public office."

They are not banned from the public policy arena but must proceed carefully. They "remain free to address issues of concern to them and to their membership, even when such issues are relevant to the campaign.... However, such discourse must focus on issues, not personalities.... In addition, exempt organizations must pay due regard to appearances, since IRS will consider complaints of citizens and other groups that an exempt organization is engaged in impermissible activity."

INTERNATIONAL

John Paul II Foundation for the Sahel — Four years after its incorporation under the auspices of the Vatican Council Cor Unum, the foundation was carrying on its work of creating local leaders "to do what needs to be done" to halt the desertification of the sub-Saharan region of Africa.

The foundation is administered by bishops of the countries most threatened by deforestation and drought: Burkina Faso, Cape Verde Islands, Gambia, Mali, Mauritania, Niger, Senegal and Chad. Its statutes state its purpose: "the training of persons who place themselves at the service of their country and of their brethren ... for the purpose of fighting desertification and its causes, and for the purpose of aiding victims of drought in the countries of the Sahel." The foundation funded 96 projects between 1984 and 1987. The foundation itself is funded by the generosity of West German and other Catholics.

Inspiration for establishment of the foundation came from the needs of the Sahelian nations and the appeal of Pope John Paul during his African visit in 1980. He said: "Let us not wait till frightening and dreadful drought returns! Let us not wait for the sand to bring death again! Let us not permit the future of these peoples to remain forever threatened!"

Anti-Discrimination Campaign in India — The

bishops of India reported that they had launched a campaign to alert lower-caste Christian converts to their civil rights, and were preparing a nationwide effort to bring about an end to discriminatory legislation. Under existing law, members of a low caste who join a religion other than Hinduism or Sikhism lose benefits which could help them improve their socio-economic status.

Church against Apartheid — Churches in South Africa were taking up the anti-apartheid cause of organizations banned by the white minority government, stated a white South African priest who predicted sharper church-state conflicts as a result. Direct church involvement in opposing racially biased laws and policies "will be increasingly the case," said Dominican Father Albert Nolan in mid-July. "Where other organizations are unable to operate, the churches will do so."

Troubled Sudan — Bishop Macram Max Gassis of El Obeid painted a gloomy potrait of Sudan as a place of civil war with no end in sight, with vast numbers of increasingly desperate refugees, and with a fundamentalist prime minister trying to impose harsh Islamic law (Shariah) on an unwilling population. Speaking in Washington July 15, he also accused the government of Prime Minister Sadiq al Mahdi of continuing the war between the mostly black Christian and animist South and the mostly Arab Moslem North in order to stay in power.

Increased Tension in Paraguay — Church-state tension increased in Paraguay in the wake of Pope John Paul's visit there in May, partially, according to observers, because of greater confidence on the past of church leaders. "The Pope's visit began something we had all been waiting for," Archbishop Ismael Blas Rolon Silvero of Asuncion said in a recent newspaper article. "Now it is up to the Paraguayan people to carry out this transformation." The growing rift between the Church and the 30-odd-year regime of President Alfredo Stroessner was highlighted by the arrest July 15 and deportation of Spanish Jesuit Father Juan de la Vega after he had given a lecture on liberation theology. One diplomat said: "The Church has decided to go for an opening up of democracy in Paraguay, and we still have to see how far Stroessner will let this challenge go."

Lithuanian Priest Released — A delayed report received by the Brooklyn-based Lithuanian Information Center said that 63-year-old Father Alfonsas Svarinskas had been released from a Soviet labor camp after serving half of a 10-year prison sentence; he was getting ready to go into exile in West Germany. The priest's latest sentence, for alleged "anti-Soviet propaganda," was his third: in 1946, he was sentenced to 10 years in prison for having "connections with Lithuanian nationalists'; in 1958, he was sentenced to six years in prison for possessing forbidden literature.

Catechists and Sects in Guatemala — Catechists have been able to counteract the influence Protestant fundamentalist sects in northern Guatemala through their witness to the Catholic faith. So stated Bishop Rodolfo Bobadilla, head of the Apostolic Vicariate of El Peten. He said "an invasion of sects (promoted by former head of government Efrain Rios Montt in 1982) had resulted in a rapid growth of evangelical fundamentalist churches in some regions of the country" but not in the Province of Peten — "due to the catechists and their work among the people." He also said: "The problem is that the sects come in with a fundamentalist preaching and alienate people from the Catholic Church with the hope of bettering their lives. They also (teach) that people (should) rely on divine Providence; and, if life is harsh, God wills it that way." There is "no commitment among the sects to the poor. There's a sense of passive acceptance. There's only individual, sentimental religious practice. There's no commitment to the social Gospel."

Violent Israeli Tactics — Latin-Rite Patriarch Michel Sabbah of Jerusalem criticized "violent" tactics used by Israeli authorities to suppress Palestinian rebellion in occupied territories. "Repressive measures never bring calm and neither do they bring peace, because violence generates violence and an always stronger resistance," he said July 23 on Vatican Radio. More than 20 people, mostly Palestinians, were reported killed since the start of demonstrations, in December, 1987.

International Briefs:

• An association of Catholics was formed in North Korea, with hopes for better church-state relations, according to an article in the July 17 edition of *Peace Newspaper,* the Seoul archdiocesan weekly.

• In its 1988 hero series of postage stamps, the government of Sri Lanka included a special stamp for Jesuit Father Ferdinand Bonnel, a pioneer educator of the early 1900s.

• Deadlocked on abortion legislation, the Canadian Parliament went on summer vacation July 28, leaving abortion in Canada free for the asking.

Public Mass in the Ukraine

Six thousand Catholics attended July 17 the first public Mass in the Ukraine in more than 41 years at the site of one of their holiest shrines near the village of Zarvanytsia, despite police efforts to stop the celebration. The observance was organized by Bishop Pawel Wasylik, one of two bishops who publicly declared in 1987 that they would practice their ministry openly. Father Kenneth Olsen, who participated in the Mass, told reporters July 27 in Amsterdam: "It was the first public gathering since the Ukrainian Catholic Church was officially outlawed in 1946" by the communist government.

In an earlier development, Ukrainian Bishop Andres Sapelak said July 7 in Rome that Ukrainian Catholics and other Christians were pressuring Soviet officials to develop a "communism with religious freedom." The Soviet Union is experiencing "a great explosion of the Christian faith, which has left those who have forcibly been imposing atheism for the last 70 years — seeking to destroy the Christian faith and the Church of Christ itself — astonished, disconcerted and intimidated."

AUGUST 1988

VATICAN

Paul VI Anniversary — The Holy Father commemorated the 10th anniversary of the death Aug. 6, 1978, of Pope Paul VI. He "was a profoundly Marian Pope," he said Aug. 7. He described his predecessor's "profound devotion to Mary" as a "stimulus" for Christians "to live in a particularly intense way this closing of the (1987-88) Marian Year."

Praise for Haitian Bishops — Pope John Paul praised the bishops of Haiti for their leadership in the "tormented period" following the 1986 overthrow of dictator Jean-Claude Duvalier. Addressing visiting bishops, he said: "You have been particularly active in accompanying your people in the quest for freedom and in the anguished search for a true democracy.... You have aided people to respect the dignity of everyone, to work for justice." (The bishop's efforts were frustrated a month later when another coup and change of government took place in an undemocratic manner.)

Invitation To Visit Hungary — It was announced Aug. 20 that the Pope had received an invitation to visit Hungary. The invitation was tendered jointly by the bishops and the government. It was expected it would take about a year to make arrangements for the trip.

Polish Labor Unrest — Labor unrest must be settled without violence, and with due respect for human rights and the nation as an "independent state," the Pope said Aug. 21. "Worried" over the situation, he appealed to pilgrims from Poland: "Let us pray for our nation. Let us pray for peace, obviously a peace based on the strength of truth and justice, and not of violence." He repeated what he had already said many times, that Poland had to solve its social problems in the context of "national sovereignty and human rights." The Pontiff spoke after several weeks of labor unrest caused by strikers in the southwestern mining region and in the port city of Szczecin. Workers were demanding higher pay and legal recognition of the independent Solidarity union movement, which was outlawed in 1981.

On Aug. 26, the Pope criticized communist one-party rule, saying: "In a state, one group or one party cannot be sovereign at the expense of all the people and their rights.... It is time to put an end to the methods of terror and violence and listen to the reasonable voices of all the citizens.... The strikes are the symptom of a disease which has been aggravated for years."

Efforts for Peace in Nicaragua — "In your desire to serve the cause of peace, you have undertaken an inestimable pastoral activity," said the Pope Aug. 22 during a meeting with 10 bishops from Nicaragua. He hailed their stalled efforts to bring lasting peace and "true democratization" to their country. "The Church offers its reconciliation services so that the conflicting parties definitively abandon the language of arms and substitute it with dialogue," he said in reference to so-far-unsuccessful attempts to have peace talks reopened. The Pope had special praise for beleaguered Cardinal Miguel Obando Bravo whose efforts to negotiate for peace between the Sandinistas and Contras had been frustrated.

The missing ingredient for peace is "full democracy," said Cardinal Obando Aug. 29 in a Vatican Radio interview. The Church wants a democracy where, "above all, there is freedom.... For us, it should be a democracy with equality of opportunity for all, with respect for human rights, where life is protected." One of the problems is disagreement on a definition of democracy on the part of both the government and the guerrillas. The Cardinal noted that a truce in effect for several months had saved "lives and suffering."

Refugees in Malawi — The Holy Father urged the local church and the international community to continue providing aid to war refugees streaming into tiny Malawi from neighboring Mozambique. Speaking to bishops from Malawi Aug. 23, he noted that the number of refugees seeking safety, food and shelter was still increasing. "I encourage you in all your endeavors to alleviate their sufferings and to help provide for their physical and spiritual well-being," he said. The Pope also called on the bishops to pay special attention to the religious instruction of young people, who need "a systematic presentation of the whole of Christian teaching," including "the whole doctrinal and moral content of the Gospel."

Violence in Burundi — The Pope appealed Aug. 24 for an end to violence in Burundi, where thousands of people had been killed in tribal and army massacres. He prayed that "reconciliation and brotherhood may prevail in people's hearts," and that "peace may return as soon as possible" to the Central African nation. The Burundian army said Aug. 22 that it had ended tribal fighting between Tutsis, the ruling minority, and the Hutus, in the wake of clashes that claimed about 5,000 dead. A senior diplomat in the country said it was impossible to verify the government claim of ending the fighting, because the area where the killings occurred was sealed off and all missionaries had left.

Catholics in Cuban Society — The Pope told visiting Cuban bishops Aug. 25 that Catholics must increase their participation in the "labor, economic and socio-political" life of their nation. He said dialogue was the way for the prelates to deal with the government in seeking to open the door to greater church influence in public life. He told the bishops to promote unity among people "in such a way that Christian witness becomes more alive, with beneficial repercussions for culture and society, and for labor, economic and socio-political relations. (The Church) must generate activities at the service of all, especially the neediest."

General Audience Topics:

• "There are two dimensions to the freedom that Christ brings: liberation from evil and liberation for good.... The freedom which Christ brings is primarily a freedom of the heart. It is not a social

or political freedom, nor a psychological freedom, although it has an impact on all of these" (Aug. 3).
• "Christ came into the world to free the human race from sin and to give every person the 'freedom of the children of God.' Whoever accepts this gift receives the forgiveness of sins and is raised to 'a new life in Christ.' In him we have become a 'new creation' " (Aug. 10).
• "The Christian spiritual life is basically an 'imitation of Christ.' Jesus is both the perfect model as well as the efficacious model for each of us" (Aug. 17).
• "Obedience is central to our imitation of Christ. As he said: 'Whoever does the will of my Father in heaven is my brother, and sister, and mother' " (Aug. 24).
• "In every event of his life, but especially during his passion, Jesus left us a perfect example of humble and selfless love. And the heroism of Christ became the perpetual model of the heroic virtues of all the saints" (Aug. 31).

The Pope Also:
• Encouraged rescue and aid efforts for victims of earthquakes in northern India and Nepal, and for flood victims in Sudan, Aug. 21.
• Expressed sadness Aug. 28 at the deaths of several scores of persons resulting from the crash of jet aircraft during an air show at the U.S. Air Force base at Ramstein, West Germany.

Vatican Briefs:
• The Vatican confirmed Aug. 12 that a PLO official had consulted with the Vatican regarding the decision of Jordanian King Hussein to cut administrative ties to the Israeli-occupied West Bank. The Vatican also stated its support for homelands for Jews and Palestinians.
• "Satisfaction" was expressed over the Aug. 20 ceasefire agreed to by Iran and Iraq after eight years of bloody warfare.

Marian Year Conclusion

Pope John Paul brought the 1987-88 Marian Year to an end with a solemn Eastern-Rite ceremony in the evening of Aug. 14 and a Mass Aug. 15 in St. Peter's Basilica. Concluding ceremonies were also held in churches throughout the world.
(See Marian Year in Retrospect.)

NATIONAL

General Absolution — U.S. bishops, by a vote of 205 to 72, approved a proposal stating that, when a bishop is faced with the question of whether to allow general absolution in a particular situation in his diocese, one criterion he should use is whether, in his pastoral judgment, penitents would otherwise not have access to the sacrament of penance for at least a month. To be effective, the proposal requires ratification by the Vatican. (See related entries: General Absolution, Penance.) The bishops' decision was reported Aug. 1.

Festival of Evangelization — About 1,700 people from 50 Christian churches attended Congress '88, an ecumenical festival of evangelization, Aug. 4 to 8 in Chicago. Cardinal Joseph L. Bernardin said in an opening address: "Evangelization leads to personal conversion, an experience that may include one or more life-changing events. But, while it establishes an intimate relationship between believer and the risen Lord, it is not exclusively a personal matter." From Jesus' table fellowship and early Christian household churches to current Sunday assemblies, Scripture and tradition show that "personal conversion always demands affiliation, community, church. Christians come to recognize the Lord both in the word and in the breaking of bread. . . . and these are actions of the community."

Another speaker said that, if Catholic parishes are to attract the unchurched and welcome back inactive Catholics, they must be permeated by an "evangelizing consciousnesses." The speaker was Gordon B. Richard, director of evangelization for the Diocese of La Crosse.

It was estimated that about 16 million inactive Catholics were among 90 million unchurched Americans.

Academic Freedom — Catholic tradition upholds academic freedom, but not in the widely held sense of "unlimited, unfettered freedom to express any thought," Bishop Donald W. Wuerl of Pittsburgh said at a national conference Aug. 5 to 7 at the University of Massachusetts. In Catholic thought, "the voice of the teaching office" of the Church is "intrinsic to the process of theological development." Bishops, theologians and the people play "distinct yet complementary" roles in discerning the faith, but it is ultimately up to the bishops to judge the "authenticity of any specific teaching proposed as the faith and teaching of the Church. . . . The perennial Catholic scholarly method recognizes the role of Scripture, its scholarly interpretation, and the function of the Church in judging the validity of the interpretation." The demands of revelation and church teaching are "part of the very nature" of theology, "not external controls imposed of it."

On the other hand, widely accepted secular definitions of academic freedom today assume: "that human reason is the ultimate arbiter of all matters under investigation; that the scientific method, that is, the study of empirical data, can alone yield truth; and that no other voice, contribution or norm can be a determinant in the process." Such views "would empty the intellectual effort in a university setting of its theological content and direction," because Christian theology "uses as its starting point revelation which, of its nature, carries us beyond the limits of unaided reason."

Meetings of Religious — "Refounding Religious Life" was the theme of the meeting of the Conference of Major Superiors of Men Aug. 10 to 14 in San Diego. Marist Brother Sean Sammon was elected to a two-year presidential term, to start in August, 1989. "Removing Racism from Our Lives" was the key to actions taken at the assembly of the Leadership Conference of Women Religious Aug. 28 to 31 in St. Paul.

Church Statistics — The number of church members in the United States remained virtually unchanged from 1985 to 1986, while the general population grew by about one per cent, according to statistics published by the National Council of

Churches. The *Yearbook of American and Canadian Churches 1988* reported that in 1986 church members made up 58.7 percent of the U.S. population. The churches with the largest numbers of members in 1986 were: Roman Catholic (52.8 million), the Southern Baptist Convention (14.6 million), United Methodist Church (9.1 million), National Baptist Convention U.S.A. (5.5 million), Church of Jesus Christ of Latter Day Saints (3.8 million).

Hispanic Youths and a New Civilization — About 2,000 participants in the first Hispanic Youth Congress in the Archdiocese of Los Angeles heard Father Virgil Elizondo say that God had placed them in "a new situation that has no precedent, to forge a new civilization that can unite the best of Latin America and the best of the United States; to form, in every sense of the word, a new man and a new woman, a new humanity." He told the youths that God had placed them "here on this great frontier between the two Americas because he wants something special from you. . . . Just as God brought his people out of Egypt, out of slavery, to make a new people, so has he brought our people to California, Arizona, Texas, New Mexico, Washington."

Vietnam Celebration — An annual Marian Day gathering gave Vietnamese Catholics from around the country their first opportunity to celebrate together the canonization June 19 of 117 martyrs of Vietnam. About 40,000 Vietnamese met in Carthage, Mo., for the 11th annual Marian Day Celebration hosted Aug. 11 to 14 by the Congregation of the Mother Co-Redemptrix, a religious community founded in Vietnam and made up of Vietnamese refugees. Bishop John J. Leibrecht of Springfield-Cape Girardeau said in a homily at Mass Aug. 11: "We recall the memory of the Vietnamese martyrs who offered themselves to the Father. They were willing to die for the faith. (They) are examples of what it means to be people of faith — even when faith is difficult."

Chavez Ends Fast — United Farm Workers leader Cesar Chavez ended a water-only fast on its 36th day at a Mass Aug. 21. Chavez undertook the fast in protest against the use of certain pesticides on California grapes, "to emphasize the dangers posed to farmworkers and consumers alike by the reckless use of deadly pesticides."

Glenmary Anniversary — The Glenmary Home Missioners, a community of 104 men ministering in poor rural areas of the U.S., began a year-long celebration Aug. 24 of the 50th anniversary of their society. Sixty-eight priests, 22 brothers and 14 candidates of the society were working in 76 counties in 12 states throughout Appalachia and the rural South and Southwest.

National Briefs:

• Catholic Relief Services announced Aug. 8 that it would suspend its annual Thanksgiving clothing collection.

• President Reagan nominated Hispanic Catholic Lauro Cavasoz to be Secretary of Education; he was president of Texas Tech University.

• In an open letter to the governor and legislators, the California Catholic Conference called the state's 1989 budget "a disaster" and urged them Aug. 11 to restore funding for a wide range of human services and needs.

• When children go through religious education programs "without learning properly of the powerful symbol and person of Mary," it is a sin of omission, said Bishop John T. Steinbock of Santa Rosa Aug. 15.

• Bishop Michael J. Sheehan said Aug. 22 that the "authenticity and significance" of messages allegedly given by the Virgin Mary to three members of a parish in Lubbock, Texas, would be investigated by a panel of experts.

The Last Temptation of Christ

Watching "The Last Temptation of Christ" felt "like a punch in the stomach," said Father John Catoir, director of The Christophers and president of the Catholic Press Association. After viewing the film, he said in a statement Aug. 12:

"What I found was an outrageous stream of distortions that amounted to a character assassination of Jesus Christ. . . . This movie comes from the world of darkness. It is offensive to the memory of Jesus Christ. To give money to the producers of such a shameful depiction of Jesus is wrong."

The film went beyond poetic license to insulting lies:

• "In his hidden life, Jesus is a carpenter who makes crosses for Roman crucifixions. He even helps nail their victims to the cross and is splattered with blood in the process."

• "Jesus seems to be a paranoid schizophrenic who, on the one hand, has illusions of grandeur and, on the other, longs to be persecuted. He allows Judas to beat him up mercilessly, acting like a deranged wimp who can't make up his own mind."

• "Jesus calls himself a liar many times in the film and begs his mother's forgiveness for being a bad son."

• "In a fantasy on the cross, he imagines himself confronting St. Paul, who is preaching the Gospel of the risen Christ, and Jesus attacks Paul, calls him a liar, claiming he was never the messiah. Paul's reply was diabolical; he says the truth doesn't matter. It's what the people need to hear. They want a messiah. They want to be saved. Paul scoffs at Jesus and says, 'We don't need you now, we have the risen Christ to offer them.'"

INTERNATIONAL

Bishops Criticize Sandinistas — The bishops of Nicaragua strongly criticized Sandinista policies in a major pastoral letter which also cited social ills brought on by years of civil war and economic crisis. At the same time, they urged Nicaraguans to avoid succumbing to depression, despite growing disillusionment with political leaders and increasing poverty. They also asked the international community to cooperate in exerting pressure for democracy and peace in the country, and appealed for high-level dialogue for peace between government and contra forces. Publication of the letter, which was dated June 29, was delayed.

Chinese Bishops and the Pope — Most government-appointed bishops in China accept the primacy of the Pope in the universal Church, according to Bishop Benedict Dong Guangqing of Wuhan. He also said that most of the bishops "want ties and relations" with the Vatican. Bishop Dong, who was elevated to the episcopacy in 1958, was the first mainland bishop elected and ordained without Vatican approval after the government-sanctioned Patriotic Association of Chinese Catholics was established and Chinese-Vatican relations were severed in 1957.

In China, there appeared to be three categories of Catholics: (1) those underground who refuse to acknowledge claims of the Patriotic Associaton; (2) those who go along, in a way, with the Association but really do not subscribe to its anti-papal tenets; and (3) those who absolutely reject any and all relationships with the Pope and the universal Church.

Radio Catolica Reopened — Employees of Radio Catolica in Managua were notified Aug. 17 that the station could resume broadcasting the next day, after being off the air — for the third time — for more than a month. Broadcasts, however, would be limited to musical and religious programs. News broadcasts would be suspended indefinitely.

Demonstration in Paraguay — Several days after the expulsion of a Spanish priest for speaking about liberation theology, about 45,000 people marched silently through the streets of Asuncion to an open-air Mass to protest against persecution. Opposition politicians described the march as the biggest demonstration in three decades against President Alfredo Stroessner.

In another report, Archbishop Ismael Rolon Silvero of Asuncion told church leaders meeting in Argentina Aug. 19 to 21, that the Paraguayan government was encouraging the establishment of churches by followers of excommunicated Archbishop Marcel Lefebvre.

State of Emergency Ended in Chile — Auxiliary Bishop Sergio Valech Aldunate of Santiago greeted "with celebration" the lifting of the state of emergency by the government of Gen. Augusto Pinochet. The Vicar General of the Vicariate of Solidarity called on the regime to "continue on this path" by repealing or modifying remaining norms restricting the basic rights of Chileans. He made the comments in a statement dated Aug. 25. The previous day, six weeks before elections for the choice of a head of government, Pinochet announced he would lift the state of emergency for the first time since he seized power in 1973.

Cuban Catholics Going Public — Catholics in Cuba were slowly being allowed greater freedom to express their faith publicly, said Archbishop Jaime Ortega Alamino of Havana late in the month. "On the part of the state, we see positive steps regarding the presence of religion in society. Today, there is a clearer possiblity for Christians to live their own faith with all the rights and duties of a citizen without feeling 'second class,' without the sometimes subtle discriminations that existed and are tending to disappear." The Archbishop was interviewed on Vatican Radio after meeting with the Pope Aug. 25.

Restrictions in Lithuania — Cardinal Vincentas Sladkevicius, president of the Lithuanian Bishops' Conference, stated that the reform policies of Mikhail Gorbachev had not loosened restrictions on Catholic activities in Lithuania. "The Church is completely yoked to the state, which controls all sectors of ecclesial organization. ... We will judge the value of 'perestroika' when we see results for church life. So far, we have not seen any improvement." The Cardinal's views were reported in the Aug. 26 edition of *Il Messaggero*.

Seminary Returned — Vatican Radio reported that the government of Mozambique returned a seminary to the Church on Aug. 30. The restitution appeared to be a first concrete step in a program the regime hoped might improve church-state relations. The seminary had been occupied by the government since the 1975 independence movement brought the Marxist-oriented government to power in the former Portuguese colony. Restoration of the seminary took place three weeks before the Pope's scheduled visit to Mozambique.

International Briefs:

• A Japanese bishop and a Maryknoll provincial asked Japanese Catholics to avoid consulting an aging American Maryknoller, Father Leo Steinbach, who claimed to have direct revelations from the Virign Mary.

• Cardinal Jean-Marie Lustiger warned priests against concelebrating Mass with a bishop ordained by schismatic Archbishop Marcel Lefebvre, saying that such celebration would involve the penalty of excommunication.

• Cardinal Bernard F. Law of Boston ordained 19 members of Opus Dei to the priesthood Aug. 20.

Lambeth Conference

Five hundred Anglican bishops from 27 autonomous provinces attended the Lambeth Conference July 18 to Aug. 7 in Canterbury, England. Actions at the conference included the following.

• Endorsement of the work of the opening round of formal talks between the Anglican and Roman Catholic Church, with approval of a Final Report.

• Agreement to admit polygamists into the church under specified conditions.

• Declaration regarding traditional teaching that sex is permissible only in marriage and that monogamous love is the Christian ideal.

• Condemnation of sectarian violence in Northern Ireland.

• Overwhelming approval of a proposal urging member churches of the Anglican Communion to respect each other's decisions on ordaining women as priests or bishops. This action raises a "serious obstacle" to "fuller communion" between the Catholic and Anglican churches, said Father Kevin McDonald, an observer at the conference and a staff member of the Vatican Secretariat for Promoting Christian Unity.

Underlying and unsettled problems of the conference and the Anglican Communion were the nature of the Church of Christ and the nature of authority in the Church.

SEPTEMBER 1988

POPE JOHN PAUL IN AFRICA

Pope John Paul traveled to Africa again Sept. 10 to 19, on visits to five countries in the southern part of the continent. His itinerary was as follows:

Sept. 10: Departure from Rome at 8:00 a.m.; arrival late in the afternoon at Zimbabwe's Harare Airport; visit with President Mugabe; meeting with bishops of the region.
Sept. 11: Meeting with the bishops of Zimbabwe; Mass; meetings with lay persons, youths and the diplomatic corps.
Sept. 12: Mass in Bulawayo; meeting with priests and Religious; address at an ecumenical prayer service.
Sept. 13: Departure from Harare and arrival at Gaborone, Botswana; visit with President Quett Masire; meeting with priests, Religious and lay persons; Mass.
Sept. 14: Departure from Gaborone and delayed arrival at Maseru, Lesotho (via South Africa, because of bad weather); meeting with King Moshoeshoe; welcoming ceremony; visit to the tomb of Father Joseph Gerard; Mass; meeting with bishops.
Sept. 15: Mass and beatification of Father Gerard; meetings with priests, Religious, seminarians, and youths; talk at an ecumenical prayer service.
Sept. 16: Departure for Manzini, Swaziland; Mass; meeting with King Mswati; meeting with the faithful. Departure for and arrival at Maputo, Mozambique; visit with President Chissano.
Sept. 17: Mass in Beira; meeting with the faithful at the airport in Nampula.
Sept. 18: Visit with the sick; Mass; ecumenical meeting; meetings with residents of a Maputo neighborhood, young people, priests, Religious, seminarians, lay persons, bishops of the country.
Sept. 19: Morning departure from Maputo and nighttime arrival at Rome's Leonardo da Vinci Airport.

HIGHLIGHTS OF THE TRIP
(By NC News Service)

Pope John Paul's trip to five southern African states was punctuated by unexpected and tragic events.

He repeatedly called for reconciliation and good will in resolving the region's deeply rooted problems. But, as he arrived in Lesotho, six people died in a bus hijacking — including the hijackers, who had demanded a conference with him.

The Pope excluded white-minority-ruled South Africa from his itinerary, at the insistence of that country's bishops, and condemned apartheid, the South African system of racial discrimination. But he briefly found himself at mid-trip the somewhat bemused guest of the South African government.

He found hope in Zimbabwe, his first stop, where black and white citizens and contending political forces appeared to be working out their differences peacefully.

While he was flying from Rome to Zimbabwe, the Pope told reporters covering his trip that apartheid is a "racist vision of human inequality" that "cannot be continued."

He praised imprisoned black anti-apartheid leader Nelson Mandela and said he hoped Mandela would be freed soon.

In Zimbabwe

At the airport in Harare, Zimbabwe, Sept. 10, the Holy Father — without naming South Africa — said "powerful political economic and ideological forces endanger the still fragile stability of countries which are only beginning to consolidate their recently acquired independence."

He also said that, while he understood why the victims of apartheid might turn to violence, "from the moral point of view it is not a solution that one wishes to propose."

He praised the government's program of national reconstruction, begun in 1980 after seven years of war.

He said Africa is looking to Zimbabwe "for a sign of a better future to be built on the basis of justice and brotherhood under God, without discrimination."

Later that day, he took a stand against controversial legislation which would reduce church control over church school policies and hiring.

"Civil law should respect the right of the responsible Catholic authorities to select the heads and the teachers of these institutions, so their Catholic character can be maintained," he told Zimbabwe's bishops.

He returned to the theme of reconciliation Sept. 12 in Bulawayo. The region's turbulent and sometimes bloody history is reflected in the city's name — which means "Place of Massacres."

Pope John Paul noted a recent political breakthrough will make southern Zimbabwe's minority Ndebele tribe a full partner in government with the majority Shona.

"You are trying to bring about the fulfillment of the prophecy of Isaiah, in which he says that people 'will hammer their swords into plowshares, their spears into sickles,' " he told participants in a Mass.

In Botswana

Apartheid underlay some of the Pope's message in Botswana. In a meeting Sept. 13 with priests, Religious and laity in the capital, Gaborone, he praised local church efforts for extending aid to refugees from neighboring South Africa.

"You have witnessed the plight of those who are subjected by law to discrimination," he said. "And I gladly support you in your desire to be close to those who are unjustly deprived of their legitimate rights and lack decent living conditions."

The Vatican press spokesman, in a mid-trip interview, said the Pope sought to provide ethical commentary on apartheid and other issues in the region, without becoming directly embroiled.

"The role of the Holy See in the political affairs of the area is not and does not want to be one of mediation in the diplomatic sense of the word," he said Sept. 13. "But, with its ethical insistence, the Holy See wants to help create a climate in which dialogue can be possible."

Unplanned Stop

The next day was one of the most unusual in any of the Pope's years of traveling.

Fog and rain forced the papal plane to land at Johannesburg, South Africa, rather than its intended stop, Maseru, Lesotho.

The Vatican, at the urging of the South African bishops, had excluded that country from the itinerary. One of their concerns was the image of the head of the Catholic Church being escorted and hosted by the government which keeps blacks, who make up the majority of South African Catholics, from full political and economic participation.

But the South Africans reacted swiftly to the unexpected arrival of the Pontiff on their territory.

Shortly after the Pope's Air Zimbabwe Boeing 707 landed at Jan Smuts airport, Foreign Minister Roelof "Pik" Botha was at the scene. Within a couple of hours, he had ordered 100 snacks for the Pope, his entourage and the press corps traveling with him; had met privately with the Pope, and had arranged a motorcade, escorted by South African police, to Maseru, 250 miles away.

In Lesotho

Meanwhile, in Maseru, four gunmen claiming membership in the rebel Lesotho Liberation Army had taken hostage a busload of Catholics traveling to attend events of the papal visit.

Within minutes after the Pope's arrival in Maseru, South African commandos called in to handle the situation shot it out with the hijackers, killing three on the spot. One died later in the hospital. Two passengers also died and 20 were wounded.

Officials said the gunmen had wanted to speak with the Pope, but the Pontiff was not told of their demand until the incident was over.

At a papal Mass in Maseru Sept. 15, a survivor of the hijacking, 49-year-old Catholic schoolteacher Mabokang Ramokoena, said, "We never thought we would be here to see him. God helped us to escape, we don't know how."

Pope John Paul said he was "saddened to learn that others on their way to join me in this pilgrimage have been the victims of a hijack that caused such anguish and ended in bloodshed."

After a Mass in which he beatified 19th-century missionary Father Joseph Gerard, he drove to nearby Queen Elizabeth II Hospital to visit the passengers wounded in the hijacking and give them rosaries.

At a meeting with youths later in the day, the Pope said it is not cowardly to spurn violence as a means of solving problems.

"There is nothing passive about non-violence," he said. "The increase of violence in the world can never be halted by responding with more of the same."

In Swaziland and Mozambique

On a brief visit to the kingdom of Swaziland Sept. 16, the Pope struck a different theme, but one he had sounded previously in Africa — Christians cannot be polygamists.

Among those listening to his sermon at a stadium in Manzini, Swaziland's capital, was the country's 20-year-old king, Mswati III — who had four wives and was becoming engaged to another woman.

The basis of stable families is a "monogamous marital union" founded on the "equal personal dignity" of men and women, Pope John Paul said.

After less than a day in Swaziland, the Pope traveled to Mozambique, a country wracked by a long and destructive civil war. Mozambique's bishops have called on the Marxist government and the opposing Mozambican National Resistance to negotiate an end to the conflict.

More than 100,000 have been killed and as many as three million made homeless by the war. Mozambique's President Joaquim Chissano praised church efforts toward helping the homeless, and described church-state relations as a condition of "progressive normalization."

Pope John Paul backed the bishops' call for negotiations during his visit to the country.

He also praised the government's recent decision to return church properties which were nationalized shortly after independence was achieved in 1974.

As many as 500,000 Mozambicans turned out to greet the Pontiff on his arrival — an unusual number even in a Catholic country. About 13 percent of the nation's 1.8 million population is Catholic.

Pope John Paul, in several of his speeches in Mozambique, sought to prod the government to open itself more to spiritual values.

In Beira, Sept. 17, he told his listeners that a society cannot "close itself to transcendence, close itself to God."

He ended his visit to Mozambique, and his southern African trip, with an appeal for peace.

In a speech to the bishops, he addressed, "from the bottom of my heart, all those involved in one way or another in this (civil) war," and urged them to "stop the killings."

COUNSEL TO BISHOPS

At a meeting with the bishops of Mozambique Sept. 18, the Holy Father called attention to: solid formation — doctrinal, spiritual, liturgical — of priests and others involved in leadership roles; catechesis at all levels for total Christian living; reestablishment of the family according to the plan of God; ecumenism and dialogue with persons preaching the teaching and practice of other religions; prayer, much prayer, for peace in Mozambique.

POPE JOHN PAUL II

(See many related entries under John Paul II in the Index.)

Cardinal-Archbishop Karol Wojtyla of Cracow was elected Bishop of Rome Oct. 16, 1978, on the seventh or eighth ballot cast on the second day of voting at a conclave of 111 cardinals. He chose the name John Paul II and was invested with the pallium, the symbol of his papal office, Oct. 22 in ceremonies attended by more than 250,000 persons in St. Peter's Square.

The 263rd successor of St. Peter as Bishop of Rome and Supreme Pastor of the Universal Church, he is the first non-Italian Pope since Adrian VI (1522-23), the first Polish Pope in the history of the Church, and the youngest at the time of his election since Pius IX (1846-78).

Early Career

Karol Wojtyla was born May 18, 1920, in Wadowice, Poland.

He began higher studies at the age of 18, with major interests in poetry and theater arts. Forced to suspend university courses because of the outbreak of World War II, he went to work in a stone quarry and a chemical plant, thereby earning the later designation of himself as the "Worker Cardinal."

He started studies for the priesthood in 1942 in the underground seminary of Cracow, whose operations had been banned after the Nazi invasion of Poland.

Ordained to the priesthood Nov. 1, 1946, he was immediately sent to Rome for studies at the Angelicum University, where he earned a doctorate in ethics.

Back home in Poland, he worked as an assistant pastor in a village parish and as a chaplain to university students while continuing studies at the Catholic University of Lublin. He was awarded another doctorate there, in moral theology.

He began writing about this time, and eventually produced more than 100 articles and several books on ethical and other themes. Phenomenology was one of his fields of expertise.

University teaching came next, in 1953, with appointment in 1954 to the position of lecturer and later to the chair of ethics at the Catholic University of Lublin, the most prestigious institute of higher learning in Poland.

Bishop and Cardinal

He was ordained Auxiliary Bishop of Cracow Sept. 28, 1958, became vicar capitular in 1962 after the death of Apostolic Administrator Eugeniusz Baziak, and was appointed Archbishop Jan. 13, 1964. He was the first residential head of the see since the death of Cardinal Adam Sapieha in 1951. Between then and 1964 the archdiocese was run by administrators because the communist government refused to permit the appointment and ministry of a residential bishop.

Archbishop Wojtyla attended all sessions of the Second Vatican Council from 1962 to 1965, and was one of the writers of the *Pastoral Constitution on the Church in the Modern World*. He also contributed input to the *Declaration on Religious Freedom* and the *Decree on the Instruments of Social Communication*.

His efforts to put into effect the directives of the council induced him to write a book, *Foundations of Renewal*, in 1972 and to start that same year an archdiocesan synod he saw concluded as Pope during his visit to Poland in 1979.

He was inducted into the College of Cardinals June 26, 1967, as one of the younger members, and subsequently served actively in the Congregation for the Sacraments and Divine Worship, the Congregation for the Clergy, and the Congregation for Catholic Education.

He also served as a theological consultant to Pope Paul VI.

He attended assemblies of the Synod of Bishops as a representative of the Polish Bishops' Conference and was a member of the Synod's permanent council.

From the beginning of his priestly career, and especially during his episcopate, the Cardinal was vigorous in the defense of human and religious rights, the rights of workers, and rights to religious education.

Close to Cardinal Wyszynski and in company with his fellow bishops, he negotiated the tightrope of Catholic survival in a country under communist control. With them, and as their spokesman at times, he was stalwart in resisting efforts of the regime to impose atheism, materialism and secularism on the people and culture of Poland.

Active Pope

Since the beginning of his pontificate, John Paul has been active as Bishop of Rome, with frequent visits to parishes and institutions of the diocese for the celebration of Mass and participation in other events. During these visits, as well as others to places of pilgrimage and historic significance in Italy, he has had perhaps more personal contact with the faithful than any other Pope. The number of attendants at weekly general audiences at the Vatican and Castel Gandolfo has been unprecedented.

Extensive Travels

By the end of September, 1988, the Pope had made 39 pastoral trips to foreign countries.

• The Pope made four trips in 1979, to: the Dominican Republic and Mexico, Jan. 5 to Feb. 1; Poland, June 2 to 10; Ireland and the United States, Sept. 29 to Oct. 7; Turkey, Nov. 28 to 30.

In Turkey, he met with Orthodox Ecumenical Patriarch Dimitrios I and, with him, announced the establishment of a commission of theologians to begin formal dialogue in quest of the union of the Roman Catholic and Orthodox Churches.

• There were four trips in 1980, to: Africa (Zaire, Congo Republic, Kenya, Ghana, Upper Volta, Ivory Coast), May 2 to 12; France, May 30 to June 2; Brazil (13 cities), June 30 to July 12; West Germany, Nov. 15 to 19.

In Africa, he spoke about the Africanization of the Church, the cultural values of Africans, and the independence they should have from alien influences of other countries and cultures.

In France, before the United Nations Educational, Scientific and Cultural Organization, he delineated with great clarity the stance of the Church on a wide variety of subjects, with special emphasis on its role in a secularized state, society and culture.

In Brazil, he declared that the Church is on the side of poor, appealed for across-the-board respect for human rights by governments and people of influence, called for measures of economic and social reform, and indicated approval of non-violent activism for the good of all peoples. He attended a plenary assembly of the bishops of the country and took part in opening ceremonies of a national Eucharistic Congress.

• In 1981, he made only one trip, to the Philippines, Guam and Japan, with stopovers in Pakistan and Alaska, Feb. 16 to 27.

Plans for additional trips in 1981 — to Lourdes, for the 42nd International Eucharistic Congress, and to Switzerland — had to be cancelled because of the attack on the Pope's life in May.

• He made seven trips in 1982, to: Africa (Nigeria, Benin, Gabon, Equatorial Guinea), Feb. 12 to 19; Portugal, May 12 to 15; Great Britain, May 28 to June 2; Argentina, June 11 and 12; Switzerland, June 15; San Marino, Aug. 29; Spain, Oct. 31 to Nov. 9.

In Portugal, at the Marian shrine at Fatima, he consecrated the world to the Blessed Virgin Mary.

• On four trips in 1983, the Pope visited: Central America (Costa Rica, Nicaragua, Panama, El Salvador, Guatemala, Belize, Honduras) and Haiti, Mar. 2 to 10; Poland, June 16 to 23; Lourdes, France, Aug. 14 and 15; Austria, Sept. 10 to 13.

• The Pope made four trips in 1984, to: South Korea, Papua New Guinea, Solomon Islands, Thailand, May 2 to 12; Switzerland, June 12 to 17; Canada, Sept. 9 to 20; Spain, Dominican Republic and Puerto Rico, Oct. 10 to 12.

• The Pope made four trips in 1985 by the middle of September, to: Venezuela, Ecuador, Peru, Trinidad and Tobago, Jan. 26 to Feb. 6; Belgium, The Netherlands and Luxembourg, May 11 to 21; Africa (Togo, Ivory Coast, Cameroon, Central African Republic, Zaire, Kenya and Morocco), Aug. 8 to 19; Liechtenstein, Sept. 8.

• In 1986, he visited India, Feb. 1 to 10; Colombia-St. Lucia, July 1 to 7; France, Oct. 4 to 7; Oceania, Nov. 18 to Dec. 1.

• Four visits in 1987 were to: Uruguay, Chile and Argentina, Mar. 31 to Apr. 12; West Germany, Apr. 30 to May 4; Poland, June 8 to 14; the United States and Canada, Sept. 10 to 19.

• In 1988, he visited Uruguay, Bolivia, Peru and Paraguay, May 7 to 18; Austria, June 23 to 27; Zimbabwe, Botswana, Lesotho, Swaziland and Mozambique, Sept. 10 to 19. (See separate entries.)

Key Writings

Encyclicals: The homilies and addresses delivered by the Pope on these trips were the equivalent of doctrinal, pastoral and social encyclical letters on a wide variety of subjects, all related to the key document of the first year of his pontificate. That was the formal encyclical, *Redemptor Hominis,* a treatise on Christian anthropology dealing with the divine and human aspects of redemption and the mission of the Church to carry on a dialogue of salvation with all peoples.

Two other encyclicals published within less than a year of each other were *Dives in Misericordia* ("On the Mercy of God") in 1980 and *Laborem Exercens* ("On Human Work") in 1981. *Slavorum Apostoli* in 1985 honored Sts. Cyril and Methodius, apostles of the Slavic peoples. *Dominum et Vivificantem* ("Lord and Giver of life") was published in 1986. *Redemptoris Mater* ("Mother of the Redeemer") was published in 1987. The Pope's seventh encyclical, *Sollicitudo Rei Socialis* ("On Social Concerns") was issued in 1988. (See separate entry.)

Other Writings: The Pope published a lengthy exhortation on the family, *Familiaris Consortio,* in December, 1981. It is an extensive synthesis of the theology of the family based not only on traditional doctrinal background but also on recommendations that emanated from the 1980 assembly of the Synod of Bishops.

Writings published in 1984 included two apostolic letters — on suffering, *Salvifici Doloris,* and on Jerusalem; an apostolic exhortation, *Redemptionis Donum,* addressed to and about Religious; a "Charter of the Rights of the Family"; and an apostolic exhortation, "Reconciliation and Penance in the Ministry of the Church." In 1986, he issued an apostolic letter on the 1600th anniversary of the conversion of St. Augustine.

Writings issued in 1988 included two apostolic letters on the millennium of Christianity in the Ukraine and the present territory of the Soviet Union. (See *Euntes in Mundum* and *Magnum Baptismi Donum.)*

Various Items

Doctrinal Concern: In December, 1980, the Pope directly confronted the controversial writings of Father Hans Kung by giving his approval to a declaration by the Congregation for the Doctrine of the Faith that he could not be regarded as a Catholic theologian.

On Aug. 6, 1983, he authorized release by the Doctrinal Congregation of a letter to bishops throughout the world in refutation of unorthodox views — especially those of Father Edward Schillebeeckx, O.P. — concerning "The Minister of the Eucharist."

The Holy Father regarded as extremely important a series of talks begun at general audiences in the summer of 1984 on marriage and sexual morality, explaining and firmly supporting traditional doctrine, with emphasis on teaching contained in the encyclical letter, *Humanae Vitae,* by Pope Paul VI.

He approved instructions on liberation theology issued by the Congregation for the Doctrine of the Faith in 1984 and 1986.

He approved the 1986 declaration of the Congregation for the Doctrine of the Faith that U.S. theologian Father Charles E. Curran is not eligible to function as a Catholic theologian.

In 1988, the Pope decreed the excommunication of dissident Archbishop Marcel Lefebvre, the prime mover in the first schism from the Church in nearly 100 years. (See Lefebvre Schism.)

Canon Law: The Pope was deeply involved in the work of completing the revision of the Code of Canon Law, which he ordered into effect as of Nov. 27, 1983. He called it, in effect, the final act of the Second Vatican Council. He emphasized its innovative force in an address Jan. 26, 1984, to personnel of the Sacred Roman Rota.

Causes of Saints: In 1988, the Pope canonized 125 saints, including 117 martyrs of Vietnam and French-born Rose Philippine Duchesne, educator and missionary to Indians in the U.S. Two among the many servants of God beatified were California missionary Junipero Serra and foundress Katharine Drexel.

Synods: The Holy Father convoked three of them in 1980.

With the Dutch bishops at the Vatican for a particular synod in January, he called for measures to cope with differences among the prelates, polarization among the people and action to remedy doctrinal and disciplinary irregularities. Later reports indicated that results of the synod were less than satisfactory.

Meeting with Ukrainian bishops in March, he named a successor to Cardinal Josyf Slipyi as the ranking Ukrainian bishop and turned down demands of some Ukrainians for a patriarchate.

With more than 200 delegates from episcopal conferences around the world, he held the fifth ordinary assembly of the Synod of Bishops.

He convoked another ordinary assembly of the Synod in 1983 and an extraordinary one that was held Nov. 25 to Dec. 8, 1985. The purpose of the 1985 assembly was to evaluate the effects and implementation of the enactments of the Second Vatican Council, on the occasion of the 20th anniversary of its conclusion. The theme of the 1987 assembly was the role and ministry of lay persons. (See separate entries, Synod of Bishops.)

Holy Year: The Holy Father proclaimed a Jubilee celebration of the 1950th anniversary of the Redemption from the Solemnity of the Annunciation of the Lord Mar. 25, 1983, to Easter Sunday, Apr. 22, 1984, and a Marian Year from Pentecost, 1987, to the solemnity of the Assumption, 1988.

Cardinals: In June, 1979, the Holy Father inducted 14 new cardinals into the Sacred College, raising its membership at that time to 135. A second group was inducted into the Sacred College Feb. 3, 1983, at which time the total membership was 138. Twenty-eight new members inducted into the College May 25, 1985, brought the membership to an all-time high of 152. Twenty-four were inducted in 1988; by late September, the total was 156.

Meetings with Bishops: In relations with the hierarchy since becoming Pope, John Paul has met with groups of bishops making required *ad limina* visits to the Vatican, for first-hand reports and admonitions regarding conditions in dioceses all over the world. He has also met with assemblies of bishops in the countries he has visited.

Ecumenism: He met with Anglican Archbishop Robert Runcie at the Canterbury Cathedral during his visit to Great Britain in May, 1982. The two prelates prayed together, renewed their baptismal promises and issued a joint statement in which they announced the formation of a new joint Catholic-Anglican theological commission for a second phase of interfaith dialogue.

Ever since the beginning of his pontificate, the Pope has maintained contact with Orthodox leaders and officials of other churches and religious bodies, and has encouraged interfaith relations at all levels.

While visiting the headquarters of the World Council of Churches in Geneva June 12, 1984, the Pope said the Church's engagement in the quest for religious unity is irreversible. At the same time, he mentioned two points of extreme significance in Catholic doctrine and practice.

The Church, he said, "entered on the hard ecumenical task bringing with it a conviction" about the role of the bishop of Rome. "It is convinced that in the ministry of the bishop of Rome it has preserved the visible pole and guarantee of unity in full fidelity to the apostolic tradition and to the faith of the Fathers."

He also reiterated doctrinal opposition to sharing the Eucharist until full unity is achieved. "It is not yet possible for us to celebrate the Eucharist together and communicate at the same table."

Nevertheless, he placed emphasis on things Christians have in common, among them, baptism, reverence for Scripture, prayer, a rediscovery of the "whole role of the Holy Spirit," and cooperation in work for social justice and human rights.

A significant interfaith event of 1986 was the papal visit to the Synagogue of Rome.

Audiences and Addresses: The Pope has delivered hundreds of addresses at general and private audiences and on special occasions. All of them have characteristically been grounded in doctrinal essentials coupled with relevance to the people being addressed or the events being commemorated.

World Affairs: In 1984, the Pope agreed to a new concordat with Italy, regulating church-state relations. He agreed also to the establishment of diplomatic relations with the United States. One hundred and 18 nations maintained diplomatic relations with the Vatican as of Sept. 20, 1987.

On his travels as well as at the Vatican, the Pope has been an outstanding advocate of human rights and dignity, of respect for life, of peace, of nuclear and conventional disarmament, of reconciliation among nations, of aid and relief for distressed peoples and nations, of people first and things second in all areas of life.

Near Tragedy: The Pope narrowly escaped death May 13, 1981, when he was fired upon at close range by Mehmet Ali Agca as he entered St. Peter's Square to address a general audience.

DATES AND EVENTS IN CHURCH HISTORY

FIRST CENTURY

c. 33: First Christian Pentecost; descent of the Holy Spirit upon the disciples; preaching of St. Peter in Jerusalem; conversion, baptism and aggregation of some 3,000 persons to the first Christian community.
St. Stephen, deacon, was stoned to death at Jerusalem; he is venerated as the first Christian martyr.

c. 34: St. Paul, formerly Saul the persecutor of Christians, was converted and baptized. After three years of solitude in the desert, he joined the college of the apostles; he made three major missionary journeys and became known as the Apostle to the Gentiles; he was imprisoned twice in Rome and was beheaded there between 64 and 67.

39: Cornelius (the Gentile) and his family were baptized by St. Peter; a significant event signalling the mission of the Church to all peoples.

42: Persecution of Christians in Palestine broke out during the rule of Herod Agrippa; St. James the Greater, the first apostle to die, was beheaded in 44; St. Peter was imprisoned for a short time; many Christians fled to Antioch, marking the beginning of the dispersion of Christians beyond the confines of Palestine. At Antioch, the followers of Christ were called Christians for the first time.

49: Christians at Rome, considered members of a Jewish sect, were adversely affected by a decree of Claudius which forbade Jewish worship there.

51: The Council of Jerusalem, in which all the apostles participated under the presidency of St. Peter, decreed that circumcision, dietary regulations, and various other prescriptions of Mosaic Law were not obligatory for Gentile converts to the Christian community. The crucial decree was issued in opposition to Judaizers who contended that observance of the Mosaic Law in its entirety was necessary for salvation.

64: Persecution broke out at Rome under Nero, the emperor said to have accused Christians of starting the fire which destroyed half of Rome.

64 or 67: Martyrdom of St. Peter at Rome during the Neronian persecution. He established his see and spent his last years there after preaching in and around Jerusalem, establishing a see at Antioch, and presiding at the Council of Jerusalem.

70: Destruction of Jerusalem by Titus.

88-97: Pontificate of St. Clement I, third successor of St. Peter as bishop of Rome, one of the Apostolic Fathers. The *First Epistle of Clement to the Corinthians,* with which he has been identified, was addressed by the Church of Rome to the Church at Corinth, the scene of irregularities and divisions in the Christian community.

95: Domitian persecuted Christians, principally at Rome.

c. 100: Death of St. John, apostle and evangelist, marking the end of the Age of the Apostles and the first generation of the Church.
By the end of the century, Antioch, Alexandria and Ephesus in the East and Rome in the West were established centers of Christian population and influence.

SECOND CENTURY

c. 107: St. Ignatius of Antioch was martyred at Rome. He was the first writer to use the expression, "the Catholic Church."

112: Emperor Trajan, in a rescript to Pliny the Younger, governor of Bithynia, instructed him not to search out Christians but to punish them if they were publicly denounced and refused to do homage to the Roman gods. This rescript set a pattern for Roman magistrates in dealing with Christians.

117-38: Persecution under Hadrian. Many *Acts of Martyrs* date from this period.

c. 125: Spread of Gnosticism, a combination of elements of Platonic philosophy and Eastern mystery religions. Its adherents claimed that its secret-knowledge principle provided a deeper insight into Christian doctrine than divine revelation and faith. One gnostic thesis denied the divinity of Christ; others denied the reality of his humanity, calling it mere appearance (Docetism, Phantasiasm).

c. 144: Excommunication of Marcion, bishop and heretic, who claimed that there was total opposition and no connection at all between the Old Testament and the New Testament, between the God of the Jews and the God of the Christians; and that the Canon (list of inspired writings) of the Bible consisted only of parts of St. Luke's Gospel and 10 letters of St. Paul. Marcionism was checked at Rome by 200 and was condemned by a council held there about 260, but the heresy persisted for several centuries in the East and had some adherents as late as the Middle Ages.

c. 155: St. Polycarp, bishop of Smyrna and disciple of St. John the Evangelist, was martyred.

c. 156: Beginning of Montanism, a form of religious extremism. Its principal tenets were the imminent second coming of Christ, denial of the divine nature of the Church and its power to forgive sin, and excessively rigorous morality. The heresy, preached by Montanus of Phrygia and others, was condemned by Pope St. Zephyrinus (199-217).

161-80: Reign of Marcus Aurelius. His persecution, launched in the wake of natural disasters, was more violent than those of his predecessors.

165: St. Justin, an important early Christian writer, was martyred at Rome.

c. 180: St. Irenaeus, bishop of Lyons and one of the great early theologians, wrote *Adversus Haereses.* He stated that the teaching and tradition of the Roman See was the standard for belief.

196: Easter Controversy, concerning the day of celebration — a Sunday, according to practice in the West, or the 14th of the month of Nisan (in the Hebrew calendar), no matter what day of the week, according to practice in the East. The controversy was not resolved at this time.

The *Didache*, whose extant form dates from the second century, is an important record of Christian belief, practice and governance in the first century.

Latin was introduced as a liturgical language in the West. Other liturgical languages were Aramaic and Greek.

The Catechetical School of Alexandria, founded about the middle of the century, gained increasing influence on doctrinal study and instruction, and interpretation of the Bible.

THIRD CENTURY

202: Persecution under Septimius Severus, who wanted to establish a simple common religion in the Empire.

206: Tertullian, a convert since 197 and the first great ecclesiastical writer in Latin, joined the heretical Montanists; he died in 230.

215: Death of Clement of Alexandria, teacher of Origen and a founding father of the School of Alexandria.

217-35: St. Hippolytus, the first antipope; he was reconciled to the Church while in prison during persecution in 235.

232-54: Origen established the School of Caesarea after being deposed in 231 as head of the School of Alexandria; he died in 254. A scholar and voluminous writer, he was one of the founders of systematic theology and exerted wide influence for many years.

c. 242: Manichaeism originated in Persia: a combination of errors based on the assumption that two supreme principles (good and evil) are operative in creation and life, and that the supreme objective of human endeavor is liberation from evil (matter). The heresy denied the humanity of Christ, the sacramental system, the authority of the Church (and state), and endorsed a moral code which threatened the fabric of society. In the 12th and 13th centuries, it took on the features of Albigensianism and Catharism.

249-51: Persecution under Decius. Many of those who denied the faith *(lapsi)* sought readmission to the Church at the end of the persecution in 251. Pope St. Cornelius agreed with St. Cyprian that *lapsi* were to be readmitted to the Church after satisfying the requirements of appropriate penance. Antipope Novatian, on the other hand, contended that persons who fell away from the Church under persecution and/or those guilty of serious sin after baptism could not be absolved and readmitted to communion with the Church. The heresy was condemned by a Roman synod in 251.

250-300: Neo-Platonism of Plotinus and Porphyry gained followers.

251: Novatian, an antipope, was condemned at Rome.

256: Pope St. Stephen I upheld the validity of baptism properly administered by heretics, in the Rebaptism Controversy.

257: Persecution under Valerian, who attempted to destroy the Church as a social structure.

258: St. Cyprian, bishop of Carthage, was martyred.

c. 260: St. Lucian founded the School of Antioch, a center of influence on biblical studies.

Pope St. Dionysius condemned Sabellianism, a form of Modalism (like Monarchianism and Patripassianism). The heresy contended that the Father, Son and Holy Spirit are not distinct divine persons but are only three different modes of being and self-manifestations of the one God. St. Paul of Thebes became a hermit.

261: Gallienus issued an edict of toleration which ended general persecution for nearly 40 years.

c. 292: Diocletian divided the Roman Empire into East and West. The division emphasized political, cultural and other differences between the two parts of the Empire and influenced different developments in the Church in the East and West. The prestige of Rome began to decline.

FOURTH CENTURY

303: Persecution broke out under Diocletian; it was particularly violent in 304.

305: St. Anthony of Heracles established a foundation for hermits near the Red Sea in Egypt.

c. 306: The first local legislation on clerical celibacy was enacted by a council held at Elvira, Spain; bishops, priests, deacons and other ministers were forbidden to have wives.

311: An edict of toleration issued by Galerius at the urging of Constantine and Licinius officially ended persecution in the West; some persecution continued in the East.

313: The *Edict of Milan* issued by Constantine and Licinius recognized Christianity as a lawful religion in the Roman Empire.

314: A council of Arles condemned Donatism, declaring that baptism properly administered by heretics is valid, in view of the principle that sacraments have their efficacy from Christ, not from the spiritual condition of their human ministers. The heresy was condemned again by a council of Carthage in 411.

318: St. Pachomius established the first foundation of the cenobitic (common) life, as compared with the solitary life of hermits in Upper Egypt.

325: Ecumenical Council of Nicaea (I). Its principal action was the condemnation of Arianism, the most devastating of the early heresies, which denied the divinity of Christ. The heresy was authored by Arius of Alexandria, a priest. Arians and several kinds of Semi-Arians propagandized their tenets widely, established their own hierarchies and churches, and raised havoc in the Church for several centuries. The council contributed to formulation of the Nicene Creed (Creed of Nicaea-Constantinople); fixed the date for the observance of Easter; passed regulations concerning clerical discipline; adopted the civil divisions of the Empire as the model for the jurisdictional organization of the Church.

326: Discovery of the True Cross on which Christ was crucified.

337: Baptism and death of Constantine.

c. 342: Beginning of a 40-year persecution in Persia.

343-44: A council of Sardica reaffirmed doctrine formulated by Nicaea I and declared also that bishops had the right of appeal to the pope as the highest authority in the Church.

361-63: Emperor Julian the Apostate waged an unsuccessful campaign against the Church in an attempt to restore paganism as the religion of the Empire.

c. 365: Persecution under Valens in the East.

c. 376: Beginning of the barbarian invasion in the West.

379: Death of St. Basil, the Father of Monasticism in the East. His writings contributed greatly to the development of rules for the life of Religious.

381: Ecumenical Council of Constantinople (I). It condemned various brands of Arianism as well as Macedonianism, which denied the divinity of the Holy Spirit; contributed to formulation of the Nicene Creed; approved a canon acknowledging Constantinople as the second see after Rome in honor and dignity.

382: The Canon of Sacred Scripture, the official list of the inspired books of the Bible, was contained in the *Decree of Pope St. Damasus* and published by a regional council of Carthage in 397; the Canon was formally defined by the Council of Trent in the 16th century.

382-c. 406: St. Jerome translated the Old and New Testaments into Latin; his work is called the Vulgate version of the Bible.

396: St. Augustine became bishop of Hippo in North Africa.

FIFTH CENTURY

410: Visigoths sacked Rome.

430: St. Augustine, bishop of Hippo for 35 years, died. He was a strong defender of orthodox doctrine against Manichaeism, Donatism and Pelagianism. The depth and range of his writings made him a dominant influence in Christian thought for centuries.

431: Ecumenical Council of Ephesus. It condemned Nestorianism, which denied the unity of the divine and human natures in the Person of Christ; defined *Theotokos* (Bearer of God) as the title of Mary, Mother of the Son of God made Man; condemned Pelagianism. The heresy of Pelagianism, proceeding from the assumption that Adam had a natural right to supernatural life, held that man could attain salvation through the efforts of his natural powers and free will; it involved errors concerning the nature of original sin, the meaning of grace and other matters. Related Semi-Pelagianism was condemned by a council of Orange in 529.

432: St. Patrick arrived in Ireland. By the time of his death in 461 most of the country had been converted, monasteries founded and the hierarchy established.

438: The *Theodosian Code,* a compilation of decrees for the Empire, was issued by Theodosius II; it had great influence on subsequent civil and ecclesiastical law.

449: The Robber Council of Ephesus, which did not have ecclesiastical sanction, declared itself in favor of the opinions of Eutyches who contended that Christ had only one, the divine, nature (Monophysitism).

451: Ecumenical Council of Chalcedon. Its principal action was the condemnation of Monophysitism (also called Eutychianism), which denied the humanity of Christ by holding that he had only one, the divine, nature.

452: Pope St. Leo the Great persuaded Attila the Hun to spare Rome.

455: Vandals sacked Rome. The decline of imperial Rome dates approximately from this time.

484: Patriarch Acacius of Constantinople was excommunicated for signing the *Henoticon,* a document which capitulated to the Monophysite heresy. The excommunication triggered a schism which lasted for 35 years.

494: Pope St. Gelasius I declared in a letter to Emperor Anastasius that the pope had power and authority over the emperor in spiritual matters.

496: Clovis, King of the Franks, was converted and became the defender of Christianity in the West. The Franks became a Catholic people.

SIXTH CENTURY

520 on: Irish monasteries flourished as centers for spiritual life, missionary training and scholarly activity.

529: The Second Council of Orange condemned Semi-Pelagianism.

c. 529: St. Benedict founded the Monte Cassino Abbey. Some years before his death in 543 he wrote a monastic rule which exercised tremendous influence on the form and style of religious life. He is called the Father of Monasticism in the West.

533: John II became the first pope to change his name. The practice did not become general until the time of Sergius IV (1009).

533-34: Emperor Justinian promulgated the *Corpus Juris Civilis* for the Roman world; like the *Theodosian Code,* it influenced subsequent civil and ecclesiastical law.

c. 545: Death of Dionysius Exiguus who was the first to date history from the birth of Christ, a practice which resulted in use of the B.C. and A.D. abbreviations. His calculations were at least four years late.

553: Ecumenical Council of Constantinople (II). It condemned the *Three Chapters,* Nestorian-tainted writings of Theodore of Mopsuestia, Theodoret of Cyrus and Ibas of Edessa.

585: St. Columban founded an influential monastic school at Luxeuil. He died in 615.

589: The most important of several councils of Toledo was held. The Visigoths renounced Arianism, and St. Leander began the organization of the Church in Spain.

590-604: Pontificate of Pope St. Gregory I the Great. He set the form and style of the papacy which prevailed throughout the Middle Ages; exerted great influence on doctrine and liturgy; was strong in support of monastic discipline and clerical celibacy; authored writings on many subjects. Gregorian Chant is named in his honor.

596: Pope St. Gregory I sent St. Augustine of Canterbury and 40 monks to do missionary work in England.

597: St. Columba died. He founded an important monastery at Iona, established schools and did notable missionary work in Scotland.

By the end of the century, monasteries of nuns were common; Western monasticism was flourishing; monasticism in the East, under the influence of Monophysitism and other factors, was losing its vigor.

SEVENTH CENTURY

613: St. Columban established the influential monastery of Bobbio in northern Italy; he died there in 615.

622: The Hegira (flight) of Mohammed from Mecca to Medina signalled the beginning of Islam which, by the end of the century, claimed almost all of the southern Mediterranean area.

628: Heraclius, Eastern Emperor, recovered the True Cross from the Persians.

649: A Lateran council condemned two erroneous formulas (*Ecthesis* and *Type*) issued by emperors Heraclius and Constans II as means of reconciling Monophysites with the Church.

664: Actions of the Synod of Whitby advanced the adoption of Roman usages in England, especially regarding the date for the observance of Easter. (See Easter Controversy.)

680-81: Ecumenical Council of Constantinople (III). It condemned Monothelitism, which held that Christ had only one will, the divine; censured Pope Honorius I for a letter to Sergius, bishop of Constantinople, in which he made an ambiguous but not infallible statement about the unity of will and/or operation in Christ.

692: Trullan Synod. Eastern-Church discipline on clerical celibacy was settled, permitting marriage before ordination to the diaconate and continuation in marriage afterwards, but prohibiting marriage following the death of the wife thereafter. Anti-Roman canons contributed to East-West alienation.

During the century, the monastic influence of Ireland and England increased in Western Europe; schools and learning declined; regulations regarding clerical celibacy became more strict in the East.

EIGHTH CENTURY

711: Moslems began the conquest of Spain.

726: Emperor Leo III, the Isaurian, launched a campaign against the veneration of sacred images and relics; called Iconoclasm (imagebreaking), it caused turmoil in the East until about 843.

731: Pope Gregory III and a synod at Rome condemned Iconoclasm, with a declaration that the veneration of sacred images was in accord with Catholic tradition.

Venerable Bede issued his *Ecclesiastical History of the English People.*

732: Charles Martel defeated the Moslems at Poitiers, halting their advance in the West.

744: The Monastery of Fulda was established by St. Sturmi, a disciple of St. Boniface; it was influential in the evangelization of Germany.

754: A council of more than 300 Byzantine bishops endorsed Iconoclast errors. This council and its actions were condemned by the Lateran synod of 769.

Stephen II (III) crowned Pepin ruler of the Franks. Pepin twice invaded Italy, in 754 and 756, to defend the pope against the Lombards. His land grants to the papacy, called the Donation of Pepin, were later extended by Charlemagne (773) and formed part of the States of the Church.

c. 755: St. Boniface (Winfrid) was martyred. He was called the Apostle of Germany for his missionary work and organization of the hierarchy there.

781: Alcuin was chosen by Charlemagne to organize a palace school, which became a center of intellectual leadership.

787: Ecumenical Council of Nicaea (II). It condemned Iconoclasm, which held that the use of images was idolatry, and Adoptionism, which claimed that Christ was not the Son of God by nature but only by adoption. This was the last council regarded as ecumenical by Orthodox Churches.

792: A council at Ratisbon condemned Adoptionism.

The famous *Book of Kells* ("The Great Gospel of Columcille") dates from the early eighth or late seventh century.

NINTH CENTURY

800: Charlemagne was crowned Emperor by Pope Leo III on Christmas Day.

Egbert became king of West Saxons; he unified England and strengthened the See of Canterbury.

813: Emperor Leo V, the Armenian, revived Iconoclasm, which persisted until about 843.

814: Charlemagne died.

843: The Treaty of Verdun split the Frankish kingdom among Charlemagne's three grandsons.

844: A Eucharistic controversy involving the writings of St. Paschasius Radbertus, Ratramnus and Rabanus Maurus occasioned the development of terminology regarding the doctrine of the Real Presence.

846: Moslems invaded Italy and attacked Rome.

847-52: Period of composition of the *False Decretals,* a collection of forged documents attributed to popes from St. Clement (88-97) to Gregory II (715-731). The *Decretals,* which strongly supported the autonomy and rights of bishops, were suspect for a long time before being repudiated entirely about 1628.

848: The Council of Mainz condemned Gottschalk for heretical teaching regarding predestination. He was also condemned by the Council of Quierzy in 853.

857: Photius displaced Ignatius as patriarch of Constantinople. This marked the beginning of the Photian Schism, a confused state of East-West relations which has not yet been cleared up by historical research. Photius, a man of exceptional ability, died in 891.

865: St. Ansgar, apostle of Scandinavia, died.

869: St. Cyril died and his brother, St. Methodius (d. 885), was ordained a bishop. The Apostles of the Slavs devised an alphabet and translated the Gospels and liturgy into the Slavonic language.

869-70: Ecumenical Council of Constantinople (IV). It issued a second condemnation of Iconoclasm, condemned and deposed Photius as patriarch of Constantinople and restored Ignatius to the patriarchate. This was the last ecumenical council held in the East. It was first called ecumenical by canonists toward the end of the 11th century.

871-c. 900: Reign of Alfred the Great, the only English king ever anointed by a pope at Rome.

TENTH CENTURY

910: William, duke of Aquitaine, founded the Benedictine Abbey of Cluny, which became a center of monastic and ecclesiastical reform, especially in France.

915: Pope John X played a leading role in the expulsion of Saracens from central and southern Italy.

955: St. Olga, of the Russian royal family, was baptized.

962: Otto I, the Great, crowned by Pope John XII, revived Charlemagne's kingdom, which became the Holy Roman Empire.

966: Mieszko, first of a royal line in Poland, was baptized; he brought Latin Christianity to Poland.

988: Conversion and baptism of St. Vladimir and the people of Kiev which subsequently become part of Russia.

993: John XV was the first pope to decree the official canonization of a saint (Ulrich) for the universal Church.

997: St. Stephen became ruler of Hungary. He assisted in organizing the hierarchy and establishing Latin Christianity in that country.

999-1003: Pontificate of Sylvester II (Gerbert of Aquitaine), a Benedictine monk and the first French pope.

ELEVENTH CENTURY

1009: Beginning of lasting East-West Schism in the Church, marked by dropping of the name of Pope Sergius IV from the Byzantine diptychs (the listing of persons prayed for during the liturgy). The deletion was made by Patriarch Sergius II of Constantinople.

1012: St. Romuald founded the Camaldolese Hermits.

1025: The Council of Arras, and other councils later, condemned the Cathari (Neo-Manichaeans, Albigenses).

1027: The Council of Elne proclaimed the Truce of God as a means of stemming violence; it involved armistice periods of varying length, which were later extended.

1038: St. John Gualbert founded the Vallombrosians.

1043-59: Constantinople patriarchate of Michael Cerularius, the key figure in a controversy concerning the primacy of the papacy. His and the Byzantine synod's refusal to acknowledge this primacy in 1054 widened and hardened the East-West Schism in the Church.

1047: Pope Clement II died; he was the only pope ever buried in Germany.

1049-54: Pontificate of St. Leo IX, who inaugurated a movement of papal, diocesan, monastic and clerical reform.

1055: Condemnation of the Eucharistic doctrine of Berengarius.

1059: A Lateran council issued new legislation regarding papal elections; voting power was entrusted to the Roman cardinals.

1066: Death of St. Edward the Confessor, king of England from 1042 and restorer of Westminster Abbey.
Defeat, at Hastings, of Harold by William I, who subsequently exerted strong influence on the life style of the Church in England.

1073-85: Pontificate of St. Gregory VII (Hildebrand). A strong pope, he carried forward programs of clerical and general ecclesiastical reform and struggled against Henry IV and other rulers to end the evils of lay investiture. He introduced the Latin liturgy in Spain and set definite dates for the observance of ember days.

1077: Henry IV, excommunicated and suspended from the exercise of imperial powers by Gregory VII, sought absolution from the pope at Canossa. Henry later repudiated this action and in 1084 forced Gregory to leave Rome.

1079: The Council of Rome condemned Eucharistic errors (denial of the Real Presence of Christ under the appearances of bread and wine) of Berengarius, who retracted.

1084: St. Bruno founded the Carthusians.

1097-99: The first of several Crusades undertaken between this time and 1265. Recovery of the Holy Places and gaining free access to them for Christians were the original purposes, but these were diverted to less worthy objectives in various ways. Results included: a Latin Kingdom of Jerusalem, 1099-1187; a military and political misadventure in the form of a Latin Empire of Constantinople, 1204-1261; acquisition, by treaties, of visiting rights for Christians in the Holy Land. East-West economic and cultural relationships increased during the period. In the religious sphere, actions of the Crusaders had the effect of increasing the alienation of the East from the West.

1098: St. Robert founded the Cistercians.

TWELFTH CENTURY

1108: Beginnings of the influential Abbey and School of St. Victor in France.

1115: St. Bernard established the Abbey of Clairvaux and inaugurated the Cistercian Reform.

1118: Christian forces captured Saragossa, Spain; the beginning of the Moslem decline in that country.

1121: St. Norbert established the original monastery of the Praemonstratensians.

1122: The Concordat of Worms *(Pactum Callixtinum)* was formulated and approved by Pope Callistus II and Emperor Henry V to settle controversy concerning the investiture of prelates. The concordat provided that the emperor could invest prelates with symbols of temporal authority but had no right to invest them with spiritual authority, which came from the Church alone, and that the emperor was not to interfere in papal elections. This was the first concordat in history.

1123: Ecumenical Council of the Lateran (I), the first of its kind in the West. It endorsed provisions of the Concordat of Worms concerning the investiture of prelates and approved reform measures in 25 canons.

1139: Ecumenical Council of the Lateran (II). It adopted measures against a schism organized by antipope Anacletus and approved 30 canons related to discipline and other matters; one of the canons stated that holy orders is an invalidating impediment to marriage.

1140: St. Bernard met Abelard in debate at the Council of Sens. Abelard, whose rationalism in theology was condemned for the first time in 1121, died in 1142 at Cluny.

1148: The Synod of Rheims enacted strict disciplinary decrees for communities of women Religious.

1152: The Synod of Kells reorganized the Church in Ireland.

1160: Gratian, whose *Decretum* became a basic text of canon law, died.

Peter Lombard, compiler of the *Four Books of Sentences,* a standard theology text for nearly 200 years, died.

1170: St. Thomas Becket, archbishop of Canterbury, who clashed with Henry II over church-state relations, was murdered in his cathedral.

1171: Pope Alexander III reserved the process of canonization of saints to the Holy See.

1179: Ecumenical Council of the Lateran (III). It enacted measures against Waldensianism and Albigensianism (see year 242 regarding Manichaeism), approved reform decrees in 27 canons, provided that popes be elected by a two-thirds vote of the cardinals.

1184: Waldenses and other heretics were excommunicated by Pope Lucius III.

THIRTEENTH CENTURY

1198-1216: Pontificate of Innocent III, during which the papacy reached its medieval peak of authority, influence and prestige in the Church and in relations with civil rulers.

1208: Innocent III called for a crusade, the first in Christendom itself, against the Albigensians; their beliefs and practices threatened the fabric of society in southern France and northern Italy.

1209: Verbal approval was given by Innocent III to a rule of life for the Order of Friars Minor, started by St. Francis of Assisi.

1212: The Second Order of Franciscans, the Poor Clares, was founded.

1215: Ecumenical Council of the Lateran (IV). It ordered annual reception of the sacraments of penance and the Eucharist; defined and made the first official use of the term transubstantiation to explain the change of bread and wine into the body and blood of Christ; adopted additional measures to counteract teachings and practices of the Albigensians and Cathari; approved 70 canons.

1216: Formal papal approval was given to a rule of life for the Order of Preachers, started by St. Dominic.

The Portiuncula Indulgence was granted by the Holy See at the request of St. Francis of Assisi.

1221: The Third Order of St. Francis (Secular Franciscan Order) for lay persons was founded.

1226: Death of St. Francis of Assisi.

1231: Pope Gregory IX authorized establishment of the Papal Inquisition for dealing with heretics. It was a creature of its time, when crimes against faith and heretical doctrines of extremists like the Cathari and Albigenses threatened the good of the Christian community, the welfare of the state and the very fabric of society. The institution, which was responsible for excesses in punishment, was most active in the second half of the century in southern France, Italy and Germany.

1245: Ecumenical Council of Lyons (I). It confirmed the deposition of Emperor Frederick II and approved 22 canons.

1247: Preliminary approval was given by the Holy See to a Carmelite rule of life.

1270: St. Louis IX, king of France, died. Beginning of papal decline.

1274: Ecumenical Council of Lyons (II). It accomplished a temporary reunion of separated Eastern Churches with the Roman Church; issued regulations concerning conclaves for papal elections; approved 31 canons.

Death of St. Thomas Aquinas, Doctor of the Church, of lasting influence.

1280: Pope Nicholas III, who made the *Breviary* the official prayer book for clergy of the Roman Church, died.

1281: The excommunication of Michael Palaeologus by Pope Martin IV ruptured the union effected with the Eastern Church in 1274.

FOURTEENTH CENTURY

1302: Pope Boniface VIII issued the bull *Unam Sanctam,* concerning the unity of the Church and the temporal power of princes, against the background of a struggle with Philip IV of France; it was the most famous medieval document on the subject.

1309-77: For a period of approximately 70 years, seven popes resided at Avignon because of unsettled conditions in Rome and other reasons; see separate entry.

1311-12: Ecumenical Council of Vienne. It suppressed the Knights Templar and enacted a number of reform decrees.

1321: Dante Alighieri died a year after completing the *Divine Comedy.*

1324: Marsilius of Padua completed *Defensor Pacis,* a work condemned by Pope John XXII as heretical because of its denial of papal primacy and the hierarchical structure of the Church, and for other reasons. It was a charter for conciliarism (an ecumenical council is superior to the pope in authority).

1337-1453: Period of the Hundred Years' War, a dynastic struggle between France and England.

1338: Four years after the death of Pope John XXII, who had opposed Louis IV of Bavaria in a years-long controversy, electoral princes declared at the Diet of Rhense that the emperor did not need papal confirmation of his title and right to rule. Charles IV later (1356) said the same thing in a *Golden Bull,* eliminating papal rights in the election of emperors.

1347-50: The Black Death swept across Europe, killing perhaps one-fourth to one-third of the total population; an estimated 40 per cent of the clergy succumbed.

1374: Petrarch, poet and humanist, died.

1377: Return of the papacy from Avignon to Rome. Beginning of the Western Schism; see separate entry.

FIFTEENTH CENTURY

1409: The Council of Pisa, without canonical authority, tried to end the Western Schism but succeeded only in complicating it by electing a third claimant to the papacy; see Western Schism.

1414-18: Ecumenical Council of Constance. It took successful action to end the Western Schism involving rival claimants to the papacy; rejected the teachings of Wycliff; condemned Hus as a heretic. One decree — passed in the earlier stages of the council but later rejected — asserted the superiority of an ecumenical council over the pope (conciliarism).

1431: St. Joan of Arc was burned at the stake.

1431-49: The Council of Basel, which began with convocation by Pope Martin V in 1431, turned into an anti-papal forum of conciliarists seeking to subject the primacy and authority of the pope to the overriding authority of an assembly of bishops. It was not an ecumenical council.

1438: The Pragmatic Sanction of Bourges was enacted by Charles VIII and the French Parliament to curtail papal authority over the Church in France, in the spirit of conciliarism. It found expression in Gallicanism and had effects lasting at least until the French Revolution.

1438-45(?): Ecumenical Council of Florence (also called Basel-Ferrara-Florence). It affirmed the primacy of the pope against the claims of conciliarists that an ecumenical council is superior to the pope. It also formulated and approved decrees of union with several separated Eastern Churches — Greek, Armenian, Jacobite — which failed to gain general or lasting acceptance.

1453: The fall of Constantinople to the Turks.

c. 1456: Gutenberg issued the first edition of the Bible printed from movable type, at Mainz, Germany.

1476: Pope Sixtus IV ordered observance of the feast of the Immaculate Conception on Dec. 8 throughout the Church.

1478: Pope Sixtus IV, at the urging of King Ferdinand of Spain, approved establishment of the Spanish Inquisition for dealing with Jewish and Moorish converts accused of heresy. The institution, which was peculiar to Spain and its colonies in America, acquired jurisdiction over other cases as well and fell into disrepute because of its procedures, cruelty and the manner in which it served the Spanish crown, rather than the accused and the good of the Church. Protests by the Holy See failed to curb excesses of the Inquisition, which lingered in Spanish history until early in the 19th century.

1492: Columbus discovered the Americas.

1493: Pope Alexander VI issued a *Bull of Demarcation* which determined spheres of influence for the Spanish and Portuguese in the Americas.

The Renaissance, a humanistic movement which originated in Italy in the 14th century, spread to France, Germany, the Low Countries and England. A transitional period between the medieval world and the modern secular world, it introduced profound changes which affected literature and the other arts, general culture, politics and religion.

SIXTEENTH CENTURY

1512-17: Ecumenical Council of the Lateran (V). It stated the relation and position of the pope with respect to an ecumenical council; acted to counteract the Pragmatic Sanction of Bourges and exaggerated claims of liberty by the Church in France; condemned erroneous teachings concerning the nature of the human soul; stated doctrine concerning indulgences. The council reflected concern for abuses in the Church and the need for reforms but failed to take decisive action in the years immediately preceding the Reformation.

1517: Martin Luther signalled the beginning of the Reformation by posting 95 theses at Wittenberg. Subsequently, he broke completely from doctrinal orthodoxy in discourses and three published works (1519 and 1520); was excommunicated on more than 40 charges of heresy (1521); remained the dominant figure in the Reformation in Germany until his death in 1546.

1519: Zwingli triggered the Reformation in Zurich and became its leading proponent there until his death in combat in 1531.

1524: Luther's encouragement of German princes in putting down the two-year Peasants' Revolt gained political support for his cause.

1528: The Order of Friars Minor Capuchin was approved as an autonomous division of the Franciscan Order; like the Jesuits, the Capuchins became leaders in the Counter-Reformation.

1530: The *Augsburg Confession* of Lutheran faith was issued; it was later supplemented by the *Smalcald Articles,* approved in 1537.

1533: Henry VIII divorced Catherine of Aragon, married Anne Boleyn, was excommunicated. In 1534 he decreed the Act of Supremacy, making the sovereign the head of the Church in England, under which Sts. John Fisher and Thomas More were executed in 1535. Despite his rejection of papal primacy and actions against monastic life in England, he generally maintained doctrinal orthodoxy until his death in 1547.

1536: John Calvin, leader of the Reformation in Switzerland until his death in 1564, issued the first edition of *Institutes of the Christian Religion*, which became the classical text of Reformed (non-Lutheran) theology.

1540: The constitutions of the Society of Jesus (Jesuits), founded by St. Ignatius of Loyola, were approved.

1541: Start of the 11-year career of St. Francis Xavier as a missionary to the East Indies and Japan.

1545-63: Ecumenical Council of Trent. It issued a great number of decrees concerning doctrinal matters opposed by the Reformers, and mobilized the Counter-Reformation. Definitions covered the Canon of the Bible, the rule of faith, the nature of justification, grace, faith, original sin and its effects, the seven sacraments, the sacrificial nature of the Mass, the veneration of saints, use of sacred images, belief in purgatory, the doctrine of indulgences, the jurisdiction of the pope over the whole Church. It initiated many reforms for renewal in the liturgy and general discipline in the Church, the promotion of religious instruction, the education of the clergy through the foundation of seminaries, etc. Trent ranks with Vatican II as the greatest ecumenical council held in the West.

1549: The first Anglican *Book of Common Prayer* was issued by Edward VI. Revised editions were published in 1552, 1559 and 1662 and later.

1553: Start of the five-year reign of Mary Tudor who tried to counteract actions of Henry VIII against the Roman Church.

1555: Enactment of the Peace of Augsburg, an arrangement of religious territorialism rather than toleration, which recognized the existence of Catholicism and Lutheranism in the German Empire and provided that citizens should adopt the religion of their respective rulers.

1558: Beginning of the reign (to 1603) of Queen Elizabeth I of England and Ireland, during which the Church of England took on its definitive form.

1559: Establishment of the hierarchy of the Church of England, with the consecration of Matthew Parker as archbishop of Canterbury.

1563: The first text of the *39 Articles* of the Church of England was issued. Also enacted were a new Act of Supremacy and Oath of Succession to the English throne.

1570: Elizabeth I was excommunicated. Penal measures against Catholics subsequently became more severe.

1571: Defeat of the Turkish armada at Lepanto staved off the invasion of Eastern Europe.

1577: The *Formula of Concord*, the classical statement of Lutheran faith, was issued; it was, generally, a Lutheran counterpart of the canons of the Council of Trent. In 1580, along with other formulas of doctrine, it was included in the *Book of Concord*.

1582: The Gregorian Calendar, named for Pope Gregory XIII, was put into effect and was eventually adopted in most countries: England delayed adoption until 1752.

SEVENTEENTH CENTURY

1605: The Gunpowder Plot, an attempt by Catholic fanatics to blow up James I of England and the houses of Parliament, resulted in an anti-Catholic Oath of Allegiance.

1610: Death of Matteo Ricci, outstanding Jesuit missionary to China, pioneer in cultural relations between China and Europe.
Founding of the first community of Visitation Nuns by Sts. Francis de Sales and Jane de Chantal.

1611: Founding of the Oratorians.

1613: Catholics were banned from Scandinavia.

1625: Founding of the Congregation of the Mission (Vincentians) by St. Vincent de Paul. He founded the Sisters of Charity in 1633.

1642: Death of Galileo, scientist, who was censured by the Congregation of the Holy Office for supporting the Copernican theory of the sun-centered planetary system.
Founding of the Sulpicians by Jacques Olier.

1643: Start of publication of the Bollandist *Acta Sanctorum*, a critical work on lives of the saints.

1648: Provisions in the Peace of Westphalia, ending the Thirty Years' War, extended terms of the Peace of Augsburg (1555) to Calvinists and gave equality to Catholics and Protestants in the 300 states of the Holy Roman Empire.

1649: Oliver Cromwell invaded Ireland and began a severe persecution of the Church there.

1653: Pope Innocent X condemned five propositions of Jansenism, a complex theory which distorted doctrine concerning the relations between divine grace and human freedom. Jansenism was also a rigoristic movement which seriously disturbed the Church in France, the Low Countries and Italy in this and the 18th century.

1673: The Test Act in England barred from public office Catholics who would not deny the doctrine of transubstantiation and receive Communion in the Church of England.

1678: Many English Catholics suffered death as a consequence of the Popish Plot, a false allegation by Titus Oates that Catholics planned to assassinate Charles II, land a French army in the country, burn London, and turn over the government to the Jesuits.

1682: The four Gallican articles, drawn up by Bossuet, asserted political and ecclesiastical immunities of France from papal control. The articles, which rejected the primacy of the pope, were declared null and void by Pope Alexander VIII in 1690.

1689: The Toleration Act granted a measure of freedom of worship to other English dissenters but not to Catholics.

EIGHTEENTH CENTURY

1704: Chinese Rites — involving the Christian adaptation of elements of Confucianism, veneration of ancestors and Chinese terminology in religion — were condemned by Clement XI.

1720: The Passionists were founded by St. Paul of the Cross.

1724: Persecution in China.

1732: The Redemptorists were founded by St. Alphonsus Liguori.

1738: Freemasonry was condemned by Clement XII and Catholics were forbidden to join, under penalty of excommunication; the prohibition was repeated by Benedict XIV in 1751 and by later popes.

1760s: Josephinism, a theory and system of state control of the Church, was initiated in Austria; it remained in force until about 1850.

1764: Febronianism, an unorthodox theory and practice regarding the constitution of the Church and relations between Church and state, was condemned for the first of several times. Proposed by an auxiliary bishop of Trier using the pseudonym Justinus Febronius, it had the effects of minimizing the office of the pope and supporting national churches under state control.

1773: Clement XIV issued a brief of suppression against the Jesuits, following their expulsion from Portugal in 1759, from France in 1764 and from Spain in 1767. Political intrigue and unsubstantiated accusations were principal factors in these developments. The ban, which crippled the society, contained no condemnation of the Jesuit constitutions, particular Jesuits or Jesuit teaching. The society was restored in 1814.

1778: Catholics in England were relieved of some civil disabilities dating back to the time of Henry VIII, by an act which permitted them to acquire, own and inherit property. Additional liberties were restored by the Roman Catholic Relief Act of 1791 and subsequent enactments of Parliament.

1789: Religious freedom in the United States was guaranteed under the First Amendment to the Constitution.

Beginning of the French Revolution which resulted in: the secularization of church property and the Civil Constitution of the Clergy in 1790; the persecution of priests, religious and lay persons loyal to papal authority; invasion of the Papal States by Napoleon in 1796; renewal of persecution from 1797-1799; attempts to dechristianize France and establish a new religion; the occupation of Rome by French troops and the forced removal of Pius VI to France in 1798.

This century is called the age of Enlightenment or Reason because of the predominating rational and scientific approach of its leading philosophers, scientists and writers with respect to religion, ethics and natural law. This approach downgraded the fact and significance of revealed religion. Also characteristic of the Enlightenment were subjectivism, secularism and optimism regarding human perfectibility.

NINETEENTH CENTURY

1809: Pope Pius VII was made a captive by Napoleon and deported to France where he remained in exile until 1814. During this time he refused to cooperate with Napoleon who sought to bring the Church in France under his own control.

The turbulence in church-state relations in France at the beginning of the century recurred in connection with the Bourbon Restoration, the July Revolution, the second and third Republics, the Second Empire and the Dreyfus case.

1814: The Society of Jesus, suppressed since 1773, was restored.

1817: Reestablishment of the Congregation for the Propagation of the Faith (Propaganda) by Pius VII was an important factor in increasing missionary activity during the century.

1820: Years-long persecution, during which thousands died for the faith, ended in China. Thereafter, communication with the West remained cut off until about 1834. Vigorous missionary work got under way in 1842.

1822: The Pontifical Society for the Propagation of the Faith, inaugurated in France by Pauline Jaricot for the support of missionary activity, was established.

1829: The Catholic Emancipation Act relieved Catholics in England and Ireland of most of the civil disabilities to which they had been subject from the time of Henry VIII.

1832: Gregory XVI, in the encyclical *Mirari vos*, condemned indifferentism, one of the many ideologies at odds with Christian doctrine which were proposed during the century.

1833: Start of the Oxford Movement which affected the Church of England and resulted in some notable conversions, including that of John Henry Newman in 1845, to the Catholic Church. Frederic Ozanam founded the Society of St. Vincent de Paul in France. The society, whose objective was works of charity, became worldwide.

1848: The *Communist Manifesto,* a revolutionary document symptomatic of socio-economic crisis, was issued.

1850: The hierarchy was reestablished in England and Nicholas Wiseman made the first archbishop of Westminster. He was succeeded in 1865 by Henry Manning, an Oxford convert and proponent of the rights of labor.

1853: The Catholic hierarchy was reestablished in Holland.

1854: Pius IX proclaimed the dogma of the Immaculate Conception in the bull *Ineffabilis Deus.*

1858: The Blessed Virgin Mary appeared to St. Bernadette at Lourdes, France; see separate entry.

1864: Pius IX issued the encyclical *Quanta cura* and the *Syllabus of Errors* in condemnation of some 80 propositions derived from the scientific mentality and rationalism of the century. The subjects in question had deep ramifications in many areas of thought and human endeavor; in religion, they explicitly and/or implicitly rejected divine revelation and the supernatural order.

1867: The first volume of *Das Kapital* was published. Together with the Communist First International, formed in the same year, it had great influence on the subsequent development of communism and socialism.

1869: The Anglican Church was disestablished in Ireland.

1869-70: Ecumenical Council of the Vatican (I). It defined papal primacy and infallibility in a dogmatic constitution on the Church; covered natural religion, revelation, faith, and the relations between faith and reason in a dogmatic constitution on the Catholic faith.

1870-71: Victor Emmanuel II of Sardinia, crowned king of Italy after defeating Austrian and papal forces, marched into Rome in 1870 and expropriated the Papal States after a plebiscite in which Catholics, at the order of Pius IX, did not vote. In 1871, Pius IX refused to accept a Law of Guarantees. Confiscation of church property and hindrance of ecclesiastical administration by the regime followed.

1871: The German Empire, a confederation of 26 states, was formed. Government policy launched a Kulturkampf whose May Laws of 1873 were designed to annul papal jurisdiction in Prussia and other states and to place the Church under imperial control. Resistance to the enactments and the persecution they legalized forced the government to modify its anti-Church policy by 1887.

1878: Beginning of the pontificate of Leo XIII, who was pope until his death in 1903. Leo is best known for the encyclical *Rerum novarum*, which greatly influenced the course of Christian social thought and the labor movement. His other accomplishments included promotion of a revival of Scholastic philosophy and the impetus he gave to scriptural studies.

1881: The first International Eucharistic Congress was held in Lille, France.

Alexander II of Russia died. His policies of Russification — as well as those of his two predecessors and a successor during the century — caused great suffering to Catholics, Jews and Protestants in Poland, Lithuania, the Ukraine and Bessarabia.

1882: Charles Darwin died. His theory of evolution by natural selection, one of several scientific highlights of the century, had extensive repercussions in the faith-and-science controversy.

1887: The Catholic University of America was founded in Washington, D.C.

1893: The U.S. apostolic delegation was set up in Washington, D.C.

TWENTIETH CENTURY

1901: Restrictive measures in France forced the Jesuits, Benedictines, Carmelites and other religious orders to leave the country. Subsequently, 14,000 schools were suppressed; religious orders and congregations were expelled; the concordat was renounced in 1905; church property was confiscated in 1906. For some years the Holy See, refusing to comply with government demands for the control of bishops' appointments, left some ecclesiastical offices vacant.

1903-14: Pontificate of St. Pius X. He initiated the codification of canon law, 1904; removed the ban against participation by Catholics in Italian national elections, 1905; issued decrees calling upon the faithful to receive Holy Communion frequently and daily, and stating that children should begin receiving the Eucharist at the age of seven, 1905 and 1910, respectively; ordered the establishment of the Confraternity of Christian Doctrine in all parishes throughout the world, 1905; condemned Modernism in the decree *Lamentabili* and the encyclical *Pascendi*, 1907.

1908: The United States and England, long under the jurisdiction of the Congregation for the Propagation of the Faith as mission territories, were removed from its control and placed under the common law of the Church.

1910: Laws of separation were enacted in Portugal, marking a point of departure in church-state relations.

1911: The Catholic Foreign Mission Society of America — Maryknoll, the first U.S.-founded society of its type — was established.

1914: Start of World War I, which lasted until 1918.

1914-22: Pontificate of Benedict XV. Much of his pontificate was devoted to seeking ways and means of minimizing the material and spiritual havoc of World War I. In 1917 he offered his services as a mediator to the belligerent nations, but his pleas for settlement of the conflict went unheeded.

1917: The Blessed Virgin Mary appeared to three children at Fatima, Portugal; see separate entry.

A new constitution, embodying repressive laws against the Church, was enacted in Mexico. Its implementation resulted in persecution in the 1920s and 1930s.

Bolsheviks seized power in Russia and set up a communist dictatorship. The event marked the rise of communism in Russian and world affairs. One of its immediate, and lasting, results was persecution of the Church, Jews and other segments of the population.

1918: The *Code of Canon Law*, in preparation for more than 10 years, went into effect in the Western Church.

1919: Benedict XV stimulated missionary work through the decree *Maximum Illud*, in which he urged the recruiting and training of native clergy in places where the Church was not firmly established.

1920-22: Ireland was partitioned by two enactments of the British government which (1) made the six counties of Northern Ireland part of the United Kingdom in 1920 and (2) gave dominion status to the Irish Free State in 1922. The Irish Free State became an independent republic in 1949.

1922-39: Pontificate of Pius XI. He subscribed to the Lateran Treaty, 1929, which settled the Roman Question created by the confiscation of the Papal States in 1871; issued the encyclical *Casti connubii*, 1930, an authoritative statement on

Christian marriage; resisted the efforts of Benito Mussolini to control Catholic Action and the Church, in the encyclical *Non abbiamo bisogno*, 1931; opposed various fascist policies; issued the encyclicals *Quadragesimo anno*, 1931, developing the social doctrine of Leo XIII's *Rerum novarum*, and *Divini Redemptoris*, 1937, calling for social justice and condemning atheistic communism; condemned anti-Semitism, 1937.

1926: The Catholic Relief Act repealed virtually all legal disabilities of Catholics in England.

1931: Leftists proclaimed Spain a republic and proceeded to disestablish the Church, confiscate church property, deny salaries to the clergy, expel the Jesuits and ban teaching of the Catholic faith. These actions were preludes to the civil war of 1936-1939.

1933: Emergence of Adolf Hitler to power in Germany. By 1935 two of his aims were clear, the elimination of the Jews and control of a single national church. Six million Jews were killed in the Holocaust. The Church was subject to repressive measures, which Pius XI protested futilely in the encyclical *Mit brennender sorge* in 1937.

1936-39: Civil war in Spain between the leftist Loyalist and rightist Franco forces. The Loyalists were defeated and one-man, one-party rule was established. Priests, Religious and lay persons fell victims to Loyalist persecution.

1939-45: World War II.

1939-58: Pontificate of Pius XII. He condemned communism, proclaimed the dogma of the Assumption of Mary in 1950, in various documents and other enactments provided ideological background for many of the accomplishments of the Second Vatican Council. (See Twentieth Century Popes.)

1940: Start of a decade of communist conquest in more than 13 countries, resulting in conditions of persecution for a minimum of 60 million Catholics as well as members of other faiths.

Persecution diminished in Mexico because of non-enforcement of anti-religious laws still on record.

1950: Pius XII proclaimed the dogma of the Assumption of the Blessed Virgin Mary.

1957: The communist regime of China established the Patriotic Association of Chinese Catholics in opposition to the Church in union with the pope.

1958-63: Pontificate of John XXIII. His principal accomplishment was the convocation of the Second Vatican Council, the twenty-first ecumenical council in the history of the Church. (See Twentieth Century Popes.)

1962-65: Ecumenical Council of the Vatican (II). It formulated and promulgated 16 documents — two dogmatic and two pastoral constitutions, nine decrees and three declarations — reflecting pastoral orientation toward renewal and reform in the Church, and making explicit dimensions of doctrine and Christian life requiring emphasis for the full development of the Church and the better accomplishment of its mission in the contemporary world.

1963-78: Pontificate of Paul VI. His main purpose and effort was to give direction and provide guidance for the authentic trends of church renewal set in motion by the Second Vatican Council. (See Twentieth Century Popes.)

1978: The thirty-four-day pontificate of John Paul I. (See Twentieth Century Popes.)

Start of the pontificate of John Paul II; see Index.

1983: The revised Code of Canon Law, embodying reforms enacted by the Second Vatican Council, went into effect in the Church of Roman Rite. (Revision of the Canon Law of Eastern Churches was still in process.)

1985: Formal ratification of a Vatican-Italy concordat replacing the Lateran Treaty of 1929.

ECUMENICAL COUNCILS

An ecumenical council is an assembly of the college of bishops, with and under the presidency of the pope, which has supreme authority over the Church in matters pertaining to faith, morals, worship and discipline.

The Second Vatican Council stated: "The supreme authority with which this college (of bishops) is empowered over the whole Church is exercised in a solemn way through an ecumenical council. A council is never ecumenical unless it is confirmed or at least accepted as such by the successor of Peter. It is the prerogative of the Roman Pontiff to convoke these councils, to preside over them, and to confirm them" *(Dogmatic Constitution on the Church*, No. 22).

Pope Presides

The pope is the head of an ecumenical council; he presides over it either personally or through legates. Conciliar decrees and other actions have binding force only when confirmed and promulgated by him. If a pope dies during a council, it is suspended until reconvened by another pope. An ecumenical council is not superior to a pope; hence, there is no appeal from a pope to a council.

Collectively, the bishops with the pope represent the whole Church. They do this not as democratic representatives of the faithful in a kind of church parliament, but as the successors of the Apostles with divinely given authority, care and responsibility over the whole Church.

Council participants with a deliberative vote are: cardinals, including those who are retired; residential patriarchs, primates, archbishops and bishops, even if they are not yet consecrated; abbots and certain other prelates, an abbot primate, abbot superiors of monastic congregations and heads of exempt clerical religious; titular bishops, on invitation. Experts in theology and canon law may be given a consultative vote. Others, including lay persons, may address a council or observe its actions, but may not vote.

Basic legislation concerning ecumenical councils is contained in Canons 337-41 of the Code of

Ecumenical Councils

Canon Law. Basic doctrinal considerations were stated by the Second Vatican Council in the *Dogmatic Constitution on the Church.*

Background

Ecumenical councils had their prototype in the Council of Jerusalem in 51, at which the Apostles under the leadership of St. Peter decided that converts to the Christian faith were not obliged to observe all the prescriptions of Old Testament law (Acts 15). As early as the second century, bishops got together in regional meetings, synods or councils to take common action for the doctrinal and pastoral good of their communities of faithful. The expansion of such limited assemblies to ecumenical councils was a logical and historical evolution, given the nature and needs of the Church.

Emperors were active in summoning or convoking the first eight councils, especially the first five and the eighth. Among reasons for intervention of this kind were the facts that the emperors regarded themselves as guardians of the faith; that the settlement of religious controversies, which had repercussions in political and social turmoil, served the cause of peace in the state; and that the emperors had at their disposal ways and means of facilitating gatherings of bishops. Imperial actions, however, did not account for the formally ecumenical nature of the councils.

Some councils were attended by relatively few bishops, and the ecumenical character of several was open to question for a time. However, confirmation and de facto recognition of their actions by popes and subsequent councils established them as ecumenical.

Role in History

The councils have played a highly significant role in the history of the Church by witnessing to and defining truths of revelation, by shaping forms of worship and discipline, and by promoting measures for the ever-necessary reform and renewal of Catholic life. In general, they have represented attempts of the Church to mobilize itself in times of crisis for self-preservation, self-purification and growth.

The first eight ecumenical councils were held in the East; the other 13, in the West. The majority of separated Eastern Churches — e.g., the Orthodox — recognize the ecumenical character of the first seven councils, which formulated a great deal of basic doctrine. Nestorians, however, acknowledge only the first two councils; the Monophysite Armenians, Syrians, and Copts acknowledge the first three.

The 21 Councils

The 21 ecumenical councils in the history of the Church are listed below, with indication of their names or titles (taken from the names of the places where they were held); the dates; the reigning and/or approving popes; the emperors who were instrumental in convoking the eight councils in the East; the number of bishops who attended, when available; the number of sessions.

Significant actions of the first 20 councils are indicated under appropriate dates in Dates and Events in Church History.

1. Nicaea I, 325: St. Sylvester I (Emperor Constantine I); attended by approximately 300 bishops; sessions held between May 20 or June 19 to near the end of August.

2. Constantinople I, 381: St. Damasus I (Emperor Theodosius I); attended by approximately 150 bishops; sessions held from May to July.

3. Ephesus, 431: St. Celestine I (Emperor Theodosius II); attended by 150 to 200 bishops; five sessions held between June 22 and July 17.

4. Chalcedon, 451: St. Leo I (Emperor Marcian); attended by approximately 600 bishops; 17 sessions held between Oct. 8 and Nov. 1.

5. Constantinople II, 553: Vigilius (Emperor Justinian I); attended by 165 bishops; eight sessions held between May 5 and June 2.

6. Constantinople III, 680-681; St. Agatho, St. Leo II (Emperor Constantine IV); attended by approximately 170 bishops; 16 sessions held between Nov. 7, 680, and Sept. 16, 681.

7. Nicaea II, 787: Adrian I (Empress Irene); attended by approximately 300 bishops; eight sessions held between Sept. 24 and Oct. 23.

8. Constantinople IV, 869-870: Adrian II (Emperor Basil I); attended by 102 bishops; six sessions held between Oct. 5, 869, and Feb. 28, 870.

9. Lateran I, 1123: Callistus II; attended by approximately 300 bishops; sessions held between Mar. 18 and Apr. 6.

10. Lateran II, 1139: Innocent II; attended by 900 to 1,000 bishops and abbots; three sessions held in April.

11. Lateran III, 1179: Alexander III; attended by at least 300 bishops; three sessions held between Mar. 5 and 19.

12. Lateran IV, 1215: Innocent III; sessions held between Nov. 11 and 30.

13. Lyons I, 1245: Innocent IV; attended by approximately 150 bishops; three sessions held between June 28 and July 17.

14. Lyons II, 1274: Gregory X; attended by approximately 500 bishops; six sessions held between May 7 and July 17.

15. Vienne, 1311-1312: Clement V; attended by 132 bishops; three sessions held between Oct. 16, 1311, and May 6, 1312.

16. Constance, 1414-1418: Gregory XII, Martin V; attended by nearly 200 bishops, plus other prelates and many experts; 45 sessions held between Nov. 5, 1414, and Apr. 22, 1418.

17. Florence (also called Basel-Ferrara-Florence), 1438-1445: Eugene IV; attended by many Latin-Rite and Eastern-Rite bishops; preliminary sessions were held at Basel and Ferrara before definitive work was accomplished at Florence.

18. Lateran V, 1512-1517: Julius II, Leo X; 12 sessions held between May 3, 1512, and Mar. 16, 1517.

19. Trent, 1545-1563: Paul III, Julius III, Pius IV; 25 sessions held between Dec. 13, 1545, and Dec. 4, 1563.

20. Vatican I, 1869-1870: Pius IX; attended by approximately 800 bishops and other prelates; four public sessions and 89 general meetings held between Dec. 8, 1869, and July 7, 1870.

VATICAN II

The Second Vatican Council, which was forecast by Pope John XXIII Jan. 25, 1959, was held in four sessions in St. Peter's Basilica.

Pope John convoked it and opened the first session, which ran from Oct. 11 to Dec. 8, 1962. Following John's death June 3, 1963, Pope Paul VI reconvened the council for the other three sessions which ran from Sept. 29 to Dec. 4, 1963; Sept. 14 to Nov. 21, 1964; Sept. 14 to Dec. 8, 1965.

A total of 2,860 Fathers participated in council proceedings, and attendance at meetings varied between 2,000 and 2,500. For various reasons, including the denial of exit from Communist-dominated countries, 274 Fathers could not attend.

The council formulated and promulgated 16 documents — two dogmatic and two pastoral constitutions, nine decrees and three declarations — all of which reflect its basic pastoral orientation toward renewal and reform in the Church. Given below are the Latin and English titles of the documents and their dates of promulgation.

- *Lumen Gentium* (Dogmatic Constitution on the Church), Nov. 21, 1964.
- *Dei Verbum* (Dogmatic Constitution on Divine Revelation), Nov. 18, 1965.
- *Sacrosanctum Concilium* (Constitution on the Sacred Liturgy), Dec. 4, 1963.
- *Gaudium et Spes* (Pastoral Constitution on the Church in the Modern World), Dec. 7, 1965.
- *Christus Dominus* (Decree on the Bishops' Pastoral Office in the Church), Oct. 28, 1965.
- *Ad Gentes* (Decree on the Church's Missionary Activity), Dec. 7, 1965.
- *Unitatis Redintegratio* (Decree on Ecumenism), Nov. 21, 1964.
- *Orientalium Ecclesiarum* (Decree on Eastern Catholic Churches), Nov. 21, 1964.
- *Presbyterorum Ordinis* (Decree on the Ministry and Life of Priests), Dec. 7, 1965.
- *Optatam Totius* (Decree on Priestly Formation), Oct. 28, 1965.
- *Perfectae Caritatis* (Decree on the Appropriate Renewal of the Religious Life), Oct. 28, 1965.
- *Apostolicam Actuositatem* (Decree on the Apostolate of the Laity), Nov. 18, 1965.
- *Inter Mirifica* (Decree on the Instruments of Social Communication), Dec. 4, 1963.
- *Dignitatis Humanae* (Declaration on Religious Freedom), Dec. 7, 1965.
- *Nostra Aetate* (Declaration on the Relationship of the Church to Non-Christian Religions), Oct. 28, 1965.
- *Gravissimum Educationis* (Declaration on Christian Education), Oct. 28, 1965.

The key documents were the four constitutions, which set the ideological basis for all the others. To date, the documents with the most visible effects are those on the liturgy, the Church, the Church in the world, ecumenism, the renewal of religious life, the life and ministry of priests, the lay apostolate.

The main business of the council was to explore and make explicit dimensions of doctrine and Christian life requiring emphasis for the full development of the Church and the better accomplishment of its mission in the contemporary world.

SUNDAY CELEBRATION IN THE ABSENCE OF A PRIEST

(Source: Newsletter of the U.S. Bishops' Committee on the Liturgy, July/August, 1988.)

A "Directory for Sunday Celebrations in the Absence of a Priest," prepared under the auspices of the Congregation for Divine Worship, was approved by Pope John Paul May 21, 1988.

In the introduction, the Directory notes that it is not always possible for a priest to celebrate the Eucharist in every Catholic community every Sunday.

The first chapter is dedicated to the meaning of Sunday; it is "a synthesis of the Church's understanding of the nature and purpose of Sunday and the divine command to worship on the Day of the Lord."

The second chapter "indicates the conditions upon which a decision can be made to have Sunday celebrations in the absence of a priest." Specifically:

- "There should be no confusion in the mind of the faithful about the difference between these celebrations and the celebration of the Eucharist."
- "The diocesan bishop . . . is to establish regulations for Sunday celebrations in the absence of a priest. All such celebrations must be approved by the bishop and be under the supervision of a pastor."
- "Sunday celebrations may be led by deacons or by suitably prepared lay people."

The third chapter explains the structure of a celebration of the Word and the distribution of Holy Communion. Specifically:

- "In no case should there be a presentation (and preparation) of the gifts or the proclamation of the Eucharistic Prayer."
- "The Opening Prayer and Prayer after Communion are taken from the *Sacramentary,* and the readings are taken from the *Lectionary for Mass.*"
- The structure of the celebration consists of Introductory Rites, Liturgy of the Word, Thanksgiving and the Lord's Prayer, the Rite of Communion and Concluding Rites.
- Regulations call for prior consecration of the Eucharist at a Mass.

Between July and December, 1987, the Bishops' Committee conducted a national survey on Sunday and weekday worship in the absence of a priest. Findings: "Seventy dioceses presently (1987) have parishes/missions which are under the administration of a deacon, a lay person or a religious sister or brother. . . . The number of such parishes/missions is 193, and a total of 201 persons is involved" (including 40 deacons, 133 Religious, 28 lay persons).

POPES

Information includes the name of the pope, in many cases his name before becoming pope, his birthplace or country of origin, the date of accession to the papacy, and the date of the end of reign which, in all but a few cases, was the date of death. Double dates indicate times of election and coronation.
Source: *"Annuario Pontificio."*

St. Peter (Simon Bar-Jona): Bethsaida in Galilee; d. c. 64 or 67.
St. Linus: Tuscany; 67-76.
St. Anacletus (Cletus): Rome; 76-88.
St. Clement: Rome; 88-97.
St. Evaristus: Greece; 97-105.
St. Alexander I: Rome; 105-115.
St. Sixtus I: Rome; 115-125.
St. Telesphorus: Greece; 125-136.
St. Hyginus: Greece; 136-140.
St. Pius I: Aquileja; 140-155.
St. Anicetus: Syria; 155-166.
St. Soter: Campania; 166-175.
St. Eleutherius: Nicopolis in Epirus; 175-189.

Up to the time of St. Eleutherius, the years indicated for the beginning and end of pontificates are not absolutely certain. Also, up to the middle of the 11th century, there are some doubts about the exact days and months given in chronological tables.

St. Victor I: Africa; 189-199.
St. Zephyrinus: Rome; 199-217.
St. Callistus I: Rome; 217-222.
St. Urban I: Rome; 222-230.
St. Pontian: Rome; July 21, 230, to Sept. 28, 235.
St. Anterus: Greece; Nov. 21, 235, to Jan. 3, 236.
St. Fabian: Rome; Jan. 10, 236, to Jan. 20, 250.
St. Cornelius: Rome; Mar., 251, to June, 253.
St. Lucius I: Rome; June 25, 253, to Mar. 5, 254.
St. Stephen I: Rome; May 12, 254, to Aug. 2, 257.
St. Sixtus II: Greece; Aug. 30, 257, to Aug. 6, 258.
St. Dionysius: July 22, 259, to Dec. 26, 268.
St. Felix I: Rome; Jan. 5, 269, to Dec. 30, 274.
St. Eutychian: Luni; Jan. 4, 275, to Dec. 7, 283.
St. Caius: Dalmatia; Dec. 17, 283, to Apr. 22, 296.
St. Marcellinus: Rome; June 30, 296, to Oct. 25, 304.
St. Marcellus I: Rome; May 27, 308, or June 26, 308, to Jan. 16, 309.
St. Eusebius: Greece; Apr. 18, 309 or 310, to Aug. 17, 309 or 310.
St. Melchiades (Miltiades): Africa; July 2, 311, to Jan. 11, 314.
St. Sylvester I: Rome; Jan. 31, 314, to Dec. 31, 335. (Most of the popes before St. Sylvester I were martyrs.)
St. Marcus: Rome; Jan. 18, 336, to Oct. 7, 336.
St. Julius I: Rome; Feb. 6, 337, to Apr. 12, 352.
Liberius: Rome; May 17, 352, to Sept. 24, 366.
St. Damasus I: Spain; Oct. 1, 366, to Dec. 11, 384.
St. Siricius: Rome; Dec. 15, or 22 or 29, 384, to Nov. 26, 399.
St. Anastasius I: Rome; Nov. 27, 399, to Dec. 19, 401.
St. Innocent I: Albano; Dec. 22, 401, to Mar. 12, 417.
St. Zozimus: Greece; Mar. 18, 417, to Dec. 26, 418.

St. Boniface I: Rome; Dec. 28 or 29, 418, to Sept. 4, 422.
St. Celestine I: Campania; Sept. 10, 422, to July 27, 432.
St. Sixtus III: Rome; July 31, 432, to Aug. 19, 440.
St. Leo I (the Great): Tuscany; Sept. 29, 440, to Nov. 10, 461.
St. Hilary: Sardinia; Nov. 19, 461, to Feb. 29, 468.
St. Simplicius: Tivoli; Mar. 3, 468, to Mar. 10, 483.
St. Felix III (II): Rome; Mar. 13, 483, to Mar. 1, 492.

He should be called Felix II, and his successors of the same name should be numbered accordingly. The discrepancy in the numerical designation of popes named Felix was caused by the erroneous insertion in some lists of the name of St. Felix of Rome, a martyr.

St. Gelasius I: Africa; Mar. 1, 492, to Nov. 21, 496.
Anastasius II: Rome; Nov. 24, 496, to Nov. 19, 498.
St. Symmachus: Sardinia; Nov. 22, 498, to July 19, 514.
St. Hormisdas: Frosinone; July 20, 514, to Aug. 6, 523.
St. John I, Martyr: Tuscany; Aug. 13, 523, to May 18, 526.
St. Felix IV (III): Samnium; July 12, 526, to Sept. 22, 530.
Boniface II: Rome; Sept. 22, 530, to Oct. 17, 532.
John II: Rome; Jan. 2, 533, to May 8, 535.

John II was the first pope to change his name. His given name was Mercury.

St. Agapitus I: Rome; May 13, 535, to Apr. 22, 536.
St. Silverius, Martyr: Campania; June 1 or 8, 536, to Nov. 11, 537 (d. Dec. 2, 537).

St. Silverius was violently deposed in March, 537, and abdicated Nov. 11, 537. His successor, Vigilius, was not recognized as pope by all the Roman clergy until his abdication.

Vigilius: Rome; Mar. 29, 537, to June 7, 555.
Pelagius I: Rome; Apr. 16, 556, to Mar. 4, 561.
John III: Rome; July 17, 561, to July 13, 574.
Benedict I: Rome; June 2, 575, to July 30, 579.
Pelagius II: Rome; Nov. 26, 579, to Feb. 7, 590.
St. Gregory I (the Great): Rome; Sept. 3, 590, to Mar. 12, 604.
Sabinian: Blera in Tuscany; Sept. 13, 604, to Feb. 22, 606.
Boniface III: Rome; Feb. 19, 607, to Nov. 12, 607.
St. Boniface IV: Abruzzi; Aug. 25, 608, to May 8, 615.
St. Deusdedit (Adeodatus I): Rome; Oct. 19, 615, to Nov. 8, 618.
Boniface V: Naples; Dec. 23, 619, to Oct. 25, 625.
Honorius I: Campania; Oct. 27, 625, to Oct. 12, 638.
Severinus: Rome; May 28, 640, to Aug. 2, 640.
John IV: Dalmatia; Dec. 24, 640, to Oct. 12, 642.
Theodore I: Greece; Nov. 24, 642, to May 14, 649.
St. Martin I, Martyr: Todi; July, 649, to Sept. 16, 655 (in exile from June 17, 653).
St. Eugene I: Rome; Aug. 10, 654, to June 2, 657.

St. Eugene I was elected during the exile of St. Martin I, who is believed to have endorsed him as pope.

St. Vitalian: Segni; July 30, 657, to Jan. 27, 672.
Adeodatus II: Rome; Apr. 11, 672, to June 17, 676.
Donus: Rome; Nov. 2, 676, to Apr. 11, 678.
St. Agatho: Sicily; June 27, 678, to Jan. 10, 681.
St. Leo II: Sicily; Aug. 17, 682, to July 3, 683.

St. Benedict II: Rome; June 26, 684, to May 8, 685.
John V: Syria; July 23, 685, to Aug. 2, 686.
Conon: birthplace unknown; Oct. 21, 686, to Sept. 21, 687.
St. Sergius I: Syria; Dec. 15, 687, to Sept. 8, 701.
John VI: Greece; Oct. 30, 701, to Jan. 11, 705.
John VII: Greece; Mar. 1, 705, to Oct. 18, 707.
Sisinnius: Syria; Jan. 15, 708, to Feb. 4, 708.
Constantine: Syria; Mar. 25, 708, to Apr. 9, 715.
St. Gregory II: Rome; May 19, 715, to Feb. 11, 731.
St. Gregory III: Syria; Mar. 18, 731, to Nov., 741.
St. Zachary: Greece; Dec. 10, 741, to Mar. 22, 752.
Stephen II (III): Rome; Mar. 26, 752, to Apr. 26, 757.

After the death of St. Zachary, a Roman priest named Stephen was elected but died (four days later) before his consecration as bishop of Rome, which would have marked the beginning of his pontificate. Another Stephen was elected to succeed Zachary as Stephen II. (The first pope with this name was St. Stephen I, 254-57.) The ordinal III appears in parentheses after the name of Stephen II because the name of the earlier elected but deceased priest was included in some lists. Other Stephens have double numbers.

St. Paul I: Rome; Apr. (May 29), 757, to June 28, 767.
Stephen III (IV): Sicily; Aug. 1 (7), 768, to Jan. 24, 772.
Adrian I: Rome; Feb. 1 (9), 772, to Dec. 25, 795.
St. Leo III: Rome; Dec. 26 (27), 795, to June 12, 816.
Stephen IV (V): Rome; June 22, 816, to Jan. 24, 817.
St. Paschal I: Rome; Jan. 25, 817, to Feb. 11, 824.
Eugene II: Rome; Feb. (May), 824, to Aug., 827.
Valentine: Rome; Aug. 827, to Sept., 827.
Gregory IV: Rome; 827, to Jan., 844.
Sergius II: Rome; Jan., 844 to Jan. 27, 847.
St. Leo IV: Rome; Jan. (Apr. 10), 847, to July 17, 855.
Benedict III: Rome; July (Sept. 29), 855, to Apr. 17, 858.
St. Nicholas I (the Great): Rome; Apr. 24, 858, to Nov. 13, 867.
Adrian II: Rome; Dec. 14, 867, to Dec. 14, 872.
John VIII: Rome; Dec. 14, 872, to Dec. 16, 882.
Marinus I: Gallese; Dec. 16, 882, to May 15, 884.
St. Adrian III: Rome; May 17, 884, to Sept., 885. Cult confirmed June 2, 1891.
Stephen V (VI): Rome; Sept., 885, to Sept. 14, 891.
Formosus: Portus; Oct. 6, 891, to Apr. 4, 896.
Boniface VI: Rome; Apr., 896, to Apr., 896.
Stephen VI (VII): Rome; May, 896, to Aug., 897.
Romanus: Gallese; Aug., 897, to Nov., 897.
Theodore II: Rome; Dec., 897, to Dec., 897.
John IX: Tivoli; Jan., 898, to Jan., 900.
Benedict IV: Rome; Jan. (Feb.), 900, to July, 903.
Leo V: Ardea; July, 903, to Sept., 903.
Sergius III: Rome; Jan. 29, 904, to Apr. 14, 911.
Anastasius III: Rome; Apr., 911, to June, 913.
Landus: Sabina; July, 913, to Feb., 914.
John X: Tossignano (Imola); Mar., 914, to May, 928.
Leo VI: Rome; May, 928, to Dec., 928.
Stephen VII (VIII): Rome; Dec., 928, to Feb., 931.
John XI: Rome; Feb. (Mar.), 931, to Dec., 935.
Leo VII: Rome; Jan. 3, 936, to July 13, 939.
Stephen VIII (IX): Rome; July 14, 939, to Oct., 942.
Marinus II: Rome; Oct. 30, 942, to May, 946.
Agapitus II: Rome; May 10, 946, to Dec., 955.
John XII (Octavius): Tusculum; Dec. 16, 955, to May 14, 964 (date of his death).
Leo VIII: Rome; Dec. 4 (6), 963, to Mar. 1, 965.
Benedict V: Rome; May 22, 964, to July 4, 966.

Confusion exists concerning the legitimacy of claims to the pontificate by Leo VIII and Benedict V. John XII was deposed Dec. 4, 963, by a Roman council. If this deposition was invalid, Leo was an antipope. If the deposition of John was valid, Leo was the legitimate pope and Benedict was an antipope.

John XIII: Rome; Oct. 1, 965, to Sept. 6, 972.
Benedict VI: Rome; Jan. 19, 973, to June, 974.
Benedict VII: Rome; Oct. 974, to July 10, 983.
John XIV (Peter Campenora): Pavia; Dec., 983, to Aug. 20, 984.
John XV: Rome; Aug., 985, to Mar., 996.
Gregory V (Bruno of Carinthia): Saxony; May 3, 996, to Feb. 18, 999.
Sylvester II (Gerbert): Auvergne; Apr. 2, 999, to May 12, 1003.
John XVII (Siccone): Rome; June, 1003, to Dec., 1003.
John XVIII (Phasianus): Rome; Jan., 1004, to July, 1009.
Sergius IV (Peter): Rome; July 31, 1009, to May 12, 1012.

The custom of changing one's name on election to the papacy is generally considered to date from the time of Sergius IV. Before his time, several popes had changed their names. After his time, this became a regular practice, with few exceptions; e.g., Adrian VI and Marcellus II.

Benedict VIII (Theophylactus): Tusculum; May 18, 1012, to Apr. 9, 1024.
John XIX (Romanus): Tusculum; Apr. (May), 1024, to 1032.
Benedict IX (Theophylactus): Tusculum; 1032, to 1044.
Sylvester III (John): Rome; Jan. 20, 1045, to Feb. 10, 1045.

Sylvester III was an antipope if the forcible removal of Benedict IX in 1044 was not legitimate.

Benedict IX (second time): Apr. 10, 1045, to May 1, 1045.
Gregory VI (John Gratian): Rome; May 5, 1045, to Dec. 20, 1046.
Clement II (Suitger, Lord of Morsleben and Hornburg): Saxony; Dec. 24 (25), 1046, to Oct. 9, 1047.

If the resignation of Benedict IX in 1045 and his removal at the December, 1046, synod were not legitimate, Gregory VI and Clement II were antipopes.

Benedict IX (third time): Nov. 8, 1047, to July 17, 1048 (d. c. 1055).
Damasus II (Poppo): Bavaria; July 17, 1048, to Aug. 9, 1048.
St. Leo IX (Bruno): Alsace; Feb. 12, 1049, to Apr. 19, 1054.
Victor II (Gebhard): Swabia; Apr. 16, 1055, to July 28, 1057.
Stephen IX (X) (Frederick): Lorraine; Aug. 3, 1057, to Mar. 29, 1058.
Nicholas II (Gerard): Burgundy; Jan. 24, 1059, to July 27, 1061.
Alexander II (Anselmo da Baggio): Milan; Oct. 1, 1061, to Apr. 21, 1073.
St. Gregory VII (Hildebrand): Tuscany; Apr. 22 (June 30), 1073, to May 25, 1085.

Bl. Victor III (Dauferius; Desiderius): Benevento; May 24, 1086, to Sept. 16, 1087. Cult confirmed July 23, 1887.

Bl. Urban II (Otto di Lagery): France; Mar. 12, 1088, to July 29, 1099. Cult confirmed July 14, 1881.

Paschal II (Raniero): Ravenna; Aug. 13 (14), 1099, to Jan. 21, 1118.

Gelasius II (Giovanni Caetani): Gaeta; Jan. 24 (Mar. 10), 1118, to Jan. 28, 1119.

Callistus II (Guido of Burgundy): Burgundy; Feb. 2 (9), 1119, to Dec. 13, 1124.

Honorius II (Lamberto): Fiagnano (Imola); Dec. 15 (21), 1124, to Feb. 13, 1130.

Innocent II (Gregorio Papareschi): Rome; Feb. 14 (23), 1130, to Sept. 24, 1143.

Celestine II (Guido): Citta di Castello; Sept. 26 (Oct. 3), 1143, to Mar. 8, 1144.

Lucius II (Gerardo Caccianemici): Bologna: Mar. 12, 1144, to Feb. 15, 1145.

Bl. Eugene III (Bernardo Paganelli di Montemagno): Pisa; Feb. 15 (18), 1145, to July 8, 1153. Cult confirmed Oct. 3, 1872.

Anastasius IV (Corrado): Rome; July 12, 1153, to Dec, 3, 1154.

Adrian IV (Nicholas Breakspear): England; Dec. 4 (5), 1154, to Sept. 1, 1159.

Alexander III (Rolando Bandinelli): Siena; Sept. 7 (20), 1159, to Aug. 30, 1181.

Lucius III (Ubaldo Allucingoli): Lucca; Sept. 1 (6), 1181, to Sept. 25, 1185.

Urban III (Uberto Crivelli): Milan; Nov. 25 (Dec. 1), 1185, to Oct. 20, 1187.

Gregory VIII (Alberto de Morra): Benevento; Oct. 21 (25), 1187, to Dec. 17, 1187.

Clement III (Paolo Scolari): Rome; Dec. 19 (20), 1187, to Mar., 1191.

Celestine III (Giacinto Bobone): Rome; Mar. 30 (Apr. 14), 1191, to Jan. 8, 1198.

Innocent IV (Lotario dei Conti di Segni); Anagni; Jan. 8 (Feb. 22), 1198, to July 16, 1216.

Honorius III (Cencio Savelli): Rome; July 18 (24), 1216, to Mar. 18, 1227.

Gregory IX (Ugolino, Count of Segni): Anagni; Mar. 19 (21), 1227, to Aug. 22, 1241.

Celestine IV (Goffredo Castiglioni): Milan; Oct. 25 (28), 1241, to Nov. 10, 1241.

Innocent IV (Sinibaldo Fieschi): Genoa; June 25 (28), 1243, to Dec. 7, 1254.

Alexander IV (Rinaldo, Count of Segni): Anagni; Dec. 12 (20), 1254, to May 25, 1261.

Urban IV (Jacques Pantaléon): Troyes; Aug. 29 (Sept. 4), 1261, to Oct. 2, 1264.

Clement IV (Guy Foulques or Guido le Gros): France; Feb. 5 (15), 1265, to Nov. 29, 1268.

Bl. Gregory X (Teobaldo Visconti): Piacenza; Sept. 1, 1271 (Mar. 27, 1272), to Jan. 10, 1276. Cult confirmed Sept. 12, 1713.

Bl. Innocent V (Peter of Tarentaise): Savoy; Jan. 21 (Feb. 22), 1276, to June 22, 1276. Cult confirmed Mar. 13, 1898.

Adrian V (Ottobono Fieschi): Genoa; July 11, 1276, to Aug. 18, 1276.

John XXI (Petrus Juliani or Petrus Hispanus): Portugal; Sept. 8 (20), 1276, to May 20, 1277.

Elimination was made of the name of John XX in an effort to rectify the numerical designation of popes named John. The error dates back to the time of John XV.

Nicholas III (Giovanni Gaetano Orsini): Rome; Nov. 25 (Dec. 26), 1277, to Aug. 22, 1280.

Martin IV (Simon de Brie): France; Feb. 22 (Mar. 23), 1281, to Mar. 28, 1285.

The names of Marinus 1 (882-84) and Marinus II (942-46) were construed as Martin. In view of these two pontificates and the earlier reign of St. Martin I (649-55), this pope was called Martin IV.

Honorius IV (Giacomo Savelli): Rome; Apr. 2 (May 20), 1285, to Apr. 3, 1287.

Nicholas IV (Girolamo Masci): Ascoli; Feb. 22, 1288, to Apr. 4, 1292.

St. Celestine V (Pietro del Murrone): Isernia; July 5 (Aug. 29), 1294, to Dec. 13, 1294; d. 1296. Canonized May 5, 1313.

Boniface VIII (Benedetto Caetani): Anagni; Dec. 24, 1294 (Jan. 23, 1295), to Oct. 11, 1303.

Bl. Benedict XI (Niccolo Boccasini): Treviso; Oct. 22 (27), 1303, to July 7, 1304. Cult confirmed Apr. 24, 1736.

Clement V (Bertrand de Got): France; June 5 (Nov. 14), 1305, to Apr. 20, 1314. (First of Avignon popes.)

John XXII (Jacques d'Euse): Cahors; Aug. 7 (Sept. 5), 1316, to Dec. 4, 1334.

Benedict XII (Jacques Fournier): France; Dec. 20, 1334 (Jan. 8, 1335), to Apr. 25, 1342.

Clement VI (Pierre Roger): France; May 7 (19), 1342, to Dec. 6, 1352.

Innocent VI (Etienne Aubert): France; Dec. 18 (30), 1352, to Sept. 12, 1362.

Bl. Urban V (Guillaume de Grimoard): France; Sept. 28 (Nov. 6), 1362, to Dec. 19, 1370. Cult confirmed Mar. 10, 1870.

Gregory XI (Pierre Roger de Beaufort): France; Dec. 30, 1370 (Jan. 5, 1371), to Mar. 26, 1378. (Last of Avignon popes.)

Urban VI (Bartolomeo Prignano): Naples; Apr. 8 (18), 1378, to Oct. 15, 1389.

Boniface IX (Pietro Tomacelli): Naples; Nov. 2 (9), 1389, to Oct. 1, 1404.

Innocent VII (Cosma Migliorati): Sulmona; Oct. 17 (Nov. 11), 1404, to Nov. 6, 1406.

Gregory XII (Angelo Correr): Venice; Nov. 30 (Dec. 19), 1406, to July 4, 1415, when he voluntarily resigned from the papacy to permit the election of his successor. He died Oct. 18, 1417. (See The Western Schism.)

Martin V (Oddone Colonna): Rome; Nov. 11 (21), 1417, to Feb. 20, 1431.

Eugene IV (Gabriele Condulmer): Venice; Mar. 3 (11), 1431, to Feb. 23, 1447.

Nicholas V (Tommaso Parentucelli): Sarzana; Mar. 6 (19), 1447, to Mar. 24, 1455.

Callistus III (Alfonso Borgia): Jativa (Valencia); Apr. 8 (20), 1455, to Aug. 6, 1458.

Pius II (Enea Silvio Piccolomini): Siena; Aug. 19 (Sept. 3), 1458, to Aug. 14, 1464.

Paul II (Pietro Barbo): Venice; Aug. 30 (Sept. 16), 1464, to July 26, 1471.

Sixtus IV (Francesco della Rovere): Savona; Aug. 9 (25), 1471, to Aug. 12, 1484.

Innocent VIII (Giovanni Battista Cibo): Genoa; Aug. 29 (Sept. 12), 1484, to July 25, 1492.

Alexander VI (Rodrigo Borgia): Jativa (Valencia); Aug. 11 (26), 1492, to Aug. 18, 1503.
Pius III (Francesco Todeschini-Piccolomini): Siena; Sept. 22 (Oct. 1, 8), 1503, to Oct. 18, 1503.
Julius II (Giuliano de la Rovere): Savona; Oct. 31 (Nov. 26), 1503, to Feb. 21, 1513.
Leo X (Giovanni de' Medici): Florence; Mar. 9 (19), 1513, to Dec. 1, 1521.
Adrian VI (Adrian Florensz): Utrecht; Jan. 9 (Aug. 31), 1522, to Sept. 14, 1523.
Clement VII (Giulio de' Medici): Florence; Nov. 19 (26), 1523, to Sept. 25, 1534.
Paul III (Alessandro Farnese): Rome; Oct. 13 (Nov. 3), 1534, to Nov. 10, 1549.
Julius III (Giovanni Maria Ciocchi del Monte): Rome; Feb. 7 (22), 1550, to Mar. 23, 1555.
Marcellus II (Marcello Cervini): Montepulciano; Apr. 9 (10), 1555, to May 1, 1555.
Paul IV (Gian Pietro Carafa): Naples; May 23 (26), 1555, to Aug. 18, 1559.
Pius IV (Giovan Angelo de' Medici): Milan; Dec. 25, 1559 (Jan. 6, 1560), to Dec. 9, 1565.
St. Pius V (Antonio-Michele Ghislieri): Bosco (Alexandria); Jan. 7 (17), 1566, to May 1, 1572. Canonized May 22, 1712.
Gregory XIII (Ugo Buoncompagni): Bologna; May 13 (25), 1572, to Apr. 10, 1585.
Sixtus V (Felice Peretti): Grottammare (Ripatransone); Apr. 24 (May 1), 1585, to Aug. 27, 1590.
Urban VII (Giovanni Battista Castagna): Rome; Sept. 15, 1590, to Sept. 27, 1590.
Gregory XIV (Niccolo Sfondrati): Cremona; Dec. 5 (8), 1590, to Oct. 16, 1591.
Innocent IX (Giovanni Antonio Facchinetti): Bologna; Oct. 29 (Nov. 3), 1591, to Dec. 30, 1591.
Clement VIII (Ippolito Aldobrandini): Florence; Jan. 30 (Feb. 9), 1592, to Mar. 3, 1605.
Leo XI (Alessandro de' Medici): Florence; Apr. 1 (10), 1605, to Apr. 27, 1605.
Paul V (Camillo Borghese): Rome; May 16 (29), 1605, to Jan. 28, 1621.
Gregory XV (Alessandro Ludovisi): Bologna; Feb. 9 (14), 1621, to July 8, 1623.
Urban VIII (Maffeo Barberini): Florence; Aug. 6 (Sept. 29), 1623, to July 29, 1644.
Innocent X (Giovanni Battista Pamfili): Rome; Sept. 15 (Oct. 4), 1644, to Jan. 7, 1655.
Alexander VII (Fabio Chigi): Siena; Apr. 7 (18), 1655, to May 22, 1667.
Clement IX (Giulio Rospigliosi): Pistoia; June 20 (26), 1667, to Dec. 9, 1669.
Clement X (Emilio Altieri): Rome; Apr. 29 (May 11), 1670, to July 22, 1676.
Bl. Innocent XI (Benedetto Odescalchi): Como; Sept. 21 (Oct. 4), 1676, to Aug. 12, 1689. Beatified Oct. 7, 1956.
Alexander VIII (Pietro Ottoboni): Venice; Oct. 6 (16), 1689, to Feb. 1, 1691.
Innocent XII (Antonio Pignatelli): Spinazzola; July 12 (15), 1691, to Sept. 27, 1700.
Clement XI (Giovanni Francesco Albani): Urbino; Nov. 23, 30 (Dec. 8), 1700, to Mar. 19, 1721.
Innocent XIII (Michelangelo dei Conti): Rome; May 8 (18), 1721, to Mar. 7, 1724.

Benedict XIII (Pietro Francesco — Vincenzo Maria — Orsini): Gravina (Bari); May 29 (June 4), 1724, to Feb. 21, 1730.
Clement XII (Lorenzo Corsini): Florence; July 12 (16), 1730, to Feb. 6, 1740.
Benedict XIV (Prospero Lambertini): Bologna; Aug. 17 (22), 1740, to May 3, 1758.
Clement XIII (Carlo Rezzonico): Venice; July 6 (16), 1758, to Feb. 2, 1769.
Clement XIV (Giovanni Vincenzo Antonio — Lorenzo — Ganganelli): Rimini; May 19, 28 (June 4), 1769, to Sept. 22, 1774.
Pius VI (Giovanni Angelo Braschi): Cesena; Feb. 15 (22), 1775, to Aug. 29, 1799.
Pius VII (Barnaba — Gregorio — Chiaramonti): Cesena; Mar. 14 (21), 1800, to Aug. 20, 1823.
Leo XII (Annibale della Genga): Genga (Fabriano); Sept. 28 (Oct. 5), 1823, to Feb. 10, 1829.
Pius VIII (Francesco Saverio Castiglioni): Cingoli; Mar. 31 (Apr. 5), 1829, to Nov. 30, 1830.
Gregory XVI (Bartolomeo Alberto — Mauro — Cappellari): Belluno; Feb. 2 (6), 1831, to June 1, 1846.
Pius IX (Giovanni M. Mastai-Ferretti): Senigallia; June 16 (21), 1846, to Feb. 7, 1878.
Leo XIII (Gioacchino Pecci): Carpineto (Anagni). Feb. 20 (Mar. 3), 1878, to July 20, 1903.
St. Pius X (Giuseppe Sarto): Riese (Treviso); Aug. 4 (9), 1903, to Aug. 20, 1914. Canonized May 29, 1954.
Benedict XV (Giacomo della Chiesa): Genoa; Sept. 3 (6), 1914, to Jan. 22, 1922.
Pius XI (Achille Ratti): Desio (Milan); Feb. 6 (12), 1922, to Feb. 10, 1939.
Pius XII (Eugenio Pacelli): Rome; Mar. 2 (12), 1939, to Oct. 9, 1958.
John XXIII (Angelo Giuseppe Roncalli): Sotto il Monte (Bergamo); Oct. 28 (Nov. 4), 1958, to June 3, 1963.
Paul VI (Giovanni Battista Montini): Concessio (Brescia); June 21 (30), 1963, to Aug. 6, 1978.
John Paul I (Albino Luciani): Forno di Canale (Belluno); Aug. 26 (Sept. 3), 1978, to Sept. 28, 1978.
John Paul II (Karol Wojtyla): Wadowice, Poland; Oct. 16 (22), 1978.

ANTIPOPES

This list of men who claimed or exercised the papal office in an uncanonical manner includes names, birthplaces and dates of alleged reigns.

Source: "Annuario Pontificio."

St. Hippolytus: Rome; 217-235; was reconciled before his death.
Novatian: Rome; 251.
Felix II: Rome; 355 to Nov. 22, 365.
Ursinus: 366-367.
Eulalius: Dec. 27 or 29, 418, to 419.
Lawrence: 498; 501-505.
Dioscorus: Alexandria; Sept. 22, 530, to Oct. 14, 530.
Theodore: ended alleged reign, 687.
Paschal: ended alleged reign, 687.
Constantine: Nepi; June 28 (July 5), 767, to 769.

Philip: July 31, 768; retired to his monastery on the same day.
John: ended alleged reign, Jan., 844.
Anastasius: Aug., 855, to Sept., 855; d. 880.
Christopher: Rome; July or Sept., 903, to Jan., 904.
Boniface VII: Rome; June, 974, to July, 974; Aug., 984, to July, 985.
John XVI: Rossano; Apr., 997, to Feb., 998.
Gregory: ended alleged reign, 1012.
Benedict X: Rome; Apr. 5, 1058, to Jan. 24, 1059.
Honorius II: Verona; Oct. 28, 1061, to 1072.
Clement III: Parma; June 25, 1080 (Mar. 24, 1084), to Sept. 8, 1100.
Theodoric: ended alleged reign, 1100; d. 1102.
Albert: ended alleged reign, 1102.
Sylvester IV: Rome; Nov. 18, 1105, to 1111.
Gregory VIII: France; Mar. 8, 1118, to 1121.
Celestine II: Rome; ended alleged reign, Dec., 1124.
Anacletus II: Rome; Feb. 14 (23), 1130, to Jan. 25, 1138.
Victor IV: Mar., 1138, to May 29, 1138; submitted to Pope Innocent II.
Victor IV: Montecelio; Sept. 7 (Oct. 4), 1159, to Apr. 20, 1164; he did not recognize his predecessor (Victor IV, above).
Paschal III: Apr. 22 (26), 1164, to Sept. 20, 1168.
Callistus III: Arezzo; Sept., 1168, to Aug. 29, 1178; submitted to Pope Alexander III.
Innocent III: Sezze; Sept. 29, 1179, to 1180.
Nicholas V: Corvaro (Rieti); May 12 (22), 1328, to Aug. 25, 1330; d. Oct. 16, 1333.

Four antipopes of the Western Schism:

Clement VII: Sept. 20 (Oct. 31), 1378, to Sept. 16, 1394.
Benedict XIII: Aragon; Sept. 28 (Oct. 11), 1394, to May 23, 1423.
Alexander V: Crete; June 26 (July 7), 1409, to May 3, 1410.
John XXIII: Naples; May 17 (25), 1410, to May 29, 1415.
Felix V: Savoy; Nov. 5, 1439 (July 24, 1440), to April 7, 1449; d. 1451.

AVIGNON PAPACY

Avignon was the residence (1309-77) of a series of French popes (Clement V, John XXII, Benedict XII, Clement VI, Innocent VI, Urban V and Gregory XI). Prominent in the period were power struggles over the mixed interests of Church and state with the rulers of France (Philip IV, John II), Bavaria (Lewis IV), England (Edward III); factionalism of French and Italian churchmen; political as well as ecclesiastical turmoil in Italy, a factor of significance in prolonging the stay of popes in Avignon. Despite some positive achievements, the Avignon papacy was a prologue to the Western Schism which began in 1378.

WESTERN SCHISM

The Western Schism was a confused state of affairs which divided Christendom into two and then three papal obediences from 1378 to 1417.

It occurred some 50 years after Marsilius theorized that a general (not ecumenical) council of bishops and other persons was superior to a pope and nearly 30 years before the Council of Florence stated definitively that no kind of council had such authority.

It was a period of disaster preceding the even more disastrous period of the Reformation.

Urban VI, following the return of the papal residence to Rome after approximately 70 years at Avignon, was elected pope Apr. 8, 1378, and reigned until his death in 1389. He was succeeded by Boniface IX (1389-1404), Innocent VII (1404-1406) and Gregory XII (1406-1415). These four are considered the legitimate popes of the period.

Some of the cardinals who chose Urban pope, dissatisfied with his conduct of the office, declared that his election was invalid. They proceeded to elect Clement VII, who claimed the papacy from 1378 to 1394. He was succeeded by Benedict XIII.

Prelates seeking to end the state of divided papal loyalties convoked the Council of Pisa which, without authority, found Gregory XII and Benedict XIII, in absentia, guilty on 30-odd charges of schism and heresy, deposed them, and elected a third claimant to the papacy, Alexander V (1409-1410). He was succeeded by John XXIII (1410-1415).

The schism was ended by the Council of Constance (1414-1418). This council, although originally called into session in an irregular manner, acquired authority after being convoked by Gregory XII in 1415. In its early irregular phase, it deposed John XXIII whose election to the papacy was uncanonical anyway. After being formally convoked, it accepted the abdication of Gregory in 1415 and dismissed the claims of Benedict XIII two years later, thus clearing the way for the election of Martin V on Nov. 11, 1417. The Council of Constance also rejected the theories of John Wycliff and condemned John Hus as a heretic.

AD LIMINA VISITS

Ad limina visits ("To the threshold" of the Holy See and the tombs of Sts. Peter and Paul) are the subjects of a 43-page directory released July 1, 1988, by the Congregation for Bishops. The purpose of the "Directory for the 'Ad limina' Visit" is to regulate not only the visit but also "the preparations which precede it" by both the bishops themselves and the various agencies of the Roman Curia.

On the part of a bishop in charge of a diocese, preparation should involve "reflection and prayer" as well as the filing of a detailed report every five years describing his diocese, its problems and its relations with "non-Catholic and non-Christian religious communities, with civil society and with public authorities."

Ad limina visits are a "visible foundation" of the unity of bishops with the successor of St. Peter and a way in which he can obtain "authoritative information on the actual situations of the various churches," as well as direct contact with bishops from all over the world.

TWENTIETH CENTURY POPES

LEO XIII

Leo XIII (Gioacchino Vincenzo Pecci) was born May 2, 1810, in Carpineto, Italy. Although all but three years of his life and pontificate were of the 19th century, his influence extended well into the 20th century.

He was educated at the Jesuit college in Viterbo, the Roman College, the Academy of Noble Ecclesiastics, and the University of the Sapienza. He was ordained to the priesthood in 1837.

He served as an apostolic delegate to two States of the Church, Benevento from 1838 to 1841 and Perugia in 1841 and 1842. Ordained titular archbishop of Damietta, he was papal nuncio to Belgium from January, 1843, until May, 1846; in the post, he had controversial relations with the government over education issues and acquired his first significant experience of industrialized society.

He was archbishop of Perugia from 1846 to 1878. He became a cardinal in 1853 and chamberlain of the Roman Curia in 1877. He was elected to the papacy Feb. 20, 1878. He died July 20, 1903.

Canonizations: He canonized 18 saints and beatified a group of English martyrs.

Church Administration: He established 300 new dioceses and vicariates; restored the hierarchy in Scotland, set up an English, as contrasted with the Portuguese, hierarchy in India; approved the action of the Congregation for the Propagation of the Faith in reorganizing missions in China.

Encyclicals: He issued 86 encyclicals, on subjects ranging from devotional to social. In the former category were *Annum Sacrum*, on the Sacred Heart, in 1899, and 11 letters on Mary and the Rosary.

Interfaith Relations: He was unsuccessful in unity overtures made to Orthodox and Slavic Churches. He declared Anglican orders invalid in the apostolic bull *Apostolicae Curae* Sept. 13, 1896.

International Relations: Leo was frustrated in seeking solutions to the Roman Question arising from the seizure of church lands by the Kingdom of Italy in 1870. He also faced anticlerical situations in Belgium and France and in the Kulturkampf policies of Bismarck in Germany.

Social Questions: Much of Leo's influence stemmed from social doctrine stated in numerous encyclicals, concerning liberalism, liberty, the divine origin of authority; socialism, in *Quod Apostolici Muneris*, 1878; the Christian concept of the family, in *Arcanum*, 1880; socialism and economic liberalism, relations between capital and labor, in *Rerum Novarum*, 1891. Two of his social encyclicals were against the African slave trade.

Studies: In the encyclical *Aeterni Patris* of Aug. 4, 1879, he ordered a renewal of philosophical and theological studies in seminaries along scholastic, and especially Thomistic, lines, to counteract influential trends of liberalism and Modernism. He issued guidelines for biblical exegesis in *Providentissimus Deus* Nov. 18, 1893, and established the Pontifical Biblical Commission in 1902.

In other actions affecting scholarship and study, he opened the Vatican Archives to scholars in 1883 and established the Vatican Observatory.

United States: He authorized establishment of the apostolic delegation in Washington, D.C. Jan. 24, 1893. He refused to issue a condemnation of the Knights of Labor. With a document entitled *Testem Benevolentiae,* he eased resolution of questions concerning what was called an American heresy in 1899.

ST. PIUS X

St. Pius X (Giuseppe Melchiorre Sarto) was born in 1835 in Riese, Italy.

Educated at the college of Castelfranco and the seminary at Padua, he was ordained to the priesthood Sept. 18, 1858. He served as a curate in Trombolo for nine years before beginning an eight-year pastorate at Salzano. He was chancellor of the Treviso diocese from November, 1875, and bishop of Mantua from 1884 until 1893. He was cardinal-patriarch of Venice from that year until his election to the papacy by the conclave held from July 31 to Aug. 4, 1903.

Aims: Pius' principal objectives as pope were "to restore all things in Christ, in order that Christ may be all and in all," and "to teach (and defend) Christian truth and law."

Canonizations, Encyclicals: He canonized four saints and issued 16 encyclicals. One of the encyclicals was issued in commemoration of the 50th anniversary of the proclamation of the dogma of the Immaculate Conception of Mary.

Catechetics: He introduced a whole new era of religious instruction and formation with the encyclical *Acerbo Nimis* of Apr. 15, 1905, in which he called for vigor in establishing and conducting parochial programs of the Confraternity of Christian Doctrine.

Catholic Action: He outlined the role of official Catholic Action in two encyclicals in 1905 and 1906. Favoring organized action by Catholics themselves, he had serious reservations about interconfessional collaboration.

He stoutly maintained claims to papal rights in the anticlerical climate of Italy. He authorized bishops to relax prohibitions against participation by Catholics in some Italian elections.

Church Administration: With the motu proprio *Arduum Sane* of Mar. 19, 1904, he inaugurated the work which resulted in the Code of Canon Law; the code was completed in 1917 and went into effect in the following year. He reorganized and strengthened the Roman Curia with the apostolic constitution *Sapienti Consilio* of June 29, 1908. While promoting the expansion of missionary work, he removed from the jurisdiction of the Congregation for the Propagation of the Faith the Church in the United States, Canada, Newfoundland, England, Ireland, Holland and Luxembourg.

International Relations: He ended traditional

prerogatives of Catholic governments with respect to papal elections, in 1904. He opposed anti-Church and anticlerical actions in several countries: Bolivia in 1905, because of anti-religious legislation; France in 1906, for its 1901 action in annulling its concordat with the Holy See, and for the 1905 Law of Separation by which it decreed separation of Church and state, ordered the confiscation of church property, and blocked religious education and the activities of religious orders; Portugal in 1911, for the separation of Church and state and repressive measures which resulted in persecution later.

In 1912 he called on the bishops of Brazil to work for the improvement of conditions among Indians.

Liturgy: "The Pope of the Eucharist," he strongly recommended the frequent reception of Holy Communion in a decree dated Dec. 20, 1905; in another decree, *Quam Singulari,* of Aug. 8, 1910, he called for the early reception of the sacrament by children. He initiated measures for liturgical reform with new norms for sacred music and the start of work on revision of the *Breviary* for recitation of the Divine Office.

Modernism: Pius was a vigorous opponent of "the synthesis of all heresies," which threatened the integrity of doctrine through its influence in philosophy, theology and biblical exegesis. In opposition, he condemned 65 of its propositions as erroneous in the decree *Lamentabili* July 3, 1907; issued the encyclical *Pascendi* in the same vein Sept. 8, 1907; backed both of these with censures; and published the Oath against Modernism in September, 1910, to be taken by all the clergy. Ecclesiastical studies suffered to some extent from these actions, necessary as they were at the time.

Pius followed the lead of Leo XIII in promoting the study of scholastic philosophy. He established the Pontifical Biblical Institute May 7, 1909.

His death, Aug. 20, 1914, was hastened by the outbreak of World War I. He was beatified in 1951 and canonized May 29, 1954. His feast is observed Aug. 21.

BENEDICT XV

Benedict XV (Giacomo della Chiesa) was born Nov. 21, 1854, in Pegli, Italy.

He was educated at the Royal University of Genoa and Gregorian University in Rome. He was ordained to the priesthood Dec. 21, 1878.

He served in the papal diplomatic corps from 1882 to 1907; as secretary to the nuncio to Spain from 1882 to 1887, as secretary to the papal secretary of state from 1887, and as undersecretary from 1901.

He was ordained archbishop of Bologna Dec. 22, 1907, and spent four years completing a pastoral visitation there. He was made a cardinal just three months before being elected to the papacy Sept. 3, 1914. He died Jan. 22, 1922. Two key efforts of his pontificate were for peace and the relief of human suffering caused by World War I.

Canonizations: Benedict canonized three saints; one of them was Joan of Arc.

Canon Law: He published the Code of Canon Law, developed by the commission set up by St. Pius X, May 27, 1917; it went into effect the following year.

Curia: He made great changes in the personnel of the Curia. He established the Congregation for the Oriental Churches May 1, 1917, and founded the Pontifical Oriental Institute in Rome later in the year.

Encyclicals: He issued 12 encyclicals. Peace was the theme of three of them. In another, published two years after the cessation of hostilities, he wrote about child victims of the war. He followed the lead of Leo XIII in *Spiritus Paraclitus,* Sept. 15, 1920, on biblical studies.

International Relations: He was largely frustrated on the international level because of the events and attitudes of the war period, but the number of diplomats accredited to the Vatican nearly doubled, from 14 to 26, between the time of his accession to the papacy and his death.

Peace Efforts: Benedict's stance in the war was one of absolute impartiality but not of uninterested neutrality. Because he would not take sides, he was suspected by both sides and the seven-point peace plan he offered to all belligerents Aug. 1, 1917, was turned down. The points of the plan were: recognition of the moral force of right; disarmament; acceptance of arbitration in cases of dispute; guarantee of freedom of the seas; renunciation of war indemnities; evacuation and restoration of occupied territories; examination of territorial claims in dispute.

Relief Efforts: Benedict assumed personal charge of Vatican relief efforts during the war. He set up an international missing persons bureau for contacts between prisoners and their families, but was forced to close it because of the suspicion of warring nations that it was a front for espionage operations. He persuaded the Swiss government to admit into the country military victims of tuberculosis.

Roman Question: Benedict prepared the way for the meetings and negotiations which led to settlement of the question in 1929.

PIUS XI

Pius XI (Ambrogio Damiano Achille Ratti) was born May 31, 1857, in Desio, Italy.

Educated at seminaries in Seviso and Milan, and at the Lombard College, Gregorian University and Academy of St. Thomas in Rome, he was ordained to the priesthood in 1879.

He taught at the major seminary of Milan from 1882 to 1888. Appointed to the staff of the Ambrosian Library in 1888, he remained there until 1911, acquiring a reputation for publishing works on palaeography and serving as director from 1907 to 1911. He then moved to the Vatican Library, of which he was prefect from 1914 to 1918. In 1919, he was named apostolic visitor to Poland in April, nuncio in June, and was made titular archbishop of Lepanto Oct. 28. He was made archbishop of Milan and cardinal June 13, 1921, before being elected to the papacy Feb. 6, 1922. He died Feb. 10, 1939.

Aim: The objective of his pontificate, as stated in the encyclical *Ubi Arcano,* Dec. 23, 1922, was to establish the reign and peace of Christ in society.

Canonizations: He canonized 34 saints, including the Jesuit Martyrs of North America, and conferred the title of Doctor of the Church on Sts. Peter Canisius, John of the Cross, Robert Bellarmine and Albertus Magnus.

Eastern Churches: He called for better understanding of the Eastern Churches in the encyclical *Rerum Orientalium* of Sept. 8, 1928, and developed facilities for the training of Eastern-Rite priests. He inaugurated steps for the codification of Eastern-Church law in 1929. In 1935 he made Syrian Patriarch Tappouni a cardinal.

Encyclicals: His first encyclical, *Ubi Arcano*, in addition to stating the aims of his pontificate, blueprinted Catholic Action and called for its development throughout the Church. In *Quas Primas*, Dec. 11, 1925, he established the feast of Christ the King for universal observance. Subjects of some of his other encyclicals were: Christian education, in *Rappresentanti in Terra*, Dec. 31, 1929; Christian marriage, in *Casti Connubii*, Dec. 31, 1930; social conditions and pressure for social change in line with the teaching in *Rerum Novarum*, in *Quadragesimo Anno*, May 15, 1931; atheistic Communism, in *Divini Redemptoris*, Mar. 19, 1937; the priesthood, in *Ad Catholici Sacerdotii*, Dec. 20, 1935.

Missions: Following the lead of Benedict XV, Pius called for the training of native clergy in the pattern of their own respective cultures, and promoted missionary developments in various ways. He ordained six native bishops for China in 1926, one for Japan in 1927, and others for regions of Asia, China and India in 1933. He placed the first 40 mission dioceses under native bishops, saw the number of native priests increase from about 2,600 to more than 7,000 and the number of Catholics in missionary areas more than double from nine million.

In the apostolic constitution *Deus Scientiarum Dominus* of May 24, 1931, he ordered the introduction of missiology into theology courses.

Interfaith Relations: Pius was negative to the ecumenical movement among Protestants but approved the Malines Conversations, 1921 to 1926, between Anglicans and Catholics.

International Relations: Relations with the Mussolini government deteriorated from 1931 on, as indicated in the encyclical *Non Abbiamo Bisogno*, when the regime took steps to curb liberties and activities of the Church; they turned critical in 1938 with the emergence of racist policies. Relations deteriorated also in Germany from 1933 on, resulting finally in condemnation of the Nazis in the encyclical *Mit Brennender Sorge*, March, 1937. Pius sparked a revival of the Church in France by encouraging Catholics to work within the democratic framework of the Republic rather than foment trouble over restoration of a monarchy. Pius was powerless to influence developments related to the civil war which erupted in Spain in July, 1936, sporadic persecution and repression by the Calles regime in Mexico, and systematic persecution of the Church in the Soviet Union. Many of the 10 concordats and two agreements reached with European countries after World War I became casualties of World War II.

Roman Question: Pius negotiated for two and one-half years with the Italian government to settle the Roman Question by means of the Lateran Agreement of 1929. The agreement provided independent status for the State of Vatican City; made Catholicism the official religion of Italy, with pastoral and educational freedom and state recognition of Catholic marriages, religious orders and societies; and provided a financial payment to the Vatican for expropriation of the former States of the Church.

PIUS XII

Pius XII (Eugenio Maria Giovanni Pacelli) was born Mar. 2, 1876, in Rome.

Educated at the Gregorian University and the Lateran University, in Rome, he was ordained to the priesthood Apr. 2, 1899.

He entered the Vatican diplomatic service in 1901, worked on the codification of canon law, and was appointed secretary of the Congregation for Ecclesiastical Affairs in 1914. Three years later he was ordained titular archbishop of Sardis and made apostolic nuncio to Bavaria. He was nuncio to Germany from 1920 to 1929, when he was made a cardinal, and took office as papal secretary of state in the following year. His diplomatic negotiations resulted in concordats between the Vatican and Bavaria (1924), Prussia (1929), Baden (1932), Austria and the German Republic (1933). He took part in negotiations which led to settlement of the Roman Question in 1929.

He was elected to the papacy Mar. 2, 1939. He died Oct. 9, 1958, at Castel Gandolfo after the 12th longest pontificate in history.

Canonizations: He canonized 34 saints, including Mother Frances X. Cabrini, the first U.S. citizen-Saint.

Cardinals: He raised 56 prelates to the rank of cardinal in two consistories held in 1946 and 1953. There were 57 cardinals at the time of his death.

Church Organization and Missions: He increased the number of dioceses from 1,696 to 2,048. He established native hierarchies in China (1946), Burma (1955) and parts of Africa, and extended the native structure of the Church in India. He ordained the first black bishop for Africa.

Communism: In addition to opposing and condemning Communism on numerous occasions, he decreed in 1949 the penalty of excommunication for all Catholics holding formal and willing allegiance to the Communist Party and its policies. During his reign the Church was persecuted in some 15 countries which fell under communist domination.

Doctrine and Liturgy: He proclaimed the dogma of the Assumption of the Blessed Virgin Mary Nov. 1, 1950 (apostolic constitution, *Munificentissimus Deus*.)

In various encyclicals and other enactments, he provided background for the *aggiornamento* introduced by his successor, John XXIII: by his formulations of doctrine and practice regarding the

Mystical Body of Christ, the liturgy, sacred music and biblical studies; by the revision of the Rites of Holy Week; by initiation of the work which led to the calendar-missal-breviary reform ordered into effect Jan. 1, 1961; by the first of several modifications of the Eucharistic fast; by extending the time of Mass to the evening. He instituted the feasts of Mary, Queen, and of St. Joseph the Worker, and clarified teaching concerning devotion to the Sacred Heart.

His 41 encyclicals and nearly 1,000 public addresses made Pius one of the greatest teaching popes. His concern in all his communications was to deal with specific points at issue and/or to bring Christian principles to bear on contemporary world problems.

Peace Efforts: Before the start of World War II, he tried unsuccessfully to get the contending nations — Germany and Poland, France and Italy — to settle their differences peaceably. During the war, he offered his services to mediate the widened conflict, spoke out against the horrors of war and the suffering it caused, mobilized relief work for its victims, proposed a five-point program for peace in Christmas messages from 1939 to 1942, and secured a generally open status for the city of Rome. After the war, he endorsed the principles and intent of the United Nations and continued efforts for peace.

United States: Pius appointed more than 200 of the 265 American bishops resident in the U.S. and abroad in 1958, erected 27 dioceses in this country, and raised seven dioceses to archiepiscopal rank.

JOHN XXIII

John XXIII (Angelo Roncalli) was born Nov. 25, 1881, at Sotte il Monte, Italy.

He was educated at the seminary of the Bergamo diocese and the Pontifical Seminary in Rome, where he was ordained to the priesthood Aug. 10, 1904.

He spent the first nine or 10 years of his priesthood as secretary to the bishop of Bergamo and as an instructor in the seminary there. He served as a medic and chaplain in the Italian army during World War I. Afterwards, he resumed duties in his own diocese until he was called to Rome in 1921 for work with the Society for the Propagation of the Faith.

He began diplomatic service in 1925 as titular archbishop of Areopolis and apostolic visitor to Bulgaria. A succession of offices followed: apostolic delegate to Bulgaria (1931-1935); titular archbishop of Mesembria, apostolic delegate to Turkey and Greece, administrator of the Latin vicariate apostolic of Istanbul (1935-1944); apostolic nuncio to France (1944-1953). On these missions, he was engaged in delicate negotiations involving Roman, Eastern-Rite and Orthodox relations; the needs of people suffering from the consequences of World War II; and unsettling suspicions arising from wartime conditions.

He was made a cardinal Jan. 12, 1953, and three days later was appointed patriarch of Venice, the position he held until his election to the papacy Oct. 28, 1958. He died of stomach cancer June 3, 1963.

John was a strong and vigorous pope whose influence far outmeasured both his age and the shortness of his time in the papacy.

Second Vatican Council: John announced Jan. 25, 1959, his intention of convoking the 21st ecumenical council in history to renew life in the Church, to reform its structures and institutions, and to explore ways and means of promoting unity among Christians. Through the council, which completed its work two and one-half years after his death, he ushered in a new era in the history of the Church.

Canon Law: He established a commission Mar. 28, 1963, for revision of the Code of Canon Law. The revised Code was promulgated in 1983.

Canonizations: He canonized 10 saints and beatified Mother Elizabeth Ann Seton, the first native of the U.S. ever so honored. He named St. Lawrence of Brindisi a Doctor of the Church.

Cardinals: He created 52 cardinals in five consistories, raising membership of the College of Cardinals above the traditional number of 70; at one time in 1962, the membership was 87. He made the college more international in representation than it had ever been, appointing the first cardinals from the Philippines, Japan and Africa. He ordered episcopal ordination for all cardinals. He relieved the suburban bishops of Rome of ordinary jurisdiction over their dioceses so they might devote all their time to business of the Roman Curia.

Eastern Rites: He made all Eastern-Rite patriarchs members of the Congregation for the Oriental Churches.

Ecumenism: He assigned to the Second Vatican Council the task of finding ways and means of promoting unity among Christians. He established the Vatican Secretariat for Promoting Christian Unity June 5, 1960. He showed his desire for more cordial relations with the Orthodox by sending personal representatives to visit Patriarch Athenagoras I June 27, 1961; approved a mission of five delegates to the General Assembly of the World Council of Churches which met in New Delhi, India, in November, 1961; removed a number of pejorative references to Jews in the Roman-Rite liturgy for Good Friday.

Encyclicals: Of the eight encyclicals he issued, the two outstanding ones were *Mater et Magistra* ("Christianity and Social Progress"), in which he recapitulated, updated and extended the social doctrine stated earlier by Leo XIII and Pius XI; and *Pacem in Terris* ("Peace on Earth"), the first encyclical ever addressed to all men of good will as well as to Catholics, on the natural-law principles of peace.

Liturgy: In forwarding liturgical reforms already begun by Pius XII, he ordered a calendar-missal-breviary reform into effect Jan. 1, 1961. He authorized the use of vernacular languages in the administration of the sacraments and approved giving Holy Communion to the sick in afternoon hours. He selected the liturgy as the first topic of major discussion by the Second Vatican Council.

Missions: He issued an encyclical on the missionary activity of the Church; established native hierarchies in Indonesia, Vietnam and Korea; and called on North American superiors of religious institutes to have one-tenth of their members assigned to work in Latin America by 1971.

Peace: John spoke and used his moral influence for peace in 1961 when tension developed over Berlin, in 1962 during the Algerian revolt from France, and later the same year in the Cuban missile crisis. His efforts were singled out for honor by the Balzan Peace Foundation. In 1963, he was posthumously awarded the U.S. Presidential Medal of Freedom.

PAUL VI

Paul VI (Giovanni Battista Montini) was born Sept. 26, 1897, at Concesio in northern Italy.

Educated at Brescia, he was ordained to the priesthood May 29, 1920. He pursued additional studies at the Pontifical Academy for Noble Ecclesiastics and the Pontifical Gregorian University. In 1924 he began 30 years of service in the Secretariat of State; as undersecretary from 1937 until 1954, he was closely associated with Pius XII and was heavily engaged in organizing informational and relief services during and after World War II.

He was ordained archbishop of Milan Dec. 12, 1954, and was inducted into the College of Cardinals Dec. 15, 1958. He was elected to the papacy June 21, 1963, two days after the conclave began. He died of a heart attack Aug. 6, 1978.

Second Vatican Council: He reconvened the Second Vatican Council after the death of John XXIII, presided over its second, third and fourth sessions, formally promulgated the 16 documents it produced, and devoted the whole of his pontificate to the task of putting them into effect throughout the Church. The main thrust of his pontificate — in a milieu of cultural and other changes in the Church and the world — was toward institutionalization and control of the authentic trends articulated and set in motion by the council.

Canonizations: He canonized 84 saints. They included groups of 22 Ugandan martyrs and 40 martyrs of England and Wales, as well as two Americans — Elizabeth Ann Bayley Seton and John Nepomucene Neumann.

Cardinals: He created 144 cardinals, and gave the Sacred College a more international complexion than it ever had before. He limited participation in papal elections to 120 cardinals under the age of 80.

Collegiality: He established the Synod of Bishops in 1965 and called it into session five times. He stimulated the formation and operation of regional conferences of bishops, and of consultative bodies on other levels.

Creed and Holy Year: On June 30, 1968, he issued a Creed of the People of God in conjunction with the celebration of a Year of Faith. He proclaimed and led the observance of a Holy Year from Christmas Eve of 1974 to Christmas Eve of 1975.

Diplomacy: He met with many world leaders, including Soviet President Nikolai Podgorny in 1967, Marshal Tito of Yugoslavia in 1971 and President Nicolas Ceausescu of Rumania in 1973. He worked constantly to reduce tension between the Church and the intransigent regimes of Eastern European countries by means of a detente type of policy called Ostpolitik. He agreed to significant revisions of the Vatican's concordat with Spain and initiated efforts to revise the concordat with Italy. More then 40 countries established diplomatic relations with the Vatican during his pontificate.

Encyclicals: He issued seven encyclicals, three of which are the best known. In *Populorum Progressio* ("Development of Peoples") he appealed to wealthy countries to take "concrete action" to promote human development and to remedy imbalances between richer and poorer nations; this encyclical, coupled with other documents and related actions, launched the Church into a new depth of involvement as a public advocate for human rights and for humanizing social, political and economic policies. In *Sacerdotalis Caelibatus* ("Priestly Celibacy") he reaffirmed the strict observance of priestly celibacy throughout the Western Church. In *Humanae Vitae* ("Of Human Life") he condemned abortion, sterilization and artificial birth control, in line with traditional teaching and in "defense of life, the gift of God, the glory of the family, the strength of the people."

Interfaith Relations: He initiated formal consultation and informal dialogue on international and national levels between Catholics and non-Catholics — Orthodox, Anglicans, Protestants, Jews, Moslems, Buddhists, Hindus, and unbelievers. He and Greek Orthodox Patriarch Athenagoras I of Constantinople nullified in 1965 the mutual excommunications imposed by their respective churches in 1054.

Liturgy: He carried out the most extensive liturgical reform in history, involving a new Order of the Mass effective in 1969, a revised church calendar in 1970, revisions and translations into vernacular languages of all sacramental rites and other liturgical texts.

Ministries: He authorized the restoration of the permanent diaconate in the Roman Rite and the establishment of new ministries of lay persons.

Peace: In 1968, he instituted the annual observance of a World Day of Peace on New Year's Day as a means of addressing a message of peace to all the world's political leaders and the peoples of all nations. The most dramatic of his many appeals for peace and efforts to ease international tensions was his plea for "No more war!" before the United Nations Oct. 4, 1965.

Pilgrimages: A "Pilgrim Pope," he made pastoral visits to the Holy Land and India in 1964, the United Nations and New York City in 1965, Portugal and Turkey in 1967, Colombia in 1968, Switzerland and Uganda in 1969, and Asia, Pacific islands and Australia in 1970. While in Manila in 1970, he was stabbed by a Bolivian artist who made an attempt on his life.

Roman Curia: He reorganized the central administrative organs of the Church in line with provisions of the apostolic constitution, *Regimini Ecclesiae Universae,* streamlining procedures for more effective service and giving the agencies a more international perspective by drawing officials and consultors from all over the world. He also instituted a number of new commissions and other bodies. Coupled with curial reorganization was a simplification of papal ceremonies.

JOHN PAUL I

John Paul I (Albino Luciani) was born Oct. 17, 1912, in Forno di Canale (now Canale d'Agordo) in northern Italy.

Educated at the minor seminary in Feltre and the major seminary of the Diocese of Belluno, he was ordained to the priesthood July 7, 1935. He pursued further studies at the Pontifical Gregorian University in Rome and was awarded a doctorate in theology. From 1937 to 1947 he was vice rector of the Belluno seminary, where he taught dogmatic and moral theology, canon law and sacred art. He was appointed vicar general of his diocese in 1947 and served as director of catechetics.

Ordained bishop of Vittorio Veneto Dec. 27, 1958, he attended all sessions of the Second Vatican Council, participated in three assemblies of the Synod of Bishops (1971, 1974 and 1977), and was vice president of the Italian Bishops' Conference from 1972 to 1975.

He was appointed archbishop and patriarch of Venice Dec. 15, 1969, and was inducted into the College of Cardinals Mar. 5, 1973.

He was elected to the papacy Aug. 26, 1978, on the fourth ballot cast by the 111 cardinals participating in the largest and one of the shortest conclaves in history. The quickness of his election was matched by the brevity of his pontificate of 33 days, during which he delivered 19 addresses. He died of a heart attack Sept. 28, 1978.

JOHN PAUL II

See separate entry.

CANONIZATIONS BY LEO XIII AND HIS SUCCESSORS

Canonization is an infallible declaration by the pope that a person who suffered martyrdom and/or practiced Christian virtue to a heroic degree is in glory with God in heaven and is worthy of public honor by the universal Church and of imitation by the faithful.

(See Canonization entry in Glossary.)

Leo XIII
(1878-1903)

1881: Clare of Montefalco, virgin (d. 1308); John Baptist de Rossi, priest (1698-1764); Lawrence of Brindisi, doctor (d. 1619).
1883: Benedict J. Labre (1748-1783).
1888: Seven Holy Founders of the Servite Order; Peter Claver, priest (1581-1654); John Berchmans (1599-1621); Alphonsus Rodriguez, lay brother (1531-1617).
1897: Anthony M. Zaccaria, founder of Barnabites (1502-1539); Peter Fourier, co-founder of Augustinian Canonesses of Our Lady (1565-1640).
1900: John Baptist de La Salle, founder of Christian Brothers (1651-1719); Rita of Cascia (1381-1457).

St. Pius X
(1903-1914)

1904: Alexander Sauli, bishop (1534-1593); Gerard Majella, lay brother (1725-1755).
1909: Joseph Oriol, priest (1650-1702); Clement M. Hofbauer, priest (1751-1820).

Benedict XV
(1914-1922)

1920: Gabriel of the Sorrowful Mother (1838-1862); Margaret Mary Alacoque, virgin (1647-1690); Joan of Arc, virgin (1412-1431).

Pius XI
(1922-1939)

1925: Therese of Lisieux, virgin (1873-1897); Peter Canisius, doctor (1521-1597); Mary Magdalen Postel, foundress of Sisterhood of Christian Schools (1756-1846); Mary Magdalen Sophie Barat, foundress of Society of the Sacred Heart (1779-1865); John Eudes, founder of Eudist Fathers (1601-1680); John Baptist Vianney (Curé of Ars), priest (1786-1859).
1930: Lucy Filippini, virgin (1672-1732); Catherine Thomas, virgin (1533-1574); Jesuit North American Martyrs (see Index); Robert Bellarmine, bishop-doctor (1542-1621); Theophilus of Corte, priest (1676-1740).
1931: Albert the Great, bishop-doctor (1206-1280) (equivalent canonization).
1933: Andrew Fournet, priest (1752-1834); Bernadette Soubirous, virgin (1844-1879).
1934: Joan Antida Thouret, foundress of Sisters of Charity of St. Joan Antida (1765-1826); Mary Michaeli, foundress of Institute of Handmaids of the Blessed Sacrament (1809-1865); Louise de Marillac, foundress of Sisters of Charity (1591-1660); Joseph Benedict Cottolengo, priest (1786-1842); Pompilius M. Pirotti, priest (1710-1756); Teresa Margaret Redi, virgin (1747-1770); John Bosco, founder of Salesians (1815-1888); Conrad of Parzham, lay brother (1818-1894).
1935: John Fisher, bishop-martyr (1469-1535); Thomas More, martyr (1478-1535).
1938: Andrew Bobola, martyr (1592-1657); John Leonardi, founder of Clerics Regular of the Mother of God (c. 1550-1609); Salvatore of Horta, lay brother (1520-1567).

Pius XII
(1939-1958)

1940: Gemma Galgani, virgin (1878-1903); Mary Euphrasia Pelletier, foundress of Good Shepherd Sisters (1796-1868).
1943: Margaret of Hungary, virgin (d. 1270) (equivalent canonization).
1946: Frances Xavier Cabrini, foundress of Missionary Sisters of the Sacred Heart (1850-1917).
1947: Nicholas of Flue, hermit (1417-1487); John of Britto, martyr (1647-1693); Bernard Realini,

priest (1530-1616); Joseph Cafasso, priest (1811-1860); Michael Garicoits, founder of Auxiliary Priests of the Sacred Heart (1797-1863); Jeanne Elizabeth des Ages, cofoundress of Daughters of the Cross (1773-1838); Louis Marie Grignon de Montfort, founder of Montfort Fathers (1673-1716); Catherine Laboure, virgin (1806-1876).

1949: Jeanne de Lestonnac, foundress of Religious of Notre Dame of Bordeaux (1556-1640); Maria Josepha Rossello, foundress of Daughters of Our Lady of Pity (1811-1880).

1950: Emily de Rodat, foundress of Congregation of the Holy Family of Villefranche (1787-1852); Anthony Mary Claret, bishop, founder of Claretians (1807-1870); Bartolomea Capitanio (1807-1833) and Vincenza Gerosa (1784-1847), foundresses of Sisters of Charity of Lovere; Jeanne de Valois, foundress of Annonciades of Bourges (1461-1504); Vincenzo M. Strambi, bishop (1745-1824); Maria Goretti, virgin-martyr (1890-1902); Mariana Paredes de Jesus, virgin (1618-1645).

1951: Maria Domenica Mazzarello, co-foundress of Daughters of Our Lady Help of Christians (1837-1881); Emilie de Vialar, foundress of Sisters of St. Joseph "of the Apparition" (1797-1856); Anthony M. Gianelli, bishop (1789-1846); Ignatius of Laconi, lay brother (1701-1781); Francis Xavier Bianchi, priest (1743-1815).

1954: Pius X, pope (1835-1914); Dominic Savio (1842-1857); Maria Crocifissa di Rosa, foundress of Handmaids of Charity of Brescia (1813-1855); Peter Chanel, priest-martyr (1803-1841); Gaspar del Bufalo, founder of Missioners of the Most Precious Blood (1786-1837); Joseph M. Pignatelli, priest (1737-1811).

1958: Herman Joseph, O. Praem., priest (1150-1241) (equivalent canonization).

John XXIII
(1958-1963)

1959: Joaquina de Vedruna de Mas, foundress of Carmelite Sisters of Charity (1783-1854); Charles of Sezze, lay brother (1613-1670).

1960: Gregory Barbarigo, bishop (1625-1697) (equivalent canonization); John de Ribera, bishop (1532-1611).

1961: Bertilla Boscardin, virgin (1888-1922).

1962: Martin de Porres, lay brother (1579-1639); Peter Julian Eymard, founder of Blessed Sacrament Fathers (1811-1868); Anthony Pucci, priest (1819-1892); Francis Mary of Camporosso, lay brother (1804-1866).

1963: Vincent Pallotti, founder of Pallottine Fathers (1795-1850).

Paul VI
(1963-1978)

1964: Charles Lwanga and Twenty-One Companions, Martyrs of Uganda (d. between 1885-1887).

1967: Benilde Romancon, Christian Brother (1805-1862).

1969: Julia Billiart, foundress of Sisters of Notre Dame of Namur (1751-1816).

1970: Maria Della Dolorato Torres Acosta, foundress of Servants Sisters of Mary (1826-1887); Leonard Murialdo, priest, founder of Congregation of St. Joseph (1828-1900); Therese Couderc, foundress of Congregation of Our Lady of the Cenacle (1805-1885); John of Avila, preacher and spiritual director (1499-1569); Nicholas Tavelic, Deodatus of Aquitaine, Peter of Narbonne and Stephen of Cuneo, martyrs (d. 1391); Forty English and Welsh Martyrs (d. 16th cent.).

1974: Teresa of Jesus Jornet Ibars, foundress of Little Sisters of Abandoned Aged (1843-1897).

1975: Vicenta Maria Lopez y Vicuna, foundress of Institute of Daughters of Mary Immaculate (1847-1890); Elizabeth Bayley Seton, foundress of Sisters of Charity in the U.S. (1774-1821); John Masias, Dominican brother-missionary (1585-1645); Oliver Plunket, archbishop-martyr (1629-1681); Justin de Jacobis, missionary bishop (1800-1860); John Baptist of the Conception, priest, reformer of the Order of the Most Holy Trinity (1561-1613).

1976: Beatrice da Silva, foundress of Congregation of the Immaculate Conception of the BVM (1424 or 1426-1490); John Ogilvie, Scottish Jesuit martyr (1579-1615).

1977: Rafaela Maria Porras y Ayllon, foundress of Handmaids of the Sacred Heart (1850-1925); John Nepomucene Neumann, bishop (1811-1860); Sharbel Makhlouf, Maronite Rite monk (1828-1898).

John Paul II
(1978-)

1982: Crispin of Viterbo, Capuchin brother (1668-1750); Maximilian Kolbe, Conventual Franciscan priest (1894-1941); Marguerite Bourgeoys, foundress of Congregation of Notre Dame (1620-1700); Jeanne Delanoue, foundress of Sisters of St. Anne of Providence of Saumur, France (1666-1736).

1983: Leopold Mandic, Capuchin priest (1866-1942).

1984: Paola Frassinetti, foundress of Sisters of St. Dorothy (1809-1892); 103 Korean Martyrs (d. between 1839-1867); Miguel Febres Cordero, of the Brothers of the Christian Schools (1854-1910).

1986: Francis Anthony Fasani, Conventual Franciscan priest (1681-1742); Giuseppe Maria Tomasi, Theatine, cardinal (1649-1713)

1987: Giuseppe Moscati, layman, physician (d. 1927); Lawrence (Lorenzo) Ruiz and Fifteen Companions (laymen, priests and religious from five countries), Martyrs of Japan (d. 1630s).

1988: Eustochia Calafato, Sicilian Poor Clare (1434-1485); 117 Martyrs of Vietnam (96 Vietnamese, 11 Spanish, 10 French; included 8 bishops, 50 priests, 1 seminarian, 58 lay persons); Roque Gonzalez (1576-1628), Alfonso Rodriguez (1598-1628) and Juan de Castillo (1598-1628), Jesuit martyrs of Paraguay; Rose Philippine Duchesne, French-born foundress of first convent of Society of the Sacred Heart in the U.S. (1796-1852); Simon de Rojas, Trinitarian priest (1552-1624); Magdalen of Canossa, foundress of Canossian Daughters of Charity (1774-1835); Maria Rosa Molas y Vollve, foundress of Sisters of Our Lady of Consolation (d. 1876).

English and Welsh Martyrs

Forty Martyrs of England and Wales, victims of persecution from 1535 to 1671, were canonized by Pope Paul Oct. 25, 1970.

The martyrs were prosecuted and executed as traitors for refusal to comply with laws enacted by Henry VIII and Elizabeth I regarding supremacy (the sovereign was proclaimed the highest authority of the Church in England, acknowledgment of papal primacy was forbidden), succession and the prohibition of native-born to study for the priesthood abroad and return to England for practice of the ministry.

John Houghton, prior of the London Charterhouse, was the first of his group to die (1535) for opposing Henry's Acts of Supremacy and Succession. Cuthbert Mayne (d. 1577) was the protomartyr of the English seminary at Douay. Margaret Clitherow (d. 1586) and Swithun Wells (d. 1591) were executed for sheltering priests. Richard Gwyn (d. 1584), poet, was the protomartyr of Wales.

Others in the group were:

John Almond, Edmund Arrowsmith, Ambrose Barlow, John Boste, Alexander Briant, Edmund Campion, Philip Evans, Thomas Garnet, Edmund Gennings;

Philip Howard, John Jones, John Kemble, Luke Kirby, Robert Lawrence, David Lewis, Ann Line, John Lloyd;

Henry Morse, Nicholas Owen, John Paine, Polydore Plasden, John Plessington, Richard Reynolds, John Rigby, John Roberts;

Alban Roe, Ralph Sherwin, Robert Southwell, John Southworth, John Stone, John Wall, Henry Walpole, Margaret Ward, Augustine Webster and Eustace White.

PAPAL ENCYCLICALS — BENEDICT XIV (1740) TO JOHN PAUL II

(Source: *The Papal Encyclicals* (5 vols.), Claudia Carlen, I.H.M.; a Consortium Book, © McGrath Publishing Co., Wilmington, N.C. Used with permission.)

An encyclical letter is a pastoral letter addressed by a pope to the whole Church. In general, it concerns matters of doctrine, morals or discipline. Its formal title consists of the first few words of the official text. A few encyclicals, notably *Pacem in terris* by John XXIII and *Ecclesiam Suam* by Paul VI, have been addressed to "all men of good will" as well as to bishops and the faithful in communion with the Church.

An encyclical epistle, which is like an encyclical letter in many respects, is addressed to part of the Church, that is, to the bishops and faithful of a particular country or area. Its contents may concern other than doctrinal, moral or disciplinary matters of universal significance; for example, the commemoration of historical events, conditions in a certain country.

The authority of encyclicals was stated by Pius XII in the encyclical *Humani generis* Aug. 12, 1950.

"Nor must it be thought that what is contained in encyclical letters does not of itself demand assent, on the pretext that the popes do not exercise in them the supreme power of their teaching authority. Rather, such teachings belong to the ordinary magisterium, of which it is true to say: 'He who hears you, hears me' (Lk. 10:16); for the most part, too, what is expounded and inculcated in encyclical letters already appertains to Catholic doctrine for other reasons. But if the supreme pontiffs in their official documents purposely pass judgment on a matter debated until then, it is obvious to all that the matter, according to the mind and will of the same pontiffs, cannot be considered any longer a question open for discussion among theologians."

The following list contains the titles and indicates the subject matter of encyclical letters and epistles. The latter are generally distinguishable by the limited scope of their titles or contents.

Benedict XIV
(1740-1758)

1740: *Ubi primum* (On the duties of bishops), Dec. 3.

1741: *Quanta cura* (Forbidding traffic in alms), June 30.

1743: *Nimiam licentiam* (To the bishops of Poland: on validity of marriages), May 18.

1745: *Vix pervenit* (To the bishops of Italy: on usury and other dishonest profit), Nov. 1.

1748: *Magnae Nobis* To the bishops of Poland: on marriage impediments and dispensations), June 29.

1749: *Peregrinantes* (To all the faithful: proclaiming a Holy Year for 1750), May 5.

Apostolica Constitutio (On preparation for the Holy Year), June 26.

1751: *A quo primum* (To the bishops of Poland: on Jews and Christians living in the same place), June 14.

1754: *Cum Religiosi* (To the bishops of the States of the Church: on catechesis), June 26.

Quod Provinciale (To the bishops of Albania: on Christians using Mohammedan names), Aug. 1.

1755: *Allatae sunt* (To missionaries of the Orient: on the observance of Oriental rites), July 26.

1756: *Ex quo primum* (To bishops of the Greek rite: on the Euchologion), Mar. 1.

Ex omnibus (To the bishops of France: on the apostolic constitution, *Unigenitus)*, Oct. 16.

Clement XIII
(1758-1769)

1758: *A quo die* (Unity among Christians), Sept. 13.

1759: *Cum primum* (On observing canonical sanctions), Sept. 17.

Appetente Sacro (On the spiritual advantages of fasting), Dec. 20.

1761: *In Dominico agro* (On instruction in the faith), June 14.

1766: *Christianae reipublicae* (On the dangers of anti-Christian writings), Nov. 25.
1768: *Summa quae* (To the bishops of Poland: on the Church in Poland), Jan. 6.

Clement XIV
(1769-1774)

1769: *Decet quam maxime* (To the bishops of Sardinia: on abuses in taxes and benefices), Sept. 21.
Inscrutabili divinae sapientiae (To all Christians: proclaiming a universal jubilee), Dec. 12.
Cum summi (Proclaiming a universal jubilee), Dec. 12.
1774: *Salutis nostrae* (To all Christians: proclaiming a universal jubilee), Apr. 30.

Pius VI
(1775-1799)

1775: *Inscrutabile* (On the problems of the pontificate), Dec. 25.
1791: *Charitas* (To the bishops of France: on the civil oath in France), Apr. 13.

Pius VII
(1800-1823)

1800: *Diu satis* (To the bishops of France: on a return to Gospel principles), May 15.

Leo XII
(1823-1829)

1824: *Ubi primum* (To all bishops: on Leo XII's assuming the pontificate), May 5.
Quod hoc ineunte (Proclaiming a universal jubilee), May 24.
1825: *Charitate Christi* (Extending jubilee to the entire Church), Dec. 25.

Pius VIII
(1829-1830)

1829: *Traditi humilitati* (On Pius VIII's program for the pontificate), May 24.

Gregory XVI
(1831-1846)

1832: *Summo iugiter studio* (To the bishops of Bavaria: on mixed marriages), May 27.
Cum primum (To the bishops of Poland: on civil obedience), June 9.
Mirari vos (On liberalism and religious indifferentism), Aug. 15.
1833: *Quo graviora* (To the bishops of the Rhineland: on the "pragmatic Constitution"), Oct. 4.
1834: *Singulari Nos* (On the errors of Lammenais), June 25.
1835: *Commissum divinitus* (To clergy of Switzerland: on Church and State), May 17.
1840: *Probe nostis* (On the Propagation of the Faith), Sept. 18.
1841: *Quas vestro* (To the bishops of Hungary: on mixed marriages), Apr. 30.
1844: *Inter praecipuas* (On biblical societies), May 8.

Pius IX
(1846-1878)

1846: *Qui pluribus* (On faith and religion), Nov. 9.
1847: *Praedecessores Nostros* (On aid for Ireland), Mar. 25.
Ubi primum (To religious superiors: on discipline for religious), June 17.
1849: *Ubi primum* (On the Immaculate Conception), Feb. 2.
Nostis et Nobiscum (To the bishops of Italy: on the Church in the Pontifical States), Dec. 8.
1851: *Exultavit cor Nostrum* (On the effects of jubilee), Nov. 21.
1852: *Nemo certe ignorat* (To the bishops of Ireland: on the discipline for clergy), Mar. 25.
Probe noscitis Venerabiles (To the bishops of Spain: on the discipline for clergy), May 17.
1853: *Inter multiplices* (To the bishops of France: pleading for unity of spirit), Mar. 21.
1854: *Neminem vestrum* (To clergy and faithful of Constantinople: on the persecution of Armenians), Feb. 2.
Optime noscitis (To the bishops of Ireland: on the proposed Catholic university for Ireland), Mar. 20.
Apostolicae Nostrae caritatis (Urging prayers for peace), Aug. 1.
1855: *Optime noscitis* (To the bishops of Austria: on episcopal meetings), Nov. 5.
1856: *Singulari quidem* (To the bishops of Austria: on the Church in Austria), Mar. 17.
1858: *Cum nuper* (To the bishops of the Kingdom of the Two Sicilies: on care for clerics), Jan. 20.
Amantissimi Redemptoris (On priests and the care of souls), May 3.
1859: *Cum sancta mater Ecclesia* (Pleading for public prayer), Apr. 27.
Qui nuper (On Pontifical States), June 18.
1860: *Nullis certe verbis* (On the need for civil sovereignty), Jan. 19.
1862: *Amantissimus* (To bishops of the Oriental rite: on the care of the churches), Apr. 8.
1863: *Quanto conficiamur moerore* (To the bishops of Italy: on promotion of false doctrines), Aug. 10.
Incredibili (To the bishops of Bogota: on persecution in New Granada), Sept. 17.
1864: *Maximae quidem* (To the bishops of Bavaria: on the Church in Bavaria), Aug. 18.
Quanta cura (Condemning current errors), Dec. 8.
1865: *Meridionali Americae* (To the bishops of South America: on the seminary for native clergy), Sept. 30.
1867: *Levate* (On the afflictions of the Church), Oct. 27.
1870: *Respicientes* (Protesting the taking of the Pontifical States), Nov. 1.
1871: *Ubi Nos* (To all bishops: on Pontifical States), May 15.

Beneficia Dei (On the twenty-fifth anniversary of his pontificate), June 4.
Saepe Venerabiles Fratres (On thanksgiving for twenty-five years of pontificate), Aug. 5.
1872: *Quae in Patriarchatu* (To bishops and people of Chaldea: on the Church in Chaldea), Nov. 16.
1873: *Quartus supra* (To bishops and people of the Armenian rite: on the Church in Armenia), Jan. 6.
Etsi multa (On the Church in Italy, Germany and Switzerland), Nov. 21.
1874: *Vix dum a Nobis* (To the bishops of Austria: on the Church in Austria), Mar. 7.
Omnem sollicitudinem (To the bishops of the Ruthenian rite: on the Greek-Ruthenian rite), May 13.
Gravibus Ecclesiae (To all bishops and faithful: proclaiming a jubilee for 1875), Dec. 24.
1875: *Quod nunquam* (To the bishops of Prussia: on the Church in Prussia), Feb. 5.
Graves ac diuturnae (To the bishops of Switzerland: on the Church in Switzerland), Mar. 23.

Leo XIII
(1878-1903)

1878: *Inscrutabili Dei consilio* (On the evils of society), Apr. 21.
Quod Apostolici muneris (On socialism), Dec. 28.
1879: *Aeterni Patris* (On the restoration of Christian philosophy), Aug. 4.
1880: *Arcanum* (On Christian marriage), Feb. 10.
Grande munus (On Sts. Cyril and Methodius), Sept. 30.
Sancta Dei civitas (On mission societies), Dec. 3.
1881: *Diuturnum* (On the origin of civil power), June 29.
Licet multa (To the bishops of Belgium: on Catholics in Belgium), Aug. 3.
1882: *Etsi Nos* (To the bishops of Italy: on conditions in Italy), Feb. 15.
Auspicato concessum (On St. Francis of Assisi), Sept. 17.
Cum multa (To the bishops of Spain: on conditions in Spain), Dec. 8.
1883: *Supremi Apostolatus officio* (On devotion to the Rosary), Sept. 1.
1884: *Nobilissima Gallorum gens* (To the bishops of France: on the religious question), Feb. 8.
Humanum genus (On Freemasonry), Apr. 20.
Superiore anno (On the recitation of the Rosary), Aug. 30.
1885: *Immortale Dei* (On the Christian constitution of states), Nov. 1.
Spectata fides (To the bishops of England: on Christian education), Nov. 27.
Quod auctoritate (Proclamation of extraordinary Jubilee), Dec. 22.
1886: *Iampridem* (To the bishops of Prussia: on Catholicism in Germany), Jan. 6.
Quod multum (To the bishops of Hungary: on the liberty of the Church), Aug. 22.
Pergrata (To the bishops of Portugal: on the Church in Portugal), Sept. 14.
1887: *Vi e ben noto* (To the bishops of Italy: on the Rosary and public life), Sept. 20.
Officio sanctissimo (To the bishops of Bavaria: on the Church in Bavaria), Dec. 22.
1888: *Quod anniversarius* (On his sacerdotal jubilee), Apr. 1.
In plurimis (To the bishops of Brazil: on the abolition of slavery), May 5.
Libertas (On the nature of human liberty), June 20.
Saepe Nos (To the bishops of Ireland: on boycotting in Ireland), June 24.
Paterna caritas (To the Patriarch of Cilicia and the archbishops and bishops of the Armenian people: on reunion with Rome), July 25.
Quam aerumnosa (To the bishops of America: on Italian immigrants), Dec. 10.
Etsi cunctas (To the bishops of Ireland: on the Church in Ireland), Dec. 21.
Exeunte iam anno (On the right ordering of Christian life), Dec. 25.
1889: *Magni Nobis* (To the bishops of the United States: on the Catholic University of America), Mar. 7.
Quamquam pluries (On devotion to St. Joseph), Aug. 15.
1890: *Sapientiae Christianae* (On Christians as citizens), Jan. 10.
Dall'alto Dell'Apostolico seggio (To the bishops and people of Italy: on Freemasonry in Italy), Oct. 15.
Catholicae Ecclesiae (On slavery in the missions), Nov. 20.
1891: *In ipso* (To the bishops of Austria: on episcopal reunions in Austria), Mar. 3.
Rerum novarum (On capital and labor), May 15.
Pastoralis (To the bishops of Portugal: on religious union), June 25.
Pastoralis officii (To the bishops of Germany and Austria: on the morality of dueling), Sept. 12.
Octobri mense (On the Rosary), Sept. 22.
1892: *Au milieu des sollicitudes* (To the bishops, clergy and faithful of France: on the Church and State in France), Feb. 16.
Quarto abeunte saeculo (To the bishops of Spain, Italy, and the two Americas: on the Columbus quadricentennial), July 16.
Magnae Dei Matris (On the Rosary), Sept. 8.
Inimica vis (To the bishops of Italy: on Freemasonry), Dec. 8.
Custodi di quella fede (To the Italian people: on Freemasonry), Dec. 8.
1893: *Ad extremas* (On seminaries for native clergy), June 24.
Constanti Hungarorum (To the bishops of Hungary: on the Church in Hungary), Sept. 2.
Laetitiae sanctae (Commending devotion to the Rosary), Sept. 8.
Non mediocri (To the bishops of Spain: on the Spanish College in Rome), Oct. 25.

Providentissimus Deus (On the study of Holy Scripture), Nov. 18.
1894: *Caritatis* (To the bishops of Poland: on the Church in Poland), Mar. 19.
Inter graves (To the bishops of Peru: on the Church in Peru), May 1.
Litteras a vobis (To the bishops of Brazil: on the clergy in Brazil), July 2.
Iucunda semper expectatione (On the Rosary), Sept. 8.
Christi nomen (On the propagation of the Faith and Eastern churches), Dec. 24.
1895: *Longinqua* (To the bishops of the United States: on Catholicism in the United States), Jan. 6.
Permoti Nos (To the bishops of Belgium: on social conditions in Belgium), July 10.
Adiutricem (On the Rosary), Sept. 5.
1896: *Insignes* (To the bishops of Hungary: on the Hungarian millennium), May 1.
Satis cognitum (On the unity of the Church), June 29.
Fidentem piumque animum (On the Rosary), Sept. 20.
1897: *Divinum illud munus* (On the Holy Spirit), May 9.
Militantis Ecclesiae (To the bishops of Austria, Germany, and Switzerland: on St. Peter Canisius), Aug. 1.
Augustissimae Virginis Mariae (On the Confraternity of the Holy Rosary), Sept. 12.
Affari vos (To the bishops of Canada: on the Manitoba school question), Dec. 8.
1898: *Caritatis studium* (To the bishops of Scotland: on the Church in Scotland), July 25.
Spesse volte (To the bishops, priests, and people of Italy: on the suppression of Catholic institutions), Aug. 5.
Quam religiosa (To the bishops of Peru: on civil marriage law), Aug. 16.
Diuturni temporis (On the Rosary), Sept. 5.
Quum diuturnum (To the bishops of Latin America: on Latin American bishops' plenary council), Dec. 25.
1899: *Annum Sacrum* (On consecration to the Sacred Heart), May 25.
Depuis le jour (To the archbishops, bishops, and clergy of France: on the education of the clergy), Sept. 8.
Paternae (To the bishops of Brazil: on the education of the clergy), Sept. 18.
1900: *Omnibus compertum* (To the Patriarch and bishops of the Greek-Melkite rite: on unity among the Greek Melkites), July 21.
Tametsi futura prospicientibus (On Jesus Christ the Redeemer), Nov. 1.
1901: *Graves de communi re* (On Christian democracy), Jan. 18.
Gravissimas (To the bishops of Portugal: on religious orders in Portugal), May 16.
Reputantibus (To the bishops of Bohemia and Moravia: on the language question in Bohemia), Aug. 20.
Urbanitatis Veteris (To the bishops of the Latin church in Greece: on the foundation of a seminary in Athens), Nov. 20.
1902: *In amplissimo* (To the bishops of the United States: on the Church in the United States), Apr. 15.
Quod votis (To the bishops of Austria: on the proposed Catholic University), Apr. 30.
Mirae caritatis (On the Holy Eucharist), May 28.
Quae ad Nos (To the bishops of Bohemia and Moravia: on the Church in Bohemia and Moravia), Nov. 22
Fin dal principio (To the bishops of Italy: on the education of the clergy), Dec. 8.
Dum multa (To the bishops of Ecuador: on marriage legislation), Dec. 24.

Saint Pius X
(1903-1914)

1903: *E supremi* (On the restoration of all things in Christ), Oct. 4.
1904: *Ad diem illum laetissimum* (On the Immaculate Conception), Feb. 2.
Iucunda sane (On Pope Gregory the Great), Mar. 12.
1905: *Acerbo nimis* (On teaching Christian doctrine), Apr. 15.
Il fermo proposito (To the bishops of Italy: on Catholic Action in Italy), June 11.
1906: *Vehementer Nos* (To the bishops, clergy, and people of France: on the French Law of Separation), Feb. 11.
Tribus circiter (On the Mariavites or Mystic Priests of Poland), Apr. 5.
Pieni l'animo (To the bishops of Italy: on the clergy in Italy), July 28.
Gravissimo officio munere (To the bishops of France: on French associations of worship), Aug. 10.
1907: *Une fois encore* (To the bishops, clergy, and people of France: on the separation of Church and State), Jan. 6.
Pascendi dominici gregis (On the doctrines of the Modernists), Sept. 8.
1909: *Communium rerum* (On St. Anselm of Aosta), Apr. 21.
1910: *Editae saepe* (On St. Charles Borromeo), May 26.
1911: *Iamdudum* (On the Law of Separation in Portugal), May 24.
1912: *Lacrimabili statu* (To the bishops of Latin America: on the Indians of South America), June 7.
Singulari quadam (To the bishops of Germany: on labor organizations), Sept. 24.

Benedict XV
(1914-1922)

1914: *Ad beatissimi Apostolorum* (Appeal for peace), Nov. 1.
1917: *Humani generis Redemptionem* (On preaching the Word of God), June 15.
1918: *Quod iam diu* (On the future peace conference), Dec. 1.
1919: *In hac tanta* (To the bishops of Germany: on St. Boniface), May 14.
Paterno iam diu (On children of central Europe), Nov. 24.

Encyclicals

1920: *Pacem, Dei munus pulcherrimum* (On peace and Christian reconciliation), May 23.
Spiritus Paraclitus (On St. Jerome), Sept. 15.
Principi Apostolorum Petro (On St. Ephrem the Syrian), Oct. 5.
Annus iam plenus (On children of central Europe), Dec. 1.
1921: *Sacra propediem* (On the Third Order of St. Francis), Jan. 6.
In praeclara summorum (To professors and students of fine arts in Catholic institutions of learning: on Dante), Apr. 30.
Fausto appetente die (On St. Dominic), June 29.

Pius XI
(1922-1939)

1922: *Ubi arcano Dei consilio* (On the peace of Christ in the Kingdom of Christ), Dec. 23.
1923: *Rerum omnium perturbationem* (On St. Francis de Sales), Jan. 26.
Studiorum Ducem (On St. Thomas Aquinas), June 29.
Ecclesiam Dei (On St. Josaphat), Nov. 12.
1924: *Maximam gravissimamque* (To the bishops, clergy, and people of France: on French diocesan associations), Jan. 18.
1925: *Quas primas* (On the feast of Christ the King), Dec. 11.
1926: *Rerum Ecclesiae* (On Catholic missions), Feb. 28.
Rite expiatis (On St. Francis of Assisi), Apr. 30.
Iniquis afflictisque (On the persecution of the Church in Mexico), Nov. 18.
1928: *Mortalium animos* (On religious unity), Jan. 6.
Miserentissimus Redemptor (On reparation to the Sacred Heart), May 8.
Rerum Orientalium (On the promotion of Oriental studies), Sept. 8.
1929: *Mens Nostra* (On the promotion of Spiritual Exercises), Dec. 20.
Quinquagesimo ante (On his sacerdotal jubilee), Dec. 23.
Rappresentanti in terra (On Christian education), Dec. 31. [Latin text, *Divini illius magistri*, published several months later with minor changes.]
1930: *Ad salutem* (On St. Augustine), Apr. 20.
Casti connubii (On Christian marriage), Dec. 31.
1931: *Quadragesimo anno* (Commemorating the fortieth anniversary of Leo XIII's *Rerum novarum:* on reconstruction of the social order), May 15.
Non abbiamo bisogno (On Catholic Action in Italy), June 29.
Nova impendet (On the economic crisis), Oct. 2.
Lux veritatis (On the Council of Ephesus), Dec. 25.
1932: *Caritate Christi compulsi* (On the Sacred Heart), May 3.
Acerba animi (To the bishops of Mexico: on persecution of the Church in Mexico), Sept. 29.
1933: *Dilectissima Nobis* (To the bishops, clergy, and people of Spain: on oppression of the Church in Spain), June 3.
1935: *Ad Catholici sacerdotii* (On the Catholic priesthood), Dec. 20.
1936: *Vigilanti cura* (To the bishops of the United States: on motion pictures), June 29.
1937: *Mit brennender Sorge* (To the bishops of Germany: on the Church and the German Reich), Mar. 14.
Divini Redemptoris (On atheistic communism), Mar. 19.
Nos es muy conocida (To the bishops of Mexico: on the religious situation in Mexico), Mar. 28.
Ingravescentibus malis (On the Rosary) Sept. 29.

Pius XII
(1939-1958)

1939: *Summi Pontificatus* (On the unity of human society), Oct. 20.
Sertum laetitiae (To the bishops of the United States: on the 150th anniversary of the establishment of the hierarchy in the United States), Nov. 1.
1940: *Saeculo exeunte octavo* (To the bishops of Portugal and its colonies: on the eighth centenary of the independence of Portugal), June 13.
1943: *Mystici Corporis Christi* (On the Mystical Body of Christ), June 29.
Divino afflante Spiritu (On promoting biblical studies, commemorating the fiftieth anniversary of *Providentissimus Deus*), Sept. 30.
1944: *Orientalis Ecclesiae* (On St. Cyril, Patriarch of Alexandria), Apr. 9.
1945: *Communium interpretes dolorum* (To the bishops of the world: appealing for prayers for peace during May), Apr. 15.
Orientales omnes Ecclesias (On the 350th anniversary of the reunion of the Ruthenian Church with the Apostolic See), Dec. 23.
1946: *Quemadmodum* (Pleading for the care of the world's destitute children), Jan. 6.
Deiparae Virginis Mariae (To all bishops: on the possibility of defining the Assumption of the Blessed Virgin Mary as a dogma of faith), May 1.
1947: *Fulgens radiatur* (On St. Benedict), Mar. 21.
Mediator Dei (On the sacred liturgy), Nov. 20.
Optatissima pax (Prescribing public prayers for social and world peace), Dec. 18.
1948: *Auspicia quaedam* (On public prayers for world peace and solution of the problem of Palestine), May 1.
In multiplicibus curis (On prayers for peace in Palestine), Oct. 24.
1949: *Redemptoris nostri cruciatus* (On the holy places in Palestine), Apr. 15.
1950: *Anni Sacri* (On the program for combat-

ting atheistic propaganda throughout the world), Mar. 12.
Summi maeroris (On public prayers for peace), July 19.
Humani generis (Concerning some false opinions threatening to undermine the foundations of Catholic doctrine), Aug. 12.
Mirabile illud (On the crusade of prayers for peace), Dec. 6.
1951: *Evangelii praecones* (On the promotion of Catholic missions), June 2.
Sempiternus Rex Christus (On the Council of Chalcedon), Sept. 8.
Ingruentium malorum (On reciting the Rosary), Sept. 15.
1952: *Orientales Ecclesias* (On the persecuted Eastern Church), Dec. 15.
1953: *Doctor Mellifluus* (On St. Bernard of Clairvaux, the last of the fathers), May 24.
Fulgens corona (Proclaiming a Marian Year to commemorate the centenary of the definition of the dogma of the Immaculate Conception), Sept. 8.
1954: *Sacra virginitas* (On consecrated virginity), Mar. 25.
Ecclesiae fastos (To the bishops of Great Britain, Germany, Austria, France, Belgium, and Holland: on St. Boniface), June 5.
Ad Sinarum gentem (To the bishops, clergy, and people of China: on the supranationality of the Church), Oct. 7.
Ad Caeli Reginam (Proclaiming the Queenship of Mary), Oct. 11.
1955: *Musicae sacrae* (On sacred music), Dec. 25.
1956: *Haurietis aquas* (On devotion to the Sacred Heart), May 15.
Luctuosissimi eventus (Urging public prayers for peace and freedom for the people of Hungary), Oct. 28.
Laetamur admodum (Renewing exhortation for prayers for peace for Poland, Hungary, and especially for the Middle East), Nov. 1.
Datis nuperrime (Lamenting the sorrowful events in Hungary and condemning the ruthless use of force), Nov. 5.
1957: *Fidei donum* (On the present condition of the Catholic missions, especially in Africa), Apr. 21.
Invicti athletae (On St. Andrew Bobola), May 16.
Le pelerinage de Lourdes (Warning against materialism on the centenary of the apparitions at Lourdes), July 2.
Miranda prorsus (On the communications field: motion picture, radio, television), Sept. 8.
1958: *Ad Apostolorum Principis* (To the bishops of China; on Communism and the Church in China), June 29.
Meminisse iuvat (On prayers for persecuted Church), July 14.

John XXIII
(1958-1963)

1959: *Ad Petri Cathedram* (On truth, unity, and peace, in a spirit of charity), June 29.
Sacerdotii Nostri primordia (On St. John Vianney), Aug. 1.
Grata recordatio (On the Rosary: prayer for the Church, missions, international and social problems), Sept. 26.
Princeps Pastorum (On the missions, native clergy, lay participation), Nov. 28.
1961: *Mater et Magistra* (On Christianity and social progress), May 15.
Aeterna Dei sapientia (On fifteenth centenary of the death of Pope St. Leo I: the see of Peter as the center of Christian unity), Nov. 11.
1962: *Paenitentiam agere* (On the need for the practice of interior and exterior penance), July 1.
1963: *Pacem in terris* (On establishing universal peace in truth, justice, charity, and liberty), Apr. 11.

Paul VI
(1963-1978)

1964: *Ecclesiam Suam* (On the Church), Aug. 6.
1965: *Mense maio* (On prayers during May for the preservation of peace), Apr. 29.
Mysterium Fidei (On the Holy Eucharist), Sept. 3.
1966: *Christi Matri* (On prayers for peace during October), Sept. 15.
1967: *Populorum progressio* (On the development of peoples), Mar. 26.
Sacerdotalis caelibatus (On the celibacy of the priest), June 24.
1968: *Humanae vitae* (On the regulation of birth), July 25.

John Paul II
(1978-)

1979: *Redemptor hominis* (On redemption and the dignity of the human race), Mar. 4.
1980: *Dives in misericordia* (On the mercy of God), Nov. 30.
1981: *Laborem exercens* (On human work), Sept. 14.
1985: *Slavorum Apostoli* (Commemorating Sts. Cyril and Methodius, on the eleventh centenary of the death of St. Methodius), June 2.
1986: *Dominum et Vivificantem* (On the Holy Spirit in the Life of the Church and the World), May 18.
1987: *Redemptoris Mater* (On the role of Mary in the mystery of Christ and her active and exemplary presence in the life of the Church), Mar. 25.
Sollicitudo Rei Socialis (On social concerns, on the twentieth anniversary of *Populorum progressio),* Dec. 30.

"Twenty years after the issuance of 'Humanae Vitae,' we see ever more clearly the prophetic wisdom of the Church's consistent teaching on marriage and responsible parenthood, and the courage of Pope Paul VI in reaffirming that teaching." So stated the U.S. Bishops' Committee for Pro-Life Activities in a commemorative statement issued July 25, just short of the anniversary of publication.

HIERARCHY OF THE CATHOLIC CHURCH

ORGANIZATION AND GOVERNMENT

As a structured society, the Catholic Church is organized and governed along lines corresponding mainly to the jurisdictions of the pope and bishops.

The pope is the supreme head of the Church. He has primacy of jurisdiction as well as honor over the entire Church.

Bishops, in union with and in subordination to the pope, are the successors of the Apostles for care of the Church and for the continuation of Christ's mission in the world. They serve the people of their own dioceses, or particular churches, with ordinary authority and jurisdiction. They also share, with the pope and each other, in common concern and effort for the general welfare of the whole Church.

Bishops of exceptional status are Eastern-Rite patriarchs who, subject only to the pope, are heads of the faithful belonging to their rites throughout the world.

Subject to the Holy Father and directly responsible to him for the exercise of their ministry of service to people in various jurisdictions or divisions of the Church throughout the world are: resident archbishops and metropolitans (heads of archdioceses), diocesan bishops, vicars and prefects apostolic (heads of vicariates apostolic and prefectures apostolic), certain abbots and prelates, apostolic administrators. Each of these, within his respective territory and according to the provisions of canon law, has ordinary jurisdiction over pastors (who are responsible for the administration of parishes), priests, Religious and lay persons.

Also subject to the Holy Father are titular archbishops and bishops, religious orders and congregations of pontifical right, pontifical institutes and faculties, papal nuncios and apostolic delegates.

Assisting the pope and acting in his name in the central government and administration of the Church are cardinals and other officials of the Roman Curia.

THE HIERARCHY

The ministerial hierarchy is the orderly arrangement of the ranks and orders of the clergy to provide for the spiritual care of the faithful, the government of the Church, and the accomplishment of the Church's total mission in the world. Persons belong to this hierarchy by virtue of ordination and canonical mission.

The term hierarchy is also used to designate an entire body or group of bishops; for example, the hierarchy of the Church, the hierarchy of the United States.

Hierarchy of Order: Consists of the pope, bishops, priests and deacons. Their purpose, for which they are ordained to holy orders, is to carry out the sacramental and pastoral ministry of the Church.

Hierarchy of Jurisdiction: Consists of the pope and bishops by divine institution, and other church officials by ecclesiastical institution and mandate, who have authority to govern and direct the faithful for spiritual ends.

The Pope

His Holiness the Pope is the Bishop of Rome, the Vicar of Jesus Christ, the successor of St. Peter, Prince of the Apostles, the Supreme Pontiff who has the primacy of jurisdiction and not merely of honor over the universal Church, the Patriarch of the West, the Primate of Italy, the Archbishop and Metropolitan of the Roman Province, the Sovereign of the State of Vatican City, Servant of the Servants of God.

Cardinals

(See Index)

Patriarchs

Patriarch, a term which had its origin in the Eastern Church, is the title of a bishop who, second only to the pope, has the highest rank in the hierarchy of jurisdiction. He is the incumbent of one of the sees listed below. Subject only to the pope, an Eastern-Rite patriarch is the head of the faithful belonging to his rite throughout the world. The patriarchal sees are so called because of their special status and dignity in the history of the Church.

The Council of Nicaea (325) recognized three patriarchs — the bishops of Alexandria and Antioch in the East, and of Rome in the West. The First Council of Constantinople (381) added the bishop of Constantinople to the list of patriarchs and gave him rank second only to that of the pope, the bishop of Rome and patriarch of the West; this action was seconded by the Council of Chalcedon (451) and was given full recognition by the Fourth Lateran Council (1215). The Council of Chalcedon also acknowledged patriarchal rights of the bishop of Jerusalem.

Eastern Rite patriarchs are as follows: one of Alexandria, for the Copts; three of Antioch, one each for the Syrians, Maronites and Greek Melkites (the latter also has the personal title of Greek Melkite patriarch of Alexandria and of Jerusalem). The patriarch of Babylonia, for the Chaldeans, and the patriarch of Sis, or Cilicia, for the Armenians, should be called, more properly, *Katholikos* — that is, a prelate delegated for a universality of causes. These patriarchs are elected by bishops of their rites: they receive approval and the pallium, symbolic of their office, from the pope.

Latin Rite patriarchates were established for Antioch, Jerusalem, Alexandria and Constantinople during the Crusades; afterwards, they became patriarchates in name only. Jerusalem, however, was reconstituted as a patriarchate by Pius IX, in virtue of the bull *Nulla Celebrior* of July 23, 1847. In 1964, the Latin titular patriarchates of Constantinople, Alexandria and Antioch, long a bone of contention in relations with Eastern Rites, were abolished.

As of Aug. 15, 1988, the patriarchs in the Church were:

The Pope, Bishop of Rome, Patriarch of the West; Stephanos II Ghattas, C.M., of Alexandria, for the Copts; Ignace Antoine II Hayek, of Antioch, for the Syrians; Maximos V Hakim, of Antioch, for the Greek Melkites (he also has the titles of Alexandria and Jerusalem for the Greek Melkites); Nasrallah Pierre Sfeir, of Antioch, for the Maronites; Michel Sabbah, of Jerusalem, for the Latin Rite; Paul II Cheikho, of Babylon, for the Chaldeans; Jean Pierre XVIII Kasparian, of Cilicia, for the Armenians.

The titular patriarchs (in name only) of the Latin Rite were: Cardinal Antonio Ribeiro, of Lisbon; Cardinal Marco Cé of Venice and Archbishop Raul Nicolau Goncalves of the East Indies (Archbishop of Goa and Damao, India). The patriarchate of the West Indies has been vacant since 1963.

Archbishops, Metropolitans

Archbishop: A bishop with the title of an archdiocese.

Coadjutor Archbishop: An assistant archbishop with right of succession.

Metropolitan: Archbishop of the principal see, an archdiocese, in an ecclesiastical province consisting of several dioceses. He has the full powers of bishop in his own archdiocese and limited supervisory jurisdiction and influence over the other (suffragan) dioceses in the province. The pallium, conferred by the pope, is the symbol of his status as a metropolitan.

Titular Archbishop: Has the title of an archdiocese which formerly existed in fact but now exists in title only. He does not have ordinary jurisdiction over an archdiocese. Examples are archbishops in the Roman Curia, papal nuncios, apostolic delegates.

Archbishop ad personam: A title of personal honor and distinction granted to some bishops. They do not have ordinary jurisdiction over an archdiocese.

Primate: A title of honor given to the ranking prelate of some countries or regions.

Bishops

Diocesan Bishop: A bishop in charge of a diocese.

Coadjutor Bishop: An assistant (auxiliary) bishop to a diocesan bishop, with right of succession to the see.

Titular Bishops: A bishop with the title of a diocese which formerly existed in fact but now exists in title only; an assistant (auxiliary) bishop to a diocesan bishop.

Episcopal Vicar: An assistant, who may or may not be a bishop, appointed by a residential bishop as his deputy for a certain part of a diocese, a determined type of apostolic work, or the faithful of a certain rite.

Eparch, Exarch: Titles of bishops of Eastern-Rite churches.

Nomination of Bishops: Nominees for episcopal ordination are selected in several ways. Final appointment and/or approval in all cases is subject to decision by the pope.

In the U.S., bishops periodically submit the names of candidates to the archbishop of their province. The names are then considered at a meeting of the bishops of the province, and those receiving a favorable vote are forwarded to the pro-nuncio for transmission to the Holy See. Bishops are free to seek the counsel of priests, religious and lay persons with respect to nominees.

Eastern-Rite churches have their own procedures and synodal regulations for nominating and making final selection of candidates for episcopal ordination. Such selection is subject to approval by the pope.

The Code of Canon Law concedes no rights or privileges to civil authorities with respect to the election, nomination, presentation or designation of candidates for the episcopate.

Ad Limina Visit: Diocesan bishops and apostolic vicars are obliged to make an *ad limina* visit ("to the threshold" of the Apostles) every five years to the tombs of Sts. Peter and Paul, have audience with the Holy Father and consult with appropriate Vatican officials. They are required to send a report on conditions in their jurisdiction to the Congregation for Bishops approximately six — and not less than three — months in advance of the scheduled visit. The most recent regulations concerning the formalities and scheduling of visits by bishops from various countries, generally every five years, were issued by the Congregation for Bishops in a decree dated June 29, 1988.

Others with Ordinary Jurisdiction

Ordinary: One who has the jurisdiction of an office: the pope, diocesan bishops, vicars general, prelates of missionary territories, vicars apostolic prefects apostolic, vicars capitular during the vacancy of a see, superiors general, abbots primate and other major superiors of men Religious.

Some prelates and abbots, with jurisdiction like that of diocesan bishops, are pastors of the people of God in territories (prelatures and abbacies) not under the jurisdiction of diocesan bishops.

Vicar Apostolic: Usually a titular bishop who has ordinary jurisdiction over a mission territory.

Prefect Apostolic: Has ordinary jurisdiction over a mission territory.

Apostolic Administrator: Usually a bishop appointed to administer an ecclesiastical jurisdiction temporarily. Administrators of lesser rank are also appointed for special and more restricted supervisory duties.

Vicar General: A bishop's deputy for the administration of a diocese. Such a vicar does not have to be a bishop.

Honorary Prelates

Honorary prelates belonging to the Pontifical Household are: Apostolic Prothonotaries, Honorary Prelates of His Holiness, and Chaplains of His Holiness. Their title is Reverend Monsignor.

SYNOD OF BISHOPS

The Synod of Bishops was chartered by Pope Paul VI Sept. 15, 1965, in a document he issued on his own initiative under the title, *Apostolica Sollicitudo*. Provisions of this *motu proprio* are contained in Canons 342 to 348 of the Code of Canon Law. According to major provisions of the Synod charter:

• The purposes of the Synod are: "to encourage close union and valued assistance between the Sovereign Pontiff and the bishops of the entire world; to insure that direct and real information is provided on questions and situations touching upon the internal action of the Church and its necessary activity in the world of today; to facilitate agreement on essential points of doctrine and on methods of procedure in the life of the Church."

• The Synod is a central ecclesiastical institution, permanent by nature.

• The Synod is directly and immediately subject to the Pope, who has authority to assign its agenda, to call it into session, and to give its members deliberative as well as advisory authority.

• In addition to a limited number of ex officio members and a few heads of male religious institutes, the majority of the members are elected by and representative of national or regional episcopal conferences. The Pope reserved the right to appoint the general secretary, special secretaries and no more than 15 per cent of the total membership.

The Pope is president of the Synod.

The secretary general is Archbishop Jan Schotte of Belgium.

An advisory council of 15 members (12 elected, three appointed by the pope) provides the secretariat with adequate staff for carrying on liaison with episcopal conferences and for preparing the agenda of synodal assemblies.

Assemblies

1. First Assembly: The first assembly was held from Sept. 29 to Oct. 29, 1967. Its objectives, as stated by Pope Paul VI, were "the preservation and strengthening of the Catholic faith, its integrity, its force, its development, its doctrinal and historical coherence." One result was a recommendation for the establishment of an international commission of theologians to assist the Congregation for the Doctrine of the Faith and to broaden approaches to theological research. Pope Paul set up the commission in 1969.

2. Pope-Bishop Relations: The second assembly, held Oct. 11 to 28, 1969, was extraordinary in character. It opened the way toward greater participation by bishops with the pope and each other in the governance of the Church. Proceedings were oriented to three main points: (1) the nature and implications of collegiality; (2) the relationship of bishops and their conferences to the pope; (3) the relationships of bishops and their conferences to each other.

3. Priesthood and Justice: The ministerial priesthood and justice in the world were the principal topics under discussion at the second ordinary assembly, Sept. 30 to Nov. 6, 1971. In one report, the Synod emphasized the primary and permanent dedication of priests in the Church to the ministry of word, sacrament and pastoral service as a full-time vocation. In another report, the assembly stated: "Action on behalf of justice and participation in the transformation of the world fully appear to us as a constitutive dimension of the preaching of the Gospel; or, in other words, of the Church's mission for the redemption of the human race and its liberation from every oppressive situation."

4. Evangelization: The assembly of Sept. 27 to Oct. 26, 1974, produced a general statement on evangelization of the modern world, covering the need for it and its relationship to efforts for total human liberation from personal and social evil. The assembly observed: "The Church does not remain within merely political, social and economic limits (elements which she must certainly take into account) but leads towards freedom under all its forms — liberation from sin, from individual or collective selfishness — and to full communion with God and with men who are like brothers. In this way the Church, in her evangelical way, promotes the true and complete liberation of all men, groups and peoples."

5. Catechetics: The fourth ordinary assembly, Sept. 30 to Oct. 29, 1977, focused attention on catechetics, with special reference to children and young people. The participants issued a "Message to the People of God," the first synodal statement issued since inception of the body, and also presented to Pope Paul VI a set of 34 related propositions and a number of suggestions.

6. Family: "A Message to Christian Families in the Modern World" and a proposal for a "Charter of Family Rights" were produced by the assembly held Sept. 26 to Oct. 25, 1980. The assembly reaffirmed the indissolubility of marriage and the contents of the encyclical letter *Humanae Vitae* (see separate entry), and urged married couples who find it hard to live up to "the difficult but loving demands" of Christ not to be discouraged but to avail themselves of the aid of divine grace. In response to synodal recommendation, Pope John Paul issued a charter of family rights late in 1983.

7. Reconciliation: Penance and reconciliation in the mission of the Church was the theme of the assembly held Sept. 29 to Oct. 29, 1983. Sixty-three propositions related to this theme were formulated on a wide variety of subjects, including: personal sin and so-called systemic or institutional sin; the nature of serious sin; the diminished sense of sin and of the need of redemption, related to decline in the administration and reception of the sacrament of penance; general absolution; individual and social reconciliation; violence and violations of human rights; reconciliation as the basis of peace and justice in society. In a statement issued Oct. 27, the Synod stressed the need of the world to become, increasingly, "a reconciled community of peoples," and said that "the Church, as sacrament of reconciliation to the world, has to be an effective sign of God's mercy."

8. Vatican II Review: The second extraordinary assembly was convened Nov. 24 to Dec. 8, 1985, for the purposes of: (1) recalling the Second Vatican Council; (2) evaluating the implementation of its enactments during the 20 years since its conclusion; (3) seeking ways and means of promoting renewal in the Church in accordance with the spirit and letter of the council.

At the conclusion of the assembly the bishops issued two documents. (1) In A Message to the People of God, they noted the need for greater appreciation of the enactments of Vatican II and for greater efforts to put them into effect, so that all members of the Church might discharge their responsibility of proclaiming the good news of salvation. (2) In a Final Report, the first of its kind published by a synodal assembly, the bishops reflected on lights and shadows since Vatican II, stating that negative developments had come from partial and superficial interpretations of conciliar enactments and from incomplete or ineffective implementation thereof. The report also covered a considerable number of subjects discussed during the assembly, ranging from the mystery of the Church to inculturation and the preferential (but not exclusive) option for the poor.

SYNOD '87: VOCATION AND MISSION OF LAY PERSONS

(Quotations are from texts circulated by the NC Documentary Service, Origins, Nov. 12, 1987: Vol. 17, No. 22).

"The Vocation and Mission of the Laity in the Church and in the World 20 Years after the Second Vatican Council," was the theme of the seventh ordinary assembly of the Synod of Bishops, held Oct. 1 to 30, 1987, at the Vatican.

The agenda of the assembly was compiled by the general secretariat of the synod from recommendations and suggestions submitted by 60 percent of the episcopal conferences throughout the world, as well as by nearly 200 church-related organizations and movements.

Synod business was conducted in three stages, with periods for: limited-time statements from the floor; group discussions of relevant subjects; full-assembly consideration and voting on topics and recommendations for the contents of a Message to the People of God, and for consideration by the Pope in a statement of his own regarding the proceedings and concerns of participants in the synod.

Fifteen of some 230 voting delegates were from the United States. Most of the delegates were elected by their respective episcopal conferences; others were appointed by the Pope (30) or were ex officio delegates.

Message to the People of God

The synodal fathers released a Message to the People of God on Oct. 29, in which they reflected on a number of subjects, including: the meaning of the term, "lay faithful"; the universal call to holiness; the strength given by the Holy Spirit; ministries and services of lay persons; the family; youth; workmen in the Church and general society; significance of the parish in the lives and service of the faithful; social-political involvement and spiritual formation.

The Message to the People of God said, in part, as follows.

"All lay faithful have a dignity which they hold in common with clerics and Religious. . . . This dignity comes from baptism, through which a person is incorporated into Christ and the community of the Church, and is called to a life of holiness."

Task of Lay Persons: "The majority of the Christian laity live out their vocation as followers and disciples of Christ in all spheres of life which we call 'the world': the family, the field of work, the local community and the like. To permeate this day-to-day living with the spirit of Christ has always been the task of the lay faithful, and it should be with still greater force their challenge today. It is in this way that they sanctify the world and collaborate in the realization of the kingdom of God. Furthermore, they are called to announce the Good News and to participate in dialogue with all."

Parish and Political Activity: Two of the significant subjects mentioned in the message were the parish and the socio-political involvement of the faithful.

"The parish in the diocese continues to be the customary place where the faithful gather to grow in holiness, to participate in the mission of the Church and to live out their ecclesial communion."

"In political activity, the primary concern of the lay faithful should be honesty, the promotion of social justice and the rights of the human person in all phases of life, the defense and recovery of various freedoms, particularly of religious freedom — so unjustly restricted in so many regions — and the constant pursuit of peace in the world.

"A similar sense of Christian involvement should bring lay people into the fields of health, culture, science, technology, work, and the means of social communication."

Recommendations to the Pope

The synod produced a set of 54 propositions which were presented to the Pope for consideration in the preparation of a statement of his own on the theme of the assembly. The recommendations were grouped under three main headings:

• Called by God to Communion with Him and to a Mission for the Salvation of the World;
• The Lay Christian within the Church;
• The Christian Lay Person in Relation to Today's Changes.

The text of the propositions was not released by the synod, but was obtained by NC News Service from an unofficial source and circulated by Origins Dec. 31, 1987 (Vol. 17, No. 29).

Homily of Pope John Paul

The secular dimension of the Church, and particularly of lay persons, was one of the subjects of the

Pope's homily at the Mass which concluded the Synod Oct. 30.

Secular Dimension of the Church: "The Church, in the words of Pope Paul VI on the (Second Vatican) Council, 'has an authentic secular dimension, inherent in her intimate nature and mission, the root of which is to be found in the mystery of the Word Incarnate and which is realized in diverse ways in her members.'

"The realization of this secular dimension, of itself common to all the baptized, is brought about in a particular way by the faithful laity. The Council called it their 'secular nature'; the faithful laity 'live in the world, in each and in all of the secular professions and occupations, and in the ordinary circumstances of family and social life, from which the very web of their existence is woven' *(Dogmatic Constitution on the Church,* No. 31).

"In this way they collaborate in the realization of the total mission of the Church, which is 'not only to bring to men the message and grace of Christ, but also to penetrate and perfect the temporal sphere with the spirit of the Gospel' *(Decree on the Apostolate of the Laity,* No. 5)."

Views of NCCB Delegates

Four elected synod delegates of the National Conference of Catholic Bishops, in a statement issued Oct. 29, cited some general synodal themes "of significance" for the Church universal:

- "the vocation and mission of the lay faithful as lived out in family, workplace and local community;
- "the hunger of laity for holiness and formation; namely, for assistance in personal and spiritual growth;
- the participation of laity in ecclesial ministries as one example of coresponsibility;
- "the inestimable value of women in the life and mission of the Church;
- "appreciation for the contribution of youth to the life of the Church, and our pledge of support for them as they face an uncertain future;
- "the centrality of the parish as a community of communities."

At the conclusion of their statement, the bishops said:

"We are committed to continued consultation with the laity . . .

"We must continue promoting the dignity, giftedness and involvement of women within Church and society . . .

"We wish also to build on the global awareness of lay vocation and mission which this Synod has strengthened."

The four elected delegates of the National Conference of Catholic Bishops were: Cardinal Joseph L. Bernardin of Chicago; Archbishop John L. May of St. Louis, conference president; Archbishop Rembert G. Weakland of Milwaukee and Bishop Stanley J. Ott of Baton Rouge.

ROMAN CURIA

The Roman Curia is the Church's network of central administrative agencies serving the Vatican and the local churches, with authority granted by the Pope.

Background

The Curia evolved gradually from advisory assemblies or synods of the Roman clergy with whose assistance the popes directed church affairs during the first 11 centuries. Its original office was the Apostolic Chancery, established in the fourth century to transmit documents. The antecedents of its permanently functioning agencies and offices were special commissions of cardinals and prelates. Its establishment in a form resembling what it is now dates from the second half of the 16th century.

Pope Paul VI initiated a four-year reorganization study in 1963 which resulted in the constitution *Regimini Ecclesiae Universae.* The document was published Aug. 18, 1967, and went into full effect in March, 1968. The stated purposes of the reorganization were to increase the efficiency of the Curia and to make it more responsive to the needs and concerns of the Universal Church.

Pope John Paul II, in the apostolic constitution *Pastor Bonus,* published June 28, 1988, and effective Mar. 1, 1989, ordered modifications of the Curia based on the broad outline of Paul VI's reorganization.

Curial Departments

Accordingly, as of Mar. 1, 1989, the Curia will consist of the Secretariat of State, nine congregations (governing agencies), three tribunals (judicial agencies), 12 councils (promotional agencies) and three offices (specialized service agencies). All agencies will have equal juridical status with authority granted by the Pope.

Agencies affected by the reorganization are:

- The Council for the Public Affairs of the Church: renamed Section for Relations with States, within the Secretariat of State; previously, a separate department.
- The Congregation for Divine Worship and the Congregation for the Sacraments: merged into one congregation.
- The Congregation for Catholic Education: renamed the Congregation for Seminaries and Institutes of Study.
- The Congregation for Religious and Secular Institutes: renamed the Congregation for Institutes of Consecrated Life and Societies of Apostolic Life.
- The Secretariats for Promoting Christian Unity, for Non-Christians and for Non-Believers: renamed, respectively, Pontifical Councils for Christian Unity, for Interreligious Dialogue and for Dialogue with Non-Believers.
- Commissions for Justice and Peace, for Health Care Workers, for Social Communications, for Migration and Tourism (renamed, for Migrants and Travelers) and for Authentic Interpretation of the Code of Canon Law (renamed, for Interpretation of Legislative Texts): made Councils. (The status

of other existing commissions and committees was not clear at the time of writing, on the basis of available sources.)

• Offices: The Prefecture of the Pontifical Household: listed with other agencies. Establishment was ordered of a Labor Office of the Holy See, to deal particularly with lay employees and employment matters.

The descriptions which follow pertain to Vatican agencies and their competencies in effect in 1988. Changes scheduled to become effective Mar. 1, 1989, are indicated where possible; all pertinent documents regarding curial revision were not available at the time of writing.

SECRETARIAT OF STATE

(As of Mar. 1, 1989, to consist of two sections: Section for General Affairs and Section for Relations with States — instead of Council for the Public Affairs of the Church.)

The Secretariat of State provides the pope with the closest possible assistance in the care of the universal Church and in dealings with all departments of the Curia.

The cardinal secretary is the key coordinator of curial operations. He has authority to call meetings of the prefects of all departments for expediting the conduct of business, for consultation and intercommunication. He handles: any and all matters entrusted to him by the pope, and ordinary matters which are not within the competence of other departments; some relations with bishops; relations with representatives of the Holy See, civil governments and their representatives, without prejudice to the competence of the Council for the Public Affairs of the Church.

The secretariat has two offices for preparing and writing letters for the pope and a Central Statistics Office. It handles work formerly done by the Apostolic Datary and the Apostolic Chancery, (care of the pope's leaden seal and the Fisherman's Ring). It has supervisory duties over the Commission for the Instruments of Social Communication, two Vatican publications, *Acta Apostolicae Sedis* and *Annuario Pontificio,* and the Vatican Personnel Office. The Prefecture of Vatican City is answerable to the secretary of state.

OFFICIALS: *Cardinal Agostino Casaroli, secretary of state; Most Rev. Edward Cassidy, assistant secretary of state.*

Council for the Public Affairs of the Church: Handles diplomatic and other relations with civil governments. With the Secretariat of State, it supervises matters concerning nunciatures and apostolic delegations. It also has supervision of the Pontifical Commission for Russia.

OFFICIALS: *Cardinal Agostino Casaroli, prefect, secretary of state; Most Rev. Angelo Sodano, secretary.*

BACKGROUND: Originated by Pius VI in 1793 as the Congregation for Extraordinary Affairs from the Kingdom of the Gauls; given wider scope by Pius VII, July 19, 1814; formerly called the Sacred Congregation for Extraordinary Ecclesiastical Affairs.

CONGREGATIONS

(As of Mar. 1, 1989, there will be nine congregations instead of 10, due to the unification of the Congregation for the Sacraments with the Congregation for Divine Worship. Two name changes are noted.)

Congregation for the Doctrine of the Faith: Has responsibility to safeguard the doctrine of faith and morals. Accordingly, it examines doctrinal questions; promotes studies thereon; evaluates theological opinions and, when necessary and after prior consultation with concerned bishops, reproves those regarded as opposed to principles of the faith; examines books on doctrinal matters and can reprove such works, if the contents so warrant, after giving authors the opportunity to defend themselves. It examines matters pertaining to the Privilege of Faith (Petrine Privilege) in marriage cases, and safeguards the dignity of the sacrament of penance. It has working relations with the Pontifical Biblical Commission and the Theological Commission

OFFICIALS: *Cardinal Joseph Ratzinger, prefect; Most Rev. Alberto Bovone, secretary.*

BACKGROUND: At the beginning of the 13th century, legates of Innocent III were commissioned as the Holy Office of the Inquisition to combat heresy; the same task was entrusted to the Dominican Order by Gregory IX in 1231 and to the Friars Minor by Innocent IV from 1243 to 1254. On July 21, 1542 (apostolic constitution *Licet*), Paul III instituted a permanent congregation of cardinals with supreme and universal competence over matters concerning heretics and those suspected of heresy. Pius IV, St. Pius V and Sixtus V further defined the work of the congregation. St. Pius X changed its name to the Congregation of the Holy Office.

Paul VI, in virtue of the motu proprio *Integrae Servandae* of Dec. 7, 1965, began reorganization of the Curia with this body, to which he gave the new title, Congregation for the Doctrine of the Faith. Its orientation is not merely negative, in the condemnation of error, but positive, in the promotion of orthodox doctrine. The right of appeal, judicial representation, and the consultation of their proper regional conference of bishops, are assured to persons accused of unorthodox doctrine. The office for the censorship of books and the Roman Index of Prohibited Books were abolished.

Congregation for the Oriental Churches: Has competence in matters concerning the persons and discipline of Eastern-Rite Churches. It has jurisdiction over territories in which the majority of Christians belong to Oriental Rites (i.e., Egypt, the Sinai Peninsula, Eritrea, Northern Ethiopia, Southern Albania, Bulgaria, Cyprus, Greece, Iran, Iraq, Lebanon, Palestine, Syria, Jordan, Turkey, Afghanistan, the part of Thrace subject to Turkey); also, over minority communities of Orientals no matter where they live. It is under mandate to consult with the Secretariat for Promoting Christian Unity on questions concerning separated Oriental Churches, and with the Secretariat for Non-Christians, especially in relations with

Moslems. It has a special commission on the liturgy and an Oriental Church Information Service.

OFFICIALS: *Cardinal D. Simon Lourdusamy, prefect; Most Rev. Miroslav Stefan Marusyn, secretary.*

Members include all Eastern Rite patriarchs and the president of the Secretariat for Promoting Christian Unity. Consultors include the secretary of the same secretariat.

BACKGROUND: Special congregations for the affairs of the Greek and other Oriental Churches were founded long before this body was created by Pius IX Jan. 6, 1862 (apostolic constitution *Romani Pontifices*), and united with the Congregation for the Propagation of the Faith. The congregation was made autonomous by Benedict XV May 1, 1917 (motu proprio *Dei Providentis*), and given wider authority by Pius XI Mar. 25, 1938 (motu proprio *Sancta Dei Ecclesia*). John XXIII appointed six patriarchs, five of Eastern Rites and one of the Roman Rite, to the congregation.

Congregation for Bishops, formerly called the Consistorial Congregation, has functions related in one way or another to bishops and the jurisdictions in which they serve. Its concerns are: the establishment and changing of dioceses, provinces, military vicariates and other jurisdictions; providing for the naming of bishops and other prelates; studying things concerning the persons, work and pastoral activity of bishops; providing for the care of bishops when they leave office; receiving and studying reports on the conditions of dioceses; general supervision of the holding and recognition of particular councils and conferences of bishops; publishing and circulating pastoral norms and guidelines through conferences of bishops. It supervises the Pontifical Commission for Latin America and the Pontifical Commission for Migration and Tourism. A central coordinating office for Military Vicars was established Feb. 2, 1985.

OFFICIALS: *Cardinal Bernardin Gantin, prefect; Most Rev. Giovanni Battista Re, secretary.*

Ex officio members are the prefects of the Council for the Public Affairs of the Church, and of the Congregations for the Doctrine of the Faith, for the Clergy, and for Catholic Education. The substitute secretaries and undersecretaries of these curial departments are ex officio consultors.

BACKGROUND: Established by Sixtus V Jan. 22, 1588 (apostolic constitution *Immensa*); given an extension of powers by St. Pius X June 20, 1908, and Pius XII Aug. 1, 1952 (apostolic constitution *Exsul Familia*).

Congregation for the Sacraments: Supervises the discipline of the sacraments without prejudice to the competencies of the Congregation for the Doctrine of the Faith and other curial departments.

(As of Mar. 1, 1989, to be united with the Congregation for Divine Worship.)

OFFICIALS: *Cardinal Eduardo Martinez Somalo, prefect; Most Rev. Lajos Kada, secretary.*

BACKGROUND: Instituted by St. Pius X, June 29, 1908, as the Congregation for the Discipline of the Sacraments; replaced by the Congregation for the Sacraments and Divine Worship by Paul VI (apostolic constitution, *Constans novis studium*, July 11, 1975); reestablished as a separate congregation by John Paul II in an autograph letter dated April 5, 1984.

Congregation for Divine Worship: Has general competence over the ritual and pastoral aspects of divine worship in the Roman and other Western rites.

(As of Mar. 1, 1989, to be united with the Congregation for the Sacraments.)

OFFICIALS: *Cardinal Eduardo Martinez Somalo, prefect; Most Rev. Virgilio Noe, secretary.*

BACKGROUND: Established by Paul VI, May 8, 1969, to replace the Congregation of Rites instituted by Pope Sixtus V in 1588; united with Congregation for the Discipline of the Sacraments by Paul VI in 1975; reestablished as a separate congregation by John Paul II in an autograph letter dated Apr. 5, 1984.

Congregation for the Causes of Saints: Handles matters connected with beatification and canonization causes (in accordance with revised procedures decreed in 1983), and the preservation of relics.

OFFICIALS: *Cardinal Angelo Felici, prefect; Most Rev. Traian Crisan, secretary.*

BACKGROUND: Established by Sixtus V in 1588 as the Congregation of Rites; affected by legislation of Pius XI in 1930; title changed and functions defined by Paul VI, 1969 (apostolic constitution *Sacra Rituum Congregatio*). It was restructured and canonization procedures were revised by John Paul II in 1983 (apostolic constitution *Divinus Perfectionis Magister*).

Congregation for the Clergy, formerly called the Congregation of the Council, handles matters concerning the persons, work and pastoral ministry of clerics and Religious who exercise their apostolate in a diocese. The International Office for Catechetics was annexed to the congregation in 1973 by Paul VI.

OFFICIALS: *Cardinal Antonio Innocenti, prefect; Most Rev. Gilberto Agustoni, secretary.*

BACKGROUND: Established by Pius IV Aug. 2, 1564 (apostolic constitution *Alias Nos*), under the title, Congregation of the Cardinals Interpreters of the Council of Trent; affected by legislation of Gregory XIII and Sixtus V.

Congregation for Religious and Secular Institutes, formerly known as the Congregation of Religious or for the Affairs of Religious, has competence over institutes of Religious, societies of the apostolic life, third orders and secular institutes. With two sections, the congregation has authority in matters related to the establishment, general direction and suppression of the various institutes; general discipline in line with their rules and constitutions; the movement toward renewal and adaptation of institutes in contemporary circumstances; the setting up and encouragement of councils and conferences of major religious superiors for intercommunication and other purposes.

(As of Mar. 1, 1989, to be called Congregation for Institutes of Consecrated Life and Societies of Apostolic Life.)

OFFICIALS: *Cardinal Jean Jerome Hamer, O.P, prefect; Most. Rev. Vincenzo Fagiolo, secretary.*

BACKGROUND: Founded by Sixtus V May 27, 1586, with the title, Congregation for Consultations of Regulars (apostolic constitution *Romanus Pontifex*); confirmed by the apostolic constitution *Immensa* Jan. 22, 1588; made part of the Congregation for Consultations of Bishops and other Prelates in 1601; made autonomous by St. Pius X in 1908.

Congregation for Catholic Education, formerly known as the Congregation of Seminaries and Universities, has supervisory competence over institutions and works of Catholic education. It carries on its work through three offices. One office handles matters connected with the direction, discipline and temporal administration of seminaries, and with the education of diocesan clergy, religious and members of secular institutes. A second office oversees Catholic universities, faculties of study and other institutions of higher learning inasmuch as they depend on the authority of the Church; encourages cooperation and mutual assistance among Catholic institutions, and the establishment of Catholic hospices and centers on campuses of non-Catholic institutions. A third office is concerned in various ways with all Catholic schools below the college-university level, with general questions concerning education and studies, and with the cooperation of conferences of bishops and civil authorities in educational matters. The congregation supervises Pontifical Works for Priestly Vocations.

(As of Mar. 1, 1989, to be called Congregation for Seminaries and Institutes of Study.)

OFFICIALS: *Cardinal William Wakefield Baum, prefect; Rev. Jose Saraiva Martins, C.M.F., secretary.*

BACKGROUND: The title and functions of the congregation were defined by Benedict XV Nov. 4, 1915; Pius XI, in 1931 and 1932, and Pius XII, in 1941 and 1949, extended its functions. Its work had previously been carried on by two other congregations erected by Sixtus V in 1588 and Leo XII in 1824.

Congregation for the Evangelization of Peoples or the Propagation of the Faith: Directs and coordinates missionary work throughout the world. Accordingly, it has competence over those matters which concern all the missions established for the spread of Christ's kingdom. These include: fostering missionary vocations; providing for the training of missionaries in seminaries; assigning missionaries to fields of work; establishing ecclesiastical jurisdictions and proposing candidates to serve them as bishops and in other capacities; encouraging the recruitment and development of indigenous clergy; mobilizing spiritual and financial support for missionary activity. In general, the varied competence of the congregation extends to most persons and affairs of the Church in areas classified as mission territories.

To promote missionary cooperation, the congregation has a Supreme Council for the Direction of Pontifical Missionary Works. Subject to this council are the general councils of the Missionary Union of the Clergy, the Society for the Propagation of the Faith, the Society of St. Peter the Apostle for Native Clergy, the Society of the Holy Childhood, the International Center of Missionary Animation and the *Fides* news agency.

OFFICIALS: *Cardinal Jozef Tomko, prefect; Most Rev. Jose T. Sanchez, secretary.*

The heads of the Secretariats for Promoting Christian Unity, for Non-Christians, and for Non-Believers are ex officio members of the congregation.

BACKGROUND: Originated as a commission of cardinals by Gregory XIII and modified by Clement VIII to promote the reconciliation of separated Eastern Christians; erected as a stable congregation by Gregory XV June 22, 1622 (apostolic constitution *Inscrutabili*).

TRIBUNALS

Apostolic Penitentiary: Has jurisdiction for the internal forum only (sacramental and non-sacramental). It issues decisions on questions of conscience; grants absolutions, dispensations, commutations, sanations and condonations; has charge of non-doctrinal matters pertaining to indulgences.

OFFICIALS: *Cardinal Luigi Dadaglio, major penitentiary; Msgr. Luigi de Magistris, regent.*

BACKGROUND: Origin dates back to the 12th century; affected by the legislation of many popes; radically reorganized by St. Pius V in 1569; jurisdiction limited to the internal forum by St. Pius X; Benedict XV annexed the Office of Indulgences to it Mar. 25, 1917.

Apostolic Signatura: The principal concerns of this supreme court of the Church are to resolve questions concerning juridical procedure and to supervise the observance of laws and rights at the highest level. It decides the jurisdictional competence of lower courts and has jurisdiction in cases involving personnel and decisions of the Rota. It is the supreme court of the State of Vatican City.

OFFICIALS: *Cardinal Achille Silvestrini, prefect; Most Rev. Zenon Grocholewski, secretary.*

BACKGROUND: A permanent office of the Signatura has existed since the time of Eugene IV in the 15th century; affected by the legislation of many popes; reorganized by St. Pius X in 1908 and made the supreme tribunal of the Church.

Roman Rota: The ordinary court of appeal for cases appealed to the Holy See. It is best known for its competence and decisions in cases concerning the validity of marriage.

OFFICIAL: *Msgr. Ernesto Fiore, dean.*

BACKGROUND: Originated in the Apostolic Chancery; affected by the legislation of many popes; reorganized by St. Pius X in 1908 and further revised by Pius XI in 1934.

SECRETARIATS

(As of Mar. 1, 1989, these three secretariats to be reconstituted as Councils: for Christian Unity, for Interreligious Dialogue and for Dialogue with Non-Believers.)

Secretariat for Promoting Christian Unity: Handles relations with members of other Christian ecclesial communities; deals with the correct interpretation and execution of the principles of ecumenism; initiates or promotes Catholic ecumenical groups and coordinates on national and international levels the efforts of those promoting Christian unity; undertakes dialogue regarding ecumenical questions and activities with churches and ecclesial communities separated from the Apostolic See; sends Catholic observer-representatives to Christian gatherings, and invites to Catholic gatherings observers of other churches; orders into execution conciliar decrees dealing with ecumenical affairs.

The Commission for Catholic-Jewish Relations is attached to the secretariat.

It has two offices, for the West and for the East. Each office is under the immediate direction of a delegate.

The prefects of the Congregation for the Oriental Churches and of the Congregation for the Evangelization of Peoples are ex officio members of the secretariat. Consultors include the secretaries of these two departments.

OFFICIALS: Cardinal Johannes Willebrands, president; Very Rev. Pierre Duprey, P.A., secretary.

BACKGROUND: Established by John XXIII June 5, 1960, as a preparatory secretariat of the Second Vatican Council; raised to commission status during the first session of the council in the fall of 1962; this status confirmed Jan. 3, 1966.

Secretariat for Non-Christians: Is concerned with persons who are not Christians but profess some kind of religious faith. Its function is to promote studies and dialogue for the purpose of increasing mutual understanding and respect between Christians and non-Christians.

The Commission for Catholic-Moslem Relations is attached to the secretariat.

The prefect of the Congregation for the Evangelization of Peoples is an ex officio member of the secretariat.

OFFICIALS: Cardinal Francis Arinze, president; Rev. Michael Louis Fitzgerald, M. Afr., secretary.

BACKGROUND: Established by Paul VI May 19, 1964.

Secretariat for Non-Believers: Studies the background and philosophy of atheism, and initiates and carries on dialogue with non-believers.

OFFICIALS: Cardinal Paul Poupard, president; Very Rev. Franc Rode, C.M., secretary.

BACKGROUND: Established by Paul VI Apr. 9, 1965.

COUNCILS, COMMISSIONS, COMMITTEES

(The categories of commission, except for several attached to congregations, and committee will lose curial status as of Mar. 1, 1989. Twelve councils will remain: nine are indicated below with an asterisk; three others are listed above under the Secretariat heading.)

Laity, Pontifical Council*: Instituted on an experimental basis by Paul VI Jan. 6, 1967; given permanent status Dec. 10, 1976 (motu proprio *Apostolatus Peragendi*); its competence covers the apostolate of the laity in the Church and the discipline of the laity as such. Members are mostly lay people from different parts of the world and involved in different apostolates. The council is headed by a cardinal. The Council for the Family is attached to the Council while retaining its own identity. Cardinal Eduardo Pironio, president; Most Rev. Paul Cordes, vice-president.

Justice and Peace, Pontifical Commission (Council, effective Mar. 1, 1989)*: Instituted by Paul VI Jan. 6, 1967, on an experimental basis; reconstituted and made a permanent body Dec. 10, 1976 (motu proprio *Iustitiam et Pacem*). Holy See's organization for examining and studying (from the point of view of doctrine, pastoral practice and the apostolate) problems connected with justice and peace and awakening the sensitivity of the people of God to their responsibility in these areas. Cardinal Roger Etchegaray, president.

Authentic Interpretation of the Code of Canon Law, Pontifical Commission (Council for Interpretation of Legislative Texts, effective Mar. 1, 1989)*: Established by John Paul II (motu proprio, *Recognito iuris canonici codice*, Jan. 2, 1984) to interpret canons of the revised Code of Canon Law and other universal laws of the Church. Cardinal Rosalio Jose Castillo Lara, S.D.B., president.

Social Communications Commission (Council, effective Mar. 1, 1989)*: Instituted on an experimental basis by Pius XII in 1948; reorganized three times in the 1950s; made permanent commission by John XXIII Feb. 22, 1959; name changed to present title Apr. 11, 1964; authorized to implement the *Decree on the Instruments of Social Communication* promulgated by the Second Vatican Council; under supervision of the Secretariat of State and the Council for the Public Affairs of the Church; Most Rev. John P. Foley, president; Cardinal Andrzej M. Deskur, president emeritus.

Migration and Tourism, Commission (Council for Migrants and Travelers, effective Mar. 1, 1989)*: Instituted by Paul VI Mar. 19, 1970, for pastoral assistance to migrants, nomads, tourists, sea and air travelers; placed under the general supervision and direction of the Congregation for Bishops; Cardinal Bernardin Gantin, president.

Cor Unum, Council*: Instituted by Paul VI July 15, 1971, to provide informational and coordinating services for Catholic aid and human development organizations and projects on a worldwide scale; Cardinal Roger Etchegaray, president.

Family, Pontifical Council*: Instituted by John Paul II May 9, 1981, replacing the Committee for the Family established Jan. 11, 1973, for "promoting the pastoral care of the family ... by putting into effect the teachings and directives of the ecclesiastical magisterium, so that Christian families may carry out the educative, evangelizing and apostolic mission to which they have been called"; has special relations with the Pontifical Council for the Laity. Cardinal Edouard Gagnon, P.S.S., president.

Culture, Pontifical Council*: Established in 1982 by Pope John Paul II to facilitate contacts between the saving message of the Gospel and the plurality of cultures. Cardinal Gabriel-Marie Garrone, head of presidential committee; Cardinal Paul Poupard, president of executive committee.

Health Care Workers, Pontifical Commission for Apostolate (Council, effective Mar. 1, 1989)*: Established in 1985 by Pope John Paul II to stimulate and foster the work of formation, study and action carried out by various international Catholic organizations in the health care field; attached to the Council for the Laity. Cardinal Eduardo Pironio, president; Most Rev. Fiorenzo Angelini, pro-president.

Revision of the Code of Oriental Canon Law: Reconstituted by Paul VI in 1972 to replace a former commission dating from July 17, 1935, "to prepare ... the reform of the Code of Oriental Canon Law, both in the sections already published by ... four motu proprios" (1,950 canons concerning marriage; processes; religious, church property and terminology; Eastern Rites and persons), "and in the remaining sections which have been completed but not published" (the balance of a total of 2,666 canons).

Latin America, Commission: Instituted by Pius XII Apr. 19, 1958; placed under supervision of the Congregation for Bishops July, 1969; Cardinal Bernardin Gantin, president.

International Eucharistic Congresses, Pontifical Committee: Instituted, 1879, by Pope Leo XIII; established as a pontifical committee with new statutes by John Paul II, Feb. 11, 1986. Cardinal Opilio Rossi, president.

Roman Curia, Disciplinary Commission: Cardinal Rosalio Jose Castillo Lara, S.D.B., president.

Council of Cardinals for Study of Organizational and Economic Problems of the Holy See: Council established in 1981 by Pope John Paul II; composed of 15 cardinals — residential archbishops — from countries outside of Italy.

Theological Commission: Instituted by Paul VI Apr. 11, 1969, as an advisory adjunct of no more than 30 theologians to the Congregation for the Doctrine of the Faith; Cardinal Joseph Ratzinger, president.

Biblical Commission: Instituted by Leo XIII Oct. 30, 1902; completely restructured by Paul VI June 27, 1971; Cardinal Joseph Ratzinger, president.

Revision and Emendation of the Vulgate, Pontifical Commission: Established in 1983 by John Paul II to replace the Abbey of St. Jerome instituted by Pius XI in 1933; Rev. Jean Mallet, O.S.B., director.

Sacred Archeology, Commission: Instituted by Pius IX Jan, 6, 1852.

Historical Sciences, Committee: Instituted by Pius XII Apr. 7, 1954, as a continuation of a commission dating from 1883; Msgr. Michele Maccarrone, president.

Ecclesiastical Archives of Italy, Commission: Instituted by Pius XII Apr. 5, 1955; Rev. Joseph Metzler, O.M.I., president.

Sacred Art in Italy, Commission: Instituted by Pius XI Sept. 1, 1924. Cardinal Egano Righi-Lambertini, honorary president.

Sanctuaries of Pompei, Loreto and Bari, Cardinalatial Commission: Originated by Leo XIII for Sanctuary of Pompei, Loreto placed under commission in 1965, St. Nicholas of Bari, 1980; under supervision of the Congregation for the Clergy; Cardinal Opilio Rossi, president.

Russia, Commission: Instituted by Pius XI Apr. 6, 1930, to handle all ecclesiastical affairs of the country; placed under supervision of the Congregation for Extraordinary Ecclesiastical Affairs (now the Council for the Public Affairs of the Church) in 1934, with jurisdiction limited to clergy and faithful of the Roman Rite; under supervision of the Council for the Public Affairs of the Church; Cardinal Achille Silvestrini, president.

Catholic-Jewish Relations, Commission: Instituted by Paul VI, Oct. 22, 1974, to promote and foster relations of a religious nature between Jews and Christians; attached to the Secretariat for Christian Unity; Cardinal Johannes Willebrands, president.

Catholic-Moslem Relations, Commission: Instituted by Paul VI, Oct. 22, 1974, to promote, regulate and interpret relations between Catholics and Moslems; attached to the Secretariat for Non-Christians; Cardinal Francis Arinze, president.

State of Vatican City, Commission: Cardinal Sebastiano Baggio, president; Most Rev. Paul Marcinkus, pro-president.

Protection of the Historical and Artistic Monuments of the Holy See, Commission: Instituted by Pius XI in 1923, reorganized by Paul VI in 1963. Most Rev. Lino Zanini, president.

Preservation of the Faith, Erection of New Churches in Rome: Instituted by Pius XI Aug. 5, 1930, to replace a commission dating from 1902; Cardinal Ugo Poletti, president.

Works of Religion, Commission: Instituted by Pius XII June 27, 1942, to bank and administer funds for works of religion; replaced an earlier administration established by Leo XIII in 1887; Most Rev. Paul C. Marcinkus, president.

Catechism Commission: Established by John Paul II, June 10, 1986, to draw up a draft catechism on which bishops of the whole church will be invited to express their views. Its work must be finished by the 1990 ordinary assembly of the Synod of Bishops. Composed of 12 cardinals and bishops. Cardinal Joseph Ratzinger, president.

OFFICES

(All offices, except the three indicated below with an asterisk, will lose curial status Mar. 1, 1989).

Apostolic Chamber*: Administers the temporal goods and rights of the Holy See between the death of one pope and the election of another, in accordance with special laws.

OFFICIALS: Cardinal Sebastiano Baggio, chamberlain of the Holy Roman Church; Most Rev. Ettore Cunial, vice-chamberlain.

BACKGROUND: Originated in the 11th century; reorganized by Pius XI in 1934.

Prefecture of the Economic Affairs of the Holy See*: A financial office which coordinates and supervises administration of the temporalities of the Holy See.

OFFICIALS: Cardinal Giuseppe Caprio, president; Msgr. Luigi Sposito, secretary.

BACKGROUND: Established by Paul VI Aug. 15, 1967.

Administration of the Patrimony of the Apostolic See*: Handles the estate of the Apostolic See under the direction of papal delegates acting with ordinary or extraordinary authorization.

OFFICIALS: Cardinal Agnelo Rossi, president; Most Rev. Lorenzo Antonetti, secretary.

BACKGROUND: Some of its functions date back to 1878; established by Paul VI Aug. 15, 1967.

Prefecture of the Pontifical Household: Oversees the papal chapel — which is at the service of the pope in his capacity as spiritual head of the Church — and the pontifical family — which is at the service of the pope as a sovereign. It arranges papal audiences, has charge of preparing non-liturgical elements of papal ceremonies, makes all necessary arrangements for papal visits and trips outside the Vatican, and settles questions of protocol connected with papal audiences and other formalities.

OFFICIAL: Most Rev. Dino Monduzzi, prefect.

BACKGROUND: Established by Paul VI Aug. 15, 1967, under the title, Prefecture of the Apostolic Palace; it supplanted the Sacred Congregation for Ceremonies founded by Sixtus V Jan. 22, 1588. The office was updated and reorganized under the present title by Paul VI, Mar. 28, 1968.

Central Statistics Office: Compiles. systematizes and analyzes information on the status and condition of the Church and the needs of its pastoral ministry, from parish to top levels.

The office is one of the organs of the Secretariat of State.

BACKGROUND: Established by Paul VI Aug. 15, 1967.

Aid Office: Distributes alms and aid to the aged, sick, handicapped and other persons in need.

OFFICIAL: Most Rev. Antonio M. Travia, director.

BACKGROUND: The office originated as a charitable office in the time of Bl. Gregory X (1271-1276).

Vatican II Archives: Preserves the acts and other documents of the Second Vatican Council.

Internationalization

As of July 15, 1988, principal officials of the Roman Curia and other agencies (cardinals unless indicated otherwise) were from the following countries: Italy (Baggio, Caprio, Casaroli, Dadaglio, Felici, Innocenti, Opilio Rossi, Silvestrini, Abps. Angelini, Bovone, Fagiolo, Noe, Re, Sodano, Bp. Monduzzi, Msgr. Fiore); France (Etchegaray, Poupard); Germany (Ratzinger, Bp. Cordes); Spain (Javierre Ortas, Martinez Somalo); United States (Baum, Abps. Foley, Marcinkus); Brazil (Agnelo Rossi); India (Lourdusamy); Poland (Abp. Grocholewski); Argentina (Pironio); Australia (Abp. Cassidy); Belgium (Hamer); Benin (Gantin); Canada (Gagnon); Czechoslovakia (Tomko); Hungary (Abp. Kada); Netherlands (Willebrands); Nigeria (Arinze); Philippines (Abp. Sanchez); Portugal (Rev. Saraiva Martins); Romania (Abp. Crisan); Switzerland (Abp. Agustoni); Ukraine (Abp. Marusyn); Venezuela (Castillo Lara).

COLLEGE OF CARDINALS

Cardinals are chosen by the pope to serve as his principal assistants and advisers in the central administration of church affairs. Collectively, they form the College of Cardinals. Provisions regarding their selection, rank, roles and prerogatives are detailed in Canons 349 to 359 of the Code of Canon Law.

History of the College

The College of Cardinals was constituted in its present form and categories of membership in the 12th century. Before that time the pope had a body of advisers selected from among the bishops of dioceses neighboring Rome, priests and deacons of Rome. The college was given definite form in 1150, and in 1179 the selection of cardinals was reserved exclusively to the pope. Sixtus V fixed the number at 70, in 1586. John XXIII set aside this rule when he increased membership at the 1959 and subsequent consistories. The number was subsequently raised to 145 by Paul VI in 1973 and to 152 by John Paul II in 1985. The number of cardinals entitled to participate in papal elections was limited to 120.

In 1567 the title of cardinal was reserved to members of the college; previously it had been used by priests attached to parish churches of Rome and by the leading clergy of other notable churches. The Code of Canon Law promulgated in 1918 decreed that all cardinals must be priests. Previously there had been cardinals who were not priests (e.g., Cardinal Giacomo Antonelli, d. 1876, Secretary of State to Pius IX, was a deacon). John XXIII provided in the motu proprio *Cum Gravissima* Apr. 15, 1962, that cardinals would henceforth be bishops; this provision is included in the revised Code of Canon Law.

Pope Paul VI placed age limits on the functions of cardinals in the apostolic letter *In-*

gravescentem Aetatem, dated Nov. 21, 1970, and effective as of Jan. 1, 1971. At 80, they cease to be members of curial departments and offices, and become ineligible to take part in papal elections. They retain membership in the College of Cardinals, however, with relevant rights and privileges.

Three Categories

All cardinals except Eastern patriarchs are aggregated to the clergy of Rome. This aggregation is signified by the assignment to each cardinal, except the patriarchs, of a titular church in Rome.

The three categories of members of the college are cardinal bishops, cardinal priests and cardinal deacons.

Cardinal bishops include the six titular bishops of the suburban sees of Rome and Eastern patriarchs.

First in rank are the titular bishops of the suburban sees, neighboring Rome: Ostia, Palestrina, Porto-Santa Rufina, Albano, Velletri-Segni, Frascati, Sabina-Poggio Mirteto. The dean of the college holds the title of the See of Ostia as well as his other suburban see. These cardinal bishops are engaged in full-time service in the central administration of church affairs in departments of the Roman Curia.

Full recognition is given in the revised Code of Canon Law to the position of Eastern patriarchs as the heads of sees of apostolic origin with ancient liturgies. They are assigned rank among the cardinals in order of seniority, following the suburban titleholders.

Cardinal priests, who were formerly in charge of leading churches in Rome, are bishops whose dioceses are outside Rome.

Cardinal deacons, who were formerly chosen according to regional divisions of Rome, are titular bishops assigned to full-time service in the Roman Curia.

The **dean** and **sub-dean** of the college are elected by the cardinal bishops — subject to approval by the pope — from among their number. The dean, or the sub-dean in his absence, presides over the college as the first among equals. Cardinals Agnelo Rossi and Sebastiano Baggio are dean and sub-dean, respectively.

Selection and Duties

Cardinals are selected by the pope and are inducted into the college in appropriate ceremonies.

Cardinals under the age of 80: elect the pope when the Holy See becomes vacant (See Papal Election; in 1059 cardinals were given the exclusive right to elect the pope.) and are major administrators of church affairs, serving in one or more departments of the Roman Curia. Cardinals in charge of agencies of the Roman Curia and Vatican City are asked to submit their resignation from office to the pope on reaching the age of 75. All cardinals enjoy a number of special rights and privileges. Their title, while symbolic of high honor, does not signify any extension of the powers of holy orders. They are called princes of the Church.

A **cardinal in pectore (petto)** is one whose selection has been made by the pope but whose name has not been disclosed; he has no title, rights or duties until such disclosure is made, at which time he takes precedence from the time of the secret selection.

BIOGRAPHIES OF CARDINALS

Biographies of the cardinals, as of Aug. 27, 1988, are given below in alphabetical order. For historical notes, order of seniority and geographical distribution of cardinals, see separate entries.

Titles of Roman Curia agencies reflect changes contained in Pope John Paul II's apostolic constitution "Pastor Bonus," published June 28, 1988, and effective March 1, 1989. (See Roman Curia.)

An asterisk indicates cardinals ineligible to take part in papal elections.

Antonelli,* Ferdinando Giuseppe, O.F.M.: b. July 14, 1896, Subbiano, Italy; solemnly professed in Order of Friars Minor, Apr. 7, 1914; ord. priest July 25, 1922; taught church history, 1928-32, and Christian archeology, 1932-65, at Antonianum; rector magnificus of Antonianum, 1937-43, 1953-59; definitor general of Friars Minor, 1939-45; held various offices in Roman Curia; secretary of Congregation of Rites, 1965-69, and Congregation for Causes of Saints, 1969-73; ord. titular archbishop of Idicra, Mar. 19, 1966; cardinal Mar. 5, 1973; titular church, San Sebastian (on the Palatine).

Aponte Martinez, Luis: b. Aug. 4, 1922, Lajas, Puerto Rico; ord. priest Apr. 10, 1950; parish priest at Ponce; ord. titular bishop of Lares and auxiliary of Ponce, Oct. 12, 1960; bishop of Ponce, 1963-64; archbishop of San Juan, Nov. 4, 1964; cardinal Mar. 5, 1973; titular church, St. Mary Mother of Providence (in Monteverde). Archbishop of San Juan. Curial membership:

Causes of Saints (congregation).

Aramburu, Juan Carlos: b. Feb. 11, 1912, Reduccion, Argentina; ord. priest in Rome, Oct. 28, 1934; ord. titular bishop of Plataea and auxiliary of Tucuman, Argentina, Dec. 15, 1946; bishop, 1953, and first archbishop, 1957, of Tucuman; titular archbishop of Torri di Bizacena and coadjutor archbishop of Buenos Aires, June 14, 1967; archbishop of Buenos Aires, Apr. 22, 1975; cardinal May 24, 1976; titular church, St. John Baptist of the Florentines. Archbishop of Buenos Aires, ordinary for Eastern Rite Catholics in Argentina without ordinaries of their own rites. Curial membership:

Oriental Churches, Divine Worship and Sacraments, Seminaries and Institutes of Study (congregations); Economic Affairs (office).

Arinze, Francis: b. Nov. 1, 1932, Eziowelle, Nigeria; ord. priest Nov. 23, 1958; ord. titular bishop of Fissiana and auxiliary of Onitsha, Aug. 29, 1965; archbishop of Onitsha, 1967-84; pro-president of Secretariat for Non-Christians, 1984; cardinal May 25, 1985; deacon, St. John (della Pigna). President of Secretariat for Non-Christians (Council for Interreligious Dialogue), 1985. Curial membership:

Evangelization of Peoples, Causes of Saints (congregations); Christian Unity, Dialogue with Non-Believers, Justice and Peace (councils).

Arns, Paulo Evaristo, O.F.M.: b. Sept. 14, 1921, Forquilhinha, Brazil; ord. priest Nov. 30, 1945; held various teaching posts; director of *Sponsa Christi*, monthly review for religious, and of the Franciscan publication center in Brazil; ord. titular bishop of Respetta and auxiliary of Sao Paulo, July 3, 1966; archbishop of Sao Paulo, Oct. 22, 1970; cardinal Mar. 5, 1973; titular church, St. Anthony of Padua (in Via Tuscolana). Archbishop of Sao Paulo. Curial membership: Divine Worship and Sacraments (congregation).

Bafile,* Corrado: b. July 4, 1903, L'Aquila, Italy; practiced law in Rome for six years before beginning studies for priesthood; ord. priest Apr. 11, 1936; served in Vatican secretariat of state, 1939-59; ord. titular archbishop of Antiochia in Pisidia, Mar. 19, 1960; apostolic nuncio to Germany, 1960-75; pro-prefect of Congregation for Causes of Saints, July 18, 1975; cardinal May 24, 1976; deacon, S. Maria (in Portico); transferred to order of cardinal priests, June 22, 1987; prefect of Congregation for Causes of Saints, 1976-80.

Baggio, Sebastiano: b. May 16, 1913, Rosa, Italy; ord. priest Dec. 21, 1935; ord. titular archbishop of Ephesus, July 26, 1953; served in Vatican diplomatic corps, 1953-69; nuncio to Chile, apostolic delegate to Canada, nuncio to Brazil; cardinal Apr. 28, 1969; archbishop of Cagliari, 1969-73; entered order of cardinal bishops as titular bishop of Velletri (now Velletri-Segni), Dec. 12, 1974; prefect of Congregation for Bishops, 1973-84. President of Pontifical Commission for Vatican City, 1984; Chamberlain (Camerlengo) of Holy Roman Church, 1985; Sub-Dean of the College of Cardinals, 1986. Curial membership: Doctrine of the Faith, Institutes of Consecrated Life and Societies of Apostolic Life, Seminaries and Institutes of Study, Evangelization of Peoples (congregations); Interpretation of Legislative Texts (council); Latin America (commission); Patrimony of Holy See (office).

Ballestrero, Anastasio Alberto, O.C.D.: b. Oct. 3, 1913, Genoa, Italy; professed in Order of Discalced Carmelites, 1929; ord. priest June 6, 1936; provincial, 1942-48, and superior general, 1955-67, of Carmelites; author of many books on Christian life; ord. archbishop of Bari, Feb. 2, 1974; archbishop of Turin, Aug. 1, 1977; cardinal June 30, 1979; titular church, S. Maria (sopra Minerva). Archbishop of Turin. Curial membership: Secretariat of State; Bishops, Institutes of Consecrated Life and Societies of Apostolic Life (congregations).

Baum, William Wakefield: b. Nov. 21, 1926, Dallas, Tex.; moved to Kansas City, Mo., at an early age; ord. priest (Kansas City-St. Joseph diocese) May 12, 1951; executive director of U.S. bishops commission for ecumenical and interreligious affairs, 1964-69; attended Second Vatican Council as *peritus* (expert adviser); ord. bishop of Springfield-Cape Girardeau, Mo., Apr. 6, 1970; archbishop of Washington, D.C., 1973-80; cardinal May 24, 1976; titular church, Holy Cross (on the Via Flaminia). Prefect of Congregation for Catholic Education (Congregation for Seminaries and Institutes of Study), 1980 (reappointed 1985); grand chancellor of Pontifical Gregorian University. Curial membership: Secretariat of State; Doctrine of the Faith, Bishops, Oriental Churches, Institutes of Consecrated Life and Societies of Apostolic Life, Evangelization of Peoples (congregations); Laity, Interpretation of Legislative Texts (councils); Patrimony of Holy See (office).

Beras Rojas,* Octavio Antonio: b. Nov. 16, 1906, Seibo, Dominican Republic; ord. priest Aug. 13, 1933; founded national Catholic youth movement; ord. titular archbishop of Euchaitae and coadjutor archbishop of Santo Domingo, Aug. 12, 1945; archbishop of Santo Domingo, 1961-81; cardinal May 24, 1976; titular church, San Sisto. Archbishop emeritus of Santo Domingo.

Bernardin, Joseph L.: b. Apr. 2, 1928, Columbia, S.C.; ord. priest (Charleston diocese) Apr. 26, 1952; ord. titular bishop of Lugura and auxiliary bishop of Atlanta, Ga., Apr. 26, 1966; general secretary, 1968-72, and president, 1974-77, of NCCB/USCC; archbishop of Cincinnati, 1972-82; archbishop of Chicago, July 10, 1982, installed Aug. 25, 1982; cardinal Feb. 2, 1983; titular church, Jesus the Divine Worker. Archbishop of Chicago. Curial membership: Divine Worship and Sacraments, Evangelization of Peoples (congregations); Christian Unity (council).

Bertoli,* Paolo: b. Feb. 1, 1908, Poggio Garfagnana, Italy; ord. priest Aug. 15, 1930; entered diplomatic service of the Holy See, serving in nunciatures in Yugoslavia, France, Haiti and Switzerland; ord. titular archbishop of Nicomedia, May 11, 1952; apostolic delegate to Turkey (1952-53), nuncio to Colombia (1953-59), Lebanon (1959-60), France (1960-69); cardinal Apr. 28, 1969; prefect of Congregation for Causes of Saints, 1969-73; entered order of cardinal bishops as titular bishop of Frascati, June 30, 1979; Chamberlain (Camerlengo) of Holy Roman Church, 1979-85.

Biffi, Giacomo: b. June 13, 1928, Milan, Italy; ord. priest Dec. 23, 1950; ord. titular bishop of Fidene and auxiliary of Milan, Jan. 11, 1976; archbishop of Bologna, Apr. 19, 1984; cardinal May 25, 1985; titular church, Sts. John the Evangelist and Petronio. Archbishop of Bologna. Curial membership: Divine Worship and Sacraments, Clergy (congregations).

Canestri, Giovanni: b. Sept. 30, 1918, Castelspina, Italy; ord. priest Apr. 12, 1941; spiritual director of Rome's seminary, 1959; ord. titular bishop of Tenedo and auxiliary to the cardinal vicar of Rome, July 30, 1961; bishop of Tortona, 1971-75; titular bishop of Monterano (personal title of archbishop) and vice regent of Rome, 1975-84; archbishop of Cagliari, 1984-87; archbishop of Genoa-Bobbio, July 6, 1987; cardinal June 28, 1988; titular church, St. Andrew of the Valley. Archbishop of Genoa-Bobbio.

Caprio, Giuseppe: b. Nov. 15, 1914, Lapio, Italy; ord. priest Dec. 17, 1938; served in diplomatic missions in China (1947-51, when Vatican diplomats were expelled by communists), Belgium (1951-54), and South Vietnam (1954-56); internuncio in China with residence at Taiwan, 1959-67; ord. titular archbishop of Apollonia, Dec. 17, 1961; pro-nuncio in India, 1967-69; secretary, 1969-77, and president, 1979-81, of Administration of Patrimony of Holy See; substitute secretary of state, 1977-79; cardinal June 30, 1979; deacon, St. Mary Auxiliatrix in Via Tuscolana. President of Prefecture of Economic Affairs of the Holy See, 1981; cardinal protodeacon, 1987. Curial membership:

Secretariat of State, Bishops, Oriental Churches, Causes of Saints, Evangelization of Peoples (congregations).

Carberry,* John J.: b. July 31, 1904, Brooklyn, N.Y.; ord. priest (Brooklyn diocese) July 28, 1929; ord. titular bishop of Elis and coadjutor bishop of Lafayette, Ind., July 25, 1956; bishop of Lafayette, Nov. 20, 1957; bishop of Columbus, Ohio, Jan. 16, 1965; archbishop of St. Louis, Mo., 1968-79; cardinal Apr. 28, 1969; titular church, St. John Baptist de Rossi (Via Latina). Archbishop emeritus of St. Louis.

Carpino,* Francesco: b. May 18, 1905, Palazzolo Acreide, Italy; ord. priest Aug. 14, 1927; ord. titular archbishop of Nicomedia and coadjutor archbishop of Monreale, Apr. 8, 1951; archbishop of Monreale, 1951-61; titular archbishop of Sardica, Jan. 19, 1961; assessor of Consistorial Congregation, 1961; pro-prefect of Congregation of the Council, Apr. 7, 1967; cardinal June 26, 1967; archbishop of Palermo, 1967-70; entered order of cardinal bishops as titular bishop of Albano, Jan. 27, 1978.

Carter, Gerald Emmett: b. Mar. 1, 1912, Montreal, Canada; ord. priest May 22, 1937; engaged in pastoral and teaching ministry in Montreal; founder and president of St. Joseph Teachers' College and co-founder and director of Thomas More Institute for adult education; ord. titular bishop of Altiburo and auxiliary bishop of London, Ont., Feb. 2, 1962; bishop of London, Ont., 1964-78; vice president, 1971-73, and president, 1975-77, of Canadian Conference of Catholic Bishops; archbishop of Toronto, Apr. 27, 1978; cardinal June 30, 1979; titular church, St. Mary (in Traspontina). Archbishop of Toronto. Curial membership:

Evangelization of Peoples (congregation); Christian Unity (council).

Casaroli, Agostino: b. Nov. 24, 1914, Castel San Giovanni, Italy; ord. priest May 27, 1937; entered service of Vatican secretariat of state, 1940; undersecretary, 1961-67, of the Congregation for Extraordinary Ecclesiastical Affairs, and secretary, 1967-79, of its successor the Council for Public Affairs of the Church; ord. titular archbishop of Cartagina, July 16, 1967; chief negotiator for the Vatican with East European communist governments; missions included visits to Hungary, Yugoslavia, Poland, Czechoslovakia, Bulgaria; headed Vatican delegations to several UN conferences and the Helsinki Conference (1975); Pro-Secretary of State and Pro-Prefect of Council for Public Affairs of the Church, Apr. 28, 1979; cardinal June 30, 1979; titular church, the Twelve Apostles; president, 1981-84, of Administration of Patrimony of Holy See and Pontifical Commission for Vatican City; entered order of cardinal bishops as titular bishop of Porto-Santa Rufina, May 25, 1985. Secretary of State, July 1, 1979 (given increased responsibility in government of Vatican City State, 1984). Curial membership:

Doctrine of the Faith, Bishops (congregations); Interpretation of Liturgical Texts (council).

Casoria, Giuseppe: b. Oct. 1, 1908, Acerra, Italy; ord. priest Dec. 21, 1930; jurist; Roman Curia official from 1937; under-secretary, 1959-69, and secretary, 1969-73, of Congregation for Sacraments and Divine Worship; secretary of Congregation for Causes of Saints, 1973-81; ord. titular bishop of Vescovia with personal title of archbishop, Feb. 13, 1972; pro-prefect of Congregation for Sacraments and Divine Worship, 1981-83; cardinal Feb. 2, 1983; deacon, St. Joseph on Via Trionfale. Prefect of Congregation for Sacraments and Divine Worship, 1983-84. Curial membership:

Doctrine of the Faith, Divine Worship and Sacraments, Oriental Churches, Causes of Saints (congregations); Interpretation of Liturgical Texts (council).

Castillo Lara, Rosalio Jose, S.D.B.: b. Sept. 4, 1922, San Casimiro, Venezuela; ord. priest Sept. 4, 1949; ord. titular bishop of Precausa, May 24, 1973; coadjutor bishop of Trujillo, 1973-76; archbishop May 26, 1982; secretary, 1975-82, and pro-president, 1982-84, of Pontifical Commission for Revision of Code of Canon Law; pro-president of Commission for Authentic Interpretation of Code of Canon Law, 1984-85; cardinal May 25, 1985; deacon, Our Lady of Coromoto (in St. John of God). President of: Pontifical Commission for Authentic Interpretation of Code of Canon Law (now the Council for the Interpretation of Liturgical Texts), 1985; Disciplinary Commission of Roman Curia, 1981. Curial membership:

Seminaries and Institutes of Study (congregation); Apostolic Signatura (tribunal); Christian Unity (council).

Cé, Marco: b. July 8, 1925, Izano, Italy; ord. priest Mar. 27, 1948; taught sacred scripture and dogmatic theology at seminary in his home diocese of Crema; rector of seminary, 1957; presided over diocesan liturgical commission, preached youth retreats; ord. titular bishop of Vulturia, May 17, 1970; auxiliary bishop of Bologna, 1970-76; general ecclesiastical assistant of Italian Catholic Action, 1976-78; patriarch of Venice, Dec. 7, 1978; cardinal June 30, 1979; titular church, St. Mark. Patriarch of Venice. Curial membership:

Divine Worship and Sacraments, Clergy, Seminaries and Institutes of Study (congregations).

Ciappi, Mario Luigi, O.P.: b. Oct. 6, 1909, Florence, Italy; ord. priest Mar. 26, 1932; papal theologian from 1955, serving Pius XII, John XXIII and Paul VI; ord. titular bishop of Misenum June 18, 1977; cardinal deacon June 27, 1977; transferred to order of cardinal priests, June 22, 1987; titular church, Sacred Heart of the Agonized Jesus. Protheologian of pontifical household. Curial membership:

Causes of Saints (congregation); Apostolic Signatura (tribunal).

Civardi,* Ernesto: b. Oct. 21, 1906, Fossarmato, Italy; ord. priest June 29, 1930; assistant rector of Pontifical Lombard Seminary in Rome; held various curial offices; undersecretary, 1953-67, and secretary, 1967-79, of the Congregation for Bishops (known as the Consistorial Congregation until 1967); ord. titular archbishop of Sardica, July 16, 1967; secretary of College of Cardinals, 1967-79; filled office of secretary at 1978 conclaves which elected Popes John Paul I and John Paul II; cardinal June 30, 1979; deacon, St. Theodore.

Clancy, Edward Bede: b. Dec. 13, 1923, Lithgow, New South Wales, Australia; ord. priest July 23, 1949; ord. titular bishop of Ard Carna and auxiliary of Sydney, Jan. 19, 1974; archbishop of Canberra, 1978-83; archbishop of Sydney, Feb. 12, 1983; cardinal June 28, 1988; titular church, Holy Mary of Vallicella. Archbishop of Sydney.

Colombo,* Giovanni: b. Dec. 6, 1902, Caronno Pertusella, Italy; ord. priest May 29, 1926; rector of Milan Seminary, 1953; ord. titular bishop of Filippopoli and auxiliary bishop of Milan, Dec. 7, 1960; archbishop of Milan, 1963-79; cardinal Feb. 22, 1965; titular church, Sts. Sylvester and Martin. Archbishop emeritus of Milan.

Cooray,* Thomas B., O.M.I.: b. Dec. 28, 1901, Periyamulla Negombo, Ceylon (now Sri Lanka); ord. priest June 23, 1929; ord. titular archbishop of Preslavo, Mar. 7, 1946; coadjutor archbishop of Colombo, Sri Lanka, 1946-47; succeeded as archbishop of Colombo, July 26, 1947 (retired 1976); cardinal Feb. 22, 1965; titular church, Sts. Nereus and Achilleus. Archbishop emeritus of Colombo, Sri Lanka.

Cordeiro, Joseph: b. Jan. 19, 1918, Bombay, India; ord. priest Aug. 24, 1946; served in educational and other diocesan posts at Karachi, Pakistan; ord. archbishop of Karachi, Aug. 24, 1958, the first native-born prelate in that see; cardinal Mar. 5, 1973; titular church, St. Andrew Apostle. Archbishop of Karachi. Curial membership: Institutes of Consecrated Life and Societies of Apostolic Life (congregation); Interreligious Dialogue (council).

Corripio Ahumada, Ernesto: b. June 29, 1919, Tampico, Mexico; ord. priest Oct. 25, 1942, in Rome, where he remained until almost the end of World War II; taught and held various positions in local seminary of Tampico, 1945-50; ord. titular bishop of Zapara and auxiliary bishop of Tampico, Mar. 19, 1953; bishop of Tampico, 1956-67; archbishop of Antequera, 1967-76; archbishop of Puebla de los Angeles, 1976-77; archbishop of Mexico City and primate of Mexico, July 19, 1977; cardinal June 30, 1979; titular church, Mary Immaculate al Tiburtino. Archbishop of Mexico City. Curial membership: Divine Worship and Sacraments, Clergy, Seminaries and Institutes of Study (congregations); Latin America (commission).

Dadaglio, Luigi: b. Sept. 28, 1914, Sezzadio, Italy; ord. priest May 22, 1937; entered diplomatic service of Holy See in 1940s; served in Haiti, the U.S., Canada, Australia, New Zealand and Colombia; ord. titular bishop of Lero with personal title of archbishop, Dec. 8, 1961; nuncio to Venezuela 1961-67; nuncio to Spain, 1967-80; secretary of Congregation for Sacraments and Divine Worship, 1980-84; pro-Major Penitentiary, 1984-85; cardinal May 25, 1985; deacon, St. Pius V. Major Penitentiary, 1985; archpriest of patriarchal Liberian Basilica. Curial membership: Secretariat of State; Bishops, Divine Worship and Sacraments, Evangelization of Peoples (congregations); Apostolic Signatura (tribunal).

Danneels, Godfried: b. June 4, 1933, Kanegem, Belgium; ord. priest Aug. 17, 1957; professor of liturgy and sacramental theology at Catholic University of Louvain, 1969-77; ord. bishop of Antwerp Dec. 18, 1977; app. archbishop of Mechelen-Brussel, Dec. 19, 1979; installed Jan. 4, 1980; elected member of general secretariat of Synod of Bishops, 1981; cardinal Feb. 2, 1983; titular church, St. Anastasia. Archbishop of Mechelen-Brussel, military ordinary of Belgium. Curial membership: Secretariat of State; Doctrine of the Faith, Bishops, Divine Worship and Sacraments, Evangelization of Peoples, Seminaries and Institutes of Study (congregations); Dialogue with Non-Believers (council).

Darmojuwono, Justin: b. Nov. 2, 1914, Godean, Indonesia; ord. priest May 25, 1947; ord. archbishop of Semarang, Apr. 6, 1964 (resigned July 3, 1981, for health reasons); cardinal June 26, 1967; titular church, Most Holy Names of Jesus and Mary. Archbishop emeritus of Semarang. Curial membership: Divine Worship and Sacraments (congregation).

Decourtray, Albert: b. Apr. 9, 1923, Wattignies, France; ord. priest June 29, 1947; ord. titular bishop of Ippona Zarito and auxiliary of Dijon, July 3, 1971; bishop of Dijon, 1974-81; archbishop of Lyon, Oct. 29, 1981; prelate of Mission of France, 1982; cardinal May 25, 1985; titular church, Most Holy Trinity (al Monte Pincio). Archbishop of Lyon, Prelate of Mission of France. Curial membership: Christian Unity, Interreligious Dialogue (councils).

De Furstenberg,* Maximilien: b. Oct. 23, 1904, Heerlen, Netherlands; ord. priest Aug. 9, 1931; ord. titular archbishop of Palto and apostolic delegate to Japan, Apr. 25, 1949; internuncio, 1952, when Japan established diplomatic relations with the Vatican; apostolic delegate to Australia, New Zealand and Oceania, Feb. 11, 1960; nuncio to Portugal, 1962-67; cardinal June 26, 1967; titular church, Most Sacred Heart of Jesus (a Castro Pretorio); prefect of the Congregation for the Oriental Churches, 1969-73. Grand Master of Equestrian Order of Holy Sepulchre of Jerusalem.

De Lubac,* Henri, S.J.: b. Feb. 20, 1896, Cambrai, France; entered Society of Jesus, October, 1913; ord. priest Aug. 22, 1927; taught fundamental theology and history of religions at the Theology Faculty of Lyons from 1929 to the early 1950s when he was dismissed because of misunderstanding of his book *The Supernatural,* intended to re-emphasize the doctrine on supernatural destiny; reinstated to his teaching post by Pope John XXIII; chief consultor of preparatory theological commission for Vatican II and *peritus* for Council itself; appointed member of International Theological Commission (1969-74) by Paul VI; cardinal Feb. 2, 1983, with permission to decline episcopal ordination; deacon, St. Mary in Domnica.

Deskur, Andrzej Marie: b. Feb. 29, 1924, Sancygniow, Poland; ord. priest Aug. 20, 1950, in France; assigned to Vatican secretariat of state, 1952; undersecretary and later secretary of Pontifical Commission for Film, Radio and TV (Social Communications), 1954-73; ord. titular bishop of Tene, June 30, 1974; archbishop, 1980; president of Pontifical Commission for Social Communications, 1974-84; cardinal May 25, 1985; deacon, St. Cesario (in Palatio). President emeritus of Council for Social Communications. Curial membership:

Causes of Saints (congregation); Health Care Workers (council).

do Nascimento, Alexandre: b. Mar. 1, 1925, Malanje, Angola; ord. priest Dec. 20, 1952, in Rome; professor of dogmatic theology in major seminary of Luanda, Angola; editor of *O Apostolada*, Catholic newspaper; forced into exile in Lisbon, Portugal, 1961-71; returned to Angola, 1971; active with student and refugee groups; professor at Pius XII Institute of Social Sciences; ord. bishop of Malanje, Aug. 31, 1975; archbishop of Lubango and apostolic administrator of Onjiva, 1977-86; held hostage by Angolan guerrillas, Oct. 15 to Nov. 16, 1982; cardinal Feb. 2, 1983; titular church, St. Mark in Agro Laurentino. Archbishop of Luanda, 1986. Curial membership:

Divine Worship and Sacraments, Evangelization of Peoples (congregations).

Duval,* Leon-Etienne: b. Nov. 9, 1903, Chenex, France; ord. priest Dec. 18, 1926; ord. bishop of Constantine, Algeria, Feb. 11, 1947; archbishop of Algiers, Feb. 3, 1954 (resigned 1988); cardinal Feb. 22, 1965; titular church, St. Balbina. Archbishop emeritus of Algiers.

Ekandem, Dominic Ignatius: b. 1917, Obio Ibiono, Nigeria; ord. priest Dec. 7, 1947; ord. titular bishop of Gerapoli di Isauri and auxiliary bishop of Calabar, Feb. 7, 1954, the first Nigerian to become a bishop; first bishop of Ikot Ekpene, Mar. 1, 1963; cardinal May 24, 1976; titular church, San Marcello. Bishop of Ikot Ekpene, superior of mission "sui juris" of Abuja. Curial membership:

Evangelization of Peoples (congregation).

Enrique y Tarancon,* Vicente: b. May 14, 1907, Burriana, Spain; ord. priest Nov. 1, 1929; ord. bishop of Solsona, Mar. 24, 1946; bishop of Oviedo, Apr. 12, 1964; archbishop of Toledo, 1969-71; cardinal Apr. 28, 1969; titular church, St. John Chrysostom; archbishop of Madrid, 1971-83. Archbishop emeritus of Madrid.

Etchegaray, Roger: b. Sept. 25, 1922, Espelette, France; ord. priest July 13, 1947; deputy director, 1961-66, and secretary general, 1966-70, of French Episcopal Conference; ord. titular bishop of Gemelle di Numidia and auxiliary of Paris, May 27, 1969; archbishop of Marseilles, 1970-84; prelate of Mission de France, 1975-82; president of French Episcopal Conference, 1979-81; cardinal June 30, 1979; titular church, St. Leo I. President, 1984, of Councils for Justice and Peace and *Cor Unum*. Curial membership:

Evangelization of Peoples, Seminaries and Institutes of Study (congregations); Apostolic Signatura (tribunal); Christian Unity (council).

Falcao, Jose Freire: b. Oct. 23, 1925, Erere, Brazil; ord. priest June 19, 1949; ord. titular bishop of Vardimissa and coadjutor of Limoeiro do Norte, June 17, 1967; bishop of Limoeiro do Norte, Aug. 19, 1967; archbishop of Teresina, Nov. 25, 1971; archbishop of Brasilia, Feb. 15, 1984; Cardinal June 28, 1988; titular church, St. Luke (Via Prenestina). Archbishop of Brasilia.

Felici, Angelo: b. July 26, 1919, Segni, Italy; ord. priest Apr. 4, 1942; in Vatican diplomatic service from 1945; ord. titular bishop of Cesariana, Sept. 24, 1967; archbishop; nuncio to Netherlands, 1967-76, Portugal, 1976-79, France, 1979-88; cardinal June 28, 1988; deacon, Sts. Blaise and Charles in Catinari. Prefect of Congregation for Causes of Saints, 1988.

Flahiff,* George B., C.S.B.: b. Oct. 26, 1905, Paris, Ont., Canada; ord. priest Aug. 17, 1930; professor of medieval history at the University of Toronto and Pontifical Institute of Medieval Studies in Toronto, 1934-54; superior general of Basilian Fathers, 1954; ord. archbishop of Winnipeg, May 31, 1961 (retired 1982); president of Canadian Conference of Bishops, 1963-65; cardinal Apr. 28, 1969; titular church, St. Mary della Salute (Primavalle). Archbishop emeritus of Winnipeg.

Freeman,* James Darcy: b. Nov. 19, 1907, Sydney, Australia; ord. priest July 13, 1930; ord. titular bishop of Ermopoli minore and auxiliary of Sydney, Jan. 24, 1957; bishop of Armidale, 1968-71; archbishop of Sydney, 1971-83; cardinal Mar. 5, 1973; titular church, St. Mary Queen of Peace. (in Ostia Mare). Archbishop emeritus of Sydney.

Fresno Larrain, Juan Francisco: b. July 26, 1914, Santiago, Chile; ord. priest Dec. 18, 1937; ord. bishop of Copiapo, Aug. 15, 1958; archbishop of La Serena, 1967-83; archbishop of Santiago, May 3, 1983; cardinal May 25, 1985; titular church, St. Mary Immaculate of Lourdes (a Boccea). Archbishop of Santiago. Curial membership:

Seminaries and Institutes of Study (congregation).

Gagnon, Edouard, P.S.S.: b. Jan. 15, 1918, Port Daniel, Que., Canada; ord. priest Aug. 15, 1940; ord. bishop of St. Paul in Alberta Mar. 25, 1969 (resigned May 3, 1972); rector of Canadian College in Rome, 1972-77; vice president-secretary of Vatican Committee for the Family, 1973-80; titular archbishop of Giustiniana Prima, July 7, 1983; pro-president of Pontifical Council for the Family, 1983; cardinal May 25, 1985; deacon, St. Elena (fuori Porta Prenestina). President of Pontifical Council for the Family, 1985. Curial membership:

Divine Worship and Sacraments, Causes of Saints (congregations); Apostolic Signatura (tribunal).

Gantin, Bernardin: b. May 8, 1922, Toffo, Dahomey (now Benin): ord. priest Jan. 14, 1951; ord. titular bishop of Tipasa di Mauritania and auxiliary bishop of Cotonou, Feb. 3, 1957; archbishop of Cotonou, 1960-71; associate secretary

(1971-73) and secretary (1973-75) of Congregation for Evangelization of Peoples; vice-president (1975) and president (1976-84) of Pontifical Commission for Justice and Peace; cardinal June 27, 1977; deacon; transferred to order of priests June 25, 1984; titular church, Sacred Heart of Christ the King; entered order of cardinal bishops as titular bishop of Palestrina, Sept. 29, 1986. Prefect of Congregation for Bishops, 1984; president of commission for Latin America and council for Migration and Tourism. Curial membership: Secretariat of State; Doctrine of the Faith, Divine Worship and Sacraments, Causes of Saints, Evangelization of Peoples, Oriental Churches, Institutes of Consecrated Life and Societies of Apostolic Life, Seminaries and Institutes of Study (congregations); Apostolic Signatura (tribunal); Dialogue with Non-Believers, Interreligious Dialogue, Social Communications (councils).

Garrone,* Gabriel-Marie: b. Oct. 12, 1901, Aix-les-Bains, France; ord. priest Apr. 11, 1925; captain during World War II, cited for bravery, taken prisoner; rector of major seminary of Chambery, 1947; ord. titular archbishop of Lemno and coadjutor of Toulouse, June 24, 1947; archbishop of Toulouse, 1956-66; titular archbishop of Torri di Numidia and pro-prefect of Congregation of Seminaries and Universities, Mar. 24, 1966; cardinal June 26, 1967; titular church, St. Sabina; prefect of Congregation for Catholic Education, 1968-80. Head of presidential committee of Pontifical Council for Culture.

Giordano, Michele: b. Sept. 26, 1930, Sant Arcangelo, Italy; ord. priest July 5, 1953; ord. titular bishop of Lari Castello and auxiliary of Matera, Feb. 5, 1972; archbishop of Matera, 1974-87; archbishop of Naples, May 9, 1987; cardinal June 28, 1988; titular church, St. Joachim. Archbishop of Naples.

Glemp, Jozef: b. Dec. 18, 1929, Inowroclaw, Poland; assigned to forced labor on German farm in Rycerzow during Nazi occupation; ord. priest May 25, 1956; studied in Rome, 1958-64; received degree in Roman and canon law from Pontifical Lateran University; secretary of primatial major seminary at Gniezno on his return to Poland, 1964; spokesman for secretariat of primate of Poland and chaplain of primate for archdiocese of Gniezno, 1967; ord. bishop of Warmia, Apr. 21, 1979; archbishop of Gniezno, July 7, 1981, with title of archbishop of Warsaw and primate of Poland; cardinal Feb. 2, 1983; titular church, St. Mary in Trastevere. Archbishop of Gniezno and Warsaw, primate of Poland, ordinary for faithful of Greek Catholic and Armenian rites in Poland. Curial membership:
Oriental Churches (congregation).

Gonzalez Martin, Marcelo: b. Jan. 16, 1918, Villanubla, Spain; ord. priest June 29, 1941; taught theology and sociology at Valladolid diocesan seminary; founded organization for construction of houses for poor; ord. bishop of Astorga, Mar. 5, 1961; titular archbishop of Case Mediane and coadjutor of Barcelona, Feb. 21, 1966; archbishop of Barcelona, 1967-71; archbishop of Toledo, Dec. 3, 1971; cardinal Mar. 5, 1973; titular church, St. Augustine. Archbishop of Toledo. Curial membership:
Clergy, Evangelization of Peoples (congregations).

Gouyon, Paul: b. Oct. 24, 1910, Bordeaux, France; ord. priest Mar. 13, 1937; ord. bishop of Bayonne, Oct. 7, 1957; titular archbishop of Pessinonte and coadjutor archbishop of Rennes, Sept. 6, 1963; archbishop of Rennes, Sept. 4, 1964 (resigned Oct. 15, 1985); cardinal Apr. 28, 1969; titular church, Nativity of Our Lord Jesus Christ (Via Gallia). Archbishop emeritus of Rennes. Curial membership:
Causes of Saints (congregation).

Gray, Gordon Joseph: b. Aug. 10, 1910, Edinburgh, Scotland; ord. priest June 15, 1935; ord. archbishop of Saint Andrews and Edinburgh, Sept. 21, 1951 (resigned May 30, 1985); chairman of International Committee for English in the Liturgy; cardinal Apr. 28, 1969; titular church, St. Clare. Archbishop emeritus of Saint Andrews and Edinburgh. Curial membership:
Divine Worship and Sacraments, Clergy, Evangelization of Peoples, (congregations).

Gregoire, Paul: b. Oct. 24, 1911, Verdun, Que., Canada; ord. priest May 22, 1937; ord. titular bishop of Curubi and auxiliary of Montreal, Dec. 27, 1961; archbishop of Montreal, Apr. 20, 1968; cardinal June 28, 1988; titular church, Our Lady of the Blessed Sacrament and the Holy Canadian Martyrs. Archbishop of Montreal.

Groër, Hans Hermann, O.S.B.: b. Oct. 13, 1919, Vienna, Austria; ord. priest Apr. 12, 1942; ord. archbishop of Vienna, Sept. 14, 1986; cardinal June 28, 1988; titular church, Sts. Joachim and Anne al Tuscolano. Archbishop of Vienna and ordinary for Byzantine-rite faithful living in Austria.

Guerri,* Sergio: b. Dec. 25, 1905, Tarquinia, Italy; ord. priest Mar. 30, 1929; ord. titular archbishop of Trevi, Apr. 27, 1969; cardinal Apr. 28, 1969; titular church, Most Holy Name of Mary; pro-president of Pontifical Commission for State of Vatican City, 1968-81.

Gulbinowicz, Henryk Roman: b. Oct. 17, 1928, Szukiszki, Poland; ord. priest June 18, 1960; ord. titular bishop of Acci and apostolic administrator of Polish territory in Lithuanian archdiocese of Vilnius (Vilna), Feb. 8, 1970; archbishop of Wroclaw, Poland, Jan. 3, 1976; cardinal May 25, 1985; titular church, Immaculate Conception of Mary (a Grottarosa). Archbishop of Wroclaw. Curial membership:
Oriental Churches, Clergy (congregations).

Hamer, Jean Jerome, O.P.: b. June 1, 1916, Brussels, Belgium; ord. priest Aug. 3, 1941; taught dogmatic and fundamental theology and ecclesiology in France and Rome, 1944-62; author of several works; secretary of Christian Unity Secretariat, 1969-73; ord. titular bishop of Lorium with personal title of archbishop June 29, 1973; secretary of Congregation for Doctrine of the Faith, 1973-84; pro-prefect of Congregation for Religious and Secular Institutes, 1984; cardinal May 25, 1985; deacon, St. Saba (al Aventino). Prefect of Congregation for Religious and Secular Institutes (Institutes of Consecrated Life and Societies of Apostolic Life), 1985. Curial membership:

Secretariat of State; Doctrine of the Faith, Bishops, Seminaries and Institutes of Study (congregations); Interpretation of Legislative Texts (council).

Hengsbach, Franz: b. Sept. 10, 1910, Velmede, Germany; ord. priest Mar. 13, 1937; ord. titular bishop of Cantano and auxiliary of Paderborn, Sept. 29, 1953; bishop of Essen, Nov. 18, 1957; cardinal June 28, 1988; titular church, Our Lady of Guadalupe. Bishop of Essen.

Hickey, James A.: b. Oct. 11, 1920, Anderson, Ind.; ord. priest (Saginaw diocese) June 15, 1946; ord. titular bishop of Taraqua and auxiliary of Saginaw, Apr. 14, 1967; rector of North American College, Rome, 1969-74; app. bishop of Cleveland, June 5, 1974; installed July 16, 1974; app. archbishop of Washington, D.C., installed Aug. 5, 1980; cardinal June 28, 1988; titular church, St. Mary Mother of the Redeemer, Archbishop of Washington, D.C.

Hume, George Basil, O.S.B.: b. Mar. 2, 1923, Newcastle-upon-Tyne, England; began monastic studies at Benedictine Abbey of St. Laurence at Ampleforth, 1941; made solemn perpetual vows as Benedictine, 1945; ord. priest July 23, 1950; abbot of Ampleforth, 1963-76; ord. archbishop of Westminster, Mar. 25, 1976; cardinal May 24, 1976; titular church, St. Silvestro (in Capite). Archbishop of Westminster. Curial membership:

Institutes of Consecrated Life and Societies of Apostolic Life (congregation); Christian Unity, Health Care Workers (councils).

Innocenti, Antonio: b. Aug. 23, 1915, Poppi, Italy; ord. priest July 17, 1938; held curial and diplomatic positions; ord. titular bishop of Eclano with personal title of archbishop, Feb. 18, 1967; nuncio to Paraguay, 1967-73; secretary of Congregation for Causes of Saints, 1973-75; secretary of Congregation for Sacraments and Divine Worship, 1975-80; nuncio to Spain, 1980-85; cardinal May 25, 1985; deacon, St. Marie (in Aquiro). Prefect of Congregation for the Clergy, 1986. Curial membership:

Secretariat of State; Bishops, Divine Worship and Sacraments, Evangelization of Peoples, Causes of Saints (congregations).

Javierre Ortas, Antonio Maria, S.D.B.: b. Feb. 21, 1921, Sietamo, Spain; ord. priest Apr. 24, 1949; leading European writer on ecumenism; ord. archbishop (titular see of Meta), June 29, 1976; Secretary of Congregation for Catholic Education, 1976-88; cardinal June 28, 1988; deacon, St. Mary Liberator (a Monte Testaccio). Librarian and Archivist of the Holy Roman Church, 1988.

Jubany Arnau, Narciso: b. Aug. 12, 1913, Santa Coloma de Farnes, Spain; ord. priest July 30, 1939; professor of law at Barcelona seminary; served on ecclesiastical tribunal; ord. titular bishop of Ortosia and auxiliary of Barcelona, Jan. 22, 1956; bishop of Gerona, 1964-71; archbishop of Barcelona, Dec. 3, 1971; cardinal Mar. 5, 1973; titular church, San Lorenzo (in Damaso). Archbishop of Barcelona. Curial membership:

Divine Worship and Sacraments, Institutes of Consecrated Life and Societies of Apostolic Life (congregations).

Khoraiche,* Antoine Pierre: b. Sept. 20, 1907, Ain-Ebel, Lebanon; ord. priest Apr. 12, 1930; ord. titular bishop of Tarsus and auxiliary bishop of Sidon of the Maronites, Oct. 15, 1950; bishop of Sidon, Nov. 25, 1957; elected patriarch of Antioch for Maronites, Feb. 3, 1975, granted ecclesial communion by Paul VI, Feb. 15, 1975 (resigned Apr. 3, 1986); advocate of reconciliation among various Lebanese ethnic and religious groups and withdrawal of foreign troops from country; cardinal Feb. 2, 1983. Patriarch emeritus of Antioch for Maronites.

Kim, Stephan Sou Hwan: b. May 8, 1922, Tae Gu, Korea; ord. priest Sept. 15, 1951; ord. bishop of Masan, May 31, 1966; archbishop of Seoul, Apr. 9, 1968; cardinal Apr. 28, 1969; titular church, St. Felix of Cantalice (Centocelle). Archbishop of Seoul, apostolic administrator of Pyeong Yang. Curial membership:

Evangelization of Peoples (congregation); Interreligious Dialogue (council).

Kitbunchu, Michael Michai: b. Jan. 25, 1929, Samphran, Thailand; ord. priest Dec. 20, 1959, in Rome; rector of metropolitan seminary in Bangkok, 1965-72; ord. archbishop of Bangkok, June 3, 1973; cardinal Feb. 2, 1983, the first from Thailand; titular church, St. Laurence in Panisperna. Archbishop of Bangkok. Curial membership:

Evangelization of Peoples (congregation).

Koenig,* Franz: b. Aug. 3, 1905, Rabenstein, Lower Austria; ord. priest Oct. 29, 1933; ord. titular bishop of Livias and coadjutor bishop of Sankt Poelten, Aug. 31, 1952; archbishop of Vienna, May 10, 1956 (resigned Sept. 16, 1985); cardinal Dec. 15, 1958; titular church, St. Eusebius; president of Secretariat for Non-Believers, 1965-80. Archbishop emeritus of Vienna.

Krol, John Joseph: b. Oct. 26, 1910, Cleveland, Ohio; ord. priest (Cleveland diocese) Feb. 20, 1937; ord. titular bishop of Cadi and auxiliary bishop of Cleveland, Sept. 2, 1953; archbishop of Philadelphia, Feb. 11, 1961, installed Mar. 22, 1961 (resigned Feb. 11, 1988); cardinal June 26, 1967; titular church, St. Mary (della Merced) and St. Adrian Martyr; vice-president, 1966-72, and president, 1972-74, of NCCB/USCC. Archbishop emeritus of Philadelphia. Curial membership:

Oriental Churches, Clergy (congregations); Economic Affairs (office).

Kuharic, Franjo: b. Apr. 15, 1919, Pribic, Yugoslavia; ord. priest July 15, 1945; ord. titular bishop of Meta and auxiliary bishop of Zagreb, May 3, 1964; apostolic administrator of archdiocese of Zagreb, 1968-70; archbishop of Zagreb, June 16, 1970; cardinal Feb. 2, 1983; titular church, St. Jerome of the Croats. Archbishop of Zagreb. Curial membership:

Secretariat of State; Bishops, Divine Worship and Sacraments, Clergy (congregations); Dialogue with Non-Believers (council).

Landazuri Ricketts, Juan, O.F.M: b. Dec. 19, 1913, Arequipa, Peru; entered Franciscans, 1933; ord. priest Apr. 16, 1939; ord. titular archbishop of Roina and coadjutor archbishop of Lima, Aug. 24,

1952; archbishop of Lima, May 2, 1955; cardinal Mar. 19, 1962; titular church, St. Mary (in Aracoeli). Archbishop of Lima. Curial membership:
Clergy, Institutes of Consecrated Life and Societies of Apostolic Life (congregations).

Law, Bernard F.: b. Nov. 4, 1931, Torreon; Mexico, the son of U.S. Air Force colonel; ord. priest (Jackson diocese) May 21, 1961; editor of Natchez-Jackson, Miss., diocesan paper, 1963-68; director of NCCB Committee on Ecumenical and Interreligious Affairs, 1968-71; ord. bishop of Springfield-Cape Girardeau, Mo., Dec. 5, 1973; archbishop of Boston, Jan. 11, 1984; cardinal May 25, 1985; titular church, St. Susanna. Archbishop of Boston. Curial membership:
Institutes of Consecrated Life and Societies of Apostolic Life, Evangelization of Peoples (congregations).

Lebrun Moratinos, Jose Ali: b. Mar. 19, 1919, Puerto Cabello, Venezuela; ord. priest Dec. 19, 1943; ord. titular bishop of Arado and auxiliary bishop of Maracaibo, Sept. 2, 1956; first bishop of Maracay, 1958-62; bishop of Valencia, 1962-72; titular archbishop of Voncaria and coadjutor archbishop of Caracas, Sept. 16, 1972; archbishop of Caracas, May 24, 1980; cardinal Feb. 2, 1983; titular church, St. Pancratius. Archbishop of Caracas. Curial membership:
Secretariat of State; Bishops, Seminaries and Institutes of Study (congregations).

Leger,* Paul Emile, S.S.: b. Apr. 26, 1904, Valleyfield, Quebec, Canada; ord. priest May 25, 1929; rector Canadian College, Rome, 1947; ord. archbishop of Montreal, Apr. 26, 1950; cardinal Jan. 12, 1953; titular church, St. Mary (of the Angels); resigned as archbishop of Montreal (Apr. 20, 1968) to become missionary to lepers; retired 1979. Archbishop emeritus of Montreal.

Lopez Trujillo, Alfonso: b. Nov. 8, 1935, Villahermosa, Colombia; ord. priest Nov. 13, 1960, in Rome; returned to Colombia, 1963; taught at major seminary; was pastoral coordinator for 1968 International Eucharistic Congress in Bogota; vicar general of Bogota, 1970-72; ord. titular bishop of Boseta (with personal title of archbishop), Mar. 25, 1971; auxiliary bishop of Bogota, 1971-72; secretary-general of CELAM, 1972-78; helped organize 1979 Puebla Conference in which Pope John Paul II participated; app. coadjutor archbishop of Medellin, 1978; archbishop of Medellin, Jan. 2, 1979; president of CELAM, 1979-83; cardinal Feb. 2, 1983; titular church, St. Prisca. Archbishop of Medellin. Curial membership:
Doctrine of the Faith, Divine Worship and Sacraments, Evangelization of Peoples (congregations); Social Communications, Migration and Tourism (councils), Latin America (commission).

Lorscheider, Aloisio, O.F.M.: b. Oct. 8, 1924, Picada Geraldo, Brazil; received in Franciscan Order, Feb. 1, 1942; ord. priest Aug. 22, 1948; professor of theology at the Antonianum, Rome, and director of Franciscan international house of studies; ord. bishop of Santo Angelo, Brazil, May 20, 1962; archbishop of Fortaleza, Mar. 26, 1973; president of CELAM, 1975-79; cardinal May 24, 1976; titular church, S. Pietro (in Montorio). Archbishop of Fortaleza. Curial membership:
Institutes of Consecrated Life and Societies of Apostolic Life (congregation); Dialogue with Non-Believers (council).

Lourdusamy, D. Simon: b. Feb. 5, 1924, Kalleri, India; ord. priest Dec. 21, 1951; ord. titular bishop of Sozusa and auxiliary of Bangalore, Aug. 22, 1962; titular archbishop of Filippi and coadjutor archbishop of Bangalore, Nov. 9, 1964; archbishop of Bangalore, 1968-71; associate secretary, 1971-73, and secretary, 1973-85, of Congregation for Evangelization of Peoples; cardinal May 25, 1985; deacon, St. Mary of Grace. Prefect of Congregation for Oriental Churches, 1985. Curial membership:
Evangelization of Peoples, Causes of Saints (congregations); Apostolic Signatura (tribunal); Christian Unity, Interreligious Dialogue, Family (councils).

Lubachivsky, Myroslav Ivan: b. June 24, 1914, Dolyna, Ukraine; ord. priest Sept. 21, 1938; began pastoral work in U.S., 1947; became U.S. citizen, 1952; ord. archbishop of Ukrainian-rite archeparchy of Philadelphia, Nov. 13, 1979; coadjutor archbishop of Lwow of the Ukrainians, Mar. 27, 1980; archbishop of Lwow and major archbishop of Ukrainians, Sept. 7, 1984; cardinal May 25, 1985; titular church, St. Sofia (a Via Boccea). Archbishop of Lwow, major archbishop of the Ukrainians (resides in Rome). Curial membership:
Oriental Churches (congregation); Dialogue with Non-Believers (council).

Lustiger, Jean-Marie: b. Sept. 17, 1926, Paris, France, of Polish-Jewish parents who emigrated to France after World War I; taken in by Catholic family in Orleans when his parents were deported during Nazi occupation (his mother died in 1943 at Auschwitz); convert to Catholicism, baptized Aug. 25, 1940; active in Young Christian Students during university days; ord. priest Apr. 17, 1954; ord. bishop of Orleans, Dec. 8, 1979; archbishop of Paris, Jan. 31, 1981; cardinal Feb. 2, 1983; titular church, Sts. Marcellinus and Peter. Archbishop of Paris, ordinary for Eastern-Rite faithful in France without ordinaries of their own. Curial membership:
Secretariat of State; Divine Worship and Sacraments, Bishops, Oriental Churches, Clergy, Institutes of Consecrated Life and Societies of Apostolic Life (congregations).

McCann,* Owen: b. June 29, 1907, Woodstock, South Africa; ord. priest Dec. 21, 1935; ord. titular bishop of Stettorio and vicar apostolic of Cape Town, May 18, 1950; first archbishop of Cape Town, Jan. 11, 1951 (retired Oct. 20, 1984); opponent of apartheid policy; cardinal Feb. 22, 1965; titular church, St. Praxedes. Archbishop emeritus of Cape Town.

Macharski, Franciszek: b. May 20, 1927, Cracow, Poland; ord. priest Apr. 2, 1950; engaged in pastoral work, 1950-56; continued theological studies in Fribourg, Switzerland, 1956-60; taught pastoral theology at the Faculty of Theology in Cracow; app. rector of archdiocesan seminary at Cracow, 1970; ord. archbishop of Cracow, Jan. 6, 1979, by Pope John Paul II; cardinal June 30, 1979; titular church, St. John at the Latin Gate. Archbishop of Cracow. Curial membership: Secretariat of State; Bishops, Clergy, Seminaries and Institutes of Study (congregations).

Malula, Joseph: b. Dec. 17, 1917, Kinshasa, Zaire; ord. priest June 9, 1946; ord. titular bishop of Attanaso and auxiliary bishop of Kinshasa, Sept. 20, 1959; archbishop of Kinshasa. July 7, 1964; cardinal Apr. 28, 1969; titular church, Ss. Protomartyrs (Via Aurelia Antica). Archbishop of Kinshasa.

Manning, Timothy: b. Nov. 15, 1909, Ballingeary, Ireland; completed studies for the priesthood at St. Patrick's Seminary, Menlo Park, Calif.; ord. priest (Los Angeles archdiocese) June 16, 1934; became American citizen, Jan. 14, 1944; ord. titular bishop of Lesvi and auxiliary of Los Angeles, Oct. 15, 1946; first bishop of Fresno, 1967-69; titular archbishop of Capri and coadjutor of Los Angeles, May 26, 1969; archbishop of Los Angeles, 1970-85; cardinal Mar. 5, 1973; titular church, Santa Lucia. Archbishop emeritus of Los Angeles. Curial membership: Institutes of Consecrated Life and Societies of Apostolic Life (congregation).

Margeot, Jean: b. Feb. 3, 1916, Quatre-Bornes, Mauritius; ord. priest Dec. 17, 1938; ord. bishop of Port Louis, May 4, 1969; cardinal June 28, 1988; titular church, St. Gabriel the Archangel all'Acqua Traversa. Bishop of Port Louis.

Martin,* Jacques: b. Aug. 26, 1908, Amiens, France; ord. priest, Oct. 14, 1934; ord. titular bishop of Neopoli di Palestrina, Feb. 11, 1964; archbishop, 1986; prefect of papal household, 1969-86; cardinal June 28, 1988; deacon, Sacred Heart of Christ the King. Prefect emeritus of Papal Household.

Martinez Somalo, Eduardo: b. Mar. 31, 1927, Bano de Rio Tobia, Spain; ord. priest Mar. 19, 1950; ord. titular bishop of Tagora, Dec. 13, 1975; archbishop; in secretariat of state from 1956; substitute (assistant) secretary of state, 1979-88; cardinal June 28, 1988; deacon, Most Holy Name of Jesus. Prefect of Congregation for Divine Worship and Sacraments, 1988.

Martini, Carlo Maria, S.J.: b. Feb. 15, 1927, Turin, Italy; entered Jesuits Sept. 25, 1944; ord. priest July 13, 1952, at the age of 25; biblical scholar; seminary professor, Chieti, Italy, 1958-61; professor and later rector, 1969-78, of Pontifical Biblical Institute; rector of Pontifical Gregorian University, 1978-79; author of theological, biblical and spiritual works; ord. archbishop of Milan, Jan. 6, 1980, by Pope John Paul II; cardinal Feb. 2, 1983; titular church, St. Cecilia. Archbishop of Milan. Curial membership: Secretariat of State; Doctrine of the Faith, Bishops, Divine Worship and Sacraments, Institutes of Consecrated Life and Societies of Apostolic Life, Seminaries and Institutes of Study, Evangelization of Peoples (congregations).

Marty,* Francois: b. May 18, 1904, Pachins, France; ord. priest June 28, 1930; ord. bishop of Saint-Flour, May 1, 1952; titular archbishop of Emesa and coadjutor archbishop of Rheims, Dec. 14, 1959; archbishop of Rheims, May 9, 1960; archbishop of Paris, 1968-81; cardinal Apr. 28, 1969; titular church, St. Louis of France. Archbishop emeritus of Paris.

Maurer,* Jose Clemente, C.SS.R.: b. Mar. 13, 1900, Puttlingen, Germany; ord. priest Sept. 19, 1925; assigned to Bolivian missions, 1926; became a Bolivian citizen; ord. titular bishop of Cea and auxiliary bishop of La Paz, Apr. 16, 1950; archbishop of Sucre, 1951-83; cardinal June 26, 1967; titular church, Most Holy Redeemer and St. Alphonsus. Archbishop emeritus of Sucre.

Mayer, Paul Augustin, O.S.B.: b. May 23, 1911, Altotting, West Germany; ord. priest Aug. 25, 1935; rector of St. Anselm's Univ., Rome, 1949-66; secretary of Congregation for Religious and Secular Institutes, 1972-84; ord. titular bishop of Satriano with personal title of archbishop, Feb. 13, 1972; pro-prefect of Congregations for Sacraments and Divine Worship, 1984; cardinal May 25, 1985; deacon, St. Anselm. Prefect of Congregation for Divine Worship and Sacraments, 1985-88. Curial membership: Secretariat of State; Doctrine of the Faith, Bishops, Institutes of Consecrated Life and Societies of Apostolic Life (congregations); Interpretation of Legislative Texts (council).

Meisner, Joachim: b. Dec. 25, 1933, Breslau, Silesia, Germany (present-day Wroclaw, Poland); ord. priest Dec. 22, 1962; regional director of Caritas; ord. titular bishop of Vina and auxiliary of apostolic administration of Erfurt-Meiningen, E. Germany, May 17, 1975; app. bishop of Berlin, Apr. 22, 1980, installed May 17, 1980 (resides in East Berlin); cardinal Feb. 2, 1983; titular church, St. Prudenziana. Bishop of Berlin. Curial membership: Divine Worship and Sacraments, Seminaries and Institutes of Study (congregations); Dialogue with Non-Believers, Justice and Peace (councils).

Munoz Vega,* Pablo, S. J.: b. May 23, 1903, Mira, Ecuador; ord. priest Apr. 15, 1933; ord. titular bishop of Ceramo and auxiliary bishop of Quito, Mar. 19, 1964; archbishop of Quito, 1967-85; cardinal Apr. 28, 1969; titular church, St. Robert Bellarmine. Archbishop emeritus of Quito.

Nasalli Rocca di Corneliano,* Mario: b. Aug. 12, 1903, Piacenza, Italy; ord. priest Apr. 9, 1927; ord. titular archbishop of Anzio, Apr. 20, 1969; cardinal Apr. 28, 1969; titular church, St. John the Baptist.

Neves, Lucas Moreira, O.P.: b. Sept. 16, 1925, Sao Joao del Rei, Brazil; ord. priest July 9, 1950; ord. titular bishop of Feradi maggiore and auxiliary of Sao Paulo, Aug. 26, 1967; assigned to Vatican, 1974; vice president of Pontifical Commission for Laity, 1974-79; secretary of Congregation for Bishops, 1979-87; archbishop; assigned titular see of Vescovia, Jan. 3, 1987; archbishop of Sao Salvador da Bahia, July 9, 1987; cardinal June 28, 1988; titular church, Sts. Boniface and Alexius. Archbishop of Sao Salvador da Bahia.

Nsubuga, Emmanuel Kiwanuka: b. Nov. 5, 1914, Kisule, Uganda; ord. priest Dec. 15, 1946; ord. bishop of Kampala, Oct. 30, 1966; cardinal May 24, 1976; titular church, S. Maria Nuova. Archbishop of Kampala. Curial membership:

Cardinals

Evangelization of Peoples (congregation).

Obando Bravo, Miguel, S.D.B.: b. Feb. 2, 1926, La Libertad, Nicaragua; ord. priest Aug. 10, 1958; ord. titular bishop of Puzia di Bizacena and auxiliary of Matagalpa, Mar. 31, 1968; archbishop of Managua, Feb. 16, 1970; cardinal May 25, 1985; titular church, St. John the Evangelist (a Spinaceta). Archbishop of Managua. Curial membership:
Clergy (congregation).

O'Connor, John J.: b. Jan. 15, 1920, Philadelphia, Pa.; ord. priest (Philadelphia archdiocese) Dec. 15, 1945; joined U.S. Navy and Marine Corps as a chaplain, 1952; overseas posts included service in South Korea and Vietnam; U.S. Navy chief of chaplains, 1975; retired from Navy June 1, 1979, with rank of rear admiral; ord. titular bishop of Curzola and auxiliary of military vicariate, May 27, 1979; bishop of Scranton, May 6, 1983; archbishop of New York, Jan. 26, 1984; cardinal May 25, 1985; titular church, Sts. John and Paul. Archbishop of New York. Curial membership:
Secretariat of State; Bishops (congregation); Social Communications, Health Care Workers (councils).

Oddi, Silvio: b. Nov. 14, 1910, Morfasso, Italy; ord. priest May 21, 1933; ord. titular archbishop of Mesembria, Sept. 27, 1953; served in Vatican diplomatic corps, 1953-69; apostolic delegate to Jerusalem, Palestine, Jordan and Cyprus, internuncio to the United Arab Republic, and nuncio to Belgium and Luxembourg; cardinal Apr. 28, 1969; titular church, St. Agatha of the Goths. Pontifical legate for Patriarchal Basilica of St. Francis of Assisi; prefect of Sacred Congregation for the Clergy, 1979-86. Curial membership:
Secretariat of State; Bishops, Oriental Churches, Causes of Saints, Evangelization of Peoples (congregations); Apostolic Signatura (tribunal); Interpretation of Legislative Texts (council); Patrimony of the Holy See (office).

O'Fiaich, Tomas: b. Nov. 3, 1923; Crossmaglen, Ireland; ord. priest July 6, 1948; lecturer, 1953, and professor, 1959, of modern history at Maynooth College; vice president, 1970, and president, 1974, of Maynooth; prolific author of scholarly works; recognized authority on early Irish Christianity; ord. archbishop of Armagh and primate of All Ireland, Oct. 2, 1977; pledged to work for the cause of peace in Northern Ireland; outspoken in his condemnation of violence; cardinal June 30, 1979; titular church, St. Patrick. Archbishop of Armagh, primate of All Ireland. Curial membership:
Secretariat of State; Bishops, Clergy, Seminaries and Institutes of Study, Evangelization of Peoples (congregations); Christian Unity (council).

Otunga, Maurice: b. January, 1923, Chebukwa, Kenya; son of pagan tribal chief; baptized 1935, at age of 12; ord. priest Oct. 3, 1950, at Rome; taught at Kisumu major seminary for three years; attaché in apostolic delegation at Mombasa, 1953-56; ord. titular bishop of Tacape and auxiliary of Kisumu, Feb. 25, 1957; bishop of Kisii, 1960-69; titular archbishop of Bomarzo and coadjutor of Nairobi, Nov. 15, 1969; archbishop of Nairobi, Oct. 24, 1971; cardinal Mar. 5, 1973; titular church, St. Gregory Barbarigo. Archbishop of Nairobi, military vicar of Kenya, 1981. Curial membership:
Divine Worship and Sacraments, Institutes of Consecrated Life and Societies of Apostolic Life, Evangelization of Peoples, Seminaries and Institutes of Study (congregations).

Padiyara, Anthony: b. Feb. 11, 1921, Manimala, India; ord. priest Dec. 19, 1945; ord. bishop of Ootacamund, Oct. 16, 1955; archbishop of Changanacherry (Syro-Malabar rite), June 14, 1970; archbishop of Ernakulam (Syro-Malabar rite), Apr. 23, 1985; cardinal June 28, 1988; titular church, St. Mary Queen of Peace (Monte Verde). Archbishop of Ernakulam of Syro-Malabar rite.

Palazzini, Pietro: b. May 19, 1912, Piobbico, Pesaro, Italy; ord. priest Dec. 6, 1934; assistant vice-rector of Pontifical Major Roman Seminary and vice-rector and bursar of Pontifical Roman Seminary for Juridical Studies; professor of moral theology at Lateran University; held various offices in Roman Curia; secretary of Congregation of Council (now Clergy), 1958-73; ord. titular archbishop of Caesarea in Cappadocia, Sept. 21, 1962; author of numerous works on moral theology and law; cardinal Mar. 5, 1973; titular church, St. Jerome. Prefect of Congregation for Causes of Saints, 1980-88. Curial membership:
Oriental Churches, Divine Worship and Sacraments, Clergy (congregations); Apostolic Signatura (tribunal); Interpretation of Legislative Texts (council).

Pappalardo, Salvatore: b. Sept. 23, 1918, Villafranca Sicula, Sicily; ord. priest Apr. 12, 1941; entered diplomatic service of secretariat of state, 1947; ord. titular archbishop of Miletus, Jan. 16, 1966; pro-nuncio in Indonesia, 1966-69; president of Pontifical Ecclesiastical Academy, 1969-70; archbishop of Palermo, Oct. 17, 1970; cardinal Mar. 5, 1973; titular church, St. Mary Odigitria of the Sicilians. Archbishop of Palermo. Curial membership:
Secretariat of State; Bishops, Oriental Churches, Clergy, Seminaries and Institutes of Study (congregations).

Paskai, Laszlo, O.F.M.: b. May 8, 1927, Szeged, Hungary; ord. priest Mar. 3, 1951; ord. titular bishop of Bavagaliana and apostolic administrator of Vezprem, Apr. 5, 1978; bishop of Vezprem Mar. 31, 1979; coadjutor archbishop of Kalocsa, Apr. 5, 1982; archbishop of Esztergom, Mar. 3, 1987; cardinal June 28, 1988; titular church, St. Theresa (al Corso d'Italia). Archbishop of Esztergom and Primate of Hungary.

Paupini,* Giuseppe: b. Feb. 25, 1907, Mondavio, Italy; ord. priest Mar. 19, 1930; ord. titular archbishop of Sebastopolis in Abasgia, Feb. 26, 1956; served in Vatican diplomatic corps, 1956-69; internuncio to Iran, 1956-57; nuncio to Guatemala and El Salvador, 1957-58, nuncio to Colombia, 1959-69; cardinal Apr. 28, 1969; titular church, All Saints Church; major penitentiary 1973-84.

Pavan,* Pietro: b. Aug. 30, 1903, Treviso, Italy; ord. priest July 8, 1928, expert at Vatican Council II; rector of Lateran University, 1969-74; chief contributor to drafting of encyclicals *Mater et*

Magistra and *Pacem in Terris:* cardinal May 25, 1985, without episcopal ordination; deacon, St. Francis of Paola (ai Monti).

Picachy, Lawrence Trevor, S.J.: b. Aug. 7, 1916, Lebong, India; ord. priest Nov. 21, 1947; dean, 1950-54, and then rector, 1954-60, of St. Francis Xavier University College, Calcutta; ord. bishop of Jamshedpur, Sept. 9, 1962; archbishop of Calcutta, May 29, 1969 (resigned 1986); cardinal May 24, 1976; titular church, Sacred Heart of Mary. Archbishop emeritus of Calcutta. Curial membership:

Divine Worship and Sacraments (congregation).

Pimenta, Simon Ignatius: b. Mar. 1, 1920, Marol, India; ord. priest Dec. 21, 1949; ord. titular bishop of Bocconia and auxiliary of Bombay, June 29, 1971; coadjutor archbishop of Bombay, Feb. 26, 1977; archbishop of Bombay, Sept. 11, 1978; cardinal June 28, 1988; titular church, Mary, Queen of the World (a torre Spaccata). Archbishop of Bombay.

Piovanelli, Silvano: b. Feb. 21, 1924, Ronta di Mugello, Italy; ord. priest July 13, 1947; ord. titular bishop of Tubune di Mauretania and auxiliary of Florence, June 24, 1982; archbishop of Florence, Mar. 18, 1983; cardinal May 25, 1985; titular church, St. Mary of Graces (Via Trionfale). Archbishop of Florence. Curial membership:

Seminaries and Institutes of Study (congregation); Dialogue with Non-Believers (council).

Pironio, Eduardo: b. Dec. 3, 1920, Nueve de Julio, Argentina; ord. priest Dec. 5, 1943; taught theology at Pius XII Seminary of Mercedes diocese, 1944-59; vicar general of diocese 1958-60; attended Second Vatican Council as *peritus*; ord. titular bishop of Ceciri, May 31, 1964; apostolic administrator of diocese of Avellaneda, 1967-72; secretary general, 1967-72, and president, 1973-75, of CELAM; bishop of Mar del Plata, 1972-75; titular archbishop of Thiges and pro-prefect of Congregation for Religious and Secular Institutes, Sept. 20, 1975; cardinal May 24, 1976; deacon, Sts. Cosmas and Damian; transferred to order of cardinal priests, June 22, 1987. Prefect of the Congregation for Religious and Secular Institutes, 1976-84. President of Pontifical Council for the Laity, 1984, and Council for Apostolate of Health Care Workers, 1985. Curial membership:

Secretariat of State; Bishops, Divine Worship and Sacraments, Seminaries and Institutes of Study, Oriental Churches (congregations); Latin America (commission); Interpretation of Legislative Texts (council).

Poletti, Ugo: b. Apr. 19, 1914, Omegna, Italy; ord. priest June 29, 1938; served in various diocesan offices at Novara; ord. titular bishop of Medeli and auxiliary of Novaro, Sept. 14, 1958; president of Pontifical Mission Aid Society for Italy, 1964-67; archbishop of Spoleto, 1967-69; titular archbishop of Cittanova, 1969; served as second viceregent of Rome, 1969-72; pro-vicar general of Rome, 1972; cardinal Mar. 5, 1973; titular church, Sts. Ambrose and Charles. Vicar general of Rome, 1973; archpriest of Patriarchal Lateran Archbasilica, 1973; grand chancellor of Lateran University. Curial membership:

Secretariat of State; Bishops, Clergy, Divine Worship and Sacraments, Oriental Churches, Institutes of Consecrated Life and Societies of Apostolic Life (congregations); Laity (council).

Poupard, Paul: b. Aug. 30, 1930, Bouzille, France; ord. priest Dec. 18, 1954; scholar; author of a number of works; ord. titular bishop of Usula and auxiliary of Paris, Apr. 6, 1979; archbishop and pro-president of the Secretariat for Non-Believers, 1980; cardinal May 25, 1985; deacon, St. Eugene. President of Secretariat for Non-Believers (Council for Dialogue with Non-Believers), 1985; president of executive committee of Pontifical Council for Culture, 1982. Curial membership:

Divine Worship and Sacraments, Evangelization of Peoples, Seminaries and Institutes of Study (congregations); Interreligious Dialogue (council).

Primatesta, Raul Francisco: b. Apr. 14, 1919, Capilla del Senor, Argentina; ord. priest Oct. 25, 1942, at Rome; taught at minor and major seminaries of La Plata; contributed to several theology reviews; ord. titular bishop of Tanais and auxiliary of La Plata, Aug. 15, 1957; bishop of San Rafael, 1961-65; archbishop of Cordoba, Feb. 16, 1965; cardinal Mar. 5, 1973; titular church, St. Mary Sorrowful Virgin. Archbishop of Cordoba, Argentina. Curial membership:

Clergy, Institutes of Consecrated Life and Societies of Apostolic Life, Divine Worship and Sacraments, Evangelization of Peoples (congregations).

Ratzinger, Joseph: b. Apr. 16, 1927, Marktl am Inn, Germany; ord. priest June 29, 1951; professor of dogmatic theology at University of Regensburg, 1969-77; member of International Theological Commission, 1969-80; ord. archbishop of Munich-Freising, May 28, 1977 (resigned Feb. 15, 1982); cardinal June 27, 1977; titular church, St. Mary of Consolation (in Tiburtina). Prefect of Congregation for Doctrine of the Faith, 1981; president of Biblical and Theological Commissions. Curial membership:

Secretariat of State; Bishops, Divine Worship and Sacraments, Oriental Churches, Clergy, Evangelization of Peoples, Seminaries and Institutes of Study (congregations); Christian Unity (council).

Razafimahatratra, Victor, S.J.: b. Sept. 8, 1921, Ambanitsilena-Ranomasina, Madagascar; entered Society of Jesus, 1945; ord. priest July 28, 1956; rector of Fianarantsoa Minor Seminary, 1960-63; superior of Jesuit residence at Ambositra, 1963-69; rector of Tananarive Major Seminary, 1969-71; ord. bishop of Farafangana, Apr. 18, 1971; archbishop of Tananarive, Apr. 10, 1976; cardinal May 24, 1976; titular church, Holy Cross in Jerusalem. Archbishop of Tananarive. Curial membership:

Evangelization of Peoples (congregation).

Revollo Bravo, Mario: b. June 15, 1919, Genoa, Italy; ord. priest Oct. 31, 1943; ord. titular bishop of Tinisa di Numidia and auxiliary of Bogota, Colombia, Dec. 2, 1973; archbishop of Nueva Pamplona, Feb. 28, 1978; archbishop of Bogota, June 25, 1984; cardinal June 28, 1988; titular church, St. Bartholomew (all' Isolo). Archbishop of Bogota.

Ribeiro, Antonio: b. May 21, 1928, Gandarela de

Basto, Portugal; ord. priest July 5, 1953; professor of fundamental theology at major seminary at Braga; ord. titular bishop of Tigillava and auxiliary of Braga, Sept. 17, 1967; patriarch of Lisbon, May 10, 1971; cardinal Mar. 5, 1973; titular church, St. Anthony of Padua (in Rome). Patriarch of Lisbon, military vicar. Curial membership: Clergy, Seminaries and Institutes of Study (congregations); Social Communications (council).

Righi-Lambertini,* Egano: b. Feb. 22, 1906, Casalecchio di Reno, Italy; ord. priest May 25, 1929; entered service of secretariat of state, 1939; served in diplomatic missions in France (1949-54), Costa Rica (1955), England (1955-57); first apostolic delegate to Korea, 1957-60; ord. titular archbishop of Doclea, Oct. 28, 1960; apostolic nuncio in Lebanon, 1960-63, Chile, 1963-67, Italy, 1967-69; France, 1969-79; while nuncio in France he also served as special envoy at the Council of Europe, 1974-79; cardinal June 30, 1979; deacon, St. John Bosco in Via Tuscolana. Honorary president of Commission on Sacred Art in Italy.

Rossi, Agnelo: b. May 4, 1913, Joaquim Egidio, Brazil; ord. priest Mar. 27, 1937; ord. bishop of Barra do Pirai, Apr. 15, 1956; archbishop of Ribeirao Preto, 1962-64; archbishop of Sao Paulo, 1964-70; cardinal Feb. 22, 1965; titular church, Mother of God; titular bishop of suburban see of Sabina-Poggia Mirteto June 25, 1984, when he entered the order of cardinal bishops, and of Ostia, Dec. 19, 1986, when he became dean of the college of cardinals; prefect of Congregation for Evangelization of Peoples, 1970-84. President of Administration of Patrimony of the Holy See, 1984; Dean of the College of Cardinals, 1986. Curial membership: Secretariat of State; Clergy, Doctrine of Faith, Bishops, Oriental Churches, Causes of Saints, Institutes of Consecrated Life and Societies of Apostolic Life, Seminaries and Institutes of Study (congregations).

Rossi, Opilio: b. May 14, 1910, New York, N.Y.; holds Italian citizenship; ord. priest for diocese of Piacenza, Italy, Mar. 11, 1933; served in nunciatures in Belgium, The Netherlands and Germany, 1938-53; ord. titular archbishop of Ancyra, Dec. 27, 1953; nuncio in Ecuador, 1953-59, Chile, 1959-61, Austria, 1961-76; cardinal May 24, 1976; deacon; transferred to order of cardinal priests, June 22, 1987; titular church, St. Lawrence (in Lucina). President of: Commission for the Sanctuaries of Pompeii, Loreto and Bari, 1984; Permanent Committee for International Eucharistic Congresses, 1983. Curial membership: Secretariat of State; Bishops, Oriental Churches, Divine Worship and Sacraments, Institutes of Consecrated Life and Societies of Apostolic Life, Clergy, Causes of Saints, Evangelization of Peoples (congregations); Apostolic Signatura (tribunal); Laity, Interpretation of Legislative Texts (councils).

Rubin, Wladyslaw: b. Sept. 20, 1917, Toki, Poland; seminary studies interrupted during World War II when he was arrested and deported to labor camp; completed studies at St. Joseph's University in Beirut; ord. priest in Beirut June 30, 1946, and served Polish community there; sent to Rome for further studies, 1949; chaplain for Polish refugees in Italy, 1953-58; rector of Polish College in Rome, 1959-64; ord. titular bishop of Serta, primate of Poland's delegate for emigration and auxiliary of Gniezno, Nov. 29, 1964; established contact with Polish emigrants throughout the world; secretary general of Synod of Bishops, 1967-79; cardinal June 30, 1979; deacon, St. Mary in Via Lata. Prefect of Congregation for Oriental Churches, 1980-85.

Rugambwa, Laurean: b. July 12, 1912, Bukongo, Tanzania; ord. priest Dec. 12, 1943; ord. titular bishop of Febiano and vicar apostolic of Lower Kagera, Feb. 10, 1952; bishop of Rutabo, Mar. 25, 1953; cardinal Mar. 28, 1960; titular church, St. Francis of Assisi (a Ripa Grande); bishop of Bukoba, 1960-68. Archbishop of Dar-es-Salaam, 1968. Curial membership: Causes of Saints (congregation).

Sabattani, Aurelio: b. Oct. 18, 1912, Casal Fiumanese, Italy; ord. priest July 26, 1935; jurist; served in various assignments in his native diocese of Imola and as judge and later an official of the regional ecclesiastical tribunal of Bologna; called to Rome in 1955 as prelate auditor of the Roman Rota; ord. titular archbishop of Justinian Prima, July 25, 1965; prelate of Loreto, 1965-71; secretary of Supreme Tribunal of Apostolic Signatura and consultor of Secretariat of State, 1971; pro-prefect of Apostolic Signatura, 1982-83; cardinal Feb. 2, 1983; deacon, St. Apollinaris. Prefect of Apostolic Signatura, 1983-88, archpriest of Patriarchal Vatican Basilica, 1983. Curial membership: Secretariat of State; Bishops, Oriental Churches (congregations); Interpretation of Legislative Texts (council).

Salazar Lopez, Jose: b. Jan. 12, 1910, Ameca, Mexico; ord. priest May 26, 1934, in Rome; instrumental in building of new seminary at Guadalajara, the largest in Mexico; vice-rector and later rector of seminary; ord. titular bishop of Prusiade and coadjutor bishop of Zamora, Aug. 20, 1961; bishop of Zamora, 1967-70; archbishop of Guadalajara, 1970-87; cardinal Mar. 5, 1973; titular church, Santa Emerentia. Archbishop emeritus of Guadalajara. Curial membership: Divine Worship and Sacraments (congregation).

Sales, Eugenio de Araujo: b. Nov. 8, 1920, Acari, Brazil; ord. priest Nov. 21, 1943; ord. titular bishop of Tibica and auxiliary bishop of Natal, Aug. 15, 1954; archbishop of Sao Salvador, 1968-71; cardinal Apr. 28, 1969; titular church, St. Gregory VII. Archbishop of Rio de Janeiro (1971), ordinary for Eastern Rite Catholics in Brazil without ordinaries of their own rites. Curial membership: Secretariat of State; Bishops, Oriental Churches, Divine Worship and Sacraments, Clergy, Evangelization of Peoples, Seminaries and Institutes of Study (congregations); Social Communications, Culture (councils).

Santos, Alexandre Jose Maria dos, O.F.M.: b. Mar. 18, 1924, Mavila, Mozambique; ord. priest July 25, 1953; first black priest; ord. archbishop of Maputo, Mar. 9, 1975; cardinal June 28, 1988; titular church, St. Frumentius (ai Prati Fiscali). Archbishop of Maputo.

Satowaki,* Joseph Asajiro: b. Feb. 1, 1904, Shittsu, Japan; ord. priest Dec. 17, 1932; served in various pastoral capacities in Nagasaki archdiocese after his ordination; apostolic administrator of Taiwan (then a Japanese possession), 1941-45; director of Nagasaki minor seminary, 1945-57; vicar general of Nagasaki, 1945; ord. first bishop of Kagoshima, May 3, 1955; archbishop of Nagasaki, Dec. 19, 1968; cardinal June 30, 1979; titular church, St. Mary of Peace. Archbishop of Nagasaki.

Scherer,* Alfred Vicente: b. Feb. 5, 1903, Bom Principio, Brazil; ord. priest Apr. 3, 1926; ord. archbishop of Porto Alegre, Feb. 23, 1947 (retired Aug. 29, 1981); cardinal Apr. 28, 1969; titular church, Our Lady of La Salette. Archbishop emeritus of Porto Alegre, Brazil.

Sensi,* Giuseppe Maria: b. May 27, 1907, Cosenza, Italy; ord. priest Dec. 21, 1929; entered Vatican diplomatic service; served in nunciatures in Hungary, Switzerland, Belgium and Czechoslovakia, 1934-49; ord. titular archbishop of Sardes, July 24, 1955; apostolic nuncio to Costa Rica, 1955; apostolic delegate to Jerusalem, 1956-62; nuncio to Ireland, 1962-67, and Portugal, 1967-76; cardinal deacon May 24, 1976; transferred to order of cardinal priests, June 22, 1987; titular church, Queen of Apostles.

Silva Henriquez,* Raul, S.D.B.: b. Sept. 27, 1907, Talca, Chile; ord. priest July 3, 1938; ord. bishop of Valparaiso, Nov. 29, 1959; archbishop of Santiago de Chile, 1961-83; cardinal Mar. 19, 1962; titular church, St. Bernard (alle Terme). Archbishop emeritus of Santiago de Chile.

Simonis, Adrianus J.: b. Nov. 26, 1931, Lisse, Netherlands; ord. priest June 15, 1957; ord. bishop of Rotterdam, Mar. 20, 1971; coadjutor archbishop of Utrecht, July 8, 1983; archbishop of Utrecht, Dec. 3, 1983; cardinal May 25, 1985; titular church, St. Clement. Archbishop of Utrecht. Curial membership:
Divine Worship and Sacraments (congregation); Christian Unity (council).

Silvestrini, Achille: b. Oct. 25, 1923, Brisighella, Italy; ord. priest July 13, 1946; official in Secretariat of State from 1953; ord. titular bishop of Novaliciana, May 27, 1979; archbishop; undersecretary, 1973-79, and secretary, 1979-88, of the Council for Public Affairs of the Church (now the section for Relations with States); cardinal June 28, 1988; deacon, St. Benedict Outside St. Paul's Gate. Prefect of Apostolic Signatura, 1988.

Sin, Jaime L.: b. Aug. 31, 1928, New Washington, Philippines; ord. priest Apr. 3, 1954; diocesan missionary in Capiz, 1954-57; app. first rector of the St. Pius X Seminary, Roxas City, 1957; ord. titular bishop of Obba and auxiliary bishop of Jaro, Mar. 18, 1967; apostolic administrator of archdiocese of Jaro, June 20, 1970; titular archbishop of Massa Lubrense and coadjutor archbishop of Jaro, Jan. 15, 1972; archbishop of Jaro, Oct. 8, 1972; archbishop of Manila, Jan. 21, 1974; cardinal May 24, 1976; titular church, S. Maria (ai Monti). Archbishop of Manila. Curial membership:
Secretariat of State; Bishops, Divine Worship and Sacraments, Clergy, Evangelization of Peoples, Seminaries and Institutes of Study (congregations); Social Communications (council); Economic Affairs (office).

Siri,* Giuseppe: b. May 20, 1906, Genoa, Italy; ord. priest Sept. 22, 1928; ord. titular bishop of Liviade and auxiliary bishop of Genoa, May 7, 1944; archbishop of Genoa (title changed to Genoa-Bobbio, 1986), 1946-87; cardinal Jan. 12, 1953; titular church, St. Mary (della Vittoria). Archbishop emeritus of Genoa-Bobbio.

Sladkevicius, Vincentas: b. Aug. 20, 1920, Zasliai, Lithuania; ord. priest Mar. 25, 1944; ord. titular bishop of Abora and auxiliary of Kaisiadorys, Dec. 25, 1957, but was not permitted to exercise his office; under house arrest 1959-82; apostolic administrator of Kaisiadorys, 1982; cardinal June 28, 1988; titular church, Holy Spirit (alla Ferratella). Apostolic Administrator of Kaisiadorys.

Stickler, Alfons, S.D.B.: b. Aug. 23, 1910, Neunkirchen, Austria; ord. priest Mar. 27, 1937; director of the Vatican Library, 1971; ord. titular bishop of Bolsena, Nov. 1, 1983, with personal title of archbishop; Pro-Librarian and Pro-Archivist, 1984; cardinal May 25, 1985; deacon, St. George (in Valabro). Librarian and Archivist of the Holy Roman Church, 1985-88. Curial membership:
Institutes of Consecrated Life and Societies of Apostolic Life, Causes of Saints (congregations); Apostolic Signatura (tribunal); Interpretation of Legislative Texts, Social Communications (councils); Patrimony of the Holy See (office).

Suenens,* Leo Josef: b. July 16, 1904, Brussels, Belgium; ord. priest Sept. 4, 1927; ord. titular bishop of Isinda, Dec. 16, 1945; auxiliary bishop of Mechelen, 1945-61; archbishop of Mechelen-Brussels, 1961-79; cardinal Mar. 19, 1962; titular church, St. Peter in Chains. Archbishop emeritus of Mechelen-Brussels.

Suquia Goicoechea, Angel: b. Oct. 2, 1916, Zaldivia, Spain; ord. priest July 7, 1940; ord. bishop of Almeria, July 16, 1966; bishop of Malaga, 1969-73; archbishop of Santiago de Compostela, 1973-83; archbishop of Madrid, Apr. 12, 1983; cardinal May 25, 1985; titular church, Great Mother of God. Archbishop of Madrid. Curial membership:
Secretariat of State; Bishops, Seminaries and Institutes of Study (congregations).

Szoka, Edmund C.: b. Sept. 14, 1927, Grand Rapids, Mich.; ord. priest (Marquette diocese), June 5, 1954; ord. first bishop of Gaylord, Mich., July 20, 1971; app. archbishop of Detroit, installed May 17, 1981; cardinal June 28, 1988; titular church, Sts. Andrew and Gregory (al Monte Celio). Archbishop of Detroit.

Taofinu'u, Pio, S.M.: b. Dec. 9, 1923, Falealupo, W. Samoa; ord. priest Dec. 8, 1954; joined Society of Mary, 1955; ord. bishop of Apia (Samoa and Tokelau), May 29, 1968, the first Polynesian bishop; cardinal Mar. 5, 1973; titular church, St. Humphrey. Archbishop of Samoa-Apia and Tokelau (Sept. 10, 1982). Curial membership:
Causes of Saints (congregation).

Thiandoum, Hyacinthe: b. Feb. 2, 1921, Poponguine, Senegal; ord. priest Apr. 18, 1949; studied at Gregorian University, Rome, 1951-53;

returned to Senegal, 1953; ord. archbishop of Dakar, May 20, 1962; cardinal May 24, 1976; titular church, S. Maria (del Popolo). Archbishop of Dakar. Curial membership:
Clergy, Institutes of Consecrecated Life and Societies of Apostolic Life (congregations); Social Communications (council).

Tomasek,* Frantisek: b. June 30, 1899, Studenka, Moravia, Czechoslovakia; ord. priest July 5, 1922; professor of pedagogy and catechetics at the theology faculty of Olomouc, 1934-39; resumed academic activity after liberation in 1945; author, *Catechism of the Catholic Religion;* ord. titular bishop of Butus and auxiliary of Olomouc, Oct. 13, 1949; only Czech bishop to attend Second Vatican Council; apostolic administrator of Prague, Feb. 18, 1965; cardinal May 24, 1976 (*in pectore*); solemnly proclaimed at June 27, 1977, consistory; titular church, Sts. Vitalis, Valeria, Gervase and Protase. Archbishop of Prague, 1978. Curial membership:
Clergy (congregation).

Tomko, Jozef: b. Mar. 11, 1924, Udavske, Slovakia; ord. priest Mar. 12, 1949; ord. titular archbishop of Doclea, Sept. 15, 1979; secretary-general of the Synod of Bishops, 1979-85; cardinal May 25, 1985; deacon, Jesus the Good Shepherd (alla Montagnola). Prefect of the Congregation for the Evangelization of Peoples, 1985. Curial membership:
Secretariat of State; Bishops, Institutes of Consecrated Life and Societies of Apostolic Life; Seminaries and Institutes of Study (congregations); Christian Unity, Interreligious Dialogue, Dialogue with Non-Believers, Interpretation of Legislative Texts (councils).

Trinh Van Can, Joseph Marie: b. Mar. 19, 1921, Trac But, Vietnam; ord. priest Dec. 3, 1949; held various offices in Hanoi archdiocese; ord. titular bishop of Ela (with personal title of archbishop) and coadjutor archbishop of Hanoi, June 2, 1963; archbishop of Hanoi, Nov. 27, 1978; cardinal June 30, 1979; titular church, St. Mary in Via. Archbishop of Hanoi. Curial membership:
Evangelization of Peoples (congregation).

Tumi, Christian Wiyghan: b. Oct. 15, 1930, Kikaikelaki, Cameroon; ord. priest Apr. 17, 1966; ord. bishop of Yagoua, Jan. 6, 1980; coadjutor archbishop of Garoua, Nov. 19, 1982; archbishop of Garoua, Mar. 17, 1984; cardinal June 28, 1988; titular church, Martyrs of Uganda (a Poggio Ameno). Archbishop of Garoua.

Tzadua, Paulos: b. Aug. 25, 1921, Addifini, Ethiopia; ord. priest Mar. 12, 1944; ord. titular bishop of Abila di Palestina and auxiliary of Addis Ababa, May 20, 1973; archbishop of Addis Ababa, Feb. 24, 1977; cardinal May 25, 1985; titular church, Most Holy Name of Mary (a Via Latina). Archbishop of Addis Ababa. Curial membership:
Oriental Churches (congregation); Dialogue with Non-Believers (council).

Ursi,* Corrado: b. July 26, 1908, Andria, Italy; ord. priest July 25, 1931; vice-rector and later rector of the Pontifical Regional Seminary of Molfetta, 1931-51; ord. bishop of Nardo, Sept. 30, 1951; archbishop of Acerenza, Nov. 30, 1961; archbishop of Naples, May 23, 1966 (resigned May 9, 1987); cardinal June 26, 1967; titular church, St. Callistus. Archbishop emeritus of Naples. Curial membership:
Seminaries and Institutes of Study (congregation).

Vachon, Louis-Albert; b. Feb. 4, 1912, Saint-Frederic, Que., Canada; ord. priest June 11, 1938; ord. titular bishop of Mesarfelta and auxiliary of Quebec, May 14, 1977; archbishop of Quebec, Mar. 20, 1981; cardinal May 25, 1985; titular church, St. Paul of the Cross (a Corviale). Archbishop of Quebec. Curial membership:
Clergy (congregation).

Vaivods,* Julijans: b. Aug. 18, 1895, Vorkova, Latvia; ord. priest Apr. 7, 1918; chaplain of various schools, 1918-23; wrote and published catechetical books and theatrical works for youth; vicar general of Liepaja, 1944; apostolic activity curtailed by political situation, he resumed writing; publications denounced as hostile to regime, he was tried and sentenced to two years' exile, 1958-60; released early but not permitted to exercise his priestly ministry for a time; vicar general of Riga, 1962; attended Vatican II, 1964; ord. titular bishop of Macriana Maior and apostolic administrator of archdiocese of Riga and diocese of Liepaja, Nov. 18, 1964, in Rome; cardinal Feb. 2, 1983; titular church, Forty Crowned Martyrs. Apostolic administrator of Riga and Liepaja.

Vidal, Ricardo J.: b. Feb. 6, 1931, Magpoc, Philippines; ord. priest Mar. 17, 1956; ord. titular bishop of Claterna and coadjutor of Melalos, Nov. 30, 1971; archbishop of Lipa, 1973; coadjutor archbishop of Cebu, Apr. 13, 1981; archbishop of Cebu, Aug. 24, 1982; cardinal May 25, 1985; titular church, Sts. Peter and Paul (in Via Ostiensi). Archbishop of Cebu. Curial membership:
Divine Worship and Sacraments (congregation); Health Care Workers (council).

Wetter, Friedrich: b. Feb. 20, 1928, Landau, West Germany; ord. priest Oct. 10, 1953; ord. bishop of Speyer, June 29, 1968; archbishop of Munich and Freising, Oct. 28, 1982; cardinal May 25, 1985; titular church, St. Stephen (al Monte Celio). Archbishop of Munich and Freising. Curial membership:
Evangelization of Peoples (congregation).

Willebrands, Johannes: b. Sept. 4, 1909, Bovenkarspel, The Netherlands; ord. priest May 26, 1934; ord. titular bishop of Mauriana, June 28, 1964; secretary of Secretariat for Christian Unity, 1960-69; cardinal Apr. 28, 1969; titular church, St. Sebastian (alle Catacombe); archbishop of Utrecht, 1975-83. President of Council for Christian Unity, 1969. Camerlengo of the College of Cardinals, 1988. Curial membership:
Doctrine of Faith, Divine Worship and Sacraments, Oriental Churches, Seminaries and Institutes of Study. Evangelization of Peoples (congregations).

Williams, Thomas Stafford: b. Mar. 20, 1930, Wellington, New Zealand; ord. priest Dec. 20, 1959, in Rome; studied in Ireland after ordination, receiving degree in social sciences; served in various pastoral assignments on his return to New Zealand; missionary in Western Samoa to 1976; ord. archbishop of Wellington, New Zealand, Dec. 20, 1979; cardinal Feb. 2, 1983; titular church, Jesus the Divine Teacher at Pineda Sacchetti. Archbishop of Wellington. Curial membership: Divine Worship and Sacraments, Evangelization of Peoples (congregations); Interreligious Dialogue (council).

Wu Cheng-Chung, John Baptist: b. Mar. 26, 1925, Shui-Tsai, mainland China; ord. priest July 6, 1952; ord. bishop of Hong Kong, July 25, 1975; cardinal June 28, 1988; titular church, Blessed Virgin Mary of Mount Carmel (a Mostacciano). Bishop of Hong Kong.

Yago, Bernard: b. July, 1916, Pass, Ivory Coast; ord. priest May 1, 1947; ord. archbishop of Abidjan, May 8, 1960, by Pope John XXIII in St. Peter's Basilica, becoming the first native member of the hierarchy of Ivory Coast; cardinal Feb. 2, 1983; titular church, St. Chrysogonus. Archbishop of Abidjan. Curial membership: Evangelization of Peoples (congregation); Christian Unity (council).

Zoungrana, Paul, P.A.: b. Sept. 3, 1917, Ouagadougou, Upper Volta (now Burkina Faso); ord. priest May 2, 1942, in the Missionaries of Africa; ord. archbishop of Ouagadougou at St. Peter's Basilica by John XXIII, May 8, 1960; cardinal Feb. 22, 1965; titular church, St. Camillus de Lellis. Archbishop of Ouagadougou. Curial membership: Divine Worship and Sacraments, Institutes of Consecrated Life and Societies of Apostolic Life, Evangelization of Peoples (congregations); Health Care Workers (council).

CATEGORIES OF CARDINALS

(As of Aug. 10, 1988.)

Information below includes categories of cardinals and dates of consistories at which they were created. Seniority or precedence usually depends on order of elevation.

Two of these cardinals were named by Pius XII (consistory of Jan. 12, 1953); 5 by John XXIII (consistories of Dec. 15, 1958, Mar. 28, 1960, and Mar. 19, 1962); 66 by Paul VI (consistories of Feb. 22, 1965, June 26, 1967, Apr. 28, 1969, Mar. 5, 1973, May 24, 1976, and June 27, 1977); 84 by John Paul II (consistories of June 30, 1979, Feb. 2, 1983, May 25, 1985, June 28, 1988).

Order of Bishops

Titular Bishops of Suburban Sees: Agnelo Rossi, dean (Feb. 22, 1965); Sebastiano Baggio, sub-dean (Apr. 28, 1969); Francesco Carpino (June 26, 1967); Paolo Bertoli (Apr. 28, 1969); Bernardin Gantin (June 27, 1977); Agostino Casaroli (June 30, 1979).

Eastern Rite Patriarch: Antoine Pierre Khoraiche (Feb. 2, 1983).

Order of Priests

1953 (Jan. 12): Giuseppe Siri, Paul Emile Leger, S.S.

1958 (Dec. 15): Franz Koenig.

1960 (Mar. 28): Laurean Rugambwa.

1962 (Mar. 19): Juan Landazuri Ricketts, O.F.M., Raul Silva Henriquez, S.D.B., Leo Josef Suenens.

1965 (Feb. 22): Thomas B. Cooray, Owen McCann, Leon-Etienne Duval, Paul Zoungrana, Giovanni Colombo.

1967 (June 26): Gabriel Garrone, Maximilien de Furstenberg, Jose Clemente Maurer, C.SS.R., John J. Krol, Corrado Ursi, Justin Darmojuwono.

1969 (Apr. 28): Alfredo Vicente Scherer, Gordon J. Gray, Silvio Oddi, Giuseppe Paupini, Francois Marty; George Flahiff, Paul Gouyon, Vicente Enrique y Tarancon, Joseph Malula, Pablo Muñoz Vega, S.J.; John J. Carberry, Stephan Sou Hwan Kim, Eugenio de Araujo Sales, Johannes Willebrands, Mario Nasalli Rocca di Corneliano, Sergio Guerri.

1973 (Mar. 5): Antonio Ribeiro, Joseph Cordeiro, Pietro Palazzini, Luis Aponte Martinez, Raul Francisco Primatesta, Salvatore Pappalardo, Ferdinando Giuseppe Antonelli, Marcelo Gonzalez Martin, Ugo Poletti, Timothy Manning, Maurice Otunga, Jose Salazar Lopez, Paulo Evaristo Arns, James Darcy Freeman, Narciso Jubany Arnau, Pio Taofinu'u.

1976 (May 24): Octavio Beras Rojas, Opilio Rossi, Giuseppe Maria Sensi, Juan Carlos Aramburu, Corrado Bafile, Hyacinthe Thiandoum, Emmanuel Nsubuga, Lawrence Trevor Picachy, Jaime L. Sin, William W. Baum, Aloisio Lorscheider, Eduardo Pironio, George Basil Hume, O.S.B., Victor Razafimahatratra, Frantisek Tomasek, Dominic Ekandem.

1977 (June 27): Joseph Ratzinger, Mario Luigi Ciappi.

1979 (June 30): Marco Ce, Joseph Marie Trinh Van Can, Ernesto Corripio Ahumada, Joseph Asajiro Satowaki, Roger Etchegaray, Anastasio Alberto Ballestrero, O.C.D., Tomas O'Fiaich, Gerald Emmett Carter, Franciszek Macharski.

1983 (Feb. 2): Bernard Yago, Franjo Kuharic, Jose Ali Lebrun Moratinos, Joseph L. Bernardin, Michael Michai Kitbunchu, Alexandre do Nascimento, Alfonso Lopez Trujillo, Godfried Danneels, Thomas Stafford Williams, Carlo Maria Martini, Jean-Marie Lustiger, Jozef Glemp, Julijans Vaivods, Joachim Meisner.

1985 (May 25): Juan Francisco Fresno Larrain, Miguel Obando Bravo, Angel Suquia Goicoechea, Ricardo Vidal, Henryk Roman Gulbinowicz, Paulus Tzadua, Myroslav Ivan Lubachivsky, Louis-Albert Vachon, Albert Decourtray, Friedrich Wetter, Silvano Piovanelli, Adrianus J. Simonis, Bernard F. Law, John J. O'Connor, Giacomo Biffi.

1988 (June 28): Paul Gregoire, Anthony Padiyara, Jose Freire Falcao, Michele Giordano, Alexandre Jose Maria dos Santos, O.F.M., Giovanni Canestri, Simon Ignatius Pimenta, Mario Revollo Bravo, Edward Bede Clancy, Lucas Moreira Neves, O.P., James Aloysius Hickey, Edmund C. Szoka, Laszlo Paskai, O.F.M., Christian Siyghan Tumi, Hans Hermann Groer, O.S.B., Franz Hengsbach, Vincentas Sladkevicius, Jean Margeot, John Baptist Wu Cheng-Chung.

Order of Deacons

1979 (June 30): Giuseppe Caprio, Egano Righi-Lambertini, Ernesto Civardi, Wladyslaw Rubin.

1983 (Feb. 2): Aurelio Sabattani, Giuseppe Casoria, Henri de Lubac.

1985 (May 25): Luigi Dadaglio, Simon D. Lourdusamy, Francis A. Arinze, Antonio Innocenti, Paul Augustin Mayer, Jean Jerome Hamer, Jozef Tomko, Andrzej Maria Deskur, Paul Poupard, Rosalio Jose Castillo Lara, Edouard Gagnon, Alfons Stickler, S.D.B., Pietro Pavan.

1988 (June 28): Eduardo Martinez Somalo, Achille Silvestrini, Angelo Felici, Antonio Maria Javierre Ortas, S.D.B., Jacques Martin.

DISTRIBUTION OF CARDINALS

As of Aug. 30, 1988, there were 157 cardinals from more than 60 countries or areas. Listed below are areas, countries, number and last names.

Europe — 80

Italy (36): Antonelli, Bafile, Baggio, Ballestrero, Bertoli, Biffi, Canestri, Caprio, Carpino, Casaroli, Casoria, Cé, Ciappi, Civardi, Colombo, Dadaglio, Felici, Giordano, Guerri, Innocenti, Martini, Nasalli Rocca di Corneliano, Oddi, Palazzini, Pappalardo, Paupini, Pavan, Piovanelli, Poletti, Righi-Lambertini, Rossi, Sabattani, Silvestrini, Sensi, Siri, Ursi.

France (9): Decourtray, De Lubac, Etchegaray, Garrone, Gouyon, Lustiger, Martin, Marty, Poupard.

Spain (6): Enrique y Tarancon, Gonzalez Martin, Javierre Ortas, Jubany Arnau, Martinez Somalo, Suquia Goicoechea.

Germany (5): Hengsbach, Mayer, Meisner, Ratzinger, Wetter.

Poland (5): Deskur, Glemp, Gulbinowicz, Macharski, Rubin.

Netherlands (3): De Furstenberg, Simonis, Willebrands.

Belgium (3): Danneels, Hamer, Suenens.

Austria (3): Groer, Koenig, Stickler.

Czechoslovakia (2): Tomasek, Tomko (Slovakia).

One from each of the following countries: England, Hume; Hungary, Paskai; Ireland, O'Fiaich; Latvia (USSR), Vaivods; Lithuania, Sladkevicius; Portugal, Ribeiro; Scotland, Gray; Yugoslavia, Kuharic.

Asia — 15

India (4): Lourdusamy, Padiyara, Picachy, Pimenta.

Philippines (2): Sin, Vidal.

One from each of the following countries: Hong Kong, Wu Cheng-Chung; Indonesia, Darmojuwono; Japan, Satowaki; Korea, Kim; Lebanon, Khoraiche; Pakistan, Cordeiro; Sri Lanka, Cooray; Thailand, Kitbunchu, Vietnam, Trinh van-Can.

Oceania — 4

Australia (2): Clancy, Freeman. One each from: New Zealand, Williams; Pacific Islands (Samoa), Taofinu'u.

Africa — 18

Nigeria (2): Arinze, Ekandem.

One from each of the following countries: Algeria, Duval; Angola, do Nascimento; Benin, Gantin; Burkina Faso, Zoungrana; Cameroon, Tumi; Ethiopia, Tzadua; Ivory Coast, Yago; Kenya, Otunga; Madagascar, Razafimahatratra; Mauritius, Margeot; Mozambique, Santos; Senegal, Thiandoum; South Africa, McCann; Tanzania, Rugambwa; Uganda, Nsubuga; Zaire, Malula.

North America — 19

United States (10): Baum, Bernardin, Carberry, Hickey, Krol, Law, Lubachivsky (head of Lwow archdiocese in Ukraine), Manning, O'Connor, Szoka.

Canada (6): Carter, Flahiff, Gagnon, Gregoire Leger, Vachon.

Mexico (2): Corripio Ahumada, Salazar Lopez.

Puerto Rico (1): Aponte Martinez.

Central and South America — 21

Brazil (7): Arns, Falcao, Lorscheider, Neves, Rossi, Sales, Scherer.

Argentina (3): Aramburu, Pironio, Primatesta.

Chile (2): Fresno Larrain, Silva Henriquez.

Colombia (2): Lopez Trujillo, Revollo Bravo.

Venezuela (2): Castillo Lara, Lebrun Moratinos.

One from each of the following countries: Bolivia, Maurer; Dominican Republic, Beras Rojas; Ecuador, Munoz Vega, S.J.; Nicaragua, Obando Bravo; Peru, Landazuri Ricketts.

INELIGIBLE TO VOTE

As of Aug. 30, 1988, 38 of the 157 cardinals were ineligible to take part in a papal election in line with the apostolic letter *Ingravescentem Aetatem* effective Jan. 1, 1971, which limited the functions of cardinals after completion of their 80th year.

Cardinals affected were: Antonelli, Bafile, Beras Rojas, Bertoli, Carberry, Carpino, Civardi, Colombo, Cooray, De Furstenberg, de Lubac, Duval, Enrique y Tarancon, Flahiff, Freeman, Garrone, Guerri, Khoraiche, Koenig, Leger, McCann, Martin, Marty, Maurer, Munoz Vega, Nasalli Rocca di Corneliano, Paupini, Pavan, Righi-Lambertini, Satowaki, Scherer, Sensi, Silva Henriquez, S.D.B., Siri, Suenens, Tomasek, Ursi, Vaivods.

Cardinal Giuseppe Casoria will become ineligible to vote after Oct. 1, 1988.

Cardinals completing their 80th year in 1989: Johannes Willebrands, Sept. 4; Mario Luigi Ciappi, Oct. 6; Timothy Manning, Nov. 15.

CARDINALS OF U.S.

As of Aug. 30, 1988, U.S. cardinals, years of elevation and sees.

John J. Krol, 1967, Philadelphia (retired 1988); John J. Carberry, 1969, St. Louis (retired 1979); Timothy Manning, 1973, Los Angeles (retired 1985); William W. Baum, 1976, Washington, D.C. (1973-80), prefect of Congregation for Seminaries and Institutes of Study, 1980; Joseph L. Bernardin,

1983, Chicago; Myroslav Lubachivsky, 1985, Lwow of the Ukrainians; Bernard F. Law, 1985, Boston; John J. O'Connor, 1985, New York; James A. Hickey, 1988, Washington; Edmund C. Szoka, 1988, Detroit.

Deceased cardinals of the United States,. Data: years of elevation, sees, years of birth and death.

John McCloskey, 1875, New York, 1810-1885; James Gibbons, 1886, Baltimore, 1834-1921; John Farley, 1911, New York, 1842-1918; William O'Connell, 1911, Boston, 1859-1944; Dennis Dougherty, 1921, Philadelphia, 1865-1951; Patrick Hayes, 1924, New York, 1867-1938; George Mundelein, 1924, Chicago, 1872-1939; John Glennon, 1946, St. Louis, 1862-1946; Edward Mooney, 1946, Detroit, 1882-1958;

Francis Spellman, 1946, New York, 1889-1967; Samuel Stritch, 1946, Chicago, 1887-1958; James F. McIntyre, 1953, Los Angeles, 1886-1979; John O'Hara, C.S.C., 1958, Philadelphia, 1888-1960; Richard Cushing, 1958, Boston, 1895-1970; Albert Meyer, 1959, Chicago, 1903-1965; Aloysius Muench, 1959, Fargo (and papal nuncio), 1889-1962; Joseph Ritter, 1961, St. Louis, 1892-1967; Francis Brennan, 1967, official of Roman Curia, 1894-1968; John P. Cody, 1967, Chicago 1907-1982; John J. Wright, 1969, prefect of Congregation for Clergy, 1909-1979; Humberto S. Medeiros, 1973, Boston, 1915-1983; Terence J. Cooke, 1969, New York, 1921-1983; Lawrence J. Shehan, 1965, Baltimore, 1898-1984; Patrick A. O'Boyle, 1967, Washington, 1896-1987; John F. Dearden, 1969, Detroit, 1907-88.

REPRESENTATIVES OF THE HOLY SEE

Papal representatives and their functions were the subject of a document entitled *Sollicitudo Omnium Ecclesiarum* which Pope Paul VI issued on his own initiative under the date of June 24, 1969.

Delegates and Nuncios

Papal representatives "receive from the Roman Pontiff the charge of representing him in a fixed way in the various nations or regions of the world.

"When their legation is only to local churches, they are known as apostolic delegates. When to this legation, of a religious and ecclesial nature, there is added diplomatic legation to states and governments, they receive the title of nuncio, pronuncio, and internuncio."

An apostolic nuncio has the diplomatic rank of ambassador extraordinary and plenipotentiary. Traditionally, because the Vatican diplomatic service has the longest uninterrupted history in the world, a nuncio has precedence among diplomats in the country to which he is accredited and serves as dean of the diplomatic corps on state occasions. Since 1965 pro-nuncios, also of ambassadorial rank, have been assigned to countries in which this prerogative is not recognized.

Other Representatives

Other representatives, who are covered in the Almanac article, Vatican Representatives to International Organizations, are clerics and lay persons "who form . . . part of a pontifical mission attached to international organizations or take part in conferences and congresses." They are variously called delegates or observers.

Service and Liaison

Representatives, while carrying out their general and special duties, are bound to respect the autonomy of local churches and bishops. Their service and liaison responsibilities include the following:

• **Nomination of Bishops:** To play a key role in compiling, with the advice of ecclesiastics and lay persons, and submitting lists of names of likely candidates to the Holy See with their own recommendations.

• **Bishops:** To aid and counsel local bishops without interfering in the affairs of their jurisdictions.

• **Episcopal Conferences:** To maintain close relations with them and to assist them in every possible way. (Papal representatives do not belong to these conferences.)

• **Religious Communities of Pontifical Rank:** To advise and assist major superiors for the purpose of promoting and consolidating conferences of men and women religious and to coordinate their apostolic activities.

• **Church-State Relations:** The thrust in this area is toward the development of sound relations with civil governments and collaboration in work for peace and the total good of the whole human family.

The mission of a papal representative begins with appointment and assignment by the pope and continues until termination of his mandate. He acts "under the guidance and according to the instructions of the cardinal secretary of state to whom he is directly responsible for the execution of the mandate entrusted to him by the Supreme Pontiff." Normally, representatives are required to retire at the age of 75.

NUNCIOS AND DELEGATES

(Sources: *Annuario Pontificio, L'Osservatore Romano, Acta Apostolicae Sedis*, NC News Service.)

Data, as of June 30, 1988, country, rank of legation (corresponding to rank of legate unless otherwise noted), name of legate (archbishop unless otherwise noted) as available.

Delegate for Papal Representatives: Archbishop Giovanni Coppa. The post was established in 1973 to coordinate papal diplomatic efforts throughout the world. The office entails responsibility for "following more closely through timely visits the activities of papal representatives . . . and encouraging their rapport with the central offices" of the Secretariat of State.

Africa, Southern (Botswana, South Africa, Namibia, Swaziland): Pretoria, South Africa, Apostolic Delegation; Ambrose De Paoli (also Pro-Nuncio to Lesotho).

Algeria: Algiers, Nunciature; Giovanni De Andrea, Pro-Nuncio (He is also Pro-Nuncio to Tunisia and Apostolic Delegate to Libya.)

Angola: Luanda, Apostolic Delegation; Fortunato Baldelli (also Pro-Nuncio to Sao Tome and Principe).
Antigua and Barbuda: Nunciature; Manuel Monteiro de Castro, Pro-Nuncio (resides in Port of Spain, Trinidad).
Antilles: Apostolic Delegation; Manuel Monteiro de Castro (resides in Port of Spain, Trinidad).
Argentina: Buenos Aires, Nunciature; Ubaldo Calabresi.
Australia: Canberra, Nunciature; Franco Brambilla, Pro-Nuncio.
Austria: Vienna, Nunciature; Michele Cecchini.
Bahamas: Nunciature; Manuel Monteiro de Castro. Pro-Nuncio (resides in Port of Spain, Trinidad).
Bangladesh: Dhaka, Nunciature; Pro-Nuncio (also serves as Apostolic Delegate to Burma.)
Barbados: Nunciature; Manuel Monteiro de Castro. Pro-Nuncio (resides in Port of Spain, Trinidad).
Belgium: Brussels, Nunciature; Angelo Pedroni (also Nuncio to Luxembourg and European Community).
Belize: Nunciature; Manuel Monteiro de Castro, Pro-Nuncio (resides in Port-of-Spain, Trinidad).
Benin (formerly Dahomey): Nunciature; Giuseppe Bertello, Pro-Nuncio (resides in Accra, Ghana).
Bolivia: La Paz, Nunciature; Santos Abril y Castello.
Botswana: See Africa, Southern.
Brazil: Brasilia, Nunciature; Carlo Furno.
Brunei: See Malaysia and Brunei.
Burkina Faso: Ouagadougou, Nunciature; Antonio Mattiazzo, Pro-Nuncio (resides in Abidjan, Ivory Coast).
Burma: See Bangladesh.
Burundi: Bujumbura, Nunciature; Pietro Sambi, Pro-Nuncio.
Cameroon: Yaounde, Nunciature; Donato Squicciarino, Pro-Nuncio (also Pro-Nuncio to Gabon and Equatorial Guinea).
Canada: Ottawa, Nunciature; Angelo Palmas, Pro-Nuncio.
Cape Verde, Republic of: Nunciature; Pablo Puente, Pro-Nuncio (resides in Dakar, Senegal).
Central African Republic: Bangui, Nunciature; Beniamino Stella, Pro-Nuncio (also Pro-Nuncio to Congo and Apostolic Delegate to Chad).
Chad: Apostolic Delegation; Beniamino Stella (resides in Bangui, Central African Republic).
Chile: Santiago, Nunciature.
China: Taipei (Taiwan), Nunciature.
Colombia: Bogota, Nunciature; Angelo Acerbi.
Congo: Brazzaville, Nunciature; Beniamino Stella, Pro-Nuncio (resides in Bangui, Central African Republic).
Costa Rica: San Jose, Nunciature; Pier Giacomo de Nicolo.
Cuba: Havana, Nunciature; Giulio Einaudi, Pro-Nuncio.
Cyprus: Nicosia, Nunciature; Carlo Curis, Pro-Nuncio (also Apostolic Delegate to Jerusalem).
Denmark: Copenhagen, Nunciature; Henri Lemaitre, Pro-Nuncio (also Pro-Nuncio to Finland, Iceland, Norway and Sweden).
Djibouti: See Red Sea Region.
Dominica: Nunciature: Manuel Monteiro de Castro, Pro-Nuncio (resides in Port-of-Spain, Trinidad).
Dominican Republic: Santo Domingo, Nunciature; Blasco Francisco Collaco (also Apostolic Delegate to Puerto Rico).
Ecuador: Quito, Nunciature; Luigi Conti.
Egypt: Cairo, Nunciature; Giovanni Moretti, Pro-Nuncio.
El Salvador: San Salvador, Nunciature; Francesco De Nittis (also Nuncio to Honduras).
Equatorial Guinea: Santa Isabel, Nunciature; Donato Squicciarino, Pro-Nuncio (resides in Yaounde, Cameroon).
Ethiopia: Addis Ababa, Nunciature; Thomas White, Pro-Nuncio.
Fiji: Nunciature; Antonio Magnoni, Pro-Nuncio (resides in New Zealand).
Finland: Helsinki, Nunciature; Henri Lemaitre, Pro-Nuncio (resides in Denmark).
France: Paris, Nunciature.
Gabon: Libreville, Nunciature; Donato Squicciarino, Pro-Nuncio (resides in Yaounde, Cameroon).
Gambia: Nunciature; Romeo Panciroli, Pro-Nuncio (resides in Monrovia, Liberia).
Germany: Bonn, Nunciature; Giuseppe Uhac.
Ghana: Accra, Nunciature; Giuseppe Bertello, Pro-Nuncio (also Pro-Nuncio to Benin and Togo).
Great Britain: London, Nunciature; Luigi Barbarito, Pro-Nuncio (also papal representative to Gibraltar).
Greece: Athens, Nunciature; Giovanni Mariani, Pro-Nuncio.
Grenada: Nunciature; Manuel Monteiro de Castro, Pro-Nuncio (resides in Port of Spain, Trinidad).
Guatemala: Guatemala City, Nunciature; Oriano Quilici.
Guinea: Conakry, Nunciature; Romeo Panciroli, Pro-Nuncio (resides in Monrovia, Liberia).
Guinea-Bissau: Nunciature; Pablo Puente, Pro-Nuncio (resides at Dakar, Senegal).
Haiti: Port-au-Prince, Nunciature; Paolo Romeo.
Honduras: Tegucigalpa, Nunciature; Francesco De Nittis (also Nuncio to El Salvador).
Iceland: Nunciature; Henri Lemaitre, Pro-Nuncio (resides in Denmark).
India: New Delhi, Nunciature; Agostino Cacciavillan, Pro-Nuncio (also Pro-Nuncio to Nepal).
Indonesia: Jakarta, Nunciature; Francesco Canalini, Pro-Nuncio.
Iran: Teheran, Nunciature; Giovanni Bulaitis, Pro-Nuncio.
Iraq: Baghdad, Nunciature; Marian Oles, Pro-Nuncio (also Pro-Nuncio to Kuwait).
Ireland: Dublin, Nunciature; Gaetano Alibrandi.
Italy: Rome, Nunciature; Luigi Poggi.
Ivory Coast: Abidjan, Nunciature; Antonio Mattiazzo, Pro-Nuncio (also Pro-Nuncio to Niger and Burkina Faso).

Jamaica: Nunciature; Manuel Monteiro de Castro, Pro-Nuncio (resides in Port of Spain, Trinidad).
Japan: Tokyo, Nunciature; William A. Carew, Pro-Nuncio.
Jerusalem, Palestine, Jordan, Israel: Jerusalem, Apostolic Delegation; Carlo Curis (also Pro-Nuncio to Cyprus).
Kenya: Nairobi, Nunciature; Clemente Faccani, Pro-Nuncio (also Pro-Nuncio to Seychelles).
Korea: Seoul, Nunciature; Ivan Dias, Pro-Nuncio.
Kuwait: Al Kuwait, Nunciature; Marian Oles, Pro-Nuncio (resides in Baghdad, Iraq).
Laos: Apostolic Delegation; Alberto Tricarico (resides in Bangkok, Thailand).
Lebanon: Beirut, Nunciature; Luciano Angeloni.
Lesotho: Maseru, Nunciature; Ambrose De Paoli, Pro-Nuncio (resides in Pretoria, S. Africa).
Liberia: Monrovia, Nunciature; Romeo Panciroli, Pro-Nuncio (also Pro-Nuncio to Gambia and Guinea and Apostolic Delegate to Sierra Leone).
Libya: Apostolic Delegation; Giovanni De Andrea (resides in Algiers, Algeria).
Liechtenstein: Nunciature; Eduardo Rovida.
Luxembourg: Nunciature; Angelo Pedroni (resides in Brussels, Belgium).
Madagascar: Tananarive, Nunciature; Agostino Marchetto, Pro-Nuncio (also Pro-Nuncio to Mauritius and Apostolic Delegate to Reunion).
Malawi: Lilongwe, Nunciature; Eugenio Sbarbaro, Pro-Nuncio (resides in Zambia).
Malaysia and Brunei: Apostolic Delegation; Alberto Tricarico (resides in Bangkok, Thailand).
Mali: Nunciature; Pablo Puente, Pro-Nuncio (resides in Dakar, Senegal).
Malta: La Valletta, Nunciature.
Mauritania: Nouakchott, Apostolic Delegation; Pablo Puente (resides in Dakar, Senegal).
Mauritius: Port Louis, Nunciature; Agostino Marchetto, Pro-Nuncio (resides in Tananarive, Madagascar).
Mexico: Mexico City, Apostolic Delegation; Girolamo Prigione.
Morocco: Rabat, Nunciature; Bernard Jacqueline, Pro-Nuncio.
Mozambique: Maputo, Apostolic Delegation; Patrick Coveney (also Pro-Nuncio to Zimbabwe).
Namibia: See Africa, Southern.
Nepal: Nunciature; Agostino Cacciavillan, Pro-Nuncio (resides in New Delhi, India).
Netherlands: The Hague, Nunciature; Audrys Juozas Backis, Pro-Nuncio.
New Zealand: Wellington, Nunciature; Antonio Magnoni, Pro-Nuncio. (He is also Pro-Nuncio to Fiji and Apostolic Delegate to Pacific Islands).
Nicaragua: Managua, Nunciature; Paolo Giglio.
Niger: Niamey, Nunciature; Antonio Mattiazzo, Pro-Nuncio (resides in Abidjan, Ivory Coast).
Nigeria: Lagos, Nunciature; Paul Fouad Tabet, Pro-Nuncio.
Norway: Nunciature; Henri Lemaitre, Pro-Nuncio (resides in Denmark).
Pacific Islands: Apostolic Delegation; Antonio Magnoni (resides in New Zealand).
Pakistan: Islamabad, Nunciature; Emanuele Gerada, Pro-Nuncio.
Panama: Panama, Nunciature; Jose Sebastian Laboa.
Papua New Guinea: Port Moresby; Nunciature; Antonio Maria Veglio, Pro-Nuncio. (He is also Pro-Nuncio to western and southern Solomon Islands.)
Paraguay: Asuncion, Nunciature; Georg Zur.
Peru: Lima, Nunciature; Luigi Dossena.
Philippines: Manila, Nunciature; Bruno Torpigliani.
Poland: Francesco Colasuonno, head of Holy See's delegation for permanent working contacts with the government of the People's Republic of Poland.
Portugal: Lisbon, Nunciature; Salvatore Asta.
Puerto Rico: See Dominican Republic.
Red Sea Region (Somalia, Djibouti, part of Arabian Peninsula): Apostolic Delegation; Luis Robles Diaz (resides in Khartoum, Sudan).
Reunion: See Madagascar.
Rwanda: Kigali, Nunciature. Giovanni Battista Morandini, Pro-Nuncio.
Saint Lucia: Nunciature; Manuel Monteiro de Castro, Pro-Nuncio (resides in Port of Spain, Trinidad).
San Marino: Nunciature; Pier Luigi Celata, Nuncio.
Sao Tome and Principe: Nunciature; Fortunato Baldelli, Pro-Nuncio (also apostolic delegate to Angola, where he resides).
Senegal: Dakar, Nunciature; Pablo Puente, Pro-Nuncio (also Pro-Nuncio to Cape Verde, Guinea-Bissau and Mali; Apostolic Delegate to Mauritania.)
Seychelles Islands: Nunciature; Clemente Faccani, Pro-Nuncio (resides in Nairobi, Kenya).
Sierra Leone: Apostolic Delegation; Romeo Panciroli (resides in Monrovia, Liberia).
Singapore: Nunciature; Alberto Tricarico, Pro-Nuncio (resides in Bangkok, Thailand).
Solomon Islands: Nunciature, Antonio Maria Veglio, Pro-Nuncio (resides in Port Moresby, Papua New Guinea).
Somalia: See Red Sea Region.
South Africa: See Africa, Southern.
Spain: Madrid, Nunciature; Mario Tagliaferri.
Sri Lanka: Colombo, Nunciature; Francois Bacque, Pro-Nuncio.
Sudan: Khartoum, Nunciature; Luis Robles Diaz, Pro-Nuncio (also Apostolic Delegate to Red Sea Region).
Swaziland: See Africa, Southern.
Sweden: Nunciature; Henri Lemaitre, Pro-Nuncio (resides in Denmark).
Switzerland: Bern, Nunciature; Eduardo Rovida.
Syria (Syrian Arab Republic): Damascus, Nunciature; Luigi Accogli, Pro-Nuncio.
Tanzania: Dar-es-Salaam, Nunciature; Gian Vincenzo Moreni, Pro-Nuncio.
Thailand: Bangkok, Nunciature; Alberto Tricarico, Pro-Nuncio (also Pro-Nuncio to Singa-

pore and Apostolic Delegate to Laos, Malaysia and Brunei).
Togo: Lome, Nunciature; Giuseppe Bertello, Pro-Nuncio (resides in Accra, Ghana).
Trinidad and Tobago: Port of Spain, Trinidad, Nunciature; Manuel Monteiro de Castro, Pro-Nuncio (also Pro-Nuncio to Antigua and Barbuda, Bahamas, Barbados, Belize, Dominica, Grenada, Jamaica, Saint Lucia and Apostolic Delegate to Antilles).
Tunisia: Tunis, Nunciature; Giovanni De Andrea, Pro-Nuncio (resides in Algiers, Algeria).
Turkey: Ankara, Nunciature; Sergio Sebastiani, Pro-Nuncio.
Uganda: Kampala, Nunciature; Karl-Joseph Rauber, Pro-Nuncio.
United States of America: Washington, D.C., Nunciature; Pio Laghi, Pro-Nuncio.
Uruguay: Montevideo, Nunciature; Andrea Cordero Lanza di Montezemolo.
Venezuela: Caracas, Nunciature; Luciano Storero.
Vietnam and Cambodia: Apostolic Delegation.
Yugoslavia: Belgrade, Nunciature; Gabriel Montalvo, Pro-Nuncio.
Zaire: Kinshasa-Gombe, Nunciature; Alfio Rapisarda, Pro-Nuncio.
Zambia: Lusaka, Nunciature; Eugenio Sbarbaro, Pro-Nuncio (also Pro-Nuncio to Malawi).
Zimbabwe: Nunciature; Patrick Coveney, Pro-Nuncio (is also Apostolic Delegate to Mozambique).

European Community: Brussels, Belgium, Nunciature; Angelo Pedroni, Nuncio.

Pro-Nuncio to U.S.

The representative of the Pope to the Church in the United States is Archbishop Pio Laghi, pro-nuncio. Archbishop Laghi was born May 21, 1922, in Castiglione, Italy. Ordained to the priesthood Apr. 20, 1946, he entered the Vatican diplomatic service in 1952. He served in Nicaragua, the U.S. (as secretary of the apostolic delegation, 1954-61) and India. He was recalled to Rome and served on the Council for the Public Affairs of the Church. He was appointed to the titular see of Mauriana and received episcopal ordination June 22, 1969. He was apostolic delegate to Jerusalem and Palestine, 1969-74, and apostolic nuncio to Argentina, 1974-80. On Dec. 10, 1980, he was appointed apostolic delegate to the United States and permanent observer to the Organization of American States.

He was named first pro-nuncio in 1984 when the U.S. and the Vatican reestablished diplomatic relations (See Index: U.S.-Vatican Relations).

The U.S. Apostolic Nunciature is located at 3339 Massachusetts Ave. N.W., Washington, D.C. 20008.

From 1893 to 1984, papal representatives to the Church in the U.S. were apostolic delegates (all archbishops): Francesco Satolli (1893-1896), Sebastiano Martinelli, O.S.A. (1896-1902), Diomede Falconio, O.F.M. (1902-1911), Giovanni Bonzano (1911-1922), Pietro Fumasoni-Biondi (1922-1933), Amleto Cicognani (1933-1958), Egidio Vagnozzi (1958-1967); Luigi Raimondi (1967-1973); Jean Jadot (1973-1980); Pio Laghi (1980-84).

DIPLOMATS AT VATICAN

(Sources: *Annuario Pontificio, L'Osservatore Romano, Acta Apostolicae Sedis*).

Listed below are countries maintaining diplomatic relations with the Vatican, dates of establishment (in some cases) and names of Ambassadors (as of June, 1988). Leaders (.....) indicate the post was vacant.

The dean of the diplomatic corps at the Vatican is Ambassador Joseph Amichia, representative of Ivory Coast from 1971, who succeeded to the post in 1983.

Algeria (1972): Abdelmadjid Alahoum.
Antigua and Barbuda (1986) ....
Argentina: Santiago Manuel de Estrado.
Australia (1973): Francis W.S. Milne.
Austria: Hans Pasch.
Bahamas (1979): ....
Bangladesh (1972): ....
Barbados (1979): ....
Belgium (1835): Baron Alexandre Paternotte de La Vaille.
Belize (1983): ....
Benin (formerly Dahomey) (1971): ....
Bolivia: Huascar Cajias Kauffmann.
Brazil: Affonso Arinos de Mello-Franco.
Burkina Faso (1973): ....
Burundi (1963): ....
Cameroon (1966): Jean Melaga.
Canada (1969): Eldon Pattyson Black.
Cape Verde (1976): ....
Central African Republic (1975): ....
Chile: Francisco Javier Cuadra Lizana.
China (Taiwan) (1966): Chow Shu-Kai.
Colombia: Julio Cesar Turbay Ayala.
Congo (1977): Jean-Marie Ewengue.
Costa Rica: ....
Cuba: Manuel Estevez Perez.
Cyprus (1973): Polys Modinos.
Denmark (1982): Troels Munk.
Dominica (1981): ....
Dominican Republic: Efrain Reyes Duluc.
Ecuador: Francisco Alfredo Salazar Alvarado.
Egypt (1966): Ahmed Ibrahim Adel.
El Salvador: Prudencio Llach Schonenberg.
Equatorial Guinea (1981): ....
Ethiopia (1969): ....
Fiji (1978): Sailosi Wai Kepa.
Finland (1966): Kaarlo Yrjo-Koskinen.
France: Bertrand Dufourcq.
Gabon (1967): Jean-Claude Labouba.
Gambia, The (1978): ....
Germany: Paul Verbeek.
Ghana (1976): Mrs. Therese Striggner Scott.
Great Britain (1982): John K.E. Broadley.
Greece (1980): .. ..
Grenada (1979): ....
Guatemala: Carlos Alfredo Escobar Armas.
Guinea (1986): ....
Guinea-Bissau (1986): Leonel Sebastiao Viera.
Haiti: Wilson Florestal.
Honduras: Oscar Acosta.

Iceland (1976): Niels P. Sigurdsson.
India: Ashoke Sen Chib.
Indonesia (1965): Hendrawan Kurniadi.
Iran (1966): Salman Ghaffari.
Iraq (1966): Wissam Chawkat Al-Zawahi.
Ireland: Brendan Dillon.
Italy: Emanuele Scammacca del Murgo e dell' Agnone.
Ivory Coast (1971): Joseph Amichia.
Jamaica (1979): Miss M.P. Durrant.
Japan (1966): Teruo Kosugi.
Kenya (1965): Simon B. Arap Bullut.
Korea (1966): Kyung Chul Kim.
Kuwait (1969): Tarek Abdul Razzak Razzoqui.
Lebanon (1966): Gazi Chidiac.
Lesotho (1967): Reginald Mokheseng Tekateka.
Liberia (1966): Willie Givens.
Liechtenstein (1985): Nikolaus de Liechtenstein.
Lithuania: Stasys Lozoraitis, Jr., first secretary.
Luxembourg (1955): Jean Wagner.
Madagascar (1967): Jean Ernest Bezaza.
Malawi (1966): Stevens Erasmus Mapunda.
Mali (1979): ....
Malta (1965): Alexander Cachia Zammit.
Mauritius: Dhurma Gian Nath.
Monaco: Cesar Charles Solamito.
Morocco: Youssef Ben Abbes.
Nepal (1983):Simha Pratap Shah.
Netherlands (1967): Seger Jan Joseph Van Voorst tot Voorst.
New Zealand (1973): Ms. Judith Catherine Trotter.
Nicaragua: Ricardo Agustin Peter Silva.
Niger (1971): ....
Nigeria (1976): Edwin Morvan Ihama.
Norway (1982): Ketil Börde.

Order of Malta (see Index): Christophe de Kallay.
Pakistan (1965): Saidulla Khan Dehlavi.
Panama: ....
Papua New Guinea (1977): ....
Paraguay: Juan Livieres Argana.
Peru: Hubert Wieland Alzamora.
Philippines (1951): Howard Q. Dee.
Portugal: João de Sa Coutinho
Rwanda (1964): Ildephonse Munyesayaka.
Saint Lucia (1984): Francis J. Carasco.
San Marino (1986): Giovanni Galassi.
Sao Tome and Principe (1984): ....
Senegal (1966): Andre Coulbary.
Seychelles (1984): ....
Singapore (1981): Francis Yeo Teng Yang.
Solomon Islands (1984): ....
Spain: Jesus Ezquerra Calvo.
Sri Lanka (1975): ....
Sudan (1972): Awad El Karim Fadulalla.
Sweden (1982): Bengt Friedman.
Syria (Arab Republic) (1966): ....
Tanzania (1968): Ahmed Diria Hassan.
Thailand (1969): ....
Togo (1981): ....
Trinidad and Tobago (1978): Maurice Oscar St. John.
Tunisia (1972): Abdelmadjid Chaker.
Turkey (1966): Selcuk Korkud.
Uganda (1966): Perezi Karukubiro-Kamunawire.
United States (1984): Frank Shakespeare.
Uruguay: Juan Jose Zorrilla.
Venezuela: Reinaldo Leandro Rodriguez.
Yugoslavia: Stefan Cigoj.
Zaire (1963): Atembina-te-Bombo.
Zambia (1965): Wilted Joseph Phiri.
Zimbabwe (1980): Ben Kufakunesu Jambga.

U.S. — VATICAN RELATIONS

The United States and the Vatican announced Jan. 10, 1984, the establishment of full diplomatic relations, thus ending a gap of 117 years in their relations. The announcement followed action by the Congress in November, 1983, to end a prohibition on diplomatic relations enacted in 1867.

William A. Wilson, a Catholic and President Ronald Reagan's personal representative to the Vatican since February, 1981, was confirmed as the U.S. ambassador by the Senate on Mar. 7, 1984; he presented his credentials to Pope John Paul on Apr. 9, 1984. He resigned in May, 1986. He was succeeded by Frank Shakespeare, also a Catholic, whose nomination by President Reagan on Sept. 26, 1986, was approved by the Senate Oct. 15; he presented his credentials to Pope John Paul Jan. 8, 1987.

Archbishop Pio Laghi, apostolic delegate to the U.S. since 1980, was named pro-nuncio by the Pope on Mar. 26, 1984.

Nature of Relations

The nature of relations was described in nearly identical statements by John Hughes, a State Department spokesman, and the Vatican.

Hughes said: "The United States of America and the Holy See, in the desire to further promote the existing mutual friendly relations, have decided by common agreement to establish diplomatic relations between them at the level of embassy on the part of the United States of America, and nunciature on the part of the Holy See, as of today, Jan. 10, 1984."

The Vatican statement said: "The Holy See and the United States of America, desiring to develop the mutual friendly relations already existing, have decided by common accord to establish diplomatic relations at the level of apostolic nunciature on the side of the Holy See and of embassy on the side of the United States beginning today, Jan. 10, 1984."

The establishment of relations was criticized as a violation of the separation-of-church-and-state principle by spokesmen for the National Council of Churches, the National Association of Evangelicals, the Baptist Joint Committee on Public Affairs, Seventh Day Adventists, Americans United for Separation of Church and State, and the American Jewish Congress.

U.S. District Judge John P. Fullam, ruling May 7, 1985, in Philadelphia, dismissed a legal challenge to U.S.-Vatican relations brought by Americans United for Separation of Church and State. He stated that Americans United and its allies in the challenge lacked legal standing to sue, and that the courts did not have jurisdiction to intervene in foreign policy decisions of the executive branch of the U.S. government. Parties to the suit brought by Americans United were the National Association of Laity, the National Coalition of American Nuns and several Protestant church organizations.

Not a Religious Issue

Bishop James W. Malone, president of the U.S. Catholic Conference, said in a statement: "This matter has been discussed at length for many years. It is not a religious issue but a public policy question which, happily, has now been settled in this context."

Russell Shaw, a conference spokesman, said the decision to send an ambassador to the Vatican was not a church-state issue and "confers no special privilege or status on the Church."

Earlier Relations

Official relations for trade and diplomatic purposes were maintained by the United States and the Papal States while the latter had the character of and acted like other sovereign powers in the international community.

Consular relations developed in the wake of an announcement, made by the papal nuncio in Paris to the American mission there Dec. 15, 1784, that the Papal States had agreed to open several Mediterranean ports to U.S. shipping.

U.S. consular representation in the Papal States began with the appointment of John B. Sartori, a native of Rome, in June, 1797. Sartori's successors as consuls were: Felix Cicognani, also a Roman, and Americans George W. Greene, Nicholas Browne, William C. Sanders, Daniel LeRoy, Horatio V. Glentworth, W.J. Stillman, Edwin C. Cushman, David M. Armstrong.

Consular officials of the Papal States who served in the U.S. were: Count Ferdinand Lucchesi, 1826 to 1829, who resided in Washington; John B. Sartori, 1829 to 1841, who resided in Trenton, N.J.; Daniel J. Desmond, 1841 to 1850, who resided in Philadelphia; Louis B. Binsse, 1850 to 1895, who resided in New York.

U.S. recognition of the consul of the Papal States did not cease when the states were absorbed into the Kingdom of Italy in 1871, despite pressure from Baron Blanc, the Italian minister. Binsse held the title until his death Mar. 28, 1895. No one was appointed to succeed him.

Diplomatic Relations

The U.S. Senate approved a recommendation, made by President James K. Polk in December, 1847, for the establishment of a diplomatic post in the Papal States. Jacob L. Martin, the first charge d'affaires, arrived in Rome Aug. 2, 1848, and presented his credentials to Pius IX Aug. 19. Martin, who died within a month, was succeeded by Lewis Cass, Jr. Cass became minister resident in 1854 and served in that capacity until his retirement in 1858.

John P. Stockton, who later became a U.S. Senator from New Jersey, was minister resident from 1858 to 1861. Rufus King was named to succeed him but, instead, accepted a commission as a brigadier general in the Army. Alexander W. Randall of Wisconsin took the appointment. He was succeeded in August, 1862, by Richard M. Blatchford who served until the following year. King was again nominated minister resident and served in that capacity until 1867 when the ministry was ended because of objections from some quarters in the U.S. and failure to appropriate funds for its continuation. J. C. Hooker, a secretary, remained in the Papal States until the end of March, 1868, closing the ministry and performing functions of courtesy.

Personal Envoys

Myron C. Taylor was appointed by President Franklin D. Roosevelt in 1939 to serve as his personal representative to Pope Pius XII and continued serving in that capacity during the presidency of Harry S. Truman until 1951. Henry Cabot Lodge was named to the post by President Richard M. Nixon in 1970, served also during the presidency of Gerald Ford, and represented President Carter at the canonization of St. John Neumann in 1977. Neither Taylor nor Lodge had diplomatic status.

Miami attorney David Walters, a Catholic, served as the personal envoy of President Jimmy Carter to the Pope from July, 1977, until his resignation Aug. 16, 1978. He was succeeded by Robert F. Wagner, also a Catholic and former mayor of New York, who served from October, 1978, to the end of the Carter presidency in January, 1981. William A. Wilson, a California businessman and Catholic, was appointed by President Ronald Reagan in February, 1981, to serve as his personal envoy to the Pope.

None of the personal envoys had diplomatic status.

President Harry S. Truman nominated Gen. Mark Clark to be ambassador to the Vatican in 1951, but withdrew the nomination at Clark's request because of controversy over the appointment.

VATICAN CITY

The State of Vatican City (Stato della Citta del Vaticano) is the territorial seat of the papacy. The smallest sovereign state in the world, it is situated within the city of Rome, embraces an area of 108.7 acres, and includes within its limits the Vatican Palace, museums, art galleries, gardens, libraries, radio station, post office, bank, astronomical observatory, offices, apartments, service facilities, St. Peter's Basilica, and neighboring buildings between the Basilica and Viale Vaticano.

The extraterritorial rights of Vatican City extend to more than 10 buildings in Rome, including the major basilicas and office buildings of various congregations of the Roman Curia, and to the **Villa of Castel Gandolfo** 15 miles southeast of the City of Rome. Castel Gandolfo is the summer residence of the Holy Father.

The government of Vatican City is in the hands of the reigning pope, who has full executive, legislative and judicial power. The administration of affairs, however, is handled by the Pontifical Commission for the State of Vatican City. The legal system is based on Canon Law; in cases where this code does not obtain, the laws of the City of Rome apply. The City is an absolutely neutral state and enjoys all the rights and privileges of a sovereign power. The Secretariat of State (Papal Secretariat) maintains diplomatic relations with other nations. The citizens of Vatican City, and they alone, owe allegiance to the pope as a temporal head of state.

Cardinals of the Roman Curia residing outside Vatican City enjoy the privileges of extraterritoriality.

The normal population is approximately 1,000. While the greater percentage is made up of priests and religious, there are several hundred lay persons living in Vatican City. They are housed in their own apartments in the City and are engaged in secretarial, domestic, trade and service occupations. About 4,000 persons are employed by the Vatican.

Services of honor and order are performed by the Swiss Guards, who have been charged with responsibility for the personal safety of popes since 1506. Additional police and ceremonial functions are under the supervision of a special office. These functions were formerly handled by the Papal Gendarmes, the Palatine Guard of Honor, and the Guard of Honor of the Pope (Pontifical Noble Guard) which Pope Paul disbanded Sept. 14, 1970.

The **Basilica of St. Peter,** built between 1506 and 1626, is the largest church in Christendom and the site of most papal ceremonies. The pope's own patriarchal basilica, however, is **St. John Lateran,** whose origins date back to 324.

St. Ann's is the parish church of Vatican City.

The vicar general of the pope for Vatican City, which is part of the diocese of Rome, is Most Rev. Peter Canisius Van Lierde, O.S.A., titular bishop of Porfireone.

The **Vatican Library,** one of five in the City, has among its holdings 70,000 manuscripts, 770,000 printed books, and 7,500 incunabula.

The independent temporal power of the pope, which is limited to the confines of Vatican City and small areas outside, was for many centuries more extensive than it is now. As late as the nineteenth century, the pope ruled 16,000 square miles of Papal States across the middle of Italy, with a population of over 3,000,000. In 1870 forces of the Kingdom of Italy occupied these lands which, with the exception of the small areas surrounding the Vatican and Lateran in Rome and the Villa of Castel Gandolfo, became part of the Kingdom by the Italian law of May 13, 1871.

The **Roman Question,** occasioned by this seizure and the voluntary confinement of the pope to the Vatican, was settled with ratification of the Lateran Agreement June 7, 1929, by the Italian government and Vatican City. The agreement recognized Catholicism as the religion of Italy and provided, among other things, a financial indemnity to the Vatican in return for the former Papal States; it became Article 7 of the Italian Constitution Mar. 26, 1947.

The Lateran Agreement was superseded by a new concordat given final approval by the Italian Chamber of Deputies Mar. 20 and formally ratified June 3, 1985.

Papal Flag

The papal flag consists of two equal vertical stripes of yellow and white, charged with the insignia of the papacy on the white stripe — a triple crown or tiara over two crossed keys, one of gold and one of silver, tied with a red cord and two tassels. The divisions of the crown represent the teaching, sanctifying and ruling offices of the pope. The keys symbolize his jurisdictional authority.

The papal flag is a national flag inasmuch as it is the standard of the Supreme Pontiff as the sovereign of the state of Vatican City. It is also universally accepted by the faithful as a symbol of the supreme spiritual authority of the Holy Father.

Vatican Radio

The declared purpose of Vatican Radio Station HVJ is "that the voice of the Supreme Pastor may be heard throughout the world by means of the ether waves, for the glory of Christ and the salvation of souls." Designed by Guglielmo Marconi, the inventor of radio, and supervised by him until his death, the station was inaugurated by Pope Pius XI in 1931. The original purpose has been extended to a wide variety of programming.

Vatican Radio operates on international wave lengths, transmits programs in 34 languages, and serves as a channel of communication between the Vatican, church officials and listeners in general in many parts of the world. The station broadcasts about 260 hours a week throughout the world. The daily English-language program for North America is broadcast on 6030 kilohertz.

The staff of 350 broadcasters and technicians includes 35 Jesuits. Studios and offices are at Palazzo Pio, Piazza Pia, 3, 00193 Rome.

1988 Vatican Stamps and Coins

The Vatican Philatelic and Numismatic Office scheduled the following issues of stamps and coins for 1988. (Issue dates are given where available.)

Stamps and Stationery: Series commemorating the centenary of the death of St. John Bosco; issued Apr. 19, 1988, in three values (500, 1,000 and 2,000 lire) on three subjects.

• Series celebrating the Marian Year 1987-1988; issued June 15, 1988, in six values (50, 300, 500, 750, 1,000 and 2,400 lire) on six subjects.

• Series commemorating the millennium of the evangelization Kievan Rus'; issued June 16, 1988, in three values (450, 650 and 2,500 lire) on three subjects.

• Series commemorating the third centenary of the death of the painter Paolo Caliari, known as "Veronese."

• Airmail series: the journeys of Pope John Paul II in 1987.

• Series celebrating the Christian solemnity of Christmas.

• New type of aerogram

• Illustrated stamped postcards

Coins: Series for the ninth year of the Pontificate of Pope John Paul II; issued Mar. 3, 1988, in seven values (10, 20, 50, 100, 200, 500 and 1,000 lire).

Papal Audiences

General audiences are scheduled weekly, on Wednesday.

In Vatican City, they are held in the Audience Hall on the south side of St. Peter's Basilica or, weather permitting, in St. Peter's Square. The hall, which was opened in 1971, has a seating capacity of 6,800 and a total capacity of 12,000.

Audiences have been held during the summer at Castel Gandolfo when the pope is there on a working vacation.

General audiences last from about 60 to 90 minutes, during which the pope gives a talk and his blessing. A résumé of the talk, which is usually in Italian, is given in several languages.

Arrangements for papal audiences are handled by an office of the Prefecture of the Apostolic Household.

American visitors can obtain passes for general audiences by applying to the Bishops' Office for United States Visitors to the Vatican, Casa Santa Maria, Via dell'Umilita, 30, 00187 Rome.

Private and group audiences are reserved for dignitaries of various categories and for special occasions.

Publications

Acta Apostolicae Sedis: The only "official commentary" of the Holy See, was established in 1908 for the publication of activities of the Holy See, laws, decrees and acts of congregations and tribunals of the Roman Curia. The first edition was published in January, 1909.

St. Pius X made *AAS* an official organ in 1908. Laws promulgated for the Church ordinarily take effect three months after the date of their publication in this commentary.

The publication, mostly in Latin, is printed by the Vatican Polyglot Press.

The immediate predecessor of this organ was *Acta Sanctae Sedis*, founded in 1865 and given official status by the Congregation for the Propagation of the Faith in 1904.

Annuario Pontificio: The yearbook of the Holy See. It is edited by the Central Statistics Office of the Church and is printed in Italian, with some portions in other languages, by the Vatican Polyglot Press. It covers the worldwide organization of the Church, lists members of the hierarchy, and includes a wide range of statistical information.

The publication of a statistical yearbook of the Holy See dates back to 1716, when a volume called *Notizie* appeared. Publication under the present title began in 1860, was suspended in 1870, and resumed again in 1872 under the title *Catholic Hierarchy*. This volume was printed privately at first, but has been issued by the Vatican Press since 1885. The title *Annuario Pontificio* was restored in 1912, and the yearbook was called an "official publication" until 1924.

L'Osservatore Romano: The daily newspaper of the Holy See. It began publication July 1, 1861, as an independent enterprise under the ownership and direction of four Catholic laymen headed by Marcantonio Pacelli, vice minister of the interior under Pope Pius IX and a grandfather of the late Pius XII. Leo XIII bought the publication in 1890, making it the "pope's" own newspaper.

The only official material in *L'Osservatore Romano* is that which appears under the heading, "Nostre Informazioni." This includes notices of appointments by the Holy See, the texts of papal encyclicals and addresses by the Holy Father and others, various types of documents, accounts of decisions and rulings of administrative bodies, and similar items. Additional material includes news and comment on developments in the Church and the world. Italian is the language most used.

The editorial board is directed by Prof. Mario Agnes. A staff of about 15 reporters covers Rome news sources. A corps of correspondents provides foreign coverage.

A weekly roundup edition in English was inaugurated in 1968. Other weekly editions are printed in French, Spanish, Portuguese, German and Polish. *L'Osservatore della Domenica* is published weekly as a supplement to the Sunday issue of the daily edition.

Vatican Press Office: The establishment of a single Vatican Press Office was announced Feb. 29, 1968, to replace service agencies formerly operated by *L'Osservatore Romano* and an office created for press coverage of the Second Vatican Council. New directives for the office were issued in 1986. Joaquin Navarro-Valls is the director.

Television: *Centro Televisivo Vaticano* (CTV) was instituted by John Paul II Oct. 23, 1983, with the rescript, *Ex Audentia*. Archbishop John P. Foley is president of the administrative council.

Vatican Polyglot Press: The official printing plant of the Vatican. The Vatican press was conceived by Marcellus II and Pius IV but was actually founded by Sixtus V on Apr. 27, 1587, to print the Vulgate and the writings of the Fathers of the Church and other authors. A Polyglot Press was established in 1626 by the Congregation for the Propagation of the Faith to serve the needs of the Oriental Church. St. Pius X merged both presses under this title. The plant has facilities for the printing of a wide variety of material in about 30 languages.

Activities of the Holy See: An annual documentary volume covering the activities of the pope — his daily work, general and special audiences, discourses and messages on special occasions, visits outside the Vatican, missionary and charitable endeavors, meetings with diplomats, heads of state and others — and activities of the congregations, commissions, tribunals and offices of the Roman Curia.

Statistical Yearbook of the Church: Issued by the Central Statistics Office of the Church, it contains principal data concerning the presence and work of the Church in the world. The first issue was published in 1972 under the title *Collection of Statistical Tables, 1969*. It is printed in corresponding columns of Italian and Latin. Some of the introductory material is printed in other languages.

VATICAN REPRESENTATIVES

(Sources: *Annuario Pontificio;* NC News Service.)

The Vatican has representatives to or is a regular member of a number of quasi-governmental and international organizations.

Governmental Organizations: United Nations (Abp. Renato Raffaele Martino, permanent observer); UN Office in Geneva and Specialized Institutes (Abp. Justo Mullor Garcia, permanent observer); International Atomic Energy Agency (Msgr. Giovanni Ceirano, permanent representative); UN Office at Vienna and UN Organization for Industrial Development (Msgr. Giovanni Ceirano, permanent observer); UN Food and Agriculture Organization (Bp. Agostino Ferrari-Toniolo, permanent observer); UN Educational, Scientific and Cultural Organization (Msgr. Lorenzo Frana, permanent observer); Council of Europe (Msgr. Luigi Bressan, special envoy with function of permanent observer); Council for Cultural Cooperation of the Council of Europe (Msgr. Luigi Bressan, delegate); Organization of American States (Abp. Pio Laghi, permanent observer, with personal title of Apostolic Nuncio); International Institute for the Unification of Private Law (Prof. Pio Ciprotti, delegate); International Committee of Military Medicine and Pharmacy (Adolphe Vander Perre, delegate), World Organization of Tourism (Rev. Pietro Fanto, permanent observer). Universal Postal Union; International Telecommunications Union; International Council on Grain; World Organization of Intellectual Property; International Union for the Protection of Literary and Artistic Works; International Union for the Protection of Industrial Property; International Organization of Telecommunication via Satellite (Intelsat); European Conference of Postal and Telecommunication Administration (CEPT).

Non-Governmental Organizations: International Committee of Historical Sciences (Msgr. Michele Maccarrone); International Committee of Paleography (Msgr. Jose Ruysschaert, delegate); International Committee of the History of Art (Prof. Carlo Pietrangeli, delegate); International Committee of Anthropological and Ethnological Sciences;

International Committee for the Neutrality of Medicine (Rev. Michel Riquet, S.J., permanent observer); International Center of Study for the Preservation and Restoration of Cultural Goods (Prof. Carlo Pietrangeli, permanent observer); International Council of Monuments and Sites (Prof. Carlo Pietrangeli, delegate); International Alliance on Tourism; International Astronomical Union; International Institute of Administrative Sciences; International Technical Committee for Prevention and Extinction of Fires; World Medical Association.

AMERICAN CHURCH

The Church of Santa Susanna was established as the national church for Americans in Rome Feb. 28, 1922, and entrusted to the Paulist Fathers who have served there continuously since then except for several years during World War II.

VATICAN-ITALIAN CONCORDAT

A new concordat on relations between the Vatican and Italy, designed to replace the one in effect since 1929, was formally ratified June 3, 1985. It bears the title, "An Agreement on the Revision of the Lateran Concordat."

The 14-article agreement ended the privileged status of the Catholic Church as the official religion of Italy. It refers, not to "the sacred character of the Eternal City of Rome," but to the "particular significance of Rome for Catholicism." It provides that Catholic religious teaching in state schools shall be optional, and makes marriage annulments by church tribunals subject to civil review before ratification by the state.

The treaty guarantees the rights of the Church to: perform its pastoral mission; oversee dioceses, other institutions, and priests; establish schools; minister in public institutions such as hospitals, correctional institutions and the armed forces.

It recognizes Sundays as holidays, along with Catholic religious feast days to be agreed upon. It provides for the protection of church buildings, and calls on Church and state to safeguard the country's historical and artistic treasures. The concordat provides also for the continuing exemption of priests, deacons and members of religious orders from military service, but requires them to perform some kind of civil service instead.

It was expected that the tax-exempt status of church organizations outside the Vatican would continue in effect.

Government subsidies to the Church and related financial issues not covered in the earlier text were the subjects of agreement reached Aug. 2, 1984, in the Italian Parliament. Substantially, the arrangement envisaged the end of subsidies in 1990, coupled with provisions for tax deductible contributions for support of the personnel and institutions of the Church.

STATISTICS OF 32 PAPAL JOURNEYS

At the end of 1986, Vatican Radio reported that Pope John Paul had made 32 trips beyond the borders of Italy. "The shortest were his one-day visits to Switzerland, San Marino and Liechtenstein. The longest was to Asia and Oceania, which lasted 14 days.

"During these 32 journeys, the Pope visited a total of 291 localities in 65 nations, delivering a total of 1,128 official addresses. The Pontiff spent a total of 216 days, 7 hours and 35 minutes of the first 2,998 days of his pontificate on these journeys, traveling a total of 465,439 kilometers. This distance equals ten times the circumference of the earth at the equator.

DOCTRINE OF THE CATHOLIC CHURCH

Following are excerpts from the first two chapters of the "Dogmatic Constitution on the Church" promulgated by the Second Vatican Council. They describe the relation of the Catholic Church to the Kingdom of God, the nature and foundation of the Church, the People of God, the necessity of membership and participation in the Church for salvation.

Additional subjects in the constitution are treated in other Almanac entries.

I. MYSTERY OF THE CHURCH

By her relationship with Christ, the Church is a kind of sacrament or sign of intimate union with God, and of the unity of all mankind (No. 1).

He (the eternal Father) planned to assemble in the holy Church all those who would believe in Christ. Already from the beginning of the world the foreshadowing of the Church took place. She was prepared for in a remarkable way throughout the history of the people of Israel and by means of the Old Covenant. Established in the present era of time, the Church was made manifest by the outpouring of the Spirit. At the end of time she will achieve her glorious fulfillment. Then . . . all just men from the time of Adam, "from Abel, the just one, to the last of the elect," will be gathered together with the Father in the universal Church (No. 2).

When the work which the Father had given the Son to do on earth (cf. Jn. 17:4) was accomplished, the Holy Spirit was sent on the day of Pentecost in order that he might forever sanctify the Church, and thus all believers would have access to the Father through Christ in the one Spirit (cf. Eph. 2:18).

The Spirit dwells in the Church and in the hearts of the faithful as in a temple (cf. 1 Cor. 3:16; 6:19). . . . The Spirit guides the Church into the fullness of truth (cf. Jn. 16:13) and gives her a unity of fellowship and service. He furnishes and directs her with various gifts, both hierarchical and charismatic, and adorns her with the fruits of His grace (cf. Eph. 4:11-12; 1 Cor. 12:4; Gal. 5:22). By the power of the Gospel he makes the Church grow, perpetually renews her, and leads her to perfect union with her Spouse (No. 4).

Foundation of the Church

The mystery of the holy Church is manifest in her very foundation, for the Lord Jesus inaugurated her by preaching the Good News, that is, the coming of God's Kingdom, which, for centuries, had been promised in the Scriptures. . . . In Christ's word, in his works, and in his presence this Kingdom reveals itself to men.

The miracles of Jesus also confirm that the Kingdom has already arrived on earth.

Before all things, however, the Kingdom is clearly visible in the very Person of Christ, Son of God and Son of Man.

When Jesus rose up again after suffering death on the cross for mankind, he manifested that he had been appointed Lord, Messiah, and Priest forever (cf. Acts 2:36; Heb. 5:6; 7:17-21), and he poured out on his disciples the Spirit promised by the Father (cf. Acts 2:33). The Church, consequently, equipped with the gifts of her Founder and faithfully guarding his precepts . . . receives the mission to proclaim and to establish among all peoples the Kingdom of Christ and of God. She becomes on earth the initial budding forth of that Kingdom. While she slowly grows, the Church strains toward the consummation of the Kingdom and, with all her strength, hopes and desires to be united in glory with her King (No. 5).

Figures of the Church

In the Old Testament the revelation of the Kingdom had often been conveyed by figures of speech. In the same way the inner nature of the Church was now to be made known to us through various images.

The Church is a sheepfold . . . a flock . . . a tract of land to be cultivated, the field of God . . . his choice vineyard . . . the true vine is Christ . . . the edifice of God . . . the house of God . . . the holy temple (whose members are) . . . living stones . . . this holy city . . . a bride . . . our Mother . . . the spotless spouse of the spotless Lamb . . . an exile (No. 6).

In the human nature which he united to himself, the Son of God redeemed man and transformed him into a new creation (cf. Gal. 6:15; 2 Cor. 5:17) by overcoming death through his own death and resurrection. By communicating his Spirit to his brothers, called together from all peoples, Christ made them mystically into his own body.

In that body, the life of Christ is poured into the believers, who, through the sacraments, are united in a hidden and real way to Christ who suffered and was glorified. Through baptism we are formed in the likeness of Christ.

Truly partaking of the body of the Lord in the breaking of the eucharistic bread, we are taken up into communion with him and with one another (No. 7).

One Body in Christ

As all the members of the human body, though they are many, form one body, so also are the faithful in Christ (cf. 1 Cor. 12:12). Also, in the building up of Christ's body there is a flourishing variety of members and functions. There is only one Spirit who . . . distributes his different gifts for the welfare of the Church (cf. 1 Cor. 12:1-11). Among these gifts stands out the grace given to the apostles. To their authority, the Spirit himself subjected even those who were endowed with charisms (cf. 1 Cor. 14).

The head of this body is Christ (No. 7).

Mystical Body of Christ

Christ, the one Mediator, established and ceaselessly sustains here on earth his holy Church, the community of faith, hope, and charity, as a visible structure. Through her he communicates truth and grace to all. But the society furnished with hierarchical agencies and the Mystical Body of Christ are not to be considered as two realities, nor are the visible assembly and the spiritual community, nor the earthly Church and the Church enriched with heavenly things. Rather they form one interlocked reality which is comprised of a divine and a human element. For this reason . . . this reality is compared to the mystery of the incarnate Word. Just as the assumed nature inseparably united to the divine Word serves him as a living instrument of salvation, so, in a similar way, does the communal structure of the Church serve Christ's Spirit, who vivifies it by way of building up the body (cf. Eph. 4:16).

This is the unique Church of Christ which in the Creed we avow as one, holy, catholic, and apostolic. After his Resurrection our Savior handed her over to Peter to be shepherded (Jn. 21:17), commissioning him and the other apostles to propagate and govern her (cf. Mt. 28:18, ff.). Her he erected for all ages as "the pillar and mainstay of the truth" (1 Tm. 3:15). This Church, constituted and organized in the world as a society, subsists in the Catholic Church, which is governed by the successor of Peter and by the bishops in union with that successor, although many elements of sanctification and of truth can be found outside of her visible structure. These elements, however, as gifts properly belonging to the Church of Christ, possess an inner dynamism toward Catholic unity.

The Church, embracing sinners in her bosom, is at the same time holy and always in need of being purified, and incessantly pursues the path of penance and renewal.

The Church, "like a pilgrim in a foreign land, presses forward . . ." announcing the cross and death of the Lord until he comes (cf. 1 Cor. 11:26) (No. 8).

II. THE PEOPLE OF GOD

At all times and among every people, God has given welcome to whosoever fears him and does what is right (cf. Acts 10:35). It has pleased God, however, to make men holy and save them not merely as individuals without any mutual bonds, but by making them into a single people, a people which acknowledges him in truth and serves him in holiness. He therefore chose the race of Israel as a people unto himself. With it he set up a covenant. Step by step he taught this people by manifesting in its history both himself and the decree of his will, and by making it holy unto himself. All these things, however, were done by way of preparation and as a figure of that new and perfect covenant which was to be ratified in Christ.

Christ instituted this New Covenant, that is to say, the New Testament, in his blood (cf. 1 Cor. 11:25), by calling together a people made up of Jew and Gentile, making them one, not according to the flesh but in the Spirit.

This was to be the new People of God . . . reborn . . . through the Word of the living God (cf. 1 Pt. 1:23) . . . from water and the Holy Spirit (cf. Jn. 3:5-6) . . . "a chosen race, a royal priesthood, a holy nation, a purchased people. . . . You who in times past were not a people, but are now the People of God" (1 Pt. 2:9-10).

That messianic people has for its head Christ. . . . Its law is the new commandment to love as Christ loved us (cf. Jn. 13:34). Its goal is the Kingdom of God, which has been begun by God himself on earth, and which is to be further extended until it is brought to perfection by him at the end of time.

This messianic people, although it does not actually include all men, and may more than once look like a small flock, is nonetheless a lasting and sure seed of unity, hope, and salvation for the whole human race. Established by Christ as a fellowship of life, charity, and truth, it is also used by him as an instrument for the redemption of all, and is sent forth into the whole world as the light of the world and the salt of the earth (cf. Mt. 5:13-16).

Israel according to the flesh . . . was already called the Church of God (Neh. 13:1; cf. Nm. 20:4; Dt. 23:1, ff.). Likewise the new Israel . . . is also called the Church of Christ (cf. Mt. 16:18). For he has bought it for himself with his blood (cf. Acts 20:28), has filled it with his Spirit, and provided it with those means which befit it as a visible and social unity. God has gathered together as one all those who in faith look upon Jesus as the author of salvation and the source of unity and peace, and has established them as the Church, that for each and all she may be the visible sacrament of this saving unity (No. 9).

Priesthood

The baptized, by regeneration and the anointing of the Holy Spirit, are consecrated into . . . a holy priesthood.

[All members of the Church participate in the priesthood of Christ, through the common priesthood of the faithful. See Priesthood of the Laity.]

Though they differ from one another in essence and not only in degree, the common priesthood of the faithful and the ministerial or hierarchical priesthood are nonetheless interrelated. Each of them in its own special way is a participation in the one priesthood of Christ (No. 10).

It is through the sacraments and the exercise of the virtues that the sacred nature and organic structure of the priestly community is brought into operation (No. 11). (See Role of the Sacraments.)

Prophetic Office

The holy People of God shares also in Christ's prophetic office. It spreads abroad a living witness to him, especially by means of a life of faith and charity and by offering to God a sacrifice of praise. . . . The body of the faithful as a whole, anointed as they are by the Holy One (cf. Jn. 2:20, 27), cannot err in matters of belief. Thanks to a supernatural sense of faith which characterizes the People as a whole, it manifests this unerring quality when, "from the bishops down to the last member of the laity," it shows universal agreement in matters of faith and morals.

God's People accepts not the word of men but the very Word of God (cf. 1 Thes. 2:13). It clings without fail to the faith once delivered to the saints (cf. Jude 3), penetrates it more deeply by accurate insights, and applies it more thoroughly to life. All this it does under the lead of a sacred teaching authority to which it loyally defers.

It is not only through the sacraments and Church ministries that the same Holy Spirit sanctifies and leads the People of God. . . . He distributes special graces among the faithful of every rank. By these gifts he makes them fit and ready to undertake the various tasks or offices advantageous for the renewal and upbuilding of the Church. . . . These charismatic gifts . . . are to be received with thanksgiving and consolation, for they are exceedingly suitable and useful for the needs of the Church.

Judgment as to their genuineness and proper use belongs to those who preside over the Church, and to whose special competence it belongs . . . to test all things and hold fast to that which is good (cf. 1 Thes. 5:12; 19-21) (No. 12).

All Are Called

All men are called to belong to the new People of God. Wherefore this People, while remaining one and unique, is to be spread throughout the whole world and must exist in all ages, so that the purpose of God's will may be fulfilled. In the beginning God made human nature one. After his children were scattered, he decreed that they should at length be united again (cf. Jn. 11:52). It was for this reason that God sent his Son . . . that he might be Teacher, King, and Priest of all, the Head of the new and universal People of the sons of God. For this God finally sent his Son's Spirit as Lord and Lifegiver. He it is who, on behalf of the whole Church and each and every one of those who believe, is the principle of their coming together and remaining together in the teaching of the apostles and in fellowship, in the breaking of bread and in prayers (cf. Acts 2:42) (No. 13).

One People of God

It follows that among all the nations of earth there is but one People of God, which takes its citizens from every race, making them citizens of a Kingdom which is of a heavenly and not an earthly nature. For all the faithful scattered throughout the world are in communion with each other in the Holy Spirit. . . . the Church or People of God . . . foster(s) and take(s) to herself, insofar as they are good, the ability, resources and customs of each people. Taking them to herself, she purifies, strengthens, and ennobles them . . . This characteristic of universality which adorns the People of God is a gift from the Lord himself. By reason of it, the Catholic Church strives energetically and constantly to bring all humanity with all its riches back to Christ its Head in the unity of his Spirit.

In virtue of this catholicity each individual part of the Church contributes through its special gifts to the good of the other parts and of the whole Church. Thus through the common sharing of gifts . . . the whole and each of the parts receive increase.

All men are called to be part of this catholic unity of the People of God. . . . And there belong to it or are related to it in various ways, the Catholic faithful as well as all who believe in Christ, and indeed the whole of mankind. For all men are called to salvation by the grace of God (No. 13).

The Catholic Church

This sacred Synod turns its attention first to the Catholic faithful. Basing itself upon sacred Scripture and tradition, it teaches that the Church . . . is necessary for salvation. For Christ, made present to us in his Body, which is the Church, is the one Mediator and the unique Way of salvation. In explicit terms he himself affirmed the necessity of faith and baptism (cf. Mk. 16:16; Jn. 3:5) and thereby affirmed also the necessity of the Church, for through baptism as through a door men enter the Church. Whosoever, therefore, knowing that the Catholic Church was made necessary by God through Jesus Christ, would refuse to enter her or to remain in her could not be saved.

They are fully incorporated into the society Church who, possessing the Spirit of Christ, accept her entire system and all the means of salvation given to her, and through union with her visible structure are joined to Christ, who rules her through the Supreme Pontiff and the bishops. This joining is effected by the bonds of professed faith, of the sacraments, of ecclesiastical government, and of communion. He is not saved, however, who, though he is part of the body of the Church, does not persevere in charity. He remains indeed in the bosom of the Church, but . . . only in a "bodily" manner and not "in his heart."

Catechumens who, moved by the Holy Spirit, seek with explicit intention to be incorporated into the Church, are by that very intention joined to her. . . . Mother Church already embraces them as her own (No. 14).

Other Christians, The Unbaptized

The Church recognizes that in many ways she is linked with those who, being baptized, are honored with the name of Christian, though they do not profess the faith in its entirety or do not preserve unity of communion with the successor of Peter.

We can say that in some real way they are joined with us in the Holy Spirit, for to them also he gives his gifts and graces, and is thereby operative among them with his sanctifying power (No. 15).

Finally, those who have not yet received the Gospel are related in various ways to the People of God. In the first place there is the people to whom the covenants and the promises were given and from whom Christ was born according to the flesh (cf. Rom. 9:4-5). On account of their fathers, this people remains most dear to God, for God does not repent of the gifts he makes nor of the calls he issues (cf. Rom. 11:28-29).

But the plan of salvation also includes those who acknowledge the Creator. In the first place among these are the Moslems. . . . Nor is God himself far distant from those who in shadows and images seek the unknown God.

Those also can attain to everlasting salvation

who through no fault of their own do not know the Gospel of Christ or his Church, yet sincerely seek God and, moved by grace, strive by their deeds to do his will as it is known to them through the dictates of conscience. Nor does divine Providence deny the help necessary for salvation to those who, without blame on their part, have not yet arrived at an explicit knowledge of God, but who strive to live a good life, thanks to his grace. Whatever goodness or truth is found among them is looked upon by the Church as a preparation for the Gospel. She regards such qualities as given by him who enlightens all men so that they may finally have life (No. 16).

THE POPE, TEACHING AUTHORITY, COLLEGIALITY

The Roman Pontiff — the successor of St. Peter as the Vicar of Christ and head of the Church on earth — has full and supreme authority over the universal Church in matters pertaining to faith and morals (teaching authority), discipline and government (jurisdictional authority).

The primacy of the pope is real and supreme power. It is not merely a prerogative of honor — that is, of his being regarded as the first among equals. Neither does primacy imply that the pope is just the presiding officer of the collective body of bishops. The pope is the head of the Church.

Catholic belief in the primacy of the pope was stated in detail in the dogmatic constitution on the Church, *Pastor Aeternus,* approved in 1870 by the fourth session of the First Vatican Council. Some elaboration of the doctrine was made in the *Dogmatic Constitution on the Church* which was approved and promulgated by the Second Vatican Council Nov. 21, 1964. The entire body of teaching on the subject is based on Scripture and tradition and the centuries-long experience of the Church.

Infallibility

The essential points of doctrine concerning infallibility in the Church and the infallibility of the pope were stated by the Second Vatican Council in the *Dogmatic Constitution on the Church,* as follows:

"This infallibility with which the divine Redeemer willed his Church to be endowed in defining a doctrine of faith and morals extends as far as extends the deposit of divine revelation, which must be religiously guarded and faithfully expounded. This is the infallibility which the Roman Pontiff, the head of the college of bishops, enjoys in virtue of his office, when, as the supreme shepherd and teacher of all the faithful who confirms his brethren in their faith (cf. Lk. 22:32), he proclaims by a definitive act some doctrine of faith or morals. Therefore his definitions, of themselves, and not from the consent of the Church, are justly styled irreformable, for they are pronounced with the assistance of the Holy Spirit, an assistance promised to him in blessed Peter. Therefore they need no approval of others, nor do they allow an appeal to any other judgment. For then the Roman Pontiff is not pronouncing judgment as a private person. Rather, as the supreme teacher of the universal Church, as one in whom the charism of the infallibility of the Church herself is individually present, he is expounding or defending a doctrine of Catholic faith.

"The infallibility promised to the Church resides also in the body of bishops when that body exercises supreme teaching authority with the successor of Peter. To the resultant definitions the assent of the Church can never be wanting, on account of the activity of that same Holy Spirit, whereby the whole flock of Christ is preserved and progresses in unity of faith.

"But when either the Roman Pontiff or the body of bishops together with him defines a judgment, they pronounce it in accord with revelation itself. All are obliged to maintain and be ruled by this revelation, which, as written or preserved by tradition, is transmitted in its entirety through the legitimate succession of bishops and especially through the care of the Roman Pontiff himself.

"Under the guiding light of the Spirit of truth, revelation is thus religiously preserved and faithfully expounded in the Church. The Roman Pontiff and the bishops, in view of their office and of the importance of the matter, strive painstakingly and by appropriate means to inquire properly into that revelation and to give apt expression to its contents. But they do not allow that there could be any new public revelation pertaining to the divine deposit of faith" (No. 25).

Authentic Teaching

The pope rarely speaks *ex cathedra* — that is, "from the chair" of St. Peter, for the purpose of making an infallible pronouncement. More often and in various ways he states authentic teaching in line with Scripture, tradition, the living experience of the Church, and the whole analogy of faith. Of such teaching, the Second Vatican Council said in its *Dogmatic Constitution on the Church* (No. 25):

"Religious submission of will and of mind must be shown in a special way to the authentic teaching authority of the Roman Pontiff, even when he is not speaking *ex cathedra*. That is, it must be shown in such a way that his supreme magisterium is acknowledged with reverence, the judgments made by him are sincerely adhered to, according to his manifest mind and will. His mind and will in the matter may be known chiefly either from the character of the documents, from his frequent repetition of the same doctrine, or from his manner of speaking."

With respect to bishops, the constitution states: "They are authentic teachers, that is, teachers endowed with the authority of Christ, who preach to the people committed to them the faith they must believe and put into practice. By the light of the Holy Spirit, they make that faith clear, bringing forth from the treasury of revelation new things and old (cf. Mt. 13:52), making faith bear fruit and vigilantly warding off any errors which threaten their flock (cf. 2 Tm. 4:1-4).

"Bishops, teaching in communion with the Roman Pontiff, are to be respected by all as witnesses to divine and Catholic truth. In matters of faith and morals, the bishops speak in the name of Christ and the faithful are to accept their teaching and adhere to it with a religious assent of soul."

Magisterium—Teaching Authority

Responsibility for teaching doctrine and judging orthodoxy belongs to the official teaching authority of the Church.

This authority is personalized in the pope, the successor of St. Peter as head of the Church, and in the bishops together and in union with the pope, as it was originally committed to Peter and to the whole college of apostles under his leadership. They are the official teachers of the Church.

Others have auxiliary relationships with the magisterium: theologians, in the study and clarification of doctrine; teachers — priests, religious, lay persons — who cooperate with the pope and bishops in spreading knowledge of religious truth; the faithful, who by their sense of faith and personal witness contribute to the development of doctrine and the establishment of its relevance to life in the Church and the world.

The magisterium, Pope Paul VI noted in an address at a general audience Jan. 11, 1967, "is a subordinate and faithful echo and secure interpreter of the divine word." It does not reveal new truths, "nor is it superior to sacred Scripture." Its competence extends to the limits of divine revelation manifested in Scripture and tradition and the living experience of the Church, with respect to matters of faith and morals and related subjects.

Official teaching in these areas is infallible when it is formally defined, for belief and acceptance by all members of the Church, by the pope, acting in the capacity of supreme shepherd of the flock of Christ; also, when doctrine is proposed and taught with moral unanimity of bishops with the pope in a solemn collegial manner, as in an ecumenical council, and/or in the ordinary course of events. Even when not infallibly defined, official teaching in the areas of faith and morals is authoritative and requires religious assent.

The teachings of the magisterium have been documented in creeds, formulas of faith, decrees and enactments of ecumenical and particular councils, various kinds of doctrinal statements, encyclical letters and other teaching instruments. They have also been incorporated into the liturgy, with the result that the law of prayer is said to be a law of belief.

Collegiality

The bishops of the Church, in union with the pope, have supreme teaching and pastoral authority over the whole Church in addition to the authority of office they have for their own dioceses.

This collegial authority is exercised in a solemn manner in an ecumenical council and can be exercised in other ways as well, "provided that the head of the college calls them to collegiate action, or at least so approves or freely accepts the united action of the dispersed bishops that it is made a true collegiate act."

This doctrine is grounded on the fact that: "Just as, by the Lord's will, St. Peter and the other apostles constituted one apostolic college, so in a similar way the Roman Pontiff as the successor of Peter, and the bishops as the successors of the apostles are joined together."

Doctrine on collegiality was stated by the Second Vatican Council in the *Dogmatic Constitution on the Church* (Nos. 22 and 23).

REVELATION

Following are excerpts from the "Constitution on Revelation" promulgated by the Second Vatican Council. They describe the nature and process of divine revelation, inspiration and interpretation of Scripture, the Old and New Testaments, and the role of Scripture in the life of the Church.

I. REVELATION ITSELF

God chose to reveal himself and to make known to us the hidden purpose of his will (cf. Eph. 1:9) by which through Christ, the Word made flesh, man has access to the Father in the Holy Spirit and comes to share in the divine nature (cf. Eph. 2:18; 2 Pt. 1:4). Through this revelation, therefore, the invisible God (cf. Col. 1:15; 1 Tm. 1:17) . . . speaks to men as friends (cf. Ex. 33:11; Jn. 15:14-15) and lives among them (cf. Bar. 3:38) so that he may invite and take them into fellowship with himself. This plan of revelation is realized by deeds and words having an inner unity: the deeds wrought by God in the history of salvation manifest and confirm the teaching and realities signified by the words, while the words proclaim the deeds and clarify the mystery contained in them. By this revelation then, the deepest truth about God and the salvation of man is made clear to us in Christ, who is the Mediator and at the same time the fullness of all revelation (No. 2).

God . . . from the start manifested himself to our first parents. Then after their fall his promise of redemption aroused in them the hope of being saved (cf. Gn. 3:15), and from that time on he ceaselessly kept the human race in his care, in order to give eternal life to those who perseveringly do good in search of salvation (cf. Rom. 2:6-7). . . . He called Abraham in order to make of him a great nation (cf. Gn. 12:2). Through the patriarchs, and after them through Moses and the prophets, he taught this nation to acknowledge himself as the one living and true God . . . and to wait for the Savior promised by him. In this manner he prepared the way for the Gospel down through the centuries (No. 3).

Revelation in Christ

Then, after speaking in many places and varied ways through the prophets, God "last of all in these days has spoken to us by his Son" (Heb. 1:1-2). . . . Jesus perfected revelation by fulfilling it through his whole work of making himself present and manifesting himself: through his words and deeds, his signs and wonders, but especially through his death and glorious resurrection from the dead and final sending of the Spirit of truth. Moreover, he confirmed with divine testimony what revelation proclaimed: that God is with us to free us from the darkness of sin and death, and to raise us up to life eternal.

The Christian dispensation, therefore, as the new and definitive covenant, will never pass away, and we now await no further new public revelation before the glorious manifestation of our Lord Jesus Christ (cf. 1 Tm. 6:14; Ti. 2:13) (No. 4).

II. TRANSMISSION OF REVELATION

God has seen to it that what he had revealed for the salvation of all nations would abide perpetually in its full integrity and be handed on to all generations. Therefore Christ the Lord, in whom the full revelation of the supreme God is brought to completion (cf. 2 Cor. 1:20; 3:16; 4:6), commissioned the apostles to preach to all men that Gospel which is the source of all saving truth and moral teaching, and thus to impart to them divine gifts. This Gospel had been promised in former times through the prophets, and Christ himself fulfilled it and promulgated it with his own lips. This commission was faithfully fulfilled by the apostles who, by their oral preaching, by example, and by ordinances, handed on what they had received from ... Christ ... or what they had learned through the prompting of the Holy Spirit. The commission was fulfilled, too, by those apostles and apostolic men who under the inspiration of the same Holy Spirit committed the message of salvation to writing (No. 7).

Tradition

But in order to keep the Gospel forever whole and alive within the Church, the apostles left bishops as their successors, "handing over their own teaching role" to them. This sacred tradition, therefore, and sacred Scripture of both the Old and the New Testament are like a mirror in which the pilgrim Church on earth looks at God (No. 7).

The apostolic preaching, which is expressed in a special way in the inspired books, was to be preserved by a continuous succession of preachers until the end of time. Therefore the apostles, handing on what they themselves had received, warn the faithful to hold fast to the traditions which they have learned.... Now what was handed on by the apostles includes everything which contributes to the holiness of life, and the increase in faith of the People of God; and so the Church, in her teaching, life, and worship, perpetuates and hands on to all generations all that she herself is, all that she believes (No. 8).

Development of Doctrine

This tradition which comes from the apostles develops in the Church with the help of the Holy Spirit. For there is a growth in the understanding of the realities and the words which have been handed down. This happens through the contemplation and study made by believers ... through the intimate understanding of spiritual things they experience, and through the preaching of those who have received through episcopal succession the sure gift of truth. For, as the centuries succeed one another, the Church constantly moves forward toward the fullness of divine truth until the words of God reach their complete fulfillment in her.

The words of the holy Fathers witness to the living presence of this tradition, whose wealth is poured into the practice and life of the believing and praying Church. Through the same tradition the Church's full canon of the sacred books is known, and the sacred writings themselves are more profoundly understood and unceasingly made active in her; ... and the Holy Spirit, through whom the living voice of the Gospel resounds in the Church, and through her, in the world, leads unto all truth those who believe and makes the word of Christ dwell abundantly in them (cf. Col. 3:16) (No. 8).

Tradition and Scripture

Hence there exist a close connection and communication between sacred tradition and sacred Scripture. For both of them, flowing from the same divine wellspring, in a certain way merge into a unity and tend toward the same end. For sacred Scripture is the word of God inasmuch as it is consigned to writing under the inspiration of the divine Spirit. To the successors of the apostles, sacred tradition hands on in its full purity God's word, which was entrusted to the apostles by Christ the Lord and the Holy Spirit. Thus, led by the light of the Spirit of truth, these successors can in their preaching preserve this word of God faithfully, explain it, and make it more widely known. Consequently, it is not from sacred Scripture alone that the Church draws her certainty about everything which has been revealed. Therefore both sacred tradition and sacred Scripture are to be accepted and venerated with the same sense of devotion and reverence (No. 9).

Sacred tradition and sacred Scripture form one sacred deposit of the word of God, which is committed to the Church (No. 10).

Teaching Authority of Church

The task of authentically interpreting the word of God, whether written or handed on, has been entrusted exclusively to the living teaching office of the Church, whose authority is exercised in the name of Jesus Christ. This teaching office is not above the word of God, but serves it, teaching only what has been handed on ... it draws from this one deposit of faith everything which it presents for belief as divinely revealed.

It is clear, therefore, that sacred tradition, sacred Scripture, and the teaching authority of the Church ... are so linked and joined together that one cannot stand without the others, and that all together and each in its own way under the action of the one Holy Spirit contribute effectively to the salvation of souls (No. 10).

III. INSPIRATION, INTERPRETATION

Those ... revealed realities ... contained and presented in sacred Scripture have been committed to writing under the inspiration of the Holy

Spirit. Holy Mother Church, relying on the belief of the apostles, holds that the books of both the Old and New Testament in their entirety, with all their parts, are sacred and canonical because, having been written under the inspiration of the Holy Spirit (cf. Jn. 20:31; 2 Tm. 3:16; 2 Pt. 1:19-21; 3:15-16) they have God as their author and have been handed on as such to the Church herself. In composing the sacred books, God chose men and, while employed by him, they made use of their powers and abilities, so that, with him acting in them and through them, they, as true authors, consigned to writing everything and only those things which he wanted (No. 11).

Inerrancy

Therefore, since everything asserted by the inspired authors or sacred writers must be held to be asserted by the Holy Spirit, it follows that the books of Scripture must be acknowledged as teaching firmly, faithfully, and without error that truth which God wanted put into the sacred writings for the sake of our salvation. Therefore "all Scripture is inspired by God and useful for teaching, for reproving, for correcting, for instruction in justice; that the man of God may be perfect, equipped for every good work" (2 Tm. 3:16-17) (No. 11).

Literary Forms

However, since God speaks in sacred Scripture through men in human fashion, the interpreter of sacred Scripture, in order to see clearly what God wanted to communicate to us, should carefully investigate what meaning the sacred writers really intended, and what God wanted to mainfest by means of their words.

The interpreter must investigate what meaning the sacred writer intended to express and actually expressed in particular circumstances as he used contemporary literary forms in accordance with the situation of his own time and culture. For the correct understanding of what the sacred author wanted to assert, due attention must be paid to the customary and characteristic styles of perceiving, speaking, and narrating which prevailed at the time of the sacred writer, and to the customs men normally followed at that period in their everyday dealings with one another (No. 12).

Analogy of Faith

No less serious attention must be given to the content and unity of the whole of Scripture, if the meaning of the sacred texts is to be correctly brought to light. The living tradition of the whole Church must be taken into account along with the harmony which exists between elements of the faith.... All of what has been said about the way of interpreting Scripture is subject finally to the judgment of the Church, which carries out the divine commission and ministry of guarding and interpreting the word of God (No. 12).

IV. THE OLD TESTAMENT

In carefully planning and preparing the salvation of the whole human race, the God of supreme love, by a special dispensation, chose for himself a people to whom he might entrust his promises. First he entered into a covenant with Abraham (cf. Gn. 15:18) and, through Moses, with the people of Israel (cf. Ex. 24:8). To this people which he had acquired for himself, he so manifested himself through words and deeds as the one true and living God that Israel came to know by experience the ways of God with men.... The plan of salvation, foretold by the sacred authors, recounted and explained by them, is found as the true word of God in the books of the Old Testament: these books, therefore, written under divine inspiration, remain permanently valuable (No. 14).

Principal Purpose

The principal purpose to which the plan of the Old Covenant was directed was to prepare for the coming both of Christ, the universal Redeemer, and of the messianic Kingdom.... Now the books of the Old Testament, in accordance with the state of mankind before the time of salvation established by Christ, reveal to all men the knowledge of God and of man and the ways in which God... deals with men. These books ... show us true divine pedagogy (No. 15).

The books of the Old Testament with all their parts, caught up into the proclamation of the Gospel, acquire and show forth their full meaning in the New Testament (cf. Mt. 5:17; Lk. 24:27; Rom. 16:25-26; 2 Cor. 3:14-16) and in turn shed light on it and explain it (No. 16).

V. THE NEW TESTAMENT

The word of God ... is set forth and shows its power in a most excellent way in the writings of the New Testament. For when the fullness of time arrived (cf. Gal. 4:4), the Word was made flesh and dwelt among us in the fullness of grace and truth (cf. Jn. 1:14). Christ established the Kingdom of God on earth, manifested his Father and himself by deeds and words, and completed his work by his death, resurrection, and glorious ascension and by the sending of the Holy Spirit. Having been lifted up from the earth, he draws all men to himself (cf. Jn. 12:32).... This mystery had not been manifested to other generations as it was now revealed to his holy apostles and prophets in the Holy Spirit (cf. Eph. 3:4-6), so that they might preach the Gospel, stir up faith in Jesus, Christ and Lord, and gather the Church together. To these realities, the writings of the New Testament stand as a perpetual and divine witness (No. 17).

The Gospels and Other Writings

The Gospels have a special preeminence ... for they are the principal witness of the life and teaching of the incarnate Word, our Savior.

The Church has always and everywhere held and continues to hold that the four Gospels are of apostolic origin. For what the apostles preached ... afterwards they themselves and apostolic men, under the inspiration of the divine Spirit, handed on to us in writing: the foundation of faith, namely, the fourfold Gospel, according to Matthew, Mark, Luke, and John (No. 18).

The four Gospels, ... whose historical character the Church unhesitatingly asserts, faithfully hand on what Jesus Christ, while living among men, really did and taught for their eternal salvation until the day he was taken up into heaven (see Acts 1:1-2). Indeed, after the ascension of the Lord the apostles handed on to their hearers what he had said and done. . . . The sacred authors wrote the four Gospels, selecting some things from the many which had been handed on by word of mouth or in writing, reducing some of them to a synthesis, explicating some things in view of the situation of their churches, and preserving the form of proclamation but always in such fashion that they told us the honest truth about Jesus. For their intention in writing was that . . . we might know "the truth" concerning those matters about which we have been instructed (cf. Lk. 1:2-4) (No. 19).

Besides the four Gospels, the canon of the New Testament also contains the Epistles of St. Paul and other apostolic writings, composed under the inspiration of the Holy Spirit. In these writings . . . those matters which concern Christ the Lord are confirmed, his true teaching is more and more fully stated, the saving power of the divine work of Christ is preached, the story is told of the beginnings of the Church and her marvelous growth, and her glorious fulfillment is foretold (No. 20).

VI. SCRIPTURE IN CHURCH LIFE

The Church has always venerated the divine Scriptures just as she venerates the body of the Lord. . . . She has always regarded the Scriptures together with sacred tradition as the supreme rule of faith, and will ever do so. For, inspired by God and committed once and for all to writing, they impart the word of God himself without change, and make the voice of the Holy Spirit resound in the words of the prophets and apostles. Therefore, like the Christian religion itself, all the preaching of the Church must be nourished and ruled by sacred Scripture (No. 21).

Easy access to sacred Scripture should be provided for all the Christian faithful. That is why the Church from the very beginning accepted as her own that very ancient Greek translation of the Old Testament which is named after seventy men (the Septuagint); and she has always given a place of honor to other translations, Eastern and Latin, especially the one known as the Vulgate. But since the word of God should be available at all times, the Church with maternal concern sees to it that suitable and correct translations are made into different languages, especially from the original texts of the sacred books. And if, given the opportunity and the approval of Church authority, these translations are produced in cooperation with the separated brethren as well, all Christians will be able to use them (No. 22).

Biblical Studies, Theology

The constitution encouraged the development and progress of biblical studies "under the watchful care of the sacred teaching office of the Church."

It noted also: "Sacred theology rests on the written word of God, together with sacred tradition, as its primary and perpetual foundation," and that "the study of the sacred page is, as it were, the soul of sacred theology" (Nos. 23, 24).

THE BIBLE

The Canon of the Bible is the Church's official list of sacred writings. These works, written by men under the inspiration of the Holy Spirit, contain divine revelation and, in conjunction with the tradition and teaching authority of the Church, constitute the rule of Catholic faith. The Canon was fixed and determined by the tradition and teaching authority of the Church.

The Catholic Canon

The Old Testament Canon of 45 books is as follows.

• **The Pentateuch,** the first five books: Genesis (Gn.), Exodus (Ex.), Leviticus (Lv.), Numbers (Nm.), Deuteronomy (Dt.).

• **Historical Books:** Joshua (Jos.), Judges (Jgs.), Ruth (Ru.) 1 and 2 Samuel (Sm.), 1 and 2 Kings (Kgs.), 1 and 2 Chronicles (Chr.), Ezra (Ezr.), Nehemiah (Neh.), Tobit (Tb.), Judith (Jdt.), Esther (Est.), 1 and 2 Maccabees (Mc.).

• **Wisdom Books:** Job (Jb.), Psalms (Ps.), Proverbs (Prv.), Ecclesiastes (Eccl.), Song of Songs (Song), Wisdom (Wis.), Sirach (Sir.).

• **The Prophets:** Isaiah (Is.), Jeremiah (Jer.), Lamentations (Lam.), Baruch (Bar.), Ezechiel (Ez.), Daniel (Dn.), Hosea (Hos.), Joel (Jl.), Amos (Am.), Obadiah (Ob.), Jonah (Jon.), Micah (Mi.), Nahum (Na.), Habakkuk (Hb.), Zephaniah (Zep.), Haggai (Hg.), Zechariah (Zec.) Malachi (Mal.).

The New Testament Canon of 27 books is as follows.

• **The Gospels** of Matthew (Mt.), Mark (Mk.), Luke (Lk.), John (Jn.)

• **The Acts of the Apostles** (Acts).

• **The Pauline Letters** — Romans (Rom.), 1 and 2 Corinthians (Cor.), Galatians (Gal.), Ephesians (Eph.), Philippians (Phil.), Colossians (Col.), 1 and 2 Thessalonians (Thes.) 1 and 2 Timothy (Tm.), Titus (Ti.), Philemon (Phlm.), Hebrews (Heb.).

• **The Catholic Letters** — James (Jas.), 1 and 2 Peter (Pt.), 1, 2 and 3 John (Jn.), Jude (Jude).

• **Revelation** (Rv.).

Developments

The Canon of the Old Testament was firm by the fifth century despite some questioning by scholars. It was stated by a council held at Rome in 382, by African councils held in Hippo in 393 and in Carthage in 397 and 419, and by Innocent I in 405.

All of the New Testament books were generally known and most of them were acknowledged as inspired by the end of the second century. The Muratorian Fragment, dating from about 200, listed most of the books recognized as canonical in later decrees. Prior to the end of the fourth cen-

The Bible

tury, however, there was controversy over the inspired character of several works — the Letter to the Hebrews, James, Jude, 2 Peter, 2 and 3 John and Revelation. Controversy ended in the fourth century and these books, along with those about which there was no dispute, were enumerated in the canon stated by the councils of Hippo and Carthage and affirmed by Innocent I in 405.

The Canon of the Bible was solemnly defined by the Council of Trent in the dogmatic decree *De Canonicis Scripturis*, Apr. 8, 1546.

Hebrew and Other Canons

The Hebrew Canon of sacred writings was fixed by tradition and the consensus of rabbis, probably by about 100 A.D. by the Synod or Council of Jamnia and certainly by the end of the second or early in the third century. It consists of the following works in three categories.

• **The Law (Torah)**, the five books of Moses: Genesis, Exodus, Leviticus, Numbers, Deuteronomy.

• **The Prophets:** former prophets — Joshua, Judges, 1 and 2 Samuel, 1 and 2 Kings; latter prophets — Isaiah, Jeremiah, Ezekiel, and 12 minor prophets (Hosea, Joel, Amos, Obadiah, Jonah, Micah, Nahum, Habakkuk, Zephaniah, Haggai, Zechariah, Malachi).

• **The Writings:** 1 and 2 Chronicles, Ezra, Nehemiah, Job, Psalms, Proverbs, Ecclesiastes, Song of Songs, Ruth, Esther, Daniel.

This Canon, embodying the tradition and practice of the Palestine community, did not include a number of works contained in the Alexandrian version of sacred writings translated into Greek between 250 and 100 B.C. and in use by Greek-speaking Jews of the Dispersion (outside Palestine). The rejected works, called apocrypha and not regarded as sacred, are: Tobit, Judith, Wisdom, Sirach, Baruch, 1 and 2 Maccabees, the last six chapters of Esther and three passages of Daniel (3:24-90; 13; 14). These books have also been rejected from the Protestant Canon, although they are included in bibles under the heading, Apocrypha.

The aforementioned books are held to be inspired and sacred by the Catholic Church. In Catholic usage, they are called deuterocanonical because they were under discussion for some time before questions about their canonicity were settled. Books regarded as canonical with little or no debate were called protocanonical. The status of both categories of books is the same in the Catholic Bible.

The Protestant Canon of the Old Testament is the same as the Hebrew.

The Old Testament Canon of some separated Eastern churches differs from the Catholic Canon.

Christians are in agreement on the Canon of the New Testament.

Languages

Hebrew, Aramaic and Greek were the original languages of the Bible. Most of the Old Testament books were written in Hebrew. Portions of Daniel, Ezra, Jeremiah, Esther, and probably the books of Tobit and Judith were written in Aramaic. The Book of Wisdom, 2 Maccabees and all the books of the New Testament were written in Greek.

Manuscripts and Versions

The original writings of the inspired authors have been lost. The Bible has been transmitted through ancient copies called manuscripts and through translations or versions.

Authoritative Greek manuscripts include the Sinaitic and Vatican manuscripts of the fourth century and the Alexandrine of the fifth century A.D.

The Septuagint and Vulgate translations are in a class by themselves.

The Septuagint version, a Greek translation of the Old Testament for Greek-speaking Jews, was begun about 250 and completed about 100 B.C. The work of several Jewish translators at Alexandria, it differed from the Hebrew Bible in the arrangement of books and included several, later called deuterocanonical, which were not acknowledged as sacred by the community in Palestine.

The Vulgate was a Latin version of the Old and New Testaments produced from the original languages by St. Jerome from about 383 to 404. It became the most widely used Latin text for centuries and was regarded as basic long before the Council of Trent designated it as authentic and suitable for use in public reading, controversy, preaching and teaching. Because of its authoritative character, it became the basis for many translations into other languages. A critical revision was completed by a pontifical commission in 1977.

Hebrew and Aramaic manuscripts of great antiquity and value have figured more significantly than before in recent scriptural work by Catholic scholars, especially since their use was strongly encouraged, if not mandated, in 1943 by Pius XII in the encyclical *Divino Afflante Spiritu*.

The English translation of the Bible in general use among Catholics until well into the 20th century was the *Douay-Rheims*, so called because of the places where it was prepared and published, the New Testament at Rheims in 1582 and the Old Testament at Douay in 1609. The translation was made from the Vulgate text. As revised and issued by Bishop Richard Challoner in 1749 and 1750, it became the standard Catholic English version for about 200 years.

A revision of the Challoner New Testament, made on the basis of the Vulgate text by scholars of the Catholic Biblical Association of America, was published in 1941 in the United States under the sponsorship of the Episcopal Committee of the Confraternity of Christian Doctrine.

New American Bible

A new translation of the entire Bible, the first ever made directly into English from the original languages under Catholic auspices, was projected in 1944 and completed in the fall of 1970 with publication of the *New American Bible*. The Episcopal Committee of the Confraternity of Christian Doctrine sponsored the NAB. The translators were members of the Catholic Biblical Association of America and several fellow scholars of other faiths. The typical edition was produced by St. Anthony Guild Press, Paterson, N.J.

The *Jerusalem Bible* is an English translation of a French version based on the original languages. It was published by Doubleday & Co., Inc., which is also working toward completion of the *Anchor Bible.*

The Protestant counterpart of the *Douay-Rheims Bible* was the *King James Bible,* called the *Authorized Version* in England. Originally published in 1611, it was in general use for more than three centuries. Its modern revisions include the *English Revised Version,* published between 1881 and 1885; the *American Revised Version,* 1901, and revisions of the New Testament (1946) and the Old Testament (1952) published in 1957 in the United States as the *Revised Standard Version.* The latest revision, a translation in the language of the present day made from Greek and Hebrew sources, is the *New English Bible,* published Mar. 16, 1970. Its New Testament portion was originally published in 1961.

New Translation of New Testament

A new translation of the New Testament (of the New American Bible published in 1970) was made public Apr. 5, 1987, in Washington, under the auspices of the U.S. Catholic Biblical Apostolate. It features gender-inclusive language where appropriate and in accord with the meaning of the original text. The 1970 New Testament remains the text approved for use in the liturgy.

Biblical Federation

In November, 1966, Pope Paul commissioned the Secretariat for Promoting Christian Unity to start work for the widest possible distribution of the Bible and to coordinate endeavors toward the production of Catholic-Protestant Bibles in all languages.

The World Catholic Federation for the Biblical Apostolate, established in 1969, sponsors a program designed to create greater awareness among Catholics of the Bible and its use in everyday life.

The U. S. Center for the Catholic Biblical Apostolate is related to the Department of Education, U.S. Catholic Conference. Address: 1312 Massachusetts Ave. N.W., Washington, D.C. 20005.

APOCRYPHA

In Catholic usage, Apocrypha are books which have some resemblance to the canonical books in subject matter and title but which have not been recognized as canonical by the Church. They are characterized by a false claim to divine authority; extravagant accounts of events and miracles alleged to be supplemental revelation; material favoring heresy (especially in "New Testament" apocrypha); minimal, if any, historical value.

Among examples of this type of literature itemized by J. McKenzie, S.J., in *Dictionary of the Bible* are: *the Books of Adam and Eve, Martyrdom of Isaiah, Testament of the Patriarchs, Assumption of Moses, Sibylline Oracles; Gospel of James, Gospel of Thomas, Arabic Gospel of the Infancy, History of Joseph the Carpenter; Acts of John, Acts of Paul, Acts of Peter, Acts of Andrew,* and numerous epistles.

Books of this type are called pseudepigrapha by Protestants.

In Protestant usage, some books of the Catholic Bible (deuterocanonical) are called apocrypha because their inspired character is rejected.

DEAD SEA SCROLLS

The Qumran Scrolls, popularly called the Dead Sea Scrolls, are a collection of manuscripts, all but one of them in Hebrew, found since 1947 in caves in the Desert of Juda west of the Dead Sea.

Among the findings were a complete text of Isaiah dating from the second century, B.C., more or less extensive fragments of other Old Testament texts (including the deuterocanonical Tobit), and a commentary on Habakkuk. Until the discovery of these materials, the oldest known Hebrew manuscripts were from the 10th century, A.D.

Also found were messianic and apocalyptic texts, and other writings describing the beliefs and practices of the Essenes, a rigoristic Jewish sect.

The scrolls, dating from about the first century before and after Christ, are important sources of information about Hebrew literature, Jewish history during the period between the Old and New Testaments, and the history of Old Testament texts. They established the fact that the Hebrew text of the Old Testament was fixed before the beginning of the Christian era and have had definite effects in recent critical studies and translations of the Old Testament. Together with other scrolls found at Masada, they are still the subject of intensive study.

BOOKS OF THE BIBLE

OLD TESTAMENT
(Dates are before Christ.)

Pentateuch

The Pentateuch is the collective title of the first five books of the Bible. Substantially, they identify the Israelites as Yahweh's Chosen People, cover their history from Egypt to the threshold of the Promised Land, contain the Mosaic Law and Covenant, and disclose the promise of salvation to come. Principal themes concern the divine promise of salvation, Yahweh's fidelity and the Covenant. Work on the composition of the Pentateuch was completed in the sixth century.

Genesis: The book of origins, according to its title in the Septuagint. In two parts, covers: religious prehistory, including accounts of the origin of the world and man, the original state of innocence and the fall, the promise of salvation, patriarchs before and after the Deluge, the Tower of Babel narrative, genealogies (first 11 chapters);

the Covenant with Abraham and patriarchal history from Abraham to Joseph (balance of the 50 chapters). Significant are the themes of Yahweh's universal sovereignty and mercy.

Exodus: Named with the Greek word for departure, is a religious epic which describes the oppression of the 12 tribes in Egypt and their departure, liberation or passover therefrom under the leadership of Moses; Yahweh's establishment of the Covenant with them, making them his Chosen People, through the mediation of Moses at Mt. Sinai; instructions concerning the tabernacle, the sanctuary and Ark of the Covenant; the institution of the priesthood. The book is significant because of its theology of liberation and redemption. In Christian interpretation, the Exodus is a figure of baptism.

Leviticus: Mainly legislative in theme and purpose, contains laws regarding sacrifices, ceremonies of ordination and the priesthood of Aaron, legal purity, the holiness code, atonement, the redemption of offerings and other subjects. Summarily, Levitical laws provided directives for all aspects of religious observance and for the manner in which the Israelites were to conduct themselves with respect to Yahweh and each other. Leviticus was the liturgical handbook of the priesthood.

Numbers: Taking its name from censuses recounted at the beginning and near the end, is a continuation of Exodus. It combines narrative of the Israelites' desert pilgrimage from Sinai to the border of Canaan with laws related to and expansive of those in Leviticus.

Deuteronomy: The concluding book of the Pentateuch, recapitulates, in the form of a testament of Moses, the Law and much of the desert history of the Israelites; enjoins fidelity to the Law as the key to good or bad fortune for the people; gives an account of the commissioning of Joshua as the successor of Moses. Notable themes concern the election of Israel by Yahweh, observance of the Law, prohibitions against the worship of foreign gods, worship of and confidence in Yahweh, the power of Yahweh in nature. The Deuteronomic Code or motif, embodying all of these elements, was the norm for interpreting Israelite history.

Joshua, Judges, Ruth

Joshua: Records the fulfillment of Yahweh's promise to the Israelites in their conquest, occupation and division of Canaan under the leadership of Joshua. It also contains an account of the return of Transjordanian Israelites and of a renewal of the Covenant. It was redacted in final form probably in the sixth century or later.

Judges: Records the actions of charismatic leaders, called judges, of the tribes of Israel between the death of Joshua and the time of Samuel, and a crisis of idolatry among the people. The basic themes are sin and punishment, repentance and deliverance; its purpose was in line with the Deuteronomic motif, that the fortunes of the Israelites were related to their observance or nonobservance of the Law and the Covenant. It was redacted in final form probably in the sixth century.

Ruth: Named for the Gentile (Moabite) woman who, through marriage with Boaz, became an Israelite and an ancestress of David (her son, Obed, became his grandfather). Themes are filial piety, faith and trust in Yahweh, the universality of messianic salvation. Dates ranging from c. 950 to the seventh century have been assigned to the origin of the book, whose author is unknown.

Historical Books

These books, while they contain a great deal of factual material, are unique in their preoccupation with presenting and interpreting it, in the Deuteronomic manner, in primary relation to the Covenant on which the nation of Israel was founded and in accordance with which community and personal life were judged.

The books are: Samuel 1 and 2, from the end of Judges (c. 1020) to the end of David's reign (c. 961); Kings 1 and 2, from the last days of David to the start of the Babylonian Exile and the destruction of the Temple (587); Chronicles 1 and 2, from the reign of Saul (c. 1020-1000) to the return of the people from the Exile (538); Ezra and Nehemiah, covering the reorganization of the Jewish community after the Exile (458-397); Maccabees 1 and 2, recounting the struggle against attempted suppression of Judaism (168-142).

Three of the books listed below — Tobit, Judith and Esther — are categorized as religious novels.

Samuel 1 and 2: A single work in concept and contents, containing episodic history of the last two Judges, Eli and Samuel, the establishment and rule of the monarchy under Saul and David, and the political consequences of David's rule. The royal messianic dynasty of David was the subject of Nathan's oracle in 2 Sm. 7. The books were edited in final form probably late in the seventh century or during the Exile.

Kings 1 and 2: Cover the last days of David and the career of Solomon, including the building of the Temple and the history of the kingdom during his reign; stories of the prophets Elijah and Elisha; the history of the divided kingdom to the fall of Israel in the North (721) and the fall of Judah in the South (587), the destruction of Jerusalem and the Temple. They reflect the Deuteronomic motif in attributing the downfall of the people to corruption of belief and practice in public and private life. They were completed probably in the sixth century.

Chronicles 1 and 2: A collection of historical traditions interpreted in such a way as to present an ideal picture of one people governed by divine law and united in one Temple worship of the one true God. Contents include genealogical tables from Adam to David, the careers of David and Solomon, coverage of the kingdom of Judah to the Exile, and the decree of Cyrus permitting the return of the people and rebuilding of Jerusalem. Both are related to and were written about 400 by the same author, the Chronicler, who composed Ezra and Nehemiah.

Ezra and Nehemiah: A running account of the return of the people to their homeland after the Exile and of practical efforts, under the leadership of Ezra and Nehemiah, to restore and reorganize the religious and political community on the basis of Israelite traditions, divine worship and observance of the Law. Events of great significance were the building of the second Temple, the building of a wall around Jerusalem and the proclamation of the Law by Ezra. This restored community was the start of Judaism. Both are related to and were written about 400 by the same author, the Chronicler, who composed Chronicles 1 and 2.

Tobit: Written in the literary form of a novel and having greater resemblance to wisdom than to historical literature, narrates the personal history of Tobit, a devout and charitable Jew in exile, and persons connected with him, viz., his son Tobiah, his kinsman Raguel and Raguel's daughter Sarah. Its purpose was to teach people how to be good Jews. One of its principal themes is patience under trial, with trust in divine Providence which is symbolized by the presence and action of the angel Raphael. It was written about 200.

Judith: Recounts, in the literary form of a historical novel or romance, the preservation of the Israelites from conquest and ruin through the action of Judith. The essential themes are trust in God for deliverance from danger and emphasis on observance of the Law. It was written probably during the Maccabean period.

Esther: Relates, in the literary form of a historical novel or romance, the manner in which Jews in Persia were saved from annihilation through the central role played by Esther, the Jewish wife of Ahasuerus; a fact commemorated by the Jewish feast of Purim. Like Judith, it has trust in divine Providence as its theme and indicates that God's saving will is sometimes realized by persons acting in unlikely ways. It may have been written near the end of the fourth century.

Maccabees 1 and 2: While related to some extent because of common subject matter, are quite different from each other.

The first book recounts the background and events of the 40-year (175-135) struggle for religious and political freedom led by Judas Maccabaeus and his brothers against the Hellenist Seleucid kings and some Hellenophiles among the Jews. Victory was symbolized by the rededication of the Temple. Against the background of opposition between Jews and Gentiles, the author equated the survival of belief in the one true God with survival of the Jewish people, thus identifying religion with patriotism. It was written probably near the year 100.

The second book supplements the first to some extent, covering and giving a theological interpretation to events from 180 to 162. It explains the feast of the Dedication of the Temple, a key event in the survival of Judaism which is commemorated in the feast of Hanukkah; stresses the primacy of God's action in the struggle for survival; and indicates belief in an afterlife and the resurrection of the body. It was completed probably about 124.

Wisdom Books

With the exceptions of Psalms and the Song of Songs, the titles listed under this heading are called wisdom books because their purpose was to formulate the fruits of human experience in the context of meditation on sacred Scripture and to present them as an aid toward understanding the problems of life. Hebrew wisdom literature was distinctive from pagan literature of the same type, but it had limitations; these were overcome in the New Testament, which added the dimensions of the New Covenant to those of the Old. Solomon was regarded as the archtype of the wise man.

Job: A dramatic, didactic poem consisting mainly of several dialogues between Job and his friends concerning the mystery involved in the coexistence of the just God, evil and the suffering of the just. It describes an innocent man's experience of suffering and conveys the truth that faith in and submission to God rather than complete understanding, which is impossible, make the experience bearable; also, that the justice of God cannot be defended by affirming that it is realized in this world. Of unknown authorship, it was composed between the seventh and fifth centuries.

Psalms: A collection of 150 religious songs or lyrics reflecting Israelite belief and piety dating from the time of the monarchy to the post-Exilic period, a span of well over 500 years. The psalms, which are a compendium of Old Testament theology, were used in the temple liturgy and for other occasions. They were of several types suitable for the king, hymns, lamentations, expressions of confidence and thanksgiving, prophecy, historical meditation and reflection, and the statement of wisdom. About one-half of them are attributed to David; many were composed by unknown authors.

Proverbs: The oldest book of the wisdom type in the Bible, consisting of collections of sayings attributed to Solomon and other persons regarding a wide variety of subjects including wisdom and its nature, rules of conduct, duties with respect to one's neighbor, the conduct of daily affairs. It reveals many details of Hebrew life. Its nucleus dates from the period before the Exile. The extant form of the book dates probably from the end of the fifth century.

Ecclesiastes: A treatise about many subjects whose unifying theme is the vanity of strictly human efforts and accomplishments with respect to the achievement of lasting happiness; the only things which are not vain are fear of the Lord and observance of his commandments. The pessimistic tone of the book is due to the absence of a concept of afterlife. It was written by an unknown author probably in the third century.

Song of Songs: A collection of love lyrics reflecting various themes, including the love of God for Israel and the celebration of ideal love and fidelity between man and woman. It was written by an unknown author after the Exile.

Wisdom: Deals with many subjects including the reward of justice; praise of wisdom, a gift of Yahweh proceeding from belief in him and the practice of his Law; the part played by him in the history of his people, especially in their liberation from Egypt; the folly and shame of idolatry. Its contents are taken from the whole sacred literature of the Jews and represent a distillation of its wisdom based on the law, beliefs and traditions of Israel. The last of the Old Testament books, it was written in the early part of the first century before Christ by a member of the Jewish community at Alexandria.

Sirach: Resembling Proverbs, is a collection of sayings handed on by a grandfather to his grandson. It contains a variety of moral instruction and eulogies of patriarchs and other figures in Israelite history. Its moral maxims apply to individuals, the family and community, relations with God, friendship, education, wealth, the Law, divine worship. Its theme is that true wisdom consists in the Law. (It was formerly called Ecclesiasticus, the Church Book, because of its extensive use by the Church for moral instruction.) It was written in Hebrew between 200 and 175, during a period of strong Hellenistic influence, and was translated into Greek after 132.

The Prophets

These books and the prophecies they contain "express judgments of the people's moral conduct, on the basis of the Mosaic alliance between God and Israel. They teach sublime truths and lofty morals. They contain exhortations, threats, announcements of punishment, promises of deliverance.... In the affairs of men, their prime concern is the interests of God, especially in what pertains to the Chosen People through whom the Messiah is to come; hence their denunciations of idolatry and of that externalism in worship which exclude the interior spirit of religion. They are concerned also with the universal nature of the moral law, with personal responsibility, with the person and office of the Messiah, and with the conduct of foreign nations" (*The Holy Bible*, Prophetic Books, CCD Edition, 1961; Preface). There are four major (Isaiah, Jeremiah, Ezekiel, Daniel) and 12 minor prophets (distinguished by the length of books), Lamentations and Baruch. Earlier prophets, mentioned in historical books, include Samuel, Gad, Nathan, Elijah and Elisha.

Before the Exile, prophets were the intermediaries through whom God communicated revelation to the people. Afterwards, prophecy lapsed and the written word of the Law served this purpose.

Isaiah: Named for the greatest of the prophets whose career spanned the reigns of three Hebrew kings from 742 to the beginning of the seventh century, in a period of moral breakdown in Judah and threats of invasion by foreign enemies. It is an anthology of poems and oracles credited to him and a number of followers deeply influenced by him. Of special importance are the prophecies concerning Immanuel (6 to 12), including the prophecy of the virgin birth (7:14). Chapters 40 to 55, called Deutero-Isaiah, are attributed to an anonymous poet toward the end of the Exile; this portion contains the Songs of the Servant. The concluding part of the book (56-66) contains oracles by later disciples. One of many themes in Isaiah concerned the saving mission of the remnant of Israel in the divine plan of salvation.

Jeremiah: Combines history, biography and prophecy in a setting of crisis caused by internal and external factors, viz., idolatry and general infidelity to the Law among the Israelites and external threats from the Assyrians, Egyptians and Babylonians. Jeremiah prophesied the promise of a new covenant as well as the destruction of Jerusalem and the Temple. His career began in 626 and ended some years after the beginning of the Exile. The book, the longest in the Bible, was edited in final form after the Exile.

Lamentations: A collection of five laments or elegies over the fall of Jerusalem and the fate of the people in Exile, written by an unknown eyewitness. They convey the message that Yahweh struck the people because of their sins and reflect confidence in his love and power to restore his converted people.

Baruch: Against the background of the already begun Exile, it consists of an introduction and several parts: an exile's prayer of confession and petition for forgiveness and the restoration of Israel; a poem praising wisdom and the Law of Moses; a lament in which Jerusalem, personified, bewails the fate of her people and consoles them with the hope of blessings to come; and a polemic against idolatry. Although ascribed to Baruch, Jeremiah's secretary, it was written by several authors probably in the second century.

Ezekiel: Named for the priest-prophet who prophesied in Babylon from 593 to 571, during the first phase of the Exile. To prepare his fellow early exiles for the impending fall of Jerusalem, he reproached the Israelites for past sins and predicted woes to come upon them. After the destruction of the city, the burden of his message was hope and promise of restoration. Ezekiel had great influence on the religion of Israel after the Exile.

Daniel: The protagonist is a young Jew, taken early to Babylon where he lived until about 538, who figured in a series of edifying stories which originated in Israelite tradition. The stories, whose characters are not purely legendary but rest on historical tradition, recount the trials and triumphs of Daniel and his three companions, and other episodes including those concerning Susannah, Bel, and the Dragon. The book is more apocalyptic than prophetic: it envisions Israel in glory to come and conveys the message that men of faith can resist temptation and overcome adversity. It states the prophetic themes of right conduct, divine control of men and events, and the final triumph of the kingdom. It was written by an unknown author in the 160's to give moral support to Jews during the persecutions of the Maccabean period.

Hosea: Consists of a prophetic parallel between Hosea's marriage and Yahweh's relations with his people. As the prophet was married to a faithless wife whom he would not give up, Yahweh was bound in Covenant with an idolatrous and unjust Israel whom he would not desert but would chastise for purification. Hosea belonged to the Northern Kingdom of Israel and began his career about the middle of the eighth century. He inaugurated the tradition of describing Yahweh's relation to Israel in terms of marriage.

Joel: Is apocalyptic and eschatological regarding divine judgment, the Day of the Lord, which is symbolized by a ravaging invasion of locusts, the judgment of the nations in the Valley of Josaphat and the outpouring of the Spirit in the messianic era to come. Its message is that God will vindicate and save Israel, in view of the prayer and repentance of the people, and will punish their enemies. It was composed about 400.

Amos: Consists of an indictment against foreign enemies of Israel; a strong denunciation of the people of Israel, whose infidelity, idolatry and injustice made them subject to divine judgment and punishment; and a messianic oracle regarding Israel's restoration. Amos prophesied in the Northern Kingdom of Israel, at Bethel, in the first half of the eighth century; chronologically, he was the first of the canonical prophets.

Obadiah: A 21-verse prophecy, the shortest and one of the sternest in the Bible, against the Edomites, invaders of southern Judah and enemies of those returning from the Exile to their homeland. It was probably composed in the fifth century.

Jonah: A parable of divine mercy with the theme that Yahweh wills the salvation of all, not just a few, men who respond to his call. Its protagonist is a disobedient prophet; forced by circumstances beyond his control to preach penance among Gentiles, he is highly successful in his mission but baffled by the divine concern for those who do not belong to the Chosen People. It was written after the Exile, probably in the fifth century.

Micah: Attacks the injustice and corruption of priests, false prophets, officials and people; announces judgment and punishment to come; foretells the restoration of Israel; refers to the saving remnant of Israel. Micah was a contemporary of Isaiah.

Nahum: Concerns the destruction of Nineveh in 612 and the overthrow of the Assyrian Empire by the Babylonians.

Habakkuk: Dating from about 605-597, concerns sufferings to be inflicted by oppressors on the people of Judah because of their infidelity to the Lord. It also sounds a note of confidence in the Lord, the Savior, and declares that the just will not perish.

Zephaniah: Exercising his ministry in the second half of the seventh century, during a time of widespread idolatry, superstition and religious degradation, he prophesied impending judgment and punishment for Jerusalem and its people. He prophesied too that a holy remnant of the people (*anawim,* mentioned also by Amos) would be spared. Zephaniah was a forerunner of Jeremiah.

Haggai: One of the first prophets after the Exile, Haggai in 520 encouraged the returning exiles to reestablish their community and to complete the second Temple (dedicated in 515), for which he envisioned greater glory, in a messianic sense, than that enjoyed by the original Temple of Solomon.

Zechariah: A contemporary of Haggai, he prophesied in the same vein. A second part of the book, called Deutero-Zechariah and composed by one or more unknown authors, relates a vision of the coming of the Prince of Peace, the Messiah of the Poor.

Malachi: Written by an anonymous author, presents a picture of life in the post-Exilic community between 516 and the initiation of reforms by Ezra and Nehemiah about 432. Blame for the troubles of the community is placed mainly on priests for failure to carry out ritual worship and to instruct the people in the proper manner; other factors were religious indifference and the influence of doubters who were scandalized at the prosperity of the wicked. The vision of a universal sacrifice to be offered to Yahweh (1:11) is interpreted in Catholic theology as a prophecy of the sacrifice of the Mass. Malachi was the last of the minor prophets.

OLD TESTAMENT DATES

c. 1800 — c. 1600: Period of the patriarchs (Abraham, Isaac, Jacob).

c. 1600: Israelites in Egypt.

c. 1250: Exodus of Israelites from Egypt.

c. 1210: Entrance of Israelites into Canaan.

c. 1210 — c. 1020: Period of the Judges.

c. 1020 — c. 1000: Reign of Saul, first king.

c. 1000 — c. 961: Reign of David.

c. 961 — 922: Reign of Solomon. Temple built during his reign.

922: Division of the Kingdom into Israel (North) and Judah (South).

721: Conquest of Israel by Assyrians.

587-538: Conquest of Judah by Babylonians. Babylonian Captivity and Exile. Destruction of Jerusalem and the Temple, 587. Captivity ended with the return of exiles, following the decree of Cyrus permitting the rebuilding of Jerusalem.

515: Dedication of the Second Temple.

458-397: Restoration and reform of the Jewish religious and political community; building of the Jerusalem wall, 439. Leaders in the movement were Ezra and Nehemiah.

168-142: Period of the Maccabees; war against Syrians.

142: Independence granted to Jews by Demetrius II of Syria.

135-37: Period of the Hasmonean dynasty.

63: Beginning of Roman rule.

37-4: Period of Herod the Great.

INTERPRETATION OF THE BIBLE

Cardinal Joseph Ratzinger, head of the Congregation for the Doctrine of the Faith, called Jan. 27, 1988, for a new look at methods used by scholars in interpreting the Bible and relating their conclusions to theology. He said the historical-critical method is in a state of "crisis" and added that scholars cannot find answers to their problems in fundamentalism. Rather, they must look at texts "in light of the total movement of history and in the light of history's central event, Jesus Christ. Only the combination of both these methods will yield understanding of the Bible." He also said most scholars have "disavowed materialist and radical feminist exegesis."

NEW TESTAMENT BOOKS
Gospels

The term Gospel is derived from the Anglo-Saxon *god-spell* and the Greek *euangelion*, meaning good news, good tidings. In Christian use, it means the good news of salvation proclaimed by Christ and the Church, and handed on in written form in the Gospels of Matthew, Mark, Luke and John.

The initial proclamation of the coming of the kingdom of God was made by Jesus in and through his Person, teachings and actions, and especially through his Passion, death and resurrection. This proclamation became the center of Christian faith and the core of the oral Gospel tradition with which the Church spread the good news by apostolic preaching for some 30 years before it was committed to writing by the Evangelists.

Nature of the Gospels

The historical truth of the Gospels was the subject of an instruction issued by the Pontifical Commission for Biblical Studies Apr. 21, 1964.

• The sacred writers selected from the material at their disposal (the oral Gospel tradition, some written collections of sayings and deeds of Jesus, eyewitness accounts) those things which were particularly suitable to the various conditions (liturgical, catechetical, missionary) of the faithful and the aims they had in mind, and they narrated these things in such a way as to correspond with those circumstances and their aims.

• The life and teaching of Jesus were not simply reported in a biographical manner for the purpose of preserving their memory but were "preached" so as to offer the Church the basis of doctrine concerning faith and morals.

• In their works, the Evangelists presented the true sayings of Jesus and the events of his life in the light of the better understanding they had following their enlightenment by the Holy Spirit. They did not transform Christ into a "mythical" Person, nor did they distort his teaching.

Passion narratives are the core of all the Gospels, covering the suffering, death and resurrection of Jesus as central events in bringing about and establishing the New Covenant. Leading up to them are accounts of the mission of John the Baptizer and the ministry of Jesus, especially in Galilee and finally in Jerusalem before the Passion. The infancy of Jesus is covered by Luke and Matthew with narratives inspired in part by appropriate Old Testament citations.

Matthew, Mark and Luke, while different in various respects, have so many similarities that they are called Synoptic; their relationships are the subject of the Synoptic Problem.

Matthew: Written probably between 80 and 100 for Jewish Christians, with clear reference to Jewish background and identification of Jesus as the divine Messiah, the fulfillment of the Old Testament. Distinctive are the use of Old Testament citations regarding the Person, activity and teaching of Jesus, and the presentation of doctrine in sermons and discourses.

Mark: The first of the Gospels, dating from about 70. Written for Gentile Christians, it is noted for the realism and wealth of concrete details with which it reveals Jesus as Son of God and Savior more by his actions and miracles than by his discourses. Theologically, it is less refined than the other Gospels.

Luke: Written about 75 for Gentile Christians. It is noted for the universality of its address, the insight it provides into the Christian way of life, the place it gives to women, the manner in which it emphasizes Jesus' friendship with sinners and compassion for the suffering.

John: Edited and arranged in final form probably between 90 and 100, is the most sublime and theological of the Gospels, and is different from the Synoptics in plan and treatment. Combining accounts of signs with longer discourses and reflections, it progressively reveals the Person and mission of Jesus — as Word, Way, Truth, Life, Light — in line with the purpose, "to help you believe that Jesus is the Messiah, the Son of God, so that through this faith you may have life in his name" (Jn. 20:31). There are questions about the authorship but no doubt about the Johannine authority and tradition behind the Gospel.

Acts of the Apostles

Acts of the Apostles: Written by Luke about 75 as a supplement to his Gospel. It describes the origin and spread of Christian communities through the action of the Holy Spirit from the resurrection of Christ to the time when Paul was placed in custody in Rome in the early 60's.

Letters (Epistles)

These letters, many of which antedated the Gospels, were written in response to existential needs of the early Christian communities for doctrinal and moral instruction, disciplinary action, practical advice, and exhortation to true Christian living.

Pauline Letters

These letters, which comprise approximately one-fourth of the New Testament, are primary and monumental sources of the development of Christian theology. Several of them may not have had Paul as their actual author, but evidence of the Pauline tradition behind them is strong. The letters to the Colossians, Philippians, Ephesians and Philemon have been called the "Captivity Letters" because of a tradition that they were written while Paul was under house arrest or another form of detention.

Romans: Written about 57 probably from Corinth on the central significance of Christ and faith in him for salvation, and the relationship of Christianity to Judaism; the condition of mankind without Christ; justification and the Christian life; duties of Christians.

Corinthians 1: Written near the beginning of 57 from Ephesus to counteract factionalism and disorders, it covers community dissensions, moral irregularities, marriage and celibacy, conduct at religious gatherings, the Eucharist, spiritual gifts (charisms) and their function in the Church, charity, the resurrection of the body.

Corinthians 2: Written later in the same year as 1 Cor., concerning Paul's defense of his apostolic life and ministry, and an appeal for a collection to aid poor Christians in Jerusalem.

Galatians: Written probably between 54 and 55 to counteract Judaizing opinions and efforts to undermine his authority, it asserts the divine origin of Paul's authority and doctrine, states that justification is not through Mosaic Law but through faith in Christ, insists on the practice of evangelical virtues, especially charity.

Ephesians: Written probably between 61 and 63, mainly on the Church as the Mystical Body of Christ.

Philippians: Written between 56 and 57 or 61 and 63 to warn the Philippians against enemies of their faith, to urge them to be faithful to their vocation and unity of belief, and to thank them for their kindness to him while he was being held in detention.

Colossians: Written probably while he was under house arrest in Rome from 61 to 63, to counteract the influence of self-appointed teachers who were watering down doctrine concerning Christ. It includes two highly important Christological passages, a warning against false teachers, and an instruction on the ideal Christian life.

Thessalonians 1 and 2: Written within a short time of each other probably in 51 from Corinth, mainly on doctrine concerning the Parousia, the second coming of Christ.

Timothy 1 and 2, Titus: Written between 65 and 67, or perhaps in the 70's, giving pastoral counsels to Timothy and Titus who were in charge of churches in Ephesus and Crete, respectively. 1 Tm. emphasizes pastoral responsibility for preserving unity of doctrine; 2 Tm. describes Paul's imprisonment in Rome.

Philemon: A private letter written between 61 and 63 to a wealthy Colossian concerning a slave, Onesimus, who had escaped from him; Paul appealed for kind treatment of the man.

Hebrews: Dating from sometime between 70 and 96, a complex theological treatise on Christology, the priesthood and sacrifice of Christ, the New Covenant, and the pattern for Christian living. Critical opinion is divided as to whether it was addressed to Judaeo or Gentile Christians.

Catholic Letters, Revelation

These seven letters have been called "catholic" because it was thought for some time, not altogether correctly, that they were not addressed to particular communities.

James: Written sometime before 62 in the spirit of Hebrew wisdom literature and the moralism of Tobit. An exhortation to practical Christian living, it is also noteworthy for the doctrine it states on good works and its citation regarding anointing of the sick.

Peter 1 and 2: The first letter may have been written between 64 and 67 or between 90 and 95; the second may date from 100 to 125. Addressed to Christians in Asia Minor, both are exhortations to perseverance in the life of faith despite trials and difficulties arising from pagan influences, isolation from other Christians and false teaching.

John 1: Written sometime in the 90's and addressed to Asian churches, its message is that God is made known to us in the Son and that fellowship with the Father is attained by living in the light, justice and love of the Son.

John 2: Written sometime in the 90's and addressed to a church in Asia, it commends the people for standing firm in the faith and urges them to perseverance.

John 3: Written sometime in the 90's, it appears to represent an effort to settle a jurisdictional dispute in one of the churches.

Jude: Written probably about 80, it is a brief treatise against erroneous teachings and practices opposed to law, authority and true Christian freedom.

Revelation: Written in the 90's along the lines of Johannine thought, it is a symbolic and apocalyptic treatment of things to come and of the struggle between the Church and evil combined with warning but hope and assurance to the Church regarding the coming of the Lord in glory.

INTERPRETATION OF THE BIBLE

According to the *Constitution on Revelation* issued by the Second Vatican Council, "the interpreter of Sacred Scripture, in order to see clearly what God wanted to communicate to us, should carefully investigate what meaning the sacred writers really intended, and what God wanted to manifest by means of their words" (No. 12).

Hermeneutics, Exegesis

This careful investigation proceeds in accordance with the rules of hermeneutics, the normative science of biblical interpretation and explanation. Hermeneutics in practice is called exegesis.

The principles of hermeneutics are derived from various disciplines and many factors which have to be considered in explaining the Bible and its parts.

These include: the original languages and languages of translation of the sacred texts, through philology and linguistics; the quality of texts, through textual criticism; literary forms and genres, through literary and form criticism; cultural, historical, geographical and other conditions which influenced the writers, through related studies; facts and truths of salvation history; the truths and analogy of faith.

Distinctive to biblical hermeneutics, which differs in important respects from literary interpretation in general, is the premise that the Bible, though written by human authors, is the work of divine inspiration in which God reveals his plan for the salvation of men through historical events and persons, and especially through the Person and mission of Christ.

Textual, Form Criticism

Textual criticism is the study of biblical texts, which have been transmitted in copies several times removed from the original manuscripts, for the purpose of establishing the real state of the original texts. This purpose is served by comparison of existing copies; by application to the texts of the disciplines of philology and linguistics; by examination of related works of antiquity; by study of biblical citations in works of the Fathers of the Church and other authors; and by other means of literary study.

Since about 1920, the sayings of Christ have been a particular object of New Testament study, the purpose being to analyze the forms of expression used by the Evangelists in order to ascertain the words actually spoken by him.

Literary Criticism

Literary criticism aims to determine the origin and kinds of literary composition, called forms or genres, employed by the inspired authors. Such determinations are necessary for decision regarding the nature and purpose and, consequently, the meaning of biblical passages. Underlying these studies is the principle that the manner of writing was conditioned by the intention of the authors, the meaning they wanted to convey, and the then-contemporary literary style, mode or medium best adapted to carry their message — e.g., true history, quasi-historical narrative, poems, prayers, hymns, psalms, aphorisms, allegories, discourses. Understanding these media is necessary for the valid interpretation of their message.

Literal Sense

The key to all valid interpretation is the literal sense of biblical passages. Regarding this matter and the relevance to it of the studies and procedures described above, Pius XII wrote the following in the encyclical *Divino Afflante Spiritu*.

"What the literal sense of a passage is, is not always as obvious in the speeches and writings of ancient authors of the East as it is in the works of our own time. For what they wished to express is not to be determined by the rules of grammar and philology alone nor solely by the context; the interpreter must, as it were, go back wholly in spirit to those remote centuries of the East and with the aid of history, archeology, ethnology, and other sciences accurately determine what modes of writing, so to speak, the authors of that ancient period would be likely to use and in fact did use. . . .

In explaining the Sacred Scripture and in demonstrating and proving its immunity from all error (the Catholic interpreter) should make a prudent use of this means, determine to what extent the manner of expression or literary mode adopted by the sacred writer may lead to a correct and genuine interpretation; and let him be convinced that this part of his office cannot be neglected without serious detriment to Catholic exegesis."

The literal sense of the Bible is the meaning in the mind of and intended by the inspired writer of a book or passage of the Bible. This is determined by the application to texts of the rules of hermeneutics. It is not to be confused with word-for-word literalism.

Typical Sense

The typical sense is the meaning which a passage has not only in itself but also in reference to something else of which it is a type or foreshadowing. A clear example is the account of the Exodus of the Israelites: in its literal sense, it narrates the liberation of the Israelites from death and oppression in Egypt; in its typical sense, it foreshadowed the liberation of men from sin through the redemptive death and resurrection of Christ. The typical sense of this and other passages emerged in the working out of God's plan of salvation history. It did not have to be in the mind of the author of the original passage.

Accommodated Senses

Accommodated, allegorical and consequent senses are figurative and adaptive meanings given to books and passages of the Bible for moral and other purposes. Such interpretations involve the danger of stretching the literal sense beyond proper proportions. Hermeneutical principles require that interpretations like these respect the integrity of the literal sense of the passages in question.

In the Catholic view, the final word on questions of biblical interpretation belongs to the teaching authority of the Church. In other views, generally derived from basic principles stated by Martin Luther, John Calvin and other reformers, the primacy belongs to individual judgment acting in response to the inner testimony of the Holy Spirit, the edifying nature of biblical subject matter, the sublimity and simplicity of the message of salvation, the intensity with which Christ is proclaimed.

Biblical Studies

The first center for biblical studies, in some strict sense of the term, was the School of Alexandria, founded in the latter half of the second century. It was noted for allegorical exegesis. Literal interpretation was a hallmark of the School of Antioch.

St. Jerome, who produced the Vulgate, and St. Augustine, author of numerous commentaries, were the most important figures in biblical studies during the patristic period. By the time of the latter's death, the Old and New Testament canons had been stabilized. For some centuries afterwards, there was little or no progress in scriptural studies, although commentaries were written, collections were made of scriptural excerpts from the writings of the Fathers of the Church, and the systematic reading of Scripture became established as a feature of monastic life.

Advances were made in the 12th and 13th centuries with the introduction of new principles and methods of scriptural analysis stemming from renewed interest in Hebraic studies and the application of dialectics.

By the time of the Reformation, the Bible had become the first book set in movable type, and more than 100 vernacular editions were in use throughout Europe.

The Council of Trent

In the wake of the Reformation, the Council of Trent formally defined the Canon of the Bible; it also reasserted the authoritative role of tradition and the teaching authority of the Church as well as Scripture with respect to the rule of faith. In the heated atmosphere of the 16th and 17th centuries, the Bible was turned into a polemical weapon; Protestants used it to defend their doctrines, and Catholics countered with citations in support of the dogmas of the Church. One result of this state of affairs was a lack of substantial progress in biblical studies during the period.

Rationalists from the 18th century on and later Modernists denied the reality of the supernatural and doctrine concerning inspiration of the Bible, which they generally regarded as a strictly human production expressive of the religious sense and experience of mankind. In their hands, the tools of positive critical research became weapons for biblical subversion. The defensive Catholic reaction to their work had the temporary effect of alienating scholars of the Church from solid advances in archeology, philology, history, textual and literary criticism.

Catholic Developments

Major influences in bringing about a change in Catholic attitude toward use of these disciplines in biblical studies were two papal encyclicals and two institutes of special study, the Ecole Biblique, founded in Jerusalem in 1890, and the Pontifical Biblical Institute established in Rome in 1909. The encyclical *Providentissimus Deus*, issued by Leo XIII in 1893, marked an important breakthrough; in addition to defending the concept of divine inspiration and the formal inspiration of the Scriptures, it encouraged the study of allied and ancillary sciences and techniques for a more fruitful understanding of the sacred writings. The encyclical *Divino Afflante Spiritu*, 50 years later, gave encouragement for the use of various forms of criticism as tools of biblical research. The documents encouraged the work of scholars and stimulated wide communication of the fruits of their study.

Great changes in the climate and direction of biblical studies have occurred in recent years. One of them has been an increase in cooperative effort among Catholic, Protestant, Orthodox and Jewish scholars. Their common investigation of the Dead Sea Scrolls is well known. Also productive has been the collaboration of Catholics and Protestants in turning out various editions of the Bible.

The development and results of biblical studies in this century have directly and significantly affected all phases of the contemporary renewal movement in the Church. Their influence on theology, liturgy, catechetics, and preaching indicate the importance of their function in the life of the Church.

APOSTLES AND EVANGELISTS

The Apostles were the men selected, trained and commissioned by Christ to preach the Gospel, to baptize, to establish, direct and care for his Church as servants of God and stewards of his mysteries. They were the first bishops of the Church.

St. Matthew's Gospel lists the Apostles in this order: Peter, Andrew, James the Greater, John, Philip, Bartholomew, Thomas, Matthew, James the Less, Jude, Simon and Judas Iscariot. Matthias was elected to fill the place of Judas. Paul became an Apostle by a special call from Christ. Barnabas was called an Apostle.

Two of the Evangelists, John and Matthew, were Apostles. The other two, Luke and Mark, were closely associated with the apostolic college.

Andrew: Born in Bethsaida, brother of Peter, disciple of John the Baptist, a fisherman, the first Apostle called; according to legend, preached the Gospel in northern Greece, Epirus and Scythia, and was martyred at Patras about 70; in art, is represented with an x-shaped cross, called St. Andrew's Cross; feast, Nov. 30; is honored as the patron of Russia and Scotland.

Barnabas: Originally called Joseph but named Barnabas by the Apostles, among whom he is ranked because of his collaboration with Paul; a Jew of the Diaspora, born in Cyprus; a cousin of Mark and member of the Christian community at Jerusalem, influenced the Apostles to accept Paul, with whom he became a pioneer missionary outside Palestine and Syria, to Antioch, Cyprus and southern Asia Minor; legend says he was martyred in Cyprus during the Neronian persecution; feast, June 11.

Bartholomew (Nathaniel): A friend of Philip; according to various traditions, preached the Gospel in Ethiopia, India, Persia and Armenia, where he was martyred by being flayed and beheaded; in art, is depicted holding a knife, an instrument of his death; feast, Aug. 24 in the Roman Rite, Aug. 25 in the Byzantine Rite.

James the Greater: A Galilean, son of Zebedee, brother of John (with whom he was called a "Son of Thunder"), a fisherman; with Peter and John, witnessed the raising of Jairus' daughter to life, the transfiguration, the agony of Jesus in the Garden of Gethsemani; first of the Apostles to die, by the sword in 44 during the rule of Herod Agrippa; there is doubt about a journey legend says he made to Spain and also about the authenticity of relics said to be his at Santiago de Compostela; in art, is depicted carrying a pilgrim's bell; feast, July 25 in the Roman Rite, Apr. 30 in the Byzantine Rite.

James the Less: Son of Alphaeus, called "Less" because he was younger in age or shorter in stature than James the Greater; one of the Catholic Epistles bears his name; was stoned to death in 62 or thrown from the top of the temple in Jerusalem and clubbed to death in 66; in art, is depicted with a club or heavy staff; feast, May 3 in the Roman Rite, Oct. 9 in the Byzantine Rite.

John: A Galilean, son of Zebedee, brother of James the Greater (with whom he was called a "Son of Thunder"), a fisherman, probably a disciple of John the Baptist, one of the Evangelists, called the "Beloved Disciple"; with Peter and James the Greater, witnessed the raising of Jairus' daughter to life, the transfiguration, the agony of Jesus in the Garden of Gethsemani; Mary was commended to his special care by Christ; the fourth Gospel, three Catholic Epistles and Revelation bear his name; according to various accounts, lived at Ephesus in Asia Minor for some time and died a natural death about 100; in art, is represented by an eagle, symbolic of the sublimity of the contents of his Gospel; feast, Dec. 27 in the Roman Rite, May 8 in the Byzantine Rite.

Jude Thaddeus: One of the Catholic Epistles, the shortest, bears his name; various traditions say he preached the Gospel in Mesopotamia, Persia and elsewhere, and was martyred; in art, is depicted with a halberd, the instrument of his death; feast, Oct. 28 in the Roman Rite, June 19 in the Byzantine Rite.

Luke: A Greek convert to the Christian community, called "our most dear physician" by Paul, of whom he was a missionary companion; author of the third Gospel and Acts of the Apostles; the place — Achaia, Bithynia, Egypt — and circumstances of his death are not certain; in art, is depicted as a man, a writer, or an ox (because his Gospel starts at the scene of temple sacrifice); feast, Oct. 18.

Mark: A cousin of Barnabas and member of the first Christian community at Jerusalem; a missionary companion of Paul and Barnabas, then of Peter; author of the Gospel which bears his name; according to legend, founded the Church at Alexandria, was bishop there and was martyred in the streets of the city; in art, is depicted with his Gospel and a winged lion, symbolic of the voice of John the Baptist crying in the wilderness, at the beginning of his Gospel; feast, Apr. 25.

Matthew: A Galilean, called Levi by Luke and John and the son of Alphaeus by Mark, a tax collector, one of the Evangelists; according to various accounts, preached the Gospel in Judea, Ethiopia, Persia and Parthia, and was martyred; in art, is depicted with a spear, the instrument of his death, and as a winged man in his role as Evangelist; feast, Sept. 21 in the Roman Rite, Nov. 16 in the Byzantine Rite.

Matthias: A disciple of Jesus whom the faithful 11 Apostles chose to replace Judas before the Resurrection; uncertain traditions report that he preached the Gospel in Palestine, Cappadocia or Ethiopia; in art, is represented with a cross and a halberd, the instruments of his death as a martyr; feast, May 14 in the Roman Rite, Aug. 9 in the Byzantine Rite.

Paul: Born at Tarsus, of the tribe of Benjamin, a Roman citizen; participated in the persecution of Christians until the time of his miraculous conversion on the way to Damascus; called by Christ, who revealed himself to him in a special way; became the Apostle of the Gentiles, among whom he did most of his preaching in the course of three major missionary journeys through areas north of Palestine, Cyprus, Asia Minor and Greece; 14 epistles bear his name; two years of imprisonment at Rome, following initial arrest in Jerusalem and confinement at Caesarea, ended with martyrdom, by beheading, outside the walls of the city in 64 or 67 during the Neronian persecution; in art, is depicted in various ways with St. Peter, with a sword, in the scene of his conversion; feasts, June 29, Jan. 25 (Roman Rite).

Peter: Simon, son of Jona, born in Bethsaida, brother of Andrew, a fisherman; called Cephas or Peter by Christ who made him the chief of the Apostles and head of the Church as his vicar; named first in the listings of Apostles in the Synoptic Gospels and the Acts of the Apostles; with James the Greater and John, witnessed the raising of Jairus' daughter to life, the transfiguration, the agony of Jesus in the Garden of Gethsemani; was the first to preach the Gospel in and around Jerusalem and was the leader of the first Christian community there; established a local church in Antioch; presided over the Council of Jerusalem in 51; wrote two Catholic Epistles to the Christians in Asia Minor; established his see in Rome where he spent his last years and was martyred by crucifixion in 64 or 65 during the Neronian persecution; in art, is depicted carrying two keys, symbolic of his primacy in the Church; feasts, June 29, Feb. 22 (Roman Rite).

Philip: Born in Bethsaida; according to legend, preached the Gospel in Phrygia where he suffered martyrdom by crucifixion; feast, May 3 in the Roman Rite, Nov. 14 in the Byzantine Rite.

Simon: Called the Cananean or the Zealot; according to legend, preached in various places in the Middle East and suffered martyrdom by being sawed in two; in art, is depicted with a saw, the instrument of his death, or a book, symbolic of his zeal for the Law; feast, Oct. 28 in the Roman Rite, May 10 in the Byzantine Rite.

Thomas (Didymus): Notable for his initial incredulity regarding the Resurrection and his subsequent forthright confession of the divinity of Christ risen from the dead; according to legend, preached the Gospel in places from the Caspian Sea to the Persian Gulf and eventually reached India where he was martyred near Madras; Thomas Christians trace their origin to him; in art, is depicted kneeling before the risen Christ, or with a carpenter's rule and square; feast, July 3 in the Roman Rite, Oct. 6 in the Byzantine Rite.

Judas

The Gospels record only a few facts about Judas, the Apostle who betrayed Christ.

The only non-Galilean among the Apostles, he was from Carioth, a town in southern Judah. He was keeper of the purse in the apostolic band. He was called a petty thief by John. He voiced dismay at the waste of money, which he said might have been spent for the poor, in connection with the anointing incident at Bethany. He took the initiative in arranging the betrayal of Christ. Afterwards, he confessed that he had betrayed an innocent man and cast into the Temple the money he had received for that action. Of his death, Matthew says that he hanged himself; the Acts of the Apostles states that he swelled up and burst open; both reports deal more with the meaning than the manner of his death — the misery of the death of a sinner.

The consensus of speculation over the reason why Judas acted as he did in betraying Christ focuses on disillusionment and unwillingness to accept the concept of a suffering Messiah and personal suffering of his own as an Apostle.

APOSTOLIC FATHERS, FATHERS, DOCTORS OF THE CHURCH

The writers listed below were outstanding and authoritative witnesses to authentic Christian belief and practice, and played significant roles in giving them expression.

Apostolic Fathers

The Apostolic Fathers were Christian writers of the first and second centuries whose writings echo genuine apostolic teaching.

Chief in importance are: St. Clement (d.c. 97), bishop of Rome and third successor of St. Peter in the papacy; St. Ignatius (50-c. 107), bishop of Antioch and second successor of St. Peter in that see, reputed to be a disciple of St. John; St. Polycarp (69-155), bishop of Smyrna and a disciple of St. John. The authors of the *Didache* and the *Epistle of Barnabas* are also numbered among the Apostolic Fathers.

Other early ecclesiastical writers included: St. Justin, martyr (100-165), of Asia Minor and Rome, a layman and apologist; St. Irenaeus (130-202), bishop of Lyons, who opposed Gnosticism; and St. Cyprian (210-258), bishop of Carthage, who opposed Novatianism.

Fathers and Doctors

The Fathers of the Church were theologians and writers of the first eight centuries who were outstanding for sanctity and learning. They were such authoritative witnesses to the belief and teaching of the Church that their unanimous acceptance of doctrines as divinely revealed has been regarded as evidence that such doctrines were so received by the Church in line with apostolic tradition and Sacred Scripture. Their unanimous rejection of doctrines branded them as heretical. Their writings, however, were not necessarily free of error in all respects.

The greatest of these Fathers were: Sts. Ambrose, Augustine, Jerome and Gregory the Great in the West; Sts. John Chrysostom, Basil the Great, Gregory of Nazianzen and Athanasius in the East.

The Doctors of the Church were ecclesiastical writers of eminent learning and sanctity who have been given this title because of the great advantage the Church has derived from their work. Their writings, however, were not necessarily free of error in all respects.

Albert the Great, St. (c. 1200-1280): Born in Swabia, Germany; Dominican; bishop of Regensburg (1260-1262); wrote extensively on logic, natural sciences, ethics, metaphysics, Scripture, systematic theology; contributed to development of Scholasticism; teacher of St. Thomas Aquinas; canonized and proclaimed doctor, 1931; named patron of natural scientists, 1941; called Doctor Universalis, Doctor Expertus; feast, Nov. 15.

Alphonsus Liguori, St. (1696-1787): Born near Naples, Italy; bishop of Saint Agatha of the Goths (1762-1775); founder of the Redemptorists; in addition to his principal work, *Theologiae Moralis,* wrote on prayer, the spiritual life and doctrinal subjects in response to controversy; canonized, 1839; proclaimed doctor, 1871; named patron of confessors and moralists, 1950; feast, Aug. 1.

Ambrose, St. (c. 340-397): Born in Trier, Germany; bishop of Milan (374-397); one of the strongest opponents of Arianism in the West; his homilies and other writings — on faith, the Holy Spirit, the Incarnation, the sacraments and other subjects — were pastoral and practical; influenced the development of a liturgy at Milan which was named for him; Father and Doctor of the Church; feast, Dec. 7.

Anselm, St. (1033-1109): Born in Aosta, Piedmont, Italy; Benedictine; archbishop of Canterbury (1093-1109); in addition to his principal work, *Cur Deus Homo,* on the atonement and reconciliation of man with God through Christ, wrote about the existence and attributes of God and defended the *Filioque* explanation of the procession of the Holy Spirit from the Father and the Son; proclaimed doctor, 1720; called Father of Scholasticism; feast, Apr. 21.

Anthony of Padua, St. (1195-1231): Born in Lisbon, Portugal; first theologian of the Franciscan Order; preacher; canonized, 1232; proclaimed doctor, 1946; called Evangelical Doctor; feast, June 13.

Athanasius, St. (c. 297-373): Born in Alexandria, Egypt; bishop of Alexandria (328-373); participant in the Council of Nicaea I while still a deacon; dominant opponent of Arians whose errors regarding Christ he refuted in *Apology against the Arians, Discourses against the Arians* and other works; Father and Doctor of the Church; called Father of Orthodoxy; feast, May 2.

Augustine, St. (354-430): Born in Tagaste, North Africa; bishop of Hippo (395-430) after conversion from Manichaeism; works include the autobiographical and mystical *Confessions, City of God,* treatises on the Trinity, grace, passages of the Bible and doctrines called into question and denied by Manichaeans, Pelagians and Donatists; had strong and lasting influence on Christian theology and philosophy; Father and Doctor of the Church; called Doctor of Grace; feast, Aug. 28.

Basil the Great, St. (c. 329-379): Born in Caesarea, Cappadocia, Asia Minor; bishop of Caesarea (370-379); wrote three books *Contra Eunomium* in refutation of Arian errors, a treatise on the Holy Spirit, many homilies and several rules for monastic life, on which he had lasting influence; Father and Doctor of the Church; called Father of Monasticism in the East; feast, Jan. 2.

Bede the Venerable, St. (c. 673-735): Born in Northumberland, England; Benedictine; in addition to his principal work, *Ecclesiastical History of the English Nation* (covering the period 597-731), wrote scriptural commentaries; regarded as probably the most learned man in Western Europe of his time; called Father of English History; feast, May 25.

Bernard of Clairvaux, St. (c. 1090-1153): Born near Dijon, France; abbot; monastic reformer, called the second founder of the Cistercian Order; mystical theologian with great influence on devotional life; opponent of the rationalism brought forward by Abelard and others; canonized, 1174; proclaimed doctor, 1830; called Mellifluous Doctor because of his eloquence; feast, Aug. 20.

Bonaventure, St. (c. 1217-1274): Born near Viterbo, Italy; Franciscan; bishop of Albano (1273-1274); cardinal; wrote *Itinerarium Mentis in Deum, De Reductione Artium ad Theologiam, Breviloquium,* scriptural commentaries, additional mystical works affecting devotional life and a life of St. Francis of Assisi; canonized, 1482; proclaimed doctor, 1588; called Seraphic Doctor; feast, July 15.

Catherine of Siena, St. (c. 1347-1380): Born in Siena, Italy; member of the Third Order of St. Dominic; mystic; authored a long series of letters, mainly concerning spiritual instruction and encouragement, to associates, and *Dialogue,* a spiritual testament in four treatises; was active in support of a crusade against the Turks and efforts to end war between papal forces and the Florentine allies; had great influence in inducing Gregory XI to return himself and the Curia to Rome in 1377, to end the Avignon period of the papacy; canonized, 1461; proclaimed the second woman doctor, Oct. 4, 1970; feast, Apr. 29.

Cyril of Alexandria, St. (c. 376-444): Born in Egypt; bishop of Alexandria (412-444); wrote treatises on the Trinity, the Incarnation and other subjects, mostly in refutation of Nestorian errors; made key contributions to the development of Christology; presided at the Council of Ephesus, 431; proclaimed doctor, 1882; feast, June 27.

Cyril of Jerusalem, St. (c. 315-386): Bishop of Jerusalem from 350; vigorous opponent of Arianism; principal work, *Catecheses,* a pre-baptismal explanation of the creed of Jerusalem; proclaimed doctor, 1882; feast, Mar. 18.

Ephraem, St. (c. 306-373): Born in Nisibis, Mesopotamia; counteracted the spread of Gnostic and Arian errors with poems and hymns of his own composition; wrote also on the Eucharist and Mary; proclaimed doctor, 1920; called Deacon of Edessa and Harp of the Holy Spirit; feast, June 9.

Francis de Sales, St. (1567-1622): Born in Savoy; bishop of Geneva (1602-1622); spiritual writer with strong influence on devotional life through treatises such as *Introduction to a Devout Life,* and *The Love of God;* canonized, 1665; proclaimed doctor, 1877; patron of Catholic writers and the Catholic press; feast, Jan. 24.

Gregory Nazianzen, St. (c. 330-c. 390): Born in Arianzus, Cappadocia, Asia Minor; bishop of Constantinople (381-390); vigorous opponent of Arianism; in addition to five theological discourses on the Nicene Creed and the Trinity for which he is best known, wrote letters and poetry; Father and Doctor of the Church; called the Christian Demosthenes because of his eloquence and, in the Eastern Church, The Theologian; feast, Jan. 2.

Gregory I, the Great, St. (c. 540-604): Born in Rome; pope (590-604): wrote many scriptural commentaries, a compendium of theology in the *Book of Morals* based on Job, *Dialogues* concerning the lives of saints, the immortality of the soul, death, purgatory, heaven and hell, and 14 books of letters; enforced papal supremacy and established the position of the pope vis-a-vis the emperor; worked for clerical and monastic reform and the observance of clerical celibacy; Father and Doctor of the Church; feast, Sept. 3.

Hilary of Poitiers, St. (c. 315-368): Born in Poitiers, France; bishop of Poitiers (c. 353-368); wrote *De Synodis,* with the Arian controversy in mind, and *De Trinitate,* the first lengthy study of the doctrine in Latin; introduced Eastern theology to the West; contributed to the development of hymnology; proclaimed doctor, 1851; called the Athanasius of the West because of his vigorous defense of the divinity of Christ against Arians; feast, Jan. 13.

Isidore of Seville, St. (c. 560-636): Born in Cartagena, Spain; bishop of Seville (c. 600-636); in addition to his principal work, *Etymologiae,* an encyclopedia of the knowledge of his day, wrote on theological and historical subjects; regarded as the most learned man of his time; proclaimed doctor, 1722; feast, Apr. 4.

Jerome, St. (c. 343-420): Born in Stridon, Dalmatia; translated the Old Testament from Hebrew into Latin and revised the existing Latin translation of the New Testament to produce the Vulgate version of the Bible; wrote scriptural commentaries and treatises on matters of controversy; regarded as Father and Doctor of the Church from the eighth century; called Father of Biblical Science; feast, Sept. 30.

John Chrysostom, St. (c. 347-407): Born in Antioch, Asia Minor; archbishop of Constantinople (398-407); wrote homilies, scriptural commentaries and letters of wide influence in addition to a classical treatise on the priesthood; proclaimed doctor by the Council of Chalcedon, 451; called the greatest of the Greek Fathers; named patron of preachers, 1909; called Golden-Mouthed because of his eloquence; feast, Sept. 13.

John Damascene, St. (c. 675-c. 749): Born in Damascus, Syria; monk; wrote *Fountain of Wisdom,* a three-part work including a history of heresies and an exposition of the Christian faith, three *Discourses against the Iconoclasts,* homilies on Mary, biblical commentaries and treatises on moral subjects; proclaimed doctor, 1890; called Golden Speaker because of his eloquence; feast, Dec. 4.

John of the Cross, St. (1542-1591): Born in Old Castile, Spain; Carmelite; founder of Discalced Carmelites; one of the greatest mystical theologians, wrote *The Ascent of Mt. Carmel — The Dark Night, The Spiritual Canticle, The Living Flame of Love;* canonized, 1726; proclaimed doctor, 1926; called Doctor of Mystical Theology; feast, Dec. 14.

Lawrence of Brindisi, St. (1559-1619): Born in Brindisi, Italy; Franciscan (Capuchin); vigorous preacher of strong influence in the post-Reformation period; 15 tomes of collected works include scriptural commentaries, sermons, homilies and doctrinal writings; canonized, 1881; proclaimed doctor, 1959; feast, July 21.

Leo I, the Great, St. (c. 400-461): Born in Tuscany, Italy; pope (440-461); wrote the *Tome of Leo,* to explain doctrine concerning the two natures and one Person of Christ, against the background of the Nestorian and Monophysite heresies; other works included sermons, letters and writings against the errors of Manichaeism and Pelagianism; was instrumental in dissuading Attila from sacking Rome in 452; proclaimed doctor, 1574; feast, Nov. 10.

Peter Canisius, St. (1521-1597): Born in Nijmegen, Holland; Jesuit; wrote popular expositions of the Catholic faith in several catechisms which were widely circulated in 20 editions in his lifetime alone; was one of the moving figures in the Counter-Reformation period, especially in southern and western Germany; canonized and proclaimed doctor, 1925; feast, Dec. 21.

Peter Chrysologus, St. (c. 400-450): Born in Imola, Italy; served as archbishop of Ravenna (c. 433-450); his sermons and writings, many of which were designed to counteract Monophysitism, were pastoral and practical; proclaimed doctor, 1729; feast, July 30.

Peter Damian, St. (1007-1072): Born in Ravenna, Italy; Benedictine; cardinal; his writings and sermons, many of which concerned ecclesiastical and clerical reform, were pastoral and practical; proclaimed doctor, 1828; feast, Feb. 21.

Robert Bellarmine, St. (1542-1621): Born in Tuscany, Italy; Jesuit; archbishop of Capua (1602-1605); wrote *Controversies,* a three-volume exposition of doctrine under attack during and after the Reformation, two catechisms and the spiritual work, *The Art of Dying Well;* was an authority on ecclesiology and Church-state relations; canonized, 1930; proclaimed doctor, 1931; feast, Sept. 17.

Teresa of Jesus (Avila), St. (1515-1582): Born in Avila, Spain; entered the Carmelite Order, 1535; in the early 1560's, initiated a primitive Carmelite, discalced-Alcantarine reform which greatly influenced men and women religious, especially in Spain; wrote extensively on spiritual and mystical subjects; principal works included her *Autobiography, Way of Perfection, The Interior Castle, Meditations on the Canticle, The Foundations, Visitation of the Discalced Nuns;* canonized, 1622; proclaimed first woman doctor, Sept. 27, 1970; feast, Oct. 15.

Thomas Aquinas, St. (1225-1274): Born near Naples, Italy; Dominican; teacher and writer on virtually the whole range of philosophy and theology; principal works were *Summa contra Gentiles,* a manual and systematic defense of Christian doctrine, and *Summa Theologiae,* a new (at that time) exposition of theology on philosophical principles; canonized, 1323; proclaimed doctor, 1567; called Doctor Communis, Doctor Angelicus, the Great Synthesizer because of the way in which he related faith and reason, theology and philosophy (especially that of Aristotle), and systematized the presentation of Christian doctrine; named patron of Catholic schools and education, 1880; feast, Jan. 28.

CREEDS

Creeds are formal and official statements of Christian doctrine. As summaries of the principal truths of faith, they are standards of orthodoxy and are useful for instructional purposes, for actual profession of the faith and for expression of the faith in the liturgy.

The classical creeds are the Apostles' Creed and the Creed of Nicaea-Constantinople. Two others are the Athanasian Creed and the Creed of Pius IV.

Apostles' Creed

Text: I believe in God, the Father almighty, Creator of heaven and earth.

And in Jesus Christ, his only Son, our Lord; who was conceived by the Holy Spirit, born of the Virgin Mary, suffered under Pontius Pilate, was crucified, died, and was buried. He descended into hell; the third day he arose again from the dead; he ascended into heaven, sits at the right hand of God, the Father almighty; from thence he shall come to judge the living and the dead.

I believe in the Holy Spirit, the holy Catholic Church, the communion of saints, the forgiveness of sins, the resurrection of the body, and life everlasting. Amen.

Background: The Apostles' Creed reflects the teaching of the Apostles but is not of apostolic origin. It probably originated in the second century as a rudimentary formula of faith professed by catechumens before the reception of baptism. Baptismal creeds in fourth-century use at Rome and elsewhere in the West closely resembled the present text, which was quoted in a handbook of Christian doctrine written between 710 and 724. This text was in wide use throughout the West by the ninth century. The Apostles' Creed is common to all Christian confessional churches in the West, but is not used in Eastern Churches.

Nicene Creed

The following translation of the Latin text of the creed was prepared by the International Committee on English in the Liturgy.

Text: We believe in one God, the Father, the Almighty, maker of heaven and earth, of all that is seen and unseen.

We believe in one Lord, Jesus Christ, the only

Son of God, eternally begotten of the Father, God from God, Light from Light, true God from true God, begotten, not made, one in Being with the Father. Through him all things were made. For us men and for our salvation he came down from heaven: by the power of the Holy Spirit he was born of the Virgin Mary, and became man. For our sake he was crucified under Pontius Pilate; he suffered, died, and was buried. On the third day he rose again in fulfillment of the Scriptures; he ascended into heaven and is seated at the right hand of the Father. He will come again in glory to judge the living and the dead, and his kingdom will have no end.

We believe in the Holy Spirit, the Lord, the giver of life, who proceeds from the Father and the Son. With the Father and the Son he is worshiped and glorified. He has spoken through the prophets.

We believe in one holy catholic and apostolic Church. We acknowledge one baptism for the forgiveness of sins. We look for the resurrection of the dead, and the life of the world to come. Amen.

Background: The Nicene Creed (Creed of Nicaea-Constantinople) consists of elements of doctrine contained in an early baptismal creed of Jerusalem and enactments of the Council of Nicaea (325) and the Council of Constantinople (381). Its strong trinitarian content reflects the doctrinal errors, especially of Arianism, it served to counteract. Theologically, it is much more sophisticated than the Apostles' Creed. Since late in the fifth century, the Nicene Creed has been the only creed in liturgical use in the Eastern Churches. The Western Church adopted it for liturgical use by the end of the eighth century.

The Athanasian Creed

The Athanasian Creed, which has a unique structure, is a two-part summary of doctrine concerning the Trinity and the Incarnation-Redemption bracketed at the beginning and end with the statement that belief in the cited truths is necessary for salvation; it also contains a number of anathemas or condemnatory clauses regarding doctrinal errors. Although attributed to St. Athanasius, it was probably written after his death, between 381 and 428, and may have been authored by St. Ambrose. It is not accepted in the East; in the West, it formerly had place in the Roman-Rite Liturgy of the Hours and in the liturgy for the Solemnity of the Holy Trinity.

Creed of Pius IV

The Creed of Pius IV, also called the Profession of Faith of the Council of Trent, was promulgated in the bull *Injunctum Nobis*, Nov. 13, 1564. It is a summary of doctrine defined by the council.

MORAL OBLIGATIONS

The basic norm of Christian morality is life in Christ. This involves, among other things, the observance of the Ten Commandments, their fulfillment in the twofold law of love of God and neighbor, the implications of the Sermon on the Mount and the whole New Testament, and membership in the Church established by Christ.

The Ten Commandments

The Ten Commandments, the Decalogue, were given by God through Moses to his Chosen People for the guidance of their moral conduct in accord with the demands of the Covenant he established with them as a divine gift.

In the traditional Catholic enumeration and according to Dt. 5:6-21, the Commandments are:

1. "I, the Lord, am your God . . . You shall not have other gods besides me. You shall not carve idols. . . ."
2. "You shall not take the name of the Lord, your God, in vain. . . ."
3. "Take care to keep holy the Sabbath day. . . ."
4. "Honor your father and your mother. . . ."
5. "You shall not kill."
6. "You shall not commit adultery."
7. "You shall not steal."
8. "You shall not bear dishonest witness against your neighbor."
9. "You shall not covet your neighbor's wife."
10. "You shall not desire your neighbor's house or field, nor his male or female slave, nor his ox or ass, nor anything that belongs to him" (summarily, his goods).

Another version of the Commandments, substantially the same, is given in Ex. 20:1-17.

The traditional enumeration of the Commandments in Protestant usage differs from the above. Thus: two commandments are made of the first, as above; the third and fourth are equivalent to the second and third, as above, and so on; and the 10th includes the ninth and 10th, as above.

The first three of the commandments deal directly with man's relations with God, viz.: acknowledgment of one true God and the rejection of false gods and idols; honor due to God and his name; observance of the Sabbath as the Lord's day.

The rest cover interpersonal relationships, viz.: the obedience due to parents and, logically, to other persons in authority, and the obligations of parents to children and of persons in authority to those under their care; respect for life and physical integrity; fidelity in marriage, and chastity; justice and rights; truth; internal respect for faithfulness in marriage, chastity, and the goods of others.

Precepts of the Church

This text of the Precepts of the Church is from *Basic Teachings for Catholic Religious Education*, copyrighted by the National Conference of Catholic Bishops and circulated by the NC Documentary Services, *Origins* (Vol. 2, No. 31).

From time to time the Church has listed certain specific duties of Catholics. Some duties expected of Catholic Christians today include the following. (Those traditionally mentioned as precepts of the Church are marked with an asterisk.)

1. To keep holy the day of the Lord's resurrection: to worship God by participating in Mass ev-

ery Sunday and holy day of obligation:* to avoid those activities that would hinder renewal of soul and body, e.g., needless work and business activities, unnecessary shopping, etc.

2. To lead a sacramental life: to receive Holy Communion frequently and the sacrament of penance regularly — minimally, to receive the sacrament of penance at least once a year (annual confession is obligatory only if serious sin is involved)* — minimally, to receive Holy Communion at least once a year between the first Sunday of Lent and Trinity Sunday.*

3. To study Catholic teaching in preparation for the sacrament of confirmation, to be confirmed, and then to continue to study and advance the cause of Christ.

4. To observe the marriage laws of the Church:* to give religious training (by example and word) to one's children; to use parish schools and religious education programs.

5. To strengthen and support the Church:* one's own parish community and parish priests; the worldwide Church and the Holy Father.

6. To do penance, including abstaining from meat and fasting from food on the appointed days.*

7. To join in the missionary spirit and apostolate of the Church.

SOCIAL DOCTRINE

Since the end of the last century, Catholic social doctrine has been formulated in a progressive manner in a number of authoritative documents. Outstanding examples are the encyclicals: *Rerum Novarum,* issued by Leo XIII in 1891; *Quadragesimo Anno,* by Pius XI in 1931; *Mater et Magistra* ("Christianity and Social Progress") and *Pacem in Terris* ("Peace on Earth"), by John XXIII in 1961 and 1963, respectively; *Populorum Progressio* ("Development of Peoples"), by Paul VI in 1967; and *Laborem Exercens* ("On Human Work"), and *Sollicitudo Rei Socialis* ("On Social Concerns") (see separate entry), by John Paul II in 1981 and 1987, respectively. Pius XII, among other accomplishments of ideological importance in the social field, made a distinctive contribution with his formulation of a plan for world peace and order in Christmas messages from 1939 to 1941, and in other documents.

These documents represent the most serious attempts in modern times to systematize the social implications of the Gospel and the rest of divine revelation as well as the socially relevant writings of the Fathers and Doctors of the Church. Their contents are theological penetrations into social life, with particular reference to human rights, the needs of the poor and those in underdeveloped countries, and humane conditions of life, freedom, justice and peace. In some respects, they read like juridical documents; underneath, however, they are Gospel-oriented and pastoral in intention.

Nature of the Doctrine

Pope John XXIII, writing in *Christianity and Social Progress,* made the following statement about the nature and scope of the doctrine stated in the encyclicals in particular and related writings in general.

"What the Catholic Church teaches and declares regarding the social life and relationships of men is beyond question for all time valid.

"The cardinal point of this teaching is that individual men are necessarily the foundation, cause, and end of all social institutions . . . insofar as they are social by nature, and raised to an order of existence that transcends and subdues nature.

"Beginning with this very basic principle whereby the dignity of the human person is affirmed and defended, Holy Church — especially during the last century and with the assistance of learned priests and laymen, specialists in the field — has arrived at clear social teachings whereby the mutual relationships of men are ordered. Taking general norms into account, these principles are in accord with the nature of things and the changed conditions of man's social life, or with the special genius of our day. Moreover, these norms can be approved by all."

The Church in the World

Even more Gospel-oriented and pastoral in a distinctive way is the *Pastoral Constitution on the Church in the Modern World* promulgated by the Second Vatican Council in 1965.

Its purpose is to search out the signs of God's presence and meaning in and through the events of this time in human history. Accordingly, it deals with the situation of men in present circumstances of profound change, challenge and crisis on all levels of life.

The first part of the constitution develops the theme of the Church and man's calling, and focuses attention on the dignity of the human person, the problem of atheism, the community of mankind, man's activity throughout the world, and the serving and saving role of the Church in the world. This portion of the document, it has been said, represents the first presentation by the Church in an official text of an organized Christian view of man and society.

The second part of the document considers several problems of special urgency: fostering the nobility of marriage and the family (see Marriage Doctrine), the proper development of culture, socio-economic life, the life of the political community, the fostering of peace (see Peace and War), and the promotion of a community of nations.

In conclusion, the constitution calls for action to implement doctrine regarding the role and work of the Church for the total good of mankind.

Excerpts

One Human Family and Community: God, who has fatherly concern for everyone, has willed that all men should constitute one family and treat one another in a spirit of brotherhood.

For this reason, love for God and neighbor is the first and greatest commandment. Sacred Scripture . . . teaches us that the love of God cannot be separated from love of neighbor. . . . To men growing daily more dependent on one another, and to a world becoming more unified every day, this truth proves to be of paramount importance (No. 24).

Human Person Is Central: Man's social nature makes it evident that the progress of the human person and the advance of society itself hinge on each other. For the beginning, the subject and the goal of all social institutions is and must be the human person, which for its part and by its very nature stands completely in need of social life. This social life is not something added on to man. Hence, through his dealings with others, through reciprocal duties and through fraternal dialogue, he develops all his gifts and is able to rise to his destiny.

Influence of Social Circumstances: But if by this social life the human person is greatly aided in responding to his destiny, even in its religious dimensions, it cannot be denied that men are often diverted from doing good and spurred toward evil by the social circumstances in which they live and are immersed from their birth. To be sure, the disturbances which so frequently occur in the social order result in part from the natural tensions of economic, political and social forms. But at a deeper level they flow from man's pride and selfishness, which contaminate even the social sphere. When the structure of affairs is flawed by the consequences of sin, man, already born with a bent toward evil, finds there new inducements to sin which cannot be overcome without strenuous efforts and the assistance of grace (No. 25).

Human Necessities: Every social group must take account of the needs and legitimate aspirations of other groups, and even of the general welfare of the entire human family.

At the same time, however, there is a growing awareness of the exalted dignity proper to the human person, since he stands above all things and his rights and duties are universal and inviolable. Therefore, there must be made available to all men everything necessary for leading a life truly human, such as food, clothing, and shelter; the right to choose a state of life freely and to found a family; the right to education, to employment, to a good reputation, to respect, to appropriate information, to activity in accord with the upright norm of one's own conscience, to protection of privacy and to rightful freedom in matters religious too.

Hence, the social order and its development must unceasingly work to the benefit of the human person if the disposition of affairs is to be subordinate to the personal realm and not contrariwise, as the Lord indicated when he said that the Sabbath was made for man, and not man for the Sabbath.

Improvement of Social Order: This social order requires constant improvement. It must be founded on truth, built on justice and animated by love; in freedom it should grow every day toward a more humane balance. An improvement in attitudes and widespread changes in society will have to take place if these objectives are to be gained.

God's Spirit, who with a marvelous providence directs the unfolding of time and renews the face of the earth, is not absent from this development. The ferment of the Gospel, too, has aroused and continues to arouse in man's heart the irresistible requirements of his dignity (No. 26).

Regard for Neighbor as Another Self: Coming down to practical and particularly urgent consequences, this Council lays stress on reverence for man; everyone must consider his every neighbor without exception as another self, taking into account first of all his life and the means necessary to living it with dignity.

In our times a special obligation binds us to make ourselves the neighbor of absolutely every person and to actively help him when he comes across our path.

Inhuman Evils: . . . Whatever is opposed to life itself, such as any type of murder, genocide, abortion, euthanasia, or willful self-destruction; whatever violates the integrity of the human person, such as mutilation, torments inflicted on body or mind, attempts to coerce the will itself; whatever insults human dignity, such as subhuman living conditions, arbitrary imprisonment, deportation, slavery, prostitution, the selling of women and children; as well as disgraceful working conditions, where men are treated as mere tools for profit rather than as free and responsible persons: all these things and others of their like are infamies indeed. They poison human society, but they do more harm to those who practice them than those who suffer from the injury. Moreover, they are a supreme dishonor to the Creator (No. 27).

Respect for Those Who Are Different: Respect and love ought to be extended also to those who think or act differently than we do in social, political and religious matters. In fact, the more deeply we come to understand their ways of thinking through such courtesy and love, the more easily will we be able to enter into dialogue with them.

Distinction between Error and Persons in Error: This love and good will, to be sure, must in no way render us indifferent to truth and goodness. Indeed, love itself impels the disciples of Christ to speak the saving truth to all men. But it is necessary to distinguish between error, which always merits repudiation, and the person in error, who never loses the dignity of being a person, even when he is flawed by false or inadequate religious notions. God alone is the judge and searcher of hearts; for that reason he forbids us to make judgments about the internal guilt of anyone.

The teaching of Christ even requires that we forgive injuries, and extends the law of love to include every enemy (No. 28).

Men Are Equal but Different: Since all men possess a rational soul and are created in God's likeness; since they have the same nature and origin, have been redeemed by Christ, and enjoy the same divine calling and destiny: the basic equality of all must receive increasingly greater recognition.

True, all men are not alike from the point of view of varying physical power and the diversity of intellectual and moral resources. Nevertheless, with respect to the fundamental rights of the person, every type of discrimination, whether social or cultural, whether based on sex, race, color, social condition, language or religion, is to be overcome and eradicated as contrary to God's intent.

Humane Conditions for All: Although rightful differences exist between men, the equal dignity of persons demands that a more humane and just condition of life be brought about. For excessive economic and social differences between the members of the one human family . . . cause scandal and militate against social justice, equity and the dignity of the human person as well as social and international peace.

Human institutions, both private and public, must labor to minister to the dignity and purpose of man. At the same time, let them put up a stubborn fight against any kind of slavery, whether social or political, and safeguard the basic rights of man under every political system. Indeed, human institutions themselves must be accommodated by degrees to the highest of all realities, spiritual ones, even though, meanwhile, a long enough time will be required before they arrive at the desired goal (No. 29).

Profound and rapid changes make it particularly urgent that no one, ignoring the trend of events or drugged by laziness, content himself with a merely individualistic morality. It grows increasingly true that the obligations of justice and love are fulfilled only if each person, contributing to the common good according to his own abilities and the needs of others, also promotes and assists the public and private institutions dedicated to bettering the conditions of human life.

Social Necessities Are Prime Duties: Let everyone consider it his sacred obligation to count social necessities among the primary duties of modern man and to pay heed to them. For the more unified the world becomes, the more plainly do the offices of men extend beyond particular groups and spread by degrees to the whole world. But this challenge cannot be met unless individual men and their associations cultivate in themselves the moral and social virtues and promote them in society. Thus, with the needed help of divine grace, men who are truly new and artisans of a new humanity can be forthcoming (No. 30).

In order for individual men to discharge with greater exactness the obligations of their conscience toward themselves and the various groups to which they belong, they must be carefully educated to a higher degree of culture through the use of the immense resources available today to the human race.

Living Conditions and Freedom: A man can scarcely arrive at the needed sense of responsibility unless his living conditions allow him to become conscious of his dignity and to rise to his destiny by spending himself for God and for others. But human freedom is often crippled when a man falls into extreme poverty, just as it withers when he indulges in too many of life's comforts and imprisons himself in a kind of splendid isolation. Freedom acquires new strength, by contrast, when a man consents to the unavoidable requirements of social life, takes on the manifold demands of human partnership and commits himself to the service of the human community.

Hence, the will to play one's role in common endeavors should be everywhere encouraged (No. 31).

Communitarian Character of Life: God did not create man for life in isolation but for the formation of social unity. So also "it has pleased God to make men holy and save them not merely as individuals, without any mutual bonds, but by making them into a single people, a people which acknowledges him in truth and serves him in holiness" (*Dogmatic Constitution on the Church,* No. 9). So from the beginning of salvation history he has chosen men not just as individuals but as members of a certain community. Revealing his mind to them, God called these chosen ones "his people" (Ex. 3:7-12) and, furthermore, made a covenant with them on Sinai.

This communitarian character is developed and consummated in the work of Jesus Christ. For the very Word made flesh willed to share in the human fellowship. He was present at the wedding of Cana, visited the house of Zacchaeus, ate with publicans and sinners. He revealed the love of the Father and the sublime vocation of man in terms of the most common of social realities and by making use of the speech and the imagery of plain everyday life. Willingly obeying the laws of his country, he sanctified those human ties, especially family ones, from which social relationships arise. He chose to lead the life proper to an artisan of his time and place.

In his preaching he clearly taught the sons of God to treat one another as brothers. In his prayers he pleaded that all his disciples might be "one." Indeed, as the Redeemer of all, he offered himself for all even to the point of death. He commanded his Apostles to preach to all peoples the Gospel message so that the human race might become the Family of God, in which the fullness of the Law would be love.

The Community Founded by Christ: As the first-born of many brethren and through the gift of his Spirit, he founded after his death and resurrection a new brotherly community composed of all those who receive him in faith and in love. This he did through his Body, which is the Church. There everyone, as members one of the other, would render mutual service according to the different gifts bestowed on each.

This solidarity must be constantly increased until that day on which it is brought to perfection. Then, saved by grace, men will offer flawless glory to God as a family beloved of God and of Christ their Brother (No. 32).

WORK

The nature of work, its relation to social issues and its significance, along with prayer, as the "way of sanctification," are among key subjects treated in Pope John Paul's third encyclical letter, *Laborem Exercens.* Following are several paragraphs from the encyclical delineating a definition of work together with capsule coverge of a number of salient points in the letter.

Social Doctrine — Work

Definition

"Through work man must earn his daily bread and contribute to the continual advance of science and technology and, above all, to elevating unceasingly the cultural and moral level of the society within which he lives in community with those who belong to the same family.

"And work means any activity by man, whether manual or intellectual, whatever its nature or circumstances; it means any human activity that can and must be recognized as work, in the midst of all the many activities of which man is capable and to which he is predisposed by his very nature, by virtue of humanity itself.

"Man is made to be in the visible universe an image and likeness of God himself, and he is placed in it in order to subdue the earth. From the beginning, therefore, he is called to work.

"Work is one of the characteristics that distinguish man from the rest of creatures, whose activity for sustaining their lives cannot be called work. Only man is capable of work and only man works, at the same time by work occupying his existence on earth. Thus, work bears a particular mark of man and of humanity, the mark of a person operating within a community of persons. And this mark decides its interior characteristics; in a sense, it constitutes its very nature."

Salient Points

Fundamental Criterion of Economics: "Respect for the objective rights of the worker . . . must constitute the adequate and fundamental criterion for shaping the whole economy, both on the level of the individual society and state and within the whole of the world economic policy as well as the systems of international relationships that derive from it."

Work and Family: "Work constitutes a foundation of the formation of family life" by providing the economic means necessary to maintain a family.

Just Wage: "A just wage is the concrete means of verifying the justice of the whole socio-economic system and, in any case, of checking that it is functioning justly."

Family Wage: A "family wage" is needed, "a single salary given to the head of the family for his work, sufficient for the needs of the family without the other spouse having to take up gainful employment outside the home," or without the need of recourse to other social provisions for aid.

Women: Women who work "should be able to fulfill their tasks in accordance with their own nature without being discriminated against and without being excluded from jobs for which they are capable." Respect is due "for their family aspirations and for their specific role in contributing, together with men, to the good of society."

Mothers: Provisions should be made for "measures such as family allowances or grants to mothers devoting themselves exclusively to their families."

Unions: Workers have the right to form a union to protect their vital interests and to be "a mouthpiece for the struggle for social justice."

"Union activity undoubtedly enters the field of politics, understood as prudent concern for the common good." But unions should not engage in partisan politics; otherwise, "they become an instrument used for other purposes."

Strike: Workers should be assured the right to strike without being subject to personal sanctions, but have the responsibility of not striking if a strike "is contrary to requirements of the common good."

Unemployment Benefits: "The obligation to provide unemployment benefits . . . is a duty springing from the fundamental principle of the common use of goods or, to put it in another way, the right to life and subsistence."

Disabled Persons: Society should provide work for disabled persons in keeping with their physical disabilities. Failure to do so means "a serious form of discrimination, that of the strong and healthy against the weak and sick."

Health Care: "The expenses involved in health care, especially in the case of accidents at work, demand that medical assistance should be easily available for workers."

Technology: It is meant to be the worker's ally but can become his enemy when mechanization supplants him or takes away "all personal satisfaction and the incentive to creativity and responsibility," thus reducing "man to the status of slave."

Haves and Have-Nots: "A disconcerting fact of immense proportions" occurs on the world scene. "While conspicuous natural resources remain unused, there are huge numbers of people who are unemployed or underemployed, and countless multitudes of people suffering from hunger." This means that there is "something wrong with the organization of work and employment" on national and international levels.

Foreign Workers: People have a right to emigrate in search of work. "The person working away from his native land, whether as a permanent emigrant or as a seasonal worker, should not be placed at a disadvantage in comparison with the workers in that society in the matter of working rights. Emigration in search of work must in no way become an opportunity for financial or social exploitation."

Marxism: Catholic social teaching "diverges radically from the program of collectivism proclaimed by Marxism and put into practice in various countries."

Private Property and Capitalism: "Christian tradition has never upheld" the right to private property "as absolute and untouchable. On the contrary, it has always understood this right common to all to use the goods of the whole creation."

"Deeply desired reforms" of capitalism "cannot be achieved by an *a priori* elimination of private ownership of the means of production." This is not sufficient to insure "satisfactory socialization" because new managers form another special group "from the fact of exercising power in society. This group . . . may carry out this task badly by claiming for itself a monopoly of the administration and disposal of the means of production and not refraining even from offending basic human rights."

Exploitation by Multinationals: "The highly industrialized countries, and even more so the businesses that direct on a large scale the means of industrial production, fix the highest possible prices for their products while trying at the same time to fix the lowest possible prices for raw materials or semi-manufactured goods."

PEACE AND WAR

The following excerpts, stating principles and objectives of social doctrine concerning peace and war, are from the "Pastoral Constitution on the Church in the Modern World" (Nos. 77 to 82) promulgated by the Second Vatican Council.

(See also: "The Challenge of Peace: God's Promise and Our Response.")

Call to Peace: This Council fervently desires to summon Christians to cooperate with all men in making secure among themselves a peace based on justice and love, and in setting up agencies of peace. This Christians should do with the help of Christ, the Author of peace (No. 77).

Conditions for Peace: Peace is not merely the absence of war. Nor can it be reduced solely to the maintenance of a balance of power between enemies. Nor is it brought about by dictatorship. Instead, it is rightly and appropriately called "an enterprise of justice" (Is. 32:7). Peace results from that harmony built into human society by its divine Founder and actualized by men as they thirst after ever greater justice.

The common good of men is in its basic sense determined by the eternal law. Still the concrete demands of this common good are constantly changing as time goes on. Hence peace is never attained once and for all, but must be built up ceaselessly. Moreover, since the human will is unsteady and wounded by sin, the achievement of peace requires that everyone constantly master his passions and that lawful authority keep vigilant.

But such is not enough. This peace cannot be obtained on earth unless personal values are safeguarded and men freely and trustingly share with one another the riches of their inner spirits and their talents. A firm determination to respect other men and peoples and their dignity, as well as the studied practice of brotherhood, are absolutely necessary for the establishment of peace. Hence peace is likewise the fruit of love, which goes beyond what justice can provide.

Renunciation of Violence: We cannot fail to praise those who renounce the use of violence in the vindication of their rights and who resort to methods of defense which are otherwise available to weaker parties too, provided that this can be done without injury to the rights and duties of others or of the community itself (No. 78).

Mass Extermination: The Council wishes to recall first of all the permanent binding force of universal natural law and its all-embracing principles. Man's conscience itself gives ever more emphatic voice to these principles. Therefore, actions which deliberately conflict with these same principles, as well as orders commanding such actions, are criminal. Blind obedience cannot excuse those who yield to them. Among such must first be counted those actions designed for the methodical extermination of an entire people, nation, or ethnic minority. These actions must be vehemently condemned as horrendous crimes. The courage of those who openly and fearlessly resist men who issue such commands merits supreme commendation.

International Agreements: On the subject of war, quite a large number of nations have subscribed to various international agreements aimed at making military activity and its consequences less inhuman. Such are conventions concerning the handling of wounded or captured soldiers, and various similar agreements. Agreements of this sort must be honored. They should be improved upon.

Conscientious Objectors: It seems right that laws make humane provisions for the case of those who for reasons of conscience refuse to bear arms, provided, however, that they accept some other form of service to the human community.

Legitimate Defense: Certainly, war has not been rooted out of human affairs. As long as the danger of war remains and there is no competent and sufficiently powerful authority at the international level, governments cannot be denied the right to legitimate defense once every means of peaceful settlement has been exhausted. Therefore, government authorities and others who share public responsibility have the duty to protect the welfare of the people entrusted to their care and to conduct such grave matters soberly.

But it is one thing to undertake military action for the just defense of the people, and something else again to seek the subjugation of other nations. Nor does the possession of war potential make every military or political use of it lawful. Neither does the mere fact that war has unhappily begun mean that all is fair between the warring parties.

Nature of Military Service: Those who are pledged to the service of their country as members of its armed forces should regard themselves as agents of security and freedom on behalf of their people. As long as they fulfill this role properly, they are making a genuine contribution to the establishment of peace (No. 79).

Total War Condemned: This most holy Synod makes its own the condemnations of total war already pronounced by recent popes, and issues the following declaration:

Any act of war aimed indiscriminately at the destruction of entire cities or of extensive areas along with their population is a crime against God and man himself. It merits unequivocal and unhesitating condemnation.

The unique hazard of modern warfare consists in this: it provides those who possess modern scientific weapons with a kind of occasion for perpetrating just such abominations. Moreover, through a certain inexorable chain of events, it can urge men on to the most atrocious decisions. That such in fact may never happen in the future, the bishops of the whole world, in unity assembled, beg all men, especially government officials and military leaders, to give unremitting thought to the awesome responsibility which is theirs before God and the entire human race (No. 80).

Retaliation and Deterrence: Scientific weapons, to be sure, are not amassed solely for use in war. The defensive strength of any nation is considered to be dependent upon its capacity for immediate retaliation against an adversary. Hence this accumulation of arms, which increases each year, also serves, in a way heretofore unknown, as a deterrent to possible enemy attack. Many regard this state of affairs as the most effective way by which peace of a sort can be maintained between nations at the present time.

Arms Race: Whatever be the case with this method of deterrence, men should be convinced that the arms race in which so many countries are engaged is not a safe way to preserve a steady peace. Nor is the so-called balance resulting from this race a sure and authentic peace. Rather than being eliminated thereby, the causes of war threaten to grow gradually stronger.

While extravagant sums are being spent for the furnishing of ever new weapons, an adequate remedy cannot be provided for the multiple miseries afflicting the whole modern world. Disagreements between nations are not really and radically healed. On the contrary, other parts of the world are infected with them. New approaches initiated by reformed attitudes must be adopted to remove this trap and to restore genuine peace by emancipating the world from its crushing anxiety.

Therefore, it must be said again: the arms race is an utterly treacherous trap for humanity, and one which injures the poor to an intolerable degree. It is much to be feared that, if this race persists, it will eventually spawn all the lethal ruin whose path it is now making ready (No. 81).

Outlaw War: It is our clear duty, then, to strain every muscle as we work for the time when all war can be completely outlawed by international consent. This goal undoubtedly requires the establishment of some universal public authority acknowledged as such by all, and endowed with effective power to safeguard, on behalf of all, security, regard for justice, and respect for rights.

Multilateral and Controlled Disarmament: But before this hoped-for authority can be set up, the highest existing international centers must devote themselves vigorously to the pursuit of better means for obtaining common security. Peace must be born of mutual trust between nations rather than imposed on them through fear of one another's weapons. Hence everyone must labor to put an end at last to the arms race, and to make a true beginning of disarmament, not indeed a unilateral disarmament, but one proceeding at an equal pace according to agreement, and backed up by authentic and workable safeguards.

In the meantime, efforts which have already been made and are still under way to eliminate the danger of war are not to be underrated. On the contrary, support should be given to the good will of the very many leaders who work hard to do away with war, which they abominate.

Public Opinion: Men should take heed not to entrust themselves only to the efforts of others, while remaining careless about their own attitudes. For government officials, who must simultaneously guarantee the good of their own people and promote the universal good, depend on public opinion and feeling to the greatest possible extent. It does them no good to work at building peace so long as feelings of hostility, contempt, and distrust, as well as racial hatred and unbending ideologies, continue to divide men and place them in opposing camps.

Hence arises a surpassing need for renewed education of attitudes and for new inspiration in the area of public opinion. Those who are dedicated to the work of education . . . should regard as their most weighty task the effort to instruct all in fresh sentiments of peace (No. 82).

THE CHALLENGE OF PEACE

Following is an excerpt from a summary of the pastoral letter, "The Challenge of Peace: God's Promise and Our Response," copyright ©1983 by the United States Catholic Conference, all rights reserved. A copy of the complete text can be ordered from the Office of Publishing Services, USCC, 1312 Massachusetts Ave. N.W., Washington, D.C. 20005.

The letter was approved by a vote of 238 to 9 at a special meeting of U.S. bishops May 2 and 3, 1983, in Chicago.

PRINCIPLES, NORMS AND PREMISES
A. On War

1. Catholic teaching begins in every case with a presumption against war and for peaceful settlement of disputes. In exceptional cases, determined by the moral principles of the just-war tradition, some uses of force are permitted.

2. Every nation has a right and duty to defend itself against unjust aggression.

3. Offensive war of any kind is not morally justifiable.

4. It is never permitted to direct nuclear or conventional weapons to "the indiscriminate destruction of whole cities or vast areas with their populations. . . ." *(Pastoral Constitution on the Church in the Modern World,* No. 80.) The intentional killing of innocent civilians or non-combatants is always wrong.

5. Even defensive response to unjust attack can cause destruction which violates the principle of proportionality, going far beyond the limits of legitimate defense. This judgment is particularly important when assessing planned use of nuclear weapons. No defensive strategy, nuclear or conventional, which exceeds the limits of proportionality is morally permissible.

B. On Deterrence

1. "In current conditions 'deterrence' based on balance, certainly not as an end in itself but as a step on the way toward a progressive disarmament, may still be judged morally acceptable. Nonetheless, in order to ensure peace, it is indispensable not to be satisfied with this minimum which is always susceptible to the real danger of explosion." (Pope John Paul II, Message to U.N.

Special Session on Disarmament, No. 8, June, 1982.)

2. No *use* of nuclear weapons which would violate the principles of discrimination or proportionality may be *intended* in a strategy of deterrence. The moral demands of Catholic teaching require resolute willingness not to intend or to do moral evil even to save our own lives or the lives of those we love.

C. The Arms Race and Disarmament

1. The arms race is one of the greatest curses on the human race; it is to be condemned as a danger, an act of aggression against the poor, and a folly which does not provide the security it promises. (Cf. *Pastoral Constitution,* No. 81; Statement of the Holy See to the United Nations, 1976.)

2. Negotiations must be pursued in every reasonable form possible; they should be governed by the "demand that the arms race should cease; that the stockpiles which exist in various countries should be reduced equally and simultaneously by the parties concerned; that nuclear weapons should be banned; and that a general agreement should eventually be reached about progressive disarmament and an effective method of control." (Pope John XXIII, *Peace on Earth,* No. 112.)

D. On Personal Conscience

1. *Military Service:* "All those who enter the military service in loyalty to their country should look upon themselves as the custodians of the security and freedom of their fellow countrymen; and when they carry out their duty properly, they are contributing to the maintenance of peace." *(Pastoral Constitution,* No. 79.)

2. *Conscientious Objection:* "Moreover, it seems just that laws should make humane provision for the case of conscientious objectors who refuse to carry arms, provided they accept some other form of community service." *(Pastoral Constitution,* No. 79.)

3. *Non-violence:* "In this same spirit we cannot but express our admiration for all who forego the use of violence to vindicate their rights and resort to other means of defense which are available to weaker parties, provided it can be done without harm to the rights and duties of others and of the community." *(Pastoral Constitution,* No. 78.)

4. *Citizens and Conscience:* "Once again we deem it opportune to remind our children of their duty to take an active part in public life, and to contribute towards the attainment of the common good of the entire human family as well as to that of their own political community. . . . In other words, it is necessary that human beings, in the intimacy of their own consciences, should so live and act in their temporal lives as to create a synthesis between scientific, technical and professional elements on the one hand, and spiritual values on the other." (Pope John XXIII, *Peace on Earth,* Nos. 146, 150.)

MORAL PRINCIPLES AND CHOICES

As bishops in the United States, assessing the concrete circumstances of our society, we have made a number of observations and recommendations in the process of applying moral principles to specific policy choices.

A. On the Use of Nuclear Weapons

1. *Counter Population Use:* Under no circumstances may nuclear weapons or other instruments of mass slaughter be used for the purpose of destroying population centers or other predominantly civilian targets. Retaliatory action which would indiscriminately and disproportionately take many wholly innocent lives, lives of people who are in no way responsible for reckless actions of their government, must also be condemned.

2. *The Initiation of Nuclear War:* We do not perceive any situation in which the deliberate initiation of nuclear war, on however restricted a scale, can be morally justified. Non-nuclear attacks by another state must be resisted by other than nuclear means.

3. *Limited Nuclear War:* Our examination of the various arguments on this question makes us highly skeptical about the real meaning of "limited." One of the criteria of the just-war teaching is that there must be a reasonable hope of success in bringing about justice and peace. We must ask whether such a reasonable hope can exist once nuclear weapons have been exchanged. The burden of proof remains on those who assert that meaningful limitation is possible. In our view the first imperative is to prevent any use of nuclear weapons and we hope that leaders will resist the notion that nuclear conflict can be limited, contained or won in any traditional sense.

B. On Deterrence

In concert with the evaluation provided by Pope John Paul II, we have arrived at a strictly conditional moral acceptance of deterrence. In this letter we have outlined criteria and recommendations which indicate the meaning of conditional acceptance of deterrence policy. We cannot consider such a policy adequate as a long-term basis for peace.

C. On Promoting Peace

1. We support immediate, bilateral, verifiable agreements to halt the testing, production and deployment of new nuclear weapons systems. This recommendation is not to be identified with any specific political initiative.

2. We support efforts to achieve deep cuts in the arsenals of both superpowers; efforts should concentrate first on systems which threaten the retaliatory forces of either major power.

3. We support early and successful conclusion of negotiations of a comprehensive test ban treaty.

4. We urge new efforts to prevent the spread of nuclear weapons in the world, and to control the conventional arms race, particularly the conventional arms trade.

5. We support, in an increasingly interdependent world, political and economic policies designed to protect human dignity and to promote the human rights of every person, especially the least among us. In this regard, we call for the establishment of some form of global authority adequate to the needs of the international common good.

LITURGY

The nature and purpose of the liturgy, along with norms for its revision, were the subject matter of the "Constitution on the Sacred Liturgy" promulgated by the Second Vatican Council. The principles and guidelines stated in this document, the first issued by the Council, are summarized here and/or are incorporated in other Almanac entries on liturgical subjects.

Nature and Purpose of Liturgy

The paragraphs under this and the following subhead are quoted directly from the "Constitution on the Sacred Liturgy."

"It is through the liturgy, especially the divine Eucharistic Sacrifice, that 'the work of our redemption is exercised.' The liturgy is thus the outstanding means by which the faithful can express in their lives, and manifest to others, the mystery of Christ and the real nature of the true Church . . ." (No. 2).

"The liturgy is considered as an exercise of the priestly office of Jesus Christ. In the liturgy the sanctification of man is manifested by signs perceptible to the senses, and is effected in a way which is proper to each of these signs; in the liturgy full public worship is performed by the Mystical Body of Jesus Christ, that is, by the Head and his members.

"From this it follows that every liturgical celebration, because it is an action of Christ the priest and of his Body the Church, is a sacred action surpassing all others. No other action of the Church can match its claim to efficacy, nor equal the degree of it" (No. 7).

"The liturgy is the summit toward which the activity of the Church is directed; at the same time it is the fountain from which all her power flows. For the goal of apostolic works is that all who are made sons of God by faith and baptism should come together to praise God in the midst of his Church, to take part in her sacrifice, and to eat the Lord's Supper.

". . . From the liturgy, therefore, and especially from the Eucharist, as from a fountain, grace is channeled into us; and the sanctification of men in Christ and the glorification of God, to which all other activities of the Church are directed as toward their goal, are most powerfully achieved" (No. 10).

Full Participation

"Mother Church earnestly desires that all the faithful be led to that full, conscious, and active participation in liturgical celebrations which is demanded by the very nature of the liturgy. Such participation by the Christian people as 'a chosen race, a royal priesthood, a holy nation, a purchased people' (1 Pt. 2:9; cf. 2:4-5), is their right and duty by reason of their baptism.

"In the restoration and promotion of the sacred liturgy, this full and active participation by all the people is the aim to be considered before all else; for it is the primary and indispensable source from which the faithful are to derive the true Christian spirit . . ." (No. 14).

"In order that the Christian people may more securely derive an abundance of graces from the sacred liturgy, holy Mother Church desires to undertake with great care a general restoration of the liturgy itself. For the liturgy is made up of unchangeable elements divinely instituted, and elements subject to change. The latter not only may but ought to be changed with the passing of time if features have by chance crept in which are less harmonious with the intimate nature of the liturgy, or if existing elements have grown less functional.

"In this restoration, both texts and rites should be drawn up so that they express more clearly the holy things which they signify. Christian people, as far as possible, should be able to understand them with ease and to take part in them fully, actively, and as befits a community . . ." (No. 21).

Norms

Norms regarding the reforms concern the greater use of Scripture; emphasis on the importance of the sermon or homily on biblical and liturgical subjects; use of vernacular languages for prayers of the Mass and for administration of the sacraments; provision for adaptation of rites to cultural patterns.

Approval for reforms of various kinds — in liturgical texts, rites, etc. — depends on the Holy See, regional conferences of bishops and individual bishops, according to provisions of law. No priest has authority to initiate reforms on his own. Reforms may not be introduced just for the sake of innovation, and any that are introduced in the light of present-day circumstances should embody sound tradition.

To assure the desired effect of liturgical reforms, training and instruction are necessary for the clergy, religious and the laity. The functions of diocesan and regional commissions for liturgy, music and art are to set standards and provide leadership for instruction and practical programs in their respective fields.

Most of the constitution's provisions regarding liturgical reforms have to do with the Roman Rite. The document clearly respects the equal dignity of all rites, leaving to the Eastern Churches control over their ancient liturgies.

(For coverage of the **Mystery of the Eucharist,** see The Mass; Other Sacraments, see separate entries.)

Sacramentals

Sacramentals, instituted by the Church, "are sacred signs which bear a resemblance to the sacraments: they signify effects, particularly of a spiritual kind, which are obtained through the Church's intercession. By them men are disposed to receive the chief effect of the sacraments, and various occasions in life are rendered holy" (No. 60).

"Thus, for well-disposed members of the faithful, the liturgy of the sacraments and sacramentals sanctifies almost every event in their lives; they are given access to the stream of divine grace which flows from the paschal mystery of the passion, death, and resurrection of Christ, the fountain from which all sacraments and sacramentals draw their power. There is hardly any proper use of material things which cannot thus be directed toward the sanctification of men and the praise of God" (No. 61).

Some common sacramentals are priestly blessings, blessed palm, candles, holy water, medals, scapulars, prayers and ceremonies of the Roman Ritual.

Liturgy of the Hours

The Liturgy of the Hours (Divine Office) is the public prayer of the Church for praising God and sanctifying the day. Its daily celebration is required as a sacred obligation by men in holy orders and by men and women religious who have professed solemn vows. Its celebration by others is highly commended and is to be encouraged in the community of the faithful.

"By tradition going back to early Christian times, the Divine Office is arranged so that the whole course of the day and night is made holy by the praises of God. Therefore, when this wonderful song of praise is worthily rendered by priests and others who are deputed for this purpose by Church ordinance, or by the faithful praying together with the priest in an approved form, then it is truly the voice of the bride addressing her bridegroom; it is the very prayer which Christ himself, together with his Body, addresses to the Father" (No. 84).

"Hence all who perform this service are not only fulfilling a duty of the Church, but also are sharing in the greatest honor accorded to Christ's spouse, for by offering these praises to God they are standing before God's throne in the name of the Church their Mother" (No. 85).

The Liturgy of the Hours, revised since 1965, was the subject of Pope Paul VI's apostolic constitution *Laudis Canticum,* dated Nov. 1, 1970. The master Latin text was published in 1971; its four volumes have been published in authorized English translation since May, 1975.

One-volume, partial editions of the Liturgy of the Hours containing Morning and Evening Prayer and other elements, have been published in approved English translation.

The revised Liturgy of the Hours consists of:

• Office of Readings, for reflection on the word of God. The principal parts are three psalms, biblical and non-biblical readings.

• Morning and Evening Prayer, called the "hinges" of the Liturgy of the Hours. The principal parts are a hymn, two psalms, an Old or New Testament canticle, a brief biblical reading, Zechariah's canticle (the *Benedictus,* morning) or Mary's canticle (the *Magnificat,* evening), responsories, intercessions and a concluding prayer.

• Daytime Prayer. The principal parts are a hymn, three psalms, a brief biblical reading and one of three concluding prayers corresponding to the time at which the prayer is offered (midmorning, midday, midafternoon).

• Night Prayer: The principal parts are one or two psalms, a brief biblical reading, Simeon's canticle *(Nunc Dimittis),* a concluding prayer and an antiphon in honor of Mary.

In the revised Liturgy of the Hours, the hours are shorter than they had been, with greater textual variety, meditation aids, and provision for intervals of silence and meditation. The psalms are distributed over a four-week period instead of a week; some psalms, entirely or in part, are not included. Additional canticles from the Old and New Testaments are assigned for Morning and Evening Prayer. Additional scriptural texts have been added and variously arranged for greater internal unity, correspondence to readings at Mass, and relevance to events and themes of salvation history. Readings include some of the best material from the Fathers of the Church and other authors, and improved selections on the lives of saints.

The book used for recitation of the Office is the **Breviary.**

For coverage of the **Liturgical Year,** see Church Calendar.

Sacred Music

"The musical tradition of the universal Church is a treasure of immeasurable value, greater even than that of any other art. The main reason for this pre-eminence is that, as sacred melody united to words, it forms a necessary or integral part of the solemn liturgy.

". . . Sacred music increases in holiness to the degree that it is intimately linked with liturgical action, winningly expresses prayerfulness, promotes solidarity, and enriches sacred rites with heightened solemnity. The Church indeed approves of all forms of true art, and admits them into divine worship when they show appropriate qualities" (No. 112).

The constitution decreed:

• Vernacular languages for the people's parts of the liturgy, as well as Latin, may be used.

• Participation in sacred song by the whole body of the faithful, and not just by choirs, is to be encouraged and brought about.

• Provisions should be made for proper musical training for clergy, religious and lay persons.

• While Gregorian Chant has a unique dignity and relationship to the Latin liturgy, other kinds of music are acceptable.

• Native musical traditions should be used, especially in mission areas.

• Various instruments compatible with the dignity of worship may be used.

Gregorian Chant: A form and style of chant called Gregorian was the basis and most highly regarded standard of liturgical music for centuries. It originated probably during the formative period of the Roman liturgy and developed in conjunction with Gallican and other forms of chant. Gregory the Great's connection with it is not clear, although it is known that he had great concern for and interest in church music. The earliest extant written versions of Gregorian Chant date from the ninth century. A thousand years later, the Benedictines of Solesmes, France, initiated a revival of chant which gave impetus to the modern liturgical movement.

Sacred Art and Furnishings

"Very rightly the fine arts are considered to rank among the noblest expressions of human genius. This judgment applies especially to religious art and to its highest achievement, which is sacred art. By their very nature both of the latter are related to God's boundless beauty, for this is the reality which these human efforts are trying to express in some way. To the extent that these works aim exclusively at turning men's thoughts to God persuasively and devoutly, they are dedicated to God and to the cause of his greater honor and glory" (No. 122).

The objective of sacred art is "that all things set apart for use in divine worship should be truly worthy, becoming, and beautiful, signs and symbols of heavenly realities. ... The Church has ... always reserved to herself the right to pass judgment upon the arts, deciding which of the works of artists are in accordance with faith, piety, and cherished traditional laws, and thereby suited to sacred purposes.

"... Sacred furnishings should worthily and beautifully serve the dignity of worship ..." (No. 122).

According to the constitution:
- Contemporary art, as well as that of the past, shall "be given free scope in the Church, provided that it adorns the sacred buildings and holy rites with due honor and reverence ..." (No. 123).
- Noble beauty, not sumptuous display, should be sought in art, sacred vestments and ornaments.
- "Let bishops carefully exclude from the house of God and from other sacred places those works of artists which are repugnant to faith, morals, and Christian piety, and which offend true religious sense either by their distortion of forms or by lack of artistic worth, by mediocrity or by pretense.
- "When churches are to be built, let great care be taken that they be suitable for the celebration of liturgical services and for the active participation of the faithful" (No. 124).
- "The practice of placing sacred images in churches so that they may be venerated by the faithful is to be firmly maintained. Nevertheless, their number should be moderate and their relative location should reflect right order. Otherwise they may create confusion among the Christian people and promote a faulty sense of devotion" (No. 125).
- Artists should be trained and inspired in the spirit and for the purposes of the liturgy.
- The norms of sacred art should be revised. "These laws refer especially to the worthy and well-planned construction of sacred buildings, the shape and construction of altars, the nobility, location, and security of the Eucharistic tabernacle, the suitability and dignity of the baptistery, the proper use of sacred images, embellishments, and vestments ..." (No. 128).

RITES

Rites are the forms and ceremonial observances of liturgical worship coupled with the total expression of the theological, spiritual and disciplinary heritages of particular churches of the East and the West.

Different rites have evolved in the course of church history, giving to liturgical worship and church life in general forms and usages peculiar and proper to the nature of worship and the culture of the faithful in various circumstances of time and place. Thus, there has been development since apostolic times in the prayers and ceremonies of the Mass, in the celebration of the sacraments, sacramentals and the Liturgy of the Hours, and in observances of the liturgical calendar. The principal sources of rites in present use were practices within the patriarchates of Rome (for the West) and Antioch, Alexandria and Constantinople (for the East). Rites are identified as Eastern or Western on the basis of their geographical area of origin in the Roman Empire.

Eastern and Roman

Eastern Rites are proper to Eastern Catholic Churches (see separate entry). The principal rites are Byzantine, Alexandrian, Antiochene, Armenian and Chaldean.

The Latin or Roman Rite prevails in the Western Church. It was derived from Roman practices and the use of Latin from the third century onward, and has been the rite in general use in the West since the eighth century. Other rites in limited use in the Western Church have been the Ambrosian (in the Archdiocese of Milan), the Mozarabic (in the Archdiocese of Toledo), the Lyonnais, the Braga, and rites peculiar to some religious orders like the Dominicans, Carmelites and Carthusians.

The purpose of the revision of rites in progress since the Second Vatican Council is to renew them, not to eliminate the rites of particular churches or to reduce all rites to uniformity. The Council reaffirmed the equal dignity and preservation of rites as follows.

"It is the mind of the Catholic Church that each individual church or rite retain its traditions whole and entire, while adjusting its way of life to various needs of time and place. Such individual churches, whether of the East or the West, although they differ somewhat among themselves in what are called rites (that is, in liturgy, ecclesiastical discipline and spiritual heritage), are, nevertheless, equally entrusted to the pastoral guidance of the Roman Pontiff, the divinely appointed successor of St. Peter in supreme government over the universal Church. They are, consequently, of equal dignity, so that none of them is superior to the others by reason of rite."

Determination of Rite

Determination of a person's rite is regulated by church law. Through baptism, a child becomes a member of the rite of his or her parents. If the parents are of different rites, the child's rite is decided by mutual consent of the parents; if there is lack of mutual consent, the child is baptized in the rite of the father. A candidate for baptism over the age of 14 can choose to be baptized in any approved rite. Catholics baptized in one rite may receive the sacraments in any of the approved ritual churches; they may transfer to another rite only with the permission of the Holy See and in accordance with other provisions of the Code of Canon Law.

MASS, EUCHARISTIC SACRIFICE AND BANQUET

Declarations of Vatican II

The Second Vatican Council made the following declarations, among others, with respect to the Mass.

"At the Last Supper, on the night when he was betrayed, our Savior instituted the Eucharistic Sacrifice of his Body and Blood. He did this in order to perpetuate the Sacrifice of the Cross throughout the centuries until he should come again, and so to entrust to his beloved spouse, the Church, a memorial of his death and resurrection: a sacrament of love, a sign of unity, a bond of charity, a paschal banquet in which Christ is consumed, the mind is filled with grace, and a pledge of future glory is given to us" (*Constitution on the Sacred Liturgy*, No. 47).

"... As often as the Sacrifice of the Cross in which 'Christ, our Passover, has been sacrificed' (1 Cor. 5:7) is celebrated on an altar, the work of our redemption is carried on. At the same time, in the sacrament of the Eucharistic bread the unity of all believers who form one body in Christ (cf. 1 Cor. 10:17) is both expressed and brought about. All men are called to this union with Christ ..." (*Dogmatic Constitution on the Church*. No. 3).

"... The ministerial priest, by the sacred power he enjoys, molds and rules the priestly people. Acting in the person of Christ, he brings about the Eucharistic Sacrifice, and offers it to God in the name of all the people. For their part, the faithful join in the offering of the Eucharist by virtue of their royal priesthood ..." (*Ibid.*, No. 10).

Declarations of Trent

Among its decrees on the Holy Eucharist, the Council of Trent stated the following points of doctrine on the Mass.

1. There is in the Catholic Church a true Sacrifice, the Mass instituted by Jesus Christ. It is the Sacrifice of his Body and Blood, Soul and Divinity, himself, under the appearances of bread and wine.

2. This Sacrifice is identical with the Sacrifice of the Cross, inasmuch as Christ is the Priest and Victim in both. A difference lies in the manner of offering, which was bloody upon the Cross and is bloodless on the altar.

3. The Mass is a propitiatory Sacrifice, atoning for sins of the living and dead for whom it is offered.

4. The efficacy of the Mass is derived from the Sacrifice of the Cross, whose superabundant merits it applies to men.

5. Although the Mass is offered to God alone, it may be celebrated in honor and memory of the saints.

6. Christ instituted the Mass at the Last Supper.

7. Christ ordained the Apostles priests, giving them power and the command to consecrate his Body and Blood to perpetuate and renew the Sacrifice.

ORDER OF MASS

The Mass consists of two principal divisions called the **Liturgy of the Word**, which features the proclamation of the Word of God, and the **Eucharistic Liturgy**, which focuses on the central act of sacrifice in the Consecration and on the Eucharistic Banquet in Holy Communion. (Formerly, these divisions were called, respectively, the **Mass of the Catechumens** and the **Mass of the Faithful**.) In addition to these principal divisions, there are ancillary introductory and concluding rites.

The following description covers the Mass as celebrated with participation by the people. This Order of the Mass was approved by Pope Paul VI in the apostolic constitution *Missale Romanum* dated Apr. 3, 1969, and promulgated in a decree issued Apr. 6, 1969, by the Congregation for Divine Worship. The assigned effective date was Nov. 30, 1969.

Introductory Rites

Entrance: The introductory rites begin with the singing or recitation of an entrance song consisting of one or more scriptural verses stating the theme of the mystery, season or feast commemorated in the Mass.

Greeting: The priest and people make the Sign of the Cross together. The priest then greets them in one of several alternative ways and they reply in a corresponding manner.

Introductory Remarks: At this point, the priest or another of the ministers may introduce the theme of the Mass.

Penitential Rite: The priest and people together acknowledge their sins as a preliminary step toward worthy celebration of the sacred mysteries. This rite includes a brief examination of conscience, a general confession of sin and plea for divine mercy in one of several ways, and a prayer for forgiveness by the priest.

Glory to God: A doxology, a hymn of praise to God, sung or said on festive occasions.

Opening Prayer: A prayer of petition offered by the priest on behalf of the worshipping community.

I. Liturgy of the Word

Readings: The featured elements of this liturgy are readings of passages from the Bible. If three readings are in order, the first is usually from the Old Testament, the second from the New Testament (Letters, Acts, Revelation), and the third from one of the Gospels; the final reading is always a selection from a Gospel. The first reading(s) is concluded with the formula, "This is the Word of the Lord," to which the people respond, "Thanks be to God." The Gospel reading is concluded with the formula, "This is the Gospel of the Lord," to which the people respond, "Praise to you, Lord Jesus Christ." Between the readings, psalm verses are sung or recited. A Gospel acclamation is either sung or omitted.

Homily: Sermon on a scriptural or liturgical subject; ideally, it should be related to the liturgical service in progress.

Creed: The Nicene profession of faith, by priest and people, on certain occasions.

Prayer of the Faithful: Litany-type prayers of petition, with participation by the people. Called general intercessions, they concern needs of the Church, the salvation of the world, public authorities, persons in need, the local community.

II. Eucharistic Liturgy

Offertory Procession: Presentation to the priest of the gifts of bread and wine, principally, by participating members of the congregation.

Offering of and Prayer over the Gifts: Consists of the prayers and ceremonies with which the priest offers bread and wine as the elements of the sacrifice to take place during the Eucharistic Prayer and of the Lord's Supper to be shared in Holy Communion.

Washing of Hands: After offering the bread and wine, the priest cleanses his fingers with water in a brief ceremony of purification.

Pray, Brethren: Prayer that the sacrifice to take place will be acceptable to God. The first part of the prayer is said by the priest; the second, by the people.

Prayer over the Gifts: A prayer of petition offered by the priest on behalf of the worshipping community.

Eucharistic Prayer

Preface: A hymn of praise, introducing the Eucharistic Prayer or Canon, sung or said by the priest following responses by the people. The Order of the Mass contains a variety of prefaces, for use on different occasions.

Holy, Holy, Holy; Blessed Is He: Divine praises sung or said by the priest and people.

Canon: The Eucharistic Prayer of the Mass whose central portion is the Consecration, when the essential act of sacrificial offering takes place with the changing of bread and wine into the Body and Blood of Christ. The prayers of the Canon, which are said by the celebrant only, commemorate principal mysteries of salvation history and include petitions for the Church, the living and dead, and remembrances of saints. There are four Eucharistic Prayers, for use on various occasions and at the option of the priest. (Additional Canons for Masses with children and for reconciliation were approved in 1975.)

Doxology: A formula of divine praise sung or said by the priest while he holds aloft the chalice containing the consecrated wine in one hand and the paten containing the consecrated host in the other.

Communion Rite

Lord's Prayer: Sung or said by the priest and people.

Prayer for Deliverance from evil: Called an **embolism** because it is a development of the final petition of the Lord's Prayer; said by the priest. It concludes with a memorial of the return of the Lord to which the people respond, "For the kingdom, the power, and the glory are yours, now and forever."

Prayer for Peace: Said by the priest, with corresponding responses by the people. The priest can, in accord with local custom, bid the people to exchange a greeting of peace with each other.

Lamb of God (*Agnus Dei*): A prayer for divine mercy sung or said while the priest breaks the consecrated host and places a piece of it into the consecrated wine in the chalice.

Communion: The priest, after saying a preparatory prayer, administers Holy Communion to himself and then to the people, thus completing the sacrifice-banquet of the Mass. (This completion is realized even if the celebrant alone receives the Eucharist.) On giving the Eucharist to the people, the priest says, "The Body of Christ," to each recipient; the customary response is "Amen." If the Eucharist is administered under the forms of bread and wine, the priest says, "The Body and Blood of Christ."

Communion Song: Scriptural verses or a suitable hymn sung or said during the distribution of Holy Communion. After Holy Communion is received, some moments may be spent in silent meditation or in the chanting of a psalm or hymn of praise.

Prayer after Communion: A prayer of petition offered by the priest on behalf of the worshipping community.

Concluding Rite

Announcements: Brief announcements to the people are in order at this time.

Dismissal: Consists of a final greeting by the priest, a blessing, and a formula of dismissal. This rite is omitted if another liturgical action immediately follows the Mass; e.g., a procession, the blessing of the body during a funeral rite.

Some parts of the Mass are changeable with the liturgical season or feast, and are called the **proper** of the Mass. Other parts are said to be **common** because they always remain the same.

Additional Mass Notes

Catholics are seriously obliged to attend Mass in a worthy manner on Sundays and holy days of obligation. Failure to do so without a proportionately serious reason is gravely wrong.

It is the custom for priests to celebrate Mass daily whenever possible. To satisfy the needs of the faithful on Sundays and holy days of obligation, they are authorized to say Mass twice (**bination**) or even three times (**trination**). Bination is also permissible on weekdays. On Christmas and All Souls' Day every priest may say three Masses.

The **fruits of the Mass**, which in itself is of infinite value, are: **general**, for all the faithful; **special (ministerial)**, for the intentions or persons specifically intended by the celebrant; **most special (personal)**, for the celebrant himself. On Sundays and certain other days pastors are obliged to offer Mass for their parishioners, or to have another priest do so. If a priest accepts a stipend or offering for a Mass, he is obliged in justice to apply the Mass for the designated intention. Mass may be applied for the living and the dead, or for any good intention.

Mass can be celebrated in several ways: e.g., with people present, without their presence (privately), with two or more priests as co-celebrants (concelebration), with greater or less solemnity.

Some of the various types of Masses are: **for the dead** (Funeral Mass or Mass of Christian Burial, Mass for the Dead — formerly called Requiem Mass); **ritual**, in connection with celebration of the sacraments, religious profession, etc.; **nuptial**, for married couples, with or after the wedding ceremony; **votive**, to honor a Person of the Trinity, a saint, or for some special intention. **Gregorian Masses** are a series of 30 Masses celebrated on 30 consecutive days for a deceased person.

On Good Friday instead of Mass, there is a celebration of the Lord's Passion consisting of a Liturgy of the Word, Veneration of the Cross and Holy Communion.

Places, Altars for Mass

The ordinary place for celebrating the Eucharist is a church or other sacred place, at a fixed or movable altar.

The altar is a table at which the Eucharistic Sacrifice is celebrated.

A *fixed altar* is attached to the floor of the church. It should be of stone, preferably, and should be consecrated. The Code of Canon Law orders observance of the custom of placing under a fixed altar relics of martyrs or other saints.

A *movable altar* can be made of any solid and suitable material, and should be blessed or consecrated.

Outside of a sacred place, Mass may be celebrated in an appropriate place at a suitable table covered with a linen cloth and corporal. An altar stone containing the relics of saints, which was formerly prescribed, is not required by regulations in effect since the promulgation Apr. 6, 1969, of *Institutio Generalis Missalis Romani*.

LITURGICAL VESTMENTS

In the early years of the Church, vestments worn by the ministers at liturgical functions were the same as the garments in ordinary popular use. They became distinctive when their form was not altered to correspond with later variations in popular style. Liturgical vestments are symbolic of the sacred ministry and add appropriate decorum to divine worship.

Mass Vestments

Alb: A body-length tunic of white fabric; a vestment common to all ministers of divine worship.

Amice: A rectangular piece of white cloth worn about the neck, tucked into the collar and falling over the shoulders; prescribed for use when the alb does not completely cover the ordinary clothing at the neck.

Chasuble: Originally, a large mantle or cloak covering the body, it is the outer vestment of a priest celebrating Mass or carrying out other sacred actions connected with the Mass.

Cincture: A cord which serves the purpose of a belt, holding the alb close to the body.

Dalmatic: The outer vestment worn by a deacon in place of a chasuble.

Stole: A long, band-like vestment worn about the neck and falling to about the knees. (A stole is used for other functions also.)

The material, form and ornamentation of the aforementioned and other vestments are subject to variation and adaptation, according to norms and decisions of the Holy See and concerned conferences of bishops. The overriding norm is that they should be appropriate for use in divine worship. The customary ornamented vestments are the chasuble, dalmatic and stole.

The minimal vestments required for a priest celebrating Mass are the alb, stole and chasuble.

Chasuble-Alb: A vestment combining the features of the chasuble and alb; for use with a stole by concelebrants and, by way of exception, by celebrants in certain circumstances.

Liturgical Colors

The colors of outer vestments vary with liturgical seasons, feasts and other circumstances. The colors and their use are:

Green: For the season of Ordinary Time; symbolic of hope and the vitality of the life of faith.

Purple: For Advent and Lent; may also be used in Masses for the dead; symbolic of penance.

Red: For the Sunday of the Passion, Good Friday, Pentecost; feasts of the Passion of Our Lord, the Apostles and Evangelists, martyrs; symbolic of the supreme sacrifice of life for the love of God.

Rose: May be used in place of purple on the Third Sunday of Advent (Gaudete Sunday) and the Fourth Sunday of Lent (Laetare Sunday); symbolic of anticipatory joy during a time of penance.

White: For the seasons of Christmas and Easter; feasts and commemorations of Our Lord, except those of the Passion; feasts and commemorations of the Blessed Virgin Mary, angels, saints who are not martyrs, All Saints (Nov. 1), St. John the Baptist (June 24), St. John the Evangelist (Dec. 27), the Chair of St. Peter (Feb. 22), the Conversion of St. Paul (Jan. 25). White, symbolic of purity and integrity of the life of faith, may generally be substituted for other colors, and can be used for funeral and other Masses for the dead.

Options are provided regarding the color of vestments used in offices and Masses for the dead. The newsletter of the U.S. Bishops' Committee on the Liturgy, in line with No. 308 of the General Instruction of the Roman Missal, announced in July, 1970: "In the dioceses of the United States, white vestments may be used, in addition to violet (purple) and black, in offices and Masses for the dead."

On more solemn occasions, better than ordinary vestments may be used, even though their color (e.g., gold) does not match the requirements of the day.

Blue: Regarding the use of blue for liturgical vestments, the National Conference of Catholic Bishops "has neither proposed nor approved the use of blue either for the season of Advent or for memorials and feasts of Mary, nor any other color." So stated the December, 1987 edition of the "Newsletter" of the U.S. Bishops' Committee on the Liturgy.

Considerable freedom is permitted in the choice of colors of vestments worn for votive Masses.

Other Vestments

Cappa Magna: Flowing vestment with a train, worn by bishops and cardinals.

Cassock: A non-liturgical, full-length, close-fitting robe for use by priests and other clerics under liturgical vestments and in ordinary use; usually black for priests, purple for bishops and other prelates, red for cardinals, white for the pope. In place of a cassock, priests belonging to religious institutes wear the habit proper to their institute.

Cope: A mantle-like vestment open in front and fastened across the chest; worn by sacred ministers in processions and other ceremonies, as prescribed by appropriate directives.

Habit: The ordinary (non-liturgical) garb of members of religious institutes, analogous to the cassock of diocesan priests; the form of habits varies from institute to institute.

Humeral Veil: A rectangular vestment worn about the shoulders by a deacon. or priest in Eucharistic processions and for other prescribed liturgical ceremonies.

Mitre: A headdress worn at some liturgical functions by bishops, abbots and, in certain cases, other ecclesiastics.

Pallium: A circular band of white wool about two inches wide, with front and back pendants, marked with six crosses, worn about the neck. It is a symbol of the fullness of the episcopal office. Pope Paul VI, in a document issued July 20, 1978, on his own initiative and entitled *Inter Eximia Episcopalis*, restricted its use to the pope and archbishops of metropolitan sees. In 1984, Pope John Paul II decreed that the pallium would ordinarily be conferred on metropolitans by the pope on the solemnity of Sts. Peter and Paul, June 29. The pallium is made from the wool of lambs blessed by the pope on the feast of St. Agnes (Jan. 21).

Rochet: A knee-length, white linen-lace garment of prelates worn under outer vestments.

Surplice: A loose, flowing vestment of white fabric with wide sleeves. For some functions, it is interchangeable with an alb.

Zucchetto: A skullcap worn by bishops and other prelates.

In a "Circular Letter concerning the Preparation and Celebration of the Easter Feasts," the Vatican was sharply critical of practices which dilute or change set norms for their celebration.

SACRED VESSELS, LINENS

Vessels

Chalice and Paten: The principal sacred vessels required for the celebration of Mass are the chalice (cup) and paten (plate) in which wine and bread, respectively, are offered, consecrated and consumed. Both should be made of solid and noble material which is not easily breakable or corruptible. Gold coating is required of the interior parts of sacred vessels subject to rust. The cup of a chalice should be made of non-absorbent material.

Vessels for containing consecrated hosts (see below) can be made of material other than solid and noble metal — e.g., ivory, more durable woods — provided the substitute material is locally regarded as noble or rather precious and is suitable for sacred use.

Sacred vessels should be blessed, according to prescribed requirements.

Vessels, in addition to the paten, for containing consecrated hosts are:

Ciborium: Used to hold hosts for distribution to the faithful and for reservation in the tabernacle.

Luna, Lunula, Lunette: A small receptacle which holds the sacred host in an upright position in the monstrance.

Monstrance, Ostensorium: A portable receptacle so made that the sacred host, when enclosed therein, may be clearly seen, as at Benediction or during extended exposition of the Blessed Sacrament.

Pyx: A watch-shaped vessel used in carrying the Eucharist to the sick.

Linens

Altar Cloth: A white cloth, usually of linen, covering the table of an altar. One cloth is sufficient. Three were used according to former requirements.

Burse: A square, stiff flat case, open at one end, in which the folded corporal can be placed; the outside is covered with material of the same kind and color as the outer vestments of the celebrant.

Corporal: A square piece of white linen spread on the altar cloth, on which rest the vessels holding the Sacred Species — the consecrated host(s) and wine — during the Eucharistic Liturgy. The corporal is similarly used whenever the Blessed Sacrament is removed from the tabernacle; e.g., during Benediction the vessel containing the Blessed Sacrament rests on a corporal.

Finger Towel: A white rectangular napkin used by the priest to dry his fingers after cleansing them following the offering of gifts at Mass.

Pall: A square piece of stiff material, usually covered with linen, which can be used to cover the chalice at Mass.

Purificator: A white rectangular napkin used for cleansing sacred vessels after the reception of Communion at Mass.

Veil: The chalice intended for use at Mass can be covered with a veil made of the same material as the outer vestments of the celebrant.

THE CHURCH BUILDING

A church is a building set aside and dedicated for purposes of divine worship, the place of assembly for a worshiping community.

A Catholic church is the ordinary place in which the faithful assemble for participation in the Eucharistic Liturgy and other forms of divine worship.

In the early years of Christianity, the first places of assembly for the Eucharistic Liturgy were private homes (Acts 2:46; Rom. 16:5; 1 Cor. 16:5; Col. 4:15) and, sometimes, catacombs. Church building began in the latter half of the second century during lulls in persecution and became widespread after enactment of the Edict of Milan in 313, when it finally became possible for the Church to emerge completely from the underground. The oldest and basic norms regarding church buildings date from about that time.

The essential principle underlying all norms for church building was reformulated by the Second Vatican Council, as follows: "When churches are to be built, let great care be taken that they be suitable for the celebration of liturgical services and for the active participation of the faithful" *(Constitution on the Sacred Liturgy*, No. 124).

This principle was subsequently elaborated in detail by the Congregation for Divine Worship in a document entitled *Institutio Generalis Missalis Romani*, which was approved by Paul VI Apr. 3 and promulgated by a decree of the congregation dated Apr. 6, 1969. Coverage of the following items reflects the norms stated in Chapter V of this document.

Main Features

Sanctuary: The part of the church where the altar of sacrifice is located, the place where the ministers of the liturgy lead the people in prayer, proclaim the word of God and celebrate the Eucharist. It is set off from the body of the church by a distinctive structural feature — e.g., elevation above the main floor — or by ornamentation. (The traditional communion rail, removed in recent years in many churches, served this purpose of demarcation.) The customary location of the sanctuary is at the front of the church; it may, however, be centrally located.

Altar: The main altar of sacrifice and table of the Lord is the focal feature of the sanctuary and entire church. It stands by itself, so that the ministers can move about it freely, and is so situated that they face the people during the liturgical action. In addition to this main altar, there may also be others; in new churches, these are ideally situated in side chapels or alcoves removed to some degree from the body of the church.

Adornment of the Altar: The altar table is covered with a suitable linen cloth. Required candelabra and a cross are placed upon or near the altar in plain sight of the people and are so arranged that they do not obscure their view of the liturgical action.

Seats of the Ministers: The seat of the celebrant, corresponding with his role as the presiding minister of the assembly, is best located behind the altar and facing the people; it is raised a bit above the level of the altar but must not have the appearance of a throne. The seats of other ministers are also located in the sanctuary.

Ambo, Pulpit, Lectern: The stand at which scriptural lessons and psalm responses are read, the word of God preached, and the prayer of the faithful offered. It is so placed that the ministers can be easily seen and heard by the people.

Places for the People: Seats and kneeling benches (pews) and other accommodations for the people are so arranged that they can participate in the most appropriate way in the liturgical action and have freedom of movement for the reception of Holy Communion. Reserved seats are out of order.

Place for the Choir: Where it is located depends on the most suitable arrangement for maintaining the unity of the choir with the congregation and for providing its members maximum opportunity for carrying out their proper function and participating fully in the Mass.

Tabernacle: The best place for reserving the Blessed Sacrament is in a chapel suitable for the private devotion of the people. If this is not possible, reservation should be at a side altar or other appropriately adorned place. In either case, the Blessed Sacrament should be kept in a tabernacle, i.e., a safe-like, secure receptacle.

Statues: Images of the Lord, the Blessed Virgin Mary and the saints are legitimately proposed for the veneration of the faithful in churches. Their number and arrangement, however, should be ordered in such a way that they do not distract the people from the central celebration of the Eucharistic Liturgy. There should be only one statue of one and the same saint in a church.

General Adornment and Arrangement of Churches: Churches should be so adorned and fitted out that they serve the direct requirements of divine worship and the needs and reasonable convenience of the people.

Other Items

Ambry: A box containing the holy oils, attached to the wall of the sanctuary in some churches.

Baptistery: The place for administering baptism. Some churches have baptisteries adjoining or near the entrance, a position symbolizing the fact that persons are initiated in the Church and incorporated in Christ through this sacrament. Contemporary liturgical practice favors placement of the baptistery near the sanctuary and altar, or the use of a portable font in the same position, to emphasize the relationship of baptism to the Eucharist, the celebration in sacrifice and banquet of the death and resurrection of Christ.

Candles: Used more for symbolical than illuminative purposes, they represent Christ, the light and life of grace, at liturgical functions. They are made of beeswax. (See Index: Paschal Candle.)

Confessional, Reconciliation Room: A booth-like structure for the hearing of confessions, with separate compartments for the priest and penitents and a grating or screen between them. The use of confessionals became general in the Roman Rite after the Council of Trent. Since the Second Vatican Council, there has been a trend in the U.S. to replace or supplement confessionals with small reconciliation rooms so arranged that priest and penitent can converse face-to-face.

Crucifix: A cross bearing the figure of the body of Christ, representative of the Sacrifice of the Cross.

Cruets: Vessels containing the wine and water used at Mass. They are placed on a credence table in the sanctuary.

Holy Water Fonts: Receptacles containing holy water, usually at church entrances, for the use of the faithful.

Sanctuary Lamp: A lamp which is kept burning continuously before a tabernacle in which the Blessed Sacrament is reserved, as a sign of the Real Presence of Christ.

LITURGICAL DEVELOPMENTS

The principal developments covered in this article are enactments of the Holy See and actions related to their implementation in the United States.

Modern Movement

Origins of the modern movement for renewal in the liturgy date back to the 19th century. The key contributing factor was a revival of liturgical and scriptural studies. Of special significance was the work of the Benedictine monks of Solesmes, France, who aroused great interest in the liturgy through the restoration of Gregorian Chant. St. Pius X approved their work in a motu proprio of 1903 and gave additional encouragement to liturgical study and development.

St. Pius X did more than any other single pope to promote early first Communion and the practice of frequent Communion, started the research behind a revised breviary, and appointed a group to investigate possible revisions in the Mass.

The movement attracted some attention in the 1920's and 30's but made little progress.

Significant pioneering developments in the U.S. during the 20's, however, were the establishment of the Liturgical Press, the beginning of publication of *Orate Fratres* (now *Worship*), and the inauguration of the League of the Divine Office by the Benedictines at St. John's Abbey, Collegeville, Minn. Later events of influence were the establishment of the Pius X School of Liturgical Music at Manhattanville College of the Sacred Heart and the organization of a summer school of liturgical music at Mary Manse College by the Gregorian Institute of America. The turning point toward real renewal was reached during and after World War II.

Pius XII gave it impetus and direction, principally through the background teaching in his encyclicals on the *Mystical Body* (1943), *Sacred Liturgy* (1947), and the *Discipline of Sacred Music* (1955), and by means of specific measures affecting the liturgy itself. His work was continued during the pontificates of John XXIII and Paul VI. The Second Vatican Council, in virtue of its *Constitution on the Sacred Liturgy,* inaugurated changes of the greatest significance.

Before and After Vatican II

The most significant liturgical changes made in the years immediately preceding the Second Vatican Council were the following:

(1) Revision of the Rites of Holy Week, for universal observance from 1956.

(2) Modification of the Eucharistic fast and permission for afternoon and evening Mass, in effect from 1953 and extended in 1957.

(3) The Dialogue Mass, introduced in 1958.

(4) Use of popular languages in administration of the sacraments.

(5) Calendar-missal-breviary reform, in effect from Jan. 1, 1961.

(6) Seven-step administration of baptism for adults, approved in 1962.

The *Constitution on the Sacred Liturgy* approved (2,174 to 4) and promulgated by the Second Vatican Council Dec. 4, 1963, marked the beginning of a profound renewal in the Church's corporate worship. Implementation of some of its measures was ordered by Paul VI Jan. 25, 1964, in the motu proprio *Sacram Liturgiam.* On Feb. 29, a special commission, the Consilium for Implementing the Constitution on the Sacred Liturgy, was formed to supervise the execution of the entire program of liturgical reform. Implementation of the program on local and regional levels was left to bishops acting through their own liturgical commissions and in concert with their fellow bishops in national conferences.

Liturgical reform in the United States has been carried out under the direction of the Liturgy Committee, National Conference of Catholic Bishops. Its secretariat, established early in 1965, is located at 1312 Massachusetts Ave. N.W., Washington, D.C. 20005.

Stages of Development

Liturgical development after the Second Vatican Council proceeded in several stages. It started with the formulation of guidelines and directives, and with the translation into vernacular languages of virtually unchanged Latin ritual texts. Then came structural changes in the Mass, the sacraments, the calendar, the Divine Office and other phases of the liturgy. These revisions were just about completed with the publication of a new order for the sacrament of penance in February, 1974. A continuing phase of development, in progress from the beginning, involves efforts to deepen the liturgical sense of the faithful, to increase their participation in worship and to relate it to full Christian life.

The master texts of all documents on liturgical reform are in Latin. Effective dates of their implementation have depended on the completion and approval of appropriate translations into vernacular languages. English translations were made by the International Committee for English in the Liturgy.

The principal features of liturgical changes and the effective dates of their introduction in the United States are covered below under topical headings. (For expanded coverage of various items, especially the sacraments, see additional entries.)

The Mass

A new Order of the Mass, supplanting the one authorized by the Council of Trent in the 16th century, was introduced in the U.S. Mar. 22, 1970. It had been approved by Paul VI in the apostolic constitution *Missale Romanum,* dated Apr. 3, 1969. Preliminary and related to it were the following developments.

Mass in English: Introduced Nov. 29, 1964. In the same year, Psalm 42 was eliminated from the prayers at the foot of the altar.

Incidental Changes: The last Gospel (prologue of John) and vernacular prayers following Mass were eliminated Mar. 7, 1965. At the same time, provision was made for the celebrant to say aloud some prayers formerly said silently.

Rubrics: An instruction entitled *Tres Abhinc Annos,* dated May 4 and effective June 29, 1967, simplified directives for the celebration of Mass, approved the practice of saying the canon aloud, altered the Communion and dismissal rites, permitted purple instead of black vestments in Masses for the dead, discontinued wearing of the maniple, and approved in principle the use of vernacular languages for the canon, ordination rites, and lessons of the Divine Office when read in choir.

Canons or Eucharistic Prayers: Three additional Eucharistic prayers authorized May 23, 1968, were approved for use in vernacular translation the following Aug. 15. They have the same basic structure as the traditional Roman Canon, whose use in English was introduced Oct. 22, 1967.

The customary Roman Canon, which dates at least from the beginning of the fifth century and has remained substantially unchanged since the seventh century, is the first in the order of listing of the Eucharistic prayers. It can be used at any time, but is the one of choice for most Sundays, some special feasts like Easter and Pentecost, and for feasts of the Apostles and other saints who are commemorated in the canon. Any preface can be used with it.

The second Eucharistic prayer, the shortest and simplest of all, is best suited for use on weekdays and various special circumstances. It has a preface of its own, but others may be used with it. This canon bears a close resemblance to the one framed by St. Hippolytus about 215.

The third Eucharistic prayer is suitable for use on Sundays and feasts as an alternative to the Roman Canon. It can be used with any preface and has a special formula for remembrance of the dead.

The fourth Eucharistic prayer, the most sophisticated of them all, presents a broad synthesis of salvation history. Based on the Eastern tradition of Antioch, it is best suited for use at Masses attended by persons versed in Sacred Scripture. It has an unchangeable preface.

Five additional Eucharistic prayers — three for Masses with children and two for Masses of reconciliation — were approved in 1974 and 1975, respectively, by the Congregation for the Sacraments and Divine Worship. The original approval for a limited period of experimentation was extended indefinitely, until further notice, according to a letter issued by the congregation Dec. 15, 1980.

Lectionary: A new compilation of scriptural readings and psalm responsories for Mass was published in 1969. The *Lectionary* contains a three-year cycle of readings for Sundays and solemn feasts, a two-year weekday cycle, and a one-year cycle for the feasts of saints, in addition to readings for a great variety of Masses, ritual Masses and Masses for various needs. There are also responsorial psalms to follow the first readings, and gospel or alleluia versicles to follow the second readings.

A second edition of the *Lectionary,* substantially the same as the first, was published in 1981. New features included an expanded introduction, extensive scriptural references and additional readings for a number of solemnities and feasts.

Sacramentary (Missal): The Vatican Polyglot Press began distribution in June, 1970, of the Latin text of a new *Roman Missal,* the first revision published in 400 years. The English translation was authorized for optional use beginning July 1, 1974; the mandatory date for use was Dec. 1, 1974.

The missal is the celebrant's book of prayers and sacramental formulas and does not include the readings of the Mass, such as the Gospel and the Epistle. It contains the texts of entrance songs, prefaces and other prayers of the Mass. The number of prefaces is four times greater than it had been. There are 10 commons (or sets of Mass prayers) of martyrs, two of doctors of the Church, and a dozen for saints or groups of saints of various kinds, such as religious, educators and mothers of families. There are Masses during which certain sacraments are administered and others for religious profession, the Church, the pope, priests, Christian unity, the evangelization of nations, persecuted Christians, and other intentions.

Mass for Special Groups: Reasons and norms for the celebration of Mass at special gatherings of the faithful were the subject of an instruction issued May 15, 1969. Two years earlier, the U.S. Bishops' Liturgy Committee went on record in support of the celebration of Mass in private homes.

Sunday Mass on Saturday: The Congregation for the Clergy, under date of Jan. 10, 1970, granted the request that the faithful, where bishops consider it pastorally necessary or useful, may satisfy the precept of participating in Mass in the late afternoon or evening hours of Saturdays and the days before holy days of obligation.

Bination and Trination: Canon 905 of the Code of

Canon Law provides that local ordinaries may permit priests to celebrate Mass twice a day (bination), for a just cause; in cases of pastoral need, they may permit priests to celebrate Mass three times a day (trination) on Sundays and holy days of obligation.

Mass in Latin: According to notices issued by the Congregation for Divine Worship June 1, 1971, and Oct. 28, 1974: (1) Bishops may permit the celebration of Mass in Latin for mixed-language groups. (2) Bishops may permit the celebration of one or two Masses in Latin on weekdays or Sundays in any church, irrespective of mixed-language groups involved (1971). (3) Priests may celebrate Mass in Latin when people are not present. (4) The approved revised Order of the Mass is to be used in Latin as well as vernacular languages. (5) By way of exception, bishops may permit older and handicapped priests to use the Council of Trent's Order of the Mass in private celebration of the holy Sacrifice. (See Permission for Tridentine Mass.)

Inter-Ritual Concelebration: The Apostolic Delegation in Washington, D.C., announced in June, 1971, that it had received authorization to permit priests of Roman and Eastern rites to celebrate Mass together in the rite of the host church. It was understood that the inter-ritual concelebrations would always be "a manifestation of the unity of the Church and of communion among particular churches."

Ordo of the Sung Mass: In a decree dated June 24 and made public Aug. 24, 1972, the Congregation for Divine Worship issued a new *Ordo of the Sung Mass* — containing Gregorian chants in Latin — to replace the *Graduale Romanum.*

Mass for Children: Late in 1973, the Congregation for Divine Worship issued special guidelines for children's Masses, providing accommodations to the mentality and spiritual growth of pre-adolescents while retaining the principal parts and structures of the Mass. The *Directory for Masses with Children* was approved by Paul VI Oct. 22 and was dated Nov. 1, 1973. Three Eucharistic prayers for Masses with children were approved by the congregation in 1974; English versions were approved June 5, 1975. Their use, authorized originally for a limited period of experimentation, was extended indefinitely Dec. 15, 1980.

Sacraments

The general use of English in administration of the sacraments was approved for the U.S. Sept. 14, 1964. Structural changes of the rites were subsequently made and introduced in the U.S. as follows.

Pastoral Care of the Sick: Revised rites, covering also administration of the Eucharist to sick persons, were approved Nov. 30, 1972, and published Jan. 18, 1973. The effective date for use of the provisional English prayer formula was Dec. 1, 1974. The mandatory effective date for use of the ritual, Pastoral Care of the Sick in English, was Nov. 27, 1983.

Baptism: New rites for the baptism of infants, approved Mar. 19, 1969, were introduced June 1, 1970.

Christian Initiation of Adults: Revised rites were issued Jan. 6, 1972, for the Christian initiation of adults — affecting preparation for and reception of baptism, the Eucharist and confirmation; also, the reception of already baptized adults into full communion with the Church. These rites, which were introduced in the U.S. on the completion of English translation, nullified a seven-step baptismal process approved in 1962.

Confirmation: Revised rites, issued Aug. 15, 1971, became mandatory in the U.S. Jan. 1, 1973. The use of a stole by persons being confirmed should be avoided, according to an item in the December, 1984, edition of the *Newsletter* of the Bishops' Committee on the Liturgy. The item said: "The distinction between the universal priesthood of all the baptized and the ministerial priesthood of the ordained is blurred when the distinctive garb (the stole) of ordained ministers is used in this manner."

Special Ministers of the Eucharist: The designation of lay men and women to serve as special ministers of the Eucharist was authorized by Paul VI in an "Instruction on Facilitating Communion in Particular Circumstances" *(Immensae Caritatis),* dated Jan. 29 and published by the Congregation for Divine Worship Mar. 29, 1973. Provisions concerning them are contained in Canons 230 and 910 of the Code of Canon Law.

Qualified lay persons may serve as special ministers for specific occasions or for extended periods in the absence of a sufficient number of priests and deacons to provide reasonable and appropriate service in the distribution of Holy Communion, during Mass and outside of Mass (to the sick and shut-ins). Appointments of ministers are made by priests with the approval of the appropriate bishop.

Holy Orders: Revised ordination rites for deacons, priests and bishops, validated by prior experimental use, were approved in 1970. The sacrament of holy orders underwent further revision in 1972 with the elimination of the Church-instituted orders of porter, reader, exorcist, acolyte and subdeacon, and of the tonsure ceremony symbolic of entrance into the clerical state. The former minor orders of reader and acolyte were changed from orders to ministries.

Matrimony: New rites, issued Mar. 19, 1969, were introduced June 1, 1970. Minor revisions had been made in 1964 in conjunction with a directive for imparting the nuptial blessing at all weddings.

Penance: Ritual revision of the sacraments was completed with the approval by Paul VI Dec. 2, 1973, of new directives for the sacrament of penance or reconciliation. The U.S. Bishops' Committee on the Liturgy set Feb. 27, 1977, as the mandatory date for use of the new rite. The committee also declared that it could be used from Mar. 7, 1976, after adequate preparation of priests and people. Earlier, authorization was given by the Holy See in 1968 for the omission of any reference to excommunication or other censures in the formula of absolution unless there was some indication that a censure had actually been incurred by a penitent.

Additional Developments

Music: An *Instruction on Music in the Liturgy*, dated Mar. 5 and effective May 14, 1967, encouraged congregational singing during liturgical celebrations and attempted to clarify the role of choirs and trained singers. More significantly, the instruction indicated that a major development under way in the liturgy was a gradual erasure of the distinctive lines traditionally drawn between the sung liturgy and the spoken liturgy, between what has been called the high Mass and the low Mass.

In the same year, the U.S. Bishops' Liturgy Committee approved the use of contemporary music, as well as guitars and other suitable instruments, in the liturgy. The Holy See authorized in 1968 the use of musical instruments other than the organ in lturgical services, "provided they are played in a manner suitable to worship."

Calendar: A revised liturgical calendar, approved by Paul VI Feb. 14 and made public May 9, 1969, went into effect in the U.S. in 1972.

Communion in Hand: Since 1969, the Holy See has approved the practice of in-hand reception of the Eucharist in regions and countries where it had the approval of the appropriate episcopal conferences. The first grant of approval was to Belgium, in May, 1969. Approval was granted the United States in June, 1977.

Liturgy of the Hours: The background, contents, scope and purposes of the revised divine Office, called the Liturgy of the Hours, were described by Paul VI in the apostolic constitution *Laudis Canticum*, dated Nov. 1, 1970. A provisional English version, incorporating basic features of the master Latin text, was published in 1971. The four complete volumes of the Hours in English have been published since May, 1975. One-volume, partial editions, intended for use by Religious and lay persons not bound to pray the Liturgy of the Hours, have also been published in approved form. Nov. 27, 1977, was set by the Congregation for Divine Worship and the National Conference of Catholic Bishops as the effective date for exclusive use in liturgical worship of the translation of the Latin text of the Office approved by the International Committee on English in the Liturgy.

Holy Week: The English version of revised Holy Week rites went into effect in 1971. They introduced concelebration of Mass, placed new emphasis on commemorating the institution of the priesthood on Holy Thursday, and modified Good Friday prayers for other Christians, Jews and other non-Christians.

Oils: The Congregation for Divine Worship issued a directive in 1971 permitting the use of other oils — from plants, seeds or coconuts — instead of the traditional olive oil in administering some of the sacraments. The directive also provided that oils could be blessed at other times than at the usual Mass of Chrism on Holy Thursday, and authorized bishops' conferences to permit priests to bless oils in cases of necessity.

Dancing and Worship: Dancing and worship was the subject of an essay which appeared in a 1975 edition of *Notitiae* (11, pp. 202-205), the official journal of the Congregation for the Sacraments and Divine Worship. The article was called a "qualified and authoritative sketch," and should be considered "an authoritative point of reference for every discussion of the matter."

The principal points of the essay were:
• "The dance has never been made an integral part of the official worship of the Latin Church."
• "If the proposal of the religious dance in the West is really to be made welcome, care will have to be taken that in its regard a place be found outside of the liturgy, in assembly areas which are not strictly liturgical. Moreover, the priests must always be excluded from the dance."

Mass for Deceased Non-Catholic Christians: The Congregation for the Doctrine of the Faith released a decree June 11, 1976, authorizing the celebration of public Mass for deceased non-Catholic Christians under certain conditions: "(1) The public celebration of the Masses must be explicitly requested by the relatives, friends, or subjects of the deceased person for a genuine religious motive. (2) In the ordinary's judgment, there must be no scandal for the faithful."

"In these cases public Mass may be celebrated, provided, however, that the name of the deceased is not mentioned in the Eucharistic Prayer, since that mention presupposes full communion with the Catholic Church."

Environment and Art in Catholic Worship: A booklet with this title was issued by the U.S. Bishops' Committee on the Liturgy in March, 1978.

Doxology: The bishops' committee called attention in August, 1978, to the directive that the Doxology concluding the Eucharistic Prayer is said or sung by the celebrant (concelebrants) alone, to which the people respond, "Amen."

Churches, Altars, Chalices: The Newsletter of the U.S. Bishops' Committee on the Liturgy reported in November, 1978, that the Congregation for Divine Worship had given provisional approval of a new English translation for the rite of dedicating churches and altars, and of a new form for the blessing of chalices.

Study of the Mass: The Bishops' Committee on the Liturgy, following approval of the project by the National Conference of Catholic Bishops in May, 1979, began a study of the function and position of some elements of the Mass, including the Gloria, the sign of peace, the penitential rite and the readings. Completion of the first phase of the study was reported in July, 1980; its product was a 175-page study document. The second phase of the project got under way in the spring of 1981 with publication of a work book entitled *The Mystery of Faith: A Study of the Structural Elements of the Order of Mass*. Another draft of the study was circulated late in 1983, for recommendations and final proposals.

Eucharistic Worship: This was the subject of two documents issued in 1980. *Dominicae Coenae* was a letter addressed by Pope John Paul to bishops throughout the world in connection with the celebration of Holy Thursday; it was dated

Feb. 24 and released Mar. 18. It was more doctrinal in content than the "Instruction on Certain Norms concerning Worship of the Eucharistic Mystery" *(Inaestimabile Donum,* "The Priceless Gift"), which was approved by the Pope Apr. 17 and published by the Congregation for the Sacraments and Divine Worship May 23. Its stated purpose was to reaffirm the clarify teaching on liturgical renewal contained in enactments of the Second Vatican Council and in several related implementing documents.

Permission for Tridentine Mass: The celebration of Mass according to the last pre-Vatican II revision of the Roman Missal approved by Pope Paul VI in 1962 (the so-called Tridentine Mass), was authorized under certain conditions by Pope John Paul. The Congregation for Divine Worship announced this authorization in a letter dated Oct. 3 and released Oct. 15, 1984.

The letter said the Pope wished "to be responsive to priests and faithful who remained attached to the so-called Tridentine Rite." Accordingly, "he grants to diocesan bishops the faculty of using an indult on behalf of such priests and faithful. The diocesan bishop may allow those who are explicitly named in a petition submitted to him to celebrate Mass by use of the 1962 *editio typica* (typical, master, edition) of the Roman Missal. The principal condition for the celebration is: "There must be unequivocal, even public, evidence that the priest and people petitioning have no ties with those who impugn the lawfulness and doctrinal soundness of the Roman Missal promulgated in 1970 by Pope Paul VI."

Spanish, a Liturgical Language: The Congregation for Divine Worship, in a letter dated Jan. 19, 1985, confirmed a decision of the U.S. bishops approving Spanish as a liturgical language in the United States.

Funeral Rites: The Order of Christian Funerals, a revision of the 1970 Rite of Funerals, was approved for use in U.S. dioceses by the National Conference of Catholic Bishops Nov. 14, 1985.

Popular Piety and Liturgy: The relation of popular piety to the liturgy was the subject of remarks by Pope John Paul at a meeting with a group of Italian bishops Apr. 24, 1986. He said, in part:

"It could be affirmed that in the lives of the faithful and of the Christian communities there is and there should be a place for forms of piety that do not strictly come under the category of liturgical celebration. This implies a requirement: these forms of piety should not be superimposed on the times for liturgical celebration; they should not be allowed to compete with the most important solemnities of the liturgical year. If there is a devotion that has a value superior to all the others, it is the devotion of the Church, namely, the cult it renders to God, its liturgical life, in the mysteries and in the seasons which follow each other in succession in the course of the year of the Lord."

"An authentic liturgical ministry will never be able to neglect the riches of popular piety, the values proper to the culture of a people, so that such riches might be illuminated, purified and introduced into the liturgy as an offering of the people."

Extended Eucharistic Exposition: In response to queries, the Secretariat of the U.S. Bishops' Committee on the Liturgy issued an advisory stating that, liturgical law permits and encourges in parish churches:

• a. exposition of the Blessed Sacrament for an extended period of time once a year, with the consent of the local Ordinary and only if suitable numbers of the faithful are expected to be present;

• b. exposition ordered by the local Ordinary, for a grave and general necessity, for a more extended period of supplication when the faithful assemble in large numbers.

With regard to perpetual exposition, this form is generally permitted only in the case of those religious communities of men or women who have the general practice of perpetual Eucharistic adoration or adoration over extended periods of time.

The Secretariat's advisory appeared in the June-July, 1986, edition of the Newsletter of the Bishops' Committee on the Liturgy.

Native American Languages; The Newsletter of the U.S. Bishops' Committee on the Liturgy reported in December, 1986, and May, 1987, respectively, that the Congregation for Divine Worship had authorized Mass translations in Navajo and Choctaw.

Communion Guidelines: The U.S. Bishops' Committee on the Liturgy, in the December, 1986, Newsletter, reported that advisories were to be included in missalettes noting that: (1) The Eucharist is to be received by Catholics only, except in certain specific cases. (2) To receive Communion worthily, a person must be in the state of grace (i.e., free of serious sin) and observe the eucharistic fast (see separate entry).

Book of Worship: The Congregation for Divine Worship has confirmed Feb. 13, 1987, the approval and authorization by the U.S. bishops of a *Book of Divine Worship* for use by communities of former members of the Episcopal Church who had been received into the full communion of the Catholic Church.

Unauthorized Eucharistic Prayers: The May, 1987, Newsletter of the U.S. Bishops' Committee on the Liturgy restated the standing prohibition against the use of any Eucharistic Prayers other than those contained in the *Sacramentary.* Specifically, the article referred to the 25 unauthorized prayers in a volume entitled *Spoken Visions.*

Special Eucharistic Ministers: The Newsletter of the U.S. Bishops' Committee on the Liturgy stated in its February, 1988, edition: "When ordinary ministers (bishops, priests, deacons) are present during a Eucharistic celebration, whether they are participating in it or not, and are not prevented from doing so, they are to assist in the distribution of Communion. Accordingly, if the ordinary ministers are in sufficient number, special ministers of the Eucharist are not allowed to distribute Communion at that Eucharistic celebration." Pope John Paul approved this decision and ordered it published June 15, 1987.

Homilist: According to the Pontifical Commission for the Authentic Interpretation of Canon Law, the diocesan bishop cannot dispense from the requirement of Canon 767, par. 1, that the homily in the liturgy be reserved to a priest or deacon. Pope John Paul approved this decision and ordered it published June 20, 1987.

Concerts in Churches: In a letter released Dec. 5, 1987, the Congregation for Divine Worship declared that churches might be used on a limited basis for concerts of sacred or religious music but not for concerts featuring secular music. "The principle that the use of the church must not offend the sacredness of the place determines the criteria by which the doors of a church may be opened to a concert of sacred or religious music, as also the concomitant exclusion of every other type of music." The congregation also said that admission to permissible concerts should be free.

Our Lady of Guadalupe: The Congregation for Divine Worship approved Jan. 8, 1988, the addition of the feast of Our Lady of Guadalupe (Dec. 12) to the proper calendar of U.S. dioceses.

Holy Week Liturgy: The Congregation for Divine Worship released Feb. 20, 1988, a "Circular Letter concerning the Preparation and Celebration of the Easter Feasts." It called the feasts the "summit of the whole liturgical year," and criticized practices which dilute or changed appropriate norms for their celebration. Singled out for blame for the abuse or ignorance of norms was the "inadequate formation given to the clergy and the faithful regarding the paschal mystery as the center of the liturgical year and of Christian life." The document set out the appropriate norms for the Lenten season, Holy Week, the Easter Triduum, Easter and the weeks following. It was particularly insistent on the proper celebration of the Easter Vigil.

RCIA: The National Conference of Catholic Bishops received notice Mar. 8, 1988, that the Congregation for Divine Worship had approved the final English translation of the Rite of Christian Initiation for Adults. The mandatory date for putting the rite into effect was Sept. 1, 1988.

SACRAMENTS

The sacraments are actions of Christ and his Church (itself a kind of sacrament) which signify grace, cause it in the act of signifying it, and confer it upon persons properly disposed to receive it. They perpetuate the redemptive activity of Christ, making it present and effective. They infallibly communicate the fruit of that activity — namely grace — to responsive persons with faith. Sacramental actions consist of the union of sensible signs (matter of the sacraments) with the words of the minister (form of the sacraments).

Christ himself instituted the seven sacraments of the New Law by determining their essence and the efficacy of their signs to produce the grace they signify.

Christ is the principal priest or minister of every sacrament; human agents — an ordained priest, baptized persons contracting marriage with each other, any person conferring emergency baptism in a proper manner — are secondary ministers. Sacraments have efficacy from Christ, not from the personal dispositions of their human ministers.

Each sacrament confers sanctifying grace for the special purpose of the sacrament; this is, accordingly, called sacramental grace. It involves a right to actual graces corresponding to the purposes of the respective sacraments.

While sacraments infallibly produce the grace they signify, recipients benefit from them in proportion to their personal dispositions. One of these is the intention to receive sacraments as sacred signs of God's saving and grace-giving action. The state of grace is also necessary for fruitful reception of the Holy Eucharist, confirmation, matrimony, holy orders and anointing of the sick. Baptism is the sacrament in which grace is given in the first instance and original sin is remitted. Penance is the secondary sacrament of reconciliation, in which persons guilty of serious sin after baptism are reconciled with God and the Church, and in which persons already in the state of grace are strengthened in that state.

Role of Sacraments

The Second Vatican Council prefaced a description of the role of the sacraments with the following statement concerning participation by all the faithful in the priesthood of Christ and the exercise of that priesthood by receiving the sacraments (*Dogmatic Constitution on the Church,* Nos. 10 and 11).

"The baptized by regeneration and the anointing of the Holy Spirit are consecrated into a spiritual house and a holy priesthood. Thus through all those works befitting Christian men they can offer spiritual sacrifice and proclaim the power of him who has called them out of darkness into his marvelous light (cf. 1 Pt. 2:4-10)."

"Though they differ from one another in essence and not only in degree, the common priesthood of the faithful and the ministerial or hierarchical priesthood (of those ordained to holy orders) are nonetheless interrelated. Each of them in its own special way is a participation in the one priesthood of Christ. The ministerial priest, by the sacred power he enjoys, molds and rules the priestly people. Acting in the Person of Christ, he brings about the Eucharistic Sacrifice, and offers it to God in the name of all the people. For their part, the faithful join in the offering of the Eucharist by virtue of their royal priesthood. They likewise exercise that priesthood by receiving the sacraments, by prayer and thanksgiving, by the witness of a holy life, and by self-denial and active charity."

"It is through the sacraments and the exercise of the virtues that the sacred nature and organic structure of the priestly community is brought into operation."

Baptism: "Incorporated into the Church through

baptism, the faithful are consecrated by the baptismal character to the exercise of the cult of the Christian religion. Reborn as sons of God, they must confess before men the faith which they have received from God through the Church."

Confirmation: "Bound more intimately to the Church by the sacrament of confirmation, they are endowed by the Holy Spirit with special strength. Hence they are more strictly obliged to spread and defend the faith both by word and by deed as true witnesses of Christ."

Eucharist: "Taking part in the Eucharistic Sacrifice, which is the fount and apex of the whole Christian life, they offer the divine Victim to God, and offer themselves along with It. Thus, both by the act of oblation and through holy Communion, all perform their proper part in this liturgical service, not, indeed, all in the same way but each in that way which is appropriate to himself. Strengthened anew at the holy table by the Body of Christ, they manifest in a practical way that unity of God's People which is suitably signified and wondrously brought about by this most awesome sacrament."

Penance: "Those who approach the sacrament of penance obtain pardon from the mercy of God for offenses committed against him. They are at the same time reconciled with the Church, which they have wounded by their sins, and which by charity, example, and prayer seeks their conversion."

Anointing of the Sick: "By the sacred anointing of the sick and the prayer of her priests, the whole Church commends those who are ill to the suffering and glorified Lord, asking that he may lighten their suffering and save them (cf. Jas. 5:14-16). She exhorts them, moreover, to contribute to the welfare of the whole People of God by associating themselves freely with the passion and death of Christ (cf. Rom. 8:17; Col. 1:24; 2 Tm. 2:11-12; 1 Pt. 4:13)."

Holy Orders: "Those of the faithful who are consecrated by holy orders are appointed to feed the Church in Christ's name with the Word and the grace of God."

Matrimony: "Christian spouses, in virtue of the sacrament of matrimony, signify and partake of the mystery of that unity and fruitful love which exists between Christ and his Church (cf. Eph. 5:32). The spouses thereby help each other to attain to holiness in their married life and by the rearing and education of their children. And so, in their state and way of life, they have their own special gift among the People of God (cf. 1 Cor. 7:7).

"For from the wedlock of Christians there comes the family, in which new citizens of human society are born. By the grace of the Holy Spirit received in baptism these are made children of God, thus perpetuating the People of God through the centuries. The family is, so to speak, the domestic Church. In it parents should, by their word and example, be the first preachers of the faith to their children. They should encourage them in the vocation which is proper to each of them, fostering with special care any religious vocation."

"Fortified by so many and such powerful means of salvation, all the faithful, whatever their condition or state, are called by the Lord, each in his own way, to that perfect holiness whereby the Father himself is perfect."

Baptism

Baptism is the sacrament of spiritual regeneration by which a person is incorporated in Christ and made a member of his Mystical Body, given grace, and cleansed of original sin. Actual sins and the punishment due for them are remitted also if the person baptized was guilty of such sins (e.g., in the case of a person baptized after reaching the age of reason). The theological virtues of faith, hope and charity are given with grace. The sacrament confers a character on the soul and can be received only once.

The matter is the pouring of water. The form is: "I baptize you in the name of the Father and of the Son and of the Holy Spirit."

The minister of solemn baptism is a bishop, priest or deacon, but in case of emergency anyone, including a non-Catholic, can validly baptize. The minister pours water on the forehead of the person being baptized and says the words of the form while the water is flowing. The water used in solemn baptism is blessed during the rite.

Baptism is conferred in the Roman Rite by immersion or infusion (pouring of water), depending on the directive of the appropriate conference of bishops, according to the Code of Canon Law. The Church recognizes as valid baptisms properly performed by non-Catholic ministers. The baptism of infants has always been considered valid and the general practice of infant baptism was well established by the fifth century. Baptism is conferred conditionally when there is doubt about the validity of a previous baptism.

Baptism is necessary for salvation. If a person cannot receive the baptism of water described above, this can be supplied by baptism of blood (martyrdom suffered for the Catholic faith or some Christian virtue) or by baptism of desire (perfect contrition joined with at least the implicit intention of doing whatever God wills that men should do for salvation).

Christian Initiation of Infants: Infants should be solemnly baptized as soon after birth as conveniently possible. In danger of death, anyone may baptize an infant. If the child survives, the ceremonies of solemn baptism should be supplied.

The sacrament is ordinarily conferred by a priest or deacon of the parents' parish.

Catholics 16 years of age and over who have received the sacraments of confirmation and the Eucharist and are practicing their faith are eligible to be sponsors or godparents. Only one is required. Two, one of each sex, are permitted. A non-Catholic Christian cannot be a godparent for a Catholic child, but may serve as a witness to the baptism. A Catholic may not be a godparent for a child baptized in a non-Catholic religion, but may be a witness.

The role of godparents in baptismal ceremonies is secondary to the role of the parents. They serve as representatives of the community of faith and with the parents request baptism for the child and perform other ritual functions. Their function after baptism is to serve as proxies for the parents if the parents should be unable or fail to provide for the religious training of the child.

At baptism every child should be given a name with Christian significance, usually the name of a saint, to symbolize newness of life in Christ.

Christian Initiation of Adults: According to the *Ordo Initiationis Christianae Adultorum* ("Rite of the Christian Initiation of Adults") issued by the Congregation for Divine Worship under date of Jan. 6, 1972, adults are prepared for baptism and reception into the Church in several stages:

- An initial period of inquiry, instruction and evangelization.
- The catechumenate, a period of formal instruction and progressive formation in and familiarity with Christian life. It starts with a statement of purpose and includes a rite in which the catechumen is signed with the cross, blessings, exorcisms, and introduction into church for celebration of the word of God.
- Immediate preparation, called a period of purification and enlightenment, from the beginning of Lent to reception of the sacraments of initiation — baptism, confirmation, Holy Eucharist — at Easter. The period is marked by scrutinies, formal giving of the creed and the Lord's Prayer, the choice of a Christian name, and a final statement of intention.
- A final phase whose objective is greater familiarity with Christian life in the Church through observances of the Easter season and association with the community of the faithful.

The mandatory date for implementation of the RCIA was Sept. 1, 1988.

The priest who baptizes a catechumen can also administer the sacrament of confirmation.

A sponsor is required for the person being baptized.

The *Ordo* also provides a simple rite of initiation for adults in danger of death and for cases in which all stages of the initiation process are not necessary, and guidelines for: (1) the preparation of adults for the sacraments of confirmation and Holy Eucharist in cases where they have been baptized but have not received further formation in the Christian life; (2) for the formation and initiation of children of catechetical age.

The Church recognizes the right of anyone over the age of seven to request baptism and to receive the sacrament after completing a course of instruction and giving evidence of good will. Practically, in the case of minors in a non-Catholic family or environment, the Church accepts them when other circumstances favor their ability to practice the faith — e.g., well-disposed family situation, the presence of another or several Catholics in the family. Those who are not in such favorable circumstances are prudently advised to defer reception of the sacrament until they attain the maturity necessary for independent practice of the faith.

Reception of Baptized Christians: Procedure for the reception of already baptized Christians into full communion with the Catholic Church is distinguished from the catechumenate, since they have received some Christian formation. Instruction and formation are provided as necessary, however; and conditional baptism is administered if there is reasonable doubt about the validity of the person's previous baptism.

In the rite of reception, the person is invited to join the community of the Church in professing the Nicene Creed and is asked to state: "I believe and profess all that the holy Catholic Church believes, teaches, and proclaims as revealed by God." The priest places his hand on the head of the person, states the formula of admission to full communion, confirms (in the absence of a bishop), gives a sign of peace, and administers Holy Communion during a Eucharistic Liturgy.

Confirmation

Confirmation is the sacrament by which a baptized person, through anointing with chrism and the imposition of hands, is endowed with the gifts and special strength of the Holy Spirit for mature Christian living. The sacrament, which completes the Christian initiation begun with baptism, confers a character on the soul and can be received only once.

According to the apostolic constitution *Divinae Consortium Naturae* dated Aug. 15, 1971, in conjunction with the *Ordo Confirmationis* ("Rite of Confirmation"): "The sacrament of confirmation is conferred through the anointing with chrism on the forehead, which is done by the imposition of the hand (matter of the sacrament), and through the words: 'N . . . . , receive the seal of the Holy Spirit, the Gift of the Father' " (form of the sacrament). On May 5, 1975, bishops' conferences in English-speaking countries were informed by the Congregation for Divine Worship that Pope Paul had approved this English version of the form of the sacrament: "Be sealed with the gift of the Holy Spirit."

The ordinary minister of confirmation in the Roman Rite is a bishop. Priests may be delegated for the purpose. A pastor can confirm a parishioner in danger of death, and a priest can confirm in ceremonies of Christian initiation and at the reception of a baptized Christian into union with the Church.

Ideally, the sacrament is conferred during the Eucharistic Liturgy. Elements of the rite include renewal of the promises of baptism, which confirmation ratifies and completes, and the laying on of hands by the confirming bishop and priests participating in the ceremony.

"The entire rite," according to the *Ordo;* "has a twofold meaning. The laying of hands upon the candidates, done by the bishop and the concelebrating priests, expresses the biblical gesture by which the gift of the Holy Spirit is invoked. . . . The anointing with chrism and the accompanying words clearly signify the effect of the Holy Spirit. Signed with the perfumed oil by the bishop's hand, the baptized person receives the indelible character, the seal of the Lord, together with the Spirit who is given and who conforms the person more perfectly to Christ and gives him the grace of spreading the Lord's presence among men."

A sponsor is required for the person being confirmed. Eligible is any Catholic 16 years of age or older who has received the sacraments of confirmation and the Eucharist and is practicing the faith. The baptismal sponsor, preferably, can also be the sponsor for confirmation. Parents may present their children for confirmation but cannot be sponsors.

In the Roman Rite, it has been customary for children to receive confirmation within a reasonable time after first Communion and confession. There is a developing trend, however, to defer confirmation until later when its significance for mature Christian living becomes more evident. In the Eastern Rites, confirmation is administered at the same time as baptism.

Eucharist

The Holy Eucharist is a sacrifice (see The Mass) and the sacrament in which Christ is present and is received under the appearances of bread and wine.

The matter is bread of wheat, unleavened in the Roman Rite and leavened in the Eastern Rites, and wine of grape. The form consists of the words of consecration said by the priest at Mass: "This is my body.... This is the cup of my blood" (according to the traditional usage of the Roman Rite).

Only a priest can consecrate bread and wine so they become the body and blood of Christ. After consecration, however, the Eucharist can be administered by deacons and, for various reasons, by religious and lay persons.

Priests celebrating Mass receive the Eucharist under the appearances of bread and wine. In the Roman Rite, others receive under the appearances of bread only, i.e., the consecrated host, or in some circumstances they may receive under the appearances of both bread and wine. In Eastern-Rite practice, the faithful generally receive a piece of consecrated leavened bread which has been dipped into consecrated wine (i.e., by intinction).

Conditions for receiving the Eucharist, commonly called Holy Communion, are the state of grace, the right intention and observance of the Eucharistic fast.

The faithful of Roman Rite are required by a precept of the Church to receive the Eucharist at least once a year, ordinarily during the Easter time.

(See Eucharistic Fast, Mass, Transubstantiation, Viaticum.)

First Communion and Confession: Children are to be prepared for and given opportunity for receiving both sacraments (Eucharist and reconciliation, or penance) on reaching the age of discretion, at which time they become subject to general norms concerning confession and Communion. This, together with a stated preference for first confession before first Communion, was the central theme of a document entitled *Sanctus Pontifex* and published May 24, 1973, by the Congregation for the Discipline of the Sacraments and the Congregation for the Clergy, with the approval of Pope Paul VI.

What the document prescribed was the observance of practices ordered by St. Pius X in the decree *Quam Singulari* of Aug. 8, 1910. Its purpose was to counteract pastoral and catechetical experiments virtually denying children the opportunity of receiving both sacraments at the same time. Termination of such experiments was ordered by the end of the 1972-73 school year.

At the time the document was issued, two- or three-year experiments of this kind — routinely deferring reception of the sacrament of penance until after the first reception of Holy Communion — were in effect in more than half of the dioceses of the U.S. They have remained in effect in many places, despite the advisory from the Vatican.

One reason stated in support of such experiments is the view that children are not capable of serious sin at the age of seven or eight, when Communion is generally received for the first time, and therefore prior reception of the sacrament of penance is not necessary. Another reason is the purpose of making the distinctive nature of the two sacraments clearer to children.

The Vatican view reflected convictions that the principle and practice of devotional reception of penance are as valid for children as they are for adults, and that sound catechetical programs can avoid misconceptions about the two sacraments.

A second letter on the same subject and in the same vein was released May 19, 1977, by the aforementioned congregations. It was issued in response to the question:

"'Whether it is allowed after the declaration of May 24, 1973, to continue to have, as a general rule, the reception of first Communion precede the reception of the sacrament of penance in those parishes in which this practice developed in the past few years.'

"The Sacred Congregations for the Sacraments and Divine Worship and for the Clergy, with the approval of the Supreme Pontiff, reply: Negative, and according to the mind of the declaration.

"The mind of the declaration is that one year after the promulgation of the same declaration, all experiments of receiving first Communion without the sacrament of penance should cease so that the discipline of the Church might be restored, in the spirit of the decree, *Quam Singulari*."

The two letters from the Vatican congregations have not produced uniformity of practice in this country. Simultaneous preparation for both sacraments is provided in some dioceses where a child has the option of receiving either sacrament first, with the counsel of parents, priests and teachers. Programs in other dioceses are geared first to reception of Communion and later to reception of the sacrament of reconciliation.

Commentators on the letters note that: they are disciplinary rather than doctrinal in content; they are subject to pastoral interpretation by bishops; they cannot be interpreted to mean that a person who is not guilty of serious sin must be required to receive the sacrament of penance before (even first) Communion.

Canon 914 of the Code of Canon Law states that sacramental confession should precede first Communion.

Holy Communion under the Forms of Bread and Wine (by separate taking of the consecrated bread and wine or by intinction, the reception of the host dipped in the wine): Such reception is permitted under conditions stated in instructions issued by the Congregation for Divine Worship (May 25, 1967; June 29, 1970), the *General Instruction on the Roman Missal* (No. 242), and directives of bishops' conferences and individual bishops.

Accordingly, Communion can be administered in this way to: persons being baptized, received into communion with the Church, confirmed, receiving anointing of the sick; couples at their wedding or jubilee; religious at profession or renewal of profession; lay persons receiving an ecclesiastical assignment (e.g., lay missionaries); participants at concelebrated Masses, retreats, pastoral commission meetings, daily Masses and, in the U.S., Masses on Sundays and holy days of obligation.

A communicant has the option of receiving the Eucharist under the form of bread alone or under the forms of bread and wine.

Holy Communion More Than Once a Day: A person who has already received the Eucharist may receive it (only) once again on the same day only during a Eucharistic celebration in which the person participates. A person in danger of death who has already received the Eucharist once or twice is urged to receive Communion again as Viaticum. Pope John Paul approved this decision, in accord with Canon 917, and ordered it published July 11, 1984.

Holy Communion and Eucharistic Devotion outside of Mass: These were the subjects of an instruction (*De Sacra Communione et de Cultu Mysterii Eucharistici extra Missam*) dated June 21 and made public Oct. 18, 1973, by the Congregation for Divine Worship.

Holy Communion can be given outside of Mass to persons unable for a reasonable cause to receive it during Mass on a given day. The ceremonial rite is modeled on the structure of the Mass, consisting of a penitential act, a scriptural reading, the Lord's Prayer, a sign or gesture of peace, giving of the Eucharist, prayer and final blessing. Viaticum and Communion to the sick can be given by extraordinary ministers (authorized lay persons) with appropriate rites.

Forms of devotion outside of Mass are exposition of the Blessed Sacrament (by men or women religious, especially, or lay persons in the absence of a priest; but only a priest can give the blessing), processions and congresses with appropriate rites.

Intercommunion: Church policy on intercommunion was stated in an "Instruction on the Admission of Other Christians to the Eucharist," dated June 1 and made public July 8, 1972, against the background of the *Decree on Ecumenism* approved by the Second Vatican Council, and the *Directory on Ecumenism* issued by the Secretariat for Promoting Christian Unity in 1967.

Basic principles related to intercommunion are:

- "There is an indissoluble link between the mystery of the Church and the mystery of the Eucharist, or between ecclesial and Eucharistic communion; the celebration of the Eucharist of itself signifies the fullness of profession of faith and ecclesial communion" (1972 Instruction).
- "Eucharistic communion practiced by those who are not in full ecclesial communion with each other cannot be the expression of that full unity which the Eucharist of its nature signifies and which in this case does not exist; for this reason such communion cannot be regarded as a means to be used to lead to full ecclesial communion" (1972 Instruction).
- The question of reciprocity "arises only with those churches which have preserved the substance of the Eucharist, the sacrament of orders and apostolic succession" (1967 Directory).
- "A Catholic cannot ask for the Eucharist except from a minister who has been validly ordained" (1967 Directory).

The policy distinguishes between separated Eastern Christians and other Christians.

With Separated Eastern Christians (e.g., Orthodox): These may be given the Eucharist (as well as penance and anointing of the sick) at their request. Catholics may receive these same sacraments from priests of separated Eastern churches if they experience genuine spiritual necessity, seek spiritual benefit, and access to a Catholic priest is morally or physically impossible. This policy (of reciprocity) derives from the facts that the separated Eastern churches have apostolic succession through their bishops, valid priests, and sacramental beliefs and practices in accord with those of the Catholic Church.

With Other Christians (e.g., members of Reformation-related churches, others): Admission to the Eucharist in the Catholic Church, according to the *Directory on Ecumenism,* "is confined to particular cases of those Christians who have a faith in the sacrament in conformity with that of the Church, who experience a serious spiritual need for the Eucharistic sustenance, who for a prolonged period are unable to have recourse to a minister of their own community and who ask for the sacrament of their own accord; all this provided that they have proper dispositions and lead lives worthy of a Christian." The spiritual need is defined as "a need for an increase in spiritual life and a need for a deeper involvement in the mystery of the Church and of its unity."

Circumstances under which Communion may be given to other properly disposed Christians are danger of death, imprisonment, persecution, grave spiritual necessity coupled with no chance of recourse to a minister of their own community.

Catholics cannot ask for the Eucharist from ministers of other Christian churches who have not been validly ordained to the priesthood.

Penance

Penance is the sacrament by which sins committed after baptism are forgiven and a person is reconciled with God and the Church.

Individual and integral confession and absolution

are the only ordinary means for the forgiveness of serious sin and for reconciliation with God and the Church.

(Other than ordinary means are perfect contrition and general absolution without prior confession, both of which require the intention of subsequent confession and absolution.)

A revised ritual for the sacrament — *Ordo Paenitentiae*, published by the Congregation of Divine Worship Feb. 7, 1974, and made mandatory in the U.S. from the first Sunday of Lent, 1977 — reiterates standard doctrine concerning the sacrament; emphasizes the social (communal and ecclesial) aspects of sin and conversion, with due regard for personal aspects and individual reception of the sacrament; prescribes three forms for celebration of the sacrament; and presents models for community penitential services.

The basic elements of the sacrament are sorrow for sin because of a supernatural motive, confession (of previously unconfessed mortal or grave sins, required; of venial sins also, but not of necessity), and reparation (by means of prayer or other act enjoined by the confessor), all of which comprise the matter of the sacrament; and absolution, which is the form of the sacrament.

The traditional words of absolution — "I absolve you from your sins in the name of the Father, and of the Son, and of the Holy Spirit" — remain unchanged at the conclusion of a petition in the new rite that God may grant pardon and peace through the ministry of the Church.

The minister of the sacrament is an authorized priest — i.e., one who, besides having the power of orders to forgive sins, also has faculties of jurisdiction granted by an ecclesiastical superior and/or by canon law.

The sacrament can be celebrated in three ways.

• For individuals: The traditional manner remains acceptable but is enriched with additional elements including: reception of the penitent and making of the Sign of the Cross; an exhortation by the confessor to trust in God; a reading from Scripture; confession of sins; manifestation of repentance; petition for God's forgiveness through the ministry of the Church and the absolution of the priest; praise of God's mercy, and dismissal in peace. Some of these elements are optional.

• For several penitents, in the course of a community celebration including a Liturgy of the Word of God and prayers, individual confession and absolution, and an act of thanksgiving.

• For several penitents, in the course of a community celebration, with general confession and general absolution. In extraordinary cases, reconciliation may be attained by general absolution without prior individual confession as, for example, under these circumstances: (1) danger of death, when there is neither time nor priests available for hearing confessions; (2) grave necessity of a number of penitents who, because of a shortage of confessors, would be deprived of sacramental grace or Communion for a lengthy period of time through no fault of their own. Persons receiving general absolution are obliged to be properly disposed and resolved to make an individual confession of the grave sins from which they have been absolved; this confession should be made as soon as the opportunity to confess presents itself and before any second reception of general absolution.

Norms regarding general absolution, issued by the Congregation for the Doctrine of the Faith in 1972, are not intended to provide a basis for convoking large gatherings of the faithful for the purpose of imparting general absolution, in the absence of extraordinary circumstances. Judgment about circumstances that warrant general absolution belongs principally to the bishop of the place, with due regard for related decisions of appropriate episcopal conferences.

Communal celebrations of the sacrament are not held in connection with Mass.

The place of individual confession, as determined by episcopal conferences in accordance with given norms, can be the traditional confessional or another appropriate setting.

A precept of the Church obliges the faithful guilty of grave sin to confess at least once a year.

The Church favors more frequent reception of the sacrament not only for the reconciliation of persons guilty of serious sins but also for reasons of devotion. Devotional confession — in which venial sins or previously forgiven sins are confessed — serves the purpose of confirming persons in penance and conversion.

Penitential Celebrations: Communal penitential celebrations are designed to emphasize the social dimensions of Christian life — the community aspects and significance of penance and reconciliation.

Elements of such celebrations are community prayer, hymns and songs, scriptural and other readings, examination of conscience, general confession and expression of sorrow for sin, acts of penance and reconciliation, and a form of non-sacramental absolution resembling the one in the penitential rite of the Mass.

If the sacrament is celebrated during the service, there must be individual confession and absolution of sin.

(See Absolution, Confession, Confessional, Confessor, Contrition, Faculties, Forgiveness of Sin, Power of the Keys, Seal of Confession, Sin.)

Anointing of the Sick

This sacrament, promulgated by St. James the Apostle (Jas. 5:13-15), can be administered to the faithful after reaching the age of reason who begin to be in danger because of illness or old age. By the anointing with blessed oil and the prayer of a priest, the sacrament confers on the person comforting grace; the remission of venial sins and inculpably unconfessed mortal sins, together with at least some of the temporal punishment due for sins; and, sometimes, results in an improved state of health.

The matter of this sacrament is the anointing with blessed oil (of the sick — olive oil, or vegetable oil if necessary) of the forehead and hands; in cases of necessity, a single anointing of another portion of the body suffices. The form is: "Through this holy anointing and his most loving mercy, may the Lord assist you by the grace of the Holy Spirit so that, when you have been freed from your sins, he may save you and in his goodness raise you up."

Anointing of the sick, formerly called extreme unction, may be received more than once, e.g., in new or continuing stages of serious illness. Ideally, the sacrament should be administered while the recipient is conscious and in conjunction with the sacraments of penance and the Eucharist. It should be administered in cases of doubt as to whether the person has reached the age of reason, is dangerously ill or dead.

The sacrament can be administered during a communal celebration in some circumstances, as in a home for the aged.

Matrimony

Coverage of the sacrament of matrimony is given in the articles, Marriage Doctrine, *Humanae Vitae*, Marriage Laws, Pastoral Ministry for Divorced and Remarried.

Holy Orders

Holy orders is the sacrament by which spiritual power and grace are given to constitute and enable an ordained minister to consecrate the Eucharist, forgive sins, perform other pastoral and ecclesiastical functions, and form the community of the People of God. Holy orders confers a character on the soul and can be received only once. The minister of the sacrament is a bishop.

Holy orders, like matrimony but in a different way, is a social sacrament. As the Second Vatican Council declared in the *Dogmatic Constitution on the Church*:

'For the nurturing and constant growth of the People of God, Christ the Lord instituted in his Church a variety of ministries, which work for the good of the whole body. For those ministers who are endowed with sacred power are servants of their brethren, so that all who are of the People of God, and therefore enjoy a true Christian dignity, can work toward a common goal freely and in an orderly way, and arrive at salvation" (No. 18).

Bishop: The fullness of the priesthood belongs to those who have received the order of bishop. Bishops, in hierarchical union with the pope and their fellow bishops, are the successors of the Apostles as pastors of the Church: they have individual responsibility for the care of the local churches they serve and collegial responsibility for the care of the universal Church (see Collegiality). In the ordination or consecration of bishops, the essential form is the imposition of hands by the consecrator(s) and the assigned prayer in the preface of the rite of ordination.

"With their helpers, the priests and deacons, bishops have . . . taken up the service of the community presiding in place of God over the flock whose shepherds they are, as teachers of doctrine, priests of sacred worship, and officers of good order" (No. 20).

Priests: A priest is an ordained minister with the power to celebrate Mass, administer the sacraments, preach and teach the word of God, impart blessings, and perform additional pastoral functions, according to the mandate of his ecclesiastical superior.

Concerning priests, the Second Vatican Council stated in the *Dogmatic Constitution on the Church* (No. 28):

"The divinely established ecclesiastical ministry is exercised on different levels by those who from antiquity have been called bishops, priests, and deacons. Although priests do not possess the highest degree of the priesthood, and although they are dependent on the bishops in the exercise of their power, they are nevertheless united with the bishops in sacerdotal dignity. By the power of the sacrament of orders, and in the image of Christ the eternal High Priest (Hb. 5:1-10; 7:24; 9:11-28), they are consecrated to preach the Gospel, shepherd the faithful, and celebrate divine worship as true priests of the New Testament. . . .

"Priests, prudent cooperators with the episcopal order as well as its aides and instruments, are called to serve the People of God. They constitute one priesthood with their bishop, although that priesthood is comprised of different functions."

In the ordination of a priest of Roman Rite, the essential matter is the imposition of hands on the heads of those being ordained by the ordaining bishop. The essential form is the accompanying prayer in the preface of the ordination ceremony. Other elements in the rite are the presentation of the implements of sacrifice — the chalice containing wine and the paten containing a host — with accompanying prayers.

Deacon: There are two kinds of deacons: those who receive the order and remain in it permanently, and those who receive the order while advancing to ordination to the priesthood. The following quotation — from Vatican II's *Dogmatic Constitution on the Church* (No. 29) — describes the nature and role of the diaconate, with emphasis on the permanent diaconate.

"At a lower level of the hierarchy are deacons, upon whom hands are imposed 'not unto the priesthood, but unto a ministry of service.' For strengthened by sacramental grace, in communion with the bishop and his group of priests, they serve the People of God in the ministry of the liturgy, of the word, and of charity. It is the duty of the deacon, to the extent that he has been authorized by competent authority, to administer baptism solemnly, to be custodian and dispenser of the Eucharist, to assist at and bless marriages in the name of the Church, to bring Viaticum to the dying, to read the sacred Scripture to the faithful, to instruct and exhort the people, to preside at the worship and prayer of the faithful, to administer sacramentals, and to officiate at funeral and burial services. (Deacons are) dedicated to duties of charity and administration."

"The diaconate can in the future be restored as a proper and permanent rank of the hierarchy. It pertains to the competent territorial bodies of bishops, of one kind or another, to decide, with the approval of the Supreme Pontiff, whether and where it is opportune for such deacons to be appointed for the care of souls. With the consent of the Roman Pontiff, this diaconate will be able to be conferred upon men of more mature age, even upon those living in the married state. It may also be conferred upon suitable young men. For them, however, the law of celibacy must remain intact" (No. 29).

The Apostles ordained the first seven deacons (Acts 6:1-6): Stephen, Philip, Prochorus, Nicanor, Timon, Parmenas, Nicholas.

Other Ministries: The Church later assigned ministerial duties to men in several other orders, as:

Subdeacon, with specific duties in liturgical worship, especially at Mass. The order, whose first extant mention dates from about the middle of the third century, was regarded as minor until the 13th century; afterwards, it was called a major order in the West but not in the East.

Acolyte, to serve in minor capacities in liturgical worship; a function now performed by Mass servers.

Exorcist, to perform services of exorcism for expelling evil spirits; a function which came to be reserved to specially delegated priests.

Lector, to read scriptural and other passages during liturgical worship; a function now generally performed by lay persons.

Porter, to guard the entrance to an assembly of Christians and to ward off undesirables who tried to gain admittance; an order of early origin and utility but of present insignificance.

Long after it became evident that these positions and functions had fallen into general disuse or did not require clerical ordination, the Holy See started a revision of the orders in 1971. By an indult of Oct. 5, the bishops of the United States were permitted to omit ordaining porters and exorcists. Another indult, dated three days later, permitted the use of revised rites for ordaining acolytes and lectors.

To complete the revision, Pope Paul VI abolished Sept. 14, 1972, the orders of porter, exorcist and subdeacon; decreed that laymen, as well as candidates for the diaconate and priesthood, can be installed (rather than ordained) in the ministries (rather than orders) of acolyte and lector; reconfirmed the suppression of tonsure and its replacement with a service of dedication to God and the Church; and stated that a man enters the clerical state on ordination to the diaconate.

PERMANENT DIACONATE

Authorization for restoration of the permanent diaconate in the Roman Rite — making it possible for men to become deacons permanently, without going on to the priesthood — was promulgated by Pope Paul VI June 18, 1967, in a document entitled *Sacrum Diaconatus Ordinem* ("Sacred Order of the Diaconate").

The Pope's action implemented the desire expressed by the Second Vatican Council for reestablishment of the diaconate as an independent order in its own right not only to supply ministers for carrying on the work of the Church but also to complete the hierarchical structure of the Church of Roman Rite.

Permanent deacons have been traditional in the Eastern Church. The Western Church, however, since the fourth or fifth century, generally followed the practice of conferring the diaconate only as a sacred order preliminary to the priesthood, and of restricting the ministry of deacons to liturgical functions.

The Pope's document, issued on his own initiative, provided:

• Qualified unmarried men 25 years of age or older may be ordained permanent deacons. They cannot marry after ordination.

• Qualified married men 35 years of age or older may be ordained permanent deacons. The consent of the wife of a prospective deacon is required. A married deacon cannot remarry after the death of his wife.

• Preparation for the diaconate includes a course of study and formation over a period of at least three years.

• Candidates who are not Religious must be affiliated with a diocese. Reestablishment of the permanent diaconate among Religious is reserved to the Holy See.

• Deacons will practice their ministry under the direction of a bishop and with the priests with whom they will be associated. (For functions, see also the description of deacon, under Holy Orders.)

Restoration of the permanent diaconate in the United States was approved by the Holy See in October, 1968. Shortly afterwards the U.S. bishops established a committee of the same name, which is chaired by Bishop William S. Skylstad of Yakima. The committee operates through a secretariat, with offices at 1312 Massachusetts Ave. N. W., Washington, D.C. 20005. Constantino J. Ferriola, Jr., permanent deacon, is executive director.

Status and Functions

Reports filed by 140 program directors indicate that, as of Oct. 31, 1987, there were in the U.S. 8,443 permanent deacons (605 more than in 1986) and 1,885 candidates (261 less than in 1986). Hispanic deacons numbered 1,109 (13 percent of the total). Black deacons numbered 314. Twenty-five dioceses had 100 or more deacons; the leaders were Chicago with 585 and Hartford with 264.

Thirty-five percent of the deacons were 51 to 60 years of age; 32 percent were 41 to 50; 21 percent were 61 to 70; 6 percent were from 32 to 40; 5 percent were from 71 to 80. Ninety-three percent were married.

Training programs of spiritual, doctrinal and pastoral formation are based on guidelines emanating from the National Conference of Catholic Bishops.

Deacons have various functions, depending on the nature of their assignments. Liturgically, they can officiate at baptisms, weddings, wake services and funerals, can preach and distribute Holy Communion. Some are engaged in religious education work. All are intended to carry out works of charity and pastoral service of one kind or another.

The majority of permanent deacons, 93 per cent of whom are married, continue in their secular work. Their ministry of service is developing in three dimensions: of liturgy, of the word, and of charity. Depending on the individual deacon's abilities and preference, he is assigned by his bishop to either a parochial ministry or to one particular field of service. The latter is the most challenging ministry to develop. Deacons are active in a variety of ministries including those to prison inmates and their families, the sick in hospitals, nursing homes and homes for the aged, alienated youth, the elderly and the poor, and in various areas of legal service to the indigent, of education and campus ministry. Sixty-five deacons (4 less than last year) have been assigned as administrators of parishes. The possibilities for diaconal ministry are under realistic assessment in a number of dioceses.

National Association of Permanent Diaconate Directors: Membership organization of directors, vicars and other staff personnel of permanent diaconate programs. Established in 1977 to promote effective communication and facilitate the exchange of information and resources of members; to develop professional expertise and promote research, training and self evaluation; to foster accountability and seek ways to promote means of implementing solutions to problems. NAPDD is governed by an executive board of elected officers. President for the 1988-89 term, James Swiler, permanent deacon, of New Orleans. Executive office: 1337 W. Ohio St., Chicago, Ill. 60622.

MARRIAGE DOCTRINE

The following excerpts, stating key points of doctrine on marriage, are from the "Pastoral Constitution on the Church in the Modern World" (Nos. 48 to 51) promulgated by the Second Vatican Council.

Conjugal Covenant

The intimate partnership of married life and love has been established by the Creator and qualified by his laws. It is rooted in the conjugal covenant of irrevocable personal consent.

God himself is the author of matrimony, endowed as it is with various benefits and purposes. All of these have a very decisive bearing on the continuation of the human race, on the personal development and eternal destiny of the individual members of a family, and on the dignity, stability, peace, and prosperity of the family itself and of human society as a whole. By their very nature, the institution of matrimony itself and conjugal love are ordained for the procreation and education of children, and find in them their ultimate crown.

Thus a man and a woman . . . render mutual help and service to each other through an intimate union of their persons and of their actions. Through this union they experience the meaning of their oneness and attain to it with growing perfection day by day. As a mutual gift of two persons, this intimate union, as well as the good of the children, imposes total fidelity on the spouses and argues for an unbreakable oneness between them (No. 48).

Sacrament of Matrimony

Christ the Lord abundantly blessed this many-faceted love. . . . The Savior of men and the Spouse of the Church comes into the lives of married Christians through the sacrament of matrimony. He abides with them thereafter so that, just as he loved the Church and handed himself over on her behalf, the spouses may love each other with perpetual fidelity through mutual self-bestowal.

Graced with the dignity and office of fatherhood and motherhood, parents will energetically acquit themselves of a duty which devolves primarily on them; namely, education, and especially religious education.

The Christian family, which springs from marriage as a reflection of the loving covenant uniting Christ with the Church, and as a participation in that covenant, will manifest to all men the Savior's living presence in the world, and the genuine nature of the Church (No. 48).

Conjugal Love

The biblical Word of God several times urges the betrothed and the married to nourish and develop their wedlock by pure conjugal love and undivided affection.

This love is an eminently human one since it is directed from one person to another through an affection of the will. It involves the good of the whole person. Therefore it can enrich the expressions of body and mind with a unique dignity, ennobling these expressions as special ingredients and signs of the friendship distinctive of marriage. This love the Lord has judged worthy of special gifts, healing, perfecting, and exalting gifts of grace and of charity.

Such love, merging the human with the divine, leads the spouses to a free and mutual gift of themselves, a gift proving itself by gentle affection and by deed. Such love pervades the whole of their lives. Indeed, by its generous activity it grows better and grows greater. Therefore it far excels mere erotic inclination, which, selfishly pursued, soon enough fades wretchedly away.

This love is uniquely expressed and perfected through the marital act. The actions within marriage by which the couple are united intimately and chastely are noble and worthy ones. Expressed in a manner which is truly human, these actions signify and promote that mutual self-giving by which spouses enrich each other with a joyful and a thankful will.

Sealed by mutual faithfulness and hallowed above all by Christ's sacrament, this love remains steadfastly true in body and in mind, in bright days or dark. It will never be profaned by adultery or divorce. Firmly established by the Lord, the unity of marriage will radiate from the equal personal dignity of wife and husband, a dignity acknowledged by mutual and total love.

The steady fulfillment of the duties of this Christian vocation demands notable virtue. For this reason, strengthened by grace for holiness of life, the couple will painstakingly cultivate and pray for constancy of love, largeheartedness, and the spirit of sacrifice (No. 49).

Fruitfulness of Marriage

Marriage and conjugal love are by their nature ordained toward the begetting and educating of children. Children are really the supreme gift of marriage and contribute very substantially to the welfare of their parents. . . . God himself . . . wished to share with man a certain special participation in his own creative work. Thus he blessed male and female, saying: "Increase and multiply" (Gn. 1:28).

Hence, while not making the other purposes of matrimony of less account, the true practice of conjugal love, and the whole meaning of the family life which results from it, have this aim: that the couple be ready with stout hearts to cooperate with the love of the Creator and the Savior, who through them will enlarge and enrich his own family day by day.

Parents should regard as their proper mission the task of transmitting human life and educating those to whom it has been transmitted. They should realize that they are thereby cooperators with the love of God the Creator, and are, so to speak, the interpreters of that love. Thus they will fulfill their task with human and Christian responsibility (No. 50).

Norms of Judgment

They will thoughtfully take into account both their own welfare and that of their children, those already born and those who may be foreseen. For this accounting they will reckon with both the material and the spiritual conditions of the times as well as of their state in life. Finally, they will consult the interests of the family group, of temporal society, and of the Church herself.

The parents themselves should ultimately make this judgment in the sight of God. But in their manner of acting, spouses should be aware that they cannot proceed arbitrarily. They must always be governed according to a conscience dutifully conformed to the divine law itself, and should be submissive toward the Church's teaching office, which authentically interprets that law in the light of the Gospel. That divine law reveals and protects the integral meaning of conjugal love, and impels it toward a truly human fulfillment.

Marriage, to be sure, is not instituted solely for procreation. Rather, its very nature as an unbreakable compact between persons, and the welfare of the children, both demand that the mutual love of the spouses, too, be embodied in a rightly ordered manner, that it grow and ripen. Therefore, marriage persists as a whole manner and communion of life, and maintains its value and indissolubility, even when offspring are lacking — despite, rather often, the very intense desire of the couple (No. 50).

Love and Life

This Council realizes that certain modern conditions often keep couples from arranging their married lives harmoniously, and that they find themselves in circumstances where at least temporarily the size of their families should not be increased. As a result, the faithful exercise of love and the full intimacy of their lives are hard to maintain. But where the intimacy of married life is broken off, it is not rare for its faithfulness to be imperiled and its quality of fruitfulness ruined. For then the upbringing of the children and the courage to accept new ones are both endangered.

To these problems there are those who presume to offer dishonorable solutions. Indeed, they do not recoil from the taking of life. But the Church issues the reminder that a true contradiction cannot exist between the divine laws pertaining to the transmission of life and those pertaining to the fostering of authentic conjugal love.

For God, the Lord of Life, has conferred on men the surpassing ministry of safeguarding life — a ministry which must be fulfilled in a manner which is worthy of men. Therefore from the moment of its conception life must be guarded with the greatest care, while abortion and infanticide are unspeakable crimes. The sexual characteristics of man and the human faculty of reproduction wonderfully exceed the dispositions of lower forms of life. Hence the acts themselves which are proper to conjugal love and which are exercised in accord with genuine human dignity must be honored with great reverence (No. 51).

Church Teaching

Therefore when there is question of harmonizing conjugal love with the responsible transmission of life, the moral aspect of any procedure does not depend solely on the sincere intentions or on an evaluation of motives. It must be determined by objective standards. These, based on the nature of the human person and his acts, preserve the full sense of mutual self-giving and human procreation in the context of true love. Such a goal cannot be achieved unless the virtue of conjugal chastity is sincerely practiced. Relying on these principles, sons of the Church may not undertake methods of regulating procreation which are found blameworthy by the teaching authority of the Church in its unfolding of the divine law.

Everyone should be persuaded that human life and the task of transmitting it are not realities bound up with this world alone. Hence they cannot be measured or perceived only in terms of it, but always have a bearing on the eternal destiny of men (No. 51).

COUPLE TO COUPLE LEAGUE

The Couple to Couple League, the largest and most complete organization of its kind in North America, is an interfaith, non-profit organization dedicated to helping couples develop the art of Natural Family Planning.

CCL serves 48 states and 13 foreign countries, and has 19,000 members and over 650 certified teaching couples. Address: P.O. Box 111184 (3621 Glenmore Ave.), Cincinnati, O. 45211.

HUMANAE VITAE

Marriage doctrine and morality were the subjects of the encyclical "Humanae Vitae" ("Of Human Life") issued by Pope Paul, July 29, 1968. Following are a number of key excerpts from the document, which was framed in the pattern of traditional teaching and statements by the Second Vatican Council.

Each and every marriage act ("quilibet matrimonii usus") must remain open to the transmission of life (No. 11).

Indeed, by its intimate structure, the conjugal act, while most closely uniting husband and wife, capacitates them for the generation of new lives, according to laws inscribed in the very being of man and of woman. By safeguarding both these essential aspects, the unitive and the procreative, the conjugal act preserves in its fullness the sense of true mutual love and its ordination toward man's most high calling to parenthood (No. 12).

It is, in fact, justly observed that a conjugal act imposed upon one's partner without regard for his or her condition and lawful desires is not a true act of love, and therefore denies an exigency of right moral order in the relationships between husband and wife. Hence, one who reflects well must also recognize that a reciprocal act of love which jeopardizes the responsibility to transmit life — which God the Creator, according to particular laws, inserted therein — is in contradiction with the design constitutive of marriage and with the will of the Author of life. To use this divine gift, destroying, even if only partially, its meaning and its purpose, is to contradict the nature both of man and of woman and of their most intimate relationship, and therefore it is to contradict also the plan of God and his will (No. 13).

Forbidden Actions

The direct interruption of the generative process already begun, and, above all, directly willed and procured abortion, even if for therapeutic reasons, are to be absolutely excluded as licit means of regulating birth.

Equally to be excluded . . . is direct sterilization, whether perpetual or temporary, whether of the man or of the woman. Similarly excluded is every action which, either in anticipation of the conjugal act, or in its accomplishment, or in the development of its natural consequences, proposes, whether as an end or as a means, to render procreation impossible.

To justify conjugal acts made intentionally infecund, one cannot invoke as valid reasons the lesser evil, or the fact that such acts would constitute a whole together with the fecund acts already performed or to follow later and hence would share in one and the same moral goodness. In truth, if it is sometimes licit to tolerate a lesser evil in order to avoid a greater evil or to promote a greater good, it is not licit, even for the gravest reasons, to do evil so that good may follow therefrom; that is, to make into the object of a positive act of the will something which is intrinsically disorder, and hence unworthy of the human person, even when the intention is to safeguard or promote individual, family or social well-being.

Consequently, it is an error to think that a conjugal act which is deliberately made infecund, and so is intrinsically dishonest, could be made honest and right by the ensemble of a fecund conjugal life (No. 14).

Family Planning

If, then, there are serious motives to space out births, which derive from the physical or psychological conditions of husband and wife, or from external conditions, the Church teaches that it is then licit to take into account the natural rhythms immanent in the generative functions, for the use of marriage in the infecund periods only, and in this way to regulate birth without offending earlier stated principles (No. 16).

Pastoral Concern

We do not at all intend to hide the sometimes serious difficulties inherent in the life of Christian married persons; for them, as for everyone else, "the gate is narrow and the way is hard that leads to life." But the hope of that life must illuminate their way, as with courage they strive to live with wisdom, justice and piety in this present time, knowing that the figure of this world passes away.

Let married couples, then, face up to the efforts needed, supported by the faith and hope which "do not disappoint . . . because God's love has been poured into our hearts through the Holy Spirit, who has been given to us." Let them implore divine assistance by persevering prayer; above all, let them draw from the source of grace and charity in the Eucharist. And, if sin should still keep its hold over them, let them not be discouraged but rather have recourse with humble perseverance to the mercy of God, which is poured forth in the sacrament of penance (No. 25).

20TH ANNIVERSARY OF HUMANAE VITAE

The following statement commemorating the 20th anniversary of Pope Paul VI's encyclical letter was issued July 25, 1988, by the Committee for Pro-Life Activities, National Conference of Catholic Bishops.

The text was circulated by the NC Documentary Service, Origins, Aug. 4, 1988 (Vol. 18, No. 10).

Twenty years ago Pope Paul VI issued the encyclical *Humanae Vitae* reaffirming the Church's teaching on conjugal love, responsible parenthood and the transmission of human life.

The encyclical reviewed the Church's teaching on marriage, family life and sexuality, advancing the Second Vatican Council's vision of conjugal love as human, total, faithful and exclusive, and ordered to the begetting and education of children. *Humanae Vitae* exalted marriage as a sacrament whose grace could transform the normal, day-to-day aspects of married life into opportunities to grow in holiness and become witnesses for Christ in the world. And it defended an inseparable link between the unitive and procreative dimensions of sexual intercourse within marriage, concluding that every such act "must remain open to the transmission of life" (*Humanae Vitae*, 11).

Issued at Critical Time

Humanae Vitae was issued at a time when there was wide concern and confusion about world population growth, when "the pill" was a relatively new scientific discovery and when people in many parts of the world were still reeling from the "sexual revolution" of the 1960s. Pope Paul was aware of the climate within which he spoke. In fact, on the document's 10th anniversary he recalled the suffering it entailed for his pontificate not only because of the seriousness of the subject, "but also, perhaps more, because of a certain climate of expectation which had given rise among Catholics and in the wider circle of public opinion to the idea of presumed concessions ... in the moral and matrimonial doctrine of the Church" (Address to the College of Cardinals, June 25, 1978).

Today's social climate is different again. Looking back over the past 20 years in our own country, we see a gradual decline in family size and an increase in divorce, both notably pronounced among Catholics, and an overwhelming assault on the sacredness of human life in judicial decisions and social policies regarding abortion. We find in our society a growing ambivalence in attitudes regarding children and an increasing tendency to equate the bond of marriage with mere cohabitation.

Special Opportunity

The 20th anniversary of *Humanae Vitae* offers Catholics a special opportunity to reflect on the encyclical's teaching and on its defense of the dignity of Christian marriage and family life.

Pope Paul VI reminded us that decisions about the transmission of human life are not merely decisions about the most efficient way to pursue a particular goal. Such decisions must be considered in light of an integral understanding of the nature and dignity of the human person, and the eternal destiny to which each of us has been called by God.

Conjugal love, that special type of love that exists between married partners, is only fully appreciated when considered in terms of its origin in a God who is love and in terms of that fundamental vocation of every human person "to love one another as God has loved us" (Jn 13:34). Marriage is much more than a universally accepted social institution. It is, in the words of Pope Paul VI, "the wise institution of the Creator to realize in mankind his design of love" (*Humanae Vitae*, 8).

Responsible Parenthood

Within this broad vision of marriage as a path to holiness, *Humanae Vitae* focused on responsible parenthood as part of the "mission" of husband and wife. This mission calls for an openness to life — more precisely, an openness to childbearing and child rearing. It is grounded in the innate value and dignity of every child from conception on — a dignity that flows from God's creative love and providential care. Each child is a unique person who, from the first moment of existence, shares in God's own life and is called to an eternal destiny with him in heaven. To parent a child is to share in a special way in God's plan of creation and redemption. As Pope John Paul II notes:

"In its most profound reality, love is essentially a gift; and conjugal love, while leading the spouses to the reciprocal 'knowledge' which makes them 'one flesh,' does not end with the couple, because it makes them capable of the greatest possible gift, the gift by which they become cooperators with God for giving life to a new human person. Thus the couple, while giving themselves to one another, give not just themselves but also the reality of children, who are a living reflection of their love, a permanent sign of conjugal unity and a loving and inseparable synthesis of their being a father and a mother" (*Familiaris Consortio*, 14).

Pope Paul VI also emphasized that, in their efforts to make responsible decisions about the timing or limiting of births, married couples should do so in full awareness of "their own duties toward God, toward themselves, toward the family and toward society, in a correct hierarchy of values" (*Humanae Vitae*, 10). Respect for the procreative dimension of human sexuality demands that one does not directly act to render procreation impossible, but allows married couples for serious reasons to reserve sexual union to the infertile periods of a woman's reproductive cycle.

Need for Grace and Good Will

Pope Paul recognized that some would find this teaching difficult — indeed, that it is only realizable with God's help, coupled with the good will of each person. In this context he recalled the mercy of Jesus, who had "compassion on the crowds," and urged married couples to make frequent recourse to prayer and to the sacraments of penance and the Eucharist. But he also recognized his responsibility to set before Catholics a clear statement of moral principle that could serve as a guide to the pursuit of Christian virtue and holiness. As Pope John Paul II has reminded us, "it is one and the same Church that is both teacher and mother" (*Familiaris Consortio*, 33) — one and the same Church that promotes moral truth and that offers care and support as well as compassion for those who find it arduous to understand and live up to that truth.

Natural Family Planning

Today the Church continues in its efforts to help married couples by making them aware of the richness of the teaching of *Humanae Vitae* and by providing them with the proper information and motivation they need to strengthen their conjugal love. Natural family planning involves individual couples intimately in decisions that are at the center of their married life. The willingness of each partner in marriage to help the other, to develop sensitivity to the other's needs and to make sacrifices that will strengthen their love helps solidify the marriage relationship. Efforts to live their sexuality in accord with the teaching of the Church brings to married couples peace of mind and conscience. It also deepens their faith and affirms their reliance on God's providential care as they meet the other responsibilities of marriage and family life.

As bishops, we reaffirm our commitment to encourage, establish and strengthen natural family planning programs so that they will be available to all married couples who desire them. Our own recent national survey on natural family planning provides assurance that efforts in this area have been fruitful. It indicates as well that the Church's teaching on responsible parenthood is important to faithful Catholic couples, and that when quality instruction is available, couples want to and can learn to practice natural family planning successfully.

Prophetic Wisdom

Twenty years after the issuance of *Humanae Vitae* we see ever more clearly the prophetic wisdom of the Church's consistent teaching on marriage and responsible parenthood, and the courage of Pope Paul VI in reaffirming that teaching. We commit ourselves to a renewed effort to explain this teaching to our Catholic people and to encourage them to develop attitudes and values enabling them to live the Church's teaching in their marriage and family relationships.

We conclude this pastoral statement by making our own the words of Pope John Paul II:

"We are not able to make the obstacles to Christian living disappear; we are not in a position to lift all the burdens that weigh upon our Christian families; and much less are we authorized to attempt to remove the cross from Christianity. But we are in a position to proclaim the great dignity of marriage, its identity as an image and symbol of God's everlasting and unbreakable covenant of love with his Church. We are able to love the family and in this pastoral love to offer it the only criterion for the real solution to the problems that it faces. This criterion is the word of God; the word of God in all its purity and power, in all its integrity and with all its demands — the word of God as transmitted by the Church" (Address to Canadian Bishops, April 23, 1983).

MARRIAGE LAWS

The Catholic Church claims jurisdiction over its members in matters pertaining to marriage, which is a sacrament. Church legislation on the subject is stated principally in 111 canons of the Code of Canon Law.

Marriage laws of the Church provide juridical norms in support of the marriage covenant. In 10 chapters, the revised Code covers: pastoral directives for preparing men and women for marriage; impediments in general and in particular; matrimonial consent; form for the celebration of marriage; mixed marriages; secret celebration of marriage; effects of marriage; separation of spouses, and convalidation of marriage.

Catholics are bound by all marriage laws of the Church. Non-Catholics, whether baptized or not, are not considered bound by these ecclesiastical laws except in cases of marriage with a Catholic. Certain natural laws, in the Catholic view, bind all men and women, irrespective of their religious beliefs; accordingly, marriage is prohibited before the time of puberty, without knowledge and free mutual consent, in the case of an already existing valid marriage bond, in the case of antecedent and perpetual impotence.

Formalities

These include, in addition to arrangements for the time and place of the marriage ceremony, doctrinal and moral instruction concerning marriage and the recording of data which verifies in documentary form the eligibility and freedom of the persons to marry. Records of this kind, which are confidential, are preserved in the archives of the church where the marriage takes place.

Premarital instructions are the subject matter of Pre-Cana Conferences.

Marital Consent

The exchange of consent to the marriage covenant, which is essential for valid marriage, must be rational, free, true and mutual.

Matrimonial consent can be invalidated by an essential defect, substantial error, the strong influence of force and fear, the presence of a condition or intention against the nature of marriage.

Form of Marriage

A Catholic is required, for validity and lawfulness, to contract marriage — with another Catholic or with a non-Catholic — in the presence of a competent priest or deacon and two witnesses.

There are two exceptions to this law. A Roman Rite Catholic (since Mar. 25, 1967) or an Eastern Rite Catholic (since Nov. 21, 1964) can contract marriage validly in the presence of a priest of a separated Eastern Rite Church, provided other requirements of law are complied with. With permission of the competent Roman-Rite or Eastern-Rite bishop, this form of marriage is lawful, as well as valid. (See Eastern Rite Laws, below.)

With these two exceptions, and aside from cases covered by special permission, the Church does not regard as valid any marriages involving Catholics which take place before non-Catholic ministers of religion or civil officials.

(An excommunication formerly in force against Catholics who celebrated marriage before a non-Catholic minister was abrogated in a decree issued by the Sacred Congregation for the Doctrine of the Faith on Mar. 18, 1966.)

The ordinary place of marriage is the parish of either Catholic party or of the Catholic party in case of a mixed marriage.

Church law regarding the form of marriage does

not affect non-Catholics in marriages among themselves. The Church recognizes as valid the marriages of non-Catholics before ministers of religion and civil officials, unless they are rendered null and void on other grounds.

The canonical form is not to be observed in the case of a marriage between a non-Catholic and a baptized Catholic who has left the Church by a formal act.

Impediments

Diriment Impediments to marriage are factors which render a marriage invalid.

• age, which obtains before completion of the 14th year for a woman and the 16th year for a man;

• impotency, if it is antecedent to the marriage and permanent (this differs from sterility, which is not an impediment);

• the bond of an existing valid marriage;

• disparity of worship, which obtains when one party is a Catholic and the other party is unbaptized;

• sacred orders;

• religious profession of the perpetual vow of chastity;

• abduction, which impedes the freedom of the person abducted;

• crime, variously involving elements of adultery, promise or attempt to marry, conspiracy to murder a husband or wife;

• blood relationship in the direct line (father-daughter, mother-son, etc.) and to the fourth degree inclusive of the collateral line (brother-sister, first cousins);

• affinity, or relationship resulting from a valid marriage, in any degree of the direct line;

• public honesty, arising from an invalid marriage or from public or notorious concubinage; it renders either party incapable of marrying blood relatives of the other in the first degree of the direct line.

• legal relationship arising from adoption; it renders either party incapable of marrying relatives of the other in the direct line or in the second degree of the collateral line.

Dispensations from Impediments: Persons hindered by impediments either may not or cannot marry unless they are dispensed therefrom in view of reasons recognized in canon law. Local bishops can dispense from the impediments most often encountered (e.g., disparity of worship) as well as others.

Decision regarding some dispensations is reserved to the Holy See.

Separation

A valid and consummated marriage of baptized persons cannot be dissolved by any human authority or any cause other than the death of one of the persons.

In other circumstances:

• 1. A valid but unconsummated marriage of baptized persons, or of a baptized and an unbaptized person, can be dissolved:

a. by the solemn religious profession of one of the persons, made with permission of the pope. In such a case, the bond is dissolved at the time of profession, and the other person is free to marry again;

b. by dispensation from the pope, requested for a grave reason by one or both of the persons. If the dispensation is granted, both persons are free to marry again.

Dispensations in these cases are granted for reasons connected with the spiritual welfare of the concerned persons.

• 2. A legitimate marriage, even consummated, of unbaptized persons can be dissolved in favor of one of them who subsequently receives the sacrament of baptism. This is the Pauline Privilege, so called because it was promulgated by St. Paul (1 Cor. 7:12-15) as a means of protecting the faith of converts. Requisites for granting the privilege are:

a. marriage prior to the baptism of either person;

b. reception of baptism by one person;

c. refusal of the unbaptized person to live in peace with the baptized person and without interfering with his or her freedom to practice the Christian faith. The privilege does not apply if the unbaptized person agrees to these conditions.

• 3. A legitimate and consummated marriage of a baptized and an unbaptized person can be dissolved by the pope in virtue of the Privilege of Faith, also called the Petrine Privilege.

Civil Divorce

Because of the unity and the indissolubility of marriage, the Church denies that civil divorce can break the bond of a valid marriage, whether the marriage involves two Catholics, a Catholic and a non-Catholic, or non-Catholics with each other.

In view of serious circumstances of marital distress, the Church permits an innocent and aggrieved party, whether wife or husband, to seek and obtain a civil divorce for the purpose of acquiring title and right to the civil effects of divorce, such as separate habitation and maintenance, and the custody of children. Permission for this kind of action should be obtained from proper church authority. The divorce, if obtained, does not break the bond of a valid marriage.

Under other circumstances — as would obtain if a marriage was invalid (see Annulment, below) — civil divorce is permitted for civil effects and as a civil ratification of the fact that the marriage bond really does not exist.

Annulment

This is a decision by a competent church authority — e.g., a bishop, a diocesan marriage tribunal, the Roman Rota — that an apparently valid marriage was actually invalid from the beginning because of the unknown or concealed existence, from the beginning, of a diriment impediment, an essential defect in consent, radical incapability for marriage, or a condition placed by one or both of the parties against the very nature of marriage.

Eastern Rite Laws

Marriage laws of the Eastern Church differ in several respects from the legislation of the Roman Rite. The regulations in effect since May 2, 1949, were contained in the motu proprio *Crebre Allatae* issued by Pius XII the previous February.

According to both the Roman Code of Canon Law and the Oriental Code, marriages between Roman Rite Catholics and Eastern Rite Catholics ordinarily take place in the rite of the groom and have canonical effects in that rite.

Regarding the form for the celebration of marriages between Eastern Catholics and baptized Eastern non-Catholics, the Second Vatican Council declared:

"By way of preventing invalid marriages between Eastern Catholics and baptized Eastern non-Catholics, and in the interests of the permanence and sanctity of marriage and of domestic harmony, this sacred Synod decrees that the canonical 'form' for the celebration of such marriages obliges only for lawfulness. For their validity, the presence of a sacred minister suffices, as long as the other requirements of law are honored" (*Decree on Eastern Catholic Churches*, No. 18).

Marriages taking place in this manner are lawful, as well as valid, with permission of a competent Eastern Rite bishop.

MIXED MARRIAGES

"Mixed Marriages" (*Matrimonia Mixta*) was the subject of: (1) a letter issued under this title by Pope Paul VI Mar. 31, 1970, and (2) a statement, *Implementation of the Apostolic Letter on Mixed Marriages*, approved by the National Conference of Catholic Bishops Nov. 16, 1970.

One of the key points in the bishops' statement referred to the need for mutual pastoral care by ministers of different faiths for the sacredness of marriage and for appropriate preparation and continuing support of parties to a mixed marriage.

Pastoral experience, which the Catholic Church shares with other religious bodies, confirms the fact that marriages of persons of different beliefs involve special problems related to the continuing religious practice of the concerned persons and to the religious education and formation of their children.

Pastoral measures to minimize these problems include instruction of a non-Catholic party in essentials of the Catholic faith for purposes of understanding. Desirably, some instruction should also be given the Catholic party regarding his or her partner's beliefs.

The Catholic party to a mixed marriage is required to declare his (her) intention of continuing practice of the Catholic faith and to promise to do all in his (her) power to share his (her) faith with children born of the marriage by having them baptized and raised as Catholics. No declarations or promises are required of the non-Catholic party, but he (she) must be informed of the declaration and promise made by the Catholic.

Notice of the Catholic's declaration and promise is an essential part of the application made to a bishop for (1) permission to marry a baptized non-Catholic, or (2) a dispensation to marry an unbaptized non-Catholic.

A mixed marriage can take place with a Nuptial Mass. (The bishops' statement added this caution: "To the extent that Eucharistic sharing is not permitted by the general discipline of the Church, this is to be considered when plans are being made to have the mixed marriage at Mass or not.")

The ordinary minister at a mixed marriage is an authorized priest, and the ordinary place is the parish church of the Catholic party. A non-Catholic minister may not only attend the marriage ceremony but may also address, pray with and bless the couple.

For appropriate pastoral reasons, a bishop can grant a dispensation from the Catholic form of marriage and can permit the marriage to take place in a non-Catholic Church with a non-Catholic minister as the officiating minister. A priest may not only attend such a ceremony but may also address, pray with and bless the couple.

"It is not permitted," however, the bishops' statement declared, "to have two religious services or to have a single service in which both the Catholic marriage ritual and a non-Catholic marriage ritual are celebrated."

PASTORAL MINISTRY FOR DIVORCED AND REMARRIED

Ministry to divorced and remarried Catholics is a difficult field of pastoral endeavor, situated as it is in circumstances tantamount to the horns of a dilemma.

At Issue

On the one side is firm church teaching on the permanence of marriage and norms against reception of the Eucharist and full participation in the life of the Church by Catholics in irregular unions.

On the other side are men and women with broken unions followed by second and perhaps happier attempts at marriage which the Church does not recognize as valid and which may not be capable of being validated because of the existence of an earlier marriage bond.

The forces at work in these circumstances are those of the Church, upholding its doctrine and practice regarding the permanence of marriage, and those of many men and women in irregular second marriages who desire full participation in the life of the Church.

Sacramental participation is not possible for those whose first marriage was valid, although there is no bar to their attendance at Mass, to sharing in other activities of the Church, or to their efforts to have children baptized and raised in the Catholic faith.

An exception to this rule is the condition of a divorced and remarried couple living in a brother-sister relationship.

There is no ban against sacramental participation by separated or divorced persons who have not attempted a second marriage.

Unverified estimates of the number of U.S. Catholics who are divorced and remarried vary between six and eight million.

Tribunal Action

What can the Church do for them and with them in pastoral ministry, is an old question charged with new urgency because of the rising number of divorced and remarried Catholics.

One way to help is through the agency of marriage tribunals charged with responsibility for investigating and settling questions concerning the validity or invalidity of a prior marriage. There are reasons in canon law justifying the Church in declaring a particular marriage null and void from the beginning, despite the short- or long-term existence of an apparently valid union.

Decrees of nullity (annulments) are not new in the history of the Church. If such a decree is issued, a man or woman is free to validate a second marriage and live in complete union with the Church.

The 1986 *Statistical Yearbook of the Church,* reported that the U.S. tribunals issued 57,681 annulments in 1986.

Reasons behind Decrees

Pastoral experience reveals that some married persons, a short or long time after contracting an apparently valid marriage, exhibit signs that point back to the existence, at the time of marriage, of latent and serious personal deficiencies which made them incapable of valid consent and sacramental commitment.

Such deficiencies might include gross immaturity and those affecting in a serious way the capacity to love, to have a true interpersonal and conjugal relationship, to fulfill marital obligations, to accept the faith aspect of marriage.

Psychological and behavioral factors like these have been given greater attention by tribunals in recent years and have provided grounds for numerous decrees of nullity.

Decisions of this type do not indicate any softening of the Church's attitude regarding the permanence of marriage. They affirm, rather, that some persons who have married were really not capable of doing so.

Serious deficiencies in the capacity for real interpersonal relationship in marriage were the reasons behind a landmark decree of nullity issued in 1973 by the Roman Rota, the Vatican high court of appeals in marriage cases. Pope John Paul referred to such deficiencies — the "grave lack of discretionary judgment," incapability of assuming "essential matrimonial rights and obligations," for example — in an address Jan. 26, 1984, to personnel of the Rota.

The tribunal way to a decree of nullity regarding a previous marriage, however, is not open to many persons in second marriages — because grounds are either lacking or, if present, cannot be verified in tribunal process.

Unacceptable Solution

One unacceptable solution of the problem, called "good conscience procedure," involves administration of the sacraments of penance and the Eucharist to divorced and remarried Catholics unable to obtain a decree of nullity for a first marriage who are living in a subsequent marriage "in good faith."

This procedure, despite the fact that it has no standing or recognition in church law, is being advocated and practiced by some priests and remarried Catholics.

Pastoral Concern

Pastoral concern for divorced and remarried persons was cited by Pope John Paul in his apostolic exhortation on the family, *Familiaris Consortium.* He called upon pastors and all members of the Church:

"Help the divorced with solicitous care to make sure that they do not consider themselves as separated from the Church, for as baptized persons they can and indeed must share in her life. They should be encouraged to listen to the word of God, to attend the Sacrifice of the Mass, to persevere in prayer, to contribute to works of charity and to community efforts of justice, to bring up their children in the Christian faith, to cultivate the spirit and practice of penance and thus implore, day by day, God's grace."

This concern is shared by hosts of priests, Religious and lay persons, as well as by numerous apostolates and support groups like the Judeans, founded in 1952, and the North American Conference of Separated and Divorced Catholics, founded in 1972.

Statistics compiled and circulated in November, 1985, by the conference indicated that 80 percent of U.S. dioceses formally included ministry to divorced persons in their family-life apostolates; 30 percent of the diocese had full-time, salaried personnel in the ministry; 25 percent of U.S. parishes had support groups for divorced persons.

Ms. K. L. Kircher is executive director of the North American Conference of Separated and Divorced Catholics, founded by Father James J. Young, C.S.P., who was its national chaplain until his death in 1986. The mailing address is: 3015 Fourth St. N.E., Washington, D.C. 20017.

Marriage Encounter brings couples together for a weekend program of events directed by a team of several couples and a priest, for the purpose of developing their abilities to communicate with each other in their life together as husband and wife. This purpose is served by direction in techniques given by the team and by private dialogue of each couple. The address of National Marriage Encounter is 4704 Jamerson Pl., Orlando, Fla. 32807. The national office of Worldwide Marriage Encounter is located at 1908 E. Highland Ave., Suite A, San Bernardino, Calif. 92404.

Catholic Engaged Encounter is designed to prepare couples for marriage by focusing attention on its sacramental aspects and by increasing their potential for communication.

THE CHURCH CALENDAR

The calendar of the Roman Church consists of an arrangement throughout the year of a series of liturgical seasons, commemorations of divine mysteries and commemorations of saints for purposes of worship.

The purposes of this calendar were outlined in the "Constitution on the Sacred Liturgy" (Nos. 102-105) promulgated by the Second Vatican Council.

Within the cycle of a year . . . (the Church) unfolds the whole mystery of Christ, not only from his incarnation and birth until his ascension, but also as reflected in the day of Pentecost, and the expectation of a blessed, hoped-for return of the Lord.

Recalling thus the mysteries of redemption, the Church opens to the faithful the riches of her Lord's powers and merits, so that these are in some way made present at all times, and the faithful are enabled to lay hold of them and become filled with saving grace (No. 102).

In celebrating this annual cycle of Christ's mysteries, holy Church honors with special love the Blessed Mary, Mother of God (No. 103).

The Church has also included in the annual cycle days devoted to the memory of the martyrs and the other saints. . . . (who) sing God's perfect praise in heaven and offer prayers for us. By celebrating the passage of these saints from earth to heaven the Church proclaims the paschal mystery as achieved in the saints who have suffered and been glorified with Christ; she proposes them to the faithful as examples who draw all to the Father through Christ, and through their merits she pleads for God's favors (No. 104).

In the various seasons of the year and according to her traditional discipline, the Church completes the formation of the faithful by means of pious practices for soul and body, by instruction, prayer, and works of penance and mercy (No. 105).

THE ROMAN CALENDAR

Norms for a revised calendar for the Western Church as decreed by the Second Vatican Council were approved by Paul VI in the *motu proprio Mysterii Paschalis* dated Feb. 14, 1969. The revised calendar was promulgated a month later by a decree of the Congregation for Divine Worship and went into effect Jan. 1, 1970, with provisional modifications. Full implementation of all its parts was delayed in 1970 and 1971, pending the completion of work on related liturgical texts. The U.S. bishops ordered the calendar into effect for 1972.

The Seasons

Advent: The liturgical year begins with the first Sunday of Advent, which introduces a season of four weeks or slightly less duration with the theme of expectation of the coming of Christ. During the first two weeks, the final coming of Christ as Lord and Judge at the end of the world is the focus of attention. From Dec. 17 to 24, the emphasis shifts to anticipation of the celebration of his Nativity on the solemnity of Christmas.

Advent has four Sundays. Since the 10th century, the first Sunday has marked the beginning of the liturgical year in the Western Church. In the Middle Ages, a kind of pre-Christmas fast was in vogue during the season.

Christmas Season: The Christmas season begins with the vigil of Christmas and lasts until the Sunday after January 6, inclusive.

The period between the end of the Christmas season and the beginning of Lent belongs to the Ordinary Time of the year. Of variable length, the pre-Lenten phase of this season includes what were formerly called the Sundays after Epiphany and the suppressed Sundays of Septuagesima, Sexagesima and Quinquagesima.

Lent: The penitential season of Lent begins on Ash Wednesday, which occurs between Feb. 4 and Mar. 11, depending on the date of Easter, and lasts until the Mass of the Lord's Supper (Holy Thursday). It has six Sundays. The sixth Sunday marks the beginning of Holy Week and is known as Passion (formerly called Palm) Sunday.

The origin of Lenten observances dates back to the fourth century or earlier.

Easter Triduum: The Easter Triduum begins with evening Mass of the Lord's Supper and ends with Evening Prayer on Easter Sunday.

Easter Season: The Easter season whose theme is resurrection from sin to the life of grace, lasts for 50 days, from Easter to Pentecost. Easter, the Sunday after the first full moon following the vernal equinox, occurs between Mar. 22 and Apr. 25. The terminal phase of the Easter season, between the solemnities of the Ascension of the Lord and Pentecost, stresses anticipation of the coming and action of the Holy Spirit.

Ordinary Time: The season of Ordinary Time begins on Monday (or Tuesday if the feast of the Baptism of the Lord is celebrated on that Monday) after the Sunday following January 6 and continues until the day before Ash Wednesday, inclusive. It begins again on the Monday after Pentecost and ends on the Saturday before the first Sunday of Advent. It consists of 33 or 34 weeks. The last Sunday is celebrated as the Solemnity of Christ the King. The overall purpose of the season is to elaborate the themes of salvation history.

Commemorations of Saints

The commemorations of saints are celebrated concurrently with the liturgical seasons and feasts of our Lord. Their purpose is to illustrate the paschal mysteries as reflected in the lives of saints, to honor them as heroes of holiness, and to appeal for their intercession.

In line with revised regulations, some former feasts were either abolished or relegated to observance in particular places by local option for one of two reasons: (1) lack of sufficient historical evidence for observance of the feasts; (2) lack of universal significance.

The commemoration of a saint, as a general rule, is observed on the day of death (*dies natalis,* day of birth to glory with God in heaven). Exceptions to this rule include the feasts of St. John the

Baptist, who is honored on the day of his birth; Sts. Basil the Great and Gregory Nazianzen, and the brother Saints, Cyril and Methodius, who are commemorated in joint feasts.

Application of this general rule in the revised calendar resulted in date changes of some observances.

Sundays and Other Holy Days

Sunday is the original Christian feast day and holy day of obligation because of the unusually significant events of salvation history which took place and are commemorated on the first day of the week — viz., the Resurrection of Christ, the key event of his life and the fundamental fact of Christianity; and the descent of the Holy Spirit upon the Apostles on Pentecost, the birthday of the Church. The transfer of observance of the Lord's Day from the Sabbath to Sunday was made in apostolic times. The Mass and Liturgy of the Hours (Divine Office) of each Sunday reflect the themes and set the tones of the various liturgical seasons.

Holy days of obligation are special occasions on which Catholics who have reached the age of reason are seriously obliged, as on Sundays, to assist at Mass: they are also to refrain from work and involvement with business which impede participation in divine worship and the enjoyment of appropriate rest and relaxation.

The holy days of obligation observed in the United States are: Christmas, the Nativity of Jesus, Dec. 25; Solemnity of Mary the Mother of God, Jan. 1; Ascension of the Lord; Assumption of Blessed Mary the Virgin, Aug. 15; All Saints' Day, Nov. 1; Immaculate Conception of Blessed Mary the Virgin, Dec. 8.

In addition to these, there are four other holy days of obligation prescribed in the general law of the Church which are not so observed in the U.S.: Epiphany, Jan. 6; St. Joseph, Mar. 19; Corpus Christi; Sts. Peter and Paul, June 29. The solemnities of Epiphany and Corpus Christi are transferred to a Sunday in countries where they are not observed as holy days of obligation.

Feasts and Commemorations

Categories of observances according to dignity and manner of observance are: solemnity (highest, corresponding to former first-class feasts); feast (corresponding to former second-class feasts); memorial (corresponding to former third-class feasts); optional memorial (observable by choice). Observances of the first three categories are universal in the Roman Rite.

Fixed observances are those which are regularly celebrated on the same calendar day each year.

Movable observances are those which are not observed on the same calendar day each year. Examples of these are Easter (the first Sunday after the first full moon following the vernal equinox), Ascension (40 days after Easter), Pentecost (50 days after Easter), Trinity Sunday (first after Pentecost), Christ the King (last Sunday of the liturgical year).

Weekdays, Days of Prayer

Weekdays are those on which no proper feast or vigil is celebrated in the Mass or Liturgy of the Hours (Divine Office). On such days, the Mass may be that of the preceding Sunday, which expresses the liturgical spirit of the season, an optional memorial, a votive Mass, or a Mass for the dead. Weekdays of Advent and Lent are in a special category of their own.

Days of Prayer: Dioceses, at times to be designated by local bishops, should observe "days or periods of prayer for the fruits of the earth, prayer for human rights and equality, prayer for world justice and peace, and penitential observance outside of Lent." So stated the *Instruction on Particular Calendars* (No. 331) issued by the Congregation for the Sacraments and Divine Worship June 24. 1970.

Days and Times of Penance

Fridays throughout the year and the time of Lent are penitential days and times throughout the Church.

The National Conference of Catholic Bishops, with Canons 1249 to 1253 of the Code of Canon Law in mind, declared as follows Nov. 18, 1966:

"Catholics in the United States are obliged to abstain from the eating of meat on Ash Wednesday and on all Fridays during the season of Lent. They are also obliged to fast on Ash Wednesday and on Good Friday. Self-imposed observance of fasting on all weekdays of Lent is strongly recommended. Abstinence from flesh meat on all Fridays of the year is especially recommended to individuals and to the Catholic community as a whole." (Friday abstinence is not in force on days celebrated as solemnities, like Christmas, Sacred Heart, etc.)

Other ways of doing penance (e.g., works of charity and exercises of piety) can be reasonably substituted for fasting and abstinence. Substantial observance of the laws of fast and abstinence is a matter of serious obligation.

This brief explanation of abstinence and fast is from the apostolic constitution *Paenitemini*, issued by Pope Paul VI Feb. 17, 1966.

Abstinence: "The law of abstinence forbids the use of meat, but not of eggs, the products of milk or condiments made of animal fat." Permissible are soup flavored with meat, meat gravy and sauces.

The law of abstinence binds persons from the completion of their 14th year — i.e., from the day after their 14th birthday throughout life.

Fasting: "The law of fasting allows only one full meal a day, but does not prohibit taking some food in the morning and evening, observing — as far as quantity and quality are concerned — approved local custom." (The order of meals is optional; i.e., the full meal may be taken in the evening instead of at midday. Also: (1) The quantity of food taken at the two lighter meals should not exceed the quantity taken at the full meal. (2) The drinking of ordinary liquids does not break the fast.)

The law of fasting binds persons from the completion of their 18th year to the beginning of their 60th year — i.e., from the day after their 18th birthday to the day after their 59th birthday.

JANUARY 1989

Prayer Intention: That religious liberty be respected everywhere, and that all believers collaborate in the search for justice and peace.

1—**Sun. Solemnity of Mary, Mother of God.** (Nm. 6:22-27; Gal. 4:4-7; Lk. 2:16-21.)
2—Mon. Sts. Basil the Great and Gregory Nazianzen, bishops-doctors; memorial.
3—Tues. Weekday.
4—Wed. St. Elizabeth Ann Seton; memorial (in U.S.).
5—Thurs. St. John Neumann, bishop; memorial (in U.S.).
6—Fri. Weekday. Bl. Andre Bessette, religious; optional memorial. [Epiphany is celebrated on a Sunday between Jan. 2 and Jan. 8 in the United States.]
7—Sat. Weekday. St. Raymond of Penyafort, priest; optional memorial.
8—**Sun. Epiphany of the Lord (in U.S.); solemnity.** (Is. 60:1-6; Eph. 3:2-3a, 5-6; Mt. 2:1-12.)
9—Mon. Baptism of the Lord; feast.
10—Tues. Weekday. (First Week of the Year.)
11—Wed. Weekday.
12—Thurs. Weekday.
13—Fri. Weekday. St. Hilary, bishop-doctor; optional memorial.
14—Sat. Weekday. BVM on Saturday; optional memorial.
15—**Second Sunday of the Year.** (Is. 62:1-5; 1 Cor. 12:4-11; Jn. 2:1-12.)
16—Mon. Weekday.
17—Tues. St. Anthony, abbot; memorial.
18—Wed. Weekday.
19—Thurs. Weekday.
20—Fri. Weekday. St. Fabian, pope-martyr, or St. Sebastian, martyr; optional memorials.
21—Sat. St. Agnes, virgin-martyr; memorial.
22—**Third Sunday of the Year.** (Neh. 8:1-4a, 5-6, 8-10; 1 Cor. 12:12-30; Lk. 1:1-4 and 4:14-21.) [St. Vincent, deacon-martyr; optional memorial.]
23—Mon. Weekday.
24—Tues. St. Francis de Sales, bishop-doctor; memorial.
25—Wed. Conversion of St. Paul; feast.
26—Thurs. Sts. Timothy and Titus, bishops; memorial.
27—Fri. Weekday. St. Angela Merici, virgin; optional memorial.
28—Sat. St. Thomas Aquinas, priest-doctor; memorial.
29—**Fourth Sunday of the Year.** (Jer. 1:4-5, 17-19; 1 Cor. 12:31 to 13:13; Lk. 4:21-30.)
30—Mon. Weekday.
31—Tues. St. John Bosco, priest; memorial.

"The freedom of individuals and of communities to profess and practice their religion is an essential element for peaceful human coexistence," declared Pope John Paul II in a message for observance of the World Day of Peace, January 1.

FEBRUARY 1989

Prayer Intention: That prayer, penance and the sacraments unite priests, Religious and lay persons in the worship of God and service to others.

1—Wed. Weekday.
2—Thurs. Presentation of the Lord; feast.
3—Fri. Weekday. St. Blase, bishop-martyr, or St. Ansgar, bishop; optional memorials.
4—Sat. Weekday. BVM on Saturday; optional memorial
5—**Fifth Sunday of the Year.** (Is 6:1-2a, 3-8; 1 Cor. 15:1-11; Lk. 5:1-11.) [St. Agatha, virgin-martyr; memorial.]
6—Mon. Sts. Paul Miki and Companions, martyrs; memorial.
7—Tues. Weekday.
8—Ash Wednesday. Beginning of Lent. *Fast and abstinence.* Ashes are blessed on this day and imposed on the forehead of the faithful to remind them of their obligation to do penance for sin and to seek spiritual renewal by means of prayer, fasting, good works, and by bearing with patience and for God's purposes the trials and difficulties of everyday life. [St. Jerome Emiliani; optional memorial.]
9—Thurs. Weekday of Lent.
10—Fri. Weekday of Lent. St. Scholastica, virgin; memorial. *Abstinence.*
11—Sat. Weekday of Lent. Our Lady of Lourdes; optional memorial.
12—**First Sunday of Lent.** (Dt. 26:4-10; Rom. 10:8-13; Lk. 4:1-13.)
13—Mon. Weekday of Lent.
14—Tues. Weekday of Lent. Sts. Cyril, monk, and Methodius, bishop; memorial.
15—Wed. Weekday of Lent.
16—Thurs. Weekday of Lent.
17—Fri. Weekday of Lent. *Abstinence.* [Seven Holy Founders of the Servite Order; optional memorial.]
18—Sat. Weekday of Lent.
19—**Second Sunday of Lent.** (Gn 15:5-12, 17-18; Phil. 3:17 to 4:1; Lk. 9:28b-36.)
20—Mon. Weekday of Lent.
21—Tues. Weekday of Lent. St. Peter Damien, bishop-doctor; optional memorial.
22—Wed. Chair of Peter, apostle; feast. Weekday of Lent.
23—Thurs. Weekday of Lent. St. Polycarp, bishop-martyr; memorial.
24—Fri. Weekday of Lent. *Abstinence.*
25—Sat. Weekday of Lent.
26—**Third Sunday of Lent.** (Ex. 3:1-8a, 13-15; 1 Cor. 10:1-6, 10-12; Lk. 13:1-9.)
27—Mon. Weekday of Lent.
28—Tues. Weekday of Lent.

February is Catholic Press Month.

The traditional blessing of throats takes place on or around the commemoration of St. Blase, February 3. The blessing includes a petition for freedom from ailments of the throat and other evils.

MARCH 1989

Prayer Intention: For the victims of conflict and violence, especially in the Middle East and in South Africa.

1—Wed. Weekday of Lent.
2—Thurs. Weekday of Lent.
3—Fri. Weekday of Lent. *Abstinence.*
4—Sat. Weekday of Lent. St. Casimir; optional memorial.
5—**Fourth Sunday of Lent.** (Jos. 5:9a, 10-12; 2 Cor. 5:17-21; Lk. 15:1-3, 11-32.)
6—Mon. Weekday of Lent.
7—Tues. Weekday of Lent. [Sts. Perpetua and Felicity, martyrs; memorial.]
8—Wed. Weekday of Lent. [St. John of God; optional memorial.]
9—Thurs. Weekday of Lent. [St. Frances of Rome; optional memorial.]
10—Fri. Weekday of Lent. *Abstinence.*
11—Sat. Weekday of Lent.
12—**Fifth Sunday of Lent.** (Is. 43:16-21; Phil. 3:8-14; Jn. 8:1-11.)
13—Mon. Weekday of Lent.
14—Tues. Weekday of Lent.
15—Wed. Weekday of Lent.
16—Thurs. Weekday of Lent.
17—Fri. Weekday of Lent. *Abstinence.* [St. Patrick, bishop; optional memorial.]
18—Sat. St. Joseph; solemnity (anticipated). [St. Cyril of Jerusalem, bishop-doctor; optional memorial.]
19—**Passion (Palm) Sunday.** (Procession — Lk. 19:28-40. Mass — Is. 50:4-7; Phil. 2:6-11; Lk. 22:14 to 23:56.)
20—Monday of Holy Week.
21—Tuesday of Holy Week.
22—Wednesday of Holy Week.
23—Thursday of Holy Week. Holy Thursday. The Easter Triduum begins with evening Mass of the Supper of the Lord. [St. Turibius, bishop; optional memorial.]
24—Friday of the Passion. Good Friday. *Fast and abstinence.*
25—Holy Saturday. The Easter Vigil.
26—**Easter Sunday; solemnity.** (Acts 10:34a, 37-43; Col. 3:1-4 or 1 Cor. 5:6b-8; Jn. 20:1-9 or Lk. 24:1-12, (evening) Lk. 24:13-35.)
27—Monday of Easter Octave.
28—Tuesday of Easter Octave.
29—Wednesday of Easter Octave.
30—Thursday of Easter Octave.
31—Friday of Easter Octave.

Liturgical events of Holy Week, and especially of the Sacred Triduum, from the evening Mass of Holy Thursday to Easter, are climactic celebrations of the Paschal Mystery of the suffering, death and resurrection of Jesus for the salvation of mankind.

One important convention of the year is that of the National Catholic Educational Association, to be held during Easter Week in Chicago.

APRIL 1989

Prayer Intention: For a progressive and balanced reduction in nuclear and conventional weapons and efficient control of the sale of arms.

1—Saturday of Easter Octave.
2—**Second Sunday of Easter.** (Acts 5:12-16; Rv. 1:9-11a, 12-13, 17-19; Jn. 20:19-31.) [St. Francis of Paola, hermit; optional memorial.]
3—Mon. Annunciation of the Lord; solemnity (transferred from Mar. 25).
4—Tues. Weekday. St. Isidore of Seville, optional memorial.
5—Wed. Weekday. St. Vincent Ferrer, priest; optional memorial.
6—Thurs. Weekday.
7—Fri. St. John Baptist de la Salle, priest; memorial.
8—Sat. Weekday.
9—**Third Sunday of Easter.** (Acts 5:27b-32, 40b-41; Rv. 5:11-14; Jn. 21:1-19.)
10—Mon. Weekday.
11—Tues. St. Stanislaus, bishop-martyr; memorial.
12—Wed. Weekday.
13—Thurs. Weekday. St. Martin I, pope-martyr; optional memorial.
14—Fri. Weekday.
15—Sat. Weekday.
16—**Fourth Sunday of Easter.** (Acts. 13:14, 43-52; Rv. 7:9, 14b-17; Jn. 10:27-30.)
17—Mon. Weekday.
18—Tues. Weekday.
19—Wed. Weekday.
20—Thurs. Weekday.
21—Fri. Weekday. St. Anselm, bishop-doctor; optional memorial.
22—Sat. Weekday.
23—**Fifth Sunday of Easter.** (Acts 14:21-27; Rv. 21:1-5a; Jn. 13:31-33a, 34-35.) [St. George, martyr; optional memorial.]
24—Mon. Weekday. St. Fidelis of Sigmaringen, priest-martyr; optional memorial.
25—Tues. St. Mark, evangelist; feast.
26—Wed. Weekday.
27—Thurs. Weekday.
28—Fri. Weekday. St. Peter Chanel, priest-martyr; optional memorial.
29—Sat. St. Catherine of Siena, virgin-doctor; memorial.
30—**Sixth Sunday of Easter.** (Acts 15:1-2, 22-29; Rv. 21:10-14, 22-23; Jn. 14:23-29.) [St. Pius V, pope; optional memorial.]

Pope John Paul's appeals for arms reduction have been repeated time and again by the bishops of the United States, as well as leaders of the Church in other countries. He observed in his latest encyclical letter: "If arms production is a serious disorder in the present world with regard to human needs and the employment of means capable of satisfying those needs, the arms trade is equally to blame."

MAY 1989

Prayer Intention: That young people, following Mary's example, respond generously to God's call with the missionary spirit of faith.

1—Mon. St. Joseph the Worker; optional memorial.
2—Tues. St. Athanasius, bishop-doctor; memorial.
3—Wed. Sts. Philip and James, apostles; feast.
4—**Thurs. Ascension of the Lord; solemnity. Holy day of obligation.** (Acts 1:1-11; Eph. 1:17-23; Lk. 24:46-53.)
5—Fri. Weekday.
6—Sat. Weekday.
7—**Seventh Sunday of Easter.** (Acts 7:55-60; Rv. 22:12-14, 16-17, 20; Jn. 17:20-26.)
8—Mon. Weekday.
9—Tues. Weekday.
10—Wed. Weekday.
11—Thurs. Weekday.
12—Fri. Weekday. Sts. Nereus and Achilleus, martyrs, or St. Pancras, martyr; optional memorials.
13—Sat. Weekday.
14—**Sun. Pentecost; solemnity.** (Acts 2:1-11; 1 Cor. 12:3b-7, 12-13; Jn. 20:19-23.) [St. Matthias, apostle; feast.]
15—Mon. Weekday. (Sixth Week of the Year.)
16—Tues. Weekday.
17—Wed. Weekday.
18—Thurs. Weekday. St. John I, pope-martyr; optional memorial.
19—Fri. Weekday.
20—Sat. Weekday. St. Bernardine of Siena, priest; or BVM on Saturday; optional memorials.
21—**Trinity Sunday; solemnity.** (Prv. 8:22-31; Rom. 5:1-5; Jn. 16:12-15.)
22—Mon. Weekday. (Seventh Week of the Year.)
23—Tues. Weekday.
24—Wed. Weekday.
25—Thurs. Weekday. St. Bede the Venerable, priest-doctor, or St. Gregory VII, pope, or St. Mary Magdalene de Pazzi, virgin; optional memorials.
26—Fri. St. Philip Neri, priest; memorial.
27—Sat. Weekday. St. Augustine of Canterbury, bishop, or BVM on Saturday; optional memorials.
28—**Sun. Corpus Christi (in U.S.); solemnity.** (Gn. 14:18-20; 1 Cor. 11:23-26; Lk. 9:11b-17).
29—Mon. Weekday. (Eighth Week of the Year.)
30—Tues. Weekday.
31—Wed. Visitation of Blessed Mary the Virgin; feast.

The solemnities of the Ascension of the Lord and Pentecost are principal celebrations of the Easter season.
  Meetings during the month include the World Conference on Mission and Evangelism, May 22 to June 1, and the annual convention of the Catholic Press Association, May 24 to 27.

JUNE 1989

Prayer Intention: That the Heart of Christ strengthen families as they witness to faith and love.

1—Thurs. St. Justin, martyr; memorial.
2—Fri. Sacred Heart of Jesus; solemnity. [Sts. Marcellinus and Peter, martyrs; optional memorial.]
3—Sat. Sts. Charles Lwanga and Companions, martyrs; memorial. [Immaculate Heart of Mary; optional memorial.]
4—**Ninth Sunday of the Year.** (1 Kgs. 8:41-43; Gal. 1:1-2, 6-10; Lk. 7:1-10.)
5—Mon. St. Boniface, bishop-martyr; memorial.
6—Tues. Weekday. St. Norbert, bishop; optional memorial.
7—Wed. Weekday.
8—Thurs. Weekday.
9—Fri. Weekday. St. Ephraem, deacon-doctor; optional memorial.
10—Sat. Weekday. BVM on Saturday; optional memorial.
11—**Tenth Sunday of the Year.** (1 Kgs. 17:17-24; Gal. 1:11-19; Lk. 7:11-17.) [St. Barnabas, apostle; memorial.]
12—Mon. Weekday.
13—Tues. St. Anthony of Padua, priest-doctor; memorial.
14—Wed. Weekday.
15—Thurs. Weekday.
16—Fri. Weekday.
17—Sat. Weekday. BVM on Saturday; optional memorial.
18—**Eleventh Sunday of the Year.** (2 Sm. 12:7-10, 13; Gal. 2:16, 19-21; Lk. 7:36 to 8:3.)
19—Mon. Weekday. St. Romuald, abbot; optional memorial.
20—Tues. Weekday.
21—Wed. St. Aloysius Gonzaga, religious; memorial.
22—Thurs. Weekday. St. Paulinus of Nola, bishop, or Sts. John Fisher, bishop-martyr, and Thomas More, martyr; optional memorials.
23—Fri. Weekday.
24—Sat. Birth of St. John the Baptist; solemnity.
25—**Twelfth Sunday of the Year.** (Zec. 12:10-11; Gal. 3:26-29; Lk. 9:18-24.)
26—Mon. Weekday.
27—Tues. Weekday. St. Cyril of Alexandria, bishop-doctor; optional memorial.
28—Wed. St. Irenaeus, bishop-martyr; memorial.
29—Thurs. Sts. Peter and Paul, apostles; solemnity.
30—Fri. Weekday. First Martyrs of the Roman Church; optional memorial.

At the time of Almanac publication, Pope John Paul was tentatively scheduled to visit five countries — Sweden, Norway, Denmark, Finland and Iceland between June 1 and 9.
  Also scheduled during the month is the semiannual meeting of the U.S. bishops' conferences at Seton Hall University.

JULY 1989

Prayer Intention: For all who suffer, and particularly for those who are incurably ill.

1—Sat. Weekday. BVM on Saturday; optional memorial.
2—**Thirteenth Sunday of the Year.** (1 Kgs. 19:16b, 19-21; Gal. 5:1, 13-18; Lk. 9:51-62.)
3—Mon. St. Thomas, apostle; feast.
4—Tues. Independence Day Votive Mass (prescribed in U.S.). Weekday. St. Elizabeth of Portugal; optional memorial.
5—Wed. Weekday. St. Anthony Zaccaria, priest; optional memorial.
6—Thurs. Weekday. St. Maria Goretti, virgin-martyr; optional memorial.
7—Fri. Weekday.
8—Sat. Weekday. BVM on Saturday; optional memorial.
9—**Fourteenth Sunday of the Year.** (Is. 66:10-14c; Gal. 6:14-18; Lk. 10:1-12, 17-20.)
10—Mon. Weekday.
11—Tues. St. Benedict, abbot; memorial.
12—Wed. Weekday.
13—Thurs. Weekday. St. Henry; optional memorial.
14—Fri. Bl. Kateri Tekakwitha, virgin; memorial (in U.S.). Weekday. St. Camillus de Lellis, priest; optional memorial.
15—Sat. St. Bonaventure, bishop-doctor; memorial.
16—**Fifteenth Sunday of the Year.** (Dt. 30:10-14; Col. 1:15-20; Lk. 10:25-37.) [Our Lady of Mt. Carmel; optional memorial.]
17—Mon. Weekday.
18—Tues. Weekday.
19—Wed. Weekday.
20—Thurs. Weekday.
21—Fri. Weekday. St. Lawrence of Brindisi, priest-doctor; optional memorial.
22—Sat. St. Mary Magdalene; memorial.
23—**Sixteenth Sunday of the Year.** (Gn. 18:1-10a; Col. 1:24-28; Lk. 10:38-42.) [St. Bridget, religious, optional memorial.]
24—Mon. Weekday.
25—Tues. St. James, apostle; feast.
26—Wed. Sts. Joachim and Anne, parents of Blessed Mary the Virgin; memorial.
27—Thurs. Weekday.
28—Fri. Weekday.
29—Sat. St. Martha; memorial.
30—**Seventeenth Sunday of the Year.** (Gn. 18:20-32; Col. 2:12-14; Lk. 11:1-13.) [St. Peter Chrysologus, bishop-doctor, optional memorial.]
31—Mon. St. Ignatius of Loyola, priest; memorial.

In accord with the prayer intention for the month are remarks of Pope John Paul, echoing those of saints, that the grace of God is in suffering; and that, without it, there can be no progress in the spiritual life. He speaks of suffering joined to the redemptive suffering of Christ.

AUGUST 1989

Prayer Intention: For a greater spirit of mutual respect and solidarity among nations, especially in Latin America.

1—Tues. St. Alphonsus Liguori, bishop-doctor; memorial.
2—Wed. Weekday. St. Eusebius of Vercelli, bishop; optional memorial.
3—Thurs. Weekday.
4—Fri. St. John Vianney, priest; memorial.
5—Sat. Weekday. Dedication of St. Mary Major Basilica; optional memorial.
6—**Sun. Transfiguration of the Lord; feast.** (Dn. 7:9-10, 13-14; 2 Pt. 1:16-19; Lk. 9:28b-36.)
7—Mon. Weekday. Sts. Sixtus II, pope, and Companions, martyrs, or St. Cajetan, priest; optional memorials. (Eighteenth Week of the Year.)
8—Tues. St. Dominic, priest; memorial.
9—Wed. Weekday.
10—Thurs. St. Lawrence, deacon-martyr; feast.
11—Fri. St. Clare, virgin; memorial.
12—Sat. Weekday. BVM on Saturday; optional memorial.
13—**Nineteenth Sunday of the Year.** (Wis. 18:6-9; Heb. 11:1-2, 8-19; Lk. 12:32-48.) [Sts. Pontian, pope, and Hippolytus, priest, martyrs; optional memorial.]
14—Mon. St. Maximilian Kolbe, priest-martyr; memorial.
15—**Tues. Assumption of Blessed Mary the Virgin; solemnity. Holy day of obligation.** (Rv. 11:19a and 12:1-6a, 10ab; 1 Cor. 15:20-26; Lk. 1:39-56.)
16—Wed. Weekday. St. Stephen of Hungary; optional memorial.
17—Thurs. Weekday.
18—Fri. Weekday.
19—Sat. Weekday. St. John Eudes, priest; optional memorial.
20—**Twentieth Sunday of the Year.** (Jer. 38:4-6, 8-10; Heb. 12:1-4; Lk. 12:49-53.) [St. Bernard of Clairvaux, abbot-doctor; memorial.]
21—Mon. St. Pius X, pope; memorial.
22—Tues. Queenship of Mary; memorial.
23—Wed. Weekday. St. Rose of Lima, virgin; optional memorial.
24—Thurs. St. Bartholomew, apostle; feast.
25—Fri. Weekday. St. Louis, or St. Joseph Calasanz, priest; optional memorials.
26—Sat. Weekday. BVM on Saturday; optional memorial.
27—**Twenty-First Sunday of the Year.** (Is. 66:18-21; Heb. 12:5-7, 11-13; Lk. 13:22-30.) [St. Monica, memorial.]
28—Mon. St. Augustine, bishop-doctor; memorial.
29—Tues. Beheading of St. John the Baptist; memorial.
30—Wed. Weekday.
31—Thurs. Weekday.

A headline event is the Pope's visit to Santiago de Compostela, Spain, for an international youth rally August 19 and 20.

SEPTEMBER 1989

Prayer Intention: That young people, inspired by the Gospel, realize their ideals of liberty, human progress and the common good.

1—Fri. Weekday.
2—Sat. Weekday. BVM on Saturday, optional memorial.
3—**Twenty-Second Sunday of the Year.** (Sir. 3:17-18, 20, 28-29; Heb. 12:18-19, 22-24a; Lk. 14:1, 7-14.) [St. Gregory the Great, pope-doctor; memorial.]
4—Mon. Labor Day Votive Mass (prescribed in U.S.). Weekday.
5—Tues. Weekday.
6—Wed. Weekday.
7—Thurs. Weekday.
8—Fri. Birth of Mary; feast.
9—Sat. St. Peter Claver, priest; memorial (in U.S.). Weekday.
10—**Twenty-Third Sunday of the Year.** (Wis. 9:13-18b; Phlm. 9b-10, 12-17; Lk. 14:24-33.)
11—Mon. Weekday.
12—Tues. Weekday.
13—Wed. St. John Chrysostom, bishop-doctor; memorial.
14—Thurs. Triumph of the Cross; feast.
15—Fri. Our Lady of Sorrows; memorial.
16—Sat. Sts. Cornelius, pope, and Cyprian, bishop, martyrs; memorial.
17—**Twenty-Fourth Sunday of the Year.** (Ex. 32:7-11, 13-14; 1 Tm. 1:12-17; Lk. 15:1-32.) [St. Robert Bellarmine, bishop-doctor; optional memorial.]
18—Mon. Weekday.
19—Tues. Weekday. St. Januarius, bishop-martyr; optional memorial.
20—Wed. Sts. Andrew Kim, priest, Paul Chong, lay apostle, and Companions, martyrs of Korea; memorial.
21—Thurs. St. Matthew, apostle-evangelist; feast.
22—Fri. Weekday.
23—Sat. Weekday. BVM on Saturday; optional memorial.
24—**Twenty-Fifth Sunday of the Year.** (Am. 8:4-7; 1 Tm. 2:1-8; Lk. 16:1-13.)
25—Mon. Weekday.
26—Tues. Weekday. Sts. Cosmas and Damian, martyrs; optional memorial.
27—Wed. St. Vincent de Paul, priest; memorial.
28—Thurs. Weekday. St. Wenceslaus, martyr, or Sts. Lawrence Ruiz and companions, martyrs; optional memorials.
29—Fri. Sts. Michael, Gabriel and Raphael, archangels; feast.
30—Sat. St. Jerome, priest-doctor; memorial.

In various writings and addresses, especially in the encyclical letter "Sollicitudo Rei Socialis," Pope John Paul mentions the need and efforts required for the realization of a civilization of work and a civilization of love of God and neighbor, through the collaboration of people.

OCTOBER 1989

Prayer Intention: For candidates to the priesthood and the religious life, especially those preparing to serve in young churches.

1—**Twenty-Sixth Sunday of the Year.** (Am. 6:1a, 4-7; 1 Tm. 6:11-16; Lk. 16:19-31.) [St. Therese of the Child Jesus, virgin; memorial.]
2—Mon. Guardian Angels; memorial.
3—Tues. Weekday.
4—Wed. St. Francis of Assisi; memorial.
5—Thurs. Weekday.
6—Fri. Weekday. Bl. Marie-Rose Durocher, virgin; optional memorial (in U.S.); St. Bruno, priest; optional memorial.
7—Sat. Our Lady of the Rosary; memorial.
8—**Twenty-Seventh Sunday of the Year.** (Hb. 1:2-3 and 2:2-4; 2 Tm. 1:6-8, 13-14; Lk. 17:5-10.)
9—Mon. Weekday. Sts. Denis, bishop, and Companions, martyrs, or St. John Leonard, priest; optional memorials.
10—Tues. Weekday.
11—Wed. Weekday.
12—Thurs. Weekday.
13—Fri. Weekday.
14—Sat. Weekday. St. Callistus I, pope-martyr; optional memorial.
15—**Twenty-Eighth Sunday of the Year.** (2 Kgs. 5:14-17; 2 Tm. 2:8-13; Lk. 17:11-19.) [St. Teresa of Jesus (Avila), virgin-doctor; memorial.]
16—Mon. Weekday. St. Hedwig, religious, or St. Margaret Mary Alacoque, virgin; optional memorials.
17—Tues. St. Ignatius of Antioch, bishop-martyr; memorial.
18—Wed. St. Luke, evangelist; feast.
19—Thurs. Sts. Isaac Jogues, John de Brebeuf, priests, and Companions, martyrs; memorial (in U.S.). Weekday. St. Paul of the Cross; optional memorial.
20—Fri. Weekday.
21—Sat. Weekday. BVM on Saturday; optional memorial.
22—**Twenty-Ninth Sunday of the Year.** (Ex. 17:8-13; 2 Tm. 3:14 to 4:2; Lk. 18:1-8.)
23—Mon. Weekday. St. John of Capistrano, priest; optional memorial.
24—Tues. Weekday. St. Anthony Mary Claret, bishop; optional memorial.
25—Wed. Weekday.
26—Thurs. Weekday.
27—Fri. Weekday.
28—Sat. Sts. Simon and Jude, apostles; feast.
29—**Thirtieth Sunday of the Year.** (Sir. 35:12-14, 16-18; 2 Tm. 4:6-8, 16-18; Lk. 18:9-14.)
30—Mon. Weekday.
31—Tues. Weekday.

"Christ in the Eucharist, Source of Peace," is the theme of the 44th International Eucharistic Congress October 5 to 8 in Seoul, Korea. The Pope expressed hope for the stimulation of ecumenical initiatives.

NOVEMBER 1989

Prayer Intention: For young nations, especially in Africa, that the aid of developed nations assist them to attain authentic progress in the full utilization of their own resources.

1—**Wed. All Saints; solemnity. Holy day of obligation.** (Rv. 7:2-4, 9-14; 1 Jn. 3:1-3; Mt. 5:1-12a.)
2—Thurs. Commemoration of All the Faithful Departed (All Souls' Day).
3—Fri. Weekday. St. Martin de Porres, religious; optional memorial.
4—Sat. St. Charles Borromeo, bishop; memorial.
5—**Thirty-First Sunday of the Year.** (Wis. 11:23 to 12:2; 2 Thes. 1:11 to 2:2; Lk. 19:1-10.)
6—Mon. Weekday.
7—Tues. Weekday.
8—Wed. Weekday.
9—Thurs. Dedication of St. John Lateran (Archbasilica of Most Holy Savior); feast.
10—Fri. St. Leo the Great, pope-doctor; memorial.
11—Sat. St. Martin of Tours, bishop; memorial.
12—**Thirty-Second Sunday of the Year.** (2 Mc. 7:1-2, 9-14; 2 Thes. 2:16 to 3:5; Lk. 20:27-38.) [St. Josaphat, bishop-martyr; memorial.]
13—Mon. St. Frances Xavier Cabrini, virgin; memorial (in U.S.).
14—Tues. Weekday.
15—Wed. Weekday. St. Albert the Great, bishop-doctor; optional memorial.
16—Thurs. Weekday. St. Margaret of Scotland, or St. Gertrude, virgin; optional memorials.
17—Fri. St. Elizabeth of Hungary, religious; memorial.
18—Sat. Weekday. Dedication of Basilicas of Sts. Peter and Paul, or BVM on Saturday; optional memorials.
19—**Thirty-Third Sunday of the Year.** (Mal. 3:19-20a; 2 Thes. 3:7-12; Lk. 21:5-19.)
20—Mon. Weekday.
21—Tues. Presentation of Blessed Mary the Virgin; memorial.
22—Wed. St. Cecilia, virgin-martyr; memorial.
23—Thurs. Thanksgiving Day Votive Mass (prescribed in U.S.). Weekday. St. Clement I, pope-martyr, or St. Columban, abbot; optional memorials.
24—Fri. Weekday.
25—Sat. Weekday. BVM on Saturday; optional memorial.
26—**Sun. Christ the King; solemnity.** (2 Sm. 5:1-3; Col. 1:12-20; Lk. 23:35-43.)
27—Mon. Weekday. (Thirty-Fourth [Last] Week of the Year.)
28—Tues. Weekday.
29—Wed. Weekday.
30—Thurs. St. Andrew, apostle; feast.

The communion of saints embraces the faithful on earth, the blessed in heaven and the souls in purgatory. We, the living, pray in honor of the saints and for the release of those in the state of purification.

DECEMBER 1989

Prayer Intention: That Our Lady and St. Joseph protect all parents and serve as their models.

1—Fri. Weekday.
2—Sat. Weekday. BVM on Saturday; optional memorial.
3—**First Sunday of Advent.** [Start of 1990 liturgical year] (Is. 2:1-5; Rom. 13:11-14; Mt. 24:37-44.) [St. Francis Xavier, priest; memorial.]
4—Mon. Weekday of Advent. St. John Damascene, priest-doctor; optional memorial.
5—Tues. Weekday of Advent.
6—Wed. Weekday of Advent. St. Nicholas, bishop; optional memorial.
7—Thurs. St. Ambrose, bishop-doctor; memorial.
8—**Fri. Immaculate Conception of Blessed Mary the Virgin. Holy day of obligation.** (Gn. 3:9-15, 20; Eph. 1:3-6, 11-12; Lk. 1:26-38.)
9—Sat. Weekday of Advent.
10—**Second Sunday of Advent.** (Is. 11:1-10; Rom. 15:4-9; Mt. 3:1-12.)
11—Mon. Weekday of Advent. St. Damasus I, pope; optional memorial.
12—Tues. Our Lady of Guadalupe; feast (in U.S.). Weekday of Advent. St. Jane Frances de Chantal, religious; optional memorial.
13—Wed. St. Lucy, virgin-martyr; memorial.
14—Thurs. St. John of the Cross, priest-doctor; memorial.
15—Fri. Weekday of Advent.
16—Sat. Weekday of Advent.
17—**Third Sunday of Advent.** (Is. 35:1-6a, 10; Jas. 5:7-10; Mt. 11:2-11.)
18—Mon. Weekday of Advent.
19—Tues. Weekday of Advent.
20—Wed. Weekday of Advent.
21—Thurs. Weekday of Advent. St. Peter Canisius, priest-doctor; optional memorial.
22—Fri. Weekday of Advent.
23—Sat. Weekday of Advent. St. John of Kanty, priest; optional memorial.
24—**Fourth Sunday of Advent.** (Is. 7:10-14; Rom. 1:1-7; Mt. 1:18-24.)
25—**Mon. Christmas. Birth of the Lord; solemnity. Holy day of obligation.** (Vigil — Is. 62:1-5; Acts 13:16-17, 22-25; Mt. 1:1-25. Midnight—Is. 9:1-6; Ti. 2:11-14; Lk. 2:1-14. At Dawn — Is. 62:11-12; Ti. 3:4-7; Lk. 2:15-20. During the Day — Is. 52:7-10; Heb. 1:1-6; Jn. 1:1-18.)
26—Tues. St. Stephen, first martyr; feast.
27—Wed. St. John, apostle-evangelist; feast.
28—Thurs. Holy Innocents, martyrs; feast.
29—Fri. Fifth Day of Christmas Octave. St. Thomas Becket, bishop-martyr; optional memorial.
30—Sat. Sixth Day of Christmas Octave.
31—**Sun. Holy Family; feast.** (Sir. 3:2-6, 12-14; Col. 3:12-21; Mt. 2:13-15, 19-23.) [St. Sylvester I, pope; optional memorial.]

The feast of the Holy Family, December 31, exemplifies family relationships.

TABLE OF MOVABLE FEASTS

Year	Ash Wednesday	Easter	Ascension	Pentecost	Weeks of Ordinary Time Before Lent		Weeks of Ordinary Time After Pent.		First Sunday of Advent
					Week	Ends	Week	Begins	
1989	Feb. 8	Mar. 26	May 4	May 14	5	Feb. 7	6	May 15	Dec. 3
1990	Feb. 28	Apr. 15	May 24	June 3	8	Feb. 27	9	June 4	Dec. 2
1991	Feb. 13	Mar. 31	May 9	May 19	5	Feb. 12	7	May 20	Dec. 1
1992	Mar. 4	Apr. 19	May 28	June 7	8	Mar. 3	10	June 8	Nov. 29
1993	Feb. 24	Apr. 11	May 20	May 30	7	Feb. 23	9	May 31	Nov. 28
1994	Feb. 16	Apr. 3	May 12	May 22	6	Feb. 15	8	May 23	Nov. 27
1995	Mar. 1	Apr. 16	May 25	June 4	8	Feb. 28	9	June 5	Dec. 3
1996	Feb. 21	Apr. 7	May 16	May 26	7	Feb. 20	8	May 27	Dec. 1
1997	Feb. 12	Mar. 30	May 8	May 18	5	Feb. 11	7	May 19	Nov. 30
1998	Feb. 25	Apr. 12	May 21	May 31	7	Feb. 24	9	June 1	Nov. 29
1999	Feb. 17	Apr. 4	May 13	May 23	6	Feb. 16	8	May 24	Nov. 28
2000	Mar. 8	Apr. 23	June 1	June 11	9	Mar. 7	10	June 12	Dec. 3
2001	Feb. 28	Apr. 15	May 24	June 3	8	Feb. 27	9	June 4	Dec. 2
2002	Feb. 13	Mar. 31	May 9	May 19	5	Feb. 12	7	May 20	Dec. 1
2003	Mar. 5	Apr. 20	May 29	June 8	8	Mar. 4	10	June 9	Nov. 30
2004	Feb. 25	Apr. 11	May 20	May 30	7	Feb. 24	9	May 31	Nov. 28
2005	Feb. 9	Mar. 27	May 5	May 15	5	Feb. 8	7	May 16	Nov. 27
2006	Mar. 1	Apr. 16	May 25	June 4	8	Feb. 28	9	June 5	Dec. 3
2007	Feb. 21	Apr. 8	May 17	May 27	7	Feb. 20	8	May 28	Dec. 2
2008	Feb. 6	Mar. 23	May 1	May 11	4	Feb. 5	6	May 12	Nov. 30
2009	Feb. 25	Apr. 12	May 21	May 31	7	Feb. 24	9	June 1	Nov. 29
2010	Feb. 17	Apr. 4	May 13	May 23	6	Feb. 16	8	May 24	Nov. 28
2011	Mar. 9	Apr. 24	June 2	June 12	9	Mar. 8	11	June 13	Nov. 27
2012	Feb. 22	Apr. 8	May 17	May 27	7	Feb. 21	8	May 28	Dec. 2

Season of Ordinary Time

Weeks between the end of the Christmas season and the beginning of Lent, and from the day after Pentecost to the last Sunday of the liturgical year, belong to the season of Ordinary Time. The table indicates the number and terminal date of the week ending the first part, and the number and starting date of the week beginning the second part, of this season. In some years, a week of this season is eliminated because of calendar conditions.

Holiday Masses

Liturgical experiments in recent years have led to the development of votive Masses for national holidays, like those introduced in the U.S. for Thanksgiving Day in 1969 and July 4 in 1972. This development is in line with a custom whereby "from the earliest times the Church has crowned many non-Christian feasts with Christian fulfillment by instituting its own liturgical festivals" to coincide with them.

Labor Day, in lieu of a special votive Mass, may be observed with celebration of the Mass of St. Joseph the Worker.

Readings at Mass

The texts of scriptural readings for Mass on Sundays, holy days and some other days are indicated under the respective dates. The third (C) cycle of readings in the Lectionary is prescribed for the 1989 liturgical year (Nov. 27, 1988, to Dec. 2, 1989); the first (A) cycle is prescribed for the 1990 liturgical year which begins with the first Sunday of Advent, Dec. 3, 1989.

Weekday cycles of readings are the first and second, respectively, for liturgical years 1989 and 1990.

Monthly Prayer Intentions

Intentions chosen and recommended by Pope John Paul II to the prayers of the faithful and circulated by the Apostleship of Prayer are given under each month of the calendar. He has expressed his desire that all Catholics make these intentions their own "in the certainty of being united with the Holy Father and praying according to his intentions and desires." These intentions represent the worldwide needs of the Church as seen through the eyes of the Pope.

HOLY DAYS AND OTHER FEASTS

The following list includes the six holy days of obligation observed in the United States and additional observances of devotional and historical significance. The dignity or rank of observances is indicated by the terms: **solemnity** (highest in rank); **feast; memorial** (for universal observance); **optional memorial** (for celebration by choice).

All Saints, Nov. 1, holy day of obligation, solemnity. Commemorates all the blessed in heaven, and is intended particularly to honor the blessed who have no special feasts. The background of the feast dates to the fourth century when groups of martyrs, and later other saints, were honored on a common day in various places. In 609 or 610, the Pantheon, a pagan temple at Rome, was consecrated as a Christian church for the honor of Our Lady and the martyrs (later all saints). In 835, Gregory IV fixed Nov. 1 as the date of observance.

All Souls, Commemoration of the Faithful Departed, Nov. 2. The dead were prayed for from the earliest days of Christianity. By the sixth century it was customary in Benedictine monasteries to hold a commemoration of deceased members of the order at Pentecost. A common commemoration of all the faithful departed on the day after All Saints was instituted in 998 by St. Odilo, of the Abbey of Cluny, and an observance of this kind was accepted in Rome in the 14th century. In 1915, Benedict XV granted priests throughout the world permission to celebrate three Masses for this commemoration. He also granted a special indulgence for the occasion.

Annunciation of the Lord (formerly, Annunciation of the Blessed Virgin Mary), Mar. 25, solemnity. A feast of the Incarnation which commemorates the announcement by the Archangel Gabriel to the Virgin Mary that she was to become the Mother of Christ (Lk. 1:26-38), and the miraculous conception of Christ by her. The feast was instituted about 430 in the East. The Roman observance dates from the seventh century, when celebration was said to be universal.

Ascension of the Lord, movable observance held 40 days after Easter, holy day of obligation, solemnity. Commemorates the Ascension of Christ into heaven 40 days after his Resurrection from the dead (Mk. 16:19; Lk. 24:51; Acts 1:2). The feast recalls the completion of Christ's mission on earth for the salvation of all people and his entry into heaven with glorified human nature. The Ascension is a pledge of the final glorification of all who achieve salvation. Documentary evidence of the feast dates from early in the fifth century, but it was observed long before that time in connection with Pentecost and Easter.

Ash Wednesday, movable observance, six and one-half weeks before Easter. It was set as the first day of Lent by Pope St. Gregory the Great (590-604) with the extension of an earlier and shorter penitential season to a total period including 40 weekdays of fasting before Easter. It is a day of fast and abstinence. Ashes, symbolic of penance, are blessed and distributed among the faithful during the day. They are used to mark the forehead with the Sign of the Cross, with the reminder: "Remember, man, that you are dust, and unto dust you shall return," or: "Repent, and believe the Good News."

Assumption, Aug. 15, holy day of obligation, solemnity. Commemorates the taking into heaven of Mary, soul and body, at the end of her life on earth, a truth of faith that was proclaimed a dogma by Pius XII on Nov. 1, 1950. One of the oldest and most solemn feasts of Mary, it has a history dating back to at least the seventh century when its celebration was already established at Jerusalem and Rome.

Baptism of the Lord, movable, usually celebrated on the Sunday after January 6, feast. Recalls the baptism of Christ by John the Baptist (Mk. 1:9-11), an event associated with the liturgy of the Epiphany. This baptism was the occasion for Christ's manifestation of himself at the beginning of his public life.

Birth of Mary, Sept. 8, feast. This is a very old feast which originated in the East and found place in the Roman liturgy in the seventh century.

Candlemas Day, Feb. 2. See Presentation of the Lord.

Chair of Peter, Feb. 22, feast. The feast, which has been in the Roman calendar since 336, is a liturgical expression of belief in the episcopacy and hierarchy of the Church.

Christmas, Birth of Our Lord Jesus Christ, Dec. 25, holy day of obligation, solemnity. Commemorates the birth of Christ (Lk. 2:1-20). This event was originally commemorated in the East on the feast of Epiphany or Theophany. The Christmas feast itself originated in the West; by 354 it was certainly kept on Dec. 25. This date may have been set for the observance to offset pagan ceremonies held at about the same time to commemorate the birth of the sun at the winter solstice. There are texts for three Christmas Masses — at midnight, dawn and during the day.

Christ the King, movable, celebrated on the last Sunday of the liturgical year, solemnity. Commemorates the royal prerogatives of Christ and is equivalent to a declaration of his rights to the homage, service and fidelity of men in all phases of individual and social life. Pius XI instituted the feast Dec. 11, 1925.

Conversion of St. Paul, Jan. 25, feast. An observance mentioned in some calendars from the 8th and 9th centuries. Pope Innocent III (1198-1216) ordered its observance with great solemnity.

Corpus Christi, movable, celebrated on the Thursday (or Sunday, as in the U.S.) following Trinity Sunday, solemnity. Commemorates the institution of the Holy Eucharist (Mt. 26:26-28). The feast originated at Liege in 1246 and was extended throughout the Church in the West by Urban IV in 1264. St. Thomas Aquinas composed the Liturgy of the Hours for the feast.

Dedication of St. John Lateran, Nov. 9, feast. Commemorates the first public consecration of a church, that of the Basilica of the Most Holy Savior by Pope St. Sylvester Nov. 9, 324. The church, as well as the Lateran Palace, was the gift of Emperor Constantine. Since the 12th century it has been known as St. John Lateran, in honor of John the Baptist after whom the adjoining baptistery was named. It was rebuilt by Innocent X (1644-55), reconsecrated by Benedict XIII in 1726, and enlarged by Leo XIII (1878-1903). This basilica is regarded as the church of highest dignity in Rome and throughout the Roman Rite.

Dedication of St. Mary Major, Aug. 5, optional memorial. Commemorates the rebuilding and dedication by Pope Sixtus III (432-40) of a church in honor of Blessed Mary the Virgin. This is the Basilica of St. Mary Major on the Esquiline Hill in Rome. An earlier building was erected during the pontificate of Liberius (352-66); according to legend, it was located on a site covered by a miraculous fall of snow seen by a nobleman favored with a vision of Mary.

Easter, movable celebration held on the first Sunday after the full moon following the vernal equinox (between Mar. 22 and Apr. 25), solemnity with an octave. Commemorates the Resurrection of Christ from the dead (Mk. 16:1-7). The observance of this mystery, kept since the first days of the Church, extends throughout the Easter season which lasts until the feast of Pentecost, a period of 50 days. Every Sunday in the year is regarded as a "little" Easter. The date of Easter determines the dates of movable feasts, such as Ascension and Pentecost, and the number of weeks before Lent and after Pentecost.

Easter Vigil, called by St. Augustine the "Mother of All Vigils," the night before Easter. Ceremonies are all related to the Resurrection and renewal-in-grace theme of Easter: blessing of the new fire, procession with the Easter Candle, singing of the Easter Proclamation (Exsultet), Liturgy of the Word with at least three Old Testament readings, the Litany of Saints, blessing of water, baptism of converts and infants, renewal of baptismal promises, Liturgy of the Eucharist. The vigil ceremonies are held after sundown.

Epiphany of the Lord, Jan. 6 or (in the U.S.) a Sunday between Jan. 2 and 8, solemnity. Commemorates the manifestations of the divinity of Christ. It is one of the oldest Christian feasts, with an Eastern origin traceable to the beginning of the third century and antedating the Western feast of Christmas. Originally, it commemorated the manifestations of Christ's divinity — or Theophany — in his birth, the homage of the Magi, and baptism by John the Baptist. Later, the first two of these commemorations were transferred to Christmas when the Eastern Church adopted that feast between 380 and 430. The central feature of the Eastern observance now is the manifestation or declaration of Christ's divinity in his baptism and at the beginning of his public life. The Epiphany was adopted by the Western Church during the same period in which the Eastern Church accepted Christmas. In the Roman Rite, commemoration is made in the Mass of the homage of the wise men from the East (Mt. 2:1-12).

Good Friday, the Friday before Easter, the second day of the Easter Triduum. Liturgical elements of the observance are commemoration of the Passion and Death of Christ in the reading of the Passion (according to John), special prayers for the Church and people of all ranks, the veneration of the Cross, and a Communion service. The celebration takes place in the afternoon, preferably at 3:00 p.m.

Guardian Angels, Oct. 2, memorial. Commemorates the angels who protect people from spiritual and physical dangers and assist them in doing good. A feast in their honor celebrated in Spain in the 16th century was extended to the whole Church by Paul V in 1608. In 1670, Clement X set Oct. 2 as the date of observance. Earlier, guardian angels were honored liturgically in conjunction with the feast of St. Michael.

Holy Family, movable observance on the Sunday after Christmas, feast. Commemorates the Holy Family of Jesus, Mary and Joseph as the model of domestic society, holiness and virtue. The devotional background of the feast was very strong in the 17th century. In the 18th century, in prayers composed for a special Mass, a Canadian bishop likened the Christian family to the Holy Family. Leo XIII consecrated families to the Holy Family. In 1921, Benedict XV extended the Divine Office and Mass of the feast to the whole Church.

Holy Innocents, Dec. 28, feast. Commemorates the infants who suffered death at the hands of Herod's soldiers seeking to kill the child Jesus (Mt. 2:13-18). A feast in their honor has been observed since the fifth century.

Holy Saturday, the day before Easter. The Sacrifice of the Mass is not celebrated, and Holy Communion may be given only as Viaticum. If possible the Easter fast should be observed until the Easter Vigil.

Holy Thursday, the Thursday before Easter. Commemorates the institution of the sacraments of the Eucharist and holy orders, and the washing of the feet of the Apostles by Jesus at the Last Supper. The Mass of the Lord's Supper in the evening marks the beginning of the Easter Triduum. Following the Mass, there is a procession of the Blessed Sacrament to a place of reposition for adoration by the faithful. At an earlier Mass of Chrism, bishops bless oils (of catechumens, chrism, the sick) for use during the year. (For pastoral reasons, diocesan bishops may permit additional Masses, but these should not overshadow the principal Mass of the Lord's Supper.)

Immaculate Conception, Dec. 8, holy day of obligation, solemnity. Commemorates the fact that Mary, in view of her calling to be the Mother of Christ and in virtue of his merits, was preserved from the first moment of her conception from original sin and was filled with grace from the very beginning of her life. She was the only person so preserved from original sin. The present form of the feast dates from Dec. 8, 1854, when Pius IX defined the dogma of the Immaculate Conception. An earlier feast of the Conception, which testified to long-existing belief in this truth, was observed in the East by the eighth century, in Ireland in the ninth, and subsequently in European countries. In 1846, Mary was proclaimed patroness of the U.S. under this title.

Immaculate Heart of Mary, Saturday following the second Sunday after Pentecost, optional memorial. On May 4, 1944, Pius XII ordered this feast observed throughout the Church in order to obtain Mary's intercession for "peace among nations, freedom for the Church, the conversion of sinners, the love of purity and the practice of virtue." Two years earlier, he consecrated the entire human race to Mary under this title. Devotion to Mary under the title of her Most Pure Heart originated during the Middle Ages. It was given great impetus in the 17th century by the preaching of St. John Eudes, who was the first to celebrate a Mass and Divine Office of Mary under this title. A feast, celebrated in various places and on different dates, was authorized in 1799.

Joachim and Ann, July 26, memorial. Commemorates the parents of Mary. A joint feast, celebrated Sept. 9, originated in the East near the end of the sixth century. Devotion to Ann, introduced in the eighth century at Rome, became widespread in Europe in the 14th century; her feast was extended throughout the Latin Church in 1584. A feast of Joachim was introduced in the West in the 15th century.

John the Baptist, Birth, June 24, solemnity. The precursor of Christ, whose cousin he was, was commemorated universally in the liturgy by the fourth century. He is the only saint, except the Blessed Virgin Mary, whose birthday is observed as a feast. Another feast, on Aug. 29, commemorates his passion and death at the order of Herod (Mk. 6:14-29).

Joseph, Mar. 19, solemnity. Joseph is honored as the husband of the Blessed Virgin Mary, the patron and protector of the universal Church and workman. Devotion to him already existed in the eighth century in the East, and in the 11th in the West. Various feasts were celebrated before the 15th century when Mar. 19 was fixed for his commemoration; this feast was extended to the whole Church in 1621 by Gregory XV. In 1955, Pius XII instituted the feast of St. Joseph the Workman for observance May 1; this feast, which may be celebrated by local option, supplanted the Solemnity or Patronage of St. Joseph formerly observed on the third Wednesday after Easter. St. Joseph was proclaimed protector and patron of the universal Church in 1870 by Pius IX.

Michael, Gabriel and Raphael, Archangels, Sept. 29, feast. A feast bearing the title of Dedication of St. Michael the Archangel formerly commemorated on this date the consecration in 530 of a church near Rome in honor of Michael, the first angel given a liturgical feast. For a while, this feast was combined with a commemoration of the Guardian Angels. The separate feasts of Gabriel (Mar. 24) and Raphael (Oct. 24) were suppressed by the calendar in effect since 1970 and this joint feast of the three archangels was instituted.

Octave of Christmas, Jan. 1. See Solemnity of Mary, Mother of God.

Our Lady of Guadalupe, Dec. 12, feast (in the U.S.). Commemorates under this title the appearances of the Blessed Virgin Mary in 1531 to an Indian, Juan Diego, on Tepayac hill outside Mexico City (see Apparitions of the Blessed Virgin Mary). The celebration, observed as a memorial in the U.S., was raised to the rank of feast at the request of the National Conference of Catholic Bishops. Approval was granted in a decree dated Jan. 8, 1988.

Our Lady of Sorrows, Sept. 15, memorial. Recalls the sorrows experienced by Mary in her association with Christ: the prophecy of Simeon (Lk. 2:34-35), the flight into Egypt (Mt. 2:13-21), the three-day separation from Jesus (Lk. 2:41-50), and four incidents connected with the Passion: her meeting with Christ on the way to Calvary, the crucifixion, the removal of Christ's body from the cross, and his burial (Mt. 27:31-61; Mk. 15:20-47; Lk. 23:26-56; Jn. 19:17-42). A Mass and Divine Office of the feast were celebrated by the Servites, especially, in the 17th century, and in 1817 Pius VII extended the observance to the whole Church.

Our Lady of the Rosary, Oct. 7, memorial. Commemorates the Virgin Mary through recall of the mysteries of the Rosary which recapitulate events in her life and the life of Christ. The feast was instituted to commemorate a Christian victory over invading Mohammedan forces at Lepanto on Oct. 7, 1571, and was extended throughout the Church by Clement XI in 1716.

Passion Sunday (formerly called **Palm Sunday**), the Sunday before Easter. Marks the start of Holy Week by recalling the triumphal entry of Christ into Jerusalem at the beginning of the last week of his life (Mt. 21:1-9). A procession and other ceremonies commemorating this event were held in Jerusalem from very early Christian times and were adopted in Rome by the ninth century, when the blessing of palm for the occasion was introduced. Full liturgical observance includes the blessing of palm and a procession before the principal Mass of the day. The Passion, by Matthew, Mark or Luke, is read during the Mass.

Pentecost, also called **Whitsunday,** movable celebration held 50 days after Easter, solemnity. Commemorates the descent of the Holy Spirit upon the Apostles, the preaching of Peter and the other Apostles to Jews in Jerusalem, the baptism and aggregation of some 3,000 persons to the Christian community (Acts 2:1-41). It is regarded as the birthday of the Catholic Church. The original observance of the feast antedated the earliest extant documentary evidence from the third century.

Peter and Paul, Sts., June 29, solemnity. Commemorates the martyrdoms of Peter by crucifixion and Paul by beheading during the Neronian persecution. This joint commemoration of the chief Apostles dates at least from 258 at Rome.

Presentation of the Lord (formerly called Purification of the Blessed Virgin Mary, also Candlemas), Feb. 2, feast. Commemorates the presentation of Jesus in the Temple — according to prescriptions of Mosaic Law (Lv. 12:2-8; Ex. 13:2; Lk. 2:22-32) — and the purification of Mary 40 days after his birth. In the East, where the feast antedated fourth century testimony regarding its existence, it was observed primarily as a feast of Our Lord; in the West, where it was adopted later, it was regarded more as a feast of Mary until the calendar in effect since 1970. Its date was set for Feb. 2 after the celebration of Christmas was fixed for Dec. 25, late in the fourth century. The blessing of candles, probably in commemoration of Christ who was the Light to enlighten the Gentiles, became common about the 11th century and gave the feast the secondary name of Candlemas.

Queenship of Mary, Aug. 22, memorial. Commemorates the high dignity of Mary as Queen of heaven, angels and men. Universal observance of the memorial was ordered by Pius XII in the encyclical *Ad Caeli Reginam*, Oct. 11, 1954, near the close of a Marian Year observed in connection with the centenary of the proclamation of the dogma of the Immaculate Conception and four years after the proclamation of the dogma of the Assumption. The original date of the memorial was May 31.

Resurrection. See Easter.

Sacred Heart of Jesus, movable observance held on the Friday after the second Sunday after Pentecost (Corpus Christi, in the U.S.), solemnity. The object of the devotion is the divine Person of Christ, whose heart is the symbol of his love for men — for whom he accomplished the work of Redemption. The Mass and Office now used on the feast were prescribed by Pius XI in 1929. Devotion to the Sacred Heart was introduced into the liturgy in the 17th century through the efforts of St. John Eudes who composed an Office and Mass for the feast. It was furthered as the result of the revelations of St. Margaret Mary Alacoque after 1675 and by the work of Claude de la Colombiere, S.J. In 1765, Clement XIII approved a Mass and Office for the feast, and in 1856 Pius IX extended the observance throughout the Roman Rite.

Solemnity of Mary, Mother of God, Jan. 1, holy day of obligation, solemnity. The calendar in effect since 1970, in accord with Eastern tradition, reinstated the Marian character of this commemoration on the octave day of Christmas. The former feast of the Circumcision, dating at least from the first half of the sixth century, marked the initiation of Jesus (Lk. 2:21) in Judaism and by analogy focused attention on the initiation of persons in the Christian religion and their incorporation in Christ through baptism. The feast of the Solemnity supplants the former feast of the Maternity of Mary observed on Oct. 11.

Transfiguration of the Lord, Aug. 6, feast. Commemorates the revelation of his divinity by Christ to Peter, James and John on Mt. Tabor (Mt. 17:1-9). The feast, which is very old, was extended throughout the universal Church in 1457 by Callistus III.

Trinity, Most Holy, movable observance held on the Sunday after Pentecost, solemnity. Commemorates the most sublime mystery of the Christian faith, i.e., that there are Three Divine Persons — Father, Son and Holy Spirit — in one God (Mt. 28:18-20). A votive Mass of the Most Holy Trinity dates from the seventh century; an Office was composed in the 10th century; in 1334, John XXII extended the feast to the universal Church.

Triumph of the Cross, Sept. 14, feast. Commemorates the finding of the cross on which Christ was crucified, in 326 through the efforts of St. Helena, mother of Constantine; the consecration of the Basilica of the Holy Sepulchre nearly 10 years later: and the recovery in 628 or 629 by Emperor Heraclius of a major portion of the cross which had been removed by the Persians from its place of veneration at Jerusalem. The feast originated in Jerusalem and spread through the East before being adopted in the West. General adoption followed the building at Rome of the Basilica of the Holy Cross "in Jerusalem," so called because it was the place of enshrinement of a major portion of the cross of crucifixion.

Visitation, May 31, feast. Commemorates Mary's visit to her cousin Elizabeth after the Annunciation and before the birth of John the Baptist, the precursor of Christ (Lk. 1:39-47). The feast had a medieval origin and was observed in the Franciscan Order before being extended throughout the Church by Urban VI in 1389. It is one of the feasts of the Incarnation and is notable for its recall of the Magnificat, one of the few New Testament canticles, which acknowledges the unique gifts of God to Mary because of her role in the redemptive work of Christ. The canticle is recited at Evening Prayer in the Liturgy of the Hours.

SAINTS

Biographical sketches of additional saints and blessed are under other Almanac titles. See Index, under name of saint. For Beatification and Canonization procedures, see those entries in the Glossary.

An asterisk with a feast date indicates that the saint is listed in the General Roman Calendar or the proper calendar for U.S. dioceses. For rank of observances, see listing in calendar for current year on preceding pages.

Adjutor (d. 1131): Norman knight; fought in First Crusade; monk-recluse after his return; legendary accounts of incidents on journey to Crusade probably account for his patronage of yachtsmen; Apr. 30.

Agatha (d. c. 250): Sicilian virgin-martyr; her intercession credited in Sicily with stilling eruptions of Mt. Etna; patron of nurses; Feb. 5*.

Agnes (d. c. 304): Roman virgin-martyr; martyred at age of 10 or 12; patron of young girls; Jan. 21*.

Aloysius Gonzaga (1568-1591): Italian Jesuit; died while nursing plague-stricken; canonized 1726; patron of youth; June 21*.

Amand (d. c. 676): Apostle of Belgium; b. France; established monasteries throughout Belgium; Feb. 6.

Andre Bessette, Bl. (Bro. Andre) (1845-1937): Canadian Holy Cross Brother; prime mover in building of St. Joseph's Oratory, Montreal; beatified May 23, 1982; Jan. 6* (U.S.).

Andre Grasset de Saint Sauveur, Bl. (1758-1792): Canadian priest; martyred in France, Sept. 2, 1792, during the Revolution; one of a group called the Martyrs of Paris who were beatified in 1926; Sept. 2.

Saints

Andrew Bobola (1592-1657): Polish Jesuit; joined Jesuits at Vilna; worked for return of Orthodox to union with Rome; martyred; canonized 1938; May 16.

Andrew Corsini (1302-1373): Italian Carmelite; bishop of Fiesoli; mediator between quarrelsome Italian states; canonized 1629; Feb. 4.

Andrew Fournet (1752-1834): French priest; cofounder with St. Jeanne Elizabeth Bichier des Anges of the Daughters of the Holy Cross of St. Andrew; canonized 1933; May 13.

Andrew Kim, Paul Chong and Companions (d. between 1839-1867): Korean martyrs (103) killed in persecutions of 1839, 1846, 1866, and 1867; among them were Andrew Kim, the first Korean priest, and Paul Chong, lay apostle; canonized May 6, 1984, during Pope John Paul II's visit to Korea; entered into General Roman Calendar, 1985, as a memorial. Sept. 20*.

Angela Merici (1474-1540): Italian secular Franciscan; foundress of Company of St. Ursula, 1535, the first teaching order of women Religious in the Church; canonized 1807; Jan. 27*.

Angelico, Bl. (Fra Angelico; John of Faesulis) (1378-1455): Dominican; Florentine painter of early Renaissance; proclaimed blessed by John Paul II, 1983; patron of artists; Feb. 18.

Anne Mary Javouhey, Bl. (1779-1851): French virgin; foundress of Institute of St. Joseph of Cluny, 1812; beatified 1950; July 15.

Ansgar (801-865): Benedictine monk; b. near Amiens; archbishop of Hamburg; missionary in Denmark, Sweden, Norway and northern Germany; apostle of Scandinavia; Feb. 3*.

Anthony (c. 251-c. 354): Abbot; Egyptian hermit; patriarch of all monks; established communities for hermits which became models for monastic life, especially in the East; friend and supporter of St. Athanasius in the latter's struggle with the Arians; Jan. 17*.

Anthony Claret (1807-1870): Spanish bishop; founder of Missionary Sons of the Immaculate Heart of Mary (Claretians), 1849; archbishop of Santiago, Cuba, 1851-57; canonized 1950; Oct. 24*.

Anthony Gianelli (1789-1846): Italian bishop; as parish priest, founded the Daughters of Our Lady of the Garden, 1829; bishop of Bobbio, 1838; canonized 1951; June 7.

Anthony Zaccaria (1502-1539): Italian priest; founder of Barnabites (Clerks Regular of St. Paul), 1530; canonized 1897; July 5*.

Apollonia (d. 249): Deaconess of Alexandria; martyred during persecution of Decius; her patronage of dentists probably rests on tradition that her teeth were broken by pincers by her persecutors; Feb. 9.

Augustine of Canterbury (d. 604 or 605): Italian missionary; apostle of the English; sent by Pope Gregory I with 40 monks to evangelize England; arrived there 597; first archbishop of Canterbury; May 27*.

Bartolomea Capitania (1807-1833): Italian foundress with Vincenza Gerosa of the Sisters of Charity of Lovere; canonized 1950; July 26.

Beatrice da Silva Meneses (1424-1490): Foundress, b. Portugal; founded Congregation of the Immaculate Conception, 1484, in Spain; canonized 1976; Sept. 1.

Benedict Joseph Labre (1748-1783): French layman; pilgrim-beggar; noted for his piety and love of prayer before the Blessed Sacrament; canonized 1883; Apr. 16.

Benedict of Nursia (c. 480-547): Abbot; founder of monasticism in Western Europe; established monastery at Monte Cassino; proclaimed patron of Europe by Paul VI in 1964; July 11*.

Benedict the Black (il Moro) (1526-1589): Sicilian Franciscan; born a slave; joined Franciscans as lay brother; appointed guardian and novice master; canonized 1807; Apr. 4.

Bernadette Soubirous (1844-1879): French peasant girl favored with series of visions of Blessed Virgin Mary at Lourdes (see Lourdes Apparitions); joined Institute of Sisters of Notre Dame at Nevers, 1866; canonized 1933; Apr. 16.

Bernard of Montjoux (or Menthon) (d. 1081): Augustinian canon; probably born in Italy; founded Alpine hospices near the two passes named for him; patron of mountaineers; May 28.

Bernardine of Feltre, Bl. (1439-1494): Italian Franciscan preacher; a founder of montes pietatis; Sept. 28.

Bernardine of Siena (1380-1444): Italian Franciscan; noted preacher and missioner; spread of devotion to Holy Name is attributed to him; represented in art holding to his breast the monogram IHS; canonized 1450; May 20*.

Blase (d. c. 316): Armenian bishop; martyr; the blessing of throats on his feast day derives from tradition that he miraculously saved the life of a boy who had half-swallowed a fish bone; Feb. 3*.

Boniface (Winfrid) (d. 754): English Benedictine; bishop; martyr; apostle of Germany; established monastery at Fulda which became center of missionary work in Germany; archbishop of Mainz; martyred near Dukkum in Holland; June 5*.

Brendan (c. 489-583): Irish abbot; founded monasteries; his patronage of sailors probably rests on a legend that he made a seven-year voyage in search of a fabled paradise; called Brendan the Navigator; May 16.

Bridget (Brigid) (c. 450-525): Irish nun; founded religious community at Kildare, the first in Ireland; patron, with Sts. Patrick and Columba, of Ireland; Feb. 1.

Bridget (Birgitta) (c. 1303-1373): Swedish mystic; widow; foundress of Order of Our Savior (Brigittines); canonized 1391; patroness of Sweden; July 23*.

Bruno (1030-1101): German monk; founded Carthusians, 1084, in France; Oct. 6*.

Cabrini, Mother: See Frances Xavier Cabrini.

Cajetan (Gaetano) of Thiene (1480-1547): Italian lawyer; religious reformer; a founder of Oratory of Divine Love, forerunner of the Theatines; canonized 1671; Aug. 7*.

Callistus I (d. 222): Pope, 217-222; martyr; condemned Sabellianism and other heresies; advocated a policy of mercy toward repentant sinners; Oct. 14*.

Camillus de Lellis (1550-1614): Italian priest;

founder of Camillians (Ministers of the Sick); canonized 1746; patron of the sick and of nurses; July 14*.

Casimir (1458-1484): Polish prince; grand duke of Lithuania; noted for his piety; buried at cathedral in Vilna, Lithuania; canonized 1521; patron of Poland and Lithuania; Mar. 4*.

Cassian of Tangier (d. 298): Roman martyr; an official court stenographer who declared himself a Christian; patron of stenographers; Dec. 3.

Catherine Laboure (1806-1876): French Religious; favored with series of visions soon after she joined Sisters of Charity of St. Vincent de Paul in Paris in 1830; first Miraculous Medal (see Index) struck in 1832 in accord with one of the visions; canonized 1947; Nov. 28.

Catherine of Bologna (1413-1463): Italian Poor Clare; mystic, writer, artist; canonized 1712; patron of artists; May 9.

Cecilia (2nd-3rd century): Roman virgin-martyr; traditional patroness of musicians; Nov. 22*.

Charles Borromeo (1538-1584): Italian cardinal; nephew of Pope Pius IV; cardinal bishop of Milan; influential figure in Church reform in Italy; promoted education of clergy; canonized 1610; Nov. 4*.

Charles Lwanga and Companions (d. between 1885 and 1887): Twenty-two Martyrs of Uganda, many of them pages of King Mwanga of Uganda, who were put to death because they denounced his corrupt lifestyle; canonized 1964; first martyrs of black Africa; June 3*.

Charles of Sezze (1616-1670): Italian Franciscan lay brother who served in humble capacities; canonized 1959; Jan. 6.

Christopher (3rd cent.): Early Christian martyr inscribed in Roman calendar about 1550; feast relegated to particular calendars because of legendary nature of accounts of his life; traditional patron of travelers; July 25.

Clare (1194-1253): Foundress of Poor Clares; b. at Assisi; was joined in religious life by her sisters, Agnes and Beatrice, and eventually her widowed mother Ortolana; canonized 1255; patroness of television; Aug. 11*.

Clement Hofbauer (1751-1820): Redemptorist priest, missionary; born in Moravia; helped spread Redemptorists north of the Alps; canonized 1909; Mar. 15.

Clement I (d. c. 100): Pope, 88-97; third successor of St. Peter; wrote important letter to Church in Corinth settling disputes there; venerated as a martyr; Nov. 23*.

Columba (521-597): Irish monk; founded monasteries in Ireland; missionary in Scotland; established monastery at Iona which became the center for conversion of Picts, Scots, and Northern English; Scotland's most famous saint; June 9.

Columban (545-615): Irish monk; scholar; founded monasteries in England and Brittany (famous abbey of Luxeuil), forced into exile because of his criticism of Frankish court; spent last years in northern Italy where he founded abbey at Bobbio; Nov. 23*.

Conrad of Parzham (1818-1894): Bavarian Capuchin lay brother; served as porter at the Marian shrine of Altotting in Upper Bavaria for 40 years; canonized 1934; Apr. 21.

Contardo Ferrini, Bl. (1859-1902): Italian secular Franciscan; model of the Catholic professor; beatified 1947; patron of universities; Oct. 20.

Cornelius (d. 253): Pope, 251-253; promoted a policy of mercy with respect to readmission of repentant Christians who had fallen away during the persecution of Decius *(lapsi)*; banished from Rome during persecution of Gallus; regarded as a martyr; Sept. 16 (with Cyprian)*.

Cosmas and Damian (d. c. 303): Arabian twin brothers, physicians; martyred during Diocletian persecution; patrons of physicians; Sept. 26*.

Crispin and Crispinian (3rd cent.): Early Christian martyrs; said to have met their deaths in Gaul; patrons of shoemakers, a trade they pursued; Oct. 25.

Crispin of Viterbo (1668-1750): Capuchin brother; canonized June 20, 1982; May 21.

Cyprian (d. 258): Early ecclesiastical writer; b. Africa; bishop of Carthage, 249-258; supported Pope St. Cornelius concerning the readmission of Christians who had apostasized in time of persecution; erred in his teaching that baptism administered by heretics and schismatics was invalid; wrote *De Unitate;* Sept. 16 (with St. Cornelius)*.

Cyril and Methodius (9th century): Greek missionaries; brothers venerated as apostles of the Slavs; Cyril (d. 869) and Methodius (d. 885) began their missionary work in Moravia in 863; developed a Slavonic alphabet; used the vernacular in the liturgy, a practice that was eventually approved; declared patrons of Europe with St. Benedict, Dec. 31, 1980; Feb. 14*.

Damasus I (d. 384): Pope, 366-384; opposed Arians and Apollinarians; commissioned St. Jerome to work on Bible translation; developed Roman liturgy; Dec. 11*.

Damian: See Cosmas and Damian.

David (5th or 6th cent.): Nothing for certain known of his life; said to have founded monastery at Menevia; patron saint of Wales; Mar. 1.

Denis and Companions (d. 3rd cent.): Denis, bishop of Paris, and two companions identified by early writers as Rusticus, a priest, and Eleutherius, a deacon; martyred near Paris; Denis is popularly regarded as the apostle and a patron saint of France; Oct. 9*.

Dismas (1st cent.): Name given to repentant thief (Good Thief) to whom Jesus promised salvation (Lk. 23:40-43); regarded as patron of prisoners; Mar. 25.

Dominic (Dominic de Guzman) (1170-1221): Spanish priest; founded the Order of Preachers (Dominicans), 1215, in France; preached against the Albigensian heresy; a contemporary of St. Francis of Assisi; canonized 1234; Aug. 8*.

Dominic Savio (1842-1857): Italian youth; pupil of St. John Bosco; died before his 15th birthday; canonized 1954; patron of choir boys; May 6.

Dunstan (c. 910-988): English monk; archbishop of Canterbury; initiated reforms in religious life; counselor to several kings; considered one of greatest Anglo-Saxon saints; patron of armorers, goldsmiths, locksmiths, jewelers (trades in which he is said to have excelled); May 17.

Dymphna (dates unknown): Nothing certain known of her life; according to legend, she was an Irish maiden murdered by her heathen father at Gheel near Antwerp, Belgium, where she had fled to escape his advances; her relics were discovered there in the 13th century; since that time cures of mental illness and epilepsy have been attributed to her intercession; patron of those suffering from mental illness; May 15.

Edith Stein, Bl. (1891-1942): German Carmelite (Teresa Benedicta of the Cross); born of Jewish parents; author and lecturer; baptized in Catholic Church, 1922; arrested with her sister Rosa in 1942 and put to death at Auschwitz; beatified 1987, by Pope John Paul II during his visit to West Germany. Aug. 10.

Edmund Campion (1540-1581): English Jesuit; convert 1573; martyred at Tyburn; canonized 1970, one of the Forty English and Welsh Martyrs; Dec. 1.

Edward the Confessor (d. 1066): King of England, 1042-66; canonized 1161; Oct. 13.

Eligius (c. 590-660): Bishop; born in Gaul; founded monasteries and convents; bishop of Noyon and Tournai; famous worker in gold and silver; Dec. 1.

Elizabeth Ann Seton (1774-1821): American foundress; convert, 1805; founded Sisters of Charity in the U.S.; beatified 1963; canonized Sept. 14, 1975; the first American-born saint; Jan. 4 (U.S.)*.

Elizabeth of Hungary (1207-1231): Became secular Franciscan after death of her husband in 1227; devoted life to poor and destitute; a patron of the Secular Franciscan Order; canonized 1235; Nov. 17*.

Elizabeth of Portugal (1271-1336): Queen of Portugal; b. Spain; retired to Poor Clare convent as a secular Franciscan after the death of her husband; canonized 1626; July 4*.

Emily de Rodat (1787-1852): French foundress of the Congregation of the Holy Family of Villefranche; canonized 1950; Sept. 19.

Emily de Vialar (1797-1856): French foundress of the Sisters of St. Joseph of the Apparition; canonized 1951; June 17.

Erasmus (Elmo) (d. 303): Life surrounded by legend; martyred during Diocletian persecution; patron of sailors; June 2.

Ethelbert (552-616): King of Kent, England; baptized by St. Augustine of Canterbury, 597; issued legal code; furthered spread of Christianity; Feb. 26.

Euphrasia Pelletier (1796-1868): French Religious; founded Sisters of the Good Shepherd at Angers, 1829; canonized 1940; Apr. 24.

Eusebius of Vercelli (283-370): Italian bishop; exiled from his see (Vercelli) for a time because of his opposition to Arianism; considered a martyr because of sufferings he endured; Aug. 2*.

Fabian (d. 250): Pope, 236-250; martyred under Decius; Jan. 20*.

Felicity: See Perpetua and Felicity.

Ferdinand III (1198-1252): King of Castile and Leon; waged successful crusade against Mohammedans in Spain; founded university at Salamanca; canonized 1671; May 30.

Fiacre (Fiachra) (d. c. 670): Irish hermit; patron of gardeners; Aug. 30.

Fidelis of Sigmaringen (Mark Rey) (1577-1622): German Capuchin; lawyer before he joined the Capuchins; missionary to Swiss Protestants; stabbed to death by peasants who were told he was agent of Austrian emperor; Apr. 24*.

Frances of Rome (1384-1440): Italian model for housewives and widows; happily married for 40 years; after death of her husband in 1436 joined community of Benedictine Oblates she had founded; canonized 1608; patron of motorists; Mar. 9*.

Frances Xavier Cabrini (Mother Cabrini) (1850-1917): American foundress; b. Italy; founded the Missionary Sisters of the Sacred Heart, 1877; settled in the U.S. 1889; became an American citizen at Seattle 1909; worked among Italian immigrants; canonized 1946, the first American citizen so honored; Nov. 13 (U.S.)*.

Francis Borgia (1510-1572): Spanish Jesuit; joined Jesuits after death of his wife in 1546; became general of the Order, 1565; Oct. 10.

Francis Caracciolo (1563-1608): Italian priest; founder with Father Augustine Adorno of the Clerks Regular Minor (Adorno Fathers); canonized 1807; June 4.

Francis Fasani (1681-1742); Italian Conventual Franciscan; model of priestly ministry, especially in service to poor and imprisoned; canonized 1986; Nov. 29.

Francis of Assisi (Giovanni di Bernardone) (1181/82-1226): Founder of the Franciscans, 1209; received stigmata 1224; canonized 1228; one of best known and best loved saints; patron of Italy, Catholic Action and ecologists; Oct. 4*.

Francis of Paola (1416-1507): Italian hermit: founder of Minim Friars; Apr. 2*.

Francis Xavier (1506-1552): Spanish Jesuit; missionary to Far East; canonized 1602; patron of foreign missions; considered one of greatest Christian missionaries; Dec. 3*.

Francis Xavier Bianchi (1743-1815): Italian Barnabite; acclaimed apostle of Naples because of his work there among the poor and abandoned; canonized 1951; Jan. 31.

Gabriel of the Sorrowful Mother (Francis Possenti) (1838-1862): Italian Passionist; died while a scholastic; canonized 1920; Feb. 27.

Gaspar (Caspar) del Bufalo (1786-1836): Italian priest; founded Missionaries of the Precious Blood, 1815; canonized 1954; Jan. 2.

Gemma Galgani (1878-1903): Italian laywoman; visionary; subject of extraordinary religious experiences; canonized 1940; Apr. 11.

Genesius (d. c. 300): Roman actor; according to legend, was converted while performing a burlesque of Christian baptism and was subsequently martyred; patron of actors; Aug. 25.

Genevieve (422-500): French nun; a patroness and protectress of Paris; events of her life not authenticated; Jan. 3.

George (d. c. 300): Martyr, probably during Diocletian persecution in Palestine; all other incidents of his life, including story of the dragon, are legendary; patron of England; Apr. 23*.

Gerard Majella (1725-1755): Italian Redemptorist lay brother; noted for supernatural occurrences in his life including bilocation and reading of consciences; canonized 1904; patron of mothers; Oct. 16.

Gertrude (1256-1302): German mystic; writer; helped spread devotion to the Sacred Heart; Nov. 16*.

Gregory VII (Hildebrand) (1020?-1085): Pope, 1075-1085; Benedictine monk; adviser to several popes; as pope, strengthened interior life of Church and fought against lay investiture; driven from Rome by Henry IV; died in exile; canonized 1584; May 25*.

Gregory Barbarigo (1626-1697): Italian cardinal; noted for his efforts to bring about reunion of separated Christians; canonized 1960; June 18.

Gregory of Nyssa (c. 335-395): Bishop; theologian; younger brother of St. Basil the Great; Mar. 9.

Gregory Thaumaturgus (c. 213-268): Bishop of Neocaesarea; missionary, famed as wonder worker; Nov. 17.

Gregory the Illuminator (257-332): Martyr; bishop; apostle and patron saint of Armenia; helped free Armenia from the Persians; Sept. 30.

Hedwig (1174-1243): Moravian noblewoman; married duke of Silesia, head of Polish royal family; fostered religious life in country; canonized 1266; Oct. 16*.

Helena (250-330): Empress; mother of Constantine the Great; associated with discovery of the True Cross; Aug. 18.

Henry (972-1024): Bavarian emperor; cooperated with Benedictine abbeys in restoration of ecclesiastical and social discipline; canonized 1146; July 13*.

Herman Joseph (1150-1241): German Premonstratensian; his visions were the subjects of artists; writer; cult approved, 1958; Apr. 7.

Hippolytus (d. c. 236): Roman priest; opposed Pope St. Callistus I in his teaching about the readmission to the Church of repentant Christians who had apostasized during time of persecution; elected antipope; exiled to Sardinia; reconciled before his martyrdom; important ecclesiastical writer; Aug. 13*.

Hubert (d. 727): Bishop; his patronage of hunters is based on legend that he was converted while hunting; Nov. 3.

Hugh of Cluny (the Great) (1024-1109): Abbot of Benedictine foundation at Cluny; supported popes in efforts to reform ecclesiastical abuses; canonized 1120; Apr. 29.

Ignatius of Antioch (d. c. 107): Early ecclesiastical writer; martyr; bishop of Antioch in Syria for 40 years; Oct. 17*.

Ignatius of Laconi (1701-1781): Italian Capuchin lay brother whose 60 years of religious life were spent in Franciscan simplicity; canonized 1951; May 11.

Ignatius of Loyola (1491-1556): Spanish soldier; renounced military career after recovering from wounds received at siege of Pampeluna (Pamplona) in 1521; founded Society of Jesus (Jesuits), 1534, at Paris; wrote *The Book of Spiritual Exercises*; canonized 1622; July 31*.

Irenaeus of Lyons (130-202): Early ecclesiastical writer; opposed Gnosticism; bishop of Lyons; traditionally regarded as a martyr; June 28*.

Isidore the Farmer (d. 1170): Spanish layman; farmer; canonized 1622; patron of farmers; May 15 (U.S.).*

Jane Frances de Chantal (1572-1641): French widow; foundress, under guidance of St. Francis de Sales, of Order of the Visitation; canonized 1767; Dec. 12*.

Januarius (Gennaro) (d. 304): Bishop of Benevento; martyred during Diocletian persecution; fame rests on liquefaction of some of his blood preserved in a phial at Naples, an unexplained phenomenon which has occurred regularly several times each year for over 400 years; declared patron of Campania region around Naples, 1980; Sept. 19*.

Jeanne Delanoue (1666-1736): French foundress of Sisters of St. Anne of Providence, 1704; canonized 1982; Aug. 16.

Jeanne (Joan) de Lestonnac (1556-1640): French foundress; widowed in 1597; founded the Religious of Notre Dame 1607; canonized 1947; Feb. 2.

Jeanne de Valois (Jeanne of France) (1464-1505): French foundress; deformed daughter of King Louis XI; was married in 1476 to Duke Louis of Orleans who had the marriage annulled when he ascended the throne as Louis XII; Jeanne retired to life of prayer; founded contemplative Annonciades of Bourges, 1504; canonized 1950; Feb. 5.

Jeanne Elizabeth Bichier des Anges (1773-1838): French Religious; co-founder with St. Andrew Fournet of Daughters of the Cross of St. Andrew, 1807; canonized 1947; Aug. 26.

Jeanne Jugan, Bl. (1792-1879): French Religious; foundress of Little Sisters of the Poor; beatified Oct. 5, 1982; Aug. 30.

Jerome Emiliani (1481-1537): Venetian priest; founded Somascan Fathers, 1532, for care of orphans; canonized 1767; patron of orphans and abandoned children; Feb. 8*.

Joan Antida Thouret (1765-1826): French Religious; founded, 1799, congregation now known as Sisters of Charity of St. Joan Antida; canonized 1934; Aug. 24.

Joan of Arc (1412-1431): French heroine, called The Maid of Orleans, La Pucelle; led French army in 1429 against English invaders besieging Orleans; captured by Burgundians the following year; turned over to ecclesiastical court on charge of heresy, found guilty and burned at the stake; her innocence was declared in 1456; canonized 1920; patroness of France; May 30.

Joaquina de Vedruna de Mas (1783-1854): Spanish foundress; widowed in 1816; after providing for her children, founded the Carmelite Sisters of Charity; canonized 1959; Aug. 28.

John I (d. 526): Pope, 523-526; martyr; May 18*.

John Baptist de la Salle (1651-1719): French priest; founder of Brothers of the Christian Schools, 1680; canonized 1900; patron of teachers; Apr. 7*.

John Berchmans (1599-1621): Belgian Jesuit

scholastic; patron of Mass servers; canonized 1888; Aug. 13.

John (Don) Bosco (1815-1888): Italian priest; founded Salesians, 1859, for education of boys and cofounded the Daughters of Mary Help of Christians for education of girls; canonized 1934; Jan. 31*.

John Capistran (1386-1456): Italian Franciscan; preacher; papal diplomat; canonized 1690; declared patron of military chaplains, Feb. 10, 1984. Oct. 23*.

John de Ribera (1532-1611): Spanish bishop and statesman; archbishop of Valencia, 1568-1611, and viceroy of that province; canonized 1960; Jan. 6.

John Eudes (1601-1680): French priest; founder of Sisters of Our Lady of Charity of Refuge, 1642, and Congregation of Jesus-Mary (Eudists), 1643; canonized 1925; Aug. 19*.

John Fisher (1469-1535): English prelate; theologian; martyr; bishop of Rochester, cardinal; refused to recognize validity of Henry VIII's marriage to Anne Boleyn; upheld supremacy of the pope; beheaded for refusing to acknowledge Henry as head of the Church; canonized 1935; June 22 (with St. Thomas More)*.

John Gualbert (d. 1073): Italian priest; founder of Benedictine congregation of Vallombrosians, 1039; canonized 1193; July 12.

John Kanty (Cantius) (1395-1473): Polish theologian; canonized 1767; Dec. 23*.

John Leonardi (1550-1609): Italian priest; worked among prisoners and the sick; founded Clerics Regular of the Mother of God; canonized 1938; Oct. 9*.

John Nepomucene (1345-1393): Bohemian priest; regarded as a martyr; canonized 1729; patron of Czechoslovakia; May 16.

John Nepomucene Neumann (1811-1860): American prelate; b. Bohemia; ordained in New York 1836; missionary among Germans near Niagara Falls before joining Redemptorists, 1840; bishop of Philadelphia, 1852; first bishop in U.S. to prescribe Forty Hours devotion in his diocese; beatified 1963; canonized June 19, 1977; Jan. 5 (U.S.)*.

John of Avila (1499-1569): Spanish priest; preacher; ascetical writer; spiritual adviser of St. Teresa of Jesus (Avila); canonized 1970; May 10.

John of Britto (1647-1693): Portuguese Jesuit; missionary in India where he was martyred; canonized 1947; Feb. 4.

John of God (1495-1550): Portuguese founder; his work among the sick poor led to foundation of Brothers Hospitallers of St. John of God, 1540, in Spain; canonized 1690; patron of sick, nurses, hospitals; Mar. 8*.

John of Matha (1160-1213): French priest; founder of the Order of Most Holy Trinity, whose original purpose was the ransom of prisoners from the Moslems; Feb. 8.

John Ogilvie (1579-1615): Scottish Jesuit; martyr; canonized 1976, the first canonized Scottish saint since 1250 (Margaret of Scotland); Mar. 10.

John Vianney (Cure of Ars) (1786-1859): French parish priest; noted confessor, spent 16 to 18 hours a day in confessional; canonized 1925; patron of parish priests; Aug. 4*.

Josaphat Kuncevyc (1584-1623): Basilian monk; b. Poland; archbishop of Polotsk, Lithuania; worked for reunion of separated Eastern Christians with Rome; martyred by mob of schismatics; canonized 1867; Nov. 12*.

Joseph Benedict Cottolengo (1786-1842): Italian priest; established Little Houses of Divine Providence (Piccolo Casa) for care of orphans and the sick; canonized 1934; Apr. 30.

Joseph Cafasso (1811-1860): Italian priest; renowned confessor; promoted devotion to Blessed Sacrament; canonized 1947; June 23.

Joseph Calasanz (1556-1648): Spanish priest; founder of Piarists (Order of Pious Schools); canonized 1767; Aug. 25*.

Joseph of Cupertino (1603-1663): Italian Franciscan; noted for remarkable incidents of levitation; canonized 1767; Sept. 18.

Joseph Pignatelli (1737-1811): Spanish Jesuit; left Spain when Jesuits were banished in 1767; worked for revival of the Order; named first superior when Jesuits were reestablished in Kingdom of Naples, 1804; canonized 1954; Nov. 28.

Julia Billiart (1751-1816): French foundress; founded Sisters of Notre Dame de Namur, 1804; canonized 1969; Apr. 8.

Justin de Jacobis (1800-1860): Italian Vincentian; bishop; missionary in Ethiopia; canonized 1975; July 31.

Justin Martyr (100-165): Early ecclesiastical writer; *Apologies for the Christian Religion, Dialog with the Jew Tryphon;* martyred at Rome; June 1*.

Kateri Tekakwitha, Bl. (1656-1680): "Lily of the Mohawks." Indian maiden born at Ossernenon (Auriesville), N.Y.; baptized Christian, Easter, 1676, by Jesuit missionary Father Jacques de Lambertville; lived life devoted to prayer, penitential practices and care of sick and aged in Christian village of Caughnawaga near Montreal where her relics are now enshrined; beatified June 22, 1980; July 14* (in U.S.).

Ladislaus (1040-1095): King of Hungary; supported Pope Gregory VII against Henry IV; canonized 1192; June 27.

Lawrence (d. 258): Widely venerated martyr who suffered death, according to a long-standing but unverifiable legend, by being fire on a gridiron; Aug. 10*.

Lawrence (Lorenzo) Ruiz and Companions (d. 1630s): Martyred in or near the city of Nagasaki, Japan; Lawrence Ruiz, first Filipino saint, and 15 companions (nine Japanese, four Spaniards, one Italian and one Frenchman); canonized 1987; Sept. 28*.

Leonard Murialdo (1828-1900): Italian priest; educator; founder Pious Society of St. Joseph of Turin, 1873; canonized 1970; Mar. 30.

Leonard of Port Maurice (1676-1751): Italian Franciscan; ascetical writer; preached missions throughout Italy; canonized 1867; patron of parish missions; Nov. 26.

Leopold Mandic (1866-1942): Croatian-born Franciscan priest, noted confessor; spent most of his priestly life in Padua, Italy; canonized, 1983, July 30.

Louis IX (1215-1270): King of France, 1226-1270; participated in Sixth Crusade; patron of Secular Franciscan Order; canonized 1297; Aug. 25*.

Louis de Montfort (1673-1716): French priest; founder of Sisters of Divine Wisdom, 1703, and Missionaries of Company of Mary, 1715; wrote *True Devotion to the Blessed Virgin*; canonized 1947; Apr. 28.

Louis Moreau, Bl. (d. 1901): Canadian bishop; headed St. Hyacinthe, Que., diocese, 1876-1901; beatified 1986; May 24.

Louise de Marillac (1591-1660): French foundress, with St. Vincent de Paul, of the Sisters of Charity; canonized 1934; Mar. 15.

Lucy (d. 304): Sicilian maiden; martyred during Diocletian persecution; one of most widely venerated early virgin-martyrs; patron of Syracuse, Sicily; invoked by those suffering from eye diseases (based on legend that she offered her eyes to a suitor who admired them); Dec. 13*.

Lucy Filippini (1672-1732): Italian educator, helped improve status of women through education; considered a founder of the Religious Teachers Filippini, 1692; canonized 1930; Mar. 25.

Madeleine Sophie Barat (1779-1865): French foundress of the Society of the Sacred Heart of Jesus; canonized 1925; May 25.

Malachy (1095-1148): Irish bishop; instrumental in establishing first Cistercian house in Ireland, 1142; canonized 1190; Nov. 3 (See Index: Prophecies of St. Malachy).

Marcellinus and Peter (d.c. 304): Early Roman martyrs; June 2*.

Margaret Clitherow (1556-1586): English martyr; convert shortly after her marriage; one of Forty Martyrs of England and Wales; canonized 1970; Mar. 25.

Margaret Mary Alacoque (1647-1690): French Religious; spread devotion to Sacred Heart in accordance with revelations made to her in 1675 (see Sacred Heart); canonized 1920; Oct. 16*.

Margaret of Cortona (1247-1297): Franciscan tertiary; reformed in 1273 following the violent death of her lover; canonized 1728; Feb. 22.

Margaret of Scotland (1050-1093): Queen of Scotland; noted for solicitude for the poor and promotion of justice; canonized 1250; Nov. 16*.

Margaret of Hungary (1242-1270): Contemplative; daughter of King Bela IV of Hungary; lived a life of self-imposed penances; canonized 1943; Jan. 18.

Maria Goretti (1890-1902): Italian virgin-martyr; a model of purity; canonized 1950; July 6*.

Mariana Paredes of Jesus (1618-1645): South American recluse; Lily of Quito; canonized, 1950; May 26.

Marie-Leonie Paradis, Bl. (1840-1912): Canadian Religious; founded Little Sisters of the Holy Family, 1880; beatified 1984; May 4.

Marie-Rose Durocher, Bl. (1811-1849): Canadian Religious; foundress of Sisters of Holy Names of Jesus and Mary; beatified 1982; Oct. 6* (in U.S.).

Martha (1st cent.): Sister of Lazarus and Mary of Bethany; Gospel accounts record her concern for homely details; patron of cooks; July 29*.

Martin I (d. 655): Pope, 649-55; banished from Rome by emperor in 653 because of his condemnation of Monothelites; considered a martyr; Apr. 13*.

Martin of Tours (316-397): Bishop of Tours; opposed Arianism and Priscillianism; pioneer of Western monasticism, before St. Benedict; Nov. 11*.

Mary Domenica Mazzarello (1837-1881): Italian foundress, with St. John Bosco, of the Daughters of Mary Help of Christians, 1872; canonized 1951; May 14.

Mary Josepha Rossello (1811-1881): Italian-born foundress of the Daughters of Our Lady of Mercy; canonized 1949; Dec. 7.

Mary Magdalen Postel (1756-1846): French foundress of the Sisters of Christian Schools of Mercy, 1807; canonized 1925; July 16.

Mary Magdalene (1st cent.): Gospels record her as devoted follower of Christ to whom he appeared after the Resurrection; her identification with Mary of Bethany (sister of Martha and Lazarus) and the woman sinner (Lk 7:36-50) has been questioned; July 22*.

Mary Magdalene dei Pazzi (1566-1607): Italian Carmelite nun; recipient of mystical experiences; canonized 1669; May 25*.

Mary Michaela Desmaisières (1809-1865): Spanish-born foundress of the Institute of the Handmaids of the Blessed Sacrament, 1848; canonized 1934; Aug. 24.

Maximilian Kolbe (1894-1941): Polish Conventual Franciscan; prisoner at Auschwitz who heroically offered his life in place of a fellow prisoner; beatified 1971, canonized 1982; Aug. 14*.

Methodius: See Index.

Miguel Febres Cordero (1854-1910): Ecuadorean Christian Brother; educator; canonized 1984; Feb. 9.

Monica (332-387): Mother of St. Augustine; model of a patient mother; her feast is observed in the Roman calendar the day before her son's; Aug. 27*.

Nereus and Achilleus (d. c. 100): Early Christian martyrs; soldiers who, according to legend, were baptized by St. Peter; May 12*.

Nicholas of Flue (1417-1487): Swiss layman; at the age of 50, with the consent of his wife and 10 children, he retreated from the world to live as a hermit; called Brother Claus by the Swiss; canonized 1947; Mar. 21.

Nicholas of Myra (4th cent.): Bishop of Myra in Asia Minor; one of most popular saints in both East and West; most of the incidents of his life are based on legend; patron of Russia; Dec. 6*.

Nicholas of Tolentino (1245-1305): Italian hermit; famed preacher; canonized 1446; Sept. 10.

Nicholas Tavelic and Companions (Deodatus of Aquitaine, Peter of Narbonne, Stephen of Cuneo) (d. 1391): Franciscan missionaries; martyred by Moslems in the Holy Land: canonized 1970; Nov. 14.

Norbert (1080-1134): German bishop; founded Canons Regular of Premontre (Premonstratensians, Norbertines), 1120; promoted reform of the clergy, devotion to Blessed Sacrament; canonized 1582; June 6*.

Odilia (d. c. 720): Benedictine abbess; according to legend she was born blind, abandoned by her family and adopted by a convent of nuns where her sight was miraculously restored; patroness of blind; Dec. 13.

Oliver Plunket (1629-1681): Irish martyr; theologian; archbishop of Armagh and primate of Ireland; beatified 1920; canonized, 1975; July 1.

Pancras (d. c. 304): Roman martyr; May 12*.

Paola Frassinetti (1809-1882): Italian Religious; foundress, 1834, of Sisters of St. Dorothy; canonized 1984; June 11.

Paschal Baylon (1540-1592): Spanish Franciscan lay brother; spent life as door-keeper in various Franciscan friaries; defended doctrine of Real Presence in Blessed Sacrament; canonized 1690; patron of all Eucharistic confraternities and congresses, 1897; May 17.

Patrick (389-461): Famous missionary of Ireland; began missionary work in Ireland about 432; organized the Church there and established it on a lasting foundation; patron of Ireland, with Sts. Bridget and Columba; Mar. 17*.

Paul Miki and Companions (d. 1597): Martyrs of Japan; Paul Miki, Jesuit, and twenty-five other priests and laymen were martyred at Nagasaki; canonized 1862, the first canonized martyrs of the Far East; Feb. 6*.

Paul of the Cross (1694-1775): Italian Religious; founder of the Passionists; canonized 1867; Oct. 19*.

Paulinus of Nola (d. 451): Bishop of Nola (Spain); writer; June 22*.

Peregrine (1260-1347): Italian Servite; invoked against cancer (he was miraculously cured of cancer of the foot after a vision); canonized 1726; May 1.

Perpetua and Felicity (d. 203): Martyrs; Perpetua was a young married woman; Felicity was a slave girl; Mar. 7*.

Peter Chanel (1803-1841): French Marist; missionary to Oceania, where he was martyred; canonized 1954; Apr. 28*.

Peter Fourier (1565-1640): French priest; cofounder with Alice LeClercq (Mother Teresa of Jesus) of the Augustinian Canonesses of Our Lady, 1598; canonized 1897; Dec. 9.

Peter Gonzalez (1190-1246): Spanish Dominican; worked among sailors; court chaplain and confessor of King St. Ferdinand of Castile; patron of sailors; Apr. 14.

Peter Julian Eymard (1811-1868): French priest; founder of the Congregation of the Blessed Sacrament (men), 1856, and Servants of the Blessed Sacrament (women), 1864; dedicated to Eucharistic apostolate; canonized 1962; Aug. 1.

Peter Nolasco (c. 1189-1258): Born in Langueduc area of present-day France; founded the Mercedarians (Order of Our Lady of Mercy), 1218, in Spain; canonized 1628; Jan. 31.

Peter of Alcantara (1499-1562): Spanish Franciscan; mystic; initiated Franciscan reform; confessor of St. Teresa of Avila; canonized 1669; Oct. 19.

Philip Benizi (1233-1285): Italian Servite; noted preacher, peacemaker; canonized 1671; Aug. 23.

Philip Neri (1515-1595): Italian Religious; founded Congregation of the Oratory; considered a second apostle of Rome because of his mission activities there; canonized 1622; May 26*.

Philip of Jesus (1571-1597): Mexican Franciscan; martyred at Nagasaki, Japan; canonized 1862; patron of Mexico City; Feb. 6*.

Pius V (1504-1572): Pope, 1566-1572; enforced decrees of Council of Trent; organized expedition against Turks resulting in victory at Lepanto; canonized 1712; Apr. 30*.

Polycarp, (2nd cent.): Bishop of Smyrna; ecclesiastical writer; martyr; Feb. 23*.

Pontian (d. c. 235): Pope, 230-235; exiled to Sardinia by the emperor; regarded as a martyr; Aug. 13 (with Hippolytus)*.

Rafaela Maria Porras y Ayllon (1850-1925): Spanish Religious; founded the Handmaids of the Sacred Heart, 1877; canonized 1977; Jan. 6.

Raymond Nonnatus (d. 1240): Spanish Mercedarian; cardinal; devoted his life to ransoming captives from the Moors; Aug. 31.

Raymond of Penyafort (1175-1275): Spanish Dominican; confessor of Gregory IX; systematized and codified canon law, in effect until 1917; master general of Dominicans, 1238; canonized 1601; Jan. 7*.

Rita of Cascia (1381-1457): Widow; cloistered Augustinian Religious of Umbria; invoked in impossible and desperate cases; May 22.

Robert Southwell (1561-1595): English Jesuit; poet; martyred at Tyburn; canonized 1970, one of the Forty English and Welsh Martyrs; Feb. 21.

Roch (1350-1379): French layman; pilgrim; devoted life to care of plague-stricken; widely venerated; invoked against pestilence; Aug. 17.

Romuald (951-1027): Italian monk; founded Camaldolese Benedictines; June 19*.

Rose of Lima (1586-1617): Peruvian Dominican tertiary; first native-born saint of the New World; canonized 1671; Aug. 23*.

Scholastica (d. c. 559): Sister of St. Benedict; regarded as first nun of the Benedictine Order; Feb. 10*.

Sebastian (3rd cent.): Roman martyr; traditionally pictured as a handsome youth with arrows; martyred; patron of athletes, archers; Jan. 20*.

Seven Holy Founders of the Servants of Mary (Buonfiglio Monaldo, Alexis Falconieri, Benedict dell'Antello, Bartholomew Amidei, Ricovero Uguccione, Gerardino Sostegni, John Buonagiunta Monetti): Florentine youths who founded Servites, 1233, in obedience to a vision; canonized 1888; Feb. 17*.

Sharbel Makhlouf (1828-1898): Lebanese Maronite monk-hermit; canonized 1977; Dec. 24.

Sixtus II and Companions (d. 258): Sixtus, pope 257-258, and four deacons, martyrs; Aug. 7*.

Stanislaus (1030-1079): Polish bishop; martyr; canonized 1253; Apr. 11*.

Stephen (d. c. 33): First Christian martyr; chosen by the Apostles as the first of the seven deacons; stoned to death; Dec. 26*.

Stephen (975-1038): King; apostle of Hungary; welded Magyars into national unity; canonized 1083; Aug. 16*.

Sylvester I (d. 335): Pope 314-335; first ecumenical council held at Nicaea during his pontificate; Dec. 31*.

Tarcisius (d. 3rd cent.): Early martyr; according to tradition, was martyred while carrying the Blessed Sacrament to some Christians in prison; patron of first communicants; Aug. 15.

Teresa Margaret Redi (1747-1770): Italian Carmelite; lived life of prayer and austere penance; canonized 1934; Mar. 11.

Teresa of Jesus Jornet Ibars (1843-1897): Spanish Religious; founded the Little Sisters of the Abandoned Aged, 1873; canonized 1974; Aug. 26.

Therese Couderc (1805-1885): French Religious; foundress of the Religious of Our Lady of the Retreat in the Cenacle, 1827; canonized 1970; Sept. 26.

Therese of Lisieux (1873-1897): French Carmelite nun; b. Therese Martin; allowed to enter Carmel at 15, died nine years later of tuberculosis; her "little way" of spiritual perfection became widely known through her spiritual autobiography; despite her obscure life, became one of the most popular saints; canonized 1925; patron of foreign missions; Oct. 1*.

Thomas Becket (1118-1170): English martyr; archbishop of Canterbury; chancellor under Henry II; murdered for upholding rights of the Church; canonized 1173; Dec. 29*.

Thomas More (1478-1535): English martyr; statesman, chancellor under Henry VIII; author of *Utopia;* opposed Henry's divorce, refused to renounce authority of the papacy; beheaded; canonized 1935; June 22 (with St. John Fisher)*.

Thorlac (1133-1193): Icelandic bishop; instituted reforms; although his cult was never officially approved, he was declared patron of Iceland, Jan. 14, 1984; Dec. 23.

Timothy (d. c. 97): Bishop of Ephesus; disciple and companion of St. Paul; martyr; Jan. 26*.

Titus (d. c. 96): Bishop; companion of St. Paul; recipient of one of Paul's epistles; Jan. 26*.

Titus Brandsma, Bl. (1881-1942): Dutch Carmelite priest; professor, scholar, journalist; denounced Nazi persecution of Jews; arrested by Nazis, Jan. 19, 1942; executed by lethal injection at Dachau, July 26, 1942; beatified 1985; July 26.

Valentine (d. 269): Priest, physician; martyred at Rome; legendary patron of lovers; Feb. 14.

Vicenta Maria Lopez y Vicuna (1847-1896): Spanish foundress of the Daughters of Mary Immaculate for domestic service; canonized 1975; Dec. 26.

Vincent (d. 304): Spanish deacon; martyr; Jan. 22*.

Vincent de Paul (1581?-1660): French priest; founder of Congregation of the Mission (Vincentians, Lazarists) and co-founder of Sisters of Charity; declared patron of all charitable organizations and works by Leo XIII; canonized 1737; Sept. 27*.

Vincent Ferrer (1350-1418): Spanish Dominican; famed preacher; Apr. 5*.

Vincent Pallotti (1795-1850): Italian priest; founded Society of the Catholic Apostolate (Pallottines), 1835; Jan. 22.

Vincent Strambi (1745-1824): Italian Passionist; bishop; reformer; canonized 1950; Sept. 25.

Vincenza Gerosa (1784-1847): Italian co-foundress of the Sisters of Charity of Lovere; canonized 1950; June 28.

Vitus (d.c. 300): Martyr; died in Lucania, southern Italy; regarded as protector of epileptics and those suffering from St. Vitus Dance (chorea); June 15.

Walburga (d. 779): English-born Benedictine Religious; belonged to group of nuns who established convents in Germany at the invitation of St. Boniface; abbess of Heidenheim; Feb. 25.

Wenceslaus (d. 935): Duke of Bohemia; martyr; patron of Bohemia; Sept. 28*.

Zita (1218-1278): Italian maid; noted for charity to poor; patron of domestics; Apr. 27.

SAINTS—PATRONS AND INTERCESSORS

A patron is a saint who is venerated as a special intercessor before God. Most patrons have been so designated as the result of popular devotion and long-standing custom. In many cases, the fact of existing patronal devotion is clear despite historical obscurity regarding its origin. The Church has made official designation of relatively few patrons; in such cases, the dates of designation are given in parentheses in the list below. The theological background of the patronage of saints includes the dogmas of the Mystical Body of Christ and the Communion of Saints.

Listed below are patron saints of occupations and professions, and saints whose intercession is sought for special needs.

Accountants: Matthew.
Actors: Genesius.
Advertisers: Bernardine of Siena (May 20, 1960).
Alpinists: Bernard of Montjoux (or Menthon) (Aug. 20, 1923).
Altar boys: John Berchmans.
Anesthetists: Rene Goupil.
Animals: Francis of Assisi.
Archers: Sebastian.
Architects: Thomas, Apostle.
Armorers: Dunstan.
Art: Catherine of Bologna.
Artists: Luke, Catherine of Bologna, Bl. Angelico (Feb. 21, 1984).
Astronomers: Dominic.
Athletes: Sebastian.
Authors: Francis de Sales.
Aviators: Our Lady of Loreto (1920), Therese of Lisieux, Joseph of Cupertino.
Bakers: Elizabeth of Hungary, Nicholas.
Bankers: Matthew.
Barbers: Cosmas and Damian, Louis.
Barren women: Anthony of Padua, Felicity.
Basket-makers: Anthony, Abbot.
Beggars: Martin of Tours.
Blacksmiths: Dunstan.
Blind: Odilia, Raphael.
Blood banks: Januarius.
Bodily ills: Our Lady of Lourdes.
Bookbinders: Peter Celestine.
Bookkeepers: Matthew.
Booksellers: John of God.
Boy Scouts: George.
Brewers: Augustine of Hippo, Luke, Nicholas of Myra.
Bricklayers: Stephen.
Brides: Nicholas of Myra.
Brushmakers: Anthony, Abbot.
Builders: Vincent Ferrer.
Butchers: Anthony (Abbot), Luke.
Cabdrivers: Fiacre.

Patron Saints

Cabinetmakers: Anne.
Cancer patients: Peregrine.
Canonists: Raymond of Peñafort.
Carpenters: Joseph.
Catechists: Viator, Charles Borromeo, Robert Bellarmine.
Catholic Action: Francis of Assisi (1916).
Chandlers: Ambrose, Bernard of Clairvaux.
Charitable societies: Vincent de Paul (May 12, 1885).
Children: Nicholas of Myra.
Children of Mary: Agnes, Maria Goretti.
Choirboys: Dominic Savio (June 8, 1956), Holy Innocents.
Church: Joseph (Dec. 8, 1870).
Clerics: Gabriel of the Sorrowful Mother.
Communications personnel: Bernardine.
Confessors: Alphonsus Liguori (Apr. 26, 1950), John Nepomucene.
Convulsive children: Scholastica.
Cooks: Lawrence, Martha.
Coopers: Nicholas of Myra.
Coppersmiths: Maurus.
Dairy workers: Brigid.
Deaf: Francis de Sales.
Dentists: Apollonia.
Desperate situations: Gregory of Neocaesarea, Jude Thaddeus, Rita of Cascia.
Dietitians (in hospitals): Martha.
Dyers: Maurice, Lydia.
Dying: Joseph.
Ecologists: Francis of Assisi (Nov. 29, 1979).
Editors: John Bosco.
Emigrants: Frances Xavier Cabrini (Sept. 8, 1950).
Engineers: Ferdinand III.
Epilepsy, Motor Diseases: Vitus, Willibrord.
Eucharistic congresses and societies: Paschal Baylon (Nov. 28, 1897).
Expectant mothers: Raymond Nonnatus, Gerard Majella.
Eye diseases: Lucy.
Falsely accused: Raymond Nonnatus.
Farmers: George, Isidore.
Farriers: John the Baptist.
Firemen: Florian.
Fire prevention: Catherine of Siena.
First communicants: Tarcisius.
Fishermen: Andrew.
Florists: Therese of Lisieux.
Forest workers: John Gualbert.
Foundlings: Holy Innocents.
Fullers: Anastasius the Fuller, James the Less.
Funeral directors: Joseph of Arimathea, Dismas.
Gardeners: Adelard, Tryphon, Fiacre, Phocas.
Glassworkers: Luke.
Goldsmiths: Dunstan, Anastasius.
Gravediggers: Anthony, Abbot.
Greetings: Valentine.
Grocers: Michael.
Hairdressers: Martin de Porres.
Happy meetings: Raphael.
Hatters: Severus of Ravenna, James the Less.
Headache sufferers: Teresa of Jesus (Avila).
Heart patients: John of God.
Hospital administrators: Basil the Great, Frances X. Cabrini.
Hospitals: Camillus de Lellis and John of God (June 22, 1886), Jude Thaddeus.
Housewives: Anne.
Hunters: Hubert, Eustachius.
Infantrymen: Maurice.
Innkeepers: Amand, Martha.
Invalids: Roch.

Jewelers: Eligius, Dunstan.
Journalists: Francis de Sales (Apr. 26, 1923).
Jurists: John Capistran.
Laborers: Isidore, James, John Bosco.
Lawyers: Ivo (Yves Helory), Genesius, Thomas More.
Learning: Ambrose.
Librarians: Jerome.
Lighthouse keepers: Venerius.
Locksmiths: Dunstan.
Maids: Zita.
Marble workers: Clement I.
Mariners: Michael, Nicholas of Tolentino.
Medical record librarians: Raymond of Peñafort.
Medical social workers: John Regis.
Medical technicians: Albert the Great.
Mentally ill: Dymphna.
Merchants: Francis of Assisi, Nicholas of Myra.
Messengers: Gabriel.
Metal workers: Eligius.
Military chaplains: John Capistran (Feb. 10, 1984).
Millers: Arnulph, Victor.
Missions, Foreign: Francis Xavier (Mar. 25, 1904), Therese of Lisieux (Dec, 14, 1927).
Missions, Black: Peter Claver (1896, Leo XIII), Benedict the Black.
Missions, Parish: Leonard of Port Maurice (Mar. 17, 1923).
Mothers: Monica.
Motorcyclists: Our Lady of Grace.
Motorists: Christopher, Frances of Rome.
Mountaineers: Bernard of Montjoux (or Menthon).
Musicians: Gregory the Great, Cecilia, Dunstan.
Notaries: Luke, Mark.
Nurses: Camillus de Lellis and John of God (1930, Pius XI), Agatha, Raphael.
Nursing and nursing service: Elizabeth of Hungary, Catherine of Siena.
Orators: John Chrysostom (July 8, 1908).
Organ builders: Cecilia.
Orphans: Jerome Emiliani.
Painters: Luke.
Paratroopers: Michael.
Pawnbrokers: Nicholas.
Pharmacists: Cosmas and Damian, James the Greater.
Pharmacists (in hospitals): Gemma Galgani.
Philosophers: Justin.
Physicians: Pantaleon, Cosmas and Damian, Luke, Raphael.
Pilgrims: James the Greater.
Plasterers: Bartholomew.
Poets: David, Cecilia.
Poison sufferers: Benedict.
Policemen: Michael.
Poor: Lawrence, Anthony of Padua.
Poor souls: Nicholas of Tolentino.
Porters: Christopher.
Possessed: Bruno, Denis.
Postal employees: Gabriel.
Priests: Jean-Baptiste Vianney (Apr. 23, 1929).
Printers: John of God, Augustine of Hippo, Genesius.
Prisoners: Dismas, Joseph Cafasso.
Protector of crops: Ansovinus.
Public relations: Bernardine of Siena (May 20, 1960).
Public relations (of hospitals): Paul, Apostle.
Radiologists: Michael (Jan. 15, 1941).
Radio workers: Gabriel.
Retreats: Ignatius Loyola (July 25, 1922).

Rheumatism: James the Greater.
Saddlers: Crispin and Crispinian.
Sailors: Cuthbert, Brendan, Eulalia, Christopher, Peter Gonzales, Erasmus, Nicholas.
Scholars: Brigid.
Schools, Catholic: Thomas Aquinas (Aug. 4, 1880), Joseph Calasanz (Aug. 13, 1948).
Scientists: Albert (Aug. 13, 1948).
Sculptors: Claude.
Seamen: Francis of Paola.
Searchers of lost articles: Anthony of Padua.
Secretaries: Genesius.
Seminarians: Charles Borromeo.
Servants: Martha, Zita.
Shoemakers: Crispin and Crispinian.
Sick: Michael, John of God and Camillus de Lellis (June 22, 1886).
Silversmiths: Andronicus.
Singers: Gregory, Cecilia.
Skaters: Lidwina.
Skiers: Bernard of Montjoux (or Menthon).
Social workers: Louise de Marillac (Feb. 12, 1960).
Soldiers: Hadrian, George, Ignatius, Sebastian, Martin of Tours, Joan of Arc.
Speleologists: Benedict.
Stenographers: Genesius, Cassian.
Stonecutters: Clement.
Stonemasons: Stephen.
Students: Thomas Aquinas.
Surgeons: Cosmas and Damian, Luke.
Swordsmiths: Maurice.
Tailors: Homobonus.
Tanners: Crispin and Crispinian, Simon.
Tax collectors: Matthew.
Teachers: Gregory the Great, John Baptist de la Salle (May 15, 1950).
Telecommunications workers: Gabriel (Jan. 12, 1951).
Television: Clare of Assisi (Feb. 14, 1958).
Television workers: Gabriel.
Tertiaries (Secular Franciscans): Louis of France, Elizabeth of Hungary.
Theologians: Augustine, Alphonsus Liguori.
Throat ailments: Blase.
Travelers: Anthony of Padua, Nicholas of Myra, Christopher, Raphael.
Travel hostesses: Bona (Mar. 2, 1962).
Universities: Blessed Contardo Ferrini.
Vocations: Alphonsus.
Watchmen: Peter of Alcantara.
Weavers: Paul the Hermit, Anastasius the Fuller, Anastasia.
Wine merchants: Amand.
Women in labor: Anne.
Women's Army Corps: Genevieve.
Workingmen: Joseph.
Writers: Francis de Sales (Apr. 26, 1923), Lucy.
Yachtsmen: Adjutor.
Young girls: Agnes.
Youth: Aloysius Gonzaga (1729, Benedict XIII; 1926, Pius XI), John Berchmans, Gabriel of the Sorrowful Mother.

Patron Saints of Places

Alsace: Odilia.
Americas: Our Lady of Guadalupe, Rose of Lima.
Angola: Immaculate Heart of Mary (Nov. 21, 1984).
Argentina: Our Lady of Lujan.
Armenia: Gregory Illuminator.
Asia Minor: John, Evangelist.
Australia: Our Lady Help of Christians.
Belgium: Joseph.

Bohemia: Wenceslaus, Ludmilla.
Borneo: Francis Xavier.
Brazil: Nossa Senhora de Aparecida, Immaculate Conception, Peter of Alcantara.
Canada: Joseph, Anne.
Chile: James the Greater, Our Lady of Mt. Carmel.
China: Joseph.
Colombia: Peter Claver, Louis Bertran.
Corsica: Immaculate Conception.
Czechoslovakia: Wenceslaus, John Nepomucene, Procopius.
Denmark: Ansgar, Canute.
Dominican Republic: Our Lady of High Grace, Dominic.
East Indies: Thomas, Apostle.
Ecuador: Sacred Heart.
El Salvador: Our Lady of Peace (Oct. 10, 1966).
England: George.
Equatorial Guinea: Immaculate Conception (May 25, 1986).
Europe: Benedict (1964), Cyril and Methodius, co-patrons (Dec. 31, 1980).
Finland: Henry.
France: Our Lady of the Assumption, Joan of Arc, Therese (May 3, 1944).
Germany: Boniface, Michael.
Gibraltar: Blessed Virgin Mary under title, "Our Lady of Europe" (May 31, 1979).
Greece: Nicholas, Andrew.
Holland: Willibrord.
Hungary: Blessed Virgin, "Great Lady of Hungary," Stephen, King.
Iceland: Thorlac (Jan. 14, 1984).
India: Our Lady of Assumption.
Ireland: Patrick, Brigid and Columba.
Italy: Francis of Assisi, Catherine of Siena.
Japan: Peter Baptist.
Korea: Joseph and Mary, Mother of the Church.
Lesotho: Immaculate Heart of Mary.
Lithuania: Casimir, Bl. Cunegunda.
Luxembourg: Willibrord.
Malta: Paul, Our Lady of the Assumption.
Mexico: Our Lady of Guadalupe.
Monaco: Devota.
Moravia: Cyril and Methodius.
New Zealand: Our Lady Help of Christians.
Norway: Olaf.
Papua New Guinea (including northern Solomon Islands): Michael the Archangel (May 31, 1979).
Paraguay: Our Lady of Assumption (July 13, 1951).
Peru: Joseph (Mar. 19, 1957).
Philippines: Sacred Heart of Mary.
Poland: Casimir, Bl. Cunegunda, Stanislaus of Cracow, Our Lady of Czestochowa.
Portugal: Immaculate Conception, Francis Borgia, Anthony of Padua, Vincent of Saragossa, George.
Russia: Andrew, Nicholas of Myra, Therese of Lisieux.
Scandinavia: Ansgar.
Scotland: Andrew, Columba.
Silesia: Hedwig.
Slovakia: Our Lady of Sorrows.
South Africa: Our Lady of Assumption (Mar. 15, 1952).
South America: Rose of Lima.
Spain: James the Greater, Teresa.
Sri Lanka (Ceylon): Lawrence.
Sweden: Bridget, Eric.
Tanzania: Immaculate Conception (Dec. 8, 1984).
United States: Immaculate Conception (1846).
Uruguay: Blessed Virgin Mary under title "La Virgen de los Treinte y Tres" (Nov. 21, 1963).
Venezuela: Our Lady of Coromoto.
Wales: David.
West Indies: Gertrude.

Emblems, Portrayals of Saints

Agatha: Tongs, veil.
Agnes: Lamb.
Ambrose: Bees, dove, ox, pen.
Andrew: Transverse cross.
Anne, Mother of the Blessed Virgin: Door.
Anthony, Abbot: Bell, hog.
Anthony of Padua: Infant Jesus, bread, book, lily.
Augustine of Hippo: Dove, child, shell, pen.
Barnabas: Stones, ax, lance.
Bartholomew: Knife, flayed and holding his skin.
Benedict: Broken cup, raven, bell, crosier, bush.
Bernard of Clairvaux: Pen, bees, instruments of the Passion.
Bernardine of Siena: Tablet or sun inscribed with IHS.
Blase: Wax, taper, iron comb.
Bonaventure: Communion, ciborium, cardinal's hat.
Boniface: Oak, ax, book, fox, scourge, fountain, raven, sword.
Bridget of Sweden: Book, pilgrim's staff.
Bridget of Kildare: Cross, flame over her head, candle.
Catherine of Ricci: Ring, crown, crucifix.
Catherine of Siena: Stigmata, cross, ring, lily.
Cecilia: Organ.
Charles Borromeo: Communion, coat of arms with word *Humilitas*.
Christopher: Giant, torrent, tree, Child Jesus on his shoulders.
Clare of Assisi: Monstrance.
Cosmas and Damian: A phial, box of ointment.
Cyril of Alexandria: Blessed Virgin holding the Child Jesus, pen.
Cyril of Jerusalem: Purse, book.
Dominic: Rosary, star.
Edmund the Martyr: Arrow, sword.
Elizabeth of Hungary: Alms, flowers, bread, the poor, a pitcher.
Francis of Assisi: Wolf, birds, fish, skull, the Stigmata.
Francis Xavier: Crucifix, bell, vessel.
Genevieve: Bread, keys, herd, candle.
George: Dragon.
Gertrude: Crown, taper, lily.
Gervase and Protase: Scourge, club, sword.
Gregory I (the Great): Tiara, crosier, dove.
Helena: Cross.
Hilary: Stick, pen, child.
Ignatius of Loyola: Communion, chasuble, book, apparition of Our Lord.
Isidore: Bees, pen.
James the Greater: Pilgrim's staff, shell, key, sword.
James the Less: Square rule, halberd, club.
Jerome: Lion.
John Berchmans: Rule of St. Ignatius, cross, rosary.
John Chrysostom: Bees, dove, pen.
John of God: Alms, a heart, crown of thorns.
John the Baptist: Lamb, head cut off on platter, skin of an animal.
John the Evangelist: Eagle, chalice, kettle, armor.
Josaphat Kuncevyc: Chalice, crown, winged deacon.
Joseph, Spouse of the Blessed Virgin: Infant Jesus, lily, rod, plane, carpenter's square.
Jude: Sword, square rule, club.
Justin Martyr: Ax, sword.
Lawrence: Cross, book of the Gospels, gridiron.
Leander of Seville: A pen.
Liborius: Pebbles, peacock.
Longinus: In arms at foot of the cross.
Louis IX of France: Crown of thorns, nails.
Lucy: Cord, eyes on a dish.
Luke: Ox, book, brush, palette.
Mark: Lion, book.
Martha: Holy water sprinkler, dragon.
Mary Magdalene: Alabaster box of ointment.
Matilda: Purse, alms.
Matthew: Winged man, purse, lance.
Matthias: Lance.
Maurus: Scales, spade, crutch.
Meinrad: Two ravens.
Michael: Scales, banner, sword, dragon.
Monica: Girdle, tears.
Nicholas: Three purses or balls, anchor or boat, child.
Patrick: Cross, harp, serpent, baptismal font, demons, shamrock.
Paul: Sword, book or scroll.
Peter: Keys, boat, cock.
Philip, Apostle: Column.
Philip Neri: Altar, chasuble, vial.
Rita of Cascia: Rose, crucifix, thorn.
Roch: Angel, dog, bread.
Rose of Lima: Crown of thorns, anchor, city.
Sebastian: Arrows, crown.
Simon Stock: Scapular.
Teresa of Jesus (Avila): Heart, arrow, book.
Therese of Lisieux: Roses entwining a crucifix.
Thomas, Apostle: Lance, ax.
Thomas Aquinas: Chalice, monstrance, dove, ox, person trampled under foot.
Vincent (Deacon): Gridiron, boat.
Vincent de Paul: Children.
Vincent Ferrer: Pulpit, cardinal's hat, trumpet, captives.

NATIONAL SHRINE

The National Shrine of the Immaculate Conception is dedicated to the honor of the Blessed Virgin Mary, who was declared patroness of the United States in 1846.

The shrine is the seventh largest religious building in the world and the largest Catholic church in the Western Hemisphere, with normal seating and standing accommodations for 6,000 persons.

More than the usual million persons per year visited the shrine during Marian Year 1987-88. Open daily, it is located adjacent to The Catholic University of America, at Michigan Ave. and Fourth St. N.E., Washington, D.C. 20017. Father Roger C. Roensch is the director of pilgrimages.

THE MOTHER OF JESUS IN CATHOLIC UNDERSTANDING

This article was written by the Rev. Eamon R. Carroll, O. Carm., member of the theological faculty of Loyola University, Chicago; author of "Understanding the Mother of Jesus" (published by M. Glazier, Wilmington, Del.; 1979).

Documents of the Second Vatican Council have provided the charter for current Catholic understanding of the Virgin Mary, Mother of Jesus. This conciliar teaching was expanded and applied in the pastoral letter, "Behold Your Mother: Woman of Faith," issued by the U.S. bishops Nov. 21, 1973. Pope Paul VI added guidelines for devotion, in the revised liturgy and with respect to the Rosary, in the letter *Marialis Cultus* ("To Honor Mary"), dated Feb. 2, 1974.

Conciliar Documents

The first conciliar document, the *Constitution on the Sacred Liturgy*, linked Mary with the life, death and exaltation of Jesus, stating: "In celebrating this annual cycle of Christ's mysteries, holy Church honors with special love blessed Mary, Mother of God, who is joined by an inseparable bond to the saving work of her Son. In her the Church holds up and admires the most excellent fruit of the redemption, and joyfully contemplates, as in a faultless manner, that which she herself wholly desires and hopes to be" (No. 103).

The eighth and final chapter of the *Dogmatic Constitution on the Church* is entitled "The Blessed Virgin Mary, Mother of God, in the Mystery of Christ and the Church." The seventh chapter deals with the communion of saints, the bond between the pilgrim Church on earth and the blessed joined to the risen Christ — what John deSatgé, an English Anglican, describes as the "mutual sharing and caring in Christ for one another." At the Eucharist, above all, "in union with the whole Church we honor Mary, the ever-Virgin Mother of Jesus Christ our Lord and God" (First Eucharistic Prayer; cf. *Constitution on the Church,* No. 50).

What Catholics believe about the Mother of Jesus is the basis for her place in their prayer life, both in the liturgy and particularly the Eucharist, and in other forms of piety, especially the Rosary. The Church's growth in insight about the Blessed Virgin comes about as Christians ponder the meaning of Mary in prayer as well as in study. The Church has come to know Mary's role by experience and by contemplation of her hidden holiness (*Constitution on the Church,* No. 64). The tradition about Mary has been transmitted by doctrinal teaching and also by life and worship, even as in her own life Mary treasured in her heart God's words and deeds (*Dogmatic Constitution on Divine Revelation,* No. 8).

Mary in the Bible

The possibility of consensus on the Virgin Mary in the Bible was the theme of a book published in 1978, entitled *Mary in the New Testament* (edited by R. E. Brown, J. A. Fitzmyer, J. Reumann and K. P. Donfried). Limiting their study to the New Testament and using critical techniques of interpretation, a team of 12 authors — Catholics, Lutherans, Anglicans and others — agreed on a biblical portrait of Mary the Virgin as the great gospel model of faith commitment.

One valuable insight centers on the "true kinsmen" incident (Mk. 3:31-35; Mt. 12:46-50; Lk. 8:19-21). One day while Jesus was preaching, word was sent to him that his "mother and brethren" wished to see him. In St. Mark, the oldest account, there is a sharp distinction between the circle of the hearers of Jesus, who were "inside" and counted as his "true family," and the relatives "outside," who failed to understand him. St. Mark does not clearly place Mary among the outsiders, but neither does he carefully distinguish her from the other relatives who did not esteem Jesus. St. Luke shifts the focus completely, placing the relatives, especially the Mother of Jesus, among the true followers, as he does also in the Acts of the Apostles by mentioning them in the Upper Room before Pentecost.

St. Luke is fond of speaking of the "word of God." At the Annunciation, Mary consented with the statement, "Be it done to me according to your word" (Lk. 1:26-38), and "the Word was made flesh" (Jn. 1:14). Jesus said in reply to the message about his visitors, "My mother and my brothers are those who hear the word of God and do it" (Lk. 8:21). St. Luke relates this event just after the parables of the sower and the seed and the lamp on the lampstand. Consistent with his high praise of the Virgin Mary in the infancy chapters, he regards Mary as the rich soil — she heard the word and brought forth fruit in abundance, the Holy One who is the Son of God. She is the pure light, rekindled by the coming of the Redeemer; she is the "woman clothed with the sun" (Rv. 12:1), for Jesus is the "sun of justice."

St. Luke alone saved one other mention of Mary during the public ministry of Jesus, in the story of the "enthusiastic woman" (Lk. 11:27-28). One day while Jesus was preaching, a woman cried out, "Blessed is the womb that bore you and the breasts that nursed you." He replied, "Still more blessed are those who hear the word of God and keep it." The obedient Mary, handmaid of the Lord, brought together opposed beatitudes — the anonymous woman's praise of her motherhood and Jesus' tribute to her faith.

In the opening chapter of St. Luke, Elizabeth did the same when, filled with the Holy Spirit, she returned Mary's greeting with the loud cry, "Of all women you are the most blessed, and blessed is the fruit of your womb." Continuing in praise of her young cousin's faith, she added: "Yes, blessed is she who has believed, for the things promised her by the Lord will be fulfilled" (Lk. 1:39-45).

Mary the Virgin

Both St. Luke and St. Matthew, whose infancy narratives differ so much otherwise, agree that Mary conceived Jesus virginally, that her Son had no human father. The Creed affirms that Jesus was "conceived of the Virgin Mary by the power of the Holy Spirit."

St. Luke writes of the virginal conception of Jesus from the standpoint of Mary. To her question, "How can this be since I know not man?" the angel replied by appealing to God's power.

St. Matthew's viewpoint is that of Joseph, who was informed in a dream-vision that Mary's child was of no human father. God accomplishes his saving purposes without dependence on the will of the flesh and the will of man (Jn. 1:13). God shows his favor where he chooses — whether for the barren Sara, wife of Abraham, or aged Elizabeth, the wife of Zechariah, or the Virgin Mary. In the words of the promise to Abraham, repeated by Gabriel to Mary, "Nothing is impossible to God" (Lk. 1:37; Gn. 18:14).

Mary and Joseph accepted as God's will the virginal conception, an unprecedented event, the sign of God sending his Son to be the Savior. Their lives were henceforth totally dedicated to the service of Jesus.

As various forms of Christian witness developed in the Church, the conviction that Mary remains always a virgin came to be held as Catholic doctrine. The Gospels leave undecided the identity of the "brethren" of Jesus. From lived experience, by the fourth century the Church had come to see Mary's life-long virginity as part of her commitment to her Son and his mission. Such "development of doctrine" remains a point of difference between Catholics and Protestants, although the great Reformers — Luther, Calvin and later John Wesley — all held that Mary was ever-Virgin.

St. Luke and St. John on Mary

Along with the role of Mary in the childhood of Jesus, St. Luke sees her as part of the fulfillment of messianic prophecy. The Second Vatican Council spoke of "the exalted daughter of Zion in whom the times are fulfilled after the long waiting for the promise, and the new economy inaugurated when the Son of God takes on human nature from her in order to free men from sin by the mysteries of his flesh." The expectations of Israel for the Messiah reach their peak in Mary of Nazareth: "She stands out among the Lord's lowly and poor who confidently look for salvation from him" (*Constitution on the Church*, No. 55).

The Gospel of St. John introduces Mary at the opening and closing of her Son's ministry, which began with the first of his signs at Cana (Jn. 2:1-11) and ended on Calvary (Jn. 19). Both scenes deal with a "third day," both turn on the "hour," not yet come at Cana but achieved in the decisive event of Calvary. In both, Jesus addresses his Mother with the unaccustomed title, "Woman." The request of Mary at Cana is for more than wine to save the wedding feast. She stands for Israel of old, symbolized by the water pots required for religious purifications; Mary stands also for the new Israel, the Church, the bride of Christ, symbolized by the abundant choice wine of the messianic banquet. The marriage feast looks forward to the hour when Christ, the bridegroom, will lay down his life in love for his bride, the Church.

When Jesus spoke from the cross to his Mother and the beloved disciple, "Woman, behold your son," and "Behold your Mother," more was meant than that the disciple should provide for Mary's care (Jn. 19:26-27). In his farewell discourse at the Last Supper, Jesus spoke of the woman in agony because her hour had come. "But when she has borne her child, she no longer remembers her pain for joy that a man has been born into the world" (Jn. 16:21). The longing of Israel for the coming of the Messiah was sometimes compared to labor pains. The "daughter of Zion" had been promised she would become the mother of all races and all nations. The words of Jesus on Calvary announced the fulfillment of that promise; Mary stands for the "woman" who is mother Church, new Israel, new People of God.

In St. John's Gospel, it is only after his words to his Mother and the disciple that Jesus, knowing "that everything was now finished," said, "I am thirsty," and then, "Now it is finished." "Then he bowed his head and delivered over his spirit" (Jn. 19:28-29).

The giving up of the spirit means both the expiring of Jesus and the giving of the Holy Spirit to the Church. The wine Mary requested at Cana was the wine of the Spirit, to be poured out at the messianic banquet. The prayer for the wine of the Spirit is answered through the self-surrender of Jesus on the cross. The triumphant Christ "gives up his spirit," and the Church comes into being. The Acts of the Apostles describes the effects of the outpouring of the Spirit at Pentecost and afterwards. What Mary requested at Cana, what she prayed for in agony at the cross of Jesus, what she sought before Pentecost in union with the Apostles and relatives and the women — all "with one accord devoted to prayer" — is the gift of the Spirit. At Nazareth Mary conceived her Son, and God became man by the power of the Holy Spirit; in the Upper Room she prayed for the Spirit that Jesus be born again in the members of his Church (*Constitution on the Church*, No. 59).

The New Eve

To the titles of Mary already familiar from the Gospels — "the Virgin," "Favored One," "Mother of Jesus," "Mother of my Lord" (Elizabeth's greeting, meaning "Mother of the Messianic King") — the early Church added other descriptions. By the mid-second century Mary was being compared to Eve. Eve was deceived by the word of the evil angel and by disobedience brought death; Mary, the obedient Virgin, heeded the message of the good angel and by her consent brought Life to the world. The title of "New Eve" became common for Mary. By the time of St. Jerome (d. 419), it was proverbial to say, "Death through Eve, life through Mary."

Immaculate Conception

Reflecting on the Blessed Virgin, Christians pondered various aspects of her holiness. The question arose of her freedom from original sin, God's gift of grace that came to be called her Immaculate Conception (not to be confused with the virginal conception of Jesus, for Mary was the child of the father and mother recalled as Joachim and Anne). It took centuries of development before the Immaculate Conception was held to be revealed by God and defined as dogma by Pius IX in 1854. The absence of clear scriptural evidence was one delaying factor; another was lack of clarity about the meaning of original sin; and most cogent was the requirement that Mary be beneficiary of the saving work of Christ. As the English Anglican John deSatgé expresses it, "Mary, who rejoiced in her Savior, was the last person to have no need of one." The Franciscan John Duns Scotus (d. 1308) suggested that Mary was kept free of original sin by a "preservative redemption" — in anticipation of the foreseen merits of Jesus Christ — the explanation eventually recognized as revealed truth.

The Assumption

The final facet of Mary's holiness is the Assumption, her union body and soul with the risen Christ in the glory of heaven, defined as dogma by Pope Pius XII in 1950. By the sixth century the feast of the Assumption was being celebrated in the East, a development from a still earlier August 15 feast that had been known as the Memory of Mary (like the birthdays into heaven of the martyrs), as the Passing of Mary, and as the Dormition or Falling Asleep of the Mother of God. There is no compelling biblical testimony; the appeal is to the concordant faith of the Church, convinced that the promise of the resurrection of the flesh in union with the risen Savior has already been fulfilled for the Mother of the Lord, who gave him human birth in her pure body and was his loyal disciple unto the end.

Model of the Church

All beliefs about the Blessed Virgin lead to Christ. God kept her free from original sin for the sake of Jesus, that she might give herself wholeheartedly to his life and work (*Constitution on the Church*, No. 56), and in consideration of his redemptive mission. Mary's Assumption is her reunion with her Son in the power of his resurrection. The Marian privileges of the Immaculate Conception and the Assumption enrich also the self-understanding of the Church, for she is the "most excellent fruit of the redemption, the spotless model of the Church," the one in whom Christians admire God's plan for his Church. "In the most holy Virgin the Church has already reached that perfection whereby she exists without spot or wrinkle (Eph. 5:27)" (*Constitution on the Church*, No. 65).

Mary Immaculate is a sign of the love of Christ for his bride, the Church; the bridegroom purifies her by his blood to make her all-holy. The preface for the Solemnity of the Immaculate Conception (December 8) addresses the Father: "You allowed no stain of sin to touch the Virgin Mary. Full of grace, she was to be a worthy Mother of your Son, your sign of favor to the Church at its beginning, and the promise of its perfection as the bride of Christ, radiantly beautiful."

Faithful to his promise, Christ has prepared a place for his bride, the Church. In Mary, daughter of the Church, now joined to Christ body and soul in glory, the pilgrim Church sees the successful completion of its own journey. The resurrection of Jesus is the central truth; the Assumption of Mary is the living sign of the Church's call to glory, to loving union with the victorious Redeemer. The preface at Mass for August 15 reads: "Today the Virgin Mother of God was taken up into heaven to be the beginning and the pattern of the Church in its perfection, and a sign of sure hope and comfort for your pilgrim people. You would not allow decay to touch her body, for she had given birth in the glory of the Incarnation to your Son, the Lord of all life." (Cf. also *Constitution on the Church*, No. 68.)

Mother of God

In 325 the first ecumenical council, at Nicaea, proclaimed that Jesus is truly Son of God. Defenders of the faith there were the first to call Mary "Mother of God." At the third ecumenical council, Ephesus, in 431, it was solemnly established that the Virgin Mary is indeed "Mother of God," for the Son to whom she gave birth is the pre-existent Second Person of the Blessed Trinity. "Mother of God" had already been used as a popular title in some parts of the Church, and after Ephesus it was adopted in the prayers of the Mass, as is still the practice in the Catholic Church and all Eastern Churches. For example. the current third Eucharistic Prayer reads: "May he (the Holy Spirit) make us an everlasting gift to you (the Father) and enable us to share in the inheritance of your saints, with Mary, the Virgin Mother of God."

Mother of the Church

When the Church began to celebrate the Assumption of Mary, it did so in the conviction Mary did not leave the members of the Church orphans when her days on earth were ended. She continues her interest for them in union with her Son, the supreme intercessor. By the time of the Council of Ephesus in 431, authors of both the East and West — like St. Ephrem of Syria (d. 373) and St. Ambrose of Italy (d. 397) — proposed Mary as the model of Christian life, and the practice of asking her to pray for her clients on earth began to appear. The feasts of the Nativity of Mary (September 8), the Annunciation (March 25) and the Presentation of Jesus (February 2, also known as the Purification of Mary or Candlemas) have been kept from the sixth and seventh centuries.

When the words of Gabriel and Elizabeth from St. Luke's infancy narrative became part of prayer, the first part of the Hail Mary, their use led to deeper awareness of Mary's holiness as well as to counting on her heavenly help — well expressed in the second part of the Hail Mary — "Holy Mary, Mother of God, pray for us sinners now and at the hour of our death," which reached its fixed form only in the fifteenth century. Mary's place in liturgical prayer and in private prayer reflected and strengthened the sense of her continuing role as loving friend in heaven of the Church on earth. People asked Mary's prayers on their behalf, recalling Mary's own "pilgrimage of faith" and trusting in her abiding maternal care.

Greek homilists like St. John of Damascus (d. ca. 749), St. Andrew of Crete (d. 740) and St. Germanus of Constantinople (d. ca. 733) sang Mary's praises and urged confidence in her loving intercession with Christ. In the West, after the upsurge of the Carolingian times (about 800), remembered for the origin of the Saturday observance in honor of Mary, came the flowering of medieval piety, as evidenced in the writings of St. Anselm (d. 1109), St. Bernard (d. 1153) and his fellow Cistercians, and the great scholastic doctors like St. Thomas Aquinas (d. 1274) and St. Bonaventure (d. 1274). The medieval authors described Mary as Mediatrix of grace, Dispensatrix of grace, spiritual Mother. Blessed Guerric, the Cistercian abbot of Igny (France, d. 1157), emphasized the maternal role of Mary in the formation of Christ in the faithful: "Like the Church of which she is a figure, Mary is Mother of all who are born to life."

Christian Unity and Mary

At the Reformation, in reaction to abuses, the invocation of the saints was rejected as harmful to confidence in Christ, the unique Mediator. Since the sixteenth century Western Christians have been sharply divided in their understanding of the communion of saints and the legitimacy of "praying to Mary." Recent events, however, hold out hope for a meeting of minds and hearts even in this sensitive area. The Second Vatican Council offered a biblical portrait of Mary without neglecting later developments in doctrine and devotion. The council described the place of Mary in words designed to meet Protestant difficulties; e.g., the much misunderstood word, Mediatrix, was used once only and was explained as completely dependent on the unique mediatorship of Christ (*Constitution on the Church*, Nos. 67, 69).

The conciliar *Decree on Ecumenism*, issued Nov. 21, 1964, spoke of the "order" or "hierarchy of truths" among Catholic doctrines, which differ in their relationship to the foundation of the faith (No. 11). The foundation is Jesus Christ, and here all Christians share a common profession of faith. The document mentioned realistically some differences that still divide Catholics and other Christians, in this "order of truths": the meaning of the Incarnation and Redemption, the mystery and ministry of the Church, and the role of Mary in the work of salvation (No. 20). The decree also said in this context: "We rejoice to see our separated brethren looking to Christ as the source and center of ecclesiastical communion. Inspired by longing for union with Christ, they feel compelled to search for unity ever more ardently, and to bear witness to their faith among all the peoples of the earth."

The formation of the Ecumenical Society of the Blessed Virgin Mary in England in 1967, and of the American branch in 1976, is an encouraging sign. The American bishops' pastoral, *"Behold Your Mother,"* appealed to the "basic reverence" of all Christians for Mary, "a veneration deeper than doctrinal differences and theological disputes" (Nos. 101-112). Pope Paul VI's major document, *Marialis Cultus*, contains an appeal to other Christians (Nos. 32 and 33). With Christians of the East, said Pope Paul, Catholics honor the Mother of God as "hope of Christians." Catholics join with Anglicans and Protestants in common praise of God, using the Virgin's own words (Lk. 1:46-55).

It may well be that the growing interest in the bonds between the Blessed Virgin and the Holy Spirit will help Christians together. The Spirit of unity inspired Mary's prophecy: "All generations will call me blessed, because he who is mighty has done great things for me" (Lk. 1:48-49).

ECUMENICAL COMMON STATEMENT ON MARY

(Courtesy of the Rev. Eamon R. Carroll, O. Carm.)

Catholic, Orthodox, Lutheran and Reformed theologians continued interfaith conversations on the role of Mary in the Communion of Saints at a Marian Congress held at Kevelaer, West Germany, in 1987. Earlier conversations, also under the auspices of the International Pontifical Marian Academy, took place at Saragossa, Spain in 1979 and Malta in 1983.

Following is a brief excerpt from the statement issued Sept. 17, 1987, by participants in the congress at Kevelaer.

Those who have reached completion in Christ — and his Mother belongs to that glad company — love in him and with him all who are still on earth. An expression of this love is their prayer for us. We should be grateful for this.

Holy Scripture bears witness to the dealings of God in saving history to and with persons, his servants in the Old Testament and the New: patriarchs, prophets, John the Baptist, Mary and the Apostles. A loving esteem for them is an ingredient of our Christian faith and contributes to its vigor and vitality. For this reason, the confessional formulas of our churches bear witness to Mary, the Virgin Mother of Jesus Christ, the Son of God. Reflection about Mary indeed serves to strengthen our belief that God shows his mercy "on those who fear him" (Luke 1:50, the Magnificat).

Our attitude as believers with respect to Mary and all the saints is essentially directed to the praise of the Eternal Father with the Son in the Holy Spirit. We recognize that Christ is the one Mediator to the Father (1 Tim. 2:5). Mary, the Mother of God, and the saints are subordinate to him. Inspired by the Holy Spirit, the people of God on earth desire to unite their praise with Christ and with all who, as the perfected ones, belong to him.

Signed by: Johannes Kalogirou (Orthodox), Wolfgang Borowsky and Dr. Hans Duefel (both

Evangelical-Lutheran), Henry Chavannes (Evangelical-Reformed), Howard Root (Anglican), and Catholics: Eamon R. Carroll, O., Carm.; Franz Courth, S.A.C.; Theodore Koehler, S.M.; Msgr. Charles Molette; Candido Pozo, S.J., and Pierre Masson, O.P. (secretary).

APPARITIONS OF THE BLESSED VIRGIN MARY

Only seven of the best known apparitions of the Blessed Virgin Mary are described briefly below.

Banneux, near Liege, Belgium: Mary appeared eight times between Jan. 15 and Mar. 2, 1933, to an 11-year-old peasant girl, Mariette Beco, in a garden behind the family cottage in Banneux, near Liege. She called herself the Virgin of the Poor, and has since been venerated as Our Lady of the Poor, the Sick, and the Indifferent. A small chapel was built by a spring near the site of the apparitions and was blessed Aug. 15, 1933. Approval of devotion to Our Lady of Banneux was given in 1949 by Bishop Louis J. Kerkhofs of Liege, and a statue of that title was solemnly crowned in 1956.

Over 100 sanctuaries throughout the world are dedicated to the honor of Our Lady of Banneux.

Beauraing, Belgium: Mary appeared 33 times between Nov. 29, 1932, and Jan. 3, 1933, to five children in the garden of a convent school in Beauraing. A chapel, which became a pilgrimage center, was erected on the spot. Reserved approval of devotion to Our Lady of Beauraing was given Feb. 2, 1943, and final approbation July 2, 1949, by Bishop Charue of Namur.

The Marian Union of Beauraing, a prayer association for the conversion of sinners, has thousands of members throughout the world (see Pro Maria Committee).

Fatima, Portugal: Mary appeared six times between May 13 and Oct. 13, 1917, to three children in a field called Cova da Iria near Fatima, north of Lisbon. She recommended frequent recitation of the Rosary; urged works of mortification for the conversion of sinners; called for devotion to herself under the title of her Immaculate Heart; asked that the people of Russia be consecrated to her under this title, and that the faithful make a Communion of reparation on the first Saturday of each month.

The apparitions were declared worthy of belief in October, 1930, after a seven-year canonical investigation, and devotion to Our Lady of Fatima was authorized under the title of Our Lady of the Rosary. In October, 1942, Pius XII consecrated the world to Mary under the title of her Immaculate Heart. Ten years later, in the first apostolic letter addressed directly to the peoples of Russia, he consecrated them in a special manner to Mary.

Fatima, with its sanctuary and basilica, ranks with Lourdes as the greatest of modern Marian shrines.

(See First Saturday Devotion.)

Guadalupe, Mexico: Mary appeared four times in 1531 to an Indian, Juan Diego, on Tepeyac hill outside of Mexico City, and instructed him to tell Bishop Zumarraga of her wish that a church be built there. The bishop complied with the request about two years later after being convinced of the genuineness of the apparition by the evidence of a miraculously painted life-size figure of the Virgin on the mantle of the Indian. The mantle bearing the picture has been preserved and is enshrined in the Basilica of Our Lady of Guadalupe, which has a long history as a center of devotion and pilgrimage in Mexico. The shrine church, originally dedicated in 1709 and subsequently enlarged, has the title of basilica.

Benedict XIV, in a decree issued in 1754, authorized a Mass and Office under the title of Our Lady of Guadalupe for celebration on Dec. 12, and named Mary the patroness of New Spain. Our Lady of Guadalupe was designated patroness of Latin America by St. Pius X in 1910 and patroness of the Americas by Pius XII in 1945.

La Salette, France: Mary appeared as a sorrowing and weeping figure Sept. 19, 1846, to two peasant children, Melanie Matthieu, 15, and Maximin Giraud, 11, at La Salette in southern France. The message she confided to them, regarding the necessity of penance, was communicated to Pius IX in 1851 and has since been known at the "secret" of La Salette. Bishop de Bruillard of Grenoble declared in 1851 that the apparition was credible, and devotion to Mary under the title of Our Lady of La Salette was authorized. The devotion has been confirmed by popes since the time of Pius IX, and a Mass and Office with this title were authorized in 1942. The shrine church was given the title of minor basilica in 1879.

Lourdes, France: Mary, identifying herself as the Immaculate Conception, appeared 18 times between Feb. 11 and July 16, 1858, to 14-year-old Bernadette Soubirous at the grotto of Massabielle near Lourdes in southern France. Her message concerned the necessity of prayer and penance for the conversion of peoples. Mary's request that a chapel be built at the grotto and spring was fulfilled in 1862 after four years of rigid examination established the credibility of the apparitions. Devotion under the title of Our Lady of Lourdes was authorized later, and a Feb. 11 feast commemorating the apparitions was instituted by Leo XIII. St. Pius X extended this feast throughout the Church in 1907.

The Church of Notre Dame was made a basilica in 1870, and the Church of the Rosary was built later. The underground Church of St. Pius X, consecrated Mar. 25, 1958, is the second largest church in the world, with a capacity of 20,000 persons.

Our Lady of the Miraculous Medal, France: Mary appeared three times in 1830 to Catherine Laboure in the chapel of the motherhouse of the Daughters of Charity of St. Vincent de Paul, Rue de Bac, Paris. She commissioned Catherine to have made the medal of the Immaculate Conception, now known as the Miraculous Medal, and to spread devotion to her under this title. In 1832, the medal was struck according to the model revealed to Catherine.

EASTERN CATHOLIC CHURCHES

The Second Vatican Council, in its "Decree on Eastern Catholic Churches", stated the following points. regarding Eastern heritage, patriarchs, sacraments and worship.

The Catholic Church holds in high esteem the institutions of the Eastern Churches, their liturgical rites, ecclesiastical traditions, and Christian way of life. For, distinguished as they are by their venerable antiquity, they are bright with that tradition which was handed down from the Apostles through the Fathers, and which forms part of the divinely revealed and undivided heritage of the universal Church (No. 1).

That Church, Holy and Catholic, which is the Mystical Body of Christ, is made up of the faithful who are organically united in the Holy Spirit through the same faith, the same sacraments, and the same government and who, combining into various groups held together by a hierarchy, form separate Churches or rites. . . . It is the mind of the Catholic Church that each individual Church or rite retain its traditions whole and entire, while adjusting its way of life to the various needs of time and place (No. 2).

Such individual Churches, whether of the East or of the West, although they differ somewhat among themselves in what are called rites (that is, in liturgy, ecclesiastical discipline, and spiritual heritage) are, nevertheless, equally entrusted to the pastoral guidance of the Roman Pontiff, the divinely appointed successor of St. Peter in supreme government over the universal Church. They are consequently of equal dignity, so that none of them is superior to the others by reason of rite (No. 3).

Eastern Heritage: Each and every Catholic, as also the baptized . . . of every non-Catholic Church or community who enters into the fullness of Catholic communion, should everywhere retain his proper rite, cherish it, and observe it to the best of his ability (No. 4).

The Churches of the East, as much as those of the West, fully enjoy the right, and are in duty bound, to rule themselves. Each should do so according to its proper and individual procedures (No. 5).

All Eastern rite members should know and be convinced that they can and should always preserve their lawful liturgical rites and their established way of life, and that these should not be altered except by way of an appropriate and organic development (No. 6).

Patriarchs: The institution of the patriarchate has existed in the Church from the earliest times and was recognized by the first ecumenical Synods.

By the name Eastern Patriarch is meant the bishop who has jurisdiction over all bishops (including metropolitans), clergy, and people of his own territory or rite, in accordance with the norms of law and without prejudice to the primacy of the Roman Pontiff (No. 7).

Though some of the patriarchates of the Eastern Churches are of later origin than others, all are equal in patriarchal dignity. Still the honorary and lawfully established order of precedence among them is to be preserved (No. 8).

In keeping with the most ancient tradition of the Church, the Patriarchs of the Eastern Churches are to be accorded exceptional respect, since each presides over his patriarchate as father and head.

This sacred Synod, therefore, decrees that their rights and privileges should be re-established in accord with the ancient traditions of each Church and the decrees of the ecumenical Synods.

The rights and privileges in question are those which flourished when East and West were in union, though they should be somewhat adapted to modern conditions.

The Patriarchs with their synods constitute the superior authority for all affairs of the patriarchate, including the right to establish new eparchies and to nominate bishops of their rite within the territorial bounds of the patriarchate, without prejudice to the inalienable right of the Roman Pontiff to intervene in individual cases (No. 9).

What has been said of Patriarchs applies as well, under the norm of law, to major archbishops, who preside over the whole of some individual Church or rite (No. 10).

Sacraments: This sacred Ecumenical Synod endorses and lauds the ancient discipline of the sacraments existing in the Eastern Churches, as also the practices connected with their celebration and administration (No. 12).

With respect to the minister of holy chrism (confirmation), let that practice be fully restored which existed among Easterners in most ancient times. Priests, therefore, can validly confer this sacrament, provided they use chrism blessed by a Patriarch or bishop (No. 13).

In conjunction with baptism or otherwise, all Eastern-Rite priests can confer this sacrament validly on all the faithful of any rite, including the Latin; licitly, however, only if the regulations of both common and particular law are observed. Priests of the Latin rite, to the extent of the faculties they enjoy for administering this sacrament, can confer it also on the faithful of Eastern Churches, without prejudice to rite. They do so licitly if the regulations of both common and particular law are observed (No. 14).

The faithful are bound on Sundays and feast days to attend the divine liturgy or, according to the regulations or custom of their own rite, the celebration of the Divine Praises. That the faithful may be able to satisfy their obligation more easily, it is decreed that this obligation can be fulfilled from the Vespers of the vigil to the end of the Sunday or the feast day (No. 15).

Because of the everyday intermingling of the communicants of diverse Eastern Churches in the same Eastern region or territory, the faculty for hearing confession, duly and unrestrictedly granted by his proper bishop to a priest of any rite, is applicable to the entire territory of the grantor, also to the places and the faithful belonging to any other rite in the same territory, unless an Ordinary of the place explicitly decides otherwise with respect to the places pertaining to his rite (No. 16).

This sacred Synod ardently desires that where it has fallen into disuse the office of the permanent diaconate be restored. The legislative authority of each individual church should decide about the subdiaconate and the minor orders (No. 17).

By way of preventing invalid marriages between Eastern Catholics and baptized Eastern non-Catholics, and in the interests of the permanence and sanctity of marriage and of domestic harmony, this sacred Synod decrees that the canonical 'form' for the celebration of such marriages obliges only for lawfulness. For their validity, the presence of a sacred minister suffices, as long as the other requirements of law are honored (No. 18).

Worship: Henceforth, it will be the exclusive right of an ecumenical Synod or the Apostolic See to establish, transfer, or suppress feast days common to all the Eastern Churches. To establish, transfer, or suppress feast days for any of the individual Churches is within the competence not only of the Apostolic See but also of a patriarchal or archiepiscopal synod, provided due consideration is given to the entire region and to other individual Churches (No. 19).

Until such time as all Christians desirably concur on a fixed day for the celebration of Easter, and with a view meantime to promoting unity among the Christians of a given area or nation, it is left to the Patriarchs or supreme authorities of a place to reach a unanimous agreement, after ascertaining the views of all concerned, on a single Sunday for the observance of Easter (No. 20).

With respect to rules concerning sacred seasons, individual faithful dwelling outside the area or territory of their own rite may conform completely to the established custom of the place where they live. When members of a family belong to different rites, they are all permitted to observe sacred seasons according to the rules of any one of these rites (No. 21).

From ancient times the Divine Praises have been held in high esteem among all Eastern Churches. Eastern clerics and religious should celebrate these Praises as the laws and customs of their own traditions require. To the extent they can, the faithful too should follow the example of their forebears by assisting devoutly at the Divine Praises (No. 22).

Origin

The Church had its beginnings in Palestine, whence it spread to other regions of the world. As it spread, certain cities or jurisdictions became key centers of Christian life and missionary endeavor — notably, Jerusalem, Alexandria, Antioch and Constantinople in the East, and Rome in the West — with the result that their practices became diffused throughout their spheres of influence. Various rites originated from these practices which, although rooted in the essentials of Christian faith, were different in significant respects because of their relationships to particular cultural patterns.

Patriarchal Jurisdictions

The main lines of Eastern Church organization and liturgy were drawn before the Roman Empire was separated into Eastern and Western divisions in 292. It was originally co-extensive with the boundaries of the Eastern Empire. Its jurisdictions were those of the patriarchates of Alexandria and Antioch (recognized as such by the Council of Nicaea in 325), and of Jerusalem and Constantinople (given similar recognition by the Council of Chalcedon in 451). These were the major parent bodies of the Eastern Rite Churches which for centuries were identifiable only with limited numbers of nationality and language groups in Eastern Europe, the Middle East and parts of Asia and Africa. Their members are now scattered throughout the world.

RITES AND FAITHFUL OF EASTERN CHURCHES

(Principal source of statistics: *Annuario Pontificio*. The statistics are for Eastern-Rite jurisdictions only, and do not include Eastern-Rite Catholics under the jurisdiction of Roman-Rite bishops. Some of the figures reported are only approximate. Some of the jurisdictions listed may be inactive because of government suppression.)

The Byzantine, Alexandrian, Antiochene, Armenian and Chaldean are the five principal rites used in their entirety or in modified form by the various Eastern churches. The number of Eastern Catholics throughout the world is more than 12 million.

Alexandrian Rite

Called the Liturgy of St. Mark, the Alexandrian Rite was modified by the Copts and Melkites, and contains elements of the Byzantine Rite of St. Basil and the liturgies of Sts. Mark, Cyril and Gregory of Nazianzen. The liturgy is substantially that of the Coptic Church, which is divided into two branches — the Coptic or Egyptian, and the Ethiopian or Abyssinian. The faithful of this rite are:

COPTS: Resumed communion with Rome about 1741; situated in Egypt, the Near East; liturgical languages are Coptic, Arabic. Jurisdictions (located in Egypt): patriarchate of Alexandria, five dioceses; 148,453.

ETHIOPIANS: Resumed comunion with Rome in 1846: situated in Ethiopia, Jerusalem, Somalia; liturgical language is Geez. Jurisdictions (located in Ethiopia): one archdiocese, two dioceses; 115,684.

Antiochene Rite

This is the source of more derived rites than any of the other parent rites. Its origin can be traced to the Eighth Book of the *Apostolic Constitutions* and to the Liturgy of St. James of Jerusalem, which ultimately spread throughout the whole patriarchate and displaced older forms based on the *Apostolic Constitutions*. The faithful of this rite are:

MALANKARESE: Resumed communion with

Rome in 1930; situated in India; liturgical languages are Syriac, Malayalam. Jurisdictions (located in India): one archdiocese, two dioceses; 272,258.

MARONITES: United to the Holy See since the time of their founder, St. Maron; have no counterparts among the separated Eastern Christians: situated throughout the world: liturgical languages are Syriac, Arabic. Jurisdictions (located in Lebanon, Cyprus, Egypt, Syria, U.S., Brazil, Australia, Canada): patriarchate of Antioch, 17 archdioceses and dioceses, one patriarchal vicariate; 1,742,025. Where no special jurisdictions exist, they are under jurisdiction of local Roman-Rite bishops.

SYRIANS: Resumed communion with Rome in 1781; situated in Asia, Africa, the Americas, Australia; liturgical languages are Syriac, Arabic. Jurisdictions (located in Lebanon, Iraq, Egypt and Syria): patriarchate of Antioch, seven archdioceses and dioceses, three patriarchal vicariates; 98,657.

Armenian Rite

Substantially, although using a different language, this is the Greek Liturgy of St. Basil; it is considered an older form of the Byzantine Rite, and incorporates some modifications from the Antiochene Rite. The faithful of this rite are:

ARMENIANS, exclusively: Resumed communion with Rome during the time of the Crusades; situated in the Near East, Europe, Africa, the Americas, Australasia: liturgical language is Classical Armenian. Jurisdictions (located in Lebanon, Iran, Iraq, Egypt, Syria, Turkey, Poland, France, Greece, Romania, Argentina (for Latin America, including Mexico), and the United States (for Canada and the U.S.): patriarchate of Cilicia, nine archdioceses and dioceses, two patriarchal vicariates, three exarchates, two ordinariates; 161,517.

Byzantine Rite

Based on the Rite of St. James of Jerusalem and the churches of Antioch, and reformed by Sts. Basil and John Chrysostom, the Byzantine Rite is proper to the Church of Constantinople. (The city was called Byzantium before Constantine changed its name; the modern name is Istanbul.) It is now used by the majority of Eastern Catholics and by the Eastern Orthodox Church (which is not in union with Rome). It is, after the Roman, the most widely used rite. The faithful of this rite are:

ALBANIANS: Resumed communion with Rome about 1628; situated in Albania; liturgical language is Albanian. Jurisdiction (located in Albania): one apostolic administration.

BULGARIANS: Resumed communion with Rome about 1861; situated in Bulgaria; liturgical language is Old Slavonic. Jurisdiction (located in Bulgaria): one apostolic exarchate.

BYELORUSSIANS, also known as WHITE RUSSIANS: Resumed communion with Rome in the 17th century; situated in Europe, the Americas, Australia; liturgical language is Old Slavonic. They have an apostolic visitator.

GEORGIANS: Resumed communion with Rome in 1861; situated in Georgia (Southern Russia), France; liturgical language is Georgian. They have an apostolic administrator.

GREEKS: Resumed communion with Rome in 1829; situated in Greece, Asia Minor, Europe; liturgical language is Greek. Jurisdictions (located in Greece and Turkey): two exarchates; 2,350.

HUNGARIANS: Descendants of Ruthenians who resumed communion with Rome in 1646; situated in Hungary, the rest of Europe, the Americas; liturgical languages are Greek, Hungarian, English. Jurisdictions (located in Hungary): one diocese and one exarchate: 272,800.

ITALO-ALBANIANS: Have never been separated from Rome; situated in Italy, Sicily, the Americas; liturgical languages are Greek, Italo-Albanian. Jurisdictions (located in Italy): two dioceses, one abbacy; 62,703.

MELKITES (GREEK CATHOLICS-MELKITES): Resumed communion with Rome during the time of the Crusades, but definitive reunion did not take place until early in the 18th century; situated in the Middle East, Asia, Africa, Europe, the Americas, Australia; liturgical languages are Greek, Arabic, English, Portuguese, Spanish. Jurisdictions (located in Syria, Lebanon, Jordan, Israel, U.S., Brazil, Canada, Australia, Mexico): patriarchate of Antioch (with patriarchal vicariates in Egypt, Sudan, Jerusalem, Iraq and Kuwait), 18 archdioceses and dioceses; 987,562.

ROMANIANS: Resumed communion with Rome in 1697; situated in Romania, the rest of Europe, the Americas; liturgical language is Modern Romanian. Jurisdictions (located in Romania and U.S.): one archdiocese, five dioceses. There were 1.5 million members in 1948 when they were forcibly incorporated into the Romanian Orthodox Church. They have a diocese (1987) in the U.S.

RUSSIANS: Resumed communion with Rome about 1905; situated in Europe, the Americas, Australia, China; liturgical language is Old Slavonic. Jurisdictions (located in Russia and China): two exarchates.

RUTHENIANS, or CARPATHO-RUSSIANS (Rusins): Resumed communion with Rome in the Union of Brest-Litovek, 1596, and the Union of Uzhorod, Apr. 24, 1646; situated in Hungary, Czechoslovakia, elsewhere in Europe, the Americas, Australia; liturgical languages are Old Slavonic, English. Jurisdictions (located in Russia and the U.S.): one archdiocese, four dioceses.

SLOVAKS: Jurisdictions (located in Czechoslovakia and Canada): two dioceses; 388,860.

UKRAINIANS, or GALICIAN RUTHENIANS: Resumed communion with Rome about 1595; situated in Europe, the Americas, Australasia; liturgical languages are Old Slavonic and Ukrainian. Jurisdictions (located in Russian Galicia, Poland, the U.S., Canada, England, Australia, Germany, France, Brazil, Argentina): major archdiocese of Lwow (Lviv), two archdioceses, 12 dioceses, four apostolic exarchates: 4.3 million. This total includes the 1943 figure of 3.6 million Ukrainian Catholics in jurisdictions subsequently forced into the Russian Orthodox Church; there are 714,000 in jurisdictions outside of Russian Galicia and Poland.

YUGOSLAVS, SERBS and CROATIANS: Resumed communion with Rome in 1611; situated in Yugoslavia, the Americas; liturgical language is Old Slavonic. Jurisdiction (located in Yugoslavia): one diocese (which also has jurisdiction over all Byzantine-Rite faithful in Yugoslavia); 48,715. They are under the jurisdiction of Ruthenian bishops elsewhere.

Chaldean Rite

This rite, listed as separate and distinct by the Congregation for the Oriental Churches, was derived from the Antiochene Rite. The faithful of this rite are:

CHALDEANS: Descendants of the Nestorians, resumed communion with Rome in 1692; situated throughout the Middle East, in Europe, Africa, the Americas; liturgical languages are Syriac, Arabic. Jurisdictions (located in Egypt, Iraq, Iran, Lebanon, Syria, Turkey, U.S.); patriarchate of Babylonia, 21 archdioceses and dioceses; 428,667. There is a patriarchal vicar for Jerusalem.

SYRO-MALABARESE: Descended from the St. Thomas Christians of India; situated mostly in the Malabar region of India; they use a Westernized and Latinized form of the Chaldean Rite in Syriac and Malayalam. Jurisdictions (located in India): two archdioceses, 19 dioceses; 3,158,252.

EASTERN JURISDICTIONS

For centuries Eastern-Rite Catholics were identifiable with a limited number of nationality and language groups in certain countries of the Middle East, Eastern Europe, Asia and Africa. The persecution of religion in the Soviet Union since 1917 and in communist-controlled countries since World War II, however — in addition to decimating and destroying the Church in those places — has resulted in the emigration of many Eastern-Rite Catholics from their homelands. This forced emigration, together with voluntary emigration, has led to the spread of Eastern Rites and their faithful to many other countries.

Europe

(Bishop Vasile Cristea, A.A., is apostolic visitor for Romanian Byzantine Rite Catholics in Europe.)

ALBANIA: Byzantine Rite, apostolic administration.

AUSTRIA: Byzantine Rite, ordinariate.

BULGARIA: Byzantine Rite (Bulgarians), apostolic exarchate.

CZECHOSLOVAKIA: Byzantine Rite (Slovakians and other Byzantine-Rite Catholics), eparchy.

FRANCE: Byzantine Rite (Ukrainians), apostolic exarchate.

Armenian Rite, eparchy (1986).

Ordinariate for all other Eastern-Rite Catholics.

GERMANY: Byzantine Rite (Ukrainians), apostolic exarchate.

GREAT BRITAIN: Byzantine Rite (Ukrainians), apostolic exarchate.

GREECE: Byzantine Rite, apostolic exarchate.

Armenian Rite, ordinariate.

HUNGARY: Byzantine Rite (Hungarians), eparchy, apostolic exarchate.

ITALY: Byzantine Rite (Italo-Albanians), two eparchies, one abbacy.

POLAND: Byzantine Rite (Ukrainian), apostolic exarchate.

Armenian Rite, archeparchy.

ROMANIA: Byzantine Rite (Romanians), metropolitan, four eparchies.

Armenian Rite, ordinariate.

RUSSIA: Byzantine Rite (Russians), apostolic exarchate; (Ruthenians), eparchy; (Ukrainians), major archeparchy, two eparchies.

YUGOSLAVIA: Byzantine Rite (Yugoslav and other Byzantine-Rite Catholics), eparchy.

Asia

CHINA: Byzantine Rite (Russians), apostolic exarchate.

CYPRUS: Antiochene Rite (Maronites), archeparchy.

INDIA: Antiochene Rite (Malankarese), metropolitan see, two eparchies.

Chaldean Rite (Syro-Malabarese), two metropolitan sees, 19 eparchies.

IRAN: Chaldean Rite (Chaldeans), two metropolitan sees, one archeparchy, one eparchy.

Armenian Rite, eparchy.

IRAQ: Antiochene Rite (Syrians), two archeparchies.

Byzantine Rite (Greek-Melkites), patriarchal vicariate.

Chaldean Rite (Chaldeans), patriarchate, two metropolitan sees, eight archeparchies and eparchies.

Armenian Rite, archeparchy.

ISRAEL (includes Jerusalem): Antiochene Rite (Syrians), patriarchal vicariate; (Maronites), patriarchal vicariate.

Byzantine Rite (Greek-Melkites), archeparchy, patriarchal vicariate.

Chaldean Rite (Chaldeans), patriarchal vicariate.

Armenian Rite, patriarchal vicariate.

JORDAN: Byzantine Rite (Greek-Melkites), archeparchy.

KUWAIT: Byzantine Rite (Greek-Melkites), patriarchal vicariate.

LEBANON: Antiochene Rite (Maronites), patriarchate, eight archeparchies and eparchies; (Syrians), patriarchate.

Byzantine Rite (Greek-Melkites), seven metropolitan and archeparchal sees.

Chaldean Rite (Chaldeans), eparchy.

Armenian Rite, patriarchate, eparchy.

SYRIA: Antiochene Rite (Maronites), two archeparchies, one eparchy; (Syrians), four archeparchies.

Byzantine Rite (Greek-Melkites), patriarchate, four metropolitan sees, one archeparchy.

Chaldean Rite (Chaldeans), eparchy.

Armenian Rite, archeparchy, eparchy, patriarchal exarchate.

TURKEY (Europe and Asia): Antiochene Rite (Syrians), patriarchal vicariate.

Byzantine Rite (Greeks), apostolic exarchate.
Chaldean Rite (Chaldeans), one archeparchy, two eparchies.
Armenian Rite, archeparchy.

Oceania

AUSTRALIA: Byzantine Rite (Ukrainians), eparchy; (Greek-Melkites), eparchy (1987).
Antiochene Rite (Maronites), eparchy.

Africa

EGYPT: Alexandrian Rite (Copts), patriarchate, five eparchies.
Antiochene Rite (Maronites), eparchy; (Syrians), eparchy.
Byzantine Rite (Greek-Melkites), patriarchal vicariate.
Chaldean Rite (Chaldeans), eparchy.
Armenian Rite, eparchy.
ETHIOPIA: Alexandrian Rite (Ethiopians), metropolitan see, two eparchies.
SUDAN: Byzantine Rite (Greek-Melkites), patriarchal vicariate.

North America

CANADA: Byzantine Rite (Ukrainians), one metropolitan, four eparchies; (Slovaks), eparchy; (Greek-Melkites), eparchy.
Armenian Rite, apostolic exarchate for Canada and the U.S. (New York is see city).
Antiochene Rite (Maronites), eparchy.
UNITED STATES: Antiochene Rite (Maronites), eparchy.
Byzantine Rite (Ukrainians), one metropolitan see, three eparchies; (Ruthenians), one metropolitan see, three eparchies; (Greek-Melkites), eparchy; (Romanians), eparchy; (Byelorussians), apostolic visitator.
Armenian Rite, apostolic exarchate for Canada and U.S. (New York is see city).
Chaldean Rite, eparchy.
MEXICO: Byzantine Rite (Greek-Melkites), eparchy (1988).
Other Eastern-Rite Catholics are under the jurisdiction of local Roman-Rite bishops. (See Eastern-Rite Catholics in the United States.)

South America

Armenian-Rite Catholics in Latin America (including Mexico) are under the jurisdiction of an apostolic exarchate (see city, Buenos Aires, Argentina).
ARGENTINA: Byzantine Rite (Ukrainians), eparchy.
Armenian Rite, apostolic exarchate (for Latin America)
Ordinariate for all other Eastern-Rite Catholics.
BRAZIL: Antiochene Rite (Maronites), eparchy.
Byzantine Rite (Greek-Melkites), eparchy; (Ukrainians), eparchy.
Ordinariate for all other Eastern-Rite Catholics.

SYNODS, ASSEMBLIES

These assemblies are collegial bodies which have pastoral authority over members of the Eastern Rite Churches.

Patriarchal Synods: Maronites: Nasrallah Pierre Sfeir, patriarch of Antioch of the Maronites.
Melkites: Maximos V Hakim, patriarch of Antioch of the Greek Catholics-Melkites.
Chaldeans: Paul II Cheikho, patriarch of Babylonia of the Chaldeans.
Copts: Stephanos II Ghattas, C.M., patriarch of Alexandria of the Copts.
Syrians: Ignace Antoine II Hayek, patriarch of Antioch of the Syrians.
Armenians: Jean Pierre XVIII Kasparian, patriarch of Cilicia of the Armenians.
Non-Patriarchal Synod: The Synod of the Ukrainian Catholic Hierarchy is an extraterritorial synod convoked with the assent of the Pope. Cardinal Myroslav Ivan Lubachivsky, major archbishop of Lwow of the Ukrainians, is president.
Assemblies: Assembly of the Catholic Hierarchy of Egypt: Stephanos II Ghattas, C.M., patriarch of Alexandria of the Copts, president.
Assembly of Catholic Patriarchs and Bishops of Lebanon: Nasrallah Pierre Sfeir, patriarch of Antioch of the Maronites, president.
Assembly of Ordinaries of the Syrian Arab Republic: Maximos V Hakim, patriarch of Antioch of the Greek Catholics-Melkites, president.
Interritual Union of the Bishops of Iraq: Paul II Cheikho, patriarch of Babylonia of the Chaldeans, president.
Syro-Malabarese Episcopal Conference (June 4, 1970): Most Rev. Anthony Padiyara, archbishop of Ernakulam, president.
Iranian Episcopal Conference (Aug. 11, 1977): Most Rev. Youhannan Semaan Issayi, metropolitan of Teheran of the Chaldeans, president.
Of the collegial bodies listed above, the patriarchal synods have the most authority. In addition to other prerogatives, they have the right to elect bishops and regulate discipline for their respective rites.

EASTERN RITES IN U.S.

(Statistics, from the *Official Catholic Directory*, unless noted otherwise, are membership figures reported by Eastern-Rite jurisdictions. Additional Eastern-Rite Catholics are included in statistics for Roman-Rite dioceses.)

Byzantine Rite

Ukrainians: There were 148,371 reported in four jurisdictions in the U.S.: the metropolitan see of Philadelphia (1924, metropolitan 1958) and the suffragan sees of Stamford, Conn. (1956), St. Nicholas of Chicago (1961) and St. Josaphat in Parma (1983).
Ruthenians: There were 274,402 reported in four jurisdictions in the U.S.: the metropolitan see of Pittsburgh (est. 1924 at Pittsburgh; metropolitan and transferred to Munhall, 1969; transferred to Pittsburgh, 1977) and the suffragan sees of Passaic, N.J. (1963), Parma, Ohio (1969) and Van Nuys, Calif. (1981). Hungarian and Croatian Byzantine Catholics in the U.S. are also under the jurisdiction of Ruthenian-Rite bishops.

Melkites (Greek Catholics-Melkites): In 1988, 25,150 were reported under the jurisdiction of the Melkite eparchy of Newton, Mass. (established as an exarchate, 1965; eparchy, 1976).

Romanians: There were 5,000 reported in 16 Romanian Catholic Byzantine Rite parishes in the U.S., under the jurisdiction of the Romanian eparchy of St. George Martyr, Canton, Ohio (established as an exarchate, 1982; eparchy, 1987).

Byelorussians: Have one parish in the U.S. — Christ the Redeemer, Chicago, Ill.

Russians: Have parishes in California (St. Andrew, El Segundo, and Our Lady of Fatima Center, San Francisco); Massachusetts (Our Lady of Kazan, Boston); New York (St. Michael's Chapel of St. Patrick's Old Cathedral). They are under the jurisdiction of local Roman-Rite bishops.

Antiochene Rite

In 1988, 51,693 Maronites were reported under the jurisdiction of the eparchy of St. Maron, Brooklyn (established at Detroit as an exarchate, 1966; eparchy, 1972; transferred to Brooklyn, 1977).

Armenian Rite

An apostolic exarchate for Canada and the United States (see city, New York) was established July 3, 1981; 33,300 in both countries *(Annuario Pontificio)*.

Chaldean Rite

In 1988, 45,000 were reported *(Annuario Pontificio)* under the jurisdiction of the eparchy of St. Thomas Apostle of Detroit (established as an exarchate, 1982; eparchy, 1986).

BYZANTINE DIVINE LITURGY

The Divine Liturgy in all rites is based on the consecration of bread and wine by the narration-reactualization of the actions of Christ at the Last Supper. Aside from this fundamental usage, there are differences between the Roman (Latin) Rite and Eastern Rites, and among the Eastern Rites themselves. Following is a general description of the Byzantine Divine Liturgy which is in widest use in the Eastern-Rite Churches.

In the Byzantine, as in all Eastern Rites, the bread and wine are prepared at the start of the Liturgy. The priest does this in a little niche or at a table in the sanctuary. Taking a round loaf of leavened bread stamped with religious symbols, he cuts out a square host and other particles while reciting verses expressing the symbolism of the action. When the bread and wine are ready, he says a prayer of offering and incenses the oblations, the altar, the icons and the people.

Liturgy of the Catechumens: At the altar a litany for all classes of people is sung by the priest. The congregation answers, "Lord, have mercy."

The Little Entrance comes next. In procession, the priest leaves the sanctuary carrying the Book of the Gospels, and then returns. He sings prayers especially selected for the day and the feast. These are followed by the solemn singing of the prayer, "Holy God, Holy Mighty One, Holy Immortal One."

The Epistle follows. The Gospel is sung or read by the priest facing the people at the middle door of the sanctuary.

An interruption after the Liturgy of the Catechumens, formerly an instructional period for those learning the faith, is clearly marked. Catechumens, if present, are dismissed with a prayer. Following this are a prayer and litany for the faithful.

Great Entrance: The Great Entrance or solemn Offertory Procession then takes place. The priest first says a long silent prayer for himself, in preparation for the great act to come. Again he incenses the oblations, the altar, the icons and people. He goes to the table on the gospel side for the veil-covered paten and chalice. When he arrives back at the sanctuary door, he announces the intention of the Mass in the prayer: "May the Lord God remember all of you in his kingdom, now and forever."

After another litany, the congregation recites the Nicene Creed.

Consecration: The most solemn portion of the sacrifice is introduced by the preface, which is very much like the preface of the Roman Rite. At the beginning of the last phrase, the priest raises his voice to introduce the singing of the Sanctus. During the singing he reads the introduction to the words of consecration.

The words of consecration are sung aloud, and the people sing "Amen" to both consecrations. As the priest raises the Sacred Species in solemn offering, he sings: "Thine of Thine Own we offer unto Thee in behalf of all and for all."

A prayer to the Holy Spirit is followed by the commemorations, in which special mention is made of the all-holy, most blessed and glorious Lady, the Mother of God and ever-Virgin Mary. The dead are remembered and then the living.

Holy Communion: A final litany for spiritual gifts precedes the Our Father. The Sacred Body and Blood are elevated with the words, "Holy Things for the Holy." The Host is then broken and commingled with the Precious Blood. The priest recites preparatory prayers for Holy Communion, consumes the Sacred Species, and distributes Holy Communion to the people under the forms of both bread and wine. During this time a communion verse is sung by the choir or congregation.

The Liturgy closes quickly after this. The consecrated Species of bread and wine are removed to the side table to be consumed later by the priest. A prayer of thanksgiving is recited, a prayer for all the people is said in front of the icon of Christ, a blessing is invoked upon all, and the people are dismissed.

BYZANTINE CALENDAR

The Byzantine-Rite calendar has many distinctive features of its own, although it shares common elements with the Roman-Rite calendar

— e.g., general purpose, commemoration of the mysteries of faith and of the saints, identical dates for some feasts. Among the distinctive things are the following.

The liturgical year begins on Sept. 1, the **Day of Indiction**, in contrast with the Latin or Roman start on the First Sunday of Advent late in November or early in December. The Advent season begins on Dec. 10.

Cycles of the Year

As in the Roman usage, the dating of feasts follows the Gregorian Calendar. Formerly, until well into this century, the Julian Calendar was used. (The Julian Calendar, which is now about 13 days late, is still used by some Eastern-Rite Churches.)

The year has several cycles, which include proper seasons, the feasts of saints, and series of New Testament readings. All of these elements of worship are contained in liturgical books of the rite.

The ecclesiastical calendar, called the **Menologion**, explains the nature of feasts, other observances and matters pertaining to the liturgy for each day of the year. In some cases, its contents include the lives of saints and the history and meaning of feasts.

The Divine Liturgy (Mass) and Divine Office for the proper of the saints, fixed feasts, and the Christmas season are contained in the **Menaion**. The **Triodion** covers the pre-Lenten season of preparation for Easter; Lent begins two days before the Ash Wednesday observance of the Roman Rite. The **Pentecostarion** contains the liturgical services from Easter to the Sunday of All Saints, the first after Pentecost. The **Evangelion** and **Apostolos** are books in which the Gospels, and Acts of the Apostles and the Epistles, respectively, are arranged according to the order of their reading in the Divine Liturgy and Divine Office throughout the year.

The cyclic progression of liturgical music throughout the year, in successive and repetitive periods of eight weeks, is governed by the **Oktoechos**, the Book of Eight Tones.

Sunday Names

Many Sundays are named after the subject of the Gospel read in the Mass of the day or after the name of a feast falling on the day — e.g., Sunday of the Publican and Pharisee, of the Prodigal Son, of the Samaritan Woman, of St. Thomas the Apostle, of the Fore-Fathers (Old Testament Patriarchs). Other Sundays are named in the same manner as in the Roman calendar — e.g., numbered Sundays of Lent and after Pentecost.

Holy Days

The calendar lists about 28 holy days. Many of the major holy days coincide with those of the Roman calendar, but the feast of the Immaculate Conception is observed on Dec. 9 instead of Dec. 8, and the feast of All Saints falls on the Sunday after Pentecost rather than on Nov. 1. Instead of a single All Souls' Day, there are five All Souls' Saturdays.

According to regulations in effect in the Byzantine-Rite (Ruthenian) Archeparchy of Pittsburgh and its suffragan sees of Passaic, Parma and Van Nuys, holy days are obligatory, solemn and simple, and attendance at the Divine Liturgy is required on five obligatory days — the feasts of the Epiphany, the Ascension, Sts. Peter and Paul, the Assumption of the Blessed Virgin Mary, and Christmas. Although attendance at the liturgy is not obligatory on 15 solemn and seven simple holy days, it is recommended.

In the Byzantine-Rite (Ukrainian) Archeparchy of Philadelphia and its suffragan sees of St. Josaphat in Parma, St. Nicholas (Chicago) and Stamford, the obligatory feasts are the Circumcision, Epiphany, Annunciation, Easter, Ascension, Pentecost, Dormition (Assumption of Mary), Immaculate Conception and Christmas.

Lent

The first day of Lent — the Monday before Ash Wednesday of the Roman Rite — and Good Friday are days of strict abstinence for persons in the age bracket of obligation. No meat, eggs, or dairy products may be eaten on these days.

All persons over the age of 14 must abstain from meat on Fridays during Lent, Holy Saturday, and the vigils of the feasts of Christmas and Epiphany; abstinence is urged, but is not obligatory, on Wednesdays of Lent. The abstinence obligation is not in force on certain "free" or "privileged" Fridays.

Synaxis

An observance without a counterpart in the Roman calendar is the synaxis. This is a commemoration, on the day following a feast, of persons involved with the occasion for the feast — e.g., Sept. 9, the day following the feast of the Nativity of the Blessed Virgin Mary, is the Synaxis of Joachim and Anna, her parents.

Holy Week

In the Byzantine Rite, Lent is liturgically concluded with the Saturday of Lazarus, the day before Palm Sunday, which commemorates the raising of Lazarus from the dead.

On the following Monday, Tuesday and Wednesday, the Liturgy of the Presanctified is prescribed.

On Holy Thursday, the Liturgy of St. Basil the Great is celebrated together with Vespers.

The Divine Liturgy is not celebrated on Good Friday.

On Holy Saturday, the Liturgy of St. Basil the Great is celebrated along with Vespers.

BYZANTINE FEATURES

Art: Named for the empire in which it developed, Byzantine art is a unique blend of imperial Roman and classic Hellenic culture with Christian inspiration. The art of the Greek Middle Ages, it reached a peak of development in the 10th or 11th century. Characteristic of its products, particularly in mosaic and painting, are majesty, dignity, refinement and grace. Its sacred paintings, called icons, are reverenced highly in all Eastern Rites.

Church Building: The classical model of Byzantine church architecture is the Church of the Holy Wisdom (Hagia Sophia), built in Constantinople in the first half of the sixth century and still standing. The square structure, extended in some cases in the form of a cross, is topped by a distinctive onion-shaped dome and surmounted by a triple-bar cross. The altar is at the eastern end of building, where the wall bellies out to form an apse. The altar and sanctuary are separated from the body of the church by a fixed or movable screen, the iconostas, to which icons or sacred pictures are attached (see below).

Clergy: The Byzantine Rite has married as well as celibate priests. In places other than the US, where married candidates have not been accepted for ordination since about 1929, men already married can be ordained to the diaconate and priesthood and can continue in marriage after ordination. Celibate deacons and priests cannot marry after ordination; neither can a married priest remarry after the death of his wife. Bishops must be unmarried.

Iconostas: A large screen decorated with sacred pictures or icons which separates the sanctuary from the nave of a church; its equivalent in the Roman Rite, for thus separating the sanctuary from the nave, is an altar rail.

An iconostas has three doors through which the sacred ministers enter the sanctuary during the Divine Liturgy: smaller (north and south) Deacons' Doors and a large central Royal Door.

The Deacons' Doors usually feature the icons of Sts. Gabriel and Michael; the Royal Door, the icons of the Evangelists — Matthew, Mark, Luke and John. To the right and left of the Royal Door are the icons of Christ the Teacher and of the Blessed Virgin Mary with the Infant Jesus. To the extreme right and left are the icons of the patron of the church and St. John the Baptist (or St. Nicholas of Myra).

Immediately above the Royal Door is a picture of the Last Supper. To the right are six icons depicting the major feasts of Christ, and to the left are six icons portraying the major feasts of the Blessed Virgin Mary. Above the picture of the Last Supper is a large icon of Christ the King.

Some icon screens also have pictures of the 12 Apostles and the major Old Testament prophets surmounted by a crucifixion scene.

Liturgical Language: In line with Eastern tradition, Byzantine practice has favored the use of the language of the people in the liturgy. Two great advocates of the practice were Sts. Cyril and Methodius, apostles of the Slavs, who devised the Cyrillic alphabet and pioneered the adoption of Slavonic in the liturgy.

Sacraments: Baptism is administered by immersion, and confirmation is conferred at the same time. The Eucharist is administered by intinction, i.e., by giving the communicant a piece of consecrated leavened bread which has been dipped into the consecrated wine. When giving absolution in the sacrament of penance, the priest holds his stole over the head of the penitent. Distinctive marriage ceremonies include the crowning of the bride and groom. Ceremonies for anointing the sick closely resemble those of the Roman Rite. Holy orders are conferred by a bishop.

Sign of the Cross: Eastern-Rite Catholics have a distinctive way of making it (see entry in the Glossary). The sign of the cross in conjunction with a deep bow, instead of a genuflection, expresses reverence for the presence of Christ in the Blessed Sacrament.

VESTMENTS, APPURTENANCES

Sticharion: A long white garment of linen or silk with wide sleeves and decorated with embroidery; formerly the vestment for clerics in minor orders, acolytes, lectors, chanters, and subdeacons; symbolic of purity.

Epitrachelion: A stole with ends sewn together, having a loop through which the head is passed; its several crosses symbolize priestly duties.

Zone: A narrow clasped belt made of the same material as the epitrachelion; symbolic of the wisdom of the priest, his strength against enemies of the Church and his willingness to perform holy duties.

Epimanikia: Ornamental cuffs; the right cuff symbolizing strength, the left, patience and good will.

Phelonion: An ample cape, long in the back and sides and cut away in front; symbolic of the higher gifts of the Holy Spirit.

Antimension: A silk or linen cloth laid on the altar for the Liturgy; it may be decorated with a picture of the burial of Christ and the instruments of his passion; the relics of martyrs are sewn into the front border.

Eileton: A linen cloth which corresponds to the Roman-Rite corporal.

Poterion: A chalice or cup which holds the wine and Precious Blood.

Diskos: A shallow plate, which may be elevated on a small stand, corresponding to the Roman-Rite paten.

Asteriskos: Made of two curved bands of gold or silver which cross each other to form a double arch; a star depends from the junction, which forms a cross; it is placed over the diskos holding the consecrated bread and is covered with a veil.

Veils: Three are used, one to cover the poterion, the second to cover the diskos, and the third to cover both.

Spoon: Used in administering Holy Communion by intinction; consecrated leavened bread is dipped into consecrated wine and spooned onto the tongue of the communicant.

All Rites Equal

The Second Vatican Council's *Decree on Eastern Catholic Churches* declared that the Latin Rite and the Eastern Rites are all "of equal dignity," and "that none of them is superior to the others by reason of rite." The decree also challenged Eastern Churches to recover their authentic liturgical, legal and spiritual traditions, and to play "a special role . . . in promoting the unity of all Christians, particularly Easterners."

SEPARATED EASTERN CHURCHES

ORTHODOX

Orthodox Churches, the largest and most widespread of the separated Eastern Churches, have much in common with their Eastern Catholic counterparts, including many matters of faith and morals, general discipline, valid orders and sacraments, and liturgy. One important difference is their acceptance of only the first seven ecumenical councils. Another is their rejection of any single supreme head of the Church. They do not acknowledge and hold communion with the pope.

Like their Catholic counterparts, Orthodox Churches are organized in jurisdictions under patriarchs. The patriarchs are the heads of approximately 15 autocephalic and several other autonomous jurisdictions organized along lines of nationality and/or language.

The Ecumenical Patriarch of Constantinople, Dimitrios I, has the primacy of honor among his equal patriarchs but his actual jurisdiction is limited to his own patriarchate. As the spiritual head of worldwide Orthodoxy, he keeps the book of the Holy Canons of the Autocephalous Churches, in which recognized Orthodox Churches are registered, and has the right to call Pan-Orthodox assemblies.

The definitive Orthodox break with Rome dates from 1054.

Top-level relations between the Churches have improved in recent years through the efforts of former Ecumenical Patriarch Athenagoras I, John XXIII, Paul VI and Patriarch Dimitrios I. Pope Paul met with Athenagoras three times before the latter's death in 1972. The most significant action of both spiritual leaders was their mutual nullification of excommunications imposed by the two Churches on each other in 1054.

The largest Orthodox body in the western hemisphere is the Greek Orthodox Archdiocese of North and South America consisting of the Archdiocese of New York, nine dioceses in the U.S., and one diocese each in Canada and South America; it is headed by Archbishop Iakovos and has an estimated membership of 1.9 million. The second largest is the Orthodox Church in America, with approximately one million members; it was given independent status by the Patriarchate of Moscow May 18, 1970, against the will of Athenagoras I who refused to register it in the book of the Holy Canons of Autocephalous Churches. An additional 650,000 or more Orthodox belong to smaller national and language jurisdictions.

Heads of Orthodox jurisdictions in this hemisphere hold membership in the Standing Conference of Canonical Orthodox Bishops in the Americas.

Jurisdictions

The principal jurisdictions of the Greek, Russian and other Orthodox Churches are as follows.

Greek: Patriarchate of Constantinople, with jurisdiction in Turkey, Crete, the Dodecanese, Western Europe, the Americas, Australia; Dimitrios I is Ecumenical Patriarch.

Patriarchate of Alexandria, with jurisdiction in Egypt and the rest of Africa; there is also a native African Orthodox Church in Kenya and Uganda.

Patriarchate of Antioch (Melkites or Syrian Orthodox), with jurisdiction in Syria, Lebanon, Iraq, Australasia, the Americas; Syrian or Arabic, in place of Greek, is the liturgical language.

Patriarchate of Jerusalem, with jurisdiction in Israel and Jordan.

Churches of Greece, Cyprus and Sinai are autocephalic but maintain relations with their fellow Orthodox.

Russian: Patriarchate of Moscow with jurisdiction centered in the Soviet Union.

Other: Patriarchate of Serbia, with jurisdiction in Yugoslavia, Western Europe, the Americas, Australasia.

Patriarchates of Rumania and Bulgaria.
Katholikate of Georgia, the Soviet Union.
Byelorussians and Ukrainian Byzantines.
Churches of Albania, China, Czechoslovakia, Estonia, Finland, Hungary, Japan, Latvia, Lithuania, Poland.

Other minor communities in various places; e.g., Korea, the U.S., Carpatho-Russia.

The Division of Archives and Statistics of the Eastern Orthodox World Foundation reported a 1970 estimate of more than 200 million Orthodox Church members throughout the world. Other sources estimate the total to be approximately 125 million.

Conference of Orthodox Bishops

The Standing Conference of Canonical Orthodox Bishops in the Americas was established in 1960 to achieve cooperation among the various Orthodox jurisdictions in the Americas. Office: 8-10 East 79th St., New York, N.Y. 10021.

Member churches of the conference are the: Albanian Orthodox Diocese of America (Ecumenical Patriarchate), American Carpatho-Russian Orthodox Greek Catholic Diocese in the U.S.A. (Ecumenical Patriarchate), Antiochian Orthodox Christian Archdiocese of North America, Bulgarian Eastern Orthodox Church, Greek Orthodox Archdiocese of North and South America (Ecumenical Patriarchate), Orthodox Church in America, Romanian Orthodox Missionary Archdiocese in America and Canada, Serbian Orthodox Church in the United States of America and Canada, Ukrainian Orthodox Church in America (Ecumenical Patriarchate).

ANCIENT CHURCHES OF THE EAST

Ancient Churches of the East, which are distinct from Orthodox Churches, were the subject of an article by Gerard Daucourt published in the Feb. 16, 1987, English edition of "L'Osservatore Romano." Following is an excerpt.

By Ancient Churches of the East one means: the Assyrian Oriental Church (formerly called Nestorian), the Armenian Church, the Coptic

Church, the Ethiopian Church, the Syrian Church (sometimes called Syro-Jacobite) and the Syrian Church of India.

After the Council of Ephesus (431), the Assyrian Oriental Church did not maintain communion with the rest of the Christian world. For reasons as much and perhaps more political than doctrinal, it did not accept the Council's teaching (that Mary is the Mother of God, in opposition to the opinion of Nestorius; see Nestorianism. For this reason, the Assyrian Oriental Church came to be called Nestorian.) It is well known that in the 16th century a great segment of the faithful of this Church entered into communion with the See of Rome and constitutes today, among the Oriental Catholic Churches, the Chaldean Patriarchate.

The Patriarch of the Assyrian Oriental Church, His Holiness Mar Denkha IV, in the course of his visit to the Holy Father and to the Church of Rome of 7 to 9 November, 1984, requested that people stop using the term "Nestorian" to designate his Church and expressed the desire that a declaration made jointly by the Pope of Rome and himself may one day serve to express the common faith of the two Churches in Jesus Christ, Son of God incarnate, born of the Virgin Mary. The labours of Catholic historians and theologians have, moreover, already contributed to showing that such a declaration would be possible.

The other Ancient Churches of the East for a long time have been designated by the term "Monophysite Churches" (see Monophysitism). It is regrettable to find this name still employed sometimes in certain publications, since already in 1951, in the encyclical *Sempiternus Rex,* on the occasion of the 15th centenary of the Council of Chalcedon, Pius XII declared with regard to the Christians of these Churches: "They depart from the right way only in terminology, when they expound the doctrine of the Incarnation of the Lord. This may be deduced from their liturgical and theological books."

In this same encyclical, Pius XII expressed the view that the separation at the doctrinal level came about "above all, through a certain ambiguity of terminology that occurred at the beginning."

Since then, two important declarations have been arrived at in line with the ecumenical stance taken by the Church at the Second Vatican Council and the labors of the theologians (particularly in the framework of the Foundation "Pro Oriente" of Vienna). One was signed by Pope Paul VI and Coptic Patriarch Shenouda III on 10 May, 1973, and the other by Pope John Paul II and the Syrian Patriarch Ignace Zakka I Iwas, on 23 June, 1984. In both of these texts, the hierarchies of the respective Churches confess one and the same faith in the mystery of the Word Incarnate. After such declarations, it is no longer possible to speak in general terms of the "Monophysite" Churches.

The Armenian Church has communicants in the Soviet Union, the Middle and Far East, the Americas.

The Coptic Church has communicants in Egypt and elsewhere.

The Ethiopian or Abyssinian Church has communicants in Africa, the Middle East, the Americas, India.

The Syrian Church has communicants in the Middle East, the Americas, India.

Members of the Assyrian Oriental Church are scattered throughout the world.

It is estimated that there are approximately 10 million or more members of these other Eastern Churches throughout the world. For various reasons, a more accurate determination is not possible.

EASTERN ECUMENISM

The Second Vatican Council, in the "Decree on Eastern Catholic Churches," pointed out the special role they have to play "in promoting the unity of all Christians, particularly Easterners." The document also stated in part as follows.

The Eastern Churches in communion with the Apostolic See of Rome have a special role to play in promoting the unity of all Christians, particularly Easterners, according to the principles of this sacred Synod's *Decree on Ecumenism* first of all by prayer, then by the example of their lives, by religious fidelity to ancient Eastern traditions, by greater mutual knowledge, by collaboration, and by a brotherly regard for objects and attitudes (No. 24).

If any separated Eastern Christian should, under the guidance of grace of the Holy Spirit, join himself to Catholic unity, no more should be required of him than what a simple profession of the Catholic faith demands. A valid priesthood is preserved among Eastern clerics. Hence, upon joining themselves to the unity of the Catholic Church, Eastern clerics are permitted to exercise the orders they possess, in accordance with the regulations established by the competent authority (No. 25).

Divine Law forbids any common worship (*communicatio in sacris*) which would damage the unity of the Church, or involve formal acceptance of falsehood or the danger of deviation in the faith, of scandal, or of indifferentism. At the same time, pastoral experience clearly shows that with respect to our Eastern brethren there should and can be taken into consideration various circumstances affecting individuals, wherein the unity of the Church is not jeopardized nor are intolerable risks involved, but in which salvation itself and the spiritual profit of souls are urgently at issue.

Hence, in view of special circumstances of time, place, and personage, the Catholic Church has often adopted and now adopts a milder policy, offering to all the means of salvation and an example of charity among Christians through participation in the sacraments and in other sacred functions and objects. With these considerations in mind, and "lest because of the harshness of our judgment we prove an obstacle to those seeking salvation," and in order to promote closer union with the Eastern Churches separated from us, this sacred Synod lays down the following policy:

In view of the principles recalled above, Eastern Christians who are separated in good faith from the Catholic Church, if they ask of their own accord and have the right dispositions, may be granted the sacraments of penance, the Eucharist, and the anointing of the sick. Furthermore, Catholics may ask for these same sacraments from those non-Catholic ministers whose Churches possess valid sacraments, as often as necessity or a genuine spiritual benefit recommends such a course of action, and when access to a Catholic priest is physically or morally impossible (Nos. 26, 27).

Again, in view of these very same principles, Catholics may for a just cause join with their separated Eastern brethren in sacred functions, things, and places (No. 28).

This more lenient policy with regard to common worship involving Catholics and their brethren of the separated Eastern Churches is entrusted to the care and execution of the local Ordinaries so that, by taking counsel among themselves and, if circumstances warrant, after consultation also with the Ordinaries of the separated Churches, they may govern relations between Christians by timely and effective rules and regulations (No. 29).

PROTESTANT CHURCHES

MEN, DOCTRINES, CHURCHES OF THE REFORMATION

Some of the leading figures, doctrines and churches of the Reformation are covered below. A companion article covers Major Protestant Churches in the United States.

John Wycliff (c. 1320-1384): English priest and scholar who advanced one of the leading Reformation ideas nearly 200 years before Martin Luther — that the Bible alone is the sufficient rule of faith — but had only an indirect influence on the 16th century Reformers. Supporting belief in an inward and practical religion, he denied the divinely commissioned authority of the pope and bishops of the Church; he also denied the Real Presence of Christ in the Holy Eucharist, and wrote against the sacrament of penance and the doctrine of indulgences. Nearly 20 of his propositions were condemned by Gregory XI in 1377; his writings were proscribed more extensively by the Council of Constance in 1415. His influence was strongest in Bohemia and Central Europe.

John Hus (c. 1369-1415): A Bohemian priest and preacher of reform who authored 30 propositions condemned by the Council of Constance. Excommunicated in 1411 or 1412, he was burned at the stake in 1415. His principal errors concerned the nature of the Church and the origin of papal authority. He spread some of the ideas of Wycliff but did not subscribe to his views regarding faith alone as the condition for justification and salvation, the sole sufficiency of Scripture as the rule of faith, the Real Presence of Christ in the Eucharist, and the sacramental system. In 1457 some of his followers founded the Church of the Brotherhood which later became known as the United Brethren or Moravian Church and is considered the earliest independent Protestant body.

Martin Luther (1483-1546): An Augustinian friar, priest and doctor of theology, the key figure in the Reformation. In 1517, as a special indulgence was being preached in Germany, and in view of needed reforms within the Church, he published at Wittenberg 95 theses concerning matters of Catholic belief and practice. Leo X condemned 41 statements from Luther's writings in 1520. Luther, refusing to recant, was excommunicated the following year. His teachings strongly influenced subsequent Lutheran theology; its statements of faith are found in the Book of Concord (1580).

Luther's doctrine included the following: The sin of Adam, which corrupted human nature radically (but not substantially), has affected every aspect of man's being. Justification, understood as the forgiveness of sins and the state of righteousness, is by grace for Christ's sake through faith. Faith involves not merely intellectual assent but an act of confidence by the will. Good works are indispensably necessary concomitants of faith, but do not merit salvation. Of the sacraments, Luther retained baptism, penance and the Holy Communion as effective vehicles of the grace of the Holy Spirit; he held that in the Holy Communion the consecrated bread and wine are the Body and Blood of Christ. The rule of faith is the divine revelation in the Sacred Scriptures. He rejected purgatory, indulgences and the invocation of the saints, and held that prayers for the dead have no efficacy. Lutheran tenets not in agreement with Catholic doctrine were condemned by the Council of Trent.

Anabaptism: Originated in Saxony in the first quarter of the 16th century and spread rapidly through southern Germany. Its doctrine included several key Lutheran tenets but was not regarded with favor by Luther, Calvin or Zwingli. Anabaptists believed that baptism is for adults only and that infant baptism is invalid. Their doctrine of the Inner Light, concerning the direct influence of the Holy Spirit on the believer, implied rejection of Catholic doctrine concerning the sacraments and the nature of the Church. Eighteen articles of faith were formulated in 1632 in Holland. Mennonites are Anabaptists.

Ulrich Zwingli (1484-1531): A priest who triggered the Reformation in Switzerland with a series of New Testament lectures in 1519, later disputations and by other actions. He held the Gospel to be the only basis of truth; rejected the Mass (which he suppressed in 1525 at Zurich), penance and other sacraments; denied papal primacy and doctrine concerning purgatory and the invocation of saints; rejected celibacy, monasticism and many traditional practices of piety. His symbolic view of the Eucharist, which was at odds with Catholic doctrine, caused an irreconcilable controversy with Luther and his followers. Zwingli was killed in a battle between the forces of Protestant and Catholic cantons in Switzerland.

John Calvin (1509-1564): French leader of the Reformation in Switzerland, whose key tenet was absolute predestination of some persons to heaven and others to hell. He rejected Catholic doctrine in 1533 after becoming convinced of a personal mission to reform the Church. In 1536 he published the first edition of *Institutes of the Christian Religion*, a systematic exposition of his doctrine which became the classic textbook of Reformed — as distinguished from Lutheran — theology. To Luther's principal theses — regarding Scripture as the sole rule of faith, the radical corruption of human nature, and justification by faith alone — he added absolute predestination, certitude of salvation for the elect, and the incapability of the elect to lose grace. His Eucharistic theory, which failed to mediate the Zwingli-Luther controversy, was at odds with Catholic doctrine. From 1555 until his death Calvin was the virtual dictator of Geneva, the capital of the non-Lutheran Reformation in Europe.

Arminianism: A modification of the rigid predestinationism of Calvin, set forth by Jacob Arminius (1560-1609) and formally stated in the *Remonstrance* of 1610. Arminianism influenced some Calvinist bodies.

Unitarianism: A 16th century doctrine which rejected the Trinity and the divinity of Christ in favor of a uni-personal God. It claimed scriptural support for a long time but became generally rationalistic with respect to "revealed" doctrine as well as in ethics and its world-view. One of its principal early proponents was Faustus Socinus (1539-1604), a leader of the Polish Brethren.

A variety of communions developed in England in the Reformation and post-Reformation periods.

Puritans: Extremists who sought church reform along Calvinist lines in severe simplicity. (Use of the term was generally discontinued after 1660.)

Presbyterians: Basically Calvinistic, called Presbyterian because church polity centers around assemblies of presbyters or elders. John Knox (c. 1513-1572) established the church in Scotland.

Congregationalists: Evangelical in spirit and seeking a return to forms of the primitive church, they uphold individual freedom in religious matters, do not require the acceptance of a creed as a condition for communion, and regard each congregation as autonomous. Robert Browne influenced the beginnings of Congregationalism.

Quakers: Their key belief is in internal divine illumination, the inner light of the living Christ, as the only source of truth and inspiration. George Fox (1624-1691) was one of their leaders in England. Called the Society of Friends, the Quakers are noted for their pacificism.

Baptists: So called because of their doctrine concerning baptism. They reject infant baptism and consider only baptism by immersion as valid. Leaders in the formation of the church were John Smyth (d. 1612) in England and Roger Williams (d. 1683) in America.

Methodists: A group who broke away from the Anglican Communion under the leadership of John Wesley (1703-1791), although some Anglican beliefs were retained. Doctrines include the witness of the Spirit to the individual and personal assurance of salvation. Wesleyan Methodists do not subscribe to some of the more rigid Calvinistic tenets held by other Methodists.

Universalism: A product of 18th-century liberal Protestantism in England. The doctrine is not Trinitarian and includes a tenet that all men will ultimately be saved.

ANGLICAN COMMUNION

This communion, which regards itself as the same apostolic Church as that which was established by early Christians in England, derived not from Reformation influences but from the renunciation of papal jurisdiction by Henry VIII (1491-1547). His Act of Supremacy in 1534 called Christ's Church an assembly of local churches subject to the prince, who was vested with fullness of authority and jurisdiction. In spite of Henry's denial of papal authority, this Act did not reject substantially other principal articles of faith. Notable changes, proposed and adopted for the reformation of the church, took place in the subsequent reigns of James VI and Elizabeth, with respect to such matters as Scripture as the rule of faith, the sacraments, the nature of the Mass, and the constitution of the hierarchy. (See Episcopal Church, Anglican Orders.)

MAJOR PROTESTANT CHURCHES IN THE UNITED STATES

There are more than 250 Protestant church bodies in the United States.

The majority of U.S. Protestants belong to the following denominations: Baptist, Methodist, Lutheran, Presbyterian, Protestant Episcopal, the United Church of Christ, the Christian Church (Disciples of Christ), Evangelicals.

See Ecumenical Dialogues, Reports and related entries for coverage of relations between the Catholic Church and other Christian churches.

Baptist Churches

(Courtesy of the Office of Communication, American Baptist Churches in the U.S.A.)

Baptist churches, comprising the largest of all American Protestant denominations, were first established by John Smyth near the beginning of the 17th century in England. The first Baptist church in America was founded at Providence by Roger Williams in 1639.

Largest of the nearly 30 Baptist bodies in the U.S. are:

The Southern Baptist Convention, 460 James Robertson Parkway, Nashville, Tenn. 37219, with 14.1 million members;

The National Baptist Convention, U.S.A., Inc., 915 Spain St., Baton Rouge, La. 70802, with 7.35 million members;

The National Baptist Convention of America, 954 Kings Rd., Jacksonville, Fla. 32204, with 2.6 million members.

The American Baptist Churches in the U.S.A., P.O. Box 851, Valley Forge, Pa. 19482, with 1.5 million members.

The total number of U.S. Baptists is more than 29 million. The world total is 33 million.

Proper to Baptists is their doctrine on baptism. Called an "ordinance" rather than a sacrament, baptism by immersion is a sign that one has experienced and decided in favor of the salvation offered by Christ. It is administered only to persons who are able to make a responsible decision. Baptism is not administered to infants.

Baptists do not have a formal creed but generally subscribe to two professions of faith formulated in 1689 and 1832 and are in general agreement with classical Protestant theology regarding Scripture as the sole rule of faith, original sin, justification through faith in Christ, and the nature of the Church. Their local churches are autonomous.

Worship services differ in form from one congregation to another. Usual elements are the reading of Scripture, a sermon, hymns, vocal and silent prayer. The Lord's Supper, called an "ordinance," is celebrated at various intervals.

Methodist Churches

(Courtesy of Joe Hale, General Secretary of the World Methodist Council.)

John Wesley (1703-1791), an Anglican clergyman, was the founder of Methodism. In 1738, following a period of missionary work in America and strongly influenced by the Moravians, he experienced a new conversion to Christ and shortly thereafter became a leader in a religious awakening in England. By the end of the 18th century, Methodism was strongly rooted also in America.

The United Methodist Church, formed in 1968 by a merger of the Methodist Church and the Evangelical United Brethren Church, is the second largest Protestant denomination in the U.S., with more than nine million members; its principal agencies are located in New York, Evanston, Ill., Nashville, Tenn., Washington, D.C., Dayton, O., and Lake Junaluska, N.C. (World Methodist Council, P.O. Box 518. 28745). The second largest body, with more than two million communicants, is the African Methodist Episcopal Church. Four other major churches in the U.S. are the African Methodist Episcopal Zion, Christian Methodist Episcopal, Free Methodist Church and the Wesleyan Church. The total Methodist membership in the U.S. is about 15.5 million.

Worldwide, there are more than 64 autonomous Methodist/Wesleyan churches in 90 countries, with a membership of more than 25 million. All of them participate in the World Methodist Council, which gives global unity to the witness of Methodist communicants.

Methodism, although it has a base in Calvinistic theology, rejects absolute predestination and maintains that Christ offers grace freely to all men, not just to a select elite. Wesley's distinctive doctrine was the "witness of the Spirit" to the individual soul and personal assurance of salvation. He also emphasized the central themes of conversion and holiness. Methodists are in general agreement with classical Protestant theology regarding Scripture as the sole rule of faith, original sin, justification through faith in Christ, the nature of the Church, and the sacraments of baptism and the Lord's Supper. Church polity is structured along episcopal lines in America, with ministers being appointed to local churches by a bishop; churches stemming from British Methodism do not have bishops but vest appointive powers within an appropriate conference. Congregations are free to choose various forms of worship services; typical elements are readings from Scripture, sermons, hymns and prayers.

Lutheran Churches

(Courtesy of Thomas Hartley Dorris, editor of Ecumenical Press Service, Box 66, CH-1211 Geneva 20, Switzerland; and other Lutheran sources.)

The origin of Lutheranism is generally traced to Oct. 31, 1517, when Martin Luther — Augustinian friar, priest, doctor of theology — tacked "95 Theses" to the door of the castle church in Wittenberg, Germany. This call to debate on the subject of indulgences and related concerns has come to symbolize the beginning of the Reformation. Luther and his supporters intended to reform the Church they knew. Though Lutheranism has come to be visible in separate denominations and national churches, at its heart it professes itself to be a confessional movement within the one, holy, catholic and apostolic Church.

The world's 60 million Lutherans form the third largest grouping of Christians, after Roman Catholics and Orthodox. About 55 million of them belong to church bodies which make up the Lutheran World Federation, headquartered in Geneva.

In the United States, Lutherans number approximately 8.5 million. About 5.3 million, in 11,000 congregations, belong to The Evangelical Lutheran Church in America, formed Jan. 1, 1988, by the uniting of The American Lutheran Church, the Association of Evangelical Lutheran Churches, and the Lutheran Church in America. The main office of the new church, the fourth largest Protestant body, is located at 8765 W. Higgins Rd., Chicago, Ill. 60631.

The Lutheran Church-Missouri Synod, with 2.7 million members, is the second-largest body of Lutherans in U.S. Its headquarters are located at 1333 S. Kirkwood Rd., St. Louis, Mo. 63122.

There are more than a dozen other U.S. Lutheran denominations, including the Wisconsin Evangelical Synod with 420,000 members. Its headquarters are located at 2929 N. Mayfair Rd., Milwaukee, Wis. 53222.

The Evangelical Lutheran Church in America and the Lutheran Church-Missouri Synod carry out their global mission relief work through Lutheran World Relief, 360 Park Ave. S., New York, N.Y. 10010.

The statements of faith which have shaped the confessional life of Lutheranism are found in the

Book of Concord. This 1580 collection includes the three ancient ecumenical creeds (Apostles', Nicene and Athanasian), Luther's *Large and Small Catechisms* (1529), the *Augsburg Confession* (1530) and the *Apology* in defense of it (1531), the *Smalcald Articles* (including the "Treatise on the Power and Primacy of the Pope") (1537), and the *Formula of Concord* (1577).

The central Lutheran doctrinal proposition is that Christians "receive forgiveness of sins and become righteous before God by grace, for Christ's sake."

Baptism and the Lord's Supper (Holy Communion, the Eucharist) are universally celebrated among Lutherans as sacramental means of grace in which the Word and promise of God are made visible by being bound to earthly elements — water, bread and wine. In baptism, a person is reborn and by God's gracious action is made a member of the Church catholic. Likewise, the Eucharist celebrates and re-presents God's gracious action. With the body and blood of Christ — "in, with, and under" the bread and wine — come the gifts of life, salvation, forgiveness.

Lutherans also treasure the Word proclaimed in the reading of the Scriptures, preaching and absolution. The Word read and preached is always part of the Eucharist. Absolution is usually imparted generally, but it may also be given individually in connection with private confession.

Although it was not the wish of the early Lutherans to deny the bishop's place as the ordinary minister of ordination, the general unwillingness of 16th century bishops to ordain Lutheran pastors led to the usual Lutheran system of presbyteral rather than episcopal ordination. Lutherans are concerned to preserve apostolic succession in life and doctrine, and generally concede the value, though not the necessity, of ordination by bishops.

Confirmation among Lutherans has been generally connected with first communion, though recent years have seen a tendency to separate the two. In the U.S., the tendency is to have first communion around grade-five age, though infant communion is not unknown. Confirmation, sometimes called affirmation of the baptismal covenant, generally occurs during the junior high school years, slightly younger than in European practice.

Lutheran jurisdictions corresponding to dioceses are called districts or synods in North America. There are more than 100 of them; each of them is headed by a bishop or president.

A visitor to a North American Lutheran parish would generally find adornments, vestments, church calendars and order of service similar to that of Episcopal or Roman Catholic congregations. Weekly celebration of the Eucharist is increasingly common and is generally stressed as the desired practice.

Presbyterian Churches

(Courtesy of Gerald W. Gillette, United Presbyterian Church in the U.S.A.; and Office of the General Assembly, Presbyterian Church in the United States.)

Presbyterians are so called because of their tradition of governing the church through a system of representative bodies composed of elders (presbyters).

Presbyterianism is a part of the Reformed Family of Churches that grew out of the theological work of John Calvin following the Lutheran Reformation, to which it is heavily indebted. Countries in which it acquired early strength and influence were Switzerland, France, Holland, Scotland and England.

Presbyterianism spread widely in this country in the latter part of the 18th century and afterwards. Presently, it has approximately 4.5 million communicants in nine bodies.

The two largest Presbyterian bodies in the country — the United Presbyterian Church in the U.S.A. and the Presbyterian Church in the United States — were reunited in June, 1983, to form the Presbyterian Church (U.S.A.), with a membership of 3.3 million.

The United Presbyterian Church in the U.S.A., with a membership of 2.5 million, was headquartered at 475 Riverside Drive, New York, N.Y. 10027. It was formed May 28, 1958, by a merger of the Presbyterian Church in the U.S.A. and the United Presbyterian Church of North America.

The Presbyterian Church in the United States, with 815,000 members, had headquarters at 341 Ponce de Leon Avenue N.E., Atlanta, Ga. 30308.

These churches, now merged, are closely allied with the Reformed Church in America, the United Church of Christ, the Cumberland Presbyterian Churches and the Associate Reformed Presbyterian Church.

In Presbyterian doctrine, baptism and the Lord's Supper, viewed as seals of the covenant of grace, are regarded as sacraments. Baptism, which is not necessary for salvation, is conferred on infants and adults The Lord's Supper is celebrated as a covenant of the Sacrifice of Christ. In both sacraments, a doctrine of the real presence of Christ is considered the central theological principle.

The Church is twofold, being invisible and also visible; it consists of all of the elect and all those Christians who are united in Christ as their immediate head.

Presbyterians are in general agreement with classical Protestant theology regarding Scripture as the sole rule of faith and practice, salvation by grace, and justification through faith in Christ.

Presbyterian congregations are governed by a session composed of elders (presbyters) elected by the communicant membership. On higher levels there are presbyteries, synods and a general assembly with various degrees of authority over local bodies; all such representative bodies are composed of elected elders and ministers in approximately equal numbers.

Worship services, simple and dignified, include sermons, prayer, reading of the Scriptures and hymns. The Lord's Supper is celebrated at intervals.

Doctrinal developments of the past several years included approval in May, 1967, by the General Assembly of the United Presbyterian Church of a contemporary confession of faith to supplement the historic Westminster Confession. The new confession emphasizes the commitment of the Church and its members to reconciliatory and apostolic works in society. A statement entitled "The Declaration of Faith" was approved in 1977 by the Presbyterian Church in the U.S. for teaching and liturgical use.

Episcopal Church

(Courtesy of The Episcopal Church Center, Office of Communication.)

The Episcopal Church, which includes dioceses in the United States, Central and South America, and elsewhere overseas, regards itself as part of the same apostolic church which was established by early Christians in England. Established in this country during the colonial period, it became independent of the jurisdiction of the Church of England when a new constitution and Prayer Book were adopted at a general convention held in 1789. It has approximately 3 million members worldwide.

Offices of the presiding bishop and the executive council are located at 815 Second Ave., New York, N.Y. 10017.

The presiding bishop is chief pastor and primate; he is elected by the House of Bishops and confirmed by the House of Deputies.

The Episcopal Church, which is a part of the Anglican Communion, regards the Archbishop of Canterbury as the "First among Equals," though not under his authority.

The Anglican Communion, worldwide, has 70 million members in 27 self-governing churches.

Official statements of belief and practice are found in the Book of Common Prayer. Scripture has primary importance with respect to the rule of faith, and some authority is attached to tradition.

An episcopal system of church government prevails, but presbyters, deacons and lay persons also have an active voice in church affairs. The levels of government are the general convention, and executive council, dioceses, and local parishes. At the parish level, the congregation has the right to select its own rector, with the consent of the bishop.

Liturgical worship is according to the Book of Common Prayer as adopted in 1979, but details of ceremonial practice vary from one congregation to another.

United Church of Christ

(Courtesy of the Rev. Carol Joyce Brun, secretary of the United Church of Christ.)

The 1,662,568-member United Church of Christ was formed in 1957 by a union of the Congregational Christian and the Evangelical and Reformed Churches. The former was originally established by the Pilgrims and the Puritans of the Massachusetts Bay Colony, while the latter was founded in Pennsylvania in the early 1700's by settlers from Central Europe. The denomination has 6,395 congregations throughout the United States.

It considers itself "a united and uniting church" and keeps itself open to all ecumenical options.

Its headquarters are located at 105 Madison Ave., New York, N.Y. 10016.

Its statement of faith recognizes Jesus Christ as "our crucified and risen Lord (who) shared our common lot, conquering sin and death and reconciling the world to himself." It believes in the life after death, and the fact that God "judges men and nations by his righteous will declared through prophets and apostles."

The United Church further believes that Christ calls its members to share in his baptism "and eat at his table, to join him in his passion and victory." Each local church is free to adopt its own methods of worship and to formulate its own covenants and confessions of faith. Some celebrate communion weekly; others, monthly or on another periodical basis. Like other Calvinistic bodies, it believes that Christ is spiritually present in the sacrament.

The United Church is governed along congregational lines, and each local church is autonomous. However, the actions of its biennial General Synod are taken with great seriousness by congregations. Between synods, a 44-member executive council oversees the work of the church.

Christian Church (Disciples of Christ)

(Courtesy of Robert L. Friedly, Vice President for Communication.)

The Christian Church (Disciples of Christ) originated early in the 1800's from two movements against rigid denominationalism led by Presbyterians Thomas and Alexander Campbell in western Pennsylvania and Barton W. Stone in Kentucky. The two movements developed separately for about 25 years before being merged in 1832.

The church, which identifies itself with the Protestant mainstream, now has approximately 1.1 million members in the U.S. and Canada. The greatest concentration of members in the U.S. is located roughly along the old frontier line, in an arc sweeping from Ohio and Kentucky through the Midwest and down into Oklahoma and Texas.

The general offices of the church are located at 222 South Downey Ave., Box 1986, Indianapolis, Ind. 46206.

The church's persistent concern for Christian unity is based on a conviction expressed in a basic document, *Declaration and Address*, dating from its founding. The document states: "The church of Christ upon earth is essentially, intentionally and constitutionally one."

The Disciples have no official doctrine or dogma. Their worship practices vary widely from more common informal services to what could almost be described as "high church" services. Membership is granted after a simple statement of belief in Jesus Christ and baptism by immersion; most congregations admit un-immersed transfers from other denominations. The Lord's Supper, generally called Communion, is always open to Christians of all persuasions. Lay men and women routinely preside over the Lord's Supper, which is celebrated each Sunday; they often preach and perform other pastoral functions as well. Distinction between ordained and non-ordained members is blurred somewhat because of the Disciples' emphasis on all members of the church as ministers.

The Christian Church is oriented to congregational government, and has a unique structure in which three levels of polity (general, regional and congregational) operate as equals rather than in a pyramid of authority. At the national or international level, it is governed by a general assembly which has voting representation direct from congregations and regions as well as all ordained clergy.

Evangelicalism

Evangelicalism, dating from 1735 in England (the Evangelical Revival) and after 1740 in the United States (the Great Awakening), has had and continues to have widespread influence in Protestant churches. It has been estimated that about 45 millon American Protestants — communicants of both large denominations and small bodies — are evangelicals.

The Bible is their rule of faith and religious practice. Being born again in a life-changing experience through faith in Christ is the promise of salvation. Missionary work for the spread of the Gospel is a normal and necessary activity. Additional matters of belief and practice are generally of a conservative character.

Fundamentalists, numbering perhaps 4.5 million, comprise an extreme right-wing subculture of evangelicalism.They are distinguished mainly by militant biblicism, belief in the absolute inerrancy of the Bible and emphasis on the Second Coming of Christ. Fundamentalism developed early in the 20th century in reaction against liberal theology and secularizing trends in mainstream and other Protestant denominations.

The Holiness or Perfectionist wing of evangelicalism evolved from Methodist efforts to preserve, against a contrary trend, the personal-piety and inner-religion concepts of John Wesley. There are at least 30 Holiness bodies in the U.S.

Pentecostals, probably the most demonstrative of evangelicals, are noted for speaking in tongues and the stress they place on healing, prophecy and personal testimony to the practice and power of evangelical faith.

Assemblies of God

Assemblies (Churches) of God form the largest body (more than 2 million members) in the Pentecostal Movement which developed from (1) the Holiness Revival in the Methodist Church after the Civil War and (2) the Apostolic Faith Movement at the beginning of the 20th century. Members share with other Pentecostals belief in the religious experience of conversion and in the baptism by the Holy Spirit that sanctifies. Distinctive to them is the emphasis they place on the charismatic gifts of the apostolic church, healing and speaking in tongues, which are signs of the "second blessing" of the Holy Spirit. The Assemblies are strongly fundamentalist in theology; are loosely organized in various districts, with democratic procedures; are vigorously evangelistic. There is considerable freedom in expressions of worship, with allowance for spontaneous demonstrations of gifts of the Spirit, sermons and hymns. The moral code is rigid.

ECUMENISM

The modern ecumenical movement, which started about 1910 among Protestants and led to formation of the World Council of Churches in 1948, developed outside the mainstream of Catholic interest for many years. It has now become for Catholics as well one of the great religious facts of our time.

The magna charta of ecumenism for Catholics is a complex of several documents which include, in the first place, the *Decree on Ecumenism* promulgated by the Second Vatican Council Nov. 21, 1964. Other enactments underlying and expanding this decree are the *Dogmatic Constitution on the Church*, the *Decree on Eastern Catholic Churches*, and the *Pastoral Constitution on the Church in the Modern World*.

VATICAN II DECREE

The following excerpts from the "Decree on Ecumenism" cover the broad theological background and principles and indicate the thrust of the Church's commitment to ecumenism, under the subheads: Elements Common to Christians, Unity Lacking, What the Movement Involves, Primary Duty of Catholics.

Men who believe in Christ and have been properly baptized are brought into a certain, though imperfect, communion with the Catholic Church. Undoubtedly, the differences that exist in varying degrees between them and the Catholic Church — whether in doctrine and sometimes in discipline, or concerning the structure of the Church — do indeed create many and sometimes serious obstacles to full ecclesiastical communion. These the ecumenical movement is striving to overcome (No. 3).

Elements Common to Christians

Moreover some, even very many, of the most significant elements or endowments which together go to build up and give life to the Church herself can exist outside the visible boundaries of the Catholic Church: the written word of God; the life of grace; faith, hope, and charity, along with other interior gifts of the Holy Spirit and visible elements. All of these, which come from Christ and lead back to Him, belong by right to the one Church of Christ (No. 3).

[In a later passage, the decree singled out a number of elements which the Catholic Church and other churches have in common but not in complete agreement: confession of Christ as Lord and God and as mediator between God and man; belief in the Trinity; reverence for Scripture as the revealed word of God; baptism and the Lord's Supper; Christian life and worship; faith in action; concern with moral questions.]

The brethren divided from us also carry out many of the sacred actions of the Christian religion. Undoubtedly, in ways that vary according to the condition of each church or community, these actions can truly engender a life of grace, and can be rightly described as capable of providing access to the community of salvation.

It follows that these separated Churches and Communities, though we believe they suffer from defects already mentioned, have by no means been deprived of significance and importance in the mystery of salvation. For the Spirit of Christ has not refrained from using them as means of salvation which derive their efficacy from the very fullness of grace and truth entrusted to the Catholic Church (No. 3).

Unity Lacking

Nevertheless, our separated brethren, whether considered as individuals or as Communities and Churches, are not blessed with that unity which Jesus Christ wished to bestow on all those whom he has regenerated and vivified into one body and newness of life — that unity which the holy Scriptures and the revered tradition of the Church proclaim. For it is through Christ's Catholic Church alone, which is the all-embracing means of salvation, that the fullness of the means of salvation can be obtained. It was to the apostolic college alone, of which Peter is the head, that we believe our Lord entrusted all the blessings of the New Covenant, in order to establish on earth the one Body of Christ into which all those should be fully incorporated who already belong in any way to God's People (No. 3).

What the Movement Involves

Today, in many parts of the world, under the inspiring grace of the Holy Spirit, multiple efforts are being expended through prayer, word, and action to attain that fullness of unity which Jesus Christ desires. This sacred Synod, therefore, exhorts all the Catholic faithful to recognize the signs of the times and to participate skillfully in the work of ecumenism.

The "ecumenical movement" means those activities and enterprises which, according to various needs of the Church and opportune occasions, are started and organized for the fostering of unity among Christians. These are:

• First, every effort to eliminate words, judgments, and actions which do not respond to the condition of separated brethren with truth and fairness and so make mutual relations between them more difficult.

• Then, "dialogue" between competent experts from different Churches and Communities [scholarly ecumenism].

• In addition, these Communions cooperate more closely in whatever projects a Christian conscience demands for the common good [social ecumenism].

• They also come together for common prayer, where this is permitted [spiritual ecumenism].

• Finally, all are led to examine their own faithfulness to Christ's will for the Church and, wherever necessary, undertake with vigor the task of renewal and reform.

It is evident that the work of preparing and reconciling those individuals who wish for full Catholic communion is of its nature distinct from ecumenical action. But there is no opposition between the two, since both proceed from the wondrous providence of God (No. 4).

Primary Duty of Catholics

In ecumenical work, Catholics must assuredly be concerned for their separated brethren, praying for them, keeping them informed about the Church, making the first approaches toward them. But their primary duty is to make an honest and careful appraisal of whatever needs to be renewed and achieved in the Catholic household itself, in order that its life may bear witness more loyally and luminously to the teachings and ordinances which have been handed down from Christ through the Apostles.

Every Catholic must . . . aim at Christian perfection (cf. Jas. 1:4; Rom. 12:1-2) and, each according to his station, play his part so that the Church . . . may daily be more purified and renewed, against the day when Christ will present her to himself in all her glory, without spot or wrinkle (cf. Eph. 5:27).

Catholics must joyfully acknowledge and esteem the truly Christian endowments from our common heritage which are to be found among our separated brethren.

Nor should we forget that whatever is wrought by the grace of the Holy Spirit in the hearts of our separated brethren can contribute to our own edification. Whatever is truly Christian never conflicts with the genuine interests of the faith; indeed, it can always result in a more ample realization of the very mystery of Christ and the Church (No. 4).

Participation in Worship

Norms concerning participation by Catholics in the worship of other Christian Churches were sketched in this conciliar decree and elaborated in a number of other documents such as: the *Decree on Eastern Catholic Churches*, promulgated by the Second Vatican Council in 1964; *Interim Guidelines for Prayer in Common*, issued June 18, 1965, by the U.S. Bishops' Committee for Ecumenical and Inter-Religious Affairs; a *Directory on Ecumenism*, published in 1967 by the Vatican Secretariat for Promoting Christian Unity; additional communications from the U.S. Bishops' Committee, and numerous sets of guidelines issued locally by and for dioceses throughout the U.S.

The norms encourage common prayer services

for Christian unity and other intentions. Beyond that, they draw a distinction between separated churches of the Reformation tradition and of the Anglican Communion and separated Eastern churches, in view of doctrine and practice the Catholic Church has in common with the latter concerning the apostolic succession of bishops, holy orders, liturgy, and other credal matters.

Full participation by Catholics in official Protestant liturgies is prohibited, because it implies profession of the faith expressed in the liturgy. Intercommunion by Catholics at Protestant liturgies is prohibited. Under certain conditions, Protestants may be given Holy Communion in the Catholic Church (see Intercommunion). A Catholic may stand as a witness, but not as a sponsor, in baptism, and as a witness in the marriage of separated Christians. Similarly, a Protestant may stand as a witness, but not as a sponsor, in a Catholic baptism, and as a witness in the marriage of Catholics.

Separated Eastern Churches

The principal norms regarding liturgical participation with separated Eastern Christians are included under Eastern Ecumenism.

ECUMENICAL AGENCIES

Vatican Secretariat

The top-level agency for Catholic ecumenical efforts is the Vatican Secretariat for Promoting Christian Unity (Council for Christian Unity, as of Mar. 1, 1989), which originated in 1960 as a preparatory commission for the Second Vatican Council. Its purposes are to provide guidance and, where necessary, coordination for ecumenical endeavor by Catholics, and to establish and maintain relations with representatives of other Christian Churches for ecumenical dialogue and action.

The secretariat, first under the direction of Cardinal Augustin Bea, S. J., and now of Cardinal Johannes Willebrands, has established firm working relations with representative agencies of other churches and the World Council of Churches. It has joined in dialogue with Orthodox Churches, the Anglican Communion, the Lutheran World Federation, the World Alliance of Reformed Churches, the World Methodist Council and other religious bodies. In the past several years, staff members and representatives of the secretariat have been involved in one way or another in nearly every significant ecumenical enterprise and meeting held throughout the world.

While the secretariat and its counterparts in other churches have focused primary attention on theological and other related problems of Christian unity, they have also begun, and in increasing measure, to emphasize the responsibilities of the churches for greater unity of witness and effort in areas of humanitarian need.

Bishops' Committee

The U.S. Bishops' Committee for Ecumenical and Interreligious Affairs was established by the American hierarchy in 1964. Its purposes are to maintain relationships with other Christian churches and other religious communities at the national level, to advise and assist dioceses in developing and applying ecumenical policies, and to maintain liaison with corresponding Vatican offices — the Secretariats for Christian Unity and Non-Christian Religions.

This standing committee of the National Conference of Catholic Bishops is chaired by Archbishop J. Francis Stafford of Denver. Operationally, the committee is assisted by the Rev. John F. Hotchkin, director; the Rev. Thaddeus Horgan, S.A., associate director; Dr. Eugene J. Fisher, executive secretary of the Secretariat for Catholic-Jewish Relations; Dr. John W. Borelli, Jr., executive secretary for Interreligious Relations.

The committee co-sponsors several national consultations with other churches and confessional families. These bring together on a regular basis Catholic representatives and their counterparts from the Episcopal Church, Evangelical Lutheran Church in America, the Lutheran Church Missouri Synod, the Polish National Catholic Church, the United Methodist Church, the Orthodox Churches, the Oriental Orthodox Churches, the Alliance of Reformed Churches (North American area), the Interfaith Witness Department of the Home Mission Board of the Southern Baptist Convention. (See Ecumenical Dialogues.)

The committee relates with the National Council of Churches of Christ, through membership in the Faith and Order Commission and through observer relationship with the Commission on Regional and Local Ecumenism, and has sponsored a joint study committee investigating the possibility of Roman Catholic membership in that body.

Advisory and other services are provided by the committee to ecumenical commissions and agencies in dioceses throughout the country.

Through its Secretariat for Catholic-Jewish Relations, the committee is in contact with several national Jewish agencies and bodies. Issues of mutual interest and shared concern are reviewed for the purpose of furthering deeper understanding between the Catholic and Jewish communities.

Through its Secretariat for Interreligious Relations, the committee promotes activity in wider areas of dialogue with other religions.

Offices of the committee are located at 1312 Massachusetts Ave. N.W. (3211 Fourth St. N.E. 20017, after March, 1989), Washington, D.C. 20005.

World Council

The World Council of Churches is a fellowship of churches which acknowledge "Jesus Christ as Lord and Savior." It is a permanent organization providing constituent members — 301 churches with some 450 million communicants in 100 countries — with opportunities for meeting, consultation and cooperative action with respect to doctrine, worship, practice, social mission, evangelism and missionary work, and other matters of mutual concern.

The WCC was formally established Aug. 23, 1948, in Amsterdam with ratification of a constitution by 147 communions. This action merged two previously existing movements — Life and Work (social mission), Faith and Order (doctrine) — which had initiated practical steps toward founding a fellowship of Christian churches at meetings held in Oxford, Edinburgh and Utrecht in 1937 and 1938. A third movement for cooperative missionary work, which originated about 1910 and, remotely, led to formation of the WCC, was incorporated into the council in 1971 under the title of the International Missionary Council (now the Commission for World Mission and Evangelism).

Additional general assemblies of the council have been held since the charter meeting of 1948: in Evanston, Ill. (1954), New Delhi, India (1961), Uppsala, Sweden (1968), Nairobi, Kenya (1975) and Vancouver, British Columbia, Canada (1983).

Between assemblies, the council operates through a central committee which meets every 12 or 18 months, and an executive committee which meets every six months.

The council continues the work of the International Missionary Council, the Commission on Faith and Order, and the Commission on Church and Society. The structure of the council has three program units: Faith and Witness, Justice and Service, Education and Renewal.

Liaison between the council and the Vatican has been maintained since 1966 through a joint working group. Roman Catholic membership in the WCC is a question officially on the agenda of this body. The Joint Commission on Society, Development and Peace (SODEPAX) was an agency of the council and the Pontifical Commission for Justice and Peace from 1968 to Dec. 31, 1980, after which another working group was formed. Roman Catholics serve individually as full members of the Commission on Faith and Order and in various capacities on other program committees of the council.

WCC headquarters are located in Geneva, Switzerland. The United States Conference for the World Council of Churches at 475 Riverside Drive, Room 1062, New York, N.Y. 10115, provides liaison between the U.S. churches and Geneva and a communications office for secular and church media relations. The WCC also maintains fraternal relations with regional, national and local councils of churches throughout the world.

The Rev. Dr. Emilio Castro, a Methodist from Uruguay, was elected secretary general in July, 1984.

WCC presidents are: Dame R. Nita Barrow, Barbados; Dr. Marga Buehrig, Switzerland; H. E. Metropolitan Gregorios, India; Bishop Dr. Johannes W. Hempel, German Democratic Republic; His Beatitude Ignatios IV, Lebanon; Most Rev. W.P.K. Makhulu, Botswana; Very Rev. Dr. Lois Wilson, Canada.

National Council of Churches

The National Council of the Churches of Christ in the U.S.A., the largest ecumenical body in the United States, is a cooperative organization of 32 Protestant, Orthodox and Anglican church bodies having about 40 million members.

The NCCC, established by the churches in 1950, was structured through the merger of 12 separate cooperative agencies. Presently, through four main program divisions and six commissions, the NCCC carries on work in behalf of member churches in home and overseas missions, Christian education, communications, disaster relief and rehabilitation, family life, stewardship, regional and local ecumenism, international affairs and other areas.

Policies of the NCCC are determined by a governing board of approximately 260 members appointed by the constituent churches. The governing board meets twice a year.

The NCCC's 1987 budget was $44.9 million, about 80 per cent of which is devoted to compassionate ministries of aid and relief to victims of disasters and endemic poverty in lands overseas.

The president and general secretary, respectively, are the Rev. Patricia A. McClurg and the Rev. Dr. Arie Brower.

NCCC headquarters are located at 475 Riverside Drive, New York, N.Y. 10115.

Consultation on Church Union

The Consultation on Church Union, officially begun in 1962, is a venture of American churches seeking a united church "truly catholic, truly evangelical, and truly reformed." The churches engaged in this process, representing 25 million Christians, are the African Methodist Episcopal Church, the African Methodist Episcopal Zion Church, the Christian Church (Disciples of Christ), the Christian Methodist Episcopal Church, the Episcopal Church, the Presbyterian Church (U.S.A.); the United Church of Christ, and the United Methodist Church. The International Council of Community Churches is also a member of COCU.

Representatives of these denominations, at a plenary session of COCU in November, 1984, approved a statement designed to serve as a theological basis for union. The 48,000-word document expressed agreement on such subjects as baptism, forms of ministry, creeds and worship. The statement was submitted to members for two years of study before further action by the plenary session of 1988.

The Rev. George Pike, a pastor of the Presbyterian Church (U.S.A.), was elected COCU president in 1984. The Rev. Gerald F. Moede is general secretary.

Offices are located at 151 Wall St., Princeton, N.J. 08540.

Graymoor Institute

The Graymoor Ecumenical Institute is a forum where issues that confront the Christian Churches are addressed, the spiritual dimensions of ecumenism are fostered, and information, documentation and developments within the ecumenical movement are published through Ecumenical Trends, a monthly journal, and Atonement, a monthly newsletter. The offices are located at 475 Riverside Dr., Rm. 528, New York, NY 10115.

U.S. ECUMENICAL DIALOGUES

(With the assistance of the Bishops' Committee for Ecumenical and Interreligious Affairs, National Conference of Catholic Bishops.)

Representatives of the Bishops' Committee for Ecumenical and Interreligious Affairs, National Conference of Catholic Bishops, have met in dialogue with representatives of other churches since the 1960s, for discussion of a wide variety of subjects related to the quest for unity among Christians.

Included in the following listing are the names of Christian churches which have been parties to dialogue, the number of dialogue sessions between initial and last available dates, and the subject of the last reported dialogue session.

American Baptist Convention (Division of Cooperative Christianity); 6 sessions between Apr. 3, 1967, and Apr. 14 and 15, 1972. Last subject: church-state relationships.

Baptists, Southern (Ecumenical Institute, Wake Forest University, and, since the 11th session, the Interfaith Witness Department, Home Mission Board, Southern Baptist Convention): 28 sessions between May 8, 1969, and Feb. 27 to Mar. 6, 1988. The last session marked the end of a 10-year conversation and produced an agreed statement entitled "How We Agree; How We Differ."

Christian Church, Disciples of Christ (Council on Christian Unity): 16 sessions between Mar. 16, 1967, and Sept. 10 to 17, 1981. Last action: completion of a report on apostolicity and catholicity in the visible unity of the church. This consultation has been resumed on the international level with the Secretariat for Promoting Christian Unity as the Catholic co-sponsoring agency.

Episcopal Church (The Anglican-Roman Catholic Consultation, Standing Commission on Ecumenical Relations: 34 sessions between June 22, 1965, and June 22 to 25, 1987. Last subjects: *Apostolicae Curae* (regarding the validity of Anglican orders), ministry, decision to begin a long-range study of authority in the Church.

Lutheran, U.S.A. (Lutheran World Ministries): 52 sessions between Mar. 16, 1965, and Sept. 21 to 24, 1988. Last action: a report on Mary and the saints.

Methodist (United Methodist Church): 25 sessions between June 28, 1966, and Mar. 8, 1988. Last action: beginning of work on an agreed statement, "Holy Living, Holy Dying."

Orthodox (Standing Conference of Canonical Orthodox Bishops of America): 38 sessions between Sept. 5, 1965, and June 2, 1988. Last action: preparation of a response to the international dialogue's Bari Document and the New York Metropolitan area's document on mixed marriage.

Orthodox, Oriental (Armenian, Coptic, Ethiopian, Indian Malabar and Syrian Orthodox Churches): 14 sessions between Jan. 27, 1978, and May 26 to 28, 1987. Last subject: Obstacles to intercommunion among churches.

Polish National Catholic Church: nine sessions between Oct. 23, 1984, and Nov. 29, 1988. Last subject: doctrine on heaven and hell.

Presbyterian and Reformed (The Roman Catholic-Presbyterian Consultation Group, North American Area Council of the World Alliance of Reformed Churches): 32 sessions between July 27, 1965, and Dec. 9, 1985. Last subject: planning for a fifth round of talks on the role of the laity.

ECUMENICAL REPORTS

(Source: Rev. John F. Hotchkin and Rev. Thaddeus Horgan, S.A., of the staff of the Bishops' Committee for Ecumenical and Interreligious Affairs, National Conference of Catholic Bishops.)

Common Declarations of Popes, Other Prelates

The following ecumenical statements, issued by several popes and prelates of other Christian churches, carry the authority given them by their signators.

Paul VI and Orthodox Ecumenical Patriarch Athenagoras I, First Common Declaration, Dec. 7, 1965: They expressed their regret for offenses the churches caused each other in the past and stated their intent to "erase from memory and the midst of the Church the sentences of excommunication which followed them." Through "this reciprocal act of justice and mutual forgiveness," they hoped the differences between the churches would be overcome, with the help of the Holy Spirit, and that their "full communion of faith, brotherly concord and sacramental life" would be restored.

Paul VI and Anglican Archbishop Michael Ramsey of Canterbury, Mar. 24, 1966: They wished "to leave in the hands of the God of mercy all that in the past has been opposed to the precept of charity." They stated their intention "to inaugurate between the Roman Catholic Church and the Anglican Communion a serious dialogue which, founded on the Gospels and on the ancient common traditions, may lead to that unity in truth for which Christ prayed."

Paul VI and Patriarch Athenagoras I, Second Common Declaration, Oct. 27, 1967: They wished "to emphasize their conviction that the restoration of full communion (between the churches) . . . is to be found within the framework of the renewal of the Church and of Christians in fidelity to the traditions of the Fathers and to the inspirations of the Holy Spirit who remains always with the Church." To this end, they called for a "dialogue of charity" at many levels between Orthodox and Catholics.

Paul VI and Vasken I, Orthodox Catholicos-Patriarch of All Armenians, May 12, 1970: They invited the people of their churches "to respond with greater fidelity to the call of the Holy Spirit stimulating them to a more profound unity," asked everyone to strive to know one another, and called for closer collaboration "in all domains of Christian life. . . . This collaboration must be based on the mutual recognition of the common Christian faith and the sacramental life, on the mutual respect of persons and their churches."

Paul VI and Mar Ignatius Jacob III, Syrian Orthodox Patriarch of Antioch, Oct. 27, 1971: They declared themselves to be "in agreement that there is no difference in the faith they profess concerning the mystery of the Word of God made flesh and become really man, even if over the centuries difficulties have arisen out of the different theological expressions by which this faith was expressed. They therefore encourage the clergy and faithful of their churches to even greater endeavors at removing the obstacles which still prevent complete communion among them."

Paul VI and Shenouda III, Coptic Orthodox Pope of Alexandria, May 10, 1973: Their common declaration recalls the common elements of the Catholic and Coptic Orthodox faith in the Trinity, the divinity and humanity of Christ, the seven sacraments, the Virgin Mary, the Church founded upon the Apostles, and the Second Coming of Christ. It recognizes that the two churches "are not able to give more perfect witness to this new life in Christ because of existing divisions which have behind them centuries of difficult history" dating back to the year 451 A.D. In spite of these difficulties, they expressed "determination and confidence in the Lord to achieve the fullness and perfection of that unity which is his gift." To that end, they announced their intention to set up a joint commission "whose function will be to guide common study in the fields of church tradition, patristics, liturgy, theology, history and practical problems." They rejected "all forms of proselytism" which disturb their respective churches.

Paul VI and Anglican Archbishop Donald Coggan of Canterbury, Apr. 29, 1977: They stated many points on which Anglicans and Roman Catholics hold the faith in common and called for greater cooperation between Anglicans and Roman Catholics. Such cooperation "is the true setting for continued dialogue and for the general extension and appreciation of its fruits, and for progress toward that goal which is Christ's will — the restoration of complete communion in faith and scramental life."

John Paul II and Orthodox Ecumenical Patriarch Dimitrios I, First Common Declaration, Nov. 30, 1979: They expressed gratitude to their predecessors "for everything they did to reconcile our churches and cause them progress in unity," and stated: "Purification of the collective memory of our churches is an important fruit of the dialogue of charity and an indispensable condition of future progress." They announced the establishment of the Catholic-Orthodox Theological Commission, an international body, responsible for theological dialogue between the churches.

John Paul II and Anglican Archbishop Robert Runcie of Canterbury, May 29, 1982: They stated their agreement to establish a new Anglican-Roman Catholic commission with the task of continuing work already begun toward the eventual resolution of doctrinal differences. The new commission was also charged with the task of studying "all that hinders the mutual recognition of the ministries of our communions, and to recommend what practical steps will be necessary when, on the basis of our unity in faith, we are able to proceed toward the restoration of full communion."

John Paul II and Ignatius Zakka I, Syrian Orthodox Patriarch of Antioch, June 23, 1984: They recalled and solemnly reaffirmed the common profession of faith made by their predecessors, Paul VI and Mar Ignatius Jacob III, in 1971. They said: "The confusions and the schisms that occurred between the churches . . . , they realize today, in no way affect or touch the substance of their faith, since these arose only because of differences in terminology and culture, and in the various formulae adopted by different theological schools to express the same matter. Accordingly, we find today no real basis for the sad divisions which arose between us concerning the doctrine of the Incarnation." On the pastoral level, they declared: "It is not rare . . . for our faithful to find access to a priest of their own church materially or morally impossible. Anxious to meet their needs and with their spiritual benefit in mind, we authorize them in such cases to ask for the sacraments of penance, Eucharist and anointing of the sick from lawful priests of either of our two sister churches, when they need them."

John Paul II and Orthodox Ecumenical Patriarch Dimitrios I, Second Common Declaration, Dec. 7, 1987: Happy at "being together as brothers," they called their meeting "a sign of the existing fraternity between the Catholic Church and the Orthodox Church." They stated their joy in "reporting the first results and positive developments of the theological dialogue" whose establishment they had announced in their first Common Declaration. The dialogue indicated that the churches can already profess together as common faith about the mystery of the Church and the connection between faith and the sacraments. They also stated that, "when unity of faith is assured, a certain diversity of expressions . . . "does not create obstacles to unity, but enriches the life of the Church and the understanding, always imperfect, of the revealed mystery . . ." They committed themselves to a "dialogue of charity" and work toward justice and peace on local, regional and world levels.

International Consultations

International interfaith consultations involving Roman Catholics (through official appointment by the Secretariat for Promoting Christian Unity) and representatives of other Christian churches have issued a great number and wide variety of reports since 1965. The statements presented here reflect the findings of the respective dialogue participants. They do not carry the formal ecclesiastical authority of the various churches; rather, they have been submitted to the churches for review and such action or response as they deem appropriate.

World Council of Churches-Vatican: The Joint Working Group established by the WCC and the Holy See in 1965 has issued five official reports, in 1965, 1967, 1969, 1975 and 1983.

The group also prepared studies on the following subjects between 1965 and 1982: joint worship at ecumenical gatherings, ecumenical dialogue, common witness and proselytism, catholicity and apostolicity, a fixed date for Easter, patterns of relationships between the Roman Catholic Church and the World Council of Churches, toward a confession of common faith, common witness, the significance and contribution of councils of churches in the ecumenical movement.

• The WCC Faith and Order Commission (with Catholics in full membership since 1968) issued the final text of a Baptism-Eucharist-Ministry statement at a meeting held in 1982 in Lima, Peru; the document represents theological convergence achieved through decades of dialogue.

International Bilateral Commissions

Anglican-Roman Catholic International Commission, sponsored by the Unity Secretariat and the Lambeth Conference, held 13 sessions during the first phase of its work, from January, 1970, to September, 1981. Its final report, published in 1982, contains statements of agreement on Eucharistic doctrine, ministry-ordination and authority in the church, plus elucidations in response to comments made by others on the work of the commission. The report is under study by provinces of the Anglican Communion and episcopal conferences of the Roman Catholic Church.

• An Anglican-Roman Catholic Preparatory Commission held three sessions in 1967 and published its Malta Report Jan. 2, 1968. Its recommendations — regarding increasing contact in prayer, worship, dialogue and mission — were endorsed in substance by Cardinal Augustin Bea, president of the Unity Secretariat, and the Lambeth Conference.

• The Anglican-Roman Catholic Commission on the Theology of Marriage and Its Application to Mixed Marriages held six sessions between April, 1968, and June, 1975. Its report contains reflections on: the theology of marriage, defective marital situations, canonical legislation regarding mixed marriages of Anglicans and Roman Catholics, the Roman Catholic requirement of the canonical form of marriage, the promise concerning the baptism and rearing of children (and a possible alternative to the promise), and pastoral care of mixed-marriage households.

• A Feb. 27 to Mar. 3, 1978, consultation co-sponsored by the Unity Secretariat and the Anglican Consultative Council issued a report on the ordination of women, named for the place of the meeting, Versailles.

Second Anglican-Roman Catholic International Commission was called into being by the Common Declaration of John Paul II and the Archbishop of Canterbury in 1982. Its first report, "Salvation and the Church," was completed in 1986; its focus is on the relation of the doctrine of salvation to faith, justification, good works and the doctrine of the Church.

The International Theological Colloquium between Baptists and Catholics was established by the Unity Secretariat and the Commission for Faith and Interchurch Cooperation of the Baptist World Alliance. The first two sessions were held in 1984 and 1985. The topic of the 1986 meeting was "The Church as the Koinonia (Fellowship) of the Spirit."

The Disciples of Christ-Roman Catholic Dialogue was organized by the Council of Christian Unity of the Christian Church (Disciples of Christ) and the U.S. Bishops' Committee for Ecumenical and Interreligious Affairs, along with participation by the Disciples' Ecumenical Consultative Council and the Unity Secretariat. Agreed accounts of five annual meetings from 1977 to 1981 cover a number of themes including the nature of the Church, unity under various aspects, faith and tradition, apostolicity and catholicity. A second stage of international dialogue has been organized for the 1983-to-1989 period.

The Evangelical-Roman Catholic Dialogue on Mission, organized by Evangelicals and the Unity Secretariat, held three sessions from 1977 to 1984, and published a report in 1986 covering the nature of mission, response in the Holy Spirit and other subjects.

The Joint Lutheran-Roman Catholic Study Commission, established by the Unity Secretariat and the Lutheran World Federation, met five times between 1967 and 1971 and made public in 1972 a report entitled, "The Gospel and the Church" (Malta Report). Its four chapters cover the Gospel in relation to tradition, the world, the office of ministry in the Church and unity of the Church.

• The subsequently established Lutheran-Roman Catholic Joint Commission held 10 sessions during the first period of its work, from 1973 to 1984. The titles of its reports are: "The Eucharist" (1978/79); "Ways to Community" (1980/81); "All Under One Christ," marking the 450th anniversary of the Augsburg Confession (1980); "The Ministry in the Church" (1981/82); "Martin Luther: Witness to Jesus Christ," marking the 500th anniversary of the birth of Luther (1983); "Facing Unity: Models, Forms and Phases of Catholic-Lutheran Church Fellowship" (1985).

• The Roman Catholic-Lutheran-Reformed Study Commission on the Theology of Marriage and the Problem of Mixed Marriages was established by the Unity Secretariat, the Lutheran World Federation and the World Alliance of Reformed Churches in 1971. In 1976, it issued a final report on the proceedings of five sessions.

The Joint Methodist-Roman Catholic Commission was inaugurated by the Unity Secretariat and the World Methodist Council in 1966. It has sponsored a series of four continuing dialogues and has prepared four reports named for the places of meetings.

• The Denver Report (1971) covers Christianity and the contemporary world, spirituality, Christian home and family, the Eucharist, ministry and authority.

• The Dublin Report (1976) includes such topics as common witness and salvation, inter-church marriages, euthanasia and other moral questions.

• The Honolulu Report (1981) covers a variety of subjects related to the general theme of an agreed statement on the Holy Spirit.

• The Nairobi Report (1986) deals with the concept of primacy and the subject of infallibility.

The International Catholic-Orthodox Theological Commission, established by the Holy See and 14 autocephalous Orthodox Churches, began its work at a first session held at Patmos/Rhodes in 1980. Subsequent sessions have been held at Munich (1982), Crete (1984) and Bari (1987). The commission's first report, "The Mystery of the Church and the Eucharist in the Light of the Most Holy Trinity," was published in 1982. Its second report, "Faith, Sacraments and the Unity of the Church," was completed June 10, 1987.

Pentecostal-Roman Catholic Conversations have been held in two series, the first of which was conducted from 1966 to 1976. A final report on this series, issued in 1976, deals with baptism in the Holy Spirit, Christian initiation and the gifts, public worship and the gifts, prayer and praise. A final report on the second series of talks, between 1977 and 1982, was published in 1984, covering speaking in tongues, faith and experience, perspectives on Mary, recognition of ministries and other subjects.

The Reformed-Roman Catholic Conversations, after preliminary meetings in 1968 and 1969, were inaugurated in 1970 by the Unity Secretariat and the World Alliance of Reformed Churches. Subjects covered in five full sessions were summarized in a final report, "The Presence of Christ in Church and World," issued in 1977. The subjects were: Christ's relationship to the Church (1970), the teaching authority of the Church (1971), the presence of Christ in the world (1972), the Eucharist (1974) and ministry (1975).

INTERFAITH STATEMENTS

The ecumenical statements listed below, and others like them, reflect the views of participants in the dialogues which produced them. They have not been formally accepted by the respective churches as formulations of doctrine or points of departure for practical changes in discipline.

• The "Windsor Statement" on Eucharistic doctrine, published Dec. 31, 1971, by the Anglican-Roman Catholic International Commission of theologians. (For text, see pages 132-33 of the 1973 *Catholic Almanac*.)

• The "Canterbury Statement" on ministry and ordination, published Dec. 13, 1973, by the same commission (For excerpts, see pages 127-30 of the 1975 *Catholic Almanac*.)

• "Papal Primacy / Converging Viewpoints," published Mar. 4, 1974, by the dialogue group sanctioned by the U.S.A. National Convention of the World Lutheran Federation and the U.S. Bishops' Committee for Ecumenical and Interreligious Affairs. (For excerpts, see pages 130-31 of the 1975 *Catholic Almanac*.)

• An "Agreed Statement on the Purpose of the Church," published Oct. 31, 1975, by the Anglican-Roman Catholic Consultation in the U.S., in which the signatories agreed on the purpose and mission of the Church "insofar as it faithfully preaches the Gospel of salvation and manifests the love of God in service." It noted that "Roman Catholics and Episcopalians believe that there is but one Church of Christ," and endorsed social action for human liberation.

• "Christian Unity and Women's Ordination," published Nov. 7, 1975, by the same consultation, in which it was said that the ordination of women (approved in principle by the Anglican Communion but not by the Catholic Church) would "introduce a new element" in dialogue but would not mean the end of consultation nor the abandonment of its declared goal of full communion and organic unity. (A similar view was expressed in an exchange of letters between Pope Paul and Anglican Archbishop Donald Coggan of Canterbury, between July 8, 1975, and Mar. 23, 1976.)

• "Holiness and Spirituality of the Ordained Ministry," issued early in 1976 by theologians of the Catholic Church and the United Methodist Church; the first statement resulting from dialogue begun in 1966.

• "Mixed Marriages," published in the spring of 1976 by the Anglican-Roman Catholic Consultation in the U.S. It was similar in some respects to the statement, "Implementation of the Apostolic Letter on Mixed Marriages," approved by the National Conference of Catholic Bishops Nov. 16, 1970. It differed in softening the statement of a Catholic party's responsibility to do everything possible to raise children in the Catholic faith and favored greater freedom for having the marriage ceremony according to the rite of another Christian church.

• "Bishops and Presbyters," published in July, 1976, by the Orthodox-Roman Catholic Consultation in the U.S., on the following points of common understanding: (1) Ordination in apostolic succession is required for pastoral office in the Church. (2) Presiding at the Eucharistic Celebration is a task belonging to those ordained to pastoral service. (3) The offices of bishop and presbyter are different realizations of the sacrament of order. (4) Those ordained are claimed permanently for the service of the Church.

• "The Principle of Economy," published by the body named above at the same time, concerning God's plan and activities in human history for salvation. The concept of "economy" was not completely defined. It appeared that Orthodox understanding precludes recognition of the validity of the sacraments of other Christian churches.

• "Venice Statement" on authority in the Church, published Jan. 20, 1977, by the Anglican-Roman Catholic International Commission of theologians. Its major headings were Christian authority, authority of the ordained ministry and of the community, authority in the community of churches, the primacy of the bishop of Rome, authority in matters of faith, conciliar and primatial authority. Differences were cited in Catholic and Anglican views with respect to scriptural passages related to claims of the Roman See to primacy of authority, the divine right of the successors of St. Peter, papal infallibility and universal jurisdiction over the Church. (For text, see pages 145-50 of the 1978 *Catholic Almanac*.)

• "Response to the Venice Statement," issued Jan. 4, 1978, by the Anglican-Roman Catholic Consultation in the U.S.A., citing additional questions regarding the sharing of authority in the Church, the nature of the primacy of Rome, and the relation of indefectibility to infallibility.

• "The Presence of Christ in Church and World," published early in 1978 by representatives of the Vatican Secretariat for Promoting Christian Unity and the World Alliance of Reformed Churches. The wide-ranging statement noted considerable degrees of mutual understanding and some agreement, along with substantial differences of view on several subjects — especially papal infallibility.

• "An Ecumenical Approach to Marriage," published in January, 1978, in the form of a report on five or more years of dialogue among representatives of the Catholic Church, the Lutheran World Federation and the World Alliance of Reformed Churches. Significant agreement was reported on doctrinal and pastoral aspects of marriage. Objections continued from the Lutheran and Reformed sides, however, with respect to the sacramental nature of marriage, and to Catholic requirements in cases of mixed marriages: (1) that the marriage normally take place with a priest as the officiating minister, and (2) that the Catholic party promise to do everything possible to raise children in the Catholic faith.

• "Teaching Authority and Infallibility in the Church," released in October, 1978, by the Catholic-Lutheran dialogue group in the U.S., noting similarities and differences between Lutheran understanding of the indefectibility of the Church and the Catholic doctrine of papal infallibility.

• "The Eucharist," reported early in 1979, in which the Roman Catholic-Lutheran Commission indicated developing convergence of views concerning the nature and sacrificial aspect of the Mass, and the significance of believing, active participation in the Eucharist.

• "The Holy Spirit," issued Feb. 12, 1979, by the International Catholic-Methodist Commission, citing points of common faith in the Holy Spirit.

• A statement on "Ministry in the Church," approved in draft form in February, 1980, and published in March, 1981, by the International Roman Catholic-Lutheran Joint Commission, regarding possible mutual recognition of ministries.

• "Baptism, Eucharist and Ministry," produced under the auspices of the Faith and Order Commission of the World Council of Churches and approved by more than 100 Christian theologians at a meeting held in Lima, Peru, in January, 1982. The Lima Document (also referred to as BEM) is an attempt to state what divided Christians can say in common about baptism, the Eucharist and ministry. It was called a significant development in the ecumenical movement by the Secretariat for Promoting Christian Unity and the Congregation for the Doctrine of the Faith; their response was reported by the NC Documentary Service, Origins, Nov. 19, 1987 (Vol. 17, No. 23). However, the Vatican agencies declared, it "does not offer a fully systematic treatment of baptism, Eucharist or ministry." Deficiencies have to do with, among other things, the notion of sacrament and the treatment of apostolic tradition and decisive authority in the church. Some passages were judged to be inconsistent with Catholic faith.

• The Final Report of the Anglican-Roman Catholic International Commission, released late in March, 1982, on the results of 12 years of dialogue. (See following article.)

• A report released June 9, 1982, by the Catholic Church-Disciples of Christ international commission concluded after five years of dialogue that the two churches already have a "unity of grace" which is "bearing fruit and which is disposing us for visible unity and urging us to move ahead to it." The report noted, however, that the two churches differ in their views of the relationship between the New Testament and later Catholic treaching embodied in liturgical texts, creeds and conciliar and papal statements.

• "Justification by Faith," issued Sept. 30, 1983, by the U.S. Lutheran-Roman Catholic dialogue group, claiming a "fundamental consensus on the Gospel."

• "Images of God: Reflections on Christian Anthropology," released Dec. 22, 1983, by the Anglican-Roman Catholic Dialogue in the United States, providing "a context in which to approach many of the difficult questions that confront" Catholic and Anglican churches.

• "Salvation and the Church," the title of an agreed statement issued Jan. 22, 1987, by the second Anglican-Roman Catholic International Commission. The statement said the two churches need not dispute the role of the church in the process of salvation, the bearing of good works on salvation, the understanding of justification and the associated concepts of righteousness and justice, and the understanding of the faith through which we are justified "insofar as this included the individual's confidence in his or her own final salvation."

• "Faith, Sacraments and the Unity of the Church," issued by the Mixed International Commission for Theological Dialogue between the Catholic Church and the Orthodox Churches in June, 1987. In two parts, the document (1) lists essential themes to be addressed before complete communion of the churches can be accomplished and (2) treats the sacraments of initiation (baptism, the Eucharist and confirmation) and their differences in the traditions of the churches.

ANGLICAN-CATHOLIC FINAL REPORT

The Anglican-Roman Catholic International Commission of theologians officially published Mar. 31, 1982, a Final Report on 12 years of dialogue concerning subjects of belief and practice which have divided the two churches for more than 400 years.

The claim to fundamental agreement made in the Final Report was questioned by Cardinal Joseph Ratzinger, prefect of the Congregation for the Doctrine of the Faith, in a letter addressed to Bishop Alan C. Clark of East Anglia, England, co-president of the Anglican-Roman Catholic International Commission.

The claim was also questioned by the Congregation for the Doctrine of the Faith in the conclusion of a set of observations, dated Mar. 29, 1982, concerning the Final Report.

"At the conclusion of its doctrinal examination, the congregation thinks that the Final Report, which represents a notable ecumenical endeavor and a useful basis for further steps on the road to reconciliation between the Catholic Church and the Anglican Communion, does not yet constitute a substantial and explicit agreement on some essential elements of Catholic faith.

- "a) because the report explicitly recognizes that one or another Catholic dogma is not accepted by our Anglican brethren (for example, Eucharistic adoration, infallibility, the Marian dogmas);
- "b) because one or another Catholic doctrine is accepted only in part by our Anglican brethren (for example, the primacy of the Bishop of Rome);
- "c) because certain formulations in the report are not explicit enough to ensure that they exclude interpretations not in harmony with the Catholic faith (for example, that which concerns the Eucharist as sacrifice, the Real Presence, the nature of the priesthood);
- "d) because certain affirmations in the report are inexact and not acceptable as Catholic doctrine (for example, the relationship between the primacy and the structure of the Church, the doctrine of 'reception' — regarding the validation of doctrine by the acceptance of the people);
- "e) finally, because some important aspects of the teaching of the Catholic Church have either not been dealt with or have been only in an indirect way (for example, apostolic succession, the rule of faith, moral teaching)."

Regarding next steps to be taken, the congregation said "the results of its examination would recommend: a) that the dialogue be continued, since there are sufficient grounds for thinking its continuation will be fruitful; b) that it be deepened in regard to the points already addressed where the results are not satisfactory; c) that it be extended to new themes, particularly those which are necessary with a view to the restoration of full church unity between the two communions."

JUDAISM

Judaism is the religion of the Old Testament and of contemporary Jews. Divinely revealed and with a patriarchal background (Abraham, Isaac, Jacob), it originated with the Mosaic Covenant, was identified with the Israelites, and achieved distinctive form and character as the religion of The Law from this Covenant and reforms initiated by Ezra and Nehemiah after the Babylonian Exile.

Judaism does not have a formal creed but its principal points of belief are clear. Basic is belief in one transcendent God who reveals himself through The Law, the prophets, the life of his people and events of history. The fatherhood of God involves the brotherhood of men. Religious faith and practice are equated with just living according to The Law. Moral conviction and practice are regarded as more important than precise doctrinal formulation and profession. Formal worship, whose principal act was sacrifice from Canaanite times to 70 A.D., is by prayer, reading and meditating upon the sacred writings, and observance of the Sabbath and festivals.

Judaism has messianic expectations of the complete fulfillment of the Covenant, the coming of God's kingdom, the ingathering of his people, final judgment and retribution for all men. Views differ regarding the manner in which these expectations will be realized — through a person, the community of God's people, an evolution of historical events, an eschatological act of God himself. Individual salvation expectations also differ, depending on views about the nature of immortality, punishment and reward, and related matters.

Sacred Books

The sacred books are the 24 books of the Masoretic Hebrew Text of The Law, the Prophets and the Writings (see The Bible). Together, they contain the basic instruction or norms for just living. In some contexts, the term Law or Torah refers only to the Pentateuch (Genesis, Exodus, Leviticus, Numbers, Deuteronomy); in others, it denotes all the sacred books and/or the whole complex of written and oral tradition.

Also of great authority are two Talmuds which were composed in Palestine and Babylon in the fourth and fifth centuries A.D., respectively. They consist of the Mishna, a compilation of oral laws, and the Gemara, a collection of rabbinical commentary on the Mishna. Midrash are collections of scriptural comments and moral counsels.

Priests were the principal official ministers during the period of sacrificial and temple worship. Rabbis were, and continue to be, teachers and leaders of prayer. The synagogue is the place of community worship. The family and home are focal points of many aspects of Jewish worship and practice.

Of the various categories of Jews, Orthodox are the most conservative in adherence to strict religious traditions. Others — Reformed, Conservative, Reconstructionist — are liberal in comparison with the Orthodox. They favor greater or less modification of religious practices in accommodation to contemporary culture and living conditions.

Principal events in Jewish life include the circumcision of males, according to prescriptions of the Covenant; the bar mitzvah which marks the coming-of-age of boys in Judaism at the age of 13; marriage; and observance of the Sabbath and festivals.

Sabbath and Festivals

Observances of the Sabbath and festivals begin at sundown of the previous calendar day and continue until the following sundown.

Judaism — Catholic-Jewish Relations

Sabbath: Saturday, the weekly day of rest prescribed in the Decalogue.

Booths (Tabernacles): A seven-to-nine-day festival in the month of Tishri (Sept.-Oct.), marked by some Jews with Covenant-renewal and reading of The Law. It originated as an agricultural feast at the end of the harvest and got its name from the temporary shelters used by workers in the fields.

Hanukkah (The Festival of Lights, the Feast of Consecration and of the Maccabees): Commemorates the dedication of the new altar in the Temple at Jerusalem by Judas Maccabeus in 165 B.C. The eight-day festival, during which candles in an eight-branch candelabra are lighted in succession, one each day, occurs near the winter solstice, close to Christmas time.

Passover: A seven-day festival commemorating the liberation of the Israelites from Egypt. The narrative of the Exodus, the Haggadah, is read at ceremonial Seder meals on the first and second days of the festival, which begins on the 14th day of Nisan (Mar.-Apr.).

Pentecost (Feast of Weeks): Observed 50 days after Passover. Some Jews regard it as commemorative of the anniversary of the revelation of The Law to Moses.

Purim: A joyous festival observed on the 14th day of Adar (Feb.-Mar.), commemorating the rescue of the Israelites from massacre by the Persians through the intervention of Esther. The festival is preceded by a day of fasting. A gift- and alms-giving custom became associated with it in medieval times.

Rosh Hashana (Feast of the Trumpets, New Year): Observed on the first day of Tishri (Sept.-Oct.), the festival focuses attention on the day of judgment and is marked with meditation on the ways of life and the ways of death. It is second in importance only to the most solemn observance of Yom Kippur, which is celebrated 10 days later.

Yom Kippur (Day of Atonement): The highest holy day, observed with strict fasting. It occurs 10 days after Rosh Hashana.

Yom HaShoah (Holocaust Memorial Day): Observed in the week after Passover; increasingly observed with joint Christian-Jewish services of remembrance.

CATHOLIC-JEWISH RELATIONS

The Second Vatican Council, in addition to the "Decree on Ecumenism" concerning the movement for unity among Christians, stated the mind of the Church on a similar matter in a "Declaration on the Relationship of the Church to Non-Christian Religions." This document, as the following excerpts indicate, backgrounds the reasons and directions of the Church's regard for the Jews. (Other portions of the document, not cited here, refer to Hindus, Buddhists and Moslems.)

Spiritual Bond

As this sacred Synod searches into the mystery of the Church, it recalls the spiritual bond linking the people of the New Covenant with Abraham's stock.

For the Church of Christ acknowledges that, according to the mystery of God's saving design, the beginnings of her faith and her election are already found among the patriarchs, Moses, and the prophets. She professes that all who believe in Christ, Abraham's sons according to faith (cf. Gal. 3:7), are included in the same patriarch's call, and likewise that the salvation of the Church was mystically foreshadowed by the Chosen People's exodus from the land of bondage.

The Church, therefore, cannot forget that she received the revelation of the Old Testament through the people with whom God in his inexpressible mercy deigned to establish the Ancient Covenant. Nor can she forget that she draws sustenance from the root of that good olive tree onto which have been grafted the wild olive branches of the Gentiles (cf. Rom.11:17-24). Indeed, the Church believes that by his cross Christ, our Peace, reconciled Jew and Gentile, making them both one in himself (cf. Eph. 2:14-16).

The Jews still remain most dear to God because of their fathers, for he does not repent of the gifts he makes nor of the calls he issues (cf. Rom. 11:28-29). In company with the prophets and the same Apostle (Paul), the Church awaits that day, known to God alone, on which all peoples will address the Lord in a single voice and "serve him with one accord" (Zeph. 3:9; Cf. Is. 66:23; Ps. 65:4; Rom. 11:11-32).

Since the spiritual patrimony common to Christians and Jews is thus so great, this sacred Synod wishes to foster and recommend that mutual understanding and respect which is the fruit above all of biblical and theological studies, and of brotherly dialogues.

No Anti-Semitism

True, authorities of the Jews and those who followed their lead pressed for the death of Christ (cf. Jn. 19:6); still, what happened in his passion cannot be blamed upon all the Jews then living, without distinction, nor upon the Jews of today. Although the Church is the new People of God, the Jews should not be presented as repudiated or cursed by God, as if such views followed from the holy Scriptures. All should take pains, then, lest in catechetical instruction and in the preaching of God's Word they teach anything out of harmony with the truth of the Gospel and the spirit of Christ.

The Church repudiates all persecutions against any man. Moreover, mindful of her common patrimony with the Jews, and motivated by the Gospel's spiritual love and by no political considerations, she deplores the hatred, persecutions, and displays of anti-Semitism directed against the Jews at any time and from any source. (No. 4).

The Church rejects, as foreign to the mind of Christ, any discrimination against men or harassment of them because of their race, color, condition of life, or religion. (No. 5).

Bishops' Secretariat

The American hierarchy's first move toward implementation of the Vatican II *Declaration on the Relationship of the Church to Non-Christian Religions (Nostra Aetate)* was to establish, in 1965, a Subcommission for Catholic-Jewish Relations in the framework of its Commission for Ecumenical and Interreligious Affairs. This subcommission was reconstituted and given the title of secretariat in September, 1967. Its moderator is Bishop William H. Keeler of Harrisburg. The Secretariat for Catholic-Jewish Relations is located at 1312 Massachusetts Ave. N.W., Washington, D.C. 20005. The executive director is Dr. Eugene J. Fisher.

According to the key norm of a set of guidelines issued by the secretariat Mar. 16, 1967 and updated Apr. 9, 1985: "The general aim of all Catholic-Jewish meetings (and relations) is to increase our understanding both of Judaism and the Catholic faith, to eliminate sources of tension and misunderstanding, to initiate dialogue or conversations on different levels, to multiply intergroup meetings between Catholics and Jews, and to promote cooperative social action."

Vatican Guidelines

In a document issued Jan. 3, 1975, the Vatican Commission for Religious Relations with the Jews offered a number of suggestions and guidelines for implementing the Christian-Jewish portion of the Second Vatican Council's *Declaration on Relations with Non-Christian Religions.*

Among "suggestions from experience" were those concerning dialogue, liturgical links between Christian and Jewish worship, the interpretation of biblical texts, teaching and education for the purpose of increasing mutual understanding, and joint social action.

The document concluded with the statement:

"On Oct. 22, 1974, the Holy Father instituted for the universal Church this Commission for Religious Relations with the Jews, joined to the Secretariat for Promoting Christian Unity. This special commission, created to encourage and foster religious relations between Jews and Catholics — and to do so in collaboration with other Christians — will be, within the limits of its competence, at the service of all interested organizations, providing information for them and helping them to pursue their task in conformity with the instructions of the Holy See.

"The commission wishes to develop this collaboration in order to implement, correctly and effectively, the express intentions of the (Second Vatican) Council."

Notes on Preaching and Catechesis

On June 24, 1985, the Vatican Commission for Religious Relations with the Jews promulgated its "Notes on the Correct Way to Present Jews and Judaism in Preaching and Catechesis in the Roman Catholic Church," with the intent of providing "a helpful frame of reference for those who are called upon in the course of their teaching assignments to speak about Jews and Judaism and who wish to do so in keeping with the current teaching of the Church in this area."

The document states emphatically that, since the relationship between the Church and the Jewish people is one "founded on the design of the God of the Covenant," Judaism does not occupy "an occasional and marginal place in catechesis," but an "essential" one that "should be organically integrated" throughout the curriculum on all levels of Catholic education.

The Notes discuss the relationship between the Hebrew Scriptures and the New Testament, focusing especially on typology, which is called "the sign of a problem unresolved." Underlined is the "eschatological dimension," that "the people of God of the Old and the New Testament are tending toward a like end in the future: the coming or return of the Messiah." Jewish witness to God's Kingdom, the Notes declare, challenges Christians to "accept our responsibility to prepare the world for the coming of the Messiah by working together for social justice . . . and reconciliation."

The Notes emphasize the Jewishness of Jesus' teaching, correct misunderstandings concerning the portrayal of Jews in the New Testament and describe the Jewish origins of Christian liturgy. One section addresses the "spiritual fecundity" of Judaism to the present, its continuing "witness — often heroic — of its fidelity to the one God," and mandates the development of Holocaust curricula and a positive approach in Catholic education to the "religious attachment which finds its roots in biblical tradition" between the Jewish people and the Land of Israel, affirming the "existence of the State of Israel" on the basis of "the common principles of international law."

Papal Statements

(Courtesy of Dr. Eugene Fisher, executive director of the Secretariat for Catholic-Jewish Relations, National Conference of Catholic Bishops; consultor to the Vatican Commission for Religious Relations with the Jews; member of the International Catholic-Jewish Liaison Committee.)

Pope John Paul, in a remarkable series of addresses beginning in 1979, has sought to promote and give shape to the development of dialogue between Catholics and Jews.

In a homily delivered June 7, 1979, at Auschwitz, which he called the "Golgotha of the Modern World," he prayed movingly for "the memory of the people whose sons and daughters were intended for total extermination."

In a key address delivered Nov. 17, 1980, to the Jewish community in Mainz, the Pope articulated his vision of the three "dimensions" of the dialogue: (1) "the meeting between the people of God of the Old Covenant . . . and the people of the New Covenant"; (2) the encounter of "mutual esteem between today's Christian churches and today's people of the Covenant concluded with Moses"; (3) the "holy duty" of witnessing to the one God in the world and "jointly to work for peace and justice."

In addressing representatives of episcopal conferences gathered in Rome from around the world, the Pope again stressed Mar. 6, 1982, the continuing validity of God's covenant with the Jewish people.

On Mar. 22, 1984, at an audience with members of the Anti-Defamation League of B'nai B'rith, the Pope commented on "the mysterious spiritual link which brings us close together, in Abraham and through Abraham, in God who chose Israel and brought forth the Church from Israel." He urged joint social action on "the great task of promoting justice and peace."

In receiving a delegation of the American Jewish Committee Feb. 14, 1985, the Holy Father confirmed that *Nostra Aetate* "remains always for us . . . a teaching which is necessary to accept not merely as something fitting, but much more as an expression of the faith, as an inspiration of the Holy Spirit, as a word of the divine wisdom."

During his historic visit to the Great Synagogue in Rome Apr. 13, 1986, the Holy Father affirmed that God's covenant with the Jewish people is "irrevocable," and stated: "The Jewish religion is not 'extrinsic' to us, but in a certain way is 'intrinsic' to our own religion. With Judaism, therefore, we have a relationship which we do not have with any other religion."

Meeting with the Jewish community in Sydney, Australia, Nov. 26, 1986, the Holy Father termed the 20th century "the century of the Shoah" (Holocaust) and called "sinful" any "acts of discrimination or persecution against Jews."

On June 14, 1987, meeting with the Jewish community of Warsaw, the Pope called the Jewish witness to the Shoah (Holocaust) a "saving warning before all of humanity" which reveals "your particular vocation, showing you (Jews) to be still the heirs of that election to which God is faithful."

A collection of Pope John Paul's addresses, *On Jews and Judaism* 1979-1986, prepared by the NCCB Secretariat was sent to the Pope Aug. 12, 1987. In a response of Aug. 17, the Pope reiterated his Warsaw statement and added: "Before the vivid memory of the extermination (Shoah), it is not permissible for anyone to pass by with indifference. . . . The suffering endured by the Jews are also for the Catholic Church a motive of sincere sorrow, especially when one thinks of the indifference and sometimes resentment which . . . have divided Jews and Christians."

Meeting with Jewish leaders Sept. 11, 1987, in Miami, the Pope praised the efforts in theological dialogue and educational reform implemented in the U.S. since the Second Vatican Council; affirmed the existence of the State of Israel "according to international law," and urged "common educational programs on the Holocaust so that never again will such a horror be possible. Never again!"

The Pope also met with Jewish leaders June 23, 1988, during his visit to Austria.

International Liaison Committee

The International Catholic-Jewish Liaison Committee was formed in 1971 and is the official link between the Commission for Religious Relations with the Jewish People and the International Jewish Committee for Interreligious Consultations. The committee meets every 18 months to examine matters of common interest.

Topics under discussion have included: mission and witness (Venice, 1977), religious education (Madrid, 1978), religious liberty and pluralism (Regensburg, 1979), religious commitment (London, 1981), the sanctity of human life in an age of violence (Milan, 1982), youth and faith (Amsterdam, 1984), the Vatican Notes on Preaching and Catechesis (Rome, 1985), and the Holocaust (Washington, D.C., 1988).

The Holy See appointed Dr. Eugene Fisher a member of the Liaison Committee Apr. 1, 1984. He is the only lay person and the only American on the eight-member committee.

In 1988, the Vatican Library published "selected documents" of the Liaison Committee under the title, *Fifteen Years of Catholic-Jewish Relations.*

U.S. Dialogue

The National Workshop on Christian-Jewish Relations, begun in 1973 by the NCCB Secretariat, draws more than 1,000 participants from around the world. Recent workshops have been held in Baltimore (1986) and Minneapolis (1987). Others are scheduled in Charleston, S.C (1989) and Chicago (1990).

Ongoing relationships are also maintained by the NCCB Secretariat with other Jewish agencies, such as the American Jewish Committee, the Anti-Defamation League of B'nai B'rith, the Union of American Hebrew Congregations and the American Jewish Congress.

Since 1984, major inter-seminary programs have been held in Dallas, Los Angeles, Chicago, Boston and elsewhere.

In June, 1988, the Bishops' Committee for Ecumenical and Interreligious affairs published in Spanish and English *Criteria for the Evaluation of Dramatizations of the Passion,* providing for the first time Catholic guidelines for passion plays.

ISLAM

Islam is the religion of Mohammed and his followers, called Moslems, or Muslims. Islam, meaning submission to God, originated with Mohammed (570-632), an Arabian, who taught that he had received divine revelation and was the last and greatest of the prophets.

Moslems believe in one God. There were six great prophets—Adam, Noah, Abraham, Moses, Jesus and Mohammed—and Mohammed was the greatest. The creed states: "There is no God but Allah and Mohammed is the prophet of Allah."

The principal duties of Moslems are to: profess the faith by daily recitation of the creed; pray five times a day facing in the direction of the holy city of Mecca; give alms; fast daily from dawn to dusk during the month of Ramadan; make a pilgrimage to Mecca once if possible.

Moslems believe in a final judgment, heaven and hell. Polygamy is practiced. Some dietary regulations are in effect. The weekly day of worship is Friday, and the principal service is at noon in a mosque. Moslems do not have an ordained ministry. The general themes of their prayer are adoration and thanksgiving.

The basis of Islamic belief is the Koran, the created word of God revealed to Mohammed by the angel Gabriel over a period of 20 years. The contents of this sacred book are complemented by the Sunna, a collection of sacred traditions, and reinforced by Ijma, the consensus of Moslems which guarantees them against error in matters of belief and practice.

There are several sects of Moslems.

Conciliar Statement

The attitude of the Church toward Islam was stated as follows in the Second Vatican Council's *Declaration on the Relationship of the Church to Non-Christian Religions* (No. 3).

"Upon the Moslems, too, the Church looks with esteem. They adore one God, living and enduring, merciful and all-powerful, Maker of heaven and earth and Speaker to men. They strive to submit wholeheartedly even to his inscrutable decrees, just as did Abraham, with whom the Islamic faith is pleased to associate itself. Though they do not acknowledge Jesus as God, they revere him as a prophet. They also honor Mary, his virgin mother; at times they call on her, too, with devotion. In addition they await the day of judgment when God will give each man his due after raising him up. Consequently, they prize the moral life, and give worship to God especially through prayer, almsgiving and fasting.

"Although in the course of the centuries many quarrels and hostilities have arisen between Christians and Moslems, this most sacred Synod urges all to forget the past and to strive sincerely for mutual understanding. On behalf of all mankind, let them make common cause of safeguarding and fostering social justice, moral values, peace and freedom."

NON-ABRAHAMIC RELIGIONS

Hinduism, Buddhism, Confucianism and some other religions can be called non-Abrahamic because — unlike Judaism, Christianity and Islam — they do not recognize Abraham as their father in faith.

Hinduism

Hinduism is the traditional religion of India with origins dating to about 5,000 B.C. Its history is complex, including original Vedic Hinduism, with a sacred literature (Veda) of hymns, incantations and other elements, and with numerous nature gods; Brahmanism, with emphasis on ceremonialism and its power over the gods; philosophical speculation, reflected in the Upanishads, with development of ideas concerning Karma, reincarnation, Brahman, and the manner of achieving salvation; the cults of Vishnu, Shiva and other deities; reforms in Hinduism and in relation to Islam and Christianity.

The principal tenets of Hinduism are open to various interpretations. Karma is the law of the deed, of sowing and reaping, of retribution. It determines the progress of a person toward liberation from the cycle of rebirths necessary for salvation. Liberation is accomplished in stages, through successive reincarnations which indicate the previous as well as the existing state of a person. The means of liberation are the practice of ceremonialism and asceticism; faith in, devotion to and worship of the gods Vishnu and Shiva in their several incarnations; and/or knowledge attained through disciplined meditation called Yoga. Salvation, according to philosophical Hinduism, consists in absorption in Brahman, the neuter world-soul. Vishnu, the sun-god, and Shiva, the destroyer or generative force of the universe, are the principal popular deities. Ancient belief in nature gods (pantheism) is reflected in sacred respect for some animals. The concept of reincarnation underlies the caste system in Indian society.

There are many sects in Hinduism, which does not have a definite creed. It lends itself easily to syncretism or amalgamation with other beliefs, as evidenced in the 15th century Sikh movement which adopted the monotheism and militancy of Islam. Hindu rituals are various and elaborate, with respect to foods, festivals, pilgrimages, marriage and other life-events.

Buddhism

Buddhism originated in the sixth century B.C. in reaction to formalism, pantheism and other trends in Hinduism. The Buddha, the Enlightened One, was Sidartha Gautama, an Indian prince, who sought to explain human suffering and evil and to find a middle way between the extremes of austerity and sensuality.

The four noble truths of Buddhism are: (1) existence involves suffering or pain; (2) suffering comes from craving: (3) craving can be overcome; (4) the way to overcome craving is to follow the "noble eightfold path" of right views, right intention, right speech, right action, right livelihood, right effort, right mindfulness and right concentration.

Karma, the deed-principle of judgment and retribution, and reincarnation are elements of Buddhism. The ultimate objective of life is Nirvana — the absorption of a person in the absolute — which ends the cycles of rebirth.

Buddhism is essentially atheistic and more of a moral philosophy and ethical system than a religion. It has a cultic element in veneration for Buddha. Monasteries, temples and shrines are places of contemplation and ritualistic observance. There are several categories of Buddhist monks and nuns.

Buddhism has many sects. Mahayana Buddhism, with an elaborate ideology, is strong in China, Korea and Japan. Hinayana Buddhism is common in Southeast Asia. Zen Buddhism is highly contemplative. Lamaism in Tibet is a combination of Buddhism and local demonolatry.

Confucianism

Confucianism is an ethical system based on the teachings of Confucius (551-479 B.C.). It is oriented toward the moral perfection of individuals and society, the attainment of the harmony of individual and social life with the harmony of the universe, through conduct governed by the relationships of humanity, justice, ritual and courtesy, wisdom, and fidelity. It exerted a strong influence on national and family life in China all these centuries.

Taoism

Taoism originated in China several centuries before the Christian era and became a fully developed religious system by the fifth century A.D. As a religion of mystery, it developed extreme polytheism, with the Jade Emperor as the highest deity; sought blessings and long life by means of alchemy; fostered superstition and witchcraft; took on organizational and other aspects of Buddhism, with several categories of priests and nuns; exerted strong ethical influence on the lower classes; split into many sects; adopted features from other religions; became the starting point of many secret societies. One of its key tenets — that the way of nature is the guide to human conduct — resulted in a form of quietism opposed to the social concern of Confucianism.

Shinto

Shinto is the way of the gods, the sum total of the cultic beliefs and practices of the ancestral religion of Japan which originated from nature and ancestor worship. Shinto is pantheistic and has many objects of devotion, the highest being the Ruler of Heaven; is practiced with detailed rituals in public shrines, which are cultic centers; has strong social influence. Sectarian Shinto has about 13 recognized sects and many offshoots. Shinto, with principal concern for this-worldly blessing, has been affected by Buddhist and Confucian influences.

Eastern Cults

Eastern cults — with their mysticism and associated disciplines and practices — have recurrent periods of vogue in the West.

GLOSSARY

A

Abbacy: A non-diocesan territory whose people are under the pastoral care of an abbot acting in general in the manner of a bishop.

Abbess: The female superior of a monastic community of nuns; e.g., Benedictines, Poor Clares, some others. Elected by members of the community, an abbess has general authority over her community but no sacramental jurisdiction.

Abbey: See Monastery.

Abbot: The male superior of a monastic community of men religious; e.g., Benedictines, Cistercians, some others. Elected by members of the community, an abbot has ordinary jurisdiction and general authority over his community. Eastern-Rite equivalents of an abbot are a *hegumen* and an *archimandrite*. A regular abbot is the head of an abbey or monastery. An abbot general or archabbot is the head of a congregation consisting of several monasteries. An abbot primate is the head of the modern Benedictine Confederation.

Ablution: A term derived from Latin, meaning washing or cleansing, and referring to the cleansing of the hands of a priest celebrating Mass, after the offering of gifts; and to the cleansing of the chalice with water and wine after Communion.

Abortion: The expulsion of a nonviable human fetus from the womb of the mother, with moral implications stemming from the humanity of the fetus from the moment of conception and its consequent right to life. Accidental expulsion, as in cases of miscarriage, is without moral fault. Direct abortion, in which a fetus is intentionally removed from the womb, constitutes a direct attack on an innocent human being, a violation of the Fifth Commandment. A person who procures a completed abortion is automatically excommunicated (Canon 1398 of the Code of Canon Law); also excommunicated are all persons involved in a deliberate and successful effort to bring about an abortion. Direct abortion is not justifiable for any reason, e.g.: therapeutic, for the physical and/or psychological welfare of the mother; preventive, to avoid the birth of a defective or unwanted child; social, in the interests of family and/or community. Indirect abortion, which occurs when a fetus is expelled during medical or other treatment of the mother for a reason other than procuring expulsion, is permissible under the principle of double effect for a proportionately serious reason; e.g., when a medical or surgical procedure is necessary to save the life of the mother.

Absolution: The act by which an authorized priest, acting as the agent of Christ and minister of the Church, grants forgiveness of sins in the sacrament of penance. The essential formula of absolution is: "I absolve you from your sins; in the name of the Father, and of the Son, and of the Holy Spirit. Amen." Priests receive the power to absolve in virtue of their ordination and the right to exercise this power in virtue of faculties of jurisdiction given them by their bishop, their religious superior, or by canon law. The faculties of jurisdiction can be limited or restricted regarding certain sins and penalties or censures. In cases of necessity, and also in cases of the absence of their own confessors, Eastern- and Roman-Rite Catholics may ask for and receive sacramental absolution from a priest of a separated Eastern Church. Separated Eastern Christians may similarly ask for and receive sacramental absolution from an Eastern- or Roman-Rite priest. Any priest can absolve a person in danger of death; in the absence of a priest with the usual faculties, this includes a laicized priest or a priest under censure. (See additional entry under Sacraments.)

Absolution, General: A blessing of the Church to which a plenary indulgence is attached, given at the hour of death, and at stated times to members of religious institutes and secular (third) orders. (See also under Penance, Sacrament.)

Accessory to Another's Sin: One who culpably assists another in the performance of an evil action. This may be done by counsel, command, provocation, consent, praise, flattery, concealment, participation, silence, defense of the evil done.

Adoration: The highest act and purpose of religious worship, which is directed in love and reverence to God alone in acknowledgment of his infinite perfection and goodness, and of his total dominion over creatures. Adoration, which is also called *latria*, consists of internal and external elements, private and social prayer, liturgical acts and ceremonies, and especially sacrifice.

Adultery: (1) Sexual intercourse between a married person and another to whom one is not married; a violation of the obligations of chastity and justice. The Sixth Commandment prohibition against adultery also prohibits all external sins of a sexual nature. (2) Any sin of impurity (thought, desire, word, action) involving a married person who is not one's husband or wife has the nature of adultery.

Adventists: Members of several Christian sects whose doctrines are dominated by belief in a more or less imminent second advent or coming of Christ upon earth for a glorious 1,000-year reign of righteousness. This reign, following victory by the forces of good over evil in a final Battle of Armageddon, will begin with the resurrection of the chosen and will end with the resurrection of all others and the annihilation of the wicked. Thereafter, the just will live forever in a renewed heaven and earth. A sleep of the soul takes place between the time of death and the day of judgment. There is no hell. The Bible, in fundamentalist interpretation, is regarded as the only rule of faith and practice. About six sects have developed in the course of the Adventist movement which originated with William Miller (1782-1849) in the United States. Miller, on the basis of calculations made from the Book of Daniel, predicted that the second advent of Christ would occur between 1843 and 1844. After the prophecy went unfulfilled, divisions occurred in the movement and the Seventh Day Adventists, whose actual formation dates from 1860, emerged as the largest single body. The observance of Saturday instead of Sunday as the Lord's Day dates from 1844.

Advent Wreath: A wreath of laurel, spruce, or similar foliage with four candles which are lighted successively in the weeks of Advent to symbolize the approaching celebration of the birth of Christ, the Light of the World, at Christmas. The wreath originated among German Protestants.

Agape: A Greek word, meaning love, love feast, designating the meal of fellowship eaten at some gatherings of early Christians. Although held in some places in connection with the Mass, the agape was not part of the Mass, nor was it of universal institution and observance. It was infrequently observed by the fifth century and disappeared altogether between the sixth and eighth centuries.

Age of Reason: (1) The time of life when one begins to distinguish between right and wrong, to understand an obligation and take on moral responsibility; seven years of age is the presumption in church law. (2) Historically, the 18th century period of Enlightenment in England and France, the age of the Encyclopedists and Deists. According to a basic thesis of the Enlightenment, human experience and reason are the only sources of certain knowledge of truth; consequently, faith and revelation are discounted as valid sources of knowledge, and the reality of supernatural truth is called into doubt and/or denied.

Aggiornamento: An Italian word having the general meaning of bringing up to date, renewal, revitalization, descriptive of the processes of spiritual renewal and institutional reform and change in the Church; fostered by the Second Vatican Council.

Agnosticism: A theory which holds that a person cannot have certain knowledge of immaterial reality, especially the existence of God and things pertaining to him. Immanuel Kant, one of the philosophical fathers of agnosticism, stood for the position that God, as well as the human soul, is unknowable on speculative grounds; nevertheless, he found practical imperatives for acknowledging God's existence, a view shared by many agnostics. The First Vatican Council declared that the existence of God and some of his attributes can be known with certainty by human reason, even without divine revelation. The word agnosticism was first used, in the sense given here, by T. H. Huxley in 1869.

Agnus Dei: A Latin phrase, meaning Lamb of God. (1) A title given to Christ, the Lamb (victim) of the Sacrifice of the New Law (on Calvary and in Mass). (2) A prayer said at Mass before the reception of Holy Communion. (3) A sacramental. It is a round paschal-candle fragment blessed by the pope. On one side it bears the impression of a lamb, symbolic of Christ. On the reverse side, there may be any one of a number of impressions; e.g., the figure of a saint, the name and coat of arms of the reigning pope. The *agnus dei* may have originated at Rome in the fifth century. The first definite mention of it dates from about 820.

Alleluia: An exclamation of joy derived from Hebrew, All hail to him who is, praise God, with various use in the liturgy and other expressions of worship.

Allocution: A formal type of papal address, as distinguished from an ordinary sermon or statement of views.

Alms: An act, gift or service of compassion, motivated by love of God and neighbor, for the help of persons in need; an obligation of charity, which is measurable by the ability of one person to give assistance and by the degree of another's need.

Glossary

Almsgiving, along with prayer and fasting, is regarded as a work of penance as well as an exercise of charity. (See Corporal and Spiritual Works of Mercy.)

Alpha and Omega: The first and last letters of the Greek alphabet, used to symbolize the eternity of God (Rv. 1:8) and the divinity and eternity of Christ, the beginning and end of all things (Rv. 21:6; 22:13). Use of the letters as a monogram of Christ originated in the fourth century or earlier.

Amen: A Hebrew word meaning truly, it is true. In the Gospels, Christ used the word to add a note of authority to his statements. In other New Testament writings, as in Hebrew usage, it was the concluding word to doxologies. As the concluding word of prayers, it expresses assent to and acceptance of God's will.

Anathema: A Greek word with the root meaning of cursed or separated and the adapted meaning of excommunication, used in church documents, especially the canons of ecumenical councils, for the condemnation of heretical doctrines and of practices opposed to proper discipline.

Anchorite: A kind of hermit living in complete isolation and devoting himself exclusively to exercises of religion and severe penance according to a rule and way of life of his own devising. In early Christian times, anchorites were the forerunners of the monastic life. The closest contemporary approach to the life of an anchorite is that of Carthusian and Camaldolese hermits.

Angels: Purely spiritual beings with intelligence and free will, whose name indicates their mission as ministers of God and ministering spirits to men. They were created before the creation of the visible universe; the devil and bad angels, who were created good, fell from glory through their own fault. In addition to these essentials of defined doctrine, it is held that angels are personal beings; they can intercede for persons; fallen angels were banished from God's glory in heaven to hell; bad angels can tempt persons to commit sin. The doctrine of guardian angels, although not explicitly defined as a matter of faith, is rooted in long-standing tradition. No authoritative declaration has ever been issued regarding choirs or various categories of angels: according to theorists, there are nine choirs, consisting of seraphim, cherubim, thrones, dominations, principalities, powers, virtues, archangels and angels. In line with scriptural usage, only three angels can be named—Michael, Raphael and Gabriel.

Angelus: A devotion which commemorates the Incarnation of Christ. It consists of three versicles, three Hail Marys and a special prayer, and recalls the announcement to Mary by the Archangel Gabriel that she was chosen to be the Mother of Christ, her acceptance of the divine will, and the Incarnation (Lk. 1:26-38). The Angelus is recited in the morning, at noon and in the evening. The practice of reciting the Hail Mary in honor of the Incarnation was introduced by the Franciscans in 1263. The *Regina Caeli,* commemorating the joy of Mary at Christ's Resurrection, replaces the Angelus during the Easter season.

Anger: Passionate displeasure arising from some kind of offense suffered at the hands of another person, frustration or other cause, combined with a tendency to strike back at the cause of the displeasure; a violation of the Fifth Commandment and one of the capital sins if the displeasure is out of proportion to the cause and or if the retaliation is unjust.

Anglican Orders: Holy orders conferred according to the rite of the Anglican Church, which Leo XIII declared null and void in the bull *Apostolicae Curae,* Sept. 13, 1896. The orders were declared null because they were conferred according to a rite that was substantially defective in form and intent, and because of a break in apostolic succession that occurred when Matthew Parker became head of the Anglican hierarchy in 1559. In making his declaration, Pope Leo cited earlier arguments against validity made by Julius III in 1553 and 1554 and by Paul IV in 1555. He also noted related directives requiring absolute ordination, according to the Catholic ritual, of convert ministers who had been ordained according to the Anglican Ordinal. Some Anglican or Episcopal clergy, however, have been validly ordained to the priesthood because of participation in their ordination by valid bishops belonging to other than the Anglican Communion; e.g., Orthodox, Old Catholic bishops.

Antichrist: The man of sin, the lawless and wicked antagonist of Christ and the work of God; a mysterious figure of prophecy mentioned in the New Testament. Supported by Satan, submitting to no moral restraints, and armed with tremendous power, Antichrist will set himself up in opposition to God, work false miracles, persecute the People of God, and employ unimaginable means to lead people into error and evil during a period of widespread defection from the Christian faith before the end of time; he will be overcome by Christ. Catholic thinkers have regarded Antichrist as a person, a caricature of Christ, who will lead a final violent struggle against God and his people; they have also applied the title to personal and impersonal forces in history hostile to God and the Church. Official teaching has said little about Antichrist. In 1318, it labeled as partly heretical, senseless, and fanciful the assertions made by the Fraticelli about his coming; in 1415, the Council of Constance condemned the Wycliff thesis that excommunications made by the pope and other prelates were the actions of Antichrist.

Antiphon: (1) A short verse or text, generally from Scripture, recited in the Liturgy of the Hours before and after psalms and canticles. (2) Any verse sung or recited by one part of a choir or congregation in response to the other part, as in antiphonal or alternate chanting.

Apologetics: The science and art of developing and presenting the case for the reasonableness of the Christian faith, by a wide variety of means including facts of experience, history, science, philosophy. The constant objective of apologetics, as well as of the total process of pre-evangelization, is preparation for response to God in faith; its ways and means, however, are subject to change in accordance with the various needs of people and different sets of circumstances.

Apostasy: (1) The total and obstinate repudiation of the Christian faith. An apostate automatically incurs a penalty of excommunication. (2) Apostasy from orders is the unlawful withdrawal from or rejection of the obligations of the clerical state by a man who has received major orders. An apostate from orders is subject to a canonical penalty. (3) Apostasy from the religious life occurs when a Religious with perpetual vows unlawfully leaves the community with the intention of not returning, or actually remains outside the community without permission. An apostate from religious life is subject to a canonical penalty.

Apostolate: The ministry or work of an apostle. In Catholic usage, the word is an umbrella-like term covering all kinds and areas of work and endeavor for the service of God and the Church and the good of people. Thus, the apostolate of bishops is to carry on the mission of the Apostles as pastors of the People of God: of priests, to preach the word of God and to carry out the sacramental and pastoral ministry for which they are ordained; of religious, to follow and do the work of Christ in conformity with the evangelical counsels and their rule of life; of lay persons, as individuals and/or in groups, to give witness to Christ and build up the kingdom of God through practice of their faith, professional competence and the performance of good works in the concrete circumstances of daily life. Apostolic works are not limited to those done within the Church or by specifically Catholic groups, although some apostolates are officially assigned to certain persons or groups and are under the direction of church authorities. Apostolate derives from the commitment and obligation of baptism, confirmation, holy orders, matrimony, the duties of one's state in life, etc.

Apostolic Succession: Bishops of the Church, who form a collective body or college, are successors to the Apostles by ordination and divine right; as such they carry on the mission entrusted by Christ to the Apostles as guardians and teachers of the deposit of faith, principal pastors and spiritual authorities of the faithful. The doctrine of apostolic succession is based on New Testament evidence and the constant teaching of the Church, reflected as early as the end of the first century in a letter of Pope St. Clement to the Corinthians. A significant facet of the doctrine is the role of the pope as the successor of St. Peter, the vicar of Christ and head of the college of bishops. The doctrine of apostolic succession means more than continuity of apostolic faith and doctrine; its basic requisite is ordination by the laying on of hands in apostolic succession.

Archangel: An angel who carries out special missions for God in his dealings with persons. Three of them are named in the Bible: Michael, leader of the angelic host and protector of the synagogue; Raphael, guide of Tobiah and healer of his father, who is regarded as the patron of travelers; Gabriel, called the angel of the Incarnation because of his announcement to Mary that she was to be the Mother of Christ.

Archdiocese: An ecclesiastical jurisdiction headed by an archbishop. An archdiocese is usually a metropolitan see, i.e., the principal one of a group of dioceses comprising a province; the other dioceses in the province are suffragan sees.

Archives: Documentary records, and the place where they are kept, of the spiritual and temporal government and affairs of the Church, a diocese, church agencies like the departments of the Roman Curia, bodies like religious institutes, and individual parishes. The collection, cataloguing, preserving, and use of these records are governed by norms stated in canon law and particular regulations. The strictest secrecy is always in effect for confidential records concerning matters of conscience, and documents of this kind are destroyed as soon as circumstances permit.

Archpriest: For some time, before and during the Middle Ages, a priest who took the place of a bishop at liturgical worship. In Europe, the term is sometimes used as an honorary title. It is also an honorary title in Eastern-Rite Churches.

Ark of the Covenant: The sacred chest of the Israelites in which were placed and carried the tablets of stone inscribed with the Ten Commandments, the basic moral precepts of the Old Covenant (Ex. 25: 10-22; 37:1-9). The Ark was also a symbol of God's presence. The Ark was probably destroyed with the Temple in 587 B.C.

Asceticism: The practice of self-discipline. In the spiritual life, asceticism — by personal prayer, meditation, self-denial, works of mortification, and outgoing interpersonal works — is motivated by love of God and contributes to growth in holiness.

Ashes: Religious significance has been associated with their use as symbolic of penance since Old Testament times. Thus, ashes of palm blessed on the previous Sunday of the Passion are placed on the foreheads of the faithful on Ash Wednesday to remind them to do works of penance, especially during the season of Lent, and that they are dust and unto dust will return. Ashes are a sacramental.

Aspergillum: A vessel or device used for sprinkling holy water. The ordinary type is a metallic rod with a bulbous tip which absorbs the water and discharges it at the motion of the user's hand.

Aspersory: A portable metallic vessel, similar to a pail, for carrying holy water.

Aspiration (Ejaculation): Short exclamatory prayer; e.g., My Jesus, mercy.

Atheism: Denial of the existence of God, finding expression in a system of thought (speculative atheism) or a manner of acting (practical atheism) as though there were no God. The Second Vatican Council, in its *Pastoral Constitution on the Church in the Modern World* (Nos. 19 to 21), noted that a profession of atheism may represent an explicit denial of God. the rejection of a wrong notion of God, an affirmation of man rather than of God, an extreme protest against evil. It said that such a profession might result from acceptance of such propositions as: there is no absolute truth; man can assert nothing, absolutely nothing, about God; everything can be explained by scientific reasoning alone; the whole question of God is devoid of meaning. The constitution also cited two opinions of influence in atheistic thought. One of them regards recognition of dependence on God as incompatible with human freedom and independence. The other views belief in God and religion as a kind of opiate which sedates man on earth, reconciling him to the acceptance of suffering, injustice, shortcomings, etc., because of hope for greater things after death, and thereby hindering him from seeking and working for improvement and change for the better here and now. All of these views, in one way or another, have been involved in the No-God and Death-of-God schools of thought in recent and remote history.

Atonement: The redemptive activity of Christ, who reconciled man with God through his Incarnation and entire life, and especially by his suffering and Resurrection. The word also applies to prayer and good works by which persons join themselves with and take part in Christ's work of reconciliation and reparation for sin.

Attributes of God: Perfections of God. God possesses — and is — all the perfections of being, without limitation. Because he is infinite, all of these perfections are one, perfectly united in him. Man, however, because of the limited power of understanding, views these perfections separately, as distinct characteristics — even though they are not actually distinct in God. God is: almighty, eternal, holy, immortal, immense, immutable, incomprehensible, ineffable, infinite, invisible, just, loving, merciful, most high, most wise, omnipotent, omniscient, omnipresent, patient, perfect, provident, supreme, true.

Avarice (Covetousness): A disorderly and unreasonable attachment to and desire for material things; called a capital sin because it involves preoccupation with material things to the neglect of spiritual goods and obligations of justice and charity.

Ave Maria: See Hail Mary.

B

Baldachino: A canopy over an altar.

Base Ecclesial Communities: The concept and operational model of basic Christian communities — *comunidades de base* — envision relatively small communities of the faithful integrated for religious and secular life, with maximum potential for liturgical and sacramental participation, pastoral ministry, apostolic activity, and for personal and social development. Communities of this type originated mainly in Latin America; thousands of them are now contributing to the vitality of parishes and dioceses in many countries throughout the world.

Pope Paul VI, in *Evangelii Nuntiandi*, stated: The name "Ecclesial Communities" can be given only to those "that appear and develop . . . within the Church, having solidarity with her life, being nourished by her teaching and united with her pastors." The name should not be attributed to those "that come together in a spirit of bitter criticism of the Church" and radically oppose the Church. Only the genuine base ecclesial communities "will be a place of evangelization for the benefit of the bigger communities, especially the individual churches . . . and will be a hope for the universal Church to the extent . . . that they constantly grow in missionary consciousness, fervor, commitment and zeal."

Beatification: A preliminary step toward canonization of a saint. It begins with an investigation of the candidate's life, writings and heroic practice of virtue, and, except in the case of martyrs, the certification of one miracle worked by God through his or her intercession. If the findings of the investigation so indicate, the pope decrees that the Servant of God may be called *Blessed* and may be honored locally or in a limited way in the liturgy. Additional procedures lead to canonization (see separate entry).

Beatific Vision: The intuitive, immediate and direct vision and experience of God enjoyed in the light of glory by all the blessed in heaven. The vision is a supernatural mystery.

Beatitude: A literary form of the Old and New Testaments in which blessings are promised to persons for various reasons. Beatitudes are mentioned 26 times in the Psalms, and in other books of the Old Testament. The best known beatitudes — identifying blessedness with participation in the kingdom of God and his righteousness, and descriptive of the qualities of Christian perfection — are those recounted in Mt. 5:3-11 and Lk. 6:20-22.

Benedictus: The canticle or hymn of Zechariah at the circumcision of St. John the Baptist (Lk. 1:68-79). It is an expression of praise and thanks to God for sending John as a precursor of the Messiah. The *Benedictus* is recited in the Liturgy of the Hours as part of the Morning Prayer.

Biglietto: A papal document of notification of appointment to the cardinalate.

Biretta: A stiff, square hat with three ridges on top worn by clerics in church and on other occasions.

Blasphemy: Any expression of insult or contempt with respect to God, principally, and to holy persons and things, secondarily; a violation of the honor due to God in the context of the First and Second Commandments.

Blasphemy of the Spirit: Deliberate resistance to the Holy Spirit, called the unforgivable sin (Mt. 12:31) because it makes his saving action impossible. Thus, the only unforgivable sin is the one for which a person will not seek pardon from God.

Blessing: Invocation of God's favor, by official ministers of the Church or by private individuals. Blessings are recounted in the Old and New Testaments, and are common in the Christian tradition. Many types of blessings are listed in the *Roman Ritual*. Private blessings, as well as those of an official kind, are efficacious. Blessings are imparted with the Sign of the Cross and appropriate prayer.

Boat: A small vessel used to hold incense which is to be placed in the censer.

Brief, Apostolic: A papal letter, less formal than a bull, signed for the pope by a secretary and impressed with the seal of the Fisherman's Ring. Simple apostolic letters of this kind are issued for beatifications and with respect to other matters.

Bull, Apostolic: The most solemn form of papal document, beginning with the name and title of the pope (e.g., John Paul II, Servant of the Servants of God), dealing with an important subject, and having attached to it either a leaden seal called a *bulla* or a red ink imprint of the device on the seal. Bulls are issued to confer the titles of bishops and cardinals, to promulgate canonizations, and for other purposes. A collection of bulls is called a *bullarium*.

Burial, Ecclesiastical: Interment with ecclesiastical rites, a right of the Christian faithful. The Church recommends burial of the bodies of the dead, but cremation is permissible if it does not involve reasons against church teaching. Ecclesiastical burial is in order for catechumens; for unbaptized children whose parents intended to have them baptized before death; and even — in the absence of their own ministers — for baptized non-Catholics unless it would be considered against their will.

C

Calumny: Harming the name and good reputation of a person by lies; a violation of obligations of justice and truth. Restitution is due for calumny.

Calvary: A knoll about 15 feet high just outside the western wall of Jerusalem where Christ was crucified, so called from the Latin *calvaria* (skull) which described its shape.

Canon: A Greek word meaning rule, norm, standard, measure. (1) The word designates the Canon of Sacred Scripture, which is the list of books recognized by the Church as inspired by the Holy Spirit. (2) In the sense of regulating norms, the word designates the Code of Canon Law enacted and promulgated by ecclesiastical authority for the orderly and pastoral administration and government of the Church. A revised Code, effective Nov. 27, 1983, consists of 1,752 canons in seven books under the titles of general norms, the people of God, the teaching mission of the Church, the sanctifying mission of the Church, temporal goods of the Church, penal law and procedural law. The antecedent of this Code was promulgated in 1917 and became effective in 1918; it consisted of 2,414 canons in five books covering general rules, ecclesiastical persons, sacred things, trials, crimes and punishments. Eastern-Rite Churches have their own canon law. (3) The term also designates the canons, (Eucharistic Prayers, anaphoras) of the Mass, the core of the liturgy. (4) Certain dignitaries of the Church have the title of Canon, and some Religious are known as Canons.

Canonization: An infallible declaration by the pope that a person, who died as a martyr and/or practiced Christian virtue to a heroic degree, is now in heaven and is worthy of honor and imitation by all the faithful. Such a declaration is preceded by the process of beatification and another detailed investigation concerning the person's reputation for holiness, writings, and (except in the case of martyrs) a miracle ascribed to his or her intercession after death. The pope can dispense from some of the formalities ordinarily required in canonization procedures (equivalent canonization), as Pope John XXIII did in the canonization of St. Gregory Barbarigo on May 26, 1960. A saint is worthy of honor in liturgical worship throughout the universal Church. From its earliest years the Church has venerated saints. Public official honor always required the approval of the bishop of the place. Martyrs were the first to be honored. St. Martin of Tours, who died in 397, was an early non-martyr venerated as a saint. The earliest canonization by a pope with positive documentation was that of St. Udalricus by Benedict VI in 973. Alexander III reserved the process of canonization to the Holy See in 1171. In 1588 Sixtus V established the Sacred Congregation of Rites for the principal purpose of handling causes for beatification and canonization: this function is now the work of the Congregation for the Causes of Saints. The official listing of saints and blessed is contained in the *Roman Martyrology* and related decrees issued after its last publication. Butler's unofficial *Lives of the Saints* (1956) contains 2,565 entries. The Church regards all persons in heaven as saints, not just those who have been officially canonized. (See Beatification, Saints, Canonizations by Leo XIII and His Successors.)

Canticle: A scriptural chant or prayer differing from the psalms. Three of the canticles prescribed for use in the Liturgy of the Hours are: the *Magnificat* (Lk. 1:46-55), the *Benedictus* (Lk. 1:68-79), and the *Nunc Dimittis* (Lk. 2:29-32).

Capital Punishment: Punishment for crime by means of the death penalty. The political community, which has authority to provide for the common good, has the right to defend itself and its members against unjust aggression and may in extreme cases punish with the death penalty persons found guilty before the law of serious crimes against individuals and a just social order. Such punishment is essentially vindictive. Its value as a crime deterrent is a matter of perennial debate. The prudential judgment as to whether or not there should be capital punishment belongs to the civic community. The U.S. Supreme Court, in a series of decisions dating from June 29, 1972, ruled against the constitutionality of statutes on capital punishment except in specific cases and with appropriate consideration, with respect to sentence, of mitigating circumstances of the crime. Capital punishment was the subject of a statement issued Mar. 1, 1978, by the Committee on Social Development and World Peace, U.S. Catholic Conference. The statement said, in part: "The use of the death penalty involves deep moral and religious questions as well as political and legal issues. In 1974, out of a commitment to the value and dignity of human life, the Catholic bishops of the United States declared their opposition to capital punishment. We continue to support this position, in the belief that a return to the use of the death penalty can only lead to the further erosion of respect for life in our society." Additional statements against capital punishment have been issued by Pope John Paul II, numerous bishops and other sources.

Capital Sins: Moral faults which, if habitual, give rise to many more sins. They are pride, covetousness, lust, anger, gluttony, envy, sloth. The opposite virtues are: humility, liberality, chastity, meekness, temperance, brotherly love, diligence.

Cardinal Virtues: The four principal moral virtues are prudence, justice, temperance and fortitude.

Catacombs: Underground Christian cemeteries in various cities of the Roman Empire and Italy, especially in the vicinity of Rome; the burial sites of many martyrs and other Christians.

Catechesis: Religious instruction and formation not only for persons preparing for baptism but also for the faithful in various stages of their spiritual development.

Catechism: A summary of Christian doctrine usually in question and answer form, used for purposes of instruction.

Catechumen: A person preparing in a program (catechumenate) of instruction and spiritual formation for baptism and reception into the Church. The Church has a special relationship with catechumens. It invites them to lead the life of the Gospel, introduces them to the celebration of the sacred rites, and grants them various prerogatives that are proper to the faithful (one of which is the right to ecclesiastical burial). (See Rite of Christian Initiation of Adults, under Baptism.)

Cathedra: A Greek word for chair, designating the chair or seat of a bishop in the principal church of his diocese, which is therefore called a cathedral (see separate entry).

Cathedraticum: The tax paid to a bishop by all churches and benefices subject to him for the support of episcopal administration and for works of charity.

Catholic: A Greek word, meaning universal, first used in the title Catholic Church in a letter written by St. Ignatius of Antioch about 107 to the Christians of Smyrna.

Celebret: A Latin word, meaning Let him celebrate, the name of a letter of recommendation issued by a bishop or other superior stating that a priest is in good standing and therefore eligible to celebrate Mass or perform other priestly functions.

Celibacy: The unmarried state of life, required in the Roman Church of candidates for holy orders and of men already ordained to holy orders, for the practice of perfect chastity and total dedication to the service of people in the ministry of the Church. Celibacy is enjoined as a condition for ordination by church discipline and law, not by dogmatic necessity. In the Roman Church, a consensus in favor of celibacy developed in the early centuries while the clergy included both celibates and men who had been married once. The first local legislation on the subject was enacted by a local council held in Elvira, Spain, about 306; it forbade bishops, priests, deacons and other ministers to have wives. Similar enactments were passed by other local councils from that time on, and by the 12th century particular laws regarded marriage by clerics in major orders to be not only unlawful but also null and void. The latter view was translated by the Second Lateran Council in 1139 into what seems to be the first written universal law making holy orders an invalidating impediment to marriage. In 1563 the Council of Trent ruled definitely on the matter and established the discipline in force in the Roman Church. Some exceptions to this discipline have been made in recent years. Several married Protestant and Episcopalian (Anglican) clergymen who became converts and were subsequently ordained to the priesthood have been permitted to continue in marriage. Married men over the age of 35 can be ordained to the permanent diaconate. Eastern Church discipline on celibacy differs from that of the Roman Church. In line with legislation enacted by the Synod of Trullo in 692 and still in force, candidates for holy orders may marry before becoming deacons and may continue in marriage thereafter, but marriage after ordination is forbidden. Eastern-Rite bishops in the U.S., however, do not ordain married candidates for the priesthood. Eastern-Rite bishops are unmarried.

Cenacle: The upper room in Jerusalem where Christ ate the Last Supper with his Apostles.

Censer: A metal vessel with a perforated cover and suspended by chains, in which incense is burned. It is used at some Masses, Benediction of the Blessed Sacrament and other liturgical functions.

Censorship of Books: An exercise of vigilance by the Church for safeguarding authentic religious teaching. Pertinent legislation in a decree issued by the Congregation for the Doctrine of the Faith Apr. 9, 1975, is embodied in the Code of Canon Law (Book III, Title IV). (1) Pre-publication clearance is required for: editions of Sacred Scripture, liturgical texts and books of private devotion, catechisms and other writings relating to catechetical instruction. Books dealing with Scripture, theology, canon law, church history and religious or moral disciplines may not be used as basic texts in educational institutions (from elementary to university levels) unless they have been published with the approval of competent church authority. (2) Pre-publication clearance is recommended for all books on the aforementioned subjects, even though they are not used as basic texts in teaching. (3) Books or other writings dealing with religion or morals may not be displayed, sold or given out in churches or oratories unless published with the approval of competent ecclesiastical authority. (4) Except for a just and reasonable cause, Catholics should not write for newspapers, magazines or periodicals which regularly and openly prove to be inimical to the Catholic religion and good morals. The approval of the local bishop is required before clerics or members of religious institutes (who also need the approval of their superior) may write for such publications. Permission to publish works of a religious character, together with the apparatus of reviewing them beforehand, falls under the authority of the bishop of the place where the writer lives or where the works are published. Clearance for publication is usually indicated by the terms *Nihil obstat* (Nothing stands in the way) issued by the censor and *Imprimatur* (Let it be printed) authorized by the bishop. The clearing of works for publication does not necessarily imply approval of an author's viewpoint or his manner of handling a subject.

Censures: Sanctions inflicted by the Church on baptized Roman Catholics for committing certain serious offenses and for being or remaining obstinate therein: excommunication (exclusion from the community of the faithful, barring a person from sacramental and other participation in the goods and offices of the community of the Church), suspension (prohibition of a cleric to exercise orders) and interdict (deprivation of the sacraments and liturgical activities). Their intended purposes are to correct and punish offenders; to deter persons from committing sins which, more seriously and openly than others, threaten the common good of the Church and its members; and to provide for the making of reparation for harm done to the community of the Church. Censures may be incurred automatically (*ipso facto*) on the commission of certain offenses for which fixed penalties have been laid down in church law (*latae sententiae*); or they may be inflicted by sentence of a judge (*ferendae sententiae*). Automatic excommunication is incurred for the offenses of abortion, apostasy, heresy and schism. Obstinacy in crime — also called contumacy, disregard of a penalty, defiance of church authority — is presumed by law in the commission of offenses for which automatic censures are decreed. The presence and degree of contumacy in other cases, for which judicial sentence is required, is subject to determination by a judge. Absolution can be obtained from any censure, provided the person repents and desists from obstinacy. Absolution may be reserved to the pope, the bishop of a place, or the major superior of an exempt clerical religious institute. In danger of death, any priest can absolve from all censures; in other cases, faculties to absolve from reserved censures can be exercised by competent authorities or given to other priests. The penal law of the Church is contained in Book VI of the Code of Canon Law.

Ceremonies, Master of: One who directs the proceedings of a rite or ceremony during the function.

Chamberlain (Camerlengo): (1) The Chamberlain of the Holy Roman Church is a cardinal who administers the property and revenues of the Holy See. On the death of the pope he becomes head of the College of Cardinals and summons and directs the conclave until a new pope is elected. (2) The Chamberlain of the College of Cardinals has charge of the property and revenues of the College and keeps the record of business transacted in consistories. (3) The Chamberlain of the Roman Clergy is the president of the secular clergy of Rome.

Chancellor: Notary of a diocese, who draws up written documents in the government of the diocese; takes care of, arranges and indexes diocesan archives, records of dispensations and ecclesiastical trials.

Chancery (1) A branch of church administration that handles written documents used in the government of a diocese. (2) The administrative office of a diocese, a bishop's office.

Chapel: A building or part of another building used for divine worship; a portion of a church set aside for the celebration of Mass or for some special devotion.

Chaplain: A priest appointed for the pastoral service of any division of the armed forces, religious communities, institutions, various groups of the faithful.

Chaplet: A term, meaning little crown, applied to a rosary or, more commonly, to a small string of beads used for devotional purposes; e.g., the Infant of Prague chaplet.

Chapter: A general meeting of delegates of religious orders for elections and the handling of other important affairs of their communities.

Charismatic Renewal: A movement which originated with a handful of Duquesne University students and faculty members in the 1966-67 academic year and spread from there to Notre Dame, Michigan State University, the University of Michigan, other campuses and cities throughout the U.S., and to well over 100 other countries.

Scriptural keys to the renewal are: Christ's promise to send the Holy Spirit upon the Apostles; the description, in the Acts of the Apostles, of the effects of the coming of the Holy Spirit upon the Apostles on Pentecost; St. Paul's explanation, in the Letter to the Romans, of the charismatic gifts (for the good of the Church and persons) the Holy Spirit would bestow on Christians; New Testament evidence concerning the effects of charismatic gifts in and through the early Church.

The personal key to the renewal is baptism of the Holy Spirit. This is not a new sacrament but the personally experienced actualization of grace already sacramentally received, principally in baptism and confirmation. The experience of baptism of the Holy Spirit is often accompanied by the reception of one or more charismatic gifts. The characteristic form of the renewal is the weekly prayer meeting, a gathering which includes periods of spontaneous prayer, singing, sharing of experience and testimony, fellowship and teaching.

The movement's International Communication Office is located at Via Feruccio, 19, 00185, Rome, Italy. The U.S. National Service Committee is located at 237 N. Michigan St., South Bend, Ind. 46601.

Charisms: Gifts or graces given by God to persons for the good of others and the Church. Examples are special gifts for apostolic work, prophecy, healing, discernment of spirits, the life of evangelical poverty, here-and-now witness to faith in various circumstances of life. The Second Vatican Council made the following statement about charisms in the *Dogmatic Constitution on the Church* (No. 12): "It is not only through the sacraments and Church ministries that the same Holy Spirit sanctifies and leads the People of God and enriches it with virtues. Allotting his gifts 'to everyone according as he will' (1 Cor. 12:11), he distributes special graces among the faithful of every rank. By these gifts he makes them fit and ready to undertake the various tasks or offices advantageous for the renewal and upbuilding of the Church, according to the words of the Apostle:

'The manifestation of the Spirit is given to everyone for profit' (1 Cor. 12:7). These charismatic gifts, whether they be the most outstanding or the more simple and widely diffused, are to be received with thanksgiving and consolation, for they are exceedingly suitable and useful for the needs of the Church. "Still, extraordinary gifts are not to be rashly sought after, nor are the fruits of apostolic labor to be presumptuously expected from them. In any case, judgment as to their genuineness and proper use belongs to those who preside over the Church, and to whose special competence it belongs, not indeed to extinguish the Spirit, but to test all things and hold fast to that which is good" (cf. 1 Thes. 5:12; 19-21).

Charity: Love of God above all things for his own sake, and love of one's neighbor as oneself because and as an expression of one's love for God; the greatest of the three theological virtues. The term is sometimes also used to designate sanctifying grace.

Chastity: Properly ordered behavior with respect to sex. In marriage, the exercise of the procreative power is integrated with the norms and purposes of marriage. Outside of marriage, the rule is self-denial of the voluntary exercise and enjoyment of the procreative faculty in thought, word or action. The vow of chastity, which reinforces the virtue of chastity with the virtue of religion, is an evangelical counsel and one of the three vows professed by Religious.

Chirograph or Autograph Letter: A letter written by a pope himself, in his own handwriting.

Christ: The title of Jesus, derived from the Greek translation *Christos* of the Hebrew term *Messiah*, meaning the Anointed of God, the Savior and Deliverer of his people. Christian use of the title is a confession of belief that Jesus is the Savior.

Christianity: The sum total of things related to belief in Christ — the Christian religion, Christian churches, Christians themselves, society based on and expressive of Christian beliefs, culture reflecting Christian values.

Christians: The name first applied about the year 43 to followers of Christ at Antioch, the capital of Syria. It was used by the pagans as a contemptuous term. The word applies to persons who profess belief in the divinity and teachings of Christ and who give witness to him in life.

Christian Science: A religious doctrine consisting of Mary Baker Eddy's interpretation and formulation of the actions and teachings of Christ. Its basic tenets reflect Mrs. Eddy's ideas regarding the reality of spirit and its control and domination of what is not spirit. The basic statement of the doctrine is contained in *Science and Health, with Key to the Scriptures,* which she first published in 1875, nine years after being saved from death and healed on reading the New Testament. Mary Baker Eddy (1821-1910) established the church in 1879, and in 1892 founded at Boston the First Church of Christ, Scientist, of which all other Christian Science churches are branches. The individual churches are self-governing and self-supporting under the general supervision of a board of directors. Services consist of readings of portions of Scripture and *Science and Health.* One of the church's publications, *The Christian Science Monitor,* has a worldwide reputation as a journal of news and opinion.

Church: (1) See several entries under Church, Catholic. The universal Church is the Church spread throughout the world. The local Church is the Church in a particular locality; e.g., a diocese. The Church embraces all of its members — on earth, in heaven, in purgatory. (2) In general, any religious body. (3) A building set aside and dedicated for divine worship.

Circumcision: A ceremonial practice symbolic of initiation and participation in the covenant between God and Abraham.

Circumincession: The indwelling of each divine Person of the Holy Trinity in the others.

Clergy: Men ordained to holy orders and commissioned for sacred ministries and assigned to pastoral and other duties for the service of the people and the Church. (1) Diocesan or secular clergy are committed to pastoral ministry in parishes and in other capacities in a particular church (diocese) under the direction of their bishop, to whom they are bound by a promise of obedience. (2) Regular clergy belong to religious institutes (orders, congregations, societies — institutes of consecrated life) and are so called because they observe the rule (*regula,* in Latin) of their respective institutes. They are committed to the ways of life and apostolates of their institutes. In ordinary pastoral ministry, they are under the direction of local bishops as well as their own superiors.

Clericalism: A term generally used in a derogatory sense to mean action, influence and interference by the Church and the clergy in matters with which they allegedly should not be concerned. Anticlericalism is a reaction of antipathy, hostility, distrust and opposition to the Church and clergy arising from real and/or alleged faults of the clergy, overextension of the role of the laity, or for other reasons.

Cloister: Part of a monastery, convent or other house of religious reserved for use by members of the institute. Houses of contemplative Religious have a strict enclosure.

Code: A digest of rules or regulations, such as the Code of Canon Law.

Collegiality: A term in use especially since the Second Vatican Council to describe the authority exercised by the College of Bishops. The bishops of the Church, in union with and subordinate to the pope — who has full, supreme and universal power over the Church which he can always exercise independently — have supreme teaching and pastoral authority over the whole Church. In addition to their proper authority of office for the good of the faithful in their respective dioceses or other jurisdictions, the bishops have authority to act for the good of the universal Church. This collegial authority is exercised in a solemn manner in an ecumenical council and can also be exercised in other ways sanctioned by the pope. Doctrine on collegiality was set forth by the Second Vatican Council in the *Dogmatic Constitution on the*

Church. (See separate entry.) By extension, the concept of collegiality is applied to other forms of participation and co-responsibility by members of a community.

Commissariat of the Holy Land: A special jurisdiction within the Order of Friars Minor, whose main purposes are the collecting of alms for support of the Holy Places in Palestine and staffing of the Holy Places and missions in the Middle East with priests and brothers. There are about 70 such commissariats in more than 30 countries. One of them has headquarters at Mt. St. Sepulchre, Washington, D.C. Franciscans have had custody of the Holy Places since 1342.

Communion of Faithful, Saints: The communion of all the People of God — on earth, in heavenly glory, in purgatory — with Christ and each other in faith, grace, prayer and good works.

Communism: The substantive principles of modern communism, a theory and system of economics and social organization, were stated about the middle of the 19th century by Karl Marx, author of *The Communist Manifesto* and, with Friedrich Engels, *Das Kapital*. The elements of Communist ideology include: radical materialism; dialectical determinism; the inevitability of class struggle and conflict, which is to be furthered for the ultimate establishment of a worldwide, classless society; common ownership of productive and other goods; the subordination of all persons and institutions to the dictatorship of the collectivity; denial of the rights, dignity and liberty of persons; militant atheism and hostility to religion, utilitarian morality. Communism in theory and practice has been the subject of many papal documents and statements. Pius IX condemned it in 1846. Leo XIII dealt with it at length in the encyclical letters *Quod Apostolici Muneris* in 1878 and *Rerum Novarum* in 1891. Pius XI wrote on the same subject in the encyclicals *Quadragesimo Anno* in 1931 and *Divini Redemptoris* in 1937. These writings have been updated and developed in new directions by Pius XII, John XXIII, Paul VI and John Paul II.

Concelebration: The liturgical act in which several priests, led by one member of the group, offer Mass together, all consecrating the bread and wine. Concelebration has always been common in churches of Eastern Rite. In the Roman Rite, it was long restricted, taking place only at the ordination of bishops and the ordination of priests. The *Constitution on the Sacred Liturgy* issued by the Second Vatican Council set new norms for concelebration, which is now relatively common in the Roman Rite.

Concordance, Biblical: An alphabetical verbal index enabling a user knowing one or more words of a scriptural passage to locate the entire text.

Concordat: A church-state treaty with the force of law concerning matters of mutual concern — e.g., rights of the Church, arrangement of ecclesiastical jurisdictions, marriage laws, education. Approximately 150 agreements of this kind have been negotiated since the Concordat of Worms in 1122.

Concupiscence: Any tendency of the sensitive appetite. The term is most frequently used in reference to desires and tendencies for sinful sense pleasure.

Confession: Sacramental confession is the act by which a person tells or confesses his sins to a priest who is authorized to give absolution in the sacrament of penance.

Confessor: A priest who administers the sacrament of penance. The title of confessor, formerly given to a category of male saints, was suppressed with publication of the calendar reform of 1969.

Confraternity: An association whose members practice a particular form of religious devotion and/or are engaged in some kind of apostolic work.

Conscience: Practical judgment concerning the moral goodness or sinfulness of an action (thought, word, desire). In the Catholic view, this judgment is made by reference of the action, its attendant circumstances and the intentions of the person to the requirements of moral law as expressed in the Ten Commandments, the summary law of love for God and neighbor, the life and teaching of Christ, and the authoritative teaching and practice of the Church with respect to the total demands of divine Revelation. A person is obliged: (1) to obey a certain and correct conscience; (2) to obey a certain conscience even if it is inculpably erroneous; (3) not to obey, but to correct, a conscience known to be erroneous or lax; (4) to rectify a scrupulous conscience by following the advice of a confessor and by other measures; (5) to resolve doubts of conscience before acting. It is legitimate to act for solid and probable reasons when a question of moral responsibility admits of argument (see Probabilism).

Conscience, Examination of: Self-examination to determine one's spiritual state before God, regarding one's sins and faults. It is recommended as a regular practice and is practically necessary in preparing for the sacrament of penance. The *particular examen* is a regular examination to assist in overcoming specific faults and imperfections.

Consistory: An assembly of cardinals presided over by the pope.

Constitution: (1) An apostolic or papal constitution is a document in which a pope enacts and promulgates law. (2) A formal and solemn document issued by an ecumenical council on a doctrinal or pastoral subject, with binding force in the whole Church; e.g., the four constitutions issued by the Second Vatican Council on the Church, liturgy, Revelation, and the Church in the modern world. (3) The constitutions of institutes of consecrated life and societies of apostolic life spell out details of and norms drawn from the various rules for the guidance and direction of the life and work of their members.

Consubstantiation: A theory which holds that the Body and Blood of Christ coexist with the substance of bread and wine in the Holy Eucharist. This theory, also called *impanation*, is incompatible with the doctrine of transubstantiation.

Contraception: Anything done by positive interference to prevent sexual intercourse from resulting in conception. Direct contraception is against the order of nature. Indirect contraception — as a secondary effect of medical treatment or other action having a necessary, good, non-contraceptive purpose — is permissible under the principle of the double effect. The practice of periodic continence is not contraception because it does not involve positive interference with the order of nature.

Contrition: Sorrow for sin coupled with a purpose of amendment. Contrition arising from a supernatural motive is necessary for the forgiveness of sin. (1) Perfect contrition is total sorrow for and renunciation of attachment to sin, arising from the motive of pure love of God. Perfect contrition, which implies the intention of doing all God wants done for the forgiveness of sin (including confession in a reasonable period of time), is sufficient for the forgiveness of serious sin and the remission of all temporal punishment due for sin. (The intention to receive the sacrament of penance is implicit — even if unrealized, as in the case of some persons — in perfect contrition.) (2) Imperfect contrition or attrition is sorrow arising from a quasi-selfish supernatural motive; e.g., the fear of losing heaven, suffering the pains of hell, etc. Imperfect contrition is sufficient for the forgiveness of serious sin when joined with absolution in confession, and sufficient for the forgiveness of venial sin even outside of confession.

Contumely: Personal insult, reviling a person in his presence by accusation of moral faults, by refusal of recognition or due respect; a violation of obligations of justice and charity.

Corporal Works of Mercy: Feeding the hungry, giving drink to the thirsty, clothing the naked, visiting the imprisoned, sheltering the homeless, visiting the sick, burying the dead.

Council, Plenary: A council held for the particular churches belonging to the same episcopal conference. Such a council can be convoked to take action related to the pastoral activity and mission of the Church in the territory. The membership of such councils is fixed by canon law; their decrees, when approved by the Holy See, are binding in the territory (see Index, Plenary Councils of Baltimore).

Councils, Provincial: Meetings of the bishops of a province. The metropolitan, or ranking archbishop, of an ecclesiastical province convenes and presides over such councils in a manner prescribed by canon law to take action related to the life and mission of the Church in the province. Acts and decrees must be approved by the Holy See before being promulgated.

Counsels, Evangelical: Gospel counsels of perfection, especially voluntary poverty, perfect chastity and obedience, which were recommended by Christ to those who would devote themselves exclusively and completely to the immediate service of God. Religious (members of institutes of consecrated life) bind themselves by public vows to observe these counsels in a life of total consecration to God and service to people through various kinds of apostolic works.

Counter-Reformation: The period of approximately 100 years following the Council of Trent, which witnessed a reform within the Church to stimulate genuine Catholic life and to counteract effects of the Reformation.

Covenant: A bond of relationship between parties pledged to each other. God-initiated covenants in the Old Testament included those with Abraham, Noah, Moses, Levi, David. The Mosaic (Sinai) covenant made Israel God's Chosen People on terms of fidelity to true faith, true worship, and righteous conduct according to the Decalogue. The New Testament covenant, prefigured in the Old Testament, is the bond people have with God through Christ. All people are called to be parties to this perfect and everlasting covenant, which was mediated and ratified by Christ. The marriage covenant seals the closest possible relationship between a man and a woman.

Creation: The production by God of something out of nothing. The biblical account of creation is contained in the first two chapters of Genesis.

Creator: God, the supreme, self-existing Being, the absolute and infinite First Cause of all things.

Creature: Everything in the realm of being is a creature, except God.

Cremation: The reduction of a human corpse to ashes by means of fire. Cremation is not in line with Catholic tradition and practice, even though it is not opposed to any article of faith. The Congregation for the Doctrine of the Faith, under date of May 8, 1963, circulated among bishops an instruction which upheld the traditional practices of Christian burial but modified anti-cremation legislation. Cremation may be permitted for serious reasons, of a private as well as public nature, provided it does not involve any contempt of the Church or of religion, or any attempt to deny, question, or belittle the doctrine of the resurrection of the body. The person may receive the last rites and be given ecclesiastical burial. A priest may say prayers for the deceased at the crematorium, but full liturgical ceremonies may not take place there. The remains must be treated with respect and placed in consecrated ground. The principal reason behind an earlier prohibition against cremation was the fact that, historically, the practice had represented an attempt to deny the doctrine of the resurrection of the body. (See Burial, Ecclesiastical.)

Crib: A devotional representation of the birth of Jesus. The custom of erecting cribs is generally attributed to St. Francis of Assisi who in 1223 obtained from Pope Honorius III permission to use a crib and figures of the Christ Child, Mary, St. Joseph, and others, to represent the mystery of the Nativity.

Crosier: The bishop's staff, symbolic of his pastoral office, responsibility and authority; used at liturgical functions.

Crypt: An underground or partly underground chamber; e.g., the lower part of a church used for worship and/or burial.

Cura Animarum: A Latin phrase, meaning care of souls, designating the pastoral ministry and responsibility of bishops and priests.

Curia: The personnel and offices through which (1) the pope administers the affairs of the universal Church, the Roman Curia (see separate entry), or (2) a bishop the affairs of a diocese, diocesan curia. The principal officials of a diocesan curia are the vicar general of the diocese, the chancellor, officials of the diocesan tribunal or court, examiners, consultors, auditors, notaries.

Custos: A religious superior who presides over a number of convents collectively called a custody. In some institutes of consecrated life a custos may be the deputy of a higher superior.

D

Deaconess: A woman officially appointed and charged by the Church to carry out service-like functions. Phoebe apparently was one (Rom. 16:1-2); a second probable reference to the office is in 1 Tm. 3:11. The office — for assistance at the baptism of women, for pastoral service to women and for works of charity — had considerable development in the third and also in the fourth century when the actual term came into use (in place of such designations as *diacona, vidua, virgo canonica*). Its importance declined subsequently with the substitution of infusion in place of immersion as the common method of baptism in the West, and with the increase of the practice of infant baptism. There is no record of the ministry of deaconess in the West after the beginning of the 11th century. The office continued, however, for a longer time in the East. The Vatican's Theological Commission, in a paper prepared in 1971, noted that there had been in the past a form of diaconal ordination for women. With a rite and purpose distinctive to women, it differed essentially from the ordination of deacons, which had sacramental effects. Several Christian churches have had revivals of the office of deaconess since the 1830s. There is a contemporary movement in support of such a revival among some Catholics.

Dean: (1) A priest with supervisory responsibility over a section of a diocese known as a deanery. The post-Vatican II counterpart of a dean is an episcopal vicar. (2) The senior or ranking member of a group.

Dean of the College of Cardinals: See Index.

Decision: A judgment or pronouncement on a cause or suit, given by a church tribunal or official with judicial authority. A decision has the force of law for concerned parties.

Declaration: (1) An ecclesiastical document which presents an interpretation of an existing law. (2) A position paper on a specific subject; e.g., the three declarations issued by the Second Vatican Council on religious freedom, non-Christian religions, and Christian education.

Decree: An edict or ordinance issued by a pope and/or by an ecumenical council, with binding force in the whole Church; by a department of the Roman Curia, with binding force for concerned parties; by a territorial body of bishops, with binding force for persons in the area; by individual bishops, with binding force for concerned parties until revocation or the death of the bishop. The nine decrees issued by the Second Vatican Council were combinations of doctrinal and pastoral statements with executive orders for action and movement toward renewal and reform in the Church.

Dedication of a Church: The ceremony whereby a church is solemnly set apart for the worship of God. The custom of dedicating churches had an antecedent in Old Testament ceremonies for the dedication of the Temple, as in the times of Solomon and the Maccabees. The earliest extant record of the dedication of a Christian church dates from early in the fourth century, when it was done simply by the celebration of Mass. Other ceremonies developed later. A church can be dedicated by a simple blessing or a solemn consecration. The rite of consecration is generally performed by a bishop.

Deism: A system of natural religion which acknowledges the existence of God but regards him as so transcendent and remote from man and the universe that divine revelation and the supernatural order of things are irrelevant and unacceptable. It developed from rationalistic principles in England in the 17th and 18th centuries, and had Voltaire, Rousseau and the Encyclopedists among its advocates in France.

Despair: Abandonment of hope for salvation arising from the conviction that God will not provide the necessary means for attaining it, that following God's way of life for salvation is impossible, or that one's sins are unforgivable; a serious sin against the Holy Spirit and the theological virtues of hope and faith, involving distrust in the mercy and goodness of God and a denial of the truths that God wills the salvation of all persons and provides sufficient grace for it. Real despair is distinguished from unreasonable fear with respect to the difficulties of attaining salvation, from morbid anxiety over the demands of divine justice, and from feelings of despair.

Detraction: Revelation of true but hidden faults of a person without sufficient and justifying reason; a violation of requirements of justice and charity, involving the obligation to make restitution when this is possible without doing more harm to the good name of the offended party. In some cases, e.g., to prevent evil, secret faults may and should be disclosed.

Devil: (1) Lucifer, Satan, chief of the fallen angels who sinned and were banished from heaven. Still possessing angelic powers, he can cause such diabolical phenomena as possession and obsession, and can tempt men to sin. (2) Any fallen angel.

Devotion: (1) Religious fervor, piety; dedication. (2) The consolation experienced at times during prayer; a reverent manner of praying.

Devotions: Pious practices of members of the Church include not only participation in various acts of the liturgy but also in other acts of worship generally called popular or private devotions. Concerning these, the Second Vatican Council said in the *Constitution on the Sacred Liturgy* (No. 13): "Popular devotions of the Christian people are warmly commended, provided they accord with the laws and norms of the Church. Such is especially the case with devotions called for by the Apostolic See. Devotions proper to the individual churches also have a special dignity. . . . These devotions should be so drawn up that they harmonize with the liturgical seasons, accord with the sacred liturgy, are in some fashion derived from it, and lead the people to it, since the liturgy by its very nature far surpasses any of them." Devotions of a liturgical type are Exposition of the Blessed Sacrament, recitation of Evening Prayer and Night Prayer of the Liturgy of the Hours. Examples of paraliturgical devotion are a Bible Service or Vigil, and the Angelus, Rosary and Stations of the Cross, which have a strong scriptural basis.

Diocese: A particular church, a fully organized ecclesiastical jurisdiction under the pastoral direction of a bishop as local Ordinary.

Discalced: Of Latin derivation and meaning without shoes, the word is applied to religious orders or congregations whose members go barefoot or wear sandals.

Disciple: A term used sometimes in reference to the Apostles but more often to a larger number of followers (70 or 72) of Christ mentioned in Lk. 10:1.

Disciplina Arcani: A Latin phrase, meaning discipline of the secret and referring to a practice of the early Church, especially during the Roman persecutions, to: (1) conceal Christian truths from those who, it was feared, would misinterpret, ridicule and profane the teachings, and persecute Christians for believing them; (2) instruct catechumens in a gradual manner, withholding the teaching of certain doctrines until the catechumens proved themselves of good faith and sufficient understanding.

Dispensation: The relaxation of a law in a particular case. Laws made for the common good sometimes work undue hardship in particular cases. In such cases, where sufficient reasons are present, dispensations may be granted by proper authorities. Bishops, religious superiors and others may dispense from certain laws; the pope can dispense from all ecclesiastical laws. No one has authority to dispense from obligations of the divine law.

Divination: Attempting to foretell future or hidden things by means of things like dreams, necromancy, spiritism, examination of entrails, astrology, augury, omens, palmistry, drawing straws, dice, cards, etc. Practices like these attribute to creatural things a power which belongs to God alone and are violations of the First Commandment.

Divine Praises: Fourteen praises recited or sung at Benediction of the Blessed Sacrament in reparation for sins of sacrilege, blasphemy and profanity. Some of these praises date from the end of the 18th century: Blessed be God. / Blessed be his holy Name. / Blessed be Jesus Christ, true God and true Man. / Blessed be the Name of Jesus. / Blessed be his most Sacred Heart. / Blessed be his most Precious Blood. / Blessed be Jesus in the most holy Sacrament of the Altar. / Blessed be the Holy Spirit, the Paraclete. / Blessed be the great Mother of God, Mary most holy. / Blessed be her holy and Immaculate Conception. / Blessed be her glorious Assumption. / Blessed be the name of Mary, Virgin and Mother. / Blessed be St. Joseph, her most chaste Spouse. / Blessed be God in his Angels and in his Saints.

Double Effect Principle: Actions sometimes have two effects closely related to each other, one good and the other bad, and a difficult moral question can arise: Is it permissible to place an action from which two such results follow? It is permissible to place the action, if: the action is good in itself and is directly productive of the good effect; the circumstances are good; the intention of the person is good; the reason for placing the action is proportionately serious to the seriousness of the indirect bad effect. For example: Is it morally permissible for a pregnant woman to undergo medical or surgical treatment for a pathological condition if the indirect and secondary effect of the treatment will be the loss of the child? The reply is affirmative, for these reasons: The action, i.e., the treatment, is good in itself, cannot be deferred until a later time without very serious consequences, and is ordered directly to the cure of critically grave pathology. By means of the treatment, the woman intends to save her life, which she has a right to do. The loss of the child is not directly sought as a means for the cure of the mother but results indirectly and in a secondary manner from the placing of the action, i.e., the treatment, which is good in itself. The double effect principle does not support the principle that the end justifies the means.

Doxology: (1) The lesser doxology, or ascription of glory to the Trinity, is the Glory be to the Father. The first part dates back to the third or fourth century, and came from the form of baptism. The concluding words, As it was in the beginning, etc., are of later origin. (2) The greater doxology, Glory to God in the highest, begins with the words of angelic praise at the birth of Christ recounted in the Infancy Narrative (Lk. 2:14). It is often recited at Mass. Of early Eastern origin, it is found in the *Apostolic Constitutions* in a form much like the present. (3) The formula of praise at the end of the Eucharistic Prayer at Mass, sung or said by the celebrant while he holds aloft the paten containing the consecrated host in one hand and the chalice containing the consecrated wine in the other.

Dulia: A Greek term meaning the veneration or homage, different in nature and degree from that given to God, paid to the saints. It includes honoring the saints and seeking their intercession with God.

Duty: A moral obligation deriving from the binding force of law, the exigencies of one's state in life, and other sources.

E

Easter Controversy: A three-phase controversy over the time for the celebration of Easter. Some early Christians in the Near East, called Quartodecimans, favored the observance of Easter on the 14th day of Nisan, the spring month of the Hebrew calendar, whenever it occurred. Against this practice, Pope St. Victor I, about 190, ordered a Sunday observance of the feast. The Council of Nicaea, in line with usages of the Church at Rome and Alexandria, decreed in 325 that Easter should be observed on the first Sunday following the first full moon of spring. Uniformity of practice in the West was not achieved until several centuries later, when the British Isles, in delayed compliance with measures enacted by the Synod of Whitby in 664, accepted the Roman date of observance. Unrelated to the controversy is the fact that some Eastern Christians, in accordance with traditional calendar practices, celebrate Easter at a different time than the Roman and Eastern-Rite churches.

Easter Duty, Season: The serious obligation binding Catholics of Roman Rite, to receive the Eucharist during the Easter season (in the U.S., from the first Sunday of Lent to and including Trinity Sunday).

Easter Water: Holy water blessed with special ceremonies and distributed on the Easter Vigil; used during Easter Week for blessing the faithful and homes.

Ecclesiology: Study of the nature, constitution, members, mission, functions, etc., of the Church.

Ecstasy: An extraordinary state of mystical experience in which a person is so absorbed in God that the activity of the exterior senses is suspended.

Ecumenism: The movement of Christians and their churches toward the unity willed by Christ. The Second Vatican Council called the movement "those activities and enterprises which, according to various needs of the Church and opportune occasions, are started and organized for the fostering of unity among Christians" (*Decree on Ecumenism,* No. 4). Spiritual ecumenism, i.e., mutual prayer for unity, is the heart of the movement. The movement also involves scholarly and pew-level efforts for the development of mutual understanding and better interfaith relations in general, and collaboration by the churches and their members in the social area.

Elevation: The raising of the host after consecration at Mass for adoration by the faithful. The custom was introduced in the Diocese of Paris about the close of the 12th century to offset an erroneous teaching of the time which held that transubstantiation of the bread did not take place until after the consecration of the wine in the chalice. The elevation of the chalice following the consecration of the wine was introduced in the 15th century.

End Justifies the Means: An unacceptable ethical principle which states that evil means may be used to produce good effects.

Envy: Sadness over another's good fortune because it is considered a loss to oneself or a detraction from one's own excellence; one of the seven capital sins, a violation of the obligations of charity.

Epikeia: A Greek word meaning reasonableness and designating a moral theory and practice, a mild interpretation of the mind of a legislator who is prudently considered not to wish positive law to bind in certain circumstances. Use of the principle is justified in practice when the lawgiver himself cannot be appealed to and when it can be prudently assumed that in particular cases, e.g., because of special hardship, he would not wish the law to be applied in a strict manner. Epikeia may not be applied with respect to acts that are intrinsically wrong or those covered by laws which automatically make them invalid.

Episcopate: (1) The office, dignity and sacramental powers bestowed upon a bishop at his ordination. (2) The body of bishops collectively.

Equivocation: (1) The use of words, phrases, or gestures having more than one meaning in order to conceal information which a questioner has no strict right to know. It is permissible to equivocate (have a broad mental reservation) in some circumstances. (2) A lie, i.e., a statement of untruth. Lying is intrinsically wrong. A lie told in joking, evident as such, is not wrong.

Eschatology: Doctrine concerning the last things: death, judgment, heaven and hell, and the final state of perfection of the people and kingdom of God at the end of time.

Eternity: The interminable, perfect possession of life in its totality without beginning or end; an attribute of God, who has no past or future but always is. Man's existence has a beginning but no end and is, accordingly, called immortal.

Ethics: Moral philosophy, the science of the morality of human acts deriving from natural law, the natural end of man, and the powers of human reason. It includes all the spheres of human activity — personal, social, economic, political, etc. Ethics is distinct from but can be related to moral theology, whose primary principles are drawn from divine revelation.

Eucharistic Congresses: Public demonstrations of faith in the Holy Eucharist. Combining liturgical services, other public ceremonies, subsidiary meetings, different kinds of instructional and inspirational elements, they are unified by central themes and serve to increase understanding of and devotion to Christ in the Eucharist, and to relate this liturgy of worship and witness to life. The first international congress developed from a proposal by Marie Marthe Tamisier of Touraine, organizing efforts of Msgr. Louis Gaston de Segur, and backing by industrialist Philibert Vrau. It was held with the approval of Pope Leo XIII at the University of Lille, France, and was attended by some 800 persons from France, Belgium, Holland, England, Spain and Switzerland. International congresses are organized by the Committee for International Eucharistic Congresses. Participants include clergy, religious and lay persons from many countries, and representatives of national and international Catholic organizations. Forty-three international congresses were held from 1881 to 1985: Lille (1881), Avignon (1882), Liege (1883), Freiburg (1885), Toulouse (1886), Paris (1888), Antwerp (1890), Jerusalem (1893), Rheims (1894), Paray-le-Monial (1897), Brussels (1898), Lourdes (1899), Angers (1901), Namur (1902), Angouleme (1904), Rome (1905), Tournai (1906), Metz (1907), London (1908), Cologne (1909), Montreal (1910), Madrid (1911), Vienna (1912), Malta (1913), Lourdes (1914), Rome (1922), Amsterdam (1924), Chicago (1926), Sydney (1928), Carthage (1930), Dublin (1932), Buenos Aires (1934), Manila (1937), Budapest (1938), Barcelona (1952), Rio de Janeiro

(1955), Munich, Germany (1960), Bombay, India (1964), Bogota, Colombia (1968), Melbourne, Australia (1973), Philadelphia (1976), Lourdes (1981), Nairobi, Kenya (1985). The 44th international congress was scheduled to be held in 1989 in Seoul, South Korea.

Eugenics: The science of heredity and environment for the physical and mental improvement of offspring. Extreme eugenics is untenable in practice because it advocates immoral means, such as compulsory breeding of the select, sterilization of persons said to be unfit, abortion, and unacceptable methods of birth regulation.

Euthanasia: Mercy killing, the direct causing of death for the purpose of ending human suffering. Euthanasia is murder and is totally illicit, for the natural law forbids the direct taking of one's own life or that of an innocent person. The use of drugs to relieve suffering in serious cases, even when this results in a shortening of life as an indirect and secondary effect, is permissible under conditions of the double effect principle. It is also permissible for a seriously ill person to refuse to follow — or for other responsible persons to refuse to permit — extraordinary medical procedures even though the refusal might entail shortening of life.

Evangelization: Proclamation of the Gospel, the Good News of salvation in and through Christ, among those who have not yet known or received it; and efforts for the progressive development of the life of faith among those who have already received the Gospel and all that it entails. Evangelization is the primary mission of the Church, in which all members of the Church are called to participate.

Evolution: Scientific theory concerning the development of the physical universe from unorganized matter (inorganic evolution) and, especially, the development of existing forms of vegetable, animal and human life from earlier and more primitive organisms (organic evolution). Various ideas about evolution were advanced for some centuries before scientific evidence in support of the main-line theory of organic evolution, which has several formulations, was discovered and verified in the second half of the 19th century and afterwards. This evidence — from the findings of comparative anatomy and other sciences — confirmed evolution within species and cleared the way to further investigation of questions regarding the processes of its accomplishment. While a number of such questions remain open with respect to human evolution, a point of doctrine not open to question is the immediate creation of the human soul by God. For some time, theologians regarded the theory with hostility, considering it to be in opposition to the account of creation in the early chapters of Genesis and subversive of belief in such doctrines as creation, the early state of man in grace, and the fall of man from grace. This state of affairs and the tension it generated led to considerable controversy regarding an alleged conflict between religion and science. Gradually, however, the tension was diminished with the development of biblical studies from the latter part of the 19th century onwards, with clarification of the distinctive features of religious truth and scientific truth, and with the refinement of evolutionary concepts. So far as the Genesis account of creation is concerned, the Catholic view is that the writer(s) did not write as a scientist but as the communicator of religious truth in a manner adapted to the understanding of the people of his time. He used anthropomorphic language, the figure of days and other literary devices to state the salvation truths of creation, the fall of man from grace, and the promise of redemption. It was beyond the competency and purpose of the writer(s) to describe creation and related events in a scientific manner.

Excommunication: A penalty or censure by which a baptized Roman Catholic is excluded from the communion of the faithful, for committing and remaining obstinate in certain serious offenses specified in canon law; e.g. heresy, schism, apostasy, abortion. As by baptism a person is made a member of the Church in which there is a communication of spiritual goods, so by excommunication he is deprived of the same spiritual goods until he repents and receives absolution. Even though excommunicated, a person is still responsible for fulfillment of the normal obligations of a Catholic. (See Censures).

Existentialism: A philosophy with radical concern for the problems of individual existence and identity viewed in particular here-and-now patterns of thought which presuppose irrationality and absurdity in human life and the whole universe. It is preoccupied with questions about freedom, moral decision and responsibility against a background of denial of objective truth and universal norms of conduct; is characterized by prevailing anguish, dread, fear, pessimism, despair; is generally atheistic, although its modern originator, Soren Kierkegaard (d. 1855), and Gabriel Marcel (d. 1973) attempted to give it a Christian orientation. Pius XII called it "the new erroneous philosophy which, opposing itself to idealism, immanentism and pragmatism, has assumed the name of existentialism, since it concerns itself only with the existence of individual things and neglects all consideration of their immutable essences" (Encyclical *Humani Generis,* Aug. 12, 1950).

Exorcism: (1) Driving out evil spirits; a rite in which evil spirits are charged and commanded on the authority of God and with the prayer of the Church to depart from a person or to cease causing harm to a person suffering from diabolical possession or obsession. The sacramental is officially administered by a priest delegated for the purpose by the bishop of the place. Elements of the rite include the Litany of Saints; recitation of the Our Father, one or more creeds, and other prayers; specific prayers of exorcism; the reading of Gospel passages and use of the Sign of the Cross. (2) Exorcisms which do not imply the conditions of either diabolical possession or obsession form part of the ceremony of baptism, and are also included in formulas for various blessings; e.g., of water.

Exposition of the Blessed Sacrament: "In churches where the Eucharist is regularly reserved, it is recommended that solemn exposition of the Blessed Sacrament for an extended period of time should take place once a year, even though the period is not strictly continuous. . . . Shorter expositions of the Eucharist (**Benediction**) are to be arranged in such a way that the blessing with the Eucharist is preceded by a reasonable time for readings of the word of God, songs, prayers and a period for silent prayer.'' So stated Vatican directives issued in 1973.

F

Faculties: Grants of jurisdiction or authority by the law of the Church or superiors (pope, bishop, religious superior) for exercise of the powers of holy orders; e.g., priests are given faculties to hear confessions, officiate at weddings; bishops are given faculties to grant dispensations, etc.

Faith: In religion, faith has several aspects. Catholic doctrine calls faith the assent of the mind to truths revealed by God, the assent being made with the help of grace and by command of the will on account of the authority and trustworthiness of God revealing. The term faith also refers to the truths that are believed (content of faith) and to the way in which a person, in response to Christ, gives witness to and expresses belief in daily life (living faith). All of these elements, and more, are included in the following statement: '' 'The obedience of faith' (Rom. 16:26; 1:5; 2 Cor. 10:5-6) must be given to God who reveals, an obedience by which man entrusts his whole self freely to God, offering 'the full submission of intellect and will to God who reveals' (First Vatican Council, *Dogmatic Constitution on the Catholic Faith,* Chap. 3), and freely assenting to the truth revealed by him. If this faith is to be shown, the grace of God and the interior help of the Holy Spirit must precede and assist, moving the heart and turning it to God, opening the eyes of the mind, and giving 'joy and ease to everyone in assenting to the truth and believing it' '' (Second Council of Orange, Canon 7) (Second Vatican Council, *Constitution on Revelation,* No. 5). Faith is necessary for salvation.

Faith, Rule of: The norm or standard of religious belief. The Catholic doctrine is that belief must be professed in the divinely revealed truths in the Bible and tradition as interpreted and proposed by the infallible teaching authority of the Church.

Fast, Eucharistic: Abstinence from food and drink, except water and medicine, is required for one hour before the reception of the Eucharist. Persons who are advanced in age or suffer from infirmity or illness, together with those who care for them, can receive Holy Communion even if they have not abstained from food and drink for an hour. A priest celebrating two or three Masses on the same day can eat and drink something before the second or third Mass without regard for the hour limit.

Father: A title of priests, who are regarded as spiritual fathers because they are the ordinary ministers of baptism, by which persons are born to supernatural life, and because of their pastoral service to people.

Fear: A mental state caused by the apprehension of present or future danger. Grave fear does not necessarily remove moral responsibility for an act, but may lessen it.

First Friday: A devotion consisting of the reception of Holy Communion on the first Friday of nine consecutive months in honor of the Sacred Heart of Jesus and in reparation for sin. (See Sacred Heart, Promises.)

First Saturday: A devotion tracing its origin to the apparitions of the Blessed Virgin Mary at Fatima in 1917. Those practicing the devotion go to confession and, on the first Saturday of five consecutive months, receive Holy Communion, recite five decades of the Rosary, and meditate on the mysteries for 15 minutes.

Fisherman's Ring: A signet ring engraved with the image of St. Peter fishing from a boat, and encircled with the name of the reigning pope. It is not worn by the pope. It is used to seal briefs, and is destroyed after each pope's death.

Forgiveness of Sin: Catholics believe that sins are forgiven by God through the mediation of Christ in view of the repentance of the sinner and by means of the sacrament of penance. (See Penance, Contrition).

Fortitude: Courage to face dangers or hardships for the sake of what is good; one of the four cardinal virtues and one of the seven gifts of the Holy Spirit.

Fortune Telling: Attempting to predict the future or the occult by means of cards, palm reading, etc.; a form of divination, prohibited by the First Commandment.

Forty Hours Devotion: A Eucharistic observance consisting of solemn exposition of the Blessed Sacrament coupled with special Masses and forms of prayer, for the purposes of making reparation for sin and praying for God's blessings of grace and peace. The devotion was instituted in 1534 in Milan. St. John Neumann of Philadelphia was the first bishop in the U.S. to prescribe its observance in his diocese. For many years in this country, the observance was held annually on a rotating basis in all parishes of a diocese. Simplified and abbreviated Eucharistic observances have taken the place of the devotion in some places.

Forum: The sphere in which ecclesiastical authority or jurisdiction is exercised. (1) External: Authority is exercised in the external forum to deal with matters affecting the public welfare of the Church and its members. Those who have such authority because of their office (e.g., diocesan bishops) are called ordinaries. (2) Internal: Authority is exercised in the internal forum to deal with matters affecting the private spiritual good of individuals. The sacramental forum is the sphere in which the sacrament of penance is administered; other exercises of jurisdiction in the internal forum take place in the non-sacramental forum.

Franciscan Crown: A seven-decade rosary used to commemorate the seven Joys of the Blessed Virgin: the Annunciation, the Visitation, the

Nativity of Our Lord, the Adoration of the Magi, the Finding of the Child Jesus in the Temple, the Apparition of the Risen Christ to his Mother, the Assumption and Coronation of the Blessed Virgin. Introduced in 1422, the Crown originally consisted only of seven Our Fathers and 70 Hail Marys. Two Hail Marys were added to complete the number 72 (thought to be the number of years of Mary's life), and one Our Father, Hail Mary and Glory be to the Father are said for the intention of the pope.

Freedom, Religious: The Second Vatican Council declared that the right to religious freedom in civil society "means that all men are to be immune from coercion on the part of individuals and of social groups and of any human power, in such wise that in matters religious no one is to be forced to act in a manner contrary to his own beliefs. Nor is anyone to be restrained from acting in accordance with his own beliefs, whether privately or publicly, whether alone or in association with others, within due limits" of requirements for the common good. The foundation of this right in civil society is the "very dignity of the human person" (*Declaration on Religious Freedom,* No. 2). The conciliar statement did not deal with the subject of freedom within the Church. It noted the responsibility of the faithful "carefully to attend to the sacred and certain doctrine of the Church" (No. 14).

Freemasons: A fraternal order which originated in London in 1717 with the formation of the first Grand Lodge of Freemasons. From England, the order spread to Europe and elsewhere. Its principles and basic rituals embody a naturalistic religion, active participation in which is incompatible with Christian faith and practice. Grand Orient Freemasonry, developed in Latin countries, is atheistic, irreligious and anticlerical. In some places, Freemasonry has been regarded as subversive of the state; in Catholic quarters, it has been considered hostile to the Church and its doctrine. In the United States, Freemasonry has been widely regarded as a fraternal and philanthropic order. For serious doctrinal and pastoral reasons, Catholics were forbidden to join the Freemasons under penalty of excommunication, according to church law before 1983. Eight different popes in 17 different pronouncements, and at least six different local councils, condemned Freemasonry. The first condemnation was made by Clement XII in 1738. Eastern Orthodox and many Protestant bodies have also opposed the order. In the U.S., there was some easing of the ban against Masonic membership by Catholics in view of a letter written in 1974 by Cardinal Franjo Seper, prefect of the Congregation for the Doctrine of the Faith. The letter was interpreted to mean that Catholics might join Masonic lodges which were not anti-Catholic. This was called erroneous in a declaration issued by the Doctrinal Congregation Feb. 17, 1981. The prohibition against Masonic membership was restated in a declaration issued by the Doctrinal Congregation Nov. 26, 1983, with the approval of Pope John Paul II, as follows. "The Church's negative position on Masonic associations . . . remains unaltered, since their principles have always been regarded as irreconcilable with the Church's doctrine. Hence, joining them remains prohibited by the Church. Catholics enrolled in Masonic associations are involved in serious sin and may not approach Holy Communion. Local ecclesiastical authorities do not have the faculty to pronounce a judgment on the nature of Masonic associations which might include a diminution of the above-mentioned judgment." This latest declaration, like the revised Code of Canon Law, does not include a penalty of excommunication for Catholics who join the Masons. Local bishops are not authorized to grant dispensations from the prohibition. The foregoing strictures against Masonic membership by Catholics were reiterated in a report by the Committee for Pastoral Research and Practice, National Conference of Catholic Bishops, released through NC News Service June 7, 1985.

Free Will: The faculty or capability of making a reasonable choice among several alternatives. Freedom of will underlies the possibility and fact of moral responsibility.

Friar: Term applied to members of mendicant orders to distinguish them from members of monastic orders. (See Mendicants.)

Fruits of the Holy Spirit: Charity, joy, peace, patience, benignity, goodness, long-animity, mildness, faith, modesty, continence, chastity.

G

Gambling: The backing of an issue with a sum of money or other valuables, which is permissible if the object is honest, if the two parties have the free disposal of their stakes without prejudice to the rights of others, if the terms are thoroughly understood by both parties, and if the outcome is not known beforehand. Gambling often falls into disrepute and may be forbidden by civil law, as well as by divine law, because of cheating, fraud and other accompanying evils.

Gehenna: Greek form of a Jewish name, *Gehinnom,* for a valley near Jerusalem, the site of Moloch worship; used as a synonym for hell.

Genuflection: Bending of the knee, a natural sign of adoration or reverence, as when persons genuflect with the right knee in passing before the tabernacle to acknowledge the Eucharistic presence of Christ.

Gethsemani: A Hebrew word meaning oil press, designating the place on the Mount of Olives where Christ prayed and suffered in agony the night before he died.

Gifts of the Holy Spirit: Supernatural habits disposing a person to respond promptly to the inspiration of grace; promised by Christ and communicated through the Holy Spirit, especially in the sacrament of confirmation. They are: wisdom, understanding, counsel, fortitude, knowledge, piety, fear of the Lord.

Gluttony: An unreasonable appetite for food and drink; one of the seven capital sins.

God: The infinitely perfect Supreme Being, uncaused and absolutely self-sufficient, eternal, the Creator and final end of all things. The one God subsists in three equal Persons, the Father and the

Son and the Holy Spirit. God, although transcendent and distinct from the universe, is present and active in the world in realization of his plan for the salvation of men, principally through Revelation, the operations of the Holy Spirit, the life and ministry of Christ, and the continuation of Christ's ministry in the Church. The existence of God is an article of faith, clearly communicated in divine Revelation. Even without this Revelation, however, the Church teaches, in a declaration by the First Vatican Council, that men can acquire certain knowledge of the existence of God and some of his attributes. This can be done on the bases of principles of reason and reflection on human experience. Non-revealed arguments or demonstrations for the existence of God have been developed from the principle of causality; the contingency of man and the universe; the existence of design, change and movement in the universe; human awareness of moral responsibility; widespread human testimony to the existence of God.

Grace: A free gift of God to persons (and angels), grace is a created sharing or participation in the life of God. It is given to persons through the merits of Christ and is communicated by the Holy Spirit. It is necessary for salvation. The principal means of grace are the sacraments (especially the Eucharist), prayer and good works. (1) Sanctifying or habitual grace makes persons holy and pleasing to God, adopted children of God, members of Christ, temples of the Holy Spirit, heirs of heaven capable of supernaturally meritorious acts. With grace, God gives persons the supernatural virtues and gifts of the Holy Spirit. The sacraments of baptism and penance were instituted to give grace to those who do not have it; the other sacraments, to increase it in those already in the state of grace. The means for growth in holiness, or the increase of grace, are prayer, the sacraments, and good works. Sanctifying grace is lost by the commission of serious sin. Each sacrament confers sanctifying grace for the special purpose of the sacrament; in this context, grace is called sacramental grace. (2) Actual grace is a supernatural help of God which enlightens and strengthens a person to do good and to avoid evil. It is not a permanent quality, like sanctifying grace. It is necessary for the performance of supernatural acts. It can be resisted and refused. Persons in the state of serious sin are given actual grace to lead them to repentance.

Grace at Meals: Prayers said before meals, asking a blessing of God, and after meals, giving thanks to God. In addition to traditional prayers for these purposes, many variations suitable for different occasions are possible, at personal option.

H

Habit: (1) A disposition to do things easily, given with grace (and therefore supernatural) and/or acquired by repetition of similar acts. (2) The garb worn by Religious.

Hagiography: Writings or documents about saints and other holy persons.

Hail Mary: A prayer addressed to the Blessed Virgin Mary; also called the *Ave Maria* (Latin equivalent of Hail Mary) and the Angelic Salutation. In three parts, it consists of the words addressed to Mary by the Archangel Gabriel on the occasion of the Annunciation, in the Infancy Narrative (Hail full of grace, the Lord is with you, blessed are you among women.); the words addressed to Mary by her cousin Elizabeth on the occasion of the Visitation (Blessed is the fruit of your womb.); a concluding petition (Holy Mary, Mother of God, pray for us sinners now and at the hour of our death. Amen.). The first two salutations were joined in Eastern Rite formulas by the sixth century, and were similarly used at Rome in the seventh century. Insertion of the name of Jesus at the conclusion of the salutations was probably made by Urban IV about 1262. The present form of the petition was incorporated into the breviary in 1514.

Heaven: The state of those who, having achieved salvation, are in glory with God and enjoy the beatific vision. The phrase, kingdom of heaven, refers to the order or kingdom of God, grace, salvation.

Hell: The state of punishment of the damned — i.e., those who die in mortal sin, in a condition of self-alienation from God and of opposition to the divine plan of salvation. The punishment of hell begins immediately after death and lasts forever.

Heresy: The obstinate post-baptismal denial or doubt by a Catholic of any truth which must be believed as a matter of divine and Catholic faith (Canon 751, of the Code of Canon Law). Formal heresy involves deliberate resistance to the authority of God who communicates revelation through Scripture and tradition and the teaching authority of the Church. Heretics automatically incur the penalty of excommunication (Canon 1364 of the Code of Canon Law). Heresies have been significant not only as disruptions of unity of faith but also as occasions for the clarification and development of doctrine. Heresies from the beginning of the Church to the 13th century are described in Dates and Events in Church History.

Hermit: See Anchorite.

Heroic Act of Charity: The completely unselfish offering to God of one's good works and merits for the benefit of the souls in purgatory rather than for oneself. Thus a person may offer to God for the souls in purgatory all the good works he performs during life, all the indulgences he gains, and all the prayers and indulgences that will be offered for him after his death. The act is revocable at will, and is not a vow. Its actual ratification depends on the will of God.

Heterodoxy: False doctrine, teaching or belief; a departure from truth.

Holy See: (1) The diocese of the pope, Rome. (2) The pope himself and/or the various officials and bodies of the Church's central administration at Vatican City — the Roman Curia — which act in the name and by authority of the pope.

Holy Spirit: God the Holy Spirit, third Person of the Holy Trinity, who proceeds from the Father and the Son and with whom he is equal in every respect; inspirer of the prophets and writers of sacred Scripture; promised by Christ to the Apostles as their advocate and strengthener; appeared in the form of a dove at the baptism of Christ and as tongues of fire at his descent upon the Apostles; soul of the Church and guarantor, by his abiding presence and action, of truth in doctrine; communicator of grace to men, for which reason he is called the sanctifier.

Holy Water: Water blessed by the Church and used as a sacramental, a practice which originated in apostolic times.

Holy Year: A year during which the pope grants the plenary Jubilee Indulgence to the faithful who fulfill certain conditions. For those who make a pilgrimage to Rome during the year, the conditions are reception of the sacraments of penance and the Eucharist, visits and prayer for the intention of the pope in the basilicas of St. Peter, St. John Lateran, St. Paul and St. Mary Major. For those who do not make a pilgrimage to Rome, the conditions are reception of the sacraments and prayer for the pope during a visit or community celebration in a church designated by the bishop of the locality. Holy Year observances have biblical counterparts in the Years of Jubilee observed at 50-year intervals by the pre-exilic Israelites — when debts were pardoned and slaves freed (Lv. 25:25-54) — and in sabbatical years observed from the end of the Exile to 70 A.D. — in which debts to fellow Jews were remitted. The practice of Christians from early times to go on pilgrimage to the Holy Land, the shrines of martyrs and the tombs of the Apostles in Rome influenced the institution of Holy Years. There was also a prevailing belief among the people that every 100th year was a year of "Great Pardon." Accordingly, even before Boniface VIII formally proclaimed the first Holy Year Feb. 22, 1300, scores of thousands of pilgrims were already on the way to or in Rome. Medieval popes embodied in the observance of Holy Years the practice of good works (reception of the sacraments of penance and the Eucharist, pilgrimages and/or visits to the tombs of the Apostles, and related actions) and spiritual benefits (particularly, special indulgences for the souls in purgatory). These and related practices, with suitable changes for celebrations in local churches, remain staple features of Holy Year observances. The first three Holy Years were observed in 1300, 1350 and 1390. Subsequent ones were celebrated at 25-year intervals except in 1800 and 1850 when, respectively, the French invasion of Italy and political turmoil made observance impossible. Pope Paul II (1464-1471) set the 25-year timetable. In 1500, Pope Alexander VI prescribed the start and finish ceremonies — the opening and closing of the Holy Doors in the major basilicas on successive Christmas Eves. All but a few of the earlier Holy Years were classified as ordinary. Several — like those of 1933 and 1983-84 to commemorate the 1900th and 1950th anniversaries of the death and resurrection of Christ — were in the extraordinary category.

Homosexuality: The condition of a person whose sexual orientation is toward persons of the same rather than the opposite sex. The condition, is not sinful in itself. Homosexual acts are seriously sinful in themselves; subjective responsibility for such acts, however, may be conditioned and diminished by compulsion and related factors.

Hope: One of the three theological virtues, by which one firmly trusts that God wills his salvation and will give him the means to attain it.

Hosanna: A Hebrew word, meaning O Lord, save, we pray.

Host, The Sacred: The bread under whose appearances Christ is and remains present in a unique manner after the consecration which takes place during Mass. (See Transubstantiation.)

Humility: A virtue which induces a person to evaluate himself at his true worth, to recognize his dependence on God, and to give glory to God for the good he has and can do.

Hyperdulia: The special veneration accorded the Blessed Virgin Mary because of her unique role in the mystery of Redemption, her exceptional gifts of grace from God, and her preeminence among the saints. Hyperdulia is not adoration; only God is adored.

Hypnosis: A mental state resembling sleep, induced by suggestion, in which the subject does the bidding of the hypnotist. Hypnotism is permissible under certain conditions: the existence of a serious reason, e.g., for anesthetic or therapeutic purposes, and the competence and integrity of the hypnotist. Hypnotism may not be practiced for the sake of amusement. Experiments indicate that, contrary to popular opinion, hypnotized subjects may be induced to perform immoral acts which, normally, they would not do.

Hypostatic Union: The union of the human and divine natures in the one divine Person of Christ.

I

Icons: Byzantine-style paintings or representations of Christ, the Blessed Virgin and other saints, venerated in the Eastern Churches where they take the place of statues.

Idolatry: Worship of any but the true God; a violation of the First Commandment.

IHS: In Greek, the first three letters of the name of Jesus — Iota, Eta, Sigma.

Immortality: The survival and continuing existence of the human soul after death.

Impurity: Unlawful indulgence in sexual pleasure. (See Chastity.)

Incardination: The affiliation of a priest to his diocese. Every secular priest must belong to a certain diocese. Similarly, every priest of a religious community must belong to some jurisdiction of his community; this affiliation, however, is not called incardination.

Incarnation: (1) The coming-into-flesh or taking of human nature by the Second Person of the Trinity. He became human as the Son of Mary, being miraculously conceived by the power of the Holy Spirit, without ceasing to be divine. His divine Person hypostatically unites his divine and human natures. (2) The supernatural mystery coextensive with Christ from the moment of his human conception and continuing through his life on earth; his sufferings and death; his resurrection from the dead and ascension to glory with the Father; his sending, with the Father, of the Holy Spirit upon the Apostles and the Church; and his unending mediation with the Father for the salvation of men.

Incense: A granulated substance which, when burnt, emits an aromatic smoke. It symbolizes the zeal with which the faithful should be consumed, the good odor of Christian virtue, the ascent of prayer to God.

Incest: Sexual intercourse with relatives by blood or marriage; a sin of impurity and also a grave violation of the natural reverence due to relatives. Other sins of impurity (desire, etc.) concerning relatives have the nature of incest.

Inculturation: This was one of the subjects of an address delivered by Pope John Paul II Feb. 15, 1982, at a meeting in Lagos with the bishops of Nigeria. "An important aspect of your own evangelizing role is the whole dimension of the inculturation of the Gospel into the lives of your people. . . . The Church truly respects the culture of each people. In offering the Gospel message, the Church does not intend to destroy or to abolish what is good and beautiful. In fact, she recognizes many cultural values and, through the power of the Gospel, purifies and takes into Christian worship certain elements of a people's customs. The Church comes to bring Christ; she does not come to bring the culture of another race. Evangelization aims at penetrating and elevating culture by the power of the Gospel. . . . It is through the Providence of God that the divine message is made incarnate and is communicated through the culture of each people. It is forever true that the path of culture is the path of man, and it is on this path that man encounters the one who embodies the values of all cultures and fully reveals the man of each culture to himself. The Gospel of Christ, the Incarnate Word, finds its home along the path of culture, and from this path it continues to offer its message of salvation and eternal life."

Index of Prohibited Books: A list of books which Catholics were formerly forbidden to read, possess or sell, under penalty of excommunication. The books were banned by the Holy See after publication because their treatment of matters of faith and morals and related subjects were judged to be erroneous or serious occasions of doctrinal error. Some books were listed in the Index by name; others were covered under general norms. The Congregation for the Doctrine of the Faith declared June 14, 1966, that the Index and its related penalties of excommunication no longer had the force of law in the Church. Persons are still obliged, however, to take normal precautions against occasions of doctrinal error.

Indifferentism: A theory that any one religion is as true and good — or false — as any other religion, and that it makes no difference, objectively, what religion one professes, if any. The theory is completely subjective, finding its justification entirely in personal choice without reference to or respect for objective validity. It is also self-contradictory, since it regards as equally acceptable — or unacceptable — the beliefs of all religions, which in fact are not only not all the same but are in some cases opposed to each other.

Indulgence: According to *The Doctrine and Practice of Indulgences,* an apostolic constitution issued by Paul VI Jan. 1, 1967, an indulgence is the remission before God of the temporal punishment due for sins already forgiven as far as their guilt is concerned, which a follower of Christ — with the proper dispositions and under certain determined conditions — acquires through the intervention of the Church. The Church grants indulgences in accordance with doctrine concerning the superabundant merits of Christ and the saints, the Power of the Keys, and the sharing of spiritual goods in the communion of saints. An indulgence is partial or plenary, depending on whether it does away with either part or all of the temporal punishment due for sin. Both types of indulgences can always be applied to the dead by way of suffrage; the actual disposition of indulgences applied to the dead rests with God. (1) Partial indulgence: Properly disposed faithful who perform an action to which a partial indulgence is attached obtain, in addition to the remission of temporal punishment acquired by the action itself, an equal remission of punishment through the intervention of the Church. (This grant was formerly designated in terms of days and years.) The proper dispositions for gaining a partial indulgence are sorrow for sin and freedom from serious sin, performance of the required good work, and the intention (which can be general or immediate) to gain the indulgence. In addition to customary prayers and other good works to which partial indulgences are attached, there are general grants of partial indulgences to the faithful who: (a) with some kind of prayer, raise their minds to God with humble confidence while carrying out their duties and bearing the difficulties of everyday life; (b) motivated by the spirit of faith and compassion, give of themselves or their goods for the service of persons in need; (c) in a spirit of penance, spontaneously refrain from the enjoyment of things which are lawful and pleasing to them. (2) Plenary indulgence: To gain a plenary indulgence, it is necessary for a person to be free of all attachment to sin, to perform the work to which the indulgence is attached, and to fulfill the three conditions of sacramental confession, Eucharistic Communion, and prayer for the intention of the pope. The three conditions may be fulfilled several days before or after the performance of the prescribed work, but it is fitting that Communion be received and prayers for the intentions of the pope be offered on the same day the work is performed. The condition of praying for the pope's intention is fully satisfied by praying one Our Father and one Hail Mary, and sometimes the Creed, but persons are free to choose other prayers. Four of the several devotional practices for which a plenary indulgence is granted are: (a) adoration of the Blessed Sacrament for at least one-half hour; (b) devout reading of sacred Scripture for at least one-half hour; (c) the Way of the Cross; (d) recitation of the Rosary in a church, public oratory or private chapel, or in a family group, a religious community or pious association. Only one plenary indulgence can be gained in a single day. The Apostolic Penitentiary issued a decree Dec. 14, 1985, granting diocesan bishops the right to impart — three times a year on solemn feasts of their choice — the papal blessing with a plenary indulgence to those who cannot be physically present but who follow the sacred rites at which the blessing is imparted by radio or television transmission. In July, 1986, publication was announced of a new and simplified *Enchiridion Indulgentiarum*, in accord with provisions of the revised Code of Canon Law.

Indult: A favor or privilege granted by competent ecclesiastical authority, giving permission to do something not allowed by the common law of the Church.

Infant Jesus of Prague: An 18-inch-high wooden statue of the Child Jesus which has figured in a form of devotion to the Holy Childhood and Kingship of Christ since the 17th century. Of uncertain origin, the statue was presented by Princess Polixena to the Carmelites of Our Lady of Victory Church, Prague, in 1628.

Infused Virtues: The theological virtues of faith, hope, and charity; principles or capabilities of supernatural action, they are given with sanctifying grace by God rather than acquired by repeated acts of a person. They can be increased by practice; they are lost by contrary acts. Natural-acquired moral virtues, like the cardinal virtues of prudence, justice, temperance, and fortitude, can be considered infused in a person whose state of grace gives them supernatural orientation.

Inquisition: A tribunal for dealing with heretics, authorized by Gregory IX in 1231 to search them out, hear and judge them, sentence them to various forms of punishment, and in some cases to hand them over to civil authorities for punishment. The Inquisition was a creature of its time when crimes against faith, which threatened the good of the Christian community, were regarded also as crimes against the state, and when heretical doctrines of such extremists as the Cathari and Albigensians threatened the very fabric of society. The institution, which was responsible for many excesses, was most active in the second half of the 13th century.

Inquisition, Spanish: An institution peculiar to Spain and the colonies in Spanish America. In 1478, at the urging of King Ferdinand, Pope Sixtus IV approved the establishment of the Inquisition for trying charges of heresy brought against Jewish (Marranos) and Moorish (Moriscos) converts. It acquired jurisdiction over other cases as well, however, and fell into disrepute because of irregularities in its functions, cruelty in its sentences, and the manner in which it served the interests of the Spanish crown more than the accused persons and the good of the Church. Protests by the Holy See failed to curb excesses of the Inquisition, which lingered in Spanish history until early in the 19th century.

I N R I: The first letters of words in the Latin inscription atop the cross on which Christ was crucified: (I)esus (N)azaraenus, (R)ex (J)udaeorum — Jesus of Nazareth, King of the Jews.

Insemination, Artificial: The implanting of human semen by some means other than consummation of natural marital intercourse. In view of the principle that procreation should result only from marital intercourse, donor insemination is not permissible.

In Sin: The condition of a person called spiritually dead because he does not possess sanctifying grace, the principle of supernatural life, action and merit. Such grace can be regained through repentance.

Instruction: A document containing doctrinal explanations, directive norms, rules, recommendations, admonitions, issued by the pope, a department of the Roman Curia or other competent authority in the Church. To the extent that they so prescribe, instructions have the force of law.

Intercommunion: The common celebration and reception of the Eucharist by members of different Christian churches; a pivotal issue in ecumenical theory and practice. Catholic participation and intercommunion in the Eucharistic liturgy of another church without a valid priesthood and with a variant Eucharistic belief is out of order. Under certain conditions, other Christians may receive the Eucharist in the Catholic Church (see additional Intercommunion entry). Intercommunion is acceptable to some Protestant churches and unacceptable to others.

Interdict: A censure imposed on persons for certain violations of church law. Interdicted persons may not take part in certain liturgical services, administer or receive certain sacraments.

Interregnum: The period of time between the death of a pope and the election of his successor. Another term applied to the period is *Sede vacante*, meaning the See (of Rome) being vacant. The main concerns during an interregnum are matters connected with the death and burial of the pope, the election of his successor, and the maintenance of ordinary routine for the proper functioning of the Roman Curia and the Diocese of Rome. Interregnum procedures follow norms contained in the apostolic constitution *Romano Pontifici Eligendo* issued by Paul VI Oct. 1, 1975. "During the vacancy of the Apostolic See," the constitution states, "the government of the Church is entrusted to the College of Cardinals for the sole dispatch of ordinary business and of matters which cannot be postponed, and for the preparation of everything necessary for the election of the new pope." The general congregation of the whole college, presided over by the dean, sub-dean or senior cardinal, has responsibility for major decisions during an interregnum. Other decisions of a routine nature are left to a particular congregation consisting of the chamberlain of the Holy Roman Church and three assistant cardinals. The chamberlain of the Holy Roman Church and the dean of the college are the key officials, with directive responsibilities before and during the electoral conclave. The chamberlain is in general charge of ordinary administration. He — or the dean prior to a chamberlain's election by the cardinals — certifies the death of the pope; orders the destruction of the Fisherman's Ring and personal seals of the pope; and sets in motion procedures, carried out in collaboration with the dean, for informing the world about the pope's death, for funeral preparations, and for summoning and supervising the conclave for the election of a new pope. Cardinals in charge of departments of the Roman Curia relinquish their offices at the death of the pope. Remaining in office, however, are the vicar of Rome, for ordinary jurisdiction over the diocese, and the major penitentiary. The substitute secretary of state or papal secretariat maintains the secretariat in a status quo. Papal representatives, such as nuncios and apostolic delegates, remain in office. The congregations, offices and tribunals of the Curia retain ordinary jurisdiction for routine affairs but may not initiate new business during an interregnum. If the pope should die during sessions of an ecumenical council or the Synod of Bishops, they would automatically be suspended. The deceased pope is buried in St. Peter's Basilica, following prescribed ceremonies and traditional customs during a mourning period of nine days. The conclave for the election of a new pope begins no sooner than 15 and no later than 20 days after the death of his predecessor. On the election of the new pope, the interregnum comes to an end.

Intinction: A method of administering Holy Communion under the dual appearances of bread and wine, in which the consecrated host is dipped in the consecrated wine before being given to the communicant. The administering of Holy Communion in this manner, which has been traditional in Eastern-Rite liturgies, was authorized in the Roman Rite for various occasions by the *Constitution on the Sacred Liturgy* promulgated by the Second Vatican Council.

Irenicism: Peace-seeking, conciliation, as opposed to polemics; an important element in ecumenism, provided it furthers pursuit of the Christian unity willed by Christ without degenerating into a peace-at-any-price disregard for religious truth.

Irregularity: An impediment to the lawful reception or exercise of holy orders. The Church instituted irregularities — which include apostasy, heresy, homicide, attempted suicide — out of reverence for the dignity of the sacraments.

Itinerarium: Prayers for a spiritually profitable journey.

J

Jansenism: Opinions developed and proposed by Cornelius Jansenius (1585-1638). He held that: human nature was radically and intrinsically corrupted by original sin; some men are predestined to heaven and others to hell; Christ died only for those predestined to heaven; for those who are predestined, the operations of grace are irresistible. Jansenism also advocated an extremely rigorous code of morals and asceticism. The errors were proscribed by Urban VIII in 1642, by Innocent X in 1653, by Clement XI in 1713, and by other popes. Despite these condemnations, the rigoristic spirit of Jansenism lingered for a long time afterwards, particularly in France.

Jehovah's Witnesses: The Witnesses, together with the Watchtower and Bible Tract Society, trace their beginnings to a Bible class organized by Charles Taze Russell in 1872 at Allegheny, Pa. They take their name from a passage in Isaiah (43:12): " 'You are my witnesses,' says Jehovah." They are generally fundamentalist and revivalist with respect to the Bible, and believe that Christ is God's Son but is inferior to God. They place great emphasis on the Battle of Armageddon (as a decisive confrontation of good and evil) that is depicted vividly in Revelation, believing that God will then destroy the existing system of things and that, with the establishment of Jehovah's Kingdom, a small band of 144,000 spiritual sons of God will go to heaven, rule with Christ, and share in some way their happiness with some others. Each Witness is considered by the society to be an ordained minister charged with the duty of spreading the message of Jehovah, which is accomplished through publications, house-to-house visitations, and other methods. The Witnesses refuse to salute the flag of any nation, regarding this as a form of idolatry, or to sanction blood transfusions even for the saving of life. There are approximately one million Witnesses in more than 22,000 congregations in some 80 countries. The freedom and activities of Witnesses are restricted in some places.

Jesus: The name of Jesus, meaning Savior in Christian usage, derived from the Aramaic and Hebrew *Yeshua* and *Joshua*, meaning *Yahweh* is salvation.

Jesus Prayer: A form of prayer dating back to the fifth century, "Lord Jesus Christ, Son of God, have mercy on me (a sinner)."

Judgment: (1) Last or final judgment: Final judgment by Christ, at the end of the world and the general resurrection. (2) Particular judgment: The judgment that takes place immediately after a person's death, followed by entrance into heaven, hell or purgatory.

Jurisdiction: Right, power, authority to rule. Jurisdiction in the Church is of divine institution; has pastoral service for its purpose; includes legislative, judicial and executive authority; can be exercised only by persons with the power of orders. (1) Ordinary jurisdiction is attached to ecclesiastical offices by law; the officeholders, called Ordinaries, have authority over those who are subject to them. (2) Delegated jurisdiction is that which is granted to persons rather than attached to offices. Its extent depends on the terms of the delegation.

Justice: One of the four cardinal virtues by which a person gives to others what is due to them as a matter of right. (See Cardinal Virtues.)

Justification: The act by which God makes a person just, and the consequent change in the spiritual status of a person, from sin to grace; the remission of sin and the infusion of sanctifying grace through the merits of Christ and the action of the Holy Spirit.

K

Kerygma: Proclaiming the word of God, in the manner of the Apostles, as here and now effective for salvation. This method of preaching or instruction, centered on Christ and geared to the facts and themes of salvation history, is designed to dispose people to faith in Christ and or to intensify the experience and practice of that faith in those who have it.

Keys, Power of the: Spiritual authority and jurisdiction in the Church, symbolized by the keys of the kingdom of heaven. Christ promised the keys to St. Peter, as head-to-be of the Church (Mt. 16:19), and commissioned him with full pastoral responsibility to feed his lambs and sheep (Jn. 21:15-17), The pope, as the successor of St. Peter, has this power in a primary and supreme manner. The bishops of the Church also have the power, in union with and subordinate to the pope. Priests share in it through holy orders and the delegation of authority. Examples of the application of the Power of the Keys are the exercise of teaching and pastoral authority by the pope and bishops, the absolving of sins in the sacrament of penance, the granting of indulgences, the imposing of spiritual penalties on persons who commit certain serious sins.

L

Laicization: The process by which a man ordained to holy orders is relieved of the obligations of orders and the ministry and is returned to the status of a lay person.

Languages of the Church: The first language in church use, for divine worship and the conduct of ecclesiastical affairs, was Aramaic, the language of the first Christians in and around Jerusalem. As the Church spread westward, Greek was adopted and prevailed until the third century when it was supplanted by Latin for official use in the West. According to traditions established very early in churches of the Eastern Rites, many different languages were adopted for use in divine worship and for the conduct of ecclesiastical affairs. The practice was, and still is, to use the vernacular or a language closely related to the common tongue of the people. In the Western Church, Latin prevailed as the general official language until the promulgation on Dec. 4, 1963, of the *Constitution on the Sacred Liturgy* by the second session of the Second Vatican Council. Since that time, vernacular languages have come into use in the Mass, administration of the sacraments, and the Liturgy of the Hours. The change was introduced in order to make the prayers and ceremonies of divine worship more informative and meaningful to all. Latin, however, remains the official language for documents of the Holy See, administrative and procedural matters.

Law: An ordinance or rule governing the activity of things. (1) Natural law: Moral norms corresponding to man's nature by which he orders his conduct toward God, neighbor, society and himself. This law, which is rooted in human nature, is of divine origin, can be known by the use of reason, and binds all men having the use of reason. The Ten Commandments are declarations and amplifications of natural law. The primary precepts of natural law, to do good and to avoid evil, are universally recognized, despite differences with respect to understanding and application resulting from different philosophies of good and evil. (2) Divine positive law: That which has been revealed by God. Among its essentials are the twin precepts of love of God and love of neighbor, and the Ten Commandments. (3) Ecclesiastical law: That which is established by the Church for the spiritual welfare of the faithful and the orderly conduct of ecclesiastical affairs. (See Canon Law.) (4) Civil law: That which is established by a socio-political community for the common good.

Liberalism: A multiphased trend of thought and movement favoring liberty, independence and progress in moral, intellectual, religious, social, economic and political life. Traceable to the Renaissance, it developed through the Enlightenment, the rationalism of the 19th century, and modernist- and existentialist-related theories of the 20th century. Evaluations of various kinds of liberalism depend on the validity of their underlying principles. Extremist positions — regarding subjectivism, libertinarianism, naturalist denials of the supernatural, and the alienation of individuals and society from God and the Church were condemned by Gregory XVI in the 1830's, Pius IX in 1864, Leo XIII in 1899, and St. Pius X in 1907. There is, however, nothing objectionable about forms of liberalism patterned according to sound principles of Christian doctrine.

Liberation Theology: Deals with the relevance of Christian faith and salvation — and, therefore, of the mission of the Church — to efforts for the promotion of human rights, social justice and human development. It originated in the religious, social, political and economic environment of Latin America, with its contemporary need for a theory and corresponding action by the Church, in the pattern of its overall mission, for human rights and integral personal and social development. Some versions of liberation theology are at variance with the body of church teaching because of their ideological concept of Christ as liberator, and also because they play down the primary spiritual nature and mission of the Church. Instructions from the Congregation for the Doctrine of the Faith — "On Certain Aspects of the Theology of Liberation" (Sept. 3, 1984) and "On Christian Freedom and Liberation" (Apr. 5, 1986) — contain warnings against translating sociology into theology and advocating violence in social activism.

Life in Outer Space: Whether rational life exists on other bodies in the universe besides earth, is a question for scientific investigation to settle. The possibility can be granted, without prejudice to the body of revealed truth.

Limbo: The limbo of the fathers was the state of rest and natural happiness after death enjoyed by the just of pre-Christian times until they were admitted to heaven following the Ascension of Christ. Belief in this matter is stated in the Apostles' Creed. The existence of a limbo for unbaptized persons of infant status — a state of rest and natural happiness — has never been formally defined.

Litany: A prayer in the form of responsive petition; e.g., St. Joseph, pray for us, etc. Examples are the litanies of Loreto (Litany of the Blessed Mother), the Holy Name, All Saints, the Sacred Heart, the Precious Blood, St. Joseph, Litany for the Dying.

Loreto, House of: A Marian shrine in Loreto, Italy, consisting of the home of the Holy Family which, according to an old tradition, was transported in a miraculous manner from Nazareth to Dalmatia and finally to Loreto between 1291 and 1294. Investigations conducted shortly after the appearance of the structure in Loreto revealed that its dimensions matched those of the house of the Holy Family missing from its place of enshrinement in a basilica at Nazareth. Among the many popes who regarded it with high honor was John XXIII, who went there on pilgrimage Oct. 4, 1962. The house of the Holy Family is enshrined in the Basilica of Our Lady.

Lust: A disorderly desire for sexual pleasure; one of the seven capital sins.

M

Magi: In the Infancy Narrative of St. Matthew's Gospel (2:1-12), three wise men from the East whose visit and homage to the Child Jesus at Bethlehem indicated Christ's manifestation of himself to non-Jewish people. The narrative teaches the universality of salvation. The traditional names of the Magi are Caspar, Melchior and Balthasar.

Magnificat: The canticle or hymn of the Virgin Mary on the occasion of her visitation to her cousin Elizabeth (Lk. 1:46-55). It is an expression of praise, thanksgiving and acknowledgment of the great blessings given by God to Mary, the Mother of the Second Person of the Blessed Trinity made Man. The Magnificat is recited in the Liturgy of the Hours as part of the Evening Prayer.

Martyr: A Greek word, meaning witness, denoting one who voluntarily suffered death for the faith or some Christian virtue.

Martyrology: A catalogue of martyrs and other saints, arranged according to the calendar. The *Roman Martyrology* contains the official list of saints venerated by the Church. Additions to the list are made in beatification and canonization decrees of the Congregation for the Causes of Saints.

Mass for the People: On Sundays and certain feasts throughout the year pastors are required to offer Mass for the faithful committed to their care. If they cannot offer the Mass on these days, they must do so at a later date or provide that another priest offer the Mass.

Master of Novices: The person in charge of the training and formation of candidates for an institute of consecrated life during novitiate.

Materialism: Theory which holds that matter is the only reality, and everything in existence is merely a manifestation of matter; there is no such thing as spirit, and the supernatural does not exist. Materialism is incompatible with Christian doctrine.

Meditation: Mental, as distinguished from vocal, prayer, in which thought, affections, and resolutions of the will predominate. There is a meditative element to all forms of prayer, which always involves the raising of the heart and mind to God.

Mendicants: A term derived from Latin and meaning beggars, applied to members of religious orders without property rights; the members, accordingly, worked or begged for their support. The original mendicants were Franciscans and Dominicans in the early 13th century; later, the Carmelites, Augustinians, Servites and others were given the mendicant title and privileges, with respect to exemption from episcopal jurisdiction and wide faculties for preaching and administering the sacrament of penance. The practice of begging is limited at the present time, although it is still allowed with the permission of competent superiors and bishops. Mendicants are supported by free will offerings and income received for spiritual services and other work.

Mercy, Divine: The love and goodness of God, manifested particularly in a time of need.

Merit: In religion, the right to a supernatural reward for good works freely done for a supernatural motive by a person in the state of and with the assistance of grace. The right to such reward is from God, who binds himself to give it. Accordingly, good works, as described above, are meritorious for salvation.

Metempsychosis: Theory of the passage or migration of the human soul after death from one body to another for the purpose of purification from guilt. The theory denies the unity of the soul and human personality, and the doctrine of individual moral responsibility.

Millennium: A thousand-year reign of Christ and the just upon earth before the end of the world. This belief of the Millenarians, Chiliasts, and some sects of modern times is based on an erroneous interpretation of Rv. 20.

Miracles: Observable events or effects in the physical or moral order of things, with reference to salvation, which cannot be explained by the ordinary operation of laws of nature and which, therefore, are attributed to the direct action of God. They make known, in an unusual way, the concern and intervention of God in human affairs for the salvation of men. The most striking examples are the miracles worked by Christ. Numbering about 35, they included his own Resurrection; the raising of three persons to life (Lazarus, the daughter of Jairus, the son of the widow of Naim); the healing of blind, leprous and other persons; nature miracles; and prophecies, or miracles of the intellectual order. The foregoing notion of miracles, which is based on the concept of a fixed order of nature, was not known by the writers of Sacred Scripture. In the Old Testament, particularly, they called some things miraculous which, according to the definition in contemporary use, may or may not have been miracles. Essentially, however, the occurrences so designated were regarded as exceptional manifestations of God's care and concern for the salvation of his people. The miracles of Christ were miracles in the full sense of the term. The Church believes it is reasonable to accept miracles as manifestations of divine power for purposes of salvation. God, who created the laws of nature, is their master; hence, without disturbing the ordinary course of things, he can — and has in the course of history before and after Christ — occasionally set aside these laws and has also produced effects beyond their power of operation. The Church does not call miraculous anything which does not admit of easy explanation; on the contrary, miracles are admitted only when the events have a bearing on the order of grace and every possible natural explanation has been tried and found wanting. (The transubstantiation — i.e., the conversion of the whole substance of bread and wine, their sensible appearances alone remaining, into the Body and Blood of Christ in the act of Consecration at Mass — is not an observable event. Traditionally, however, it has been called a miracle.)

Missal: A liturgical book of Roman Rite also called the *Sacramentary,* containing the celebrant's prayers of the Mass, along with general instructions and ceremonial directives. The Latin text of the new *Roman Missal,* replacing the one authorized by the Council of Trent in the 16th century, was published by the Vatican Polyglot Press in 1970. Its use in English was made mandatory in the U.S. from Dec. 1, 1974. Readings and scriptural responsories formerly in the missal are contained in the *Lectionary.*

Missiology: Study of the missionary nature, constitution and activity of the Church in all aspects: theological reasons for missionary activity, laws and instructions of the Holy See, history of the missions, social and cultural background, methods, norms for carrying on missionary work.

Mission: (1) Strictly, it means being sent to perform a certain work, such as the mission of Christ to redeem mankind, the mission of the Apostles and the Church and its members to perpetuate the prophetic, priestly and royal mission of Christ. (2) A place where: the Gospel has not been proclaimed; the Church has not been firmly established; the Church, although established, is weak. (3) An ecclesiastical territory with the simplest kind of canonical organization, under the jurisdiction of the Congregation for the Evangelization of Peoples. (4) A church or chapel without a resident priest. (5) A special course of sermons and spiritual exercises conducted in parishes for the purpose of renewing and deepening the spiritual life of the faithful and for the conversion of lapsed Catholics.

Modernism: The "synthesis of all heresies," which appeared near the beginning of the 20th century. It undermines the objective validity of religious beliefs and practices which, it contends, are products of the subconscious developed by mankind under the stimulus of a religious sense. It holds that the existence of a personal God cannot be demonstrated, the Bible is not inspired, Christ is not divine, nor did he establish the Church or institute the sacraments. A special danger lies in modernism, which is still influential, because it uses Catholic terms with perverted meanings. St. Pius X condemned 65 propositions of modernism in 1907 in the decree *Lamentabili* and issued the encyclical *Pascendi* to explain and analyze its errors.

Monastery: The dwelling place, as well as the community thereof, of monks belonging to the Benedictine and Benedictine-related orders like the Cistercians and Carthusians; also, the Augustinians and Canons Regular. Distinctive of monasteries are: their separation from the world; the enclosure or cloister; the permanence or stability of attachment characteristic of their members; autonomous government in accordance with a monastic rule, like that of St. Benedict in the West or of St. Basil in the East; the special dedication of its members to the community celebration of the liturgy as well as to work that is suitable to the surrounding area and the needs of its people. Monastic superiors of men have such titles as abbot and prior; of women, abbess and prioress. In most essentials, an abbey is the same as a monastery.

Monk: A member of a monastic order — e.g., the Benedictines, the Benedictine-related Cistercians and Carthusians, and the Basilians, who bind themselves by religious profession to stable attachment to a monastery, the contemplative life and the work of their community. In popular use, the title is wrongly applied to many men religious who really are not monks.

Monotheism: Belief in and worship of one God.

Morality: Conformity or difformity of behavior to standards of right conduct. (See Moral Obligations, Commandments of God, Precepts of the Church, Conscience, Law.)

Mormons: Members of the Church of Jesus Christ of Latter-Day Saints. The church was established by Joseph Smith (1805-1844) at Fayette, N.Y., three years after he said he had received from an angel golden tablets containing the *Book of the Prophet Mormon.* This book, the Bible, *Doctrine and Covenants,* and *The Pearl of Great Price,* are the basic doctrinal texts of the church. Characteristic of the Mormons are strong belief in the revelations of their leaders, among whom was Brigham Young; a strong community of religious-secular concern; a dual secular and spiritual priesthood, and vigorous missionary activity. The headquarters of the church are located at Salt Lake City, Utah, where the Mormons first settled in 1847.

Mortification: Acts of self-discipline, including prayer, hardship, austerities and penances undertaken for the sake of progress in virtue.

Motu Proprio: A Latin phrase designating a document issued by a pope on his own initiative. Documents of this kind often concern administrative matters.

Mysteries of Faith: Supernatural truths whose existence cannot be known without revelation by God and whose intrinsic truth, while not contrary to reason, can never be wholly understood even after revelation. These mysteries are above reason, not against reason. Among them are the divine mysteries of the Trinity, Incarnation and Eucharist. Some mysteries — e.g., concerning God's attributes — can be known by reason without revelation, although they cannot be fully understood.

N

Necromancy: Supposed communication with the dead; a form of divination.

Non-Expedit: A Latin expression. It is not expedient (fitting, proper), used to state a prohibition or refusal of permission.

Novena: A term designating public or private devotional practices over a period of nine consecutive days; or, by extension, over a period of nine weeks, in which one day a week is set aside for the devotions.

Novice: A man or woman preparing, in a formal period of trial and formation called a novitiate, for membership in an institute of consecrated life. The novitiate lasts a minimum of 12 and a maximum of 24 months; at its conclusion, the novice professes temporary vows of poverty, chastity and obedience. Norms require that certain periods of time be spent in the house of novitiate: the first three months, one solid period of six months, the final month before the profession of temporary commitment. Periods of apostolic work are also required, to acquaint the novice with the apostolate(s) of the institute. A novice is not bound by the obligations of the professed members of the institute, is free to leave at any time, and may be discharged at the discretion of competent superiors. The immediate superior of a novice is a master or mistress of novices.

Nun (1) Strictly, a member of a religious order of women with solemn vows (moniales). (2) In general, all women religious, even those in simple vows who are more properly called sisters.

Nunc Dimittis: The canticle or hymn of Simeon at the sight of Jesus at the Temple on the occasion of his presentation (Lk. 2:29-32). It is an expression of joy and thanksgiving for the blessing of having lived to see the Messiah. It is prescribed for use in the Night Prayer of the Liturgy of the Hours.

O

Oath: Calling upon God to witness the truth of a statement. Violating an oath, e.g., by perjury in court, or taking an oath without sufficient reason, is a violation of the honor due to God.

Obedience: Submission to one in authority. General obligations of obedience fall under the Fourth Commandment. The vow of obedience professed by religious is one of the evangelical counsels.

Obsession, Diabolical: The extraordinary state of one who is seriously molested by evil spirits in an external manner. Obsession is more than just temptation.

Occultism: Practices involving ceremonies, rituals, chants, incantations, other cult-related activities intended to affect the course of nature, the lives of practitioners and others, through esoteric powers of magic, diabolical or other forces; one of many forms of superstition.

Octave: A period of eight days given over to the celebration of a major feast such as Easter.

Oils, Holy: The oils consecrated by bishops on Holy Thursday or another suitable day, and by priests under certain conditions for use in certain sacraments and consecrations. (1) The oil of catechumens (olive or vegetable oil), used at baptism; also, poured with chrism into the baptismal water blessed in Easter Vigil ceremonies. (2) Chrism (olive or vegetable oil mixed with balm), used at baptism, in confirmation, at the ordination of a priest and bishop, in the dedication of churches and altars. (3) Oil of the sick (olive or vegetable oil) used in anointing the sick.

Old Catholics — Several sects, including: (1) the Church of Utrecht, which severed relations with Rome in 1724; (2) the National Polish Church in the U.S., which had its origin near the end of the 19th century; (3) German, Austrian and Swiss Old Catholics, who broke away from union with Rome following the First Vatican Council in 1870 because they objected to the dogma of papal infallibility. The formation of the Old Catholic communion of Germans, Austrians and Swiss began in 1870 at a public meeting held in Nuremberg under the leadership of A. Dollinger. Four years later episcopal succession was established with the ordination of an Old Catholic German bishop by a prelate of the Church of Utrecht. In line with the "Declaration of Utrecht" of 1889, they accept the first seven ecumenical councils and doctrine formulated before 1054, but reject communion with the pope and a number of other Catholic doctrines and practices. They have a valid priesthood and valid sacraments. *The Oxford Dictionary of the Christian Church* notes that they have recognized Anglican ordinations since 1925, that they have had full communion with the Church of England since 1932, and that their bishops, using their own formula, have taken part in the ordination of Anglican bishops. This communion does not recognize the "Old Catholic" status of several smaller sects calling themselves such. In turn, connection with it is disavowed by the Old Roman Catholic Church headquartered in Chicago, which contends that it has abandoned the traditions of the Church of Utrecht. The United States is the only English-speaking country with Old Catholic communities.

Opus Dei: Opus Dei was founded by Msgr. Josemaria Escriva de Balaguer in 1928 in Madrid with the aim of spreading throughout all sectors of society a profound awareness of the universal call to holiness and apostolate (of Christian witness and action) in the ordinary circumstances of life, and, more specifically, through one's professional work. The institution was fully approved by the Vatican as a secular institute in 1950. On Aug. 5, 1982, Pope John Paul II confirmed and ordered publication of a declaration concerning the erection of the then secular institute into the Prelature of the Holy Cross and Opus Dei. The 1988 edition of *Annuario Pontificio* reported that the prelature had 1,265 priests (51 newly ordained) and 354 major seminarians. Also, there were 74,370 lay persons — men and women, married and single, of every class and social condition — of about 80 nationalities. In the United States, members of Opus Dei, along with non-member associates, conduct apostolic works corporately in major cities in the East and Midwest, Texas and on the West Coast.

Elsewhere, members are engaged in universities, vocational institutes, training schools for farmers and numerous other apostolic initiatives. An information office is located at 330 Riverside Drive, New York, N.Y. 10025.

Oratory: A chapel.

Ordinariate: An ecclesiastical jurisdiction for special purposes and people. Examples are military ordinariates for armed services personnel (in accord with provisions of the apostolic constitution *Spirituali militum curae,* Apr. 21, 1986) and Eastern-Rite ordinariates in places where Eastern-Rite dioceses do not exist.

Ordination: The consecration of sacred ministers for divine worship and the service of people in things pertaining to God. The power of ordination comes from Christ and the Church, and must be conferred by a minister capable of communicating it.

Organ Transplants: The transplanting of organs from one person to another is permissible provided it is done with the consent of the concerned parties and does not result in the death or essential mutilation of the donor. Advances in methods and technology have increased the range of transplant possibilities in recent years.

Original Sin: The sin of Adam (Gn. 2:8—3:24), personal to him and passed on to all persons as a state of privation of grace. Despite this privation and the related wounding of human nature and weakening of natural powers, original sin leaves unchanged all that man himself is by nature. The scriptural basis of the doctrine was stated especially by St. Paul in 1 Cor. 15:21ff., and Romans 5:12-21. Original sin is remitted by baptism and incorporation in Christ, through whom grace is given to persons. Pope John Paul, while describing original sin during a general audience Oct. 1, 1986, called it "the absence of sanctifying grace in nature which has been diverted from its supernatural end."

O Salutaris Hostia: The first three Latin words, O Saving Victim, of a Benediction hymn.

Ostpolitik: Policy adopted by Pope Paul VI in an attempt to improve the situation of Eastern European Catholics through diplomatic negotiations with their governments.

Oxford Movement: A movement in the Church of England from 1833 to about 1845 which had for its objective a threefold defense of the church as a divine institution, the apostolic succession of its bishops, and the Book of Common Prayer as the rule of faith. The movement took its name from Oxford University and involved a number of intellectuals who authored a series of influential *Tracts for Our Times.* Some of its leading figures — e.g., F. W. Faber, John Henry Newman and Henry Edward Manning — became converts to the Catholic Church. In the Church of England, the movement affected the liturgy, historical and theological scholarship, the status of the ministry, and other areas of ecclesiastical life.

P

Paganism: A term referring to non-revealed religions, i.e., religions other than Christianity, Judaism and Mohammedanism.

Palms: Blessed palms are a sacramental. They are blessed and distributed on the Sunday of the Passion in commemoration of the triumphant entrance of Christ into Jerusalem. Ashes of the burnt palms are used on Ash Wednesday.

Pange Lingua: First Latin words, Sing, my tongue, of a hymn in honor of the Holy Eucharist, used particularly on Holy Thursday and in Eucharistic processions.

Pantheism: Theory that all things are part of God, divine, in the sense that God realizes himself as the ultimate reality of matter or spirit through being and/or becoming all things that have been, are, and will be. The theory leads to hopeless confusion of the Creator and the created realm of being, identifies evil with good, and involves many inherent contradictions.

Papal Election: The pope is elected by members of the College of Cardinals in a secret conclave or meeting convened ordinarily in secluded quarters of the Vatican Palace between 15 and 20 days after the death of his predecessor. Cardinals under the age of 80, totaling no more than 120, are eligible to participate in a papal election. Following are some of the principal regulations decreed by Paul VI Oct. 1, 1975, in the apostolic constitution *Romano Pontifici Eligendo.* The ordinary manner of election is by scrutiny, with two votes each morning and afternoon in the Sistine Chapel until one of the candidates receives a two-thirds plus one vote majority. Alternative methods, which can be adopted by unanimous agreement of the cardinals in difficult cases, are provided for: (1) by delegation, in which the cardinals designate a limited number (nine to 15) to make the choice; (2) by changing the majority rule from two-thirds plus one vote to an absolute majority plus one; (3) by limiting final choice, if the procedure in force becomes protracted, to one between the two candidates who received the largest numbers of votes, but not a required majority, in the most recent balloting. An unusual manner of election is by acclamation or inspiration — that is, by spontaneous, unanimous choice without any need for normal voting procedure. The elected candidate is asked by the dean of the college if he accepts the election. If he does so and is already a bishop, he immediately becomes the bishop of Rome and pope, and signifies the name by which he will be called. The cardinals then pledge their obedience to him before the senior cardinal deacon proclaims his election to the world from the main balcony of the Vatican and the new pope imparts his blessing *Urbi et Orbi* (to the City and the World). If the candidate is not a bishop, he is so ordained before receiving the pledge of obedience and being proclaimed pope. The subsequent coronation of the pope is a ceremonial recognition of the fact of his election. The pope is elected for life. If one should resign, a new pope would be elected in accordance with the foregoing regulations. Rigid rules govern the conclave — its personnel, freedom from internal and external influence and interference, absolute secrecy (with a ban on recording devices and a prohibition against any disclosures). Ordinarily, the first indication that a new pope has been elected is a plume of white smoke rising from the Vatican on burning of the last ballots. Early methods of electing a pope — with various degrees of participation by the clergy and people of Rome and others — were set aside by Pope Nicholas II, who decreed in 1059 that cardinal bishops would be the electors. Further modification of the process was decreed by the Lateran Council in 1179 (that election would take place by a two-thirds majority vote of the cardinals) and by Pope Gregory X in 1274 (regarding a secluded conclave arrangement for elections).

Paraclete: A title of the Holy Spirit meaning, in Greek, Advocate, Consoler.

Parental Duties: All duties related to the obligation of parents to provide for the welfare of their children. These obligations fall under the Fourth Commandment.

Parish: A community of the faithful served by a pastor charged with responsibility for providing them with full pastoral service. Most parishes are territorial, embracing all of the faithful in a certain area of a diocese: some are personal or national, for certain classes of people, without strict regard for their places of residence.

Parousia: The coming, or saving presence, of Christ which will mark the completion of salvation history and the coming to perfection of God's kingdom at the end of the world.

Paschal Candle: A large candle, symbolic of the risen Christ, blessed and lighted on the Easter Vigil and placed at the Gospel side of the altar until Ascension Day. It is ornamented with five large grains of incense, representing the wounds of Christ, inserted in the form of a cross; the Greek letters Alpha and Omega, symbolizing Christ the beginning and end of all things, at the top and bottom of the shaft of the cross; and the figures of the current year of salvation in the quadrants formed by the cross.

Paschal Precept: Church law requiring reception of the Eucharist in the Easter season (see separate entry) unless, for a just cause, once-a-year reception takes place at another time.

Passion of Christ: Sufferings of Christ, recorded in the four Gospels.

Pastor: An ordained minister charged with responsibility for the doctrinal, sacramental and related service of people committed to his care; e.g., a bishop for the people in his diocese, a priest for the people of his parish.

Pater Noster: The initial Latin words, Our Father, of the Lord's Prayer.

Peace, Sign of: A gesture of greeting — e.g., a handshake — exchanged by the ministers and participants at Mass.

Pectoral Cross: A cross worn on a chain about the neck and over the breast by bishops and abbots as a mark of their office.

Penance or Penitence: (1) The spiritual change or conversion of mind and heart by which a person turns away from sin, and all that it implies, toward God, through a personal renewal under the influence of the Holy Spirit. In the apostolic constitution *Paenitemini*, Pope Paul VI called it "a religious, personal act which has as its aim love and surrender to God." Penance involves sorrow and contrition for sin, together with other internal and external acts of atonement. It serves the purposes of reestablishing in one's life the order of God's love and commandments, and of making satisfaction to God for sin. A divine precept states the necessity of penance for salvation: "Unless you do penance, you shall all likewise perish" (Lk. 13:3) . . . "Be converted and believe in the Gospel" (Mk. 1:15). In the penitential discipline of the Church, the various works of penance have been classified under the headings of prayer (interior), fasting and almsgiving (exterior). The Church has established minimum requirements for the common and social observance of the divine precept by Catholics — e.g., by requiring them to fast and/or abstain on certain days of the year. These observances, however, do not exhaust all the demands of the divine precept, whose fulfillment is a matter of personal responsibility; nor do they have any real value unless they proceed from the internal spirit and purpose of penance. Related to works of penance for sins actually committed are works of mortification. The purpose of the latter is to develop — through prayer, fasting, renunciations and similar actions — self-control and detachment from things which could otherwise become occasions of sin. (2) Penance is a virtue disposing a person to turn to God in sorrow for sin and to carry out works of amendment and atonement. (3) The sacrament of penance and sacramental penance.

Perjury: Taking a false oath, lying under oath, a violation of the honor due to God.

Persecution, Religious: A campaign waged against a church or other religious body by persons and governments intent on its destruction. The best known campaigns of this type against the Christian Church were the Roman persecutions which occurred intermittently from about 54 to the promulgation of the Edict of Milan in 313, The most extensive persecutions took place during the reigns of Nero, the first major Roman persecutor, Domitian, Trajan, Marcus Aurelius, and Diocletian. Besides the Roman persecutions, the Catholic Church has been subject to many others, including those of the 20th century in Communist-controlled countries.

Personal Prelature: A special-purpose jurisdiction — for particular pastoral and missionary work, etc., — consisting of secular priests and deacons and open to lay persons willing to dedicate themselves to its apostolic works. The prelate in charge is an Ordinary, with the authority of office; he can establish a national or international seminary, incardinate its students and promote them to holy orders under the title of service to the prelature. The prelature is constituted and governed according to statutes laid down by the Holy See. Statutes define its relationship and mode of operation with the bishops of territories in which members live and work. Opus Dei is a personal prelature.

Peter's Pence: A collection made each year among Catholics for the maintenance of the pope and his works of charity. It was originally a tax of a penny on each house, and was collected on St. Peter's day, whence the name. It originated in England in the eighth century.

Petition: One of the four purposes of prayer. In prayers of petition, persons ask of God the blessings they and others need.

Pharisees: Influential class among the Jews, referred to in the Gospels, noted for their self-righteousness, legalism, strict interpretation of the Law, acceptance of the traditions of the elders as well as the Law of Moses, and beliefs regarding angels and spirits, the resurrection of the dead and judgment. Most of them were laymen, and they were closely allied with the Scribes; their opposite numbers were the Sadducees. The Pharisaic and rabbinical traditions had a lasting influence on Judaism following the destruction of Jerusalem in 70 A.D.

Pious Fund: Property and money originally accumulated by the Jesuits to finance their missionary work in Lower California. When the Jesuits were expelled from the territory in 1767, the fund was appropriated by the Spanish Crown and used to support Dominican and Franciscan missionary work in Upper and Lower California. In 1842 the Mexican government took over administration of the fund, incorporated most of the revenue into the national treasury, and agreed to pay the Church interest of six per cent a year on the capital so incorporated. From 1848 to 1967 the fund was the subject of lengthy negotiations between the U.S. and Mexican governments because of the latter's failure to make payments as agreed. A lump-sum settlement was made in 1967 with payment by Mexico to the U.S. government of more than $700,000, to be turned over to the Archdiocese of San Francisco.

Polytheism: Belief in and worship of many gods or divinities, especially prevalent in pre-Christian religions.

Poor Box: Alms-box; found in churches from the earliest days of Christianity.

Pope Joan: Alleged name of a woman falsely said to have been pope from 855-858, the years of the reign of Benedict III. The myth was not heard of before the 13th century.

Portiuncula: (1) Meaning little portion (of land), the Portiuncula was the chapel of Our Lady of the Angels near Assisi, Italy, which the Benedictines gave to St. Francis early in the 13th century. He repaired the chapel and made it the first church of the Franciscan Order. It is now enshrined in the Basilica of St. Mary of the Angels in Assisi. (2) The Portiuncula Indulgence, or Pardon of Assisi, was authorized by Honorius III. Originally, it could be gained for the souls in purgatory only in the chapel of Our Lady of the Angels; by later concessions, it could be gained also in other Franciscan and parish churches. The Portiuncula Indulgence can be gained once from noon to midnight of Aug. 1 and once on Aug. 2, or on the following Sunday with permission of the bishop of the place. The conditions are, in addition to freedom from attachment to sin: reception of the sacraments of penance and the Eucharist on or near the day; a visit to a parish church on the day, during which the Our Father and Creed are offered for the intentions of the pope.

Possession, Diabolical: The extraordinary state of a person who is tormented from within by evil spirits who exercise strong influence over his powers of mind and body.

Postulant: One of several names used to designate a candidate for membership in a religious institute during the period before novitiate.

Poverty: (1) The quality or state of being poor, in actual destitution and need, or being poor in spirit. In the latter sense, poverty means the state of mind and disposition of persons who regard material things in proper perspective as gifts of God for the support of life and its reasonable enrichment, and for the service of others in need. It means freedom from unreasonable attachment to material things as ends in themselves, even though they may be possessed in small or large measure. (2) One of the evangelical counsels professed as a public vow by members of an institute of consecrated life. It involves the voluntary renunciation of rights of ownership and of independent use and disposal of material goods; or, the right of independent use and disposal, but not of the radical right of ownership. Religious institutes provide their members with necessary and useful goods and services from common resources. The manner in which goods are received and/or handled by religious is determined by poverty of spirit and the rule and constitutions of their institute.

Pragmatism: Theory that the truth of ideas, concepts and values depends on their utility or capacity to serve a useful purpose rather than on their conformity with objective standards; also called utilitarianism.

Prayer: The raising of the mind and heart to God in adoration, thanksgiving, reparation and petition. Prayer, which is always mental because it involves thought and love of God, may be vocal, meditative, private and personal, social, and official. The official prayer of the Church as a worshipping community is called the liturgy.

Precepts: Commands or orders given to individuals or communities in particular cases; they establish law for concerned parties. Preceptive documents are issued by the pope, departments of the Roman Curia and other competent authority in the Church.

Presence of God: A devotional practice of increasing one's awareness of the presence and action of God in daily life.

Presumption: A violation of the theological virtue of hope, by which a person striving for salvation either relies too much on his own capabilities or expects God to do things which he cannot do, in keeping with his divine attributes, or does not will to do, according to his divine plan. Presumption is the opposite of despair.

Preternatural Gifts: Exceptional gifts, beyond the exigencies and powers of human nature, enjoyed by Adam in the state of original justice: immunity from suffering and death, superior knowledge, integrity or perfect control of the passions. These gifts were lost as the result of original sin;

their loss, however, implied no impairment of the integrity of human nature.

Pride: Unreasonable self-esteem; one of the seven capital sins.

Prie-Dieu: A French phrase, meaning pray God, designating a kneeler or bench suitable for kneeling while at prayer.

Priesthood of the Laity: Lay persons share in the priesthood of Christ in virtue of the sacraments of baptism and confirmation. They are not only joined with Christ for a life of union with him but are also deputed by him for participation in his mission, now carried on by the Church, of worship, teaching, witness and apostolic works. St. Peter called Christians "a royal priesthood" (1 Pt. 2:9) in this connection. St. Thomas Aquinas declared: "The sacramental characters (of baptism and confirmation) are nothing else than certain sharings of the priesthood of Christ, derived from Christ himself." The priesthood of the laity differs from the official ministerial priesthood of ordained priests and bishops — who have the power of holy orders for celebrating the Eucharist, administering the other sacraments, and providing pastoral care. The ministerial priesthood, by divine commission, serves the universal priesthood. (See Role of Sacraments.)

Primary Option: The life-choice of a person for or against God which shapes the basic orientation of moral conduct. A primary option for God does not preclude the possibility of serious sin.

Prior: A superior or an assistant to an abbot in a monastery.

Privilege: A favor, an exemption from the obligation of a law. Privileges of various kinds, with respect to ecclesiastical laws, are granted by the pope, departments of the Roman Curia and other competent authority in the Church.

Probabilism: A moral system for use in cases of conscience which involve the obligation of doubtful laws. There is a general principle that a doubtful law does not bind. Probabilism, therefore, teaches that it is permissible to follow an opinion favoring liberty, provided the opinion is certainly and solidly probable. Probabilism may not be invoked when there is question of: a certain law or the certain obligation of a law; the certain right of another party; the validity of an action; something which is necessary for salvation.

Pro-Cathedral: A church used as a cathedral.

Promoter of the Faith: An official of the Congregation for the Causes of Saints, whose role in beatification and canonization procedures is to establish beyond reasonable doubt the validity of evidence regarding the holiness of prospective saints and miracles attributed to their intercession.

Prophecies of St. Malachy: These so-called prophecies, listing the designations of 102 popes and 10 antipopes, bear the name they have because they have been falsely attributed to St. Malachy, bishop of Armagh, who died in 1148. Actually, they are forgeries by an unknown author and came to light only in the last decade of the 16th century. The first 75 prophecies cover the 65 popes and 10 antipopes from Celestine II (1143-1144) to Gregory XIV (1590-91), and are exact with respect to names, coats of arms, birthplaces, and other identifying characteristics. This portion of the work, far from being prophetic, is the result of historical knowledge or hindsight. The 37 designations following that of Gregory are vague, fanciful, and subject to wide interpretation. According to the prophecies, John Paul II, from the Labor of the Sun, will have only two successors before the end of the world.

Prophecy: (1) The communication of divine revelation by inspired intermediaries, called prophets, between God and his people. Old Testament prophecy was unique in its origin and because of its ethical and religious content, which included disclosure of the saving will of Yahweh for the people, moral censures and warnings of divine punishment because of sin and violations of the Law and Covenant, in the form of promises, admonitions, reproaches and threats. Although Moses and other earlier figures are called prophets, the period of prophecy is generally dated from the early years of the monarchy to about 100 years after the Babylonian Exile. From that time on the written Law and its interpreters supplanted the prophets as guides of the people. Old Testament prophets are cited in the New Testament, with awareness that God spoke through them and that some of their oracles were fulfilled in Christ. John the Baptist is the outstanding prophetic figure in the New Testament. Christ never claimed the title of prophet for himself, although some people thought he was one. There were prophets in the early Church, and St. Paul mentioned the charism of prophecy in 1 Cor. 14:1-5. Prophecy disappeared after New Testament times. Revelation is classified as the prophetic book of the New Testament. (2) In contemporary non-scriptural usage, the term is applied to the witness given by persons to the relevance of their beliefs in everyday life and action.

Province: (1) A territory comprising one archdiocese called the metropolitan see and one or more dioceses called suffragan sees. The head of the archdiocese, an archbishop, has metropolitan rights and responsibilities over the province. (2) A division of a religious order under the jurisdiction of a provincial superior.

Prudence: Practical wisdom and judgment regarding the choice and use of the best ways and means of doing good; one of the four cardinal virtues.

Punishment Due for Sin: The punishment which is a consequence of sin. It is of two kinds: (1) Eternal punishment is the punishment of hell, to which one becomes subject by the commission of mortal sin. Such punishment is remitted when mortal sin is forgiven. (2) Temporal punishment is a consequence of venial sin and/or forgiven mortal sin; it is not everlasting and may be remitted in this life by means of penance. Temporal punishment unremitted during this life is remitted by suffering in purgatory.

Purgatory: The state or condition in which those who have died in the state of grace, but with some attachment to sin, suffer for a time before they are admitted to the glory and happiness of heaven. In this state and period of passive suffering, they are purified of unrepented venial sins, satisfy the demands of divine justice for temporal punishment due for sins, and are thus converted to a state of worthiness of the beatific vision.

R

Racism: A theory which holds that any one or several of the different races of the human family are inherently superior or inferior to any one or several of the others. The teaching denies the essential unity of the human race, the equality and dignity of all men because of their common possession of the same human nature, and the participation of all men in the divine plan of redemption. It is radically opposed to the virtue of justice and the precept of love of neighbor. Differences of superiority and inferiority which do exist are the result of accidental factors operating in a wide variety of circumstances, and are in no way due to essential defects in any one or several of the branches of the one human race. The theory of racism, together with practices related to it, is incompatible with Christian doctrine.

Rash Judgment: Attributing faults to another without sufficient reason; a violation of the obligations of justice and charity.

Rationalism: A theory which makes the mind the measure and arbiter of all things, including religious truth. A product of the Enlightenment, it rejects the supernatural, divine revelation, and authoritative teaching by any church.

Recollection: Meditation, attitude of concentration or awareness of spiritual matters and things pertaining to salvation and the accomplishment of God's will.

Relativism: Theory which holds that all truth, including religious truth, is relative, i.e., not absolute, certain or unchanging; a product of agnosticism, indifferentism, and an unwarranted extension of the notion of truth in positive science. Relativism is based on the tenet that certain knowledge of any and all truth is impossible. Therefore, no religion, philosophy or science can be said to possess the real truth; consequently, all religions, philosophies and sciences may be considered to have as much or as little of truth as any of the others.

Relics: The physical remains and effects of saints, which are considered worthy of veneration inasmuch as they are representative of persons in glory with God. Catholic doctrine proscribes the view that relics are not worthy of veneration. In line with norms laid down by the Council of Trent and subsequent enactments, discipline concerning relics is subject to control by the Congregation for the Causes of Saints.

Religion: The adoration and service of God as expressed in divine worship and in daily life. Religion is concerned with all of the relations existing between God and man, and between man and man because of the central significance of God. Objectively considered, religion consists of a body of truth which is believed, a code of morality for the guidance of conduct, and a form of divine worship. Subjectively, it is a person's total response, theoretically and practically, to the demands of faith; it is living faith, personal engagement, self-commitment to God. Thus, by creed, code and cult, a person orders and directs his life in reference to God and, through what the love and service of God implies, to his fellow men and all things.

Reliquary: A vessel for the preservation and exposition of a relic; sometimes made like a small monstrance.

Reparation: The making of amends to God for sin committed; one of the four ends of prayer and the purpose of penance.

Rescript: A written reply by an ecclesiastical superior regarding a question or request; its provisions bind concerned parties only. Papal dispensations are issued in the form of rescripts.

Reserved Case: A sin or censure, absolution from which is reserved to religious superiors, bishops, the pope, or confessors having special faculties. Reservations are made because of the serious nature and social effects of certain sins and censures.

Restitution: An act of reparation for an injury done to another. The injury may be caused by taking and/or retaining what belongs to another or by damaging either the property or reputation of another. The intention of making restitution, usually in kind, is required as a condition for the forgiveness of sins of injustice, even though actual restitution is not possible.

Ring: In the Church a ring is worn as part of the insignia of bishops, abbots, et al.; by sisters to denote their consecration to God and the Church. The wedding ring symbolizes the love and union of husband and wife.

Ritual: A book of prayers and ceremonies used in the administration of the sacraments and other ceremonial functions. In the Roman Rite, the standard book of this kind is the Roman Ritual.

Rogito: The official notarial act or document testifying to the burial of a pope.

Rosary: A form of mental and vocal prayer centered on mysteries or events in the lives of Jesus and Mary. Its essential elements are meditation on the mysteries and the recitation of a number of decades of Hail Marys, each beginning with the Lord's Prayer. Introductory prayers may include the Apostles' Creed, an initial Our Father, three Hail Marys and a Glory be to the Father; each decade is customarily concluded with a Glory be to the Father; at the end, it is customary to say the Hail, Holy Queen and a prayer from the liturgy for the feast of the Blessed Virgin Mary of the Rosary. The **Mysteries of the Rosary,** which are the subject of meditation, are: (1) Joyful — the Annunciation to Mary that she was to be the Mother of Christ, her visit to Elizabeth, the birth of Jesus, the presentation of Jesus in the Temple, the finding of Jesus in the Temple. (2) Sorrowful — Christ's agony in the Garden of Gethsemani, scourging at the pillar, crowning with thorns, carrying of the Cross to Calvary, and crucifixion. (3) Glorious — the Resurrection and Ascension of Christ, the descent of the Holy Spirit upon the Apostles, Mary's Assumption into heaven and her crowning as Queen of angels and men. The complete Rosary, called the Dominican Rosary, consists of 15 decades. In customary practice, only five decades are usually said at one time. Rosary beads are used to aid in counting the prayers without distraction. The Rosary originated through the coalescence of popular devotions to Jesus and Mary from the 12th century onward. Its present form dates from about the 15th century. Carthusians contributed greatly toward its development; Dominicans have been its greatest promoters.

S

Sabbath: The seventh day of the week, observed by Jews and Sabbatarians as the day for rest and religious observance.

Sacramentary: One of the first liturgical books, containing the celebrant's part of the Mass and rites for administration of the sacraments. The earliest book of this kind, the Leonine Sacramentary, dates from the middle or end of the sixth century. The *Sacramentary* in current use is the same as the *Roman Missal*.

Sacrarium: A basin with a drain leading directly into the ground; standard equipment of a sacristy.

Sacred Heart, Enthronement: An acknowledgment of the sovereignty of Jesus Christ over the Christian family, expressed by the installation of an image or picture of the Sacred Heart in a place of honor in the home, accompanied by an act of consecration.

Sacred Heart, Promises: Twelve promises to persons having devotion to the Sacred Heart of Jesus, which were communicated by Christ to St. Margaret Mary Alacoque in a private revelation in 1675: (1) I will give them all the graces necessary in their state in life. (2) I will establish peace in their homes. (3) I will comfort them in all their afflictions. (4) I will be their secure refuge during life and, above all, in death. (5) I will bestow abundant blessing upon all their undertakings. (6) Sinners shall find in my Heart the source and the infinite ocean of mercy. (7) By devotion to my Heart tepid souls shall grow fervent. (8) Fervent souls shall quickly mount to high perfection. (9) I will bless every place where a picture of my Heart shall be set up and honored. (10) I will give to priests the gift of touching the most hardened hearts. (11) Those who promote this devotion shall have their names written in my Heart, never to be blotted out. (12) I will grant the grace of final penitence to those who communicate (receive Holy Communion) on the first Friday of nine consecutive months.

Sacrilege: Violation of and irreverence toward a person, place or thing that is sacred because of public dedication to God; a sin against the virtue of religion. Personal sacrilege is violence of some kind against a cleric or religious, or a violation of chastity with a cleric or religious. Local sacrilege is the desecration of sacred places. Real sacrilege is irreverence with respect to sacred things, such as the sacraments and sacred vessels.

Sacristy: A utility room where vestments, church furnishings and sacred vessels are kept and where the clergy vest for sacred functions.

Sadducees: The predominantly priestly party among the Jews in the time of Christ, noted for extreme conservatism, acceptance only of the Law of Moses, and rejection of the traditions of the elders. Their opposite numbers were the Pharisees.

Saints, Cult of: The veneration, called dulia, of holy persons who have died and are in glory with God in heaven; it includes honoring them and petitioning them for their intercession with God. Liturgical veneration is given only to saints officially recognized by the Church; private veneration may be given to anyone thought to be in heaven. The veneration of saints is essentially different from the adoration given to God alone; by its very nature, however, it terminates in the worship of God. According to the Second Vatican Council's *Dogmatic Constitution on the Church* (No. 50): "It is supremely fitting . . . that we love those friends and fellow heirs of Jesus Christ, who are also our brothers and extraordinary benefactors, that we render due thanks to God for them and 'suppliantly invoke them and have recourse to their prayers, their power and help in obtaining benefits from God through his Son, Jesus Christ, our Lord, who is our sole Redeemer and Savior.' For by its very nature every genuine testimony of love which we show to those in heaven tends toward and terminates in Christ, who is the 'crown of all saints.' Through him it tends toward and terminates in God, who is wonderful in his saints and is magnified in them."

Salvation: The liberation of persons from sin and its effects, reconciliation with God in and through Christ, the attainment of union with God forever in the glory of heaven as the supreme purpose of life and as the God-given reward for fulfillment of his will on earth. Salvation-in-process begins and continues in this life through union with Christ in faith professed and in action; its final term is union with God and the whole community of the saved in the ultimate perfection of God's kingdom. The Church teaches that: God wills the salvation of all men; men are saved in and through Christ; membership in the Church established by Christ, known and understood as the community of salvation, is necessary for salvation; men with this knowledge and understanding who deliberately reject this Church, cannot be saved. The Catholic Church is the Church founded by Christ. (See below, Salvation outside the Church.)

Salvation History: The facts and the record of God's relations with men, in the past, present and future, for the purpose of leading them to live in accordance with his will for the eventual attainment after death of salvation, or everlasting happiness with him in heaven. The essentials of salvation history are: God's love for all men and will for their salvation; his intervention and action in the world to express this love and bring about their salvation; the revelation he made of himself and the covenant he established with the Israelites in the Old Testament; the perfecting of this revelation and the new covenant of grace through Christ in the New Testament; the continuing action-for-salvation carried on in and through the Mystical

Body of Christ, the Church; the communication of saving grace to men through the merits of Christ and the operations of the Holy Spirit in the here-and-now circumstances of daily life and with the cooperation of men themselves.

Salvation outside the Church: The Second Vatican Council covered this subject summarily in the following manner: "Those also can attain to everlasting salvation who through no fault of their own do not know the Gospel of Christ or his Church, yet sincerely seek God and, moved by grace, strive by their deeds to do his will as it is known to them through the dictates of conscience. Nor does divine Providence deny the help necessary for salvation to those who, without blame on their part, have not yet arrived at an explicit knowledge of God, but who strive to live a good life, thanks to his grace. Whatever good or truth is found among them is looked upon by the Church as a preparation for the Gospel. She regards such qualities as given by him who enlightens all men so that they may finally have life" *(Dogmatic Constitution on the Church,* No. 16).

Satanism: Worship of the devil, a blasphemous inversion of the order of worship which is due to God alone.

Scandal: Conduct which is the occasion of sin to another person.

Scapular: (1) A part of the habit of some religious orders like the Benedictines and Dominicans; a nearly shoulder-wide strip of cloth worn over the tunic and reaching almost to the feet in front and behind. Originally a kind of apron, it came to symbolize the cross and yoke of Christ. (2) Scapulars worn by lay persons as a sign of association with religious orders and for devotional purposes are an adaptation of monastic scapulars. Approved by the Church as sacramentals, they consist of two small squares of woolen cloth joined by strings and are worn about the neck. They are given for wearing in a ceremony of investiture or enrollment. There are nearly 20 scapulars for devotional use: the five principal ones are generally understood to include those of Our Lady of Mt. Carmel (the brown Carmelite Scapular), the Holy Trinity, Our Lady of the Seven Dolors, the Passion, the Immaculate Conception.

Scapular Medal: A medallion with a representation of the Sacred Heart on one side and of the Blessed Virgin Mary on the other. Authorized by St. Pius X in 1910, it may be worn or carried in place of a scapular by persons already invested with a scapular.

Scapular Promise: According to a legend of the Carmelite Order, the Blessed Virgin Mary appeared to St. Simon Stock in 1251 at Cambridge and declared that wearers of the brown Carmelite Scapular would be saved from hell and taken to heaven by her on the first Saturday after death. The validity of the legend has never been the subject of official decision by the Church. Essentially, it expresses belief in the intercession of Mary and the efficacy of sacramentals in the context of truly Christian life.

Schism: Derived from a Greek word meaning separation, the term designates formal and obstinate refusal by a baptized Catholic, called a *schismatic,* to be in communion with the pope and the Church. The canonical penalty is excommunication. One of the most disastrous schisms in history resulted in the definitive separation of the Church in the East from union with Rome about 1054.

Scholasticism: The term usually applied to the Catholic theology and philosophy which developed in the Middle Ages.

Scribes: Hebrew intellectuals noted for their knowledge of the Law of Moses, influential from the time of the Exile to about 70 A.D. Many of them were Pharisees. They were the antecedents of rabbis and their traditions, as well as those of the Pharisees, had a lasting influence on Judaism following the destruction of Jerusalem in 70 A.D.

Scruple: A morbid, unreasonable fear and anxiety that one's actions are sinful when they are not, or more seriously sinful than they actually are. Compulsive scrupulosity is quite different from the transient scrupulosity of persons of tender or highly sensitive conscience, or of persons with faulty moral judgment.

Seal of Confession: The obligation of secrecy which must be observed regarding knowledge of things learned in connection with the confession of sin in the sacrament of penance. The seal covers matters whose revelation would make the sacrament burdensome. Confessors are prohibited, under penalty of excommunication, from making any direct revelation of confessional matter; this prohibition holds, outside of confession, even with respect to the person who made the confession unless the person releases the priest from the obligation. Persons other than confessors are obliged to maintain secrecy, but not under penalty of excommunication. General, non-specific discussion of confessional matter does not violate the seal.

Secularism: A school of thought, a spirit and manner of action which ignores and/or repudiates the validity or influence of supernatural religion with respect to individual and social life. In describing secularism in their annual statement in 1947, the bishops of the United States said in part: "... There are many men — and their number is daily increasing — who in practice live their lives without recognizing that this is God's world. For the most part they do not deny God. On formal occasions they may even mention his name. Not all of them would subscribe to the statement that all moral values derive from merely human conventions. But they fail to bring an awareness of their responsibility to God into their thought and action as individuals and members of society. This, in essence, is what we mean by secularism."

See: Another name for diocese or archdiocese.

Seminary: A house of study and formation for men, called seminarians, preparing for the priesthood. Traditional seminaries date from the Council of Trent in the middle of the 16th century; before that time, candidates for the priesthood were variously trained in monastic schools, universities under church auspices, and in less formal ways. At the present time, seminaries are undergoing considerable change for the improvement of academic and formation programs and procedures.

Sermon on the Mount: A compilation of sayings of Our Lord in the form of an extended discourse in Matthew's Gospel (5:1 to 7:27) and, in a shorter discourse, in Luke (6:17-49). The passage in Matthew, called the "Constitution of the New Law," summarizes the living spirit of believers in Christ and members of the kingdom of God. Beginning with the Beatitudes and including the Lord's Prayer, it covers the perfect justice of the New Law, the fulfillment of the Old Law in the New Law of Christ, and the integrity of internal attitude and external conduct with respect to love of God and neighbor, justice, chastity, truth, trust and confidence in God.

Seven Last Words of Christ: Words of Christ on the Cross. (1) "Father, forgive them; for they do not know what they are doing." (2) To the penitent thief: "I assure you: today you will be with me in Paradise." (3) To Mary and his Apostle John: "Woman, there is your son . . . There is your mother." (4) "My God, my God, why have you forsaken me?" (5) "I am thirsty." (6) "Now it is finished." (7) "Father, into your hands I commend my spirit."

Shrine, Crowned: A shrine approved by the Holy See as a place of pilgrimage. The approval permits public devotion at the shrine and implies that at least one miracle has resulted from devotion at the shrine. Among the best known crowned shrines are those of the Virgin Mary at Lourdes and Fatima. Shrines with statues crowned by Pope John Paul in 1985 in South America were those of Our Lady of Coromoto, patroness of Venezuela, in Caracas, and Our Lady of Carmen of Paucartambo in Cuzco, Peru.

Shroud of Turin: A strip of brownish linen cloth, 14 feet, three inches in length and three feet, seven inches in width, bearing the front and back imprint of a human body. A tradition dating from the seventh century, which has not been verified beyond doubt, claims that the shroud is the fine linen in which the body of Christ was wrapped for burial. The early history of the shroud is obscure. It was enshrined at Lirey, France, in 1354 and was transferred in 1578 to Turin, Italy, where it has been kept in the cathedral down to the present time. Scientific investigation, which began in 1898, seems to indicate that the markings on the shroud are those of a human body. The shroud, for the first time since 1933, was placed on public view from Aug. 27 to Oct. 8, 1978, and was seen by an estimated 3.3 million people. Scientists conducted intensive studies of it for several days after the end of public viewing. The shroud, which had been the possession of the House of Savoy, was willed to Pope John Paul II in 1983.

Sick Calls: When a person is confined at home by illness or other cause and is unable to go to church for reception of the sacraments, a parish priest should be informed and arrangements made for him to visit the person at home. Such visitations are common in pastoral practice, both for special needs and for providing persons with regular opportunities for receiving the sacraments. If a priest cannot make the visitation, arrangements can be made for a deacon or Eucharistic minister to bring Holy Communion to the homebound or bedridden person.

Sign of the Cross: A sign, ceremonial gesture or movement in the form of a cross by which a person confesses faith in the Holy Trinity and Christ, and intercedes for the blessing of himself, other persons, and things. In Roman-Rite practice, a person making the sign touches the fingers of the right hand to his forehead, below the breast, left shoulder and right shoulder while saying: "In the name of the Father, and of the Son, and of the Holy Spirit." The sign is also made with the thumb on the forehead, the lips, and the breast. For the blessing of persons and objects, a large sign of the cross is made by movement of the right hand. In Eastern-Rite practice, the sign is made with the thumb and first two fingers of the right hand joined together and touching the forehead, below the breast, the right shoulder and the left shoulder; the formula generally used is the doxology, "O Holy God, O Holy Strong One, O Immortal One." The Eastern manner of making the sign was general until the first half of the 13th century; by the 17th century, Western practice involved the whole right hand and the reversal of direction from shoulder to shoulder.

Signs of the Times: Contemporary events, trends and features in culture and society, the needs and aspirations of people, all the factors that form the context in and through which the Church has to carry on its saving mission. The Second Vatican Council spoke on numerous occasions about these signs and the relationship between them and a kind of manifestation of God's will, positive or negative, and about subjecting them to judgment and action corresponding to the demands of divine revelation through Scripture, Christ, and the experience, tradition and teaching authority of the Church.

Simony: The deliberate intention and act of selling and/or buying spiritual goods or material things so connected with the spiritual that they cannot be separated therefrom; a violation of the virtue of religion, and a sacrilege, because it wrongfully puts a material price on spiritual things, which cannot be either sold or bought. In church law, actual sale or purchase is subject to censure in some cases. The term is derived from the name of Simon Magus, who attempted to buy from Sts. Peter and John the power to confirm people in the Holy Spirit (Acts 8:4-24).

Sin: (1) Actual sin is rejection of God manifested by free and deliberate violation of his law by thought, word or action. (a) Mortal sin — involving serious matter, sufficient reflection and full consent — results in total alienation from God, making a person dead to sanctifying grace, incapable of performing meritorious supernatural acts and subject to everlasting punishment. (b) Venial sin — involving less serious matter, reflection and consent — does not have such serious consequences. (2) Original sin is the sin of Adam, with consequences for all men. (See separate entry.)

Sins against the Holy Spirit: Despair of salvation, presumption of God's mercy, impugning the known truths of faith, envy at another's spiritual good, obstinacy in sin, final impenitence. Those guilty of such sins stubbornly resist the influence of grace and, as long as they do so, cannot be forgiven.

Sins, Occasions of: Circumstances (persons, places, things, etc.) which easily lead to sin. There is an obligation to avoid voluntary proximate occasions of sin, and to take precautions against the dangers of unavoidable occasions.

Sins That Cry to Heaven for Vengeance: Willful murder, sins against nature, oppression of the poor, widows and orphans, defrauding laborers of their wages.

Sister: Any woman religious, in popular speech; strictly, the title applies only to women Religious belonging to institutes whose members never professed solemn vows. Most of the institutes whose members are properly called Sisters were established during and since the 19th century. Women Religious with solemn vows, or belonging to institutes whose members formerly professed solemn vows, are properly called nuns.

Sisterhood: A generic term referring to the whole institution of the life of women religious in the Church, or to a particular institute of women religious.

Situation Ethics: A subjective, individualistic ethical theory which denies the binding force of ethical principles as universal laws and preceptive norms of moral conduct, and proposes that morality is determined only by situational conditions and considerations and the intention of the person. In an instruction issued on the subject in May, 1956, the Congregation for the Holy Office said: "It ignores the principles of objective ethics. This 'New Morality,' it is claimed, is not only the equal of objective morality, but is superior to it. The authors who follow this system state that the ultimate determining norm for activity is not the objective order as determined by the natural law and known with certainty from this law. It is instead some internal judgment and illumination of the mind of every individual by which the mind comes to know what is to be done in a concrete situation. This ultimate decision of man is, therefore, not the application of the objective law to a particular case after the particular circumstances of a 'situation' have been considered and weighed according to the rules of prudence, as the more important authors of objective ethics teach; but it is, according to them, immediate, internal illumination and judgment. With regard to its objective truth and correctness, this judgment, at least in many things, is not ultimately measured, is not to be measured or is not measurable by any objective norm found outside man and independent of his subjective persuasion, but it is fully sufficient in itself.... Much that is stated in this system of 'Situation Ethics' is contrary to the truth of reality and to the dictate of sound reason. It gives evidence of relativism and modernism, and deviates far from the Catholic teaching handed down through the ages."

Slander: Attributing to a person faults which he does not have; a violation of the obligations of justice and charity, for which restitution is due.

Sloth: One of the seven capital sins; spiritual laziness, involving distaste and disgust for spiritual things; spiritual boredom, which saps the vigor of spiritual life. Physical laziness is a counterpart of spiritual sloth.

Sorcery: A kind of black magic in which evil is invoked by means of diabolical intervention; a violation of the virtue of religion.

Soteriology: The division of theology which treats of the mission and work of Christ as Redeemer.

Species, Sacred: The appearances of bread and wine (color, taste, smell, etc.) which remain after the substance has been changed at the Consecration of the Mass into the Body and Blood of Christ. (See Transubstantiation.)

Spiritism: Attempts to communicate with spirits and departed souls by means of seances, table tapping, ouija boards, and other methods; a violation of the virtue of religion. Spiritualistic practices are noted for fakery.

Spiritual Works of Mercy: Works of spiritual assistance, motivated by love of God and neighbor, to persons in need: counseling the doubtful, instructing the ignorant, admonishing sinners, comforting the afflicted, forgiving offenses, bearing wrongs patiently, praying for the living and the dead.

Stational Churches, Days: Churches, especially in Rome, where the clergy and lay people were accustomed to gather with their bishop on certain days for the celebration of the liturgy. The 25 early titular or parish churches of Rome, plus other churches, each had their turn as the site of divine worship in practices which may have started in the third century. The observances were rather well developed toward the latter part of the fourth century, and by the fifth they included a Mass concelebrated by the pope and attendant priests. On some occasions, the stational liturgy was preceded by a procession from another church called a collecta. There were 42 Roman stational churches in the eighth century, and 89 stational services were scheduled annually in connection with the liturgical seasons. Stational observances fell into disuse toward the end of the Middle Ages. Some revival was begun by John XXIII in 1959 and continued by

Stations of the Cross: A series of meditations on the sufferings of Christ: his condemnation to death and taking up of the Cross; the first fall on the way to Calvary; meeting his Mother; being assisted by Simon of Cyrene, and by Veronica who wiped his face; the second fall; meeting the women of Jerusalem; the third fall; being stripped and nailed to the Cross; his death; the removal of his body from the Cross and his burial. Depictions of these scenes are mounted in most churches, chapels and in some other places, beneath small crosses. A person making the Way of the Cross passes before these Stations, or stopping points, pausing at each for meditation. If the Stations are made by a group of people, only the leader has to pass from Station to Station. Prayer for the intentions of the pope is required for gaining the indulgence granted for the Stations. Those unable to make the Stations in the ordinary manner, because they are impeded from visiting a church or other place where the Stations are, can still practice the devotion by meditating on the sufferings of Christ; praying the Our Father, Hail Mary and Glory for each Station and five times in commemoration of the wounds of Christ; and praying for the intentions of the pope. This practice has involved the use of a Stations Crucifix. The Stations originated, remotely, from the practice of Holy Land pilgrims who visited the actual scenes of incidents in the Passion of Christ. Representations elsewhere of at least some of these scenes were known as early as the fifth century. Later, the Stations evolved in connection with and as a consequence of strong devotion to the Passion in the 12th and 13th centuries. Franciscans, who were given custody of the Holy Places in 1342, promoted the devotion widely; one of them, St. Leonard of Port Maurice, became known as the greatest preacher of the Way of the Cross in the 18th century. The general features of the devotion were fixed by Clement XII in 1731.

Statutes: Virtually the same as decrees (see separate entry), they almost always designate laws of a particular council or synod rather than pontifical laws.

Stigmata: Marks of the wounds suffered by Christ in his crucifixion, in hands and feet by nails, and side by the piercing of a lance. Some persons, called stigmatists, have been reported as recipients or sufferers of marks like these. The Church, however, has never issued any infallible declaration about their possession by anyone, even in the case of St. Francis of Assisi whose stigmata seem to be the best substantiated and may be commemorated in the Roman-Rite liturgy. Ninety percent of some 300 reputed stigmatists have been women. Judgment regarding the presence, significance, and manner of causation of stigmata would depend, among other things, on irrefutable experimental evidence.

Stipend, Mass: An offering given to a priest for applying the fruits of the Mass according to the intention of the donor. The offering is a contribution to the support of the priest. The disposition of the fruits of the sacrifice, in line with doctrine concerning the Mass in particular and prayer in general, is subject to the will of God. In the early Christian centuries, when Mass was not offered for the intentions of particular persons, the participants made offerings of bread and wine for the sacrifice and their own Holy Communion, and of other things useful for the support of the clergy and the poor. Some offerings may have been made as early as the fourth century for the celebration of Mass for particular intentions, and there are indications of the existence of this practice from the sixth century when private Masses began to be offered. The earliest certain proof of stipend practice, however, dates from the eighth century. By the 11th century, along with private Mass, it was established custom.

Stole Fee: An offering given on certain occasions; e.g., at a baptism, wedding, funeral, for the support of the clergy who administer the sacraments and perform other sacred rites.

Stoup: A vessel used to contain holy water.

Suffragan See: Any diocese, except the archdiocese, within a province.

Suicide: The taking of one's own life; a violation of God's dominion over human life. Ecclesiastical burial is denied to persons who deliberately commit suicide while in full possession of their faculties; it is permitted in cases of doubt.

Supererogation: Good and virtuous actions which go beyond the obligations of duty and the requirements enjoined by God's law as necessary for salvation. Examples of these works are the profession and observance of the evangelical counsels of poverty, chastity, and obedience, and efforts to practice charity to the highest degree.

Supernatural: Above the natural; that which exceeds and is not due or owed to the essence, exigencies, requirements, powers and merits of created nature. While man has no claim on supernatural things and does not need them in order to exist and act on a natural level, he does need them in order to exist and act in the higher order or economy of grace established by God for his salvation. God has freely given to man certain things which are beyond the powers and rights of his human nature. Examples of the supernatural are: grace, a kind of participation by man in the divine life, by which man becomes capable of performing acts meritorious for salvation; divine revelation by which God manifests himself to man and makes known truth that is inaccessible to human reason alone; faith, by which man believes divine truth because of the authority of God who reveals it through Sacred Scripture and tradition and the teaching of his Church.

Superstition: A violation of the virtue of religion, by which God is worshipped in an unworthy manner or creatures are given honor which belongs to God alone. False, vain, or futile worship involves elements which are incompatible with the honor and respect due to God, such as error, deception, and bizarre practices. Examples are: false and exaggerated devotions, chain prayers and allegedly unfailing prayers, the mixing of unbecoming practices in worship. The second kind of superstition attributes to persons and things powers and honor which belong to God alone. Examples are: idolatry, divination, magic, spiritism, necromancy.

Suspension: A censure by which a cleric is forbidden to exercise some or all of his powers of orders and jurisdiction, or to accept the financial support of his benefices.

Swearing: Taking an oath; calling upon God to witness the truth of a statement; a legitimate thing to do for serious reasons and under proper circumstances, as in a court of law. To swear without sufficient reason is to dishonor God's name; to swear falsely in a court of law is perjury.

Swedenborgianism: A doctrine developed in and from the writings of Emmanuel Swedenborg (1688-1772), who claimed that during a number of visions he had in 1745 Christ taught him the spiritual sense of Sacred Scripture and commissioned him to communicate it to others. He held that, just as Christianity succeeded Judaism, so his teaching supplemented Christianity. He rejected belief in the Trinity, original sin, the Resurrection, and all the sacraments except baptism and the Eucharist. His followers are members of the Church of the New Jerusalem or of the New Church.

Syllabus, The: (1) When not qualified, the term refers to the list of 80 errors accompanying Pope Pius IX's encyclical *Quanta Cura,* issued in 1864. (2) The *Syllabus* of St. Pius X in the decree *Lamentabili,* issued by the Holy Office July 4, 1907, condemning 65 heretical propositions of modernism. This schedule of errors was followed shortly by that pope's encyclical *Pascendi,* the principal ecclesiastical document against modernism, issued Sept. 8, 1907.

Synod, Diocesan: Meeting of representative persons of a diocese — priests, religious, lay persons — with the bishop, called by him for the purpose of considering and taking action on matters affecting the life and mission of the Church in the diocese. Persons taking part in a synod have consultative status; the bishop alone is the legislator, with power to authorize synodal decrees. According to canon law, every diocese should have a synod every 10 years.

T

Te Deum: The opening Latin words, Thee, God, of a hymn of praise and thanksgiving prescribed for use in the Office of Readings of the Liturgy of the Hours on many Sundays, solemnities and feasts.

Temperance: Moderation, one of the four cardinal virtues.

Temptation: Any enticement to sin, from any source: the strivings of one's own faculties, the action of the devil, other persons, circumstances of life, etc. Temptation itself is not sin. Temptation can be avoided and overcome with the use of prudence and the help of grace.

Thanksgiving: An expression of gratitude to God for his goodness and the blessings he grants; one of the four ends of prayer.

Theism: A philosophy which admits the existence of God and the possibility of divine revelation; it is generally monotheistic and acknowledges God as transcendent and also active in the world. Because it is a philosophy rather than a system of theology derived from revelation, it does not include specifically Christian doctrines, like those concerning the Trinity, the Incarnation and Redemption.

Theological Virtues: The virtues which have God for their direct object: faith, or belief in God's infallible teaching; hope, or confidence in divine assistance; charity, or love of God. They are given to a person with grace in the first instance, through baptism and incorporation in Christ.

Theology: Knowledge of God and religion, deriving from and based on the data of divine Revelation, organized and systematized according to some kind of scientific method. It involves systematic study and presentation of the truths of divine Revelation in Sacred Scripture, tradition, and the teaching of the Church. The Second Vatican Council made the following declaration about theology and its relation to divine Revelation: "Sacred theology rests on the written word of God, together with sacred tradition, as its primary and perpetual foundation. By scrutinizing in the light of faith all truth stored up in the mystery of Christ, theology is most powerfully strengthened and constantly rejuvenated by that word. For the sacred Scriptures contain the word of God and, since they are inspired, really are the word of God; and so the study of the sacred page is, as it were, the soul of sacred theology" *(Constitution on Revelation.* No. 24). Theology has been divided under various subject headings. Some of the major fields have been: dogma (systematic theology), moral, pastoral, ascetics (the practice of virtue and means of attaining holiness and perfection), mysticism (higher states of religious experience). Other subject headings include ecumenism (Christian unity, interfaith relations), ecclesiology (the nature and constitution of the Church), Mariology (doctrine concerning the Blessed Virgin Mary), the sacraments, etc.

Tithing: Contribution of a portion of one's income, originally one-tenth, for purposes of religion and charity. The practice is mentioned 46 times in the Bible. In early Christian times, tithing was adopted in continuance of Old Testament practices of the Jewish people, and the earliest positive church legislation on the subject was enacted in 567. Catholics are bound in conscience to contribute to the support of their church, but the manner in which they do so is not fixed by law. Tithing, which amounts to a pledged contribution of a portion of one's income, has aroused new attention in recent years in the United States.

Titular Sees: Dioceses where the Church once flourished but which later were overrun by pagans or Moslems and now exist only in name or title. Bishops without a territorial or residential diocese of their own; e.g., auxiliary bishops, are given titular sees.

Transfinalization, Transignification: Terms coined to express the sign value of consecrated bread and wine with respect to the presence and action of Christ in the Eucharistic sacrifice and the spiritually vivifying purpose of the Eucharistic banquet in Holy Communion. The theory behind the terms has strong undertones of existential and "sign" philosophy, and has been criticized for its openness to interpretations at variance with the doctrine of transubstantiation and the abiding presence of Christ under the appearances of bread and wine after the sacrifice of the Mass and Communion have been completed. The terms, if used as substitutes for transubstantiation, are unacceptable; if they presuppose transubstantiation, they are acceptable as clarifications of its meaning.

Transubstantiation: "The way Christ is made present in this sacrament (Holy Eucharist) is none other than by the change of the whole substance of the bread into his Body, and of the whole substance of the wine into his Blood (in the Consecration at Mass) . . . this unique and wonderful change the Catholic Church rightly calls transubstantiation" (encyclical *Mysterium Fidei* of Paul VI, Sept. 3, 1965). The first official use of the term was made by the Fourth Council of the Lateran in 1215. Authoritative teaching on the subject was issued by the Council of Trent.

Treasury of the Church: The superabundant merits of Christ and the saints from which the Church draws to confer spiritual benefits, such as indulgences.

Triduum: A three-day series of public or private devotions.

U-Z

Usury: Excessive interest charged for the loan and use of money; a violation of justice.

Veronica: A word resulting from the combination of a Latin word for true, *vera*, and a Greek word for image, *eikon*, designating a likeness of the face of Christ or the name of a woman said to have given him a cloth on which he caused an imprint of his face to appear. The veneration at Rome of a likeness depicted on cloth dates from about the end of the 10th century; it figured in a popular devotion during the Middle Ages, and in the Holy Face devotion practiced since the 19th century. A faint, indiscernible likeness said to be of this kind is preserved in St. Peter's Basilica. The origin of the likeness is uncertain, and the identity of the woman is unknown. Before the 14th century, there were no known artistic representations of an incident concerning a woman who wiped the face of Christ with a piece of cloth while He was carrying the Cross to Calvary.

Viaticum: Holy Communion given to those in danger of death. The word, derived from Latin, means provision for a journey through death to life hereafter.

Vicar General: A priest or bishop appointed by the bishop of a diocese to serve as his deputy, with ordinary executive power, in the administration of the diocese.

Virginity: Observance of perpetual sexual abstinence. The state of virginity, which is embraced for the love of God by religious with a public vow or by others with a private vow, was singled out for high praise by Christ (Mt. 19:10-12) and has always been so regarded by the Church. In the encyclical *Sacra Virginitas,* Pius XII stated: "Holy virginity and that perfect chastity which is consecrated to the service of God is without doubt among the most perfect treasures which the founder of the Church has left in heritage to the society which he established." Paul VI approved in 1970 a rite in which women can consecrate their virginity "to Christ and their brethren" without becoming members of a religious institute. The *Ordo Consecrationis Virginum,* a revision of a rite promulgated by Clement VII in 1596, is traceable to the Roman liturgy of about 500.

Virtue: A habit or established capability for performing good actions. Virtues are *natural* (acquired and increased by repeating good acts) and/or *supernatural* (given with grace by God).

Vocation: A call to a way of life. Generally, the term applies to the common call of all men, from God, to holiness and salvation. Specifically, it refers to particular states of life, each called a vocation, in which response is made to this universal call; viz., marriage, the religious life and/or priesthood, the single state freely chosen or accepted for the accomplishment of God's will. The term also applies to the various occupations in which persons make a living. The Church supports the freedom of each individual in choosing a particular vocation, and reserves the right to pass on the acceptability of candidates for the priesthood and religious life. Signs or indicators of particular vocations are many, including a person's talents and interests, circumstances and obligations, invitations of grace and willingness to respond thereto.

Vow: A promise made to God with sufficient knowledge and freedom, which has as its object a moral good that is possible and better than its voluntary omission. A person who professes a vow binds himself or herself by the virtue of religion to fulfill the promise. The best known examples of vows are those of poverty, chastity and obedience professed by religious (see Evangelical Counsels, individual entries). Public vows are made before a competent person, acting as an agent of the Church, who accepts the profession in the name of the Church, thereby giving public recognition to the person's dedication and consecration to God and divine worship. Vows of this kind are either solemn, rendering all contrary acts invalid as well as unlawful; or simple, rendering contrary acts unlawful. Solemn vows are for life; simple vows are for a definite period of time or for life. Vows professed without public recognition by the Church are called private vows. The Church, which has authority to accept and give public recognition to vows, also has authority to dispense persons from their obligations for serious reasons.

Week of Prayer for Christian Unity: Eight days of prayer, from Jan. 18 to 25, for the union of all men in the Church established by Christ. On the initiative of Father Paul James Francis, S.A., of Graymoor, N.Y., it originated in 1908 as the Chair of Unity Octave. In recent years, its observance on an interfaith basis has increased greatly.

Witness, Christian: Practical testimony or evidence given by Christians of their faith in all circumstances of life — by prayer and general conduct, through good example and good works, etc.; being and acting in accordance with Christian belief; actual practice of the Christian faith.

Agrimissio is a service office established for the purpose of assisting missionaries in rural development work in agriculture. Founded in 1970 by Msgr. Luigi Ligutti, late honorary president, it is sponsored by the Union of Superiors General (of male religious), the International Union of Superiors General (of female religious). It promotes cooperation among missionaries, the Rome headquarters of religious orders, governmental and non-governmental organizations.

Headquarters are located at the Palazzo S. Calisto, 00120, Vatican City.

THE CHURCH IN COUNTRIES THROUGHOUT THE WORLD

(Principal sources for statistics: *Statistical Yearbook of the Church, 1986* (the most recent edition); *Annuario Pontificio, 1988*. Figures are as of Dec. 31, 1986, unless indicated otherwise. For 1988 events, see Index entries for individual countries.)

An asterisk indicates that the country has full diplomatic relations with Vatican City (see pages 173-74).

Abbreviations (in order in which they appear): archd. — archdiocese; dioc. — diocese; ap. ex. — apostolic exarchate; prel. — prelature; abb. — abbacy; v.a. — vicariate apostolic; p.a. — prefecture apostolic; a.a. — apostolic administration; mil. ord. — military ordinariate; card. — cardinal; abp. — archbishops; bp. — bishops (diocesan and titular); priests (dioc. — diocesan or secular priests; rel. — those belonging to religious orders); p.d. — permanent deacons; sem. — major seminarians, diocesan and religious; bros. — brothers; srs. — sisters; bap. — baptisms; Caths. — Catholic population; tot. pop. — total population; (AD), apostolic delegate (see page 170).

Afghanistan

People's Republic in south-central Asia; capital, Kabul. Christianity antedated Moslem conquest in the seventh century but was overcome by it. All inhabitants are subject to the law of Islam. Christian missionaries are prohibited. Population (est.), 18,610,000.

Albania

Archd., 2; dioc., 3; abb., 1; a.a. 1; bp., 3 (impeded). Tot. pop., 3,020,000.

Communist people's republic in the Balkans, bordering the Adriatic Sea; capital, Tirana. Christianity was introduced before the middle of the fourth century. The Byzantine-Rite Church broke from unity with Rome following the schism of 1054. A large percentage of the population was forcibly Islamized following the invasion (15th century) and long centuries of occupation by the Ottoman Turks. Many Catholics fled to southern Italy, Sicily and Greece. At the time of the communist take-over in 1945, an estimated 68 per cent of the population was Moslem; 19 per cent, Orthodox and 13 per cent, Roman Catholic. The Catholic Church prevailed in the north. It fell victim, as did all religions, to systematic persecution by the government: non-Albanian missionaries were expelled; death, prison sentences and other repressive measures were enacted against church personnel and laity; Catholic schools and churches were closed and used for other purposes, and lines of communication with the Holy See were cut off. In 1967, the government, declaring it had eliminated all religion in the country, proclaimed itself the first atheist state in the world. Despite this, there are reports of a clandestine Catholic community in the country.

Algeria*

Archd., 1; dioc., 3; card., 1; abp., 2; bp., 4 parishes, 73; priests, 167 (67 dioc., 100 rel.); p.d., 2; sem. 1; bros., 19; srs., 430; bap., 26; Caths., 63,000 (.28%); tot. pop., 22,420,000.

Republic in northwest Africa: capital, Algiers. Christianity, introduced at an early date, succumbed to Vandal devastation in the fifth century and Moslem conquest in 709, but survived for centuries in small communities into the 12th century. Missionary work was unsuccessful except in service to traders, military personnel and captives along the coast. Church organization was established after the French gained control of the territory in the 1830s. A large number of Catholics were among the estimated million Europeans who left the country after it secured independence from France July 5, 1962. Sunni-Moslem is the state religion.

Andorra

Parishes, 7; priests, 21 (13 dioc., 8 rel.); srs., 19; bap., 350; Caths., 42,000 (84%); tot. pop., 50,000.

Autonomous principality in the Pyrenees, under the rule of co-princes — the French head of state and the bishop of Urgel, Spain; capital, Andorra la Vella. Christianity was introduced at an early date. Catholicism is the state religion. The principality is under the ecclesiastical jurisdiction of the Spanish diocese of Urgel.

Angola

Archd., 3; dioc., 11; card., 1 (native); abp., 2 (native); bp., 12 (9 native); parishes, 262; priests, 323 (110 dioc., 213 rel.); p.d., 1; sem., 214; bros., 48; srs., 877; catechists, 14,074; bap., 78,002; Caths., 4,783,000 (53.2%); tot. pop., 8,980,000. (AD)

People's Republic in West Africa; capital, Luanda. Evangelization by Catholic missionaries, from Portugal, dating from 1491, reached high points in the 17th and 18th centuries. Independence from Portugal in 1975 left the Church with a heavy loss of personnel when about half of the foreign missionaries fled the country. Two ecclesiastical provinces were established in 1977; all but two of the ordinaries are Angolan; the first Angolan cardinal (Alexandre do Nascimento) was named in 1983.

Anguilla

Parish, 1; priest, 1 (rel.); bap., 3; Caths., 100; tot. pop., 7,000. (AD)

Self-governing British island territory in the Caribbean; capital, The Valley. Under ecclesiastical jurisdiction of St. John's-Basseterre diocese, Antigua.

Antigua and Barbuda*

Dioc., 1; bp., 1; parishes, 2; priests, 4 (1 dioc., 3 rel.); bros., 5; srs., 13; bap., 71; Caths., 7,000 (8.7%); tot. pop., 80,000.

Arabian Peninsula

Christianity, introduced in various parts of the peninsula in early Christian centuries, succumbed to Islam in the seventh century. The native population is entirely Moslem. The only Christians are foreign workers mainly from the Philippines, India and Korea. Most of the peninsula is under the ecclesiastical jurisdiction of the Vicariate Apostolic of Arabia with its seat in Abu Dhabi, United Arab Emirates. See individual countries: Bahrain, Oman, Qatar, Saudi Arabia, United Arab Emirates, North Yemen, and South Yemen.

Argentina*

Archd., 13; dioc., 45; prel., 3; ap. ex., 1 (for Armenians of Latin America); ord., 1; mil. ord.; card., 3; abp., 13; bp., 77; parishes, 2,308; priests, 5,572 (2,804 dioc., 2,768 rel.); p.d., 122; sem., 2,104; bros., 1,148; srs., 11,678; bap., 610,725; Caths., 28,855,000 (93%); tot. pop., 31,030,000

Republic in southeast South America, bordering on the Atlantic; capital, Buenos Aires. Priests were with the Magellan exploration party and the first Mass in the country was celebrated Apr. 1, 1519. Missionary work began in the 1530s, diocesan organization in the late 1540s, and effective evangelization about 1570. Independence from Spain was proclaimed in 1816. Since its establishment in the country, the Church has been influenced by Spanish cultural and institutional forces, antagonistic liberalism, government interference and opposition; the latter reached a climax during the last five years of the first presidency of Juan Peron (1946-1955). Widespread human rights violations including the disappearance of thousands of people marked the period of military rule from 1976 to December, 1983, when an elected civilian government took over. The bishops' conference published in book form in September, 1983, communiques they had sent to the military government during those years concerning human right abuses. Catholicism is the state religion.

Australia*

Archd., 7; dioc. (1988), 24; mil. ord.; card. (1988), 2; abp., 8; bp., 40; parishes, 1,431; priests, 3,787 (2,190 dioc., 1,597 rel.); p.d., 14; sem., 385; bros., 1,979; srs., 10,521; bap., 73,124; Caths., 4,304,000 (26.9%); tot. pop. 15,970,000.

Commonwealth; island continent southeast of Asia; capital, Canberra. The first Catholics in the country were Irish under penal sentence, 1795-1804; the first public Mass was celebrated May 15, 1803. Official organization of the Church dates from 1820. The country was officially removed from mission status in March, 1976.

Austria*

Archd., 2; dioc., 7; abb., 1; ord., 1; mil. ord.; card. (1988), 3; abp., 1; bp., 14; parishes, 3,076; priests, 5,691 (3,244 dioc., 2,447 rel.); p.d., 185; sem., 636; bros., 605; srs., 9,793; bap., 77,572; Caths., 6,469,000 (85.4%); tot. pop., 7,570,000.

Republic in central Europe; capital, Vienna. Christianity was introduced by the end of the third century, strengthened considerably by conversion of the Bavarians from about 600, and firmly established in the second half of the eighth century. Catholicism survived and grew stronger as the principal religion in the country in the post-Reformation period, but suffered from Josephinism in the 18th century. Although liberated from much government harassment in the aftermath of the Revolution of 1848, it came under pressure again some 20 years later in the Kulturkampf. During this time the Church became involved with a developing social movement. The Church faced strong opposition from Socialists after World War I and suffered persecution from 1938 to 1945 during the Nazi regime. Some Church-state matters are regulated by a concordat originally concluded in 1934. (See Index for papal visit.)

Azores

North Atlantic island group 750 miles west of Portugal, of which it is part. Christianity was introduced in the second quarter of the 15th century. The diocese of Angra was established in 1534. Statistics are included in Portugal.

Bahamas*

Dioc., 1; bp., 1; parishes, 30; priests, 37 (11 dioc., 26 rel.); p.d., 4; sem., 7; bros., 5; srs., 51; bap., 1,896; Caths., 44,000 (18.6%); tot. pop., 236,000.

Independent (July 10, 1973) island group consisting of some 700 (30 inhabited) small islands southeast of Florida and north of Cuba; capital, Nassau. On Oct. 12, 1492, Columbus landed on one of these islands, where the first Mass was celebrated in the New World. Organization of the Catholic Church in the Bahamas dates from about the middle of the 19th century.

Bahrain

Parishes, 2; priests, 3 (1 dioc., 2 rel.); srs., 9; bap., 340; Caths., 12,000; tot. pop., 420,000. (AD)

Island state in Persian Gulf; capital, Manama. Under ecclesiastical jurisdiction of Arabia vicariate apostolic.

Balearic Islands

Spanish province consisting of an island group in the western Mediterranean. Statistics are included in those for Spain.

Bangladesh*

Archd., 1; dioc., 4; abp., 1 (native); bp., 4 (native); parishes, 56; priests, 202 (66 dioc., 136 rel.); sem., 87; bros., 58; srs., 639; bap., 5,291; Caths., 184,000 (.17%); tot. pop. 100,620,000.

Formerly the eastern portion of Pakistan. Officially constituted as a separate nation Dec. 16, 1971; capital, Dhaka. Islam is the principal religion; freedom of religion is granted. There were Jesuit, Dominican and Augustinian missionaries in the area in the 16th century. A vicariate apostolic (of Bengali) was established in 1834; the hierarchy was erected in 1950.

Barbados*

Dioc., 1; bp., 1; parishes, 6; priests, 10 (3 dioc., 7 rel.); p.d., 2; sem., 3; bros., 5; srs., 18; bap., 172; Caths., 11,000 (4%); tot. pop., 275,000.

Parliamentary democracy (independent since 1966), easternmost of the Caribbean islands; capital, Bridgetown. About 70 per cent of the people are Anglicans.

Belgium*

Archd., 1; dioc., 7; mil. ord.; card., 3; abp., 1; bp., 19; parishes, 4,072; priests, 11,286 (6,988 dioc., 4,298 rel.); p.d., 344; sem., 444; bros., 2,007; srs., 27,224; bap., 90,143; Caths., 8,848,000 (89.2%); tot. pop., 9,910,000.

Constitutional monarchy in northwestern Europe; capital, Brussels. Christianity was introduced about the first quarter of the fourth century and major evangelization was completed about 730. During the rest of the medieval period the Church had firm diocesan and parochial organization, generally vigorous monastic life, and influential monastic and cathedral schools. Lutherans and Calvinists made some gains during the Reformation period but there was a strong Catholic restoration in the first half of the 17th century, when the country was under Spanish rule. Jansenism disturbed the Church from about 1640 into the 18th century. Josephinism, imposed by an Austrian regime, hampered the Church late in the same century. Repressive and persecutory measures were enforced during the Napoleonic conquest. Freedom came with separation of Church and state in the wake of the Revolution of 1830, which ended the reign of William I. Thereafter, the Church encountered serious problems with philosophical liberalism and political socialism. Catholics have long been engaged in strong educational, social and political movements. Except for one five-year period (1880-1884), Belgium has had diplomatic relations with Vatican City since 1835.

Belize*

Dioc., 1; bp., 1; parishes, 12; priests, 38 (11 dioc., 27 rel.); p.d., 1; sem., 4; bros., 8; srs., 83; bap., 2,914; Caths., 106,000 (62.3%); tot. pop., 170,000.

Formerly British Honduras. Independent (Sept. 21, 1981) republic on east coast of Central America; capital, Belmopan. Its history has points in common with Guatemala, where evangelization began in the 16th century.

Benin*

Archd., 1; dioc., 5; card., 1 (native); abp., 2 (native); bp., 5 (native); parishes, 123; priests, 207 (125 dioc., 82 rel.); sem., 119; bros., 20; srs., 380; bap., 23,842; Caths., 781,000 (19.3%); tot. pop., 4,040,000.

Formerly Dahomey. People's republic in west Africa, bordering on the Atlantic; capital, Porto Novo. Missionary work was very limited from the 16th to the 18th centuries. Effective evangelization dates from 1861. The hierarchy was established in 1955. The majority of Christians are Catholics.

Bermuda

Dioc., 1; bp., 1; parishes, 7; priests, 8 (1 dioc., 7 rel.); p.d., 1; sem., 2; srs., 3; bap., 126; Caths., 9,000 (15%); tot. pop., 60,000. (AD)

British dependency, consisting of 360 islands (20 of them inhabited) nearly 600 miles east of Cape Hatteras; capital, Hamilton. Catholics were not permitted until about 1800. Occasional pastoral care was provided the few Catholics there by visiting priests during the 19th century. Early in the 1900s priests from Halifax began serving the area. A prefecture apostolic was set up in 1953. The first bishop assumed jurisdiction in 1956 when it was made a vicariate apostolic; diocese established, 1967.

Bhutan

Parishes, 3; priests, 7 (2 dioc., 5 rel.); bro., 1; srs., 8; bap., 12; Caths., 400; tot. pop, 1,420,000.*

Kingdom in the Himalayas, northeast of India; capital, Thimphu. Most of the population are Buddhists. Jesuits (1963) and Salesians (1965) were invited to country to direct schools. Salesians were expelled in February, 1982, on disputed charges of proselytism. Jesuits and some Sisters remained *(Fides)*. Ecclesiastical jurisdiction is under the Darjeeling diocese, India.

Bolivia*

Archd., 4; dioc., 4; prel., 2; v.a., 6; mil. ord.; card., 1; abp., 7; bp., 23; parishes, 468; priests, 833 (221 dioc., 612 rel.); p.d., 27; sem., 313; bros., 180; srs., 1,694; bap., 191,875; Caths., 6,134,000 (93.6%); tot. pop., 6,550,000.

Republic in central South America; capital, Sucre; seat of government, La Paz. Catholicism, the official religion, was introduced in the 1530s and the first bishopric was established in 1552. Effective evangelization among the Indians, slow to start, reached high points in the middle of the 18th and the beginning of the 19th centuries and was resumed about 1840. Independence from Spain was proclaimed in 1825, at the end of a campaign that started in 1809. Church-state relations are regulated by a 1951 concordat with the Holy See. In recent years, human rights violations in conditions of political, economic and social turmoil have occasioned strong protests by members of the hierarchy and other people of the Church. (See Index for papal visit.)

Botswana

Dioc., 1; bp., 1 (native); parishes, 22; priests, 36 (3 dioc., 33 rel.); p.d., 1; sem., 5; bros., 5; srs., 65; bap., 1,906; Caths., 44,000 (3.9%); tot. pop., 1,130,000. (AD)

Republic (independent since 1966) in southern Africa; capital, Gaborone. (See Index for papal visit.)

Brazil*

Archd., 36; dioc., 191; prel. (1988), 14; abb., 2; ord., 1; mil. ord.; card. (1988), 7; abp., 48; bp., 309; parishes, 7,353; priests, 13,832 (5,944 dioc., 7,888 rel.); p.d., 472; sem., 6,049; bros., 2,476; srs., 37,647; bap., 2,715,694; Caths., 122,676,000 (90%); tot. pop., 138,490,000.

Federal republic in northeast South America; capital, Brasilia. One of several priests with the discovery party celebrated the first Mass in the country Apr. 26, 1500. Evangelization began some years later and the first diocese was erected in 1551. During the colonial period, which lasted until 1822, evangelization made some notable progress — especially in the Amazon region between 1680 and 1750 — but was seriously hindered by government policy and the attitude of colonists regarding Amazon Indians the missionaries tried to protect from exploitation and slavery. The Jesuits were suppressed in 1782 and other missionaries expelled as well. Liberal anti-Church influence grew in strength. The government gave minimal support but exercised maximum control over the Church. After the proclamation of independence from Portugal in 1822 and throughout the regency, government control was tightened and the Church suffered greatly from dissident actions of ecclesiastical brotherhoods, Masonic anti-clericalism and general decline in religious life. Church and state were separated by the constitution of 1891, proclaimed two years after the end of the empire. The Church carried into the 20th century a load of inherited liabilities and problems amid increasingly difficult political, economic and social conditions affecting the majority of the population. A number of bishops, priests, religious and lay persons have been active in movements for social and religious reform.

Brunei

Parishes, 3; priests, 5 (2 dioc., 3 rel.); srs., 4; bap., 102; Caths., 5,000; tot. pop., 240,000.

Independent state (1984) on the northern coast of Borneo; capital, Bandar Seri Begawan. Under ecclesiastical jurisdiction of Miri diocese, Malaysia.

Bulgaria

Dioc., 2; ap. ex., 1; bp., 2. No statistics available. In 1968 there were approximately 65,000 Catholics. Tot. pop., 8,960,000.

People's republic in southeastern Europe on the eastern part of the Balkan peninsula; capital, Sofia. Christianity was introduced before 343 but disappeared with the migration of Slavs into the territory. The baptism of Boris I about 865 ushered in a new period of Christianity which soon became involved in switches of loyalty between Constantinople and Rome. Through it all the Byzantine, and later Orthodox, element remained stronger and survived under the rule of Ottoman Turks into the 19th century. The few modern Latin Catholics in the country are traceable to 17th century converts from heresy. The Byzantines are products of a reunion movement of the 19th century. In 1947 the constitution of the new republic decreed the separation of Church and state. Catholic schools and institutions were abolished and foreign religious banished in 1948. A year later the apostolic delegate was expelled. Ivan Romanoff, vicar general of Plovdiv, died in prison in 1952. Bishop Eugene Bossilkoff, imprisoned in 1948, was sentenced to death in 1952; his fate remained unknown until 1975 when the Bulgarian government informed the Vatican that he had died in prison shortly after being sentenced. Roman and Bulgarian Rite vicars apostolic were permitted to attend the Second Vatican Council from 1962 to 1965. All church activity is under surveillance and/or control by the government, which professes to be atheistic. Pastoral and related activities are strictly limited. Most of the population is Orthodox. There was some improvement in Bulgarian-Vatican relations in 1975, following a visit of Bulgarian President Todor Zhivkov to Pope Paul VI June 19 and talks between Vatican and Bulgarian representatives at the Helsinki Conference in late July. The needs of the church in Bulgaria were outlined by Pope John Paul II in a private audience with the Bulgarian foreign minister in December, 1978. In 1979, the Sofia-Plovdiv vicariate apostolic was raised to a diocese and a bishop was appointed for the vacant see of Nicopoli.

Burkina Faso*

Archd., 1; dioc., 8; card., 1 (native); bp., 10 (native); parishes, 106; priests, 396 (197 dioc., 199 rel.); sem., 146; bros., 124; srs., 634; bap., 30,767; Caths., 688,000 (10.1%); tot. pop., 6,750,000.

Formerly Upper Volta. Republic inland in western Africa; capital, Ouagadougou. White Fathers (now known as Missionaries of Africa) started the first missions in 1900 and 1901. White Sisters began work in 1911. A minor and a major seminary were established in 1926 and 1942, respectively. The first native bishop in modern times from West Africa was ordained in 1956 and the first cardinal created in 1965. The hierarchy was established in 1955.

Burma

Archd., 2; dioc., 6; p.a., 1; abp., 2 (native); bp., 10 (9 native); parishes, 166; priests, 267 (248 dioc., 19 rel.); sem., 192; bros., 56; srs., 848; bap., 27,264; Caths., 430,000 (1.09%); tot. pop., 39,410,000. (AD)

Union of Burma, a socialist republic in southeast Asia, on the Bay of Bengal; capital, Rangoon. Christianity was introduced about 1500. Small-scale evangelization had limited results from the middle of the 16th century until the 1850s when effective organization of the Church began. The hierarchy was established in 1955. Buddhism was declared the state religion in 1961, but the state is now officially secular. In 1965, church schools and hospitals were nationalized. In 1966, all foreign missionaries who had entered the country after 1948 for the first time were forced to leave when the government refused to renew their work

Burundi*

Archd., 1; dioc., 6; abp., 1 (native); bp., 6 (native); parishes, 105; priests, 223 (159 dioc., 64 rel.); sem., 160; bros., 140; srs., 575; bap., 84,837; Caths., 2,774,000 (57.1%); tot. pop., 4,850,000.

Republic since 1966, near the equator in east-central Africa; capital, Bujumbura. The first permanent Catholic mission station was established late in the 19th century. Large numbers of persons were received into the Church following the ordination of the first Burundi priests in 1925. The first native bishop was appointed in 1959. In 1972-73, the country was torn by tribal warfare between the Tutsis, the ruling minority, and the Hutus. Since 1979, approximately 100 Catholic missionaries have been expelled. In 1986, seminaries were nationalized. (See Index for recent developments.)

Cambodia (Kampuchea)

V.a., 1; p.a., 2. No statistics available. Catholics numbered 13,835 in 1973. Tot. pop., 7,490,000.

People's republic in southeast Asia, bordering on the Gulf of Siam, Thailand, Laos and Vietnam; capital Phnom Penh. Evangelization dating from the second half of the 16th century had limited results, more among Vietnamese than Khmers. Thousands of Catholics of Vietnamese origin were forced to flee in 1970 because of Khmer hostility. The status of the Church remained uncertain following the Khmer Rouge take-over in April, 1975. Foreign missionaries were expelled immediately. Local clergy and religious were sent to work the land; whether they would be able to minister to the faithful was not known. Buddhism is the state religion.

Cameroon*

Archd., 4; dioc., 13; card. (1988), 1 (native); abp., 3 (native); bp., 15 (12 native); parishes, 439; priests, 847 (389 dioc., 458 rel.); p.d., 27; sem., 323; bros., 190; srs., 1,280; bap., 80,618; Caths., 2,883,000 (27.5%); tot. pop., 10,450,000.

Republic in west Africa, bordering on the Gulf of Guinea; capital, Yaounde. Effective evangelization began in the 1890s, although Catholics had been in the country long before that time. In the 40-year period from 1920 to 1960, the number of Catholics increased from 60,000 to 700,000. The first native priests were ordained in 1935. Twenty years later the first native bishops were ordained and the hierarchy established. In 1982, three new ecclesiastical provinces and one diocese were established.

Canada*

Archd., 18; dioc., 54; abb., 1; ap. ex., 1; mil. ord.; card. (1988), 6 (3 head archdioceses; 1 is Curia official; 2 are retired); abp., 25 (15 archdiocesan, 2 head eparchies with personal title of abp.; 1 coadjutor, 7 retired); bp., 96 (51 diocesan, 1 coadjutor; 22 auxiliary, 1 abbot ordinary; 21 retired); parishes 5,878; priests, 11,838 (7,075 dioc., 4,763 rel.); p.d., 513; sem., 911; bros., 3,935; srs., 33,536; bap., 171,717; Caths., 11,732,000 (45.8%); tot. pop., 25,610,000. (Principal sources: 1988 Directory of Canadian Conference of Catholic Bishops; Statistical Yearbook of the Church.)

Independent federation comprising the northern half of North America; capital, Ottawa. (See Index for news events and pages 374-84.)

Canary Islands

Two Spanish provinces, consisting of seven islands, off the northwest coast of Africa. Evangelization began about 1400. Almost all of the one million inhabitants are Catholics. Statistics are included in those for Spain.

Cape Verde*

Dioc., 1; bp., 1; parishes, 30; priests, 43 (12 dioc., 31 rel.); sem., 5; bros., 5; srs., 72; bap., 10,128; Caths., 310,000 (93.9%); tot. pop., 330,000.

Independent (July 5, 1975) island group in the Atlantic 300 miles west of Senegal; formerly a Portuguese overseas province; capital, Praia, San Tiago Island. Evangelization began some years before the establishment of the first diocese in 1532.

Carolines and Marshalls

Dioc., 1; bp., 2; parishes, 25; priests, 32 (2 dioc., 30 rel.); p.d., 21; sem., 9; bros., 4; srs., 47; bap., 2,423; Caths., 62,000 (46.6%); tot. pop., 133,000.

Federated States of Micronesia (Caroline archipelago) and the Republic of the Marshall Islands. U.S. trust territories in the southwest Pacific. Effective evangelization began in the late 1880s. Under ecclesiastical jurisdiction of Carolines-Marshall diocese.

Cayman Islands

Parish, 1; priests, 1 (dioc.); srs., 2; bap., 8; Caths. 200; tot. pop., 9,000. (AD)

British dependency in Caribbean; capital, George Town on Grand Cayman. Under ecclesiastical jurisdiction of Kingston diocese, Jamaica.

Central African Republic*

Archd., 1; dioc., 5; abp., 1 (native); bp., 6 (1 nat.); parishes, 90; priests, 225 (60 dioc., 165 rel.); p.d., 1; sem., 82; bros., 53; srs., 269; bap., 23,363; Caths., 450,000 (16.4%); tot. pop., 2,740,000.

Former French colony (independent since 1960) in central Africa; capital, Bangui. Effective evangelization dates from 1894. The region was organized as a mission territory in 1909. The first native priest was ordained in 1938. The hierarchy was organized in 1955.

Ceuta

Spanish possession (city) on the northern tip of

Chad

Archd., 1; dioc., 3; abp., 1; bp., 3 (1 native); parishes, 95; priests, 181 (27 dioc., 154 rel.); sem., 65; bros., 43; srs., 238; bap., 10,102; Caths., 321,000 (6.2%); tot. pop., 5,140,000. (AD)

Republic (independent since 1960) in north-central Africa; former French possession; capital, N'Djamena. Evangelization began in 1929, leading to firm organization in 1947 and establishment of the hierarchy in 1955.

Chile*

Archd., 5; dioc. (1987), 16; prel., 2; v.a., 2; mil. ord.; card., 2; abp., 6; bp., 33; parishes, 831; priests, 2,192 (855 dioc., 1,337 rel.); p.d., 205; sem., 870; bros., 385; srs., 4,454; bap., 174,238; Caths., 10,482,000 (85%); tot. pop., 12,330,000.

Republic on the southwestern coast of South America; capital, Santiago. Priests were with the Spanish conquistadores on their entrance into the territory early in the 16th century. The first parish was established in 1547 and the first bishopric in 1561. Overall organization of the Church took place later in the century. By 1650 most of the peaceful Indians in the central and northern areas were evangelized. Missionary work was more difficult in the southern region. Church activity was hampered during the campaign for independence, 1810 to 1818, and through the first years of the new government, to 1830. Later gains were made, into this century, but hindering factors were shortages of native clergy and religious and attempts by the government to control church administration through the patronage system in force while the country was under Spanish control. Separation of Church and state were decreed in the constitution of 1925. Church-state relations were strained during the regime of Marxist president Salvator Allende Gossens (1970-73). He was overthrown in a bloody coup and was reported to have committed suicide Sept. 11, 1973. Conditions have remained unsettled under the military government which assumed control after the coup. The Chilean bishops have issued numerous statements strongly critical of the military government's human rights violations, urging the release of political prisoners and a return to civilian rule.

China

Archd., 20; dioc., 92; p.a., 29. No Catholic statistics are available. In 1949 there were between 3,500,000-4,000,000 Catholics, about .7 per cent of the total population. Tot. pop. 1,052,754,000.

People's republic in eastern part of Asia (mainland China under communist control since 1949); capital, Peking (Beijing). Christianity was introduced by Nestorians who had some influence on part of the area from 635 to 845 and again from the 11th century until 1368. John of Monte Corvino started a Franciscan mission in 1294; he was ordained an archbishop about 1307. Missionary activity involving more priests increased for a while thereafter but the Franciscan mission ended in 1368. The Jesuit Matteo Ricci initiated a remarkable period of activity in the 1580s. By 1700 the number of Catholics was reported to be 300,000. The Chinese Rites controversy, concerning the adaptation of rituals and other matters to Chinese traditions and practices, ran throughout the 17th century, ending in a negative decision by mission authorities in Rome. Bl. Francis de Capillas, the protomartyr of China, was killed in 1648. Persecution, a feature of Chinese history as recurrent as changes in dynasties, occurred several times in the 18th century and resulted in the departure of most missionaries from the country. The Chinese door swung open again in the 1840s and progress in evangelization increased with an extension of legal and social tolerance. At the turn of the 20th century, however, the Boxer Rebellion took one or the other kind of toll among an estimated 30,000 victims. Missionary work in the 1900s reached a new high in every respect before the disaster of persecution initiated by Communists before and especially since they established the republic in 1949. The Reds began a savage persecution as soon as they came into power. Among its results were the expulsion of over 5,000 foreign missionaries, 510 of whom were American priests, brothers and nuns; the arrest, imprisonment and harassment of all members of the native religious, clergy and hierarchy; the forced closing of 3,932 schools, 216 hospitals, 781 dispensaries, 254 orphanages, 29 printing presses and 55 periodicals; denial of the free exercise of religion to all the faithful; the detention of hundreds of priests, religious and lay persons in jail and their employment in slave labor; the proscription of the Legion of Mary and other Catholic Action groups for "counter-revolutionary activities" and "crimes against the new China"; complete outlawing of missionary work and pastoral activity. The government formally established a Patriotic Association of Chinese Catholics in July, 1957. Relatively few priests and lay persons joined the organization, which was condemned by Pius XII in 1958. The government formed the nucleus of what it hoped might become the hierarchy of a schismatic Chinese church in 1958 by "electing" 26 bishops and having them consecrated validly but illicitly between Apr. 13, 1958, and Nov. 15, 1959, without the permission or approval of the Holy See. By 1983, an estimated 60 bishops were consecrated in this manner. In March, 1960, Bishop James E. Walsh, M.M., the last American missionary in China, was sentenced and placed in custody for a period of 20 years. He was released in the summer of 1970. (He died in 1981.) Activity of the Patriotic Association and official policy of the government are in direct opposition to any connection between the Church in China and the Vatican. Bishop Ignatius Kung Pin-Mei, imprisoned for 30 years, was paroled in 1985. (See Index for recent developments.)

Colombia*

Archd., 12; dioc., 36; prel., 2; v.a., 8; p.a.,

6; mil. ord., card., 2 (preceding figures as of July 1, 1988); abp., 14; bp., 65; parishes, 2,639; priests, 5,568 (3,592 dioc., 1,976 rel.); p.d., 53; sem., 2,908; bros.; 873; srs., 18,469; bap., 783,142; Caths., 27,731,000 (95%); tot. pop., 29,190,000.

Republic in northwest South America, with Atlantic and Pacific borders; capital, Bogota. Evangelization began in 1508. The first two dioceses were established in 1534. Vigorous development of the Church was reported by the middle of the 17th century despite obstacles posed by the multiplicity of Indian languages, government interference through patronage rights and otherwise, rivalry among religious orders and the small number of native priests among the predominantly Spanish clergy. Some persecution, including the confiscation of property, followed in the wake of the proclamation of independence from Spain in 1819. The Church was affected in many ways by the political and civil unrest of the nation through the 19th century and into the 20th. Various aspects of Church-state relations are regulated by a concordat with the Vatican signed July 12, 1973, and ratified July 2, 1975. The new concordat replaced one which had been in effect with some modifications since 1887. Guerrilla warfare aimed at Marxist-oriented radical social reform and redistribution of land has plagued the country since the 1960s, posing problems for the Church which backed reforms but rejected actions of radical groups.

Comoros

A.a., 1; parishes, 2; priests, 2 (rel.); srs., 8; bap., 15; Caths., 1,000 (.2%); tot. pop., 480,000. (AD)

Consists of main islands of Grande Comore, Anjouan and Moheli in Indian Ocean off southeast coast of Africa; capital, Moroni, Grande Comore Island. Former French territory; independent (July 6, 1975). The majority of the population is Moslem. An apostolic administration was established in 1975.

Congo*

Archd., 1; dioc. (1988), 5; abp., 1 (native); bp., 5 (native); parishes, 114; priests, 148 (60 dioc., 88 rel.); sem., 131; bros., 47; srs., 251; bap., 8,048; Caths., 857,000 (47.8%); tot. pop., 1,790,000.

People's republic (independent since 1960) in west central Africa; former French possession; capital, Brazzaville. Small-scale missionary work with little effect preceded modern evangelization dating from the 1880s. The work of the Church has been affected by political instability, Communist influence, tribalism and hostility to foreigners. The hierarchy was established in 1955.

Cook Islands

Dioc., 1; bp., 1; parishes, 14; priests, 10 (2 dioc., 8 rel.); sem., 5; bros., 4; srs., 7; bap., 97; Caths., 3,000; tot. pop., 17,000.

Self-governing territory of New Zealand, an archipelago of small islands in Oceania. Evangelization by Protestant missionaries started in 1821, resulting in a predominantly Protestant population. The first Catholic missionary work began in 1894. The hierarchy was established in 1966.

Costa Rica*

Archd., 1; dioc., 3; v.a., 1; abp., 1; bp., 5; parishes, 198; priests, 479 (292 dioc., 187 rel.); sem., 368; bros., 47; srs., 886; bap., 73,880; Caths., 2,365,000 (88.5%); tot. pop., 2,670,000.

Republic in Central America; capital, San Jose. Evangelization began about 1520 and proceeded by degrees to real development and organization of the Church in the 17th and 18th centuries. The republic became independent in 1838. Twelve years later church jurisdiction also became independent with the establishment of a bishopric in the present capital.

Cuba*

Archd., 2; dioc., 5; abp., 2; bp., 6; parishes, 231; priests, 208 (118 dioc., 90 rel.); sem., 29; bros., 21; srs., 251; bap., 32,162; Caths. 4,227,000 (41.2%); tot. pop., 10,250,000.

Republic under Communist dictatorship, south of Florida; capital, Havana. Effective evangelization began about 1514, leading eventually to the predominance of Catholicism on the island. Native vocations to the priesthood and religious life were unusually numerous in the 18th century but declined in the 19th. The island became independent of Spain in 1902 following the Spanish-American War. Fidel Castro took control of the government Jan. 1, 1959. In 1961, after Cuba was officially declared a socialist state, the University of Villanueva was closed, 350 Catholic schools were nationalized and 136 priests expelled. A greater number of foreign priests and religious had already left the country. Freedom of worship and religious instruction are limited to church premises and no social action is permitted the Church, which survives under surveillance. A new constitution approved in 1976 guaranteed freedom of conscience but restricted its exercise.

Cyprus*

Archd., 1 (Maronite); abp., 1 (resides in Lebanon); parishes, 10; priests, 21 (6 dioc., 15 rel.); bros., 3; srs., 99; bap., 100; Caths., 8,000 (1.2%); tot. pop., 670,000.

Republic in the eastern Mediterranean; capital, Nicosia. Christianity was preached on the island in apostolic times and has a continuous history from the fourth century. Latin and Eastern rites were established but the latter prevailed and became Orthodox after the schism of 1054. Roman and Orthodox Christians have suffered under many governments, particularly during the period of Turkish dominion from late in the 16th to late in the 19th centuries, and from differences between the 80 per cent Greek majority and the Turkish minority. About 80 per cent of the population are Orthodox. Maronite-Rite Catholics are under the jurisdiction of the archdiocese of Cyprus (of the Maronites), whose archbishop resides in Lebanon. Roman-Rite Catholics are under the jurisdiction of the Roman-Rite patriarchate of Jerusalem.

Czechoslovakia

Archd., 3; dioc., 10; card., 2 (1 heads archiepiscopal see, 1 is curia official); bp. (1988), 9 (2 head sees; 3 are apostolic administrators; 2 are auxiliaries; 2 are impeded); parishes, 4,418; priests, 3,558 (3,099 dioc., 459 rel.); sem., 506; bros., 37; srs., 6,154; bap., 96,140; Caths., 10,709,000 (68.9%); tot. pop., 15,530,000.

Federal socialist republic (since 1969) in Central Europe, consisting of the Czech Socialist Republic, capital Prague; and the Slovak Socialist Republic, capital Bratislava. The republics have local autonomy but are subordinate to the Federal Assembly at Prague made up of representatives from both regions. The Czech and Slovak regions of the country have separate religious and cultural backgrounds. Christianity was introduced in Slovakia in the 8th century by Irish and German missionaries and the area was under the jurisdiction of German bishops. In 863, at the invitation of the Slovak ruler Rastislav who wanted to preserve the cultural and liturgical heritage of the people, Sts. Cyril and Methodius began pastoral and missionary work in the region, ministering to the people in their own language. The saints introduced Old Slovak (Old Church Slavonic) into the liturgy and did so much to evangelize the territory that they are venerated as the apostles of Slovakia. A diocese established at Nitra in 880 had a continuous history except for a century ending in 1024. The Church in Slovakia was severely tested by the Reformation and political upheavals. After World War I, when it became part of the Republic of Czechoslovakia, it was 75 per cent Catholic. In the Czech lands, the martyrdom of Prince Wenceslaus in 929 triggered the spread of Christianity. Prague has had a continuous history as a diocese since 973. A parish system was organized about the 13th century in Bohemia and Moravia, the land of the Czechs. Mendicant orders strengthened relations with the Latin Rite in the 13th century. In the next century the teachings of John Hus in Bohemia brought trouble to the Church in the forms of schism and heresy, and initiated a series of religious wars which continued for decades following his death at the stake in 1415. Church property was confiscated, monastic communities were scattered and even murdered, ecclesiastical organization was shattered, and so many of the faithful joined the Bohemian Brethren that Catholics became a minority. The Reformation, with the way prepared by the Hussites and cleared by other factors, affected the Church seriously. A Counter Reformation got under way in the 1560s and led to a gradual restoration through the thickets of Josephinism, the Enlightenment, liberalism and troubled politics. In 1920, two years after the establishment of the Republic of Czechoslovakia, the schismatic Czechoslovak Church was proclaimed at Prague, resulting in numerous defections from the Catholic Church in the Czech region. In Ruthenia, 112,000 became Russian Orthodox between 1918 and 1930. Vigorous persecution of the church began in Slovakia before the end of World War II when Communists mounted a 1944 offensive against bishops, priests and religious. In 1945, church schools were nationalized, youth organizations were disbanded, the Catholic press was curtailed, the training of students for the priesthood was seriously impeded. Msgr. Josef Tiso, president of the Slovak Republic, was tried for "treason" in December, 1947, and was executed the following April. Between 1945 and 1949 approximately 10 per cent of the Slovak population spent some time in jail or a concentration camp. Persecution began later in the Czech part of the country, following the accession of the Gottwald regime to power early in 1948. Hospitals, schools and property were nationalized and Catholic organizations were liquidated. A puppet organization was formed in 1949 to infiltrate the Church and implement an unsuccessful plan for establishing a schismatic church. In the same year Archbishop Josef Beran of Prague was placed under house arrest. (He left the country in 1965, was made a cardinal, and died in 1969 in Rome.) A number of theatrical trials of bishops and priests were staged in 1950. All houses of religious were taken over between March, 1950, and the end of 1951. Pressure was applied on the clergy and faithful of the Eastern Rite in Slovakia to join the Orthodox Church. Diplomatic relations with Vatican City were terminated in 1950. About 3,000 priests were deprived of liberty in 1951 and attempts were made to force "peace priests" on the people. In 1958 it was reported that 450 to 500 priests were in jail; an undisclosed number of religious and Byzantine-Rite priests had been deported; two bishops released from prison in 1956 were under house arrest; one bishop was imprisoned at Leopoldov and two at the Mirov reformatory. In Bohemia, Moravia and Silesia, five of six dioceses were without ruling bishops; one archbishop and two bishops were active but subject to "supervision"; most of the clergy refused to join the "peace priests." In 1962 only three bishops were permitted to attend the first session of the Second Vatican Council. From January to October, 1968, Church-state relations improved to some extent under the Dubcek regime: a number of bishops were reinstated; some 3,000 priests were engaged in the pastoral ministry, although 1,500 were still barred from priestly work; the "peace priests" organization was disbanded; the Eastern-Rite Church, with 147 parishes, was reestablished. In 1969, an end was ordered to rehabilitation trials for priests and religious, but no wholesale restoration of priests and religious to their proper ways of life and work was in prospect. In 1972, the government ordered the removal of nuns from visible but limited apostolates to farms and mental hospitals where they would be out of sight. In 1973, the government allowed the ordination of four bishops — one in the Czech region and three in the Slovak region. Reports from Slovakia late in the same year stated that authorities there had placed severe restrictions on the education of seminarians and the functioning of priests. Government restrictions continued to hamper the work of priests and nuns in recent years. Signatories of the human rights declaration called Charter 77 have been particular objects of government repression and retribution. In December, 1983, the Czechoslovakian foreign minister met with the Pope at Vatican City — the first meeting of a high Czech official with a pope since the country came under communist rule. In 1984, two Vatican officials visited Czechoslovakia. Despite the communication breakthrough, there was no indication of any change of policy toward the Church in the country. In 1988, three new bishops were ordained in Czechoslovakia — the first since 1973.

Denmark*

Dioc., 1; bp., 1; parishes, 50; priests, 107 (40 dioc., 67 rel.); p.d., 1; sem., 3; bros., 3; srs., 375; bap., 354; Caths., 26,000 (.5%); tot. pop., 5,120,000.

Includes the Faroe Islands and Greenland. Constitutional monarchy in northwestern Europe, north of West Germany; capital, Copenhagen. Christianity was introduced in the ninth century and the first diocese for the area was established in 831. Intensive evangelization and full-scale organization of the Church occurred from the second half of the 10th century and ushered in a period of great development and influence in the 12th and 13th centuries. Decline followed, resulting in almost total loss to the Church during the Reformation when Lutheranism became the national religion. Catholics were considered foreigners until religious freedom was legally assured in 1849. Modern development of the Church dates from the second half of the 19th century. About 95 per cent of the population are Evangelical Lutherans.

Djibouti

Dioc., 1; parishes, 7; priests, 6 (rel.); bros., 7; srs., 26; bap., 19; Caths., 9,000; tot. pop., 460,000. (AD)

Formerly French Territory of Afars and Issas. Independent (1977) republic in east Africa, on the Gulf of Aden; capital, Djibouti. Christianity in the area, formerly part of Ethiopia, antedated but was overcome by the Arab invasion of 1200. Modern evangelization, begun in the latter part of the 19th century, had meager results. The hierarchy was established in 1955.

Dominica*

Dioc., 1; bp., 1; parishes, 14; priests, 32 (6 dioc., 26 rel.); sem., 2; bros., 5; srs., 35; bap., 1,111; Caths., 57,000 (77%); tot. pop., 74,000.

Independent (Nov. 3, 1978) state in Caribbean; capital, Roseau. Evangelization began in 1642.

Dominican Republic*

Archd., 1; dioc., 8; card., 1; abp., 1; bp., 9; parishes, 250; priests, 539 (156 dioc., 383 rel.); p.d., 80; sem., 380; bros., 70; srs., 1,414; bap., 103,997; Caths., 5,902,000 (91.9%); tot. pop., 6,420,000.

Caribbean republic on the eastern two-thirds of the island of Hispaniola, bordering on Haiti; capital, Santo Domingo. Evangelization began shortly after discovery by Columbus in 1492 and church organization, the first in America, was established by 1510. Catholicism is the state religion.

Ecuador*

Archd., 3; dioc., 10; prel., 2; v.a., 7; p.a., 1; mil. ord., card., 1; abp., 3; bp., 27; parishes, 932; priests, 1,564 (675 dioc., 889 rel.); p.d., 16; sem., 427; bros., 361; srs., 4,011; bap., 208,699; Caths., 9,027,000 (93.5%); tot. pop., 9,650,000.

Republic on the west coast of South America, includes Gallapogos Islands; capital, Quito. Evangelization began in the 1530s. The first diocese was established in 1545. A synod, one of the first in the Americas, was held in 1570 or 1594. Multiphased missionary work, spreading from the coastal and mountain regions into the Amazon, made the Church highly influential during the colonial period. The Church was practically enslaved by the constitution enacted in 1824, two years after Ecuador, as part of Colombia, gained independence from Spain. Some change for the better took place later in the century, but from 1891 until the 1930s the Church labored under serious liabilities imposed by liberal governments. The concordat of 1866 was violated; foreign missionaries were barred from the country for some time; the property of religious orders was confiscated; education was taken over by the state; traditional state support was refused; legal standing was denied; attempts to control church offices were made through insistence on rights of patronage. A period of harmony and independence for the Church began after agreement was reached on Church-state relations in 1937.

Egypt*

Patriarchate, 2 (Alexandria for the Copts and for the Melkites); dioc., 9; v.a. (1988), 1; patriarch, 1; abp., 1; bp., 11; parishes, 200; priests, 373 (178 dioc., 195 rel.); sem., 111; bros., 60; srs., 1,543; bap., 3,254; Caths., 174,000 (.35%); tot. pop., 49,610,000.

Arab Republic in northeastern Africa, bordering on the Mediterranean; capital, Cairo. Alexandria was the influential hub of a Christian community established by the end of the second century; it became a patriarchate and the center of the Coptic Church, and had great influence on the spread of Christianity in various parts of Africa. Monasticism developed from desert communities of hermits in the third and fourth centuries. Arianism was first preached in Egypt in the 320s. In the fifth century, the Coptic church went Monophysite through failure to accept doctrine formulated by the Council of Chalcedon in 451 with respect to the two natures of Christ. The country was thoroughly Arabized after 640 and was under the rule of Ottoman Turks from 1517 to 1798. English influence was strong during the 19th century. A monarchy established in 1922 lasted about 30 years, ending with the proclamation of a republic in 1953-54. By that time Egypt had become the leader of pan-Arabism against Israel. It waged two unsuccessful wars against Israel in 1948-49 and 1967. Between 1958 and 1961 it was allied with Syria and Yemen, in the United Arab Republic. In 1979, following negotiations initiated by Pres. Anwar el-Sadat in

1977, Egypt and Israel signed a peace agreement. Islam, the religion of some 90 percent of the population, is the state religion.

El Salvador*

Archd., 1; dioc. (1988), 7; mil. ord.; abp., 1; bp., 10; parishes, 241; priests, 378 (192 dioc., 186 rel.); sem., 214; bros., 104; srs., 1,011; bap., 97,001; Caths., 4,547,000 (92.6%); tot. pop., 4,910,000.

Republic in Central America; capital, San Salvador. Evangelization affecting the whole territory followed Spanish occupation in the 1520s. The country was administered by the captaincy general of Guatemala until 1821 when independence from Spain was declared and it was annexed to Mexico. El Salvador joined the Central American Federation in 1825, decreed its own independence in 1841 and became a republic formally in 1856. In recent years, Church efforts to achieve social justice have resulted in persecution of the Church. Archbishop Oscar Romero of San Salvador, peace advocate and outspoken champion of human rights, was murdered Mar. 24, 1980, while celebrating Mass. (See Index for recent events.)

England*

Archd., 4; dioc., 15; ap. ex., 1; mil. ord. (Great Britain); card., 1; abp., 3; bp., 33; parishes, 2,560; priests, 5,729 (3,793 dioc., 1,936 rel.); p.d., 138; sem., 490; bros., 893; srs., 11,676; bap., 77,545; Caths., 3,895,000 (8.5%); tot. pop., 45,574,000 (1988 Annuario Pontificio).

Center of the United Kingdom of Great Britain (England, Scotland, Wales) and Northern Ireland, off the northwestern coast of Europe; capital, London. The arrival of St. Augustine of Canterbury and a band of monks in 597 marked the beginning of evangelization. Real organization of the Church took place some years after the Synod of Whitby, held in 663. Heavy losses were sustained in the wake of the Danish invasion in the 780s, but recovery starting from the time of Alfred the Great and dating especially from the middle of the 10th century led to Christianization of the whole country and close Church-state relations. The Norman Conquest of 1066 opened the Church in England to European influence. The 13th century was climactic, but decline had already set in by 1300 when the country had an all-time high of 17,000 religious. In the 14th century, John Wycliff presaged the Protestant Reformation. Henry VIII, failing in 1529 to gain annulment of his marriage to Catherine of Aragon, refused to acknowledge papal authority over the Church in England, had himself proclaimed its head, suppressed all houses of religious, and persecuted persons — Sts. Thomas More and John Fisher, among others — for not subscribing to the Oath of Supremacy and Act of Succession. He held the line on other-than-papal doctrine, however, until his death in 1547. Doctrinal aberrations were introduced during the reign of Edward VI (1547-53), through the Order of Communion, two books of Common Prayer, and the Articles of the Established Church. Mary Tudor's attempted Catholic restoration (1553-58) was a disaster, resulting in the deaths of more than 300 Protestants. Elizabeth (1558-1603) firmed up the Established Church with formation of a hierarchy, legal enactments and multi-phased persecution. One hundred and 11 priests and 62 lay persons were among the casualties of persecution during the underground Catholic revival which followed the return to England of missionary priests from France and The Lowlands. Several periods of comparative toleration ensued after Elizabeth's death. The first of several apostolic vicariates was established in 1685; this form of church government was maintained until the restoration of the hierarchy and diocesan organization in 1850. The revolution of 1688 and subsequent developments to about 1781 subjected Catholics to a wide variety of penal laws and disabilities in religious, civic and social life. The situation began to improve in 1791, and from 1801 Parliament frequently considered proposals for the repeal of penal laws against Catholics. The Act of Emancipation restored citizenship rights to Catholics in 1829. Restrictions remained in force for some time afterwards, however, on public religious worship and activity. The hierarchy was restored in 1850. Since then the Catholic Church, existing side by side with the Established Churches of England and Scotland, has followed a general pattern of growth and development.

Equatorial Guinea*

Archd., 1; dioc., 2; abp., 1 (native); bp., 2 (native); parishes, 43; priests, 71 (29 dioc., 42 rel.); p.d. 1; sem., 24; bros., 25; srs., 163; bap., 10,868; Caths., 317,000 (79.2%); tot. pop., 400,000.

Republic on the west coast of Africa, consisting of Rio Muni on the mainland and the islands of Fernando Po and Annobon in the Gulf of Guinea: capital, Malabo (Santa Isabel). Evangelization began in 1841. The country became independent of Spain in 1968. The Church was severely repressed during the 11-year rule of Pres. Macias (Masie) Nguema. Developments since his overthrow (August 1979) indicated some measure of improvement. An ecclesiastical province was established in October, 1982.

Estonia

Baltic republic forcibly absorbed by the U.S.S.R. in 1941; capital Tallinn. Catholicism was introduced in the 11th and 12th centuries. Jurisdiction over the area was made directly subject to the Holy See in 1215. Lutheran penetration was general in the Reformation period and Russian Orthodox influence was strong from early in the 18th century until 1917 when independence was attained. The first of several apostolic administrators was appointed in 1924. The small Catholic community was hard hit during and since Russian occupation in 1941. The Russian take-over of Estonia has not been recognized by the Holy See or the United States.

Ethiopia*

Archd., 1; dioc., 2; v.a., 5; p.a., 1; card., 1;

abp., 1; bp., 8; parishes, 254; priests, 484 (168 dioc., 316 rel.); p.d., 4; sem., 167; bros., 79; srs., 850; bap., 16,271; Caths., 276,000 (.6%); tot. pop., 44,930,000.

People's republic (Marxist) in northeast Africa; capital, Addis Ababa. The country was evangelized by missionaries from Egypt in the fourth century and had a bishop by about 340. Following the lead of its parent body, the Egyptian (Coptic) Church, the Church in the area succumbed to the Monophysite heresy in the sixth century. Catholic influence was negligible for centuries. An ordinariate for the Ethiopian Rite was established in Eritrea in 1930. An apostolic delegation was set up in Addis Ababa in 1937 and several jurisdictions were organized, some under the Congregation for the Oriental Churches and others under the Congregation for the Evangelization of Peoples. Most of the Catholics in the country are in the former Italian colony of Eritrea. The first Ethiopian cardinal (Abp. Paulos Tzadua of Addis Ababa) was named in 1985.

Falkland Islands

P.a., 1; parish, 1; priests, 2 (rel.); bap., 2; Caths., 200; tot. pop., 2,000.

British colony off the southern tip of South America; capital, Port Stanley. The islands are called Islas Malvinas by Argentina which also claims sovereignty.

Faroe Islands

Parish, 1; priest, 1 (rel.); srs., 11; Caths., 100; tot. pop., 46,000.

Self-governing island group in North Atlantic; Danish possession. Under ecclesiastical jurisdiction of Copenhagen diocese.

Fiji*

Archd., 1; abp., 1 (native); parishes, 33; priests, 89 (15 dioc., 74 rel.); sem., 68; bros., 43; srs., 165; bap., 2,382; Caths., 59,000 (8.3%); tot. pop., 706,000.

Independent island group (100 inhabited) in the southwest Pacific; capital, Suva. Marist missionaries began work in 1844 after Methodism had been firmly established. A prefecture apostolic was organized in 1863. The hierarchy was established in 1966.

Finland*

Dioc., 1; bp., 1; parishes, 5; priests, 17 (2 dioc., 15 rel.); p.d., 1; bros., 3; srs., 32; bap., 58; Caths., 4,000 (.08%); tot. pop., 4,920,000.

Republic in northern Europe; capital, Helsinki. Swedes evangelized the country in the 12th century. The Reformation swept the country, resulting in the prohibition of Catholicism in 1595, general reorganization of ecclesiastical life and affairs, and dominance of the Evangelical Lutheran Church. Catholics were given religious liberty in 1781 but missionaries and conversions were forbidden by law. The first Finnish priest since the Reformation was ordained in 1903 in Paris. A vicariate apostolic for Finland was erected in 1920 (made a diocese in 1955). A law on religious liberty, enacted in 1923, banned the foundation of monasteries.

France*

Archd., 18; dioc., 76; prel., 1; ap. ex., 1; ord., 1; mil. ord.; card., 9; abp., 34; bp., 158; parishes, 37,071; priests, 35,101 (27,477 dioc., 7,624 rel.); p.d., 337; sem., 1,600; bros., 4,917; srs., 72,707; bap., 487,520; Caths., 46,867,000 (84.6%); tot. pop., 55,390,000.

Republic in western Europe; capital, Paris. Christianity was known around Lyons by the middle of the second century. By 250 there were 30 bishoprics. The hierarchy reached a fair degree of organization by the end of the fourth century. Vandals and Franks subsequently invaded the territory and caused barbarian turmoil and doctrinal problems because of their Arianism. The Frankish nation was converted following the baptism of Clovis about 496. Christianization was complete by some time in the seventh century. From then on the Church, its leaders and people, figured in virtually every important development — religious, cultural, political and social — through the periods of the Carolingians, feudalism, the Middle Ages and monarchies to the end of the 18th century. The great University of Paris became one of the intellectual centers of the 13th century. Churchmen and secular rulers were involved with developments surrounding the Avignon residence of the popes and curia from 1309 until near the end of the 14th century and with the disastrous Western Schism that followed. Strong currents of Gallicanism and conciliarism ran through ecclesiastical and secular circles in France; the former was an ideology and movement to restrict papal control of the Church in the country, the latter sought to make the pope subservient to a general council. Calvinism invaded the country about the middle of the 16th century and won a strong body of converts. Jansenism with its rigorous spirit and other aberrations appeared in the next century, to be followed by the highly influential Enlightenment. The Revolution which started in 1789 and was succeeded by the Napoleonic period completely changed the status of the Church, taking a toll of numbers by persecution and defection and disenfranchising the Church in practically every way. Throughout the 19th century the Church was caught up in the whirl of imperial and republican developments and made the victim of official hostility, popular indifference and liberal opposition. In this century, the Church has struggled with problems involving the heritage of the Revolution and its aftermath, the alienation of intellectuals, liberalism, the estrangement of the working classes because of the Church's former identification with the ruling class, and the massive needs of contemporary society.

French Guiana

Dioc., 1; bp., 1; parishes, 23; priests, 25 (5 dioc., 20 rel.); bros., 3; srs., 103; bap., 1,682; Caths., 65,000; tot. pop., 87,000. (AD)

French overseas department on the northeast coast of South America; capital, Cayenne. Catholicism was introduced in the 17th century. The

French Polynesia

Archd., 1; *dioc.*, 1; *abp.*, 1 *(native)*; *bp.*, 1; *parishes*, 76; *priests*, 33 (10 *dioc.*, 23 *rel.*); *p.d.*, 10; *sem.*, 5; *bros.*, 36; *srs.*, 61; *bap.*, 1,545; *Caths.*, 61,000; *tot. pop.*, 177,000. (AD)

French overseas territory in the southern Pacific, including Tahiti and the Marquesas Islands; capital, Papeete. The first phase of evangelization in the Marquesas Islands, begun in 1838, resulted in 216 baptisms in 10 years. A vicariate was organized in 1848 but real progress was not made until after the baptism of native rulers in 1853. Persecution caused missionaries to leave the islands several times. By the 1960s, more than 95 per cent of the population was Catholic. Isolated attempts to evangelize Tahiti were made in the 17th and 18th centuries. Two Picpus Fathers began missionary work in 1831. A vicariate was organized in 1848. By 1908, despite the hindrances of Protestant opposition, disease and other factors, the Church had firm roots.

Gabon*

Archd., 1; *dioc.*, 3; *abp.*, 1 *(native)*; *bp.*, 3 *(native)*; *parishes*, 63; *priests*, 107 (32 *dioc.*, 75 *rel.*); *sem.*, 8; *bros.*, 31; *srs.*, 159; *bap.*, 9,472; *Caths.*, 615,000 (52.5%); *tot. pop.*, 1,170,000.

Republic on the west coast of central Africa; capital, Libreville. Sporadic missionary effort took place before 1881 when effective evangelization began. The hierarchy was established in 1955.

The Gambia*

Dioc., 1; *bp.*, 1; *parishes*, 14; *priests*, 21 (4 *dioc.*, 17 *rel.*); *sem.* 4; *bros.*, 4; *srs.*, 40; *bap.*, 745; *Caths.*, 14,000 (2%); *tot. pop.*, 660,000.

Republic (1970) on the northwestern coast of Africa, smallest state in Africa; capital, Banjui. The country was under the jurisdiction of a vicariate apostolic until 1931. The hierarchy was established in 1957.

Germany

West Germany*: *Archd.*, 5; *dioc.*, 16 *(also part of the Berlin diocese)*; *ap., ex.*, 1; *mil. ord.*; *card.*, 4; *abp.*, 3; *bp.*, 60; *parishes*, 11,944; *priests*, 21,782 (16,407 *dioc.*, 5,385 *rel.*); *p.d.*, 1,174; *sem.*, 3,407; *bros.*, 2,541; *srs.*, 54,046; *bap.*, 262,039; *Caths.*, 28,324,000 (46.3%); *tot. pop.*, 61,050,000.

East Germany: *Dioc.*, 2 *(Dresden-Meissen and Berlin, since most of its territory lies in East Germany)*; *a.a.*, 1 *(Gorlitz; there are also 3 territories with apostolic administrators)*; *card.*, 1 *(Joachim Meisner, bishop of Berlin)*; *bps.*, 9; *parishes*, 888; *priests*, 1,371 (1,148 *dioc.*, 223 *rel.*); *p.d.*, 58; *sem.*, 164; *bros.*, 61; *srs.*, 2,622; *bap.*, 8,939; *Caths.*, 1,291,000 (7.7%); *tot. pop.*, 16,620,000.

Country in northern Europe partitioned in 1949 into the Communist German Democratic Republic in the East (capital, East Berlin) and the German Federal Republic in the West (capital, Bonn). Christianity was introduced in the third century, if not earlier. Trier, which became a center for missionary activity, had a bishop by 400. Visigoth invaders introduced Arianism in the fifth century but were converted in the seventh century by the East Franks, Celtic and other missionaries. St. Boniface, the apostle of Germany, established real ecclesiastical organization in the eighth century. The Church had great influence during the Carolingian period. Bishops from that time onward began to act in dual roles as pastors and rulers, a state of affairs which led inevitably to confusion and conflict in Church-state relations and perplexing problems of investiture. The Church developed strength and vitality through the Middle Ages but succumbed to abuses which antedated and prepared the ground for the Reformation. Luther's actions from 1517 made Germany a confessional battleground. Religious strife continued until conclusion of the Peace of Westphalia at the end of the Thirty Years' War in 1648. Nearly a century earlier the Peace of Augsburg (1555) had been designed, without success, to assure a degree of tranquillity by recognizing the legitimacy of different religious confessions in different states, depending on the decisions of princes. The implicit principle that princes should control the churches emerged in practice into the absolutism and Josephinism of subsequent years. St. Peter Canisius and his fellow Jesuits spearheaded a Counter Reformation in the second half of the 16th century. Before the end of the century, however, 70 per cent of the population of north and central Germany were Lutheran. Calvinism also had established a strong presence. The Church gained internal strength in a defensive position. Through much of the 19th century, however, its influence was eclipsed by Protestant intellectuals and other influences. It suffered some impoverishment also as a result of shifting boundaries and the secularization of property shortly after 1800. It came under direct attack in the Kulturkampf of the 1870s but helped to generate the opposition which resulted in a dampening of the campaign of Bismarck against it. Despite action by Catholics on the social front and other developments, discrimination against the Church spilled over into the 20th century and lasted beyond World War I. Catholics in politics struggled with others to pull the country through numerous postwar crises. The dissolution of the Center Party, agreed to by the bishops in 1933 without awareness of the ultimate consequences, contributed negatively to the rise of Hitler to supreme power. Church officials protested the Nazi anti-Church and anti-Semitic actions, but to no avail. After World War II Christian leadership had much to do with the recovery of Western Germany. East Germany, gone Communist under Russian auspices, initiated a program of control and repression of the Church in 1948 and 1949. With no prospect of success for measures designed to split bishops, priests, religious and lay persons, the regime has concentrated most of its attention on mind control, especially of the younger generation, by the elimination of religious schools, curtailment of freedom for religious instruction and formation, severe restriction of the religious press, and the substitution since the mid-50s of youth initiation and Communist ceremonies for the rites of baptism, confirmation, marriage, and funerals. Bishops are generally forbidden to travel outside the Republic. The number of priests is decreasing, partly because of reduced seminary enrollments ordered by the government since 1958. In 1973, the Vatican appointed three apostolic administrators and one auxiliary (all titular bishops) for the areas of three West German dioceses located in East Germany.

Ghana*

Archd., 2; dioc., 7; abp., 2 (native); bp., 7 (native); parishes, 183; priests, 550 (328 dioc., 222 rel.); sem., 335; bros., 139; srs., 558; bap., 48,633; Caths., 1,736,000 (12.3%); tot. pop., 14,040,000.

Republic on the western coast of Africa, bordering on the Gulf of Guinea; capital, Accra. Priests visited the country in 1482, 11 years after discovery by the Portuguese, but missionary effort — hindered by the slave trade and other factors — was slight until 1880 when systematic evangelization began. A prefecture apostolic was set up in 1879. The hierarchy was established in 1950.

Gibraltar

Dioc., 1; bp., 1; parishes, 5; priests, 10 (9 dioc., 1 rel.); sem., 2; srs., 18; bap., 310; Caths., 20,000; tot. pop., 28,000.

British dependency on the tip of the Spanish Peninsula on the Mediterranean. Evangelization took place after the Moors were driven out near the end of the 15th century. The Church was hindered by the British who acquired the colony in 1713. Most of the Catholics were, and are, Spanish and Italian immigrants and their descendants. A vicariate apostolic was organized in 1817. The diocese was erected in 1910.

Greece*

Archd., 4; dioc., 4; v.a., 1; ap. ex., 1; ord., 1; abp., 3; bp., 2; parishes, 79; priests, 97 (53 dioc., 44 rel.); p.d., 1; sem., 2; bros., 40; srs., 152; bap., 359; Caths., 51,000 (.5%); tot. pop., 9,970,000.

Republic in southeastern Europe on the Balkan Peninsula; capital, Athens. St. Paul preached the Gospel at Athens and Corinth on his second missionary journey and visited the country again on his third tour. Other Apostles may have passed through also. Two bishops from Greece attended the First Council of Nicaea. After the division of the Roman Empire, the Church remained Eastern in rite and later broke ties with Rome as a result of the schism of 1054. A Latin-Rite jurisdiction was set up during the period of the Latin Empire of Constantinople, 1204-1261, but crumbled afterwards. Unity efforts of the Council of Florence had poor results. The country now has Greek Catholic and Latin jurisdictions. The Greek Orthodox Church is predominant.

Greenland (Kalaallit Nunaat)

Priest, 1 (rel.); srs., 2; Caths., 100; tot. pop., 54,000.

Danish island province northeast of North America; granted self rule in 1979; capital, Nuuk (Godthaab). Catholicism was introduced about 1000. The first diocese was established in 1124 and a line of bishops dated from then until 1537. The first known churches in the western hemisphere, dating from about the 11th century, were on Greenland; the remains of 19 have been unearthed. The departure of Scandinavians and spread of the Reformation reduced the Church to nothing. The Moravian Brethren evangelized the Eskimos from the 1720s to 1901. By 1930 the Danish Church — Evangelical Lutheran — was in full possession. Since 1930 priests have been in Greenland, which is part of the Copenhagen diocese.

Grenada*

Dioc., 1; bp., 1; parishes, 20; priests, 21 (7 dioc., 14 rel.); p.d., 4; sem., 2; bros., 5; srs., 28; bap., 1,467; Caths., 75,000; tot. pop., 110,000.

Independent island state in the West Indies; capital, St. George's.

Guadeloupe

Dioc., 1; bp., 1; parishes, 43; priests, 72 (42 dioc., 30 rel.); sem., 14; bros., 6; srs., 203; bap., 5,291; Caths., 302,000; tot. pop., 333,000 (AD).

French overseas department in the Leeward Islands of the West Indies; capital, Basse-Terre. Catholicism was introduced in the islands in the 16th century.

Guam

Archd., 1; archbp., 1 (native); parishes, 24; priests, 43 (13 dioc., 30 rel.); p.d., 7; sem., 8; bros., 10; srs., 142; bap., 2,153; Caths., 141,000; tot. pop., 155,000.

Outlying area of U.S. in the southwest Pacific; capital, Agana. The first Mass was offered in the Mariana Islands in 1521. The islands were evangelized by the Jesuits, from 1668, and other missionaries. The first native Micronesian bishop was ordained in 1970. The Agana diocese, which had been a suffragan of San Francisco, was made a metropolitan see in 1984.

Guatemala*

Archd., 1; dioc., 8; prel., 2; v.a. (1988), 2; abp., 1; bp., 14; parishes, 347; priests, 670 (227 dioc., 443 rel.); p.d., 3; sem., 460; bros., 189; srs., 1,290; bap., 234,709; Caths. 7,081,000 (86.4%); tot. pop. 8,190,000.

Republic in Central America; capital, Guatemala City. Evangelization dates from the beginning of Spanish occupation in 1524. The first diocese, for all Central American territories administered by the captaincy general of Guatemala, was established in 1534. The country became independent in 1839, following annexation to Mexico in 1821, secession in 1823 and membership in the Central American Federation from 1825. In 1870, a government installed by a liberal revolution repudiated the concordat of 1853 and took active measures against the Church. Separation of Church and state was decreed; religious orders were suppressed and their property seized; priests and religious were exiled; schools were secularized. Full freedom was subsequently granted. The country has been in a virtual state of civil war in recent years, with violence and repression directed at all segments of the population, including the Church which has been subjected to persecution. From 1980 to 1985 an estimated 60,000 people were reported killed or missing. The inauguration in January, 1986, of Vinicio Cerezo as president of the country's first civilian government in 20 years was greeted with the hope that he would promote a more just society.

Guinea*

Archd., 1; dioc., 1; p.a., 1; abp., 1 (native); bp., 1 (native); parishes, 28; priests, 25 (24 dioc., 1 rel.); sem., 21; bros., 2; srs., 23; bap., 1,381; Caths., 54,000 (.86%); tot. pop., 6,220,000.

Republic on the west coast of Africa; capital, Conakry. Occasional missionary work followed exploration by the Portuguese about the middle of the 15th century; organized effort dates from 1877. The hierarchy was established in 1955. Following independence from France in 1958, Catholic schools were nationalized, youth organizations banned and missionaries restricted. Foreign missionaries were expelled in 1967. Archbishop Tchidimbo of Conakry, sentenced to life imprisonment in 1971 on a charge of conspiring to overthrow the government, was released in August, 1979; he resigned his see. Private schools, suppressed by the government for more than 20 years, were again authorized in 1984.

Guinea-Bissau*

Dioc., 1; bp., 1; parishes, 23; priests, 52 (2 dioc., 50 rel.); p.d., 1; sem., 13; bros., 11; srs., 56; bap., 2,214; Caths., 50,000 (5.4%); tot. pop., 910,000.

Formerly Portuguese Guinea. Independent state on the west coast of Africa; capital, Bissau. Catholicism was introduced in the second half of the 15th century but limited missionary work, hampered by the slave trade, had meager results. Missionary work in this century dates from 1933. A prefecture apostolic was established in 1955 (made a diocese in 1977).

Guyana

Dioc., 1; bp., 1; parishes, 30; priests, 41 (8 dioc., 33 rel.); sem., 2; bro., 1; srs., 40; bap., 1,334; Caths., 94,000 (9.4%); tot. pop., 1,000,000. (AD)

Republic on the northern coast of South America; capital, Georgetown. In 1899 the Catholic Church and other churches were given equal status with the Church of England and the Church of Scotland, which had sole rights up to that time. Most of the Catholics are Portuguese. The Georgetown diocese was established in 1956, 10 years before Guyana became independent of England. The first native bishop was appointed in 1971. Schools were nationalized in 1976. Increased government interference was reported in 1980-81.

Haiti*

Archd. (1988), 2; dioc., 6; abp. (1988), 2; bp., 9; parishes, 207; priests, 453 (258 dioc., 195 rel.); p.d., 2; sem., 219; bros., 253; srs., 895; bap., 99,676; Caths., 4,798,000 (89.5%); tot. pop. 5,360,000.

Caribbean republic on the western third of Hispaniola adjacent to the Dominican Republic; capital, Port-au-Prince. Evangelization followed discovery by Columbus in 1492. Capuchins and Jesuits did most of the missionary work in the 18th century. From 1804, when independence was declared, until 1860, the country was in schism. Relations were regularized by a concordat concluded in 1860, when an archdiocese and four dioceses were established. Factors hindering the development of the Church have been a shortage of native clergy, inadequate religious instruction and the prevalence of voodoo. Political upheavals in the 1960s had serious effects on the Church. In 1984, a new concordat was concluded replacing the one in effect since 1860.

Honduras*

Archd., 1; dioc. (1988), 6; abp., 1; bp., 9; parishes, 120; priests, 258 (75 dioc., 183 rel.); p.d., 3; sem., 105; bros., 23; srs., 364; bap., 77,158; Caths., 4,266,000 (94.5%); tot. pop., 4,510,000.

Republic in Central America; capital, Tegucigalpa. Evangelization preceded establishment of the first diocese in the 16th century. Under Spanish rule and after independence from 1823, the Church held a favored position until 1880 when equal legal status was given to all religions. Harassment of priests and nuns working among peasants and Salvadoran refugees was reported in recent years.

Hong Kong

Dioc., 1; card. (1988), 1; parishes, 53; priests, 341 (74 dioc., 267 rel.); sem., 38; bros., 66; srs., 738; bap., 4,611; Caths., 267,000; tot. pop., 5,530,000.

British crown colony at the mouth of the Canton River, adjacent to the southeast Chinese province of Kwangtung. Most of the territory, leased from China, is scheduled for return in 1997. A prefecture apostolic was established in 1841. Members of the Pontifical Institute for Foreign Missions began work there in 1858. The Hong Kong diocese was erected in 1946.

Hungary

Archd., 3; dioc., 8; abb., 1; ap. ex., 1; card. (1988), 1; abp., 2; bp., 10; parishes, 2,266; priests, 2,985 (2,775 dioc., 210 rel.); p.d., 3; sem., 337; bros., 152; srs., 94; bap., 65,831; Caths., 6,508,000 (61.2%); tot. pop., 10,630,000.

People's republic in east central Europe; capital, Budapest. The early origins of Christianity in the country, whose territory was subject to a great deal of change, is not known. Magyars accepted

Christianity about the end of the 10th century. St. Stephen I (d. 1038) promoted its spread and helped to organize some of its historical dioceses. Bishops early became influential in politics as well as in the Church. For centuries the country served as a buffer for the Christian West against barbarians from the East, notably the Mongols in the 13th century. Religious orders, whose foundations started from the 1130s, provided the most effective missionaries, pastors and teachers. Outstanding for years were the Franciscans and Dominicans; the Jesuits were noted for their work in the Counter-Reformation from the second half of the 16th century onwards. Hussites and Waldensians prepared the way for the Reformation which struck at almost the same time as the Turks. The Reformation made considerable progress after 1526, resulting in the conversion of large numbers to Lutheranism and Calvinism by the end of the century. Most of them or their descendants returned to the Church later, but many Magyars remained staunch Calvinists. Turks repressed the churches, Protestant as well as Catholic, during a reign of 150 years but they managed to survive. Domination of the Church was one of the objectives of government policy during the reigns of Maria Theresa and Joseph II in the second half of the 18th century; their Josephinism affected Church-state relations until the first World War. More than 100,000 Eastern-Rite schismatics were reunited with Rome about the turn of the 18th century. Secularization increased in the second half of the 19th century, which also witnessed the birth of many new Catholic organizations and movements to influence life in the nation and the Church. Catholics were involved in the social chaos and anti-religious atmosphere of the years following World War I, struggling with their compatriots for religious as well as political survival. After World War II Communist strength, which had manifested itself with less intensity earlier in the century, was great long before it forced the legally elected president out of office in 1947 and imposed a Soviet type of constitution on the country in 1949. The campaign against the Church started with the disbanding of Catholic organizations in 1946. In 1948, "Caritas," the Catholic charitable organization, was taken over and all Catholic schools, colleges and institutions were suppressed. Interference in church administration and attempts to split the bishops preceded the arrest of Cardinal Mindszenty on Dec. 26, 1948, and his sentence to life imprisonment in 1949. (He was free for a few days during the unsuccessful uprising of 1956. He then took up residence at the U.S. Embassy in Budapest where he remained until September, 1971, when he was permitted to leave the country. He died in 1975 in Vienna.) In 1950, religious orders and congregations were suppressed and 10,000 religious were interned. At least 30 priests and monks were assassinated, jailed or deported. About 4,000 priests and religious were confined in jail or concentration camps. The government sponsored a national "Progressive Catholic" church and captive organizations for priests and "Catholic Action," which attracted only a small minority. Signs were clear in 1965 and 1966 that a 1964 agreement with the Holy See regarding episcopal appointments had settled nothing. Six bishops were appointed by the Holy See and some other posts were filled, but none of the prelates were free from government surveillance and harassment. Four new bishops were appointed by the Holy See in January and ordained in Budapest in February, 1969; three elderly prelates resigned their sees. Shortly thereafter, peace priests complained that the "too Roman" new bishops would not deal with them. Talks between Vatican and Hungarian representatives during the past several years have resulted in the appointment of diocesan bishops to fill long-vacant sees.

Iceland*

Dioc., 1; bp., 1; parishes, 3; priests, 11 (7 dioc., 4 rel.); sem., 1; srs., 46; bap., 33; Caths., 2,000; tot. pop., 244,000.

Island republic between Norway and Greenland; capital, Reykjavik. Irish hermits were there in the eighth century. Missionaries subsequently evangelized the island and Christianity was officially accepted about 1000. The first bishop was ordained in 1056. The Black Death had dire effects and spiritual decline set in during the 15th century. Lutheranism was introduced from Denmark between 1537 and 1552 and made the official religion. Some Catholic missionary work was done in the 19th century. Religious freedom was granted to the few Catholics in 1874. A vicariate was erected in 1929 (made a diocese in 1968).

India*

Patriarchate, 1 (titular of East Indies); archd., 19; dioc. (1988), 100; p.a., 1; card. (1988), 4; patriarch, 1; abp., 22; bp., 106; parishes, 5,827; priests, 13,205 (7,801 dioc., 5,404 rel.); p.d., 22; sem., 6,709; bros., 2,646; srs., 57,316; bap., 288,558; Caths., 13,162,000 (1.7%); tot. pop. 766,140,000.

Republic on the subcontinent of south central Asia; capital, New Delhi. Long-standing tradition credits the Apostle Thomas with the introduction of Christianity in the Kerala area. Evangelization followed the establishment of Portuguese posts and the conquest of Goa in 1510. Jesuits, Franciscans, Dominicans, Augustinians and members of other religious orders figured in the early missionary history. An archdiocese for Goa, with two suffragan sees, was set up in 1558. Five provincial councils were held between 1567 and 1606. The number of Catholics in 1572 was estimated to be 280,000. This figure rose to 800,000 in 1700 and declined to 500,000 in 1800. Missionaries had some difficulties with the British East India Co. which exercised virtual government control from 1757 to 1858. They also had trouble because of a conflict that developed between policies of the Portuguese government, which pressed its rights of patronage in episcopal and clerical appointments, and the Congregation for the Propagation of the Faith, which sought greater freedom of action in the same appointments. This struggle eventuated in the schism of Goa between 1838 and 1857. In 1886, when the number of Catholics was estimated to be one million, the hierarchy for India and Ceylon was restored. Jesuits contributed greatly to the development of Catholic education from the second half of the 19th century. A large percentage of the Catholic population is located around Goa and Kerala and farther south. The country is predominantly Hindu. So-called anti-conversion laws in effect in several states have had a restrictive effect on pastoral ministry and social service.

Indonesia*

Archd., 7; dioc., 26; mil. ord.; card., 1; abp., 7; bps., 29; parishes, 758; priests, 1,814 (359 dioc., 1,455 rel.); p.d., 11; sem., 1,743; bros., 723; srs., 4,369; bap., 163,553; Caths., 4,253,000 (2.5%); tot. pop., 166,940,000.

Eastern Timor (former Portuguese Timor annexed by Indonesia in 1976): Dioc., 1; parishes, 21; priests, 52 (23 dioc., 29 rel.); sem., 13; bros., 8; srs., 60; bap., 26,077; Caths., 535,000; tot. pop., 680,000.

Republic southeast of Asia, consisting of some 3,000 islands including Kalimantan (most of Borneo), Sulawesi (Celebes), Java, the Lesser Sundas, Moluccas, Sumatra, Timor and West Irian (Irian Jaya, western part of New Guinea); capital, Jakarta. Evangelization by the Portuguese began about 1511. St. Francis Xavier, greatest of the modern missionaries, spent some 14 months in the area. Christianity was strongly rooted in some parts of the islands by 1600. Islam's rise to dominance began at this time. The Dutch East Indies Co., which gained effective control in the 17th century, banned evangelization by Catholic missionaries for some time but Dutch secular and religious priests managed to resume the work. A vicariate of Batavia for all the Dutch East Indies was set up in 1841. About 90 per cent of the population is Moslem. The hierarchy was established in 1961.

Iran*

Archd., 4; dioc., 2; abp., 3; bp., 1; parishes, 29; priests, 24 (6 dioc., 18 rel.); p.d., 11; sem., 2; srs., 42, bap., 244; Caths., 14,000 (.03%); tot. pop., 45,910,000.

Islamic republic (Persia until 1935) in southwestern Asia, between the Caspian Sea and the Persian Gulf; capital, Teheran. Some of the earliest Christian communities were established in this area outside the (then) Roman Empire. They suffered persecution in the fourth century and were then cut off from the outside world. Nestorianism was generally professed in the late fifth century. Islam became dominant after 640. Some later missionary work was attempted but without success. Religious liberty was granted in 1834, but Catholics were the victims of a massacre in 1918. Islam is the religion of perhaps 98 per cent of the population. In 1964 the country had approximately 120,000 Orthodox Oriental Christians (not in union with Rome). Catholics belong to the Latin, Armenian and Chaldean rites.

Iraq*

Patriarchate, 1; archd., 9; dioc., 5; patriarch, 1; abp., 13; bp., 3; parishes, 109; priests, 138 (108 dioc., 30 rel.); p.d., 3; sem., 52; bros., 23; srs., 393; bap., 5,694; Caths., 402,000 (2.4%); tot. pop., 16,450,000.

Republic in southwestern Asia, between Iran and Saudi Arabia; capital, Baghdad. Some of the earliest Christian communities were established in the area, whose history resembles that of Iran. Catholics belong to the Armenian, Chaldean, Latin and Syrian rites; Chaldeans are most numerous. Islam is the religion of some 90 per cent of the population.

Ireland*

Archd., 4; dioc., 22; card., 1; abp., 3; bp., 33; parishes, 1,342; priests, 5,941 (3,732 dioc., 2,209 rel.); p.d., 2; sem., 1,020; bap., 73,796 (preceding figures include Northern Ireland); Caths., (approx.), 3,406,560 (94%); tot. pop., 3,624,000.

Republic in the British Isles; capital, Dublin. St. Patrick, who is venerated as the apostle of Ireland, evangelized parts of the island for some years after the middle of the fifth century. Conversion of the island was not accomplished, however, until the seventh century or later. Celtic monks were the principal missionaries. The Church was organized along monastic lines at first, but a movement developed in the 11th century for the establishment of jurisdiction along episcopal lines. By that time many Roman usages had been adopted. The Church gathered strength during the period from the Norman Conquest of England to the reign of Henry VIII despite a wide variety of rivalries, wars, and other disturbances. Henry introduced an age of repression of the faith which continued for many years under several of his successors. The Irish suffered from proscription of the Catholic faith, economic and social disabilities, subjection to absentee landlords and a plantation system designed to keep them from owning property, and actual persecution which took an uncertain toll of lives up until about 1714. Most of those living in the northern part of Ireland became Anglican and Presbyterian in the 1600s but the south remained strong in faith. Some penal laws remained in force until emancipation in 1829. Nearly 100 years later Ireland was divided by two enactments which made Northern Ireland, consisting of six counties, part of the United Kindgom (1920) and gave dominion status to the Irish Free State, made up of the other 26 counties (1922). This state (Eire, in Gaelic) was proclaimed the Republic of Ireland in 1949. The Catholic Church predominates but religious freedom is guaranteed for all.

Northern Ireland

Tot. pop., 1,578,000; Catholics comprise about one third. (Other statistics are included in Ireland).

Part of the United Kingdom, it consists of six of the nine counties of Ulster in the northeast corner of Ireland; capital, Belfast. History is given under Ireland. For recent developments, see Index.

Israel

Patriarchates, 2 (Jerusalem for Latins; patriarchal vicariate for Greek-Melkites); archd., 1; patriarch, 1; abp., 2; bp., 1; parishes, 85; priests, 368 (78 dioc., 290 rel.); p.d., 3; sem., 62; bros., 144; srs., 963; bap., 1,833; Caths., 81,000; tot. pop., 4,300,000. (AD)

Parliamentary democracy in the Middle East, at the eastern end of the Mediterranean; capitals, Jerusalem and Tel Aviv (diplomatic). Israel was the birthplace of Christianity, the site of the first Christian communities. Some persecution was suffered in the early Christian era and again during the several hundred years of Roman control. Moslems conquered the territory in the seventh century and, except for the period of the Kingdom of Jerusalem established by Crusaders, remained in control most of the time up until World War I. The Church survived in the area, sometimes just barely, but it did not prosper greatly or show any notable increase in numbers. The British took over the protectorate of the area after World War I. Partition into Israel for the Jews and Palestine for the Arabs was approved by the United Nations in 1947. War broke out a year later with the proclamation of the Republic of Israel. The Israelis won the war and 50 percent more territory than they had originally been ceded. War broke out again for six days in June, 1967, and in October, 1973, resulting in a Middle East crisis which persists to the present time. Caught in the middle of the conflict are hundreds of thousands of dispossessed Palestinian refugees. Judaism is the faith professed by about 85 percent of the inhabitants; approximately one-third of them are considered observants. Most of the Arab minority are Moslems.

Italy*

Patriarchate, 1; archd. (metropolitans), 38; archd. and dioc., (approx.), 172; prel., 2; abb., 7; mil. ord.; card. (1988), 36; abp., and bp., 406 (216 residential, 32 coadjutors or auxiliaries, remainder in other offices or retired); parishes, 26,234; priests, 60,769 (39,510 dioc., 21,259 rel.); p.d., 608; sem., 6,010; bros., 5,534; srs., 137,431; bap., 529,494; Caths., 56,116,000 (98%); tot. pop., 57,200,000.

Republic in southern Europe; capital, Rome. A Christian community was formed early at Rome, probably by the middle of the first century. St. Peter established his see there. He and St. Paul suffered death for the faith there in the 60s. The early Christians were persecuted at various times there, as in other parts of the empire, but the Church developed in numbers and influence, gradually spreading out from towns and cities in the center and south to rural areas and the north. Organization, in the process of formation in the second century, developed greatly between the fifth and eighth centuries. By the latter date the Church had already come to grips with serious problems, including doctrinal and disciplinary disputes that threatened the unity of faith, barbarian invasions, and the need for the pope and bishops to take over civil responsibilities because of imperial default. The Church has been at the center of life on the peninsula throughout the centuries. It emerged from underground in 313, with the Edict of Milan, and rose to a position of prestige and lasting influence. It educated and converted the barbarians, preserved culture through the early Middle Ages and passed it on to later times, suffered periods of decline and gained strength through recurring reforms, engaged in military combat for political reasons and intellectual combat for the preservation and development of doctrine, saw and patronized the development of the arts, experienced all human strengths and weaknesses in its members, knew triumph and the humiliation of failure. For long centuries, from the fourth to the 19th, the Church was a temporal as well as spiritual power. This temporal aspect complicated its history in Italy. Since the 1870s, however, when the Papal States were annexed by the Kingdom of Italy, the history became simpler — but remained complicated — as the Church, shorn of temporal power, began to find new freedom for the fulfillment of its spiritual mission. In 1985, a new concordat was ratified between the Vatican and Italy, replacing one in effect since 1929.

Ivory Coast (Côte d'Ivoire)*

Archd., 1; dioc. (1988), 10; card., 1 (native); bp., 11 (native); parishes, 176; priests, 398 (155 dioc., 243 rel.); sem., 129; bros., 102; srs., 553; bap., 25,816; Caths., 1,044,000 (10.2%); tot. pop., 10,160,000.

Republic in western Africa; capital, Abidjan. The Holy Ghost Fathers began systematic evangelization in 1895. The first native priests from the area were ordained in 1934. The hierarchy was set up in 1955; the first native cardinal (Bernard Yago) was named in 1983.

Jamaica*

Archd., 1; dioc., 1; abp., 1; bp., 1; parishes, 70; priests, 93 (22 dioc., 71 rel.); p.d., 5; sem., 20; bros., 13; srs., 198; bap., 2,286; Caths., 229,000 (9.6%); tot. pop., 2,370,000.

Republic in the West Indies; capital, Kingston. Franciscans and Dominicans evangelized the island from about 1512 until 1655. Missionary work was interrupted after the English took possession but was resumed by Jesuits about the turn of the 19th century. A vicariate apostolic was organized in 1837. The hierarchy was established in 1967.

Japan*

Archd., 3; dioc., 13; p.a., 1; card., 1; abp., 2; bp., 17; parishes, 821; priests, 1,946 (571 dioc., 1,375 rel.); p.d., 4; sem., 228; bros., 387; srs., 7,006; bap., 10,072; Caths., 435,000 (.35%); tot. pop., 121,490,000.

Archipelago in the northwest Pacific; capital, Tokyo. Jesuits began evangelization in the middle of the 16th century and about 300,000 converts, most of them in Kyushu, were reported at the end of the century. The Nagasaki Martyrs were victims of persecution in 1597. Another persecution took some 4,000 lives between 1614 and 1651. Missionaries, banned for two centuries, returned about the middle of the 19th century and found Christian communities still surviving in Nagasaki and other places in Kyushu. A vicariate was organized in 1866. Religious freedom was guaranteed in 1889. The hierarchy was established in 1891.

Jerusalem

The entire city, site of the first Christian community, has been under Israeli control since the Israeli-Arab war of June, 1967. There are two patriarchates of Jerusalem, Melkite and Latin. (AD)

Jordan

Archd., 1; abp., 1; parishes, 63; priests, 65 (52 dioc., 13 rel.); p.d., 3; sem. 6; bros., 8; srs., 212; bap., 1,189; Caths., 53,000 (1.4%); tot. pop., 3,660,000. (AD)

Constitutional monarchy in the Middle East; capital, Amman. Christianity there dates from apostolic times. Survival of the faith was threatened many times under the rule of Moslems from 636 and Ottoman Turks from 1517 to 1918, and in the Islamic Emirate of Trans-Jordan from 1918 to 1949. Since the creation of Israel, some 500,000 Palestinian refugees, some of them Christians, have been in Jordan. Islam is the state religion but religious freedom is guaranteed for all. The Greek Melkite-Rite Archdiocese of Petra and Philadelphia is located in Jordan. Latin (Roman)-Rite Catholics are under the jurisdiction of the Latin patriarchate of Jerusalem.

Kenya*

Archd., 1; dioc. (1988), 17; mil. ord.; card., 1 (native); bp., 16 (11 native); parishes, 442; priests, 1,041 (404 dioc., 637 rel.); p.d., 4; sem., 835; bros., 273; srs., 2,253; bap., 237,417; Caths., 4,380,000 (20.7%); tot. pop., 21,160,000.

Republic in eastern Africa bordering on the Indian Ocean; capital, Nairobi. Systematic evangelization by the Holy Ghost Fathers began in 1892, nearly 40 years after the start of work by Protestant missionaries. The hierarchy was established in 1953.

Kiribati

Dioc., 1; bp., 1; parishes, 21; priests, 12 (2 dioc., 10 rel.); sem., 8; bros., 13; srs., 59; bap., 1,543; Caths., 33,000 (52.3%); tot. pop., 63,000.

Former British colony (Gilbert Islands) in Oceania; became independent July 12, 1979; capital, Bairiki on Tarawa. French Missionaries of the Sacred Heart began work in the islands in 1888. A vicariate for the islands was organized in 1897. The hierarchy was established in 1966.

Korea

North Korea: Dioc., 2; abb., 1; bp., 1 (exiled); tot. pop., 20,380,000. No recent Catholic statistics available; there were an estimated 100,000 Catholics reported in 1969.

South Korea*: Archd., 3; dioc., 11; mil. ord.; card., 1; abp., 2; bp., 14; parishes, 713; priests, 1,336 (1,012 dioc., 324 rel.); sem.,
1,419; bros., 268; srs., 4,572; bap., 175,407; Caths. 2,093,000 (5%); tot. pop., 41,570,000.

Peninsula in eastern Asia, east of China, divided into the (Communist) Democratic People's Republic in the North, formed May 1, 1948, with Pyongyang as its capital; and the Republic of Korea in the South, with Seoul as the capital. Some Catholics may have been in Korea before it became a "hermit kingdom" toward the end of the 16th century and closed its borders to foreigners. The real introduction to Catholicism came in 1784 through lay converts. A priest arriving in the country in 1794 found 4,000 Catholics there who had never seen a priest. A vicariate was erected in 1831 but was not manned for several years thereafter. There were 15,000 Catholics by 1857. Four persecutions in the 19th century took a terrible toll; several thousands died in the last one, 1866-69. (One-hundred and three martyrs of this period were canonized by Pope John Paul II during his 1984 apostolic visit to the country.) Freedom of religion was granted in 1883 when Korea opened its borders. Progress was made thereafter. The hierarchy was established in 1962. Since the war of 1950-1953, there have been no signs of Catholic life in the North, which has been blanketed by a news blackout. In July, 1972, both Koreas agreed to seek peaceful means of reunification. Bishop Tji of Won Ju, South Korea, convicted and sentenced to 15 years' imprisonment in 1974 on a charge of inciting to rebellion, was released in February, 1975.

Kuwait*

V.a., 1; bp., 1; parishes, 6; priests, 8 (4 dioc., 4 rel.); srs., 31; bap., 704; Caths., 57,000; tot. pop., 1,790,000.

Constitutional monarchy (sultanate or sheikdom) in southwest Asia bordering on the Persian Gulf. Remote Christian origins probably date to apostolic times. Islam is the predominant and official religion.

Laos

V.a., 4; bp., 3; No statistics available. Catholics numbered 35,000 (1% of the total population) in 1974. Tot. pop., 4,220,000. (AD)

People's republic in southeast Asia, surrounded by China, Vietnam, Kampuchea, Thailand and Burma; capital, Vientiane. Systematic evangelization by French missionaries started about 1881; earlier efforts ended in 1688. The first mission was established in 1885 by Father Xavier Guégo. A vicariate apostolic was organized in 1899 when there were 8,000 Catholics and 2,000 catechumens in the country. Most of the foreign missionaries were expelled following the communist take-over in 1975. Buddhism is the state religion.

Latvia

Archd., 1; dioc., 1; card., 1 (Julijans Vaivods, named in 1983); bp. (1988), 3 (titular, 1 is impeded); parishes, 179; priests, 102 (95 dioc., 7 rel.); sem., 72; bap., 5,467; Caths., 504,000; tot. pop. 2,606,000.

Baltic republic forcibly absorbed by the U.S.S.R. in the early 1940s; capital, Riga. Catholicism was introduced late in the 12th century. Lutheranism became the dominant religion after 1530. Catholics were free to practice their faith during the long period of Russian control and during independence from 1918 to 1940. The relatively small Catholic community has been repressed since the start of Soviet occupation. The Russian take-over of Latvia has not been recognized by the Holy See or the United States.

Lebanon*

Archd. 11 (1 Armenian, 3 Maronite, 7 Greek Melkite); dioc., 6 (1 Chaldean, 5 Maronite); v.a., 1 (Latin); card., 1 (Patr. Antoine Khoraiche of Maronites); patriarchs, 3 (patriarchs of Antioch of the Maronites, Antioch of the Syrians and Cilicia of the Armenians who reside in Lebanon); abp. and bp., 23; parishes, 989; priests, 1,392 (656 dioc., 736 rel.); p.d., 3; sem., 256; bros., 90; srs., 3,147; bap., 15,973; Caths., 1,459,000; tot. pop., 2,710,000.

Republic in the Middle East, north of Israel; capital, Beirut. Christianity, introduced in apostolic times, was firmly established by the end of the fourth century and has remained so despite heavy Moslem influence since early in the seventh century. The country is the center of the Maronite Rite. During the past 10 years the country has been torn by violence and often heavy fighting among rival political-religious factions drawn along Christian-Moslem lines. (See Index for recent developments.)

Lesotho*

Archd., 1; dioc., 3; abp., 1 (native); bp., 3 (native); parishes, 77; priests, 135 (25 dioc., 110 rel.); sem., 67; bros., 46; srs., 702; bap., 24,335; Caths., 653,000 (41.8%); tot. pop., 1,560,000.

Constitutional monarchy, an enclave in the southeastern part of the Republic of South Africa; capital, Maseru. Oblates of Mary Immaculate, the first Catholic missionaries in the area, started evangelization in 1862. A prefecture apostolic was organized in 1894. The hierarchy was established in 1951. (See Index for papal visit.)

Liberia*

Archd., 1; dioc., 2; abp., 1 (native); bp., 2 (native); parishes, 51; priests, 59 (12 dioc., 47 rel.); p.d., 5; sem., 30; bros., 36; srs., 111; bap. 3,028; Caths., 66,000 (2.9%); tot. pop., 2,220,000.

Republic in western Africa, bordering on the Atlantic; capital, Monrovia. Missionary work and influence, dating interruptedly from the 16th century, were slight before the Society of African Missions undertook evangelization in 1906. The hierarchy was established in 1982.

Libya

V.a., 3; p.a., 1; bp., 2; parishes, 2; priests, 9 (rel.); srs., 110; bap., 294; Caths., 38,000 (1%); tot. pop., 3,740,000. (AD)

Arab state in northern Africa, on the Mediterranean between Egypt and Tunisia; capital, Tripoli. Christianity was probably preached in the area at an early date but was overcome by the spread of Islam from the 630s. Islamization was complete by 1067 and there has been no Christian influence since then. The Catholics in the country belong to the foreign colony. Islam is the state religion.

Liechtenstein*

Parishes, 10; priests, 35 (19 dioc., 16 rel); bros., 8; srs., 102; bap., 350; Caths., 22,000; tot. pop., 25,000.

Constitutional monarchy in central Europe, in the Alps and on the Rhine between Switzerland and Austria; capital, Vaduz. Christianity in the country dates from the fourth century; the area has been under the jurisdiction of Chur, Switzerland, since about that time. The Reformation had hardly any influence in the country. Catholicism is the state religion but religious freedom for all is guaranteed by law.

Lithuania

Archd., 2 (Kaunas and Vilna, which includes territory in political confines of Poland); dioc., 4; prel., 1; card. (1988), 1; abp., 1 (titular); bp., 4 (none residential); parishes 630; priests, 664 (655 dioc., 9 rel.); sem., 129; bros., 21; srs., 337; Caths., 2,651,000 (79.9%); tot. pop., 3,315,000.

Baltic republic forcibly absorbed and under Soviet domination since 1945; captial, Vilna (Vilnius). Catholicism was introduced in 1251 and a short-lived diocese was established by 1260. Effective evangelization took place between 1387 and 1417, when Catholicism became the state religion. Losses to Lutheranism in the 16th century were overcome. Efforts of czars to "russify" the Church between 1795 and 1918 were strongly resisted. Concordat relations with the Vatican were established in 1927, nine years after independence from Russia and 13 years before the start of another kind of Russian control with the following results, among others: all convents closed since 1940; four seminaries shut down; appointment to one seminary (Kaunas) only with government approval; priests restricted in pastoral ministry and subject to appointment by government officials; no religious services outside churches; no religious press; religious instruction banned; parish installations and activities controlled by directives enacted in 1976; two bishops — Vincentas Sladkevicius and Julijonas Steponavicius — forbidden to act as bishops and relegated to remote parishes in 1957 and 1961, respectively; arrest, imprisonment or detention in Siberia for four bishops, 185 priests, 275 lay persons between 1945 and 1955. Despite such developments and conditions, there remains a strong and vigorous underground Church in Lithuania, where the Soviet government finds its repressive potential limited by the solidarity of popular resistance. In July, 1982, Rev. Antanas Vaicius was ordained apostolic administrator of the Telsiai diocese and Klaipeda prelature. Auxiliary Bishop Vincentas Sladkevicius, of

Kaisiadorys, under severe government restrictions since 1957, was allowed to return to his see in 1982 following his appointment as apostolic administrator. (He was made a cardinal in 1988.) In 1983, four of the five bishops were allowed to go to Rome for their *ad limina* visit. The Soviet take-over of Lithuania is not recognized by the Holy See or the United States.

Luxembourg*

Archd. (1988), 1; abp., 1; parishes, 273; priests, 391 (295 dioc., 96 rel.); p.d., 2; sem., 20; bros., 25; srs., 1,085; bap., 3,575; Caths. 348,000 (94%); tot. pop., 366,000.

Constitutional monarchy in western Europe, between Belgium, Germany and France; capital, Luxembourg. Christianity, introduced in the fifth and sixth centuries, was firmly established by the end of the eighth century. A full-scale parish system was in existence in the ninth century. Monastic influence was strong until the Reformation, which had minimal influence in the country. The Church experienced some adverse influence from the currents of the French Revolution.

Macau (Macao)

Dioc., 1; bp., 2; parishes, 6; priests, 69 (38 dioc., 31 rel.); sem., 7; bros., 16; srs., 168; bap., 446; Caths., 20,000; tot. pop., 400,000.

Portuguese-administered territory in southeast Asia across the Pearl River estuary from Hong Kong; scheduled to revert to China in 1999. Christianity was introduced by the Jesuits in 1557. Diocese was established in 1576. Macau served as a base for missionary work in Japan and China.

Madagascar*

Archd., 3; dioc., 14; card., 1 (native); abp., 2 (native); bp., 15 (12 native); parishes, 247; priests, 695 (176 dioc., 519 rel.); p.d., 1; sem., 355; bros., 370; srs., 1,913; bap., 72,749; Caths., 2,292,000 (22.2%); tot. pop. 10,300,000.

Republic (Malagasy Republic) off the eastern coast of Africa; capital, Antananarivo. Missionary efforts were generally fruitless from early in the 16th century until the Jesuits were permitted to start open evangelization about 1845. A prefecture apostolic was set up in 1850 and a vicariate apostolic in the north was placed in charge of the Holy Ghost Fathers in 1898. There were 100,000 Catholics by 1900. The first native bishop was ordained in 1936. The hierarchy was established in 1955.

Madeira Islands

Portuguese province, an archipelago 340 miles west of the northwestern coast of Africa; capital, Funchal. Catholicism has had a continuous history since the first half of the 15th century. The diocese of Funchal was established in 1514. Statistics are included in Portugal.

Malawi*

Archd., 1; dioc., 6; abp., 1 (native); bp., 6 (4 native); parishes, 131; priests, 375 (152 dioc., 223 rel.); sem., 185; bros., 151; srs., 593; bap., 58,132; Caths., 1,495,000 (20.5%); tot. pop., 7,280,000.

Republic in the interior of eastern Africa; capital, Lilongwe. Missionary work, begun by Jesuits in the late 16th and early 17th centuries, was generally ineffective until the end of the 19th century. The Missionaries of Africa (White Fathers) arrived in 1889 and later were joined by others. A vicariate was set up in 1897. The hierarchy was established in 1959.

Malaysia

Archd., 2; dioc., 5; abp., 2 (native); bp., 5 (native); parishes, 152; priests, 235 (169 dioc., 66 rel.); p.d., 2; sem., 81; bros., 96; srs., 448; bap., 20,820; Caths., 475,000 (2.9%); tot. pop., 16,110,000. (AD)

Parliamentary democracy in southeastern Asia; federation of former states of Malaya, Sabah (former Br. North Borneo), and Sarawak; capital, Kuala Lumpur. Christianity, introduced by Portuguese colonists about 1511, was confined almost exclusively to Malacca until late in the 18th century. The effectiveness of evangelization increased from then on because of the recruitment and training of native clergy. Singapore (see separate entry), founded in 1819, became a center for missionary work. Seventeen thousand Catholics were in the Malacca diocese in 1888. Effective evangelization in Sabah and Sarawak began in the second half of the 19th century. The hierarchy was established in 1973.

Maldives

Republic, an archipelago 400 miles southwest of India and Ceylon; capital, Male. No serious attempt was ever made to evangelize the area, which is completely Moslem. Population, 190,000.

Mali*

Archd., 1; dioc., 5; abp., 1 (native); bp., 5 (3 native); parishes, 42; priests, 133 (24 dioc., 109 rel.); sem., 44; bros., 23; srs., 121; bap., 3,237; Caths., 78,000 (.9%); tot. pop., 8,440,000.

Republic, inland in western Africa; capital, Bamako. Catholicism was introduced late in the second half of the 19th century. Missionary work made little progress in the midst of the predominantly Moslem population. A vicariate was set up in 1921. The hierarchy was established in 1955.

Malta*

Archd., 1; dioc., 1; abp., 1; bp., 1; parishes, 78; priests, 1,001 (536 dioc., 465 rel.); sem., 101; bros., 109; srs., 1,449; bap., 5,226; Caths., 340,000 (98.8%); tot. pop., 344,000.

Republic 58 miles south of Sicily; capital, Valletta. Early catacombs and inscriptions are evidence of the early introduction of Christianity. St. Paul was shipwrecked on Malta in 60. Saracens controlled the island(s) from 870 to 1090, a period of difficulty for the Church. The line of bishops extends from 1090 to the present. Church-state conflict developed in recent years over passage of government-sponsored legislation affecting Catholic schools and church-owned property. An agree-

The Marianas

Dioc., 1; bp., 1; parishes, 9; priests, 7 (6 dioc., 1 rel.); p.d., 3; sem., 2; bap., 661; Caths., 29,000; tot. pop., 32,000.

Northern Mariana Islands, U.S. Trust territory in Pacific (scheduled to become a U.S. commonwealth).

Martinique

Archd., 1; abp., 1; parishes, 47; priests, 83 (40 dioc., 43 rel.); sem., 3; bros., 12; srs., 215; bap., 4,995; Caths., 290,000; tot. pop., 330,000.

French overseas department in the West Indies, about 130 miles south of Guadeloupe; capital, Fort-de-France. Catholicism was introduced in the 16th century. The hierarchy was established in 1967.

Mauritania

Dioc., 1; bp., 1; parishes, 7; priests, 11 (3 dioc., 8 rel.); bros., 2; srs., 35; bap., 51; Caths., 6,000 (.3%); tot. pop., 1,950,000. (AD)

Islamic republic on the northwest coast of Africa; capital, Nouakchott. With few exceptions, the Catholics in the country are members of the foreign colony.

Mauritius*

Dioc., 1; card. (1988), 1; parishes, 44; priests, 88 (50 dioc., 38 rel.); sem., 8; bros., 36; srs., 289; bap., 6,236; Caths., 280,000 (28.2%); tot. pop., 990,000.

Self-governing island state 500 miles east of Madagascar; capital, Port Louis. Catholicism was introduced by Vincentians in 1722. Port Louis, made a vicariate in 1819 and a diocese in 1847, was a jumping-off point for missionaries to Australia, Madagascar and South Africa.

Mayotte

French overseas island territory, in Indian Ocean off southeast coast of Africa; formerly part of Comoros. Statistics included in Comoros.

Melilla

Spanish possession in northern Africa. Statistics are included in those for Spain.

Mexico

Archd., 12; dioc. (1988), 57; prel., 7; v.a. (1988), 1; card., 2; abp., 11; bp., 77; parishes, 4,540; priests, 10,653 (7,603 dioc., 3,050 rel.); p.d., 110; sem., 4,960; bros., 1,271; srs., 24,906; bap., 2,080,533; Caths., 76,498,000 (96.1%); tot. pop., 79,560,000. (AD)

Republic in Middle America (United States of Mexico); capital, Mexico City. Christianity was introduced early in the 16th century. Mexico City, made a diocese in 1530, became the missionary and cultural center of the whole country. Missionary work, started in 1524 and forwarded principally by Franciscans, Dominicans, Augustinians and Jesuits, resulted in the baptism of all persons in the central plateau by the end of the century. Progress there and in the rest of the country continued in the following century but tapered off and went into decline in the 18th century, for a variety of reasons ranging from diminishing government support to relaxations of Church discipline. The wars of independence, 1810-21, in which some Catholics participated, created serious problems of adjustment for the Church. Social problems, political unrest and government opposition climaxed in the constitution of 1917 which practically outlawed the Church. Persecution took serious tolls of life and kept the Church underground, under Calles, 1924-1928, again in 1931, and under Cardenas in 1934. President Camacho, 1940-1946, ended persecution and instituted a more lenient policy. The Church, however, still labors under legal and practical disabilities. The Mexican president has a personal envoy to the Vatican.

Monaco*

Archd., 1; abp., 1; parishes, 5; priests, 28 (13 dioc., 15 rel.); p.d., 1; sem., 5; bros., 14; srs., 39; bap., 210; Caths., 25,000; tot. pop., 27,000.

Constitutional monarchy, an enclave on the Mediterranean coast of France near the Italian border; capital, Monaco-Ville. Christianity was introduced before 1000. Catholicism is the official religion but freedom is guaranteed for all.

Mongolia

People's republic in north central Asia; capital Ulaanbaatar. Christianity was introduced by Oriental Orthodox. Some Franciscans were in the country in the 13th and 14th centuries, en route to China. Limited evangelization efforts from the 18th century had little success among the Mongols in Outer Mongolia, where Buddhism has predominated for hundreds of years. No Christians were known to be there in 1953. There may be a few Catholics in Inner Mongolia. No foreign missionaries have been in the country since 1953. Population, 1,940,000.

Montserrat

Parish, 1; priest, 1 (dioc.); p.d.; 1; srs., 5; bap., 28; Caths., 1,000; tot. pop., 12,000.

British island possession in Caribbean; capital, Plymouth. Under ecclesiastical jurisdiction of St. John's-Basseterre diocese, Antigua.

Morocco*

Archd., 2; abp., 2; parishes, 49; priests, 76 (20 dioc., 56 rel.); bros., 10; srs., 320; bap., 118; Caths., 41,000 (.18%); tot. pop., 22,480,000.

Constitutional monarchy in northwest Africa with Atlantic and Mediterranean coastlines; capital, Rabat. Christianity was known in the area by the end of the third century. Bishops from Morocco attended a council at Carthage in 484. Catholic life survived under Visigoth and, from 700, Arab rule; later it became subject to influence from the Spanish, Portuguese and French. Islam is the state religion. The hierarchy was established in 1955.

Mozambique

Archd., 3; dioc., 6; card. (1988), 1 (native); abp. 2 (1 native); bp., 6 (5 native); parishes, 271; priests, 272 (23 dioc., 249 rel.); sem., 45; bros., 70; srs., 514; bap., 36,523; Caths., 1,882,000 (13.2%); tot. pop., 14,170,000. (AD)

People's republic in southeast Africa, bordering on the Indian Ocean; former Portuguese territory (independent, 1975); capital, Maputo (formerly Lourenco Marques). Christianity was introduced by Portuguese Jesuits about the middle of the 16th century. Evangelization continued from then until the 18th century when it went into decline largely because of the Portuguese government's expulsion of the Jesuits. Conditions worsened in the 1830s, improved after 1881, but deteriorated again during the anticlerical period from 1910 to 1925. Conditions improved in 1940, the year Portugal concluded a new concordat with the Holy See and the hierarchy was established. Outspoken criticism by missionaries of Portuguese policies in Mozambique resulted in Church-state tensions in the years immediately preceding independence. Tension continues to be a factor, although to a smaller degree, in relations between the Church and the Marxist-oriented government in power since 1975. The first two native bishops were ordained March 9, 1975. Two ecclesiastical provinces were established in 1984. (See Index for papal visit.)

Namibia (South West Africa)

V.a., 2; bp., 2 (1 native); parishes, 52; priests, 57 (3 dioc., 54 rel.); p.d., 23; sem., 9; bros., 44; srs., 313; bap., 8,982; Caths., 208,000 (13%); tot. pop., 1,590,000. (AD)

Territory in South Africa in dispute between the Republic of South Africa and the United Nations; capital, Windhoek. The area shares the history of South Africa.

Nauru

Parish, 1; priest, 1 (rel.); srs., 5; bap., 148; Caths., 3,000; tot. pop., 8,000.

Independent republic in western Pacific; capital, Yaren. Forms part of the Tarawa and Nauru diocese (Kiribati).

Nepal*

Mission "sui juris," 1; parishes, 17; priests, 30 (3 dioc.; 27 rel.); bros., 8; srs., 42; bap., 72; Caths., 2,000; tot. pop., 17,130,607.

Constitutional monarchy, the only Hindu kingdom in the world, in central Asia south of the Himalayas between India and Tibet; capital, Kathmandu. Little is known of the country before the 15th century. Some Jesuits passed through from 1628 and some sections were evangelized in the 18th century, with minimal results, before the country was closed to foreigners. Conversions from Hinduism, the state religion, are not recognized in law. Christian missionary work is not allowed.

Netherlands*

Archd., 1; dioc., 6; mil ord.; card. (1988), 3; bp., 11; parishes, 1,780; priests 5,856 (2,250 dioc., 3,606 rel.); p.d., 66; sem., 249; bros., 2,602; srs., 19,605; bap., 50,720; Caths., 5,611,000 (38.5%); tot. pop., 14,560,000.

Constitutional monarchy in northwestern Europe; capital, Amsterdam (seat of the government, The Hague). Evangelization, begun about the turn of the sixth century by Irish, Anglo-Saxon and Frankish missionaries, resulted in Christianization of the country by 800 and subsequent strong influence on The Lowlands. Invasion by French Calvinists in 1572 brought serious losses to the Catholic Church and made the Reformed Church dominant. Catholics suffered a practical persecution of official repression and social handicap in the 17th century. The schism of Utrecht occurred in 1724. Only one-third of the population was Catholic in 1726. The Church had only a skeleton organization from 1702 to 1853, when the hierarchy was reestablished. Despite this upturn, cultural isolation was the experience of Catholics until about 1914. From then on new vigor came into the life of the Church, and a whole new climate of interfaith relations began to develop. Before and for some years following the Second Vatican Council, the thrust and variety of thought and practice in the Dutch Church moved it to the vanguard position of "progressive" renewal. A particular synod of Dutch bishops held at the Vatican in January, 1980, and aimed at internal improvement of the Church in the Netherlands, had disappointing results, according to reports in 1981.

Netherlands Antilles

Dioc., 1; bp., 1; parishes, 47; priests, 54 (14 dioc., 40 rel.); sem., 1; bros., 38; srs., 125; bap., 3,820; Caths., 199,000 (76%); tot. pop., 260,000. (AD)

Autonomous part of The Netherlands. Consists of two groups of islands in the Caribbean: Curacao, Aruba and Bonaire, off the northern coast of Venezuela; and St. Eustatius, Saba and the southern part of St. Maarten, southeast of Puerto Rico; capital, Willemstad on Curacao. Christianity was introduced in the 16th century.

New Caledonia

Archd., 1; abp., 1; parishes, 36; priests, 49 (8 dioc., 41 rel.); sem., 8; bros., 56; srs., 195; bap., 1,773; Caths., 94,000; tot. pop., 145,000.

French territory consisting of several islands in Oceania east of Queensland, Australia; capital, Noumea. Catholicism was introduced in 1843, nine years after Protestant missionaries began evangelization. A vicariate was organized in 1847. The hierarchy was established in 1966.

New Zealand*

Archd., 1; dioc., 5; mil. ord.; card., 1; bp., 8; parishes, 279; priests, 728 (409 dioc., 319 rel.); sem., 64; bros., 243; srs., 1,690; bap., 7,499; Caths. 485,000 (14.9%); tot. pop., 3,250,000.

Independent nation in Commonwealth, a group of islands in Oceania 1,200 miles southeast of Australia: capital, Wellington. Protestant missionaries were the first evangelizers. On North Island, Catholic missionaries started work before the establishment of two dioceses in 1848; their work among the Maoris was not organized until about 1881. On South Island, whose first resident priest arrived in 1840, a diocese was established in 1869. These three jurisdictions were joined in a province in 1896. The Marists were the outstanding Catholic missionaries in the area.

Nicaragua*

Archd., 1; dioc., 4; prel., 2; v.a., 1; card., 1; bp., 9; parishes, 196; priests, 347 (124 dioc., 223 rel.); p.d., 28; sem., 114; bros., 71; srs., 584; bap., 83,270; Caths., 2,985,000 (88.3%); 3,380,000.

Republic in Central America: capital, Managua. Evangelization began shortly after the Spanish conquest about 1524 and eight years later the first bishop took over jurisdiction of the Church in the country. Jesuits were leaders in missionary work during the colonial period, which lasted until the 1820s. Evangelization endeavor increased after establishment of the republic in 1838. In this century it was extended to the Atlantic coastal area where Protestant missionaries had begun work about the middle of the 1900s. Many church leaders, clerical and lay, supported the aims but not necessarily all the methods of the revolution which forced the resignation and flight July 17, 1979, of Anastasio Somoza Debayle, whose family had controlled the government since the early 1930s. (See Index for recent events.)

Niger*

Dioc., 1; bp., 1; parishes, 21; priests, 36 (6 dioc., 30 rel.); bros., 9; srs., 80; bap., 293; Caths., 15,000 (.2%); tot. pop., 6,700,000.

Republic in west central Africa; capital, Niamey. The first mission was set up in 1831. A prefecture apostolic was organized in 1942 and the first diocese was established in 1961. The country is predominantly Moslem.

Nigeria*

Archd., 3; dioc. (1988), 29; mission "sui juris," 1; card., 2; abp., 3 (native); bp., 27 (23 native); parishes, 751; priests, 1,648 (1,139 dioc., 509 rel.); p.d., 5; sem., 2,238; bros., 194; srs., 1,709; bap., 280,619; Caths., 7,499,000 (7.6%); tot. pop., 98,520,000.

Republic in western Africa; capital, Lagos. The Portuguese introduced Catholicism in the coastal region in the 15th century. Capuchins did some evangelization in the 17th century but systematic missionary work did not get under way along the coast until about 1840. A vicariate for this area was organized in 1870. A prefecture was set up in 1911 for missions in the northern part of the country where Islam was strongly entrenched. From 1967, when Biafra seceded, until early in 1970 the country was torn by civil war. The hierarchy was established in 1950.

Niue

Parish, 1; priest, 1 (rel.); bap. 14; Caths., 200; tot. pop., 4,000.

New Zealand self-governing territory in South Pacific. Under ecclesiastical jurisdiction of Rarotonga diocese, Cook Islands.

Norway*

Dioc., 1; prel., 2; bp., 2; parishes, 28; priests, 58 (15 dioc., 43 rel.); sem., 10; bros., 4; srs., 282; bap., 404; Caths., 20,000 (.47%); tot. pop., 4,170,000.

Constitutional monarchy in northern Europe, the western part of the Scandinavian peninsula; capital, Oslo. Evangelization begun in the ninth century by missionaries from England and Ireland put the Church on a firm footing about the turn of the 11th century. The first diocese was set up in 1153 and development of the Church progressed until the Black Death in 1349 inflicted losses from which it never recovered. Lutheranism, introduced from outside in 1537 and furthered cautiously, gained general acceptance by about 1600 and was made the state religion. Legal and other measures crippled the Church, forcing priests to flee the country and completely disrupting normal activity. Changes for the better came in the 19th century, with the granting of religious liberty in 1845 and the repeal of many legal disabilities in 1897. Norway was administered as a single apostolic vicariate from 1892 to 1932, when it was divided into three jurisdictions under the supervision of the Congregation for the Propagation of the Faith.

Oman

Parishes, 2; priests, 3 (1 dioc., 2 rel.); bap., 103; Caths., 10,000; tot. pop., 1,400,000.

Independent monarchy in eastern corner of Arabian Peninsula; capital, Muscat. Under ecclesiastical jurisdiction of Arabia vicariate apostolic.

Pakistan*

Archd., 1; dioc., 5; card., 1 (native); bp., 6 (native); parishes, 84; priests, 261 (96 dioc., 165 rel.); p.d., 2; sem., 109; bros., 43; srs., 656; bap., 20,706; Caths., 608,000 (.6%); tot. pop., 99,160,000.

Islamic republic in southwestern Asia; capital, Islamabad. (Formerly included East Pakistan which became the independent nation of Bangladesh in 1971.) Islam, firmly established in the eighth century, is the state religion. Christian evangelization of the native population began about the middle of the 19th century, years after earlier scattered attempts. The hierarchy was established in 1950.

Panama*

Archd., 1; dioc., 3; prel., 1; v.a., 1; abp., 1; bp., 5; parishes, 166; priests, 290 (93 dioc., 197 rel.); p.d., 10; sem., 108; bros., 49; srs., 469; bap., 36,209; Caths., 1,935,000 (86.7%); tot. pop., 2,230,000.

Republic in Central America; capital, Panama. Catholicism was introduced by Franciscan missionaries and evangelization started in 1514. The Panama diocese, oldest in the Americas, was set up at the same time. The Catholic Church has favored status and state aid for missions, charities and parochial schools, but religious freedom is guaranteed to all religions.

Papua New Guinea*

Archd., 4; dioc., 14; abp., 4; bp., 16; parishes, 305; priests, 496 (77 dioc., 419 rel.); p.d., 12; sem., 185; bros., 337; srs., 1,022; bap., 35,752; Caths., 1,133,000 (33.3%); tot. pop., 3,400,000.

Independent (Sept. 16, 1975) republic (formerly under Australian administration) in southwest Pacific. Consists of the eastern half of the southwestern Pacific island of New Guinea and the Northern Solomon Islands; capital, Port Moresby. Marists began evangelization about 1844 but were handicapped by many factors, including "spheres of influence" laid out for Catholic and Protestant missionaries. A prefecture apostolic was set up in 1896 and placed in charge of the Divine Word Missionaries. The territory suffered greatly during World War II. Hierarchy was established for New Guinea and adjacent islands in 1966.

Paraguay*

Archd., 1; dioc., 8; prel., 2; v.a., 2; mil. ord.; abp., 1; bp., 14; parishes, 327; priests, 557 (185 dioc., 372 rel.); p.d., 23; sem., 323; bros., 88; srs., 1,114; bap., 101,935; Caths., 3,505,000 (92%); tot. pop., 3,810,000.

Republic in central South America; capital, Asuncion. Catholicism was introduced in 1542, evangelization began almost immediately. A diocese erected in 1547 was occupied for the first time in 1556. On many occasions thereafter dioceses in the country were left unoccupied because of political and other reasons. Jesuits who came into the country after 1609 devised the reductions system for evangelizing the Indians, teaching them agriculture, husbandry, trades and other useful arts, and giving them experience in property use and community life. The reductions were communes of Indians only, under the direction of the missionaries. About 50 of them were established in southern Brazil, Uruguay and northeastern Argentina as well as in Paraguay. They had an average population of three to four thousand. At their peak, some 30 reductions had a population of 100,000. Political officials regarded the reductions with disfavor because they did not control them and feared that the Indians trained in them might foment revolt and upset the established colonial system under Spanish control. The reductions lasted until about 1768 when their Jesuit founders and directors were expelled from Latin America. Church-state relations following independence from Spain in 1811 were tense as often as not because of government efforts to control the Church through continued exercise of Spanish patronage rights and by other means. The Church as well as the whole country suffered a great deal during the War of the Triple Alliance from 1865-70. After that time, the Church had the same kind of experience in Paraguay as in the rest of Latin America with forces of liberalism, anticlericalism, massive educational needs, poverty, a shortage of priests and other personnel. Most recently church leaders have been challenging the government to initiate long-needed economic and social reforms. (See Index for papal visit.)

Peru*

Archd., 7; dioc., 14; prel., 12; v.a., 8; mil. ord.; card., 1; abp., 6; bp., 44; parishes, 1,360; priests, 2,378 (1,018 dioc., 1,360 rel.); p.d., 53; sem., 1,062; bros., 450; srs., 4,716; bap., 472,649; Caths., 18,574,000 (92%); tot. pop., 20,210,000.

Republic on the western coast of South America; capital, Lima. An effective diocese became operational in 1537, five years after the Spanish conquest. Evangelization, already under way, developed for some time after 1570 but deteriorated before the end of the colonial period in the 1820s. The first native-born saint of the new world was a Peruvian, Rose of Lima, a Dominican tertiary who died in 1617 and was canonized in 1671. In the new republic founded after the wars of independence the Church experienced problems of adjustment and many of the difficulties that cropped up in other South American countries: government efforts to control it through continuation of the patronage rights of the Spanish crown; suppression of houses of religious and expropriation of church property; religious indifference and outright hostility. The Church was given special status but was not made the established religion. Repressive measures by the government against labor protests have been condemned by Church leaders in the past several years. (See Index for papal visit.)

Philippines*

Archd., 16; dioc., 49; prel., 5; v.a., 5; mil. ord.; card., 2; abp., 14; bp., 78; parishes, 2,293; priests, 5,203 (3,129 dioc., 2,074 rel.); p.d., 5; sem., 5,217; bros., 382; srs., 8,774; bap., 1,432,652; Caths., 46,186,000 (84%); tot. pop., 55,000,000.

Republic, an archipelago of 7,000 islands off the southeast coast of Asia; capital, Quezon City (de facto, Manila). Systematic evangelization was begun in 1564 and resulted in firm establishment of the Church by the 19th century. During the period of Spanish rule, which lasted from the discovery of the islands by Magellan in 1521 to 1898, the Church experienced difficulties with the patronage system under which the Spanish crown tried to control ecclesiastical affairs through episcopal and other appointments. This system ended in 1898 when the United States gained possession of the islands and instituted a policy of separation of Church and state. Anticlericalism flared late in the 19th century. The Aglipayan schism, an attempt to set up a nationalist church, occurred a few years later, in 1902. The government of Ferdinand Marcos, under attack by people of the church for a number of years for violations of human rights, was replaced in 1986.

Poland

Archd., 7; dioc., 21; card., 5; abp., 1; bp., 90; parishes, 8,431; priests, 21,280 (16,603 dioc., 4,677 rel.); p.d., 2; sem., 8,246; bros.,

1,598; srs., 24,973; bap., 635,843; Caths., 35,596,000 (95%); tot. pop., 37,460,000.

People's republic in eastern Europe; capital, Warsaw. The first traces of Christianity date from the second half of the ninth century. Its spread was accelerated by the union of the Slavs in the 10th century. The first bishopric was set up in 968. The Gniezno archdiocese, with suffragan sees and a mandate to evangelize the borderlands as well as Poland, was established in 1000. Steady growth continued thereafter, with religious orders and their schools playing a major role. Some tensions with the Orthodox were experienced. The Reformation, supported mainly by city dwellers and the upper classes, peaked from about the middle of the 16th century, resulting in numerous conversions to Lutheranism, the Reformed Church and the Bohemian Brethren. A successful Counter-Reformation, with the Jesuits in a position of leadership, was completed by about 1632. The movement served a nationalist as well as religious purpose; in restoring religious unity to a large degree, it united the country against potential invaders, the Swedes, Russians and Turks. The Counter-Reformation had bad side effects, leading to the repression of Protestants long after it was over and to prejudice against Orthodox who returned to allegiance with Rome in 1596 and later. The Church, in the same manner as the entire country, was adversely affected by the partitions of the 18th and 19th centuries. Russification hurt the Orthodox who had reunited with Rome and the Latins who were in the majority. Germans extended their Kulturkampf to the area they controlled. The Austrians exhibited some degree of tolerance. In the republic established after World War I the Church reorganized itself, continued to serve as a vital force in national life, and enjoyed generally harmonious relations with the state. Progressive growth was strong until 1939 when disaster struck in the form of invasion by German and Russian forces and six years of war. In 1945, seven years before the adoption of a Soviet-type of constitution, the Communist-controlled government initiated a policy that included a constant program of atheistic propaganda; a strong campaign against the hierarchy and clergy; the imprisonment in 1948 of 700 priests and even more religious; rigid limitation of the activities of religious; censorship and curtailment of the Catholic press and Catholic Action; interference with church administration and appointments of the clergy; the "deposition" of Cardinal Wyszynski in 1953 and the imprisonment of other members of the hierarchy; the suppression of "Caritas," the Catholic charitable organization; promotion of "Progressive Catholic" activities and a small minority of "patriotic priests." Establishment of the Gomulka regime, the freeing of Cardinal Wyszynski in October, 1956, and the signing of an agreement two months later by bishops and state officials, led to some improvement of conditions. The underlying fact, however, was that the regime conceded to Catholics only so much as was necessary to secure support of the government as a more tolerable evil than the harsh and real threat of a Russian-imposed puppet government like that in Hungary. This has been the controlling principle in Church-state relations. Auxiliary Bishop Ladislaw Rubin of Gniezno sketched the general state of affairs in March, 1968. He said that there was no sign that the government had any intention of releasing its oppressive grip on the Church. As evidence of the "climate of asphyxiation" in the country he cited: persistent questioning of priests by officials concerning their activities; the prohibition against Catholic schools, hospitals and charitable works; the financial burden of a 60 per cent tax on church income. Cardinal Wyszynski denounced "enforced atheism" in a Lenten pastoral in the same year. In May, 1969, the bishops drafted a list of grievances against the government which, they said, were "only some examples of difficulties which demonstrated the situation of the Church in our homeland." The grievances were: refusal of permits to build new churches and establish new parishes; refusal of permission "for the organization of new religion classes"; pressure on Catholics who attend religious ceremonies; censorship and the lack of an independent Catholic daily newspaper; lack of representation in public life; restriction of "freedom to conduct normal pastoral work" in the western portion of the country. There was a move toward improvement in Church-state relations in 1971-72. In 1973, the Polish bishops issued a pastoral letter urging Catholics to resist the official atheism imposed by the government. In 1974 the bishops expressed approval of renewed Vatican efforts at regularizing Church-state relations but insisted that they (the bishops) be consulted on every step of the negotiations. The bishops have continued their sharp criticism of anti-religious policies and human rights violations of the government. Regular contacts on a working level were initiated by the Vatican and Poland in 1974, but regular diplomatic relations have not been established. Cardinal Karol Wojtyla of Cracow was elected to the papacy in 1978. Church support was strong for the independent labor movement, Solidarity, which was recognized by the government in August, 1980, but outlawed in December, 1981, when martial law was imposed. The prevailing church-state condition is one of tension, affected by three principal internal factors: (1) the need of the government for social order, which is impossible to achieve without the moderating influence of the Church; (2) pressure by the Church for freedom from restraints on its pastoral, education, and social mission; (3) mutual resistance to Soviet intervention.

Portugal*

Patriarchate, 1; archd., 2; dioc., 17; mil. ord.; card., 1; abp., 2; bp., 29; parishes, 4,337; priests, 4,626 (3,537 dioc., 1,089 rel.); p.d., 13; sem., 619; bros., 498; srs., 7,588; bap., 125,930; Caths., 9,553,000 (92.8%); tot. pop., 10,290,000.

Republic in the western part of the Iberian peninsula; capital, Lisbon. Christianity was introduced before the fourth century. From the fifth century to early in the eighth century the Church experienced difficulties from the physical invasion of barbarians and the intellectual invasion of doctrinal errors in the forms of Arianism, Priscillianism and Pelagianism. The Church survived under the rule of Arabs from about 711 and of the Moors until 1249. Ecclesiastical life was fairly vigorous from 1080 to 1185, and monastic influence became strong. A decline set in about 1450. Several decades later Portugal became the jumping-off place for many missionaries to newly discovered colonies. The Reformation had little effect in the country. Beginning about 1750, Pombal, minister of foreign affairs and prime minister, mounted a frontal attack on the Jesuits whom he succeeded in expelling from Portugal and the colonies. His anti-Jesuit campaign successful Pombal also attempted, and succeeded to some extent, in controlling the Church in Portugal until his fall from power about 1777. Liberal revolutionaries with anti-Church policies made the 19th century a difficult one for the Church. Similar policies prevailed in Church-state relations in this century until the accession of Salazar to power in 1928. In 1940 he concluded a concordat with the Holy See which regularized Church-state relations but still left the Church in a subservient condition. The prevailing spirit of church authorities in Portugal has been conservative. In 1971 several priests were tried for subversion for speaking out against colonialism and for taking part in guerrilla activities in Angola. A military coup of Apr. 25, 1974, triggered a succession of chaotic political developments which led to an attempt by Communists, after receiving only 18 per cent of the votes cast in a national election, to take over the government in the summer of 1975.

Puerto Rico

Archd., 1; dioc., 4; card., 1; bp., 9; parishes, 299; priests, 755 (309 dioc., 446 rel.); p.d., 254; sem., 197; bros., 82; srs., 1,554; bap., 45,519; Caths., 2,763,000 (78.9%); tot. pop., 3,500,000. (AD)

A U.S. commonwealth, the smallest of the Greater Antilles, 885 miles southeast of the southern coast of Florida; capital, San Juan. Following its discovery by Columbus in 1493, the island was evangelized by Spanish missionaries and remained under Spanish ecclesiastical as well as political control until 1898 when it became a possession of the United States. The original diocese, San Juan, was erected in 1511. The present hierarchy was established in 1960.

Qatar

Parish, 1; priest, 2 (1 dioc., 1 rel.); bap., 73; Caths., 5,000; tot. pop., 330,000.

Independent state in the Persian Gulf; capital, Doha. Under ecclesiastical jurisdiction of Arabia vicariate apostolic.

Reunion

Dioc., 1; bp., 1; parishes, 73; priests, 112 (58 dioc., 54 rel.); p.d., 1; sem., 16; bros., 40; srs., 430; bap., 11,313; Caths., 488,000 (90.3%); tot. pop., 540,000. (AD)

French overseas department, 450 miles east of Madagascar; capital, Saint-Denis. Catholicism was introduced in 1667 and some intermittent missionary work was done through the rest of the century. A prefecture apostolic was organized in 1712. Vincentians began work there in 1817 and were joined later by Holy Ghost Fathers.

Rhodes

Greek island in the Aegean Sea, 112 miles from the southwestern coast of Asia Minor. A diocese was established about the end of the third century. A bishop from Rhodes attended the Council of Nicaea in 325. Most of the Christians followed the Eastern Churches into schism in the 11th century and became Orthodox. Turks controlled the island from 1522 to 1912. The small Catholic population, for whom a diocese existed from 1328 to 1546, lived in crossfire between Turks and Orthodox. After 1719 Franciscans provided pastoral care for the Catholics, for whom an archdiocese was erected in 1928. Statistics are included in Greece.

Romania

Archd., 2; dioc., 9; ord., 1; bp., 3; parishes, 659; priests, 940 (880 dioc., 60 rel.); sem., 221; bros., 13; srs., 160; bap., 19,425; Caths., 1,492,000 (6.4%); tot. pop., 23,170,000. (Statistics are for Latin-rite dioceses.)

Socialist republic in southeastern Europe; capital, Bucharest. Latin Christianity, introduced in the third century, all but disappeared during the barbarian invasions. The Byzantine Rite was introduced by the Bulgars about the beginning of the eighth century and established firm roots. It eventually became Orthodox, but a large number of its adherents returned later to union with Rome. Attempts to reintroduce the Latin Rite on any large scale have been unsuccessful. Communists took over the government following World War II, forced the abdication of Michael I in 1947, and enacted a Soviet type of constitution in 1952. By that time a campaign against religion was already in progress. In 1948 the government denounced a concordat concluded in 1929, nationalized all schools and passed a law on religions which resulted in the disorganization of Church administration. The 1.5 million-member Romanian Byzantine Rite Church, by government decree, was incorporated into the Romanian Orthodox Church, and the Orthodox bishops then seized the cathedrals of Roman Catholic bishops. Five of the six Latin Rite bishops were immediately disposed of by the government, and the last was sentenced to 18 years' imprisonment in 1951, when a great many arrests of priests and laymen were made. Religious orders were suppressed in 1949. Since 1948 more than 50 priests have been executed and 200 have died in prison. One hundred priests were reported in prison at the end of 1958. Some change for the better in Church-state relations was reported after the middle of the summer of 1964, although restrictions were still in effect. About 1,200 priests were engaged in parish work in August, 1965.

Rwanda*

Archd., 1; dioc., 7; abp., 1 (native); bp., 7 (6 native); parishes, 109; priests, 513 (280 dioc., 233 rel.); p.d., 1; sem., 203; bap., 117,926; Caths., 2,764,000 (44%); tot. pop., 6,270,000.

Republic in east central Africa; capital, Kigali. Catholicism was introduced about the turn of the 20th century. The hierarchy was established in 1959. Intertribal warfare between the ruling Hutus (90 per cent of the population) and the Tutsis (formerly the ruling aristocracy) plagued the country for a number of years.

Saint Christopher and Nevis

Parishes, 4; priests, 4 (1 dioc., 3 rel.); bros., 2; srs., 6; bap., 49; Caths., 5,000; tot. pop., 45,000. (AD)

Independent (Sept. 19, 1983) island states in West Indies; capital, Basseterre, on St. Christopher; Charlestown, on Nevis. Under ecclesiastical jurisdiction of St. John's-Basseterre diocese, Antigua.

Saint Helena

Mission "sui juris," 1; priest, 1 (superior of the mission); Caths., 140; tot. pop., 6,240. (1988 Annuario Pontificio.)

Comprises British Island possessions of St. Helena, Ascension and Tristan da Cunha in the South Atlantic; formerly under ecclesiastical jurisdiction of Cape Town archdiocese (South Africa).

Saint Lucia*

Archd., 1; abp., 1; parishes, 22; priests, 30 (10 dioc., 20 rel.); p.d., 1; sem., 3; bros., 2; srs., 40; bap., 3,191; Caths., 115,000; tot. pop., 144,000.

Independent (Feb. 22, 1979) island state in West Indies; capital, Castries.

Saint Pierre and Miquelon

V.a., 1; bp., 1; parishes, 3; priests, 3 (rel.); bros., 3; srs., 11; bap., 94; Caths., 6,000; tot. pop., 6,000.

French overseas department, two groups of islands near the southwest coast of Newfoundland; capital, St. Pierre. Catholicism was introduced about 1689.

Saint Vincent and the Grenadines

Parishes, 6; priests, 7 (3 dioc., 4 rel.); bros., 8; srs., 8; bap., 156; Caths., 14,000; tot. pop., 100,000.

Independent State (1979) in West Indies; capital, Kingstown. Under ecclesiastical jurisdiction of Bridgetown-Kingstown diocese, Barbados.

American Samoa

Dioc., 1;bp., 1; parishes 7; priests, 9 (6 dioc., 3 rel.); sem., 2; bros., 8; srs., 14; bap., 314; Caths., 7,000; tot. pop., 32,000.

Unincorporated U.S. territory in southwestern Pacific, consisting of six small islands; seat of government, Pago Pago on the Island of Tutuila.

Samoa-Pago Pago diocese established in 1982.

Western Samoa

Archd., 1; card., 1; bp., 1; parishes, 19; priests, 41 (18 dioc., 23 rel.); sem., 23; bros., 20; srs., 123; bap., 1,440; Caths., 34,000; tot. pop., 157,000.

Independent state in the southwestern Pacific; capital, Apia. Catholic missionary work began in 1845. Most of the missions now in operation were established by 1870 when the Catholic population numbered about 5,000. Additional progress was made in missionary work from 1896. The first Samoan priest was ordained in 1892. A diocese was established in 1966; elevated to a metropolitan see in 1982.

San Marino*

Parishes, 11; priests, 25 (12 dioc., 13 rel.); bro., 1; srs., 29; bap., 368; Caths., 22,000; tot. pop., 22,000.

Republic, a 24-square-mile enclave in northeastern Italy; capital, San Marino. The date of initial evangelization is not known, but a diocese was established by the end of the third century. Ecclesiastically, it forms part of the diocese of San Marino-Montefeltro in Italy.

Sao Tome and Principe*

Dioc., 1; bp., 1; parishes, 12; priests, 9 (1 dioc., 8 rel.); sem. 11; bros., 3; srs., 20; bap., 2,147; Caths., 94,000 (85.4%); tot. pop., 110,000.

Independent republic (July 12, 1975), consisting of two islands off the western coast of Africa in the Gulf of Guinea; former Portuguese territory; capital, Sao Tome. Evangelization was begun by the Portuguese who discovered the islands in 1471-72. The Sao Tome diocese was established in 1534.

Saudi Arabia

Parishes, 5; priests, 4 (1 dioc., 3 rel.); srs., 20; bap., 227; Caths., 320,000; tot. pop., 12,010,000.

Monarchy occupying four-fifths of Arabian peninsula; capital, Riyadh. Under ecclesiastical jurisdiction of Arabia vicariate apostolic.

Scotland

Archd., 2; dioc., 6; card., 1; abp., 2; bp., 9; parishes, 479; priests, 980 (762 dioc., 218 rel.); p.d., 4; sem., 130; bros., 107; srs., 1,045; bap., 13,236; Caths., 804,000 (15.3%); tot. pop., 5,239,000. (1988 Annuario Pontificio.)

Part of the United Kingdom, in the northern British Isles; capital, Edinburgh. Christianity was introduced by the early years of the fifth century. The arrival of St. Columba and his monks in 563 inaugurated a new era of evangelization which reached into remote areas by the end of the sixth century. He was extremely influential in determining the character of the Celtic Church, which was tribal, monastic, and in union with Rome. Considerable disruption of church activity resulted from Scandinavian invasions in the late eighth and ninth centuries. By 1153 the Scottish

Church took a turn away from its insularity and was drawn into closer contact with the European community. Anglo-Saxon religious and political relations, complicated by rivalries between princes and ecclesiastical superiors, were not always the happiest. Religious orders expanded greatly in the 12th century. From shortly after the Norman Conquest of England to 1560 the Church suffered adverse effects from the Hundred Years' War, the Black Death, the Western Schism and other developments. In 1560 parliament abrogated papal supremacy over the Church in Scotland and committed the country to Protestantism in 1567. The Catholic Church was proscribed, to remain that way for more than 200 years, and the hierarchy was disbanded. Defections made the Church a minority religion from that time on. Presbyterian church government was ratified in 1690. Priests launched the Scottish Mission in 1653, incorporating themselves as a mission body under a prefect apostolic and working underground to serve the faithful in much the same way their confreres did in England. About 100 heather priests, trained in clandestine places in the heather country, were ordained by the early 19th century. Catholics got some relief from legal disabilities in 1793 and more later. Many left the country about that time. Some of their numbers were filled subsequently by immigrants from Ireland. The hierarchy was restored in 1878. Scotland, though predominantly Protestant, has a better record for tolerance than Northern Ireland.

Senegal*

Archd., 1; dioc., 4; p.a., 1; card., 1 (native); bp., 4 (native); parishes, 80; priests, 241 (98 dioc., 143 rel.); sem., 78; bros., 139; srs., 546; bap., 10,207 Caths., 287,000 (4.3%); tot. pop., 6,610,000.

Republic in western Africa; capital, Dakar. The country had its first contact with Catholicism through the Portuguese some time after 1460. Some incidental missionary work was done by Jesuits and Capuchins in the 16th and 17th centuries. A vicariate for the area was placed in charge of the Holy Ghost Fathers in 1779. More effective evangelization efforts were accomplished after the Senegambia vicariate was established in 1955.

Seychelles*

Dioc., 1; bp., 1 (native); parishes, 17; priests, 20 (9 dioc., 11 rel.); sem., 3; bros., 9; srs., 58; bap., 1,530; Caths., 60,000; tot. pop., 70,000.

Independent (1976) group of 92 islands in the Indian Ocean 970 miles east of Kenya; capital, Victoria. Catholicism was introduced in the 18th century. A vicariate apostolic was organized in 1852. All education in the islands was conducted under Catholic auspices until 1954.

Sierra Leone

Archd., 1; dioc., 2; abp., 1 (native); bp., 2; parishes, 31; priests, 125 (24 dioc., 101 rel.); sem., 51; bros., 16; srs., 110; bap., 3,020; Caths., 76,000 (2%); tot. pop., 3,670,000. (AD)

Republic on the western coast of Africa; capital, Freetown. Catholicism was introduced in 1858. Members of the African Missions Society, the first Catholic missionaries in the area, were joined by Holy Ghost Fathers in 1864. Protestant missionaries were active in the area before their Catholic counterparts. Educational work had a major part in Catholic endeavor. The hierarchy was established in 1950.

Singapore*

Archd., 1; abp., 1 (native); parishes, 26; priests, 113 (71 dioc., 42 rel.); sem., 31; bros., 46; srs., 244; bap., 3,116; Caths., 105,000 (4%); tot. pop., 2,590,000.

Independent island republic off the southern tip of the Malay Peninsula; capital, Singapore. Christianity was introduced in the area by Portuguese c olonists about 1511. Singapore was founded in 1819; the first parish church was built in 1846.

Solomon Islands*

Archd., 1; dioc., 2; abp., 1; bp., 2; parishes, 26; priests, 36 (10 dioc., 26 rel.); p.d. 1; sem., 12; bros., 25; srs., 114; bap., 2,200; Caths., 56,000 (19.6%); tot. pop., 285,000.

Independent (July 7, 1978) island group in Oceania; capital, Honiara, on Guadalcanal. Evangelization of the Southern Solomons, begun earlier but interrupted because of violence against them, was resumed by the Marists in 1898. A vicariate apostolic was organized in 1912. A similar jurisdiction was set up for the Western Solomons in 1959. World War II caused a great deal of damage to mission installations.

Somalia

Dioc., 1; bp., 1; parishes, 2; priests, 4 (rel.); bro., 1; srs., 70; bap., 10; Caths., 2,000; tot. pop., 4,760,000. (AD)

Republic on the eastern coast of Africa; capital, Mogadishu. The country has been Moslem for centuries. Pastoral activity has been confined to immigrants. Schools and hospitals were nationalized in 1972, resulting in the departure of some foreign missionaries.

South Africa

Archd., 4; dioc. (1988), 20; abb., 1; p.a. (1988), 1; mil. ord.; card., 1; abp., 3; bp., 21; parishes, 805; priests, 1,052 (279 dioc., 773 rel.); p.d., 115; sem., 220; bros., 315; srs., 3,466; bap., 68,116; Caths., 2,602,000 (7.8%); tot. pop., 33,220,000. (AD)

Republic in the southern part of Africa; capitals, Cape Town (legislative), Pretoria (administrative) and Bloemfontein (judicial). Christianity was introduced by the Portuguese who discovered the Cape of Good Hope in 1488. Boers, who founded Cape Town in 1652, expelled Catholics from the region. There was no Catholic missionary activity from that time until the 19th century. After a period of British opposition, a bishop established residence in 1837 and evangelization got under way thereafter among the Bantus and white immigrants. In recent years church authorities have strongly protested the white supremacy policy of apartheid which seriously infringes the human rights of the native Blacks and impedes the Church from carrying out its pastoral, educational and social service functions. The hierarchy was established in 1951.

Spain*

Archd., 13; dioc., 52; mil. ord.; card. (1988), 6; abp., 9; bp., 65; parishes, 21,424; priests, 30,845 (20,282 dioc., 10,563 rel.); p.d., 112; sem., 3,388; bros., 6,683; srs., 76,875; bap., 417,011; Caths., 37,852,000 (97.8%); tot. pop., 38,670,000.

Constitutional monarchy on the Iberian peninsula in southwestern Europe; capital, Madrid. Christians were on the peninsula by 200; some of them suffered martyrdom during persecutions of the third century. A council held in Elvira about 304/6 enacted the first legislation on clerical celibacy in the West. Vandals invaded the peninsula in the fifth century, bringing with them an Arian brand of Christianity which they retained until their conversion following the baptism of their king Reccared, in 589. One of the significant developments of the seventh century was the establishment of Toledo as the primatial see. The Visigoth kingdom lasted to the time of the Arab invasion, 711-14. The Church survived under Moslem rule but experienced some doctrinal and disciplinary irregularities as well as harassment. Reconquest of most of the peninsula was accomplished by 1248; unification was achieved during the reign of Ferdinand and Isabella. The discoveries of Columbus and other explorers ushered in an era of colonial expansion in which Spain became one of the greatest mission-sending countries in history. In 1492, in repetition of anti-Semitic actions of 694, the expulsion of unbaptized Jews was decreed, leading to mass baptisms but a questionable number of real conversions in 1502. (The Jewish minority numbered about 165,000.) Activity by the Inquisition followed. Spain was not seriously affected by the Reformation. Ecclesiastical decline set in about 1650. Anti-Church actions authorized by a constitution enacted in 1812 resulted in the suppression of religious and other encroachments on the leaders, people and goods of the Church. Political, religious and cultural turmoil recurred during the 19th century and into the 20th. A revolutionary republic was proclaimed in 1931, triggering a series of developments which led to civil war from 1936 to 1939. During the conflict, which pitted leftist Loyalists against the forces of Francisco Franco, 6,632 priests and religious and an unknown number of lay persons perished in addition to thousands of victims of combat. One-man, one-party rule, established after the civil war and with rigid control policies with respect to personal liberties and social and economic issues, continued for more than 35 years before giving way after the death of Franco to democratic reforms. The Catholic Church, long the established religion, was disestablished under a new constitution providing guarantees of freedom for other religions as well. Disestablishment was ratified with modifications of a 1976 revision of the earlier concordat of 1953.

Sri Lanka*

Archd., 1; dioc., 9; card., 1; abp., 1; bp., 10; parishes, 320; priests, 680 (401 dioc., 279 rel.); p.d., 1; sem., 250; bros., 234; srs., 2,148; bap., 27,115; Caths., 1,391,000 (8.6%); tot. pop., 16,120,000.

Independent socialist republic, island southeast of India (formerly Ceylon); capital, Colombo. Effective evangelization began in 1543 and made great progress by the middle of the 17th century. The Church was seriously hampered during the Dutch period from about 1650 to 1795. Anti-Catholic laws were repealed by the British in 1806. The hierarchy was established in 1886. Leftist governments and other factors have worked against the Church since the country became independent in 1948. The high percentage of indigenous clergy and religious has been of great advantage to the Church.

Sudan*

Archd., 2; dioc., 7; abp., 2 (native); bp., 5 (native); parishes, 97; priests, 237 (57 dioc., 180 rel.); p.d., 1; sem., 85; bros., 48; srs., 311; bap., 18,071; Caths., 1,606,000 (7.2%); tot. pop., 22,180,000.

Republic in northeastern Africa, the largest country on the continent; capital, Khartoum. Christianity was introduced from Egypt and gained acceptance in the sixth century. Under Arab rule, it was eliminated in the northern region. No Christians were in the country in 1600. Evangelization attempts begun in the 19th century in the south yielded hard-won results. By 1931 there were nearly 40,000 Catholics there, and considerable progress was made by missionaries after that time. In 1957, a year after the republic was established, Catholic schools were nationalized. An act restrictive of religious freedom went into effect in 1962, resulting in the harassment and expulsion of foreign missionaries. By 1964 all but a few Sudanese missionaries had been forced out of the southern region. The northern area, where Islam predominates, is impervious to Christian influence. Late in 1971 some missionaries were allowed to return to work in the South. Southern Sudan was granted regional autonomy within a unified country in March, 1972, thus ending often bitter fighting between the North and South dating back to 1955. The hierarchy was established in 1974. The imposition of Islamic penal codes in 1984 was a cause of concern to all Christian churches.

Suriname

Dioc., 1; bp., 1; parishes, 17; priests, 33 (5 dioc., 28 rel.); sem., 1; bros., 20; srs., 73; bap., 2,172; Caths., 81,000 (21.3%); tot. pop., 380,000. (AD)

Independent (Nov. 25, 1975) state in northern South America (formerly Dutch Guiana); capital, Paramaribo, Catholicism was introduced in 1683. Evangelization began in 1817.

Swaziland

Dioc., 1; bp., 1 (native); priests, 36 (3 dioc., 33 rel.); sem., 2; bros., 8; srs., 90; bap., 647; Caths., 40,000 (5.9%); tot. pop., 650,000. (AD)

Monarchy in southern Africa; almost totally surrounded by South Africa; capital, Mbabane. Missionary work was entrusted to the Servites in 1913. A prefecture apostolic was organized in 1923. The hierarchy was established in 1951. (See Index for papal visit.)

Sweden*

Dioc., 1; bp., 1; parishes, 36; priests, 100 (41 dioc., 59 rel.); p.d., 6; sem., 19; bros., 8; srs., 259; bap., 1.066; Caths., 120,000 (1.4%); tot. pop., 8,379,000.

Constitutional monarchy in northwestern Europe; capital, Stockholm. Christianity was introduced by St. Ansgar, a Frankish monk, in 829/30. The Church became well established in the 12th century and was a major influence at the end of the Middle Ages. Political and other factors favored the introduction and spread of the Lutheran Church which became the state religion in 1560. The Augsburg Confession of 1530 was accepted by the government; all relations with Rome were severed; monasteries were suppressed; the very presence of Catholics in the country was forbidden in 1617. A decree of tolerance for foreign Catholics was issued about 1781. Two years later a vicariate apostolic was organized for the country. In 1873 Swedes were given the legal right to leave the Lutheran Church and join another Christian church. (Membership in the Lutheran Church is presumed by law unless notice is given of membership in another church.) In 1923 there were only 11 priests and five churches in the country. Since 1952 Catholics have enjoyed almost complete religious freedom. The hierarchy was reestablished in 1953. Hindrances to growth of the Church are the strongly entrenched established church, limited resources, a clergy shortage and the size of the country.

Switzerland

Dioc., 6; abb., 2; bp., 10; parishes, 1,702; priests, 3,952 (2,332 dioc., 1,620 rel.); p.d., 35; sem., 221; bros., 349; srs., 9,411; bap., 33,860; Caths., 3,072,000 (47.2%); tot. pop., 6,500,000. (Nuncio)

Confederation in central Europe; capital, Bern. Christianity was introduced in the fourth century or earlier and was established on a firm footing before the barbarian invasions of the sixth century. Constance, established as a diocese in the seventh century, was a stronghold of the faith against the pagan Alamanni, in particular, who were not converted until some time in the ninth century. During this period of struggle with the barbarians, a number of monasteries of great influence were established. The Reformation in Switzerland was triggered by Zwingli in 1519 and furthered by him at Zurich until his death in battle against the Catholic cantons in 1531. Calvin set in motion the forces that made Geneva the international capital of the Reformation and transformed it into a theocracy. Catholics mobilized a Counter-Reformation in 1570, six years after Calvin's death. Struggle between Protestant and Catholic cantons was a fact of Swiss life for several hundred years. The Helvetic Constitution enacted at the turn of the 19th century embodied anti-Catholic measures and consequences, among them the dissolution of 130 monasteries. The Church was reorganized later in the century to meet the threats of liberalism, radicalism and the Kulturkampf. In the process, the Church, even though on the defensive, gained the strength and cohesion that characterizes it to the present time. The six dioceses in the country are immediately subject to the Holy See. In 1973, constitutional articles banning Jesuits from the country and prohibiting the establishment of convents and monasteries were repealed.

Syria*

Patriarchates, 3 (Antioch of Maronites, Greek Melkites and Syrians; patriarchs of Maronites and Syrians reside in Lebanon); Archd., 12 (1 Armenian, 2 Maronite, 5 Greek-Melkite, 4 Syrian); dioc., 3 (Armenian, Chaldean, Maronite); v.a., 1 (Latin); patriarch, 1; abp., 12; bp., 5; parishes, 188; priests, 211 (134 dioc., 77 rel.); p.d., 2; sem., 45; bros., 10; srs., 399; bap., 2,490; Caths., 270,000 (2.5%); tot. pop., 10,610,000.

Arab socialist republic in southwest Asia; capital, Damascus. Christian communities were formed in apostolic times. It is believed that St. Peter established a see at Antioch before going to Rome. Damascus became a center of influence. The area was the place of great men and great events in the early history of the Church. Monasticism developed there in the fourth century. So did the Monophysite and Monothelite heresies to which portion of the Church succumbed. Byzantine Syrians who remained in communion with Rome were given the name Melkites. Christians of various persuasions — Jacobites, Orthodox and Melkites — were subject to various degrees of harassment from the Arabs who took over in 638 and from the Ottoman Turks who isolated the country and remained in control from 1516 to the end of World War II.

Taiwan

Archd., 1; dioc., 6; abp., 2; bp., 6; parishes, 446; priests, 760 (226 dioc., 534 rel.); sem., 90; bros., 80; srs., 1,160; bap., 4,548; Caths., 290,000 (1.48%); tot. pop., 19,466,000.

Location of the Nationalist Government of the Republic of China*, an island 100 miles off the southern coast of mainland China (also known as Formosa); capital, Taipei. Attempts to introduce Christianity in the 17th century were unsuccessful. Evangelization in the 19th century resulted in some 1,300 converts in 1895. Missionary endeavor was hampered by the Japanese who occupied the island following the Sino-Japanese war of 1894-95. Nine thousand Catholics were reported in 1938. Great progress was made in missionary endeavor among the Chinese who emigrated to the island following the Communist take-over of the mainland in 1949. The hierarchy was established in 1952.

Tanzania*

Archd., 4; dioc., 25; card., 1 (native); abp., 3 (native); bp., 23 (22 native) (preceding figures as of Jan. 1, 1988); parishes, 677; priests, 1,495 (861 dioc., 634 rel.); p.d. 2; sem., 612; bros., 384; srs., 4,709; bap., 167,560; Caths., 4,719,000 (21%); tot. pop., 22,460,000.

Republic (consisting of former Tanganyika on the eastern coast of Africa and former Zanzibar, an island group off the eastern coast); capital, Dar es Salaam. The first Catholic mission in the former Tanganyikan portion of the republic was manned by Holy Ghost Fathers in 1868. The hierarchy was established there in 1953. Zanzibar was the landing place of Augustinians with the Portuguese in 1499. Some evangelization was attempted between then and 1698 when the Arabs expelled all priests from the territory. There was no Catholic missionary activity from then until the 1860s. The Holy Ghost Fathers arrived in 1863 and were entrusted with the mission in 1872. Zanzibar was important as a point of departure for missionaries to Tanganyika, Kenya and other places in East Africa. A vicariate for Zanzibar was set up in 1906.

Thailand*

Archd., 2; dioc., 8; card., 1 (native); abp., 1 (native); bp., 8 (native); parishes, 269; priests, 473 (234 dioc., 239 rel.); sem., 243; bros., 129; srs., 1,199; bap., 6,165; Caths., 216,000 (.4%); tot. pop., 52,090,000.

Constitutional monarchy in southeastern Asia (formerly Siam); capital, Bangkok. The first Christians in the region were Portuguese traders who arrived early in the 16th century. A number of missionaries began arriving in 1554 but pastoral care was confined mostly to the Portuguese until the 1660s. Evangelization of the natives got under way from about that time. A seminary was organized in 1665, a vicariate was set up four years later, and a point of departure was established for missionaries to Tonkin, Cochin China and China. Persecution and death for some of the missionaries ended evangelization efforts in 1688. It was resumed, however, and made progress from 1824 onwards. In 1881 missionaries were sent from Siam to neighboring Laos. The hierarchy was established in 1965. Abp., Michai Kitbunchu was named the first Thai cardinal in 1983.

Togo*

Archd., 1; dioc., 3; abp., 1 (native); bp., 2 (native); parishes, 86; priests, 247 (127 dioc., 120 rel.); sem., 143; bros., 83; srs., 326; bap., 23,822; Caths., 669,000 (21.9%); tot. pop., 3,050,000.

Republic on the western coast of Africa; capital, Lome. The first Catholic missionaries in the area, where slave raiders operated for nearly 200 years, were members of the African Missions Society who arrived in 1563. They were followed by Divine Word Missionaries in 1914, when a prefecture apostolic was organized. At that time the Catholic population numbered about 19,000. The African Missionaries returned after their German predecessors were deported following World War I. The first native priest was ordained in 1922. The hierarchy was established in 1955.

Tokelau

Parish, 1; p.d., 1; srs., 4; catechist, 5; bap., 22; Caths., 1,000; tot. pop., 2,000. (AD)

Pacific islands administered by New Zealand. Forms part of Samoa-Apia and Tokelau archdiocese, Western Samoa.

Tonga

Dioc., 1; bp., 1 (native); parishes, 13; priests, 22 (13 dioc., 9 rel.); sem., 16; bros., 12; srs., 61; bap., 528; Caths., 13,000 (13.4%); tot. pop., 97,000.

Polynesian monarchy in the southwestern Pacific, consisting of about 150 islands; capital Nuku'alofa. Marists started missionary work in 1842, some years after Protestants had begun evangelization. By 1880 the Catholic population numbered about 1,700. A vicariate was organized in 1937. The hierarchy was established in 1966.

Trinidad and Tobago*

Archd., 1; abp., 1; parishes, 60; priests, 119 (29 dioc., 90 rel.); sem., 27; bros., 20; srs., 189; bap., 9,140; Caths., 400,000 (33.3%); tot. pop., 1,200,000.

Independent nation, consisting of two islands in the Caribbean; capital, Port-of-Spain. The first Catholic church in Trinidad was built in 1591, years after several missionary ventures had been launched and a number of missionaries killed. Capuchins were there from 1618 until about 1802. Missionary work continued after the British gained control early in the 19th century. Cordial relations have existed between the Church and state, both of which have manifested their desire for the development of native clergy.

Tunisia*

Prel., 1; abp., 1; parishes, 15; priests, 48 (20 dioc., 28 rel.); sem., 1; bros., 7; srs., 212; bap., 23; Caths., 15,000 (.2%); tot. pop., 7,230,000.

Republic on the northern coast of Africa; capital, Tunis. There were few Christians in the territory until the 19th century. A prefecture apostolic was organized in 1843 and the Carthage archdiocese was established in 1884. The Catholic population in 1892 consisted of most of the approximately 50,000 Europeans in the country. When Tunis became a republic in 1956, most of the Europeans left the country. The Holy See and the Tunisian government concluded an agreement in 1964 which changed the Carthage archdiocese into a prelacy and handed over some ecclesiastical property to the republic. A considerable number of Moslem students are in Catholic schools, but the number of Moslem converts to the Church has been small.

Turkey*

Patriarchate, 1 (Cilicia for the Armenians,

the patriarch resides in Lebanon); archd., 3; dioc., 2; v.a., 2; mission "sui juris," 1; ap. ex., 1; abp., 4; bp., 2; parishes, 62; priests, 72 (14 dioc., 58 rel.); p.d., 2; sem., 2; bros., 23; srs., 142; bap., 150; Caths., 17,000 (.03)%); tot. pop., 50,300,000.

Republic in Asia Minor and southeastern Europe, capital, Ankara. Christian communities were established in apostolic times, as attested in the Acts of the Apostles, some of the Letters of St. Paul, and Revelation. The territory was the scene of heresies and ecumenical councils, the place of residence of Fathers of the Church, the area in which ecclesiastical organization reached the dimensions of more than 450 sees in the middle of the seventh century. The region remained generally Byzantine except for the period of the Latin occupation of Constantinople from 1204 to 1261, but was conquered by the Ottoman Turks in 1453 and remained under their domination until establishment of the republic in 1923. Christians, always a minority, numbered more Orthodox than Latins; they were all under some restriction during the Ottoman period. They suffered persecution in the 19th and 20th centuries, the Armenians being the most numerous victims. Turkey is overwhelmingly Moslem. Catholics are tolerated to a degree.

Turks and Caicos Islands

Mission "sui juris," 1; parish, 1; priest, 1 (rel.); bap., 19; Caths., 2,000; tot. pop., 14,000. (AD, Antilles)

British possession in West Indies; capital, Grand Turk.

Tuvalu

Mission "sui juris," 1; priest, 1 (rel.); bap., 3; Caths., 100; tot. pop., 9,000.

Independent state (1978) in Oceania, consisting of 9 islands (formerly Ellice Islands); capital, Funafuti.

Uganda*

Archd., 1; dioc., 13; mil. ord., card., 1 (native); bp., 16 (15 native); parishes, 330; priests, 1,074 (748 dioc., 326 rel.); p.d., 2; sem., 581; bros., 318; srs., 2,271; bap., 230,448; Caths., 6,663,000 (41.6%); tot. pop., 16,020,000.

Republic in eastern Africa; capital, Kampala. The Missionaries of Africa (White Fathers) were the first Catholic missionaries, starting in 1879. Persecution broke out from 1885 to 1887, taking a toll of 22 Catholic martyrs, who were canonized in 1964, and a number of Anglican victims. (Pope Paul honored all those who died for the faith during a visit to Kampala in 1969.) By 1888, there were more than 8,000 Catholics. Evangelization was resumed in 1894, after being interrupted by war, and proceeded thereafter. The first native African bishop was ordained in 1939. The hierarchy was established in 1953. The Church was suppressed during the erratic regime of Pres. Idi-Amin, who was deposed in the spring of 1979.

Union of Soviet Socialist Republics

Union of 15 Soviet Socialist Republics in northern Eurasia, from the Baltic Sea to the Pacific; Russian capital, Moscow. The Orthodox Church has been predominant in Russian history. It developed from the Byzantine Church before 1064. Some of its members subsequently established communion with Rome as the result of reunion movements but most of them remained Orthodox. The government has always retained some kind of general or particular control of this church. Latins, always a minority, had a little more freedom. From the beginning of the Communist government in 1917, all churches of whatever kind — including Jews and Moslems — became the targets of official campaigns designed to negate their influence on society and/or to eliminate them entirely. An accurate assessment of the situation of the Catholic Church in Russia is difficult to make. Its dimensions, however, can be gauged from the findings of a team of research specialists made public by the Judiciary Committee of the U.S. House of Representatives in 1964. It was reported: "The fate of the Catholic Church in the USSR and countries occupied by the Russians from 1917 to 1959 shows the following: (a) the number killed: 55 bishops; 12,800 priests and monks; 2.5 million Catholic believers; (b) imprisoned or deported: 199 bishops; 32,000 priests and 10 million believers; (c) 15,700 priests were forced to abandon their priesthood and accept other jobs; and (d) a large number of seminaries and religious communities were dissolved; 1,600 monasteries were nationalized, 31,779 churches were closed. 400 newspapers were prohibited, and all Catholic organizations were dissolved." Several Latin Rite churches are open; e.g., in Moscow, Leningrad, Odessa and Tiflis. An American chaplain is stationed in Moscow to serve Catholics at the U.S. embassy there. Recent reports indicate that, despite repression and attempts at Sovietization, the strongholds of Catholicism in the USSR are Lithuania (incorporated in the USSR in 1940, together with Estonia and Latvia) and the Ukraine. No Catholic statistics are available for the USSR. See separate entries for Estonia, Latvia, Lithuania. Population, 279,904,000. (See Index for Ukrainian Millennium.)

United Arab Emirates

V.a., 1; bp., 1; parishes, 4; priests, 10 (4 dioc., 6 rel.); sem. 3; srs., 26; bap., 694; Caths., 60,000; tot. pop., 1,380,000.

Independent state along Persian Gulf; capital, Abu Dhabi.

United States*

See Catholic History in the United States, Statistics of the Church in the United States.

Uruguay*

Archd., 1; dioc., 9; abp., 1; bp., 12; parishes, 223; priests, 703 (196 dioc., 507 rel.); p.d., 32; sem., 81; bros., 144; srs., 2,029; bap., 43,497; Caths., 2,381,000 (78.9%); tot. pop., 3,016,000.

Republic (called the Eastern Republic of Uruguay) on the southeast coast of South America; capital, Montevideo. The Spanish established a settlement in 1624 and evangelization followed.

Missionaries followed the reduction pattern to reach the Indians, form them in the faith and train them in agriculture, husbandry, other useful arts, and the experience of managing property and living in community. Montevideo was made a diocese in 1878. The constitution of 1830 made Catholicism the religion of the state and subsidized some of its activities, principally the missions to the Indians. Separation of Church and state was provided for in the constitution of 1917. (See Index for papal visit.)

Vanuatu

Dioc., 1; bp., 1; parishes, 23; priests, 21 (3 dioc., 18 rel.); p.d., 1; sem., 11; bros., 10; srs., 66; bap., 600; Caths., 18,000 (15%); tot. pop., 128,000.

Independent (July 29, 1980) island group in the southwest Pacific, about 500 miles west of Fiji (formerly New Hebrides); capital, Vila. Effective, though slow, evangelization by Catholic missionaries began about 1887. A vicariate apostolic was set up in 1904. The hierarchy was established in 1966.

Vatican City

See separate entry.

Venezuela*

Archd., 6; dioc., 18; v.a., 4; card., 2; abp., 4; bp., 33; parishes, 1,016; priests, 2,005 (898 dioc., 1,107 rel.); p.d., 29, sem., 700; bros., 285; srs., 3,930; bap., 372,159; Caths., 16,317,000 (91.7%); tot. pop., 17,790,000.

Republic in northern South America; capital, Caracas. Evangelization began in 1513-14 and involved members of a number of religious orders who worked in assigned territories, developing missions into pueblos or towns and villages of Indian converts. Nearly 350 towns originated as missions. Fifty-four missionaries met death by violence from the start of missionary work until 1817. Missionary work was seriously hindered during the wars of independence in the second decade of the 19th century and continued in decline through the rest of the century as dictator followed dictator in a period of political turbulence. Restoration of the missions got under way in 1922. The first diocese was established in 1531. Most of the bishops have been native Venezuelans. The first diocesan synod was held in 1574. Church-state relations are regulated by an agreement concluded with the Holy See in 1964.

Vietnam

Archd., 3; dioc., 22; card., 1; abp., 2; bp., 31. No statistics are available. There were 2,749,475 Catholics (6.4% of the total population) in 1974. Pop., 60,920,000. (AD)

Country in southeastern Asia, reunited officially July 2, 1976, as the Socialist Republic of Vietnam; capital, Hanoi. Previously, from 1954, partitioned into the Democratic Peoples' Republic of Vietnam in the North (capital, Hanoi) and the Republic of Vietnam in the South (capital, Saigon). Catholicism was introduced in 1533 but missionary work was intermittent until 1615 when Jesuits arrived to stay. One hundred thousand Catholics were reported in 1639. Two vicariates were organized in 1659. A seminary was set up in 1666 and two native priests were ordained two years later. A congregation of native women religious formed in 1670 is still active. Severe persecution broke out in 1698, three times in the 18th century, and again in the 19th. Between 100,000 and 300,000 persons suffered in some way from persecution during the 50 years before 1883 when the French moved in to secure religious liberty for the Catholics. Most of the 117 beatified Martyrs of Vietnam were killed during this 50-year period. After the French were forced out of Vietnam in 1954, the country was partitioned at the 17th parallel. The North went Communist and the Viet Cong, joined by North Vietnamese regular army troops in 1964, fought to gain control of the South. In 1954 there were approximately 1,114,000 Catholics in the North and 480,000 in the South. More than 650,000 fled to the South to avoid the government repression that silenced the Church in the North. In South Vietnam, the Church continued to develop during the war years. Fragmentary reports about the status of the Church since the end of the war in 1975 have been ominous. Freedom of religious belief, promised by the Revolutionary Government in May, 1975, shortly after its capture of Saigon (Ho Chi Min City), is denied in practice. Late in 1983, the government initiated support for a "patriotic" Catholic church analogous to the communist-sponsored church in China. The hierarchy was established in 1960. The apostolic delegation, formerly in Saigon, was transferred to Hanoi in 1976; it is presently vacant.

Virgin Islands

Dioc., 1 (St. Thomas, suffragan of Washington, D.C.); bp., 1; parishes, 7; priests, 27 (6 dioc., 21 rel.); p.d., 15; bros., 3; srs., 14; bap., 665; Caths., 30,000; tot. pop., 121,000.

Organized unincorporated U.S. territory, about 34 miles east of Puerto Rico; capital, Charlotte Amalie on St. Thomas (one of the three principal islands). The islands were discovered by Columbus in 1493 and named for St. Ursula and her virgin companions. Missionaries began evangelization in the 16th century. A church on St. Croix dates from about 1660; another, on St. Thomas, from 1774. The Baltimore archdiocese had jurisdiction over the islands from 1804 to 1820 when it was passed on to the first of several places in the Caribbean area. Some trouble arose over a pastoral appointment in the 19th century, resulting in a small schism. The Redemptorists took over pastoral care in 1858; normal conditions have prevailed since.

British Virgin Islands

Parish, 1; priests, 2 (rel.); catechists, 2; bap., 18; Caths., 400; tot. pop., 10,000.

British possession in Caribbean; capital, Road Town.

Wales

Archd., 1; dioc., 2; abp., 1; bp., 2; parishes, 169; priests, 304 (176 dioc., 128 rel.); p.d., 6;

sem., 32; bros., 28; srs., 622; bap., 3,116; Caths., 151,491 (5.1%); tot. pop., 2,951,100 (1988 Annuario Pontificio.)

Part of the United Kingdom, on the western part of the island of Great Britain. Celtic missionaries completed evangelization by the end of the sixth century, the climax of what has been called the age of saints. Welsh Christianity received its distinctive Celtic character at this time. Some conflict developed when attempts were made — and proved successful later — to place the Welsh Church under the jurisdiction of Canterbury; the Welsh opted for direct contact with Rome. The Church made progress despite the depredations of Norsemen in the eighth and ninth centuries. Norman infiltration occurred near the middle of the 12th century, resulting in a century-long effort to establish territorial dioceses and parishes to replace the Celtic organizational plan of monastic centers and satellite churches. The Western Schism produced split views and allegiances. Actions of Henry VIII in breaking away from Rome had serious repercussions. Proscription and penal laws crippled the Church, resulted in heavy defections in which more than 91 persons died for the faith. Methodism prevailed by 1750. Modern Catholicism came to Wales with Irish immigrants in the 19th century, when the number of Welsh Catholics was negligible. Catholic emancipation was granted in 1829. The hierarchy was restored in 1850.

Wallis and Futuna Islands

Dioc., 1; bp., 1 (native); parishes, 5; priests, 15 (10 dioc., 5 rel.); sem., 2; bros., 7; srs., 42; bap., 350; Caths., 14,000 (almost the entire population).

French overseas territory in the southwestern Pacific; capital Mata-Utu. Marists, who began evangelizing the islands in 1836-7, were the first Catholic missionaries. The entire populations of the two islands were baptized by the end of 1842 (Wallis) and 1843 (Futuna). The first missionary to the latter island was killed in 1841. Most of the priests on the islands are native Polynesians. The hierarchy was established in 1966.

Western Sahara

P.a., 1; parishes, 2; priests, 2 (rel.); Caths., 200; tot. pop., 160,000.

Former Spanish overseas province (Spanish Sahara) on the northwestern coast of Africa. Territory is under control of Morocco. Islam is the religion of non-Europeans. A prefecture apostolic was established in 1954 for the European Catholics there.

North Yemen

Parishes, 3; priests, 3 (rel.); srs., 25; bap., 19; Caths., 3,000; tot. pop., 7,050,000.

Arab republic in southwestern Arabia; capital, Sanaa. Christians perished in the first quarter of the sixth century. Moslems have been in control since the seventh century. The state religion is Islam. In 1973, for the first time in 1,400 years, Catholic personnel — priests, religious, lay persons — were invited to work in the country as staff of a government hospital; they were not to engage in proselytizing. Under ecclesiastical jurisdiction of Arabia vicariate apostolic.

South Yemen

Parish, 1; priest, 1 (rel); Caths., 500; tot. pop., 2,360,000.

People's Democratic Republic of Yemen in the southern part of the Arabian peninsula; capital, Aden. No Christian community has existed there since the Moslem conquest of the seventh century. Catholics are from other countries. Under ecclesiastical jurisdiction of Arabia vicariate apostolic.

Yugoslavia*

Archd., 8; dioc., 15; card., 1; abp., 7; bp., 25; parishes, 2,840; priests, 4,270 (2,728 dioc., 1,542 rel.); p.d., 5; sem., 812; bros., 224; srs., 6,099; bap., 79,965; Caths., 6,955,000 (29.9%); tot. pop., 23,270,000.

Socialist republic in southeastern Europe; capital, Belgrade. Christianity was introduced from the seventh to ninth centuries in the regions which were combined to form the nation after World War I. Since these regions straddled the original line of demarcation for the Western and Eastern Empires (and churches), and since the Reformation had little lasting effect, the Christians are nearly all either Roman Catholics or Byzantines (some in communion with Rome, the majority Orthodox). Yugoslavia was proclaimed a Socialist republic in 1945. Repression of religion became government policy. Between May, 1945, and December, 1950, persecution took the following toll: almost two-thirds of 22 dioceses lost their bishops; about 348 priests were killed; 200 priests were under arrest and in prison; 12 of 18 seminaries were closed; the Catholic press was confiscated; religious instruction was suppressed in all schools; 300 religious houses and institutions were confiscated, and nuns and other religious driven out; all Church property was expropriated; the ministry of priests was severely restricted and subject to government interference; many thousands of the faithful shared the fate of priests and religious in death, imprisonment and slave labor. Cardinal Stepinac, arrested in 1946 and the symbol of the Church under persecution in Yugoslavia, died Feb. 10, 1960. In an agreement signed June 25, 1966, the government recognized the Holy See's spiritual jurisdiction over the Church in the country and guaranteed to bishops the possibility of maintaining contact with Rome in ecclesiastical and religious matters. The Holy See confirmed the principle that the activity of ecclesiastics, in the exercise of priestly functions, must take place within the religious and ecclesiastical sphere, and that abuse of these functions for political ends would be illegal. Less than two months after the agreement was signed, a group of exiled Croatian priests issued a statement in which they accused the Yugoslav government of failing to abide by it. According to others, an improvement was noticeable.

Zaire*
Archd., 6; dioc., 41; card., 1 (native); abp., 5 (native); bp., 45 (43 native); parishes, 1,106; priests, 2,756 (1,120 dioc., 1,636 rel.); p.d., 3; sem., 2,640; bros., 888; srs., 5,090; bap., 509,588; Caths., 15,011,000 (48.6%); tot. pop., 30,850,000.

CATHOLIC WORLD STATISTICS

(Principal sources: *Statistical Yearbook of the Church, 1986*, the latest edition; *Annuario Pontificio, 1988*. Figures are as of Dec. 31, 1986, unless indicated otherwise.)

	Africa	North America[1]	South America	Asia	Europe	Oceania	WORLD TOTALS
Patriarchates[2]	2	1	—	8	2	—	13
Archdioceses	59	78	87	101	141	18	484
Dioceses	318	320	349	254	468	53	1,762
Prelatures	1	13	38	5	6	—	63
Abbacies	1	1	2	—	11	—	15
Exarchates/Ords.	—	2	3	1	8	—	14
Vicariates Apostolic	13	7	37	11	1	—	69
Prefectures	7	—	9	2	—	—	18
Independent Missions	2	1	—	2	—	1	6
Ap. Admin.	1	1	—	4	—	—	6
Mil. Ord.	3	4	8	3	9	2	29
Cardinals[3]	18	21	19	15	80	4	157
Patriarchs[2]	1	—	—	7	1	—	9
Archbishops	86	109	119	142	255	26	737[4]
Bishops	380	652	647	399	984	76	3,138[4]
Priests	18,353	83,984	35,305	29,324	230,487	5,433	402,886
Diocesan	8,070	51,167	16,406	15,591	159,682	2,794	253,710
Religious	10,283	32,817	18,899	13,733	70,805	2,639	149,176
Perm. Deacons	209	9,053	1,032	74	3,106	70	13,544
Brothers	5,214	13,831	6,414	5,548	30,929	2,805	64,741
Sisters	38,579	185,826	89,958	95,877	483,563	14,355	908,158
Maj. Seminarians	10,708	15,068	14,840	16,885	29,197	813	87,511
Sec. Insts., Men (Mbrs.)	87	31	3	26	318	1	466
Sec. Insts., Women (Mbrs.)	391	1,640	2,729	975	27,981	41	33,757
Lay Missionaries	1,329	264	341	437	—	146	2,517
Catechists	216,026	12,787	11,613	68,776	277	6,596	316,075
Parishes	8,434	32,499	17,528	13,593	137,092	2,350	211,496[5]
Elem./Primary Schools[6]	21,049	12,771	8,185	11,981	19,433	2,451	75,870
Students[6]	7,116,748	3,803,856	3,464,410	4,095,567	3,610,334	487,609	22,578,524
Secondary Schools	3,523	3,559	4,901	7,085	10,117	689	29,874
Students	990,029	1,507,529	1,968,415	3,677,205	3,373,762	312,676	11,829,616
Students in Higher Insts.[7]	10,529	265,143	102,223	500,219	130,660	1,898	1,010,672
Social Service Facilities	11,286	9,957	17,989	14,621	28,829	1,168	83,850
Hospitals	925	1,073	1,155	1,012	1,703	160	6,028
Dispensaries	3,369	1,712	2,434	2,787	2,161	155	12,618
Leprosariums	318	12	45	341	5	3	724
Homes for Aged/Handic.	362	1,239	1,360	716	6,829	192	10,698
Orphanages	594	610	1,194	2,089	2,382	176	7,045
Nurseries	688	535	2,592	1,415	2,319	22	7,571
Matrimonial Advice Ctrs.	858	1,278	1,096	859	2,467	192	6,750
Social Educ. Ctrs.	1,123	1,458	1,797	1,912	1,653	100	8,043
Other Institutions	3,049	2,040	6,316	3,490	9,310	168	24,373
Baptisms	2,457,254	4,196,886	5,679,353	2,246,420	3,166,922	134,571	17,881,406
Under Age 7	1,677,090	4,039,128	5,446,146	1,914,162	3,132,957	118,079	16,327,562
Over Age 7	780,164	157,758	233,207	332,258	33,965	16,492	1,553,844
Marriages	209,009	967,892	1,125,412	430,994	1,268,907	33,768	4,035,982
Between Catholics	178,238	841,636	1,110,972	385,927	1,184,238	19,148	3,720,159
Mixed Marriages	30,771	126,256	14,440	45,067	84,669	14,620	315,823
Catholic Pop.[8]	74,988,000	184,556,000	245,922,000	73,428,000	278,935,000	6,550,000	864,379,000
World Population	571,946,000	404,210,000	273,535,000	2,924,557,000	700,085,000	24,784,000	4,899,117,000

[1]Includes Middle America. [2]For listing and description, see pages 143-44. [3]As of Aug. 30, 1988; see page 169. [4]Figures for the hierarchy (cardinals, archbishops and bishops) included 2,336 ordinaries, 640 coadjutors or auxiliaries, 162 with offices in the Roman Curia, 50 in other offices, 839 retired). [5]156,790 have parish priests; 51,564 are administered by another priest; 198 are entrusted to permanent deacons; 103, to Brothers; 808 to women Religious; 868 to lay people; 1,165 are vacant. [6]Does not include kindergartens which numbered 46,671, with 4,540,240 pupils. [7]There are also approximately 121,020 students in universities for ecclesiastical studies and 1,413,276 other university students. [8]Percentages of Catholics in world population: Africa, 13.1; North America (Caths., 65,302,000; tot. pop., 267,330,000), 24.4; Middle America (Caths., 119,254,000; tot. pop., 136,880,000), 87.1; South America, 89.9; Asia, 2.5; Europe, 39.8; Oceania, 26.4; World, 17.6. (Catholic totals do not include those in areas that could not be surveyed, estimated to be 15 million.)

Republic in south central Africa; (formerly the Congo); capital, Kinshasa. Christianity was introduced in 1484 and evangelization began about 1490. The first native bishop in black Africa was ordained in 1518. Subsequent missionary work was hindered by faulty methods of instruction and formation, inroads of the slave trade, wars among the tribes, and Portuguese policy based on the patronage system and having all the trappings of anticlericalism in the 18th and 19th centuries. Modern evangelization started in the second half of the 19th century. The hierarchy was established in 1959. In the civil disorders which followed independence in 1960, some missions and other church installations were abandoned, thousands of people reverted to tribal religions and many priests and religious were killed. Church-state tensions have developed in recent years because of the Church's criticism of the anti-Christian thrust of Pres. Mobutu's "Africanization" policies.

Zambia*

Archd., 2; dioc., 7; abp., 2 (native); bp., 7 (6 native); parishes, 224; priests, 549 (143 dioc., 406 rel.); p.d., 1; sem., 131; bros., 162; srs., 802; bap., 56,889; Caths., 1,973,000 (28.6%); tot. pop., 6,900,000.

Republic in central Africa; capital, Lusaka. Portuguese priests did some evangelizing in the 16th and 17th centuries but no results of their work remained in the 19th century. Jesuits began work in the south in the 1880s and White Fathers in the north and east in 1895. Evangelization of the western region began for the first time in 1831. The number of Catholics doubled in the 20 years following World War II.

Zimbabwe*

Archd., 1; dioc., 5; abp., 1 (native); bp., 5 (2 native); parishes, 129; priests, 313 (76 dioc., 237 rel.); p.d., 7; sem., 52; bros., 105; srs., 988; bap., 33,596; Caths., 742,000 (8.8%); tot. pop., 8,410,000.

Independent republic (Apr. 18, 1980) in south central Africa (formerly Rhodesia); capital, Harare (Salisbury). Earlier unsuccessful missionary ventures preceded the introduction of Catholicism in 1879. Missionaries began to make progress after 1893. The hierarchy was established in 1955; the first black bishop was ordained in 1973. In 1969, four years after the government of Ian Smith made a unilateral declaration of independence from England, a new constitution was enacted for the purpose of assuring continued white supremacy over the black majority. Catholic and Protestant prelates in the country protested vigorously against the constitution and related enactments as opposed to human rights of the blacks and restrictive of the Church's freedom to carry out its pastoral, educational and social service functions. The Smith regime was ousted in 1979 after seven years of civil war in which at least 25,000 people were killed. (See Index for papal visit.)

Pope John Paul's trip to Africa Sept. 10 to 19, 1988, was his fourth to that continent and the 39th outside Italy since the beginning of his pontificate in October, 1978.

EPISCOPAL CONFERENCES

(Principal source: *Annuario Pontificio*.)

Episcopal conferences, organized and operating under general norms and particular statutes approved by the Holy See, are official bodies in and through which the bishops of a given country or territory act together as pastors of the Church.

Listed below according to countries or regions are titles and addresses of conferences and names and sees of presidents (archbishops unless otherwise noted).

Africa, North: Conference Episcopale Regionale du Nord de l'Afrique (CERNA), 13 rue Khelifa-Boukhalfa, Algiers, Algeria. Henri Teissier (Coadjutor, Algiers).

Africa, South: Southern African Catholic Bishops' Conference (SACBC), P.O. Box 941, Pretoria 0001, S. Africa. Bp. Wilfred Fox Napier, O.F.M. (Kokstad).

Angola and Sao Tome: Conferencia Episcopal de Angola e Sao Tome (CEAST), C.P. 87 Luanda, Angola. Manuel F. da Costa (Lubango).

Antilles: Antilles Episcopal Conference, P.O. Box 43, 21 Hopefield Ave., Kingston 6, Jamaica. Samuel E. Carter, S.J. (Kingston in Jamaica).

Arab Countries: Conference des Eveques Latins dans les Regions Arabes (CELRA), Latin Patriarchate, P.O. Box 14152, Jerusalem (Old City). Patriarch Michel Sabbah (Jerusalem).

Argentina: Conferencia Episcopal Argentina (CEA), Calle Suipacha 1032, 1088 Buenos Aires. Card. Raul Francisco Primatesta (Cordoba).

Australia: Australian Episcopal Conference, P.O. Box 368, Canberra, A.C.T., 2601. Card. Edward Bede Clancy (Sydney).

Austria: Osterreichische Bischofskonferenz, Rotenturmstrasse 2, A1010 Vienna. Karl Berg (Salzburg).

Bangladesh: Catholic Bishops' Conference (CBCB), P.O. Box 3, Dhaka-2. Michael Rozario (Dhaka).

Belgium: Bisschoppenconferentie van Belgie — Conference Episcopale de Belgique, Aartsbisdom, Wollemarkt 15, B-2800 Mechelen. Card. Godfried Danneels (Mechelen-Brussel).

Benin: Conference Episcopale du Benin, B.P. 491, Cotonou. Christophe Adimou (Cotonou).

Bolivia: Conferencia Episcopal de Bolivia (CEB), Casilla 2309, La Paz. Bp. Julio Terrazas Sandoval, C.SS.R. (Oruro).

Brazil: Conferencia Nacional dos Bispos do Brasil (CNBB), C.P. 13-2067, 70401 Brasilia, D.F. Bp. Jose Ivo Lorscheiter (Santa Maria).

Bulgaria: Ulitza Pashovi 10-B, Sofia VI. Bp. Metodio Dimitrow Stratiew, A.A. (Apostolic Exarch, Sofia).

Burkina Faso and Niger: Conference des Eveques de Bourkina Faso et du Niger, B.P. 1195, Ouagadougou, Burkina Faso. Bp. Anselme Titanma Sanon (Bobo-Dioulasso).

Burma: Burma Catholic Bishops' Conference

(BCBC), 292 Prome Rd., Sanchaung P.O., Rangoon. Bp. Paul Zinghtung Grawng (Myitkyina).
Burundi: Conference Episcopale du Burundi, B. P. 1390, Bujumbura. Bp. Evariste Ngoyagoye (Bubanza).
Cameroon: Conference Episcopale Nationale du Cameroun (CENC), P.O. Box 272, Garoua. Card. Christian Wiyghan Tumi (Garoua).
Canada: See Canadian Conference of Catholic Bishops.
Central African Republic: Conference Episcopale Centrafricaine (CECA), B.P. 798, Bangui. Joachim N'Dayen (Bangui).
Chad: Conference Episcopale du Tchad, B.P. 456, N'Djamena. Charles Vandame, S.J. (N'Djamena).
Chile: Conferencia Episcopal de Chile (CECH), Casilla 517-V, Correo 21, Santiago. Bp. Carlos Gonzalez Cruchaga (Talca).
China (Republic of China, Taiwan): Regional Episcopal Conference of China, P.O. Box 36603, Taipeh 10552, Taiwan. Bp. Paul Shan Kuo-hsi, S.J. (Hwalien).
Colombia: Conferencia Episcopal de Colombia, Apartado 7448, Carrera 8 , N. 84-87, Bogota D.E. Card. Alfonso Lopez Trujillo (Medellin).
Congo: Conference Episcopale du Congo, B.P. 2301, Brazzaville. Barthelemy Batantu (Brazzaville).
Costa Rica: Conferencia Episcopal de Costa Rica (CECOR), Apartado 3187, San Jose. Roman Arrieta Villalobos (San Jose de Costa Rica).
Cuba: Conferencia Episcopal de Cuba (CEC), Apartado 594, Calle Habana 152. Bp. Adolfo Rodriguez Herrera (Camaguey).
Dominican Republic: Conferencia del Episcopado Dominicano (CED), Apartado 186, Santo Domingo. Nicolas de Jesus Lopez Rodriguez (Santo Domingo).
Ecuador: Conferencia Episcopal Ecuatoriana, Apartado 1081, Avenida America 1866 y Lagasca, Quito. Antonio Gonzalez Zumarraga (Quito).
El Salvador: Conferencia Episcopal de El Salvador (CEDES). 15 Av. Norte 1420, Col. Layce, Apartado 1310, San Salvador. Bp. Marco Rene Revelo Contreras (Santa Ana).
Equatorial Guinea: Apartado 106, Malabo. Rafael Nze Abuy, C.M.F. (Malabo).
Ethiopia: Conferenza Episcopale di Etiopia, P.O. Box 21903, Addis Ababa. Card. Paulos Tzadua (Addis Ababa).
France: Conference Episcopale Francaise, 106 rue du Bac, 75341 Paris CEDEX 07. Card. Albert Decourtray (Lyon).
Gabon: Conference Episcopale du Gabon, B.P. 230, Franceville. Bp. Felicien-Patrice Makouaka (Franceville).
Gambia, Liberia and Sierra Leone: Inter-Territorial Episcopal Conference, P.O. Box 893, Freetown, Sierra Leone. Bp. Michael J. Cleary, C.S.Sp. (Banjui, Gambia).
Germany: Deutsche Bischofskonferenz, Kaiserstrasse 163, D-5300 Bonn. Bp. Karl Lehmann (Mainz). Berliner Bischofskonferenz, Franzosische Strasse 234, DDR-1086 Berlin. Card. Joachim Meisner (Berlin, Bp.)

Ghana: Ghana Bishops' Conference, National Catholic Secretariat, P.O. Box 9712 Airport, Accra. Peter Poreku Dery (Tamale).
Great Britain: Bishops' Conference of England and Wales, Archbishop's House, Ambrosden Avenue, Westminster, London, SWIP IQJ. Card. George Basil Hume, O.S.B. (Westminster). Bishops' Conference of Scotland, 18 Park Circus, Glasgow G3 6BE. Thomas Winning (Glasgow).
Greece: Conferenza Episcopale di Grecia, Archeveche Catholique, 49100 Kerkyra. Antonio Varthalitis, A.A. (Corfu, Zante and Cefalonia.)
Guatemala: Conferencia Episcopal de Guatemala (CEG), 26 Calle 8-90, zona 12, Ciudad de Guatemala. Bp. Victor Hugo Martinez Contreras (Quetzaltenango).
Guinea: Conference Episcopale de la Guinee, B.P. 1006 Bis, Conakry. Robert Sarah (Conakry).
Haiti: Conference Episcopale de Haiti (CEH). C.P. 22, Cap Haitien, Haiti. Francois Gayot, S.M.M. (Cap Haitien).
Honduras: Conferencia Episcopal de Honduras (CEH), Arzobispado, Apartado 106, Tegucigalpa. Hector Enrique Santos Hernandez, S.D.B. (Tegucigalpa).
Hungary: Magyar Puspoki Kar Konferenciaja, Berenyi Zsigmond u. 2, Pf. 25, H-2501 Esztergom. Card. Lazlo Paskai (Esztergom).
India: Catholic Bishops' Conference of India (CBCI), CBCI Centre, Ashok Place, Goldakkhana, New Delhi-110001. Benedict Varghese Gregorios Thangalathil (Trivandrum).
Indian Ocean: Conference Episcopale de l'Ocean Indian (CEDOI) (includes Islands of Mauritus, Seychelles, Comore and La Reunion), rue Mgr. Gonin, Port-Louis, Mauritius. Card. Jean Margeot (Port-Louis).
Indonesia: General Conference of the Ordinaries of Indonesia (Majelis Agung Waligereja Indonesia — MAWI), Taman Cut Mutiah 10, Jakarta II/14. Bp. Francis Xavier Sudartanto Hadisumarta, O. Carm. (Malang).
Ireland: Episcopal Meetings, "Ara Coeli," Armagh BT61 7QY. Card. Tomas O'Fiaich (Armagh).
Italy: Conferenza Episcopale Italiana (CEI), Circonvallazione Aurelia, 50, 00165 Roma. Card. Ugo Poletti (Vicar General, Rome).
Ivory Coast: Conference Episcopale de la Cote d'Ivoire, B.P. 1287, Abidjan. Card. Bernard Yago (Abidjan).
Japan: Japan Catholic Bishops' Conference, Catholic Center, 10-1 Rokubancho, Chiyoda-Ku, Tokyo 102. Peter Seiichi Shirayanagi (Tokyo).
Kenya: Kenya Episcopal Conference (KEC), P.O. Box 938, Nakuru. Bp. Raphael S. Ndingi Mwana's Nzeki (Nakuru).
Korea: Catholic Conference of Korea, Box 16, Seoul. Bp. Angelo Nam Sou Kim (Su Won).
Laos and Cambodia: Conference Episcopale du Laos et du Cambodge, Centre Catholique, Thakhek, Khammouane, Laos. Bp. Jean-Baptiste Outhay (vicar apostolic, Savannakhet).
Latvia: Pils Jela, 2, Riga 226650. Card. Julijans Vaivods (Ap. Admin., Riga and Liepaja).
Lesotho: Lesotho Catholic Bishops' Conference,

P.O. Box 200, Maseru 100. Bp. Paul Khoari (Leribe).
Liberia: See Gambia, Liberia and Sierra Leone.
Lithuania: Vilniaus gatve 4, 233000 Kaunas. Bp. Liudas Povilonis (Ap. Admin., Kaunas and Vilkaviskis).
Madagascar: Conference Episcopale du Madagascar, 102 bis, Av. Marechal Joffre, Antanimena, B. P 667, Antananarivo. Albert Joseph Tsiahoana (Diego-Suarez).
Malawi: Episcopal Conference of Malawi, Catholic Secretariat of Malawi, P.O. Box 30384, Lilongwe 3. James Chiona (Blantyre).
Malaysia-Singapore-Brunei: Catholic Bishops' Conference of Malaysia-Singapore-Brunei, (BCMSB), Archbishop's House, 31 Victoria St., Singapore 0718. Anthony Soter Fernandez (Kuala Lumpur).
Mali: Conference Episcopale du Mali, B.P. 298, Bamako. Bp. Jean-Marie Cisse (Sikasso).
Malta: Conferenza Episcopale Maltese, Archbishop's Curia, Floriana. Joseph Mercieca (Malta).
Mexico: Conferencia del Episcopado Mexicano (CEM), Apartado 118-055, Col. Tepeyac Insurgentes, 07050 Mexico D.F. Sergio Obeso Rivera (Jalapa).
Mozambique: Conferencia Episcopal de Mocambique (CEM), C.P. 286, Maputo. Bp. Paulo Mandlate, S.S.S. (Tete).
Netherlands: Nederlandse Bisschoppenconferentie, Postbus 13049, NL-3507 LA, Utrecht. Card. Adrianus J. Simonis (Utrecht).
New Zealand: New Zealand Episcopal Conference, P.O. Box 198, Wellington. Card. Thomas Stafford Williams (Wellington).
Nicaragua: Conferencia Episcopal de Nicaragua, Apartado Postal 92, Ferreteria Lang, Zona 3, Las Piedrecitas, Managua. Card. Miguel Obando Bravo (Managua).
Niger: See Burkina Faso.
Nigeria: Catholic Bishops Conference of Nigeria, P.O. Box 951, 6 Force Rd., Lagos. Anthony O. Okogie (Lagos).
Pacific: Conference des Eveques du Pacifique (CE PAC), P.O. Box 109, Suva (Fiji). Bp. Francis Roland Lambert (Port-Vila).
Pakistan: Pakistan Episcopal Conference, St. Patrick's Cathedral, Karachi 3. Card. Joseph Cordeiro (Karachi).
Panama: Conferencia Episcopal de Panama (CEP), Apartado 386, Panama 1. Marcos Gregorio McGrath, C.S.C. (Panama).
Papua New Guinea and Solomon Islands: Bishops' Conference of Papua New Guinea and Solomon Islands, Southern Highlands, P.O. Box 106, North Solomons Province, Kieta. Bp. Gerard-Joseph Deschamps, S.M.M. (Daru-Kiunga).
Paraguay: Conferencia Episcopal Paraguaya (CEP), Calle Alberdi 782, Casilla Correo 1436, Asuncion. Ismael Blas Rolon Silvero, S.D.B. (Asuncion).
Peru: Conferencia Episcopal Peruana, Apartado 310, Rio de Janeiro 488, Lima 1. Card. Juan Landazuri Ricketts, O.F.M. (Lima).
Philippines: Catholic Bishops' Conference of the Philippines (CBCP), P.O. Box 3601, 470 General Luna St., Manila 2800. Leonardo Z. Legaspi (Caceres).
Poland: Konferencja Episkopatu Polski, Skwer Kardynala Stefana Wyszynskiego 6, 01-015 Warsaw. Card. Jozef Glemp (Gniezno and Warsaw).
Portugal: Conferencia Episcopal Portuguesa, Campo dos martires da Patria, 43-1 Esq., 1198 Lisbon. Card. Antonio Ribeiro (Lisbon).
Puerto Rico: Conferencia Episcopal Puertorriquena (CEP), Apartado 205, Estacion 6, Ponce 00732. Bp. Juan Fremiot Torres Olivier (Ponce).
Rhodesia: See Zimbabwe.
Romania: Vacant.
Rwanda: Conference Episcopale du Rwanda (C.Ep.R.), B.P. 357, Kigali. Bp. Joseph Ruzindana (Byumba).
Scandinavia: Conferentia Episcopalis Scandiae, Akersveien 5, P.B. 8270 Hammersborg, N-0129 Oslo 1, Norway. Bp. Paul Verschuren, S.C.I. (Helsinki).
Senegal, Mauritania and Cape Verde: Conference Episcopale du Senegal, de la Mauritanie et du Cap Vert., B.P. 5082, Dakar, Fann. Senegal. Bp. Theodore Adrien Sarr (Kaolack, Senegal).
Sierra Leone: See Gambia, Liberia and Sierra Leone.
Spain: Conferencia Episcopal Espanola, Calle Anastro 1, 28033 Madrid. Card. Angel Suquia Goicoechea (Madrid).
Sri Lanka: Catholic Bishops' Conference of Sri Lanka, 19 Balcombe Place, Cotta Rd., Colombo 8. Bp. Frank Marcus Fernando (Chilaw).
Sudan: Sudan Episcopal Conference (SEC), P.O. Box 49, Khartoum. Gabriel Zubeir Wako (Khartoum).
Switzerland: Conference des Eveques Suisses, Secretariat, av. Moleson 30, CH-1700 Fribourg 1. Bp. Henri Schwery (Sion).
Tanzania: Tanzania Episcopal Conference (TEC), P.O. Box 2133, Mansfield St., Dar-es-Salaam. Anthony Mayala (Mwanza).
Thailand: Conference des Eveques de Thailand, 57 Oriental Ave., Praetham Bldg., Bangrak, Bangkok 10500. Card. Michael Michai Kitbunchu (Bangkok).
Togo: Conference Episcopale du Togo, B.P. 348, Lome. Robert Dosseh-Anyron (Lome).
Turkey: Conferenza Episcopale di Turchia, Olcek Sokak 83, Harbiye, Istanbul. Bp. Gauthier Pierre Dubois, O.F.M. Cap. (V.A., Istanbul).
Uganda: Uganda Episcopal Conference, P.O. Box 2886, Kampala. Bp. Emmanuel Wamala (Kiyinda-Mityana).
United States: See National Conference of Catholic Bishops.
Uruguay: Conferencia Episcopal Uruguaya (CEU), Avenida Uruguay 1319, Montevideo. Jose Gottardi Cristelli, S.D.B. (Montevideo).
Venezuela: Conferencia Episcopal de Venezuela (CEV), Apartado 4897, Torre a Madrices, Edificio Juan XXIII, Piso 4, Caracas 1010-A. Card. Jose Ali Lebrun Moratinos (Caracas).
Vietnam: Conference Episcopale du Vietnam, 40 Pho Nha Chung, Hanoi. Card. Joseph-Marie Trinh van-Can (Hanoi).

Yugoslavia: Biskupska Konferencija Jugoslavije, Kaptol 31, 41000, Zagreb. Card. Franjo Kuharic (Zagreb).
Zaire: Conference Episcopale du Zaire (CEZ), B.P. 3258, Kinshasa-Gombe. Bp. Monsengwo Pasinya (Kisangani, auxiliary).
Zambia: Zambia Episcopal Conference, P.O. Box 31965, Lusaka. Bp. James Spaita (Mansa).
Zimbabwe: Zimbabwe Catholic Bishops' Conference (ZCBC), P.O. Box 8135, Causeway, Harare. Bp. Alescio Churu Muchabaiwa (Mutare).

Territorial Conferences

(Source: *Annuario Pontificio*.)
Territorial as well as national episcopal conferences have been established in some places. Some conferences of this kind are still in the planning stage.

Africa: Symposium of Episcopal Conferences of Africa and Madagascar (SECAM) (Symposium des Conferences Episcopales d'Afrique et de Madagascar, SCEAM): Bp. Gabriel Gonsum Gonaka, Jos, Nigeria, president. Address: Secretariat, P.O. Box 7530, Accra North, Ghana.
Association of Episcopal Conferences of Central Africa (Association des Conferences Episcopales de l'Afrique Centrale, ACEAC): Bp. Ngabu, Goma, Zaire, president. Address: B.P. 20511, Kinshasa, Zaire.
Association of Member Episcopal Conferences in Eastern Africa (AMECEA): Represents Ethiopia, Kenya, Malawi, Sudan, Tanzania, Uganda and Zambia. The Seychelles was accepted as an affiliate member in 1979, Bp. Denis Harold De Jong, Ndola, Zambia, president. Address: P.O. Box 21191, Nairobi, Kenya.
Regional Episcopal Conference of French-Speaking West Africa (Conference Episcopale Regionale de l'Afrique de l'Ouest Francophone, CERAO): Bp. Bernard Agre, Man, Ivory Coast, president. Address: Secretariat General, B.P. 22, Abidjan 08, Ivory Coast.
Association of Episcopal Conferences of Anglophone West Africa (AECAWA): Abp. John Kodwo Amissah, Cape Coast, Ghana, president. Address: P.O. Box 297, Monrovia, Liberia.
Association of Episcopal Conferences of Congo, Central African Republic and Chad (ACECCT): Abp. Joachim N'Dayen, Bangui, Central African Republic, president. Address: Secretariat, B.P. 1518, Bangui, Central African Republic.
Inter-Regional Meeting of Bishops of Southern Africa (IMBISA): Abp. Jaime Pedro Goncalves, Beira, Mozambique, president. Address: 4 Bayswater Rd., Highlands Harare, Zimbabwe.
Asia: Federation of Asian Bishops' Conferences (FABC): Represents 14 Asian episcopal conferences (excluding the Middle East). Established in 1970; statutes approved experimentally Dec. 6, 1972. Abp. Henry Sebastian D'Souza, Calcutta, India, secretary general. Address: P.O. Box 2984, Hong Kong.
Europe: Council of European Bishops' Conferences (Consilium Conferentiarum Episcopalium Europae, CCEE): Card. Carlo Maria Martini, S.J., Milan, Italy, president. Address of secretariat: Klosterhof 6b, CH-9000 St. Gallen, Switzerland.
Commission of the Episcopates of the European Community (Commissio Episcopatuum Communitatis Europaeae, COMECE): Established in 1980; represents episcopates of states which belong to European Community. Abp.-Bp. Jean Hengen, Luxembourg, president. Address of secretariat: 13 Avenue Pere Damien, B-1150 Brussels, Belgium.
Central and South America: Latin American Bishops' Conference (Consejo Episcopal LatinoAmericano, CELAM): Established in 1956; statutes approved Nov. 9, 1974. Represents 22 Latin American national bishops' conferences. Bp. Dario Castrillon Hoyos, Pereira, Colombia, president. Address of the secretariat: Calle 78, no. 11-17, Apartado Aereo 5278, Bogota, Colombia.
Episcopal Secretariat of Central America and Panama (Secretariado Episcopal de America Central y Panama, SEDAC): Statutes approved experimentally Sept. 26, 1970. Abp. Arturo Rivera Damas, S.D.B., San Salvador, president. Address of secretariat: Calle S. Jose y Avenida Las Americas, Urbanizacion Isidro Menendez, San Salvador, El Salvador.

INTERNATIONAL CATHOLIC ORGANIZATIONS

(Principal sources: Conference of International Catholic Organizations; Pontifical Council for the Laity; Almanac survey.)

Guidelines

International organizations wanting to call themselves "Catholic" are required to meet standards set by the Vatican's Council for the Laity and to register with and get the approval of the Papal Secretariat of State, according to guidelines dated Dec. 3 and published in *Acta Apostolicae Sedis* under date of Dec. 23, 1971.

Among conditions for the right of organizations to "bear the name Catholic" are:

• leaders "will always be Catholics," and candidates for office will be approved by the Secretariat of State;

• adherence by the organization to the Catholic Church, its teaching authority and teachings of the Gospel;

• evidence that the organization is really international with a universal outlook and that it fulfills its mission through its own management, meetings and accomplishments.

The guidelines also stated that leaders of the organizations "will take care to maintain necessary reserve as regards taking a stand or engaging in public activity in the field of politics or trade unionism. Abstention in these fields will normally be the best attitude for them to adopt during their term of office."

The guidelines were in line with a provision stated by the Second Vatican Council in the *Decree on the Apostolate of the Laity:* "No project may claim the name 'Catholic' unless it has obtained the consent of the lawful church authority."

They made it clear that all organizations are not obliged to apply for recognition, but that the Church "reserves the right to recognize as linked with her mission and her aims those organizations or movements which see fit to ask for such recognition."

Conference

Conference of International Catholic Organizations: A permanent body for collaboration among various organizations which seek to promote the development of international life along the lines of Christian principles. Eleven international Catholic organizations participated in its foundation and first meeting in 1927 at Fribourg, Switzerland. In 1951, the conference established its general secretariat and adopted governing statutes which were approved by the Vatican Secretariat of State in 1953.

The permanent secretariat is located at 37-39 rue de Vermont, CH-1202 Geneva, Switzerland. Other office addresses are: 1 rue Varembe, CH-1211 Geneva 20, Switzerland (Information Center); 9, rue Cler, F-75007 Paris, France (International Catholic Center for UNESCO); ICO Information Center, 323 East 47th St., New York, N.Y. 10017.

International Organizations

International Catholic organizations are listed below. Information includes name, date and place of establishment (when available), address of general secretariat. An asterisk indicates that the organization is a member of the Conference of International Catholic Organizations. Approximately 30 of the organizations have consultative status with other international or regional non-governmental agencies.

Apostleship of Prayer (1849): Borgo Santo Spirito 5, I-00193 Rome, Italy. National secretariat in most countries. (See Index.)

Apostolatus Maris (Apostleship of the Sea) (1922, Glasgow, Scotland): Pontifical Commission for Migration and Tourism, Piazza San Calisto 16, 00153 Rome, Italy. (See Index.)

L'Arche Communities: B.P. 35, 60350 Cuise Lamotte, France.

Associationes Juventutis Salesianae (Associations of Salesian Youth) (1847): Via della Pisana, 1111, 00163 Rome, Italy.

Blue Army of Our Lady of Fatima: (See Index.)

Caritas Internationalis* (1951, Rome, Italy): Piazza San Calisto 16, I-00153, Rome, Italy. Coordinates and represents its 117 national member organizations (in 113 countries) operating in the fields of development, emergency aid, social action.

Catholic International Education Office* (1952): 60, rue des Eburons, B-1040 Brussels, Belgium.

Catholic International Federation for Physical and Sports Education (1911; present name, 1957): 5, rue Cernuschi, F-75017 Paris, France.

Catholic International Union for Social Service* (1925, Milan, Italy): rue de la Poste 111, B-1030 Brussels, Belgium (general secretariat).

Christian Fraternity of the Sick and Handicapped: 9, Avenue de la Gare, CH-1630, Bulle, Switzerland.

"Communione e Liberazione" Fraternity (1955, Milan, Italy): Via Marcello Malpighi 2, 00161 Rome, Italy. Catholic renewal movement.

European Forum of National Committees of the Laity: 12 Brookwood Lawn Artane, Dublin 5, Ireland.

"Focolare Movement" or "Work of Mary" (1943, Trent, Italy): Via di Frascati, 304, I-00040 Rocca di Papa (Rome), Italy. (See Index: Focolare Movement.)

Foi et Lumiere: 8 rue Serret, 75015 Paris, France.

Inter Cultural Association, formerly International Catholic Auxiliaries (1937, Belgium): 91, rue de la Servette, CH-1202 Geneva, Switzerland.

International Association of Charities of St. Vincent de Paul* (1617, Chatillon les Dombes, France): 38, rue d'Alsace-Lorraine, B-1050 Brussels, Belgium. (See Index: St. Vincent de Paul Society.)

International Association of Children of Mary (1847): 67 rue de Sèvres, F-75006 Paris, France.

International Catholic Association for Service to Young Women* (1897): 37-39, rue de Vermont, CH-1202 Geneva, Switzerland. Welfare of Catholic girls living away from home.

International Catholic Child Bureau* (1948, in Paris): 65, rue de Lausanne, CH-1202 Geneva, Switzerland.

International Catholic Conference of Guiding* (1965): Rue Paul-Emile Janson, 35, B-1050 Brussels, Belgium. Founded by member bodies of interdenominational World Association of Guides and Girl Scouts.

International Catholic Conference of Scouting* (1948): 21, rue de Dublin, B-1050 Brussels, Belgium.

International Catholic Migration Commission* (1951): 37-39 rue de Vermont, C.P. 96, CH-1211 Geneva 20, Switzerland. Coordinates activities worldwide on behalf of refugees and migrants, both administering programs directly and supporting the efforts of national affiliated agencies.

International Catholic Organization for Cinema and Audiovisual* (1928, The Hague, The Netherlands): Rue de l'Orme, 8, B-1040 Brussels, Belgium (general secretariat). Federation of national Catholic film offices.

International Catholic Rural Association (1962, Rome): Piazza San Calisto, 00153 Rome, Italy. International body for agricultural and rural organizations.

International Catholic Union of Esperanto: Via Berni 9, 00185 Rome, Italy.

International Catholic Union of the Press*: 37-39 rue de Vermont, Case Postale 197, CH-1211 Geneva 20 CIC, Switzerland. Coordinates and represents at the international level the activities of Catholics and Catholic federations or associations in the field of press and information. Has five specialized branches: International Federation of Catholic Dailies and Periodicals (1928); International Federation of Catholic Journalists (1927); International Federation of Catholic Press Agencies (1950); International Catholic Association of Teachers and Scientific or Technical Research Workers on Information (1968); Federation of Church Press Associations (1974).

International Centre for Studies in Religious Education LUMEN VITAE* (1934-35, Louvain, Belgium, under name Catechetical Documentary Centre; present name, 1956): 184, rue Washington, B-1050 Brussels, Belgium. Also referred to as Lumen Vitae Centre; concerned with all aspects of religious formation.

International Committee of Catholic Nurses and Medical Social Workers* (1933): Piazza San Calisto 16, 00153 Rome, Italy.

International Cooperation for Socio-Economic Development (1965, Rome, Italy): Avenue des ARTS-1, 2, Boite 6, 1040 Brussels, Belgium.

International Federation of Catholic Medical Associations (1954): Palazzo San Calisto, I-00120 Vatican City.

International Federation of Catholic Men* (Unum Omnes) (1948): Piazza San Calisto 16, 00153 Rome, Italy.

International Federation of Catholic Parochial Youth Communities* (1962, Rome, Italy): Kipdorp 30, B-2000 Antwerp, Belgium.

International Federation of Catholic Pharmacists* (1954): 59, Bergstrasse, B-4700 Eupen, Belgium.

International Federation of Catholic Rural Movements* (1964, Lisbon, Portugal): 92, rue Africaine, B-1050 Brussels, Belgium.

International Federation of Catholic Universities* (1949): 78A, rue de Sevres, F-75341 Paris Cedex 7, France.

International Federation of the Catholic Associations of the Blind: FIDACA, Chamblioux 18, CH-1700 Fribourg, Switzerland. Coordinates actions of Catholic groups and assciations for the blind and develops their apostolate.

International Military Apostolate (1967): Gablenzgasse 62, A-1160 Vienna, Austria. Comprised of organizations of military men.

International Movement of Apostolate of Children* (1929, France): 8, rue Duguay-Trouin, F-75006 Paris, France.

International Movement of Apostolate in Middle and Upper Classes* (1963): Piazza San Calisto 16, 00153 Rome, Italy. Evangelization of adults of the independent milieus (that part of population known as old or recent middle class, aristocracy, bourgeoisie or "white collar").

International Movement of Catholic Agricultural and Rural Youth* (1954, Annevoie, Belgium): Tiensevest 68, B-3000 Leuven, Belgium (permanent secretariat).

International Young Catholic Students* (1946, Fribourg, Switzerland; present name, 1954): 171 rue de Rennes, F-75006 Paris, France.

International Young Christian Workers* (1925, Belgium): 11, rue Plantin, B-1070 Brussels, Belgium.

Legion of Mary (1921, Dublin, Ireland): De Montfort House, North Brunswick St., Dublin, Ireland. (See Index.)

Medicus Mundi Internationalis: (1964,

Bensberg. Germany FR): P.O. Box 1547, 6501 BM Nijmegen, Netherlands. Promote health and medico-social services, particularly in developing countries; recruit essential health and medical personnel for developing countries; contribute to training of medical and auxiliary personnel; undertake research in the field of health.

NOVALIS, Marriage Preparation Center: University of St. Paul, 1 rue Stewart, Ottawa 2, Ont. Canada.

Our Lady's Teams (Equipes Notre-Dame) (1937, France): 49, rue de la Glacière, F-75013 Paris, France. Movement for spiritual formation of couples.

Pax Christi International (1950): Plantin en Moretuslei, 174, B. 2038, Antwerpen, Belgium. International Catholic peace movement. Originated in Lourdes, France in 1948 by French and German Catholics to reconcile enemies from World War II; spread to Italy and Poland and acquired its international title when it merged with the English organization Pax. (See Index: Pax Christi USA.)

Pax Romana* (1921, Fribourg, Switzerland, divided into two branches, 1947):

Pax Romana — IMCS* (International Movement of Catholic Students) (1921): 171, rue de Rennes, F-75006, Paris, France. For undergraduates.

Pax Romana — ICMICA* (International Catholic Movement for Intellectual and Cultural Affairs) (1947): 37-39 rue de Vermont, Case Postale n 85, CH-1211 Geneva 20 CIC, Switzerland. For Catholic intellectuals and professionals.

Pro Sanctity Movement: Piazza S. Andrea della Valle 3, 00166 Rome, Italy.

St. Joan's International Alliance (1911, in England, as Catholic Women's Suffrage Society): 15 London Rd., Canterbury, Kent CT2 8LR, England. Associate member of ICO.

Salesian Cooperators (1876): Don Bosco College, Newton, N.J. 07860. Third Salesian family founded by St. John Bosco. Members commit themselves to an apostolate at the service of the Church, giving particular attention to youth in the Salesian spirit and style.

Secular Franciscan Order (1221, first Rule approved): Via Piemonte, 70, 00187, Rome, Italy. (See Index.)

Secular Fraternity of Charles de Foucauld: Katharinenweg 4, B4700 Eupen, Belgium.

Serra International (1953, in U.S.): (See Index.)

Society of St. Vincent de Paul* (1833, Paris): 5, rue du Pré-aux-Clercs, F-75007 Paris, France.

The Grail (1921, Nijmegen, The Netherlands): Duisburgerstrasse 470, D-4330, Mulheim, West Germany. (See Index.)

Third Order of St. Dominic (1285): Convento Santa Sabina, Piazza Pietro d'Illiria, Aventino, I-00153 Rome, Italy. (See Index.)

Unda: International Catholic Association for Radio and Television* (1928, Cologne, Germany): rue de l'Orme, 12, B-1040 Brussels, Belgium. (See Index.)

Unio Internationalis Laicorum in Servitio Ecclesiae (1965, Aachen, Germany): Postfach 990125, Am Kielshof 2, 5000 Cologne, Germany 91. Consists

of national and diocesan associations of persons who give professional services to the Church.
Union of Adorers of the Blessed Sacrament (1937): Largo dei Monti Parioli 3, I-00197, Rome, Italy.
World Catholic Federation for the Biblical Apostolate (1969, Rome): Mittelstrasse, 12, P.O. Box 601, D-7000, Stuttgart 1, Germany.
World Federation of Christian Life Communities* (1953): 8, Borgo Santo Spirito, 00193 Rome, Italy. First Sodality of Our Lady founded in 1563.
World Movement of Christian Workers* (1961): 90, rue des Palais, 1210 Brussels, Belgium.
World Organization of Former Students of Catholic Schools (1967, Rome): Largo Nazareno 25, I-00187 Rome, Italy.
World Union of Catholic Philosophical Societies (1948, Amsterdam, The Netherlands): The Catholic University of America, Washington, D.C. 20064.
World Union of Catholic Teachers* (1951): Piazza San Calisto 16, 00153 Rome, Italy.
World Union of Catholic Women's Organizations* (1910): 20, rue Notre Dame des Champs, F-75006 Paris, France.

Regional Organizations

European Federation for Catholic Adult Education (1963, Lucerne, Switzerland): Kapuzinestrasse 84, A-4020 Linz, Austria.
European Forum of National Committees of the Laity (1968): 12, Brookwood Lawn Artane, Dublin 5, Ireland.
Movimiento Familiar Cristiano (1949-50, Montevideo and Buenos Aires): Carrera 17 n. 4671, Bogota, D.E., Colombia. Christian Family Movement of Latin America.

THE CATHOLIC CHURCH IN CANADA

The first date in the remote background of the Catholic history of Canada was July 7, 1534, when a priest in the exploration company of Jacques Cartier celebrated Mass on the Gaspe Peninsula.

Successful colonization and the significant beginnings of the Catholic history of the country date from the foundation of Quebec in 1608 by Samuel de Champlain and French settlers. Montreal was established in 1642.

The earliest missionaries were Franciscan Recollects and Jesuits who arrived in 1615 and 1625, respectively. They provided some pastoral care for the settlers but worked mainly among the 100,000 Indians — Algonquins, Hurons and Iroquois — in the interior and in the Lake Ontario region. Eight of the Jesuit missionaries, killed in the 1640s, were canonized in 1930. (See Index: Jesuit North American Martyrs.) Sulpician Fathers, who arrived in Canada late in the 1640s, played a part in the great missionary period which ended about 1700.

Kateri Tekakwitha, "Lily of the Mohawks," who was baptized in 1676 and died in 1680, was declared "Blessed" June 22, 1980.

The communities of women religious with the longest histories in Canada are the Canonesses of St. Augustine, since 1637; the Ursulines, since 1639; and the Hospitallers of St. Joseph, since 1642. Communities of Canadian origin are the Congregation of Notre Dame, founded by St. Marguerite Bourgeoys in 1658, and the Grey Nuns, formed by Bl. Marie Marguerite d'Youville in 1738.

Mother Marie (Guyard) of the Incarnation, an Ursuline nun, was one of the first three women missionaries to New France; called "Mother of the Church in Canada," she was declared "Blessed" June 22, 1980.

Start of Church Organization

Ecclesiastical organization began with the appointment in 1658 of Francois De Montmorency-Laval, "Father of the Church in Canada," as vicar apostolic of New France. He was the first bishop of Quebec from 1674 to 1688, with jurisdiction over all French-claimed territory in North America. He was declared "Blessed" June 22, 1980.

In 1713, the French Canadian population numbered 18,000. In the same year, the Treaty of Utrecht ceded Acadia, Newfoundland and the Hudson Bay Territory to England. The Acadians were scattered among the American Colonies in 1755.

The English acquired possession of Canada and its 70,000 French-speaking inhabitants in virtue of the Treaty of Paris in 1763. Anglo-French and Anglican-Catholic differences and tensions developed. The pro-British government at first refused to recognize the titles of church officials, hindered the clergy in their work and tried to install a non-Catholic educational system. Laws were passed which guaranteed religious liberties to Catholics (Quebec Act of 1774, Constitutional Act of 1791, legislation approved by Queen Victoria in 1851), but it took some time before actual respect for these liberties matched the legal enactments. The initial moderation of government antipathy toward the Church was caused partly by the loyalty of Catholics to the Crown during the American Revolution and the War of 1812.

Growth

The 15 years following the passage in 1840 of the Act of Union, which joined Upper and Lower Canada, were significant. New communities of men and women religious joined those already in the country. The Oblates of Mary Immaculate, missionaries par excellence in Canada, advanced the penetration of the West which had been started in 1818 by Abbe Provencher. New jurisdictions were established, and Quebec became a metropolitan see in 1844. The first Council of Quebec was held in 1851. The established Catholic school system enjoyed a period of growth.

Laval University was inaugurated in 1854 and canonically established in 1876.

Archbishop Elzear-Alexandre Taschereau of Quebec was named Canada's first cardinal in 1886.

The apostolic delegation to Canada was set up in 1899. It became a nunciature October 16, 1969, with the establishment of diplomatic relations with the Vatican.

Early in this century, Canada had eight ecclesiastical provinces, 23 dioceses, three vicariates apostolic, 3,500 priests, 2.4 million Catholics, about 30 communities of men religious, and 70 or more communities of women religious. The Church in Canada was phased out of mission status and removed from the jurisdiction of the Congregation for the Propagation of the Faith in 1908.

Diverse Population

The greatest concentration of Catholics is in the eastern portion of the country. In the northern and western portions, outside metropolitan centers, there are some of the most difficult parish and mission areas in the world. Bilingual (English-French) differences in the general population are reflected in the Church; for example, in the parallel structures of the Canadian Conference of Catholic Bishops, which was established in 1943. Quebec is the center of French cultural influence. Many language groups are represented among Catholics, who include about 211,265 members of Eastern Rite in a metropolitan see, six eparchies and an apostolic exarchate.

Education, a past source of friction between the Church and the government, is administered by the civil provinces in a variety of arrangements authorized by the Canadian Constitution. Denominational schools have tax support in one way in Quebec and Newfoundland, and in another way in Alberta, Ontario and Saskatchewan. Several provinces provide tax support only for public schools, making private financing necessary for separate church-related schools.

ECCLESIASTICAL JURISDICTIONS OF CANADA

Provinces

Names of ecclesiastical provinces and metropolitan sees in bold face: suffragan sees in parentheses.

Edmonton (Calgary, St. Paul).
Grouard-McLennan (Mackenzie-Ft. Smith, Prince George, Whitehorse).
Halifax (Antigonish, Charlottetown, Yarmouth).
Keewatin-LePas (Churchill-Hudson Bay, Labrador-Schefferville, Moosonee).
Kingston (Alexandria-Cornwall, Peterborough, Sault Ste. Marie).
Moncton (Bathurst, Edmundston, St. John).
Montreal (Joliette, St. Jean-Longueuil, St. Jerome, Valleyfield).
Ottawa (Gatineau-Hull, Hearst, Mont-Laurier, Pembroke, Rouyn-Noranda, Timmins).
Quebec (Amos, Chicoutimi, Ste.-Anne-de-la-Pocatiere, Trois Rivieres).
Regina (Gravelbourg, Prince Albert, Saskatoon, Abbey of St. Peter).
Rimouski (Baie-Comeau, Gaspe).
St. Boniface (no suffragans).
St. John's (Grand Falls, St. George).
Sherbrooke (Nicolet, St. Hyacinthe).
Toronto (Hamilton, London, St. Catharines, Thunder Bay).
Vancouver (Kamloops, Nelson, Victoria).
Winnipeg — Ukrainian (Edmonton, New Westminster, Saskatoon, Toronto).
Jurisdictions immediately subject to the Holy See: Roman-Rite Archdiocese of Winnipeg, Byzantine-Rite Eparchy of Sts. Cyril and Methodius for Slovaks, Byzantine-Rite Eparchy of St. Sauveur de Montreal for Greek Melkites; Antiochene-Rite Eparchy of St. Maron of Montreal for Maronites.

Archdioceses, Archbishops

Edmonton, Alta. (St. Albert, 1871; archdiocese, transferred Edmonton, 1912): Joseph N. MacNeil, archbishop, 1973.
Grouard-McLennan, Alta. (v.a. Athabaska-Mackenzie, 1862; Grouard, 1927; archdiocese Grouard-McLennan, 1967); Henri Legare, O.M.I., archbishop, 1972.
Halifax, N.S. (1842; archdiocese, 1852): James M. Hayes, archbishop, 1967.
Keewatin-Le Pas, Man. (v.a., 1910; archdiocese, 1967): Peter-Alfred Sutton, O.M.I., archbishop, 1986.
Kingston, Ont. (1826; archdiocese, 1889): Francis J. Spence, archbishop, 1982.
Moncton, N.B. (1936): Donat Chiasson, archbishop, 1972.
Montreal, Que. (1836; archdiocese, 1886): Cardinal Paul Gregoire, archbishop, 1968. Andre Cimichella, O.S.M., Gerard Tremblay, P.S.S., Jude Saint-Antoine, Jean-Claude Turcotte, Leonard Crowley, auxiliaries.
Ottawa, Ont. (Bytown, 1847, name changed, 1854; archdiocese, 1886): Joseph Aurele Plourde, archbishop, 1967. Gilles Belisle, Brendan M. O'Brien, auxiliaries.
Quebec, Que. (v.a., 1658; diocese, 1674; archdiocese, 1819; metropolitan, 1844; primatial see, 1956): Cardinal Louis-Albert Vachon, archbishop, 1981. Jean-Paul Labrie, Maurice Couture, Marc Leclerc, Pierre Morissette, auxiliaries.
Regina, Sask. (1910; archdiocese, 1915): Charles A. Halpin, archbishop, 1973.
Rimouski, Que. (1867; archdiocese, 1946): Gilles Ouellet, P.M.E., archbishop, 1973.
St. Boniface, Man. (1847; archdiocese, 1871): Antoine Hacault, archbishop, 1974.
St. John's, Nfld. (p.a., 1784; v.a., 1796; diocese, 1847; archdiocese, 1904): Alphonsus Penney, archbishop, 1979.
Sherbrooke, Que. (1874; archdiocese, 1951); J.-M. Fortier, archbishop, 1968.
Toronto, Ont. (1841; archdiocese, 1870): Cardinal G. Emmett Carter, archbishop, 1978. Aloysius M. Ambrozic, coadjutor. Michael Pearse Lacey, Robert B. Clune, Leonard J. Wall, auxiliaries.
Vancouver, B. C. (v.a. British Columbia, 1863; diocese New Westminster, 1890; archdiocese Vancouver, 1908): James F. Carney, archbishop, 1969.

Winnipeg, Man. (1915): Adam Exner, O.M.I, archbishop, 1982.
Winnipeg, Man. (Ukrainian Byzantine Rite) (Ordinariate of Canada, 1912; ap. ex. Central Canada, 1948; ap. ex. Manitoba, 1951; archdiocese Winnipeg, 1956): Maxim Hermaniuk, C.Ss.R., archeparch, 1956. Myron Daciuk, O.S.B.M., auxiliary.

Dioceses, Bishops

Alexandria-Cornwall, Ont. (1890): Eugene Philippe LaRocque, bishop, 1974.
Amos, Que. (1938): Gerard Drainville, bishop, 1978.
Antigonish, N.S. (Arichat, 1844; transferred, 1886): Colin Campbell, bishop, 1987.
Baie-Comeau, Que. (p.a., 1882; v.a., 1905; diocese Gulf of St. Lawrence, 1945; name changed, to Hauterive, 1960; present title, 1986): Vacant as of May 6, 1988.
Bathurst, N.B. (Chatham, 1860; transferred, 1938): Arsène Richard, bishop, 1986.
Calgary, Alta. (1912): Paul J. O'Byrne, bishop, 1968.
Charlottetown, P.E.I. (1829): James H. MacDonald, C.S.C., bishop, 1982.
Chicoutimi, Que. (1878): Jean-Guy Couture, bishop, 1979. Roch Pedneault, auxiliary.
Churchill-Hudson Bay, Man. (p.a., 1925; v.a. Hudson Bay, 1931; diocese Churchill, 1967; Churchill-Hudson Bay, 1968): Reynald Rouleau, O.M.I., bishop, 1987.
Edmonton, Alta. (Ukrainian Byzantine Rite) (ap. ex., 1948; diocese, 1956): Martin Greschuk, eparch, 1986.
Edmundston, N.B. (1944): Gerard Dionne, bishop, 1983.
Gaspe, Que. (1922): Bertrand Blanchet, bishop, 1973.
Gatineau-Hull, Que. (1963 as Hull; name changed, 1982); Roger Ebacher, bishop, 1988.
Grand Falls, Nfld. (Harbour Grace, 1856; present title, 1964): Joseph Faber MacDonald, bishop, 1980.
Gravelbourg, Sask. (1930): Noel Delaquis, bishop, 1974.
Hamilton, Ont. (1856): Anthony Tonnos, bishop, 1984. Matthew Ustrzycki, auxiliary.
Hearst, Ont. (p.a., 1918; v.a., 1920; diocese, 1938): Roger Despatie, bishop, 1973.
Joliette, Que. (1904): Rene Audet, bishop, 1968.
Kamloops, B.C. (1945): Lawrence Sabatini, C.S., bishop, 1982.
Labrador City (Nfld.)-Schefferville, Que. (v.a. Labrador, 1945; diocese, 1967): Henri Goudreault, O.M.I., 1987.
London, Ont. (1855; transferred Sandwich, 1859; London, 1869): John Sherlock, bishop, 1978. Frederick Henry, auxiliary.
Mackenzie-Fort Smith, N.W.T. (v.a. Mackenzie, 1901; diocese Mackenzie-Fort Smith, 1967): Denis Croteau, O.M.I., bishop, 1986.
Mont-Laurier, Que. (1913): Jean Gratton, bishop, 1978.
Moosonee, Ont. (v.a. James Bay, 1938; diocese Moosonee, 1967): Jules LeGuerrier, O.M.I., bishop, 1967.
Nelson, B.C. (1936): Wilfred Emmett Doyle, bishop, 1958.
New Westminster, B.C. (Ukrainian Byzantine Rite) (1974): Jerome Chimy, O.S.B.M., eparch, 1974.
Nicolet, Que. (1885): Albertus Martin, bishop, 1950. Raymond Saint-Gelais, coadjutor, 1988.
Pembroke, Ont. (v.a. 1882; diocese, 1898): Joseph R. Windle, bishop, 1971.
Peterborough, Ont. (1882): James L. Doyle, bishop, 1976.
Prince Albert, Sask. (v.a., 1890; diocese, 1907): Blaise Morand, bishop, 1983.
Prince George, B.C. (p.a., 1908; v.a. Yukon and Prince Rupert, 1944; diocese Prince George, 1967): Hubert P. O'Connor, O.M.I., bishop, 1986.
Rouyn-Noranda, Que. (1973): Jean-Guy Hamelin, bishop, 1974.
St. Catharines, Ont. (1958): Thomas B. Fulton, bishop, 1978.
St. George's, Nfld. (p.a., 1870; v.a., 1890; diocese, 1904): Raymond J. Lahey, bishop, 1986.
St. Hyacinthe, Que. (1852): Louis-de-Gonzague Langevin, bishop, 1979.
Saint-Jean-Longueuil, Que. (1933 as St.-Jean-de-Quebec; named changed, 1982): Bernard Hubert, bishop, 1978. Jacques Berthelet, auxiliary.
St. Jerome, Que. (1951): Charles Valois, bishop, 1977.
Saint John, N.B. (1842): J. Edward Troy, bishop, 1986.
St. Maron of Montreal (Maronites) (1982): Archeparch Elias Shaheen, eparch, 1982.
St. Paul in Alberta (1948): Raymond Roy, bishop, 1972.
St. Sauveur de Montreal (Greek Melkites) (ap. ex. 1980; eparchy, 1984): Archeparch Michel Hakim, 1980.
Sts. Cyril and Methodius, Toronto, Ont. (Slovakian Byzantine Rite) (1980): Michael Rusnak, C.Ss.R., eparch, 1981.
Sainte-Anne-de-la-Pocatiere, Que. (1951): Andre Gaumond, bishop, 1985.
Saskatoon, Sask. (1933): James P. Mahoney, bishop, 1967.
Saskatoon, Sask. (Ukrainian Byzantine Rite) (ap. ex., 1951; diocese, 1956): Basil (Wasyl) Filevich, eparch, 1984.
Sault Ste. Marie, Ont. (1904): Marcel Gervais, bishop, 1985. Bernard F. Pappin, Jean-Louis Plouffe, auxiliaries.
Thunder Bay, Ont. (Ft. William, 1952; transferred, 1970): John A. O'Mara, bishop, 1976.
Timmins, Ont. (v.a. Temiskaming, 1908; diocese Haileybury, 1915; present title, 1938): Jacques Landriault, bishop, 1971.
Toronto, Ont. (Ukrainian Byzantine Rite) (ap. ex., 1948; diocese, 1956): Isidore Borecky, eparch, 1948.
Trois-Rivieres, Que. (1852): Laurent Noel, bishop, 1975. Martin Veillette, auxiliary.
Valleyfield, Que. (1892): Robert Lebel, bishop, 1976.
Victoria, B.C. (diocese Vancouver Is., 1846;

Canadian Ecclesiastical Jurisdictions — Statistics

archdiocese, 1903; diocese Victoria, 1908): Remi J. De Roo, bishop, 1962.
Whitehorse, Y.T. (v.a., 1944; diocese 1967): Thomas Lobsinger, O.M.I., bishop, 1987.
Yarmouth, N.S. (1953): Austin-Emile Burke, bishop, 1968.
Military Ordinariate of Canada (1951): André Valée, P.M.E., military ordinary, 1988.
Abbacy of St. Peter, Muenster, Sask. (1921): Jerome Weber, O.S.B. (blessed, 1960).

An **Apostolic Exarchate for Armenian-Rite Catholics in Canada and the United States** was established in July, 1981, with headquarters in New York City. Nerses Mikaël Setian, exarch.

Dioceses with Interprovincial Lines

The following dioceses, indicated by + in the table, have interprovincial lines.

Churchill-Hudson Bay includes part of Northwest Territories.
Keewatin-Le Pas includes part of Manitoba and Saskatchewan provinces.
Labrador City-Schefferville includes the Labrador region of Newfoundland and the northern part of Quebec province.
MacKenzie-Fort Smith, Northwest Territories, includes part of Alberta and Saskatchewan provinces.
Moosonee, Ont., includes part of Quebec province.
Pembroke, Ont., includes one county of Quebec province.
Whitehorse, Y.T., includes part of British Columbia.

STATISTICS OF THE CATHOLIC CHURCH IN CANADA

(Principal source: *1988 Directory of the Canadian Conference of Catholic Bishops;* Catholic population statistics are those reported in the 1981 Canadian census. Permanent deacon statistics are from the *1988 Annuario Pontificio*. Archdioceses are indicated by an asterisk. For dioceses marked +, see Canadian Dioceses with Interprovincial Lines.)

Canada's 10 civil provinces and two territories are divided into 17 ecclesiastical provinces consisting of 17 metropolitan sees (archdioceses) and 52 suffragan sees (51 dioceses and one territorial abbacy); there are also one archdiocese, and three eparchies immediately subject to the Holy See. (See listing of Ecclesiastical Provinces elsewhere in this section.)

This table presents a regional breakdown of Catholic statistics. In some cases, the totals are approximate because diocesan boundaries fall within several civil provinces.

Civil Province Diocese	Cath. Pop.	Dioc. Priests	Rel. Priests	Total Priests	Perm. Deacs.	Brothers	Sisters	Parishes
Newfoundland	207,705	115	30	145	—	73	449	235
*St. John's	109,345	52	18	70	—	53	314	94
Grand Falls	42,075	32	—	32	—	11	53	45
Labrador City-Schefferville+	12,793	2	11	13	—	3	31	35
St. George's	43,492	29	1	30	—	6	51	61
Prince Edward Island								
Charlottetown	56,551	73	2	75	1	—	199	61
Nova Scotia	304,613	272	61	333	25	16	948	227
*Halifax	124,007	75	31	106	23	3	381	59
Antigonish	144,011	177	10	187	—	8	497	126
Yarmouth	36,595	20	20	40	2	5	70	42
New Brunswick	363,303	300	86	386	2	40	1,079	265
*Moncton	96,527	79	40	119	—	26	360	64
Bathurst	114,474	79	23	102	—	7	314	69
Edmundston	54,227	55	10	65	—	7	170	37
St. John	98,075	87	13	100	2	—	235	95
Quebec	5,471,650	3,860	2,511	6,371	197	3,246	22,722	1,899
*Montreal	1,566,942	730	1,006	1,736	51	1,146	7,120	291
*Quebec	851,318	723	493	1,216	56	552	5,464	276
*Rimouski	167,748	193	67	260	—	42	926	119
*Sherbrooke	222,972	270	123	393	9	182	1,359	142
Amos	106,825	80	23	103	—	19	232	72
Baie-Comeau	108,994	62	28	90	5	39	215	50
Chicoutimi	277,334	260	77	337	8	95	850	95
Gaspe	104,229	94	16	110	1	6	239	63
Gatineau-Hull	186,217	77	73	150	—	23	368	62
Joliette	151,129	129	47	176	2	134	513	58
Mont Laurier	67,500	62	38	100	—	41	197	59
Nicolet	113,066	207	41	248	13	142	963	85

Civil Province Diocese	Cath. Pop.	Dioc. Priests	Rel. Priests	Total Priests	Perm. Deacs.	Brothers	Sisters	Parishes
Quebec								
Rouyn-Noranda	54,848	32	21	53	—	10	139	43
Ste.-Anne-de-la-Pocatiere	93,922	178	7	185	2	16	370	54
St. Hyacinthe	274,053	224	108	332	27	273	1,447	115
St. Jean-Longueuil	461,642	148	80	228	—	121	632	89
St. Jerome	257,233	107	118	225	5	136	298	67
Trois Rivieres	238,485	181	100	281	14	192	1,055	94
Valleyfield	167,193	103	45	148	4	77	335	65
Ontario	2,929,303	1,476	1,197	2,673	206	361	4,750	1,203
*Kingston	87,067	75	13	88	1	—	240	69
*Ottawa	287,777	159	232	391	10	95	1,133	113
*Toronto	1,124,558	343	556	899	89	169	957	231
Alexandria-Cornwall	55,890	45	9	54	6	9	111	34
Hamilton	386,697	147	132	279	2	28	535	149
Hearst	34,391	36	3	39	1	—	50	37
London	346,241	243	106	349	—	21	634	174
Moosonee+	1,878	1	11	12	1	4	8	11
Pembroke+	64,044	80	6	86	3	6	276	72
Peterborough	62,887	89	3	92	2	—	182	68
St. Catharines	126,662	63	39	102	—	3	83	49
Sault Ste. Marie	224,469	127	54	181	82	11	377	104
Thunder Bay	71,634	30	22	52	1	3	81	58
Timmins	55,108	38	11	49	8	12	83	34
Manitoba	253,346	146	185	331	33	62	948	330
*Keewatin-LePas+	35,775	1	27	28	1	6	39	55
*St. Boniface	66,000	98	70	168	11	40	575	110
*Winnipeg	148,215	47	74	121	21	14	325	152
Churchill-Hudson Bay+	3,356	—	14	14	—	2	9	13
Saskatchewan	268,687	179	129	308	—	27	798	376
*Regina	122,661	75	33	108	—	2	325	175
Gravelbourg	17,136	25	4	29	—	—	70	40
Prince Albert	55,826	40	20	60	—	4	139	78
Saskatoon	64,299	39	48	87	—	1	179	62
St. Peter-Muenster (Abb.)	8,765	—	24	24	—	20	85	21
Alberta	564,091	224	234	458	3	46	871	396
*Edmonton	252,482	104	121	225	—	36	582	179
*Grouard-McLennan	40,547	8	39	47	1	2	52	68
Calgary	219,025	86	69	155	1	8	165	77
St. Paul	52,037	26	5	31	1	—	72	72
British Columbia	522,264	170	166	336	1	41	571	324
*Vancouver	275,083	91	100	191	—	25	307	72
Kamloops	49,273	14	11	25	1	6	39	80
Nelson	62,225	28	15	43	—	—	54	54
Prince George	56,977	5	21	26	—	6	38	60
Victoria	78,706	32	19	51	—	4	133	58
Yukon Territory								
Whitehorse+	7,373	2	16	18	—	1	10	24
Northwest Territories								
MacKenzie-Ft. Smith+	15,017	2	25	27	—	11	33	45
Eastern Rite (Ukrainians)	207,080	177	65	242	45	7	152	390
*Winnipeg	49,000	32	14	46	13	1	40	110
Edmonton	41,065	27	12	39	6	3	18	75
New Westminster	7,000	16	4	20	2	—	6	19
Saskatoon	26,815	18	17	35	3	—	42	130
Toronto	83,200	84	18	102	21	3	46	56

Civil Province Diocese	Cath. Pop.	Dioc. Priests	Rel. Priests	Total Priests	Perm. Deacs.	Brothers	Sisters	Parishes
Other Eastern Rites								
St. Maron of Montreal (Maronites)	60,000	7	6	13	—	—	6	11
St. Sauveur-Montreal (Greek Melkites)	50,000	3	6	9	—	—	—	10
Sts. Cyril and Methodius-Toronto (Slovaks)	15,000	5	4	9	—	—	—	11
Armenian Exarchate	12,000	—	—	—	—	—	—	—
Military Ordinariate	79,931	55	20	75	—	—	—	70
TOTALS 1988	11,375,914*	7,075	4,763	11,838	513	3,935	33,536	5,878
Totals 1987	11,375,914*	7,017	4,777	11,794	470	3,684	35,087	5,932

* 1981 Canadian census. The *1986 Statistical Yearbook of the Church* reported a Catholic population of 11,732,000 as of December 31, 1986.

PERCENTAGE OF CATHOLICS*

Catholic population statistics are from the 1981 Canadian census; total population figures are 1985 estimates.

The table presents a regional breakdown of Catholic percentage in total population. In some cases, the Catholic totals are approximate because diocesan boundaries fall within several civil provinces. See Index: Canadian Dioceses with Interprovincial Lines.

Civil Province Territory	Cath. Pop.	Total Pop.	Cath. Pct.
Alberta	564,091	2,337,500	24.1
British Columbia	522,264	2,883,000	18.1
Manitoba	253,346	1,065,000	23.8
New Brunswick	363,303	717,200	50.6
Newfoundland	207,705	578,900	35.9
Nova Scotia	304,613	878,300	34.6
Ontario	2,929,303	9,023,900	32.4
Prince Edward Is.	56,551	126,800	44.6
Quebec	5,471,650	6,562,200	83.3
Saskatchewan	268,687	1,016,400	26.4
Yukon	7,373	22,800	32.3
Northwest Territories	15,017	50,500	29.7
Eastern Rites	332,080	—	—
Military Ordinariate	79,931	—	—
TOTALS	11,375,914	25,262,500	45.0

*The 1986 *Statistical Yearbook of the Church* (figures as of Dec. 31, 1986) reported 11,732,000 Catholics (45.8%) in a total population of 25,610,000.

CANADIAN CONFERENCE OF CATHOLIC BISHOPS

The Canadian Conference of Catholic Bishops was established Oct. 12, 1943, as a permanent voluntary association of the bishops of Canada, was given official approval by the Holy See in 1948, and acquired the status of an episcopal conference after the Second Vatican Council.

The CCCB acts in two ways: (1) as a strictly ecclesiastical body through which the bishops act together with pastoral authority and responsibility for the Church throughout the country; (2) as an operational secretariat through which the bishops act on a wider scale for the good of the Church and society.

At the top of the CCCB organizational table are the president, an executive committee, a permanent council and a plenary assembly. The membership consists of all the bishops of Canada.

Departments and Offices

The CCCB's work is planned and co-ordinated by a Pastoral Team of 14 members — six bishops and six staff members (lay and clergy) and the two general secretaries.

The CCCB's nine episcopal commissions undertake study and projects in special areas of pastoral work. Six serve nationally (social affairs, canon law/inter-rite, ministries, missions, ecumenism, theology); three relate to French and English sectors (social communications, Christian education, liturgy).

The general secretariat consists of a French and an English general secretary and their assistants and directors of public relations.

Administrative services for purchasing, archives and library, accounting, personnel, publications, printing and distribution are supervised by directors who relate to the general secretaries.

Various advisory councils and committees with mixed memberships of lay persons, religious, priests and bishops also serve the CCCB on a variety of topics.

Operations

Meetings for the transaction of business are held at least once a year by the plenary assembly, six times a year by the executive committee, and four times a year by the permanent council.

Archbishop James M. Hayes of Halifax, N.S., is president of the CCCB; Bishop Robert Lebel of Valleyfield, Que., is vice-president.
Secretariat is located at 90 Parent Ave., Ottawa, K1N 7B1, Canada.

The Catholic Church Extension Society of Canada supports home missions. Address: 67 Bond St., Toronto, Ontario M5B 1X5.

The Catholic Women's League of Canada, with a membership of more than 125,000. Address: 3081 Ness Ave., Winnipeg, Man. R2Y 2G3.

BIOGRAPHIES OF CANADIAN BISHOPS

(Sources: Almanac survey; *1988 Directory of Canadian Conference of Catholic Bishops; Annuario Pontificio.* Data as of Aug. 1, 1988.)

Ambrozic, Aloysius M.: b. Jan. 27, 1930; ord. priest June 4, 1955; ord. titular bishop of Valabria and auxiliary bishop of Toronto, May 27, 1976; coadjutor archbishop of Toronto, May 28, 1986.

Audet, Lionel: b. May 22, 1908, Ste. Marie de Beauce, Que.; ord. priest July 8, 1934; ord. titular bishop of Tibari and auxiliary bishop of Quebec, May 1, 1952; retired Mar. 26, 1983.

Audet, Rene: b. Jan. 18, 1920, Montreal, Que.; ord. priest May 30, 1948; ord. titular bishop of Chonochora and auxiliary bishop of Ottawa, July 31, 1963; bishop of Joliette, Jan. 3, 1968.

Baudoux, Maurice: b. July 10, 1902, Louviere, Belgium; ord. priest July 17, 1929; ord. bishop of St. Paul in Alberta, Oct. 28, 1948; titular archbishop of Preslavus and coadjutor archbishop of St. Boniface, Mar. 4, 1952; archbishop of St. Boniface, Sept. 14, 1955; retired Sept. 7, 1974.

Belisle, Gilles: b. Oct. 7, 1923, Clarence Creek, Ont.; ord. priest Feb. 2, 1950; ord. titular bishop of Uccula and auxiliary bishop of Ottawa, June 21, 1977.

Berthelet, Jacques, C.S.V.: b. Oct. 24, 1934, Montreal, Que.; ord. priest June 16, 1962; ord. titular bishop of Lamsorti and auxiliary of Saint-Jean-Longueuil, Mar. 21, 1987.

Blais, Leo: b. Apr. 28, 1904, Dollar Bay, Mich.; ord. priest June 14, 1930; ord. bishop of Prince Albert, Aug. 28, 1952; titular bishop of Geron and auxiliary bishop of Montreal, 1959; retired 1964. Bishop emeritus of Prince Albert.

Blanchet, Bertrand: b. Sept. 19, 1932, Saint Thomas de Montmagny, Que.; ord. priest May 20, 1956; ord. bishop of Gaspe, Dec. 8, 1973.

Borecky, Isidore: b. Oct. 1, 1911, Ostrovec, Ukraine; ord. priest July 17, 1938; ord. titular bishop of Amathus in Cypro and exarch of Toronto, May 27, 1948; eparch of Toronto (Ukrainians), Nov. 3, 1956.

Burke, Austin-Emile: b. Jan. 11, 1922, Sluice Point, N.S.; ord. priest Mar. 25, 1950; ord. bishop of Yarmouth, May 14, 1968.

Campbell, Colin: b. June 12, 1931, Antigonish, N.S.; ord. priest May 26, 1956; ord. bishop of Antigonish, Mar. 19, 1987.

Carew, William A.: b. Oct. 23, 1922, St. John's, Nfld., ord. priest June 15, 1947; ord. titular archbishop of Telde, Jan. 4, 1970; nuncio to Rwanda and Burundi, 1970-74; apostolic delegate to Jerusalem and Palestine and pro-nuncio to Cyprus, 1974-83; pro-nuncio to Japan, Aug. 30, 1983.

Carney, James F.: b. June 28, 1915, Vancouver, B.C.; ord. priest Mar. 21, 1942; ord. titular bishop of Obori and auxiliary bishop of Vancouver, Feb. 11, 1966; archbishop of Vancouver, Jan. 8, 1969.

Carter, Alexander: b. Apr. 16, 1909, Montreal, Que.; ord. priest June 6, 1936; ord. titular bishop of Sita and coadjutor bishop of Sault Ste. Marie, Feb. 2, 1957; bishop of Sault Ste. Marie, Nov. 22, 1958; retired May 8, 1985.

Carter, G. Emmett: (See Cardinals, Biographies.)

Charbonneau, Paul E.: b. May 4, 1922, Ste. Therese de Blainville, Que.; ord. priest May 31, 1947; ord. titular bishop of Thapsus and auxiliary bishop of Ottawa, Jan. 18, 1961; first bishop of Hull, May 21, 1963; retired Apr. 12, 1973, because of ill health.

Chiasson, Donat: b. Jan. 2, 1930, Paquetville, N.B.; ord. priest May 6, 1956; ord. archbishop of Moncton, June 1, 1972.

Chimy, Jerome I., O.S.B.M.: b. Mar. 12, 1919, Radway, Alta.; ord. priest, June 29, 1944; ord. first eparch of New Westminster, B.C., for the Ukrainians, Sept. 5, 1974.

Cimichella, Andre, O.S.M.: b. Feb. 21, 1921, Grotte Santo Stefano, Italy; ord. priest May 26, 1945; ord. titular bishop of Quiza and auxiliary of Montreal, July 16, 1964.

Clune, Robert B.: b. Sept. 18, 1920, Toronto, Ont.; ord. priest May 26, 1945; ord. titular bishop of Lacubaza and auxiliary bishop of Toronto, June 21, 1979.

Coderre, Gerard-Marie: b. Dec. 19, 1904, St. Jacques de Montcalm, Que.; ord. priest May 30, 1931; ord. titular bishop of Aegae and coadjutor bishop of St.-Jean-de-Quebec, Sept. 12, 1951; bishop of St.-Jean-de-Quebec, (now Saint-Jean-Longueuil; Feb. 3, 1955; retired May 3, 1978.

Couture, Jean-Guy: b. May 6, 1929, St.-Jean-Baptiste de Quebec, Que.; ord. priest May 30, 1953; ord. bishop of Hauterive (now Baie-Comeau), Que., Aug. 15, 1975; bishop of Chicoutimi, Apr. 5, 1979.

Couture, Maurice, R.S.V.: b. Nov. 3, 1926, Saint-Pierre-de-Broughton, Que.; ord. priest June 17, 1951; ord. titular bishop of Talaptula and auxiliary bishop of Quebec, Oct. 22, 1982.

Couturier, Gerard: b. Jan. 12, 1913, St. Louis du Ha Ha, Que; ord. priest Mar. 25, 1938; ord. bishop of Hauterive (now Baie-Comeau), Feb. 28, 1957; resigned Sept. 7, 1974.

Croteau, Denis, O.M.I: b. Oct. 23, 1932, Thetford Mines, Que., ord. priest Aug. 31, 1958; ord. bishop of MacKenzie-Fort Smith, June 8, 1986.

Crowley, Leonard: b. Dec. 28, 1921, Montreal, Que.; ord. priest May 31, 1947; ord. titular bishop of Mons and auxiliary bishop of Montreal, Mar. 24, 1971.

Daciuk, Myron, O.S.B.M.: b. Nov. 16, 1919, Mundare, Alta; ord. priest June 10, 1945; ord. titular bishop of Thyatira and auxiliary eparch of Winnipeg (Ukrainians), Oct. 14, 1982.

Decosse, Aime: b. June 21, 1903, Somerset, Man.; ord. priest July 4, 1926; ord. bishop of Gravelbourg, Jan. 20, 1954; retired May 12, 1973.

Delaquis, Noel: b. Dec. 25, 1934, Notre-Dame-de-Lourdes, Man.; ord. priest June 5, 1958; ord. bishop of Gravelbourg, Feb. 19, 1974.

De Roo, Remi J.: b. Feb. 24, 1924, Swan Lake, Man.; ord. priest June 8, 1950; ord. bishop of Victoria, Dec. 14, 1962.

Despatie, Roger: b. Apr. 12, 1927, Sudbury, Ont.; ord. priest Apr. 12, 1952; ord. titular bishop of Usinaza and auxiliary bishop of Sault Ste. Marie, June 28, 1968; bishop of Hearst, Feb. 8, 1973.

Dionne, Gerard: b. June 19, 1919, Saint-Basile, N.B.; ord. priest May 1, 1948; ord. titular bishop of Garba and auxiliary bishop of Sault Ste. Marie, Apr. 8, 1975; bishop of Edmundston, Nov. 17, 1983.

Doyle, James L.: b. June 20, 1929, Chatham, Ont.; ord. priest June 12, 1954; ord. bishop of Peterborough June 28, 1976.

Doyle, W. Emmett: b. Feb. 18, 1913, Calgary, Alta.; ord. priest June 5, 1938; ord. bishop of Nelson, Dec. 3, 1958.

Drainville, Gerard: b. May 20, 1930, L'Isle-du-Pas, Que.; ord. priest May 30, 1953; ord. bishop of Amos, June 12, 1978.

Dumouchel, Paul, O.M.I.: b. Sept. 19, 1911, St. Boniface, Man.; ord. priest June 24, 1936; ord. titular bishop of Sufes and vicar apostolic of Keewatin, May 24, 1955; archbishop of Keewatin-Le Pas, July 13, 1967; retired 1986.

Ebacher, Roger: b. Oct. 6, 1936, Amos, Que.; ord. priest May 27, 1961; ord. bishop of Hauterive, July 31, 1979; title of see changed to Baie-Comeau, 1986; bishop of Gatineau-Hull, May 6, 1988.

Exner, Adam, O.M.I.: b. Dec. 24, 1928, Killaly, Sask.; ord. priest July 7, 1957; ord. bishop of Kamloops, B.C., Mar. 12, 1974; archbishop of Winnipeg, April, 1982.

Filevich, Basil (Wasyl): b. Jan. 13, 1918; ord. priest Apr. 12, 1942; ord. eparch of Ukrainian eparchy of Saskatoon Feb. 27, 1984.

Flahiff, George F.: (See Cardinals Biographies.)

Fortier, Jean-Marie: b. July 1, 1920, Quebec, Que.; ord. priest June 16, 1944; ord. titular bishop of Pomaria and auxiliary bishop of Ste. Anne-de-la-Pocatiere, Jan. 23, 1961; bishop of Gaspe, Jan. 19, 1965; archbishop of Sherbrooke, Apr. 20, 1968.

Fulton, Thomas B.: b. Jan. 13, 1918, St. Catharines, Ont.; ord. priest June 7, 1941; ord. titular bishop of Cursola and auxiliary bishop of Toronto, Jan. 6, 1969; bishop of St. Catharines, July 7, 1978.

Gagnon, Edouard, P.S.S.: (See Cardinals, Biographies.)

Gaumond, Andre: b. June 3, 1936, St. Thomas de Montmagny, Que.; ord. priest May 27, 1961; ord. bishop of Ste. Anne-de-la-Pocatiere, Aug. 15, 1985.

Gervais, Marcel A.: b. Sept. 21, 1931, Elie, Man.; ord. priest May 31, 1958; ord. titular bishop of Rosmarkaeum and auxiliary bishop of London, Ont., June 11, 1980; bishop of Sault Ste. Marie, May 8, 1985.

Gilbert, Arthur J.: b. Oct. 26, 1915, Oromocto, N.B.; ord. priest June 3, 1943; ord. bishop of St. John, N.B., June 19, 1974; retired Apr. 2, 1986.

Goudreault, Henri, O.M.I.: b. Apr. 30, 1928, Belle-Vallee, Ont.; ord. priest June 17, 1956; ord. bishop of Labrador City-Schefferville, June 17, 1987.

Gratton, Jean: b. Dec. 4, 1924, Wendover, Ont.; ord. priest Apr. 27, 1952; ord. bishop of Mont Laurier, June 29, 1978.

Gregoire, Paul: (See Cardinals, Biographies.)

Greschuk, Martin: b. Nov. 7, 1923, Innisfree, Alta.; ord. priest June 11, 1950; ord. titular bishop of Nazianus and auxiliary eparch of Edmonton of the Ukrainians, Oct. 3, 1974; apostolic administrator "sede plena" of Edmonton, Apr. 14, 1984; eparch of Edmonton of the Ukrainians, May 7, 1986.

Hacault, Antoine: b. Jan. 17, 1926, Bruxelles, Man.; ord. priest May 20, 1951; ord. titular bishop of Media and coadjutor of St. Boniface, Sept. 8, 1964; archbishop of St. Boniface, Sept. 7, 1974.

Hakim, Michel: b. Apr. 21, 1921, Magdouche, South Lebanon; ord. priest Nov. 10, 1947; ord. archbishop of Saida of Greek Melkites, Sept. 10, 1977; app. titular archbishop of Caesarea in Cappadocia and apostolic exarch of Greek Melkite Catholics in Canada, Oct. 13, 1980; first eparch (with personal title of archbishop), Sept. 1, 1984, when exarchate was raised to eparchy with title St. Sauveur de Montreal.

Halpin, Charles A.: b. Aug. 30, 1930, St. Eustache, Man.; ord. priest May 27, 1956; ord. archbishop of Regina, Nov. 26, 1973.

Hamelin, Jean-Guy: b. Oct. 8, 1925, St. Severin-de-Proulxville, Que.; ord. priest June 11, 1949; ord. first bishop of Rouyn-Noranda, Que., Feb. 9, 1974.

Hayes, James M.: b. May 27, 1924, Halifax, N.S.; ord. priest June 15, 1947; ord. titular bishop of Reperi and apostolic administrator of Halifax, Apr. 20, 1965; archbishop of Halifax, June 22, 1967. President of Canadian Conference of Catholic Bishops, 1987-.

Henry, Frederick: b. Apr. 11, 1943, London, Ont.; ord. priest May 25, 1968; ord. titular bishop of Carinola and auxiliary bishop of London, Ont., June 24, 1986.

Hermaniuk, Maxim, C.Ss.R.: b. Oct. 30, 1911, Nove Selo, Ukraine; ord. priest Sept. 4, 1938; ord. titular bishop of Sinna and exarch of Manitoba (Ukrainians), June 29, 1951; archeparch of Winnipeg (Ukrainians), Nov. 3, 1956.

Hubert, Bernard: b. June 1, 1929, Beloeil, Que.; ord. priest May 30, 1953; ord. bishop of St. Jerome, Sept. 12, 1971; coadjutor bishop of Saint-Jean-de-Quebec, 1977; succeeded as bishop of Saint-Jean-de-Quebec, May 3, 1978; title of see changed to Saint-Jean-Longueuil, 1982. President of Canadian Conference of Catholic Bishops, 1985-87.

Labrie, Jean-Paul: b. Nov. 4, 1922, Laurieville, Que.; ord. priest May 20, 1951; ord. titular bishop of Urci and auxiliary bishop of Quebec, May 14, 1977.

Lacey, Michael Pearse: b. Nov. 27, 1916, Toronto, Ont.; ord. priest May 23, 1943; ord. titular bishop of Diana and auxiliary bishop of Toronto, June 21, 1979.

Lacroix, Fernand, C.J.M.: b. Oct. 16, 1919, Quebec; ord. priest Feb. 10, 1946; ord. bishop of Edmundston, Oct. 20, 1970; retired May 31, 1983.

Lahey, Raymond: b. May 29, 1940, St. John's Nfld.; ord. priest June 13, 1963; ord. bishop of St. George's, Nfld., Aug. 3, 1986.

Landriault, Jacques: b. Sept. 23, 1921, Alfred, Ont.; ord. priest Feb. 9, 1947; ord. titular bishop of Cadi and auxiliary bishop of Alexandria, July 25, 1962; bishop of Hearst, May 27, 1964; app. bishop of Timmins, Mar. 24, 1971.

Langevin, Louis-de-Gonzague, P.B.: b. Oct. 31, 1921, Oka, Que.; ord. priest Feb. 2, 1950; ord. titular bishop of Rosemarkie and auxiliary of St. Hyacinthe Sept. 23, 1974; bishop of St. Hyacinthe, July 18, 1979.

LaRocque, Eugene-Philippe: b. Mar. 27, 1927, Windsor, Ont.; ord. priest June 7, 1952; ord. bishop of Alexandria, Ont., Sept. 3, 1974; title of see changed to Alexandria-Cornwall, 1976.

Lebel, Robert: b. Nov. 8, 1924, Trois-Pistoles, Que.; ord. priest June 18, 1950; ord. titular bishop of Alinda and auxiliary of St. Jean de Quebec, May 12, 1974; bishop of Valleyfield, Mar. 26, 1976.

LeBlanc, Camille-Andre: b. Aug. 25, 1898, Barachois, N.B.; ord. priest Apr. 5, 1924; ord. bishop of Bathurst, Sept. 8, 1942; retired Jan. 8, 1969.

Leclerc, Marc: b. Jan. 9, 1933, Saint-Gregoire de Montmorency, Que; ord. priest, May 31, 1958; ord. titular bishop of Eguga and auxiliary bishop of Quebec, Oct. 22, 1982.

Legare, Henri, O.M.I.: b. Feb. 20, 1918, Willow Bunch, Sask.; ord. priest June 29, 1943; ord. first bishop of Labrador-Schefferville, Sept. 9, 1967; archbishop of Grouard-McLennan, Nov. 21, 1972. President of Canadian Conference of Catholic Bishops, 1981-83.

Leger, Paul-Emile: (See Cardinals, Biographies).

Leguerrier, Jules, O.M.I.: b. Feb. 18, 1915, Clarence Creek, Ont.; ord. priest June 19, 1943; ord. titular bishop of Bavagaliana and vicar apostolic of James Bay, June 29, 1964; first bishop of Moosonee, July 13, 1967.

Lemieux, Marie Joseph, O.P.: b. May 10, 1902, Quebec, Que.; ord. priest Apr. 15, 1928; ord. bishop of Sendai, Japan, June 29, 1936; titular bishop of Calydon, 1941; apostolic administrator of Gravelbourg, 1942; bishop of Gravelbourg, Apr. 15, 1944; archbishop of Ottawa, 1953-66; titular archbishop of Salde, Nov. 16, 1966, apostolic nuncio. Retired. Archbishop emeritus of Ottawa.

Levesque, Louis: b. May 27, 1908, Amqui, Que.; ord. priest June 26, 1932; ord. bishop of Hearst, Aug. 15, 1952; titular archbishop of Egnatia and coadjutor of Rimouski, Apr. 13, 1964; archbishop of Rimouski, Feb. 25, 1967; retired May 14, 1973.

Lobsinger, Thomas J., O.M.I.: b. Nov. 17, 1927, Ayton, Ont.; ord. priest May 29, 1954; ord. bishop of Whitehorse, Y.T., Oct. 1, 1987.

MacDonald, James H., C.S.C.: b. Apr. 28, 1925, Wycogama, N.S.; ord. priest June 29, 1953; ord. titular bishop of Gibba and auxiliary bishop of Hamilton April 17, 1978; app. bishop of Charlottetown, Aug. 12, 1982.

MacDonald, Joseph Faber: b. Jan. 20, 1932, Little Pond, P.E.I.; ord. priest Mar. 9, 1963; ord. bishop of Grand Falls, Mar. 19, 1980.

MacNeil, Joseph N.: b. Apr. 15, 1924, Sydney, N.S.; ord. priest May 23, 1948; ord. bishop of St. John, N.B., June 24, 1969; archbishop of Edmonton, July 6, 1973. President Canadian Conference of Catholic Bishops, 1979-81.

Mahoney, James P.: b. Dec. 7, 1927, Saskatoon, Sask.; ord. priest June 7, 1952; ord. bishop of Saskatoon, Dec. 13, 1967.

Martin, Albertus: b. Oct. 4, 1913, Southbridge, Mass.; ord. priest May 18, 1939; ord. titular bishop of Bassiana and coadjutor bishop of Nicolet, Oct. 7, 1950; bishop of Nicolet, Nov. 8, 1950.

Morand, Blaise E.: b. Sept. 12, 1932, Tecumseh, Ont.; ord. priest Mar. 22, 1958; ord. coadjutor bishop of Prince Albert, June 29, 1981; bishop of Prince Albert, Apr. 9, 1983.

Morin, Laurent: b. Feb. 14, 1908, Montreal, Que.; ord. priest May 27, 1934; ord. titular bishop of Arsamosata and auxiliary bishop of Montreal, Oct. 30, 1955; bishop of Prince Albert, Feb. 28, 1959; retired Apr. 9, 1983.

Morissette, Pierre: b. Thetford-Mines, Que., Nov. 22, 1944; ord. priest June 8, 1968; ord. titular bishop of Mesarfelta and auxiliary of Quebec, June 12, 1987.

Noel, Laurent: b. Mar. 19, 1920, Saint-Just-de-Bretenieres, Que.; ord. priest June 16, 1944; ord. titular bishop of Agathopolis and auxiliary bishop of Quebec, Aug. 29, 1963; bishop of Trois Rivieres, Nov. 5, 1975.

O'Brien, Brendan M.: b. Sept. 28, 1943, Ottawa, Ont.; ord. priest June 1, 1968; ord. titular bishop of Numana and auxiliary of Ottawa, June 29, 1987.

O'Byrne, Paul J.: b. Dec. 12, 1922, Calgary, Alta.; ord. priest Feb. 21, 1948; ord. bishop of Calgary, Aug. 22, 1968.

O'Connor, Hubert P., O.M.I.: b. Feb. 17, 1928, Huntingdon, Que.; ord. priest June 5, 1955; ord. bishop of Whitehorse, Dec. 8, 1971; bishop of Prince George, June, 1986.

O'Grady, John Fergus, O.M.I.: b. July 27, 1908, Macton, Ont.; ord. priest June 29, 1934; ord. titular bishop of Aspendus and vicar apostolic of Prince Rupert, Mar. 7, 1956; first bishop of Prince George, July 13, 1967; retired June, 1986.

O'Mara, John A.: b. Nov. 17, 1924, Buffalo, N.Y.; ord. priest June 1, 1951; ord. bishop of Thunder Bay, June 29, 1976.

Ouellet, Gilles, P.M.E.: b. Aug. 14, 1922, Bromptonville, Que.; ord. priest June 30, 1946; ord. bishop of Gaspe, Nov. 23, 1968; app. archbishop of Rimouski, Apr. 27, 1973. President Canadian Conference of Catholic Bishops, 1977-79.

Ouellette, Andre: b. Feb. 4, 1913, Salem, Mass.; ord. priest June 11, 1938; ord. titular bishop of Carre and auxiliary bishop of Mont-Laurier, Feb. 25, 1957; bishop of Mont-Laurier, Mar. 27, 1965; retired Feb. 15. 1978.

Pappin, Bernard F.: b. July 10, 1928, Westmeath, Ont.; ord. priest May 27, 1954; ord. titular bishop of Aradi and auxiliary bishop of Sault Ste. Marie, Apr. 11, 1975.

Pare, Marius: b. May 22, 1903, Montmagny, Que.; ord. priest July 3, 1927; ord. titular bishop of Aegae and auxiliary bishop of Chicoutimi, May 1, 1956; bishop of Chicoutimi, Feb. 18, 1961; retired Apr. 5, 1979.

Pedneault, Roch: b. Apr. 10, 1927, Saint Joseph d'Alma, Que.; ord. priest Feb. 8, 1953; ord. titular bishop of Aggersel and auxiliary of Chicoutimi, Que., June 29, 1974.

Penney, Alphonsus L.: b. Sept. 17, 1924, St. John's, Nfld.; ord. priest June 29, 1949; ord. bishop of Grand Falls, Jan. 18, 1973; archbishop of St. John's, Nfld., Apr. 5, 1979.

Piche, Paul, O.M.I.: b. Sept. 14, 1909, Gravelbourg, Sask.; ord. priest Dec. 23, 1934; ord. titular bishop of Orcistus and vicar apostolic of Mackenzie, June 11, 1959; first bishop of Mackenzie-Fort Smith, July 13, 1967; retired Feb. 6, 1986.

Plouffe, Jean-Louis: b. Oct. 29, 1940, Ottawa, Ont.; ord. priest June 12, 1965; ord. titular bishop of Lamzella and auxiliary of Sault Ste. Marie, Feb. 26, 1987.

Plourde, Joseph-Aurele: b. Jan. 12, 1915, St. Francois de Madawaska, N.B.; ord. priest May 7, 1944; ord. titular bishop of Lapda and auxiliary bishop of Alexandria, Aug. 26, 1964; archbishop of Ottawa, Jan. 2, 1967.

Power, William E.: b. Sept. 27, 1915; Montreal, Que.; ord. priest June 7, 1941; ord. bishop of Antigonish, July 20, 1960 (retired Dec. 12, 1986); president Canadian Conference of Catholic Bishops, 1971-73.

Richard, Arsène: b. May 9, 1935, St-Louis-de-Kent, N.B.; ord. priest June 11, 1960; ord. bishop of Bathurst Nov. 20, 1985.

Rouleau, Reynald, O.M.I.: b. Nov. 30, 1935, Saint-Jean-de-Dieu, Que.; ord. priest Feb. 2, 1963; ord. bishop of Churchill-Hudson Bay, July 29, 1987.

Routhier, Henri, O.M.I.: b. Feb. 28, 1900, Pincher Creek, Alta.; ord. priest Sept. 7, 1924; ord. titular bishop of Naissus and coadjutor vicar apostolic of Grouard, Sept. 8, 1945; vicar apostolic of Grouard, 1953; archbishop of Grouard-McLennan, July 13, 1967; retired Nov. 21, 1972.

Roy, Raymond: b. May 3, 1919, St. Boniface, Man.; ord. priest May 31, 1947; ord. bishop of St. Paul in Alberta, July 18, 1972.

Rusnak, Michael, C.SS.R.: b. Aug. 21, 1921, Beaverdale, Pa.; ord. priest July 4, 1949; ord. titular bishop of Tzernicus and auxiliary eparch of Toronto eparchy and apostolic visitator to Slovak Catholics of Byzantine rite in Canada, Jan. 2, 1965; first eparch of Sts Cyril and Methodius Eparchy for Slovaks of Byzantine Rite, Feb. 28, 1981.

Ryan, Joseph F.: b. Mar. 1, 1897, Dundas, Ont.; ord. priest May 21, 1921; ord. bishop of Hamilton, Oct. 19, 1937; retired Mar. 27, 1973.

Sabatini, Lawrence, C.S.: b. May 15, 1930, Chicago, Ill.; ord. priest Mar. 19, 1957; ord. titular bishop of Nasai and auxiliary bishop of Vancouver, Sept. 21, 1978; bishop of Kamloops, Sept. 30, 1982.

Saint-Antoine, Jude: b. Oct. 29, 1930, Montreal, Que.; ord. priest May 31, 1956; ord. titular bishop of Scardona and auxiliary bishop of Montreal, May 22, 1981. Episcopal vicar of west central region.

Saint-Gelais, Raymond: b. Mar. 23, 1936, Baie St. Paul, Que.; ord. priest June 12, 1960; ord. titular bishop of Diana and auxiliary bishop of St. Jerome, July 31, 1980; app. coadjutor bishop of Nicolet, February, 1988.

Sanschagrin, Albert, O.M.I.: b. Aug. 5, 1911, Saint-Tite, Que.; ord. priest May 24, 1936; ord. titular bishop of Bagi and coadjutor bishop of Amos Sept. 14, 1957; bishop of Saint-Hyacinthe, June 13, 1967; retired July 18, 1979.

Setian, Nerses Mikaël: Apostolic Exarch of Armenian Catholics in Canada and the U.S. (see Index).

Shaheen, Elias: b. July 20, 1914, Ebrine, Patriarchate of Antioch of Maronites; ord. priest Mar. 25, 1939; ord. first eparch of St. Maron of Montreal for the Maronites, Nov. 7, 1982; personal title of archeparch, 1985.

Sherlock, John M.: b. Jan. 20, 1926, Regina, Sask.; ord. priest June 3, 1950; ord. titular bishop of Macriana and auxiliary of London, Ont., Aug. 28, 1974; bishop of London, July 7, 1978. President of the Canadian Conference of Catholic Bishops, 1983-85.

Skinner, Patrick J., C.J.M.: b. Mar. 9, 1904, St. John's, Nfld.; ord. priest May 30, 1929; ord. titular bishop of Zenobia and auxiliary bishop of St. John's, Mar. 17, 1950; archbishop of St. John's, Mar. 23, 1951; retired Apr. 5, 1979.

Spence, Francis J.: b. June 3, 1926, Perth, Ont.; ord. priest Apr. 16, 1950; ord. titular bishop of Nova and auxiliary bishop of the military vicariate, June 15, 1967; bishop of Charlottetown, Aug. 15, 1970; military vicar of Canada, 1982-88; archbishop of Kingston, May, 1982.

Sutton, Peter Alfred, O.M.I.: b. Oct. 18, 1934, Chandler, Que.; ord. priest Oct. 22, 1960; ord. bishop of Labrador-Schefferville, July 18, 1974; coadjutor archbishop of Keewatin-Le Pas, Feb. 5, 1986; archbishop of Keewatin-LePas, Nov. 7, 1986.

Tessier, Maxime: b. Oct. 9, 1906, St. Sebastien, Que.; ord. priest June 14, 1930; ord. titular bishop of Christopolis and auxiliary bishop of Ottawa, Aug. 2, 1951; coadjutor bishop of Timmins, 1953; bishop of Timmins, May 8, 1955; retired Mar. 24, 1971.

Tonnos, Anthony: b. Aug. 1, 1935, Port Colborne, Ont.; ord. priest May 27, 1961; ord. titular bishop of Nazionia and auxiliary bishop of Hamilton, July 12, 1983; app. bishop of Hamilton, May 5, 1984.

Tremblay, Gerard, P.S.S.: b. Oct. 27, 1918, Montreal, Que.; ord. priest June 16, 1946; ord. titular bishop of Trisipa and auxiliary bishop of Montreal, May 22, 1981.

Troy, J. Edward: b. Sept. 3, 1931, Chatham, N.B.; ord. priest May 28, 1959; ord. coadjutor bishop of St. John, N.B., May 22, 1984; bishop of St. John, N.B., Apr. 2, 1986.

Turcotte, Jean-Claude: b. June 26, 1936, Montreal, Que.; ord. priest May 24, 1959; ord. titular bishop of Suas and auxiliary bishop of Montreal, June 29, 1982.

Ustrzycki, Matthew: b. Mar. 25, 1932, Saint Catharines, Ont.; ord. priest May 30, 1959; ord. titular bishop of Nationa and auxiliary of Hamilton, July 3, 1985.

Vachon, Louis-Albert: (See Cardinals, Biographies.)

Vallée, Andre, P.M.E.: b. July 31, 1930, Sainte-Anne-de-Perade, Que.; ord. priest June 24, 1956; ord. titular bishop of Sufasar and bishop of the Military Ordinariate of Canada, Jan. 28, 1988.

Valois, Charles: b. Apr. 24, 1924, Montreal, Que.; ord. priest June 3, 1950; ord. bishop of St. Jerome, June 29, 1977.

Veillette, Martin: b. Nov. 16, 1936, Saint-Zephirin de Courval, Que., ord. priest June 12, 1960; ord. titular bishop of Valabria and auxiliary of Trois-Rivieres, Dec. 13, 1986.

Wall, Leonard J.: b. Sept. 27, 1924, Windsor, Ont.; ord. priest June 11, 1949; ord. titular bishop of Leptiminus and auxiliary bishop of Toronto, June 21, 1979.

Weber, Jerome, O.S.B.: b. Sept. 14, 1915, Muenster, Sask., Canada; ord. priest June 8, 1941; app. abbot-ordinary of St. Peter Muenster, Apr. 6, 1960; abbatial blessing, Aug. 24, 1960.

Wilhelm, Joseph L: b. Nov. 16, 1909, Walkerton, Ont.; ord. priest June 9, 1934; ord. titular bishop of Saccaea and auxiliary bishop of Calgary, Aug. 22, 1963; archbishop of Kingston, Dec. 14, 1966; retired Mar. 12, 1982.

Windle, Joseph R.: b. Aug. 28, 1917, Ashdad, Ont.; ord. priest May 16, 1943; ord. titular bishop of Uzita and auxiliary bishop of Ottawa, Jan. 18, 1961; coadjutor bishop of Pembroke, 1969; bishop of Pembroke, Feb. 15, 1971.

CANADIAN SHRINES

Our Lady of the Cape (Cap de la Madeleine), Queen of the Most Holy Rosary: The Three Rivers, Quebec, parish church, built of fieldstone in 1714 and considered the oldest stone church on the North American continent preserved in its original state, was rededicated June 22, 1888, as a shrine of the Queen of the Most Holy Rosary. Thereafter, the site increased in importance as a pilgrimage and devotional center, and in 1904 St. Pius X decreed the crowning of a statue of the Blessed Virgin which had been donated 50 years earlier to commemorate the dogma of the Immaculate Conception. In 1909, the First Plenary Council of Quebec declared the church a shrine of national pilgrimage. In 1964, the church at the shrine was given the status and title of minor basilica.

St. Anne de Beaupre: The devotional history of this shrine in Quebec, began with the reported cure of a cripple, Louis Guimont, on Mar. 16, 1658, the starting date of construction work on a small chapel of St. Anne. The original building was successively enlarged and replaced by a stone church which was given the rank of minor basilica in 1888. The present structure, a Romanesque-Gothic basilica, houses the shrine proper in its north transept. The centers of attraction are an eight-foot-high oaken statue and the great relic of St. Anne, a portion of her forearm.

St. Joseph's Oratory: The massive oratory basilica standing on the western side of Mount Royal and overlooking the city of Montreal had its origin in a primitive chapel erected there by Blessed Andre Bessette, C.S.C., in 1904. Eleven years later, a large crypt was built to accommodate an increasing number of pilgrims, and in 1924 construction work was begun on the large church. A belfry, housing a 60-bell carillon and standing on the site of the original chapel, was dedicated May 15, 1955, as the first major event of the jubilee year observed after the oratory was given the rank of minor basilica.

Martyrs' Shrine: A shrine commemorating several of the Jesuit Martyrs of North America who were killed between 1642 and 1649 in the Ontario and northern New York area is located on the former site of old Fort Sainte Marie. Before its location was fixed near Midland, Ont., in 1925, a small chapel had been erected in 1907 at old Mission St. Ignace to mark the martyrdom of Fathers Jean de Brebeuf and Gabriel Lalemant. This sanctuary has a U.S. counterpart in the Shrine of the North American Martyrs near Auriesville, N.Y.

CANADIAN CATHOLIC PUBLICATIONS

(Sources: *Catholic Press Directory*, Canadian Conference of Catholic Bishops.)

Newspapers

B. C. Catholic, The, w; 150 Robson St., Vancouver, B.C. V6B 2A7.

Catholic New Times (national), biweekly; 80 Sackville St., Toronto, Ont. M5A 3E5.

Catholic Register, The (national), w; 67 Bond St., Toronto, Ont. M5B 1X6. Lay edited.

Catholic Times, The, 10 times a year; 2005 St. Marc St., Montreal, Que. H3H 2G8.

Diocesan News, m; P.O. Box 1689, Charlottetown, P.E.I. C1A 7N4.

Diocesan Review, The, m; 16 Hammond Dr., Corner Brook, Nfld. A2H 2W2.

Hamilton Diocesan News, 3 times a year; 700 King St. West, Hamilton, Ont. L8P 1C7.

L'Informateur Catholique, semimonthly; 1915 Est-Boulevard Gouin, Montreal, Que. H2B 1W7.

Monitor, The, m; P.O. Box 986, St. John's, Nfld. A1C 5M3.

New Freeman, The, w; 1 Bayard Dr., St. John, N.B. E2L 3L5.

Northwestern Ontario Catholic, m; 486 Erindale Cres., Thunder Bay, Ont. P7C 5BC.

Our Diocese, bm; P.O. Box 397, Grand Falls, Nfld. A2A 2J8.

Pastoral Reporter, The, 4 times a year; 1916 Second St. S.W., Calgary. Alta. T2S 1S3.

Prairie Messenger, w; Box 190, Muenster, Sask. S0K 2Y0.

Teviskes, Ziburiai (Lithuanian), w; 2185 Stavebank Rd., Mississauga, Ont. L5C 1T3.

Western Catholic Reporter, w; 10562 109th St., Edmonton, Alta. T5H 3B2.

Magazines

Annals of St. Anne de Beaupre, m; Box 1000, Ste. Anne de Beaupre, Que. G0A 3C0; Basilica of St. Anne.

Apostolat, bm; 460 Primiere Rue, Richelieu, Que. J3L 4B5, Oblates of Mary Immaculate.

Bread of Life, The, 6 times a year; Box 4068, Sta. D, Hamilton, Ont. L8V 4L5.

Bulletin (French-English), q; 324 E. Laurier St., Ottawa, Ont. K1N 6P6. Canadian Religious Conference. Newsletter.

Canadian Catholic Review, 11 times a year; 1437 College Dr., Saskatoon, Saskatchewan S7N 0W6.

Canadian League, The, 4 times a year; 3081 Ness Ave., Winnipeg, Man. R2Y 2G3. Catholic Women's League of Canada.

Casket, The, w; 88 College St., Antigonish, N.S. B2G 2L7.

Chesterton Review, q; 1437 College Dr., Saskatoon, Sask. S7N 0W6.

Companion of St. Francis and St. Anthony, m; P.O. Box 535, Sta. F., Toronto, Ont. M4Y 2L8; Conventual Franciscan Fathers.

Compass — A Jesuit Journal, 4 times a year; 1709 Bloor St. West, Toronto, Ont. M6P 1B2.

Fatima Crusader, The, 4 times a year, P.O. Box 602, Fort Erie, Ont. L2A 5X3.

Global Village Voice, The, 4 times a year; 3028 Danforth Ave., Toronto, Ont. M4C 1N2. Canadian Catholic Organization for Development and Peace.

Grail: An Ecumenical Journal, q; Univ. of St. Jerome's College, Waterloo, Ont. N2L 3G3.

Home Missions, q; 67 Bond St., Suite 101, Toronto, Ont. M5B 1X5.

Indian Record, 4 times a year; 503-480 Aulneau St., Winnipeg, Man. R2H 2V2.

Kateri (English-French), q; P.O. Box 70, Kahnawake, Que. J0L 1B0.

Martyrs' Shrine Message, q; Midland, Ont. L4R 4K5. Newsletter.

Messager de Saint Antoine, Le, 10 times a year; Lac-Bouchette, Que. G0W 1V0.

Messenger of the Sacred Heart, m; 661 Greenwood Ave., Toronto, Ont. M4J 4B3. Apostleship of Prayer.

Missions Etrangeres, 6 times a year; 180 Place Juge-Desnoyers, Laval, Que. H7G 1A4.

Oratory, 6 times a year; 3800 Ch. Reine-Marie, Montreal, Que. H3V 1H6.

Our Family, m; P.O. Box 249, Battleford, Sask.; S0M 0E0; Oblates of Mary Immaculate.

Prete et Pasteur, m; 4450 St. Hubert St., Montreal, Que. H2J 2W9.

Redeemer's Voice (Ukrainian-English), m; 165 Catherine St., P.O. Box 220, Yorkton, Sask. S3N 2V7.

Regard de Foi, 6 times a year; 5875 Est. rue Sherbrooke, Montreal, Que. H1N 1B6.

Relations, 10 times a year; 8100 Blvd. Saint-Laurent, Montreal Que. H2P 2L9; Jesuit Fathers.

Restoration, 10 times a year; Madonna House, Combermere, Ont., K0J 1L0.

Sainte Anne de Beaupre, m; P.O. Box 1000, Que. G0A 3C0.

Scarboro Missions, m; 2685 Kingston Rd., Scarboro, Ont. M1M 1M4.

Spiritan Missionary News, 4 times a year; 1440 McQueen Rd., Edmonton, Alta. T5N 3L2.

Unity, bm; 308 Young St., Montreal, Que. H3C 2G2.

Vox Benedictina, q; 409 Garrison Crescent, Saskatoon, Saskatchewan S7H 2Z9.

MISSIONARIES TO THE AMERICAS

Allouez, Claude Jean (1622-1689): French Jesuit; missionary in Canada and midwestern U.S.; preached to 20 different tribes of Indians and baptized over 10,000; vicar general of Northwest.

Altham, John (1589-1640): English Jesuit; missionary among Indians in Maryland.

Anchieta, Jose de, Bl. (1534-1597): Portuguese Jesuit, b. Canary Islands; missionary in Brazil; writer; beatified 1980; feast, June 9.

Andreis, Felix de (1778-1820): Italian Vincentian; missionary and educator in western U.S.

Aparicio, Sebastian, Bl. (1502-1600): Franciscan brother, born Spain; settled in Mexico, c. 1533; worked as road builder and farmer before becoming Franciscan at about the age of 70; beatified, 1787; feast, Feb. 25.

Badin, Stephen T. (1768-1853): French missioner; came to U.S., 1792, when Sulpician seminary in Paris was closed; ordained, 1793, Baltimore, the first priest ordained in U.S.; missionary in Kentucky, Ohio and Michigan; bought land on which Notre Dame University now stands; buried on its campus.

Baraga, Frederic (1797-1868): Slovenian missionary bishop in U.S.; studied at Ljubljana and Vienna, ordained, 1823; came to U.S., 1830; missionary to Indians of Upper Michigan; first bishop of Marquette, 1857-1868; wrote Chippewa grammar, dictionary, prayer book and other works.

Bertran, Louis, St. (1526-1581): Spanish Dominican; missionary in Colombia and Caribbean, 1562-69; canonized, 1671; feast, Oct. 9.

Betancur, Pedro de San Jose, Bl. (1626-1667): Secular Franciscan, b. Canary Islands; arrived in Guatemala, 1651; established hospital, school and homes for poor; beatified 1980; feast, Apr. 25.

Bourgeoys, Marguerite, St. (1620-1700): French foundress, missionary; settled in Canada, 1653; founded Congregation of Notre Dame, 1658; beatified, 1950; canonized 1982; feast, Jan. 12.

Brebeuf, John de, St. (1593-1649): French Jesuit; missionary among Huron Indians in Canada; martyred by Iroquois, Mar. 16, 1649; canonized, 1930; one of Jesuit North American martyrs; feast, Oct. 19.

Cancer de Barbastro, Louis (1500-1549): Spanish Dominican; began missionary work in Middle America, 1533; killed at Tampa Bay, Fla.

Castillo, John de, St. (1596-1628): Spanish Jesuit; worked in Paraguay Indian mission settlements (reductions); martyred; beatified, 1934; canonized, 1988; feast, Nov. 17.

Catala, Magin (1761-1830): Spanish Franciscan; worked in California mission of Santa Clara for 36 years.

Chabanel, Noel, St. (1613-1649): French Jesuit; missionary among Huron Indians in Canada; murdered by renegade Huron, Dec. 8, 1649; canonized, 1930; one of Jesuit North American martyrs; feast, Oct. 19.

Chaumonot, Pierre Joseph (1611-1693): French Jesuit; missionary among Indians in Canada.

Claver, Peter, St. (1581-1654): Spanish Jesuit; missionary among Negroes of South America and West Indies; canonized, 1888; patron of Catholic missions among black people; feast, Sept. 9.

Daniel, Anthony, St. (1601-1648): French Jesuit; missionary among Huron Indians in Canada; martyred by Iroquois, July 4, 1648; canonized, 1930; one of Jesuit North American martyrs; feast, Oct. 19.

De Smet, Pierre Jean (1801-1873): Belgian-born Jesuit; missionary among Indians of northwestern U.S.; served as intermediary between Indians and U.S. government; wrote on Indian culture.

Duchesne, Rose Philippine, St. (1769-1852): French nun; educator and missionary in the U.S.; established first convent of the Society of the Sacred Heart in the U.S., at St. Charles, Mo. (later Florissant); founded schools for girls; did missionary work among Indians; beatified, 1940; canonized, 1988; feast, Nov. 17.

Farmer, Ferdinand (family name, Steinmeyer) (1720-1786): German Jesuit; missionary in Philadelphia, where he died; one of the first missionaries in New Jersey.

Flaget, Benedict J. (1763-1850): French Sulpician bishop; came to U.S., 1792; missionary and educator in U.S.; first bishop of Bardstown, Ky. (now Louisville); 1810-32; 1833-50.

Gallitzin, Demetrius (1770-1840): Russian prince, born The Hague; convert, 1787; ordained priest at Baltimore, 1795; frontier missionary, known as Father Smith; Gallitzin, Pa., named for him.

Garnier, Charles, St. (c. 1606-1649): French Jesuit; missionary among Hurons in Canada; martyred by Iroquois, Dec. 7, 1649; canonized, 1930; one of Jesuit North American martyrs; feast, Oct. 19.

Gibault, Pierre (1737-1804): Canadian missionary in Illinois and Indiana; aided in securing states of Ohio, Indiana, Illinois, Michigan and Wisconsin for the Americans during Revolution.

Gonzalez, Roch, St. (1576-1628): Paraguayan Jesuit; worked in Paraguay Indian mission settlements (reductions); martyred; beatified, 1934; canonized, 1988; feast, Nov. 17.

Goupil, Rene, St. (1607-1642): French lay missionary; had studied surgery at Orleans, France; missionary companion of St. Isaac Jogues among the Hurons; martyred, Sept. 29, 1642; canonized, 1930; one of Jesuit North American martyrs; feast, Oct. 19.

Gravier, Jacques (1651-1708): French Jesuit; missionary among Indians of Canada and midwestern U.S.

Hennepin, Louis (d. c. 1701): Belgian-born Franciscan missionary and explorer of Great Lakes region and Upper Mississippi, 1675-81, when he returned to Europe; first European to see and describe Niagara Falls.

Jesuit North American Martyrs: Isaac Jogues, Anthony Daniel, John de Brebeuf, Gabriel Lalemant, Charles Garnier, Noel Chabanel (Jesuit priests), and Rene Goupil and John Lalande (lay missionaries) who were martyred between Sept. 29, 1642, and Dec. 9, 1649, in the missions of New France; canonized June 29, 1930; feast, Oct. 19. See separate entries.

Jogues, Isaac, St. (1607-1646): French Jesuit; missionary among Indians in Canada; martyred near present site of Auriesville, N.Y., by Mohawks, Oct. 18, 1646; canonized, 1930; one of Jesuit North American martyrs; feast, Oct. 19.

Kino, Eusebio (1645-1711): Italian Jesuit; missionary and explorer in U.S.; arrived Southwest, 1681; established 25 Indian missions, took part in 14 exploring expeditions in northern Mexico, Arizona and southern California; helped develop livestock raising and farming in the area. He was selected in 1965 to represent Arizona in Statuary Hall.

Lalande, John, St. (d. 1646): French lay missionary, companion of Isaac Jogues; martyred by Mohawks at Auriesville, N.Y., Oct. 19, 1646; canonized, 1930; one of Jesuit North American martyrs; feast, Oct. 19.

Lalemant, Gabriel, St. (1610-1649): French Jesuit; missionary among the Hurons in Canada; martyred by the Iroquois, Mar. 17, 1649; canonized, 1930; one of Jesuit North American martyrs; feast, Oct. 19.

Lamy, Jean Baptiste (1814-1888): French prelate; came to U.S., 1839; missionary in Ohio and Kentucky; bishop in Southwest from 1850; first bishop (later archbishop) of Santa Fe, 1850-1885. He was nominated in 1951 to represent New Mexico in Statuary Hall.

Las Casas, Bartolome (1474-1566): Spanish Dominican; missionary in Haiti, Jamaica and Venezuela; reformer of abuses against Indians and black people; bishop of Chalapas, Mexico, 1544-47; historian.

Laval, Francoise de Montmorency, Bl. (1623-1708): French-born missionary bishop in Canada; named vicar apostolic of Canada, 1658; first bishop of Quebec, 1674; jurisdiction extended over all French-claimed territory in New World; beatified 1980; feast, May 6.

Manogue, Patrick (1831-1895): Missionary bishop in U.S., b. Ireland; migrated to U.S.; miner in

California; studied for priesthood at St. Mary's of the Lake, Chicago, and St. Sulpice, Paris; ordained, 1861; missionary among Indians of California and Nevada; coadjutor bishop, 1881-84, and bishop, 1884-86, of Grass Valley; first bishop of Sacramento, 1886-1895, when see was transferred there.

Margil, Antonio (1657-1726): Spanish Franciscan; missionary in Middle America; apostle of Guatemala; established missions in Texas.

Marie of the Incarnation, Bl. (Marie Guyard Martin) (1599-1672): French widow; joined Ursuline Nuns; arrived in Canada, 1639; first superior of Ursulines in Quebec; missionary to Indians; writer; beatified 1980; feast, Apr. 30.

Marquette, Jacques (1637-1675): French Jesuit; missionary and explorer in America; sent to New France, 1666; began missionary work among Ottawa Indians on Lake Superior, 1668; accompanied Joliet down the Mississippi to mouth of the Arkansas, 1673, and returned to Lake Michigan by way of Illinois River; made a second trip over the same route; his diary and map are of historical significance. He was selected in 1895 to represent Wisconsin in Statuary Hall.

Massias (Macias), John de, St. (1585-1645); Dominican brother, a native of Spain; entered Dominican Friary at Lima, Peru, 1622; served as doorkeeper until his death; beatified, 1837; canonized 1975; feast, Sept. 16.

Mazzuchelli, Samuel C. (1806-1864): Italian Dominican; missionary in midwestern U.S.; called builder of the West; writer.

Membre, Zenobius (1645-1687): French Franciscan; missionary among Indians of Illinois; accompanied LaSalle expedition down the Mississippi (1681-1682) and Louisiana colonizing expedition (1684) which landed in Texas; murdered by Indians.

Nerinckx, Charles (1761-1824): Belgian priest; missionary in Kentucky; founded Sisters of Loretto at the Foot of the Cross.

Nobrega, Manoel (1517-1570): Portuguese Jesuit; leader of first Jesuit missionaries to Brazil, 1549.

Padilla, Juan de (d. 1542): Spanish Franciscan; missionary among Indians of Mexico and southwestern U.S.; killed by Indians in Kansas; protomartyr of the U.S.

Palou, Francisco (c. 1722-1789): Spanish Franciscan; accompanied Junipero Serra to Mexico, 1749; founded Mission Dolores in San Francisco; wrote history of the Franciscans in California.

Pariseau, Mother Mary Joseph (1833-1902): Canadian Sister of Charity of Providence; missionary in state of Washington from 1856; founded first hospitals in northwest territory; artisan and architect. Represents Washington in National Statuary Hall.

Peter of Ghent (d. 1572): Belgian Franciscan brother; missionary in Mexico for 49 years.

Porres, Martin de, St. (1579-1639): Peruvian Dominican oblate; his father was a Spanish soldier and his mother a black freedwoman from Panama; called wonder worker of Peru; beatified, 1837; canonized, 1962; feast, Nov. 3.

Quiroga, Vasco de (1470-1565): Spanish missionary in Mexico; founded hospitals; bishop of Michoacan, 1537.

Ravalli, Antonio (1811-1884): Italian Jesuit; missionary in far-western United States, mostly Montana, for 40 years.

Raymbaut, Charles (1602-1643): French Jesuit; missionary among Indians of Canada and northern U.S..

Richard, Gabriel (1767-1832): French Sulpician; missionary in Illinois and Michigan; a founder of University of Michigan; elected delegate to Congress from Michigan, 1823; first priest to hold seat in the House of Representatives.

Rodriguez, Alfonso, St. (1598-1628): Spanish Jesuit; missionary in Paraguay; martyred; beatified, 1934; canonized, 1988; feast, Nov. 17.

Rosati, Joseph (1789-1843): Italian Vincentian; missionary bishop in U.S. (vicar apostolic of Mississippi and Alabama, 1822; coadjutor of Louisiana and the Two Floridas, 1823-26; administrator of New Orleans, 1826-29; first bishop of St. Louis, 1826-1843).

Sahagun, Bernardino de (c. 1500-1590): Spanish Franciscan; missionary in Mexico for over 60 years; expert on Aztec archaeology.

Seelos, Francis X. (1819-1867): Redemptorist missionary, born Bavaria; ordained, 1844, at Baltimore; missionary in Pittsburgh and New Orleans.

Serra, Junipero, Bl. (1713-1784): Spanish Franciscan, b. Majorca; missionary in America; arrived Mexico, 1749, where he did missionary work for 20 years; began work in Upper California in 1769 and established nine of the 21 Franciscan missions along the Pacific coast; baptized some 6,000 Indians and confirmed almost 5,000; a cultural pioneer of California. Represents California in Statuary Hall. He was declared venerable May 9, 1985, and was beatified Sept. 25, 1988; feast, Aug. 28.

Seghers, Charles J. (1839-1886): Belgian missionary bishop in North America; Apostle of Alaska; archbishop of Oregon City (now Portland), 1880-1884; murdered by berserk companion while on missionary journey.

Solanus, St. Francis (1549-1610): Spanish Franciscan; missionary in Paraguay, Argentina and Peru; wonder worker of the New World; canonized, 1726; feast, July 14.

Sorin, Edward F. (1814-1893): French priest; member of Congregation of Holy Cross; sent to U.S. in 1841; founder and first president of the University of Notre Dame; missionary in Indiana and Michigan.

Todadilla, Anthony de (1704-1746): Spanish Capuchin; missionary to Indians of Venezuela; killed by Motilones.

Turibius de Mogrovejo, St. (1538-1606): Spanish archbishop of Lima, Peru, c. 1580-1606; canonized 1726; feast, Mar. 23.

Twelve Apostles of Mexico (early 16th century): Franciscan priests; arrived in Mexico, 1524: Fathers Martin de Valencia (leader), Francisco de Soto, Martin de la Coruna, Juan Suares, Antonio de Ciudad Rodrigo, Toribio de Benevente, Garcia de Cisneros, Luis de Fuensalida, Juan de

Ribas, Francisco Ximenes; Brothers Andres de Coroboda, Juan de Palos.

Valdivia, Luis de (1561-1641): Spanish Jesuit; defender of Indians in Peru and Chile.

Vasques de Espinosa, Antonio (early 17th century): Spanish Carmelite; missionary and explorer in Mexico, Panama and western coast of South America.

Vieira, Antonio (1608-1687): Portuguese Jesuit; preacher; missionary in Peru and Chile; protector of Indians against exploitation by slave owners and traders; considered foremost prose writer of 17th-century Portugal.

White, Andrew (1579-1656): English Jesuit; missionary among Indians in Maryland.

Wimmer, Boniface (1809-1887): German Benedictine; missionary among German immigrants in the U.S..

Youville, Marie Marguerite d', Bl. (1701-1771): Canadian widow; foundress of Sisters of Charity (Grey Nuns), 1738, at Montreal; beatified, 1959; feast, Dec. 23.

Zumarraga, Juan de (1468-1548): Spanish Franciscan; missionary; first bishop of Mexico; introduced first printing press in New World, published first book in America, a catechism for Aztec Indians; extended missions in Mexico and Central America; vigorous opponent of exploitation of Indians; approved of devotions at Guadalupe; leading figure in early church history in Mexico.

FRANCISCAN MISSIONS

The 21 Franciscan missions of Upper California were established during the 54-year period from 1769 to 1822. Located along the old El Camino Real, or King's Highway, they extended from San Diego to San Francisco and were the centers of Indian civilization, Christianity and industry in the early history of the state.

Fray Junipero Serra was the great pioneer of the missions of Upper California. He and his successor as superior of the work, Fray Fermin Lasuen, each directed the establishment of nine missions. One hundred and 46 priests of the Order of Friars Minor, most of them Spaniards, labored in the region from 1769 to 1845; 67 of them died at their posts, two as martyrs. The regular time of mission service was 10 years.

The missions were secularized by the Mexican government in the 1830's but were subsequently restored to the Church by the U.S. government. They are now variously used as the sites of parish churches, a university, houses of study and museums.

The names of the missions and the order of their establishment were as follows:

San Diego de Alcala, San Carlos Borromeo (El Carmelo), San Antonio de Padua, San Gabriel Arcangel, San Luis Obispo de Tolosa, San Francisco de Asis (Dolores), San Juan Capistrano;

Santa Clara de Asis, San Buenaventura, Santa Barbara, La Purisima Concepcion de Maria Santisima, Santa Cruz, Nuestra Senora de la Soledad, San Jose de Guadalupe;

San Juan Bautista, San Miguel Arcangel, San Fernando Rey de Espana, San Luis Rey de Francia, Santa Ines, San Rafael Arcangel, San Francisco Solano de Sonoma (Sonoma).

SHRINES AND PLACES OF HISTORIC INTEREST IN THE UNITED STATES

(Principal source: Catholic Almanac Survey.)

Listed below, according to state, are shrines, other centers of devotion and some places of historic interest with special significance for Catholics. The list is necessarily incomplete because of space limitations.

Information includes: name and location of shrine or place of interest, date of foundation, sponsoring agency or group, and address for more information.

Alabama: St. Jude Church of the City of St. Jude, Montgomery (1934; dedicated, 1938); Mobile Archdiocese. Address: 2048 W. Fairview Ave., Montgomery, Ala. 36196.

• Shrine of the Most Blessed Trinity, Holy Trinity (1924); Missionary Servants of the Most Blessed Trinity. Address: Holy Trinity, Ala. 36859.

Arizona: Chapel of the Holy Cross, in Oak Creek Canyon, Sedona (1956); Phoenix Diocese: P.O. Box 1043, Sedona, Ariz. 86336.

• Mission San Francis Xavier del Bac, near Tucson (1700); National Historic Landmark; Franciscan Friars and Tucson Diocese; Address: Route 11, Box 645, Tucson, Ariz. 85746.

• Shrine of St. Joseph of the Mountains, Yarnell (1939); Catholic Action League of Arizona. Address: P.O. Box 98, Yarnell, Ariz. 65362.

California: Mission San Diego del Alcala (July 16, 1769); first of the 21 Franciscan missions of Upper California; Minor Basilica; National Historic Landmark; San Diego Diocese. Address: 1018 San Diego Mission Rd., San Diego 92108.

• Carmel Mission (Mission San Carlos Borromeo del Rio Carmelo), Carmel by the Sea (June 3, 1770); Monterey Diocese. Address: 3080 Rio Rd., Carmel, Calif. 93923.

• Old Mission San Luis Obispo de Tolosa, San Luis Obispo (Sept. 1, 1772); Monterey Diocese (Parish Church). Address: P.O. Box 1483, San Luis Obispo, Calif. 93402.

• San Gabriel Mission, San Gabriel (Sept. 8, 1771); Los Angeles Archdiocese (Parish Church, staffed by Claretians). Address: 537 W. Mission, San Gabriel, Calif. 91776.

• Mission San Francisco de Asis (Oct. 9, 1776) and Mission Dolores Basilica (1860s); San Francisco Archdiocese. Address: 3321 Sixteenth St., San Francisco, Calif. 94114.

• Mission San Juan Capistrano, San Juan Capistrano (Nov. 1, 1776); Orange Diocese. Address: 31882 Camino Capistrano, Suite 218, San Juan Capistrano, Calif. 92675.

• Old Mission Santa Barbara, Santa Barbara (Dec. 4, 1786); National Historic Landmark; Franciscan Friars. Address: 2201 Laguna St., Santa

Shrines, Historical Places

Barbara, Calif. 93105.
• Old Mission San Juan Bautista, San Juan Bautista (June 24, 1797); Monterey Diocese (Parish Church). Address: P.O. Box 410, San Juan Bautista, Calif. 95045.
• Mission San Miguel, San Miguel (July 25, 1797); Franciscan Friars. Address: P.O. Box 69, San Miguel, Calif. 93451.
• Old Mission Santa Ines, Solvang (1804); Los Angeles Archdiocese (Parish Church). Address: P.O. Box 408, Solvang, Calif. 93463.
Franciscan Friars founded 21 missions in California. Ten are listed above; for the others, see p. 388.
• Shrine of Our Lady of Sorrows, Colusa (1883): Sacramento Diocese. Address: c/o Our Lady of Lourdes Church, 745 Ware Ave., Colusa, Calif. 95932.

Connecticut: Lourdes in Litchfield (Shrine Grotto of Our Lady of Lourdes), Litchfield (1958); Montfort Missionaries. Address: P.O. Box 667, Litchfield, Conn. 06759.
• Shrine of the Infant of Prague, New Haven (1945); Dominican Friars. Address: P.O. Box 1202, 5 Hillhouse Ave., New Haven, Conn. 06505.

District of Columbia: Mount St. Sepulchre, Franciscan Monastery of the Holy Land (1897; church dedicated, 1899); Order of Friars Minor. Address: 1400 Quincy St. N.E., Washington, D.C. 20017.
• National Shrine of the Immaculate Conception. See Index for separate entry.

Florida: Our Lady of La Leche Shrine and Mission of Nombre de Dios, Saint Augustine (1565); St. Augustine Diocese. Address: P.O. Box 3845, St. Augustine, Fla. 32084.
• Our Lady of Guadalupe, Patroness of Unborn, Miami (1981; dedicated, 1984); Respect Life Apostolate, Miami Archdiocese. Address: P.O. Box 3235, Miami, Fla. 33169.

Illinois: Holy Family Log Church, Cahokia (1799); Belleville Diocese (Parish Church). Address: 116 Church St., Cahokia, Ill. 62206.
• National Shrine of Our Lady of the Snows, Belleville (1958); Missionary Oblates of Mary Immaculate. Address: 9500 W. Illinois, Rt. 15, Belleville, Ill. 62223.
• National Shrine of St. Jude, Chicago (1929); located in Our Lady of Guadalupe Church, founded and staffed by Claretians. Address: 221 W. Madison St., Chicago, Ill. 60606.
• Shrine of St. Jude Thaddeus, Chicago (1929) located in St. Pius V Church, staffed by Dominicans, Central Province. Address: 1909 S. Ashland Ave., Chicago, Ill. 60608.

Indiana: Our Lady of Monte Cassino Shrine, St. Meinrad (1870); Benedictines. Address: St. Meinrad Archabbey, St. Meinrad, Ind. 47577.
• Old Cathedral (Basilica of St. Francis Xavier), Vincennes (1826, parish records go back to 1749); Evansville Diocese. Minor Basilica, 1970. Address: 205 Church St., Vincennes, Ind. 47591.

Iowa: Grotto of the Redemption, West Bend (1912); Sts. Peter and Paul Church, Sioux City Diocese. Mailing address: P.O. Box 376, West Bend, Iowa 50597.

Louisiana: National Shrine of Our Lady of Prompt Succor, New Orleans (1810); located in the Chapel of the Ursuline Convent (a National Historic Landmark). Address: 2635 State St., New Orleans, La. 70118.
• Shrine of St. Roch, New Orleans (1876); located in St. Roch's *Campo Santo* (Cemetery); New Orleans Archdiocese. Address: 1725 St. Roch Ave., New Orleans, La. 70117.

Maryland: National Shrine of St. Elizabeth Ann Seton, Emmitsburg (1975); Daughters of Charity of St. Vincent de Paul. Address: 333 South Seton Ave., Emmitsburg, Md. 21727.
• St. Francis Xavier Shrine, "Old Bohemia", near Warwick (1704), located in Wilmington, Del., Diocese; restoration under auspices of Old Bohemia Historical Society, Inc. Address: P.O. Box 61, Warwick, Md. 21912.
• St. Anthony Shrine, Emmitsburg (1893); attached to St. Anthony Parish, Baltimore Archdiocese. Address: 16150 St. Anthony Rd., Emmitsburg, Md. 21727.

Massachusetts: National Shrine of Our Lady of La Salette, Ipswich (1945); Missionaries of Our Lady of La Salette. Address: 315 Topsfield Rd., Ipswich, Mass. 01938.
• Our Lady of Fatima Shrine, Holliston (1950); Xaverian Missionaries. Address: 101 Summer St. Holliston, Mass. 01746.
• St. Anthony Shrine, Boston (1947); downtown Service Church with shrine; Boston Archdiocese and Franciscans of Holy Name Province. Address: 100 Arch St., Boston, Mass. 02107.
• Saint Clement's Eucharistic Shrine, Boston (1945); Boston Archdiocese, staffed by Oblates of Virgin Mary. Address: 1105 Boylston St., Boston, Mass. 02215.

Missouri: National Shrine of Our Lady of the Miraculous Medal, Perryville; located in St. Mary of the Barrens Church (1837); Vincentians. Address: 1811 W. St. Joseph St., Perryville, Mo. 63775.
• Shrine of Our Lady of Sorrows, Starkenburg (1887; shrine building, 1910); Jefferson City Diocese. Address: c/o Risen Savior Parish, Rhineland, Mo. 65069.

New Hampshire: Our Lady of Grace, Colebrook (1948); Oblates of Mary Immaculate. Address: R.R. 1, Box 521, Colebrook, N.H. 03576.
• Shrine to Our Lady of La Salette, Enfield (1951); Missionaries of Our Lady of La Salette. Address: Rt. 4A, P.O. Box 420, Enfield, N.H. 03748.

New Jersey: National Blue Army Shrine of Immaculate Heart of Mary, Washington (1978); World Apostolate of Fatima (The Blue Army). Address: Washington, N.J. 07882.

- Shrine of St. Joseph, Stirling (1924); Missionary Servants of the Most Blessed Trinity. Address: 1050 Long Hill Rd., Stirling, N.J. 07980.

New Mexico: St. Augustine Mission, Isleta (1613); Santa Fe Archdiocese. Address: P.O. Box 463, Isleta, N. Mex. 87022.
- San Miguel Chapel, Santa Fe (1610); Private Chapel; Brothers of the Christian Schools. Address: c/o 100 Diringo Rd., Santa Fe, N. Mex. 87501.

New York: National Shrine of Bl. Kateri Tekakwitha, Fonda (1938); Order of Friars Minor Conventual. Address: P.O. Box 627, Fonda, N.Y. 12068.
- Infant Jesus Shrine, North Tonawanda (1958); Society of the Catholic Apostolate. Address: 3452 Niagara Falls Blvd., N. Tonawanda, N.Y. 14120.
- Marian Shrine (National Shrine of Mary Help of Christians), West Haverstraw (1953); Salesians of St. John Bosco. Address: Filor's Lane, W. Haverstraw, N.Y. 10993.
- National Shrine of St. Frances Xavier Cabrini, New York (1938); Missionary Sisters of the Sacred Heart. Address: 701 Fort Washington Ave., New York, N.Y. 10040.
- Original Shrine of St. Ann in New York City (1892); located in St. Jean Baptiste Church; Blessed Sacrament Fathers. Address: 184 E. 76th St., New York, N.Y. 10021.
- Our Lady of Fatima Shrine, Youngstown (1954); Barnabite Fathers. Address: 1023 Swan Rd., Youngstown, N.Y. 14174.
- Our Lady of Victory National Shrine, Lackawanna (1926); Minor Basilica; Our Lady of Victory Homes of Charity. Address: 767 Ridge Rd., Lackawanna, N.Y. 14218.
- Shrine Church of Our Lady of Mt. Carmel, Brooklyn (1888); Brooklyn Diocese (Parish Church). Address: 275 N. 8th St., Brooklyn, N.Y. 11218.
- Shrine of Our Lady of Martyrs, Auriesville (1885); Society of Jesus. Address: Auriesville, N.Y. 12016.
- Shrine of Our Lady of the Island, Eastport (1975); Montfort Missionaries. Address: Box 31, Eastport, L.I., 11941.

Ohio: Basilica and National Shrine of Our Lady of Consolation, Carey (1867); Minor Basilica; Toledo Diocese; staffed by Conventual Franciscan Fathers. Address: 315 Clay St., Carey, O. 43316.
- National Shrine of Our Lady of Lebanon, North Jackson (1965); St. Maron diocese (Brooklyn). Address: 2759 N. Lipkey Rd., N. Jackson, O. 44451.
- Our Lady of Czestochowa, Garfield Heights (1939); Sisters of St. Joseph, Third Order of St. Francis. Address: 12215 Granger Rd., Garfield Hts., O. 44125.
- Our Lady of Fatima, Ironton (1954); Watterson Council of Knights of Columbus. Address: P.O. Box, 112, Ironton, O. 45638.
- Our Lady Queen of the Most Holy Rosary, Parma Heights (1936); Sisters of the Incarnate Word. Address: 6618 Pearl Rd., Parma Hts., O. 44130.
- St. Anthony Shrine, Cincinnati (1888); Franciscan Friars, St. John Baptist Province. Address: 5000 Colerain Ave., Cincinnati, O. 45223.
- Shrine of the Holy Relics, Maria Stein (1892); Sisters of the Precious Blood. Address: 2291 St. John's Rd., Maria Stein, O. 45860.
- Sorrowful Mother Shrine, Bellevue (1850); Society of the Precious Blood. Address: 4106 State Rt. 269, Bellevue, O. 44811.

Oklahoma: National Shrine of the Infant Jesus of Prague, Prague (1949); Oklahoma City Archdiocese. Address: P.O. Box 488, Prague, Okla. 74864.

Oregon: The Grotto (National Sanctuary of Our Sorrowful Mother), Portland (1924); Servite Friars. Address: P.O. Box 20008, Portland, Ore. 97220.

Pennsylvania: Basilica of the Sacred Heart of Jesus (1741; present church, 1787); Minor Basilica; Harrisburg Diocese. Address: 30 Basilica Dr., Hanover, Pa. 17331.
- National Shrine Center of Our Lady of Guadalupe, Mother of the Americas, Allentown (1974); located in Immaculate Conception Church; Allentown Diocese. Address: 501 Ridge Ave., Allentown, Pa. 18102.
- National Shrine of Our Lady of Czestochowa (1955); Order of St. Paul the Hermit (Pauline Fathers). Address: P.O. Box 151, Doylestown, Pa. 18901.
- National Shrine of St. John Neumann, Philadelphia (1860); Redemptorist Fathers, St. Peter's Church. Address: 1019 N. 5th St., Philadelphia, Pa. 19123.
- National Shrine of the Sacred Heart, Harleigh (1975); Scranton Diocese. Address: P.O. Box 500, Harleigh, Pa. 18225.
- Old St. Joseph's National Shrine, a unit of the Independence National Historical Park, Philadelphia (1733); Philadelphia Archdiocese (Parish Church). Address: 321 Willings Alley, Philadelphia, Pa. 19106.
- St. Ann's Monastery Shrine, Scranton (1902); Passionist Community. Address: 1230 St. Ann's St., Scranton, Pa. 18504.
- St. Anthony's Chapel, Pittsburgh (1883); Pittsburgh Diocese; St. Anthony's Chapel Committee. Address: 1700 Harpster St., Pittsburgh, Pa. 15212.
- Shrine of St. Walburga, Greensburg (1974); Sisters of St. Benedict. Address: 1001 Harvey Ave., Greensburg, Pa. 15601.

Texas: Virgen de San Juan del Valle Shrine, San Juan (1949); Brownsville Diocese; staffed by Oblates of Mary Immaculate. Address: P.O. Box 747, San Juan, Tex. 78589.

Vermont: St. Anne's Shrine, Isle La Motte (1666); Burlington Diocese, conducted by Edmundites. Address: West Shore Rd., Isle La Motte, Vt. 05463.

Wisconsin: Holy Hill — Shrine of Mary, Help of Christians (1857); Discalced Carmelite Fathers. Address: 1525 Carmel Rd., Hubertus, Wis. 53033.
- National Shrine of St. Joseph, De Pere (1889); Norbertine Fathers. Address: 1016 N. Broadway, De Pere, Wis. 54115.

THE CATHOLIC CHURCH IN THE UNITED STATES

The starting point of the mainstream of Catholic history in the United States was Baltimore at the end of the Revolutionary War, although before that time Catholic explorers had traversed much of the country and missionaries had done considerable work among the Indians in the Southeast, Northeast and Southwest. (See Index: Chronology of Church in U.S.)

Beginning of Organization

Father John Carroll's appointment as superior of the American missions on June 9, 1784, was the first step toward organization of the Church in this country.

At that time, according to a report he made to Rome in 1785, there were approximately 25,000 Catholics in the general population of four million. Many of them had been in the Colonies for several generations. Among them were such outstanding figures as Charles Carroll, a member of the Continental Congress and signer of the Declaration of Independence; Thomas FitzSimons of Philadelphia and Oliver Pollock, the Virginia agent, who raised funds for the militia; Commander John Barry, father of the American Navy, and numerous high-ranking army officers. For the most part, however, Catholics were an unknown minority laboring under legal and social handicaps.

Father Carroll, the cousin of Charles Carroll, was named the first American bishop in 1789 and placed in charge of the Diocese of Baltimore, whose boundaries were coextensive with those of the United States. He was ordained in England Aug. 15, 1790, and installed in his see the following Dec. 12.

Ten years later, Father Leonard Neale became his coadjutor and the first bishop ordained in the United States. Bishop Carroll became an archbishop in 1808 when Baltimore was designated a metropolitan see and the new dioceses of Boston, New York, Philadelphia and Bardstown were established. These jurisdictions were later subdivided, and by 1840 there were, in addition to Baltimore, 15 dioceses, 500 priests and 663,000 Catholics in the general population of 17 million.

Priests and First Seminaries

The original number of 24 priests noted in Bishop Carroll's 1785 report was gradually augmented with the arrival of others from France, after the Civil Constitution on the Clergy went into effect there, and other countries. Among the earliest arrivals were several Sulpicians who established the first seminary in the U.S., St. Mary's, Baltimore, in 1791. By 1815, 30 alumni of the school had been ordained to the priesthood. By that time, two additional seminaries were in operation: Mt. St. Mary's, established in 1809 at Emmitsburg, Md., and St. Thomas, founded two years later, at Bardstown, Ky. These and similar institutions founded later played key roles in the development and growth of the American clergy.

Early Schools

Early educational enterprises included the establishment in 1791 of a school at Georgetown which later became the first Catholic university in the U.S.; the opening of a secondary school for girls, conducted by Visitation Nuns, in 1799 at Georgetown; and the start of a similar school in the first decade of the 19th century at Emmitsburg, Md., by Saint Elizabeth Ann Seton and the Sisters of Charity of St. Joseph, the first religious community of American foundation.

By the 1840s, which saw the beginnings of the present public school system, more than 200 Catholic elementary schools, half of them west of the Alleghenies, were in operation. From this start, the Church subsequently built the greatest private system of education in the world.

Trusteeism

The initial lack of organization in ecclesiastical affairs, nationalistic feeling among Catholics and the independent action of some priests were factors involved in several early crises.

In Philadelphia, some German Catholics, with the reluctant consent of Bishop Carroll, founded Holy Trinity, the first national parish in the U.S. They refused to accept the pastor appointed by the bishop and elected their own. This and other abuses led to formal schism in 1796, a condition which existed until 1802 when they returned to canonical jurisdiction. Philadelphia was also the scene of the Hogan Schism, which developed in the 1820s when Father William Hogan, with the aid of lay trustees, seized control of St. Mary's Cathedral. His movement, for churches and parishes controlled by other than canonical procedures and run in extralegal ways, was nullified by a decision of the Pennsylvania Supreme Court in 1822.

Similar troubles seriously disturbed the peace of the Church in other places, principally New York, Baltimore, Buffalo, Charleston and New Orleans.

Dangers arising from the exploitation of lay control were gradually diminished with the extension and enforcement of canonical procedures and with changes in civil law about the middle of the century.

Bigotry

Bigotry against Catholics waxed and waned during the 19th century and into the 20th. The first major campaign of this kind, which developed in the wake of the panic of 1819 and lasted for about 25 years, was mounted in 1830 when the number of Catholic immigrants began to increase to a noticeable degree. Nativist anti-Catholicism generated a great deal of violence, represented by climaxes in loss of life and property in Charlestown, Mass., in 1834, and in Philadelphia 10 years later. Later bigotry was fomented by the Know-Nothings, in the 1850s; the Ku Klux Klan, from 1866; the American Protective Association, from 1887, and the Guardians of Liberty. Perhaps the last eruption of virulently overt anti-Catholicism occurred during the campaign of Alfred E. Smith for the presidency in 1928. Observers feel the issue was muted to a considerable extent in the political area with the election of John F. Kennedy to the presidency in 1960.

Growth and Immigration

Between 1830 and 1900, the combined factors of natural increase, immigration and conversion raised the Catholic population to 12 million. A large percentage of the growth figure represented immigrants: some 2.7 million, largely from Ireland, Germany and France, between 1830 and 1880; and another 1.25 million during the 1880s when Eastern and Southern Europeans came in increasing numbers. By the 1860s the Catholic Church, with most of its members concentrated in urban areas, was one of the largest religious bodies in the country.

The efforts of progressive bishops to hasten the acculturation of Catholic immigrants occasioned a number of controversies, which generally centered around questions concerning national or foreign-language parishes. One of them, called Cahenslyism, arose from complaints that German Catholic immigrants were not being given adequate pastoral care.

Immigration continued after the turn of the century, but its impact was more easily cushioned through the application of lessons learned earlier in dealing with problems of nationality and language.

Councils of Baltimore

The bishops of the growing U.S. dioceses met at Baltimore for seven provincial councils between 1829 and 1849.

In 1846, they proclaimed the Blessed Virgin Mary patroness of the United States under the title of the Immaculate Conception, eight years before the dogma was proclaimed.

After the establishment of the Archdiocese of Oregon City in 1846 and the elevation to metropolitan status of St. Louis, New Orleans, Cincinnati and New York, the first of the three plenary councils of Baltimore was held.

The first plenary assembly was convoked on May 9, 1852, with Archbishop Francis P. Kenrick of Baltimore as papal legate. The bishops drew up regulations concerning parochial life, matters of church ritual and ceremonies, the administration of church funds and the teaching of Christian doctrine.

The second plenary council, meeting from Oct. 7 to 21, 1866, under the presidency of Archbishop Martin J. Spalding, formulated a condemnation of several current doctrinal errors and established norms affecting the organization of dioceses, the education and conduct of the clergy, the management of ecclesiastical property, parochial duties and general education.

Archbishop (later Cardinal) James Gibbons called into session the third plenary council which lasted from Nov. 9 to Dec. 7, 1884. Among highly significant results of actions taken by this assembly were the preparation of the line of Baltimore catechisms which became a basic means of religious instruction in this country; legislation which fixed the pattern of Catholic education by requiring the building of elementary schools in all parishes; the establishment of the Catholic University of America in Washington, D.C., in 1889; and the determination of six holy days of obligation for observance in this country.

The enactments of the three plenary councils have had the force of particular law for the Church in the United States.

The Holy See established the Apostolic Delegation in Washington, D.C., on Jan. 24, 1893.

Slavery

In the Civil War period, as before, Catholics reflected attitudes of the general population with respect to the issue of slavery. Some supported it, some opposed it, but none were prominent in the Abolition Movement. Gregory XVI had condemned the slave trade in 1839, but no contemporary pope or American bishop published an official document on slavery itself. The issue did not split Catholics in schism as it did Baptists, Methodists and Presbyterians.

Catholics fought on both sides in the Civil War. Five hundred members of 20 or more sisterhoods served the wounded of both sides.

One hundred thousand of the four million slaves emancipated in 1863 were Catholics; the highest concentrations were in Louisiana, about 60,000, and Maryland, 16,000. Three years later, their pastoral care was one of the subjects covered in nine decrees issued by the Second Plenary Council of Baltimore. The measures had little practical effect with respect to integration of the total Catholic community, predicated as they were on the proposition that individual bishops should handle questions regarding segregation in churches and related matters as best they could in the pattern of local customs.

Long entrenched segregation practices continued in force through the rest of the 19th century and well into the 20th. The first effective efforts to alter them were initiated by Cardinal Joseph Ritter of St. Louis in 1947, Cardinal (then Archbishop) Patrick O'Boyle of Washington in 1948, and Bishop Vincent Waters of Raleigh in 1953.

Friend of Labor

The Church became known during the 19th century as a friend and ally of labor in seeking justice for the working man. Cardinal Gibbons journeyed to Rome in 1887, for example, to defend and prevent a condemnation of the Knights of Labor by Leo XIII. The encyclical *Rerum Novarum* was hailed by many American bishops as a confirmation, if not vindication, of their own theories. Catholics have always formed a large percentage of union membership, and some have served unions in positions of leadership.

The American Heresy

Near the end of the century some controversy developed over what was characterized as Americanism or the phantom heresy. It was alleged that Americans were discounting the importance of contemplative virtues, exalting the practical virtues, and watering down the purity of Catholic doctrine for the sake of facilitating convert work.

The French translation of Father Walter Elliott's *Life of Isaac Hecker,* which fired the controversy, was one of many factors that led to the issuance of Leo XIII's *Testem Benevolentiae* in January, 1899, in an attempt to end the matter. It was the first time the orthodoxy of the Church in the U.S. was called into question.

Schism

In the 1890s, serious friction developed between Poles and Irish in Scranton, Buffalo and Chicago, resulting in schism and the establishment of the Polish National Church. A central figure in the affair was Father Francis Hodur, who was excommunicated by Bishop William O'Hara of Scranton in 1898. Nine years later, his ordination by an Old Catholic Archbishop of Utrecht gave the new church its first bishop.

Another schism of the period led to formation of the American Carpatho-Russian Orthodox Greek Catholic Church.

Coming of Age

In 1900, there were 12 million Catholics in the total U.S. population of 76 million, 82 dioceses in 14 provinces, and 12,000 priests and members of about 40 communities of men Religious. Many sisterhoods, most of them of European origin and some of American foundation, were engaged in Catholic educational and hospital work, two of their traditional apostolates.

The Church in the United States was removed from mission status with promulgation of the apostolic constitution *Sapienti Consilio* by Pope St. Pius X on June 29, 1908.

Before that time, and even into the early 1920s, the Church in this country received financial assistance from mission-aid societies in France, Bavaria and Austria. Already, however, it was making increasing contributions of its own. At the present time, it is one of the major national contributors to the worldwide Society for the Propagation of the Faith.

American foreign missionary personnel increased from 14 or less in 1906 to an all-time high in 1968 of 9,655 priests, brothers, sisters, seminarians, and lay persons. The first missionary seminary in the U.S. was in operation at Techny, Ill., in 1909, under the auspices of the Society of the Divine Word. Maryknoll, the first American missionary society, was established in 1911 and sent its first priests to China in 1918. Despite these contributions, the Church in the U.S. has not matched the missionary commitment of some other nations.

Bishops' Conference

A highly important apparatus for mobilizing the Church's resources was established in 1917 under the title of the National Catholic War Council. Its name was changed to National Catholic Welfare Conference several years later, but its objectives remained the same: to serve as an advisory and coordinating agency of the American bishops for advancing works of the Church in fields of social significance and impact — education, communications, immigration, social action, legislation, youth and lay organizations.

The forward thrust of the bishops' social thinking was evidenced in a program of social reconstruction they recommended in 1919. By 1945, all but one of their twelve points had been enacted into legislation.

The NCWC was renamed the United States Catholic Conference (USCC) in November, 1966, when the hierarchy also organized itself as a territorial conference with pastoral-juridical authority under the title, National Conference of Catholic Bishops. The USCC is carrying on the functions of the former NCWC.

Pastoral Concerns

The potential for growth of the Church in this country by immigration was sharply reduced but not entirely curtailed after 1921 with the passage of restrictive federal legislation. As a result, the Catholic population became more stabilized and, to a certain extent and for many reasons, began to acquire an identity of its own.

Some increase from outside has taken place in the past 50 years, however; from Canada, from Central and Eastern European countries, and from Puerto Rico and Latin American countries since World War II. This influx, while not as great as that of the 19th century and early 20th, has enriched the Church here with a sizable body of Eastern-Rite Catholics for whom eight ecclesiastical jurisdictions were established between 1924 and 1969. It has also created a challenge for pastoral care of millions of Hispanics in urban centers and in agricultural areas where migrant workers are employed.

The Church continues to grapple with serious pastoral problems in rural areas, where about 600 counties are no-priest land. The National Catholic Rural Life Conference was established in 1922 in an attempt to make the Catholic presence felt on the land, and the Glenmary Society since its foundation in 1939 has devoted itself to this single apostolate. Religious communities and diocesan priests are similarly engaged.

Other challenges lie in the cities and suburbs where 75 percent of the Catholic population lives. Conditions peculiar to each segment of the metropolitan area have developed in recent years as the flight to the suburbs has not only altered some traditional aspects of parish life but has also, in combination with many other factors, left behind a complex of special problems in inner city areas.

Contemporary Factors

The Church in the U.S. is in a stage of transition from a relatively stable and long established order of life and action to a new order of things. Some of the phenomena of this period are:

• differences in trends and emphasis in theology, and in interpretation and implementation of direc-

tives of the Second Vatican Council, resulting in situations of conflict;
• the changing spiritual formation, professional education, style of life and ministry of priests and Religious (men and women), which are altering influential patterns of pastoral and specialized service;
• vocations to the priesthood and religious life, which are generally in decline;
• departures from the priesthood and religious life which, while small percentage-wise, are numerous enough to be a matter of serious concern;
• decline of traditional devotional practices, along with the emergence of new ones.
• exercise of authority along the lines of collegiality and subsidiarity;
• structure and administration, marked by a trend toward greater participation in the life and work of the Church by its members on all levels, from the parish on up;
• alienation from the Church, leading some persons into the catacombs of an underground church, "anonymous Christianity" and religious indifferentism;
• education, undergoing crisis and change in Catholic schools and seeking new ways of reaching out to the young not in Catholic schools and to adults;
• social witness in ministry to the world, which is being shaped by the form of contemporary needs — e.g., race relations, poverty, the peace movement, the Third World;
• ecumenism, involving the Church in interfaith relations on a wider scale than before.

BACKGROUND DATES IN U.S. CATHOLIC CHRONOLOGY

Dates in this section refer mostly to earlier "firsts" and developments in the background of Catholic history in the United States. For other dates, see various sections of the Almanac.

Alabama

1540: Priests crossed the territory with De Soto's expedition.
1560: Five Dominicans in charge of mission at Santa Cruz des Nanipacna.
1682: La Salle claimed territory for France.
1704: First parish church established at Fort Louis de la Mobile under the care of diocesan priests.
1829: Mobile diocese established (redesignated Mobile-Birmingham, 1954-69).
1830: Spring Hill College, Mobile, established.
1834: Visitation Nuns established an academy at Summerville.
1969: Birmingham diocese established.
1980: Mobile made metropolitan see.

Alaska

1779: Mass celebrated for first time on shore of Port Santa Cruz on lower Bucareli Bay on May 13 by Franciscan Juan Riobo.
1868: Alaska placed under jurisdiction of Vancouver Island.
1879: Father John Althoff became first resident missionary.
1886: Archbishop Charles J. Seghers, "Apostle of Alaska," murdered by a guide; had surveyed southern and northwest Alaska in 1873 and 1877, respectively.
Sisters of St. Ann first nuns in Alaska.
1887: Jesuits enter Alaska territory.
1894: Alaska made prefecture apostolic.
1902: Sisters of Providence opened hospital at Nome.
1916: Alaska made vicariate apostolic.
1917: In first ordination in territory, Rev. G. Edgar Gallant raised to priesthood.
1951: Juneau diocese established.
1962: Fairbanks diocese established.
1966: Anchorage archdiocese established.

Arizona

1539: Franciscan Marcos de Niza explored the state.
1540: Franciscans Juan de Padilla and Marcos de Niza accompanied Coronado expedition through the territory.
1629: Spanish Franciscans began work among Moqui Indians.
1632: Franciscan Martin de Arvide killed by Indians.
1680: Franciscans Jose de Espeleta, Augustin de Santa Maria, Jose de Figueroa and Jose de Trujillo killed in Pueblo Revolt.
1700: Jesuit Eusebio Kino, who first visited the area in 1692, established mission at San Xavier del Bac, near Tucson. In 1783, under Franciscan administration, construction was begun of the Mission Church of San Xavier del Bac near the site of the original mission; it is still in use as a parish church.
1767: Jesuits expelled; Franciscans took over 10 missions.
1828: Spanish missionaries expelled by Mexican government.
1863: Jesuits returned to San Xavier del Bac briefly.
1869: Sisters of Loretto arrived to conduct schools at Bisbee and Douglas.
1897: Tucson diocese established.
1969: Phoenix diocese established.

Arkansas

1541: Priests accompanied De Soto expedition through the territory.
1673: Marquette visited Indians in east.
1686: Henri de Tonti established trading post, first white settlement in territory.
1700-1702: Fr. Nicholas Foucault working among Indians.
1805: Bishop Carroll of Baltimore appointed Administrator Apostolic of Arkansas.
1838: Sisters of Loretto opened first Catholic school.
1843: Little Rock diocese established. There were about 700 Catholics in state, two churches, one priest.

1851: Sisters of Mercy founded St. Mary's Convent in Little Rock.

California

1542: Cabrillo discovered Upper (Alta) California; name of priest accompanying expedition unknown.
1602: On Nov. 12 Carmelite Andres de la Ascencion offered first recorded Mass in California on shore of San Diego Bay.
1697: Missionary work in Lower and Upper Californias entrusted to Jesuits.
1767: Jesuits expelled from territory. Spanish Crown confiscated their property, including the Pious Fund for Missions. Upper California missions entrusted to Franciscans.
1769: Franciscan Junipero Serra began establishment of Franciscan missions in California, in present San Diego.
1775: Franciscan Luis Jayme killed by Indians at San Diego Mission.
1779: Diocese of Sonora, Mexico, which included Upper California, established.
1781: On Sept. 4 an expedition from San Gabriel Mission founded present city of Los Angeles — Pueblo "de Nuestra Senora de los Angeles."
Franciscans Francisco Hermenegildo Garces, Juan Antonio Barreneche, Juan Marcello Diaz and Jose Matias Moreno killed by Indians.
1812: Franciscan Andres Quintana killed at Santa Cruz Mission.
1822: Dedication on Dec. 8 of Old Plaza Church, "Assistant Mission of Our Lady of the Angels."
1833: Missions secularized, finally confiscated.
1840: Pope Gregory XVI established Diocese of Both Californias.
1846: Peter H. Burnett, who became first governor of California in 1849, received into Catholic Church.
1848: Mexico ceded California to the United States.
1850: Monterey diocese erected; title changed to Monterey-Los Angeles, 1859; and to Los Angeles-San Diego, 1922.
1851: University of Santa Clara chartered.
Sisters of Notre Dame de Namur opened women's College of Notre Dame at San Jose; chartered in 1868; moved to Belmont, 1923.
1852: Baja California detached from Monterey diocese.
1853: San Francisco archdiocese established.
1855: Negotiations inaugurated to restore confiscated California missions to Church.
1868: Grass Valley diocese established; transferred to Sacramento in 1886.
1922: Monterey-Fresno diocese established; became separate dioceses, 1967.
1934: Sesquicentennial of Serra's death observed; Serra Year officially declared by Legislature and Aug. 24 observed as Serra Day.
1936: Los Angeles made archdiocese. San Diego diocese established.
1952: Law exempting non-profit, religious-sponsored elementary and secondary schools from taxation upheld in referendum, Nov. 4.
1953: Archbishop James Francis McIntyre of Los Angeles made cardinal by Pius XII.
1962: Oakland, Santa Rosa and Stockton dioceses established.
1973: Archbishop Timothy Manning of Los Angeles made cardinal by Pope Paul VI.
1976: Orange diocese established.
1978: San Bernardino diocese established.
1981: San Jose diocese established.
Byzantine-Rite eparchy of Van Nuys established.

Colorado

1858: First parish in Colorado established.
1864: Sisters of Loretto at the Foot of the Cross, first nuns in the state, established academy at Denver.
1868: Vicariate Apostolic of Colorado and Utah established.
1887: Denver diocese established.
1888: Regis College founded.
1941: Denver made archdiocese.
Pueblo diocese established.
1983: Colorado Springs diocese established.

Connecticut

1651: Probably first priest to enter state was Jesuit Gabriel Druillettes; ambassador of Governor of Canada, he participated in a New England Colonial Council at New Haven.
1756: Catholic Acadians, expelled from Nova Scotia, settled in the state.
1791: Rev. John Thayer, first native New England priest, offered Mass at the Hartford home of Noah Webster, his Yale classmate.
1808: Connecticut became part of Boston diocese.
1818: Religious freedom established by new constitution, although the Congregational Church remained, in practice, the state church.
1829: Father Bernard O'Cavanaugh became first resident priest in state.
Catholic Press of Hartford established.
1830: First Catholic church in state dedicated at Hartford.
Father James Fitton (1805-81), New England missionary, was assigned to Hartford for six years. He ministered to Catholics throughout the state.
1843: Hartford diocese established.
1882: Knights of Columbus founded by Father Michael J. McGivney.
1942: Fairfield University founded.
1953: Norwich and Bridgeport dioceses established. Hartford made archdiocese.
1956: Byzantine Rite Exarchate of Stamford established; made eparchy, 1958.

Delaware

1730: Mount Cuba, New Castle County, the scene of Catholic services.
1750: Jesuit mission at Apoquiniminck administered from Maryland.
1772: First permanent parish established at Coffee Run.
1792: French Catholics from Santo Domingo settled near Wilmington.
1816: St. Peter's Church, later the cathedral of the diocese, erected at Wilmington.

1830: Daughters of Charity opened school and orphanage at Wilmington.
1868: Wilmington diocese established.
1869: Visitation Nuns established residence in Wilmington.

District of Columbia

1641: Jesuit Andrew White evangelized Anacosta Indians.
1774: Father John Carroll ministered to Catholics.
1789: Georgetown, first Catholic college in U.S., established.
1791: Pierre Charles L'Enfant designed the Federal City of Washington. His plans were not fully implemented until the early 1900s.
1792: James Hoban designed the White House.
1794: Father Anthony Caffrey began St. Patrick's Church, first parish church in the new Federal City.
1801: Poor Clares opened school for girls in Georgetown.
1802: First mayor of Washington, appointed by President Jefferson, was Judge Robert Brent.
1889: Catholic University of America founded.
1893: Apostolic Delegation established; became an Apostolic Nunciature in 1984 with the establishment of full diplomatic relations between the U.S. and the Vatican.
1919: National Catholic Welfare Conference (now the United States Catholic Conference) organized by American hierarchy to succeed National Catholic War Council.
1920: Cornerstone of National Shrine of Immaculate Conception laid.
1939: Washington made archdiocese of equal rank with Baltimore, under direction of same archbishop.
1947: Washington archdiocese received its own archbishop, was separated from Baltimore; became a metropolitan see in 1965.
1967: Archbishop Patrick A. O'Boyle of Washington made cardinal by Pope Paul VI.
1976: Archbishop William Baum of Washington made a cardinal by Pope Paul VI; transferred to Roman Curia in 1980 as prefect of Sacred Congregation for Catholic Education (now the Congregation for Seminaries and Institutes of Study).
1988: Archbishop James A. Hickey of Washington made a cardinal by Pope John Paul II.

Florida

1513: Ponce de Leon discovered Florida.
1521: Missionaries accompanying Ponce de Leon and other explorers probably said first Masses within present limits of U.S.
1528: Franciscans landed on western shore.
1539: Twelve missionaries landed with De Soto at Tampa Bay.
1549: Dominican Luis Cancer de Barbastro and two companions slain by Indians near Tampa Bay.
1565: City of St. Augustine, oldest in U.S., founded by Pedro Menendez de Aviles, who was accompanied by four secular priests. America's oldest mission, Nombre de Dios, was established.
Father Martin Francisco Lopez de Mendoza Grajales became the first parish priest of St. Augustine, where the first parish in the U.S. was established.
1572: St. Francis Borgia, general of the Society, withdrew Jesuits from Florida.
1606: Bishop Juan de las Cabeyas de Altamirano, O.P., conducted the first episcopal visitation in the U.S..
1620: The chapel of Nombre de Dios was dedicated to Nuestra Senora de la Leche y Buen Parto (Our Nursing Mother of the Happy Delivery); oldest shrine to the Blessed Mother in the U.S.
1704: Destruction of Florida's northern missions by English and Indian troops led by Governor James Moore of South Carolina. Franciscans Juan de Parga, Dominic Criodo, Tiburcio de Osorio, Augustine Ponze de Leon, Marcos Delgado and two Indians, Anthony Enixa and Amador Cuipa Feliciano, were slain by the invaders.
1735: Bishop Francis Martinez de Tejadu Diaz de Velasco, auxiliary of Santiago, was the first bishop to take up residence in U.S., at St. Augustine.
1793: Florida and Louisiana were included in Diocese of New Orleans.
1857: Eastern Florida made a vicariate apostolic.
1870: St. Augustine diocese established.
1917: Convent Inspection Bill passed; repealed 1935.
1958: Miami diocese established.
1968: Miami made metropolitan see; Orlando and St. Petersburg dioceses established.
1976: Pensacola-Tallahassee diocese established.
1984: Palm Beach and Venice dioceses established.

Georgia

1540: First priests to enter were chaplains with De Soto. They celebrated first Mass within territory of 13 original colonies.
1566: Pedro Martinez, first Jesuit martyr of the New World, was slain by Indians on Cumberland Island.
1569: Jesuit mission was opened at Guale Island by Father Antonio Sedeno.
1572: Jesuits withdrawn from area.
1595: Five Franciscans assigned to Province of Guale.
1597: Five Franciscan missionaries (Fathers Pedro de Corpa, Blas de Rodriguez, Miguel de Anon, Francisco de Berascolo and Brother Antonio de Badajoz) killed in coastal missions. Their cause for beatification was formally opened in 1984.
1606: Bishop Altamirano, O.P., conducted visitation of the Georgia area.
1612: First Franciscan province in U.S. erected under title of Santa Elena; it included Georgia, South Carolina and Florida.
1655: Franciscans had nine flourishing missions among Indians.
1742: Spanish missions ended as result of English

conquest at Battle of Bloody Marsh.
1796: Augustinian Father Le Mercier was first post-colonial missionary to Georgia.
1798: Catholics granted right of refuge.
1800: First church erected in Savannah on lot given by city council.
1810: First church erected in Augusta on lot given by State Legislature.
1850: Savannah diocese established; became Savannah-Atlanta, 1937; divided into two separate sees, 1956.
1864: Father Emmeran Bliemel, of the Benedictine community of Latrobe, Pa., was killed at the battle of Jonesboro while serving as chaplain of the Confederate 10th Tennessee Artillery.
1962: Atlanta made metropolitan see.

Hawaii

1825: Pope Leo XII entrusted missionary efforts in Islands to Sacred Hearts Fathers.
1827: The first Catholic missionaries arrived — Fathers Alexis Bachelot, Abraham Armand and Patrick Short, along with three lay brothers. After three years of persecution, the priests were forcibly exiled.
1836: Father Arsenius Walsh, SS. CC., a British subject, was allowed to remain in Islands but was not permitted to proselytize or conduct missions.
1839: Hawaiian government signed treaty with France granting Catholics freedom of worship and same privileges as Protestants.
1844: Vicariate Apostolic of Sandwich Islands (Hawaii) erected.
1873: Father Damien de Veuster of the Sacred Hearts Fathers arrived in Molokai and spent the remainder of his life working among lepers.
1941: Honolulu diocese established, made a suffragan of San Francisco.

Idaho

1840: Jesuit Pierre de Smet preached to the Flathead and Pend d'Oreille Indians; probably offered first Mass in state.
1842: Jesuit Nicholas Point opened a mission among Coeur d'Alene Indians near St. Maries.
1863: Secular priests sent from Oregon City to administer to incoming miners.
1867: Sisters of Holy Names of Jesus and Mary opened first Catholic school at Idaho City.
1868: Idaho made a vicariate apostolic.
1870: First church in Boise established.
Church lost most of missions among Indians of Northwest Territory when Commission on Indian Affairs appointed Protestant missionaries to take over.
1893: Boise diocese established.

Illinois

1673: Jesuit Jacques Marquette, accompanying Joliet, preached to Indians.
1674: Father Marquette set up a cabin for saying Mass in what later became City of Chicago.
1675: Father Marquette established Mission of the Immaculate Conception among Kaskaskia Indians, near present site of Utica; transferred to Kaskaskia, 1703.
1679: La Salle brought with him Franciscans Louis Hennepin, Gabriel de la Ribourde, and Zenobius Membre.
1680: Father Ribourde was killed by Kickapoo Indians.
1689: Jesuit Claude Allouez died after 32 years of missionary activity among Indians of Midwest; he had evangelized Indians of 20 different tribes. Jesuit Jacques Gravier succeeded Allouez as vicar general of Illinois.
1699: Mission established at Cahokia, first permanent settlement in state.
1730: Father Gaston, a diocesan priest, was killed at the Cahokia Mission.
1763: Jesuits were banished from the territory.
1778: Father Pierre Gibault championed Colonial cause in the Revolution and aided greatly in securing states of Ohio, Indiana, Illinois, Michigan and Wisconsin for Americans.
1827: The present St. Patrick's Parish at Ruma, oldest English-speaking Catholic congregation in state, was founded.
1833: Visitation Nuns established residence in Kaskaskia.
1843: Chicago diocese established.
1853: Quincy diocese established; transferred to Alton, 1857; Springfield, 1923.
1860: Quincy College founded.
1877: Peoria diocese established.
1880: Chicago made archdiocese.
1887: Belleville diocese established.
1894: Franciscan Sisters of Bl. Kunegunda (now the Franciscan Sisters of Chicago) founded by Mother Marie Therese (Josephine Dudzik).
1908: Rockford diocese established.
First American Missionary Congress held in Chicago.
1924: Archbishop Mundelein of Chicago made cardinal by Pope Pius XI.
1926: The 28th International Eucharistic Congress, first held in U.S., convened in Chicago.
1946: Blessed Frances Xavier Cabrini, former resident of Chicago, was canonized; first U.S. citizen raised to dignity of altar.
Archbishop Samuel A. Stritch of Chicago made cardinal by Pope Pius XII.
1948: Joliet diocese established.
1958: Cardinal Stritch appointed Pro-Prefect of the Sacred Congregation for the Propagation of the Faith — the first U.S.-born prelate to be named to the Roman Curia.
1959: Archbishop Albert G. Meyer of Chicago made cardinal by Pope John XXIII.
1961: Eparchy of St. Nicholas of the Ukrainians established at Chicago.
1967: Archbishop John P. Cody of Chicago made cardinal by Pope Paul VI.
1983: Archbishop Joseph L. Bernardin of Chicago made cardinal by Pope John Paul II.

Indiana

1679: Recollects Louis Hennepin and Gabriel de la Ribourde passed through state.
1686: Land near present Notre Dame University at

South Bend given by French government to Jesuits for mission.

1749: Beginning of the records of St. Francis Xavier Church, Vincennes. These records continue with minor interruptions to the present.

1778: Father Gibault aided George Rogers Clark in campaign against British in conquest of Northwest Territory.

1824: Sisters of Charity of Nazareth, Ky., opened St. Clare's Academy in Vincennes.

1825: Laying of cornerstone of third church of St. Francis Xavier, which later (from 1834-98) was the cathedral of the Vincennes diocese. The church was designated a minor basilica in 1970 and is still in use as a parish church.

1834: Vincennes diocese established with Simon Gabriel Brute as bishop; title changed to Indianapolis, 1898.

1840: Sisters of Providence founded St. Mary-of-the-Woods College for women.

1842: University of Notre Dame founded by Holy Cross Father Edward Sorin and Brothers of St. Joseph on land given the diocese of Vincennes by Father Stephen Badin.

1853: First Benedictine community established in state at St. Meinrad. It became an abbey in 1870 and an archabbey in 1954.

1857: Fort Wayne diocese established; changed to Fort Wayne-South Bend, 1960.

1944: Indianapolis made archdiocese. Lafayette and Evansville dioceses established.

1957: Gary diocese established.

Iowa

1673: A Peoria village on Mississippi was visited by Father Marquette.

1679: Fathers Louis Hennepin and Gabriel de la Ribourde visited Indian villages.

1836: First permanent church, St. Raphael's, founded at Dubuque by Dominican Samuel Mazzuchelli.

1837: Dubuque diocese established.

1838: St. Joseph's Mission founded at Council Bluffs by Jesuit Father De Smet.

1843: Sisters of Charity of the Blessed Virgin Mary were first sisterhood in state.

Sisters of Charity opened Clarke College, Dubuque.

1850: First Trappist Monastery in state, Our Lady of New Melleray, was begun.

1881: Davenport diocese established.

1882: St. Ambrose College, Davenport, established.

1893: Dubuque made archdiocese.

1902: Sioux City diocese established.

1911: Des Moines diocese established.

Kansas

1542: Franciscan Juan de Padilla, first martyr of the United States, was killed in central Kansas.

1858: St. Benedict's College founded.

1863: Sisters of Charity opened orphanage at Leavenworth, and St. John's Hospital in following year.

1877: Leavenworth diocese established; transferred to Kansas City in 1947.

1887: Dioceses of Concordia (transferred to Salina in 1944) and Wichita established.

1888: Oblate Sisters of Providence opened an orphanage for Negro boys at Leavenworth, first west of Mississippi.

1951: Dodge City diocese established.

1952: Kansas City made archdiocese.

Kentucky

1775: First Catholic settlers came to Kentucky.

1787: Father Charles Maurice Whelan, first resident priest, ministered to settlers in the Bardstown district.

1793: Father Stephen T. Badin began missionary work in Kentucky.

1806: Dominican Fathers built Priory at St. Rose of Lima.

1808: Bardstown diocese established with Benedict Flaget as its first bishop; transferred to Louisville, 1841.

1811: Rev. Guy I. Chabrat first priest ordained west of the Allegheny Mountains.

St. Thomas Seminary founded.

1812: Sisters of Loretto founded by Rev. Charles Nerinckx; first religious community in the United States without foreign affiliation.

Sisters of Charity of Nazareth founded, the second native community of women founded in the West.

1814: Nazareth College for women established.

1816: Cornerstone of St. Joseph's Cathedral, Bardstown, laid.

1836: Hon. Benedict J. Webb founded *Catholic Advocate* first Catholic weekly newspaper in Kentucky.

1848: Trappist monks took up residence in Gethsemani.

1849: Cornerstone of Cathedral of the Assumption laid at Louisville.

1852: Know-Nothing troubles in state.

1853: Covington diocese established.

1937: Louisville made archdiocese. Owensboro diocese established.

1988: Lexington diocese established.

Louisiana

1682: La Salle's expedition, accompanied by two priests, completed discoveries of De Soto at mouth of Mississippi. LaSalle named territory Louisiana.

1699: French Catholics founded colony of Louisiana.

First recorded Mass offered Mar. 3, by Franciscan Father Anastase Douay.

1706: Father John Francis Buisson de St. Cosme was killed near Donaldsonville.

1717: Franciscan Anthony Margil established first Spanish mission in north central Louisiana.

1718: City of New Orleans founded by Jean Baptiste Le Moyne de Bienville.

1720: First resident priest in New Orleans was the French Recollect Prothais Boyer.

1725: Capuchin Fathers opened school for boys.

1727: Ursuline Nuns founded convent in New Orleans, oldest convent in what is now U.S.; they conducted a school, hospital and orphan asylum.

1793: New Orleans diocese established.
1850: New Orleans made archdiocese.
1853: Natchitoches diocese established; transferred to Alexandria in 1910; became Alexandria-Shreveport in 1977; redesignated Alexandria, 1986.
1892: Sisters of Holy Family, a black congregation, established at New Orleans.
1912: Loyola University of South established.
1918: Lafayette diocese established.
1925: Xavier University established in New Orleans.
1961: Baton Rouge diocese established.
1962: Catholic schools on all levels desegregated in New Orleans archdiocese.
1977: Houma-Thibodaux diocese established.
1980: Lake Charles diocese established.
1986: Shreveport diocese established.

Maine

1604: First Mass in territory celebrated by Father Nicholas Aubry, accompanying De Monts' expedition which was authorized by King of France to begin colonizing region.
1605: Colony founded on St. Croix Island; two secular priests served as chaplains.
1613: Four Jesuits attempted to establish permanent French settlement near mouth of Kennebec River.
1619: French Franciscans began work among settlers and Indians; driven out by English in 1628.
1630: New England made a prefecture apostolic in charge of French Capuchins.
1633: Capuchin Fathers founded missions on Penobscot River.
1646: Jesuits established Assumption Mission on Kennebec River.
1688: Church of St. Anne, oldest in New England, built at Oldtown.
1704: English soldiers destroyed French missions.
1724: English forces again attacked French settlements, killed Jesuit Sebastian Rale.
1853: Portland diocese established.
1854: Know-Nothing uprising resulted in burning of church in Bath.
1856: Anti-Catholic feeling continued; church at Ellsworth burned.
1864: Sisters of Congregation of Notre Dame from Montreal opened academy at Portland.
1875: James A. Healy, first bishop of Negro blood consecrated in U.S., became second Bishop of Portland.

Maryland

1634: Maryland established by Lord Calvert. Two Jesuits among first colonists.
First Mass offered on Island of St. Clement in Lower Potomac by Jesuit Father Andrew White.
St. Mary's founded by English and Irish Catholics.
1641: St. Ignatius Parish founded by English Jesuits at Chapel Point, near Port Tobacco.
1649: Religious Toleration Act passed by Maryland Assembly. It was repealed in 1654 by Puritan-controlled government.
1651: Cecil Calvert, second Lord Baltimore, gave Jesuits 10,000 acres for use as Indian mission.
1658: Lord Baltimore restored Toleration Act.
1672: Franciscans came to Maryland under leadership of Father Massius Massey.
1688: Maryland became royal colony as a result of the Revolution in England; Anglican Church became the official religion (1692); Toleration Act repealed; Catholics disenfranchised and persecuted until 1776.
1704: Jesuits founded St. Francis Xavier Mission, Old Bohemia, to serve Catholics of Delaware, Maryland and southeastern Pennsylvania; its Bohemia Academy established in the 1740s was attended by sons of prominent Catholics in the area.
1784: Father John Carroll appointed prefect apostolic for the territory embraced by new Republic.
1789: Baltimore became first diocese established in U.S., with John Carroll as first bishop.
1790: Carmelite Nuns founded convent at Port Tobacco, the first in the English-speaking Colonies.
1791: First Synod of Baltimore held.
St. Mary's Seminary, first seminary in U.S., established.
1793: Rev. Stephen T. Badin first priest ordained by Bishop Carroll.
1800: Jesuit Leonard Neale became first bishop consecrated in present limits of U.S..
1806: Cornerstone of Assumption Cathedral, Baltimore, was laid.
1808: Baltimore made archdiocese.
1809: St. Joseph's College, first women's college in U.S., founded.
Sisters of Charity of St. Joseph founded by St. Elizabeth Ann Seton; first native American sisterhood.
1821: Assumption Cathedral, Baltimore, formally opened.
1829: Oblate Sisters of Providence, a Negro congregation, established at Baltimore.
First Provincial Council of Baltimore held; six others followed, in 1833, 1837, 1840, 1843, 1846 and 1849.
1836: Roger B. Taney appointed Chief Justice of Supreme Court by President Jackson.
1852: First of the three Plenary Councils of Baltimore convened. Subsequent councils were held in 1866 and 1884.
1855: German Catholic Central Verein founded.
1886: Archbishop James Gibbons of Baltimore made cardinal by Pope Leo XIII.
1965: Archbishop Lawrence Shehan of Baltimore made cardinal by Pope Paul VI.

Massachusetts

1630: New England made a prefecture apostolic in charge of French Capuchins.
1647: Massachusetts Bay Company enacted an anti-priest law.
1732: Although Catholics were not legally admitted to colony, a few Irish families were in Boston; a priest was reported working among them.
1755-56: Acadians landing in Boston were denied services of a Catholic priest.

1775: General Washington discouraged Guy Fawkes Day procession in which pope was carried in effigy, and expressed surprise that there were men in his army "so void of common sense as to insult the religious feelings of the Canadians with whom friendship and an alliance are being sought."
1780: The Massachusetts State Constitution granted religious liberty, but required a religious test to hold public office and provided for tax to support Protestant teachers of piety, religion and morality.
1788: First public Mass said in Boston on Nov. 2 by Abbe de la Poterie, first resident priest.
1803: Church of Holy Cross erected in Boston with financial aid given by Protestants headed by John Adams.
1808: Boston diocese established.
1831: Irish Catholic immigration increased.
1832: St. Vincent's Orphan Asylum, oldest charitable institution in Boston, opened by Sisters of Mercy.
1834: Ursuline Convent in Charlestown burned by a Nativist mob.
1843: Holy Cross College founded.
1855: Catholic militia companies disbanded; nunneries' inspection bill passed.
1859: St. Mary's, first parochial school in Boston, opened.
1860: Portuguese Catholics from Azores settled in New Bedford.
1870: Springfield diocese established.
1875: Boston made archdiocese.
1904: Fall River diocese established.
1911: Archbishop O'Connell of Boston made cardinal by Pope Pius X.
1950: Worcester diocese established.
1958: Archbishop Richard J. Cushing of Boston made cardinal by Pope John XXIII.
1966: Apostolic Exarchate for Melkites in the U.S. established, with headquarters in Boston; made an eparchy (Newton) in 1976.
1973: Archbishop Humberto S. Medeiros of Boston made cardinal by Pope Paul VI.
1985: Archbishop Bernard F. Law of Boston made a cardinal by Pope John Paul II.

Michigan

1641: Jesuits Isaac Jogues and Charles Raymbaut preached to Chippewas; named the rapids Sault Sainte Marie.
1660: Jesuit Rene Menard opened first regular mission in Lake Superior region.
1668: Father Marquette founded Sainte Marie Mission at Sault Sainte Marie.
1671: Father Marquette founded St. Ignace Mission at Michilimackinac.
1701: Fort Pontchartrain founded on present site of Detroit and placed in command of Antoine de la Mothe Cadillac. The Chapel of Sainte-Anne-de-Detroit founded.
1706: Franciscan Father Delhalle killed by Indians at Detroit.
1823: Father Gabriel Richard elected delegate to Congress from Michigan territory; he was the first priest chosen for the House of Representatives.
1833: Father Frederic Baraga celebrated first Mass in present Grand Rapids.
Detroit diocese established, embracing whole Northwest Territory.
1843: *Western Catholic Register* founded at Detroit.
1845: St. Vincent's Hospital, Detroit, opened by Sisters of Charity.
1848: Cathedral of Sts. Peter and Paul, Detroit, consecrated.
1853: Vicariate Apostolic of Upper Michigan established.
1857: Sault Ste. Marie diocese established; later transferred to Marquette.
1877: University of Detroit founded.
1882: Grand Rapids diocese established.
1897: Nazareth College for women founded.
1937: Detroit made archdiocese. Lansing diocese established.
1938: Saginaw diocese established.
1946: Archbishop Edward Mooney of Detroit created cardinal by Pope Pius XII.
1949: Opening of St. John's Theological (major) Seminary at Plymouth; this was first seminary in U.S. serving an entire ecclesiastical province (Detroit).
1966: Apostolic Exarchate for Maronites in the United States established, with headquarters in Detroit; made an eparchy in 1972; transferred to Brooklyn, 1977.
1969: Archbishop John Dearden of Detroit made cardinal by Pope Paul VI.
1971: Gaylord and Kalamazoo dioceses established.
1982: Apostolic Exarchate for Chaldean-Rite Catholics in United States established. Detroit designated see city; made an eparchy, 1985, under title St. Thomas Apostle of Detroit.
1988: Archbishop Edmund C. Szoka of Detroit made a cardinal by Pope John Paul II.

Minnesota

1680: Falls of St. Anthony discovered by Franciscan Louis Hennepin.
1727: First chapel, St. Michael the Archangel, erected near town of Frontenac and placed in charge of French Jesuits.
1732: Fort St. Charles built; Jesuits ministered to settlers.
1736: Jesuit Jean Pierre Aulneau killed by Indians.
1839: Swiss Catholics from Canada settled near Fort Snelling; Bishop Loras of Dubuque, accompanied by Father Pellamourgues, visited the Fort and administered sacraments.
1841: Father Lucian Galtier built Church of St. Paul, thus forming nucleus of modern city of same name.
1850: St. Paul diocese established.
1851: Sisters of St. Joseph arrived in state.
1857: St. John's University founded.
1888: St. Paul made archdiocese; name changed to St. Paul and Minneapolis in 1966.
1889: Duluth, St. Cloud and Winona dioceses established.

Mississippi

1540: Chaplains with De Soto expedition entered territory.
1682: Franciscans Zenobius Membre and Anastase Douay preached to Taensa and Natchez Indians. Father Membre offered first recorded Mass in the state on Mar. 29, Easter Sunday.
1698: Priests of Quebec Seminary founded missions near Natchez and Fort Adams.
1702: Father Nicholas Foucault murdered by Indians near Fort Adams.
1721: Missions practically abandoned, with only Father Juif working among Yazoos.
1725: Jesuit Mathurin de Petit carried on mission work in northern Mississippi.
1729: Indians tomahawked Jesuit Paul du Poisson near Fort Rosalie; Father Jean Souel shot by Yazoos.
1736: Jesuit Antoine Senat burned at stake by Chickasaws.
1822: Vicariate Apostolic of Mississippi and Alabama established.
1825: Mississippi made a separate vicariate apostolic.
1837: Natchez diocese established; became Natchez-Jackson in 1956; transferred to Jackson in 1977.
1848: Sisters of Charity opened orphan asylum and school in Natchez.
1977: Biloxi diocese established.

Missouri

1700: Jesuit Gabriel Marest established a mission among Kaskaskia Indians near St. Louis.
1734: French Catholic miners and traders settled Old Mines and Sainte Genevieve.
1750: Jesuits visited French settlers.
1762: Mission established at St. Charles.
1767: Carondelet mission established.
1770: First church founded at St. Louis.
1811: Jesuits established Indian mission school at Florissant.
1818: Bishop Dubourg arrived at St. Louis, with Vincentians Joseph Rosati and Felix de Andreis. St. Louis University, the diocesan (Kenrick) seminary and the Vincentian Seminary in Perryville trace their origins to them.
1826: St. Louis diocese established.
1828: Sisters of Charity opened first hospital west of the Mississippi, at St. Louis.
1832: *The Shepherd of the Valley,* first Catholic paper west of the Mississippi.
1845: First conference of Society of St. Vincent de Paul in U.S. founded at St. Louis.
1847: St. Louis made archdiocese.
1865: A Test Oath Law passed by State Legislature (called Drake Convention) to crush Catholicism in Missouri. Law declared unconstitutional by Supreme Court in 1866.
1867: College of St. Teresa for women founded at Kansas City.
1868: St. Joseph diocese established.
1880: Kansas City diocese established.
1909: Crookston diocese established.
1957: New Ulm diocese established.
1946: Archbishop John J. Glennon of St. Louis made cardinal by Pope Pius XII.
1956: Kansas City and St. Joseph dioceses combined into one see. Jefferson City and Springfield-Cape Girardeau dioceses established.
1961: Archbishop Joseph E. Ritter of St. Louis made cardinal by Pope John XXIII.
1969: Archbishop John J. Carberry of St. Louis made cardinal by Pope Paul VI.

Montana

1743: Pierre and Francois Verendrye, accompanied by Jesuit Father Coquart, may have explored territory.
1833: Indian missions handed over to care of Jesuits by Second Provincial Council of Baltimore.
1840: Jesuit Pierre De Smet began missionary work among Flathead and Pend d'Oreille Indians.
1841: St. Mary's Mission established by Father De Smet and two companions on the Bitter Root River in present Stevensville.
1845: Jesuit Antonio Ravalli arrived at St. Mary's Mission; Ravalli County named in his honor.
1859: Fathers Point and Hoecken established St. Peter's Mission near the Great Falls.
1869: Sisters of Charity founded a hospital and school in Helena.
1884: Helena diocese established.
1904: Great Falls diocese established; redesignated Great Falls-Billings in 1980.
1910: Carroll College founded.
1935: Rev. Joseph M. Gilmore became first Montana priest elevated to hierarchy.

Nebraska

1541: Coronado expedition, accompanied by Franciscan Juan de Padilla, reached the Platte River.
1673: Father Marquette visited Nebraska Indians.
1720: Franciscan Juan Miguel killed by Indians near Columbus.
1855: Father J. F. Tracy administered to Catholic settlement of St. Patrick and to Catholics in Omaha.
1856: Land was donated by Governor Alfred Cumming for a church in Omaha.
1857: Nebraska vicariate apostolic established.
1878: Creighton University established.
1881: Poor Clares, first contemplative group in state, arrived in Omaha.
Duchesne College established.
1885: Omaha diocese established.
1887: Lincoln diocese established.
1912: Kearney diocese established; name changed to Grand Island, 1917.
1917: Father Edward Flanagan founded Boy's Town for homeless boys, an institution which gained national and international recognition in subsequent years.
1945: Omaha made archdiocese.

Nevada

1774: Franciscan missionaries passed through Nevada on way to California missions.

1860: First parish, serving Genoa, Carson City and Virginia City, established.
1862: Rev. Patrick Manogue appointed pastor of Virginia City. He established a school for boys and girls, an orphanage and hospital.
1871: Church erected at Reno.
1931: Reno diocese established; name changed to Reno-Las Vegas, 1977.

New Hampshire

1630: Territory made part of a prefecture apostolic embracing all of New England.
1784: State Constitution included a religious test which barred Catholics from public office; local support was provided for public Protestant teachers of religion.
1818: The Barber family of Claremont was visited by their son Virgil (converted to Catholicism in 1816) accompanied by Father Charles Ffrench, O.P. The visit led to the conversion of the entire Barber family.
1823: Father Virgil Barber, minister who became a Jesuit priest, built first Catholic church and school at Claremont.
1830: Church of St. Aloysius dedicated at Dover.
1853: New Hampshire made part of the Portland diocese.
1858: Sisters of Mercy began to teach school at St. Anne's, Manchester.
1877: Catholics obtained full civil liberty and rights.
1884: Manchester diocese established.
1893: St. Anselm's College opened; St. Anselm's Abbey canonically erected.
1937: Francis P. Murphy became first Catholic governor of New Hampshire.

New Jersey

1668: William Douglass of Bergen was refused a seat in General Assembly because he was a Catholic.
1672: Fathers Harvey and Gage visited Catholics in Woodbridge and Elizabethtown.
1701: Tolerance granted to all but "papists."
1744: Jesuit Theodore Schneider of Pennsylvania visited German Catholics of New Jersey.
1762: Fathers Ferdinand Farmer and Robert Harding working among Catholics in state.
1765: First Catholic community organized in New Jersey at Macopin in Passaic County.
1776: State Constitution tacitly excluded Catholics from office.
1799: Foundation of first Catholic school in state, St. John's at Trenton.
1814: First church in Trenton erected.
1820: Father Richard Bulger, of St. John's, Paterson, first resident pastor in state.
1844: Catholics obtained full civil liberty and rights.
1853: Newark diocese established.
1856: Seton Hall University established.
1878: John P. Holland, teacher at St. John's School, Paterson, invented first workable submarine.
1881: Trenton diocese established.
1937: Newark made archdiocese. Paterson and Camden dioceses established.
1947: U.S. Supreme Court ruled on N.J. bus case, permitting children attending non-public schools to ride on buses and be given other health services provided for those in public schools.
1957: Seton Hall College of Medicine and Dentistry established: the first medical school in state; it was run by Seton Hall until 1965.
1963: Byzantine Eparchy of Passaic established.
1981: Metuchen diocese established.

New Mexico

1539: Territory explored by Franciscan Marcos de Niza.
1581: Franciscans Agustin Rodriguez, Juan de Santa Maria and Francisco Lopez named the region "New Mexico"; they later died at hands of Indians.
1598: Juan de Onate founded a colony at Chamita, where first chapel in state was built.
1609-10: Santa Fe founded.
1631: Franciscan Pedro de Miranda was killed by Indians.
1632: Franciscan Francisco Letrado was killed by Indians.
1672: Franciscan Pedro de Avila y Ayala was killed by Indians.
1675: Franciscan Alonso Gil de Avila was killed by Indians.
1680: Pueblo Indian revolt; 21 Franciscan missionaries massacred; missions destroyed.
1692: Franciscan missions refounded and expanded.
1696: Indians rebelled, five more Franciscan missionaries killed.
1850: Jean Baptiste Lamy appointed head of newly established Vicariate Apostolic of New Mexico.
1852: Sisters of Loretto arrived in Santa Fe.
1853: Santa Fe diocese established.
1859: Christian Brothers arrived, established first school for boys in New Mexico (later St. Michael's College).
1865: Sisters of Charity started first orphanage and hospital in Santa Fe. It was closed in 1966.
1875: Santa Fe made archdiocese.
1939: Gallup diocese established.
1982: Las Cruces diocese established.

New York

1524: Giovanni da Verrazano was first white man to enter New York Bay.
1642: Jesuits Isaac Jogues and Rene Goupil were mutilated by Mohawks; Rene Goupil was killed by them shortly afterwards. Dutch Calvinists rescued Father Jogues.
1646: Jesuit Isaac Jogues and John Lalande were martyred by Iroquois at Ossernenon, now Auriesville.
1654: The Onondagas were visited by Jesuits from Canada.
1655: First permanent mission established near Syracuse.
1656: Church of St. Mary erected on Onondaga Lake, in first French settlement within state.
Kateri Tekakwitha, "Lily of the Mohawks," was born at Ossernenon, now Auriesville (d. in Cana-

da, 1680). She was beatified in 1980.

1658: Indian uprisings destroyed missions among Cayugas, Senecas and Oneidas.

1664: English took New Amsterdam. Freedom of conscience allowed by the Duke of York, the new Lord Proprietor.

1667: Missions were restored under protection of Garaconthie, Onondaga chief.

1678: Franciscan Louis Hennepin, first white man to describe Niagara Falls, celebrated Mass there.

1682: Thomas Dongan appointed governor by Duke of York.

1683: English Jesuits came to New York, later opened a school.

1700: Although Assembly enacted a bill calling for religious toleration of all Christians in 1683, other penal laws were now enforced against Catholics; all priests were ordered out of the province.

1709: French Jesuit missionaries obliged to give up their central New York missions.

1741: Because of an alleged popish plot to burn city of New York, four whites were hanged and 11 blacks burned at stake.

1774: Elizabeth Bayley Seton, foundress of the American Sisters of Charity, was born in New York City on Aug. 28. She was canonized in 1975.

1777: State Constitution gave religious liberty, but the naturalization law required an oath to renounce allegiance to any foreign ruler, ecclesiastical as well as civil.

1785: Cornerstone was laid for St. Peter's Church, New York City, first permanent structure of Catholic worship in state.

Trusteeism began to cause trouble at New York.

1806: Anti-Catholic 1777 Test Oath for naturalization repealed.

1808: New York diocese established.

1828: New York State Legislature enacted a law upholding sanctity of seal of confession.

1834: First native New Yorker to become a secular priest, Rev. John McCloskey, was ordained.

1836: John Nepomucene Neumann arrived from Bohemia and was ordained a priest in Old St. Patrick's Cathedral, New York City. He was canonized in 1977.

1841: Fordham University and Manhattanville College established.

1847: Albany and Buffalo dioceses established.

1850: New York made archdiocese.

1853: Brooklyn diocese established.

1856: Present St. Bonaventure University and Christ the King Seminary founded at Allegany.

1858: Cornerstone was laid of second (present) St. Patrick's Cathedral, New York City. The cathedral was completed in 1879.

1868: Rochester diocese established.

1872: Ogdensburg diocese established.

1875: Archbishop John McCloskey of New York made first American cardinal by Pope Pius IX.

1878: Franciscan Sisters of Allegany were first native American community to send members to foreign missions.

1880: William R. Grace was first Catholic mayor of New York City.

1886: Syracuse diocese established.

1889: Mother Frances Xavier Cabrini arrived in New York City to begin work among Italian immigrants. She was canonized in 1946.

1911: Archbishop John M. Farley of New York made cardinal by Pope Pius X.

Catholic Foreign Mission Society of America (Maryknoll) opened a seminary for foreign missions, the first of its kind in U.S. The Maryknollers were also unique as the first U.S.-established foreign mission society.

1917: Military Ordinariate established with headquarters at New York; transferred to Washington, D.C., in 1985.

1919: Alfred E. Smith became first elected Catholic governor.

1924: Archbishop Patrick Hayes of New York made cardinal by Pope Pius XI.

1930: Jesuit Martyrs of New York and Canada were canonized on June 29.

1946: Archbishop Francis J. Spellman of New York made cardinal by Pope Pius XII.

1957: Rockville Centre diocese established.

1969: Archbishop Terence Cooke of New York made cardinal by Pope Paul VI.

1981: Apostolic Exarchate for Armenian-Rite Catholics in the United States and Canada established. New York designated see city.

1985: Archbishop John J. O'Connor of New York made cardinal by Pope John Paul II.

North Carolina

1526: The Ayllon expedition attempted to establish a settlement on Carolina coast.

1540: De Soto expedition, accompanied by chaplains, entered state.

1776: State Constitution denied office to "those who denied the truths of the Protestant religion."

1805: The few Catholics in state were served by visiting missionaries.

1821: Bishop John England of Charleston celebrated Mass in the ballroom of the home of William Gaston at New Bern, marking the start of organization of the first parish, St. Paul's, in the state.

1835: William Gaston, State Supreme Court Justice, succeeded in having the article denying religious freedom repealed.

1852: First Catholic church erected in Charlotte.

1868: North Carolina vicariate apostolic established.

Catholics obtained full civil liberty and rights.

1874: Sisters of Mercy arrived, opened an academy, several schools, hospitals and an orphanage.

1876: Benedictine priory and school (later Belmont Abbey College) founded at Belmont; priory designated an abbey in 1884.

1910: Belmont Abbey established as an abbacy nullius; abbacy nullius status suppressed in 1977.

1924: Raleigh diocese established.

1971: Charlotte diocese established.

North Dakota

1742: Pierre and Francois Verendrye, accom-

panied by Jesuit Father Coquart, explored territory.
1818: Canadian priests ministered to Catholics in area.
1840: Jesuit Father De Smet made first of several trips among Mandan and Gros Ventre Indians.
1848: Father George Belcourt, first American resident priest in territory, reestablished Pembina Mission.
1874: Grey Nuns arrived at Fort Totten to conduct a school.
1889: Jamestown diocese established; transferred to Fargo in 1897.
1893: Benedictines founded St. Gall Monastery at Devil's Lake. (It was moved to Richardton in 1899 and became an abbey in 1903.)
1909: Bismarck diocese established.
1959: Archbishop Aloysius J. Muench, bishop of Fargo, made cardinal by Pope John XXIII.

Ohio

1749: Jesuits in expedition of Céleron de Blainville preached to Indians.
First religious services were held within present limits of Ohio. Jesuit Joseph de Bonnecamps celebrated Mass at mouth of Little Miami River and in other places.
1751: First Catholic settlement founded among Huron Indians near Sandusky by Jesuit Father de la Richardie.
1790: Benedictine Pierre Didier ministered to French immigrants.
1812: Bishop Flaget of Bardstown visited and baptized Catholics of Lancaster and Somerset Counties.
1818: Dominican Father Edward Fenwick (later first bishop of Cincinnati) built St. Joseph's Church and established first Dominican convent in Ohio.
1821: Cincinnati diocese established.
1831: Xavier University founded.
1843: Members of Congregation of Most Precious Blood arrived in Cincinnati from Switzerland.
1845: Cornerstone laid for St. Peter's Cathedral, Cincinnati.
1847: Cleveland diocese established.
1850: Cincinnati made archdiocese.
Marianists opened St. Mary's Institute, now University of Dayton.
1865: Sisters of Charity opened hospital in Cleveland, first institution of its kind in city.
1868: Columbus diocese established.
1871: Ursuline College for women opened at Cleveland.
1910: Toledo diocese established.
1935: Archbishop John T. McNicholas, O.P., founded the Institutum Divi Thomae in Cincinnati for fundamental research in natural sciences.
1943: Youngstown diocese established.
1944: Steubenville diocese established.
1969: Byzantine Rite Eparchy of Parma (for Ruthenians) established.
1982: Apostolic Exarchate for Romanian Byzantine-Rite Catholics in the United States established. Canton designated see city. Raised to an eparchy (St. George Martyr) 1987.
1983: Byzantine Rite Eparchy of Saint Josaphat in Parma (for Ukrainians) established.

Oklahoma

1540: De Soto expedition, accompanied by chaplains, explored territory.
1541: Coronado expedition, accompanied by Franciscan Juan de Padilla, explored state.
1630: Spanish Franciscan Juan de Salas labored among Indians.
1700: Scattered Catholic families were visited by priests from Kansas and Arkansas.
1874: First Catholic church built by Father Smyth at Atoka.
1876: Prefecture Apostolic of Indian Territory established with Benedictine Isidore Robot as its head.
1886: First Catholic day school for Choctaw and white children opened by Sisters of Mercy at Krebs.
1891: Vicariate Apostolic of Oklahoma and Indian Territory established.
1905: Oklahoma diocese established; title changed to Oklahoma City and Tulsa, 1930.
1917: Benedictine Heights College for women founded.
Carmelite Sisters of St. Theresa of the Infant Jesus founded at Oklahoma City.
1972: Oklahoma City made archdiocese. Tulsa diocese established.

Oregon

1603: Vizcaino explored northern Oregon coast.
1774: Franciscan missionaries accompanied Juan Perez on his expedition to coast, and Heceta a year later.
1811: Catholic Canadian trappers and traders with John J. Astor expedition founded first American settlement — Astoria.
1834: Indian missions in Northwest entrusted to Jesuits by Holy See.
1838: Abbe Blanchet appointed vicar general to Bishop of Quebec with jurisdiction over area which included Oregon Territory.
1839: First Mass celebrated at present site of St. Paul.
1843: Oregon vicariate apostolic established.
St. Joseph's College for boys opened.
1844: Jesuit Pierre de Smet established Mission of St. Francis Xavier near St. Paul.
Sisters of Notre Dame de Namur, first to enter Oregon, opened an academy for girls.
1846: Vicariate made an ecclesiastical province with Bishop Blanchet as first Archbishop of Oregon City (now Portland).
Walla Walla diocese established; suppressed in 1853.
1847: First priest was ordained in Oregon.
1848: First Provincial Council of Oregon.
1857: Death of Dr. John McLoughlin, "Father of Oregon."
1865: Rev. H. H. Spalding, a Protestant missionary, published the Whitman Myth to hinder work of Catholic missionaries.
1874: Catholic Indian Mission Bureau established.

U.S. Background Dates

1875: St. Vincent's Hospital, first in state, opened at Portland.
1903: Baker diocese established.
1922: Anti-private school bill sponsored by Scottish Rite Masons was passed by popular vote, 115,506 to 103,685.
1925: U.S. Supreme Court declared Oregon anti-private school bill unconstitutional.
1953: First Trappist monastery on West Coast established in Willamette Valley north of Lafayette.

Pennsylvania

1673: Priests from Maryland ministered to Catholics in the Colony.
1682: Religious toleration was extended to members of all faiths.
1729: Jesuit Joseph Greaton became first resident missionary of Philadelphia.
1734: St. Joseph's Church, first Catholic church in Philadelphia, was opened by Father Greaton.
1741: Jesuit Fathers Schneider and Wappeler ministered to German immigrants.
Conewego Chapel, a combination chapel and dwelling, was built by Father William Wappeler, S.J., a priest sent to minister to the German Catholic immigrants who settled in the area in the 1730's.
1782: St. Mary's Parochial School opened at Philadelphia.
1788: Holy Trinity Church, Philadelphia, was incorporated; first exclusively national church organized in U.S.
1797: Augustinian Matthew Carr founded St. Augustine parish, Philadelphia.
1799: Prince Demetrius Gallitzin (Father Augustine Smith) built church in western Pennsylvania, at Loretto.
1808: Philadelphia diocese established.
1814: St. Joseph's Orphanage was opened at Philadelphia; first Catholic institution for children in U.S.
1842: University of Villanova founded by Augustinians.
1843: Pittsburgh diocese established.
1844: Thirteen persons killed, two churches and a school burned in Know-Nothing riots at Philadelphia.
1846: First Benedictine Abbey in New World founded near Latrobe by Father Boniface Wimmer.
1852: Redemptorist John Nepomucene Neumann became fourth bishop of Philadelphia. He was beatified in 1963 and canonized in 1977.
1853: Erie diocese established.
1868: Scranton and Harrisburg dioceses established.
1871: Chestnut Hill College, first for women in state, founded.
1875: Philadelphia made archdiocese.
1901: Altoona-Johnstown diocese established.
1913: Byzantine Rite Apostolic Exarchate of Philadelphia established; became metropolitan see, 1958.
1921: Archbishop Dennis Dougherty made cardinal by Pope Benedict XV.
1924: Byzantine Rite Apostolic Exarchate of Pittsburgh established; made an eparchy in 1963; raised to metropolitan status and transferred to Munhall, 1969; transferred back to Pittsburgh in 1977.
1951: Greensburg diocese established.
1958: Archbishop John O'Hara, C.S.C., of Philadelphia made cardinal by Pope John.
1961: Allentown diocese established.
1967: Archbishop John J. Krol of Philadelphia made cardinal by Pope Paul VI.
1969: Bishop John J. Wright of Pittsburgh made cardinal by Pope Paul VI and transferred to Curia post.
1976: The 41st International Eucharistic Congress, the second held in the U.S., convened in Philadelphia, August 1-8.
1985: Major Archbishop Myroslav Lubachivsky of the Ukrainians, former metropolitan of Byzantine-rite Philadelphia archeparchy (1979-80), made cardinal by Pope John Paul II.

Rhode Island

1663: Colonial Charter granted freedom of conscience.
1719: Laws denied Catholics the right to hold public office.
1829: St. Mary's Church, Pawtucket, was first Catholic church in state.
1837: Parochial schools inaugurated in state.
First Catholic church in Providence was built.
1851: Sisters of Mercy began work in Rhode Island.
1872: Providence diocese established.
1900: Trappists took up residence in state.
1917: Providence College founded.

South Carolina

1569: Jesuit Juan Rogel was the first resident priest in the territory.
1573: First Franciscans arrived in southeastern section.
1606: Bishop Altamirano conducted visitation of area.
1655: Franciscans had two missions among Indians; later destroyed by English.
1697: Religious liberty granted to all except "papists."
1790: Catholics given right to vote.
1820: Charleston diocese established.
1822: Bishop England founded *U.S. Catholic Miscellany*, first Catholic paper of a strictly religious nature in U.S.
1830: Sisters of Our Lady of Mercy, first in state, took up residence at Charleston.
1847: Cornerstone of Cathedral of St. John the Baptist, Charleston, was laid.
1861: Cathedral and many institutions destroyed in Charleston fire.

South Dakota

1842: Father Augustine Ravoux began ministrations to French and Indians at Fort Pierre, Vermilion and Prairie du Chien; printed devotional book in Sioux language the following year.
1867: Parish organized among the French at Jefferson.

1878: Benedictines opened school for Sioux children at Fort Yates.
1889: Sioux Falls diocese established.
1902: Lead diocese established; transferred to Rapid City, 1930.
1950: Mount Marty College for women founded.
1952: Blue Cloud Abbey, first Benedictine foundation in state, was dedicated.

Tennessee

1541: Cross planted on shore of Mississippi by De Soto; accompanying the expedition were Fathers John de Gallegos and Louis De Soto.
1682: Franciscan Fathers Membre and Douay accompanied La Salle to present site of Memphis; may have offered the first Masses in the territory.
1800: Catholics were served by priests from Bardstown, Ky.
1822: Non-Catholics assisted in building church in Nashville.
1837: Nashville diocese established.
1843: Sisters of Charity opened a school for girls in Nashville.
1921: Sisters of St. Dominic opened Siena College for women at Memphis; closed in 1971.
1940: Christian Brothers College founded at Memphis.
1970: Memphis diocese established.
1988: Knoxville diocese established.

Texas

1541: Missionaries with Coronado expedition probably entered territory.
1553: Dominicans Diego de la Cruz, Hernando Mendez, Juan Ferrer, Brother Juan de Mina killed by Indians.
1675: Bosque-Larios missionary expedition entered region; Father Juan Larios offered first recorded high Mass.
1682: Mission Corpus Christi de Isleta (Ysleta) founded by Franciscans near El Paso, first mission in present-day Texas.
1690: Mission San Francisco de los Tejas founded in east Texas.
1703: Mission San Francisco de Solano founded on Rio Grande; rebuilt in 1718 as San Antonio de Valero or the Alamo.
1717: Franciscan Antonio Margil founded six missions in northeast.
1720: San Jose y San Miguel de Aguayo Mission founded by Fray Antonio Margil de Jesus.
1721: Franciscan Brother Jose Pita killed by Indians at Carnezeria.
1728: Site of San Antonio settled.
1738: Construction of San Fernando Cathedral at San Antonio.
1744: Mission church of the Alamo built.
1750: Franciscan Francisco Xavier was killed by Indians; so were Jose Ganzabal in 1752, and Alonzo Ferrares and Jose San Esteban in 1758.
1793: Mexico secularized missions.
1825: Governments of Cohuila and Texas secularized all Indian missions.
1838-39: Irish priests ministered to settlements of Refugio and San Patricio.
1841: Vicariate of Texas established.
1847: Ursuline Sisters established their first academy in territory at Galveston.
Galveston diocese established.
1852: Oblate Fathers and Franciscans arrived in Galveston to care for new influx of German Catholics.
St. Mary's College founded at San Antonio.
1854: Know-Nothing Party began to stir up hatred against Catholics.
1858: Texas Legislature passed law entitling all schools granting free scholarships and meeting state requirements to share in school fund.
1874: San Antonio diocese established.
Vicariate of Brownsville established.
1881: St. Edward's College founded: became first chartered college in state in 1889.
Sisters of Charity founded Incarnate Word College at San Antonio.
1890: Dallas diocese established; changed to Dallas-Ft. Worth, 1953; made two separate dioceses, 1969.
1912: Corpus Christi diocese established.
1914: El Paso diocese established.
1926: San Antonio made archdiocese. Amarillo diocese established.
1947: Austin diocese established.
1959: Galveston diocese redesignated Galveston-Houston.
1961: San Angelo diocese established.
1965: Brownsville diocese established.
1966: Beaumont diocese established.
1982: Victoria diocese established.
1983: Lubbock diocese established.
1986: Tyler diocese established.

Utah

1776: Franciscans Silvestre de Escalante and Atanasio Dominguez reached Utah (Salt) Lake; first white men known to enter the territory.
1858: Jesuit Father De Smet accompanied General Harney as chaplain on expedition sent to settle troubles between Mormons and U.S. Government.
1866: On June 29 Father Edward Kelly offered first Mass in Salt Lake City in Mormon Assembly Hall.
1886: Utah vicariate apostolic established.
1891: Salt Lake City diocese established.
1926: College of St. Mary-of-the-Wasatch for women was founded.

Vermont

1609: Champlain expedition passed through territory.
1666: Captain La Motte built fort and shrine of St. Anne on Isle La Motte; Sulpician Father Dollier de Casson celebrated first Mass.
1668: Bishop Laval of Quebec (beatified in 1980), administered confirmation in region; this was the first area in northeastern U.S. to receive an episcopal visit.
1710: Jesuits ministered to Indians near Lake Champlain.
1793: Discriminatory measures against Catholics were repealed.

1830: Father Jeremiah O'Callaghan became first resident priest in state.
1853: Burlington diocese established.
1854: Sisters of Charity of Providence arrived to conduct St. Joseph's Orphanage at Burlington.
1904: St. Michael's College founded.
1951: First Carthusian foundation in America established at Whitingham.

Virginia

1526: Dominican Antonio de Montesinos offered first Mass on Virginia soil.
1561: Dominicans visited the coast.
1571: Father John Baptist de Segura and seven Jesuit companions killed by Indians.
1642: Priests outlawed and Catholics denied right to vote.
1689: Capuchin Christopher Plunket was captured and exiled to a coastal island where he died in 1697.
1776: Religious freedom granted.
1791: Father Jean Dubois arrived at Richmond with letters from Lafayette. The House of Delegates was placed at his disposal for celebration of Mass.
1796: A church was built at Alexandria.
1820: Richmond diocese established.
1822: Trusteeism created serious problems in diocese; Bishop Kelly resigned the see.
1848: Sisters of Charity opened an orphan asylum at Norfolk.
1866: School Sisters of Notre Dame and Sisters of Charity opened academies for girls at Richmond.
1974: Arlington diocese established.

Washington

1774: Spaniards explored the region.
1838: Fathers Blanchet and Demers, "Apostles of the Northwest," were sent to territory by archbishop of Quebec.
1840: Cross erected on Whidby Island, Puget Sound.
1843: Vicariate Apostolic of Oregon, including Washington, was established.
1844: Mission of St. Paul founded at Colville.
Six Sisters of Notre Dame de Namur began work in area.
1850: Nesqually diocese established; transferred to Seattle, 1907.
1856: Providence Academy, the first permanent Catholic school in the Northwest, was built at Fort Vancouver by Mother Joseph Pariseau of the Sisters of Charity of Providence.
1887: Gonzaga University founded.
1913: Spokane diocese established.
1951: Seattle made archdiocese. Yakima diocese established.

West Virginia

1749: Father Joseph de Bonnecamps, accompanying the Bienville expedition, may have offered first Mass in the territory.
1821: First Catholic church in Wheeling.
1838: Sisters of Charity founded school at Martinsburg.
1848: Visitation Nuns established academy for girls in Wheeling.
1850: Wheeling diocese established; name changed to Wheeling-Charleston, 1974.
Wheeling Hospital incorporated, the oldest Catholic charitable institution in territory.
1955: Wheeling College established.

Wisconsin

1661: Jesuit Rene Menard, first known missionary in the territory, was killed or lost in the Black River district.
1665: Jesuit Claude Allouez founded Mission of the Holy Ghost at La Pointe Chegoimegon, now Bayfield; was the first permanent mission in region.
1673: Father Marquette and Louis Joliet traveled from Green Bay down the Wisconsin and Mississippi rivers.
1762: Suppression of Jesuits in French Colonies closed many missions for 30 years.
1843: Milwaukee diocese established.
1853: St. John's Cathedral, Milwaukee, was built.
1864: State charter granted for establishment of Marquette University. First students admitted, 1881.
1868: Green Bay and La Crosse dioceses established.
1875: Milwaukee made archdiocese.
1905: Superior diocese established.
1946: Madison diocese established.

Wyoming

1840: Jesuit Pierre de Smet offered first Mass near Green River.
1851: Father De Smet held peace conference with Indians near Fort Laramie.
1867: Father William Kelly, first resident priest, arrived in Cheyenne and built first church a year later.
1873: Father Eugene Cusson became first resident pastor in Laramie.
1875: Sisters of Charity of Leavenworth opened school and orphanage at Laramie.
1884: Jesuits took over pastoral care of Shoshone and Arapaho Indians.
1887: Cheyenne diocese established.
1949: Weston Memorial Hospital opened near Newcastle.

Puerto Rico

1493: Island discovered by Columbus on his second voyage; he named it San Juan de Borinquen (the Indian name for Puerto Rico).
1509: Juan Ponce de Leon, searching for gold, colonized the island and became its first governor; present population descended mainly from early Spanish settlers.
1511: Diocese of Puerto Rico established as suffragan of Seville, Spain; Bishop Alonso, Manso, sailing from Spain in 1512, became first bishop to take up residence in New World.
1645: Synod held in Puerto Rico to regulate frequency of Masses according to distances people had to walk.
1898: Puerto Rico ceded to U.S. (became self-gov-

erning Commonwealth in 1952); inhabitants granted U.S. citizenship in 1917.
1924: Diocese of Puerto Rico renamed San Juan de Puerto Rico and made immediately subject to the Holy See; Ponce diocese established.
1948: Catholic University of Puerto Rico founded at Ponce through efforts of Bishop James E. McManus, C.SS.R., 1947-63.
1960: San Juan made metropolitan see. Arecibo diocese established.
1964: Caguas diocese established.
1973: Archbishop Luis Aponte Martinez of San Juan made first native Puerto Rican cardinal by Pope Paul VI.
1976: Mayaguez diocese established.
Virgin of Providence officially approved as Patroness of Puerto Rico by Pope Paul VI.

CATHOLICS IN PRESIDENTS' CABINETS

Roger B. Taney, Attorney General 1831-33, Secretary of Treasury 1833-34; app. by Andrew Jackson.

James Campbell, Postmaster General 1853-57; app. by Franklin Pierce.

John B. Floyd, Secretary of War 1857-61; app. by James Buchanan.

Joseph McKenna, Attorney General 1897-98; app. by William McKinley.

Robert J. Wynne, Postmaster General 1904-05; app. by Theodore Roosevelt.

Charles Bonaparte, Secretary of Navy 1905-06, Attorney General 1906-09; app. by Theodore Roosevelt.

James A. Farley, Postmaster General 1933-40; app. by Franklin D. Roosevelt.

Frank Murphy, Attorney General 1939-40; app. by Franklin D. Roosevelt.

Frank C. Walker, Postmaster General 1940-45; app. by Franklin D. Roosevelt.

Robert E. Hannegan, Postmaster General 1945-47; app. by Harry S. Truman.

J. Howard McGrath, Attorney General 1949-52; app. by Harry S. Truman.

Maurice J. Tobin, Secretary of Labor; 1949-53; app. by Harry S. Truman.

James P. McGranery, Attorney General 1952-53; app. by Harry S. Truman.

Martin P. Durkin, Secretary of Labor 1953; app. by Dwight D. Eisenhower.

James P. Mitchell, Secretary of Labor 1953-61; app. by Dwight D. Eisenhower.

Robert F. Kennedy, Attorney General 1961-65; app. by John F. Kennedy, reapp. by Lyndon B. Johnson.

Anthony Celebrezze, Secretary of Health, Education and Welfare 1962-65; app. by John F. Kennedy, reapp. by Lyndon B. Johnson.

John S. Gronouski, Postmaster General 1963-65; app. by John F. Kennedy, reapp. by Lyndon B. Johnson.

John T. Connor, Secretary of Commerce 1965-67; app. by Lyndon B. Johnson.

Lawrence O'Brien, Postmaster General 1965-68; app. by Lyndon B. Johnson.

Walter J. Hickel, Secretary of Interior 1969-71; app. by Richard M. Nixon.

John A. Volpe, Secretary of Transportation 1969-72; app. by Richard M. Nixon.

Maurice H. Stans, Secretary of Commerce, 1969-72; app. by Richard M. Nixon.

Peter J. Brennan, Secretary of Labor, 1973-75; app. by Richard M. Nixon, reapp. by Gerald R. Ford.

William E. Simon, Secretary of Treasury, 1974-76; app. by Richard M. Nixon, reapp. by Gerald R. Ford.

Joseph A. Califano, Jr., Secretary of Health, Education and Welfare, 1977-79; app. by Jimmy Carter.

Benjamin Civiletti, Attorney General, 1979-81; app. by Jimmy Carter.

Moon Landrieu, Secretary of Housing and Urban Development, 1979-81; app. by Jimmy Carter.

Edmund S. Muskie, Secretary of State, 1980-81; app. by Jimmy Carter.

Alexander M. Haig, Secretary of State, 1981-82; app. by Ronald Reagan.

Raymond J. Donovan, Secretary of Labor, 1981-84; app. by Ronald Reagan.

Margaret M. Heckler, Secretary of Health and Human Services, 1983-85; app. by Ronald Reagan.

William J. Bennett, Secretary of Education, 1985-88; app. by Ronald Reagan.

Ann Dore McLaughlin, Secretary of Labor, 1988; app. by Ronald Reagan.

Lauro F. Cavazos, Secretary of Education, 1988; app. by Ronald Reagan.

Men who became Catholics after leaving Cabinet posts: Thomas Ewing, Secretary of Treasury under William A. Harrison, and Secretary of Interior under Zachary Taylor; Luke E. Wright, Secretary of War under Theodore Roosevelt; Albert B. Fall, Secretary of Interior under Warren G. Harding.

CATHOLICS IN STATUARY HALL

Statues of 13 Catholics deemed worthy of national commemoration by the donating states are among those enshrined in National Statuary Hall and other places in the U.S. Capitol. The Hall, formerly the chamber of the House of Representatives, was erected by Act of Congress July 2, 1864.

Donating states, names and years of placement are listed. An asterisk indicates placement of a statue in the Hall itself.

Arizona: Rev. Eusebio Kino, S. J., missionary, 1965.
California: Rev. Junipero Serra, O. F. M.* missionary, 1931. (Beatified 1988.)
Hawaii: Father Damien, missionary, 1969.
Illinois: Gen. James Shields, statesman, 1893.
Louisiana: Edward D. White, Justice of the U.S. Supreme Court (1894-1921), 1955.
Maryland: Charles Carroll,* statesman, 1901.
Nevada: Patrick A. McCarran,* statesman, 1960.
New Mexico: Dennis Chavez, statesman, 1966. (Archbishop Jean B. Lamy, pioneer prelate of Santa Fe, was nominated for Hall honor in 1951.)
North Dakota: John Burke,* U.S. treasurer, 1963.
Oregon: Dr. John McLoughlin, pioneer, 1953.
Washington: Mother Mary Joseph Pariseau, pioneer missionary and humanitarian.
West Virginia: John E. Kenna, statesman, 1901.
Wisconsin: Rev. Jacques Marquette, S.J., missionary, explorer, 1895.

CATHOLIC SUPREME COURT JUSTICES

Roger B. Taney, Chief Justice 1836-64; app. by Andrew Jackson.
Edward D. White, Associate Justice 1894-1910, app. by Grover Cleveland; Chief Justice 1910-21, app. by William H. Taft.
Joseph McKenna, Associate Justice 1898-1925; app. by William McKinley.
Pierce Butler, Associate Justice 1923-39; app. by Warren G. Harding.
Frank Murphy, Associate Justice 1940-49; app. by Franklin D. Roosevelt.
William Brennan, Associate Justice 1956-; app. by Dwight D. Eisenhower.
Antonin Scalia, Associate Justice 1986-; app. by Ronald Reagan.
Anthony M. Kennedy, Associate Justice 1988- ; app. by Ronald Reagan.
Sherman Minton, Associate Justice from 1949 to 1956, became a Catholic several years before his death in 1965.

CHURCH-STATE DECISIONS OF THE SUPREME COURT

(Among sources of this listing of U.S. Supreme Court decisions was *The Supreme Court on Church and State,* Joseph Tussman, editor; Oxford University Press, New York, 1962.)
(See News Events for 1987-88 decisions.)

Terrett v. Taylor, 9 Cranch 43 (1815): The Court declared unconstitutional an act of the Virginia Legislature which denied property rights to Protestant Episcopal churches in the state. Religious corporations, like other corporations, have rights to their property.

Vidal v. Girard's Executors, 2 Howard 205 (1844): The Court upheld the will of Stephen Girard, which barred ministers of any religion from serving as faculty members or visitors in a school he established for orphans.

Watson v. Jones, 13 Wallace 679 (1872): The Court declared that a member of a religious organization may not appeal to secular courts against a decision made by a church tribunal within the area of its competence.

Reynolds v. United States, 98 US 145 (1879): The Court declared, in reference to the Mormon practice of polygamy, that one may not knowingly violate by external practices the law of the land on religious grounds, since such conduct would make the professed doctrines of belief superior to federal or state law. One must keep the external practice of religion within the framework of laws enacted for the common welfare. This was the first decision rendered on the Free Exercise Clause of the First Amendment.

Davis v. Beason, 133 US 333 (1890): The Court upheld the denial of the right of Mormons to vote in Idaho if they refused to sign a registration oath stating that they were not bigamists or polygamists and would not encourage or preach bigamy or polygamy.

Church of Latter-Day Saints v. United States, 136 US 1 (1890): The Court upheld an Act of Congress which annulled the charter of the Corporation of the Church of Jesus Christ of Latter-Day Saints, and declared "forfeited to the government all its real estate except a small portion used exclusively for public worship" (Tussman, *op. cit.*, p. 33). The Court held that the Corporation continually used its power to violate US laws prohibiting polygamy.

Church of the Holy Trinity v. United States, 143 US 457 (1892): The Court declared it is not "a misdemeanor for a church of this country to contract for the services of a Christian minister residing in another nation" (from the text of the decision).

Bradfield v. Roberts, 175 US 291 (1899): The Court denied that an appropriation of government funds for an institution (Providence Hospital, Washington, D.C.) run by Roman Catholic sisters violated the No Establishment Clause of the First Amendment.

Pierce v. Society of Sisters, 268 US 510 (1925): The Court denied that a state can require children to attend public schools only. The Court held that the liberty of the Constitution forbids standardization by such compulsion, and that the parochial schools involved had claims to protection under the Fourteenth Amendment.

Cochran v. Board of Education, 281 US 370 (1930): The Court upheld a Louisiana statute providing textbooks at public expense for children attending public or parochial schools. The Court held that the children and state were beneficiaries of the appropriations, with incidental secondary benefit going to the schools.

United States v. MacIntosh, 283 US 605 (1931): The Court denied that anyone can place allegiance to the will of God above his allegiance to the government, since such a person could make his own interpretation of God's will the decisive test as to whether he would or would not obey the nation's law. The Court stated that the nation, which has a duty to survive, can require citizens to bear arms in its defense.

Hamilton v. Regents of University of California, 293 US 245 (1934): The Court rejected a "claim to exemption from R.O.T.C. based on conscientious objection to war" (Tussman *op. cit.*, p. 64). If such an exemption were allowed, the liberties of the objector might be extended to the point of refusal to pay taxes in furtherance of a war or any other end condemned by his conscience. This would be an undue exaltation of the right of private judgment.

Cantwell v. Connecticut, 310 US 296 (1940): The Court declared that the right to religious freedom is violated by a statute requiring a person to secure a permit from a government official before soliciting money for alleged religious purposes from someone not of his or her sect. Such a practice would constitute censorship of religion.

Minersville School District v. Gobitis, 310 US 586 (1940): The Court upheld the right of a state to require the salute to the national flag from school children, even from those who refused to do so for sincere religious reasons.

Jones v. City of Opelika, 316 US 584 (1942): The court upheld licensing ordinances in three municipalities against "the claim by Jehovah's Witnesses that they interfere with the free exercise of religion" (Tussman, op. cit., p. 91).

Murdock v. Commonwealth of Pennsylvania, 319 US 105 (1943): In a reversal of the decision handed down in Jones v. City of Opelika, the Court declared the licensing unconstitutional since it violated a freedom guaranteed under the First Amendment. The selling of religious literature by traveling preachers does not make evangelism the equivalent of a commercial enterprise taxable by the State.

Jones v. City of Opelika, 316 US 584 105 (1943): The Court declared that the Constitution denies a city the right to control the expression of men's minds and denies also the right of men to win others to their views through a program of taxes levied against such activity.

Douglas v. City of Jeannette, 319 US 157 (1943): The Court again upheld the proselytizing rights of Jehovah's Witnesses, ruling unconstitutional the action of any public authority in regulating or taxing such activity.

West Virginia State Board of Education v. Barnette, 319 US 624 (1943): In a reversal of the decision handed down in Minersville School District v. Gobitis, the Court declared unconstitutional a state statute requiring of all children a salute to the national flag and a pledge of allegiance which a child may consider contrary to sincere religious beliefs.

Prince v. Commonwealth of Massachusetts, 321 US 158 (1944): The Court upheld a "child-labor regulation against the claim that it prevents a child from performing her religious duty" (Tussman, op. cit., p. 170). The Court asserted a general principle that the state has a wide range of power for limiting parental freedom and authority in things affecting the child's welfare.

United States v. Ballard, 322 US 78 (1944): The Court upheld the general principle that "the truth of religious claims is not for secular authority to determine" (Tussman, op. cit., p. 181).

In Re Summers, 325 US 561 (1945): The Court upheld "the denial, to an otherwise qualified applicant, of admission to the bar on the basis of the applicant's religiously motivated 'conscientious scruples against participation in war' " (Tussman, op. cit., p. 192). The petitioner was barred because he could not in good faith take the prescribed oath to support the Constitution of Illinois which required service in the state militia in times of necessity.

Girouard v. United States, 328 US 61 (1946): In a ruling related to that handed down in United States v. MacIntosh, the Court affirmed the opinion that the refusal of an alien to bear arms does not deny him citizenship.

Everson v. Board of Education, 330 US 1 (1947): The Court upheld the constitutionality of a New Jersey statute authorizing free school bus transportation for parochial as well as public school students. The Court expressed the opinion that the benefits of public welfare legislation, included under such bus transportation, do not run contrary to the concept of separation of Church and State.

McCollum v. Board of Education, 333 US 203 (1948): The Court declared unconstitutional a program for releasing children, with parental consent, from public school classes so they could receive religious instruction on public school premises from representatives of their own faiths.

Zorach v. Clauson, 343 US 306 (1952): The Court upheld the constitutionality of a New York statute permitting, on a voluntary basis, the release during school time of students from public school classes for religious instruction given off public school premises.

Kedroff v. St. Nicholas Cathedral, 344 US 94 (1952): The Court ruled against an action of New York in taking "control of St. Nicholas Cathedral away from the Moscow hierarchy" (Tussman, op. cit., p. 292), on the ground that the controversy involved a matter of church government.

Fowler v. Rhode Island, 345 US 67 (1953): The Court upheld the right of a Jehovah's Witness to preach in a public park against a city ordinance which forbade such preaching. The Court held that the ordinance, as construed and applied, discriminated against the Witness and therefore amounted to preferment by the state of other religious groups.

Torcaso v. Watkins, 367 US 488 (1961): The Court declared unconstitutional a Maryland requirement that one must make a declaration of belief in the existence of God as part of the oath of office for notaries public.

McGowan v. Maryland, 81 Sp Ct 1101; **Two Guys from Harrison v. McGinley,** 81 Sp Ct 1135; **Gallagher v. Crown Kosher Super Market,** 81 Sp Ct 1128; **Braunfield v. Brown,** 81 Sp Ct 1144 (1961): The Court ruled that Sunday closing laws do not violate the No Establishment of Religion Clause of the First Amendment, even though the laws were religious in their inception and still have some religious overtones. The Court held that, "as presently written and administered, most of them, at least, are of a secular rather than of a religious character, and that presently they bear no relationship to establishment of religion as those words are used in the Constitution of the United States."

Engel v. Vitale, 370 US 42 (1962): The Court declared that the voluntary recitation in public schools of a prayer composed by the New York State Board of Regents is unconstitutional on the ground that it violates the No Establishment of Religion Clause of the First Amendment.

Abington Township School District v. Schempp and **Murray v. Curlett,** 83 Sp Ct 1560 (1963): The Court ruled that Bible reading and recitation of the Lord's Prayer in public schools, with voluntary participation by students, are unconstitutional on the ground that they violate the No Establishment of Religion Clause of the First Amendment.

Sherbert v. Verner, 83 A Sp Ct 1790 (1963): The

Court ruled that individuals of any religious faith may not, because of their faith or lack of it, be deprived of the benefits of public welfare legislation.

Chamberlin v. Dade County, 83 Sp Ct 1864 (1964): The Court reversed a decision of the Florida Supreme Court concerning the constitutionality of prayer and devotional Bible reading in public schools during the school day, as sanctioned by a state statute which specifically related the practices to a sound public purpose.

Board of Education v. Allen, No. 660 (1968): The Court declared constitutional the New York school book loan law which requires local school boards to purchase books with state funds and lend them to parochial and private school students.

Flast v. Cohen, No. 416 (1968): The Court held that individual taxpayers can bring suits to challenge federal expenditures on grounds that they violate the principle of separation of Church and State even though generally taxpayers cannot challenge federal expenditures in court.

Walz v. Tax Commission of New York (1970): The Court upheld the constitutionality of a New York statute exempting church-owned property from taxation.

Earle v. DiCenso, Robinson v. DiCenso, Lemon v. Kurtzman, Tilton v. Richardson (1971): In Earle v. DiCenso and Robinson v. DiCenso, the Court ruled unconstitutional a 1969 Rhode Island statute which provided salary supplements to teachers of secular subjects in parochial schools; in Lemon v. Kurtzman, the Court ruled unconstitutional a 1968 Pennsylvania statute which authorized the state to purchase services for the teaching of secular subjects in nonpublic schools. The principal argument against constitutionality in these cases was that the statutes and programs at issue entailed excessive entanglement of government with religion. In Tilton v. Richardson, the Court held that this argument did not apply to a prohibitive degree with respect to federal grants, under the Higher Education Facilities Act of 1963, for the construction of facilities for nonreligious purposes by four church-related institutions of higher learning, three of which were Catholic, in Connecticut.

Amish Decision (1972): In a case appealed on behalf of Yoder, Miller and Yutzy, the Court ruled that Amish parents were exempt from a Wisconsin statute requiring them to send their children to school until the age of 16. The Court said in its decision that secondary schooling exposed Amish children to attitudes, goals and values contrary to their beliefs, and substantially hindered "the religious development of the Amish child and his integration into the way of life of the Amish faith-community at the crucial adolescent state of development."

Committee for Public Education and Religious Liberty, et al., v. Nyquist, et al., No. 372-694 (1973): The Court ruled that provisions of a 1972 New York statute were unconstitutional on the grounds that they were violative of the No Establishment Clause of the First Amendment and had the "impermissible effect" of advancing the sectarian activities of church-affiliated schools. The programs ruled unconstitutional concerned: (1) maintenance and repair grants, for facilities and equipment, to ensure the health, welfare and safety of students in nonpublic, non-profit elementary and secondary schools serving a high concentration of students from low income families; (2) tuition reimbursement ($50 per grade school child, $100 per high school student) for parents (with income less than $5,000) of children attending nonpublic elementary or secondary schools; tax deduction from adjusted gross income for parents failing to qualify under the above reimbursement plan, for each child attending a nonpublic school.

Sloan, Treasurer of Pennsylvania, et al., v. Lemon, et al., No. 72-459 (1973): The Court ruled unconstitutional a Pennsylvania Parent Reimbursement Act for Nonpublic Education which provided funds to reimburse parents (to a maximum of $150) for a portion of tuition expenses incurred in sending their children to nonpublic schools. The Court held that there was no significant difference between this and the New York tuition reimbursement program (above), and declared that the Equal Protection Clause of the Fourteenth Amendment cannot be relied upon to sustain a program held to be violative of the No Establishment Clause.

Levitt, et al., v. Committee for Public Education and Religious Liberty, et al., No. 72-269 (1973): The Court ruled unconstitutional the Mandated Services Act of 1970 under which New York provided $28 million ($27 per pupil from first to seventh grade, $45 per pupil from seventh to 12th grade) to reimburse nonpublic schools for testing, recording and reporting services required by the state. The Court declared that the act provided "impermissible aid" to religion in contravention of the No Establishment Clause.

In related decisions handed down June 25, 1973, the Court: (1) affirmed a lower court decision against the constitutionality of an Ohio tax credit law benefiting parents with children in nonpublic schools; (2) reinstated an injunction against a parent reimbursement program in New Jersey; (3) affirmed South Carolina's right to grant construction loans to church-affiliated colleges, and dismissed an appeal contesting its right to provide loans to students attending church-affiliated colleges (**Hunt v. McNair, Durham v. McLeod**).

Wheeler v. Barrera (1974): The Court ruled that nonpublic school students in Missouri must share in federal funds for educationally deprived students on a comparable basis with public school students under Title I of the Elementary and Secondary Education Act of 1965.

Norwood v. Harrison (93 S. Ct. 2804): The Court ruled that public assistance which avoids the prohibitions of the "effect" and "entanglement" tests (and which therefore does not substantially promote the religious mission of sectarian schools) may be confined to the secular functions of such schools.

Wiest v. Mt. Lebanon School District (1974):

The Court upheld a lower court ruling that invocation and benediction prayers at public high school commencement ceremonies do not violate the principle of separation of Church and state.

Meek v. Pittenger (1975): The Court ruled unconstitutional portions of a Pennsylvania law providing auxiliary services for students of nonpublic schools; at the same time, it ruled in favor of provisions of the law permitting textbook loans to students of such schools. In denying the constitutionality of auxiliary services, the Court held that they had the "primary effect of establishing religion" and involved "excessive entanglement" of Church and state officials with respect to supervision; objection was also made against providing such services only on the premises of non-public schools and only at the request of such schools.

Roemer v. Board of Public Works of Maryland, 96 S. Ct. 2337 (1976): The Court ruled that a Maryland statute which authorized state funds to any private institution meeting certain minimal criteria was constitutional. The Court said the statute met the test previously outlined in Lemon v. Kurtzman because the colleges were not pervasively sectarian and the aid was in fact intended only for secular purposes.

Serbian Eastern Orthodox Diocese v. Milivojevich, 96 S. Ct. 2372 (1976): The Court held unconstitutional the decision of the Illinois Supreme Court that the Serbian Orthodox Church had arbitrarily removed one of its bishops and that its reorganization of the diocese was beyond the power of the church. The Court declared that the First Amendment does not permit civil courts to make ecclesiastical decisions.

TWA, Inc., v. Hardison, 75-1126; **International Association of Machinists and Aero Space Workers v. Hardison,** 75-1385 (1977): The Court ruled that federal civil rights legislation does not require employers to make more than minimal efforts to accommodate employees who want a particular working day off as their religion's Sabbath Day, and that an employer cannot accommodate such an employee by violating seniority systems determined by a union collective bargaining agreement. The Court noted that its ruling was not a constitutional judgment but an interpretation of existing law.

Wolman v. Walter (1977): The Court ruled constitutional portions of an Ohio statute providing tax-paid textbook loans and some auxiliary services (standardized and diagnostic testing, therapeutic and remedial services, off school premises) for nonpublic school students. It decided that other portions of the law, providing state funds for non-public school field trips and instructional materials (audio-visual equipment, maps, tape recorders), were unconstitutional.

Clergymen (1978): The Court struck down the last state ban against the holding of public office by clergymen, nullifying the 182-year-old provision of the Tennessee constitution which held that involvement in politics might affect the clergy's "dedication to God and the care of souls."

Lay Teachers (1979): The Court ruled that lay teachers in church-related schools are not covered by the National Labor Relations Act. The decision was based, not on church-state grounds, but on the lack of any affirmative decision of the Congress to include such teachers in coverage of the law.

Church Property (1979): The Court ruled, in Jones v. Wolf, that civil courts are not always bound to yield to decisions of church courts in settling local church property disputes.

Parochiaid (1979): The Court decided, in Byrne v. Public Funds for Public Schools, against the constitutionality of a 1976 New Jersey law providing state income tax deductions for tuition paid by parents of students attending parochial and other private schools.

Religious Belief v. Union (1979): The Court supported the claim of a San Diego man that his right to religious freedom was violated when he was fired from his job because his Seventh Day Adventist beliefs prevented him from belonging to a union.

Student Bus Transportation (1979): The Court upheld a Pennsylvania law providing bus transportation at public expense for students to non-public schools up to 10 miles away from the boundaries of the public school districts in which they lived.

Reimbursement (1980): The Court upheld the constitutionality of a 1974 New York law providing direct cash payment to non-public schools for the costs of state-mandated testing and record-keeping.

Solicitation of Funds (1980): The Court struck down a Schaumburg, Ill., ordinance permitting the solicitation of funds only by groups spending a specific percentage of their funds for charitable purposes.

Remedial Teaching (1980): The Court refused to hear an appeal from a lower court ruling in support of a New York law permitting the use of federal funds to pay for remedial teaching in non-public schools.

Ten Commandments (1980): The Court struck down a 1978 Kentucky law requiring the posting of the Ten Commandments in public school classrooms in the state.

Christmas Carols (1980): The Court refused to hear an appeal from a lower court ruling permitting the singing of Christmas carols in public school holiday programs in Sioux Falls, S.D.

Highway Prayer (1981): The Court ruled that North Carolina could not publish a prayer for highway safety on official state maps.

Unemployment Benefits (1981): The Court decided, in Thomas v. Review Board, that a worker who, for religious reasons, quits his job rather than help to produce armaments cannot be denied state unemployment benefits.

Unemployment Taxes (1981): The Court ruled, in St. Martin Evangelical Lutheran Church v. South Dakota, that church-run schools do not have to pay state unemployment compensation taxes for their employees, because the relevant 1976 law did not "reveal any clear intent to repeal" their tax-exempt status.

Campus Worship (1981): The Court ruled, in Widmar v. Vincent, that the University of Missouri

Church-State Decisions — Church Tax Exemption

at Kansas City could not deny student religious groups the use of campus facilities for worship services. The Court also, in Brandon v. Board of Education of Guilderland Schools, declined without comment to hear an appeal for reversal of lower court decisions denying a group of New York high school students the right to meet for prayer on public school property before the beginning of the school day.

Americans United (1982): The Court ruled that Americans United for the Separation of Church and State did not have legal standing to challenge in court the transfer of government property to a Protestant college in Pennsylvania.

Social Security Taxes (1982): The Court ruled that Amish businessmen must pay Social Security taxes for their employees even if such payments violate their religious beliefs.

Unification Church (1982): The Court struck down a Minnesota law, aimed at the Unification Church, which required detailed financial reports from religious groups which raise more than half of their funds from non-members.

No Meeting on Public School Property (1983): By refusing to hear an appeal in Lubbock v. Lubbock Civil Liberties Union, the Court upheld a lower court ruling against a public policy of permitting student religious groups to meet on public school property before and after school hours.

Tuition Tax Deduction (1983): In Mueller v. Allen, the Court upheld a Minnesota law allowing parents of students in public and non-public (including parochial) schools to take a tax deduction for the expenses of tuition, textbooks and transportation. Maximum allowable deductions were $500 per child in elementary school and $700 per child in grades seven through 12.

Pay for Chaplain (1983): The Court ruled in Marsh v. Chambers that it was not against the Constitution for the Nebraska Legislature to pay a chaplain to open each day's session with a prayer.

Christmas Nativity Scene (1984): The Court ruled 5-to-4 in Lynch v. Donnelly that the First Amendment does not mandate "complete separation of church and state," and that, therefore, the sponsorship of a Christmas nativity scene by the City of Pawtucket, R.I., was not unconstitutional. The case involved a scene included in a display of Christmas symbols sponsored by the city in a park owned by a non-profit group. The majority opinion said "the Constitution (does not) require complete separation of church and state; it affirmatively mandates accommodation, not merely tolerance, of all religions and forbids hostility toward any. Anything less" would entail callous indifference not intended by the Constitution. Moreover, "such hostility would bring us into 'war with our national tradition as embodied in the First Amendment's guaranty of the free exercise of religion.' " (The additional quotation was from the 1948 decision in McCollum v. Board of Education.)

Christmas Nativity Scene (1985): The Court upheld a lower court ruling that the Village of Scarsdale, N.Y., must make public space available for the display of privately sponsored nativity scenes.

Wallace v. Jaffree, No. 83-812 (1985): The Court ruled against the constitutionality of a 1981 Alabama law calling for a public-school moment of silence that specifically included optional prayer.

Thornton v. Caldor, No. 83-1158 (1985): The Court ruled against the validity of a Connecticut law providing employees an unqualified right not to work on the Sabbath of their choice.

Grand Rapids v. Ball, No. 83-990, and **Aguilar v. Felton,** No. 84-237 (1985): The Court ruled against the constitutionality of programs in Grand Rapids and New York City allowing public school teachers to teach remedial entitlement subjects (under the Elementary and Secondary Education Act of 1965) in private schools, many of which were Catholic.

Alamo Foundation v. Secretary of Labor, No. 83-1935 (1985): The Court ruled that religious organizations running commercial businesses must pay employees the minimum wage.

CHURCH TAX EXEMPTION

The exemption of church-owned property was ruled constitutional by the U.S. Supreme Court May 4, 1970, in the case of Walz v. The Tax Commission of New York.

Suit in the case was brought by Frederick Walz, who purchsed in June, 1967, a 22-by-29-foot plot of ground in Staten Island valued at $100 and taxable at $5.24 a year. Shortly after making the purchase, Walz instituted a suit in New York State, contending that the exemption of church property from taxation authorized by state law increased his own tax rate and forced him indirectly to support churches in violation of his constitutional right to freedom of religion under the First Amendment. Three New York courts dismissed the suit, which had been instituted by mail. The Supreme Court, judging that it had probable jurisdiction, then took the case.

In a 7-1 decison affecting church-state relations in every state in the nation, the Court upheld the New York law under challenge.

FOR AND AGAINST

Chief Justice Warren E. Burger, who wrote the majority opinion, said that Congress from its earliest days had viewed the religion clauses of the Constitution as authorizing statutory real estate tax exemption to religious bodies. He declared: "Nothing in this national attitude toward religious tolerance and two centuries of uninterrupted freedom from taxation has given the remotest sign of leading to an established church or religion, and on the contrary it has operated affirmatively to help guarantee the free exercise of all forms of religious beliefs."

Justice William O. Douglas wrote in dissent that the involvement of government in religion as typified in tax exemption may seem inconsequential but: "It is, I fear, a long step down the establishment path. . . . Perhaps I have been misinformed. But, as I read the Constitution and the philosophy, I gathered that independence was the price of liberty."

Burger rejected Douglas' "establishment" fears. If tax exemption is the first step toward establishment, he said, "the second step has been long in coming."

The basic issue centered on the following question: Is there a contradiction between federal constitutional provisions against the establishment of religion, or the use of public funds for religious purposes, and state statutes exempting church property from taxation?

In the Walz' decision, the Supreme Court ruled that there is no contradiction.

Legal Background

The U.S. Constitution makes no reference to tax exemption.

There was no discussion of the issue in the Constitutional Convention nor in debates on the Bill of Rights.

In the Colonial and post-Revolutionary years, some churches had established status and were state-supported. This state of affairs changed with enactment of the First Amendment, which laid down no-establishment as the federal norm. This norm was adopted by the states which, however, exempted churches from tax liabilities.

No establishment, no hindrance, was the early American view of Church-state relationships.

This view, reflected in custom law, was not generally formulated in statute law until the second half of the 19th century, although specific tax exemption was provided for churches in Maryland in 1798, in Virginia in 1800, and in North Carolina in 1806.

The first major challenge to church property exemption was initiated by the Liberal League in the 1870s. It reached the point that President Grant included the recommendation in a State of the Union address in 1875, stating that church property should bear its own proportion of taxes. The plea fell on deaf ears in Congress, but there was some support for the idea at state levels. The exemption, however, continued to survive various challenges.

About 36 state constitutions contain either mandatory or permissive provisions for exemption.

THE WALL OF SEPARATION

Thomas Jefferson, in a letter written to the Danbury (Conn.) Baptist Association Jan. 1, 1802, coined the metaphor, "a wall of separation between Church and State," to express a theory concerning interpretation of the religion clauses of the First Amendment: "Congress shall make no law respecting an establishment of religion or prohibiting the free exercise thereof."

The metaphor was cited for the first time in judicial proceedings in 1879, in the opinion by Chief Justice Waite in Reynolds v. United States. It did not, however, figure substantially in the decision.

In 1947 the wall of separation gained acceptance as a constitutional rule, in the decision handed down in Everson v. Board of Education. Associate Justice Black, in describing the principles involved in the No Establishment Clause, wrote:

"Neither a state nor the Federal Government can set up a church. Neither can pass laws which aid one religion, aid all religions, or prefer one religion over another. Neither can force nor influence a person to go to or to remain away from church against his will or force him to profess a belief or disbelief in any religion. No person can be punished for entertaining or professing religious beliefs or disbeliefs, for church attendance or nonattendance. No tax in any amount, large or small, can be levied to support any religious activities or institutions, whatever they may be called, or whatever form they may adopt to teach or practice religion. Neither a state nor the Federal Government can, openly or secretly, participate in the affairs of any religious organizations or groups and vice versa. In the words of Jefferson, the clause against establishment of religion by law was intended to erect 'a wall of separation between Church and State.' "

Mr. Black's associates agreed with his statement of principles, which were framed without reference to the Freedom of Exercise Clause. They disagreed, however, with respect to application of the principles, as the split decision in the case indicated. Five members of the Court held that the benefits of public welfare legislation — in this case, free bus transportation to school for parochial as well as public school students — did not run contrary to the concept of separation of Church and State embodied in the First Amendment.

Inside and outside the legal profession, opinion is divided concerning the wall of separation and the balance of the religion clauses.

The view of absolute separationists, carried to the extreme, would make government the adversary of religion. The bishops of the United States, following the McCollum decision in 1948, said that the wall metaphor had become for some persons the "shibboleth of doctrinaire secularism."

Proponents of governmental neutrality toward religion are of the opinion that such neutrality should not be so interpreted as to prohibit incidental aid to religious institutions providing secular services.

1987-88 CASES

Religion-related cases before the U.S. Supreme Court in the 1987-88 term included the following.

• In a 4-to-4 ruling issued with no written opinion, the Court upheld Dec. 14, 1987, a lower court decision against an Illinois law requiring an unmarried girl under the age of 18 to notify both parents 24 hours before having an abortion. The U.S. Catholic Conference and other pro-life advocates had filed friend-of-the-court briefs urging that the law be upheld.

On an 8-to-1 vote June 20, 1988, the Court upheld the right of the U.S. Catholic Conference to challenge subpoenas for church documents as part of ongoing efforts by Abortion Rights Mobilization to force the federal government to revoke the Catholic Church's tax exempt status because of alleged improper political activity. The ruling did not deal with a church-state issue.

• The Court ruled 5-to-3 that building a road through a forest revered by Indians did not violate their religious rights.

U.S. CATHOLIC JURISDICTIONS, HIERARCHY, STATISTICS

The organizational structure of the Catholic Church in the United States consists of 33 provinces with as many archdioceses (metropolitan sees); 150 suffragan sees (dioceses); four Eastern-Rite jurisdictions immediately subject to the Holy See — the eparchies of St. Maron (Maronites), Newton (Melkites), St. Thomas Apostle of Detroit (Chaldeans) and St. George Martyr of Canton, Ohio (Romanians); and the Military Services Archdiocese. An Armenian-Rite apostolic exarchate for the United States and Canada has its seat in New York. Each of these jurisdictions is under the direction of an archbishop or bishop, called an ordinary, who has apostolic responsibility and authority for the pastoral service of the people in his care.

The structure includes the territorial episcopal conference known as the National Conference of Catholic Bishops. In and through this body, which is strictly ecclesiastical and has defined juridical authority, the bishops exercise their collegiate pastorate over the Church in the entire country (see Index).

Related to the NCCB is the United States Catholic Conference, a civil corporation and operational secretariat through which the bishops, in cooperation with other members of the Church, act on a wider-than-ecclesiastical scale for the good of the Church and society in the United States (see Index).

The representative of the Holy See to the Church in this country is an Apostolic Pro-Nuncio.

ECCLESIASTICAL PROVINCES

(Sources: *The Official Catholic Directory*, NC News Service.)

The 33 ecclesiastical provinces bear the names of archdioceses, i.e., of metropolitan sees.

Anchorage: Archdiocese of Anchorage and suffragan sees of Fairbanks, Juneau. Geographical area: Alaska.

Atlanta: Archdiocese of Atlanta (Ga.) and suffragan sees of Savannah (Ga.); Charlotte and Raleigh (N.C.), Charleston (S.C.). Geographical area: Georgia, North Carolina, South Carolina.

Baltimore: Archdiocese of Baltimore (Md.) and suffragan sees of Wilmington (Del.); Arlington and Richmond (Va.); Wheeling-Charleston (W. Va.). Geographical area: Maryland (except five counties), Delaware, Virginia, West Virginia.

Boston: Archdiocese of Boston (Mass.) and suffragan sees of Fall River, Springfield and Worcester (Mass.); Portland (Me.); Manchester (N.H.); Burlington (Vt.). Geographical area: Massachusetts, Maine, New Hampshire, Vermont.

Chicago: Archdiocese of Chicago and suffragan sees of Belleville, Joliet, Peoria, Rockford, Springfield. Geographical area: Illinois.

Cincinnati: Archdiocese of Cincinnati and suffragan sees of Cleveland, Columbus, Steubenville, Toledo, Youngstown. Geographical area: Ohio.

Denver: Archdiocese of Denver (Colo.) and suffragan sees of Colorado Springs and Pueblo (Colo.); Cheyenne (Wyo.). Geographical area: Colorado, Wyoming.

Detroit: Archdiocese of Detroit and suffragan sees of Gaylord, Grand Rapids, Kalamazoo, Lansing, Marquette, Saginaw. Geographical area: Michigan.

Dubuque: Archdiocese of Dubuque and suffragan sees of Davenport, Des Moines, Sioux City. Geographical area: Iowa.

Hartford: Archdiocese of Hartford (Conn.) and suffragan sees of Bridgeport and Norwich (Conn.); Providence (R.I.). Geographical area: Connecticut, Rhode Island.

Indianapolis: Archdiocese of Indianapolis and suffragan sees of Evansville, Fort Wayne-South Bend, Gary, Lafayette. Geographical area: Indiana.

Kansas City (Kans.): Archdiocese of Kansas City and suffragan sees of Dodge City, Salina, Wichita. Geographical area: Kansas.

Los Angeles: Archdiocese of Los Angeles and suffragan sees of Fresno, Monterey, Orange, San Bernardino, San Diego. Geographical area: Southern and Central California.

Louisville: Archdiocese of Louisville (Ky.) and suffragan sees of Covington, Lexington and Owensboro (Ky.); Knoxville, Memphis and Nashville (Tenn.). Geographical area: Kentucky, Tennessee.

Miami: Archdiocese of Miami and suffragan sees of Orlando, Palm Beach, Pensacola-Tallahassee, St. Augustine, St. Petersburg, Venice. Geographical area: Florida.

Milwaukee: Archdiocese of Milwaukee and suffragan sees of Green Bay, La Crosse, Madison, Superior. Geographical area: Wisconsin.

Mobile: Archdiocese of Mobile, Ala., and suffragan sees of Birmingham (Ala.); Biloxi and Jackson (Miss.). Geographical area: Alabama, Mississippi.

Newark: Archdiocese of Newark and suffragan sees of Camden, Metuchen, Paterson, Trenton. Geographical area: New Jersey.

New Orleans: Archdiocese of New Orleans and suffragan sees of Alexandria, Baton Rouge, Houma-Thibodaux, Lafayette, Lake Charles and Shreveport. Geographical area: Louisiana.

New York: Archdiocese of New York and suffragan sees of Albany, Brooklyn, Buffalo, Ogdensburg, Rochester, Rockville Centre, Syracuse. Geographical area: New York.

Oklahoma City: Archdiocese of Oklahoma City (Okla.) and suffragan sees of Tulsa (Okla.) and Little Rock (Ark.). Geographical area: Oklahoma, Arkansas.

Omaha: Archdiocese of Omaha and suffragan sees of Grand Island, Lincoln. Geographical area: Nebraska.

Philadelphia: Archdiocese of Philadelphia and suffragan sees of Allentown, Altoona-Johnstown,

Erie, Greensburg, Harrisburg, Pittsburgh, Scranton. Geographical area: Pennsylvania.

Philadelphia (Byzantine Rite, Ukrainians): Metropolitan See of Philadelphia (Byzantine Rite) and Eparchies of St. Josaphat in Parma (Ohio), St. Nicholas of the Ukrainians in Chicago and Stamford, Conn. The jurisdiction extends to all Ukrainian Catholics in the U.S. from the ecclesiastical province of Galicia in the Ukraine.

Pittsburgh (Byzantine Rite, Ruthenians): Metropolitan See of Pittsburgh, Pa. and Eparchies of Passaic (N.J.), Parma (Ohio), Van Nuys (Calif.).

Portland: Archdiocese of Portland (Ore.) and suffragan sees of Baker (Ore.); Boise (Ida.); Great Falls-Billings and Helena (Mont.). Geographical area: Oregon, Idaho, Montana.

St. Louis: Archdiocese of St. Louis and suffragan sees of Jefferson City, Kansas City-St. Joseph, Springfield-Cape Girardeau. Geographical area: Missouri.

St. Paul and Minneapolis: Archdiocese of St. Paul and Minneapolis (Minn.) and suffragan sees of Crookston, Duluth, New Ulm, St. Cloud and Winona (Minn.); Bismarck and Fargo (N.D.); Rapid City and Sioux Falls (S.D.). Geographical area: Minnesota, North Dakota, South Dakota.

San Antonio: Archdiocese of San Antonio (Tex.) and suffragan sees of Amarillo, Austin, Beaumont, Brownsville, Corpus Christi, Dallas, El Paso, Fort Worth, Galveston-Houston, Lubbock, San Angelo, Tyler and Victoria (Tex.). Geographical area: Texas.

San Francisco: Archdiocese of San Francisco (Calif.) and suffragan sees of Oakland, Sacramento, San Jose, Santa Rosa and Stockton (Calif.); Honolulu (Hawaii); Reno-Las Vegas (Nev.); Salt Lake City (Utah). Geographical area: Northern California, Nevada, Utah, Hawaii.

Santa Fe: Archdiocese of Santa Fe (N.M.) and suffragan sees of Gallup and Las Cruces (N.M.); Phoenix and Tucson (Ariz.). Geographical area: New Mexico, Arizona.

Seattle: Archdiocese of Seattle and suffragan sees of Spokane, Yakima. Geographical area: Washington.

Washington: Archdiocese of Washington, D.C., and suffragan see of St. Thomas (Virgin Islands). Geographical area: District of Columbia, five counties of Maryland, Virgin Islands.

ARCHDIOCESES, DIOCESES, ARCHBISHOPS, BISHOPS

(Sources: *The Official Catholic Directory;* NC News Service. As of Aug. 15, 1988.)

Information includes name of diocese, year of foundation (as it appears on the official document erecting the see), present ordinaries (year of installation), auxiliaries and former ordinaries (for biographies, see Index).

Archdioceses are indicated by an asterisk.

Albany, N.Y. (1847): Howard J. Hubbard, bishop, 1977.

Former bishops: John McCloskey, 1847-64; John J. Conroy, 1865-77; Francis McNeirny, 1877-94; Thomas M. Burke, 1894-1915; Thomas F. Cusack, 1915-18; Edmund F. Gibbons, 1919-54; William A. Scully, 1954-69; Edwin B. Broderick, 1969-76.

Alexandria, La. (1853): John C. Favalora, bishop, 1986.

Established at Natchitoches, transferred to Alexandria 1910; title changed to Alexandria-Shreveport, 1977; redesignated Alexandria, 1986, when Shreveport was made a diocese.

Former bishops: Augustus M. Martin, 1853-75; Francis X. Leray, 1877-79, administrator, 1879-83; Anthony Durier, 1885-1904; Cornelius Van de Ven, 1904-32; Daniel F. Desmond, 1933-45; Charles P. Greco, 1946-73; Lawrence P. Graves, 1973-82; William B. Friend, 1983-86.

Allentown, Pa. (1961): Thomas J. Welsh, bishop, 1983.

Former bishop: Joseph McShea, 1961-83.

Altoona-Johnstown, Pa. (1901): Joseph V. Adamek, bishop, 1987.

Established as Altoona, name changed, 1957.

Former bishops: Eugene A. Garvey, 1901-20; John J. McCort, 1920-36; Richard T. Guilfoyle, 1936-57; Howard J. Carroll, 1958-60; J. Carroll McCormick, 1960-66; James J. Hogan, 1966-86.

Amarillo, Tex. (1926): Leroy T. Matthiesen, bishop, 1980.

Former bishops; Rudolph A. Gerken, 1927-33; Robert E. Lucey, 1934-41; Laurence J. Fitzsimon, 1941-58; John L. Morkovsky, 1958-63; Lawrence M. De Falco, 1963-79.

Anchorage,* Alaska (1966): Francis T. Hurley, archbishop, 1976.

Former archbishop: Joseph T. Ryan, 1966-75.

Arlington, Va. (1974): John R. Keating, bishop, 1983.

Former bishop: Thomas J. Welsh, 1974-83.

Atlanta,* Ga. (1956; archdiocese, 1962): Eugene A. Marino, S.S.J., archbishop, 1988.

Former ordinaries: Francis E. Hyland, 1956-61; Paul J. Hallinan, first archbishop, 1962-68; Thomas A. Donnellan, 1968-87.

Austin, Tex. (1947): John E. McCarthy, bishop, 1986.

Former bishop: Louis J. Reicher, 1947-71; Vincent M. Harris, 1971-86.

Baker, Ore. (1903): Thomas J. Connolly, bishop, 1971.

Established as Baker City, name changed, 1952.

Former bishops: Charles J. O'Reilly, 1903-18; Joseph F. McGrath, 1919-50; Francis P. Leipzig, 1950-71.

Baltimore,* Md. (1789; archdiocese, 1808): William D. Borders, archbishop, 1974. P. Francis Murphy, William C. Newman, John H. Ricard, S.S.J. auxiliaries.

Former ordinaries: John Carroll, 1789-1815, first archbishop; Leonard Neale, 1815-17; Ambrose Marechal, S.S., 1817-28; James Whitfield, 1828-34; Samuel Eccleston, S.S., 1834-51; Francis P. Kenrick, 1851-63; Martin J. Spalding, 1864-72; James R. Bayley, 1872-77; Cardinal James Gibbons, 1877-1921; Michael J. Curley, 1921-47; Francis P. Keough, 1947-61; Cardinal Lawrence J. Shehan, 1961-74.

Baton Rouge, La. (1961): Stanley J. Ott, bishop, 1983.

Former bishops: Robert E. Tracy, 1961-74; Joseph V. Sullivan, 1974-82.
Beaumont, Tex. (1966): Bernard J. Ganter, bishop, 1977.
Former bishops: Vincent M. Harris, 1966-71; Warren L. Boudreaux, 1971-77.
Belleville, Ill. (1887): James P. Keleher, bishop, 1984.
Former bishops: John Janssen, 1888-1913; Henry Althoff, 1914-47; Albert R. Zuroweste, 1948-76; William M. Cosgrove, 1976-81; John N. Wurm, 1981-84.
Biloxi, Miss. (1977): Joseph Lawson Howze, bishop, 1977.
Birmingham, Ala. (1969): Raymond J. Boland, bishop, 1988.
Former bishop: Joseph G. Vath, 1969-87.
Bismarck, N. Dak. (1909): John F. Kinney, bishop, 1982.
Former bishops: Vincent Wehrle, O.S.B., 1910-39; Vincent J. Ryan, 1940-51; Lambert A. Hoch, 1952-56; Hilary B. Hacker, 1957-82.
Boise, Ida. (1893): Vacant as of Aug. 20, 1988.
Former bishops: Alphonse J. Glorieux, 1893-1917; Daniel M. Gorman, 1918-27; Edward J. Kelly, 1928-56; James J. Byrne, 1956-62; Sylvester Treinen, 1962-88.
Boston,* Mass. (1808; archdiocese, 1875): Cardinal Bernard F. Law, archbishop, 1984. Lawrence J. Riley, John J. Mulcahy, Daniel A. Hart, Alfred C. Hughes, Robert J. Banks, Roberto O. Gonzalez, O.F.M., auxiliaries.
Former ordinaries: John L. de Cheverus, 1810-23; Benedict J. Fenwick, S.J., 1825-46; John B. Fitzpatrick, 1846-66; John J. Williams, 1866-1907, first archbishop; Cardinal William O'Connell, 1907-44; Cardinal Richard Cushing, 1944-70; Cardinal Humberto Medeiros, 1970-83.
Bridgeport, Conn. (1953): Vacant as of Aug. 11, 1988.
Former bishops: Lawrence J. Shehan, 1953-61; Walter W. Curtis, 1961-68.
Brooklyn, N.Y. (1853): Francis J. Mugavero, bishop, 1968. Joseph M. Sullivan, Rene A. Valero, auxiliaries.
Former bishops: John Loughlin, 1853-91; Charles E. McDonnell, 1892-1921; Thomas E. Molloy, 1921-56; Bryan J. McEntegart, 1957-68.
Brownsville, Tex. (1965): John J. Fitzpatrick, bishop, 1971.
Former bishops: Adolph Marx, 1965; Humberto S. Medeiros, 1966-70.
Buffalo, N.Y. (1847): Edward D. Head, bishop, 1973. Donald W. Trautman, auxiliary.
Former bishops: John Timon, C.M., 1847-67; Stephen V. Ryan, C.M., 1868-96; James E. Quigley, 1897-1903; Charles H. Colton, 1903-15; Dennis J. Dougherty, 1915-18; William Turner, 1919-36; John A. Duffy, 1937-44; John F. O'Hara, C.S.C., 1945-51; Joseph A. Burke, 1952-62; James McNulty, 1963-72.
Burlington, Vt. (1853): John A. Marshall, bishop, 1972.
Former bishops: Louis De Goesbriand, 1853-99; John S. Michaud, 1899-1908; Joseph J. Rice, 1910-38; Matthew F. Brady, 1938-44; Edward F. Ryan, 1945-56; Robert F. Joyce, 1957-71.

Camden, N.J. (1937): George H. Guilfoyle, bishop, 1968. James L. Schad, auxiliary.
Former bishops: Bartholomew J. Eustace, 1938-56; Justin J. McCarthy, 1957-59; Celestine J. Damiano, 1960-67.
Charleston, S.C. (1820): Ernest L. Unterkoefler, bishop, 1964.
Former bishops: John England, 1820-42; Ignatius W. Reynolds, 1844-55; Patrick N. Lynch, 1858-82; Henry P. Northrop, 1883-1916; William T. Russell, 1917-27; Emmet M. Walsh, 1927-49; John J. Russell, 1950-58; Paul J. Hallinan, 1958-62; Francis F. Reh, 1962-64.
Charlotte, N.C. (1971): John F. Donoghue, bishop, 1984.
Former bishop: Michael J. Begley, 1972-84.
Cheyenne, Wyo. (1887): Joseph Hart, bishop, 1978.
Former bishops: Maurice F. Burke, 1887-93; Thomas M. Lenihan, 1897-1901; James J. Keane, 1902-11; Patrick A. McGovern, 1912-51; Hubert M. Newell, 1951-78.
Chicago,* Ill. (1843; archdiocese, 1880): Cardinal Joseph L. Bernardin, archbishop, 1982. Alfred L. Abramowicz, O. Carm., Placido Rodriguez, C.M.F., Timothy J. Lyne, Wilton D. Gregory, Thad J. Jakubowski, John R. Gorman, auxiliaries.
Former ordinaries: William Quarter, 1844-48; James O. Van de Velde, S.J., 1849-53; Anthony O'Regan, 1854-58; James Duggan, 1859-70; Thomas P. Foley, administrator, 1870-79; Patrick A. Feehan, 1880-1902, first archbishop; James E. Quigley, 1903-15; Cardinal George Mundelein, 1915-39; Cardinal Samuel Stritch, 1939-58; Cardinal Albert Meyer, 1958-65; Cardinal John Cody, 1965-82.
Cincinnati,* Ohio (1821; archdiocese, 1850): Daniel E. Pilarczyk, archbishop, 1982. James H. Garland, auxiliary.
Former ordinaries: Edward D. Fenwick, O.P., 1822-32; John B. Purcell, 1833-83, first archbishop; William H. Elder, 1883-1904; Henry Moeller, 1904-1925; John T. McNicholas, O.P., 1925-50; Karl J. Alter, 1950-69; Paul F. Leibold, 1969-72; Joseph L. Bernardin, 1972-82.
Cleveland, Ohio (1847): Anthony M. Pilla, bishop, 1980. Gilbert I. Sheldon, James P. Lyke, O.F.M., A. Edward Pevec, A. James Quinn, auxiliaries.
Former bishops: L. Amadeus Rappe, 1847-70; Richard Gilmour, 1872-91; Ignatius F. Horstmann, 1892-1908; John P. Farrelly, 1909-21; Joseph Schrembs, 1921-45; Edward F. Hoban, 1945-66; Clarence G. Issenmann, 1966-74; James A. Hickey, 1974-80.
Colorado Springs, Colo. (1983): Richard C. Hanifen, bishop, 1984.
Columbus, Ohio (1868): James A. Griffin, bishop, 1983.
Former bishops: Sylvester H. Rosecrans, 1868-78; John A. Watterson, 1880-99; Henry Moeller, 1900-03; James J. Hartley, 1904-44; Michael J. Ready, 1944-57; Clarence Issenmann, 1957-64; John J. Carberry, 1965-68; Clarence E. Elwell, 1968-73; Edward J. Herrmann, 1973-82.

Corpus Christi, Tex. (1912): Rene H. Gracida, bishop, 1983.
Former bishops: Paul J. Nussbaum, C.P., 1913-20; Emmanuel B. Ledvina, 1921-49; Mariano S. Garriga, 1949-65; Thomas J. Drury, 1965-83.
Covington, Ky. (1853): William A. Hughes, bishop, 1979.
Former bishops: George A. Carrell, S.J., 1853-68; Augustus M. Toebbe, 1870-84; Camillus P. Maes, 1885-1914; Ferdinand Brossart, 1916-23; Francis W. Howard, 1923-44; William T. Mulloy, 1945-59; Richard Ackerman, C.S.Sp., 1960-78.
Crookston, Minn. (1909): Victor H. Balke, bishop, 1976.
Former bishops: Timothy Corbett, 1910-38; John H. Peschges, 1938-44; Francis J. Schenk, 1945-60; Laurence A. Glenn, 1960-70; Kenneth J. Povish, 1970-75.

Dallas, Tex. (1890): Thomas Tschoepe, bishop, 1969.
Established 1890, as Dallas, title changed to Dallas-Ft. Worth 1953; redesignated Dallas, 1969, when Ft. Worth was made diocese.
Former bishops: Thomas F. Brennan, 1891-92; Edward J. Dunne, 1893-1910; Joseph P. Lynch, 1911-54; Thomas K. Gorman, 1954-69.
Davenport, Ia. (1881): Gerald F. O'Keefe, bishop, 1966.
Former bishops: John McMullen, 1881-83; Henry Cosgrove, 1884-1906; James Davis, 1906-26; Henry P. Rohlman, 1927-44; Ralph L. Hayes, 1944-66.
Denver,* Colo. (1887; archdiocese, 1941): J. Francis Stafford, archbishop, 1986.
Former ordinaries: Joseph P. Machebeuf, 1887-89; Nicholas C. Matz, 1889-1917; J. Henry Tihen, 1917-31; Urban J. Vehr, 1931-67, first archbishop; James V. Casey, 1967-86.
Des Moines, Ia. (1911): William H. Bullock, bishop, 1987.
Former bishops: Austin Dowling, 1912-19; Thomas W. Drumm, 1919-33; Gerald T. Bergan, 1934-48; Edward C. Daly, O.P., 1948-64; George J. Biskup, 1965-67; Maurice J. Dingman, 1968-86.
Detroit,* Mich. (1833; archdiocese, 1937): Cardinal Edmund C. Szoka, archbishop, 1981. Thomas J. Gumbleton, Walter J. Schoenherr, Moses B. Anderson, S.S.E., Patrick R. Cooney, Dale J. Melczek, auxiliaries.
Former ordinaries: Frederic Rese, 1833-71; Peter P. Lefevere, administrator, 1841-69; Caspar H. Borgess, 1871-88; John S. Foley, 1888-1918; Michael J. Gallagher, 1918-37; Cardinal Edward Mooney, 1937-58, first archbishop; Cardinal John F. Dearden, 1958-80.
Dodge City, Kans. (1951): Stanley G. Schlarman, bishop, 1983.
Former bishops: John B. Franz, 1951-59; Marion F. Forst, 1960-76; Eugene J. Gerber, 1976-82.
Dubuque,* Iowa (1837; archdiocese, 1893): Daniel W. Kucera, O.S.B., archbishop, 1984. Francis J. Dunn, William E. Franklin, auxiliaries.
Former ordinaries: Mathias Loras, 1837-58; Clement Smyth, O.C.S.O., 1858-65; John Hennessy, 1866-1900, first archbishop; John J. Keane, 1900-11; James J. Keane, 1911-29; Francis J. Beckman, 1930-46; Henry P. Rohlman, 1946-54; Leo Binz, 1954-61; James J. Byrne, 1962-83.
Duluth, Minn. (1889): Robert H. Brom, bishop, 1983.
Former bishops: James McGolrick, 1889-1918; John T. McNicholas, O.P., 1918-25; Thomas A. Welch, 1926-59; Francis J. Schenk, 1960-69; Paul F. Anderson, 1969-82.
El Paso, Tex. (1914): Raymundo J. Pena, bishop, 1980.
Former bishops: Anthony J. Schuler, S.J., 1915-42; Sidney M. Metzger, 1942-78. Patrick F. Flores, 1978-79.
Erie, Pa. (1853): Michael J. Murphy, bishop, 1982.
Former bishops: Michael O'Connor, 1853-54; Josue M. Young, 1854-66; Tobias Mullen, 1868-99; John E. Fitzmaurice, 1899-1920; John M. Gannon, 1920-66; John F. Whealon, 1966-69; Alfred M. Watson, 1969-82.
Evansville, Ind. (1944): Francis Raymond Shea, bishop, 1970.
Former bishops: Henry J. Grimmelsman, 1944-65; Paul F. Leibold, 1966-69.
Fairbanks, Alaska (1962): Michael J. Kaniecki, S.J., bishop, 1985.
Former bishops: Francis D. Gleeson, S.J., 1962-68; Robert L. Whelan, S.J., 1968-85.
Fall River, Mass. (1904): Daniel A. Cronin, bishop, 1970.
Former bishops: William Stang, 1904-07; Daniel F. Feehan, 1907-34; James E. Cassidy, 1934-51; James L. Connolly, 1951-70.
Fargo, N. Dak. (1889): James S. Sullivan, bishop, 1985.
Established at Jamestown, transferred, 1897.
Former bishops: John Shanley, 1889-1909; James O'Reilly, 1910-34; Aloysius J. Muench, 1935-59; Leo F. Dworschak, 1960-70; Justin A. Driscoll, 1970-84.
Fort Wayne-South Bend, Ind. (1857): John M. D'Arcy, bishop, 1985. Joseph R. Crowley, auxiliary.
Established as Fort Wayne, name changed, 1960.
Former bishops: John H. Luers, 1858-71; Joseph Dwenger, C.Pp. S., 1872-93; Joseph Rademacher, 1893-1900; Herman J. Alerding, 1900-24; John F. Noll, 1925-56; Leo A. Pursley, 1957-76; William E. McManus, 1976-85.
Fort Worth, Tex. (1969): Joseph P. Delaney, bishop, 1981.
Former bishop: John J. Cassata, 1969-80.
Fresno, Calif. (1967): Joseph J. Madera, M.Sp.S., bishop, 1980.
Formerly Monterey-Fresno, 1922.
Former bishops (Monterey-Fresno): John J. Cantwell, administrator, 1922-24; John B. MacGinley, first bishop, 1924-32; Philip G. Sher, 1933-53; Aloysius J. Willinger, 1953-67.
Former bishops (Fresno): Timothy Manning, 1967-69; Hugh A. Donohoe, 1969-80.
Gallup, N. Mex. (1939): Jerome J. Hastrich, bishop, 1969. Donald Pelotte, S.S.S., coadjutor.
Former bishop: Bernard T. Espelage, O.F.M., 1940-69.
Galveston-Houston, Tex. (1847): Joseph A. Fiorenza, bishop, 1985. Enrique San Pedro, S.J.,

U.S. Ecclesiastical Jurisdictions

Curtis J. Guillory, S.V.D., auxiliaries.
Established as Galveston, name changed, 1959.
Former bishops: John M. Odin, C.M., 1847-61; Claude M. Dubuis, 1862-92; Nicholas A. Gallagher, 1892-1918; Christopher E. Byrne, 1918-50; Wendelin J. Nold, 1950-75; John L. Morkovsky, 1975-84.

Gary, Ind. (1956): Norbert F. Gaughan, bishop, 1984.
Former bishop: Andrew G. Grutka, 1957-84.

Gaylord, Mich. (1971): Robert J. Rose, bishop, 1981.
Former bishop: Edmund C. Szoka, 1971-81.

Grand Island, Neb. (1912): Lawrence McNamara, bishop, 1978.
Established at Kearney, transferred, 1917.
Former bishops: James A. Duffy, 1913-31; Stanislaus V. Bona, 1932-44; Edward J. Hunkeler, 1945-51; John L. Paschang, 1951-72; John J. Sullivan, 1972-77.

Grand Rapids, Mich. (1882): Joseph M. Breitenbeck, bishop, 1969. Joseph C. McKinney, auxiliary.
Former bishops: Henry J. Richter, 1883-1916; Michael J. Gallagher, 1916-18; Edward D. Kelly, 1919-26; Joseph G. Pinten, 1926-40; Joseph C. Plagens, 1941-43; Francis J. Haas, 1943-53; Allen J. Babcock, 1954-69.

Great Falls-Billings, Mont. (1904): Anthony J. Milone, bishop, 1988.
Established as Great Falls; name changed, 1980.
Former bishops: Mathias C. Lenihan, 1904-30; Edwin V. O'Hara, 1930-39; William J. Condon, 1939-67; Eldon B. Schuster, 1968-77; Thomas J. Murphy, 1978-87.

Green Bay, Wis. (1868): Adam J. Maida, bishop, 1984. Robert F. Morneau, auxiliary.
Former bishops: Joseph Melcher, 1868-73; Francis X. Krautbauer, 1875-85; Frederick X. Katzer, 1886-91; Sebastian G. Messmer, 1892-1903; Joseph J. Fox, 1904-14; Paul P. Rhode, 1915-45; Stanislaus V. Bona, 1945-67; Aloysius J. Wycislo, 1968-83.

Greensburg, Pa. (1951): Anthony G. Bosco, bishop, 1987.
Former bishops: Hugh L. Lamb, 1951-59; William G. Connare, 1960-87.

Harrisburg, Pa. (1868): William H. Keeler, bishop, 1984.
Former bishops: Jeremiah F. Shanahan, 1868-86; Thomas McGovern, 1888-98; John W. Shanahan,1899-1916; Philip R. McDevitt, 1916-35; George L. Leech, 1935-71; Joseph T. Daley, 1971-83.

Hartford,* Conn. (1843; archdiocese, 1953): John F. Whealon, archbishop, 1969. Peter A. Rosazza, Paul S. Loverde, auxiliaries.
Former ordinaries: William Tyler, 1844-49; Bernard O'Reilly, 1850-56; F. P. MacFarland, 1858-74; Thomas Galberry, O.S.A., 1876-78; Lawrence S. McMahon, 1879-93; Michael Tierney, 1894-1908; John J. Nilan, 1910-34; Maurice F. McAuliffe, 1934-44; Henry J. O'Brien, 1945-68, first archbishop.

Helena, Mont. (1884): Elden F. Curtiss, bishop, 1976.
Former bishops: John B. Brondel, 1884-1903; John P. Carroll, 1904-25; George J. Finnigan, C.S.C., 1927-32; Ralph L. Hayes, 1933-35; Joseph M. Gilmore, 1936-62; Raymond Hunthausen, 1962-75.

Honolulu, Hawaii (1941): Joseph A. Ferrario, bishop, 1982.
Former bishops: James J. Sweeney, 1941-68; John J. Scanlan, 1968-81.

Houma-Thibodaux, La. (1977): Warren L. Boudreaux, bishop, 1977.

Indianapolis,* Ind. (1834; archdiocese, 1944): Edward T. O'Meara, archbishop, 1980.
Established at Vincennes, transferred, 1898.
Former ordinaries: Simon G. Bruté, 1834-39; Celestine de la Hailandiere, 1839-47; John S. Bazin, 1847-48; Maurice de St. Palais, 1849-77; Francis S. Chatard, 1878-1918; Joseph Chartrand, 1918-33; Joseph E. Ritter, 1934-46, first archbishop; Paul C. Schulte, 1946-70; George J. Biskup, 1970-79.

Jackson, Miss. (1837): William R. Houck, bishop, 1984.
Established at Natchez; title changed to Natchez-Jackson, 1956; transferred to Jackson, 1977 (Natchez made titular see).
Former bishops: John J. Chanche, S.S., 1841-52; James Van de Velde, S.J., 1853-55; William H. Elder, 1857-80; Francis A. Jansens, 1881-88; Thomas Heslin, 1889-1911; John E. Gunn, S.M., 1911-24; Richard O. Gerow, 1924-67; Joseph B. Brunini, 1968-84.

Jefferson City, Mo. (1956): Michael F. McAuliffe, bishop, 1969.
Former bishop: Joseph Marling, C.Pp.S., 1956-69.

Joliet, Ill. (1948): Joseph L. Imesch, bishop, 1979. Raymond J. Vonesh, Roger L. Kaffer, auxiliaries.
Former bishops: Martin D. McNamara, 1949-66. Romeo Blanchette, 1966-79.

Juneau, Alaska (1951): Michael H. Kenny, bishop, 1979.
Former bishops: Dermot O'Flanagan, 1951-68; Joseph T. Ryan, administrator, 1968-71; Francis T. Hurley, 1971-76, administrator, 1976-79.

Kalamazoo, Mich. (1971): Paul V. Donovan, bishop, 1971.

Kansas City,* Kans. (1877; archdiocese, 1952): Ignatius J. Strecker, archbishop, 1969.
Established as vicariate apostolic, 1850, became Diocese of Leavenworth, 1877, transferred to Kansas City 1947.
Former ordinaries: J. B. Miege, vicar apostolic, 1851-74; Louis M. Fink, O.S.B., vicar apostolic, 1874-77, first bishop, 1877-1904; Thomas F. Lillis, 1904-10; John Ward, 1910-29; Francis Johannes, 1929-37; Paul C. Schulte, 1937-46; George J. Donnelly, 1946-50; Edward Hunkeler, 1951-69, first archbishop.

Kansas City-St. Joseph, Mo. (Kansas City, 1880; St. Joseph, 1868; united 1956): John J. Sullivan, bishop, 1977.
Former bishops: John J. Hogan, 1880-1913; Thomas F. Lillis, 1913-38; Edwin V. O'Hara, 1939-56; John P. Cody, 1956-61; Charles H. Helmsing, 1962-77.
Former bishops (St. Joseph): John J. Hogan, 1868-80, administrator, 1880-93; Maurice F. Burke, 1893-1923; Francis Gilfillan, 1923-33; Charles H. Le Blond, 1933-56.

Knoxville, Tenn. (1988): Anthony J. O'Connell, bishop, 1988.

La Crosse, Wis. (1868): John J. Paul, bishop, 1983.
Former bishops: Michael Heiss, 1868-80; Kilian C. Flasch, 1881-91; James Schwebach, 1892-1921; Alexander J. McGavick, 1921-48; John P. Treacy, 1948-64; Frederick W. Freking, 1965-83.

Lafayette, Ind. (1944): William L. Higi, bishop, 1984.
Former bishops: John G. Bennett, 1944-57; John J. Carberry, 1957-65; Raymond J. Gallagher, 1965-82; George A. Fulcher, 1983-84.

Lafayette, La. (1918): Gerard L. Frey, bishop, 1973. Harry J. Flynn, coadjutor, 1986.
Former bishops: Jules B. Jeanmard, 1918-56; Maurice Schexnayder, 1956-72.

Lake Charles, La. (1980): Jude Speyrer, bishop, 1980.

Lansing, Mich. (1937): Kenneth J. Povish, bishop, 1975.
Former bishops: Joseph H. Albers, 1937-65; Alexander Zaleski, 1965-75.

Las Cruces, N. Mex. (1982): Ricardo Ramirez, C.S.B., bishop, 1982.

Lexington, Ky. (1988): James Kendrick Williams, bishop, 1988.

Lincoln, Neb. (1887): Glennon P. Flavin, bishop, 1967.
Former bishops: Thomas Bonacum, 1887-1911; J. Henry Tihen, 1911-17; Charles J. O'Reilly, 1918-23; Francis J. Beckman, 1924-30; Louis B. Kucera, 1930-57; James V. Casey, 1957-67.

Little Rock, Ark. (1843): Andrew J. McDonald, bishop, 1972.
Former bishops: Andrew Byrne, 1844-62; Edward Fitzgerald, 1867-1907; John Morris, 1907-46; Albert L. Fletcher, 1946-72.

Los Angeles,* Calif. (1840; archdiocese, 1936): Roger M. Mahony, archbishop, 1985. John J. Ward, Juan A. Arzube, Carl Fisher, S.S.J., Armando Ochoa, Patrick Ziemann, auxiliaries.
Founded as diocese of Two Californias, 1840; became Monterey diocese, 1850; Baja California detached from Monterey diocese, 1852; title changed to Monterey-Los Angeles, 1859; Los Angeles-San Diego, 1922; became archdiocese under present title, 1936 (San Diego became separate see).
Former ordinaries: Francisco Garcia Diego y Moreno, O.F.M., 1840-46; Joseph S. Alemany, O.P., 1850-53; Thaddeus Amat, C.M., 1854-78; Francis Mora, 1878-96; George T. Montgomery, 1896-1903; Thomas J. Conaty, 1903-15; John J. Cantwell, 1917-47, first archbishop; Cardinal James McIntyre, 1948-70; Cardinal Timothy Manning, 1970-85.

Louisville,* Ky. (1808; archdiocese, 1937): Thomas C. Kelly, O.P., archbishop, 1982.
Established at Bardstown, transferred, 1841.
Former ordinaries: Benedict J. Flaget, S.S. 1810-32; John B. David, S.S., 1832-33; Benedict J. Flaget, S.S., 1833-50; Martin J. Spalding, 1850-64; Peter J. Lavialle, 1865-67; William G. McCloskey, 1868-1909; Denis O'Donaghue, 1910-'24; John A. Floersh, 1924-67, first archbishop; Thomas J. McDonough, 1967-81.

Lubbock, Tex. (1983): Michael J. Sheehan, bishop, 1983.

Madison, Wis. (1946): Cletus F. O'Donnell, bishop, 1967. George O. Wirz, auxiliary.
Former bishop: William P. O'Connor, 1946-67.

Manchester, N.H. (1884): Odore J. Gendron, bishop, 1975. Joseph Gerry, O.S.B., auxiliary.
Former bishops: Denis M. Bradley, 1884-1903; John B. Delany, 1904-06; George A. Guertin, 1907-32; John B. Peterson, 1932-44; Matthew F. Brady, 1944-59; Ernest J. Primeau, 1960-74.

Marquette, Mich. (1857): Mark F. Schmitt, bishop, 1978.
Former bishops: Frederic Baraga, 1857-68; Ignatius Mrak, 1869-78; John Vertin, 1879-99; Frederick Eis, 1899-1922; Paul J. Nussbaum, C.P., 1922-35; Joseph C. Plagens, 1935-40; Francis Magner, 1941-47; Thomas L. Noa, 1947-68; Charles A. Salatka, 1968-77.

Memphis, Tenn. (1970): Daniel M. Buechlein, O.S.B., bishop, 1987.
Former bishops: Carroll T. Dozier, 1971-82; J. Francis Stafford, 1982-86.

Metuchen, N.J. (1981): Edward T. Hughes, bishop, 1987.
Former bishop: Theodore E. McCarrick, 1981-86.

Miami,* Fla. (1958; archdiocese, 1968): Edward A. McCarthy, archbishop, 1977. Agustin A. Roman, Norbert M. Dorsey, C.P., auxiliaries.
Former ordinary: Coleman F. Carroll, 1958-77, first archbishop.

Milwaukee,* Wis. (1843; archdiocese, 1875): Rembert G. Weakland, O.S.B., archbishop, 1977. Leo J. Brust, Richard J. Sklba, auxiliaries.
Former ordinaries: John M. Henni, 1844-81, first archbishop; Michael Heiss, 1881-90; Frederick X. Katzer, 1891-1903; Sebastian G. Messmer, 1903-30; Samuel A. Stritch, 1930-39; Moses E. Kiley, 1940-53; Albert G. Meyer, 1953-58; William E. Cousins, 1959-77.

Mobile,* Ala. (1829; archdiocese, 1980): Oscar H. Lipscomb, first archbishop, 1980.
Founded as Mobile, 1829; title changed to Mobile-Birmingham, 1954; redesignated Mobile, 1969.
Former bishops: Michael Portier, 1829-59; John Quinlan, 1859-83; Dominic Manucy, 1884; Jeremiah O'Sullivan, 1885-96; Edward P. Allen, 1897-1926; Thomas J. Toolen, 1927-69; John L. May, 1969-80.

Monterey in California (1967): Thaddeus A. Shubsda, bishop, 1982.
Formerly Monterey-Fresno, 1922. (Originally established in 1850, see Los Angeles listing.)
Former bishops (Monterey-Fresno): John J. Cantwell, administrator, 1922-24; John B. MacGinley, first bishop, 1924-32; Philip G. Scher, 1933-53; Aloysius J. Willinger, 1953-67.
Former bishop (Monterey): Harry A. Clinch, 1967-82.

Nashville, Tenn. (1837): James D. Niedergeses, bishop, 1975.
Former bishops: Richard P. Miles, O.P., 1838-60; James Whelan, O.P., 1860-64; Patrick A. Feehan, 1865-80; Joseph Rademacher, 1883-93; Thomas S. Byrne, 1894-1923; Alphonse J. Smith, 1924-35; William L. Adrian, 1936-69; Joseph A. Durick, 1969-75.

U.S. Ecclesiastical Jurisdictions

Newark,* N.J. (1853; archdiocese, 1937): Theodore E. McCarrick, archbishop, 1986. Jerome Pechillo, T.O.R., Robert F. Garner, Joseph A. Francis, S.V.D., Dominic A. Marconi, David Arias, O.A.R., James T. McHugh, John M. Smith, auxiliaries.

Former ordinaries: James R. Bayley, 1853-72; Michael A. Corrigan, 1873-80; Winand M. Wigger, 1881-1901; John J. O'Connor, 1901-27; Thomas J. Walsh, 1928-52, first archbishop; Thomas A. Boland, 1953-74; Peter L. Gerety, 1974-86.

New Orleans,* La. (1793; archdiocese, 1850): Philip M. Hannan, archbishop, 1965. Harold R. Perry, S. V. D., auxiliary. Nicholas D'Antonio, O.F.M., vicar general.

Former ordinaries: Luis Penalver y Cardenas, 1793-1801; John Carroll, administrator, 1809-15; W. Louis Dubourg, S.S., 1815-25; Joseph Rosati, C.M., administrator, 1826-29; Leo De Neckere, C.M., 1829-33; Anthony Blanc, 1835-60, first archbishop; Jean Marie Odin, C.M., 1861-70; Napoleon J. Perche, 1870-83; Francis X. Leray, 1883-87; Francis A. Janssens, 1888-97; Placide L. Chapelle, 1897-1905; James H. Blenk, S.M., 1906-17; John W. Shaw, 1918-34; Joseph F. Rummel, 1935-64; John P. Cody, 1964-65.

Newton, Mass. (Melkite Rite) (1966; eparchy, 1976): Archbishop Joseph Tawil, exarch, 1969, first eparch, 1976. John A. Elya, auxiliary.

Former ordinary: Justin Najmy, 1966-68.

New Ulm, Minn. (1957): Raymond A. Lucker, bishop, 1975.

Former bishop: Alphonse J. Schladweiler, 1958-75.

New York,* N.Y. (1808; archdiocese, 1850): Cardinal John J. O'Connor, archbishop, 1984. Patrick V. Ahern, James P. Mahoney, Anthony F. Mestice, Austin B. Vaughan, Francisco Garmendia, Emerson J. Moore, Edward M. Egan, William J. McCormack, auxiliaries.

Former ordinaries: Richard L. Concanen, O.P., 1808-10; John Connolly, O.P., 1814-25; John Dubois, S.S., 1826-42; John J. Hughes, 1842-64, first archbishop; Cardinal John McCloskey, 1864-85; Michael A. Corrigan, 1885-1902; Cardinal John Farley, 1902-18; Cardinal Patrick Hayes, 1919-38; Cardinal Francis Spellman, 1939-67; Cardinal Terence J. Cooke, 1968-83.

Norwich, Conn. (1953): Daniel P. Reilly, bishop, 1975.

Former bishops: Bernard J. Flanagan, 1953-59; Vincent J. Hines, 1960-75.

Oakland, Calif. (1962): John S. Cummins, bishop, 1977.

Former bishop: Floyd L. Begin, 1962-77.

Ogdensburg, N.Y. (1872): Stanislaus J. Brzana, bishop, 1968.

Former bishops: Edgar P. Wadhams, 1872-91; Henry Gabriels, 1892-1921; Joseph H. Conroy, 1921-39; Francis J. Monaghan, 1939-42; Bryan J. McEntegart, 1943-53; Walter P. Kellenberg, 1954-57; James J. Navagh, 1957-63; Leo R. Smith, 1963; Thomas A. Donnellan, 1964-68.

Oklahoma City,* Okla. (1905; archdiocese, 1972): Charles A. Salatka, archbishop, 1977.

Former ordinaries: Theophile Meerschaert, 1905-24; Francis C. Kelley, 1924-48; Eugene J. McGuinness, 1948-57; Victor J. Reed, 1958-71; John R. Quinn, 1971-77, first archbishop.

Omaha,* Nebr. (1885; archdiocese, 1945): Daniel E. Sheehan, archbishop, 1969.

Former ordinaries: James O'Gorman, O.C.S.O., 1859-74, vicar apostolic; James O'Connor, vicar apostolic, 1876-85, first bishop, 1885-90; Richard Scannell, 1891-1916; Jeremiah J. Harty, 1916-27; Francis Beckman, administrator, 1926-28; Joseph F. Rummel, 1928-35; James H. Ryan, 1935-47, first archbishop; Gerald T. Bergan, 1948-69.

Orange, Calif. (1976): Norman F. McFarland, bishop, 1986.

Former bishop: William R. Johnson, 1976-86.

Orlando, Fla. (1968): Thomas J. Grady, bishop, 1974.

Former bishop: William Borders, 1968-74.

Owensboro, Ky. (1937): John J. McRaith, bishop, 1982.

Former bishops: Francis R. Cotton, 1938-60, Henry J. Soenneker, 1961-82.

Palm Beach, Fla. (1984): Thomas V. Daily, bishop, 1984.

Parma, Ohio (Byzantine Rite) (1969): Andrew Pataki, eparch, 1984.

Former bishop: Emil Mihalik, 1969-84.

Passaic, N.J. (Byzantine Rite) (1963): Michael J. Dudick, eparch, 1968. George M. Kuzma, auxiliary.

Former bishop: Stephen Kocisko, 1963-68.

Paterson, N.J. (1937): Frank J. Rodimer, bishop, 1978.

Former bishops: Thomas H. McLaughlin, 1937-47; Thomas A. Boland, 1947-52; James A. McNulty, 1953-63; James J. Navagh, 1963-65; Lawrence B. Casey, 1966-77.

Pensacola-Tallahassee, Fla. (1975): J. Keith Symons, bishop, 1983.

Former bishop: Rene H. Gracida, 1975-83.

Peoria, Ill. (1877): Edward W. O'Rourke, bishop, 1971. John J. Myers, Coadjutor, 1987.

Former bishops: John L. Spalding, 1877-1908; Edmund M. Dunne, 1909-29; Joseph H. Schlarman, 1930-51; William E. Cousins, 1952-58; John B. Franz, 1959-71.

Philadelphia,* Pa. (1808; archdiocese, 1875): Anthony J. Bevilacqua, archbishop, 1988. John J. Graham, Martin J. Lohmuller, Louis A. De Simone, auxiliaries.

Former ordinaries: Michael Egan, O.F.M., 1810-14; Henry Conwell, 1820-42; Francis P. Kenrick, 1842-51; John N. Neumann, C.SS.R., 1852-60; James F. Wood, 1860-83, first archbishop; Patrick J. Ryan, 1884-1911; Edmond F. Prendergast, 1911-18; Cardinal Dennis Dougherty, 1918-51; Cardinal John O'Hara, C.S.C., 1951-60; Cardinal John Krol, 1961-88.

Philadelphia,* Pa. (Byzantine Rite, Ukrainians) (1924; metropolitan, 1958): Stephen Sulyk, archbishop, 1981. Michael Kuchmiak, auxiliary.

Former ordinaries: Stephen Ortynsky, O.S.B.M., 1907-16; Constantine Bohachevsky, 1924-61; Ambrose Senyshyn, O.S.B.M., 1961-76; Joseph Schmondiuk, 1977-78; Myroslav J.

Lubachivsky, 1979-80, apostolic administrator, 1980-81.

Phoenix, Ariz. (1969): Thomas J. O'Brien, bishop, 1982.
Former bishops: Edward A. McCarthy, 1969-76; James S. Rausch, 1977-81.

Pittsburgh,* Pa. (Byzantine Rite, Ruthenians) (1924; metropolitan, 1969): Stephen J. Kocisko, eparch, 1968, first metropolitan, 1969. John M. Bilock, auxiliary.
Former ordinaries: Basil Takach 1924-48; Daniel Ivancho, 1948-54; Nicholas T. Elko, 1955-67.

Pittsburgh, Pa. (1843): Donald W. Wuerl, bishop, 1988. John B. McDowell, auxiliary.
Former bishops: Michael O'Connor, 1843-53, 1854-60; Michael Domenec, C.M., 1860-76; J. Tuigg, 1876-89; Richard Phelan, 1889-1904; J.F. Regis Canevin, 1904-20; Hugh C. Boyle, 1921-55; John F. Dearden, 1950-58; John J. Wright, 1959-69; Vincent M. Leonard, 1969-83; Anthony J. Bevilacqua, 1983-88.

Portland, Me. (1853): Edward C. O'Leary, bishop, 1974. Amedee W. Proulx, auxiliary.
Former bishops: David W. Bacon, 1855-74; James A. Healy, 1875-1900; William H. O'Connell, 1901-06; Louis S. Walsh, 1906-24; John G. Murray, 1925-31; Joseph E. McCarthy, 1932-55; Daniel J. Feeney, 1955-69; Peter L. Gerety, 1969-74.

Portland,* Ore. (1846): William J. Levada, archbishop, 1986. Paul E. Waldschmidt, C.S.C., Kenneth D. Steiner, auxiliaries.
Established as Oregon City, name changed, 1928.
Former ordinaries: Francis N. Blanchet, 1846-80 vicar apostolic, first archbishop; Charles J. Seghers, 1880-84; William H. Gross, C.SS.R., 1885-98; Alexander Christie, 1899-1925; Edward D. Howard, 1926-66; Robert J. Dwyer, 1966-74; Cornelius M. Power, 1974-86.

Providence, R.I. (1872): Louis E. Gelineau, bishop, 1972. Kenneth A. Angell, auxiliary.
Former bishops: Thomas F. Hendricken, 1872-86; Matthew Harkins, 1887-1921; William A. Hickey, 1921-33; Francis P. Keough, 1934-47; Russell J. McVinney, 1948-71.

Pueblo, Colo. (1941): Arthur N. Tafoya, bishop, 1980.
Former bishops: Joseph C. Willging, 1942-59; Charles A. Buswell, 1959-79.

Raleigh, N.C. (1924): F. Joseph Gossman, bishop, 1975.
Former bishops: William J. Hafey, 1925-37; Eugene J. McGuinness, 1937-44; Vincent S. Waters, 1945-75.

Rapid City, S. Dak. (1902): Charles J. Chaput, O.F.M. Cap., bishop, 1988.
Established at Lead, transferred, 1930.
Former bishops: John Stariha, 1902-09; Joseph F. Busch, 1910-15; John J. Lawler, 1916-48; William T. McCarty, C.SS.R., 1948-69; Harold J. Dimmerling, 1969-87.

Reno-Las Vegas, Nev. (1931): Daniel F. Walsh, bishop, 1987.
Established at Reno; title changed to Reno-Las Vegas, 1976.
Former bishops: Thomas K. Gorman, 1931-52;

Robert J. Dwyer, 1952-66; Joseph Green, 1967-74; Norman F. McFarland, 1976-86.

Richmond, Va. (1820): Walter F. Sullivan, bishop, 1974. David E. Foley, auxiliary.
Former bishops: Patrick Kelly, 1820-22; Richard V. Whelan, 1841-50; John McGill, 1850-72; James Gibbons, 1872-77; John J. Keane, 1878-88; Augustine Van de Vyver, 1889-1911; Denis J. O'Connell, 1912-26; Andrew J. Brennan, 1926-45; Peter L. Ireton, 1945-58; John J. Russell, 1958-73.

Rochester, N.Y. (1868): Matthew H. Clark, bishop, 1979. Dennis W. Hickey, auxiliary.
Former bishops: Bernard J. McQuaid, 1868-1909; Thomas F. Hickey, 1909-28; John F. O'Hern, 1929-33; Edward F. Mooney, 1933-37; James E. Kearney, 1937-66; Fulton J. Sheen, 1966-69; Joseph L. Hogan, 1969-78.

Rockford, Ill. (1908): Arthur J. O'Neill, bishop, 1968.
Former bishops: Peter J. Muldoon, 1908-27; Edward F. Hoban, 1928-42; John J. Boylan, 1943-53; Raymond P. Hillinger, 1953-56; Loras T. Lane, 1956-68.

Rockville Centre, N.Y. (1957): John R. McGann, bishop, 1976. James Daly, Alfred R. Markiewicz, auxiliaries.
Former bishop: Walter P. Kellenberg, 1957-76.

Sacramento, Calif. (1886): Francis A. Quinn, bishop, 1979. Alphonse Gallegos, O.A.R., auxiliary.
Former bishops: Patrick Manogue, 1886-95; Thomas Grace, 1896-1921; Patrick J. Keane, 1922-28; Robert J. Armstrong, 1929-57; Joseph T. McGucken, 1957-62; Alden J. Bell, 1962-79.

Saginaw, Mich. (1938): Kenneth E. Untener, bishop, 1980.
Former bishops: William F. Murphy, 1938-50; Stephen S. Woznicki, 1950-68; Francis F. Reh, 1969-80.

St. Augustine, Fla. (1870): John J. Snyder, bishop, 1979.
Former bishops: Augustin Verot, S.S., 1870-76; John Moore, 1877-1901; William J. Kenny, 1902-13; Michael J. Curley, 1914-21; Patrick J. Barry, 1922-40; Joseph P. Hurley, 1940-67; Paul F. Tanner, 1968-79.

St. Cloud, Minn. (1889): Jerome Hanus, O.S.B., bishop, 1987.
Former bishops: Otto Zardetti, 1889-94; Martin Marty, O.S.B., 1895-96; James Trobec, 1897-1914; Joseph F. Busch, 1915-53; Peter Bartholome, 1953-68; George H. Speltz, 1968-87.

St. George Martyr, Canton, Ohio (Byzantine Rite, Romanians) (1982; eparchy, 1987): Louis Puscas, exarch, 1983; first eparch, 1987.

St. Josaphat in Parma, Ohio (Byzantine Rite, Ukrainians) (1983): Robert M. Moskal, bishop, 1984.

St. Louis,* Mo. (1826; archdiocese, 1847): John L. May, archbishop, 1980. Charles R. Koester, Edward J. O'Donnell, J. Terry Steib, auxiliaries.
Former ordinaries: Joseph Rosati, C.M., 1827-43; Peter R. Kenrick, 1843-95, first archbishop; John J. Kain, 1895-1903; Cardinal John Glennon, 1903-46; Cardinal Joseph Ritter, 1946-67; Cardinal John J. Carberry, 1968-79.

St. Maron, Brooklyn, N.Y. (Maronite Rite)

(1966; diocese, 1971): Francis Zayek (titular archbishop), exarch, 1966, first eparch, 1972. John Chedid, auxiliary.
Established at Detroit; transferred to Brooklyn, 1977.
St. Nicholas in Chicago (Byzantine Rite Eparchy of St. Nicholas of the Ukrainians) (1961): Innocent H. Lotocky, O.S.B.M., bishop, 1981.
Former bishop: Jaroslav Gabro, 1961-80.
St. Paul and Minneapolis,* Minn. (1850; archdiocese, 1888): John R. Roach, archbishop, 1975. J. Richard Ham, M.M., Robert J. Carlson, auxiliaries.
Former ordinaries: Joseph Cretin, 1851-57; Thomas L. Grace, O.P., 1859-84; John Ireland, 1884-1918, first archbishop; Austin Dowling, 1919-30; John G. Murray, 1931-56; William O. Brady, 1956-61; Leo Binz, 1962-75.
St. Petersburg, Fla. (1968): W. Thomas Larkin, bishop, 1979.
Former bishop: Charles McLaughlin, 1968-78.
St. Thomas the Apostle of Detroit (Chaldean Rite) (1982; eparchy, 1985): Ibrahim N. Ibrahim, exarch, 1982; first eparch, 1985.
Salina, Kans. (1887): George K. Fitzsimons, bishop, 1984.
Established at Concordia, transferred, 1944.
Former bishops: Richard Scannell, 1887-91; John J. Hennessy, administrator, 1891-98; John F. Cunningham, 1898-1919; Francis J. Tief, 1921-38; Frank A. Thill, 1938-57; Frederick W. Freking, 1957-64; Cyril J. Vogel, 1965-79; Daniel W. Kucera, O.S.B., 1980-84.
Salt Lake City, Utah (1891): William K. Weigand, bishop, 1980.
Former bishops: Lawrence Scanlan, 1891-1915; Joseph S. Glass, C.M., 1915-26; John J. Mitty, 1926-32; James E. Kearney, 1932-37; Duane G. Hunt, 1937-60; J. Lennox Federal, 1960-80.
San Angelo, Tex. (1961): Michael D. Pfeifer, O.M.I., bishop, 1985.
Former bishops: Thomas J. Drury, 1962-65; Thomas Tschoepe, 1966-69; Stephen A. Leven, 1969-79; Joseph A. Fiorenza, 1979-84.
San Antonio,* Tex. (1874; archdiocese, 1926): Patrick F. Flores, archbishop, 1979. Bernard F. Popp, auxiliary.
Former ordinaries: Anthony D. Pellicer, 1874-80; John C. Neraz, 1881-94; John A. Forest, 1895-1911; John W. Shaw, 1911-18; Arthur Jerome Drossaerts, 1918-40, first archbishop; Robert E. Lucey, 1941-69; Francis Furey, 1969-79.
San Bernardino, Calif. (1978): Phillip F. Straling, bishop, 1978.
San Diego, Calif. (1936): Leo T. Maher, bishop, 1969. Gilbert Espinoza Chavez, auxiliary.
Former bishops: Charles F. Buddy, 1936-66; Francis J. Furey, 1966-69.
San Francisco,* Calif. (1853): John R. Quinn, archbishop, 1977.
Former ordinaries: Joseph S. Alemany, O.P., 1853-84; Patrick W. Riordan, 1884-1914; Edward J. Hanna, 1915-35; John Mitty, 1935-61; Joseph T. McGucken, 1962-77.
San Jose, Calif. (1981): R. Pierre DuMaine, first bishop, 1981.

Santa Fe,* N. Mex. (1850; archdiocese, 1875): Robert Sanchez, archbishop, 1974.
Former ordinaries: John B. Lamy, 1850-85, first archbishop; John B. Salpointe, 1885-94; Placide L. Chapelle, 1894-97; Peter Bourgade, 1899-1908; John B. Pitaval, 1909-18; Albert T. Daeger, O.F.M., 1919-32; Rudolph A. Gerken, 1933-43; Edwin V. Byrne, 1943-63; James P. Davis, 1964-74.
Santa Rosa, Calif. (1962): John T. Steinbock, bishop, 1987.
Former bishops: Leo T. Maher, 1962-69; Mark J. Hurley, 1969-86.
Savannah, Ga. (1850): Raymond W. Lessard, bishop, 1973.
Former bishops: Francis X. Gartland, 1850-54; John Barry, 1857-59; Augustin Verot, S.S., 1861-70; Ignatius Persico, O.F.M. Cap., 1870-72; William H. Gross, C.SS.R., 1873-85; Thomas A. Becker, 1886-99; Benjamin J. Keiley, 1900-22; Michael Keyes, S.M., 1922-35; Gerald P. O'Hara, 1935-59; Thomas J. McDonough, 1960-67; Gerard L. Frey, 1967-72.
Scranton, Pa. (1868): James C. Timlin, bishop, 1984. Francis X. Di Lorenzo, auxiliary.
Former bishops: William O'Hara, 1868-99; Michael J. Hoban, 1899-1926; Thomas C. O'Reilly, 1928-38; William J. Hafey, 1938-54; Jerome D. Hannan, 1954-65; J. Carroll McCormick, 1966-83; John J. O'Connor, 1983-84.
Seattle,* Wash. (1850; archdiocese, 1951): Raymond G. Hunthausen, archbishop, 1975. Thomas J. Murphy, coadjutor, 1987.
Established as Nesqually, name changed, 1907.
Former ordinaries; Augustin M. Blanchet, 1850-79; Aegidius Junger, 1879-95; Edward J. O'Dea, 1896-1932; Gerald Shaughnessy, S.M., 1933-50; Thomas A. Connolly, first archbishop, 1950-75.
Shreveport, La. (1986): William B. Friend, bishop, 1986.
Sioux City, Ia. (1902): Lawrence D. Soens, bishop, 1983.
Former bishops: Philip J. Garrigan, 1902-19; Edmond Heelan, 1919-48; Joseph M. Mueller, 1948-70; Frank H. Greteman, 1970-83.
Sioux Falls, S. Dak. (1889): Paul V. Dudley, bishop, 1978.
Former bishops: Martin Marty, O.S.B., 1889-94; Thomas O'Gorman, 1896-1921; Bernard J. Mahoney, 1922-39; William O. Brady, 1939-56; Lambert A. Hoch, 1956-78.
Spokane, Wash. (1913): Lawrence H. Welsh, bishop, 1978.
Former bishops: Augustine F. Schinner, 1914-25; Charles D. White, 1927-55; Bernard J. Topel, 1955-78.
Springfield, Ill. (1853): Daniel L. Ryan, bishop, 1984.
Established at Quincy, transferred to Alton 1857; transferred to Springfield 1923.
Former bishops: Henry D. Juncker, 1857-68; Peter J. Baltes, 1870-86; James Ryan, 1888-1923; James A. Griffin, 1924-48; William A. O'Connor, 1949-75; Joseph A. McNicholas, 1975-83.
Springfield, Mass. (1870): Joseph F. Maguire, bishop, 1977. Leo E. O'Neil, auxiliary.

Former bishops: Patrick T. O'Reilly, 1870-92; Thomas D. Beaven, 1892-1920; Thomas M. O'Leary, 1921-49; Christopher J. Weldon, 1950-77.

Springfield-Cape Girardeau, Mo. (1956): John J. Leibrecht, bishop, 1984.

Former bishops: Charles Helmsing, 1956-62; Ignatius J. Strecker, 1962-69; William Baum, 1970-73; Bernard F. Law, 1973-84.

Stamford, Conn. (Byzantine Rite, Ukrainians) (1956); Basil Losten, eparch, 1977.

Former eparchs: Ambrose Senyshyn, O.S.B.M., 1956-61; Joseph Schmondiuk, 1961-77.

Steubenville, Ohio (1944): Albert H. Ottenweller, bishop, 1977.

Former bishop: John K. Mussio, 1945-77.

Stockton, Calif. (1962): Donald W. Montrose, bishop, 1986.

Former bishops: Hugh A. Donohoe, 1962-69; Merlin J. Guilfoyle, 1969-79; Roger M. Mahony, 1980-85.

Superior, Wis. (1905): Raphael M. Fliss, bishop, 1985.

Former bishops: Augustine F. Schinner, 1905-13; Joseph M. Koudelka, 1913-21; Joseph G. Pinten, 1922-26; Theodore M. Reverman, 1926-41; William P. O'Connor, 1942-46; Albert G. Meyer, 1946-53; Joseph Annabring, 1954-59; George A. Hammes, 1960-85.

Syracuse, N.Y. (1886): Joseph T. O'Keefe, bishop, 1987. Thomas J. Costello, auxiliary.

Former bishops: Patrick A. Ludden, 1887-1912; John Grimes, 1912-22; Daniel J. Curley, 1923-32; John A. Duffy, 1933-37; Walter A. Foery, 1937-70; David F. Cunningham, 1970-76; Frank J. Harrison, 1976-87.

Toledo, Ohio (1910): James R. Hoffman, bishop, 1980. Robert Donnelly, auxiliary.

Former bishops: Joseph Schrembs, 1911-21; Samuel A. Stritch, 1921-30; Karl J. Alter, 1931-50; George J. Rehring, 1950-67; John A. Donovan, 1967-80.

Trenton, N.J. (1881): John C. Reiss, bishop, 1980. Edward U. Kmiec, auxiliary.

Former bishops: Michael J. O'Farrell, 1881-94; James A. McFaul, 1894-1917; Thomas J. Walsh, 1918-28; John J. McMahon, 1928-32; Moses E. Kiley, 1934-40; William A. Griffin, 1940-50; George W. Ahr, 1950-79.

Tucson, Ariz. (1897): Manuel D. Moreno, bishop, 1982.

Former bishops: Peter Bourgade, 1897-99; Henry Granjon, 1900-22; Daniel J. Gercke, 1923-60; Francis J. Green, 1960-81.

Tulsa, Okla. (1972): Eusebius J. Beltran, bishop, 1978.

Former bishop: Bernard J. Ganter, 1973-77.

Tyler, Tex. (1986): Charles E. Herzig, bishop, 1987.

Van Nuys, Calif. (Byzantine Rite, Ruthenians) (1981): Thomas V. Dolinay, bishop, 1982.

Venice, Fla. (1984): John J. Nevins, bishop, 1984.

Victoria, Tex. (1982): Charles Grahmann, bishop, 1982.

Washington,* **D.C.** (1939): Cardinal James A. Hickey, archbishop, 1980. Alvaro Corrada del Rio, S.J., auxiliary.

Former ordinaries: Michael J. Curley, 1939-47; Cardinal Patrick O'Boyle, 1948-73; Cardinal William Baum, 1973-80.

Wheeling-Charleston, W. Va. (1850): Francis B. Schulte, bishop, 1985. Bernard W. Schmitt, auxiliary.

Established as Wheeling; name changed, 1974.

Former bishops: Richard V. Whelan, 1850-74; John J. Kain, 1875-93; Patrick J. Donahue, 1894-1922; John J. Swint, 1922-62; Joseph H. Hodges, 1962-85.

Wichita, Kans. (1887): Eugene J. Gerber, bishop, 1982.

Former bishops: John J. Hennessy, 1888-1920; Augustus J. Schwertner, 1921-39; Christian H. Winkelmann, 1940-46; Mark K. Carroll, 1947-67; David M. Maloney, 1967-82.

Wilmington, Del. (1868): Robert E. Mulvee, bishop, 1985. James C. Burke, O.P., vicar for urban affairs.

Former bishops: Thomas A. Becker, 1868-86; Alfred A. Curtis, 1886-96; John J. Monaghan, 1897-1925; Edmond Fitzmaurice, 1925-60; Michael Hyle, 1960-67; Thomas J. Mardaga, 1968-84.

Winona, Minn. (1889): John G. Vlazny, bishop, 1987.

Former bishops: Joseph B. Cotter, 1889-1909; Patrick R. Heffron, 1910-27; Francis M. Kelly, 1928-49; Edward A. Fitzgerald, 1949-69; Loras J. Watters, 1969-86.

Worcester, Mass. (1950): Timothy J. Harrington, bishop, 1983. George E. Rueger, auxiliary.

Former bishops: John J. Wright, 1950-59; Bernard J. Flanagan, 1959-83.

Yakima, Wash. (1951): William Skylstad, bishop, 1977.

Former bishops: Joseph P. Dougherty, 1951-69; Cornelius M. Power, 1969-74; Nicholas E. Walsh, 1974-76.

Youngstown, Ohio (1943): James W. Malone, bishop, 1968. Benedict C. Franzetta, auxiliary.

Former bishops: James A. McFadden, 1943-52; Emmet M. Walsh, 1952-68.

Apostolic Exarchate for Armenian-Rite Catholics in the United States and Canada, New York, N.Y. (1981); Nerses Mikael Setian, exarch, 1981.

Archdiocese for the Military Services, U.S.A., Washington, D.C. (1957; restructured, 1985): Archbishop Joseph T. Ryan, military ordinary, 1985. Lawrence J. Kenney, Francis X. Roque, Joseph T. Dimino, Angelo T. Acerro, O.S.B., John G. Nolan, auxiliaries.

Military vicar appointed, 1917; canonically established, 1957, as U.S. Military Vicariate under jurisdiction of New York archbishop; name changed, restructured as independent jurisdiction, 1985.

Former military vicars: Cardinal Patrick Hayes, 1917-38; Cardinal Francis Spellman, 1939-67; Cardinal Terence J. Cooke, 1968-83; Cardinal John J. O'Connor, apostolic administrator, 1984-85.

Cardinal John Dearden was a "true man of the Church," said the Pope in a message read at the prelate's funeral Aug. 5, 1988 in Detroit.

MISSIONARY BISHOPS

Africa

Namibia (South West Africa): Keetmanshoop (vicariate apostolic), Edward F. Schlotterback, O.S.F.S.
South Africa: Keimos-Upington (diocese), John Minder, O.S.F.S.
Tanzania: Arusha (diocese), Dennis V. Durning, C.S.Sp.

Asia

Indonesia: Agats (diocese), Alphonse A. Sowada, O.S.C.
Iraq: Mossul (Chaldean-rite archdiocese), George Garmo.
Korea: Inchon (diocese), William J. McNaughton, M.M.
Philippines: Cotabato (archdiocese), Philip F. Smith, O.M.I.
Jolo (vicariate apostolic), Georges Dion, O.M.I.

Central America, West Indies

Dominican Republic: San Juan de la Maguana (diocese), Ronald G. Connors, C.SS.R.
Honduras: Comayagua (diocese), Gerald Scarpone, O.F.M.
Nicaragua: Bluefields (vicariate apostolic), Salvator Schlaefer Berg, O.F.M.Cap., vicar apostolic; Paul Schmitz, O.F.M. Cap., auxiliary.
Virgin Islands: St. Thomas (diocese), Sean O'Malley, O.F.M. Cap.

North America

Mexico: Mexico City (archdiocese), Ricardo Watty Urquidi, M.Sp.S., auxiliary.

Europe

Iceland: Reykjavik (diocese), Alfred Jolson, S.J.

Oceania

American Samoa: Samoa-Pago Pago (diocese), John Quinn Weitzel, M.M.
Caroline and Marshall Islands: Carolines-Marshalls (diocese), Martin J. Neylon, S.J.
Papua New Guinea: Mendi (diocese), Firmin Schmidt, O.F.M.Cap.
Wewak (diocese), Raymond P. Kalisz, S.V.D.
Vanuatu (New Hebrides): Port Vila (diocese), Francis Lambert, S.M.

South America

Bolivia: Coroico (diocese), Thomas R. Manning, O.F.M.
Pando (vicariate apostolic), Luis Morgan Casey.
Santa Cruz (archdiocese), Charles A. Brown, M.M., auxiliary.
Brazil: Abaetetuba (diocese), Angelo Frosi, S.X.
Belem do Para (archdiocese), Jude Prost, O.F.M., auxiliary.
Itaituba (prelacy), Capistran Heim, O.F.M.
Jatai (diocese), Benedict D. Coscia, O.F.M., bishop; Michael P. Mundo, auxiliary.
Paranagua (diocese), Bernard Nolker, C.SS.R.
Ruy Barbosa (diocese), Matthias W. Schmidt, O.S.B.
Sao Paulo (archdiocese), Alfred Novak, C.SS.R., auxiliary.
Sao Salvador da Bahia (archdiocese), Thomas W. Murphy, C.SS.R., auxiliary.
Peru: Chulucanas (prelacy), John C. McNabb Conway, O.S.A.

CATHOLIC POPULATION OF THE UNITED STATES

(Source: *The Official Catholic Directory, 1988*; figures as of Jan. 1, 1988. Archdioceses are indicated by an asterisk; for dioceses marked +, see Dioceses with Interstate Lines. Figures for the Chaldean-rite diocese of St. Thomas Apostle of Detroit are from the *Annuario Pontificio, 1988*, and are not included in Eastern Rite totals.)

Section, State Diocese	Catholics	Dioc. Priests	Rel. Priests	Total Priests	Perm. Deacons	Bros.	Sisters	Parishes
NEW ENGLAND	5,552,926	3,826	2,021	5,847	743	829	11,358	1,700
Maine, Portland	279,000	213	84	297	5	37	698	145
New Hampshire, Manchester	295,930	291	96	387	16	88	1,039	130
Vermont, Burlington	147,816	152	57	209	31	23	339	97
Massachusetts	2,842,040	1,881	1,370	3,251	261	454	5,770	778
*Boston	1,807,312	1,103	1,073	2,176	151	245	3,950	403
Fall River	350,000	204	140	344	36	34	518	112
Springfield	352,703	254	75	329	27	24	640	135
Worcester	332,025	320	82	402	47	151	662	128
Rhode Island, Providence	625,170	368	145	513	73	145	1,004	159
Connecticut	1,362,970	921	269	1,190	357	82	2,508	391
*Hartford	824,297	503	79	582	261	53	1,452	223
Bridgeport	331,761	272	117	389	48	5	715	91
Norwich+	206,912	146	73	219	48	24	341	77
MIDDLE ATLANTIC	13,424,319	8,975	4,036	13,011	1,608	1,587	29,517	3,891
New York	6,771,854	4,080	2,116	6,196	836	968	13,636	1,693
*New York	1,839,204	953	1,248	2,201	260	369	4,857	410
Albany	408,648	364	160	524	79	88	1,200	198

Section, State Diocese	Catholics	Dioc. Priests	Rel. Priests	Total Priests	Perm. Deacons	Bros.	Sisters	Par- ishes
New York								
Brooklyn	1,474,927	836	220	1,056	130	202	1,945	219
Buffalo	793,452	550	249	799	70	53	1,931	281
Ogdensburg	169,645	190	34	224	39	24	305	122
Rochester	386,390	334	84	418	65	82	934	161
Rockville Centre	1,337,498	482	40	522	151	119	1,839	130
Syracuse	362,090	371	81	452	42	31	625	172
New Jersey	**3,072,758**	**1,874**	**731**	**2,605**	**584**	**307**	**4,836**	**707**
*Newark	1,359,787	787	343	1,130	219	165	2,019	241
Camden	373,704	359	57	416	65	16	468	127
Metuchen	475,000	179	66	245	75	39	604	108
Paterson	355,578	288	197	485	75	38	1,084	108
Trenton	508,689	261	68	329	150	49	661	123
Pennsylvania	**3,579,707**	**3,021**	**1,189**	**4,210**	**188**	**312**	**11,045**	**1,491**
*Philadelphia	1,351,177	897	510	1,407	58	206	4,844	302
Allentown	250,084	300	85	385	32	19	852	153
Altoona-Johnstown	144,563	183	86	269	5	16	113	122
Erie	214,178	266	26	292	1	1	670	127
Greensburg	215,202	180	104	284	—	8	412	116
Harrisburg	218,212	179	65	244	64	12	701	111
Pittsburgh	835,790	607	203	810	24	44	2,422	318
Scranton	350,501	409	110	519	4	6	1,031	242
SOUTH ATLANTIC	**3,348,897**	**2,397**	**2,036**	**4,433**	**890**	**459**	**6,386**	**1,391**
Delaware, Wilmington+	134,598	126	95	221	42	34	387	56
Maryland, *Baltimore	438,016	401	352	753	163	110	1,564	160
District of Columbia								
*Washington+	395,016	349	676	1,025	154	73	1,050	135
Virginia	347,490	270	137	407	72	37	662	176
Arlington	215,213	95	91	186	61	26	263	58
Richmond	132,277	175	46	221	11	11	399	118
West Virginia								
Wheeling-Charleston	107,379	132	63	195	28	5	420	128
North Carolina	140,288	143	88	231	28	12	309	130
Charlotte	70,786	73	57	130	24	6	188	65
Raleigh	69,502	70	31	101	4	6	121	65
South Carolina, Charleston	75,382	75	66	141	30	30	220	84
Georgia	216,368	164	141	305	110	37	344	113
*Atlanta	154,928	97	101	198	74	25	159	65
Savannah	61,440	67	40	107	36	12	185	48
Florida	1,494,360	737	418	1,155	263	121	1,430	409
*Miami	596,650	219	146	365	72	58	432	105
Orlando	208,000	106	38	144	45	3	143	64
Palm Beach	146,630	67	56	123	25	4	204	42
Pensacola-Tallahassee	49,571	78	14	92	45	—	75	47
St. Augustine	85,920	90	15	105	10	1	120	48
St. Petersburg	281,317	109	101	210	47	45	338	61
Venice	126,272	68	48	116	19	10	118	42
EAST NORTH CENTRAL	**10,263,129**	**7,373**	**3,733**	**11,106**	**1,820**	**1,545**	**25,280**	**4,288**
Ohio	2,219,167	1,881	736	2,617	454	348	5,929	963
*Cincinnati	542,681	424	317	741	113	200	1,668	254
Cleveland	815,331	607	211	818	100	87	2,120	244
Columbus	198,607	220	80	300	45	6	562	109
Steubenville	50,419	144	12	156	—	8	118	77
Toledo	335,775	253	75	328	158	9	1,074	165
Youngstown	276,354	233	41	274	38	38	387	114
Indiana	695,551	713	415	1,128	99	236	2,205	448
*Indianapolis	203,800	195	141	336	—	67	867	142
Evansville	83,766	122	11	133	22	2	351	73
Ft. Wayne-South Bend	150,848	132	169	301	36	123	665	90
Gary	177,324	142	62	204	38	34	182	80
Lafayette	79,813	122	32	154	3	10	140	63

U.S. Catholic Statistics

Section, State Diocese	Catholics	Dioc. Priests	Rel. Priests	Total Priests	Perm. Deacons	Bros.	Sisters	Parishes
Illinois	**3,535,524**	**2,123**	**1,486**	**3,609**	**754**	**561**	**8,072**	**1,133**
*Chicago	2,350,000	1,179	1,049	2,228	503	390	4,946	437
Belleville	122,230	153	36	189	28	11	363	129
Joliet	435,000	210	157	367	104	115	948	114
Peoria	224,009	242	83	325	47	5	461	177
Rockford	225,514	166	78	244	72	17	501	99
Springfield	178,771	173	83	256	—	23	853	177
Michigan	**2,281,181**	**1,259**	**469**	**1,728**	**268**	**171**	**3,788**	**843**
*Detroit	1,484,443	579	321	900	153	135	2,119	331
Gaylord	87,863	66	18	84	7	4	115	85
Grand Rapids	150,432	142	31	173	17	3	457	91
Kalamazoo	96,461	62	26	88	21	9	298	51
Lansing	223,395	152	40	192	45	17	520	86
Marquette	79,487	122	9	131	4	—	114	85
Saginaw	159,100	136	24	160	21	3	165	114
Wisconsin	**1,531,706**	**1,397**	**627**	**2,024**	**245**	**229**	**5,286**	**901**
*Milwaukee	622,824	576	400	976	135	138	3,002	268
Green Bay	360,156	282	157	439	77	68	881	219
La Crosse	230,945	241	19	260	20	10	672	194
Madison	236,213	205	28	233	—	11	554	138
Superior	81,568	93	23	116	13	2	177	82
EAST SOUTH CENTRAL	**729,879**	**970**	**350**	**1,320**	**262**	**267**	**3,546**	**688**
Kentucky	**376,688**	**499**	**123**	**622**	**113**	**117**	**2,388**	**292**
*Louisville	206,403	234	89	323	95	108	1,341	130
Covington	115,203	187	20	207	18	8	735	87
Lexington	No separate statistics available.							
Owensboro	55,082	78	14	92	—	1	312	75
Tennessee	**127,220**	**168**	**52**	**220**	**89**	**57**	**385**	**125**
Knoxville	No separate statistics available.							
Memphis	47,967	74	16	90	31	45	139	39
Nashville	79,253	94	36	130	58	12	246	86
Alabama	**126,774**	**162**	**116**	**278**	**43**	**32**	**440**	**152**
*Mobile	66,548	94	61	155	22	13	263	77
Birmingham	60,226	68	55	123	21	19	177	75
Mississippi	**99,197**	**141**	**59**	**200**	**17**	**61**	**333**	**119**
Biloxi	54,857	64	27	91	7	49	63	44
Jackson	44,340	77	32	109	10	12	270	75
WEST NORTH CENTRAL	**3,420,294**	**3,842**	**1,455**	**5,297**	**739**	**711**	**12,932**	**2,952**
Minnesota	**1,097,821**	**925**	**330**	**1,255**	**148**	**190**	**3,305**	**726**
*St. Paul and Minneapolis	620,558	367	144	511	110	86	1,502	220
Crookston	41,303	49	15	64	1	3	252	42
Duluth	88,380	89	21	110	12	1	143	100
New Ulm	68,283	108	5	113	3	—	113	93
St. Cloud	152,912	159	135	294	22	68	742	147
Winona	126,385	153	10	163	—	32	553	124
Iowa	**510,388**	**816**	**63**	**879**	**142**	**34**	**1,980**	**553**
*Dubuque	216,792	325	41	366	51	24	1,309	233
Davenport	103,824	173	16	189	29	10	369	116
Des Moines	87,419	124	5	129	35	—	176	85
Sioux City	102,353	194	1	195	27	—	126	119
Missouri	**788,048**	**884**	**634**	**1,518**	**241**	**347**	**3,836**	**497**
*St. Louis	527,254	531	422	953	127	216	3,087	245
Jefferson City	87,903	124	23	147	50	17	126	95
Kansas City-St. Joseph	124,130	147	129	276	61	57	441	93
Springfield-Cape Girardeau	48,761	82	60	142	3	57	182	64
North Dakota	**173,436**	**213**	**60**	**273**	**58**	**26**	**494**	**185**
Bismarck	74,098	79	40	119	31	22	211	70
Fargo	99,338	134	20	154	27	4	283	115
South Dakota	**146,906**	**182**	**73**	**255**	**34**	**35**	**508**	**278**
Rapid City	36,274	44	36	80	22	19	86	121
Sioux Falls	110,632	138	37	175	12	16	422	157

Section, State Diocese	Catholics	Dioc. Priests	Rel. Priests	Total Priests	Perm. Deacons	Bros.	Sisters	Parishes
Nebraska	329,925	440	173	613	107	48	882	322
*Omaha	200,036	220	154	374	107	38	619	138
Grand Island	53,373	92	2	94	—	—	106	51
Lincoln	76,516	128	17	145	—	10	157	133
Kansas	373,770	382	122	504	9	31	1,927	391
*Kansas City	174,986	118	69	187	—	21	993	123
Dodge City	39,254	61	9	70	7	—	158	59
Salina	60,228	66	30	96	—	9	306	97
Wichita	99,302	137	14	151	2	1	470	112
WEST SOUTH CENTRAL	4,844,072	2,128	1,533	3,661	1,151	590	5,944	1,664
Arkansas, Little Rock	69,416	104	62	166	46	45	364	85
Louisiana	1,404,411	733	480	1,213	257	273	1,759	496
*New Orleans	554,837	266	276	542	134	199	1,139	144
Alexandria	48,350	65	14	79	9	6	72	47
Baton Rouge	206,374	91	55	146	21	17	144	73
Houma-Thibodaux	126,000	58	11	69	23	10	31	40
Lafayette	338,536	159	75	234	42	36	223	120
Lake Charles	89,616	47	29	76	21	2	43	36
Shreveport	40,698	47	20	67	7	3	107	36
Oklahoma	143,226	174	71	245	71	32	387	151
*Oklahoma City	87,666	102	41	143	41	25	178	67
Tulsa	55,560	72	30	102	30	7	209	84
Texas	3,227,019	1,117	920	2,037	777	240	3,434	932
*San Antonio	577,721	166	220	386	166	125	1,094	135
Amarillo	36,749	48	11	59	24	1	142	34
Austin	193,308	114	57	171	37	32	135	93
Beaumont	83,811	55	20	75	16	1	68	40
Brownsville	544,906	55	62	117	48	10	160	61
Corpus Christi	330,920	86	66	152	31	27	317	81
Dallas	200,796	104	74	178	96	3	229	55
El Paso	201,643	82	54	136	27	9	264	53
Fort Worth	145,542	59	46	105	27	10	143	81
Galveston-Houston	650,000	185	231	416	185	18	615	144
Lubbock	51,657	28	15	43	30	—	45	33
San Angelo	66,192	59	30	89	48	1	43	49
Tyler	28,774	18	17	35	30	2	68	27
Victoria	115,000	58	17	75	12	1	111	46
MOUNTAIN	2,000,919	1,204	780	1,984	491	227	2,767	858
Montana	130,194	192	37	229	16	5	243	123
Great Falls-Billings	66,092	86	26	112	3	5	149	66
Helena	64,102	106	11	117	13	—	94	57
Idaho, Boise	70,642	102	22	124	32	2	85	68
Wyoming, Cheyenne+	60,120	56	7	63	2	6	61	36
Colorado	485,236	268	229	497	117	48	938	195
*Denver	331,486	157	165	322	98	32	572	112
Colorado Springs	65,000	30	21	51	14	3	208	27
Pueblo	88,750	81	43	124	5	13	158	56
New Mexico	459,863	229	189	418	135	99	575	199
*Santa Fe	297,600	136	107	243	95	85	328	91
Gallup+	37,263	64	36	100	16	11	173	60
Las Cruces	125,000	29	46	75	24	3	74	48
Arizona	577,920	256	206	462	160	40	652	147
Phoenix	309,385	130	122	252	105	23	280	84
Tucson	268,535	126	84	210	55	17	372	63
Utah, Salt Lake City	69,944	54	50	104	24	19	98	43
Nevada, Reno-Las Vegas	147,000	47	40	87	5	8	115	47
PACIFIC	7,091,462	2,888	2,475	5,363	697	834	8,838	1,614
Washington	434,606	367	192	559	122	59	1,145	251
*Seattle	309,420	217	176	393	80	48	685	133
Spokane	75,132	97	5	102	31	10	412	78
Yakima	50,054	53	11	64	11	1	48	40

U.S. Catholic Statistics

Section, State Diocese	Catholics	Dioc. Priests	Rel. Priests	Total Priests	Perm. Deacons	Bros.	Sisters	Parishes
Oregon	282,390	215	257	472	6	91	810	161
*Portland	251,700	170	248	418	5	90	756	129
Baker	30,690	45	9	54	1	1	54	32
California	6,137,006	2,193	1,863	4,056	478	622	6,483	1,059
*Los Angeles	2,753,952	604	676	1,280	137	196	2,375	285
*San Francisco	386,000	245	282	527	13	42	1,067	103
Fresno	311,664	121	42	163	2	14	182	86
Monterey	148,693	75	34	109	2	35	285	45
Oakland	440,110	172	200	372	53	90	515	87
Orange	448,937	149	86	235	42	13	415	52
Sacramento	290,835	179	73	252	59	45	273	95
San Bernardino	360,993	150	80	230	59	20	202	90
San Diego	392,709	268	89	357	70	35	449	98
San Jose	348,773	97	250	347	18	90	528	46
Santa Rosa	107,068	87	19	106	7	36	121	41
Stockton	147,272	46	32	78	16	6	71	31
Alaska	45,940	50	49	99	60	11	92	77
*Anchorage	22,928	24	20	44	13	4	45	20
Fairbanks	16,217	11	27	38	38	7	36	49
Juneau	6,795	15	2	17	9	—	11	8
Hawaii, Honolulu	191,520	63	114	177	31	51	308	66
EASTERN RITES	530,616	577	118	695	57	20	344	550
*Philadelphia	77,098	67	11	78	2	1	107	81
St. Nicholas	17,000	33	13	46	8	1	11	32
Stamford	42,274	50	22	72	4	4	51	51
St. Josaphat (Parma)	11,999	36	3	39	1	—	8	35
*Pittsburgh	152,651	73	10	83	—	12	132	85
Parma	25,597	49	3	52	—	—	15	45
Passaic	87,231	99	18	117	11	1	14	93
Van Nuys	8,923	28	3	31	6	—	2	15
St. Maron (Maronites)	51,693	76	7	83	11	1	1	53
Newton (Melkites)	25,150	44	20	64	14	—	3	37
St. Thomas Apostle of Detroit (Chaldean)	45,000	10	—	10	—	—	9	10
St. George Martyr (Romanian)	5,000	18	1	19	—	—	—	16
Armenian (Ap. Ex.)	26,000	4	7	11	—	—	—	7
MILITARY ARCHDIOCESE	2,290,349	611	194	805	54	—	—	—
TOTALS 1988	53,496,862	34,791	18,731	53,522	8,512	7,069	106,912	19,596
Totals 1987	52,893,217	34,471	18,911	53,382	7,981	7,418	112,489	19,546
Totals 1978	49,836,176	35,766	22,719	58,485	2,498	8,460	129,391	18,625

Dioceses with Interstate Lines

Diocesan lines usually fall within a single state and in some cases include a whole state.

The following dioceses, with their statistics as reported in tables throughout the Almanac, are exceptions.

Norwich, Conn., includes Fisher's Island, N.Y.

Wilmington, Del., includes all of Delaware and nine counties of Maryland.

Washington, D.C., includes five counties of Maryland.

Gallup, N.M., has jurisdiction over several counties of Arizona.

Cheyenne, Wyo., includes all of Yellowstone National Park.

HUMAN DEVELOPMENT CAMPAIGN

The Campaign for Human Development was inaugurated by the U.S. Catholic Conference in November, 1969, to combat injustice, oppression, alienation and poverty in this country by funding self-help programs begun and carried out by the poor or by the poor and non-poor working together.

The campaign got under way with a collection taken up in all parishes throughout the country on Nov. 22, 1970. Seventy-five percent of the money contributed in this and subsequent annual collections was placed in a national fund principally for funding self-help projects and also for educational purposes; 25 percent remained in the dioceses where it was collected.

From 1970 to 1987, the campaign raised more than $140 million in contributions from U.S. Catholics, and approximately $103 million was disbursed by the national office.

The national office is located at 1312 Massachusetts Ave. N.W., Washington, D.C. 20005.

PERCENTAGE OF CATHOLICS IN U.S. POPULATION

(Source: *The Official Catholic Directory, 1988*; figures are as of Jan. 1, 1988. Total general population figures at the end of the table are U.S. Census Bureau estimates for Jan. 1 of the respective years. Archdioceses are indicated by an asterisk; for dioceses marked +, see Dioceses with Interstate Lines.)

Section, State Diocese	Catholic Pop.	Total Pop.	Cath. Pct.	Section, State Diocese	Catholic Pop.	Total Pop.	Cath. Pct.
NEW ENGLAND	5,552,926	12,600,561	44	Georgia	216,368	6,630,555	3
Maine, Portland	279,000	1,124,660	25	*Atlanta	154,928	4,457,143	3
New Hampshire				Savannah	61,440	2,173,412	3
Manchester	295,930	1,027,008	29	Florida	1,494,360	11,748,250	13
Vermont, Burlington	147,816	541,000	27	*Miami	596,650	3,146,000	19
Massachusetts	2,842,040	5,679,393	50	Orlando	208,000	2,290,600	9
*Boston	1,807,312	3,704,700	49	Palm Beach	146,630	1,071,081	14
Fall River	350,000	540,000	65	Pensacola-Tallahassee	49,571	1,012,500	5
Springfield	352,703	790,725	45	St. Augustine	85,920	1,138,000	8
Worcester	332,025	643,968	52	St. Petersburg	281,317	2,046,369	14
Rhode Island, Providence	625,170	986,000	63	Venice	126,272	1,043,700	12
Connecticut	1,362,970	3,242,500	42	**EAST NORTH**			
*Hartford	824,297	1,793,080	46	**CENTRAL**	10,263,129	41,516,316	25
Bridgeport	331,761	842,570	39	Ohio	2,219,167	10,764,839	21
Norwich+	206,912	606,850	34	*Cincinnati	542,681	2,728,200	20
MIDDLE ATLANTIC	13,424,319	37,622,284	36	Cleveland	815,331	2,776,200	29
				Columbus	198,607	2,006,700	10
New York	6,771,854	18,047,118	38	Steubenville	50,419	535,225	9
*New York	1,839,204	5,037,429	37	Toledo	335,775	1,486,614	23
Albany	408,648	1,472,684	28	Youngstown	276,354	1,231,900	22
Brooklyn	1,474,927	4,216,500	35	Indiana	695,551	5,360,025	13
Buffalo	793,452	1,599,000	50	*Indianapolis	203,800	2,127,915	10
Ogdensburg	169,645	396,245	43	Evansville	83,766	466,821	18
Rochester	386,390	1,446,355	27	Ft. Wayne-S. Bend	150,848	1,065,500	14
Rockville Centre	1,337,498	2,671,342	50	Gary	177,324	651,739	27
Syracuse	362,090	1,207,563	30	Lafayette	79,813	1,048,050	8
New Jersey	3,072,758	7,595,800	40	Illinois	3,535,524	11,490,981	31
*Newark	1,359,787	2,737,300	50	*Chicago	2,350,000	5,707,300	41
Camden	373,704	1,202,400	31	Belleville	122,230	861,986	14
Metuchen	475,000	1,036,900	46	Joliet	435,000	1,270,000	34
Paterson	355,578	1,003,700	35	Peoria	224,009	1,501,917	15
Trenton	508,689	1,615,500	31	Rockford	225,514	1,016,100	22
Pennsylvania	3,579,707	11,979,366	30	Springfield	178,771	1,133,678	16
*Philadelphia	1,351,177	3,736,800	36	Michigan	2,281,181	9,010,107	25
Allentown	250,084	1,032,206	24	*Detroit	1,484,443	4,230,200	35
Altoona-Johnstown	144,563	643,800	22	Gaylord	87,863	401,200	22
Erie	214,178	886,000	24	Grand Rapids	150,432	906,483	17
Greensburg	215,202	721,210	30	Kalamazoo	96,461	867,500	11
Harrisburg	218,212	1,801,300	12	Lansing	223,395	1,575,000	14
Pittsburgh	835,790	2,165,361	39	Marquette	79,487	316,304	25
Scranton	350,501	992,689	35	Saginaw	159,100	713,420	22
				Wisconsin	1,531,706	4,890,364	31
SOUTH ATLANTIC	3,348,897	41,321,988	8	*Milwaukee	622,824	2,011,900	31
				Green Bay	360,156	873,671	41
Delaware, Wilmington+	134,598	814,300	17	La Crosse	230,945	751,203	31
Maryland, *Baltimore	438,016	2,508,947	17	Madison	236,213	944,852	25
District of Columbia				Superior	81,568	308,738	26
*Washington+	395,016	2,188,000	18	**EAST SOUTH**			
Virginia	347,490	5,856,990	6	**CENTRAL**	729,879	14,456,390	5
Arlington	215,213	1,682,800	13				
Richmond	132,277	4,174,190	3	Kentucky	376,688	3,697,674	10
West Virginia				*Louisville	206,403	1,301,024	16
Wheeling-Charleston	107,379	1,919,000	6	Covington	115,203	1,630,900	7
North Carolina	140,288	6,230,946	2	Lexington	No separate statistics available.		
Charlotte	70,786	3,337,000	2	Owensboro	55,082	765,750	7
Raleigh	69,502	2,893,946	2	Tennessee	127,220	4,745,400	3
South Carolina				Knoxville	No separate statistics available.		
Charleston	75,382	3,425,000	2	Memphis	47,967	1,326,000	4

U.S. Catholic Statistics

Section, State Diocese	Catholic Pop.	Total Pop.	Cath. Pct.	Section, State Diocese	Catholic Pop.	Total Pop.	Cath. Pct.
Tennessee				Texas			
Nashville	79,253	3,419,400	2	Austin	193,308	1,623,183	12
Alabama	126,774	3,464,335	4	Beaumont	83,811	512,650	16
*Mobile	66,548	1,422,835	5	Brownsville	544,906	681,132	80
Birmingham	60,226	2,041,500	3	Corpus Christi	330,920	658,670	50
Mississippi	99,197	2,548,981	4	Dallas	200,796	2,424,900	8
Biloxi	54,857	638,981	9	El Paso	201,643	636,563	32
Jackson	44,340	1,910,000	2	Fort Worth	145,542	1,900,100	8
				Galveston-Houston	650,000	3,715,950	17
WEST NORTH CENTRAL	**3,420,294**	**17,273,264**	**20**	Lubbock	51,657	501,000	10
				San Angelo	66,192	604,958	11
				Tyler	28,774	1,167,000	2
Minnesota	1,097,821	4,072,371	27	Victoria	115,000	223,100	52
*St. Paul and				**MOUNTAIN**	**2,000,919**	**12,835,667**	**16**
Minneapolis	620,558	2,173,572	29	Montana	130,194	766,553	17
Crookston	41,303	239,045	17	Great Falls-Billings	66,092	351,858	19
Duluth	88,380	425,987	21	Helena	64,102	414,695	15
New Ulm	68,283	291,014	23	Idaho, Boise	70,642	1,002,000	7
St. Cloud	152,912	409,791	37	Wyoming, Cheyenne+	60,120	482,088	12
Winona	126,385	532,962	24	Colorado	485,236	3,239,671	15
Iowa	510,388	2,895,039	18	*Denver	331,486	2,281,471	15
*Dubuque	216,792	995,648	22	Colorado Springs	65,000	480,700	14
Davenport	103,824	733,591	14	Pueblo	88,750	477,500	19
Des Moines	87,419	675,500	13	New Mexico	459,863	1,543,585	30
Sioux City	102,353	490,300	21	*Santa Fe	297,600	825,000	36
Missouri	788,048	4,954,295	16	Gallup+	37,263	355,340	10
*St. Louis	527,254	1,959,500	27	Las Cruces	125,000	363,245	34
Jefferson City	87,903	737,020	12	Arizona	577,920	3,121,200	19
Kansas City-St. Joseph	124,130	1,260,051	10	Phoenix	309,385	2,150,200	14
Springfield-				Tucson	268,535	971,000	28
Cape Girardeau	48,761	997,724	5	Utah, Salt Lake City	69,944	1,678,000	4
North Dakota	173,436	677,689	26	Nevada, Reno-Las Vegas	147,000	1,002,570	15
Bismarck	74,098	287,289	26	**PACIFIC**	**7,091,462**	**36,093,925**	**20**
Fargo	99,338	390,400	25	Washington	434,606	4,400,826	10
South Dakota	146,906	698,316	21	*Seattle	309,420	3,423,700	9
Rapid City	36,274	202,816	18	Spokane	75,132	584,626	13
Sioux Falls	110,632	495,500	22	Yakima	50,054	392,500	13
Nebraska	329,925	1,567,902	21	Oregon	282,390	2,690,550	10
*Omaha	200,036	750,259	27	*Portland	251,700	2,338,600	11
Grand Island	53,373	306,000	17	Baker	30,690	351,950	9
Lincoln	76,516	511,643	15	California	6,137,006	27,538,436	22
Kansas	373,770	2,407,652	16	*Los Angeles	2,753,952	9,364,000	29
*Kansas City	174,986	952,000	18	*San Francisco	386,000	1,650,000	23
Dodge City	39,254	228,252	17	Fresno	311,664	1,775,614	18
Salina	60,228	342,800	18	Monterey	148,693	743,467	20
Wichita	99,302	884,600	11	Oakland	440,110	1,948,520	23
				Orange	448,937	2,216,800	20
WEST SOUTH CENTRAL	**4,844,072**	**26,531,927**	**18**	Sacramento	290,835	2,309,995	13
				San Bernardino	360,993	2,117,400	17
Arkansas, Little Rock	69,416	2,360,000	3	San Diego	392,709	2,467,915	16
Louisiana	1,404,411	4,444,421	32	San Jose	348,773	1,401,600	25
*New Orleans	554,837	1,433,355	39	Santa Rosa	107,068	704,600	15
Alexandria	48,350	431,400	11	Stockton	147,272	838,525	18
Baton Rouge	206,374	774,431	27	Alaska	45,940	401,769	11
Houma-Thibodaux	126,000	202,000	62	*Anchorage	22,928	205,000	11
Lafayette	338,536	561,977	60	Fairbanks	16,217	126,000	13
Lake Charles	89,616	270,500	33	Juneau	6,795	70,769	10
Shreveport	40,698	770,758	5	Hawaii, Honolulu	191,520	1,062,344	18
Oklahoma	143,226	3,106,100	5	**EASTERN RITES**	**530,616**	—	—
*Oklahoma City	87,666	1,849,600	5	**MILITARY**			
Tulsa	55,560	1,256,500	4	**ARCHDIOCESE**	**2,290,000**	—	—
Texas	3,227,019	16,621,406	19	**TOTALS 1988**	**53,496,862**	**244,427,098**	**22**
*San Antonio	577,721	1,611,700	36	Totals 1987	52,893,217	242,085,811	22
Amarillo	36,749	360,500	10	Totals 1978	49,836,176	216,287,455	23

INFANT BAPTISMS AND CONVERTS IN THE UNITED STATES

(Source: *The Official Catholic Directory, 1988;* figures as of Jan. 1, 1988. Archdioceses are indicated by an asterisk; for dioceses marked +, see Dioceses with Interstate Lines. Figure for the Chaldean-rite diocese of St. Thomas the Apostle of Detroit is from the *Annuario Pontificio, 1988,* and is not included in Eastern Rite totals.)

Section, State Diocese	Infant Baptisms	Converts
NEW ENGLAND	85,654	2,637
Maine, Portland	3,909	346
New Hampshire, Manchester	5,664	142
Vermont, Burlington	2,194	143
Massachusetts	45,547	1,165
*Boston	29,565	584
Fall River	5,682	128
Springfield	5,122	216
Worcester	5,178	237
Rhode Island, Providence	7,413	154
Connecticut	20,927	687
*Hartford	12,352	340
Bridgeport	5,240	153
Norwich+	3,335	194
MIDDLE ATLANTIC	230,194	12,182
New York	128,133	5,124
*New York	32,302	1,344
Albany	8,494	256
Brooklyn	40,124	776
Buffalo	9,503	509
Ogdensburg	2,524	310
Rochester	6,937	760
Rockville Centre	20,906	664
Syracuse	7,343	505
New Jersey	48,958	2,173
*Newark	18,240	509
Camden	7,168	710
Metuchen	6,626	194
Paterson	7,520	309
Trenton	9,404	451
Pennsylvania	53,103	4,885
*Philadelphia	20,865	1,645
Allentown	4,007	190
Altoona-Johnstown	2,039	265
Erie	3,425	368
Greensburg	2,712	338
Harrisburg	3,882	619
Pittsburgh	10,897	1,054
Scranton	5,276	406
SOUTH ATLANTIC	66,457	8,684
Delaware, Wilmington+	2,814	175
Maryland, *Baltimore	8,783	1,123
District of Columbia, *Washington+	7,101	713
Virginia	7,740	944
Arlington	4,673	411
Richmond	3,067	533
West Virginia, Wheeling-Charleston	1,559	580
North Carolina	2,846	655
Charlotte	1,417	310
Raleigh	1,429	345
South Carolina, Charleston	1,688	413
Georgia	4,219	1,083
*Atlanta	2,979	686
Savannah	1,240	397
Florida	29,707	2,998
*Miami	14,110	677
Orlando	4,044	633
Pensacola-Tallahassee	1,000	275
Palm Beach	3,022	335
St. Augustine	1,722	280
St. Petersburg	3,761	572
Venice	2,048	226
EAST NORTH CENTRAL	160,335	19,564
Ohio	34,673	5,406
*Cincinnati	9,149	1,689
Cleveland	11,511	1,605
Columbus	3,659	518
Steubenville	1,090	278
Toledo	5,436	781
Youngstown	3,828	535
Indiana	11,632	2,919
*Indianapolis	3,989	1,165
Evansville	1,335	230
Ft. Wayne-South Bend	2,589	819
Gary	2,268	298
Lafayette	1,451	407
Illinois	57,666	5,169
*Chicago	36,153	2,100
Belleville	2,010	471
Joliet	8,455	589
Peoria	3,523	777
Rockford	4,376	491
Springfield	3,149	741
Michigan	31,807	3,976
*Detroit	17,604	1,789
Gaylord	1,345	178
Grand Rapids	3,220	420
Kalamazoo	1,484	330
Lansing	4,047	744
Marquette	1,436	148
Saginaw	2,671	367
Wisconsin	24,557	2,094
*Milwaukee	10,698	769
Green Bay	4,775	290
La Crosse	3,967	443
Madison	3,604	299
Superior	1,513	293
EAST SOUTH CENTRAL	13,210	3,836
Kentucky	6,563	1,442
*Louisville	3,461	653
Covington	2,072	497
Lexington	No separate statistics available.	
Owensboro	1,030	292
Tennessee	2,513	936
Knoxville	No separate statistics available.	
Memphis	950	319
Nashville	1,563	617
Alabama	2,242	836
*Mobile	1,207	390
Birmingham	1,035	446

U.S. Catholic Statistics

Section, State Diocese	Infant Baptisms	Converts
Mississippi	1,892	622
Biloxi	1,124	281
Jackson	768	341
WEST NORTH CENTRAL	**66,914**	**10,748**
Minnesota	21,679	1,849
*St. Paul and Minneapolis	12,351	1,054
Crookston	794	79
Duluth	1,411	117
New Ulm	1,379	137
St. Cloud	3,284	186
Winona	2,460	276
Iowa	9,877	1,721
*Dubuque	3,924	526
Davenport	2,213	567
Des Moines	1,721	349
Sioux City	2,019	279
Missouri	14,202	3,179
*St. Louis	9,584	1,721
Jefferson City	1,414	400
Kansas City-St. Joseph	2,481	565
Springfield-Cape Girardeau	723	493
North Dakota	3,522	312
Bismarck	1,687	103
Fargo	1,835	209
South Dakota	3,229	518
Rapid City	932	176
Sioux Falls	2,297	342
Nebraska	6,707	1,611
*Omaha	4,239	892
Grand Island	1,070	221
Lincoln	1,398	498
Kansas	7,698	1,558
*Kansas City	3,175	653
Dodge City	1,017	125
Salina	1,183	245
Wichita	2,323	535
WEST SOUTH CENTRAL	**100,313**	**7,776**
Arkansas, Little Rock	1,370	459
Louisiana	23,321	1,525
*New Orleans	8,215	719
Alexandria	851	123
Baton Rouge	3,001	—
Houma-Thibodaux	2,067	65
Lafayette	6,788	232
Lake Charles	1,685	193
Shreveport	714	193
Oklahoma	2,833	837
*Oklahoma City	1,845	521
Tulsa	988	316
Texas	72,789	4,955
*San Antonio	13,569	380
Amarillo	1,030	108
Austin	3,833	667
Beaumont	1,439	282
Brownsville	7,367	72
Corpus Christi	6,874	232
Dallas	5,706	835
El Paso	7,057	88
Fort Worth	4,243	558
Galveston-Houston	14,129	1,311
Lubbock	2,206	50
San Angelo	2,546	168
Tyler	880	129
Victoria	1,910	75
MOUNTAIN	**43,471**	**4,502**
Montana	2,418	834
Great Falls	1,386	206
Helena	1,032	628
Idaho, Boise	1,866	383
Wyoming, Cheyenne+	1,394	247
Colorado	11,368	1,122
*Denver	8,776	799
Colorado Springs	1,225	162
Pueblo	1,367	161
New Mexico	9,655	514
*Santa Fe	6,386	266
Gallup+	1,043	153
Las Cruces	2,226	95
Arizona	12,288	747
Phoenix	6,878	645
Tucson	5,410	102
Utah, Salt Lake City	1,694	317
Nevada, Reno-Las Vegas	2,788	338
PACIFIC	**156,798**	**9,965**
Washington	8,590	1,576
*Seattle	5,558	1,027
Spokane	1,423	396
Yakima	1,609	153
Oregon	3,821	915
*Portland	3,264	768
Baker	557	147
California	139,002	7,085
*Los Angeles	61,726	2,129
*San Francisco	6,892	445
Fresno	11,367	421
Monterey	3,750	264
Oakland	7,485	560
Orange	12,256	723
Sacramento	7,231	561
San Bernardino	5,508	501
San Diego	9,446	682
San Jose	7,642	471
Santa Rosa	2,185	163
Stockton	3,514	165
Alaska	1,307	169
*Anchorage	704	130
Fairbanks	481	23
Juneau	122	16
Hawaii, Honolulu	4,078	220
EASTERN RITES	**3,643**	**286**
*Philadelphia	404	12
St. Nicholas	255	6
Stamford	294	8
St. Josaphat (Parma)	179	23
*Pittsburgh	870	102
Parma	247	28
Passaic	571	33
Van Nuys	66	11
St. Maron (Maronites)	577	53
Newton (Melkites)	—	—
St. Thomas Apostle of Detroit (Chaldeans)	767	—
St. George Martyr (Romanian)	45	10
Armenians (Ap. Ex.)	135	—
MILITARY ARCHDIOCESE	**10,958**	**1,559**
TOTALS 1988	**937,947**	**81,739**
Totals 1987	941,898	80,703
Totals 1978	890,677	78,598

STATISTICAL SUMMARY OF THE CHURCH IN THE U.S.

(Principal source: *The Official Catholic Directory, 1988.* Comparisons, where given, are with figures reported in the previous edition of the *Directory.*)

Catholic Population: 53,496,862; increase, 603,645. Percent of total population, 21.88.

Jurisdictions: 34 archdioceses (includes Military Archdiocese), 154 dioceses, 1 apostolic exarchate (New York-based Armenian exarchate for U.S. and Canada).

Cardinals: 10 (5 head archiepiscopal sees in U.S., 1, in Europe; 1 is a Roman Curia official; 3 are retired). As of Sept. 1, 1988.

Archbishops: 58. Diocesan, in U.S., 34 (includes 5 cardinals and the Military Archbishop); coadjutor, 1; retired, 15 (includes 3 cardinals); outside U.S., 8 (includes 1 cardinal). As of Sept. 1, 1988.

Bishops: 391. Diocesan, in U.S., 150 (2 are titular archbishops); coadjutors, 2; exarch, 1; auxiliaries, 107; retired, 97; serving outside U.S., 34. As of Sept. 1, 1988.

Priests: 53,522; increase, 140. Diocesan, 34,791 (increase, 320); religious order priests (does not include those assigned overseas), 18,731 (decrease, 180).

Permanent Deacons: 8,512; increase, 531.

Brothers: 7,069; decrease, 349.

Sisters: 106,912; decrease, 5,577.

Seminarians: 7,512. Diocesan seminarians, 4,981; religious order seminarians, 2,531.

Infant Baptisms: 937,947; decrease, 3,951.
Converts: 81,739; increase, 1,036.
Marriages: 341,622; decrease, 818.
Deaths: 453,290; increase, 22,938.
Parishes: 19,596; increase, 50.
Seminaries, Diocesan: 74; decrease, 2.
Religious Seminaries: 176; increase, 13.
Colleges and Universities: 233; decrease, 5. Students, 563,799; increase, 7,462.
High Schools: 1,391; decrease, 17. Students, 708,189; decrease, 46,525.
Elementary Schools: 7,659; decrease, 113. Students, 1,989,466; decrease, 41,132.
Teachers: 163,232; decrease, 6,714. Priests, 3,483 (decrease, 255); brothers, 2,139 (decrease, 126); scholastics, 140 (decrease, 59); sisters, 23,153 (decrease, 3,421); laity, 134,317 (decrease, 2,853).
Public School students in Religious Instruction Programs: 3,849,607; decrease, 11,433. High school students, 904,775 (decrease, 83,677); elementary school students, 3,044,832 (increase, 72,244).
Hospitals: 646; patients treated, 40,039,956.
Dispensaries: 162; patients treated, 1,509,143.
Homes for Special Care: 688; patients treated, 109,723.
Child Welfare Centers: 722; total assisted, 75,680.
Nurseries: 245; total assisted, 23,509.
Special Social Centers: 1,542; total assisted, 4,979,995.

CATHEDRALS IN THE UNITED STATES

A cathedral is the principal church in a diocese, the one in which the bishop has his seat (*cathedra*). He is the actual rector, although many functions of the church, which usually serves a parish, are the responsibility of a priest serving as the administrator. Because of the dignity of a cathedral, the dates of its dedication and its patronal feast are observed throughout a diocese.

The pope's cathedral, the Basilica of St. John Lateran, is the highest-ranking church in the world.

(Archdioceses are indicated by asterisk.)

Albany, N.Y.: Immaculate Conception.
Alexandria, La.: St. Francis Xavier.
Allentown, Pa.: St. Catherine of Siena.
Altoona-Johnstown, Pa.: Blessed Sacrament (Altoona); St. John Gualbert (Johnstown Co-Cathedral).
Amarillo, Tex.: St. Laurence.
Anchorage,* Alaska: Holy Family.
Arlington, Va: St. Thomas More.
Atlanta,* Ga.: Christ the King.
Austin, Tex.: St. Mary (Immaculate Conception).
Baker, Ore.: St. Francis de Sales.
Baltimore,* Md.: Mary Our Queen; Basilica of the Assumption of the Blessed Virgin Mary (Co-Cathedral).
Baton Rouge, La.: St. Joseph.
Beaumont, Tex.: St. Anthony (of Padua).
Belleville, Ill.: St. Peter.
Biloxi, Miss.: Nativity of the Blessed Virgin Mary.
Birmingham, Ala.: St. Paul.
Bismarck, N.D.: Holy Spirit.
Boise, Ida.: St. John the Evangelist.
Boston,* Mass.: Holy Cross.
Bridgeport, Conn.: St. Augustine.
Brooklyn, N.Y.: St. James (Minor Basilica).
Brownsville, Tex.: Immaculate Conception.
Buffalo, N.Y.: St. Joseph.
Burlington, Vt.: Immaculate Conception.
Camden, N.J.: Immaculate Conception.
Charleston, S.C.: St. John the Baptist.
Charlotte, N.C.: St. Patrick.
Cheyenne, Wyo.: St. Mary.
Chicago,* Ill.: Holy Name (of Jesus).
Cincinnati,* Ohio: St. Peter in Chains.
Cleveland, Ohio: St. John the Evangelist.
Colorado Springs, Colo: St. Mary.
Columbus, Ohio: St. Joseph.
Corpus Christi, Tex.: Corpus Christi.
Covington, Ky.: Basilica of the Assumption.
Crookston, Minn.: Immaculate Conception.
Dallas, Tex.: Cathedral-Santuario de Guadalupe.
Davenport, Ia.: Sacred Heart.
Denver,* Colo.: Immaculate Conception (Minor Basilica).
Des Moines, Ia.: St. Ambrose.
Detroit,* Mich.: Most Blessed Sacrament.
Dodge City, Kans.: Sacred Heart.
Dubuque,* Ia.: St. Raphael.
Duluth, Minn.: Our Lady of the Rosary.
El Paso, Tex.: St. Patrick.

Cathedrals

Erie, Pa.: St. Peter.
Evansville, Ind.: Most Holy Trinity (Pro-Cathedral).
Fairbanks, Alaska: Sacred Heart.
Fall River, Mass.: St. Mary of the Assumption.
Fargo, N.D.: St. Mary.
Fort Wayne-S. Bend, Ind.: Immaculate Conception (Fort Wayne); St. Matthew (South Bend Co-Cathedral).
Fort Worth, Tex.: St. Patrick.
Fresno, Calif.: St. John (the Baptist).
Gallup, N.M.: Sacred Heart.
Galveston-Houston, Tex.: St. Mary (Minor Basilica, Galveston); Sacred Heart (Houston Co-Cathedral).
Gary, Ind.: Holy Angels.
Gaylord, Mich.: St. Mary, Our Lady of Mt. Carmel.
Grand Island, Nebr.: Nativity of Blessed Virgin Mary.
Grand Rapids, Mich.: St. Andrew.
Great Falls-Billings, Mont.: St. Ann (Great Falls); St. Patrick (Billings Co-Cathedral).
Green Bay, Wis.: St. Francis Xavier.
Greensburg, Pa.: Blessed Sacrament.
Harrisburg, Pa.: St. Patrick.
Hartford,* Conn.: St. Joseph.
Helena, Mont.: St. Helena.
Honolulu, Hawaii: Our Lady of Peace; St. Theresa of the Child Jesus (Co-Cathedral).
Houma-Thibodaux, La.: St. Francis de Sales (Houma); St. Joseph (Thibodaux Co-Cathedral).
Indianapolis,* Ind.: Sts. Peter and Paul.
Jackson, Miss.: St. Peter.
Jefferson City, Mo.: St. Joseph.
Joliet, Ill.: St. Raymond Nonnatus.
Juneau, Alaska: Nativity of the Blessed Virgin Mary.
Kalamazoo, Mich.: St. Augustine.
Kansas City,* Kans.: St. Peter the Apostle.
Kansas City-St. Joseph, Mo.: Immaculate Conception (Kansas City); St. Joseph (St. Joseph Co-Cathedral).
Knoxville, Tenn.: Sacred Heart of Jesus.
La Crosse, Wis.: St. Joseph.
Lafayette, Ind.: St. Mary.
Lafayette, La.: St. John the Evangelist.
Lake Charles, La.: Immaculate Conception.
Lansing, Mich.: St. Mary.
Las Cruces, N. Mex.: Immaculate Heart of Mary.
Lexington, Ky.: Christ the King.
Lincoln, Nebr.: Cathedral of the Risen Christ.
Little Rock, Ark.: St. Andrew.
Los Angeles,* Calif.: St. Vibiana.
Louisville,* Ky.: Assumption.
Lubbock, Tex.: Christ the King.
Madison, Wis.: St. Raphael.
Manchester, N.H.: St. Joseph.
Marquette, Mich.: St. Peter.
Memphis, Tenn.: Immaculate Conception.
Metuchen, N.J.: St. Francis (of Assisi).
Miami,* Fla.: St. Mary (Immaculate Conception).
Milwaukee,* Wis.: St. John.
Mobile,* Ala.: Immaculate Conception (Minor Basilica).
Monterey, Calif.: San Carlos Borromeo.
Nashville, Tenn.: Incarnation.
Newark,* N.J.: Sacred Heart.
New Orleans,* La.: Cathedral (Basilica) of St. Louis.
Newton, Mass. (Melkite Rite): Our Lady of the Annunciation (Boston).
New Ulm, Minn.: Holy Trinity.
New York,* N.Y.: St. Patrick.
Norwich, Conn.: St. Patrick.
Oakland, Calif.: St. Francis de Sales.
Ogdensburg, N.Y.: St. Mary (Immaculate Conception).
Oklahoma City,* Okla.: Our Lady of Perpetual Help.
Omaha,* Nebr.: St. Cecilia.
Orange, Calif.: Holy Family.
Orlando, Fla.: St. James.
Owensboro, Ky.: St. Stephen.
Palm Beach, Fla.: St. Ignatius Loyola, Palm Beach Gardens.
Parma, Ohio (Byzantine Rite): St. John the Baptist.
Passaic, N.J. (Byzantine Rite): St. Michael.
Paterson, N.J.: St. John the Baptist.
Pensacola-Tallahassee, Fla.: Sacred Heart (Pensacola); St. Thomas More (Tallahassee Co-Cathedral).
Peoria, Ill.: St. Mary.
Philadelphia,* Pa.: Sts. Peter and Paul (Minor Basilica).
Philadelphia,* Pa. (Byzantine Rite): Immaculate Conception.
Phoenix, Ariz.: Sts. Simon and Jude.
Pittsburgh,* Pa. (Byzantine Rite): St. John the Baptist, Munhall.
Pittsburgh, Pa.: St. Paul.
Portland, Me.: Immaculate Conception.
Portland,* Ore.: Immaculate Conception.
Providence, R.I.: Sts. Peter and Paul.
Pueblo, Colo.: Sacred Heart.
Raleigh, N.C.: Sacred Heart.
Rapid City, S.D.: Our Lady of Perpetual Help.
Reno-Las Vegas, Nev.: St. Thomas Aquinas (Reno), Guardian Angel (Las Vegas Co-Cathedral).
Richmond, Va.: Sacred Heart.
Rochester, N.Y.: Sacred Heart.
Rockford, Ill.: St. Peter.
Rockville Centre, N.Y.: St. Agnes.
Sacramento, Calif.: Blessed Sacrament.
Saginaw, Mich.: St. Mary.
St. Augustine, Fla.: St. Augustine (Minor Basilica).
St. Cloud, Minn.: St. Mary.
St. George Martyr, Canton, Ohio (Byzantine Rite, Romanians): St. George (Pro-Cathedral).
St. Josaphat in Parma, Ohio (Byzantine Rite): St. Josaphat.
St. Louis,* Mo.: St. Louis.
St. Maron, Brooklyn, N.Y. (Maronite Rite): Our Lady of Lebanon.
St. Nicholas in Chicago (Byzantine Rite): St. Nicholas.
St. Paul and Minneapolis,* Minn.: St. Paul (St.

Paul); Basilica of St. Mary (Minneapolis Co-Cathedral).
St. Petersburg, Fla.: St. Jude the Apostle.
St. Thomas the Apostle of Detroit (Chaldean Rite): Our Lady of Chaldeans Cathedral (Mother of God Church), Southfield, Mich.
Salina, Kans.: Sacred Heart.
Salt Lake City, Utah: The Madeleine.
San Angelo, Tex.: Sacred Heart.
San Antonio,* Tex.: San Fernando.
San Bernardino, Calif: Our Lady of the Rosary.
San Diego, Calif.: St. Joseph.
San Francisco,* Calif.: St. Mary (Assumption).
San Jose, Calif.: St. Patrick.
Santa Fe,* N.M.: San Francisco de Asis.
Santa Rosa, Calif.: St. Eugene.
Savannah, Ga.: St. John the Baptist.
Scranton, Pa.: St. Peter.
Seattle,* Wash.: St. James.
Shreveport, La.: St. John Berchmans.
Sioux City, Ia.: Epiphany.
Sioux Falls, S.D.: St. Joseph.
Spokane, Wash.: Our Lady of Lourdes.
Springfield, Ill.: Immaculate Conception.
Springfield, Mass.: St. Michael.
Springfield-Cape Girardeau, Mo.: St. Agnes (Springfield); St. Mary (Cape Girardeau Co-Cathedral).
Stamford, Conn. (Byzantine Rite): St. Vladimir.
Steubenville, Ohio: Holy Name.
Stockton, Calif: Annunciation.
Superior, Wis.: Christ the King.
Syracuse, N.Y.: Immaculate Conception.
Toledo, Ohio: Queen of the Most Holy Rosary.
Trenton, N.J.: St. Mary (Assumption).
Tucson, Ariz.: St. Augustine.
Tulsa, Okla.: Holy Family.
Tyler, Tex.: Immaculate Conception.
Van Nuys, Calif. (Byzantine Rite): St. Mary.
Venice, Fla: Epiphany.
Victoria, Tex.: Our Lady of Victory.
Washington,* D.C.: St. Matthew.
Wheeling-Charleston, W. Va.: St. Joseph (Wheeling); Sacred Heart (Charleston Co-Cathedral).
Wichita, Kans.: Immaculate Conception.
Wilmington, Del.: St. Peter.
Winona, Minn.: Sacred Heart.
Worcester, Mass.: St. Paul.
Yakima, Wash.: St. Paul.
Youngstown, Ohio: St. Columba.
Apostolic Exarchate for Romanian Catholics of Byzantine Rite in U.S.: St. George, Canton, O. (Pro-Cathedral).
Apostolic Exarchate for Armenian-Rite Catholics in the U.S. and Canada: St. Ann (110 E. 12th St., New York, N.Y. 10003).

BASILICAS IN U.S. AND CANADA

Basilica is a title assigned to certain churches because of their antiquity, dignity, historical importance or significance as centers of worship. Major basilicas have the papal altar and holy door, which is opened at the beginning of a Jubilee Year; minor basilicas enjoy certain ceremonial privileges.

Among the major basilicas are the patriarchal basilicas of St. John Lateran, St. Peter, St. Paul Outside the Walls and St. Mary Major in Rome; St. Francis and St. Mary of the Angels in Assisi, Italy.

The patriarchal basilica of St. Lawrence, Rome, is a minor basilica.

The dates in the listings below indicate when the churches were designated as basilicas.

Minor Basilicas in U.S., Puerto Rico, Guam
Alabama: Mobile, Cathedral of the Immaculate Conception (Mar. 10, 1962).
Arizona: Phoenix, St. Mary's (Immaculate Conception) (Sept. 11, 1985).
California: San Francisco, Mission Dolores (Feb. 8, 1952); Carmel, Old Mission of San Carlos (Feb. 5, 1960); Alameda, St. Joseph (Jan. 21, 1972); San Diego, Mission San Diego de Alcala (Nov. 17, 1975).
Colorado: Denver, Cathedral of the Immaculate Conception (Nov. 3, 1979).
Florida: St. Augustine, Cathedral of St. Augustine (Dec. 4, 1976).
Illinois: Chicago, Our Lady of Sorrows (May 4, 1956), Queen of All Saints (Mar. 26, 1962).
Indiana: Vincennes, Old Cathedral (Mar. 14, 1970).
Iowa: Dyersville, St. Francis Xavier (May 11, 1956).
Kentucky: Trappist, Our Lady of Gethsemani (May 3, 1949); Covington, Cathedral of Assumption (Dec. 8, 1953).
Louisiana: New Orleans, St. Louis King of France (Dec. 9, 1964).
Maryland: Baltimore, Assumption of the Blessed Virgin Mary (Sept. 1, 1937).
Massachusetts: Roxbury, Perpetual Help ("Mission Church") (Sept. 8, 1954).
Michigan: Grand Rapids, St. Adalbert (Aug. 22, 1979).
Minnesota: Minneapolis. St. Mary (Feb. 1, 1926).
Missouri: Conception, Basilica of Immaculate Conception (Sept. 14, 1940); St. Louis, St. Louis King of France (Jan. 27, 1961).
New York: Brooklyn, Our Lady of Perpetual Help (Sept. 5, 1969), Cathedral-Basilica of St. James (June 22, 1982); Lackawanna, Our Lady of Victory (1926); Youngstown, Blessed Virgin Mary of the Rosary of Fatima (Oct. 7, 1975).
Ohio: Carey, Shrine of Our Lady of Consolation (Oct. 21, 1971).
Pennsylvania: Latrobe, St. Vincent Basilica, Benedictine Archabbey (Aug. 22, 1955); Conewago, Basilica of the Sacred Heart (June 30, 1962); Philadelphia, Sts. Peter and Paul (Sept. 27, 1976).
Texas: Galveston, St. Mary Cathedral (Aug. 11, 1979).
Wisconsin: Milwaukee, St. Josaphat (Mar. 10, 1929).
Puerto Rico: San Juan, Cathedral of San Juan (Jan. 25, 1978).
Guam: Agana, Cathedral of Dulce Nombre de Maria (Sweet Name of Mary) (1985).

Minor Basilicas in Canada

Alberta: Edmonton, Cathedral Basilica of St. Joseph (Mar. 15, 1984).
Manitoba: St. Boniface, Cathedral Basilica of St. Boniface (June 10, 1949).
Newfoundland: St. John's, Cathedral Basilica of St. John the Baptist.
Nova Scotia: Halifax, St. Mary's Basilica (June 14, 1950).
Ontario: Ottawa, Basilica of Notre Dame; London, St. Peter's Cathedral (Dec. 13, 1961).
Prince Edward Island: Charlottetown, Basilica of St. Dunstan.
Quebec: Sherbrooke, Cathedral Basilica of St. Michael (July 31, 1959). Montreal, Cathedral Basilica of Our Lady Queen of the World; St. Joseph of Mount Royal; Basilica of Notre Dame (Feb. 15, 1982). Cap-de-la-Madeleine, Basilica of Our Lady of the Cape (Aug. 15, 1964). Quebec, Basilica of Notre Dame; St. Anne de Beaupre, Basilica of St. Anne.

CHANCERY OFFICES OF U.S. ARCHDIOCESES AND DIOCESES

A chancery office, under this or another title, is the central administrative office of an archdiocese or diocese.

(Archdioceses are indicated by asterisk.)

Albany, N.Y.: 465 State St., Box 6480. 12206.
Alexandria, La.: 4400 Gardner Hwy., P.O. Box 7417, Alexandria. 71306.
Allentown, Pa.: 202 N. 17th St., P.O. Box F. 18105.
Altoona-Johnstown, Pa.: Box 126, Logan Blvd., Hollidaysburg, Pa. 16648.
Amarillo, Tex.: 1800 N. Spring St., P.O. Box 5644. 79117.
Anchorage,* Alaska: P.O. Box 2239. 99510.
Arlington, Va.: 200 N. Glebe Rd. 22203.
Atlanta,* Ga.: Catholic Center, 680 W. Peachtree St. N.W. 30308.
Austin, Tex.: N. Congress and 16th, P.O. Box 13327. Capitol Sta. 78711.
Baker, Ore.: 911 S.E. Armour, Bend 97702.
Baltimore,* Md.: 320 Cathedral St. 21201.
Baton Rouge, La.: P.O. Box 2028. 70821.
Beaumont, Tex.: 703 Archie St., P.O. Box 3948. 77704.
Belleville, Ill.: 222 S. Third St., 62220.
Biloxi, Miss.: P.O. Box 1189. 39533.
Birmingham, Ala.: P.O. Box 2086. 35201.
Bismarck, N.D.: 420 Raymond St., Box 1575. 58502.
Boise, Ida.: Box 769. 83701.
Boston,* Mass.: 2121 Commonwealth Ave., Brighton, Mass. 02135.
Bridgeport, Conn.: The Catholic Center, 238 Jewett Ave. 06606.
Brooklyn, N.Y.: 75 Greene Ave., P.O. Box C. 11202.
Brownsville, Tex.: P.O. Box 2279. 78522.
Buffalo, N.Y.: 795 Main St. 14203.
Burlington, Vt.: 351 North Ave. 05401.
Camden, N.J.: 1845 Haddon Ave., P.O. Box 709, 01801.
Charleston, S.C.: 119 Broad St., P.O. Box 818. 29402.
Charlotte, N.C.: P.O. Box 36776. 28236.
Cheyenne, Wyo.: Box 426. 82003.
Chicago,* Ill.: 155 E. Superior St., P.O. Box 1979. 60690.
Cincinnati,* O.: 100 E. 8th St. 45202.
Cleveland, O.: Chancery Bldg., 1027 Superior Ave. 44114.
Colorado Springs, Colo.: 29 W. Kiowa. 80903.
Columbus, O.: 198 E. Broad St. 43215.
Corpus Christi, Tex.: 620 Lipan St. P.O. Box 2620, 78403.
Covington, Ky.: 1140 Madison Ave., P.O. Box 192. 41012.
Crookston, Minn.: 1200 Memorial Dr., P.O. Box 610. 56716.
Dallas, Tex.: 3915 Lemmon Ave., P.O. Box 190507. 75219.
Davenport, Ia.: St. Vincent Center, 2706 Gaines St. 52804.
Denver,* Colo.: 200 Josephine St. 80206.
Des Moines, Ia.: P.O. Box 1816. 50306.
Detroit,* Mich.: 1234 Washington Blvd. 48226.
Dodge City, Kans.: 910 Central Ave., P.O. Box 849. 67801.
Dubuque,* Ia.: 1229 Mt. Loretta Ave., Box 479. 52001.
Duluth, Minn.: 215 W. 4th St. 55806.
El Paso, Tex.: 499 St. Matthews St. 79907.
Erie, Pa.: 205 W. 9th St. 16501.
Evansville, Ind.: P.O. Box 4169. 47711.
Fairbanks, Alaska: 1316 Peger Rd. 99709.
Fall River, Mass.: 47 Underwood St., Box 2577. 02722.
Fargo, N.D.: 1310 Broadway, Box 1750. 58107.
Fort Wayne-South Bend, Ind.: P.O. Box 390, Fort Wayne. 46801.
Fort Worth, Tex.: 800 W. Loop, 820 South. 76108.
Fresno, Calif.: P.O. Box 1668, 1550 N. Fresno St. 93717.
Gallup, N. Mex.: 711 S. Puerco Dr., P.O. Box 1338. 87301.
Galveston-Houston, Tex.: 1700 San Jacinto St., Houston. 77002.
Gary, Ind.: 9292 Broadway, Merrillville. 46410.
Gaylord, Mich.: 1665 M-32 West, Seton Bldg. 49735.
Grand Island, Nebr.: 311 W. 17th St., P.O. Box 996. 68802.
Grand Rapids, Mich.: 660 Burton St., S.E. 49507.
Great Falls-Billings, Mont.: P.O. Box 1399, Great Falls. 59403.
Green Bay, Wis.: Box 66. 54305.
Greensburg, Pa.: 723 E. Pittsburgh St. 15601.
Harrisburg, Pa.: P.O. Box 2153. 17105.
Hartford,* Conn.: 134 Farmington Ave. 06105.
Helena, Mont.: 515 North Ewing, P.O. Box 1729. 59624.
Honolulu, Hawaii: 1184 Bishop St. 96813.
Houma-Thibodaux, La.: P.O. Box 9077, Houma, La. 70361.
Indianapolis,* Ind.: 1400 N. Meridian St., P.O. Box 1410, 46206.
Jackson, Miss.: 237 E. Amite St., P.O. Box 2248. 39225.
Jefferson City, Mo.: 605 Clark Ave. P.O. Box 417. 65101.
Joliet, Ill.: 425 Summit St. 60435.

Juneau, Alaska: 419 6th St. 99801.
Kalamazoo, Mich.: 215 N. Westnedge Ave., P.O. Box 949. 49005.
Kansas City,* Kans.: 2220 Central Ave., P.O. Box 2328. 66110.
Kansas City-St. Joseph, Mo.: P.O. Box 419037, Kansas City. 64141.
Knoxville, Tenn.: 711 Northshore Dr. 37919. (address of cathedral).
La Crosse, Wis.: 3710 East Ave., Box 4004. 54602.
Lafayette in Indiana: P.O. Box 260. 47902.
Lafayette, La.: P.O. Drawer 3387. 70502.
Lake Charles, La.: P.O. Box 3223. 70602.
Lansing, Mich.: 300 W. Ottawa. 48933.
Las Cruces, N. Mex.: P.O. Box 16318. 88004.
Lexington, Ky.: P.O. Box 12350. 40582.
Lincoln, Nebr.: P.O. Box 80328. 68501.
Little Rock, Ark.: 2415 N. Tyler St. P.O. Box 7239. 72217.
Los Angeles,* Calif.: 1531 W. 9th St. 90015.
Louisville,* Ky.: 212 E. College St., P.O. Box 1073. 40201.
Lubbock, Tex.: P.O. Box 98700. 79499.
Madison, Wis.: 15 E. Wilson St., P.O. Box 111. 53701.
Manchester, N. H.: 153 Ash St., P.O. Box 310. 03105.
Marquette, Mich.: 444 S. Fourth St., P.O. Box 550. 49855.
Memphis, Tenn.: P.O. Box 41679. 38174.
Metuchen, N.J.: P.O. Box 191. 08840.
Miami,* Fla.: 9401 Biscayne Blvd., Miami Shores. 33138.
Milwaukee,* Wis.: P.O. Box 2018. 53201.
Mobile,* Ala.: 400 Government St., P.O. Box 1966. 36633.
Monterey, Calif.: P.O. Box 2048. 93942.
Nashville, Tenn.: 2400 21st Ave. S. 37212.
Newark,* N.J.: 31 Mulberry St. 07102.
New Orleans,* La.: 7887 Walmsley Ave. 70125.
Newton, Mass. (Melkite Rite): 19 Dartmouth St., W. Newton, Mass. 02165.
New Ulm, Minn.: 1400 Sixth North St. 56073.
New York,* N.Y.: 1011 First Ave. 10022.
Norwich, Conn.: 201 Broadway, P.O. Box 587. 06360.
Oakland, Calif.: 2900 Lakeshore Ave. 94610.
Ogdensburg, N.Y.: 622 Washington St., P.O. Box 369. 13669.
Oklahoma City,* Okla.: P.O. Box 32180. 73123.
Omaha,* Nebr.: 100 N. 62nd St. 68132.
Orange, Calif.: 2811 E. Villa Real Dr. 92667.
Orlando, Fla.: P.O. Box 1800. 32802.
Owensboro, Ky.: 4005 Frederica St. 42301.
Palm Beach, Fla.: 8895 N. Military Trail, Bldg. C 201, Palm Beach Gardens 33418.
Parma, Ohio (Byzantine Rite): 1900 Carlton Rd. 44134.
Passaic, N.J. (Byzantine Rite): 445 Lackawanna Ave., W. Paterson. 07424.
Paterson, N.J.: 777 Valley Rd., Clifton. 07013.
Pensacola-Tallahassee, Fla.: P.O. Drawer 17329, Pensacola. 32522.
Peoria, Ill.: 607 N.E. Madison Ave., P.O. Box 1406. 61655.
Philadelphia,* Pa.: 222 N. 17th St. 19103.

Philadelphia,* Pa. (Byzantine Rite): 827 N. Franklin St. 19123.
Phoenix, Ariz.: 400 E. Monroe St. 85004.
Pittsburgh,* Pa. (Byzantine Rite): 54 Riverview Ave. 15214.
Pittsburgh, Pa.: 111 Blvd. of the Allies. 15222.
Portland, Me.: 510 Ocean Ave., P.O. Box 6750. 04101.
Portland in Oregon*: 2838 E. Burnside St. 97214.
Providence, R.I.: One Cathedral Sq. 02903.
Pueblo, Colo.: 1001 N. Grand Ave. 81003.
Raleigh, N.C.: 300 Cardinal Gibbons Dr. 27606.
Rapid City, S.D.: 606 Cathedral Dr., P.O. Box 678. 57709.
Reno-Las Vegas, Nev.: P.O. Box 1211, Reno. 89504.
Richmond, Va.: 811 Cathedral Pl., Suite C. 23220.
Rochester, N.Y.: 1150 Buffalo Rd. 14624.
Rockford, Ill.: 1245 N. Court St. 61103.
Rockville Centre, N.Y.: 50 N. Park Ave. 11570.
Sacramento, Calif.: 1119 K St., P.O. Box 1706. 95808.
Saginaw, Mich.: 5800 Weiss St. 48603.
St. Augustine, Fla.: P.O. Box 24000, Jacksonville, Fla. 32241.
St. Cloud, Minn.: P.O. Box 1248. 56302.
St. George Martyr, Canton, Ohio (Byzantine Rite, Romanian): 1121 44th St. N.E., Canton, O. 44714.
St. Josaphat in Parma, Ohio (Byzantine Rite): P.O. Box 347180, Parma. 44134.
St. Louis,* Mo.: 4445 Lindell Blvd. 63108.
St. Maron (Maronite Rite), Brooklyn, N.Y.: 8120 15th Ave., Brooklyn. 11228.
St. Nicholas in Chicago (Byzantine Rite): 2245 W. Rice St. 60622.
St. Paul and Minneapolis,* Minn.: 226 Summit Ave., St. Paul. 55102.
St. Petersburg, Fla.: P.O. Box 40200. 33743.
St. Thomas the Apostle of Detroit (Chaldean Rite): 25585 Berg Rd., Southfield, Mich. 48034.
Salina, Kans.: P.O. Box 980. 67402.
Salt Lake City, Utah: 27 C St. 84103.
San Angelo, Tex.: 804 Ford, P.O. Box 1829. 76902.
San Antonio,* Tex.: P.O. Box 28410. 78228.
San Bernardino, Calif.: 1450 North D St. 92405.
San Diego, Calif.: P.O. Box 80428. 92138.
San Francisco,* Calif.: 445 Church St. 94114.
San Jose, Calif.: 7600 St. Joseph Ave., Los Altos. 94022.
Santa Fe,* N. Mex.: 4000 St. Joseph's Pl. N.W., Albuquerque. 87120.
Santa Rosa, Calif.: P.O. Box 1297. 95402.
Savannah, Ga.: P.O. Box 8789. 31412.
Scranton, Pa.: 300 Wyoming Ave. 18503.
Seattle,* Wash.: 910 Marion St. 98104.
Shreveport, La.: 2500 Line Ave. 71104.
Sioux City, Ia.: P.O. Box 3379. 51102.
Sioux Falls, S.D.: Box 5033. 57117.
Spokane, Wash.: 1023 W. Riverside Ave. 99201.
Springfield, Illinois: P.O. Box 1667. 62705.
Springfield, Mass.: P.O. Box 1730. 01101.
Springfield-Cape Girardeau, Mo.: P.O. Box 50690, Springfield. 65805.
Stamford, Conn. (Byzantine Rite): 161 Glenbrook Rd. 06902.
Steubenville, Ohio: P.O. Box 969. 43952.

Chancery Offices — National Catholic Conferences   439

Stockton, Calif.: P.O. Box 4237. 95204.
Superior, Wis.: Box 969. 54880.
Syracuse, N.Y.: P.O. Box 511. 13201.
Toledo, Ohio: P.O. Box 985. 43696.
Trenton, N.J.: P.O. Box 5309. 08638.
Tucson, Ariz.: 192 S. Stone Ave., Box 31. 85702.
Tulsa, Okla.: P.O. Box 2009. 74101.
Tyler, Tex.: 1920 Sybil Lane. 75703.
Van Nuys, Calif. (Byzantine Rite): 18024 Parthenia St., Northride, Calif. 91325.
Venice, Fla.: P.O. Box 2006. 34284.
Victoria, Tex.: P.O. Box 4708. 77903.
Washington,* D.C.: P.O. Box 29260. 20017.
Wheeling-Charleston, W. Va.: 1300 Byron St., P.O. Box 230, Wheeling. 26003.
Wichita, Kans.: 424 N. Broadway. 67202.
Wilmington, Del.: P.O. Box 2030. 19899.
Winona, Minn.: P.O. Box 588. 55987.
Worcester, Mass.: 49 Elm St. 01609.
Yakima, Wash.: 5301-A Tieton Dr. 98908.
Youngstown, Ohio: 144 W. Wood St. 44503.
Military Archdiocese: 962 Wayne Ave., Silver Spring, Md. 20910.
Armenian-Rite Apostolic Exarchate for the United States and Canada: 110 E. 12th St., New York, N.Y. 10003.

NATIONAL CATHOLIC CONFERENCES

The two conferences described below are related in membership and directive control but distinct in nature, purpose and function.

The National Conference of Catholic Bishops (NCCB) is a strictly ecclesiastical body in and through which the bishops of the United States act together, officially and with authority as pastors of the Church. It is the sponsoring organization of the United States Catholic Conference.

The United States Catholic Conference (USCC) is a civil corporation and operational secretariat in and through which the bishops, together with other members of the Church, act on a wider scale for the good of the Church and society. It is sponsored by the National Conference of Catholic Bishops.

The principal officers of both conferences are: Archbishop John L. May, president; Archbishop Daniel E. Pilarczyk, vice president; Archbishop Daniel W. Kucera, O.S.B., treasurer; Bishop Eugene A. Marino, S.S.J., secretary.

The membership of the Administrative Committee of the NCCB and the Administrative Board of the USCC is identical.

Headquarters of both conferences are located at 1312 Massachusetts Ave. N.W., Washington, D.C. 20005. (3221 - 4th St., N.E., Washington, D.C. 20017, after March, 1989).

NCCB

The National Conference of Catholic Bishops, established by action of the U.S. hierarchy Nov. 14, 1966, is a strictly ecclesiastical body with defined juridical authority over the Church in this country. It was set up with the approval of the Holy See and in line with directives from the Second Vatican Council. Its constitution was formally ratified during the November, 1967, meeting of the U.S. hierarchy.

The NCCB is a development from the Annual Meeting of the Bishops of the United States, whose pastoral character was originally approved by Pope Benedict XV Apr. 10, 1919.

The address of the Conference is 1312 Massachusetts Ave. N.W., Washington, D.C. 20005. Rev. Msgr. Daniel F. Hoye is general secretary.

Pastoral Council

The conference, one of many similar territorial conferences envisioned in the conciliar *Decree on the Pastoral Office of Bishops in the Church* (No. 38), is "a council in which the bishops of a given nation or territory (in this case, the United States) jointly exercise their pastoral office to promote the greater good which the Church offers mankind, especially through the forms and methods of the apostolate fittingly adapted to the circumstances of the age."

Its decisions, "provided they have been approved legitimately and by the votes of at least two-thirds of the prelates who have a deliberative vote in the conference, and have been recognized by the Apostolic See, are to have juridically binding force only in those cases prescribed by the common law or determined by a special mandate of the Apostolic See, given either spontaneously or in response to a petition of the conference itself."

All bishops who serve the Church in the U.S., its territories and possessions, have membership and voting rights in the NCCB.

Officers, Committees

The conference operates through a number of bishops' committees with functions in specific areas of work and concern. Their basic assignments are to prepare materials on the basis of which the bishops, assembled as a conference, make decisions, and to put suitable action plans into effect.

The principal officers are: Archbishop John L. May, president; Archbishop Daniel E. Pilarczyk, vice president; Archbishop Daniel W. Kucera, O.S.B., treasurer; Bishop Eugene A. Marino, S.S.J., secretary.

These officers, with several other bishops, hold positions on executive-level committees — Executive Committee, the Committee on Budget and Finance, the Committee on Personnel and Administrative Services, and the Committee on Priorities and Plans. They also, with other bishops, serve on the NCCB Administrative Board.

The standing committees and their chairmen (Archbishops and Bishops) are as follows.

American Board of Catholic Missions, Thomas V. Daily.
American College, Louvain, Robert E. Mulvee.
Bishops' Welfare Emergency Relief, John L. May.
Black Catholics, John H. Ricard, S.S.J.
Boundaries of Dioceses and Provinces, John L. May.

Canonical Affairs, John R. Keating.
Church in Latin America, Ricardo Ramirez, C.S.B.
Doctrine, Raymond W. Lessard.
Ecumenical and Interreligious Affairs, J. Francis Stafford.
Hispanic Affairs, Raymundo J. Pena.
Human Values, R. Pierre Du Maine.
Laity, John S. Cummins.
Liaison with Priests, Religious and Laity, Andrew J. McDonald.
Liturgy, Joseph P. Delaney.
Marriage and Family Life, Howard J. Hubbard.
Migration, Theodore E. McCarrick.
Missions, J. Terry Steib, S.V.D.
North American College, Rome, James A. Griffin.
Pastoral Research and Practices, John R. Quinn.
Permanent Diaconate, William S. Skylstad.
Priestly Formation, James P. Keleher.
Priestly Life and Ministry, Thomas J. Murphy.
Pro-Life Activities, Cardinal Joseph Bernardin.
Selection of Bishops, John L. May.
Vocations, John G. Vlazny.
Women in Society and in the Church, Joseph L. Imesch.
Ad hoc committees and their chairmen are as follows.
Bicentennial of Establishment of U.S. Hierarchy, William D. Borders.
Bishops Life and Ministry, John F. Kinney.
Campaign for Human Development, Arthur N. Tafoya.
Catholic Charismatic Renewal, Joseph McKinney.
Economic Concerns of the Holy See, John E. McCarthy.
Evangelization, William R. Houck.
Farm Labor, Roger M. Mahony.
Implementation of Pastoral on U.S. Economy, William S. Skylstad.
Inter-Rite, William H. Keeler.
Liaison Committee with NC News, Thomas J. Grady.
Moral Evaluation of Deterrence, Cardinal Joseph Bernardin.
1990 Special Assembly, John J. McRaith.
Nomination of Conference Offices, Anthony F. Mestice.
Observance of the Fifth Centenary of the Evangelization of the Americas, Edward A. McCarthy.
Pastoral Response to the Challenge of Proselytism, Anthony J. Bevilacqua.
Planning for General Meetings, William H. Bullock.
Religious Life and Ministry, John J. Leibrecht.
Writing Committee for the Pastoral on Women in Society and in the Church, Joseph L. Imesch.

Cardinal John Dearden was the first president of the National Conference of Catholic Bishops and the U.S. Catholic Conference (1966 to 1971). He was influential in "Call to Action" developments following the Second Vatican Council.

USCC

The United States Catholic Conference, Inc. (USCC), is the operational secretariat and service agency of the National Conference of Catholic Bishops for carrying out the civic-religious work of the Church in this country. It is a civil corporation related to the NCCB in membership and directive control but distinct from it in purpose and function.

The address of the Conference is 1312 Massachusetts Ave. N.W., Washington, D.C. 20005. Rev. Msgr. Daniel F. Hoye is general secretary.

Service Secretariat

The USCC, as of Jan. 1, 1967, took over the general organization and operations of the former National Catholic Welfare Conference, Inc., whose origins dated back to the National Catholic War Council of 1917. The council underwent some change after World War I and was established on a permanent basis Sept. 24, 1919, as the National Catholic Welfare Council to serve as a central agency for organizing and coordinating the efforts of U.S. Catholics in carrying out the social mission of the Church in this country. In 1923, its name was changed to National Catholic Welfare Conference, Inc., and clarification was made of its nature as a service agency of the bishops and the Church rather than as a conference of bishops with real juridical authority in ecclesiastical affairs.

The Official Catholic Directory states that the USCC assists "the bishops in their service to the Church in this country by uniting the people of God where voluntary collective action on a broad interdiocesan level is needed. The USCC provides an organizational structure and the resources needed to insure coordination, cooperation, and assistance in the public, educational and social concerns of the Church at the national, regional, state and, as appropriate, diocesan levels."

Officers, Departments

The principal officers of the USCC are Archbishop John L. May, president; Archbishop Daniel E. Pilarczyk, vice president; Archbishop Daniel W. Kucera, O.S.B., treasurer; Bishop Eugene A. Marino, S.S.J., secretary. These officers, with several other bishops, hold positions on executive-level committees — the Executive Committee; the Committee on Priorities and Plans; the Committee on Budget and Finance; the Committee on Personnel and Administration. They also serve on the Administrative Board.

The Executive Committee, organized in 1969, is authorized to handle matters of urgency between meetings of the Administrative Board and the general conference, to coordinate items for the agenda of general meetings, and to speak in the name of the USCC.

The major departments and their chairmen (Archbishops and Bishops) are: Communications, Anthony G. Bosco; Education, Francis B. Schulte; Social Development and World Peace, Joseph M. Sullivan (Committee on Domestic Policy), Roger

M. Mahony (Committee on International Policy). Each department is supervised by a committee composed of an equal number of episcopal and non-episcopal members, including lay persons.

A national Advisory Council of bishops, priests, men and women religious, lay men and women advises the Administrative Board on overall plans and operations of the USCC.

The administrative general secretariat, in addition to other duties, supervises staff-service offices of Finance, General Counsel, Government Liaison, Priorities and Plans, Management Information Services, Human Resources, General Services, Research, Publishing and Promotion Services.

Most of the organizations and associations affiliated with the USCC are covered in separate Almanac entries.

NCCB-USCC REGIONS

I. Maine, Vermont, New Hampshire, Massachusetts, Rhode Island, Connecticut.

II. New York. III. New Jersey, Pennsylvania.

IV. Delaware, District of Columbia, Florida, Georgia, Maryland, North Carolina, South Carolina, Virgin Islands, Virginia, West Virginia.

V. Alabama, Kentucky, Louisiana, Mississippi, Tennessee.

VI. Michigan, Ohio.

VII. Illinois, Indiana, Wisconsin.

VIII. Minnesota, North Dakota, South Dakota.

IX. Iowa, Kansas, Missouri, Nebraska.

X. Arkansas, Oklahoma, Texas.

XI. California, Hawaii, Nevada. XII. Idaho, Montana, Alaska, Washington, Oregon.

XIII. Utah, Arizona, New Mexico, Colorado, Wyo.

1987 MEETING OF THE U.S. BISHOPS

Approximately 300 bishops attended the annual meeting of the National Conference of Catholic Bishops and the U.S. Catholic Conference Nov. 16 to 19, 1987, in Washington, D.C.

Presidential Address

Pope John Paul's 1987 visit to the United States was the principal theme of the presidential address by Archbishop John L. May of St. Louis.

He said the Pope "saw a Church alive, dynamic and vibrant." And, "when the visit was over, Pope John Paul spoke of the 'profound bond between American Catholicism and the universal Church.'"

Archbishop May said the major impressions of the Pope were related to:

• The liturgical vitality of the Church: "If there is one aspect of post-conciliar American experience where we have grown, it is the liturgical renewal.... No one should question the fidelity and authenticity of our life of worship."

• The depth of ecumenical and interfaith relations: "I know that he was deeply touched in South Carolina to experience the peace and harmony in a pluralistic society of many denominations walking together under one common banner: In God We Trust. He said of his reception in predominantly Protestant Columbia, 'This could never happen in Europe.'"

• The multicultural dimensions of Catholicism in the United States: "There is no mistaking the Hispanic presence, and there can be no minimizing the Hispanic challenge.... Certainly, no black Catholic leader will soon forget that magical hour in New Orleans" when the Holy Father met with black Catholics.

• The vitality of lay involvement in the Church: "I believe the Holy Father saw a Church also alive with generous men and women who, in different ways and through different institutional responses, work hard to build up the body of Christ."

Archbishop May also singled out "four dominant themes" of the visit.

1. "The importance of family life," with emphasis on conjugal and family love, and the indissolubility of marriage.

2. The need for social justice, for "solidarity with and respect for all life."

3. "The papal challenge to American Catholics 'to risk being countercultural,'" especially in resisting widespread "selfishness, sexual license and excess, neglect of the poor."

4. "The need for encouraging our young people to consider the priesthood and religious life," while emphasizing at the same time "a broader notion of vocation as a call to all the faithful to transform the world."

In a later intervention, Archbishop May gave a brief report on the 1987 assembly of the Synod of Bishops. He singled out concern for the role of women in the Church as a significant topic of discussion at the synod, even though it was not one of the subjects among the recommendations submitted to Pope John Paul at the conclusion of the assembly.

Business Items

Budget: Authorization was given for a 1988 NCCB-USCC budget of $29.5 million.

Central America: The bishops adopted a statement in which they: called for consideration of the problems of all Central America countries; called the policy of support for the contras in Nicaragua "morally flawed"; repeated their conviction that conflicts in the region should be resolved through negotiation, not through arms; said the region should not be allowed to serve as a battleground for the superpowers; urged "fellow Catholics ... to consider how they might best bring moral perspectives to bear on the human anguish of today's Central America."

Clinics in Schools: In a statement of opposition, the bishops said: "The provision of contraceptive and abortion services through public school-based clinics is morally objectionable, and is open to question even on practical grounds as a response to the problem of teen-age pregnancy." The bishops were critical of clinical and educational programs that "treat sex as a purely physiological reality or implicitly condone it as a form of recreation."

The statement also said: "School-based clinics that clearly separate themselves from the agenda of contraceptive advocates may provide part of an effective response to the health needs of young people.... A comprehensive response to the problem of teen-age sexual activity and pregnancy must include efforts to strengthen the traditional character-forming task of the schools, to improve social and economic opportunities for young people in low-income areas, to support parents in their difficult task of passing on healthy values to their children, and to establish programs of education promoting the values of chastity and fidelity."

Collection for Religious: The bishops approved an annual national collection, for a period of 10 years or less, to raise funds for the retirement needs of Religious, especially nuns. It was estimated that the amount needed would be approximately $2.5 billion.'

Election: Archbishop Daniel W. Kucera of Dubuque was elected to a three-year term as treasurer of the NCCB-USCC.

Hispanics: The bishops approved a national pastoral program for ministry among Hispanics with emphasis on the development of small ecclesial communities, parish renewal, family and youth ministry, and leadership formation. Backgrounding the program were recommendations and initiatives stemming from three national meetings (*encuentros*) and the 1983 pastoral letter entitled "The Hispanic Presence: Challenge and Commitment."

Market Loss: A stock market loss of $6.7 million was reported in the wake of Wall St. developments of Oct. 19, 1987. The total value of the conference portfolio had been $69.7 million. Despite the loss, current value was greater than that of the original investment.

Marriage Rite: A rite for use in interfaith marriages was approved, with a request for ratification by the Congregation for Divine Worship.

Our Lady of Guadalupe: The bishops voted to elevate, from memorial to feast, the liturgical observance in honor of Our Lady of Guadalupe, patroness of the Americas. The action required the approval of the Congregation for Divine Worship.

Priests: The bishops approved "Norms for Priests in Their Third Age," to provide for their needs in retirement.

Religious: Approval was given for the establishment of a tri-conference commission to deal with bishop-religious relations, consisting of five members each from the National Conference of Catholic Bishops, the Conference of Major Superiors of Men and the Leadership Conference of Women Religious.

Also approved was the formation of a 5-member NCCB committee on Religious Life and Ministry.

Unfinished Business: These items included a statement on bishop-theologian relationships, for the resolution of doctrinal and related issues, and an unfinished committee report regarding the morality of nuclear deterrence. The bishops were also advised that a statement on AIDS was still being developed and would be circulated when completed.

BISHOPS' MEETING OF JUNE 24 TO 27, 1988

Nearly 300 bishops attended the semiannual meeting of the National Conference of Catholic Bishops and the U.S. Catholic Conference June 24 to 27, 1988, in Collegeville, Minn.

Business Items

The bishops took action on the following items.

AIDS: Approved a motion "to appoint an ad hoc committee to prepare a new, updated statement on the AIDS crisis which will respond to the new facts, fears and efforts which have emerged in recent months.... The committee will have the benefit of the extant broad statement on AIDS ('The Many Faces of AIDS — A Gospel Response'), the discussions which have taken place since its publication (in December, 1987), dialogue with the Congregation for the Doctrine of the Faith, and participation by all the bishops in open, plenary session." (See separate entry.)

Episcopal Conferences: Were critical of a draft statement from Vatican sources regarding the theological foundation, collegial concept and teaching mandate of episcopal conferences; agreed to form a committee to frame a response, as solicited by the Vatican.

General Absolution: Debated at length but reached an inconclusive vote on a time-norm for its use in the U.S. (See separate entry.)

Nuclear Deterrence: Issued a report critical of President Reagan's Strategic Defense Initiative, urging that it not be deployed; stood by their "strictly conditioned moral acceptance" of nuclear deterrence, related to no bombing of civilians and progress toward a maximum degree of disarmament. (See The Challenge of Peace: God's Promise and Our Response.)

Retired Religious: Agreed on a plan for the allocation and distribution of an estimated $20 mil-

---

PAPAL COMMENT ON DRAFT OF PASTORAL LETTER

At a meeting with a group of American bishops Sept. 2, 1988, the Pope said their draft statement on women's issues was a sensitive document. He went on to say that the whole Church needs to make a "great prayerful reflection" about the dignity and vocation of women. "The Church is determined to place her full teaching ... at the service of the cause of women in the modern world — to help clarify their correlative rights and duties, while defending their feminine dignity and vocation. ... The importance of true Christian feminism is so great that every effort must be made to present the principles on which this cause is based." He said the complementary nature of men and women is an essential concept regarding the specific rights of women.

lion a year they expect to collect in the nation's parishes to help meet the critical retirement needs of men and women Religious.

Statutes and Bylaws: Approved updated statutes and bylaws governing the National Conference of Catholic Bishops and the U.S. Catholic Conference.

Television: Approved a two-year contract to use the Eternal World Television Network as the cable network for programs produced by the bishops' conference; turned down a proposal to pursue negotiations toward joining a new ecumenical cable TV netwok called VISN; approved proposals to improve their own national communications posture, especially in further development of their Catholic Telecommunications Network of America.

Women: Discussed the first draft of a pastoral letter on the concerns of women and offered suggestions to improve it. (See separate entry.)

CATHOLIC RELIEF SERVICES

Catholic Relief Services is the official overseas aid and development agency of American Catholics; it is a separately incorporated organization of the U.S. Catholic Conference.

CRS was founded in 1943 by the bishops of the United States to help civilians in Europe and North Africa caught in the disruption and devastation of World War II.

As conditions in Europe improved in the late 1940s and early 1950s, the works conducted by CRS spread to other continents and areas — Asia, Africa and Latin America.

Although best known for its record of disaster response, compassionate aid to refugees and commitment to reconstruction and rehabilitation, CRS places primary focus on long-term development projects designed to help people to help themselves and to determine their own future.

Administrative funding for CRS comes from an annual collection, the Catholic Relief Services Annual Appeal (known variously as Bishops' Relief or American Catholic Overseas Aid Appeal), held during Lent in most of the 18,000 Catholic parishes of the U.S.

Major support is derived from private, individual donors through direct contributions and through a program of sacrificial giving called Operation Rice Bowl. Funds are also received from philanthropic foundations and humanitarian organizations in the U.S. and Europe.

Assistance is received from the U.S. Government in several forms: foodstuffs available under Title II of Public Law 480, ocean-freight subsidies for government food and other privately generated relief supplies, and grants for both emergency programs and community development projects.

In 1987, the CRS global program in 70 countries employed 1,100 people and was valued at $250 million.

Lawrence Pezzullo is executive director.

CRS headquarters are located at 1011 First Ave., New York, N.Y. 10022.

STATE CATHOLIC CONFERENCES

These conferences are agencies of bishops and dioceses in the various states. Their general purposes are to develop and sponsor cooperative programs designed to cope with pastoral and common-welfare needs, and to represent the dioceses before governmental bodies, the public, and in private sectors. Their membership consists of representatives from the dioceses in the states — bishops, clergy and lay persons in various capacities.

The **National Association of State Catholic Conference Directors** maintains liaison with the general secretariat of the United States Catholic Conference.

Arizona Catholic Conference, 400 E. Monroe St., Phoenix, Ariz. 85004; exec. dir., Rev. Msgr. Edward J. Ryle.

California Catholic Conference, Cathedral Square, 1010 11th St., Suite 200, Sacramento, Calif. 95814; exec. dir., Rev. William J. Wood, S.J.

Colorado Catholic Conference, 200 Josephine St., Denver, Colo. 80206; exec. dir., Sr. Loretto Anne Madden, S.L.

Connecticut Catholic Conference, 134 Farmington Ave., Hartford, Conn. 06105; exec. dir., William Wholean.

Florida Catholic Conference, P.O. Box 1571, Tallahassee, Fla. 32302; exec. dir., Thomas A. Horkan, Jr.

Georgia Catholic Conference, Suite 2129, First Atlanta Tower, Atlanta, Ga. 30383; exec. dir., Cheatham E. Hodges, Jr.

Illinois, Catholic Conference of, 500 North Clark St., Chicago, Ill. 60610; 300 E. Monroe St., Springfield, Ill. 62701; exec. dir., Jimmy M. Lago.

Indiana Catholic Conference, 1400 N. Meridian St., P.O. Box 1410, Indianapolis, Ind. 46206.

Iowa Catholic Conference, 818 Insurance Exchange Building, Des Moines, Iowa 50309; exec. dir., Timothy McCarthy.

Kansas Catholic Conference, 702 Commercial National Bank Bldg., Kansas City, Kan. 66101; exec. dir., Robert Runnels, Jr.

Kentucky Catholic Conference, P.O. Box 1073, Louisville, Ky. 40201; exec. dir., Ken Dupre.

Louisiana Catholic Conference, P.O. Box 52948, New Orleans, La. 70152; exec. dir., Emile Comar (Office of Governmental Programs and Planning); FNB Tower, Box 19, 666 Jefferson St., Lafayette, La. 70501; exec. dir., Ralph Guidroz (Office of Church Ministry).

Maryland Catholic Conference, 309 Cathedral St., Baltimore, Md. 21201; exec. dir., Richard J. Dowling.

Massachusetts Catholic Conference, 60 School St., Boston, Mass. 02108; exec. dir., Gerald D. D'Avolio, Esq.

Michigan Catholic Conference, 505 N. Capitol Ave., Lansing, Mich. 48933; exec. dir., Sr. Monica Kostielney.

Minnesota Catholic Conference, 475 University Ave. W., St. Paul, Minn. 55103; exec. dir., Rev. Msgr. James D. Habiger.

Missouri Catholic Conference, P.O. Box 1022,

600 Clark Ave., Jefferson City, Mo. 65102; exec. dir., Louis C. DeFeo, Jr.
Montana Catholic Conference, P.O. Box 1708, Helena, Mont. 59624; exec. dir., John L. Ortwein.
Nebraska Catholic Conference, 521 S. 14th St., Lincoln, Nebr. 68508; exec. dir., James R. Cunningham.
New Jersey Catholic Conference, 211 N. Warren St., Trenton, N.J. 08618; exec. dir., William F. Bolan, Jr.
New York State Catholic Conference, 119 Washington Ave., Albany, N.Y. 12210; exec. dir., J. Alan Davitt.
North Dakota Catholic Conference, 227 West Broadway Suite No. 2, Bismarck, N. Dak. 58501; exec. dir., Sr. Paula Ringuette, P.B.V.M.
Ohio, Catholic Conference of, 35 E. Gay St., Suite 502, Columbus, Ohio 43215; exec. dir., M. Desmond Ryan.
Oregon Catholic Conference, 2838 E. Burnside, Portland, Ore. 97214; exec. dir., Robert J. Castagna.
Pennsylvania Catholic Conference, 223 North St., Box 2835, Harrisburg, Pa. 17105; exec. dir., Howard J. Fetterhoff.
Texas Catholic Conference, 3001 S. Congress Ave., Austin, Tex. 78704; exec. dir., Bro. Richard Daly, C.S.C.
Washington State Catholic Conference, 1402 Third Ave., Seattle, Wash. 98101; exec. dir. Ned Dolejsi.
Wisconsin Catholic Conference, 30 W. Mifflin St., Suite 302, Madison, Wis. 53703; exec. dir., Charles M. Phillips.

BIOGRAPHIES OF AMERICAN BISHOPS

(Sources: Almanac survey, *The Official Catholic Directory,* NC News Service. As of Aug. 15, 1988. For former bishops of the U.S., see "American Bishops of the Past," elsewhere in this section.)

Information includes: date and place of birth; educational institutions attended; date of ordination to the priesthood with, where applicable, name of archdiocese (*) or diocese in parentheses; date of episcopal ordination; episcopal appointments; date of resignation.

A

Abramowicz, Alfred L.: b. Jan. 27, 1919, Chicago, Ill.; educ. St. Mary of the Lake Seminary (Mundelein, Ill.), Gregorian Univ. (Rome); ord. priest (Chicago*) May 1, 1943; ord. titular bishop of Paestum and auxiliary bishop of Chicago, June 13, 1968.

Acerra, Angelo Thomas, O.S.B.: b. Nov. 7, 1925, Memphis, Tenn.; educ. St. Benedict's (Atchison, Kans.), Catholic Univ. (Washington, D.C.), St. Mary's Univ. (San Antonio, Tex.), Univ. of Northern Colorado (Greeley, Colo.), Angelicum (Rome); ord. priest May 20, 1950; ord. titular bishop of Lete and auxiliary bishop of the Military Services archdiocese, Nov. 29, 1983; vicar for the Far East.

Ackerman, Richard Henry, C.S.Sp.: b. Aug. 30, 1903, Pittsburgh, Pa.; educ. Duquesne Univ. (Pittsburgh, Pa.), St. Mary's Scholasticate (Norwalk, Conn.), Univ. of Fribourg (Switzerland); ord. priest Aug. 28, 1926; ord. titular bishop of Lares and auxiliary bishop of San Diego, May 22, 1956; app. bishop of Covington, Apr. 4, 1960; resigned Nov. 28, 1978.

Adamek, Joseph V.: b. Aug. 13, 1935, Bannister, Mich.; educ. Michigan State Univ. (East Lansing), Nepomucene College and Lateran Univ. (Rome); ord. priest (for Nitra diocese, Czechoslovakia), July 3, 1960; incardinated in Saginaw diocese; ord. bishop of Altoona-Johnstown, May 20, 1987.

Ahern, Patrick V.: b. Mar. 8, 1919, New York, N.Y.; educ. Manhattan College and Cathedral College (New York City), St. Joseph's Seminary (Yonkers, N.Y.), St. Louis Univ. (St. Louis, Mo.), Notre Dame Univ. (Notre Dame, Ind.); ord. priest (New York*) Jan. 27, 1945; ord. titular bishop of Naiera and auxiliary bishop of New York, Mar. 19, 1970.

Ahr, George William: b. June 23, 1904, Newark, N.J.; educ. St. Vincent College (Latrobe, Pa.), Seton Hall College (S. Orange, N.J.), North American College (Rome); ord. priest (Newark*) July 29, 1928; ord. bishop of Trenton, Mar. 20, 1950; resigned June 23, 1979.

Anderson, Moses B., S.S.E.: b. Sept. 9, 1928, Selma, Ala.; educ. St. Michael's College (Winooski, Vt.), St. Edmund Seminary (Burlington, Vt.), Univ. of Legon (Ghana); ord. priest May 30, 1958; ord. titular bishop of Vatarba and auxiliary bishop of Detroit, Jan. 27, 1983.

Angell, Kenneth A.: b. Aug. 3, 1930, Providence, R.I.; educ. St. Mary's Seminary (Baltimore, Md.); ord. priest (Providence) May 26, 1956; ord. titular bishop of Septimunicia and auxiliary bishop of Providence, R.I., Oct. 7, 1974.

Apuron, Anthony Sablan, O.F.M. Cap.: b. Nov. 1, 1945, Agana, Guam; educ. St. Anthony College and Capuchin Seminary (Hudson, N.H.), Capuchin Seminary (Garrison, N.Y.), Maryknoll Seminary (New York), Notre Dame Univ. (Notre Dame, Ind.); ord. priest Aug. 26, 1972, in Guam; ord. titular bishop of Muzuca in Proconsulari and auxiliary bishop of Agana, Guam (U.S. Trust Territory), Feb. 19, 1984; archbishop of Agana, Mar. 10, 1986.

Arias, David, O.A.R.: b. July 22, 1929, Leon, Spain; educ. St. Rita's College (San Sebastian, Spain), Our Lady of Good Counsel Theologate (Granada, Spain), Teresianum Institute (Rome, Italy); ord. priest May 31, 1952; ord. titular bishop of Badie and auxiliary bishop of Newark, Apr. 7, 1983; episcopal vicar for Hispanic affairs.

Arkfeld, Leo, S.V.D.: b. Feb. 4, 1912, Butte, Nebr.; educ. Divine Word Seminary (Techny, Ill.), Sacred Heart College (Girard, Pa.); ord. priest Aug. 15, 1943; ord. titular bishop of Bucellus and vicar apostolic of Central New Guinea, Nov. 30, 1948; name of vicariate changed to Wewak, May 15, 1952; first bishop of Wewak, Nov. 15, 1966; app. archbishop of Madang, Papua New Guinea, Dec.

19, 1975; resigned Dec. 31, 1987.

Arliss, Reginald, C.P.: b. Sept. 8, 1906, East Orange, N.J.; educ. Immaculate Conception Seminary (Jamaica, N.Y.) and other Passionist houses of study; ord. priest Apr. 28, 1934; missionary in China for 16 years, expelled 1951; missionary in Philippines; rector of the Pontifical Philippine College Seminary in Rome, 1961-69; ord. titular bishop of Cerbali and prelate of Marbel, Philippines (now a diocese), Jan. 30, 1970; resigned from titular see and prelature, Oct. 1, 1981.

Arzube, Juan A.: b. June 1, 1918, Guayaquil, Ecuador; educ. Rensselaer Polytechnic Institute (Troy, N.Y.), St. John's Seminary (Camarillo, Calif.); ord. priest (Los Angeles*) May 5, 1954; ord. titular bishop of Civitate and auxiliary bishop of Los Angeles, Mar. 25, 1971.

B

Balke, Victor: b. Sept. 29, 1931, Meppen, Ill.; educ. St. Mary of the Lake Seminary (Mundelein, Ill.), St. Louis Univ. (St. Louis, Mo.); ord. priest (Springfield, Ill.) May 24, 1958; ord. bishop of Crookston, Sept. 2, 1976.

Baltakis, Paul Antanas, O.F.M.: b. Jan. 1, 1925, Troskunai, Lithuania; educ. seminaries of the Franciscan Province of St. Joseph (Belgium); ord. priest Aug. 24, 1952, in Belgium; served in U.S. as director of Lithuanian Cultural Center, New York, and among Lithuanian youth; head of U.S. Lithuanian Franciscan Vicariate, Kennebunkport, Maine, from 1979; ord. titular bishop of Egara, Sept. 24, 1984; assigned to pastoral assistance to Lithuanian Catholics living outside Lithuania.

Banks, Robert J.: b. Feb. 26, 1928, Winthrop, Mass.; educ. St. John's Seminary (Brighton, Mass.), Gregorian Univ., Lateran Univ. (Rome); ord. priest (Boston*) Dec. 20. 1952, in Rome; rector of St. John's Seminary, Brighton, Mass., 1971-81; vicar general of Boston archdiocese, 1984; ord. titular bishop of Taraqua and auxiliary bishop of Boston, Sept. 19, 1985.

Baum, William W.: (See Cardinals, Biographies.)

Begley, Michael J.: b. Mar. 12, 1909, Mattineague, Mass.; educ. Mt. St. Mary Seminary (Emmitsburg, Md.); ord. priest (Raleigh) May 26, 1934; ord. first bishop of Charlotte, N.C., Jan. 12, 1972; retired May 29, 1984.

Beltran, Eusebius J.: b. Aug. 31, 1934, Ashley, Pa.; educ. St. Charles Seminary (Philadelphia, Pa.); ord. priest (Atlanta*) May 14, 1960; ord. bishop of Tulsa, Apr. 20, 1978.

Bernardin, Joseph L.: (See Cardinals, Biographies.)

Bevilacqua, Anthony J.: b. June 17, 1923, Brooklyn, N.Y.; educ. Cathedral College (Brooklyn, N.Y.), Immaculate Conception Seminary (Huntington, N.Y.), Gregorian Univ. (Rome), Columbia Univ. and St. John's Univ. (New York); ord. priest (Brooklyn) June 11, 1949; ord. titular bishop of Aquae Albae in Byzacena and auxiliary bishop of Brooklyn, Nov. 24, 1980; app. bishop of Pittsburgh Oct. 7, 1983, installed Dec. 11, 1983; archbishop of Philadelphia, Feb. 11, 1988.

Bilock, John M.: b. June 20, 1916, McAdoo, Pa.; educ. St. Procopius College and Seminary (Lisle, Ill.); ord. priest (Pittsburgh,* Byzantine Rite) Feb. 3, 1946; vicar general of Byzantine archdiocese of Munhall, 1969; ord. titular bishop of Pergamum and auxiliary bishop of Munhall, May 15, 1973; title of see changed to Pittsburgh, 1977.

Boccella, John H., T.O.R.: b. June 25, 1912, Castelfranci, Italy; came to U.S. at the age of two; educ. St. Francis College and Seminary (Loretto, Pa.), Angelicum Univ. (Rome), Catholic Univ. (Washington, D.C.); ord. priest Mar. 29, 1941; minister general of Third Order Regular, 1947-65; ord. archbishop of Izmir, Turkey, Apr. 17, 1968; transferred to titular see of Ephesus, Dec. 7, 1978 (resides in Rome).

Boland, Ernest B., O.P.: b. July 10, 1925, Providence, R.I.; educ. Providence College (Rhode Island), Dominican Houses of Study (Somerset, Ohio; Washington, D.C.); ord. priest June 9, 1955; ord. bishop of Multan, Pakistan, July 25, 1966; resigned Oct. 20, 1984.

Boland, Raymond J.: b. Feb. 8, 1932, Tipperary, Ireland; educ. National Univ. of Ireland and All Hallows Seminary (Dublin); ord. priest (Washington*) July 16, 1957, in Dublin; vicar general and chancellor of Washington archdiocese; ord. bishop of Birmingham, Ala., Mar. 25, 1988.

Borders, William D.: b. Oct. 9, 1913, Washington, Ind.; educ. St. Meinrad Seminary (St. Meinrad, Ind.), Notre Dame Seminary (New Orleans, La.), Notre Dame Univ. (Notre Dame, Ind.); ord. priest (New Orleans*) May 18, 1940; ord. first bishop of Orlando, June 14, 1968; app. archbishop of Baltimore, Apr. 2, 1974, installed June 26, 1974.

Bosco, Anthony G.: b. Aug. 1, 1927, New Castle, Pa.; educ. St. Vincent Seminary (Latrobe, Pa.), Lateran Univ. (Rome); ord. priest (Pittsburgh) June 7, 1952; ord. titular bishop of Labicum and auxiliary of Pittsburgh, June 30, 1970; app. bishop of Greensburg, Apr. 14, 1987, installed June 30, 1987.

Boudreaux, Warren L.: b. Jan. 25, 1918, Berwick, La.; educ. St. Joseph's Seminary (St. Benedict, La.), St. Sulpice Seminary (Paris, France), Notre Dame Seminary (New Orleans, La.), Catholic Univ. (Washington, D.C.); ord. priest (Lafayette, La.) May 30, 1942; ord. titular bishop of Calynda and auxiliary bishop of Lafayette, La., July 25, 1962; app. bishop of Beaumont, June 5, 1971; app. first bishop of Houma-Thibodaux, installed June 5, 1977.

Breitenbeck, Joseph M.: b. Aug. 3, 1914, Detroit, Mich.; educ. University of Detroit, Sacred Heart Seminary (Detroit, Mich.), North American College and Lateran Univ. (Rome), Catholic Univ. (Washington, D.C.); ord. priest (Detroit*) May 30, 1942; ord. titular bishop of Tepelta and auxiliary bishop of Detroit, Dec. 20, 1965; app. bishop of Grand Rapids, Oct. 15, 1969, installed Dec. 2, 1969.

Brizgys, Vincas: b. Nov. 10, 1903, Plyniai, Lithuania; ord. priest June 5, 1927; ord. titular bishop of Bosano and auxiliary bishop of Kaunas, Lithuania, May 10, 1940; taken into custody and deported to Germany, 1944; liberated by Americans, 1945; U.S. citizen, 1958.

Broderick, Edwin B.: b. Jan. 16, 1917, New York, N.Y.; educ. Cathedral College (New York City), St. Joseph's Seminary (Yonkers, N.Y.), Fordham Univ. (New York City); ord. priest (New York*) May 30, 1942; ord. titular bishop of Tizica and auxiliary of New York, Apr. 21, 1967; bishop of Albany, 1969-76; executive director of Catholic Relief Services, 1976-82. Bishop emeritus of Albany.

Brom, Robert H.: b. Sept. 18, 1938, Arcadia, Wis.; educ. St. Mary's College (Winona, Minn.), Gregorian Univ. (Rome); ord. priest (Winona) Dec. 18, 1963, in Rome; ord. bishop of Duluth, May 23, 1983.

Brown, Charles A., M.M.: b. Aug. 20, 1919, New York, N.Y.; educ. Cathedral College (New York City), Maryknoll Seminary (Maryknoll, N.Y.); ord. priest June 9, 1946; ord. titular bishop of Vallis and auxiliary bishop of Santa Cruz, Bolivia, Mar. 27, 1957.

Brunini, Joseph B.: b. July 24, 1909, Vicksburg, Miss.; educ. Georgetown Univ. (Washington, D.C.), North American College (Rome), Catholic Univ. (Washington, D.C.); ord. priest (Jackson) Dec. 5, 1933; ord. titular bishop of Axomis and auxiliary bishop of Natchez-Jackson, Jan. 29, 1957; apostolic administrator of Natchez-Jackson, 1966; app. bishop of Natchez-Jackson, Dec. 2, 1967, installed Jan. 29, 1968; title of see changed to Jackson, 1977; retired Jan. 24, 1984.

Brust, Leo J.: b. Jan. 7, 1916, St. Francis, Wis.; educ. St. Francis Seminary (Milwaukee, Wis.), Canisianum (Innsbruck, Austria), Catholic Univ. (Washington, D.C.); ord. priest (Milwaukee*) May 30, 1942; ord. titular bishop of Suelli and auxiliary bishop of Milwaukee. Oct. 16, 1969.

Brzana, Stanislaus J.: b. July 1, 1917, Buffalo, N.Y.; educ. Christ the King Seminary (St. Bonaventure, N.Y.), Gregorian Univ. (Rome); ord. priest (Buffalo) June 7, 1941; ord, titular bishop of Cufruta and auxiliary bishop of Buffalo, June 29, 1964; bishop of Ogdensburg, Oct. 22, 1968.

Buechlein, Daniel M., O.S.B.: b. Apr. 20, 1938; educ. St. Meinrad College and Seminary (St. Meinrad, Ind.), St. Anselm Univ. (Rome); solemn profession as Benedictine monk, Aug. 15, 1963; ord. priest (St. Meinrad Archabbey) May 3, 1964; ord. bishop of Memphis, Mar. 2, 1987.

Bullock, William H.: b. Apr. 13, 1927, Maple Lake, Minn.; educ. St. Thomas College and St. Paul Seminary (St. Paul, Minn.), Notre Dame Univ. (Notre Dame, Ind.); ord. priest (St. Paul-Minneapolis*) June 7, 1952; ord. titular bishop of Natchez and auxiliary bishop of St. Paul and Minneapolis, Aug. 12, 1980; app. bishop of Des Moines, Feb. 10, 1987, installed Apr. 2, 1987.

Burke, James C., O.P.: b. Nov. 30, 1926, Philadelphia, Pa.; educ. King's College (Wilkes-Barre, Pa.), Providence College (R.I.); ord. priest June 8, 1956; ord. titular bishop of Lamiggiga and prelate of Chimbote, Peru, May 25, 1967, resigned from prelature (now a diocese), June 8, 1978. Titular bishop of Lamiggiga. Vicar for urban affairs, Wilmington, Del., diocese Aug. 31, 1978.

Buswell, Charles A.: b. Oct. 15, 1913, Homestead, Okla.; educ. St. Louis Preparatory Seminary (St. Louis, Mo.), Kenrick Seminary (Webster Groves, Mo.), American College, Univ. of Louvain (Belgium); ord. priest (Oklahoma City*) July 9, 1939; ord. bishop of Pueblo, Sept. 30, 1959; resigned Sept. 18, 1979.

Byrne, James J.: b. July 28, 1908, St. Paul, Minn.; educ. Nazareth Hall Preparatory Seminary and St. Paul Seminary (St. Paul, Minn.), Univ. of Minnesota (Minneapolis, Minn.); Louvain Univ. (Belgium); ord. priest (St. Paul-Minneapolis*) June 3, 1933; ord. titular bishop of Etenna and auxiliary bishop of St. Paul, July 2, 1947; app. bishop of Boise, June 16, 1956; app. archbishop of Dubuque, Mar. 19, 1962, installed May 8, 1962; retired Aug. 23, 1983.

C

Camacho, Tomas Aguon: b. Sept. 18, 1933, Chalon Kanoa, Saipan; educ. St. Patrick's Seminary (Menlo Park, Calif.); ord. priest June 14, 1961; ord. first bishop of Chalon Kanoa, Northern Marianas (U.S. Trust Territory), Jan. 13, 1985.

Carberry, John J.: (See Cardinals, Biographies.)

Carlson, Robert J.: b. June 30, 1944, Minneapolis, Minn.; educ. Nazareth Hall and St. Paul Seminary (St. Paul, Minn.), Catholic Univ. (Washington, D.C.): ord. priest (St. Paul-Minneapolis*) May 23, 1970; ord. titular bishop of Avioccala and auxiliary bishop of St. Paul and Minneapolis, Jan. 11, 1984; vicar of eastern vicariate.

Casey, Luis Morgan: b. June 23, 1935, Portageville, Mo.; ord. priest (St. Louis*) Apr. 7, 1962; missionary in Bolivia from 1965; ord. titular bishop of Mibiarca and auxiliary of La Paz, Jan. 28, 1984; vicar apostolic of Pando, Bolivia, April, 1988.

Cassata, John J.: b. Nov. 8, 1908, Galveston, Tex.; educ. St. Mary's Seminary (La Porte, Tex.), North American College, Urban Univ. and Gregorian Univ. (Rome); ord. priest (Galveston-Houston) Dec. 8, 1932; ord. titular bishop of Bida and auxiliary bishop of Dallas-Fort Worth, June 5, 1968; app. bishop of Fort Worth, Aug. 27, 1969, installed Oct. 21, 1969; retired Sept. 16, 1980.

Chaput, Charles J., O.F.M. Cap.: b. Sept. 26, 1944, Concordia, Kans.; educ. St. Fidelis College (Herman, Pa.), Capuchin College and Catholic Univ. (Washington, D.C.), Univ. of San Francisco; solemn vows as Capuchin, July 14, 1968; ord. priest Aug. 29, 1970; ord. bishop of Rapid City, S.D., July 26, 1988, the second priest of Native American ancestry ordained a bishop in the U.S.

Chavez, Gilbert Espinoza: b. May 9, 1932, Ontario, Calif.; educ. St. Francis Seminary (El Cajon, Calif.), Immaculate Heart Seminary (San Diego), Univ. of California; ord. priest (San Diego) Mar. 19, 1960; ord. titular bishop of Magarmel and auxiliary of San Diego, June 21, 1974.

Chedid, John: b. July 4, 1923, Eddid, Lebanon; educ. seminaries in Lebanon and Pontifical Urban College (Rome); ord. priest Dec. 21, 1951, in Rome; ord. titular bishop of Callinico and auxiliary bishop of St. Maron of Brooklyn for the Maronites, Jan. 25, 1981.

Clark, Matthew H.: b. July 15, 1937, Troy, N.Y.; educ. St. Bernard's Seminary (Rochester, N.Y.), Gregorian Univ. (Rome); ord. priest (Albany) Dec. 19, 1962; ord. bishop of Rochester, May 27,

1979; installed June 26, 1979.
Clavel Mendez, Tomas Alberto: b. Dec. 21, 1921, Canazas, Panama; ord. priest Dec. 7, 1947; ord. bishop of David, Panama, July 24, 1955; archbishop of Panama, 1964; resigned Dec. 30, 1968; vicar for Spanish Speaking in Orange diocese, California.
Clinch, Harry A.: b. Oct. 27, 1908, San Anselmo, Calif.; educ. St. Joseph's College (Mountain View, Calif.), St. Patrick's Seminary (Menlo Park, Calif.); ord. priest (Monterey-Fresno) June 6, 1936; ord. titular bishop of Badiae and auxiliary bishop of Monterey-Fresno, Feb. 27, 1957; app. first bishop of Monterey in California, installed Dec. 14, 1967; resigned Jan. 19, 1982.
Coggin, Walter A., O.S.B.: b. Feb. 10, 1916, Richmond, Va.; ord. priest June 19, 1943; app. abbot ordinary of abbacy nullius of Mary Help of Christians, Belmont N.C., 1959; blessed Mar. 28, 1960; resigned 1970.
Cohill, John Edward, S.V.D.: b. Dec. 13, 1907, Elizabeth, N.J.; educ. Divine Word Seminary (Techny, Ill.); ord. priest Mar. 20, 1936; ord. first bishop of Goroko, Papua New Guinea, Mar. 11, 1967; resigned Aug. 30, 1980.
Comber, John W., M.M.: b. Mar. 12, 1906, Lawrence, Mass.; educ. St. John's Preparatory College (Danvers, Mass.), Boston College (Boston, Mass.), Maryknoll Seminary (Maryknoll, N.Y.); ord. priest Feb. 1, 1931; superior general of Maryknoll, 1956-66; ord. titular bishop of Foratiana, Apr. 9, 1959.
Connare, William G.: b. Dec. 11, 1911, Pittsburgh, Pa.; educ. Duquesne Univ. (Pittsburgh, Pa.), St. Vincent Seminary (Latrobe, Pa.); ord. priest (Pittsburgh) June 14, 1936; ord. bishop of Greensburg, May 4, 1960; retired Jan. 20, 1987.
Connolly, Thomas Arthur: b. Oct. 5, 1899, San Francisco, Calif.; educ. St. Patrick's Seminary (Menlo Park, Calif.), Catholic Univ. (Washington, D.C.); ord. priest (San Francisco*) June 11, 1926; ord. titular bishop of Sila and auxiliary bishop of San Francisco, Aug. 24, 1939; app. coadjutor bishop of Seattle, Feb. 28, 1948; succeeded as bishop of Seattle, May 18, 1950; first archbishop of Seattle, June 23, 1951; retired Feb. 25, 1975.
Connolly, Thomas J.: b. July 18, 1922, Tonopah, Nev.; educ. St. Patrick's Seminary (Menlo Park, Calif.), Catholic Univ. (Washington, D.C.), Lateran Univ. (Rome); ord. priest (Reno-Las Vegas) Apr. 8, 1947; ord. bishop of Baker, June 30, 1971.
Connors, Ronald G., C.SS.R.: b. Nov. 1, 1915, Brooklyn, N.Y.; ord. priest June 22, 1941; ord. titular bishop of Equizetum and coadjutor bishop of San Juan de la Maguana, Dominican Republic, July 20, 1976; succeeded as bishop of San Juan de la Maguana, July 20, 1977.
Cooney, Patrick R.: b. Mar. 10, 1934, Detroit, Mich.; educ. Sacred Heart Seminary (Detroit), Gregorian Univ. (Rome), Notre Dame Univ. (Notre Dame, Ind.); ord. priest (Detroit*) Dec. 20, 1959; ord. titular bishop of Hodelm and auxiliary bishop of Detroit, Jan. 27, 1983.
Corrada del Rio, Alvaro, S.J.: b. May 13, 1942, Santurce, Puerto Rico; entered Society of Jesus, 1960, at novitiate of St. Andrew-on-Hudson (Poughkeepsie, N.Y.); educ. Jesuit seminaries, Fordham Univ. (New York), Institut Catholique (Paris); ord. priest July 6, 1974, in Puerto Rico; pastoral coordinator of Northeast Catholic Hispanic Center, New York, 1982-85; ord. titular bishop of Rusticiana and auxiliary bishop of Washington, D.C., Aug. 4, 1985.
Coscia, Benedict Dominic, O.F.M.: b. Aug. 10, 1922, Brooklyn, N.Y.; educ. St. Francis College (Brooklyn, N.Y.), Holy Name College (Washington, D.C.); ord. priest June 11, 1949; ord. bishop of Jatai, Brazil, Sept. 21, 1961.
Cosgrove, William M.: b. Nov. 26, 1916, Canton, Ohio; educ. John Carroll Univ. (Cleveland, O.); ord. priest (Cleveland) Dec. 18, 1943; ord. titular bishop of Trisipa and auxiliary bishop of Cleveland, Sept. 3, 1968; app. bishop of Belleville, installed Oct. 28, 1976; retired May 19, 1981.
Costello, Thomas J.: b. Feb. 23, 1929, Camden, N.Y.; educ. Niagara Univ. (Niagara Falls, N.Y.), St. Bernard's Seminary (Rochester, N.Y.), Catholic Univ. (Washington, D.C.); ord. priest (Syracuse) June 5, 1954; ord. titular bishop of Perdices and auxiliary bishop of Syracuse Mar. 13, 1978.
Cotey, Arnold R., S.D.S.: b. June 15, 1921, Milwaukee, Wis.; educ. Divine Savior Seminary (Lanham, Md.), Marquette Univ. (Milwaukee, Wis.); ord. priest June 7, 1949; ord. first bishop of Nachingwea, Tanzania, Oct. 20, 1963; retired Nov. 11, 1983.
Cousins, William E.: b. Aug. 20, 1902, Chicago, Ill.; educ. Quigley Seminary (Chicago, Ill.), St. Mary of the Lake Seminary (Mundelein, Ill.); ord. priest (Chicago*) Apr. 23, 1927; ord. titular bishop of Forma and auxiliary bishop of Chicago, Mar. 7, 1949; app. bishop of Peoria, May 21, 1952; archbishop of Milwaukee, Jan. 27, 1959; retired Jan. 17, 1977.
Cronin, Daniel A.: b. Nov. 14, 1927, Newton, Mass.; educ. St. John's Seminary (Boston, Mass.), North American College and Gregorian Univ. (Rome); ord. priest (Boston*) Dec. 20, 1952; attaché apostolic nunciature (Addis Ababa), 1957-61; served in papal Secretariat of State, 1961-68; ord. titular bishop of Egnatia and auxiliary bishop of Boston, Sept. 12, 1968; bishop of Fall River, Dec. 16, 1970.
Crowley, Joseph R.: b. Jan. 12, 1915, Fort Wayne, Ind.; educ. St. Mary's College (St. Mary, Ky.), St. Meinrad Seminary (St. Meinrad, Ind.); served in US Air Force, 1942-46; ord. priest (Ft. Wayne-S. Bend) May 1, 1953; editor of *Our Sunday Visitor* 1958-67; ord. titular bishop of Maraguis and auxiliary bishop of Fort Wayne-South Bend, Aug. 24, 1971.
Cummins, John S.: b. Mar. 3, 1928, Oakland, Calif.; educ. St. Patrick's Seminary (Menlo Park, Calif.), Catholic Univ. (Washington, D.C.), Univ. of California; ord. priest (San Francisco*) Jan. 24, 1953; executive director of the California Catholic Conference 1971-76; ord. titular bishop of Lambaesis and auxiliary bishop of Sacramento, May 16, 1974; app. bishop of Oakland, installed June 30, 1977.
Curtis, Walter W.: b. May 3, 1913, Jersey City,

N.J.; educ. Fordham Univ. (New York City), Seton Hall Univ. (South Orange, N.J.), Immaculate Conception Seminary (Darlington, N.J.), North American College and Gregorian Univ. (Rome), Catholic Univ. (Washington, D.C.); ord. priest (Newark*) Dec. 8, 1937; ord. titular bishop of Bisica and auxiliary bishop of Newark, Sept. 24, 1957; app. bishop of Bridgeport, 1961, installed Nov. 21, 1961; retired June 28, 1988.

Curtiss, Elden F.: b. June 16, 1932, Baker, Ore.; educ. St. Edward Seminary College and St. Thomas Seminary (Kenmore, Wash.); ord. priest (Baker) May 24, 1958; ord. bishop of Helena, Mont., Apr. 28, 1976.

D

Daily, Thomas V.: b. Sept. 23, 1927, Belmont, Mass.; educ. Boston College, St. John's Seminary (Brighton, Mass.); ord. priest (Boston*) Jan. 10, 1952; missionary in Peru for five years as a member of the Society of St. James the Apostle; ord. titular bishop of Bladia and auxiliary bishop of Boston, Feb. 11, 1975; app. first bishop of Palm Beach, Fla., July 17, 1984, installed Oct. 24, 1984.

Daly, James: b. Aug. 14, 1921, New York, N.Y.; educ. Cathedral College (Brooklyn, N.Y.), Immaculate Conception Seminary (Huntington, L.I.); ord. priest (Buffalo) May 22, 1948; ord. titular bishop of Castra Nova and auxiliary bishop of Rockville Centre, May 9, 1977.

Danglmayr, Augustine: b. Dec. 11, 1898, Muenster, Tex.; educ. Subiaco College (Arkansas), St. Mary's Seminary (La Porte, Tex.), Kenrick Seminary (St. Louis, Mo.); ord. priest (Dallas) June 10, 1922; ord. titular bishop of Olba, Oct. 7, 1942; auxiliary bishop of Dallas-Ft. Worth, 1942-69.

D'Antonio, Nicholas, O.F.M.: b. July 10, 1916, Rochester, N.Y.; educ. St. Anthony's Friary (Catskill, N.Y.); ord. priest June 7, 1942; ord. titular bishop of Giufi Salaria and prelate of Olancho, Honduras, July 25, 1966; resigned 1977; app. vicar general of New Orleans archdiocese and episcopal vicar for Spanish Speaking, August, 1977.

D'Arcy, John M.: b. Aug. 18, 1932, Brighton, Mass.; educ. St. John's Seminary (Brighton, Mass.), Angelicum Univ. (Rome); ord. priest (Boston*) Feb. 2, 1957; spiritual director of St. John's Seminary; ord. titular bishop of Mediana and auxiliary bishop of Boston, Feb. 11, 1975; app. bishop of Fort Wayne-South Bend, Feb. 26, 1985, installed May 1, 1985.

Deksnys, Antanas L.: b. May 9, 1906, Buteniskiai, Lithuania; educ. Metropolitan Seminary and Theological and Philosophical Faculty at Vytautas the Great Univ. (all at Kaunas, Lithuania), Univ. of Fribourg (Switzerland); ord. priest May 30, 1931; served in U.S. parishes at Mt. Carmel, Pa., and East St. Louis, Ill.; ord. titular bishop of Lavellum, June 15, 1969; assigned to pastoral work among Lithuanians in Western Europe; retired June 5, 1984.

Delaney, Joseph P.: b. Aug. 29, 1934, Fall River, Mass.; educ. Cardinal O'Connell Seminary (Boston, Mass.), Theological College (Washington, D.C.), North American College (Rome), Rhode Island College (Providence, R.I.); ord. priest (Fall River) Dec. 18, 1960; ord. bishop of Fort Worth, Tex., Sept. 13, 1981.

Dempsey, Michael J., O.P.: b. Feb. 22, 1912, Providence, R.I.; entered Order of Preachers (Dominicans), Chicago province, 1935; ord. priest June 11, 1942; ord. bishop of Sokoto, Nigeria, Aug. 15, 1967; resigned Dec. 31, 1984.

Denning, Joseph P.: b. Jan. 4, 1907, Flushing, L.I.; educ. Cathedral College (Brooklyn, N.Y.), Immaculate Conception Seminary (Huntington, L.I.), St. Mary's Seminary (Baltimore, Md.); ord. priest (Brooklyn) May 21, 1932; ord. titular bishop of Mallus and auxiliary bishop of Brooklyn, Apr. 22, 1959; resigned Apr. 13, 1982.

De Palma, Joseph A., S.C.J.: b. Sept. 4, 1913, Walton, N.Y.; ord. priest May 20, 1944; superior general of Congregation of Priests of the Sacred Heart, 1959-67; ord. first bishop of De Aar, South Africa, July 19, 1967; retired Nov. 18, 1987.

De Paoli, Ambrose: b. Aug. 19, 1934, Jeannette, Pa., moved to Miami at age of nine; educ. St. Joseph Seminary (Bloomfield, Conn.), St. Mary of the West Seminary (Cincinnati, O.), North American College and Lateran Univ. (Rome); ord. priest (Miami*) Dec. 18, 1960, in Rome; served in diplomatic posts in Canada, Turkey, Africa and Venezuela; ord. titular archbishop of Lares, Nov. 20, 1983, in Miami; apostolic pro-nuncio to Sri Lanka, 1983-88; apostolic delegate in southern Africa and pro-nuncio to Lesotho, 1988.

De Simone, Louis A.: b. Feb. 21, 1922, Philadelphia, Pa.; educ. Villanova Univ. (Villanova, Pa.), St. Charles Borromeo Seminary (Overbrook, Pa.); ord. priest (Philadelphia*) May 10, 1952; ord. titular bishop of Cillium and auxiliary bishop of Philadelphia, Aug. 12, 1981.

DiLorenzo, Francis X.: b. Apr. 15, 1942, Philadelphia, Pa.; educ. St. Charles Borromeo Seminary (Philadelphia), Univ. of St. Thomas (Rome); ord. priest (Philadelphia*) May 18, 1968; ord. titular bishop of Tigia and auxiliary bishop of Scranton, Mar. 8, 1988.

Dimino, Joseph T.: b. Jan. 7, 1923, New York, N.Y.; educ. Cathedral College (New York, N.Y.), St. Joseph's Seminary (Yonkers, N.Y.), Catholic Univ. (Washington, D.C.); ord. priest (New York*) June 4, 1949; ord. titular bishop of Carini and auxiliary bishop of the Military Services archdiocese, May 10, 1983.

Dingman, Maurice J.: b. Jan. 20, 1914, St. Paul, Ia.; educ. St. Ambrose College (Davenport, Ia.), North American College and Gregorian Univ. (Rome), Catholic Univ. (Washington, D.C.); ord. priest (Davenport) Dec. 8, 1939; ord. bishop of Des Moines, June 19, 1968; retired Oct. 14, 1986.

Dion, Georges E., O.M.I.: b. Sept. 25, 1911, Central Falls, R.I.; educ. Holy Cross College (Worcester, Mass.), Oblate Juniorate (Colebrook, N.H.), Oblate Scholasticates (Natick, Mass., and Ottawa, Ont.); ord. priest June 24, 1936; ord. titular bishop of Arpaia and vicar apostolic of Jolo, Philippines Apr. 23, 1980.

Dolinay, Thomas V.: b. July 24, 1923, Uniontown, Pa.; educ. St. Procopius College (Lisle, Ill.); ord. priest (Pittsburgh*, Byzantine Rite)

May 16, 1948; editor *Eastern Catholic Life*, 1966-82; ord. titular bishop of Tiatira and auxiliary bishop of Byzantine-Rite diocese of Passaic, Nov. 23, 1976; app. first bishop Byzantine-Rite diocese of Van Nuys, Calif., Dec. 3, 1981, installed Mar. 9, 1982.

Donnelly, Robert William: b. Mar. 22, 1931, Toledo, O.; educ. St. Meinrad Seminary College (St. Meinrad, Ind.), Mount St. Mary's in the West Seminary (Norwood, O.); ord. priest (Toledo) May 25, 1957; ord. titular bishop of Garba and auxiliary bishop of Toledo, May 3, 1984.

Donoghue, John F.: b. Aug. 9, 1928, Washington, D.C.; educ. St. Mary's Seminary (Baltimore, Md.); Catholic Univ. (Washington, D.C.); ord. priest (Washington*) June 4, 1955; chancellor and vicar general of Washington archdiocese, 1973-84; ord. bishop of Charlotte, N.C., Dec. 18, 1984.

Donovan, John A.: b. Aug. 5, 1911, Chatham, Ont., Canada; educ. Sacred Heart Seminary (Detroit, Mich.), North American College and Gregorian Univ. (Rome); ord. priest (Detroit*) Dec. 8, 1935; ord. titular bishop of Rhasus and auxiliary bishop of Detroit, Oct. 26, 1954; app. bishop of Toledo, installed Apr. 18, 1967; retired July 29, 1980.

Donovan, Paul V.: b. Sept. 1, 1924, Bernard, Iowa; educ. St. Gregory's Seminary (Cincinnati, Ohio), Mt. St. Mary's Seminary (Norwood, Ohio), Lateran Univ. (Rome); ord. priest (Lansing) May 20, 1950; ord. first bishop of Kalamazoo, Mich., July 21, 1971.

Dorsey, Norbert M., C.P.: b. Dec. 14, 1929, Springfield, Mass.; educ. Passionist seminaries, (eastern U.S. province), Pontifical Institute of Sacred Music and Gregorian Univ. (Rome, Italy); professed in Passionists, Aug. 15, 1949; ord priest Apr. 28, 1956; assistant general of Passionists, 1976-86; ord. titular bishop of Mactaris and auxiliary bishop of Miami, Mar. 19, 1986.

Drury, Thomas J.: b. Jan. 4, 1908, Co. Sligo, Ireland; educ. St. Benedict's College (Atchison, Kans.), Kenrick Seminary (St. Louis, Mo.); ord. priest (Amarillo) June 2, 1935; ord. first bishop of San Angelo, Tex., Jan. 24, 1962; app. bishop of Corpus Christi, installed Sept. 1, 1965; resigned May 24, 1983.

Dudick, Michael J.: b. Feb. 24, 1916, St. Clair, Pa.; educ. St. Procopius College and Seminary (Lisle, Ill.); ord. priest (Passaic, Byzantine Rite) Nov. 13, 1945; ord. bishop of Byzantine Rite Eparchy of Passaic, Oct. 24, 1968.

Dudley, Paul: b. Nov. 27, 1926, Northfield, Minn.; educ. Nazareth College and St. Paul Seminary (St. Paul, Minn.); ord. priest (St. Paul-Minneapolis*) June 2, 1951; ord. titular bishop of Ursona and auxiliary bishop of St. Paul and Minneapolis, Jan. 25, 1977; app. bishop of Sioux Falls, installed Dec. 13, 1978.

Duhart, Clarence James, C.SS.R.: b. Mar. 23, 1912, New Orleans, La.; ord, priest June 29, 1937; ord. bishop of Udon Thani, Thailand, Apr. 21, 1966; resigned Oct. 2, 1975.

DuMaine, (Roland) Pierre: b. Aug. 2, 1931, Paducah, Ky.; educ. St. Joseph's College (Mountain View, Calif.), St. Patrick's College and Seminary (Menlo Park, Calif.), Univ. of California (Berkeley), Catholic Univ. (Washington, D.C.); ord. priest (San Francisco*) June 15, 1957; ord. titular bishop of Sarda and auxiliary bishop of San Francisco, June 29, 1978; app. first bishop of San Jose, Jan. 27, 1981; installed Mar. 18, 1981.

Dunn, Francis J.: b. Mar. 22, 1922, Elkader, Ia.; educ. Loras College (Dubuque, Ia.), Kenrick Seminary (St. Louis, Mo.), Angelicum (Rome, Italy); ord. priest (Dubuque*) Jan. 11, 1948; chancellor of Dubuque, Aug. 27, 1960; ord. titular bishop of Turris Tamallani and auxiliary bishop of Dubuque, Aug. 27, 1969, app. vicar general, Aug. 28, 1969.

Durick, Joseph Aloysius: b. Oct. 13, 1914, Dayton, Tenn.; educ. St. Bernard Minor Seminary (St. Bernard, Ala.), St. Mary's Seminary (Baltimore, Md.), Urban Univ. (Rome); ord. priest (Mobile*) May 23, 1940; ord. titular bishop of Cerbal and auxiliary bishop of Mobile-Birmingham, Mar. 24, 1955; app. coadjutor bishop of Nashville, Tenn., installed Mar. 3, 1964; apostolic administrator, 1966; bishop of Nashville, Sept. 10, 1969; resigned Apr. 4, 1975, to work with inmates of Federal correctional institutions and their families.

Durning, Dennis V., C.S.Sp.: b. May 18, 1923, Germantown, Pa.; educ. St. Mary's Seminary (Ferndale, Conn.); ord. priest June 3, 1949; ord. first bishop of Arusha, Tanzania, May 28, 1963.

E

Egan, Edward M.: b. Apr. 2, 1932, Oak Park, Ill.; educ. Quigley Preparatory Seminary (Chicago, Ill.), St. Mary of the Lake Seminary (Mundelein, Ill.), Gregorian Univ. (Rome); ord. priest (Chicago*) Dec. 15, 1957, in Rome; judge of Roman Rota, 1972-85; ord. titular bishop of Allegheny and auxiliary bishop of New York, May 22, 1985.

Elko, Nicholas T.: b. Dec. 14, 1909, Donora, Pa.; educ. Duquesne Univ. (Pittsburgh, Pa.), Seminary of Uzhorod (Czechoslovakia), Louvain Univ. (Belgium); ord. priest (Pittsburgh*, Byzantine Rite) Sept. 30, 1934; ord. titular bishop of Apollonias and apostolic administrator of Byzantine-Rite exarchy of Pittsburgh, Mar. 6, 1955; succeeded as exarch of Pittsburgh, Sept. 5, 1955; became eparch when Pittsburgh was raised to eparchy, July, 1963; app. titular archbishop of Dara, 1967, and ordaining prelate for Byzantine Rite in Rome; head of Oriental liturgical commission; app. auxiliary bishop of Cincinnati, Aug. 10, 1971; resigned Apr. 16, 1985.

Elya, John A., B.S.O.: b. Sept. 16, 1928, Maghdouche, Lebanon; educ. diocesan monastery (Sidon, Lebanon), Gregorian Univ. (Rome, Italy); professed as member of Basilian Salvatorian Order, 1949; ord. priest Feb. 17, 1952, in Rome; came to U.S., 1958; ord. titular bishop of Abilene of Syria and auxiliary bishop of Melkite-Rite diocese of Newton, Mass., June 29, 1986.

F

Favalora, John C.: b. Dec. 5, 1935, New Orleans, La.; educ. St. Joseph Seminary (St. Benedict, La.), Notre Dame Seminary (New Orleans, La.), Gregorian Univ. (Rome), Catholic Univ. of America (Washington, D.C.), Xavier Univ. and Tulane

Univ. (New Orleans); ord. priest (New Orleans*) Dec. 20, 1961; ord. bishop of Alexandria, La., July 29, 1986.

Federal, Joseph Lennox: b. Jan. 13, 1910, Greensboro, N.C.; educ. Belmont Abbey College (Belmont Abbey, N.C.), Niagara Univ. (Niagara Falls, N.Y.), Univ. of Fribourg (Switzerland), North American College and Gregorian Univ. (Rome); ord. priest (Raleigh) Dec. 8, 1934; ord. titular bishop of Appiaria and auxiliary bishop of Salt Lake City, Apr. 11, 1951; app. coadjutor with right of succession, May, 1958; bishop of Salt Lake City, Mar. 31, 1960; retired Apr. 22, 1980.

Ferrario, Joseph A.: b. Mar. 3, 1926, Scranton, Pa.; educ. St. Charles College (Catonsville, Md.), St. Mary's Seminary (Baltimore, Md.), Catholic Univ. (Washington, D.C.); Univ. of Scranton; ord. priest (Honolulu) May 19, 1951; ord. titular bishop of Cuse and auxiliary bishop of Honolulu Jan. 13, 1978; bishop of Honolulu, May 13, 1982.

Fiorenza, Joseph A.: b. Jan. 25, 1931, Beaumont, Tex.; educ. St. Mary's Seminary (LaPorte, Tex.); ord. priest (Galveston-Houston) May 29, 1954; ord. bishop of San Angelo, Oct. 25, 1979; app. bishop of Galveston-Houston, Dec. 18, 1984, installed Feb. 18, 1985.

Fisher, Carl, S.S.J.: b. Nov. 24, 1945, Pascagoala, Miss.; educ. Epiphany Apostolic College (Newburgh, N.Y.) St. Joseph's Seminary, Oblate College and American Univ. (Washington, D.C.), Loyola Univ. (New Orleans, La.), Princeton Univ. (Princeton, N.J.); ord. priest June 2, 1973; ord. titular bishop of Tlos and auxiliary bishop of Los Angeles, Feb. 23, 1987.

Fitzpatrick, John J.: b. Oct. 12, 1918, Trenton, Ont., Canada; educ. Urban Univ. (Rome), Our Lady of the Angels Seminary (Niagara Falls, N.Y.); ord. priest (Buffalo) Dec. 13, 1942; ord. titular bishop of Cenae and auxiliary bishop of Miami, Aug. 28, 1968; bishop of Brownsville, Tex., May 28, 1971.

Fitzsimons, George K.: b. Sept. 4, 1928, Kansas City, Mo.; educ. Rockhurst College (Kansas City, Mo.), Immaculate Conception Seminary (Conception, Mo.); ord. priest (Kansas City-St. Joseph) Mar. 18, 1961; ord. titular bishop of Pertusa and auxiliary bishop of Kansas City-St. Joseph, July 3, 1975; app. bishop of Salina, Apr. 3, 1984.

Flanagan, Bernard Joseph: b. Mar. 31, 1908, Proctor, Vt.; educ. Holy Cross College (Worcester, Mass.), North American College (Rome), Catholic Univ. (Washington, D.C.); ord. priest (Hartford*) Dec. 8, 1931; ord. first bishop of Norwich, Nov. 30, 1953; app. bishop of Worcester, installed, Sept. 24, 1959; resigned Apr. 12, 1983.

Flavin, Glennon P.: b. Mar. 2, 1916, St. Louis, Mo.; educ. Kenrick Seminary (St. Louis, Mo.); ord. priest (St. Louis*) Dec. 20, 1941; ord. titular bishop of Joannina and auxiliary bishop of St. Louis, May 30, 1957; app. bishop of Lincoln, installed Aug. 17, 1967.

Fliss, Raphael M.: b. Oct. 25, 1930, Milwaukee, Wis.; educ. St. Francis Seminary (Milwaukee, Wis.), Catholic University (Washington, D.C.), Pontifical Lateran Univ. (Rome); ord. priest (Milwaukee*) May 26, 1956; ord. coadjutor bishop of Superior with right of succession, Dec. 20, 1979; bishop of Superior, June 27, 1985.

Flores, Patrick F.: b. July 26, 1929, Ganado, Tex.; educ. St. Mary's Seminary (Houston, Tex.); ord. priest (Galveston-Houston) May 26, 1956; ord. titular bishop of Itolica and auxiliary bishop of San Antonio, May 5, 1970 (first Mexican-American bishop); app. bishop of El Paso, Apr. 4, 1978, installed May 29, 1978; app. archbishop of San Antonio 1979; installed Oct. 13, 1979.

Flynn, Harry J.: b. May 2, 1933, Schenectady, N.Y.; educ. Siena College (Loudonville, N.Y.), Mt. St. Mary's College (Emmitsburg, Md.); ord. priest (Albany) May 28, 1960; ord. coadjutor bishop of Lafayette, La., June 24, 1986.

Foley, David E.: b. Feb. 3, 1930, Worcester, Mass.; educ. St. Charles College (Catonsville, Md.), St. Mary's Seminary (Baltimore, Md.); ord. priest (Washington*) May 26, 1952; ord. titular bishop of Octaba and auxiliary bishop of Richmond, June 27, 1986.

Foley, John Patrick: b. Nov. 11, 1935, Sharon Hill, Pa.; educ. St. Joseph's Preparatory School (Philadelphia, Pa.), St. Joseph's College (now University) (Philadelphia, Pa.), St. Charles Borromeo Seminary (Overbrook, Pa.), St. Thomas Univ. (Rome), Columbia School of Journalism (New York); ord. priest (Philadelphia*) May 19, 1962; assistant editor (1967-70) and editor (1970-84) of *The Catholic Standard and Times*, Philadelphia archdiocesan paper; ord. titular archbishop of Neapolis in Proconsulari, May 8, 1984, in Philadelphia; app. to five-year term as president of the Pontifical Commission (Council) for Social Communications, Apr. 5, 1984; is also president of the council of administration of the Vatican Television Center.

Forst, Marion F.: b. Sept. 3, 1910, St. Louis, Mo.; educ. St. Louis Preparatory Seminary (St. Louis, Mo.), Kenrick Seminary (Webster Groves, Mo.); ord. priest (St. Louis*) June 10, 1934; ord. bishop of Dodge City, Mar. 24, 1960; app. titular bishop of Scala and auxiliary bishop of Kansas City, Kans. Oct. 16, 1976; retired Dec. 23, 1986. Bishop emeritus of Dodge City.

Francis, Joseph A., S.V.D.: b. Sept. 30, 1923, Lafayette, La.; educ. St. Augustine Seminary (Bay St. Louis, Miss.), St. Mary Seminary (Techny, Ill.), Catholic Univ. (Washington, D.C.); ord. priest Oct. 7, 1950; president Conference of Major Superiors of Men, 1974-76, and the National Black Catholic Clergy Caucus; ord. titular bishop of Valliposita and auxiliary bishop of Newark, June 25, 1976.

Franklin, William Edwin: b. May 3, 1930, Parnell, Iowa; educ. Loras College and Mt. St. Bernard Seminry (Dubuque, Iowa); ord. priest (Dubuque*) Feb. 4, 1956; ord. titular bishop of Surista and auxiliary bishop of Dubuque, Apr. 1, 1987.

Franz, John B.: b. Oct. 29, 1896, Springfield, Ill.; educ. Quincy College (Quincy, Ill.), Kenrick Seminary (Webster Groves, Mo.), Catholic Univ. (Washington, D.C.); ord. priest (Springfield, Ill.) June 13, 1920; ord. first bishop of Dodge City, Aug. 29, 1951; app. bishop of Peoria, installed Nov. 4, 1959; resigned May 24, 1971.

Franzetta, Benedict C.: b. Aug. 1, 1921, East Liverpool, O.; educ. St. Charles College (Catonsville, Md.), St. Mary Seminary (Cleveland, O.); ord. priest (Youngstown) Apr. 29, 1950; ord. titular bishop of Oderzo and auxiliary bishop of Youngstown, Sept. 4, 1980.

Freking, Frederick W.: b. Aug. 11, 1913, Heron Lake, Minn.; educ. St. Mary's College (Winona, Minn.), North American College and Gregorian Univ. (Rome), Catholic Univ. (Washington, D.C.); ord. priest (Winona) July 31, 1938; ord. bishop of Salina, Nov. 30, 1957; app. bishop of La Crosse, Dec. 30, 1964, installed Feb. 24, 1965; resigned May 10, 1983.

Frey, Gerard L.: b. May 10, 1914, New Orleans, La.; educ. Notre Dame Seminary (New Orleans, La.); ord. priest (New Orleans*) Apr. 2, 1938; ord. bishop of Savannah, Aug. 8, 1967; app. bishop of Lafayette, La., Nov. 7, 1972, installed Jan 7, 1973.

Friend, William. .: b. Oct. 22, 1931, Miami, Fla.; educ. St. Mary's College (St. Mary, Ky.), Mt. St. Mary Seminary (Emmitsburg, Md.), Catholic Univ. (Washington, D.C.), Notre Dame Univ. (Notre Dame, Ind.); ord. priest (Mobile*) May 7, 1959; ord. titular bishop of Pomaria and auxiliary bishop of Alexandria-Shreveport, La., Oct. 30, 1979; app. bishop of Alexandria-Shreveport, Nov. 17, 1982, installed Jan 11, 1983; app. first bishop of Shreveport, June, 1986; installed July 30, 1986.

Frosi, Angelo, S. X.: b. Jan. 31, 1924, Baffano Cremona, Italy; ord. priest May 6, 1948; U.S. citizen; ord. titular bishop of Magneto, May 1, 1970, and prelate of Abaete do Tocantins, Brazil; app. first bishop of Abaetetuba, Brazil, Sept. 17, 1981.

Furlong, Philip J.: b. Dec. 8, 1892, New York, N.Y.; educ. Cathedral College (New York, N.Y.), St. Joseph's Seminary (Yonkers, N.Y.); ord. priest (New York*) May 18, 1918; ord. titular bishop of Araxa and auxiliary to military vicar, Jan. 25, 1956. Retired 1971.

G

Gallagher, Raymond J.: b. Nov. 19, 1912, Cleveland, Ohio; educ. John Carroll Univ. and Our Lady of the Lake Seminary (Cleveland, O.); ord. priest (Cleveland) Mar. 25, 1939; secretary of the National Conference of Catholic Charities 1961-65; ord. bishop of Lafayette in Indiana, Aug. 11, 1965; resigned Oct. 26, 1982.

Gallegos, Alphonse, O.A.R.: b. Feb. 20, 1931, Albuquerque, N. Mex., ord. priest May 24, 1958; ord. titular bishop of Sasabe and auxiliary bishop of Sacramento, Nov. 4, 1981.

Ganter, Bernard J.: b. July 17,1928, Galveston, Tex.; educ. Texas A & M Univ. (College Sta., Tex.), St. Mary's Seminary (La Porte, Tex.), Catholic Univ. (Washington, D.C.); ord. priest (Galveston-Houston) May 22, 1952; chancellor of Galveston-Houston diocese, 1966-73; ord. first bishop of Tulsa, Feb. 7, 1973; app. bishop of Beaumont, Tex., Oct. 18, 1977, installed Dec. 13, 1977.

Garland, James H.: b. Dec. 13, 1931, Wilmington, Ohio; educ. Wilmington College (Ohio), Ohio State Univ. (Columbus, O.); Mt. St. Mary's Seminary (Cincinnati, O.), Catholic Univ. (Washington, D.C.); ord. priest (Cincinnati*) Aug. 15, 1959; ord. titular bishop of Garriana and auxiliary bishop of Cincinnati, July 25, 1984; director of department of social services.

Garmendia, Francisco: b. Nov. 6, 1924, Lozcano, Spain; ord. priest June 29, 1947, in Spain; came to New York in 1964; became naturalized citizen; ord. titular bishop of Limisa and auxiliary bishop of New York, June 29, 1977. Vicar for Spanish pastoral development in New York archdiocese.

Garmo, George: b. Dec. 8, 1921, Telkaif, Iraq; educ. St. Peter Chaldean Patriarchal Seminary (Mossul, Iraq), Pontifical Urban Univ. (Rome); ord. priest Dec. 8, 1945; pastor of Chaldean parish in Detroit archdiocese, 1960-64, 1966-80; ord. archbishop of Chaldean-Rite archdiocese of Mossul, Iraq, Sept. 14, 1980.

Garner, Robert F.: b. Apr. 27, 1920, Jersey City, N.J.; educ. Seton Hall Univ. (S. Orange, N.J.), Immaculate Conception Seminary (Darlington, N.J.); ord. priest (Newark*) June 15, 1946; ord. titular bishop of Blera and auxiliary bishop of Newark, June 25, 1976.

Gaughan, Norbert F.: b. May 30, 1921, Pittsburgh, Pa.; educ. St. Vincent College (Latrobe, Pa.), Univ. of Pittsburgh; ord. priest (Pittsburgh) Nov. 4, 1945; ord. titular bishop of Taraqua and auxiliary bishop of Greensburg, June 26, 1975; app. bishop of Gary, July 24, 1984, installed Oct. 1, 1984.

Gelineau, Louis E.: b. May 3, 1928, Burlington, Vt.; educ. St. Michael's College (Winooski, Vt.), St. Paul's Univ. Seminary (Ottawa, Ont.), Catholic Univ. (Washington, D.C.); ord. priest (Hartford*) June 5, 1954; ord. bishop of Providence, R.I., Jan. 26, 1972.

Gendron, Odore: b. Sept. 13, 1921, Manchester, N.H.; educ. St. Charles Borromeo Seminary (Sherbrooke, Que., Canada), Univ. of Ottawa, St. Paul Univ. Seminary (Ottawa, Ont., Canada); ord. priest (Manchester) May 31, 1947; ord. bishop of Manchester, Feb. 3, 1975.

Gerber, Eugene J.: b. Apr. 30, 1931, Kingman, Kans.; educ. St. Thomas Seminary (Denver, Colo.), Wichita State Univ.; Catholic Univ. (Washington, D.C.), Angelicum (Rome); ord. priest (Wichita) May 19, 1959; ord. bishop of Dodge City, Dec. 14, 1976; app. bishop of Wichita, Nov. 17, 1982.

Gerbermann, Hugo, M.M.: b. Sept. 11, 1913, Nada, Tex.; educ. St. John's Minor and Major Seminary (San Antonio, Tex.), Maryknoll Seminary (Maryknoll, N.Y.); ord. priest Feb. 7, 1943; missionary work in Ecuador and Guatemala; ord. titular bishop of Amathus and prelate of Huehuetenango, Guatemala, July 22, 1962; first bishop of Huehuetenango, Dec. 23, 1967; app. titular bishop of Pinkel and auxiliary bishop of San Antonio, July 24, 1975; resigned June 30, 1982.

Gerety, Peter L.: b. July 19, 1912, Shelton, Conn.; educ. Sulpician Seminary (Paris, France); ord. priest (Hartford*) June 29, 1939; ord. titular bishop of Crepedula and coadjutor bishop of Portland, Me., with right of succession, June 1, 1966; app. apostolic administrator of Portland, 1967; bishop of Portland, Me., Sept. 15, 1969; app. archbishop of Newark, Apr. 2, 1974; installed June 28, 1974; retired June 3, 1986.

Gerrard, James J.: b. June 9, 1897, New Bedford,

Mass.; educ. St. Laurent College (Montreal, Que.), St. Bernard's Seminary (Rochester, N.Y.); ord. priest (Fall River) May 26, 1923; ord. titular bishop of Forma and auxiliary bishop of Fall River, Mar. 19, 1959. Retired January, 1976.

Gerry, Joseph, O.S.B.: b. Sept. 12, 1928, Millinocket, Me.; educ. St. Anselm Abbey Seminary (Manchester, N.H.), Univ. of Toronto (Canada), Fordham Univ. (New York); ord. priest June 12, 1954; abbot of St. Anselm Abbey, Manchester, N.H., 1972; ord. titular bishop of Praecausa and auxiliary of Manchester, Apr. 21, 1986.

Glennie, Ignatius T., S.J.: b. Feb. 5, 1907, Mexico City; educ. Mt. St. Michael's Scholasticate (Spokane, Wash.), Pontifical Seminary (Kandy, Ceylon), St. Mary's College (Kurdeong, India); entered Society of Jesus, 1924; ord. priest Nov. 21, 1938; ord. bishop of Trincomalee, Ceylon, Sept. 21, 1947; title of see changed to Trincomalee-Batticaloa (Sri Lanka), 1967; resigned Feb. 15, 1974.

Gonzalez, Roberto O., O.F.M.: b. June 2, 1950, Elizabeth, N.J.; educ. St. Joseph Seraphic Seminary (Callicoon, N.Y.), Siena College (Loudonville, N.Y.), Washington Theological Union (Silver Spring, Md.), Fordham Univ. (New York, N.Y.); solemnly professed in Franciscan Order, 1976; ord. priest May 8, 1977; ord. titular bishop of Ursona and auxiliary bishop of Boston, Oct. 3, 1988.

Gorman, John R.: b. Dec. 11, 1925, Chicago, Ill.; educ. Quigley Preparatory Seminary, Mundelein Seminary, Loyola Univ. (Chicago, Ill.); ord. priest May 1, 1956 (Chicago*); ord. titular bishop of Catula and auxiliary bishop of Chicago, Apr. 11, 1988.

Gossman, F. Joseph: b. Apr. 1, 1930, Baltimore, Md.: educ. St. Charles College (Catonsville, Md.), St. Mary's Seminary (Baltimore, Md.), North American College (Rome), Catholic Univ. (Washington, D.C.); ord. priest (Baltimore*) Dec. 17, 1955; ord. titular bishop of Agunto and auxiliary bishop of Baltimore, Sept. 11, 1968; named urban vicar, June 13, 1970; app. bishop of Raleigh April 8, 1975.

Gottwald, George J.: b. May 12, 1914, St. Louis, Mo.; educ. Kenrick Seminary (Webster Groves, Mo.); ord. priest (St. Louis*) June 9, 1940; ord. titular bishop of Cedamusa and auxiliary bishop of St. Louis, Aug. 8, 1961; resigned Aug. 2, 1988.

Gracida, Rene H.: b. June 9, 1923, New Orleans, La.; educ. Rice Univ. and Univ. of Houston (Houston, Tex.), Univ. of Fribourg (Switzerland); ord. priest (Miami*) May 23, 1959; ord. titular bishop of Masuccaba and auxiliary bishop of Miami, Jan. 25, 1972; app. first bishop of Pensacola-Tallahassee, Oct. 1, 1975, installed Nov. 6, 1975; app. bishop of Corpus Christi, May 24, 1983, installed July 11, 1983.

Grady, Thomas J.: b. Oct. 9, 1914, Chicago, Ill.; educ. St. Mary of the Lake Seminary (Mundelein, Ill.), Gregorian Univ. (Rome), Loyola Univ. (Chicago, Ill.); ord. priest (Chicago*) Apr. 23, 1938; ord. titular bishop of Vamalla and auxiliary bishop of Chicago, Aug. 24, 1967; app. bishop of Orlando, Fla., Nov. 11, 1974, installed Dec. 16, 1974.

Graham, John J.: b. Sept. 11, 1913, Philadelphia, Pa.; educ. St. Charles Borromeo Seminary (Philadelphia, Pa.), Pontifical Roman Seminary (Rome, Italy); ord. priest (Philadelphia*) Feb. 26, 1938; ord. titular bishop of Sabrata and auxiliary bishop of Philadelphia, Jan. 7, 1964.

Grahmann, Charles V.: b. July 15, 1931, Halletsville, Tex.; educ. The Assumption-St. John's Seminary (San Antonio, Tex.); ord. priest (San Antonio*) Mar. 17, 1956; ord. titular bishop of Equilium and auxiliary bishop of San Antonio, Aug. 20, 1981; app. first bishop of Victoria, Tex., Apr. 13, 1982.

Graves, Lawrence P.: b. May 4, 1916, Texarkana, Ark.; educ. St. John's Seminary (Little Rock, Ark.), North American College (Rome), Catholic Univ. (Washington, D.C.); ord. priest (Little Rock) June 11, 1942; ord. titular bishop of Vina and auxiliary bishop of Little Rock, Apr. 25, 1969; app. bishop of Alexandria, May 22, 1973, installed Sept. 18, 1973; title of see changed to Alexandria-Shreveport, Jan. 12, 1977; resigned July 20, 1982.

Graziano, Lawrence, O.F.M.: b. Apr. 5, 1921, Mt. Vernon, N.Y.; educ. Mt. Alvernia Seminary (Wappingers Falls, N.Y.); ord. priest Jan. 26, 1947; ord. titular bishop of Limata and auxiliary bishop of Santa Ana, El Salvador, Sept. 21, 1961; app. coadjutor bishop of San Miguel, El Salvador, with right of succession, 1965; bishop of San Miguel, Jan. 10, 1968; resigned June 27, 1969.

Green, Francis J.: b. July 7, 1906, Corning, N.Y.; educ. St. Patrick's Seminary (Menlo Park, Calif.); ord. priest (Tucson) May 15, 1932; ord. titular bishop of Serra and auxiliary bishop of Tucson, Sept. 17, 1953; named coadjutor of Tucson with right of succession, May 11, 1960; bishop of Tucson, Oct. 26, 1960; retired July 27, 1981.

Gregory, Wilton D.: b. Dec. 7, 1947, Chicago, Ill.; educ. Quigley Preparatory Seminary South, Niles College of Loyola Univ. (Chicago, Ill.), St. Mary of the Lake Seminary (Mundelein, Ill.), Pontifical Liturgical Institute, Sant'Anselmo (Rome); ord. priest (Chicago*) May 9, 1973; ord. titular bishop of Oliva and auxiliary bishop of Chicago, Dec. 13, 1983.

Griffin, James A.: b. June 13, 1934, Fairview Park, O.; educ. St. Charles College (Baltimore, Md.), Borromeo College (Wicklife, O.); St. Mary Seminary (Cleveland, O.); Lateran Univ. (Rome); Cleveland State Univ.; ord. priest (Cleveland) May 28, 1960; ord. titular bishop of Holar and auxiliary bishop of Cleveland, Aug. 1, 1979; app. bishop of Columbus, Feb. 8, 1983.

Grutka, Andrew G.: b. Nov. 17, 1908, Joliet, Ill.; educ. St. Procopius College and Seminary (Lisle, Ill.), Urban Univ. and Gregorian Univ. (Rome); ord. priest (Ft. Wayne-S. Bend) Dec. 5, 1933; app. moderator of lay activities in Gary diocese, 1955; app. first bishop of Gary, Feb. 25, 1957; app. member of Pontifical Marian Academy, Jan. 5, 1970; retired July 24, 1984.

Guilfoyle, George H.: b. Nov. 13, 1913, New York, N.Y.; educ. Georgetown Univ. (Washington, D.C.), Fordham Univ. (New York City), St. Joseph's Seminary (Dunwoodie, N.Y.), Columbia Univ. Law School (New York City); ord. priest (New York*) Mar. 25, 1944; ord. titular bishop of Marazane and auxiliary bishop of New York, Nov.

30, 1964; app. bishop of Camden, installed Mar. 4, 1968.

Guillory, Curtis J., S.V.D.: b. Sept. 1, 1943, Lafayette, La.; educ. Divine Word College (Epworth, Iowa), Chicago Theological Union (Chicago), Creighton Univ. (Omaha, Neb.); ord. priest Dec. 16, 1972; ord. titular bishop of Stagno and auxiliary bishop of Galveston-Houston, Feb 19, 1988.

Gumbleton, Thomas J.: b. Jan. 26, 1930, Detroit, Mich.; educ. St. John Provincial Seminary (Detroit, Mich.), Pontifical Lateran Univ. (Rome); ord. priest (Detroit*) June 2, 1956; ord. titular bishop of Ululi and auxiliary bishop of Detroit, May 1, 1968.

H

Hacker, Hilary B.: b. Jan. 10, 1913, New Ulm, Minn.; educ. St. Paul Seminary (St. Paul, Minn.), Gregorian Univ. (Rome); ord. priest (St. Paul-Minneapolis*) June 4, 1938; ord. bishop of Bismarck, N. Dak., Feb. 27, 1957; resigned June 30, 1982.

Hackett, John F.: b. Dec. 7, 1911, New Haven, Conn.; educ. St. Thomas Seminary (Bloomfield, Conn.), Seminaire Ste. Sulpice (Paris); ord. priest (Hartford*) June 29, 1936; ord. titular bishop of Helenopolis in Palaestina and auxiliary bishop of Hartford, Mar. 19, 1953; retired Dec. 16, 1986.

Ham, J. Richard, M.M.: b. July 11, 1921, Chicago, Ill.; educ. Maryknoll Seminary (New York); ord. priest June 12, 1948; missionary to Guatemala, 1958; ord. titular bishop of Puzia di Numidia and auxiliary bishop of Guatemala, Jan. 6, 1968; resigned see 1979; app. vicar for Hispanic ministry in St. Paul and Minneapolis archdiocese, January, 1980; auxiliary bishop of St. Paul and Minneapolis, October, 1980.

Hammes, George A.: b. Sept. 11, 1911, St. Joseph Ridge, Wis.; educ. St. Lawrence Seminary (Mt. Calvary. Wis.), St. Louis Preparatory Seminary (St. Louis, Mo.), Kenrick Seminary (Webster Groves, Mo.), Sulpician Seminary, Catholic Univ. (Washington, D.C.); ord. priest (LaCrosse) May 22, 1937; ord. bishop of Superior, May 24, 1960; resigned June 29, 1985.

Hanifen, Richard C.: b. June 15, 1931, Denver, Colo,; educ. Regis College and St. Thomas Seminary (Denver, Colo.), Catholic Univ. (Washington, D.C.), Lateran Univ. (Rome); ord. priest (Denver*) June 6, 1959; ord. titular bishop of Abercorn and auxiliary bishop of Denver, Sept. 20, 1974; app. first bishop of Colorado Springs, 1983; installed Jan. 30, 1984.

Hannan, Philip M.: b. May 20, 1913, Washington, D.C.; educ. St. Charles College (Catonsville, Md.), Catholic Univ. (Washington, D.C.), North American College (Rome); ord. priest (Washington*) Dec. 8, 1939; ord. titular bishop of Hieropolis and auxiliary bishop of Washington, D.C., Aug. 28, 1956; app. archbishop of New Orleans, installed Oct. 13, 1965.

Hanus, Jerome George, O.S.B.: b. May 25, 1940, Brainard, Nebr.; educ. Conception Seminary (Conception, Mo.), St. Anselm Univ. (Rome), Princeton Theological Seminary (Princeton, N.J.); ord. priest (Conception Abbey, Mo.) July 30, 1966; abbot of Conception Abbey, 1977-87; president of Swiss American Benedictine Congregation, 1984-87; ord. bishop of St. Cloud, Aug. 24, 1987.

Harper, Edward, C.SS.R.: b. July 23, 1910, Brooklyn, N.Y.; educ. Redemptorist Houses of Study; ord. priest June 18, 1939; ord. titular bishop of Heraclea Pontica and first prelate of Virgin Islands, Oct. 6, 1960; became first bishop, 1977, when prelacy was made diocese of St. Thomas; retired Oct. 16, 1985.

Harrington, Timothy J.: b. Dec. 19, 1918, Holyoke, Mass.; educ. Holy Cross College (Worcester, Mass.), Grand Seminary (Montreal, Que.), Boston College School of Social Work; ord. priest (Springfield, Mass.*) Jan. 19, 1946; ord. titular bishop of Rusuca and auxiliary bishop of Worcester, Mass., July 2, 1968; app. bishop of Worcester, Sept. 1, 1983, installed Oct. 13, 1983.

Harrison, Frank J.: b. Aug. 12, 1912; Syracuse, N.Y.; educ. Notre Dame Univ. (Notre Dame, Ind.), St. Bernard's Seminary (Rochester, N.Y.), ord. priest (Syracuse) June 4, 1937; ord. titular bishop of Aquae in Numidia and auxiliary bishop of Syracuse, Apr. 22, 1971; app. bishop of Syracuse, Nov. 9, 1976, installed Feb. 6, 1977; retired June 16, 1987.

Hart, Daniel A.: b. Aug. 24, 1927, Lawrence, Mass.; educ. St. John's Seminary (Brighton, Mass.); ord. priest (Boston*) Feb. 2, 1953; ord. titular bishop of Tepelta and auxiliary bishop of Boston, Oct. 18, 1976.

Hart, Joseph: b. Sept. 26, 1931, Kansas City, Missouri; educ. St. John Seminary (Kansas City, Mo.), St. Meinrad Seminary (Indianapolis, Ind.); ord. priest (Kansas City-St. Joseph) May 1, 1956; ord. titular bishop of Thimida Regia and auxiliary bishop of Cheyenne, Wyo., Aug. 31, 1976; app. bishop of Cheyenne, installed June 12, 1978.

Hastrich, Jerome J.: b. Nov. 13, 1914, Milwaukee, Wis.; educ. Marquette Univ., St. Francis Seminary (Milwaukee, Wis.); ord. priest (Milwaukee*) Feb. 9, 1941; ord. titular bishop of Gurza and auxiliary bishop of Madison, Sept. 3, 1963; app. bishop of Gallup, N.Mex., Sept. 3, 1969.

Head, Edward D.: b. Aug. 5, 1919, White Plains, N.Y.; educ. Cathedral College, St. Joseph's Seminary, Columbia Univ. (New York City); ord. priest (New York*) Jan. 27, 1945; director of New York Catholic Charities; ord. titular bishop of Ardsratha and auxiliary bishop of New York, Mar. 19, 1970; app. bishop of Buffalo, Jan. 23, 1973, installed Mar. 19, 1973.

Heim, Capistran F., O.F.M.: b. Jan. 21, 1934, Catskill, N.Y.; educ. Franciscan Houses of Study; ord. priest Dec. 18, 1965; missionary in Brazil; ord. first bishop of prelature of Itaituba, Brazil, Sept. 17, 1988; installed Oct. 2, 1988.

Helmsing, Charles H.: b. Mar. 23, 1908, Shrewsbury, Mo.; educ. St. Louis Preparatory Seminary (St. Louis, Mo.), Kenrick Seminary (Webster Groves, Mo.); ord. priest (St. Louis*) June 10, 1933; ord. titular bishop of Axomis and auxiliary bishop of St. Louis, Apr. 19, 1949; first bishop of Springfield-Cape Girardeau, Aug. 24, 1956; bishop of Kansas City-St. Joseph, 1962, installed Apr. 3, 1962; resigned June 25, 1977.

Herrmann, Edward J.: b. Nov. 6, 1913, Baltimore, Md.; educ. Mt. St. Mary's Seminary (Emmitsburg, Md.), Catholic Univ. (Washington, D.C.); ord. priest (Washington*) June 12, 1947; ord. titular bishop of Lamzella and auxiliary bishop of Washington, D.C., Apr. 26, 1966; app. bishop of Columbus, June 26, 1973; resigned Sept. 18, 1982.

Herzig, Charles E.: b. Aug. 14, 1929, San Antonio, Tex.; educ. St. Mary's Univ., St. John's Seminary and Our Lady of the Lake Univ. (San Antonio, Tex.); ord. priest (San Antonio*) May 31, 1955; ord. first bishop of Tyler, Tex. Feb. 24, 1987.

Hettinger, Edward Gerhard: b. Oct. 14, 1902, Lancaster, O.; educ. St. Vincent's College (Beatty, Pa.); ord. priest (Columbus) June 2, 1928; ord. titular bishop of Teos and auxiliary bishop of Columbus, Feb. 24, 1942; retired Oct. 18, 1977.

Hickey, Dennis W.: b. Oct. 28, 1914, Dansville, N.Y.; educ. Colgate Univ. and St. Bernard's Seminary (Rochester, N.Y.); ord. priest (Rochester) June 7, 1941; ord. titular bishop of Rusuccuru and auxiliary bishop of Rochester, N.Y., Mar. 14, 1968.

Hickey, James A.: (See Cardinals, Biographies.)

Higi, William L.: b. Aug. 29, 1933, Anderson, Ind.; educ. Our Lady of the Lakes Preparatory Seminary (Wawasee, Ind.), Mt. St. Mary of the West Seminary and Xavier Univ. (Cincinnati, O.); ord. priest (Lafayette, Ind.) May 30, 1959; ord. bishop of Lafayette, Ind., June 6, 1984.

Hines, Vincent J.: b. Sept. 14, 1912, New Haven, Conn.; educ. St. Thomas Seminary (Bloomfield, Conn.), St. Sulpice Seminary (Paris), Lateran Univ. (Rome); ord. priest (Hartford*) May 2, 1937; ord. bishop of Norwich, Conn., Mar. 17, 1960; retired June 17, 1975.

Hoch, Lambert A.: b. Feb. 6, 1903, Elkton, S.D.; educ. Creighton Univ. (Omaha, Nebr.), St. Paul Seminary (St. Paul, Minn.); ord. priest (Sioux Falls) May 30, 1928; ord. bishop of Bismarck, Mar. 25, 1952; app. bishop of Sioux Falls Dec. 5, 1956; retired June 13, 1978.

Hodapp, Robert L., S.J.: b. Oct. 1, 1910. Mankato, Minn.; educ. St. Stanislaus Seminary (Florissant, Mo.), St. Louis Univ. (St. Louis, Mo.); ord. priest June 18, 1941; ord. bishop of Belize (now Belize City-Belmopan), June 26, 1958; retired Nov. 11, 1983.

Hoffman, James R.: b. June 12, 1932, Fremont, O.; educ. Our Lady of the Lake Minor Seminary (Wawasee, Ind.), St. Meinrad College (St. Meinrad, Ind.); Mt. St. Mary Seminary (Norwood, O.); Catholic Univ. (Washington, D.C.); ord. priest (Toledo) July 28, 1957; ord. titular bishop of Italica and auxiliary bishop of Toledo, June 23, 1978; bishop of Toledo, Dec. 16, 1980.

Hogan, James J.: b. Oct. 17, 1911, Philadelphia, Pa.; educ. St. Charles College (Catonsville, Md.), St. Mary's Seminary (Baltimore), Gregorian Univ. (Rome), Catholic Univ. (Washington, D.C.); ord. priest (Trenton) Dec. 8, 1937; ord. titular bishop of Philomelium and auxiliary bishop of Trenton, Feb. 25, 1960; app. bishop of Altoona-Johnstown, installed July 6, 1966; retired Nov. 4, 1986.

Hogan, Joseph L.: b. Mar. 11, 1916, Lima, N.Y.; educ. St. Bernard's Seminary (Rochester, N.Y.), Canisius College (Buffalo, N.Y.), Angelicum (Rome); ord. priest (Rochester) June 6, 1942; ord. bishop of Rochester, Nov. 28, 1969; resigned Nov. 28, 1978.

Houck, William Russell: b. June 26, 1926, Mobile Ala.; educ. St. Bernard Junior College (Cullman, Ala.), St. Mary's Seminary College and St. Mary's Seminary (Baltimore, Md.), Catholic Univ. (Washington, D.C.); ord. priest (Mobile*) May 19, 1951; ord. titular bishop of Alessano and auxiliary bishop of Jackson, Miss., May 27, 1979, by Pope John Paul II; app. bishop of Jackson, Apr. 11, 1984, installed June 5, 1984.

Howze, Joseph Lawson E.: b. Aug. 30, 1923, Daphne, Ala.; convert to Catholicism, 1948; educ. St. Bonaventure Univ. (St. Bonaventure, N.Y.); ord. priest (Raleigh) May 7, 1959; ord. titular bishop of Massita and auxiliary bishop of Natchez-Jackson, Jan. 28, 1973; app. first bishop of Biloxi, Miss., Mar. 8, 1977; installed June 6, 1977.

Hubbard, Howard J.: b. Oct. 31, 1938, Troy, N.Y.; educ. St. Joseph's Seminary (Dunwoodie, N.Y.); North American College and Gregorian Univ. (Rome), Catholic Univ. (Washington, D.C.); ord. priest (Albany) Dec. 18, 1963; ord. bishop of Albany, Mar. 27, 1977.

Hughes, Alfred C.: b. Dec. 2, 1932, Boston, Mass.; educ. St. John Seminary (Brighton, Mass), Gregorian Univ. (Rome); ord. priest (Boston*) Dec. 15, 1957, in Rome; ord. titular bishop of Maximiana in Byzacena and auxiliary bishop of Boston, Sept. 14, 1981.

Hughes, Edward T.: b. Nov. 13, 1920, Lansdowne, Pa.; educ. St. Charles Seminary, Univ. of Pennsylvania (Philadelphia); ord. priest (Philadelphia*) May 31, 1947; ord. titular bishop of Segia and auxiliary bishop of Philadelphia, July 21, 1976; app. bishop of Metuchen, Dec. 11, 1986.

Hughes, William A.: b. Sept. 23, 1921, Youngstown, O.; educ. St. Charles College (Catonsville, Md.), St. Mary's Seminary (Cleveland, O.) Notre Dame Univ. (Notre Dame, Ind.); ord. priest (Youngstown) Apr. 6, 1946; ord. titular bishop of Inis Cathaig and auxiliary bishop of Youngstown, Sept. 12, 1974; app. bishop of Covington, installed May 8, 1979.

Hunthausen, Raymond G.: b. Aug. 21, 1921, Anaconda, Mont.; educ. Carroll College (Helena, Mont.), St. Edward's Seminary (Kenmore, Wash.), St. Louis Univ. (St. Louis, Mo.), Catholic Univ. (Washington, D.C.), Fordham Univ. (New York City), Notre Dame Univ. (Notre Dame, Ind.); ord. priest (Helena) June 1, 1946; ord. bishop of Helena, Aug. 30, 1962; app. archbishop of Seattle, Feb. 25, 1975.

Hurley, Francis T.: b. Jan. 12, 1927, San Francisco, Calif.; educ. St. Patrick's Seminary (Menlo Park, Calif.), Catholic Univ. (Washington, D.C.); ord. priest (San Francisco*) June 16, 1951; assigned to NCWC in Washington, D.C., 1957; assistant (1958) and later (1968) associate secretary of NCCB and USCC; ord. titular bishop of Daimlaig and auxiliary bishop of Juneau, Alaska, Mar. 19, 1970; app. bishop of Juneau, July 20, 1971, installed Sept. 8, 1971; app. archbishop of Anchorage, May 4, 1976, installed July 8, 1976.

Hurley, Mark J.: b. Dec. 13, 1919, San Francisco,

Calif.; educ. St. Patrick's Seminary (Menlo Park, Calif.), Univ. of California (Berkeley), Catholic Univ. (Washington, D.C.), Lateran Univ. (Rome), Univ. of Portland (Portland, Ore.); ord. priest (San Francisco*) Sept. 23, 1944; ord. titular bishop of Thunusuda and auxiliary bishop of San Francisco, Jan. 4, 1968; app. bishop of Santa Rosa, Nov. 19, 1969; resigned Apr. 15, 1986.

I-J

Ibrahim, Ibrahim N.: b. Oct. 1, 1937, Telkaif, Mosul, Iraq.; educ. Patriarchal Seminary (Mosul, Iraq), St. Sulpice Seminary (Paris, France); ord. priest Dec. 30, 1962, in Baghdad, Iraq; ord. titular bishop of Anbar and apostolic exarch for Chaldean-Rite Catholics in the United States, Mar. 8, 1982, in Baghdad; installed in Detroit, Apr. 18, 1982; app. first eparch, Aug. 3, 1985, when exarchate was raised to eparchy of St. Thomas Apostle of Detroit.

Imesch, Joseph L.: b. June 21, 1931, Detroit, Mich.; educ. Sacred Heart Seminary (Detroit, Mich.), North American College, Gregorian Univ. (Rome); ord. priest (Detroit*) Dec. 16, 1956; ord. titular bishop of Pomaria and auxiliary bishop of Detroit, Apr. 3, 1973; app. bishop of Joliet, June 30, 1979.

Jakubowski, Thad J.: b. Apr. 5, 1924, Chicago, Ill.; educ. Mundelein Seminary, St. Mary of the Lake Univ., Loyola Univ. (Chicago); ord priest May 3, 1950 (Chicago*); ord. titular bishop of Plestia and auxiliary bishop of Chicago, Apr. 11, 1988.

Jolson, Alfred, S.J.: b. June 18, 1928, Bridgeport, Conn.; educ. Weston College (Weston, Mass.), Gregorian Univ. (Rome); ord. priest June 14, 1958; app. Bishop of Reykjavik, Iceland, Dec. 12, 1987.

Joyce, Robert F.: b. Oct. 7, 1896, Proctor, Vt.; educ. Univ. of Vermont (Burlington, Vt.), Grand Seminary (Montreal, Canada); ord. priest (Hartford*) May 26, 1923; ord. titular bishop of Citium and auxiliary bishop of Burlington, Oct. 28, 1954; installed as bishop of Burlington, Feb. 26, 1957; resigned Dec. 14, 1971.

K

Kaffer, Roger L.: b. Aug. 14, 1927, Joliet, Ill.; educ. Quigley Preparatory Seminary (Chicago, Ill.), St. Mary of the Lake Seminary (Mundelein, Ill.), Gregorian Univ. (Rome); ord. priest (Joliet) May 1, 1954; ord. titular bishop of Dusa and auxiliary bishop of Joliet, June 26, 1985.

Kalisz, Raymond P., S.V.D.: b. Sept. 25, 1927, Melvindale, Mich.; educ. St. Mary's Seminary (Techny, Ill.); ord. priest Aug. 15, 1954; ord. bishop of Wewak, Papua New Guinea, August 15, 1980.

Kaniecki, Michael Joseph, S.J.: b. Apr. 13, 1935, Detroit Mich.; joined Jesuits 1953; educ. Xavier Univ. (Milford, O.), Mt. St. Michael's Seminary (Spokane, Wash.), Regis College (Willowdale, Ont.); ord. priest June 5, 1965; ord. coadjutor bishop of Fairbanks, May 1, 1984; bishop of Fairbanks, June 1, 1985.

Keating, John Richard: b. July 20, 1934, Chicago, Ill.; educ. Quigley Preparatory Seminary (Chicago, Ill.), St. Mary of the Lake Seminary (Mundelein, Ill.), Gregorian Univ. (Rome); ord. priest (Chicago*) Dec. 20, 1958; ord. bishop of Arlington, Aug. 4, 1983.

Keeler, William Henry: b. Mar. 4, 1931, San Antonio, Tex.; educ. St. Charles Seminary (Overbrook, Pa.), North American College, Pontifical Gregorian Univ. (Rome); ord. priest (Harrisburg) July 17, 1955; ord. titular bishop of Ulcinium and auxiliary bishop of Harrisburg, Sept. 21, 1979; app. bishop of Harrisburg, Nov. 15, 1983; installed Jan. 4, 1984.

Keleher, James P.: b. July 31, 1931, Chicago, Ill.; educ. Quigley Preparatory Seminary (Chicago, Ill.), St. Mary of the Lake Seminary (Mundelein, Ill.); ord. priest (Chicago*) Apr. 12, 1958; ord. bishop of Belleville, Dec. 11, 1984.

Kelly, Thomas C., O.P.: b. July 14, 1931, Rochester, N.Y.; educ. Providence College (Providence, R.I.), Immaculate Conception College (Washington, D.C.), Angelicum (Rome); professed in Dominicans, Aug. 26, 1952; secretary, apostolic delegation, Washington, D.C., 1965-71; associate general secretary, 1971-77, and general secretary, 1977-81, NCCB/USCC; ord. titular bishop of Tusurus and auxiliary bishop of Washington, D.C., Aug. 15, 1977; app. archbishop of Louisville, Dec. 28, 1981, installed Feb. 18, 1982.

Kenney, Lawrence J.: b. Aug. 30, 1930, New Rochelle, N.Y.; educ. Cathedral College (New York, N.Y.), St. Joseph's Seminary (Yonkers, N.Y.), Iona College (New Rochelle, N.Y.); ord. priest (New York*) June 2, 1956; ord. titular bishop of Holar and auxiliary bishop of the Military Services archdiocese, May 10, 1983.

Kenny, Michael H.: b. June 26, 1937, Hollywood, Calif.; educ. St. Joseph College (Mountain View, Calif.), St. Patrick's Seminary (Menlo Park, Calif.), Catholic Univ. (Washington, D.C.); ord. priest (Santa Rosa) Mar. 30, 1963; ord. bishop of Juneau, May 27, 1979.

Kinney, John F.: b. June 11, 1937, Oelwein, Iowa; educ. Nazareth Hall and St. Paul Seminaries (St. Paul, Minn.); Pontifical Lateran University (Rome); ord. priest (St. Paul-Minneapolis*) Feb. 2, 1963; ord. titular bishop of Caorle and auxiliary bishop of St. Paul and Minneapolis, Jan. 25, 1977; app. bishop of Bismarck June 30, 1982.

Kmiec, Edward U.: b. June 4, 1936, Trenton, N.J.; educ. St. Charles College (Catonsville, Md.), St. Mary's Seminary (Baltimore, Md.), Gregorian Univ. (Rome); ord. priest (Trenton) Dec. 20, 1961; ord. titular bishop of Simidicca and auxiliary bishop of Trenton, Nov. 3, 1982.

Kocisko, Stephen: b. June 11, 1915, Minneapolis, Minn.; educ. Nazareth Hall Minor Seminary (St. Paul, Minn.), Pontifical Ruthenian College, Urban Univ. (Rome); ord. priest (Pittsburgh*, Byzantine Rite) Mar. 30, 1941; ord. titular bishop of Teveste and auxiliary bishop of apostolic exarchate of Pittsburgh, Oct. 23, 1956; installed as first eparch of the eparchy of Passaic, Sept. 10, 1963; app. eparch of Byzantine-Rite diocese of Pittsburgh, installed Mar. 5, 1968; app. first metropolitan of Munhall, installed June 11, 1969; title of see changed to Pittsburgh, 1977.

Koester, Charles R.: b. Sept. 16, 1915, Jefferson City, Mo.; educ. Conception Academy (Conception, Mo.), St. Louis Preparatory Seminary and Kenrick Seminary (St. Louis, Mo.), North American College (Rome); ord. priest (St. Louis*) Dec. 20, 1941; ord. titular bishop of Suacia and auxiliary bishop of St. Louis, Feb. 11, 1971.

Krawczak, Arthur H.: b. Feb. 2, 1913, Detroit, Mich.; educ. Sacred Heart Seminary, Sts. Cyril and Methodius Seminary (Orchard Lake, Mich.), Catholic Univ. (Washington, D.C.); ord. priest (Detroit*) May 18, 1940; ord. titular bishop of Subbar and auxiliary bishop of Detroit, Apr. 3, 1973; retired Aug. 17, 1982.

Krol, John J.: (See Cardinals, Biographies.)

Kucera, Daniel, O.S.B.: b. May 7, 1923, Chicago, Ill.; educ. St. Procopius College (Lisle, Ill.), Catholic Univ. (Washington, D.C.); professed in Order of St. Benedict, June 16, 1944; ord. priest May 26, 1949; abbot, St. Procopius Abbey, 1964-71; pres. Illinois Benedictine College, 1959-65 and 1971-76; ord. titular bishop of Natchez and auxiliary bishop of Joliet, July 21, 1977; app. bishop of Salina, Mar. 5, 1980, installed May 7, 1980; app. archbishop of Dubuque, installed Feb. 23, 1984.

Kuchmiak, Michael, C.SsR.: b. Feb. 5, 1923, Obertyn, Horodenka, Western Ukraine; left during World War II; educ. St. Josaphat Ukrainian Seminary (Rome, Italy), St. Mary's Seminary (Meadowvale, Ont., Canada); ord. priest May 13, 1956; in the U.S. from 1967; ord. titular bishop of Agathopolis and auxiliary bishop of Ukrainian metropolitan of Philadelphia, Apr. 27, 1988.

Kupfer, William F., M.M.: b. Jan. 28, 1909, Brooklyn, N.Y.; educ. Cathedral College (Brooklyn, N.Y.), Maryknoll Seminary (Maryknoll, N.Y.); ord. priest June 11, 1933; missionary in China; app. prefect apostolic of Taichung, Taiwan, 1951; ord. first bishop of Taichung, July 25, 1962; retired Sept. 3, 1986.

Kuzma, George M.: b. July 24, 1925, Widber, Pa.; educ. St. Francis Seminary (Loretto, Pa.), St. Procopius College (Lisle, Ill.), Sts. Cyril and Methodius Byzantine Catholic Seminary, Duquesne Univ. (Pittsburgh, Pa.); ord. priest (Pittsburgh*, Byzantine Rite), May 5, 1955; ord. titular bishop of Telmisso and auxiliary bishop of Byzantine Rite eparchy of Passaic, 1987.

L

Lambert, Francis, S.M.: b. Feb. 7, 1921, Lawrence, Mass.; educ. Marist Seminary (Framingham, Mass.); ord. priest, June 29, 1946; served in Marist missions in Oceania; provincial of Marist Oceania province, 1971; ord. bishop of Port Vila, Vanuatu (New Hebrides), Mar. 20, 1977.

Larkin, W. Thomas: b. Mar. 31, 1923, Mt. Morris, N.Y.; educ. St. Andrew Seminary and St. Bernard Seminary (Rochester, N.Y.); Angelicum Univ. (Rome); ord. priest (St. Augustine) May 15, 1947; ord. bishop of St. Petersburg, May 27, 1979.

Law, Bernard F.: (See Cardinals, Biographies.)

Leibrecht, John J.: b. Aug. 30, 1930, Overland, Mo.; educ. Catholic Univ. (Washington, D.C.); ord. priest (St. Louis*) Mar. 17, 1956; superintendent of schools of St. Louis archdiocese, 1962-1981; ord. bishop of Springfield-Cape Girardeau, Mo., Dec. 12, 1984.

Leonard, Vincent M.: b. Dec. 11, 1908, Pittsburgh, Pa.; educ. Duquesne Univ. (Pittsburgh, Pa.), St. Vincent Seminary (Latrobe, Pa.); ord. priest (Pittsburgh) June 16, 1935; ord. titular bishop of Arsacal and auxiliary bishop of Pittsburgh, Apr. 21, 1964; app. bishop of Pittsburgh, installed July 2, 1969; resigned June 30, 1983.

Lessard, Raymond W.: b. Dec. 21, 1930, Grafton, N.D.; educ. St. Paul Seminary (St. Paul, Minn.), North American College (Rome); ord. priest (Fargo) Dec. 16, 1956; served on staff of the Congregation for Bishops in the Roman Curia, 1964-73; ord. bishop of Savannah, Apr. 27, 1973.

Levada, William J.: b. June 15, 1936, Long Beach, Calif.; educ. St. John's College (Camarillo, Calif.), Gregorian Univ. (Rome); ord. priest (Los Angeles*) Dec. 20, 1961; ord. titular bishop of Capri and auxiliary bishop of Los Angeles, May 12, 1983; app. archbishop of Portland, Ore., July 3, 1986.

Lipscomb, Oscar H.: b. Sept. 21, 1931, Mobile, Ala.; educ. McGill Institute, St. Bernard College (Cullman, Ala.), North American College and Gregorian Univ. (Rome), Catholic Univ. (Washington, D.C.); ord. priest (Mobile*) July 15, 1956; ord. first archbishop of Mobile, Nov. 16, 1980.

Lohmuller, Martin J.: b. Aug. 21, 1919, Philadelphia, Pa.; educ. St. Charles Borromeo Seminary (Philadelphia, Pa.), Catholic Univ. (Washington, D.C.); ord. priest (Philadelphia*) June 3, 1944; ord. titular bishop of Ramsbury and auxiliary bishop of Philadelphia, Apr. 2, 1970.

Losten, Basil: b. May 11, 1930, Chesapeake City, Md.; educ. St. Basil's College (Stamford, Conn.), Catholic University (Washington, D.C.); ord. priest (Philadelphia*, Byzantine Rite) June 10, 1957; ord. titular bishop of Arcadiopolis in Asia and auxiliary bishop of Ukrainian archeparchy of Philadelphia, May 25, 1971; app. apostolic administrator of archeparchy, 1976; app. bishop of Ukrainian eparchy of Stamford, Sept. 20, 1977.

Lotocky, Innocent Hilarius, O.S.B.M.: b. Nov. 3, 1915, Petlykiwci, Ukraine; educ. seminaries in Ukraine, Czechoslovakia and Austria; ord. priest Nov. 24, 1940; ord. bishop of St. Nicholas of Chicago for the Ukrainians, Mar. 1, 1981.

Loverde, Paul S.: b. Sept. 3, 1940, Framingham, Mass.; educ. St. Thomas Seminary (Bloomfield, Conn.), St. Bernard Seminary (Rochester, N.Y.), Gregorian Univ. (Rome), Catholic Univ. (Washington, D.C.); ord. priest (Norwich), Dec. 18, 1965; ord. titular bishop of Ottabia and auxiliary bishop of Hartford, Apr. 12, 1988.

Lubachivsky, Myroslav I.: (See Cardinals, Biographies.)

Lucker, Raymond A.: b. Feb. 24, 1927, St. Paul, Minn.; educ. St. Paul Seminary (St. Paul, Minn.); University of Minnesota (Minneapolis), Angelicum (Rome); ord. priest (St. Paul-Minneapolis*) June 7, 1952; director of USCC department of education, 1968-71; ord. titular bishop of Meta and auxiliary bishop of St. Paul and Minneapolis, Sept. 8, 1971; app. bishop of New Ulm, Dec. 23, 1975, installed Feb. 19, 1976.

Lyke, James Patterson, O.F.M.: b. Feb. 18, 1939, Chicago, Ill.; educ. Quincy College (Quincy, Ill.), Antonianum (Rome), Union Graduate School (Cincinnati, O.); professed in Order of Friars Minor, June 21, 1963; ord. priest June 24, 1966; president of National Black Catholic Clergy Caucus; ord. titular bishop of Furnos Maior and auxiliary bishop of Cleveland, Aug. 1, 1979.

Lynch, George E.: b. Mar. 4, 1917, New York, N.Y.; educ. Fordham Univ. (New York), Mt. St. Mary's Seminary (Emmitsburg, Md.), Catholic Univ. (Washington, D.C.); ord. priest (Raleigh) May 29, 1943; ord. titular bishop of Satafi and auxiliary of Raleigh Jan. 6, 1970; retired Apr. 16, 1985.

Lyne, Timothy J.: b. Mar. 21, 1919, Chicago, Ill.; educ. Quigley Preparatory Seminary, St. Mary of the Lake Seminary (Mundelein, Ill.); ord. priest (Chicago*) May 1, 1943; ord. titular bishop of Vamalla and auxiliary bishop of Chicago, Dec. 13, 1983.

M

McAuliffe, Michael F.: b. Nov. 22, 1920, Kansas City, Mo.; educ. St. Louis Preparatory Seminary (St. Louis, Mo.), Catholic Univ. (Washington, D.C.): ord. priest (Kansas City-St. Joseph) May 31, 1945; ord. bishop of Jefferson City, Aug. 18, 1969.

McCarrick, Theodore E.: b. July 7, 1930, New York, N.Y.; educ. Fordham Univ. (Bronx, N.Y.), St. Joseph's Seminary (Dunwoodie, N.Y.), Catholic Univ. (Washington, D.C.); ord. priest (New York*) May 31, 1958; dean of students Catholic Univ. of America, 1961-68; pres., Catholic Univ. of Puerto Rico, 1965-69; secretary to Cardinal Cooke, 1970; ord. titular bishop of Rusubisir and auxiliary bishop of New York, June 29, 1977; app. first bishop of Metuchen, N.J., Nov. 19, 1981, installed Jan. 31, 1982; app. archbishop of Newark, June 3, 1986, installed July 25, 1986.

McCarthy, Edward A.: b. Apr. 10, 1918, Cincinnati, O.; educ. Mt. St. Mary Seminary (Norwood, O.), Catholic Univ. (Washington, D.C.), Lateran and Angelicum (Rome); ord. priest (Cincinnati*) May 29, 1943; ord. titular bishop of Tamascani and auxiliary bishop of Cincinnati, June 15, 1965; first bishop of Phoenix, Ariz., Dec. 2, 1969; app. coadjutor archbishop of Miami, Fla., July 7, 1976; succeeded as archbishop of Miami, July 26, 1977.

McCarthy, John E., b. June 21, 1930, Houston, Tex.; educ. Univ. of St. Thomas (Houston, Tex.); ord. priest (Galveston-Houston) May 26, 1956; assistant director Social Action Dept. USCC, 1967-69; executive director Texas Catholic Conference; ord. titular bishop of Pedena and auxiliary bishop of Galveston-Houston, Mar. 14, 1979; app. bishop of Austin, Dec. 19, 1985, installed Feb. 25, 1986.

McCormack, William J.: b. Jan. 24, 1924, New York, N.Y.; educ. Christ the King Seminary, St. Bonaventure Univ. (St. Bonaventure, N.Y.); ord. priest (New York*) Feb. 21, 1959; national director of the Society for the Propagation of the Faith, 1980- ; ord. titular bishop of Nicives and auxiliary bishop of New York, June 6, 1987.

McCormick, J. Carroll: b. Dec. 15, 1907, Philadelphia, Pa.; educ. College Ste. Marie (Montreal),

St. Charles Seminary (Overbrook, Pa.), Minor and Major Roman Seminary (Rome); ord. priest (Philadelphia*) July 10, 1932; ord. titular bishop of Ruspae and auxiliary bishop of Philadelphia, Apr. 23, 1947; app. bishop of Altoona-Johnstown, installed Sept. 21, 1960; app. bishop of Scranton, installed May 25, 1966; resigned Feb. 15, 1983.

McDonald, Andrew J.: b. Oct. 24, 1923, Savannah, Ga.; educ. St. Mary's Seminary (Baltimore, Md.), Catholic Univ. (Washington, D.C.), Lateran Univ. (Rome); ord. priest (Savannah) May 8, 1948; ord. bishop of Little Rock, Sept. 5, 1972.

McDonald, William J.: b. June 17, 1904, Mooncoin, Ireland; educ. St. Kieran's College and Seminary (Kilkenny, Ireland), Catholic Univ. (Washington, D.C.); ord. priest (San Francisco*) June 10, 1928; rector of Catholic Univ. of America, 1957-67; ord. titular bishop of Aquae Regiae and auxiliary bishop of Washington, May 19, 1964; app. auxiliary bishop of San Francisco, July 26, 1967; retired June 5, 1979.

McDonough, Thomas J.: b. Dec. 5, 1911, Philadelphia, Pa.; educ. St. Charles Seminary (Overbrook, Pa.), Catholic Univ. (Washington, D.C.); ord. priest (Philadelphia*) May 26, 1938; ord. titular bishop of Thenae and auxiliary bishop of St. Augustine, Apr. 30, 1947; app. auxiliary bishop of Savannah, Jan. 2, 1957; named bishop of Savannah, installed Apr. 27, 1960; app. archbishop of Louisville, installed May 2, 1967; resigned Sept. 29, 1981.

McDowell, John B.: b. July 17, 1921, New Castle, Pa.; educ. St. Vincent College, St. Vincent Theological Seminary (Latrobe, Pa.), Catholic Univ. (Washington, D.C.); ord. priest (Pittsburgh) Nov. 4, 1945; superintendent of schools, Pittsburgh diocese, 1955-70; ord. titular bishop of Tamazuca, and auxiliary bishop of Pittsburgh, Sept. 8, 1966.

McFarland, Norman F.: b. Feb. 21, 1922, Martinez, Calif.; educ. St. Patrick's Seminary (Menlo Park, Calif.), Catholic Univ. (Washington, D.C.); ord. priest (San Francisco*) June 15, 1946; ord. titular bishop of Bida and auxiliary bishop of San Francisco, Sept. 8, 1970; apostolic administrator of Reno, 1974; app. bishop of Reno, Feb. 10, 1976, installed Mar. 31, 1976; title of see changed to Reno-Las Vegas; app. bishop of Orange, Calif., Dec. 29, 1986; installed Feb. 24, 1987.

McGann, John R.: b. Dec. 2, 1924, Brooklyn, N.Y.; educ. Cathedral College (Brooklyn, N.Y.), Immaculate Conception Seminary (Huntington, L.I.); ord. priest (Rockville Centre) June 3, 1950; ord. titular bishop of Morosbisdus and auxiliary bishop of Rockville Centre, Jan. 7, 1971; vicar general and episcopal vicar; app. bishop of Rockville Centre May 3, 1976, installed June 24, 1976.

McGarry, Urban, T.O.R.: b. Nov. 11, 1911, Warren, Pa.; ord. priest Oct. 3, 1942, in India; prefect apostolic of Bhagalpur, Aug. 7, 1956; ord. first bishop of Bhagalpur, India, May 10, 1965; resigned Nov. 30, 1987.

McHugh, James T.: b. Jan. 3, 1932, Orange, N.J. educ. Immaculate Conception Seminary (Darlington, N.J.), Fordham Univ. (New York, N.Y.), Catholic Univ. (Washington, D.C.), Angelicum (Rome, Italy); ord. priest May 25, 1957

(Newark*); assistant director. 1965-67, and director, 1967-75, of Family Life Division, USCC; director, 1972-78, of NCCB Office for Pro-Life Activities; special advisor to Mission of Permanent Observer of Holy See to UN; ord. titular bishop of Morosbisdo and auxiliary of Newark, Jan. 25, 1988.

McKinney, Joseph C.: b. Sept. 10, 1928, Grand Rapids, Mich.: educ. St. Joseph's Seminary (Grand Rapids, Mich.), Seminaire de Philosophie (Montreal, Canada), Urban Univ. (Rome, Italy); ord. priest (Grand Rapids) Dec. 20, 1953; ord. titular bishop of Lentini and auxiliary bishop of Grand Rapids, Sept. 26, 1968.

McLaughlin, Bernard J.: b. Nov. 19, 1912, Buffalo, N.Y.; educ. Urban Univ. (Rome, Italy); ord. priest (Buffalo) Dec. 21, 1935, at Rome; ord. titular bishop of Mottola and auxiliary bishop of Buffalo, Jan. 6, 1969; resigned Jan. 5, 1988.

McManus, William E.: b. Jan. 27, 1914, Chicago, Ill.; educ. St. Mary of the Lake Seminary (Mundelein, Ill.), Catholic Univ. (Washington, D.C.); ord. priest (Chicago*) Apr. 15, 1939; ord. titular bishop of Mesarfelta and auxiliary bishop of Chicago, Aug. 24, 1967; app. bishop of Fort Wayne-South Bend, Aug. 31, 1976, installed Oct. 19, 1976; retired Feb. 26, 1985.

McNabb Conway, John C., O.S.A.: b. Dec. 11, 1925, Beloit, Wis.; educ. Villanova Univ. (Villanova, Pa.), Augustinian College and Catholic Univ. (Washington, D.C.), De Paul Univ. (Chicago, Ill.); ord. priest May 24, 1952; ord. titular bishop of Saia Maggiore, June 17, 1967 (resigned titular see, Dec. 27, 1977); prelate of Chulucanas, Peru, 1967.

McNamara, Lawrence D.: b. Aug. 5, 1928, Chicago, Ill.; educ. St. Paul Seminary (St. Paul, Minn.), Catholic Univ. (Washington, D.C.); ord. priest (Kansas City-St. Joseph) May 30, 1953; executive director of Campaign for Human Development 1973-77; ord. bishop of Grand Island, Nebr., Mar. 28, 1978.

McNaughton, William J., M.M.: b. Dec. 7, 1926, Lawrence, Mass.; educ. Maryknoll Seminary (Maryknoll, N.Y.); ord. priest June 13, 1953; ord. titular bishop of Thuburbo Minus and vicar apostolic of Inchon, Korea, Aug. 24, 1961; title changed to bishop of Inchon, Mar. 10, 1962.

McRaith, John Jeremiah: b. Dec. 6, 1934, Hutchinson, Minn.; educ. St. John Preparatory School (Collegeville, Minn.), Loras College, St. Bernard Seminary (Dubuque, Ia); ord. priest (New Ulm) Feb. 21, 1960; exec. dir. of Catholic Rural Life Conference, 1971-78; ord. bishop of Owensboro, Ky., Dec. 15, 1982.

McShea, Joseph M.: b. Feb. 22, 1907, Latimer, Pa.; educ. St. Charles Seminary (Philadelphia, Pa.), Major Pontifical Roman Seminary (Rome); ord. priest (Philadelphia*) Dec. 6, 1931; ord. titular bishop of Mina and auxiliary bishop of Philadelphia, Mar. 19, 1952; app. first bishop of Allentown, installed Apr. 11, 1961; resigned Feb. 8, 1983.

Madera, Joseph J., M.Sp.S.: b. Nov. 27, 1927, San Francisco, Calif.; educ. Domus Studiorum of the Missionaries of the Holy Spirit (Coyoacan, D.F. Mexico); ord. priest June 15, 1957; ord. coadjutor bishop of Fresno, Mar. 4, 1980; bishop of Fresno, July 1, 1980.

Maguire, John J.: b. Dec. 11, 1904, New York, N.Y.; educ. Cathedral College (New York City), St. Joseph's Seminary (Dunwoodie, N.Y.), North American College (Rome); ord. priest (New York*) Dec. 22, 1928; ord. titular bishop of Antiphrae and auxiliary bishop of New York, June 29, 1959; app. titular archbishop of Tabalta and coadjutor archbishop of New York, Sept. 15, 1965; retired Jan. 8, 1980.

Maguire, Joseph F.: b. Sept. 4, 1919, Boston, Mass.; educ. Boston College, St. John's Seminary (Boston, Mass.); ord. priest (Boston*) June 29, 1945; ord. titular bishop of Macteris and auxiliary bishop of Boston, Feb. 2, 1972; app. coadjutor bishop of Springfield, Mass., Apr. 13, 1976; succeeded as bishop of Springfield, Mass., Oct. 15, 1977.

Maher, Leo T.: b. July 1, 1915, Mount Union, Ia.; educ. St. Joseph's College (Mountain View, Calif.); St. Patrick's Seminary (Menlo Park, Calif.); ord. priest (San Francisco*) Dec. 18, 1943; ord. first bishop of Santa Rosa, April 5, 1962; bishop of San Diego, Oct. 4, 1969.

Mahoney, James P.: b. Aug. 16, 1925, Kingston, N.Y.; educ. St. Joseph's Seminary (Dunwoodie, N.Y.); ord. priest (New York*) May 19, 1951; ord. titular bishop of Ipagro and auxiliary bishop of New York, Sept. 15, 1972.

Mahony, Roger M.: b. Feb. 27, 1936, Hollywood, Calif.; educ. St. John's Seminary (Camarillo, Calif.), National Catholic School of Social Service (Catholic Univ., Washington, D.C.); ord. priest (Fresno) May 1, 1962; ord. titular bishop of Tamascani and auxiliary bishop of Fresno, Mar. 19, 1975; app. bishop of Stockton, installed Apr. 25, 1980; archbishop of Los Angeles, July 16, 1985, installed Sept. 5, 1985.

Maida, Adam J.: b. Mar. 18, 1930, East Vandergrift, Pa.; educ. St. Vincent College (Latrobe, Pa.). St. Mary Univ. (Baltimore, Md.), Lateran Univ. (Rome), Duquesne Univ. (Pittsburgh, Pa.); ord. priest (Pittsburgh) May 26, 1956; ord. bishop of Green Bay, Jan. 25, 1984.

Malone, James W.: b. Mar. 8, 1920, Youngstown, O.; educ. St. Charles Preparatory Seminary (Catonsville, Md.), St. Mary's Seminary (Cleveland, O.), Catholic Univ. (Washington, D.C.); ord. priest (Youngstown) May 26, 1945; ord. titular bishop of Alabanda and auxiliary bishop of Youngstown, Mar. 24, 1960; apostolic administrator, 1966; bishop of Youngstown, installed June 20, 1968; president of NCCB/USCC, 1983-86.

Maloney, Charles G.: b. Sept. 9, 1912, Louisville, Ky.; educ. St. Joseph's College (Rensselaer, Ind.), North American College (Rome); ord. priest (Louisville*) Dec. 8, 1937; ord. titular bishop of Capsa and auxiliary bishop of Louisville, Feb. 2, 1955; resigned Jan. 8, 1988.

Maloney, David M.: b. Mar. 15, 1912, Littleton, Colo.; educ. St. Thomas Seminary (Denver, Colo.), Gregorian Univ. and Apollinare Univ. (Rome); ord. priest (Denver*) Dec. 8, 1936; ord. titular bishop of Ruspe and auxiliary bishop of Denver, Jan. 4, 1961; app. bishop of Wichita, Kans., Dec. 6, 1967; resigned July 16, 1982.

Manning, Thomas R., O.F.M.: b. Aug. 29, 1922, Baltimore, Md.; educ. Duns Scotus College (Southfield, Mich.), Holy Name College (Washington, D.C.); ord. priest June 5, 1948; ord. titular bishop of Arsamosata, July 14, 1959 (resigned titular see Dec. 30, 1977); prelate of Coroico, Bolivia, July 14, 1959; became first bishop, 1983, when prelature was raised to diocese.

Manning, Timothy: (See Cardinals, Biographies.)

Marcinkus, Paul C.: b. Jan. 15, 1922, Cicero, Ill.; ord. priest (Chicago*) May 3, 1947; served in Vatican secretariat from 1952; ord. titular bishop of Orta, Jan. 6, 1969; secretary (1968-71) and president (1971-) of Institute for Works of Religion (Vatican Bank); titular archbishop, Sept. 26, 1981; pro-president of Pontifical Commission for the State of Vatican City.

Marconi, Dominic A.: b. Mar. 13, 1927, Newark, N.J.; educ. Seton Hall Univ. (S. Orange, N.J.), Immaculate Conception Seminary (Darlington, N.J.), Catholic Univ. (Washington, D.C.); ord. priest (Newark*) May 30, 1953; ord. titular bishop of Bure and auxiliary bishop of Newark, June 25, 1976.

Marino, Eugene A., S.S.J.: b. May 29, 1934, Biloxi, Miss.; educ. Epiphany Apostolic College and Mary Immaculate Novitiate (Newburgh, N.Y.), St. Joseph's Seminary (Washington, D.C.), Catholic Univ. (Washington, D.C.), Loyola Univ. (New Orleans, La.), Fordham Univ. (New York City); ord. priest June 9, 1962; ord. titular bishop of Walla Walla and auxiliary bishop of Washington, D.C., Sept. 12, 1974; archbishop of Atlanta, installed May 5, 1988.

Markiewicz, Alfred J.: b. May 17, 1928, Brooklyn, N.Y.; educ. St. Francis College (Brooklyn, N.Y.), Immaculate Conception Seminary (Huntington, N.Y.); ord. priest (Brooklyn) June 6, 1953; ord. titular bishop of Afufenia and auxiliary bishop of Rockville Centre, Sept. 17, 1986. Vicar for Nassau.

Marshall, John A.: b. Apr. 26, 1928, Worcester, Mass.; educ. Holy Cross College (Worcester, Mass.), Sulpician Seminary (Montreal), North American College and Gregorian Univ. (Rome), Assumption College (Worcester); ord. priest (Worcester) Dec. 19, 1953; ord. bishop of Burlington, Jan. 25, 1972.

Matthiesen, Leroy Theodore: b. June 11, 1921, Olfen, Tex.; educ. Josephinum College (Columbus, O.), Catholic Univ. (Washington, D.C.), Register School of Journalism; ord. priest (Amarillo) Mar. 10, 1946; ord. bishop of Amarillo, May 30, 1980.

May, John L.: b. Mar. 31, 1922, Evanston, Ill.; educ. St. Mary of the Lake Seminary (Mundelein, Ill.); ord. priest (Chicago*) May 3, 1947; general secretary and vice-president of the Catholic Church Extension Society, 1959; ord. titular bishop of Tagarbala and auxiliary bishop of Chicago, Aug. 24, 1967; bishop of Mobile, Ala., Sept. 29, 1969; app. archbishop of St. Louis, installed Mar. 25, 1980; president of NCCB/USCC, 1986-.

Melczek, Dale J.: b. Nov. 9, 1938, Detroit, Mich.; educ. St. Mary's College (Orchard Lake, Mich.), St. John's Provincial Seminary (Plymouth, Mich.), Univ. of Detroit; ord. priest (Detroit*) June 6, 1964; ord. titular bishop of Trau and auxiliary bishop of Detroit, Jan. 27, 1983; vicar general; regional bishop of northwest region of Detroit archdiocese.

Mendez, Alfred, C.S.C.: b. June 3, 1907, Chicago, Ill.; educ. Notre Dame Univ. (Notre Dame, Ind.), Institute of Holy Cross (Washington, D.C.); ord. priest June 24, 1935; ord. first bishop of Arecibo, Puerto Rico, Oct. 28, 1960; resigned Jan. 24, 1974.

Mestice, Anthony F.: b. Dec. 6, 1923, New York, N.Y.; educ. St. Joseph Seminary (Yonkers, N.Y.); ord. priest (New York*) June 4, 1949; ord. titular bishop of Villa Nova and auxiliary bishop of New York, Apr. 27, 1973.

Michaels, James E., S.S.C.: b. May 30, 1926, Chicago, Ill.; educ. Columban Seminary (St. Columban, Neb.), Gregorian Univ. (Rome); ord. priest Dec. 21, 1951; ord. titular bishop of Verbe and auxiliary bishop of Kwang Ju, Korea, Apr. 14, 1966; app. auxiliary bishop of Wheeling, Apr. 3, 1973; title of see changed to Wheeling-Charleston, 1974; resigned Sept. 22, 1987.

Milone, Anthony: b. Sept. 24, 1932, Omaha, Nebr.; educ. North American College (Rome); ord. priest (Omaha*) Dec. 15, 1957, in Rome; ord. titular bishop of Plestia and auxiliary bishop of Omaha, Jan. 6, 1982; app. bishop of Great Falls-Billings, Dec. 14, 1987, installed Feb. 23, 1988.

Minder, John, O.S.F.S.: b. Nov. 1, 1923, Philadelphia, Pa.; educ. Catholic Univ. (Washington, D.C.); ord. priest June 3, 1950; ord. bishop of Keimos (renamed Keimos-Upington, 1985), South Africa, Jan. 10, 1968.

Montrose, Donald: b. May 13, 1923, Denver, Colo.; educ. St. John's Seminary (Camarillo, Calif.); ord. priest (Los Angeles*) May 7, 1949; ord. titular bishop of Forum Novum and auxiliary bishop of Los Angeles, May 12, 1983; app. bishop of Stockton, Dec. 17, 1985.

Moore, Emerson John: b. May 16, 1938, New York, N.Y.; educ. Cathedral College (New York City), St. Joseph's Seminary (Yonkers, N.Y.); New York University, Columbia Univ. School of Social Work (New York City); ord. priest (New York*) May 30, 1964; ord. auxiliary bishop of Curubi and auxiliary bishop of New York, Sept. 8, 1982.

Moran, William J.: b. Jan. 15, 1906, San Francisco, Calif.; educ. St. Patrick's Seminary (Menlo Park, Calif.); ord. priest (San Francisco*) June 20, 1931; Army chaplain, 1933; ord. titular bishop of Centuria and auxiliary bishop to the military vicar, Dec. 13, 1965; retired Jan. 15, 1981.

Moreno, Manuel D.: b. Nov. 27, 1930, Placentia, Calif.; educ. Univ. of California (Los Angeles), Our Lady Queen of Angels (San Fernando, Calif.), St. John's Seminary (Camarillo, Calif.); ord. priest (Los Angeles*) Apr. 25, 1961; ord. titular bishop of Tanagra and auxiliary bishop of Los Angeles, Feb. 19, 1977; bishop of Tucson, Jan. 12, 1982, installed Mar. 11, 1982.

Morkovsky, John Louis: b. Aug. 16, 1909, Praha, Tex.; educ. St. John's Seminary (San Antonio, Tex.), North American College, Urban Univ. and

Gregorian Univ. (Rome), Catholic Univ. (Washington, D.C.); ord. priest (San Antonio*) Dec. 5, 1933; ord titular bishop of Hieron and auxiliary bishop of Amarillo, Feb. 22, 1956; app. bishop of Amarillo, Aug. 27, 1958; titular bishop of Tigava and coadjutor bishop of Galveston-Houston with right of succession, June 11, 1963; apostolic administrator; president Texas Conference of Churches, 1970-72; bishop of Galveston-Houston, Apr. 22, 1975; retired Aug. 21, 1984.

Morneau, Robert F.: b. Sept. 10, 1938, New London, Wis.; educ. St. Norbert's College (De Pere, Wis.), Sacred Heart Seminary (Oneida, Wis.), Catholic Univ. (Washington, D.C.); ord. priest (Green Bay) May 28, 1966; ord. titular bishop of Massa Lubrense and auxiliary bishop of Green Bay, Feb. 22, 1979.

Moskal, Robert M.: b. Oct. 24, 1937, Carnegie, Pa.; educ. St. Basil Minor Seminary (Stamford, Conn.), St. Josaphat Seminary and Catholic Univ. (Washington, D.C.); ord. priest (Philadelphia*, Byzantine Rite) Mar. 25, 1963; ord. titular bishop of Agatopoli and auxiliary bishop of the Ukrainian-Rite archeparchy of Philadelphia, Oct. 13, 1981; app. first bishop of St. Josaphat in Parma, Dec. 5, 1983.

Mugavero, Francis John: b. June 8, 1914, Brooklyn, N.Y.; educ. Cathedral College (Brooklyn, N.Y.), Immaculate Conception Seminary (Huntington, N.Y.), Seminary of the Immaculate Conception (New York City); ord. priest (Brooklyn) May 18, 1940; ord. bishop of Brooklyn, Sept. 12, 1968.

Mulcahy, John J.: b. June 26, 1922, Dorchester, Mass.; educ. St. John's Seminary (Brighton, Mass.); ord. priest (Boston*) May 1, 1947; rector Pope John XXIII Seminary for Delayed Vocations, 1969-73; ord. titular bishop of Penafiel and auxiliary bishop of Boston, Feb. 11, 1975.

Mulrooney, Charles R.: b. Jan. 13, 1906, Brooklyn, N.Y.; educ. Cathedral College (Brooklyn, N.Y.), St. Mary's Seminary (Baltimore, Md.), Sulpician Seminary (Washington, D.C.); ord. priest (Brooklyn) June 10, 1930; ord. titular bishop of Valentiniana and auxiliary bishop of Brooklyn, Apr. 22, 1959; retired Jan. 13, 1981.

Mulvee, Robert E.: b. Feb. 15, 1930, Boston, Mass.; educ. St. Thomas Seminary (Bloomfield, Conn.), University Seminary (Ottawa, Ont., Canada), American College (Louvain, Belgium), Lateran Univ. (Rome); ord. priest (Manchester) June 30, 1957; ord. titular bishop of Summa and auxiliary bishop of Manchester, N.H., Apr. 14, 1977; app. bishop of Wilmington, Del., Feb. 19, 1985.

Mundo, Michael P.: b. July 25, 1937, New York, N.Y.; educ. Fordham Univ. (Bronx, N.Y.), St. Jerome's College (Kitchener, Ont., Canada), St. Francis Seminary (Loretto, Pa.); ord. priest (Camden) May 19, 1962; missionary in Brazil from 1963; ord. titular bishop of Blanda Julia and auxiliary bishop of Jataí, Brazil, June 2, 1978.

Murphy, Michael J.: b. July 1, 1915, Cleveland, O.; educ. Niagara Univ. (Niagara Falls, N.Y.); North American College (Rome), Catholic Univ. (Washington, D.C.); ord. priest (Cleveland) Feb. 28, 1942; ord. titular bishop of Ariendela and auxiliary bishop of Cleveland, June 11, 1976; app. coadjutor bishop of Erie, Nov. 20, 1978; bishop of Erie, July 16, 1982.

Murphy, Philip Francis: b. Mar. 25, 1933, Cumberland, Md.; educ. St. Mary Seminary (Baltimore, Md.), North American College (Rome); ord. priest (Baltimore*) Dec. 20, 1958; ord. titular bishop of Tacarata and auxiliary bishop of Baltimore, Feb. 29, 1976.

Murphy, T. Austin: b. May 11, 1911, Baltimore, Md.; educ. St. Charles College (Catonsville, Md.), St. Mary's Seminary (Baltimore, Md.); ord. priest (Baltimore*) June 10, 1937; ord. titular bishop of Appiaria and auxiliary bishop of Baltimore, July 3, 1962; retired May 29, 1984.

Murphy, Thomas J.: b. Oct. 3, 1932, Chicago, Ill.; educ. Quigley Preparatory Seminary (Chicago, Ill.), St. Mary of the Lake Seminary (Mundelein, Ill.); ord. priest (Chicago*) Apr. 12, 1958; ord. bishop of Great Falls, Mont. Aug. 21, 1978; title of see changed to Great Falls-Billings, 1980; app. coadjutor archbishop of Seattle, May 27, 1987.

Murphy, Thomas W., C.SS.R.: b. Dec. 17, 1917, Omaha, Nebr.; educ. St. Joseph's College (Kirkwood, Mo.); ord. priest June 29, 1943; ord. first bishop of Juazeiro, Brazil, Jan. 2, 1963; resigned Dec. 29, 1973; app. titular bishop of Sululos and auxiliary bishop of Sao Salvador da Bahia, Brazil, Jan. 31, 1974.

Myers, John Joseph: b. July 26, 1941, Ottawa, Ill.; educ. Loras College (Dubuque, Ia.), North American College and Gregorian Univ. (Rome), Catholic Univ. of America (Washington, D.C.); ord. priest (Peoria) Dec. 17, 1966, in Rome; ord. coadjutor bishop of Peoria, Sept. 3, 1987.

N

Nelson, Knute Ansgar, O.S.B.: b. Oct. 1, 1906, Copenhagen, Denmark; educ. Abbey of Maria Laach (Germany), Brown Univ. (Providence, R.I.); professed in the Order of St. Benedict, May 30, 1932; ord. priest May 22, 1937; became an American citizen, Mar. 4, 1941; ord. titular bishop of Bilta and coadjutor bishop of Stockholm, Sweden, Sept. 8, 1947; succeeded as bishop of Stockholm, Oct. 1, 1957; retired; titular bishop of Dura, 1962.

Nevins, John J.: b. Jan. 19, 1932, New Rochelle, N.Y.; educ. Iona College (New Rochelle, N.Y.), Catholic Univ. (Washington, D.C.); ord. priest (Miami*) June 6, 1959; ord. titular bishop of Rusticana and auxiliary bishop of Miami, Mar. 24, 1979; app. first bishop of Venice, Fla., July 17, 1984; installed Oct. 25, 1984.

Newman, William C.: b. Aug. 16, 1928, Baltimore, Md.; educ. St. Mary Seminary (Baltimore, Md.). Catholic Univ. (Washington, D.C.), Loyola College (Baltimore, Md.); ord. priest (Baltimore*) May 29, 1954; ord. titular bishop of Numluli and auxiliary bishop of Baltimore, July 2, 1984.

Neylon, Martin J., S.J.: b. Feb. 13, 1920, Buffalo, N.Y.; ord. priest June 18, 1950; ord. titular bishop of Libertina and coadjutor vicar apostolic of the Caroline and Marshall Islands, Feb. 2, 1970; vicar apostolic of Caroline and Marshall Is., Sept. 20, 1971; first bishop of Carolines-Marshalls when vic-

Niedergeses, James D.: b. Feb. 2, 1917, Lawrenceburg, Tenn.; educ. St. Bernard College (St. Bernard, Ala.), St. Ambrose College (Davenport, Ia.), Mt. St. Mary Seminary of the West and Athenaeum (Cincinnati, Ohio); ord. priest (Nashville) May 20, 1944; ord. bishop of Nashville, May 20, 1975.

Nolan, John G.: b. Mar. 15, 1924, Mechanicsville, N.Y.; educ. Siena College (Loudonville, N.Y.), St. Charles College (Catonsville, Md.), St. Mary's Seminary (Baltimore, Md.); Catholic Univ. (Washington, D.C.), Fordham Univ. (New York, N.Y.); ord. priest June 11, 1949 (Albany); ord. titular bishop of Natchez and auxiliary bishop of Military Services archdiocese; vicar general for Europe.

Nolker, Bernard, C.SS.R.: b. Sept. 25, 1912, Baltimore, Md.; educ. St. Mary's College (North East, Pa.), St. Mary's College (Ilchester, Md.), Mt. St. Alphonsus Seminary (Esopus, N.Y.); ord. priest June 18, 1939; ord. first bishop of Paranagua, Brazil, Apr. 25, 1963.

Novak, Alfred, C.SS.R.: b. June 2, 1930, Dwight, Nebr.; educ. Immaculate Conception Seminary (Oconomowoc, Wis.); ord. priest July 2, 1956; ord. titular bishop of Vardimissa and auxiliary bishop of Sao Paulo, Brazil, May 25, 1979.

O

O'Brien, Thomas Joseph: b. Nov. 29, 1935, Indianapolis, Ind.; educ. St. Meinrad High School Seminary, St. Meinrad College Seminary (St. Meinrad, Ind.); ord. priest (Tucson) May 7, 1961; ord. bishop of Phoenix, Jan. 6, 1982.

Ochoa, Armando: b. Apr. 3, 1943, Oxnard, Calif.; educ. Ventura College (Ventura, Calif.), St. John's College and St. John's Seminary (Camarillo, Calif.); ord. priest (Los Angeles*) May 23, 1970; ord. titular bishop of Sitifi and auxiliary bishop of Los Angeles, Feb. 23, 1987.

O'Connell, Anthony J.: b. May 10, 1938, Lisheen, Co. Clare, Ireland; came to U.S. at the age of 20; educ. Mt. St. Joseph College (Cork, Ire.), Mungret College (Limerick, Ire.), Kenrick Seminary (St. Louis, Mo.); ord. priest (Jefferson City) Mar. 30, 1963; ord. first bishop of Knoxville, Tenn., Sept. 8, 1988.

O'Connor, John J.: (See Cardinals, Biographies.)

O'Donnell, Cletus F.: b. Aug. 22, 1917, Waukon, Ia.; educ. St. Mary Seminary (Mundelein, Ill.), Catholic Univ. (Washington, D.C.); ord. priest (Chicago*) May 3, 1941; ord. titular bishop of Abritto and auxiliary bishop of Chicago, Dec. 21, 1960; app. bishop of Madison, Feb. 22, 1967, installed Apr. 25, 1967.

O'Donnell, Edward J.: b. July 4, 1931, St. Louis, Mo.; educ. St. Louis Preparatory Seminary and Kenrick Seminary (St. Louis, Mo.); ord. priest (St. Louis*) Apr. 6, 1957; ord. titular bishop of Britania and auxiliary bishop of St. Louis, Feb. 10, 1984.

O'Keefe, Gerald F.: b. Mar. 30, 1918, St. Paul, Minn.; educ. College of St. Thomas, St. Paul Seminary (St. Paul, Minn.); ord. priest (St. Paul-Minneapolis*) Jan. 29, 1944; ord. titular bishop of Candyba and auxiliary bishop of St. Paul July 2, 1961; bishop of Davenport, Oct. 20, 1966, installed Jan. 4, 1967.

O'Keefe, Joseph Thomas: b. Mar. 12, 1919, New York, N.Y.; educ. Cathedral College (New York City), St. Joseph's Seminary (Yonkers, N.Y.), Catholic Univ. (Washington, D.C.); ord. priest (New York*) Apr. 17, 1948; ord. titular bishop of Tre Taverne and auxiliary bishop of New York, Sept. 8, 1982; app. bishop of Syracuse, June 16, 1987, installed Aug. 3, 1987.

O'Leary, Edward C.: b. Aug. 21, 1920, Bangor, Me.; educ. Holy Cross College (Worcester, Mass.), St. Paul's Seminary (Ottawa, Canada); ord. priest (Portland, Me.) June 15, 1946; ord. titular bishop of Moglena and auxiliary bishop of Portland, Me., Jan. 25, 1971; app. bishop of Portland, installed Dec. 18, 1974.

O'Malley, Sean, O.F.M. Cap.: b. June 29, 1944, Lakewood, O.; educ. St. Fidelis Seminary (Herman, Pa.), Capuchin College and Catholic Univ. (Washington, D.C.); ord. priest Aug. 29, 1970; episcopal vicar of priests serving Spanish speaking in Washington archdiocese, 1978-84; executive director of Spanish Catholic Center, Washington, from 1973; ord. coadjutor bishop of St. Thomas, Virgin Islands, Aug. 2, 1984; bishop of St. Thomas, Oct. 16, 1985.

O'Meara, Edward T.: b. Aug. 3, 1921, St. Louis, Mo.; educ. Cardinal Glennon College and Kenrick Seminary (St. Louis, Mo.), Angelicum (Rome); ord. priest (St. Louis*) Dec. 21, 1946; national director of Society for the Propagation of the Faith, 1967-80; ord. titular bishop of Thisiduo and auxiliary bishop of St. Louis, Feb. 13, 1972; app. archbishop of Indianapolis, installed Jan. 10, 1980.

O'Neil, Leo E.: b. Jan. 31, 1928, Holyoke, Mass.; educ. Maryknoll Seminary (Maryknoll, N.Y.), St. Anselm's College (Manchester, N.H.), Grand Seminary (Montreal, Canada); ord. priest (Springfield, Mass.) June 4, 1955; ord. titular bishop of Bencenna and auxiliary bishop of Springfield, Mass., Aug. 22, 1980.

O'Neill, Arthur J.: b. Dec. 14, 1917, East Dubuque, Ill.; educ. Loras College (Dubuque, Ia.), St. Mary's Seminary (Baltimore, Md.); ord. priest (Rockford) Mar. 27, 1943; ord. bishop of Rockford, Oct. 11, 1968.

O'Rourke, Edward W.: b. Oct. 31, 1917, Downs, Ill.; educ. St. Mary's Seminary (Mundelein, Ill.), Aquinas Institute of Philosophy and Theology (River Forest, Ill.); ord. priest (Peoria) May 28, 1944; exec. dir. National Catholic Rural Life Conference, 1960-71; ord. bishop of Peoria, July 15, 1971.

Ott, Stanley J.: b. June 29, 1927, Gretna, La.; educ. Notre Dame Seminary (New Orleans, La.), North American College and Gregorian Univ. (Rome); ord. priest (New Orleans*) Dec. 8, 1951; ord. titular bishop of Nicives and auxiliary bishop of New Orleans, June 29, 1976; app. bishop of Baton Rouge, Jan 17, 1983, installed Mar. 24, 1983.

Ottenweller, Albert H.: b. Apr. 5, 1916, Stanford, Mont.; educ. St. Joseph's Seminary (Rensselaer, Ind.), Catholic Univ. (Washington,

D.C.); ord. priest (Toledo) June 19, 1943; ord. titular bishop of Perdices and auxiliary bishop of Toledo, May 29, 1974; app. bishop of Steubenville, Oct. 11, 1977, installed Nov. 22, 1977.

P

Paschang, John L.: b. Oct. 5, 1895, Hemingford, Nebr.; educ. Conception College (Conception, Mo.), St. John Seminary (Collegeville, Minn.), Catholic Univ. (Washington, D.C.); ord. priest (Omaha*) June 12, 1921; ord. bishop of Grand Island, Oct. 9, 1951; resigned July 25, 1972.

Pataki, Andrew: b. Aug. 30, 1927, Palmerton, Pa.; educ. St. Vincent College (Latrobe, Pa.), St. Procopius College, St. Procopius Seminary (Lisle, Ill.), Sts. Cyril and Methodius Byzantine Catholic Seminary (Pittsburgh, Pa.), Gregorian Univ. and Oriental Pontifical Institute (Rome, Italy); ord. priest (Pittsburgh,* Byzantine Rite) Feb. 24, 1952; ord. titular bishop of Telmisso and auxiliary bishop of Byzantine diocese of Passaic, Aug. 23, 1983; vicar general; episcopal vicar of Pennsylvania; app. bishop of Ruthenian Byzantine diocese of Parma, July 3, 1984.

Paul, John J.: b. Aug. 17, 1918, La Crosse, Wis.; educ. Loras College (Dubuque, Iowa), St. Mary's Seminary (Baltimore, Md.), Marquette Univ. (Milwaukee, Wis.), ord. priest (Lincoln) Jan. 24, 1943; ord. titular bishop of Lambaesis and auxiliary bishop of La Crosse, Aug. 4, 1977; app. bishop of La Crosse, Oct. 18, 1983, installed Dec. 5, 1983.

Pearce, George H., S.M.: b. Jan. 9, 1921, Brighton, Mass.; educ. Marist College and Seminary (Framington, Mass.); ord. priest Feb. 2, 1947; ord. titular bishop of Attalea in Pamphylia and vicar apostolic of the Samoa and Tokelau Islands, June 29, 1956; title changed to bishop of Apia, June 21, 1966; app. archbishop of Suva, Fiji Islands, June 22, 1967; resigned Apr. 10, 1976.

Pechillo, Jerome, T.O.R.: b. May 16, 1919, Brooklyn, N.Y.; educ. Catholic Univ. (Washington, D.C.); ord. priest June 10, 1947; ord. titular bishop of Novasparsa and prelate of Coronel Oviedo, Paraguay, Jan. 25, 1966; app. auxiliary bishop of Newark, N.J., Mar. 6, 1976.

Pelotte, Donald E., S.S.S.: b. Apr. 13, 1945, Waterville, Me.; educ. Eymard Seminary and Junior College (Hyde Park, N.Y.), John Carroll Univ. (Cleveland, O.), Fordham Univ. (Bronx, N.Y.); ord. priest Sept. 2, 1972; ord. coadjutor bishop of Gallup, May 6, 1986. First priest of Native American ancestry to be named U.S. bishop.

Pena, Raymundo J.: b. Feb. 19, 1934, Robstown, Tex.; educ. Assumption Seminary (San Antonio, Tex.); ord. priest (Corpus Christi) May 25, 1957; ord. titular bishop of Trisipa and auxiliary bishop of San Antonio, Dec. 13, 1976; app. bishop of El Paso, Apr. 29, 1980.

Perry, Harold R., S.V.D.: b. Oct. 9, 1916, Lake Charles, La.; educ. St. Augustine Seminary (Bay St. Louis, Miss.), St. Mary's Seminary (Techny, Ill.); ord. priest Jan. 6, 1944; app. provincial of southern province of Society of the Divine Word, 1964; ord. titular bishop of Mons in Mauretania and auxiliary bishop of New Orleans, Jan. 6, 1966.

Pevec, A. Edward: b. Apr. 16, 1925, Cleveland, O.; educ. St. Mary's Seminary, John Carroll Univ. (Cleveland, O.); ord. priest (Cleveland) Apr. 29, 1950; ord. titular bishop of Mercia and auxiliary bishop of Cleveland, July 2, 1982.

Pfeifer, Michael, O.M.I.: b. May 18, 1937, Alamo, Tex.; educ. Oblate school of theology (San Antonio, Tex.); ord. priest Dec. 21, 1964; provincial of southern province of Oblates of Mary Immaculate, 1981; ord. bishop of San Angelo, July 26, 1985.

Pilarczyk, Daniel E.: b. Aug. 12, 1934, Dayton, Ohio; educ. St. Gregory's Seminary (Cincinnati, O.), Urban Univ. (Rome), Xavier Univ. and Univ. of Cincinnati (Cincinnati, O.); ord. priest (Cincinnati*) Dec. 20, 1959; ord. titular bishop of Hodelm and auxiliary bishop of Cincinnati, Dec. 20, 1974; app. archbishop of Cincinnati, Oct. 30, 1982; installed Dec. 20, 1982.

Pilla, Anthony M.: b. Nov. 12, 1932, Cleveland, O.; educ. St. Gregory College Seminary (Cincinnati, O.), Borromeo College Seminary (Wickliffe, O.), St. Mary Seminary and John Carroll Univ. (Cleveland, O.); ord. priest (Cleveland) May 23, 1959; ord. titular bishop of Scardona and auxiliary bishop of Cleveland, Aug. 1, 1979; app. apostolic administrator of Cleveland, 1980; bishop of Cleveland, Nov. 13, 1980.

Pinger, Henry A., O.F.M.: b. Aug. 16, 1897, Lindsay, Nebr.; educ. Our Lady of Angels Seminary (Cleveland, O.), St. Anthony's Seminary (St. Louis, Mo.); professed in the Order of Friars Minor, June 18, 1918; ord. priest June 27, 1924; ord. titular bishop of Capitolias and vicar apostolic of Chowtsun, China, Sept. 21, 1937; title changed to bishop of Chowtsun, Apr. 11, 1946; imprisoned by Reds in 1951, released in 1956; expelled; bishop emeritus of Chowtsun.

Popp, Bernard F.: b. Dec. 6, 1917, Nada, Tex.; educ. St. John's Seminary and St. Mary's Univ. (San Antonio, Tex.); ord. priest (San Antonio*) Feb. 24, 1943; ord. titular bishop of Capsus and auxiliary bishop of San Antonio, July 25, 1983.

Povish, Kenneth J.: b. Apr. 19, 1924, Alpena, Mich.; educ. St. Joseph's Seminary (Grand Rapids, Mich.), Sacred Heart Seminary (Detroit, Mich.), Catholic Univ. (Washington, D.C.); ord. priest (Saginaw) June 3, 1950; ord. bishop of Crookston, Sept. 29, 1970; app. bishop of Lansing, Oct. 8, 1975, installed Dec. 11, 1975.

Power, Cornelius M.: b. Dec. 18, 1913, Seattle, Wash.; educ. St. Patrick's College (Menlo Park, Calif.), St. Edward's Seminary (Kenmore, Wash.), Catholic Univ. (Washington, D.C.); ord. priest (Seattle*) June 3, 1939; ord. bishop of Yakima, May 1, 1969, installed May 20, 1969; app. archbishop of Portland, Ore., Jan. 22, 1974, installed Apr. 17, 1974; retired 1986.

Primeau, Ernest J.: b. Sept. 17, 1909, Chicago, Ill.; educ. Loyola Univ. (Chicago, Ill.), St. Mary of the Lake Seminary (Mundelein, Ill.), Lateran Univ. (Rome); ord. priest (Chicago*) Apr. 7, 1934; ord. bishop of Manchester, Feb. 25, 1960; resigned Jan. 30, 1974; director of Villa Stritch, Rome, 1974-79.

Prost, Jude, O.F.M.: b. Dec. 6, 1915, Chicago,

Ill.; educ. Our Lady of the Angels Seminary (Cleveland, O.), St. Joseph's Seminary (Teutopolis, Ill.); ord. priest June 24, 1942; ord. titular bishop of Fronta and auxiliary bishop of Belem do Para, Brazil, Nov. 1, 1962.

Proulx, Amedee W.: b. Aug. 31, 1932, Sanford, Me.; educ. St. Hyacinthe Seminary (Quebec), St. Paul Univ. Seminary (Ottawa), Catholic Univ. (Washington, D.C.); ord. priest (Portland, Me.) May 31, 1958; ord. titular bishop of Clipia and auxiliary bishop of Portland, Me., Nov. 12, 1975.

Pursley, Leo A.: b. Mar. 12, 1902, Hartford City, Ind.; educ. Mt. St. Mary's Seminary (Cincinnati, O.); ord. priest (Ft. Wayne-S. Bend) June 11, 1927; ord. titular bishop of Hadrianapolis in Pisidia and auxiliary bishop of Fort Wayne, Sept. 19, 1950; app. apostolic administrator of Fort Wayne, Mar. 9, 1955; installed as bishop of Fort Wayne, Feb. 26, 1957; title of see changed to Fort Wayne-South Bend, 1960; resigned Aug. 31, 1976.

Puscas, Louis: b. Sept. 13, 1915, Aurora, Ill.; educ. Quigley Preparatory Seminary (Chicago, Ill.), seminary in Oradea-Mare (Romania), Propaganda Fide Seminary (Rome), Illinois Benedictine College (Lisle, Ill.); ord. priest (Erie) May 14, 1942; ord. titular bishop of Leuce and first exarch of apostolic exarchate for Romanians of the Byzantine Rite in the U.S., June 26, 1983 (seat of the exarchate is Canton, Ohio); app. first eparch, Apr. 11, 1987, when exarchate was raised to eparchy of St. George Martyr.

Q

Quinn, Alexander James: b. Apr. 8, 1932, Cleveland, O.; educ. St. Charles College (Catonsville, Md.), St. Mary Seminary (Cleveland, O.), Lateran Univ. (Rome), Cleveland State Univ.; ord. priest (Cleveland) May 24, 1958; ord. titular bishop of Socia and auxiliary bishop of Cleveland, Dec. 5, 1983; vicar of western region of Cleveland diocese.

Quinn, Francis A.: b. Sept. 11, 1921, Los Angeles, Calif.; educ. St. Joseph's College (Mountain View, Calif.), St. Patrick's Seminary (Menlo Park, Calif.), Catholic Univ. (Washington, D.C.); Univ. of California (Berkley); ord. priest (San Francisco*) June 15, 1946; ord. titular bishop of Numana and auxiliary bishop of San Francisco, June 29, 1978; app. bishop of Sacramento Dec. 18, 1979.

Quinn, John R.: b. Mar. 28, 1929, Riverside, Calif.; educ. St. Francis Seminary (El Cajon, Calif.), North American College (Rome); ord. priest (San Diego) July 19, 1953; ord. titular bishop of Thisiduo and auxiliary bishop of San Diego, Dec. 12, 1967; bishop of Oklahoma City and Tulsa, Nov. 30, 1971; first archbishop of Oklahoma City, Dec. 19, 1972; app. archbishop of San Francisco Feb. 22, 1977, installed Apr. 26, 1977; president NCCB/USCC, 1977-80.

R

Ramirez, Ricardo, C.S.B.: b. Sept. 12, 1936, Bay City, Tex.; educ. Univ. of St. Thomas (Houston, Tex.), Univ. of Detroit (Detroit, Mich.), St. Basil's Seminary (Toronto, Ont.); Seminario Concilium (Mexico City, Mexico), East Asian Pastoral Institute (Manila, Philippines); ord. priest Dec. 10, 1966; ord titular bishop of Vatarba and auxiliary of San Antonio, Dec. 6, 1981; app. first bishop of Las Cruces, N. Mex., Aug. 17, 1982; installed Oct. 18, 1982.

Raya, Joseph M.: b. July 20, 1917, Zahle, Lebanon; educ. St. Louis College (Paris, France), St. Anne's Seminary (Jerusalem); ord. priest July 20, 1941; came to U.S., 1949, became U.S. citizen; ord. archbishop of Acre, Israel, of the Melkites, Oct. 20, 1968; resigned Aug. 20, 1974; assigned titular metropolitan see of Scytopolis.

Regan, Joseph W., M.M.: b. Apr. 5, 1905, Boston, Mass.; educ. Boston College (Boston, Mass.), St. Bernard's Seminary (Rochester, N.Y.), Maryknoll Seminary (Maryknoll, N.Y.); ord. priest Jan. 27, 1929; missionary in China 15 years; in Philippines since 1952; ord. titular bishop of Isinda and prelate of Tagum, Philippine Islands, Apr. 25, 1962; resigned May 16, 1980.

Reh, Francis F.: b. Jan. 9, 1911, New York, N.Y.; educ. St. Joseph's Seminary (Dunwoodie, N.Y.), North American College and Gregorian Univ. (Rome); ord. priest (New York*) Dec. 8, 1935; ord. bishop of Charleston, S.C., June 29, 1962; named titular bishop of Macriana in Mauretania, 1964; rector of North American College, 1964-68; bishop of Saginaw, installed Feb. 26, 1969; resigned Apr. 28, 1980.

Reilly, Daniel P.: b. May 12, 1928, Providence, R.I.; educ. Our Lady of Providence Seminary (Warwick, R.I.), St. Brieuc Major Seminary (Cotes du Nord, France); ord. priest (Providence) May 30, 1953; ord. bishop of Norwich, Aug. 6, 1975.

Reilly, Thomas F., C.SS.R.: b. Dec. 20, 1908, Boston, Mass.; educ. Mt. St. Alphonsus Seminary (Esopus, N.Y.), Catholic Univ. (Washington, D.C.); ord. priest June 10, 1933; ord. titular bishop of Themisonium and prelate of San Juan de la Maguana, Dominican Republic, Nov. 30, 1956; first bishop of San Juan de la Maguana, Nov. 21, 1969; retired July 20, 1977.

Reiss, John C.: b. May 13, 1922, Red Bank, N.J.; educ. Catholic Univ. (Washington, D.C.), Immaculate Conception Seminary (Darlington, N.J.); ord. priest (Trenton) May 31, 1947; ord. titular bishop of Simidicca and auxiliary bishop of Trenton, Dec. 12, 1967; app. bishop of Trenton, Mar. 11, 1980.

Riashi, Georges, B.C.O.: b. Nov. 25, 1933, Kaa-el-Rim, Lebanon; ord. priest Apr. 4, 1965; parish priest of Our Lady of Redemption Parish, Warren, Mich. (Newton Greek-Catholic Melkite eparchy); U.S. citizen; ord. first bishop of eparchy of St. Michael's of Sydney (Australia) for Greek-Catholic Melkites, July 19, 1987.

Ricard, John H., S.S.J.: b. Feb. 29, 1940, Baton Rouge, La.; educ. St. Joseph's Seminary (Washington, D.C.), Tulane Univ. (New Orleans, La.); ord. priest May 25, 1968; ord. titular bishop of Rucuma and auxiliary of Baltimore, July 2, 1984; urban vicar, Baltimore.

Rigali, Justin: b. Apr. 19, 1935, Los Angeles, Calif.; educ. St. John's Seminary (Camarillo, Calif.); ord. priest (Los Angeles*) Apr. 25, 1961; in Vatican diplomatic service from 1964; ord. titular archbishop of Bolsena, Sept. 14, 1985, by Pope John

Paul II; president of the Pontifical Ecclesiastical Academy.

Riley, Lawrence J.: b. Sept. 6, 1914; Boston, Mass.; educ. Boston College and St. John's Seminary (Boston, Mass.), North American College and Gregorian Univ. (Rome), Catholic Univ. (Washington, D.C.); ord. priest (Boston*) Sept. 21, 1940; ord. titular bishop of Daimlaig and auxiliary bishop of Boston, Feb. 2, 1972.

Roach, John R.: b. July 31, 1921, Prior Lake, Minn.; educ. St. Paul Seminary (St. Paul, Minn.), Univ. of Minnesota (Minneapolis); ord. priest (St. Paul and Minneapolis*) June 18, 1946; ord. titular bishop of Cenae and auxiliary bishop of St. Paul and Minneapolis, Sept. 8, 1971; app. archbishop of St. Paul and Minneapolis, May 28, 1975; vice-president NCCB/USCC, 1977-80; president, 1980-83.

Rodimer, Frank J.: b. Oct. 25, 1927, Rockaway, N.J.; educ. Seton Hall Prep (South Orange, N.J.), St. Charles College (Catonsville, Md.), St. Mary's Seminary (Baltimore, Md.), Immaculate Conception Seminary (Darlington, N.J.), Catholic Univ. (Washington, D.C.); ord. priest (Paterson) May 19, 1951; ord. bishop of Paterson, Feb. 28, 1978.

Rodriguez, Migúel, C.SS.R.: b. Apr. 18, 1931, Mayaguez, P.R.; educ. St. Mary's Minor Seminary (North East, Pa.), Mt. St. Alphonsus Major Seminary (Esopus, N.Y.); ord. priest June 22, 1958; ord. bishop of Arecibo, P.R., Mar. 23, 1974.

Rodriguez, Placido, C.M.F.: b. Oct. 11, 1940, Celaya, Guanajuato, Mexico; educ. Claretian Novitate (Los Angeles, Calif.), Claretville Seminary College (Calabasas, Calif.), Catholic Univ. (Washington, D.C.), Loyola Univ. (Chicago, Ill.); ord. priest May 23, 1968; ord. titular bishop of Fuerteventura and auxiliary bishop of Chicago, Dec. 13, 1983.

Roman, Agustin A.: b. May 5, 1928, San Antonio de los Banos, Havana, Cuba; educ. San Alberto Magno Seminary (Matanzas, Cuba), Missions Etrangeres (Montreal, Canada), Barry College (Miami, Fla.); ord. priest July 5, 1959, Cuba; vicar for Spanish speaking in Miami archdiocese, 1976; ord. titular bishop of Sertei and auxiliary bishop of Miami, Mar. 24, 1979.

Roque, Francis: b. Oct. 9, 1928, Providence R.I.; educ. St. John's Seminary (Brighton, Mass.); ord. priest (Providence) Sept. 19, 1953; became chaplain in U.S. Army 1961; ord. titular bishop of Bagai and auxiliary bishop of Military Services archdiocese, May 10, 1983.

Rosazza, Peter Anthony: b. Feb. 13, 1935, New Haven, Conn.; educ. St. Thomas Seminary (Bloomfield, Conn.), Dartmouth College (Hanover, N.H.), St. Bernard's Seminary (Rochester, N.Y.), St. Sulpice (Issy, France); ord. priest (Hartford*) June 29, 1961; ord. titular bishop of Oppido Nuovo and auxiliary bishop of Hartford, June 24, 1978.

Rose, Robert John: b. Feb. 28, 1930, Grand Rapids, Mich.; educ. St. Joseph's Seminary (Grand Rapids, Mich.), Seminaire de Philosophie (Montreal, Canada), Pontifical Urban University (Rome), Univ. of Michigan (Ann Arbor, Mich.); ord. priest (Grand Rapids) Dec. 21, 1955; ord. bishop of Gaylord, Dec. 6, 1981.

Rudin, John J., M.M.: b. Nov. 27, 1916, Pittsfield, Mass.; educ. Maryknoll Seminary (Maryknoll, N.Y.), Gregorian Univ. (Rome); ord. priest June 11, 1944; ord. first bishop of Musoma, Tanzania, Oct. 3, 1957; retired Jan. 12, 1979.

Rueger, George E.: b. Sept. 3, 1933, Framingham, Mass; educ. Holy Cross College (Worcester, Mass.), St. John's Seminary (Brighton), Harvard University (Cambridge, Mass.); ord. priest (Worcester), Jan. 6, 1958; ord. titular bishop of Maronana and auxiliary bishop of Worcester Feb. 25, 1987.

Russell, John J.: b. Dec. 1, 1897, Baltimore, Md.; educ. St. Charles College (Catonsville, Md.), St. Mary's Seminary (Baltimore, Md.), North American College (Rome); ord. priest (Baltimore*) July 8, 1923; ord. bishop of Charleston, Mar. 14, 1950; bishop of Richmond, July 3, 1958; retired Apr. 30, 1973.

Ryan, Daniel L.: b. Sept. 28, 1930, Mankato, Minn.; educ. St. Procopius Seminary (Lisle, Ill.), Lateran Univ. (Rome); ord. priest (Joliet) May 3, 1956; ord. titular bishop of Surista and auxiliary bishop of Joliet, Sept. 30, 1981; app. bishop of Springfield, Ill., Nov. 22, 1983, installed Jan. 18, 1984.

Ryan, James C., O.F.M.: b. Nov. 17, 1912, Chicago, Ill.; educ. St. Joseph's Seraphic Seminary (Westmont, Ill.), Our Lady of the Angels Seminary (Cleveland, O.); ord. priest June 24, 1938; ord. titular bishop of Margo and prelate of Santarem, Brazil, April 9, 1958; first bishop of Santarem, Dec. 4, 1979; retired Nov. 27, 1985.

Ryan, Joseph T.: b. Nov. 1, 1913, Albany, N.Y.; educ. Manhattan College (New York City); ord. priest (Albany) June 3, 1939; national secretary of Catholic Near East Welfare Assn. 1960-65; ord. first archbishop of Anchorage, Alaska, Mar. 25, 1966; app. titular archbishop of Gabi and coadjutor archbishop of the military ordinariate, Oct. 24, 1975, installed Dec. 13, 1975; app. military vicar of U.S. military archdiocese, Mar. 16, 1985, installed Apr. 30, 1985, at National Shrine of the Immaculate Conception, Washington, D.C.

S

Salatka, Charles A.: b. Feb. 26, 1918, Grand Rapids, Mich.; educ. St. Joseph's Seminary (Grand Rapids, Mich.), Catholic Univ. (Washington, D.C.), Lateran Univ. (Rome); ord. priest (Grand Rapids) Feb. 24, 1945; ord. titular bishop of Cariana and auxiliary bishop of Grand Rapids, Mich., Mar. 6, 1962; app. bishop of Marquette, installed Mar. 25, 1968; app. archbishop of Oklahoma City, Sept. 27, 1977; installed Dec. 15, 1977.

Sanchez, Robert: b. Mar. 20, 1934, Socorro, N.M.; educ. Immaculate Heart Seminary (Santa Fe, N.M.), Gregorian Univ. (Rome), Catholic Univ. (Washington, D.C.); ord. priest (Santa Fe*) Dec. 20, 1959; ord. archbishop of Santa Fe, N.M., July 25, 1974.

San Pedro, Enrique, S.J.: b. Mar. 9, 1926, Havana, Cuba; educ. Cuba, Spain, Philippines, Leopold-Franzens Univ. (Innsbruck, Austria); Pontifical Biblical Institute (Rome), ord. priest Mar. 18, 1957; taught Scripture and did missionary work in Vietnam, 1965-75, when he was expelled; visiting Scripture professor at St. Vincent de Paul Regional Seminary, Florida, from 1981; ord. titular bishop of Siccesi and auxiliary bishop of Galveston-Houston, June 29, 1986.

Scanlan, John J.: b. May 24, 1906, County Cork, Ireland; educ. National Univ. of Ireland (Dublin), All Hallows College (Dublin); ord. priest (San Francisco*) June 22, 1930; U.S. citizen 1938; ord. titular bishop of Cenae and auxiliary bishop of Honolulu, Sept. 21, 1954; bishop of Honolulu, installed May 1, 1968; retired June 30, 1981.

Scarpone, Gerald, O.F.M.: b. Oct. 1, 1928, Watertown, Mass.; ord. priest June 24, 1956; ord. coadjutor bishop of Comayagua, Honduras, Feb. 21, 1979; succeeded as bishop of Comayagua, May 30, 1979.

Schad, James L.: b. July 20, 1917, Philadelphia, Pa.; educ. St. Mary's Seminary (Baltimore, Md.); ord. priest (Camden) Apr. 10, 1943; ord. titular bishop of Panatoria and auxiliary bishop of Camden, Dec. 8, 1966.

Schladweiler, Alphonse: b. July 18, 1902, Milwaukee, Wis.; educ. St. Joseph College (Teutopolis, Ill.), St. Paul's Seminary (St. Paul, Minn.), Univ. of Minnesota (Minneapolis, Minn.); ord. priest (St. Paul and Minneapolis*) June 9, 1929; ord. first bishop of New Ulm, Jan. 29, 1958; retired Dec. 23, 1975.

Schlaefer Berg, Salvator, O.F.M. Cap.: b. June 27, 1920, Campbellsport, Wis.; ord. priest June 5, 1946; missionary in Bluefields, Nicaragua from 1947; ord. titular bishop of Fiumepiscense and vicar apostolic of Bluefields, Nicaragua, Aug. 12, 1970.

Schlarman, Stanley Gerard: b. July 27, 1933, Belleville, Ill.; educ. St. Henry Prep Seminary (Belleville, Ill.), Gregorian Univ. (Rome), St. Louis Univ. (St. Louis, Mo.); ord. priest (Belleville) July 13, 1958, Rome; ord. titular bishop of Capri and auxiliary bishop of Belleville, May 14, 1979; app. bishop of Dodge City, Mar. 1, 1983.

Schlotterback, Edward F., O.S.F.S.: b. Mar. 2, 1912, Philadelphia, Pa.; educ. Catholic Univ. (Washington, D.C.); ord. priest Dec. 17, 1938; ord. titular bishop of Balanea and vicar apostolic of Keetmanshoop, Namibia, June 11, 1956.

Schmidt, Firmin M., O.F.M.Cap.: b. Oct. 12, 1918, Catherine, Kans.; educ. Catholic Univ. (Washington, D.C.); ord. priest June 2, 1946; app. prefect apostolic of Mendi, Papua New Guinea, Apr. 3, 1959; ord. titular bishop of Conana and first vicar apostolic of Mendi, Dec. 15, 1965; became first bishop of Mendi when vicariate apostolic was raised to a diocese, Nov. 15, 1966.

Schmidt, Matthias W., O.S.B.: b. Apr. 21, 1931, Nortonville, Kans.; professed St. Benedict's Abbey (Atchison, Kans.), July 11, 1952; ord. priest May 30, 1957; missionary to Brazil, Feb. 5, 1961; ord. titular bishop of Mutugenna and auxiliary bishop of Jatai, Goias, Brazil, Sept. 10, 1972; bishop of Ruy Barbosa, Bahia, Brazil, May 14, 1976.

Schmitt, Bernard W.: b. Aug. 17, 1928, Wheeling, W. Va.; educ. St. Joseph College (Catonsville, Md.). St. Mary's Seminary (Baltimore), Ohio Univ. (Athens, O.). ord. priest May 28, 1955 (Wheeling-Charleston); ord. titular bishop of Walla Walla and auxiliary bishop of Wheeling-Charleston, Aug. 1, 1988.

Schmitt, Mark: b. Feb. 14, 1923, Algoma, Wis., educ. Salvatorian Seminary (St. Nazianz, Wis.), St. John's Seminary (Collegeville, Minn.); ord. priest (Green Bay) May 22, 1948; ord. titular bishop of Ceanannus Mor and auxiliary bishop of Green Bay, June 24, 1970; app. bishop of Marquette, Mar. 21, 1978, installed May 8, 1978.

Schmitz, Paul, O.F.M. Cap.: b. Dec. 4, 1943, Fond du Lac, Wis.; ord. priest Sept. 3, 1970; missionary in Nicaragua from 1970; superior of vice province of Capuchins in Central America (headquartered in Managua), 1982-84; ord. titular bishop of Elepla and auxiliary bishop of the vicariate apostolic of Bluefields, Nicaragua, Sept. 17, 1984.

Schoenherr, Walter J.: b. Feb. 28, 1920, Detroit, Mich.; educ. Sacred Heart Seminary (Detroit, Mich.), Mt. St. Mary Seminary (Norwood, O.); ord. priest (Detroit*) Oct. 27, 1945; ord. titular bishop of Timidana and auxiliary bishop of Detroit, May 1, 1968.

Schuck, James A., O.F.M.: b. Jan. 17, 1913, Treverton, Pa.; educ. St. Joseph's Seminary (Callicoon, N.Y.), St. Bonaventure's University (St. Bonaventure, N.Y.). Holy Name College (Washington, D.C.); ord. priest June 11, 1940; ord. titular bishop of Avissa, Feb. 24, 1959 (resigned titular see May 26, 1978); prelate of Cristalandia, Brazil, 1959; resigned May 11, 1988.

Schulte, Francis B.: b. Dec. 23, 1926, Philadelphia, Pa.; educ. St. Charles Borromeo Seminary (Overbrook, Pa.): ord. priest (Philadelphia*) May 10, 1952; ord. titular bishop of Afufenia and auxiliary bishop of Philadelphia, Aug. 12, 1981; app. bishop of Wheeling-Charleston, June 4, 1985.

Schuster, Eldon B.: b. Mar. 10, 1911, Calio, N. Dak.; educ. Loras College (Dubuque, Ia.), Catholic Univ. (Washington, D.C.), Oxford Univ. (England), St. Louis Univ. (St. Louis, Mo.); ord. priest (Great Falls) May 27, 1937; ord. titular bishop of Amblada and auxiliary bishop of Great Falls, Mont., Dec. 21, 1961; app. bishop of Great Falls, Dec. 2, 1967, installed Jan. 23, 1968; resigned Dec. 28, 1977.

Setian, Nerses Mikail: b. Oct. 18,1918, Sebaste, Turkey; educ. Armenian Pontifical College and Gregorian Univ. (Rome); ord. priest Apr. 13, 1941, in Rome; ord. titular bishop of Ancira of the Armenians and first exarch of the apostolic exarchate for Armenian-Rite Catholics in Canada and the United States (see city New York), Dec. 5, 1981.

Shea, Francis R.: b. Dec. 4, 1913, Knoxville, Tenn.; educ. St. Mary's Seminary (Baltimore, Md.), North American College (Rome), Peabody College (Nashville, Tenn.); ord. priest (Nashville) Mar. 19, 1939; ord. bishop of Evansville, Ind., Feb. 3, 1970.

Sheehan, Daniel E.: b. May 14, 1917, Emerson, Nebr.; educ. Creighton Univ. (Omaha, Nebr.), Kenrick Seminary (Webster Groves, Mo.), Catholic Univ. (Washington, D.C.): ord. priest (Omaha*) May 23, 1942; ord. titular bishop of Capsus and auxiliary bishop of Omaha, Mar. 19,

1964; app. archbishop of Omaha, installed Aug. 11, 1969.

Sheehan, Michael J.: b. July 9, 1939, Wichita, Kans.; educ. Assumption Seminary (San Antonio, Tex.), Gregorian Univ. and Lateran Univ. (Rome); ord. priest (Dallas) July 12, 1964; ord. first bishop of Lubbock, Tex., June 17, 1983.

Sheldon, Gilbert I.: b. Sept. 20, 1926, Cleveland, O.; educ. John Carroll Univ. and St. Mary Seminary (Cleveland, O.); ord. priest (Cleveland) Feb. 28, 1953; ord. titular bishop of Taparura and auxiliary bishop of Cleveland, June 11, 1976.

Shubsda, Thaddeus A.: b. Apr. 2, 1925, Los Angeles, Calif.; educ. St. John's Seminary (Camarillo, Calif.); ord. priest (Los Angeles*) Apr. 26, 1950; ord. titular bishop of Trau and auxiliary bishop of Los Angeles, Feb. 19, 1977; app. bishop of Monterey, June 1, 1982.

Sklba, Richard J.: b. Sept. 11, 1935, Racine, Wis.; educ. Old St. Francis Minor Seminary (Milwaukee, Wis.), North American College, Gregorian Univ., Pontifical Biblical Institute, Angelicum (Rome); ord. priest (Milwaukee*) Dec. 20, 1959; ord. titular bishop of Castra and auxiliary bishop of Milwaukee, Dec. 19, 1979.

Skylstad, William: b. Mar. 2, 1934, Omak, Wash.; educ. Pontifical College Josephinum (Worthington, Ohio), Washington State Univ. (Pullman, Wash.), Gonzaga Univ. (Spokane, Wash.); ord. priest (Spokane) May 21, 1960; ord. bishop of Yakima, May 12, 1977.

Smith, John M.: b. June 23, 1935, Orange, N.J.; educ. Immaculate Conception Seminary (Darlington, N.J.), Seton Hall Univ. (South Orange, N.J.), Catholic Univ. (Washington, D.C.); ord. priest May 27, 1961 (Newark*); ord. titular bishop of Tre Taverne and auxiliary bishop of Newark, Jan. 25, 1988.

Smith, Philip F., O.M.I.: b. Oct. 16, 1924, Lowell, Mass.; ord. priest Oct. 29, 1950; ord. titular bishop of Lamfua and vicar apostolic of Jolo, Philippine Islands, Sept. 8, 1972; app. coadjutor archbishop of Cotabato, Philippines, April 11, 1979; archbishop of Cotabato, Mar. 14, 1980.

Snyder, John J.: b. Oct. 25, 1925, New York, N.Y.; educ. Cathedral College (Brooklyn, N.Y.), Immaculate Conception Seminary (Huntington, N.Y.); ord. priest (Brooklyn) June 9, 1951; ord. titular bishop of Forlimpopli and auxiliary bishop of Brooklyn, Feb. 2, 1973; app. bishop of St. Augustine, installed Dec. 5, 1979.

Soens, Lawrence D.: b. Aug. 26, 1926, Iowa City, Ia.; educ. Loras College (Dubuque, Ia.), St. Ambrose College (Davenport, Ia.), Kenrick Seminary (St. Louis, Mo.), Univ. of Iowa; ord. priest (Davenport) May 6, 1950; ord. bishop of Sioux City, Aug. 17, 1983.

Sowada, Alphonse A., O.S.C.: b. June 23, 1933, Avon, Minn.; educ. Holy Cross Scholasticate (Fort Wayne, Ind.), Catholic Univ. (Washington, D.C.); ord. priest May 31, 1958; missionary in Indonesia from 1958; ord. bishop of Agats, Indonesia, Nov. 23, 1969.

Speltz, George H.: b. May 29, 1912, Altura, Minn.; educ. St. Mary's College, St. Paul's Seminary (St. Paul, Minn.), Catholic Univ. (Washington, D.C.); ord. priest (St. Cloud) June 2, 1940; ord. titular bishop of Claneus and auxiliary bishop of Winona, Mar. 25, 1963; app. coadjutor bishop of St. Cloud, Apr. 4, 1966; bishop of St. Cloud, Jan. 31, 1968; retired Jan. 13, 1987.

Speyrer, Jude: b. Apr. 14, 1929, Leonville, La.; educ. St. Joseph Seminary (Covington, La.), Notre Dame Seminary (New Orleans, La.), Gregorian Univ. (Rome), Univ. of Fribourg (Switzerland); ord. priest (Lafayette, La.) July 25, 1953; ord. first bishop of Lake Charles, La., Apr. 25, 1980.

Stafford, James Francis: b. July 26, 1932, Baltimore, Md.; educ. St. Mary's Seminary (Baltimore, Md.), North American College and Gregorian Univ. (Rome); ord. priest (Baltimore*) Dec. 15, 1957; ord. titular bishop of Respecta and auxiliary bishop of Baltimore, Feb. 29, 1976; app. bishop of Memphis, Nov. 17, 1982; app. archbishop of Denver, June 3, 1986, installed July 30, 1986.

Steib, J. (James) Terry, S.V.D.: b. May 17, 1940, Vacherie, La.; educ. Divine Word seminaries (Bay St. Louis, Miss., Conesus, N.Y., Techny, Ill.), Xavier Univ. (New Orleans, La.); ord. priest Jan. 6, 1967; ord. titular bishop of Fallaba and auxiliary bishop of St. Louis, Feb. 10, 1984.

Steinbock, John T.: b. July 16, 1937, Los Angeles, Calif.; educ. Los Angeles archdiocesan seminaries; ord. priest (Los Angeles*) May 1, 1963; ord. titular bishop of Midila and auxiliary bishop of Orange, Calif., July 14, 1984; app. bishop of Santa Rosa, Jan. 27, 1987.

Steiner, Kenneth Donald: b. Nov. 25, 1936, David City, Nebr.; educ. Mt. Angel Seminary (St. Benedict, Ore.), St. Thomas Seminary (Seattle, Wash.); ord. priest (Portland,* Ore.) May 19, 1962; ord. titular bishop of Avensa and auxiliary bishop of Portland, Ore., Mar. 2, 1978.

Straling, Phillip F.: b. Apr. 25, 1933, San Bernardino, Calif.; educ. Immaculate Heart Seminary, St. Francis Seminary, Univ. of San Diego and San Diego State University (San Diego, Calif.), North American College (Rome); ord. priest (San Diego) Mar. 19, 1959; ord. first bishop of San Bernardino, Nov. 6, 1978.

Strecker, Ignatius J.: b. Nov. 23, 1917, Spearville, Kans.; educ. St. Benedict's College (Atchison, Kans.), Kenrick Seminary (Webster Groves, Mo.), Catholic Univ. (Washington, D.C.); ord. priest (Wichita) Dec. 19, 1942; ord. bishop of Springfield-Cape Girardeau, Mo., June 20, 1962; archbishop of Kansas City, Kans., Oct. 28, 1969.

Sullivan, James S.: b. July 23, 1929, Kalamazoo, Mich.; educ. Sacred Heart Seminary (Detroit, Mich.), St. John Provincial Seminary (Plymouth, Mich.); ord. priest (Lansing) June 4, 1955; ord. titular bishop of Siccessi and auxiliary bishop of Lansing, Sept. 21, 1972; app. bishop of Fargo, Apr. 2, 1985; installed May 30, 1985.

Sullivan, John J.: b. July 5, 1920, Horton, Kans.; educ. Kenrick Seminary (St. Louis, Mo.); ord. priest (Oklahoma City*) Sept. 23, 1944; vice-president of Catholic Church Extension Society and national director of Extension Lay Volunteers, 1961-68; ord. bishop of Grand Island, Sept. 19, 1972; app. bishop of Kansas City-St. Joseph, June 27, 1977, installed Aug. 17, 1977.

Sullivan, Joseph M.: b. Mar. 23, 1930, Brooklyn, N.Y.; educ. Immaculate Conception Seminary (Huntington, N.Y.), Fordham Univ. (New York); ord. priest (Brooklyn) June 2, 1956; ord. titular bishop of Suliana and auxiliary bishop of Brooklyn, Nov. 24, 1980.

Sullivan, Walter F.: b. June 10, 1928, Washington, D.C.; educ. St. Mary's Seminary (Baltimore, Md.), Catholic Univ. (Washington, D.C.); ord. priest (Richmond) May 9, 1953; ord. titular bishop of Selsea and auxiliary bishop of Richmond, Va., Dec. 1, 1970; app. bishop of Richmond, June 4, 1974.

Sulyk, Stephen: b. Oct. 2, 1924, Balnycia, Western Ukraine; migrated to U.S. 1948; educ. Ukrainian Catholic Seminary of the Holy Spirit (Hirschberg, Germany), St. Josaphat's Seminary and Catholic Univ. (Washington, D.C.); ord. priest (Philadelphia,* Byzantine Rite) June 14, 1952; ord. archbishop of the Ukrainian-Rite archeparcy of Philadelphia, Mar. 1, 1981.

Symons, J. Keith: b. Oct. 14, 1932, Champion, Mich.; educ. St. Thomas Seminary (Bloomfield, Conn.), St. Mary Seminary (Baltimore, Md.); ord. priest (St. Augustine) May 18, 1958; ord. titular bishop of Siguitanus and auxiliary bishop of St. Petersburg, Mar. 19, 1981; app. bishop of Pensacola-Tallahassee, Oct. 4, 1983, installed Nov. 8, 1983.

Szoka, Edmund C.: (See Cardinals, Biographies.)

T

Tafoya, Arthur N.: b. Mar. 2, 1933, Alameda, N.M.; educ. St. Thomas Seminary (Denver, Colo.), Conception Seminary (Conception, Mo.); ord. priest (Santa Fe*) May 12, 1962; ord. bishop of Pueblo, Sept. 10, 1980.

Tanner, Paul F.: b. Jan. 15, 1905, Peoria, Ill.; educ. Marquette Univ. (Milwaukee, Wis.), Kenrick Seminary (Webster Groves, Mo.), St. Francis Seminary (Milwaukee, Wis.), Catholic Univ. (Washington, D.C.): ord. priest (Milwaukee*) May 30, 1931; assistant director NCWC Youth Department 1940-45; assistant general secretary of NCWC 1945-58; general secretary of NCWC (now USCC) 1958-68; ord. titular bishop of Lamasba, Dec. 21, 1965; bishop of St. Augustine, Mar. 27, 1968; resigned Apr. 21, 1979.

Tawil, Joseph: b. Dec. 25, 1913, Damascus, Syria; ord. priest July 20, 1936; ord. titular archbishop of Mira and patriarchal vicar for eparchy of Damascus of the Patriarchate of Antioch for the Melkites, Jan. 1, 1960; apostolic exarch for faithful of the Melkite rite in the U.S., Oct. 31, 1969; app. first eparch with personal title of archbishop when exarchate was raised to eparchy, July 15, 1976; title of see changed to Newton, 1977.

Timlin, James C.: b. Aug. 5, 1927, Scranton, Pa.; educ. St. Charles College (Catonsville, Md.), St. Mary's Seminary (Baltimore, Md.), North American College (Rome); ord. priest (Scranton) July 16, 1951; ord. titular bishop of Gunugo and auxiliary bishop of Scranton, Sept. 21, 1976; app. bishop of Scranton, Apr. 24, 1984.

Trautman, Donald W.: b. June 24, 1936, Buffalo, N.Y.; educ. Our Lady of Angels Seminary (Niagara Falls, N.Y.), Theology Faculty (Innsbruck, Austria), Pontifical Biblical Institute (Rome), Catholic Univ. (Washington, D.C.); ord. priest (Buffalo) Apr. 7, 1962, in Innsbruck; ord. titular bishop of Sassura and auxiliary of Buffalo, Apr. 16, 1985.

Treinen, Sylvester: b. Nov. 19, 1917, Donnelly, Minn.; educ. Crosier Seminary (Onamia, Minn.), St. Paul Seminary (St. Paul, Minn.); ord. priest (Bismarck) June 11, 1946; ord. bishop of Boise, July 25, 1962; resigned Aug. 17, 1988.

Tschoepe, Thomas: b. Dec. 17, 1915, Pilot Point, Tex.; educ. Pontifical College Josephinum (Worthington, O.); ord. priest (Dallas) May 30, 1943; ord. bishop of San Angelo, Tex., Mar. 9, 1966; app. bishop of Dallas, Tex., Aug. 27, 1969.

U-V

Untener, Kenneth E.: b. Aug. 3, 1937, Detroit, Mich.; educ. Sacred Heart Seminary (Detroit, Mich.), St. John's Provincial Seminary (Plymouth, Mich.), Gregorian Univ. (Rome); ord. priest (Detroit*) June 1, 1963; ord. bishop of Saginaw, Nov. 24, 1980.

Unterkoefler, Ernest L.: b. Aug. 17, 1917, Philadelphia, Pa.; educ. Catholic Univ. (Washington, D.C.); ord. priest (Richmond) May 18, 1944; ord. titular bishop of Latopolis and auxiliary bishop of Richmond, Va., Feb. 22, 1962; app. bishop of Charleston, Dec. 12, 1964, installed Feb. 22, 1965.

Valero, René A.: b. Aug. 15, 1930, New York, N.Y.; educ. Cathedral College, Immaculate Conception Seminary (Huntington, N.Y.), Fordham Univ. (New York); ord. priest (Brooklyn) June 2, 1956; ord. titular bishop of Turris Vicus and auxiliary bishop of Brooklyn, Nov. 24, 1980.

Vaughan, Austin B.: b. Sept. 27, 1927, New York, N.Y.; educ. North American College and Gregorian Univ. (Rome), ord. priest (New York*) Dec. 8, 1951; pres. Catholic Theological Society of America, 1967; rector of St. Joseph's Seminary (Dunwoodie, N.Y.), 1973; ord. titular bishop of Cluain Iraird and auxiliary bishop of New York, June 29, 1977.

Veigle, Adrian J.M., T.O.R.: b. Sept. 15, 1912, Lilly, Pa.; educ. St. Francis College (Loretto, Pa.), Pennsylvania State College; ord. priest May 22, 1937; ord. titular bishop of Gigthi June 9, 1966 (resigned titular see May 26, 1978); prelate of Borba, Brazil, 1966; retired July 6, 1988.

Vlazny, John G.: b. Feb. 22, 1937, Chicago, Ill.; educ. Quigley Preparatory Seminary (Chicago, Ill.), St. Mary of the Lake Seminary (Mundelein, Ill.), Gregorian Univ. (Rome), Univ. of Michigan, Loyola Univ. (Chicago, Ill.); ord. priest (Chicago*) Dec. 20, 1961; ord. titular bishop of Stagno and auxiliary bishop of Chicago, Dec. 13, 1983; episcopal vicar; app. bishop of Winona, Minn., May 19, 1987.

Vonesh, Raymond J.: b. Jan. 25, 1916, Chicago, Ill.; educ. St. Mary of the Lake Seminary (Mundelein, Ill.). Gregorian Univ. (Rome); ord. priest (Chicago*) May 3, 1941; ord. titular bishop of Vanariona and auxiliary bishop of Joliet, Ill., Apr. 3, 1968.

W

Waldschmidt, Paul E., C.S.C.: b. Jan. 7, 1920, Evansville, Ind.; educ. Notre Dame Univ. (Notre Dame, Ind.), Holy Cross College (Washington, D.C.), Laval Univ. (Quebec), Angelicum (Rome), Louvain (Belgium), Sorbonne (Paris), ord. priest June 24, 1946; president University of Portland, 1962-77; ord. titular bishop of Citium and auxiliary bishop of Portland, Ore., Mar. 2, 1978.

Walsh, Daniel Francis: b. Oct. 2, 1937, San Francisco, Calif.; educ. St. Joseph Seminary (Mountain View, Calif.), St. Patrick Seminary (Menlo Park, Calif.) Catholic Univ. (Washington, D.C.); ord. priest (San Francisco*) Mar. 30, 1963; ord. titular bishop of Tigia and auxiliary bishop of San Francisco, Sept. 24, 1981; app. bishop of Reno-Las Vegas, June 9, 1987.

Walsh, Nicolas E.: b. Oct. 20, 1916, Burnsville, Minn.; educ. St. Paul Seminary (St. Paul, Minn.), Catholic Univ. (Washington, D.C.), Pontifical Palafoxianum Seminary (Puebla, Mexico), Register College of Journalism (Denver, Colo.); ord. priest (Boise) June 6, 1942; first editor of *Idaho Register;* diocesan vicar for Mexican Americans; ord. bishop of Yakima, Oct. 28, 1974; app. titular bishop of Bolsena and auxiliary bishop of Seattle, Aug. 10, 1976; retired Sept. 6, 1983. Bishop emeritus of Yakima.

Ward, John J.: b. Sept. 28, 1920, Los Angeles, Calif.; educ. St. John's Seminary (Camarillo, Calif.), Catholic Univ. (Washington, D.C.); ord. priest (Los Angeles*) May 4, 1946; ord. titular bishop of Bria and auxiliary of Los Angeles, Dec. 12, 1963.

Watson, Alfred M.: b. July 11, 1907, Erie, Pa.; educ. St. Mary's Seminary (Baltimore, Md.), Catholic Univ. (Washington, D.C.); ord. priest (Erie) May 10, 1934; ord. titular bishop of Nationa and auxiliary bishop of Erie, June 29, 1965; app. bishop of Erie, 1969, installed May 13, 1969; resigned July 16, 1982.

Watters, Loras J.: b. Oct. 14, 1915, Dubuque, Ia.; educ. Loras College (Dubuque, Ia.), Gregorian Univ. (Rome), Catholic Univ. (Washington, D.C.); ord. priest (Dubuque*) June 7, 1941; ord. titular bishop of Fidoloma and auxiliary bishop of Dubuque, Aug. 26, 1965; bishop of Winona, installed Mar. 13, 1969; retired Oct. 14, 1986.

Watty Urquidi, Ricardo, M.Sp.S.: b. July 16, 1938, San Diego, Calif.; ord. priest June 8, 1968; ord. titular bishop of Macomedes and auxiliary bishop of Mexico City, July 19, 1980.

Weakland, Rembert G., O.S.B.: b. Apr. 2, 1927, Patton, Pa.; joined Benedictines, 1945; ord. priest June 24, 1951; abbot-primate of Benedictine Confederation, 1967-77; ord. archbishop of Milwaukee, Nov. 8, 1977.

Weigand, William K.: b. May 23, 1937, Bend, Ore.; educ. Mt. Angel Seminary (St. Benedict, Ore.), St. Edward's Seminary and St. Thomas Seminary (Kenmore, Wash.); ord. priest (Boise) May 25, 1963; ord. bishop of Salt Lake City, Nov. 17, 1980.

Weitzel, John Quinn, M.M.: b. May 10, 1928, Chicago, Ill.; educ. Maryknoll Seminary (Maryknoll, N.Y.); ord. priest Nov. 5, 1955, missionary to Samoa, 1979; ord. bishop of Samoa-Pago Pago, American Samoa, Oct. 29, 1986.

Welsh, Lawrence H.: b. Feb. 1, 1935, Winton, Wyo.; educ. Univ. of Wyoming (Laramie, Wyo.), St. John's Seminary (Collegeville, Minn.), Catholic Univ. (Washington, D.C.); ord. priest (Rapid City) May 26, 1962; ord. bishop of Spokane, Dec. 14, 1978.

Welsh, Thomas J.: b. Dec. 20, 1921, Weatherly, Pa.; educ. St. Charles Borromeo Seminary (Philadelphia, Pa.), Catholic Univ. (Washington, D.C.); ord. priest (Philadelphia*) May 30, 1946; ord. titular bishop of Scattery Island and auxiliary bishop of Philadelphia, Apr. 2, 1970; app. first bishop of Arlington, Va., June 4, 1974, installed Aug. 13, 1974; app. bishop of Allentown, Feb. 8, 1983, installed Mar. 21, 1983.

Whealon, John F.: b. Jan. 15, 1921, Barberton, O.; educ. St. Charles College (Catonsville, Md.), St. Mary's Seminary (Cleveland, O.); ord. priest (Cleveland) May 26, 1945; ord. titular bishop of Andrapa and auxiliary bishop of Cleveland, July 6, 1961; app. bishop of Erie, Dec. 9, 1966, installed Mar. 7, 1967; archbishop of Hartford, installed Mar. 19, 1969.

Whelan, Robert L., S.J.: b. Apr. 16, 1912, Wallace, Ida.; educ. St. Michael's College (Spokane, Wash.), Alma College (Alma, Calif.); ord. priest June 17, 1944; ord. titular bishop of Sicilibba and coadjutor bishop of Fairbanks, Alaska, with right of succession, Feb. 22, 1968; bishop of Fairbanks, Nov. 30, 1968; retired June 1, 1985.

Wildermuth, Augustine F., S.J.: b. Feb. 20, 1904, St. Louis, Mo.; educ. St. Stanislaus Seminary (Florissant, Mo.), St. Michael's Scholasticate (Spokane, Wash.), Sacred Heart College (Shembaganur, S. India), St. Mary's College (Kurseong, India), Gregorian Univ. (Rome); entered Society of Jesus, 1922; ord. priest July 25, 1935; ord. bishop of Patna, India, Oct. 28, 1947; retired Mar. 6, 1980.

Williams, James Kendrick: b. Sept. 5, 1936, Athertonville, Ky.; educ. St. Mary's College (St. Mary's, Ky.), St. Maur's School of Theology (South Union, Ky.); ord. priest (Louisville*) May 25, 1963; ord. titular bishop of Catula and auxiliary bishop of Covington, June 19, 1984; first bishop of Lexington, Ky., installed Mar. 2, 1988.

Wirz, George O.: b. Jan. 17, 1929, Monroe, Wis.; educ. St. Francis Seminary and Marquette Univ. (Milwaukee, Wis.); Cath. Univ. (Washington, D.C.); ord. priest (Madison) May 31, 1952; ord. titular bishop of Municipa and auxiliary bishop of Madison, Mar. 9, 1978.

Wuerl, Donald: b. Nov. 12, 1940, Pittsburgh, Pa.; educ. Catholic Univ. of America (Washington, D.C.), North American College, Angelicum (Rome); ord. priest (Pittsburgh) Dec. 17, 1966, in Rome; ord. titular bishop of Rosemarkie Jan. 6, 1986, in Rome; auxiliary bishop of Seattle, 1986-87; app. bishop of Pittsburgh Feb. 11, 1988, installed Mar. 25, 1988.

Wycislo, Aloysius John: b. June 17, 1908, Chicago, Ill.; educ. St. Mary's Seminary (Mundelein, Ill.), Catholic Univ. (Washington, D.C.); ord. priest (Chicago*) Apr. 4, 1934; ord. titular bishop of Stadia and auxiliary bishop of Chicago, Dec. 21,

1960; app. bishop of Green Bay, installed Apr. 16, 1968; resigned May 10, 1983.

Z

Zayek, Francis: b. Oct. 18, 1920, Manzanillo, Cuba; ord. priest Mar. 17, 1946; ord. titular bishop of Callinicum and auxiliary bishop for Maronites in Brazil, Aug. 5, 1962; named apostolic exarch for Maronites in U.S., with headquarters in Detroit; installed June 11, 1966; first eparch of St. Maron of Detroit, Mar. 25, 1972; see transferred to Brooklyn, June 27, 1977; given personal title of archbishop, Dec. 22, 1982.

Ziemann, G. Patrick: b. Sept. 13, 1941, Pasadena, Calif.; educ. St. John's College Seminary and St. John's Seminary (Camarillo, Calif.), Mt. St. Mary's College (Los Angeles, Calif.); ord. priest (Los Angeles*) Apr. 29, 1967; ord. titular bishop of Obba and auxiliary bishop of Los Angeles, Feb. 23, 1987.

U.S. BISHOPS OVERSEAS

Cardinal William W. Baum, prefect of the Congregation for Catholic Education (Seminaries and Institutes of Study, effective Mar. 1, 1989); Cardinal Myroslav Ivan Lubachivsky, archbishop of Lwow and major archbishop of Ukrainians; Archbishop Ambrose De Paoli, apostolic delegate to southern Africa and pro-nuncio to Lesotho; Archbishop John P. Foley, president of the Pontifical Commission (Council, effective Mar. 1, 1989) for Social Communications; Archbishop Paul C. Marcinkus, president of Institute for Works of Religion (Vatican Bank) and pro-president of Pontifical Commission for the State of Vatian City; Archbishop Justin Rigali, president of Pontifical Ecclesiastical Academy; Most Rev. Georges Riashi, B.C.O., bishop of eparchy of St. Michael of Sydney (Australia) for Greek-Catholic Melkites.

(See also Missionary Bishops.)

BISHOP-BROTHERS

(The asterisk indicates brothers who were bishops at the same time.)

There have been nine pairs of brother-bishops in the history of the U.S. hierarchy.

Living: Francis T. Hurley,* archbishop of Anchorage and Mark J. Hurley,* bishop emeritus of Santa Rosa.

Deceased: Francis Blanchet* of Oregon City (Portland) and Augustin Blanchet* of Walla Walla; John S. Foley of Detroit and Thomas P. Foley of Chicago; Francis P. Kenrick,* apostolic administrator of Philadelphia, bishop of Philadelphia and Baltimore, and Peter R. Kenrick* of St. Louis; Matthias C. Lenihan of Great Falls and Thomas M. Lenihan of Cheyenne; James O'Connor, vicar apostolic of Nebraska and bishop of Omaha, and Michael O'Connor of Pittsburgh and Erie; Jeremiah F. and John W. Shanahan, both of Harrisburg; Sylvester J. Espelage, O.F.M.,* of Wuchang, China, who died 10 days after the ordination of his brother, Bernard T. Espelage,* O.F.M., of Gallup; Coleman F. Carroll* of Miami and Howard Carroll* of Altoona-Johnstown.

RETIRED U.S. PRELATES

Information, as of Aug. 15, 1988, includes name of the prelate and see held at the time of retirement or resignation; archbishops are indicated by an asterisk. Most of the prelates listed below resigned their sees because of age in accordance with church law. See Index: Biographies, U.S. Bishops.

Forms of address of retired residential prelates (unless they have a titular see): *Archbishop or Bishop Emeritus of* (last see held); *Former Archbishop or Bishop of* (last see held).

Richard H. Ackerman, C.S.Sp. (Covington), George W. Ahr (Trenton), Leo Arkfeld, S.V.D.* (Madang, Papus New Guinea), Reginald Arliss, C.P. (Marbel, Philippines, prelate), Michael J. Begley (Charlotte), John H. Boccella, T.O.R.* (Izmir, Turkey), Ernest B. Boland, O.P. (Multan, Pakistan), Edwin B. Broderick (Albany), Joseph Brunini (Jackson), James C. Burke, O.P. (Chimbote, Peru, prelate), Charles A. Buswell (Pueblo), James J. Byrne* (Dubuque), Cardinal John Carberry* (St. Louis), John J. Cassata (Fort Worth), Harry A. Clinch (Monterey), John E. Cohill, S.V.D. (Goroka, Papua New Guinea), John W. Comber, M.M. (Foratiano, titular see), William G. Connare (Greensburg), Thomas Connolly* (Seattle), William M. Cosgrove (Belleville), Arnold R. Cotey, S.D.S. (Nachingwea, Tanzania), William E. Cousins* (Milwaukee), Walter W. Curtis (Bridgeport), Augustine Danglmayr (Ft. Worth, auxiliary), Nicholas D'Antonio, O.F.M. (Olancho, Honduras).

Antanas L. Deksnys (Lavellum, titular see), Michael J. Dempsey, O.P. (Sokoto, Nigeria), Joseph P. Denning (Brooklyn, auxiliary), Joseph A. DePalma, S.C.J. (DeAar, South Africa), Maurice Dingman (Des Moines), John A. Donovan (Toledo), Thomas J. Drury (Corpus Christi), Clarence J. Duhart, C.SS.R. (Udon Thani, Thailand), Joseph A. Durick (Nashville), Nicholas T. Elko* (Cincinnati, auxiliary), J. Lennox Federal (Salt Lake City), Bernard J. Flanagan (Worcester), Marion F. Forst (Dodge City), John B. Franz (Peoria), Frederick W. Freking (La Crosse), Philip J. Furlong (Military Vicariate, auxiliary).

Raymond J. Gallagher (Lafayette, Ind.), Hugo Gerbermann, M.M. (San Antonio, auxiliary), Peter L. Gerety* (Newark), James J. Gerrard (Fall River, auxiliary), Ignatius T. Glennie, S.J. (Trincomalee-Batticaloa, Sri Lanka), George J. Gottwald (St. Louis, auxiliary), Lawrence P. Graves (Alexandria-Shreveport), Lawrence Graziano, O.F.M. (San Miguel, El Salvador), Francis J. Green (Tucson), Andrew G. Grutka (Gary).

Hilary B. Hacker (Bismarck), John F. Hackett (Hartford, auxiliary), George A. Hammes (Superior), Edward Harper, C.SS.R. (St. Thomas, V.I.), Frank H. Harrison (Syracuse), Charles H. Helmsing (Kansas City-St. Joseph), Edward J. Herrmann (Columbus), Edward G. Hettinger (Columbus, auxiliary), Vincent J. Hines (Norwich), Lambert A. Hoch (Sioux Falls), Robert L. Hodapp, S.J. (Belize), James J. Hogan (Altoona-Johnstown), Joseph L. Hogan (Rochester), Mark J. Hurley

(Santa Rosa), Robert F. Joyce (Burlington), Arthur H. Krawczak (Detroit, auxiliary), Cardinal John Krol* (Philadelphia), William F. Kupfer, M.M. (Taichung, Taiwan), Vincent M. Leonard (Pittsburgh), George E. Lynch (Raleigh, auxiliary). J. Carroll McCormick (Scranton), William McDonald (San Francisco, auxiliary), Thomas J. McDonough* (Louisville), Bernard J. McLaughlin (Buffalo, auxiliary), William E. McManus (Fort Wayne-South Bend), Joseph H. McShea (Allentown), John J. Maguire* (New York, coadjutor), Charles G. Maloney (Louisville, auxiliary), David M. Maloney (Wichita), Cardinal Timothy Manning* (Los Angeles), Alfred Mendez, C.S.C. (Arecibo, P.R.), James E. Michaels (Wheeling-Charleston, auxiliary), William J. Moran (Military Vicariate, delegate), John L. Morkovsky (Galveston-Houston), Charles R. Mulrooney (Brooklyn, auxiliary), T. Austin Murphy (Baltimore, auxiliary), Knute Ansgar Nelson, O.S.B. (Stockholm, Sweden).

John L. Paschang (Grand Island), George H. Pearce, S.M.* (Suva, Fiji Islands), Henry A. Pinger, O.F.M. (Chowtsun, China), Cornelius M. Power* (Portland, Ore.), Ernest J. Primeau (Manchester), Leo A. Pursley (Fort Wayne-South Bend), Joseph M. Raya* (Acre), Joseph W. Regan, M.M. (Tagum, P.I., Prelate), Francis F. Reh (Saginaw). Thomas F. Reilly, C.SS.R. (San Juan de la Maguana, Dominican Republic), John J. Rudin, M.M. (Musoma, Tanzania), John J. Russell (Richmond), James C. Ryan, O.F.M. (Santarem, Brazil), John J. Scanlan (Honolulu), Alphonse Schladweiler (New Ulm), Eldon B. Schuster (Great Falls). George H. Speltz (St. Cloud), Paul F. Tanner (St. Augustine), Sylvester Treinen (Boise), Adrian Veigle, T.O.R. (Borba, Brazil, Prelate), Nicolas Walsh (Yakima), Alfred M. Watson (Erie), Loras J. Watters (Winona), Robert L. Whelan (Fairbanks), Augustine Wildermuth, S.J. (Patna, India), Aloysius J. Wycislo (Green Bay).

AMERICAN BISHOPS OF THE PAST

Information includes: dates; place of birth if outside the U.S.; date of ordination to the priesthood; titular see in parentheses of bishops who were not ordinaries; indication, where applicable, of date of resignation.

Abbreviation code: abp., archbishop; bp., bishop; v.a., vicar apostolic; aux., auxiliary bishop; coad., coadjutor; ord., ordained; res., resigned.

A

Adrian, William L. (1883-1972): ord. Apr. 15, 1911; bp. Nashville, 1936-69 (res.).
Albers, Joseph (1891-1965): ord. June 17, 1916; aux. Cincinnati (Lunda), 1929-37; first bp. Lansing, 1937-65.
Alemany, Joseph Sadoc, O.P. (1814-88): b. Spain; ord. Mar. 11, 1837; bp. Monterey, 1850-53; first abp. San Francisco, 1853-84 (res.).
Alencastre, Stephen P., SS.CC. (1876-1940): b. Madeira; ord. Apr. 5, 1902; coad. v.a. Sandwich Is. (Arabissus), 1924-36; v.a. Sandwich (Hawaiian) Is., 1936-40.
Alerding, Herman J. (1845-1924): b. Germany; ord. Sept. 22, 1869; bp. Fort Wayne, 1900-24.
Allen, Edward P. (1853-1926): ord. Dec. 17, 1881; bp. Mobile, 1897-1926.
Alter, Karl J. (1885-1977): ord. June 4, 1910; bp. Toledo, 1931-50; abp. Cincinnati, 1950-69 (res.).
Althoff, Henry (1873-1947): ord. July 26, 1902; bp. Belleville, 1914-47.
Amat, Thaddeus, C.M. (1811-78): b. Spain; ord. Dec. 23, 1837; bp. Monterey (title changed to Monterey-Los Angeles, 1859), 1854-78.
Anderson, Joseph (1865-1927): ord. May 20, 1892; aux. Boston (Myrina), 1909-27.
Anderson, Paul F. (1917-87): ord. Jan. 6, 1943; coad. bp. Duluth (Polignana), 1968-69; bp. Duluth, 1969-82 (res.); aux. Sioux Falls, 1983-87.
Anglim, Robert, C.SS.R. (1922-73): ord. Jan. 6, 1948; prelate Coari, Brazil (Gaguari), 1966-73.
Annabring, Joseph (1900-59): b. Hungary; ord.

May 3, 1927; bp. Superior, 1954-59.
Appelhans, Stephen A., S.V.D. (1905-51): ord. May 5, 1932; v.a. East New Guinea (Catula), 1948-51.
Armstrong, Robert J. (1884-1957): ord. Dec. 10, 1910; bp. Sacramento, 1929-57.
Arnold, William R. (1881-1965): ord. June 13, 1908; delegate of U.S. military vicar (Phocaea), 1945-65.
Atkielski, Roman R. (1898-1969): ord. May 30, 1931; aux. Milwaukee (Stobi), 1947-69.

B

Babcock, Allen J. (1898-1969): ord. Mar. 7, 1925; aux. Detroit (Irenopolis), 1947-54; bp. Grand Rapids, 1954-69.
Bacon, David W. (1815-74): ord. Dec. 13, 1838; first bp. Portland, Me., 1855-74.
Baldwin, Vincent J. (1907-79): ord. July 26, 1931; aux. Rockville Centre (Bencenna), 1962-79.
Baltes, Peter J. (1827-86): b. Germany; ord. May 31, 1852; bp. Alton (now Springfield), Ill., 1870-86.
Baraga, Frederic: See Index.
Barron, Edward (1801-54): b. Ireland; ord. 1829; v.a. The Two Guineas (Constantina), 1842-44 (res.) missionary in U.S.
Barry, John (1799-1859): b. Ireland; ord. Sept. 24, 1825; bp. Savannah, 1857-59.
Barry, Patrick J. (1868-1940): b. Ireland; ord. June 9, 1895; bp. St. Augustine, 1922-40.
Bartholome, Peter W. (1893-1982): ord. June 12, 1917; coad. St. Cloud (Lete), 1942-53; bp. St. Cloud, 1953-68 (res.).
Baumgartner, Apollinarls, O.F.M. Cap. (1899-1970): ord. May 30, 1926; v.a. Guam (Joppa), 1945-65; first bp. Agana, Guam, 1965-70.
Bayley, James Roosevelt (1814-77): convert, 1842; ord. Mar. 2, 1843; first bp. Newark, 1853-72; abp. Baltimore, 1872-77.
Bazin, John S. (1796-1848): b. France; ord. July

22, 1822; bp. Vincennes (now Indianapolis), 1847-48.

Beaven, Thomas D. (1851-1920): ord. Dec. 18, 1875; bp. Springfield, Mass., 1892-1920.

Becker Thomas A. (1832-99): ord. June 18, 1859; first bp. Wilmington, 1868-86; bp. Savannah, 1886-99.

Beckman, Francis J. (1875-1948): ord. June 20, 1902; bp. Lincoln, 1924-30; abp. Dubuque, 1930-46 (res.).

Begin, Floyd L. (1902-77): ord. July 31, 1927; aux. Cleveland (Sala), 1947-62; first bp. Oakland, 1962-77.

Bell, Alden J. (1904-82): b. Canada; ord. May 14, 1932; aux. Los Angeles (Rhodopolis), 1956-62; bp. Sacramento, 1962-79 (res.).

Benincasa, Pius A. (1913-86): ord. Mar. 27, 1937; aux. Buffalo (Buruni), 1964-86.

Benjamin, Cletus J. (1909-61): ord. Dec. 8, 1935; aux. Philadelphia (Binda), 1960-61.

Bennett, John G. (1891-1957): ord. June 27, 1914; first bp. Lafayette, Ind. 1944-57.

Bergan, Gerald T. (1892-1972): ord. Oct. 28, 1915; bp. Des Moines, 1934-48; abp. Omaha, 1948-69 (res.).

Bernarding, George, S.V.D. (1912-87): ord. Aug. 13, 1939; first v.a. Mount Hagen, Papua New Guinea (Belabitene), 1960-66; first bp., 1966-82, and first abp., 1982-87 (res.), Mount Hagen.

Bidawid, Thomas M. (1910-71): b. Iraq; ord. May 15, 1935; U.S. citizen; first abp. Ahwaz, Iran (Chaldean Rite), 1968-70; Chaldean patriarchal vicar for United Arab Republic, 1970-71.

Binz, Leo (1900-79): ord. Mar. 15, 1924; coad. bp. Winona (Pinara) 1942-49; coad. abp. Dubuque (Silyum), 1949-54; abp. Dubuque, 1954-61; abp. St. Paul and Minneapolis, 1962-75 (res.).

Biskup, George J. (1911-79): ord. Mar. 19, 1937; aux. Dubuque (Hemeria), 1957-65; bp. Des Moines, 1965-67; coad. abp. Indianapolis (Tamalluma), 1969-70; abp. Indianapolis, 1970-79 (res.).

Blanc, Anthony (1792-1860): b. France; ord. July 22, 1916; bp. New Orleans, 1835-50; first abp. New Orleans, 1850-60.

Blanchet (brothers): Augustin M. (1797-1887): b. Canada; ord. June 3, 1821; bp. Walla Walla, 1846-50; first bp. Nesqually (now Seattle), 1850-79 (res.). **Francis N.** (1795-1883): b. Canada; ord. July 19, 1819; v.a. Oregon Territory (Philadelphia, Adrasus), 1843-46; first abp. Oregon City (now Portland), 1846-80 (res.).

Blanchette, Romeo R. (1913-82): ord. Apr. 3, 1937; aux. Joliet (Maxita), 1965-66; bp. Joliet, 1966-79 (res.).

Blenk, James H., S.M. (1856-1917): b. Germany; ord. Aug. 16, 1885; bp. San Juan, 1899-1906; abp. New Orleans, 1906-17.

Boardman, John J. (1894-1978): ord. May 21, 1921; aux. Brooklyn (Gunela), 1952-77 (res.).

Boeynaems, Libert H., SS.CC. (1857-1926): b. Belgium; ord. Sept. 11, 1881; v.a. Sandwich (Hawaiian) Is. (Zeugma), 1903-26.

Bohachevsky, Constantine (1884-1961): b. Austrian Galicia; ord. Jan. 31, 1909; ap. ex. Ukrainian Byzantine Catholics in U.S. (Amisus), 1924-58; first metropolitan of Byzantine Rite archeparchy of Philadelphia, 1958-61.

Boileau, George, S.J. (1912-65): ord. June 13, 1948; coad. bp. Fairbanks (Ausuccura), 1964-65.

Bokenfohr, John, O.M.I. (1903-82): ord. July 11, 1927; bp. Kimberley, S. Africa, 1963-74 (res,).

Boland, Thomas A. (1896-1979): ord. Dec. 23, 1922; aux. Newark (Irina), 1940-47; bp. Paterson, 1947-52; abp. Newark, 1953-74 (res.).

Bona, Stanislaus (1888-1967): ord. Nov. 1, 1912; bp. Grand Island, 1932-44; coad. bp. Green Bay (Mela), 1944-45; bp. Green Bay, 1945-67.

Bonacum, Thomas (1847-1911): b. Ireland; ord. June 18, 1870; bp. Lincoln, 1887-1911.

Borgess, Caspar H. (1826-90): b. Germany; ord. Dec. 8, 1848; coad. bp. and ap. admin. Detroit (Calydon), 1870-71; bp. Detroit, 1871-87 (res.).

Bourgade, Peter (1845-1908): b. France; ord. Nov. 30, 1869; v.a. Arizona (Thaumacus), 1885-97; first bp. Tucson, 1897-99; abp. Santa Fe, 1899-1908.

Boylan, John J. (1889-1953): ord. July 28, 1915; bp. Rockford, 1943-53.

Boyle, Hugh C. (1873-1950): ord. July 2, 1898; bp. Pittsburgh, 1921-50.

Bradley, Denis (1846-1903):b. Ireland; ord. June 3, 1871; first bp. Manchester, 1884-1903.

Brady, John (1842-1910): b. Ireland; ord. Dec. 4, 1864; aux. Boston (Alabanda), 1891-1910.

Brady, Matthew F. (1893-1959): ord. June 10, 1916; bp. Burlington, 1938-44 bp. Manchester, 1944-59.

Brady, William O. (1899-1961): ord. Dec. 21, 1923; bp. Sioux Falls, 1939-56; coad. abp. St. Paul (Selymbria), June-Oct, 1956; abp. St. Paul, 1956-61.

Brennan, Andrew J. (1877-1956): ord. Dec. 17, 1904; aux. Scranton (Thapsus), 1923-26; bp. Richmond, 1926-45 (res.).

Brennan, Francis J. (1894-1968): ord. Apr. 3, 1920; judge (1940-59) and dean (1959-67) of Roman Rota; ord. bp. 1967; cardinal 1967.

Brennan, Thomas F. (1853-1916): b. Ireland; ord. July 14, 1880; first bp. Dallas, 1881-93; aux. St. John's, Newfoundland (Usula), 1893-1905 (res.).

Broderick, Bonaventure (1868-1943): ord. July 26, 1896; aux. Havana, Cuba (Juliopolis), 1903-05 (res.).

Brondel, John B. (1842-1903): b. Belgium; ord. Dec. 17, 1864; bp. Vancouver Is., 1879-84; first bp. Helena, 1884-1903.

Brossart, Ferdinand (1849-1930): b. Germany; ord. Sept. 1, 1892; bp. Covington, 1916-23 (res.).

Brute, Simon G. (1779-1839): b. France; ord. June 11, 1808; first bp. Vincennes (now Indianapolis), 1834-39.

Buddy, Charles F. (1887-1966): ord. Sept. 19, 1914; first bp. San Diego, 1936-66.

Burke, Joseph A. (1886-1962): ord. Aug. 3, 1912; aux. Buffalo (Vita), 1943-52; bp. Buffalo, 1952-62.

Burke, Maurice F. (1845-1923): b. Ireland; ord. May 22, 1875; first bp. Cheyenne, 1887-93; bp. St. Joseph, 1893-1923.

Burke, Thomas M. (1840-1915): b. Ireland; ord. June 30, 1864; bp. Albany, 1894-1915.

Busch, Joseph F. (1866-1953): ord. July 28, 1889; bp. Lead (now Rapid City), 1910-15; bp. St. Cloud, 1915-53.

Byrne, Andrew (1802-62): b. Ireland; ord. Nov. 11, 1827; first bp. Little Rock, 1844-62.
Byrne, Christopher E. (1867-1950): ord. Sept. 23, 1891; bp. Galveston, 1918-50.
Byrne, Edwin V. (1891-1963): ord. May 22, 1915; first bp. Ponce, 1925-29; bp. San Juan, 1929-43; abp. Santa Fe, 1943-63.
Byrne, Leo C. (1908-74): ord. June 10, 1933; aux. St. Louis (Sabadia), 1954-61; coad. bp. Wichita, 1961-67; coad. abp. (Plestra) St. Paul and Minneapolis, 1967-74.
Byrne, Patrick J., M.M. (1888-1950): ord. June 23, 1915; apostolic delegate to Korea (Gazera), 1949-50.
Byrne, Thomas S. (1841-1923): ord. May 22, 1869; bp. Nashville, 1894-1923.

C

Caesar, Raymond R., S.V.D. (1932-87): ord. June 4, 1961; coad. bp. Goroka, Papua New Guinea, 1978-80; bp. Goroka, 1980-87.
Caillouet, L. Abel (1900-84): ord. May 7, 1925; aux. New Orleans (Setea), 1947-76 (res.).
Canevin, J. F. Regis (1853-1927): ord. June 4, 1879; coad. bp. Pittsburgh (Sabrata), 1903-04; bp. Pittsburgh, 1904-21 (res.).
Cantwell, John J. (1874-1947): b. Ireland; ord. June 18, 1899; bp. Monterey-Los Angeles, 1917-22; bp. Los Angeles-San Diego, 1922-36; first abp. Los Angeles, 1936-47.
Carrell, George A., S.J. (1803-68): ord. Dec. 20, 1827; first bp. Covington, 1853-68.
Carroll (brothers) **Coleman F.** (1905-77): ord. June 15, 1930; aux. Pittsburgh (Pitanae), 1953-58; first bp. Miami, 1958-68 and first abp., 1968-77. **Howard J.** (1902-60): ord. Apr. 2, 1927; bp. Altoona-Johnstown, 1958-60.
Carroll, James J. (1862-1913): ord. June 15, 1889; bp. Nueva Segovia, P.I., 1908-12 (res.).
Carroll, John (1735-1815): ord. Feb. 14, 1761; first bishop of the American hierarchy; first bp., 1789-1808, and first abp., 1808-15, of Baltimore.
Carroll, John P. (1864-1925): ord. July 7, 1886; bp. Helena, 1904-25.
Carroll, Mark K. (1896-1985): ord. June 10, 1922; bp. Wichita, 1947-67 (res.).
Cartwright, Hubert J. (1900-58): ord. June 11, 1927; coad. bp. Wilmington (Neve), 1956-58.
Caruana, George (1882-1951): b. Malta; ord. Oct. 28, 1905; bp. Puerto Rico (name changed to San Juan, 1924), 1921-25; ap. del. Mexico (Sebastea in Armenia), 1925-27; internuncio to Haiti, 1927-35; nuncio to Cuba, 1935-47 (res.).
Casey, James V. (1914-86): ord. Dec. 8, 1939; aux. Lincoln (Citium), Apr.-June, 1957; bp. Lincoln, 1957-67; abp. Denver 1967-86.
Casey, Lawrence B. (1905-77): ord. June 7, 1930; aux. Rochester (Cea), 1953-66; bp. Paterson, 1966-77.
Cassidy, James E. (1869-1951): ord. Sept. 8, 1898; aux. Fall River (Ibora), 1930-34; bp. Fall River, 1934-51.
Chabrat, Guy Ignatius, S.S. (1787-1868): b. France; ord. Dec. 21, 1811; coad. bp. Bardstown (Bolina), 1834-47 (res.).
Chanche, John J., S.S. (1795-1852): ord. June 5, 1819; bp. Natchez (now Jackson), 1841-52.
Chapelle, Placide L. (1842-1905): b. France; ord. June 28, 1865; coad. abp. Santa Fe (Arabissus), 1891-94; abp. Santa Fe, 1894-97; abp. New Orleans 1897-1905.
Chartrand, Joseph (1870-1933): ord. Sept. 24, 1892; coad. bp. Indianapolis (Flavias), 1910-18; bp. Indianapolis, 1918-33.
Chatard, Francis S. (1834-1918): ord. June 14, 1862; bp. Vincennes (now Indianapolis — title changed in 1898), 1878-1918.
Cheverus, John Lefebvre de (1768-1836): b. France; ord. Dec. 18, 1790; bp. Boston, 1810-23 (returned to France, made cardinal 1836).
Christie, Alexander (1848-1925): ord. Dec. 22, 1877; bp. Vancouver Is., 1898-99; abp. Oregon City (now Portland), 1899-1925.
Clancy, William (1802-47): b. Ireland; ord. May 24, 1823; coad. bp. Charleston (Oreus), 1834-37; v.a. British Guiana, 1837-43.
Cody, John P. (1907-82): ord. Dec. 8, 1931; aux. St. Louis (Apollonia), 1947-54; coad. bp. St. Joseph, Mo., 1954-55; bp. Kansas City-St. Joseph, 1956-61; coad. abp. 1961-62; ap. admin., 1962-64, and abp., 1964-65, New Orleans; abp. Chicago, 1965-82; cardinal, 1967.
Collins, John J., S.J. (1856-1934): ord. Aug. 29, 1891; v.a. Jamaica (Antiphellus), 1907-18 (res.).
Collins, Thomas P., M.M. (1915-73): ord. June 21, 1942; v.a. Pando, Bolivia (Sufetula), 1961-68 (res.).
Colton, Charles H. (1848-1915): ord. June 10, 1876; bp. Buffalo, 1903-15.
Conaty, Thomas J. (1847-1915): b. Ireland; ord. Dec. 21, 1872; rector of Catholic University, 1896-1903; tit. bp. Samos, 1901-03; bp. Monterey-Los Angeles (now Los Angeles), 1903-15.
Concanen, Richard L., O.P. (1747-1810): b. Ireland; ord. Dec. 22, 1770; first bp. New York, 1808-10 (detained in Italy, never reached his see).
Condon, William J. (1895-1967): ord. Oct. 14, 1917; bp. Great Falls, 1939-67.
Connolly, James L. (1894-1986): ord. Dec. 21, 1923; coad bp. Fall River (Mylasa), 1945-51; bp. Fall River, 1951-70 (res.).
Connolly, John, O.P. (1750-1825): b. Ireland; ord. Sept. 24, 1774; bp. New York, 1814-25.
Conroy, John J. (1819-95): b. Ireland; ord. May 21, 1842; bp. Albany, 1865-77 (res.).
Conroy, Joseph H. (1858-1939): ord. June 11, 1881; aux. Ogdensburg (Arindela), 1912-21; bp. Ogdensburg, 1921-39.
Conwell, Henry (1748-1842): b. Ireland; ord. 1776; bp. Philadelphia, 1820-42.
Cooke, Terence J. (1921-83): ord. Dec. 1, 1945; aux. New York (Summa), 1965-68; abp. New York, 1965-83; cardinal 1969.
Corbett, Timothy (1858-1939): ord. June 12, 1886; first bp. Crookston, 1910-38 (res.).
Corrigan, Joseph M. (1879-1942): ord. June 6, 1903; rector of Catholic University, 1936-42; tit. bp. Bilta, 1940-42.
Corrigan, Michael A. (1839-1902): ord. Sept. 19, 1863; bp. Newark, 1873-80; coad. abp. New York (Petra), 1880-85; abp. New York, 1885-1902.
Corrigan, Owen (1849-1929): ord. June 7, 1873;

aux. Baltimore (Macri), 1908-29.
Cosgrove, Henry (1834-1906): ord. Aug. 27, 1857; bp. Davenport, 1884-1906.
Costello, Joseph A. (1915-78): ord. June 7, 1941; aux. Newark (Choma), 1963-78.
Cote, Philip, S.J. (1896-1970): ord. Aug. 14, 1927; v.a. Suchow, China (Polystylus), 1935-46; first bp. Suchow, 1946-70 (imprisoned by Chinese Communists, 1951; expelled from China, 1953; ap. admin. Islands of Quemoy and Matsu, 1969-70.
Cotter, Joseph B. (1844-1909): b. England; ord. May 3, 1871; first bp. Winona, 1889-1909.
Cotton, Francis R. (1895-1960): ord. June 17, 1920; first bp. Owensboro, 1938-60.
Cowley, Leonard P. (1913-73): ord. June 4, 1938; aux. St. Paul and Minneapolis (Pertusa), 1958-73.
Crane, Michael J. (1863-1928): ord. June 15, 1889; aux. Philadelphia (Curium), 1921-28.
Cretin, Joseph (1799-1857): b. France; ord. Dec. 20, 1823; bp. St. Paul, 1851-57.
Crimont, Joseph R., S.J. (1858-1945): b. France; ord. Aug. 26, 1888; v.a. Alaska (Ammaedara), 1917-45.
Crowley, Timothy J., C.S.C. (1880-1945): b. Ireland; ord. Aug. 2, 1906; coad. bp. Dacca (Epiphania), 1927-29; bp. Dacca, 1929-45.
Cunningham, David F. (1900-79): ord. June 12, 1926; aux., 1950-67, and coad. bp., 1967-79, Syracuse (Lampsacus); bp. Syracuse, 1970-76 (res.).
Cunningham, John F. (1842-1919): b. Ireland; ord. Aug. 8, 1865; bp. Concordia, 1898-1919.
Curley, Daniel J. (1869-1932): ord. May 19, 1894; bp. Syracuse, 1923-32.
Curley, Michael J. (1879-1947): b. Ireland; ord. Mar. 19, 1904; bp. St. Augustine, 1914-21; abp. Baltimore, 1921-39; title changed to abp. Baltimore and Washington, 1939-47.
Curtis, Alfred A. (1831-1908): convert, 1872; ord. Dec. 19, 1874; bp. Wilmington, 1886-96 (res.).
Cusack, Thomas F. (1862-1918): ord. May 30, 1885; aux. New York (Temiscyra), 1904-15; bp. Albany, 1915-18.
Cushing, Richard J. (1895-1970): ord. May 26, 1921; aux. Boston (Mela), 1939-44; abp. Boston, 1944-70; cardinal 1958.

D

Daeger, Albert T., O.F.M. (1872-1932): ord. July 25, 1896; abp. Santa Fe, 1919-32.
Daley, Joseph T. (1915-83): ord. June 7, 1941; aux. Harrisburg (Barca), 1964-67; coad., 1967-71, and bp., 1971-83, Harrisburg.
Daly, Edward C., O.P. (1894-1964): ord. June 12, 1921; bp. Des Moines, 1948-64.
Damiano, Celestine (1911-67): ord. Dec. 21, 1935; apostolic delegate to South Africa (Nicopolis in Epiro), 1952-60; bp. Camden, 1960-67.
Danehy, Thomas J., M.M. (1914-59): ord. Sept. 17, 1939; ap. admin. v.a. Pando, Bolivia (Bita), 1953-59.
Dargin, Edward V. (1898-1981): ord. Sept. 23, 1922; aux. New York (Amphipolis), 1953-73 (res.).
David, John B., S.S. (1761-1841): b. France; ord. Sept. 24, 1785; coad. bp. Bardstown (Mauricastrum), 1819-32; bp. Bardstown (now Louisville), 1832-33 (res.).

Davis, James (1852-1926): b. Ireland; ord. June 21, 1878; coad. bp. Davenport (Milopotamus), 1904-06; bp. Davenport, 1906-26.
Davis, James P. (1904-88): ord. May 19, 1929; bp. 1943-60, and first abp., 1960-64, San Juan, P.R.; abp. Santa Fe, 1964-74 (res.).
Dearden, John F. (1907-88): ord. Dec. 8, 1932; coad. bp. Pittsburgh (Sarepta), 1948-50; bp. Pittsburgh, 1950-58; abp. Detroit, 1958-80 (res.); cardinal 1969.
De Cheverus, John L.: See Cheverus, John
De Falco, Lawrence M. (1915-79): ord. June 11, 1942; bp. Amarillo, 1963-79 (res.).
De Goesbriand, Louis (1816-99): b. France; ord. July 13, 1840; first bp. Burlington, 1853-99.
De la Hailandiere, Celestine (1798-1882): b. France; ord. May 28, 1825; bp. Vincennes (now Indianapolis), 1839-47 (res.).
Delany, John B. (1864-1906): ord. May 23, 1891; bp. Manchester, 1904-06.
Demers, Modeste (1809-71): b. Canada; ord. Feb. 7, 1836; bp. Vancouver Is., 1846-71.
Dempsey, Michael R. (1918-74): ord. May 1, 1943; aux. Chicago (Truentum), 1968-74.
De Neckere, Leo, C.M. (1799-1833): b. Belgium; ord. Oct. 13, 1822; bp. New Orleans, 1829-33.
De Saint Palais, Maurice (1811-77): b. France; ord. May 28, 1836; bp. Vincennes (now Indianapolis), 1849-77.
Desmond, Daniel F. (1884-1945): ord. June 9, 1911; bp. Alexandria, 1933-45.
Dimmerling, Harold J. (1914-87): ord. May 2, 1940; bp. Rapid City, 1969-87.
Dinand, Joseph N., S.J. (1869-1943): ord. June 25, 1903; v.a. Jamaica (Selinus), 1927-29 (res.).
Dobson, Robert (1867-1942): ord. May 23, 1891; aux. Liverpool, Eng. (Cynopolis), 1922-42.
Domenec, Michael, C.M. (1816-78): b. Spain; ord. June 30, 1839; bp. Pittsburgh, 1860-76; bp. Allegheny, 1876-77 (res.).
Donaghy, Frederick A., M.M. (1903-88): ord. Jan. 29, 1929; v.a. Wuchow, China (Setea), 1939; first bp. Wuchow, 1946, expelled from China, 1955.
Donahue, Joseph P. (1870-1959): ord. June 8, 1895; aux. New York (Emmaus), 1945-59.
Donahue, Patrick J. (1849-1922): b. England; ord. Dec. 19, 1885; bp. Wheeling, 1894-1922.
Donahue, Stephen J. (1893-1982): ord. May 22, 1918; aux. New York (Medea), 1934-69 (res.).
Donnellan, Thomas A. (1914-87): ord. June 3, 1939; bp. Ogdensburg, 1964-68; abp. Atlanta, 1968-87.
Donnelly, George J. (1889-1950): ord. June 12, 1921; aux. St. Louis (Coela), 1940-46; bp. Leavenworth (now Kansas City — title changed in 1947), 1946-50.
Donnelly, Henry E. (1904-67): ord. Aug. 17, 1930; aux. Detroit (Tymbrias), 1954-67.
Donnelly, Joseph F. (1909-77): ord. June 29, 1934; aux. Hartford (Nabala), 1965-77.
Donohoe, Hugh A. (1905-87): ord. June 14, 1930; aux. bp. San Francisco (Taium), 1947-62; first bp. Stockton, 1962-69; bp. Fresno, 1969-80 (res.).
Doran, Thomas F. (1856-1916): ord. July 4, 1880; aux. Providence (Halicarnassus), 1915-16.
Dougherty, Dennis (1865-1951): ord. May 31,

1890; bp. Nueva Segovia, P.I., 1903-08; bp. Jaro, P.I., 1908-15; bp. Buffalo, 1915-18; abp. Philadelphia, 1918-51; cardinal, 1921.
  Dougherty, John J. (1907-86): ord. July 23, 1933; aux. Newark (Cotena), 1963-82 (res.).
  Dougherty, Joseph P. (1905-70): ord. June 14, 1930; first bp. Yakima, 1951-69; aux. Los Angeles (Altino), 1969-70.
  Dowling, Austin (1868-1930): ord. June 24, 1891; first bp. Des Moines, 1912-19; abp. St. Paul, 1919-30.
  Dozier, Carroll T. (1911-85): ord. Mar. 19, 1937; first bp. Memphis, 1971-82 (res.).
  Driscoll, Justin A. (1920-84): ord. July 28, 1945; bp. Fargo, 1970-84.
  Drossaerts, Arthur J. (1862-1940): b. Holland; ord. June 15, 1889; bp. San Antonio 1918-26; first abp. San Antonio, 1926-40.
  Drumm, Thomas W. (1871-1933): b. Ireland; ord. Dec. 21, 1901; bp. Des Moines, 1919-33.
  Dubois, John, S.S. (1764-1842): b. France; ord. Sept. 28, 1787; bp. New York, 1826-42.
  Dubourg, Louis William, S.S. (1766-1833): b. Santo Domingo; ord. 1788; bp. Louisiana and the Two Floridas (now New Orleans), 1815-25; returned to France; bp. Montauban, 1826-33; abp. Besancon 1833.
  Dubuis, Claude M. (1817-1895): b. France; ord. June 1, 1844; bp. Galveston, 1862-92 (res.).
  Dufal, Peter, C.S.C. (1822-98): b. France; ord. Sept. 29, 1852; v.a. Eastern Bengal (Delcon), 1860-78; coad. bp. Galveston, 1878-80 (res.).
  Duffy, James A. (1873-1968): ord. May 27, 1899; bp. Kearney (see transferred to Grand Island, 1917), 1913-31 (res.).
  Duffy, John A. (1884-1944): ord. June 13, 1908; bp. Syracuse, 1933-37; bp. Buffalo, 1937-44.
  Duggan, James (1825-99): b. Ireland; ord. May 29, 1847; coad. bp. St. Louis (Gabala), 1857-59; bp. Chicago, 1859-80 (res.). Inactive from 1869 because of illness.
  Dunn, John J. (1869-1933): ord. May 30, 1896; aux. New York (Camuliana), 1921-33.
  Dunne, Edmund M. (1864-1929): ord. June 24, 1887; bp. Peoria, 1909-29.
  Dunne, Edward (1848-1910): b. Ireland; ord. June 29, 1871; bp. Dallas, 1893-1910.
  Durier, Anthony (1832-1904): b. France; ord. Oct. 28, 1856; bp. Natchitoches (now Alexandria), La., 1885-1904.
  Dwenger, Joseph, C.Pp.S. (1837-93): ord. Sept. 4, 1859; bp. Fort Wayne, 1872-93.
  Dworschak, Leo F. (1900-76): ord. May 29, 1926; coad. bp. Rapid City (Tium), 1946-47; aux. Fargo, 1947-60; bp. Fargo, 1960-70 (res.).
  Dwyer, Robert J. (1908-76): ord. June 11, 1932; bp. Reno, 1952-66; abp. Portland, Ore., 1966-74 (res.).

E

  Eccleston, Samuel, S.S. (1801-51): ord. Apr. 24, 1825; coad. bp. Baltimore (Thermae), Sept.-Oct., 1834; abp. Baltimore, 1834-51.
  Egan, Michael, O.F.M. (1761-1814): b. Ireland; first bp. Philadelphia, 1810-14.
  Eis, Frederick (1843-1926): b. Germany; ord.
Oct. 30, 1870; bp. Sault Ste. Marie and Marquette (now Marquette), 1899-1922 (res.).
  Elder, William (1819-1904): ord. Mar. 29, 1846; bp. Natchez (now Jackson), 1857-80; coad. bp. Cincinnati (Avara), 1880-83; abp. Cincinnati, 1883-1904.
  Elwell, Clarence E. (1904-73): ord. Mar. 17, 1929; aux. Cleveland (Cone) 1962-68; bp. Columbus, 1968-73.
  Emmet, Thomas A., S.J. (1873-1950): ord. July 30, 1909; v.a. Jamaica (Tuscamia), 1930-49 (res.).
  England, John (1786-1842): b. Ireland; ord. Oct. 11, 1808; first bp. Charleston, 1820-42.
  Escalante, Alonso Manuel, M.M. (1906-67): b. Mexico; ord. Feb. 1, 1931; v.a. Pando, Bolivia (Sora), 1943-60 (res.).
  Espelage (brothers): **Bernard T., O.F.M.** (1892-1971): ord. May 16, 1918; bp. Gallup, 1940-69 (res.). **Sylvester J., O.F.M.** (1877-1940): ord. Jan. 18, 1900; v.a. Wuchang, China (Oreus), 1930-40.
  Etteldorf, Raymond P. (1911-86): ord. Dec. 8, 1937; apostolic delegate, 1969-73, and nuncio, 1973-74, to New Zealand (Tindari); pro-nuncio to Ethiopia, 1947-82.
  Eustace, Bartholomew J. (1887-1956): ord. Nov. 1, 1914; bp. Camden, 1938-56.
  Evans, George R. (1922-85): ord. May 31, 1947; aux. Denver (Tubyza), 1969-85.

F

  Fahey, Leo F. (1898-1950): ord. May 29, 1926; coad. bp. Baker City (Ipsus), 1948-50.
  Farley, John (1842-1918): b. Ireland; ord. June 11, 1870; aux. New York (Zeugma), 1895-1902; abp. New York, 1902-18; cardinal 1911.
  Farrelly, John P. (1856-1921): ord. Mar. 22, 1880; bp. Cleveland, 1909-21.
  Fearns, John M. (1897-1977): ord. Feb. 19, 1922; aux. New York (Geras), 1957-72 (res.).
  Fedders, Edward L., M.M. (1913-73): ord. June 11, 1944; prelate Juli, Peru (Antiochia ad Meadrum), 1963-73.
  Feehan, Daniel F. (1855-1934): ord. Dec. 29, 1879; bp. Fall River, 1907-34.
  Feehan, Patrick A. (1829-1902): b. Ireland; ord. Nov. 1, 1852; bp. Nashville, 1865-80; first abp. Chicago, 1880-1902.
  Feeney, Daniel J. (1894-1969): ord. May 21, 1921; aux. Portland, Me. (Sita), 1946-52; coad. bp. Portland, 1952-55; bp. Portland, 1955-69.
  Feeney, Thomas J., S.J. (1894-1955): ord. June 23, 1927; v.a. Caroline and Marshall Is. (Agnus), 1951-55.
  Fenwick, Benedict J., S.J. (1782-1846): ord. June 11, 1808; bp. Boston, 1825-46.
  Fenwick, Edward D., O.P. (1768-1832): ord. Feb. 23, 1793; first bp. Cincinnati, 1822-32.
  Fink, Michael, O.S.B. (1834-1904): b. Germany; ord. May 28, 1857; coad. v.a., 1871-74, and v.a. 1874-77, Kansas and Indian Territory (Eucarpia); first bp. Leavenworth (now Kansas City), 1877-1904.
  Finnigan, George, C.S.C. (1885-1932): ord. June 13, 1915; bp. Helena, 1927-32.
  Fitzgerald, Edward (1833-1907): b. Ireland; ord. Aug. 22, 1857; bp. Little Rock, 1867-1907.

Fitzgerald, Edward A. (1893-1972): ord. July 25, 1916; aux. Dubuque (Cantanus), 1946-49; bp. Winona, 1949-69 (res.).
Fitzgerald, Walter J., S.J. (1883-1947): ord. May 16, 1918; coad. v.a. Alaska (Tymbrias), 1939-45; v.a. Alaska, 1945-47.
Fitzmaurice, Edmond (1881-1962): b. Ireland; ord. May 28, 1904; bp. Wilmington, 1925-60 (res.).
Fitzmaurice, John E. (1837-1920): b. Ireland; ord. Dec. 21, 1862; coad. bp. Erie (Amisus), 1898-99; bp. Erie, 1899-1920.
Fitzpatrick, John B. (1812-66): ord. June 13, 1840; aux. Boston (Callipolis), 1843-46; bp. Boston, 1846-66.
Fitzsimon, Laurence J. (1895-1958): ord. May 17, 1921; bp. Amarillo, 1941-58.
Flaget, Benedict, S.S.: See Index.
Flaherty, J. Louis (1910-75): ord. Dec. 8, 1936; aux. Richmond (Tabudo), 1966-75.
Flannelly, Joseph F. (1894-1973): ord. Sept. 1, 1918; aux. New York (Metelis), 1948-70 (res.).
Flasch, Kilian C. (1831-91): b. Germany; ord. Dec. 16, 1859; bp. La Crosse, 1881-91.
Fletcher, Albert L. (1896-1979): ord. June 4, 1920; aux. Little Rock (Samos), 1940-46; bp. Little Rock, 1946-72 (res.).
Floersh, John (1886-1968): ord. June 10, 1911; coad. bp. Louisville (Lycopolis), 1923-24; bp. Louisville, 1924-37; first abp. Louisville, 1937-67 (res.).
Flores, Felixberto C. (1921-85): b. Gaum; ord. Apr. 30, 1949; ap. admin. Agana, Guam (Stonj), 1970-72; bp. 1977-84, and first abp. Agana, 1984-85.
Foery, Walter A. (1890-1978): ord. June 10, 1916; bp. Syracuse, 1937-70 (res.).
Foley (brothers): **John S.** (1833-1918): ord. Dec. 20, 1856; bp. Detroit, 1888-1918. **Thomas** (1822-79): ord. Aug. 16, 1846; coad. bp. and ap. admin. Chicago (Pergamum), 1870-79.
Foley, Maurice P. (1867-1919): ord. July 25, 1891; bp. Tuguegarao, P.I., 1910-16; bp. Jaro, P.I., 1916-19.
Ford, Francis X., M.M. (1892-1952): ord. Dec. 5, 1917; v.a. Kaying, China (Etenna), 1935-46; first bp. Kaying, 1946-52.
Forest, John A. (1838-1911): b. France; ord. Apr. 12, 1863; bp. San Antonio, 1895-1911.
Fox, Joseph J. (1855-1915): ord. June 7, 1879; bp. Green Bay, 1904-14 (res.).
Fulcher, George A. (1922-84): ord. Feb. 28, 1948; aux. Columbus (Morosbisdus), 1976-83; bp. Lafayette, 1983-84.
Furey, Francis J. (1905-79): ord. Mar. 15, 1930; aux. Philadelphia (Temnus), 1960-63; coad bp. San Diego, 1963-66; bp. San Diego, 1966-69; abp. San Antonio, 1969-79.

G

Gabriels, Henry (1838-1921): b. Belgium; ord. Sept. 21, 1861; bp. Ogdensburg, 1892-1921.
Gabro, Jaroslav (1919-80): ord. Sept. 27, 1945; bp. St. Nicholas of Chicago (Byzantine Rite, Ukrainians), 1961-80.
Galberry, Thomas, O.S.A. (1833-78): b. Ireland; ord. Dec. 20, 1856; bp. Hartford, 1876-78.
Gallagher, Michael J. (1866-1937): ord. Mar. 19, 1893; coad. bp. Grand Rapids (Tiposa in Mauretania), 1915-16; bp. Grand Rapids, 1916-18;

bp. Detroit, 1918-37.
Gallagher, Nicholas (1846-1918): ord. Dec. 25, 1868; coad. bp. Galveston (Canopus), 1882-92; bp. Galveston, 1892-1918.
Gannon, John M. (1877-1968): ord. Dec. 21, 1901; aux. Erie (Nilopolis), 1918-20; bp. Erie, 1920-66 (res.).
Garcia Diego y Moreno, Francisco, O.F.M. (1785-1846): b. Mexico; ord. Nov. 14, 1808; bp. Two Californias (now Los Angeles), 1840-46.
Garriga, Mariano S. (1886-1965): ord. July 2, 1911; coad. bp. Corpus Christi (Syene), 1936-49; bp. Corpus Christi, 1949-65.
Garrigan, Philip (1840-1919): b. Ireland; ord. June 11, 1870; first bp. Sioux City, 1902-19.
Gartland, Francis X. (1808-54): b. Ireland; ord. Aug. 5, 1832; first bp. Savannah, 1850-54.
Garvey, Eugene A. (1845-1920): ord. Sept. 22, 1869; first bp. Altoona (now Altoona-Johnstown), 1901-20.
Gercke, Daniel J. (1874-1964): ord. June 1, 1901; bp. Tucson, 1923-60 (res.).
Gerken, Rudolph A. (1887-1943): ord. June 10, 1917; first bp. Amarillo, 1927-33; abp. Santa Fe, 1933-43.
Gerow, Richard O. (1885-1976): ord. June 5, 1909; bp. Natchez-Jackson (now Jackson), 1924-67 (res.).
Gibbons, Edmund F. (1868-1964): ord. May 27, 1893; bp. Albany, 1919-54 (res.).
Gibbons, James (1834-1921): ord. June 30, 1861; v.a. North Carolina (Adramyttium), 1868-72; bp. Richmond, 1872-77; coad. Baltimore (Jonopolis), May-Oct., 1877; abp. Baltimore, 1877-1921; cardinal 1886.
Gilfillan, Francis (1872-1933): b. Ireland; ord. June 24, 1895; coad. bp. St. Joseph (Spiga), 1922-23; bp. St. Joseph, 1923-33.
Gill, Thomas E. (1908-73): ord. June 10, 1933; aux. Seattle (Lambesis) 1956-73.
Gilmore, Joseph M. (1893-1962): ord. July 25, 1915; bp. Helena, 1936-62.
Gilmour, Richard (1824-91): b. Scotland; ord. Aug. 30, 1852; bp. Cleveland, 1872-91.
Girouard, Paul J., M.S. (1898-1964): ord. July 26, 1927; first bp. Morondava, Madagascar, 1956-64.
Glass, Joseph S., C.M. (1874-1926): ord. Aug. 15, 1897; bp. Salt Lake City, 1915-26.
Gleeson, Francis D., S.J. (1895-1983): ord. July 29, 1926; v.a. Alaska (Cotenna), 1948-62; first bp. Fairbanks, 1962-68 (res.).
Glenn, Lawrence A. (1900-85): ord. June 11, 1927; aux. Duluth (Tuscamia), 1956-60; bp. Crookston, 1960-70 (res.).
Glennon, John J. (1862-1946): b. Ireland; ord. Dec. 20, 1884; coad. bp. Kansas City, Mo. (Pinara), 1896-1903; coad. St. Louis, April-Oct., 1903; abp. St. Louis, 1903-46; cardinal 1946.
Glorieux, Alphonse J. (1844-1917): b. Belgium; ord. Aug. 17, 1867; v.a. Idaho (Apollonia), 1885-93; bp. Boise, 1893-1917.
Gorman, Daniel (1861-1927): ord. June 24, 1893; bp. Boise, 1918-27.
Gorman, Thomas K. (1892-1980): ord. June 23, 1917; first bp. Reno, 1931-52; coad. bp. Dallas-Ft.

Worth (Rhasus), 1952-54; bp. Dallas-Fort Worth (now Dallas), 1954-69 (res.).
Grace, Thomas (1841-1921): b. Ireland; ord. June 24, 1876; bp. Sacramento, 1896-1921.
Grace, Thomas L., O.P. (1814-97): ord. Dec. 21, 1839; bp. St. Paul, 1859-84 (res.).
Graner, Lawrence L., C.S.C. (1901-82): ord. June 24, 1928; bp. Dacca, 1947-50, and first abp., 1950-67 (res.).
Granjon, Henry (1863-1922): b. France; ord. Dec. 17, 1887; bp. Tucson, 1900-22.
Greco, Charles P. (1894-1987): ord. July 25, 1918; bp. Alexandria, La., 1946-73 (res.).
Green, Joseph J. (1917-82): ord. July 14, 1946; aux. Lansing (Trisipa), 1962-67; bp. Reno 1967-74 (res.).
Grellinger, John B. (1899-1984): ord. priest July 14, 1929; aux. Green Bay (Syene), 1949-74 (res.).
Greteman, Frank H. (1907-87): ord. Dec. 8, 1932; aux. Sioux City (Vissala), 1965-70; bp. Sioux City, 1970-83 (res.).
Griffin, James A. (1883-1948): ord. July 4, 1909; bp. Springfield, Ill., 1924-48.
Griffin, William A. (1885-1950): ord. Aug. 15, 1910; aux. Newark (Sanavus), 1938-40; bp. Trenton, 1940-50.
Griffin, William R. (1883-1944): ord. May 25, 1907; aux. La Crosse (Lydda), 1935-44.
Griffiths, James H. (1903-64): ord. Mar. 12, 1927; aux. New York and delegate of U.S. military vicar (Gaza), 1950-64.
Grimes, John (1852-1922): b. Ireland; ord. Feb. 19, 1882; coad. bp. Syracuse (Hemeria), 1909-12; bp. Syracuse, 1912-22.
Grimmelsman, Henry J. (1890-1972); ord. Aug. 15, 1915; first bp. Evansville, 1945-65 (res.).
Gross, William H., C.SS.R. (1837-98): ord. Mar. 21, 1863; bp. Savannah, 1873-85; abp. Oregon City (now Portland), 1885-98.
Guertin, George A. (1869-1932): ord. Dec. 17, 1892; bp. Manchester, 1907-32.
Guilfoyle, Richard T. (1892-1957): ord. June 2, 1917; bp. Altoona (now Altoona-Johnstown), 1936-57.
Guilfoyle, Merlin J. (1908-81): ord. June 10, 1933; aux. San Francisco (Bulla), 1950-69; bp. Stockton, 1969-79 (res.).
Gunn, John E., S.M. (1863-1924): b. Ireland; ord. Feb. 2, 1890; bp. Natchez (now Jackson), 1911-24.

H

Haas, Francis J. (1889-1953): ord. June 11, 1913; bp. Grand Rapids, 1943-53.
Hafey, William (1888-1954): ord. June 16, 1914; first bp. Raleigh, 1925-37; coad. bp. Scranton (Appia), 1937-38; bp. Scranton, 1938-54.
Hagan, John R. (1890-1946): ord. Mar. 7, 1914; aux. Cleveland (Limata), 1946.
Hagarty, Paul L., O.S.B. (1909-84): ord. June 6, 1936; v.a. Bahamas (Arba), 1950-60; first bp. Nassau, Bahamas, 1960-81 (res.).
Haid, Leo M., O.S.B. (1849-1924): ord. Dec. 21, 1872; v.a. N. Carolina (Messene), 1888-1910; abbot Mary Help of Christians abbacy, 1910-24.
Hallinan, Paul J. (1911-68): ord. Feb. 20, 1937; bp. Charleston, 1958-62; first abp. Atlanta, 1962-68.

Hanna, Edward J. (1860-1944): ord. May 30, 1885; aux. San Francisco (Titiopolis). 1912-15; abp. San Francisco, 1915-35 (res.).
Hannan, Jerome D. (1896-1965): ord. May 22, 1921; bp. Scranton, 1954-65.
Harkins, Matthew (1845-1921): ord. May 22, 1869; bp. Providence, 1887-1921.
Harris, Vincent M. (1913-88): ord. Mar. 19, 1938; first bp. Beaumont, 1966-71; coad. bp. Austin (Rotaria), Apr. 27-Nov. 16, 1971; bp. Austin, 1971-85 (res.).
Hartley, James J. (1858-1944): ord. July 10, 1882; bp. Columbus, 1904-44.
Harty, Jeremiah J. (1853-1927): ord. Apr. 28, 1878; abp. Manila, 1903-16; abp. Omaha, 1916-27.
Hayes, James T., S.J. (1889-1980): ord. June 29, 1921; bp. of Cagayan, Philippines, 1933-51; first abp. Cagayan, 1951-70 (res.).
Hayes, Nevin W., O. Carm. (1922-88): ord. June 8, 1946; prelate Sicuani, Peru (Nova Sinna), 1965-70; aux. bp. Chicago, 1971-88.
Hayes, Patrick J. (1867-1938): ord. Sept. 8, 1892; aux. New York (Thagaste), 1914-19; abp. New York, 1919-38; cardinal 1924.
Hayes, Ralph L. (1884-1970): ord. Sept. 19, 1909; bp. Helena 1933-35; rector North American College (Hieropolis) 1935-44; bp. Davenport, 1944-66 (res.).
Healy, James A. (1830-1900): ord. June 10, 1854; bp. Portland 1875-1900.
Heelan, Edmond (1868-1948): b. Ireland; ord. June 24, 1890; aux. Sioux City (Gerasa), 1919-20; bp. Sioux City, 1920-48.
Heffron, Patrick (1860-1927): ord. Dec. 22, 1884; bp. Winona, 1910-27.
Heiss, Michael (1818-90): b. Germany; ord. Oct. 18, 1840; bp. La Crosse, 1868-80; coad. abp. Milwaukee (Hadrianopolis), 1880-81; abp. Milwaukee, 1881-90.
Hendrick, Thomas A. (1849-1909): ord. June 7, 1873; bp. Cebu, P.I., 1904-09.
Hendricken, Thomas F. (1827-86): b. Ireland; ord. Apr. 25, 1853; bp. Providence, 1872-86.
Hennessy, John (1825-1900): b. Ireland; ord. Nov. 1, 1850; bp. Dubuque, 1866-93; first abp. Dubuque, 1893-1900.
Hennessy, John J. (1847-1920): b. Ireland; ord. Nov. 28, 1869; first bp. Wichita, 1888-1920; ap. admin. Concordia (now Salina), 1891-98.
Henni, John M. (1805-81): b. Switzerland; ord. Feb. 2, 1829; first bp. Milwaukee, 1844-75; first abp. Milwaukee, 1875-81.
Henry, Harold W., S.S.C. (1909-76): ord. Dec. 21, 1932; v.a. Kwang Ju, Korea (Coridala), 1957-62; first abp. Kwang Ju, 1962-71; ap. admin. p.a. Cheju-Do, Korea (Thubunae), 1971-76.
Heslin, Thomas (1845-1911): b. Ireland; ord. Sept. 8, 1869; bp. Natchez (now Jackson), 1889-1911.
Heston, Edward L. (1907-73): ord. Dec. 22, 1934; sec. Sacred Congregation for Religious and Secular Institutes, 1969-71; pres. Pontifical Commission for Social Communications, 1971-73; tit. abp. Numidea, 1972.
Hickey, David F., S.J. (1882-1973): ord. June 27, 1917; v.a. Belize, Br. Honduras (Bonitza), 1948-56;

first bp. Belize, 1956-57 (res.); tit. abp. Cabasa, 1957-73.

Hickey, Thomas F. (1861-1940): ord. Mar. 25, 1884; coad. bp. Rochester (Berenice), 1905-09; bp. Rochester, 1909-28 (res.).

Hickey, William A. (1869-1933): ord. Dec. 22, 1893; coad. bp. Providence (Claudiopolis), 1919-21; bp. Providence, 1921-33.

Hillinger, Raymond P. (1904-71): ord. Apr. 2, 1932; bp. Rockford, 1953-56; aux. Chicago (Derbe), 1956-71.

Hoban, Edward F. (1878-1966): ord. July 11, 1903; aux. Chicago (Colonia), 1921-28; bp. Rockford, 1928-42; coad. bp. Cleveland (Lystra), 1942-45; bp. Cleveland, 1945-66.

Hoban, Michael J. (1853-1926): ord. May 22, 1880; coad. bp. Scranton (Halius), 1896-99; bp. Scranton, 1899-1926.

Hodges, Joseph H. (1911-85): ord. Dec. 8, 1935; aux. Richmond (Rusadus), 1952-61; coad. Wheeling, 1961-62; bp. Wheeling (now Wheeling-Charleston), 1962-85.

Hogan, John J. (1829-1913): b. Ireland; ord. Apr. 10, 1852; first bp. St. Joseph, 1868-80; first bp. Kansas City, 1880-1913.

Horstmann, Ignatius (1840-1908): ord. June 10, 1865; bp. Cleveland, 1892-1908.

Howard, Edward D. (1877-1983): ord. June 12, 1906; aux. Davenport (Isauropolis), 1924-26; abp. Oregon City (title changed to Portland, 1928), 1926-66 (res.).

Howard, Francis W. (1867-1944): ord. June 16, 1891; bp. Covington, 1923-44.

Hughes, John J. (1797-1864): b. Ireland; ord. Oct. 15, 1826; coad. bp. New York (Basilinopolis), 1837-42; bp. New York, 1842-50, and first abp., 1850-64.

Hunkeler, Edward J. (1894-1970): ord. June 14, 1919; bp. Grand Island, 1945-51; bp. Kansas City, Kans. 1951-52; first abp. Kansas City, 1952-69 (res.).

Hunt, Duane G. (1884-1960): ord. June 27, 1920; bp. Salt Lake City, 1937-60.

Hurley, Joseph P. (1894-1967): ord. May 29, 1919; bp. St. Augustine, 1940-67.

Hyland, Francis E. (1901-68): ord. June 11, 1927; aux. Savannah-Atlanta (Gomphi), 1949-56; bp. Atlanta, 1956-61 (res.).

Hyle, Michael W. (1901-67): ord. Mar. 12, 1927; coad. bp. Wilmington, 1958-60; bp. Wilmington, 1960-67.

I

Iranyi, Ladislaus A., Sch. P. (1923-87): ord. Mar. 13, 1948; U.S. citizen, ord. bp. (Castel Mediano), July 27, 1983, for spiritual care of Hungarian Catholics living outside Hungary.

Ireland, John (1838-1918): b. Ireland; ord. Dec. 21, 1861; coad. bp. St. Paul (Marobea), 1875-84; bp. St. Paul, 1884-88, and first abp. St. Paul, 1888-1918.

Ireton, Peter L. (1882-1958): ord. June 20, 1906; coad. bp. Richmond (Cyme), 1935-45; bp. Richmond, 1945-58.

Issenmann, Clarence G. (1907-82): ord. June 29, 1932; aux. Cincinnati (Phytea), 1954-57; bp. Columbus, 1957-64; coad. bp. Cleveland (Filaca), 1964-66; bp. Cleveland, 1966-74 (res.).

J

Janssen, John (1835-1913): b. Germany; ord. Nov. 19, 1858; first bp. Belleville, 1888-1913.

Janssens, Francis A. (1843-97): b. Holland; ord. Dec. 21, 1867; bp. Natchez (now Jackson) 1881-88; abp. New Orleans, 1888-97.

Jeanmard, Jules B. (1879-1957): ord. June 10, 1903; first bp. Lafayette, La., 1918-56 (res.).

Johannes, Francis (1874-1937): b. Germany; ord. Jan. 3, 1897; coad. bp. Leavenworth (Thasus), 1928-29; bp. Leavenworth (now Kansas City), 1929-37.

Johnson, William R. (1918-86): ord. May 28, 1944; aux. Los Angeles (Blera), 1971-76; first bp. Orange, 1976-86.

Jones, William A., O.S.A. (1865-1921): ord. Mar. 15, 1890; bp. San Juan, 1907-21.

Juncker, Henry D. (1809-68): b. Lorraine (France); ord. Mar. 16, 1834; first bp. Alton (now Springfield), Ill., 1857-68.

Junger, Aegidius (1833-95): b. Germany; ord. June 27, 1862; bp. Nesqually (now Seattle), 1879-95.

K

Kain, John J. (1841-1903): ord. July 2, 1866; bp. Wheeling, 1875-93; coad. abp. St. Louis (Oxyrynchus), 1893-95; abp. St. Louis, 1895-1903.

Katzer, Frederick X. (1844-1903): b. Austria; ord. Dec. 21, 1866; bp. Green Bay, 1886-91; abp. Milwaukee, 1891-1903.

Keane, James J. (1856-1929): ord. Dec. 23, 1882; bp. Cheyenne, 1902-11; abp. Dubuque, 1911-29.

Keane, John J. (1839-1918): b. Ireland; ord. July 2, 1866; bp. Richmond, 1878-88; rector of Catholic University, 1888-97; consultor of Congregation for Propagation of the Faith, 1897-1900; abp. Dubuque, 1900-11 (res.).

Keane, Patrick J. (1872-1928): b. Ireland; ord. June 20, 1895; aux. Sacramento (Samaria), 1920-22; bp. Sacramento, 1922-28.

Kearney, James E. (1884-1977): ord. Sept. 19, 1908; bp. Salt Lake City, 1932-37; bp. Rochester, 1937-66 (res.).

Kearney, Raymond A. (1902-56): ord. Mar. 12, 1927; aux. Brooklyn (Lysinia), 1935-56.

Keiley, Benjamin J. (1847-1925): ord. Dec. 31, 1873; bp. Savannah, 1900-22 (res.).

Kelleher, Louis F. (1889-1946): ord. Apr. 3, 1915; aux. Boston (Thenae), 1945-46.

Kellenberg, Walter P. (1901-86): ord. June 2, 1928; aux. New York (Joannina), 1953-54; bp. Ogdensburg, 1954-57; first bp. Rockville Centre, 1957-76 (res.).

Kelley, Francis C. (1870-1948): b. Canada; ord. Aug. 23, 1893; bp. Oklahoma, 1924-48.

Kelly, Edward D. (1860-1926): ord. June 16, 1886; aux. Detroit (Cestrus), 1911-19; bp. Grand Rapids, 1919-26.

Kelly, Edward J. (1890-1956): ord. June 2, 1917; bp. Boise, 1928-56.

Kelly, Francis M. (1886-1950): ord. Nov. 1, 1912; aux. Winona (Mylasa), 1926-28; bp. Winona, 1928-49 (res.).

Kelly, Patrick (1779-1829): b. Ireland; ord. July 18, 1802; first bp. Richmond, 1820-22 (returned to Ireland; bp. Waterford and Lismore, 1822-29).

Kennally, Vincent, S.J. (1895-1977): ord. June 20, 1928; v.a. Caroline and Marshall Islands (Sassura), 1957-71 (res.).

Kennedy, Thomas F. (1858-1917): ord. July 24, 1887; rector North American College, 1901-17; tit. bp. Hadrianapolis, 1907-15; tit. abp. Seleucia, 1915-17.

Kenny, William J. (1853-1913): ord. Jan. 15, 1879; bp. St. Augustine, 1902-13.

Kenrick (brothers): **Francis P.** (1796-1863): b. Ireland; ord. Apr. 7, 1821; coad. bp. Philadelphia (Aratha), 1830-42; bp. Philadelphia, 1842-51; abp. Baltimore, 1851-63. **Peter** (1806-96): b. Ireland; ord. Mar. 6, 1832; coad. bp. St. Louis (Adrasus), 1841-43; bp. 1843-47, and first abp. 1847-95, St. Louis (res.).

Keough, Francis P. (1890-1961): ord. June 10, 1916; bp. Providence, 1943-47; abp. Baltimore, 1947-61.

Keyes, Michael, S.M. (1876-1959): b. Ireland; ord. June 21, 1907; bp. Savannah, 1922-35 (res.).

Kiley, Moses E. (1876-1953): b. Nova Scotia; ord. June 10, 1911; bp. Trenton, 1934-40; abp. Milwaukee, 1940-53.

Killeen, James (1917-78): ord. May 30, 1942; aux. Military Vicariate (Valmalla), 1975-78.

Klonowski, Henry T. (1898-1977): ord. Aug. 8, 1920; aux. Scranton (Daldis), 1947-73 (res.).

Kogy, Lorenz S., O.M. (1895-1963): b. Georgia, Russia; ord. Nov. 15, 1917; U.S. citizen, 1944; patriarchal vicar for Armenian diocese of Beirut (Comana), 1951-63.

Koudelka, Joseph (1852-1921): b. Austria; ord. Oct. 8, 1875; aux. Cleveland (Germanicopolis), 1908-11; aux. Milwaukee, 1911-13; bp. Superior, 1913-21.

Kowalski, Rembert, O.F.M. (1884-1970): ord. June 22, 1911; v.a. Wuchang, China (Ipsus), 1942-46; first bp. Wuchang, 1946-70 (in exile from 1953).

Kozlowski, Edward (1860-1915): b. Poland; ord. June 29, 1887; aux. Milwaukee (Germia), 1914-15.

Krautbauer, Francix X. (1824-85): b. Germany; ord. July 16, 1850; bp. Green Bay, 1875-85.

Kucera, Louis B. (1888-1957): ord. June 8, 1915; bp. Lincoln, 1930-57.

L

Lamb, Hugh (1890-1959): ord. May 29, 1915; aux. Philadelphia (Helos), 1936-51; first bp. Greensburg, 1951-59.

Lamy, Jean B.: See Index.

Lane, Loras (1910-68): ord. Mar. 19, 1937; aux. Dubuque (Bencenna), 1951-56; bp. Rockford, 1956-68.

Lane, Raymond A., M.M. (1894-1974): ord. Feb. 8, 1920; v.a. Fushun, Manchukuo (Hypaepa), 1940-46; sup. gen. Maryknoll, 1946-56.

Lardone, Francesco (1887-1980): b. Italy; ord. June 29, 1910; U.S. citizen 1937; nuncio to various countries (tit. abp. Rhizaeum), 1949-66 (res.).

Laval, John M. (1854-1937): b. France; ord. Nov. 10, 1877; aux. New Orleans (Hierocaesarea), 1911-37.

Lavialle, Peter J. (1819-67): b. France; ord. Feb. 12, 1844; bp. Louisville, 1865-67.

Lawler, John J. (1862-1948): ord. Dec. 19, 1885; aux. St. Paul (Hermopolis), 1910-16; bp. Lead (now Rapid City), 1916-48.

Le Blond, Charles H. (1883-1958): ord. June 29, 1909; bp. St. Joseph, 1933-56 (res.).

Ledvina, Emmanuel (1868-1952): ord. Mar. 18, 1893; bp. Corpus Christi, 1921-49 (res.).

Leech, George L. (1890-1985): ord. May 29, 1920; aux. Harrisburg (Mela), Oct.-Dec., 1935; bp. Harrisburg, 1935-71 (res.).

Lefevere, Peter P. (1804-69): b. Belgium; ord. Nov. 30, 1831; coad. bp. and admin. Detroit (Zela), 1841-69.

Leibold, Paul F. (1914-72): ord. May 18, 1940; aux. Cincinnati (Trebenna), 1958-66; bp. Evansville, 1966-69; abp. Cincinnati, 1969-72.

Leipzig, Francis P. (1895-1981): ord. Apr. 17, 1920; bp. Baker, 1950-71 (res.).

Lenihan (brothers): **Mathias C.** (1854-1943): ord. Dec. 20, 1879; first bp. Great Falls, 1904-30 (res.). **Thomas M.** (1844-1901): b. Ireland; ord. Nov. 19, 1868; bp. Cheyenne, 1897-1901.

Leray, Francis X. (1825-87): b. France; ord. Mar. 19, 1852; bp. Natchitoches (now Alexandria, La.), 1877-79; coad. bp. New Orleans and admin. of Natchitoches (Jonopolis), 1879-83; abp. New Orleans, 1883-87.

Leven, Stephen A. (1905-83): ord. June 10, 1928; aux. San Antonio (Bure), 1956-69; bp. San Angelo, 1969-79 (res.).

Ley, Felix, O.F.M. Cap. (1909-72): ord. June 14, 1936; ap. admin. Ryukyu Is. (Caporilla), 1968-72.

Lillis, Thomas F. (1861-1938): ord. Aug. 15, 1885; bp. Leavenworth (now Kansas City, Kans.), 1904-10; coad. bp. Kansas City, Mo. (Cibyra), 1910-13; bp. Kansas City, Mo., 1913-38.

Lootens, Louis (1827-98): b. Belgium; ord. June 14, 1851; v.a. Idaho and Montana (Castabala), 1868-75 (res.).

Loras, Mathias (1792-1858): b. France; ord. Nov. 12, 1815; first bp. Dubuque, 1837-58.

Loughlin, John (1817-91): b. Ireland; ord. Oct. 18, 1840; first bp. Brooklyn, 1853-91.

Lowney, Denis M. (1863-1918): b. Ireland; ord. Dec. 17, 1887; aux. Providence (Hadrianopolis), 1917-18.

Lucey, Robert E. (1891-1977): ord. May 14, 1916; bp. Amarillo, 1934-41; abp. San Antonio, 1941-69 (res.).

Ludden, Patrick A. (1838-1912): b. Ireland; ord. May 21, 1865; first bp. Syracuse, 1887-1912.

Luers, John (1819-71): b. Germany; ord. Nov. 11, 1846; first bp. Fort Wayne, 1858-71.

Lynch, Joseph P. (1872-1954): ord. June 9, 1900; bp. Dallas, 1911-54.

Lynch, Patrick N. (1817-82): b. Ireland; ord. Apr. 5, 1840; bp. Charleston, 1858-82.

Lyons, Thomas W. (1923-88): ord. May 22, 1948; aux. bp. Washington, D.C. (Mortlach), 1974-88.

M

McAuliffe, Maurice F. (1875-1944): ord. July 29,

1900; aux. Hartford (Dercos), 1923-34; bp. Hartford, 1934-44.
McCafferty, John E. (1920-80): ord. Mar. 17, 1945; aux. Rochester (Tanudaia), 1968-80.
McCarthy, Joseph E. (1876-1955): ord. July 4, 1903; bp. Portland, Me., 1932-55.
McCarthy, Justin J. (1900-59): ord. Apr. 16, 1927; aux. Newark (Doberus), 1954-57; bp. Camden, 1957-59.
McCarty, William T., C.SS.R. (1889-1972): ord. June 10, 1915; military delegate (Anea), 1943-47; coad. bp. Rapid City, 1947-48; bp. Rapid City, 1948-69 (res.).
McCauley, Vincent J., C.S.C. (1906-82): ord. June 24, 1943; first bp. Fort Portal, Uganda, 1961-72 (res.).
McCloskey, James P. (1870-1945): ord. Dec. 17, 1898; bp. Zamboanga, P.I., 1917-20; bp. Jaro, P.I., 1920-45.
McCloskey, John (1810-85): ord. Jan. 12, 1834; coad. bp. New York (Axiere), 1843-47; first bp. Albany, 1847-64; abp. New York, 1864-85; first U.S. cardinal 1875.
McCloskey, William G. (1823-1909): ord. Oct. 6, 1852; bp. Louisville, 1868-1909.
McCormick, Patrick J. (1880-1953): ord. July 6, 1904; aux. Washington (Atenia), 1950-53.
McCort, John J. (1860-1936): ord. Oct. 14, 1883; aux. Philadelphia (Azotus), 1912-20; bp. Altoona, 1920-36.
McDevitt, Gerald V. (1917-80): ord. May 30, 1942; aux. Philadelphia (Tigias), 1962-80.
McDevitt, Philip R. (1858-1935): ord. July 14, 1885; bp. Harrisburg, 1916-35.
McDonnell, Charles E. (1854-1921): ord. May 19, 1878; bp. Brooklyn, 1892-1921.
McDonnell, Thomas J. (1894-1961): ord. Sept. 20, 1919; aux. New York (Sela), 1947-51; coad. bp. Wheeling, 1951-61.
McEleney, John J., S.J. (1895-1986): ord. June 18, 1930; v.a. Jamaica (Zeugma), 1950-56; bp. Kingston, 1956-67; abp. Kingston 1967-70 (res.)
McEntegart, Bryan (1893-1968): ord. Sept. 8, 1917; bp. Ogdensburg, 1943-53; rector Catholic University (Aradi), 1953-57; bp. Brooklyn, 1957-68.
McFadden, James A. (1880-1952): ord. June 17, 1905; aux. Cleveland (Bida), 1932-43; first bp. Youngstown, 1943-52.
MacFarland, Francis P. (1819-74): ord. May 1, 1845; bp. Hartford, 1858-74.
McFaul, James A. (1850-1917): b. Ireland; ord. May 26, 1877; bp. Trenton, 1894-1917.
McGavick, Alexander J. (1863-1948): ord. June 11, 1887; aux. Chicago (Marcopolis), 1899-1921; bp. La Crosse, 1921-48.
McGeough, Joseph F. (1903-70): ord. Dec. 20, 1930; internuncio Ethiopia, 1957-60; apostolic delegate (Hemesa) S. Africa, 1960-67; nuncio Ireland, 1967-69.
McGill, John (1809-72): ord. June 13, 1835; bp. Richmond, 1850-72.
MacGinley, John B. (1871-1969): b. Ireland; ord. June 8, 1895; bp. Nueva Caceres, 1910-24; first bp. Monterey-Fresno, 1924-32 (res.).
McGolrick, James (1841-1918): b. Ireland; ord. June 11, 1867; first bp. Duluth, 1889-1918.
McGovern, Patrick A. (1872-1951): ord. Aug. 18, 1895; bp. Cheyenne, 1912-51.
McGovern, Thomas (1832-98): b. Ireland; ord. Dec. 27, 1861; bp. Harrisburg, 1888-98.
McGrath, Joseph F. (1871-1950): b. Ireland; ord. Dec. 21, 1895; bp. Baker City (now Baker), 1919-50.
McGucken, Joseph T. (1902-84): ord. Jan. 15, 1928; aux. Los Angeles (Sanavus), 1940-55; coad. bp. Sacramento, 1957-62; abp. San Francisco, 1962-77 (res.).
McGuinness, Eugene (1889-1957): ord. May 22, 1915; bp. Raleigh, 1937-44; coad. bp. Oklahoma City and Tulsa (Ilium), 1944-48; bp. Oklahoma City and Tulsa, 1948-57.
McGurkin, Edward A., M.M. (1905-83): ord. Sept. 14, 1930; bp. Shinyanga, Tanzania, 1956-75 (res.).
McIntyre, James F. (1886-1979): ord. May 21, 1921; aux. New York (Cirene), 1941-46; coad. abp. New York (Palto), 1946-48; abp. Los Angeles, 1948-70 (res.); cardinal, 1953.
MacKenzie, Eric F. (1893-1969): ord. Oct. 20, 1918; aux. Boston (Alba), 1950-69.
McLaughlin, Charles B. (1913-78): ord. June 6, 1941; aux. Raleigh (Risinium), 1964-68; first bp. St. Petersburg, 1968-78.
McLaughlin, Thomas H. (1881-1947): ord. July 26, 1904; aux. Newark (Nisa), 1935-37; first bp. Paterson, 1937-47.
McMahon, John J. (1875-1932): ord. May 20, 1900; bp. Trenton, 1928-32.
McMahon, Lawrence S. (1835-93): ord. Mar. 24, 1860; bp. Hartford, 1879-93.
McManaman, Edward P. (1900-64): ord. Mar. 12, 1927; aux. Erie (Floriana), 1948-64.
McManus, James E., C.SS.R. (1900-76): ord. June 19, 1927; bp. Ponce, P.R., 1947-63; aux. New York (Banda), 1963-70 (res.).
McMullen, John (1832-83): b. Ireland; ord. June 20, 1858; first bp. Davenport, 1881-83.
McNamara, John M. (1878-1960): ord. June 21, 1902; aux. Baltimore (Eumenia), 1928-47; aux. Washington, 1947-60.
McNamara, Martin D. (1898-1966): ord. Dec. 23, 1922; first bp. Joliet, 1949-66.
McNeirny, Francis (1828-94): ord. Aug. 17, 1854; coad. bp. Albany (Rhesaina), 1872-77; bp. Albany, 1877-94.
McNicholas, John T., O.P. (1877-1950): b. Ireland; ord. Oct. 10, 1901; bp. Duluth, 1918-25; abp. Cincinnati, 1925-50.
McNicholas, Joseph A. (1923-83): ord. June 7, 1949; aux. St. Louis (Scala), 1969-75; bp. Springfield, Ill., 1975-83.
McNulty, James A. (1900-72): ord. July 12, 1925; aux. Newark (Methone), 1947-53; bp. Paterson, 1953-63; bp. Buffalo, 1963-72.
McQuaid, Bernard J. (1823-1909): ord. Jan. 16, 1848; first bp. Rochester, 1868-1909.
McSorley, Francis J., O.M.I. (1913-71): ord. May 30, 1939; v.a. Jolo, P.I. (Sozusa), 1958-71.
McVinney, Russell J. (1898-1971): ord. July 13, 1924; bp. Providence, 1948-71.
Machebeuf, Joseph P. (1812-89): b. France; ord. Dec. 17, 1836; v.a. Colorado and Utah (Epiphania), 1868-87; first bp. Denver, 1887-89.

Maes, Camillus P. (1846-1915): b. Belgium; ord. Dec. 19, 1868; bp. Covington, 1885-1915.
Maginn, Edward J. (1897-1984): b. Scotland; ord. June 10, 1922; aux. Albany (Curium), 1957-72 (res.).
Magner, Francis (1887-1947): ord. May 17, 1913; bp. Marquette, 1941-47.
Mahoney, Bernard (1875-1939): ord. Feb. 27, 1904; bp. Sioux Falls, 1922-39.
Maloney, Thomas F. (1903-62): ord. July 13, 1930; aux. Providence (Andropolis), 1960-62.
Manogue, Patrick: See Index.
Manucy, Dominic (1823-85): ord. Aug. 15, 1850; v.a. Brownsville (Dulma), 1874-84; bp. Mobile, Mar.-Sept., 1884 (res.); reappointed v.a. Brownsville (Maronea) (now diocese of Corpus Christi), 1884-85.
Mardaga, Thomas J. (1913-84): ord. May 14, 1940; aux. Baltimore (Mutugenna), 1967-68; bp. Wilmington, 1968-84.
Marechal, Ambrose, S.S. (1766-1828): b. France; ord. June 2, 1792; abp. Baltimore, 1817-28.
Markham, Thomas F. (1891-1952): ord. June 2, 1917; aux. Boston (Acalissus), 1950-52.
Marling, Joseph M., C.Pp.S. (1904-79): ord. Feb. 21, 1929; aux. Kansas City, Mo. (Thasus), 1947-56; first bp. Jefferson City, 1956-69 (res.).
Martin, Augustus M. (1803-75): b. France; ord. May 31, 1828; first bp. Natchitoches (now Alexandria), 1853-75.
Marty, Martin, O.S.B. (1834-96): b. Switzerland; ord. Sept. 14, 1856; v.a. Dakota (Tiberias), 1880-89; first bp. Sioux Falls, 1889-95; bp. St. Cloud, 1895-96.
Marx, Adolph (1915-65): b. Germany; ord. May 2, 1940; aux. Corpus Christi (Citrus), 1956-65; first bp. Brownsville, 1965.
Matz, Nicholas C. (1850-1917): b. France; ord. May 31, 1874; coad. bp. Denver (Telmissus), 1887-89; bp. Denver, 1889-1917.
Mazzarella, Bernardino N., O.F.M. (1904-79): ord. June 5, 1931; prelate Olancho, Honduras (Hadrianopolis in Pisidia), 1957-63; first bp. Comayagua, Honduras, 1963-79.
Medeiros, Humberto S. (1915-83): b. Azores; U.S. citizen, 1940; ord. June 15, 1946; bp. Brownsville, 1966-70; abp. Boston, 1970-83; cardinal 1973.
Meerschaert, Theophile (1847-1924): b. Belgium; ord. Dec. 23, 1871; v.a. Oklahoma and Indian Territory (Sidyma), 1891-1905; first bp. Oklahoma, 1905-24.
Melcher, Joseph (1806-73): b. Austria; ord. Mar. 27, 1830; first bp. Green Bay, 1868-73.
Messmer, Sebastian (1847-1930): b. Switzerland; ord. July 23, 1871; bp. Green Bay, 1892-1903; abp. Milwaukee, 1903-30.
Metzger, Sidney M. (1902-86): ord. Apr. 3, 1926; aux. Santa Fe (Birtha), 1940-41; coad. bp. El Paso, 1941-42; bp. El Paso, 1942-78 (res.).
Meyer, Albert (1903-65): ord. July 11, 1926; bp. Superior, 1946-53; abp. Milwaukee, 1953-58; abp. Chicago, 1958-65; cardinal, 1959.
Michaud, John S. (1843-1908): ord. June 7, 1873; coad. bp. Burlington (Modra), 1892-99; bp. Burlington, 1899-1908.
Miege, John B., S.J. (1815-84): b. France; ord. Sept. 12, 1844; v.a. Kansas and Indian Territory (now Kansas City) (Messene), 1851-74 (res.).
Mihalik, Emil J. (1920-84): ord. Sept. 21, 1945; first bp. Parma (Byzantine Rite, Ruthenians), 1969-84.
Miles, Richard P., O.P. (1791-1860): ord. Sept. 21, 1816; first bp. Nashville, 1838-60.
Minihan, Jeremiah F. (1903-73): ord. Dec. 21, 1929; aux. Boston (Paphus), 1954-73.
Misner, Paul B., C.M. (1891-1938): ord. Feb. 23, 1919; v.a. Yukiang, China (Myrica), 1935-38.
Mitty, John J. (1884-1961): ord. Dec. 22, 1906; bp. Salt Lake, 1926-32; coad. abp. San Francisco (Aegina), 1932-35; abp. San Francisco, 1935-61.
Moeller, Henry (1849-1925): ord. June 10, 1876; bp. Columbus, 1900-03; coad. abp. Cincinnati (Areopolis), 1903-04; abp. Cincinnati, 1904-25.
Molloy, Thomas E. (1884-1956): ord. Sept. 19, 1908; aux. Brooklyn (Lorea), 1920-21; bp. Brooklyn, 1921-56.
Monaghan, Francis J. (1890-1942): ord. May 29, 1915; coad. bp. Ogdensburg (Mela), 1936-39; bp. Ogdensburg, 1939-42.
Monaghan, John J. (1856-1935): ord. Dec. 18, 1880; bp. Wilmington, 1897-1925 (res.).
Montgomery, George T. (1847-1907): ord. Dec. 20, 1879; coad. bp. Monterey-Los Angeles (Thmuis), 1894-96; bp. Monterey-Los Angeles (now Los Angeles), 1896-1903; coad. abp. San Francisco (Auxum), 1903-07.
Mooney, Edward (1882-1958): ord. Apr. 10, 1909; ap. del. India (Irenopolis), 1926-31; ap. del. Japan, 1931-33; bp. Rochester, 1933-37; first abp. Detroit, 1937-58; cardinal, 1946.
Moore, John (1835-1901): b. Ireland; ord. Apr. 9, 1860; bp. St. Augustine, 1877-1901.
Mora, Francis (1827-1905): b. Spain; ord. Mar. 19, 1856; coad. bp. Monterey-Los Angeles (Mosynopolis), 1873-78; bp. Monterey-Los Angeles (now Los Angeles), 1878-96 (res.).
Morris, John (1866-1946): ord. June 11, 1892; coad. bp. Little Rock (Acmonia), 1906-07; bp. Little Rock, 1907-46.
Morrow, Louis La Ravoire, S.D.B., (1892-1987): ord. May 21, 1921; bp. Krishnagar, India 1939-69 (res.).
Mrak, Ignatius (1810-1901): b. Austria; ord. July 31, 1837; bp. Sault Ste. Marie and Marquette (now Marquette), 1869-78 (res.).
Mueller, Joseph M. (1894-1981): ord. June 14, 1919; coad. bp. Sioux City (Sinda), 1947-48; bp. Sioux City, 1948-70 (res.).
Muench, Aloysius (1889-1962): ord. June 8, 1913; bp. Fargo, 1935-59 (res.); apostolic visitator to Germany, 1946; nuncio to Germany 1951-59; cardinal 1959.
Muldoon, Peter J. (1862-1927): ord. Dec. 18, 1886; aux. Chicago (Tamasus), 1901-08; first bp. Rockford, 1908-27.
Mullen, Tobias (1818-1900): b. Ireland; ord. Sept. 1, 1844; bp. Erie, 1868-99 (res.).
Mulloy, William T. (1892-1959): ord. June 7, 1916; bp. Covington, 1945-59.
Mundelein, George (1872-1939): ord. June 8, 1895; aux. Brooklyn (Loryma), 1909-15; abp. Chicago, 1915-39; cardinal, 1924.

Murphy, Joseph A., S.J. (1857-1939): b. Ireland; ord. Aug. 26, 1888; v.a. Belize, Br. Honduras (Birtha), 1923-39.
Murphy, William F. (1885-1950): ord. June 13, 1908; first bp. Saginaw, 1938-50.
Murray, John G. (1877-1956): ord. Apr. 14, 1900; aux. Hartford (Flavias), 1920-25; bp. Portland, 1925-31; abp. St. Paul, 1931-56.
Mussio, John K. (1902-78): ord. Aug. 15, 1935; bp. Steubenville, 1945-77 (res.).

N

Najmy, Justin, O.S.B.M. (1898-1968): b. Syria; ord. Dec. 25, 1926; ap. ex. Melkites (Augustopolis in Phrygia), 1966-68.
Navagh, James J. (1901-65): ord. Dec. 21, 1929; aux. Raleigh (Ombi), 1952-57; bp. Ogdensburg, 1957-63; bp. Paterson, 1963-65.
Neale, Leonard (1746-1817): ord. June 5, 1773; coad. bp. Baltimore (Gortyna), 1800-15; abp. Baltimore, 1815-17.
Neraz, John C. (1828-94): b. France; ord. Mar. 19, 1853; bp. San Antonio, 1881-1894.
Neumann, John, St.: See Index.
Newell, Hubert M. (1904-87): ord. June 15, 1930; coad. bp. Cheyenne (Zapara), 1947-51; bp. Cheyenne, 1951-78 (res.).
Newman, Thomas A., M.S. (1903-78): ord. June 29, 1929; first bp. Prome, Burma, 1961-75 (res.).
Niedhammer, Matthew A., O.F.M. Cap. (1901-70): ord. June 8, 1927; v.a. Bluefields, Nicaragua (Caloe), 1943-70.
Nilan, John J. (1855-1934): ord. Dec. 2, 1878; bp. Hartford, 1910-34.
Noa, Thomas L. (1892-1977): ord. Dec. 23, 1916; coad. bp. Sioux City (Salona), 1946-47; bp. Marquette, 1947-68 (res.).
Nold, Wendelin J. (1900-81): ord. Apr. 11, 1925; coad. bp. Galveston (Sasima), 1948-50; bp. Galveston-Houston, 1950-75 (res.).
Noll, John F. (1875-1956): ord. June 4, 1898; bp. Fort Wayne, 1925-56 (pers. tit. abp., 1953).
Northrop, Henry P. (1842-1916): ord. June 25, 1865; v.a. North Carolina (Rosalia), 1881-83; bp. Charleston, 1883-1916.
Noser, Adolph, S.V.D. (1900-81): ord. Sept. 27, 1925; v.a. Accra, British W. Africa (now Ghana) (Capitolias), 1947-50; bp. Accra, 1950-53; v.a. Alexishafen, New Guinea (Hierpiniana), 1953-66; abp. Madang, Papua New Guinea, 1966-75 (res.).
Nussbaum, Paul J., C.P. (1870-1935): ord. May 20, 1894; first bp. Corpus Christi, 1913-20 (res.); bp. Sault Ste. Marie and Marquette (now Marquette), 1922-35.

O

O'Boyle, Patrick A. (1896-1987): ord. May 21, 1921; abp. Washington, D.C., 1948-73 (res.); cardinal 1967.
O'Brien, Henry J. (1896-1976): ord. July 8, 1923; aux. Hartford (Sita), 1940-45; bp. Hartford, 1945-53, and first abp. Hartford, 1953-68 (res.).
O'Brien, William D. (1878-1962): ord. July 11, 1903; aux. Chicago (Calynda), 1934-62.
O'Connell, Denis J. (1849-1927): b. Ireland; ord. May 26, 1877; aux. San Francisco (Sebaste), 1908-12; bp. Richmond, 1912-26 (res.).
O'Connell, Eugene (1815-91): b. Ireland; ord. May 21, 1842; v.a. Marysville (Flaviopolis), 1861-68; first bp. Grass Valley, 1868-84 (res.).
O'Connell, William H. (1859-1944): ord. June 7, 1884; bp. Portland, 1901-06; coad. bp. Boston (Constantia), 1906-07; abp. Boston, 1907-44; cardinal, 1911.
O'Connor (brothers), **James** (1823-90): b. Ireland; ord. Mar. 25, 1848; v.a. Nebraska (Dibon), 1876-85; first bp. Omaha, 1885-90. **Michael, S.J.** (1810-72): b. Ireland; ord. June 1, 1833; first bp. Pittsburgh, 1843-53; first bp. Erie, 1853-54; bp. Pittsburgh, 1854-60 (resigned, joined Jesuits).
O'Connor, John J. (1855-1927): ord. Dec. 22, 1877; bp. Newark, 1901-27.
O'Connor, Martin J. (1900-86): ord. Mar. 15, 1924; aux. Scranton (Thespia), 1943-46; rector North American College, Rome, 1946-64; abp., 1959 (Laodicea); nuncio to Malta, 1965-69; pres. Pontifical Commission for Social Communications, 1964-71.
O'Connor, William A. (1903-83): ord. Sept. 24, 1927; bp. Springfield, Ill., 1949-75 (res.).
O'Connor, William P. (1886-1973): ord. Mar. 10, 1912; bp. Superior, 1942-46; first bp. Madison, 1946-67 (res.).
O'Dea, Edward J. (1856-1932): ord. Dec. 23, 1882; bp. Nesqually (now Seattle — title changed in 1907), 1896-1932.
Odin, John M., C.M. (1800-70): b. France; ord. May 4, 1823; v.a. Texas (Claudiopolis), 1842-47; first bp. Galveston, 1847-61; abp. New Orleans, 1861-70.
O'Donaghue, Denis (1848-1925): ord. Sept. 6, 1874; aux. Indianapolis (Pomaria), 1900-10; bp. Louisville, 1910-24 (res.).
O'Dowd, James T. (1907-50): ord. June 4, 1932; aux. San Francisco (Cea), 1948-50.
O'Farrell, Michael J. (1832-94): b. Ireland; ord. Aug. 18, 1855; first bp. Trenton, 1881-94.
O'Flanagan, Dermot (1901-73): b. Ireland; ord. Aug. 27, 1929; first bp. Juneau, 1951-68 (res.).
O'Gara, Cuthbert, C.P. (1886-1968): b. Canada; ord. May 26, 1915; v.a. Yuanling, China (Elis), 1934-46; first bp. Yuanling 1946-68 (imprisoned, 1951, and then expelled, 1953, by Chinese Communists).
O'Gorman, James, O.C.S.O. (1804-74): b. Ireland; ord. Dec. 18, 1843; v.a. Nebraska (now Omaha) (Raphanea), 1859-74.
O'Gorman, Thomas (1843-1921): ord. Nov. 5, 1865; bp. Sioux Falls, 1896-1921.
O'Hara, Edwin V. (1881-1956): ord. June 9, 1905; bp. Great Falls, 1930-39; bp. Kansas City, Mo., 1939-56 (title changed to Kansas City-St. Joseph, 1956).
O'Hara, Gerald P. (1888-1963): ord. Apr. 3, 1920; aux. Philadelphia (Heliopolis), 1929-35; bp. Savannah (title changed to Savannah-Atlanta in 1937), 1935-59 (res.); regent of Rumania nunciature, 1946-50 (expelled); nuncio to Ireland, 1951-54; ap. del. to Gret Britain, 1954-63; tit. abp. Pessinus, 1959-63.
O'Hara, John F., C.S.C. (1886-1960): ord. Sept. 9, 1916; delegate of U.S. military vicar (Mylasa),

1940-45; bp. Buffalo, 1945-51; abp. Philadelphia, 1951-60; cardinal, 1958.

O'Hara, William (1816-99): b. Ireland; ord. Dec. 21, 1842; first bp. Scranton, 1868-99.

O'Hare, William F., S.J. (1870-1926): ord. June 25, 1903; v.a. Jamaica (Maximianopolis), 1920-26.

O'Hern, John F. (1874-1933): ord. Feb. 17, 1901; bp. Rochester, 1929-33.

O'Leary, Thomas (1875-1949): ord. Dec. 18, 1897; bp. Springfield, Mass., 1921-49.

Olwell, Quentin, C.P. (1898-1972): ord. Feb. 4, 1923; prelate Marbel, P.I. (Thabraca), 1961-69 (res.).

O'Regan, Anthony (1809-66): b. Ireland; ord. Nov. 29, 1834; bp. Chicago, 1854-58 (res.).

O'Reilly, Bernard (1803-56): b. Ireland; ord. Oct. 16, 1831; bp. Hartford, 1850-56.

O'Reilly, Charles J. (1860-1923): b. Canada; ord. June 29, 1890; first bp. Baker City (now Baker), 1903-18; bp. Lincoln; 1918-23.

O'Reilly, James (1855-1934): b. Ireland; ord. June 24, 1880; bp. Fargo, 1910-34.

O'Reilly, Patrick T. (1833-92): b. Ireland; ord. Aug. 15, 1857; first bp. Springfield, Mass., 1870-92.

O'Reilly, Peter J. (1850-1924): b. Ireland; ord. June 24, 1877; aux. Peoria (Lebedus), 1900-24.

O'Reilly, Thomas C. (1873-1938): ord. June 4, 1898; bp. Scranton, 1928-38.

Ortynsky, Stephen, O.S.B.M. (1866-1916): b. Poland; ord. July 18, 1891; first Ukrainian Byzantine Rite bishop in U.S. (Daulia), 1907-16.

O'Shea, John A., C.M. (1887-1969): ord. May 30, 1914; v.a. Kanchow, China (Midila), 1928-46; first bp. Kanchow, 1949-69 (expelled by Chinese Communists, 1953).

O'Shea, William F., M.M. (1884-1945): ord. Dec. 5, 1917; v.a. Heijon, Japan (Naissusz), 1939-45; prisoner of Japanese 1941-42.

O'Sullivan, Jeremiah (1842-96): b. Ireland; ord. June 30, 1868; bp. Mobile, 1885-96.

P

Pardy, James V., M.M. (1898-1983): ord. Jan. 26, 1930; v.a. Cheong-Ju, Korea (Irenopolis), 1958-62; first bp. Cheong-Ju, 1962-69 (res.).

Paschang, Adolph J., M.M. (1895-1968): ord. May 21, 1921; v.a. Kong Moon, China (Sasima), 1937-46; first bp. Kong Moon, 1946-68 (expelled by Communists, 1951).

Pellicer, Anthony (1824-80): ord. Aug. 15, 1850; first bp. San Antonio, 1874-80.

Penalver y Cardenas, Luis (1749-1810): b. Cuba; ord. Apr. 4, 1772; first bp. Louisiana and the Two Floridas (now New Orleans), 1793-1801; abp. Guatemala, 1801-06 (res.).

Perche, Napoleon J. (1805-83): b. France; ord. Sept. 19, 1829; abp. New Orleans, 1870-83.

Pernicone, Joseph M. (1903-85): b. Sicily; ord. Dec. 18, 1926; aux. New York (Hadrianapolis) 1954-78 (res.).

Persico, Ignatius, O.F.M. Cap. (1823-95): b. Italy; ord. Jan. 24, 1846; bishop from 1854; bp. Savannah-Atlanta, 1870-72; cardinal, 1893.

Peschges, John H. (1881-1944): ord. Apr. 15, 1905; bp. Crookston, 1938-44.

Peterson, John B. (1871-1944): ord. Sept. 15, 1899; aux. Boston (Hippos), 1972-32: bp. Manchester, 1932-44.

Phelan, Richard (1828-1904): b. Ireland; ord. May 4, 1854; coad. bp. Pittsburgh (Cibyra), 1885-89; bp. Pittsburgh, 1889-1904.

Pinten, Joseph G. (1867-1945): ord. Nov. 1, 1890; bp. Superior, 1922-26; bp. Grand Rapids, 1926-40 (res.).

Pitaval, John B. (1858-1928): b. France; ord. Dec. 24, 1881; aux. Santa Fe (Sora), 1902-09; abp. Santa Fe, 1909-18 (res.).

Plagens, Joseph C. (1880-1943): b. Poland; ord. July 5, 1903; aux. Detroit (Rhodiapolis), 1924-35; bp. Sault Ste. Marie and Marquette (title changed to Marquette, 1937), 1935-40; bp. Grand Rapids, 1941-43.

Portier, Michael (1795-1859): b. France; ord. May 16. 1818; v.a. Two Floridas and Alabama (Olena), 1826-29; first bp. Mobile, 1829-59.

Prendergast, Edmond (1843-1918): b. Ireland; ord. Nov. 17, 1865; aux. Philadelphia (Scilium), 1897-1911; abp. Philadelphia, 1911-18.

Purcell, John B. (1800-83): b. Ireland; ord. May 20, 1826; bp., 1833-50, and first abp., 1850-83, Cincinnati.

Q

Quarter, William (1806-48): b. Ireland; ord. Sept. 19, 1829; first bp. Chicago, 1844-48.

Quigley, James F. (1855-1915): b. Canada; ord. Apr. 13, 1879; bp. Buffalo, 1897-1903; abp. Chicago, 1903-15.

Quinlan, John (1826-83): b. Ireland; ord. Aug. 30, 1852; bp. Mobile, 1859-83.

Quinn, William Charles, C.M. (1905-60): ord. Oct. 11, 1931; v.a. Yukiang, China (Halicarnassus), 1940-46; first bp. Yukiang, 1946-60 (expelled by Chinese Communists, 1951).

R

Rademacher, Joseph (1840-1900): ord. Aug. 2, 1863; bp. Nashville, 1883-93; bp. Fort Wayne, 1893-1900.

Rappe, Louis Amadeus (1801-77): b. France; ord. Mar. 14, 1829; first bp. Cleveland, 1847-70 (res.).

Rausch, James S. (1928-81): ord. June 2, 1956; aux. St. Cloud (Summa), 1973-77; bp. Phoenix, 1977-81.

Ready, Michael J. (1893-1957): ord. Sept. 14, 1918; bp. Columbus, 1944-57.

Reed, Victor J. (1905-71): ord. Dec. 21, 1929; aux. Oklahoma City and Tulsa (Limasa), 1957-58; bp. Oklahoma City and Tulsa, 1958-71.

Rehring, George J. (1890-1976): ord. Mar. 28, 1914; aux. Cincinnati (Lunda), 1937-50; bp. Toledo, 1950-67 (res.).

Reicher, Louis J. (1890-1984): ord. Dec. 6, 1918; first bp. Austin, 1948-71 (res.).

Reilly, Edmond J. (1897-1958): ord. Apr. 1, 1922; aux. Brooklyn (Nepte), 1955-58.

Rese, Frederic (1791-1871): b. Germany; ord. Mar. 15, 1823; first bp. Detroit, 1833-71. Inactive from 1841 because of ill health.

Reverman, Theodore (1877-1941): ord. July 26, 1901; bp. Superior, 1926-41.

Reynolds, Ignatius A. (1798-1855): ord. Oct. 24, 1823; bp. Charleston, 1844-55.
Rhode, Paul P. (1871-1945): b. Poland; ord. June 17, 1894; aux. Chicago (Barca), 1908-15; bp. Green Bay, 1915-45.
Rice, Joseph J. (1871-1938): ord. Sept. 29, 1894; bp. Burlington, 1910-38.
Rice, William A., S.J. (1891-1946): ord. Aug. 27, 1925; v.a. Belize, Br. Honduras (Rusicade), 1939-46.
Richter, Henry J. (1838-1916): b. Germany; ord. June 10, 1865; first bp. Grand Rapids, 1883-1916.
Riley, Thomas J. (1900-1977): ord. May 20, 1927; aux. Boston (Regiae), 1956-76 (res.).
Riordan, Patrick W. (1841-1914): b. Canada; ord. June 10, 1865; coad. abp. San Francisco (Cabasa), 1883-84; abp. San Francisco, 1884-1914.
Ritter, Joseph E. (1892-1967): ord. May 30, 1917; aux. Indianapolis (Hippos), 1933-34; bp., 1934-44, and first abp. Indianapolis, 1944-46; abp. St. Louis, 1946-67; cardinal 1961.
Robinson, Pascal C., O.F.M. (1870-1948): b. Ireland; ord. Dec. 21, 1901; ap. visitor to Palestine, Egypt, Syria and Cyprus (Tyana), 1927-29; ap. nuncio to Ireland, 1929-48.
Rohlman, Henry P. (1876-1957): b. Germany; ord. Dec. 21, 1901; bp. Davenport, 1927-44; coad. abp. Dubuque (Macra), 1944-46; abp. Dubuque, 1946-54 (res.).
Rooker, Frederick Z. (1861-1907): ord. July 25, 1888; bp. Jaro, P.I., 1903-07.
Ropert, Gulstan F., SS.CC. (1839-1903): b. France; ord. May 26, 1866; v.a. Sandwich (now Hawaiian) Is. (Panopolis), 1892-1903.
Rosati, Joseph, C.M.: See Index.
Rosecrans, Sylvester (1827-78): ord. June 5, 1853; aux. Cincinnati (Pompeiopolis), 1862-68; first bp. Columbus, 1868-78.
Rouxel, Gustave A. (1840-1908): b. France, ord. Nov. 4, 1863; aux. New Orleans (Curium), 1899-1908.
Rummel, Joseph (1876-1964): b. Germany; ord. May 24, 1902; bp. Omaha, 1928-35; abp. New Orleans, 1935-64.
Ruocco, Joseph J. (1922-80): ord. May 6, 1948; aux. Boston (Polignano), 1975-80.
Russell, William T. (1863-1927): ord. June 21, 1889; bp. Charleston, 1917-27.
Ryan, Edward F. (1879-1956): ord. Aug. 10, 1905; bp. Burlington, 1945-56.
Ryan, Gerald J. (1923-85): ord. June 3, 1950; aux. Rockville Centre (Munatiana), 1977-85.
Ryan, James (1848-1923): b. Ireland; ord. Dec. 24, 1871; bp. Alton (now Springfield), Ill., 1888-1923.
Ryan, James H. (1886-1947): ord. June 5, 1909; rector Catholic University, 1928-35; tit. bp. Modra, 1933-35; bp., 1935-45, and first abp. Omaha, 1945-47.
Ryan, Patrick J. (1831-1911): b. Ireland; ord. Sept. 8, 1853; coad. bp. St. Louis (Tricomia), 1872-84; abp. Philadelphia, 1884-1911.
Ryan, Stephen, C.M. (1826-96): b. Canada; ord. June 24, 1849; bp. Buffalo, 1868-96.
Ryan, Vincent J. (1884-1951): ord. June 7, 1912; bp. Bismarck, 1940-41.

S

Salpointe, John B. (1825-98): b. France; ord. Dec. 20, 1851; v.a. Arizona (Dorylaeum), 1869-84; coad. abp. Santa Fe (Anazarbus), 1884-85; abp. Santa Fe, 1885-94 (res.).
Scanlan, Lawrence (1843-1915): b. Ireland; ord. June 28, 1868; v.a. Utah (Laranda), 1887-91; bp. Salt Lake (now Salt Lake City), 1891-1915.
Scannell, Richard (1845-1916): b. Ireland; ord. Feb. 26, 1871; first bp. Concordia (now Salina), 1887-91; bp. Omaha, 1891-1916.
Schenk, Francis J. (1901-69): ord. June 13, 1926; bp. Crookston, 1945-60; bp. Duluth, 1960-69.
Scher, Philip G. (1880-1953): ord. June 6, 1904; bp. Monterey-Fresno, 1933-53.
Schexnayder, Maurice (1895-1981): ord. Apr. 11, 1925; aux. Lafayette (Tuscamia), 1951-56; bp. Lafayette, La., 1956-72 (res.).
Schierhoff, Andrew B. (1922-87): ord. Apr. 14, 1948; aux. La Paz, Bolivia (Gerenza), 1969-82; v.a. Pando, Bolivia, 1982-87.
Schinner, Augustine (1863-1937): ord. Mar. 7, 1886; first bp. Superior, 1905-13; first bp. Spokane, 1914-25 (res.).
Schlarman, Joseph H. (1879-1951): ord. June 29, 1904; bp. Peoria, 1930-51.
Schmitt, Adolph G., C.M.M. (1905-76): b. Bavaria; U.S. citizen 1945; v.a. Bulawayo (Nasai), Rhodesia, 1951-55; first bp. Bulawayo, 1955-74 (res.). Murdered by terrorists.
Schmondiuk, Joseph (1912-1978): ord. Mar. 29, 1936; aux. Philadelphia exarchate (Zeugma in Syria), 1956-61; eparch Stamford, 1961-77; abp. Philadelphia, 1977-78.
Schott, Lawrence F. (1907-63): ord. July 15, 1935; aux. Harrisburg (Eluza), 1956-63.
Schrembs, Joseph (1866-1945): b. Germany; ord. June 29, 1889; aux. Grand Rapids (Sophene), 1911; first bp. Toledo, 1911-21; bp. Cleveland, 1921-45.
Schuler, Anthony J., S.J. (1869-1944): ord. June 27, 1901; first bp. El Paso, 1915-42 (res.).
Schulte, Paul (1890-1984): ord. June 11, 1915; bp. Leavenworth, 1937-46; abp. Indianapolis, 1946-70 (res.).
Schwebach, James (1847-1921): b. Luxembourg; ord. June 16, 1870; bp. La Crosse, 1892-1921.
Schwertner, August J. (1870-1939): ord. June 12, 1897; bp. Wichita, 1921-39.
Scully, William (1894-1969): ord. Sept. 20, 1919; coad. bp. Albany (Pharsalus), 1945-54; bp. Albany, 1954-69.
Sebastian, Jerome D. (1895-1960): ord. May 25, 1922; aux. Baltimore (Baris in Hellesponto), 1954-60.
Seghers, Charles J.: See Index.
Seidenbusch, Rupert, O.S.B. (1830-95): b. Germany; ord. June 22, 1853; v.a. Northern Minnesota (Halia), 1875-88 (res.).
Senyshyn, Ambrose, O.S.B.M. (1903-76): b. Galicia; ord. Aug. 23, 1931; aux. Ukrainian Catholic Diocese of U.S. (Maina), 1942-56; first bp. Stamford (Byzantine Rite), 1958-61; abp. Philadelphia (Byzantine Rite), 1961-76.
Seton, Robert J. (1839-1927): b. Italy, ord. Apr.

15, 1865; tit. abp. Heliopolis, 1903-27. Grandson of St. Elizabeth Seton.
Shahan, Thomas J. (1857-1932): ord. June 3, 1882; rector, Catholic University of America, 1909-27; tit. bp. Germanicopolis, 1914-32.
Shanahan (brothers): **Jeremiah F.** (1834-86): ord. July 3, 1859; first bp. Harrisburg, 1868-86. **John W.** (1846-1916): ord. Jan. 2, 1869; bp. Harrisburg, 1899-1916.
Shanley, John (1852-1909): ord. May 30, 1874; first bp. Jamestown (see transferred to Fargo in 1897), 1889-1909.
Shanley, Patrick H., O.C.D. (1896-1970): b. Ireland; ord. Dec. 21, 1930; U.S. citizen; prelate Infanta, P.I. (Sophene), 1953-60 (res.).
Shaughnessy, Gerald, S.M. (1887-1950): ord. June 20, 1920; bp. Seattle, 1933-50.
Shaw, John W. (1861-1934): ord. May 26, 1888; coad. bp. San Antonio (Castabala), 1910-11; bp. San Antonio, 1911-18; abp. New Orleans, 1918-34.
Sheehan, Edward T., C.M. (1888-1933): ord. June 7, 1916, v.a. Yukiang, China (Calydon), 1929-33.
Sheen, Fulton J. (1895-1979): ord. Sept. 20, 1919; aux. New York (Caesarina), 1951-66; bp. Rochester, 1966-69 (res.); tit. abp. Newport.
Shehan, Lawrence J. (1898-1984): ord. Dec. 23, 1922; aux. Baltimore and Washington (Lidda), 1945-53; bp. Bridgeport, 1953-61; coad. abp. Baltimore (Nicopolis ad Nestum), Sept.-Dec., 1961; abp. Baltimore, 1961-74 (res.); cardinal 1965.
Sheil, Bernard J. (1886-1969); ord. May 21, 1910; aux. bp. Chicago (Pegae), 1928-69; tit. abp. Selge, 1959-69.
Smith, Alphonse (1883-1935): ord. Apr. 18, 1908; bp. Nashville, 1924-35.
Smith, Eustace, O.F.M. (1908-75): ord. June 12, 1934; v.a. Beirut, Lebanon (Apamea Cibotus), 1958-73 (res.).
Smith, Leo R. (1905-63): ord. Dec. 21, 1929; aux. Buffalo (Marida), 1952-63; bp. Ogdensburg, 1963.
Smyth, Clement, O.C.S.O. (1810-65): b. Ireland; ord. May 29, 1841; coad. bp. Dubuque (Thennesus), 1857-58; bp. Dubuque, 1858-65.
Soenneker, Henry J. (1907-87): Ord. May 26, 1934; bp. Owensboro, 1961-82 (res.).
Spalding, John F. (1840-1916): ord. Dec. 19, 1863, first bp. Peoria, 1876-1908 (res.).
Spalding, Martin J. (1810-72): ord. Aug. 13, 1834; aux. Louisville (Lengone), 1848-50; bp. Louisville, 1850-64; abp. Baltimore, 1864-72.
Spellman, Francis J. (1889-1967): ord. May 14, 1916; aux. Boston (Sila), 1932-39; abp. New York, 1939-67; cardinal 1946.
Spence, John S. (1909-73): ord. Dec. 5, 1933; aux. Washington (Aggersel), 1964-73.
Stang, William (1854-1907): b. Germany; ord. June 15, 1878; first bp. Fall River, 1904-07.
Stanton, Martin W. (1897-1977): ord. June 14, 1924; aux. Newark (Citium) 1957-72 (res.).
Stariha, John (1845-1915): b. Austria; ord. Sept. 19, 1869; first bp. Lead (now Rapid City), 1902-09 (res.).
Steck, Leo J. (1898-1950): ord. June 8, 1924; aux. Salt Lake City (Ilium), 1948-50.
Stemper, Alfred M., M.S.C. (1913-84): ord. June 26, 1940; v.a. Kavieng (Eleutheropolis), 1957-66; first bp. Kavieng, 1966-80 (res.).
Stock, John (1918-72): ord. Dec. 4, 1943; aux. Philadelphia (Ukrainian Rite) (Pergamum), 1971-72.
Stritch, Samuel (1887-1958): ord. May 21, 1909; bp. Toledo, 1921-30; abp. Milwaukee, 1930-39; abp. Chicago, 1939-58; cardinal 1946.
Sullivan, Bernard, S.J. (1889-1970): ord, June 26, 1921; bp. Patna, India, 1929-46 (res.).
Sullivan, Joseph V. (1919-82): ord. June 1, 1946; aux. Kansas City-St. Joseph (Tagamuta), 1964-74; bp. Baton Rouge, 1974-82.
Swanstrom, Edward E. (1903-85): ord. June 2, 1928; aux. New York (Arba), 1960-78 (res.).
Sweeney, James S. (1898-1968): ord. June 20, 1925; first bp. Honolulu, 1941-68.
Swint, John J. (1879-1962): ord. June 23, 1904; aux. Wheeling (Sura), 1922; bp. Wheeling, 1922-62.

T

Takach, Basil (1879-1948): b. Austria-Hungary; ord. Dec. 12, 1902; first ap. ex. Pittsburgh Byzantine Rite (Zela), 1924-48.
Tarasevitch, Vladimir L, O.S.B. (1921-86): b. Byelorussia (White Russia); ord. May 26, 1949; ap. visitator (with residence in Chicago) for Byelorussians outside Soviet Union (Mariamme), 1983-86.
Taylor, John E., O.M.I. (1914-76): ord. May 25, 1940; bp. Stockholm, Sweden, 1962-76.
Thill, Francis A. (1893-1957): ord. Feb. 28, 1920; bp. Concordia (title changed to Salina in 1944), 1938-57.
Tief, Francis J. (1881-1965): ord. June 11, 1908; bp. Concordia (now Salina), 1921-38 (res.).
Tierney, Michael (1839-1908): b. Ireland; ord. May 26, 1866; bp. Hartford, 1894-1908.
Tihen, J. Henry (1861-1940): ord. Apr. 26, 1886; bp. Lincoln, 1911-17; bp. Denver, 1917-31 (res.).
Timon, John, C.M. (1797-1867): ord. Sept. 23, 1826; first bp. Buffalo, 1847-67.
Toebbe, Augustus M. (1829-84): b. Germany; ord. Sept. 14, 1854; bp. Covington, 1870-84.
Toolen, Thomas J. (1886-1976): ord. Sept. 27, 1910; bp. (pers. tit. abp., 1954), Mobile, 1927-69 (res.).
Topel, Bernard J. (1903-86): ord. June 7, 1927; coad. bp. Spokane (Binda), Sept. 21-25, 1955; bp. Spokane, 1955-78 (res.).
Tracy, Robert E. (1909-80): ord. June 12, 1932; aux. Lafayette, La. (Sergentiza), 1959-61; first bp. Baton Rouge, 1961-74 (res.).
Treacy, John P. (1890-1964): ord. Dec. 8, 1918; coad. bp. La Crosse (Metelis), 1945-48; bp. La Crosse, 1948-64.
Trobec, James (1838-1921): b. Austria; ord. Sept. 8, 1865; bp. St. Cloud, 1897-1914 (res.).
Tuigg, John (1820-89): b. Ireland; ord. May 14, 1850; bp. Pittsburgh, 1876-89.
Turner, William (1871-1936): b. Ireland; ord. Aug. 13, 1893; bp. Buffalo, 1919-36.
Tyler, William (1806-49): ord. June 3, 1829; first bp. Hartford, 1844-49.

V

Van de Velde, James O., S.J. (1795-1855): b. Belgium; ord. Sept. 16, 1827; bp. Chicago, 1849-53; bp. Natchez (now Jackson), 1953-55.

Van de Ven, Cornelius (1865-1932): b. Holland; ord. May 31, 1890; bp. Natchitoches (title changed to Alexandria, 1910), 1904-32.

Van de Vyver, Augustine (1844-1911): b. Belgium; ord. July 24, 1870; bp. Richmond, 1889-1911.

Vath, Joseph G. (1918-87): ord. June 7, 1941; aux. Mobile-Birmingham (Novaliciana), 1966-69; first bp. Birmingham, 1969-87.

Vehr, Urban J. (1891-1973): ord. May 29, 1915; bp. 1931-41, and first abp. Denver, 1941-67 (res.).

Verdaguer, Peter (1835-1911): b. Spain; ord. Dec. 12, 1862; v.a. Brownsville (Aulon), 1890-1911.

Verot, Augustin, S.S. (1805-76): b. France; ord. Sept. 20, 1828; v.a. Florida (Danaba), 1856-61; bp. Savannah, 1961-70; bp. St. Augustine, 1870-76.

Vertin, John (1844-99): b. Austria; ord. Aug. 31, 1866; bp. Sault Ste. Marie and Marquette (now Marquette), 1879-99.

Vogel, Cyril J. (1905-79): ord. June 7, 1931; bp. Salina, 1965-79.

W

Wade, Thomas, S.M. (1893-1969): ord. June 15, 1922; v.a. Northern Solomons (Barbalissus), 1930-69.

Wadhams, Edgar (1817-91): convert, 1846; ord. Jan. 15, 1850; first bp. Ogdensburg, 1872-91.

Walsh, Emmet (1892-1968): ord. Jan. 15, 1916; bp. Charleston, 1927-49; coad. bp. Youngstown (Rhaedestus), 1949-52; bp. Youngstown, 1952-68.

Walsh, James A., M.M. (1867-1936): ord. May 20, 1892; co-founder (with Thomas F. Price) of Maryknoll, first U.S. established foreign mission society and first sponsor of a U.S. foreign mission seminary; superior of Maryknoll, 1911-36; tit. bp. Syene, 1933-36.

Walsh, James E., M.M. (1891-1981): ord. Dec. 7, 1915; v.a. Kongmoon, China (Sata), 1927-36; superior of Maryknoll, 1936-46; general secretary, Catholic Central Bureau, Shanghai, China, 1948; imprisoned by Chinese communists, 1958-70.

Walsh, Louis S. (1858-1924): ord. Dec. 23, 1882; bp. Portland, Me., 1906-24.

Walsh, Thomas J. (1873-1952): ord. Jan. 27, 1900; bp. Trenton, 1918-28; bp., 1928-37, and first abp. 1937-52, Newark.

Ward, John (1857-1929): ord. July 17, 1884; bp. Leavenworth (now Kansas City), 1910-29.

Waters, Vincent S. (1904-74): ord. Dec. 8, 1931; bp. Raleigh, 1945-74.

Watterson, John A. (1844-99): ord. Aug. 9, 1868; bp. Columbus, 1880-99.

Wehrle, Vincent, O.S.B. (1855-1941): b. Switzerland; ord. Apr. 23, 1882; first bp. Bismarck, 1910-39 (res.).

Welch, Thomas A. (1884-1959): ord. June 11, 1909; bp. Duluth, 1926-59.

Weldon, Christopher J. (1905-82): ord. Sept. 21, 1939; bp. Springfield, Mass., 1950-77 (res.).

Whelan, James O.P. (1822-78): b. Ireland; ord. Aug. 2, 1846; coad. bp. Nashville (Marcopolis), 1859-60; bp. Nashville, 1860-64 (res.).

Whelan, Richard V. (1809-74): ord. May 1, 1831; bp. Richmond, 1841-50; bp. Wheeling, 1850-74.

White, Charles (1879-1955): ord. Sept. 24, 1910; bp. Spokane, 1927-55.

Whitfield, James (1770-1834): b. England; ord. July 24, 1809; coad. bp. Baltimore (Apollonia), 1828; abp. Baltimore, 1828-34.

Wigger, Winand (1841-1901): ord. June 10, 1865; bp. Newark, 1881-1901.

Willging, Joseph C. (1884-1959): ord. June 20, 1908; first bp. Pueblo, 1942-59.

Williams, John J. (1822-1907): ord. May 17, 1845; bp., 1866-75, and first abp., 1875-1907, Boston.

Willinger, Aloysius J., C.SS.R. (1886-1973): ord. July 2, 1911; bp. Ponce, P.R., 1929-46; coad. bp. Monterey-Fresno, 1946-53; bp. Monterey-Fresno, 1953-67 (res.).

Winkelmann, Christian H. (1883-1946): ord. June 11, 1907; aux. St. Louis (Sita), 1933-39; bp. Wichita, 1939-46.

Wood, James F. (1813-83): convert, 1836; ord. Mar. 25, 1844; coad. bp. Philadelphia (Antigonea), 1857-60; bp., 1860-75, and first abp., 1875-83, Philadelphia.

Woznicki, Stephen (1894-1968): ord. Dec. 22, 1917; aux. Detroit (Peltae), 1938-50; bp. Saginaw, 1950-68.

Wright, John J. (1909-79): ord. Dec. 8, 1935; aux. Boston (Egee), 1947-50; bp. Worcester, 1950-59; bp. Pittsburgh, 1959-69; cardinal, 1969; prefect Congregation of the Clergy, 1969-79.

Wurm, John N. (1927-84): ord. Apr. 3, 1954; aux. St. Louis (Plestia), 1976-81; bp. Belleville, 1981-84.

Y-Z

Young, Josue (1808-66): ord. Apr. 1, 1838; bp. Erie, 1854-66.

Zaleski, Alexander, M. (1906-75): ord. July 12, 1931; aux. Detroit (Lybe), 1950-64; coad. bp. Lansing, 1964-65; bp. Lansing 1966-75.

Zardetti, Otto (1847-1902): b. Switzerland; ord. Aug. 21, 1870; first bp. St. Cloud, 1889-94; abp. Bucharest, Rumania, 1894-95 (res.).

Zuroweste, Albert R. (1901-87): ord. June 8, 1924; bp. Belleville, 1948-76 (res.).

THE AMERICAN COLLEGE, LOUVAIN

The American College was founded by the bishops of the United States in 1857 as a house of formation for U.S. seminarians and as a residence for graduate priest students pursuing courses in theology and related subjects at The Catholic Universities of Leuven and Louvain-la-Neuve (dating from 1425) in Belgium.

The college is administered by an American rector and staff, and operates under the auspices of a special committee of the National Conference of Catholic Bishops headed by Bishop Robert F. Mulvee. The rector is: Msgr. Thomas P. Ivory of Newark, N.J. The address is: The American College of Louvain, Naamsestraat 100, 3000 Leuven, Belgium. The student body is representative of various dioceses of the United States.

BLACK CATHOLICS IN THE UNITED STATES

National Office

The National Office for Black Catholics, organized in July, 1970, is a central agency with the general purposes of promoting active and full participation by black Catholics in the Church and of making more effective the presence and ministry of the Church in the black community.

Its operations are in support of the aspirations and calls of black Catholics for a number of objectives, including the following:

- representation and voice for blacks among bishops and others with leadership and decision-making positions in the Church;
- promoting vocations to the priesthood and religious life;
- sponsoring programs of evangelization, pastoral ministry, education and liturgy on a national level;
- recognition of the black heritage in liturgy, community life, theology and education.

James McConduit is president of the NOBC.

The NOBC office is located at 3025 Fourth St. N.E., Washington, D.C. 20017.

Clergy Caucus

The National Black Catholic Clergy Caucus, founded in 1968 in Detroit, is a fraternity of approximately 750 black priests, permanent deacons and brothers pledged to mutual support in their vocations and ministries.

The Caucus develops programs of spiritual, theological, educational and ministerial growth for its members, to counteract the effects of institutionalized racism within the Church and American society. A bimonthly newsletter is published.

The NBCCC office is located at 1419 V St. N.W., Washington, D.C. 20009.

Committee and Secretariat

The National Conference of Catholic Bishops established a **Committee on Black Catholics** in 1987 and placed it under the direction of Auxiliary Bishop John Ricard of Baltimore. The purpose of the committee is to take the lead in efforts to put into effect the three-year national pastoral program fashioned by the National Black Catholic Congress in May, 1987.

Priorities of the pastoral plan include evangelization of black people, unchurched or churched, the study of black history and culture, ways of being authentically black and truly Catholic, leadership training and pastoral ministry, and outreach to communities through schools and parishes.

Also established as a service agency to the committee was a **Secretariat for Black Catholics** under

---

TABLE

(Source: *Statistical Profile of Black Catholics, 1984*, published by the Josephite Pastoral Center, 1200 Varnum St. N.E., Washington, D.C. 20017.)

State	Black Cath. Population	Total Black Pop.	Cath. Pct. Black Pop.
Alabama	15,500	996,335	1.6
Alaska	350	13,643	2.6
Arizona	1,184	73,718	1.6
Arkansas	1,600	373,768	.4
California	102,895	1,819,281	5.7
Colorado	4,235	101,703	4.2
Connecticut	10,774	217,465	5.0
Delaware	2,000	154,086	1.3
District of Columbia	75,000	779,487	9.6
Florida	82,880	1,342,688	6.2
Georgia	12,000	1,465,181	.8
Hawaii	100	17,364	.6
Idaho	50	2,716	1.8
Illinois	113,550	1,675,398	6.8
Indiana	15,076	414,785	3.6
Iowa	956	41,700	2.3
Kansas	9,107	126,127	7.2
Kentucky	9,243	259,477	3.6
Louisiana	210,799	1,238,242	17.0
Maine	100	3,128	3.2
Maryland	25,074	569,328	4.4
Massachusetts	27,108	221,279	12.3
Michigan	62,785	1,199,023	5.2
Minnesota	6,230	53,344	11.7
Mississippi	9,731	887,206	1.1
Missouri	50,625	514,276	9.8
Montana	55	1,786	3.1
Nebraska	1,255	48,390	2.6
Nevada	1,800	50,999	3.5
New Hampshire	250	3,990	6.3
New Jersey	25,433	925,066	2.7
New Mexico	770	25,276	3.0
New York	205,500	2,401,974	8.6
North Carolina	4,684	1,318,857	.4
North Dakota	175	2,568	6.8
Ohio	20,754	1,076,748	1.9
Oklahoma	9,000	204,674	4.4
Oregon	3,025	37,060	8.2
Pennsylvania	49,717	1,046,810	4.7
Rhode Island	2,758	27,584	10.0
South Carolina	7,000	948,623	.7
South Dakota	120	2,144	5.6
Tennessee	10,000	725,942	1.4
Texas	71,397	1,710,175	4.2
Utah	200	9,225	2.2
Vermont	53	1,135	4.7
Virginia	10,500	1,008,668	1.0
Washington	4,812	105,574	4.6
West Virginia	700	65,051	1.1
Wisconsin	15,093	182,592	8.3
Wyoming	100	3,364	3.0
TOTALS 1984	**1,294,103**	**26,495,023**	**4.9**
Totals 1975	916,854	22,549,815	4.0

the executive direction of Beverly Carroll. One of its objectives is the establishment of a network of black agencies, including the National Black Catholic Clergy Caucus, the National Black Sisters' Conference, National Black Catholic Administrators, Knights and Ladies of St. Peter Claver.

The committee and secretariat have offices at 1312 Massachusetts Ave. N.W., Washington, D.C. 20005.

Bishops

There were twelve black bishops in 1988: Archbishop Eugene A. Marino, S.S.J., of Atlanta, Bishop Joseph L. Howze of Biloxi, and Auxiliary Bishops Joseph A. Francis, S.V.D., of Newark, Harold R. Perry, S.V.D., of New Orleans, James P. Lyke, O.F.M., of Cleveland, Emerson Moore of New York, Moses Anderson of Detroit, Wilton D. Gregory of Chicago, J. Terry Steib, S.V.D., of St. Louis, John H. Ricard, S.S.J., of Baltimore, Carl Fisher, S.S.J., of Los Angeles and Curtis J. Guillory of Galveston-Houston.

Josephite Pastoral Center

The Josephite Pastoral Center was established in September, 1968, as an educational and pastoral service agency for the Josephites in their mission work, specifically in the black community. St. Joseph's Society of the Sacred Heart, the sponsoring body, has about 185 priests and 20 brothers in 80 mostly southern parishes in 18 dioceses.

The staff of the center includes Father John G. Harfmann, S.S.J., director, and Maria M. Lannon, associate director. The center is located at St. Joseph Seminary, 1200 Varnum St. N.E., Washington, D.C. 20017.

Various dioceses have agencies like New York's Office of Black Ministry for pastoral and related service to the black community.

HISPANICS

The U.S. Census Bureau, reporting in September, 1987, estimated that, as of the previous March, the Hispanic population was 18.8 milion, a 4.3 million increase since the last census in 1980. The greatest growth and highest concentrations of Spanish speaking were in the Southwest, California, Illinois, New York and Florida. Most of the Hispanics were from Central and South America. The number of undocumented aliens was variously estimated from two to four million.

Most persons of Hispanic origin in the United States have been baptized in the Catholic Church and comprise, probably, between 25 and 30 per cent of the Catholic population.

Bishops

As of August, 1988, there were 20 bishops of Hispanic origin in the United States; all were named since 1970 (for biographies, see Index). Eight were heads of archdioceses or dioceses: Archbishops Robert F. Sanchez (Santa Fe) and Patrick F. Flores (San Antonio); Bishops Raymundo J. Pena (El Paso), Ricardo Ramirez, C.S.B. (Las Cruces), Rene H. Gracida (Corpus Christi), Joseph J. Madera (Fresno), Arthur N. Tafoya (Pueblo) and Manuel D. Moreno (Tucson). Twelve were auxiliary bishops: Juan Arzube and Armando Ochoa (Los Angeles), Gilbert Espinoza Chavez (San Diego), Alphonse Gallegos, O.A.R. (Sacramento), Francisco Garmendia (New York), Agustin Roman (Miami), Rene Valero (Brooklyn), David Arias, O.A.R. (Newark), Placido Rodriguez, C.M.F. (Chicago), Alvaro Corrada del Rio, S.J. (Washington, D.C.), Enrique San Pedro, S.J. (Galveston-Houston) and Roberto O. Gonzalez, O.F.M. (Boston).

Hispanic priests and nuns in the U.S. number about 1,600 and 2,000, respectively, according to an estimate made in June, 1988, by Father Gary Riebe Estrella, S.V.D., director of a Hispanic vocational recruitment program.

Pastoral ministry to Hispanics varies, depending on differences among the people and the availability of personnel to carry it out.

Pastoral Patterns

The pattern in cities with large numbers of Spanish-speaking is built around special and bilingual churches, centers or other agencies where pastoral and additional forms of service are provided in a manner suited to the needs, language and culture of the people. Services in some places are extensive and include legal advice, job placement, language instruction, recreational and social assistance, specialized counseling, replacement services. In many places, however, even where there are special ministries, the needs are generally greater than the means required to meet them.

Some of the urban dwellers have been absorbed into established parishes and routines of church life and activity. Many Spanish-speaking communities, especially those with migrants, remain in need of special ministries.

An itinerant form of ministry best meets the needs of the thousands of migrant workers who follow the crops.

Special ministries for the Spanish-speaking have been in operation for a long time in dioceses of the Southwest. The total number of dioceses with such ministries is more than 108.

Pastoral ministry to Hispanics was the central concern of three national meetings, *Encuentros,* held in 1972, 1977 and 1985. In line with recommendations emanating from these meetings, particular emphasis has since been focused on five general areas: evangelization, education, leadership development, youth ministry and social justice.

The U.S. bishops, at their annual meeting in November, 1983, approved and subsequently published a pastoral letter on Hispanic Ministry under the title, "The Hispanic Presence: Challenge and Commitment." (For text, see pp. 46-49 of the 1985 *Catholic Almanac.*)

Secretariat for Hispanic Affairs

The national secretariat was established by the U.S. Catholic Conference for service in promoting and coordinating pastoral ministry to the Spanish-speaking. Its basic orientation is toward integral evangelization, combining religious ministry with development efforts in programs geared to the culture and needs of Hispanics. Its concerns are urban and migrant Spanish-speaking people; communications and publications in line with secretariat purposes and the service of people; bilingual and bicultural religious and general education; liaison for and representation of Hispanics with church, civic and governmental agencies.

The secretariat publishes a bimonthly newsletter, *En Marcha,* available on request to interested parties.

Paul Sedillo, Jr., is director of the national office at 1312 Massachusetts Ave. N.W., Wasington, D.C. 20005.

The secretariat has working relationships with regional offices in the Northeast, Southeast, Midwest, Southwest, Far West, Northwest and Mountain States. Each office shares the objectives of the secretariat. In addition, the Northeast, Southeast and Midwest offices have established pastoral institutes for formation, training and program development.

The Northeast regional office, officially the Northeast Hispanic Catholic Center, was established in 1976 and is supported by bishops in 14 states from Maine to Virginia. The office consists of professional staff members in the fields of pastoral work, communications, evangelization, research, development and publications. It has established the Conference of Diocesan Directors of the Hispanic Apostolate, Association of Hispanic Deacons, Regional Youth Task Force and a regional committee of Diocesan Coordinators of Religious Educators for the Hispanics. The executive director is Mario J. Paredes. The center is located at 1011 First Ave., New York, N.Y. 10022.

The Southeast regional office serves 25 dioceses in Tennessee, North and South Carolina, Florida, Georgia, Mississippi, Alabama and Louisiana. Its South East Pastoral Institute offers an academic degree in pastoral ministry, reaches out to communities throughout the region with its Evangelization Mobile Team and distributes audio-visual and print resources for Hispanic ministry. Father Mario Vizcaino, Sch. P., is director of the region and institute. The office is located at 2900 S.W. 87th Ave., Miami, Fla. 33265.

Five states of the Midwest (Ohio, Indiana, Illinois, Michigan, Wisconsin) are served by a Midwest Hispanic Catholic Commission. The executive director of the commission is Olga Villa Parra. The mailing address is P.O. Box 703 (Holy Cross Annex), Notre Dame, Ind. 46556.

In the Southwest, a regional office serving Arkansas, Oklahoma, and Texas was being reorganized in 1987; reopening was scheduled for 1988.

A regional office serving the Mountain States (Arizona, New Mexico, Utah, Colorado and Wyoming) is under the direction of Mr. Primitivo Romero, office for Hispanic Affairs, 400 E. Monroe, Phoenix, Ariz. 85004.

California and Nevada are served by the Far West office, which is a component of the California Catholic Conference. The regional director is Father Ricardo A. Chavez. The office is located at 1010 11th St., Suite 200, Sacramento Calif. 95814.

A regional office serving the northwestern corner of the U.S. is under the direction of Sister Dolorita Martinez, O.P. Its Mobile Pastoral Institute, under the direction of Mr. Alejandro Aguilera, has outreach to communities in Idaho, Montana, Oregon, Washington and Alaska. The office is located at 5301-F Tieton Dr., Yakima, Wash. 98908.

PADRES

In the Southwest, 55 Mexican-American priests organized PADRES in February, 1970, to help the Church identify more closely with the pastoral, social, economic and educational needs of the Spanish-speaking. The present membership exceeds 500, mainly in California, Texas, New Mexico and on the East Coast. PADRES is an acronym for the Spanish title, "Padres Asociados para Derechos Religiosos, Educativos y Sociales."

Leadership development of Hispanos is one of the principal concerns of PADRES, now a national organization with membership open to priests, brothers and deacons working in Hispanic ministry. Seminarians and others interested in working with the Hispanic community are eligible for honorary membership. Father Ramon Gaitan, O.A.R., is the national president. The office is located at 2216 E. 108th St., Los Angeles, Calif. 90059.

(Two other organizations of priests are *La Asociacion de Sacerdotes Hispanos* in New York and Miami.)

Mexican American Cultural Center

This national center, specializing in pastoral studies and language education, was founded in 1972 to provide programs focused on ministry among Hispanics and personnel working with Hispanics in the U.S. and Latin America. Courses — developed according to the see-judge-act methodology — include culture, faith development, Scripture, theology, and praxis; some are offered in Spanish, others in English. Intensive language classes are offered in Spanish and English as second languages, with emphasis on pastoral usage.

The center also conducts workshops for the development of leadership skills. Faculty members serve as resource personnel for pastoral centers, dioceses and parishes throughout the U.S. The center offers master-degree programs in pastoral ministry in cooperation with Incarnate Word College, San Antonio, and Boston College. Participants attending summer study weeks can obtain a *Certificado de Pastoralista.*

A National Resource Center for Hispanic Ministry has information available on personnel and resources for the Hispanic apostolate, as well as a distribution center for the circulation of pastoral materials in the U.S. and Latin America.

Father Rosendo Urrabazo, C.M.F., is president of the center which is located at 3019 W. French Place, San Antonio, Tex. 78228.

RELIGIOUS

Institutes of Consecrated Life

Religious orders and congregations are special societies in the Church — institutes of consecrated life — whose members, called Religious, commit themselves, by public vows to observance of the evangelical counsels of poverty, chastity and obedience in a community kind of life in accordance with rules and constitutions approved by church authority.

Secular institutes (covered in its own Almanac entry) are also institutes of consecrated life.

The particular goal of each institute and the means of realizing it in practice are stated in the rule and constitutions proper to the institute. Local bishops can give approval for rules and constitutions of institutes of diocesan rank. Pontifical rank belongs to institutes approved by the Holy See. General jurisdiction over all Religious is exercised by the Congregation for Religious and Secular Institutes. General legislation concerning Religious is contained in Canons 573 to 709 in Book II, Part III, of the Code of Canon Law.

All institutes of consecrated life are commonly called religious orders, despite the fact that there are differences between orders and congregations. The best known orders include the Benedictines, Trappists, Franciscans, Dominicans, Carmelites and Augustinians, for men; and the Carmelites, Benedictines, Poor Clares, Dominicans of the Second Order and Visitation Nuns, for women. The orders are older than the congregations, which did not appear until the 16th century.

Contemplative institutes are oriented to divine worship and service within the confines of their communities, by prayer, penitential practices, other spiritual activities and self-supporting work. Examples are the Trappists and Carthusians, the Carmelite and Poor Clare nuns. Active institutes are geared for pastoral ministry and various kinds of apostolic work. Mixed institutes combine elements of the contemplative and active ways of life. While most institutes of men and women can be classified as active, all of them have contemplative aspects.

Clerical communities of men are those whose membership is predominantly composed of priests.

Non-clerical or lay institutes of men are the various brotherhoods.

Societies of Apostolic Life

Some of the institutes of men listed below have a special kind of status because their members, while living a common life like that which is characteristic of Religious, do not profess the vows of Religious. Examples are the Maryknoll Fathers, the Oratorians of St. Philip Neri, the Paulists and Sulpicians. They are called societies of apostolic life and are the subject of Canons 731 to 746 in the Code of Canon Law.

RELIGIOUS INSTITUTES OF MEN IN THE UNITED STATES

(Sources: *Official Catholic Directory;* Catholic Almanac survey.)

Africa, Missionaries of (M. Afr.): Founded 1868 at Algiers by Cardinal Charles M. Lavigerie; known as White Fathers until 1984. Generalate, Rome Italy; U.S. headquarters, 1624 21st St. N.W., Washington, D.C. 20009. Missionary work in Africa.

African Missions, Society of, S.M.A.: Founded 1856, at Lyons, France, by Bishop Melchior de Marion Brésillac. Generalate, Rome, Italy; American provincialate, 23 Bliss Ave., Tenafly, N.J. 07670. Missionary work.

Assumptionists (Augustinians of the Assumption), AA.: Founded 1845, at Nimes, France, by Rev. Emmanuel d'Alzon; in U.S., 1946. General house, Rome, Italy; U.S. province, 328 Adams St., Milton, Mass. 02186. Educational, parochial, ecumenical, retreat, foreign mission work.

Atonement, Franciscan Friars of the, S.A.: Founded as an Anglican Franciscan community in 1898 at Garrison, N.Y., by Rev. Paul Wattson. Community corporately received into the Catholic Church in 1909. Motherhouse, St. Paul Friary, Graymoor, Garrison N.Y. 10524. Ecumenical, mission, retreat and charitable works.

Augustinian Recollects, O.A.R.: Founded 1588: in U.S., 1944. General motherhouse, Rome, Italy. Missionary, parochial, education work.

St. Augustine Province (1944), 29 Ridgeway Ave., W. Orange, N.J. 07052.

St. Nicholas Province (Madrid): U.S. Delegate, 2800 Schurz Ave., Bronx, N.Y. 10465.

Augustinians (Order of St. Augustine), O.S.A.: Established canonically in 1256 by Pope Alexander IV; in U.S., 1796. General motherhouse, Rome, Italy.

St. Thomas of Villanova Province (1796), P.O. Box 338, Villanova, Pa. 19085.

Our Mother of Good Counsel Province (1941), Tolentine Center, 20300 Governors Hwy., Olympia Fields, Ill. 60461.

St. Augustine Province (1969), 1605 28th St., San Diego, Calif. 92102.

Good Counsel Vice-Province, St. Augustine Preparatory School, Richland, N.J. 08350.

U.S. Address of King City, Ont., Canada, Province: 3103 Arlington Ave., Bronx, N.Y. 10463.

U.S. Vicariate of Castile, Spain, Province (1963), Vicar, 3648-61st St., Port Arthur, Tex. 77642.

Barnabites (Clerics Regular of St. Paul), C.R.S.P.: Founded 1530, in Milan, Italy, by St. Anthony M. Zaccaria; in U.S., 1952. Historical motherhouse, Church of St. Barnabas (Milan). Generalate, Rome, Italy; North American province, 1023 Swann Rd., Youngstown, N.Y. 14174. Parochial, educational, mission work.

Basil the Great, Order of St. (Basilian Order of

St. Josaphat), O.S.B.M.: General motherhouse, Rome, Italy; U.S. province, 31-12 30th St., Long Island City, N.Y. 11106. Parochial work among Byzantine Ukrainian Rite Catholics.

Basilian Fathers (Congregation of the Priests of St. Basil), C.S.B.: Founded 1822, at Annonay, France. General motherhouse, 20 Humewood Dr., Toronto, Ont. M6C 2W2, Canada. Educational, parochial work.

Basilian Salvatorian Fathers: Founded 1684, at Saida, Lebanon, by Eftimios Saifi; in U.S., 1953. General motherhouse, Saida, Lebanon; American headquarters, 30 East St., Methuen, Mass. 01844. Educational, parochial work among Eastern Rite peoples.

Benedictine Monks (Order of St. Benedict), O.S.B.: Founded 529, in Italy, by St. Benedict of Nursia; in U.S., 1846.
• American Cassinese Congregation (1855). Pres., Rt. Rev. John Eidenschink, O.S.B., Chaplain, Mother of Mèrcy Nursing Home, Albany, Minn. 56307. Abbeys and Priories belonging to the congregation:
St. Vincent Archabbey, Latrobe, Pa. 15650; St. John's Abbey, Collegeville, Minn. 56321; St. Benedict's Abbey, Atchison, Kans. 66002; St. Mary's Abbey, Delbarton, Morristown, N.J. 07960; Newark Abbey, 528 Dr. Martin Luther King, Jr., Blvd., Newark, N.J. 07102; Belmont Abbey, Belmont, N.C. 28012; St. Bernard Abbey, Cullman, Ala. 35055; St. Procopius Abbey, 5601 College Rd., Lisle, Ill. 60532; St. Gregory's Abbey, Shawnee, Okla. 74801; St. Leo Abbey, St. Leo, Fla. 33574; Assumption Abbey, Richardton, N. Dak. 58652;
St. Bede Abbey, Peru, Ill. 61354; St. Martin's Abbey, Lacey, Wash. 98503; Holy Cross Abbey, P.O. Box 351, Canon City, Colo. 81212; St. Anselm's Abbey, Manchester, N.H. 03102; St. Andrew's Abbey, 2900 Martin Luther King Dr., Cleveland, O. 44104; Holy Trinity Priory, P.O. Box 990, Butler, Pa. 16003; St. Maur Priory, 4615 N. Michigan Rd., Indianapolis, Ind. 46208; St. Mark's Priory, South Union, Ky. 42283; Benedictine Priory, 6502 Seawright Dr., Savannah, Ga. 31406; Woodside Priory, 302 Portola Rd., Portola Valley, Calif. 94025.
• Swiss-American Congregation (1870). Abbeys and priory belonging to the congregation:
St. Meinrad Archabbey, St. Meinrad, Ind. 47577; Conception Abbey, Conception, Mo. 64433; Mt. Michael Abbey, Elkhorn, Nebr. 68022; New Subiaco Abbey, Subiaco, Ark. 72865; St. Joseph's Abbey, St. Benedict, La. 70457; Mt. Angel Abbey, St. Benedict, Ore. 97373; Marmion Abbey, Butterfield Rd., Aurora, Ill. 60504;
St. Benedict's Abbey, Benet Lake, Wis. 53102; Glastonbury Abbey, 16 Hull St., Hingham, Mass. 02043; Westminster Abbey, Mission, B.C., Canada; St. Pius X Abbey, Columbia, Mo. 65203; Blue Cloud Abbey, Marvin, S. Dak. 57251; Corpus Christi Abbey, HCR2, Box 6300, Sandia, Tex. 78383; Prince of Peace Abbey, 650 Benet Hill Rd., Oceanside, Calif. 92054.
• English Benedictine Congregation: St. Anselm's Abbey, 4501 S. Dakota Ave. N.E., Washington, D.C. 20017; Abbey of St. Gregory, Cory's Lane, Portsmouth, R.I. 02871; Priory of St. Mary and St. Louis, 500 S. Mason Rd., St. Louis, Mo. 63141.
• Congregation of St. Ottilien for Foreign Missions, St. Paul's Abbey, Newton, N.J. 07860; Christ the King Priory, Schuyler, Neb. 68661.
• Congregation of the Annunciation, St. Andrew Priory, Valyermo, Calif. 93563.
• Houses not in Congregations: Mount Saviour Monastery, Pine City, N.Y. 14871; Conventual Priory of St. Gabriel the Archangel, Weston, Vt. 05161.

Benedictines, Olivetan, O.S.B.: General motherhouse, Siena, Italy. U.S. monasteries, Our Lady of Guadalupe Abbey, Pecos, N. Mex. 87552; Holy Trinity Monastery, P.O. Box 298, St. David, Ariz. 85630; Benedictine Monastery of Hawaii, P.O. Box 490, Waialua, Hawaii 96791; Monastery of the Risen Christ, P.O. Box 3931, San Luis Obispo, Calif. 93403.

Benedictines, Sylvestrine, O.S.B.: Founded 1231, in Italy by Sylvester Gozzolini. General motherhouse, Rome, Italy; U.S. foundations: 17320 Rosemont Rd., Detroit, Mich. 48219; 2711 E. Drahner Rd., Oxford, Mich. 48051; 1697 State Highway 3, Clifton, N.J. 07012.

Bethlehem Missionaries, Society of, S.M.B.: Founded 1921, at Immensee, Switzerland, by Rt. Rev. Canon Peter Bondolfi. General motherhouse, Immensee, Switzerland; U.S. headquarters, 5630 E. 17th Ave., Denver, Colo. 80220. Foreign mission work.

Blessed Sacrament, Congregation of the, S.S.S.: Founded 1856, at Paris, France, by St. Pierre Julien Eymard; in U.S., 1900. General motherhouse, Rome, Italy; U.S. province, 5384 Wilson Mills Rd., Cleveland, O. 44143. Eucharistic apostolate.

Brigittine Monks (Order of the Most Holy Savior), O.Ss.S.: Monastery of Our Lady of Consolation, 23300 Walker Lane, Amity, Ore. 97101.

Camaldolese Congregation, Cam. O.S.B.: Founded 1012, at Camaldoli, near Arezzo, Italy, by St. Romuald; in U.S. 1958. General motherhouse, Arezzo, Italy; U.S. foundation, Immaculate Heart Hermitage, Big Sur, Calif. 93920.

Camaldolese Hermits of the Congregation of Monte Corona, Er. Cam.: Founded 1520, from Camaldoli, Italy, by Bl. Paul Giustiniani. General motherhouse, Frascati (Rome), Italy; U.S. foundation, Holy Family Hermitage, Rt. 2, Box 36, Bloomingdale, O. 43910.

Camillian Fathers and Brothers (Order of St. Camillus; Order of Servants of the Sick), O.S.Cam.: Founded 1582, at Rome, by St. Camillus de Lellis; in U.S., 1923. General motherhouse, Rome, Italy; North American province, 10213 W. Wisconsin Ave., Wauwatosa, Wis. 53226.

Carmelites (Order of Our Lady of Mt. Carmel), O. Carm.: General motherhouse, Rome, Italy. Educational, charitable work.
Most Pure Heart of Mary Province (1864), 45 E. Dundee Rd., Barrington, Ill. 60010.
St. Elias Province (1931), P.O. Box 868, Middletown, N.Y. 10940.
Mt. Carmel Hermitage, Pineland, R.D. 1, Box

Men Religious

36, New Florence, Pa. 15944 (immediately subject to Prior General.)

Carmelites, Order of Discalced, O.C.D.: Established 1562, a Reform Order of Our Lady of Mt. Carmel; in U.S., 1924. Generalate, Rome, Italy. Spiritual direction, retreat, parochial work.

St. Therese of Oklahoma Province (1935), 1125 S. Walker St., P.O. Box 26127, Oklahoma City, Okla. 73126.

Immaculate Heart of Mary Province (1947), P.O. Box 67, Hubertus, Wis. 53033.

Western Province, Central Office, (1924), St. Therese Church, 510 N. El Molino St., Alhambra, Calif. 91801.

Polish Province of the Holy Spirit, 1628 Ridge Rd., Munster, Ind. 46321.

Carthusians, Order of, O. Cart.: Founded 1084, in France, by St. Bruno; in U.S., 1951. General motherhouse, St. Pierre de Chartreuse, France; U.S. charterhouse, Arlington, Vt. 05250. Cloistered contemplatives; semi-eremitic.

Charity, Servants of (Guanellians), S.C.: Founded 1908, in Italy, by Bl. Luigi Guanella. General motherhouse, Rome, Italy; U.S. headquarters, Don Guanella Seminary, 1779 S. Sproul Rd., Springfield, Pa. 19064.

Christ, Society of, S.Ch.: Founded 1932, General Motherhouse, Poznan, Poland; U.S.-Canadian Province, 3000 Eighteen Mile Rd., Sterling Heights, Mich. 48311.

Cistercians, Order of, O. Cist.: Founded 1098, by St. Robert. Headquarters, Rome, Italy.

Our Lady of Spring Bank Abbey, Rt. 3, Box 159, Sparta, Wis. 54656.

Our Lady of Dallas Monastery, 1 Cistercian Rd., Irving, Tex. 75039.

Cistercian Monastery of Our Lady of Fatima, Hainesport-Mt. Laurel Rd., Mt. Laurel, N.J. 08054.

Cistercian Conventual Priory, St. Mary's Priory, R.D. 1, Box 206, New Ringgold, Pa. 17960.

Cistercians of the Strict Observance, Order of (Trappists), O.C.S.O.: Founded 1098, in France, by St. Robert; in U.S., 1848. Generalate, Rome, Italy.

Our Lady of Gethsemani Abbey (1848), Trappist P.O., Ky. 40051.

Our Lady of New Melleray Abbey (1849), Dubuque, Iowa 52001.

St. Joseph's Abbey (1825), Spencer, Mass. 01562.

Holy Spirit Monastery (1944), 2625 Hwy. 212, Conyers, Ga. 30208.

Our Lady of Guadalupe Abbey (1947), Lafayette, Ore. 97127.

Our Lady of the Holy Trinity Abbey (1947), Huntsville, Utah 84317.

Abbey of the Genesee (1951), Piffard, N.Y. 14533.

Our Lady of Mepkin Abbey (1949), HC 69, Box 800, Moncks Corner, S. Car. 29461.

Our Lady of the Holy Cross Abbey (1950), Rt. 2, Box 3870, Berryville, Va. 22611.

Our Lady of the Assumption Abbey (1950), Rt. 5, Box 193, Ava, Mo. 65608.

Abbey of New Clairvaux (1955), Vina, Calif. 96092.

St. Benedict's Monastery (1956), 1012 Monastery Rd., Snowmass, Colo. 81654.

Claretians (Missionary Sons of the Immaculate Heart of Mary), C.M.F.: Founded 1849, at Vich, Spain, by St. Anthony Mary Claret. General headquarters, Rome, Italy. Missionary, parochial, educational, retreat work.

Western Province, 1414 Fair Oaks Ave., S. Pasadena, Calif. 91030.

Eastern Province, 400 N. Euclid Ave. Oak Park, Ill. 60302.

Clerics Regular Minor (Adorno Fathers) C.R.M.: Founded 1588, at Naples, Italy, by Ven. Augustine Adorno and St. Francis Caracciolo. General motherhouse, Rome, Italy; U.S. address, 575 Darlington Ave., Ramsey, N.J. 07446.

Columban, Society of St. (St. Columban Foreign Mission Society, S.S.C.): Founded 1918. General headquarters, Dublin, Ireland. U.S. headquarters, St. Columbans, Nebr. 68056. Foreign mission work.

Comboni Missionaries of the Heart of Jesus (Verona Fathers), M.C.C.J.: Founded 1867, in Italy by Bp. Daniele Comboni; in U.S., 1940. General motherhouse, Rome, Italy; North American headquarters, Comboni Mission Center, 8108 Beechmont Ave., Cincinnati, O. 45230. Mission work in Africa and the Americas.

Consolata Society for Foreign Missions, I.M.C.: Founded 1901, at Turin, Italy, by Father Joseph Allamano. General motherhouse, Rome, Italy; U.S. headquarters, P.O. Box 5550, Lincoln Hwy., Somerset, N.J. 08873.

Crosier Fathers (Canons Regular of the Order of the Holy Cross), O.S.C.: Founded 1210, in Belgium by Bl. Theodore De Celles. Generalate, Rome, Italy; U.S. Province of St. Odilia, 3204 E. 43rd St., Minneapolis, Minn. 55406. Mission, retreat, educational work.

Cross, Priests of the Congregation of Holy, C.S.C.: Founded 1837, in France; in U.S., 1841. Generalate, Rome, Italy. Educational and pastoral work; home missions and retreats; foreign missions; social services and apostolate of the press.

Indiana Province (1841), 1304 E. Jefferson Blvd., South Bend, Ind. 46617.

Eastern Province (1952), 835 Clinton Ave., Bridgeport, Conn. 06604.

Southern Province (1968), 2111 Brackenridge St., Austin, Tex. 78704.

Divine Word, Society of the, S.V.D.: Founded 1875, in Holland, by Bl. Arnold Janssen. North American Province founded 1897 with headquarters in Techny, Ill. General motherhouse, Rome, Italy.

Province of Bl. Joseph Freinademetz (Chicago Province) (1985, from merger of Eastern and Northern provinces), 1985 Waukegan Rd., Techny, Ill. 60082.

St. Augustine's Province (Southern Province) (1940), 201 Ruella Ave., Bay St. Louis, Miss. 39520.

St. Therese Province (Western Province) (1964), 2737 Pleasant Ave., Riverside, Calif. 92507.

Dominicans (Order of Friars Preachers), O.P.: Founded early 13th century by St. Dominic de Guzman. General headquarters, Santa Sabina,

Rome, Italy. Preaching, teaching, missions, research, parishes.

St. Joseph Province (1806), 869 Lexington Ave., New York, N.Y. 10021.

Holy Name of Jesus Province (1912), 5877 Birch Ct., Oakland, Calif. 94618.

St. Albert the Great Province (1939), 1909 S. Ashland Ave., Chicago, Ill. 60608.

Southern Dominican Province (1979), 3407 Napoleon Ave., New Orleans, La. 70125.

Spanish Province, U.S. foundation (1933), P.O. Box 279, San Diego, Tex. 78384.

Edmund, Society of St., S.S.E.: Founded 1843, in France, by Fr. Jean Baptiste Muard. General motherhouse, Edmundite Generalate, Fairholt, S. Prospect St., Burlington, Vt. 05401. Educational, missionary work.

Eudists (Congregation of Jesus and Mary), C.J.M.: Founded 1643, in France, by St. John Eudes. General motherhouse, Rome, Italy; North American province, 6125 Première Ave., Charlesbourg, Quebec G1H 2V9, Canada; U.S. community, 71 Burke Dr., Buffalo, N.Y. 14215. Parochial, educational, pastoral, missionary work.

Francis, Third Order Regular of St., T.O.R.: Founded 1221, in Italy; in U.S., 1910. General motherhouse, Rome, Italy. Educational, parochial, missionary work.

Most Sacred Heart of Jesus Province (1910), 601 Pitcairn Pl., Pittsburgh, Pa. 15232.

Immaculate Conception Province (1925), P.O. Box 29655, Brookland Sta., Washington, D.C. 20017.

Commissariat of the Spanish Province (1924), 301 Jefferson Ave., Waco, Tex. 76702.

Francis de Sales, Oblates of St., O.S.F.S.: Founded 1871, by Fr. Louis Brisson. General motherhouse, Rome, Italy. Educational, missionary, parochial work.

Wilmington-Philadelphia Province (1906), 2200 Kentmere Parkway, Box 1452, Wilmington, Del. 19899.

Toledo-Detroit Province (1966), Box 4683, Toledo, Ohio 43620.

Franciscans (Order of Friars Minor), O.F.M.: A family of the First Order of St. Francis (of Assisi) founded in 1209 and established as a separate jurisdiction in 1517; in U.S., 1844. General headquarters, Rome, Italy. English-speaking conference: 3140 Meramec St., St. Louis, Mo. 63118. Preaching, missionary, educational, parochial, charitable work.

St. John the Baptist Province (1844), 1615 Vine St., Cincinnati, Ohio 45210.

Sacred Heart Province (1858), 3140 Meramec St., St. Louis, Mo. 63118.

Assumption of the Blessed Virgin Mary Province (1887), Pulaski, Wis. 54162.

Most Holy Name of Jesus Province (1901), 135 W. 31st St., New York, N.Y. 10001.

St. Barbara Province (1915), 1500 34th Ave., Oakland, Calif. 94601.

Immaculate Conception Province (1855), 147 Thompson St., New York, N.Y. 10012.

Our Lady of Guadalupe Province (1985), Box 12315, Albuquerque, N.M. 87105.

Holy Cross Custody (1912), 1400 Main St., P.O. Box 608, Lemont, Ill. 60439.

Most Holy Savior Custody, 232 S. Home Ave., Pittsburgh, Pa. 15202.

St. John Capistran Custody (1928), 1290 Hornberger Ave., Roebling, N.J. 08554.

St. Stephen King, Transylvanian Custody (1948), 517 S. Belle Vista Ave., Youngstown, Ohio 44509.

Holy Family Croatian Custody, (1927), 4848 S. Ellis Ave., Chicago, Ill. 60615.

St. Casimir Lithuanian Vice-Province, P.O. Box 980, Kennebunkport, Me. 04046.

Holy Gospel Province (Mexico), U.S. foundation, 2400 Marr St., El Paso, Tex. 79903.

Saints Francis and James Province (Jalisco, Mexico), U.S. foundation, 504 E. Santa Clara St., Hebbronville, Tex. 78361.

Commissariat of the Holy Land, Mt. St. Sepulchre, 1400 Quincy St. N.E., Washington, D.C. 20017.

St. Mary of the Angels Custody, Byzantine Slavonic Rite, P.O. Box 270, Sybertsville, Pa. 18251.

Academy of American Franciscan History, P.O. Box 34440, West Bethesda, Md. 20817.

Franciscans (Order of Friars Minor Capuchin), O.F.M. Cap.: A family of the First Order of St. Francis (of Assisi) founded in 1209 and established as a separate jurisdiction in 1528. General motherhouse, Rome, Italy. Missionary, parochial work, chaplaincies.

St. Joseph Province (1857), 1740 Mt. Elliott Ave., Detroit, Mich. 48207.

St. Augustine Province (1873), 220 37th St., Pittsburgh, Pa. 15201.

St. Mary Province (1952), 30 Gedney Park Dr., White Plains, N.Y. 10605.

Province of the Stigmata (1918), P.O. Box 6279, Hoboken, N.J. 07030.

Western American Capuchin Province, Our Lady of the Angels, 453 Miller Ave., S., San Francisco, Calif. 94080.

Sts. Adalbert and Stanislaus Province (Warsaw, Poland), Manor Dr., Oak Ridge, N.J. 07438.

Province of Mid-America (1977), St. Elizabeth Friary, 1060 St. Francis Way, Denver, Colo. 80204.

Texas Capuchin Fraternity (Province of Navarre, Spain), 720 N. Blvd. Terr., Dallas, Tex. 75211.

Franciscans (Order of Friars Minor Conventual), O.F.M. Conv.: A family of the First Order of St. Francis (of Assisi) founded in 1209 and established as a separate jurisdiction in 1517; first U.S. foundation, 1852. General curia, Rome, Italy. Missionary, educational, parochial work.

Immaculate Conception Province (1852), P.O. Box 830, Union City, N.J. 07087.

St. Anthony of Padua Province (1906), 1300 Dundalk Ave., Baltimore, Md. 21222.

St. Bonaventure Province (1939), 6107 Kenmore Ave., Chicago, Ill. 60660.

Our Lady of Consolation Province (1926), Mt. St. Francis, Ind. 47146.

Our Lady of Guadalupe Custody (vice-province), Holy Cross Friary, P.O. Box 158, Mesilla Park, N.M. 88047.

St. Joseph of Cupertino Province (1981), P.O. Box 820, Arroyo Grande, Calif. 93420.

Men Religious

Glenmary Missioners (The Home Missioners of America): Founded 1939, in U.S. General headquarters, P.O. Box 465618, Cincinnati, Ohio 45246. Home mission work.

Holy Family, Congregation of the Missionaries of the, M.S.F.: Founded 1895, in Holland, by Rev. John P. Berthier. General motherhouse, Rome, Italy; U.S. provincial house, 10415 Midland Blvd., St. Louis, Mo. 63114. Belated vocations for the missions.

Holy Family, Sons of the, S.F.: Founded 1864, at Barcelona, Spain, by Bl. Jose Mañanet y Vives; in U.S., 1920. General motherhouse, Barcelona, Spain; U.S. address, 401 Randolph Rd., Silver Spring, Md. 20904.

Holy Ghost Fathers, C.S.Sp.: Founded 1703, in Paris, by Claude Francois Poullart des Places; in U.S., 1872. Generalate, Rome, Italy. Missions, education.

Eastern Province (1872), 6230 Brush Run Rd., Bethel Park, Pa. 15102.

Western Province (1968), 919 Briarcliff, San Antonio, Tex. 78213.

Holy Ghost Fathers of Ireland (1971), U.S. delegates: 4849 37th St., Long Island City, N.Y. 11101 (East); St. Cecilia Church, 2555 17th Ave., San Francisco, Calif. 94116. (West); St. John Baptist Church, 1139 Dryades St., New Orleans, La. 70113.

Holy Spirit, Missionaries of the, M.Sp.S.: Founded 1914, at Mexico City, Mexico, by Felix Rougier. General motherhouse, Mexico City; U.S. headquarters, Our Lady of Guadalupe, 500 N. Juanita Ave., Oxnard, Calif. 93030. Missionary work.

Jesuits (Society of Jesus), S.J.: Founded 1534, in France, by St. Ignatius of Loyola; received papal approval, 1540; first U.S. province, 1833. Generalate, Rome, Italy; U.S. national office, Jesuit Conference, 1424 16th St. N.W., Suite 300, Washington, D.C. 20036. Missionary, educational, literary work.

Maryland Province (1833), 5704 Roland Ave., Baltimore, Md. 21210.

New York Province (1943), 501 E. Fordham Rd., Bronx, N.Y. 10458.

Missouri Province (1863), 4511 W. Pine Blvd., St. Louis, Mo. 63108.

New Orleans Province (1907), 500 S. Jefferson Davis Pkwy., New Orleans, La. 70119.

California Province (1909), 300 College Ave., P.O. Box 519, Los Gatos, Calif. 95031.

New England Province (1926), 761 Harrison Ave., Boston, Mass. 02118.

Chicago Province, 2050 N. Clark St., Chicago, Ill. 60614.

Oregon Province (1932), 2222 N.W. Hoyt, Portland, Ore. 97210.

Detroit Province (1955), 7303 W. Seven Mile Rd., Detroit, Mich. 48221.

Wisconsin Province (1955), 1434 W. State St., Milwaukee, Wis. 53233.

Province of Mexico, U.S. address, P.O. Box 17950, El Paso, Tex. 79917.

Province of the Antilles (1947), U.S. address, 1339 S.W. 9 Terrace, Miami, Fla. 33184.

Joseph, Congregation of St., C.S.J.: General motherhouse, Rome, Italy; U.S. vice province, 12021 Mayfield Rd., Cleveland, O. 44106. Parochial, missionary, educational work.

Joseph, Oblates of St., O.S.J.: Founded 1878, in Italy, by Bishop Joseph Marello. General motherhouse, Rome, Italy. Parochial, educational work.

Eastern Province, Route 315, Pittston, Pa. 18640.

California Province, 1333-58th St., Sacramento, Calif. 95819.

Josephite Fathers, C.J.: General motherhouse, Ghent, Belgium; U.S. foundation, 989 Brookside Ave., Santa Maria, Calif. 93454.

Josephites (St. Joseph's Society of the Sacred Heart), S.S.J.: Founded 1866, in England, by Cardinal Vaughan; in U.S., 1871. General motherhouse, 1130 N. Calvert St., Baltimore, Md. 21202. Work in black missions.

LaSalette, Missionaries of Our Lady of, M.S.: Founded 1852, by Msgr. de Bruillard; in U.S., 1892. Motherhouse, Rome, Italy.

Our Lady of Seven Dolors Province (1934), P.O. Box 6127, Hartford, Conn. 06106.

Immaculate Heart of Mary Province (1945), P.O. Box 538, Attleboro, Mass. 02703.

Mary Queen Province (1958), 4650 S. Broadway, St. Louis, Mo. 63111.

Mary Queen of Peace Province (1967), 1607 E. Howard Ave., Milwaukee, Wis. 53207.

Lateran, Canons Regular of the, C.R.L.: General house, Rome, Italy; U.S. address: 2317 Washington Ave., Bronx, N.Y. 10458.

Legionaries of Christ, L.C.: Founded 1941, in Mexico, by Rev. Marcial Maciel; in U.S., 1965. General headquarters, Rome, Italy; U.S. novitiate, 475 Oak Ave., Cheshire, Conn. 06410.

Marian Fathers and Brothers, M.I.C.: Founded 1673; U.S. foundation, 1913. General motherhouse, Rome, Italy. Educational, parochial, mission, publication work.

St. Casimir Province (1913), 6336 S. Kilbourn Ave., Chicago, Ill. 60629.

St. Stanislaus Kostka Province (1948), Eden Hill, Stockbridge, Mass. 01262.

Marianists (Society of Mary; Brothers of Mary), S.M.: Founded 1817, at Bordeaux, France, by Rev. William-Joseph Chaminade; in U.S., 1849. General motherhouse, Rome, Italy. Educational work.

Cincinnati Province (1849), 4435 E. Patterson Rd., Dayton, Ohio 45430.

St. Louis Province (1908), 4538 Maryland Ave., St. Louis, Mo. 63156.

Pacific Province (1948), 22825 San Juan Rd., Cupertino, Calif. 95015.

New York Province (1961), 4301 Roland Ave., Baltimore, Md. 21210.

Province of Meribah (1976), 240 Emory Rd., Mineola, N.Y. 11501.

Mariannhill, Congregation of the Missionaries of, C.M.M.: Trappist monastery, begun in 1882 by Abbot Francis Pfanner in Natal, South Africa, became an independent modern congregation in 1909; in U.S., 1920. Generalate, Rome, Italy; U.S.-Canadian province (1938), Our Lady of Grace Monastery, 23715 Ann Arbor Trail, Dearborn Hts., Mich. 48127. Foreign mission work.

Marist Fathers (Society of Mary), S.M.: Founded 1816, at Lyons, France, by Jean Claude Colin; in

U.S., 1863. General motherhouse, Rome, Italy. Educational, foreign mission, pastoral work.

Washington Province (1924), 815 Varnum St., N.E., Washington D.C. 20017.

Northeast Province (1924), 15 Notre Dame Ave., Cambridge, Mass. 02140.

San Francisco Western Province (1962), 625 Pine St., San Francisco, Calif. 94108.

Maronite Monks (Cloistered Penitents of St. Francis), **O.P.C.:** Most Holy Trinity Monastery, Dugway Rd., Petersham, Mass. 01366.

Mary Immaculate, Oblates of, O.M.I.: Founded 1816, in France, by Bl. Charles Joseph Eugene de Mazenod; in U.S., 1849. General house, Rome, Italy. U.S. consulate, 707 Jefferson St., Oakland, Calif. 94607. Parochial, foreign mission, educational work; ministry to marginal.

Southern U.S. Province (1904), 334 W. Kings Hwy., San Antonio, Tex. 78212.

Our Lady of Hope, Eastern Province (1883), 350 Jamaicaway, Boston, Mass. 02130.

St. John the Baptist Province (1921), 45 Kenwood Ave., Worcester, Mass. 01605.

Central Province (1924), 267 E. 8th St., St. Paul, Minn. 55101.

Western Province (1953), 290 Lenox Ave., Oakland, Calif. 94610.

Maryknoll (Catholic Foreign Mission Society of America), M.M.: Founded 1911, in U.S., by Frs. Thomas F. Price and James A. Walsh. General Center, Maryknoll, N.Y. 10545.

Mekhitarist Order of Vienna, C.M.Vd.: Established 1773. General headquarters, Vienna, Austria. U.S. address, Our Lady Queen of Martyrs Church, 1327 Pleasant Ave., Los Angeles, Calif. 90033. Work among Armenians in U.S..

Mercedarians (Order of Our Lady of Mercy), O. de M.: Founded 1218, in Spain, by St. Peter Nolasco. General motherhouse, Rome, Italy; U.S. headquarters, 8692 Lake St., LeRoy, N.Y. 14482.

Mercy, Congregation of Priests of (Fathers of Mercy), C.P.M.: Founded 1808, in France, by Rev. Jean Baptiste Rauzan; in U.S., 1839. General mission house, Cold Spring, N.Y. 10516. Mission work.

Mill Hill Missionaries (St. Joseph's Society for Foreign Missions), M.H.M.: Founded 1866, in England, by Cardinal Vaughan; in U.S., 1951. International headquarters, London, England; American headquarters, 1377 Nepperhan Ave., Yonkers, N.Y. 10703.

Missionaries of St. Charles, Congregation of the, C.S.: Founded 1887, at Piacenza, Italy, by Bishop John Baptist Scalabrini. General motherhouse, Rome, Italy.

St. Charles Borromeo Province (1888), 27 Carmine St., New York, N.Y. 10014.

St. John Baptist Province (1903), 546 N. East Ave., Oak Park, Ill. 60302.

Missionaries of the Holy Apostles, M.Ss.A.: Founded 1962, Washington, D.C., by Very Rev. Eusebe M. Menard. North American headquarters, 33 Prospect Hill Rd., Cromwell, Conn. 06416.

Missionhurst — CICM (Congregation of the Immaculate Heart of Mary): Founded 1862, at Scheut, Brussels, Belgium, by Very Rev. Theophile Verbist. General motherhouse, Rome, Italy; U.S. province, 4651 N. 25th St., Arlington, Va. 22207. Home and foreign mission work.

Montfort Missionaries (Missionaries of the Company of Mary), S.M.M.: Founded 1715, by St. Louis Marie Grignon de Montfort; in U.S., 1948. General motherhouse, Rome, Italy; U.S. province, 101-18 104th St., Ozone Park, N.Y. 11416. Mission work.

Mother Co-Redemptrix, Congregation of, C.M.C.: Founded 1953 at Lein-Thuy, Vietnam (North), by Fr. Dominic Mary Tran Dinh Thu; in U.S., 1975. General house, Hochiminhville, Vietnam; U.S. provincial house, 1900 Grand Ave., Carthage, Mo. 64836. Work among Vietnamese Catholics in U.S.

Oblates of the Virgin Mary, O.M.V.: Founded 1815, in Italy. Generalate, Rome, Italy; U.S. address: St. Peter Chanel Rectory, 21611 Juan Ave., Hawaii Gardens, Calif. 90716.

Oratorians (Congregation of the Oratory of St. Philip Neri), C.O.: Founded 1575, at Rome, by St. Philip Neri. A confederation of autonomous houses. U.S. addresses: P.O. Box 11586, Rock Hill, S.C. 29731; P.O. Box 1688, Monterey, Calif. 93940; 4040 Bigelow Blvd., Pittsburgh, Pa. 15213; P.O. Drawer 11, Pharr, Tex. 78577.

Pallottines (Society of the Catholic Apostolate), S.A.C.: Founded 1835, at Rome, by St. Vincent Pallotti. Generalate, Rome, Italy. Charitable, educational, parochial, mission work.

Immaculate Conception Province (1953), P.O. Box 573, Pennsauken, N.J. 08110.

Mother of God Province (1946), 5424 W. Blue Mound Rd., Milwaukee, Wis. 53208.

Irish Province (1909), U.S. address: 3352 4th St., Wyandotte, Mich. 48192.

Queen of Apostles Province (1909), 448 E. 116th St., New York, N.Y. 10029.

Christ the King Province, 3452 Niagara Falls, Blvd., N. Tonawanda, N.Y. 14120.

Paraclete, Servants of the, s.P.: Founded 1947, Santa Fe, N.M., archdiocese. Generalate and U.S. motherhouse, Via Coeli, Jemez Springs, N.M. 87025. Devoted to care of priests.

Paris Foreign Missions Society, M.E.P.: Founded 1662, at Paris, France. Headquarters, Paris, France; U.S. establishment, 930 Ashbury St., San Francisco, Calif. 94117. Mission work and training of native clergy.

Passionists (Congregation of the Passion), C.P.: Founded 1720, in Italy, by St. Paul of the Cross. General motherhouse, Rome, Italy.

St. Paul of the Cross Province (Eastern Province) (1852), 80 David St., South River, N.J. 08882.

Holy Cross Province (Western Province), 5700 N. Harlem Ave., Chicago, Ill. 60631.

Patrick's Missionary Society, St., S.P.S.: Founded 1932, at Wicklow, Ireland, by Msgr. Patrick Whitney; in U.S., 1953. International headquarters, Kiltegan Co., Wicklow, Ireland. U.S. foundations: 70 Edgewater Rd., Cliffside Park, N.J. 07010; 19536 Eric Dr., Saratoga, Calif. 95070; 1347 W. Granville Ave., Chicago, Ill. 60660.

Pauline Fathers (Order of St. Paul the First Hermit), O.S.P.P.E.: Founded 1215; established in

U.S., 1955. General motherhouse, Czestochowa, Jasna Gora, Poland; U.S. province, P.O. Box 2049, Doylestown, Pa. 18901.

Pauline Fathers and Brothers (Society of St. Paul for the Apostolate of Communications), S.S.P.: Founded 1914, by Very Rev. James Alberione; in U.S., 1932. Motherhouse, Rome, Italy; American province (1932), 6746 Lake Shore Rd., Derby, N.Y. 14047. Social communications work.

Paulists (Missionary Society of St. Paul the Apostle), C.S.P.: Founded 1858, in New York, by Fr. Isaac Thomas Hecker. General offices, 86 Dromore Rd., Scarsdale, N.Y. 10583. Missionary, ecumenical, pastoral work.

Piarists (Order of the Pious Schools), Sch.P.: Founded 1617, at Rome, Italy, by St. Joseph Calasanctius. General motherhouse, Rome, Italy. American province, 4605 Bayview Dr., Fort Lauderdale, Fla. 33308. New York-Puerto Rico vice-province (Calasanzian Fathers), P.O. Box 29254, Rio Piedras, P.R. 00929. California delegation, 3951 Rogers St., Los Angeles, Calif. 90063. Educational work.

Pontifical Institute for Foreign Missions, P.I.M.E.: Founded 1850, in Italy, at request of Pope Pius IX. General motherhouse, Rome, Italy; U.S. headquarters, 17330 Quincy Ave., Detroit, Mich. 48221. Foreign mission work.

Precious Blood, Society of, C.Pp.S.: Founded 1815, in Italy, by St. Gaspar del Bufalo. General motherhouse, Rome, Italy.

Cincinnati Province, 431 E. Second St., Dayton, O. 45402.

Kansas City Province, Liberty, Mo. 64068.

Pacific Province, 1850 Church Lane, San Pablo, Calif. 94806.

Atlantic Province, 207 S. Garfield, E. Rochester, N.Y. 14445.

Premonstratensians (Order of the Canons Regular of Premontre; Norbertines), O. Praem.: Founded 1120, at Premontre, France, by St. Norbert. Generalate, Rome, Italy. Educational, parish work.

St. Norbert Abbey, 1016 N. Broadway, DePere, Wis. 54115.

Daylesford Abbey, 220 S. Valley Rd., Paoli, Pa. 19301.

St. Michael's Abbey, 1042 Star Route, Orange, Calif. 92667.

Providence, Sons of Divine, F.D.P.: Founded 1893, at Tortona, Italy, by Bl. Luigi Orione; in U.S., 1933. General motherhouse, Rome, Italy; U.S. address, 111 Orient Ave., E. Boston, Mass. 02128.

Redemptorists (Congregation of the Most Holy Redeemer), C.SS.R.: Founded 1732, in Italy, by St. Alphonsus Mary Liguori. Generalate, Rome, Italy. Mission work.

Baltimore Province (1850), 7509 Shore Rd., Brooklyn, N.Y. 11209.

St. Louis Province (1875), Box 6, Glenview, Ill. 60025.

Oakland Province (1952), 3696 Clay St., San Francisco, Calif. 94118.

New Orleans Vice-Province, 1527 3rd St., New Orleans, La., 70130.

Richmond Vice-Province, (1942), 313 Hillman St., P.O. Box 1558, New Smyrna Beach, Fla. 32070.

Resurrectionists (Congregation of the Resurrection), C.R.: Founded 1836, in France, under direction of Bogdan Janski. Motherhouse, Rome, Italy.

U.S. Province, 2250 N. Latrobe Ave., Chicago, Ill. 60639.

Ontario Kentucky Province, Resurrection College, Westmont Rd., N., Waterloo, Ont. N2L 3G7, Canada.

Rogationist Fathers, R.C.J.: Founded 1926. General motherhouse, Rome, Italy. U.S. addresses: P.O. Box 248, Mendota, Calif. 93640; P.O. Box 335, Sanger, Calif. 93657.

Rosminians (Institute of Charity), I.C.: Founded 1828, in Italy, by Antonio Rosmini-Serbati. General motherhouse, Rome, Italy; U.S. address, 2327 W. Heading Ave., Peoria, Ill. 61604. Charitable work.

Sacred Heart, Missionaries of the, M.S.C.: Founded 1854, by Rev. Jules Chevelier. General motherhouse, Rome, Italy; U.S. province, P.O. Box 270, Aurora, Ill. 60507.

Sacred Heart of Jesus, Congregation of the (Sacred Heart Fathers and Brothers), S.C.J.: Founded 1877, in France. General motherhouse, Rome, Italy; U.S. provincial office: P.O. Box 289, Hales Corners, Wis. 53130. Educational, preaching, mission work.

Sacred Hearts, Fathers of the (Picpus Fathers), SS.CC.: Founded 1805, in France, by Fr. Coudrin. General motherhouse, Rome, Italy. Mission, educational work.

Eastern Province (1946), 3 Adams St. (Box 111), Fairhaven, Mass. 02719.

Western Province (1970), 32481 Sage Rd., Hemet, Calif. 92343.

Hawaiian Province, Box 797, Kaneohe, Oahu, Hawaii 96744.

Sacred Hearts of Jesus and Mary, Missionaries of the, M.SS.CC.: Founded 1833, in Naples, Italy, by Ven. Cajetan Errico. General motherhouse, Rome, Italy; U.S. headquarters, 2249 Shore Rd., Linwood, N.J. 08221.

Salesians of St. John Bosco (Society of St. Francis de Sales), S.D.B.: Founded 1859, by St. John (Don) Bosco. Generalate, Rome, Italy.

St. Philip the Apostle Province (1902), 148 Main St., New Rochelle, N.Y. 10802.

San Francisco Province (1926), 1100 Franklin St., San Francisco, Calif. 94109.

Salvatorians (Society of the Divine Savior), S.D.S.: Founded 1881, in Rome, by Fr. Francis Jordan; in U.S., 1896. General headquarters, Rome, Italy; U.S. province, 1735 Hi-Mount Blvd., Milwaukee, Wis. 53208. Educational, parochial, mission work; campus ministries, chaplaincies.

Scalabrinians: See Missionaries of St. Charles, Congregation of the.

Servites (Order of Friar Servants of Mary), O.S.M.: Founded 1233, at Florence, Italy, by Seven Holy Founders. Generalate, Rome, Italy. General apostolic ministry.

Eastern Province (1967) 3401 S. Home Ave., Berwyn, Ill. 60402.

Western Province (1967), 5210 Somerset St., Buena Park, Calif. 90621.

Somascan Fathers, C.R.S.: Founded 1534, at Somasca, Italy, by St. Jerome Emiliani. General motherhouse, Rome, Italy; U.S. address, Pine Haven Boys Center, River Rd., P.O. 162, Suncook, N.H. 03275.

Sons of Mary Missionary Society (Sons of Mary, Health of the Sick), F.M.S.I.: Founded 1952, in the Boston archdiocese, by Rev. Edward F. Garesche, S.J. Headquarters, 567 Salem End Rd., Framingham, Mass. 01701. Dedicated to health of the sick; medical, catechetical and social work in home and foreign missions.

Stigmatine Fathers and Brothers (Congregation of the Sacred Stigmata), C.S.S.: Founded 1816, by Bl. Gaspare Bertoni. General motherhouse, Rome, Italy; North American Province, 554 Lexington St., Waltham, Mass. 02154. Parish work.

Sulpicians (Society of Priests of St. Sulpice), S.S.: Founded 1641, at Paris, by Rev. Jean Jacques Olier. General motherhouse, Paris, France; U.S. province, 5408 Roland Ave., Baltimore, Md. 21210. Education of seminarians and priests.

Theatines (Congregation of Clerics Regular): C.R.: Founded 1524, at Rome, by St. Cajetan. General motherhouse, Rome, Italy; U.S. headquarters, 1050 S. Birch St., Denver, Colo. 80222.

Trappists: See Cistercians of the Strict Observance.

Trinitarians (Order of the Most Holy Trinity), O.SS.T.: Founded 1198, by St. John of Matha; in U.S., 1911. General motherhouse, Rome, Italy; U.S. headquarters, P.O. Box 5719, Baltimore, Md. 21208.

Trinity Missions (Missionary Servants of the Most Holy Trinity), S.T.: Founded 1929, by Fr. Thomas Augustine Judge. Generalate, 1215 N. Scott St., Arlington, Va. 22209. Home mission work.

Viatorian Fathers (Clerics of St. Viator), C.S.V.: Founded 1831, in France, by Fr. Louis Joseph Querbes. General motherhouse, Rome, Italy. Province of Chicago (1882), 1212 E. Euclid St., Arlington Hts., Ill. 60004. Educational work.

Vincentians (Congregation of the Mission; Lazarists), C.M.: Founded 1625, in Paris, by St. Vincent de Paul; in U.S., 1818. General motherhouse, Rome, Italy. Educational work.

Eastern Province (1867), 500 E. Chelten Ave., Philadelphia, Pa. 19144.

Midwest Province (1888), 42 Henrietta Pl., St. Louis, Mo. 63104.

New England Province (1975), 1109 Prospect Ave., W. Hartford, Conn. 06105.

American Italian Branch, Our Lady of Pompei Church, 3600 Claremont St., Baltimore, Md. 21224.

American Spanish Branch (Barcelona, Spain), 234 Congress St., Brooklyn, N.Y. 11201.

American Spanish Branch (Zaragoza, Spain), Holy Agony Church, 1834 3rd Ave., New York, N.Y. 10029.

Western Province (1975), 650 W. 23rd St., Los Angeles, Calif. 90007.

Southern Province (1975), 1302 Kipling St., Houston, Tex. 77006.

Vocationist Fathers (Society of Divine Vocations), S.D.V.: Founded 1920, in Italy; in U.S., 1962. General motherhouse, Naples, Italy; U.S. address, 170 Broad St., Newark, N.J. 07104.

Xaverian Missionary Fathers, S.X.: Founded 1895, by Archbishop Conforti, at Parma, Italy. General motherhouse, Rome, Italy; U.S. province, 12 Helene Ct., Wayne, N.J. 07470. Foreign mission work.

INSTITUTES OF BROTHERS

Alexian Brothers, C.F.A.: Founded 14th century in western Germany and Belgium during the Black Plague. Motherhouse, Aachen, Germany; generalate, Signal Mountain, Tenn. 37377. Hospital and general health work.

Bethany, Brothers of: Founded in 1984. Holy Trinity Monastery, Dunhamtown Rd., Palmer, Mass. 01069.

Charity, Brothers of, F.C.: Founded 1807, in Belgium, by Canon Peter J. Triest. General motherhouse, Rome, Italy: American District (1963), Emeric House, 13 Wren Ct., Edison, N.J. 08820. Charitable, educational work.

Christian Brothers, Congregation of, C.F.C. (formerly Christian Brothers of Ireland): Founded 1802 at Waterford, Ireland, by Edmund Ignatius Rice. General motherhouse, Rome, Italy. Educational work.

American Province, Eastern U.S. (1916), 21 Pryer Terr., New Rochelle, N.Y. 10804. 354.

Brother Rice Province, Western U.S. (1966), 9237 S. Avalon Ave., Chicago, Ill. 60619.

Christian Instruction, Brothers of (La Mennais Brothers), F.I.C.: Founded 1817, at Ploermel, France, by Abbe Jean Marie de la Mennais and Abbe Gabriel Deshayes. General motherhouse, Rome, Italy; American province, Notre Dame Institute, Alfred, Me. 04002.

Christian Schools, Brothers of the (Christian Brothers), F.S.C.: Founded 1680, at Reims, France, by St. Jean Baptiste de la Salle. General motherhouse, Rome, Italy; U.S. Conference, 100 De La Salle Dr., Romeoville, Ill. 60441. Educational, charitable work.

Baltimore Province (1845), Box 29, Adamstown, Md. 21710.

Chicago Province (1966), 200 De La Salle Dr., Romeoville, Ill. 60441.

New York Province (1848), 820 Newman Springs Rd., Lincroft, N.J. 07738.

Long Island-New England Province (1957), Christian Brothers Center, 635 Ocean Ave., Narragansett, R.I. 02882.

St. Louis Province (1849), 2101 Rue de la Salle, Glencoe, Mo. 63038.

San Francisco Province (1868), P.O. Box A-D, Saint Mary's College, Moraga, Calif. 94575.

New Orleans-Santa Fe Province (1921), De La Salle Christian Brothers, 1522 Breaux Bridge Rd., Lafayette, La. 70501.

St. Paul-Minneapolis Province (1963), 807 Summit Ave., St. Paul, Minn. 55105.

Cross, Congregation of Holy, C.S.C.: Founded 1837, in France, by Rev. Basil Moreau; U.S. prov-

Men Religious

ince, 1841. Generalate, Rome, Italy. Educational, social work; missions.

Midwest Province (1841), Box 460, Notre Dame, Ind. 46556.

Southwest Province (1956), St. Edward's University, Austin, Tex. 78704.

Eastern Province (1956), 85 Overlook Circle, New Rochelle, N.Y. 10804.

Francis, Brothers of Poor of St., C.F.P.: Founded 1857. Motherhouse, Aachen, Germany; U.S. province, 105 Valley St., Burlington, Ia. 52601. Educational work, especially with poor and emotionally disturbed youth.

Francis Xavier, Brothers of St. (Xaverian Brothers), C.F.X.: Founded 1839, in Belgium, by Theodore J. Ryken. Generalate, Twickenham, Middlesex, England. Educational work.

Sacred Heart Province, 10516 Summit Ave., Kensington, Md. 20895.

St. Joseph Province, 704 Brush Hill Rd., Milton, Mass. 02186.

Franciscan Brothers of Brooklyn, O.S.F.: Founded in Ireland; established at Brooklyn, 1858. Generalate, 135 Remsen St., Brooklyn, N.Y. 11201. Educational work.

Franciscan Brothers of Christ the King, O.S.F.: Founded 1961. General motherhouse, 1401 Central Ave., Bettendorf, Iowa 52722.

Franciscan Brothers of the Good News, O.S.F.: Founded 1970 in Archdiocese of New York. Central hermitage, Mount Road, Cummington, Mass. 01026. Combine volunteer works of mercy with contemplative life of prayer in hermitages.

Franciscan Brothers of the Holy Cross, F.F.S.C.: Founded 1862, in Germany. Generalate, Hausen, Linz Rhein, West Germany; U.S. region, R.R. 1, Springfield, Ill. 62707. Educational work.

Franciscan Missionary Brothers of the Sacred Heart of Jesus, O.S.F.: Founded 1927, in the St. Louis, Mo., archdiocese. Motherhouse, R.R. 3, Box 39, Eureka, Mo. 63025. Care of aged, infirm, homeless men and boys.

Good Shepherd, Society of Brothers of the, B.G.S.: Founded 1951, by Bro. Mathias Barrett. Motherhouse, P.O. Box 389, Albuquerque, N.M. 87102. Operate shelters and refuges for aged and homeless; homes for handicapped men and boys, alcoholic rehabilitation center.

Holy Eucharist, Brothers of the, F.S.E.: Founded in U.S., 1957. Generalate, P.O. Box 25, Plaucheville, La. 71362. Teaching, social, clerical, nursing work.

Immaculate Heart of Mary, Brothers of the, F.I.C.M.: Founded 1948, at Steubenville, Ohio, by Bishop John K. Mussio. Motherhouse, Villa Maria, 609 N. 7th St., Steubenville, Ohio 43952. Educational, charitable work.

John of God, Brothers of the Hospitaller Order of St., O.H.: Founded 1537, in Spain. General motherhouse, Rome, Italy; American province, 2425 S. Western Ave., Los Angeles, Calif. 90018; Irish Province of Immaculate Conception, 532 Delsea Dr., Westville Grove, N.J. 08093. Nursing work and related fields.

Little Brothers of Jesus: Generalate, London, England; U.S. foundation, 2833 Cochrane, Detroit, Mich. 48216.

Little Brothers of St. Francis, L.B.S.F.: Founded 1970 in Archdiocese of Boston. General fraternity, 785-789 Parker St., Roxbury (Boston), Mass. 02120. Combine contemplative life with evangelical street ministry

Marist Brothers, F.M.S.: Founded 1817, in France, by Bl. Marcellin Champagnat. General motherhouse, Rome, Italy. Educational, social, catechetical work.

Esopus Province, 1241 Kennedy Blvd., Bayonne, N.J. 07002 (office).

Poughkeepsie Province, 252 School St., Watertown, Mass. 02172.

Mercy, Brothers of, F.M.M.: Founded 1856, in Germany. General motherhouse, Montabaur, Germany. American headquarters, 4520 Ransom Rd., Clarence, N.Y. 14031. Hospital work.

Mercy, Brothers of Our Lady of, C.F.M.M.: Founded 1844, in The Netherlands by Abp. J. Zwijsen. Generalate, Tilburg, The Netherlands; U.S. region, 7140 Ramsgate Ave., Los Angeles, Calif. 90045.

Patrician Brothers (Brothers of St. Patrick), F.S.P.: Founded 1808, in Ireland, by Bishop Daniel Delaney; U.S. novitiate, 7820 Bolsa Ave., Midway City, Calif. 92655. Educational work.

Pius X, Brothers of St.: Founded 1952, at La Crosse, Wis., by Bishop John P. Treacy. Motherhouse, 3710 East Ave. S., La Crosse, Wis. 54601. Education.

Presentation Brothers of Mary, F.P.M.: Founded 1802, at Waterford, Ireland, by Edmund Ignatius Rice. General motherhouse, Cork, Ireland. U.S. foundation (Canadian Province), 368 S. Ellsworth, Marshall, Mo. 65340.

Rosary, Brothers of the Holy, F.S.R.: Founded 1956, in U.S., Motherhouse and novitiate, 1725 S. McCarran Blvd., Reno, Nev. 89502.

Sacred Heart, Brothers of the, S.C.: Founded 1821, in France, by Rev. Andre Coindre. General motherhouse, Rome, Italy, Educational work.

New Orleans Province (1847), P.O. Box 89, Bay St. Louis, Miss. 39520.

New England Province (1945), R.R. 1, Box A51, Pascoag, R.I. 02859.

New York Province (1960), P.O. Box 68, Belvidere, N.J. 07823.

SEMINARY STUDY

Bishop John A. Marshall of Burlington reported in July, 1988, that a Vatican-commissioned study of 221 U.S. seminaries was nearly complete. A Vatican report on post-college seminaries said they were "basically good," with praise for seminary leadership, community life, liturgies, pastoral formation, attention to spiritual life and preparation for priestly celibacy. However, it was noted that in some seminaries there was confusion and even dissent with regard to authoritative teaching in moral theology, inadequate preparation of students in philosophy, a need for better recruitment of minority students, and lack of clarity about the distinctiveness of the priesthood.

MEMBERSHIP OF RELIGIOUS INSTITUTES OF MEN

(Principal source: *Annuario Pontificio.* Statistics as of Jan. 1, 1987, unless indicated otherwise.)

Listed below are world membership statistics of institutes of men of pontifical right with 500 or more members; the number of priests is in parentheses. Also listed are institutes with less than 500 members with houses in the United States.

Institute	Members
Jesuits (18,077)	26,236
Franciscans (Friars Minor) (13,385)	19,738
Salesians (10,904)	17,161
Franciscans (Capuchins) (8,150)	11,867
Benedictines (5,622)	9,293
Brothers of Christian Schools	9,045
Dominicans (5,123)	6,829
Redemptorists (5,633)	6,344
Marist Brothers	6,295
Oblates of Mary Immaculate (4,207)	5,688
Society of the Divine Word (3,408)	5,567
Franciscans (Conventuals) (2,639)	4,133
Vincentians (3,422)	3,808
Holy Spirit (Holy Ghost), Congregation (2,797)	3,597
Discalced Carmelites (2,333)	3,567
Augustinians (2,588)	3,311
Claretians (1,859)	2,936
Passionists (2,155)	2,796
Trappists (1,312)	2,762
Missionaries of Africa (2,355)	2,718
Priests of the Sacred Heart (1,862)	2,609
Missionaries of the Sacred Heart of Jesus (1,747)	2,483
Christian Brothers	2,456
Pallottines (1,503)	2,219
Carmelites (Ancient Observance) (1,500)	2,028
Holy Cross, Congregation (885)	1,965
Marianists (595)	1,926
Combonian Missionaries of the Heart of Jesus (1,310)	1,868
Brothers of the Sacred Heart (62)	1,750
Marists (1,447)	1,741
Hospitallers of St. John of God (134)	1,638
Piarists (1,240)	1,587
Carmelites of BVM (938)	1,531
Brothers of Christian Instruction of Ploermel (4)	1,516
Congregation of the Immaculate Heart of Mary (Missionhurst) (1,162)	1,490
Cistercians (Common Observance) (828)	1,391
Sacred Hearts, Congregation (Picpus) (1,121)	1,379
Brothers of Christian Instruction of St. Gabriel (32)	1,345
Premonstratensians (973)	1,329
Montfort Missionaries (959)	1,255
Salvatorians (809)	1,242
Society of African Missions (1,085)	1,200
Augustinians (Recollects) (882)	1,182
Society of St. Paul (554)	1,161
Blessed Sacrament, Congregation of (1985) (771)	1,133
Little Workers of Divine Providence (779)	1,130
Servants of Mary (848)	1,129
Assumptionists (880)	1,098
Ministers of Sick (Camillians) (648)	1,073
Missionaries of Holy Family (727)	1,048
Viatorians (418)	1,041
Consolata Missionaries (789)	993
Legionaries of Christ (193)	964
Xaverian Missionaries (685)	941
LaSalette Missionaries (629)	933
Franciscans (Third Order Regular)(587)	894
Canons Regular of St. Augustine (676)	868
Oblates of St. Francis de Sales (657)	857
Mill Hill Missionaries (735)	851
Columbans (774)	832
Maryknollers (702)	820
Brothers of Charity (Ghent)	787
Scalabrinians (603)	781
Mercedarians (524)	778
Congregation of St. Joseph (547)	732
Missionaries of the Most Precious Blood (550)	727
Pontifical Institute for Foreign Missions (567)	622
Missionaries of St. Francis de Sales of Annecy (328)	603
Trinitarians (397)	591
Brothers of the Immaculate Conception (5)	586
Crosier Fathers and Brothers (405)	545
Eudists (426)	544
Brothers of Our Lady Mother of Mercy	523
Servants of Charity (360)	521
Paris Foreign Mission Society (509)	511
Society of Christ (287)	494
Somascans (311)	485
Resurrection, Congregation of (338)	476
Oratorians (338)	461
Sulpicians (457)	457
Barnabites (339)	446
Marian Fathers and Brothers (222)	436
Oblates of St. Joseph (282)	432
St. Patrick's Mission Society (382)	430
Congr. of St. Basil (Canada) (395)	423
Stigmatine Fathers and Brothers (334)	420
Mariannhill Missionaries (242)	414
Rosminians (291)	403
Carthusians (205)	397
Xaverian Brothers	386
Order of St. Paul the First Hermit (151)	344
Missionaries of the Holy Spirit (238)	319
Order of St. Basil the Great (Basilians of St. Josaphat) (199)	307
Rogationists (188)	305
Bethlehem Missionaries (231)	294
Little Brothers of Jesus (74)	267
Paulists (228)	260
Vocationist Fathers (161)	212
Brothers of St. Patrick	211
Atonement Friars (126)	203
Josephites (St. Joseph's Society of the Sacred Heart—S.S.J.) (160)	186
Sons of the Holy Family (129)	177

Missionary Servants of the Most Holy
  Trinity (120) 167
Presentation Brothers 161
Alexian Brothers (2) 158
Theatines (98) 152
Josephites (C.J.) (107) 149
Basilian Salvatorian Fathers *(1977)* (84) 121
Bros. of Poor of St. Francis (4) 116
Glenmary Missioners (70) 109
Brothers of Mercy 93

Society of St. Edmund (77) 91
Camaldolese (30) 88
Congr. of Sacerdotal Fraternity (39) 75
Franciscan Bros. of Holy Cross (3) 68
Brothers of the Good Shepherd 62
Clerics Regular Minor (Adorno
  Fathers) (33) 38
Servants of Holy Paraclete *(1985)* (29) ... 35
Mekhitarist Order of Vienna (20) 22
Fathers of Mercy (6) 12

RELIGIOUS INSTITUTES OF WOMEN IN THE UNITED STATES

(Sources: *Official Catholic Directory;* Catholic Almanac survey.)

Adorers of the Blood of Christ, A.S.C.: Founded 1834, in Italy; in U.S., 1870. General motherhouse, Rome, Italy. U.S. provinces: Rt. 1, Box 115, Red Bud, Ill. 62278; 1400 South Sheridan, Wichita, Kans. 67213; Columbia, Pa. 17512. Education, retreats, social services, pastoral ministry.

Africa, Missionary Sisters of Our Lady of (Sisters of Africa), M.S.O.L.A.: Founded 1869, at Algiers, Algeria, by Cardinal Lavigerie; in U.S., 1929. General motherhouse, Frascati, Italy; U.S. headquarters, 5335 16th St., N.W., Washington, D.C. 20011. Medical, educational, catechetical and social work in Africa.

Agnes, Sisters of St., C.S.A.: Founded 1858, in U.S., by Caspar Rehrl. General motherhouse, 475 Gillett St., Fond du Lac, Wis. 54935. Education, health care, social services.

Ann, Sisters of St., S.S.A.: Founded 1834, in Italy; in U.S., 1952. General motherhouse, Rome, Italy; U.S. headquarters, Mount St. Ann, Ebensburg, Pa. 15931.

Anne, Sisters of St., S.S.A.: Founded 1850, at Vaudreuil, Que., Canada; in U.S., 1866. General motherhouse, Lachine, Que., Canada; U.S. address, 720 Boston Post Rd., Marlboro, Mass. 01752. Retreat work, pastoral ministry, religious education.

Anthony, Missionary Servants of St., M.S.S.A.: Founded 1929, in U.S., by Rev. Peter Baque. General motherhouse, 100 Peter Baque Rd., San Antonio, Tex. 78209. Social work.

Apostolate, Sisters Auxiliaries of the, S.A.A.: Founded 1903, in Canada; in U.S., 1911. General motherhouse, 689 Maple Terr., Monongah, W. Va. 26554. Education, nursing.

Assumption, Little Sisters of the, L.S.A.: Founded 1865, in France; in U.S., 1891. General motherhouse, Paris, France; U.S. provincialate, 214 E. 30th St., New York, N.Y. 10016. Social work, nursing, family life education.

Assumption, Religious of the, R.A.: Founded 1839, in France; in U.S., 1919. Generalate, Paris, France; North American province, 21 Otsego Rd., Worcester, Mass. 01609. Educational work.

Assumption of the Blessed Virgin, Sisters of the, S.A.S.V.: Founded 1853, in Canada; in U.S., 1891. General motherhouse, Nicolet, Que., Canada; U.S. province, 316 Lincoln St., Worcester, Mass. 01605. Education, mission, pastoral ministry.

Augustinian Cloistered Nuns, O.S.A.: Established in Spain in 13th century; U.S. foundation, Convent of Our Mother of Good Counsel, 4328 W. Westminster Pl., St. Louis, Mo. 63108.

Augustinian Sisters, Servants of Jesus and Mary, Congregation of, O.S.A.: Generalate, Rome, Italy; U.S. foundation, St. John School, Brandenburg, Ky. 40108.

Basil the Great, Sisters of the Order of St. (Byzantine Rite), O.S.B.M.: Founded fourth century, in Cappadocia, by St. Basil the Great and his sister St. Macrina; in U.S., 1911. Generalate, Rome, Italy; U.S. motherhouses: Philadelphia Ukrainian Byzantine Rite, 710 Fox Chase Rd., Philadelphia, Pa. 19111; Pittsburgh Ruthenian Byzantine Rite, Mount St. Macrina P.O. Box 878, Uniontown, Pa. 15401. Education, health care.

Benedict, Sisters of the Order of St., O.S.B.: Our Lady of Mount Caritas Monastery (founded 1979, Ashford, Conn.), Seckar Rd., Ashford, Conn. 06278. Contemplative.

Benedict, Sisters of the Order of St. (of the Congregation of Solesmes), O.S.B.: U.S. establishment, 1981, in Burlington diocese. Monastery of the Immaculate Heart of Mary, Westfield, Vt. 05874. Cloistered, papal enclosure.

Benedictine Nuns, O.S.B.: St. Scholastica Priory, Box 606, Petersham, Mass. 01366. Cloistered.

Benedictine Nuns of the Primitive Observance, O.S.B.; Founded c. 529, in Italy; in U.S., 1948. Abbey of Regina Laudis, Flanders Rd., Bethlehem, Conn. 06751. Cloistered.

Benedictine Sisters, O.S.B.: Founded c. 529, in Italy; in U.S., 1852. General motherhouse, Eichstatt, Bavaria, Germany. U.S. addresses: St. Vincent's Archabbey, Latrobe, Pa. 15650; St. Emma's Retreat House and Convent, 1001 Harvey St., Greensburg, Pa. 15601; St. Walburga Convent, 6717 S. Boulder Rd., Boulder, Colo. 80303.

Benedictine Sisters (Bedford, N.H.), **O.S.B.:** Founded 1627, in Lithuania as cloistered community; reformed 1918 as active community; established in U.S. 1957, by Mother M. Raphaela Simonis. Regina Pacis, 333 Wallace Rd., Bedford, N.H. 03102.

Benedictine Sisters, Missionary, O.S.B.: Founded 1885. Generalate, Rome, Italy; U.S. motherhouse, 300 N. 18th St., Norfolk, Nebr. 68701.

Benedictine Sisters, Olivetan, O.S.B.: Founded 1887, in U.S.. General motherhouse, Holy Angels Convent, P.O. Drawer 130, Jonesboro, Ark. 72403. Educational, hospital work.

Benedictine Sisters of Perpetual Adoration of Pontifical Jurisdiction, Congregation of the, O.S.B.: Founded in U.S., 1874, from Maria Rickenbach, Switzerland. General motherhouse, 8300 Morganford Rd., St. Louis, Mo. 63123.

Benedictine Sisters of Pontifical Jurisdiction, O.S.B.: Founded c. 529, in Italy. No general motherhouse in U.S.. Three federations.

• Federation of St. Scholastica (1922). Pres., Sister Johnette Putnam, O.S.B., St. Scholastica Priory, 238 Rio Vista, Jefferson, La. 70121. Motherhouses belonging to the federation:

Mt. St. Scholastica, Atchison, Kans. 66002; Benedictine Sisters of Elk Co., St. Joseph's Convent, St. Mary's, Pa. 15857; Mt. St. Benedict Priory, 6101 E. Lake Rd., Erie, Pa. 16511; Benedictine Sisters of Chicago, St. Scholastica Priory, 7430 Ridge Blvd., Chicago, Ill. 60645; Sacred Heart Priory, 1910 Maple Ave., Lisle, Ill. 60532; Our Lady of Sorrows belonging to the federation, 5900 W. 147th St., Oak Forest, Ill. 60452; St. Walburga Priory, 851 N. Broad St., Elizabeth, N.J. 07208; Benedictine Sisters, Mt. St. Mary Priory, 4530 Perrysville Ave., Pittsburgh, Pa. 15229;

Red Plains Priory, 1132 N.W. 32nd, Oklahoma City, Okla. 73118; St. Joseph's Convent, 2200 S. Lewis, Tulsa, Okla. 74114; St. Gertrude's Priory, Ridgely, Md. 21660; St. Walburga Monastery, Villa Madonna, 2500 Amsterdam Rd., Covington, Ky. 41016; Sacred Heart Convent, Cullman, Ala. 35056; St. Scholastica Priory, Box 1118, Covington, La. 70434; Holy Family Priory, Benet Lake, Wis. 53102; St. Benedict's Convent, Bristow, Va. 22013; St. Scholastica Convent, P.O. Box 700, Boerne, Tex. 78006; St. Lucy's Priory, Glendora, Calif. 91740; Holy Name Priory, St. Leo, Fla. 33574; Benet Hill Priory, 2555 N. Chelton Rd., Colorado Springs, Colo. 80909; Queen of Heaven Convent (Byzantine Rite), 8640 Squires Lane N.E., Warren, O. 44484; Emmanuel Monastery, 2229 W. Joppa Rd., Lutherville, Md. 21093.

• Federation of St. Gertrude the Great (1937). Pres., Sister Anselm Hammerling, O.S.B. Address: c/o Mount Saint Benedict Priory, 620 E. Summit Ave., Crookston, Minn. 56716. Motherhouses belonging to the federation:

Mother of God Priory, Watertown, S. Dak. 57201; Sacred Heart Convent, 1005 W. 8th St., Yankton, S. Dak. 57078; Mt. St. Benedict Convent, E. Summit Ave., Crookston, Minn. 56716; Sacred Heart Priory, Richardton, N. Dak. 58652; Convent of St. Martin, R.R. 4, Box 1660, Rapid City, S. Dak. 57702; Convent of the Immaculate Conception, 802 E. 10th St., Ferdinand, Ind. 47532; Priory of St. Gertrude, Cottonwood, Ida. 83522;

St. Benedict Priory, Fox Bluff, Box 5070, Madison, Wis. 53705; Queen of Angels Priory, 840 S. Main St., Mt. Angel, Ore. 97362; St. Scholastica's Convent, Albert Pike and Rogers Ave., Fort Smith, Ark. 72913; Our Lady of Peace Convent, 1511 Wilson, Columbia, Mo. 65201; Queen of Peace Priory, Belcourt, N. Dak. 58316. Convent of Our Lady of Grace, Beech Grove, Ind. 46107; Holy Spirit Monastery, 22791 Pico St., Grand Terrace, Calif. 92324.

• Federation of St. Benedict (1947). Pres., Sister Margaret Michaud, O.S.B., St. Bede Priory, P.O. Box 66, Eau Claire, Wis. 54702. Motherhouses belonging to the federation:

St. Benedict's Convent, St. Joseph, Minn. 56374; St. Scholastica Priory, Kenwood Ave., Duluth, Minn. 55811; St. Bede Priory, 1190 Priory Rd., Eau Claire, Wis. 54702; St. Mary Priory, Nauvoo, Ill. 62354; Annunciation Priory, 7520 University Dr., Bismarck, N. Dak. 58501; St. Paul's Priory, 2675 Larpenteur Ave. E., St. Paul, Minn. 55109; St. Placid Priory, 320 College St. N.E., Lacey, Wash. 98506.

Bethany, Sisters of, C.V.D.: Founded 1928, in El Salvador; in U.S. 1949. General motherhouse, Santa Tecla, El Salvador. U.S. address: 850 N. Hobart Blvd., Los Angeles, Calif. 90029.

Bethlemita Sisters, Daughters of the Sacred Heart of Jesus, S.C.I.F.: Founded 1861, in Guatemala. Motherhouse, Bogota, Colombia; U.S. address, St. Joseph Residence, 330 W. Pembroke St., Dallas, Tex. 75208.

Blessed Virgin Mary, Institute of the (Loreto Sisters), I.B.V.M.: Founded 17th century in Belgium; in U.S., 1954. Motherhouse, Rathfarnham, Dublin, Ireland; U.S. addresses: 6351 N. 27th Ave., Phoenix, Ariz. 85017; 810 Patrick Lane, Prescott, Ariz. 86301; 202 S. Kendrick, Flagstaff, Ariz. 86001.

Blessed Virgin Mary, Institute of the (Loretto Sisters), I.B.V.M.: Founded 1609, in Belgium; in U.S., 1880. U.S. address, Loretto Convent, Box 508, Wheaton, Ill. 60189. Educational work.

Bon Secours, Sisters of, C.B.S.: Founded 1824, in France; in U.S., 1881. Generalate, Rome, Italy; U.S. provincial house, Marriottsville Rd., Marriottsville, Md. 21104. Hospital work.

Brigid, Congregation of St., C.S.B.: Founded 1807, in Ireland; in U.S., 1953. U.S. regional house, 5118 Loma Linda Dr., San Antonio, Tex. 78201.

Brigittine Sisters (Order of the Most Holy Savior), O.SS.S.: Founded 1344, at Vadstena, Sweden, by St. Bridget; in U.S., 1957. General motherhouse, Rome, Italy; U.S. address, Vikingsborg, Runkenhage Rd., Darien, Conn. 06820.

Carmel, Congregation of Our Lady of Mount, O. Carm.: Founded 1825, in France; in U.S., 1833. Generalate, P.O. Box 476, Lacombe, La. 70445. Education, social services, pastoral ministry, retreat work.

Carmel, Institute of Our Lady of Mount, O. Carm.: Founded 1854, in Italy; in U.S., 1947. General motherhouse, Rome, Italy; U.S. novitiate, 5 Wheatland St., Peabody, Mass. 01960. Apostolic work.

Carmel Community, C.C.: Founded 1975, Columbus, O. Address, 100 Noe-Bixby Rd., Columbus, O. 43213. Contemplative.

Carmelite Missionaries of St. Theresa, C.M.S.T.: Founded 1903, in Mexico. General motherhouse, Mexico City, Mexico; U.S. foundation, 9548 Deertrail Dr., Houston, Tex. 70038.

Carmelite Nuns, Discalced, O.C.D.: Founded 1562, Spain. First foundation in U.S. in 1790, at Charles County, Md.; this monastery was moved to Baltimore. Monasteries in U.S. are listed below, according to states.

Alabama: 716 Dauphin Island Pkwy., Mobile 36606. Arkansas: 7201 W. 32nd St., Little Rock 72204. California: 215 E. Alhambra Rd., Alhambra

91801; 27601 Highway 1, Carmel 93923; 68 Rincon Rd., Kensington 94707; 3361 E. Ocean Blvd., Long Beach 90803; 6981 Teresian Way, Georgetown 95634; 5158 Hawley Blvd., San Diego 92116; 721 Parker Ave., San Francisco 94118; 530 Blackstone Dr., San Rafael 94903; 1000 Lincoln St., Santa Clara 95050. Colorado: 6138 S. Gallup St., Littleton 80120. Georgia: Coffee Bluff, 11 W. Back St., Savannah 31419; Illinois: River Rd. and Central, Des Plaines 60016. Indiana: 2500 Cold Springs Rd., Indianapolis 46222; 63 Allendale Pl., Terre Haute 47802. Iowa: Eldridge 52748; 2901 S. Cecilia St., Sioux City 51106. Kentucky: 1740 Newburg Rd., Louisville 40205. Louisiana: 1250 Carmel Ave., Lafayette 70507; 1611 Mirabeau Ave., New Orleans 70122. Maryland: 1318 Dulaney Valley Rd., Towson, Baltimore 21204; R.R. 4, Box 4035A, LaPlata, Md. 20646. Massachusetts: 61 Mt. Pleasant Ave., Roxbury, Boston 02119; 15 Mt. Carmel Rd., Danvers 01923; Sol-E-Mar Rd., S. Dartmouth 02748. Michigan: 16630 Wyoming Ave., Detroit 48221; 1036 Valley Ave. N.W., Grand Rapids 49504; U.S. 2 Highway, P.O. Box 397, Iron Mountain 49801; 3501 Silver Lake Rd., Traverse City 49684. Minnesota: 8251 De Montreville Trail N., Lake Elmo 55042. Mississippi: 2155 Terry Rd., Jackson 39204. Missouri: 2201 W. Main St., Jefferson City 65101; 9150 Clayton Rd., Ladue, St. Louis Co. 63124; 424 E. Republic Rd., Springfield 65807. Nevada: 1950 La Fond Dr., Reno 89509. New Hampshire: 275 Pleasant St., Concord, 03301. New Jersey: P.O. Box 785, Flemington 08822; 189 Madison Ave., Morristown 07960. New Mexico: Mt. Carmel Rd., Santa Fe 87501. New York: 745 St. John's Pl., Brooklyn 11216; 139 De Puyster Ave., Beacon 12508; 75 Carmel Rd., Buffalo 14214; 1931 W. Jefferson Rd., Pittsford 14534; 68 Franklin Ave., Saranac Lake 12983; 428 Duane Ave., Schenectady 12304. Ohio: 3176 Fairmount Blvd., Cleveland Heights 44118. Oklahoma: 20,000 N. County Line Rd., Piedmont 73078. Oregon: 87609 Green Hill Rd., Eugene 97402. Pennsylvania: Elysburg 17824; 510 E. Gore Rd., Erie 16509; R.D. 6, Box 28, Center Dr., Latrobe 15650; P.O. Box 57, Loretto 15940; 66th Ave. and Old York Rd. (Oak Lane), Philadelphia 19126; Byzantine Rite, R.D. No. 1, Box 245, Sugarloaf 18249. Rhode Island: Watson Ave. at Nayatt Rd., Barrington 02806. Texas: 600 Flowers Ave., Dallas 75211; 5801 Mt. Carmel Dr., Arlington 76017; 1100 Parthenon Pl., Roman Forest, New Caney 77357. 6301 Culebra and St. Joseph Way, San Antonio 78238. Utah: 5714 Holladay Blvd., Salt Lake City 84121. Vermont: Beckley Hill, Barre, 05641. Washington: 2215 N.E. 147th St., Seattle 98155. Wisconsin: W267 N2517 Meadowbrook Rd., Pewaukee 53072.

Carmelite Nuns of the Ancient Observance (Calced Carmelites), O. Carm.: Founded 1452, in The Netherlands; in U.S., 1930, from Naples, Italy, convent (founded 1856). U.S. monasteries: Carmelite Monastery of St. Therese, R.D. 3, Box 551, Coopersburg, Pa. 18036; Carmel of Mary, Wahpeton, N.D. 58075; Carmel of the Sacred Heart, 430 Laurel Ave., Hudson, Wis. 54016. Papal enclosure.

Carmelite Sisters (Corpus Christi), O. Carm.: Founded 1908, in England; in U.S., 1920. General motherhouse, Tunapuna, Trinidad, W.I. U.S. addresses: Carmelite Retreat House, 21 Battery St., Newport, R.I. 02840; Mt. Carmel Home, 412 W. 18th St., Kearney, Nebr. 68847. Home and foreign mission work.

Carmelite Sisters for the Aged and Infirm, O. Carm.: Founded 1929, at New York, by Mother M. Angeline Teresa, O. Carm. Motherhouse, Avila-on-Hudson, Germantown, N.Y. 12526. Social work, nursing and educating in the field of gerontology.

Carmelite Sisters of Charity, C.a.Ch.: Founded 1826 at Vich, Spain, by St. Joaquina de Vedruna. General motherhouse, Rome, Italy; U.S. address, 701 Beacon Rd., Silver Spring, Md. 20903.

Carmelite Sisters of St. Therese of the Infant Jesus, C.S.T.: Founded 1917, in U.S.. General motherhouse, 1300 Classen Dr., Oklahoma City, Okla. 73103. Educational work.

Carmelite Sisters of the Divine Heart of Jesus, D.C.J.: Founded 1891, in Germany; in U.S., 1912. General motherhouse, Sittard, Netherlands. U.S. provincial houses: 1230 Kavanaugh Pl., Milwaukee, Wis. 52313 (Northern Province); 10341 Manchester Rd., St. Louis, Mo. 63122 (Central Province); 8585 La Mesa Blvd., La Mesa, Calif. 92041 (South Western Province). Social services, mission work.

Carmelite Sisters of the Most Sacred Heart of Los Angeles, O.C.D.: Founded 1904, in Mexico. General motherhouse, Guadalajara, Mexico; U.S. provincialate and novitiate, 920 E. Alhambra Rd., Alhambra, Calif. 91801. Social services, retreat and educational work.

Casimir, Sisters of St., S.S.C.: Founded 1907, in U.S. by Mother Maria Kaupas. General motherhouse, 2601 W. Marquette Rd., Chicago, Ill. 60629. Education, missions, social services.

Cenacle, Congregation of Our Lady of the Retreat in the, R.C.: Founded 1826, in France; in U.S., 1892. Generalate, Rome, Italy. Eastern Province: 154-27 Horace Harding Expressway, Flushing, N.Y. 11367; Midwestern Province, 513 Fullerton Pkwy., Chicago, Ill. 60614.

Charity, Daughters of Divine, F.D.C.: Founded 1868, at Vienna, Austria; in U.S., 1913. General motherhouse, Rome, Italy. U.S. provinces: 205 Major Ave., Staten Island, N.Y. 10305; 39 N. Portage Path, Akron, O. 44303; 1315 N. Woodward Ave., Bloomfield Hills, Mich. 48013. Education, social services.

Charity, Little Missionary Sisters of, P.M.C.: Founded 1915, in Italy by Bl. Luigi Orione; in U.S., 1949. General motherhouse, Rome, Italy; U.S. address, 120 Orient Ave., East Boston, Mass. 02128.

Charity, Missionaries of, M.C.: Founded 1950, in Calcutta, India, by Mother Teresa; first U.S. foundation 1971. General motherhouse, 54A Acharya Jagadish C. Bose Road, Calcutta 16, India. U.S. address, 335 E. 145th St., Bronx, N.Y. 10451. Service of the poor.

Charity, Religious Sisters of, R.S.C.: Founded 1815, in Ireland; in U.S., 1953. Motherhouse, Dublin, Ireland; U.S. headquarters, Marycrest Manor, 10664 St. James Dr., Culver City, Calif. 90230.

Charity, Sisters of (of Seton Hill), S.C.: Founded 1870, at Altoona, Pa., from Cincinnati foundation. Administrative Offices, De Paul Center, Mt. Thor Rd., Greensburg, Pa. 15601. Educational, hospital, social, foreign mission work.

Charity, Sisters of (Grey Nuns of Montreal), S.G.M.: Founded 1737, in Canada by Bl. Marie Marguerite d'Youville; in U.S., 1855. General administration, Montreal, Que. H2Y 2L7, Canada; U.S. provincial house, 10 Pelham Rd., Lexington, Mass. 02173.

Charity, Sisters of (of Leavenworth), S.C.L.: Founded 1858, in U.S.. Motherhouse, 4200 S. 4th St., Leavenworth, Kans. 66048.

Charity, Sisters of (of Nazareth), S.C.N.: Founded 1812, in U.S.. General motherhouse, Nazareth P. O., Nelson Co., Ky. 40048.

Charity, Sisters of (of St. Augustine), C.S.A.: Founded 1851, at Cleveland, O. Motherhouse, 5232 Broadview Rd., Richfield, O. 44286.

Charity, Sisters of Christian, S.C.C.: Founded 1849, in Paderborn, Germany, by Bl. Pauline von Mallinckrodt; in U.S., 1873. General motherhouse, Rome, Italy. U.S. provinces: Mallinckrodt Convent, Mendham, N.J. 07945; Maria Immaculata Convent, 1041 Ridge Rd., Wilmette, Ill. 60091, Education, health services, other apostolic work.

Charity, Vincentian Sisters of, V.S.C.: Founded 1835, in Austria; in U.S., 1902. General motherhouse, 8200 McKnight Rd., Pittsburgh, Pa. 15237.

Charity, Vincentian Sisters of, V.S.C.: Founded 1928, at Bedford, O. General motherhouse, 1160 Broadway, Bedford, O. 44146.

Charity at Ottawa, Sisters of (Grey Nuns of the Cross), S.C.O.: Founded 1845, at Ottawa, Canada; in U.S., 1857. General motherhouse, Ottawa, Canada; U.S. provincial house, 975 Varnum Ave., Lowell, Mass. 01854. Educational, hospital work, extended health care.

Charity of Canossa, Daughters of, Canossian Sisters: Founded 1808 in Verona, Italy. General motherhouse, Rome, Italy; U.S. provincial house, 5625 Isleta Blvd. S.W., Albuquerque, N.M. 87105.

Charity of Cincinnati, Ohio, Sisters of, S.C.: Founded 1809; became independent community, 1852. General motherhouse, Mt. St. Joseph, Ohio 45051. Educational, hospital, social work.

Charity of Our Lady, Mother of Mercy, Sisters of, S.C.M.M.: Founded 1832, in Holland; in U.S., 1874. General motherhouse, Den Bosch, Netherlands; U.S. provincialate, 520 Thompson Ave., East Haven Conn. 06512.

Charity of Our Lady of Mercy, Sisters of, O.L.M.: Founded 1829, in Charleston, S.C. Generalate and motherhouse, 424 Fort Johnson Rd., James Island, Charleston, S.C. 29412. Education, campus ministry, social services.

Charity of Quebec, Sisters of (Grey Nuns), S.C.Q.: Founded 1849, at Quebec; in U.S., 1890. General motherhouse, 2655 rue Le Pelletier, Beauport, Quebec GIC 3X7, Canada; U.S. address, 359 Summer St., New Bedford, Mass. 02740. Social work.

Charity of St. Elizabeth, Sisters of (Convent, N.J.), S.C.: Founded 1859, at Newark, N. J. Generalate, Convent Station, N. J. 07961. Education, pastoral ministry, social services.

Charity of St. Hyacinthe, Sisters of (Grey Nuns), S.C.S.H.: Founded 1840, at St. Hyacinthe, Canada; in U.S., 1878. General motherhouse, 16470 Avenue Bourdages, SUD, St. Hyacinthe, Quebec J2T 4J8, Canada; U.S. regional house, 98 Campus Ave., Lewiston, Me. 04240.

Charity of St. Joan Antida, Sisters of, S.C.S.J.A.: Founded 1799, in France; in U.S., 1932. General motherhouse, Rome, Italy; U.S. provincial house, 8560 N. 76th Pl., Milwaukee, Wis. 53223.

Charity of St. Louis, Sisters of, S.C.S.L.: Founded 1803, in France; in U.S., 1910. Generalate, Rome, Italy; U.S. provincialate, 149 S. Catherine St., Plattsburgh, N.Y. 12901.

Charity of St. Vincent de Paul, Daughters of, D.C.: Founded 1633, in France; in U.S. 1809, at Emmitsburg, Md., by St. Elizabeth Ann Seton. General motherhouse, Paris, France. U.S. provinces: Emmitsburg, Md. 21727; 7800 Natural Bridge Rd., St. Louis, Mo. 63121; 9400 New Harmony Rd., Evansville, Ind. 47712; 96 Menands Rd., Albany, N.Y. 12204; 26000 Altamont Rd., Los Altos Hills, Calif. 94022.

Charity of St. Vincent de Paul, Sisters of, S.V.Z.: Founded 1845, in Croatia; in U.S., 1955. General motherhouse, Zagreb, Yugoslavia; U.S. foundation, 171 Knox Ave., West Seneca, N.Y. 14224.

Charity of St. Vincent de Paul, Sisters of, Halifax, S.C.H.: Founded 1856, at Halifax, N. S., from Emmitsburg, Md., foundation. Generalate, Mt. St. Vincent, Halifax, N. S., Canada. U.S. addresses: Commonwealth of Massachusetts, 125 Oakland St., Wellesley Hills, Mass. 02181; Boston Province, 26 Phipps St., Quincy, Mass. 02169; New York Province, 410 Grant Ave., Brooklyn, N.Y. 11208. Educational, hospital, social work.

Charity of St. Vincent de Paul, Sisters of, New York, S.C.: Founded 1817, from Emmitsburg, Md. General motherhouse, Mt. St. Vincent on Hudson, New York, N.Y. 10471. Educational, hospital work.

Charity of the Blessed Virgin Mary, Sisters of, B.V.M.: Founded 1833, in U.S. by Mary Frances Clarke. General motherhouse, Mt. Carmel, 1100 Carmel Dr., Dubuque, Ia. 52001. Education, pastoral ministry, social services.

Charity of the Immaculate Conception of Ivrea, Sisters of, S.C.I.C.: Founded 18th century, in Italy; in U.S., 1961. General motherhouse, Rome, Italy; U.S. address, Immaculate Virgin of Miracles Convent, R.D. 2, Box 348, Mt. Pleasant, Pa. 15666.

Charity of the Incarnate Word, Congregation of the Sisters of, C.C.V.I.: Founded 1869, at San Antonio, Tex., by Bishop C. M. Dubuis. Provincialate, 2128 Stone Moss Lane, Grapevine, Tex. 76051.

Charity of the Incarnate Word, Congregation of the Sisters of (Houston, Tex.), C.C.V.I.: Founded 1866, in U.S., by Bishop C. M. Dubuis. General motherhouse, 6510 Lawndale Ave., Houston, Tex. 77023. Educational, hospital, social work.

Charity of the Sacred Heart, Daughters of, F.C.S.C.J.: Founded 1823, at La Salle de Vihiers, France; in U.S., 1905. General motherhouse, La Salle de Vihiers, France; U.S. address, Sacred

Heart Province, Littleton, N.H. 03561.

Charles Borromeo, Missionary Sisters of St. (Scalabrini Srs.): Founded 1895, in Italy; in U.S., 1941. American novitiate, 1414 N. 37th Ave., Melrose Park, Ill. 60601.

Child Jesus, Sisters of the Poor, P.C.J.: Founded 1844, at Aix-la-Chapelle, Germany; in U.S., 1924. General motherhouse, Simpelveld, Netherlands, American provincialate, 4567 Olentangy River Rd., Columbus, O. 43214.

Chretienne, Sisters of Ste., S.S.CH.: Founded 1807, in France; in U.S., 1903. General motherhouse, Metz, France; U.S. provincial house, 297 Arnold St., Wrentham, Mass. 02093. Educational, hospital, mission work.

Christ the King, Sister Servants of, S.S.C.K.: Founded 1936, in U.S. General motherhouse, Loretto Convent, Mt. Calvary, Wis. 53057. Social services.

Christian Doctrine, Sisters of Our Lady of, R.C.D.: Founded 1910, in New York. Central office, 23 Haskell Ave., Suffern, N.Y. 10901.

Christian Education, Religious of, R.C.E.: Founded 1817, in France; in U.S., 1905. General motherhouse, Farnborough, England; U.S. provincial residence, 36 Hillcrest Rd., Belmont, Mass. 02178.

Church, Daughters of the: Founded in Italy; U.S. foundation, 1965. General house, Rome; U.S. address, 1029 Arosa Ave., Charlotte, N.C. 28203. Parish work, Spanish apostolate, teaching.

Cistercian Nuns, O. Cist.: Headquarters, Rome, Italy; U.S. address, Valley of Our Lady Monastery, E. 11096 Yanke Dr., Prairie du Sac, Wis. 53578.

Cistercian Nuns of the Strict Observance, Order of, O.C.S.O.: Founded 1125, in France, by St. Stephen Harding; in U.S., 1949. U.S. addresses: Mt. St. Mary's Abbey, 300 Arnold St., Wrentham, Mass. 02093; Our Lady of the Santa Rita Abbey, HCR 929, Sonoita, Ariz. 85637; Our Lady of the Redwoods Abbey, Whitethorn, Calif. 95489. Abbey of Our Lady of the Mississippi, R.R. 3, Dubuque, Ia. 52001; Our Lady of the Angels Monastery, Rt. 2, Box 288-A, Crozet, Va. 22932.

Clare, Sisters of St., O.S.C.: General motherhouse, Dublin, Ireland; U.S. foundation, St. Clare's Convent, 174 Tamarisk, Redlands, Calif. 92373.

Clergy, Congregation of Our Lady, Help of the, C.L.H.C.: Founded 1961, in U.S. Motherhouse, Maryvale Convent, Rt. 1, Box 164, Vale, N.C. 28168.

Clergy, Servants of Our Lady Queen of the, S.R.C.: Founded 1929, in Canada; in U.S., 1934. General motherhouse, 54, St. Jean, Rimouski, Que. G5L 1X1 Canada.

Colettines: See Franciscan Poor Clare Nuns.

Columban, Missionary Sisters of St., S.S.C.: Founded 1922, in Ireland; in U.S., 1930. General motherhouse, Wicklow, Ireland; U.S. region, 1250 W. Loyola Ave., Chicago, Ill. 60626.

Comboni Missionary Sisters (Missionary Sisters of Verona), C.M.S.: Founded 1872, in Italy; in U.S., 1950. U.S. address, 1307 S. Lakeside Ave., Richmond, Va. 23288.

Consolata Missionary Sisters, M.C.: Founded 1910, in Italy; in U.S., 1954. General motherhouse, Turin, Italy; U.S. headquarters, 6801 Belmont Rd., Belmont, Mich. 49306.

Cross, Daughters of the, D.C.: Founded 1640, in France; in U.S., 1855. General motherhouse, 1000 Fairview St., Shreveport, La. 71104. Educational work.

Cross, Daughters of, of Liege, F.C.: Founded 1833, in Liege, Belgium; in U.S., 1958. U.S. address, 165 W. Eaton Ave., Tracy, Calif. 95376.

Cross, Sisters, Lovers of the Holy (Phat Diem): Founded 1670, in Vietnam; in U.S. 1976. U.S. address, Holy Cross Convent, Mary Immaculate Seminary, 300 Cheryville Rd., Northampton, Pa. 18067.

Cross, Sisters of the Holy, C.S.C.: Founded 1841, at Le Mans, France, established 1847, in Canada; in U.S., 1881. General motherhouse, St. Laurent, Montreal, Que., Canada; U.S. provincial house, Fairview Rd., Pittsfield, N.H. 03263. Educational work.

Cross, Sisters of the Holy, Congregation of, C.S.C.: Founded 1841, at Le Mans, France; in U.S., 1843. General motherhouse, Saint Mary's, Notre Dame, Ind. 46556. Education, health care, social services, pastoral ministry.

Cross and Passion, Sisters of the (Passionist Sisters), C.P.: Founded 1852; in U.S., 1924. General motherhouse, Northampton, England; U.S. address: Holy Family Convent, One Wright Lane, N. Kingstown, R.I. 02852.

Cyril and Methodius, Sisters of Sts., SS.C.M.: Founded 1909, in U.S., by Rev. Matthew Jankola. General motherhouse, Danville, Pa. 17821. Education, care of aged.

Disciples of the Divine Master, Sister, P.D.D.M.: Founded 1924; in U.S., 1948. General motherhouse, Rome, Italy; U.S. headquarters, 60 Sunset Ave., Staten Island, N.Y. 10314.

Divine Compassion, Sisters of, R.D.C.: Founded 1886, in U.S. General motherhouse, 52 N. Broadway, White Plains, N.Y. 10603. Education, other ministries.

Divine Love, Sisters Oblates to, R.O.D.A.: Founded 1923, in Italy; in U.S., 1947. General motherhouse, Rome, Italy; U.S. provincial house, St. Clare's Convent, 1925 Hone Ave., Bronx, N.Y. 10461.

Divine Spirit, Congregation of the, C.D.S.: Founded 1956, in U.S., by Archbishop John M. Gannon. Motherhouse, 409 W. 6th St., Erie, Pa. 16507. Education, social services.

Dominicans

Nuns of the Order of Preachers (Dominican Nuns), O.P.: Founded 1206 by St. Dominic at Prouille, France. Cloistered, contemplative. Two branches in the United States:

• Dominican Nuns having perpetual adoration. First monastery established 1880, in Newark, N.J., from Oullins, France, foundation (1868). Seven autonomous monasteries.

St. Dominic, 375 13th Ave., Newark, N.J. 07103; Corpus Christi, 1230 Lafayette Ave., Bronx, N.Y. 10474; Blessed Sacrament, 29575 Middlebelt Rd., Farmington Hills, Mich. 48018; Holy Name, 3020

Erie Ave., Cincinnati, O. 45208; Monastery of the Angels, 1977 Carmen Ave., Los Angeles, Calif. 90068; Corpus Christi, 215 Oak Grove Ave., Menlo Park, Calif. 94025; Infant Jesus, 1501 Lotus Lane, Lufkin, Tex. 75901.

• Dominican Nuns devoted to the perpetual Rosary. First monastery established 1891, in Union City, N.J., from Calais, France, foundation (1880). Twelve autonomous monasteries (some also observe perpetual adoration).

Dominican Nuns of Perpetual Rosary, 14th and West Sts., Union City, N.J. 07087; 217 N. 68th St., Milwaukee, Wis. 53213; Perpetual Rosary, 1500 Haddon Ave., Camden, N.J. 08103; Our Lady of the Rosary, 335 Doat St., Buffalo, N.Y. 14211; Our Lady of the Rosary, 543 Springfield Ave., Summit, N.J. 07901; Mother of God, 1430 Riverdale St., W. Springfield, Mass. 01089; Perpetual Rosary, 802 Court St., Syracuse, N.Y. 13208; Immaculate Heart of Mary, 1834 Lititz Pike, Lancaster, Pa. 17601; Mary the Queen, 1310 W. Church St., Elmira, N.Y. 14905; St. Jude, Marbury, Ala. 36051; Our Lady of Grace, North Guilford, Conn. 06437; St. Dominic, 4901 16th St. N.W., Washington, D.C. 20011.

Dominican Rural Missionaries, O.P.: Founded 1932, in France; in U.S., 1951, at Abbeville, La. General motherhouse, Luzarches, France; U.S. address, 1318 S. Henry St., Abbeville, La. 70510.

Dominican Sisters of Bethany, Congregation, O.P.: Founded 1866, in France. Motherhouse, France; U.S. novitiate, 401 Lindell Ave., Leominster, Mass. 04153.

Dominican Sisters of Charity of the Presentation, O.P.: Founded 1684, in France; in U.S., 1906. General motherhouse, Tours, France; U.S. headquarters, 3012 Elm St., Dighton, Mass. 02715. Hospital work.

Dominican Sisters of Our Lady of the Rosary and of St. Catherine of Siena (Cabra): Founded 1644 in Ireland. General motherhouse, Cabra, Dublin, Ireland. U.S. regional house, 2943 St. Bernard Ave., New Orleans, La. 70119.

Dominican Sisters of the Roman Congregation of St. Dominic, O.P.: Founded 1621, in France; in U.S., 1904. General motherhouse, Rome, Italy; U.S. province, 2624 Fillmore St., Davenport, Ia. 52804. Educational work.

Eucharistic Missionaries of St. Dominic, O.P.: Founded 1927, in Louisiana. General motherhouse, 1101 Aline St., New Orleans, La. 70115. Parish work, social services.

Maryknoll Sisters of St. Dominic, M.M.: Founded 1912, in New York. Center, Maryknoll, N.Y. 10545.

Religious Missionaries of St. Dominic, O.P.: General motherhouse, Rome, Italy. U.S. foundations: Box 157, Alice, Texas 78332.

Sisters of St. Dominic, O.P.: Thirty congregations in the U.S. Educational, hospital work. Names of congregations are given below, followed by the date of foundation, and location of motherhouse.

St. Catharine of Siena, 1822. St. Catharine, Ky. 40061.

St. Mary of the Springs, 1830. Columbus Ohio 43219.

Most Holy Rosary, 1847. Sinsinawa, Wis. 53824.

Most Holy Name of Jesus, 1850. 1520 Grand Ave., San Rafael, Calif. 94901.

Holy Cross, 1853. Albany Ave., Amityville, N.Y. 11701.

Most Holy Rosary, 1859. Mt. St. Mary on Hudson, Newburgh, N.Y. 12550.

St. Cecilia, 1860. 801 Dominican Dr., Nashville, Tenn. 37208.

St. Mary, 1860. 580 Broadway, New Orleans, La. 70118.

St. Catherine of Siena, 1862. 5635 Erie St., Racine, Wis. 53402.

Our Lady of the Sacred Heart, 1873. 1237 W. Monroe St., Springfield, Ill. 62704.

Our Lady of the Rosary, 1876. Sparkill, N.Y. 10976.

Queen of the Holy Rosary, 1876. Mission San Jose, Calif. 94539.

Most Holy Rosary, 1892. 1257 Siena Heights Dr., Adrian, Mich. 49221.

Our Lady of the Sacred Heart, 1877. 2025 E. Fulton St., Grand Rapids, Mich. 49503.

St. Dominic, 1878. Blauvelt, N.Y. 10913.

Immaculate Conception (Dominican Sisters of the Sick Poor), 1879. Ossining, N.Y. 10562. Social work.

St. Catherine de Ricci, 1880. 2850 N. Providence Rd., Media, Pa. 19063.

Sacred Heart of Jesus, 1881. Mt. St. Dominic, Caldwell, N.J. 07006.

Sacred Heart, 1882. 6501 Almeda Rd., Houston, Tex. 77021.

St. Thomas Aquinas, 1888. 423 E. 152nd St., Tacoma, Wash. 98445.

Holy Cross, 1890. P.O. Box 280, Edmonds, Wash. 98020.

St. Catherine of Siena, 1891. 37 Park St., Fall River, Mass. 02721.

St. Rose of Lima (Servants of Relief for Incurable Cancer), 1896. Hawthorne, N.Y. 10532.

Immaculate Conception, 1902. 3600 Broadway, Great Bend, Kans. 67530.

St. Catherine of Siena, 1911. 4600 93rd St., Kenosha, Wis. 53140.

St. Rose of Lima, 1923. 775 Drahner Rd., Oxford, Mich. 48051.

Immaculate Conception, 1929. 9000 W. 81st St., Justice, Ill. 60458.

Immaculate Heart of Mary, 1929. Our Lady of the Elms Convent, Akron, Ohio 44313.

Immaculate Heart of Mary Province (Dominican Sisters of Spokane). W. 3102 Fort George Wright Dr., Spokane, Wash. 99204.

Dominican Sisters of Oakford (St. Catherine of Siena), 1889. Motherhouse, Oakford, Natal, South Africa. U.S. regional house, 1965. Villa Siena, 1855 Miramonte Ave., Mountain View, Calif. 94040.

(End, Listing of Dominicans)

Dorothy, Institute of the Sisters of St., S.S.D.: Founded 1834, in Italy; by St. Paola Frassinetti; in U.S., 1911. General motherhouse, Rome, Italy;

U.S. provincialate, Mt. St. Joseph, Ferry Rd., Bristol, R.I. 02809.

Eucharist, Religious of the, R.E.: Founded 1857, in Belgium; in U.S., 1900. General motherhouse, Belgium; U.S. foundation, 2907 Ellicott Terr., N.W., Washington, D.C. 20008.

Eucharistic Missionary Sisters, E.M.S.: Founded 1943, in Mexico. Motherhouse, 943 S. Soto St., Los Angeles, Calif. 90023.

Family, Congregation of the Sisters of the Holy, S.S.F.: Founded 1842, in U.S. General motherhouse, 6901 Chef Menteur Hwy., New Orleans, La. 70126. Educational, hospital work.

Family, Little Sisters of the Holy, P.S.S.F.: Founded 1880, in Canada; in U.S., 1900. General motherhouse, Sherbrooke, Que., Canada. U.S. novitiate, 285 Andover St., Lowell, Mass. 01852.

Family, Sisters of the Holy, S.H.F.: Founded 1872, in U.S. General motherhouse, P.O. Box 3248, Mission San Jose, Calif. 94539. Educational, social work.

Family of Nazareth, Sisters of the Holy, C.S.F.N.: Founded 1875, in Italy; in U.S., 1885. General motherhouse, Rome, Italy. U.S. provinces: 353 N. River Rd., Des Plaines, Ill. 60016; Grant and Torresdale Aves., Torresdale, Philadelphia, Pa. 19114; 285 Bellevue Rd., Pittsburgh, Pa. 15229; Marian Heights, 1428 Monroe Turnpike, Monroe, Conn. 06468; 1814 Egyptian Way, Box 530959, Grand Prairie, Tex. 75053.

Filippini, Religious Teachers, M.P.F.: Founded 1692, in Italy; in U.S., 1910. General motherhouse, Rome, Italy; U.S. provinces: St. Lucy Filippini Province, Villa Walsh, Morristown, N.J. 07960; Queen of Apostles Province, 474 East Rd., Bristol, Conn. 06010. Educational work.

Francis de Sales, Oblate Sisters of St., O.S.F.S.: Founded 1866, in France; in U.S., 1951. General motherhouse, Troyes, France; U.S. headquarters, Villa Aviat Convent, Childs, Md. 21916. Educational, social work.

Franciscans

Bernardine Sisters of the Third Order of St. Francis, O.S.F.: Founded 1457, at Cracow, Poland; in U.S., 1894. Generalate, 647 Spring Mill Rd., Villanova, Pa. 19085. Educational, hospital, social work.

Capuchin Sisters of St. Clare (Madres Clarisas Capuchinas): U.S. establishment, 1981, Amarillo diocese. Convent of the Blessed Sacrament and Our Lady of Guadalupe, 4201 N.E. 18th St., Amarillo, Tex. 79107. Cloistered.

Congregation of the Servants of the Holy Infancy of Jesus, O.S.F.: Founded 1855, in Germany; in U.S., 1929. General motherhouse, Wuerzburg, Germany; American motherhouse, Villa Maria, P.O. Box 708, North Plainfield, N.J. 07061.

Congregation of the Third Order of St. Francis of Mary Immaculate, O.S.F.: Founded 1865, in U.S., by Fr. Pamphilus da Magliano, O.F.M. General motherhouse, 520 Plainfield Ave., Joliet, Ill. 60435. Educational and pastoral work.

Daughters of St. Francis of Assisi, D.S.F.: Founded 1890, in Austria-Hungary; in U.S., 1946. Provincial motherhouse, 507 N. Prairie St., Lacon, Ill. 61540. Nursing, CCD work.

Felician Sisters (Congregation of the Sisters of St. Felix), C.S.S.F.: Founded 1855, in Poland; in U.S., 1874. General motherhouse, Rome, Italy. U.S. provinces: 36800 Schoolcraft Rd., Livonia, Mich. 48150; 600 Doat St., Buffalo, N.Y. 14211; 3800 Peterson Ave., Chicago, Ill. 60659; 260 South Main St., Lodi, N.J. 07644; 1500 Woodcrest Ave., Coraopolis, Pa. 15108; 1315 Enfield St., Enfield, Conn. 06082; 4210 Meadowlark Lane, S.E., Rio Rancho, N. Mex. 87174.

Franciscan Handmaids of the Most Pure Heart of Mary, F.H.M.: Founded 1917, in U.S.. General motherhouse, 15 W. 124th St., New York, N.Y. 10027. Educational, social work.

Franciscan Hospitaller Sisters of the Immaculate Conception, F.H.I.C.: Founded 1876, in Portugal; in U.S., 1960. General motherhouse, Lisbon, Portugal; U.S. novitiate, 300 S. 17th St., San Jose, Calif. 95112.

Franciscan Missionaries of Mary, F.M.M.: Founded 1877, in India; in U.S., 1904. General motherhouse, Rome, Italy; U.S. provincialate, 225 E. 45th St., New York, N.Y. 10017. Mission work.

Franciscan Missionaries of Our Lady, O.S.F.: Founded 1854, at Calais, France; in U.S., 1913. General motherhouse, Desvres, France; U.S. provincial house, 4200 Essen Lane, Baton Rouge, La. 70809. Hospital work.

Franciscan Missionaries of St. Joseph (Mill Hill Sisters), F.M.S.J.: Founded 1883, at Rochdale, Lancashire, England; in U.S., 1952. Generalate, Manchester, England; U.S. headquarters, Franciscan House, 1006 Madison Ave., Albany, N.Y. 12208.

Franciscan Missionary Sisters for Africa, O.S.F.: American foundation, 1953. Generalate, Ireland; U.S. headquarters, 172 Foster St., Brighton, Mass. 02135.

Franciscan Missionary Sisters of Assisi, F.M.S.A.: First foundation in U.S., 1961. General motherhouse, Assisi, Italy; U.S. address, St. Francis Convent, 1039 Northampton St., Holyoke, Mass. 01040.

Franciscan Missionary Sisters of Our Lady of Sorrows, O.S.F.: Founded 1939, in China, by Bishop Rafael Palazzi, O.F.M.; in U.S., 1949. U.S. address, 3600 S.W. 170th Ave., Beaverton, Ore. 97006. Educational, social, domestic, retreat and foreign mission work.

Franciscan Missionary Sisters of the Divine Child, F.M.D.C.: Founded 1927, at Buffalo, N.Y., by Bishop William Turner. General motherhouse, 6380 Main St., Williamsville, N.Y. 14221. Educational, social work.

Franciscan Missionary Sisters of the Immaculate Conception, O.S.F.: Founded 1874, in Mexico; in U.S., 1926. U.S. provincial house, 11306 Laurel Canyon Blvd., San Fernando, Calif. 91340.

Franciscan Missionaries of the Immaculate Heart of Mary, F.M.I.H.M.: Founded at Cairo, Egypt by Bl. Catarino di S. Rosa (Costanzo Troiano). Generalate, Rome, Italy; U.S. address, Ave Maria House, 3501 Good Intent Rd., Deptford, N.J. 08096.

Franciscan Missionary Sisters of the Infant Jesus, F.M.I.J.: Generalate, Rome, Italy. U.S. provincialate, 1215 Kresson Rd., Cherry Hill, N.J. 08003.

Franciscan Missionary Sisters of the Sacred Heart, F.M.S.C.: Founded 1860, in Italy; in U.S., 1865. Generalate, Rome, Italy; U.S. provincialate, 250 South St., Peekskill, N.Y. 10566. Educational and social welfare apostolates and specialized services.

Franciscan Poor Clare Nuns (Poor Clares, Order of St. Clare, Poor Clares of St. Colette), P.C., O.S.C., P.C.C.: Founded 1212, at Assisi, Italy, by St. Francis of Assisi; in U.S., 1875. Proto-monastery, Assisi, Italy. Addresses of autonomous motherhouses in U.S. are listed below.
3626 N. 65th Ave., Omaha, Nebr. 68104; 720 Henry Clay Ave., New Orleans, La. 70118; 6825 Nurrenbern Rd., Evansville, Ind. 47712; 1310 Dellwood Ave., Memphis Tenn. 38127; 920 Centre St., Jamaica Plain, Mass. 02130; 201 Crosswicks St., Bordentown, N.J. 08505; 1271 Langhorne-Newton Rd., Langhorne, Pa. 19047; 4419 N. Hawthorne St., Spokane, Wash. 99205; 142 Hollywood Ave., Bronx, N.Y. 10465; 421 S. 4th St., Sauk Rapids, Minn. 56379; 8650 Russell Ave. S., Minneapolis, Minn. 55431; 3501 Rocky River Dr., Cleveland, O. 44111;
89th and Kean Ave., Hickory Hills, Ill. 60457; 280 State Park Dr., Aptos, Calif. 95003; 2111 S. Main St., Rockford, Ill. 61102; 215 E. Los Olivos St., Santa Barbara, Calif. 93105; 460 River Rd., W. Andover, Mass. 01810; 809 E. 19th St., Roswell, N. Mex. 88201; 28210 Natoma Rd., Los Altos Hills, Calif. 94022; 1916 N. Pleasantburg Dr., Greenville, S.C. 29609; 28 Harpersville Rd., Newport News, Va. 23601; 1175 N. County Rd. 300 W., Kokomo, Ind. 46901; 4000 Sherwood Blvd., Delray Beach, Fla. 33445; 200 Marycrest Dr., St. Louis, Mo. 63129.

Franciscan Sisters, Daughters of the Sacred Hearts of Jesus and Mary, O.S.F.: Founded 1860, in Germany; in U.S., 1872. Generalate, Rome, Italy; U.S. motherhouse, P.O. Box 667, Wheaton, Ill. 60189. Educational, hospital, foreign mission, social work.

Franciscan Sisters of Allegany, N.Y., O.S.F.: Founded 1859, at Allegany, N.Y., by Fr. Pamphilus da Magliano, O.F.M. General motherhouse Allegany, N.Y. 14706. Educational, hospital, foreign mission work.

Franciscan Sisters of Baltimore, O.S.F.: Founded 1868, in England; in U.S., 1881. General motherhouse, 3725 Ellerslie Ave., Baltimore, Md. 21218. Educational work; social services.

Franciscan Sisters of Chicago, O.S.F.: Founded 1894, in U.S., by Mother Mary Therese (Josephine Dudzik). General motherhouse, 1220 Main St., Lemont, Ill. 60439. Educational work, social services.

Franciscan Sisters of Christian Charity, O.S.F.: Founded 1869, in U.S. Holy Family Convent, 2409 S. Alverno Rd., Manitowoc, Wis. 54220. Educational, hospital work.

Franciscan Sisters of Little Falls, Minn., O.S.F.: Founded 1891, in U.S. General motherhouse, Little Falls, Minn. 56345. Health, education, social services, pastoral ministry, mission work.

Franciscan Sisters of Mary: Established, 1987, through unification of the Sisters of St. Mary of the Third Order of St. Francis (founded 1872, St. Louis) and the Sisters of St. Francis of Maryville, Mo. (founded 1894). Address of general superior: 1100 Bellevue Ave., St. Louis, Mo. 63117. Health care, social services.

Franciscan Sisters of Mary Immaculate of the Third Order of St. Francis of Assisi, F.M.I.: Founded 16th century, in Switzerland; in U.S., 1932. General motherhouse, Bogota, Colombia; U.S. provincial house, 4301 N.E. 18th Ave., Amarillo, Tex. 79107. Education.

Franciscan Sisters of Our Lady of Perpetual Help, O.S.F.: Founded 1901, in U.S., from Joliet, Ill., foundation. General motherhouse, 201 Brotherton Lane, St. Louis, Mo. 63135. Educational, hospital work.

Franciscan Sisters of Peace, F.S.P.: Established 1986, in U.S., as archdiocesan community, from Franciscan Missionary Sisters of the Sacred Heart. Headquarters, 20 Ridge St., Haverstraw, N.Y. 10927.

Franciscan Sisters of Ringwood, F.S.R.: Founded 1927, at Passaic, N.J. General motherhouse, Mt. St. Francis, Ringwood, N.J. 07456. Educational work.

Franciscan Sisters of St. Elizabeth, F.S.S.E.: Founded 1866, at Naples, Italy; in U.S., 1919. General motherhouse, Rome; U.S. novitiate, 449 Park Rd., Parsippany, N.J. 07054. Educational work, social services.

Franciscan Sisters of St. Joseph, F.S.S.J.: Founded 1897, in U.S. General motherhouse, 5286 S. Park Ave., Hamburg, N.Y. 14075. Educational, hospital work.

Franciscan Sisters of St. Joseph (of Mexico): U.S. foundation, St. Paul College, 3015 4th St., Washington, D.C. 20017.

Franciscan Sisters of the Atonement, Third Order Regular of St. Francis (Graymoor Sisters), S.A.: Founded 1898, in U.S., as Anglican community; entered Church, 1909. General motherhouse, Graymoor, Garrison P.O., N.Y. 10524. Mission work.

Franciscan Sisters of the Blessed Virgin Mary of the Holy Angels, O.S.F.: Founded 1863, at Neuwied, Germany; in U.S., 1923. General motherhouse, Rhine, Germany; U.S. motherhouse, 1388 Prior Ave. S., St. Paul, Minn. 55116. Educational, hospital, social work.

Franciscan Sisters of the Immaculate Conception, O.S.F.: Founded in Germany; in U.S., 1928. General motherhouse, Kloster, Bonlanden, Germany; U.S. province, 291 W. North St., Buffalo, N.Y. 14201.

Franciscan Sisters of the Immaculate Conception, O.S.F.: Founded 1901, in U.S. General motherhouse, 1000 30th St., Rock Island, Ill. 61201. Health care.

Franciscan Sisters of the Immaculate Conception, Missionary, O.S.F.: Founded 1873, in U.S. General motherhouse, Rome, Italy; U.S. address, 790 Centre St., Newton, Mass. 02158. Educational work.

Franciscan Sisters of the Immaculate Conception and St. Joseph for the Dying, O.S.F.: Founded 1919, in U.S. General motherhouse, 485 Church St., Monterey, Calif. 93940.

Franciscan Sisters of the Poor, S.F.P.: Founded 1845, at Aachen, Germany, by Bl. Frances Schervier; in U.S., 1858. Community service center, 191 Joralemon St., Brooklyn, N.Y. 11201. Hospital, social work and foreign missions.

Franciscan Sisters of the Sacred Heart, O.S.F.: Founded 1866, in Germany; in U.S., 1876. General motherhouse, St. Francis Woods, R.R. 4, Mokena, Ill. 60448. Education, health care, other service ministries.

Hospital Sisters of the Third Order of St. Francis, O.S.F.: Founded 1844, in Germany; in U.S., 1875. General motherhouse, Muenster, Germany; U.S. motherhouse, Box 19431, Springfield, Ill. 62794. Hospital work.

Institute of the Franciscan Sisters of the Eucharist, F.S.E.: Founded 1973. Motherhouse, 405 Allen Ave., Meriden, Conn. 06450.

Little Franciscan Sisters of Mary, P.F.M.: Founded 1889, in U.S. General motherhouse, Baie St. Paul, Que., Canada. U.S. region, 55 Moore Ave., Worcester, Mass. 01602. Educational, hospital, social work.

Missionaries of the Third Order of St. Francis of Our Lady of the Prairies, O.L.P.: Founded 1960, in U.S. General motherhouse, Powers Lake, N.D. 58773.

Missionary Sisters of the Immaculate Conception of the Mother of God, S.M.I.C.: Founded 1910, in Brazil; in U.S., 1922, U.S. provincialate, P.O. Box 3026, Paterson, N.J. 07509. Mission, educational, health work, social services.

Mothers of the Helpless, M.D.: Founded 1873, in Spain; in U.S., 1916. General motherhouse, Valencia, Spain; U.S. address, Sacred Heart Residence, 432 W. 20th St., New York, N.Y. 10011.

Philip Neri Missionary Teachers, Sisters of St., R.F.: Founded 1858, in Spain; in U.S., 1956. General house, Madrid, Spain; U.S. address: Sisters of St. Philip Neri, St. Albert's Convent, 1259 St. Alberts St., Reno, Nev. 89503.

Poor Clares of Perpetual Adoration, P.C.P.A.: Founded 1854, at Paris, France; in U.S., 1921, at Cleveland, Ohio. U.S. monasteries: 4200 N. Market Ave., Canton, O. 44714; 2311 Timlin Rd., Portsmouth, O. 45662; 4108 Euclid Ave., Cleveland, O. 44103; 3900 13th St. N.E., Washington, D.C. 20017; 5817 Old Leeds Rd., Birmingham, Ala. 35210. Contemplative, cloistered, perpetual adoration.

School Sisters of St. Francis, O.S.F.: Founded 1874, in U.S. General motherhouse, 1501 S. Layton Blvd., Milwaukee, Wis. 53215.

School Sisters of St. Francis (Bethlehem, Pa.), O.S.F.: Founded in Austria, 1843; in U.S., 1913. General motherhouse, Rome, Italy; U.S. province, 395 Bridle Path Rd., Bethlehem, Pa. 18017. Educational, mission work.

School Sisters of St. Francis, (Pittsburgh, Pa.), O.S.F.: Established 1913, in U.S. Motherhouse, Mt. Assisi Convent, 934 Forest Ave., Pittsburgh, Pa. 15202. Education, health care services and related ministries.

School Sisters of the Third Order of St. Francis (Panhandle, Tex.), O.S.F.: Founded 1845, in Austria; in U.S., 1931. General motherhouse, Vienna, Austria; U.S. center and novitiate, Sancta Maria Convent, Panhandle, Tex. 79068. Educational, social work.

Sisters of Charity of Our Lady, Mother of the Church, S.C.M.C.: Established 1970, in U.S. Motherhouse, Baltic, Conn. 06330. Teaching, nursing, care of aged, and dependent children.

Sisters of Mercy of the Holy Cross, S.C.S.C.: Founded 1856, in Switzerland; in U.S. 1912. General motherhouse, Ingenbohl, Switzerland; U.S. provincial house, Holy Cross Convent, 5710 Elysian Fields Ave., New Orleans, La. 70122.

Sisters of Our Lady of Mercy (Mercedarians), S.O.L.M.: General motherhouse, Rome, Italy; U.S. addresses: Most Precious Blood, 133 27th Ave., Brooklyn, N.Y. 11214; St. Edward School, Pine Hill, N.J. 08021.

Sisters of St. Elizabeth, S.S.E.: Founded 1931, at Milwaukee, Wis. General motherhouse, 745 N. Brookfield Rd., Brookfield, Wis. 53005.

Sisters of St. Francis (Clinton, Iowa), O.S.F.: Founded 1868, in U.S. General motherhouse, Bluff Blvd. and Springdale Dr., Clinton, Ia. 57232. Educational, hospital, social work.

Sisters of St. Francis (Maryville, Mo.), O.S.F.: See Franciscan Sisters of Mary.

Sisters of St. Francis (Millvale, Pa.), O.S.F.: Founded 1865, Pittsburgh, Pa. General motherhouse, 146 Hawthorne Rd., Millvale P.O., Pittsburgh, Pa. 15209. Educational, hospital work.

Sisters of St. Francis (Hastings-on-Hudson), O.S.F.: Founded 1893, in New York. General motherhouse, Hastings-on-Hudson, N.Y. 10706. Education, parish ministry, social services.

Sisters of St. Francis of Christ the King, O.S.F.: Founded 1864, in Austria. General motherhouse, Rome, Italy; U.S. provincial house, 1600 Main St., Lemont, Ill. 60439. Educational work, home for aged.

Sisters of St. Francis of Penance and Christian Charity, O.S.F.: Founded 1835, in Holland; in U.S., 1874. General motherhouse, Rome, Italy. U.S. provinces: 4421 Lower River Rd., Stella Niagara, N.Y. 14144; 2851 W. 52nd Ave., Denver, Colo. 80221; 3910 Bret Harte Dr., P.O. Box 1028, Redwood City, Calif. 94064.

Sisters of St. Francis of Philadelphia, O.S.F.: Founded 1855, at Philadelphia, by Mother Mary Francis Bachmann and St. John N. Neumann. General motherhouse, Convent of Our Lady of the Angels, Glen Riddle-Aston, Pa. 19014. Education, health care, social services.

Sisters of St. Francis of Savannah, Mo., O.S.F.: Founded 1850, in Austria; in U.S., 1922. Provincial house, La Verna Heights, Savannah, Mo. 64485. Educational, hospital work.

Sisters of St. Francis of the Congregation of Our Lady of Lourdes, O.S.F.: Founded 1916, in U.S. General motherhouse, 6832 Convent Blvd., Sylvania, O. 43560. Education, health care, social services, pastoral ministry.

Sisters of St. Francis of the Holy Cross, O.S.F.: Founded 1881, in U.S., by Rev. Edward Daems, O.S.C. General motherhouse, 3025 Bay Settlement

Rd., Green Bay, Wis. 54301. Educational, nursing work, pastoral ministry, foreign missions.

Sisters of St. Francis of the Holy Eucharist, O.S.F.: Founded 1378, in Switzerland; in U.S., 1893. General motherhouse, 2100 N. Noland Rd., Independence, Mo. 64050. Education, health care, social services, foreign missions.

Sisters of St. Francis of the Holy Family, O.S.F.: U.S. foundation, 1875. Motherhouse, Mt. St. Francis, 3390 Windsor Ave., Dubuque, Ia. 52001. Varied apostolates.

Sisters of St. Francis of the Immaculate Conception, O.S.F.: Founded 1890, in U.S. General motherhouse, 2408 W. Heading Ave., Peoria, Ill. 61604. Education, care of aging, pastoral ministry.

Sisters of St. Francis of the Immaculate Heart of Mary, O.S.F.: Founded 1241, in Bavaria; in U.S., 1913. General motherhouse, Rome, Italy; U.S. motherhouse, Hankinson, N.D. 58041. Education, social services.

Sisters of St. Francis of the Martyr St. George, O.S.F.: Founded 1859, in Germany; in U.S., 1923. General motherhouse, Thuine, West Germany; U.S. provincial house, St. Francis Convent, 2120 Central Ave., Alton, Ill. 62002. Education, social services, foreign mission work.

Sisters of St. Francis of the Perpetual Adoration, O.S.F.: Founded 1863, in Germany; in U.S., 1875. General motherhouse, Olpe, Germany. U.S. provinces: Box 766, Mishawaka, Ind. 46544; P.O. Box 1060, Colorado Springs, Colo. 80901. Educational, hospital work.

Sisters of St. Francis of the Providence of God, O.S.F.: Founded 1922, in U.S., by Msgr. M. L. Krusas. General motherhouse, Grove and McRoberts Rds., Pittsburgh, Pa. 15234. Education, varied apostolates.

Sisters of St. Francis of the Third Order Regular, O.S.F.: Founded 1861, at Buffalo, N.Y., from Philadelphia foundation. General motherhouse, 400 Mill St., Williamsville, N.Y. 14221. Educational, hospital work.

Sisters of St. Joseph of the Third Order of St. Francis, S.S.J.: Founded 1901, in U.S. Administrative office, P.O. Box 688, South Bend, Ind. 46624. Education, health care, social services.

Sisters of St. Mary of the Third Order of St. Francis, S.S.M.: See Franciscan Sisters of Mary.

Sisters of the Infant Jesus, I.J.: Founded 1662, at Rouen, France; in U.S., 1950. Motherhouse, Paris, France. Generalate, Rome, Italy. U.S. address: 20 Reiner St., Colma, Calif. 94014.

Sisters of the Sorrowful Mother (Third Order of St. Francis), S.S.M.: Founded 1883, in Italy; in U.S., 1889. General motherhouse, Rome, Italy. U.S. provinces: 6618 N. Teutonia Ave., Milwaukee, Wis. 53209; 9 Pocono Rd., Denville, N.J. 07834; Tulsa Provincialate, 17600 E. 51st St. S., Broken Arrow, Okla. 74012. Educational, hospital work.

Sisters of the Third Franciscan Order, O.S.F.: Founded 1860, at Syracuse, N.Y. Generalate offices, 100 Michaels Ave., Syracuse, N.Y. 13208. Educational, hospital work.

Sisters of the Third Order of St. Francis, O.S.F.: Founded 1877, in U.S., by Bishop John L. Spalding. Motherhouse, Edgewood Hills, E. Peoria, Ill. 61611. Hospital work.

Sisters of the Third Order of St. Francis (Oldenburg, Ind.), O.S.F.: Founded 1851, in U.S. General motherhouse, Convent of the Immaculate Conception, Oldenburg, Ind. 47036. Education, social services, pastoral ministry, foreign missions.

Sisters of the Third Order of St. Francis of Assisi, O.S.F.: Founded 1849, in U.S. General motherhouse, 3221 S. Lake Dr., Milwaukee, Wis. 53207. Education, other ministries.

Sisters of the Third Order of St. Francis of Penance and Charity, O.S.F.: Founded 1869, in U.S., by Rev. Joseph Bihn. Motherhouse, St. Francis Convent, St. Francis Ave., Tiffin, O. 44883. Education, social services.

Sisters of the Third Order of St. Francis of the Perpetual Adoration, F.S.P.A.: Founded 1849, in U.S. Generalate, 912 Market St., La Crosse, Wis. 54601. Education, health care.

Sisters of the Third Order Regular of St. Francis of the Congregation of Our Lady of Lourdes, O.S.F.: Founded 1877, in U.S. General motherhouse, Assisi Heights, Rochester, Minn. 55901. Education, health care, social services.

(End, Listing of Franciscans)

Good Shepherd Sisters (Servants of the Immaculate Heart of Mary), S.C.I.M.: Founded 1850, in Canada; in U.S., 1882. General motherhouse, Quebec, Canada; Provincial House, Bay View, Saco, Maine 04072. Educational, social work.

Good Shepherd, Sisters of Our Lady of Charity of the, R.G.S.: Founded 1641, in France; in U.S., 1843. Generalate, Rome, Italy. U.S. provinces: 2849 Fischer Pl., Cincinnati, O. 45211; 82-31 Doncaster Pl., Jamaica, N.Y. 11432; 504 Hexton Hill Rd., Silver Spring, Md. 20904; 7654 Natural Bridge Rd., Normandy, Mo. 63121; 5100 Hodgson Rd., St. Paul, Minn. 55112.

Graymoor Sisters: See Franciscan Sisters of the Atonement.

Grey Nuns of the Sacred Heart, G.N.S.H.: Founded 1921, in U.S. General motherhouse, 1750 Quarry Rd., Yardley, Pa. 19067.

Guadalupe, Sisters of, O.L.G.: Founded 1946, in Mexico City. General motherhouse, Mexico City, Mexico; U.S. address, St. Mary's College, Winona, Minn. 55987.

Guardian Angel, Sisters of the Holy, S.A.C.: Founded 1839, in France. General motherhouse, Madrid, Spain; U.S. foundation, 1245 S. Van Ness, Los Angeles, Calif. 90019.

Handmaids of Mary Immaculate, A.M.I.: Founded 1952 in Helena, Mont. Address: Mountain View Rd., Washington, N.J. 07882.

Handmaids of the Precious Blood, Congregation of, H.P.B.: Founded 1947, at Jemez Springs, N.M. Motherhouse and novitiate, Cor Jesu Monastery, Jemez Springs, N.M. 87025.

Helpers, Society of, H.H.S.: Founded 1856, in France; in U.S., 1892. General motherhouse, Paris, France; American province, 303 W. Barry Ave., Chicago, Ill. 60657.

Hermanas Catequistas Guadalupanas, H.C.G.: Founded 1923, in Mexico; in U.S., 1950. General motherhouse, Mexico; U.S. foundation, 4110 S. Flores, San Antonio, Tex. 78214.

Hermanas Josefinas, H.J.: General motherhouse, Mexico; U.S. foundation, Assumption Seminary, 2600 W. Woodlawn Ave., P.O. Box 28240, San Antonio, Tex. 78284. Domestic work.

Hermit Sisters of Christ in Solitude: Hermitage of Christ the King, 6501 Orchard Station Road, Sebastopol, Calif. 95472.

Holy Child Jesus, Society of the, S.H.C.J.: Founded 1846, in England; in U.S., 1862. General motherhouse, Rome, Italy. U.S. province: 460 Shadeland Ave., Drexel Hill, Pa. 19026.

Holy Faith, Congregation of the Sisters of the, C.H.F.: Founded 1856, in Ireland; in U.S., 1953. General motherhouse, Dublin, Ireland; U.S. regional superior, 1205 Corning St., Los Angeles, Calif. 90035.

Holy Heart of Mary, Servants of the, S.S.C.M.: Founded 1860, in France; in U.S., 1889. General motherhouse, Montreal, Que., Canada; U.S. province, 145 S. 4th Ave., Kankakee, Ill. 60901. Educational, hospital, social work.

Holy Names of Jesus and Mary, Sisters of the, S.N.J.M.: Founded 1843, in Canada; in U.S., 1859. Generalate, Longueuil Que., Canada. U.S. addresses: Oregon Province, Box 25, Marylhurst, Ore. 97036; California Province, P.O. Box 907, Los Gatos, Calif. 95031; New York Province, 1061 New Scotland Rd., Albany, N.Y. 12208; Washington Province, W. 2911 Ft. Wright Dr., Spokane, Wash. 99204.

Holy Spirit, Community of the: Founded 1970 in San Diego, Calif. Address: 6680 Reservoir Lane, San Diego, Calif. 92115.

Holy Spirit, Daughters of the, D.H.S.: Founded 1706, in France; in U.S., 1902. Generalate, Bretagne, France; U.S. motherhouse, 72 Church St., Putnam, Conn. 06260. Educational work, district nursing; pastoral ministry.

Holy Spirit, Mission Sisters of the, M.SS.Sp.: Founded 1932, at Cleveland, O. Motherhouse, 1030 N. River Rd., Saginaw, Mich. 48603.

Holy Spirit, Missionary Sisters, Servants of the: Founded 1889, in Holland; in U.S., 1901. Generalate, Rome, Italy; U.S. motherhouse, Convent of the Holy Spirit, Techny, Ill. 60082.

Holy Spirit, Sisters of the, C.S.Sp.: Founded 1890, in Rome, Italy; in U.S., 1929. General motherhouse, 10102 Granger Rd., Garfield Hts., Ohio 44125. Educational, social, nursing work.

Holy Spirit, Sisters of the, S.H.S.: Founded 1913, in U.S., by Most Rev. J. F. Regis Canevin. General motherhouse, 5246 Clarwin Ave., Ross Township, Pittsburgh, Pa. 15229. Educational, nursing work; care of aged.

Holy Spirit and Mary Immaculate, Sisters of, S.H.Sp.: Founded 1893, in U.S. Motherhouse, 301 Yucca St., San Antonio, Tex. 78203. Education, hospital work.

Holy Spirit of Perpetual Adoration, Sister Servants of the: Founded 1896, in Holland; in U.S., 1915. Generalate, West Germany; U.S. Province, 2212 Green St., Philadelphia, Pa. 19130.

Home Mission Sisters of America (Glenmary Sisters): Founded 1952, in U.S. Motherhouse, Morning Star, P.O. Box 39188, Cincinnati, O. 45239.

Home Visitors of Mary, Sisters, H.V.M.: Founded 1949, in Detroit, Mich. Motherhouse, 356 Arden Park, Detroit, Mich. 48202.

Humility of Mary, Congregation of, C.H.M.: Founded 1854, in France; in U.S., 1864. U.S. address, Humility of Mary Center, Davenport, Ia. 52804.

Humility of Mary, Sisters of the, H.M.: Founded 1854, in France; in U.S., 1864. U.S. address, Villa Maria Community Center, Villa Maria, Pa. 16155.

Immaculate Conception, Little Servant Sisters of the: Founded 1850, in Poland; in U.S., 1926. General motherhouse, Poland; U.S. provincial house, 184 Amboy Ave., Woodbridge, N.J. 07095. Education, social services, African missions.

Immaculate Conception, Sisters of the, R.C.M.: Founded 1892, in Spain; in U.S., 1962. General motherhouse, Madrid, Spain; U.S. address, 2250 Franklin, San Francisco, Calif. 94109.

Immaculate Conception, Sisters of the, C.I.C.: Founded 1874, in U.S. General motherhouse, 4920 Kent Ave., Metairie, La. 70006.

Immaculate Conception of the Blessed Virgin Mary, Sisters of the (Lithuanian): Founded 1918, at Mariampole, Lithuania; in U.S., 1936. U.S. headquarters, Immaculate Conception Convent, Putnam, Conn. 06260.

Immaculate Heart of Mary, Missionary Sisters, I.C.M.: Founded 1897, in India; in U.S., 1919. Generalate, Rome, Italy; U.S. address, 1710 N. Glebe Rd., Arlington, Va. 22207. Educational social, foreign mission work.

Immaculate Heart of Mary, Sisters of the: Founded 1848, in Spain; in U.S., 1878. General motherhouse, Rome, Italy. U.S. province, 4100 Sabino Canyon Rd., Tucson, Ariz. 85715. Educational work.

Immaculate Heart of Mary, Sisters of the (California Institute of the Most Holy and Immaculate Heart of the B.V.M.), I.H.M.: Founded 1848, in Spain; in U.S., 1871. Generalate. 3431 Waverly Dr., Los Angeles, Calif. 90027.

Immaculate Heart of Mary, Sisters, Servants of the, I.H.M.: Founded 1845, at Monroe, Mich., by Rev. Louis Florent Gillet. Three independent branches: Generalate, 610 W. Elm St., Monroe, Mich. 48161; Villa Maria, Immaculata, Pa. 19345; Immaculate Heart of Mary Generalate, Marywood, Scranton, Pa. 18509.

Incarnate Word and Blessed Sacrament, Congregation of, V.I.: Founded 1625, in France; in U.S., 1853. Incarnate Word Convent, 3400 Bradford Pl., Houston, Tex. 77028.

Incarnate Word and Blessed Sacrament, Congregation of the, of the Archdiocese of San Antonio, I.W.B.S.: Motherhouses: 1101 Northeast Water St., Victoria, Tex. 77901; 2930 S. Alameda, Corpus Christi, Tex. 78404.

Incarnate Word and Blessed Sacrament, Sisters of the, S.I.W.: Founded 1625, in France; in U.S. 1853. Motherhouse, 6618 Pearl Rd., Parma Heights, Cleveland, O. 44130.

Infant Jesus, Congregation of the (Nursing Sisters of the Sick Poor), C.I.J.: Founded 1835, in France; in U.S., 1905. General motherhouse, 310

Prospect Park W., Brooklyn, N.Y. 11215.

Jeanne d'Arc, Sisters of Ste.: Founded 1914, in U.S., by Rev. Marie Clement Staub, A.A. General motherhouse, 1505, rue de l'Assomption Sillery, Que. G1S 4T3, Canada. U.S. novitiate, 2121 Commonwealth Ave., Brighton, Mass. 02135. Spiritual and temporal service of priests.

Jesus, Daughters of, F.I.: Founded 1871, in Spain; in U.S., 1950. General motherhouse, Rome, Italy; U.S. address, 2021 Stuart Ave., Baton Rouge, La. 70808.

Jesus, Daughters of (Filles de Jesus), F.J.: Founded 1834, in France; in U.S., 1904. General motherhouse, Kermaria, Locmine, France; U.S. address, 123 West Blvd., Lewiston, Mont. 59457. Educational, hospital, parish and social work.

Jesus, Little Sisters of: Founded 1939, in Sahara; in U.S., 1952. General motherhouse, Rome, Italy; U.S. headquarters, 700 Irving St. N.E., Washington, D.C. 20017.

Jesus, Servants of, S.J.: Founded 1974, in U.S. Central Office, 9075 Big Lake Rd., P.O. Box 128, Clarkston, Mich. 48016.

Jesus, Society of the Sisters, Faithful Companions of, F.C.J.: Founded 1820, in France; in U.S., 1896. General motherhouse, Kent, England. U.S. convents: 20 Atkins St., Providence, R.I. 02908; St. Philomena Convent, Cory's Lane, Portsmouth, R.I. 02871.

Jesus Crucified, Congregation of: Founded 1930, in France; in U.S., 1955. General motherhouse, Brou, France; U.S. foundations: Regina Mundi Priory, Devon, Pa. 19333; St. Paul's Priory, 61 Narragansett, Newport, R.I. 02840.

Jesus Crucified and the Sorrowful Mother, Poor Sisters of, C.J.C.: Founded 1924, in U.S., by Rev. Alphonsus Maria, C.P. Motherhouse, 261 Thatcher St., Brockton, Mass. 02402. Education, nursing homes, catechetical centers.

Jesus-Mary, Religious of, R.J.M.: Founded 1818, at Lyons, France; in U.S., 1877. General motherhouse, Rome, Italy; U.S. province, 8908 Riggs Rd., Hyattsville, Md. 20783. Educational work.

Jesus, Mary and Joseph, Missionaries of, M.J.M.J.: Founded 1942, in Spain; in U.S., 1956. General motherhouse, Madrid, Spain; U.S. regional house, 12940 Up River Rd., Corpus Christi, Tex. 78410.

John the Baptist, Sisters of St., C.S.J.B.: Founded 1878, in U.S., 1906. General motherhouse, Rome, Italy; U.S. provincialate, Anderson Hill Rd., Purchase, N.Y. 10577. Education, parish and retreat work; social services.

Joseph, Missionary Servants of St., M.S.S.J.: Founded 1874, in Spain; in U.S., 1957. General motherhouse, Salamanca, Spain; U.S. address, 203 N. Spring St., Falls Church, Va. 22046.

Joseph, Poor Sisters of St.: Founded 1880, in Argentina. General motherhouse, Muniz, Buenos Aires, Argentina; U.S. addresses, Casa Belen, 305 E. 4th St., Bethlehem, Pa. 78015; Casa Nazareth, 330 S. Spruce St., Reading, Pa. 19602; St. Gabriel Convent, 4319 Sano St., Alexandria, Va. 22312.

Joseph, Religious Daughters of St., F.S.J.: Founded 1875, in Spain. General motherhouse, Spain; U.S. foundation, 319 N. Humphreys Ave., Los Angeles, Calif. 90022.

Joseph, Religious Hospitallers of St., R.H.S.J.: Founded 1636, in France; in U.S., 1894. Generalate, Montreal, Que., Canada; U.S. address, Holy Family Convent, 438 College St., Burlington, Vt. 05401. Hospital work.

Joseph, Sisters of St., C.S.J.: Founded 1650, in France; in U.S., 1836, at St. Louis. U.S. independent motherhouses:

637 Cambridge St., Brighton, Mass. 02135; 1515 W. Ogden Ave., La Grange Park, Ill., 60525; 480 S. Batavia St., Orange, Calif. 92668; Mt. St. Joseph Convent, Chestnut Hill, Philadelphia, Pa. 19118.

St. Joseph Convent, Brentwood, N.Y. 11717; 23 Agassiz Circle, Buffalo, N.Y. 14214; Avila Hall, Clement Rd., Rutland, Vt. 05701; 3430 Rocky River Dr., Cleveland, O. 44111; R.R. No. 3, Box 291A, Tipton, Ind. 46072; Motherhouse and novitiate, Nazareth, Mich. 49074; 1425 Washington St., Watertown, N.Y. 13601; Mt. Gallitzin Academy and Motherhouse, Baden, Pa. 15005; 819 W. 8th St., Erie, Pa. 16502.

4095 East Ave., Rochester, N.Y. 14610; 215 Court St., Concordia, Kans. 66901; Mont Marie, Holyoke, Mass. 01040; 1412 E. 2nd St., Superior, Wis. 54880; Pogue Run Rd., Wheeling, W. Va. 26003; 3700 E. Lincoln St., Wichita, Kans. 67218.

Joseph, Sisters of St. (Lyons, France), C.S.J.: Founded 1650, in France; in U.S., 1906. General motherhouse, Lyons, France; U.S. provincialate, 93 Halifax St., Winslow, Me. 04901. Educational, hospital work.

Joseph, Sisters of St., of Peace, C.S.J.P.: Founded 1884, in England; in U.S. 1885. Generalate, 1225 Newton St. N.E., Washington, D.C. 20017. Educational, hospital, social service work.

Joseph of Carondelet, Sisters of St., C.S.J.: Founded 1650, in France; in U.S., 1836, at St. Louis, Mo. U.S. headquarters, 2307 S. Lindbergh Blvd., St. Louis, Mo. 63131.

Joseph of Chambery, Sisters of St.: Founded 1650, in France; in U.S., 1885. Generalate, Rome, Italy; U.S. provincial house, 27 Park Rd., West Hartford, Conn. 06119. Educational, hospital, social work.

Joseph of Cluny, Sisters of St., S.J.C.: Founded 1807, in France. Generalate, Paris, France; U.S. provincial house, Brenton Rd., Newport, R.I. 02840.

Joseph of Medaille, Sisters of, C.S.J.: Founded 1650, in France; in U.S., 1855. Became an American congregation Nov. 30, 1977. Central office, 1821 Summit Rd., Cincinnati, Ohio 45237.

Joseph of St. Augustine, Fla., Sisters of St., S.S.J.: General motherhouse, 241 St. George St., P.O. Box 3056, St. Augustine, Fla. 32085. Educational, hospital, pastoral, social work.

Joseph of St. Mark, Sisters of St., S.S.J.S.M.: Founded 1845, in France; in U.S., 1937. General motherhouse, 21800 Chardon Rd., Euclid, Cleveland, O. 44117. Nursing homes.

Joseph the Worker, Sisters of St., S.J.W.: General motherhouse, St. Joseph Convent, 143 S. Main St., Walton, Ky. 41094.

Lamb of God, Sisters of the, A.D.: Founded

1945, in France; in U.S., 1958. General motherhouse, France; U.S. address, Rt. 1, Box 260, Philpot, Ky 42366.

Living Word, Sisters of the, S.L.W.: Founded 1975, in U.S. Motherhouse, The Center, 7200 N. Osceola Ave., Chicago, Ill. 60648. Education, hospital, parish ministry work.

Loretto at the Foot of the Cross, Sisters of, S.L.: Founded 1812 in U.S., by Rev. Charles Nerinckx. General motherhouse, Nerinx, Ky. 40049. Educational work.

Louis, Congregation of Sisters of St., S.S.L.: Founded 1842, in France; in U.S., 1949. General motherhouse, Monaghan, Ireland; U.S. regional house, 22300 Mulholland Dr., Woodland Hills, Calif. 91364. Educational, medical, parish, foreign mission work.

Marian Sisters of the Diocese of Lincoln: Founded 1954. Motherhouse, Marycrest, R.R. 1, Box 108, Waverly, Nebr. 68462.

Marian Society of Dominican Catechists, O.P.: Founded 1954 in Louisiana. General motherhouse, P.O. Box 176, Boyce, La. 71409. Community of Alexandria-Shreveport, La., diocese.

Marianites of Holy Cross, Congregation of the Sisters, M.S.C.: Founded 1841, in France; in U.S., 1843. Motherhouse, Le Mans, Sarthe, France. North American headquarters, 4123 Woodland Dr., New Orleans, La. 70114.

Marist Sisters, Congregation of Mary, S.M.: Founded 1824, in France. General motherhouse, Rome, Italy; U.S. convents: St. Albert the Great, 4855 Parker, Dearborn Hts., Mich. 48125; St. Barnabas, 16103 Chesterfield, E. Detroit, Mich. 48021; Our Lady of the Snows, 4810 S. Leamington, Chicago, Ill. 60638.

Maronite Antonine Sisters: Established in U.S., 1966. U.S. address, 2961 N. Lipkey Rd., North Jackson, Ohio 44451.

Marthe, Sisters of Sainte (of St. Hyacinthe), S.M.S.H.: Founded 1883, in Canada; in U.S., 1929. General motherhouse 675 ouest, rue St.-Pierre, Hyacinthe, Que., J2T IN7 Canada.

Mary, Company of, O.D.N.: Founded 1607, in France; in U.S., 1926. General motherhouse, Rome, Italy; U.S. motherhouse, 16791 E. Main St., Tustin, Calif. 92680.

Mary, Daughters of the Heart of, D.H.M.: Founded 1790, in France; in U.S., 1851. Generalate, Paris, France; U.S. provincialate, 1339 Northampton St., Holyoke, Mass. 01040. Education retreat work.

Mary, Little Company of, Nursing Sisters, L.C.M.: Founded 1877, in England; in U.S., 1893. General motherhouse, Rome, Italy; U.S. provincial house, 9350 S. California Ave., Evergreen Park, Ill. 60642.

Mary, Missionary Sisters of the Society of (Marist Sisters), S.M.S.M.: Founded 1845, at St. Brieuc, France; in U.S., 1922. General motherhouse, Rome, Italy; U.S. provincial house, 357 Grove St., Waltham, Mass. 02154. Foreign missions.

Mary, Servants of, O.S.M.: Founded 13th century, in Italy; in U.S., 1893. Generalate, Rome, Italy; U.S. provincial motherhouse, 7400 Military Ave., Omaha, Nebr. 68134.

Mary, Servants of (Servite Sisters), O.S.M.: Founded 13th century, in Italy; in U.S., 1912. General motherhouse, Our Lady of Sorrows Convent, Ladysmith, Wis. 54848.

Mary, Servants of, of Blue Island (Mantellate Sisters), O.S.M.: Founded 1861, in Italy; in U.S., 1916. Generalate, Rome, Italy; U.S. motherhouse, 13811 S. Western Ave., Blue Island, Ill. 60406. Educational work.

Mary, Sisters of St., of Oregon, S.S.M.O.: Founded 1886, in Oregon, by Bishop William H. Gross, C.Ss.R. General motherhouse, 4440 S.W. 148th Ave., Beaverton, Ore. 97007. Educational, nursing work.

Mary, Sisters Servants of (Trained Nurses), S.M.: Founded 1851, at Madrid, Spain; in U.S., 1914. General motherhouse, Rome, Italy; U.S. motherhouse, 800 N. 18th St., Kansas City, Kans. 66102. Home nursing.

Mary and Joseph, Daughters of, D.M.J.: Founded 1817, in Belgium; in U.S., 1926. Generalate, Rome, Italy; American provincialate, 5300 Crest Rd., Rancho Palos Verdes, Calif. 90274.

Mary Help of Christians, Daughters of (Salesian Sisters of St. John Bosco), F.M.A.: Founded 1872, in Italy, by St. John Bosco and St. Mary Dominic Mazzarello; in U.S., 1908. General motherhouse, Rome, Italy; U.S. provincial house, 655 Belmont Ave., Haledon, N.J. 07508. Education, youth work.

Mary Immaculate, Daughters of (Marianist Sisters), F.M.I.: Founded 1816, in France, by Very Rev. William-Joseph Chaminade. General motherhouse, Rome, Italy; U.S. foundation, 251 W. Ligustrum Dr., San Antonio, Tex. 78228. Educational work.

Mary Immaculate, Religious of, R.M.I.: Founded 1876, in Spain; in U.S., 1954. Generalate, Rome, Italy; U.S. foundation, Villa Maria, 719 Augusta St., San Antonio, Tex. 78215.

Mary Immaculate, Sister Servants of, S.S.M.I.: Founded 1878 in Poland. General motherhouse, Mariowka, Poland; American provincialate, 1220 Tugwell Dr., Catonsville, Md. 21228.

Mary Immaculate, Sisters of, S.M.I.: Founded 1948, in India, by Bishop Louis LaRavoire Morrow; in U.S., 1981. General motherhouse, Bengal, India; U.S. address, R.D. 5, Box 1231, Leechburg, Pa. 15656.

Mary Immaculate, Sisters Servants of, S.S.M.I: Founded 1892, in Ukraine; in U.S., 1935. General motherhouse, Rome, Italy; U.S. province, Immaculate Conception Province, Table Rock, Sloatsburg, N.Y. 10974. Educational, hospital work.

Mary of Namur, Sisters of St., S.S.M.N.: Founded 1819, at Namur, Belgium; in U.S., 1863. General motherhouse, Namur, Belgium. U.S. provinces: 3756 Delaware Ave., Kenmore, N.Y. 14217; 3300 Hemphill St., Ft. Worth, Tex. 76110.

Mary of Providence, Daughters of St., D.S.M.P.: Founded 1872, at Como, Italy; in U.S., 1913. General motherhouse, Rome, Italy; U.S. provincial house, 4200 N. Austin Ave., Chicago, Ill. 60634. Special education for mentally handicapped.

Mary of the Immaculate Conception, Daughters of, D.M.: Founded 1904, in U.S., by Msgr. Lucian Bojnowski. General motherhouse, 314 Osgood Ave., New Britain, Conn. 06053. Educational, hospital work.

Mary Queen, Congregation of, C.M.R.: Founded in Vietnam; established in U.S., 1979. U.S. region, 535 S. Jefferson, Springfield, Mo. 65806.

Mary Reparatrix, Society of, S.M.R.: Founded 1857, in France; in U.S., 1908. Generalate, Rome, Italy. U.S. province, 225 E. 234th St., Bronx, N.Y. 10470.

Medical Mission Sisters (Society of Catholic Medical Missionaries, Inc.), S.C.M.M.: Founded 1925, in U.S., by Mother Anna Dengel. Generalate, London, Eng.; U.S. headquarters, 8400 Pine Rd., Philadelphia, Pa. 19111. Medical work, health education, especially in mission areas.

Medical Missionaries of Mary, M.M.M.: Founded 1937, in Ireland, by Mother Mary Martin; in U.S., 1950. General motherhouse, Drogheda, Ireland; U.S. headquarters, 563 Minneford Ave., City Island, Bronx, N.Y. 10464. Medical aid in missions.

Medical Sisters of St. Joseph, M.S.J.: Founded 1946, in India; first U.S. foundation, 1985. General motherhouse, Kerala, S. India; U.S. address, 3213 E. Grand, Wichita, Kans. 67218. Health care apostolate.

Mercedarian Missionaries of Berriz, M.M.B.: Founded 1930, in Spain; in U.S., 1946. General motherhouse, Rome, Italy. U.S. headquarters, 918 E. 9th St., Kansas City, Mo. 64106.

Mercy, Daughters of Our Lady of, D.M.: Founded 1837, in Italy, by St. Mary Joseph Rossello; in U.S., 1919. General motherhouse, Savona, Italy; U.S. motherhouse, Villa Rossello, Catawba Ave., Newfield, N.J. 08344. Educational, hospital work.

Mercy, Missionary Sisters of Our Lady of, M.O.M.: Founded 1938, in Brazil; in U.S., 1955. General motherhouse, Brazil; U.S. address, 388 Franklin St., Buffalo, N.Y. 14202.

Mercy, Sisters of, R.S.M.: Founded 1831, in Ireland, by Mother Mary Catherine McAuley. U.S. motherhouses:

634 New Scotland Ave., Albany, N.Y. 12208; 273 Willoughby Ave., Brooklyn, N.Y. 11205; S. 5245 Murphy Rd., Orchard Park, N.Y. 14127; 100 Mansfield Ave., Burlington, Vt. 05401; 1125 Prairie Dr., N.E., Cedar Rapids, Ia. 52402; 444 E. Grandview Blvd., Erie, Pa. 16504; 249 Steele Rd., W. Hartford, Conn. 06117.

21 Searles Rd., Windham, N.H. 03087; Sisters of Mercy, Merion, Pa. 10966; 3333 Fifth Ave., Pittsburgh, Pa. 15213; 605 Stevens Ave., Portland, Me. 04103; Sacred Heart Convent, Belmont, N. Car. 28012; 1437 Blossom Rd., Rochester, N.Y. 14610; 535 Sacramento St., Auburn, Calif. 95603.

2300 Adeline Dr., Burlingame, Calif. 94010; U.S. Route 22 at Terrill Rd., Watchung, N.J. 07060; 101 Barry Rd., Worcester, Mass. 01609.

Mercy, Sisters of, of the Union in the United States of America, R.S.M.: Founded 1831 in Ireland, by Mother M. Catherine McAuley; union formed in 1929. Central headquarters, 1320 Fenwick Lane, Suite 610, Silver Spring, Md. 20910. U.S. provinces:

P.O. Box 11448, Baltimore, Md. 21239; 10024 S. Central Park Ave., Chicago, Ill. 60642; 2301 Grandview Ave., Cincinnati, Ohio 45206; 29000 Eleven Mile Rd., Farmington Hills, Mich. 48024; 541 Broadway, Dobbs Ferry, N.Y. 10522; 1801 S. 72nd St., Omaha, Nebr. 68124; R.D. 3, Cumberland, R.I. 02864; 2039 N. Geyer Rd., St. Louis, Mo. 63131; Dallas, Pa. 18612.

Mercy, Sisters of, Daughters of Christian Charity of St. Vincent de Paul, S.M.D.C.: Founded 1842, in Hungary; U.S. foundation, Rt. 1, Box 353, Hewitt, N.J. 07421.

Mercy of the Blessed Sacrament, Sisters of: Founded 1910 in Mexico. U.S. foundation, 555 E. Mountain View, Barstow, Calif. 92311.

Mill Hill Sisters; See Franciscan Missionaries of St. Joseph.

Minim Sisters of Mary Immaculate, C.F.M.M.: Founded 1886, in Mexico; in U.S. 1926. General motherhouse, Leon, Guanajuato, Mexico; U.S. address, Our Lady of Lourdes Academy, Box 1856, Nogales, Ariz. 85621.

Misericordia Sisters, S.M.: Founded 1848, in Canada; in U.S., 1887. General motherhouse. 12435 Ave. Misericorde, Montreal H4J 2J3, Canada; U.S. address, 820 Jungles Ave., Aurora, Ill. 60505. Social work with unwed mothers and their children; hospital work.

Mission Helpers of the Sacred Heart, M.H.S.H.: Founded 1890, in U.S. General motherhouse, 1001 W. Joppa Rd., Baltimore, Md. 21204. Religious education, evangelization.

Missionary Catechists of the Sacred Hearts of Jesus and Mary (Violetas), M.C.: Founded 1918, in Mexico; in U.S., 1943. Motherhouse, Tlalpan, Mexico; U.S. address, 209 W. Murray St., Victoria, Tex. 77901.

Missionary Sisters of the Catholic Apostolate (Pallottine Missionary Sisters), S.A.C.: Founded in Rome, 1838; in U.S., 1912. Generalate, Rome, Italy; U.S. provincialate, Rt. 2, 15270 Old Halls Ferry Rd., Florissant, Mo. 63034.

Mother of God, Missionary Sisters of the, M.S.M.G.: Byzantine, Ukrainian Rite, Stamford. Motherhouse, 711-719 N. Franklin St., Philadelphia, Pa. 19123.

Mother of God, Sisters Poor Servants of the, S.M.G.: Founded 1869, in London, England; in U.S., 1947. General motherhouse, Mayfield, Roehampton, London. U.S. addresses: Maryfield Nursing Home, Greensboro Rd., High Point, N.C. 27260; St. Mary's Hospital, 916 Virginia Ave., Norton, Va. 24273; Holy Spirit School, 1800 Geary St., Philadelphia, Pa. 19145. Hospital, educational work.

Nazareth, Poor Sisters of: Founded in England; U.S. foundation, 1924. General motherhouse, Hammersmith, London, England; U.S. novitiate, 3333 Manning Ave., Los Angeles, Calif. 90064. Social services, education.

Notre Dame, School Sisters of, S.S.N.D.: Founded 1833, in Germany; in U.S., 1847. General motherhouse, Rome, Italy. U.S. motherhouse, 1233 N. Marshall St., Milwaukee, Wis. 53202. Provinces: 6401 N. Charles St., Baltimore, Md. 21212; 320 E. Ripa Ave., St. Louis, Mo. 63125; Good Counsel Hill, Mankato, Minn. 56001; 345 Belden Hill Rd., Wilton, Conn. 06897; P.O. Box 227275, Dallas, Tex. 75222; 1431 Euclid Ave., Berwyn, Ill. 60402.

Notre Dame, Sisters of, S.N.D.: Founded 1850, at Coesfeld, Germany; in U.S., 1874. General motherhouse, Rome, Italy. U.S. provinces: 13000 Auburn Rd., Chardon, O. 44024; 1601 Dixie Highway, Covington, Ky. 41011; 3837 Secor Rd., Toledo, O. 43623; 1776 Hendrix Ave., Thousand Oaks, Calif. 91360.

Notre Dame, Sisters of the Congregation of, C.N.D.: Founded 1653, in Canada; in U.S., 1860. General motherhouse, Montreal, Que., Canada; U.S. province, 223 West Mountain Rd., Ridgefield, Conn. 06877. Education.

Notre Dame de Namur, Sisters of, S.N.D.: Founded 1803, in France; in U.S., 1840. General motherhouse, Rome, Italy. U.S. provinces: P.O. Box 112, Boston, Mass. 02117; 54 Jeffrey's Neck Rd., Ipswich, Mass. 01938; 1561 N. Benson Rd., Fairfield, Conn. 06431; P.O. Box 813, 5025 Ilchester Rd., Ellicott City, Md. 21043; 701 E. Columbia Ave., Cincinnati, O. 45215; 14800 Bohlman Rd., Saratoga, Calif. 95070. Educational work.

Notre Dame de Sion, Congregation of, N.D.S.: Founded 1843, in France; in U.S., 1892. Generalate, Rome, Italy; U.S. provincial house, 3823 Locust St., Kansas City, Mo. 64109. Creation of better understanding and relations between Christians and Jews.

Notre Dame Sisters: Founded 1853, in Czechoslovakia; in U.S., 1910. General motherhouse, Javornik, Czechoslovakia; U.S. motherhouse, 3501 State St., Omaha, Nebr. 68112. Educational work.

Our Lady of Charity, North American Union of Sisters of, Eudist Sisters (Sisters of Our Lady of Charity of the Refuge), O.L.C.: Founded 1641, in Caen, France, by St. John Eudes; in U.S., 1855. Autonomous houses were federated in 1944 and in May, 1978, the North American Union of the Sisters of Our Lady of Charity was established. General motherhouse and administrative center, Box 327, Wisconsin Dells, Wis. 53965. Primarily devoted to re-education and rehabilitation of women and girls in residential and non-residential settings.

Two independent monasteries; 1125 Malvern Ave., Hot Springs, Ark. 71901; 620 Roswell Rd. N.W., Carrollton, O. 44615.

Our Lady of Sorrows, Sisters of, O.L.S.: Founded 1839, in Italy; in U.S., 1947. General motherhouse, Rome, Italy; U.S. headquarters, 9494 Norris Ferry Rd., Shreveport, La. 71106.

Our Lady of the Garden, Sisters of, O.L.G.: Founded 1829, in Italy, by St. Anthony Mary Gianelli. Motherhouse, Rome, Italy; U.S. address, St. Brendan School, 445½ Whalley Ave., New Haven, Conn. 06511.

Our Lady of Victory Missionary Sisters, O.L.V.M.: Founded 1922, in U.S. Motherhouse, Victory Noll, Box 109, Huntington, Ind. 46750. Educational, social work.

Pallottine Sisters of the Catholic Apostolate, C.S.A.C.: Founded 1843, at Rome, Italy; in U.S., 1889. General motherhouse, Rome; U.S. motherhouse, St. Patrick's Villa, Harriman Heights, Harriman, N.Y. 10926. Educational work.

Parish Visitors of Mary Immaculate, P.V.M.I.: Founded 1920, in New York. General motherhouse, Box 658, Monroe, N.Y. 10950. Mission work.

Passion of Jesus Christ, Religious of (Passionist Nuns), C.P.: Founded 1771, in Italy, by St. Paul of the Cross; in U.S., 1910. U.S. convents: 2715 Churchview Ave., Pittsburgh, Pa. 15227; 631 Griffin Pond Rd., Clarks Summit, Pa. 18411; 1420 Benita Ave., Owensboro, Ky. 42301; 1151 Donaldson Hwy., Erlanger, Ky. 41018; 15700 Clayton Rd., Ellisville, Mo. 63011. Contemplatives.

Passionist Sisters: See Cross and Passion, Sisters of the.

Paul, Angelic Sisters of St.: Founded 1535, in Milan, Italy; U.S. address, Fatima Shrine, Swan Rd., Youngstown, N.Y. 14174.

Paul, Daughters of St. (Missionary Sisters of the Media of Communication), D.S.P.: Founded 1915, at Alba, Piedmont, Italy; in U.S., 1932. General motherhouse, Rome, Italy; U.S. provincial house, 50 St. Paul's Ave., Jamaica Plain, Mass. 02130. Apostolate of the communications arts.

Paul of Chartres, Sisters of St., S.P.C.: Founded 1696, in France. General house, Rome, Italy; U.S. address, 1300 County Rd. 492, Marquette, Mich. 49855.

Peter Claver, Missionary Sisters of St., S.S.P.C.: Founded 1894; in U.S., 1914. General motherhouse, Rome, Italy; U.S. address, 667 Woods Mill Rd. S., Chesterfield, Mo. 63017.

Pious Schools, Sisters of, Sch. P.: Founded 1829 in Spain; in U.S., 1954. General motherhouse, Rome, Italy; U.S. headquarters, 9925 Mason Ave., Chatsworth, Calif. 91311.

Poor, Little Sisters of the, L.S.P.: Founded 1839, in France by Bl Jeanne Jugan; in U.S., 1868. General motherhouse, St. Pern, France. U.S. provinces: 110-30 221st St., Queens Village, N.Y. 11429; 601 Maiden Choice Lane, Baltimore, Md. 21228; 2325 N. Lakewood Ave.; Chicago, Ill. 60614. Care of aged.

Poor Clare Missionary Sisters (Misioneras Clarisas), M.C.: Founded Mexico. General motherhouse, Rome, Italy; U.S. novitiate, 1019 N. Newhope, Santa Ana, Calif. 92703.

Poor Clare Nuns: See Franciscan Poor Clare Nuns.

Poor Handmaids of Jesus Christ (Ancilla Domini Sisters), P.H.J.C.: Founded 1851, in Germany by Bl. Mary Kasper; in U.S., 1868. General motherhouse, Dernbach, Westerwald, Germany; U.S. motherhouse, Ancilla Domini Convent, Donaldson, Ind. 46513. Educational, hospital work, social services.

Precious Blood, Daughters of Charity of the Most: Founded 1872, at Pagani, Italy; in U.S., 1908. General motherhouse, Rome, Italy; U.S. convent, 1482 North Ave., Bridgeport, Conn. 06604.

Precious Blood, Missionary Sisters of the, C.P.S.: Founded 1885, at Mariannhill, South Africa; in U.S., 1925. Generalate, Rome, Italy; U.S. novitiate, New Holland Ave., P.O. Box 97,

Shillington, Pa. 19607. Home and foreign mission work.

Precious Blood, Sisters Adorers of the, A.P.B.: Founded 1861, in Canada; in U.S., 1890. General motherhouses, Canada. U.S. autonomous monasteries: 54th St. and Fort Hamilton Pkwy., Brooklyn, N.Y. 11219; 700 Bridge St., Manchester, N.H. 03104; 7408 S.E. Alder St., Portland, Ore. 97215; 166 State St., Portland, Me. 04101; 1106 State St., Lafayette, Ind. 47905; 400 Pratt St., Watertown, N.Y. 13601. Cloistered, contemplative.

Precious Blood, Sisters of the, C.Pp.S.: Founded 1834, in Switzerland; in U.S., 1844. Generalate, 4000 Denlinger Rd., Dayton, Ohio 45426. Education, health care, other ministries.

Precious Blood, Sisters of the Most, C.Pp.S.: Founded 1845, in Steinerberg, Switzerland; in U.S., 1870. General motherhouse, 204 N. Main St., O'Fallon, Mo. 63366. Education, other ministries.

Presentation, Sisters of Mary of the, S.M.P.: Founded 1829, in France; in U.S., 1903. General motherhouse, Broons, Cotes-du-Nord, France. U.S. address, Maryvale Novitiate, Valley City, N. Dak. 58072. Educational, hospital work.

Presentation of Mary, Sisters of the, P.M.: Founded 1796, in France by Bl Marie Rivier; in U.S., 1873. General motherhouse, Castel Gandolfo, Italy. U.S. provincial houses: 495 Mammoth Rd., Manchester, N.H. 03104; 209 Lawrence St., Methuen, Mass. 01844.

Presentation of the B.V.M., Sisters of the, P.B.V.M.: Founded 1775, in Ireland; in U.S., 1854, in San Francisco. U.S. motherhouses: 2360 Carter Rd., Dubuque, Ia. 52001; R.D. 2, Box 33, Newburgh, N.Y. 12550; 8931 Callaghan Rd., San Antonio, Tex. 78230; 2340 Turk Blvd., San Francisco, Calif. 94118; St. Colman's Convent, Watervliet, N.Y. 12189. 1101 32nd Ave., S. Fargo, N. Dak. 58103; 250 S. Davis Dr., P.O. Box 1113, Warner Robbins, Ga. 31093; 1500 N. Main, Aberdeen, S. Dak. 57401; 1300 E. Cedar, Globe, Ariz. 85501; 1555 E. Dana, Mesa, Ariz. 85201; 366 South St., Fitchburg, Mass. 01420; 419 Woodrow Rd., Annadale, Staten Island, N.Y. 10312.

Presentation of the Blessed Virgin Mary, Sisters of, of Union: Founded in Ireland, 1775; union established in Ireland, 1976; first U.S. vice province, 1979. Generalate, Kildare, Ireland. U.S. addresses: 349 Oak Ave., San Bruno, Calif. 94066 (vice provincialate); Presentation Convent, 4410 Cleary Ave., Matairie, La. 70002 (Southeastern Region).

Providence, Daughters of Divine, F.D.P.: Founded 1832, Italy; in U.S., 1964. General motherhouse, Rome, Italy; U.S. address, 1625 Missouri St., Chalmette, La. 70043.

Providence, Missionary Catechists of Divine, M.C.D.P.: Founded 1930, as a filial society; adjunct branch of Sisters of Divine Providence (Helotes, Tex.). Administrative house, 4650 Eldridge Ave., San Antonio, Tex. 78337.

Providence, Oblate Sisters of, O.S.P.: Founded 1829, in U.S. General motherhouse, 701 Gun Rd., Baltimore, Md. 21227. Educational work.

Providence, Sisters of, S.P.: Founded 1861, in Canada; in U.S., 1873. General motherhouse, Our Lady of Victory Convent, Holyoke, Mass. 01040.

Providence, Sisters of, S.P.: Founded 1843, in Canada; in U.S., 1854. General motherhouse, Montreal, Canada. U.S. provinces: P.O. Box C-11038, Seattle, Wash. 98111; 9 E. 9th Ave., Spokane, Wash. 99202; 353 N. River Rd., Des Plaines, Ill. 60616.

Providence, Sisters of (of St. Mary-of-the-Woods), S.P.: Founded 1806, in France; in U.S., 1840. Generalate, St. Mary-of-the-Woods, Ind. 47876.

Providence, Sisters of Divine, C.D.P.: Founded 1762, in France; in U.S., 1866. Generalate, Box 197, Helotes, Tex. 78023. Educational, hospital work.

Providence, Sisters of Divine, C.D.P.: Founded 1851, in Germany; in U.S., 1876. Generalate, Rome, Italy. U.S. provinces: 9000 Babcock Blvd., Allison Park, Pa. 15101; 8351 Florissant Rd., St. Louis, Mo. 63121; Box 2, Rte. 80, Kingston, Mass. 02364. Educational, hospital work.

Providence, Sisters of Divine (of Kentucky), C.D.P.: Founded 1762, in France; in U.S., 1889. General motherhouse, Fenetrange, France; U.S. province, St. Anne Convent, Melbourne, Ky. 41059. Education, social services, other ministries.

Redeemer, Oblates of the Most Holy, O.SS.R.: Founded 1864, in Spain. General motherhouse, Spain; U.S. foundation, 60-80 Pond St., Jamaica Plain, Mass. 02130.

Redeemer, Order of the Most Holy, O.SS.R.: Founded 1731, by St. Alphonsus Liguori; in U.S., 1957. U.S. addresses: Mother of Perpetual Help Monastery, Esopus, N.Y. 12429; St. Alphonsus Monastery, Liguori, Mo. 63057.

Redeemer, Sisters of the Divine, S.D.R.: Founded 1849, in Niederbronn, France; in U.S., 1912. General motherhouse, Rome, Italy; U.S. province, 999 Rock Run Road, Elizabeth, Pa. 15037. Educational, hospital work; care of the aged.

Redeemer, Sisters of the Holy, C.S.R.: Founded 1849, in Alsace; in U.S., 1924. General motherhouse, Wuerzburg, Germany; U.S. provincial house, Huntingdon Valley, Pa. 19006. Personalized medical care in hospitals, homes for aged, private homes; retreat work.

Reparation of the Congregation of Mary, Sisters of, S.R.C.M.: Founded 1903, in U.S. Motherhouse, St. Zita's Villa, Monsey, N.Y. 10952.

Resurrection, Sisters of the, C.R.: Founded 1891, in Italy; in U.S., 1900. General motherhouse, Rome, Italy. U.S. provinces: 7432 Talcott Ave., Chicago, Ill. 60631; Mt. St. Joseph, Castleton-on-Hudson, N.Y. 12033. Education, nursing.

Rita, Sisters of St., O.S.A.: General motherhouse, Wurzburg, Germany. U.S. foundation, St. Monica's Convent, 3920 Green Bay Rd., Racine, Wis. 53404.

Rosary, Congregation of Our Lady of the Holy, R.S.R.: Founded 1874, in Canada; in U.S., 1899. General motherhouse, Rimouski, Que., Canada. U.S. regional house, 20 Thomas St., Portland, Me. 04102. Educational work.

Rosary, Missionary Sisters of the Holy, M.S.H.R.: Founded 1924, in Ireland; in U.S., 1954. Motherhouse, Dublin, Ireland. U.S. regional mailing address, P.O. Box 304, Bryn Mawr, Pa. 19010. African missions.

Sacrament, Missionary Sisters of the Most Blessed, M.SS.S.: General motherhouse, Madrid, Spain; U.S. foundation: 1111 Wordin Ave., Bridgeport, Conn. 06605.

Sacrament, Nuns of the Perpetual Adoration of the Blessed, A.P.: Founded 1807 in Rome, Italy; in U.S., 1925. U.S. monasteries: 145 N. Cotton Ave., El Paso, Tex. 79901; 771 Ashbury St., San Francisco, Calif. 94117.

Sacrament, Oblate Sisters of the Blessed, O.S.B.S.: Founded 1935, in U.S.; motherhouse, St. Sylvester Convent, Marty, S.D. 57361. Care of American Indians.

Sacrament, Religious Sisters of the Blessed, R.M.S.S.: Founded 1910, in Mexico; in U.S., 1926. General motherhouse, Mexico City, Mexico; U.S. convent, 222 W. Cevallos St., San Antonio, Tex. 78204.

Sacrament, Servants of the Blessed, S.S.S.: Founded 1858, in France, by St. Pierre Julien Eymard; in U.S., 1947. General motherhouse, Rome, Italy; American vice-provincial house, 101 Silver St., Waterville, Me. 04901. Contemplative.

Sacrament, Sisters of the Blessed, for Indians and Colored People, S.B.S.: Founded 1891, in U.S., by Bl. Katharine Drexel. General motherhouse, St. Elizabeth's Convent, Bensalem, Pa. 19020.

Sacrament, Sisters of the Most Holy, M.H.S.: Founded 1851, in France; in U.S., 1872. Generalate, 409 W. St. Mary Blvd. (P.O. Box 30727), Lafayette, La. 70503.

Sacrament, Sisters Servants of the Blessed, S.S.B.S.: Founded 1904, in Mexico. General motherhouse, Guadalajara, Mexico. U.S. address, Our Lady of Guadalupe School, 536 Rockwood Ave., Calexico, Calif. 92231.

Sacramentine Nuns (Religious of the Order of the Blessed Sacrament and Our Lady), O.S.S.: Founded 1639, in France; in U.S., 1912. U.S. monasteries: 23 Park Ave., Yonkers, N.Y. 10703; US 31, Conway, Mich. 49722. Perpetual adoration of the Holy Eucharist.

Sacred Heart, Daughters of Our Lady of the: Founded 1882, in France; in U.S., 1955. General motherhouse, Rome, Italy; U.S. address, 424 E. Browning Rd., Bellmawr, N.J. 08031. Educational work.

Sacred Heart, Missionary Sisters of the (Cabrini Sisters), M.S.C.: Founded 1880, in Italy, by St. Frances Xavier Cabrini; in U.S., 1889. General motherhouse, Rome, Italy; U.S. provinces: 222 E. 19th St., New York, N.Y. 10003 (Eastern); 434 W. Deming Pl., Chicago, Ill. 60614 (Western). Educational, health, social and catechetical work.

Sacred Heart, Religious of the Apostolate of the, R.A.: General motherhouse, Madrid, Spain; U.S. address, 1310 W. 42nd Pl., Hialiah, Fla., 33012.

Sacred Heart, Society Devoted to the, S.D.S.H.: Founded 1940, in Hungary; in U.S., 1956. U.S. motherhouse, 2121 W. Olive Dr., Burbank, Calif. 91506. Educational work.

Sacred Heart, Society of the, R.SC.J.: Founded 1800, in France; in U.S., 1818. Generalate, Rome, Italy. U.S. provincial house, 4389 W. Pine Blvd., St. Louis, Mo. 63108. Educational work.

Sacred Heart of Jesus, Apostles of, A.S.C.J.: Founded 1894, in Italy; in U.S., 1902. General motherhouse, Rome, Italy; U.S. motherhouse, 265 Benham St., Hamden, Conn. 06514. Educational, social work.

Sacred Heart of Jesus, Handmaids of the, A.C.J.: Founded 1877, in Spain. General motherhouse, Rome, Italy; U.S. province, 616 Coopertown Rd., Haverford, Pa. 19041. Educational, retreat work.

Sacred Heart of Jesus, Missionary Sisters of the Most (Hiltrup), M.S.C.: Founded 1899, in Germany; in U.S., 1908. General motherhouse, Rome, Italy; U.S. province, Hyde Park, Reading, Pa. 19605. Education, health care, pastoral ministry.

Sacred Heart of Jesus, Oblate Sisters of the, O.S.H.J.: Founded 1894; in U.S., 1949. General motherhouse, Rome, Italy; U.S. headquarters, 50 Warner Rd., Hubbard, Ohio 44425. Educational, social work.

Sacred Heart of Jesus, Servants of the Most, S.S.C.J.: Founded 1894, in Poland; in U.S., 1959. General motherhouse, Cracow, Poland; U.S. address, R.D. 1, Box 429, Portage, Pa. 15946. Education, health care, social services.

Sacred Heart of Jesus, Sisters of the, S.S.C.J.: Founded 1816, in France; in U.S., 1903. General motherhouse, St. Jacut, Brittany, France; U.S. provincial house, 5922 Blanco Rd., San Antonio, Tex. 78216. Educational, hospital, domestic work.

Sacred Heart of Jesus and of the Poor, Servants of the (Mexican), S.S.H.J.P.: Founded 1885, in Mexico; in U.S., 1907. General motherhouse, Apartado 92, Puebla, Pue., Mexico; U.S. address, 237 Tobin Pl., El Paso, Tex. 79905.

Sacred Heart of Jesus for Reparation, Congregation of the Handmaids of the: Founded 1918, in Italy; in U.S., 1958. U.S. address, Sunshine Park, R.D. 3, Steubenville, Ohio 43952.

Sacred Heart of Mary, Religious of the, R.S.H.M.: Founded 1848, in France; in U.S., 1877. Generalate, Rome, Italy. U.S. provinces: 50 Wilson Park Dr., Tarrytown, N.Y. 10591; 8008 Loyola Blvd., Los Angeles, Calif. 90045.

Sacred Hearts, Religious of the Holy Union of the, S.U.S.C.: Founded 1826, in France; in U.S., 1886. Generalate, Rome, Italy. U.S. provinces: 550 Rock St., Fall River, Mass. 02720; Main St., Groton, Mass. 01450. Varied ministries.

Sacred Hearts and of Perpetual Adoration, Sisters of the, SS.CC.: Founded 1797, in France; in U.S., 1908. General motherhouse, Rome, Italy; U.S. provinces: 3253 Wailele Rd., Kaneohe, Hawaii 96816 (Pacific); 3115 Queens Chapel Rd. (Apts. 301-302); Mt. Rainier, Md. 20822 (East Coast). Varied ministries.

Sacred Hearts of Jesus and Mary, Sisters of the, S.H.J.M.: Established 1953, in U.S. General motherhouse, Essex, England; U.S. address, 310 San Carlos Ave., El Cerrito, Calif. 94530.

Savior, Company of the, C.S.: Founded 1952, in Spain; in U.S., 1962. General motherhouse, Madrid, Spain; U.S. foundation, 820 Clinton Ave., Bridgeport, Conn. 06604.

Savior, Sisters of the Divine, S.D.S.: Founded 1888, in Italy; in U.S., 1895. General motherhouse, Rome, Italy; U.S. province, 4311 N. 100th St., Milwaukee, Wis. 53222. Educational, hospital work.

Social Service, Sisters of, S.S.S.: Founded in Hungary, 1923, by Sr. Margaret Slachta. U.S. address, 440 Linwood Ave., Buffalo, N.Y. 14209. Social work.

Social Service, Sisters of, of Los Angeles, S.S.S.: Founded 1908, in Hungary; in U.S., 1926. General motherhouse, 1120 Westchester Pl., Los Angeles, Calif. 90019.

Teresa of Jesus, Society of St., S.T.J.: Founded 1876, in Spain; in U.S., 1910. General motherhouse, Rome, Italy; U.S. provincial house, 154 Fair Ave., San Antonio, Tex. 78223.

Thomas of Villanova, Congregation of Sisters of St., S.S.T.V.: Founded 1661, in France; in U.S., 1948. General motherhouse, Neuilly-sur-Seine, France; U.S. foundation W. Rocks Rd., Norwalk, Conn. 06851.

Trinity, Missionary Servants of the Most Blessed, M.S.B.T.: Founded 1912, in U.S., by Very Rev. Thomas A. Judge. General motherhouse, 3501 Solly Ave., Philadelphia, Pa. 19136. Educational, social work; health services.

Trinity, Sisters of the Most Holy, O.Ss.T.: Founded 1198, in Rome; in U.S., 1920. General motherhouse, Rome, Italy; U.S. address, Immaculate Conception Province, 21281 Chardon Rd., Euclid, Ohio 44117. Educational work.

Ursula of the Blessed Virgin, Society of the Sisters of St., S.U.: Founded 1606, in France; in U.S., 1902. General motherhouse, France; U.S. novitiate, Linwood Rd., Rhinebeck, N.Y. 12572. Educational work.

Ursuline Nuns (Roman Union), O.S.U.: Founded 1535, in Italy; in U.S., 1727. Generalate, Rome, Italy. U.S. provinces: 323 E. 198th St., Bronx, N.Y. 10458; Crystal Heights Rd., Crystal City, Mo. 63019; 639 Angela Dr., Santa Rosa, Calif. 95401; 71 Lowder St., Dedham, Mass. 02026,

Ursuline Nuns of the Congregation of Paris, O.S.U.: Founded 1535, in Italy; in U.S., 1727, in New Orleans. U.S. motherhouses: St. Martin, O. 45170; 901 E. Miami St., Paola, Kans. 66071; 3115 Lexington Rd., Louisville, Ky. 40206; 2600 Lander Rd., Cleveland, O. 44124; Maple Mount, Ky. 42356; 436 W. Delaware, Toledo, O. 43610; 4250 Shields Rd., Canfield, O. 44406; 1339 E. McMillan St., Cincinnati, O. 45206.

Ursuline Nuns of the Congregation of Tildonk, Belgium, O.S.U.: Founded 1535, in Italy; Tildonk congregation, 1832; in U.S., 1924. Generalate, Tildonk, Belgium; U.S. address, 81-15 Utopia Parkway, Jamaica, N.Y. 11432. Educational, foreign mission work.

Ursuline Sisters of Belleville, O.S.U.: Founded 1535, in Italy; in U.S., 1910; established as diocesan community, 1983. Central house, 1026 N. Douglas Ave., Belleville, Ill. 62221. Educational work.

Ursuline Sisters (Irish Ursuline Union), O.S.U.: Generalate, Dublin, Ireland; U.S. address, 1973 Torch Hill Rd., Columbus, Ga. 31903.

Venerini Sisters, Religious, M.P.V.: Founded 1685, in Italy; in U.S., 1909. General motherhouse, Rome, Italy; U.S. provincialate; 23 Edward St., Worcester, Mass. 01605.

Vincent de Paul, Sisters: See Charity of St. Vincent de Paul, Sisters of.

Visitation Nuns, V.H.M.: Founded 1610, in France; in U.S. (Georgetown, D.C.), 1799. Contemplative, educational work. Two federations in U.S.

First Federation of North America. Major pontifical enclosure. Pres., Mother Mary Jozefa Kowalewski, Monastery of the Visitation, 2002 Bancroft Pkwy., Wilmington, Del. 19806. Addresses of monasteries belonging to the federation: 2300 Springhill Ave., Mobile, Ala. 36607; 2002 Bancroft Pkwy., Wilmington, Del. 19806; 2209 E. Grace St., Richmond, Va. 23223; 5820 City Ave., Philadelphia, Pa. 19131; 1745 Parkside Blvd., Toledo, O. 43607; 2055 Ridgedale Dr., Snellville, Ga. 30278.

Second Federation of North America. Constitutional enclosure. Pres., Rev. Mother Mary Philomena Tisinger, Visitation Monastery, 1500 35th St., Washington, D.C. 20007. Addresses of monasteries belonging to the federation: 1500 35th St., Washington, D.C. 20007; 3020 N. Ballas Rd., St. Louis, Mo. 63131; 200 E. Second St., Frederick, Md. 21701; Mt. St. Chantal Monastery of the Visitation, Wheeling, W. Va. 26003; Ridge Blvd. and 89th St., Brooklyn, N.Y. 11209; 1600 Murdoch Ave., Parkersburg, W. Va. 26101; 2000 Sixteenth Ave., Rock Island, Ill. 61201; 2475 Dodd Rd., Mendota Heights, St. Paul, Minn. 55120; 3200 S.W. Dash Point Rd., Federal Way, Wash. 98003.

Visitation of the Congregation of the Immaculate Heart of Mary, Sisters of the, S.V.M.: Founded 1952, in U.S. Motherhouse, 900 Alta Vista St., Dubuque, Ia. 52001. Educational work, parish ministry.

Vocation Sisters, V.S.: Founded 1945, in England; in U.S. 1977. Motherhouse, England; U.S. house, 6611 South St., Falls, Church, Va. 22042.

Vocationist Sisters (Sisters of the Divine Vocations): Founded 1921, in Italy; in U.S., 1967. General motherhouse, Naples, Italy; U.S. foundation, Perpetual Help Nursery, 172 Broad St., Newark, N.J. 07104.

Wisdom, Daughters of, D.W.: Founded 1703, in France, by St. Louis Marie Grignion de Montfort; in U.S., 1904. General motherhouse, Vendee, France; U.S. province, P.O. Box 430, Islip, N.Y. 11751. Education, health care, parish ministry, social services.

Xaverian Missionary Society of Mary, Inc., X.M.M.: Founded 1945, in Italy; in U.S., 1954. General motherhouse, Parma, Italy; U.S. address, 242 Salisbury St., Worcester, Mass. 01609.

Xavier Mission Sisters (Catholic Mission Sisters of St. Francis Xavier), X.M.S.: Founded 1946, at Warren, Mich., by Cardinal Edward Mooney. General motherhouse, 37179 Moravian Dr., Mount Clemens, Mich. 48043. Educational, hospital, social work in missions.

In May, 1988, Mother Mary Assumpta Long was reelected president of the Forum of Major Superiors.

ORGANIZATIONS OF RELIGIOUS

Conferences

Conferences of major superiors of religious institutes, dating from the 1950s and encouraged by the Code of Canon Law (canons 708, 709), have been established in 19 countries of Europe, 14 in North and Central America, 10 in South America, 30 in Africa and 20 in Asia and Oceania.

Conference of Major Superiors of Men: Founded in 1956; established officially Mar. 23, 1960, by decree of the Congregation for Religious and Secular Institutes. Its purposes are to promote the spiritual and apostolic welfare of men Religious, provide liaison opportunities among Religious and with church officials, and serve as a national voice for the corporate views of superiors. Membership, 269 major superiors representing institutes with a combined membership of approximately 30,000. President Bro. Sean Sammon, F.M.S.; executive director, Rev. Roland J. Faley, T.O.R. National office: 8808 Cameron St., Silver Spring, Md. 20910.

Leadership Conference of Women Religious: Organized in the late 1950s as the Conference of Major Superiors of Women (name changed, 1971); approved by the Congregation for Religious and Secular Institutes June 13, 1962. Its purpose is to promote the spiritual and apostolic calling and works of sisterhoods in the U.S. Membership, approximately 700. President, Sister Helen Garvey, B.V.M.; executive director, Sister Janet Roesener, C.S.J. National secretariat: 8808 Cameron St., Silver Spring, Md. 20910.

International Union of Superiors General (Women): Established in 1965; approved by the Congregation for Religious and Secular Institutes, 1967. President, Sister Helen McLaughlin, R.S.C.J. Address: Adolfo Gandiglio, 27, 00151, Rome, Italy.

Union of Superiors General (Men): Established in 1957. President, Father John Vaughn, O.F.M. Address: Via dei Penitenzieri 19, 00193 Rome, Italy.

Latin American Confederation of Religious: Established in 1959, approved by the Congregation for Religious and Secular Institutes, 1967. President, Father Luis Ugalde Olalde, S.J. Address: Av. Berrizbeitia 14, el Paraiso, Qta. Santa Tecla, Caracas 1020-A Venezuela.

Union of European Conferences of Major Superiors: Established Dec. 25, 1983. President, Sister Frances Delcourt, S.A.; secretary, Father Leonhard Gregotsch, M.I. Address: Freyung 6/1-3, A-1010, Vienna, Austria.

World Conference of Secular Institutes: Established May 23, 1974. Address: Via deglia Ombrellari 40, 00193 Rome, Italy.

Association of Contemplative Sisters (1969): Its principal purpose is development of the contemplative life-style for effective service to the Church. Membership, approximately 400. President, Sister Mary Lavin, O.C.D. Central office: 3176 Fairmount Blvd., Cleveland, Ohio 44118.

Consortium Perfectae Caritatis (Women) (1971): To encourage the development of religious life in line with Vatican II guidelines and related directives. President, Sister Mary Elise Krantz, S.N.D.; coordinator, Rev. James A. Viall. Mailing address: P.O. Box 1856, Middleburg, Va. 22117.

Institute on Religious Life (1974). To foster more effective understanding and implementation of teachings of the Church on religious life, promote vocations to religious life and the priesthood, and promote growth in sanctity of all the faithful according to their state in life. Executive director, Rev. James Downey. National office, 4200 N. Austin Ave., Chicago, Ill. 60634.

National Assembly of Religious Brothers (1972): To publicize the unique vocations of brothers, to further communication among brothers and provide liaison with various organizations of the Church. Executive secretary, Bro. Thomas A. Hickey, M.M., National office, 1307 S. Wabash Ave., Suite 201, Chicago, Ill. 60605.

National Black Sisters' Conference (1968): To determine priorities in service to Black people, promote Black vocations and the development of religious life in the unique Black life-style. Executive director, Sister Marie de Porres Taylor, S.N.J.M. National office, 3014 Lake Shore Ave., Oakland, Calif. 94610.

National Conference of Vicars for Religious (1967): National organization of diocesan officials concerned with relations between their respective dioceses and religious communities engaged therein. President, Rev. Robert C. Nash, 1300 Byron St., P.O. Box 230, Wheeling, W. Va. 26003; secretary, Sr. Barbara A. Ginther, S.C., P.O. Box 43022, St. Petersburg, Fla. 33743.

National Religious Vocation Conference (NRVC) (1988, with merger of National Sisters Vocation Conference and National Conference of Religious Vocation Directors): Service organization of men and women committed to the fostering and discernment of vocations, Executive director, Bro. Joseph Samson, F.S.C. Address: 1307 S. Wabash Ave., No. 350, Chicago, Ill. 60605.

Religious Formation Conference (1953): Originally Sister Formation Conference; membership now includes men and persons belonging to non-canonical religious groups. Executive director, Sister Peggy Nichols, C.S.J. National office: 1234 Massachusetts Ave. N.W., Washington, D.C. 20005.

SECULAR INSTITUTES

(Sources: Almanac survey; United States Conference of Secular Institutes; *Annuario Pontificio*.)

Secular institutes are societies of men and women living in the world who dedicate themselves to observe the evangelical counsels and to carry on apostolic works suitable to their talents and opportunities in the areas of their everyday life.

"Secular institutes are not religious communities but they carry with them in the world a profession of evangelical counsels which is genuine and complete, and recognized as such by the Church. This profession confers a consecration on men and women, laity and clergy, who reside in the world. For this reason they should chiefly strive for total self-dedication to God, one inspired by perfect charity. These institutes should preserve their proper and particular character, a secular one, so that they may everywhere measure up successfully to that apostolate which they were designed to exercise, and which is both in the world and, in a sense, of the world" (*Decree on the Appropriate Renewal of Religious Life,* No. 11; Second Vatican Council).

Secular institutes are under the jurisdiction of the Congregation for Religious and Secular Institutes. General legislation concerning them is contained in Canons 710 to 730 of the Code of Canon Law.

A secular institute reaches maturity in several stages. It begins as an association of the faithful, technically called a pious union, with the approval of a local bishop. Once it has proved its viability, he can give it the status of an institute of diocesan right, in accordance with norms and permission emanating from the Congregation for Religious and Secular Institutes. On issuance of a separate decree from this congregation, an institute of diocesan right becomes an institute of pontifical right.

Secular institutes, which originated in the latter part of the 18th century, were given full recognition and approval by Pius XII Feb. 2, 1947, in the apostolic constitution *Provida Mater Ecclesia.* On Mar. 25 of the same year a special commission for secular institutes was set up within the Congregation for Religious. Institutes were commended and confirmed by Pius XII in a motu proprio of Mar. 12, 1948, and were the subject of a special instruction issued a week later, Mar. 19, 1948.

The **United States Conference of Secular Institutes** (CSI) was established in October, 1972, following the organization of the World Conference of Secular Institutes in Rome. Its membership is open to all canonically erected secular institutes with members living in the United States. The conference was organized to offer secular institutes an opportunity to exchange experiences, to do research in order to help the Church carry out its mission, and to search for ways and means to make known the existence of secular institutes in the U.S. Address: c/o Claudette Cyr, president, 121 Greenwood St., Watertown, Conn. 06795.

Institutes in the U.S.

Caritas Christi: Originated in Marseilles, 1937; for women. Established as a secular institute of pontifical right Mar. 19, 1955. Address: P.O. Box 162, River Forest, Ill. 60305.

Company of St. Paul: Originated in Milan, Italy, 1920; for lay people and priests. Approved as a secular institute of pontifical right June 30, 1950. Address: 52 Davis Ave., White Plains, N.Y. 10605.

Company of St. Ursula, Secular Institute of St. Angela Merici: Founded in Brescia, Italy, 1535; for women. Approved as a secular institute of pontifical right 1958. Addresses: Lina Moser, President, Via Rosmini 128, 38100 Trento, Italy; Juline Lamb, 2937 Hemphill St., Fort Worth, Tex. 76110. International membership of 3,000.

DeSales Secular Institute: Founded in Vienna, Austria, 1940; for women. Pontifical right, 1964. Address: Mary Robinson, 420 Biddle St., Chesapeake City, Md. 21915.

Diocesan Laborer Priests: Approved as a secular institute of pontifical right, 1952. The specific aim of the institute is the promotion, sustenance and cultivation of apostolic, religious and priestly vocations. Address: Rev. Jose M. Ambros, 3706 15th St. N.E., Washington, D.C. 20017.

Don Bosco Volunteers: Founded 1917; for women. Approved as a secular institute of pontifical right Aug. 5, 1978. Address: Don Bosco Volunteers, 202 Union Ave., Paterson, N.J. 07502. International membership of 900 in 25 countries.

Handmaids of Divine Mercy: Founded in Bari, Italy, 1951; for women. Approved as an institute of pontifical right 1972. Address: Mary I. DiFonzo, 2410 Hughes Ave., Bronx, N.Y. 10458. International membership of 980.

Institute of Secular Missionaries: Founded in Vitoria, Spain, 1939; for women. Approved as a secular institute, 1955. Address: 2710 Ruberg Ave., Cincinnati, O. 45211, Att. E. Dilger.

Institute of the Heart of Jesus: Originated in France Feb. 2, 1791; restored Oct. 29, 1918; for diocesan priests and lay people. Received final approval from the Holy See as a secular institute of pontifical right Feb. 2, 1952. Rev. Andre Loisel, superior general. Addresses: Central House, 202 Avenue du Maine, Pavillion 4, 75014 Paris, France; U.S. address, Rev. Msgr. John A. Esseff, 300 Wyoming Ave., Scranton, Pa. 18503. International membership of approximately 1,400.

Missionaries of the Kingship of Christ the King: Under this title are included three distinct and juridically separate institutes founded by Agostino Gemelli, O.F.M. (1878-1959).

(1) Women Missionaries of the Kingship of Christ — Founded in 1919, in Italy; definitively approved as an institute of pontifical rite 1953. Established in 15 countries. U.S. branch established 1950. Age at time of entrance, 21 to 40.

(2) Men Missionaries of the Kingship of Christ — Founded 1928, in Italy, as an institute of diocesan right. U.S. branch established 1962.

(3) Priest Missionaries of the Kingship of Christ — Established in U.S., 1954; approved as institute of pontifical right July 15, 1978. For diocesan priests.

Addresses: Rev. Stephen Hartdegen, O.F.M., 1650 St. Camillus Dr., Silver Spring, Md. 20903 (for Men Missionaries); Rev. Jeffrey Bridges, O.F.M., 1500-34th Ave., Oakland, Calif. 94601 (for Women Missionaries).

Oblate Missionaries of Mary Immaculate: Founded, 1952; approved as a secular institute of diocesan right Feb. 2, 1962, and of pontifical right Mar. 25, 1984; for women. Addresses: Oblate Missionaries of Mary Immaculate, 121 Greenwood St., Watertown, Conn. 06795; P.O. Box 303, Manville,

Secular Institutes — Associations

R.I. 02838; 7535 Boulevard Parent, Trois Rivieres, P. Q. G9A 5E1, Canada. International membership.

Opus Spiritus Sancti: Originated in West Germany, 1952; for diocesan priests and unmarried deacons. Formally acknowledged by Rome in 1977. Address: Rev. Ronald J. Reicks, P.O. Box 337, Whittemore, Ia. 50598.

Rural Parish Workers of Christ the King: Founded in 1942; for women. An approved lay institute of apostolic action of the Archdiocese of St. Louis. Dedicated to the glory of God in service of neighbor, especially in rural areas. Address: Box 552, Rt. 1, Cadet, Mo. 63630.

Schoenstatt Sisters of Mary: Originated in Schoenstatt, Germany, 1926; for women. Established as a secular institute of diocesan right May 20, 1948; of pontifical right Oct. 18, 1948. Addresses: Schoenstatt Sisters of Mary, W. 284 N. 404 Cherry Lane, Waukesha, Wis. 53188; House Schoenstatt, Star Rt. 1, Box 100, Rockport, Tex. 78382. International membership of more than 2,800.

Secular Institute of Pius X: Originated in Manchester, N.H., 1940; for priests and laymen. Approved as a secular institute, 1959 (first secular institute of diocesan right founded in the U.S. to be approved by the Holy See). Also admits married and unmarried men as associate members. Addresses: Lynchville Park, Goffstown, N.H. 03045. C.P. 1815, Quebec City, P.Q. G1K 7K7, Canada.

Servitium Christi Secular Institute of the Blessed Sacrament: Founded in Holland, 1952; for women. Approved as a secular institute of diocesan right May 8, 1963. Address: Miss Olympia Panagatos, 250 E. 77th St., Apt. 3B, New York, N.Y. 10021.

Society of Our Lady of the Way: Originated, 1936; for women. Approved as a secular institute of pontifical right Jan. 3, 1953. Addresses: 147 Dorado Terr., San Francisco, Calif. 94112; P.O. Box 412, Stamford, Conn. 06904; 1116 Cook Ave., Apt. 27, Lakewood, O. 44107. International membership, 300.

Teresian Institute: Founded in Spain 1911 by Pedro Poveda. Approved as an institute of pontifical right Jan. 11, 1924. Mailing Address: P.O. Box 14-3407, Coral Gables, Fla. 33114.

Voluntas Dei Institute: Originated in Canada, 1958 by Father L. M. Parent; for secular priests, laymen and couples. Approved as a secular institute of pontifical right, July 12, 1987. Established in 14 countries. Mailing address: 6477, Lemay St., Montreal, Que. H1T 2L6, Canada.

The *Annuario Pontificio* lists the following secular institutes of pontifical right which are not established in the U.S.:

For men: Christ the King; Institute of Our Lady of Life; Institute of Prado; Priests of the Sacred Heart of Jesus.

For women: Alliance in Jesus through Mary; Apostles of the Sacred Heart; Catechists of Mary, Virgin and Mother; Catechists of the Sacred Heart of Jesus (Ukrainian); Cordimarian Filiation; Daughters of the Nativity of Mary; Daughters of the Queen of the Apostles; Daughters of the Sacred Heart; Evangelical Crusade; Faithful Servants of Jesus; Handmaids of Our Mother of Mercy; Institute of the Blessed Virgin Mary (della Strada); Institute of Notre Dame du Travail; Institute of Our Lady of Life; Institute of St. Boniface; Little Apostles of Charity; Life and Peace in Christ Jesus; Missionaries of Royal Priesthood; Missionaries of the Sick; Oblates of Christ the King; Oblates of the Sacred Heart of Jesus; Servants of Jesus the Priest; Servite Secular Institute; Union of the Daughters of God; Workers of Divine Love; Workers of the Cross; Handmaids of Holy Church; Augustinian Auxiliary Missionaries; Heart of Jesus; Apostolic Missionaries of Charity; Combonian Secular Missionaries; Missionaries of the Gospel; Little Franciscan Family; Secular Servants of Jesus Christ Priest.

Associations

Caritas: Originated in New Orleans, 1950; for women. Follow guidelines of secular institutes. Small self-supporting groups who live and work among the poor and oppressed; work in Louisiana and Guatemala. Address: Box 308, Abita Springs, La. 70420.

Daughters of Our Lady of Fatima: Originated in Lansdowne, Pa., 1949; for women. Received diocesan approval, Jan., 1952. Address: Fatima House, Rolling Hills Rd., Ottsville, Pa. 18942.

Focolare Movement: Founded in Trent, Italy, in 1943, by Chiara Lubich and a small group of companions; for men and women. Approved as an association of the faithful, 1962. It is not a secular institute by statute; however, vows are observed by its totally dedicated core membership of 4,000 who live in small communities called Focolare (Italian word for "hearth") centers. There are 16 resident centers in the U.S. and two in Canada. GEN (New Generation) is the youth organization of the movement. An estimated 70,000 are affiliated with the movement in the U.S. and Canada; 1,200,000, worldwide. Publications include *Living City*, monthly; *GEN II* and *GEN III* for young people and children. Five week-long summer conventions, called "Mariapolis" ("City of Mary"), are held annually. Address for information: P.O. Box 496, New York, N.Y. 10021 (indicate men's or women's branch).

Institute of Apostolic Oblates: Founded in Rome, Italy, 1947; for women. Address: 2125 W. Walnut Ave., Fullerton, Calif. 92633.

Jesus Caritas — Fraternity of Priests: An international association of priests who strive to live in the spirit of Charles de Foucauld, combining an active life with a contemplative calling. U.S. address for information: Rev. Donald Hanchon, 924 E. 2nd St., Monroe, Mich. 48161.

Madonna House Apostolate: Originated in Toronto, Canada, 1930; for priests and lay persons. Public association of the faithful. Address: Madonna House, Combermere, Ontario, Canada K0J 1L0 — Jean Fox (women), Albert Osterberger (men), Rev. Robert Pelton (priests). International membership and missions.

Pax Christi: Lay institute of men and women

dedicated to witnessing to Christ, with special emphasis on service to the poor in Mississippi. Addresses: St. Francis Center, 708 Ave. I, Greenwood, Miss. 38930; LaVerna House, 2108 Altawoods Blvd., Jackson, Miss. 39204.

SECULAR ORDERS

Secular orders (commonly called third orders) are societies of the faithful living in the world who seek to deepen their Christian life and apostolic commitment in association with and according to the spirit of various religious institutes. The orders are called "third" because their foundation followed the establishment of the first (for men) and second (for women) religious orders with which they are associated.

Augustine, Third Order Secular of St.: Founded, 13th century; approved Nov. 7, 1400.

Carmelites, Lay (Third Order of Our Lady of Mt. Carmel): Rule for laity approved by Pope Nicholas V, Oct. 7, 1452. Address: Lay Carmelite Office, Aylesford, 8501 Bailey Rd., Darien, Ill. 60559. Approximately 160 communities and 6,400 members in the U.S. and Canada.

Carmelites, The Secular Order of Discalced (formerly the Third Order Secular of the Blessed Virgin Mary of Mt Carmel and of St. Teresa of Jesus): Rule based on the Carmelite reform established by St. Teresa and St. John of the Cross, 16th century; approved Mar. 23, 1594. Revised rule approved May 10, 1979. Office of National Secretariat, U.S.A.; P.O. Box 3079, San Jose, Calif. 95156. Approximately 22,245 throughout the world; 3,000 in U.S.

Dominican Laity: Founded in the 13th century. Addresses of provincial coordinators: 487 Michigan Ave. N.E., Washington, D.C. 20017; 1909 S. Ashland Ave., Chicago, Ill. 60608; 5890 Birch Ct., Oakland, Calif. 94618; 3175 Hathaway Ct. N.E., Atlanta, Ga. 30341.

Franciscan Order, Secular (SFO): Founded, 1209 by St. Francis of Assisi; approved Aug. 30, 1221. National minister, James David Lynch, 4143 "J" St., Juniata Park, Philadelphia, Pa. 19124. Approximately 780,000 throughout the world; 40,000 in U.S.

Mary, Third Order of: Founded, Dec. 8, 1850; rule approved by the Holy See, 1857. Addresses of provincial directors: 815 Varnum St. N.E., Washington, D.C. 20017; 7 Harvard St., P.O. Box 66, Charlestown, Mass. 02129; 566 Bush St., San Francisco, Calif. 94108. Approximately 14,000 in the world, 5,600 in U.S.

Mary, Secular Order of Servants of (Servite): Founded, 1233; approved, 1304. Revised rule approved 1986. Address: Assistant for Secular Order, 3401 S. Home Ave., Berwyn, Ill. 60402.

Mercy, Secular Third Order of Our Lady of (Mercedarian): Founded, 1219 by St. Peter Nolasco; approved the same year.

Norbert, Third Order of St.: Founded, 1122 by St. Norbert; approved by Pope Honorius II, 1126. Address: St. Norbert Abbey, De Pere, Wis. 54115.

Trinity, Third Order Secular of the Most Holy: Founded 1198; approved, 1219.

Oblates of St. Benedict are lay persons affiliated with a Benedictine abbey or monastery who strive to direct their lives, as circumstances permit, according to the spirit and Rule of St. Benedict.

MISSIONARY ACTIVITY OF THE CHURCH

UNITED STATES OVERSEAS MISSIONARIES

Data on U.S. overseas missionary personnel in the following tables were gathered by, and are reproduced with permission of, the United States Catholic Mission Association, 3029 Fourth St., Washington, D.C. 20017.

For additional information about the Church in mission areas, see News Events and other Almanac entries.

Field Distribution, 1988

Under this and following headings, Alaska, Hawaii, etc., are considered abroad because they are outside the 48 contiguous states.

Africa: 984 (485 men; 499 women). Largest numbers in Kenya, 200; Tanzania, 145; Ghana, 95; Zambia, 74; Liberia, 56.

Near East: 72 (55 men; 17 women). Largest numbers in Israel, 42; Egypt, 18; Cyprus, 5.

Far East: 1,332 (883 men; 449 women). Largest numbers in Philippines, 336; Japan, 282; Taiwan, 165; Korea, 128; India, 89; Hong Kong, 82.

Oceania: 584 (288 men; 296 women). Largest groups in Hawaii, 193; Papua New Guinea, 180; Australia, 58; Caroline Islands, 49; Mariana Islands, 41; Samoa, 16.

Europe: 27 (14 men; 13 women). Largest groups in Denmark, 8; Finland, 8; Sweden, 7.

North America: 289 (130 men; 159 women). Largest groups in Alaska, 161; Canada, 123.

Caribbean Islands: 466 (253 men; 213 women). Largest groups in Puerto Rico, 171; Jamaica, 113; Dominican Republic, 50; Haiti, 44; Bahamas, 41.

Central America: 818 (445 men; 373 women). Largest groups in Mexico, 259; Guatemala, 215.

South America: 1,491 (760 men; 731 women). Largest groups in Peru, 459; Brazil, 410; Bolivia, 197; Chile, 190.

TOTAL: 6,063 (3,313 men; 2,750 women).

Men Religious, 1988

Ninety-one mission-sending groups had 2,974 priests and brothers in overseas assignments.

Jesuits: 504 in 43 countries; largest group, 74 in the Philippines.

Maryknoll Missionaries: 496 in 27 countries; largest group, 45 in Tanzania.

Franciscans (O.F.M.): 200 in 26 countries; largest group, 54 in Brazil.

Divine Word Missionaries: 161 in 19 countries; largest group, 43 in Papua New Guinea.
Oblates of Mary Immaculate: 133 in 17 countries; largest group, 25 in Brazil.
Redemptorists: 126 in 9 countries; largest group, 49 in Brazil.
Capuchins (O.F.M. Cap): 124 in 12 countries; largest group, 29 in Papua New Guinea.
Congregation of Holy Cross: 106 in 15 countries; largest group, 24 in Bangladesh.
Marianists: 92 in 13 countries; largest group, 23 in Hawaii.
Benedictines: 80 in 13 countries; largest group, 22 in Guatemala.
Columbans: 63 in 12 countries; largest group, 23 in the Philippines.
Dominicans: 58 in 12 countries; largest group, 13 in Pakistan.
Conventual Franciscans (O.F.M. Conv): 57 in 10 countries; largest group, 13 in Canada.
Brothers of the Christian Schools: 54 in 17 countries; largest group, 11 in the Philippines.
Passionists: 49 in 12 countries; largest group, 16 in the Philippines.
Vincentians: 39 in 8 countries; largest group, 17 in Panama.
Holy Ghost Fathers: 37 in 7 countries; largest group, 18 in Tanzania.
La Salette Missionaries: 37 in 8 countries; largest group, 13 in Argentina.
Congregation of Christian Brothers: 28 in 5 countries; largest group, 12 in Peru.
Marist Fathers: 26 in 9 countries; largest group, 9 in Hawaii.
Marist Brothers: 26 in 6 countries; largest group, 9 in the Philippines.
Augustinians: 26 in 3 countries; largest group, 16 in Peru.
Missionaries of the Sacred Heart: 25 in 4 countries; largest group, 18 in Papua New Guinea.
Salesians: 25 in 9 countries; largest group, 11 in Canada.
Society of the Precious Blood: 18 in 3 countries; largest group, 9 in Chile.
Missionhurst-CICM: 18 in 8 countries; largest group, 4 in Dominican Republic.
Xaverian Missionary Fathers: 18 in 7 countries; largest group, 6 in Brazil.

Sixty-four other mission-sending institutes had 17 or less members in overseas assignments.

Diocesan Priests, 1988

Two hundred diocesan priests from 91 dioceses were in overseas assignments in 1988.

The largest groups were from Boston (18 in 3 countries), Cleveland (8 in 2 countries), Jefferson City (7 in 1 country), and St. Louis (6 in 1 country).

Sixty of the diocesan priests in overseas assignments were members of the Missionary Society of St. James the Apostle, founded by Cardinal Richard J. Cushing of Boston in 1958. Its director is Rev. Msgr. John J. Moriarty, 24 Clark St., Boston, Mass. 02109.

Twenty-nine other diocesan priests in overseas assignments were working as Priest Associates with the Maryknoll Fathers, whose headquarters are in Maryknoll, New York 10545.

Sisters, 1988

Two hundred and 43 mission-sending groups had 2,495 sisters in overseas assignments.

Maryknoll Sisters: 390 in 26 countries; largest group, 50 in Hawaii.
School Sisters of Notre Dame: 111 in 18 countries; largest group, 14 in Guatemala.
Marist Sisters: 66 in 11 countries; largest groups, 11 each in Papua New Guinea and Peru.
Sisters of St. Joseph of Carondelet: 59 in 8 countries; largest group, 25 in Hawaii.
Daughters of Charity: 57 in 9 countries; largest group, 23 in Bolivia.
Sisters of Notre Dame de Namur: 54 in 10 countries; largest group, 14 in Kenya.
Medical Mission Sisters: 49 in 13 countries; largest group, 15 in Ghana.
Sisters of the Holy Cross: 44 in 6 countries; largest group, 17 in Brazil.
Benedictine Sisters: 42 in 12 countries: largest group, 10 in Colombia.
Sisters, Servants of the Immaculate Heart of Mary (Philadelphia): 37 in 2 countries; larger group, 24 in Peru.
Ursulines of the Roman Union: 37 in 14 countries; largest group, 8 in Thailand.
Franciscan Missionaries of Mary: 32 in 17 countries; largest group, 5 in Liberia.
Sisters of Mercy of the Union in the U.S.A.: 31 in 8 countries; largest group, 10 in Jamaica.
Sisters of the Holy Family of Nazareth: 29 in 4 countries; largest group, 16 in Australia.
Sisters of the Third Franciscan Order (Syracuse): 28 in 3 countries; largest group, 18 in Hawaii.
Sisters of Our Lady of the Good Shepherd: 27 in 9 countries; largest groups, 6 each in Hong Kong and Hawaii.
Sisters, Servants of the Immaculate Heart of Mary (Monroe): 25 in 8 countries; largest groups, 5 each in Puerto Rico and South Africa.
Religious of the Sacred Heart: 24 in 9 countries; largest group, 9 in Japan.
Servants of the Holy Spirit: 24 in 8 countries; largest group, 7 in Ghana.
Sisters of Notre Dame: 23 in 2 countries; larger group, 13 in Papua New Guinea.
Franciscan Sisters of Allegany: 21 in 2 countries; larger group, 15 in Jamaica.
Sisters of the Assumption B.V.M.: 21 in 3 countries; largest group, 17 in Canada.
Sisters of St. Joseph (Brentwood): 20 in 4 countries; largest group, 17 in Puerto Rico.
Little Sisters of the Poor: 19 in 11 countries; largest group, 4 in India.
Adorers of the Blood of Christ: 19 in 4 countries; largest group, 10 in Liberia.

Two hundred and 18 other mission-sending institutes had 17 or less members in overseas assignments.

Lay Volunteers, 1988

Three hundred and 94 lay volunteers of 42 sponsoring organizations were in overseas assignments in 1988.

Maryknoll Lay Missioners: 115 in 20 countries; largest group, 20 in Venezuela.

Jesuit International Volunteers: 36 in 4 countries; largest group, 18 in the Caroline Islands.

Lay Mission Helpers/Mission Doctors: 32 in 8 countries; largest group, 12 in Papua New Guinea.

Jesuit Volunteer Corps: 29 in Alaska.

Volunteer Missionary Movement: 19 in 6 countries; largest groups, 6 in Papua New Guinea.

Christian Foundation for Children: 18 in 5 countries; largest group, 9 in Venezuela.

Holy Cross Associates: 12 in 4 countries; largest group, 5 in Chile.

Covenant House: 10 in 2 countries; larger group, 6 in Guatemala.

Catholic Medical Mission Board: 10 in 5 countries; largest group, 3 in Malawi. (This figure

U.S. OVERSEAS MISSIONARIES, 1960-1988

Year	Diocesan Priests	Religious Priests	Religious Brothers	Religious Sisters	Seminarians	Lay Persons	Total
1960	14	3018	575	2827	170	178	6782
1962	31	3172	720	2764	152	307	7146
1964	80	3438	782	3137	157	532	8126
1966	215	3731	901	3706	201	549	9303
1968	282	3727	869	4150	208	419	9655
1970	373	3117	666	3824	90	303	8373
1972+	246	3182	634	3121	97	376	7656
1973	237	3913*		3012		529	7691
1974	220	3084	639	2916	101	458	7418
1975	197	3023	669	2850	65	344	7148
1976	193	2961	691	2840	68	257	7010
1977	182	2882	630	2781	42	243	6760
1978	166	2830	610	2673	43	279	6601
1979	187	2800	592	2568	50	258	6455
1980	188	2750	592	2592	50	221	6393
1981	187	2702	584	2574	43	234	6324
1982	178	2668	578	2560	44	217	6245
1983	174	2668	569	2540	48	247	6246
1984	187	2603	549	2492	40	263	6134
1985	171	2500	558	2505	30	292	6056
1986	204	2473	532	2481	30	317	6037
1987	200	2394	570	2505	53	351	6073
1988	200	2420	504	2495	50	394	6063

+A corrected total for 1972 should read 7937, indicating losses of 436 from 1970 to 1972 and 246 from 1972 to 1973.
*Includes religious brothers and seminarians.

FIELD DISTRIBUTION BY AREAS, 1960-1988

Year	Africa	Far East	Near East	Oceania	Europe	N. Amer.	Carib. Is.	Cent. Amer.	S. Amer.	Total
1960	781	1959	111	986	203	337	991	433	981	6782
1962	901	2110	75	992	93	224	967	537	1247	7146
1964	1025	2332	122	846	69	220	1056	660	1796	8126
1966	1184	2453	142	953	38	211	1079	857	2386	9303
1968	1157	2470	128	1027	33	251	1198	936	2455	9655
1970	1141	2137	39	900	38	233	1067	738	2080	8373
1972	1107	1955	59	826	39	234	819	728	1889	7656
1973	1229	1962	54	811	40	253	796	763	1783	7691
1974	1121	1845	60	883	43	241	757	752	1716	7418
1975	1065	1814	71	808	37	252	698	734	1669	7148
1976	1042	1757	68	795	34	313	671	712	1618	7010
1977	1003	1659	62	784	34	296	629	702	1591	6760
1978	966	1601	57	769	34	339	593	705	1537	6601
1979	923	1562	65	743	37	332	562	686	1545	6455
1980	909	1576	65	711	35	294	548	699	1556	6393
1981	946	1529	70	696	36	315	511	693	1528	6324
1982	956	1501	62	673	32	319	522	669	1511	6245
1983	990	1468	68	640	34	346	517	650	1533	6246
1984	967	1420	84	644	29	329	513	650	1498	6134
1985	986	1366	78	650	31	312	500	692	1441	6056
1986	944	1356	73	631	28	306	495	743	1461	6037
1987	971	1335	76	635	27	283	499	762	1485	6073
1988	984	1332	72	584	27	289	466	818	1491	6063

represents those whose term of service was for at least one year. In addition, 64 short-term volunteers served in 13 countries during the year.)

Dominican Apostolic Volunteers: 9 in 2 countries; larger group, 8 in the Bahamas.

Auxiliary Missionaries of the Assumption: 9 in 4 countries; largest group, 3 in El Salvador.

Diocese of Davenport: 8 in 4 countries; largest group, 4 in Mexico.

The other thirty sponsoring organizations had 7 members or less in overseas assignments.

U.S. MISSION ASSOCIATION

The United States Catholic Mission Association, juridically established Sept. 1, 1981, continues the activities and functions of the former U.S. Catholic Mission Council.

According to existing bylaws approved by the general assembly May 25, 1982, the USCMA is "open to all those who seek to promote global mission in community with others. It is envisioned to be an experience of the renewed Church, in which all members are equal. The methods of decision-making, of financial support, and of committee service reflect the underlying ecclesiology." The purpose of the association is the "promotion of global mission. Its primary focus is cross-cultural mission, with special emphasis on international justice."

Typical activities of the association are educational efforts related to the Church's teaching about its missionary nature, sponsorship of conferences on theological and pastoral foundations of missionary endeavor, liaison and cooperation with missionary bodies of other Christian churches, training programs and refresher courses for departing and returning missionaries, and general mission animation. The USCMA is responsible for gathering and publishing annual statistical data on U.S. missionary personnel overseas. It publishes the data in the annual, *Mission Handbook.* Ten times a year, the association publishes *Mission Intercom,* a newsletter with brief information on the life and activities of the Church in the six continents.

The president of the association is Rev. John P. Fischer and the executive director is Rev. Joseph R. Lang, M.M. The office is located at 3029 Fourth St. N.E., Washington, D.C. 20017.

HOME MISSIONS

The expression "home missions" is applied to places in the U.S. where the local church does not have its own resources, human and otherwise, which are needed to begin or, if begun, to survive and grow. These areas share the name "missions" with their counterparts in foreign lands because they too need outside help to provide the personnel and means for making the Church present and active there in carrying out its mission for the salvation of people.

Dioceses in the Southeast, the Southwest, and the Far West are most urgently in need of outside help to carry on the work of the Church. Millions of persons live in counties in which there are no resident priests. Many others live in rural areas beyond the reach and influence of a Catholic center. According to recent statistics compiled by the Glenmary Research Center, there are approximately 545 priestless counties in the United States. Many states generally thought to be well off from a pastoral standpoint include areas in which the Catholic Church and the ministry of priests are virtually unknown.

About 20 per cent of the total U.S. population and less than three per cent of the Catholic population live within the boundaries of the 17 "most missionary" dioceses of the country. A "Survey of the Catholic Weakness" conducted by the National Catholic Rural Life Conference disclosed that the Catholic Church ranked near the bottom of about 40 religious bodies in percentage of rural membership.

Mission Workers

A number of forces are at work to meet the pastoral needs of these missionary areas and to establish permanent churches and operating institutions where they are required. In many dioceses, one or more missions and stations are attended from established parishes and are gradually growing to independent status. Priests, brothers and sisters belonging to scores of religious institutes are engaged full-time in the home missions. Lay persons, some of them in affiliation with special groups and movements, are also involved.

The Society for the Propagation of the Faith, which conducts an annual collection for mission support in all parishes of the U.S., allocates 40 per cent of this sum for disbursement to home missions through the American Board of Catholic Missions.

The Catholic Church Extension Society (see separate article) disburses millions of dollars each year for mission work.

Special mission support is the purpose of the Commission for the Catholic Missions among the Colored People and the Indians.

Various mission-aid societies frequently undertake projects in behalf of the home missions.

The **Glenmary Home Missioners,** founded by Father W. Howard Bishop in 1939, is the only home mission society established for the sole purpose of carrying out the pastoral ministry in small towns and rural districts of the United States. Glenmary serves in many areas where at least 20 per cent of the people live in poverty and less than one per cent are Catholic. With 70 priests and 22 professed brothers as of May, 1988, the Glenmary Missioners had 37 parishes and 39 missions in the archdioceses of Atlanta and Cincinnati, and in the dioceses of Birmingham, Charlotte, Covington, Dallas, Jackson, Lexington, Little Rock, Nashville, Owensboro, Richmond, Savannah, Tulsa, Tyler and Wheeling-Charleston. National headquarters are located at 4119 Glenmary Trace, Fairfield, O. The mailing address is P.O. Box 465618, Cincinnati, O. 45246.

Organizations

The Commission for Catholic Missions among the Colored People and the Indians (Black and Indian Mission Office): Organized officially in 1885 by decree of the Third Plenary Council of Baltimore. Provides financial support for religious works among Blacks and Indians in 133 archdioceses and dioceses through funds raised by an annual collection in all parishes of the U.S. on the first Sunday of Lent, the designated Sunday. In 1987, $6.1 million was raised. Archbishop William D. Borders is president of the board; Msgr. Paul A. Lenz is secretary. Headquarters: 2021 H St. N.W., Washington, D.C. 20006.

Bureau of Catholic Indian Missions: Established in 1874 as the representative of Catholic Indian missions before the federal government and the public; made permanent organization in 1884 by Third Plenary Council of Baltimore. After a remarkable history of rendering important services to the Indian people, the bureau continues to represent the Catholic Church in the U.S. in her apostolate to the American Indian. Concerns are evangelization, catechesis, liturgy, family life, education, advocacy. Archbishop William D. Borders is president of the board; Msgr. Paul A. Lenz is secretary. Address: 2021 H St., Washington, D.C. 20006.

Latest statistics of the bureau reported 285,354 Catholics (19 percent) in a total Indian population of 1,486,000. Among dioceses with the largest numbers of Catholic Indians: Santa Fe (archdiocese), 41,000; Gallup, N.M., 32,000; Tuscon, Ariz., 21,000; Santa Rosa, Calif., 16,000; Rapid City, S.D., 15,000; Great Falls-Billings, Mont., 14,000.

Catholic Negro-American Mission Board (1907): Support priests and sisters in southern states and provide monthly support to sisters and lay teachers in the poorest Black schools. In 1987, over $350,000 was allocated to 36 needy schools. Archbishop William D. Borders is president of the board; Msgr. Paul A. Lenz is executive director; Patricia L. O'Rourke, administrator. Address: 2021 H St. N.W., Washington, D.C. 20005.

The Catholic Church Extension Society (1905): Established with papal approval for the purpose of preserving and extending the Church in rural and isolated parts of the U.S. and its dependencies principally through the collection and disbursement of funds for mission work. Since the time of its founding, more than $125 million have been received and expended for this purpose. Disbursements, made at the requests of bishops in 90 designated mission dioceses, exceeded $11 million for fiscal year 1986-87. The society also distributes evangelization and catechetical materials. Works of the society are supervised by a 12-member board of governors: Cardinal Joseph Bernardin, archbishop of Chicago, chancellor; Very Rev. Edward J. Slattery, president; five bishops, one sister and four laymen. Headquarters: 35 E. Wacker Drive, Chicago, Ill. 60601.

National Catholic Rural Life Conference: Founded in 1923 through the efforts of Bishop Edwin V. O'Hara for the purpose of promoting the general welfare of rural people by a program of extensive services, publications and rural-related activities. The conference has approximately 2,000 members among rural pastors, farmers, teachers, sociologists, economists, agricultural agents and officials. There are 114 officially appointed diocesan rural life directors. Most Rev. John R. Roach, archbishop of St. Paul-Minneapolis, is president. National headquarters: 4625 N.W. Beaver Dr., Des Moines, Ia. 50310.

Rural Ministry Institute: The Edwin Vincent O'Hara Institute for Rural Ministry Education was founded in 1978 to provide training and other resource services for priests, seminarians, religious and lay persons beginning or already involved in rural ministry. Sister Dolores Brinkel, S.C.L., is director. Address: 3700 Oakview Terr., N.E., Washington, D.C. 20017.

Tekakwitha Conference: Established in 1939, as a missionary priest advisory group in the Fargo, N.D., diocese. It became (1946-77) a missionary priest support group and, since 1977, a gathering of Catholic Native peoples together with men and women — clerical, Religious and lay — who minister with Native Catholic communities. The primary focus is evangelization, with specific emphasis on development of Native ministry and leadership. Other areas of priority include catechesis, liturgy, family life, social justice ministry, chemical dependency, youth ministry, spirituality and Native Catholic dialogue. The annual Conference, regional conferences and local Kateri Circles serve as opportunities for exchange of ideas, approaches, prayer and mutual support. Publications include a quarterly Newsletter. The Conference provides a Basic Directions in Native Ministry Institute to orient new mission personnel, a four-year Native Catechesis Formation Program and other summer course offerings. The conference has a nine-member board of directors, the majority of whom are Native people. Most Rev. John F. Kinney of Bismarck is episcopal moderator; Rev. Gilbert F. Hemauer, O.F.M. Cap., is executive director; Rev. John Hascall, O.F.M. Cap., is president. Address: P.O. Box 6759, Great Falls, Mont. 59406.

APPALACHIA COMMITTEE

The 600-member Catholic Committee of Appalachia consists of bishops, priests, religious and lay persons engaged in pastoral and social justice ministry in the 13-state region. Appalachia has been defined by Congress as including all of West Virginia and parts of Alabama, Georgia, Kentucky, Maryland, Mississippi, New York, North Carolina, Ohio, Pennsylvania, South Carolina, Tennessee and Virginia. The committee is the Catholic Caucus of the Commission on Religious in Appalachia, an interfaith group.

Address: P.O. Box 953, Whiteburg, Ky 41858.

Bishop William A. Hughes of Covington said May 18, 1985, that the 10th anniversary of a pastoral letter on powerlessness in Appalachia called for a "rededication" to the poor of the region. The original appeal was contained in "This Land Is Home to Me: A Pastoral Letter on Powerlessness in Appalachia," issued by the bishops of the region.

EDUCATION

LEGAL STATUS OF CATHOLIC EDUCATION

The right of private schools to exist and operate in the United States is recognized in law. It was confirmed by the U.S. Supreme Court in 1925 when the tribunal ruled (Pierce v. Society of Sisters, see Church-State Decisions of the Supreme Court) that an Oregon state law requiring all children to attend public schools was unconstitutional.

Private schools are obliged to comply with the education laws in force in the various states regarding such matters as required basic curricula, periods of attendance, and standards for proper accreditation.

The special curricula and standards of private schools are determined by the schools themselves. Thus, in Catholic schools, the curricula include not only the subject matter required by state educational laws but also other fields of study, principally, education in the Catholic faith.

The Supreme Court has ruled that the First Amendment to the U.S. Constitution, in accordance with the No Establishment of Religion Clause of the First Amendment, prohibits direct federal and state aid from public funds to church-affiliated schools. (See several cases in Church-State Decisions of the Supreme Court.)

Public Aid

This prohibition does not extend to all child-benefit and public-purpose programs of aid to students of non-public elementary and secondary schools.

Statutes authorizing such programs have been ruled constitutional on the grounds that they:

- have a "secular legislative purpose";
- neither inhibit nor advance religion as a "principal or primary effect";
- do not foster "excessive government entanglement with religion."

Aid programs considered constitutional have provided bus transportation, textbook loans, school lunches and health services, and "secular, neutral or non-ideological services, facilities and materials provided in common to all school children," public and non-public.

The first major aid to education program in U.S. history containing provisions benefitting nonpublic school students was enacted by the 89th Congress and signed into law by President Lyndon B. Johnson Apr. 11, 1965. The Elementary and Secondary Education Act was designed to avoid the separation of Church and state impasse which had blocked all earlier aid proposals pertaining to nonpublic, and especially church-affiliated, schools. The objective of the program, under public control, is to serve the public purpose by aiding disadvantaged pupils in nonpublic as well as public schools.

In a highly significant 5-to-4 decision June 29, 1983, the U.S. Supreme Court upheld the constitutionality of a Minnesota tuition tax credit for the parents of students attending parochial, other private and public schools. The majority opinion rejected arguments that the law benefitted religion in an unconstitutional manner, and said that the program did not involve excessive church-state entanglement. Supporters of the measure called it sound tax policy.

With respect to college and university education in church-affiliated institutions, the Supreme Court has upheld the constitutionality of statutes providing student loans and, under the Federal Higher Education Facilities Act of 1963, construction loans and grants for secular-purpose facilities.

Catholic schools are exempt from real estate taxation in all of the states. Since Jan. 1, 1959, nonprofit parochial and private schools have also been exempt from several federal excise taxes.

Shared and Released Time

In a shared time program of education, students enrolled in Catholic or other church-related schools take some courses (e.g., religion, social studies, fine arts) in their own schools and others (e.g., science, mathematics, industrial arts) in public schools. Such a program has been given serious consideration in recent years by Catholic and other educators. Its constitutionality has not been seriously challenged, but practical problems — relating to teacher and student schedules, transportation, adjustment to new programs, and other factors — are knotty.

Several million children of elementary and high school age of all denominations have the opportunity of receiving religious instruction on released time. Under released time programs they are permitted to leave their public schools during school hours to attend religious instruction classes held off the public school premises. They are released at the request of their parents. Public school authorities merely provide for their dismissal, and take no part in the program.

NCEA

The National Catholic Educational Association, founded in 1904, is a voluntary organization of educational institutions and individuals concerned with Catholic education in the U.S. Its objectives are to promote and encourage the principles and ideals of Christian education and formation by suitable service and other activities.

The NCEA has 18,000 institutional and individual members. Its official publication is *Momentum*. Numerous service publications are issued to members.

Archbishop John Roach of St. Paul and Minneapolis, is chairman of the association. Sister Catherine T. McNamee, C.S.J., is president.

Headquarters are located at: 1077 30th St. N.W., Washington, D.C. 20007.

The well-attended annual convention of the association is held during Easter Week.

CATHOLIC SCHOOLS AND STUDENTS IN THE UNITED STATES

(Source: *The Official Catholic Directory, 1988;* figures as of Jan. 1, 1988. Archdioceses are indicated by an asterisk.)

Section, State Diocese	Univs. Colleges	Students	High Schools	Students	Elem. Schools	Students
NEW ENGLAND	25	58,722	116	56,083	499	120,681
Maine, Portland	1	555	3	914	21	4,580
New Hampshire, Manchester	4	4,555	6	2,168	28	6,477
Vermont, Burlington	3	3,136	3	932	11	2,089
Massachusetts	9	30,285	64	30,308	224	60,369
*Boston	4	19,883	48	20,394	144	38,475
Fall River	1	2,944	4	2,930	25	6,242
Springfield	1	880	4	3,008	32	10,703
Worcester	3	6,578	8	3,976	23	4,949
Rhode Island, Providence	2	8,075	11	5,198	61	14,406
Connecticut	6	12,116	29	16,563	154	32,760
*Hartford	3	2,067	14	8,230	89	18,687
Bridgeport	2	9,949	10	5,383	44	10,069
Norwich	1	100	5	2,950	21	4,004
MIDDLE ATLANTIC	63	180,274	339	204,394	1,970	556,051
New York	29	96,601	147	88,518	852	244,341
*New York	12	49,406	63	32,827	268	81,118
Albany	3	7,711	11	3,668	52	11,294
Brooklyn	2	20,465	22	23,298	170	67,982
Buffalo	6	12,865	18	7,517	118	26,086
Ogdensburg	2	690	3	766	25	4,437
Rochester	—	—	8	5,157	71	14,792
Rockville Centre	2	2,837	15	12,256	90	29,130
Syracuse	2	2,627	7	3,029	58	9,502
New Jersey	7	17,141	84	49,666	422	112,219
*Newark	4	14,210	40	19,341	186	47,175
Camden	—	—	11	11,299	64	16,962
Metuchen	—	—	9	4,455	44	12,230
Paterson	2	981	13	5,284	65	15,825
Trenton	1	1,950	11	9,287	63	20,027
Pennsylvania	27	66,532	108	66,210	696	199,491
*Philadelphia	11	32,629	48	40,470	254	101,968
Allentown	2	2,084	9	4,068	64	14,058
Altoona-Johnstown	2	2,396	3	1,420	35	6,671
Erie	3	6,232	9	3,356	47	13,396
Greensburg	2	2,062	2	1,160	47	7,669
Harrisburg	—	—	10	3,994	47	11,088
Pittsburgh	3	9,608	16	7,799	142	32,464
Scranton	4	11,521	11	3,943	60	12,177
SOUTH ATLANTIC	15	44,196	125	60,718	536	146,001
Delaware, Wilmington	—	—	7	4,293	29	9,487
Maryland, *Baltimore	4	10,304	23	14,642	84	23,957
District of Columbia, *Washington	3	20,273	25	9,381	85	22,147
Virginia	2	2,947	16	5,597	57	15,620
Arlington	2	2,947	5	3,441	30	9,192
Richmond	—	—	11	2,156	27	6,428
West Virginia, Wheeling-Charleston	1	941	9	1,776	33	5,188
North Carolina	2	1,029	3	1,118	32	7,087
Charlotte	2	1,029	2	858	15	3,618
Raleigh	—	—	1	260	17	3,469
South Carolina, Charleston	—	—	4	1,293	29	4,952
Georgia	—	—	7	4,047	30	8,507
*Atlanta	—	—	2	1,909	14	4,498
Savannah	—	—	5	2,138	16	4,009

School Statistics

Section, State Diocese	Univs. Colleges	Students	High Schools	Students	Elem. Schools	Students
Florida	3	8,702	31	18,571	157	49,056
*Miami	2	7,581	12	9,013	53	19,528
Orlando	—	—	4	1,722	26	7,126
Palm Beach	—	—	4	2,597	15	4,608
Pensacola-Tallahassee	—	—	1	381	9	2,293
St. Augustine	—	—	2	1,215	16	4,630
St. Petersburg	1	1,121	5	2,633	30	8,649
Venice	—	—	3	1,010	8	2,222
EAST NORTH CENTRAL	52	127,370	291	162,186	2,010	519,950
Ohio	11	26,797	84	47,538	485	142,231
*Cincinnati	4	16,075	22	14,627	117	37,446
Cleveland	3	5,915	25	16,578	153	51,216
Columbus	1	1,220	13	5,054	51	12,940
Steubenville	1	1,400	3	885	17	2,717
Toledo	1	807	15	7,235	92	24,142
Youngstown	1	1,380	6	3,159	55	13,770
Indiana	10	15,975	24	11,913	198	42,740
*Indianapolis	3	1,942	9	4,583	71	14,835
Evansville	—	—	5	1,743	28	5,248
Ft. Wayne-South Bend	5	12,110	4	2,680	43	9,885
Gary	1	993	4	2,411	36	9,373
Lafayette	1	930	2	496	20	3,399
Illinois	15	44,468	94	61,848	611	179,212
*Chicago	9	34,811	57	44,327	348	116,911
Belleville	1	855	4	1,965	49	8,409
Joliet	3	6,915	9	6,004	61	17,501
Peoria	—	—	8	3,079	50	12,722
Rockford	—	—	8	3,739	44	11,145
Springfield	2	1,887	8	2,734	59	12,524
Michigan	7	17,219	59	27,564	323	81,252
*Detroit	5	13,764	39	20,065	155	48,051
Gaylord	—	—	4	561	19	3,167
Grand Rapids	1	2,648	4	2,175	45	8,275
Kalamazoo	1	807	3	775	21	4,094
Lansing	1	—	6	3,158	41	10,339
Marquette	—	—	—	—	10	1,820
Saginaw	—	—	3	830	32	5,506
Wisconsin	9	22,911	30	13,323	393	74,515
*Milwaukee	5	18,352	13	7,935	162	36,548
Green Bay	2	2,424	8	2,615	90	16,541
La Crosse	1	1,075	7	2,036	75	10,592
Madison	1	1,060	2	737	46	7,628
Superior	—	—	—	—	20	3,206
EAST SOUTH CENTRAL	8	9,010	52	21,098	268	61,750
Kentucky	5	6,023	25	11,209	146	33,842
*Louisville	3	4,196	10	6,734	73	18,649
Covington	1	1,095	11	3,183	50	10,674
Lexington			No separate statistics available.			
Owensboro	1	732	4	1,292	23	4,519
Tennessee	2	1,982	11	4,281	39	9,733
Knoxville			No separate statistics available.			
Memphis	1	1,642	6	2,256	14	4,115
Nashville	1	340	5	2,025	25	5,618
Alabama	1	1,005	6	2,679	50	10,914
*Mobile	1	1,005	3	1,662	26	6,359
Birmingham	—	—	3	1,017	24	4,555
Mississippi	—	—	10	2,929	33	7,261
Biloxi	—	—	6	2,061	16	2,800
Jackson	—	—	4	868	17	4,461

Section, State Diocese	Univs. Colleges	Students	High Schools	Students	Elem. Schools	Students
WEST NORTH CENTRAL	32	62,622	154	54,387	892	187,890
Minnesota	8	22,756	23	9,726	224	45,544
*St. Paul and Minneapolis	3	15,349	12	7,370	111	27,017
Crookston	—	—	1	115	11	1,563
Duluth	1	1,649	—	—	14	1,889
New Ulm	—	—	3	468	25	3,688
St. Cloud	2	3,716	3	773	37	6,548
Winona	2	2,042	4	1,000	26	4,839
Iowa	7	9,157	29	8,938	144	30,511
*Dubuque	3	4,344	11	3,476	57	13,877
Davenport	3	3,630	7	1,233	36	4,986
Des Moines	—	—	2	1,614	19	4,213
Sioux City	1	1,183	9	2,615	32	7,435
Missouri	5	16,092	44	20,313	277	64,143
*St. Louis	3	11,686	31	15,260	177	45,422
Jefferson City	—	—	2	763	35	5,630
Kansas City-St. Joseph	2	4,406	8	3,628	42	10,383
Springfield-Cape Girardeau	—	—	3	662	23	2,708
North Dakota	2	1,474	5	1,582	32	3,646
Bismarck	1	1,336	4	1,218	18	1,511
Fargo	1	138	1	364	14	2,135
South Dakota	2	1,123	5	1,377	28	4,736
Rapid City	—	—	2	386	3	718
Sioux Falls	2	1,123	3	991	25	4,018
Nebraska	2	7,083	32	7,305	91	19,314
*Omaha	2	7,083	19	5,330	61	13,836
Grand Island	—	—	7	831	7	1,047
Lincoln	—	—	6	1,144	23	4,431
Kansas	6	4,937	16	5,146	96	19,996
*Kansas City	3	2,752	7	2,825	40	10,115
Dodge City	1	908	—	—	12	1,488
Salina	1	659	5	781	12	1,866
Wichita	1	618	4	1,540	32	6,527
WEST SOUTH CENTRAL	11	22,886	119	44,160	490	140,082
Arkansas, Little Rock	—	—	6	1,752	34	5,570
Louisiana	3	7,861	59	25,409	192	72,963
*New Orleans	3	7,861	28	16,860	87	39,195
Alexandria	—	—	3	565	9	2,468
Baton Rouge	—	—	8	2,801	29	11,673
Houma-Thibodaux	—	—	3	941	12	4,102
Lafayette	—	—	12	2,844	32	10,087
Lake Charles	—	—	2	505	10	2,679
Shreveport	—	—	3	893	13	2,759
Oklahoma	1	325	4	1,942	30	5,499
*Oklahoma City	1	325	2	871	16	3,004
Tulsa	—	—	2	1,071	14	2,495
Texas	7	14,700	50	15,057	234	56,050
*San Antonio	4	7,844	10	2,968	50	13,181
Amarillo	—	—	1	76	8	1,242
Austin	1	2,676	2	345	17	3,105
Beaumont	—	—	1	522	8	1,666
Brownsville	—	—	2	768	7	1,839
Corpus Christi	—	—	6	1,410	23	5,030
Dallas	1	2,555	7	2,615	28	8,158
El Paso	—	—	3	1,000	11	3,564
Fort Worth	—	—	4	1,442	13	3,417
Galveston-Houston	1	1,625	9	3,286	46	10,344
Lubbock	—	—	—	—	3	561
San Angelo	—	—	—	—	3	774
Tyler	—	—	1	116	5	823
Victoria	—	—	4	509	12	2,346

School Statistics

Section, State Diocese	Univs. Colleges	Students	High Schools	Students	Elem. Schools	Students
MOUNTAIN	5	8,354	34	12,532	185	41,791
Montana	2	2,738	3	825	18	2,630
Great Falls-Billings	1	1,358	2	460	14	1,911
Helena	1	1,380	1	365	4	719
Idaho, Boise	1	68	1	360	12	1,713
Wyoming, Cheyenne	—	—	1	95	6	1,089
Colorado	1	5,548	8	2,255	48	10,649
*Denver	1	5,548	6	2,045	37	8,812
Colorado Springs	—	—	—	—	5	1,064
Pueblo	—	—	2	210	6	773
New Mexico	1	—	6	1,706	36	7,066
*Santa Fe	1	—	4	1,531	20	4,491
Gallup	—	—	2	175	11	1,893
Las Cruces	—	—	—	—	5	682
Arizona	—	—	10	4,786	45	13,210
Phoenix	—	—	6	3,234	24	7,175
Tucson	—	—	4	1,552	21	6,035
Utah, Salt Lake City	—	—	2	1,105	9	2,330
Nevada, Reno-Las Vegas	—	—	3	1,400	11	3,104
PACIFIC	21	49,973	155	91,906	764	208,493
Washington	3	7,985	10	5,814	78	17,274
*Seattle	2	4,868	8	4,782	55	12,993
Spokane	1	3,117	2	1,032	16	2,792
Yakima	—	—	—	—	7	1,489
Oregon	2	4,802	9	3,064	47	8,250
*Portland	2	4,802	8	2,974	43	7,422
Baker	—	—	1	90	4	828
California	15	34,569	127	79,454	603	174,522
*Los Angeles	5	8,772	56	43,579	233	70,281
*San Francisco	3	8,357	17	8,441	69	21,133
Fresno	—	—	2	1,049	23	5,309
Monterey	—	—	5	1,215	14	3,404
Oakland	3	4,120	10	5,849	56	15,055
Orange	1	100	6	4,164	36	13,043
Sacramento	—	—	9	3,353	44	10,995
San Bernardino	—	—	2	1,159	29	8,084
San Diego	1	5,600	5	2,974	44	12,260
San Jose	2	7,620	6	4,804	29	8,900
Santa Rosa	—	—	7	1,758	14	2,985
Stockton	—	—	2	1,109	12	3,073
Alaska	—	—	1	169	4	720
*Anchorage	—	—	—	—	2	273
Fairbanks	—	—	1	169	1	358
Juneau	—	—	—	—	1	89
Hawaii, Honolulu	1	2,617	8	3,405	32	7,727
EASTERN RITES	1	392	6	725	45	6,777
*Philadelphia	1	392	1	310	15	2,325
St. Nicholas (Chicago)	—	—	1	74	2	422
Stamford	—	—	3	206	6	564
St. Josaphat (Parma)	—	—	—	—	2	404
*Pittsburgh	—	—	—	—	6	1,259
Parma	—	—	—	—	4	498
Passaic	—	—	1	135	5	569
Van Nuys	—	—	—	—	1	36
St. Maron (Maronites)	—	—	—	—	—	—
Newton	—	—	—	—	—	—
St. Thomas Apostle of Detroit (Chaldeans)	—	—	—	—	—	—
Armenians	—	—	—	—	4	700
Romanians	—	—	—	—	—	—
MILITARY ARCHDIOCESE	—	—	—	—	—	—
TOTALS 1988	233	563,799	1,391	708,189	7,659	1,989,466
Totals 1987	238	556,337	1,408	754,714	7,772	2,030,598
Totals 1978	238	457,498	1,572	869,268	8,299	2,402,778

SCHOOL STATISTICS

The status of Catholic educational institutions and programs in the United States at the beginning of 1988, 1987 and 1978 was reflected in figures (as of Jan. 1) reported by The Official Catholic Directory, 1988.

Schools and Students

Colleges and Universities: 233 (5 less than 1987 and 1978).

College and University Students: 563,799 (7,462 more than 1987; 106,301 more than 1978).

High Schools: 1,391 (17 less than 1987; 181 less than 1978).

High School Students: 708,189 (46,525 less than 1987; 161,079 less than 1978).

Public High School Students Receiving Religious Instruction: 804,775 (83,677 less than 1987; 204,864 less than in 1978).

Elementary Schools: 7,659 (113 less than 1987; 640 less than 1978).

Elementary School Students: 1,989,466 (41,132 less than 1987; 413,312 less than 1978).

Public Elementary School Students Receiving Religious Instruction: 3,044,832 (72,244 more than 1987; 596,925 less than 1978).

Teachers

Lay Teachers: 134,317 (2,853 less than 1987; 20,129 more than 1978).

Sisters: 23,153 (3,421 less than 1987; 23,517 less than 1978).

Priests: 3,483 (255 less than 1987; 2,929 less than 1978).

Brothers: 2,139 (126 less than 1987; 1,380 less than 1978).

Scholastics: 140 (59 less than 1987; 68 less than 1978).

RELIGIOUS EDUCATION

Religious Education/Catechesis/CCD (Confraternity of Christian Doctrine): Its objective is the catechesis of persons from early childhood through adult life.

The modern expansion of catechesis dates from publication of the encyclical letter *Acerbo Nimis* by Pope St. Pius X in 1905. His directive, that CCD programs be established in every parish, was incorporated in the 1917 Code of Canon Law, reaffirmed by the Second Vatican Council in the *Decree on the Bishops' Pastoral Office in the Church*, and given direction by the publication of the *National Catechetical Directory* in 1971.

Programs for catechesis are parish-based. Policies are developed by parish boards or commissions, and responsibility for administering programs rests ideally with a coordinator or director who is a trained professional. On the diocesan level, religious education is coordinated by a director with a staff operating under the title of an office of religious education or a similar title.

On the national level, Religious Education/Catechetical Ministry/CCD (formerly called the National Center for the Confraternity of Christian Doctrine is situated in the Division of Catechesis/Faith Formation within the Department of Education of the United States Catholic Conference. On the international level, it participates in programs which find their roots with the Vatican congregations that deal with religious education or catechesis. Publications include an annual Catechetical Sunday booklet and other materials related to various facets of catechesis/religious education.

Offices are located at 1312 Massachusetts Ave. N.W., Washington, D.C. 20005.

UNIVERSITIES AND COLLEGES IN THE UNITED STATES

(Sources: Almanac survey; *The Official Catholic Directory*.)

Listed below are institutions of higher learning established under Catholic auspices. Some of them are now independent.

Information includes: name of each institution; indication of male (m), female (w), coeducational (c) student body; name of founding group or group with which the institution is affiliated; year of foundation; number of students, in parentheses.

Albertus Magnus College (c): 700 Prospect St., New Haven, Conn. 06511. Dominican Sisters; 1925 (553).

Allentown College of St. Francis de Sales (c): Center Valley, Pa. 18034. Oblates of St. Francis de Sales; 1965 (1,205).

Alvernia College (c): Reading, Pa. 19607. Bernardine Sisters; 1958 (879).

Alverno College (w): 3401 S. 39th St. Milwaukee, Wis. 53215. School Sisters of St. Francis; 1887; independent (1,982).

Anna Maria College (c): Sunset Lane, Paxton, Mass. 01612. Sisters of St. Anne; 1946; independent (1,230).

Aquinas College (c): 1607 Robinson Rd. S.E., Grand Rapids, Mich. 49506. Sisters of St. Dominic; 1922; independent (2,648).

Assumption College (c): 500 Salisbury St., Worcester, Mass. 01609. Assumptionist Fathers; 1904 (2,939).

Avila College (c): 11901 Wornall Rd., Kansas City, Mo. 64145. Sisters of St. Joseph of Carondelet; 1916 (1,506).

Barat College (c): 700 Westleigh Rd., Lake Forest, Ill. 60045. Society of the Sacred Heart; 1919; independent (635).

Barry University (c): 11300 N.E. 2nd Ave., Miami, Fla. 33161. Dominican Sisters (Adrian, Mich.); 1940 (4,713).

Bellarmine College (c): Newburg Rd., Louisville, Ky. 40205; Louisville archdiocese, 1950 (2,676).

Belmont Abbey College (c): Belmont, N.C. 28012. Benedictine Fathers; 1876 (1,029).

Benedictine College (c): Atchison, Kans. 66002. Benedictines, 1971 (808).

Boston College (University Status) (c): Chestnut Hill, Mass. 02167. Jesuit Fathers; 1863 (14,310).

Brescia College (c): 120 W. 7th St., Owensboro,

Universities and Colleges

Ky. 42301. Ursuline Sisters; 1950 (732).

Briar Cliff College (c): 3303 Rebecca St., Sioux City, Ia. 51104. Sisters of St. Francis of the Holy Family; 1930 (1,183).

Cabrini College (c): Radnor, Pa. 19087. Missionary Srs. of Sacred Heart; 1957; private (872).

Caldwell College (c): Caldwell, N.J. 07006. Dominican Sisters; 1939 (827).

Calumet College of St. Joseph (c): 2400 New York Ave., Whiting, Ind. 46394. Society of the Precious Blood, 1951 (993).

Canisius College (c): 2001 Main St., Buffalo, N.Y. 14208. Jesuit Fathers; 1870; independent (4,400).

Cardinal Stritch College (c): 6801 N. Yates Rd., Milwaukee, Wis. 53217. Sisters of St. Francis of Assisi; 1937; independent (2,400).

Carlow College (w): 3333 5th Ave., Pittsburgh, Pa. 15213. Sisters of Mercy; 1929 (1,237).

Carroll College (c): Helena, Mont. 59625. Diocesan; 1909 (1,380).

Catholic University of America, The (c): 620 Michigan Ave. N.E., Washington, D.C. 20064. Hierarchy of the United States; 1887. Pontifical University (6,688).

Catholic University of Puerto Rico (c): Ponce, P.R. Hierarchy of Puerto Rico; 1948; Pontifical University (11,762).

Chaminade University of Honolulu (c): 3140 Waialae Ave., Honolulu, Hawaii 96816. Marianists; 1955 (1,011).

Chestnut Hill College (w): Philadelphia, Pa. 19118. Sisters of St. Joseph; 1924 (1,239).

Christendom College (c): Rt. 3, Box 87, Front Royal, Va. 22630. Founded 1977 (147).

Christian Brothers College (c): 650 E. Parkway S., Memphis, Tenn. 38104. Brothers of the Christian Schools; 1871 (1,642).

Clarke College (c): 1550 Clarke Dr., Dubuque, Iowa 52001. Sisters of Charity, BVM; 1843 (802).

Creighton University (c): California St. at 24th, Omaha, Neb. 68178. Jesuit Fathers; 1878; independent (5,666).

Dallas, University of (c): 1845 E. Northgate, Irving, Tex. 75062. Dallas diocese; 1956; independent (2,540).

Dayton, University of (c): 300 College Park Ave., Dayton, Ohio 45409. Marianists; 1850 (10,700).

DePaul University (c): 25 E. Jackson Blvd., Chicago, Ill. 60604. Vincentians; 1898 (13,688).

Detroit, University of (c): 4001 W. McNichols Rd. at Livernois, Detroit, Mich. 48221. Jesuit Fathers; 1877 (6,101).

Dominican College of Blauvelt (c): Orangeburg, N.Y. 10962. Dominican Sisters; 1952; independent (1,442).

Dominican College of San Rafael (c): 1520 Grand Ave.; San Rafael, Calif. 94901. Dominican Sisters; 1890; independent (714).

Duquesne University (c): 600 Forbes Ave., Pittsburgh, Pa. 15282. Congregation of the Holy Ghost; 1878 (6,616).

D'Youville College (c): 320 Porter Ave., Buffalo, N.Y. 14201. Grey Nuns of the Sacred Heart; 1908; independent. (1,202).

Edgewood College (c): 855 Woodrow St., Madison, Wis. 53711. Dominican Sisters; 1927 (1,060).

Emmanuel College (w): 400 The Fenway, Boston, Mass. 02115. Sisters of Notre Dame de Namur; independent (953).

Fairfield University (c): North Benson Rd., Fairfield, Conn. 06430. Jesuits; 1942 (4,949).

Felician College (w): S. Main St., Lodi, N.J. 07644. Felician Sisters; 1942 (545). Coed in nursing and evening programs.

Fontbonne College (c): 6800 Wydown Blvd., St. Louis, Mo. 63105. Sisters of St. Joseph of Carondelet; 1917; independent (998).

Fordham University (c): Fordham Rd. and Third Ave., New York, N.Y. 10458. Society of Jesus (Jesuits); 1841; independent (13,110).

Gannon University (c): University Square, Erie, Pa. 16541. Diocese of Erie; 1933 (4,096).

Georgetown University (c): 37th and O Sts. N.W., Washington, D.C. 20057. Jesuit Fathers; 1789 (11,985).

Georgian Court College (w): Lakewood, N.J. 08701. Sisters of Mercy; 1908 (1,774). Coed in evening and graduate divisions.

Gonzaga University (c): Spokane, Wash. 99258. Jesuit Fathers; 1887 (3,117).

Great Falls, College of (c): 1301 20th St. S., Great Falls, Mont. 59405. Sisters of Providence; 1932 (1,358).

Gwynedd-Mercy College (c): Gwynedd Valley, Pa. 19437. Sisters of Mercy; 1948; independent (1,980).

Holy Cross, College of the (c): Worcester, Mass. 01610. Jesuit Fathers; 1843 (2,595).

Holy Family College (c): Grant and Frankford Aves., Philadelphia, Pa. 19114. Sisters of Holy Family of Nazareth; 1954 (1,620).

Holy Names College (c): 3500 Mountain Blvd., Oakland, Calif. 94619. Sisters of the Holy Names of Jesus and Mary; 1868 (600).

Illinois Benedictine College (c): Lisle, Ill. 60532. Benedictine Fathers of St. Procopius Abbey; 1887 (2,366).

Immaculata College (w): Immaculata, Pa. 19345. Sisters, Servants of the Immaculate Heart of Mary; 1920 (1,981).

Incarnate Word College (c): 4301 Broadway, San Antonio, Tex. 78209. Sisters of Charity of the Incarnate Word; 1881 (1,905).

Iona College (c): 715 North Ave., New Rochelle, N.Y. 10801. Congregation of Christian Brothers; 1940; independent (5,803).

John Carroll University (c): North Park and Miramar Blvds., Cleveland, Ohio. 44118. Jesuits; 1886 (3,583).

Kansas Newman College (formerly Sacred Heart College) (c): 3100 McCormick Ave., Wichita, Kans. 67213. Sisters Adorers of the Blood of Christ; 1933 (765).

King's College (c): Wilkes-Barre, Pa. 18711. Holy Cross Fathers; 1946 (2,289).

La Roche College (c): 9000 Babcock Blvd., Pittsburgh, Pa. 15237. Sisters of Divine Providence; 1963 (1,755)

La Salle University (c): 20th St. and Olney Ave.,

Philadelphia, Pa. 19141. Brothers of the Christian Schools; 1863 (6,400)

Le Moyne College (c): Syracuse, N.Y. 13214. Jesuit Fathers; 1946; independent (2,133).

Lewis University (c): Romeoville, Ill. 60441. Christian Brothers; 1932 (3,390).

Loras College (c): 1450 Alta Vista St., Dubuque, Ia. 52004. Archdiocese of Dubuque; 1839 (1,978).

Lourdes College (c): Sylvania, Ohio 43560. Sisters of St. Francis; 1958 (807).

Loyola College (c): 4501 N. Charles St., Baltimore, Md. 21210, Jesuits; 1852; combined with Mt. St. Agnes College, 1971 (5,607).

Loyola Marymount University (c): Loyola Blvd. at W. 80th St., Los Angeles, Calif. 90045. Society of Jesus; Religious of Sacred Heart of Mary, Sisters of St. Joseph of Orange; 1911 (6,430).

Loyola University (c): 6363 St. Charles Ave., New Orleans, La. 70118. Jesuit Fathers; 1912 (4,966).

Loyola University of Chicago (c): 820 N. Michigan Ave., Chicago, Ill. 60611. Jesuit Fathers; 1870 (14,072).

Madonna College (c): 36600 Schoolcraft Rd., Livonia, Mich. 48150. Felician Sisters; 1947 (3,992).

Magdalen College (c): 270 D.W. Highway So., Bedford, N.H. 03102; Magdalen College Corporation; 1973 (44).

Mallinckrodt College (c): 1041 Ridge Rd., Wilmette, Ill. 60091. Sisters of Christian Charity 1918 (251).

Manhattan College (c): 4513 Manhattan College Pkwy., New York, N.Y. 10471. Brothers of the Christian Schools; 1853; independent (4,500). Cooperative program with College of Mt. St. Vincent.

Marian College (c): Fond du Lac, Wis. 54935. Sisters of St. Agnes; 1936 (680).

Marian College (c): 3200 Cold Spring Rd., Indianapolis, Ind. 46222. Sisters of St. Francis (Oldenburg, Ind.); 1851; independent (1,099).

Marist College (c): Poughkeepsie, N.Y. 12601. Marist Brothers of the Schools; 1946; independent (4,451).

Marquette University (c): 615 N. 11th St., Milwaukee, Wis. 53233. Jesuit Fathers; 1881; independent (12,000).

Mary, University of (c): 7500 University Dr., Bismarck, N.D. 58501. Benedictine Sisters; 1959 (1,336).

Marycrest College (c): 1607 W. 12th St., Davenport, Iowa 52804. Congregation of the Humility of Mary; 1939; independent (1,140).

Marygrove College (c): 8425 W. McNichols Rd., Detroit, Mich. 48221. Sisters, Servants of the Immaculate Heart of Mary; 1910 (1,237).

Marylhurst College (c): Marylhurst, Ore. 97036. Srs. of Holy Names of Jesus and Mary; 1893; independent (2,501).

Marymount College (w): Tarrytown, N.Y. 10591. Religious of the Sacred Heart of Mary; 1907; independent (1,233). Coed in weekend degree programs.

Marymount College of Kansas (c): Box 5050, Salina, Kans. 67401. Salina diocese; 1922 (659).

Marymount University (c): 2807 N. Glebe Rd., Arlington, Va. 22207. Religious of the Sacred Heart of Mary; 1950; independent (2,800).

Marymount Manhattan College (w): 221 E. 71st St., New York, N.Y. 10021. Religious of the Sacred Heart of Mary; 1936; independent (1,245).

Marywood College (w): Scranton, Pa. 18509. Sisters, Servants of the Immaculate Heart of Mary; 1915; independent (3,081). Coed in graduate division.

Mater Dei College (c): Riverside Dr., Ogdensburg, N.Y. 13669. Sisters of St. Joseph; 1960; independent (580).

Mercy College of Detroit (c): 8200 W. Outer Dr., Detroit, Mich. 48219. Sisters of Mercy; 1941 (2,241).

Mercyhurst College (c): 501 E. 38th St., Erie, Pa. 16546. Sisters of Mercy; 1926 (1,895).

Merrimack College (c): North Andover, Mass. 01845. Augustinians; 1947 (2,284).

Misericordia (College Misericordia) (c): Dallas, Pa. 18612. Religious Sisters of Mercy of the Union; 1924 (1,268).

Molloy College (c): 1000 Hempstead Ave., Rockville Centre, N.Y. 11570. Dominican Sisters; 1955; independent (1,390).

Mount Marty College (c): Yankton, S.D. 57078. Benedictine Sisters; 1936 (631).

Mount Mary College (w): 2900 W. Menomonee River Pkwy., Milwaukee, Wis. 53222. School Sisters of Notre Dame; 1913 (1,352).

Mt. Mercy College (c): 1330 Elmhurst Dr. N.E., Cedar Rapids, Ia. 52402. Sisters of Mercy; 1928 (1,564).

Mt. St. Clare College (c): Bluff Blvd. and Springdale Dr., Clinton, Ia. 52732. Clinton Franciscans; 1928 (360).

Mt. St. Joseph on the Ohio, College of (c): Mt. St. Joseph, Ohio 45051. Sisters of Charity; 1920 (2,322).

Mt. St. Mary College (c): Newburgh, N.Y. 12550. Dominican Sisters; 1959; independent (1,176).

Mount St. Mary College (c): Emmitsburg, Md. 21727. Diocesan Clergy; 1808; independent (1,400).

Mount St. Mary's College (w): 12001 Chalon Rd., Los Angeles, Calif. 90049 and 10 Chester Pl., Los Angeles, Calif. 90007 (Doheny Campus). Sisters of St. Joseph of Carondelet; 1925 (1,292). Coed in music, nursing and graduate programs.

Mt. St. Vincent, College of (c): Mt. St. Vincent-on-Hudson, New York, N.Y. 10471. Sisters of Charity; 1847; independent (1,200). Cooperative program with Manhattan College.

Mundelein College (w): 6363 N. Sheridan Rd., Chicago, Ill. 60660. Sisters of Charity of the Blessed Virgin Mary; 1929 (1,182).

Nazareth College in Kalamazoo (c): 3333 Gull Rd., Kalamazoo, Mich. 49001. Sisters of St. Joseph; 1924; independent (807).

Neumann College (formerly Our Lady of Angels) (c): Aston, Pa. 19014. Sisters of St. Francis; 1965 (1,000).

New Rochelle, College of (w): 29 Castle Pl., New Rochelle, N.Y. 10801 (main campus). Ursuline Nuns; 1904; independent (4,496). Coed in nursing, graduate, new resources divisions.

Niagara University (c): Niagara Univ., N.Y.

Universities and Colleges 533

14109. Vincentian Fathers; 1856 (3,278).

Notre Dame, College of (c): 1500 Ralston Ave., Belmont, Calif. 94002. Sisters of Notre Dame de Namur; 1868; independent (1,061).

Notre Dame, University of (c): Notre Dame, Ind. 46556. Congregation of Holy Cross; 1842 (9,500).

Notre Dame College (w): 4545 College Rd., Cleveland, Ohio 44121. Sisters of Notre Dame; 1922 (745).

Notre Dame College (w): Manchester, N.H. 03104. Sisters of the Holy Cross; 1950 (788).

Notre Dame of Maryland, College of (w): 4701 N. Charles St., Baltimore, Md. 21210. School Sisters of Notre Dame; 1873 (2,116).

Ohio Dominican College (c): Columbus, Ohio 43219. Dominican Sisters of St. Mary of the Springs; 1911 (1,120).

Our Lady of Holy Cross College (c): 4123 Woodland Dr., New Orleans, La. 70114. Congregation of Sisters Marianites of Holy Cross; 1916 (536).

Our Lady of the Elms, College of (w): Chicopee, Mass. 01013. Sisters of St. Joseph; 1928 (880).

Our Lady of the Lake University of San Antonio (c): 411 S.W. 24th St., San Antonio, Tex. 78285. Sisters of Divine Providence; 1911 (1,758).

Parks College of Saint Louis University (c): Cahokia, Ill. 62206. Jesuits; 1927; independent (855).

Portland, University of (c): 5000 N. Willamette Blvd., Portland, Ore. 97203. Holy Cross Fathers; 1901; independent (2,426).

Providence College (c): River Ave. and Eaton St., Providence, R.I. 02918. Dominican Friars; 1917 (3,700).

Quincy College (c): 1800 College Ave., Quincy, Ill. 62301. Franciscan Friars; 1859 (1,425).

Regis College (c): W. 50th Ave. and Lowell Blvd. Denver, Colo. 80221. Jesuit Fathers; 1887 (3,780).

Regis College (w): Weston, Mass. 02193. Sisters of St. Joseph; 1927; independent (1,086).

Rivier College (w): Nashua, N.H. 03060. Sisters of the Presentation of Mary; 1933; independent (2,481). Coed schools of nursing, continuing education and graduate studies.

Rockhurst College (c): 5225 Troost Ave., Kansas City, Mo. 64110. Jesuit Fathers; 1910 (2,906).

Rosary College (c): 7900 Division St., River Forest, Ill. 60305. Dominican Sisters; 1901 (1,542).

Rosemont College (w): Rosemont, Pa. 19010. Society of the Holy Child Jesus; 1921 (612).

Sacred Heart University (c): Fairfield (P.O. Bridgeport), Conn. 06606. Diocese of Bridgeport; 1963; independent (5,000).

St. Ambrose College (c): Davenport, Ia. 52803. Diocese of Davenport; 1882 (2,122).

Saint Anselm College (c): Manchester N.H. 03102. Benedictine Monks; 1889 (1,897).

Saint Benedict, College of (w): 37 S. College Ave., St. Joseph, Minn. 56379. Benedictine Sisters; 1913 (1,788).

St. Bonaventure University (c): St. Bonaventure, N.Y. 14778. Franciscan Friars; 1856; independent (2,507).

St. Catherine, College of (w): 2004 Randolph St., St. Paul, Minn. 55105. Sisters of St. Joseph of Carondelet; 1905 (2,701).

St. Edward's University (c): 3001 S. Congress Ave., Austin, Tex. 78704. Holy Cross Brothers; 1885; independent (2,676).

St. Elizabeth, College of (w): Convent Station, N.J. 07961. Sisters of Charity; 1899; independent (969).

St. Francis, College of (c): 500 N. Wilcox St., Joliet, Ill. 60435. Sisters of St. Francis of Mary Immaculate; 1925; independent (1,100).

St. Francis College (c): 180 Remsen St., Brooklyn Heights, N.Y. 11201. Franciscan Brothers; 1884; private, independent in the Franciscsan tradition (2,400).

St. Francis College (c): 2701 Spring St., Fort Wayne, Ind. 46808. Sisters of St. Francis; 1890 (1,215).

St. Francis College (c): Loretto, Pa. 15940. Franciscan Friars; 1847; independent (1,746).

St. John's University (c): Grand Central and Utopia Pkwys., Jamaica, N.Y. 11439 (Main Campus); 300 Howard Ave., Grymes Hill, Staten Island, N.Y. 10301 (Staten Island Campus). Vincentian Fathers; 1870 (19,248).

St. John's University (m): Collegeville, Minn. 56321. Benedictines; 1857 (1,928). Coed in graduate school.

St. Joseph, College of (c): Clement Rd., Rutland, Vt. 05701. Sisters of St. Joseph; 1954; independent (398).

Saint Joseph College (w): 1678 Asylum Ave., West Hartford, Conn. 06117. Sisters of Mercy; 1932 (1,573). Coed in graduate school and in McAuley Program Weekend College.

Saint Joseph's College (c): Windham, Me. 04062. Sisters of Mercy; 1912 (555).

Saint Joseph's College (c): Rensselaer, Ind. 47978. Society of the Precious Blood; 1889 (930).

St. Joseph's College (c): 245 Clinton Ave., Brooklyn, N.Y. 11205 (338) and 155 Roe Blvd., Patchogue, N.Y. 11772 (1,445). Sisters of St. Joseph; 1916; independent.

St. Joseph's University (c): 5600 City Ave., Philadelphia, Pa. 19131. Jesuit Fathers; 1851 (5,649).

Saint Leo College (c): Saint Leo, Fla. 33574. Order of St. Benedict; 1889; independent (1,100).

St. Louis University (c): 221 N. Grand Blvd., St. Louis, Mo. 63103. Jesuit Fathers; 1818 (10,000).

Saint Martin's College (c): Lacey, Wash. 98503. Benedictine Monks; 1895 (577).

St. Mary, College of (w): 1901 S. 72nd St., Omaha, Neb. 68124. Sisters of Mercy; 1923; independent (1,276).

Saint Mary College (c): Leavenworth, Kans. 66048. Sisters of Charity of Leavenworth; 1923 (1,137).

St. Mary of the Plains College (c): Dodge City, Kans. 67801. Sisters of St. Joseph of Wichita; 1952 (908).

St. Mary-of-the-Woods College (w): St. Mary-of-the-Woods, Ind. 47876. Sisters of Providence; 1840 (701).

Saint Mary's College (w): Notre Dame, Ind. 46556. Sisters of the Holy Cross; 1844 (1,826).

St. Mary's College (c): Orchard Lake, Mich. 48033. Secular Clergy; 1885 (250).

St. Mary's College (c): Moraga, Calif. 94575. Brothers of the Christian Schools; 1863 (3,646).

St. Mary's College (c): Winona, Minn. 55987. Brothers of the Christian Schools; 1912 (1,676).

St. Mary's University (c): One Camino Santa Maria, San Antonio, Tex. 78284. Society of Mary (Marianists); 1852 (3,386).

St. Michael's College (c): Winooski, Vt. 05404. Society of St. Edmund; 1904 (1,737).

St. Norbert College (c): De Pere, Wis. 54115. Norbertine Fathers; 1898; independent (1,804).

St. Peter's College (c): 2641 Kennedy Blvd., Jersey City, N.J. 07306. Jesuit Fathers; independent; 1872 (3,575).

Saint Rose, College of (c): 432 Western Ave., Albany, N.Y. 12203. Sisters of St. Joseph of Carondelet; 1920; independent (3,146).

St. Scholastica, College of (c): 1200 Kenwood Ave., Duluth, Minn. 55811. Benedictine Sisters; 1912; independent (1,649).

Saint Teresa, College of (w): Winona, Minn. 55987. Sisters of St. Francis; 1907 (366).

St. Thomas, College of (c): St. Paul, Minn. 55105. Archdiocese of St. Paul; 1885 (8,396).

St. Thomas, University of (c): 3812 Montrose Blvd., Houston, Tex. 77006. Basilian Fathers; 1947 (1,625).

St. Thomas Aquinas College (c): Sparkill, N.Y. 10976. Dominican Sisters of Sparkill; 1952; independent, corporate board of trustees (2,132).

St. Thomas University (c): 16400 N.W. 32nd Ave., Opa Locka, Fla. 33054. Augustinian Fathers; 1962 (3,200).

Saint Vincent College (c): Latrobe, Pa. 15650. Benedictine Fathers; 1846 (1,230).

St. Xavier College (c): 3700 W. 103rd St., Chicago, Ill. 60655. Sisters of Mercy; chartered 1847 (2,591).

Salve Regina — The Newport College (c): Ochre Point Ave., Newport, R.I. 02840. Sisters of Mercy; 1934 (2,360).

San Diego, University of (c): Alcala Park, San Diego, Calif. 92110. San Diego diocese and Religious of the Sacred Heart; 1949; independent (5,264).

San Francisco, University of (c): Ignation Heights, San Francisco, Calif. 94117. Jesuit Fathers; 1855 (6,582).

Santa Clara University (c): Santa Clara, Calif. 95053. Jesuit Fathers; 1851; independent (7,550).

Santa Fe, College of (c): Santa Fe, N. Mex. 87501. Brothers of the Christian Schools; 1947 (1,300).

Scranton, University of (c): Scranton, Pa. 18510. Society of Jesus; 1888 (4,800).

Seattle University (c): Broadway and East Madison, Seattle, Wash. 98122. Jesuit Fathers; 1891 (4,400).

Seton Hall University (c): South Orange, N.J. 07079. Diocesan Clergy; 1856 (9,411).

Seton Hill College (w): Greensburg, Pa. 15601. Sisters of Charity of Seton Hill; 1883 (832).

Siena College (c): Loudonville, N.Y. 12211. Franciscan Friars; 1937 (2,913, day; 704, evening).

Siena Heights College (c): Adrian, Mich. 49221. Dominican Sisters; 1919 (1,551).

Silver Lake College of Holy Family (c): 2406 S. Alverno Rd., Manitowoc, Wis. 54220. Franciscan Sisters of Christian Charity; 1935 (620).

Spalding University (c): 851 S. 4th Ave., Louisville, Ky. 40203. Sisters of Charity of Nazareth; 1814; independent (1,255).

Spring Hill College (c): Mobile, Ala. 36608. Jesuit Fathers; 1830 (1,005).

Steubenville, Franciscan University of (c): Steubenville, Ohio 43952. Franciscan Fathers; 1946 (1,395).

Stonehill College (c): North Easton, Mass. 02357. Holy Cross Fathers; 1948; independent (2,949).

Thomas Aquinas College (c): 10000 N. Ojai Rd., Santa Paula, Calif. 93060. Founded 1971 (135).

Thomas More College (c): Crestview Hills, Covington, Ky. 41017. Diocese of Covington; 1921 (1,095).

Trinity College (w/c): Colchester Ave., Burlington, Vt. 05401. Sisters of Mercy; 1925 (1,001).

Trinity College (w): Michigan Ave. and Franklin St. N.E., Washington, D.C. 20017. Sisters of Notre Dame de Namur; 1897 (744). Coed in graduate school.

Ursuline College (w): 2550 Lander Rd., Cleveland, Ohio 44124. Ursuline Nuns; 1871 (1,370).

Villa Maria College (w): 2551 W. Lake Rd., Erie, Pa. 16505. Sisters of St. Joseph; 1925 (602).

Villanova University (c): Villanova, Pa. 19085. Order of St. Augustine; 1842 (12,119).

Viterbo College (c): La Crosse, Wis. 54601. Franciscan Sisters of Perpetual Adoration; 1890 (1,075).

Walsh College (c): 2020 Easton St. N.W., Canton, Ohio 44720. Brothers of Christian Instruction; 1958 (1,380).

Wheeling Jesuit College (c): 316 Washington Ave., Wheeling, W. Va. 26003. Jesuit Fathers; 1954 (1,030).

Xavier University (c): 3800 Victory Pkwy., Cincinnati, Ohio 45207. Jesuit Fathers; 1831 (6,785).

Xavier University of Louisiana (c): 7325 Palmetto St., New Orleans, La. 70125. Sisters of Blessed Sacrament; 1925; lay-Religious administration board (2,211).

Catholic Junior Colleges

Ancilla College (c): Donaldson, Ind. 46513. Ancilla Domini Sisters; 1937 (420).

Aquinas Junior College (c): Harding Rd., Nashville, Tenn. 37205. Dominican Sisters; 1961 (340).

Assumption College for Sisters: Hilltop Rd., Mendham, N.J. 07945. Sisters of Christian Charity; 1953 (18).

Castle Junior College: Searles Rd., Windham, N.H. 03087. Sisters of Mercy (122).

Chatfield College (c): St. Martin, O. 45118. Ursulines; 1971 (350).

Donnelly College (c): 608 N. 18th St., Kansas City, Kans. 66102. Archdiocesan College; 1949 (800).

Don Bosco Technical Institute (m): 1151 San

Gabriel Blvd., Rosemead, Calif. 91770. Salesians; 1969 (275).

Elizabeth Seton College (c): 1061 N. Broadway, Yonkers, N.Y. 10701. Sisters of Charity; 1960; independent (1,100).

Felician College (c): 3800 W. Peterson Ave., Chicago, Ill. 60659. Felician Sisters (325).

Harriman College (c): Harriman Heights Rd., Harriman, N.Y. 10926. Independent (300).

Hilbert College (c): 5200 S. Park Ave., Hamburg, N.Y. 14075. Franciscan Sisters of St. Joseph; 1957; independent (647).

Holy Cross Junior College (c): Notre Dame, Ind. 46556. Brothers of Holy Cross; 1966 (372).

Manor Junior College (w): Fox Chase Manor, Jenkintown, Pa. 19046. Sisters of St. Basil the Great; 1947 (450).

Maria College (c): 700 New Scotland Ave., Albany, N.Y. 12208. Sisters of Mercy; 1963 (948).

Maria Regina College (w): 1024 Court St., Syracuse, N.Y. 13208. Franciscan Sisters; 1963; independent (627).

Marymount Palos Verdes College (c): Rancho Palos Verdes, Calif. 90274. Religious of the Sacred Heart of Mary; independent (795).

Mt. Aloysius Junior College (c): Cresson, Pa. 16630. Sisters of Mercy; 1939 (571).

Presentation College (c): Aberdeen, S.D. 57401. Sisters of the Presentation; 1951 (405).

St. Catharine College (c); St. Catharine, Ky. 40061. Dominican Sisters; 1931 (265).

St. Gertrude, College of (c): Cottonwood, Ida. 83522. Benedictine Sisters.

St. Gregory's College (c): Shawnee, Okla. 74801. Benedictine Monks; 1876 (325).

St. Mary's College of O'Fallon (c): 200 N. Main St., O'Fallon, Mo. 63366. Sisters of the Most Precious Blood; 1921.

St. Mary's College (c): 2500 S. 6th St., Minneapolis, Minn. 55454. Sisters of St. Joseph of Carondelet (680).

Springfield College in Illinois (c): 1500 N. Fifth St., Springfield, Ill. 62702. Ursuline Nuns; 1929 (567).

Trocaire College (c): 110 Red Jacket Pkwy., Buffalo, N.Y. 14220. Sisters of Mercy; 1958; independent (954).

Villa Julie College (c): Green Spring Valley Rd., Stevenson, Md. 21153. Sisters of Notre Dame de Namur; 1952; independent (1,181).

Villa Maria College of Buffalo (c): 240 Pine Ridge Rd., Buffalo, N.Y. 14225. Felician Srs.; 1960; independent (566).

CAMPUS MINISTRY

Campus ministry is an expression of the Church's special desire to be present to all who are involved in higher education and to further dialogue between the Church and the academic community. In the words of the U.S. bishops' 1985 pastoral letter entitled "Empowered by the Spirit," this ministry is "the public presence and service through which properly prepared baptized persons are empowered by the Spirit to use their talents and gifts on behalf of the Church in order to be sign and instrument of the Kingdom in the academic world."

Campus ministry, carried on by lay, Religious and ordained ministers, gathers members of the Church on campus to form the faith community, appropriate the faith, form Christian consciences, educate for justice and facilitate religious development.

The dimensions and challenge of this ministry are evident from, among other things, the numbers involved: approximately 550,000 Catholics on more than 230 Catholic college and university campuses; about four million on several thousand non-Catholic private and public institutions; 1,200 or more campus ministers.

In many dioceses, the activities of ministers are coordinated by a local diocesan director. Two professional organizations serve the ministry on the national level:

The National Association of Diocesan Directors of Campus Ministry; Father George Schroeder, president, is located at 845 Fairfax St., Denver, Colo. 80220.

The Catholic Campus Ministers Association, with a membership of 1,100, is headquartered at 300 College Park Ave., Dayton, O. 45469; the executive director is Donald R. McCrabb.

In the U.S. Catholic Conference, Christian Brother Peter Clifford is the staff assistant for campus ministry. His responsibilities are the maintenance of liaison between the campus ministers' organizations and the U.S. bishops, and providing continuing support for the ministry on college and university campuses. He is located at 1312 Massachusetts Ave. N.W., Washington, D.C. 20005.

DIOCESAN AND INTERDIOCESAN SEMINARIES

(Sources: Almanac survey; *Official Catholic Directory;* NC News Service.)

Information, according to states, includes names of archdioceses and dioceses, and names and addresses of seminaries. Types of seminaries, when not clear from titles, are indicated in most cases. Interdiocesan seminaries are generally conducted by religious orders for candidates for the priesthood from several dioceses. The list does not include houses of study reserved for members of religious communities. Archdioceses are indicated by an asterisk.

California: Los Angeles* — St. John's Seminary (major), 5012 E. Seminary Rd., Camarillo. 93010; St. John's Seminary College, 5118 E. Seminary Rd., Camarillo. 93010; Seminary of Our Lady, Queen of Angels (minor, high school), P.O. Box 1071, San Fernando, 91341.

San Diego — St. Francis Seminary (college residence), 1667 Santa Paula Dr., San Diego 92111.

San Francisco* — St. Patrick's Seminary (major), 320 Middlefield Rd., Menlo Park. 94025.

San Jose — St. Joseph's College, P.O. Box 7009, Mountain View 94039.

Colorado: Denver* — St. Thomas Theological Seminary (major), 1300 S. Steele St., Denver 80210.

Connecticut: Hartford* — St. Thomas Seminary (college formation program), 467 Bloomfield Ave., Bloomfield. 06002.

Norwich — Holy Apostles College and Seminary (adult vocations), 33 Prospect Hill Rd., Cromwell 06416.

Stamford Byzantine Rite — Ukrainian Catholic Seminary: St. Basil College (minor), 195 Glenbrook Rd., Stamford 06902; St. Basil's Preparatory School (minor), 39 Clovelly Rd., Stamford 06902.

District of Columbia: Washington* — Theological College, The Catholic University of America, 401 Michigan Ave., N.E. 20017.

St. Josaphat's Seminary, 201 Taylor St. N.E., Washington 20017. (Major house of formation serving the four Ukrainian Byzantine-rite dioceses in the U.S.)

Florida: Miami*, Palm Beach, St. Petersburg, Venice — St. John Vianney College Seminary, 2900 S.W. 87th Ave., Miami 33165; St. Vincent de Paul Regional Seminary (major), 10701 S. Military Trail, Boynton Beach. 33436.

Illinois: Chicago* — Quigley Preparatory Seminary (North), 103 East Chestnut St., Chicago 60611; Quigley Preparatory Seminary (South), 7740 South Western Ave., Chicago 60620; Niles College of Loyola University, 7135 N. Harlem Ave., Chicago 60631; Mundelein Seminary, University of St. Mary of the Lake, Mundelein. 60060.

Indiana: Indianapolis* — St. Meinrad Seminary, College and School of Theology (interdiocesan), St. Meinrad. 47577.

Iowa: Davenport — St. Ambrose College Seminary, 518 W. Locust St., Davenport 52803.

Dubuque* — Seminary of St. Pius X, Loras College, Dubuque 52001.

Louisiana: New Orleans* — Notre Dame Seminary Graduate School of Theology, 2901 S. Carrollton Ave., New Orleans 70118; St. Joseph Seminary College (interdiocesan), St. Benedict 70457.

Maryland: Baltimore* — St. Mary's Seminary and University, 5400 Roland Ave., Baltimore 21210; Mt. St. Mary's Seminary, Emmitsburg. 21727.

Massachusetts: Boston* — St. John's Seminary School of Theology, 127 Lake St., Brighton. 02135; St. John's Seminary, College of Liberal Arts, 197 Foster St., Brighton 02135; Pope John XXIII National Seminary (for ages 30-60), 558 South Ave., Weston. 02193.

Melkite Eparchy of Newton — St. Gregory the Theologian Seminary, 233 Grant Ave., Newton 02159.

Michigan: Detroit* — Sacred Heart Major Seminary (college and theologate), 2701 Chicago Blvd., Detroit 48206; The Orchard Lake Schools (Sts. Cyril and Methodius Seminary, St. Mary's College, St. Mary's Preparatory — graduate, undergraduate, secondary; independent, primarily serving Polish-American community), Orchard Lake 48033.

Grand Rapids — Christopher House, 723 Rosewood Ave., S.E., Grand Rapids 49506.

Minnesota: Seminary of the Diocese of St. Cloud, St. John's University, Collegeville. 56321.

St. Paul and Minneapolis* — St. Paul Seminary School of Divinity of the College of St. Thomas, 2260 Summit Ave., St. Paul. 55105; St. John Vianney College Seminary, 2115 Summit Ave., St. Paul. 55105.

Winona — Immaculate Heart of Mary Seminary, Terrace Heights, St. Mary's College, Winona 55987.

Missouri: Jefferson City — St. Thomas Aquinas Preparatory Seminary, 245 N. Levering Ave., P.O. Box 858, Hannibal. 63401.

St. Louis* — St. Louis Roman Catholic Theological Seminary (Kenrick Seminary), 5200 Glennon Dr., St. Louis 63119; Cardinal Glennon College (House of Formation), 5200 Glennon Dr., St. Louis 63119; St. Louis Preparatory Seminary, 5200 Shrewsbury Ave., St. Louis 63119.

Montana: Helena — Borromeo Pre-Seminary Program, Carroll College, Helena 59625.

New Jersey: Newark* — Immaculate Conception Seminary — college seminary; major seminary; graduate school — Seton Hall University, South Orange Ave., South Orange 07079.

New Mexico: Gallup — Cristo Rey College and High School Seminary, 205 E. Wilson, Gallup 87301.

Santa Fe* — Immaculate Heart of Mary Seminary, Mt. Carmel Rd., Santa Fe 87501.

New York: Brooklyn — Cathedral Preparatory Seminary of the Immaculate Conception, 56-25 92nd St., Elmhurst. 11373; Cathedral Seminary Residence of the Immaculate Conception, 7200 Douglaston Parkway, Douglaston. 11362.

Buffalo — Christ the King Seminary (interdiocesan theologate), 711 Knox Rd., East Aurora. 14052.

New York* — St. Joseph's Seminary (major), 201 Seminary Ave., Yonkers. 10704; St. John Neumann Residence (college), 5655 Arlington Ave., Riverdale 10471. Cathedral Preparatory Seminary, 555 West End Ave., New York 10024.

Ogdensburg — Wadhams Hall Seminary College (interdiocesan), Riverside Dr., Ogdensburg 13669.

Rockville Centre — Seminary of the Immaculate Conception, Lloyd Harbor, Huntington, L.I. 11743.

St. Maron Diocese, Brooklyn — Our Lady of Lebanon Maronite Seminary, 7164 Alaska Ave. N.W., Washington, D.C. 20012.

Syracuse — Syracuse-Aquinas House, 702 Danforth St., Syracuse 13208.

North Dakota: Fargo — Cardinal Muench Seminary, 100 35th Ave. N.E., Fargo 58102.

Ohio: Cincinnati* — Mt. St. Mary's Seminary of the West, 6616 Beechmont Ave., Cincinnati. 45230 (division of the Athenaeum of Ohio).

Cleveland — St. Mary Seminary, 1227 Ansel Rd., Cleveland 44108; Borromeo College of Ohio, 28700 Euclid Ave. Wickliffe. 44092.

Columbus — Pontifical College Josephinum (national), theologate and college, Columbus. 43235.

Oregon: Portland* — Mt. Angel Seminary (college, pre-theology program, graduate school of theology, St. Benedict 97373.

Pennsylvania: Allentown — Mary Immaculate Seminary (interdiocesan; pre-theology program), Northampton 18067.

Erie — St. Mark's Seminary, 429 E. Grandview

Blvd., Erie 16504.(College formation and pre-theology.)
Greensburg — St. Vincent Seminary School of Theology (interdiocesan), Latrobe 15650.
Philadelphia* — Theological Seminary of St. Charles Borromeo, Overbrook. 19151. (College, pre-theology program, theologate, religious studies program.)
Pittsburgh Byzantine Rite (Ruthenians)* — Byzantine Catholic Seminary of Sts. Cyril and Methodius, 3605 Perrysville Ave., Pittsburgh. 15214.
Pittsburgh — St. Paul Seminary, 2900 Noblestown Rd. 15205.
Scranton — St. Pius X Seminary (college and pre-theology formation; interdiocesan), Dalton. 18414.

Rhode Island: Providence — St. Vincent House of Formation (college students), 485 Mount Pleasant Ave., Providence 02908.

Texas: Corpus Christi — Corpus Christi Academy (residential pre-seminary program) and St. John Vianney House of Studies (college-age students interested in the priesthood), Saratoga Blvd., 3036 Saratoga Blvd., Corpus Christi 78415.
Dallas — Holy Trinity Seminary (college and pre-theology), P.O. Box 160309, Irving. 75016.
El Paso — St. Charles Seminary College, P.O. Box 17548, El Paso 79917.
Galveston-Houston — St. Mary's Seminary (major), 9845 Memorial Dr., Houston. 77024.
San Antonio* — Assumption Seminary (theologate), 2600 W. Woodlawn Ave., San Antonio 78228.

Washington: Spokane — Bishop White Seminary, College Formation Program, E. 429 Sharp Ave., Spokane 99202.

Wisconsin: Madison — Holy Name Seminary (High School), 3577 High Point Rd., Madison 53719.
Milwaukee* — St. Francis Seminary, School of Pastoral Ministry, and St. Francis Seminary, College Formation Program, 3257 S. Lake Dr., Milwaukee 53207. Sacred Heart School of Theology (interdiocesan), P.O. Box 429, Hales Corner, Wis. 53130.

PONTIFICAL UNIVERSITIES

(Principal source: *Annuario Pontificio*.)

These universities, listed according to country of location, have been canonically erected and authorized by the Congregation for Catholic Education to award degrees in stated fields of study.

New laws and norms governing ecclesiastical universities and faculties were promulgated in the apostolic constitution *Sapientia Christiana*, issued Apr. 15, 1979.

Argentina: Pontifical Catholic University of S. Maria of Buenos Aires (June 16, 1960): Juncal 1912, 1116 Buenos Aires.

Belgium: Catholic University of Louvain (Dec. 9, 1425; 1834), with autonomous institutions for French- (Louvain) and Flemish- (Leuven) speaking: Place de l'Universite I, 1348 Louvain-La-Neuve (French); Naamsestraat 22B, 3000 Leuven (Flemish).

Brazil: Pontifical Catholic University of Rio de Janeiro (Jan. 20, 1947): Rua Marques de Sao Vicente 225, 22451. Rio de Janeiro, RJ.
Pontifical Catholic University of Minas Gerais (June 5, 1983): Av. Dom Jose Gaspar 500, C.P. 2686, 30000 Belo Horizonte MG.
Pontifical Catholic University of Parana (Aug. 6, 1985): Rua Imaculada Conceicao, 1155 — Prado Velho — 80000 Curitiba PA.
Pontifical Catholic University of Rio Grande do Sul (Nov. 1, 1950): Praca Dom. Sebastiao 2, 90000 Porto Alegre, RS.
Pontifical Catholic University of Sao Paulo (Jan. 25, 1947): Rua Monte Alegre 984, 05014 Sao Paulo.
Pontifical University of Campinas (Sept. 8, 1956): Rua Marechal Deodoro 1099, 13100 Campinas, Sao Paulo.

Canada: Laval University (Mar. 15, 1876): Case Postale 460, Quebec G1K 7P4.
St. Paul University (formerly University of Ottawa) (Feb. 5, 1889): 223, Rue Main, Ottawa, K1S 1C4, Ontario.
University of Sherbrooke (Nov. 21, 1957): Chemin Ste.-Catherine, Cite Universitaire, Sherbrooke, Que. J1K 2R1.

Chile: Pontifical Catholic University of Chile (June 21, 1888): Avenida Bernardo O'Higgins 340, Casilla 114D, Santiago.
Catholic University of Valparaiso (Nov. 1, 1961): Avenida Brasil 2950, Casilla 4059, Valparaiso.

Colombia: Bolivarian Pontifical Catholic University (Aug. 16, 1945): Calle 52, N. 43-53, Medellin.
Pontifical Xaverian University (July 31, 1937): Carrera 7, N. 40-76, Apartado 56710, Bogota D.E.; Apartado 8264, Cali (Cali campus).

Cuba: Catholic University of St. Thomas of Villanueva (May 4, 1957): Avenida Quenta 16,660, Mariano, Havana. Taken over by the Castro government in May, 1961.

Dominican Republic: Pontifical Catholic University "Mother and Teacher" (Sept. 9, 1987): Santiago de Los Caballeros.

Ecuador: Pontifical Catholic University of Ecuador (July 16, 1954): Doce de Octubre, N. 1076, Apartado 2184, Quito.

Ethiopia: University of Asmara (Sept. 8, 1960): Via Menelik II, 45, Post Office Box 1220, Asmara.

France: Catholic University of Lille (Nov. 18, 1875): Boulevard Vauban 60, 59046 Lille.
Catholic Faculties of Lyon (Nov. 22, 1875): 25, Rue du Plat, 69288 Lyon.
Catholic Institute of Paris (Aug. 11, 1875): 21, Rue d'Assas, 75270 Paris.
Catholic Institute of Toulouse (Nov. 15,1877): Rue de la Fonderie 31, 31068 Toulouse.
Catholic University of the West (Sept. 16, 1875): 3, Place Andre Leroy, B.P. 808, 49005 Angers.

Germany: Eichstatt Catholic University (Apr. 1, 1980): Ostenstrasse 26, D-8078, Eichstatt, Federal Republic of Germany.

Guatemala: Rafael Landivar University (Oct. 18, 1961): 17 Calle 8-64, Z 10 Guatemala.

Ireland: St. Patrick's College (Mar. 29, 1896): Maynooth, Co. Kildare.

Italy: Catholic University of the Sacred Heart (Dec. 25, 1920): Largo Gemelli 1, 20123 Milan.

Japan: *Jochi Daigaku* (Sophia University) (Mar. 29, 1913): Chiyoda-Ku, Kioi-cho 7, Tokyo.

Lebanon: St. Joseph University of Beirut (Mar. 25, 1881): Rue de l'Universite St.-Joseph, Boite Postale 293, Beyrouth.

Netherlands: Nijmegen Roman Catholic University (June 29, 1923): Wilhelminasingel 13, Nijmegen.

Panama: University of S. Maria La Antigua (May 27, 1965): Apartado 2143, Panama 1.

Paraguay: Catholic University of Our Lady of the Assumption (Feb. 2, 1965): Independencia Nacional y Comuneros, Casilla 1718, Asuncion.

Peru: Pontifical Catholic University of Peru (Sept. 30, 1942): Apartado 1761, Lima.

Philippines: Pontifical University of Santo Tomas (Nov. 20, 1645): Espana Street, Manila 2806.

Poland: Catholic University of Lublin (July 25, 1920): Aleje Raclawickie 14, Skr. Poczt. 279, 20-950, Lublin.

Pontifical Academy of Theology of Krakow (Dec. 8, 1981): Ul. Podzamcze 8, 31-003 Krakow.

Portugal: Portuguese Catholic University (Nov. 1, 1967): Palma de Cima, 1600 Lisbon.

Puerto Rico: Catholic University of Puerto Rico (Aug. 15, 1972): Ponce, Puerto Rico 00731.

Spain: Catholic University of Navarra (Aug. 6, 1960): Ciudad Universitaria, Pamplona.

Pontifical University "Comillas" (Mar. 29, 1904): Apartado Postal 3082, 28080 Madrid.

Pontifical University of Salamanca (Sept. 25, 1940): Apartado 541, 37080 Salamanca.

University of Deusto (Aug. 10, 1963): Avenida de las Universidades, 28, 48007 Bilbao.

Taiwan (China): Fu Jen Catholic University (Nov. 15, 1923, at Peking; reconstituted at Taipeh, Sept. 8, 1961): Hsinchuang, Taipeh Hsien 242.

United States: Catholic University of America (Mar. 7, 1889): 620 Michigan Ave. N.E., Washington, D.C. 20064.

Georgetown University (Mar. 30, 1833): 37th and O Sts. N.W., Washington, D.C. 20057.

Niagara University (June 21, 1956): Niagara University P.O., N.Y. 14109.

Uruguay: Catholic University of Uruguay "Damaso Antonio Larranaga" (Jan. 25, 1985): Avda. 8 de Octubre 2738, Montevideo.

Venezuela: Catholic University "Andres Bello" (Sept. 29, 1963): Esquina Jesuitas, Apartado 422, Caracas.

ECCLESIASTICAL FACULTIES

(Principal source: *Annuario Pontificio*)

These faculties in Catholic seminaries and universities, listed according to country of location, have been canonically erected and authorized by the Sacred Congregation for Catholic Education to award degrees in stated fields of study. In addition to those listed here, there are other faculties of theology or philosophy in state universities and for members of certain religious orders only.

Argentina: Faculties of Philosophy and Theology, San Miguel (Sept. 8, 1932).

Australia: Institute of Theology, Sydney (Feb. 2, 1954).

Austria: Theological Faculty, Linz (Dec. 25, 1978).

Brazil: Ecclesiastical Faculty of Philosophy "John Paul II," Rio de Janeiro Aug. 6, 1981.

Philosophical and Theological Faculties of the Company of Jesus, Belo Horizonte (July 15, 1941 and Mar. 30, 1945).

Canada: Pontifical Institute of Medieval Studies, Toronto (Oct. 18, 1939).

Dominican Faculty of Theology of Canada, Ottawa (1965; Nov. 15, 1975).

Regis College — Toronto Section of the Jesuit Faculty of Theology in Canada, Toronto (Feb. 17, 1956; Dec. 25, 1977).

College of Immaculate Conception — Montreal Section of Jesuit Faculties in Canada (Sept. 8, 1932).

France: Centre Sevres — Faculties of Theology and Philosophy of the Jesuits, Paris (Sept. 8, 1932).

Germany: Theological Faculty, Paderborn (June 11, 1966).

Theological Faculty of the Major Episcopal Seminary, Trier (Sept. 8, 1955)

Philosophical Faculty, Munich (1932; Oct. 25, 1971).

Theological-Philosophical Faculty, Frankfurt (1932; June 7, 1971).

Theological Faculty, Fulda (Dec. 22, 1978).

Great Britain: Heythrop College, University of London, London (Nov. 1, 1964). Theology, philosophy.

India: "Jnana Deepa" (Pontifical Athenaeum), Institute of Philosophy and Religion, Poona (July 27, 1926).

Pontifical Institute of Theology and Philosophy at the Pontifical Interritual Seminary of St. Joseph, Alwaye, Kerala (Feb. 24, 1972).

"Vidyajyoti," Institute of Religious Studies, Faculty of Theology, Delhi (1932; Dec. 9, 1974).

Dharmaram Pontifical Institute of Theology and Philosophy, Bangalore (Jan. 6, 1976; Dec. 8, 1983).

Faculty of Theology, Ranchi (Aug. 15, 1982).

Pontifical Oriental Institute of Religious Studies, Kottayam (July 3, 1982).

St. Peter's Pontifical Institute of Theology, Bangalore (Jan. 6, 1976).

"Satya Nilayam," Institute of Philosophy and Culture. Faculty of Philosophy, Madras (Sept. 8, 1932; Dec. 15, 1976).

Indonesia: Wedabhakti Pontifical Faculty of Theology, Yogyakarta (Nov. 1, 1984).

Israel: French Biblical and Archeological School, Jerusalem (founded 1890; approved Sept. 17, 1892; canonically approved to confer Doctorate in Biblical Science, June 29, 1983).

Italy: Interregional Theological Faculty, Milan (Aug. 8, 1935; restructured 1969).

Pontifical Theological Faculty of Sardinia, Cagliari, (Aug. 5, 1927).

Pontifical Ambrosian Institute of Sacred Music, Milan (Mar. 12, 1940).

Theological Faculty of Sicily, Palermo (Dec. 8, 1980).

Theological Faculty of Southern Italy, Naples.

Two sections: St. Thomas Aquinas Capodimonte (Oct. 31, 1941) and St. Louis Posillipo (Mar. 16, 1918). Pastoral Ignatian Institute, Messina (July 31, 1972).
Faculty of Philosophy "Aloisianum," Gallarate (1937; Mar. 20, 1974).
Ivory Coast: Catholic Institute of West Africa, Abidjan (Aug. 12, 1975).
Japan: Faculty of Theology, Nagoya (May 25, 1984).
Lebanon: Faculty of Theology, University of the Holy Spirit, Kaslik (May 30, 1982).
Madagascar: Superior Institute of Theology, at the Regional Seminary of Antananarivo, Ambatoroka-Antananarivo (Apr. 21, 1960).
Malta: Faculty of Theology, Tal-Virtu (Nov. 22, 1769), with Institute of Philosophy and Human Studies (Sept. 8, 1984).
Mexico: Theological Faculty of Mexico (June 29, 1982) and Philosophy (Jan. 6, 1986), Mexico City.
Nigeria: Catholic Institute of West Africa, Port Harcourt (Nov. 30, 1981).
Peru: Pontifical and Civil Faculty of Theology, Lima (July 25, 1571).
Poland: Theological Faculty, Poznan (1969; pontifical designation, June 2, 1974).
Philosophical Faculty, Krakow (1932; Sept. 20, 1984).
Theological Faculty, Warsaw (1932; Sept. 26, 1984).
Spain: Theological Faculty of Catalunya, (Mar. 7, 1968), with the Institutes of Fundamental Theology (Dec. 28, 1984) and Liturgy (Aug. 15, 1986), Barcelona.
Theological Faculty, Granada (1940; July 31, 1973).
Theological Faculty of the North, of the Metropolitan Seminary of Burgos and the Diocesan Seminary of Vitoria (Feb. 6, 1967).
Theological Faculty "San Vicente Ferrer" (two sections), Valencia (Jan. 23, 1974).
Switzerland: Theological Faculty, Chur (Jan. 1, 1974).
Theological Faculty, Luzerne (Dec. 25, 1973).
United States: St. Mary's Seminary and University. School of Theology, Baltimore (May 1, 1822).
St. Mary of the Lake Faculty of Theology, Mundelein, Ill. (Sept. 30, 1929).
Weston School of Theology, Cambridge, Mass. (Oct. 18, 1932).
The Jesuit School of Theology, Berkeley, Calif. (Feb. 2, 1934, as "Alma College," Los Gatos, Calif.).
Faculty of Philosophy and Letters, St. Louis, Mo. (Feb. 2, 1934).
St. Michael's Institute, Jesuit School of Philosophy and Letters, Spokane, Wash. (Feb. 2, 1934).
Pontifical Faculty of Theology of the Immaculate Conception, Washington, D.C. (Nov. 15, 1941).
International Marian Research Institute (IMRI), U.S. branch of Pontifical Theological Faculty "Marianum," University of Dayton, Dayton, O. 45469 (affil. 1976, inc. 1983).
Vietnam: Theological Faculty of the Pontifical National Seminary of St. Pius X, Dalat (July 31, 1965). Activities suppressed.

The Pontifical College Josephinum (Theologate and College) at Columbus, Ohio, is a national pontifical seminary. Established Sept. 1, 1888, it is immediately subject to the Holy See.

PONTIFICAL UNIVERSITIES AND INSTITUTES IN ROME
(Source: *Annuario Pontificio.*)

Pontifical Gregorian University (1552): Piazza della Pilotta, 4, 00187 Rome. Associated with the university are:

The **Pontifical Biblical Institute** (May 7, 1909): Via della Pilotta, 25, 00187 Rome.

The **Pontifical Institute of Oriental Studies** (Oct. 15, 1917): Piazza S. Maria Maggiore, 7, 00185 Rome.

Pontifical Lateran University (1773). Piazza S. Giovanni in Laterano, 4, 00184 Rome.

Pontifical Urban University (1627): Via Urbano VIII, 16, 00165 Rome.

Pontifical University of St. Thomas Aquinas (Angelicum) (1580), of the Order of Preachers: Largo Angelicum, 1, 00184 Rome.

Pontifical University Salesianum (May 3, 1940; university designation May 24, 1973), of the Salesians of Don Bosco: Piazza dell' Ateneo Salesiano, 1, 00139 Rome. Associated with the university is the **Pontifical Institute of Higher Latin Studies,** known as the **Faculty of Christian and Classical Letters** (Feb. 22, 1964).

Pontifical Athenaeum of St. Anselm (1687), of the Benedictines: Piazza dei Cavalieri di Malta, 5, 00153 Rome.

Pontifical Athenaeum "Antonianum" (of St. Anthony) (May 17, 1933), of the Order of Friars Minor: Via Merulana, 124, 00185 Rome.

Pontifical Institute of Sacred Music (1911; May 24, 1931): Via di Torre Rossa, 21, 00165 Rome.

Pontifical Institute of Christian Archeology (Dec. 11, 1925): Via Napoleone III, 1, 00185 Rome.

Pontifical Theological Faculty "St. Bonaventure" (Dec. 18, 1587), of the Order of Friars Minor Conventual: Via del Serafico, 1, 00142 Rome.

Pontifical Theological Faculty, Pontifical Institute of Spirituality "Teresianum" (1935), of the Discalced Carmelites: Piazza San Pancrazio, 5-A, 00152 Rome.

Pontifical Theological Faculty "Marianum" (1398), of the Servants of Mary: Viale Trente Aprile, 6, 00153 Rome.

Pontifical Institute of Arabic and Islamic Studies (1926), of the Missionaries of Africa: Piazza S. Apollinare, 49, 00186 Rome.

Pontifical Faculty of Educational Science "Auxilium" (June 27, 1970), of the Daughters of Mary, Help of Christians: Via Cremolino, 141, 00166 Rome.

Pontifical Institute "Regina Mundi" (1954): Lungotevere Tor di Nona, 7, 00186 Rome.

PONTIFICAL ACADEMY OF SCIENCES

(Sources: *Annuario Pontificio,* NC News Service. Membership as of July 1, 1988.)

The Pontifical Academy of Sciences was constituted in its present form by Pius XI Oct. 28, 1936, in virtue of *In Multis Solaciis,* a document issued on his own initiative.

The academy is the only supranational body of its kind in the world, with a pope-selected, life-long membership of outstanding mathematicians and experimental scientists from many countries. The normal complement of 70 members was increased in 1985-86 by John Paul II who appointed 15 scientists to the Academy. There are additional honorary and supernumerary members. Non-Catholics as well as Catholics belong to the academy.

Purposes of the academy are to honor pure science and its practitioners, to promote the freedom of pure science and to foster research.

The academy traces its origin to the *Linceorum Academia* (Academy of the Lynxes — its symbol) founded in Rome Aug. 17, 1603. Pius IX reorganized this body and gave it a new name — *Pontificia Accademia dei Nuovi Lincei* — in 1847. It was taken over by the Italian state in 1870 and called the *Accademia Nationale dei Lincei.* Leo XIII reconstituted it with a new charter in 1887. Pius XI designated the Vatican Gardens as the site of academy headquarters in 1922 and gave it its present title and status in 1936. In 1940, Pius XII gave the title of Excellency to its members; John XXIII extended the privilege to honorary members in 1961.

Members in U.S.

Scientists in the U.S. who presently hold membership in the Academy are listed below according to year of appointment.

1936 (Oct. 28): Franco Rasetti, professor emeritus of physics at Johns Hopkins University, Baltimore, Md.; George Speri-Sperti, president and director of the Institute Divi Thomae in the Athanaeum of Ohio.

1964 (Sept. 24): William Wilson Morgan, professor emeritus of astronomy at the University of Chicago.

1974 (June 24): Rita Levi-Montalcini, professor emeritus of biology at Washington University, St. Louis, Mo.; Marshall Warren Nirenberg, professor of genetics and biochemistry at the National Institutes of Health, Bethesda, Md.

1975 (Dec. 2): George Palade, professor of cellular biology at Yale University, New Haven, Conn.; Victor Weisskopf, professor of physics at the Massachusetts Institute of Technology, Cambridge, Mass.

1978 (Apr. 17): David Baltimore, professor of biology, Har Gobind Khorana, professor of biochemistry, and Alexander Rich, professor of biophysics — all at the Massachusetts Institute of Technology, Cambridge, Mass.; Roger Walcott Sperry, professor of psychobiology, California Institute of Technology, Pasadena, Calif.

1981 (May 12): Christian Anfinsen, professor of biochemistry at Johns Hopkins University, Baltimore, Md.

1983 (Jan. 26): Charles Townes, professor of physics at the University of California at Berkeley.

1986 (June 9): Beatrice Mintz, chief researcher, Cancer Research Institute of Philadelphia; Maxine Singer, director of biochemistry laboratory, Biologic and Diagnostic Division of National Cancer Institute, Bethesda, Md.

Members in Other Countries

Other members of the Academy are listed below according to country of location; dates of their selection are given in parentheses.

Austria: Hans Tuppy (Apr. 10, 1970); Walter Thirring (June 9, 1986).

Belgium: Christian de Duve (Apr. 10, 1970).

Brazil: Carlos Chagas (Aug. 18, 1961); Johanna Dobereiner (Apr. 17, 1978); Crodowaldo Pavan (Apr. 17, 1978).

Canada: Gerhard Herzberg (Sept. 24, 1964); John Charles Polanyi (June 9, 1986).

Chile: Hector Croxatto Rezzio (Dec. 2, 1975).

Denmark: Bengt Georg Stromgren (Dec. 2, 1975); Aage Bohr (Apr. 17, 1978).

France: Pierre Raphael Lepine (Sept. 24, 1964); Louis Leprince-Ringuet (Aug. 18, 1961); Marcel Roche (Apr. 10, 1970); Jerome Lejeune (June 24, 1974); Andre Blanc-LaPierre (Apr. 17, 1978), Anatole Abragam (May 12, 1981), Andre Lichnerowicz (May 12, 1981), Bernard Pullman (May 12, 1981); Paul Germain (June 9, 1986).

Germany: Rudolf L. Mossbauer (Apr. 10, 1970), Manfred Eigen (May 12, 1981).

Great Britain: Hermann Alexander Bruck (Apr. 5, 1955); Alan Lloyd Hodgkin (Apr. 22, 1968); Alfred R. Ubbelohde (Apr. 22, 1968); Percy C. C. Garnham (Apr. 10, 1970); George Porter (June 24, 1974); Max Ferdinand Perutz (May 12, 1981); Stanley Keith Runcorn (Sept. 12, 1981); Stephen William Hawking (Jan. 7, 1986).

Hungary: Janos Szentagothai (May 12, 1981).

India: Mambilliralathil Govind Kumar Menon (May 12, 1981).

Israel: Michael Sela (Dec. 2, 1975).

Italy: Giovanni Battista Marini-Bettolo (Apr. 22, 1968); Giampietro Puppi (Apr. 17, 1978), Ennio De Giorgi (May 12, 1981), Abdus Salam (May 12, 1981); Nicola Cabibbo (June 9, 1986).

Japan: Kenichi Fukui (Dec. 14, 1985).

Kenya: Thomas R. Odhiambo (May 12, 1981); Daniel Adzei Bekoe (Sept. 26, 1983).

Mexico: Marcos Moshinsky (June 9, 1986).

Netherlands: Jan Hendrik Oort (Aug. 18, 1961).

Pakistan: Salimuzzaman Siddiqui (Sept. 24, 1964).

Poland: Stanislaw Lojasiewicz (Feb. 12, 1983); Czeslaw Olech (June 9, 1986).

Spain: Manuel Lora Tamayo (Sept. 24, 1964); Severo Ochoa (June 24, 1974).

Sweden: Sven Horstadius (Aug. 18, 1961); Sune Bergstrom (Dec. 14, 1985); Kai Siegbahn (Dec. 14, 1985).

Switzerland: John Carew Eccles (Apr. 8, 1961), Thomas Adeoyo Lambo (June 24, 1974), Werner Arber (May 12, 1981); Vladimir Prélog (Dec. 14, 1985); Carlo Rubbia (Dec. 14, 1985); Albert Eschenmoser (June 9, 1986).

Zaire: Wa Kalengo Malu (Sept. 26, 1983).

Ex officio members: Rev. George V. Coyne, S.J., director of Vatican Observatory (Sept. 2, 1978); Very Rev. Leonard E. Boyle, O.P., prefect of the Vatican Library (May 24, 1984); Very Rev. Joseph Metzler, O.M.I., prefect of the Secret Vatican Archives (May 24, 1984).

Honorary members: Silvio Ranzi, professor emeritus of biology and zoology of the University of Milan (May 12, 1981); Enrico di Rovasenda, O.P., civil engineer and doctor of theology; former chancellor of the Pontifical Academy of Science (Nov. 13, 1986).

President: Carlos Chagas (Nov. 9, 1972).

SOCIAL SERVICES

Catholic Charities USA (formerly National Conference of Catholic Charities): Established in 1910 to help advance and promote the charitable programs and activities of Catholic community and social service agencies in the United States. As the central and national organization for this purpose, it services member agencies and institutions by consultation, information and assistance in planning and evaluating social service programs under Catholic auspices.

The principal fields of service in which Catholic Charities agencies are engaged are family counseling, child welfare, services for unmarried mothers, community services, day care centers, neighborhood center programs, and care of the aged. Community organization, social action and parish social ministry are also functions of Catholic Charities.

The organization conducts research with respect to service to the aging, community self-help programs, the institutional care of children, and other social service projects. It represents the Catholic philosophy of social service to government agencies and personnel, and to professional organizations in the field. Its publications include *Charities USA*, a monthly membership magazine, and *Social Thought*, a scholarly quarterly co-sponsored with the National School of Social Service of the Catholic University of America.

Membership includes more than 900 local agencies and branches, 1,000 institutions and 4,000 individuals.

Rev. Thomas J. Harvey is executive director of the conference, with offices at 1319 F St. N.W., Washington, D.C. 20004.

The Society of St. Vincent de Paul, originally called the Conference of Charity: An association of Catholic lay men and women devoted to personal service of the poor through the spiritual and corporal works of mercy. The first conference was formed at Paris in 1833 by Frederic Ozanam and his associates.

The first conference in the U.S. was organized in 1845 at St. Louis. There are now approximately 4,700 units of the society in this country, with a membership of about 60,000.

In the fiscal year 1985-86, members of the society in this country have distributed among poor persons financial and other forms of assistance valued at approximately $75,000,000.

Besides person-to-person assistance, increasing emphasis is being given to stores and rehabilitation workshops of the society through which persons with marginal income can purchase refurbished goods at minimal cost. Handicapped persons are employed in renovating goods and store operations. The society also operates food centers, shelters, criminal justice and other programs.

Address of the National Council: 4140 Lindell Blvd., St. Louis, Mo. 63108. John F. Coppinger, president; Rita W. Porter, executive director.

Catholic Health Association of the United States is the national organization of Catholic hospitals and long-term care facilities, their sponsoring organizations and systems, and other health and related agencies and services operated as Catholic. It is an ecclesial community participating in the mission of the Catholic Church through its members' ministry of healing. CHA witnesses this ministry by providing leadership both within the Church and within the broader society and through its programs of education, facilitation and advocacy.

Comprised of more than 1,000 organizational and personal members, CHA maintains its headquarters office at 4455 Woodson Road, St. Louis, Mo. 63134, and its government services office at 1776 K Street N.W., Suite 204, Washington, D.C. 20006.

National Association of Catholic Chaplains: Founded in 1965. Membership is approximately 3,400.

Sister Helen Hayes, O.S.F., is executive director. Address: 3501 S. Lake Dr., P.O. Box 3018, Milwaukee Wis. 53201.

FACILITIES FOR RETIRED AND AGED PERSONS

(Sources: Almanac survey, *The Official Catholic Directory.*)

This list covers residence, health care and other facilities for the retired and aged under Catholic auspices. Information includes name, type of facility if not evident from the title, address, and total capacity (in parentheses); unless noted otherwise, facilities are for both men and women. Many facilities for the aged offer intermediate nursing care.

Alabama: Allen Memorial Home (Skilled Nursing), 735 S. Washington Ave., Mobile 36603 (94).

Cathedral Place, 351 Conti St., Mobile 36602 (190).

Sacred Heart Residence Little Sisters of the Poor, 1655 McGill Ave., Mobile 36604 (120).

Seton Haven, 3721 Wares Ferry Rd., Montgomery 36193 (106).

Villa Mercy (Skilled Nursing Facility, Hospice, Home Health Agency), P.O. Box 1090, Daphne 36526. Specialized hospital, not restricted to elderly.

Arizona: Villa Maria Geriatric Center (Skilled Nursing Facility and Apartments), 4310 E. Grant Rd., Tucson 85712 (93 beds, 50 apartments). Members of the Holy Cross Health System.

Arkansas: Benedictine Manor (Retirement Home), 2nd and Grand Sts., Box 2249, Hot Springs 71914 (92).

California: Alexis Apartments of St. Patrick's Parish, 756 Mission St. 94103; 390 Clementina St., San Francisco 94103 (220).
Casa Manana Inn, 3700 N. Sutter St., Stockton 95204 (175).
Cathedral Plaza, 1551 Third Ave., San Diego 92101 (222 apartments).
Ellis Seniors Residence, 3263 First Ave., Sacramento 95817 (18).
Francis of Assisi Community, 145 Guerrero St., San Francisco 94103 (117). For elderly and handicapped.
Guadalupe Plaza, 4142 42nd St., San Diego 92105 (127 apartments).
Jeanne d'Arc Manor, 85 S. Fifth St., San Jose 95112 (91). For elderly and handicapped.
La Paz Villas, 43-555 Deep Canyon Dr., Palm Desert 92260 (30 units).
Little Flower Haven (Residential Care Facility for Retired), 8585 La Mesa Blvd., La Mesa 92041 (75).
Little Sisters of the Poor, 300 Lake St., San Francisco 94118 (118).
Little Sisters of the Poor, Jeanne Jugan Residence, 2100 South Western Ave., San Pedro, Calif. 90732 (110).
Madonna Residence (Low-Income women over 60), 1055 Pine St., San Francisco 94109 (57).
Marian Residence (Retirement Home), 124 S. College Dr., Santa Maria 93454 (58).
Mercy Retirement and Care, 3431 Foothill Blvd., Oakland 94601 (130).
Mother Gertrude Balcazar Home for Senior Citizens, 11320 Laurel Canyon Blvd., San Fernando 91340 (114).
Nazareth House (Residential, Skilled and Intermediate Care), 2121 N. 1st St., Fresno 93703 (91).
Nazareth House, 3333 Manning Ave., Los Angeles 90064 (138).
Nazareth House (Retirement Home), 245 Nova Albion Way, Terra Linda, San Rafael 94903 (145).
Nazareth House Retirement Home, 6333 Rancho Mission Rd., San Diego 92108 (122).
Our Lady of Fatima Villa (Skilled Nursing Facility, Women), 20400 Saratoga/Los Gatos Rd., Saratoga 95070 (85).
St. Bernardine Plaza (Retirement Home), 550 W. 5th St., San Bernardino 92401 (150 units).
St. Francis Home (Elderly and Retired Women), 1718 W. 6th St., Santa Ana 92703 (80).
St. John of God Nursing Hospital and Residence, 2035 W. Adams Blvd., Los Angeles 90018.
St. John's Plaza, 8150 Broadway, Lemon Grove 92045 (100 apartments).
Vigil Light Apartments, 1945 Long Dr., Santa Rosa 95405 (56).
Villa Scalabrini (Retirement Center), 10631 Vinedale St., Sun Valley 91352 (130 residence; 58 nursing).
Villa Siena (Residence and Intermediate Care), 1855 Miramonte Ave., Mountain View 94040 (50, residence; 20, skilled nursing care).

Colorado: Francis Heights, Inc., 2626 Osceola St., Denver 80212 (400 units; 431 residents).
Gardens at St. Elizabeth (Congregate Housing and Assisted Living), 2825 W. 32nd Ave., Denver 80211 (250).
Little Sisters of the Poor, 3629 W. 29th Ave., Denver 80211 (22 skilled care; 68 intermediate care, 14 independent living).

Connecticut: Augustana Homes (Residence), Simeon Rd., Bethel 06801.
Carmel Ridge Estates, Gramco Management Co., 525 Palisade Ave., Bridgeport 06610 (36 units).
Matulaitis Nursing Home, Thurber Rd., Putnam 06260 (119).
Monsignor Bojnowski Manor, Inc. (Skilled Nursing Facility), 50 Pulaski St., New Britain 06053 (60).
Notre Dame Convalescent Home, 76 West Rocks Rd., Norwalk 06851 (60).
Regina Pacis Villa (Residence), RFD No. 1, Pomfret Center 06259 (16).
St. Joseph Guest Home (Women, Employed and Retired), 311 Greene St., New Haven 06511 (62).
St. Joseph's Home for the Aged, 88 Jackson St., Willimantic 06226 (37).
St. Joseph's Manor, Carmelite Srs. for Aged and Infirm, 6448 Main St., Trumbull 06611 (294).
St. Joseph's Residence, Little Sisters of the Poor, 1365 Enfield St., Enfield, Conn. 06082 (94)
St. Lucian's Home for the Aged, 532 Burritt St., New Britain 06053 (54).
St. Mary's Home (Residence and Health Care Facility), 291 Steele Rd., W. Hartford 06117 (177).
Teresian Towers, Gramco Management Co., 525 Palisade Ave., Bridgeport 16610 (50 units).
Villa Maria Rest Home for the Aged, West St., Thompson 06277 (24).

Delaware: The Antonian, 1701 W. 10th St., Wilmington 19805 (136 apartments).
Jeanne Jugan Residence, Little Sisters of the Poor, 185 Salem Church Rd., Newark 19713 (123).
Marydale Retirement Village, 135 Jeandell Dr., Newark 19713 (108 apartments).
St. Patrick's House, Inc., 14th and French Sts., Wilmington 19801 (14).

District of Columbia: Jeanne Jugan Residence — St. Joseph' Villa, Little Sisters of the Poor, 4200 Harewood Rd., N.E. Washington 20017 (117).

Florida: All Saints Home for the Aged, 2040 Riverside Ave., Jacksonville 32204 (60).
Carroll Manor (Retirement Apartments), 3667 S.

Miami Ave., Miami 33133 (236 apartments).
Casa Calderon, Inc. (Retirement Apartments), 800 W. Virginia St., Tallahassee 32304 (111).
Cor Jesu Retirement Center, 4918 N. Habana Ave., Tampa 33614 (75).
Haven of Our Lady of Peace (Residence and Health Care Facility), 5203 N. 9th Ave., Pensacola 32504 (87).
Maria Manor Health Care Center, 10300 4th St. N., St. Petersburg 33702 (274).
Marian Towers, Inc. (Retirement Apartments), 17505 North Bay Rd., Miami Beach 33160.
Noreen McKeen Residence for Geriatric Care, 315 Flagler Dr. S., W. Palm Beach 33401.
Opa Locka Village, Inc., 13201 N.W. 28 Avenue, Opa Locka 33054 (113 apartments).
Palmer House, Inc., 1225 S.W. 107th Ave., Miami 33174 (120 apartments).
Pennsylvania Retirement Residence, 208 Evernia St., W. Palm Beach 33401 (190).
St. Andrew Towers (Retirement Apartments), 2700 N.W. 99th Ave., Coral Springs 33065.
St. Dominic Gardens, 5849 N.W. 7th St., Miami 33126.
St. Elizabeth Gardens, Inc. (Retirement Apartments), 801 N.E. 33rd St., Pompano Beach 33064.
St. John's Rehabilitation Hospital/St. John Health Care Center, 3075 N.W. 35th Ave., Lauderdale Lakes 33311. (Under construction.)
Stella Maris House, Inc., 8636 Harding Ave., Miami Beach 33141 (136 apartments).

Illinois: Addolorato Villa (Home for Aged), 555 McHenry Rd., Wheeling 60090 (98).
Alvernia Manor (Sheltered Care), 1598 Main St., Lemont 60439 (50).
Carmelite Carefree Village, 8419 Bailey Rd., Darien 60559 (96 units, 115 residents).
Cortland Manor Retirement Home, 1900 N. Karlov, Chicago 60639. (52).
Holy Family Health Center, 2380 Dempster, Des Plaines 60016 (362).
Holy Family Villa (Intermediate Care Facility), 123rd St. and Father Linkus Dr., Lemont 60439 (99).
Jugan Terrace, Little Sisters of the Poor, 2300 N. Racine, Chicago 60614 (50 apartments).
Little Sisters of the Poor Center for the Aging, 2325 N. Lakewood Ave., Chicago, Ill. 60614 (120).
Maria Care Center, 350 S. First St., Red Bud 62278 (112).
Marian Heights Apartments (Elderly, Handicapped), 20 Oak St., Alton 62002 (141).
Marian Park, Inc., 2126 W. Roosevelt Rd., Wheaton 60187 (117 apartments).
Maryhaven, Inc. (Intermediate Care Facility), 1700 E. Lake Ave., Glenview 60025 (147).
Mayslake Village (Retirement Apartments), 1801 35th St., Oak Brook 60521 (630 apartments).
Mercy Residence at Tolentine Center, 20300 Governors Hwy., Olympia Fields 60461 (52).
Meredith Memorial Home, 16 S. Illinois St., Belleville 62220 (90).
Merkle-Knipprath Nursing Home, Rt. 1, Franciscan Brothers. Clifton 60927 (100).
Mother Theresa Home (Sheltered and Intermediate Care), 1270 Main St., Lemont 60439 (57).
Nazarethville (Intermediate and Sheltered Care), 300 River Rd., Des Plaines 60016 (83).
Our Lady of Angels Retirement Home, 1201 Wyoming, Joliet 60435 (100).
Our Lady of the Snows Apartment Community (Retirement Apartment Community; Health Care Program), 9500 W. Ill., Rt. 15, Belleville 62223 (230).
Pope John Paul I Apartments (Elderly and Handicapped), 1 Pope John Paul Plaza, Springfield 62703 (150).
Resurrection Nursing Pavilion (Skilled Care), 1001 N. Greenwood 60068 (295).
Resurrection Retirement Community, 7262 W. Peterson Ave., Chicago, 60631 (311 apartments).
Rosary Hill Home, 9000 W. 81st St., Justice 60458 (50).
St. Andrew Home (Retirement Residence), 7000 N. Newark Ave., Niles 60648 (198).
St. Benedict Home, 6930 W. Touhy Ave., Niles 60648 (52).
St. James Healthcare Center, 1251 Richton Rd., Crete 60417 (110).
St. Joseph's Home (Sheltered and Intermediate Care), 3306 S. 6th St. Rd., Springfield 62703 (133).
St. Joseph's Home (Sheltered and Intermediate Care), 2223 W. Heading Ave., Peoria 61604 (200).
St. Joseph's Home for the Aged, 659 E. Jefferson St., Freeport 61032 (106).
St. Joseph's Home for the Elderly, 80 W. Northwest Hwy., Palatine 60067 (137).
St. Joseph Home of Chicago, Inc., 2650 N. Ridgeway Ave., Chicago 60647 (173).
St. Patrick's Residence (Sheltered and Intermediate Care), 22 E. Clinton St., Joliet 60431 (197).
Villa Saint Cyril (Intermediate Care), 1111 St. John's Ave., Highland Park 60035 (80).
Villa Scalabrini (Sheltered, Intermediate and Skilled), 480 N. Wolf Rd., Northlake 60164 (265).

Indiana: Little Company of Mary Health Facility (Comprehensive Nursing), Route 421 San Pierre 46374 (180).
Providence Retirement Home, 703 E. Spring St., New Albany 47150 (95).
Regina Continuing Care Center (Skilled Nursing and Intermediate Care Facility), 3900 Washington Ave., Evansville 47715 (154).
Sacred Heart Home (Comprehensive Nursing), R.R. 2, Box 2A, Avilla 46710 (133). LaVerna Terrace, same address; independent living for senior citizens, handicapped and disabled (51 units).
St. Anne Home (Residence and Comprehensive Nursing), 1900 Randalia Dr., Ft. Wayne 46805 (205).
St. Anthony Medical Center and St. Anthony Home, Inc.; 201 Franciscan Rd., Crown Point 46307 (219).
St. Augustine Home for the Aged, Little Sisters of the Poor, 2345 W. 86th St., Indianapolis 46260 (77).
St. John's Home for the Aged, Little Sisters of the Poor, 1236 Lincoln Ave., Evansville 47714 (104).

St. Paul Hermitage (Residential and Intermediate Care Nursing), 501 N. 17th St., Beech Grove 46107 (105).

Iowa: The Alverno Health Care Facility (Intermediate Care), 849 13th Ave. N., Clinton 52732 (136).
Bishop Drumm Retirement Center, 5387 Winwood Dr., Johnston 50131 (120 beds; 87 apartments).
Hallmar-Mercy Hospital, 701 Tenth St. S.E., Cedar Rapids 52403 (62).
Holy Spirit Retirement Home (Intermediate Care), 1701 W. 25th St., Sioux City 51103 (94).
Kahl Home for the Aged and Infirm (Intermediate Care Facility), 1101 W. 9th St., Davenport 52804 (141).
The Marian Home, 2400 6th Ave. North, Fort Dodge 50501 (Intermediate Care, 97) and Marian Village (Apartments), 2320 6th Ave. North, Fort Dodge 50501.
Mary of the Angels Home (Women, Employed and Retired), 605 Bluff St., Dubuque 52001 (70).
Padre Pio Health Care Center, Stonehill Care Center (Residence, Nursing Home), 3485 Windsor, Dubuque 52001 (250).
Ritter Home for Retired Women, 1837 Sunnyside Ave., Burlington 52601 (6).
St. Anthony Nursing Home (Intermediate Care), 406 E. Anthony St., Carroll 51401 (80).
St. Francis Continuation Care and Nursing Home Center, Burlington 52601 (29 skilled nursing; 59 intermediate care).

Kansas: Catholic Care Center (Skilled Care Facility), 3411 E. Zimmerly, Wichita 67218 (151 beds, 13 apartments).
Mt. Joseph (Intermediate Care Facility), 1110 W. 11, R.R. 1, Concordia 66901 (125 nursing; 12 apartments).
St. John Rest Home (Intermediate Care Facility), 701 Seventh St., Victoria 67671 (90 nursing).
St. John's New Horizons (Assisted Living Complex), 2205 Canterbury Dr., Hays 67601 (48 apartments).
St. John's of Hays (Skilled Facility), 2403 Canterbury Rd., Hays 67601 (60 nursing; 12 apartments).
St. Joseph Home (Skilled Care Facility), 759 Vermont Ave., Kansas City 66101 (201 nursing; 36 apartments).
Villa Maria, Inc. (Intermediate Care Facility), 116 S. Central, Mulvane 67110 (66).

Kentucky: Bishop Soenneker Home, 9545 Ky. 144, Philpot 42366 (60).
Carmel Home (Residence, Adult Day Care, Respite Care and Nursing Care), 2501 Old Hartford Rd., Owensboro 42303 (111).
Carmel Manor (Personal Care Home), Carmel Manor Rd., Ft. Thomas, 41075 (99).
Madonna Manor Intermediate Care Nursing Home, 2344 Amsterdam Rd., Covington 41016 (60). (Cottages for Senior Citizens: 49, with 56 apartments).
St. Charles Care Center and Village, 500 Farrell Dr., Covington 41011 (147).

Louisiana: Annunciation Inn, 1220 Spain St., New Orleans 70117 (106 residential units).
Bethany M.H.S. Health Care Center (Women), P.O. Box 2308, Lafayette 70502 (42).
Chateau de Notre Dame (Residence and Nursing Home), 2832 Burdette St., New Orleans 70125 (110 residential units, 180 nursing beds).
Christopher Inn Apartments, 2110 Royal St., New Orleans 70116 (144 residential units).
Consolata Home (Nursing Home), 2319 E. Main St., New Iberia 70560 (114).
Lafon Nursing Home of the Holy Family, 6900 Chef Menteur Hwy., New Orleans 70126 (171).
Mary-Joseph Residence for the Elderly, 4201 Woodland Dr., New Orleans 70131 (122).
Metairie Manor, 4929 York St., Metairie 70001 (200 residential units).
Nazareth Inn, 9630 Haynes Blvd., New Orleans 70127 (270 apartments).
Ollie Steele Burden Manor (Nursing Home), 4200 Essen Lane, Baton Rouge 70809 (65).
Our Lady of Prompt Succor Home (Skilled Nursing Care), 751 E. Prudhomme Lane, Opelousas 70570 (80).
Our Lady's Manor, Inc., 402 Monroe St., Alexandria 71301 (104 apartments).
Place Dubourg, 201 Rue Dubourg, LaPlace 70068 (115 residential units).
Rouquette Lodge, 4300 Hwy 22, Mandeville 70448 (119 residential units).
St. John Berchman's Manor, 3400 St. Anthony St., New Orleans 70122 (150 residential units).
St. Joseph's Home (Nursing Home), 2301 Sterlington Rd., Monroe 71201 (122).
St. Margaret's Daughters Home (Nursing Home, Women), 6220 Chartres St., New Orleans 70117 (112).
St. Martin Manor, 1501 N. Johnson St., New Orleans 70116 (140 residential units).
Villa St. Maurice, 500 St. Maurice Ave., New Orleans 70117. (110 residential units).
Village du Lac, Inc., 1404 Carmel Ave., Lafayette 70501 (200). For handicapped and elderly.
Wynhoven Apartments (Residence for Senior Citizens), 4600 - 10th St., Marrero 70072 (350).

Maine: Deering Pavilion (Apartments for Senior Citizens), 880 Forest Ave., Portland 04103 (200 units).
Marcotte Nursing Home-D'Youville Pavilion, 102 Campus Ave., Lewiston 04240 (280).
Mt. St. Joseph (Nursing Home), Highwood St., Waterville 04901 (77).
St. Andre Health Care Facility, Inc. (Nursing Home), 407 Pool St., Biddeford 04005 (96).
St. Joseph's Manor (Nursing Home), 1133 Washington Ave., Portland 04103 (200).
Seton Village, Inc., 1 Carver St., Waterville 04901 (140 housing units).

Maryland: Cardinal Shehan Center for the Aging, Inc., 2300 Dulaney Valley Rd., Towson 21204.
Carroll Manor (Residence and Nursing Home), 4922 La Salle Rd., Hyattsville 20782 (232).
Little Sisters of the Poor, St. Martin's Home (for

Facilities for the Retired and Aged

the Aged), 601 Maiden Choice Lane, Baltimore 21228 (120).

Sacred Heart Home (Women), 5805 Queens Chapel Rd., Hyattsville 20782 (102).

St. Joseph Nursing Home, 1222 Tugwell Dr., Baltimore 21228 (40).

Villa Rosa (Nursing Home), 3800 Lottsford Vista Rd., Mitchellville 20716 (101).

Massachusetts: Beaven-Kelly Home for Elderly (Rest Home), 1245 Main St., Holyoke 01040 (55).

Catholic Memorial Home (Nursing Home), 2446 Highland Ave., Fall River 02720 (288).

Don Orione Nursing Home, 111 Orient Ave., East Boston 02128 (194). Adult day care center (30).

D'Youville Manor (Nursing Home), 981 Varnum Ave., Lowell 01854 (196). Day care program (20).

Jeanne Jugan Residence, Little Sisters of the Poor (Nursing Home), 186 Highland Ave., Somerville 02143 (95). Jeanne Jugan Pavilion, 190 Highland Ave., Somerville 02143 (apartments, 27; residents, 30).

Madonna Manor (Nursing Home), 85 N. Washington St., N. Attleboro 02760 (121).

Marian Manor, for the Aged and Infirm (Nursing Home), 130 Dorchester St., S. Boston, 02127 (376).

Marian Manor of Taunton (Nursing Home), 33 Summer St., Taunton 02780 (83).

Maristhill Nursing Home, 66 Newton St., Waltham 02154 (120).

Mary Immaculate Nursing/Restorative Center, Bennington St., Lawrence 01841 (250).

Mary Immaculate Residential Community, 189 Maple St., Lawrence 01841 (304 apartments). Adult Day Health Care Center (36), Social Day Care (30).

Mt. St. Vincent Nursing Home, Holy Family Rd., Holyoke 01040 (125).

Our Lady's Haven (Nursing Home), 71 Center St., Fairhaven 02719 (110).

Sacred Heart Nursing Home, 359 Summer St., New Bedford 02740 (217).

St. Joseph Manor Nursing Home, 215 Thatcher St., Brockton 02402 (120).

St. Joseph's Manor, 321 Centre St., Dorchester, Boston 02122. (Under renovation; scheduled to open in 1989 as nursing home.)

St. Luke's Home (Rest Home, Women), 85 Spring St., Springfield 01105 (92).

St. Patrick's Manor (Nursing Home), 863 Central St., Framingham 01701 (292).

Michigan: Bishop Noa Home for Senior Citizens, Escanaba 49829 (109).

Burtha M. Fisher Home, Little Sisters of the Poor (Residence and Nursing Home), 17550 Southfield Rd., Detroit 48235 (123).

Casa Maria (Residence), 600 Maple Vista, Imlay City 48444 (96).

Kundig Center (Residence), 3300 Jefferies Freeway, Detroit 48208 (168). Rooms and apartments.

Lourdes Nursing Home (Skilled Facility), 2300 Watkins Lake Rd., Pontiac 48054 (108).

Madonna Villa Senior Residence, 17825 Fifteen Mile Rd., Fraser, 48026 (90).

Marian Hall (Residence), 529 Detroit St., Flint 48502 (124).

Marian-Oakland West, 29250 W. Ten Mile Rd., Farmington Hills 48024 (100). Rooms and apartments.

Marian Place (Residence), 408 W. Front St., Monroe 48161 (52).

Marycrest Manor (Skilled Nursing Facility), 15475 Middlebelt Rd., Livonia 48154 (55).

Marydale Center for Senior Citizens (Board and Apartments), 3147 Tenth Ave., Port Huron 48060 (71).

Maryhaven (Residence), 11350 Reeck Rd., Southgate 48195 (93).

St. Ann's Home, (Residence and Nursing Home), 2161 Leonard St. N.W., Grand Rapids 49504 (112).

St. Catherine Cooperative House, 1641 Webb Ave., Detroit 48206 (12).

St. Elizabeth Briarbank (Women, Residence), 1315 N. Woodward Ave., Bloomfield Hills 48013 (54).

St. Francis Home (Nursing Home), 915 N. River Rd., Saginaw 48603 (100).

St. Joseph's Home for the Aged, 4800 Cadieux Rd., Detroit 48224 (104).

St. Jude Home, Inc. (Residence), 2270 Marwood, Pontiac 48054.

Stapleton Center (Residence), 9341 Agnes St., Detroit 48214 (65).

Villa Elizabeth (Nursing Home), 2100 Leonard St. N.E., Grand Rapids 49505 (136). Country Villa (Assisted Living Apartments), 2110 Leonard N.E., Grand Rapids 49505 (48 units).

Villa Francesca (Residence, Women), 565 W. Long Lake Rd., Bloomfield Hills 48013 (18).

Villa Marie (Board and Apartments), 15131 Newburgh Rd., Livonia 48154 (100).

Minnesota: Alverna Apartments, 300 8th Ave. S.E., Little Falls 56345 (63).

Assumption Home, 715 North First St., Cold Spring 56320 (Skilled nursing beds, 95). Respite care.

Benedictine Health Center, 935 Kenwood Ave., Duluth 55811 (Nursing home, 120; day care, 25). St. Anthony Center for Ambulatory Confused, 1028 E. 8th St., Duluth 55811 (Day care, 15). Respite care.

Divine Providence Community Home (Intermediate Care), 700 Third Ave. N.W., Sleepy Eye 56085 (58).

Divine Providence Home (Skilled Nursing Home), Ivanhoe 56142 (51).

John Paul Apartments, 200 8th Ave. N., Cold Spring 56320 (61).

Little Sisters of the Poor, Holy Family Residence (Skilled Nursing and Intermediate Care), 330 S. Exchange St., St. Paul 55102 (120).

Madonna Towers (Retirement Apartments and Nursing Home), 4001 19th Ave. N.W., Rochester 55901 (200).

Mary Rondorf Retirement Home, 222 N. 5th St., Staples 56479 (50).

Mille Laks Nursing Home, 200 N. Elm, Onamia 56359 (80).

Mother of Mercy Nursing Home and Retirement Center, Albany 56307 (117).

Regina Nursing Home and Retirement Residence, Hastings 55033. Nursing home (61); retirement home (70); boarding care (16).

Sacred Heart Hospice (Skilled and Intermediate Nursing Care), 1200 Twelfth St. S.W., Austin 55912 (59).

St. Ann's Residence, 330 E. 3rd St., Duluth 55805 (200).

St. Anne Hospice, Inc. (Nursing Home), 1347 W. Broadway, Winona 55987 (121).

St. Benedict's Center (Nursing Home), 1810 Minnesota Blvd. S.E., St. Cloud 56304 (222). Skilled and intermediate nursing, adult day care, respite care. Benedict Village (Retirement Apartments), 2000 15th Ave. S.E., St. Cloud 56304.

St. Elizabeth's Hospital and Nursing Home, 1200-5th Grant Blvd., Wabasha 55981 (52). Assisted living apartments (20).

St. Francis Home, 501 Oak St., Breckenridge 56520 (124).

St. Mary's Home (Nursing Home), 1925 Norfolk Ave., St. Paul 55116 (140).

St. Mary's Hospital and Nursing Home, Winsted 55395 (95).

St. Mary's Hospital and Nursing Home, Detroit Lakes 56501 (103).

St. Mary's Rehabilitation Center, 2512 S. 7th St., Minneapolis 55454.

St. Mary's Villa (Nursing Home), Pierz 56364 (101).

St. Otto's Home (Nursing Home), Little Falls 56345 (159).

St. William's Nursing Home, Parkers Prairie 56361 (70).

Villa of St. Francis Nursing Home, Morris 56267 (144).

Villa St. Vincent (Skilled Nursing Home and Residence), 516 Walsh St., Crookston 56716. Nursing home (80); residence (95).

Mississippi: Santa Maria Retirement Apartments, 305 E. Beach Blvd., Biloxi, 39530.

Villa Maria Retirement Apartments, 921 Porter Ave., Ocean Springs 39564.

Missouri: Cathedral Square Towers, 444 W. 12th St., Kansas City 64105. Apartments for elderly and handicapped.

Chariton Apartments (Retirement Apartments), 4249 Michigan Ave., St. Louis 63111 (122 units; 143 residents).

DePaul Health Center — St. Anne's Division (Skilled Nursing), 12349 DePaul Dr., Bridgeton 63044 (86).

LaVerna Heights Retirement Home (Women), 104 E. Park Ave., Savannah 64485 (40).

LaVerna Village Apartments, 1000-1005 Hall Ave., Savannah 64485 (20).

LaVerna Village Nursing Home, 904 Hall Ave., Savannah 64485 (120).

Little Sisters of the Poor (Home for Aged), 3225 N. Florissant Ave., St. Louis 63107 (165).

Mary, Queen and Mother Center (Skilled-Intermediate Nursing Care), 7601 Watson Rd., St. Louis 63119 (220).

Mercy Villa (Nursing Home), Division of St. John's Regional Health Center, 1100 E. Montclair, Springfield 65807 (150).

Mother of Good Counsel Home (Skilled Nursing, Women), 6825 Natural Bridge Rd., Northwoods, 63121 (110).

Our Lady of Mercy Home (Residence and Nursing Home), 918-24 E. 9th St., Kansas City 64106 (153).

Our Lady of Mercy Country Home, Box 451, R.R. No. 4, Liberty 64038 (56).

Price Memorial Skilled Nursing Facility Forby Rd., P.O. Box 476, Eureka 63025 (120).

St. Agnes Home for the Elderly, 10341 Manchester Rd., Kirkwood 63122 (130).

St. Joseph Hill Infirmary, Inc., (Nursing Care Facility, Men), St. Joseph Road, Eureka 63025 (130).

St. Joseph's Home, 723 First Capitol Dr., St. Charles 63301 (100).

St. Joseph's Home for the Aged, 1306 W. Main St., Jefferson City 65109 (75).

Nebraska: Madonna Centers, 2200 S. 52nd St., Lincoln 68506 (252).

Mercy Care Center (Health Care), 1870 S. 75th St., Omaha 68124 (250).

Mt. Carmel Home, Keens' Memorial (Nursing Home), 412 W. 18th St., Kearney 68847 (76).

New Cassel Retirement Center, 900 N. 90th St., Omaha 68114. (156).

St. Joseph's Home (Residential Care), 320 E. Decatur St., West Point 68788 (70).

St. Joseph's Nursing Home, 401 N. 18th St., Norfolk 68701 (75).

St. Joseph's Villa, David City 68632. (65).

New Hampshire: Mount Carmel Nursing Home, 235 Myrtle St., Manchester 03104 (120).

St. Ann Home, 195 Dover Point Rd., Dover 03820 (53).

St. Francis Home (Nursing Home), Court St., Laconia 03246 (51). Apartments (24).

St. Teresa Manor (Nursing Home), 519 Bridge St., Manchester 03104 (51).

St. Vincent de Paul Nursing Home, 29 Providence Ave., Berlin 03570 (80).

New Jersey: Holy Family Residence (Women), 44 Rifle Camp Rd., P.O. Box 536, W. Paterson 07424 (64).

Little Sisters of the Poor, St. Joseph Home, 140 Shepherd Lane, Totowa 07512 (183; also, 18 independent living units).

McCarrick Care Center, 15 Dellwood Lane, Somerset 08873 (124).

Mater Dei Nursing Home, RD 3, Box 164, Rt. 40, P.O. Newfield 08344 (64).

Morris Hall, Home for the Aged (Residence and Skilled Nursing Home), 2361 Lawrenceville Rd., Lawrenceville 08648 (115).

Mount St. Andrew Villa (Residence), 55 W. Midland Ave., Paramus 07652 (56).

Our Lady's Residence (Nursing Home), Glendale and Clematis Aves., Pleasantville 08232 (104).

St. Ann's Home for the Aged (Skilled and In-

Facilities for the Retired and Aged

termediate Nursing Care Home, Women), 198 Old Bergen Rd., Jersey City 07305 (106). Adult Medical Day Care.
St. Joseph's Home (Women), 240 Longhouse Dr., Hewitt 07421.
St. Joseph's Rest Home for Aged Women, 46 Preakness Ave., Paterson 07522 (35).
St. Joseph's Senior Residence (Sheltered Care), 1 St. Joseph Terr., Woodbridge 07095 (60).
St. Mary's Catholic Home (Skilled Nursing Home), 1730 Kresson Rd., Cherry Hill 08003 (215).
St. Vincent's Nursing Home, 45 Elm St., Montclair 07042 (135).
Villa Maria (Residence and Infirmary, Women), 641 Somerset St., N. Plainfield 07061 (70).

New Mexico: Good Shepherd Manor (Residential Care for Aged Persons), Little Brothers of the Good Shepherd, P.O. Box 10248, Albuquerque 87184 (40).

New York: Bernardine Apartments, 417 Churchill Ave., Syracuse 13205.
Brothers of Mercy Sacred Heart Home (Residence) 4520 Ransom Rd., Clarence 14031 (82).
Brothers of Mercy Nursing Home, 10570 Bergtold Rd., Clarence 14031 (240). Brothers of Mercy Housing Co., Inc. (Apartments), 10500 Bergtold Rd., Clarence 14031 (100 units).
Carmel Richmond Nursing Home, 88 Old Town Rd., Staten Island 10304 (300).
Consolation Residence (Skilled Nursing and Health Related), 111 Beach Dr., West Islip 11795 (250).
Ferncliff Nursing Home, 52 River Rd., Rhinebeck 12572 (320).
Frances Schervier Home and Hospital, 2975 Independence Ave., Bronx 10463 (364). Frances Schervier Long Term Health Care Program, same address (150 slots). Frances Schervier Housing Development Fund Corporation, 2995 Independence Ave., Bronx 10463 (154 units).
Good Samaritan Nursing Home (Skilled Nursing), 101 Elm St., Sayville, N.Y. 11782 (100).
Holy Family Home, 410 Mill St., Williamsville 14221 (87).
Kateri Residence (Skilled Nursing), 150 Riverside Dr., New York 10024 (520).
Little Sisters of the Poor, Jeanne Jugan Residence (Skilled Nursing and Health Related), 3200 Baychester Ave., Bronx 10475 (120).
Little Sisters of the Poor, Holy Family Home, 1740-84th St., Brooklyn 11214 (105).
Little Sisters of the Poor, Queen of Peace Residence, 110-30 221st St., Queens Village 11429 (165).
Madonna Home of Mercy Hospital (Nursing Home and Extended Care Facility) (140), and Mercy Hospital Health Related Facility (Residence) (58), Watertown 13601.
Madonna Residence, Inc. (Skilled Nursing and Health Related), 1 Prospect Park W., Brooklyn, 11215 (290).
Mary Manning Walsh Home (Nursing Home), 1339 York Ave., New York 10021 (362).
Mercy Healthcare Center (Skilled Nursing Facility), Tupper Lake 12986 (54).

Mt. Loretto Nursing Home, (Skilled Nursing Facility), Sisters of the Resurrection, R.D., 3, Amsterdam 12010 (82).
Nazareth Nursing Home and Health Related Facility (Women), 291 W. North St., Buffalo 14201 (125).
Our Lady of Hope Residence (Home for the Aged), Little Sisters of the Poor, 1 Jeanne Jugan Lane, Latham 12210 (146).
Ozanam Hall of Queens Nursing Home, Inc. (Skilled Nursing and Health-Related Facilities), 42-41 201st St., Bayside 11361 (432).
Providence Rest, 3304 Waterbury Ave., Bronx 10465 (200).
Resurrection Rest Home (Nursing Home and Health Related Facility, Women), Castleton 12033 (48).
Sacred Heart Home (Skilled Nursing Facility), 8 Mickle St., Plattsburgh 12901 (89).
St. Ann's Home / The Heritage (Skilled Nursing), 1500 Portland Ave., Rochester 14621.
St. Clare Manor, 543 Locust St., Lockport 14094 (28).
St. Columban's on the Lake (Retirement Home), Silver Creek 14136 (50).
St. Elizabeth Home (Residence), 5539 Broadway, Lancaster 14086 (102).
St. Francis Home (Nursing and Health Related Facility), 147 Reist St., Williamsville 14221 (142).
St. Joseph Manor, W. State St., Olean 14760 (22).
St. Joseph Nursing Home, 2535 Genesee St., Utica 13501 (120).
St. Joseph's Guest Home, Missionary Sisters of St. Benedict,, 350 Cuba Hill Rd., Huntington 11743 (48).
St. Joseph's Home (Nursing Home), 420 Lafayette St., Ogdensburg 13669 (82).
St. Joseph's Villa (Residence), 38 Prospect Ave., Catskill 12414 (60).
St. Luke Manor, 17 Wiard St., Batavia 14020 (20).
St. Mary's Manor, 515 Sixth St., Niagara Falls 14301 (119).
St. Patrick's Home for the Aged and Infirm, 66 Van Cortland Park S., Bronx 10463 (225).
St. Vincent's Home for the Aged, 319 Washington Ave., Dunkirk 14048 (34).
Terence Cardinal Cooke Health Care Center (Skilled Nursing), 1249 Fifth Ave., New York 10029 (237).
Teresian House, Washington Ave. Extension, Albany 12203 (300).
Uihlein Mercy Center (Nursing Home), Lake Placid 12946 (156).

North Carolina: Maryfield Nursing Home (115 beds) and Maryfield Acres (16 retirement homes), Greensboro Rd., High Point 27260.

North Dakota: Carrington Health Center (Nursing Home), Carrington 58421 (38).
Manor St. Joseph Home for Aged and Infirm; Edgeley 58433 (40).
Marillac Manor (Retirement Apartments), 1016 N. 28th St., Bismarck 58501 (42 apartments).
St. Anne's Guest Home (Retirement), 524 N. 17th St., Grand Forks 58201 (56) Apartments (30).

St. Vincent's Nursing Home, 1021 N. 26th St., Bismarck 58501 (98).

Ohio: Archbishop Leibold Home for the Aged, Little Sisters of the Poor, 476 Riddle Rd., Cincinnati 45220 (125).
Assumption Nursing Home, 550 W. Chalmers Ave., Youngstown 44511 (126).
Francesca Residence (Retirement), 39 N. Portage Path, Akron 44303 (45).
Franciscan Terrace at St. Clare Center (Nursing Home, Rest Home, Apartments), Franciscan Sisters of the Poor, 100 Compton Rd., Cincinnati 45215 (171).
House of Loreto (Nursing Home), 2812 Harvard Ave. N.W., Canton 44709 (98).
Jennings Hall, Inc. (Intermediate Care Facility), 10204 Granger Rd., Garfield Heights 44125 (100).
Little Sisters of the Poor, Sacred Heart Home, 4900 Navarre Ave., Oregon 43616 (126).
Little Sisters of the Poor, Sts. Joseph and Mary Home for Aged, 4291 Richmond Rd., Cleveland 44122 (140).
The Maria-Joseph Living Care Center, 4830 Salem Ave., Dayton 45416 (440).
Mount Alverna (Residence for Aged), 6765 State Rd., Cleveland 44134 (200).
Mt. St. Joseph (Skilled Nursing Facility, Dual Certified), 21800 Chardon Rd., Cleveland 44117 (100).
Nazareth Towers, 300 E. Rich St., Columbus 43215. Hi-rise apartments for independent living (208).
St. Augustine Manor (Nursing Home), 7800 Detroit Ave., Cleveland 44102 (194).
St. Edward Nursing Home, 3131 Smith Rd., Akron 44313 (100).
St. Francis Home, Inc. (Residence and Nursing Care), 182 St. Francis Ave., Tiffin 44883 (116).
St. Francis Rehabilitation Hospital and Nursing Home, 401 N. Broadway St., Green Springs 44836 (186).
St. Joseph's Hospice (Nursing Home), 2308 Reno Dr., Louisville 44641 (100).
St. Margaret Hall (Residence and Nursing Facility), 1960 Madison Rd., Cincinnati 45206 (145).
St. Raphael Home (Nursing Home), 1550 Roxbury Rd., Columbus 43212 (80).
St. Rita's Home (Skilled Nursing Home), 880 Greenlawn Ave., Columbus 43223 (100).
St. Theresa Home for the Aged, 6760 Belkenton Pl., Cincinnati 45236 (100).
Schroder Manor (Residence, Skilled Nursing Care and Independent Living Units), Franciscan Sisters of the Poor, 1302 Millville Ave., Hamilton 45013 (173).
The Siena Home (Nursing Home, Intermediate Care), 235 W. Orchard Spring Dr., Dayton 45415 (99).
The Villa Sancta Anna Home for the Aged, Inc., 25000 Chagrin Blvd., Beachwood 44122 (68).

Oklahoma: Franciscan Villa, 17110 E. 51st St. S., Broken Arrow 74012. Intermediate nursing care (60); apartments (66).

St. Ann's Nursing Home, 3825 N.W. 19th St., Oklahoma City 73107 (82).

Oregon: Benedictine Nursing Center and Home Health Agency, S. Main St., Mt. Angel 97362 (127).
Evergreen Court Retirement Apartments, 451 O'Connell St., North Bend 97459 (72).
Maryville Nursing Home, 14645 S.W. Farmington, Beaverton 97007 (137).
Mt. St. Joseph's Residence and Extended Care Center, 3060 S.E. Stark St., Portland 97214 (290).
St. Catherine's Residence and Nursing Center, 3959 Sheridan Ave., North Bend 97459 (166).
St. Elizabeth Health Care Center, 3985 Midway Dr., Box 1046, Baker 97814 (80).

Pennsylvania: Ascension Manor I (Senior Citizen Housing), 911 N. Franklin St., Philadelphia 19123 (140 units).
Ascension Manor II (Senior Citizen Housing), 970 N. 7th St., Philadelphia 19123 (140 units).
Benetwood Apartments for Elderly and Handicapped, 640 Troupe Rd., Erie 16421 (75).
Bethlehem Retirement Village, 100 W. Wissahickon Ave., Flourtown 19031. Apartments for well elderly. (100).
Christ the King Manor, 1100 W. Long Ave., Du Bois 15801 (160).
Corpus Christi Residence, 7165 Churchland St., Pittsburgh 15206 (27).
Garvey Manor (Nursing Home), Logan Blvd., Hollidaysburg, 16648 (150).
Holy Family Apartments (Low Income), Clay and Valley Sts., New Philadelphia 17959 (11).
Holy Family Home, Little Sisters of the Poor, 5300 Chester Ave., Philadelphia 19143 (130).
Holy Family Manor (Skilled and Intermediate Nursing Facility), 1200 Spring St., Bethlehem 18018 (200).
Holy Family Residence (Residential Care Facility), 417 Hayes St., Bethlehem 18015 (15).
Holy Family Residence (Residential Care Facility), 217 Garden St., Easton 18042 (14).
Holy Family Residence (Personal Care Facility), 570 Wood St., Emmaus 18049 (14).
Holy Family Residence (Personal Care Facility), 900 W. Market St., Orwigsburg 17961 (22).
Immaculate Mary Home, (Skilled and Intermediate Nursing Care), Holme Circle and Welsh Rd., Philadelphia 19136 (296).
John XXIII Home, 2250 Shenango Freeway, Hermitage 16148 (142).
Little Flower Manor Nursing Home (Skilled Nursing), 1201 Springfield Rd., Darby 19023 (122).
Little Flower Manor of Diocese of Scranton, (Long-Term Skilled Nursing Care Facility), 200 S. Meade St., Wilkes-Barre 18702 (133).
Little Sisters of the Poor, 1028 Benton Ave. N.S., Pittsburgh 15212 (127).
Little Sisters of the Poor, Holy Family Residence, 2500 Adams Ave., Scranton 18509 (82).
Maria Joseph Manor, R.D. 4, Box 3, Danville 17821 (94).
Marian Hall Home for the Aged (Women), 934 Forest Ave., Pittsburgh 15202.
Marian Manor (Intermediate Care), 2695

Facilities for the Retired and Aged

Winchester Dr., Pittsburgh 15220 (170).
Mount Macrina Manor (Skilled Nursing Facility), 520 W. Main St., Uniontown 15401 (54).
Neumann Apartments (Low Income), 25 N. Nichols St., St. Clair 17970 (25).
Queen of Angels Apartments (Low Income), 22 Rothermel St., Hyde Park, Reading 19605 (45).
Queen of Peace Apartments (Low Income), 777 Water St., Pottsville 17901 (65).
Redeemer Village (Senior Citizen Housing), Huntingdon Pike, Huntingdon Valley 19006 (200 apartments).
Sacred Heart Manor (Nursing Home and Personal Care), 6445 Germantown Ave., Philadelphia 19119 (142).
St. Anne Home, R.D. 2, Columbia 17512 (Nursing home, 121; personal care, 14; independent living, 32 cottages).
St. Anne Home for the Elderly (Nursing Facility), 685 Angela Dr., Greensburg 15601 (125).
St. Basil's Home for Aged Women (Residential), Box 878, Uniontown 15401 (14).
St. Ignatius Nursing Home, 4401 Haverford Ave., Philadelphia 19104 (176).
St. John Neumann Nursing Home, 10400 Roosevelt Blvd. Philadelphia 19116 (218).
St. Joseph Home for the Aged (Residential and Skilled Nursing Facility), 1182 Holland Rd., Holland 18966 (96).
St. Joseph Nursing and Health Care Center (Skilled Nursing Facility), 5324 Penn Ave., Pittsburgh 15224 (158).
St. Joseph's House of Hospitality (Low Income Senior Citizen Residence for Men and Women), 1635 Bedford Ave., Pittsburgh 15219 (65).
St. Joseph's Manor (Skilled Nursing Facility), 1616 Huntingdon Pike, Meadowbrook 19046 (250).
St. Joseph's Residence, 1111½ S. Cascade St., New Castle 16101.
St. Leonard's Home Inc., 601 N. Montgomery St., Hollidaysburg 16648 (21).
St. Mary of Providence Center, R.D. 2, Box 145, Elverson 19520 (Senior Citizen Housing, 30 units).
St. Mary's Home of Erie, 607 E. 26th St., Erie 16504. Residential and personal care (131); skilled and intermediate nursing care (193); day care (23).
Saint Mary's Manor (Residential, Personal Care and Nursing Care), 701 Lansdale Ave., Lansdale 19446 (160).
St. Mary's Villa Nursing Home, Elmhurst 18416 (121).
Villa de Marillac Nursing Home, 5300 Stanton Ave., Pittsburgh 15206 (50).
Villa St. Teresa (Residence, Women), 1215 Springfield Rd., Darby 19023 (53).
Villa Teresa (Nursing Home), 1051 Avila Rd., Harrisburg 17109 (184).
Vincentian Home for the Chronically Ill., Perrymont Rd., Pittsburgh 15237 (219).

Rhode Island: Jeanne Jugan Residence of the Little Sisters of the Poor, 964 Main St., Pawtucket 02860 (120).
Saint Antoine Residence (Home for the Aged), 400 Mendon Rd., North Smithfield 02895 (243).

St. Clare Home, 309 Spring St., Newport 02840 (44).
St. Francis House, 167 Blackstone St., Woonsocket 02895 (50).
Scalabrini Villa (Convalescent, Rest — Nursing Home). 860 N. Quidnessett Rd., North Kingstown 02852 (70).

South Carolina: Carter-May Home, 1660 Ingram Rd., Charleston 29407 (12). Personal care home for elderly ladies.

South Dakota: Brady Memorial Home (Skilled Nursing Facility), 500 S. Ohlman St., Mitchell 57301 (60). Independent living units (9). Respite care; day care.
Maryhouse, Inc. (Skilled Nursing Facility), 717 E. Dakota, Pierre 57501 (105).
Mother Joseph Manor (Intermediate Care and Skilled Nursing Facility), 1002 North Jay St., Aberdeen 57401 (30 intermediate; 50 skilled). Apartment units (7). Adult day care program. Respite nursing care.
St. William's Home for the Aged (Intermediate Care, 60), and Angela Hall (Supervised Living, 15), 901 E. Virgil, Box 432, Milbank 57252.
Tekakwitha Nursing Home (Skilled and Intermediate Care). Sisseton 57262 (101). Tekakwitha Housing Corp. (Independent Living), same address (24 units).
Wilge Memorial Home (Intermediate Care), 619 N. Kittridge, Mitchell 57301 (19).

Tennessee: Alexian Village of Tennessee (Retired Men and Women), 100 James Blvd., Signal Mountain 37377 (150) and Health Care Center (124).
Ave Maria Home, 2805 Charles Bryan Rd., Memphis 38134 (73).
St. Mary Manor, 1771 Highway 45 Bypass, Jackson 38305.
St. Peter Manor, 108 N. Aubrundale, Memphis 38104.
St. Peter Villa (Nursing Home), 141 N. McLean, Memphis 38104.

Texas: Casa Housing for Elderly and Handicapped, 3201 Sondra Dr., Fort Worth 76107 (200).
Casa Brendan and Casa II Housing for the Elderly and Handicapped, 1302 Hyman St., Stephenville 76401 (86).
Home for Aged Women-Men, 920 S. Oregon St., El Paso 79901 (24).
John Paul II Nursing Home (Intermediate Care and Personal Care), 215 Tilden St., Kenedy 78219.
Laboure Care Center (Skilled Nursing Facility), 1950 Record Crossing Rd., Dallas 75235.
Mother of Perpetual Help Home (Intermediate Care Facility), 519 E. Madison Ave., Brownsville 78520 (37).
Mt. Carmel Home (Personal Care Home), 4130 S. Alameda St., Corpus Christi 78411 (92).
Nuestro Hogar Apartment Complex for Elderly and Handicapped, 709 Magnolia St., Arlington 76010 (65).
The Regis Retirement Home and St. Elizabeth

Nursing Home, 400 Austin Ave., Waco 76701 (420).
St. Ann's Home (Skilled Nursing Facility), P.O. Box 1179, Panhandle 79068 (52).
St. Anthony Center (Skilled Nursing, Rehabilitation, Geriatric), 6301 Almeda Rd., Houston 77021 (372).
St. Dominic Nursing Home, 6502 Grand Ave., Houston 77021 (120).
St. Dominic Residence Hall, 2401 E. Holcombe Blvd., Houston 77021 (80).
St. Francis Nursing Home (Home for Aged and Convalescents), 2717 N. Flores St., San Antonio 78212 (143).
St. Francis Village, Inc. (Retired and Elderly), 1 Chapel Plaza, Crowley 76036 (415).
St. Joseph Residence, 330 W. Pembroke St., Dallas 75208 (49).
San Juan Nursing Home, Inc. (Skilled and Intermediate Care Facility), P.O. Box 1238, San Juan 78589 (124).
Villa Maria, Inc., 3146 Saratoga Blvd., Corpus Christi 78415. Apartments.

Utah: St. Joseph Villa (Skilled and Intermediate Care Facility), 475 Ramona Ave., Salt Lake City 84115 (175).

Vermont: Loretto Home for Aged, 59 Meadow St., Rutland 05701 (57).
Michaud Memorial Manor (Home for Aged), Derby Line 05830 (24).
St. Joseph's Home for Aged, 243 N. Prospect St., Burlington 05401 (52).

Virginia: Madonna Home, 814 W. 37th St., Norfolk 23508 (15).
Marywood, 1261 Marywood Lane, Marywood 23229 (123).
McGrath Apartments, 2425 Tate Springs Rd., Lynchburg 24504 (89 units).
Russell House, 900 First Colonial Rd., Virginia Beach 23454 (127).
St. Francis Home, 2511 Wise St., Richmond 23225 (31).
St. Joseph's Home for the Aged, Little Sisters of the Poor, 1503 Michael Rd., Richmond 23229 (100).

Washington: Cathedral Plaza Apartments (Retirement Apartments), W. 1120 Sprague Ave., Spokane 99204 (150).
The Delaney, W. 242 Riverside Ave., Spokane 99201 (84).
The De Paul and Mt. St. Vincent, 4831 35th Ave. S.W., Seattle 98126 (118).
Fahy Garden Apartments, W. 1411 Dean Ave., Spokane 99201 (31).
Fahy West Apartments, W. 1523 Dean Ave., Spokane 99201 (55).
The Josephinum (Retirement Home), 1902 2nd Ave., Seattle 98101 (228).
The O'Malley, E. 707 Mission, Spokane 99202 (100).
St. Joseph Nursing Home, 1006 North H St., Aberdeen 98520 (34).
St. Joseph Care Center (Skilled Long-Term Care), West 20 — 90th Ave., Spokane 99204 (103).

West Virginia: Knights of St. George Home/William Penn Home, Wellsburg 26070 (52).
Welty Home for the Aged (Women), 21 Washington Ave., Wheeling 26003 (44).

Wisconsin: Alexian Village of Milwaukee (Retirement Community/Skilled Nursing Home), 7979 W. Glenbrook Rd., Milwaukee 53223 (329 apartments; 61 skilled nursing).
Bethany-St. Joseph Health Care Center, 2501 Shelby Rd., La Crosse 54601 (226).
Clement Manor (Retirement Community and Skilled Nursing), 3939 S. 92nd St., Greenfield 53228 (164 skilled nursing; 99 apartments). Senior day care.
Divine Savior Nursing Home, 715 W. Pleasant St., Portage 53901 (111).
Franciscan Care Center, 2915 North Meade St., Appleton 54911.
Franciscan Villa (Skilled Nursing Home), 3601 S. Chicago Ave., S. Milwaukee 53172 (150).
Hope Nursing Home, 438 Ashford Ave., Lomira 53048 (42).
McCormick Memorial Home for the Aged, 212 Iroquois St., Green Bay 54301 (72).
Marian Catholic Home, 3333 W. Highland Blvd., Milwaukee 53208 (360).
Marian Center of Racine, Inc., 3801 Spring St., Racine 53405 (53).
Marian Franciscan Nursing Center, 9632 W. Appleton Ave., Milwaukee 53225.
Maryhill Manor Nursing Home, 501 Madison Ave., Niagara 54151 (45).
Milwaukee Catholic Home, Inc., 2462 N. Prospect Ave., Milwaukee 53211 (44 skilled nursing beds; 168 apartments).
Nazareth House (Skilled Nursing Facility), Stoughton 53589 (100).
St. Ann Rest Home (Intermediate Care Facility, Women), 2020 S. Muskego Ave., Milwaukee 53204 (54).
St. Anne's Home for the Elderly (Aged Poor), 3800 N. 92nd St., Milwaukee 53222 (116).
St. Camillus Campus (Skilled Care Nursing Home, Retirement Community, Community Based Residential Facility, Home Health), 10100 West Bluemound Road, Wauwatosa 53226 (188 skilled nursing, 200 apartments, 40 CBRF apartments).
St. Catherine Infirmary (Nursing Home), 5635 Erie St., Racine 53402 (41).
St. Elizabeth Nursing Home, 502 St. Lawrence Ave., Janesville 53545 (43).
St. Elizabeth's Home (Intermediate Care; Women), 745 N. Brookfield Rd., Brookfield 53005 (16).
St. Francis Home, 620 S. 11th St., La Crosse 54601 (95).
St. Francis Home (Skilled Nursing Facility), 1800 New York Ave., Superior 54880 (192).
St. Francis Home (Skilled Nursing), 365 Gillett St., Fond du Lac 54935 (70).
St. Francis Manor (Retirement Residence), 3553 S. 41st St., Milwaukee 53221 (125).
St. Joan Antida Home (Women), 6640 W. Beloit Rd., W. Allis 53219 (76).

St. Joseph's Home, 705 Clyman St., Watertown 53094 (28).
St. Joseph's Home, 9244 29th Ave., Kenosha 53140 (93).
St. Joseph's Home, 5301 W. Lincoln Ave., W. Allis 53219 (124).
St. Joseph's Nursing Home, 464 S. St. Joseph Ave., Arcadia 54612 (75).
St. Joseph's Nursing Home, 2902 East Ave. S., La Crosse 54601 (80).
St. Joseph's Nursing Home, 400 Water Ave., Hillsboro 54634 (65).
St. Joseph Residence, Inc. (Nursing Home), 1925 Division St., New London 54961 (107).
St. Mary's Home for the Aged (Residence and Nursing Care), 2005 Division St., Manitowoc 54220 (256).
St. Mary's Nursing Home (Skilled Nursing and Respite Care), 3516 W. Center St., Milwaukee 53210 (130).
St. Monica's Senior Citizens Home, 3920 N. Green Bay Rd., Racine 53404 (125).
St. Paul Home (Intermediate and Skilled Nursing Home), 509 W. Wisconsin Ave., Kaukauna 54130 (52). St. Paul Manor, same address (8). For well elderly.
Villa Clement (Nursing Home), 9047 W. Greenfield Ave., W. Allis 53214 (190).
Villa Loretto Nursing Home, Mount Calvary 53057 (52).

FACILITIES FOR HANDICAPPED CHILDREN AND ADULTS

Sources: Almanac survey; *Directory of Catholic Special Facilities and Programs for Handicapped Children and Adults,* published by the National Catholic Educational Association; *Official Catholic Directory.*

This listing covers facilities and programs with educational and training orientation. Information about other services for the handicapped can generally be obtained from the Catholic Charities Office or its equivalent (c/o Chancery Office) in any diocese. (See Index for listing of addresses of chancery offices in the U.S.)

Abbreviation code: b, boys; c, coeducational; d, day; g, girls; r, residential. Other information includes chronological age for admission. The number in parentheses at the end of an entry indicates total capacity or enrollment.

Deaf and Hard of Hearing

California: St. Joseph's Center for Deaf and Hard of Hearing, 37588 Fremont Blvd., Fremont 94536.

Louisiana: Chinchuba Institute (d,c; parent-infant through 16 yrs.), 1131 Barataria Blvd., Marrero. 70072 (101).

Massachusetts: Boston School for the Deaf (r,d,c; 3-21 yrs.), 800 N. Main St., Randolph. 02368 (135). Psycho-Education Center (PEC) for emotionally disturbed deaf children (r, d; 3-10 yrs.).

Missouri: St. Joseph Institute for the Deaf (r,d,c; birth to 15 yrs.), 1483 82nd Blvd., St. Louis 63132 (150).

New York: Cleary School for the Deaf (d,c; infancy through high school), 301 Smithtown Blvd., Lake Ronkonkoma, L.I. 11779 (105).
St. Francis de Sales School for the Deaf (d,c; parent-infant programs through age 14), 260 Eastern Parkway, Brooklyn 11225.
St. Joseph's School for the Deaf (d,c; birth-14 yrs.), 1000 Hutchinson River Pkwy, Bronx. 10465 (180).
St. Mary's School for the Deaf (r,d,c; birth to 21 yrs.), 2253 Main St., Buffalo. 14214 (220).

Ohio: St. Rita School for the Deaf (r,d,c; 4-21 yrs.), 1720 Glendale-Milford Rd., Cincinnati. 45215 (125).

Pennsylvania: Abp. Ryan Memorial Institute for Deaf (d,c; parent-infant programs through 8th grade), 3509 Spring Garden St., Philadelphia. 19104 (62).
De Paul Institute (d,c; birth-21 yrs.), Castlegate Ave., Pittsburgh. 15226 (132).

Emotionally And/Or Socially Maladjusted

This listing includes facilities for abused, abandoned and neglected as well as emotionally disturbed children and youth.

California: Hanna Boys Center (r; 9-14 yrs. at intake; school goes to 10th grade), Box 100, Sonoma. 95476 (72).
Rancho San Antonio (r,b; 12-16 yrs.), 21000 Plummer St., Chatsworth. 91311 (118).

Colorado: Mt. St. Vincent Home (r,c; 5-13 yrs.), 4159 Lowell Blvd., Denver. 80211 (45).

Connecticut: Highland Heights — St. Francis Home for Children (r,d,c; 4-17 yrs.), 651 Prospect St., New Haven. 06511 (70).
Mt. St. John (r,b; 11-16 yrs.), Kirtland St., Deep River. 06417 (75).

Delaware: Our Lady of Grace Home for Children (r,c; 6-12 yrs.), 487 Chestnut Hill Rd., Newark 19713 (16).

Georgia: Village of St. Joseph (r,d,c; 6-16 yrs.), 2969 Butner Rd. S.W., Atlanta 30331 (39 r; 48 d). Residential treatment center and therapeutic special school for children with emotional problems, behavior disorders, learning disabilities.

Illinois: Charles I. Doyle, S.J., Center and Day School of Loyola University (d, c; pre-school to 12 yrs.), 1043 Loyola Ave., Chicago 60626 (25 in day school, unlimited in guidance center).
Guardian Angel (r,b;d,c; 5-17 yrs.), 1550 Plainfield Rd., Joliet 60435 (20 r, 40 d).
St. Joseph Carondelet Child Center (r,b; 5-14 yrs. and d,c; 4-18 yrs.); 739 E. 35th St., Chicago 60616 (28 r, 45 d).

Indiana: Gibault School for Boys (r; 10-16 yrs.), 5901 Dixie Bee Rd., Terre Haute. 47802 (104).
Hoosier Boys Town (r; 9-18 yrs.), Schererville. 46375 (65).

Kentucky: Boys' Haven (r; 13-18 yrs.), 3201 Bardstown Rd., Louisville. 40205 (36).
Maryhurst School (r,g; 13-17 yrs.), 1015 Dorsey Lane, Louisville 40223 (42).

Louisiana: Hope Haven — Madonna Manor Residential Treatment Center (r,b; 5-18 yrs.), 1101 Barataria Blvd., Marrero 70072 (162).

Maison Marie Group Home (r,g; 13-18 yrs.), 3020 Independence St., Metairie 70006 (12).

Maryland: Good Shepherd Center (r,d,g; 14-18 yrs.), 4100 Maple Ave., Baltimore. 21227 (90r, 15d).

Massachusetts: McAuley Nazareth Home for Boys (r; 6-14 yrs.), 77 Mulberry St., Leicester. 01524 (27).

Our Lady of Providence Children's Center/The Brightside for Families and Children (r,d,c; 5-15 yrs.), 2112 Riverdale St., W. Springfield. 01089 (50). Diagnostic treatment program also.

St. Vincent Home (r,c 6-18 yrs.), 2425 Highland Ave., Fall River 02720 (62 b; 10 g). Residential treatment center.

Michigan: Barat House, Barat Human Services, League of Catholic Women (r,g; 13-17 yrs.), 5250 John R. St., Detroit. 48202 (24).

Boysville of Michigan, Inc. (r; 13-18 yrs.), 8744 Clinton-Macon Rd., Clinton. 49236 (180).

Don Bosco Hall (r,b; 13-17 years.), 10001 Petoskey Ave., Detroit. 48204 (30).

St. John's Home (r,c; 9-16 yrs.), 385 E. Leonard N.E., Grand Rapids 49503 (40).

St. Vincent Home for Children (r,c; 10-16 yrs.), 2800 W. Willow St., Lansing 48917 (30).

Vista Maria (r,d, g; 11-17 yrs.), 20651 W. Warren Ave., Dearborn Heights. 48127 (152 r; 10 d).

Minnesota: St. Cloud Children's Home (r,c; 8-17 yrs.), 1726 7th Ave. S., St. Cloud. 56301 (72).

Missouri: Child Center of Our Lady (r,c; 4-12 yrs. — d,c; 4-17 yrs.), 7900 Natural Bridge Rd., St. Louis. 63121 (79).

Marillac Home for Children (r,d,c; 4-14 yrs.), P.O. Box 1037, Kansas City. 64141 (28 r; 60 d).

Marygrove (r,c; 6-18 yrs.), 2705 Mullanphy Lane, Florissant. 63031 (87).

Nebraska: Father Flanagan's Boys' Home (r; c; 9-18 yrs.), Boys Town, Nebr. 68010 (550).

Nevada: Home of Good Shepherd-St. Yves School for Girls (r,g; 13-17 yrs.), 7000 North Jones Blvd., Las Vegas, 89131 (30).

New Jersey: Christopher House (c; 18 and over), 55 N. Clinton Ave., Trenton 08607 (90). Psychiatric day treatment.

Collier Group Home (r,g; 14-18 yrs.), 47 Reckless Pl., Red Bank 07701 (10).

Collier School (d,c; 13-18 yrs.), Wickatunk 07765.

Guidance Clinic of Catholic Welfare Bureau (c), 39 N. Clinton Ave., Trenton 08607. Psychiatric counseling for children and adults.

Mt. St. Joseph Children's Center (r,d,c; 6-12 yrs.), Shepherd Lane, Totowa 07512 (32).

New Jersey's Boystown (r,b; adolescents), 499 Belgrove Dr., Kearny 07032.

New York: The Astor Home for Children (r,d,c; 5-12 yrs.), 36 Mill St., Rhinebeck 12572 (75). Group Homes (7-18 yrs.), 1967 Turnbull Ave., Bronx 10473 (52). Child Guidance Clinics/Day Treatment (Rhinebeck, Poughkeepsie, Beacon, Bronx). Head start — Day Care (Poughkeepsie, Beacon, Red Hook, Dover, Millerton).

Baker Hall (r,d,b; 10-18 yrs.), 150 Martin Rd., Lackawanna. 14218 (250). Special services, institution, group homes, foster homes, preventive services, special education school.

LaSalle School (r,d,b; 12-18 yrs.), 391 Western Ave., Albany. 12203 (145). Also conducts a group home and prevention programs.

Madonna Heights Services (r,d,g; 11-17 yrs.), Burrs Lane, Huntington. 11743 (110). Also conducts group homes on Long Island and outpatient programs.

Saint Anne Institute (r,d,g; 12-18 yrs.), 160 N. Main Ave., Albany. 12206 (140). Critical level, preventive services, group home. Sex abuse prevention programs.

St. Catherine Center for Children (r,c; birth to 12 yrs. and d,c; 3-12 yrs.), 30 N. Main St., Albany 12203 (150). Also conducts group home and specialized foster care programs.

St. Helena's Services-Euphrasian Residence (r,g; 12-17 yrs.), 120 W. 60th St., New York. 10023 (20).

St. John's of Rockaway Beach (r,b; 10-18 yrs.), 144 Beach 111th St., Rockaway Park. 11694 (100). Also conducts group homes in Far Rockaway and Richmond Hill.

North Dakota: Home on the Range for Boys (r; 12-18 yrs.), Box 41, Sentinel Butte. 58654 (52).

Ohio: Diocesan Child Guidance Center, Inc. (d,c; preschool) Outpatient counseling program (c; 2-18 yrs.), 840 W. State St., Columbus 43222.

Marycrest (r,g; 13-17 yrs.), 7800 Brookside Rd., Independence. 44131 (70).

Parmadale/St. Anthony's Family Services Village (r,c; 9-18 yrs.), 6753 State Rd., Parma 44134.

Rosemont (r,g;d,c; 12-18 yrs.), 2440 Dawnlight Ave., Columbus 43211 (150).

Oregon: St. Mary's Home for Boys (r; 9-17 yrs.), 16535 S.W. Tualatin Valley Highway, Beaverton 97006 (50).

Pennsylvania: De LaSalle in Towne (d,b; 12-17 yrs.), 25 S. Van Pelt St., Philadelphia 19103 (110).

De LaSalle Vocational Day Treatment (b; 15-17 yrs.), P.O. Box 344 — Street Rd. and Bristol Pike, Bensalem 19020 (120).

Gannondale School for Girls (r; 12-17 yrs.), 4635 E. Lake Rd., Erie 16511 (57).

Harborcreek School for Boys (r; 10-17 yrs.), 5712 Iroquois Ave., Harborcreek 16421 (135). Also conducts group homes.

Lourdesmont Good Shepherd Youth and Family Services (r,g;d,c; 13-17 yrs.), 537 Venard Rd., Clarks Summit 18411 (100).

Pauline Auberle Foundation, Auberle Home (r,c; 7-18 yrs.), 1101 Hartman St., McKeesport 15132 (57). Residential and emergency shelter programs.

St. Gabriel Hall (r,b; 12-17 yrs.), P.O. Box 13, Audobon 19407 (220). Also conducts group homes.

St. Michael's School (r,b; d,c; 12-17 yrs.), Hoban Heights, Tunkhannock 18657 (120). Also conducts group homes, day treatment program.

Tennessee: DeNeuville Heights School for Girls (r; 12-18 yrs.), 3060 Baskin St., Memphis 38127 (52).

Texas: St. Joseph Youth Center (r,c; 13-17 yrs.), 901 S. Madison St., Dallas 75208 (52).

Washington: Morning Star Boys Ranch

Facilities for the Handicapped 553

(Spokane Boys' Ranch, Inc.), (r,b; 9-18 yrs.), Box 8087 Manito Station, Spokane 99203 (30).

Wisconsin: Eudes Family Programs at Our Lady of Charity Center (r,c; 10-17 yrs.), 2640 West Point Rd., Green Bay 54304 (24).

St. Aemilian Child Care Center, Inc. (r,d,b; 6-16 yrs.), 8901 W. Capitol Dr., Milwaukee 53222 (68).

St. Charles, Inc. (r,d,c; 12-18 yrs.), 151 S. 84th St., Milwaukee 53214 (63).

Wyoming: St. Joseph's Children's Home (r,c; 6-17 yrs.), P.O. Box 1117, Torrington 82240 (48). Also conducts group home.

Developmentally Handicapped

This listing includes facilities for children, youth and adults with learning disabilities and/or mental retardation.

Alabama: Father Walter Memorial Child Care Center (r,c; birth-12 yrs.), 2815 Forbes Dr., Montgomery 36199 (44). Skilled nursing facility.

California: Child Study Center (d,c; birth-18 yrs.), 1339 - 20th St., Santa Monica. 90404 (80). Also conducts a developmental nursery (birth-3 yrs.) and a private school program for children (3-9 yrs.).

Helpers of the Mentally Retarded, Inc., 2626 Fulton St., San Francisco 94118. Conducts three homes: Helpers Home for Girls (18 years and older), 2608 Fulton St. and 2626 Fulton St., San Francisco 94118; Helpers Home for Men (18 years and older), 2750 Fulton St., San Francisco 94118.

St. Madeleine Sophie's Training Center (d,c; 18 yrs. and older), 2111 E. Madison Ave., El Cajon 92021 (110).

St. Vincent's (r,d,c; 8-18 yrs.), P.O. Drawer V, 4200 Calle Real, Santa Barbara 93102 (102).

Tierra Consolidated Systems, Inc. (d,c; 18 yrs. and older), 9919 Sunland Blvd., Sunland 91040 (200) and 14123 Valerio St., Van Nuys 91405 (28).

Connecticut: Gengras Center (d,c; 8-21 yrs.), St. Joseph College, 1678 Asylum Ave., W. Hartford 06117 (75).

Special Education Office, Diocese of Bridgeport, 238 Jewett Ave., Bridgeport 06606.

Villa Maria Education Center (d,c), 159 Sky Meadow Dr., Stamford 06903 (31). For children with learning disabilities.

District of Columbia: Lt. Joseph P. Kennedy Jr. Institute (d,c; 5-85 yrs.), 801 Buchanan St. N.E., Washington 20017 (400). Also conducts group homes, continuing education and life skills training programs, contract employment and job placement.

St. Gertrude's School of Arts and Crafts (r,d,g; 6-19 yrs.), 4801 Sargent Rd. N.E., Washington 20017 (40).

Florida: Harbor House, 700-2 Arlington Rd., Jacksonville 32211. Residence for mentally retarded adults.

Marian Center Services for Developmentally Handicapped and Mentally Retarded (r,d,c), 15701 Northwest 37th Ave., Opa Locka 33054. Offers variety of services.

Morning Star School (d,c; 4-12 yrs.), 725 Mickler Rd., Jacksonville 32211 (100). For children with learning disabilities.

Morning Star School (d,c; 3-12 yrs.), 954 Leigh Ave., Orlando 32804 (45).

Morning Star School (d,c; 6-13 yrs.), 4661 - 80th Ave., N., Pinellas Park 33565 (50). For children with learning disabilities and other learning handicaps.

Illinois: Bartlett Learning Center (r,d,c; 3-21 yrs.), 801 W. Bartlett Rd., Bartlett 60103 (116).

Good Shepherd Manor (r,b; 18 yrs. and older), Little Brothers of the Good Shepherd, P.O. Box 260, Momence. 60954 (120).

Heart of Mercy Village (r,c; 21-33 yrs.), 6300 N. Ridge Ave., Chicago 60660 (40).

Lt. Joseph P. Kennedy, Jr., School (r,d,c; 6-21 yrs.) and Job Training Center (c; 16 yrs. and older), 123rd and Wolf Rd., Palos Park 60464 (101).

Misericordia Home South (r,c), 2916 W. 47th St., Chicago 60632 (117).

Misericordia Home North (r,c; 4-21 yrs.), 6300 North Ridge, Chicago 60660 (125).

Mt. St. Joseph (mentally handicapped women; 20-45 yrs.), 24955 N. Highway 12, Lake Zurich 60047 (160).

St. Francis School for Exceptional Children (r,c; 2-12 yrs.), 1209 S. Walnut Ave., Freeport 61032 (36).

St. Jude Special Education Center (d,c), 2nd and Spring Ave., Aviston 62216.

St. Mary of Providence (r,d,g; 4-21 yrs.), 4200 N. Austin Ave., Chicago 60634 (110).

St. Rose Day School (d,c; 3-21 yrs.), 4911 S. Hoyne Ave., Chicago 60609 (60). For mentally handicapped children.

St. Vincent Community Living Facility (adults, over 18 yrs.) (20), and St. Vincent Supported Living Arrangement (adults, over 18 yrs.) (20), 659 E. Jefferson St., Freeport 61032.

Special Education Program of the East St. Louis Deanery (d,c; 5-16 yrs.), 8213 Church Lane, East St. Louis 62203 (50).

Indiana: Marian Day Program (d,c; 6-16 yrs.), 700 Herndon Dr., Evansville 47711 (35).

Providence House (r, men; 18 yrs. and up), 520 W. 9th St., Jasper 47546 (66).

St. Bavo Special Class (d,c; 6-15 yrs.), 512 W. 8th St., Mishawaka 46544 (12).

Kansas: Lakemary Center, Inc. (r,d,c; 3-16 yrs.), 100 Lakemary Dr., Paola 66071 (72r,35d).

Kentucky: Ursuline-Pitt School (d,c), 2117 Payne St., Louisville 40206 (75).

Ursuline Speech Clinic (d,c; 3 yrs.-adult), 3105 Lexington Rd., Louisville 40206 (105).

Louisiana: Department of Special Education, Archdiocese of New Orleans, St. Michael Special School, 1522 Chippewa St., New Orleans 70130.

Holy Angels Residential Facility (r,c; teen-age, 14 yrs. and older), 10450 Ellerbe Rd., Shreveport 71106 (180).

Our Lady of Fatima School (d,c; 6-21 yrs.), 2315 Johnston St., Lafayette 70503 (50).

Padua House (r,c; birth-21 yrs.), 200 Beta St., Belle Chase 70037 (44).

Regina Caeli Center (d,c; 6-16 yrs.), P.O. Box 5950, Drew Station, Lake Charles. 70606 (36).

St. Jude the Apostle, 1430 Claire Ave., Gretna 70053. Group home.

St. Mary's Training School (r,c: 3-22 yrs.), P.O. Drawer 7768, Alexandria 71306 (152).

Sts. Mary and Elizabeth, 720 N. Elm St., Metairie 70003. Group home.

St. Peter the Fisherman, 235 Airport Dr., Slidell 70458. Group home.

St. Rosalie, 119 Kass St., Gretna 70056. Group home.

Maryland: The Benedictine School for Exceptional Children (r,c; 6-21 yrs.), Ridgely 21660 (100). Also conducts Habilitation Center (r,c; 17 yrs. and older) (50) and 5 community-based homes (21 yrs. and older).

Francis X. Gallagher Services (r), 2520 Pot Spring Rd., Timonium 21093 (180). Adult day activity programs.

St. Elizabeth School and Habilitation Center (d,c; 12-21 yrs.), 801 Argonne Dr., Baltimore 21218 (125).

St. Francis School for Special Education (d,c; 3-13 yrs.), 2226 Maryland Ave., Baltimore 21218 (60).

Massachusetts: Cardinal Cushing School and Training Center (r,d,c; 10-22 yrs.), Hanover 02339 (130 r; 40 d).

Mercy Centre for Developmental Disabilities (d,c; 3-22 yrs. and over), 25 West Chester St., Worcester 01605 (172).

St. Coletta Day School (d,c; 5-22 yrs.), 85 Washington St., Braintree 02184 (132).

Michigan: Our Lady of Providence Center (r,d,g; 5-17 yrs., child caring; 18-26, adult foster care), 16115 Beck Rd., Northville. 48167 (100).

St. Louis Center and School (r,d,b; 6-18 yrs. child care; 18-26 yrs. adult foster care), 16195 Old U.S. 12, Chelsea 48118 (68).

Minnesota: Mother Teresa Home (r,c; 18 yrs. and older), 101-10th Ave. N., Cold Spring 56320 (14).

St. Elizabeth Home (r,c; 18 yrs. and older), 306 15th Ave. N., St. Cloud 56301 (14).

St. Francis Home (r,c; 9-12 yrs.) 25-2nd St. N., Waite Park 56387 (6).

Missouri: Department of Special Education, Archdiocese of St. Louis, 4472 Lindell Blvd., St. Louis. 63108. Conducts 43 special day classes (c; 5-16 yrs.).

Good Shepherd Manor (residential for developmentally disabled men; 16 yrs. and up), Little Brothers of the Good Shepherd, 3220 E. 23rd St., Kansas City 64127 (43).

Mt. Carmel Group Home (r,c; 16-21 yrs.), 8757 Annetta Ave., St. Louis 63147.

St. Casimir Group Home (r; young women, 16-21 yrs.), 10735 Vorhof Dr., St. Louis 63136.

St. Joseph's Vocational Center (d,c; 15-21 yrs.), 5341 Emerson Ave., St. Louis 63120 (150).

St. Mary's Special School (r,c; 5-16 yrs.), 5341 Emerson Ave., St. Louis 63120 (135).

Universal Sheltered Workshop (c, adults), 6912 W. Florissant Ave., St. Louis 63136. Sheltered employment (80).

Vogelweid Learning Center (d,c; 5-18 yrs.), 314 W. High St., Jefferson City 65101 (30).

Nebraska: Madonna School for Exceptional Children (d,c; 5-21 yrs.), 2537 N. 62nd St., Omaha 68104 (65).

Villa Marie School (r,d,c; 7-16 yrs.), P. O. Box 80328, Lincoln 68501 (17).

New Jersey: Alhambra Child Study Center (d,c; 5-12 yrs.), 31 Centre St., Newark 07102 (35).

Archbishop Boland Rehabilitation Center (d,c; 16-60 yrs.), 450 Market St. Newark 07105 (350).

Archbishop Damiano School (d,c; 5-21 yrs.), 532 Delsea Dr., Westville Grove 08093.

Catholic Communities Services, Archdiocese of Newark, 17 Mulberry St., Newark 07102. Services include: Alhambra Child Study Center, Archbishop Boland Rehabilitation Center, Mt. Carmel Guild, St. Anthony's and St. Patrick's Special Education Schools (see separate entries).

Department of Special Education, Diocese of Camden, 1845 Haddon Ave., Camden 08108. Services include: Archbishop Damiano School (above), and full time programs at 6 Catholic Schools; adult evening classes (18-65 yrs.); religious education programs.

Department of Special Education, Diocese of Paterson. Murray House (r; adults), 389 Main St., Paterson 07501. Also conducts four other adult group homes and one adult opportunity center.

Felician School for Exceptional Children (r,d,c; 2½-14 yrs.), 260 S. Main St., Lodi 07644 (120).

McAuley School for Exceptional Children (d,c; 5-9 yrs.), 1633 Rt. 22 at Terrill Rd., N. Plainfield 07061 (40).

Mt. Carmel Guild Special Education School (d,c; 6-12 yrs.), 550 E. Broad St., Westfield 07079 (35).

St. Anthony's Special Education School (d,c; 10-20 yrs.), 25 N. 7th St., Belleville 07109 (40).

Sr. Georgine Learning Center (d,c; 6-17 yrs.), 544 Chestnut Ave., Trenton 08611 (30).

St. Patrick's Special Education School (d,c; 6-17 yrs.), 72 Central Ave., Newark 07102 (50).

New Mexico: St. Joseph's Manor (r,b; 18-35 yrs.), P.O. Box 610, Bernalillo 87004. Little Brothers of the Good Shepherd, P.O. Box 610, Bernalillo 87004. Twenty-four-hour adult care center for mentally retarded men.

New York: Cantalician Center for Learning (d,c; birth-21 yrs.), 3233 Main St., Buffalo 14214. Infant and pre-school; elementary and secondary; workshop.

Catholic Charities/Community Residence Program (r,c; 21 years and up), 143 Schleigel Blvd., Amityville 11701. Conducts four residences for retarded adults (Christopher Residence; Neumann Residence for Deaf Retarded; Alhambra House; Seton Residence.)

Cobb Memorial School (r,d,c; 6-10 yrs.), Altamont 12009 (40).

L'Arche (r, adults), 1701 James St., Syracuse 13206 (12). Long-term facility for mentally retarded adults following philosophy of Jean Vanier and L'Arche movement.

Maryhaven Center of Hope (r,d,c; pre-school to adult), Myrtle Ave., Port Jefferson 11777. Offers variety of services.

Mercy Home for Children (r,c), 273 Willoughby

Ave., Brooklyn 11205 (40). Also conducts four group homes.

Office for Disabled Persons, Diocese of Brooklyn, 191 Joralemon St., Brooklyn 11201. Services include day care center and community residences for retarded adults.

Office for Disabled Persons, Archdiocese of New York, 1011 First Ave., New York 10022. Services include consultation and referral, summer camp for adults, variety of services for deaf and blind of all ages, day camp for children.

School of the Holy Childhood (d,c; 5-21 yrs.), 100 Groton Parkway, Rochester 14623 (94). Adult program, 18-50 yrs.

North Carolina: Holy Angels (r,c; birth to 18 yrs.), Belmont 28012 (46).

Ohio: Good Shepherd Manor (residential care and programming for developmentally disabled men 22 years and older), Little Brothers of the Good Shepherd, P.O. Box 387, Wakefield 45687 (97).

Julie Billiart School (d,c; 6-12 yrs.), 4982 Clubside Rd., Cleveland 44124 (130). Non-graded school for children with learning problems.

Mary Immaculate School (d,c; 7-14 yrs.), 3837 Secor Rd., Toledo 43623 (60). For children with learning disabilities.

Mt. Aloysius (r, men; 21 yrs. and over), Little Brothers of the Good Shepherd, P.O. Box 598, New Lexington 43764 (80).

Our Lady of Angels-St. Joseph Center (d,c; 6-16 yrs.), 2346 W. 14th St., Cleveland 44113 (80).

Our Lady of the Elms Special School (d,c; 4-14 yrs.), Dominican Sisters, 1230 W. Market St., Akron 44313 (65).

Rose Mary, The Johanna Graselli Rehabilitation and Education Center (r,c; 3-12 yrs.), 19350 Euclid Ave., Cleveland 44117 (40).

St. John's Villa (r,c,b, 6-14 yrs; g, 6-18 yrs., continued care, g, 18 yrs. and over), 620 Roswell Rd. N.W., Carrollton 44615 (182).

Oregon: Emily School for Multi-Handicapped Children (d,c; 2½-5 yrs.), 830 N.E. 47th Ave., Portland 97213 (12).

Providence Children's Nursing Center (r, c; birth-10 yrs.; nursing care), 830 N. E. 47th Ave., Portland 97213 (54).

Pennsylvania: Clelian Heights School for Exceptional Children (r,d,c; 5-21 yrs.), R.D. 9, Box 607, Greensburg 15601 (140). Also conducts re-socialization program (r,d,c; young adults).

Divine Providence Village (r, women), 686 Old Marple Rd., Springfield 19064 (96).

Don Guanella School (r,b; d,c; 6-21 yrs.) and C. K. Center (r,c; adults, post-school age), 1797 S. Sproul Rd., Springfield 19064.

McGuire Memorial (r,d,c; infancy to 7 yrs.), 2119 Mercer Rd., New Brighton 15066 (99).

Mercy Day School: Center for Special Learning (d,c; 2-21 yrs.) and infant stimulation), 830 S. Woodward St., Allentown 18103 (76).

Our Lady of Confidence Day School (d,c; 4½-21 yrs.), 10th and Lycoming Sts., Philadelphia 19140 (140).

St. Anthony School for Exceptional Children (r,d,c; 5-21 yrs.), 13th St. and Hulton Rd., Oakmont 15139 (135).

St. Joseph Center for Special Learning (d,c; 4.7-21 yrs.), 619 Mahantongo St., Pottsville 17901 (50).

St. Joseph's Center (r,c; birth-17 yrs.), 2010 Adams Ave., Scranton 18509 (93).

St. Katherine School (d,c; 4-21 yrs.), William Rd. and Bowman Ave., Philadelphia 19151 (150)

Tennessee: Madonna Day School for Retarded Children (d,c; 5-16 yrs.), 4189 Leroy, Memphis 38108 (52).

St. Bernard School for Exceptional Children, (c; 4-8 yrs.), 2021 21st Ave. S., Nashville 37212 (25).

Texas: Notre Dame of Dallas Special School (d,c; 3-16 yrs.), 1451 E. Northgate Dr., Irving 75062. Notre Dame Vocational Center (d,c; 16 yrs. and over), same address, provides work-study program for exceptional people over 16.

Virginia: St. Coletta School (d,c; 3-25 yrs.), 1305 N. Jackson St., Arlington 22201 (25). For developmentally disabled.

St. Mary's Infant Home (r,c; 3 days-9 yrs.), 317 Chapel St., Norfolk 23504 (50).

Wisconsin: St. Coletta School, W4955, Jefferson. Academic or school program (c; 6-18 yrs.); Habilitation Program to prepare adolescents and young adults for gainful employment in community; employment for limited number of post adolescents; Alverno Personal Care Program; Coletta-James Transitional Group Home.

St. Coletta Day School (c; 8-16 yrs.), 1725 N. 54th St., Milwaukee. 53208 (12).

Orthopedically Handicapped

Alabama: Father Harold Purcell Memorial (r,c; birth to 14 yrs.), 2048 W. Fairview Ave., Montgomery 36108 (52). Skilled nursing home.

Pennsylvania: St. Edmond's Home for Crippled Children (r,c; birth-16 yrs.)., 320 S. Roberts Rd., Rosemont 19010 (40).

Visually Handicapped

Maine: Visually Handicapped Services (Diocesan Human Relations Services), 87 High St., Portland 04101; 15 Vaughn St., Caribou 04736; 382 Sabattus St., Lewiston 04240; 224 Main St., Waterville. Itinerant teacher and other services.

New Jersey: St. Joseph's School for the Multiple Handicapped Blind (r,d,c; 3-21 yrs.), 253 Baldwin Ave., Jersey City 07306 (27).

New York: Lavelle School for the Blind (r,d,c; 3-21 yrs.), 221st St. and Paulding Ave., Bronx 10469 (120).

Pennsylvania: St. Lucy Day School (d,c; pre-K to 8th grade — 3½-14 yrs.), 929 S. Farragut St., Philadelphia. 19143. Also has part-time program for infants and toddlers (birth to 3 yrs.).

At the annual conference of the National Catholic Office for **Persons with Disabilities** July 25, 1988, awards were presented to the Office of Pastoral Ministry with Handicapped Persons, Buffalo, N.Y., the Office of Ministry with Persons with Disabilities, Springfield, Ill., and the Catholic Commission for the Handicapped, St. Louis.

OTHER SOCIAL SERVICES

Cancer Hospitals or Homes: The following homes or hospitals specialize in the care of cancer patients. They are listed according to state.

Our Lady of Perpetual Help Home, Servants of Relief for Incurable Cancer, 760 Washington St., S.W., Atlanta, Ga. 30315 (54).

Rose Hawthorne Lathrop Home, Servants of Relief for Incurable Cancer, 1600 Bay St., Fall River, Mass. 02724 (35).

Our Lady of Good Counsel Free Cancer Home, Servants of Relief for Incurable Cancer, 2076 St. Anthony Ave., St. Paul, Minn. 55104 (40).

Calvary Hospital, Inc., 1740 Eastchester Rd., Bronx, N.Y. 10461 (200). Sponsored by Catholic Charities, Department of Health and Hospitals, Archdiocese of New York.

St. Rose's Home (Free Home, owned and operated by the Servants of Relief for Incurable Cancer), 71 Jackson St., New York, N.Y. 10002 (60).

Rosary Hill Home, Servants of Relief for Incurable Cancer, 600 Linda Ave., Hawthorne, N.Y. 10532 (72).

Holy Family Home, Servants of Relief for Incurable Cancer, 6707 State Rd., Parma, O. 44134 (50).

Sacred Heart Free Home for Incurable Cancer, Servants of Relief for Incurable Cancer, 1315 W. Hunting Park Ave., Philadelphia, Pa. 19140 (45).

Drug Abuse: Rehabilitation centers and outpatient clinics have been established in several dioceses. Facilities include:

Alpha House for Drug Rehabilitation (women; 30 beds — 25 adults, 5 children), and Dismas House for Drug Rehabilitation (men; 78 beds), 396 Straight St., Paterson, N.J. 07501 (residential rehabilitation programs). Cedar Outpatient Clinic and Cedar Day Care Center, 101-105 Cedar St., Paterson, N.J. 07501 (outpatient services). Straight and Narrow Hospital for Detoxification (20 beds).

Daytop Village, Inc., 54 W. 40th St., New York, N.Y. 10018. Msgr. William B. O'Brien. Seven residential facilities and eight outreach centers in New York.

New Hope Manor, 218 Hillside Rd., Barryville, N.Y. 12719. Long-term residential substance abuse treatment center for teen-age girls and women ages 13-26. Three-month residential half-way house after primary treatment; six-month after-care program.

St. Joseph's Hospital, L. E. Phillips Center for the Chemically Dependent, 2661 County Trunk I, Chippewa Falls, Wis. 54729 (46). Residential and outpatient. Adult and adolescent programs. Hospital Sisters of the Third Order of St. Francis.

St. Luke's Center, 3290 N.W. 7th St., Miami, Fla. 33125. Residential and outpatient detoxification programs for drug abusers; day care services for children of addicts in treatment. Miami DARE, same address, trains parents, youth, priests and teachers as prevention volunteers in the area of substance abuse.

Transitus House for Chemically Dependent Women. 1830 Wheaton St., Chippewa Falls, Wis. 54729 (21). Six month residential transitional living after primary treatment. Hospital Sisters of the Third Order of St. Francis.

Alcoholics: Some priests and religious throughout the U.S. are committed in a special way to the personal rehabilitation and pastoral care of alcoholics through participation in Alcoholics Anonymous and other programs. Facilities for the rehabilitation of alcoholics include:

Matt Talbot Inn, 2270 Professor St., Cleveland, Ohio 44113 (capacity 23 men; Halfway House; residential treatment for male alcoholics).

Straight and Narrow Hospital for Alcoholism (20 beds), and Straight and Narrow Rehabilitation Center for Male Alcoholics (30 beds), 396 Straight St., Paterson, N.J. 07501. McNulty House for Male Alcoholics (10 beds), 101 Cedar St., Paterson, N.J. 07501. Straight and Narrow Alcohol Abuse Services (outpatient services), 896 E. 19th St., Paterson, N.J. 07501. Intoxicated Drivers Resource Center, 184 First St., Passaic, N.J. 07055.

Sacred Heart Rehabilitation Center, Inc., 569 E. Elizabeth St., Detroit, Mich. 48201 (10 beds, detoxification; 70 beds, early treatment); 400 Stoddard Rd., Memphis, Mich. 48041 (120 beds, advance treatment). Both facilities serve male and female live-in clients. Outpatient services available for male and female clients.

The National Clergy Conference on Alcoholism and Related Drug Problems, 1200 Varnum St., N.E., Washington, D.C. 20017, offers educational material to those involved in pastoral ministry on ways of dealing with problems related to alcoholism and medication dependency.

Convicts: Priests serve as full- or part-time chaplains in penal and correctional institutions throughout the country. Limited efforts have been made to assist in the rehabilitation of released prisoners in Halfway House establishments.

Dining Rooms; Facilities for Homeless: Representative of places where meals are provided, and in some cases lodging and other services as well, are:

St. Anthony's Dining Room, 121 Golden Gate Ave., San Francisco, Calif. 94102. Founded in 1950. Over 2,000 complete meals served free daily; more than 18 million since its founding. Clothing, temporary shelter and basic medical care also provided. Rehabilitation program (farm and urban).

St. Vincent de Paul Free Dining Room, 675 23rd St., Oakland, Calif. 94604. Administered by Daughters of Charity of St. Vincent de Paul, under sponsorship of St. Vincent de Paul Society. Hot meals served at lunch time 7 days a week; clothing, lodging provided those in need.

St. Vincent's Dining Room, 505 W. 3rd St., Reno, Nev. 89503.

St. Vincent Dining Room, 1501 N. Main St., Las Vegas, Nev. 89101. Hot meal every day at noon.

Good Shepherd Refuge, Little Brothers of the Good Shepherd, 601 2nd St. S.W., Albuquerque, N.M. 87102.

Holy Name Centre for Homeless Men, Inc., 18 Bleeker St., New York, N.Y. 10012. A day shelter for alcoholic, homeless men. Provides social services and aid to transients and those in need. Affiliated with New York Catholic Charities.

St. Francis Inn, 2441 Kensington Ave., Philadelphia, Pa. 19125. Serves hot meals. Temporary shelter for men and women. Two thrift shops.

St. John's Hospice for Men, staffed by Little Brothers of the Good Shepherd, 1221 Race St., Philadelphia, Pa. 19107. Founded in 1963. Hot breakfast and dinner served to all in need; accommodations for 35 men for night shelter; clothing distributed daily to needy.

Camillus House, Little Brothers of the Good Shepherd, 726 N.E. First Ave., Miami, Fla. 33132. Breakfast and dinner served to all in need; accommodations for 70 men for night lodging; clothing distributed daily. Free medical clinic 5 days and 3 nights a week.

Shelters: Facilities for runaways, the abused, exploited and homeless include:

Anthony House, under sponsorship of St. Anthony's Guild (see Index). Four locations: 246 2nd St., Jersey City, N.J. 07302 (for homeless women and children); 38 E. Roosevelt Ave., Roosevelt, N.Y. 11575 (with St. Vincent de Paul Society — for homeless men); P.O. Box 880, Zellwood, Fla. 32798 (for migrant workers and their families); 2130 N. Hancock St., Philadelphia, Pa. 19122 (for homeless youth).

Covenant House, 460 W. 41st St., New York, N.Y. 10036. Non-sectarian. President, Rev. Bruce Ritter, O.F.M. Conv. Provides shelter and services for homeless, runaway and exploited youth under the age of 21, in New York, Houston, Ft. Lauderdale, New Orleans, Anchorage, Toronto (Canada), Tegucigalpa (Honduras) and Antigua (Guatemala).

Crescent House, Associated Catholic Charities, 1231 Prytania St., New Orleans, La. 70130. Provides temporary shelter, counseling and advocacy for battered women and their children.

The Dwelling Place, 409 W. 40th St., New York, N.Y. 10018. For homeless women.

The Good Shepherd Shelter, 1114 W. Grace St., Chicago, Ill. 60613. For abused women with children.

Good Shepherd Shelter, 2561 Venice Blvd., Los Angeles, Calif. 90019. For battered women with children.

Good Shepherd Gracenter, Convent of the Good Shepherd, 503 Cambridge, San Francisco, Calif. 94134. Transitional residential program for women in need who want to change their lives.

Mercy Hospice, Sisters of Mercy, 334 S. 13th St., Philadelphia, Pa. 19107. Temporary shelter and relocation assistance for homeless women and children.

Mt. Carmel House, Carmelite Sisters, 471 G Pl., N.W., Washington, D.C. 20001. For homeless women.

Ozanam Inn, 843 Camp St., New Orleans, La. 70130. Under sponsorship of the St. Vincent de Paul Society. Hospice for homeless men.

St. Christopher Inn, Graymoor, Garrison, N.Y. 10524. Temporary shelter for homeless and needy men.

Siena/Francis House, Inc. P.O. Box 217 D.T.S., Omaha, Nebr. 68102. Two facilities: Siena House, 804 N. 19th St., Omaha, Nebr. 68102 (for homeless and abused women or women with children; provides 24-hour assistance and advocacy services); Francis House, 1902 Cuming St., Omaha, Nebr. 68102 (temporary shelter for homeless men).

Unwed Mothers: Residential and care services for unwed mothers are available in many dioceses.

ORGANIZATIONS

(See separate article for a listing of facilities for the handicapped.)

Blind

The Carroll Center for the Blind (formerly the Catholic Guild for All the Blind): Located at 770 Centre St., Newton, Mass. 02158, the center conducts diagnostic evaluation and rehabilitation programs for blind people over 16 years of age, and maintains programs in community services for all ages, volunteer and special services, computer access training, low-vision training and professional training. It offers a large range of services for blind people who are not in residence, and maintains an office of public education and information. The executive director is Rachel Rosenbaum.

Xavier Society for the Blind: The Society is located at 154 E. 23rd St., New York, 10010. Founded in 1900 by Rev. Joseph Stadelman, S.J., it is a center for publications for the blind and partially sighted and for the deaf blind and maintains a circulating library of approximately 7,000 volumes in Braille, large type and on tape. Its many publications include *The Catholic Review,* a monthly selection of articles of current interest from the Catholic press presented for the visually handicapped in Braille, on tape, and in large print. All services provided for the visually impaired are free. The director of Xavier is Rev. Anthony F. La Bau, S.J.

The Deaf

According to the National Catholic Office for the Deaf, there are approximately 95,000 Catholics among the total deaf population of 410,522. (The deaf were defined by the 1974 National Census of the Deaf Population as "those persons who could not hear and understand speech and who had lost — or never had — that ability prior to 19 years of age.) Reported statistics indicated: Students in Catholic schools for the deaf, 1,969; teachers, 570 (147 were religious). Personnel involved in out-of-school pastoral ministry to the deaf included: priests, 90 (35 full-time, 55 part-time); permanent deacons, 9 (part-time); sisters, 65 (40 full-time, 25 part-time); brothers, 3 (2 full-time, 1 part-time); lay people, 53 (23 full-time, 30 part-time).

Organizations involved in work for the deaf include the following.

International Catholic Deaf Association: Established by deaf adults in Toronto, Canada, in 1949, the association has more than 5,000 members in 124 chapters, mostly in the U.S. It is the only international lay association founded and controlled by deaf Catholic adults. The ICDA publishes *The Deaf Catholic* bimonthly, sponsors regional conferences, workshops and an annual convention. The executive secretary is Robert L. Bates, 814 Thayer Ave., Silver Spring, Md. 20910.

National Catholic Office for the Deaf: Formally established in 1976, at Washington, D.C., to provide pastoral service to those who teach deaf children and adults, to the parents of deaf children, to pastors of deaf persons, and to organizations of the deaf. The office develops liturgical and religious education materials; organizes workshops, pastoral weeks, community weeks, leadership programs, cursillos; and serves as a clearinghouse for information concerning ministry to the deaf. It publishes *Listening,* a pastoral service for the hearing impaired, five times a year. The executive director is Sister Alverna Hollis, O.P. Address: 814 Thayer Ave., Silver Spring, Md. 20910.

Mentally Retarded

National Apostolate with Mentally Retarded Persons: Established in 1968 to promote the full participation in the Church by persons who are mentally retarded. It publishes the *NAMRP Quarterly* and a monthly newsletter, and has available a bibliography on religious education for mentally retarded persons. Father Richard Hockman, C.S.C., is president of the apostolate; the executive director is Charles M. Luce, P.O. Box 4711, Columbia, S.C. 29240.

Service Agencies

National Catholic Office for Persons with Disabilities: Established in 1982 to assist dioceses in developing pastoral services with handicapped persons. The executive director is Sister Rita Baum, S.S.J. Address: P.O. Box 29113, Washington, D.C. 20017.

Special Education Department, National Catholic Educational Association: Established in 1954 to coordinate under one agency information and service functions for all areas of special education under Catholic auspices. The executive director is Sr. Suzanne Hall, S.N.D. de N. Address: 1077 30th St. N.W., Washington, D.C. 20007.

RETREATS, SPIRITUAL RENEWAL PROGRAMS

There is great variety in retreat and renewal programs, with orientations ranging from the traditional to teen encounters. Central to all of them are celebration of the liturgy and deepening of a person's commitment to faith and witness in life.

Features of many of the forms are as follows.

Traditional Retreats: Centered around conferences and the direction of a retreat master; oriented to the personal needs of the retreatants; including such standard practices as participation in Mass, reception of the sacraments, private and group prayer, silence and meditation, discussions.

Team Retreat: Conducted by a team of several leaders or directors (priests, religious, lay persons) with division of subject matter and activities according to their special skills and the nature and needs of the group.

Closed Retreat: Involving withdrawal for a period of time — overnight, several days, a weekend — from everyday occupations and activities.

Open Retreat: Made without total disengagement from everyday involvements, on a part-time basis.

Private Retreat: By one person, on a kind of do-it-yourself basis with the one-to-one assistance of a director.

Special Groups: With formats and activities geared to particular groups; e.g., members of Alcoholics Anonymous, vocational groups and apostolic groups.

Marriage Encounters: Usually weekend periods of husband-wife reflection and dialogue; introduced into the U.S. from Spain in 1967.

Charismatic Renewal: Featuring elements of the movement of the same name; "Spirit-oriented"; communitarian and flexible, with spontaneous and shared prayer, personal testimonies of faith and witness.

Christian Community: Characterized by strong community thrust.

Teens Encounter Christ (TEC), SEARCH: Formats adapted to the mentality and needs of youth, involving experience of Christian faith and commitment in a community setting.

Christian Maturity Seminars: Similar to teen encounters in basic concept but different to suit persons of greater maturity.

Cursillo: see separate entry.

Movement for a Better World: see separate entry.

Conference

Retreats International Inc.: The first organization for promoting retreats in the U.S. was started in 1904 in New York. Its initial efforts and the gradual growth of the movement led to the formation in 1927 of the National Catholic Laymen's Retreat Conference, the forerunner of the men's division of Retreats International. The women's division developed from the National Laywomen's Retreat Movement which was founded in Chicago in 1936. The men's and women's divisions merged July 9, 1977. The services of the organization include an annual summer institute for retreat and pastoral ministry, regional conferences for retreat center leadership and area meetings of directors and key leadership in the retreat movement. The officers are: Auxiliary Bishop Robert Morneau of Green Bay, episcopal advisor; Mr. Dave Ramey, president; Rev. Thomas W. Gedeon, S.J., executive director. National office: Box 1067, Notre Dame, Ind. 46556.

NORTH AMERICAN COLLEGE

The North American College was founded by the bishops of the United States in 1859 as a residence and house of formation for U.S. seminarians and graduate students in Rome. The first ordination of an alumnus took place June 14, 1862. Pontifical status was granted the college by Leo XIII Oct. 25, 1884. Students at the college study theology principally at the Pontifical Gregorian University.

HOUSES OF RETREAT AND RENEWAL

(Principal sources: Almanac survey; *1988 Directory of Retreat Ministry Centers* of Retreats International; *The Official Catholic Directory*.)

Abbreviation code: m, men; w, women; mc, married couples; y, youth. Houses and centers without code generally offer facilities to most groups. An asterisk after an abbreviation indicates that the facility is primarily for the group designated but that special groups are also accommodated. Houses furnish information concerning the types of programs they offer.

Alabama: Blessed Trinity Shrine Retreat, Holy Trinity 36859.
Visitation Sacred Heart Retreat House, 2300 Spring Hill Ave., Mobile 36607.

Alaska: Holy Spirit Retreat House, 10980 Hillside Dr., Anchorage 99516.

Arizona: Franciscan Renewal Center, 5802 E. Lincoln Dr., Box 220, Scottsdale 85252.
Mount Claret Cursillo Center, 4633 N. 54th St., Phoenix 85018.
Our Lady of Solitude House of Prayer, P.O. Box 1140, Black Canyon City 85324.
Redemptorist Picture Rocks Retreat House, 7101 W. Picture Rocks Rd., Tucson 85743.

Arkansas: Little Portion Franciscan Hermitage, Rt. 3, Box 608, Eureka Springs 72632.
St. Scholastica Retreat Center, P.O. Box 3489, Ft. Smith, 72913.

California: Angela Center, 535 Angela Dr., Santa Rosa 95401.
Christ the King Retreat Center, 6520 Van Maren Lane, Citrus Heights 95621.
Christian Brothers Retreat House, 2233 Sulphur Springs Ave., St. Helena 94574.
Claretian Retreat Center, 1119 Westchester Pl., Los Angeles 90019.
De Paul Center, 1105 Bluff Rd., Montebello 90640.
El Carmelo Retreat House, P.O. Box 446, Redlands 92373.
Heart of Jesus Retreat Center, 2927 S. Greenville St., Santa Ana 92704.
Holy Spirit Retreat Center, 4316 Lanai Rd., Encino 91436.
Holy Transfiguration Monastery, Monks of Mt. Tabor (Ukrainian Byzantine), 17001 Tomki Rd., Redwood Valley, Calif. 95470.
Jesuit Retreat House, 662 University Ave., Box 128, Los Altos 94023.
Madonna of Peace Renewal Center (y), P.O. Box 71, Copperopolis 95228.
Manresa Retreat House, 801 E. Foothill Blvd., P.O. Box K, Azusa 91702.
Mary and Joseph Retreat Center, 5300 Crest Rd., Rancho Palos Verdes 90274.
Mater Dolorosa Retreat Center, 700 N. Sunnyside Ave., Sierra Madre 91024.
Mercy Center, 2300 Adeline Dr., Burlingame 94010.
Mother of Mercy Convent, 20301 Elkwood St., Canoga Park 91306.
Mount Alverno Retreat and Conference Center, 3910 Bret Harte Dr., Redwood City 94061.
Mount Mary Immaculate Center for Spiritual Growth, 3254 Gloria Terr., Lafayette 94549.
New Camaldoli Immaculate Heart Hermitage, Big Sur 93920.
Old Mission Retreat, P.O. Box 409, San Luis Rey 92068.
Our Lady of Trust Spirituality Center, 205 S. Pine St., Fullerton 92633. For day use.
Poverello of Assisi Retreat House, 1519 Woodworth St., San Fernando 91340.
Presentation Education and Retreat Center, 19480 Bear Creek Rd., Los Gatos 95030.
Prince of Peace Abbey, 650 Benet Hill Rd., Oceanside 92054.
Sacred Heart Retreat House (w*), 920 E. Alhambra Rd., Alhambra 91801.
St. Andrew's Priory Retreat House, Valyermo 93563.
St. Anthony's Retreat House, P.O. Box 249, Three Rivers 93271.
St. Clare's Retreat, 2381 Laurel Glen Rd. Soquel 95073.
St. Francis Retreat, P.O. Box 1070, San Juan Bautista 95045.
St. Francis Salesian Retreat (Camp St. Francis) (y), 2400 E. Lake Ave., Watsonville 95076.
St. Joseph's Salesian Youth Center (St. Dominic Savio Retreat House) (y), 8301 Arroyo Dr., Rosemead 91770.
St. Mary's Seminary and Retreat House, 1964 Las Conoas Rd., Santa Barbara 93105.
San Damiano Retreat, P.O. Box 767, Danville 94526.
San Miguel Retreat House, P.O. Box 69, San Miguel 93451.
Santa Sabina Center, 1520 Grand Ave., San Rafael 94901.
Serra Retreat, 3401 S. Serra Rd., Box 127, Malibu 90265.
Starcross Community, House of Prayer, Annapolis, Calif. 95412.
Villa Maria del Mar, Santa Cruz. Mailing address, 2-1918 E. Cliff Dr., Santa Cruz 95062.
Villa Maria — House of Prayer (w), 1252 N. Citrus Dr., La Habra 90631.

Colorado: Benet Hill Center, 2577 N. Chelton Rd., Colorado Springs 80909. Primarily day center.
Bethlehem Center, 12550 Zuni, North Glenn 80234.
Convent of St. Walburga, 6717 S. Boulder Rd., Boulder 80303.
Julie Penrose Center (formerly El Pomar), 1661 Mesa Ave., Colorado Springs 80906.
Sacred Heart Retreat House, Box 185, Sedalia 80135.
Spiritual Life Institute (individuals only), Nada

Hermitage. Crestone 81131. Private desert retreats with minimal direction.

Connecticut: Archdiocesan Spiritual Life Center. 467 Bloomfield Ave., Bloomfield 06002.
Cenacle Center for Meditation and Spiritual Renewal, P.O. Box 550,Middletown 06457.
Edmundite Apostolate and Conference Center, Enders Island, Mystic 06355.
Emmaus Spiritual Life Center, 24 Maple Ave., Uncasville 06382.
Holy Family Retreat, 303 Tunxis Rd., West Hartford 06107.
Immaculata Retreat House, 289 Windham Rd., Willimantic 06226.
Mercy Center, P.O. Box 191, 167 Neck Rd., Madison 06443.
Montfort Missionaries Retreat Center, P.O. Box 667, Litchfield 06759.
My Father's House, Box 22, North Moodus Rd., Moodus 06469.
Our Lady of Calvary Retreat (w*), 31 Colton St., Farmington 06032.
Trinita Ecumenical Retreat Center, Town Hill Rd., New Hartford 06057.
Villa Maria Retreat House, 159 Sky Meadow Dr., Stamford 06903.

Delaware: St. Francis Renewal Center, 1901 Prior Rd., Wilmington 19809.

District of Columbia: Washington Retreat House (w*), 4000 Harewood Rd. N.E., Washington 20017.

Florida: Cenacle Spiritual Life Center, 1400 S. Dixie Highway, Lantana 33462.
Dominican Retreat House, Inc., 7275 S.W. 124th St., Miami 33156.
Franciscan Center, 3010 Perry Ave., Tampa 33603.
Holy Name Priory, P.O. Drawer H, St. Leo 33574.
Our Lady of Florida Spiritual Center, 1300 US Hwy. No. 1, North Palm Beach 33408.
Pilgrim Center of St. Leo Abbey, P.O. Drawer "C", St. Leo 33574.
Saint John Neumann Renewal Center, 685 Miccosukee Rd., Tallahassee 32303.

Georgia: Ignatius House, 6700 Riverside Dr. N.W., Atlanta 30328.

Idaho: Nazareth, 4450 N. Five Mile Rd., Boise 83704.

Illinois: Aylesford Carmelite Spiritual Center, I-55 at Cass Ave. N., Darien 60559.
Bellarmine Hall (m*), Box 268, Barrington 60010.
Bishop Lane Retreat House, 7708 E. McGregor Rd., Rockford 61102.
Cabrini Retreat Center (m, w, y), 9430 Golf Rd., Des Plaines 60016.
Cenacle Retreat House, 513 Fullerton Parkway, Chicago 60614.
Cenacle Retreat and Conference Center, P.O. Box 340, Warrenville 60555.
Divine Word International, 2001 Waukegan Rd., Techny 60082.
Franciscan Apostolic Center, Sangamon Ave. Rd., P.O. Box 19431, Springfield 62794.
King's House, N. 66th St., Belleville 62223.
King's House of Retreats, Box 165, Henry 61537.
La Salle Manor, Christian Brothers Retreat House, Plano 60545.
National Shrine of Our Lady of the Snows, 9500 W. Illinois Route 15, Belleville 62223.
Sacred Heart Center, 3000 Central Rd., Rolling Meadows 60008.
St. Francis Retreat, House at Mayslake, 1717 31st St., Oak Brook 60521.
St. Joseph Retreat Center, 353 N. River Rd., Des Plaines 60016.
St. Mary's Retreat House, P.O. Box 608, 1400 Main St., Lemont 60439.
Tolentine Center, 20300 Governors Highway, Olympia Fields 60461.
Villa Desiderata Retreat House, 3015 N. Bayview Lane, McHenry 60050.
Villa Center for Renewal, 35 W. 076 Villa Maria Rd., St. Charles 60174.
Villa Redeemer Retreat Center, P.O. Box 6, Glenview 60025.

Indiana: Alverna Center, 8140 Spring Mill Rd., Indianapolis 46260.
Beech Grove Benedictine Center, 1402 Southern Ave., Beech Grove 46107.
Franciscan Retreat, P.O. Box 500, Cedar Lake 46303.
John XXIII Center, 407 W. McDonald St., Hartford City 47348.
Kordes Enrichment Center, R.R. 3, Box 200, Ferdinand 47532.
Lindenwood Retreat and Ministry Center, P.O. Box 1, Donaldson 46513.
Mount Saint Francis Retreat Center, Mount Saint Francis 47146.
Our Lady of Fatima Retreat Center, Notre Dame 46556.
Our Lady of Fatima Retreat House, 5353 E. 56th St., Indianapolis 46226.
St. Jude Guest House, St. Meinrad 47577.
Saint Maur Hospitality Center, 4615 N. Michigan Rd., Indianapolis 46208.
Sarto Retreat House, 4200 N. Kentucky Ave., Evansville 47711.
Solitude of St. Joseph, Box 164, Notre Dame, Ind. 46556.

Iowa: American Martyrs Retreat House, 2209 N. Union Rd., P.O. Box 605, Cedar Falls 50613.
Colette Renewal Center, 3380 Windsor Ave., Dubuque 52001.
Emmanuel House of Prayer and Retreat Center, 925 Kirkwood Ave., Iowa City 52240.

Kansas: Manna House of Prayer, 323 East 5th St., Box 675, Concordia 66901.
Villa Christi Retreat Center, 3033 W. Second St., Wichita 67203.

Houses of Retreat and Renewal

Kentucky: Catherine Spalding Center, P.O. Box 24, Nazareth 40048.
Flaget Center, 1935 Lewiston Pl., Louisville 40216.
Marydale Retreat Center, 945 Donaldson Hwy., Erlanger 41018.
Our Lady of Gethsemani (m, private), The Guestmaster, Abbey of Gethsemani, Trappist 40051.

Louisiana: Abbey Christian Life Center, St. Joseph's Abbey, St. Benedict 70457.
Ave Maria Retreat House, Route 1, Box 0368 AB, Marrero 70072.
Cenacle Retreat House (w*), 5500 St. Mary St., P.O. Box 8115, Metairie 70011.
Jesuit Spirituality Center, P.O. Box C, Grand Coteau 70541.
Lumen Christi Retreat Center, 100 Lumen Christi Lane, Hwy. 311, Schriever 70395.
Manresa House of Retreats (m), P.O. Box 89, Convent 70723.
Maryhill Renewal Center, 600 Maryhill Rd., Pineville 71360.
Our Lady of the Oaks Retreat House, P.O. Drawer D, Grand Coteau 70541.
Regina Coeli Retreat Center, Rt. 7, P.O. Box 515, Covington 70433.

Maine: Marie Joseph Spiritual Center, RFD 2, Biddeford 04005.
St. Paul's Center, Oblate Fathers Retreat House (French-English), 136 State St., Augusta 04330.

Maryland: Bon Secours Spiritual Center, Marriottsville 21104.
CYO Retreat Center, 5625 Edson Lane, Rockville 20852.
Christian Brothers Spiritual Center, 2535 Buckeyestown Pike, Adamstown 21710.
Loyola Retreat House-on-Potomac, Faulkner 20632.
Manresa Retreat House, P.O. Box 9, Annapolis 21404.
Monsignor Clare J. O'Dwyer Youth Retreat House, 15523 York Rd., Sparks 21152.
Villa Cortona, 7007 Bradley Blvd., Bethesda 20817.

Massachusetts: Calvary Retreat Center, Passionist Community, 59 South St., Shrewsbury 01545.
Campion Renewal Center, 319 Concord Rd., Weston 02193.
Cenacle Retreat House, 200 Lake St., Brighton, Boston 02135.
Eastern Point Retreat House, Gonzaga Hall, Gloucester 01930.
Espousal Center, 554 Lexington St., Waltham 02154.
Esther House of Spiritual Renewal, Sisters of St. Anne, 1015 Pleasant St., Worcester 01602.
Genesis Spiritual Life Center, 53 Mill St., Westfield 01085.
Glastonbury Abbey (Benedictine Monks), 16 Hull St., Hingham 02043.
Holy Cross Fathers Retreat House, 490 Washington St., N. Easton 02356.
Jesuit Center, Sullivan Square, Charlestown, Boston 02129.
La Salette Center for Christian Living, 947 Park St., Attleboro 02703.
LaSalette Retreat House, 315 Topsfield Rd., Ipswich 01938.
Marian Center, 1365 Northampton St., Holyoke 01040. Day and evening programs.
Mater Dei Retreat House (boys), Old Groveland Rd., Bradford 01830.
Miramar Retreat Center, Duxbury, 02331.
Mother of Sorrows Retreat House, 110 Monastery Ave., W. Springfield 01089.
Mt. Carmel Christian Life Center, Oblong Rd., Box 613, Williamstown 01267.
Retreat Center, 339 Jerusalem Rd., Cohasset 02025.
Sacred Heart Retreat House, Salesians of St. John Bosco, P.O. Box 271, Ipswich 01938.
St. Benedict Priory (Benedictine), Still River-Harvard 01467. Self-directed.
St. Joseph's Abbey Retreat House (m) (Trappist Monks), Spencer 01562.
St. Stephen Priory Spiritual Life Center (Dominican), 20 Glen St., Box 370, Dover, Mass. 02030.

Michigan: Augustine Center, Conway 49722.
Capuchin Retreat, Box 188, Washington 48094.
Colombiere Retreat/Conference Center, Box 139, 9075 Big Lake Rd., Clarkston 48016.
Manresa Jesuit Retreat House, 1390 Quarton Rd., Bloomfield Hills 48013.
Marygrove Retreat Center, Garden 49835.
Portiuncula in the Pines, 703 E. Main St., De Witt 48820.
Queen of Angels Retreat, Box 2026, 3400 S. Washington Blvd., Saginaw 48605.
Retreat Center (w*), Sisters of Mary Reparatrix, 13600 Virgil Ave., Detroit 48223.
St. Basil's Center, 3990 Giddings Rd., Auburn Hills 48055.
St. Clare Capuchin Retreat (y*), 1975 N. River Rd., St. Clair 48079.
St. Lazare Retreat House, 18600 W. Spring Lake Rd., Box 462, Spring Lake 49456.
St. Mary's Retreat House (w*), 775 W. Drahren Rd., Oxford 48051.
St. Paul of the Cross Retreat Center, 23333 Schoolcraft, Detroit 48223.

Minnesota: Benedictine Center, St. Paul's Priory, 2675 E. Larpenteur Ave., St. Paul 55109.
The Cenacle, 1221 Wayzata Blvd., Wayzata 55391.
Center for Spiritual Development, Box 538, 211 Tenth St., Bird Island 55310.
Christ the King Retreat House, 621 First Ave. S., Buffalo 55313.
Christian Brothers Retreat Center, 15525 St. Croix Trail North, Marine-on-St. Croix 55047.
The Dwelling Place, 116 S.E. Eighth Ave., Little Falls 56345.
Franciscan Retreats, Conventual Franciscan Friars, 16385 St. Francis Lane, Prior Lake 55372.

Jesuit Retreat House, 8243 De Montreville Trail North, Lake Elmo 55042.
Maryhill Retreat Center, Society of Daughters of the Heart of Mary, 260 Summit Ave., St. Paul 55102.
Minneapolis Catholic Youth Center (y, mc), 2120 Park Ave. S., Minneapolis 55404.
Villa Maria Center, Ursuline Sisters, Frontenac 55026.

Missouri: Cenacle Retreat House, 900 S. Spoede Rd., St. Louis 63131.
Christina House Hermitages, Abbey Lane, P.O. Box 619, Pevely 63070.
Maria Fonte Solitude (private; individual hermitages), P.O. Box 322, High Ridge 63049.
Marianist Apostolic Center, P.O. Box 718, Eureka 63025.
Our Lady of Assumption Abbey (m, w), Trappists, Rt. 5, Box 193, Ava 65608.
Our Lady's Retreat House, Passionist Community, 3036 Bellerive Dr., St. Louis 63121.
Pallottine Renewal Center, 15270 Old Halls Ferry Rd., Florissant 63034.
Queen of Heaven Solitude (private, individual hermitages), Rt. 1, Box 107A, Marionville 65705.
White House Retreat, 7400 Christopher Dr., St. Louis 63129.

Montana: Christhaven - Diocesan Retreat Center, P.O. Box 948, Anaconda 59711.
Emmaus Retreat House, Box 407, Havre 59501.
Ursuline Retreat Center, 2300 Central Ave., Great Falls 59401.

Nebraska: Crosier Renewal Center, 223 E. 14th St., P.O. Box 789, Hastings 68901.
Good Counsel, R.R. 1, Box 110, Waverly 68462.
St. Columban's Conference Center, St. Columbans 68056.

New Hampshire: The Common - St. Joseph Monastery, Discalced Carmelite Friars, 174 Old Street Rd., Peterborough 03458.
La Salette Conference and Retreat Center, Enfield 03748.
New Hampshire Monastery, Hundred Acres, New Boston 03070.
Oblates of Mary Immaculate Retreat House, Hudson 03051.
St. Francis Retreat Center, 860 Central Rd., Rye Beach 03871.

New Jersey: Bethlehem Hermitage, Pleasant Hill Rd., Box 315, Chester 07930.
Blackwood Center, St. Pius X House, Box 216, Blackwood 08012.
Carmel Retreat House, 1071 Ramapo Valley Rd., Mahwah 07430.
Cenacle Retreat House, 411 River Rd., Highland Park 08904.
Felician Retreat House, Windemere Ave., Mt. Arlington 07856.
Good Shepherd Center, 74 Kahdena Rd., Morristown 07960.
Loyola House of Retreats, 161 James St., Morristown 07960.
Marianist Christian Family Living Center (families), Cape and Yale Ave., Cape May Point 08212.
Maris Stella, 7201 Long Beach Blvd., Harvey Cedars 08008.
Mt. St. Francis Retreat House, Sloatsburg Rd., Ringwood 07456. Facilities only.
Queen of Peace Retreat House, St. Paul's Abbey, P.O. Box 7, Newton 07860.
St. Joseph by the Sea Retreat House, 400 Rte. 35 N., South Mantoloking 08738.
St. Joseph's Villa (w, guest and retreat house), Srs. of St. John the Baptist, Peapack 07977.
San Alfonso Retreat House, 755 Ocean Ave., Long Branch 07740.
Sanctuary of Mary, R.R. 1, Box 106, Branchville 07826. Days of Recollection.
Stella Maris Retreat House, 981 Ocean Ave., Elberon 07740.
Trinity Ministries Center, 1292 Long Hill Rd., Stirling 07980.
Villa Pauline Retreat and Guest House (w*), Hilltop Rd., Mendham 07945.
Xavier Center, Convent Station 07961.

New Mexico: Dominican Retreat House, 5825 Coors Rd. S.W., Albuquerque 87105.
Holy Cross Retreat, Conventual Franciscan Friars, P.O. Box 158, Mesilla Park 88047.
Our Lady of Guadalupe Abbey, Pecos 87552.
Sacred Heart Retreat, P.O. Box 1989, Gallup 87301.

New York: At Home Retreats, 310 Cenacle Rd., Lake Ronkonkoma 11779.
Bethany Retreat House, County Road 105, Highland Mills 10930.
Bethlehem Retreat House (m*), Abbey of the Genesee, Piffard 14533.
Bishop Molloy Retreat House, 86-45 Edgerton Blvd., Jamaica, L.I. 11432.
Blessed Kateri Retreat House, National Kateri Shrine, P.O. Box 627, Fonda, N.Y. 12068.
Cabrini-on-the-Hudson, West Park, N.Y. 12493.
Cardinal Spellman Retreat House, Passionist Community, 5801 Palisade Ave., Bronx (Riverdale) 10471.
Cenacle Center for Spiritual Renewal, 310 Cenacle Rd., Lake Ronkonkoma 11779.
The Cenacle: Center for Spiritual Renewal, 693 East Ave., Rochester 14607.
Cenacle Retreat House, State Rd., P.O. Box 467, Bedford Village 10506.
Christ the King Retreat House, 500 Brookford Rd., Syracuse 13224.
Cormaria Retreat House, Sag Harbor, L.I. 11963.
Diocesan Cursillo Center (Spanish), 118 Congress St., Brooklyn 11201.
Dominican Retreat House, 1945 Union St., Schenectady 12309.
Don Bosco Retreat Center, Filor's Lane, West Haverstraw 10993.
Graymoor Christian Unity Center, Graymoor, Garrison 10524.
Island Retreat (June-Sept.), Bluff Island, Tupper Lake 12986.
Jesuit Retreat House, North American Martyrs Shrine, Auriesville 12016.

Houses of Retreat and Renewal

Little Portion Retreat House, 292 E. 151st St., Bronx 10451.
Monastery of the Precious Blood (w), Ft. Hamilton Parkway and 54th St., Brooklyn 11219.
Mount Alvernia Retreat House, Box 858, Wappingers Falls 12590.
Mount Manresa Retreat House, 239 Fingerboard Rd., Staten Island 10305.
Notre Dame Retreat House (m*), Box 342, Foster Rd., Canandaigua 14424.
Our Lady of Hope Center, 434 River Rd., Newburgh 12550.
Regina Maria Retreat House, 77 Brinkerhoff St., Plattsburgh 12901.
St. Andrew's House, 89 A St. Andrew's Rd., Walden 12586.
St. Columban Center, Diocese of Buffalo, 6892 Lake Shore Rd., P.O. Box 816, Derby 14047.
St. Gabriel Retreat House (y, mc), 64 Burns Rd., P.O. Box P, Shelter Island 11965.
St. Ignatius Renewal Center, Diocese of Buffalo, 6969 Strickler Rd., Clarence Center 14032. Poustinia available.
St. Ignatius Retreat House, Searington Rd., Manhasset, L.I. 11030.
St. Josaphat's Retreat House, Basilian Monastery, East Beach Rd., Glen Cove 11542.
St. Joseph Center (Spanish Center), 523 W. 142nd St., New York 10031.
St. Mary's Villa, Sloatsburg 10974.
St. Ursula Center, Middle Rd. and Blue Point Ave., Blue Point 11715.
Stella Maris Retreat Center, 130 E. Genesee St., Skaneateles 13152.
Stella Niagara Center of Renewal, 4421 Lower River Rd., Stella Niagara 14144.
Tagaste Monastery Retreat House (m, y), Suffern 10901.

North Carolina: Avila Retreat Center, 711 Mason Rd., Durham 27712.
Living Waters Catholic Reflection Center, Rt. 1, Box 476, Maggie Valley 28751.
Maryhurst Retreat House, P.O. Box 38, Pinehurst 28374.

North Dakota: Queen of Peace Retreat, Redemptorist Fathers, 1310 N. Broadway, Fargo 58102.

Ohio: Bergamo, 4400 Shakertown Rd., Dayton 45430.
Friarhurst Retreat House, 8136 Wooster Pike, Cincinnati 45227.
Jesuit Renewal Center, 5361 S. Milford Rd., Milford 45150.
Jesuit Retreat House, 5629 State Rd., Cleveland 44134.
Loyola of the Lakes, 700 Killinger Rd., Clinton 44216.
Maria Stein Center, 2365 St. Johns Rd., Maria Stein 45860.
Milford Retreat House, Box 348, Milford 45150.
Our Lady of Consolation Renewal Center, 320 West St., Carey 43316.
Our Lady of the Pines, 1250 Tiffin St., Fremont 43420.

Sacred Heart, 3128 Logan Ave., Box 6074, Youngstown 44501.
St. Anthony Pilgrim House, 321 Clay St., Carey 43316.
St. Joseph Christian Life Center, 18485 Lake Shore Blvd., Cleveland 44119.
Shrine Center for Renewal, Diocese of Columbus, 5277 E. Broad St., Columbus 43213.

Oklahoma: St. Gregory's Abbey, Shawnee 74801.

Oregon: Franciscan Renewal Center, 0858 S.W. Palatine Hill Rd., Portland 97219.
Loyola Retreat House (Jesuit Center for Spiritual Renewal), 3220 S.E. 43rd St., Portland 97206.
Mt. Angel Abbey Guest-Retreat Center, St. Benedict 97373.
Our Lady of Peace Retreat (m, w); 3600 S. W. 170th Ave., Beaverton 97006.
St. Rita Retreat Center, P.O. Box 310, Gold Hill 97525.
Shalom Prayer Center, Benedictine Sisters, Mt. Angel 97362.
Trappist Abbey Retreat (private), P.O. Box 97, Lafayette 97127.

Pennsylvania: Byzantine Catholic Seminary (m), 3605 Perrysville Ave., Pittsburgh 15214.
Cenacle Retreat House, 4721 Fifth Ave., Pittsburgh 15213.
Dominican Retreat House, Ashbourne Rd. and Juniper Ave., Elkins Park 19117.
Fatima House, Rolling Hills Rd., Ottsville 18942.
Gilmary Diocesan Center, Flaugherty Run Rd., Coraopolis 15108.
Jesuit Center for Spiritual Growth, Box 223, Church Rd., Wernersville 19565.
Maria Wald Retreat House, Convent of the Precious Blood, Box 97, New Holland Ave., Shillington 19607.
Mount St. Macrina Retreat Center, Mt. St. Macrina, Box 878, Uniontown 15401.
Our Lady of Fatima Center, Griffin Rd., Box 163, Elmhurst 18416.
Precious Blood Spirituality Center, St. Joseph Convent, Columbia 17512.
St. Alphonsus Retreat House (m*), Box 218, Tobyhanna 18466 (1,200).
St. Emma Retreat House, 1001 Harvey St., Greensburg 15601.
St. Fidelis Retreat Center, Herman 16039.
St. Francis Center, 900 W. Market St., Orwigsburg 17961.
St. Francis Center for Renewal, Monocacy Manor, 395 Bridle Path Rd., Bethlehem 18017.
St. Francis Retreat House, 3918 Chipman Rd., Easton 18042.
St. Gabriel's Retreat House (w*), 631 Griffin Pond Rd., Clarks Summit 18411.
St. Joseph's in the Hills (m), 313 Warren Ave., Malvern 19355.
St. Paul of the Cross Retreat House, 148 Monastery Ave., Pittsburgh 15203.
Saint Raphaela Mary Retreat House, 616 Coopertown Rd., Haverford 19041.

St. Vincent Archabbey, Latrobe 15650.
Villa of Our Lady Retreat Center (w, mc, y), HCR No. 1, Box 41, Mt. Pocono 18344.

Rhode Island: Carmel Renewal Center, 21 Battery St., Newport 02840.
Ephpheta House — A Center for Renewal, 10 Manville Hill Rd; mailing address, P.O. Box 1, Manville 02838.
Father Marot CYO Center (y), 53 Federal St., Woonsocket 02895.
Our Lady of Peace Spiritual Life Center, Ocean Rd., Narragansett 02882.
St. Dominic Savio Youth Center (y*), Broad Rock Rd., Box 67, Peace Dale 02883.

South Carolina: The Oratory, 434 Charlotte Ave., Box 11586, Rock Hill 29730.
Springbank Retreat Center, Rt. 2, Box 180, Kingstree 29556.

South Dakota: St. Martin's Community Center, R.R. 4, Box 1660, Rapid City 57702.
Sioux Spiritual Center (for Native Americans), Diocese of Rapid City, Howes Star Route Box 271, Plainview 57748.

Tennessee: House of the Lord, 1306 Dellwood Ave., Memphis 38127.

Texas: Bishop DeFalco Retreat Center, 2100 N. Spring, Amarillo 79107.
Catholic Renewal Center of North Texas, 4503 Bridge St., Ft. Worth 76103.
Cenacle Retreat House, 420 N. Kirkwood, Houston 77079.
Christian Holiday House and Renewal Center, Oblates of Mary Immaculate, P.O. Box 635, Dickinson 77539.
Holy Family Retreat Center, 9920 N. Major Dr., Beaumont 77706.
Holy Name Retreat Center, 430 Bunker Hill Rd., Houston 77024.
Montserrat Jesuit Retreat House, P.O. Box 398, Lake Dallas 75065.
Mount Tabor Retreat House, 12940 Up River Rd., Corpus Christi 78410.
Moye Center, Box M, Castroville 78009.
Our Lady of the Pillar Marianist Retreat Center, 2507 N.W. 36th St., San Antonio 78228.
Saint Joseph Retreat House (Casa San Jose), 127 Oblate Dr., San Antonio 78216.
San Juan Retreat House, Diocese of Brownsville, P.O. Box 998, San Juan 78589.

Utah: Our Lady of the Holy Trinity Retreat House (m), Huntsville 84317.
Our Lady of the Mountains, 1794 Lake St., Ogden 84401.

Virginia: Dominican Retreat, 7103 Old Dominion Dr., McLean 22101.
The Franciscan Center, P.O. Box 825, Winchester 22601.
Holy Family Retreat House, Redemptorist Fathers, 1414 N. Mallory St., Hampton 23663.
Missionhurst CICM Mission Center, 4651 N. 25th St., Arlington 22207.
Retreat House, Holy Cross Abbey, Rt. 2, Box 3870, Berryville 22611.

Washington: Camp Field Retreat Center, P.O. Box 128, Leavenworth 98826.
Immaculate Heart Retreat House, S. 6910 Ben Burr Rd., Spokane 99223.
Redemptorist Palisades Retreat, P.O. Box 3739, Federal Way 98063.
Visitation Retreat Center (w), 3200 S.W. Dash Point Rd., Federal Way 98023.

West Virginia: Bishop Hodges Pastoral Center, P.O. Box 60, Huttonsville, 26273.
Cenacle Retreat House, 1114 Virginia St. E., Charleston 25301.
John XXIII Pastoral Center, 100 Hodges Rd., Charleston, W. Va. 25314.
Paul VI Pastoral Center, 667 Stone and Shannon Rd., Wheeling 26003.
Priest Field Pastoral Center, Rt. 1, Box 133, Kearneysville 25430.

Wisconsin: Archdiocesan Retreat Center, 3501 S. Lake Dr., P.O. Box 2018, Milwaukee 53201.
Cardoner Jesuit Retreat Center, 1501 S. Layton Blvd., Milwaukee 53215.
Chapel House of Prayer, Route 1, New Franken, Wis. 54229.
Holy Cross Center for Spiritual Growth, 503 S. Center Ave., Merrill 54452.
Holy Name Retreat House, Chambers Island; mailing address, 1825 Riverside Drive, P.O. Box 1825, Green Bay 54305.
Jesuit Retreat House, 4800 Fahrnwald Rd., Oshkosh 54901.
Marynook — House of the Lord (ecumenically owned retreat and conference center), 500 S. 12th St., P.O. Box 9, Galesville 54630.
Monte Alverno Retreat Center, 1000 N. Ballard Rd., Appleton 54911.
Perpetual Help Retreat Center, 1800 N. Timber Trail Lane, Oconomowoc 53066.
St. Anthony Retreat Center, 500 E. 4th St., Marathon 54448.
St. Benedict Center (ecumenical retreat and conference center), Fox Bluff, P.O. Box 5070, Madison 53705.
St. Francis Friary and Retreat Center, 503 S. Browns Lake Dr., Burlington 53105.
St. Joseph's Retreat Center, Bailey's Harbor 54202.
St. Vincent Pallotti Center, Rt. 3, Box 61, Elkhorn 53121.
Schoenstatt Center, W. 284 N. 698 Cherry Lane, Waukesha 53186.

Antioch is the name of a program designed to enable youths to develop as Christians, as the followers of Christ were first called by the people of Antioch in the year 43. Antioch, with peer leadership and participation, combines on weekends opportunities for religious instruction and formation, sacramental practice and personal counseling.

LAY PERSONS AND THEIR APOSTOLATE

RIGHTS AND OBLIGATIONS OF ALL THE FAITHFUL

The following rights are listed in Canons 208-223 of the revised Code of Canon Law; additional rights are specified in other canons.

They are all equal in dignity because of their baptism and regeneration in Christ.

They are bound always to preserve communion with the Church.

According to their condition and circumstances, they should strive to lead a holy life and promote the growth and holiness of the Church.

They have the right and duty to work for the spread of the divine message of salvation to all peoples of all times and places.

They are bound to obey declarations and orders given by their pastors in their capacity as representatives of Christ, teachers of the faith and rectors of the Church.

They have the right to make known their needs, especially their spiritual needs, to pastors of the Church.

They have the right, and sometimes the duty, of making known to pastors and others of the faithful their opinions about things pertaining to the good of the Church.

They have the right to receive help from their pastors, from the spiritual goods of the Church and especially from the word of God and the sacraments.

They have the right to divine worship performed according to prescribed rules of their rite, and to follow their own form of spiritual life in line with the doctrine of the Church.

They have the right to freely establish and control associations for good and charitable purposes, to foster the Christian vocation in the world, and to hold meetings related to the accomplishment of these purposes.

They have the right to promote and support apostolic action but may not call it "Catholic" unless they have the consent of competent authority.

They have a right to a Christian education.

They have a right to freedom of inquiry in sacred studies, in accordance with the teaching authority of the Church.

They have a right to freedom in the choice of their state of life.

No one has the right to harm the good name of another person or to violate his or her right to maintain personal privacy.

They have the right to vindicate the rights they enjoy in the Church, and to defend themselves in a competent ecclesiastical forum.

They have the obligation to provide for the needs of the Church, with respect to things pertaining to divine worship, apostolic and charitable works, and the reasonable support of ministers of the Church.

They have the obligation to promote social justice and to help the poor from their own resources.

In exercising their rights, the faithful should have regard for the common good of the Church and for the rights and duties of others.

Church authority has the right to monitor the exercise of rights proper to the faithful, with the common good in view.

RIGHTS AND OBLIGATIONS OF LAY PERSONS

In addition to rights and obligations common to all the faithful and those stated in other canons, lay persons are bound by the obligations and enjoy the rights specified in these canons (224-231).

Lay persons, like all the faithful, are called by God to the apostolate in virtue of their baptism and confirmation. They have the obligation and right, individually or together in associations, to work for the spread and acceptance of the divine message of salvation among people everywhere; this obligation is more urgent in those circumstances in which people can hear the Gospel and get to know Christ only through them (lay persons).

They are bound to bring an evangelical spirit to bear on the order of temporal things and to give Christian witness in carrying out their secular pursuits.

Married couples are obliged to work for the building up of the people of God through their marital and family life.

Parents have the most serious obligation to provide for the Christian education of their children according to the doctrine handed down by the Church.

Lay persons have the same civil liberty as other citizens. In the use of this liberty, they should take care that their actions be imbued with an evangelical spirit. They should attend to the doctrine proposed by the magisterium of the Church but should take care that, in questions of opinion, they do not propose their own opinion as the doctrine of the Church.

Qualified lay persons are eligible to hold and perform the duties of ecclesiastical offices open to them in accord with the provisions of law.

Properly qualified lay persons can assist pastors of the Church as experts and counselors.

Lay persons have the obligation and enjoy the right to acquire knowledge of doctrine commensurate with their capacity and condition.

They have the right to pursue studies in the sacred sciences in pontifical universities or facilities and in institutes of religious sciences, and to obtain academic degrees.

If qualified, they are eligible to receive from ecclesiastical authority a mandate to teach sacred sciences.

Lay men can be invested by liturgical rite and in a stable manner in the ministries of lector and acolyte.

Lay persons, by temporary assignment, can

fulfill the office of lector in liturgical actions; likewise, all lay persons can perform the duties of commentator or cantor.

In cases of necessity and in the absence of the usual ministers, lay persons — even if not lectors or acolytes — can exercise the ministry of the word, lead liturgical prayers, confer baptism and distribute Communion, according to the prescripts of law.

Lay persons who devote themselves permanently or temporarily to the service of the Church are obliged to acquire the formation necessary for carrying out their duties in a proper manner.

They have a right to remuneration for their service which is just and adequate to provide for their own needs and those of their families; they also have a right to insurance, social security and health insurance.

SPECIAL APOSTOLATES AND GROUPS

Apostleship of the Sea: An international Catholic organization for the moral, social and spiritual welfare of seafarers and those involved in the maritime industry. It was founded in 1920 in Glasgow, Scotland, and formally approved by the Holy See in 1922. It is promoted and directed by the Pontifical Commission for Migrants and Tourism, Piazza San Calisto 16, Rome, Italy 00153. The U.S. unit is the Apostleship of the Sea in the United States, an affiliate of the NCCB-USCC, established in 1947. It serves port chaplains in 63 U.S. ports on the seacoasts, the Great Lakes, Alaska, Hawaii and American Samoa. Operations include a hospitality and welcoming program as well as counseling and spiritual services carried on by individual port chaplains through Catholic maritime clubs. Recent developments have emphasized the interfaith cooperation on the port level in seamen's ministry. The episcopal promoter of the conference is Most Rev. Rene Gracida, P.O. Box 2620, Corpus Christi, Tex. 78403. Rev. Raymond F. Rau is national director. Address of the national office is P.O. Box 4787, Corpus Christi, Tex. 78469. Also affiliated with the Apostleship of the Sea in the United States is the **National Catholic Conference for Seafarers.** The president is Rev. Msgr. Elmo Romagosa, 4219 Constance St., New Orleans, La. 70115.

Augustinian Volunteers (1983): Founded by Rev. Patrick H. O'Neill, O.S.A., to promote values of social justice by direct service to those who do not have access to educational, cultural, social and economic resources throughout the State of Florida. Volunteers, 21 years of age and older, serve for a one-year period. There are currently nine volunteers serving in urban and rural settings. Address: P.O. Box 702, Goldenrod, Fla. 32733.

Auxiliaries of Our Lady of the Cenacle (1878, France): An association of Catholic laywomen, under the direction of the Congregation of Our Lady of the Cenacle, who serve God through their own professions and life styles by means of vows. Members live a fully secular life consecrated according to the spirituality of the Cenacle and pursue individual apostolates. They number approximately 150 throughout the world. U.S. regional director: Sister Barbara Whittemore, r.c., 310 Cenacle Rd., Lake Ronkonkoma, N.Y. 11779.

Catholic Central Union of America (1855): One of the oldest Catholic lay organizations in the U.S., the Union is devoted to the development and vigor of Christian principles in personal, social, cultural, economic and civic life. It was the first society ever given an official mandate for Catholic Action by a committee of the American bishops, in 1936. The Central Bureau in St. Louis is the center for the separate but coordinated direction of the National Catholic Women's Union. The headquarters is also a publishing house (*Social Justice Review,* other publications), a library of German-Americana and Catholic Americana, a clearinghouse for information, and a center for works of charity. Aid is given to the missions, and maintenance. Union membership is approximately 8,100. Address: 3835 Westminster Place, St. Louis, Mo. 63108.

Catholic Medical Mission Board (1928): Founded by Dr. Paluel Flagg and the Rev. Edward Garesche, S.J. Its purposes are to gather and ship medical supplies for the sick poor in mission lands, and to recruit and assign medical and paramedical personnel to overseas mission hospitals and dispensaries. Since its foundation, it has shipped approximately 54 million pounds of supplies. In 1987, more than $12 million in medicines were shipped to 2,080 mission distribution centers in 46 countries. Also in 1987, 74 medical volunteers were placed in 16 countries. Rev. Joseph J. Walter, S.J., is the director. Office: 10 W. 17th Street, New York, N.Y. 10011.

Catholic Movement for Intellectual and Cultural Affairs of Pax Romana: The U.S. affiliate of Pax Romana — ICMICA (see International Catholic Organizations). *The Notebook* is published quarterly. The president is Edward J. Kirchner, 31 Chesterfield Road, Stamford, Conn. 06902.

Center for Applied Research in the Apostolate (CARA): A non-profit research center serving the planning needs of the Catholic Church. CARA gathers empirical data (from attitudinal surveys, demographic projections, etc.) for use by bishops, diocesan agencies, parishes and congregations of men and women religious. Francis Gillespie, S.J., is president. Offices are located at 3700 Oakview Terrace, N.E., Washington, D.C. 20017.

Christian Family Movement (CFM) (1947): Originating in Chicago and having a membership of married couples and individuals, its purpose is to Christianize family life and create communities conducive to Christian family life. Since 1968, CFM in the U.S. has included couples from all Christian churches. The International Confederation of Christian Family Movements embraces a worldwide membership. Executive directors, Gary and Kay Aitchison, Box 272, Ames, Iowa 50010.

Christian Life Communities: Formerly known as Sodalities of Our Lady, they are groups of men and women, adults and youth, joined with other people involved in living their full Christian vocation and commitment in the world. The governing principles and operating norms of Sodalities, revised in the spirit of documents of the Second Vatican Council, were promulgated and approved by Pope Paul VI in 1971. The Spiritual Exercises of St. Ignatius remain a specific source and characteristic of the spirituality of the movement. Christian Life Communities are located in more than 60 countries; the U.S. Federation is comprised of approximately 150 communities. National office: 6301 Lindell Blvd., St. Louis, Mo. 63108. The World Federation office is located in Rome.

Cursillo Movement: An instrument of Christian renewal designed to form and stimulate persons to engage in apostolic action individually and in the organized apostolate, in accordance with the mission which individuals have to transform the environments in which they live into Christian environments. The movement originated in Spain, where the first cursillo was held near Palma, Mallorca, in 1949. It was introduced in the U.S. in 1957 and is functioning in more than 180 dioceses. The method of the movement involves a three-day weekend called a cursillo and a follow-up program known as the post-cursillo.

The weekend is an intensive experience in Christian community living centered on Christ and built around 15 talks (10 by laymen, five by priests), active participation in discussions and related activities, the celebration of the liturgy. The follow-up program focuses on small weekly reunions of three to five persons and larger group reunions, called ultreyas, in which participants share experiences and insights derived from their prayer life, study and apostolic action. The movement operates within the framework of diocesan and parish pastoral plans, and functions autonomously in each diocese under the direction of the bishop. Responsibility for growth and effectiveness rests with a diocesan leaders' school, a diocesan secretariat, or both. Bishop James S. Sullivan of Fargo, N. Dak., is episcopal advisor to the movement. Gerald P. Hughes is executive director of the National Cursillo Center, P.O. Box 210226, Dallas, Tex. 75211.

Frontier Apostolate (1956): Volunteers for a minimum of two years' service in their professional line (teachers, secretaries, houseparents, etc.) in the Diocese of Prince George, British Columbia, Canada. More than 2,600 have served since the start of the corps by Bishop Fergus O'Grady. There are about 150 men and women from 8 different countries actively engaged in works throughout the diocese. Address: Bishop O'Connor, O.M.I., College Rd., P.O. Box 7000, Prince George, B.C., Canada V2N 3Z2.

Grail, The (1921): An international movement of women concerned about the full development of all peoples, working in education, religious, social and cultural areas. Founded by Rev. Jacques van Ginneken, S.J., in The Netherlands, it was introduced in the U.S. in 1940. The Grail is at work in: Australia, Brazil, Canada, Costa Rica, Egypt, France, Germany, India, Italy, Kenya, The Netherlands, Nigeria, Philippines, Portugal, South Africa. Tanzania, Uganda, United States. U.S. headquarters: Grailville, Loveland, Ohio 45140. International Secretariat: Duisburger Strasse 470, 4330 Mulheim, West Germany.

International Liaison of Lay Volunteers in Mission (1963): The U.S. Catholic network of lay mission programs acts as a clearinghouse for promotion, recruitment and referral of lay missioners who serve interdenominationally in church missions and public and private volunteer agencies throughout the world. The organization also assists mission agencies to facilitate participation by lay persons in ministries of the Church. Publications include *The Response,* an annual directory of lay mission opportunities and a quarterly newsletter. Sister Ellen Cavanaugh, R.S.M., is the executive director. National office: 4121 Harewood Rd. N.E., P.O. Box 29149, Washington, D.C. 20017.

Jesuit Volunteer Corps (1956): Sponsored by the Society of Jesus in the U.S. Men and women volunteers work throughout the U.S. serving the poor directly and working for structural change. They live a simple life-style in community and seek to develop spiritually. Address for information: 18th and Thompson Sts., Philadelphia, Pa. 19121.

Lay Mission-Helpers Association (1955): It trains and assigns men and women for work in overseas apostolates for periods of three years. Approximately 600 members of the association have served in overseas assignments since 1955. The Rev. Msgr. Joseph Alzugaray is director of the association. Headquarters: 1531 West Ninth St., Los Angeles, Calif. 90015.

The **Mission Doctors Association** recruits, trains and sends Catholic physicians and their families to mission hospitals and clinics throughout the world for tours of two to three years. Address: 1531 W. Ninth St., Los Angeles, Calif. 90015.

Legion of Mary (1921): Founded in Dublin, its purposes are the sanctification of its members and spiritual service to others. It is one of the largest lay organizations in the Church. U.S. address for information: The Legion of Mary, St. Louis Regional Senatus, Box 1313, St. Louis, Mo. 63188. The supreme governing body has offices at De Montfort House, North Brunswick St., Dublin 7, Ireland.

Movement for a Better World (1952): An international movement founded by Rev. Riccardo Lombardi, S.J. The U.S. promoting group, like its counterparts in other countries, conducts various types of renewal programs with a distinctive communitarian thrust for the purpose of motivating Christian witness and action for making a better world in accordance with the plan of God. Address for information: Sr. Mary Byrnes, 102 Magnolia Ave., Jersey City, N.J. 07306. The movement is a non-governmental organization with the United Nations.

Movimiento Familiar Cristiano — USA (MFC) (1969): Movement of Catholic Hispanic families united in their efforts to promote the human and Christian virtues of the family so that it may become a force that forms persons, transmits the faith and contributes to the total development of the community. National president couple, Baldomero and Mavi Torres. Rev. Eduardo Villa is national spiritual director. Address: P.O. Box 610, Roma, Tex. 78584.

Pax Christi USA (1973): U.S. section of Pax Christi (see International Catholic Organizations). Founded to establish peacemaking as a priority for the American Catholic Church, to work for disarmament, primacy of conscience, a just world order, education for peace, and alternatives to violence. *Pax Christi USA* is published quarterly; membership, 9,000. Sr. Mary Lou Kownacki, O.S.B., is national coordinator. Address: 348 E. 10th St., Erie, Pa. 16503.

Regis College Lay Apostolate (1950): Founded by Sister Mary John Sullivan, C.S.J., it enlists college graduates for a year of teaching service in home and overseas missions. More than 250 lay apostles from Regis College and more than 400 from other colleges have served since the beginning of the program. Headquarters: Regis College, Weston, Mass. 02193

Southwest Volunteer Apostolate (1970): Places volunteers for work among the Indians and Spanish-speaking of the Diocese of Gallup. Mailing address: P. O. Box 626, Gallup, N.M. 87301.

Center of Concern (1971): An independent, public-interest group engaged in analysis, education and advocacy relating to issues of global concern. Address: 3700 13th St. N.E., Washington, D.C. 20017.

CATHOLIC YOUTH ORGANIZATIONS

Boy Scouts in the Catholic Church: The National Catholic Committee on Scouting works with the Boy Scouts of America in developing the character and spiritual life of 600,000 members in units chartered to Catholic and non-Catholic organizations. *Boy's Life*. Committee Chairman, Marvin L. Smith, 4416 Basswood Lane, Bellaire, Tex. 77401.

Camp Fire, Inc. (1910): 4601 Madison Ave., Kansas City, Mo. 64112. The National Catholic Committee for Girl Scouts and Camp Fire, a standing committee of the National Federation for Catholic Youth Ministry, cooperates with Camp Fire. To help young people learn and grow in their individual ways through participation in enjoyable activities. Open to youth up to 21 years of age. Membership: approximately 500,000 (no exact statistics available on number of Catholics participating).

Catholic Forester Youth Program, Catholic Order of Foresters: 425 W. Shuman Blvd., Naperville, Ill. 60566. To develop Christian leadership and promote the moral, intellectual, social and physical growth of its youth members. *Catholic Forester*. Membership: youth up to 16 years of age — about 19,000 in 799 local courts in U.S. the High Chief Ranger is John A. Gorski.

Catholic Youth Organization (CYO): Name of parish-centered diocesan Catholic youth programs throughout the country. CYO promotes a program of spiritual, social and physical activities. The original CYO was organized by Bishop Bernard Sheil of Chicago in 1930.

Columbian Squires (1925): One Columbus Plaza, New Haven, Conn. 06507. Junior organization of the Knights of Columbus. To train and develop leadership through active participation in a well-organized program of activities. Membership: Catholic young men, 12-18 years old. More than 22,000 in over 900 circles (local units) active in the U.S., Canada, Puerto Rico, Mexico, Guam and the Philippines. *Squires Newsletter,* monthly.

Girl Scouts of the U.S.A.: 830 Third Ave., New York, N.Y. 10022. Girls from archdioceses and dioceses in the U.S. and its possessions participate in Girl Scouting. The National Catholic Committee for Girl Scouts and Camp Fire, a standing committee of the National Federation for Catholic Youth Ministry, cooperates with Girl Scouts of the U.S.A. *Girl Scout Leader*. Membership: approximately three million (no exact statistics available on number of Catholic girls participating).

Holy Childhood Association (Pontifical Association of the Holy Childhood) (1843): 1720 Massachusetts Ave. N.W., Washington, D.C. 20036. The official children's mission-aid society of the Church; provides financial assistance to children in 94 developing countries. Produces mission and global education material for teachers and students in Catholic schools and religious education programs. *It's Our World,* four times a year in three editions. National Director, Rev. Francis W. Wright, C.S.Sp.

Junior Catholic Daughters of the Americas: 10 W. 71st St., New York, N.Y. 10023. A major department of the Catholic Daughters of the Americas. To promote development of the whole person, service to others, spiritual growth. Membership: Juniors (11 to 18 years old); Juniorettes (6 to 10 years old).

Knights of the Altar International (1938): P.O. Box 5476, Lakeland, Fla. 33807 (national office). Society for altar boys. *Young Heralds,* 6 times a year. Membership: 3,000 units in the U.S. and foreign countries.

National Catholic Forensic League (1952): To develop articulate Catholic leaders through an inter-diocesan program of speech and debate activities. *Newsletter,* quarterly. Membership: 600 schools; membership open to Catholic, private and public schools through the local diocesan league. Secretary-Treasurer, Richard Gaudette, 21 Nancy Rd., Milford, Mass. 01757.

National Catholic Young Adult Ministry Association (1982): 3900-A Harewood Rd. N.E., Washington, D.C. 20017. To strengthen the professional competence of those engaged in young adult ministry. President, Rev. Ken Stonecipher.

National Christ Child Society Inc. (1887): 5100 Wisconsin Ave. N.W., Washington, D.C. 20016. Founder, Mary V. Merrick. A non-profit association of Catholic volunteers dedicated to the service of needy children and youth regardless of race or creed. The service has been expanded to include underprivileged adults. Membership: approximately 8,000 adult and junior members in 34 cities in U.S. President, Mrs. Frank J. Wear.

**National Federation for Catholic Youth Ministry (1982): 3900-A Harewood Rd. N.E., Washington, D.C. 20017. To foster the development of youth ministry in the United States through CYO and other expressions of ministry to, with, by and for youth. *Catholic Teen,* monthly. Executive Director, Jim Knowles.

St. Dominic Savio Club (1950): Marian Shrine, Filor's Lane, West Haverstraw, N.Y. 10993. A character-building, leadership and public service program conducted in Catholic schools, CCD classes and home/neighborhood units. *Savio Notes,* quarterly. Membership: students in grades three through twelve — more than 1,500,000 since its founding. Director, Rev. Peter Malloy, S.D.B. members in U.S., Canada and nine foreign countries.

Young Christian Students: 7436 W. Harrison, Forest Park, Ill. 60130. A student movement for Christian personal and social change. Membership: 500 in high schools and parishes.

COLLEGE SOCIETIES

Alpha Sigma Nu (1915): Marquette Univ., 1324 W. Wisconsin Ave., Milwaukee, Wis. 53233 (national headquarters). National honor society of the 28 Jesuit colleges and universities of the U.S.; members chosen on the basis of scholarship, loyalty and service; 1,400 student and 25,000 alumni members. Member, Association of College Honor Societies. Gamma Pi Epsilon (1924) merged with Alpha Sigma Nu in 1973 to form society open to men and women. Executive Director, Ann J. Panlener.

Delta Epsilon Sigma (1939): Barry University, Miami Shores, Fla. 33161. National scholastic honor society for students, faculty and alumni of colleges and universities with a Catholic tradition. Membership: 40,000 in 100 chapters. Secretary, Dr. J. Patrick Lee.

Kappa Gamma Pi (1926): A national Catholic college honor society for graduates who, in addition to academic excellence, have shown outstanding leadership in extra-curricular activities. *Kappa Gamma Pi News,* five times a year. Membership: approximately 29,000 in 127 colleges; 20 alumnae chapters in metropolitan areas. Executive Secretary, Marjorie Durbin, 2415 Hillcrest Dr., Stow, Ohio 44224.

Phi Kappa Theta: 3901 W. 86th St., Indianapolis, Ind. 46268. National social fraternity with a Catholic heritage. Merger (1959) of Phi Kappa Fraternity, founded at Brown Univ. in 1889, and Theta Kappa Phi Fraternity, founded at Lehigh Univ. in 1919. *The Temple Magazine* quarterly, and newsletter, *The Sun.* Membership: 2,500 undergraduate and 40,000 alumni in 58 collegiate and 15 alumni chapters. Executive Director, Douglas D. Dilling.

National Catholic Student Coalition: The U.S. affiliate of Pax Romana — IMCS (see International Catholic Organizations). Publishes *The Catholic Collegian.* Address: c/o CCMA Executive Office, 300 College Park, Dayton, Ohio 45469.

ASSOCIATIONS, MOVEMENTS, SOCIETIES IN THE U.S.

(Principal source: Almanac survey.)
See *Index for other associations, movements and societies covered elsewhere.*

Academy of American Franciscan History (1944), Box 34440, Bethesda, Md. 20817. Dir., Rev. James McManamon, O.F.M.

Albanian Catholic Information Center (1966), Box 1217 University, Santa Clara, Calif. 95053; To encourage and restore religious freedom in Albania and to promote Albania's religious and cultural heritage. Director, Rev. Leo G. Neal, O.F.M. Conv. *Albanian Catholic Bulletin,* annually; circulation 1,500 in North and South America, Europe, Australia, Japan and New Zealand. Editor, Gjon Sinishta.

American Benedictine Academy (1947). To promote Benedictine values in contemporary culture. Pres., Sr. Ruth Fox, O.S.B., Sacred Heart Priory, Richardton, N.D. 58652.

American Catholic Correctional Chaplains Association (1952), 350 in 475 institutions. Pres., Rev. Francis Menie; Sec., Rev. John Noe, Federal Correctional Institution, Ashland, Ky. 41101.

American Catholic Historical Association (1919), Catholic University of America, Washington, D.C. 20064. *The Catholic Historical Review,* quarterly. Sec.-Treas., Rev. Robert Trisco.

American Catholic Philosophical Association (1926), Catholic University of America, Washington, D.C. 20064. *New Scholasticism,* quarterly, *Proceedings,* annually.

American Committee on Italian Migration (1952), 352 W. 44th St., New York, N.Y. 10036; 6,000. *ACIM Newsletter* and *ACIM Nuova Via,* 6 times a year. Sec., Rev. Joseph A. Cogo, C.S.

American Friends of the Vatican Library (1981), 157 Lakeshore Rd., Grosse Point Farms, Mich. 48236. Sponsored by the Catholic Library Association. To assist in supporting the Vatican Library: *AMICI,* newsletter.

Ancient Order of Hibernians in America, Inc. (1836); 120,000. *National Hibernian Digest,* bimonthly. Nat. Sec., Thomas McNabb, 31 Logan St., Auburn, N.Y. 13021.

Apostleship of Prayer (1844-France; 1861-U.S.): 3 Stephen Ave., New Hyde Park, N.Y. 11040. Promotes Daily Offering and Sacred Heart devotion.

Apostolate for Family Consecration (1975), St. Joseph Center, 6305 Third Ave., P.O. Box 220, Kenosha, Wis. 53141; 26,000 members. Family reinforcement by transforming neighborhoods into God-centered communities in the spirit of Pope John Paul II. Pres., Jerome F. Coniker.

Archconfraternity of Christian Mothers (Christian Mothers) (1881), 220 37th St., Pittsburgh, Pa. 15201; over 3,500 branches. Dir., Rev. Bertin Roll, O.F.M. Cap.

Archconfraternity of the Holy Ghost (1912), Holy Ghost Fathers, 2401 Bristol Pike, Bensalem, Pa. 19020 (U.S. headquarters). Nat. Dir., Rev. Albert Seichepine, C.S.Sp.

Archdiocese for the Military Services Seminary

Education Fund (1988), 962 Wayne Ave., Suite 500, Silver Spring, Md., 20910. Bishp Angelo T. Acerra, President.

Association for Religious and Value Issues in Counseling (1962), division of American Association for Counseling and Development. *Counseling and Values,* 2 times a year. Address, 5999 Stevenson Ave., Alexandria, Va. 22304.

Association for Social Economics (formerly the Catholic Economic Association) (1941), Marquette University, Milwaukee, Wis. 53233; 1,300. *Review of Social Economy,* quarterly.

Association of Catholic Diocesan Archivists (1983), c/o 7200 Douglaston Parkway, Douglaston, N.Y. 11362; To work for establishment of an archival program in every American diocese. *ACDA Bulletin,* twice a year. Pres., Rev. Harry M. Culkin, Diocese of Brooklyn.

Association of Catholic Trade Unionists (1937), 12 Holly Hills Dr., Woodstock, N.Y. 12498. Exec. Sec., John C. Donohue.

Association of Marian Helpers (1944), Stockbridge, Mass. 01263; 1,050,000, mostly in U.S. *The Marian Helpers Bulletin,* quarterly.

Association of Romanian Catholics of America (1948), 4309 Olcott Ave., E. Chicago, Ind. 46312.

Beginning Experience (1973), 2701 W. Chicago Blvd., Detroit, Mich. 48206; 140 teams throughout the world. Weekend program to help divorced, widowed and separated start a new beginning in their lives. Exec. Dir., Sr. Tarianne DeYonker, O.P.

Calix Society (1947), 7601 Wayzata Blvd., Minneapolis, Minn. 55426; 2,000 members in U.S. and Canada; *Chalice,* bimonthly. Association of Catholic alcoholics maintaining their sobriety through affiliation with and participation in Alcoholics Anonymous. Dir., R. D. Dickinson.

Canon Law Society of America (1939), Catholic University, Washington, D.C. 20064. To further research and study in canon law; 1,850. Exec. Coord., Rev. Edward G. Pfnausch.

Cardinal Mindszenty Foundation (CMF) (1958), P.O. Box 11321, St. Louis, Mo. 63105. To combat communism with knowledge and facts. Exec. Dir., Eleanor Schlafly.

Catholic Aid Association (1878), 3499 N. Lexington Ave., St. Paul, Minn. 55126; 80,000. *Catholic Aid News,* monthly. Fraternal life insurance society. Pres., F. L. Spanier.

Catholic Alumni Clubs International (1957), To advance social, cultural and spiritual well-being of members. Membership limited to single Catholics with professional education; 7,000 in 47 clubs in U.S. International chaplain, Rev. John Urell; Pres., Donald Luebbering. Address, White Flint Mall, P.O. Box 2801, Kensington, Md. 20895.

Catholic Biblical Association of America (1936), Catholic University of America, Washington, D.C. 20064; 1,122. *The Catholic Biblical Quarterly; Old Testament Abstracts,* monograph series.

Catholic Book Publishers Association (1987), c/o Michael Glazier, Inc. 1935 W. 4th St., Wilmington, Del. 19805. Pres., Michael Glazier.

Catholic Center, The, 721 Second St., N.E., Washington, D.C. 20002. Conducts training and information programs to prepare Catholics for public activism. Dir., Angela Grimm.

Catholic Commission on Intellectual and Cultural Affairs (CCICA) (1946), P.O. Box 21, Notre Dame, Ind. 46556; 262. Exec. Dir., Dr. Konrad Schaum.

Catholic Daughters of the Americas (1903), 10 W. 71st St., New York, N.Y. 10023; 155,000. *Share Magazine.* Nat. Regent, Miss Rayola McLaughlin.

Catholic Family Life Insurance (1868), 1572 E. Capitol Dr., Milwaukee, Wis. 53211; 41,000. *The Family Friend,* quarterly. Pres., David L. Springob.

Catholic Golden Age: National Headquarters, Scranton, Pa. 18503; 800,000. *CGA World Magazine,* quarterly. For Catholics over 50 years of age. Pres., Thomas D. Hinton.

Catholic Guardian Society (1913), 1011 First Ave., New York, N.Y. 10022. Exec. Dir., James P. O'Neill.

Catholic Home Bureau for Dependent Children (1898), 1011 First Ave., New York, N.Y. 10022. Exec. Dir., Sr. Una McCormack.

Catholic Interracial Council of New York, Inc. (1934), 16 W. 36th St., New York, N.Y. 10018. To promote racial and social justice. *Interracial Review,* quarterly. Exec. Dir., John J. Garra.

Catholic Knights of America (1877), 1850 Dalton St., Cincinnati, O. 45214; 7,800. *Catholic Knights of America Journal,* monthly. Fraternal insurance society.

Catholic Knights of Ohio (1891): 16010 Detroit Ave., Lakewood, O. 44107; 12,000 in Ohio and Kentucky. *The Messenger,* monthly. Fraternal insurance society. Pres., Victor D. Huss.

Catholic Kolping Society of America (1923), 22515 Masonic Blvd., St. Clair Shores, Mich. 48082. *Kolping Banner,* monthly. International society concerned with spiritual, educational and physical development of members.

Catholic Lawyers' Guild. Organization usually on a diocesan basis, under different titles.

Catholic League (1943), 1200 N. Ashland Ave., Chicago, Ill. 60622. Exec. Dir., Most Rev. Alfred Abramowicz.

Catholic Library Association (1921), 461 W. Lancaster Avenue, Haverford, Pa., 19041; 2,210. *Catholic Library World,* bimonthly; *Catholic Periodical and Literature Index.* Pres., Irma C. Godfrey; Exec. Dir., Bro. John T. Corrigan, C.F.X.

Catholic Near East Welfare Association (1926), 1011 First Ave., New York, N.Y. 10022. A papal agency for humanitarian and pastoral support, under the jurisdiction of the Congregation for the Oriental Churches. Missionary service for all Near and Middle East countries, India and Ethiopia. Acting Sec. Gen., Rev. Msgr. Robert L. Stern.

Catholic One Parent Organization (COPO): To give widows and widowers an opportunity to meet others in the same situation, blending social and spiritual programs. Organized in various dioceses.

Catholic Order of Foresters (1883), 425 W.

Shuman Blvd., Naperville, Ill. 60566; 150,000. *The Catholic Forester,* bimonthly. Fraternal insurance society. High Chief Ranger, John A. Gorski.

Catholic Pamphlet Society (1938), 500 Maryvale Dr., Cheektowago, N.Y. 14225. Parish pamphlet rack distributors. Dir., Rev. Walter O. Kern.

Catholic Peace Fellowship (1964), 339 Lafayette St., New York, N.Y. 10012; 5,500, *CPF Bulletin.* Peace education and direct action projects, development of the nonviolent tradition within the Catholic Church; draft counseling and nonviolence training. Coord., Bill O'Fenloch.

Catholic Press Association of the U.S., Inc. (1911), 119 N. Park Ave., Rockville Centre, N.Y. 11570. *The Catholic Journalist* monthly; *Catholic Press Directory,* annually. Pres., Rev. John T. Catoir; interim exec. dir., Regina A. Salzman.

Catholic Theological Society of America (1946), Office of Secretary, Loyola University, Chicago, Ill. 60626; 1,200. *Proceedings,* annually. Pres. (1988-89), Rev. John Boyle.

Catholic War Veterans (1935), 419 N. Lee St., Alexandria, Va. 22314; 500 posts, *Catholic War Veteran,* bimonthly.

Catholic Worker Movement (1933), 36 E. First St., New York, N.Y. 10003. *The Catholic Worker,* 8 times a year. Lay apostolate founded by Peter Maurin and Dorothy Day; has Houses of Hospitality in over 60 U.S. cities and several communal farms in various parts of the country. Promotes pacifism, personalism, voluntary poverty and anarchism in that it is decentralist, and believes in what the popes have termed the principle of subsidiarity, urging decentralization in the school system, community control, and in the economic field credit unions, cooperatives and unions of workers and mutual aid.

Catholic Workman (Katolicky Delnik) (1891), P.O. Box 47, New Prague, Minn. 56071; 16,007. *Catholic Workman,* monthly. Fraternal and insurance society.

Catholics United for Spiritual Action, Inc. (CUSA) (1947), 63 Wall St., New York, N.Y. 10005 (legal office); 1,200. An apostolate for the disabled. Admin. Leader, Miss Anna Marie Sopko, 176 W. 8th St., Bayonne, N.J. 07002 (national central office).

Catholics United for the Faith (1968), 45 Union Ave., New Rochelle, N.Y. 10801; 15,000 worldwide, *Lay Witness,* monthly. Lay apostolate founded in response to Vatican II's call to the laity. Pres., James Likoudis.

Central Association of the Miraculous Medal (1915), 475 E. Chelten Ave., Philadelphia, Pa. 19144. *Miraculous Medal,* quarterly. Dir., Rev. Robert P. Cawley, C.M.

Chaplains' Aid Association, Inc. (1917), 962 Wayne Ave., Silver Spring, Md. 20910. Pres., Most Rev. Joseph T. Ryan.

Christopher Movement (1945), 12 E. 48th St., New York, N.Y. 10017. Without formal organization or meetings, the movement stimulates personal initiative and responsible action in line with Christian principles, particularly in the fields of education, government, family life and communications. Christopher radio and TV programs are broadcast by more than 805 radio and TV stations; 750,000 copies of *Christopher News Notes* are distributed 10 times a year without subscription fee; 160 weekly newspapers carry Christopher columns. Dir., Rev. John Catoir.

Citizens for Educational Freedom (1959): Nonsectarian group concerned with parents' right to educational choice by means of tuition tax credits and vouchers. Exec. dir., Sr. Renee Oliver, O.S.U., 1611 N. Kent St., Arlington, Va. 22209.

Confraternity Home Study Services, 1701 W. St. Joseph St., Perryville, Mo. 63775.

Confraternity of Catholic Clergy (1976), 21-72 43rd St., Astoria, N.Y. 11105 (national office). Association of priests pledged to pursuit of personal holiness, loyalty to the Pope, theological study and adherence to authentic teachings of the Catholic faith. Pres., Rev. Msgr. Nelson Logal.

Confraternity of the Immaculate Conception of Our Lady of Lourdes (1874), Box 561, Notre Dame, Ind. 46556. Distributors of Lourdes water.

Confraternity of the Most Holy Rosary: See Rosary Altar Society.

Convert Movement Our Apostolate (CMOA) (1945), formerly Convert Makers of America, c/o Our Lady of Grace Rectory, 430 Avenue W, Brooklyn, N.Y. 11223. *Bulletin* quarterly. To train and assist lay persons on a parish level to discuss and present the Faith to interested persons on a one-to-one basis. Dir., Msgr. Erwin A. Juraschek.

Czech Catholic Union of Texas (K.J.T.) (1889), 214 Colorado St., La Grange, Tex. 78945; 17,500. *Nasinec,* weekly, and *K. J. T. News,* monthly. Fraternal and insurance society. Pres., Laddie Matula, Sr.

Damien-Dutton Society for Leprosy Aid, Inc. (1944), 616 Bedford Ave., Bellmore, N.Y. 11710; 25,000. *Damien Dutton Call,* quarterly. Provides medicine, rehabilitation and research for conquest of leprosy. Pres., Howard E. Crouch, Dir., Sr. Mary Augustine, S.M.S.M.

Daughters of Isabella (1897), P.O. Box 9585, New Haven, Conn. 06535; 120,000. To unite Catholic women into a fraternal order for spiritual benefits and to promote higher ideals within society.

Edith Stein Guild, Inc. (1955), Our Lady of Victory Church, 60 William St., New York, N.Y. 10005; quarterly newsletter. Promotes Judaeo-Christian understanding, extends friendship to Catholics of Jewish background, spreads knowledge of life and writings of Bl. Edith Stein (Sister Benedicta of the Cross).

Enthronement of the Sacred Heart in the Home (1907), 3 Adams St., Fairhaven, Mass. 02719; over 2,500,000.

Eymard League (1948), 5384 Wilson Mills Rd., Cleveland, O. 44143; approximately 24,000.

Families for Prayer (1982), 775 Madison Ave., Albany, N.Y. 12208. *Let's Pray Together,* weekly. Conducts family-centered parish renewal programs. Dir., Rev. John J. Gurley, C.S.C.

Family Rosary, Inc., The (1942), Executive Park Drive, Albany, N.Y. 12203. Pres., Rev. Patrick Peyton, C.S.C.

Federation of Diocesan Liturgical Commissions (FDLC) (1969), P.O. Box 29039, Washington, D.C. 20017. Voluntary association of personnel from diocesan liturgical commissions of the U.S. The main purpose is promotion of the liturgy as the heart of Christian life, especially in the parish community. Exec. Sec., Rev. Michael J. Spillane.

Fellowship of Catholic Scholars (1977), Prof. William May, president, Catholic University of America, Washington, D.C. 20064; 700 members. Interdisciplinary research and publications of Catholic scholars in accord with the magisterium of the Catholic Church.

First Catholic Slovak Ladies' Association, USA (1892), 24950 Chagrin Blvd., Beachwood, Ohio 44122; 102,000. *Fraternally Yours*, monthly. Fraternal insurance society. Pres., Anna S. Granchay.

First Catholic Slovak Union (Jednota) (1890), FCSU Corporate Center, 6611 Rockside Rd., Independence, Ohio 44131; 96,206. *Jednota*, weekly. Sec./Treas., Cyril M. Ferenchak.

Franciscan Apostolate of the Way of the Cross (1949), 103 Arch St., Boston, Mass. 02107. Distributes religious materials to the sick and shut-in. Dir., Rev. Robert Lynch, O.F.M.

Free the Fathers (1983), 1120 Appleton Circle, Signal Mountain, Tenn. 37377. To work for the freedom of bishops and priests imprisoned in China. Pres., John M. Davies.

Gabriel Richard Institute (1949), 2315 Orleans Ave., Detroit, Mich. 48207. Conducts Christopher leadership courses in 18 dioceses.

Gelasian Guild (1976), Association of Catholic attorneys working with the USCC; concerned with scholarly study of legal questions affecting Church-state relations. Pres., Rev. Charles Whelan, S.J., 106 W. 56th St., New York, N.Y. 10019.

Guard of Honor of the Immaculate Heart of Mary (1932), 135 West 31st St., New York, N.Y. 10001. An archconfraternity approved by the Holy See whose members cultivate devotion to the Blessed Virgin Mary, particularly through a daily Guard Hour of Prayer.

Guild of Our Lady of Ransom (1948), c/o St. Timothy's Rectory, 650 Nichols St., Norwood, Mass. 02062. Boston archdiocesan ministry for spiritual aid and rehabilitation of inmates of penal institutions. Exec. Dir., Rev. Dr. Joseph P. McDermott.

Guild of St. Paul (1937), 230 Waller Ave., Lexington, Ky. 40503; For converts. Nat. Spir. Dir., Rev. Msgr. Leonard Nienaber.

Holy Name Society: Founded in 1274 by Blessed John Vercelli, master general of the Dominicans, to promote reverence for the Holy Name of Jesus; this is still the principal purpose of the society, which also develops lay apostolic programs in line with directives of the Second Vatican Council. Introduced in the U.S. by Dominican Father Charles H. McKenna in 1870-71, the society has about 5 million members on diocesan and parochial levels. With approval of the local bishop and pastor, women as well as men may be members.

Holy Name Society, National Association (NAHNS) (1970), P.O. Box 26038, Baltimore, Md. 21224. *Holy Name Newsletter*, monthly. Association of diocesan and parochial Holy Name Societies.

Hungarian Catholic League of America, Inc. (1945), 30 E. 30th St., New York, N.Y. 10016. Member of the National Catholic Resettlement Council. *Catholic Hungarian Sunday*, weekly. Pres., Rev. Msgr. John S. Sabo.

International Institute of the Heart of Jesus (1972), 7700 Blue Mound Rd., Milwaukee Wis. 53213 (business office); Delegacion Latino- americana, IIHJ, Apartado Aereo 3047, Transv. 28 No. 35A-25, Bogota 1, Colombia (president's office). Promote awareness and appreciation of the mystery of the Heart of Christ and establish an international forum for the apostolate. Pres., Rev. Roger Vekemans, S.J.

Italian Catholic Federation, Central Council (1924), 1801 Van Ness Ave., San Francisco, Calif. 94109; 25,000; *Bollettino*, monthly.

John Carroll Society, The (1951), 1722 Eye St., Washington, D.C. 20006. Pres., James E. Murray, Esq.

Judean Society, Inc., The (1966), 1075 Space Park Way No. 336, Mt. View, Calif. 94043; over 800. International organization for divorced Catholic women. Self-help, mutual-help counseling groups. Foundress/Internatl., Dir., Frances A. Miller.

Knights of Peter Claver (1909), and **Ladies of St. Peter Claver** (1922), 1825 Orleans Ave., New Orleans, La. 70116. 17,000. *The Claverite*, biannually. Fraternal and aid society. National Chaplain, Most Rev. Joseph A. Francis, S.V.D.

Knights of St. John, Supreme Commandery (1886), 6517 Charles Ave., Parma, O. 44129; Sup. Sec., Brig. Gen. Salvatore La Bianca.

Knights of the Immaculata (Militia Immaculatae, M.I.) (1917), National Center, 1600 W. Park Ave., Libertyville, Ill. 60048; canonically established with international headquarters in Rome. A pious association for evangelization and catechesis beginning with members' own inner renewal, through the intercession of the Blessed Virgin Mary.

Ladies of Charity of the United States, Association of (1960), 7806 Natural Bridge Rd., P.O. Box 5730, St. Louis, Mo. 63121; 40,000 in U.S. International Association founded by St. Vincent de Paul in 1617.

Latin Liturgy Association (1975), Office of Chairman, Prof. Anthony Lo Bello, Box 29, Dept. of Mathematics, Allegheny College, Meadville, Pa. 16335; 2,000. To promote the use of the Latin language and music in the approved rites of the Church.

Lithuanian Groups: Ateitininkai, members of Lithuanian Catholic Federation Ateitis (1910), 7235 Sacramento Ave., Chicago, Ill. 60629; to promote Catholic action and uphold Lithuanian heritage among youth; *Ateitis*, bimonthly; Pres., Juozas Polikaitis. Knights of Lithuania (1913), educa-

Associations, Movements, Societies

tional-fraternal organization; *Vytis,* monthly; Pres., Loretta T. Stukas, 234 Sunlit Dr., Watchung, N.J. 07060. Lithuanian Catholic Alliance (1886), 73 S. Washington St., Wilkes-Barre, Pa. 18701; 118 branches; *Garsas,* monthly; fraternal insurance organization; Pres., Thomas E. Mack. Lithuanian Roman Catholic Federation of America (1906), umbrella organization for Lithuanian parishes and organizations; *The Observer,* monthly; Pres., Saulius Kuprys, 4545 W. 63rd St., Chicago, Ill. 60629. Lithuanian Roman Catholic Priests' League (1909): religious-professional association, Pres., Albert Contons, 50 Orton-Marotta Way, Boston, Mass. 02127. Lithuanian Catholic Religious Aid, Inc. (1961), 351 Highland Blvd., Brooklyn, N.Y. 11207; to assist persecuted Catholics in Lithuania; Chairman, Most Rev. Vincent Brizgys; Pres., Most Rev. Paul Baltakis; Exec. Dir., Rev. Casimir Pugevicius.

Little Flower Mission League (1957), P.O. Box 25, Plaucheville, La. 71362. Sponsored by the Brothers of the Holy Eucharist.

Little Flower Society (1923), 1313 Frontage Rd.; Darien, Ill. 60559; 200,000 Nat. Dir., Rev. Terrence L. Sempowski, O. Carm.

Liturgical Conference, The, 1017 12th St. N.W., Washington, D.C. 20005. *Liturgy, Accent on Worship, Homily Service.* Education, research and publication programs for renewing and enriching Christian liturgical life. Ecumenical. Exec. Dir., Rachel Reeder.

Loyal Christian Benefit Association (1890), P.O. Box 13005, Erie, Pa. 16514; 56,623. *The Fraternal Leader,* quarterly.

Marian Movement of Priests (1972), P.O. Box 8, St. Francis, Me. 04774 (U.S.); Via Mercalli, 23, 20122 Milano, Italy (internatl. headquarters); 20,000 clergy, religious and laity (U.S.). Spiritual renewal through consecration to the Immaculate Heart of Mary. Pres. Rev. Albert G. Roux.

Mariological Society of America (1949), Sec., Rev. Theodore A. Koehler, S.M., Marian Library, University of Dayton, Dayton, O. 45469; 400. *Marian Studies,* annually. Founded by Rev. Juniper B. Carol, O.F.M., and other priest-scholars to promote greater appreciation of and scientific research in Marian theology.

Maryheart Crusaders, The (1964), 22 Button St., Meriden, Conn. 06450; 3,000. To reunite fallen-away Catholics and promote religious education for adults. Pres., Louise D'Angelo.

Men of the Sacred Heart (1964), Shrine of the Sacred Heart, Harleigh, Pa. 18225. Promote enthronement of Sacred Heart.

Missionary Association of Catholic Women (1916), 3501 S. Lake Dr., P.O. Box 2018, Milwaukee, Wis. 53201. Pres., Donald J. Mueller.

Missionary Cenacle Apostolate (MCA) (1909), General Office, Colleen Green, 12902 View Ridge Rd., Santa Ana, Calif. 92705; 600. To foster spiritual and apostolic life of the laity through prayer, instruction, example and service.

Missionary Vehicle Association, Inc. (MIVA America) (1971), 1326 Perry St., N.E., Washington, D.C. 20017. To raise funds and distribute them annually as vehicle grants to missionaries working with the poor in Third World countries. Nat. Dir., Rev. Philip De Rea, M.S.C.

Morality in Media, Inc. (1962), 475 Riverside Dr., New York, N.Y. 10115; 50,000 members. Newsletter, bimonthly; *The Obscenity Law Bulletin,* bimonthly. To stop traffic in pornography constitutionally and effectively, and promote principles of love, truth and taste in the media. A major project is the National Obscenity Law Center which provides legal information for prosecutors and other attorneys. Pres., Rev. Paul J. Murphy, S.J.

National Assembly of Religious Women (NARW): Founded as the National Assembly of Women Religious, 1970; title changed, 1980. A movement of feminist women committed to prophetic tasks of giving witness, raising awareness and engaging in public action and advocacy for justice in church and society. Address: 1307 S. Wabash Ave., Room 206, Chicago, Ill. 60605.

National Association of Church Personnel Administrators (1973), 100 E. 8th St., Cincinnati, O. 45202. Pres., Sr. Elizabeth Wendelin, S.C.N.; Exec. Dir., Sr. Christine Matthews, O.P.

National Association of Diocesan Ecumenical Officers, Pres., Rev. John H. McDonnell, 4807 Staunton Ave. S.E., Charleston, W. Va. 25304.

National Association of Pastoral Musicians (1976), 225 Sheridan St., N.W., Washington, D.C. 20011; 8,700. *Pastoral Music,* six times a year. For clergy and musicians. Pres. and Exec. Dir., Rev. Virgil C. Funk.

National Association of Priest Pilots (1964), Pres., Rev. John Hemann, 510 First Ave. N.W., Cedar Rapids, Ia. 52405.

National Catholic Bandmasters' Association (1953), Box 1023, Notre Dame University, Notre Dame, Ind. 46556. *The School Musician Magazine.*

National Catholic Cemetery Conference (1949), 710 N. River Rd., Des Plaines, Ill. 60016. *The Catholic Cemetery,* monthly. Exec. Dir., Leo A. Droste.

National Catholic Conference for Interracial Justice (NCCIJ) (1960), 1200 Varnum St. N.E., Washington, D.C. 20017. Stresses moral dimension of civil rights, intercultural cooperation and interracial justice programming in each diocese/organization. Exec. Dir. Mr. Jerome B. Ernst.

National Catholic Development Conference (1968), 86 Front St., Hempstead, N.Y. 11550. Professional association of organizations and individuals engaged in raising funds for Catholic charitable activities. Pres., Msgr. Robert C. Wurtz; Exec. Dir., George T. Holloway.

National Catholic Disaster Relief Committee (under the direction of Catholic Charities USA), 1319 F St. N.W., Washington, D.C. 20004. Staff coordinator, Bro. Joseph Berg, C.S.C.

National Catholic Pharmacists Guild of the United States (1962), 400 members; *The Catholic Pharmacist.* Exec. Dir., John P. Winkelmann, 1012 Surrey Hills Dr., St. Louis, Mo. 63117.

National Catholic Society of Foresters (1891),

446 E. Ontario St., Chicago, Ill. 60611; 70,951; *National Catholic Forester,* quarterly. A fraternal insurance society. Pres., Miss Rosemary Trettin.

National Catholic Stewardship Council (1962), 1 Columbia Place, Albany, N.Y. 12207. To promote the concept of Christian stewardship.

National Catholic Women's Union (1916), 3835 Westminster Pl., St. Louis, Mo. 63108; 10,500.

National Center for the Laity (1977), 1 E. Superior St., No. 311, Chicago, Ill. 60611. *Initiatives,* six times a year. To promote and implement the vision of Vatican II: That the laity are the Church in the modern world as they attend to their occupational, family and neighborhood responsibilities. Pres., Gregory Pierce.

National Center for Urban Ethnic Affairs (1971): P.O. Box 20, Cardinal Station, Washington, D.C. 20064. Research and action related to the Church's concern for cultural pluralism and urban neighborhoods. An affiliate of the USCC. Pres., Dr. John A. Kromkowski.

National Clergy Conference on Alcoholism and Related Drug Problems, 1200 Varnum St. N.E., Washington, D.C. 20017. Exec. Dir., Rev. John F. X. O'Neill.

National Committee of Catholic Laymen, The (1977), 150 E. 35th St., Room 840, New York, N.Y. 10016. Lobbying and publishing organization representing "orthodox" Catholics who strongly support Pope John Paul II; *catholic eye,* monthly. Pres., J.P. McFadden.

National Conference of Airport Chaplains, O'Hare International Airport, P.O. Box 66353, Chicago, Ill. 66353.

National Conference of Diocesan Directors of Religious Education: 3021 4th St. N.E., Washington, D.C. 20017.

National Conference of Diocesan Vocation Directors (NCDVD) (1961), 1307 S. Wabash, Suite 350, Chicago, Ill. 60605. To provide diocesan vocation personnel with information and services regarding: awareness and discernment of vocations to the diocesan or religious priesthood and the religious life for both men and women; formation of diocesan priesthood candidates. Exec. Dir., Edward J. Griswold.

National Council for Catholic Evangelization (1983), 1007 Varnum St. N.E., Washington, D.C. 20017. To promote evangelization as the "primary and essential mission of the Church," in accordance with *Evangelii Nuntiandi,* the 1975 apostolic exhortation of Pope Paul VI. Exec. Dir., Dorothy L. Armstrong.

National Council of Catholic Laity (1971), 5664 Midforest Lane, Cincinnati, Ohio 45233. Formed by the National Council of Catholic Men and the National Council of Catholic Women to provide direction and guidance to existing and new lay organizations. It sponsors conferences and is a contact agency for information about specialized groups in the Church.

National Council of Catholic Men, 4712 Randolph Dr., Annandale, Va. 22003. A federation of Catholic organizations through which Catholic men may be heard nationally on matters of common interest. NCCM is a constituent of the National Council of Catholic Laity.

National Council of Catholic Women (1920), 1312 Massachusetts Ave. N.W., Washington, D.C. 20005. A federation of some 8,000 organizations of Catholic women in the U.S. NCCW unites Catholic organizations and individual Catholic women of the U.S., develops their leadership potential, assists them to act upon current issues in the Church and society, provides a medium through which Catholic women may speak and act upon matters of common interest, and relates to other national and international organizations in the solution of present-day problems. It is an affiliate of the World Union of Catholic Women's Organizations. The official bimonthly publication is *Catholic Woman.*

National Federation of Catholic Physicians' Guilds (1927), 850 Elm Grove, Suite 11, Elm Grove, Wis. 53122; 4,800 in 92 autonomous guilds in U.S. and Canada, *Linacre Quarterly.* Exec. Dir., Robert H. Herzog.

National Federation of Priests' Councils (1968), 1307 S. Wabash Ave., Chicago, Ill. 60605. To give priests' councils a representative voice in matters of presbyteral, pastoral and ministerial concern to the U.S. and the universal Church.

National Federation of Spiritual Directors (1972). Pres., Rev. Noah Caseyr, O.S.B.; St. Meinrad College, St. Meinrad, Ind. 47577.

National Guild of Catholic Psychiatrists, Inc. (1949). Integration of psychiatry and Roman Catholic theology. *The Bulletin.* Mailing address: Exec. Sec., 120 Hill St., Whitinsville, Mass. 01588.

National Organization for Continuing Education of Roman Catholic Clergy, Inc. (1973). Membership, 151 dioceses, 85 religious provinces, 71 affiliated institutions. Pres., Rev. Watter Dolan, O.F.M., 3140 Meramec St., St. Louis, Mo. 63118; Exec. Dir., Rev. Jerome Thompson, Catholic Theological Union, 5401 S. Cornell, Chicago, Ill. 60615 (national office).

NETWORK (1971), 806 Rhode Island Ave. N.E., Washington, D.C. 20018. A Catholic social justice lobby.

Nocturnal Adoration Society of the United States (1882), 1335 W. Harrison St., Chicago, Ill. 60607. 57,000. Nat. Dir., Rev. Thomas E. Waldie, S.S.S.

North American Academy of Liturgy, c/o Dr. David Truemper, Valparaiso Univ., Valparaiso, Ind. 46383. *Proceedings,* annually. Foster liturgical research, publication and dialogue on a scholarly level. Pres., Horace T. Allen, Jr.

North American Conference of Separated and Divorced Catholics (1972), Exec. Dir., Ms. Kathleen L. Kircher, 1100 S. Goodman St., Rochester, N.Y. 14620; Natl. Chaplain, Christopher Witt, C.S.P., 3115 Bremerton Pl., La Jolla, Calif. 92037.

Order of the Alhambra (1904), 4200 Leeds Ave., Baltimore, Md. 21229. 11,000 in U.S. and Canada. Fraternal society dedicated to assisting mentally handicapped children. Supreme Commander, Thomas J. Smith.

Paulist National Catholic Evangelization Association (1977), 3031 Fourth St., N.E., Washington, D.C. 20017; 190,000, *Share the Word,* bimonthly magazine; weekly "Share the Word" television program. To work with unchurched and alienated Catholics; to develop, test and document contemporary ways in which Catholic parishes and dioceses can evangelize unchurched and inactive. Exec. Dir., Rev. Alvin A. Illig, C.S.P.

Perpetual Eucharistic Adoration, P.O. Box 84595, Los Angeles, Calif. 90073. Promote program of Perpetual Eucharistic adoration in parishes throughout the world.

Philangeli (Friends of the Angels) (1949 in England; 1956 in U.S.), Viatorian Fathers, 1115 E. Euclid St., Arlington Heights, Ill. 60004; approximately 870,000 in 60 countries. To encourage devotion to the angels.

Pious Union of Prayer (1898), St. Joseph's Home, P.O. Box 288, Jersey City, N.J. 07303; 31,000. *St. Joseph's Messenger and Advocate of the Blind,* quarterly.

Pontifical Mission for Palestine (1949), c/o Catholic Near East Welfare Association, 1011 First Ave., New York, N.Y. 10022. Field offices in Rome, Italy, Beirut, Lebanon, Jerusalem, and Amman, Jordan. The papal relief agency for 1.8 million Palestinian refugees in Lebanon, Syria, Jordan, and the Gaza Strip. Distributes food, clothing, other essentials; maintains medical clinics, orphanages, libraries, refugee camp schools and chapels, the Pontifical Mission Center for the Blind (Gaza), the Pontifical Mission Libraries (Jerusalem, Bethlehem, Nazareth, Amman), the Epheta Institute for Deaf-Mutes (Bethlehem). Acting Pres., Rev. Msgr. Robert L. Stern.

Pontifical Missionary Union (1916), 366 Fifth Ave., New York, N.Y. 10001. To promote mission awareness among clergy, religious, candidates to priestly and religious life, and others engaged in pastoral ministry of the Church. Nat. Dir., Most Rev. William J. McCormack.

Priests' Eucharistic League (1887), 184 E. 76th St., New York, N.Y. 10021; 17,500. *Emmanuel,* 10 issues a year. Nat. Dir., Rev. James Feeley, S.S.S.,

Pro Ecclesia Foundation (1970), 509 Madison Ave., New York, N.Y. 10022. *Pro Ecclesia,* bimonthly. To answer attacks against Church and promote Church teachings. Pres., Dr. Timothy A. Mitchell.

Pro Maria Committee (1952), 22 Second Ave., Lowell, Mass. 01854. Promote devotion to Our Lady of Beauraing (See Index).

Pro Sanctity Movement. A worldwide force of laity organized to spread God's call of all persons to holiness. Addresses: 205 S. Pine Dr., Fullerton, Calif. 92633; 730 E. 87th St., Brooklyn, N.Y. 11236; 5310 S. 52nd St., Omaha, Nebr. 68117.

The Providence Association of the Ukrainian Catholics in America (Ukrainian Catholic Fraternal Benefit Society) (1912), 817 N. Franklin St., Philadelphia, Pa. 19123. *America* (Ukrainian-English).

Raskob Foundation for Catholic Activities, Inc. (1945), Kennett Pike and Montchanin Rd., P.O. Box 4019, Wilmington, Del. 19807. Pres., Gerard S. Garey.

Reparation Society of the Immaculate Heart of Mary, Inc. (1946), 100 E. 20th St., Baltimore, Md. 21218. *Fatima Findings,* monthly. Dir. Rev. John Ryan, S.J.

Rosary Apostolate 141 E. 65th St., New York, N.Y. 10021. Dir., Rev. Damian Myett, O.P.

Rosary League (1901), Franciscan Sisters of the Atonement, Graymoor, Garrison, N.Y. 10524.

Sacred Heart League, Walls, Miss. 38686; 1,200,000. Promote devotion to the Sacred Heart. Its program services include the Sacred Heart Auto League for careful, prayerful driving and the Apostolate of the Printed Word. Pres., Rev. Robert Hess, S.C.J.

St. Ansgar's Scandinavian Catholic League (1910), 40 W. 13th St., New York, N.Y. 10011; 1,000. *St. Ansgar's Bulletin,* annually. Financial support for Church in Scandinavia.

St. Anthony's Guild (1924), Paterson, N.J. 07509. *The Anthonian.* Dir., Rev. Kevin E. Mackin, O.F.M.

St. Jude League (1929), 205 W. Monroe St., Chicago, Ill. 60606. *St. Jude Journal,* bi-monthly. Dir., Rev. Mark J. Brummel, C.M.F.

St. Margaret of Scotland Guild, Inc. (1938), Graymoor, Garrison, N.Y. 10524; 800. Moderator, Bro. Pius MacIsaac, S.A.

St. Martin de Porres Guild (1935), 141 E. 65th St., New York, N.Y. 10021. Dir., Rev. Damian Myett, O.P.

St. Thomas Aquinas Foundation of the Dominican Fathers of the United States (STAF). Mod., Very Rev. Thomas H. McBrien, O.P., Providence College, Providence, R.I. 02918

Serra International (1938), 22 W. Monroe St., Chicago, Ill. 60603; 16,500 members in 518 clubs in 29 countries. *Serran,* bimonthly. Fosters vocations to the priesthood, and religious life, trains Catholic lay leadership. Formally aggregated to the Pontifical Society for Priestly Vocations, 1951. Pres., Rizal V. Pangilinan, M.D.

Slovak Catholic Federation (1911): Founded by Rev. Joseph Murgas to promote and coordinate religious activities among Slovak Catholic fraternal societies, religious communities and Slovak ethnic parishes in their effort to address themselves to the special needs of Slovak Catholics in the U.S. and Canada. Pres., Edward M. Matash, 210 Monroe St., Linden, N.J. 07036; Sec., Mr. John Mizenko, 32283 Sedgefield Oval, Solon, Ohio 44139.

Slovak Catholic Sokol (1905), 205 Madison St., Passaic, N.J. 07055; 48,500. *Slovak Catholic Falcon,* weekly. Pres., Stephen J. Hruska.

Society for the Propagation of the Faith (1822), 366 Fifth Ave., New York, N.Y. 10001; established in 174 dioceses. Church's principal instrument for promoting mission awareness and generating financial support for the missions. General fund for ordinary and extraordinary subsidies for all mission dioceses. *Mission,* 4 times a year; *Director's Newsletter,* monthly. Is subject to Congregation for the Evangelization of Peoples. Nat.

Dir.. Most Rev. William J. McCormack.

Society of St. Peter the Apostle (1889), 366 Fifth Ave., New York, N.Y. 10001; 174 dioceses. Church's central fund for support of seminaries, seminarians and novices in all mission dioceses. Nat. Dir., Most Rev. William J. McCormack.

Society of the Divine Attributes (1974). Contemplative prayer society; 3,000 members worldwide (lay, clerical and religious). Spir. Dir. Rev. Ronald D. Lawler, O.F.M. Cap., 225 Jerome St., Brooklyn, N.Y. 11207.

Spiritual Life Institute of America (1960), Box 119, Crestone, Colo. 81131. *Desert Call,* seasonal. An eremetical movement to foster the contemplative spirit in America. Founder, Rev. William McNamara, O.C.D. Second foundation: *Nova Nada,* Primitive Wilderness Hermitage, Kemptville, Nova Scotia, Canada B0W 1Y0.

Theresians of the United States (1961), 5326 E. Pershing Ave., Scottsdale, Ariz. 85254; 5,000. Spiritual, educational and ministerial organization of Christian women. Exec. Dir., Patricia Mullen, S.F.C.C.

United Societies of U.S.A. (1903), 613 Sinclair St., McKeesport, Pa. 15132; 3,500 members. *Prosvita-Enlightenment,* monthly newspaper.

United States Catholic Historical Society (1884). No. 3 Downing Drive, E. Brunswick, N.J. 08816. 500. *U.S. Catholic Historian,* quarterly. Preserve U.S. Catholic history and culture, Pres. Dr. Brian Butler.

Western Catholic Union (1877), W.C.U. Bldg., 506-510 Maine St., Quincy, Ill. 62301; 25,025 members. *Western Catholic Union Record,* bimonthly.

Women for Faith and Family (1984), P.O. Box 8326, St. Louis, Mo. 63132. *Voices,* seasonal. To provide Catholic women with a means of expressing unity with the teachings of the Catholic Church through the "Affirmation for Catholic Women" (over 40,000 signatures worldwide).

Word of God Institute (1972), 487 Michigan Ave. N.E., Washington, D.C. 20017. For renewed biblical preaching, Bible sharing and evangelization. Dir., Rev. John Burke, O.P.

World Apostolate of Fatima (The Blue Army) (1946), Washington, N.J. 07882; worldwide membership. *Soul,* bimonthly. U.S. Pres., Most Rev. Jerome Hastrich, bishop of Gallup, N. Mex.

Young Ladies' Institute (1887), P.O. Box 64087, San Francisco, Calif. 94164. Grand Sec. Miss Loretto O'Rourke.

Young Men's Institute (1883), 50 Oak St., San Francisco, Calif. 94102; 4,500. *Institute Journal,* bimonthly. Grand Sec., R. A. Bettencourt.

The Catholic League for Religious and Civil Rights, founded in 1973, serves the Catholic community as an anti-defamation and civil-rights agency. Father Virgil C. Blum, S.J., is president and founder of the league, which is headquartered at 1100 W. Wells St., Milwaukee, Wis. 53233. The league also has 15 local chapters across the country

Knights of Columbus

The Knights of Columbus, which originated as a fraternal benefit society of Catholic men, was founded by Father Michael J. McGivney and chartered by the General Assembly of Connecticut Mar. 29, 1882.

In line with their general purpose to be of service to the Church, the Knights are active in many apostolic works and community programs.

Since January, 1947, the Knights have sponsored a program of Catholic advertising in secular publications with national circulation. This has brought some 7.5 million inquiries and led to more than 800,000 enrollments in courses in the Catholic faith. In more recent years the Knights have broadened this program to include other media for spreading Christian and religious ideals. In 1975 the Knights also undertook funding of the up-link costs for telecasting papal ceremonies throughout the world via satellite.

K. of C. scholarship funds — two at the Catholic University of America, another for disbursement at other Catholic colleges in the U.S., one at Canadian colleges and others for the Philippines, Mexico and Puerto Rico — have provided college educations for about 1,700 students since 1914.

With funding from the Knights of Columbus, a North American Campus of the John Paul II Institute for Studies on Marriage and Family — a pontifical graduate school affiliated with Lateran University — opened in 1988 at the Dominican House of Studies, Washington, D.C.

The order promotes youth activity through sponsorship of the Columbian Squires and through cooperation with other organized youth groups.

Recent programs undertaken by the Knights include: promotion of vocations to the priesthood and religious life; promotion of rosary devotion with free distribution of more than 100,000 rosaries a year; securing aid for private schools; efforts to halt the increased killing of the unborn; assistance to the retarded and other disadvantaged people.

The Knights have formed an association with the Bishops in the United States, Canada and Mexico to help protect the lives of the unborn and to disseminate information on responsible family planning. Assistance also has been provided to the Eternal Word Television Network to help spread positive values over the airwaves and to Morality in Media to assist that organization in its battle to contain the spread of pornography.

In 1987, local units of the Knights contributed more than $68 million to charitable and benevolent causes, and gave more than 25 million hours of community service.

K. of C. membership, as of Feb. 29, 1988, was 1,446,951 in 8,807 councils in the U.S., Canada, the Philippines, Mexico, Puerto Rico, Panama, Guatemala, Guam, the Dominican Republic and the Virgin Islands.

The Knights' publication, *Columbia,* has the largest circulation (over 1.4 million) of any Catholic monthly in North America.

Virgil C. Dechant is Supreme Knight.

International headquarters are located at One Columbus Plaza, New Haven, Conn. 06507.

COMMUNICATIONS

CATHOLIC PRESS STATISTICS

The 1988 *Catholic Press Directory*, published by the Catholic Press Association, reported a total of 665 periodicals in North America with a circulation of 28,297,117. The figures included 196 newspapers with a circulation of 5,763,779; 289 magazines with a circulation of 18,572,449; 139 newsletters with a circulation of 3,237,136, and 41 other-language periodicals (newspapers and magazines) with a circulation of 723,753.

Newspapers in the U.S.

There were 179 newspapers in the United States, with a circulation 5,524,759. Six of these had national circulation; 159 were diocesan newspapers; 14 were Eastern rite publications.

National newspapers included: *National Catholic Register*, founded 1900; *Our Sunday Visitor*, founded 1912; *National Catholic Reporter*, founded 1964; *Catholic Twin Circle*, founded 1967 and *The Wanderer*.

The oldest Catholic newspaper in the United States is *The Pilot* of Boston, established in 1829 (under a different title).

Magazines in U.S.

The *Catholic Press Directory* reported 267 magazines in the U.S. with a circulation of 17,643,837. In addition, there were 138 newsletters, circulation, 3,231,536.

America and *Commonweal* are the only weekly and biweekly magazines, respectively, of general interest.

The monthly magazine with the largest circulation is *Columbia*, the official organ of the Knights of Columbus.

Other-Language Publications: There were an additional 27 publications (newspapers and magazines) in the U.S. in languages other than English with a circulation of 397,581.

Canadian Statistics

There were 17 newspapers in Canada with a circulation of 239,020. These included two national newspapers (*The Catholic Register*, founded 1857; *Catholic New Times*, founded 1976) and 11 diocesan. There were 22 magazines, with a circulation of 928,612; one newsletter, circulation 5,600 and 14 publications in languages other than English, circulation 326,172.

CATHOLIC NEWSPAPERS AND MAGAZINES IN THE U.S.

(Sources: *Catholic Press Directory; The Catholic Journalist*; Almanac survey; NC News Service.)

Abbreviation code: a, annual; bm, bimonthly; m, monthly; q, quarterly; w, weekly.

Circulation figures for some of these newspapers and magazines are given in the article, Catholic Press Statistics.

Newspapers

Acadiana Catholic, m; P.O. Box 3223, Lafayette, La. 70502; Lafayette diocese.

Agua Viva, m; P.O. Box 16318, Las Cruces, N. Mex. 88004; Las Cruces diocese.

Alaskan Shepherd, 6 times a year; 1312 Peger Rd., Fairbanks, Alaska 99709; Fairbanks diocese.

America (Ukrainian-English), daily; 817 N. Franklin St., Philadelphia, Pa. 19123.

Anchor, The w; P.O. Box 7, Fall River, Mass. 02722; Fall River diocese.

Arkansas Catholic, w; P.O. Box 7417, Little Rock, Ark. 72217.

Arlington Catholic Herald, w; 200 N. Glebe Rd., Suite 614, Arlington, Va. 22203; Arlington diocese.

Bayou Catholic, The, w; P.O. Box 9077, Houma, La. 70361; Houma-Thibodaux diocese.

Beacon, The, w; P.O. Box 1887, Clifton, N.J. 07015. Paterson diocese.

Bishop's Bulletin, m; P.O. Box 665, Yankton, S. Dak. 57078.

Bolletino, m; 1801 Van Ness Ave., San Francisco, Calif. 94109; Central Council of Italian Catholic Federation.

Byzantine Catholic World, biweekly; 3643 Perrysville Ave., Pittsburgh, Pa. 15214; Pittsburgh Byzantine archdiocese.

Catholic Accent, w; P.O. Box 850, Greensburg, Pa. 15601; Greensburg diocese.

Catholic Advance, The, w; 424 N. Broadway, Wichita, Kans. 67202; Wichita diocese.

Catholic Advocate, The, w; 37 Evergreen Pl., E. Orange, N.J. 07018; Newark archdiocese.

Catholic Banner, w; P.O. Box 818, Charleston, S.C. 29402; Charleston diocese.

Catholic Bulletin, w; 244 Dayton Ave., St. Paul, Minn. 55102; St. Paul and Minneapolis archdiocese.

Catholic Calendar, bm; 834 Ryan St., Lake Charles, La. 70601; one page in local newspaper; Lake Charles diocese.

Catholic Chronicle, biweekly; P.O. Box 1866, Toledo, O. 43603; Toledo diocese.

Catholic Commentary, w; P.O. Box 2239, Anchorage, Alaska 99510; one-page supplement in local newspaper; Anchorage archdiocese.

Catholic Commentator, The, biweekly; P.O. Box 14746, Baton Rouge, La. 70898; Baton Rouge diocese.

Catholic East Texas, 1920 Sybil Lane, Tyler, Tex. 75703. Tyler diocese.

Catholic Exponent, biweekly; 25 East Boardman St., Room 330, Youngstown, O. 44503; Youngstown diocese.

Catholic Free Press, w; 47 Elm St., Worcester, Mass. 01609; Worcester diocese.

Catholic Herald, The, m; 514 El Paso Blvd., Manitou Springs, Colo. 80829; Colorado Springs diocese.

Catholic Herald, w; P.O. Box 1572, Milwaukee, Wis. 53201; Milwaukee archdiocese.

Catholic Herald — Madison Edition, w; P.O. Box 5913, Madison, Wis. 53705.

Catholic Herald — Superior Edition, w; P.O. Box 969, Superior, Wis. 54880.

Catholic Herald, w; 5890 Newman Ct., Sacramento, Calif. 95819; Sacramento diocese.

Catholic Hungarian's Sunday, w; 1739 Mahoning Ave., Youngstown, O. 44509.

Catholic Key to the News, w; P.O. Box 419037, Kansas City, Mo. 64141; Kansas City-St. Joseph diocese.

Catholic Lantern, m; P.O. Box 4237, Stockton, Calif. 95204; Stockton diocese.

Catholic Light, biweekly; P.O. Box 708, Scranton, Pa. 18501; Scranton diocese.

Catholic Lighthouse, biweekly; P.O. Box 4708, Victoria, Tex. 77903; Victoria diocese.

Catholic Mentor, m; 6747 Pennywell Dr., Nashville, Tenn. 37205.

Catholic Messenger, w; P.O. Box 460, Davenport, Ia. 52805; Davenport diocese.

Catholic Mirror Interim, 4 times a year; P.O. Box 10372, Des Moines, Ia. 50306. Des Moines diocese.

Catholic Missourian, w; P.O. Box 1107, Jefferson City, Mo. 65102; Jefferson City diocese.

Catholic New York, w; P.O. Box 5133, New York, N.Y. 10150; New York archdiocese.

Catholic Observer, biweekly; Box 1570, Springfield, Mass. 01101; Springfield diocese.

Catholic Outlook, m; 215 W. 4th St., Duluth, Minn. 55806; Duluth diocese.

Catholic Post, The, w; P.O. Box 1722, Peoria, Ill. 61656; Peoria diocese.

Catholic Register, biweekly; Box 126-C, Logan Blvd., Hollidaysburg, Pa. 16648; Altoona-Johnstown diocese.

Catholic Review, w; P.O. Box 777, Baltimore, Md. 21203; Baltimore archdiocese.

Catholic Sentinel, w; 5536 N.E. Hassalo St., Portland, Ore. 97213; Portland archdiocese, Baker diocese.

Catholic Spirit, The, m; P.O. Box 13327, Capitol Sta., Austin, Tex. 78711; Austin diocese.

Catholic Spirit, The, w; P.O. Box 951, Wheeling, W. Va. 26003; Wheeling-Charleston diocese.

Catholic Standard, w; P.O. Box 4464, Washington, D.C. 20017; Washington archdiocese.

Catholic Standard and Times, w; 222 N. 17th St., Philadelphia, Pa. 19103; Philadelphia archdiocese; Allentown diocese.

Catholic Star Herald, w; 1845 Haddon Ave., Camden, N.J. 08101; Camden diocese.

Catholic Sun, The, biweekly; 400 E. Monroe, Phoenix, Ariz. 85004; Phoenix diocese.

Catholic Sun, The, w; 257 E. Onondaga St., Syracuse, N.Y. 13202; Syracuse diocese.

Catholic Telegraph, w; 100 E. 8th St., Cincinnati, O. 45202; Cincinnati archdiocese.

Catholic Times, w; P.O. Box 636, Columbus, O. 43216; Columbus diocese.

Catholic Times, w; 514 E. Lawrence St., Springfield, Ill. 62703; Springfield diocese.

Catholic Transcript, w; 785 Asylum Ave., Hartford, Conn. 06105; Hartford archdiocese, Bridgeport and Norwich dioceses.

Catholic Twin Circle, w; 6404 Wilshire Blvd., Suite 900, Los Angeles, Calif. 90048.

Catholic Universe Bulletin, biweekly; 1027 Superior Ave. N.E., Cleveland, O. 44114; Cleveland diocese.

Catholic Virginian, biweekly; Box 26843, Richmond, Va. 23261; Richmond diocese.

Catholic Voice, The, biweekly; 2918 Lakeshore Ave., Oakland, Calif. 94610; Oakland diocese.

Catholic Voice, The, w; P.O. Box 4010, Omaha, Nebr. 68104; Omaha archdiocese.

Catholic Week, w; P.O. Box 349, Mobile, Ala. 36601; Mobile archdiocese.

Catholic Weekly, The, w; P.O. Box 1405, Saginaw, Mich. 48605; Saginaw and Gaylord dioceses.

Catholic Weekly, The, w; P.O. Box 167, Flint, Mich. 48501; Lansing diocese.

Catholic Witness, The, w; P.O. Box 2555, Harrisburg, Pa. 17105; Harrisburg diocese.

Central Washington Catholic, 6 times a year; 5301-A Tieton Dr., Yakima, Wash. 98908. Yakima diocese.

Challenge, The, semimonthly; 66 Portland Ave., Dover, N.H. 03820. St. Maron diocese.

Chicago Catholic, The, w; 1144 W. Jackson, Chicago, Ill. 60607; Chicago archdiocese.

Chicago Catolico, El, m; 155 E. Superior St., Chicago, Ill. 60611.

Chronicle of Catholic Life, m; 1001 N. Grand Ave., Pueblo, Colo. 81003; Pueblo diocese.

Church Today, biweekly; P.O. Box 7417, Alexandria, La. 71306; Alexandria and Shreveport dioceses.

Church World, w; Industry Rd., P.O. Box 698, Brunswick, Me. 04011; Portland diocese.

Clarion Herald, w; 523 Natchez St., New Orleans, La. 70130; New Orleans archdiocese.

Common Sense, w; 1325 Jefferson Ave., Memphis, Tenn. 38104; Memphis diocese.

Community, w; P.O. Box 24000, Jacksonville, Fla. 32241; one-page weekly in Sunday editions of two daily newspapers; St. Augustine diocese.

Compass, The, w; Box 1825, Green Bay, Wis. 54305; Green Bay diocese.

Courier, The, m; P.O. Box 949, Winona, Minn. 55987; Winona diocese.

Courier-Journal, w; 1150 Buffalo Rd., Rochester, N.Y. 14624; Rochester diocese.

Criterion, The, w; P.O. Box 1717, Indianapolis, Ind. 46206; Indianapolis archdiocese.

Dakota Catholic Action, 9 times a year; P.O. Box 1137, Bismarck, N.D. 58502; Bismarck diocese.

Darbininkas (The Worker) (Lithuanian), w; 341 Highland Blvd., Brooklyn, N.Y. 11207; Lithuanian Franciscan Fathers.

Denver Catholic Register, w; P.O. Box 1620, Denver, Colo. 80201; Denver archdiocese.

Dialog, The, w; P.O. Box 2208, Wilmington, Del. 19899; Wilmington diocese.

Diocese of Orange Bulletin, m; 2811 E. Villa Real Dr., Orange, Calif. 92667.

Newspapers

Diocese of Van Nuys Newsletter, bm; 5335 Sepulveda Blvd., Van Nuys, Calif. 91411; Van Nuys Byzantine-Rite diocese.

Draugas (Lithuanian), daily; 4545 W. 63rd St., Chicago, Ill. 60629; Lithuanian Catholic Press Society.

East Texas Catholic, The, biweekly; P.O. Box 222, Port Neches, Tex. 77651; Beaumont diocese.

Eastern Catholic Life, w; 445 Lackawanna Ave., W. Paterson, N.J. 07424; Passaic Byzantine eparchy.

Eastern Oklahoma Catholic, biweekly; Box 520, Tulsa, Okla. 74101; Tulsa diocese.

Evangelist, The, w; 39 Philip St., Albany, N.Y. 12207; Albany diocese.

Fairfield County Catholic, m; 238 Jewett Ave., Bridgeport, Conn. 06606; Bridgeport diocese.

Florida Catholic, The, w; P.O. Box 3551, Orlando, Fla. 32802; Orlando diocese. Publishes editions for Palm Beach, Pensacola-Tallahassee, St. Petersburg and Venice dioceses.

Georgia Bulletin, w; 680 W. Peachtree St. N.W., Atlanta, Ga. 30308; Atlanta archdiocese.

Glasilo KSK Jednote (Amerikanski Slovenec) (Slovenian), semimonthly; 2439 Glenwood Ave., Joliet, Ill. 60435; American Slovenian Catholic Union.

Globe, The, w; 1825 Jackson St., Sioux City, Ia. 51105; Sioux City diocese.

Gulf Pine Catholic, w; P.O. Box 1189, Biloxi, Miss. 39533; Biloxi diocese.

Hawaii Catholic Herald, w; 1184 Bishop St., Honolulu, H.I. 96813; Honolulu diocese.

Heraldo Catolico, El (Spanish), bm; P.O. Box 19312, Sacramento, Calif. 95819; Sacramento and Stockton dioceses.

Hlas Naroda (Voice of the Nation) (Czech-English), w; 2657-59 S. Lawndale Ave., Chicago. 60623.

Horizons, semimonthly; 1900 Carlton Rd., Parma, O. 44134; Parma diocese.

Idaho Register, w; P.O. Box 2835, Boise, Idaho 83701; Boise diocese.

Inland Catholic, w; P.O. Box 2788, San Bernardino, Calif. 92406. San Bernardino diocese.

Inland Register, every 3 weeks; P.O. Box 48, Spokane, Wash. 99210; Spokane diocese.

Inside Passage, biweekly; 419 6th St., Juneau, Alaska 99801; Juneau diocese.

Intermountain Catholic, w; P.O. Box 2489, Salt Lake City, Utah 84110; Salt Lake City diocese.

Jednota (Slovak-Eng.), w; Jednota and Rosedale Aves., Middletown, Pa. 17057; First Catholic Slovak Union.

Joliet Catholic Explorer, w; 98 N. Independence Blvd., Rt. 53 and Airport Rd., Romeoville, Ill. 60441. Joliet diocese.

Katolicky Sokol (Catholic Falcon) (Slovak-English), w; 205 Madison St., Passaic, N.J. 07055; Slovak Catholic Sokol.

Lake Shore Visitor, w; P.O. Box 4047, Erie, Pa. 16512; Erie diocese.

Leaven, The, w; P.O. Box 2329, Kansas City, Kans. 66110; Kansas City archdiocese.

Long Island Catholic, The, w; P.O. Box 700, Hempstead, N.Y. 11551; Rockville Centre diocese.

Mensajero Catolico, El (Spanish), m; P.O. Box 1572, Milwaukee, Wis. 53201; Milwaukee archdiocese.

Message, The, w; P.O. Box 4169, Evansville, Ind. 47711; Evansville diocese.

Messenger, The, w; P.O. Box 327, Belleville, Ill. 62222; Belleville diocese.

Messenger, The, w; P.O. Box 268, Covington, Ky. 41012; Covington diocese.

Michigan Catholic, The, w; 305 Michigan Ave., Detroit, Mich. 48226; Detroit archdiocese.

Mirror, The, w; M.P.O. Box 847, Springfield, Mo. 65801; Springfield-Cape Girardeau diocese.

Mississippi Today, w; P.O. Box 2130, Jackson, Miss. 39225; Jackson diocese.

Monitor, The, w; P.O. Box 3095, Trenton, N.J. 08619; Trenton and Metuchen dioceses.

Montana Catholic, The, m; P.O. Box 1729, Helena, Mont. 59624; Helena diocese.

Narod Polski (Polish Nation) (Polish-Eng.) semimonthly; 984 Milwaukee Ave., Chicago, Ill. 60622.

National Catholic Register, w; 6404 Wilshire Blvd., Suite 900, Los Angeles, Calif. 90048.

National Catholic Reporter, The, w; P.O. Box 419281, Kansas City, Mo. 64141.

New Earth, The, m; P.O. Box 1750, Fargo, N.D. 58107; Fargo diocese.

New Star, The, biweekly; 2208 W. Chicago Ave., Chicago, Ill. 60622; St. Nicholas of Chicago Ukrainian diocese.

Newsletter, The, 6 times a year; 215 N. Westnedge, Kalamazoo, Mich. 49001; Kalamazoo diocese.

North Carolina Catholic, w; 300 Cardinal Gibbons Dr., Raleigh, N.C. 27606 and 1524 E. Morehead St., Charlotte, N.C. 28207; Raleigh and Charlotte dioceses.

North Country Catholic, w; Box 326, Ogdensburg, N.Y. 13669; Ogdensburg diocese.

North Texas Catholic, w; 800 West Loop 820 South, Fort Worth, Tex. 76108; Fort Worth diocese.

Northwest Indiana Catholic, w; 9292 Broadway, Merrillville, Ind. 46410; Gary diocese.

Northwestern Kansas Register, w; P.O. Box 1038, Salina, Kans. 67402; Salina diocese.

Nuevo Amanecer, m; P.O. Box 155, Brooklyn, N.Y. 11243; for Hispanic Catholic community of Brooklyn diocese.

Observer, The, biweekly; P.O. Box 2079, Monterey, Calif. 93942; Monterey diocese.

Observer, The, biweekly; 921 W. State St., Rockford, Ill. 61102; Rockford diocese.

One Voice, w; P.O. Box 10822, Birmingham, Ala. 35202; Birmingham diocese.

Our Northland Diocese, biweekly; P.O. Box 610, Crookston, Minn. 56716; Crookston diocese.

Our Sunday Visitor, w; 200 Noll Plaza, Huntington, Ind. 46750; national edition and official publication for 3 dioceses.

People of God, m; 1800 Martha N.E., Albuquerque, N. Mex. 87112; Santa Fe archdiocese.
Pilot, The, w; 49 Franklin St., Boston, Mass. 02110; Boston archdiocese.
Pittsburgh Catholic, The, w; 100 Wood St., Suite 500, Pittsburgh, Pa. 15222; Pittsburgh diocese.
Polish American Journal, m; 774 Fillmore Ave., Buffalo, N.Y. 14212.
Pregonero, El (Spanish), w; P.O. Box 4464; Washington, D.C. 20017.
Progress, The, w; 910 Marion St., Seattle, Wash. 98104; Seattle archdiocese.
Providence Visitor, The, w; 184 Broad St., Providence, R.I. 02903. Providence diocese.

Record, The, w; 701 W. Jefferson St., Louisville, Ky. 40202; Louisville archdiocese.
Redwood Crozier, The, biweekly, 547 B St., Santa Rosa, Calif. 95401; Santa Rosa diocese.
Register, The, biweekly; P.O. Box 1668, Fresno, Calif. 93717; Fresno diocese.

St. Cloud Visitor, w; P. O. Box 1068, St. Cloud, Minn. 56302; St. Cloud diocese.
St. Louis Review, w; 462 N. Taylor Ave., St. Louis, Mo. 63108; St. Louis archdiocese.
San Francisco Catholic, m; 441 Church St., San Francisco, Calif. 94114; San Francisco archdiocese.
Sooner Catholic, The, biweekly; P.O. Box 32180, Oklahoma City, Okla. 73123; Oklahoma City archdiocese.
South Plains Catholic, biweekly; 5802 22nd St., Lubbock, Tex. 79407; Lubbock diocese.
South Texas Catholic, w; 1200 Lantana St., Corpus Christi, Tex. 78407; Corpus Christi diocese.
Southern Cross, The, w; P.O. Box 81869, San Diego, Calif. 92138; San Diego diocese.
Southern Cross, The, w; 601 E. 6th St., Waynesboro, Ga. 30830; Savannah diocese.
Southern Nebraska Register, w; P.O. Box 80329, Lincoln, Nebr. 68501; Lincoln diocese.
Southwest Catholic, m; 834 Ryan St., Lake Charles, La. 70601 Lake Charles diocese.
Southwest Kansas Register, w; P.O. Box 1317, Dodge City, Kans. 67801; Dodge City diocese.
Sower, biweekly; 161 Glenbrook Rd., Stamford, Conn. 06902. Stamford Ukrainian diocese.
Steubenville Register, w; P.O. Box 160, Steubenville, O. 43952; Steubenville diocese.
Sunday Visitor, The w; P.O. Box 1603, Lafayette, Ind. 47902; Lafayette diocese.

Tablet, w; 1 Hanson Pl., Brooklyn, N.Y. 11243; Brooklyn diocese.
Tennessee Register, The, w; 2400 21st Ave. S., Nashville, Tenn. 37212; Nashville diocese.
Texas Catholic, w; P.O. Box 190347, Dallas, Tex. 75219; Dallas diocese.
Texas Catholic Herald, The, semi-monthly; 1700 San Jacinto St., Houston, Tex. 77002; Galveston-Houston diocese.

Tidings, The, w; 1530 W. 9th St., Los Angeles, Calif. 90015; Los Angeles archdiocese.
Times Review, The, w; P.O. Box 4004, La Crosse, Wis. 54602; La Crosse diocese.
Today's Catholic, w; P.O. Box 11169, Fort Wayne, Ind. 46856; Fort Wayne-S. Bend diocese.
Today's Catholic, biweekly; P.O. Box 28410, San Antonio, Tex. 78228; San Antonio archdiocese.

Upper Peninsula Catholic, biweekly; P.O. Box 548, Marquette, Mich. 49855; Marquette diocese.

Valley Catholic, m; 7600 St. Joseph Ave., Los Altos, Calif. 94022; San Jose diocese.
Vermont Catholic Tribune, biweekly; 351 North Ave., Burlington, Vt. 05401; Burlington diocese.
Visitante de Puerto Rico, El (Spanish), w; Apartado 41305, Est Minillas, San Juan, P.R. 00904. Puerto Rican Catholic Conference.
Voice, The, biweekly; P.O. Box 38-1059, Miami, Fla. 33238; Miami archdiocese.
Voice of the Southwest, w; P.O. Box 1338, Gallup, N. Mex. 87301; Gallup diocese.
Voz Catolica, La (Spanish); biweekly; 9401 Biscayne Blvd., Miami, Fla. 33138; Miami archdiocese.

Wanderer, The, w; 201 Ohio St., St. Paul, Minn. 55107.
The Way, (Ukrainian-Eng.), biweekly; 827 N. Franklin St., Philadelphia, Pa. 19123; Philadelphia archeparchy.
West Nebraska Register, w; P.O. Box 608, Grand Island, Nebr. 68802; Grand Island diocese.
West River Catholic, m; P.O. Box 678, Rapid City, S. Dak. 57709; Rapid City diocese.
West Texas Angelus, biweekly; P.O. Box 1829, San Angelo, Tex. 76902; San Angelo diocese.
West Texas Catholic, semimonthly; P.O. Box 5644, Amarillo, Tex. 79117; Amarillo diocese.
Western Kentucky Catholic, m; 4005 Frederica St., Owensboro, Ky. 42301.
Western New York Catholic, m; 795 Main St., Buffalo, N.Y. 14203; Buffalo diocese.
Witness, The, w; P.O. Box 917, Dubuque, Ia. 52004; Dubuque archdiocese.
World Observer, biweekly; 921 State St., Rockford, Ill. 61102.
Wyoming Catholic Register, m; P.O. Box 4279, Casper, Wyo. 82604; Cheyenne diocese.

Magazines, Other Periodicals

Act, 10 times a year; R.D. 9, Box 512, Greensburg, Pa. 15601; Christian Family Movement.
ADRIS Newsletter, q; Department of Theology, Fordham University, Bronx, N.Y. 10458. Association for the Development of Religious Information Services.
AIM (Aids in Ministry), q; P.O. Box 2703, Schiller Park, Ill. 60176.
Albanian Catholic Bulletin (Buletini Katholik Shqiptar), a; P.O. Box 1217, (University), Santa Clara, Calif. 95053; Albanian Catholic Information Center.
America, w; 106 W. 56th St., New York, N.Y. 10019. Jesuits of U.S. and Canada.

American Benedictine Review, q; Assumption Abbey, Richardson, N.D. 58652.
American Midland Naturalist, q; Notre Dame, Ind. 46556.
Americas, The, q; Box 34440, Bethesda, Md. 20817; Academy of American Franciscan History.
Angel Guardian Home Quarterly, The, q; 6301 12th Ave., Brooklyn, N.Y. 11219.
Anthonian, The, q; Paterson, N.J. 07509; St. Anthony's Guild.
Anthropological Quarterly, q; 620 Michigan Ave. N.E., Washington, D.C. 20064.
Apostolate of Our Lady, m; 315 Clay St., Carey, O. 43316; Our Lady of Consolation National Shrine.
Apostolate of the Little Flower, bm; P.O. Box 5280, San Antonio, Tex. 78201; Discalced Carmelite Fathers.
Archeparchal Bulletin, m; 827 N. Franklin St., Philadelphia, Pa. 19123; Philadelphia archeparchy.
Atchison Benedictine Community News, q; Mount St. Scholastica Convent, 801 S. 8th St., Atchison, Kans. 66002.
Ateitis (The Future) (Lithuanian), bm; 7235 S. Sacramento Ave., Chicago, Ill. 60629; for youth.
Aylesford Carmelite Newsletter, q; P.O. Box 65, Darien, Ill. 60559.

Benedictine Orient, bm; 2400 Maple Ave., Lisle, Ill. 60532.
Benedictines, semiannually; Mt. St. Scholastica, Atchison, Kans. 66002.
Bible Today, The, bm; Liturgical Press, Collegeville, Minn. 56321.
Biblical Theology Bulletin, q; St. John's Univ., Theology Dept., Jamaica, N.Y. 11432.
BLUEPRINT for Social Justice, 10 times a year; Institute of Human Relations, Loyola University, Box 12, New Orleans, La. 70118.
Bringing Religion Home, m; 205 W. Monroe St., Chicago, Ill. 60606.
Brothers, 5 times a year; 555 Cardinal Dr., Thibodaux, La. 70301; National Assembly of Religious Brothers.

Call Board, The, 5 times a year; 165 W. 46th St., Suite 710, New York, N.Y. 10036; Catholic Actors' Guild.
Camillian/Newsletter — National Association of Catholic Chaplains, bm; 3257 S. Lake Dr., Milwaukee, Wis. 53207.
Caring Community, The, m; 115 E. Armour Blvd., Kansas City, Mo. 64111.
Carmelite Review, The, m; 29 N. Broadway, Joliet, Ill. 60435; Canadian-American Province of Carmelite Order.
Catechist, The, 8 times a year; 2451 E. River Rd., Dayton, O. 45439.
Catechist's Connection, The, 10 times a year; 115 E. Armour Blvd., Kansas City, Mo. 64111.
Catechumenate, 6 times a year; 1800 N. Hermitage Ave., Chicago, Ill. 60622.
Catholic Aid News, m; 3499 Lexington Ave., St. Paul, Minn. 55146.
Catholic Answer, The, bm; 200 Noll Plaza, Huntington, Ind. 46750.

Catholic Biblical Quarterly, q; Catholic University of America, Washington, D.C. 20064; Catholic Biblical Assn.
Catholic Campus Ministry Newsletter, 10 times a year; 300 College Park Ave., Dayton, O. 45469.
Catholic Cemetery, The, m; 710 N. River Rd., Des Plaines, Ill. 60016; National Catholic Cemetery Conference.
Catholic Communicator, The, q; 9 Loudoun St. S.E., Leesburg, Va. 22075; Catholic Home Study Institute.
Catholic Digest, The, m; P.O. Box 64090, St. Paul, Minn. 55164.
Catholic Evangelization, bm; 3031 Fourth St. N.E., Washington, D.C. 20017.
Catholic Family, The, q; P.O. Box 331389, Fort Worth, Tex. 76163.
Catholic Forester Magazine, bm; 425 W. Shuman Blvd., Naperville, Ill. 60566; Catholic Order of Foresters.
CGA World, q; National Headquarters, 400 Lackawanna Ave., Scranton, Pa. 18503. Catholic Golden Age.
Catholic Health World, semimonthly; 4455 Woodson Rd., St. Louis, Mo. 63134.
Catholic Historical Review, q; 620 Michigan Ave. N.E., Washington, D.C. 20064; American Catholic Historical Assn.
Catholic Journalist, The, m; 119 N. Park Ave., Rockville Centre, N.Y. 11570; Catholic Press Association.
C.K. of A. Journal, m; 1850 Dalton St., Cincinnati, O. 45214; Catholic Knights of America.
Catholic Lawyer, q; St. John's University, Jamaica, N.Y. 11439; St. Thomas More Institute for Legal Research.
Catholic League Newsletter, m; 1100 W. Wells St., Milwaukee, Wis. 53233; Catholic League for Religious and Civil Rights.
Catholic Library World, 6 times a year; 461 W. Lancaster Ave., Haverford, Pa. 19041; Catholic Library Association.
Catholic Life Magazine, m (exc. July-Aug.); 35750 Moravian Dr., Fraser, Mich. 48026; PIME Missionaries.
Catholic Near East Magazine, q; 1011 First Ave., New York, N.Y. 10022; Catholic Near East Welfare Assn.
Catholic Periodical and Literature Index, bm; 461 W. Lancaster Ave., Haverford, Pa. 19041; Catholic Library Association.
Catholic Pharmacist, a; 1012 Surrey Hills Dr., St. Louis, Mo. 63117; National Catholic Pharmacists Guild.
Catholic Press Directory, a; 119 N. Park Ave. Rockville Centre, N.Y. 11570; Catholic Press Assn.
Catholic Quote, m; Valparaiso, Nebr. 68065; Rev. Jerome Pokorny.
Catholic Review (Braille), m; 154 E. 23rd St., New York, N.Y. 10010; Xavier Society for the Blind.
Catholic Rural Life, 5 times a year; 4625 N.W. Beaver Dr., Des Moines, Ia. 50310; National Catholic Rural Life Conference.
Catholic Singles Magazine, bm; 8408 S. Muskegon, Chicago, Ill. 60617.

Catholic Teen Magazine, m (Sept.-June); 3900-A Harewood Rd. N.E., Washington, D.C.; National Federation for Catholic Youth Ministry.
Catholic Trends, biweekly; 1312 Massachusetts Ave. N.W., Washington, D.C. 20005; NC News Service.
Catholic University of America Law Review, q; Washington, D.C. 20064.
Catholic Update, m; 1615 Republic St., Cincinnati, O. 45210.
Catholic War Veteran, bm; 419 N. Lee St., Alexandria, Va. 22314.
Catholic Woman, bm; 1312 Massachusetts Ave. N.W., Washington, D.C. 20005. National Council of Catholic Women.
Catholic Worker, 8 times a year; 36 E. First St., New York, N.Y. 10003.
Catholic Workman, m; 111 W. Main, P.O. Box 47, New Prague, Minn. 56071.
Catholic Youth Ministry, q; P.O. Box 215, Weston, Vt. 05161.
Celebration, m; 11211 Monticello Ave., Silver Spring, Md. 20902; National Catholic Reporter Publishing Co.
Charism; 3 times a year; 4435 E. Patterson Rd., Dayton, O. 45430; Society of Mary.
Chariscenter USA Newsletter, 10 times a year; P.O. Box 1065, Notre Dame, Ind. 46556.
Charities USA, m; 1319 F St. N.W., Washington, D.C. 20004.
Chicago Studies, 3 times a year; P.O. Box 665, Mundelein, Ill. 60060; Civitas Dei Foundation.
CFC Newsletter, 4 times a year; 13001 Wornall Rd., Kansas City, Mo. 64145. Christian Foundation for Children.
Christian Renewal News, P.O. Box 467, La Puente, Calif. 91747. Apostolate of Christian Renewal.
Christopher News Notes, 7 times a year; 12 E. 48th St., New York, N.Y. 10017; The Christophers, Inc.
Chronicle of Catholic Church in Lithuania, 6 times a year; 351 Highland Blvd., Brooklyn, N.Y. 11207; Lithuanian Catholic Religious Aid.
Church, q; 299 Elizabeth St., New York, N.Y. 10012; National Pastoral Life Center.
Cistercian Studies, q; Abbey of Gethsemani, Trappist, Ky. 40051; international review dedicated to monastic and contemplative spirituality.
Clarion, The, 5 times a year; Box 159, Alfred, Me. 04002; Brothers of Christian Instruction.
Columban Mission, m (exc. June, Aug.); St. Columbans, Nebr. 68056; Columban Fathers.
Columbia, m; One Columbus Plaza, P.O. Drawer 1670, New Haven, Conn. 06507; Knights of Columbus.
Columbian, The, biweekly; 188 W. Randolph St., Chicago, Ill. 60601.
Comboni Missions, q; 8108 Beechmont Ave., Cincinnati, O. 45230.
Commitment, q; 1200 Varnum St. N.E., Washington, D.C. 20017; National Catholic Conference for Interracial Justice.
Commonweal, biweekly; 15 Dutch St., New York, N.Y. 10038.
Communio — International Catholic Review, q; P.O. Box 1046, Notre Dame, Ind. 46556.
Company, q; 3441 N. Ashland Ave., Chicago, Ill. 60657. National Jesuit Magazine.
Consecrated Life, semi-annually; 4200 N. Austin Ave., Chicago, Ill. 60634; Institute on Religious Life. English edition of *Informationes,* official publication of Congregation for Religious and Secular Institutes.
Consolata Missionaries, bm; P.O. Box 5550, Somerset, N.J. 08873.
Contact, q; 555 Albany Ave., Amityville, N.Y. 11701; Sisters of St. Dominic.
Context, 22 issues a year; 205 W. Monroe St., Chicago, Ill. 60606.
Cord, The, m; P.O. Drawer F, St. Bonaventure, N.Y. 14778; Franciscan Institute.
Counseling and Values, 2 times a year; College of Education, Univ. of Iowa, Iowa City, Ia. 52242.
Crescat, 3 times a year; Belmont Abbey, Belmont, N.C. 28012; Benedictine Monks.
Crisis, 11 times a year; P.O. Box 1006, Notre Dame, Ind. 46556. Journal of lay Catholic opinion.
Critic, The, 4 times a year; 223 W. Erie, Chicago, Ill. 60610. Thomas More Assn.
Cross Currents, q; Mercy College, 555 Broadway, Dobbs Ferry, N.Y. 10522.
Crossroads Series, The, m; 1089 Elm St., W. Springfield, Mass. 01089.
Crusader's Almanac, The, biannually; 1400 Quincy St. N.E., Washington, D.C. 20017; Commissariat of the Holy Land.
CRUX of the News, w; 75 Champlain St., Albany, N.Y. 12204.

Damien-Dutton Call, q; 616 Bedford Ave., Bellmore, N.Y. 11710.
Dare, q; 1011 First Ave., New York, N.Y. 10022. New York archdiocesan Office of Substance Abuse Ministry.
Deaf Blind Weekly, The (Braille), w; 154 E. 23rd St., New York, N.Y. 10010; Xavier Society for the Blind.
DeSales World, The 4 times a year; 2200 Kentmere Pkwy., Wilmington, Del. 19899.
Desert Call, q; Box 260, Crestone, Colo. 81131; Spiritual Life Institute of America.
Diaconate, bm; 1937 Tenth Ave. N., P.O. Box 9501, Lake Worth, Fla. 33466.
Diakonia, 3 times a year; Univ. of Scranton, Scranton, Pa. 18510.
Dimensions, m; 86 Front St., Hempstead, N.Y. 11550; National Catholic Development Conference.
Divine Word Missionaries, q; Techny, Ill. 60082.

Ecumenical Trends, m (exc. Aug.); 475 Riverside Dr., Room 528, New York, N.Y. 10115. Friars of the Atonement.
Ecumenist, The, 6 times a year; Paulist Press, 997 MacArthur Blvd., Mahwah, N.J. 07430.
Educating in Faith, q; 2021 H St. N.W., Washington, D.C. 20006. Catholic Negro-American Mission Board.
Eglute (The Little Fir Tree) (Lithuanian), m; Putnam, Conn. 06260; Srs. of Immaculate Conception. For children ages 5-10.
Emmanuel, m (bm July-Aug.); 184 E. 76th St.,

New York, N.Y. 10021; Blessed Sacrament Fathers.
Envoy, 6 times a year; Duquesne Univ., Pittsburgh, Pa. 15282; Institute of Formative Spirituality.
Envoy, q; Office of Public Affairs, Catholic University of America, Washington, D.C. 20064.
Eucharistic Minister, m; 115 E. Armour, Kansas City, Mo. 64111.
Extension, 10 times a year; 35 E. Wacker Dr., Suite 400, Chicago, Ill. 60601; Catholic Church Extension Society.

Faith and Reason, q. Route 3, Box 87, Front Royal, Va. 22630; Christendom College.
Family, m; 50 St. Paul's Ave., Boston, Mass. 02130; Daughters of St. Paul.
Family Friend, q; P.O. Box 11563, Milwaukee, Wis. 53211; Catholic Family Life Insurance.
Family of Mary Update, 3 times a year; 4435 E. Patterson Rd., Dayton, O. 45430. Society of Mary.
Family Spirit, q; 3943 W. End Rd., Downers Grove, Ill. 60515. Worldwide Marriage Encounter.
Fatima Findings, m; 100 E. 20th St., Baltimore, Md. 21218; Reparation Society of the Immaculate Heart of Mary.
Fellowship of Catholic Scholars Newsletter, q; St. John's University, Jamaica, N.Y. 11439.
Festivals, 6 times a year; 160 E. Virginia St. No. 290, San Jose, Calif. 95112.
Fidelity, m; 206 Marquette Ave., South Bend, Ind. 46617.
Flame, The, 4 times a year; Barry Univ., 11300 N.E. 2nd Ave., Miami Shores, Fla. 33161.
Fonda Tekakwitha News, q; P.O. Box 627, Fonda, N.Y. 12068.
Food for the Poor, 3 times a year; 1301 W. Copans Rd., Pompano Beach, Fla. 33064.
F.M.A. Focus, q; 274-280 W. Lincoln Ave., Mt. Vernon, N.Y. 10550; Franciscan Mission Associates.
Franciscan Reporter, q; 3140 Meramec St., St. Louis, Mo. 63118.
Franciscan Studies, a; St. Bonaventure, N.Y. 14778; Franciscan Institute.
Fraternal Leader, q; P.O. Box 13005; Erie, Pa. 16514; Loyal Christian Benefit Association.
Fraternally Yours (Zenska Jednota) (Eng.-Slovak), m; 24950 Chagrin Blvd., Beachwood, O. 44122; First Catholic Slovak Ladies Assn.
Frontline Report, bm; 23 Bliss Ave., Tenafly, N.J. 07670.
Fund Raising Forum, m; 86 Front St., Hempstead, N.Y. 11550; National Catholic Development Conference.

Garsas (The Sound) (Lithuanian-English), m; 341 Highland Blvd., Brooklyn, N.Y. 11207; Lithuanian Roman Catholic Alliance of America.
Generation, m; 205 W. Monroe St., Chicago, Ill. 60606.
Glenmary Challenge, The, q; P.O. Box 465618, Cincinnati, O. 45246; Glenmary Home Missioners.
God's Anchor, 4 times a year; 264 Elm St., Holyoke, Mass. 01040.

God's Word Today, m; Box 40664, St. Petersburg, Fla. 33743.
Good News, m; P.. Box 9501; Lake Worth, Fla. 33466; Sunday Publications, Inc.
Good News for Children, 24 times during school year; 2451 E. River Rd., Dayton, Ohio 45439.
Good Shepherd (Dobry Pastier) (Slovak and English), a; 645 Rhode Island, Gary, Ind. 46402; Slovak Catholic Federation of America.
Guadalupe Missioners Newsletter, m; 4714 W. 8th St., Los Angeles, Calif. 90005.
Guide to Religious Ministries, A, a; 210 Main St., New Rochelle, N.Y. 10801.

Happiness, q; 567 Salem End Rd., Framingham, Mass. 01701; Sons of Mary, Health of the Sick.
Harmony, 3 times a year; 8300 Morganford Rd., St. Louis, Mo. 63123; Benedictine Srs. of Perpetual Adoration.
Healing Times, The, q; 191 Joralemon St., Brooklyn, N.Y. 11201.
Health Progress, m; 4455 Woodson Rd., St. Louis, Mo. 63134; Catholic Health Association.
Hearts Aflame, bm; Blue Army, Mountain View Rd., Washington, N.J. 07882. For youth (14-16).
Hispanic American Pastoral Studies, semiannually; 1011 First Ave., New York, N.Y. 10022; Northeast Pastoral Center for Hispanics.
Holy Name Newsletter, m; 100 Clyde Morris Blvd., No. 155, Ormond Beach, Fla. 32074; National Association of the Holy Name Society.
Homiletic and Pastoral Review, m; 86 Riverside Dr., New York, N.Y. 10024.
Horizons, biannual; Villanova University, Villanova, Pa. 19085. College Theology Society.
Human Development, q; Jesuit Educational Center, 53 Park Pl., New York, N.Y. 10007.
Human Life Issues, q; University of Steubenville, Steubenville, O. 43952.

IDEA Ink, q; P.O. Box 4010, Madison, Wis. 53711.
In a Word, m; Bay Saint Louis, Miss. 39520; Society of the Divine Word.
In Between, 6 times a year; 1257 E. Siena Hts. Dr., Adrian, Mich. 49221; Adrian Dominican Sisters.
INFO, q; Eden Hill, Stockbridge, Mass. 01262.
In-Formation, 8 times a year; 1234 Massachusetts Ave., N.W., Washington, D.C. 20005; Religious Formation Conference.
Inner Horizons, q; 50 St. Paul's Avenue, Jamaica Plain, Boston, Mass. 02130; Daughters of St. Paul.
Institute Journal, bm; 50 Oak St., San Francisco, Calif. 94102; Young Men's Institute.
International Philosophical Quarterly; Fordham University, Bronx, N.Y. 10458.
International Review — Natural Family Planning, q; University of Steubenville, Steubenville, Ohio 43952.
It's Our World, 4 times a year; 1720 Massachusetts Ave. N.W., Washington, D.C. 20036. Holy Childhood Association.

Jesuit Blackrobe, semiannually; 3601 W. Fond

du Lac Ave., Milwaukee, Wis. 53216.

Jesuit Bulletin, 4 times a year; 4511 W. Pine Blvd., St. Louis, Mo. 63108; Jesuit Seminary Aid Association.

Josephite Harvest, The, q; 1130 N. Calvert St., Baltimore, Md. 21202; Josephite Missionaries.

Jurist, The, semiannually; Catholic University of America, Washington, D.C. 20064; Department of Canon Law.

Kinship, q; P.O. Box 39188, Cincinnati, O. 45239; Glenmary Sisters.

Knights of St. John, q; 6517 Charles Ave., Cleveland, O. 44129.

Kolping Banner, m; 115-14 227th St., Cambria Heights., N.Y. 11411; Catholic Kolping Society.

Kosmos Magazine, 6 times a year; 3700 Oakview Terr. N.E., Washington, D.C. 20017.

Laivas (Lithuanian), bm; 4545 W. 63rd St., Chicago, Ill. 60629.

Land of Cotton, q; 2048 W. Fairview Ave., Montgomery, Ala. 39196; City of St. Jude.

Law Briefs, m; 1312 Massachusetts Ave. N.W., Washington, D.C. 20005; Office of General Counsel, USCC.

Law Reports, m; 4455 Woodson Rd., St. Louis, Mo. 63134; Catholic Health Association.

Laywitness, m; 45 Union Ave., New Rochelle, N.Y. 10801; Catholics United for the Faith.

Leaven, q; Convent of the Holy Spirit, Techny, Ill. 60082.

Leaves, bm; 23715 Ann Arbor Trail, Dearborn Heights, Mich. 48127; Mariannhill Mission Society.

Let's Pray Together, w; 775 Madison Ave., Albany, N.Y. 12208; Families for Prayer.

Liguorian, m; 1 Liguori Dr., Liguori, Mo. 63057; Redemptorists.

Linacre Quarterly, q; 850 Elm Grove Rd., Elm Grove, Wis. 53122; Federation of Catholic Physicians Guilds.

Link, The, 6 times a year; Teleport One, The Teleport Staten Island, N.Y. 10314; Catholic Telecommunications Network of America.

Listening, 5 times a year; 814 Thayer Ave., Silver Spring, Md. 20910. National Catholic Office for the Deaf.

Liturgy, q; 806 Rhode Island Ave. N.E. Washington, D.C. 20018. Liturgical Conference.

Living City, m; P.O. Box 496, New York, N.Y. 10021; Focolare Movement.

Living Light, The, q; 1312 Massachusetts Ave. N.W., Washington, D.C. 20005; Department of Education, USCC.

Living Prayer, bm; Beckley Hill, R.R. 2, Box 4784, Barre, Vt. 05641; Assn. of Contemplative Sisters.

Marian Helpers Bulletin, q; Eden Hill, Stockbridge, Mass. 01262; Association of Marian Helpers and of the Congregation of Marians.

Marian Library Studies, a; Marian Library, Dayton, O. 45369.

Marian Studies, a; Marian Library, Dayton, O. 45469; Mariological Society of America (proceedings).

Marriage and Family Living, m; Abbey Press, St. Meinrad, Ind. 47577.

Marriage Encounter, m; 955 Lake Dr., St. Paul, Minn. 55120; International Marriage Encounter.

Maryknoll, m; Maryknoll, N.Y. 10545; Catholic Foreign Mission Society.

Mary's Shrine, q; Michigan Ave. and 4th St. N.E., Washington, D.C. 20017.

Medical Mission News, bm; 10 W. 17th St., New York, N.Y. 10011; Catholic Medical Mission Board, Inc.

Medical Mission Sisters News, 4 times a year; 8400 Pine Road, Philadelphia, Pa. 19111.

Men of Malvern, bm; Malvern, Pa. 19355; Laymen's Retreat League of Philadelphia.

Messenger of Our Lady, bm; 9380 C1 Forestwood Lane, Manassas, Va. 22110. For youth.

Messenger of St. Joseph's Union, The, 3 times a year; 108 Bedell St., Staten Island, N.Y. 10309.

Mid-America, 3 times a year; Loyola University, Chicago, Ill. 60626.

Miesiecznik Franciszkanski (Polish), m; 165 E. Pulaski St., Pulaski, Wis. 54162; Franciscan Fathers.

Migration World, 5 times a year; 209 Flagg Pl., Staten Island, N.Y. 10304; Center for Migration Studies.

Miraculous Medal, The, q; 475 E. Chelten Ave., Philadelphia, Pa. 19144; Central Association of the Miraculous Medal.

Mission, 4 times a year; 366 Fifth Ave., New York, N.Y. 10001; Society for Propagation of the Faith.

Mission, q; 1663 Bristol Pike, Bensalem, Pa. 19020; Sisters of the Blessed Sacrament.

Mission Handbook, a; 1233 Lawrence St. N.E.; Washington, D.C. 20017. United States Catholic Mission Association.

Mission Helper, The, q; 1001 W. Joppa Rd., Baltimore, Md. 21204; Mission Helpers of the Sacred Heart.

Missionhurst, 6 times a year; 4651 N. 25th St., Arlington, Va. 22207; Immaculate Heart of Mary Mission Society, Inc.

Mission Intercom, 10 times a year; 1233 Lawrence St., N.E., Washington, D.C. 20017; U.S. Catholic Mission Association.

Mission of the Immaculata, The, biweekly; 1600 W. Park Ave., Libertyville, Ill. 60048; Conventual Franciscan Friars.

Missionaries of Africa Report, bm; 1622 21st St. N.W., Washington, D.C. 20009; Society of Missionaries of Africa (White Fathers).

Modern Liturgy, 9 times a year; Resource Publications, 160 E. Virginia St., San Jose, Calif. 95112.

Modern Schoolman, The, q; 3700 W. Pine Blvd., St. Louis, Mo. 63108; St. Louis University.

Momentum, 4 times a year; Suite 100, 1077 30th St., N.W., Washington, D.C. 20007; National Catholic Educational Asssociation.

Mountain Spirit, The, 6 times a year; 322 Crab Orchard Rd., Lancaster, Ky. 40446; ecumenical; Christian Appalachian Project.

Mustard Seed, m; 1615 Vine St., Cincinnati, O. 45210; Franciscans.

My Daily Visitor, bm; 200 Noll Plaza, Hunting-

Magazines

ton, Ind. 46750; Our Sunday Visitor, Inc.
My Friend, 10 times a year; 50 St. Paul's Ave., Jamaica Plain, Boston, Mass. 02130; for children.

National Catholic Forester, q; 446 E. Ontario, Chicago, Ill. 60611.
NCSC News, bm; 1 Columbia Pl., Albany, N.Y. 12207. National Catholic Stewardship Council.
National Directory of Catholic Higher Education, a; 210 North Ave., New Rochelle, N.Y. 10801.
National Jesuit News, m; Gonzaga Univ., Spokane, Wash. 99258.
Network, bm; 806 Rhode Island Ave. N.E., Washington, D.C. 20018; Network.
Nevada Catholic Newsletter, m; P.O. Box 1211, Reno, Nev. 89504; Reno-Las Vegas diocese.
New Catholic World, bm; 997 Macarthur Blvd., Mahwah, N.J. 07430.
New Covenant, m; P.O. Box 400, Steubenville, O. 43952; Catholic Charismatic Renewal.
New Heaven/New Earth, m; 107 S. Greenlawn Ave., South Bend, Ind. 46617.
New Oxford Review, 10 issues a year; 1069 Kains Ave., Berkeley, Calif. 94706.
New Scholasticism, q; 715 Memorial Library, Notre Dame, Ind. 46556. American Catholic Philosophical Association.
New Theology Review, q; 1935 W. 4th St., Wilmington, Del. 19805.
News/Views, 5 times a year; 1307 S. Wabash Ave., Chicago, Ill. 60605; National Sisters Vocation Conference.
News and Views, q; 3900 Westminster Pl.; St. Louis, Mo. 63108; Sacred Heart Program.
Newsletter of the Bureau of Catholic Indian Missions, 10 times a year; 2021 H St. N.W., Washington, D.C. 20006.
North American Voice of Fatima, bm; 1023 Swann Rd., Youngstown, N.Y. 14174.
Notre Dame Magazine, 4 times a year; Notre Dame Univ., Notre Dame, Ind. 46556.
Notebook, The, 4 times a year; 31 Chesterfield Rd., Stamford, Conn. 06902. Catholic Movement for Intellectual and Cultural Affairs.

Oblate World and Voice of Hope, bm; 350 Jamaica Way, Boston, Mass. 02130; Oblates of Mary Immaculate.
Oblates, bm; 15 S. 59th St., Belleville, Ill. 62222; Oblate Fathers.
Observer, The, m; 4545 W. 63rd St., Chicago, Ill. 60629; Lithuanian Roman Catholic Federation of America.
Old Testament Abstracts, 3 times a year; Catholic University of America, Washington, D.C. 20064.
Origins, 48 times a year; 1312 Massachusetts Ave., N.W., Washington, D.C. 20005; NC News Service.
Our Lady's Digest, q; Box 777, Twin Lakes, Wis. 53181; La Salette Fathers.
Overview, m; 223 W. Erie St., Chicago, Ill. 60610; Thomas More Assn.

Pacer, biweekly, and **Pacer Bulletin,** m; 500 17th Ave., Seattle, Wash. 98124; Providence Medical Center.

Padres' Trail, 4 times a year; Box 645, St. Michael, Ariz. 86511; Franciscan Fathers.
Parish Communication, q; P.O. Box 215, Weston, Vt. 05161.
Parish Family Digest, bm; 200 Noll Plaza, Huntington, Ind. 46750.
Passionists' Compassion, The, q; 526 Monastery Pl., Union City, N.J. 07087.
Pastoral Life, m; Route 224, Canfield, Ohio 44406; Society of St. Paul.
Pastoral Music, bm; 225 Sheridan St., N.W. Washington, D.C. 20011; National Association of Pastoral Musicians.
Paulist, q; 997 Macarthur Blvd., Mahwah, N.J. 07430.
Philosophy Today, q; Carthagena Station, Celina, Ohio 45822.
Piarist Newsletter, 2 times a year; 363 N. Valley Forge Rd., Devon, Pa. 19333.
Pilgrim, q; Jesuit Fathers, Auriesville, N.Y. 12016; Shrine of North American Martyrs.
Pope Speaks, The, q; Our Sunday Visitor, Inc., 200 Noll Plaza, Huntington, Ind. 46750.
Praying, 6 times a year; 115 E. Armour Blvd., Kansas City, Mo. 64111.
Priest, The, 11 times a year; 200 Noll Plaza, Huntington, Ind. 46750; Our Sunday Visitor, Inc.
Probe, bm (Sept.-June); 1307 S. Wabash Ave., Chicago, Ill. 60605; NARW.
Proceedings, a; Catholic Univ. of America, 403 Adm. Bldg., Washington, D.C. 20064; American Catholic Philosophical Assn.
Professional Placement Newsnotes, bm; 10 W. 17th St., New York, N.Y. 10011; Catholic Medical Mission Board, Inc.
Program Supplement, 18 times a year; Columbus Plaza, New Haven, Conn. 06507; Knights of Columbus.

Quarterly, The, 2021 H St. N.W., Washington, D.C. 20006; Commission for Catholic Missions Among the Colored People and the Indians.
Queen; bm; 26 S. Saxon Ave., Bay Shore, N.Y. 11706; Montfort Fathers.

Reign of the Sacred Heart, m; Hales Corners, Wis. 53130.
Religion Teacher's Journal, m (Sept.-May); P.O. Box 180, Mystic, Conn. 06355.
Religious Life, m (bm, May-Aug.); 4200 N. Austin Ave., Chicago, Ill. 60634; Institute on Religious Life.
RSCJ Newsletter, bm; 785 Centre St., Newton, Mass. 02158. Religious of Sacred Heart.
Renascence, q; Marquette University, Milwaukee, Wis. 53233.
Respect Life Report, m; 1312 Massachusetts Ave. N.W., Washington, D.C. 20005; Committee for Pro-Life Activities, NCCB.
Response, The, a; 810 Rhode Island Ave. N.E., Washington, D.C. 20018; International Liaison of Lay Volunteers.
Review for Religious, bm; Room 428, 3601 Lindell Blvd., St. Louis, Mo. 63108.
Review of Politics, q; Box B, Notre Dame, Ind. 46556.

Review of Social Economy, Marquette University, Marquette, Wis. 53233. Association for Social Economics.
Revista Maryknoll (Spanish-English), m; Maryknoll, N.Y. 10545; Catholic Foreign Mission Society of America.
Roze Maryi (Polish), m; Eden Hill, Stockbridge, Mass. 01262; Marian Helpers Center.

SCJ News, 9 times a year; P.O. Box 289, Hales Corners, Wis. 53130; Sacred Heart Fathers and Brothers.
Sacred Heart Newsletter, 2 times a year; 317 Leroy Ave., Buffalo, N.Y. 14214.
Sacred Music, q; 548 Lafond Ave., St. Paul, Minn. 55103.
St. Anthony Messenger, m; 1615 Republic St., Cincinnati, O. 45210; Franciscan Fathers.
St. Anthony's Newsletter, m; Mt. St. Francis, Ind. 47146.
St. Joseph's Messenger and Advocate of the Blind, q; St. Joseph Home, P.O. Box 288, Jersey City, N.J. 07303.
St. Paul's Family Magazine, q; P.O. Box 772, Ft. Scott, Kans. 66701.
Salesian Bulletin, bm; 148 Main St., New Rochelle, N.Y. 10802; Salesian Fathers.
Salesian Missions of St. John Bosco, q; 148 Main St., New Rochelle, N.Y. 10802.
Salt, m; 205 W. Monroe St., Chicago, Ill. 60606; Claretians.
Salvatorian Newsletter, The, 6 times a year; 1303 Milwaukee Dr., Salvatorian Center, Wis. 53062.
Savio Notes, bm; Filors Lane, W. Haverstraw, N.Y. 10993; St. Dominic Savio Clubs International.
Scalabrinians, 3 times a year; 25 Carmine St., New York, N.Y. 10014.
School Guide, a; 210 North Ave., New Rochelle, N.Y. 10801.
School Sister, The, 3 times a year; 1233 N. Marshall St., Milwaukee, Wis. 53202; Sisters of Notre Dame.
SCRC Vision, The, m; 2810 Artesia Blvd., Redondo Beach, Calif. 90278; Southern California Renewal Communities.
Scripture in Church, q; P.O. Box 9, Northport, N.Y. 11768.
Senior Update, m; 1615 Republic St., Cincinnati, O. 45210.
Serenity, q; 601 Maiden Choice Lane, Baltimore, Md. 21228; Little Sisters of the Poor.
Serran, The, bm; 22 W. Monroe St., Chicago, Ill. 60603; Serra International.
Share the Word, bm; 3031 Fourth St. N.E., Washington, D.C. 20017; Paulist Catholic Evangelist Center.
Shepherd's Call, The, q; P.O. Box 7775, Albuquerque, N.M. 87194; Brothers of Good Shepherd.
Silent Advocate, q; St. Rita School for the Deaf, 1720 Glendale-Milford Rd., Cincinnati, O. 45215.
Sister Miriam Teresa League of Prayer Bulletin, q; League Headquarters, Convent Station, N.J. 07961.
SC News, 10 times a year; 2208 Dixie Highway, Louisville, Ky. 40210; Sisters of Charity of Nazareth.

SSM Network, q; 1100 Bellevue Ave., St. Louis, Mo. 63117. Sisters of St. Mary.
Sisters Today, m (exc. July-Aug.); Liturgical Press, Collegeville, Minn. 56321.
Social Justice Review, bm; 3835 Westminster Pl., St. Louis, Mo. 63108; Catholic Central Union of America.
Social Thought, q; 1319 F St. N.W., Washington, D.C. 20004; Catholic Charities USA.
Sophia, bm; P.O. Box 265, Newton Centre, Mass. 02159; Newton Melkite eparchy.
Soul, bm; Mountain View Rd., Washington, N.J. 07882; Blue Army.
Spinnaker, q; 610 W. Elm, Monroe, Mich. 48161; IHM Sisters.
Spirit, biannually; Seton Hall University, South Orange, N.J. 07079; poetry magazine.
Spirit and Life, 6 times a year; 8300 Morganford Rd., St. Louis, Mo. 63123; Benedictine Srs. of Perpetual Adoration.
Spiritual Book News, 8 times a year; Notre Dame, Ind. 46556.
Spiritual Life, q; 2131 Lincoln Rd. N.E., Washington, D.C. 20002; Discalced Carmelite Friars.
Spirituality Today (formerly Cross and Crown), q; 7200 W. Division, River Forest, Ill. 60605; Dominican Fathers.
Squires Newsletter, m; Columbus Plaza, New Haven, Conn. 06507; Columbian Squires.
Star, 10 times a year; 16 W. Bijou, Colorado Springs, Colo. 80903.
Studies in the Spirituality of Jesuits, 5 times a year; 3700 W. Pine Blvd., St. Louis, Mo. 63108.
Sword Magazine, 2 times a year; 29 N. Broadway, Joliet, Ill. 60435. Carmelites.

Tekakwitha Conference Newsletter, q; P.O. Box 6759, Great Falls, Mont. 59406.
Theological Studies, q; Georgetown Univ., 37th and O Sts., N.W., Washington, D.C. 20057.
Theology Digest, q; 3634 Lindell Blvd., St. Louis, Mo. 63108.
Theresian, The, 4 times a year; 5326 E. Pershing Ave., Scottsdale, Ariz. 85254.
Thirsting for Justice, q; 1312 Massachusetts Ave. N.W. Washington, D.C. 20005, Campaign for Human Development.
30 Days, m; Ignatius Press, 2515 McAllister St., San Francisco, Calif. 94118.
This Week, w; 135 W. 31st St., New York, N.Y. 10001; Franciscan Communications Office, Holy Name Province.
Thomist, The, q; 487 Michigan Ave. N.E., Washington, D.C. 20017; Dominican Fathers.
Thought, q; Fordham University Press, Box L, Bronx, N.Y. 10458; Fordham University.
Today's Catholic Teacher, m (Sept.-May); 2451 E. River Rd., Suite 200, Dayton, O. 45439.
Today's Parish, m (Sept.-May); P.O. Box 180, Mystic, Conn. 06355.
Touchstone, 4 times a year; 1307 S. Wabash Ave., Chicago, Ill. 60605; National Federation of Priests' Councils.
Tracings, q; Gamelin St., Holyoke, Mass. 01040; Sisters of Providence.
Trinity Missions Magazine, q; 9001 New Hamp-

shire Ave., Silver Springs, Md. 20903.

Trinity Review, bm; 3606 Coolcrest Dr., P.O. Box 169, Jefferson, Md. 21755.

Ultreya Magazine, m; 4500 W. Davis St., Dallas, Tex. 75211. Cursillo Movement.

Unda USA Newsletter, 6 times a year; P.O. Box 59, Akron, O. 45469.

L'Union (French), bm; 1 Social St., Woonsocket, R.I. 02895.

UNIREA, The Union (Romanian and English), m; 4309 Olcott Ave., East Chicago, Ind. 46312.

Universitas, q; 221 N. Grand, Room 303, St. Louis, Mo. 63103; St. Louis University.

U.S. Catholic, m; 205 W. Monroe St., Chicago, Ill. 60606; Claretian Fathers and Brothers.

U.S. Catholic Historian, q; P.O. Box 16229, Baltimore, Md. 21210.

U.S. Dominican, q; 1909 S. Ashland Ave., Chicago, Ill. 60608.

U.S. Parish, m; 205 W. Monroe St., Chicago, Ill. 60606.

Venture, 26 times during school year; 2451 E. River Rd., Dayton, O. 45439, Intermediate grades.

Veritas, bm; P.O. Box 8033, Syracuse, N.Y. 13217. Catholic youth magazine.

Vision, 2 times a year; P.O. Box 28185, San Antonio, Tex. 78228. Mexican American Cultural Center.

Visions, 24 times during school year; 2451 E. River Rd., Dayton, O. 45439. For junior high school students.

Vocation News, q; 26 Brentford Ct., Camarillo, Calif. 93010.

Voices, seasonal; P.O. Box 8326, St. Louis, Mo. 63132; Women for Faith and Family.

Waif's Messenger, q; 1140 W. Jackson Blvd., Chicago, Ill. 60607; Mission of Our Lady of Mercy.

Washington Theological Union Newsletter, q; 9001 New Hampshire Ave., Silver Spring, Md 20903.

Way — of St. Francis, bm; 109 Golden Gate Ave., San Francisco, Calif. 94102; Franciscan Friars of California, Inc.

Wheeling College Chronicle, 3 times a year; 316 Washington Ave., Wheeling, W. Va. 26003.

Word Among Us, The, m; 12625 Glen Rd., Potomac, Md. 20854.

Word One, 5 times a year; 205 W. Monroe St., Chicago, Ill. 60606; Claretians.

Word of God, w; 2187 Victory Blvd., Staten Island, N.Y. 10314; Society of St. Paul.

World Lithuanian Catholic Directory, biannually; 351 Highland Blvd., Brooklyn, N.Y. 11207.

Worship, 6 times a year; St. John's Abbey, Collegeville, Minn. 56321.

Xaverian Missions Newsletter, bm; 101 Summer St., Holliston, Mass. 01746; Xaverian Missionary Fathers.

Your Edmundite Missions Newsletter, bm; 1428 Broad St., Selma, Ala. 36701; Southern Missions of Society of St. Edmund.

Youth Update, m; 1615 Republic St., Cincinnati, Ohio 45210.

Zeal Magazine, q; P.O. Box 86, Allegany, N.Y. 14706; Franciscan Sisters of Allegany.

BOOKS

The Official Catholic Directory, annual, P. J. Kenedy and Sons, 3004 Glenview Rd., Wilmette, Ill. 60091. First edition, 1817.

The Catholic Almanac, annual; Our Sunday Visitor, Inc., 200 Noll Plaza, Huntington, Ind. 46750, publisher; editorial offices, 620 Route 3, Clifton, N.J. 07014. First edition, 1904.

BOOK CLUBS

Catholic Book Club (1928), 106 W. 56th St., New York, N.Y. 10019. Sponsors the Campion Award.

Catholic Digest Book Club (1954), Catholic Digest Magazine, P.O. Box 64090, St. Paul, Minn. 55164.

Thomas More Book Club (1939), Thomas More Association, 223 W. Erie St., Chicago, Ill. 60610.

FOREIGN CATHOLIC PERIODICALS

Principal source: Catholic Almanac survey. Included are English-language Catholic periodicals published outside the U.S.

African Ecclesial Review (AFER), bm; Gaba Publications, P.O. Box 4002, Eldoret, Kenya.

Australasian Catholic Record, q; St. Patrick's Seminary, Manly, New South Wales, Australia.

Christ to the World, bm; Via di Propaganda 1-C, 00187, Rome, Italy.

Doctrine and Life, m, and **Supplement to Doctrine and Life,** bm; Dominican Publications, St. Saviour's, Dublin 1, Ireland.

Downside Review, q; Downside Abbey, Stratton on Fosse, Bath, BA3 4RH, England.

East Asian Pastoral Review, q; East Asian Pastoral Institute, P.O. Box 221 U.P. Campus, 1101 Quezon City, Philippines.

Eastern Churches Review, semi-annual; 9 Alfred St., Oxford, England.

Faith Today, 10 times a year; Dominican Publications, St. Saviour's, Dublin 1, Ireland.

Furrow, m; St. Patrick's College, Maynooth, Ireland.

Heythrop Journal q; Heythrop College, 11 Cavendish Sq., London W1M, OAN, England (Editorial Office).

Holy Land Review, q; P.O. Box 186, 91001 Jerusalem, Israel. Illustrated.

Irish Biblical Studies, q; Union Theological College, Belfast BT7 1JT, N. Ireland.

Irish Theological Quarterly, q; St. Patrick's College, Maynooth, Ireland.

L'Osservatore Romano, w; Vatican City. (See Index.)

Louvain Studies, q; St. Michielsstraat 2, B-3000, Leuven, Belgium.

Lumen Vitae (French, with English summaries), q; International Center for Studies in Religious Education, 186, rue Washington, 1050 Brussels, Belgium.

Maynooth Review, q; St. Patrick's College, Maynooth, Ireland.

Mediaeval Studies, annual; Pontifical Institute of Mediaeval Studies, 59 Queen's Park Crescent East, Toronto, Ont., Canada M5S 2C4.

Month, m; 114 Mount St., London, WIY, 6AH, England.

Music and Liturgy, q; The Editor, St. Thomas More Centre, The Burroughs, London NW4 4TY, England.

New Blackfriars, m; edited by English Dominicans, Blackfriars, Oxford, OX1 3LY, England.

Omnis Terra (English Edition), m; Pontifical Missionary Union, Congregation for the Evangelization of Peoples, 1, Via di Propaganda, 00187 Rome, Italy.

One in Christ, q; Edited at: Turvey Abbey, Turvey, Beds. MK43 8DE, England.

Priests and People (formerly The Clergy Review), 10 times a year; 48 Great Peter St., London, SW1P 2HB, England.

Recusant History, biannual; Catholic Record Society, 12 Melbourne Pl., Wolsingham, Durham DL13 3EH, England.

Social Studies, q; St. Patrick's College, Maynooth, Ireland.

Spearhead, 5 times a year; Gaba Publications, P.O. Box 4002, Eldoret, Kenya.

Tablet, The w; 48 Great Peter St., London, SW1P 2HB, England.

Teilhard Review, The, 3 times a year; The Teilhard Centre for the Future of Man, 23 Kensington Square, London W8 5 HN, England.

Way, The, q; 114 Mount St., London W1Y 6AN, England.

CATHOLIC NEWS AGENCIES

(Sources: International Catholic Union of the Press, Geneva; Catholic Press Association, U.S.)

Argentina: Agencia Informativa Catolica Argentina (AICA), av. Rivadavia, 413,4⁰ Casilla de Correo Central 2886, 1020 Buenos Aires.

Austria: Katholische Presse-Agentur (Kathpress), Singerstrasse 6.2, 1010 Vienna 1.

Belgium: Centre d'Information de Presse (CIP), 1 Bd. Charlemagne, 1041 Bruxelles (Brussels).

Germany: Katholische Nachrichten Agentur (KNA), Adenauer Allee 134, 5300 Bonn 1.

Great Britain: Catholic Information Office of England and Wales (CIOEW), 38/40 Eccleston Square, London SW1V 1PD.

Greece: Agence TYPOS Rue Acharnon 246, Athenes 815.

Hong Kong: UCA-News, P.O. Box 69.626, Kwun Tong (Hong Kong).

Hungary: Magyar Kurir, Karolyi w 4-8, Postafiok 41, Budapest V.

India: South Asia Religious News (SAR-News), P.O. Box 4228, New Delhi 110.048.

Italy: Servizio Informazioni Settimanali (SIS-Roma) 1, via della Conciliazione, I-00193 Roma.

Centrum Informationis Catolicae (CIC-Roma), via Domenico Silveri, 30, I-00165 Roma.

Switzerland: Katholische Internationale Presse-Agentur (KIPA), Case Postale 1054 CH 1701, Fribourg.

Centre International de Reportages et d'Information Culturelle (CIRIC), 10, av. de la Gare-des-Eaux Vives, CH-1207 Geneva.

United States of America: NC News Service (NC), 1312 Massachusetts Ave. N.W., Washington, D.C. 20005. Name to be changed to Catholic News Service (CNS).

Yugoslavia: Aktusinosti Krscanska Sadasnjost (AKSA), Marulicev TRG 14, Zagreb p.p. 02-748.

Zaire: Documentation et Information Africaine (DIA), B.P. 2598, Kinshasa I.

Missions: Agenzia Internationale Fides (AIF), Palazzo di Propagande Fide, Via di Propaganda I-c, 00187 Rome, Italy.

U.S. PRESS SERVICES

Catholic News Service (CNS), established in 1920 (NC News Service), provides a worldwide daily news report by satellite throughout the U.S. and Canada and by wire and computer links into several foreign countries, and by mail to other clients, serving Catholic periodicals and broadcasters including Vatican Radio in about 40 countries. CNS also provides feature and photo services and a weekly religious education tabloid insert, "Faith Today." It publishes "Origins," a weekly documentary service, and "Catholic Trends," a fortnightly newsletter. CNS maintains a full-time bureau in Rome. It is a division of the United States Catholic Conference, with offices at 1312 Massachusetts Ave. N.W., Washington, D.C. 20005. The director and editor-in-chief is Richard W. Daw.

Religious News Service (RNS) provides domestic and foreign religious news in daily photos and features; RNS was inaugurated in 1933 by the National Conference of Christians and Jews as an independent news agency. In 1983, it was taken over by the United Methodist Reporter, a chain of newspapers with headquarters in Dallas, Tex. Mailing address: P.O. Box 1015, Radio City Station, New York, N.Y. 10101.

Spanish-Language Service: A weekly news summary provided by Catholic News Service is used by a number of Catholic newspapers. Some papers carry features of their own in Spanish.

Office of Public Affairs

The Office of Public Affairs of the United States Catholic Conference/National Conference of Catholic Bishops serves as the official source of information for both the USCC and NCCB, especially in relating to the news media. The office relates directly to the NCCB/USCC General Secretariat.

The office prepares and distributes news releases; handles inquiries from the press; arranges news media coverage of bishops' meetings; offers public information and public relations counsel on a day-to-day basis to the office of the general secretary of the USCC and the NCCB, and to other agencies and staff members; performs a number of special research and writing functions on behalf of the conferences and their staffs.

The office also provides services to diocesan information offices, Unda-USA and other agencies.

William Ryan is acting secretary of the office, which is located at 1312 Massachusetts Ave. N.W., Washington, D.C. 20005.

Other Communications Offices

International Mission Radio Association: Rev. Jude Bradley, O.S.B., treasurer-administrator, St. Paul's Abbey, Newton, N.J. 07860.

Jesuits in Communication (JESCOM): Rev. James J. Conn, S.J., executive secretary, Suite 300, 1424 16th St. N.W., Washington, D.C. 20036.

Maryknoll Media Relations: Rev. Donald Doherty, M.M., director, Maryknoll Fathers and Brothers, Maryknoll, N.Y. 10545.

National Franciscan Communications Conference: Rev. James J. Gardiner, S.A., president, St. Joseph's Church, 371 Sixth Ave., New York, N.Y. 10014.

CATHOLIC WRITERS' MARKET

(Source: Almanac survey.)

Editors call the following suggestions to the attention of writers:

Manuscripts should be typewritten, double-spaced, on one side of the page.

Writers should know the editorial policy, purpose and style of the publication to which they submit manuscripts. Sample copies may easily be obtained, often for the mere cost of postage. Some editors suggest that writers send outlines of proposed material, in order to facilitate editorial decision and direction. "Timely" copy should be submitted considerably in advance of the date of proposed publication; some editors advise a period of three months. Authors are urged to avoid sermonizing. Writers should not expect extensive criticism of their work, although they should profit from advice and direction when these are given. Editors are not required to state their reasons for rejecting manuscripts. Replies regarding the acceptance or rejection of copy are usually made within a few weeks.

All writers should send to editors stamped, self-addressed envelopes for the return of material. Those who write to Canadian editors may use international reply coupons, not U.S. stamps.

Payment is made on acceptance or publication. Rates are sometimes variable because of the reputation of the writer, the quality and length of the manuscript, the amount of editorial work required for its final preparation.

America: 106 W. 56th St., New York, N.Y. 10019. Ed., Rev. George W. Hunt, S.J. Weekly, circulation 33,000; $25 per year.

ARTICLES on important public issues evaluated scientifically and morally; serious and authenticated articles on family life, education, religion, and social and political issues with ethical or religious implications; occasionally, "thought" pieces; 1,000-2,000 words — 6¢ a word. VERSE, short and modern, befitting a Catholic publication but not necessarily religious—$7.50 and up. No fiction.

Annals of St. Anne de Beaupre, The: P.O. Box 1000, St. Anne de Beaupre, Que., Canada G0W 3C0. Ed., Roch Achard, C.Ss.R. Monthly, circulation 50,000; $7.00 per year.

Official organ of St. Anne de Beaupre Shrine.

ARTICLES of general Catholic interest, promoting Christian family values. FICTION and SHORT STORIES with a religious dimension: 700-1,200 words — 3 to 4¢ a word. Payment on acceptance.

BLUEPRINT for Social Justice: Institute of Human Relations, Loyola University, Box 12, New Orleans, La. 70118. Ed., Arthur J. Gallese. Ten times a year, circulation 3,000; sent free on request.

ARTICLES analyzing current justice issues in economics, labor, peace and human rights; length, 3,200 words.

Catechist: 2451 E. River Rd., Dayton, O. 45439. Ed., Patricia Fischer. Monthly August through April (exc. Dec.), circulation 45,620; $15.95 per year.

ARTICLES of interest to teachers of religion in parochial schools and CCD programs: 1,200-1,800 words — rate varies. PHOTOGRAPHS, black and white — rate varies. Payment on publication.

Catholic Digest: P.O. Box 64090, St. Paul, Minn. 55164. Ed., Henry Lexau. Monthly, circulation 600,000; $12.97 per year.

ARTICLES of close-to-home interest for average Catholic — rates vary; most frequent payments are $200 for originals, $100 for reprints; payment on acceptance. FILLERS, short features and jokes — rates vary; payment on publication. Cover pictures — $150. No fiction or verse. No queries necessary.

Columban Mission: St. Columbans, Nebr. 68056. Ed., Rev. Richard Steinhilber. Monthly (exc. June, Aug.); circulation 228,975; $5 per year.

ARTICLES mostly from missions or staff written: occasionally accept feature or factual articles on social and religious aspects of Asian and Latin American life: 2,000 words — $100 and up. PHOTOGRAPHS of Asian and Latin American subjects and photo stories — $10 each.

Columbia: Columbus Plaza, New Haven, Conn. 06507. Ed., Richard McMunn. Monthly, circulation 1,409,117; $6 per year. Official organ of the Knights of Columbus.

ARTICLES on K of C councils dealing with current events, social problems, Catholic apostolic activities: 1,000-1,500 words (must be accompanied by color glossy photos or transparencies) — up to $500. CARTOONS, pungent, wordless humor — $50. COVERS — up to $1,000. No fiction.

Commonweal: 15 Dutch St., New York, N.Y. 10038. Ed., Margaret O'Brien Steinfels. Biweekly, circulation 18,500; $32 per year.

ARTICLES, political, religious and literary subjects: 1,000-3,000 words — 3¢ a word. VERSE, serious poetry of high literary merit — about 50¢ a line.

Crusader's Almanac: Franciscan Monastery, 1400 Quincy St. N.E., Washington, D.C. 20017. Ed., Rev. Kevin Treston, O.F.M. Biannually, circulation 85,000; free.

ARTICLES about the Holy Land, Bible and Crusades given preference — 1¢ a word.

Emmanuel: 184 E. 76th Street, New York, N.Y. 10021. Editor-in-Chief, Rev. James Feeley, S.S.S. Monthly (combined Jan.-Feb., July-Aug. issues), circulation 7,000; $18 per year.

ARTICLES, spirituality for those in Church ministry, Eucharistic, pastoral, theological, Scriptural: 2,000-3,000 words — $100.

Extension: 35 E. Wacker Dr., Chicago, Ill. 60601. Ed., Brad Collins. Ten times a year, circulation, 90,000; free.

ARTICLES featuring U.S. home missioners, their work and the cultures and issues of the people they serve in poor, rural and remote parts of the U.S. Also, short catechetical and inspirational articles; 800-2,000 words — rate varies. Queries required before submitting material. PHOTOGRAPHS — black-and-white and color related to U.S. home missions — rate varies.

Health Progress: 4455 Woodson Rd., St. Louis, Mo. 63134. Ten issues per year. Circulation 13,881; $35 per year (U.S. and Canada); $40 (foreign).

Official journal of the Catholic Health Association of the United States.

ARTICLES, health-care oriented; administrative procedures and theories; hospital departmental services; 1,500-3,000 words — payment by agreement. BOOK REVIEWS, hospital oriented — payment by agreement.

Liguorian: One Liguori Dr., Liguori, Mo. 63057. Ed., Norman J. Muckerman, C.SS.R. Monthly, circulation over 500,000; $12 per year.

STORIES with a Christian influence yet without maudlin sentimentality; 1,500-2,000 words — 10-12¢ a word. ARTICLES on family, Scripture, liturgy; material for older readers and those under 21 needed; 1,500-2,000 words — 10-12¢ a word. POETRY, $25. ILLUSTRATIONS and BOOK REVIEWS on assignment only.

Marriage and Family Living: St. Meinrad, Ind. 47577. Man. Ed., Kass Dotterweich. Monthly, circulation 35,000; $14.95 per year.

ARTICLES: aimed at nurturing and enriching husband-wife and parent-child relationships: should focus on marriage or family issues with a moral, religious, or spiritual slant. Two types preferred: (1) informative, by an accredited author writing on a subject of expertise and experience; (2) personal experience, sharing an enlightening experience as a married person/parent. 300 — 2,000 words — 7¢ a word. POETRY: any style and length — $15.

Maryknoll: Maryknoll, N.Y. 10545. Ed., Moises Sandoval. Monthly, circulation more than 800,000.

ARTICLES must apply in some way to the hopes and aspirations, the culture, the problems and challenges of peoples in Asia, Africa and Latin America: 1,000-1,500 words — average payment, $100. Outline wanted before submission of material. PHOTOS: More interested in photo stories than in individual black and whites and color transparencies. Photo stories — up to $150, black and white; up to $200, color. Individual photos — $20, black and white; $50, color. Transparencies returned after use. Query before sending photos.

Messenger of the Sacred Heart, The: 661 Greenwood Ave., Toronto, Ont., Canada, M4J 4B3. Eds., Rev. F. J. Power, S.J., Alfred De Manche. Monthly, circulation 16,000; $7 per year.

ARTICLES and FICTION with a religious theme or moral about people, adventure, heroism, humor: maximum, 1,500 words — 2¢ a word. Payment upon acceptance.

Miraculous Medal, The: 475 E. Chelten Ave., Philadelphia, Pa. 19144. Ed., Rev. Robert P. Cawley, C.M. Quarterly, circulation 81,000.

FICTION, of general interest. Catholic in principle: 1,500-2,000 words — 2¢ a word and up. VERSE, religious in theme or turn; preferably about Our Lady: maximum 20 lines — 50¢ a line and up. Payment on acceptance. No articles.

Modern Liturgy: 160 E. Virginia St., No. 290, San Jose, Calif. 95112. Ed. Kenneth Guentert. Nine issues a year, circulation, 15,000; $40 per year.

FICTION: parables, fantasy, fables; 1,000 words. ARTICLES: how-to, sample services, skills for liturgical artists; 1,200 words. BOOK REVIEWS appropriate for liturgy. Pays in sample copies, subscriptions and advertising credit.

My Daily Visitor: 200 Noll Plaza, Huntington, Ind. 46750. Ed., Jacquelyn M. Eckert. Bimonthly, circulation 35,000; $8 per year.

A pocket-sized booklet of reflections for each day of the month.

MATERIAL: Daily reflections based on readings from the Mass, spiritual meditation, the feast of the day or the liturgical season: maximum 165 words per page (each day's reflection is printed on a separate page) — $200 for series of reflections.

New Catholic World: 997 Macarthur Blvd., Mahwah, N.J. 07430. Mng. Ed., Laurie Felknor. Bimonthly, circulation 14,000; $10 per year. Thematic issues.

ARTICLES, related to themes of issue (query editor): about 1,800-2,000 words. Rates of payment supplied.

Our Family: Box 249,Dept. C, Battleford, Sask., Canada SOM OEO. Monthly, circulation 14,265; $15.98 per year; $19.98 in U.S.

FICTION, adult only; stories that reflect lives, problems and concerns of audience; anything true to human nature; no sentimentality or blatant moralizing; stories with "woven in" Christian message: 1,000-2,000 words — 7¢ to 10¢ a word. ARTICLES related to family living; religion, education, social, biographical, marriage, courtship, domestic, institutional: 1,000-2,000 words — 7¢ to 10¢ a word. POETRY, in the market for many more poems; should deal with man in search for himself, for God, for others, for love, for meaning in life, for commitment: 8-30 lines — 75¢-$1.00 per line. PHOTOS — purchased with manuscript as package (extra payment for photos); also in search of individual photos for editorial use. FILLERS — anecdotes of inspirational value, straight exposition, short humor.

Our Sunday Visitor Magazine: 200 Noll Plaza, Huntington, Ind. 46750. Ed., Robert P. Lockwood. Weekly, circulation 220,000; $20 per year.

ARTICLES, no limitation on subjects other than those imposed by good taste and orthodoxy. Picture and text stories, profiles of individuals and organizations; articles that reflect moral, cultural, historical, social, economic and certain political concerns about the U.S. and the world; articles on current problems. Practical, factual and anecdotal material is sought: 750-1,000 words — $75-$100, usual payment. Queries are preferred to unsolicited completed manuscripts. PHOTOGRAPHS, picture stories preferred rather than individual photos. Picture stories (color) — $100 and up. No fiction or poetry.

Parish Family Digest: 200 Noll Plaza, Huntington, Ind. 46750. Ed.,George P. Foster. Bimonthly, circulation 150,000.

ARTICLES of timely interest to the young and growing Catholic family as a unit of the Catholic parish — personality profiles, interviews, social concerns, education, humor, inspiration and family and parish-family interrelationships; 1,000 words or less — 5¢ a word. REPRINTS — 3¢ a word. CARTOONS — $10 each for exclusives. FILLERS — $5 each for exclusives based on personal experience. No poetry.

Pastoral Music: 225 Sheridan St. N.W., Washington, D.C. 20011. Ed. Dr. Gordon E. Truitt. Bimonthly, circulation 8,000; $18 per year.

FICTION and ARTICLES — 4¢ a word.

Priest, The: 200 Noll Plaza, Huntington, Ind. 46750. Ed., Rev. Owen Campion. Eleven issues a year, circulation 12,000; $16.50 per year.

ARTICLES of benefit to priests, permanent deacons and seminarians in any of the following areas: priestly spirituality, contemporary theology, liturgy, apostolate and ministry, pastoral notes, Scripture. Controversial subject matter acceptable provided it does not go beyond the realm of orthodoxy or respect for authority or demands of fraternal charity: 6-15 double-spaced pages — $25 to $100 (about $6 per manuscript page).

Queen of All Hearts: 26 S. Saxon Ave., Bay Shore, N.Y. 11706. Ed., Rev. James McMillan, S.M.M.; Mng. Ed., Rev. Roger M. Charest S.M.M. Bimonthly; circulation 6,000; $10 per year (U.S.), $11 (Canada and foreign).

FICTION: short stories, preferably with a Marian theme: 1,000-2,000 words. ARTICLES on Marian theology, spirituality and devotion. Payment varies. VERSE with Marian theme — payment, two years' subscription. No artwork or fillers.

Religion Teacher's Journal: Twenty-Third Publications, P.O. Box 180, Mystic, Conn. 06355. Ed., Gwen Costello. Seven issues a year, circulation 40,000; $14.95 per year.

ARTICLES on catechesis, methods, theology, sample programs, how-to ideas, etc.; maximum length, 6 typewritten, double-spaced pages — $100 maximum. ILLUSTRATIONS, black and white — $20 each; covers/color slides — $50.

Review for Religious: Room 428, 3601 Lindell Blvd., St. Louis, Mo. 63108. Ed., David L. Fleming, S.J. Bimonthly, circulation 17,133; $12 per year.

ARTICLES, of interest to religious: 3,000-6,000 words — $6 per printed page.

St. Anthony Messenger: 1615 Republic St., Cincinnati, O. 45210. Ed., Rev. Norman Perry, O.F.M. Monthly, circulation 409,000; $14 per year.

FICTION: Written out of a totally Christian background, illuminating the truth of human nature for adults. No preachiness, sentimentality. FACT ARTICLES: 3,000-3,500 words. Outstanding personalities (must be based on personal interview). Information and comment on major movements in the Church: application of Christian faith to daily life; real-life solutions in the areas of a) family life, education; b) personal living (labor, leisure, art, psychology, spirituality). Human interest narrative. Humor. Photos and picture stories. Query letters welcome.

St. Joseph's Messenger and Advocate of the Blind: St. Joseph's Home, P.O. Box 288, Jersey City, N.J. 07303. Ed., Sr. Ursula Maphet, C.S.J. Quarterly, circulation 31,000; $4 per year.

FICTION, and ARTICLES, contemporary, mainstream themes, 500-1,500 words — 1¢ to 3¢ a word.

Social Justice Review: 3835 Westminster Pl., St. Louis, Mo. 63108. Bimonthly, circulation 1,050; $15 per year.

ARTICLES: research, editorial and review: 2,000-4,000 words — 2¢ a word. No fiction.

Spiritual Life: 2131 Lincoln Rd., N.E., Washington, D.C. 20002. Ed., Rev. Steven Payne, O.C.D. Quarterly, circulation 17,000; $9 per year.

ARTICLES, must follow scope of magazine: 3,000-5,000 words — rate varies. Sample copy and writers' guidelines sent upon request when accompanied by SASA (6" x 9" or larger).

Spirituality Today: 7200 W. Division St., River Forest, Ill. 60305. Ed., Rev. Richard John Woods, O.P. Quarterly, circulation 4,000; $11 per year.

ARTICLES concerning any phase of the spiritual life: minimum 3,000-4,000 words — 1¢ a word. No fiction or poetry. Query first.

Today's Catholic Teacher: 2451 E. River Rd., Suite 200, Dayton, O. 45439. Monthly Sept. through May (exc. Dec.), circulation 60,000; $14.95 per year.

ARTICLES of professional and personal interest to teachers, administrators, pastors, parish councils and school board members concerning Catholic schools (all subject areas) and CCD programs: 900-1,200 words, 1,500-3,000 words — $15-$75. Premium payment for superior content and writing presentation. Black and white photos helpful. Payment on publication.

Today's Parish: Twenty-Third Publications, P.O. Box 180, Mystic, Conn. 06355. Ed., Mary Carol Kendzia. Seven issues a year, circulation 16,000; $20 per year.

ARTICLES related to all aspects of parish life and ministry; minimum 1,200-1,500 words — $100 to $150. PHOTOS — $20; four-color cover photos $50.

Worship: St. John's Abbey, Collegeville, Minn. 56321. Ed., Rev. R. Kevin Seasoltz, O.S.B. Bimonthly, circulation 6,500; $18 per year; $20, foreign.

ARTICLES related to the engagement of the magazine in ongoing study of both the theoretical and pastoral dimensions of liturgy; examines historical traditions of worship in their doctrinal context, the experience of worship in Christian churches, the findings of contemporary theology, psychology and sociology insofar as they have a bearing on public worship: 4,500-7,000 words.

RADIO, TELEVISION, THEATRE

Radio and Television

Christopher Radio Program: 14-minute interview series, "Christopher Closeup," weekly, on 90 stations; "Christopher Minutes," daily, on 615 stations. Address: 12 E. 48th St., New York, N.Y. 10017.

Christopher TV Series, "Christopher Closeup": Originated in 1952. Half-hour and quarter-hour interviews in color, weekly, on 100 commercial and cable stations, American Forces Network outlets, CTNA and EWTN. Address: 12 E. 48th St., New York, N.Y. 10017.

For Our Times (TV): Originated in April 1979, this weekly half-hour series produced by CBS in a unique joint cooperative consultation with the Department of Communication, NCCB/USCC, the National Council of Churches and the New York Board of Rabbis focuses on the ethical and social challenges confronting American society today. Format: documentary and studio discussion (CBS-TV).

Guideline (Radio): Produced by Rev. Joseph Fenton, S.M., of the Department of Communication, NCCB/USCC. Weekly program designed to set forth the teachings of the Catholic Church and to discuss issues the Church faces in the contemporary world; heard on approximately 100 stations (NBC).

On This Rock (Radio): Produced in cooperation with the Department of Communication, NCCB/USCC. A 15-minute weekly program currently employing a youth-oriented music and commentary format; heard on more than 950 stations (ABC).

Sacred Heart Program (Radio, TV): Originated in 1939, operated by the Jesuits. Produces and syndicates nationally one TV program and nine radio programs each week on approximately 1,800 stations. Address: 3900 Westminster Place, St. Louis, Mo. 63108.

Religious Specials (TV): The NCCB/USCC Department of Communication produces four one-hour Catholic specials a year and additional seasonal liturgical services. The specials use a variety of formats and are broadcast on the ABC and NBC television networks.

Theatre

Catholic University Drama Department: Established in 1937. Offers B.A., M.A. and M.F.A. degree programs in playwriting, directing and acting. Produces four or five plays in The Hartke Theatre and four to six plays in the Callan Theatre each year. Affiliated with National Players and Olney Theatre. Chairman of the department, William H. Graham. Address: Catholic University of America, Washington, D.C. 20064.

National Players: An operation of the Olney Theatre Corp. It originated in 1949 and is the oldest classical touring company in the U.S.

Olney Theatre Corporation: A non-profit organization. It operates Olney Theatre, Olney, Md., an Equity theatre designated the State Summer Theatre of Maryland in 1978.

Catholic Actors' Guild of America, Inc.: Established in 1914 to provide material and spiritual assistance to people in the theatre. Has more than 500 members; publishes *The Call Board* bimonthly. Address: 165 W. 46th St., Suite 710, New York, N.Y. 10036.

Communications Services

Black Catholic Televangelization Network, 5247 Sheridan Ave., Detroit, Mich. 48213.

Catholic Views Broadcasts, Inc., 86 Riverside Dr., New York, N.Y. 10024.

Dabar Productions, 40 E. Center St., Akron, O. 44308. Sponsored by Unda-USA; produces *Real to Reel*, TV magazine program, and other Catholic TV projects.

Eternal Word Television Network, Inc., 5817 Old Leeds Rd., Birmingham, Ala. 35210. Mother M. Angelica, P.C.P.A., foundress. More than 10 million viewers.

Father Justin Rosary Hour (Polish): Station F — Box 217, Buffalo, N.Y. 14212. Rev. Cornelian Dende, O.F.M. Conv., director. Aired over more than 45 stations in U.S. and Canada.

Father Peyton's Family Theater Productions: Video cassettes, films for TV, for sale and rental. Address: 7201 Sunset Blvd., Hollywood, Calif. 90046.

Franciscan Advertising and Media Enterprises (F.A.M.E.): Produces and distributes media and advertising programs for religious education and evangelization. Address: 620 Route 3, Clifton, N.J. 07014.

Franciscan Communications: An award-winning religious producer of quality films, videos, filmstrips, media kits, phonograph records, audio cassettes and print materials for catechetical use in parishes and schools worldwide, distributed under the trade name TeleKETICS. Also produces public service spot messages for radio and TV. Address: 1229 South Santee St., Los Angeles, Calif. 90015.

Heart of the Nation, 2525 N. Naomi St., Burbank, Calif. 91504.

Hispanic Telecommunications Network, Inc. (HTN): Produces *Nuestra Familia*, a national weekly Spanish-language TV series. It also produces and distributes quality pastoral teaching videos. Address: 130 Lewis, San Antonio, Tex. 78212.

Life Broadcasting Network, 175 Crossways Park West, Woodbury, N.Y. 11797.

Mary Productions: Originated in 1950. Offers royalty-free scripts for stage, film, radio and tape production. Audio and video tapes of lives of the saints and historical characters. Traveling theatre company. Address: Mary Productions, Tomaso Pl., Apt. 212, Oakdale Dr., Middletown, N.J. 07748.

Oblate Media and Communication Corporation: 5901 West Main, Suite A, Belleville, Ill. 62223.

Passionist Communications, Inc.: Present Sunday Mass on TV seen in U.S. and available to dioceses and channels; publish "TV Prayer Guide," semi-annually. Address: 117 Harmon Ave., P.O. Box 440, Pelham, N.Y. 10803.

Paulist Communications: Contracts with dioceses and parishes to provide public service programs and spot series free to radio stations and scripts to priest-broadcasters; contacts stations for dioceses. Address: 2257 Barry Ave., Los Angeles, Calif. 90064.

Paulist Productions: Producers and distributors of the INSIGHT Film Series (available for TV) and educational film series. Purchase and rental information available. Address: P.O. Box 1057, Pacific Palisades, Calif. 90272.

Share the Word Television, 3031 Fourth St. N.E., Washington, D.C. 20017.

That's the Spirit Productions, Inc.: Produces "That's the Spirit," a family show, in cooperation with Passionist Fathers. Available to dioceses, organizations or channels. Address: P.O. Box 440, Pelham, N.Y. 10803.

Catholic Telecommunications Network of America (CTNA): Satellite communications network of the Church in U.S.; 106 affiliates. Address: Teleport One, The Teleport, Staten Island, N.Y. 10311.

Catholic Television Network (CTN): Instructional TV operations have been established in the following archdioceses and dioceses. Archdioceses are indicated by an asterisk.

Boston,* Mass.: Mr. Dennis Correira, Director, 55 Chapel, Box 56, Newton 02160.

Brooklyn, N.Y.: Rev. Msgr. Michael J. Dempsey, Director, 1712 10th Ave., 11215.

Chicago,* Ill.: Mr. Kenneth P. Murr, Director, 2001 W. Devon Ave. 60659.

Detroit,* Mich.: Rev. Robert Humitz, Director, 305 Michigan Ave., Detroit, Mich. 48226.

Los Angeles,* Calif.: Mr. Tom Mossman, 1520 W. Ninth St. 90015.

New York,* N.Y.: Sr. M. Irene Fugazy, Director, Seminary Ave., Yonkers, N.Y. 10704.

Orange, Calif.: Rev. Jerome Henson, Director, 2811 E. Villa Real Dr., Orange, Calif. 92667.

Rockville Centre, N.Y.: Rev. Msgr. Thomas Hartman, Director, 1345 Admiral Lane, Uniondale, N.Y. 11553.

San Bernardino, Calif.: Ms. Clare Colella, Director, 1450 N. D St., San Bernardino, Calif. 92405.

San Francisco,* Calif. (Bay Area): Mr. John Rohrbach, 324 Middlefield Rd., Menlo Park, Calif. 94025.

Youngstown, O.: Rev. James Korda, P.O. Box 430, Canfield, O. 44406.

Unda-USA: A national professional Catholic association for broadcasters and allied communicators organized in 1972. It succeeded the Catholic Broadcasters Association of America which in 1948 had replaced the Catholic Forum of the Air organized in 1938. It is a member of the international Catholic association for radio and television known as Unda (the Latin word for "wave," symbolic of air waves of communication). Subgroups include Catholic Television Network, the Association of Catholic TV/Radio Syndicators, the Catholic Telecommunications Network of America and the USCC Communications Dept. Unda-USA publishes a newsletter six times a year for members, produces "Real to Reel," a Catholic TV magazine, sponsors an annual general assembly and presents the Gabriel Awards annually for excellence in broadcasting. President, Sr. Angela Ann Zukowski, M.H.S.H.; executive director, Patrick J. DiSalvatore. National office: 40 East Center St., Akron, O. 44308.

The Catholic Communications Foundation (CCF) was established by the Catholic Fraternal Benefit Societies in 1966 to lend support and assistance to development of the communications apostolate of the Church. The CCF, promotes the development of diocesan communications capabilities and funds a scholarship program at the Annual Institute for Religious Communications. CCF officers include Bishop Anthony G. Bosco, chairman of the board. Address: MPO Box 2600, Niagara Falls, N.Y. 14302.

ECONOMIC JUSTICE: A PASTORAL MESSAGE

Following are excerpts from the pastoral message issued by the bishops of the United States in conjunction with their voluminous pastoral letter, "Economic Justice for All: Social Teaching and the U.S. Economy." The pastoral letter, six years in the making, was approved in its third draft by a vote of 225 to 9 Nov. 13, 1986, during the annual meeting of the National Conference of Catholic Bishops and the U.S. Catholic Conference. The drafting committee was headed by Archbishop Rembert G. Weakland of Milwaukee.

These excerpts, stating principal moral themes with respect to the economy, are from the text circulated by the NC Documentary Service, Origins, Nov. 27, 1986 (Vol. 16, No. 24). Subheads have been added.

This letter is a personal invitation to Catholics in the United States to use the resources of our faith, the strength of our economy and the opportunities of our democracy to shape a society which better protects the dignity and basic rights of our sisters and brothers both in this land and around the world.

We write to share our teaching, to raise questions, to challenge one another to live our faith in the world. We write as heirs of the biblical prophets who summons us "to do justice, to love kindness and to walk humbly with our God" (Mi. 6:8); and we write as followers of Jesus, who told us in the Sermon on the Mount: "Blessed are the poor in spirit.... Blessed are the lowly.... Blessed are those who hunger and thirst for justice.... You are the salt of the earth.... You are the light of the world" (Mt. 5:1-6, 13-14).

The challenge for us is to discover in our own place and time what it means to be "poor in spirit" and "the salt of the earth," and what it means to serve, "the least among us."

Moral Principles

• Every economic decision and institution must be judged in light of whether it protects or under-

mines the dignity of the human person.
- Human dignity can be realized and protected only in community.
- All people have a right to participate in the economic life of society.
- All members of society have a special obligation to the poor and vulnerable.
- Human rights are the minimum conditions for life in community.
- Society as a whole, acting through public and private institutions, has the moral responsibility to enhance human dignity and protect human rights.

Moral Vision

These six moral principles are not the only ones presented in the pastoral letter, but they give an overview of the moral vision that we are trying to share. This vision of economic life cannot exist in a vacuum; it must be translated into concrete measures. Our pastoral letter spells out some specific applications of Cathòlic moral principles.
- We call for a new national commitment to full employment.
- We say it is a social and moral scandal that one of every seven Americans is poor, and we call for concerted efforts to eradicate poverty.
- The fulfillment of the basic needs of the poor is of the highest priority.
- We urge that all economic policies be evaluated in light of their impact on the life and stability of the family.
- We support measures to halt the loss of family farms and to resist the growing concentration in the ownership of agricultural resources.
- We specify ways in which the United States can do far more to relieve the plight of poor nations and assist in their development.
- We also reaffirm church teaching on the rights of workers, collective bargaining, private property, subsidiarity and equal opportunity.

We know that some of our specific recommendations are controversial. As bishops, we do not claim to make these prudential judgments with the same kind of authority that marks our declarations of principle. But we feel obliged to teach by example how Christians can undertake concrete analysis and make specific judgments on economic issues. The Church's teachings cannot be left at the level of appealing generalities.

In the pastoral letter, we suggest that the time has come for a "new American experiment" to implement economic rights, to broaden the sharing of economic power and to make economic decisions more accountable to the common good. This new experiment can create new structures of economic partnership and participation within firms, at the regional level, for the whole nation and across borders.

Conversion and Action

We should not be surprised if we find Catholic social teaching to be demanding. The Gospel is demanding. We know that, at times, in order to remain truly a community of Jesus' disciples, we will have to say no to certain aspects in our culture, to certain trends and ways of acting that are opposed to a life of faith, love and justice. Changes in our hearts lead naturally to a desire to change how we act.
- With what care, human kindness and justice do I conduct myself at work?
- How will my economic decisions to buy, sell, invest, divest, hire or fire serve human dignity and the common good?
- In what career can I best exercise my talents so as to fill the world with the Spirit of Christ?
- How do my economic choices contribute to the strength of my family and community, to the values of my children, to a sensitivity to those in need?
- In this consumer society, how can I develop a healthy detachment from things and avoid the temptation to assess who I am by what I have?
- How do I strike a balance between labor and leisure that enlarges my capacity for friendships, for family life, for community?
- What government policies should I support to attain the well-being of all, especially the poor and vulnerable?

The pursuit of economic justice takes believers into the public arena, testing the policies of government by the principles of our teaching. We ask you to become more informed and active citizens, using your voices and votes to speak for the voiceless, to defend the poor and vulnerable, and to advance the common good. We are called to shape a constituency of conscience, measuring every policy by how it touches the least, the lost and the left out among us. This letter calls us to conversion and common action, to new forms of stewardship, service and citizenship.

We believe that the Christian view of life, including economic life, can transform the lives of individuals, families, schools and our whole culture. We believe that with your prayers, reflection, service and action our economy can be shaped so that human dignity prospers and the human person is served.

PUBLISHERS

(Principal source: *Catholic Press Directory.*)

Abbey Press, St. Meinrad, Ind. 47577.
ACTA, 4848 N. Clark St., Chicago, Ill. 60640.
Affirmation Books, 109 Woodland St., Natick, Mass. 02215.
Alba House, 2187 Victory Blvd., Staten Island, N.Y. 10314.
Alleluia Press, 672 Franklin Turnpike, Allendale, N.J. 07401.
American Catholic Press, 1223 Rossell Ave., Oak Park, Ill. 60302.
Ave Maria Press, Notre Dame, Ind. 46556.
Benziger Publishing Co., 15319 Chatsworth St., Mission Hills, Calif. 91345.
Wm. C. Brown Company Publishers, 2460 Kerper Blvd., Dubuque, Ia. 52001.
Catholic Book Publishing, 257 W. 17th St., New York, N.Y. 10011.

Catholic Health Association of the U.S., 4455 Woodson Rd., St. Louis, Mo. 63134.
Catholic Home Study Institute, 9 Loudoun St. S.E., Leesburg, Va. 22075.
Catholic University of America Press, 620 Michigan Ave. N.E., Washington, D.C. 20064.
Christian Classics, Inc., 73 West Main St., P.O. Box 30, Westminster, Md. 21157.
Christophers, 14 E. 48th St., New York, N.Y. 10017.
Claretian Publications, 205 W. Monroe St., Chicago, Ill. 60606.
Costello Publishing Co., Box 9, Northport, N.Y. 11768.
Crossroad Publishing Co., 370 Lexington Ave., New York, N.Y. 10017.
Daughters of St. Paul, 50 St. Paul's Ave., Jamaica Plain, Boston, Mass. 02130.
Dimension Books, Inc., 1 Summit St., Rockaway, N.J. 07866.
Don Bosco Multimedia, 475 North Ave., Box T, New Rochelle, N.Y. 10802.
Doubleday and Co., Inc., 245 Park Ave., New York, N.Y. 10167.
Fordham University Press, University Box L, Bronx, N.Y. 10458.
Franciscan Herald Press, 1434 W. 51st St. Chicago, Ill. 60609.
Georgetown University Press, Georgetown Univ., Washington, D.C. 20057.
The K.S. Giniger Co., Inc., 1133 Broadway, Suite 1301, New York, N.Y. 10010.
Michael Glazier, Inc., 1935 Fourth St., Wilmington, Del. 19805.
Ignatius Press, P.O. Box 18990, San Francisco, Calif. 94118.
Liguori Publications, One Liguori Dr., Liguori, Mo. 63057.
The Liturgical Press, St. John's Abbey, Collegeville, Minn. 56321.
Living Flame Press, 325 Rabro Dr., Hauppauge, N.Y. 11788.
Loyola University Press, 3441 N. Ashland Ave., Chicago, Ill. 60657.
Lumen Christi Press, 2229 Pech Rd., Houston, Tex. 77055.
McGrath Publishing Co., 6231 Leesburg Pike, Suite 404, Falls Church, Va. 22044.
Marquette University Press, 1324 W. Wisconsin Ave., Milwaukee, Wis. 53233.
Montfort Publications, 29 S. Saxon Ave., Bayshore, N.Y. 11706.
New City Press, 206 Skillman Ave., Brooklyn, N.Y. 11211.

Orbis Books, Maryknoll, N.Y. 10545.
Our Sunday Visitor, Inc., 200 Noll Plaza, Huntington, Ind. 46750.
Pastoral Press, 225 Sheridan St. N.W., Washington, D.C. 20011.
Paulist Press, 997 Macarthur Blvd., Mahwah, N.J. 07430.
Peter Li, Inc. (Pflaum Press Imprint), 2451 East River Rd., Dayton, O. 45439.
Pope John Center, 186 Forbes Rd., Braintree, Mass. 02184.
Pueblo Publishing Co., 100 W. 32nd St., New York, N.Y. 10001.
Regina Press, 145 Sherwood Ave., Farmingdale, N.Y. 11735.
Resource Publications, Inc., 160 E. Virginia St., No. 290, San Jose, Calif. 95112.
William H. Sadlier, Inc., 11 Park Place, New York, N.Y. 10007.
St. Anthony Messenger Press, 1615 Republic St., Cincinnati, O. 45210.
St. Bede's Publications, P.O. Box 545, Petersham, Mass. 01366.
Saint Mary's Press, Terrace Heights, Winona, Minn. 55987.
Scepter Press, 481 Main St., Suite 401, New Rochelle, N.Y. 10801.
Servant Publications, Box 8617, Ann Arbor, Mich. 48107.
Silver Burdett and Ginn Company, 250 James St. CN-1918. Morristown. N.J. 07960.
Templegate Publishers, 302 E. Adams St., Springfield, Ill. 62705.
Thomas More Association, 223 W. Erie St., Chicago, Ill. 60610.
Thomas Nelson Publishers (Catholic Bible Press imprint), P.O. Box 141000, Nashville, Tenn. 37214.
Trinity Communications, 9380 C1 Forestwood Lane, Manassas, Va. 22110.
Twenty-Third Publications, 185 Willow St., P.O. Box 180, Mystic, Conn. 06355.
USCC Office of Publishing Services, 1312 Massachusetts Ave. N.W., Washington, D.C. 20005.
U.S. Catholic Historical Society, 3 Downing Dr., E. Brunswick, N.J. 08816.
University of Notre Dame Press, P.O. Box L, Notre Dame, Ind. 46556.
University of Scranton Press, Scranton, Pa. 18510.
Winston-Derek Publishers, Inc., P.O. Box 90883, Nashville, Tenn. 37209.
Winston Press, Inc., 600 First Ave. N., Suite 800, Minneapolis, Minn. 55403.

HONORS AND AWARDS

PONTIFICAL ORDERS

The Pontifical Orders of Knighthood are secular orders of merit whose membership depends directly on the pope. Details regarding the various orders are handled by a special agency in the Secretariat of Briefs, an office in the Papal Secretariat of State.

Supreme Order of Christ (Militia of Our Lord Jesus Christ): The highest of the five pontifical orders of knighthood, the Supreme Order of Christ was approved Mar. 14, 1319, by John XXII as a continuation in Portugal of the suppressed Order of Templars. Members were religious with vows and a rule of life until the order lost its religious character toward the end of the 15th century. Since that time it has existed as an order of merit. Paul VI, in 1966, restricted awards of the order to Christian heads of state.

Order of the Golden Spur (Golden Militia): Although the original founder is not certainly known, this order is one of the oldest knighthoods. Indiscriminate bestowal and inheritance diminished its prestige, however, and in 1841 Gregory XVI replaced it with the Order of St. Sylvester and gave it the title of Golden Militia. In 1905 St. Pius X restored the Order of the Golden Spur in its own right, separating it from the Order of St. Sylvester. Paul VI, in 1966, restricted awards of the order to Christian heads of state.

Order of Pius IX: Founded by Pius IX June 17, 1847, the order is awarded for outstanding services for the Church and society, and may be given to non-Catholics as well as Catholics. The title to nobility formerly attached to membership was abolished by Pius XII in 1939. In 1957 Pius XII instituted the Class of the Grand Collar as the highest category of the order; in 1966, Paul VI restricted this award to heads of state "in solemn circumstances." The other three classes are of Knights of the Grand Cross, Knight Commanders with and without emblem, and Knights. The new class was created to avoid difficulties in presenting papal honors to Christian or non-Christian leaders of high merit.

Order of St. Gregory the Great: First established by Gregory XVI in 1831 to honor citizens of the Papal States, the order is conferred on persons who are distinguished for personal character and reputation, and for notable accomplishment. The order has civil and military divisions, and three classes of knights.

Order of St. Sylvester: Instituted Oct. 31, 1841, by Gregory XVI to absorb the Order of the Golden Spur, this order was divided into two by St. Pius X in 1905, one retaining the name of St. Sylvester and the other assuming the title of Golden Militia. Membership consists of three degrees: Knights of the Grand Cross, Knight Commanders with and without emblem, and Knights.

ECCLESIASTICAL ORDER

Equestrian Order of the Holy Sepulchre of Jerusalem: The order traces its origin to Godfrey of Bouillon who instituted it in 1099. It took its name from the Basilica of the Holy Sepulchre where its members were knighted. After the fall of the Latin Kingdom of Jerusalem and the consequent departure of the knights from the Holy Land, national divisions were established in various countries.

The order was reorganized by Pius IX in 1847 when he reestablished the Latin Patriarchate of Jerusalem and placed the order under the jurisdiction of its patriarch. In 1888, Leo XIII confirmed permission to admit women — Ladies of the Holy Sepulchre — to all degrees of rank. Pius X reserved the office of grand master to himself in 1907; Pius XII gave the order a cardinal patron in 1940 and, in 1949, transferred the office of grand master from the pope to the cardinal patron. Pope John XXIII approved updated constitutions in 1962; the latest statutes were approved by Paul VI in 1977.

The purposes of the order are strictly religious and charitable. Members are committed to sustain and aid the charitable, cultural and social works of the Catholic Church in the Holy Land, particularly in the Latin Patriarchate of Jerusalem.

The order is composed of knights and ladies grouped in three classes: class of Knights of the Collar and Ladies of the Collar; Class of Knights (in four grades); Class of Ladies (in four grades). Members are appointed by the cardinal grand master according to procedures outlined in the constitution.

Under the present constitution, the order is divided into national lieutenancies, largely autonomous, with international headquarters in Rome. Cardinal Maximilien de Furstenberg is the grand master of the order; the official church in Rome, given to the order in 1945 by Pius XII, is S. Onofrio on the Janiculum Hill.

There are five lieutenancies of the order in the United States and one in Puerto Rico.

ORDER OF MALTA

The Sovereign Military Hospitaller Order of St. John of Jerusalem of Rhodes and of Malta traces its origin to a group of men who maintained a Christian hospital in the Holy Land in the 11th century. The group was approved as a religious order — the Hospitallers of St. John — by Paschal II in 1113.

The order, while continuing its service to the poor, principally in hospital work, assumed military duties in the twelfth century and included knights, chaplains and sergeants-at-arms among its members. All the knights were professed monks with the vows of poverty, chastity and obedience. Headquarters were located in the Holy Land until the last decade of the 13th century and on Rhodes after 1308 (whence the title, Knights of Rhodes).

After establishing itself on Rhodes, the order became a sovereign power like the sea republics of Italy and the Hanseatic cities of Germany, flying its own flag, coining its own money, floating its own navy, and maintaining diplomatic relations with many nations.

The order was forced to abandon Rhodes in 1522 after the third siege of the island by the Turks under Sultan Suliman I. Eight years later, the Knights were given the island of Malta, where they remained as a bastion of Christianity until near the end of the 18th century. Headquarters have been located in Rome since 1834.

The title of Grand Master of the Order, in abeyance for some time, was restored by Leo XIII in 1879. A more precise definition of both the religious and the sovereign status of the order was embodied in a new constitution of 1961 and a code issued in 1966.

Religious aspects of the order are subject to regulation by the Holy See. At the same time the sovereignty of the order, which is based on international law, is recognized by the Holy See and by 48 countries with which full diplomatic relations are maintained.

The four main classifications of members are: Knights of Justice, who are religious with the vows of poverty, chastity and obedience; Knights of Obedience, who make a solemn promise to strive for Christian perfection; Knights of Honor and Devotion and of Grace and Devotion — all of noble lineage; and Knights of Magistral Grace. There are also chaplains, Dames and Donats of the order.

The order, with five grand priories, three subpriories and 38 national associations, is devoted to hospital and charitable work of all kinds in some 77 countries.

The Grand Master, who is the head of the order, has the title of Most Eminent Highness with the rank of Cardinal. He must be of noble lineage and under solemn vows for a minimum period of 10 years, if under 50.

The present Grand Master is Fra' Andrew Willoughby Ninian Bertie, member of the British aristocracy, who was elected for life Apr. 8, 1988, by the Council of State. His election was approved by the Pope.

The address of headquarters of the order is Via Condotti, 68, Palazzo Malta, 00187 Roma, Italia.

PAPAL MEDALS

Pro Ecclesia et Pontifice: This decoration ("For the Church and the Pontiff") had its origin in 1888 as a token of the golden sacerdotal jubilee of Leo XIII; he bestowed it on those who had assisted in the observance of his jubilee and on persons responsible for the success of the Vatican Exposition. The medal, cruciform in shape, bears the likenesses of Sts. Peter and Paul, the tiara and the papal keys, the words *Pro Ecclesia et Pontifice,* and the name of the present pontiff, all on the same side; it is attached to a ribbon of yellow and white, the papal colors. Originally, the medal was issued in gold, silver or bronze. It is awarded in recognition of service to the Church and the papacy.

Benemerenti: Several medals ("To a well-deserving person") have been conferred by popes for exceptional accomplishment and service. The medals, which are made of gold, silver or bronze, bear the likeness and name of the reigning pope on one side; on the other, a laurel crown and the letter "B."

These two medals may be given by the pope to both men and women. Their bestowal does not convey any title or honor of knighthood.

AMERICAN CATHOLIC AWARDS

Aquinas Medal, by the American Catholic Philosophical Association for outstanding contributions to the field of Catholic philosophy. Quentin Lauer (1985), Armand Maurer (1987).

Bellarmine Medal (1955), by Bellarmine College (Louisville, Ky.), to persons in national or international affairs who, in controversial matters, exemplify the characteristics of St. Robert Bellarmine in charity, justice and temperateness. Ambassador Philip C. Habib (1984).

Berakah Award (1976), by the North American Academy of the Liturgy, to recognize distinguished contribution to the professional work of liturgy by a liturgist or person of an allied vocation. Aelred Tegels, O.S.B., and Michael Marx, O.S.B. (1988).

Borromeo Award (1960), by Carroll College (Helena, Mont.), for zeal, courage and devotion in the spirit of St. Charles Borromeo. Mrs. Martha Burke (1987).

Brent Award (1976), by the Diocese of Arlington, Va., for distinguished service to fellowman. Dr. George W. Johnson (1987).

Campion Award (1955), by the Catholic Book Club for distinguished service in Catholic letters. Robert Giroux (1988).

Cardinal Gibbons Medal (1949) by the Alumni Association of The Catholic University of America for distinguished and meritorious service to the Church, the United States or The Catholic University of America. Mildred Jefferson (1985).

Cardinal Spellman Award (1947), by the Catholic Theological Society for outstanding achievement in the field of theology. Raymond E. Brown, S.S. (1971). See John Courtney Murray Award.

Cardinal Wright Award (1980), by the Fellowship of Catholic Scholars to a Catholic adjudged to have done an outstanding service for the Church. Rev. John F. Harvey, O.S.F.S. (1988). Special award, 1988: **Cardinal Patrick O'Boyle Award,** for defense of the Faith. Rev. John T. Ford, S.J.

The Catholic University of America Patronal Medal (1974), by the University in cooperation with the National Shrine of the Immaculate Conception for outstanding contributions to the Catholic Church and in promoting interest and devotion to Mary, patroness of the University. Cardinal John Krol (1986), Most Rev. Thomas J. Grady (1987).

Cecilia Medal (1952), by the Music Department of Boys Town (Nebr.) for outstanding work in liturgical music. Evelyn Letter (1980).

Christian Culture Award (1941), by Assumption University (Canada) to outstanding exponents of Christian ideals. Mrs. Louise Summerhill (1988).

College of New Rochelle Pope John XXIII Award (1963), by College of New Rochelle (N.Y.) to those whose lives are witnesses "to the centrality of human dignity in the creation of peace." Sisters Mary Collins, O.S.B., M. Patrice Murphy, S.C., Marie Augusta Neal, S.N.D. deN., Elaine Roulet, C.S.J., Mary Luke Tobin, S.L. (1985).

Compostela Award, The (1982), by the Cathedral-Basilica of St. James (Diocese of Brooklyn) to men and women whose lives represent the noblest ideals of the cathedral tradition of fidelity to justice, truth, beauty and peace. Mother M. Angelica, P.C.P.A., Horton Foote, Fred Rogers, Mercedes Arzu Wilson (1988).

Damien-Dutton Award (1953), by the Damien-Dutton Society for service toward conquest of leprosy or for the promotion of better understanding of social problems connected with the disease. Mr. Herbert Kober (1988).

Edith Stein Award (1955), by the Edith Stein Guild for service toward better understanding between Christians and Jews. Dr. Eugene Fisher (1983).

Emmanuel D'Alzon Medal (1954), by Assumptionists to persons exemplifying the ideals of their founder. Mother Helene-Marie Bories, R.A., and Cardinal Johannes Willebrands (1980).

Father McKenna Award (1950), by the national headquarters of the Holy Name Society, for outstanding service to the society's ideals. Rev. John Morley (1981).

Fidelitas Medal (1949), by Orchard Lake Schools (Sts. Cyril and Methodius Seminary, St. Mary's College, St. Mary's Preparatory), to an outstanding American Catholic of Polish descent for fidelity in serving God and country. Abp. Edmund C. Szoka (1987).

Franciscan International Award (1958), by the Conventual Franciscans (Prior Lake, Minn.) for outstanding contributions in the education of children. Sesame Street Staff (1987).

George M. Cohan Award (1970), by the Catholic Actors Guild of America, Inc., Joel Gray (1988).

Good Samaritan Award (1968), by the National Catholic Development Conference to recognize the concern for one's fellowman exemplified by the Good Samaritan. Sr. Elaine Roulet (1987); Bro. Cesare Bullo, S.D.B. (1988).

Hoey Awards (1942), by the Catholic Interracial Council of New York, to persons who have worked to combat racism and have promoted social and interracial justice. Clara Hale, James Hoge, Cleveland Robinson (1986); Robert L. Biblo, Sonny Hall, Thomas L. Jacobs, Most Rev. Joseph M. Sullivan (1987).

Honor et Veritas Award (1959), by the Catholic War Veterans to outstanding Americans. Dr. Timothy A. Mitchell (1987).

Howard R. Marraro Prize (1973), by the American Catholic Historical Association for a book on Italian history or Italo-American history or relations. Gary Ross Mormino (1987).

Insignis Medal (1951), by Fordham University for extraordinary distinction in the service of God and humanity. Dr. Paul J. Reiss (1985).

John Courtney Murray Award (1972), by the Catholic Theological Society for distinguished achievement in theology. Originated in 1947 as the Cardinal Spellman Award. Richard Sklba (1988).

John Gilmary Shea Prize (1944), by the American Catholic Historical Association for scholarly works on the history of the Catholic Church broadly considered. James M. Powell (1987).

John La Farge Memorial Award for Interracial Justice (1965), by the Catholic Interracial Council of New York. Presented annually to leading citizens of the community regardless of race, color or creed for promoting social and interracial justice. Ralph P. Davidson, David N. Dinkins, Archbishop Iakovos, John J. Sweeney, Mario Cuomo (1987), Lenore Miller, Bp. Emerson J. Moore, Robert F. Wagner, Jr., William S. Woodside (1988).

King Award (1971), by the U.S. Catholic Historical Society for significant contribution in the study of the history of the Catholic Church in the U.S. Elisa A. Carrillo (1976).

Laetare Medal (1883), by the University of Notre Dame for distinguished accomplishment for Church or nation by an American Catholic. Eunice Kennedy Shriver (1988).

Lumen Christi Award (1978) by the Catholic Church Extension Society to persons making an outstanding contribution in service to the American home missions. Rev. Joseph Valine, O.P. (1988).

The Manhattan College De La Salle Medal, by Manhattan College, for significant contribution to the moral, cultural and educational life of the nation. Maurice R. Greenberg (1988).

Marianist Award (1949), by the University of Dayton for outstanding service in America to the Mother of God (until 1966); for outstanding contributions to mankind (from 1967); for outstanding scholarship by a Roman Catholic (from 1986). Timothy O'Meara (1988).

Marian Library Medal (1953), by the Marian Library of the University of Dayton. Awarded annually (until 1967) to encourage books in English on the Blessed Virgin Mary. Awarded every four years (from 1971), at the time of an International Mariological Congress, to a scholar for Mariological studies. Heinrich M. Koester, S.A.C. (1987).

Mater et Magistra Award (1963), by the College of Mt. St. Joseph on the Ohio to women for social action in the pattern and spirit of the encyclical *Mater et Magistra*. Mother Teresa (1974).

Mendel Medal (1928), by Villanova University for scientists. Dr. Alfred M. Bongiovanni (1968).

Msgr. John P. Monaghan Social Action Award by the Assn. of Catholic Trade Unionists; originally (1948), the Quadragesimo Anno Medal. Vincent McDonnell (1970).

O'Reilly-Conway Medal (1979), by *The Pilot*, Boston archdiocesan newspaper, for distinctive contributions to journalism. Rev. Peter V. Conley (1987).

Paulist Award for Lay Evangelization (1979), by the Paulist Fathers to Catholic laity for significant contribution in ministry of evangelizing inactive Catholics and the unchurched in the U.S. Chet and Thelma Stokloza (1988).

Pax Christi Award (1963), by St. John's University (Collegeville, Minn.), to honor persons of strong faith whose lives exemplify the importance of spiritual values and concern for the welfare of others. Rev. Albert C. Outler (1987).

Peace Award (1950), by the Secular Franciscan Order. Pope John Paul II (1986).

Peter Guilday Prize (1972), by the American Catholic Historical Association for articles accepted by the editors of the *Catholic Historical Review* which are the first scholarly publications of their authors. Vincent J. McNally (1980).

Pius XII Marian Award (1955), by the Montfort Missionaries for promotion of the devotion of consecration to the Immaculate Heart of Mary. Mr. and Mrs. Thomas F. Larkin, Jr. (1973).

Poverello Medal (1949), by The University of Steubenville (Ohio), "in recognition of great benefactions to humanity, exemplifying in our age the Christ-like spirit of charity which filled the life of St. Francis of Assisi." James D. Lynch, S.F.O., March, and Charles W. Colson, December (1986).

Regina Medal (1959), by the Catholic Library Association for outstanding contributions to children's literature. Katherine Paterson (1988).

Role of Law Award (1973), by the Canon Law Society of America, to recognize a canon lawyer who embodies a pastoral attitude and is committed to research and study. Rev. James A. Coriden (1987).

St. Bonaventure University Justice and Peace Medal (1981), by St. Bonaventure University (St. Bonaventure, N.Y.). Sister Joan Malone, O.S.F. (1983).

St. Francis de Sales Award (1958), by the Catholic Press Association for distinguished contribution to Catholic journalism. Henry Libersat, Jr. and James A. Doyle (Special Award) (1988).

St. Francis Xavier Medal (1954), by Xavier University (Cincinnati) to persons exemplifying the spirit of St. Francis Xavier. Rev. Edward R. Brueggeman, S.J. (1987).

St. Vincent de Paul Medal (1948), by St. John's University (Jamaica, N.Y.), for outstanding service to Catholic charities. John J. Farrell (1985).

Serra Award of the Americas (1947), by the Academy of American Franciscan History for service to Inter-American good will. Prof. Richard E. Greenleaf (1986).

Signum Fidei Medal (1942), by the Alumni Association of La Salle University (Phila.) for noteworthy contributions to the advancement of humanitarian principles in keeping with Christian tradition. Rev. Bruce Ritter, O.F.M. Conv. (1988).

Soteriological Award (1967), by the Confraternity of the Passion (Third Order of the Passionists, Corpus Christi Residence, 80 David St., South River, N.J. 08882), for outstanding exemplification of sharing in the Passion of Christ in contemporary society. Doris Froelich (1984), Rev. Jude Meade, C.P. (1985).

Sword of Loyola (1964), by Loyola University of Chicago to person or persons exemplifying Ignatius of Loyola's courage, dedication and service. Rev. Theodore M. Hesburgh, C.S.C. (1986), Frank Considine (1988).

U.S. Catholic Award (1978), by editors of *U.S. Catholic* magazine for furthering the cause of women in the Church. Donna Hanson (1988).

Vercelli Medal (1947), by the Holy Name Society for distinguished service to ideals of the society. John Farmerie (1983), Leo H. Nuedling, John Kovach (1985), Kenneth J. Livaudais (1986).

1988 CPA AWARDS

Catholic Press Association Awards for material published in 1987 were presented during the annual CPA convention held May 25-27, 1988, in Boston, Mass. Some of the awards are listed below.

Newspapers — General Excellence

National Newspapers: *National Catholic Register* (first place); *National Catholic Reporter* (second place). *Catholic Twin Circle* and *Our Sunday Visitor* (third place, tie).

Diocesan Newspapers, to 17,000 circulation: *The Catholic Observer*, Springfield, Mass. (first place); *The Catholic Herald*, Colorado Springs, Colo. (second); *The Montana Catholic*, Helena, Mont. (third).

Diocesan Newspapers, 17,001 to 40,000 circulation: *Acadiana Catholic*, Lafayette, La. (first place); *The Florida Catholic*, Orlando, and *The Florida Catholic*, St. Petersburg (second, tie); *The Catholic Post*, Peoria, Ill. (third).

Diocesan Newspapers, 40,001 and over circulation: *The Catholic Review*, Baltimore, Md. (first place); *Catholic New York*, New York, N.Y. (second); *The Voice*, Miami, Fla. (third).

First, second and third place awards were presented in 19 other categories.

Magazines — General Excellence

General Interest: *America* (first place); *New Catholic World* (second place); *Commonweal* (third place).

Mission: *The Mountain Spirit* (first place); *Kinship* (second); *Catholic Near East* (third).

Religious Order: *National Jesuit News* (first place); *In Between* (second); *The Carmelite Review* (third).

Professional and Special Interest: *Church* (first place); *Catholic Rural Life* (second); *U.S. Catholic Historian* (third).

Magazines for Clergy and Religious: *Chicago Studies* (first place); *The Priest* (second); *Emmanuel* (third).

Scholarly: *Theological Studies* (first place); *Thought* (second); *Horizons* (third).

Devotional/Inspirational: *The Bible Today* (first place); *Spirituality Today* (second); *Praying* (third).

Newsletters, General Interest: *U.S. Parish* (first place); *Context* (second); *Catholic Update* (third).

Newsletters, Special Interest: *CRS News* (first place); *SCJ News* (second); *Missionaries of Africa Report* (third).

First, second and third place awards were presented in 14 other categories.

Spanish-Language Awards

General Excellence: *Chicago Catolico* and *Revista Maryknoll*, (first place, tie); *La Voz Catolica*, Miami, Fla. (second place); *El Mensajero Catolico*, Milwaukee, Wis., and *El Heraldo Catolico*, Sacramento, Calif. (third place, tie).

Books — First Place Awards

Popular Presentation of Catholic Faith: Paulist Press, Mahwah, N.J., *The Catholic Faith: An Introduction*, by Lawrence S. Cunningham.

Spirituality: Orbis Books, Maryknoll, N.Y., *Passion of Christ, Passion of the World*, by Leonardo Boff.

Theology: Twenty-Third Publications, Mystic, Conn., *The Creed*, by Bernard L. Marthaler.

Scripture: Orbis Books, Maryknoll, N.Y., *On Exodus*, by George Pixley.

Liturgical/Pastoral Ministry: The Liturgical Press, Collegeville, Minn., *Alternative Futures for Worship Series* (7 volumes), edited by Bernard J. Lee, Regis A. Duffy, Mark Searle, Peter E. Fink, Bernard Cooke, Michael Cowan.
Professional: Sheed and Ward, Kansas City, Mo., *Future of Catholic Leadership: Responses to the Priest Shortage,* by Dean Hoge.
Educational: Twenty-Third Publications, Mystic, Conn., *Leading Students into Scripture,* by Mary Kathleen Glavich, S.N.D.
Design and Production: Loyola University Press, Chicago, Ill., *Land of the Spotted Eagle: A Portrait of the Reservation Sioux,* by Harry W. Paige and Don Doll, S.J.

1988 CHRISTOPHER AWARDS

Christopher Awards are given each year to recognize the creative writers, producers and directors who have achieved artistic excellence in films, books and television specials affirming the highest values of the human spirit.
The 1988 awards were presented as follows:
Books for Adults: *An Echo in My Heart,* by Alois O'Toole, C.F.X.; *Anne Frank Remembered: The Story of the Woman Who Helped To Hide the Frank Family,* by Miep Gies with Alison Leslie Gold; *Dorothy Day: A Radical Devotion,* by Robert Coles, M.D.; *Emergency Doctor,* by Edward Ziegler in cooperation with Lewis R. Goldfrank, M.D.; *Iron and Silk,* by Mark Salzman; *Life and Death in Shanghai,* by Nien Cheng; *Song in a Weary Throat: An American Pilgrimage,* by Pauli Murray; *Wilbur and Orville: A Biography of the Wright Brothers,* by Fred Howard.
Books for Young People: *Heckedy Peg,* by Audrey Wood; *Humphrey's Bear,* by Jan Wahl (ages 6 to 8); *The Gold Cadillac,* by Mildred D. Taylor (ages 9 to 12); *Into a Strange Land: Unaccompanied Refugee Youth in America,* by Brent and Melissa Ashabranner (ages 12 and up).
Television Specials: Producers, directors and writers of: "ABC News Closeup: Alcohol and Cocaine: The Secret of Addiction"; "Capital to Capital: An ABC News Special"; "December Flower" (PBS); "Eye on the Sparrow" (NBC); "Eyes on the Prize: America's Civil Rights Years, 1954-65" (PBS); "The Father Clements Story" (NBC); "Kids Like These" (CBS); "Monsignor Quixote" (PBS); "The Secret Garden" (CBS); "Twenty Years on the Road with Charles Kuralt: A CBS News Special."
James Keller Youth Award: Father Bruce Ritter, O.F.M. Conv., founder of Covenant House.

DEATHS SEPTEMBER 1987 TO SEPTEMBER 1988

Cardinals: Bernard Jan **Alfrink**, 87, Dec. 17, 1987, Netherlands; John F. **Dearden**, 80, Aug. 1, 1988, Detroit, Mich.; Louis Jean **Guyot**, 83, Aug. 1, 1988, Bordeaux, France; Joseph **Hoeffner**, 80, Oct. 16, 1987, Cologne, Germany; Hermann **Volk**, 84, July 1, 1988, Mainz, Germany.

Archbishops: George E. **Bernarding**, 75, Dec. 21, 1987, Pittsburgh, Pa.; William E. **Cousins**, 86, Sept. 14, 1988, Milwaukee, Wis.; James P. **Davis**, 83, Mar. 4, 1988, Albuquerque, N.M.; Thomas A. **Donnellan**, 73, Oct. 15, 1987, Atlanta, Ga.; Philippe **Nguyen Kim Dien**, 67, June 8, 1988, Hue, Vietnam.

Bishops: Eduardo **Dalmau**, 94, Nov. 19, 1987, Miami, Fla.; Harold J. **Dimmerling**, 73, Dec. 13, 1987, Rapid City, S.D.; Evelio **Dominguez Recinos**, 78, Apr. 20, 1988, Tegucigalpa, Honduras; Frederick A. **Donaghy**, M.M., 85, Feb. 5, 1988, Ossining, N.Y.; Hugh A. **Donohoe**, 82, Oct. 26, 1987, Fresno, Calif.; Julius **Gabris**, 73, Nov. 13, 1987, Trnava (Slovakia), Czechoslovakia. Vincent M. **Harris**, 74, Mar. 31, 1988, Houston, Tex.; Nevin W. **Hayes**, 66, July 12, 1988, Chicago, Ill.; Thomas W. **Lyons**, 64, Mar. 25, 1988, Baltimore, Md.; Eugene **Maillat**, P.A., 66, July 5, 1988, Fribourg, Switzerland; Henry J. **Soenneker**, 80, Sept. 24, 1987, Owensboro, Ky.; Horacio Olave **Velandia**, 44, Mar. 17, 1988, near Zulia, Colombia (plane crash).

Floyd **Anderson**, 81, Jan. 13, 1988, Alexandria, Va.; Chester A. **Beatty**, 74, May 5, 1988, Brooklyn, N.Y.; Rev. Fidelis **Benedik**, C.P., 85, Aug. 29, 1988, Chicago, Ill.; Msgr. Josiah G. **Chatham**, 73, May 4, 1988, Jackson, Miss.; Pres. **Chiang Ching-Kuo**, 77, Jan. 13, 1988, Taiwan; Rev. John R. **Connery**, S.J., 74, Dec. 22, 1987, Evanston, Ill.; John E. **Cosgrove**, 65, June 16, 1988, Silver Spring, Md.; Dennis **Day**, 72, June 22, 1988, Los Angeles, Calif.; Fra Angelo **de Mojana** di Cologna, 82, Jan. 18, 1988, Rome, Italy;

Rev. Paul **Faulkner**, M.H.M., 67, Feb. 21, 1988, Innsbruck, Austria; Woody **Herman**, 74, Oct. 29, 1987, Los Angeles, Calif.; Mary **Hinton**, 75, May 28, 1988, Scranton, Pa.; Dennis J. **Horan**, 56, May 1, 1988, Chicago, Ill.; George **Kemon**, Jr., 65, May, 1988, Dade City, Fla.; Joseph K. **Kozak**, 77, July 15, 1988, Chicago, Ill.; Thomas A.J. **Lewis**, 86, May 20, 1988, Ojai, Calif.; Joseph **Lichten** (Jewish pioneer promoter of Catholic-Jewish dialogue), 81, Dec. 15, 1987, Rome, Italy;

Clare Booth **Luce**, 84, Oct. 9, 1987, Washington, D.C.; Sr. Janemarie **Luecke**, O.S.B., 63, Nov. 17, 1987, Oklahoma City, Okla.; Sean **MacBride**, 83, Jan. 15, 1988, Dublin, Ireland; Rev. Paul E. **McKeever**, 64, Jan. 10, 1988, Huntington, N.Y.; Raimondo **Manzini**, 87, Jan. 14, 1988, Rome, Italy; Rev. Silvester **Mooney**, O.S.B., 102, Sept. 5, 1988, Douai Abbey, England; Rev. Harold **Mulqueen**, S.J., 93, Jan. 31, 1988, Bronx, N.Y.; William **Porter**, 73, Mar. 16, 1988, Hawthorne, N.Y.; Anglican Archbishop Michael **Ramsey**, 83, Apr. 23, 1988, London, England.

Arthur J. **Rooney**, Sr., 87, Aug. 25, 1988, Pittsburgh, Pa.; Rev. George D. **Ruggieri**, S.J., 62, Dec. 1, 1987, Moorestown, N.J.; Rev. Carl **Schmitz**, C.P., 70, Apr. 7, 1988, Bolul, Philippines; Sr. Sharon **Sullivan**, O.S.F., 43, July 17, Jackson, Miss.; Rev. Hans Urs **von Balthasar**, 82, June 26, 1988, Basel, Switzerland; Edward Bennett **Williams,**, 68, Aug. 13, 1988, Washington, D.C.; Abbot Bonaventure **Zerr**, O.S.B., 51, June 22, 1988, St. Benedict, Ore.